Irving Layton, b. 1912
Robert Hayden, 1913–1980
Tillie Olsen, b. 1913
Muriel Rukeyser, 1913–1980
Karl Shapiro, b. 1913
Barbara Howes, b. 1914
Randall Jarrell, 1914–1965
Dudley Randall, b. 1914
Henry Reed, 1914–1986
William Stafford, b. 1914
Dylan Thomas, 1914–1953
Tom Whitecloud, 1914–1972
Isabella Gardner, 1915–1981
Arthur Miller, b. 1915
Américo Parédes, b. 1915
Orson Welles, 1915–1985
Gwendolyn Brooks, b. 1917
Arthur Laurents, b. 1918
Shirley Jackson, 1919–1965
Doris Lessing, b. 1919
May Swenson, 1919–1989
Edwin Morgan, b. 1920
Howard Nemerov, 1920–1991
Mary Ellen Solt, b. 1920
James Emanuel, b. 1921
Mona Van Duyn, b. 1921
Richard Wilbur, b. 1921
Philip Larkin, 1922–1985
Grace Paley, b. 1922
James Dickey, b. 1923
Mari Evans, b. 1923
Richard Hugo, 1923–1982
Edward Field, b. 1924
Mary Noël Kernan, b. ca. 1924
Vassar Miller, b. 1924
Donald Justice, b. 1925
Carolyn Kizer, b. 1925
Maxine Kumin, b. 1925
Flannery O'Connor, 1925–1964
Gerald Stern, b. 1925
A. R. Ammons, b. 1926
Allen Ginsberg, b. 1926
James Merrill, b. 1926
Frank O'Hara, 1926–1966
W. D. Snodgrass, b. 1926
David Wagoner, b. 1926
W. S. Merwin, b. 1927
James Wright, 1927–1980
Edward Albee, b. 1928
Maya Angelou, b. 1928
Donald Hall, b. 1928
Cynthia MacDonald, b. 1928
Gabriel García Márquez, b. 1928
Cynthia Ozick, b. 1928
Anne Sexton, 1928–1974
John Hollander, b. 1929
X. J. Kennedy, b. 1929
Jon Silkin, b. 1930
John Engels, b. 1931
Etheridge Knight, 1931-1991
Alice Munro, b. 1931
Judith Viorst, b. 1931
Joanne Greenberg, b. 1932
Linda Pastan, b. 1932
Sylvia Plath, 1932–1963
John Updike, b. 1932

Erne
Imar
Jo
Joanne
Audre Lorde, b. 1934
Marge Piercy, b. 1934
Sonia Sanchez, b. 1934
Mark Strand, b. 1934
Paul Zimmer, b. 1934
Betty Keller, b. 1935
Lucille Clifton, b. 1936
Stephen Dixon, b. 1936
Andre Dubus, b. 1936
John Haines, b. 1936
H. S. (Sam) Hamod, b. 1936
Marvin Bell, b. 1937
Judith Minty, b. 1937
Luis Omar Salinas, b. 1937
Diane Wakoski, b. 1937
Dan Georgakas, b. 1938
Michael S. Harper, b. 1938
Virginia Scott, b. 1938
Margaret Atwood, b. 1939
Toni Cade Bambara, b. 1939
Seamus Heaney, b. 1939
Joseph Brodsky, b. 1940
William Heyen, b. 1940
Billy Collins, b. 1941
Simon Ortiz, b. 1941
Tino Villanueva, b. 1941
Marilyn Hacker, b. 1942
Sharon Olds, b. 1942
Dave Smith, b. 1942
Nikki Giovanni, b. 1943
Jim Northrup, b. 1943
James Tate, b. 1943
Alice Walker, b. 1944
Joy Williams, b. 1944
Daniel Halpern, b. 1945
Carol Muske, b. 1945
Brenda Serotte, b. 1946
Maura Stanton, b. 1946
Leonard Adamé, b. 1947
Roberta Hill, b. 1947
Jane Shore, b. 1947
Alan Lightman, b. 1948
Heather McHugh, b. 1948
Leslie Marmon Silko, b. 1948
Gary Soto, b. 1948
Shelly Wagner, b. 1948
Olga Broumas, b. 1949
Katha Pollitt, b. 1949
Bruce Weigl, b. 1949
Carolyn Forché, b. 1950
Chase Twichell, b. 1950
Rita Dove, b. 1952
Beth Henley, b. 1952
Naomi Shihab Nye, b. 1952
David Wojahn, b. 1953
Sandra Cisneros, b. 1954
Irene Zabytko, b. 1954
Cathy Song, b. 1955
Lorrie Moore, b. 1957

**FOURTH
EDITION**

LITERATURE

*An Introduction
to Reading
and Writing*

Edgar V. Roberts
Lehman College
The City University of New York

Henry E. Jacobs

PRENTICE HALL, Englewood Cliffs, New Jersey 07632

Library of Congress Cataloging-in-Publication Data

Roberts, Edgar V.
    Literature : an introduction to reading and writing / Edgar
V. Roberts, Henry E. Jacobs. – 4th ed.
        p.   cm.
    Includes indexes.
    ISBN 0-13-097510-9 (case)
    1. Literature.   2. Exposition (Rhetoric)   3. Literature—
Collections. 4. College readers.   I. Jacobs, Henry E.   II. Title.
PN45.R575   1995
  808´.0668—dc20   94-20463
                                      CIP

Acquisitions Editor: Alison Reeves
Project Managers: Hilda Tauber/Andrew Roney
Development Editor: Barbara Muller
Buyer: Tricia Kenny
Interior and cover design: Joanne Kaiser/Tom Nery
Design Director: Paula Martin
Photo Research: Barbara Scott
Director Image Resource Center: Lori Morris-Nantz
Editorial assistant: Lee Mamunes
Cover photo: *Birch Tree*, Comstock © 1993

Credits and copyright acknowledgments appear on pp. xlvi–lii,
which constitute an extension of the copyright page. Photo credits appear
on pp. 1712–1713, which also constitute an extension of the copyright page.

©1995, 1992, 1989, 1987 by Prentice-Hall, Inc.
A Paramount Communications Company
Englewood Cliffs, New Jersey 07632

Printed in the United States of America
10 9 8 7 6 5 4 3 2 1

ISBN 0-13-097510-9

Prentice-Hall International (UK) Limited, *London*
Prentice-Hall of Australia Pty. Limited, *Sydney*
Prentice-Hall Canada Inc., *Toronto*
Prentice-Hall Hispanoamericana, S.A., *Mexico*
Prentice-Hall of India Private Limited, *New Delhi*
Prentice-Hall of Japan, Inc., *Tokyo*
Simon & Schuster Asia Pte. Ltd., *Singapore*
Editora Prentice-Hall do Brasil, Ltda., *Rio de Janeiro*

CONTENTS

POETRY

18   TONE: THE CREATION OF ATTITUDE IN POETRY   678

21   SYMBOLISM AND ALLUSION: WINDOWS TO A WIDE EXPANSE OF MEANING

24   THREE POETIC CAREERS: JOHN DONNE, EMILY DICKINSON, AND ROBERT FROST   **865**

25   ADDITIONAL POEMS   910

DRAMA

APPENDICES

Thematic Table
of Contents

For analytical purposes, the following alternative table of contents groups the selections into twenty separate thematic categories. The subject headings are advisory at best; they are *not* meant to dictate approaches or interpretations. Although many works belong naturally and easily within the niches we have provided, some of the works defy exclusive classification. We have accordingly assigned such works to two or more of the classifications.

For convenience, we have shortened a few of the titles. Thus we refer to "A Refusal to Mourn" by Dylan Thomas, and to "That Time of Year" by Shakespeare, and so on, using recognizable short titles whenever possible rather than the full titles that appear in the regular table of contents, the text itself, and the index.

HUSBANDS AND WIVES

Stories

Poems

Plays

THE INDIVIDUAL AND SOCIETY

Stories

Poems

Plays

*The works by Chioles, Ozick, Zabytko, Eberhart, Georgakas, Jarrell, Kernan, Layton, Quasimodo, and Radnóti are concerned with issues of World War II. More specifically concerned with the Holocaust are works by Ozick, Zabytko, Kernan, Layton, Quasimodo, and Radnóti. The works by Zabytko, Northrup, Weigl, and Wojahn are concerned with the Vietnamese War. Crane's poem concerns European wars that he covered as a news correspondent in the 1890s. The poems by Dickinson and Whitman are derived from the Civil War, while the works by Hemingway, Hardy, Owen, Sassoon, and Seeger are related to World War I. Forché's poem concerns the civil war in El Salvador during the 1980s. Clark's story and Nash's poem refer to the effects of immensely destructive future wars.

Preface to the Fourth Edition

Like the past editions of *Literature: An Introduction to Reading and Writing*, the fourth edition is a carefully chosen anthology. There are fifty-four stories, 366 poems, and sixteen dramatic works. Each work is suitable for discussion either alone or in comparison. Nine stories, thirty-five poems, and one play are new, and one play has been restored from the first and second editions.

The book is unique among anthologies, however, because it is dedicated throughout to the interlocking processes of writing and reading. Because writing is a major mode of thinking, it is an essential reinforcement of reading. Students who write about what they read learn their assignments well. As they plan and develop their essays, paragraphs, and answers, they necessarily grow as thinkers. Such a combined approach is the essential quality of *Literature: An Introduction to Reading and Writing*.

The fourth edition reaffirms another principle to which the book is dedicated—flexibility. The earlier editions have been used for introduction-to-literature courses, genre courses, and both composition and composition-and-literature courses. Flexibility and adaptability have been the key to this variety. Instructors may use the book for classroom discussion, panel discussions, essay or paragraph-length assignments, and special topics not covered in class. Students may find incentives for understanding and writing about literature through questions, study and writing guides, and also through many suggestions for strengthening their own writing—in both essays and examinations.

While we stress the value of our book as a teaching tool, we also emphasize that literature is to be enjoyed and loved. Sometimes we neglect the truth that study and delight are complementary, and that intellectual stimulation and emotional enjoyment develop not only from the immediate responses of amusement, involvement, and sympathy, but also from the understanding, contemplation, and confidence generated by expanding skills and knowledge. We therefore hope that the selections in the fourth edition of *Literature: An Introduction to Reading and Writing* will teach students about humanity, about their own perceptions, feelings, and lives, and about the timeless patterns of human existence. We hope they will take delight in such discoveries, and grow as they make them. We see the book as a stepping stone to lifelong understanding and joy in great literature.

Features and Innovations

Most of the works chosen here are by American, British, and Canadian authors, but also represented are writers of France, Italy, Norway, South America, ancient Greece and Rome, and Russia. As one might expect, we have included a number of writers with secure places in the history of literature, such as Sophocles, Shakespeare, Wordsworth, Keats, Poe, Dickinson, Ibsen, Frost, Hemingway, Lowell, Welty, Miller, Olds, Plath, and Williams. We have also chosen authors who are less well known, along with authors, such as Northrup and Zabytko, from a variety of cultural and ethnic groups. The anthology includes works by men and women, blacks and whites, Hispanics and Native Americans, conservatives and liberals, heterosexuals and gays/Lesbians, people with strong religious convictions and others who are indifferent to religion. At the suggestion of a number of readers for making the "Stories for Study" and "Poems for Study" within the fiction and poetry chapters easier to use, these selections are now arranged alphabetically, by authors' last names, rather than chronologically, as in the past.

In the fourth edition, all the chapter introductions have been reorganized, rewritten, revised, clarified, and generally strengthened. The sections marked "Questions for Discovering Ideas" and "Strategies for Organizing Ideas" have also been revised and refocused, with the goal of helping students concentrate on writing assignments.

We have also integrated many new art reproductions and illustrations into the chapter discussions. We hope that these reproductions, together with others that instructors might add, will encourage comparison-and-contrast discussions and essays about the relationship of literature and art.

Of particular note is that we have included a new "career" chapter on fiction, thus matching the chapter on "Poetic Careers" (Chapter 24) of the first three editions. The new Chapter 11 includes four stories by Edith Wharton. Each of these chapters contains brief introductions and selective bibliographies for further study.

Organization

Because of the successful classroom use of the first three editions of *Literature: An Introduction to Reading and Writing*, the organization of the fourth edition has remained the same. We have arranged the sections in the commonly accepted order of fiction, poetry, and drama. This organization gives instructors the flexibility to choose assignments from any section and permits students to analyze various aspects of literature one at a time and in depth. Each major section begins with a comprehensive chapter. If time is short, these chapters may be assigned in lieu of the detailed chapters to give students an overview of the respective genres. In the fiction and poetry sections, the detailed chapters cover elements such as character, setting, tone, imagery, symbolism, and theme. In the section on drama, the detailed chapters deal with major categories such as tragedy and comedy. As in the first three editions, both the fiction and poetry sections conclude with a chapter containing many additional works for further study.

To make *Literature: An Introduction to Reading and Writing* as flexible as possible, we have added the "Thematic Table of Contents" that had previously been included only in our Instructor's Manual. In this table, which follows the full Table of Contents, twenty thematic topics are provided, such as *Women and Men; Faith and Doubt; Conformity and Rebellion; The Role of Women; Race, Ethnicity, and Nationality;* and *Innocence and Experience*. Under these topics, generous numbers of stories, poems, and plays are listed (many in a number of categories), so that entire thematic units may be created should instructors wish to use them. In the fourth edition a number of works have been added which pertain to the Second World War and the Holocaust—in observation of the recent commemoration of the fiftieth anniversary of the armed uprising in the Warsaw Ghetto. Instructors using the works as a unit may wish to relate them to films like *The Diary of Anne Frank; Europa, Europa; Escape from Sobibor;* and *Schindler's List.*

THE FICTION SECTION.   In the fiction section the number of stories has been increased to fifty-four. We emphasize that twenty-seven of the stories are by women, making the story selections one of the most balanced to be found in any comprehensive anthology.

To strengthen the connection between reading and dramatization, a number of stories are included that are available on videocassettes. These may be used as teaching tools for support and interpretation. In addition, for unique comparison we include two versions of the same subject matter—a short story and a one-act play—by the same author: Susan Glaspell's "A Jury of Her Peers" and *Trifles* (in the drama section).

Responding to requests by instructors and students, we have added brief biographies of the fiction writers as headnotes to each story, along with photographs (when available). The intention of these new biographies is to provide location, education, noteworthy details, special honors, and brief references to other works by the same authors.

THE POETRY SECTION.   The poetry section is confined almost exclusively to poems in English, by men and women alike—academicians and business people, professionals and amateurs, prize recipients and some who will eventually be recipients, some aristocrats and some ex-slaves. The poems have been chosen for their excellence—with the few exceptions being included for illustrative purposes.

The thirteen poetry chapters are arranged according to particular characteristics or techniques (e.g., symbolism, form, myth), in the expectation that the book will be used to teach these important aspects of poetry. But the selections are also comprehensive enough to permit valid observations about the history of poetry in both England and the United States.

Because the poetry section may often be used for reference as well as study and writing assignments, the comprehensiveness of the chapter on prosody has been preserved, although a short exposition of special rhythms has been separately designated so that instructors may emphasize it (or pass it by) if they wish.

We have added biographies of each of the anthologized poets so that the poetry section may be parallel with the drama and fiction sections. To avoid being cumbersome, we have included these biographies in a new appendix (E). Because biographical material about Shakespeare is included in the drama section, and also because some of the anthologized poets also wrote stories (Crane, Poe, Walker), Appendix E refers the reader to appropriate pages elsewhere in the text where the relevant biographies are contained.

THE DRAMA SECTION. The drama section, which includes fourteen complete plays, has also been revised to emphasize its usefulness for students. The introductions for both tragedy and comedy have been entirely rewritten and updated; indeed, all the introductions have been redesigned to make them more comprehensive than in the past. Of special note is the addition of Langston Hughes's important and powerful play *Mulatto* (1935), together with a discussion of Hughes's place in African-American drama.

Five of the longer plays from the previous edition have been retained because they are important in an introductory study of drama (*Oedipus the King, Hamlet, A Midsummer Night's Dream, Death of a Salesman, The Glass Menagerie*). Added to these is Ibsen's *A Doll House*, which brings the total of longer plays to six. At a mid-point with regard to length are *Love Is the Doctor* and *Mulatto*. In an anthology of this scope, the six short plays (*Am I Blue, The Bear, Before Breakfast, Tea Party, The Sandbox, Trifles*) are valuable because they may be covered within a single classroom period and may be enlivened by having parts acted out by students. Indeed, Keller's *Tea Party* is brief enough to permit both reading and discussion in a single hour.

At the suggestion of a number of instructors who like to use films, a unique feature of the third edition—the chapter on film—is retained, and an introduction matches those in the other chapters. We have kept the scenes from *Citizen Kane*, by Welles and Mankiewicz, and *The Turning Point* by Laurents. With these film-script selections, the drama section now contains sixteen separate works.

THE APPENDICES. The text includes five appendices, on the topics of: (A) Examinations, (B) Comparison-contrast essays, (C) Research essays, including an emphasis on computer-based online bibliographical research, (D) Current critical approaches to literature, and (E) Biographies of poets included in the poetry section. Of these, D and E are new. Appendix E has already been described. Of particular note, Appendix D contains brief descriptions of critical approaches that have proved important in twentieth-century literary studies, such as New Criticism, structuralism, and feminism, as well as Deconstruction and Reader-Response criticism. A number of the writing topics at the ends of the twenty-five detailed chapters suggest how students may effectively connect relevant critical approaches to individual works.

The Apparatus

QUESTIONS. Following each selection in most of the chapters are study questions designed to help students explore and understand the selection. Some questions are factual and may be quickly answered. Others provoke extended thought and classroom discussion and may also serve for both in-class and out-of-class writing assignments. At the ends of twenty-six chapters we include a number of more general "Writing Topics." These are designed to promote comparison and contrast and to suggest creative-writing assignments (for example, "Write a poem," or "Compose a short scene"). Unique about the creative-writing topics is that students are asked not only to write creatively, but also to analyze their own creative processes.

DATES. To place the various works in historical context, we include the life dates for all authors. Because some contemporary authors are private and elusive, however, it has been necessary to make a very small number of informed estimates. All the authors are listed together chronologically on the inside front covers. Along with the title of each anthologized work, we give the date of publication, along with a date of composition, when known, in parentheses.

NUMBERING. For convenient reference, we have adopted a regular style of numbering the selections by fives, as follows:

Stories:	every fifth *paragraph.*
Poems:	every fifth *line.*
Poetic plays:	every fifth *line,* starting at *1* with each new scene and act.
Prose plays:	every fifth *speech,* starting at *1* with each new scene and act.

GLOSSES. For the poetry and poetic plays, we provide brief *marginal* glosses wherever they are needed. For all works, including poetry, we supply explanatory *footnotes* when necessary. Words and phrases that are glossed or footnoted are highlighted by a small degree sign (°).

In the introductory discussions to the various chapters, key terms and concepts are **boldfaced**, and these are gathered alphabetically and explained briefly, with relevant page numbers in the text, in a comprehensive glossary at the back of the book. To emphasize their importance, the terms in the glossary are also listed, with page numbers, in the inside back cover.

SEPARATE SUB-DISCUSSIONS WITHIN THE CHAPTERS. In some of the chapters and appendices (particularly in Chapter 1), separately framed sections contain brief discussions of a number of important and related matters. The topics chosen for this treatment—such as the use of tenses in discussing a work, the use of authorial names, the concept of decorum, and the use of computerized library reference systems—were based on feedback from instructors and students.

Writing About Literature

The integration of reading literature and writing essays, a major goal of the book, begins in Chapter 1. As in the second and third editions, Guy de Maupassant's famous story "The Necklace" is printed along with sample marginal comments to illustrate the process of active response. The comments are then embodied within an expanding set of prewriting activities: journal entries, brainstorming and freewriting, general observations, selected details focusing on a major aspect for development, an essay outline, and an early draft of an essay that has evolved out of the preliminary work. Following this section is an extensive analysis of revising—sharpening the focus, stressing pertinent evidence, and refining language. A revision of the earlier draft is then included to demonstrate how greater breadth, emphasis, and clarity are achieved by application of the principles developed throughout Chapter 1.

In the detailed chapters, each of our "Writing About..." guides following the selections is designed to help students progress from reading to responding and thinking, and then to planning and writing. Taken with the introductory discussions, these guides give students comprehensive assistance for thinking and writing. Of major importance is that the guides stress the actual *process* of writing: responding to a work, raising questions about it, organizing thoughts, selecting supporting details, planning the form for an essay, and writing effectively.

Beyond all this, in these writing sections we do not simply *say* what can be done with a topic of literary study, but we also *show* ways in which it might be done. Each section concludes with a sample essay exemplifying the strategies and methods brought out in the chapter. Following the essay is an analytical commentary, showing how the writing principles of the discussion have been carried out. The emphasis throughout these sections is the openness of the writing process along with the unique nature of writing for each topic—together with the need to produce completed drafts for submission.

Reading and Writing Now and in the Future

The techniques acquired in the systematic use of the fourth edition of *Literature: An Introduction to Reading and Writing* will help students in every course they may ever take and in whatever profession they follow. Students will always *read*—if not the authors contained here, then other authors, and certainly newspapers, legal documents, magazine articles, technical reports, business proposals, and much more. Although students may never again be required to write about topics like setting, structure, or poetic rhythm, they will certainly find a future need to *write*.

Indeed, the more effectively students learn to write about literature during their literature courses, the better they will be able to write later on—no matter what the topic. It is undeniable that the power to analyze problems and make convincing written and oral presentations is a major quality of leadership and success in all fields. To acquire the skills of disciplined reading and strong writing is therefore the best possible preparation that students can make for the future, whatever it may hold.

ACKNOWLEDGMENTS

As the book goes into the fourth edition, I wish to acknowledge the many people who have offered helpful advice, information, and suggestions. To name them, as Dryden says in *Absalom and Achitophel*, is to praise them. They are Professors Eileen Allman, David Bady, Alice Griffin, Robert Halli, Karen Holt, Claudia Johnson, Matthew Marino, Ruth Milberg-Kaye, Nancy Miller, Michael Paull, Dan Rubey, Scott Westrem, Mardi Valgemae, Matthew Winston, and Ruth Zerner, and also Christel Bell, Linda Bridgers, Catherine Davis, Edward Hoeppner, Anna F. Jacobs, Eleanor Tubbs, Rex Butt, Nanette Roberts, April Roberts, David Roberts, and Eve Zarin. The skilled assistance of Jonathan Roberts has been essential and invaluable at every stage of all the editions.

A number of other people have provided sterling guidance for the preparation of the fourth edition. They are Professors Susan H. Aylworth (Cal State U. at Chico), Kristin Berkey-Abbot (Trident Technical College), Jean W. Cash (James Madison U.), Bruce Henricksen (Loyola University), Will Hochman (U. of Southern Colorado), William H. Lay (Kalamazoo Valley Community College), Harriet McDuffie (U. of South Carolina), Clarinda H. Raymond (Towson State U.), Stephen John Roth (St. Thomas Aquinas), Judith P. Saunders (Marist College), Mitchell E. Summerlin (Calhoun Community College), and Deborah S. Workman (Dyke College).

I wish especially to thank Alison Reeves, English Editor of Prentice Hall. Her understanding and creativity have made working with her the greatest of pleasures. I also thank Phil Miller, Editor-in-Chief, Humanities, and Bill Oliver and Kate Morgan Jackson, former Prentice Hall English Editors, for their imagination, foresight, support, and patience in the development and revision of this project. Of major importance has been the work of Ray Mullaney, Editor-in-Chief, Development, for his pioneering work with the text and for his continued work and support. I am deeply grateful to Barbara Muller, development editor of the fourth edition, for the insight and intelligence of her many suggestions for improvement, chapter by chapter. Special words of thanks are reserved for Hilda Tauber and Andrew Roney of Prentice Hall, who have devoted their knowledge, intelligence, diligence, and skill to the many tasks needed to bring a book of this size to fruition. Additional thanks are due to Gina Sluss, for her constant support and enthusiasm, and to Kara Hado and Lee Mamunes.

It is with continued sadness that I speak of my associate, Professor Henry E. Jacobs (1946–1986) of the University of Alabama. His energy and creativity were essential in the planning and writing of the first edition. All later editions represent an extended collaboration, even though the edition I now offer is different in many details from what we would have presented together.

EDGAR V. ROBERTS
Lehman College
The City University of New York

Credits

John Chioles. "Before the Firing Squad" by John Chioles. Copyright © 1983 by John Chioles. Reprinted by permission of PEN Syndicated Fiction Project.

Sandra Cisneros. "The House on Mango Street" from *The House on Mango Street* by Sandra Cisneros. Copyright © 1989 by Sandra Cisneros, Vintage Books/Random House 1991. Reprinted by permission of Sasan Bergholz Literary Services, New York, NY.

Walter Van Tilburg Clark. "The Portable Phonograph" by Walter Van Tilburg Clark. Copyright 1941, © 1969 by Walter Van Tilburg Clark. Reprinted by permission of International Creative Management, Inc.

Lucille Clifton. "homage to my hips" from *Good Woman: Poems and a Memoir 1969–1980* by Lucille Clifton. Copyright © 1987 by Lucille Clifton. Reprinted by permission of Curtis Brown Ltd.

Lucille Clifton. "this morning" and "the poet" from *Good Woman: Poems and a Memoir 1969–1980* by Lucille Clifton. Copyright © 1987 by Lucille Clifton. Reprinted by permission of BOA Editions, Ltd., 92 Park Ave., Brockport, NY 14420.

John Collier. "The Chaser" by John Collier. Copyright © 1940, © renewed 1967 by John Collier. Reprinted by permission of Harold Matson Company, Inc.

Billy Collins. "Schoolville" from *The Apple That Astonished Paris* by Billy Collins. Published by The University of Arkansas. Reprinted by permission of the publisher.

Countee Cullen. "Yet Do I Marvel" from *On These I Stand* by Countee Cullen. Copyright 1925 by Harper & Row, Publishers, Inc., renewed 1953 by Ida M. Cullen. Reprinted by permission of HarperCollins Publishers.

e. e. cummings. "Buffalo Bill's", "in Just-", "a politician is an arse upon", "if there are any heavens", "she being Brand" and "next to of course god america i" from *Complete Poems, 1904–1962* by e. e. cummings, edited by George J. Firmage. Copyright © 1923, 1925, 1926, 1931, 1935, 1938, 1939, 1940, 1944, 1945, 1946, 1947, 1948, 1949, 1950, 1951, 1952, 1953, 1954, 1955, 1956, 1957, 1958, 1959, 1960, 1961, 1962 by e. e. cummings. Copyright © 1961, 1963, 1966, 1967, 1968 by Marion Morehouse Cummings. Copyright © 1972, 1973, 1974, 1975, 1976, 1977, 1978, 1979, 1980, 1981, 1982, 1983, 1984, 1985, 1986, 1987, 1988, 1989, 1990, 1991 by the Trustees for the e. e. cummings Trust. By permission of Liveright Publishing Corporation.

James Dickey. "The Performance" and "The Lifeguard" from *Poems 1957–1967* by James Dickey. Copyright © 1967 by James Dickey. Reprinted by permission of Wesleyan University Press and University Press of New England.

James Dickey. "Kudzu" from *Helmets* by James Dickey. Copyright © 1964 by James Dickey. Reprinted by permission of Wesleyan University Press and University Press of New England.

Emily Dickinson. "I Cannot Live With You", "I Heard a Fly Buzz—When I Died", "I Like to See It Lap the Miles", "I Taste a Liquor Never Brewed", "Much Madness Is Divinest Sense", "One Need Not Be a Chamber—To Be Haunted", "The Soul Selects Her Own Society", "Success Is Counted Sweetest", "There's a Certain Slant of Light", "Because I Could Not Stop for Death", "Going to Him! Happy Letter!", "I Died for Beauty—but Was Scarce", "I'm Nobody! Who Are You?", "I Never Felt At Home—Below—," "This World Is Not Conclusion" and "A Word Made Flesh Is Seldom" from *The Poems of Emily Dickinson*, ed. by Thomas H. Johnson. Cambridge, Mass.: The Belknap Press of Harvard University Press. Copyright © 1951, 1955, 1983 by the President and Fellows of Harvard College. Reprinted by permission of the publishers and the Trustees of Amherst College.

Emily Dickinson. "After Great Pain, a Formal Feeling Comes", "My Triumph Lasted Till the Drums" and "The Heart is the Capital of the Mind" from *The Complete Poems of Emily Dickinson*, ed. by Thomas H. Johnson. Copyright 1929, 1935 by Martha Dickinson Bianchi; Copyright © renewed 1957, 1963 by Mary L. Hampson. By permission of Little, Brown and Company.

Stephen Dixon. "All Gone" by Stephen Dixon. Reprinted by permission of Johns Hopkins University Press.

H. D. (Hilda Doolittle). "Heat" from *Selected Poems* by H. D. (Hilda Doolittle). Copyright © 1957, Grove Press. "Pear Tree" from *The Collected Poems 1912–1944* by Hilda Doolittle. Copyright by the Estate of Hilda Doolittle. Reprinted by permission of New Directions Publishing Corporation.

Rita Dove. "O" from *The Yellow House on the Corner* by Rita Dove. Copyright © 1980 by Rita Dove. Reprinted by permission of Carnegie-Mellon University Press.

Andre Dubus. "The Curse" from *Selected Stories of Andre Dubus.* Copyright © 1988 by Andre Dubus. Reprinted by permission of David R. Godine, Publisher.

Richard Eberhart. "The Fury of Aerial Bombardment" and "The Groundhog" from *Collected Poems 1930–1986* by Richard Eberhart. Copyright © 1960, 1976, 1988 by Richard Eberhart. Reprinted by permission of Oxford University Press, Inc.

T. S. Eliot. "Sweeney Among the Nightingales", "The Love Song of J. Alfred Prufrock", "Eyes That Last I Saw in Tears" and "Preludes" from *Collected Poems 1909–1962* by T. S. Eliot. Copyright 1936 by Harcourt Brace & Company. Copyright © 1964, 1963 by T. S. Eliot. Reprinted by permission of Harcourt Brace & Company and Faber and Faber Ltd. "Macavity: The Mystery Cat" from *Old Possum's Book of Practical Cats* by T. S. Eliot. Copyright 1939 by T. S. Eliot and renewed 1967 by Esme Valerie Eliot. Reprinted by permission of Harcourt Brace & Company and Faber and Faber Ltd.

James Emanuel. "The Negro" by James Emanuel. Copyright © 1968. Reprinted by permission of Broadside Press.

John Engles. "Naming the Animals" from *Vivaldi in Early Fall* by John Engles. Copyright © 1981 by John Engles. Reprinted by permission of The University of Georgia Press.

Mari Evans. "I Am a Black Woman" from *I am a Black Woman* by Mari Evans. Published by William Morrow & Company, Inc. Reprinted by permission of the author.

William Faulkner. "Barn Burning" from *Collected Stories of William Faulkner.* Copyright 1939 and renewed © 1967 by Estelle Faulkner and Jill Faulkner Summers. Reprinted by permission of Random House, Inc.

Edward Field. "Icarus" from *Stand Up, Friend, with Me* by Edward Field. Copyright © 1963 by Field/Grove Press. Reprinted by permission of Grove Press.

Carolyn Forché. "Because One Is Always Forgotten" from *The Country Between Us* by Carolyn Forché. Copyright © 1981 by Carolyn Forché. Reprinted by permission of HarperCollins Publishers.

Robert Frost. "A Line-Storm Song", "The Oven Bird" and "The Strong Are Saying Nothing" from *The Poetry of Robert Frost*, ed. by Edward Connery Lathem. Copyright 1936, 1944, © 1962 by Robert Frost. Copyright © 1964 by Lesley Frost Ballantine. Copyright 1916, 1934, © 1969 by Henry Holt and Company, Inc. Reprinted by permission of Henry Holt and Company, Inc.

Robert Frost. "Stopping By Woods On a Snowy Evening", "Desert Places", "Acquainted With The Night", "A Considerable Speck", "Design", "Fire and Ice", "Mending Wall", "Misgiving", "Nothing Gold Can Stay", "The Tuft of Flowers" from *The Poetry of Robert Frost,* edited by Edward Connery Lathem. Copyright 1923, 1928, 1930, 1936, 1939, © 1969 by Henry Holt and Company, Inc. Copyright © 1964, 1967, 1970 by Lesley Frost Ballantine. Copyright 1942, 1951, © 1956, 1958, 1962 by Robert Frost. Reprinted by permission of Henry Holt and Company, Inc.

Ernest J. Gaines. "The Sky is Gray" from *Bloodline* by Ernest J. Gaines. Copyright © 1963 by Ernest J. Gaines. Used by permission of Doubleday, a division of Bantam Doubleday Dell Publishing Group, Inc.

Gabriel García Márquez. "A Very Old Man with Enormous Wings" from *Collected Stories* by Gabriel García Márquez. Copyright © 1971 by Gabriel García Márquez. Reprinted by permission of HarperCollins Publishers.

1

Introduction: Reading, Responding, and Writing About Literature

WHAT IS LITERATURE, AND WHY DO WE STUDY IT?

Literature refers to compositions that tell stories, dramatize situations, express emotions, and analyze and advocate ideas. Before the invention of writing, literary works were necessarily spoken or sung, and were retained only as long as living people performed them. In some societies, the oral tradition of literature still exists, with many poems and stories designed exclusively for spoken delivery. Even in our modern age of writing and printing, much literature is still heard aloud rather than read silently. Parents delight their children with stories and poems; poets and story writers read their works directly before live audiences; and plays and scripts are interpreted on stages and before cameras for the benefit of a vast public.

No matter how we assimilate literature, we gain much from it. In truth, readers often cannot explain why they enjoy reading, for goals and ideals are not easily articulated. There are, however, areas of general agreement about the value of systematic and extensive reading.

Literature helps us grow, both personally and intellectually. It provides an objective base for knowledge and understanding. It links us with the broader cultural, philosophic, and religious world of which we are a part. It enables us to recognize human dreams and struggles in different places and times that we would never otherwise know. It helps us develop mature sensibility and compassion for the condition of *all* living things—human, animal, and vegetable. It gives us the knowledge and perception to appreciate the beauty of order and arrangement, just as a well-structured song or a beautifully painted canvas can. It provides the comparative basis from which we can see worthiness in the aims of all people, and it therefore helps us see beauty in the world around us. It exercises our emotions through interest, concern, tension, excitement, hope, fear, regret, laughter, and sympathy. Through our cumulative experience in reading, literature shapes our goals and values by clarifying our own identities—both positively, through acceptance of the admirable in human beings, and negatively, through rejection of the sinister. It enables us to develop a perspective on events occurring locally and globally, and thereby it gives us understanding and control. It encourages us to assist creative, talented people who need recognition and support. It is one of the shaping influences of life. Literature makes us human.

TYPES OF LITERATURE: THE GENRES

Literature may be classified into four categories or *genres:* (1) prose fiction, (2) poetry, (3) drama, and (4) nonfiction prose. Usually the first three are classed as **imaginative literature.**

The genres of imaginative literature have much in common, but they also have distinguishing characteristics. **Prose fiction**, or **narrative fiction**, includes **myths, parables, romances, novels**, and **short stories**. Originally, *fiction* meant anything made up, crafted, or shaped, but today the word refers to prose stories based in the author's imagination. The essence of fiction is **narration**, the relating or recounting of a sequence of events or actions. Works of fiction usually focus on one or a few major characters who undergo a change of attitude or character as they interact with other characters and deal with problems. While fiction, like all imaginative literature, may introduce true historical details, it is not real history. Its main purpose is to interest, stimulate, instruct, and divert, not to create a precise historical record.

Poetry expresses a conversation or interchange that is grounded in the most deeply felt experiences of human beings. Poetry exists in many formal and informal shapes, from the brief **haiku** to the extensive **epic**. More economical than prose fiction in its use of words, poetry relies heavily on **imagery, figurative language,** and **sound.**

Drama is literature designed to be performed by actors. Like fiction, drama may focus on a single character or a small number of characters, and it enacts fictional events as if they were happening in the present, to be witnessed by an audience. Although most modern plays use prose dialogue, in the belief that dramatic speech should be as lifelike as possible, many plays from the past, like those of ancient Greece and Renaissance England, are in poetic form.

Nonfiction prose is the literary genre that consists of news reports, feature articles, essays, editorials, textbooks, historical and biographical works, and the like, all of which describe or interpret facts and present judgments and opinions. Major goals of nonfiction prose are truth in reporting and logic in reasoning. Whereas in imaginative literature the aim is truth to life and human nature, in nonfiction prose the goal is truth to the factual world of news, science, and history.

READING LITERATURE AND RESPONDING TO IT ACTIVELY

Do not expect a cursory reading of a literary work to produce full understanding. After a first reading, it may be embarrassingly difficult to answer pointed questions or to say anything intelligent about the work. A more careful, active reading gives us the understanding to develop well-considered answers. Obviously, we must first follow the work and understand its details, but just as importantly we must respond to the words, get at the ideas, and understand the implications of what is happening. We must apply our own experiences to verify the accuracy and truth of the situation and incidents, and we must articulate our own emotional responses to the characters and their problems.

To illustrate such active responding, the following story, "The Necklace" (1884), by the French writer Guy de Maupassant,* is printed with the sorts of marginal annotations that any reader might make during original and follow-up readings. Many observations, particularly at the beginning, are *assimilative*; that is, they do little more than record details about the action. But as the story progresses the comments reflect conclusions about the story's developing meaning. Toward the end, the comments are full rather than minimal, for they result not only from first responses, but also from considered thought. Here, then, is Maupassant's "The Necklace":

GUY DE MAUPASSANT   (1850–1893)

The Necklace   *1884*

Translated by Edgar V. Roberts

She was one of those pretty and charming women, born, as if by an error of destiny, into a family of clerks and copyists. She had no dowry, no prospects, no way of getting known, courted, loved, married by a rich and distinguished man. She finally settled for a marriage with a minor clerk in the Ministry of Education.

> "She" is pretty but poor. Apparently there is no other life for her than marriage. Without connections, she has no entry into high society, and marries an insignificant clerk.

She was a simple person, without the money to dress well, but she was as unhappy as if she had gone through bankruptcy, for women have neither rank nor race. In place of high birth or important family connections, they can rely only on their beauty, their grace, and their charm. Their inborn finesse, their elegant taste, their engaging personalities,

> She is unhappy.

> A view of women that excludes the possibility of a career. In 1884, women had little else than their

---

* Maupassant, an apostle of Gustave Flaubert, was one of the major nineteenth-century French naturalists. He was an especially careful writer, devoting great attention to reality and economy of detail. His stories are focused on the difficulties and ironies of existence among not only the Parisian middle class, as in "The Necklace," but also among both peasants and higher society. Two of his better-known novels are *A Life* (1883) and *A Good Friend* (1885). Among his other famous stories are "The Rendez-vous" and "The Umbrella." "The Necklace" is notable for its concluding ironic twist, and for this reason is perhaps the best known of his stories.

which are their only power, make working-class women the equals of the grandest ladies.

She suffered constantly, feeling herself destined for all delicacies and luxuries. She suffered because of her grim apartment with its drab walls, threadbare furniture, ugly curtains. All such things, which most other women in her situation would not even have noticed, tortured her and filled her with despair. The sight of the young country girl who did her simple housework awakened in her only a sense of desolation and lost hopes. She daydreamed of large, silent anterooms, decorated with oriental tapestries and lighted by high bronze floor lamps, with two elegant valets in short culottes dozing in large armchairs under the effects of forced-air heaters. She visualized large drawing rooms draped in the most expensive silks, with fine end tables on which were placed knickknacks of inestimable value. She dreamed of the perfume of dainty private rooms, which were designed only for intimate tête-à-têtes with the closest friends, who because of their achievements and fame would make her the envy of all other women.

When she sat down to dinner at her round little table covered with a cloth that had not been washed for three days, in front of her husband who opened the kettle while declaring ecstatically, "Ah, good old boiled beef! I don't know anything better," she dreamed of expensive banquets with shining place settings, and wall hangings depicting ancient heroes and exotic birds in an enchanted forest. She imagined a gourmet-prepared main course carried on the most exquisite trays and served on the most beautiful dishes, with whispered gallantries which she would hear with a sphinxlike smile as she dined on the pink meat of a trout or the delicate wing of a quail.

5   She had no decent dresses, no jewels, nothing. And she loved nothing but these; she believed herself born only for these. She burned with the desire to please, to be envied, to be attractive and sought after.

She had a rich friend, a comrade from convent days, whom she did not want to see anymore because she suffered so much when she returned home. She would weep for the entire day afterward with sorrow, regret, despair, and misery.

Well, one evening, her husband came home glowing and carrying a large envelope.

"Here," he said, "this is something for you."

She quickly tore open the envelope and took out a card engraved with these words:

The Minister of Education and Mrs. George Ramponneau request that Mr. and Mrs. Loisel do them the

Margin notes:
personalities to get ahead.

She suffers because of her cheap belongings, wanting expensive things. She dreams of wealth and of how other women would envy her if she had all these fine things. But these luxuries are unrealistic and unattainable for her.

Her husband's taste is for plain things, while she dreams of expensive gourmet food. He has adjusted to his status. She has not.

She lives for her unrealistic dreams, and these increase her frustration.

She even thinks of giving up a rich friend because she is so depressed after visiting her.

A new section in the story.

An invitation to dinner at the Ministry of Education. A big plum.

honor of coming to dinner at the Ministry of Education on the evening of January eighth.

Instead of being delighted, as her husband had hoped, she threw the invitation spitefully on the table, muttering:

"What do you expect me to do with this?"

"But honey, I thought you'd be glad. You never get to go out, and this is a special occasion! I had a lot of trouble getting the invitation. Everyone wants one; the demand is high and not many clerks get invited. Everyone important will be there."

She looked at him angrily and stated impatiently:

"What do you expect me to wear to go there?"

He had not thought of that. He stammered:

"But your theater gown. That seems nice to me . . ."

He stopped, amazed and bewildered, as his wife began to cry. Large tears fell slowly from the corners of her eyes to her mouth. He said falteringly:

"What's wrong? What's the matter?"

But with a strong effort she had recovered, and she answered calmly as she wiped her damp cheeks:

"Nothing, except that I have nothing to wear and therefore can't go to the party. Give your invitation to someone else at the office whose wife will have nicer clothes than mine."

Distressed, he responded:

"Well, all right, Mathilde. How much would a new dress cost, something you could use at other times, but not anything fancy?"

She thought for a few moments, adding things up and thinking also of an amount that she could ask without getting an immediate refusal and a frightened outcry from the frugal clerk.

Finally she responded tentatively:

"I don't know exactly, but it seems to me that I could get by on four hundred francs."

He blanched slightly at this, because he had set aside just that amount to buy a shotgun for Sunday lark-hunts the next summer with a few friends in the Plain of Nanterre.

However, he said:

"All right, you've got four hundred francs, but make it a pretty gown."

As the day of the party drew near, Mrs. Loisel seemed sad, uneasy, anxious, even though her gown was all ready. One evening her husband said to her:

"What's the matter? You've been acting funny for several days."

She answered:

Marginal notes:

10

It only upsets her.

She declares that she hasn't anything to wear. He tries to persuade her that her theater gown might do for the occasion.

15

20

Her name is Mathilde.

He volunteers to pay for a new dress.

She is manipulating him.

25

The gown will cost him his next summer's vacation. (He doesn't seem to have included her in his plans.)

A new section, the third in the story. The day of the party is near.

30

"It's awful, but I don't have any jewels to wear, not a single gem, nothing to dress up my outfit. I'll look like a beggar. I'd almost rather not go to the party."

He responded:

"You can wear a corsage of cut flowers. This year it's all the rage. For only ten francs you can get two or three gorgeous roses."

35   She was not convinced.

"No . . . there's nothing more humiliating than looking shabby in the company of rich women."

But her husband exclaimed:

"God, but you're silly! Go to your friend Mrs. Forrestier, and ask her to lend you some jewelry. You know her well enough to do that."

She uttered a cry of joy:

40   "That's right. I hadn't thought of that."

The next day she went to her friend's house and described her problem.

Mrs. Forrestier went to her mirrored wardrobe, took out a large jewel box, opened it, and said to Mrs. Loisel:

"Choose, my dear."

She saw bracelets, then a pearl necklace, then a Venetian cross of finely worked gold and gems. She tried on the jewelry in front of a mirror, and hesitated, unable to make up her mind about each one. She kept asking:

45   "Do you have anything else?"

"Certainly. Look to your heart's content. I don't know what will please you most."

Suddenly she found, in a black satin box, a superb diamond necklace, and her heart throbbed with desire for it. Her hands shook as she picked it up. She fastened it around her neck, watched it gleam at her throat, and looked at herself ecstatically.

Then she asked, haltingly and anxiously:

"Could you lend me this, nothing but this?"

50   "Why yes, certainly."

She jumped up, hugged her friend joyfully, then hurried away with her treasure.

The day of the party came. Mrs. Loisel was a success. She was prettier than anyone else, stylish, graceful, smiling, and wild with joy. All the men saw her, asked her name, sought to be introduced. All the important administrators stood in line to waltz with her. The Minister himself eyed her.

She danced joyfully, passionately, intoxicated with pleasure, thinking of nothing but the moment, in the triumph of her beauty, in the glory of her success, on cloud nine with happiness made up of all the admiration, of all the aroused desire, of this victory so complete and so sweet to the heart of any woman.

Marginal notes:

Now she complains that she doesn't have any nice jewelry. She is manipulating him again.

She has a very good point, but there seems to be no way out.

He proposes a solution: borrow jewelry from Mrs. Forrestier, who is apparently the rich friend mentioned earlier.

Mathilde will have her choice of jewels.

A "superb" diamond necklace.

This is what she wants, just this.

She leaves with the "treasure."

A new section.

The party. Mathilde is a huge success.

Another judgment about women. Don't men want admiration, too?

She did not leave until four o'clock in the morning. Her husband, since midnight, had been sleeping in a little empty room with three other men whose wives had also been enjoying themselves.

Loisel, with other husbands, is bored, while the wives are having a ball.

5 He threw over her shoulders the shawl that he had brought for the trip home, a modest everyday wrap, the poverty of which contrasted sharply with the elegance of her evening gown. She felt it and hurried away to avoid being noticed by the other women who luxuriated in rich furs.

Ashamed of her wrap, she rushes away to avoid being seen.

Loisel tried to hold her back:

"Wait a minute. You'll catch cold outdoors. I'll call a cab."

But she paid no attention and hurried down the stairs. When they reached the street they found no carriages. They began to look for one, shouting at cabmen passing by at a distance.

They walked toward the Seine, desperate, shivering. Finally, on a quay, they found one of those old night-going buggies that are seen in Paris only after dark, as if they were ashamed of their wretched appearance in daylight.

A comedown after the nice evening. They take a wretched-looking buggy home.

It took them to their door, on the Street of Martyrs, and they sadly climbed the stairs to their flat. For her, it was finished. As for him, he could think only that he had to begin work at the Ministry of Education at ten o'clock.

"Street of Martyrs." Is this name significant?

Loisel is down-to-earth.

She took the shawl off her shoulders, in front of the mirror, to see herself once more in her glory. But suddenly she cried out. The necklace was no longer around her neck!

Her husband, already half undressed, asked:

"What's wrong?"

She turned toward him frantically:

SHE HAS LOST THE NECKLACE!

"I . . . I . . . I no longer have Mrs. Forrestier's necklace."

He stood up bewildered:

"What! . . . How! . . . It's not possible!"

And they looked in the folds of the gown, in the folds of the shawl, in the pockets, everywhere. They found nothing.

They can't find it.

He asked:

"You're sure you still had it when you left the party?"

"Yes. I checked it in the vestibule of the Ministry."

"But if you had lost it in the street, we would have heard it fall. It must be in the cab."

"Yes, probably. Did you notice the number?"

"No. Did you see it?"

"No."

Overwhelmed, they looked at each other. Finally, Loisel got dressed again:

"I'm going out to retrace all our steps," he said, "to see if I can find the necklace that way."

And he went out. She stayed in her evening dress, without the energy to get ready for bed, stretched out in a chair, drained of strength and thought.

He goes out to search for the necklace.

Her husband came back at about seven o'clock. He had found nothing.

But is unsuccessful.

80   He went to Police Headquarters and to the newspapers to announce a reward. He went to the small cab companies, and finally he followed up even the slightest hopeful lead.

He really tries. He is doing his best.

She waited the entire day, in the same enervated state, in the face of this frightful disaster.

Loisel came back in the evening, his face pale and haggard. He had found nothing.

"You'll have to write to your friend," he said, "that you broke a clasp on her necklace and that you are having it fixed. That will give us time to look around."

Loisel's plan to explain delaying the return. He takes charge, is resourceful.

She wrote as he dictated.

85   At the end of a week they had lost all hope.

Things are hopeless.

And Loisel, looking five years older, declared:

"We'll have to see about replacing the jewels."

The next day they took the case which had contained the necklace and went to the jeweler whose name was inside. He looked at his books:

They hunt for a replacement.

"I wasn't the one, Madam, who sold the necklace. I only made the case."

90   Then they went from jeweler to jeweler, searching for a necklace like the other one, racking their memories, both of them sick with worry and anguish.

In a shop in the Palais-Royal, they found a necklace of diamonds that seemed to them exactly like the one they were looking for. It was priced at forty thousand francs. They could buy it for thirty-six thousand.

A new diamond necklace will cost 36,000 francs.

They got the jeweler to promise not to sell it for three days. And they made an agreement that he would buy it back for thirty-four thousand francs if the original was recovered before the end of February.

They make a deal with the jeweler. (Is Maupassant hinting that things might work out for them?)

Loisel had saved eighteen thousand francs that his father had left him. He would have to borrow the rest.

It will take all of Loisel's inheritance plus another 18,000 francs that must be borrowed at enormous rates of interest.

He borrowed, asking a thousand francs from one, five hundred from another, five louis° here, three louis there. He wrote promissory notes, undertook ruinous obligations, did business with finance companies and the whole tribe of loan sharks. He compromised himself for the remainder of his days, risked his signature without knowing whether he would be able to honor it, and, terrified by anguish over the future, by the black misery that was about to descend on him, by the prospect of all kinds of physical deprivations and moral tortures, he went to get the new necklace, and put down thirty-six thousand francs on the jeweler's counter.

° *louis:* a gold coin worth twenty francs.

5   Mrs. Loisel took the necklace back to Mrs. Forrestier, who said with an offended tone:

"You should have brought it back sooner; I might have needed it."

Mrs. Forrestier complains about the delay.

She did not open the case, as her friend feared she might. If she had noticed the substitution, what would she have thought? What would she have said? Would she not have taken her for a thief?

Is this enough justification for not telling the truth? It seems to be for the Loisels.

Mrs. Loisel soon discovered the horrible life of the needy. She did her share, however, completely, heroically. That horrifying debt had to be paid. She would pay. They dismissed the maid; they changed their address; they rented an attic flat.

A new section, the fifth.

She learned to do the heavy housework, dirty kitchen jobs. She washed the dishes, wearing away her manicured fingernails on greasy pots and encrusted baking dishes. She handwashed dirty linen, shirts, and dish towels that she hung out on the line to dry. Each morning, she took the garbage down to the street, and she carried up water, stopping at each floor to catch her breath. And, dressed in cheap house dresses, she went to the fruit dealer, the grocer, the butchers, with her basket under her arms, haggling, insulting, defending her measly cash penny by penny.

They suffer to repay their debts. Loisel works late at night. Mathilde accepts a cheap attic flat, and does all the heavy housework herself to save on domestic help.

She pinches pennies, and haggles with the local merchants.

They had to make installment payments every month, and, to buy more time, to refinance loans.

They struggle to meet payments.

The husband worked evenings to make fair copies of tradesmen's accounts, and late into the night he made copies at five cents a page.

Mr. Loisel moonlights to make extra money.

And this life lasted ten years.

At the end of ten years, they had paid back everything—everything—including the extra charges imposed by loan sharks and the accumulation of compound interest.

The last section. For ten years they endure. They have finally paid back the entire debt.

Mrs. Loisel looked old now. She had become the strong, hard, and rude woman of poor households. Her hair unkempt, with uneven skirts and rough, red hands, she spoke loudly, washed floors with large buckets of water. But sometimes, when her husband was at work, she sat down near the window, and she dreamed of that evening so long ago, of that party, where she had been so beautiful and so admired.

Mrs. Loisel (how come the narrator does not say "Mathilde"?) is roughened and aged by the work. But she has behaved "heroically" (¶ 98), and has shown her mettle.

What would life have been like if she had not lost that necklace? Who knows? Who knows? Life is so peculiar, so uncertain. How little a thing it takes to destroy you or to save you!

A moral? Our lives are shaped by small, uncertain things; we hang by a thread.

Well, one Sunday, when she had gone for a stroll along the Champs-Elysées to relax from the cares of the

A scene on the Champs-Elysées. She sees Jeanne Forrestier, after ten years.

week, she suddenly noticed a woman walking with a child. It
was Mrs. Forrestier, still youthful, still beautiful, still attractive.

Mrs. Loisel felt moved. Would she speak to her? Yes,
certainly. And now that she had paid, she could tell all. Why
not?

She walked closer.

"Hello, Jeanne."

110   The other gave no sign of recognition and was astonished to be addressed so familiarly by this working-class
woman. She stammered:

"But . . . Madam! . . . I don't know . . . You must have
made a mistake."

"No. I'm Mathilde Loisel."

Her friend cried out.

"Oh! . . . My poor Mathilde, you've changed so much."   Jeanne notes Mathilde's
115   "Yes. I've had some tough times since I saw you last; in   changed appearance.
fact, hardships . . . and all because of you! . . ."

"Of me . . . how so?"

"You remember the diamond necklace that you lent   Mathilde tells Jeanne
me to go to the party at the Ministry of Education?"   everything.

"Yes. What then?"

"Well, I lost it."

120   "How, since you gave it back to me?"

"I returned another exactly like it. And for ten years
we've been paying for it. You understand that this wasn't easy
for us, who have nothing. . . . Finally it's over, and I'm
damned glad."

Mrs. Forrestier stopped her.

"You say that you bought a diamond necklace to replace mine?"

"Yes, you didn't notice it, eh? It was exactly like yours."   SURPRISE! The lost neck-
125   And she smiled with proud and childish joy.   lace was *not* real diamonds, and the Loisels
Mrs. Forrestier, deeply moved, took both her hands.   slaved for no reason at all.
"Oh, my poor Mathilde! But mine was only costume   But hard work and sacrifice probably brought out
jewelry. At most, it was worth only five hundred francs! . . ."   better qualities in
Mathilde than she other-
wise might have shown. Is
this the moral of the story?

READING AND RESPONDING IN A JOURNAL

The marginal comments demonstrate the active reading-responding process
you should apply with everything you read. Use the margins in your text to
record your comments and questions, but also keep a **journal** for lengthier
responses. Your journal, which may be a notebook or a computer file, will be
immeasurably useful to you as you shape your initial impressions into
thoughtful analysis.

In keeping your journal, the objective is to learn assigned works inside and out, and then to say perceptive things about them. To achieve this goal, you need to read the work more than once. You will need a good note-taking system so that as you read, you can develop a "memory bank" of your own knowledge about a work. You can draw from this fund of ideas when you begin to write.

GUIDELINES FOR READING

1. Observations for Basic Understanding
    a. Explain words, situations, and concepts. Write down words that are new or not immediately clear. If you find a passage that you do not quickly understand, decide whether the problem arises from unknown words. Use your dictionary and record the relevant meanings in your journal, but be sure that these meanings clarify your understanding. Make note of special difficulties so that you may ask your instructor about them.
    b. Determine what is happening. For a story or play, where do the actions take place? What do they show? Who is involved? Who is the major figure? Why is he/she major? What relationships do the characters have with each other? What concerns do the characters have? What do they do? Who says what to whom? How do the speeches advance the action and reveal the characters? For a poem, what is the situation? Who is talking, and to whom? What does the speaker say about the situation? Why does the poem end as it does and where it does?
    c. Trace developing patterns. Make an outline or scheme for the story or main idea: What conflicts appear? Do these conflicts exist between people, groups, or ideas? How does the author resolve them? Is one force, idea, or side the winner? Why? How do you respond to the winner, or loser?
    d. Use separate cards to write out in full some of the passages that you think are interesting, well written, and important. Keep these passages within easy reach, and when riding public transportation, walking to class, or otherwise not occupying your time, memorize them.
    e. Always, note any questions, so you can use them in class and in your own further study.
2. Notes on First Impressions
    a. In your marginal notations, record your first responses to the work. What did you think was funny, memorable, noteworthy, or otherwise striking? Did you laugh, smile, worry, get scared, feel a thrill, learn a great deal, feel proud, find a lot to think about? In your journal, record these responses and explain them more fully.
    b. Describe interesting characterizations, events, techniques, and ideas. If you like a character or idea, explain what you like, and do the same for characters and ideas you don't like. Is there anything else in the work that you especially like or dislike? Are parts easy or difficult to understand? Why? Are there any surprises? What was your reaction to them? Be sure to use your own words when writing your explanations.

Specimen Journal Entries

The following entries suggest how the guidelines may help you in your first writing attempts. The important issue is not the order of observation, which follows the time sequence of the story, but rather that there are enough observations and responses to be useful later, both for additional study and for a developing essay. Notice that the entries are not only comments, but also questions.

JOURNAL ENTRIES ON MAUPASSANT'S "THE NECKLACE"

Early in the story, Mathilde seems spoiled. She is poor, or at least lower middle class, but is unable to face her own situation.

As a dreamer, she seems harmless. Her daydreams about a fancy home, with all the expensive belongings, are not unusual. Most people dream about being well off.

She is embarrassed by her husband's taste for plain food. The story contrasts her taste for trout and quail with Loisel's cheaper favorites.

Only when the Loisels get the invitation does Mathilde seem especially difficult. Her wish for an expensive dress (the cost of Loisel's entire vacation), and then her wanting the jewelry, are problems.

Her success at the party shows that she has the charm the story-teller talks about in paragraph 2. She seems never to have had any other chance to exert her power.

The worst part of her personality is shown when she hurries away from the party because she is ashamed of her everyday shawl. It is Mathilde's unhappiness and unwillingness to adjust to her modest means that cause the financial downfall of the Loisels. It is her fault.

Borrowing the money to replace the necklace shows that both Loisel and Mathilde have a strong sense of honor. Making up for the loss is good, even if it destroys them financially.

There are some nice touches, like Loisel's seeming to be five years older (paragraph 86), and his staying with the other husbands of women enjoying themselves (paragraph 54). These are well done.

It's too bad that Loisel and Mathilde don't confess to Jeanne that the jewels are lost. Their pride or their honor stops them—or perhaps their fear of being accused of theft.

Their ten years of slavish work (paragraphs 98–102) show how they have come down in life. Mathilde does all her work by hand, so she really does pitch in, and is heroic.

Mathilde becomes loud and frumpy when living in the attic flat (paragraph 98), but she also develops strength. She does what she has to. The earlier apartment and the elegance of her imaginary rooms had brought out her limitations.

The setting of the Champs-Elysées also reflects her character, for she feels free there to tell Jeanne about the disastrous loss and sacrifice (paragraph 121), producing the surprise ending.

The narrator's thought about how "little a thing it takes to destroy you or save you" (paragraph 105) is full of thought. The necklace is little, but it makes a huge problem. This creates the story's irony.

Questions: Is this story more about the surprise ending or about the character of Mathilde? Is she to be condemned or admired? Does the outcome stem from the little things that make us or break us, as the narrator suggests, or on the difficulty of rising above one's economic class, which seems true, or both? What do the speaker's remarks about women's status mean? (Remember, the story was published in 1884.) This probably isn't relevant, but wouldn't Jeanne, after hearing about the substitution, give the full value of the necklace to the Loisels, and wouldn't they then be pretty well off?

These are reasonable, if fairly full, remarks and observations about "The Necklace." Use your journal similarly for *all* reading assignments. If your assignment is simply to learn about a work, general notes like these should be enough. If you are preparing for a test, you might write pointed observations more in line with what is happening in your class, and also write and answer your own questions (see Appendix A, *Taking Examinations on Literature*). If you have a writing assignment, these entries can help you focus more closely on your topic—such as character, idea, or setting. Whatever your purpose, always use a journal when you read, and put into it as many details and responses as you can. Your journal will then be invaluable in helping you develop your ideas and refresh your memory.

WRITING ESSAYS ON LITERARY TOPICS

Writing is the sharpened, focused expression of thought and study. It begins with the search for something to say—an idea. Not all ideas are equal; some are better than others, and getting good ideas is an ability that you will develop the more you think and write. As you discover ideas and write them down, you will also improve your perceptions and increase your critical faculties.

Learning to think and write about literature will also prepare you to write about other topics. Because literature itself contains the subject material, though not in a systematic way, of philosophy, religion, psychology, sociology, and politics, learning to analyze literature and to write about it will also improve your capacity to deal with these and other disciplines.

At the outset, it is important to realize that writing is a process that, for most of us, begins in uncertainty. When you read a complete, polished, well-formed piece of writing, you might initially believe that the writer wrote this perfect version in only one draft, and never needed to make any changes and improvements in it at all. Nothing could be further from the truth, for writing becomes presentable only by considerable thought and work.

If you could see the early drafts of writing you admire, you would be surprised—but you might also be encouraged—to see that good writers are also human, and that their first versions are messy, uncertain, vague, tangential, tentative, and incomplete. They may not even like these first drafts. But then they build on this first work: They discard some details, add others, chop paragraphs in half and reassemble the parts elsewhere, throw out much (and then maybe recover some of it), revise or completely rewrite sentences, change words, correct misspellings, and add new material to tie all parts together and make them flow smoothly.

For good and not-so-good writers alike, the writing task follows three basic stages. The first—*discovering ideas*—shares many of the qualities of ordinary conversation. Usually, conversation is random and disorganized. It shifts from topic to topic, often without any apparent cause, and it is repetitive. In discovering ideas for writing, your process is much the same, for you jump from idea to idea, and do not necessarily identify the connections or bridges between them. By the next step, however—*creating the early, rough draft of an essay*—your thought should be less like ordinary conversation and more like classroom discussion. Such discussions generally stick to a point, but they are also free and spontaneous, and digressions often occur. At the final stage—*preparing a finished essay*—your thinking must be sharply focused, and your writing must be concise and highly organized.

If you find that writing a finished essay seems halting and digressive, remember that *it is important just to start*—no matter how unacceptable your first efforts seem. Make the beginning, and force yourself to come to grips with the materials. Beginning to write does not commit you to your first ideas. They are not holy and untouchable just because they are on paper or on your computer screen. You may throw them out in favor of new ideas. You may also cross out words, or move sections around, as you wish. But if you keep your first thoughts buried in your mind, you will have nothing to work with. It is essential to accept the uncertainties in the writing process and make them work *for* you rather than *against* you.

DISCOVERING IDEAS

Ideas cannot be known and shaped until they take a written form. Thus, the first act of the writing process is to uncover, discover, and drag out of your mind and reading responses all the observations you can make about a particular topic. Write down anything and everything that occurs to you about the work. If you have questions you can't answer, write them down and plan to answer them later. In your attempts to discover ideas, use the following prewriting techniques.

Brainstorming

Brainstorming is an informal way to describe your own written but private no-holds-barred conversation about what you write. The technique is essential in the early writing process. When you begin brainstorming you let your mind play over all the possibilities you generate as you consider the work, or over a particular element of the work, or over your own earlier responses to it. In effect, you are conversing with yourself to develop ideas by writing down all your thoughts, whether they fall into patterns or seem disjointed, unlikely, or even ridiculous. (This is also sometimes called **freewriting.**) At this time, do not try to organize or criticize your thoughts. Later you can decide which ideas to keep and which to throw out. For now, *the goal is to get all your ideas on paper or on the computer screen.* As you develop your essay, you may, at any time, return to the brainstorming process to initiate and develop any new ideas that you think you will need.

Focusing on Specific Topics

DEVELOPING SUBJECTS FROM BRAINSTORMING AND NOTETAKING. Although the idea of brainstorming is to be totally free about the topics, you will soon need to direct your mind into specific channels. Once you start focusing on definite topics, your thinking becomes analogous to classroom discussion. Let us assume that in brainstorming you produce a topic that you find especially interesting. You might then start to focus on this topic, and write as much as you can about it. The following examples show how a writer may zero in on the topic "honor" once the word comes up in freewriting:

> Mathilde could have gone to her friend and told her she lost the necklace. But she didn't. Did her honor stop her?
>
> What is honor? doing what you think you should even if you don't want to, or if it's hard. Or is it pride? Was she too proud or too honorable to tell her friend? Does having honor mean going a harder way, when either would probably be okay? Do you have to suffer to be honorable? Does pride or honor produce a choice for suffering?
>
> Mathilde wants others to envy her, to find her attractive. Later she tells Loisel that she would feel humiliated at the party with rich women unless she wore jewelry. Maybe M. was more concerned about her own good name than the necklace. Having a good reputation seems like it has something to do with honor. So it could be mainly a public thing. When I think of good name, though, I think more of personal qualities than appearance.
>
> Duty. Is it the same as honor? Was her duty to work so hard? In the Middle Ages, it was the duty of knights to defend a lady's honor (her good name?) by fighting, or going out to spear dragons . . . or is all this myth?
>
> Honor is a part of myths, I think. They both seem bigger than any one life or person. Honor is just an idea or feeling—can an idea of honor be larger than a life, take over someone's life?

This writer is trying to figure out what honor is and whether Mathilde behaves honorably throughout the story. Although the last two paragraphs depart from the story somewhat, this diversion is perfectly acceptable, for in brainstorming a writer expresses ideas as they arise. If the ideas amount to something, they may be used in the developing essay, but if they don't, they may be discarded. The important principle in brainstorming is to record all ideas—*incomplete thoughts and bad grammar (and spelling) included*—with no initial concern about how they might seem to a reader. The notes are for your use only.

BUILDING ON YOUR ORIGINAL NOTES.   An essential way to focus your mind is to use your journal notes as a mine for likely topics. For example, one of the notes on p. 12 brings up the topic of the attic flat in "The Necklace." With this note as a start, you can develop a number of ideas, as in the following:

> The attic flat is important. Before, in her apartment, M. was dreamier and less practical, she was delicate, but after losing necklace, no way. She becomes a worker when in the flat. She can do a lot more now.
>
> M. gives up her servant, climbs stairs carrying buckets of water, washes greasy pots, throws water around to clean floors, does all the wash by hand.
>
> While she gets stronger, she also gets loud and frumpy—argues with shopkeepers to get the lowest prices. She stops caring for herself. A reversal here, from incapable and well groomed to capable and coarse. The attic flat is the location of this reversal.

Notice that just a sentence in an original note can help you discover thoughts that you did not originally have. This act of stretching your mind in the focusing process leads you to put elements of the story together in ways that create support for the assertions that build essays. Even in an assertion as basic as "The attic flat is important," the process itself, which is a form of concentrated thought, leads you creatively forward.

RAISING AND ANSWERING QUESTIONS.   Another major way to discover ideas about a work is to raise questions as you read, and then to try answering them. The *Guidelines for Reading* will help you formulate questions, but you may also raise specific questions like these (assuming that you are considering a story:

- What explanations need to be made about the characters? Which actions, scenes, and situations invite interpretation? Why so?
- What assumptions do the characters and speakers reveal about life and humanity generally, about themselves, the people around them, their families, their friends, and about work, the economy, religion, politics, and the state of the world?
- What are their manners or customs?
- What kinds of words do they use: formal or informal words, slang or profanity?
- What literary conventions and devices have you discovered, and how do these add to the work? (If an author addresses readers directly, for example, that is a **convention**; if a comparison is used, this is a **device** which might be either a **metaphor** or a **simile**.)

Of course you may raise other questions as you re-read the piece, or you may be left with one or two major questions that you decide to pursue.

USING THE PLUS-MINUS, PRO-CON, OR EITHER-OR METHOD. A common method of discovering ideas is to develop a set of contrasts: plus-minus, pro-con, either-or. Let us suppose a pro-con method of considering the character of Mathilde in "The Necklace": whether she should be "admired" (pro) or "condemned" (con).

ADMIRED?	*CONDEMNED?*
After she cries when they get the invitation, she recovers with a "strong effort"—maybe she doesn't want her husband to feel bad.	She only wants to be envied and admired for being attractive (end of 1st part), not for more important qualities.
She does really score a great victory at the dance. She does have the power to charm and captivate.	She wastes her time in daydreaming about things she can't have, and whines about her unhappiness.
Once she lost the necklace, "she did her share . . . completely, heroically" (¶ 98) to make up for the loss.	She manipulates her husband into giving her a lot of money for a party dress, but they live poorly.
Even when she is poor, she still dreams about that single shining moment. She really gets worse than she deserves.	She assumes that her friend would think she was a thief if she knew she was returning a different necklace.
At the end, she confesses the loss to her friend.	She gets loud and coarse, and haggles about pennies, thus undergoing a total cheapening of her character.

Once you begin putting contrasting ideas side by side, new discoveries will occur to you. Filling the columns almost demands that you list as many contrasting positions as you can, and that you think about how the story material supports each position. The notes will be useful regardless of how you choose to organize the essay. You may develop either column in a full essay. Or you might use the notes to support the idea that Mathilde is too complex to be wholly admired or condemned. You might even introduce an entirely new idea, such as that Mathilde is more to be pitied than either condemned or admired. In short, arranging materials in the "either-or" pattern is a powerful way to discover ideas that can lead to ways of development that you might not otherwise find.

TRACING DEVELOPING PATTERNS. You can also discover ideas by making an outline, list, or scheme for the story or main idea. What conflicts appear? Do these conflicts exist between people, groups, or ideas? How does the author resolve them? Is one force, idea, or side the winner? Why? How do you respond to the winner, or loser?

Using this method, you might make a list similar to this one.

Beginning: M. is a fish out of water. Dreams of wealth, but her life is drab and her husband is ordinary.

Fantasies—make her even more dissatisfied—almost punishes herself by thinking of lavish rooms

Her character relates to the places in the story: the Street of the Martyrs, the dinner party scene, the attic flat. Also the places she dreams of—she fills them with the most expensive things she can imagine.

They get the dinner invitation—she pouts and whines. Her husband feels discomfort, but she doesn't really harm him. She does manipulate him into buying her an expensive party dress, though.

Her dream world hurts her real life when her desire for wealth causes her to borrow the necklace. Losing the necklace is just plain bad luck.

The attic flat brings out her potential coarseness. But she also develops a spirit of sacrifice and cooperation. She loses, but she's actually a winner.

These observations all focus on Mathilde's character. However, you might trace other patterns you find in the work. If you start planning an essay about one of these other patterns, be sure to account for all the actions and scenes that relate to your topic. Otherwise, you may miss a piece of evidence that can lead you to a new viewpoint.

THINKING BY WRITING. No matter what method of discovering ideas you use, it is important to realize that *unwritten thought is incomplete thought.* Make a practice of writing notes about your reactions and any questions that occur to you. They may lead you later to the most startling discoveries you will make about a work

DRAFTING THE ESSAY

As you use the brainstorming and focusing techniques for discovering ideas, you are also beginning to draft your essay. Although you will need to revise your ideas—as connections among them become more clear, and as you re-examine the work for support for the ideas you are developing—you already have many of the raw materials you need for developing your topic.

Developing a Central Idea

By definition, an essay is *a fully developed and organized set of paragraphs that are directly connected to a central idea.* Everything in an essay should contribute to the reader's understanding of the idea. To achieve unity and completeness, each paragraph refers to the central idea and demonstrates how selected details from the work relate to it and support it. The central idea helps the writer control and shape the essay, and it provides guidance to the reader.

A successful essay about literature is a brief but thorough (not exhaustive) examination of a literary work in light of a particular element, such as *point of view, imagery,* or *symbolism.* Typical central ideas might be (1) that a character is strong and tenacious, or (2) that the point of view makes the action seem "distant and objective," or (3) that one work is different from or better than another. In essays on these topics, all points must be tied to these ideas. Thus, it is a fact that Mathilde Loisel in "The Necklace" endures ten years of slavish work and sacrifice. This fact is not relevant to an essay on her character, however, unless you connect it by showing how it demonstrates one of her major traits—in this case, her strength and tenacity.

Look through all of your ideas for one or two that catch your eye for development. If you have used more than one prewriting technique, the chances are that you have already discovered at least a few ideas that are more thought-provoking, or important, than the others.

Once you choose one that interests you, write it as a complete sentence. The *complete sentence* is important, for a simple phrase, such as "setting and character," does not focus thought the way a sentence does. A sentence will move the topic toward new exploration and discovery because it combines a topic with an outcome, such as "The setting is related to Mathilde's character." You may choose to be even more specific: "Mathilde's strengths and weaknesses are connected to the real and imaginary places in the story."

WRITING BY HAND OR BY WORD PROCESSOR

As we have emphasized, *thinking and writing are inseparable processes.* It is therefore essential to get ideas into a *visible form* so that you may develop them further. For many people, *handwriting* is a psychological necessity in this process. In noting handwritten responses to a work, be sure to use *only one side* of your paper or notecards. This will enable you to spread your materials out and overview them when the time comes to begin writing.

Other students prefer word processors. The word processor can help you develop ideas, for it enables you to eliminate unworkable thoughts and replace them with others. You can move sentences and paragraphs tentatively into new contexts, test out how they look, and move them somewhere else if you choose. If you see questionable spellings, you may check them out with a dictionary and make corrections on the screen. (Because spelling is often an element of grading, find out whether your instructor will let you use a spell-check program.)

Studies have shown that errors and awkward sentences frequently are found at the bottoms of pages prepared by hand or with a conventional typewriter. The reason is that writers hesitate to make improvements when they get near the end of a page because they want to avoid the dreariness of starting the page over. Word processors eliminate this difficulty completely. Changes can be made anywhere in the draft, at any time, without damage to the appearance of the final draft.

In addition, with the rapid printers available today, you can print drafts, even in the initial and tentative stages. Using your printed draft, you can make additional notes, marginal corrections, and suggestions for further development. With the marked-up draft for guidance, you can go back to the word processor and implement your changes and improvements, repeating this process as often as necessary. This facility makes the machine an additional incentive for improvement, right up to your final draft.

Regardless of your writing method, it is important to realize that *unwritten thought is incomplete thought*. Therefore, somewhere in the composing process, it is vital to prepare a complete draft of what you have written. Even with the word processor's screen, you see only a small part and cannot lay everything out at once. A clean, readable draft permits you to gather everything together and to make even more improvements through the act of revision.

With a single, central idea for your essay, you have a standard for accepting, rejecting, rearranging, and changing the ideas you have been developing. You may now choose to draft a few paragraphs to see whether your idea seems valid. Or, you may decide that it would be more helpful to make an outline or list before you attempt to support your ideas in a rough draft. In either case, you need to use your notes for evidence to connect to your central idea. If you need more ideas, use any of the brainstorming-prewriting techniques to discover them. If you need more details, jot them down as you re-read the work.

Using the central idea that the story's settings are related to Mathilde's changing character might produce paragraphs like the following:

> The original apartment in the Street of Martyrs, and the dream world of wealthy places, both show negative sides of her character. The real-life apartment, though livable, is shabby. The furnishings all bring out her discontent. The shabbiness makes her think only of luxuriousness, and her one servant girl makes her dream of many servants. The luxury of her dream life heightens her unhappiness.

> Mathilde's character is coarsened during the ten years of repayment. She gives up her domestic help, and does all the heavy housework herself. She climbs stairs carrying heavy buckets of water, and throws water around to clean floors. She washes greasy and encrusted pots and pans, takes out the garbage, and does the clothes and dishes by hand. She gives up caring for her hair and hands, and wears the cheapest clothing possible. She becomes loud and argumentative, and spends much time haggling with shopkeepers to save as much money as she can. Whatever delicacy and attractiveness she had, she loses.

> Her Sunday walk to the Champs-Elysées is in character. This is a fashionable street, and her walk to it is similar to her earlier daydreams about wealth, for it is on this wide street that wealthy people stroll and flaunt themselves. Her meeting with Jeanne there is accidental, but it also brings out her sense of pride; that is, she confesses to the loss of the necklace, having seen things through to the complete repayment of all indebtedness. The Champs-Elysées thus brings out the surprise and irony of the story, and Mathilde's going there is totally in character, in keeping with her earlier dreams of a luxurious life.

Notice that the first and second paragraphs come directly from earlier notes. The third paragraph was written after the central idea was established. The central idea is not stated, but each paragraph helps to demonstrate how the setting relates to Mathilde's character. No attempt has been made to connect the paragraphs or make the draft read well. Even in this "discovery" draft, however, where the purpose is to write initial thoughts about the central idea, many details from the story are given in support. In the final draft, this support will be essential.

Creating a Thesis Statement

Using the central idea for guidance, you can now decide which of the earlier observations and ideas can be developed further. Your goal is to establish a number of major topics to support the central idea, and to express them in a **thesis statement**—a sentence that, like a plan, lists the major topics in the order of development in the essay. Suppose you choose three ideas from the discovery stage of development. If you put the central idea at the left and the list of topics at the right, you have the shape of the thesis statement.

CENTRAL IDEA	TOPICS
The setting of "The Necklace" reflects Mathilde's character.	1. Real-life apartment
	2. Dream surroundings
	3. Attic flat

This arrangement leads to the following thesis statement:

> Mathilde's character development is related to her first apartment, her dream-life mansion rooms, and her attic flat.

You can revise the thesis statement at any stage of the writing process if you find you do not have enough evidence from the work to support it. Or perhaps a new topic may occur to you, and you can include it, appropriately, as a part of your thesis statement.

As we have seen, the central idea is the glue of the essay. The thesis statement lists the parts to be fastened together—that is, the topics in which the central idea is to be demonstrated and argued. To alert the audience to the essay's structure, the thesis statement is often placed at the end of the introductory paragraph.

WRITING A FIRST DRAFT

To write a first draft, you support the points of your thesis statement with your notes and discovery materials. You may alter, reject, and rearrange ideas and details as you wish, as long as you change the thesis statement to account for the changes (a major reason why most writers write their introductions last). The thesis statement above contains three topics (it could be two, or four, or more), which will be used in forming the body of the essay.

Just as the organization of the entire essay is based on the thesis, the form of each paragraph is based on its **topic sentence**. A topic sentence is an assertion about how a topic from the predicate of the thesis statement supports the central idea. The first topic in our example is the relationship of Mathilde's character to her first apartment, and the resulting paragraph should emphasize this relationship. If you choose her trait of being constantly dissatisfied, you can then form a topic sentence by connecting the trait with the location, as follows:

> Details about the first apartment explain her dissatisfaction and depression.

Beginning with this sentence, the paragraph can show how items in the apartment, such as the furniture, the curtains, and the unwashed tablecloth, feed Mathilde's dissatisfaction.

Usually you will devote a single paragraph to each topic. However, if your topic is difficult, long, and heavily detailed, you may divide it into two or more subtopics, each devoted to single paragraphs. Should you make this division, your topic then is really a section, and each paragraph in the section should have its own topic sentence.

Once you choose your thesis statement, you can use the statement to focus your observations and conclusions. Let us see how we can sharpen the second paragraph of the discovery draft.

ORIGINAL PARAGRAPH	*RESHAPED PARAGRAPH*
Mathilde's character is coarsened during the ten years of repayment. She gives up her domestic help, and does all the heavy housework herself. She climbs stairs carrying heavy buckets of water, and throws water around to clean floors. She washes greasy and encrusted pots and pans, takes out the garbage, and does the clothes and dishes by hand. She gives up caring for her hair and hands, and wears the cheapest clothing possible. She becomes loud and argumentative, and spends much time haggling with shopkeepers to save as much money as she can. Whatever delicacy and attractiveness she had, she loses.	The attic flat reflects the coarsening of Mathilde's character. Maupassant emphasizes the burdens she endures to save money, such as mopping the floors, cleaning greasy and encrusted pots and pans, taking out the garbage, and handwashing clothes and dishes. This work makes her rough and coarse, an effect that is heightened by her giving up care of her hair and hands, her wearing the cheapest dresses possible, and her becoming loud and penny-pinching in haggling with the local shopkeepers. If at the beginning she is delicate and attractive, at the end she is unpleasant and coarse.

Notice that details from the story are substantially the same in each paragraph, but while the paragraph on the left is unfocused, the right-hand paragraph connects the details to Mathilde's housework in the attic flat. The paragraph on the right shows how details from a work may substantiate a unifying central idea.

Developing an Outline

So far we have been developing an *outline*—that is, a skeletal plan of organization for the essay. Some writers never use formal outlines at all, preferring to make informal lists of ideas, while others rely on them constantly. Still other writers insist that they cannot make an outline until they have finished their essays. Regardless of your preference, *your finished essay should have a tight structure.* At some point, therefore, you should create a guiding outline to develop or to shape your essay.

The outline we have been developing here is the **analytical sentence outline**. This type is easier to create than it sounds. It consists of the following:

1. An *introduction,* including the central idea and the thesis statement. Some instructors require a fusion of the two in the final draft. Therefore, make sure you follow your instructor's directions.
2. *Topic sentences* within each paragraph of the body, usually at the beginning. It is also acceptable to include a topic sentence elsewhere in a paragraph, but if you relocate it, be sure that your details make it follow naturally and logically. Usually you may devote a single paragraph to each topic. However, if your topic is difficult, long, and heavily detailed, you may divide it into two or more subtopics, each devoted to single paragraphs.
3. A *conclusion.*

When applied to the subject we have been developing, the outline looks like this:

TITLE: How Setting in "The Necklace" Is Related to the Character of Mathilde

1. **INTRODUCTION**
    a. *Central Idea:* Setting is used to show Mathilde's character.
    b. *Thesis Statement:* Her character development is related to her first apartment, her dream-life mansion rooms, and her attic flat.
2. **BODY:** *Topic sentences* a, b, and c (and d, e, f, if necessary)
    a. Details about her first apartment explain her dissatisfaction and depression.
    b. Her dream-life images of wealth are like the apartment because they too make her unhappy.
    c. The attic flat reflects the coarsening of her character.

3.   **CONCLUSION**
      Topic sentence. All details in the story, particularly the setting, are focused on the
      character of Mathilde.

The *conclusion* may be a summary of the body; it may evaluate the main
idea; it may briefly suggest further points of discussion; or it may be a reflection on the details of the body.

Using the Outline

The sample essays to be developed in this book are organized according to the principles of the analytical sentence outline. To emphasize the
shaping effect of these outlines, all central ideas, thesis statements, and topic
sentences are underlined. In your own writing, you may underline these
"skeletal" sentences as a check on your organization. Unless your instructor
requires the underlines, however, remove them in your final drafts.

SAMPLE ESSAY, DRAFT 1

The following essay is a first draft of the topic we have been developing. Although it is relatively advanced, it shows how even working from an outline
leaves much yet to do to produce a finished essay. Because the draft omits a
topic and some details that will be included in the final draft (pp. 35-36), it
reveals the need to make improvements through additional brainstorming
and discovery-prewriting techniques. Nevertheless, as it stands, it is an acceptable piece of writing.

How Setting in "The Necklace" Is Related to the Character of Mathilde°

[1]   In "The Necklace" Guy de Maupassant does not give much detail about
the setting. He does not even describe the necklace itself, which is the central
object in his plot, but he says only that it is "superb" (¶ 47). Rather, he uses
the setting to reflect the character of the central figure, Mathilde Loisel.* All his
details are presented to bring out her traits. Her character development is related to her first apartment, her dream-life mansion rooms, and her attic flat.†

[2]   Details about her first apartment explain her dissatisfaction and depression. The walls are "drab," the furniture "threadbare," and the curtains "ugly" (¶
3). There is only a simple country girl to do the housework. The tablecloth is
not changed daily, and the best dinner dish is boiled beef. Mathilde has no
evening clothes, only a theater dress that she does not like. These details
show her dissatisfaction with life with her low-salaried husband.

Her dream-life images of wealth are like the apartment because they too

---

° See pp 3–10 for this story.
* Central idea.
† Thesis sentence.

[3] make her unhappy. In her daydreams, the rooms are large, filled with expensive furniture and bric-a-brac, and draped in silk. She imagines private rooms for intimate talks, and big dinners with delicacies like trout and quail. With dreams of such a rich home, she feels even more despair about her modest apartment on the Street of Martyrs in Paris.

[4] The attic flat reflects the coarsening of Mathilde's character. Maupassant emphasizes the burdens she endures to save money, such as mopping the floors, cleaning greasy and encrusted pots and pans, taking out the garbage, and handwashing dishes and clothes. This work makes her rough and coarse, a fact also shown by her giving up care of her hair and hands, her wearing the cheapest dresses possible, and her becoming loud and penny-pinching in haggling with the local shopkeepers. If at the beginning she is delicate and attractive, at the end she is unpleasant and coarse.

[5] In summary, Maupassant focuses everything in the story, including the setting, on the character of Mathilde. Anything extra is not needed, and he does not include it. Thus he says little about the big party scene, but emphasizes the necessary detail that Mathilde was a great "success" (¶ 52), because this detail brings out some of her early attractiveness and charm (despite her more usual unhappiness). In "The Necklace," Maupassant uses setting as a means to his end—the story of Mathilde and her needless sacrifice.

Commentary on the Essay

You might notice that several parts need more thought. For example, paragraph 2 contains a series of short, unconnected comments. Also, the last sentence of that paragraph implies that Mathilde's dissatisfaction relates mainly to her husband, which is not what the writer had intended. Paragraph 4 focuses too much on Mathilde's coarseness and not enough on her sacrifice and cooperation. Finally, there is not enough support in this draft for the contention (in paragraph 5) that *everything* in the story focuses on Mathilde's character. To discover how these issues may be more fully considered, compare this first draft to draft 2 of the essay on pp. 35-36.

REVISING THE ESSAY

After finishing your first draft, you may wonder what more you can do. You have read the work several times, discovered ideas to write about through brainstorming techniques, made an outline of your ideas, and written at least one full draft. How can you do better?

The best way to begin is to observe that *a major mistake writers make when writing about literature is to do no more than retell a story or reword an idea.* Retelling a story shows only that you have read it, not that you have thought about it. Writing a good essay requires you to arrange your thoughts into a pattern that can be followed by a perceptive reader.

Using Your Own Order of References

There are many ways to escape the trap of summarizing stories and to set up your own pattern of development. One is to stress *your own* order when referring to parts of a work. Do not treat details as they happen, but rearrange them to suit your own thematic plans. Rarely, if ever, should you begin by talking about a work's opening; it is better to talk first about the conclusion or middle. As you examine your first draft, if you find that you have followed the chronological order of the work instead of stressing your own order, you may use one of the prewriting techniques to figure out new ways to connect your materials. The principle is that you should introduce references to the work only to support the points you wish to make.

Using Literary Material as Evidence

Whenever you write, your position is like that of a detective using clues as evidence for building a case, or of a lawyer using evidence as support for an **argument**. It is vital to use evidence convincingly so that your readers can follow your ideas. Let us look at two examples to see how writing may be improved by the pointed use of details. These are from drafts of a longer essay on the character of Mathilde.

1

The major extenuating detail about Mathilde is that she seems to be isolated, locked away from other people. She and her husband do not speak to each other much, except about external things. He speaks about his liking for boiled beef, and she states that she cannot accept the big invitation because she has no nice dresses. Once she gets the dress, she complains because she has no jewelry. Even when borrowing the necklace from Jeanne Forrestier, she does not say much. When she and her husband discover that the necklace is lost, they simply go over the details, and Loisel dictates a letter of explanation, which she writes in her own hand. Even when she meets Jeanne on the Champs-Elysées, she does not say a great deal about her life, but only goes through enough details about the loss and replacement of the necklace to make Jeanne exclaim about the needlessness of the ten-year sacrifice.

2

The major flaw of Mathilde's character is that she is withdrawn and uncommunicative, apparently unwilling or unable to form an intimate relationship. For example, she and her husband do not speak to each other much, except about external things such as his taste for boiled beef and her lack of a party dress and jewelry. With such an uncommunicative marriage, one might suppose that she would be more open with her close friend, Jeanne Forrestier, but Mathilde does not say much even to her. This flaw hurts her greatly, because if she were more open she might have explained the loss and avoided the horrible sacrifice. This lack of openness, along with her self-indulgent dreaminess, is her biggest defect.

A comparison of these paragraphs shows that the first has more words than the second (158 to 121), but that it is more appropriate for a rough than a final draft because the writer is doing little more than retell the story. The paragraph is cluttered with details that do not support any conclusions. If you examine it for what you might learn about Maupassant's actual use of Mathilde's solitary traits in "The Necklace," you will find that it gives you no help at all. The writer needs to consider why these details should be shared, and revise the paragraph according to the central idea.

On the other hand, the details in the second paragraph all support the declared topic. Phrases like "for example," "but even here," and "this lack" show that the writer of paragraph 2 has assumed that the audience knows the story and now wants help in interpretation. Paragraph 2 therefore guides readers *by connecting the details to the topic.* It uses these details *as evidence,* not as a retelling of actions. By contrast, paragraph 1 recounts a number of relevant actions, but does not *connect* them to the topic. More details, of course, could have been added to the second draft, but they are unnecessary because the paragraph demonstrates the point with the details used. There are many qualities that make good writing good, but one of the most important is evident here: *In good writing, details are used only as evidence in an original pattern of thought.*

USE THE PRESENT TENSE OF VERBS
WHEN REFERRING TO ACTIONS AND IDEAS

Literary works spring into life with each and every reading. You may thus assume that everything happening takes place in the present, and, when writing about literature you should use the *present tense of verbs.* It is correct to say "Mathilde and her husband *work* and *economize* (not "*worked* and *economized*") for ten years to pay off the 18,000-franc debt which they *undertake* (not "*undertook*") to pay for the lost necklace."

When you consider an author's ideas, the present tense is also proper, on the principle that the words of an author are just as alive and current today (and tomorrow) as they were at the moment of writing, even though this same author has been dead for hundreds or even thousands of years.

Because it is incorrect to shift tenses inappropriately, you may encounter a problem when you refer to actions that have occurred prior to the time of the main action. An instance is Hemingway's "Soldier's Home," in which the main character is discontented and unsettled as a result of his combat experiences in Europe during World War I. In such a situation it is important to keep details in order, and thus you may use the past tense as long as you keep the relationship clear between past and present, as in this example: "Krebs **cannot settle down** because he **is always thinking** [present tense] about the actions he **went through** [past tense] during the fighting in Europe." This use of the past influencing the present is acceptable because it corresponds to the cause-and-effect relationship brought out in the story.

A problem also arises when you introduce historical or biographical details about a work or author. It is appropriate to use the *past tense* for such details as long as they actually do belong to the past. Thus it is correct to state that "Shakespeare **lived** from 1564 to 1616," or that "Shakespeare **wrote** *Hamlet* in about 1599–1600." It is also permissible to mix past and present tenses when you are treating historical facts about a literary work and are also considering it as a living text. Of prime importance is to keep things straight. Here is an example showing how past and present tenses may be used when appropriate:

> Because *Hamlet* **was** first **performed** in about 1600, Shakespeare most probably **wrote** it shortly before this time. In the play, a tragedy, Shakespeare **treats** an act of vengeance, but more importantly he **demonstrates** the difficulty of ever learning the exact truth. The hero, Prince Hamlet, **is** the focus of this difficulty, for the task of revenge **is assigned** to him by the Ghost of his father. Though the Ghost **claims** that his brother, Claudius, **is** his murderer, Hamlet **is** not able to verify this claim.

Here, the historical details are presented in the past tense, while all details about the play *Hamlet*, including Shakespeare as the creating author whose ideas and words are still alive, are considered in the present.

As a general principle, you will be right most of the time if you use the present tense exclusively for literary details and the past tense for historical details. When in doubt, however, *consult your instructor.*

Keeping to Your Point

To show another distinction between first and second draft writing, let us consider a third example. The following paragraph, in which the writer assumes an audience that is interested in the relationship of economics and politics to literature, is drawn from an essay on "The Idea of Economic Determinism in 'The Necklace.'" In this paragraph the writer shows how economics are related to a number of incidents from the story. The idea is to assert that Mathilde's difficulties result not from character but rather from financial restrictions:

> More important than chance in governing life is the idea that people are controlled by economic circumstances. Mathilde, as is shown at the story's opening, is born poor. Therefore she doesn't get the right doors opened for her, and her marriage is to a minor clerk. With a vivid imagination and a burning desire for luxury, seeming to be born only for the wealthy life, her poor home brings out her daydreams of expensive surroundings. She taunts her husband, Loisel, when he brings the big invitation, because she does not have a suitable (read "expensive") dress. Once she gets the dress it is jewelry that she lacks, and she borrows that and loses it. The loss of the necklace is the greatest trouble, because it forces the Loisels to borrow deeply and to lead an impoverished life for ten years.

This paragraph begins with an effective topic sentence, indicating that the writer has a good plan. The remaining part, however, shows how easily writers may be diverted from their objective. The flaw is that the material of the paragraph, while accurate, *is not tied to the topic.* Once the second sentence is under way, the paragraph gets lost in a retelling of events, and the fine opening sentence is left behind. The paragraph therefore shows that writers cannot assume that detail alone will make an intended meaning clear. They must do the connecting themselves, to make sure that all relationships are explicitly clear. *This point cannot be overstressed.*

Let us see how the problem may be treated. If the ideal paragraph can be schematized with line drawings, we might say that the paragraph's topic should be a straight line, moving toward and reaching a specific goal (explicit meaning), with an exemplifying line moving away from the straight line briefly to bring in evidence, but returning to the line after each new fact to demonstrate the relevance of the fact. Thus, the ideal scheme looks like this, with a straight line touched a number of times by an undulating line:

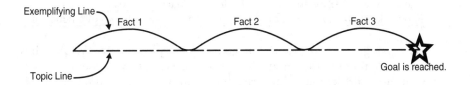

Notice that the exemplifying line, waving to illustrate how documentation or exemplification is to be used, always returns to the topic line. A scheme for the faulty paragraph on "The Necklace," however, would look like this, with the line never returning, but flying out into space:

How might the faulty paragraph be improved? The best way is to remind the reader again and again of the topic, and to use examples from the text in support.

Consistently with our model diagram, each time the topic is mentioned, the undulating line merges with the straight, or central-idea line. This relationship of topic to illustrative examples should prevail no matter what subject you write about. If you are analyzing *point of view,* for example, you should keep connecting your material to the speaker, or narrator, and the same applies to topics like character, theme, or setting. According to this principle, we might revise the paragraph on economic determinism in "The

Necklace" as follows. (Parts of sentences stressing the relationship of the examples to the topic of the paragraph are underlined.)

> More important than chance in governing life is the idea that people are con-
> trolled by economic circumstances. <u>As illustration</u>, the speaker begins by em-
> phasizing that Mathilde, the main character, is born poor. Therefore she does-
> n't get the right doors opened for her, and her marriage is to a minor clerk. <u>In
> keeping with the idea</u>, her vivid imagination and burning desire for luxury (she
> seems to have been born only for the wealthy life) feed on her weakness of char-
> acter as she feels deep unhappiness and depression because of the contrast be-
> tween her daydreams of expensive surroundings and the poor home she actu-
> ally has. <u>These straitened economic circumstances</u> inhibit her relationship with
> her husband, and she taunts him when he brings the big invitation because she
> does not have a suitable (read "expensive") dress. As a merging of her unreal-
> istic dream life with actual reality, <u>her borrowing of the necklace suggests the
> impossibility of overcoming economic restrictions</u>. In the context of the idea,
> the ten-year sacrifice to pay for the lost necklace <u>demonstrates that lack of
> money keeps people down, destroying their dreams and hopes of a better life.</u>

The paragraph now reaches the goal of the topic sentence. While it has also been lengthened, the length has been caused not by inessential detail but by phrases and sentences that give form and direction. You might object that if you lengthened all your paragraphs in this way, your essays would grow too bulky. The answer is to reduce the number of major points and para-graphs, on the theory that *it is better to develop a few topics pointedly than to develop many pointlessly*. Revising for the purpose of strengthening central and topic ideas requires that you either throw out some topics or else incorporate them as sub-points in the topics you keep. To control your writing in this way can result only in improvement.

CHECKING DEVELOPMENT AND ORGANIZATION

One of the first requirements of a good essay, then, is to stick to a point. An-other major step toward excellence is to make your central idea expand and grow. The word *growth* is a metaphor describing the creation of new insights, the disclosure of ideas that were not at first noticeable, and the expression of new, fresh, and original interpretations.

An argument against this idea might be that you cannot be original when you are writing about someone else's work. "The author has said every-thing," might go the argument, "and therefore you can do little more than follow the story." This claim presupposes that you have no choice in selecting material, and no opportunity to make individual thoughts and original con-tributions.

But you do have choices and opportunities for originality. One obvious area of originality is the development and formulation of your central idea.

For example, a natural first response to "The Necklace" is that "It is about a woman who loses a borrowed necklace and endures hardship to help pay for it." Because this response refers only to events in the story and not to any idea, an area of thought might be introduced if the hardship is called "needless." This idea would require an explanation of the differences between needed and unneeded hardships. The application of these differences to the heroine's plight would produce an original essay. Even better and more original insights could result if the topic of the budding essay were to connect the dreamy, withdrawn traits of the main character to her misfortunes and also to general misfortunes. A resulting central idea might be that "People themselves create their own difficulties." Such an idea would require the writer to define not only the personal but also the representative nature of Mathilde's experiences, an avenue of exploration that could produce much in the way of a fresh, original essay about "The Necklace."

You can also develop your ability to treat your subject freshly and originally if you plan the body of the essay to build up to what you think is your most important and incisive idea. As examples of such planning, the following brief topic outlines suggest how each central idea may be widened and expanded:[*]

A. **Mathilde as a growing character** (*Character*, Chapter 4)
   1. Mathilde has normal daydreams about a better life.
   2. She takes a risk to make her daydreams seem real.
   3. She develops by facing her mistake and working hard to correct it.
B. **The idea of economic determinism** (*Idea or Theme*, Chapter 10)
   1. Mathilde's economic class inhibits her wishes.
   2. Her husband's low income is a damper on her character.
   3. The ten-year hardship is her punishment for trying to live beyond her means.
C. **The development of irony in the story** (*Tone*, Chapters 8, 18)
   1. Mathilde's dissatisfaction is heightened by her dreams.
   2. The loss of the necklace ironically makes the Loisels seem poorer than they really are.
   3. Mathilde's failure to confess the loss to Jeanne makes the sacrifice needless.
D. **The symbolic value of the necklace** (*Symbolism and Allegory*, Chapters 9, 21)
   1. The necklace symbolizes economic wealth and ease.
   2. Its falseness symbolizes the discrepancy between appearance and reality.
   3. Restoring the necklace symbolizes the value of sacrifice and work.

[*] The critical basis for some of these topics is discussed in Appendix D, on the various critical approaches to literature. Thus the study of character is considered with the description of the psychological approach. The economic topic is described under the category of the Marxian-economic approach. The consideration of irony fits into the formalist category, as does the topic of symbolism.

These outlines indicate how a subject may be enlarged if the exemplifying topics are treated in an increasing order of importance. Outlines A and D, for example, both move toward ideas about moral values, while outline B moves toward a broad consideration of the story, and outline C suggests a climax based on the story's situational irony. These possible patterns show how two primary standards of excellence in writing—organization and growth—can be met.

Clearly, then, an important goal in writing is the development of your central idea. Constantly adhere to your topic, and constantly develop it. Nurture it and make it grow. Admittedly, in a short essay you will be able to move only a short distance with an idea, but you *should never be satisfied to leave the idea exactly where you found it.* To the degree that you can learn to develop your ideas, you will receive recognition for increasingly superior writing.

WRITE WITH YOUR READERS IN MIND

In preparing to write, you need to decide how much detail to select and discuss, and this requires that you gauge the needs of your readers. For example, if you assume that they have not read the work you are writing about, you will need to include a short summary as background for them. Otherwise, they may not understand your argument.

Consider, too, any special interests or concerns of your readers. If your readers are specially concerned about politics, sociology, religion, or psychology, you need to select and develop your materials accordingly.

Your instructor will let you know who your audience is. Usually, it will be your instructor or the members of your class. They will be familiar with the work and will not expect you to retell the story. Rather they will look to you as an explainer or interpreter. Thus, you may introduce details from the work only if they exemplify your central idea, and omit details that do not.

USING EXACT, COMPREHENSIVE, AND FORCEFUL LANGUAGE

In addition to being organized and well developed, the best writing is expressed in *exact, comprehensive,* and *forceful* language. At first, sentences and paragraphs are usually weak, and you need to rethink them, reword them, and re-arrange them.

Always ask yourself whether your sentences really *mean* what you intend, or whether you can make them more exact and therefore stronger. For example, consider these two sentences from essays about "The Necklace":

> It seems as though the main character's dreams of luxury cause her to respond as she does in the story.

> This incident, although it may seem trivial or unimportant, has substantial significance in the creation of the story; by this I mean the incident which occurred is essentially what the story is all about.

These sentences are inexact and vague, and therefore unhelpful; neither of them goes anywhere. The first is satisfactory up to the verb "cause," but then it falls apart because the writer has lost sight of the meaning. It is best to describe *what* that response is, rather than to be satisfied with nothing more than that there *is* a response. To make the sentence more exact, we may make the following revision:

> Mathilde's dreams of luxury make it impossible for her to accept her own possessions, and therefore she goes beyond her means to attend the party.

With this revision, the writer could consider the meaning of the story's early passages, and could contrast the ideas there with those in the latter part. Without the revision, it is not clear where the writer might go.

The second sentence is vague because again the writer has lost sight of the topic. If we adopt the principle of aiming toward exactness, however, we may bring the dead sentence to life:

> The accidental loss of the necklace, which is trivial though costly, supports the narrator's claim that major turns in life are produced not by earthshaking events, but rather by minor ones.

In addition to exactness, it is vital to make sentences—all sentences, but particularly thesis and topic sentences—complete and comprehensive. As an example, consider the following sentence, which was written in a student essay as a central idea about "The Necklace":

> The idea in "The Necklace" is how Mathilde and her husband respond to the loss of the necklace.

This sentence merely summarizes the story. It needs additional rethinking and rephrasing to make it more comprehensive, as in the these two revisions:

> Maupassant's surprise ending of "The Necklace" symbolizes the need for always being truthful.

> In "The Necklace" Maupassant shows that hard work and responsibility are basic and necessary in life.

Both new sentences are connected to how the Loisels respond to the loss of the necklace, although they point toward differing treatments. The first concerns the virtue shown by the Loisels in their sacrifice. Because the second sentence includes the word *symbolizes*, an essay stemming from it would stress the Loisels' mistake in not confessing the loss. In dealing with the symbolic meaning of their failure, such an essay would focus on the negative aspects of their characters, while an essay developed from the first sentence would stress their positive aspects. Either of the revised sentences, therefore, is more comprehensive than the original sentence, and would help a writer develop a thoughtful and accurate composition.

USING THE NAMES OF AUTHORS

For both men and women writers, you should typically include the author's *full name* in the *first sentence* of your essay. Here are a few model first sentences:

> Shirley Jackson's "The Lottery" is a story featuring both suspense and horror.

> "The Lottery," by Shirley Jackson, is a story featuring both suspense and horror.

For all later references, use only last names, such as *Steinbeck, Munro, Crane,* or *Porter.* However, for the "giants" of literature, you should use the last names exclusively. In referring to writers like Shakespeare and Milton, for example, there is no need ever to include *William* or *John.*

In spite of today's informal standards, do not use an author's first name, as in "**Shirley** skillfully creates suspense and horror in 'The Lottery.'" Also, do not use a familiar title before the names of dead authors, such as "**Ms.** Jackson's 'The Lottery' is a suspenseful horror story," or "**Mr.** Shakespeare's idea is that information is uncertain." Use the last names alone.

As with all conventions, of course, there are exceptions. If you are referring to a childhood work of a writer, the first name is appropriate, but shift to the last name when referring to the writer's mature works. If your writer has a professional or a noble title, such as "**Judge** O'Connor," "**Governor** Cross, "**Lord** Byron" or "**Lady** Winchelsea," it is not improper to use the title. Even then, however, the titles are commonly omitted for males, so that most references to Lord Byron and Lord Tennyson should be simply to "Byron" and "Tennyson."

Referring to living authors is somewhat problematical. Some journals and newspapers, like the *New York Times*, use the respectful titles **Mr.** and **Ms.** in their reviews. Scholarly journals, however, which are likely to remain on library shelves for many decades, follow the general principle of beginning with the entire name and then using only the last name for subsequent references.

Of course it is never easy to create fine sentences, but as a mode of improvement, you might create some self-testing mechanisms:

- *For responses and impressions.* Do not say simply, "The story's ending left me with a definite impression," but *state* what the impression is: "The story's ending surprised me and also made me sympathetic to Mathilde."

- *For ideas.* Try to make the idea clear and direct. Do not say "Mathilde is living in a poor household," but rather get at an idea like this one: "The story of Mathilde shows that poor circumstances reduce the quality of life."

- *For critical commentary.* Do not rest with a statement such as "I found 'The Necklace' interesting," but try to describe *what* was interesting and *why* it was interesting: "I found 'The Necklace' interesting because it shows how chance may either make or destroy people's lives."

Good writing begins with attempts, like these, to rephrase sentences to make them really say something. If you always name and pin down descriptions, responses, and judgments, no matter how difficult the task seems, your sentences can be strong because you will be making them exact.

SAMPLE ESSAY, DRAFT 2

The following essay, a revision of the draft on pp. 24–25, includes changes that create greater emphasis and unity. Compared to the early draft, it creates more introductory detail, includes another topic, and reshapes each of the paragraphs to stress the relationship of central idea to topic. Within the limits of a short assignment, the essay illustrates all the principles of organization and unity we have been discussing.

Maupassant's Use of Setting in "The Necklace" to Show the Character of Mathilde

[1]
In "The Necklace" Guy de Maupassant uses setting to reflect the character and development of the main figure, Mathilde Loisel.* As a result, his setting is not particularly vivid or detailed. He does not even provide a description of the ill-fated necklace—the central object in the story—but states only that it is "superb" (¶ 47). He includes only enough description to illuminate his central character, Mathilde. Her changing character may be related to the first apartment, the dream-life mansion rooms, the attic flat, and the public street.†

[2]
Details about the modest apartment of the Loisels on the Street of Martyrs indicate Mathilde's peevish lack of adjustment to life. Though everything is serviceable, she is unhappy with the "drab" walls, "threadbare" furniture, and "ugly" curtains (¶ 3). She has domestic help, but wants more servants than the simple country girl who does the household chores. Her dissatisfaction is also shown by details of her irregularly cleaned tablecloth and the plain and inelegant boiled beef that her husband adores. Even her best formal, which she wears for the theater, makes her unhappy. All these details of the apartment establish that Mathilde's dominant character trait at the start of the story is maladjustment. She therefore seems unpleasant and unsympathetic.

[3]
Like the real-life apartment, the impossibly expensive setting of her daydreams strengthens her unhappiness and her avoidance of reality. All the rooms of her fantasies are large and expensive, draped in silk and filled with nothing but the best furniture and bric-a-brac. Maupassant gives us the following description of her dream world:

> She imagined a gourmet-prepared main course carried on the most exquisite trays and served on the most beautiful dishes, with whispered gallantries which she would hear with a sphinxlike smile as she dined on the pink meat of a trout or the delicate wing of a quail. (¶ 4)

---

* Central idea.
† Thesis sentence.

With dreams like this filling her mind, her despair is even greater. Ironically, this despair, together with her inability to live with reality, brings about her undoing. It makes her agree to borrow the necklace (which is just as unreal as her daydreams of wealth), and losing the necklace drives her into the reality of giving up her apartment and moving into the attic flat.

[4]   Also ironically, the attic flat is related to the coarsening of her character while at the same time it brings out her best qualities of cooperativeness and honesty. Maupassant emphasizes the drudgery of the work she endures to maintain the flat, such as walking up many stairs, washing floors with large buckets of water, cleaning greasy and encrusted pots and pans, taking out the garbage, handwashing clothes, and haggling loudly with local tradespeople. All this reflects her coarsening and loss of sensibility, also shown by her giving up hair and hand care, and wearing the cheapest dresses. The things she does, however, make her heroic (¶ 98). As she cooperates to help her husband pay back the loans, her dreams of a mansion fade and all she has left is the memory of that one happy evening at the Minister of Education's reception. Thus the attic flat brings out her physical change for the worse at the same time that it also brings out her psychological and moral change for the better.

[5]   Her walk on the Champs-Elysées illustrates another combination of traits—self-indulgence and frankness. The Champs-Elysées is the most fashionable street in Paris, and her walk to it is similar to her earlier indulgences in her dreams of wealth. She is, in effect, seeing how the upper-class people are living. But it is on this street where she meets Jeanne, and it is her frankness in confessing the loss and replacement to Jeanne that makes her, finally, completely honest. While the walk thus serves as the occasion for the story's concluding surprise and irony, Mathilde's being on the Champs-Elysées is totally in character, in keeping with her earlier reveries about luxury.

[6]   Other details in the story also have a similar bearing on Mathilde's character. For example, the story mentions little about the party scene, but emphasizes only that she was a great "success" (¶ 52)—a judgment that shows her ability to shine if given the chance. After she and Loisel accept the fact that the necklace cannot be found, Maupassant includes details about the Parisian streets, the visits to loan sharks, and the jewelry and jewelry-case shops, in order to bring out Mathilde's sense of honesty and pride as she "heroically" prepares to live the life of the poor. Thus, in "The Necklace," Maupassant uses setting to highlight Mathilde's maladjustment, her needless misfortune, her loss of youth and beauty, and finally her growth as a responsible human being.

Commentary on the Essay

Several improvements to the first draft (pp. 24-25) may be seen here. The language of paragraph 2 has been revised to show more clearly that Mathilde's dissatisfaction does not seem appropriate. In paragraph 3, the irony of the story is brought out, and the writer has connected the details to the central idea in a richer pattern of ideas, showing the effects of Mathilde's despair. In paragraph 6, the fact that Mathilde "shines" at the dinner party is interpreted according to the central idea. Finally, the conclusion is now much more specific, summarizing the change in Mathilde's character rather than saying simply that the setting reveals her "needless sacrifice." In short, the second draft reflects the complexity of "The Necklace" better than the first draft. Because the writer keeps thinking about and revising the first-draft ideas about the story, the final essay is insightful, tightly structured, and forcefully written.

ESSAY COMMENTARIES

Throughout this book, the sample essays are followed by short commentaries which show how the essays embody the chapter's instruction and guidelines. For each essay in which a number of possible approaches are suggested, the commentary points out which one is employed, and when a sample essay uses two or more approaches, the commentary makes this fact clear. In addition, each commentary singles out one of the paragraphs for detailed analysis of its strategy and use of detail. It is hoped that the commentaries will help you develop the insight necessary to use the essays as aids in your own study and writing.

To sum up, follow these guidelines whenever you do any kind of writing:

- Keep returning to your points.
- Use material from the work you are studying as evidence to support your argument; do not retell the story.
- Include no details from the work unless you have clearly connected them to your points.
- Develop your topic; make it bigger than it was when you began.
- Always strive to make your statements exact, comprehensive, and forceful.

RESPONDING TO LITERATURE: LIKES AND DISLIKES

People read literature because they like it. It is therefore worth considering those qualities that, at the simplest level, produce responses of pleasure and, in addition, of displeasure. You either like or dislike a poem, story, or play, but if you say no more than that you have not said much. Writing about likes and dislikes requires you to explain the reasons for your responses. In short, your discussion should be *informed and informative* rather than *uninformed and unexplained.*

Sometimes a first response is that a work is "boring." This reaction is usually a mask covering an incomplete and superficial first reading. It is neither informative nor informed. As you study most works, however, you will be drawn into them and become *interested* and *involved.* To be interested in a work is to be taken into it emotionally; to be involved suggests that your emotions become almost wrapped up in the characters, problems, and outcomes of a work. Both "interest" and "involvement" describe genuine responses to reading. Once you get interested and involved, your reading ceases to be a task or assignment, and becomes a pleasure.

Using Your Journal to Record Responses

No one can tell you what you should or should not like; liking is your own concern. While your experience of reading is still fresh, therefore, you should use your journal (discussed earlier, pp. 10-13) to record not only your observations about a work, but also your responses. Be frank in your judgment. Write down your likes and dislikes, and try to explain the reasons for your response, even if these are brief and incomplete. If, after later thought and fuller understanding, you change or modify your first impressions , record these changes too. Here is a journal entry that explains a favorable response to Guy de Maupassant's "The Necklace":

> I like "The Necklace" because of the surprise ending. It isn't that I like Mathilde's bad luck, but I like the way Maupassant hides the most important fact in the story until the end. Mathilde does all that work and sacrifice for no reason at all, and the surprise ending makes this point strongly.

This paragraph could be expanded as a part of a developing essay. It is a clear statement of liking, followed by references to likable things in the work. This response pattern, which can be simply phrased as "I like [dislike] this work *because* . . .," is a useful way to begin journal entries because it always requires that a response be followed with an explanation. If at first you cannot write any full sentences detailing the causes of your responses, at least make a brief list of the things you like or dislike. If you write nothing, you will probably forget your reactions. Recovering them later, either for discussion or writing, will be difficult.

Responding Favorably

Usually you can equate your interest in a work with liking it. You can be more specific about favorable responses by citing one or more of the following:

- You like and admire the characters and what they do and stand for.
- You learn something new—something you had never known or thought before.
- You gain new insights into things that you already knew.
- You learn about characters and customs of different places, times, and ways of life.
- You get interested and involved in the outcome of the action or ideas, and do not want to put the work down until you have finished it.

- You feel happy or thrilled because of reading the work.
- You are amused and laugh often as you read.
- You like the author's presentation.
- You find that some of the ideas and expressions are beautiful and worth remembering.

Obviously, if you have none of these responses, or find a character or incident that is distasteful, you will not like the work.

Responding Unfavorably

Although so far we have dismissed *boring* and stressed *interest, involvement,* and *liking,* it is important to know that disliking all or part of a work is normal and acceptable. You do not need to hide this response. Here, for example, are two short journal responses expressing dislike for Maupassant's "The Necklace":

1. I do not like "The Necklace" because Mathilde seems spoiled, and I don't think she is worth reading about.
2. "The Necklace" is not an adventure story, and I like reading only adventure stories.

These are both legitimate responses because they are based on a clear standard of judgment. The first stems from a distaste for one of the main character's unlikable traits; the second, from a preference for rapidly moving stories that evoke interest in the dangers that main characters face and overcome.

Here is a paragraph-length journal entry that might be developed from the first response. Notice that the reasons for dislike are explained. They would need only slightly more development for use in an essay:

> I do not like "The Necklace" because Mathilde seems spoiled and I do not think she is worth reading about. She is a phony. She nags her husband because he is not rich. She never tells the truth. I dislike her for hurrying away from the party because she is afraid of being seen in her shabby coat. She is foolish and dishonest for not telling Jeanne Forrestier about losing the necklace. It is true that she works hard to pay the debt, but she also puts her husband through ten years of hardship. If Mathilde had faced facts, she might have had a better life. I do not like her and cannot like the story because of her.

As long as you include reasons for your dislike, as in this journal paragraph, you can use them again when developing your essay. In further consideration, you will surely also expand thoughts, include new details, pick new topics for development as paragraphs, and otherwise modify your journal entry. You might even change your mind. However, even if you do not, it is better to record your original responses and reasons honestly than to force yourself to say you like something that you do not like.

Putting Dislikes into a Larger Context

While it is important to be honest about disliking a work, it is more important to broaden your perspective and expand your taste. For example, a dislike based on the preference for only mystery or adventure stories, if generally applied, would cause a person to dislike most works of literature. This attitude seems unnecessarily self-limiting.

If negative responses are put in a larger context, it is possible to expand the capacity to like and appreciate. For instance, some readers might be preoccupied with their own concerns and therefore be uninterested in remote or "irrelevant" literary figures. However, if by reading about literary characters they can gain insight into general problems of life, and therefore their own concerns, they can find something to like in just about any work of literature. Other readers might like sports and therefore not read anything but the daily sports pages. But what probably interests them about sports is competition, so if competition or conflict can be found in a literary work, they might discover something to like in that work.

As an example, let us consider again the dislike based on a preference for adventure stories, and see if this preference can be widened. Here are some reasons for liking adventures:

1. Adventure has fast action.
2. It has danger and tension, and therefore interest.
3. It has daring, active, and successful characters.
4. It has obstacles which the characters work hard to overcome.

No one could claim that the first three points apply to "The Necklace," but the fourth point is promising. Mathilde, the major character, works hard to overcome an obstacle: She pitches in to help her husband pay the large debt. If you like adventures because the characters try to gain worthy goals, then you can also like "The Necklace" for the same reason. The principle here is clear: If a reason for liking a favorite work or type of work can be found in another work, then there is reason to like that new work.

The following paragraph shows a possible application of this "bridging" process of extending preferences. (The sample essay [p. 43] is also developed along these lines.)

> I usually like only adventure stories, and therefore I disliked "The Necklace" at first because it is not adventure. But one of my reasons for liking adventure is that the characters work hard to overcome difficult obstacles, like finding buried treasure or exploring new places. Mathilde, Maupassant's main character in "The Necklace," also works hard to overcome an obstacle—helping to pay back the money and interest for the borrowed 18,000 francs used as part of the payment for the replacement necklace. I like adventure characters because they stick to things and win out. I see the same toughness in Mathilde. Her problems get more interesting as the story moves on after a slow beginning. I came to like the story.

In this way, an accepted principle of liking can be applied to another work where it also applies. A person who adapts principles in this open-minded way can redefine dislikes and may consequently expand the ability to like and appreciate many kinds of literature.

An equally open-minded way to develop understanding and widen taste is to put dislikes in the following light: An author's creation of an *unlikable* character, situation, attitude, or expression may be deliberate. Your dislike might then result from the author's *intentions*. A first task of study is therefore to understand and explain the intention or plan. As you put the plan into your own words, you may find that you can like a work with unlikable things in it. Here is paragraph that traces this pattern of thinking, based again on "The Necklace":

> Maupassant apparently wants the reader to dislike Mathilde, and I do. At first, he shows her being unrealistic and spoiled. She lies to everyone and nags her husband. Her rushing away from the party so that no one can see her shabby coat is a form of lying. But I like the story itself because Maupassant makes another kind of point. He does not hide her bad qualities, but makes it clear that she herself is the cause of her trouble. If people like Mathilde never face the truth, they will get into bad situations. This is a good point, and I like the way Maupassant makes it. The entire story is therefore worth liking even though I still do not like Mathilde.

Both of these ways are honest to the original negative reactions. In the first paragraph, the writer applies one of his principles of liking to include "The Necklace." In the second, the writer considers her initial dislike in the context of the work, and discovers a basis for liking the story as a whole while still disliking the main character. The main concern in both responses is to keep an open mind despite initial dislike, and then to see if the unfavorable response can be more fully and broadly considered.

However, if you decide that your dislike overbalances any reasons you can find for liking, then you should explain your dislike. As long as you relate your response to the work accurately, and measure it by a clear standard of judgment, your dislike of even a commonly liked work is not unacceptable. The important issue is not so much that you like or dislike a particular work *but that you develop your own abilities to analyze and express your ideas.*

WRITING ABOUT RESPONSES: LIKES AND DISLIKES

In writing about your responses, rely on your initial informed reactions. It is not easy to reconstruct your first responses after a lapse of time, so you will need your journal observations to guide the prewriting stage. Develop your essay by stressing those characters, incidents, and ideas that interest (or do not interest) you in the work.

Always relate the details of the work to the point you are making about your ongoing responses. Stress your involvement in the work as you bring out evidence from it. You can show your attitudes by indicating approval (or disapproval), by commenting favorably (or unfavorably) on the details, by indicating things that seem new (or shopworn) and particularly instructive (or wrong), and by giving assent to (or dissent from) ideas or expressions of feeling.

Organizing Your Essay

INTRODUCTION. Begin by describing briefly the conditions that influence your response. Your central idea should be why you like or dislike the work. The thesis sentence should list the major causes of your response, which are to be developed in the body.

BODY. The most common approach is to consider specific details that you like or dislike. The list on pages 38-39 may help you articulate your responses. For example, you may have admired a particular character, or maybe you got so interested in the story that you could not put it down. Also, it may be that a major idea, a fresh insight, or a particular outcome is the major point that you wish to develop. The sample paragraph on page 000 shows a surprise ending as the cause of a favorable response.

A second approach (see p. 40) is to explain any changes in your responses about the work (i.e., negative to positive and vice versa). This approach requires that you isolate the causes of the change, but it does *not* require you to retell the story from beginning to end. (1) One way to deal with such a change—the "bridge" method of transferring preference from one type of work to another—is shown in the sample essay (p. 43). (2) Another way is to explain a change in terms of a new awareness or understanding that you did not have on a first reading. Thus your first response to Poe's "The Masque of the Red Death" might be unfavorable or neutral because the story seems unnecessarily sensational and lurid. But further consideration might lead you to discover new insights that change your mind, like the futility of challenging death, or the impossibility of stopping an epidemic. Your essay would then explain how these new insights have caused you to start liking the story.

CONCLUSION. Here you might summarize the reasons for your major response. You might also face any issues brought up by a change or modification of your first reactions. For example, if you have always held certain assumptions about your taste but like the work despite these assumptions, you may wish to talk about your own change or development. This topic is personal, but in an essay about likes or dislikes, discovery about yourself is legitimate and worthy.

SAMPLE ESSAY

Some Reasons for Liking Maupassant's "The Necklace"°

[1]
To me, the most likable kind of reading is adventure. There are many reasons for my preference, but an important one is that adventure characters work hard to overcome obstacles. Because Guy de Maupassant's "The Necklace" is not adventure, I did not like it at first. But in one respect the story is like adventure: The major character Mathilde, with her husband Loisel, works hard for ten years to overcome a difficult obstacle. Thus, because Mathilde does what adventure characters also do, the story is likable.* Mathilde's appeal results from her hard work, strong character, sad fate, and also from the way our view of her changes.†

[2]
Mathilde's hard work makes her seem good. Once she and her husband are faced with the huge debt of 18,000 francs, she works like a slave to pay it back. She gives up her servant and moves to a cheaper place. She does the household drudgery, wears cheap clothes, and bargains with shopkeepers for the lowest prices. Just like the characters in adventure stories, who do hard and unpleasant things, she does what she has to, and this makes her admirable.

[3]
Her strong character shows her endurance, a likable trait. At first she is nagging and fussy, and she always dreams about wealth and tells lies, but she changes and gets better. She recognizes her blame in losing the necklace, and she has the toughness to help her husband redeem the debt. She sacrifices "heroically" (¶ 98) by giving up her comfortable way of life, even though in the process she also loses her youth and beauty. Her jobs are not the exotic and glamorous ones of adventure stories, but her force of character makes her as likable as an adventure heroine.

[4]
Her sad fate also makes her likable. In adventure stories the characters often suffer as they do their jobs. Mathilde also suffers, but in a different way, because her suffering is permanent while the hardships of adventure characters are temporary. This fact makes her pitiable, and even more so because all her sacrifices are not necessary. This unfairness about her life invites the reader to take her side.

[5]
The most important quality promoting admiration is the way in which Maupassant shifts our view of Mathilde. As she goes deeper into her hard life, Maupassant stresses her work and not the innermost thoughts he reveals at the beginning. In other words, the view into her character at the start, when she dreams about wealth, invites dislike, while the focus at the end is on her achievements, with never a complaint—even though she still has golden memories, as the narrator tells us:

> But sometimes, when her husband was at work, she sat down near the window, and she dreamed of that evening so long ago, of that party, where she had been so beautiful and so admired. (¶104)

° See pp 3–10 for this story.
* Central idea.
† Thesis sentence.

A major quality of Maupassant's changed emphasis is that these recollections do not lead to anything unfortunate. Thus his shift in focus, from Mathilde's dissatisfaction to her sharing of responsibility and sacrifice, encourages the reader to like her.

[6]   "The Necklace" is not an adventure story, but Mathilde has some of the good qualities of adventure characters . Also, the surprise revelation that the lost necklace was false is an unforgettable twist which makes her more deserving than she seems at first. Maupassant has arranged the story so that the reader finally admires Mathilde. "The Necklace" is a skillful and likable story.

Commentary on the Essay

This essay demonstrates how a reader may develop appreciation by transferring or "bridging" a preference for one type of work to a work that does not belong to the type (described on pp. 40-41). In the essay, the bridge is an already established taste for adventure stories, and the grounds for liking "The Necklace" is that Mathilde, the main character, shares the admirable qualities of adventure heroes and heroines.

In paragraph 1, the introduction, the grounds for transferring preference are established. Paragraph 2 deals with Mathilde's capacity to work hard, while paragraph 3 considers the equally admirable quality of endurance. The fourth paragraph describes how Mathilde's condition evokes sympathy and pity. These paragraphs hence explain the story's appeal by asserting that the main character is similar to admirable characters from works of adventure.

Paragraph 5 shows that Maupassant, as the story unfolds, alters the reader's perceptions of Mathilde from bad to good. For this reason paragraph 5 marks a new direction from paragraphs 2, 3, and 4, because it moves away from the topic material itself—Mathilde's character—to Maupassant's *technique* in handling the topic material.

Paragraph 6, the conclusion, restates the comparison, and also introduces the surprise ending as an additional reason for liking "The Necklace." With the body and conclusion together, therefore, the essay establishes five separate reasons for approval. Three of these, which are derived directly from the main character, constitute the major grounds for liking the story, while two are related to Maupassant's techniques as an author.

Throughout the essay, the central idea is brought out in words and expressions like "likable," "Mathilde's appeal," "strong character," "she does what she has to," "pitiable," and "take her side" Many of these expressions were first made in the writer's journal, and, mixed as they are with details from the story, they make for continuity. It is this thematic development, together with details from the story as supporting evidence, that shows how an essay on the responses of liking and disliking may be both informed and informative.

FICTION

Henri Matisse, Harmony in Red, (1808-9), Hermitage, Leningrad, (ARS/SPADEM), George Roos/Art Resource, NY.

2

Fiction: An Overview

Fiction originally meant anything made up or shaped. As we understand the word now, it refers to prose stories—short or long—a meaning it has retained since its first recorded use in this sense in 1599. Fiction is distinguished from the works it imitates, such as *historical accounts, reports, biographies, autobiographies, letters,* and *personal memoirs* and *meditations.* While fiction may often resemble these forms, it has a separate identity because it originates not in historical facts but in the creative, imaginative powers. Writers of fiction may include historically accurate details, but their primary goal is to tell a story and say something significant about life.

The essence of fiction, as opposed to drama, is **narration**, the recounting or telling of a sequence of events or actions. The earliest works of fiction relied almost exclusively on narration, with speeches or dialogue being reported rather than quoted directly. Much recent fiction includes extended passages of dialogue, thereby becoming more *dramatic* even though narration is still the primary mode.

Fiction is rooted in ancient legends and myths. Local priests narrated stories about their gods and heroes, as shown in some of the narratives of ancient Egypt. In the course of history, traveling storytellers would appear in a court or village to entertain listeners with tales of adventure in faraway countries. Although many of these were fictionalized accounts of events and people who may not ever have existed, they were largely accepted as fact or history. An especially long tale, an **epic**, was recited over a period of days. To aid their memories, the storytellers chanted their tales in poetry, often perhaps accompanying themselves on a stringed instrument, to impress and entertain their listeners.

Legends and epics also reinforced the local religions and power structures. Myths of gods like Zeus and Athena (Greece), Jupiter and Minerva (Rome), and Baal and Ishtar (Mesopotamia) abounded, together with stories of famous men and women like Oedipus, Helen of Troy, Hercules, Achilles,

Odysseus, Penelope, Utu-Napishtim, Joseph, David, and Ruth. The ancient Macedonian king and general Alexander the Great (356–323 B.C.) developed many of his ideas about nobility and valor from *The Iliad,* Homer's epic about the Trojan War—and, we might add, from discussing the epic with his tutor, Aristotle.

Perhaps nowhere is the moralistic-argumentative aspect of ancient storytelling better illustrated than in the **fables** of Aesop, a Greek who wrote in the sixth century B.C., and in the **parables** of Jesus as told in the Gospels of the New Testament. In these works, a short narrative provides an illustration of a religious, philosophic, or psychological conclusion. A Roman story of the first century A.D., "The Widow of Ephesus," by Gaius Petronius (included in this chapter), illustrates this type of persuasive intention, in which the use of narrative events for a rhetorical and persuasive purpose is made clear right at the beginning.

Starting about 800 years ago, storytelling in Western civilization was developed to a fine art by writers such as Marie de France, a Frenchwoman who wrote in England near the end of the twelfth century, Giovanni Boccaccio (Italian, 1313–1375), and Geoffrey Chaucer (English, ca. 1340–1400). William Shakespeare (1564–1616) drew heavily on history and legend for the stories and characters in his plays.

MODERN FICTION

Fiction in the modern sense of the word did not begin to flourish until the late seventeenth and eighteenth centuries, when human beings of all social stations and ways of life became important literary topics. As one writer put it in 1709, human nature was not simple, and could be explained only with reference to many complex motives like "passion, humor, caprice, zeal, faction, and a thousand other springs."[1] Thus began the individual and psychological concerns that characterize fiction today. Indeed, fiction is strong because it is so real and personal. Most characters have both first and last names; the countries and cities in which they live are modeled on real places; and their actions and interactions are like those which readers themselves have experienced, could experience, or could easily imagine themselves experiencing.

Along with attention to character, fiction is also concerned with the place of individuals in their environments. In the simplest sense, environment is a backdrop or setting within which characters speak, move, and act. But more broadly, environment comprises the social, economic, and political conditions which affect the outcomes of people's lives. Fiction is usually about the interactions among people, but it also involves these larger interactions—either directly or indirectly. Indeed, in a typical work of fiction

[1] Anthony Ashley Cooper, Third Earl of Shaftesbury, *Sensus Communis,* Part III, Section iii.

there are always many forces, both small and large, that influence the ways in which characters meet and deal with their problems.

The first true works of fiction in Europe, however, were less concerned with society or politics than adventure. These were the lengthy Spanish and French **romances** of the sixteenth and seventeenth centuries. (The French word for "novel" is still *roman*.) In English the word **novel** was borrowed from French and Italian to describe these works and to distinguish them from medieval and classical romances as something that was *new* (the meaning of *novel*). In England the word **story** was used along with *novel* in reference to the new literary form.

The increased levels of education and literacy in the eighteenth century facilitated the development of fiction. During the times of Shakespeare (1564–1616) and Dryden (1631–1700), the only way a writer could make a living from writing was to have a play accepted at a theater, and then receive either a direct payment or the proceeds of an "author's benefit." The paying audiences, however, were limited to people who lived within a short distance of the theater or who had the leisure and money to stay in town during the theater season.

Once great numbers of people could read for themselves, the paying audience for literature expanded. A writer could write a novel and receive money for it from a publisher, who could then profit from a wide sale. Readers could pick up the book when they wished and finish it when they chose. Reading a novel could even be a social event, for people would read to each other as a means of sharing the experience. With this wider audience, authors could make a career out of writing. Fiction had arrived as a major genre of literature.

THE SHORT STORY

Because novels were long, they took a long time to read—hours, days, even weeks. American writer Edgar Allan Poe (1809–1849) addressed this problem and developed a theory of the **short story,** which he described in a review of Nathaniel Hawthorne's *Twice-Told Tales.* Poe was convinced that "worldly interests" prevented people from gaining the "totality" of comprehension and response that he believed reading should provide. A short, concentrated story (he called it "a brief prose tale" which could be read at a single sitting) was ideal for producing this kind of powerful impression.

In the wake of the taste for short fiction that Poe created, many writers have worked in the form. Today, innumerable stories are printed in periodicals, such as *Story* magazine, and collections, such as *American Short Story Masterpieces.* Some of the more well-established writers, such as William Faulkner, Ernest Hemingway, Shirley Jackson, Guy de Maupassant, Flannery O'Connor, Alice Walker, and Eudora Welty, to name only a small number, have collected their works and published them in single volumes.

ELEMENTS OF FICTION I: VERISIMILITUDE AND *DONNÉE*

Fiction, along with drama, has a basis in **realism** or **verisimilitude**. That is, the situations or characters, though they are the **invention** of writers, are similar to those that many human beings experience, know, or think. Even **fantasy**, the creation of events that are dreamlike or fantastic, is anchored in the real world, however remotely. This connection of art and life has led some critics to label fiction, and also drama, as an art of **imitation**. Shakespeare's Hamlet states that an actor attempts to portray real human beings in realistic situations (to "hold a mirror up to Nature").

The same may also be said about writers of fiction, with the provisos that reality is not easily defined and that authors can follow many paths in imitating it. What counts in fiction is the way in which authors establish the *ground rules* for their works, whether with realistic or nonrealistic characters, places, actions, and physical and chemical laws. The assumption that authors make about the nature of their story material is called a **postulate** or a **premise**—what Henry James called a *donnée* (something given). The *donnée* of some stories is to resemble the everyday world as much as possible. Eudora Welty's "A Worn Path" is such a story. It tells of a woman's walking journey through a wooded area to the streets of a town, and then to the interior of a building. The events of the story are common; they could happen in life just as Welty presents them.

Once a *donnée* is established, it governs the directions in which the story moves. Jackson's "The Lottery," for example, contains a premise or *donnée* that may be phrased like this: "Suppose that a small, ordinary town held a lottery in which the prize was not money but a ritual punishment." Everything in Jackson's story follows from this premise. At first we seem to be reading about innocent actions in a rural American community. By the end, however, in accord with the premise, the story shifts from this everyday, realistic level into a nightmarish act of cruelty.

In such ways authors may lead us into remote, fanciful, and symbolic levels of reality. In Clark's "A Portable Phonograph," for example, the futuristic *donnée* is that world civilization has been destroyed in a global war. In Poe's "The Masque of the Red Death," the phantasmagoric *donnée* is that Death may assume a human shape and claim all the revelers at a bizarre party. Literally nothing is out of bounds as long as the author makes clear the premise for the action, as in Pickthall's "The Worker in Sandalwood," where the *donnée* is that miracles may overcome ordinary reality.

Scenes and actions such as these, which are not realistic in our ordinary sense of the word, are normal in stories *as long as they follow the author's own stated or implied ground rules.* You may always judge a work by the standard of whether it is consistent with the premise, or the *donnée*, created by the writer.

In addition to referring to various levels of reality, the word *donnée* may also be taken more broadly. In *futuristic* and *science fiction*, for example, there is an assumption or *donnée* of certain situations and technological developments (e.g., interstellar space travel) that are not presently in existence. In a *love story*, the *donnée* is that two people meet and overcome an obstacle of some sort (usually not a serious one) on the way to fulfilling their love. Interesting variations of this type may be seen in Lawrence's "The Horse Dealer's Daughter," Munro's "The Found Boat," Dixon's "All Gone," and Joyce's "Araby."

There are of course other types. An *apprenticeship* or *growth story*, for example, is about the growth of a major character, such as Jackie in "First Confession," Sarty in "Barn Burning," and Emily in "I Stand Here Ironing." In the *detective story*, a mysterious event is posited, and then the detective draws conclusions from the available evidence. A variation on the detective story may be seen in Glaspell's "A Jury of Her Peers," in which the correct detective work is done by two women, not by the police investigator who should be doing it right.

In addition to setting levels of reality and fictional types, authors may use other controls or springboards as their *données*. Sometimes an initial situation may be the occasion from which the story develops (such as the social worker calling the mother to express concern about the daughter in Olsen's "I Stand Here Ironing"). Or the key may be a pattern of behavior (the boy's reactions to the people around him in O'Connor's "First Confession"), or a lie, as in Anderson's "I'm a Fool," or a lunchtime conversation, as in Atwood's "Rape Fantasies." There is always a shaping force, or a *donnée*, that guides the actions, and often a number of such controls operate at the same time.

ELEMENTS OF FICTION II: CHARACTER, PLOT, STRUCTURE, AND THEME

Works of fiction share a number of common elements, which we discuss in detail in subsequent chapters. The more significant ones are *character, plot, structure*, and *theme*.

Character

Stories, like plays, are about characters—characters who, though not real people, are drawn from life. A **character**, also discussed in detail in Chapter 4, is a reasonable facsimile of a human being, with all the good and bad traits of being human.[2] A story is usually concerned with a major problem that a character must face. This may involve interaction with another char-

---

[2] Even the beings from other worlds and the lifelike robots and computers that we meet in science fiction, along with animals who populate beast fables and modern comics and films, interest us only as they exhibit human characteristics. Thus, Yogi Bear prefers honey to berries; a supremely intelligent computer with a conflicting program turns destructive; and an alien of superhuman strength riding on a spaceship tries to destroy all the human passengers. But we all know human beings with a sweet tooth; we all know that internal conflicts can produce unpredictable and destructive results; and who would say that the desire for power is not human?

acter, with a difficult situation, or with an idea or general circumstances that force action. The character may win, lose, or tie. He or she may learn and be the better for the experience or may miss the point and be unchanged.

Earlier we mentioned that modern fiction has accompanied the development of a psychological interest in human beings. Psychology itself has grown out of the philosophical and religious idea that people are not evil by nature, but rather that they have many inborn capacities—some for good and others for bad. People are not free of problems, and they make many mistakes in their lives, but they nevertheless are important and interesting, and are therefore worth writing about, whether male or female; young or old; white, black, tan, or yellow; rich or poor; worker or industrialist; traveler or resident; aviator, performer, mother, daughter, homemaker, prince, general, bartender, or checkout clerk.

It would therefore seem that there is nothing that is beyond the scope of fiction. A married couple struggling under an enormous debt, a woman meditating about her daughter's growth, a young boy learning about sin and forgiveness, a young man regretting that he cannot admit a lie, a woman surrounded by insensitive and self-seeking men, a man preserving love despite overwhelming odds, a woman learning to cope with her son's handicap—all these are important because human beings are important. In fiction you may expect characters from every area of life, and, because we all share the same capacities for concern, involvement, sympathy, happiness, sorrow, exhilaration, and disappointment, you should be able to interest yourself in characters and the ways they deal with their circumstances.

Plot

In a well-done story, all the **actions** or **incidents**, **speeches**, **thoughts**, and **observations** are linked together to make up an entirety, sometimes called an **organic unity**. The essence of this unity is the development and resolution of a **conflict**—or conflicts—in which the **protagonist**, or central character, is engaged. The pattern in which the protagonist meets and resolves the conflict is called the **plot**, which has been compared to the story's *map, scheme,* or *blueprint.* The plot is based on the interactions of causes and effects as they develop **sequentially** or **chronologically**. That is, the story's actions follow one another in time as the protagonist meets and tries to overcome the forces of opposition.

Often the protagonist's struggle is directed against another character—an **antagonist.** Just as often, however, the struggle may occur between the protagonist and opposing groups, forces, ideas, and choices—all of which make up a collective antagonist. The conflict may be carried out wherever human beings spend their lives, such as a kitchen, a bedroom, a restaurant, a town square, a farm, an estate, a workshop, or a battlefield. The conflict may also take place internally, within the mind of the protagonist.

Structure

Structure refers to the way a plot is assembled. Chronologically, all stories are similar because they all move from beginning to end in accord with the time it takes for causes to produce effects. But authors choose many different ways to develop their plots. While some stories are told in chronological order, others may get pieced together through out-of-sequence and widely separated episodes, speeches, remembrances, dreams, nightmares, periods of delirium, fragments of letters, overheard conversations, and the like. In dealing with structure, therefore, we deal with the *arrangement* and *development* of individual stories. Usually we study an entire story, but we may also direct our attention toward a smaller aspect of arrangement.

Theme

Fiction necessarily embodies issues and ideas. Even stories written for entertainment alone are based in an idea or position. Thus, writers of comic works are committed to the idea that human difficulties can be treated with humor. More serious works may force characters to make difficult moral choices, in the thought that in a losing situation the only winner is the one who maintains honor and self-respect. Mystery and suspense stories rest on the belief that problems have solutions, even if they may not at first seem apparent. Writers may deal with the triumphs and defeats of life, the admirable and the despicable, the humorous and the pathetic, but whatever their goal, they are always expressing ideas about human experience.

In fiction, ideas take the form of an underlying **theme** or **central idea**, which helps to tie the work together. Often the author makes the theme obvious, as in the Aesop fable in which a man uses an ax to kill a fly on his son's forehead. It does not take much imagination to state the theme of this fable. A major theme in Maupassant's "The Necklace" is that people may be destroyed or made fortunate by the most insignificant and unpredictable of events. The accidental loss of the borrowed necklace is just such an event; this misfortune ruins the lives of both Mathilde and her husband for the following ten years.

The process of determining and describing the themes or ideas in stories is probably never complete; there is always another theme that we may discuss. Thus in "The Necklace," one might note the additional themes that adversity brings out worth, that telling the truth is better than concealing it, that envy often produces ill fortune, or that good fortune is never recognized until it is lost. Indeed, one of the ways in which we may judge stories is to determine the degree to which they embody a number of valid and important themes.

ELEMENTS OF FICTION III: THE WRITER'S TOOLS

Narration

Writers have a number of modes of presentation, or "tools," which they may use in writing their stories. The principal tool (and the heart of fiction) is **narration**, the reporting of actions in chronological sequence. The object of narration is, as much as possible, to *render* the story, to make it clear and to bring it alive to the reader's imagination. The essence of narration is the movement of sentences through time. The reading and comprehension of a narration cannot be done in a single view, as with works of painting and sculpture. Jacques-Louis David's painting *The Death of Socrates*, for example, is like a narrative because it tells a story—an actual historical occurrence. As related by Plato in the dialogue *Phaedo*, Socrates takes the cup of hemlock which he will drink as the means of carrying out his own execution. But it is *only* this moment of time that David is able to capture in his painting. In contrast, the writer of narrative may include all the events leading up to and following such a moment, for a narration moves in a continuous line, from word to word, scene to scene, action to action, and speech to speech. As a result of this sequential movement, the reader's comprehension must necessarily also be sequential.

The Death of Socrates, Jacques Louis David, The Metropolitan Museum of Art, Wolfe Fund, 1931.

Style

The medium of fiction and of all literature is language, and the manipulation of language—the **style**—is a primary skill of the writer. A mark of a good style is *active verbs*, and nouns that are **specific** and **concrete.** Even with the most active and graphic diction possible, writers can never render their incidents and scenes exactly, but they may be judged on how vividly they tell their stories.

Point of View

One of the most important ways in which writers knit their stories together, and also an important way in which they try to interest and engage readers, is the careful control of **point of view** (See Chapter 5, pp. 180–229). Point of view is the **voice** of the story, the speaker who does the narrating. It is the way the reality of a story is made to seem authentic. It may be regarded as the story's *focus*, the *angle of vision* from which things are not only seen and reported but also judged.

A story may be told by a fictitious "observer" who tells us what he or she saw, heard, concluded, and thought. This **speaker,** or **narrator**—terms that are interchangeable— may sometimes seem to be the author speaking directly using an **authorial voice**, but just as often the speaker is an independent character—a **persona** with characteristics that separate him or her from the author. Sometimes the narrator is a participant in the story. Stories told in these ways have **first-person** points of view, for the speaker uses the "I" personal pronoun in referring to his or her position as an observer or commentator.

The other important point of view is the **third person**.[3] The third-person point of view may be (1) **limited**, with the focus being on one particular character and what he or she does, says, hears, thinks, and otherwise experiences, (2) **omniscient**, with the possibility that the thoughts and behaviors of all the characters are open and fully known by the speaker, and (3) **dramatic**, or **objective**, in which the story is confined *only* to the reporting of actions and speeches, with no commentary and no revelation of the thoughts of any of the characters unless the characters themselves make these revelations dramatically.

Understanding point of view often requires subtlety— indeed, it may be one of the most difficult of all concepts in the study of fiction. In fuller perspective, therefore, we may think of it as the *total position* from which things are viewed, understood, and communicated. The position might be simply physical: *Where was the speaker located when the events occurred,* or *Does the speaker give us a close or distant view of the events?* The position might also be personal or philosophical: *Do the events illustrate a personal opinion* (Maupassant's "The

---

[3] The possibilities of a second-person point of view are discussed in Chapter 5.

Necklace"), or *embody a philosophical judgment* (Hawthorne's "Young Goodman Brown"), or *argue for a theological viewpoint* ("The Prodigal Son")?

Point of view is one of the many ways in which authors make fiction vital. By controlling point of view, an author helps us make reasonable inferences about the story's actions. Authors use point of view to raise some of the same questions in their fiction that perplex us in life. We need to evaluate what fictional narrators as well as real people tell us, for what they say is affected by their limitations, attitudes, opinions, and degree of candidness. The narrator of Petronius's "The Widow of Ephesus," for example, declares that his story illustrates the weakness and inconstancy of women. But doesn't he really tell us more about his own limitations than about the limitations of women? The narrator of Twain's "Luck" is convinced that his hero is a total fool, and he tells the story to make us similarly convinced. But could we make a case that he might also be somewhat jealous of his boob hero, enough perhaps to omit some of the explanations that might give us a rounder picture? For readers, the perception of a fictional point of view can be as complex as life itself, and it may be as difficult—in fiction as in life—to evaluate our sources of information.

Description

Together with narration, an important aspect of fiction is **description,** which brings scenes and feelings readily to the imagination of readers. Description can be both physical (places and persons) and psychological (an emotion or set of emotions). Description can interrupt action, so many writers include only as much as is necessary to highlight actions, as in Tillie Olsen's "I Stand Here Ironing," where we find a minimum of physical description, although all of us can imagine where a woman doing the week's ironing might be and what she might look like.

Other writers create extensive descriptions. Edgar Allan Poe presents detailed scenes not only to locate his actions, but also to evoke tension and excitement. Alice Munro imaginatively creates an entire nineteenth-century town in her story "Meneseteung." By the time we finish the story we have a sense of what life in her imaginary town was like over a period of several decades.

Mood and **atmosphere** are important adjuncts of descriptive writing, and to the degree that descriptions are evocative, they may reach the level of **metaphor** and **symbolism**. These characteristics of fiction are a property of all literature, and you will also encounter them in your considerations of poetry and drama.

Dialogue

Another major tool of the writer of fiction is **dialogue**. By definition, dialogue is the conversation of two people, but more than two characters may participate. The major medium of the dramatist, dialogue is just one of the means by which the fiction writer makes a story vivid and dramatic. Straight narration and description can do no more than make a secondhand assertion that a character's thoughts and responses exist, but dialogue makes everything real and firsthand.

Dialogue is hence a means of *rendering* rather than presenting. If characters feel pain or declare love, their own words may be taken as the expression of what is on their minds. Some dialogue may be terse and minimal, like that in Hemingway. Other dialogue may be expanded, depending on the situation, the personalities of the characters, and the author's intent. Dialogue may be about anything, including future plans, reactions to the past, indications of emotion, and political, social, philosophic, or religious ideas.

The language of dialogue indicates the intelligence, articulateness, educational levels, or emotional states of the speakers. Hence the author might use *grammatical mistakes, faulty pronunciation,* or *slang* to show a character of limited or disadvantaged background or a character who is trying to be seen in that light. *Dialect* shows the region from which the speaker comes, just as an *accent* indicates a place of national origin. *Jargon* and *cliché* suggest self-inflation or intellectual limitations—usually reasons for laughter. The use of *private, intimate expressions* might show people who are close to each other emotionally. Speech that is interrupted by *voiced pauses* (e.g., "er," "ah," "um," "you know"), or speech characterized by *inappropriate words* might show a character who is unsure or not in control. There are many possibilities in dialogue, but no matter what qualities you find, writers include dialogue to enable you to know their characters better.

Commentary

Writers may also include **commentary**, **analysis**, or **interpretation**, in the expectation that readers need insight or into the characters and actions. When fiction was new, authors often expressed such commentary directly. Henry Fielding (1707–1754) divided his novels into "books," and included a chapter of personal and philosophic commentary at the beginning of each of these. In the next century, George Eliot (1819–1880) included many extensive passages of commentary in her novels.

Later writers have kept commentary at a minimum, preferring instead to concentrate on direct action and dialogue, and leaving it to readers to draw their own conclusions about meaning. In first-person narrations, however, you may expect the narrators to make their own personal comments, as in Olsen's "I Stand Here Ironing," and Zabytko's "Home Soil." Observations made by dramatic speakers in works like these may be accepted at face value, but you should recognize that anything the speakers say is also a mode of character disclosure. Such commentary is therefore just as much a part of the story as the narrative incidents.

Tone and Irony

In every story one may consider **tone**, that is, the ways in which the author conveys attitudes about the story material and toward the readers. In "The Necklace," for example, Maupassant presents the bitter plight of Mathilde and her husband. *Pity* is thus an appropriate word for the author's attitude, and it is appropriate also for the reader's response. Maupassant also shows that Mathilde has brought her misfortune on herself, so the attitude is one of at least partial *satisfaction* that justice has been done. But Mathilde works hard and unselfishly; hence *admiration* tempers any inclination to condemn her. Finally, the story's conclusion shows that Mathilde's years of hard labor were unnecessary. Therefore, *regret* enters into the response. In a discussion of the tone of the story, it would be necessary to describe *how the author's presentation of material shapes these varying attitudes.*

Because Mathilde's sacrifice for a period of ten years is unnecessary, her situation is *ironic.* Generally, **irony** refers to language and situations that are inappropriate or opposite from normal expectations. **Situational irony** refers to circumstances in which punishments do not fit crimes, or in which rewards are not earned. Forces are beyond human comprehension or control. The characteristic of **dramatic irony** is that a character may perceive his or her situation in a limited way while both readers and other characters see things more broadly. In Collier's "The Chaser," the major character believes that his future life will be happy, but Collier's irony contradicts this expectation. In **verbal irony,** which applies to language, what is *meant* is distinct from what is *said.* Thus Maupassant in "The Necklace" does not *say* that Mathilde's husband is a crashing bore during the big party, but by asserting that he had been sleeping "in a little empty room with three other men whose wives had also been enjoying themselves," Maupassant makes the point with ironic force.

Symbolism and Allegory

In fiction, even an apparently ordinary thing may be understood as a **symbol;** that is, it may stand for something beyond itself. Many symbols are **universally** recognized, as with the cane in Hawthorne's "Young Goodman Brown." Because Hawthorne describes it as resembling the serpent associated with Satan, the cane symbolizes the Devil himself. Other symbols are **contextual;** that is, they become symbolic only in their individual works, as with Sammy's walking out on his job in "A & P" to protest the way the girls in swimsuits are treated. Within the context of the story, his action may be taken as a symbol of freedom and personal behavior.

When a story, in addition to maintaining its own narrative integrity, may be closely applied to another, parallel, set of situations, it is an **allegory.** "Young Goodman Brown" may be considered as an allegory of the development of hatred, distrust, and paranoia. Most stories are not allegories, however, even though they may contain sections that have allegorical parallels.

Thus, the narrative of Mathilde's long servitude in Maupassant's "The Necklace" is similar to the lives and activities of many people who carry out tasks for mistaken or meaningless reasons. For this reason, "The Necklace" may be considered allegorically, even though it is not a complete allegory.

These, then, are the major tools of writers of fiction. For analytical purposes, one or another of them may be considered separately so that the artistic achievement of a particular author may be recognized. It is also important to realize that authors may use all the tools simultaneously. The story may be told by a character who is a witness, and thus it has a **first-person point of view.** The major **character,** the **protagonist,** goes through a series of **actions** as a result of a carefully arranged **plot.** Because of this plot, together with the author's chosen method of **narration,** the story will follow a certain kind of arrangement, or **structure,** such as a straightforward **sequence** or a disjointed series of **episodes.** One thing that the action may demonstrate is the **theme** or **central idea.** The writer's **style** may be manifested in **ironic** expressions. The description of the character's actions may reveal **irony of situation,** while at the same time this situation is made vivid through **dialogue** in which the character is a participant. Because the plight of the character is like the plight of many persons in the world, it is an **allegory,** and the character herself or himself may be considered as a **symbol.**

Throughout the story, no matter what characteristics we are considering, it is most important to realize that a work of fiction is an entirety, a unity. Any reading of a story should be undertaken not to break things down into parts, but to understand and assimilate the work *as a whole.* The separate analysis of various topics, to which this book is committed, is thus the means to that end, not the end itself. Finally, the study of fiction, like the study of all literature, is designed to foster our growth and our understanding of the human condition.

 STORIES FOR STUDY

GAIUS PETRONIUS (d. A.D. 66)

> *History records very little about Petronius except that he was unfortunate enough to have lived at the time of the Emperor Nero, who (according to Tacitus) for political and personal reasons directed him to commit suicide. Readers might wonder why Petronius did not escape, but in the ancient Roman Empire, there was nowhere to go. In addition, the refusal to obey the emperor would have deprived his heirs of all money and property. The story included here is one of the best known sections of Petronius's* The Satyricon, *a lengthy novelistic work partially preserved in manuscript. Because* The Satyricon *is about adventures encountered when traveling, it enables the writer to vary the narrative fabric by introducing digressionary episodes and stories, of which "The Widow of Ephesus" is one of the most famous examples.*
> *The story of the Widow appears after a brawl that occurs on board the ship of Lichas, a wealthy sea captain whom Encolpius, the narrator, had once robbed. Among the listen-*

ers is Lichas's lover Tryphena, a courtesan with whom Encolpius once had a brief affair.
Encolpius and his friends, one of whom is Eumolpus, an elderly poet and raconteur, fight
against Lichas and his crew. After the fight ends and the combatants settle down, there is
general levity on the ship, and everyone settles down to listen to Eumolpus's story.

The Widow of Ephesus _____ (First Century A.D.)

(From The Satyricon, Chs. 108–113)

An English version by Edgar V. Roberts

We shook hands, chatted happily, and sang loudly while the entire ship rang with our
noise. Sea birds landed on the yard-arms, and Eumolpus, who was drinking too much
wine, decided to amuse us with a few stories. He began by insulting women. He called
them weak because he claimed they were impetuous in love and would neglect even
their own children while having an illicit affair. Moreover, he said that no woman he
had ever known had the moral strength to resist a handsome man. He insisted that
he did not get his ideas from legend or from historical accounts about evil women.
Rather, he himself had actually seen what he was talking about, and he offered to tell
us a true story in illustration. We immediately urged him on, and gave him our complete attention. This is the tale he told:

"Once upon a time in the city of Ephesus, on the Coast of Asia Minor, there
lived a virtuous woman whose marital fidelity was so famous that women came from
far and near just to get a glimpse of her. In the course of time, her husband got sick
and died, and the newly widowed lady, all by herself, arranged his funeral and burial.
At the funeral she was not satisfied only to follow the cortège in the usual way, by tearing her hair and beating her breasts. No, she actually accompanied the dead body
right into the tomb, and after the coffin was placed in the vault in the custom of the
Greeks, she began a vigil beside it, weeping and wailing both day and night.

"She was so rigorous in her duty that she neglected to eat, and she therefore became weaker by the hour. Neither her parents nor her closest relatives could persuade her to return home. Even the local politicians and judges could not convince
her. She snubbed them, and so, with their dignity ruffled, they gave up trying.

"By this time this most amazing woman was already in the fifth day of her fast,
to the sorrow of everyone in town, who believed that she would die at any moment.
At her side was her faithful handmaiden, who shed as many tears as the mournful
Widow did. This maiden also attended to practical matters such as refuelling and re-
lighting the torch whenever it was about to go out. Through all the city of Ephesus,
from one end to another, no one talked about anything else. All the people from
richest to poorest acknowledged the Widow as the supreme example of wifely love
and duty. They had never seen or heard of anyone like her.

"But regular business in Ephesus also went on, and one day the Provincial Governor sentenced some local hoodlums to be crucified in the grounds next to the tomb
in which the Widow stood vigil. On the night of the crucifixion a soldier was stationed

there to keep away all relatives or friends who might have wanted to steal the bodies in order to bury them properly.

"As he stood guard, he saw the torchlight from the Widow's tomb, and he also heard her heartbreaking outcries. Now, curiosity is a weakness of humankind, and this soldier was typically human. He went down the stairs into the sepulchre to take a look. Imagine his shock at the sight of this pretty woman and the corpse of her husband! At first he thought he was seeing ghosts, or apparitions out of the Kingdom of Hades! But when he saw how the Widow mourned, and how she had scarred her face with her fingernails, he understood that she was near death. He therefore ran up to his station and got his supper, which he carried to her. He pleaded with the sorrowing woman to stop tearing herself apart with sobs. 'The same inescapable fate waits for all human beings,' he said, 'the final trip of all to the home of the dead.' He racked his brain for other customary words of condolence which are intended to heal the broken hearts of the bereaved.

"But the Widow, who was upset rather than consoled by this unexpected stranger, only tore at her bosom more violently, ripping out some of her hair and throwing it on the corpse. The soldier then kept repeating his soothing words, while at the same time he tempted her with the tasty food and drink of his supper. The first to yield was the Widow's handmaiden, who, beguiled by the aromatic bouquet of the wine, gratefully accepted his generous offer.

"Brought back to life by the wine and the food, the handmaiden joined the soldier in his siege against the fortress of her mistress's self-sacrifice. She cried out, 'What good can it do anyone if you starve yourself to death, if you bury yourself alive, or if you yourself speed up your own last breath before your time has truly come? Remember what the poet Virgil said:

Do you believe that ashes or buried ghosts can feel?°

My Lady, come back to life, please! Give up this crazy notion of wifely duty and, as long as you are able, enjoy the light of the sun once more. Even your dead husband, if he could speak, would advise you to get on with your life.'

"Nobody is deaf when told to eat or continue staying alive, and so the Widow, starving after her long fast, finally gave way. She refreshed herself with the food just as vigorously as her handmaiden had done.

"But everybody knows that one appetite follows another, and it should come as   10
no surprise that the soldier began wooing the Widow with the same tempting words he had used to rescue her from starvation. Although she was unparalleled for modesty, she recognized that he was an unusually handsome young man. He was also persuasive, and in addition the Widow's handmaiden quoted another line of Virgil to help him in his cause:

Would you hold out against a pleasure-giving passion?°

Do . . . feel: Aeneid, IV.34
Would . . . passion: Aeneid, IV.38

"Why make the story last longer? This woman stopped resisting, and she accepted the young soldier's love just as she had accepted his food. They spent the night together—and after that the next night, and the next, and the next. Naturally they kept the door of the tomb barred and bolted so that any strangers or friends passing by would conclude that the faithful wife had died upon the body of her husband.

"The soldier was enchanted both by the beauty of his new sweetheart and by their secret affair, and he bought her a few small presents out of his small pay. Every night, as soon as it was dark, he would steal away to the tomb with his gifts, and would stay there until morning.

"But one evening the parents of one of the crucified thieves took advantage of him. They watched him abandon his post to enjoy his night of love, and then they hurried to their son's cross, carried his body away, and had the final ceremony for the dead performed over it. When morning came and the soldier saw that the cross was empty, he fell into a cold sweat because he knew that the punishment for his dereliction of duty would be death. He told the Widow, and swore that he could not wait for the sentence of a court martial. He would, he said, commit suicide for his folly by falling on his sword. He then asked the Widow to put his body in the tomb after he was dead—as the final resting place not only for her husband, but also for him, her lover. The Widow, however, was resourceful as well as virtuous and dutiful.

"'No,' she cried, 'heaven forbid that I should be forced by bad luck to stand vigil at the same time beside the bodies of the only two men in the world that I ever loved. I would rather hang up a dead man on the cross than permit a living man to die.'

"After these words she told him to take her husband's corpse from the vault, carry it to the empty cross, and nail it up. The soldier readily agreed to this practical scheme, and the next day everyone in town was asking how on earth the dead man had been able to climb onto the cross!"

As Eumolpus was finishing his story, Tryphena blushed until her face was red, and she tried to hide her embarrassment. The sailors were so amused that they rolled on the deck with laughter. While they laughed, Lichas sternly declared that the Provincial Governor should not have permitted such a farce. Indeed, Lichas said that the Governor's duty was to have restored the husband's corpse to the tomb, and then to have executed the Widow herself on the cross.

QUESTIONS

1. Who tells the story? How is he introduced? What do you learn about him? What point does he make about his story?
2. Since there is an audience, some of whom react when the narrator is finished, what is their effect on the story?
3. What is the Widow's main virtue? How does she show this virtue upon her husband's death? What does abandoning her wish for self-sacrifice show about her?
4. Should the story be taken as a joke, as it apparently was intended, at the expense of the female protagonist? What values might make it still seem a joke? What values might make it seem more serious? In light of the misogynistic theme, to what degree are you able to like the story?

JOHN UPDIKE (b. 1932)

Updike was brought up in Pennsylvania during the Great Depression. His parents were diligent about his education, however, and in 1950 he received a scholarship for study at Harvard, graduating in 1954. He worked for The New Yorker *for two years before deciding to devote himself exclusively to his own writing. In 1959, he published his first story collection,* The Same Door, *and his first novel,* The Poorhouse Fair. *In 1960, with* Rabbit, Run, *he began his Rabbit chronicles. In 1981 he received the Pulitzer Prize for* Rabbit Is Rich. *His collected poems were published in 1993.*

A & P° —————————————————— *1961*

In walks these three girls in nothing but bathing suits. I'm in the third checkout slot, with my back to the door, so I don't see them until they're over by the bread. The one that caught my eye first was the one in the plaid green two-piece. She was a chunky kid, with a good tan and a sweet broad soft-looking can with those two crescents of white just under it, where the sun never seems to hit, at the top of the backs of her legs. I stood there with my hand on a box of HiHo crackers trying to remember if I rang it up or not. I ring it up again and the customer starts giving me hell. She's one of these cash-register-watchers, a witch about fifty with rouge on her cheekbones and no eyebrows, and I know it made her day to trip me up. She'd been watching cash registers for fifty years and probably never seen a mistake before.

By the time I got her feathers smoothed and her goodies into a bag—she gives me a little snort in passing, if she'd been born at the right time they would have burned her over in Salem—by the time I get her on her way the girls had circled around the bread and were coming back, without a pushcart, back my way along the counters, in the aisle between the checkouts and the Special bins. They didn't even have shoes on. There was this chunky one, with the two-piece—it was bright green and the seams on the bra were still sharp and her belly was still pretty pale so I guessed she just got it (the suit)—there was this one, with one of those chubby berry-faces, the lips all bunched together under her nose, this one, and a tall one, with black hair that hadn't quite frizzed right, and one of these sunburns right across under the eyes, and a chin that was too long—you know, the kind of girl other girls think is very "striking" and "attractive" but never quite makes it, as they very well know, which is why they like her so much—and then the third one, that wasn't quite so tall. She was the queen. She kind of led them, the other two peeking around and making their shoulders round. She didn't look around, not this queen, she just walked straight on slowly, on these long white prima-donna legs. She came down a little hard on her heels, as if she didn't walk in her bare feet that much, putting down her heels and then letting the weight move along to her toes as if she was testing the floor with every step, putting a little deliberate extra action into it. You never know for sure how girls' minds work (do you really think it's a mind in there or just a little buzz like a bee in a glass jar?)

A & P: "The Great Atlantic and Pacific Tea Company," a large grocery chain still flourishing in twenty-four states with more than 1150 stores.

but you got the idea she had talked the other two into coming in here with her, and now she was showing them how to do it, walk slow and hold yourself straight.

She had on a kind of dirty-pink—beige, maybe, I don't know—bathing suit with a little nubble all over it and, what got me, the straps were down. They were off her shoulders looped loose around the cool tops of her arms, and I guess as a result the suit had slipped a little on her, so all around the top of the cloth there was this shining rim. If it hadn't been there you wouldn't have known there could have been anything whiter than those shoulders. With the straps pushed off, there was nothing between the top of the suit and the top of her head except just *her*, this clean bare plane of the top of her chest down from the shoulder bones like a dented sheet of metal tilted in the light. I mean, it was more than pretty.

She had sort of oaky hair that the sun and salt had bleached, done up in a bun that was unraveling, and a kind of prim face. Walking into the A & P with your straps down, I suppose it's the only kind of face you *can* have. She held her head so high her neck, coming up out of those white shoulders, looked kind of stretched, but I didn't mind. The longer her neck was, the more of her there was.

She must have felt in the corner of her eye me and over my shoulder Stokesie in the second slot watching, but she didn't tip. Not this queen. She kept her eyes moving across the racks, and stopped, and turned so slow it made my stomach rub the inside of my apron, and buzzed to the other two, who kind of huddled against her for relief, and then they all three of them went up the cat-and-dog-food-breakfast-cereal-macaroni-rice-raisins-seasonings-spreads-spaghetti-soft-drinks-crackers-and-cookies aisle. From the third slot I look straight up this aisle to the meat counter, and I watched them all the way. The fat one with the tan sort of fumbled with the cookies, but on second thought she put the package back. The sheep pushing their carts down the aisle—the girls were walking against the usual traffic (not that we have one-way signs or anything)—were pretty hilarious. You could see them, when Queenie's white shoulders dawned on them, kind of jerk, or hop, or hiccup, but their eyes snapped back to their own baskets and on they pushed. I bet you could set off dynamite in an A & P and the people would by and large keep reaching and checking oatmeal off their lists and muttering "Let me see, there was a third thing, began with A, asparagus, no ah, yes, applesauce!" or whatever it is they do mutter. But there was no doubt, this jiggled them. A few houseslaves in pin curlers even looked around after pushing their carts past to make sure what they had seen was correct.

You know, it's one thing to have a girl in a bathing suit down on the beach, where what with the glare nobody can look at each other much anyway, and another thing in the cool of the A & P, under the fluorescent lights, against all those stacked packages, with her feet paddling along naked over our checkerboard green-and-cream rubber-tile floor.

"Oh Daddy," Stokesie said beside me. "I feel so faint."

"Darling," I said. "Hold me tight." Stokesie's married, with two babies chalked up on his fuselage already, but as far as I can tell that's the only difference. He's twenty-two, and I was nineteen this April.

"Is it done?" he asks, the responsible married man finding his voice. I forgot to say he thinks he's going to be manager some sunny day, maybe in 1990 when it's called the Great Alexandrov and Petrooshki° Tea Company or something.

Great Alexandrov and Petrooshki: Apparently a reference to the possibility that someday Russia might rule the United States.

What he meant was, our town is five miles from the beach, with a big summer colony out on the Point, but we're right in the middle of town, and the women generally put on a shirt or shorts or something before they get out of the car into the street. And anyway these are usually women with six children and varicose veins mapping their legs and nobody, including them, could care less. As I say, we're right in the middle of town, and if you stand at our front doors you can see two banks and the Congregational church and the newspaper store and three real-estate offices and about twenty-seven old freeloaders tearing up Central Street because the sewer broke again. It's not as if we're on the Cape,° we're north of Boston and there's people in this town haven't seen the ocean for twenty years.

The girls had reached the meat counter and were asking McMahon something. He pointed, they pointed, and they shuffled out of sight behind a pyramid of Diet Delight peaches. All that was left for us to see was old McMahon patting his mouth and looking after them sizing up their joints. Poor kids, I began to feel sorry for them, they couldn't help it.

Now here comes the sad part of the story, at least my family says it's sad, but I don't think it's so sad myself. The store's pretty empty, it being Thursday afternoon, so there was nothing much to do except lean on the register and wait for the girls to show up again. The whole store was like a pinball machine and I didn't know which tunnel they'd come out of. After a while they come around out of the far aisle, around the light bulbs, records at discount of the Caribbean Six or Tony Martin Sings or some such gunk you wonder they waste the wax on, sixpacks of candy bars, and plastic toys done up in cellophane that fall apart when a kid looks at them anyway. Around they come, Queenie still leading the way, and holding a little gray jar in her hand. Slots Three through Seven are unmanned and I could see her wondering between Stokes and me, but Stokesie with his usual luck draws an old party in baggy gray pants who stumbles up with four giant cans of pineapple juice (what do these bums *do* with all that pineapple juice? I've often asked myself) so the girls come to me. Queenie puts down the jar and I take it into my fingers icy cold. Kingfish Fancy Herring Snacks in Pure Sour Cream: 49¢. Now her hands are empty, not a ring or a bracelet, bare as God made them, and I wonder where the money's coming from. Still with that prim look she lifts a folded dollar bill out of the hollow at the center of her nubbed pink top. The jar went heavy in my hand. Really, I thought that was so cute.

Then everybody's luck begins to run out. Lengel comes in from haggling with a truck full of cabbages on the lot and is about to scuttle into that door marked MANAGER behind which he hides all day when the girls touch his eye. Lengel's pretty dreary, teaches Sunday school and the rest, but he doesn't miss that much. He comes over and says, "Girls, this isn't the beach."

Queenie blushes, though maybe it's just a brush of sunburn I was noticing for the first time, now that she was so close. "My mother asked me to pick up a jar of herring snacks." Her voice kind of startled me, the way voices do when you see the people first, coming out so flat and dumb yet kind of tony, too, the way it ticked over "pick up" and "snacks." All of a sudden I slid right down her voice into her living room. Her father and the other men were standing around in ice-cream coats and bow ties and the women were in sandals picking up herring snacks on toothpicks off a big glass

the Cape: Cape Cod, the southeastern area of Massachusetts, a place of many resorts and beaches.

plate and they were all holding drinks the color of water with olives and sprigs of mint in them. When my parents have somebody over they get lemonade and if it's a real racy affair Schlitz in tall glasses with "They'll Do It Every Time"° cartoons stenciled on.

"That's all right," Lengel said. "But this isn't the beach." His repeating this struck me as funny, as if it had just occurred to him, and he had been thinking all these years the A & P was a great big dune and he was the head lifeguard. He didn't like my smiling—as I say he doesn't miss much—but he concentrates on giving the girls that sad Sunday-school-superintendent stare.

Queenie's blush is no sunburn now, and the plump one in plaid, that I liked better from the back—a really sweet can—pipes up, "We weren't doing any shopping. We just came in for the one thing."

"That makes no difference," Lengel tells her, and I could see from the way his eyes went that he hadn't noticed she was wearing a two-piece before. "We want you decently dressed when you come in here."

"We *are* decent," Queenie says suddenly, her lower lip pushing, getting sore now that she remembers her place, a place from which the crowd that runs the A & P must look pretty crummy. Fancy Herring Snacks flashed in her very blue eyes.

"Girls, I don't want to argue with you. After this come in here with your shoulders covered. It's our policy." He turns his back. That's policy for you. Policy is what the kingpins want. What the others want is juvenile delinquency.

All this while, the customers had been showing up with their carts but, you know, sheep, seeing a scene, they had all bunched up on Stokesie, who shook open a paper bag as gently as peeling a peach, not wanting to miss a word. I could feel in the silence everybody getting nervous, most of all Lengel, who asks me, "Sammy, have you rung up their purchase?"

I thought and said "No" but it wasn't about that I was thinking. I go through the punches, 4, 9, GROC, TOT—it's more complicated than you think, and after you do it often enough, it begins to make a little song, that you hear words to, in my case "Hello (*bing*) there, you (*gung*) hap-py *pee*-pul (*splat*)!"—the *splat* being the drawer flying out. I uncrease the bill, tenderly as you may imagine, it just having come from between the two smoothest scoops of vanilla I had ever known were there, and pass a half and a penny into her narrow pink palm, and nestle the herrings in a bag and twist its neck and hand it over, all the time thinking.

The girls, and who'd blame them, are in a hurry to get out, so I say "I quit" to Lengel quick enough for them to hear, hoping they'll stop and watch me, their unsuspected hero. They keep right on going, into the electric eye; the door flies open and they flicker across the lot to their car, Queenie and Plaid and Big Tall Goony-Goony (not that as raw material she was so bad), leaving me with Lengel and a kink in his eyebrow.

"Did you say something, Sammy?"

"I said I quit."

"I thought you did."

"You didn't have to embarrass them."

"It was they who were embarrassing us."

I started to say something that came out "Fiddle-de-doo." It's a saying of my grandmother's, and I know she would have been pleased.

"I don't think you know what you're saying," Lengel said.

"They'll Do It Every Time": syndicated daily and Sunday cartoon created by Jimmy Hatlo.

"I know you don't," I said. "But I do." I pull the bow at the back of my apron   30
and start shrugging it off my shoulders. A couple customers that had been heading
for my slot begin to knock against each other, like scared pigs in a chute.

Lengel sighs and begins to look very patient and old and gray. He's been a
friend of my parents for years. "Sammy, you don't want to do this to your Mom and
Dad," he tells me. It's true, I don't. But it seems to me that once you begin a gesture
it's fatal not to go through with it. I fold the apron, "Sammy" stitched in red on the
pocket, and put it on the counter, and drop the bow tie on top of it. The bow tie is
theirs, if you've ever wondered. "You'll feel this for the rest of your life," Lengel says,
and I know that's true, too, but remembering how he made that pretty girl blush
makes me so scrunchy inside I punch the No Sale tab and the machine whirs "pee-
pul" and the drawer splats out. One advantage to this scene taking place in summer,
I can follow this up with a clean exit, there's no fumbling around getting your coat
and galoshes, I just saunter into the electric eye in my white shirt that my mother
ironed the night before, and the door heaves itself open, and outside the sunshine is
skating around on the asphalt.

I look around for my girls, but they're gone, of course. There wasn't anybody
but some young married screaming with her children about some candy they didn't
get by the door of a powder-blue Falcon° station wagon. Looking back in the big windows, over the bags of peat moss and aluminum lawn furniture stacked on the pavement, I could see Lengel in my place in the slot, checking the sheep through. His face
was dark gray and his back stiff, as if he'd just had an injection of iron, and my stomach kind of fell as I felt how hard the world was going to be to me hereafter.

QUESTIONS

1. Consider the first eleven paragraphs as exposition, in which you learn about the
   location, the issues, and the participants of the conflict. Is there anything
   inessential? Do you learn enough to understand the story? On the basis of your
   conclusions, consider the nature of fictional exposition.
2. From Sammy's language what do you learn about his view of himself? About his
   educational and class level? The first sentence, for example, is grammatically incorrect in Standard English but not uncommon in colloquial English. Point out
   and explain similar passages.
3. Indicate evidence in the narration that Sammy is an experienced "girl watcher."
   What is his estimation of the intelligence of most girls? Is this judgment consistent with what he finally does?
4. Why does Sammy say "I quit" so abruptly? What do you think he means at the
   end by saying that the world is going to be hard to him afterwards?

Falcon: small car that had recently been introduced by the Ford Motor Company.

ALICE WALKER (b. 1944)

Walker was born in Georgia and attended Sarah Lawrence College, graduating in 1965. In addition to teaching at Yale, Wellesley, and other schools, she has edited and published fiction, poetry, and biography, and received a Guggenheim Fellowship in 1977. Her main hobby is gardening. For her collection of poems Revolutionary Petunias *(1973), she received a Wall Book Award nomination. Her best known novel,* The Color Purple *(1982), was made into a movie that won an Academy Award for 1985.*

Everyday Use ————————————————— *1973*

for your grandmama

I will wait for her in the yard that Maggie and I made so clean and wavy yesterday afternoon. A yard like this is more comfortable than most people know. It is not just a yard. It is like an extended living room. When the hard clay is swept clean as a floor and the fine sand around the edges lined with tiny, irregular grooves, anyone can come and sit and look up into the elm tree and wait for the breezes that never come inside the house.

Maggie will be nervous until after her sister goes: she will stand hopelessly in corners, homely and ashamed of the burn scars down her arms and legs, eying her sister with a mixture of envy and awe. She thinks her sister has held life always in the palm of one hand, that "no" is a word the world never learned to say to her.

You've no doubt seen those TV shows° where the child who has "made it" is confronted, as a surprise, by her own mother and father, tottering in weakly from backstage. (A pleasant surprise, of course: What would they do if parent and child came on the show only to curse out and insult each other?) On TV mother and child embrace and smile into each other's faces. Sometimes the mother and father weep, the child wraps them in her arms and leans across the table to tell how she would not have made it without their help. I have seen these programs.

Sometimes I dream a dream in which Dee and I are suddenly brought together on a TV program of this sort. Out of a dark and soft-seated limousine I am ushered into a bright room filled with many people. There I meet a smiling, gray, sporty man like Johnny Carson who shakes my hand and tells me what a fine girl I have. Then we are on the stage and Dee is embracing me with tears in her eyes. She pins on my dress a large orchid, even though she has told me once that she thinks orchids are tacky flowers.

In real life I am a large, big-boned woman with rough, man-working hands. In the winter I wear flannel nightgowns to bed and overalls during the day. I can kill and clean a hog as mercilessly as a man. My fat keeps me hot in zero weather. I can work outside all day, breaking ice to get water for washing; I can eat pork liver cooked over the open fire minutes after it comes steaming from the hog. One winter I knocked a

———

TV shows: In the early days of television, a popular show was "This Is Your Life," which the narrator describes exactly here.

bull calf straight in the brain between the eyes with a sledge hammer and had the meat hung up to chill before nightfall. But of course all this does not show on television. I am the way my daughter would want me to be: a hundred pounds lighter, my skin like an uncooked barley pancake. My hair glistens in the hot bright lights. Johnny Carson has much to do to keep up with my quick and witty tongue.

But that is a mistake, I know even before I wake up. Who ever knew a Johnson with a quick tongue? Who can even imagine me looking a strange white man in the eye? It seems to me I have talked to them always with one foot raised in flight, with my head turned in whichever way is farthest from them. Dee, though. She would always look anyone in the eye. Hesitation was no part of her nature.

"How do I look, Mama?" Maggie says, showing just enough of her thin body enveloped in pink skirt and red blouse for me to know she's there, almost hidden by the door.

"Come out into the yard," I say.

Have you ever seen a lame animal, perhaps a dog run over by some careless person rich enough to own a car, sidle up to someone who is ignorant enough to be kind to him? That is the way my Maggie walks. She has been like this, chin on chest, eyes on ground, feet in shuffle, ever since the fire that burned the other house to the ground.

Dee is lighter than Maggie, with nicer hair and a fuller figure. She's a woman now, though sometimes I forget. How long ago was it that the other house burned? Ten, twelve years? Sometimes I can still hear the flames and feel Maggie's arms sticking to me, her hair smoking and her dress falling off her in little black papery flakes. Her eyes seemed stretched open, blazed open by the flames reflected in them. And Dee, I see her standing off under the sweet gum tree she used to dig gum out of; a look of concentration on her face as she watched the last dingy gray board of the house fall in toward the red-hot brick chimney. Why don't you do a dance around the ashes? I'd wanted to ask her. She had hated the house that much.

I used to think she hated Maggie, too. But that was before we raised the money, the church and me, to send her to Augusta° to school. She used to read to us without pity; forcing words, lies, other folks' habits, whole lives upon us two, sitting trapped and ignorant underneath her voice. She washed us in a river of make-believe, burned us with a lot of knowledge we didn't necessarily need to know. Pressed us to her with the serious way she read, to shove us away at just the moment, like dimwits, we seemed about to understand.

Dee wanted nice things. A yellow organdy dress to wear to her graduation from high school; black pumps to match a green suit she'd made from an old suit somebody gave me. She was determined to stare down any disaster in her efforts. Her eyelids would not flicker for minutes at a time. Often I fought off the temptation to shake her. At sixteen she had a style of her own: and knew what style was.

I never had an education myself. After second grade the school was closed down. Don't ask me why: in 1927 colored asked fewer questions than they do now. Sometimes Maggie reads to me. She stumbles along good-naturedly, but can't see well. She knows she is not bright. Like good looks and money, quickness passed her by. She will marry John Thomas (who has mossy teeth in an earnest face) and then

10

Augusta: city in eastern Georgia, the location of Paine College.

I'll be free to sit here and I guess just sing church songs to myself. Although I never was a good singer. Never could carry a tune. I was always better at a man's job. I used to love to milk till I was hooked in the side° in '49. Cows are soothing and slow and don't bother you, unless you try to milk them the wrong way.

I have deliberately turned my back on the house. It is three rooms, just like the one that burned, except the roof is tin; they don't make shingle roofs any more. There are no real windows, just some holes cut in the sides, like the portholes on a ship, but not round and not square, with rawhide holding the shutters up on the outside. This house is in a pasture, too, like the other one. No doubt when Dee sees it she will want to tear it down. She wrote me once that no matter where we "choose" to live, she will manage to come see us. But she will never bring her friends. Maggie and I thought about this and Maggie asked me, "Mama, when did Dee ever *have* any friends?"

She has a few. Furtive boys in pink shirts hanging about on washday after school. Nervous girls who never laughed. Impressed with her they worshiped the well-turned phrase, the cute shape, the scalding humor that erupted like bubbles in lye. She read to them.

When she was courting Jimmy T she didn't have much time to pay to us, but turned all her faultfinding power on him. He *flew* to marry a cheap city girl from a family of ignorant flashy people. She hardly had time to recompose herself.

When she comes I will meet—but there they are!

Maggie attempts to make a dash for the house, in her shuffling way, but I stay her with my hand. "Come back here," I say. And she stops and tries to dig a well in the sand with her toe.

It is hard to see them clearly through the strong sun. But even the first glimpse of leg out of the car tells me it is Dee. Her feet were always neat-looking, as if God himself had shaped them with a certain style. From the other side of the car comes a short, stocky man. Hair is all over his head a foot long and hanging from his chin like a kinky mule tail. I hear Maggie suck in her breath. "Uhnnnh," is what it sounds like. Like when you see the wriggling end of a snake just in front of your foot on the road. "Uhnnnh."

Dee next. A dress down to the ground, in this hot weather. A dress so loud it hurts my eyes. There are yellows and oranges enough to throw back the light of the sun. I feel my whole face warming from the heat waves it throws out. Earrings gold, too, and hanging down to her shoulders. Bracelets dangling and making noises when she moves her arm up to shake the folds of the dress out of her armpits. The dress is loose and flows, and as she walks closer, I like it. I hear Maggie go "Uhnnnh" again. It is her sister's hair. It stands straight up like the wool on a sheep. It is black as night and around the edges are two long pigtails that rope about like small lizards disappearing behind her ears.

"Wa-su-zo-Tean-o!"° she says, coming on in that gliding way the dress makes her move. The short stocky yellow with the hair to his navel is all grinning and he follows up with "Asalamalakim,° my mother and my sister!" He moves to hug Maggie but she falls back, tight up against the back of my chair. I feel her trembling there and when I look up I see the perspiration falling off her chin.

---

hooked in the side: kicked by a cow.
Wa-su-zo-Tean-o: greeting used by Black Muslims.
Asalamalakim: Muslim salutation meaning "Peace be with you."

"Don't get up," says Dee. Since I am stout it takes something of a push. You can see me trying to move a second or two before I make it. She turns, showing white heels through her sandals, and goes back to the car. Out she peeks next with a Polaroid. She stoops down quickly and lines up picture after picture of me sitting there in front of the house with Maggie cowering behind me. She never takes a shot without making sure the house is included. When a cow comes nibbling around the edge of the yard she snaps it and me and Maggie *and* the house. Then she puts the Polaroid in the back seat of the car, and comes up and kisses me on the forehead.

Meanwhile Asalamalakim is going through motions with Maggie's hand. Maggie's hand is as limp as a fish, and probably as cold, despite the sweat, and she keeps trying to pull it back. It looks like Asalamalakim wants to shake hands but wants to do it fancy. Or maybe he don't know how people shake hands. Anyhow, he soon gives up on Maggie.

"Well," I say, "Dee."

"No, Mama," she says. "Not 'Dee,' Wangero Leewanika Kemanjo!"   25

"What happened to 'Dee'?" I wanted to know.

"She's dead," Wangero said. "I couldn't bear it any longer, being named after the people who oppress me."

"You know as well as me you was named after your aunt Dicie," I said. Dicie is my sister. She named Dee. We called her "Big Dee" after Dee was born.

"But who was *she* named after?" asked Wangero.

"I guess after Grandma Dee," I said.   30

"And who was she named after?" asked Wangero.

"Her mother," I said, and saw Wangero was getting tired. "That's about as far back as I can trace it," I said. Though, in fact, I probably could have carried it back beyond the Civil War through the branches.

"Well," said Asalamalakim, "there you are."

"Uhnnnh," I heard Maggie say.

"There I was not," I said, "before 'Dicie' cropped up in our family, so why   35
should I try to trace it that far back?"

He just stood there grinning, looking down on me like somebody inspecting a Model A car.° Every once in a while he and Wangero sent eye signals over my head.

"How do you pronounce this name?" I asked.

"You don't have to call me by it if you don't want to," said Wangero.

"Why shouldn't I?" I asked. "If that's what you want us to call you, we'll call you."

"I know it might sound awkward at first," said Wangero.   40

"I'll get used to it," I said. "Ream it out again."

Well, soon we got the name out of the way. Asalamalakim had a name twice as long and three times as hard. After I tripped over it two or three times he told me to just call him Hakim-a-barber. I wanted to ask him was he a barber, but I didn't really think he was, so I didn't ask.

"You must belong to those beef-cattle peoples down the road," I said. They said "Asalamalakim" when they met you, too, but they didn't shake hands. Always too busy: feeding the cattle, fixing the fences, putting up salt-lick shelters,° throwing down hay.

Model A car: The Ford car that replaced the Model T in the late 1920s. The Model A was proverbial for its quality and durability.
salt-lick shelters: shelters built to prevent rain from dissolving the large blocks of rock salt set up on poles for cattle.

When the white folks poisoned some of the herd the men stayed up all night with rifles in their hands. I walked a mile and a half just to see the sight.

Hakim-a-barber said, "I accept some of their doctrines, but farming and raising
cattle is not my style." (They didn't tell me, and I didn't ask, whether Wangero (Dee)
had really gone and married him.)

We sat down to eat and right away he said he didn't eat collards and pork was
unclean. Wangero, though, went on through the chitlins and corn bread, the greens
and everything else. She talked a blue streak over the sweet potatoes. Everything delighted her. Even the fact that we still used the benches her daddy made for the table
when we couldn't afford to buy chairs.

"Oh, Mama!" she cried. Then turned to Hakim-a-barber. "I never knew how
lovely these benches are. You can feel the rump prints," she said, running her hands
underneath her and along the bench. Then she gave a sigh and her hand closed over
Grandma Dee's butter dish. "That's it!" she said. "I knew there was something I
wanted to ask you if I could have." She jumped up from the table and went over in
the corner where the churn stood, the milk in it clabber° by now. She looked at the
churn and looked at it.

"This churn top is what I need," she said. "Didn't Uncle Buddy whittle it out of
a tree you all used to have?"

"Yes," I said.

"Uh huh," she said happily. "And I want the dasher, too."

"Uncle Buddy whittle that, too?" asked the barber.

Dee (Wangero) looked up at me.

"Aunt Dee's first husband whittled the dash," said Maggie so low you almost
couldn't hear her. "His name was Henry, but they called him Stash."

"Maggie's brain is like an elephant's," Wangero said, laughing. "I can use the
churn top as a centerpiece for the alcove table," she said, sliding a plate over the
churn, "and I'll think of something artistic to do with the dasher."

When she finished wrapping the dasher the handle stuck out. I took it for a moment in my hands. You didn't even have to look close to see where hands pushing the
dasher up and down to make butter had left a kind of sink in the wood. In fact, there
were a lot of small sinks; you could see where thumbs and fingers had sunk into the
wood. It was beautiful light yellow wood, from a tree that grew in the yard where Big
Dee and Stash had lived.

After dinner Dee (Wangero) went to the trunk at the foot of my bed and started
rifling through it. Maggie hung back in the kitchen over the dishpan. Out came
Wangero with two quilts. They had been pieced by Grandma Dee and then Big Dee
and me had hung them on the quilt frames on the front porch and quilted them. One
was in the Lone Star pattern. The other was Walk Around the Mountain. In both of
them were scraps of dresses Grandma Dee had worn fifty and more years ago. Bits and
pieces of Grandpa Jarrell's Paisley shirts. And one teeny faded blue piece, about the
size of a penny matchbox, that was from Great Grandpa's Ezra's uniform that he wore
in the Civil War.

"Mama," Wangero said sweet as a bird. "Can I have these old quilts?"

I heard something fall in the kitchen, and a minute later the kitchen door
slammed.

clabber: curdled, turned sour.

"Why don't you take one or two of the others?" I asked. "These old things was just done by me and Big Dee from some tops your grandma pieced before she died."

"No," said Wangero. "I don't want those. They are stitched around the borders by machine."

"That'll make them last better," I said. 60

"That's not the point," said Wangero. "These are all pieces of dresses Grandma used to wear. She did all this stitching by hand. Imagine!" She held the quilts securely in her arms, stroking them.

"Some of the pieces, like those lavender ones, come from old clothes her mother handed down to her," I said, moving up to touch the quilts. Dee (Wangero) moved back just enough so that I couldn't reach the quilts. They already belonged to her.

"Imagine!" she breathed again, clutching them closely to her bosom.

"The truth is," I said, "I promised to give them quilts to Maggie, for when she marries John Thomas."

She gasped like a bee had stung her. 65

"Maggie can't appreciate these quilts!" she said. "She'd probably be backward enough to put them to everyday use."

"I reckon she would," I said. "God knows I been saving 'em for long enough with nobody using 'em. I hope she will!" I didn't want to bring up how I had offered Dee (Wangero) a quilt when she went away to college. Then she had told me they were old-fashioned, out of style.

"But they're *priceless*!" she was saying now, furiously; for she has a temper. "Maggie would put them on the bed and in five years they'd be in rags. Less than that!"

"She can always make some more," I said. "Maggie knows how to quilt."

Dee (Wangero) looked at me with hatred. "You just will not understand. The 70
point is these quilts, *these* quilts!"

"Well," I said, stumped. "What would *you* do with them?"

"Hang them," she said. As if that was the only thing you *could* do with quilts.

Maggie by now was standing in the door. I could almost hear the sound her feet made as they scraped over each other.

"She can have them, Mama," she said, like somebody used to never winning anything, or having anything reserved for her. "I can 'member Grandma Dee without the quilts."

I looked at her hard. She had filled her bottom lip with checkerberry snuff and 75
it gave her face a kind of dopey, hangdog look. It was Grandma Dee and Big Dee who taught her how to quilt herself. She stood there with her scarred hands hidden in the folds of her skirt. She looked at her sister with something like fear but she wasn't mad at her. This was Maggie's portion. This was the way she knew God to work.

When I looked at her like that something hit me in the top of my head and ran down to the soles of my feet. Just like when I'm in church and the spirit of God touches me and I get happy and shout. I did something I never had done before: hugged Maggie to me, then dragged her on into the room, snatched the quilts out of Miss Wangero's hands and dumped them into Maggie's lap. Maggie just sat there on my bed with her mouth open.

"Take one or two of the others," I said to Dee.

But she turned without a word and went out to Hakim-a-barber.

"You just don't understand," she said, as Maggie and I came out to the car.

"What don't I understand?" I wanted to know.

"Your heritage," she said. And then she turned to Maggie, kissed her, and said, "You ought to try to make something of yourself, too, Maggie. It's really a new day for us. But from the way you and Mama still live you'd never know it."

She put on some sunglasses that hid everything above the tip of her nose and her chin.

Maggie smiled; maybe at the sunglasses. But a real smile, not scared. After we watched the car dust settle I asked Maggie to bring me a dip of snuff. And then the two of us sat there just enjoying, until it was time to go in the house and go to bed.

QUESTIONS

1. Describe the narrator. Who is she? What is she like? Where and how does she live? What kind of life has she had? How does the story bring out her judgments about her two daughters?
2. Describe the narrator's daughters. How are they different physically and mentally? How have their lives been different?
3. Why did Dee change her name to "Wangero?" How is this change important, and how is it reflected in her attitude toward the family artifacts?
4. Describe the importance of the phrase "everyday use" (paragraph 66). How does this phrase highlight the conflicting values in the story?

JOY WILLIAMS (b. 1944)

Williams was born in Massachusetts, and graduated from Marietta College and the University of Iowa. While still in her twenties she published her first stories. Among her novels are State of Grace *(1973),* The Changeling *(1978), and* Breaking and Entering *(1988). Her story collection* Taking Care, *including the title story "Taking Care," appeared in 1982. Her varied interests are shown by the fact that she has published a history and guide to the Keys of Florida, her adopted home state. Among her distinctions are a judgeship of the PEN/Faulkner Award for Fiction, a Wallace Stegner Fellowship, and a Guggenheim Fellowship.*

Taking Care _____ *1982*

Jones, the preacher, has been in love all his life. He is baffled by this because as far as he can see, it has never helped anyone, even when they have acknowledged it, which is not often. Jones's love is much too apparent and arouses neglect. He is like an animal in a traveling show who, through some aberration, wears a vital organ outside the skin, awkward and unfortunate, something that shouldn't be seen, certainly something that shouldn't be watched working. Now he sits on a bed beside his wife in the self-care unit of a hospital fifteen miles from their home. She has been committed here for tests. She is so weak, so tired. There is something wrong with her blood. Her arms are covered with bruises where they have gone into the veins. Her hip, too, is blue and swollen where they have drawn out samples of bone marrow. All of this is frightening. The doctors are severe and wise, answering Jones's questions in a way that makes him feel hopelessly deaf. They have told him that there really is no such thing as a disease of the blood, for the blood is not a living tissue but a passive vehicle for the transportation of food, oxygen and waste. They have told him that abnormalities in the blood corpuscles, which his wife seems to have, must be regarded as symptoms of disease elsewhere in the body. They have shown him, upon request, slides and charts of normal and pathological blood cells which look to Jones like canapés. They speak (for he insists) of leukocytosis,° myelocytes° and megaloblasts.° None of this takes into account the love he has for his wife! Jones sits beside her in this dim pleasant room, wearing a grey suit and his clerical collar, for when he leaves her he must visit other parishioners who are patients here. This part of the hospital is like a motel. One may wear one's regular clothes. The rooms have ice-buckets, rugs and colorful bedspreads. How he wishes that they were traveling and staying overnight, this night, in a motel. A nurse comes in with a tiny paper cup full of pills. There are three pills, or rather, capsules, and they are not for his wife but for her blood. The cup is the smallest of its type that Jones has ever seen. All perspective, all sense of time and scale seem abandoned in this hospital. For example, when Jones turns to kiss his wife's hair, he nicks the air instead.

Jones and his wife have one child, a daughter, who, in turn, has a single child, a girl, born one-half year ago. Jones's daughter has fallen in with the stars and is using the heavens, as Jones would be the first to admit, more than he ever has. It has, however, brought her only grief and confusion. She has left her husband and brought the baby to Jones. She has also given him her dog. She is going to Mexico where soon, in the mountains, she will have a nervous breakdown. Jones does not know this, but his daughter has seen it in the stars and is going out to meet it. Jones quickly agrees to care for both the baby and the dog, as this seems to be the only thing his daughter needs from him. The day of the baby's birth is secondary to the position of the planets and the terms of houses, quadrants and gradients.° Her symbol is a bareback rider. To Jones, this is a graceful thought. It signifies audacity. It also means luck. Jones slips a twenty dollar bill in the pocket of his daughter's suitcase and drives her to the airport. The plane taxis down the runway and Jones waves, holding all their luck in his arms.

One afternoon, Jones had come home and found his wife sitting in the garden, weeping. She had been transplanting flowers, putting them in pots before the first frost came. There was dirt on her forehead and around her mouth. Her light clothes felt so heavy. Their weight made her body ache. Each breath was a stone she had to swallow. She cried and cried in the weak autumn sunshine. Jones could see the veins throbbing in her neck. "I'm dying," she said. "It's taking me months to die." But after he had brought her inside, she insisted that she felt better and made them both a cup of tea while Jones potted the rest of the plants and carried them down cellar. She lay on the sofa and Jones sat beside her. They talked quietly with one another. Indeed, they were almost whispering, as though they were in a public place surrounded by strangers instead of in their own house with no one present but themselves. "It's the season," Jones said. "In fall everything slows down, retreats. I'm feeling tired myself.

leukocytosis: elevated number of white blood cells.
myelocytes: nuclei of nerve cells.
megaloblasts: damaged red blood cells characteristic of anemia and leukemia.
planets . . . gradients: terms used by believers in astrology to determine the future.

We need iron. I'll go to the druggist right now and buy some iron tablets." His wife agreed. She wanted to go with him, for the ride. Together they ride, through the towns, for miles and miles, even into the next state. She does not want to stop driving. They buy sandwiches and milkshakes and eat in the car. Jones drives. They have to buy more gasoline. His wife sits close to him, her eyes closed, her head tipped back against the seat. He can see the veins beating on in her neck. Somewhere there is a dreadful sound, almost audible. "First I thought it was my imagination," his wife said. "I couldn't sleep. All night I would stay awake, dreaming. But it's not in my head. It's in my ears, my eyes. They ache. Everything. My tongue. My hair. The tips of my fingers are dead." Jones pressed her cold hand to his lips. He thinks of something mad and loving better than he—running out of control, deeply in the darkness of his wife. "Just don't make me go to the hospital," she pleaded. Of course she will go there. The moment has already occurred.

Jones is writing to his daughter. He received a brief letter from her this morning, telling him where she could be reached. The foreign postmark was so large that it almost obliterated Jones's address. She did not mention either her mother or the baby, which makes Jones feel peculiar. His life seems increate as his God's life, perhaps even imaginary. His daughter tells him about the town in which she lives. She does not plan to stay there long. She wants to travel. She will find out exactly what she wants to do and then she will come home again. The town is poor but interesting and there are many Americans there her own age. There is a zoo right on the beach. Almost all the towns, no matter how small, have little zoos. There are primarily eagles and hawks in cages. And what can Jones reply to that? He writes *Every thing is fine here. We are burning wood from the old apple tree in the fire place and it smells wonderful. Has the baby had her full series of polio shots? Take care.* Jones uses this expression constantly, usually in totally unwarranted situations, as when he purchases pipe cleaners or drives through toll booths. Distracted, Jones writes off the edge of the paper and onto the blotter. He must begin again. He will mail this on the way to the hospital. They have been taking X-rays for three days now but the pictures are cloudy. They cannot read them. His wife is now in a real sickbed with high metal sides. He sits with her while she eats her dinner. She asks him to take her good nightgown home and wash it with a bar of Ivory. They won't let her do anything now, not even wash out a few things. *You must take care.*

Jones is driving down a country road. It is the first snowfall of the season and he wants to show it to the baby who rides beside him in a small cushioned car seat all her own. Her head is almost on a level with his and she looks earnestly at the landscape, sometimes smiling. They follow the road that winds tightly between fields and deep pine woods. Everything is white and clean. It has been snowing all afternoon and is doing so still, but very very lightly. Fat snowflakes fall solitary against the windshield. Sometimes the baby reaches out for them. Sometimes she gives a brief kick and cry of joy. They have done their errands. Jones has bought milk and groceries and two yellow roses which lie wrapped in tissue and newspaper in the trunk, in the cold. He must buy two on Saturday as the florist is closed on Sunday. He does not like to do this but there is no alternative. The roses do not keep well. Tonight he will give one to his wife. The other he will pack in sugar water and store in the refrigerator. He can only hope that the bud will remain tight until Sunday when he brings it into the terrible heat of the hospital. The baby rocks against the straps of her small carrier. Her lips are pursed as she watches intently the fields, the grey stalks of crops growing out of the snow, the trees. She is warmly dressed and she wears a knitted orange cap. The cap is twenty-three years old, the age of her mother. Jones found it just the other day. It has faded almost to pink on one side. At one time, it must have been stored in the sun. Jones, driving, feels almost gay. The snow is so beautiful. Everything is white. Jones is an educated man. He has read Melville, who said that white is the colorless all-color of atheism from which we shrink.° Jones does not believe this. He sees a holiness in snow, a promise. He hopes that his wife will know that it is snowing even though she is separated from the window by a curtain. Jones sees something moving across the snow, a part of the snow itself running. Although he is going slowly, he takes his foot completely off the accelerator. "Look, darling, a snowshoe rabbit." At the sound of his voice, the baby stretches open her mouth and narrows her eyes in soundless glee. The hare is splendid. So fast! It flows around invisible obstructions, something out of a kind dream. It flies across the ditch, its paws like paddles, faintly yellow, the color of raw wood. "Look, sweet," cries Jones, "How big he is!" But suddenly the hare is curved and falling, round as a ball, its feet and head tucked closely against its body. It strikes the road and skids upside down for several yards. The car passes around it, avoids it. Jones brakes and stops, amazed. He opens the door and trots back to the animal. The baby twists about in her seat as well as she can and peers after him. It is as though the animal had never been alive at all. Its head is broken in several places. Jones bends to touch its fur, but straightens again, not doing so. A man emerges from the woods, swinging a shotgun. He nods at Jones and picks the hare up by the ears. As he walks away, the hare's legs rub across the ground. There are small crystal stains on the snow. Jones returns to the car. He wants to apologize but he does not know to whom or for what. His life has been devoted to apologetics.° It is his profession. He is concerned with both justification and remorse. He has always acted rightly, but nothing has ever come of it. He gets in the car, starts the engine. "Oh, sweet," he says to the baby. She smiles at him, exposing her tooth. At home that night, after the baby's supper, Jones reads a story to her. She is asleep, panting in her sleep, but Jones tells her the story of al-Boraq,° the milk-white steed of Mohammed, who could stride out of the sight of mankind with a single step.

Jones sorts through a collection of records, none of which have been opened. They are still wrapped in cellophane. The jacket designs are subdued, epic. Names, instruments and orchestras are mentioned confidently. He would like to agree with their importance, for he knows that they have worth, but he is not familiar with the references. His daughter brought these records with her. They had been given to her by an older man, a professor she had been having an affair with. Naturally, this pains Jones. His daughter speaks about the men she has been involved with but no longer cares about. Where did these men come from? Where were they waiting and why have they gone? Jones remembers his daughter when she was a little girl, helping him rake leaves. What can he say? For years on April Fool's Day, she would take tobacco out of his humidor and fill it with corn flakes. Jones is full of remorse and astonishment. When he saw his daughter only a few weeks ago, she was thin and nervous. She had torn out almost all her eyebrows with her fingers from this nervousness. And her lashes. The roots of her eyes were white, like the bulbs of flowers. Her fingernails were

colorless . . . shrink: quotation from Chapter 42, "The Whiteness of the Whale," of *Moby Dick* (1851) by Herman Melville (1819–1891).

apologetics: the explanation and defense of religion, here, specifically, of Christianity.

al-Boraq: According to the Koran, the angel Gabriel brought the prophet Mohammed to the Islamic Seventh Heaven (made up of divine light) on the mystical horse *Borak* or *al-Borak* ("lightning").

crudely bitten, some bleeding below the quick. She was tough and remote, wanting only to go on a trip for which she had a ticket. What can he do? He seeks her in the face of the baby but she is not there. All is being both continued and resumed, but the dream is different. The dream cannot be revived. Jones breaks into one of the albums, blows the dust from the needle, plays a record. Outside it is dark. The parsonage is remote and the only buildings nearby are barns. The river cannot be seen. The music is Bruckner's *Te Deum.*° Very nice, Dedicated to God. He plays the other side. A woman, Kathleen Ferrier,° is singing in German. Jones cannot understand the words but the music stuns him. *Kindertotenlieder.*° It is devastating. In college he had studied only scientific German, The vocabulary of submarines, dirigibles and steam engines. Jones plays the record again and again, searching for his old grammar. At last he finds it. The wings of insects are between some of the pages. There are notes in pencil, written in his own young hand.

RENDER:
A. WAS THE TEACHER SATISFIED WITH YOU TODAY?
B. NO. HE IS NOT. MY ESSAY WAS GOOD BUT IT WAS NOT COPIED WELL.
C. I AM SORRY YOU WERE NOT INDUSTRIOUS THIS TIME FOR YOU GENERALLY ARE.

These lessons are neither of life or death. Why was he instructed in them? In the hospital, his wife waits to be translated, no longer a woman, the woman whom he loves, but a situation. Her blood moves mysteriously as constellations. She is under scrutiny and attack and she has abandoned Jones. She is a swimmer waiting to get on with the drowning. Jones is on the shore. In Mexico, his daughter walks along the beach with two men. She is acting out a play that has become her life. Jones is on the mountaintop. The baby cries and Jones takes her from the crib to change her. The dog paws the door. Jones lets him out. He settles down with the baby and listens to the record. He still cannot make out many of the words. The baby wiggles restlessly on his lap. Her eyes are a foal's eyes, navy-blue. She has grown in a few weeks to expect everything from Jones. He props her on one edge of the couch and goes to her small toy box where he keeps a bear, a few rattles and balls. On the way, he opens the door and the dog immediately enters. His heavy coat is cold, fragrant with ice. He noses the baby and she squeals.

Oft denk' ich, sie sind nur ausgegangen
Bald werden sie wieder nach Hause gelangen°

Jones selects a bright ball and pushes it gently in her direction.

Bruckner: Anton Bruckner (1824–1896), Austrian composer and organist. His *Te Deum* for chorus, soloists, and orchestra was completed in 1884.

Kathleen Ferrier: celebrated English contralto (1912–1953), who died of cancer.

Kindertotenlieder: "Songs on the Death of Children" (1901, 1904), a cycle of five songs for voice and orchestra by Gustav Mahler (1860–1911), Austrian composer and conductor. Mahler's elder daughter died three years after he completed the work.

Oft . . . gelangen: opening two lines of the fourth song in Mahler's *Kindertotenlieder,* from a poem by Friedrich Rückert (1788–1866): "Often I think they've just gone outside/They'll get back home again soon!"

It is Sunday morning and Jones is in the pulpit. The church is very old but the walls of the sanctuary have recently been painted a pale blue. In the cemetery adjoining, some of the graves are three hundred years old. It has become a historical landmark and no one has been buried there since World War I. There is a new place, not far away, which the families now use. Plots are marked not with stones but with small tablets, and immediately after any burial, workmen roll grassed sod over the new graves so that there is no blemish on the grounds, not even for a little while. Present for today's service are seventy-eight adults, eleven children and the junior choir. Jones counts them as the offertory is received. The church rolls say that there are three hundred fifty members but as far as Jones can see, everyone is here today. This is the day he baptizes the baby. He has made arrangements with one of the ladies to hold her and bring her up to the font at the end of the first hymn. The baby looks charming in a lacy white dress. Jones has combed her fine hair carefully, slicking it in a curl with water, but now it has dried and it sticks up awkwardly like the crest of a kingfisher. Jones bought the dress in Mammoth Mart, an enormous store which has a large metal elephant dressed in overalls dancing on the roof. He feels foolish at buying it there but he had gone to several stores and that is where he saw the prettiest dress. He blesses the baby with water from the silver bowl. He says, *We are saved not because we are worthy. We are saved because we are loved.* It is a brief ceremony. The baby, looking curiously at Jones, is taken out to the nursery. Jones begins his sermon. He can't remember when he wrote it, but here it is, typed, in front of him. *There is nothing wrong in what one does but there is something wrong in what one becomes.* He finds this questionable but goes on speaking. He has been preaching for thirty-four years. He is gaunt with belief. But his wife has a red cell count of only 2.3 millions. It is not enough! She is not getting enough oxygen! Jones is giving his sermon. Somewhere he has lost what he was looking for. He must have known once, surely. The congregation sways, like the wings of a ray in water. It is Sunday and for patients it is a holiday. The doctors don't visit. There are no tests or diagnoses. Jones would like to leave, to walk down the aisle and out into the winter, where he would read his words into the ground. Why can't he remember his life! He finishes, sits down, stands up to present communion. Tiny cubes of bread lie in a slumped pyramid. They are offered and received. Jones takes his morsel, hacked earlier from a sliced enriched loaf with his own hand. It is so dry, almost wicked. The very thought now sickens him. He chews it over and over again, but it lies unconsumed, like a muscle in his mouth.

Jones is waiting in the lobby for the results of his wife's operation. Has there ever been a time before dread? He would be grateful even to have dread back, but it has been lost, for a long time, in rapid possibility, probability and fact. The baby sits on his knees and plays with his tie. She woke very early this morning for her orange juice and then gravely, immediately, spit it all up. She seems fine now, however, her fingers exploring Jones's tie. Whenever he looks at her, she gives him a dazzling smile. He has spent most of the day fiercely cleaning the house, changing the bed-sheets and the pages of the many calendars that hang in the rooms, things he should have done a week ago. He has dusted and vacuumed and pressed all his shirts. He has laundered all the baby's clothes, soft small sacks and gowns and sleepers which froze in his hands the moment he stepped outside. And now he is waiting and watching his wristwatch. The tumor is precisely this size, they tell him, the size of his clock's face.

Jones has the baby on his lap and he is feeding her. The evening meal is lengthy and complex. First he must give her vitamins, then, because she has a cold, a dropper of liquid aspirin. This is followed by a bottle of milk, eight ounces, and a portion of strained vegetables. He gives her a rest now so that the food can settle. On his hip, she rides through the rooms of the huge house as Jones turns lights off and on. He comes back to the table and gives her a little more milk, a half jar of strained chicken and a few spoonfuls of dessert, usually cobbler, buckle or pudding. The baby enjoys all equally. She is good. She eats rapidly and neatly. Sometimes she grasps the spoon, turns it around and thrusts the wrong end into her mouth. Of course there is nothing that cannot be done incorrectly. Jones adores the baby. He sniffs her warm head. Her birth is a deep error, an abstraction. Born in wedlock but out of love. He puts her in the playpen and tends to the dog. He fills one dish with water and one with horse-meat. He rinses out the empty can before putting it in the wastebasket. The dog eats with great civility. He eats a little meat and then takes some water, then meat, then water. When the dog has finished, the dishes are as clean as though they'd been washed. Jones now thinks about his own dinner. He opens the refrigerator. The ladies of the church have brought brownies, venison, cheese and apple sauce. There are turkey pies, pork chops, steak, haddock and sausage patties. A brilliant light exposes all this food. There is so much of it. It must be used. A crust has formed around the punctures in a can of Pet. There is a clear bag of chicken livers stapled shut. There are large brown eggs in a bowl. Jones stares unhappily at the beads of moisture on cartons and bottles, at the pearls of fat on the cold cooked stew. He sits down. The room is full of lamps and cords. He thinks of his wife, her breathing body deranged in tubes, and begins to shake. All objects here are perplexed by such grief.

Now it is almost Christmas and Jones is walking down by the river, around an abandoned house. The dog wades heavily through the snow, biting it. There are petals of ice on the tree limbs and when Jones lingers under them, the baby puts out her hand and her mouth starts working because she would like to have it, the ice, the branch, everything. His wife will be coming home in a few days, in time for Christmas. Jones has already put up the tree and brought the ornaments down from the attic. He will not trim it until she comes home. He wants very much to make a fine occasion out of opening the boxes of old decorations. The two of them have always enjoyed this greatly in the past. Jones will doubtlessly drop and smash a bauble, for he does every year. He tramps through the snow with his small voyager. She dangles in a shoulder sling, her legs wedged around his hip. They regard the rotting house seriously. Once it was a doctor's home and offices but long before Jones's time, the doctor, who was very respected, had been driven away because a town girl accused him of fathering her child. The story goes that all the doctor said was, "Is that so?" This incensed the town and the girl's parents, who insisted that he take the child as soon as it was born. He did and he cared for the child very well even though his practice was ruined and no one had anything to do with him. A year later the girl told the truth—that the actual father was a young college boy whom she was now going to marry. They wanted the child back, and the doctor willingly returned the infant to them. Of course it is a very old, important story. Jones has always appreciated it, but now he is annoyed at the man's passivity. He wife's sickness has changed everything for Jones. He will continue to accept but he will no longer surrender. Surely things are different for Jones now.

For insurance purposes, Jones's wife is brought out to the car in a wheelchair. She is thin and beautiful. Jones is grateful and confused. He has a mad wish to tip the orderly. Have so many years really passed? Is this not his wife, his love, fresh from giving birth? Isn't everything about to begin? In Mexico, his daughter wanders disinterestedly through a jewelry shop where she picks up a small silver egg. It opens on a hinge and inside are two figures, a bride and groom. Jones puts the baby in his wife's arms. At first the baby is alarmed because she cannot remember this person very well and she reaches for Jones, whimpering. But soon she is soothed by his wife's soft voice and she falls asleep in her arms as they drive. Jones has readied everything carefully for his wife's homecoming. The house is clean and orderly. For days he has restricted himself to only one part of the house so that his clutter will be minimal. Jones helps his wife up the steps to the door. Together they enter the shining rooms.

QUESTIONS

1. Describe the character of Jones. What is his major trait? How do you learn about it? Why does he continue to practice his profession and care for his family?

2. On the basis of this story, what can you say about the use of tenses in a narration? Why is the story told mainly in the present tense? What is the relationship here between past and present tense?

3. Explain why there are so few paragraphs in the story and why they are rather long. Why do you think Williams does not use more dialogue?

4. Explore the sad or depressing references and situations in the story (e.g., the ill wife, the dead rabbit, the daughter abandoning her child, the songs on the death of children). In the light of such references, how does the story make you think and feel?

THE PRÉCIS OR ABRIDGMENT

A **précis** (*pray-SEE*) is a concise summary, in your own words, of a written work. The closely related word *precise* helps to explain that a précis emphasizes just the most significant details. Other words for précis are *abridgment, paraphrase, abstract, condensation,* and *epitome*. *Epitome* (*ee-PIT-uh-me*) from the Greek for a "cutting away" so that only the essential parts remain, is a particularly helpful explanation of the objective of a précis.

Uses of the Précis

Beyond enabling you to follow a story with accuracy, the précis is important in study, research, and speaking and writing. One of the best ways to study any work is to write a précis of it, for the process forces you to grasp each of the parts. Précis writing can be used in taking notes, preparing for exams, establishing and clarifying facts, studying for classroom discussion, and reinforcing details and ideas learned in the past. The object of a précis should be not to retell all a story's details, but only enough to give the highlights, so that any reader will know the main sections of the work. Although you may sometimes need to condense an entire plot or epitomize an entire argument, most often you will refer to no more than parts of works, because your arguments will depend on a number of separate interpretations.

GUIDELINES FOR PRÉCIS WRITING

The following guidelines will help you in developing a précis.

1. SELECTION. Only essential details belong in a précis. For example, at the opening of the story "Everyday Use," Walker describes the narrator as a large woman who has lived a very hard life. We learn that she can kill animals for food and survival. She is fully capable of taking care of herself and her family. Including all these details would needlessly lengthen a précis of "Everyday Use." Instead it is sufficient to say no more than "Mrs. Johnson is a strong woman," because this fact is the most vital one about her. Concentrating on just the essentials enables you to achieve the shortening required of a précis. Thus a 5,000-word story might be epitomized in 100, 300, or 600 words, with the amount of detail being governed by the desired length. Regardless of the length of your précis, however, base your selection of detail on your judgment of its importance.

2. ACCURACY. All details in a précis should be both correct and accurate. Avoid misstatement, and avoid using words that give a misleading impression of the original. In "The Necklace," for example, Mathilde cooperates with her husband for ten years to repay their 18,000-franc debt. In a précis it would be possible to say no more than she "works" during this time. The word *works* is misleading, however, for it may be interpreted to mean that Mathilde gets paid for outside employment. In fact she does not. What Maupassant tells us is that Mathilde gives up her servant girl and then does all the heavy housework herself as part of her general economizing in her *own* household, not in the houses of others.

As important as the need to condense long sections of a story accurately is the need to be comprehensive. In reference to Walker's "Everyday Use," there is a concluding dispute between the mother (the narrator) and her visiting daughter about the daughter's request for two homemade quilts. Wangero wants them to adorn a wall, while the mother refuses on the grounds that she has promised them to her other daughter for "everyday use" during her approaching marriage. These details are complex, and they represent the climax of the major conflict in the story. In a précis it is important not only to explain the claims but also to present enough language to highlight the conflict. Thus, accurate and comprehensive language might be: "Mrs. Johnson hesitates, having already promised the quilts to Maggie for use when she gets married. Though Maggie offers to give Wangero the quilts, Mrs. Johnson insists on her original promise. Wangero then objects, claiming that the quilts will be spoiled by 'everyday use' and that her mother misunderstands the value of the family heritage." This language explains the details accurately and comprehensively—the goal of précis writing.

3. DICTION. A précis should be an original essay and therefore it should be written *in your own words*, not those of the work you are abridging. The best way to ensure original wording is to read the work, take note of the major actions and situations, and then put the work out of reach as you write. In that way you can avoid the temptation to borrow words.

However, if a number of words from the text find their way into the précis even after you have tried to keep them out, then you must use quotation marks to set them off. As long as direct quotations are kept to a minimum, they are permissible. Too many quoted words, however, indicate that your précis is not original.

4. OBJECTIVITY. A précis should be scrupulously factual. Avoid explanatory or introductory material unless it is a true part of the story. Just as you need to *include* judgments and interpretations in other kinds of writing about literature, you need to *avoid* them in a précis. Here is a comparative example of what to do and what to avoid:

WHAT TO DO	*WHAT TO AVOID*
Mrs. Johnson, a strong woman living on her Southern farm with her younger daughter, Maggie, is waiting for a visit by her elder daughter, Dee. Dee is returning from her home in the city, and the mother has cleaned and swept the house and yard in order to make a good impression.	Walker opens the story by building up the contrast that will soon be made apparent. Her narrator, Mrs. Johnson, is a plain, down-to-earth woman who has worked hard all her life and whose basic value is her home and possessions. The contrast is her daughter Dee, whose visit she is waiting for. Dee has left home and lived a sophisticated life in the city. Mrs. Johnson takes pride in her home, while Dee will regard the home and her mother's belongings as being of no more use than to be put on display.

The right-hand paragraph starts with a topic sentence, to which the following sentences adhere. Such writing is commendable elsewhere, but not in a précis. The left-hand paragraph is better writing *as a précis*, for it presents a selection of details only as they appear in the story, without introductory sentences. In the story there are no such introductions.

5. SENTENCES. Because a précis should be concise and factual, it is tempting to write sentences that are like short bursts of machine-gun fire. Sentences of this kind are often called "choppy," or "bumpy." Here is an example of choppy sentences:

Dee comes in a car. She is dressed flamboyantly. She is with a strange man. He is short and bearded. She greets her mother and sister with foreign phrases. The man does, too. She immediately begins taking pictures. She snaps her mother with her sister in the background. She also takes pictures of wandering cows. She makes sure to get the house in all the shots. She kisses her mother then, on the forehead.

An entire essay consisting of sentences like these might make readers feel as though they have been machine-gunned. Although you want to include detail, you also need to shape and organize your sentences. Here is a more acceptable set of sentences revised to contain the same information:

When Dee comes, she is flamboyantly dressed, and gets out of the car with a strange, short, and bearded man. Both Dee and the man greet Mrs. Johnson and Maggie with foreign phrases. Before embracing her mother, Dee gets her Polaroid camera and takes pictures of her mother, her sister, and wandering cows, taking care to include the house in all her shots. Only then does she kiss her mother, and then only on the forehead.

This revision blends the shorter sentences together while still attempting to cover the essential details from the story. The phrase "only then" beginning the last sentence gets at Dee's ridiculous behavior without calling it ridiculous. Even though sentences in a précis must be almost rigidly factual, try to make them as graceful as possible.

WRITING A PRÉCIS

Your writing task is to condense the original work with the least possible distortion. Thus it is necessary to keep intact the arrangement and sequence of the original. Let us suppose that a work has a surprise ending, like that in "The Necklace." In a précis, it is important to keep the same order and withhold the conclusion until the very end. It is appropriate, however, to introduce essential details of circumstance, such as names and places, at the beginning of the précis, even though these details are not brought out immediately in the story. For example, Maupassant does not name Mathilde right away, and he never says that she is French, but a précis of "The Necklace" would be obscure without these details.

If your assignment is a very short précis, say 100 to 150 words, you might confine everything to only one paragraph. For a longer précis, the normal principle of devoting a separate paragraph to each topic applies. If each major division, episode, scene, action, or section of the story (or play) is considered a topic, then the précis may be divided into paragraphs devoted to each of the divisions.

SAMPLE ESSAY

A Précis of Alice Walker's "Everyday Use"*

[1] Mrs. Johnson, a strong woman living on her southern farm with her younger daughter, Maggie, is waiting for a visit by her elder daughter, Dee. Dee is returning from her home in the city, and the mother has cleaned and swept the house and yard in order to make a good impression.

[2] As she waits, she thinks of how independent Dee has been in the past, and of how self-confident and sophisticated she may be now. She contrasts Dee with Maggie, who is awkward, homely, and burn-scarred, and who has never left home. She also contrasts Dee with herself, thinking of Dee's many opportunities for self-improvement while she herself has never had any opportunities at all.

[3] When Dee comes, she is flamboyantly dressed, and gets out of the car with a strange, short, and bearded man. Both Dee and the man greet Mrs. Johnson with foreign phrases. Before embracing her mother, Dee gets her Polaroid camera, and takes pictures of her mother, her sister, and wandering cows, taking care to get the house in all her shots. Only then does she kiss her mother, and then only on the forehead.

[4] Dee soon explains that she no longer wishes to be called "Dee," but that she has taken a new name, "Wangero Leewanika Kemanjo," which she regards as her own, and not the name that previous oppressors had given her. The man she is with has an incomprehensible name, which the family understands as "Hakim-a-Barber," which he has also taken in keeping with his present philosophy.

[5] Once greetings are past, the family sits down to eat. Wangero (Dee) is impressed with the artistic qualities of the homemade furniture, and asks for the family butter churn and dasher for display in her present home. After dinner, Wangero also asks for two homemade quilts that had been in the family for years. Mrs. Johnson hesitates, having already promised the quilts to Maggie for use when she gets married. Though Maggie offers to give Wangero the quilts, Mrs. Johnson insists on her original promise. Wangero then objects, claiming that the quilts will be spoiled by "everyday use" and that her mother misunderstands the value of the family heritage. Wangero hurriedly leaves with Hakim, while Mrs. Johnson and Maggie remain together, enjoying their snuff, until bedtime.

Commentary on the Essay

This précis, about 400 words long, illustrates the selection of major actions and the omission of interesting but inessential detail. Thus, the phrase "a strong black woman" contains four words, and it condenses more than 150 words of detailed description in paragraph 5 of the story. By contrast, paragraph 3 of the sample essay deals with a relatively short paragraph of the story

---

* See p. 68 for this story.

(paragraph 22). This amount of detail, however, is important because it indicates, right at Dee's entrance, her confused attitudes about her mother and the farm; the farm seems more to her like something for a scrapbook or for a wall than for real living. It is this confusion on Dee's part that underlies the major conflict of the story.

To demonstrate omissions, some materials that disclose things about Hakim's character and philosophy, to be found in paragraphs 43 through 45 of the story, are left out entirely from the précis, because they are not essential to the main characters—namely, the three women.

Each of the five paragraphs in the précis is devoted to comparable sections of "Everyday Use." Paragraphs 1 and 2 describe the story up to the appearance of Dee and her man. Paragraph 3 details Dee's activity at her entrance. Paragraph 4 treats the conversation and narrative from paragraph 24 through 44 of the story. The last paragraph condenses the dinner and post-dinner scene, featuring Dee's requests to take away family heirlooms, including the vitally important quilts.

The paragraphs of the précis require not only fidelity to the narrative development of the story, but also unity of subject matter. Thus, paragraph 1 is unified by the speaker's expectations, while paragraph 2 is unified by her contrast of her two daughters and also her contrast of herself with her returning daughter. Each of the other paragraphs is similarly unified—paragraph 3 by Dee's photography, paragraph 4 by the use of new names, and paragraph 5 by the conflicting attitudes about the disposal of family heirlooms. In any précis, similar attempts should be made to unify paragraphs.

WRITING TOPICS

1. Consider Williams's "Taking Care" as a narrative. To what extent is the author's concern less to tell a story than to reveal a character? If the major quality of a fully developed character in short fiction is adaptation to change, how does the story make Jones's adaptation apparent?

2. Consider the intention of Eumolpus for recounting the tale of "The Widow of Ephesus." In light of what the Widow finally does with her husband's dead body, do you believe that the story bears out this intention? Why does Petronius show how particular characters respond to the story? Why doesn't the main character, the narrator Encolpius, comment on the story?

3. Describe the mixture of narration and dialogue in Walker's "Everyday Use." Why do you think there is a great deal of dialogue from paragraph 24 to the end? On the basis of the mixture of dialogue and narration, what conclusions can you draw about the use that fiction makes of these elements?

4. Study the speeches of Wangero, or Dee, in "Everyday Use" and write an essay taking her point of view. That is, base your analysis not on Mrs. Johnson but rather on Wangero, and consider Mrs. Johnson as a victim of economic injustice and racial prejudice.

5. Compare how "A & P" and "The Widow of Ephesus" deal with women. Are the stories friendly or hostile to women? What level of understanding do they

show of the roles that women play in the social worlds from which they are derived? What evidence of sympathy do you find in the stories?

6. Write a story based on a historical period you believe you know well, being as factually accurate as you can. Introduce your own fictional characters as important "movers and shakers" in your episode, dealing with their public or personal affairs, or both. While you may wish to model your characters and episodes on historical persons, you are free to exercise your imagination completely.

3

Plot and Structure: The Development and Organization of Stories

WHAT IS PLOT?

Stories are made up mostly of **actions** or **incidents** that follow each other sequentially. Finding a sequential or **narrative** order, however, is only the first step toward the more important consideration—the **plot**, or the controls governing the development of the actions.

The English novelist E. M. Forster, in *Aspects of the Novel*, presents a memorable illustration of plot. To show a bare set of actions, he uses the following: "The king died, and then the queen died." He points out, however, that this sequence does not form a plot because it lacks *motivation* and *causation*, which he introduces in his next example: "The king died, and then the queen died of grief." With the phrase "of grief," which shows that one thing (grief) controls or overcomes another (the normal desire to live), motivation and causation enter the sequence to form a plot. In a well-plotted story, things precede or follow each other not simply because time ticks away, but more importantly because *effects* follow *causes*. In a good story nothing is irrelevant or accidental; everything is related and causative.

Conflict

The controlling impulse in a connected pattern of causes and effects is **conflict,** which refers generally to people or circumstances that a character (often the **protagonist**) must face and try to overcome (often the **antagonist**). Conflict brings out the extremes of human energy, causing characters to engage in the decisions, actions, responses, and interactions that make up most stories.

In its most elemental form, a conflict is the opposition of two people. Their conflict may take the shape of envy, hatred, anger, argument, avoidance, gossip, lies, fighting, and many other forms and actions. Conflicts may also exist between groups, although conflicts between individuals are more identifiable and therefore more suitable for stories. Conflicts may also be abstract, such as when an individual opposes larger forces like natural objects, ideas, modes of behavior, public opinion, and the like. A difficult or even impossible *choice* —a **dilemma**—is a natural conflict for an individual person. A conflict may also be brought out in ideas and opinions that may clash. In short, conflict shows itself in many ways.

CONFLICT, DOUBT, TENSION, AND INTEREST. Conflict is the major element of plot because opposing forces arouse *curiosity*, cause *doubt*, create *tension*, and produce *interest*. The same responses are the lifeblood of athletic competition. Consider which kind of game is more interesting: (1) One team gets so far ahead that the winner is no longer in doubt. (2) Both teams are so evenly matched that the winner is in doubt even in the final seconds. Obviously, every game should be a tense contest between teams of comparable strength. The same applies to conflicts in stories. There should be uncertainty about a protagonist's success, for unless there is doubt there is no tension, and without tension there is no interest.

PLOT IN OPERATION. To see a plot in operation, let us build on Forster's description. Here is a bare plot for a story of our own: "John and Jane meet, fall in love, and get married." This is a plot because it shows cause and effect (they get married *because* they fall in love), but with no conflict, the plot is not interesting. However, let us introduce conflicting elements in this common "boy meets girl" story:

> John and Jane meet at school and fall in love. They go together for two years, and plan to marry, but a problem arises. Jane wants a career first, and after marriage she wants to be an equal contributor to the family. John understands Jane's wishes, but he wants to get married first and let her finish her studies and have her career after they have children. Jane believes that John's plan is not for her because it constitutes a trap from which she will never escape. This conflict interrupts their plans, and they part in regret and anger. Even though they still love each other, both marry other people and build separate lives and careers. Neither is happy even though they like and respect their spouses. The years pass, and, after children and grandchildren, Jane and John meet again. He is now divorced and she is a widow. Because their earlier conflict is no longer a barrier, they marry and try to make up for the past. Even their new happiness, however, is tinged with regret and reproach because of their earlier conflict, their unhappy solution, their lost years, and their increasing age.

Here we have a true plot because our original "boy-meets-girl" story outline contains a major conflict, from which a number of related conflicts develop. These conflicts lead to attitudes, choices, and outcomes that make the story interesting. The situation is lifelike; the conflicts rise out of realistic aims and hopes; the outcome is true to life.

THE STRUCTURE OF FICTION

Structure describes how the writer arranges and places materials in accord with the general ideas and purpose of the work. The importance of structure may be seen graphically in the art of the painter. For example, Claude Lorrain's *Seaport, with the Setting Sun* (1639) presents a lifelike scene comprising a harbor, ships, boats, and buildings, and a shore on which people are engaging in various activities. Because the distant and glowing sun is the ultimate center of attention, and also the controlling source of light, the painting seems arranged to emphasize both the variety and complexity of earthly life. Clearly, Claude has placed his objects and figures to emphasize that, despite human preoccupations with business, architecture, and navigation, the source of existence is remote, vast, and mysterious, like the sun. There are also other contrasts—namely those between the fighting figures, the buildings and ships, and the land, sea, and sky.

Similarly, in most fiction there is a major conflict, together with other, related ones. While *plot* is concerned with the conflict or conflicts, *structure* defines layout—the way a story is shaped. Structure is about matters such as placement, balance, recurring themes, true and misleading conclusions, sus-

Seaport at Sunset, Claude Lorrain, Louvre, Lauros-Giraudon/Art Resource, NY.

pense, and the imitation of models or forms like reports, letters, conversations, confessions. Thus a story might be divided up into parts, or it might move from countryside to city, or it might develop relationships between two people from their first introduction to their falling in love. To study structure is to study these arrangements and the purposes for which they are made.

FORMAL CATEGORIES OF STRUCTURE

Many aspects of structure are common to all genres of literature. Particularly for stories and plays, however, the following aspects form a skeleton, a pattern of development.

EXPOSITION. Exposition is the laying out, the putting forth, of the materials in the story—the main characters, their backgrounds, their characteristics, interests, goals, limitations, potentials, and basic assumptions. It may not be limited to the story's beginning, where it is most expected, but may be found anywhere. Thus, intricacies, twists, turns, false leads, blind alleys, surprises, and other quirks may be introduced to interest, perplex, intrigue, and otherwise please readers. Whenever something new arises, to the degree that it is new it is a part of exposition.

COMPLICATION. The complication is the *onset* of the major conflict—the plot. The major participants are the protagonist and antagonist, together with whatever ideas and values they represent, such as good—evil, freedom—suppression, independence—dependence, love—hate, intelligence—stupidity, knowledge—ignorance, and the like.

CRISIS. The crisis (Greek for *turning point*) is the separation between what has gone before and what will come after, usually a decision or action undertaken to resolve the conflict. The crisis is that point in which curiosity, uncertainty, and tension are greatest. Usually the crisis is followed closely by the next stage, the *climax*. Often, in fact, the two happen so closely that they are considered to be the same.

CLIMAX. Because the **climax** (Greek for *ladder*) is a consequence of the crisis, it is the story's *high point*, which may take the shape of a decision, an action, an affirmation or denial, or an illumination or realization. It is the logical conclusion of the preceding actions; no new major developments follow it. In most stories, the climax occurs at or close to the end. For example, in Crane's "The Blue Hotel," the climax is the Swede's verbal and physical encounter with the gambler. Everything that happens prior to this confrontation leads to it: the Swede's nervousness and suspicion, his behavior at the card table, his exultation after the fist fight, his leaving the Blue Hotel, and his heavy drinking. The primitive "honor" his bullying ignites in the gambler brings his story to its sudden and disastrous end.

RESOLUTION, or DÉNOUEMENT. The **resolution** (a releasing or untying) or **dénouement** (untying) is the finishing of things after the climax. The resolution of "The Blue Hotel" is composed of the gambler's retreat, the focus on the dead Swede, the news of the gambler's sentence, and the concluding conversation between the cowboy and the Easterner. Once the climax has occurred, there is a relaxation of tension and uncertainty, and most authors untie things as quickly as possible to avoid losing their readers' interest. Thus, Welty ends "A Worn Path," with the main character beginning her long walk home; Poe ends "The Masque of the Red Death" by asserting the "illimitable dominion" of the Red Death itself; and Twain ends "Luck" with the simple statement that the main character is a fool. Once the conflicts are finished, in other words, a brief action underscores the finality.

FORMAL AND ACTUAL STRUCTURE

The structure just described is a *formal* one, an ideal pattern that moves directly from beginning to end. Most stories, however, present a *real* structure that departs from the formal pattern to greater or lesser degrees. A mystery story, for example, may hold back crucial details of exposition (because the goal is to mystify); a suspense story may keep the protagonist ignorant but provide readers with abundant details in order to maximize concern and tension about the outcome.

More realistic, less "artificial" stories might also contain structural variations. For example, Welty's "A Worn Path" produces a *double take* because of unique structuring. During most of the story, Phoenix's conflicts are against age, poverty, and environment. At the end, however, we are introduced to an additional difficulty—a new conflict—which enlarges our responses to include not just concern but also heartfelt anguish. "A Worn Path" is just one example of how a structural variation maximizes a story's impact.

There are many other possible variants in structure. One of these is the **flashback,** in which present circumstances are explained by the selective introduction of past events. The moment at which the flashback is introduced may be a part of the resolution of the plot, and the flashback might lead you into a moment of climax, but then go from there to develop the details that are more properly part of the exposition. Let us again consider our brief plot about John and Jane, and use the flashback method of structuring the story.

> Jane is now old, and a noise outside causes her to remember the argument that forced her to part with John many years before. They were deeply in love, but their disagreement about her wishes for a career split them apart. Then she pic-

tures in her mind the years she and John have spent happily together after they married. She then contrasts her present happiness with her memory of her earlier, less happy marriage, and from there she recalls her youthful years of courtship with John before their disastrous conflict developed. Then she looks over at John, reading in a chair, and smiles. John smiles back, and the two embrace. Even then, Jane has tears on her face.

In this structure the action begins and remains in the present. Important parts of the past flood the protagonist's memory in flashback, though not in the order in which they happened. Flashbacks might be used structurally in other ways. Alice Munro's "Meneseteung" consists of a series of flashbacks that the narrator imagines in order to describe a probable life for the protagonist. Tillie Olsen's "I Stand Here Ironing" takes place as the narrator stands at her ironing board, but the story develops through flashbacks—memories of her daughter's growth. In short, a technique like flashback creates a unique story that departs significantly from a formal structural pattern.

Each story has a unique structure. Simple geography, for example, may govern a story's development, as in Whitecloud's "Blue Winds Dancing" (a ride from California to Wisconsin), Munro's "The Found Boat" (from a spring flood to an exploration on and beside a river), and Welty's "A Worn Path" (a walk from country to town). Parts or scenes might be carried on through conversations, as in "The Blue Hotel" and "Everyday Use," or through a ceremony witnessed by a major character, as in "Young Goodman Brown." A story may unfold in an apparently accidental way, with the characters drawing significant conclusions as they make vital discoveries about the major characters, as in Glaspell's "A Jury of Her Peers." Or there might be a dream sequence, as in Pickthall's "The Worker in Sandalwood." The possible variations are extensive.

 ## STORIES FOR STUDY

STEPHEN CRANE (1871–1900)

Born in New Jersey, Crane began writing stories at the age of eight, and by the time he was sixteen he was helping his brothers write for newspapers. He attended a number of colleges, but did not graduate. While at Syracuse University he completed his first novel, Maggie: A Girl of the Streets, *which he published with borrowed money in 1893. During the remainder of his brief and turbulent life he worked as a writer and war correspondent. He spent a year in the West, and two of his better known stories, "The Bride Comes to Yellow Sky" and "The Blue Hotel," came out of this experience. His best-known novel,* The Red Badge of Courage, *was published in 1895. "The Blue Hotel" was included in* The Monster and Other Stories *in 1899.*

The Blue Hotel ———————————————————————— *1899*

I

The Palace Hotel at Fort Romper was painted a light blue, a shade that is on the legs of a kind of heron, causing the bird to declare its position against any background. The Palace Hotel, then, was always screaming and howling in a way that made the dazzling winter landscape of Nebraska seem only a grey swampish hush. It stood alone on the prairie, and when the snow was falling the town two hundred yards away was not visible. But when the traveller alighted at the railway station he was obliged to pass the Palace Hotel before he could come upon the company of low clapboard houses which composed Fort Romper, and it was not to be thought that any traveller could pass the Palace Hotel without looking at it. Pat Scully, the proprietor, had proved himself a master of strategy when he chose his paints. It is true that on clear days, when the great transcontinental expresses, long lines of swaying Pullmans, swept through Fort Romper, passengers were overcome at the sight, and the cult that knows the brown-reds and the subdivisions of the dark greens of the East expressed shame, pity, horror, in a laugh. But to the citizens of this prairie town and to the people who would naturally stop there, Pat Scully had performed a feat. With this opulence and splendour, these creeds, classes, egotisms, that streamed through Romper on the rails day after day, they had no colour in common.

As if the displayed delights of such a blue hotel were not sufficiently enticing, it was Scully's habit to go every morning and evening to meet the leisurely trains that stopped at Romper and work his seductions upon any man that he might see wavering, gripsack in hand.

One morning, when a snow-crusted engine dragged its long string of freight cars and its one passenger coach to the station, Scully performed the marvel of catching three men. One was a shaky and quick-eyed Swede, with a great shining cheap valise; one was a tall bronzed cowboy, who was on his way to a ranch near the Dakota line; one was a little silent man from the East, who didn't look it, and didn't announce it. Scully practically made them prisoners. He was so nimble and merry and kindly that each probably felt it would be the height of brutality to try to escape. They trudged off over the creaking board sidewalks in the wake of the eager little Irishman. He wore a heavy fur cap squeezed tightly down on his head. It caused his two red ears to stick out stiffly, as if they were made of tin.

At last, Scully, elaborately, with boisterous hospitality, conducted them through the portals of the blue hotel. The room which they entered was small. It seemed to be merely a proper temple for an enormous stove, which, in the centre, was humming with godlike violence. At various points on its surface the iron had become luminous and glowed yellow from the heat. Beside the stove Scully's son Johnnie was playing High-Five° with an old farmer who had whiskers both grey and sandy. They were quarreling. Frequently the old farmer turned his face toward a box of sawdust—coloured brown from tobacco juice—that was behind the stove, and spat with an air of great impatience and irritation. With a loud flourish of words Scully destroyed the game of cards, and bustled his son upstairs with part of the baggage of the new guests. He himself conducted them to three basins of the coldest water in the world. The cowboy and the Easterner burnished themselves fiery red with this water, until it seemed to be

---

High-Five: the most commonly played card game in the United States before it was replaced in popularity by poker.

some kind of metal-polish. The Swede, however, merely dipped his fingers gingerly and with trepidation. It was notable that throughout this series of small ceremonies the three travellers were made to feel that Scully was very benevolent. He was conferring great favours upon them. He handed the towel from one to another with an air of philanthropic impulse.

Afterward they went to the first room, and, sitting about the stove, listened to   5
Scully's officious clamour at his daughters, who were preparing the midday meal. They reflected in the silence of experienced men who tread carefully amid new people. Nevertheless, the old farmer, stationary, invincible in his chair near the warmest part of the stove, turned his face from the sawdust-box frequently and addressed a glowing commonplace to the strangers. Usually he was answered in short but adequate sentences by either the cowboy or the Easterner. The Swede said nothing. He seemed to be occupied in making furtive estimates of each man in the room. One might have thought that he had the sense of silly suspicion which comes to guilt. He resembled a badly frightened man.

Later, at dinner, he spoke a little, addressing his conversation entirely to Scully. He volunteered that he had come from New York, where for ten years he had worked as a tailor. These facts seemed to strike Scully as fascinating, and afterward he volunteered that he had lived at Romper for fourteen years. The Swede asked about the crops and the price of labour. He seemed barely to listen to Scully's extended replies. His eyes continued to rove from man to man.

Finally, with a laugh and a wink, he said that some of these Western communities were very dangerous; and after his statement he straightened his legs under the table, tilted his head, and laughed again, loudly. It was plain that the demonstration had no meaning to the others. They looked at him wondering and in silence.

II

As the men trooped heavily back into the front room, the two little windows presented views of a turmoiling sea of snow. The huge arms of the wind were making attempts—mighty, circular, futile—to embrace the flakes as they sped. A gate-post like a still man with a blanched face stood aghast amid this profligate fury. In a hearty voice Scully announced the presence of a blizzard. The guests of the blue hotel, lighting their pipes, assented with grunts of lazy masculine contentment. No island of the sea could be exempt in the degree of this little room with its humming stove. Johnnie, son of Scully, in a tone which defined his opinion of his ability as a card-player, challenged the old farmer of both grey and sandy whiskers to a game of High-Five. The farmer agreed with a contemptuous and bitter scoff. They sat close to the stove, and squared their knees under a wide board. The cowboy and the Easterner watched the game with interest. The Swede remained near the window, aloof, but with a countenance that showed signs of an inexplicable excitement.

The play of Johnnie and the grey-beard was suddenly ended by another quarrel. The old man arose while casting a look of heated scorn at his adversary. He slowly buttoned his coat, and then stalked with fabulous dignity from the room. In the discreet silence of all other men the Swede laughed. His laughter rang somehow childish. Men by this time had begun to look at him askance, as if they wished to inquire what ailed him.

A new game was formed jocosely. The cowboy volunteered to become the part-   10
ner of Johnnie, and they all then turned to ask the Swede to throw in his lot with the

little Easterner. He asked some questions about the game, and, learning that it wore many names, and that he had played it when it was under an alias, he accepted the invitation. He strode toward the men nervously, as if he expected to be assaulted. Finally, seated, he gazed from face to face and laughed shrilly. This laugh was so strange that the Easterner looked up quickly, the cowboy sat intent and with his mouth open, and Johnnie paused, holding the cards with still fingers.

Afterward there was a short silence. Then Johnnie said, "Well, let's get at it. Come on now!" They pulled their chairs forward until their knees were bunched under the board. They began to play, and their interest in the game caused the others to forget the manner of the Swede.

The cowboy was a board-whacker. Each time that he held superior cards he whanged them, one by one, with exceeding force, down upon the improvised table, and took the tricks with a glowing air of prowess and pride that sent thrills of indignation into the hearts of his opponents. A game with a board-whacker in it is sure to become intense. The countenances of the Easterner and the Swede were miserable whenever the cowboy thundered down his aces and kings, while Johnnie, his eyes gleaming with joy, chuckled and chuckled.

Because of the absorbing play none considered the strange ways of the Swede. They paid strict heed to the game. Finally, during a lull caused by a new deal, the Swede suddenly addressed Johnnie: "I suppose there have been a good many men killed in this room." The jaws of the others dropped and they looked at him.

"What in hell are you talking about?" said Johnnie.

The Swede laughed again his blatant laugh, full of a kind of false courage and defiance. "Oh, you know what I mean all right," he answered.

"I'm a liar if I do!" Johnnie protested. The card was halted, and the men stared at the Swede. Johnnie evidently felt that as the son of the proprietor he should make a direct inquiry. "Now, what might you be drivin' at, mister?" he asked. The Swede winked at him. It was a wink full of cunning. His fingers shook on the edge of the board. "Oh, maybe you think I have been to nowheres. Maybe you think I'm a tenderfoot?"

"I don't know nothin' about you," answered Johnnie, "and I don't give a damn where you've been. All I got to say is that I don't know what you're driving at. There hain't never been nobody killed in this room."

The cowboy, who had been steadily gazing at the Swede, then spoke. "What's wrong with you, mister?"

Apparently it seemed to the Swede that he was formidably menaced. He shivered and turned white near the corners of his mouth. He sent an appealing glance in the direction of the little Easterner. During these moments he did not forget to wear his air of advanced pot-valour. "They say they don't know what I mean," he remarked mockingly to the Easterner.

The latter answered after prolonged and cautious reflection. "I don't understand you," he said, impassively.

The Swede made a movement then which announced that he thought he had encountered treachery from the only quarter where he had expected sympathy, if not help. "Oh, I see you are all against me. I see———"

The cowboy was in a state of deep stupefaction. "Say," he cried, as he tumbled the deck violently down upon the board, "say, what are you gittin' at, hey?"

The Swede sprang up with the celerity of a man escaping from a snake on the floor. "I don't want to fight!" he shouted, "I don't want to fight!"

The cowboy stretched his long legs indolently and deliberately. His hands were in his pockets. He spat into the sawdust-box. "Well, who the hell thought you did?" he inquired.

The Swede backed rapidly toward a corner of the room. His hands were out protectingly in front of his chest, but he was making an obvious struggle to control his fright. "Gentlemen," he quavered. "I suppose I am going to be killed before I can leave this house! I suppose I am going to be killed before I can leave this house!" In his eyes was the dying-swan° look. Through the windows could be seen the snow turning blue in the shadow of dusk. The wind tore at the house, and some loose thing beat regularly against the clapboards like a spirit tapping.

A door opened, and Scully himself entered. He paused in surprise as he noted the tragic attitude of the Swede. Then he said. "What's the matter here?"

The Swede answered him swiftly and eagerly: "These men are going to kill me."

"Kill you!" ejaculated Scully. "Kill you! What are you talkin'?"

The Swede made the gesture of a martyr.

Scully wheeled sternly upon his son. "What is this, Johnnie?"

The lad had grown sullen. "Damned if I know," he answered. "I can't make no sense of it." He began to shuffle the cards, fluttering them together with an angry snap. "He says a good many men have been killed in this room, or something like that. And he says he's goin' to be killed here too. I don't know what ails him. He's crazy, I shouldn't wonder."

Scully then looked for explanation to the cowboy, but the cowboy simply shrugged his shoulders.

"Kill you?" said Scully again to the Swede. "Kill you? Man, you're off your nut."

"Oh, I know," burst out the Swede. "I know what will happen. Yes, I'm crazy—yes. Yes, of course, I'm crazy—yes. But I know one thing—" There was a sort of sweat of misery and terror upon his face. "I know I won't get out of here alive."

The cowboy drew a deep breath, as if his mind was passing into the last stages of dissolution. "Well, I'm doggoned," he whispered to himself.

Scully wheeled suddenly and faced his son. "You've been troublin' this man!"

Johnnie's voice was loud with its burden of grievance. "Why, good Gawd, I ain't done nothin' to 'im."

The Swede broke in. "Gentlemen, do not disturb yourselves. I will leave this house. I will go away, because"—he accused them dramatically with his glance—"because I do not want to be killed."

Scully was furious with his son. "Will you tell me what is the matter, you young divil? What's the matter, anyhow? Speak out!"

"Blame it!" cried Johnnie in despair, "don't I tell you I don't know? He—he says we want to kill him, and that's all I know. I can't tell what ails him."

The Swede continued to repeat: "Never mind, Mr. Scully; never mind. I will leave this house. I will go away, because I do not wish to be killed. Yes, of course, I am crazy—yes. But I know one thing! I will go away. I will leave this house. Never mind, Mr. Scully; never mind, I will go away."

"You will not go 'way," said Scully. "You will not go 'way until I hear the reason of this business. If anybody has troubled you I will take care of him. This is my house. You are under my roof, and I will not allow any peaceable man to be troubled here." He cast a terrible eye upon Johnnie, the cowboy, and the Easterner.

dying swan: Proverbially, a swan sings its most beautiful notes when it is about to die.

"Never mind, Mr. Scully; never mind. I will go away. I do not wish to be killed."
The Swede moved toward the door which opened upon the stairs. It was evidently his
intention to go at once for his baggage.

"No, no," shouted Scully peremptorily; but the white-faced man slid by him and
disappeared. "Now," said Scully severely, "what does this mane?"°

Johnnie and the cowboy cried together: "Why, we didn't do nothin' to 'im!"

Scully's eyes were cold. "No," he said, "you didn't?"

Johnnie swore a deep oath. "Why, this is the wildest loon I ever see. We didn't
do nothin' at all. We were just sittin' here playin cards, and he————"

The father suddenly spoke to the Easterner. "Mr. Blanc," he asked, "what has
these boys been doin'?"

The Easterner reflected again. "I didn't see anything wrong at all," he said at
last, slowly.

Scully began to howl, "But what does it mane?" He stared ferociously at his son.
"I have a mind to lather you for this, me boy."

Johnnie was frantic. "Well, what have I done?" he bawled at his father.

III

"I think you are tongue-tied," said Scully finally to his son, the cowboy, and the
Easterner; and at the end of this scornful sentence he left the room.

Upstairs the Swede was swiftly fastening the straps of his great valise. Once his
back happened to be half turned toward the door, and, hearing a noise there, he
wheeled and sprang up, uttering a loud cry. Scully's wrinkled visage showed grimly in
the light of the small lamp he carried. This yellow effulgence, streaming upward,
coloured only his prominent features, and left his eyes, for instance, in mysterious
shadow. He resembled a murderer.

"Man! man!" he exclaimed, "have you gone daffy?"

"Oh, no! Oh, no!" rejoined the other. "There are people in this world who
know pretty nearly as much as you do—understand?"

For a moment they stood gazing at each other. Upon the Swede's deathly pale
cheeks were two spots brightly crimson and sharply edged, as if they had been carefully painted. Scully placed the light on the table and sat himself on the edge of the
bed. He spoke ruminatively. "By cracky, I never heard of such a thing in my life. It's
a complete muddle. I can't, for the soul of me, think how you ever got this idea into
your head." Presently he lifted his eyes and asked: "And did you sure think they were
going to kill you?"

The Swede scanned the old man as if he wished to see into his mind. "I did,"
he said at last. He obviously suspected that this answer might precipitate an outbreak.
As he pulled on a strap his whole arm shook, the elbow wavering like a bit of paper.

Scully banged his hand impressively on the footboard of the bed. "Why, man,
we're goin' to have a line of ilictric street-cars in this town next spring."

"'A line of electric street-cars,'" repeated the Swede, stupidly.

"And," said Scully, "there's a new railroad goin' to be built down from Broken
Arm to here. Not to mention the four churches and the smashin' big brick
schoolhouse. Then there's the big factory, too. Why, in two years Romper'll be a
met-tro-*pol*-is."

mane: mean. Scully speaks with a slight Irish brogue (see paragraph 114).

Having finished the preparation of his baggage, the Swede straightened himself. "Mr. Scully," he said, with sudden hardihood, "how much do I owe you?"

"You don't owe me anythin'," said the old man, angrily.

"Yes, I do," retorted the Swede. He took seventy-five cents from his pocket and tendered it to Scully; but the latter snapped his fingers in disdainful refusal. However, it happened that they both stood gazing in a strange fashion at three silver pieces on the Swede's open palm.

"I'll not take your money," said Scully at last. "Not after what's been goin' on here." Then a plan seemed to strike him. "Here," he cried, picking up his lamp and moving toward the door. "Here! Come with me a minute."

"No," said the Swede, in overwhelming alarm.   65

"Yes," urged the old man. "Come on! I want you to come and see a picter—just across the hall—in my room."

The Swede must have concluded that his hour was come. His jaw dropped and his teeth showed like a dead man's. He ultimately followed Scully across the corridor, but he had the step of one hung in chains.

Scully flashed the light high on the wall of his own chamber. There was revealed a ridiculous photograph of a little girl. She was leaning against a balustrade of gorgeous decoration, and the formidable bang to her hair was prominent. The figure was as graceful as an upright sled-stake, and, withal, it was of the hue of lead. "There," said Scully, tenderly, "that's the picter of my little girl that died. Her name was Carrie. She had the purtiest hair you even saw! I was that fond of her, she———"

Turning then, he saw that the Swede was not contemplating the picture at all, but, instead, was keeping keen watch on the gloom in the rear.

"Look, man!" cried Scully, heartily. "That's the picter of my little gal that died.   70
Her name was Carrie. And then here's the picter of my oldest boy, Michael. He's a lawyer in Lincoln, an' doin' well. I gave that boy a grand eddication, and I'm glad for it now. He's a fine boy. Look at 'im now. Ain't he bold as blazes, him there in Lincoln, an honoured an' respicted gintleman! An honoured and respicted gintleman," concluded Scully with a flourish. And, so saying, he smote the Swede jovially on the back.

The Swede faintly smiled.

"Now," said the old man, "there's only one more thing." He dropped suddenly to the floor and thrust his head beneath the bed. The Swede could hear his muffled voice. "I'd keep it under me piller if it wasn't for that boy Johnnie. Then there's the old woman———Where is it now? I never put it twice in the same place. Ah, now come out with you!"

Presently he backed clumsily from under the bed, dragging with him an old coat rolled into a bundle. "I've fetched him," he muttered. Kneeling on the floor, he unrolled the coat and extracted from its heart a large yellow-brown whiskey-bottle.

His first maneuver was to hold the bottle up to the light. Reassured, apparently, that nobody had been tampering with it, he thrust it with a generous movement toward the Swede.

The weak-kneed Swede was about to eagerly clutch this element of strength, but   75
he suddenly jerked his hand away and cast a look of horror upon Scully.

"Drink," said the old man affectionately. He had risen to his feet, and now stood facing the Swede.

There was a silence. Then again Scully said: "Drink!"

The Swede laughed wildly. He grabbed the bottle, put it to his mouth; and as his lips curled absurdly around the opening and his throat worked, he kept his glance, burning with hatred, upon the old man's face.

IV

After the departure of Scully the three men, with the card-board still upon their knees, preserved for a long time an astounded silence. Then Johnnie said: "That's the dod-dangedest Swede I ever see."

"He ain't no Swede," said the cowboy, scornfully.

"Well, what is he then?" cried Johnnie. "What is he then?"

"It's my opinion," replied the cowboy deliberately, "he's some kind of a Dutchman." It was a venerable custom of the country to entitle as Swedes all light-haired men who spoke with a heavy tongue. In consequence the idea of the cowboy was not without its daring. "Yes, sir," he repeated. "It's my opinion this feller is some kind of Dutchman."

"Well, he says he's a Swede, anyhow," muttered Johnnie, sulkily. He turned to the Easterner: "What do you think, Mr. Blanc?"

"Oh, I don't know," replied the Easterner.

"Well, what do you think makes him act that way?" asked the cowboy.

"Why, he's frightened." The Easterner knocked his pipe against the rim of the stove. "He's clear frightened out of his boots."

"What at?" cried Johnnie, and the cowboy together.

The Easterner reflected over his answer.

"What at?" cried the others again.

"Oh, I don't know, but it seems to me this man has been reading dime novels, and he thinks he's right out in the middle of it—the shootin' and stabbin' and all."

"But," said the cowboy, deeply scandalized, "this ain't Wyoming, ner none of them places. This is Nebrasker."

"Yes," added Johnnie, "an' why don't he wait till he gits *out West?*"

The travelled Easterner laughed. "It isn't different there even—not in these days. But he thinks he's right in the middle of hell."

Johnnie and the cowboy mused long.

"It's awful funny," remarked Johnnie at last.

"Yes," said the cowboy. "This is a queer game. I hope we don't git snowed in, because then we'd have to stand this here man bein' around with us all the time. That wouldn't be no good."

"I wish pop would throw him out," said Johnnie.

Presently they heard a loud stamping on the stairs, accompanied by ringing jokes in the voice of old Scully, and laughter, evidently from the Swede. The men around the stove stared vacantly at each other. "Gosh!" said the cowboy. The door flew open, and old Scully, flushed and anecdotal, came into the room. He was jabbering at the Swede, who followed him, laughing bravely. It was the entry of two roisterers from a banquet hall.

"Come now," said Scully sharply to the three seated men, "move up and give us a chance at the stove." The cowboy and the Easterner obediently sidled their chairs to make room for the new-comers. Johnnie, however, simply arranged himself in a more indolent attitude, and then remained motionless.

"Come! Git over, there," said Scully.

"Plenty of room on the other side of the stove," said Johnnie.

"Do you think we want to sit in the draught?" roared the father.

But the Swede here interposed with a grandeur of confidence. "No, no. Let the boy sit where he likes," he cried in a bullying voice to the father.

"All right! All right!" said Scully, deferentially. The cowboy and the Easterner exchanged glances of wonder.

The five chairs were formed in a crescent about one side of the stove. The Swede began to talk; he talked arrogantly, profanely, angrily. Johnnie, the cowboy, and the Easterner maintained a morose silence, while old Scully appeared to be receptive and eager, breaking in constantly with sympathetic ejaculations.

Finally the Swede announced that he was thirsty. He moved in his chair, and said that he would go for a drink of water.

"I'll git it for you," cried Scully at once.

"No," said the Swede contemptuously. "I'll get it for myself." He arose and stalked with the air of an owner off into the executive parts of the hotel.

As soon as the Swede was out of hearing Scully sprang to his feet and whispered intensely to the others: "Upstairs he thought I was tryin' to poison 'im."

"Say," said Johnnie, "this makes me sick. Why don't you throw 'im out in the snow?"

"Why, he's all right now," declared Scully. "It was only that he was from the East, and he thought this was a tough place. That's all. He's all right now."

The cowboy looked with admiration upon the Easterner. "You were straight," he said. "You were on to that there Dutchman."

"Well," said Johnnie to his father, "he may be all right now, but I don't see it. Other time he was scared, but now he's too fresh."

Scully's speech was always a combination of Irish brogue and idiom, Western twang and idiom, and scraps of curiously formal diction taken from the storybooks and newspapers. He now hurled a strange mass of language at the head of his son. "What do I keep? What do I keep? What do I keep?" he demanded, in a voice of thunder. He slapped his knee impressively, to indicate that he himself was going to make reply, and that all should heed. "I keep a hotel," he shouted. "A hotel, do you mind? A guest under my roof has sacred privileges. He is to be intimidated by none. Not one word shall he hear that would prijudice him in favor of goin' away. I'll not have it. There's no place in this here town where they can say they iver took in a guest of mine because he was afraid to stay here." He wheeled suddenly upon the cowboy and the Easterner. "Am I right?"

"Yes, Mr. Scully," said the cowboy, "I think you're right."

"Yes, Mr. Scully," said the Easterner, "I think you're right."

V

At six-o'clock supper, the Swede fizzed like a fire-wheel. He sometimes seemed on the point of bursting into riotous song, and in all his madness he was encouraged by old Scully. The Easterner was encased in reserve; the cowboy sat in wide-mouthed amazement, forgetting to eat, while Johnnie wrathily demolished great plates of food. The daughters of the house, when they were obliged to replenish the biscuits, approached as warily as Indians, and, having succeeded in their purpose, fled with ill-concealed trepidation. The Swede domineered the whole feast, and he gave it the appearance of a cruel bacchanal. He seemed to have grown suddenly taller; he gazed, brutally disdainful, into every face. His voice rang through the room. Once when he jabbed out harpoon-fashion with his fork to pinion a biscuit, the weapon nearly impaled the hand of the Easterner, which had been stretched quietly out for the same biscuit.

After supper, as the men filed toward the other room, the Swede smote Scully ruthlessly on the shoulder. "Well, old boy, that was a good, square meal." Johnnie looked hopefully at his father; he knew that shoulder was tender from an old fall; and, indeed, it appeared for a moment as if Scully was going to flame out over the matter, but in the end he smiled a sickly smile and remained silent. The others understood from his manner that he was admitting his responsibility for the Swede's new viewpoint.

Johnnie, however, addressed his parent in an aside. "Why don't you license somebody to kick you downstairs?" Scully scowled darkly by way of reply.

When they were gathered about the stove, the Swede insisted on another game of High-Five. Scully gently deprecated the plan at first, but the Swede turned a wolfish glare upon him. The old man subsided, and the Swede canvassed the others. In his tone there was always a great threat. The cowboy and the Easterner both remarked indifferently that they would play. Scully said that he would presently have to go to meet the 6.58 train, and so the Swede turned menacingly upon Johnnie. For a moment their glances crossed like blades, and then Johnnie smiled and said, "Yes, I'll play."

They formed a square, with the little board on their knees. The Easterner and the Swede were again partners. As the play went on, it was noticeable that the cowboy was not board-whacking as usual. Meanwhile, Scully, near the lamp, had put on his spectacles and, with an appearance curiously like an old priest, was reading a newspaper. In time he went out to meet the 6.58 train, and, despite his precautions, a gust of polar wind whirled into the room as he opened the door. Besides scattering the cards, it chilled the players to the marrow. The Swede cursed frightfully. When Scully returned, his entrance disturbed a cosy and friendly scene. The Swede again cursed. But presently they were once more intent, their heads bent forward and their hands moving swiftly. The Swede had adopted the fashion of board-whacking.

Scully took up his paper and for a long time remained immersed in matters which were extraordinarily remote from him. The lamp burned badly, and once he stopped to adjust the wick. The newspaper, as he turned from page to page, rustled with a slow and comfortable sound. Then suddenly he heard three terrible words: "You are cheatin'!"

Such scenes often prove that there can be little of dramatic import in environment. Any room can present a tragic front: any room can be comic. This little den was now hideous as a torture-chamber. The new faces of the men themselves had changed it upon the instant. The Swede held a huge fist in front of Johnnie's face, while the latter looked steadily over it into the blazing orbs of his accuser. The Easterner had grown pallid: the cowboy's jaw had dropped in that expression of bovine amazement which was one of his important mannerisms. After the three words, the first sound in the room was made by Scully's paper as it floated forgotten to his feet. His spectacles had also fallen from his nose, but by a clutch he had saved them in air. His hand, grasping the spectacles, now remained poised awkwardly and near his shoulder. He stared at the card-players.

Probably the silence was while a second elapsed. Then, if the floor had been suddenly twitched out from under the men they could not have moved quicker. The five had projected themselves headlong toward a common point. It happened that Johnnie, in rising to hurl himself upon the Swede, had stumbled slightly because of his curiously instinctive care for the cards and the board. The loss of the moment allowed time for the arrival of Scully, and also allowed the cowboy time to give the Swede a great push which sent him staggering back. The men found tongue together, and hoarse shouts of rage, appeal, or fear burst from every throat. The cowboy pushed and jostled feverishly at the Swede, and the Easterner and Scully clung wildly to Johnnie; but through the smoky air, above the swaying bodies of the peace-compellers, the eyes of the two warriors ever sought each other in glances of challenge that were at once hot and steely.

Of course the board had been overturned, and now the whole company of   125
cards was scattered over the floor, where the boots of the men trampled the fat and painted kings and queens as they gazed with their silly eyes at the war that was waging above them.

Scully's voice was dominating the yells. "Stop now! Stop, I say! Stop, now— "Johnnie, as he struggled to burst through the rank formed by Scully and the Easterner, was crying. "Well, he says I cheated! He says I cheated! I won't allow no man to say I cheated! If he says I cheated, he's a ——— ———!"

The cowboy was telling the Swede, "Quit, now! Quit, d'ye hear———"

The screams of the Swede never ceased: "He did cheat! I saw him! I saw him———"

As for the Easterner, he was importuning in a voice that was not heeded: "Wait a moment, can't you? Oh, wait a moment. What's the good of a fight over a game of cards? Wait a moment———"

In this tumult no complete sentences were clear. "Cheat"—"Quit"—"He   130
says"—these fragments pierced the uproar and rang out sharply. It was remarkable that, whereas Scully undoubtedly made the most noise, he was the least heard of any of the riotous band.

Then suddenly there was a great cessation. It was as if each man had paused for breath; and although the room was still lighted with the anger of men, it could be seen that there was no danger of immediate conflict, and at once Johnnie, shouldering his way forward, almost succeeded in confronting the Swede. "What did you say I cheated for? What did you say I cheated for? I don't cheat, and I won't let no man say I do!"

The Swede said, "I saw you! I saw you!"

"Well," cried Johnnie, "I'll fight any man what says I cheat!"

"No, you won't," said the cowboy. "Not here."

"Ah, be still, can't you?" said Scully, coming between them.   135

The quiet was sufficient to allow the Easterner's voice to be heard. He was repeating, "Oh, wait a moment, can't you? What's the good of a fight over a game of cards? Wait a moment!"

Johnnie, his red face appearing above his father's shoulder, hailed the Swede again. "Did you say I cheated?"

The Swede showed his teeth. "Yes."

"Then," said Johnnie, "we must fight."

"Yes, fight," roared the Swede. He was like a demoniac. "Yes, fight! I'll show you   140
what kind of a man I am! I'll show you who you want to fight! Maybe you think I can't fight! Maybe you think I can't! I'll show you, you skin, you card-sharp! Yes, you cheated! You cheated! You cheated!"

"Well, let's go at it, then, mister," said Johnnie coolly.

The cowboy's brow was beaded with sweat from his efforts in intercepting all sorts of raids. He turned in despair to Scully. "What are you goin' to do now?"

A change had come over the Celtic visage of the old man. He now seemed all eagerness; his eyes glowed.

"We'll let them fight," he answered stalwartly. "I can't put up with it any longer. I've stood this damned Swede till I'm sick. We'll let them fight."

VI

The men prepared to go out of doors. The Easterner was so nervous that he had great difficulty in getting his arms into the sleeves of his new leather coat. As the cowboy drew his fur cap down over his ears his hands trembled. In fact, Johnnie and old Scully were the only ones who displayed no agitation. These preliminaries were conducted without words.

Scully threw open the door. "Well, come on," he said. Instantly a terrific wind caused the flame of the lamp to struggle at its wick, while a puff of black smoke sprang from the chimney-top. The stove was in mid-current of the blast, and its voice swelled to equal the roar of the storm. Some of the scarred and bedabbled cards were caught up from the floor and dashed helplessly against the farther wall. The men lowered their heads and plunged into the tempest as into a sea.

No snow was falling, but great whirls and clouds of flakes, swept up from the ground by the frantic winds, were streaming southward with the speed of bullets. The covered land was blue with the sheen of an unearthly satin, and there was no other hue save where, at the low, black railway station—which seemed incredibly distant—one light gleamed like a tiny jewel. As the men floundered into a thigh-deep drift, it was known that the Swede was bawling out something. Scully went to him, put a hand on his shoulder, and projected an ear. "What's that you say?" he shouted.

"I say," bawled the Swede again. "I won't stand much show against this gang, I know you'll all pitch on me."

Scully smote him reproachfully on the arm. "Tut, man!" he yelled. The wind tore the words from Scully's lips and scattered them far alee.

"You are all a gang of———" boomed the Swede, but the storm also seized the remainder of this sentence.

Immediately turning their backs upon the wind, the men had swung around a corner to the sheltered side of the hotel. It was the function of the little house to preserve here, amid this great devastation of snow, an irregular V-shape of heavily encrusted grass, which crackled beneath the feet. One could imagine the great drifts piled against the windward side. When the party reached the comparative peace of this spot it was found that the Swede was still bellowing.

"Oh, I know what kind of a thing this is! I know you'll all pitch on me. I can't lick you all!"

Scully turned upon him panther-fashion. "You'll not have to whip all of us. You'll have to whip my son Johnnie. An' the man what troubles you durin' that time will have me to dale with."

The arrangements were swiftly made. The two men faced each other, obedient to the harsh commands of Scully, whose face, in the subtly luminous gloom, could be seen set in the austere impersonal lines that are pictured on the countenances of the Roman veterans. The Easterner's teeth were chattering, and he was hopping up and down like a mechanical toy. The cowboy stood rock-like.

The contestants had not stripped off any clothing. Each was in his ordinary at- 155 tire. Their fists were up, and they eyed each other in a calm that had the elements of leonine cruelty in it.

During this pause, the Easterner's mind, like a film, took lasting impressions of three men—the iron-nerved master of the ceremony; the Swede, pale, motionless, terrible; and Johnnie, serene yet ferocious, brutish yet heroic. The entire prelude had in it a tragedy greater than the tragedy of action, and this aspect was accentuated by the long, mellow cry of the blizzard, as it sped the tumbling and wailing flakes into the black abyss of the south.

"Now!" said Scully.

The two combatants leaped forward and crashed together like bullocks. There was heard the cushioned sound of blows, and of a curse squeezing out from between the tight teeth of one.

As for the spectators, the Easterner's pent-up breath exploded from him with a pop of relief, absolute relief from the tension of the preliminaries. The cowboy bounded into the air with a yowl. Scully was immovable as from supreme amazement and fear at the fury of the fight which he himself had permitted and arranged.

For a time the encounter in the darkness was such a perplexity of flying arms 160 that it presented no more detail than would a swiftly revolving wheel. Occasionally a face, as if illumined by a flash of light, would shine out, ghastly and marked with pink spots. A moment later, the men might have been known as shadows, if it were not for the involuntary utterance of oaths that came from them in whispers.

Suddenly a holocaust of warlike desire caught the cowboy, and he bolted forward with the speed of a broncho. "Go it, Johnnie! go it! Kill him! Kill him!"

Scully confronted him. "Kape back," he said; and by his glance the cowboy could tell that this man was Johnnie's father.

To the Easterner there was a monotony of unchangeable fighting that was an abomination. This confused mingling was eternal to his sense, which was concentrated in a longing for the end, the priceless end. Once the fighters lurched near him, and as he scrambled hastily backward he heard them breathe like men on the rack.

"Kill him, Johnnie! Kill him! Kill him! Kill him!" The cowboy's face was contorted like one of those agony masks in museums.

"Keep still," said Scully, icily. 165

Then there was a sudden loud grunt, incomplete, cut short, and Johnnie's body swung away from the Swede and fell with sickening heaviness to the grass. The cowboy was barely in time to prevent the mad Swede from flinging himself upon his prone adversary. "No, you don't," said the cowboy, interposing an arm. "Wait a second."

Scully was at his son's side. "Johnnie! Johnnie, me boy!" His voice had a quality of melancholy tenderness. "Johnnie! Can you go on with it?" He looked anxiously down into the bloody, pulpy face of his son.

There was a moment of silence, and then Johnnie answered in his ordinary voice, "Yes, I—it—yes."

Assisted by his father he struggled to his feet. "Wait a bit now till you git your wind," said the old man.

A few paces away the cowboy was lecturing the Swede. "No, you don't! Wait a 170 second!"

The Easterner was plucking at Scully's sleeve. "Oh, this is enough," he pleaded. "This is enough! Let it go as it stands. This is enough!"

"Bill," said Scully, "git out of the road." The cowboy stepped aside. "Now." The combatants were actuated by a new caution as they advanced toward collision. They glared at each other, and then the Swede aimed a lightning blow that carried with it his entire weight. Johnnie was evidently half stupid from weakness, but he miraculously dodged, and his fist sent the over-balanced Swede sprawling.

The cowboy, Scully, and the Easterner burst into a cheer that was like a chorus of triumphant soldiery, but before its conclusion the Swede has scuffed agilely to his feet and come in berserk abandon at his foe. There was another perplexity of flying arms, and Johnnie's body again swung away and fell, even as a bundle might fall from a roof. The Swede instantly staggered to a little wind-waved tree and leaned upon it, breathing like an engine, while his savage and flamelit eyes roamed from face to face as the men bent over Johnnie. There was a splendour of isolation in his situation at this time which the Easterner felt once when, lifting his eyes from the man on the ground, he beheld that mysterious and lonely figure, waiting.

"Are you any good yet, Johnnie?" asked Scully in a broken voice.

The son gasped and opened his eyes languidly. After a moment he answered, "No—I ain't—any good—any—more." Then, from shame, and bodily ill, he began to weep, the tears furrowing down through the blood-stains on his face. "He was too—too—too heavy for me."

Scully straightened and addressed the waiting figure.

"Stranger," he said, evenly, "it's all up with our side." Then his voice changed into that vibrant huskiness which is commonly the tone of the most simple and deadly announcements. "Johnnie is whipped."

Without replying, the victor moved off on the route to the front door of the hotel.

The cowboy was formulating new and unspellable blasphemies. The Easterner was startled to find that they were out in a wind that seemed to come direct from the shadowed arctic floes. He heard again the wail of the snow as it was flung to its grave in the south. He knew now that all this time the cold had been sinking into him deeper and deeper, and he wondered that he had not perished. He felt indifferent to the condition of the vanquished man.

"Johnnie, can you walk?" asked Scully.

"Did I hurt—hurt him any?" asked the son.

"Can you walk, boy? Can you walk?"

Johnnie's voice was suddenly strong. There was a robust impatience in it. "I asked you whether I hurt him any!"

"Yes, yes, Johnnie," answered the cowboy, consolingly; "he's hurt a good deal."

They raised him from the ground, and as soon as he was on his feet he went tottering off, rebuffing all attempts at assistance. When the party rounded the corner they were fairly blinded by the pelting of the snow. It burned their faces like fire. The cowboy carried Johnnie through the drift to the door. As they entered, some cards again rose from the floor and beat against the wall.

The Easterner rushed to the stove. He was so profoundly chilled that he almost dared to embrace the glowing iron. The Swede was not in the room. Johnnie sank into a chair and, folding his arms on his knees, buried his face in them. Scully, warming one foot and then the other at a rim of the stove, muttered to himself with Celtic mournfulness. The cowboy had removed his fur cap, and with a dazed and rueful air he was running one hand through his tousled locks. From overhead they could hear the creaking of boards, as the Swede tramped here and there in his room.

The sad quiet was broken by the sudden flinging open of a door that led toward the kitchen. It was instantly followed by an inrush of women. They precipitated themselves upon Johnnie amid a chorus of lamentation. Before they carried their prey off to the kitchen, there to be bathed and harangued with that mixture of sympathy and abuse which is a feat of their sex, the mother straightened herself and fixed old Scully with an eye of stern reproach, "Shame be upon you, Patrick Scully!" she cried. "Your own son, too. Shame be upon you!"

"There, now! Be quiet, now!" said the old man, weakly.

"Shame be upon you, Patrick Scully!" The girls, rallying to this slogan, sniffed disdainfully in the direction of those trembling accomplices, the cowboy and the Easterner. Presently they bore Johnnie away, and left the three men to dismal reflection.

VII

"I'd like to fight this here Dutchman myself," said the cowboy, breaking a long   190
silence.

Scully wagged his head sadly. "No, that wouldn't do. It wouldn't be right. It wouldn't be right."

"Well, why wouldn't it?" argued the cowboy. "I don't see no harm in it."

"No," answered Scully, with mournful heroism. "It wouldn't be right. It was Johnnie's fight, and now we mustn't whip the man just because he whipped Johnnie."

"Yes, that's true enough," said the cowboy; "but—he better not get fresh with me, because I couldn't stand no more of it."

"You'll not say a word to him," commanded Scully, and even then they heard   195
the tread of the Swede on the stairs. His entrance was made theatric. He swept the door back with a bang and swaggered to the middle of the room. No one looked at him. "Well," he cried, insolently, at Scully, "I s'pose you'll tell me now how much I owe you?"

The old man remained stolid. "You don't owe me nothin'."

"Huh!" said the Swede, "huh! Don't owe 'im nothin'."

The cowboy addressed the Swede. "Stranger, I don't see how you come to be so gay around here."

Old Scully was instantly alert. "Stop!" he shouted, holding his hand forth, fingers upward. "Bill, you shut up!"

The cowboy spat carelessly into the sawdust-box. "I didn't say a word, did I?" he   200
asked.

"Mr. Scully," called the Swede, "how much do I owe you?" It was seen that he was attired for departure, and that he had his valise in his hand.

"You don't owe me nothin'," repeated Scully in the same imperturbable way.

"Huh!" said the Swede. "I guess you're right. I guess if it was any way at all, you'd owe me somethin'. That's what I guess." He turned to the cowboy. "'Kill him! Kill him! Kill him!'" he mimicked, and then guffawed victoriously. "'Kill him!'" He was convulsed with ironical humour.

But he might have been jeering the dead. The three men were immovable and silent, staring with glassy eyes at the stove.

The Swede opened the door and passed into the storm, giving one derisive   205
glance backward at the still group.

As soon as the door was closed, Scully and the cowboy leaped to their feet and began to curse. They trampled to and fro, waving their arms and smashing into the air with their fists. "Oh, but that was a hard minute!" wailed Scully. "That was a hard minute! Him there leerin' and scoffin'! One bang at his nose was worth forty dollars to me that minute! How did you stand it, Bill?"

"How did I stand it?" cried the cowboy in a quivering voice. "How did I stand it? Oh!"

The old man burst into sudden brogue. "I'd loike to take that Swade," he wailed, "and hould 'im down on a shtone flure and bate 'im to a jelly wid a shtick!"

The cowboy groaned in sympathy. "I'd like to git him by the neck and hammer him"—he brought his hand down on a chair with a noise like a pistol-shot—"hammer that there Dutchman until he couldn't tell himself from a dead coyote!"

"I'd bate 'im until he————"

"I'd show *him* some things————"

And then together they raised a yearning, fanatic cry—"Oh-o-oh! if we only could————"

"Yes!"

"Yes!"

"And then I'd————"

"O-o-oh!"

VIII

The Swede, tightly gripping his valise, tacked across the face of the storm as if he carried sails. He was following a line of little naked, gasping trees which, he knew, must mark the way of the road. His face, fresh from the pounding of Johnnie's fists, felt more pleasure than pain in the wind and the driving snow. A number of square shapes loomed upon him finally, and he knew them as the houses of the main body of the town. He found a street and made travel along it, leaning heavily upon the wind whenever, at a corner, a terrific blast caught him.

He might have been in a deserted village. We picture the world as thick with conquering and elate humanity, but here, with the bugles of the tempest pealing, it was hard to imagine a peopled earth. One viewed the existence of man then as marvel, and conceded a glamour of wonder to these lice which were caused to cling to a whirling, fire-smitten, ice-locked, disease-stricken, space-lost bulb. The conceit of man was explained by this storm to be the very engine of life. One was a coxcomb not to die in it. However, the Swede found a saloon.

In front of it an indomitable red light was burning, and the snowflakes were made blood-colour as they flew through the circumscribed territory of the lamp's shining. The Swede pushed open the door of the saloon and entered. A sanded expanse was before him, and at the end of it four men sat about a table drinking. Down one side of the room extended a radiant bar, and its guardian was leaning upon his elbows listening to the talk of the men at the table. The Swede dropped his valise upon the floor and, smiling fraternally upon the barkeeper, said, "Gimme some whisky, will you?" The man placed a bottle, a whisky-glass, and a glass of ice-thick water upon the bar. The Swede poured himself an abnormal portion of whisky and drank it in three gulps. "Pretty bad night," remarked the bartender, indifferently. He was making the pretension of blindness which is usually a distinction of his class; but it could have been seen that he was furtively studying the half-erased blood-stains on the face of the Swede. "Bad night," he said again.

"Oh, it's good enough for me," replied the Swede, hardily, as he poured him-   220
self some more whisky. The barkeeper took his coin and manoeuvred it through its
reception by the highly nickelled cash-machine. A bell rang; a card labelled "20 cts."
had appeared.

"No," continued the Swede, "this isn't too bad weather. It's good enough for
me."

"So?" murmured the barkeeper, languidly.

The copious drams made the Swede's eyes swim, and he breathed a trifle heavier. "Yes, I like this weather. I like it. It suits me." It was apparently his design to impart a deep significance to these words.

"So?" murmured the bartender again. He turned to gaze dreamily at the scroll-
like birds and bird-like scrolls which had been drawn with soap upon the mirrors in
back of the bar.

"Well, I guess I'll take another drink," said the Swede, presently. "Have some-   225
thing?"

"No, thanks; I'm not drinkin'," answered the bartender. Afterward he asked,
"How did you hurt your face?"

The Swede immediately began to boast loudly. "Why, in a fight. I thumped the
soul out of a man down here at Scully's hotel."

The interest of the four men at the table was at last aroused.

"Who was it?" said one.

"Johnnie Scully," blustered the Swede. "Son of the man what runs it. He will be   230
pretty near dead for some weeks, I can tell you. I made a nice thing of him. I did. He
couldn't get up. They carried him in the house. Have a drink?"

Instantly the men in some subtle way encased themselves in reserve. "No,
thanks," said one. The group was of curious formation. Two were prominent local
business men; one was the district attorney; and one was a professional gambler of the
kind known as "square." But a scrutiny of the group would not have enabled an observer to pick the gambler from the men of more reputable pursuits. He was, in fact,
a man so delicate in manner, when among people of fair class, and so judicious in his
choice of victims, that in the strictly masculine part of the town's life he had come to
be explicitly trusted and admired. People called him a thoroughbred. The fear and
contempt with which his craft was regarded were undoubtedly the reason why his
quiet dignity shone conspicuous above the quiet dignity of men who might be merely
hatters, billiard-markers, or grocery clerks. Beyond an occasional unwary traveller who
came by rail, this gambler was supposed to prey solely upon reckless and senile farmers, who, when flush with good crops, drove into town in all the pride and confidence
of an absolutely invulnerable stupidity. Hearing at times in circuitous fashion of the
despoilment of such a farmer, the important men of Romper invariably laughed in
contempt of the victim, and if they thought of the wolf at all, it was with a kind of
pride at the knowledge that he would never dare think of attacking their wisdom and
courage. Besides, it was popular that this gambler had a real wife and two real children in a neat cottage in a suburb, where he led an exemplary home life; and when
any one even suggested a discrepancy in his character, the crowd immediately vocif-
erated descriptions of this virtuous family circle. Then men who led exemplary home
lives, and men who did not lead exemplary home lives, all subsided in a bunch, remarking that there was nothing more to be said.

However, when a restriction was placed upon him—as, for instance, when a strong clique of members of the new Pollywog Club refused to permit him, even as a spectator, to appear in the rooms of the organization—the candour and gentleness with which he accepted the judgment disarmed many of his foes and made his friends more desperately partisan. He invariably distinguished between himself and a respectable Romper man so quickly and frankly that his manner actually appeared to be a continual broadcast compliment.

And one must not forget to declare the fundamental fact of his entire position in Romper. It is irrefutable that in all affairs outside his business, in all matters that occur eternally and commonly between man and man, this thieving cardplayer was so generous, so just, so moral, that, in a contest, he could have put to flight the consciences of nine tenths of the citizens of Romper.

And so it happened that he was seated in this saloon with the two prominent local merchants and the district attorney.

The Swede continued to drink raw whisky, meanwhile babbling at the barkeeper and trying to induce him to indulge in potations. "Come on. Have a drink. Come on. What—no? Well, have a little one, then. By gawd, I've whipped a man tonight, and I want to celebrate. I whipped him good, too. Gentlemen," the Swede cried to the men at the table, "have a drink?"

"Ssh!" said the barkeeper.

The group at the table, although furtively attentive, had been pretending to be deep in talk, but now a man lifted his eyes toward the Swede and said, shortly, "Thanks. We don't want any more."

At this reply the Swede ruffled out his chest like a rooster. "Well," he exploded, "it seems I can't get anybody to drink with me in this town. Seems so, don't it? Well!"

"Ssh!" said the barkeeper.

"Say," snarled the Swede, "don't you try to shut me up. I won't have it. I'm a gentleman, and I want people to drink with me. And I want 'em to drink with me now. *Now*—do you understand?" He rapped the bar with his knuckles.

Years of experience had calloused the bartender. He merely grew sulky. "I hear you," he answered.

"Well," cried the Swede, "listen hard then. See those men over there? Well, they're going to drink with me, and don't you forget it. Now you watch."

"Hi!" yelled the barkeeper, "this won't do!"

"Why won't it?" demanded the Swede. He stalked over to the table, and by chance laid his hand upon the shoulder of the gambler. "How about this?" he asked wrathfully. "I asked you to drink with me."

The gambler simply twisted his head and spoke over his shoulder. "My friend, I don't know you."

"Oh, hell!" answered the Swede, "come and have a drink."

"Now, my boy," advised the gambler, kindly, "take your hand off my shoulder and go 'way and mind your own business." He was a little, slim man, and it seemed strange to hear him use this tone of heroic patronage to the burly Swede. The other men at the table said nothing.

"What! You won't drink with me, you little dude? I'll make you, then! I'll make you!" The Swede had grasped the gambler frenziedly at the throat, and was dragging him from his chair. The other men sprang up. The barkeeper dashed around the corner of his bar. There was a great tumult, and then was seen a long blade in the hand of the gambler. It shot forward, and a human body, this citadel of virtue, wisdom, power, was pierced as easily as if it had been a melon. The Swede fell with a cry of supreme astonishment.

The prominent merchants and the district attorney must have at once tumbled out of the place backward. The bartender found himself hanging limply to the arm of a chair and gazing into the eyes of a murderer.

"Henry," said the latter, as he wiped his knife on one of the towels that hung   250
beneath the bar rail, "you tell 'em where to find me. I'll be home, waiting for 'em."
Then he vanished. A moment afterward the barkeeper was in the street dinning through the storm for help and, moreover, companionship.

The corpse of the Swede, alone in the saloon, had its eyes fixed upon a dreadful legend that dwelt atop the cash-machine: "This registers the amount of your purchase."

IX

Months later, the cowboy was frying pork over the stove of a little ranch near the Dakota line, when there was a quick thud of hoofs outside, and presently the Easterner entered with the letters and the papers.

"Well," said the Easterner at once, "the chap that killed the Swede has got three years. Wasn't much, was it?"

"He has? Three years?" The cowboy poised his pan of pork, while he ruminated upon the news. "Three years. That ain't much."

"No. It was a light sentence," replied the Easterner as he unbuckled his spurs.   255
"Seems there was a good deal of sympathy for him in Romper.

"If the bartender had been any good," observed the cowboy, thoughtfully, "he would have gone in and cracked that there Dutchman on the head with a bottle in the beginnin' of it and stopped all this here murderin'."

"Yes, a thousand things might have happened," said the Easterner, tartly.

The cowboy returned his pan of pork to the fire, but his philosophy continued. "It's funny, ain't it? If he hadn't said Johnnie was cheatin' he'd be alive this minute. He was an awful fool. Game played for fun, too. Not for money. I believe he was crazy."

"I feel sorry for that gambler," said the Easterner.

"Oh, so do I," said the cowboy. "He don't deserve none of it for killin' who he   260
did."

"The Swede might not have been killed if everything had been square."

"Might not have been killed?" exclaimed the cowboy. "Everythin' square? Why, when he said that Johnnie was cheatin' and acted like such a jackass? And then in the saloon he fairly walked up to git hurt?" With these arguments the cowboy browbeat the Easterner and reduced him to rage.

"You're a fool!" cried the Easterner, viciously. "You're a bigger jackass than the Swede by a million majority. Now let me tell you one thing. Let me tell you something. Listen! Johnnie *was* cheating!"

"'Johnnie,'" said the cowboy, blankly. There was a minute of silence, and then he said, robustly, "Why, no. The game was only for fun."

"Fun or not," said the Easterner, "Johnnie was cheating. I saw him. I know it. I   265
saw him. And I refused to stand up and be a man. I let the Swede fight it out alone. And you—you were simply puffing around the place wanting to fight. And then old Scully himself! We are all in it! This poor gambler isn't even a noun. He is a kind of

an adverb. Every sin is the result of collaboration. We, five of us, have collaborated in the murder of this Swede. Usually there are from a dozen to forty women really involved in every murder, but in this case it seems to be only five men—you, I, Johnnie, old Scully; and that fool of an unfortunate gambler came merely as a culmination, the apex of a human movement, and gets all the punishment."

The cowboy, injured and rebellious, cried out blindly into this fog of mysterious theory: "Well, I didn't do anythin', did I?"

QUESTIONS

1. Describe the conflict in the story. Why is the Swede the major antagonist? How could he be seen as protagonist, instead of antagonist? Why do the others stress his identity as a Swede, and why is he never named?

2. Consider the Easterner's analysis (paragraph 90) as a plausible explanation of the Swede's behavior before the fight. How fully does this analysis explain these actions? How could the analysis be used in an argument that "The Blue Hotel" is a critique of conventional, dime-store views of the wild west?

3. Analyze the structure of the story. What relationship do the parts of abstract formal structure (described on pp. 90–92) have to the part divisions marked by Crane himself? Why is most of the story about events at the Blue Hotel, and why do events at the saloon, where the murder occurs, occupy only a small section? Explain, in relation to the story's structure, why we do not learn until the very end that Johnny actually *was* cheating.

4. How adequately does the Easterner's "noun-adverb" analysis in the concluding paragraphs explain the events of the story? Could such events be stopped at a certain point, or are they inevitable regardless of the Easterner's theory about collaborative control and responsibility?

EUDORA WELTY (b. 1909)

One of the major Southern writers, Welty was born in Jackson, Mississippi. She attended the Mississippi State College for Women and the University of Wisconsin, and began her writing career during the Great Depression. By 1943 she had published two major story collections, Curtain of Green *(1941, including "A Worn Path") and* The Wide Net *(1943). She is the author of many stories, and was awarded the Pulitzer Prize in 1973 for her short novel* The Optimist's Daughter *(1972). "A Worn Path" received an O. Henry Award in 1941.*

A Worn Path _____ *1941*

It was December—a bright frozen day in the early morning. Far out in the country there was an old Negro woman with her head tied in a red rag, coming along a path through the pinewoods. Her name was Phoenix Jackson. She was very old and small and she walked slowly in the dark pine shadows, moving a little from side to side in her steps, with the balanced heaviness and lightness of a pendulum in a grandfather clock. She carried a thin, small cane made from an umbrella, and with this she kept tapping the frozen earth in front of her. This made a grave and persistent noise in the still air, that seemed meditative like the chirping of a solitary little bird.

She wore a dark striped dress reaching down to her shoe tops, and an equally long apron of bleached sugar sacks, with a full pocket: all neat and tidy, but every time she took a step she might have fallen over her shoelaces, which dragged from her unlaced shoes. She looked straight ahead. Her eyes were blue with age. Her skin had a pattern all its own of numberless branching wrinkles and as though a whole little tree stood in the middle of her forehead, but a golden color ran underneath, and the two knobs of her cheeks were illuminated by a yellow burning under the dark. Under the rag her hair came down on her neck in the frailest of ringlets, still black, and with an odor like copper.

Now and then there was a quivering in the thicket. Old Phoenix said, "Out of my way, all you foxes, owls, beetles, jack rabbits, coons and wild animals! . . . Keep out from under these feet, little bob-whites. . . . Keep the big wild hogs out of my path. Don't let none of those come running my direction. I got a long way." Under her small black-freckled hand her cane, limber as a buggy whip, would switch at the brush as if to rouse up any hiding things.

On she went. The woods were deep and still. The sun made the pine needles almost too bright to look at, up where the wind rocked. The cones dropped as light as feathers. Down in the hollow was the mourning dove—it was not too late for him.

The path ran up a hill. "Seem like there is chains about my feet, time I get this far," she said, in the voice of argument old people keep to use with themselves. "Something always take a hold of me on this hill—pleads I should stay." 5

After she got to the top she turned and gave a full, severe look behind her where she had come. "Up through pines," she said at length. "Now down through oaks."

Her eyes opened their widest, and she started down gently. But before she got to the bottom of the hill a bush caught her dress.

Her fingers were busy and intent, but her skirts were full and long, so that before she could pull them free in one place they were caught in another. It was not possible to allow the dress to tear. "I in the thorny bush," she said. "Thorns, you doing your appointed work. Never want to let folks pass, no sir. Old eyes thought you was a pretty little *green* bush."

Finally, trembling all over, she stood free, and after a moment dared to stoop for her cane.

"Sun so high!" she cried, leaning back and looking, while the thick tears went over her eyes. "The time getting all gone here." 10

At the foot of this hill was a place where a log was laid across the creek.

"Now comes the trial," said Phoenix.

Putting her right foot out, she mounted the log and shut her eyes. Lifting her skirt, leveling her cane fiercely before her, like a festival figure in some parade, she began to march across. Then she opened her eyes and she was safe on the other side.

"I wasn't as old as I thought," she said.

But she sat down to rest. She spread her skirts on the bank around her and folded her hands over her knees. Up above her was a tree in a pearly cloud of mistletoe. She did not dare to close her eyes, and when a little boy brought her a plate with 15 a slice of marble-cake on it she spoke to him. "That would be acceptable," she said. But when she went to take it there was just her own hand in the air.

So she left that tree, and had to go through a barbed-wire fence. There she had to creep and crawl, spreading her knees and stretching her fingers like a baby trying to climb the steps. But she talked loudly to herself: she could not let her dress be torn now, so late in the day, and she could not pay for having her arm or leg sawed off if she got caught fast where she was.

At last she was safe through the fence and risen up out in the clearing. Big dead trees, like black men with one arm, were standing in the purple stalks of the withered cotton field. There sat a buzzard.

"Who you watching?"

In the furrow she made her way along.

"Glad this is not the season for bulls," she said, looking sideways, "and the good Lord made his snakes to curl up and sleep in the winter. A pleasure I don't see no two-headed snake coming around that tree, where it come once. It took a while to get by him, back in the summer."

She passed through the old cotton and went into a field of dead corn. It whispered and shook and was taller than her head. "Through the maze now," she said, for there was no path.

Then there was something tall, black, and skinny there, moving before her.

At first she took it for a man. It could have been a man dancing in the field. But she stood still and listened, and it did not make a sound. It was as silent as a ghost.

"'Ghost," she said sharply, "who be you the ghost of? For I have heard of nary death close by."

But there was no answer—only the ragged dancing in the wind.

She shut her eyes, reached out her hand, and touched a sleeve. She found a coat and inside that an emptiness, cold as ice.

"You scarecrow," she said. Her face lighted. "I ought to be shut up for good," she said with laughter. "My senses is gone. I too old, I the oldest people I ever know. Dance, old scarecrow," she said, "while I dancing with you."

She kicked her foot over the furrow, and with mouth drawn down, shook her head once or twice in a little strutting way. Some husks blew down and whirled in steamers about her skirts.

Then she went on, parting her way from side to side with the cane, through the whispering field. At last she came to the end, to a wagon track where the silver grass blew between the red ruts. The quail were walking around like pullets, seeming all dainty and unseen.

"Walk pretty," she said. "This is the easy place. This the easy going."

She followed the track, swaying through the quiet bare fields, through the little strings of trees silver in their dead leaves, past cabins silver from weather, with the doors and windows boarded shut, all like old women under a spell sitting there. "I walking in their sleep," she said, nodding her head vigorously.

In a ravine she went where a spring was silently flowing through a hollow log. Old Phoenix bent and drank. "Sweet-gum makes the water sweet," she said, and drank more. "Nobody know who made this well, for it was here when I was born."

The track crossed a swampy part where the moss hung as white as lace from every limb. "Sleep on, alligators, and blow your bubbles." Then the track went into the road.

Deep, deep the road went down between the high green-colored banks. Overhead the live-oaks met, and it was as dark as a cave.

A black dog with a lolling tongue came up out of the weeds by the ditch. She   35
was meditating, and not ready, and when he came at her she only hit him a little with
her cane. Over she went in the ditch, like a little puff of milkweed.

Down there, her sense drifted away. A dream visited her, and she reached her
hand up, but nothing reached down and gave her a pull. So she lay there and
presently went to talking. "Old woman," she said to herself, "that black dog come up
out of the weeds to stall you off, and now there he sitting on his fine tail smiling at
you."

A white man finally came along and found her—a hunter, a young man, with
his dog on a chain.

"Well, Granny!" he laughed. "What are you doing there?"

"Lying on my back like a June-bug waiting to be turned over, mister," she said,
reaching up her hand.

He lifted her up, gave her a swing in the air, and set her down. "Anything bro-   40
ken, Granny?"

"No sir, them old dead weeds is springy enough," said Phoenix, when she had
got her breath. "I thank you for your trouble."

"Where do you live, Granny?" he asked, while the two dogs were growling at
each other.

"Away back yonder, sir, behind the ridge. You can't even see it from here."

"On your way home?"

"No sir, I goin to town."   45

"Why, that's too far! That's as far as I walk when I come out myself, and I get
something for my trouble." He patted the stuffed bag he carried, and there hung
down a little closed claw. It was one of the bob-whites, with its beak hooked bitterly to
show it was dead. "Now you go on home, Granny!"

"I bound to go to town, mister," said Phoenix. "The time come around."

He gave another laugh, filling the whole landscape. "I know you old colored
people! Wouldn't miss going to town to see Santa Claus!"

But something held old Phoenix very still. The deep lines in her face went into
a fierce and different radiation. Without warning, she had seen with her own eyes a
flashing nickel fall out of the man's pocket onto the ground.

"How old are you, Granny?" he was saying.   50

"There is no telling, mister," she said, "no telling."

Then she gave a little cry and clapped her hands and said, "Git on away from
here, dog! Look! Look at that dog!" She laughed as if in admiration. "He ain't scared
of nobody. He a big black dog." She whispered, "Sic him!"

"Watch me get rid of that cur," said the man. "Sic him, Pete! Sic him!"

Phoenix heard the dogs fighting, and heard the man running and throwing
sticks. She even heard a gunshot. But she was slowly bending forward by that time, further and further forward, the lids stretched down over her eyes, as if she were doing
this in her sleep. Her chin was lowered almost to her knees. The yellow palm of her
hand came out from the fold of her apron. Her fingers slid down and along the
ground under the piece of money with the grace and care they would have in lifting
an egg from under a setting hen. Then she slowly straightened up, she stood erect,

and the nickel was in her apron pocket. A bird flew by. Her lips moved. "God watching me the whole time. I come to stealing."

The man came back, and his own dog panted about them. "Well, I scared him off that time," he said, and then he laughed and lifted his gun and pointed it at Phoenix.

She stood straight and faced him.

"Doesn't the gun scare you?" he said, still pointing it.

"No, sir. I seen plenty go off closer by, in my day, and for less than what I done," she said, holding utterly still.

He smiled, and shouldered the gun. "Well, Granny," he said, "you must be a hundred years old, and scared of nothing. I'd give you a dime if I had any money with me. But you take my advice and stay home, and nothing will happen to you."

"I bound to go on my way, mister," said Phoenix. She inclined her head in the red rag. Then they went in different directions, but she could hear the gun shooting again and again over the hill.

She walked on. The shadows hung from the oak trees to the road like curtains. Then she smelled wood-smoke, and smelled the river, and she saw a steeple and the cabins on their steep steps. Dozens of little black children whirled around her. There ahead was Natchez shining. Bells were ringing. She walked on.

In the paved city it was Christmas time. There were red and green electric lights strung and crisscrossed everywhere, and all turned on in the daytime. Old Phoenix would have been lost if she had not distrusted her eyesight and depended on her feet to know where to take her.

She paused quietly on the sidewalk where people were passing by. A lady came along in the crowd, carrying an armful of red-, green-, and silver-wrapped presents; she gave off perfume like the red roses in hot summer, and Phoenix stopped her.

"Please, missy, will you lace up my shoe?" She held up her foot.

"What do you want, Grandma?"

"See my shoe," said Phoenix. "Do all right for out in the country, but wouldn't look right to go in a big building."

"Stand still then, Grandma," said the lady. She put her packages down on the sidewalk beside her and laced and tied both shoes tightly.

"Can't lace 'em with a cane," said Phoenix. "Thank you, missy. I doesn't mind asking a nice lady to tie up my shoe, when I gets out on the street."

Moving slowly and from side to side, she went into the big building, and into a tower of steps, where she walked up and around and around until her feet knew to stop.

She entered a door, and there she saw nailed up on the wall the document that had been stamped with the gold seal and framed in the gold frame, which matched the dream that was hung up in her head.

"Here I be," she said. There was a fixed and ceremonial stiffness over her body.

"A charity case, I suppose," said an attendant who sat at the desk before her.

But Phoenix only looked above her head. There was sweat on her face, the wrinkles in her skin shone like a bright net.

"Speak up, Grandma," the woman said, "What's your name? We must have your history, you know. Have you been here before? What seems to be the trouble with you?"

Old Phoenix only gave a twitch to her face as if a fly were bothering her.

"Are you deaf?" cried the attendant.

But then the nurse came in.

"Oh, that's just old Aunt Phoenix," she said. "She doesn't come for herself— she has a little grandson. She makes these trips just as regular as clockwork. She lives away back off the Old Natchez Trace." She bent down. "Well, Aunt Phoenix, why don't you just take a seat? We won't keep you standing after your long trip." She pointed.

The old woman sat down, both upright in the chair.

"Now, how is the boy?" asked the nurse.   80

Old Phoenix did not speak.

"I said, how is the boy?"

But Phoenix only waited and stared straight ahead, her face very solemn and withdrawn into rigidity.

"Is his throat any better?" asked the nurse. "Aunt Phoenix, don't you hear me? Is your grandson's throat any better since the last time you came for the medicine?"

With her hands on her knees, the old woman waited, silent, erect, and motion-   85
less, just as if she were in armor.

"You mustn't take up our time this way, Aunt Phoenix," the nurse said. "Tell us quickly about your grandson, and get it over. He isn't dead, is he?"

At last there came a flicker and then a flame of comprehension across her face, and she spoke.

"My grandson. It was my memory had left me. There I sat and forgot why I made my long trip."

"Forgot?" the nurse frowned. "After you came so far?"

Then Phoenix was like an old woman begging a dignified forgiveness for wak-   90
ing up frightened in the night. "I never did go to school, I was too old at the Surren- der," she said in a soft voice. "I'm an old woman without an education. It was my mem- ory fail me. My little grandson, he is just the same, and I forgot it in the coming."

"Throat never heals, does it?" said the nurse, speaking in a loud, sure voice to old Phoenix. By now she had a card with something written on it, a little list. "Yes. Swallowed lye. When was it—January—two, three years ago—"

Phoenix spoke unasked now. "No missy, he not dead, he just the same. Every little while his throat begin to close up again, and he not able to swallow. He not get his breath. He not able to help himself. So the time come around, and I go on an- other trip for the soothing medicine."

"All right. The doctor said as long as you came to get it, you could have it," said the nurse. "But it's an obstinate case."

"My little grandson, he sit up there in the house all wrapped up, waiting by him- self," Phoenix went on. "We is the only two left in the world. He suffer and it don't seem to put him back at all. He got a sweet look. He going to last. He wear a little patch quilt and peep out holding his mouth open like a little bird. I remembers so plain now. I not going to forget him again, no, the whole enduring time. I could tell him from all the others in creation."

"All right." The nurse was trying to hush her now. She brought her a bottle of   95
medicine. "Charity," she said, making a check mark in a book.

Old Phoenix held the bottle close to her eyes, and then carefully put it into her pocket.

"I thank you," she said.

"It's Christmas time, Grandma," said the attendant. "Could I give you a few pennies out of my purse?"

"Five pennies is a nickel," said Phoenix stiffly.

"Here's a nickel," said the attendant.   1(

Phoenix rose carefully and held out her hand. She received the nickel and then fished the other nickel out of her pocket and laid it beside the new one. She stared at her palm closely, with her head on one side.

Then she gave a tap with her cane on the floor.

"This is what come to me to do," she said, "I going to the store and buy my child a little windmill they sells, made out of paper. He going to find it hard to believe there such a thing in the world. I'll march myself back where he waiting, holding it straight up in this hand."

She lifted her free hand, gave a little nod, turned around, and walked out of the doctor's office. Then her slow step began on the stairs, going down.

QUESTIONS

1. From the description of Phoenix, what do you conclude about her economic condition? How do you know that she has taken the path through the woods before? Is she accustomed to being alone? What do you make of her speaking to animals, and of her imagining a boy offering her a piece of cake? What does her speech show about her education and background?

2. Describe the plot of the story. With Phoenix as the protagonist, what are the obstacles ranged against her? How might Phoenix be considered to be in the grip of large and indifferent social and political forces?

3. Comment on the meaning of this dialogue between Phoenix and the hunter:

    "Doesn't the gun scare you?" he said, still pointing it.

    "No, sir, I seen plenty go off closer by, in my day, and for less than what I done," she said, holding utterly still.

4. A number of responses might be made to this story, among them admiration for Phoenix, pity for her and her grandson and for the downtrodden generally, anger at her impoverished condition, and apprehension about her approaching senility. Do you share in any of these responses? Do you have any others?

TOM WHITECLOUD (1914–1972)

Thomas St. Germain Whitecloud was born in New York City. However, he spent much of his youth in the Lac du Flambeau Indian Reservation near Woodruff, Wisconsin, the town mentioned in paragraph 20 of "Blue Winds Dancing." After attending colleges in New Mexico and California, he received his degree in Medicine from Tulane University. He lived in Louisiana and Texas throughout his medical career, and at the time of his death he was a consultant for the Texas Commission on Alcoholism and Drug Abuse for Indians. "Blue Winds Dancing," which may be considered as either a story or fictionalized autobiographical fragment, received a prize in 1938 from both Scribner's Magazine, where it was published, and the Phi Beta Kappa National Honor Society.

Blue Winds Dancing ————————————————————————— *1938*

There is a moon out tonight. Moon and stars and clouds tipped with moonlight. And there is a fall wind blowing in my heart. Ever since this evening, when against a fading sky I saw geese wedge southward. They were going home. . . . Now I try to study, but against the pages I see them again, driving southward. Going home.

Across the valley there are heavy mountains holding up the night sky, and beyond the mountains there is home. Home, and peace, and the beat of drums, and blue winds dancing over snow fields. The Indian lodge will fill with my people, and our gods will come and sit among them. I should be there then. I should be at home.

But home is beyond the mountains, and I am here. Here where fall hides in the valleys, and winter never comes down from the mountains. Here where all the trees grow in rows; the palms stand stiffly by the roadsides, and in the groves the orange trees line in military rows, and endlessly bear fruit. Beautiful, yes; there is always beauty in order, in rows of growing things! But it is the beauty of captivity. A pine fighting for existence on a windy knoll is much more beautiful.

In my Wisconsin, the leaves change before the snows come. In the air there is the smell of wild rice and venison cooking; and when the winds come whispering through the forests, they carry the smell of rotting leaves. In the evenings, the loon calls, lonely; and birds sing their last songs before leaving. Bears dig roots and eat late fall berries, fattening for their long winter sleep. Later, when the first snows fall, one awakens in the morning to find the world white and beautiful and clean. Then one can look back over his trail and see the tracks following. In the woods there are tracks of deer and snowshoe rabbits, and long streaks where partridges slide to alight. Chipmunks make tiny footprints on the limbs and one can hear squirrels busy in hollow trees, sorting acorns. Soft lake waves wash the shores, and sunsets burst each evening over the lakes, and make them look as if they were afire.

That land which is my home! Beautiful, calm—where there is no hurry to get anywhere, no driving to keep up in a race that knows no ending and no goal. No classes where men talk and talk and then stop now and then to hear their own words come back to them from the students. No constant peering into the maelstrom of one's mind; no worries about grades and honors; no hysterical preparing for life until that life is half over; no anxiety about one's place in the thing they call Society.

I hear again the ring of axes in deep woods, the crunch of snow beneath my feet. I feel again the smooth velvet of ghost-birch bark. I hear the rhythm of the drums. . . . I am tired. I am weary of trying to keep up this bluff of being civilized. Being civilized means trying to do everything you don't want to, never doing anything you want to. It means dancing to the strings of custom and tradition; it means living in houses and never knowing or caring who is next door. These civilized white men want us to be like them—always dissatisfied—getting a hill and wanting a mountain.

Then again, maybe I am not tired. Maybe I'm licked. Maybe I am just not smart enough to grasp these things that go to make up civilization. Maybe I am just too lazy to think hard enough to keep up.

Still, I know my people have many things that civilization has taken from the whites. They know how to give; how to tear one's piece of meat in two and share it with one's brother. They know how to sing—how to make each man his own songs and sing them; for their music they do not have to listen to other men singing over a radio. They know how to make things with their hands, how to shape beads into design and make a thing of beauty from a piece of birch bark.

But we are inferior. It is terrible to have to feel inferior; to have to read reports of intelligence tests, and learn that one's race is behind. It is terrible to sit in classes and hear men tell you that your people worship sticks of wood—that your gods are all false, that the Manitou forgot your people and did not write them a book.

I am tired. I want to walk again among the ghost-birches. I want to see the leaves turn in autumn, the smoke rise from the lodgehouses, and to feel the blue winds. I want to hear the drums; I want to hear the drums and feel the blue whispering winds.

There is a train wailing into the night. The trains go across the mountains. It would be easy to catch a freight. They will say he has gone back to the blanket; I don't care. The dance at Christmas. . . .

A bunch of bums warming at a tiny fire talk politics and women and joke about the Relief and the WPA and smoke cigarettes. These men in caps and overcoats and dirty overalls living on the outskirts of civilization are free, but they pay the price of being free in civilization. They are outcasts. I remember a sociology professor lecturing on adjustment to society; hobos and prostitutes and criminals are individuals who never adjusted, he said. He could learn a lot if he came and listened to a bunch of bums talk. He would learn that work and a woman and a place to hang his hat are all the ordinary man wants. These are all he wants, but other men are not content to let him want only these. He must be taught to want radios and automobiles and a new suit every spring. Progress would stop if he did not want these things. I listen to hear if there is any talk of communism or socialism in the hobo jungles. There is none. At best there is a sort of disgusted philosophy about life. They seem to think there should be a better distribution of wealth, or more work, or something. But they are not rabid about it. The radicals live in the cities.

I find a fellow headed for Albuquerque, and talk road-talk with him. "It is hard to ride fruit cars. Bums break in. Better to wait for a cattle car going back to the Middle West, and ride that." We catch the next east-bound and walk the tops until we find a cattle car. Inside, we crouch near the forward wall, huddle, and try to sleep. I feel peaceful and content at last. I am going home. The cattle car rocks. I sleep.

Morning and the desert. Noon and the Salton Sea, lying more lifeless than a mirage under a somber sun in a pale sky. Skeleton mountains rearing on the skyline, thrusting out of the desert floor, all rock and shadow and edges. Desert. Good country for an Indian reservation. . . .

Yuma and the muddy Colorado. Night again, and I wait shivering for the dawn.

Phoenix. Pima country. Mountains that look like cardboard sets on a forgotten stage. Tucson, Papago country. Giant cacti that look like petrified hitchhikers along the highways. Apache country. At El Paso my road-buddy decides to go on to Houston. I leave him, and head north to the mesa country. Las Cruces and the terrible Organ Mountains, jagged peaks that instill fear and wondering. Albuquerque. Pueblos along the Rio Grande. On the boardwalk there are some Indian women in colored sashes selling bits of pottery. The stone age offering its art to the twentieth century. They hold up a piece and fix the tourist with black eyes until, embarrassed, he buys or turns away. I feel suddenly angry that my people should have to do such things for a living. . . .

Santa Fe trains are fast, and they keep them pretty clean of bums. I decide to hurry and ride passenger coaltenders. Hide in the dark, judge the speed of the train as it leaves, and then dash out, and catch it. I hug the cold steel wall of the tender and think of the roaring fire in the engine ahead, and of the passengers back in the dining car reading their papers over hot coffee. Beneath me there is a blur of rails. Death would come quick if my hands should freeze and I fall. Up over the Sangre De Cristo range, around cliffs and through canyons to Denver. Bitter cold here, and I must watch out for Denver Bob. He is a railroad bull who has thrown bums from fast freights. I miss him. It is too cold, I suppose. On north to the Sioux country.

Small towns lit for the coming Christmas. On the streets of one I see a beam-shouldered young farmer gazing into a window filled with shining silver toasters. He is tall and wears a blue shirt buttoned, with no tie. His young wife by his side looks at him hopefully. He wants decorations for his place to hang his hat to please his woman. . . .

Northward again. Minnesota, and great white fields of snow; frozen lakes, and dawn running into dusk without noon. Long forests wearing white. Bitter cold, and one night the northern lights. I am nearing home.

I reach Woodruff at midnight. Suddenly I am afraid, now that I am but twenty miles from home. Afraid of what my father will say, afraid of being looked on as a stranger by my own people. I sit by a fire and think about myself and all other young Indians. We just don't seem to fit in anywhere—certainly not among the whites, and not among the older people. I think again about the learned sociology professor and his professing. So many things seem to be clear now that I am away from school and do not have to worry about some man's opinion of my ideas. It is easy to think while looking at dancing flames.

Morning, I spend the day cleaning up, and buying some presents for my family with what is left of my money. Nothing much, but a gift is a gift, if a man buys it with his last quarter. I wait until evening, then start up the track toward home.

Christmas Eve comes in on a north wind. Snow clouds hang over the pines, and the night comes early. Walking along the railroad bed, I feel the calm peace of snow-bound forests on either side of me. I take my time; I am back in a world where time does not mean so much now. I am alone; alone but not nearly so lonely as I was back on the campus at school. Those are never lonely who love the snow and the pines; never lonely when the pines are wearing white shawls and snow crunches coldly un-derfoot. In the woods I know there are the tracks of deer and rabbit; I know that if I leave the rails and go into the woods I shall find them. I walk along feeling glad be-cause my legs are light and my feet seem to know that they are home. A deer comes out of the woods ahead of me, and stands silhouetted on the rails. The North, I feel, has welcomed me home. I watch him and am glad that I do not wish for a gun. He goes into the woods quietly, leaving only the design of his tracks in the snow. I walk on. Now and then I pass a field, white under the night sky, with houses at the far end. Smoke comes from the chimneys of the houses, and I try to tell what sort of wood each is burning by the smoke; some burn pine, others aspen, others tamarack. There is one from which comes black coal smoke that rises lazily and drifts out over the tops of the trees. I like to watch houses and try to imagine what might be happening in them.

Just as a light snow begins to fall I cross the reservation boundary; somehow it seems as though I have stepped into another world. Deep woods in a white-and-black winter night. A faint trail leading to the village.

The railroad on which I stand comes from a city sprawled by a lake—a city with a million people who walk around without seeing one another; a city sucking the life from all the country around; a city with stores and police and intellectuals and crim-inals and movies and apartment houses; a city with its politics and libraries and zoos.

20

Laughing, I go into the woods. As I cross a frozen lake I begin to hear the drums. Soft in the night the drums beat. It is like the pulse beat of the world. The white line of the lake ends at a black forest, and above the trees the blue winds are dancing.

I come to the outlying houses of the village. Simple box houses, etched black in the night. From one or two windows soft lamplight falls on the snow. Christmas here, too, but it does not mean much; not much in the way of parties and presents. Joe Sky will get drunk. Alex Bodidash will buy his children red mittens and a new sled. Alex is a Carlisle man, and tries to keep his home up to white standards. White standards. Funny that my people should be ever falling farther behind. The more they try to imitate whites the more tragic the result. Yet they want us to be imitation white men. About all we imitate well are their vices.

The village is not a sight to instill pride, yet I am not ashamed; one can never be ashamed of his own people when he knows they have dreams as beautiful as white snow on a tall pine.

Father and my brother and sister are seated around the table as I walk in. Father stares at me for a moment, then I am in his arms, crying on his shoulder. I give them the presents I have brought, and my throat tightens as I watch my sister save carefully bits of red string from the packages. I hide my feelings by wrestling with my brother when he strikes my shoulder in token of affection. Father looks at me, and I know he has many questions, but he seems to know why I have come. He tells me to go alone to the lodge, and he will follow.

I walk along the trail to the lodge, watching the northern lights forming in the heavens. White waving ribbons that seem to pulsate with the rhythm of the drums. Clean snow creaks beneath my feet, and a soft wind sighs through the trees, singing to me. Everything seems to say, "Be happy! You are home now—you are free. You are among friends—we are your friends; we, the trees, and the snow, and the lights." I follow the trail to the lodge. My feet are light, my heart seems to sing to the music, and I hold my head high. Across white snow fields blue winds are dancing.

Before the lodge door I stop, afraid, I wonder if my people will remember me. I wonder—"Am I Indian, or am I white?" I stand before the door a long time. I hear the ice groan on the lake, and remember the story of the old woman under the ice, trying to get out, so she can punish some runaway lovers. I think to myself, "If I am white I will not believe that story; If I am Indian, I will know that there is an old woman under the ice." I listen for a while, and I know that there is an old woman under the ice. I look again at the lights, and go in.

Inside the lodge there are many Indians. Some sit on benches around the walls, others dance in the center of the floor around a drum. Nobody seems to notice me. It seems as though I were among a people I have never seen before. Heavy women with long hair. Women with children on their knees—small children that watch with intent black eyes the movements of the dancers, whose small faces are solemn and serene. The faces of the old people are serene, too, and their eyes are merry and bright. I look at the old men. Straight, dressed in dark trousers and beaded velvet vests, wearing soft moccasins. Dark, lined faces intent on the music. I wonder if I am at all like them. They dance on, lifting their feet to the rhythm of the drums swaying lightly, looking upward. I look at their eyes, and am startled at the rapt attention to the rhythm of the music.

The dance stops. The men walk back to the walls, and talk in low tones or with their hands. There is little conversation, yet everyone seems to be sharing some se-cret. A woman looks at a small boy wandering away, and he comes back to her.

Strange, I think and then remember. These people are not sharing words—they are sharing a mood. Everyone is happy. I am so used to white people that it seems strange so many people could be together without someone talking. These In-dians are happy because they are together, and because the night is beautiful out-side, and the music is beautiful. I try hard to forget school and white people, and be one of these—my people. I try to forget everything but the night, and it is a part of me that I am one with my people and we are all a part of something universal. I watch eyes, and see now that the old people are speaking to me. They nod slightly, imperceptibly, and their eyes laugh into mine. I look around the room. All the eyes are friendly; they all laugh. No one questions my being here. The drums begin to beat again, and I catch the invitation in the eyes of the old men. My feet begin to lift to the rhythm, and I look out beyond the walls into the night and see the lights. I am happy. It is beautiful. I am home.

QUESTIONS

1. Describe the first section of the story in terms of the structure. Could a case be made that this first section contains its own crisis and climax and that the rest of the story is really a resolution?
2. What do you learn in the first section about the conflict in the attitudes of the narrator? What is his attitude about "civilization"? What values make him think this way? If he is the protagonist, who or what is the antagonist?
3. What does the narrator mean by saying, "I am alone; alone but not nearly so lonely as I was back on the campus at school"?
4. What is meant by the dancing of the blue winds—what kind of wisdom? What is the place for such wisdom in a computerized, industrialized society?

WRITING ABOUT THE PLOT OF A STORY

An essay about plot is an analysis of the conflict and its developments. The organization of the essay should not be modeled on sequential sections and principal events, however, because these invite only a retelling of the story. Instead, the organization is to be developed from the important ele-ments of conflict. Ask yourself the following questions as you look for ideas about plot for your essay.

Questions for Discovering Ideas

*   Who are the protagonist and antagonist, and how do their characteristics put them in conflict? How would you describe the conflict?
*   How does the action develop from the conflict?
*   If the conflict stems from contrasting ideas or values, what are these, and how are they brought out?

- Does the major character face a dilemma? What is the dilemma? How does the character deal with it?

- How do the major characters achieve (or not achieve) their major goal(s)? What obstacles do they overcome? What obstacles overcome them?

- At the end, are the characters happy or unhappy, satisfied or dissatisfied, changed or about the same, enlightened or ignorant? How has the resolution of the major conflict produced these results?

Strategies for Organizing Ideas

To keep your essay brief, you need to be selective. Rather than detailing everything a character does, for example, stress the major elements in his or her conflict. Such an essay on Eudora Welty's "A Worn Path" might emphasize Phoenix as she encounters the various obstacles both in the woods and in town. When there is a conflict between two major characters, the obvious approach is to focus equally on both. For brevity, however, emphasis might be placed on just one. Thus, an essay on the plot of "The Blue Hotel" might stress the things we learn about the Swede that are important to his being a major participant in the conflict.

In addition, the plot may be analyzed more broadly in terms of impulses, goals, values, issues, and historical perspectives. Thus, you might emphasize the elements of chance working against Mathilde in Maupassant's "The Necklace," as a contrast to her dreams about wealth. A discussion of the plot of Poe's "The Masque of the Red Death" might stress the haughtiness of Prospero, the major character, because the plot could not develop without his egotism.

The conclusion may contain a brief summary of the points you have made. It is also a fitting location for a brief consideration of the effect or *impact* produced by the conflict. Additional ideas might focus on whether the author has arranged actions and dialogue to direct your favor toward one side or the other, or whether the plot is possible or impossible, serious or comic, fair or unfair, powerful or indifferent, and so on.

SAMPLE ESSAY

The Plot of Eudora Welty's "A Worn Path"°

[1] At first, the complexity of Eudora Welty's plot in "A Worn Path" is not clear. The main character is Phoenix Jackson, an old, poor, and frail woman; the story seems to be no more than a record of her walk to Natchez through the woods from her rural home. By the story's end, however, the plot is clear:

° See page 112 for this story.

It consists of the brave attempts of a courageous, valiant woman to carry on against overwhelming forces.* Her determination despite the great odds against her gives the story its impact. The powers ranged against her are old age, poverty, environment, and illness.†

[2]   Old age as a silent but overpowering antagonist is shown in signs of Phoenix's increasing senility. Not her mind but her feet tell her where to find the medical office in Natchez. Despite her inner strength, she is unable to explain her errand when the nursing attendant asks her. Instead she sits dumbly and unknowingly for a time, until "a flame of comprehension" comes across her face (¶ 87). Against the power of advancing age, Phoenix is slowly losing. The implication is that she soon will lose entirely.

[3]   An equally crushing opponent is her poverty. She cannot afford to ride to town, but must walk. She has no money, and acquires her ten cents for the paper windmill by stealing and begging. The "soothing medicine" she gets for her grandson (¶ 92) is given to her out of charity. Despite the boy's need for advanced medical care, she has no money to provide it, and the story therefore shows that her guardianship is doomed.

Closely connected to her poverty is the way through the woods, which during her walk seems to be an almost active opponent. The long hill tires her, the thorn bush catches her clothes, the log endangers her balance as she crosses the creek, and the barbed-wire fence threatens to puncture her skin. Another danger on her way is the stray dog, which topples her over. Apparently not afraid, however, Phoenix carries on a cheerful monologue:

[4]   "Out of my way, all you foxes, owls, beetles, jack rabbits, coons and wild animals! . . . Keep out from under these feet, little bobwhites. . . . Keep the big wild hogs out of my path. Don't let none of these come running my direction. I got a long way." (¶ 3)

She prevails for the moment as she enters Natchez, but all the hazards of her walk are still there, waiting for her to return.

[5]   The force against Phoenix which shows her plight most clearly and pathetically is her grandson's incurable illness. His condition highlights her helplessness, for she is his only support. Her difficulties would be enough for one person alone, but with the grandson the odds against her are doubled. Despite her care, there is nothing anyone can do for the grandson but take the long worn path to get something to help him endure his pain.

[6]   This brief description of the conflicts in "A Worn Path" only hints at the story's power. Welty layers the details to bring out the full range of the conditions against Phoenix, who cannot win despite her determination and devotion. The most hopeless fact, the condition of the invalid grandson, is not revealed until she reaches the medical office, and this delayed final revelation makes one's heart go out to her. The plot is strong because it is so real, and Phoenix is a pathetic but memorable protagonist struggling against overwhelming odds.

---

* Central idea.
† Thesis sentence.

Commentary on the Essay

The strategy of this essay is to explain the elements of plot in "A Worn Path" selectively, without duplicating the story's narrative order. Thus the third aspect of conflict, the woods, might be introduced first if the story's narrative order were to be followed, but it is deferred while the more personal elements of old age and poverty are considered first. It is important to note that the essay does not consider other characters as part of Phoenix's conflict. Rather Phoenix's antagonist takes the shape of impersonal and unconquerable forces, like the grandson's illness.

Paragraph 1 briefly describes how one's first impressions are changed by the story's end. The thesis sentence anticipates the body by listing the four topics about to be treated. Paragraph 2 concerns Phoenix's old age; paragraph 3 her poverty; paragraph 4 the woods; and paragraph 5, her grandson's illness. The concluding paragraph (6) points out that in this set of conflicts the protagonist cannot win, except as she lives out her duty and her devotion to help her grandson. Continuing the theme of the introduction, the last paragraph also accounts for the power of the plot: By building up to Phoenix's personal strength against unbeatable forces, the story evokes sympathy and admiration.

WRITING ABOUT STRUCTURE IN A STORY

Your essay should concern the story's arrangement and shape. In form, the essay should not follow the part-by-part unfolding of the narrative or argument. Rather it should explain why things are where they are: "Why is this here and not there?" is the fundamental question you need to answer. Thus it is possible to begin with a consideration of a work's crisis, and then to consider how the exposition and complication have built up to it. A vital piece of information, for example, might have been withheld in the earlier exposition (as in Jackson's "The Lottery" and Welty's "A Worn Path"), and introduced only at the crisis; thus the crisis might be heightened because there would have been less suspense if the detail had been introduced earlier. Consider the following questions as you examine the story's structure.

Questions for Discovering Ideas

- If spaces or numbers divide the story into sections or parts, what structural importance do these parts have?
- If there are no marked divisions, what major sections can you discover? (You might make divisions according to places where actions occur, or various times of day, or changing weather, or increasingly important events.)
- If the story departs in major ways from the formal structure of exposition, complication, crisis, climax, and resolution, what purpose do these departures have?

- What variations in chronological order, if any, appear in the story (e.g., gaps in the time sequence, flashbacks)? What effects are achieved by these variations?
- Does the story withhold any crucial details of exposition? Why? What effect is achieved?
- About a major part or important action (such as the climax): Where does it begin? End? How is it related to the other formal structural elements, such as the crisis? Is the climax an action, a realization, or a decision? To what degree does it relieve the work's tension? What is the effect of the climax on your understanding of the characters involved in it? How is this effect related to the arrangement of the climax?

Strategies for Organizing Ideas

Your essay should discuss why a story is arranged the way it is—to reveal the nature of a character's situation, or to create surprise, or to bring out maximum humor.

You can also discuss the structure of no more than a part of the story, such as the climax, or the complication.

The essay is best developed in concert or agreement with what the work contains. The location of scenes is an obvious organizing element. Thus, an essay on the structure of "A Worn Path" might be based on the countryside, the town, and the medical building, where the actions of the story occur. Hawthorne's "Young Goodman Brown" and Mansfield's "Miss Brill" both take place outside (a dark forest for one and a sunny public park for the other). Maupassant's "The Necklace" begins in interiors and concludes outdoors. The locations of Updike's "A & P" are the aisles and the checkout counter of a supermarket. A structural study of any of these works might be based on these locations and their effect on the plot.

Other ways to consider structure may be derived from a work's notable aspects, such as the growing suspense and horrible conclusion of Jackson's "The Lottery," or the revelation about the father's sinister past in Zabytko's "Home Soil."

The conclusion should highlight the main parts of your essay. You may also deal briefly with the relationship of structure to the plot. If the work you have analyzed departs from chronological order, you might stress the effects of this departure. Your aim should be to focus on the success of the work as it has been brought about by the author's choices in development.

SAMPLE ESSAY

The Structure of Eudora Welty's "A Worn Path"°

[1]   On the surface, Eudora Welty's "A Worn Path" is structured simply. The narrative is not difficult to follow, and things move sequentially. The main char-

---

° See page 112 for this story.

acter is Phoenix Jackson, an old and poor woman. She walks from her rural home in Mississippi through the woods to Natchez to get a free bottle of medicine for her grandson, who is a hopeless invalid. Everything takes place in just a few hours. This action is only the frame, however, for a skillfully and powerfully structured plot.* The masterly control of structure is shown in the story's locations, and in the way in which the delayed revelation produces both mystery and complexity.†

[2] The locations in the story coincide with the increasing difficulties that Phoenix encounters. The first and most obvious worn path is the rural woods with all its natural difficulties. For most people the obstacles would not be challenging, but for an old woman they are formidable. In Natchez, the location of the next part of the story, Phoenix's inability to bend over to tie her shoe demonstrates the lack of flexibility of old age. In the medical office, where the final scene takes place, two major difficulties of the plot are brought out. One is Phoenix's increasing senility, and the other is the disclosure that her grandson is an incurable invalid. This set of oppositions, the major conflicts in the plot, thus coincide with locations or scenes and show the powerful forces opposing Phoenix.

The strongest of these conditions, the revelation about the grandson, makes the story something like a mystery. Because detail about the boy is delayed until the end, the reader wonders for most of the story what bad thing might happen next. In fact, some parts of the story are false leads. For example, the episode with the hunter's dog is threatening, but it leads nowhere; Phoenix, with the aid of the hunter, is unharmed. That she picks up and keeps the nickel dropped by the hunter might seem at first to be cause for punishment. In fact, she thinks it does, as this scene with the hunter shows:

[3]
. . . he laughed and lifted his gun and pointed it at Phoenix.
She stood straight and faced him.
"Doesn't the gun scare you?" he said, still pointing it.
"No, sir, I seen plenty go off closer by, in my day, and for less than what I done," she said, holding utterly still. (paragraphs 55-58)

But the young hunter does not notice that the coin is missing, and he does not accuse her. Right up to the moment of her entering the medical building, therefore, the reader is still wondering what might happen.

[4] Therefore the details about the grandson, carefully concealed until the end, make the story more complex than it at first seems. Because of this concluding revelation, the reader must do a double take, and reconsider what has gone on before. Phoenix's difficult walk into town must be seen not as an ordinary errand but as a hopeless mission of mercy. Her character also bears reevaluation: She is not just a funny old woman who speaks to the woods and animals, but she is a brave and pathetic woman carrying on against crushing odds. These conclusions are not apparent for most of the story, and the late emergence of the carefully concealed details makes "A Worn Path" both forceful and powerful.

* Central idea.
† Thesis sentence.

[5]   Thus the parts of "A Worn Path," while simple at first, are skillfully arranged. The key to the double take and reevaluation is Welty's withholding of the crucial detail of exposition until the very end. The result is that parts of the exposition and complication, through the speeches of the attendant and the nurse, merge with the climax near the story's end. In some respects, the detail makes it seem as though Phoenix's entire existence is a crisis, although she is not aware of this condition as she leaves the office to buy the paper windmill. It is this complex buildup and emotional peak that make the structure of "A Worn Path" the creation of a master writer.

Commentary on the Essay

To highlight the differences between essays on plot and structure, the topic of this sample essay is Welty's "A Worn Path," also analyzed in the sample essay on plot (p. 124). While both essays are concerned with the conflicts of the story, the essay on plot concentrates on the opposing forces, while the essay on structure focuses on the placement and arrangement of the story's details. Notice that neither essay retells the story, event by event. Instead, these are analytical essays that explain the *conflict* (for plot) and the *arrangement and layout* (for structure). In both essays, the assumption is that the reader has read "A Worn Path"; hence there is no need in the essay to tell the story again.

The introductory paragraph points out that the masterly structure accounts for the story's power. Paragraph 2 develops the topic that the geographical locations are arranged climactically to demonstrate the forces against the major character. Paragraph 3 considers how the early exposition about the grandson creates uncertainty about the issues and direction of the story. As supporting evidence, the paragraph cites two important details—the danger from the hunter's dog and the theft of his nickel—as structural false leads about Phoenix's troubles. Paragraph 4 deals with the complexity brought about by the delayed information: the necessary reevaluation of Phoenix' character and her mission to town. The concluding paragraph also considers this complexity, accounting for the story's power by pointing out how a number of plot elements merge near the end to bring things out swiftly and powerfully.

WRITING TOPICS

1. Compare "Everyday Use" (Chapter 2) and "Blue Winds Dancing" as stories developing plots about clashing social and racial values. In what ways are the plots similar and different?
2. What kind of story might "A Worn Path" be, structurally, if the detail about the invalid grandson were introduced at the start, before Phoenix begins her walk to town?
3. Compare the structuring of the interior scenes in "The Blue Hotel," "A Worn Path," and "Blue Winds Dancing." How do these scenes bring out the various conflicts of the stories? How do characters in the interiors contribute to plot de-

velopments? What is the relationship of these characters to the major themes of the stories?

4. Select a circumstance in your life that caused you doubt, difficulty, and conflict. Making yourself anonymous (give yourself a fictitious name and put yourself in a fictitious location), write a brief *story* about the occasion, stressing how your conflict began, how it affected you, and how you resolved it. You might choose to describe the details in chronological order, or you might begin the story in the present tense, and introduce details in flashback.

5. Consider those aspects of "A Worn Path" that seem socially and politically significant. You might consider questions such as whether elderly women like Phoenix are living in such remote areas today, whether her grandson should be left entirely in her care, whether she should be near public transportation so that she would not need to walk great distances to attend to her needs. You might also consider her as a representative of a group suffering discrimination, and treat her as an example of the need for legislation that would improve her condition.

4

Characters:
The People in Fiction

Fiction has flourished along with the study of psychology, which has produced psychological pioneers like Freud, Jung and Skinner. In this intellectual milieu, writers of fiction have chosen not only to create narratives, but also to embody materials that increase understanding of human nature. Psychologists, in turn, have influenced the study of literature. It is well known that Freud used many literary works, including plays by Shakespeare, to buttress some of his psychological conclusions, and films like *Spellbound*, *The Snake Pit*, and *Final Analysis* have popularized the relationships between literary character and the science of psychology. Without doubt, the presentation and understanding of character has become a major aim of fiction and drama.

In fiction, a **character** may be defined as a verbal representation of a human being. Through action, speech, description, and commentary, authors portray characters who are worth caring about, rooting for, and even loving, although there are also characters you may laugh at, dislike, or even hate.

In a story emphasizing a major character, you may expect that each action or speech, no matter how small, is part of a total presentation of that complex combination of both the inner and outer self that constitutes a human being. Whereas in life things may "just happen," in stories all actions, interactions, speeches, and observations are deliberate. Thus, you read about important actions like a long period of work and sacrifice (Maupassant's "The Necklace"), the taking of a regular journey of mercy (Welty's "A Worn Path"), the first solo airplane flight around the world (Thurber's "The Greatest Man in the World"), or a young boy's disobedience of his father (Faulkner's "Barn Burning"). By making such actions interesting, authors help you understand and appreciate their major characters.

CHARACTER TRAITS

In studying a literary character, begin by determining the character's outstanding traits. A **trait** is a quality of mind or habitual mode of behavior, such as never repaying borrowed money, or avoiding eye contact, or always thinking oneself the center of attention. If we look at the facial expression of Verocchio's bust of Lorenzo de' Medici, for example, we may recognize traits of pride and ruthlessness, and perhaps cruelty. Sometimes, of course, the traits we encounter are minor and therefore negligible. But often a trait may be a person's *primary* characteristic (not only in fiction but also in life). Thus, characters may be ambitious or lazy, serene or anxious, aggressive or fearful, thoughtful or inconsiderate, open or secretive, confident or self-doubting, kind or cruel, quiet or noisy, visionary or practical, careful or careless, impartial or biased, straightforward or underhanded, "winners" or "losers," and so on.

With this sort of list, to which you may add at will, you can analyze and develop conclusions about character. For example, in studying Mathilde in Maupassant's "The Necklace" (pp. 3–10), you would note that at the beginning she dreams of unattainable wealth and comfort, and that she is so swept up in her visions that she scorns her comparatively good life with her reliable but dull husband. It is fair to say that this aversion to reality is her major trait. It is also a major weakness, because Maupassant shows how her dream life

Bust of Lorenzo de'Medici by Andrea del Verrochio, National Gallery of Art, Washington, DC, Samuel H. Kress Collection.

harms her real life. By contrast, the narrator of Anderson's "I'm a Fool" indulges in retrospection about many mistakes he made when courting a young woman. Although his mistakes make him conclude that he has been a fool, his increasing self-knowledge indicates character strength. By similarly analyzing the actions, speeches, and thoughts in the characters you encounter, you can draw conclusions about their qualities and strengths.

DISTINGUISHING BETWEEN CIRCUMSTANCES AND TRAITS

When you study a fictional person, distinguish between circumstances and character, for circumstances have value *only if they demonstrate important traits.* Thus, if Sam wins a lottery, it is a fortunate circumstance, but the win does not say much about his character—not much, that is, unless we also learn that he has been spending hundreds of dollars each week for lottery tickets. In other words, making the effort to win a lottery *is* a character trait, while winning (or losing) *is not.*

Or, let us suppose that an author stresses the neatness of one character and the sloppiness of another. If you accept the premise that people care for their appearance according to choice—and that choices indicate character—you can use these details to make conclusions about self-esteem or the lack of it. In short, when reading about fictional characters, look beyond circumstances, actions, and appearances and *determine what these things show about character.* Always try to get from the outside to the inside, for it is the *internal* quality that determines the *external* behavior.

TYPES OF CHARACTERS: ROUND AND FLAT

No writer can present an entire life history of a protagonist; nor can each character in a story get "equal time" for development. Accordingly, some characters grow to be full and alive, while others remain shadowy. The British novelist and critic E. M. Forster, in his critical work *Aspects of the Novel,* calls the two major types "round" and "flat."

ROUND CHARACTERS. The basic trait of **round characters** is that they *recognize, change with,* or *adjust to* circumstances. The round character—usually the main figure in a story—profits from experience and undergoes a *change* or *alteration,* which may be shown in (1) an action or actions, (2) the realization of new strength and therefore the affirmation of previous decisions, (3) the acceptance of a new condition, or (4) the discovery of unrecognized truths.

Because round they usually play a major role in a story, round characters are often called the **hero** or **heroine.** Many main characters are anything but heroic, however, and it is therefore preferable to use the more neutral word **protagonist**. The protagonist is central to the action, moves against an **antagonist,** and exhibits the ability to adapt to new circumstances.

To the degree that round characters are both individual and sometimes unpredictable, and because they undergo change or growth, they are **dynamic.** Minnie Wright, in Glaspell's "A Jury of Her Peers," is dynamic. We learn that as a young woman she was happy and musical, but she has been deprived and blighted by her marriage of twenty years. Finally, one outrageous action by her husband so enrages her that she breaks out of her subservient role and commits an act of violence. Her action shows her as a character undergoing radical, dynamic change.

FLAT CHARACTERS. In contrast, **flat characters** do not grow. They remain the same because they may be stupid or insensitive or lacking in knowledge or insight. They end where they begin and are **static,** not dynamic. But flat characters are not therefore worthless, for they usually highlight the development of the round characters, as with the male characters in Glaspell's "A Jury of Her Peers." Usually, flat characters are minor (e.g., relatives, acquaintances, functionaries), although not all minor characters are necessarily flat.

Sometimes flat characters are prominent in certain types of literature, such as cowboy, police, and detective stories, where the focus is less on character than on performance. Such characters might be lively and engaging, even though they do not develop or change. They must be strong, tough, and clever enough to perform recurring tasks like solving a crime, overcoming a villain, or finding a treasure. The term **stock character** refers to characters in these repeating situations. To the degree that stock characters have many common traits, they are **representative** of their class, or group. Such characters, with variations in names, ages, and sexes, have been constant in literature since the ancient Greeks. Some regular stock characters are the insensitive father, the interfering mother, the sassy younger sister or brother, the greedy politician, the resourceful cowboy or detective, the overbearing or henpecked husband, the submissive or nagging wife, the angry police captain, the lovable drunk, and the town do-gooder.

Stock characters stay flat as long as they merely perform their roles and exhibit conventional and unindividual traits. When they possess no attitudes except those of their class, they are labeled **stereotype,** because they all seem to be cast from the same mold or printing matrix.

When authors bring characters into focus, however, no matter what roles they perform, they emerge from flatness and move into roundness. For example, though most of us would consider the character of a checkout clerks as flat, the clerk Sammy in Updike's "A & P," is a round, not flat, character; an incident at the checkout counter causes him to grow. Minnie Wright in "A Jury of Her Peers," who has led an ordinary, dull life for most of her years—a flat role—through a dynamic process breaks out of that role.

Sarty of "Barn Burning," is just a little boy, but he grows morally in opposition to his father's criminal acts. In sum, the ability to grow and develop, to be altered by circumstances, makes characters round; absence of these traits makes characters flat.

HOW IS CHARACTER DISCLOSED IN FICTION?

Authors use five ways to present their characters. Remember that you must use your own knowledge and experience to make judgments about the qualities of the characters being revealed.

1. *Actions.* What characters *do* is our best way to understand what they *are.* For example, walking in the woods is recreation for most people, and it shows little about their characters. But Phoenix's walk through the woods (Welty's "A Worn Path") is difficult and dangerous for her. Her walk, seen within the context of her age and her mission, may be taken as an expression of a loving, responsible character. Similar strength may be seen when a character faces psychological difficulties, as in Joy William's "Taking Care." For Jones, the central character who is also a minister, all aspects of life are going badly—with his wife, his daughter, and his own religious faith. Despite these incentives to despair, however, he preserves his caring and loving role, thus showing a character of great devotion and determination.

As with ordinary human beings, fictional characters do not necessarily understand how they may be changing or why they do the things they do. Nevertheless, their actions express their characters. For example, Sarty of Faulkner's "Barn Burning" is developing a sense of rightness and responsibility, but he does not show the knowledge that is causing his growth. Similarly, Fritz in Chioles's "Firing Squad" disobeys a military order to save the villagers. Although Fritz's action is unplanned and spontaneous, it clearly shows his growing conscience and sense of morality.

Actions may also signal qualities such as naiveté, weakness, deceit, a scheming personality, strong inner conflicts, or a realization or growth of some sort. Most of the actions of Abner Snopes in Faulkner's "Barn Burning" indicate a character of suspicion and resentment. A strong inner conflict and almost immediate growth may be seen in the two women in Glaspell's "A Jury of Her Peers." They have an obligation to the law, but they feel a stronger obligation to the accused killer, Minnie Wright. Hence they cover up the incriminating evidence, an action that indicates their roundness and depth.

2. *Descriptions, both personal and environmental.* Appearance and environment reveal much about a character's social and economic status, of course, but they also tell us more about character traits. A desire for elegance is a trait of Mathilde in Maupassant's "The Necklace." Although her unrealizable taste is destructive, it also brings out her strength of character. In Walker's "Everyday Use," the mother and younger daughter devote great care to the

appearance of their poor and unpretentious house, and their self-esteem is shown in this care.

3. *Dramatic statements and thoughts.* Although the speeches of most characters are functional—essential to keep the story moving along—they provide material from which you can draw conclusions. When Jackie Smurch of "The Greatest Man in the World" speaks, for example, he reveals his self-inflated and greedy nature. The three men in "A Jury of Her Peers" speak straightforwardly and directly, and these speeches suggest that their characters are similarly orderly. Their constant ridicule of the two women, however, indicates their limitations.

Often, characters use speech to hide their motives, though we as readers should see through such a ploy. For example, the old man in Collier's "The Chaser" is a schemer, and we learn this from his indirect and manipulative language to the youthful and romantic young man, Alan Austen. To Alan, the old man seems concerned and helpful, but to us he is lurid and cynical.

4. *Statements by other characters.* By studying what characters say about each other, you can enhance your understanding of the character being discussed. Thus the two women talking about Phoenix's condition in "A Worn Path" tell us much about her difficult life, but more importantly they provide a basis for conclusions about Phoenix's great strength.

Ironically, the characters doing the talking often indicate something other than what they intend, perhaps because of prejudice, stupidity, or foolishness. Nora's words about Jackie in O'Connor's "First Confession," for example, reveal that Jackie is just a normal little boy, but they also show Nora's own limited judgment. In Walker's "Everyday Use," Wangero's criticism of her mother's ways also expresses her own developing insensitivity and prejudice.

5. *Statements by the author speaking as storyteller or observer.* What the author, speaking with the authorial voice, says about a character is usually accurate, and the authorial voice can be accepted factually. However, when the authorial voice *interprets* actions and characteristics, as in Hawthorne's "Young Goodman Brown," the author himself or herself assumes the role of a reader or critic, and any opinions may be questioned. For this reason, authors frequently avoid interpretations and devote their skill to arranging events and speeches so that readers may draw their own conclusions.

REALITY AND PROBABILITY: VERISIMILITUDE

Characters in fiction should be true to life. That is, their actions, statements, and thoughts must all be what human beings are *likely* to do, say, and think under the conditions presented in the story. The standard is that of **verisimilitude, probability,** or **plausibility.** That is, there may be persons *in life* who perform tasks or exhibit characteristics that are difficult or seemingly impossible (such as always throwing the touchdown pass, getting A+'s on every test, always being cheerful and helpful, or always understanding the needs of others). Such characters *in fiction* would not be true to life, however, because they do not fit within *normal* or *usual* behavior.

One should therefore distinguish between what characters may *possibly* do and what they *most frequently* or *most usually* do. Thus, in "The Necklace," it is possible that Mathilde could be truthful and tell her friend Jeanne Forrestier about the lost necklace. In light of her pride, honor, and respectability, however, it is more in character for her and her husband to hide the loss, borrow money for a replacement, and endure the consequences for ten years. Granted the possibilities of the story (either self-sacrifice or the admission of a fault), the decision she makes with her husband is the more *probable* one.

Nevertheless, probability does not rule out surprise or even exaggeration. It is unusual that young Sarty tries to inform on his father in Faulkner's "Barn Burning," but it is not improbable because he has been developing a sense of morality throughout the story. Likewise, in Porter's "The Jilting of Granny Weatherall," the accomplishments of Granny—such as having fenced 100 acres of farming land all by herself—do not seem impossible even though they do seem unlikely. But we learn that when she was young she became almost compulsively determined to overcome the betrayal of her unfaithful lover. It is therefore not improbable that she would be capable of monumental achievements.

There are many ways of rendering probability in character. Works that attempt to mirror life—realistic, naturalistic, or "slice of life" stories like Welty's "A Worn Path"—set up a pattern of everyday probability. Less realistic conditions establish different frameworks of probability, in which characters are *expected* to be unusual. Such an example is Hawthorne's "Young Goodman Brown." Because a major way to explain this story is that Brown is having a nightmarish psychotic trance, his bizarre and unnatural responses are probable, just as Phoenix Jackson's speeches, influenced as they are by her approaching senility, are probable in "A Worn Path."

You might also encounter works containing *supernatural* figures, like the visiting boy in Pickthall's "The Worker in Sandalwood" and the woodland guide in "Young Goodman Brown." You may wonder whether such characters are probable or improbable. Usually, gods and goddesses like the little boy embody qualities of the best and most moral human beings (but see García Márquez's "A Very Old Man with Enormous Wings"), and devils like Hawthorne's guide take on attributes of the worst. However, you might remember that the devil is often given dashing and engaging qualities so that he may deceive gullible sinners and lead them into hell. The friendliness of Brown's guide is therefore a probable trait. In judging characters of this or any type, your best criterion is probability, consistency, and believability.

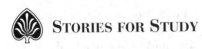

STORIES FOR STUDY

JOHN CHIOLES (b. 1940)

A Greek-American, Chioles is known for his collection Twenty Contemporary Greek Poets *(1979), which he edited with Dionos Siotis. His volume* Athens, Capital City *(1985) describes the history, art, and architecture of Athens. "Before the Firing Squad" was included in* The Available Press / PEN Short Story Collection *(1985), with an introduction by Anne Tyler.*

Before the Firing Squad _____ *1985*

The sound at first was a low moan, and you knew the momentum would build as soon as the hand-cranked siren, managed by teenaged boys, would pick up speed. No matter where I was, my knees turned to jelly, my pulse quickened, instinctively I would look up the hill to the bell tower of the church feeling betrayed that I could not be up there; at least there, watching the crank turn, the sound didn't frighten me. But the watch at the bell tower was for the older boys. You had to be at least twelve. From atop, where the giant bell hung, the boys kept a lookout for movement of vehicles; on a clear day they could see seven kilometers in the distance, beyond the bend.

Their convoys came from the main road. The moment they turned the bend that brings you full face with the town, their approach would echo against the side of the mountain. A hollow reverberation. The siren had by then stopped, to be replaced now by the rumbling of their trucks and heavy artillery. A moan of a different kind. The boys would run from the bell tower down the narrow streets to their homes. In no time, the dissonance of the enemy, something as ugly, efficient, and foreign to these parts as the unclean death they brought, appeared and disappeared, taking away the sun, leaving behind clouds of dust. They rarely stopped. But if they did, it could only bring down the reign of terror on all our heads. Mostly, though, they rode through on their way to Mani,° where they would embark on ships bound for North Africa. To that end, they would ride roughshod over the Arkadian mountains.° What interested them most was to make sure they passed through the towns and hamlets without incident or delay, ready to crush any attempt at interference.

Their garrison of twelve soldiers stationed in the town wore mustard-colored uniforms, not the sinister black kind° worn by the ones in the convoys. These soldiers seemed very young and curiously happy. Everyone said they spoke a softer kind of German, without the harsh sounds of those northern peoples; most of them knew ancient Greek even, and liked the lilting songs of Homer. Their weapons were limited and not always in evidence. The whole town was ready to swear that these youths had never fought even a skirmish, let alone been in a war. My father used to call them Hitler's boy-soldiers, sent to promote a peaceful occupation, playing on the conscience of the partisans, counting on their decency. And, a curious thing, these young

---

Mani . . . Arkadian mountains: Places in southern Greece. The time of the story is envisioned as 1944, during the closing days of the German occupation of Greece.

mustard-colored . . . black kind: The mustard-colored uniforms are those of the regular German army. The black uniforms belong to the Waffen *SS,* whose members were infamous for their cruelty.

soldiers were never ambushed; none of them died in the everyday activity along these mountains, the daily sabotaging of the main artery, the only asphalt road leading down to the sea. While killing was the order of the day during that spring—ten towns-people executed for the death of one dark-uniformed German—these twelve had become practically the mascots of the town.

"I don't want you talking to this Fritz so much," Father said one day. "Everybody treats him like one of us. It isn't right." All the nice Germans we called Fritz and all the mean ones Ludwig; except that Fritz was really the name of my friend.

"He's harmless," I said. "And sometimes he brings his ration of chocolate and   5 biscuits to share."

"He's the enemy," Father retorted the way he did when he would have no more discussion.

But the siren prevented any further talk. They came late in the afternoon of that day. My father was caught unawares. One convoy had already passed earlier, and he had run to the mountain and back again. They rarely had more than one a day. His reflexes were so swift that he practically knocked me over when he jumped to his feet.

"Put your warm sweater on and let's go." He had never taken me with him before. Women and children never ran to the mountain. The siren was for the men, whether they were part of the road sabotage teams or not. My father often stayed in the mountains for days; we never knew what he did there. "Hurry, we have no time. We'll take the back way so Fritz will not spot us. Your mother will know I've taken you with me."

The small garrison, our German mascots, lived across the street from us. They had requisitioned the best two-storied house, using the ground floor as offices and the second floor as living quarters. They were fully aware of the siren, but they pretended it came from the partisan stronghold in the mountain. Some said they even welcomed it; it gave them time to put on battle outfits, grab their guns, and move, a fierce-looking patrol, along the road. They never asked about the men of each household; their frequent absences from home they were content to believe had to do with working in the fields and vineyards. So Fritz had never asked about my father. Much like any of my friends, he was shy in his presence and avoided passing by whenever it was obvious Father was at home. Often he would come over to show us photos of his parents and his sisters, tell my mother how homesick he was, express joy or sadness whenever he would receive mail from home. And always my mother would find something to give him by way of comfort, a bunch of grapes or chestnuts or a few raisins. But whenever Father was at home it was understood he would never come over. He seemed no more than a boy and was treated much like the rest of us.

"Run faster! They're getting greedy today, and they could be mean." As we ran   10 through brush foliage I would scrape my legs and thought how nice it will be when I get to wear long trousers in another year or so.

"When we get on top I'll pick some wild tea leaves and camomile buds for Mother. We don't have to come right back, do we?"

"We'll stay as long as we have to. Till they're gone." My father's furrowed brow told me this was not a usual run. The enemy was changing its routine; that meant everything would become unpredictable.

"Whoever is not alert, and doesn't expect the worst, will never know the unexpected when it comes his way," my father was saying to his friends when we reached the thick forest of pines. Below us, like ants in the distance, carefully covered heavy artillery rolled along the asphalt road. The atmosphere was highly charged. An unusually large number of people had taken to the mountain. The mood had changed as the sun went away and a cold mid-afternoon chill set in. All the world turned dark green and it smelled of rain, even the canvas covering the moving guns and trucks below took on the color of running oil in the absence of the sun.

"It's best to do nothing for a couple of days. They'll have patrols everywhere," one of the older men was saying to Father.

"We could've blown the far bridge yesterday. We should have been warned about this."

"Maybe this is only the beginning of moving out their heavy stuff. It's up to us."

My presence in this adult conversation went unnoticed. Yet I knew I should not be hearing what was being said. So I slipped away quietly. Nearby, some goats beat their grazing rhythm on the bushes; they made the acanthus bob up and down. I had no time to wonder why the goats seemed so nervous. Just then I stepped on a dried branch which flew up at me, my feet got tangled, and I came tumbling a good ten meters down the slope. Though I was stunned, I felt hardly any pain. But the fear was real, for I heard the pounding of a machine-gun and felt the whistle of bullets flying above my head. I stayed down, hardly breathing. The machine-gun, rattling but unable to pin down movement in the vast forest, moved on along a horizontal line, then stopped.

As the moan of the convoy became more distant, I felt my father's hand lifting me up. I was more ashamed than hurting. Not until I stood upright did I see the blood running down my leg and a whole patch of skin from my knee hanging upside down.

"It's nothing," my father said, and quickly used his handkerchief to patch it up.

"It doesn't hurt any," I said.

"It will. Why did you come this far? Didn't we say we never come into full view of the road?"

"I fell down."

"You'll be all right. I'm going to have to send you home with your cousins. Your mother should take care of that knee."

I said nothing but followed sheepishly the downward path, my father's handkerchief tied behind my left knee. He had made the knot too tight and I felt a numbing pain but did not let on to my older cousins. Father had whispered something to them, that they should take care of me, I guessed, so I did not want to show I needed looking after.

At home there was commotion; our window was open. Mother had been putting my baby sister to sleep; she had lit the oil lamp. Across the way, the German soldiers were playing phonograph records, their usual sad music. (Only, Fritz had told me many times that their music was not at all funereal as the townspeople thought—it was happy and exultant, he'd say; still, it sounded sad to me.) Nobody got wind that I limped into the house at dusk. Stealth was always my strong point.

When Mother saw me, there was an uproar and a lot to answer for. I explained quickly, and, seeing that my wound was still bleeding, she softened her tone as to the mystery of my whereabouts all afternoon.

"Here, sit down. Let's have a look."

I clenched my teeth while she cleaned the whole knee with a sponge. It stung good and sharp now.

"You must be starved, too. Fritz has brought you a surprise. Uncover that bowl on the table. It's all for you."

A bowl of food, rice with bits of chicken, cubed chunks of meat in a thick white   30
soup. Never had I eaten anything so tasty before. It came from a fancy tin that my friend received on special occasions. If each of us had to cherish one memory of food that would make our taste buds water, Fritz's bowl of chicken with rice on that evening would be mine. I felt no pain from the leg while I ate to my heart's content, nor did I notice that he had come to the window, looking in, and already my mother had silently shown him my knee. In no time, he returned with a first-aid kit and set about to dress the wound. He spoke admonishingly to me in German, but also found the right phrases in Greek to let me know he was unhappy with me.

"Children don't become partisans, you know." But his smile gave him away. He only meant I should be careful. Then he became serious again. Whenever he looked serious his eyebrows went from the straw color of his hair to a darker shade and he looked older. Even his eyes did not keep their blue but went dark like the sea.

It seemed a cloud hung over the fate of the twelve German soldiers of our town. They would be transferred soon. They might be taken to the front lines. Everything was becoming very unpredictable, he was telling my mother. I had never seen Fritz so sad before. He hung his head low as he pulled out of his trouser pocket a letter he had just received from his mother. She lived, he told us, in a big city in his country that was being bombed constantly now, and they had even less to eat than we did.

"I do not know if I will see them again."

"You will, you will. All this will soon be over and you'll get to go home. You'll see," my mother consoled as best she could.

The next morning the news was out. The whole town became concerned. If   35
they left, would they be replaced by the black-uniformed ones? What would be in store for us? The neighborhood around us began to treat them like departing friends; they offered them sweets, dried fruits and nuts, and whatever parting hospitality they could. In their turn, the boy-soldiers responded with moist eyes, uncertain, and very scared of the weeks ahead. My mother always said, remembering those last few hours, not one of them looked a day over sixteen.

An old philosopher who dwelled along the dusty plains of Asia Minor once said there will come a Great Year whose summer will be a World Conflagration. That's just what happened to us that summer. On the very day they came to collect their soldiers and depart for good, they also set fire to nearly every house in the town.

Activity along the mountains had been fierce lately. The far bridge had been blown up; so had the narrow pass beyond. The siren howled urgently at full speed on that day. When they turned the bend they began to slow down, rolling into town at a snail's pace to cover for their foot soldiers, who darted off the road, torches in hand, setting fire to every house, every barn, every haystack in sight. That way they took a long time to get to us who lived near the square; but we had seen the smoke and the flames and we knew what was in store for us.

My mother refused to run away, hoping, with children in hand, she might at least save the house. But as the confusion around us got worse, the shooting in all directions, the trails of smoke, the terror-filled sounds of homes bursting open under the flame—no one could possibly be reasoned with, no one caught up in such careening panic. Every black Ludwig looked like a madman in passionate play with fire. During these terrible moments Fritz was nowhere to be seen.

We stood at the door of our house and watched the commotion all around us, until a burst from an automatic hit near our feet and we were routed and shown the way to the open space in the middle of the square. While she held the baby and I held on to her sleeve, my mother shuffled us to the gathering place. We never looked behind. But we knew. All around the square the trucks were moving slowly, never at rest, making a terrible din, which drowned out the cries of the dozen or so women and children huddled in the middle. We were shoved against them, and for the first time I saw a number of our town mascots, the boy-soldiers, armed to the teeth, some guarding us, some being given stern orders by an officer while others were already jumping onto the moving trucks with all their gear.

The officer pointed in our direction and began to scream an order to his subordinates. Three of them rushed over to our group and kneaded us all into a straight line. I saw to my horror that Fritz was one of them. His eyes were dark and furious, hardly anyone recognized him; his whole body and movements had taken on a different shape. I felt a crushing disappointment. He looked old now like the others.

Their mission accomplished, the three ran back to the officer. He gave them what seemed final instructions and climbed into the cab of his moving truck. The three raced to set up just ahead of us a machine-gun with tripod at the front of the barrel. One of them brought the ammunition, and I saw Fritz reach into the box and bring out a magazine, which he loaded onto the gun. Just then, whistles began blowing, those piercing kind they use at train platforms to signal an imminent departure. They didn't want to remain sitting targets for the partisans, so they had to make haste.

Suddenly the motors got louder; speed was only seconds away. Fritz, now arguing with the other two soldiers, appeared even more fierce. They were pushing to get behind the machine-gun, but he seemed to win out. While they rushed to jump on the trucks, he fell on his belly and hugged the gun, groping for the trigger. We were all frozen with fear. I searched for his eyes in utter disbelief. Time fled and backtracked toward me again. I was aware only that the trucks were moving faster, that Fritz was frozen in his place, his right hand now on the ground, too far from the latch of the trigger. Then in a flash he jumped up, lifted the gun from its tripod, and let it sing half across the sky, while in the same motion he chased the last truck, leaping headfirst into it. His torso, writhing wildly to get his weight into the truck, was the last thing I saw of Fritz, who had in those last dancerlike movements transformed his body once more into the boy that he really was, waving good-bye at us with his legs.

QUESTIONS

1. Who are the "town mascots"? What is their relationship to the townspeople? How is this relationship ironic?

2. Describe Fritz's character. What is his relationship to the narrator's family? What does Fritz's treatment of the narrator's injury show about him?

3. What does Fritz do in the final scene of the story? What does his action show about him? What does it show, generally, about war?

WILLIAM FAULKNER (1897–1962)

Faulkner spent his childhood in Mississippi and became one of the foremost American novelists of the twentieth century. He twice received the Pulitzer Prize (in 1955 and 1963), and he also received the Nobel Prize for Literature in 1949. Throughout his extensive fiction about the special world he called "Yoknapatawpha County," he treats life in the southern United States as a symbol of humankind generally, emphasizing the decline of civilization and culture in the wake of the Civil War. Often he deals with degraded, sullen, and degenerate characters, and in this respect Abner Snopes of "Barn Burning" is typical. The loyalty he tries to exact from his son Sarty is one which excludes any allegiance to morality. Faulkner also uses the topic of the Snopes family in The Hamlet *(1940),* The Town *(1957), and* The Mansion *(1960).*

Barn Burning _____ *1939*

The store in which the Justice of the Peace's court was sitting smelled of cheese. The boy, crouched on his nail keg at the back of the crowded room, knew he smelled cheese, and more; from where he sat he could see the ranked shelves close-packed with the solid, squat, dynamic shapes of tin cans whose labels his stomach read, not from the lettering which meant nothing to his mind but from the scarlet devils and the silver curve of fish—this, the cheese which he knew he smelled and the hermetic meat° which his intestines believed he smelled coming in intermittent gusts momentary and brief between the other constant one, the smell and sense just a little of fear because mostly of despair and grief, the old fierce pull of blood. He could not see the table where the Justice sat and before which his father and his father's enemy (*our enemy* he thought in that despair; *ourn! mine and his both! He's my father!*) stood, but he could hear them, the two of them that is, because his father had said no word yet:

"But what proof have you, Mr. Harris?"

"I told you. The hog got into my corn. I caught it up and sent it back to him. He had no fence that would hold it. I told him so, warned him. The next time I put the hog in my pen. When he came to get it I gave him enough wire to patch up his pen. The next time I put the hog up and kept it. I rode down to his house and saw the wire I gave him still rolled on to the spool in his yard. I told him he could have the hog when he paid me a dollar pound fee. That evening a nigger came with the dollar and got the hog. He was a strange nigger. He said, 'He say to tell you wood and hay kin burn.' I said, 'What?' 'That what he say to tell you,' the nigger said. 'Wood and hay kin burn.' That night my barn burned. I got the stock out but I lost the barn."

"Where is the nigger? Have you got him?"

"He was a strange nigger, I tell you. I don't know what became of him."   5

"But that's not proof. Don't you see that's not proof?"

"Get that boy up here. He knows." For a moment the boy thought too that the man meant his older brother until Harris said. "Not him. The little one. The boy," and, crouching, small for his age, small and wiry like his father, in patched and faded jeans even too small for him, with straight, uncombed, brown hair and eyes gray and

hermetic meat: canned meat.

wild as storm scud, he saw the men between himself and the table part and become a lane of grim faces, at the end of which he saw the Justice, a shabby, collarless, graying man in spectacles, beckoning him. He felt no floor under his bare feet; he seemed to walk beneath the palpable weight of the grim turning faces. His father, stiff in his black Sunday coat donned not for the trial but for the moving, did not even look at him. *He aims for me to lie,* he thought, again with that frantic grief and despair. *And I will have to do hit.*

"What's your name, boy?" the Justice said.

"Colonel Sartoris Snopes," the boy whispered.

"Hey?" the Justice said. "Talk louder. Colonel Sartoris? I reckon anybody named for Colonel Sartoris in this country can't help but tell the truth, can they?" The boy said nothing. *Enemy! Enemy!* he thought; for a moment he could not even see, could not see that the Justice's face was kindly nor discern that his voice was troubled when he spoke to the man named Harris: "Do you want me to question this boy?" But he could hear, and during those subsequent long seconds there was absolutely no sound in the crowded little room save that of quiet and intent breathing it was as if he had swung outward at the end of a grape vine, over a ravine, and at the top of the swing had been caught in a prolonged instant of mesmerized gravity, weightless in time.

"No!" Harris said violently, explosively. "Damnation! Send him out of here!" Now time, the fluid world, rushed beneath him again, the voices coming to him again through the smell of cheese and sealed meat, the fear and despair and the old grief of blood:

"This case is closed. I can't find against you, Snopes, but I can give you advice. Leave this country and don't come back to it."

His father spoke for the first time, his voice cold and harsh, level, without emphasis: "I aim to. I don't figure to stay in a country among people who . . ." he said something unprintable and vile, addressed to no one.

"That'll do," the Justice said, "Take your wagon and get out of this country before dark. Case dismissed."

His father turned, and he followed the stiff black coat, the wiry figure walking a little stiffly, from where a Confederate provost's man's musket ball had taken him in the heel on a stolen horse thirty years ago, followed the two backs now, since his older brother had appeared from somewhere in the crowd, no taller than the father but thicker, chewing tobacco steadily, between the two lines of grim-faced men and out of the store and across the worn gallery and down the sagging steps and among the dogs and half-grown boys in the mild May dust, where as he passed a voice hissed:

"Barn burner!"

Again he could not see, whirling; there was a face in a red haze, moonlike, bigger than the full moon, the owner of it half again his size, he leaping in the red haze toward the face, feeling no blow, feeling no shock when his head struck the earth, scrabbling up and leaping again, feeling no blow this time either and tasting no blood, scrabbling up to see the other boy in full flight and himself already leaping into pursuit as his father's hand jerked him back, the harsh, cold voice speaking above him: "Go get in the wagon."

It stood in a grove of locusts and mulberries across the road. His two hulking sisters in their Sunday dresses and his mother and her sister in calico and sunbonnets were already in it, sitting on and among the sorry residue of the dozen and more movings which even the boy could remember—the battered stove, the broken beds and chairs, the clock inlaid with mother-of-pearl, which would not run, stopped at some fourteen minutes past two o'clock of a dead and forgotten day and time, which had been his mother's dowry. She was crying, though when she saw him she drew her sleeve across her face and began to descend from the wagon. "Get back," the father said.

"He's hurt, I got to get some water and wash his . . ."

"Get back in the wagon." his father said. He got in too, over the tail-gate. His father mounted to the seat where the older brother already sat and struck the gaunt mules two savage blows with the peeled willow, but without heat. It was not even sadistic; it was exactly that same quality which in later years would cause his descendants to over-run the engine before putting a motor car into motion, striking and reining back in the same movement. The wagon went on, the store with its quiet crowd of grimly watching men dropped behind; a curve in the road hid it. *Forever* he thought. *Maybe he's done satisfied now, now that he has . . .* stopping himself, not to say it aloud even to himself. His mother's hand touched his shoulder.

"Does hit hurt?" she said.

"Naw," he said. "Hit don't hurt. Lemme be."

"Can't you wipe some of the blood off before hit dries?"

"I'll wash tonight," he said. "Lemme be, I tell you."

The wagon went on. He did not know where they were going. None of them ever did or ever asked, because it was always somewhere, always a house of sorts waiting for them a day or two days or even three days away. Likely his father had already arranged to make a crop on another farm before he . . . Again he had to stop himself. He (the father) always did. There was something about his wolflike independence and even courage when the advantage was at least neutral which impressed strangers, as if they got from his latent ravening ferocity not so much a sense of dependability as a feeling that his ferocious conviction in the rightness of his own actions would be of advantage to all whose interest lay with his.

That night they camped, in a grove of oaks and beeches where a spring ran. The nights were still cool and they had a fire against it, of a rail lifted from a nearby fence and cut into lengths—a small fire, neat, niggard almost, a shrewd fire; such fires were his father's habit and custom always, even in freezing weather. Older, the boy might have remarked this and wondered why not a big one; why should not a man who had not only seen the waste and extravagance of war, but who had in his blood an inherent prodigality with material not his own, have burned everything in sight? Then he might have gone a step farther and thought that that was the reason; that niggard blaze was the living fruits of nights passed during those four years in the woods hiding from all men, blue or grey, with his strings of horses (captured horses, he called them). And older still, he might have divined the true reason: that the element of fire spoke to some deep mainspring of his father's being, as the element of steel or of powder spoke to other men, as the one weapon for the preservation of integrity, else breath were not worth the breathing, and hence to be regarded with respect and used with discretion.

But he did not think this now and he had seen those same niggard blazes all his life. He merely ate his supper beside it and was already half asleep over his iron plate when his father called him, and once more he followed the stiff back, the stiff and ruthless limp, up the slope and on to the starlit road where, turning, he could see his father against the stars but without face or depth—a shape black, flat, and bloodless as though cut from tin in the iron folds of the frockcoat which had not been made for him, the voice harsh like tin and without heat like tin:

"You were fixing to tell them. You would have told him." He didn't answer. His father struck him with the flat of his hand on the side of the head, hard but without heat, exactly as he had struck the two mules at the store, exactly as he would strike either of them with any stick in order to kill a horse fly, his voice still without heat or anger: "You're getting to be a man. You got to learn. You got to learn to stick to your own blood or you ain't going to have any blood to stick to you. Do you think either of them, any man there this morning, would? Don't you know all they wanted was a chance to get at me because they knew I had them beat? Eh?" Later, twenty years later, he was to tell himself, "If I had said they wanted only truth, justice, he would have hit me again." But now he said nothing. He was not crying. He just stood there. "Answer me," his father said.

"Yes," he whispered. His father turned.

"Get on to bed. We'll be there tomorrow."

Tomorrow they were there. In the early afternoon the wagon stopped before a paintless two-room house identical almost with the dozen others it had stopped before even in the boy's ten years, and again, as on the other dozen occasions, his mother and aunt got down and began to unload the wagon, although his two sisters and his father and brother had not moved.

"Likely hit ain't fitten for hawgs," one of the sisters said.

"Nevertheless, fit it will and you'll hog it and like it," his father said. "Get out of them chairs and help your Ma unload."

The two sisters got down, big, bovine, in a flutter of cheap ribbons; one of them drew from the jumbled wagon bed a battered lantern, the other a worn broom. His father handed the reins to the older son and began to climb stiffly over the wheel. "When they get unloaded, take the team to the barn and feed them." Then he said, and at first the boy thought he was still speaking to his brother: "Come with me."

"Me?" he said.

"Yes," his father said. "You."

"Abner," his mother said. His father paused and looked back—the harsh level stare beneath the shaggy, graying, irascible brows.

"I reckon I'll have a word with the man that aims to begin tomorrow owning me body and soul for the next eight months."

They went back up the road. A week ago—or before last night, that is—he would have asked where they were going, but not now. His father had struck him before last night but never before had he paused afterward to explain why; it was as if the blow and the following calm, outrageous voice still rang, repercussed, divulging nothing to him save the terrible handicap of being young, the light weight of his few years, just heavy enough to prevent his soaring free of the world as it seemed to be ordered but not heavy enough to keep footed solid in it, to resist it and try to chance the course of its events.

Presently he could see the grove of oaks and cedars and the other flowering trees and shrubs where the house would be, though not the house yet. They walked beside a fence massed with honeysuckle and Cherokee roses and came to a gate swinging open between two brick pillars, and now, beyond a sweep of drive, he saw the house for the first time and at that instant he forgot his father and the terror and despair both, and even when he remembered his father again (who had stopped) the terror and despair did not return. Because, for all the twelve movings, they had sojourned until now in a poor country, a land of small farms and fields and houses, and he had never seen a house like this before. *Hit's big as a courthouse* he thought quietly, with a surge of peace and joy whose reason he could not have thought into words, being too young for that: *They are safe from him. People whose lives are a part of this peace and dignity are beyond his touch, he no more to them than a buzzing wasp: capable of stinging for a little moment but that's all; the spell of this peace and dignity rendering even the barns and stable and cribs which belong to it impervious to the puny flames he might contrive* . . . this, the peace and joy, ebbing for an instant as he looked again at the stiff black back, the stiff and implacable limp of the figure which was not dwarfed by the house, for the reason that it had never looked big anywhere and which now, against the serene columned backdrop, had more than ever that impervious quality of something cut ruthlessly from tin, depthless, as though, sidewise to the sun, it would cast no shadow. Watching him, the boy remarked the absolutely undeviating course which his father held and saw the stiff foot come squarely down in a pile of fresh droppings where a horse had stood in the drive and which his father could have avoided by a simple change of stride. But it ebbed only for a moment, though he could not have thought this into words either, walking on in the spell of the house, which he could even want but without envy, without sorrow, certainly never with that ravening and jealous rage which unknown to him walked in the ironlike black coat before him: *Maybe he will feel it too. Maybe it will even change him now from what maybe he couldn't help but be.*

They crossed the portico. Now he could hear his father's stiff foot as it came down on the boards with clocklike finality, a sound out of all proportion to the displacement of the body it bore and which was not dwarfed either by the white door before it, as though it had attained to a sort of vicious and ravening minimum not to be dwarfed by anything—the flat, wide, black hat, the formal coat of broadcloth which had once been black but which had now that friction-glazed greenish cast of the bodies of old house flies, the lifted sleeve which was too large, the lifted hand like a curled claw. The door opened so promptly that the boy knew the Negro must have been watching them all the time, an old man with neat grizzled hair, in a linen jacket, who stood barring the door with his body, saying "Wipe yo foots, white man, fo you come in here. Major ain't home nohow."

"Get out of my way, nigger," his father said, without heat too, flinging the door back and the Negro also and entering, his hat still on his head. And now the boy saw the prints of the stiff foot on the doorsill and saw them appear on the pale rug behind the machinelike deliberation of the foot which seemed to bear (or transmit) twice the weight which the body compassed. The Negro was shouting "Miss Lula! Miss Lula!" somewhere behind them, then the boy, deluged as though by a warm wave by a suave turn of carpeted stair and a pendant glitter of chandeliers and a mute gleam of gold frames, heard the swift feet and saw her too, a lady—perhaps he had never seen her like before either—in a gray, smooth gown with lace at the throat and an apron tied at the waist and the sleeves turned back, wiping cake or biscuit dough from her hands with a towel as she came up the hall, looking not at his father at all but at the tracks on the blond rug with an expression of incredulous amazement.

"I tried," the Negro cried. "I tole him to . . ."

"Will you please go away?" she said in a shaking voice. "Major de Spain is not at home. Will you please go away?"

His father had not spoken again. He did not speak again. He did not even look at her. He just stood stiff in the center of the rug, in his hat, the shaggy iron-gray brows twitching slightly above the pebble-colored eyes as he appeared to examine the house with brief deliberation. Then with the same deliberation he turned; the boy watched him pivot on the good leg and saw the stiff foot drag round the arc of the turning, leaving a final long and fading smear. His father never looked at it, he never once looked down at the rug. The Negro held the door. It closed behind them, upon the hysteric and indistinguishable woman-wail. His father stopped at the top of the steps and scraped his boot clean on the edge of it. At the gate he stopped again. He stood for a moment, planted stiffly on the stiff foot, looking back at the house. "Pretty and white, ain't it?" he said. "That's sweat. Nigger sweat. Maybe it ain't white enough yet to suit him. Maybe he wants to mix some white sweat with it."

Two hours later the boy was chopping wood behind the house within which his mother and aunt and the two sisters (the mother and aunt, not the two girls, he knew that; even at this distance and muffled by walls the flat loud voices of the two girls emanated an incorrigible idle inertia) were setting up the stove to prepare a meal, when he heard the hooves and saw the linen-clad man on a fine sorrel mare, whom he recognized even before he saw the rolled rug in front of the Negro youth following on a fat bay carriage horse—a suffused, angry face vanishing, still at full gallop, beyond the corner of the house where his father and brother were sitting in the two tilted chairs; and a moment later, almost before he could have put the axe down, he heard the hooves again and watched the sorrel mare go back out of the yard, already galloping again. Then his father began to shout one of the sisters' names, who presently emerged backward from the kitchen door dragging the rolled rug along the ground by one end while the other sister walked behind it.

"If you ain't going to tote, go on and set up the wash pot," the first said.

"You, Sarty!" the second shouted. "Set up the wash pot!" His father appeared at the door, framed against that shabbiness, as he had been against that other bland perfection, impervious to either, the mother's anxious face at his shoulder.

"Go on," the father said. "Pick it up." The two sisters stooped, broad, lethargic; stooping, they presented an incredible expanse of pale cloth and a flutter of tawdry ribbons.

"If I thought enough of a rug to have to git hit all the way from France I wouldn't keep hit where folks coming in would have to tromp on hit," the first said. They raised the rug.

"Abner," the mother said. "Let me do it."

"You go back and git dinner," his father said. "I'll tend to this."

From the woodpile through the rest of the afternoon the boy watched them, the rug spread flat in the dust beside the bubbling wash pot, the two sisters stooping over it with that profound and lethargic reluctance, while the father stood over them in turn, implacable and grim, driving them though never raising his voice again. He could smell the harsh homemade lye they were using; he saw his mother come to the door once and look toward them with an expression not anxious now but very like despair; he saw his father turn, and he fell to with the axe and saw from the corner of his eye his father raise from the ground a flattish fragment of field stone and examine it and return to the pot, and this time his mother actually spoke: "Abner. Abner. Please don't. Please, Abner."

Then he was done too. It was dusk; the whippoorwills had already begun. He could smell coffee from the room where they would presently eat the cold food remaining from the mid-afternoon meal, though when he entered the house he realized they were having coffee again because there was a fire on the hearth, before which the rug now lay spread over the backs of the two chairs. The tracks of his father's foot were gone. Where they had been were now long, water-cloudy scoriations resembling the sporadic course of a Lilliputian mowing machine.

It still hung there while they ate the cold food and then went to bed, scattered   55
without order or claim up and down the two rooms, his mother in one bed, where his
father would later lie, the older brother in the other, himself, the aunt, and the two
sisters on pallets on the floor. But his father was not in bed yet. The last thing the boy
remembered was the depthless, harsh silhouette of the hat and coat bending over the
rug and it seemed to him that he had not even closed his eyes when the silhouette
was standing over him, the fire almost dead behind it, the stiff foot prodding him
awake. "Catch up the mule," his father said.

When he returned with the mule his father was standing in the black door, the
rolled rug over his shoulder. "Ain't you going to ride?" he said.

"No. Give me your foot."

He bent his knee into his father's hand, the wiry, surprising power flowed
smoothly, rising, he rising with it, on to the mule's bare back (they had owned a saddle once; the boy could remember it though not when or where) and with the same
effortlessness his father swung the rug up in front of him. Now in the starlight they
retraced the afternoon's path, up the dusty road rife with honeysuckle, through the
gate and up the black tunnel of the drive to the lightless house, where he sat on the
mule and felt the rough warp of the rug drag across his thighs and vanish.

"Don't you want me to help?" he whispered. His father did not answer and now
he heard again that stiff foot striking the hollow portico with that wooden and clocklike deliberation, that outrageous overstatement of the weight it carried. The rug,
hunched, not flung (the boy could tell that even in the darkness) from his father's
shoulder, struck the angle of wall and floor with a sound unbelievably loud, thunder-
ous, then the foot again, unhurried and enormous; a light came on in the house and
the boy sat, tense, breathing steadily and quietly and just a little fast, though the foot
itself did not increase its beat at all, descending the steps now; now the boy could see
him.

"Don't you want to ride now?" he whispered. "We kin both ride now," the light   60
within the house altering now, flaring up and sinking. *He's coming down the stairs now,*
he thought. He had already ridden the mule up beside the horse block; presently his
father was up behind him and he doubled the reins over and slashed the mule across
the neck, but before the animal could begin to trot the hard, thin arm came round
him, the hard, knotted hand jerking the mule back to a walk.

In the first red rays of the sun they were in the lot, putting plow gear on the
mules. This time the sorrel mare was in the lot before he heard it at all, the rider collarless and even bareheaded, trembling, speaking in a shaking voice as the woman in
the house had done, his father merely looking up once before stooping again to the
hame he was buckling, so that the man on the mare spoke to his stooping back:

"You must realize you have ruined that rug. Wasn't there anybody here, any of
your women . . ." He ceased, shaking, the boy watching him, the older brother leaning now in the stable door, chewing, blinking slowly and steadily at nothing apparently. "It cost a hundred dollars. But you never had a hundred dollars. You never will.
So I'm going to charge you twenty bushels of corn against your crop. I'll add it in your
contract and when you come to the commissary you can sign it. That won't keep Mrs.
de Spain quiet but maybe it will teach you to wipe your feet off before you enter her
house again."

Then he was gone. The boy looked at his father, who still had not spoken or
even looked up again, who was now adjusting the logger-head in the hame.

"Pap," he said. His father looked at him—the inscrutable face, the shaggy brows beneath which the gray eyes glinted coldly. Suddenly the boy went toward him, fast, stopping as suddenly. "You done the best you could!" he cried. "If he wanted hit done different why didn't he wait and tell you how? He won't git no twenty bushels! He won't git none! We'll get hit and hide hit! I kin watch . . ."

"Did you put the cutter back in that straight stock like I told you?"

"No, sir," he said.

"Then go do it."

That was Wednesday. During the rest of that week he worked steadily, at what was within his scope and some which was beyond it, with an industry that did not need to be driven nor even commanded twice; he had this from his mother, with the difference that some at least of what he did he liked to do, such as splitting wood with the half-size axe which his mother and aunt had earned, or saved money somehow, to present him with at Christmas. In company with the two older women (and on one afternoon even one of the sisters), he built pens for the shoat and the cow which were a part of his father's contract with the landlord, and one afternoon, his father being absent, gone somewhere on one of the mules, he went to the field.

They were running a middle buster now, his brother holding the plow straight while he handled the reins, and walking beside the straining mule, the rich black soil shearing cool and damp against his bare ankles, he thought *Maybe this is the end of it. Maybe even that twenty bushels that seems hard to have to pay for just a rug will be a cheap price for him to stop forever and always from being what he used to be*; thinking, dreaming now, so that his brother had to speak sharply to him to mind the mule: *Maybe he even won't collect the twenty bushels. Maybe it will all add up and balance and vanish—corn, rug, fire; the terror and grief, the being pulled two ways like between two teams of horses—gone, done with forever and ever.*

Then it was Saturday; he looked up from beneath the mule he was harnessing and saw his father in the black coat and hat. "Not that," his father said. "The wagon gear." And then, two hours later, sitting in the wagon bed behind his father and brother on the seat, the wagon accomplished a final curve, and he saw the weathered paintless store with its tattered tobacco- and patent-medicine posters and the tethered wagons and saddle animals below the gallery. He mounted the gnawed steps behind his father and brother, and there again was the lane of quiet, watching faces for the three of them to walk through. He saw the man in spectacles sitting at the plank table and he did not need to be told this was a Justice of the Peace; he sent one glare of fierce, exultant, partisan defiance at the man in collar and cravat now, whom he had seen but twice in his life, and that on a galloping horse, who now wore on his face an expression not of rage but of amazed unbelief which the boy could not have known was at the incredible circumstance of being sued by one of his own tenants, and came and stood against his father and cried at the Justice: "He ain't done it! He ain't burnt . . ."

"Go back to the wagon," his father said.

"Burnt?" the Justice said. "Do I understand this rug was burned too?"

"Does anybody here claim it was?" his father said. "Go back to the wagon." But he did not, he merely retreated to the rear of the room, crowded as that other had been, but not to sit down this time, instead, to stand pressing among the motionless bodies, listening to the voices:

"And you claim twenty bushels of corn is too high for the damage you did to the rug?"

"He brought the rug to me and said he wanted the tracks washed out of it. I 75 washed the tracks out and took the rug back to him."

"But you didn't carry the rug back to him in the same condition it was in before you made the tracks on it."

His father did not answer, and now for perhaps half a minute there was no sound at all save that of breathing, the faint, steady suspiration of complete and intent listening.

"You decline to answer that, Mr. Snopes?" Again his father did not answer. "I'm going to find against you, Mr. Snopes. I'm going to find that you were responsible for the injury to Major de Spain's rug and hold you liable for it. But twenty bushels of corn seems a little high for a man in your circumstances to have to pay. Major de Spain claims it cost a hundred dollars. October corn will be worth about fifty cents. I figure that if Major de Spain can stand a ninety-five-dollar loss on something he paid cash for, you can stand a five-dollar loss you haven't earned yet. I hold you in damages to Major de Spain to the amount of ten bushels of corn over and above your contract with him, to be paid to him out of your crop at gathering time. Court adjourned."

It had taken no time hardly, the morning was but half begun. He thought they would return home and perhaps back to the field, since they were late, far behind all other farmers. But instead his father passed on behind the wagon, merely indicating with his hand for the older brother to follow with it, and crossed the road toward the blacksmith shop opposite, pressing on after his father, overtaking him, speaking, whispering up at the harsh, calm face beneath the weathered hat: "He won't git no ten bushels neither. He won't git one. We'll . . ." until his father glanced for an instant down on him, the face absolutely calm, the grizzled eyebrows tangled above the cold eyes, the voice almost pleasant, almost gentle:

"You think so? Well, we'll wait till October anyway." 80

The matter of the wagon—the setting of a spoke or two and the tightening of the tires—did not take long either, the business of the tires accomplished by driving the wagon into the spring branch behind the shop and letting it stand there, the mules nuzzling into the water from time to time, and the boy on the seat with the idle reins, looking up the slope and through the sooty tunnel of the shed where the slow hammer rang and where his father sat on an upended cypress bolt, easily, either talking or listening, still sitting there when the boy brought the dripping wagon up out of the branch and halted it before the door.

"Take them on to the shade and hitch," his father said. He did so and returned. His father and the smith and a third man squatting on his heels inside the door were talking, about crops and animals; the boy, squatting too in the ammoniac dust and hoof-parings and scales of rust, heard his father tell a long and unhurried story out of the time before the birth of the older brother even when he had been a professional horsetrader. And then his father came up beside him where he stood before a tattered last year's circus poster on the other side of the store, gazing rapt and quiet at the scarlet horses, the incredible poisings and convolutions of tulle and tights and the painted leers of comedians, and said, "It's time to eat."

But not at home. Squatting beside his brother against the front wall, he watched his father emerge from the store and produce from a paper sack a segment of cheese and divided it carefully and deliberately into three with his pocket knife and produce crackers from the same sack. They all three squatted on the gallery and ate slowly, without talking; then in the store again, they drank from a tin dipper tepid water smelling of the cedar bucket and of living beech trees. And still they did not go home. It was a horse lot this time, a tall rail fence upon and along which men stood and sat and out of which one by one horses were led, to be walked and trotted and then cantered back and forth along the road while the slow swapping and buying went on and the sun began to slant westward, they—the three of them—watching and listening, the older brother with his muddy eyes and his steady inevitable tobacco, the father commenting now and then on certain of the animals, to no one in particular.

It was after sundown when they reached home. They ate supper by lamplight, then, sitting on the doorstep, the boy watched the night fully accomplish, listening to the whippoorwills and the frogs, when he heard his mother's voice: "Abner! No! No! Oh, God, Oh, God, Abner!" and he rose, whirled, and saw the altered light through the door where a candle stub now burned in a bottle neck on the table and his father, still in the hat and coat, at once formal and burlesque as though dressed carefully for some shabby and ceremonial violence, emptying the reservoir of the lamp back into the five-gallon kerosene can from which it had been filled, while the mother tugged at his arm until he shifted the lamp to the other hand and flung her back, not savagely or viciously, just hard, into the wall, her hands flung out against the wall for balance, her mouth open and in her face the same quality of hopeless despair as had been in her voice. Then his father saw him standing in the door.

"Go to the barn and get that can of oil we were oiling the wagon with," he said. The boy did not move. Then he could speak.

"What . . ." he cried. "What are you . . ."

"Go get that oil," his father said. "Go."

Then he was moving, running, outside the house, toward the stable: this the old habit, the old blood which he had not been permitted to choose for himself, which had been bequeathed him willy nilly and which had run for so long (and who knew where, battening on what of outrage and savagery and lust) before it came to him. *I could keep on,* he thought. *I could run on and on and never look back, never need to see his face again. Only I can't. I can't,* the rusted can in his hand now, the liquid sloshing in it as he ran back to the house and into it, into the sound of his mother's weeping in the next room, and handed the can to his father.

"Ain't you going to even send a nigger?" he cried. "At least you sent a nigger before!"

This time his father didn't strike him. The hand came even faster than the blow had, the same hand which had set the can on the table with almost excruciating care flashing from the can toward him too quick for him to follow it, gripping him by the back of his shirt and on to tiptoe before he had seen it quit the can, the face stooping at him in breathless and frozen ferocity, the cold, dead voice speaking over him to the older brother who leaned against the table, chewing with that steady, curious, sidewise motion of cows:

"Empty the can into the big one and go on. I'll catch up with you."

"Better tie him up to the bedpost," the brother said.

"Do like I told you," the father said. Then the boy was moving, his bunched shirt and the hard, bony hand between his shoulder-blades, his toes just touching the floor, across the room and into the other one, past the sisters sitting with spread heavy thighs in the two chairs over the cold hearth, and to where his mother and aunt sat side by side on the bed, the aunt's arms about the mother's shoulders.

"Hold him," the father said. The aunt made a startled movement. "Not you," the father said. "Lennie. Take hold of him. I want to see you do it." His mother took him by the wrist. "You'll hold him better than that. If he gets loose don't you know what he is going to do? He will go up yonder." He jerked his head toward the road. "Maybe I'd better tie him."

"I'll hold him," his mother whispered. 95

"See you do then." Then his father was gone, the stiff foot heavy and measured upon the boards, ceasing at last.

Then he began to struggle. His mother caught him in both arms, he jerking and wrenching at them. He would be stronger in the end, he knew that. But he had not time to wait for it. "Lemme go!" he cried. "I don't want to have to hit you!"

"Let him go!" the aunt said. "If he don't go, before God, I am going up there myself!"

"Don't you see I can't?" his mother cried. "Sarty! Sarty! No! No! Help me, Lizzie!"

Then he was free. His aunt grasped at him but it was too late. He whirled, run- 100 ning, his mother stumbled forward on to her knees behind him, crying to the nearer sister: "Catch him, Net! Catch him!" But that was too late too, the sister (the sisters were twins, born at the same time, yet either of them now gave the impression of be- ing, encompassing as much living meat and volume and weight as any other two of the family) not yet having begun to rise from the chair, her head, face, alone merely turned, presenting to him in the flying instant an astonishing expanse of young fe- male features untroubled by any surprise even, wearing only an expression of bovine interest. Then he was out of the room, out of the house, in the mild dust of the star- lit road and the heavy rifeness of honeysuckle, the pale ribbon unspooling with ter- rific slowness under his running feet, reaching the gate at last and turning in, run- ning, his heart and lungs drumming, on up the drive toward the lighted house, the lighted door. He did not knock, he burst in, sobbing for breath, incapable for the mo- ment of speech; he saw the astonished face of the Negro in the linen jacket without knowing when the Negro had appeared.

"De Spain!" he cried, panted. "Where's . . ." then he saw the white man too emerging from a white door down the hall. "Barn!" he cried. "Barn!"

"What?" the white man said. "Barn?"

"Yes!" the boy cried. "Barn!"

"Catch him!" the white man shouted.

But it was too late this time too. The Negro grasped his shirt, but the entire 105 sleeve, rotten with washing, carried away, and he was out that door too and in the drive again, and had actually never ceased to run even while he was screaming into the white man's face.

Behind him the white man was shouting. "My horse! Fetch my horse!" and he thought for an instant of cutting across the park and climbing the fence into the road, but he did not know the park nor how high the vine-massed fence might be and he dared not risk it. So he ran on down the drive, blood and breath roaring; presently he was in the road again though he could not see it. He could not hear either: the galloping mare was almost upon him before he heard her, and even then he held his course, as if the very urgency of his wild grief and need must in a moment more find him wings, waiting until the ultimate instant to hurl himself aside and into the weed- choked roadside ditch as the horse thundered past and on, for an instant in furious silhouette against the stars, the tranquil early summer night sky which, even before the shape of the horse and rider vanished, strained abruptly and violently upward: a

long, swirling roar incredible and soundless, blotting the stars, and he springing up
and into the road again, running again, knowing it was too late yet still running even
after he heard the shot and, an instant later, two shots, pausing now without knowing
he had ceased to run, crying "Pap! Pap!," running again before he knew he had begun to run, stumbling, tripping over something and scrabbling up again without ceasing to run, looking backward over his shoulder at the glare as he got up, running on
among the invisible trees, panting, sobbing, "Father! Father!"

At midnight he was sitting on the crest of a hill. He did not know it was midnight and he did not know how far he had come. But there was no glare behind him
now and he sat now, his back toward what he had called home for four days anyhow,
his face toward the dark woods which he would enter when breath was strong again,
small, shaking steadily in the chill darkness, hugging himself into the remainder of
his thin, rotten shirt, the grief and despair now no longer terror and fear but just grief
and despair. *Father. My father*, he thought. "He was brave!" he cried suddenly, aloud
but not loud, no more than a whisper: "He was! He was in the war! He was in Colonel
Sartoris' cav'ry!" not knowing that his father had gone to that war a private in the fine
old European sense, wearing no uniform, admitting the authority of and giving fidelity to no man or army or flag, going to war as Malbrouck° himself did: for booty—
it meant nothing and less than nothing to him if it were enemy booty or his own.

The slow constellations wheeled on. It would be dawn and then sun-up after a
while and he would be hungry. But that would be tomorrow and now he was only
cold, and walking would cure that. His breathing was easier now and he decided to
get up and go on, and then he found that he had been asleep because he knew it was
almost dawn, the night almost over. He could tell that from the whippoorwills. They
were everywhere now among the dark trees below him, constant and inflectioned and
ceaseless, so that, as the instant for giving over to the day birds drew nearer and
nearer, there was no interval at all between them. He got up. He was a little stiff, but
walking would cure that too as it would the cold, and soon there would be the sun.
He went on down the hill, toward the dark woods within which the liquid silver voices
of the birds called unceasing—the rapid and urgent beating of the urgent and quir-
ing heart of the late spring night. He did not look back.

QUESTIONS

1. Explain why Sarty's character is round rather than flat. In what ways does he
    change and grow? What conflicts does he face? What does he learn? How does
    he feel about the things his father does? Why does he leave and "not look back"
    at the end?

2. In the Bible, 2 Samuel, Chapters 2 and 3, Abner, the cousin of King Saul, is a
    powerful commander, warrior, and king maker. He is loyal to the son of King
    Saul and fights against the supporters of King David. Abner's death makes it
    possible for David to become uncontested ruler. Why do you think that
    Faulkner chose the name *Abner* for the father of the Snopes family? What ac-
    tions of Abner Snopes make him seem heroic? Antiheroic? Why?

Malbrouck: hero of an old French ballad ("Malbrouck s'en va-t-en guerre"). The original
Malbrouck, the English Duke of Marlborough (1650–1722) had been accused of profiteering
during Queen Anne's War (1702–13).

3.   When and where is the story occurring? How does Faulkner convey this information to you?
4.   Describe the characters of Sarty's mother and sisters. What do you learn about them? To what extent do any of them exhibit growth or development?
5.   At the story's end, who is the rider of the horse? Who fires the three shots? Why does Faulkner not tell us the result of the shooting? (In Book I of *The Hamlet,* Faulkner explains that Abner and his other son, Flem, escape.)

SUSAN GLASPELL (1882–1948)

For a brief biography, please see Chapter 26.

A Jury of Her Peers° ——————————————————— 1917

When Martha Hale opened the storm-door and got a cut of the north wind, she ran back for her big woolen scarf. As she hurriedly wound that round her head her eye made a scandalized sweep of her kitchen. It was no ordinary thing that called her away—it was probably further from ordinary than anything that had ever happened in Dickson County. But what her eye took in was that her kitchen was in no shape for leaving: her bread all ready for mixing, half the flour sifted and half unsifted.

She hated to see things half done; but she had been at that when the team from town stopped to get Mr. Hale, and then the sheriff came running in to say his wife wished Mrs. Hale would come too—adding, with a grin, that he guessed she was getting scary and wanted another woman along. So she had dropped everything right where it was.

"Martha!" now came her husband's impatient voice. "Don't keep folks waiting out here in the cold."

She again opened the storm-door, and this time joined the three men and the one woman waiting for her in the big two-seated buggy.

After she had the robes tucked around her she took another look at the woman who sat beside her on the back seat. She had met Mrs. Peters the year before at the county fair, and the thing she remembered about her was that she didn't seem like a sheriff's wife. She was small and thin and didn't have a strong voice. Mrs. Gorman, sheriff's wife before Gorman went out and Peters came in, had a voice that somehow seemed to be backing up the law with every word. But if Mrs. Peters didn't look like a sheriff's wife, Peters made it up in looking like a sheriff. He was to a dot the kind of man who could get himself elected sheriff—a heavy man with a big voice, who was particularly genial with the law-abiding, as if to make it plain that he knew the difference between criminals and non-criminals. And right there it came into Mrs. Hale's mind, with a stab, that this man who was so pleasant and lively with all of them was going to the Wrights' now as a sheriff.

"The country's not very pleasant this time of year," Mrs. Peters at last ventured, as if she felt they ought to be talking as well as the men.

Mrs. Hale scarcely finished her reply, for they had gone up a little hill and could

5

Glaspell's play *Trifles,* with which this story may be compared, appears in Chapter 26.

see the Wright place now, and seeing it did not make her feel like talking. It looked very lonesome this cold March morning. It had always been a lonesome-looking place. It was down in a hollow, and the poplar trees around it were lonesome-looking trees. The men were looking at it and talking about what had happened. The county attorney was bending to one side of the buggy, and kept looking steadily at the place as they drew up to it.

"I'm glad you came with me," Mrs. Peters said nervously, as the two women were about to follow the men in through the kitchen door.

Even after she had her foot on the door-step, her hand on the knob, Martha Hale had a moment of feeling she could not cross that threshold. And the reason it seemed she couldn't cross it now was simply because she hadn't crossed it before. Time and time again it had been in her mind, "I ought to go over and see Minnie Foster"—she still thought of her as Minnie Foster, though for twenty years she had been Mrs. Wright. And then there was always something to do and Minnie Foster would go from her mind. But *now* she could come.

The men went over to the stove. The women stood close together by the door. Young Henderson, the county attorney, turned around and said, "Come up to the fire, ladies."

Mrs. Peters took a step forward, then stopped. "I'm not—cold," she said.

And so the two women stood by the door, at first not even so much as looking around the kitchen.

The men talked for a minute about what a good thing it was the sheriff had sent his deputy out that morning to make a fire for them, and then Sheriff Peters stepped back from the stove, unbuttoned his outer coat, and leaned his hands on the kitchen table in a way that seemed to mark the beginning of official business. "Now, Mr. Hale," he said in a sort of semi-official voice, "before we move things about, you tell Mr. Henderson just what it was you saw when you came here yesterday morning."

The county attorney was looking around the kitchen.

"By the way," he said, "has anything been moved?" He turned to the sheriff. "Are things just as you left them yesterday?"

Peters looked from cupboard to sink; from that to a small worn rocker a little to one side of the kitchen table.

"It's just the same."

"Somebody should have been left here yesterday," said the county attorney.

"Oh—yesterday," returned the sheriff, with a little gesture as of yesterday having been more than he could bear to think of. "When I had to send Frank to Morris Center for that man who went crazy—let me tell you. I had my hands full *yesterday*. I knew you could get back from Omaha by today, George, and as long as I went over everything here myself—"

"Well, Mr. Hale," said the county attorney, in a way of letting what was past and gone go, "tell just what happened when you came here yesterday morning."

Mrs. Hale, still leaning against the door, had that sinking feeling of the mother whose child is about to speak a piece. Lewis often wandered along and got things mixed up in a story. She hoped he would tell this straight and plain, and not say unnecessary things that would just make things harder for Minnie Foster. He didn't begin at once, and she noticed that he looked queer—as if standing in that kitchen and having to tell what he had seen there yesterday morning made him almost sick.

"Yes, Mr. Hale?" the county attorney reminded.

"Harry and I had started to town with a load of potatoes," Mrs. Hale's husband began.

Harry was Mrs. Hale's oldest boy. He wasn't with them now, for the very good reason that those potatoes never got to town yesterday and he was taking them this morning, so he hadn't been home when the sheriff stopped to say he wanted Mr. Hale to come over to the Wright place and tell the county attorney his story there, where he could point it all out. With all Mrs. Hale's other emotions came the fear now that maybe Harry wasn't dressed warm enough—they hadn't any of them realized how that north wind did bite.

"We come along this road," Hale was going on, with a motion of his hand to the road over which they had just come, "and as we got in sight of the house I says to Harry, 'I'm goin' to see if I can't get John Wright to take a telephone.' You see," he explained to Henderson, "unless I can get somebody to go in with me they won't come out this branch road except for a price *I* can't pay. I'd spoke to Wright about it once before; but he put me off, saying folks talked too much anyway, and all he asked was peace and quiet—guess you know about how much he talked himself. But I thought maybe if I went to the house and talked about it before his wife, and said all the women-folks liked the telephones, and that in this lonesome stretch of road it would be a good thing—well, I said to Harry that that was what I was going to say— though I said at the same time that I didn't know as what his wife wanted made much difference to John—"

Now there he was!—saying things he didn't need to say. Mrs. Hale tried to catch her husband's eye, but fortunately the county attorney interrupted with:

"Let's talk about that a little later, Mr. Hale. I do want to talk about that, but I'm anxious now to get along to just what happened when you got here."

When he began this time, it was very deliberately and carefully:

"I didn't see or hear anything. I knocked at the door. And still it was all quiet inside. I knew they must be up—it was past eight o'clock. So I knocked again, louder, and I thought I heard somebody say, ' Come in.' I wasn't sure—I'm not sure yet. But I opened the door—this door," jerking a hand toward the door by which the two women stood. "and there, in that rocker"—pointing to it—"sat Mrs. Wright."

Everyone in the kitchen looked at the rocker. It came into Mrs. Hale's mind that that rocker didn't look in the least like Minnie Foster—the Minnie Foster of twenty years before. It was a dingy red, with wooden rungs up the back, and the middle rung was gone, and the chair sagged to one side.

"How did she—look?" the county attorney was inquiring.

"Well," said Hale, "she looked—queer."

"How do you mean—queer?"

As he asked it he took out a note-book and pencil. Mrs. Hale did not like the sight of that pencil. She kept her eye fixed on her husband, as if to keep him from saying unnecessary things that would go into that note-book and make trouble.

Hale did speak guardedly, as if the pencil had affected him too.

"Well, as if she didn't know what she was going to do next. And kind of— done up."

"How did she seem to feel about your coming?"

"Why, I don't think she minded—one way or other. She didn't pay much attention. I said, 'Ho' do, Mrs. Wright? It's cold, ain't it?' And she said. 'Is it?'—and went on pleatin' at her apron.

25

30

35

"Well, I was surprised. She didn't ask me to come up to the stove, or to sit down, but just set there, not even lookin' at me. And so I said: 'I want to see John.'

"And then she—laughed. I guess you would call it a laugh.

"I thought of Harry and the team outside, so I said, a little sharp, 'Can I see John?' 'No,' says she—kind of dull like. 'Ain't he home?' says I. Then she looked at me. 'Yes,' says she, 'he's home.' 'Then why can't I see him?' I asked her, out of patience with her now. ''Cause he's dead' says she, just as quiet and dull—and fell to pleatin' her apron. 'Dead?' says, I, like you do when you can't take in what you've heard.

"She just nodded her head, not getting a bit excited, but rockin' back and forth.

"'Why—where is he?' says I, not knowing *what* to say.

"She just pointed upstairs—like this"—pointing to the room above.

"I got up, with the idea of going up there myself. By this time I—didn't know what to do. I walked from there to here; then I says: 'Why, what did he die of?'

"'He died of a rope around his neck,' says she; and just went on pleatin' at her apron."

Hale stopped speaking, and stood staring at the rocker, as if he were still seeing the woman who had sat there the morning before. Nobody spoke; it was as if every one were seeing the woman who had sat there the morning before.

"And what did you do then?" the county attorney at last broke the silence.

"I went out and called Harry. I thought I might—need help. I got Harry in, and we went upstairs." His voice fell almost to a whisper. "There he was—lying over the—"

"I think I'd rather have you go into that upstairs," the county attorney interrupted, "where you can point it all out. Just go on now with the rest of the story."

"Well, my first thought was to get that rope off. It looked—"

He stopped, his face twitching.

"But Harry, he went up to him, and he said. 'No, he's dead all right, and we'd better not touch anything.' So we went downstairs.

"She was still sitting that same way. 'Has anybody been notified?' I asked. 'No,' says she, unconcerned.

"'Who did this, Mrs. Wright?' said Harry. He said it businesslike, and she stopped pleatin' at her apron. 'I don't know,' she says. 'You don't *know*?' says Harry. 'Weren't you sleepin' in the bed with him?' 'Yes,' says she, 'but I was on the inside.' 'Somebody slipped a rope round his neck and strangled him, and you didn't wake up?' says Harry. 'I didn't wake up,' she said after him.

"We may have looked as if we didn't see how that could be, for after a minute she said, 'I sleep sound.'

"Harry was going to ask her more questions, but I said maybe that weren't our business; maybe we ought to let her tell her story first to the coroner or the sheriff. So Harry went fast as he could over to High Road—the Rivers' place, where there's a telephone."

"And what did she do when she knew you had gone for the coroner?" The attorney got his pencil in his hand all ready for writing.

"She moved from that chair to this one over here"—Hale pointed to a small chair in the corner—"and just sat there with her hands held together and looking down. I got a feeling that I ought to make some conversation, so I said I had come in to see if John wanted to put in a telephone; and at that she started to laugh, and then she stopped and looked at me—scared."

At the sound of a moving pencil the man who was telling the story looked up. 60

"I dunno—maybe it wasn't scared," he hastened: "I wouldn't like to say it was. Soon Harry got back, and then Dr. Lloyd came, and you, Mr. Peters, and so I guess that's all I know that you don't."

He said that last with relief, and moved a little, as if relaxing. Everyone moved a little. The county attorney walked toward the stair door.

"I guess we'll go upstairs first—then out to the barn and around there."

He paused and looked around the kitchen.

"You're convinced there was nothing important here?" he asked the sheriff. 65 "Nothing that would—point to any motive?"

The sheriff too looked all around, as if to re-convince himself.

"Nothing here but kitchen things," he said, with a little laugh for the insignificance of kitchen things.

The county attorney was looking at the cupboard—a peculiar, ungainly structure, half closet and half cupboard, the upper part of it being built in the wall, and the lower part just the old-fashioned kitchen cupboard. As if its queerness attracted him, he got a chair and opened the upper part and looked in. After a moment he drew his hand away sticky.

"Here's a nice mess," he said resentfully.

The two women had drawn nearer, and now the sheriff's wife spoke. 70

"Oh—her fruit," she said, looking to Mrs. Hale for sympathetic understanding. She turned back to the county attorney and explained: "She worried about that when it turned so cold last night. She said the fire would go out and her jars might burst."

Mrs. Peters' husband broke into a laugh.

"Well, can you beat the women! Held for murder, and worrying about her preserves!"

The young attorney set his lips.

"I guess before we're through with her she may have something more serious 75 than preserves to worry about."

"Oh, well," said Mrs. Hale's husband, with good-natured superiority, "women are used to worrying over trifles."

The two women moved a little closer together. Neither of them spoke. The county attorney seemed suddenly to remember his manners—and think of his future.

"And yet," said he, with the gallantry of a young politician. "for all their worries, what would we do without the ladies?"

The women did not speak, did not unbend. He went to the sink and began washing his hands. He turned to wipe them on the roller towel—whirled it for a cleaner place.

"Dirty towels! Not much of a housekeeper, would you say, ladies?" 80

He kicked his foot against some dirty pans under the sink.

"There's a great deal of work to be done on a farm," said Mrs. Hale stiffly.

"To be sure. And yet"—with a little bow to her—"I know there are some Dickson County farm-houses that do not have such roller towels." He gave it a pull to expose its full length again.

"Those towels get dirty awful quick. Men's hands aren't always as clean as they might be."

"Ah, loyal to your sex, I see," he laughed. He stopped and gave her a keen look. "But you and Mrs. Wright were neighbors. I suppose you were friends, too."

Martha Hale shook her head.

"I've seen little enough of her of late years. I've not been in this house—it's more than a year."

"And why was that? You didn't like her?"

"I liked her well enough," she replied with spirit. "Farmers' wives have their hands full, Mr. Henderson. And then—" She looked around the kitchen.

"Yes?" he encouraged.

"It never seemed a very cheerful place," said she, more to herself than to him.

"No," he agreed; "I don't think anyone would call it cheerful. I shouldn't say she had the home-making instinct."

"Well, I don't know as Wright had, either," she muttered.

"You mean they didn't get on very well?" he was quick to ask.

"No; I don't mean anything," she answered, with decision. As she turned a little away from him, she added: "But I don't think a place would be any the cheerfuller for John Wright's bein' in it."

"I'd like to talk to you about that a little later, Mrs. Hale," he said. "I'm anxious to get the lay of things upstairs now."

He moved toward the stair door, followed by the two men.

"I suppose anything Mrs. Peters does'll be all right?" the sheriff inquired. "She was to take in some clothes for her, you know—and a few little things. We left in such a hurry yesterday."

The county attorney looked at the two women whom they were leaving alone there among the kitchen things.

"Yes—Mrs. Peters," he said, his glance resting on the woman who was not Mrs. Peters, the big farmer woman who stood behind the sheriff's wife. "Of course Mrs. Peters is one of us," he said, in a manner of entrusting responsibility. "And keep your eye out, Mrs. Peters, for anything that might be of use. No telling; you women might come upon a clue to the motive—and that's the thing we need."

Mr. Hale rubbed his face after the fashion of a showman getting ready for a pleasantry.

"But would the women know a clue if they did come upon it?" he said; and, having delivered himself of this, he followed the others through the stair door.

The women stood motionless and silent, listening to the footsteps, first upon the stairs, then in the room above them.

Then, as if releasing herself from something strange. Mrs. Hale began to arrange the dirty pans under the sink, which the county attorney's disdainful push of the foot had deranged.

"I'd hate to have men comin' into my kitchen," she said testily—"snoopin' round and criticizin'."

"Of course it's no more than their duty," said the sheriff's wife, in her manner of timid acquiescence.

"Duty's all right," replied Mrs. Hale bluffly; "but I guess that deputy sheriff that come out to make the fire might have got a little of this on." She gave the roller towel a pull. "Wish I'd thought of that sooner! Seems mean to talk about her for not having things slicked up, when she had to come away in such a hurry."

She looked around the kitchen. Certainly it was not "slicked up." Her eye was held by a bucket of sugar on a low shelf. The cover was off the wooden bucket, and beside it was a paper bag—half full.

Mrs. Hale moved toward it.

"She was putting this in there," she said to herself—slowly. 110

She thought of the flour in her kitchen at home—half sifted, half not sifted. She had been interrupted, and had left things half done. What had interrupted Minnie Foster? Why had that work been left half done? She made a move as if to finish it,—unfinished things always bothered her,—and then she glanced around and saw that Mrs. Peters was watching her—and she didn't want Mrs. Peters to get that feeling she had got of work begun and then—for some reason—not finished.

"It's a shame about her fruit," she said, and walked toward the cupboard that the county attorney had opened, and got on the chair, murmuring: "I wonder if it's all gone."

It was a sorry enough looking sight, but "Here's one that's all right," she said at last. She held it toward the light. "This is cherries, too." She looked again. "I declare I believe that's the only one."

With a sigh, she got down from the chair, went to the sink, and wiped off the bottle.

"She'll feel awful bad, after all her hard work in the hot weather. I remember 115 the afternoon I put up my cherries last summer."

She set the bottle on the table, and, with another sigh, started to sit down in the rocker. But she did not sit down. Something kept her from sitting down in that chair. She straightened—stepped back, and, half turned away, stood looking at it, seeing the woman who had sat there "pleatin' at her apron."

The thin voice of the sheriff's wife broke in upon her: "I must be getting those things from the front-room closet." She opened the door into the other room, started in, stepped back. "You coming with me, Mrs. Hale?" she asked nervously. "You—you could help me get them."

They were soon back—the stark coldness of that shut-up room was not a thing to linger in.

"My!" said Mrs. Peters, dropping the things on the table and hurrying to the stove.

Mrs. Hale stood examining the clothes the woman who was being detained in 120 town had said she wanted.

"Wright was close!"° she exclaimed, holding up a shabby black skirt that bore the marks of much making over. "I think maybe that's why she kept so much to herself. I s'pose she felt she couldn't do her part; and then, you don't enjoy things when you feel shabby. She used to wear pretty clothes and be lively—when she was Minnie Foster, one of the town girls, singing in the choir. But that—oh, that was twenty years ago."

With a carefulness in which there was something tender, she folded the shabby clothes and piled them at one corner of the table. She looked up at Mrs. Peters, and there was something in the other woman's look that irritated her.

"She don't care," she said to herself. "Much difference it makes to her whether Minnie Foster had pretty clothes when she was a girl."

Then she looked again, and she wasn't so sure; in fact, she hadn't at any time

close: that is, frugal, tightfisted.

been perfectly sure about Mrs. Peters. She had that shrinking manner, and yet her eyes looked as if they could see a long way into things.

"This all you was to take in?" asked Mrs. Hale.

"No," said the sheriff's wife; "she said she wanted an apron. Funny thing to want," she ventured in her nervous little way, "for there's not much to get you dirty in jail, goodness knows. But I suppose just to make her feel more natural. If you're used to wearing an apron—. She said they were in the bottom drawer of this cupboard. Yes—here they are. And then her little shawl that always hung on the stair door."

She took the small gray shawl from behind the door leading upstairs, and stood a minute looking at it.

Suddenly Mrs. Hale took a quick step toward the other woman.

"Mrs. Peters!"

"Yes, Mrs. Hale?"

"Do you think she—did it?"

A frightened look blurred the other thing in Mrs. Peters' eyes.

"Oh, I don't know," she said, in a voice that seemed to shrink away from the subject.

"Well, I don't think she did," affirmed Mrs. Hale stoutly. "Asking for an apron, and her little shawl. Worryin' about her fruit."

"Mr. Peters says—." Footsteps were heard in the room above; she stopped, looked up, then went on in a lowered voice: "Mr. Peters says—it looks bad for her. Mr. Henderson is awful sarcastic in a speech, and he's going to make fun of her saying she didn't—wake up."

For a moment Mrs. Hale had no answer. Then, "Well, I guess John Wright didn't wake up—when they was slippin' that rope under his neck," she muttered.

"No, it's *strange*," breathed Mrs. Peters. "They think it was such a—funny way to kill a man."

She began to laugh; at sound of the laugh, abruptly stopped.

"That's just what Mr. Hale said," said Mrs. Hale, in a resolutely natural voice. "There was a gun in the house. He says that's what he can't understand."

"Mr. Henderson said, coming out, that what was needed for the case was a mo- tive. Something to show anger—or sudden feeling."

"Well, I don't see any signs of anger around here," said Mrs. Hale, "I don't—" She stopped. It was as if her mind tripped on something. Her eye was caught by a dish- towel in the middle of the kitchen table. Slowly she moved toward the table. One half of it was wiped clean, the other half messy. Her eyes made a slow, almost unwilling turn to the bucket of sugar and the half empty bag beside it. Things begun—and not finished.

After a moment she stepped back, and said, in that manner of releasing herself: "Wonder how they're finding things upstairs? I hope she had it a little more red up° up there. You know,"—she paused, and feeling gathered,—"it seems kind of *sneaking*: locking her up in town and coming out here to get her own house to turn against her!"

"But, Mrs. Hale," said the sheriff's wife, "the law is the law."

"I s'pose 'tis," answered Mrs. Hale shortly.

red up: neat.

She turned to the stove, saying something about that fire not being much to brag of. She worked with it a minute, and when she straightened up she said aggressively:

"The law is the law—and a bad stove is a bad stove. How'd you like to cook on this?"—pointing with the poker to the broken lining. She opened the oven door and started to express her opinion of the oven; but she was swept into her own thoughts, thinking of what it would mean, year after year, to have that stove to wrestle with. The thought of Minnie Foster trying to bake in that oven—and the thought of her never going over to see Minnie Foster—.

She was startled by hearing Mrs. Peters say: "A person gets discouraged—and loses heart."

The sheriff's wife had looked from the stove to the sink—to the pail of water which had been carried in from outside. The two women stood there silent, above them the footsteps of the men who were looking for evidence against the woman who had worked in that kitchen. That look of seeing into things, of seeing through a thing to something else, was in the eyes of the sheriff's wife now. When Mrs. Hale next spoke to her, it was gently:

"Better loosen up your things, Mrs. Peters. We'll not feel them when we go out."   150

Mrs. Peters went to the back of the room to hang up the fur tippet she was wearing. A moment later she exclaimed, "Why, she was piecing a quilt," and held up a large sewing basket piled high with quilt pieces.

Mrs. Hale spread some of the blocks on the table.

"It's log-cabin pattern," she said, putting several of them together, "Pretty, isn't it?"

They were so engaged with the quilt that they did not hear the footsteps on the stairs. Just as the stair door opened Mrs. Hale was saying:

"Do you suppose she was going to quilt it or just knot it?"   155

The sheriff threw up his hands.

"They wonder whether she was going to quilt it or just knot it!"

There was a laugh for the ways of women, a warming of hands over the stove, and then the county attorney said briskly:

"Well, let's go right out to the barn and get that cleared up."

"I don't see as there's anything so strange," Mrs. Hale said resentfully, after the   160
outside door had closed on the three men—"our taking up our time with little things while we're waiting for them to get the evidence. I don't see as it's anything to laugh about."

"Of course they've got awful important things on their minds," said the sheriff's wife apologetically.

They returned to an inspection of the block for the quilt. Mrs. Hale was looking at the fine, even sewing, and preoccupied with thoughts of the woman who had done that sewing, when she heard the sheriff's wife say, in a queer tone:

"Why, look at this one."

She turned to take the block held out to her.

"The sewing," said Mrs. Peters, in a troubled way, "All the rest of them have   165
been so nice and even—but—this one. Why, it looks as if she didn't know what she was about!"

Their eyes met—something flashed to life, passed between them; then, as if with an effort, they seemed to pull away from each other. A moment Mrs. Hale sat there, her hands folded over that sewing which was so unlike all the rest of the sewing. Then she had pulled a knot and drawn the threads.

"Oh, what are you doing, Mrs. Hale?" asked the sheriff's wife, startled.

"Just pulling out a stitch or two that's not sewed very good," said Mrs. Hale mildly.

"I don't think we ought to touch things," Mrs. Peters said, a little helplessly.

"I'll just finish up this end," answered Mrs. Hale, still in that mild, matter-of-fact fashion.

She threaded a needle and started to replace bad sewing with good. For a little while she sewed in silence. Then, in that thin, timid voice, she heard:

"Mrs. Hale!"

"Yes, Mrs. Peters?"

"What do you suppose she was so—nervous about?"

"Oh, *I* don't know," said Mrs. Hale, as if dismissing a thing not important enough to spend much time on. "I don't know as she was—nervous. I sew awful queer sometimes when I'm just tired."

She cut a thread, and out of the corner of her eye looked up at Mrs. Peters. The small, lean face of the sheriff's wife seemed to have tightened up. Her eyes had that look of peering into something. But next moment she moved, and said in her thin, indecisive way:

"Well, I must get those clothes wrapped. They may be through sooner than we think. I wonder where I could find a piece of paper—and string."

"In that cupboard, maybe," suggested to Mrs. Hale, after a glance around.

One piece of the crazy sewing remained unripped. Mrs. Peter's back turned, Martha Hale now scrutinized that piece, compared it with the dainty, accurate sewing of the other blocks. The difference was startling. Holding this block made her feel queer, as if the distracted thoughts of the woman who had perhaps turned to it to try and quiet herself were communicating themselves to her.

Mrs. Peters' voice roused her.

"Here's a bird-cage," she said. "Did she have a bird, Mrs. Hale?"

"Why, I don't know whether she did or not." She turned to look at the cage Mrs. Peters was holding up. "I've not been here in so long." She sighed. "There was a man round last year selling canaries cheap—but I don't know as she took one. Maybe she did. She used to sing real pretty herself."

Mrs. Peters looked around the kitchen.

"Seems kind of funny to think of a bird here." She half laughed—an attempt to put up a barrier. "But she must have had one—or why would she have a cage? I wonder what happened to it."

"I suppose maybe the cat got it," suggested Mrs. Hale, resuming her sewing.

"No; she didn't have a cat. She's got that feeling some people have about cats—being afraid of them. When they brought her to our house yesterday, my cat got in the room, and she was real upset and asked me to take it out."

"My sister Bessie was like that," laughed Mrs. Hale.

The sheriff's wife did not reply. The silence made Mrs. Hale turn round. Mrs. Peters was examining the bird-cage.

"Look at this door," she said slowly. "It's broke. One hinge has been pulled apart."

Mrs. Hale came nearer.   190

"Looks as if someone must have been—rough with it."

Again their eyes met—startled, questioning, apprehensive. For a moment neither spoke nor stirred. Then Mrs. Hale, turning away, said brusquely:

"If they're going to find any evidence, I wish they'd be about it. I don't like this place."

"But I'm awful glad you came with me, Mrs. Hale." Mrs. Peters put the bird-cage on the table and sat down. "It would be lonesome for me—sitting here alone."

"Yes, it would, wouldn't it?" agreed Mrs. Hale, a certain determined naturalness   195
in her voice. She had picked up the sewing, but now it dropped in her lap, and she murmured in a different voice: "But I tell you what I *do* wish, Mrs Peters. I wish I had come over sometimes when she was here. I wish—I had."

"But of course you were awful busy, Mrs. Hale. Your house—and your children."

"I could've come," retorted Mrs. Hale shortly. "I stayed away because it weren't cheerful—and that's why I ought to have come. I"—she looked around—"I've never liked this place. Maybe because it's down in a hollow and you don't see the road. I don't know what it is, but it's a lonesome place, and always was. I wish I had come over to see Minnie Foster sometimes. I can see now—" She did not put it into words.

"Well, you mustn't reproach yourself," counseled Mrs. Peters. "Somehow, we just don't see how it is with other folks till—something comes up."

"Not having children makes less work," mused Mrs. Hale, after a silence, "but it makes a quiet house—and Wright out to work all day—and no company when he did come in. Did you know John Wright, Mrs. Peters?"

"Not to know him. I've seen him in town. They say he was a good man."   200

"Yes—good," conceded John Wright's neighbor grimly. "He didn't drink, and kept his word as well as most, I guess, and paid his debts. But he was a hard man, Mrs. Peters. Just to pass the time of day with him—." She stopped, shivered a little. "Like a raw wind that gets to the bone." Her eye fell upon the cage on the table before her, and she added, almost bitterly: "I should think she would've wanted a bird!"

Suddenly she leaned forward, looking intently at the cage. "But what do you s'pose went wrong with it?"

"I don't know," returned Mrs. Peters; "unless it got sick and died."

But after she said it she reached over and swung the broken door. Both women watched it as if somehow held by it.

"You didn't know—her?" Mrs. Hale asked, a gentler note in her voice.   205

"Not till they brought her yesterday," said the sheriff's wife.

"She—come to think of it, she was kind of like a bird herself. Real sweet and pretty, but kind of timid and—fluttery. How—she—did—change."

That held her for a long time. Finally, as if struck with a happy thought and relieved to get back to everyday things, she exclaimed:

"Tell you what, Mrs. Peters, why don't you take the quilt in with you? It might take up her mind."

"Why, I think that's a real nice idea, Mrs. Hale," agreed the sheriff's wife, as if   210
she too were glad to come into the atmosphere of a simple kindness. "There couldn't possibly be any objection to that, could there? Now, just what will I take? I wonder if her patches are in here—and her things?"

They turned to the sewing basket.

"Here's some red," said Mrs. Hale, bringing out a roll of cloth. Underneath that was a box. "Here, maybe her scissors are in here—and her things." She held it up. "What a pretty box! I'll warrant that was something she had a long time ago—when she was a girl."

She held it in her hand a moment; then, with a little sigh, opened it.

Instantly her hand went to her nose.

"Why—!"

Mrs. Peters drew nearer—then turned away.

"There's something wrapped up in this piece of silk," faltered Mrs. Hale.

"This isn't her scissors," said Mrs. Peters, in a shrinking voice.

Her hand not steady, Mrs. Hale raised the piece of silk. "Oh, Mrs. Peters!" she cried. "It's—"

Mrs. Peters bent closer.

"It's the bird," she whispered.

"But, Mrs. Peters!" cried Mrs. Hale. "*Look* at it! Its *neck*—look at its neck! It's all—other side *to*."

She held the box away from her.

The sheriff's wife again bent closer.

"Somebody wrung its neck," said she, in a voice that was slow and deep.

And then again the eyes of the two women met—this time clung together in a look of dawning comprehension, of growing horror. Mrs. Peters looked from the dead bird to the broken door of the cage. Again their eyes met. And just then there was a sound at the outside door.

Mrs. Hale slipped the box under the quilt pieces in the basket, and sank into the chair before it. Mrs. Peters stood holding to the table. The county attorney and the sheriff came in from outside.

"Well, ladies," said the county attorney, as one turning from serious things to little pleasantries, "have you decided whether she was going to quilt it or knot it?"

"We think," began the sheriff's wife in a flurried voice, "that she was going to—knot it."

He was too preoccupied to notice the change that came in her voice on that last.

"Well, that's very interesting, I'm sure," he said tolerantly. He caught sight of the bird-cage. "Has the bird flown?"

"We think the cat got it," said Mrs. Hale in a voice curiously even.

He was walking up and down, as if thinking something out.

"Is there a cat?" he asked absently.

Mrs. Hale shot a look up at the sheriff's wife.

"Well, not *now*," said Mrs. Peters. "They're superstitious, you know; they leave."

She sank into her chair.

The county attorney did not heed her. "No sign at all of anyone having come in from the outside," he said to Peters, in the manner of continuing an interrupted conversation. "Their own rope. Now let's go upstairs again and go over it, piece by piece. It would have to have been someone who knew just the—"

The stair door closed behind them and their voices were lost.

The two women sat motionless, not looking at each other, but as if peering into something and at the same time holding back. When they spoke now it was as if they were afraid of what they were saying, but as if they could not help saying it.

"She liked the bird," said Martha Hale, low and slowly. "She was going to bury it in that pretty box."

"When I was a girl," said Mrs. Peters, under her breath, "my kitten—there was a boy took a hatchet, and before my eyes—before I could get there—" She covered her face an instant. "If they hadn't held me back I would have"—she caught herself, looked upstairs where footsteps were heard, and finished weakly—"hurt him."

Then they sat without speaking or moving.

"I wonder how it would seem," Mrs. Hale at last began, as if feeling her way over strange ground—"never to have had any children around?" Her eyes made a slow sweep of the kitchen, as if seeing what that kitchen had meant through all the years. "No, Wright wouldn't like the bird," she said after that—"a thing that sang. She used to sing. He killed that too." Her voice tightened.

Mrs. Peters moved uneasily.   245

"Of course we don't know who killed the bird."

"I knew John Wright," was Mrs. Hale's answer.

"It was an awful thing was done in this house that night, Mrs. Hale," said the sheriff's wife. "Killing a man while he slept—slipping a thing round his neck that choked the life out of him."

Mrs. Hale's hand went out to the bird cage.

"His neck. Choked the life out of him."   250

"We don't *know* who killed him," whispered Mrs. Peters wildly. "We don't *know*."

Mrs. Hale had not moved. "If there had been years and years of—nothing, then a bird to sing to you, it would be awful—still—after the bird was still."

It was as if something within her not herself had spoken, and it found in Mrs. Peters something she did not know as herself.

"I know what stillness is," she said, in a queer, monotonous voice. "When we homesteaded in Dakota, and my first baby died—after he was two years old—and me with no other then—"

Mrs. Hale stirred.   255

"How soon do you suppose they'll be through looking for the evidence?"

"I know what stillness is," repeated Mrs. Peters, in just that same way. Then she too pulled back. "The law has got to punish crime, Mrs. Hale," she said in her tight little way.

"I wish you'd seen Minnie Foster," was the answer, "when she wore a white dress with blue ribbons, and stood up there in the choir and sang."

The picture of that girl, the fact that she had lived neighbor to that girl for twenty years, and had let her die for lack of life, was suddenly more than she could bear.

"Oh, I *wish* I'd come over here once in a while!" she cried. "That was a crime!   260
Who's going to punish that?"

"We mustn't take on," said Mrs. Peters, with a frightened look toward the stairs.

"I might 'a' *known* she needed help! I tell you, it's *queer*, Mrs. Peters. We live close together, and we live far apart. We all go through the same things—it's all just a different kind of the same thing! If it weren't—why do you and I *understand?* Why do we *know*—what we know this minute?"

She dashed her hand across her eyes. Then, seeing the jar of fruit on the table, she reached for it and choked out:

"If I was you I wouldn't *tell* her her fruit was gone! Tell her it *ain't*. Tell her it's all right—all of it. Here—take this in to prove it to her! She—she may never know whether it was broke or not."

She turned away.   265

Mrs. Peters reached out for the bottle of fruit as if she were glad to take it—as if touching a familiar thing, having something to do, could keep her from something else. She got up, looked about for something to wrap the fruit in, took a petticoat from the pile of clothes she had brought from the front room, and nervously started winding that round the bottle.

"My!" she began, in a high, false voice, "it's a good thing the men couldn't hear us! Getting all stirred up over a little thing like a—dead canary." She hurried over that. "As if that could have anything to do with—with—My, wouldn't they *laugh?*"

Footsteps were heard on the stairs.

"Maybe they would," muttered Mrs. Hale—"maybe they wouldn't."

"No, Peters," said the county attorney incisively; "it's all perfectly clear, except the reason for doing it. But you know juries when it comes to women. If there was some definite thing—something to show. Something to make a story about. A thing that would connect up with this clumsy way of doing it."

In a covert way Mrs. Hale looked at Mrs. Peters. Mrs. Peters was looking at her. Quickly they looked away from each other. The outer door opened and Mr. Hale came in.

"I've got the team° round now," he said. "Pretty cold out there."

"I'm going to stay here awhile by myself," the county attorney suddenly announced. "You can send Frank out for me, can't you?" he asked the sheriff. "I want to go over everything. I'm not satisfied we can't do better."

Again, for one brief moment, the two women's eyes found one another.

The sheriff came up to the table.

"Did you want to see what Mrs. Peters was going to take in?"

The county attorney picked up the apron. He laughed.

"Oh, I guess they're not very dangerous things the ladies have picked out."

Mrs. Hale's hand was on the sewing basket in which the box was concealed. She felt that she ought to take her hand off the basket. She did not seem able to. He picked up one of the quilt blocks which she had piled on to cover the box. Her eyes felt like fire. She had a feeling that if he took up the basket she would snatch it from him.

But he did not take it up. With another little laugh, he turned away, saying:

"No; Mrs. Peters doesn't need supervising. For that matter, a sheriff's wife is married to the law. Ever think of it that way, Mrs. Peters?"

Mrs. Peters was standing beside the table. Mrs. Hale shot a look up at her; but she could not see her face. Mrs. Peters had turned away. When she spoke, her voice was muffled.

"Not—just that way," she said.

"Married to the law!" chuckled Mrs. Peters' husband. He moved toward the door into the front room, and said to the county attorney:

"I just want you to come in here a minute, George. We ought to take a look at these windows."

"Oh—windows," said the county attorney scoffingly.

"We'll be right out, Mr. Hale," said the sheriff to the farmer, who was still waiting by the door.

Hale went to look after the horses. The sheriff followed the county attorney into

team: team of horses pulling the buggy in which the group had come.

the other room. Again—for one final moment—the two women were alone in that kitchen.

Martha Hale sprang up, her hands tight together, looking at that other woman, with whom it rested. At first she could not see her eyes, for the sheriff's wife had not turned back since she turned away at that suggestion of being married to the law. But now Mrs. Hale made her turn back. Her eyes made her turn back. Slowly, unwillingly, Mrs. Peters turned her head until her eyes met the eyes of the other woman. There was a moment when they held each other in a steady, burning look in which there was no evasion nor flinching. Then Martha Hale's eyes pointed the way to the basket in which was hidden the thing that would make certain the conviction of the other woman—that woman who was not there and yet who had been there with them all through that hour.

For a moment Mrs. Peters did not move. And then she did it. With a rush forward, she threw back the quilt pieces, got the box, tried to put it in her handbag. It was too big. Desperately she opened it, started to take the bird out. But there she broke—she could not touch the bird. She stood there helpless, foolish.   290

There was the sound of a knob turning in the inner door. Martha Hale snatched the box from the sheriff's wife, and got it in the pocket of her big coat just as the sheriff and the county attorney came back into the kitchen.

"Well, Henry," said the county attorney facetiously, "at least we found out that she was not going to quilt it. She was going to—what is it you call it, ladies?"

Mrs. Hale's hand was against the pocket of her coat.

"We call it—knot it, Mr. Henderson."

QUESTIONS

1. Who is the central character? That is, on whom does the story focus?
2. Describe the differences between Mrs. Hale and Mrs. Peters, in terms of their status, backgrounds, and comparative strengths of character.
3. Why do the two women not voice their conclusions about the murderer? How does Glaspell show that they both know the murderer's identity, the reasons, and the method? Why do they both "cover up" at the story's conclusion?

JAMES THURBER (1894–1961)

Thurber was born in Ohio and made his reputation as a writer and cartoonist with The New Yorker. *Late in his life he was troubled with increasing blindness. His stories and drawings are often centered upon quiet, unassuming men yearning to free themselves from the shackles that inhibit their "freedom." Ironically, "The Greatest Man in the World" gives us a view of an individual from an opposite viewpoint. The major character, Jacky Smurch, wishes to assert himself in the world, much like Walter Mitty and Erwin Martin in the stories "The Secret Life of Walter Mitty" and "The Catbird Seat." But, unlike these fellow Thurber characters who remain private, Smurch is thrust into public prominence, and his private wishes are measured against standards of publicly acceptable behavior.*

The Greatest Man in the World ————————————————— *1935*

Looking back on it now, from the vantage point of 1950, one can only marvel that it hadn't happened long before it did. The United States of America had been, even since Kitty Hawk,° blindly constructing the elaborate petard by which, sooner or later, it must be hoist.° It was inevitable that some day there would come roaring out of the skies a national hero of insufficient intelligence, background, and character successfully to endure the mounting orgies of glory prepared for aviators who stayed up a long time or flew a great distance. Both Lindbergh° and Byrd,° fortunately for national decorum and international amity, had been gentlemen; so had our other famous aviators. They wore their laurels gracefully, withstood the awful weather of publicity, married excellent women, usually of fine family, and quietly retired to private life and the enjoyment of their varying fortunes. No untoward incidents, on a worldwide scale, marred the perfection of their conduct on the perilous heights of fame. The exception to the rule was, however, bound to occur and it did, in July, 1937, when Jack ("Pal") Smurch, erstwhile mechanics' helper in a small garage in Westfield, Iowa, flew a second-hand, single-motored Bresthaven Dragon-Fly III monoplane all the way around the world, without stopping.

Never before in the history of aviation had such a flight as Smurch's ever been dreamed of. No one had even taken seriously the weird floating auxiliary gas tanks, invention of the mad New Hampshire professor of astronomy, Dr. Charles Lewis Gresham, upon which Smurch placed full reliance. When the garage worker, a slightly built, surly, unprepossessing young man of twenty-two appeared at Roosevelt Field in early July, 1937, slowly chewing a great quid of scrap tobacco, and announced "Nobody ain't seen no flyin' yet," the newspapers touched briefly and satirically upon his projected twenty-five-thousand-mile flight. Aeronautical and automotive experts dismissed the idea curtly, implying that it was a hoax, a publicity stunt. The rusty, battered, second-hand plane wouldn't go. The Gresham auxiliary tanks wouldn't work. It was simply a cheap joke.

Smurch, however, after calling on a girl in Brooklyn who worked in the flap-folding department of a large paper-box factory, a girl whom he later described as his "sweet patootie," climbed nonchalantly into his ridiculous plane at dawn of the memorable seventh of July, 1937, spat a curve of tobacco juice into the still air, and took off, carrying with him only a gallon of bootleg gin and six pounds of salami.

When the garage boy thundered out over the ocean the papers were forced to record, in all seriousness, that a mad, unknown young man—his name was variously misspelled—had actually set out upon a preposterous attempt to span the world in a rickety, one-engined contraption, trusting to the long-distance refueling device of a crazy schoolmaster. When, nine days later, without having stopped once, the tiny place appeared above San Francisco Bay, headed for New York, spluttering and chok-

----

Kitty Hawk: in North Carolina, the location of the first heavier-than-air flight by the Wright brothers in 1903.
   petard . . . hoist: that is, to be destroyed by one's own cleverness. See *Hamlet*, Act III, scene iv, lines 206–207.
   Lindbergh: Charles A. Lindbergh (1902–1974), considered to be America's greatest aviation hero, made the first solo trans-Atlantic flight in May 1927.
   Byrd: Richard E. Byrd, "Admiral Byrd" (1888–1957), made the first flight to the North Pole in 1926, and the first airmail flight to France in June 1927.

ing, to be sure, but still magnificently and miraculously aloft, the headlines, which long since had crowded everything else off the front page—even the shooting of the Governor of Illinois by the Vileti gang—swelled to unprecedented size, and the news stories began to run to twenty-five and thirty columns. It was noticeable, however, that the accounts of the epoch-making flight touched rather lightly upon the aviator himself. This was not because facts about the hero as a man were too meagre, but because they were too complete.

Reporters, who had been rushed out to Iowa when Smurch's plane was first sighted over the little French coast town of Serly-le-Mar, to dig up the story of the great man's life, had promptly discovered that the story of his life could not be printed. His mother, a sullen short-order cook in a shack restaurant on the edge of a tourists' camping ground near Westfield, met all enquiries as to her son with an angry, "Ah, the hell with him; I hope he drowns." His father appeared to be in jail somewhere for stealing spotlights and laprobes from tourists' automobiles; his younger brother, a weak-minded lad, had but recently escaped from the Preston, Iowa Reformatory and was already wanted in several Western towns for the theft of money-order blanks from post offices. These alarming discoveries were still piling up at the very time that Pal Smurch, the greatest hero of the twentieth century, blear-eyed, dead for sleep, half-starved, was piloting his crazy junk-heap high above the region in which the lamentable story of his private life was being unearthed, headed for New York under greater glory than any man of his time had ever known.

The necessity for printing some account in the papers of the young man's career and personality had led to a remarkable predicament. It was of course impossible to reveal the facts, for a tremendous popular feeling in favor of the young hero had sprung up, like a grass fire, when he was halfway across Europe on his flight around the globe. He was, therefore, described as a modest chap, taciturn, blond, popular with his friends, popular with girls. The only available snapshot of Smurch, taken at the wheel of a phony automobile in a cheap photo studio at an amusement park, was touched up so that the little vulgarian looked quite handsome. His twisted leer was smoothed into a pleasant smile. The truth was, in this way, kept from the youth's ecstatic compatriots; they did not dream that the Smurch family was despised and feared by its neighbors in the obscure Iowa town, nor that the hero himself, because of numerous unsavory exploits, had come to be regarded in Westfield as a nuisance and a menace. He had, the reporters discovered, once knifed the principal of his high school—not mortally, to be sure, but he had knifed him; and on another occasion, surprised in the act of stealing an altar-cloth from a church, he had bashed the sacristan over the head with a pot of Easter lilies; for each of these offences he had served a sentence in the reformatory.

Inwardly, the authorities, both in New York and in Washington, prayed that an understanding Providence might, however awful such a thing seemed, bring disaster to the rusty, battered plane and its illustrious pilot, whose unheard-of flight had aroused the civilized world to hosannas of hysterical praise. The authorities were convinced that the character of the renowned aviator was such that the limelight of adulation was bound to reveal him to all the world, as a congenital hooligan mentally and morally unequipped to cope with his own prodigious fame. "I trust," said the Secretary of State, at one of many secret Cabinet meetings called to consider the national dilemma, "I trust that his mother's prayer will be answered," by which he referred to Mrs. Emma Smurch's wish that her son might be drowned. It was, however, too late for that—Smurch had leaped the Atlantic and then the Pacific as if they were millponds. At three minutes after two o'clock in the afternoon of 17 July, 1937, the garage boy brought his idiotic plane into Roosevelt Field for a perfect three-point landing.

It had, of course, been out of the question to arrange a modest little reception for the greatest flier in the history of the world. He was received at Roosevelt Field with such elaborate and pretentious ceremonies as rocked the world. Fortunately, however, the worn and spent hero promptly swooned, had to be removed bodily from his plane, and was spirited from the field without having opened his mouth once. Thus he did not jeopardize the dignity of this first reception, a reception illuminated by the presence of the Secretaries of War and the Navy, Mayor Michael J. Moriarity of New York, the Premier of Canada, Governors Fanniman, Groves, McFeely, and Critchfield, and a brilliant array of European diplomats. Smurch did not, in fact, come to in time to take part in the gigantic hullabaloo arranged at City Hall for the next day. He was rushed to a secluded nursing home and confined to bed. It was nine days before he was able to get up, or to be more exact, before he was permitted to get up. Meanwhile the greatest minds in the country, in solemn assembly, had arranged a secret conference of city, state and government officials, which Smurch was to attend for the purpose of being instructed in the ethics and behavior of heroism.

On the day that the little mechanic was finally allowed to get up and dress and, for the first time in two weeks, took a great chew of tobacco, he was permitted to receive the newspapermen—this by way of testing him out. Smurch did not wait for questions. "Youse guys," he said—and the *Times* man winced—"youse guys can tell the cock-eyed world dat I put it over on Lindbergh, see? Yeh—an' made an ass o' them two frogs." The "two frogs" was a reference to a pair of gallant French fliers who, in attempting a flight only halfway round the world, had, two weeks before, unhappily been lost at sea. The *Times* man was bold enough, at this point, to sketch out for Smurch the accepted formula for interviews in cases of this kind; he explained that there should be no arrogant statements belittling the achievements of other heroes, particularly heroes of foreign nations. "Ah, the hell with that," said Smurch. "I did it, see? I did it, an' I'm talkin' about it." And he did talk about it.

None of this extraordinary interview was, of course, printed. On the contrary, the newspapers, already under the disciplined direction of a secret directorate created for the occasion and composed of statesmen and editors, gave out to a panting and restless world that "Jacky," as he had been arbitrarily nicknamed, would consent to say only that he was very happy and that anyone could have done what he did. "My achievement has been, I fear, slightly exaggerated," the *Times* man's article had him protest, with a modest smile. These newspaper stories were kept from the hero, a restriction which did not serve to abate the rising malevolence of his temper. The situation was, indeed, extremely grave, for Pal Smurch was, as he kept insisting, "rarin' to go." He could not much longer be kept from a nation clamorous to lionize him. It was the most desperate crisis the United States of America had faced since the sinking of the *Lusitania.*°

On the afternoon of the twenty-seventh of July, Smurch was spirited away to a conference-room in which were gathered mayors, governors, government officials, behaviorist psychologists, and editors. He gave them each a limp, moist paw and a brief

---

Lusitania: British liner sunk by a German submarine in 1915. More than a thousand people were killed, including 128 Americans.

unlovely grin. "Hah ya?"° he said. When Smurch was seated, the Mayor of New York arose and, with obvious pessimism, attempted to explain what he must say and how he must act when presented to the world, ending his talk with a high tribute to the hero's courage and integrity. The Mayor was followed by Governor Fanniman of New York, who, after a touching declaration of faith, introduced Cameron Spottiswood, Second Secretary of the American Embassy in Paris, the gentlemen selected to coach Smurch in the amenities of public ceremonies. Sitting in a chair, with a soiled yellow tie in his hand and his shirt open at the throat, unshaved, smoking a rolled cigarette, Jack Smurch listened with a leer on his lips. "I get ya, I get ya," he cut in nastily. "Ya want me to ack like a softy, huh? Ya want me to ack like that—baby-faced Lindbergh, huh? Well, nuts to that, see?" Everyone took in his breath sharply; it was a sigh and a hiss. "Mr. Lindbergh," began a United States Senator, purple with rage, "and Mr. Byrd—" Smurch, who was paring his nails with a jacknife, cut in again, "Byrd!" he exclaimed. "Aw fa God's sake, dat big—" Somebody shut off his blasphemies with a sharp word. A newcomer had entered the room. Everyone stood up, except Smurch, who, still busy with his nails, did not even glance up. "Mr. Smurch," said someone sternly, "the President of the United States!" It had been thought that the presence of the Chief Executive might have a chastening effect upon the young hero, and the former had been, thanks to the remarkable co-operation of the press, secretly brought to the obscure conference room.

A great, painful silence fell. Smurch looked up, waved a hand at the President. "How ya comin?" he asked, and began rolling a fresh cigarette. The silence deepened. Someone coughed in a strained way. "Geez it's hot, ain't it?" said Smurch. He loosened two more shirt buttons, revealing a hairy chest and the tattooed word "Sadie" enclosed in a stenciled heart. The great and important men in the room, faced by the most serious crisis in recent American history, exchanged worried frowns. Nobody seemed to know how to proceed. "Come awn, come awn," said Smurch. "Let's get the hell out of here! When do I start cuttin' in on de parties, huh? And what's they goin' to be *in* it?" He rubbed a thumb and a forefinger together meaningly. "Money!" exclaimed a state senator, shocked, pale. "Yeh, money," said Pal, flipping his cigarette out of a window, "an' big money." He began rolling a fresh cigarette. "Big money," he repeated, frowning over the rice paper. He tilted back in his chair, and leered at each gentlemen, separately, the leer of an animal that knows its power, the leer of a leopard loose in a bird-and-dog shop. "Aw, fa God's sake, let's get some place where it's cooler," he said. "I been cooped up plenty for three weeks!"

Smurch stood up and walked over to an open window, where he stood staring down into the street, nine floors below. The faint shouting of newsboys floated up to him. He made out his name. "Hot dog!" he cried, grinning, ecstatic. He leaned out over the sill. "You tell 'em, babies!" he shouted down. "Hot diggity dog!" In the tense little knot of men standing behind him, a quick, mad impulse flared up. An unspoken word of appeal, of command, seemed to ring through the room. Yet it was deadly silent. Charles K. I. Brand, secretary to the Mayor of New York City, happened to be standing nearest Smurch; he looked inquiringly at the President of the United States. The President, pale, grim, nodded shortly. Brand, a tall, powerfully built man, once a tackle at Rutgers, stepped forward, seized the greatest man in the world by his left shoulder and the seat of his pants, and pushed him out of the window.

Hah ya: "How are you?"

"My God, he's fallen out the window!" cried a quick-witted editor.

"Get me out of here!" cried the President. Several men sprang to his side and he was hurriedly escorted out of a door toward a side-entrance of the building. The editor of the Associated Press took charge, being used to such things. Crisply he ordered certain men to leave, others to stay; quickly he outlined a story which all the papers were to agree on, sent two men to the street to handle that end of the tragedy, commanded a Senator to sob and two Congressmen to go to pieces nervously. In a word, he skillfully set the stage for the gigantic task that was to follow, the task of breaking to a grief-stricken world the sad story of the untimely, accidental death of its most illustrious and spectacular figure.

The funeral was, as you know, the most elaborate, the finest, the solemnest, and the saddest ever held in the United States of America. The monument in Arlington Cemetery, with its clean white shaft of marble and the simple device of a tiny plane on its base, is a place for pilgrims, in deep reverence, to visit. The nations of the world paid lofty tributes to little Jacky Smurch, America's greatest hero. At a given hour there were two minutes of silence throughout the nation. Even the inhabitants of the small, bewildered town of Westfield, Iowa, observed this touching ceremony; agents of the Department of Justice saw to that. One of them was especially assigned to stand grimly in the doorway of a little shack restaurant on the edge of the tourists' camping ground just outside the town. There, under his stern scrutiny, Mrs. Emma Smurch bowed her head above two hamburger steaks sizzling on her grill—bowed her head and turned away, so that the Secret Service man could not see the twisted, strangely familiar, leer on her lips.

QUESTIONS

1. Describe Jacky Smurch. What do you learn about him from his actions, the words of others, and his statements? Is he flat or round?
2. How probable is it that a person in Smurch's position would refuse to undergo the changes required of his new success? How probable that someone would push him out the window if he didn't? From your answers, what conclusions can you make about the story's level of realism?
3. Describe the humor of the story. What does Thurber ask you to laugh at? How is the laughter produced? How is the conflict linked to the humor?
4. What serious purpose underlies the story? To what degree is it true that public relations require people to adjust their character to what is expected of them? What might happen if politicians, for example, did not scrupulously control the "image" they project before the public?

WRITING ABOUT CHARACTERS

Usually you will write about a major character, although you might also study a minor character or characters. After your customary overview, begin taking notes. List as many traits as you can, and also determine how the author presents details about the character; that is, actions, appearance, speeches, comments by others, authorial explanations. If there are unusual traits, determine what they show.

Questions for Discovering Ideas

- Describe the importance of the character to the story's principal action. Is the character the protagonist or antagonist?
- How do the protagonist and antagonist interact with each other? How do their qualities produce reactions and changes?
- What actions bring out important traits of the character? To what degree is the character *creating* or just *responding* to events?
- Characterize the protagonist's actions: Are they good or bad, intelligent or stupid, deliberate or spontaneous? How do they help you understand the protagonist?
- Characterize the character's traits, both major and minor. To what extent do the traits permit you to judge the character? What is your judgment?
- What descriptions (if any) of the character's appearance do you discover in the story? What does the appearance demonstrate about the character?
- In what ways is the character's major trait a strength—or a weakness? As the story progresses, to what degree does the trait become more (or less) prominent?
- Is the character round (dynamic)? How does the character recognize, change with, or adjust to circumstances?
- If the character is minor (flat or static), what function does he or she perform in the story (for example, by doing a task, or by bringing out qualities of the major character)?
- If a character is a stereotype, to what type does he or she belong? To what degree does the character stay in the stereotypical role or rise above it? How?
- What do any of the other characters do, say, or think to give you insight into the character? What does the character say or think about himself or herself? What does the storyteller or narrator say? How valid are their comments and insights? How helpful in providing insights into the character?
- Is the character lifelike or unreal? Consistent or inconsistent? Believable or not believable?

Strategies for Organizing Ideas

Consider one of the following approaches to organize your ideas:

1. *Organization around central traits or major characteristics,* such as "unquestioning devotion and service" (Phoenix of "A Worn Path") or "the habit of seeing the world only on one's own terms" (Miss Brill of "Miss Brill," Snopes of "Barn Burning"). This kind of structure would show how the work embodies the trait. For example, a trait may be brought out, in one part, through speeches that characters make about the major character (as at the end of Mansfield's "Miss Brill"), and in another part through that character's own speeches and actions. Studying the trait thus enables you to focus on the differing ways in which the author presents the character, and it also enables you to focus on separate parts of the work.

2. *Organization around a character's growth or change.* Such an essay would describe a character's traits at the story's opening, and then analyze changes or developments. *It is important to stress the actual alterations as they emerge, but at the same time to avoid retelling the story.* It is also important not only to describe the changing traits, but also to analyze how they are brought out within the work (such as the narrator's desire to reconnect himself with his own Indian identity in Whitecloud's "Blue Winds Dancing," or Minnie Wright's action to overcome her long ordeal).

3. *Organization around central actions, objects, or quotations that reveal primary characteristics.* Certain key incidents may stand out, along with objects closely associated with the character being analyzed. There may be key quotations spoken by the character or by someone else in the work. Show how the things you choose serve as signposts or keys to understanding the character. See the sample essay for an illustration of this type of development.

4. *Organization around qualities of a flat character or characters.* If the character is flat (such as the sisters in "Barn Burning" or the cowboy in "The Blue Hotel"), your essay might develop topics like the function and relative significance of the character, the group the character represents, the relationship of the flat character to the round ones, the importance of this relationship, and any additional qualities or traits. For a flat character you should explain the circumstances or defects that keep the character from being round, and the importance of these shortcomings in the author's presentation of human character.

In the conclusion, you might show how the character's traits are related to the work as a whole. If the person was good but came to a bad end, does this misfortune make him or her seem especially worthy? If the person suffers, does this fact suggest any attitudes about the class or type of which he or she is a part? Or does it illustrate the author's general view of human life? Or both? Do the characteristics explain why the person helps or hinders other characters? How does your essay help in clearing up first-reading misunderstandings? These and similar questions are appropriate for your conclusion.

SAMPLE ESSAY

The Character of Minnie Wright in Glaspell's "A Jury of Her Peers"°

[1]   Minnie Wright is Susan Glaspell's major character in "A Jury of Her Peers." We learn about her, however, not from seeing and hearing her, for she does not act or speak, but rather from the secondhand evidence provided by the major characters. Lewis Hale, the neighboring farmer, tells about Minnie's behavior on the morning when her husband, John, was found strangled in his bed. Martha Hale, Hale's wife, tells about Minnie's young womanhood and

° For the text of this story, see pp. 155–69.

about how she became alienated from her nearest neighbors because of John's stingy and unfriendly ways. Both Martha and Mrs. Peters, the Sheriff's wife, make observations about her based on the condition of her kitchen. From this information we get a full portrait of Minnie, who has changed from passivity to destructive assertiveness.* Her change in character is indicated by her clothing, her dead canary, and her unfinished patchwork quilt.†

[2]

The clothes that Minnie has worn in the past and in the present indicate her character as a person of charm who has withered under neglect and contempt. Martha mentions Minnie's attractive and colorful dresses as a young woman, even recalling a white dress with blue ribbons (¶ 258). Martha also recalls that Minnie, when young, was "sweet and pretty, but kind of timid and—fluttery" (¶ 208). In the light of these recollections, Martha observes that Minnie had changed, and changed for the worse, during her twenty years of marriage with John Wright, who is characterized as a "raw wind that gets to the bone" (¶ 202). As more evidence for Minnie's acceptance of her drab life, Mrs. Peters says that Minnie asks for no more than an apron and shawl when under arrest in the sheriff's home. This modest clothing, as contrasted with the colorful dresses of her youth, suggests her suppression of spirit.

[3]

Minnie's dead canary, however, while indicating her love of music, also shows the end of her suppression and the emergence of her rage. For nineteen years of marriage Minnie endures her cheerless farm home, the contempt of her husband, her life of solitude, the abandonment of her early enjoyment of singing, a general lack of pretty things, and the recognition that she could not share the social life of the local farm women as an equal. But her buying the canary (¶ 183) suggests the reemergence of her love of song, just as it also suggests her growth toward self-assertion. That her husband wrings the bird's neck may thus be seen as the cause not only of immediate grief (shown by the dead bird in a "pretty box" (¶¶ 214–226) but also of the anger that marks her change from a stock, obedient wife to a person angry enough to kill.

[4]

Like her love of song, her unfinished quilt indicates her creativity. In twenty years on the farm, never having had children, she has nothing creative to do except for needlework like the quilt. Mrs. Hale comments on the beauty of Minnie's log-cabin design (¶ 154), and observes the colorful patches of cloth in her sewing basket (¶ 213). The inference is that even though Minnie's life has been bleak, she has been able to indulge her characteristic love of color and form—and also of warmth, granted the purpose of a quilt.

[5]

Ironically, the quilt also shows Minnie's creativity in the murder of her husband. Both Mrs. Hale and Mrs. Peters interpret the breakdown of her stitching on the quilt as signs of distress about the dead canary and also of her nervousness in planning revenge (¶ 166). Further, even though nowhere in the story is it said that John is strangled with a quilting knot, no other conclusion is possible. Both Mrs. Hale and Mrs. Peters agree that Minnie probably intended to knot the quilt rather than sew it in a quilt stitch, and Glaspell pointedly causes the men to learn this detail also, even though they scoff at it and ignore it. In other words, we learn that Minnie's only outlet for creativity—

* Central idea
† Thesis sentence

needlework—has enabled her to perform the murder in the only way she can, by strangling John with a slip-proof quilting knot. Even though her plan for the murder is deliberate (Mrs. Peters reports that the arrangement of the rope was "a funny way to kill" [¶ 137]), Minnie is not cold or remorseless. Her passivity after the crime demonstrates that planning to evade guilt, beyond simple denial, is not in her character. She is not so diabolically creative that she plans or even understands the irony of strangling her husband just as he killed the bird by wringing its neck. Glaspell, however, has made the irony plain.

[6]

It is important to emphasize again that we learn about Minnie from others. Indeed, Glaspell describes her as "that woman who was not there and yet who had been there with them all through that hour" (¶ 290). Undeniably, then, Minnie is fully realized, round, and poignant. For the greater part of her adult life, she has been representative of women whose capacities for growth and expression are stunted by the grind of life and the cruelty and insensitivity of others. She patiently accepts her drab and colorless marriage that is so different from her youthful expectations. Amid the dreary farm surroundings, she suppresses her grudges, just as she suppresses her prettiness, colorfulness, and creativity. In short, she has been nothing more than a flat character. But the killing of the canary causes her to change and to destroy her husband in an assertive rejection of her stock role as the suffering wife. She is a patient woman whose patience finally reaches the breaking point.

Commentary on the Essay

The strategy of this essay is to use details from the story to support the central idea that Minnie Wright is a round, developing character. Hence the essay illustrates one of the types in the third approach described on p. 176. Other plans of organization could also have been chosen, such as the qualities of acquiescence, fortitude, and potential for anger (no. 1), the change in Minnie from submission to vengefulness (no. 2), or the reported actions of Minnie's singing, knotting quilts, and sitting in the kitchen on the morning after the murder (another type of no. 3).

Because of the unusual fact that Minnie does not appear in the story, but is described only in the words of the major characters, the introductory paragraph deals with the way information is given about her. The essay thus highlights how Glaspell uses methods 2 and 4 (see page 176) as the ways of rendering the story's main character, while omitting methods 1 and 3.

The body is developed through inferences made from details in the story, namely Minnie's clothing (paragraph 2), her canary (3), and her quilt (4 and 5). The last paragraph, 6, summarizes a number of these details, and it also considers how Minnie transcends the stock qualities of her role as a farm wife, and gains roundness as a result of this outbreak.

WRITING TOPICS

1. Compare the ways in which actions (or speeches, or the comments of others) are used to bring out the character traits of Sarty of "Barn Burning" and Fritz of "Firing Squad."

2. Write a brief essay comparing the changes or developments of two major or *round* characters in stories included in this chapter. You might deal with issues such as what the characters are like at the beginning, what conflicts they confront, deal with, or avoid, what qualities are brought out which signal the changes or developments, and so on.

3. Compare the qualities and functions of two or more *flat* characters (e.g., the narrator's father in "Firing Squad," the twins in "Barn Burning"). How do they bring out qualities of the major characters? What do you discover about their own character traits?

4. Topics for brief essays:

    a. Why does Jacky Smurch not try to fit the role of "The Greatest Man in the World"? Does this absence of change make him a flat character? Consider the possibility that his absence of change indicates the roundness of his character.

    b. Why does Abner Snopes burn barns? What qualities of character do these actions reveal? In the light of your assessment of his character, how might Abner justify to himself his role as an arsonist?

    c. Consider this proposition: To friends who haven't seen us for a time, we are round, but to ourselves and most other people, we are flat.

5. Using Sarty, Minnie Wright, and Fritz as examples, describe the effects of circumstance on character. Under the rubric "circumstance" you may consider elements such as education, family, economic and social status, wartime conditions, and geographic isolation.

6. Write a brief story about an important decision you have made (e.g., picking a school, beginning or leaving a job, declaring a major, ending a friendship, etc.). Show how your own qualities of character (to the extent that you understand them), together with your own experiences, have gone into the decision. You may write more comfortably if you give yourself another name and describe your actions in the third person.

Point of View: The Position or Stance of the Narrator or Speaker

Point of View refers to the position and stance of the **voice**, or **speaker**, that authors adopt for their works. It supposes a living **narrator** or **persona** who tells stories, presents arguments, or expresses attitudes such as love, anger, or excitement. Practically, point of view involves the actual physical location of this speaker and his or her position to see and record the main actions and ideas. More abstractly and psychologically, point of view may be considered as the centralizing or guiding intelligence in a work—the mind that filters the fictional experience and presents only the most important details to create the maximum possible impact. It may also be considered as a way of seeing, the perspective into which the work of art is cast. As we noted in Chapter 3, Claude Lorrain's painting *Seaport with the Setting Sun* (p. 90) puts all the buildings, ships, landscape, and foreground figures into the perspective of the distant sun's mysterious glow. By contrast, Matisse's *Harmony in Red / La desserte* (p. 45) abandons the illusion of three dimensions while creating a perspective in which all the objects—chair, table, designs, still life, woman, wall, and window view—are dominated not by dimensionality but rather by the color red.

Bear in mind that authors, like painters, try not only to make their works vital and interesting, but also to bring their *presentations* alive. The situation is like that of actors performing a play: The actors are always themselves, but in their roles they *impersonate* the characters they act, and temporarily *become* them.

Authors, too, impersonate characters who do the talking, with the difference that authors also *create* these impersonations, like Sammy of Updike's "A & P," the young man in Anderson's "I'm a Fool," and the unnamed speaker of Hawthorne's "Young Goodman Brown." Thus Updike creates Sammy as a real person telling readers about an important event in his own life. We read Sammy's words, and we know that Sammy is a distinct though fictional character, but because Updike is the author we know that Updike is the one putting the words in Sammy's mouth. Unlike Sammy, Hawthorne's speaker tells a story about someone else, and is not easily separated from the author, even though the words we read may be different from those that Hawthorne himself might have chosen to use in his own person. The speaker is Hawthorne's authorial *creation* or *impersonation* for "Young Goodman Brown."

AN EXERCISE IN POINT OF VIEW: REPORTING AN ACCIDENT

As an exercise to show that point of view is derived from lifelike situations, let us imagine that there has been an accident; two cars, driven by Alice and Bill, have collided. How might this accident be reported by a number of people? What would Alice say? What would Bill say?

Now assume that Frank, who is Bill's best friend, and Mary, who knows neither Bill nor Alice, were witnesses. What might Frank say about who was responsible? What might Mary say? Further, assume that you are a reporter for a local newspaper, and are sent to report on the accident. You know none of the people involved. How will your report differ from the other reports? And finally, to what degree are all the statements designed to persuade listeners and readers of the correctness of the details and claims made in the respective reports?

The differences in the various accident reports may be explained in terms of point of view. Obviously, because both Alice and Bill are deeply involved—each of them is a major participant, or what may be called a *major mover*—they will arrange their words to make themselves seem blameless. Frank, because he is Bill's best friend, will likely report things in Bill's favor. Mary will favor neither Alice nor Bill, but let us assume that she did not look at the colliding cars until she heard the crash; therefore her report will be restricted because she did not *actually see* everything. Most likely, *your* account as an impartial reporter will be the most reliable and objective of all, because your major interest is to learn all the details and report the truth accurately, with no concern about the personal interests of either Alice or Bill.

Above all, however, each person's report will have the "hidden agenda" of making herself or himself seem honest, objective, intelligent, impartial, and thorough. The ramifications of telling a story are far reaching, and the consideration of the various interests and situations can become quite subtle. On the one hand, point of view is intertwined with the many interests and wishes of humanity at large, and, on the other, it is linked to the enormous difficulty of uncovering and determining truth.

CONDITIONS THAT AFFECT POINT OF VIEW

Point of view depends on two major factors. First is *the situation of the narrator as an observer.* How much is she or he privileged to know? How accurate and complete is his or her observation? What are the narrator's particular qualifications or limitations to be an observer or commentator? Second is *the narrator's closeness, distance, and involvement in the actions.* From what position, both physical and psychological, does the narrator observe the action? Are the narrator's words colored by any particular interest or direct involvement in the action itself or in the outcome? Does the narrator seem to have any persuasive purpose, beyond serving as the recorder or observer? In a story, the author develops point of view in light of these same considerations. Anderson's speaker in "I'm a Fool" is a young man filled with regrets about having lied to a young woman he truly loves. Munro's speaker in "Meneseteung" declares the wish to "rescue" the memories of long-forgotten lives. For these reasons, these narrators show their own involvements and concerns about the events they describe. The speaker in Jackson's "The Lottery," however, does not seem personally involved in the action. This narrator listens, sees, and reports, but is not involved personally in the cruel actions in the story's country village.

KINDS OF POINTS OF VIEW

In the various works you read you will encounter a wide variety of points of view. To begin your analysis, first determine the work's grammatical voice. Then you should study the ways in which the subject, characterization, dialogue, and form interact with the point of view.

First-Person Point of View

If the voice of the work is an "I," the author is using the **first-person point of view**—the impersonation of a fictional narrator or speaker. In our hypothetical accident, both Alice and Bill are first-person speakers. In literature, Sammy of Updike's "A & P" and the unnamed speaker of Anderson's "I'm a Fool" are also first-person speakers; in Twain's "Luck" there are two separate first-person speakers (the first "I" introduces the second "I").

Of all the points of view, the first person is potentially the most independent of the author, for such a speaker is often given a unique identity, with name, job, and economic and social positions (like Sammy). Quite often, however, the author may create a relatively neutral, uninvolved narrator who still uses the first-person voice, as with the speaker of Poe's "The Masque of the Red Death." A unique first-person narrator is the speaker of Munro's "Meneseteung." The story depends on the curiosity and sympathetic imagination of this narrator, who begins normally enough by describing her examination of various documents relating to the major character. Soon however, the narrator shifts into an imaginative reconstruction of events leading up to a major event in the character's life. Though the narrator reports no first-hand material except for having visited the location of the story, she nevertheless is deeply involved, since the story results entirely from her power to articulate her imaginative vision of what the major character might have experienced.

First-person speakers might report events as though they have acquired their knowledge in a number of ways:

What they have *done, said, heard,* and *thought* (firsthand experience).

What they have *observed* others do and say (firsthand witness).

What *others have told them* (second-hand testimony and hearsay).

What they are able to *reconstruct* from the information they might have been able to find (hypothetical or imaginative information).

What they are able to *imagine* a character or characters might do or think, given the situation.

When you encounter a first-person narrative, determine the narrator's position and ability, prejudices or self-interest, and judgment of their readers or listeners. When they describe their own experiences they have great authority and sometimes great power. Whatever their involvement, however, they are to be seen as one of the means by which authors create an authentic, life-like aura around their stories.

Second-Person Point of View

The **second-person point of view,** the least common of the points of view, offers the writer two major possibilities. In the first, a narrator tells a present and involved listener what he or she has done and said at a past time. The actions might be a simple retelling of events, as when a parent tells a child about an action of the child during infancy, or a doctor tells a patient with amnesia about events before the causative injury. The actions might also be subject to dispute and interpretation, as when a prosecuting attorney describes a crime for which a defendant is on trial, or a spouse lists grievances against an alienated spouse in a custody or divorce case.

The second possibility is more complex. Some narrators seem to be addressing a "you" but are instead referring mainly to themselves, and to listeners only tangentially, in preference to an "I." A clever variation of the "you" point of view may be seen in Lorrie Moore's "How to Become a Writer" (p. 205), in which the narrator is apparently narrating her own experiences under the guise of giving commands to a listener aspiring to the writer's craft.

In addition, some narrators follow the usage—common in colloquial speech—of the indefinite "you." In such a narration, speakers use "you" to refer not to a specific reader or listener but rather to anyone at all—in this way avoiding the more formal use of words like "one," "a person," or "people." (Incidentally, the selection of "you" is non-gender specific, because it eliminates the need for the pronouns "he," "she," "he or she," and the like.)

Third-Person Point of View

If events in the work are described in the third person (*he, she, it, they*), the author is using the **third-person point of view.** It is not always easy to characterize the voice in this point of view. Sometimes the speaker may use an "I" (as in Poe's "The Masque of the Red Death") and be seemingly identical with the author, but at other times the author may create a distinct **authorial voice,** as in Mansfield's "Miss Brill." There are three variants of the third-person point of view: *dramatic* or *objective, omniscient,* and *limited omniscient.*

DRAMATIC OR OBJECTIVE. The most direct presentation of action and dialogue is the **dramatic** or **objective point of view** (also called **third-person objective**). It is the basic method of rendering action and speech which all the points of view share. The narrator of the dramatic point of view is an unidentified speaker who reports things in a way that is analogous to a hovering or tracking motion-picture camera, or to what some critics have called "a fly on the wall (or tree)." Somehow, the narrator is always on the spot—within rooms, forests, village squares, and moving vehicles, or even in outer space—to tell us what is happening and what is being said.

The dramatic presentation is limited only to what is said and what happens. There is no attempt to draw conclusions or make interpretations, because the presupposition underlying the dramatic point of view is that readers, like a jury, can form their own interpretations if they are given the right evidence. Thus Jackson's "The Lottery" (the subject of the sample essay, pp. 227–28)—a powerful example of the dramatic point of view—is an objective story about a bizarre small-town lottery. We the readers draw many conclusions about this story (such as that people are tradition bound, insensitive, cruel, and so on), but because of the dramatic point of view Jackson does not *state* any of these conclusions for us.

OMNISCIENT. The third-person point of view is **omniscient** (all-knowing) when the speaker not only presents action and dialogue, but also is able to report what goes on in the minds of the characters. The real world does not permit us to *know* absolutely what other people are thinking. However, we are always making assumptions about the mental activities of others, and these assumptions are the basis of the omniscient point of view. Authors use it freely but judiciously to explain responses, thoughts, feelings, and plans—an additional dimension that aids in the development of character. For example, in Munro's "Meneseteung," the speaker assumes omniscience to explain the responses and thoughts of her major character, and therefore to communicate the character's loneliness and also her inaction.

LIMITED, OR LIMITED OMNISCIENT. More common than the omniscient point of view is the *limited third person*, or **limited omniscient third-person point of view,** in which the author confines or *limits* attention to a major character. In our accident case, Frank, being Bill's friend, would be sympathetic to Bill, and thus his report of the collision would likely be third-person limited, with Bill as the center of interest. In a story, the central figure on whom things are focused is the **point-of-view character,** such as Miss Brill in Mansfield's "Miss Brill," Sarty in Faulkner's "Barn Burning," and Goodman Brown in Hawthorne's "Young Goodman Brown." Virtually everything in these stories is there because the point-of-view characters see it, hear it, respond to it, think about it, do it or share in it, try to control it, or are controlled by it.

MINGLING POINTS OF VIEW

In some works, an author may shift the point of view in order to sustain interest, create suspense, or put the burden of response entirely upon readers. For example, Mansfield in "Miss Brill" interrupts the limited omniscient focus on Miss Brill's thoughts and reactions immediately after she is insulted. The last paragraphs are objective until the last sentence, when the limited omniscient point of view is resumed. The result is that Miss Brill is made totally alone in her grief, cut off; readers can no longer share her sorrow as they earlier share her observations about the characters in the park. A similar shift occurs at the end of Hawthorne's "Young Goodman Brown," where the narrator objectively and almost brutally summarizes Brown's gloomy, loveless life after his nightmare about evil.

POINT OF VIEW AND VERB TENSE

Usually *point of view* refers to the ways narrators and speakers perceive and report actions and speeches. In the broadest sense, however, point of view may be considered as a total way of rendering truth, and for this reason the *tense* chosen by the narrators is important. In most narrations, especially traditional ones, the *past tense* prevails: The actions happened in the past, and they are now over. It is important to note, however, that the inclusion of dialogue, even in a past-tense narrative, is a dramatic means of moving the story into the present. The dialogue concluding "The Necklace" performs such a function in that story. In addition, the narrator may emphasize the narrative's meaning—also a means of transferring tense from past to present. For example, the narrator of "I'm a Fool" is constantly adding his own judgments, and the speaker of "Meneseteung" draws similar conclusions about reviving the memory of remote and vanished lives. In "Raymond's Run" the narrator makes many comments (some of them in the future tense to indicate continuity) alongside the story's basic past tense narrative. As we note in Chapter 9, the narrators of *parables* and *fables* perceive past-tense stories as vehicles for teaching lessons in philosophy and religion.

In recent years, a number of writers have increasingly used the *present tense* as the principal time reference in stories. With the present tense, the story is rendered as a virtual play, being unfolded moment by moment. In "Blue Winds Dancing," for instance, Whitecloud employs the present tense to emphasize the immediate experience of the narrator's return home. Williams uses the present tense in "Taking Care" as a means not only of emphasizing the immediacy of the main character's situation, but also of demonstrating the challenges he will be facing in the future. In "Meneseteung," Munro effectively uses the present tense to bring alive the revived actions and words of her long-dead characters.

Some writers intermingle the present and past tenses to show how time itself may be merged within the human consciousness, as in Zabytko's "Home Soil," where the present tense both at the beginning and end of the story underlines the narrator's pain about the events he describes. The intermingling of tenses may not only show the fusion of past, present, and future within a character's mind, but also demonstrate how that character perceives the social world, including the listeners and/or readers. For example, in Updike's "A & P," Sammy's mixing of tenses shows the vividness of his memory of events in the store (past), and it also shows his friendliness and informality (present).

GUIDELINES FOR POINTS OF VIEW

The following guidelines summarize and further classify the types of points of view. Use them to distinguish differences and shades of variation in stories and poems

1. **First Person ("I" and "me").** First-person speakers are involved to at least some degree in the actions of the work. Such narrators may have (1) complete understanding, (2) partial or incorrect understanding, or (3) no understanding at all.
   a. *Major participant*
      i. Telling his or her own story and thoughts as a major mover.
      ii. Telling a story about others and also about herself or himself as one of the major movers.
      iii. Telling a story mainly about others, and about himself or herself only tangentially.
   b. *Minor participant, telling a story about events experienced and witnessed*
   c. *Nonparticipating but identifiable speaker who learns about events in other ways (e.g., listening to participants, examining documents, hearing news reports). The narrator tells the story as a report, or as a combination report and reconstruction.*

2. **Second person ("you").** Occurs (a) when the speaker (e.g., parent, psychologist) knows more about a character's actions than the character himself or herself or else (b) when the speaker (e.g., lawyer, spouse, friend, sports umpire) is explaining to another person (the "you") that person's disputable actions and statements. The speaker may also use "you" to mean (c) himself or herself, or else (d) anyone at all.

3. **Third person ("she," "he," "it," "they").** The speaker is outside the action and is mainly a reporter of actions and speeches. Some speakers may have unique and distinguishing traits even though no separate identity is claimed for them ("the unnamed third-person narrator"). In other third-person narratives, speakers who are not separately identifiable may represent the words and views of the authors themselves ("the authorial voice").
   a. *Dramatic or third-person objective.* The narrator reports only what can be seen and heard. The thoughts of characters are included only if they are spoken or written (dialogue, reported or overheard conversation, letters, reports, etc.).
   b. *Omniscient.* Omniscient speaker sees all, reports all, knows and explains, when necessary, the inner workings of the minds of any or all characters.
   c. *Limited, or limited omniscient.* The focus is on the actions, responses, thoughts, and feelings of a single major character. The narration may involve primarily what the character does, and it may also probe deeply within the consciousness of the character.

STORIES FOR STUDY

SHERWOOD ANDERSON (1876–1941)

Anderson was a native of Ohio. His early years showed no particular career objective: He worked at many odd jobs and served in the Spanish-American War. He married and worked briefly as manager of a paint factory. Soon, however, he deserted his family and moved to Chicago to pursue a career in writing. In 1916 he published his first book, a semi-autobiographical novel entitled Windy McPherson's Son, *which established him as a master of naturalistic fiction (i.e., things never work out right). His major triumph was* Winesburg, Ohio, *published in 1919. In this collection of 23 stories, conflict develops from the characters' attempts (usually unsuccessful) to fit into society's norms and patterns. "I'm a Fool," which shares these conflicts, is taken from the collection* Horses and Men *(1924).*

I'm a Fool _____1924

It was a hard jolt for me, one of the most bitterest I ever had to face. And it all came about through my own foolishness, too. Even yet sometimes, when I think of it, I want to cry or swear or kick myself. Perhaps, even now, after all this time, there will be a kind of satisfaction in making myself look cheap by telling of it.

It began at three o'clock one October afternoon as I sat in the grandstand at the fall trotting and pacing meet at Sandusky, Ohio.

To tell the truth, I felt a little foolish that I should be sitting in the grand-stand at all. During the summer before I had left my home town with Harry Whitehead and, with a nigger named Burt, had taken a job as swipe° with one of the two horses Harry was campaigning through the fall race meets that year. Mother cried and my sister Mildred, who wanted to get a job as a schoolteacher in our town that fall, stormed and scolded about the house all during the week before I left. They both thought it something disgraceful that one of our family should take a place as a swipe with race horses. I've an idea Mildred thought my taking the place would stand in the way of her getting the job she'd been working so long for.

But after all I had to work, and there was no other work to be got. A big lumbering fellow of nineteen couldn't just hang around the house and I had got too big to mow people's lawns and sell newspapers. Little chaps who could get next to·people's sympathies by their sizes were always getting jobs away from me. There was one fellow who kept saying to everyone who wanted a lawn mowed or a cistern cleaned that he was saving money to work his way through college, and I used to lay awake nights thinking up ways to injure him without being found out. I kept thinking of wagons running over him and bricks falling on his head as he walked along the street. But never mind him.

_____

swipe: a groom and general handyman; the narrator describes a swipe's duties in paragraph 7.

I got the place with Harry and I liked Burt fine. We got along splendid together. He was a big nigger with a lazy sprawling body and soft, kind eyes, and when it came to a fight he could hit like Jack Johnson.° He had Bucephalus, a big black pacing stallion that could do 2.09 or 2.10 if he had to, and I had a little gelding named Doctor Fritz that never lost a race all fall when Harry wanted him to win.

We set out from home late in July, in a box car with the two horses and after that, until late November, we kept moving along to the race meets and the fairs. It was a peachy time for me, I'll say that. Sometimes now I think that boys who are raised regular in houses, and never have a fine nigger like Burt for best friend, and go to high schools and college, and never steal anything, or get drunk a little, or learn to swear from fellows who know how, or come walking up in front of a grand stand in their shirt sleeves and with dirty horsy pants on when the races are going on and the grand stand is full of people all dressed up—What's the use of talking about it? Such fellows don't know nothing at all. They've never had no opportunity.

But I did. Burt taught me how to rub down a horse and put the bandages on after a race and steam a horse out and a lot of valuable things for any man to know. He could wrap a bandage on a horse's leg so smooth that if it had been the same color you would think it was his skin, and I guess he'd have been a big driver, too, and got to the top like Murphy and Walter Cox and the others if he hadn't been black.

Gee whizz! it was fun. You got to a county-seat town, maybe say on a Saturday or Sunday, and the fair began the next Tuesday and lasted until Friday afternoon. Doctor Fritz would be, say, in the 2.25 trot on Tuesday afternoon and on Thursday afternoon Bucephalus would knock 'em cold in the "free-for-all" pace. It left you a lot of time to hang around and listen to horse talk, and see Burt knock some yap cold that got too gay,° and you'd find out about horses and men and pick up a lot of stuff you could use all the rest of your life, if you had some sense and salted down what you heard and felt and saw.

And then at the end of the week when the race meet was over, and Harry had run home to tend up to his livery-stable business, you and Burt hitched the two horses to carts and drove slow and steady across country, to the place for the next meeting, so as to not overheat the horses, etc., etc., you know.

Gee whizz! Gosh amighty! the nice hickory-nut and beechnut and oaks and other kinds of trees along the roads, all brown and red, and the good smells, and Burt singing a song called "Deep River,"° and the country girls at the windows of houses and everything. You can stick your colleges up your nose for all me. I guess I know where I got my education.

Why, one of those little burgs of towns you came to on the way, say now on a Saturday afternoon, and Burt says, "Let's lay up here." And you did.

And you took the horses to a livery stable and fed them, and you got your good clothes out of a box and put them on.

And the town was full of farmers gaping, because they could see you were racehorse people, and the kids maybe never see a nigger before and was afraid and run away when the two of us walked down their main street.

And that was before prohibition and all that foolishness, and so you went into a saloon, the two of you, and all the yaps come and stood around, and there was al-

Jack Johnson: (1878–1946), the first black heavyweight champion, 1910–1915.
gay: high spirited as a result of being drunk.
"Deep River": well-known spiritual.

ways some one pretended he was horsy and knew things and spoke up and began asking questions, and all you did was to lie and lie all you could about what horses you
had, and I said I owned them, and then some fellow said, "Will you have a drink of
whisky?" and Burt knocked his eye out the way he could say, offhand like, "Oh, well,
all right, I'm agreeable to a little nip. I'll split a quart with you." Gee whizz!

But that isn't what I want to tell my story about. We got home late in November
and I promised mother I'd quit the race horses for good. There's a lot of things
you've got to promise a mother because she don't know any better.

And so, there not being any work in our town any more than when I left there
to go to the races, I went off to Sandusky and got a pretty good place taking care of
horses for a man who owned a teaming and delivery and storage and coal and real-
estate business there. It was a pretty good place with good eats, and a day off each
week, and sleeping on a cot in a big barn, and mostly just shoveling in hay and oats
to a lot of big good-enough skates of horses that couldn't have trotted a race with a
toad. I wasn't dissatisfied and I could send money home.

And then, as I started to tell you, the fall races come to Sandusky and I got the
day off and I went. I left the job at noon and had on my good clothes and my new
brown derby hat I'd bought the Saturday before, and a stand-up collar.

First of all I went downtown and walked about with the dudes. I've always
thought to myself, "Put up a good front," and so I did it. I had forty dollars in my
pockets and so I went into the West House, a big hotel, and walked up to the cigar
stand. "Give me three twenty-five cent cigars," I said. There was a lot of horsemen and
strangers and dressed-up people from other towns standing around in the lobby and
in the bar, and I mingled amongst them. In the bar there was a fellow with a cane and
a Windsor tie on, that it made me sick to look at him. I like a man to be a man and
dressed up, but not to go put on that kind of airs. So I pushed him aside, kind of
rough, and had me a drink of whisky. And then he looked at me, as though he
thought maybe he'd get gay, but he changed his mind and didn't say anything. And
then I had another drink of whisky, just to show him something, and went out and
had a hack out to the races, all to myself, and when I got there I bought myself the
best seat I could get up in the grandstand, but didn't go in for any of these boxes.
That's putting on too many airs.

And so there I was, sitting up in the grandstand as gay as you please and looking down on the swipes coming out with their horses, and with their dirty horsy pants
on and the horseblankets swung over their shoulders, same as I had been doing all
the year before. I liked one thing about the same as the other, sitting up there and
feeling grand and being down there and looking up at the yaps and feeling grander
and more important, too.

One thing's about as good as another, if you take it just right. I've often said
that.

Well, right in front of me, in the grandstand that day, there was a fellow with a
couple of girls and they was about my age. The young fellow was a nice guy, all right.
He was the kind maybe that goes to college and then comes to be a lawyer or maybe
a newspaper editor or something like that, but he wasn't stuck on himself. There are
some of that kind are all right and he was one of the ones.

He had his sister with him and another girl and the sister looked around over
his shoulder, accidental at first, not intending to start anything—she wasn't that
kind—and her eyes and mine happened to meet.

You know how it is. Gee, she was a peach! She had on a soft dress, kind of a blue stuff and it looked carelessly made, but was well sewed and made and everything. I knew that much. I blushed when she looked right at me and so did she. She was the nicest girl I've ever seen in my life. She wasn't stuck on herself and she could talk proper grammar without being like a schoolteacher or something like that. What I mean is, she was O.K. I think maybe her father was well-to-do, but not rich to make her chesty because she was his daughter, as some are. Maybe he owned a drug store or a dry-goods store in their home town, or something like that. She never told me and I never asked.

My own people are all O.K. too, when you come to that. My grandfather was Welsh and over in the old country, in Wales he was—but never mind that.

The first heat of the first race come off and the young fellow setting there with   25
the two girls left them and went down to make a bet. I knew what he was up to, but he didn't talk big and noisy and let everyone around know he was a sport, as some do. He wasn't that kind. Well, he come back and I heard him tell the two girls what horse he'd bet on, and when the heat trotted they all half got to their feet and acted in the excited, sweaty way people do when they've got money down on a race, and the horse they bet on is up there pretty close at the end, and they think maybe he'll come on with a rush, but he never does because he hasn't got the old juice in him, come right down to it.

And then, pretty soon, the horses came out for the 2.18 pace and there was a horse in it I knew. He was a horse Bob French had in his string but Bob didn't own him. He was a horse owned by a Mr. Mathers down at Marietta, Ohio.

This Mr. Mathers had a lot of money and owned some coal mines or something and he had a swell place out in the country, and he was stuck on race horses, but was a Presbyterian or something, and I think more than likely his wife was one, too, maybe a stiffer one than himself. So he never raced his horses hisself, and the story round the Ohio race tracks was that when one of his horses got ready to go to the races he turned him over to Bob French and pretended to his wife he was sold.

So Bob had the horses and he did pretty much as he pleased and you can't blame Bob, at least, I never did. Sometimes he was out to win and sometimes he wasn't. I never cared much about that when I was swiping a horse. What I did want to know was that my horse had the speed and could go out in front, if you wanted him to.

And, as I'm telling you, there was Bob in this race with one of Mr. Mathers' horses, was named "About Ben Ahem"° or something like that, and was fast as a streak. He was a gelding and had a mark of 2.21, but could step in .08 or .09.

Because when Burt and I were out, as I've told you, the year before, there was   30
a nigger Burt knew, worked for Mr. Mathers and we went out there one day when we didn't have no race on at the Marietta Fair and our boss Harry was gone home.

And so everyone was gone to the fair but just this one nigger and he took us all through Mr. Mathers' swell house and he and Burt tapped a bottle of wine Mr. Mathers had hid in his bedroom, back in a closet, without his wife knowing, and he showed us this Ahem horse. Burt was always stuck on being a driver but didn't have much chance to get to the top, being a nigger, and he and the other nigger gulped the whole bottle of wine and Burt got a little lit up.

So the nigger let Burt take this About Ben Ahem and step him a mile in a track

---

"About Ben Ahem": more likely "Abou Ben Adhem," from the poem "Abou Ben Adhem and the Angel" (1834) by Leigh Hunt (1784–1859).

Mr. Mathers had all to himself, right there on the farm. And Mr. Mathers had one child, a daughter, kinda sick and not very good looking, and she came home and we had to hustle to get About Ben Ahem stuck back in the barn.

I'm only telling you to get everything straight. At Sandusky, that afternoon I was at the fair, this young fellow with the two girls was fussed, being with the girls and losing his bet. You know how a fellow is that way. One of them was his girl and the other his sister. I had figured that out.

"Gee whizz," I say to myself, "I'm going to give him the dope."

He was mighty nice when I touched him on the shoulder. He and the girls were nice to me right from the start and clear to the end. I'm not blaming them.

And so he leaned back and I give him the dope on About Ben Ahem. "Don't bet a cent on this first heat because he'll go like an oxen hitched to a plow, but when the first heat is over go right down and lay on your pile." That's what I told him.

Well, I never saw a fellow treat any one sweller. There was a fat man sitting beside the little girl, that had looked at me twice by this time, and I at her, and both blushing, and what did he do but have the nerve to turn and ask the fat man to get up and change places with me so I could set with his crowd.

Gee whizz, craps amighty. There I was. What a chump I was to go and get gay up there in the West House bar, and just because that dude was standing there with a cane and that kind of a necktie on, to go and get all balled up and drink that whisky, just to show off.

Of course she would know, me setting right beside her and letting her smell of my breath. I could have kicked myself right down out of that grand stand and all around that race track and made a faster record than most of the skates of horses they had there that year.

Because that girl wasn't any mutt of a girl. What wouldn't I have give right then for a stick of chewing gum to chew, or a lozenger, or some licorice, or most anything. I was glad I had those twenty-five cent cigars in my pocket and right away I give that fellow one and lit one myself. Then that fat man got up and we changed places and there I was, plunked right down beside her.

They introduced themselves and the fellow's best girl, he had with him, was named Miss Elinor Woodbury, and her father was a manufacturer of barrels from a place called Tiffin, Ohio. And the fellow himself was named Wilbur Wessen and his sister was Miss Lucy Wessen.

I suppose it was their having such swell names that got me off my trolley. A fellow, just because he has been a swipe with a race horse, and works taking care of horses for a man in the teaming, delivery, and storage business isn't any better or worse than any one else. I've often thought that, and said it too.

But you know how a fellow is. There's something in that kind of nice clothes, and the kind of nice eyes she had, and the way she had looked at me, awhile before, over her brother's shoulder, and me looking back at her, and both of us blushing.

I couldn't show her up for a boob, could I?

I made a fool of myself, that's what I did. I said my name was Walter Mathers from Marietta, Ohio, and then I told all three of them the smashingest lie you ever heard. What I said was that my father owned the horse About Ben Ahem and that he had let him out to this Bob French for racing purposes, because our family was proud and had never gone into racing that way, in our own name, I mean, and Miss Lucy Wessen's eyes were shining, and I went the whole hog.

I told about our place down at Marietta, and about the big stables and the grand brick house we had on a hill, up above the Ohio River, but I knew enough not to do it in no bragging way. What I did was to start things and then let them drag the rest out of me. I acted just as reluctant to tell as I could. Our family hasn't got any barrel factory, and since I've known us, we've always been pretty poor, but not asking anything of any one at that, and my grandfather, over in Wales—but never mind that.

We set there talking like we had known each other for years and years, and I went and told them that my father had been expecting maybe this Bob French wasn't on the square, and had sent me up to Sandusky on the sly to find out what I could.

And I bluffed it through I had found out all about the 2.18 pace, in which About Ben Ahem was to start.

I said he would lose the first heat by pacing like a lame cow and then he would come back and skin 'em alive after that. And to back up what I said I took thirty dollars out of my pocket and handed it to Mr. Wilbur Wessen and asked him, would he mind, after the first heat, to go down and place it on About Ben Ahem for whatever odds he could get. What I said was that I didn't want Bob French to see me and none of the swipes.

Sure enough the first heat come off and About Ben Ahem went off his stride, 50 up the back stretch, and looked like a wooden horse or a sick one, and come in to be last. Then this Wilbur Wessen went down to the betting place under the grand stand and there I was with the two girls, and when that Miss Woodbury was looking the other way once, Lucy Wessen kinda, with her shoulder you know, kinda touched me. Not just tucking down, I don't mean. You know how a woman can do. They get close, but not getting gay either. You know what they do. Gee whizz.

And then they give me a jolt. What they had done, when I didn't know, was to get together, and they had decided Wilbur Wessen would bet fifty dollars, and the two girls had gone and put in ten dollars each, of their own money, too. I was sick then, but I was sicker later.

About the gelding, About Ben Ahem, and their winning their money, I wasn't worried a lot about that. It came out O.K. Ahem stepped the next three heats like a bushel of spoiled eggs going to market before they could be found out, and Wilbur Wessen had got nine to two for the money. There was something else eating at me.

Because Wilbur come back, after he had bet the money, and after that he spent most of his time talking to that Miss Woodbury, and Lucy Wessen and I was left alone together like on a desert island. Gee, if I'd only been on the square or if there had been any way of getting myself on the square. There ain't any Walter Mathers, like I said to her and them, and there hasn't ever been one, but if there was, I bet I'd go to Marietta, Ohio, and shoot him tomorrow.

There I was, big boob that I am. Pretty soon the race was over, and Wilbur had gone down and collected our money, and we had a hack downtown, and he stood us a swell supper at the West House, and a bottle of champagne beside.

And I was with the girl and she wasn't saying much, and I wasn't saying much 55 either. One thing I know. She wasn't stuck on me because of the lie about my father being rich and all that. There's a way you know . . . Craps amighty. There's a kind of girl you see just once in your life, and if you don't get busy and make hay, then you're gone for good and all, and might as well go jump off a bridge. They give you a look from inside of them somewhere, and it ain't no vamping, and what it means is—you want that girl to be your wife, and you want nice things around her like flowers and swell clothes, and you want her to have the kids you're going to have, and you want good music played and no ragtime. Gee whizz.

There's a place over near Sandusky, across a kind of bay, and it's called Cedar Point. And after we had supper we went over to it in a launch, all by ourselves. Wilbur and Miss Lucy and that Miss Woodbury had to catch a ten o'clock train back to Tiffin, Ohio, because, when you're out with girls like that you can't get careless and miss any trains and stay out all night, like you can with some kinds of Janes.

And Wilbur blowed himself to the launch and it cost him fifteen cold plunks, but I wouldn't never have knew if I hadn't listened. He wasn't no tin horn kind of a sport.

Over at the Cedar Point place, we didn't stay around where there was a gang of common kind of cattle at all.

There was big dance halls and dining places for yaps, and there was a beach you could walk along and get where it was dark, and we went there.

She didn't talk hardly at all and neither did I, and I was thinking how glad I was my mother was all right, and always made us kids learn to eat with a fork at the table, and not swill soup, and not be noisy and rough like a gang you see around a race track that way.

Then Wilbur and his girl went away up the beach and Lucy and I sat down in a dark place, where there was some roots of old trees the water had washed up, and after that the time, till we had to go back in the launch and they had to catch their trains, wasn't nothing at all. It went like winking your eye.

Here's how it was. The place we were setting in was dark, like I said, and there was the roots from that old stump sticking up like arms, and there was a watery smell, and the night was like—as if you could put your hand out and feel it—so warm and soft and dark and sweet like an orange.

I most cried and I most swore and I most jumped up and danced, I was so mad and happy and sad.

When Wilbur come back from being alone with his girl, and she saw him coming, Lucy she says, "We got to go to the train now," and she was most crying too, but she never knew nothing I knew, and she couldn't be so all busted up. And then, before Wilbur and Miss Woodbury got up to where we was, she put her face up and kissed me quick, and put her head up against me and she was all quivering and—Gee whizz.

Sometimes I hope I have cancer and die. I guess you know what I mean. We went in the launch across the bay to the train like that, and it was dark, too. She whispered and said it was like she and I could get out of the boat and walk on water, and it sounded foolish, but I knew what she meant.

And then quick we were right at the depot, and there was a big gang of yaps, the kind that goes to the fairs, and crowded and milling around like cattle, and how could I tell her? "It won't be long because you'll write and I'll write you." That's all she said.

I got a chance like a hay barn afire. A swell chance I got.

And maybe she would write me, down at Marietta that way, and the letter would come back, and stamped on the front of it by the U.S.A. "there ain't any such guy," or something like that, whatever they stamp on a letter that way.

And me trying to pass myself off for a big-bug and a swell—to her, as decent a little body as God ever made. Craps amighty—swell chance I got!

And then the train come in, and she got on it, and Wilbur Wessen, he come and shook hands with me, and that Miss Woodbury was nice too and bowed to me, and I at her, and the train went and I busted out and cried like a kid.

Gee, I could have run after the train and made Dan Patch° look like a freight train after a wreck but, socks amighty, what was the use? Did you ever see such a fool?

I'll bet you what—if I had an arm broke right now or a train had run over my foot—I wouldn't go to no doctor at all. I'd go set down and let her hurt and hurt—that's what I'd do.

I'll bet you what—if I hadn't a drunk that booze I'd never been such a boob as to go tell such a lie—that couldn't never be made straight to a lady like her.

I wish I had that fellow right here that had on a Windsor tie and carried a cane. I'd smash him for fair. Gosh darn his eyes. He's a big fool—that's what he is.

And if I'm not another you just go find me one and I'll quit working and be a   75
bum and give him my job. I don't care nothing for working, and earning money, and saving it for no such boob as myself.

QUESTIONS

1. Describe the point of view of "I'm a Fool." How completely does the narrator describe himself? What is the level and effect of the narrator's diction? Why, in paragraphs 8 and 11–14, does he shift to the second-person point of view?
2. What changes does the narrator undergo during the events of the story?
3. Compare the characters of Lucy and the narrator. How successful might a match have been between the two if the narrator had not made things impossible by his false stories about himself?
4. Describe the importance of location and background. How does the narrator's familiarity with racing enable him to impress the Wessens?

SHIRLEY JACKSON (1919–1965)

Jackson was a native of California. She graduated from Syracuse University in New York, and lived much of her life in Vermont. Although her life was short, she was a successful writer of novels, short stories, biographies, and children's fiction. Her stories often depict unusual, unreal, or bizarre events in common settings, of which "The Lottery" is a major example. She wrote the story in only two hours and submitted it to The New Yorker *without major revisions. When it was published many readers raised questions about how to interpret the conclusion. Jackson steadfastly refused to explain, leaving readers to decide for themselves.*

Dan Patch: one of the fastest pace horses. Dan Patch still held records at the time of the story. Proverbial for his speed, his records were not broken until well into the 1930s.

The Lottery ————————————————————————————————————*1948*

The morning of June 27th was clear and sunny, with the fresh warmth of a full summer day; the flowers were blossoming profusely and the grass was richly green. The people of the village began to gather in the square, between the post office and the bank, around ten o'clock; in some towns there were so many people that the lottery took two days and had to be started on June 26th, but in this village, where there were only about three hundred people, the whole lottery took less than two hours, so it could begin at ten o'clock in the morning and still be through in time to allow the villagers to get home for noon dinner.

The children assembled first, of course. School was recently over for the summer, and the feeling of liberty sat uneasily on most of them; they tended to gather together quietly for a while before they broke into boisterous play, and their talk was still of the classroom and the teacher, of books and reprimands. Bobby Martin had already stuffed his pockets full of stones, and the other boys soon followed his example, selecting the smoothest and roundest stones; Bobby and Harry Jones and Dickie Delacroix—the villagers pronounced this name "Dellacroy"—eventually made a great pile of stones in one corner of the square and guarded it against the raids of the other boys. The girls stood aside, talking among themselves, looking over their shoulders at the boys, and the very small children rolled in the dust or clung to the hands of their older brothers or sisters.

Soon the men began to gather, surveying their own children, speaking of planting and rain, tractors and taxes. They stood together, away from the pile of stones in the corner, and their jokes were quiet and they smiled rather than laughed. The women, wearing faded house dresses and sweaters, came shortly after their menfolk. They greeted one another and exchanged bits of gossip as they went to join their husbands. Soon the women, standing by their husbands, began to call to their children, and the children came reluctantly, having to be called four or five times. Bobby Martin ducked under his mother's grasping hand and ran, laughing, back to the pile of stones. His father spoke up sharply, and Bobby came quickly and took his place between his father and his oldest brother.

The lottery was conducted—as were the square dances, the teen-age club, the Halloween program—by Mr. Summers, who had time and energy to devote to civic activities. He was a round-faced, jovial man and he ran the coal business, and people were sorry for him, because he had no children and his wife was a scold. When he arrived in the square, carrying the black wooden box, there was a murmur of conversation among the villagers, and he waved and called, "Little late today, folks." The postmaster, Mr. Graves, followed him, carrying a three-legged stool, and the stool was put in the center of the square and Mr. Summers set the black box down on it. The villagers kept their distance, leaving a space between themselves and the stool, and when Mr. Summers said, "Some of you fellows want to give me a hand?" there was a hesitation before two men, Mr. Martin and his oldest son, Baxter, came forward to hold the box steady on the stool while Mr. Summers stirred up the papers inside it.

The original paraphernalia for the lottery had been lost long ago, and the black box now resting on the stool had been put into use even before Old Man Warner, the oldest man in town, was born. Mr. Summers spoke frequently to the villagers about making a new box, but no one liked to upset even as much tradition as was represented by the black box. There was a story that the present box had been made with some pieces of the box that had preceded it, the one that had been constructed when the first people settled down to make a village here. Every year, after the lottery, Mr. Summers began talking again about a new box, but every year the subject was allowed to fade off without anything's being done. The black box grew shabbier each year; by now it was no longer completely black but splintered badly along one side to show the original wood color, and in some places faded or stained.

Mr. Martin and his oldest son, Baxter, held the black box securely on the stool until Mr. Summers had stirred the papers thoroughly with his hand. Because so much of the ritual had been forgotten or discarded, Mr. Summers had been successful in having slips of paper substituted for the chips of wood that had been used for generations. Chips of wood, Mr. Summers had argued, had been all very well when the village was tiny, but now that the population was more than three hundred and likely to keep on growing, it was necessary to use something that would fit more easily into the black box. The night before the lottery, Mr. Summers and Mr. Graves made up the slips of paper and put them in the box, and it was then taken to the safe of Mr. Summers' coal company and locked up until Mr. Summers was ready to take it to the square next morning. The rest of the year, the box was put away, sometimes one place, sometimes another; it had spent one year in Mr. Graves's barn and another year underfoot in the post office, and sometimes it was set on a shelf in the Martin grocery and left there.

There was a great deal of fussing to be done before Mr. Summers declared the lottery open. There were the lists to make up—of heads of families, heads of households in each family, members of each household in each family. There was the proper swearing-in of Mr. Summers by the postmaster, as the official of the lottery; at one time, some people remembered, there had been a recital of some sort, performed by the official of the lottery, a perfunctory, tuneless chant that had been rattled off duly each year; some people believed that the official of the lottery used to stand just so when he said or sang it, others believed that he was supposed to walk among the people, but years and years ago this part of the ritual had been allowed to lapse. There had been, also, a ritual salute, which the official of the lottery had had to use in addressing each person who came up to draw from the box, but this also had changed with time, until now it was felt necessary only for the official to speak to each person approaching. Mr. Summers was very good at all this; in his clean white shirt and blue jeans, with one hand resting carelessly on the black box, he seemed very proper and important as he talked interminably to Mr. Graves and the Martins.

Just as Mr. Summers finally left off talking and turned to the assembled villagers, Mrs. Hutchinson came hurriedly along the path to the square, her sweater thrown over her shoulders, and slid into place in the back of the crowd. "Clean forgot what day it was," she said to Mrs. Delacroix, who stood next to her, and they both laughed softly. "Thought my old man was out back stacking wood," Mrs. Hutchinson went on, "and then I looked out the window and the kids was gone, and then I remembered it was the twenty-seventh and came a-running." She dried her hands on her apron, and Mrs. Delacroix said, "You're in time, though. They're still talking away up there."

Mrs. Hutchinson craned her neck to see through the crowd and found her husband and children standing near the front. She tapped Mrs. Delacroix on the arm as a farewell and began to make her way through the crowd. The people separated good-humoredly to let her through; two or three people said, in voices just loud enough to be heard across the crowd, "Here comes your Missus, Hutchinson," and "Bill, she made it after all." Mrs. Hutchinson reached her husband, and Mr. Summers, who had been waiting, said cheerfully, "Thought we were going to have to get on without you, Tessie." Mrs. Hutchinson said, grinning, "Wouldn't have me leave m'dishes in the sink, now, would you, Joe?," and soft laughter ran through the crowd as the people stirred back into position after Mrs. Hutchinson's arrival.

"Well, now," Mr. Summers said soberly, "guess we better get started, get this over with, so's we can go back to work. Anybody ain't here?"

"Dunbar," several people said. "Dunbar, Dunbar."

Mr. Summers consulted his list. "Clyde Dunbar," he said. "That's right. He's broke his leg, hasn't he? Who's drawing for him?"

"Me, I guess," a woman said, and Mr. Summers turned to look at her. "Wife draws for her husband," Mr. Summers said. "Don't you have a grown boy to do it for you, Janey?" Although Mr. Summers and everyone else in the village knew the answer perfectly well, it was the business of the official of the lottery to ask such questions formally. Mr. Summers waited with an expression of polite interest while Mrs. Dunbar answered.

"Horace's not but sixteen yet," Mrs. Dunbar said regretfully. "Guess I gotta fill in for the old man this year."

"Right," Mr. Summers said. He made a note on the list he was holding. Then he asked, "Watson boy drawing this year?"

A tall boy in the crowd raised his hand. "Here," he said. "I'm drawing for m'mother and me." He blinked his eyes nervously and ducked his head as several voices in the crowd said things like "Good fellow, Jack," and "Glad to see your mother's got a man to do it."

"Well," Mr. Summers said, "guess that's everyone. Old Man Warner make it?"

"Here," a voice said, and Mr. Summers nodded.

A sudden hush fell on the crowd as Mr. Summers cleared his throat and looked at the list. "All ready?" he called. "Now, I'll read the names—heads of families first—and the men come up and take a paper out of the box. Keep the paper folded in your hand without looking at it until everyone has had a turn. Everything clear?"

The people had done it so many times that they only half listened to the directions; most of them were quiet, wetting their lips, not looking around. Then Mr. Summers raised one hand high and said, "Adams." A man disengaged himself from the crowd and came forward. "Hi, Steve," Mr. Summers said, and Mr. Adams said, "Hi, Joe." They grinned at one another humorlessly and nervously. Then Mr. Adams reached into the black box and took out a folded paper. He held it firmly by one corner as he turned and went hastily back to his place in the crowd, where he stood a little apart from his family, not looking down at his hand.

"Allen," Mr. Summers said. "Anderson. . . . Bentham."

"Seems like there's no time at all between lotteries any more," Mrs. Delacroix said to Mrs. Graves in the back row. "Seems like we got through with the last one only last week."

"Time sure goes fast," Mrs. Graves said.

"Clark. . . . Delacroix."

"There goes my old man," Mrs. Delacroix said. She held her breath while her husband went forward.

"Dunbar," Mr. Summers said, and Mrs. Dunbar went steadily to the box while one of the women said, "Go on, Janey," and another said, "There she goes."

"We're next," Mrs. Graves said. She watched while Mr. Graves came around from the side of the box, greeted Mr. Summers gravely, and selected a slip of paper from the box. By now, all through the crowd there were men holding the small folded papers in their large hands, turning them over and over nervously. Mrs. Dunbar and her two sons stood together, Mrs. Dunbar holding the slip of paper.

"Harburt. . . . Hutchinson."

"Get up there, Bill," Mrs. Hutchinson said, and the people near her laughed.

"Jones."

"They do say," Mr. Adams said to Old Man Warner, who stood next to him, "that over in the north village they're talking of giving up the lottery."

Old Man Warner snorted. "Pack of crazy fools," he said. "Listening to the young folks, nothing's good enough for *them*. Next thing you know, they'll be wanting to go back to living in caves, nobody work any more, live *that* way for a while. Used to be a saying about 'Lottery in June, corn be heavy soon.' First thing you know, we'd all be eating stewed chickweed and acorns. There's *always* been a lottery," he added petulantly. "Bad enough to see young Joe Summers up there joking with everybody."

"Some places have already quit lotteries," Mrs. Adams said.

"Nothing but trouble in *that*," Old Man Warner said stoutly. "Pack of young fools."

"Martin." And Bobby Martin watched his father go forward. "Overdyke. . . . Percy."

"I wish they'd hurry," Mrs. Dunbar said to her older son. "I wish they'd hurry."

"They're almost through," her son said.

"You get ready to run tell Dad," Mrs. Dunbar said.

Mr. Summers called his own name and then stepped forward precisely and selected a slip from the box. Then he called, "Warner."

"Seventy-seventh year I been in the lottery," Old Man Warner said as he went through the crowd. "Seventy-seventh time."

"Watson." The tall boy came awkwardly through the crowd. Someone said, "Don't be nervous, Jack," and Mr. Summers said, "Take your time, son."

"Zanini."

After that, there was a long pause, a breathless pause, until Mr. Summers, holding his slip of paper in the air, said, "All right, fellows." For a minute, no one moved, and then all the slips of paper were opened. Suddenly, all the women began to speak at once, saying, "Who is it?" "Who's got it?" "Is it the Dunbars?" "Is it the Watsons?" Then the voices began to say, "It's Hutchinson. It's Bill," "Bill Hutchinson's got it."

"Go tell your father," Mrs. Dunbar said to her older son.

People began to look around to see the Hutchinsons. Bill Hutchinson was standing quiet, staring down at the paper in his hand. Suddenly, Tessie Hutchinson shouted to Mr. Summers, "You didn't give him time enough to take any paper he wanted. I saw you. It wasn't fair!"

"Be a good sport, Tessie," Mrs. Delacroix called, and Mrs. Graves said, "All of us took the same chance."

"Shut up, Tessie," Bill Hutchinson said.

"Well, everyone," Mr. Summers said, "that was done pretty fast, and now we've got to be hurrying a little more to get done in time." He consulted his next list. "Bill," he said, "you draw for the Hutchinson family. You got any other households in the Hutchinsons?"

"There's Don and Eva," Mrs. Hutchinson yelled. "Make *them* take their chance!"

"Daughters draw with their husbands' families, Tessie," Mr. Summers said gently. "You know that as well as anyone else."

"It wasn't *fair*," Tessie said.

"I guess not, Joe," Bill Hutchinson said regretfully. "My daughter draws with her husband's family, that's only fair. And I've got no other family except the kids."

"Then, as far as drawing for families is concerned, it's you," Mr. Summers said in explanation, "and as far as drawing for households is concerned, that's you, too. Right?"

"Right," Bill Hutchinson said.

"How many kids, Bill?" Mr. Summers asked formally.

"Three," Bill Hutchinson said. "There's Bill, Jr., and Nancy, and little Dave. And Tessie and me."

"All right, then," Mr. Summers said. "Harry, you got their tickets back?"

Mr. Graves nodded and held up the slips of paper. "Put them in the box, then," Mr. Summers directed. "Take Bill's and put it in."

"I think we ought to start over," Mrs. Hutchinson said, as quietly as she could. "I tell you it wasn't *fair*. You didn't give him time enough to choose. *Every*body saw that."

Mr. Graves had selected the five slips and put them in the box, and he dropped all the papers but those onto the ground, where the breeze caught them and lifted them off.

"Listen, everybody," Mrs. Hutchinson was saying to the people around her.

"Ready, Bill?" Mr. Summers asked, and Bill Hutchinson, with one quick glance around at his wife and children, nodded.

"Remember," Mr. Summers said, "take the slips and keep them folded until each person has taken one. Harry, you help little Dave." Mr. Graves took the hand of the little boy, who came willingly with him up to the box. "Take a paper out of the box, Davy," Mr. Summers said. Davy put his hand into the box and laughed. "Take just *one* paper," Mr. Summers said. "Harry, you hold it for him." Mr. Graves took the child's hand and removed the folded paper from the tight fist and held it while little Dave stood next to him and looked up at him wonderingly.

"Nancy next," Mr. Summers said. Nancy was twelve, and her school friends breathed heavily as she went forward, switching her skirt, and took a slip daintily from the box. "Bill, Jr.," Mr. Summers said, and Billy, his face red and his feet over-large, nearly knocked the box over as he got a paper out. "Tessie," Mr. Summers said. She hesitated for a minute, looking around defiantly, and then set her lips and went up to the box. She snatched a paper out and held it behind her.

"Bill," Mr. Summers said, and Bill Hutchinson reached into the box and felt around, bringing his hand out at last with the slip of paper in it.

The crowd was quiet. A girl whispered, "I hope it's not Nancy," and the sound of the whisper reached the edges of the crowd.

"It's not the way it used to be," Old Man Warner said clearly. "People ain't they way they used to be."

"All right," Mr. Summers said. "Open the papers. Harry, you open little Dave's."

Mr. Graves opened the slip of paper and there was a general sigh through the crowd as he held it up and everyone could see that it was blank. Nancy and Bill, Jr., opened theirs at the same time, and both beamed and laughed, turning around to the crowd and holding their slips of paper above their heads.

"Tessie," Mr. Summers said. There was a pause, and then Mr. Summers looked   70
at Bill Hutchinson, and Bill unfolded his paper and showed it. It was blank.

"It's Tessie," Mr. Summers said, and his voice was hushed. "Show us her paper,
Bill."

Bill Hutchinson went over to his wife and forced the slip of paper out of her
hand. It had a black spot on it, the black spot Mr. Summers had made the night before with the heavy pencil in the coal-company office. Bill Hutchinson held it up, and
there was a stir in the crowd.

"All right, folks," Mr. Summers said. "Let's finish quickly."

Although the villagers had forgotten the ritual and lost the original black box,
they still remembered to use stones. The pile of stones the boys had made earlier was
ready; there were stones on the ground with the blowing scraps of paper that had
come out of the box. Mrs. Delacroix selected a stone so large she had to pick it up
with both hands and turned to Mrs. Dunbar. "Come on," she said. "Hurry up."

Mrs. Dunbar had small stones in both hands, and she said, gasping for breath,   75
"I can't run at all. You'll have to go ahead and I'll catch up with you."

The children had stones already, and someone gave little Davy Hutchinson a
few pebbles.

Tessie Hutchinson was in the center of a cleared space by now, and she held
her hands out desperately as the villagers moved in on her. "It isn't fair," she said. A
stone hit her on the side of the head.

Old Man Warner was saying, "Come on, come on, everyone." Steve Adams was
in the front of the crowd of villagers with Mrs. Graves beside him.

"It isn't fair, it isn't right," Mrs. Hutchinson screamed, and then they were upon
her.

QUESTIONS

1. Describe the point of view of the story. What seems to be the position from
   which the narrator sees and describes the events? How much extra information
   does the narrator provide?
2. What would the story be like if it were done with an omniscient point of view?
   With the first person? Could the story be as suspenseful as it is? In what other
   ways might the story be different with another point of view?
3. Does the conclusion of "The Lottery" seem to come as a surprise? In retrospect,
   what hints earlier in the story tell about what is to come?
4. A scapegoat, in the ritual of purification described in the Old Testament, was
   an actual goat that was released into the wilderness after having been ceremo-
   nially heaped with the "iniquities" of the people (Leviticus 16:22). What traces
   of such a ritual are suggested in "The Lottery"? Can you think of any other
   kinds of rituals that are retained today even though their purpose is now remote or even nonexistent?
5. Is "The Lottery" a horror story or a surprise story, or neither or both? Explain.

KATHERINE MANSFIELD (1888–1923)

Mansfield was born in New Zealand but spent most of her brief adult life in England, where her stories earned a reputation for originality and experimentation. She treats topics of crucial importance in the lives of individuals, such as those in the stories "Bliss" and "The Garden Party." In "Miss Brill," an insignificant woman, who sustains herself with fancies and daydreams, is subjected to the crisis of shattering, callously cruel words. Mansfield's artistry is pointed and skillful, and the ending quizzically leaves readers wondering how the heroine will deal with her grief.

Miss Brill° ⸺⸺⸺⸺⸺⸺⸺⸺⸺⸺⸺*1920*

Although it was so brilliantly fine—the blue sky powdered with gold and great spots of light like white wine splashed over the Jardins Publiques°—Miss Brill was glad that she had decided on her fur. The air was motionless, but when you opened your mouth there was just a faint chill, like a chill from a glass of iced water before you sip, and now and again a leaf came drifting—from nowhere, from the sky. Miss Brill put up her hand and touched her fur. Dear little thing! It was nice to feel it again. She had taken it out of its box that afternoon, shaken out the moth-powder, given it a good brush, and rubbed the life back into the dim little eyes. "What has been happening to me?" said the sad little eyes. Oh, how sweet it was to see them snap at her again from the red eiderdown! . . . But the nose, which was of some black composition, wasn't at all firm. It must have had a knock, somehow. Never mind—a little dab of black sealing-wax when the time came—when it was absolutely necessary. . . . Little rogue! Yes, she really felt like that about it. Little rogue biting its tail just by her left ear. She could have taken it off and laid it on her lap and stroked it. She felt a tingling in her hands and arms, but that came from walking, she supposed. And when she breathed, something light and sad—no, not sad, exactly—something gentle seemed to move in her bosom.

There were a number of people out this afternoon, far more than last Sunday. And the band sounded louder and gayer. That was because the Season had begun. For although the band played all the year round on Sundays, out of season it was never the same. It was like some one playing with only the family to listen; it didn't care how it played if there weren't any strangers present. Wasn't the conductor wearing a new coat, too? She was sure it was new. He scraped with his foot and flapped his arms like a rooster about to crow, and the bandsmen sitting in the green rotunda blew out their cheeks and glared at the music. Now there came a little "flutey" bit—very pretty!—a little chain of bright drops. She was sure it would be repeated. It was; she lifted her head and smiled.

Only two people shared her "special" seat: a fine old man in a velvet coat, his hands clasped over a huge carved walking-stick, and a big old woman, sitting upright,

---

Miss Brill: Brill is the name of a common deep-sea flatfish.
Jardins Publiques: public gardens or park. The setting of the story is apparently a French seaside town.

with a roll of knitting on her embroidered apron. They did not speak. This was disappointing, for Miss Brill always looked forward to the conversation. She had become really quite expert, she thought, at listening as though she didn't listen, at sitting in other people's lives just for a minute while they talked round her.

She glanced, sideways, at the old couple. Perhaps they would go soon. Last Sunday, too, hadn't been as interesting as usual. An Englishman and his wife, he wearing a dreadful Panama hat and she button boots. And she'd gone on the whole time about how she ought to wear spectacles; she knew she needed them; but that it was no good getting any; they'd be sure to break and they'd never keep on. And he'd been so patient. He'd suggested everything—gold rims, the kind that curved round your ears, little pads inside the bridge. No, nothing would please her. "They'll always be sliding down my nose!" Miss Brill had wanted to shake her.

The old people sat on the bench, still as statues. Never mind, there was always the crowd to watch. To and fro, in front of the flower-beds and the band rotunda, the couples and groups paraded, stopped to talk, to greet, to buy a handful of flowers from the old beggar who had his tray fixed to the railings. Little children ran among them, swooping and laughing; little boys with big white silk bows under their chins, little girls, little French dolls, dressed up in velvet and lace. And sometimes a tiny staggerer came suddenly rocking into the open from under the trees, stopped, stared, as suddenly sat down "flop," until its small high-stepping mother, like a young hen, rushed scolding to its rescue. Other people sat on the benches and green chairs, but they were nearly always the same, Sunday after Sunday, and—Miss Brill had often noticed—there was something funny about nearly all of them. They were odd, silent, nearly all old, and from the way they stared they looked as though they'd just come from dark little rooms or even—even cupboards!

Behind the rotunda the slender trees with yellow leaves down drooping, and through them just a line of sea, and beyond the blue sky with gold-veined clouds.

Tum-tum-tum tiddle-um! tiddle-um! tum tiddle-um tum ta! blew the band.

Two young girls in red came by and two young soldiers in blue met them, and they laughed and paired and went off arm-in-arm. Two peasant women with funny straw hats passed, gravely, leading beautiful smoke-coloured donkeys. A cold, pale nun hurried by. A beautiful woman came along and dropped her bunch of violets, and a little boy ran after to hand them to her, and she took them and threw them away as if they'd been poisoned. Dear me! Miss Brill didn't know whether to admire that or not! And now an ermine toque° and a gentleman in grey met just in front of her. He was tall, stiff, dignified, and she was wearing the ermine toque she'd bought when her hair was yellow. Now everything, her hair, her face, even her eyes, was the same colour as the shabby ermine, and her hand, in its cleaned glove, lifted to dab her lips, was a tiny yellowish paw. Oh, she was so pleased to see him—delighted! She rather thought they were going to meet that afternoon. She described where she'd been—everywhere, here, there, along by the sea. The day was so charming—didn't he agree? And wouldn't he, perhaps? ... But he shook his head, lighted a cigarette, slowly breathed a great deep puff into her face, and, even while she was still talking and laughing, flicked the match away and walked on. The ermine toque was alone; she smiled more brightly than ever. But even the band seemed to know what she was feeling and played more softly, played tenderly, and the drum beat, "The Brute! The

5

---

ermine toque: close-fitting hat made of the white fur of an ermine; here the phrase stands for the woman wearing the hat.

Brute!" over and over. What would she do? What was going to happen now? But as Miss Brill wondered, the ermine toque turned, raised her hand as though she'd seen some one else, much nicer, just over there, and pattered away. And the band changed again and played more quickly, more gaily than ever, and the old couple on Miss Brill's seat got up and marched away, and such a funny old man with long whiskers hobbled along in time to the music and was nearly knocked over by four girls walking abreast.

Oh, how fascinating it was! How she enjoyed it! How she loved sitting here, watching it all! It was like a play. It was exactly like a play. Who could believe the sky at the back wasn't painted? But it wasn't till a little brown dog trotted on solemn and then slowly trotted off, like a little "theatre" dog, a little dog that had been drugged, that Miss Brill discovered what it was that made it so exciting. They were all on the stage. They weren't only the audience, not only looking on; they were acting. Even she had a part and came every Sunday. No doubt somebody would have noticed if she hadn't been there; she was part of the performance after all. How strange she'd never thought of it like that before! And yet it explained why she made such a point of starting from home at just the same time each week—so as not to be late for the performance—and it also explained why she had quite a queer, shy feeling at telling her English pupils how she spent her Sunday afternoons. No wonder! Miss Brill nearly laughed out loud. She was on the stage. She thought of the old invalid gentleman to whom she read the newspaper four afternoons a week while he slept in the garden. She had got quite used to the frail head on the cotton pillow, the hollowed eyes, the open mouth and the high pinched nose. If he'd been dead she mightn't have noticed for weeks; she wouldn't have minded. But suddenly he knew he was having the paper read to him by an actress! "An actress!" The old head lifted; two points of light quivered in the old eyes. "An actress—are ye?" And Miss Brill smoothed the newspaper as though it were the manuscript of her part and said gently: "Yes, I have been an actress for a long time."

The band had been having a rest. Now they started again. And what they played was warm, sunny, yet there was just a faint chill—a something, what was it?—not sadness—no, not sadness—a something that made you want to sing. The tune lifted, lifted, the light shone; and it seemed to Miss Brill that in another moment all of them, all the whole company, would begin singing. The young ones, the laughing ones who were moving together, they would begin, and the men's voices, very resolute and brave, would join them. And then she too, she too, and the others on the benches— they would come in with a kind of accompaniment—something low, that scarcely rose or fell, something so beautiful—moving. . . . And Miss Brill's eyes filled with tears and she looked smiling at all the other members of the company. Yes, we understand, we understand, she thought—though what they understood she didn't know.

Just at that moment a boy and girl came and sat down where the old couple had been. They were beautifully dressed; they were in love. The hero and heroine, of course, just arrived from his father's yacht. And still soundlessly singing, still with that trembling smile, Miss Brill prepared to listen.

"No, not now," said the girl, "Not here, I can't."

"But why? Because of that stupid old thing at the end there?" asked the boy. "Why does she come here at all—who wants her? Why doesn't she keep her silly old mug at home?"

"It's her fu-fur which is so funny," giggled the girl. "It's exactly like a fried whiting."

"Ah, be off with you!" said the boy in an angry whisper. Then: "Tell me, ma pe- 15
tite chérie—"

"No, not here," said the girl. "Not *yet*."

On her way home she usually bought a slice of honeycake at the baker's. It was
her Sunday treat. Sometimes there was an almond in her slice, sometimes not. It
made a great difference. If there was an almond it was like carrying home a tiny present—a surprise—something that might very well not have been there. She hurried
on the almond Sundays and struck the match for the kettle in quite a dashing way.

But to-day she passed the baker's by, climbed the stairs, went into the little dark
room—her room like a cupboard—and sat down on the red eiderdown. She sat there
for a long time. The box that the fur came out of was on the bed. She unclasped the
necklet quickly; quickly, without looking, laid it inside. But when she put the lid on
she thought she heard something crying.

QUESTIONS

1. Describe the point of view of "Miss Brill." Who says, in paragraph 1, "Dear little
   thing!" about the fur? How do you justify your conclusion about the source of
   this and similar insights that appear throughout the story?
2. Would this story be possible if told in the first person by Miss Brill herself? What
   might it have been like if told by a walker in the park who observed Miss Brill
   and overheard the conversation about her by the boy and girl?
3. A shift in the point of view occurs when the boy and girl sit down and Miss Brill
   overhears them. Describe the nature of this shift. Why do you think Mansfield
   made the change at this point?
4. In relation to the point of view, explain the last sentence of the story: "But when
   she put the lid on she thought she heard something crying."

LORRIE MOORE (b. 1957)

*One of the youngest writers represented in this book, Lor-
rie Moore teaches at the University of Wisconsin. She was
born in upstate New York, and received a Master of Fine
Arts degree from Cornell. Following her first collection of
stories,* Self Help *(1985), from which "How to Become a
Writer" is taken, she published her first novel,* Anagrams, *in 1986. A recent work is* Like Life *(1991), a
collection of eight stories taking its title from the last story,
a grim portrait of life in a polluted, deteriorating future.
She has received awards from the NEH and the Rockefeller
Foundation. Her fiction has been heralded for its combination of wry humor, deep feeling, and impending tragedy.*

How to Become a Writer ───────────────────── *1985*

First, try to be something, anything, else. A movie star/astronaut. A movie star/mis-
sionary. A movie star/kindergarten teacher. President of the World. Fail miserably. It

is best if you fail at an early age—say, fourteen. Early, critical disillusionment is necessary so that at fifteen you can write long haiku sequences about thwarted desire. It is a pond, a cherry blossom, a wind brushing against sparrow wing leaving for mountain. Count the syllables. Show it to your mom. She is tough and practical. She has a son in Vietnam and a husband who may be having an affair. She believes in wearing brown because it hides spots. She'll look briefly at your writing, then back up at you with a face blank as a donut. She'll say: "How about emptying the dishwasher?" Look away. Shove the forks in the fork drawer. Accidentally break one of the freebie gas station glasses. This is the required pain and suffering. This is only for starters.

In your high school English class look only at Mr. Killian's face. Decide faces are important. Write a villanelle about pores. Struggle. Write a sonnet. Count the syllables: nine, ten, eleven, thirteen. Decide to experiment with fiction. Here you don't have to count syllables. Write a short story about an elderly man and woman who accidentally shoot each other in the head, the result of an inexplicable malfunction of a shotgun which appears mysteriously in their living room one night. Give it to Mr. Killian as your final project. When you get it back, he has written on it: "Some of your images are quite nice, but you have no sense of plot." When you are home, in the privacy of your own room, faintly scrawl in pencil beneath his black-inked comments: "Plots are for dead people, pore-face."

Take all the babysitting jobs you can get. You are great with kids. They love you. You tell them stories about old people who die idiot deaths. You sing them songs like "Blue Bells of Scotland," which is their favorite. And when they are in their pajamas and have finally stopped pinching each other, when they are fast asleep, you read every sex manual in the house, and wonder how on earth anyone could ever do those things with someone they truly loved. Fall asleep in a chair reading Mr. McMurphy's *Playboy*. When the McMurphys come home, they will tap you on the shoulder, look at the magazine in your lap, and grin. You will want to die. They will ask you if Tracey took her medicine all right. Explain, yes, she did, that you promised her a story if she would take it like a big girl and that seemed to work out just fine. "Oh, marvelous," they will exclaim.

Try to smile proudly.

Apply to college as a child psychology major.

As a child psychology major, you have some electives. You've always liked birds. Sign up for something called "The Ornithological Field Trip." It meets Tuesdays and Thursdays at two. When you arrive at Room 134 on the first day of class, everyone is sitting around a seminar table talking about metaphors. You've heard of these. After a short, excruciating while, raise your hand and say diffidently, "Excuse me, isn't this Bird-watching One-oh-one?" The class stops and turns to look at you. They seem to all have one face—giant and blank as a vandalized clock. Someone with a beard booms out, "No, this is Creative Writing." Say: "Oh—right," as if perhaps you knew all along. Look down at your schedule. Wonder how the hell you ended up here. The computer, apparently, has made an error. You start to get up to leave and then don't. The lines at the registrar this week are huge. Perhaps you should stick with this mistake. Perhaps your creative writing isn't all that bad. Perhaps it is fate. Perhaps this is what your dad meant when he said, "It's the age of computers, Francie, it's the age of computers."

Decide that you like college life. In your dorm you meet many nice people. Some are smarter than you. And some, you notice, are dumber than you. You will continue, unfortunately, to view the world in exactly these terms for the rest of your life.

The assignment this week in creative writing is to narrate a violent happening. Turn in a story about driving with your Uncle Gordon and another one about two old people who are accidentally electrocuted when they go to turn on a badly wired desk lamp. The teacher will hand them back to you with comments: "Much of your writing is smooth and energetic. You have, however, a ludicrous notion of plot." Write another story about a man and a woman who, in the very first paragraph, have their lower torsos accidentally blitzed away by dynamite. In the second paragraph, with the insurance money, they buy a frozen yogurt stand together. There are six more paragraphs. You read the whole thing out loud in class. No one likes it. They say your sense of plot is outrageous and incompetent. After class someone asks you if you are crazy.

Decide that perhaps you should stick to comedies. Start dating someone who is funny, someone who has what in high school you called a "really great sense of humor" and what now your creative writing class calls "self-contempt giving rise to comic form." Write down all of his jokes, but don't tell him you are doing this. Make up anagrams of his old girlfriend's name and name all of your socially handicapped characters with them. Tell him his old girlfriend is in all of your stories and then watch how funny he can be, see what a really great sense of humor he can have.

Your child psychology advisor tells you you are neglecting courses in your major. What you spend the most time on should be what you're majoring in. Say yes, you understand.   10

In creative writing seminars over the next two years, everyone continues to smoke cigarettes and ask the same things: "But does it work?" "Why should we care about this character?" "Have you earned this cliché?" These seem like important questions.

On days when it is your turn, you look at the class hopefully as they scour your mimeographs for a plot. They look back up at you, drag deeply, and then smile in a sweet sort of way.

You spend too much time slouched and demoralized. Your boyfriend suggests bicycling. Your roommate suggests a new boyfriend. You are said to be self-mutilating and losing weight, but you continue writing. The only happiness you have is writing something new, in the middle of the night, armpits damp, heart pounding, something no one has yet seen. You have only those brief, fragile, untested moments of exhilaration when you know: you are a genius. Understand what you must do. Switch majors. The kids in your nursery project will be disappointed, but you have a calling, an urge, a delusion, an unfortunate habit. You have, as your mother would say, fallen in with a bad crowd.

Why write? Where does writing come from? These are questions to ask yourself. They are like: Where does dust come from? Or: Why is there war? Or: If there's a God, then why is my brother now a cripple?

These are questions that you keep in your wallet, like calling cards. These are questions, your creative writing teacher says, that are good to address in your journals but rarely in your fiction.

The writing professor this fall is stressing the Power of the Imagination. Which means he doesn't want long descriptive stories about your camping trip last July. He wants you to start in a realistic context but then to alter it. Like recombinant DNA. He wants you to let your imagination sail, to let it grow big-bellied in the wind. This is a quote from Shakespeare.

Tell your roommate your great idea, your great exercise of imaginative power: a transformation of Melville to contemporary life. It will be about monomania and the fish-eat-fish world of life insurance in Rochester, New York. The first line will be "Call me Fishmeal," and it will feature a menopausal suburban husband named Richard, who because he is so depressed all the time is called "Mopey Dick" by his witty wife Elaine. Say to your roommate: "Mopey Dick, get it?" Your roommate looks at you, like a buddy, and puts an arm around your burdened shoulders. "Listen, Francie," she says, slow as speech therapy. "Let's go out and get a big beer."

The seminar doesn't like this one either. You suspect they are beginning to feel sorry for you. They say: "You have to think about what is happening. Where is the story here?"

The next semester the writing professor is obsessed with writing from personal experience. You must write from what you know, from what has happened to you. He wants deaths, he wants camping trips. Think about what has happened to you. In three years there have been three things: you lost your virginity; your parents got divorced; and your brother came home from a forest ten miles from the Cambodian border with only half a thigh, a permanent smirk nestled into one corner of his mouth.

About the first you write: "It created a new space, which hurt and cried in a voice that wasn't mine, 'I'm not the same anymore, but I'll be okay.'"

About the second you write an elaborate story of an old married couple who stumble upon an unknown land mine in their kitchen and accidentally blow themselves up. You call it: "For Better or for Liverwurst."

About the last you write nothing. There are no words for this. Your typewriter hums. You can find no words.

At undergraduate cocktail parties, people say, "Oh, you write? What do you write about?" Your roommate, who has consumed too much wine, too little cheese, and no crackers at all, blurts: "Oh, my god, she always writes about her dumb boyfriend."

Later on in life you will learn that writers are merely open, helpless texts with no real understanding of what they have written and therefore must half-believe anything and everything that is said of them. You, however, have not yet reached this stage of literary criticism. You stiffen and say, "I do not," the same way you said it when someone in the fourth grade accused you of really liking oboe lessons and your parents really weren't just making you take them.

Insist you are not very interested in any one subject at all, that you are interested in the music of language, that you are interested in—in—syllables, because they are the atoms of poetry, the cells of the mind, the breath of the soul. Begin to feel woozy. Stare into your plastic wine cup.

"Syllables?" you will hear someone ask, voice trailing off, as they glide slowly toward the reassuring white of the dip.

Begin to wonder what you do write about. Or if you have anything to say. Or if there even is such a thing as a thing to say. Limit these thoughts to no more than ten minutes a day; like sit-ups, they can make you thin.

You will read somewhere that all writing has to do with one's genitals. Don't dwell on this. It will make you nervous.

Your mother will come visit you. She will look at the circles under your eyes and hand you a brown book with a brown briefcase on the cover. It is entitled: *How to Become a Business Executive.* She has also brought the *Names for Baby* encyclopedia you asked for; one of your characters, the aging clown–school teacher, needs a new name. You mother will shake her head and say: "Francie, Francie, remember when you were going to be a child psychology major?"

Say: "Mom, I like to write."   30

She'll say: "Sure you like to write. Of course. Sure you like to write."

Write a story about a confused music student and title it: "Schubert Was the One with the Glasses, Right?" It's not a big hit, although your roommate likes the part where the two violinists accidentally blow themselves up in a recital room. "I went out with a violinist once," she says, snapping her gum.

Thank god you are taking other courses. You can find sanctuary in nineteenth-century ontological snags and invertebrate courting rituals. Certain globular mollusks have what is called "Sex by the Arm." The male octopus, for instance, loses the end of one arm when placing it inside the female body during intercourse. Marine biologists call it "Seven Heaven." Be glad you know these things. Be glad you are not just a writer. Apply to law school.

From here on in, many things can happen. But the main one will be this: you decide not to go to law school after all, and, instead, you spend a good, big chunk of your adult life telling people how you decided not to go to law school after all. Somehow you end up writing again. Perhaps you go to graduate school. Perhaps you work odd jobs and take writing courses at night. Perhaps you are working on a novel and writing down all the clever remarks and intimate personal confessions you hear during the day. Perhaps you are losing your pals, your acquaintances, your balance.

You have broken up with your boyfriend. You now go out with men who, in-   35
stead of whispering "I love you," shout: "Do it to me, baby." This is good for your writing.

Sooner or later you have a finished manuscript more or less. People look at it in a vaguely troubled sort of way and say, "I'll bet becoming a writer was always a fantasy of yours, wasn't it?" Your lips dry to salt. Say that of all the fantasies possible in the world, you can't imagine being a writer even making the top twenty. Tell them you were going to be a child psychology major. "I bet," they always sigh, "you'd be great with kids." Scowl fiercely. Tell them you're a walking blade.

Quit classes. Quit jobs. Cash in old savings bonds. Now you have time like warts on your hands. Slowly copy all of your friends' addresses into a new address book.

Vacuum. Chew cough drops. Keep a folder full of fragments.

An eyelid darkening sideways.
World as conspiracy.
Possible plot? A woman gets on a bus.
Suppose you threw a love affair and nobody came.

At home drink a lot of coffee. At Howard Johnson's order the cole slaw. Consider how it looks like the soggy confetti of a map: where you've been, where you're going—"You Are Here," says the red star on the back of the menu.

Occasionally a date with a face blank as a sheet of paper asks you whether writers often become discouraged. Say that sometimes they do and sometimes they do. Say it's a lot like having polio.

"Interesting," smiles your date, and then he looks down at his arm hairs and starts to smooth them, all, always, in the same direction.

QUESTIONS

1. To whom does the "you" in the story refer? How strong a case may be made that the "you" refers really to "I," and that Francie is actually telling a story about herself?
2. In light of the title, how adequate are Francie's "directions" for becoming a writer?
3. Describe some of the comic elements of the story. What serious ideas about the development of a writer's profession undergird the story's humor?

ALICE MUNRO (b. 1931)

Munro was brought up in Ontario, twenty miles east of Lake Huron—a site not far from the imaginary village portrayed in "Meneseteung, " and also within the same locale as the town of Jubilee explored in Something I've Been Meaning to Tell You, *from which the story "The Found Boat" is selected (see Chapter 7). "Meneseteung" was first published in* The New Yorker *in 1988, and was also included in* The Best Short Stories of 1989. *Margaret Atwood, in her introduction to this volume, praised "Meneseteung" and called it one of Munro's very best. It is a story of great imaginative strength, for in it Munro develops an entire life for her heroine, endowing* this life with a sense of total believability and a powerful mood of sympathy and compassion. Munro included the story in her 1990 collection of stories, Friend of My Youth.

Meneseteung ———————————————————————————*1988*

I

Columbine, bloodroot,
And wild bergamot,
Gathering armfuls,
Giddily we go.

Offerings, the book is called. Gold lettering on a dull-blue cover. The author's full name underneath: Almeda Joynt Roth. The local paper, the *Vidette*, referred to her as "our poetess." There seems to be a mixture of respect and contempt, both for her calling and for her sex—or for their predictable conjuncture. In the front of the book is a photograph, with the photographer's name in one corner, and the date: 1865. The book was published later, in 1873.

The poetess has a long face; a rather long nose; full, somber dark eyes, which seem ready to roll down her cheeks like giant tears; a lot of dark hair gathered around her face in droopy rolls and curtains. A streak of gray hair plain to see, although she is, in this picture, only twenty-five. Not a pretty girl but the sort of woman who may age well, who probably won't get fat. She wears a tucked and braid-trimmed dark dress or jacket, with a lacy, floppy arrangement of white material—frills or a bow—filling the deep V at the neck. She also wears a hat, which might be made of velvet, in a dark color to match the dress. It's the untrimmed, shapeless hat, something like a soft beret, that makes me see artistic intentions, or at least a shy and stubborn eccentricity, in this young woman, whose long neck and forward-inclining head indicate as well that she is tall and slender and somewhat awkward. From the waist up, she looks like a young nobleman of another century. But perhaps it was the fashion.

"In 1854," she writes in the preface to her book, "my father brought us—my mother, my sister Catherine, my brother William, and me—to the wilds of Canada West (as it then was). My father was a harness-maker by trade, but a cultivated man who could quote by heart from the Bible, Shakespeare, and the writings of Edmund Burke. He prospered in this newly opened land and was able to set up a harness and leather-goods store, and after a year to build the comfortable house in which I live (alone) today. I was fourteen years old, the eldest of the children, when we came into this country from Kingston,° a town whose handsome streets I have not seen again but often remember. My sister was eleven and my brother nine. The third summer that we lived here, my brother and sister were taken ill of a prevalent fever and died within a few days of each other. My dear mother did not regain her spirits after this blow to our family. Her health declined, and after another three years she died. I then became housekeeper to my father and was happy to make his home for twelve years, until he died suddenly one morning at his shop.

"From my earliest years I have delighted in verse and I have occupied myself—and sometimes allayed my griefs, which have been no more, I know, than any sojourner on earth must encounter—with many floundering efforts at its composition. My fingers, indeed, were always too clumsy for crochetwork, and those dazzling productions of embroidery which one sees often today—the overflowing fruit and flower

---

Kingston: city in southeastern Ontario, on the St. Lawrence. The town of Meneseteung is visualized as being about 200 miles west of Kingston.

baskets, the little Dutch boys, the bonneted maidens with their watering cans—have likewise proved to be beyond my skill. So I offer instead, as the product of my leisure hours, these rude posies, these ballads, couplets, reflections."

Titles of some of the poems: "Children at Their Games," "The Gypsy Fair," "A Visit to My Family," "Angels in the Snow," "Champlain at the Mouth of the Meneseteung," "The Passing of the Old Forest," and "A Garden Medley." There are some other, shorter, poems, about birds and wildflowers and snowstorms. There is some comically intentioned doggerel about what people are thinking about as they listen to the sermon in church.

"Children at Their Games": The writer, a child, is playing with her brother and sister—one of those games in which children on different sides try to entice and catch each other. She plays on in the deepening twilight, until she realizes that she is alone, and much older. Still she hears the (ghostly) voices of her brother and sister calling. *Come over, come over, let Meda come over.* (Perhaps Almeda was called Meda in the family, or perhaps she shortened her name to fit the poem.)

"The Gypsy Fair": The Gypsies have an encampment near the town, a "fair," where they sell cloth and trinkets, and the writer as a child is afraid that she may be stolen by them, taken away from her family. Instead, her family has been taken away from her, stolen by Gypsies she can't locate or bargain with.

"A Visit to My Family": A visit to the cemetery, a one-sided conversation.

"Angels in the Snow": The writer once taught her brother and sister to make "angels" by lying down in the snow and moving their arms to create wing shapes. Her brother always jumped up carelessly, leaving an angel with a crippled wing. Will this be made perfect in Heaven, or will he be flying with his own makeshift, in circles?

"Champlain° at the Mouth of the Meneseteung": This poem celebrates the popular, untrue belief that the explorer sailed down the eastern shore of Lake Huron and landed at the mouth of the major river.

"The Passing of the Old Forest": A list of all the trees—their names, appearance, and uses—that were cut down in the original forest, with a general description of the bears, wolves, eagles, deer, waterfowl.

"A Garden Medley": Perhaps planned as a companion to the forest poem. Catalogue of plants brought from European countries, with bits of history and legend attached, and final Canadianness resulting from this mixture.

The poems are written in quatrains or couplets. There are a couple of attempts at sonnets, but mostly the rhyme scheme is simple—*abab* or *abcb*. The rhyme used is what was once called "masculine" ("shore"/"before"), though once in a while it is "feminine" ("quiver"/"river"). Are those terms familiar anymore?° No poem is unrhymed.

II

> While roses cold as snow
> Bloom where those "angels" lie.
> Do they but rest below
> Or, in God's wonder, fly?

Champlain: The explorer Samuel de Champlain (1567–1635), a founder of Quebec, had traveled to the eastern regions of Lake Huron in 1615.
anymore: See Chapter 19, on Prosody.

In 1879, Almeda Roth was still living in the house at the corner of Pearl and Dufferin streets, the house her father had built for his family. The house is there today; the manager of the liquor store lives in it. It's covered with aluminum siding; a closed-in porch has replaced the veranda. The woodshed, the fence, the gates, the privy, the barn—all these are gone. A photograph taken in the eighteen-eighties shows them all in place. The house and fence look a little shabby, in need of paint, but perhaps that is just because of the bleached-out look of the brownish photograph. The lace-curtained windows look like white eyes. No big shade tree is in sight, and, in fact, the tall elms that overshadowed the town until the nineteen-fifties, as well as the maples that shade it now, are skinny young trees with rough fences around them to protect them from the cows. Without the shelter of those trees, there is a great exposure—back yards, clotheslines, woodpiles, patchy sheds and barns and privies—all bare, exposed, provisional looking. Few houses would have anything like a lawn, just a patch of plantains and anthills and raked dirt. Perhaps petunias growing on top of a stump, in a round box. Only the main street is graveled; the other streets are dirt roads, muddy or dusty according to season. Yards must be fenced to keep animals out. Cows are tethered in vacant lots or pastured in back yards, but sometimes they get loose. Pigs get loose, too, and dogs roam free or nap in a lordly way on the boardwalks. The town has taken root, it's not going to vanish, yet it still has some of the look of an encampment. And, like an encampment, it's busy all the time—full of people, who, within the town, usually walk wherever they're going; full of animals, which leave horse buns, cowpats, dog turds, that ladies have to hitch up their skirts for; full of the noise of building and of drivers shouting at their horses and of the trains that come in several times a day.

I read about that life in the *Vidette*.

The population is younger than it is now, than it will ever be again. People past fifty usually don't come to a raw, new place. There are quite a few people in the cemetery already, but most of them died young, in accidents or childbirth or epidemics. It's youth that's in evidence in town. Children—boys—rove through the streets in gangs. School is compulsory for only four months a year, and there are lots of occasional jobs that even a child of eight or nine can do—pulling flax, holding horses, delivering groceries, sweeping the boardwalk in front of stores. A good deal of time they spend looking for adventures. One day they follow an old woman, a drunk nicknamed Queen Aggie. They get her into a wheelbarrow and trundle her all over town, then dump her into a ditch to sober her up. They also spend a lot of time around the railway station. They jump on shunting cars and dart between them and dare each other to take chances, which once in a while result in their getting maimed or killed. And they keep an eye out for any strangers coming into town. They follow them, offer to carry their bags, and direct them (for a five-cent piece) to a hotel. Strangers who don't look so prosperous are taunted and tormented. Speculation surrounds all of them—it's like a cloud of flies. Are they coming to town to start up a new business, to persuade people to invest in some scheme, to sell cures or gimmicks, to preach on the street corners? All these things are possible any day of the week. Be on your guard, the *Vidette* tells people. These are times of opportunity and danger. Tramps, confidence men, hucksters, shysters, plain thieves, are traveling the roads, and particularly the railroads. Thefts are announced: money invested and never seen again, a pair of trousers taken from the clothesline, wood from the woodpile, eggs from the henhouse. Such incidents increase in the hot weather.

Hot weather brings accidents, too. More horses run wild then, upsetting bug-

15

gies. Hands caught in the wringer while doing the washing, a man lopped in two at the sawmill, a leaping boy killed in a fall of lumber at the lumberyard. Nobody sleeps well. Babies wither with summer complaint, and fat people can't catch their breath. Bodies must be buried in a hurry. One day a man goes through the streets ringing a cowbell and calling "Repent! Repent!" It's not a stranger this time, it's a young man who works at the butcher shop. Take him home, wrap him in cold wet cloths, give him some nerve medicine, keep him in bed, pray for his wits. If he doesn't recover, he must go to the asylum.

Almeda Roth's house faces on Dufferin Street, which is a street of considerable respectability. On this street merchants, a mill owner, an operator of salt wells, have their houses. But Pearl Street, which her back windows overlook and her back gate opens onto, is another story. Workmen's houses are adjacent to hers. Small but decent row houses—that is all right. Things deteriorate toward the end of the block, and the next, last one becomes dismal. Nobody but the poorest people, the unrespectable and undeserving poor, would live there at the edge of a boghole (drained since then), called the Pearl Street Swamp. Bushy and luxuriant weeds grow there, makeshift shacks have been put up, there are piles of refuse and debris and crowds of runty children, slops are flung from doorways. The town tries to compel these people to build privies, but they would just as soon go in the bushes. If a gang of boys goes down there in search of adventure, it's likely they'll get more than they bargained for. It is said that even the town constable won't go down Pearl Street on a Saturday night. Almeda Roth has never walked past the row housing. In one of those houses lives the young girl Annie, who helps her with her housecleaning. That young girl herself, being a decent girl, has never walked down to the last block or the swamp. No decent woman ever would.

But that same swamp, lying to the east of Almeda Roth's house, presents a fine sight at dawn. Almeda sleeps at the back of the house. She keeps to the same bedroom she once shared with her sister Catherine—she would not think of moving to the larger front bedroom, where her mother used to lie in bed all day, and which was later the solitary domain of her father. From her window she can see the sun rising, the swamp mist filling with light, the bulky, nearest trees floating against that mist and the trees behind turning transparent. Swamp oaks, soft maples, tamarack, butternut.

III

> Here where the river meets the inland sea,
> Spreading her blue skirts from the solemn wood,
> I think of birds and beasts and vanished men,
> Whose pointed dwellings on these pale sands stood.

One of the strangers who arrived at the railway station a few years ago was Jarvis Poulter, who now occupies the house next to Almeda Roth's—separated from hers by a vacant lot, which he has bought, on Dufferin Street. The house is plainer than the Roth house and has no fruit trees or flowers planted around it. It is understood that this is a natural result of Jarvis Poulter's being a widower and living alone. A man may keep his house decent, but he will never—if he is a proper man—do much to decorate it. Marriage forces him to live with more ornament as well as sentiment, and it protects him, also, from the extremities of his own nature—from a frigid parsimony or a luxuriant sloth, from squalor, and from excessive sleeping, drinking, smoking, or freethinking.°

> In the interests of economy, it is believed, a certain estimable gentleman of our town persists in fetching water from the public tap and supplementing his fuel supply by picking up the loose coal along the railway track. Does he think to repay the town or the railway company with a supply of free salt?

This is the *Vidette*, full of shy jokes, innuendo, plain accusation, that no newspaper would get away with today. It's Jarvis Poulter they're talking about—though in other passages he is spoken of with great respect, as a civil magistrate, an employer, a churchman. He is close, that's all. An eccentric, to a degree. All of which may be a result of his single condition, his widower's life. Even carrying his water from the town tap and filling his coal pail along the railway track. This is a decent citizen, prosperous: a tall—slightly paunchy?—man in a dark suit with polished boots. A beard? Black hair streaked with gray. A severe and self-possessed air, and a large pale wart among the bushy hairs of one eyebrow? People talk about a young, pretty, beloved wife, dead in childbirth or some horrible accident, like a house fire or a railway disaster. There is no ground for this, but it adds interest. All he has told them is that his wife is dead.

He came to this part of the country looking for oil. The first oil well in the world was sunk in Lambton County, south of here, in the eighteen-fifties. Drilling for oil, Jarvis Poulter discovered salt. He set to work to make the most of that. When he walks home from church with Almeda Roth, he tells her about his salt wells. They are twelve hundred feet deep. Heated water is pumped down into them, and that dissolves the salt. Then the brine is pumped to the surface. It is poured into great evaporator pans over slow, steady fires, so that the water is steamed off and the pure, excellent salt remains. A commodity for which the demand will never fail.

"The salt of the earth," Almeda says.

"Yes," he says, frowning. He may think this disrespectful. She did not intend it so. He speaks of competitors in other towns who are following his lead and trying to hog the market. Fortunately, their wells are not drilled so deep, or their evaporating is not done so efficiently. There is salt everywhere under this land, but it is not so easy to come by as some people think.

Does that not mean, Almeda says, that there was once a great sea?

Very likely, Jarvis Poulter says. Very likely. He goes on to tell her about other enterprises of his—a brickyard, a lime kiln. And he explains to her how this operates, and where the good clay is found. He also owns two farms, whose woodlots supply the fuel for his operations.

> Among the couples strolling home from church on a recent, sunny Sabbath morning we noted a certain salty gentleman and literary lady, not perhaps in their first youth but by no means blighted by the frosts of age. May we surmise?

25

Freethinking: an intellectual movement, begun in the eighteenth century, emphasizing reason and denying the authority of religion and the supernatural. In the nineteenth century, there were organized groups in America devoted to freethinking.

This kind of thing pops up in the *Vidette* all the time.

May they surmise, and is this courting? Almeda Roth has a bit of money, which her father left her, and she has her house. She is not too old to have a couple of children. She is a good enough housekeeper, with the tendency toward fancy iced cakes and decorated tarts which is seen fairly often in old maids. (Honorable mention at the Fall Fair.) There is nothing wrong with her looks, and naturally she is in better shape than most married women of her age, not having been loaded down with work and children. But why was she passed over in her earlier, more marriageable years, in a place that needs women to be partnered and fruitful? She was a rather gloomy girl— that may have been the trouble. The deaths of her brother and sister and then of her mother, who lost her reason, in fact, a year before she died, and lay in her bed talking nonsense—those weighed on her, so she was not lively company. And all that reading and poetry—it seemed more of a drawback, a barrier, an obsession, in the young girl than in the middle-aged woman, who needed something, after all, to fill her time. Anyway, it's five years since her book was published, so perhaps she has got over that. Perhaps it was the proud, bookish father, encouraging her?

Everyone takes it for granted that Almeda Roth is thinking of Jarvis Poulter as a husband and would say yes if he asked her. And she is thinking of him. She doesn't want to get her hopes up too much, she doesn't want to make a fool of herself. She would like a signal. If he attended church on Sunday evenings, there would be a chance, during some months of the year, to walk home after dark. He would carry a lantern. (There is as yet no street lighting in town.) He would swing the lantern to light the way in front of the lady's feet and observe their narrow and delicate shape. He might catch her arm as they step off the boardwalk. But he does not go to church at night.

Nor does he call for her, and walk with her *to* church on Sunday mornings. That would be a declaration. He walks her home, past his gate as far as hers; he lifts his hat then and leaves her. She does not invite him to come in—a woman living alone could never do such a thing. As soon as a man and woman of almost any age are alone together within four walls, it is assumed that anything may happen. Spontaneous combustion, instant fornication, an attack of passion. Brute instinct, triumph of the senses. What possibilities men and women must see in each other to infer such dangers. Or, believing in the dangers, how often they must think about the possibilities.

When they walk side by side she can smell his shaving soap, the barber's oil, his pipe tobacco, the wool and linen and leather smell of his manly clothes. The correct, orderly, heavy clothes are like those she used to brush and starch and iron for her father. She misses that job—her father's appreciation, his dark, kind authority. Jarvis Poulter's garments, his smell, his movement, all cause the skin on the side of her body next to him to tingle hopefully, and a meek shiver raises the hairs on her arms. Is this to be taken as a sign of love? She thinks of him coming into her—*their*—bedroom in his long underwear and his hat. She knows this outfit is ridiculous, but in her mind he does not look so; he has the solemn effrontery of a figure in a dream. He comes into the room and lies down on the bed beside her, preparing to take her in his arms. Surely he removes his hat? She doesn't know, for at this point a fit of welcome and submission overtakes her, a buried gasp. He would be her husband.

One thing she has noticed about married women, and that is how many of them have to go about creating their husbands. They have to start ascribing preferences, opinions, dictatorial ways. Oh, yes, they say, my husband is very particular. He won't touch turnips. He won't eat fried meat. (Or he will only eat fried meat.) He likes me to wear blue (brown) all the time. He can't stand organ music. He hates to see a woman go out bareheaded. He would kill me if I took one puff of tobacco. This way, bewildered, sidelong-looking men are made over, made into husbands, heads of households. Almeda Roth cannot imagine herself doing that. She wants a man who doesn't have to be made, who is firm already and determined and mysterious to her. She does not look for companionship. Men—except for her father—seem to her deprived in some way, incurious. No doubt that is necessary, so that they will do what they have to do. Would she herself, knowing that there was salt in the earth, discover how to get it out and sell it? Not likely. She would be thinking about the ancient sea. That kind of speculation is what Jarvis Poulter has, quite properly, no time for.

Instead of calling for her and walking her to church, Jarvis Poulter might make another, more venturesome declaration. He could hire a horse and take her for a drive out to the country. If he did this, she would be both glad and sorry. Glad to be beside him, driven by him, receiving this attention from him in front of the world. And sorry to have the countryside removed for her—filmed over, in a way, by his talk and preoccupations. The countryside that she has written about in her poems actually takes diligence and determination to see. Some things must be disregarded. Manure piles, of course, and boggy fields full of high, charred stumps, and great heaps of brush waiting for a good day for burning. The meandering creeks have been straightened, turned into ditches with high, muddy banks. Some of the crop fields and pasture fields are fenced with big, clumsy uprooted stumps, others are held in a crude stitchery of rail fences. The trees have all been cleared back to the woodlots. And the woodlots are all second growth. No trees along the roads or lanes or around the farmhouses, except a few that are newly planted, young and weedy looking. Clusters of log barns—the grand barns that are to dominate the countryside for the next hundred years are just beginning to be built—and mean-looking log houses, and every four or five miles a ragged little settlement with a church and school and store and a blacksmith shop. A raw countryside just wrenched from the forest, but swarming with people. Every hundred acres is a farm, every farm has a family, most families have ten or twelve children. (This is the country that will send out wave after wave of settlers—it's already starting to send them—to northern Ontario and the West.) It's true that you can gather wildflowers in spring in the woodlots, but you'd have to walk through herds of horned cows to get to them.

35

IV

The Gypsies have departed.
Their camping-ground is bare.
Oh, boldly would I bargain now
At the Gypsy Fair.

Almeda suffers a good deal from sleeplessness, and the doctor has given her bromides and nerve medicine. She takes the bromides, but the drops gave her dreams that were too vivid and disturbing, so she has put the bottle by for an emergency. She told the doctor her eyeballs felt dry, like hot glass, and her joints ached. Don't read so much, he said, don't study; get yourself good and tired out with housework, take exercise. He believes that her troubles would clear up if she got married. He believes this in spite of the fact that most of his nerve medicine is prescribed for married women.

So Almeda cleans house and helps clean the church, she lends a hand to friends who are wallpapering or getting ready for a wedding, she bakes one of her famous cakes for the Sunday-school picnic. On a hot Saturday in August she decides to make some grape jelly. Little jars of grape jelly will make fine Christmas presents, or offerings to the sick. But she started late in the day and the jelly is not made by nightfall. In fact, the hot pulp has just been dumped into the cheesecloth bag, to strain out the juice. Almeda drinks some tea and eats a slice of cake with butter (a childish indulgence of hers), and that's all she wants for supper. She washes her hair at the sink and sponges off her body, to be clean for Sunday. She doesn't light a lamp. She lies down on the bed with the window wide open and a sheet just up to her waist, and she does feel wonderfully tired. She can even feel a little breeze.

When she wakes up, the night seems fiery hot and full of threats. She lies sweating on her bed, and she has the impression that the noises she hears are knives and saws and axes—all angry implements chopping and jabbing and boring within her head. But it isn't true. As she comes further awake she recognizes the sounds that she has heard sometimes before—the fracas of a summer Saturday night on Pearl Street. Usually the noise centers on a fight. People are drunk, there is a lot of protest and encouragement concerning the fight, somebody will scream "Murder!" Once, there was a murder. But it didn't happen in a fight. An old man was stabbed to death in his shack, perhaps for a few dollars he kept in the mattress.

She gets out of bed and goes to the window. The night sky is clear, with no moon and with bright stars. Pegasus° hangs straight ahead, over the swamp. Her father taught her that constellation—automatically, she counts its stars. Now she can make out distinct voices, individual contributions to the row. Some people, like herself, have evidently been wakened from sleep. "Shut up!" they are yelling. "Shut up that caterwauling or I'm going to come down and tan the arse off yez!"

But nobody shuts up. It's as if there were a ball of fire rolling up Pearl Street, shooting off sparks—only the fire is noise, it's yells and laughter and shrieks and curses, and the sparks are voices that shoot off alone. Two voices gradually distinguish themselves—a rising and falling howling cry and a steady throbbing, low-pitched stream of abuse that contains all those words which Almeda associates with danger and depravity and foul smells and disgusting sights. Someone—the person crying out, "Kill me! Kill me now!"—is being beaten. A woman is being beaten. She keeps crying, "Kill me! Kill me!" and sometimes her mouth seems choked with blood. Yet there is something taunting and triumphant about her cry. There is something theatrical about it. And the people around are calling out, "Stop it! Stop that!" or "Kill her! Kill her!" in a frenzy, as if at the theater or a sporting match or a prizefight. Yes, thinks Almeda, she has noticed that before—it is always partly a charade with these people; there is a clumsy sort of parody, an exaggeration, a missed connection. As if anything they did—even a murder—might be something they didn't quite believe but were powerless to stop.

Now there is the sound of something thrown—a chair, a plank?—and of a woodpile or part of a fence giving way. A lot of newly surprised cries, the sound of running, people getting out of the way, and the commotion has come much closer. Almeda can see a figure in a light dress, bent over and running. That will be the woman. She has got hold of something like a stick of wood or a shingle, and she turns and flings it at the darker figure running after her.

Pegasus: a constellation that is at its highest point (in early evening) in autumn. Its location here, in summer, indicates the lateness of the hour.

"Ah, go get her!" the voices cry. "Go baste her one!"

Many fall back now; just the two figures come on and grapple, and break loose again, and finally fall down against Almeda's fence. The sound they make becomes very confused—gagging, vomiting, grunting, pounding. Then a long, vibrating, choking sound of pain and self-abasement, self-abandonment, which could come from either or both of them.

Almeda has backed away from the window and sat down on the bed. Is that the sound of murder she has heard? What is to be done, what is she to do? She must light a lantern, she must go downstairs and light a lantern—she must go out into the yard, she must go downstairs. Into the yard. The lantern. She falls over on her bed and pulls the pillow to her face. In a minute. The stairs, the lantern. She sees herself already down there, in the back hall, drawing the bolt of the back door. She falls asleep.

She wakes, startled, in the early light. She thinks there is a big crow sitting on her windowsill, talking in a disapproving but unsurprised way about the events of the night before. "Wake up and move the wheelbarrow!" it says to her, scolding, and she understands that it means something else by "wheelbarrow"—something foul and sorrowful. Then she is awake and sees that there is no such bird. She gets up at once and looks out the window.

Down against her fence there is a pale lump pressed—a body.

Wheelbarrow.

She puts a wrapper over her nightdress and goes downstairs. The front rooms are still shadowy, the blinds down in the kitchen. Something goes *plop, plup*, in a leisurely, censorious way, reminding her of the conversation of the crow. It's just the grape juice, straining overnight. She pulls the bolt and goes out the back door. Spiders have draped their webs over the doorway in the night, and the hollyhocks are drooping, heavy with dew. By the fence, she parts the sticky hollyhocks and looks down and she can see.

A woman's body heaped up there, turned on her side with her face squashed down into the earth. Almeda can't see her face. But there is a bare breast let loose, brown nipple pulled long like a cow's teat, and a bare haunch and leg, the haunch bearing a bruise as big as a sunflower. The unbruised skin is grayish, like a plucked, raw drumstick. Some kind of nightgown or all-purpose dress she has on. Smelling of vomit. Urine, drink, vomit.

Barefoot, in her nightgown and flimsy wrapper, Almeda runs away. She runs around the side of her house between the apple trees and the veranda; she opens the front gate and flees down Dufferin Street to Jarvis Poulter's house, which is the nearest to hers. She slaps the flat of her hand many times against the door.

"There is the body of a woman," she says when Jarvis Poulter appears at last. He is in his dark trousers, held up with braces, and his shirt is half unbuttoned, his face unshaven, his hair standing up on his head. "Mr. Poulter, excuse me. A body of a woman. At my back gate."

He looks at her fiercely. "Is she dead?"

His breath is dank, his face creased, his eyes bloodshot.

"Yes. I think murdered," says Almeda. She can see a little of his cheerless front hall. His hat on a chair. "In the night I woke up. I heard a racket down on Pearl Street," she says, struggling to keep her voice low and sensible. "I could hear this—pair. I could hear a man and a woman fighting."

He picks up his hat and puts it on his head. He closes and locks the front door, and puts the key in his pocket. They walk along the boardwalk and she sees that she

45

50

55

is in her bare feet. She holds back what she feels a need to say next—that she is responsible, she could have run out with a lantern, she could have screamed (but who needed more screams?), she could have beat the man off. She could have run for help then, not now.

They turn down Pearl Street, instead of entering the Roth yard. Of course the body is still there. Hunched up, half bare, the same as before.

Jarvis Poulter doesn't hurry or halt. He walks straight over to the body and looks down at it, nudges the leg with the toe of his boot, just as you'd nudge a dog or a sow.

"You," he says, not too loudly but firmly, and nudges again.

Almeda tastes bile at the back of her throat.

"Alive," says Jarvis Poulter, and the woman confirms this. She stirs, she grunts weakly.

Almeda says, "I will get the doctor." If she had touched the woman, if she had forced herself to touch her, she would not have made such a mistake.

"Wait," says Jarvis Poulter. "Wait. Let's see if she can get up."

"Get up, now," he says to the woman. "Come on. Up, now. Up."

Now a startling thing happens. The body heaves itself onto all fours, the head is lifted—the hair all matted with blood and vomit—and the woman begins to bang this head, hard and rhythmically, against Almeda Roth's picket fence. As she bangs her head she finds her voice, and lets out an open-mouthed yowl, full of strength and what sounds like an anguished pleasure.

"Far from dead," says Jarvis Poulter. "And I wouldn't bother the doctor."

"There's blood," says Almeda as the woman turns her smeared face.

"From her nose," he says. "Not fresh." He bends down and catches the horrid hair close to the scalp to stop the head banging.

"You stop that now," he says. "Stop it. Gwan home now. Gwan home, where you belong." The sound coming out of the woman's mouth has stopped. He shakes her head slightly, warning her, before he lets go of her hair. "Gwan home!"

Released, the woman lunges forward, pulls herself to her feet. She can walk. She weaves and stumbles down the street, making intermittent, cautious noises of protest. Jarvis Poulter watches her for a moment to make sure that she's on her way. Then he finds a large burdock leaf, on which he wipes his hand. He says, "There goes your dead body!"

The back gate being locked, they walk around to the front. The front gate stands open. Almeda still feels sick. Her abdomen is bloated; she is hot and dizzy.

"The front door is locked," she says faintly. "I came out by the kitchen." If only he would leave her, she could go straight to the privy. But he follows. He follows her as far as the back door and into the back hall. He speaks to her in a tone of harsh joviality that she has never before heard from him. "No need for alarm," he says. "It's only the consequences of drink. A lady oughtn't to be living alone so close to a bad neighborhood." He takes hold of her arm just above the elbow. She can't open her mouth to speak to him, to say thank you. If she opened her mouth she would retch.

What Jarvis Poulter feels for Almeda Roth at this moment is just what he has not felt during all those circumspect walks and all his own solitary calculations of her probable worth, undoubted respectability, adequate comeliness. He has not been able to imagine her as a wife. Now that is possible. He is sufficiently stirred by her loosened hair—prematurely gray but thick and soft—her flushed face, her light clothing, which nobody but a husband should see. And by her indiscretion, her agitation, her foolishness, her need?

"I will call on you later," he says to her. "I will walk with you to church."

At the corner of Pearl and Dufferin streets last Sunday morning there was discovered, by a lady resident there, the body of a certain woman of Pearl Street, thought to be dead but only, as it turned out, dead drunk. She was roused from her heavenly—or otherwise—stupor by the firm persuasion of Mr. Poulter, a neighbour and a Civil magistrate, who had been summoned by the lady resident. Incidents of this sort, unseemly, troublesome, and disgraceful to our town, have of late become all too common.

V

I sit at the bottom of sleep,
As on the floor of the sea.
And fanciful Citizens of the Deep
Are graciously greeting me.

As soon as Jarvis Poulter has gone and she has heard her front gate close, Almeda rushes to the privy. Her relief is not complete, however, and she realizes that the pain and fullness in her lower body come from an accumulation of menstrual blood that has not yet started to flow. She closes and locks the back door. Then, remembering Jarvis Poulter's words about church, she writes on a piece of paper, "I am not well, and wish to rest today." She sticks this firmly into the outside frame of the little window in the front door. She locks that door, too. She is trembling, as if from a great shock or danger. But she builds a fire, so that she can make tea. She boils water, measures the tea leaves, makes a large pot of tea, whose steam and smell sicken her further. She pours out a cup while the tea is still quite weak and adds to it several dark drops of nerve medicine. She sits to drink it without raising the kitchen blind. There, in the middle of the floor, is the cheesecloth bag hanging on its broom handle between the two chair backs. The grape pulp and juice has stained the swollen cloth a dark purple. *Plop, plup* into the basin beneath. She can't sit and look at such a thing. She takes her cup, the teapot, and the bottle of medicine into the dining room.

She is still sitting there when the horses start to go by on the way to church, stirring up clouds of dust. The roads will be getting hot as ashes. She is there when the gate is opened and a man's confident steps sound on her veranda. Her hearing is so sharp she seems to hear the paper taken out of the frame and unfolded—she can almost hear him reading it, hear the words in his mind. Then the footsteps go the other way, down the steps. The gate closes. An image comes to her of tombstones—it makes her laugh. Tombstones are marching down the street on their little booted feet, their long bodies inclined forward, their expressions preoccupied and severe. The church bells are ringing.

Then the clock in the hall strikes twelve and an hour has passed.

The house is getting hot. She drinks more tea and adds more medicine. She knows that the medicine is affecting her. It is responsible for her extraordinary languor, her perfect immobility, her unresisting surrender to her surroundings. That is all right. It seems necessary.

Her surroundings—some of her surroundings—in the dining room are these: walls covered with dark green garlanded wallpaper, lace curtains and mulberry velvet curtains on the windows, a table with a crocheted cloth and a bowl of wax fruit, a pink-ish-gray carpet with nosegays of blue and pink roses, a sideboard spread with embroidered runners and holding various patterned plates and jugs and the silver tea things. A lot of things to watch. For every one of these patterns, decorations, seems charged with life, ready to move and flow and alter. Or possibly to explode. Almeda Roth's occupation throughout the day is to keep an eye on them. Not to prevent their alteration so much as to catch them at it—to understand it, to be a part of it. So much is going on in this room that there is no need to leave it. There is not even the thought of leaving it.

Of course, Almeda in her observations cannot escape words. She may think she can, but she can't. Soon this glowing and swelling begins to suggest words—not specific words but a flow of words somewhere, just about ready to make themselves known to her. Poems, even. Yes, again, poems. Or one poem. Isn't that the idea—one very great poem that will contain everything and, oh, that will make all the other poems, the poems she has written, inconsequential, mere trial and error, mere rags? Stars and flowers and birds and trees and angels in the snow and dead children at twilight—that is not the half of it. You have to get in the obscene racket on Pearl Street and the polished toe of Jarvis Poulter's boot and the plucked-chicken haunch with its blue-black flower. Almeda is a long way now from human sympathies or fears or cozy household considerations. She doesn't think about what could be done for that woman or about keeping Jarvis Poulter's dinner warm and hanging his long underwear on the line. The basin of grape juice has overflowed and is running over her kitchen floor, staining the boards of the floor, and the stain will never come out.

She has to think of so many things at once—Champlain and the naked Indians and the salt deep in the earth but as well as the salt the money, the money-making intent brewing forever in heads like Jarvis Poulter's. Also, the brutal storms of winter and the clumsy and benighted deeds on Pearl Street. The changes of climate are often violent, and if you think about it there is no peace even in the stars. All this can be borne only if it is channeled into a poem, and the word "channeled" is appropriate, because the name of the poem will be—it *is*—"The Meneseteung." The name of the poem is the name of the river. No, in fact it is the river, the Meneseteung, that is the poem—with its deep holes and rapids and blissful pools under the summer trees and its grinding blocks of ice thrown up at the end of winter and its desolating spring floods. Almeda looks deep, deep into the river of her mind and into the tablecloth, and she sees the crocheted roses floating. They look bunchy and foolish, her mother's crocheted roses—they don't look much like real flowers. But their effort, their floating independence, their pleasure in their silly selves, does seem to her so admirable. A hopeful sign. *Meneseteung.*

She doesn't leave the room until dusk, when she goes out to the privy again and discovers that she is bleeding, her flow has started. She will have to get a towel, strap it on, bandage herself up. Never before, in health, has she passed a whole day in her nightdress. She doesn't feel any particular anxiety about this. On her way through the kitchen she walks through the pool of grape juice. She knows that she will have to mop it up, but not yet, and she walks upstairs leaving purple footprints and smelling her escaping blood and the sweat of her body that has sat all day in the closed hot room.

No need for alarm.

For she hasn't thought that crocheted roses could float away or that tombstones could hurry down the street. She doesn't mistake that for reality, and neither does she mistake anything else for reality, and that is how she knows that she is sane.

VI

I dream of you by night,
I visit you by day.
Father, Mother,
Sister, Brother,
Have you no word to say?

April 22, 1903. At her residence, on Tuesday last, between three and four   85
o'clock in the afternoon, there passed away a lady of talent and refinement
whose pen, in days gone by, enriched our local literature with a volume of sensitive, eloquent verse. It is a sad misfortune that in later years the mind of this
fine person had become somewhat clouded and her behaviour, in consequence, somewhat rash and unusual. Her attention to decorum and to the care
and adornment of her person had suffered, to the degree that she had become,
in the eyes of those unmindful of her former pride and daintiness, a familiar
eccentric, or even, sadly, a figure of fun. But now all such lapses pass from memory and what is recalled is her excellent published verse, her labours in former
days in the Sunday school, her dutiful care of her parents, her noble womanly
nature, charitable concerns, and unfailing religious faith. Her last illness was of
mercifully short duration. She caught cold, after having become thoroughly wet
from a ramble in the Pearl Street bog. (It has been said that some urchins
chased her into the water, and such is the boldness and cruelty of some of our
youth, and their observed persecution of this lady, that the tale cannot be entirely discounted.) The cold developed into pneumonia, and she died, attended
at the last by a former neighbour, Mrs. Bert (Annie) Friels, who witnessed her
calm and faithful end.

January, 1904. One of the founders of our community, an early maker
and shaker of this town, was abruptly removed from our midst on Monday
morning last, whilst attending to his correspondence in the office of his company. Mr. Jarvis Poulter possessed a keen and lively commercial spirit, which was
instrumental in the creation of not one but several local enterprises, bringing
the benefits of industry, productivity, and employment to our town.

I looked for Almeda Roth in the graveyard. I found the family stone. There was
just one name on it—Roth. Then I noticed two flat stones in the ground, a distance
of a few feet—six feet?—from the upright stone. One of these said "Papa," the other
"Mama." Farther out from these I found two other flat stones, with the names William
and Catherine on them. I had to clear away some overgrowing grass and dirt to see
the full name of Catherine. No birth or death dates for anybody, nothing about being dearly beloved. It was a private sort of memorializing, not for the world. There
were no roses, either—no sign of a rosebush. But perhaps it was taken out. The
grounds keeper doesn't like such things, they are a nuisance to the lawnmower, and
if there is nobody left to object he will pull them out.

I thought that Almeda must have been buried somewhere else. When this plot
was bought—at the time of the two children's deaths—she would still have been expected to marry, and to lie finally beside her husband. They might not have left room
for her here. Then I saw that the stones in the ground fanned out from the upright
stone. First the two for the parents, then the two for the children, but these were
placed in such a way that there was room for a third, to complete the fan. I paced out

from "Catherine" the same number of steps that it took to get from "Catherine" to "William," and at this spot I began pulling grass and scrabbling in the dirt with my bare hands. Soon I felt the stone and knew that I was right. I worked away and got the whole stone clear and I read the name "Meda." There it was with the others, staring at the sky.

I made sure I had got to the edge of the stone. That was all the name there was—Meda. So it was true that she was called by that name in the family. Not just in the poem. Or perhaps she chose her name from the poem, to be written on her stone.

I thought that there wasn't anybody alive in the world but me who would know this, who would make the connection. And I would be the last person to do so. But perhaps this isn't so. People are curious. A few people are. They will be driven to find things out, even trivial things. They will put things together, knowing all along that they may be mistaken. You see them going around with notebooks, scraping the dirt off gravestones, reading microfilm, just in the hope of seeing this trickle in time, making a connection, rescuing one thing from the rubbish.

QUESTIONS

1. What do you learn about the speaker of this story? How does what you learn—particularly in paragraph 90—explain the narrator's concern with the story of Meda and Jarvis? How intimately does the speaker reveal the mind of Meda?
2. What "facts" form the springboard for the story? As the speaker explains it, what firsthand experiences does she have with the places of the story? What effect do her experiences have on your perceptions of the characters?
3. Particularly considering paragraphs 14, 16, 31, and 85, explain the story's shifting or developing narration. You might deal with tense, documentation, and the degree of the speaker's involvement in the developing story.
4. Describe the character development of Meda Roth. What effect does her poetry have on how you understand her? Why does the episode of the beaten woman, and its immediate aftermath, cause a change in her attitude toward Jarvis?
5. Who is the subject of paragraphs 72–73? What is the effect of these paragraphs on Meda's story? Explain how one might claim that these paragraphs (a) interrupt the story, or (b) are integral to it.

WRITING ABOUT POINT OF VIEW

Your goal is to explain how point of view contributes to making the work exactly as it is. In prewriting, therefore, consider language, authority and opportunity for observation, the involvement or detachment of the speaker, the selection of detail, interpretive commentaries, and narrative development. The following questions will help you get started.

Questions for Discovering Ideas

- How is the narration made to seem real and probable? Are the actions and speeches reported authentically, as they might be seen and reported in life? How much of the story seems to result from the imaginative or creative powers of the narrator?

- To what extent does the point of view make the work interesting and effective, or uninteresting and ineffective?

- Is the narrator identifiable? What is she or he like? What qualities of character influence the narration?

- How does the narrator perceive the time of the actions? If the predominant tense is the past, what relationship, if any, does the speaker establish between the past and the present (e.g., drawing lessons, providing explanations). If the tense is present, what effect does this tense have on your understanding of the story?

First-Person Point of View

- What situation prompts the speaker to tell the story or explain the situation? What is the speaker's background?

- Is the speaker talking to the reader, a listener, or herself? How does her audience affect what she is saying? Is the level of language appropriate to her and the situation? How much does she tell about herself?

- To what degree is the narrator involved in the action (i.e., as a major participant, minor participant, or nonparticipating observer)? Does he make himself the center of humor or admiration? How? Does he seem aware of changes he undergoes?

- Does the speaker criticize other characters? Why? Does she seem to report fairly and accurately what others have told her?

Second-Person Point of View

- What is the situation that prompts the use of the second person? How does the speaker acquire the authority to explain things to the listener? How directly involved is the listener? If the listeners are indefinite, why does the speaker choose to use the "you" as the basis of the narration?

Third-Person Point of View

- Does the author seem to be speaking in an authorial voice, or has the author adopted a special but unnamed voice for the work?

- What is the speaker's level of language? Are actions, speeches, and explanations made fully or sparsely?

- From what apparent vantage point does the speaker report action and speeches? Does this vantage point make the characters seem distant or close? How much sympathy does the speaker express for the characters?

- To what degree is your interest centered on a particular character? Does the speaker give you thoughts and responses of this character (limited third person)?

- If the work is third-person omniscient, how extensive is this omniscience (e.g., all the characters or just a few)? Generally, what limitations or free-doms can be attributed to this point of view?

- What special kinds of knowledge does the narrator assume that the listen-ers or readers possess (e.g., art, religion, history, navigation, music, etc.)?

Strategies for Organizing Ideas

Your object is to develop your analysis of how the point of view deter-mines such aspects as situation, form, general content, and language. The questions in the preceding section will help you decide how the point of view interacts with these other elements.

An excellent way to strengthen your argument is to explore how some other point of view might affect the work you are considering (see paragraph 4 of the sample essay). Anderson's "I'm a Fool," for example, uses a first-per-son narrator—a young man telling about the greatest mistake in his life. You might consider whether this story could work with a third-person narration. A third-person limited narration would certainly state that the protagonist is self-critical and repentant. The first-person is superior, however, because we learn, first hand, about the narrator's actual feelings. Indeed, the story seems totally dependent on the use of the first-person narrator. Conversely, Mans-field's "Miss Brill" employs the third-person limited point of view, with the speaker presenting an intimate portrait of the major character, but also pre-serving an objective and ironic distance. If Miss Brill herself were the narra-tor, we would get the intimacy that encourages us to sympathize with her, but we would lose the distance which permits us to see her objectively.

You can see that this approach requires creative imagination, for you must speculate about a point of view that is not present. Considering alter-native points of view deeply, however, will greatly enhance your analytical and critical abilities.

In your conclusion, evaluate the success of the point of view: Is it con-sistent, effective, truthful? What does the writer gain or lose (if anything) by the selection of point of view?

DISTINGUISH POINT OF VIEW FROM OPINION

Be careful to distinguish between *point of view* and *opinions* or *beliefs*. Point of view refers to the dramatic situation occasioning the speaking of a work, in-cluding language, audience, and perspective on events and characters (includ-ing tense), whereas an opinion is a thought about something. In examining point of view, then, you should draw conclusions about how the speaking situation of the work actually *creates* the work. Philosophical and religious opinions belong to the consideration of ideas, but bear on point of view *only if they influence what the narrator says.*

SAMPLE ESSAY

Shirley Jackson's Dramatic Point of View in "The Lottery"°

[1] The dramatic point of view in Shirley Jackson's "The Lottery" is essential to her success in rendering horror in the midst of the ordinary.* The story, however, is not only one of horror: It may also be called a surprise story, an allegory, or a portrayal of human insensitivity and cruelty. But the validity of all other claims for "The Lottery" hinges on the author's control over point of view to make the events develop out of a seemingly everyday, matter-of-fact situation—a control that could not be easily maintained with another point of view. The success of Jackson's point of view is achieved through her characterization, selection of details, and diction.†

[2] Because of the dramatic point of view, Jackson succeeds in presenting the villagers as ordinary folks attending a normal, festive event—in contrast to the horror of their real purpose. The contrast depends on Jackson's speaker, who is emotionally uninvolved and who tells only enough about the 300 townsfolk and their customs to permit the conclusion that they are normal, common people. The principal character is a local housewife, Tessie Hutchinson, but the speaker presents little about her except that she is just like everyone else—an important characteristic when she, like any other person being singled out for punishment, objects not to the lottery itself but to the "unfairness" of the drawing. The same commonness applies also to the other characters, whose brief conversations are recorded but not analyzed. This detached, reportorial method of making the villagers seem common and one-dimensional is fundamental to Jackson's dramatic point of view, and the cruel twist of the ending depends on the method.

[3] While there could be much description, Jackson's speaker omits some of the important details to conceal the lottery's horrible purpose. For example, the speaker presents enough information about the lottery to permit readers to understand its rules, but does not disclose that the winning prize is instant death. The short saying "Lottery in June, corn be heavy soon" is mentioned as a remnant of a long-forgotten ritual, but the speaker does not explain anything more about this connection with scapegoatism and human sacrifice (¶ 32). None of these references seems unusual as the narrator first presents them, and it is only the conclusion that reveals, in reconsideration, their shocking ghastliness.

[4] Without doubt, a point of view other than the dramatic would spoil Jackson's concluding horror, because it would require more explanatory detail. A first-person speaker, for example, would not be credible without explaining the situation and revealing feelings that would give away the ending. Such an "I" speaker would need to say something like "The little boys gathered rocks but seemed not to be thinking about their forthcoming use in the execution." But

° Please see pp. 196–201 for this story.
* Central Idea.
† Thesis sentence.

how would such detail affect the reader's response to the horrifying conclusion? Similarly, an omniscient narrator would need to include details about people's reactions (how could he or she be omniscient otherwise?). A more suitable alternative might be a limited omniscient point of view confined to, say, a stranger in town, or to one of the local children. But any intelligent stranger would be asking "giveaway" questions, and any child but a tiny tot would know about the lottery's horrible purpose. Either hypothetical point-of-view character would therefore require revealing the information too soon. The only possible conclusion is that the point of view that Jackson chose—the dramatic—is best for this story. Because it permits her naturally to hold back crucial details, it is essential for the suspenseful delay of horror.

Appropriate both to the suspenseful ending and also to the simple character of the villagers is the speaker's language. The words are accurate and descriptive but not elaborate. When Tessie Hutchinson appears, for example, she dries "her hands on her apron" (¶ 8)—words that define her role as a housewife. Most of these simple, bare words may be seen as part of Jackson's technique of withholding detail to delay the reader's understanding. A prime example is the pile of stones, which is in truth a thoughtless and cruel preparation for the stoning, yet this conclusion cannot be drawn from the easy words describing it (¶ 2):

[5]   Bobby Martin had already stuffed his pockets full of stones, and the other boys soon followed his example, selecting the smoothest and roundest stones; Bobby and Harry Jones and Dickie Delacroix—the villagers pronounced this name "Dellacroy"—eventually made a great pile of stones in one corner of the square and guarded it against the raids of the other boys.

Both the nicknames and the connotation of boyhood games divert attention and obscure the horrible purpose of the stones. Even at the end, the speaker uses the word "pebbles" to describe the stones given to Tessie's son Davy (¶ 76). The implication is that Davy is playing a game, not a participant in killing his own mother!

Such masterly control over point of view is a major cause of Jackson's success in "The Lottery." Her narrative method is to establish the appearance of everyday, uneventful reality, which she maintains up to the beginning of the last scene. She is so successful that a reader's first response to the stoning is that "such a killing could not take place among such common, earthy folks."

[6]   Yet it is this reality that validates Jackson's vision. Horror is not to be found on moors and in haunted castles, but among everyday people like Jackson's 300 villagers. Without her control of the dramatic point of view, there could be little of this power of suggestion, and it would not be possible to claim such success for the story.

Commentary on the Essay

The strategy of this essay is to describe how Jackson's dramatic point of view is fundamental to her success in building toward the shocking horror of the ending. Words of tribute throughout the essay are "success," "control," "essential," "appropriate," and "masterly." The introductory paragraph sets out three areas for exploration in the body: character, detail, and diction.

The body begins with Paragraph 2, in which the aim is *not* to present a full character study (since the essay is not about character but point of view), but rather to discuss the ways in which the dramatic point of view *enables* the characters to be rendered. The topic of the paragraph is that the villagers are to be judged not as complete human beings but as "ordinary folks."

The second part of the body (paragraphs 3 and 4) emphasizes how the sparseness of detail aids Jackson in deferring conclusions about the horror of the drawing. Paragraph 4, which continues the topic of paragraph 3, shows how talking about alternative points of view may aid understanding of the story's actual point of view (see p. 226). The material for the paragraph is derived from notes speculating about whether Jackson's technique of withholding detail to build toward the concluding horror (the topic of paragraph 3) could be maintained with differing points of view. A combination of analysis and imagination is therefore at work in the paragraph.

The third section of the body (paragraph 5) emphasizes the idea that the flat, colorless diction defers awareness of what is happening; therefore the point of view is vital in the story's surprise and horror. The concluding paragraph (6) emphasizes the way in which general response to the story, and also its success, are conditioned by the detached, dramatic point of view.

WRITING TOPICS

1. Write a short narrative from the point of view of one of these characters:
   a. Lucy Wessen in "I'm a Fool": How I met and lost the most wonderful man.
   b. The baker in "Miss Brill": *My favorite customer.*
   c. Old Man Warner in "The Lottery": *People ain't the way they used to be.*
   d. Jarvis Poulter in "Meneseteung": Why did Meda Roth not want me to take her to church?
2. How would the story "Meneseteung" be affected if told by the narrators in "I'm a Fool," "How to Become a Writer," or "The Lottery"?
3. Recall a childhood occasion on which you were punished, and write an explanation of the punishment as though you were the adult who was in the position of punishing you. Be sure to consider your childhood self objectively, in the third person. Present things from the viewpoint of the adult, and try to determine how the adult would have learned about your action, judged it, and decided on your punishment.
4. Consider the proposition that people never speak without showing their motives, and that therefore we need to judge all things that we are told.

6

Setting: Place, Objects, and Culture in Stories

Like all human beings, fictional characters do not exist in isolation. Just as they become human by interacting with other characters, they gain identity because of their cultural and political allegiances, their possessions, their jobs, and the locations where they live and move and have their being. Stories must therefore necessarily include descriptions of places, objects, and backgrounds—the **setting.**

WHAT IS SETTING?

Setting is the natural, manufactured, political, cultural, and temporal environment, including everything that characters know and own. Characters may be either helped or hurt by their surroundings, and they may fight about possessions and goals. Further, as characters speak with each other, they reveal the degree to which they share the customs and ideas of their times.

Types of Settings

NATURE AND THE OUTDOORS. The natural world is an obvious location for the action of many narratives and plays. It is therefore important to note natural surroundings (hills, valleys, mountains, meadows, fields, trees, lakes, streams), living creatures (birds, dogs, horses, snakes), and also the conditions in which things happen (sunlight, darkness, calm, wind, rain, snow, storm, heat, cold)—any or all of which may influence character and action.

OBJECTS OF HUMAN MANUFACTURE AND CONSTRUCTION. To reveal or highlight qualities of character, and also to make fiction lifelike, authors include details about buildings and objects of human manufacture and construction. Houses, both interiors and exteriors, are common, as are possessions such as walking sticks, fences, park benches, toys, automobiles, phonograph records, necklaces, hair ribbons, cash registers, and so on. In Maupassant's "The Necklace," the loss of a comfortable home brings out the best in a character by causing her to adjust to her economic reversal, whereas in Lawrence's "The Horse Dealer's Daughter," such a loss leads a character to suicidal depression. A shabby but neat house reveals strength of character in Walker's "Everyday Use." In Greenberg's "And Sarah Laughed," the major character's life within the solitude of a farm setting influences her to reach out for a new form of communication.

Objects also enter directly into fictional action and character. A jar of herring is a major cause of conflict in "A & P"; a broken birdcage reveals the pathetic husband–wife relationship in "A Jury of Her Peers"; a furpiece leads to heartbreak in "Miss Brill." O'Connor uses a few pieces of candy to demonstrate a child's liberation from guilt in "First Confession." And Welty uses a bottle of medicine to represent the beauty of a character's love as well as the goal of her journey in "A Worn Path."

CULTURAL CONDITIONS AND ASSUMPTIONS. Just as physical setting influences characters, so do cultural conditions and assumptions. In García Márquez's "A Very Old Man with Enormous Wings," for example, the characters live in a small South American village, and the premises of their lives are therefore vastly different from our own. The broad cultural setting of Jackson's "The Lottery" is made up of two incompatible cultural assumptions: the primitive belief that the fertility of the earth requires human sacrifice and the modern scientific belief that such rituals are meaningless and savage. In Clark's "The Portable Phonograph," we see that an artistic and peaceful way of life breaks down when the culture on which it depends has been destroyed.

THE LITERARY USES OF SETTING

Authors use setting to create meaning, just as painters include backgrounds and objects to render ideas. The contrasting settings of Boucher's portrait of *Madame de Pompadour*, for example, and Hopper's *Automat* demonstrate how the same subject—a single female figure—may show divergent views of human life, one elegant and pampered, the other ordinary and forlorn (see pp. 232 and 233). Writers manipulate literary locations in a comparable way. For example, in Welty's "A Worn Path" and Hawthorne's "Young Goodman Brown," woodland paths that are difficult to trace and filled with obstacles are a major topographical feature. These are central to the time and circumstances of the stories, but they also convey the idea that life is difficult and uncertain. Similarly, in Glaspell's "A Jury of Her Peers," the fixtures and utensils in the kitchen of the Wright farm indicate that midwestern homesteads early in the twentieth century were bleak and oppressive.

Madame de Pompadour, François Boucher, The Wallace Collection, London, England.

Important Purposes of Setting

To study the setting in a story, discover the important details, and then try to explain their function. Depending on the author's purpose, the amount of detail may vary. Poe provides graphic and colorful details in "The Masque of the Red Death," so that we may follow, almost visually, the weird and bizarre action at the story's end. In some stories the setting is so intensely present, like the woods in Welty's "A Worn Path," that it is almost literally an additional participant in the action.

Automat, 1927, Edward Hopper, Des Moines Art Center, Permanent Collection, 1958.2.

SETTING AND CREDIBILITY. One of the major purposes of setting in fiction is to lend **realism,** or **verisimilitude** to the story. As the description of location and objects becomes particular and detailed, the events of the work become more believable. "The House on Mango Street," for example, provides one such example of this technique; in this story, Cisneros gives us representative details about a number of ramshackle residences that her speaker's family has lived in. Even futuristic, symbolic, and fantastic stories, as well as ghost stories, seem more believable if they include places and objects from everyday experience. Hawthorne's "Young Goodman Brown" and Poe's "The Masque of the Red Death" are such stories. Though they make no pretenses at everyday realism, their credibility is enhanced because their settings are so realistic.

SETTING AND CHARACTER. Setting may intersect with character as a means by which authors underscore the importance of place, circumstance, and time on human growth and change. Glaspell's setting in "A Jury of Her Peers" is the kitchen of the lonely, dreary Wright farm. The kitchen is a place of such hard work, oppression, and unrelieved joylessness that it explains the extinguishing of Minnie's early brightness and promise, and also helps us understand her angry act. (A blending of setting and character as seen in Maupassant's "The Necklace" is explored in the two versions of the sample essay in Chapter 1).

The way characters respond and adjust to setting can reveal their strength or weakness. In Jackson's "The Lottery," for example, a number of townspeople question the custom of the lottery, but they still participate in the concluding mob action. Their acquiescence demonstrates their lack of thought and sensitivity. In Updike's "A & P," Sammy shows strength and decisiveness by protesting the store manager's straight-laced and inflexible disciplinary action.

SETTING AND ORGANIZATION. Authors often use setting to organize the story, as in Jackson's "The Lottery." All the story's actions take place in the village square, "between the post office and the bank" (paragraph 1), beginning at ten o'clock in the morning and ending almost exactly at noon—in other words, according to a pattern of before, during, and immediately after the lottery drawing. In Maupassant's "The Necklace," Mathilde and her husband move from a respectable apartment to a cheap attic flat. The story's final scene is believable because Mathilde takes a nostalgic walk on the *Champs Élysées,* the most fashionable street in Paris. Without this shift of setting, she could not have encountered Jeanne Forrestier again, for their usual ways of life would no longer bring them together.

Another organizational application of place, time, and object is the **framing** or **enclosing setting,** when an author opens with a particular description and then returns to the same setting at the end. An example is Welty's "A Worn Path," which begins with the major character walking toward Natchez and ends with her walking away from it. The use of objects as a frame may be seen in Mansfield's "Miss Brill," which opens and closes with references to the heroine's shabby furpiece. In such ways, framing creates a formal completeness, just as it may underscore the author's ideas about the human condition.

SETTING AND SYMBOL. If the scenes and materials of setting are highlighted or emphasized, they also may be taken as symbols through which the author expresses ideas (see also Chapter 9). For example, the shawl in Ozick's "The Shawl" has the ordinary function of providing cover, warmth, and nourishment for the baby, Magda. Because it is so prominent, however, it also suggests or symbolizes the attempt to preserve future generations, and because its loss also produces a human loss, it symbolizes the helplessness of Nazi extermination camp victims. In Updike's "A & P," the reference to the local Congregational church symbolizes the decorum and restraint that the people of the town—including those shopping at the A & P—are expected to exercise.

SETTING AND ATMOSPHERE. Setting also helps to create **atmosphere** or **mood.** Most actions *require* no more than a functional description of setting. Thus, taking a walk in a forest needs just the statement that there are trees. However, if you find descriptions of shapes, light and shadows, animals, wind, and sounds, you may be sure that the author is creating an atmosphere or mood for the action (as in Hawthorne's "Young Goodman Brown"). There are many ways to develop moods. Descriptions of bright colors (red, orange, yellow) may contribute to a mood of happiness. Darker or shaded colors, like those in Poe's "The Masque of the Red Death," may invoke gloom or augment hysteria. References to smells and sounds further bring the setting to life by asking additional sensory responses from the reader. The setting of a story in a small town or large city, or green or snow-covered fields, or middle-class or lower-class residences, may evoke responses to these places that contribute to the work's atmosphere.

SETTING AND IRONY. Just as setting may reinforce character and theme, so it may ironically establish expectations that are the opposite of what occurs. At the beginning of "The Lottery," for example, Jackson describes the folksiness of the assembling townspeople—details that make the conclusion ironic, for it is just these real, everyday folks who participate in the final horror. A bizarre irony is created by Poe in "The Masque of the Red Death," when Prince Prospero seals off his palace to prevent the plague but at the same moment seals the "Red Death" within his walls.

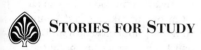

STORIES FOR STUDY

SANDRA CISNEROS (b. 1954)

Cisneros, a Mexican-American, was born in Illinois and now lives in Texas. She has been a "poet in the schools" in addition to teaching and also working as a college recruiter. She has held two NEA fellowships. Currently she serves a number of colleges as a visiting writer. The House on Mango Street, which includes the story by the same name, was Cisneros's first book. Originally published in 1983, it was reissued in 1991, when her second book of stories, Woman Hollering Creek and Other Stories, *was published.*

The House on Mango Street ———————————————— *1983*

We didn't always live on Mango Street. Before that we lived on Loomis on the third floor, and before that we lived on Keeler. Before Keeler it was Paulina, and before that I can't remember. But what I remember most is moving a lot. Each time it seemed there'd be one more of us. By the time we got to Mango Street we were six— Mama, Papa, Carlos, Kiki, my sister Nenny and me.

The house on Mango Street is ours and we don't have to pay rent to anybody or share the yard with the people downstairs or be careful not to make too much noise and there isn't a landlord banging on the ceiling with a broom. But even so, it's not the house we'd thought we'd get.

We had to leave the flat on Loomis quick. The water pipes broke and the landlord wouldn't fix them because the house was too old. We had to leave fast. We were using the washroom next door and carrying water over in empty milk gallons. That's why Mama and Papa looked for a house, and that's why we moved into the house on Mango Street, far away, on the other side of town.

They always told us that one day we would move into a house, a real house that would be ours for always so we wouldn't have to move each year. And our house would have running water and pipes that worked. And inside it would have real stairs, not hallway stairs, but stairs inside like the houses on T.V. And we'd have a basement and at least three washrooms so when we took a bath we didn't have to tell everybody. Our house would be white with trees around it, a great big yard and grass growing without a fence. This was the house Papa talked about when he held a lottery ticket and this was the house Mama dreamed up in the stories she told us before we went to bed.

But the house on Mango Street is not the way they told it at all. It's small and red with tight little steps in front and windows so small you'd think they were holding their breath. Bricks are crumbling in places, and the front door is so swollen you have to push hard to get in. There is no front yard, only four little elms the city planted by the curb. Out back is a small garage for the car we don't own yet and a small yard that looks smaller between the two buildings on either side. There are stairs in our house, but they're ordinary hallway stairs, and the house has only one washroom, very small. Everybody has to share a bedroom—Mama and Papa, Carlos and Kiki, me and Nenny.

Once when we were living on Loomis, a nun from my school passed by and saw me playing out front. The laundromat downstairs had been boarded up because it had been robbed two days before and the owner had painted on the wood YES WE'RE OPEN so as not to lose business.

Where do you live? she asked.

There, I said pointing up to the third floor.

You live *there*?

There. I had to look to where she pointed—the third floor, the paint peeling, wooden bars Papa had nailed on the windows so we wouldn't fall out. You live *there*? The way she said it made me feel like nothing. *There.* I lived *there.* I nodded.

I knew then I had to have a house. A real house. One I could point to. But this isn't it. The house on Mango Street isn't it. For the time being, Mama says. Temporary, says Papa. But I know how those things go.

QUESTIONS

1. Why is the speaker concerned with the nature of the houses she has lived in? What feeling does she show about these houses?

2. Describe the house on Mango Street. How does the condition of this house and the other houses explain the economic circumstances of the speaker's family?

3. What is the speaker like as a character? How do you learn about her? How much do you learn?

WALTER VAN TILBURG CLARK (1909–1971)

*Clark was born in Maine, but spent most of his life as a Professor of English in the western
United States. His best-known novel,* The Ox-Bow Incident *(1940), which was popularized as a movie, deals with fairness and justice on the Nevada frontier. His other major
novel was* The City of Trembling Leaves *(1945), a haunting story of initiation about
a young man whose ambition it is to be a composer. "The Portable Phonograph" appeared
in 1942, early in World War II, when American forces were being regularly defeated by the
Japanese armies and navies in the South Pacific , and two years before the allies invaded
France. The atomic bomb was not known at this time, and hence the desolation envisioned
in the story is the result of the "conventional" weaponry of bombs and tanks. Clark's stories
were collected in* The Watchful Gods *(1950).*

The Portable Phonograph ———————————————————— *1942*

The red sunset, with narrow, black cloud strips like threats across it, lay on the curved
horizon of the prairie. The air was still and cold, and in it settled the mute darkness
and greater cold of night. High in the air there was wind, for through the veil of the
dusk the clouds could be seen gliding rapidly south and changing shapes. A sensation
of torment, of two-sided, unpredictable nature, arose from the stillness of the earth
air beneath the violence of the upper air. Out of the sunset, through the dead, matted grass and isolated weed stalks of the prairie, crept the narrow and deeply rutted
remains of a road. In the road, in places, there were crusts of shallow, brittle ice.
There were little islands of an old oiled pavement in the road too, but most of it was
mud, now frozen rigid. The frozen mud still bore the toothed impress of great tanks,
and a wanderer on the neighboring undulations might have stumbled, in this light,
into large, partially filled-in and weed-grown cavities, their banks channeled and beginning to spread into badlands. These pits were such as might have been made by
falling meteors, but they were not. They were the scars of gigantic bombs, their raw-
ness already made a little natural by rain, seed and time. Along the road there were
rakish remnants of fence. There was also, just visible, one portion of tangled and multiple barbed wire still erect, behind which was a shelving ditch with small caves, now
very quiet and empty, at intervals in its back wall. Otherwise there was no structure or
remnant of a structure visible over the dome of the darkling earth, but only, in sheltered hollows, the darker shadows of young trees trying again.

Under the wuthering arch of the high wind a V of wild geese fled south. The
rush of their pinions sounded briefly, and the faint, plaintive notes of their expedi-
tionary talk. Then they left a still greater vacancy. There was the smell and expectation of snow, as there is likely to be when the wild geese fly south. From the remote
distance, toward the red sky, came faintly the protracted howl and quick yap-yap of a
prairie wolf.

North of the road, perhaps a hundred yards, lay the parallel and deeply in-
trenched course of a small creek, lined with leafless alders and willows. The creek was
already silent under ice. Into the bank above it was dug a sort of cell, with a single
opening, like the mouth of a mine tunnel. Within the cell there was a little red of fire,
which showed dully through the opening, like a reflection or a deception of the imagination. The light came from the chary burning of four blocks of poorly aged peat,
which gave off a petty warmth and much acrid smoke. But the precious remnants of
wood, old fence posts and timbers from the long-deserted dugouts, had to be saved
for the real cold, for the time when a man's breath blew white, the moisture in his

nostrils stiffened at once when he stepped out, and the expansive blizzards paraded for days over the vast open, swirling and settling and thickening, till the dawn of the cleared day when the sky was a thin blue-green and the terrible cold, in which a man could not live for three hours unwarmed, lay over the uniformly drifted swell of the plain.

Around the smoldering peat four men were seated cross-legged. Behind them, traversed by their shadows, was the earth bench, with two old and dirty army blankets, where the owner of the cell slept. In a niche in the opposite wall were a few tin utensils which caught the glint of the coals. The host was rewrapping in a piece of daubed burlap, four fine, leather-bound books. He worked slowly and very carefully, and at last tied the bundle securely with a piece of grass-woven cord. The other three looked intently upon the process, as if a great significance lay in it. As the host tied the cord, he spoke. He was an old man, his long, matted beard and hair gray to nearly white. The shadows made his brows and cheekbones appear gnarled, his eyes and cheeks deeply sunken. His big hands, rough with frost and swollen by rheumatism, were awkward but gentle at their task. He was like a prehistoric priest performing a fateful ceremonial rite. Also his voice had in it a suitable quality of deep, reverent despair, yet perhaps, at the moment, a sharpness of selfish satisfaction.

"When I perceived what was happening," he said, "I told myself, 'It is the end. I cannot take much; I will take these.'

"Perhaps I was impractical," he continued. "But for myself, I do not regret, and what do we know of those who will come after us? We are the doddering remnant of a race of mechanical fools. I have saved what I love; the soul of what was good in us here; perhaps the new ones will make a strong enough beginning not to fall behind when they become clever."

He rose with slow pain and placed the wrapped volumes in the niche with his utensils. The others watched him with the same ritualistic gaze.

"Shakespeare, the Bible, *Moby Dick*,° *The Divine Comedy*,"° one of them said softly. "You might have done worse; much worse."

"You will have a little soul left until you die," said another harshly. "That is more than is true of us. My brain becomes thick, like my hands." He held the big, battered hands, with their black nails, in the glow to be seen.

"I want paper to write on," he said. "And there is none."

The fourth man said nothing. He sat in the shadow farthest from the fire, and sometimes his body jerked in its rags from the cold. Although he was still young, he was sick, and coughed often. Writing implied a greater future than he now felt able to consider.

The old man seated himself laboriously, and reached out, groaning at the movement, to put another block of peat on the fire. With bowed heads and averted eyes, his three guests acknowledged his magnanimity.

"We thank you, Doctor Jenkins, for the reading," said the man who had named the books.

They seemed then to be waiting for something. Doctor Jenkins understood, but was loath to comply. In an ordinary moment he would have said nothing. But the words of *The Tempest*,° which he had been reading, and the religious attention of the three, made this an unusual occasion.

Moby Dick: by Herman Melville (1819–1891), a classic American novel published in 1851.
The Divine Comedy: by Dante (1265–1321), regarded as the supreme poem of the Italian Renaissance, circulated about 1300.
The Tempest: Shakespeare's last play, first performed about 1611.

"You wish to hear the phonograph,"° he said grudgingly.   15

The two middle-aged men stared into the fire, unable to formulate and expose the enormity of their desire.

The young man, however, said anxiously, between suppressed coughs, "Oh, please," like an excited child.

The old man rose again in his difficult way, and went to the back of the cell. He returned and placed tenderly upon the packed floor, where the firelight might fall upon it, an old, portable phonograph in a black case. He smoothed the top with his hand, then opened it. The lovely green-felt-covered disk became visible.

"I have been using thorns as needles," he said. "But tonight, because we have a musician among us"—he bent his head to the young man, almost invisible in the shadow—"I will use a steel needle. There are only three left."

The two middle-aged men stared at him in speechless adoration. The one with   20
the big hands, who wanted to write, moved his lips, but the whisper was not audible.

"Oh, don't," cried the young man, as if he were hurt. "The thorns will do beautifully."

"No," the old man said. "I have become accustomed to the thorns—but they are not really good. For you, my young friend, we will have good music tonight.

"After all," he added generously, and beginning to wind the phonograph, which creaked, "they can't last forever."

"No, nor we," the man who needed to write said harshly. "The needle, by all means."

"Oh, thanks," said the young man. "Thanks," he said again, in a low, excited   25
voice, and then stifled his coughing with a bowed head.

"The records, though," said the old man when he had finished winding, "are a different matter. Already they are very worn. I do not play them more than once a week. One, once a week, that is what I allow myself.

"More than a week I cannot stand it; not to hear them," he apologized.

"No, how could you?" cried the young man. "And with them here like this."

"A man can stand anything," said the man who wanted to write, in his harsh, antagonistic voice.

"Please, the music," said the young man.

"Only the one," said the old man. "In the long run we will remember more that   30
way."

He had a dozen records with luxuriant gold and red seals. Even in that light the others could see that the threads of the records were becoming worn. Slowly he read out the titles, and the tremendous, dead names of the composers and the artists and the orchestras. The three worked upon the names in their minds, carefully. It was difficult to select from such a wealth what they would at once most like to remember. Finally the man who wanted to write named Gershwin's "New York."°

"Oh, no," cried the sick young man, and then could say nothing more because he had to cough. The others understood him, and the harsh man withdrew his selection and waited for the musician to choose.

---

phonograph: Early phonographs, in use before electrically driven record players, had to be wound up by hand. They played records at a speed of 78 revolutions per minute, and used steel needles that had to be changed very often. The phonograph is especially valuable to the characters in this story because they have no electricity.

George Gershwin (1898–1937): American composer who wrote in the jazz idiom, not in the classical manner.

The musician begged Doctor Jenkins to read the titles again, very slowly, so that he could remember the sounds. While they were read, he lay back against the wall, his eyes closed, his thin, horny hand pulling at his light beard, and listened to the voices and the orchestras and the single instruments in his mind.

When the reading was done he spoke despairingly. "I have forgotten," he complained. "I cannot hear them clearly.

"There are things missing," he explained.

"I know," said Doctor Jenkins. "I thought that I knew all of Shelley° by heart. I should have brought Shelley."

"That's more soul than we can use," said the harsh man. "*Moby Dick* is better.

"By God, we can understand that," he emphasized.

The doctor nodded.

"Still," said the man who had admired the books, "we need the absolute if we are to keep a grasp on anything.

"Anything but these sticks and peat clods and rabbit snares," he said bitterly.

"Shelley desired an ultimate absolute," said the harsh man. "It's too much," he said. "It's no good; no earthly good."

The musician selected a Debussy° nocturne. The others considered and approved. They rose to their knees to watch the doctor prepare for the playing, so that they appeared to be actually in an attitude of worship. The peat glow showed the thinness of their bearded faces, and the deep lines in them, and revealed the condition of their garments. The other two continued to kneel as the old man carefully lowered the needle onto the spinning disk, but the musician suddenly drew back against the wall again, with his knees up, and buried his face in his hands.

At the first notes of the piano the listeners were startled. They stared at each other. Even the musician lifted his head in amazement, but then quickly bowed it again, strainingly, as if he were suffering from a pain he might not be able to endure. They were all listening deeply, without movement. The wet, blue-green notes tinkled forth from the old machine, and were individual, delectable presences in the cell. The individual, delectable presences swept into a sudden tide of unbearably beautiful dissonance, and then continued fully the swelling and ebbing of that tide, the dissonant inpourings, and the resolutions, and the diminishments, and the little, quiet wavelets of interlude lapping between. Every sound was piercing and singularly sweet. In all the men except the musician, there occurred rapid sequences of tragically heightened recollection. He heard nothing but what was there. At the final, whispering disappearance, but moving quietly, so that the others would not hear him and look at him, he let his head fall back in agony, as if it were drawn there by the hair, and clenched the fingers of one hand over his teeth. He sat that way while the others were silent, and until they began to breathe again normally. His drawn-up legs were trembling violently.

Quickly Doctor Jenkins lifted the needle off, to save it, and not to spoil the recollection with scraping. When he had stopped the whirling of the sacred disk, he courteously left the phonograph open and by the fire, in sight.

Percy Bysshe Shelley (1792–1822): English poet who wrote poems about the soul, intellectual beauty, and mutability.

Claude Debussy (1862–1918): French composer. His "Nocturne" for piano was first published in 1890.

The others, however, understood. The musician rose last, but then abruptly, and went quickly out at the door without saying anything. The others stopped at the door and gave their thanks in low voices. The doctor nodded magnificently.

"Come again," he invited, "in a week. We will have the 'New York.'"

When the two had gone together, out toward the rimmed road, he stood in the entrance, peering and listening. At first there was only the resonant boom of the wind overhead, and then, far over the dome of the dead, dark plain, the wolf cry lamenting. In the rifts of clouds the doctor saw four stars flying. It impressed the doctor that one of them had just been obscured by the beginning of a flying cloud at the very moment he heard what he had been listening for, a sound of suppressed coughing. It was not near by, however. He believed that down against the pale alders he could see the moving shadow.

With nervous hands he lowered the piece of canvas which served as his door, and pegged it at the bottom. Then quickly and quietly, looking at the piece of canvas frequently, he slipped the records into the case, snapped the lid shut, and carried the phonograph to his couch. There, pausing often to stare at the canvas and listen, he dug earth from the wall and disclosed a piece of board. Behind this there was a deep hole in the wall, into which he put the phonograph. After a moment's consideration, he went over and reached down his bundle of books and inserted it also. Then, guardedly, he once more sealed up the hole with the board and the earth. He also changed his blankets, and the grass-stuffed sack which served as a pillow, so that he could lie facing the entrance. After carefully placing two more blocks of peat on the fire, he stood for a long time watching the stretched canvas, but it seemed to billow naturally with the first gusts of a lowering wind. At last he prayed, and got in under his blankets, and closed his smoke-smarting eyes. On the inside of the bed, next to the wall, he could feel with his hand, the comfortable piece of lead pipe.

50

QUESTIONS

1. What kind of environment is described in the first three paragraphs of this story? What has happened before the story opens? To what extent do these paragraphs establish the tone and atmosphere of the story?

2. The first three descriptive paragraphs are loaded with adjectives. In the first, for example, we find *narrow, black, still, cold, mute, dead, isolated, shallow, brittle, old, frozen, tangled, quiet,* and *empty*. What do most of these adjectives contribute to the establishment of setting and, in turn, mood?

3. How is "the host's" home described? What do the details tell us about the host, humanity, and existence in the world of the story?

4. What record do the men choose to hear? What do the phonograph and the music represent to these men?

5. What does Dr. Jenkins do with his things after the men leave? How does he readjust his bed? Why does he do these things?

JOANNE GREENBERG (b. 1932)

Greenberg, a resident of Colorado, graduated from American University in Washington and also attended the University of London. Under the pseudonym "Hannah Green," she achieved wide recognition in 1964 with the novel I Never Promised You a Rose Garden, *which describes the struggles of a teenage girl against schizophrenia. In 1977, the story was made into a successful film, featuring Kathleen Quinlan. Greenberg's fiction reflects her deep concern for "problems of the less fortunate." She is a member of the National Association for the Deaf and has taught sign language. As a writer she has been prolific, producing nearly a dozen novels. "And Sarah Laughed" is taken from her collection* Rites of Passage *(1972).*

And Sarah Laughed° ————————————————— 1972

She went to the window every fifteen minutes to see if they were coming. They would be taking the new highway cutoff; it would bring them past the south side of the farm; past the unused, dilapidated outbuildings instead of the orchards and fields that were now full and green. It would look like a poor place to the new bride. Her first impression of their farm would be of age and bleached-out, dried-out buildings on which the doors hung open like a row of gaping mouths that said nothing.

All day, Sarah had gone about her work clumsy with eagerness and hesitant with dread, picking up utensils to forget them in holding, finding them two minutes later a surprise in her hand. She had been planning and working ever since Abel wrote to them from Chicago that he was coming home with a wife. Everything should have been clean and orderly. She wanted the bride to know as soon as she walked inside what kind of woman Abel's mother was—to feel, without a word having to be said, the house's dignity, honesty, simplicity, and love. But the spring cleaning had been late, and Alma Yoder had gotten sick—Sarah had had to go over to the Yoders and help out.

Now she looked around and saw that it was no use trying to have everything ready in time. Abel and his bride would be coming any minute. If she didn't want to get caught shedding tears of frustration, she'd better get herself under control. She stepped over the pile of clothes still unsorted for the laundry and went out on the back porch.

The sky was blue and silent, but as she watched, a bird passed over the fields crying. The garden spread out before her, displaying its varying greens. Beyond it, along the creek, there was a row of poplars. It always calmed her to look at them. She looked today. She and Matthew had planted those trees. They stood thirty feet high now, stately as figures in a procession. Once—only once and many years ago—she had tried to describe in words the sounds that the wind made as it combed those trees on its way west. The little boy to whom she had spoken was a grown man now, and he was bringing home a wife. Married....

Ever since he had written to tell them he was coming with his bride, Sarah had been going back in her mind to the days when she and Matthew were bride and

And Sarah Laughed: See Genesis 18:12.

groom and then mother and father. Until now, it hadn't seemed so long ago. Her life had flowed on past her, blurring the early days with Matthew when this farm was strange and new to her and when the silence of it was sharp and bitter like pain, not dulled and familiar like an echo of old age.

Matthew hadn't changed much. He was a tall, lean man, but he had had a boy's spareness then. She remembered how his smile came, wavered and went uncertainly, but how his eyes had never left her. He followed everything with his eyes. Matthew had always been a silent man; his face was expressionless and his body stiff with reticence, but his eyes had sought her out eagerly and held her and she had been warm in his look.

Sarah and Matthew had always known each other—their families had been neighbors. Sarah was a plain girl, a serious "decent" girl. Not many of the young men asked her out, and when Matthew did and did again, her parents had been pleased. Her father told her that Matthew was a good man, as steady as any woman could want. He came from honest, hardworking people and he would prosper any farm he had. Her mother spoke shyly of how his eyes woke when Sarah came into the room, and how they followed her. If she married him, her life would be full of the things she knew and loved, an easy, familiar world with her parents' farm not two miles down the road. But no one wanted to mention the one thing that worried Sarah: the fact that Matthew was deaf. It was what stopped her from saying yes right away; she loved him, but she was worried about his deafness. The things she feared about it were the practical things: a fall or a fire when he wouldn't hear her cry for help. Only long after she had put those fears aside and moved the scant two miles into his different world, did she realize that the things she had feared were the wrong things.

Now they had been married for twenty-five years. It was a good marriage—good enough. Matthew was generous, strong, and loving. The farm prospered. His silence made him seem more patient, and because she became more silent also, their neighbors saw in them the dignity and strength of two people who do not rail against misfortune, who are beyond trivial talk and gossip; whose lives needed no words. Over the years of help given and meetings attended, people noticed how little they needed to say. Only Sarah's friend Luita knew that in the beginning, when they were first married, they had written yearning notes to each other. But Luita didn't know that the notes also were mute. Sarah had never shown them to anyone, although she kept them all, and sometimes she would go up and get the box out of her closet and read them over. She had saved every scrap, from questions about the eggs to the tattered note he had left beside his plate on their first anniversary. He had written it when she was busy at the stove and then he'd gone out and she hadn't seen it until she cleared the table.

The note said: "I love you derest wife Sarah. I pray you have happy day all day your life."

When she wanted to tell him something, she spoke to him slowly, facing him, and he took the words as they formed on her lips. His speaking voice was thick and hard to understand and he perceived that it was unpleasant. He didn't like to use it. When he had to say something, he used his odd, grunting tone, and she came to understand what he said. If she ever hungered for laughter from him or the little meaningless talk that confirms existence and affection, she told herself angrily that Matthew talked through his work. Words die in the air; they can be turned one way or another, but Matthew's work prayed and laughed for him. He took good care of her and the boys, and they idolized him. Surely that counted more than all the words—words that meant and didn't mean—behind which people could hide.

10

Over the years she seldom noticed her own increasing silence, and there were times when his tenderness, which was always given without words, seemed to her to make his silence beautiful.

She thought of the morning she had come downstairs feeling heavy and off balance with her first pregnancy—with Abel. She had gone to the kitchen to begin the day, taking the coffeepot down and beginning to fill it when her eye caught something on the kitchen table. For a minute she looked around in confusion. They had already laid away what the baby would need: diapers, little shirts and bedding, all folded away in the drawer upstairs, but here on the table was a bounty of cloth, all planned and scrimped for and bought from careful, careful study of the catalogue— yards of patterned flannel and plissé, coat wool and bright red corduroy. Sixteen yards of yellow ribbon for bindings. Under the coat wool was cloth Matthew had chosen for her; blue with a little gray figure. It was silk, and there was a card on which was rolled precisely enough lace edging for her collar and sleeves. All the long studying and careful planning, all in silence.

She had run upstairs and thanked him and hugged him, but it was no use showing delight with words, making plans, matching cloth and figuring which pieces would be for the jacket and which for sleepers. Most wives used such fussing to tell their husbands how much they thought of their gifts. But Matthew's silence was her silence too.

When he had left to go to the orchard after breakfast that morning, she had gone to their room and stuffed her ears with cotton, trying to understand the world as it must be to him, with no sound. The cotton dulled the outside noises a little, but it only magnified all the noises in her head. Scratching her cheek caused a roar like a downpour of rain; her own voice was like thunder. She knew Matthew could not hear his own voice in his head. She could not be deaf as he was deaf. She could not know such silence ever.

So she found herself talking to the baby inside her, telling it the things she would have told Matthew, the idle daily things: Didn't Margaret Amson look peaked in town? Wasn't it a shame the drugstore had stopped stocking lump alum—her pickles wouldn't be the same.

Abel was a good baby. He had Matthew's great eyes and gentle ways. She chattered to him all day, looking forward to his growing up, when there would be confidences between them. She looked to the time when he would have his own picture of the world, and with that keen hunger and hope she had a kind of late blooming into a beauty that made people in town turn to look at her when she passed in the street holding the baby in the fine clothes she had made for him. She took Abel everywhere, and came to know a pride that was very new to her, a plain girl from a modest family who had married a neighbor boy. When they went to town, they always stopped over to see Matthew's parents and her mother.

Mama had moved to town after Pa died. Of course they had offered to have Mama come and live with them, but Sarah was glad she had gone to a little place in town, living where there were people she knew and things happening right outside her door. Sarah remembered them visiting on a certain spring day, all sitting in Mama's new front room. They sat uncomfortably in the genteel chairs, and Abel crawled around on the floor as the women talked, looking up every now and then for his father's nod of approval. After a while he went to catch the sunlight that was glancing off a crystal nut dish and scattering rainbow bands on the floor. Sarah smiled down at him. She too had a radiance, and, for the first time in her life, she knew it. She was wearing the dress she had made from Matthew's cloth—it became her and she knew that too, so she gave her joy freely as she traded news with Mama.

Suddenly they heard the fire bell ringing up on the hill. She caught Matthew's eye and mouthed, "Fire engines," pointing uphill to the firehouse. He nodded.

In the next minutes there was the strident, off-key blare as every single one of Arcadia's volunteer firemen—his car horn plugged with a matchstick and his duty before him—drove hellbent for the firehouse in an ecstasy of bell and siren. In a minute the ding-ding-ding-ding careened in deafening, happy privilege through every red light in town.

"Big bunch of boys!" Mama laughed. "You can count two Saturdays in good weather when they don't have a fire, and that's during the hunting season!"   20

They laughed. Then Sarah looked down at Abel, who was still trying to catch the wonderful colors. A madhouse of bells, horns, screaming sirens had gone right past them and he hadn't cried, he hadn't looked, he hadn't turned. Sarah twisted her head sharply away and screamed to the china cats on the whatnot shelf as loud as she could, but Abel's eyes only flickered to the movement and then went back to the sun and its colors.

Mama whispered, "Oh, my dear God!"

Sarah began to cry bitterly, uncontrollably, while her husband and son looked on, confused, embarrassed, unknowing.

The silence drew itself over the season and the seasons layered into years. Abel was a good boy; Matthew was a good man.

Later, Rutherford, Lindsay, and Franklin Delano came. They too were silent.   25
Hereditary nerve deafness was rare, the doctors all said. The boys might marry and produce deaf children, but it was not likely. When they started to school, the administrators and teachers told her that the boys would be taught specially to read lips and to speak. They would not be "abnormal," she was told. Nothing would show their handicap, and with training no one need know that they were deaf. But the boys seldom used their lifeless voices to call to their friends; they seldom joined games unless they were forced to join. No one but their mother understood their speech. No teacher could stop all the jumping, turning, gum-chewing schoolboys, or remember herself to face front from the blackboard to the sound-closed boys. The lip-reading exercises never seemed to make plain differences—"man," "pan," "began."

But the boys had work and pride in the farm. The seasons varied their silence with colors—crows flocked in the snowy fields in winter, and tones of golden wheat darkened across acres of summer wind. If the boys couldn't hear the bedsheets flapping on the washline, they could see and feel the autumn day. There were chores and holidays and the wheel of birth and planting, hunting, fishing, and harvest. The boys were familiar in town; nobody ever laughed at them, and when Sarah met neighbors at the store, they praised her sons with exaggerated praise, well meant, saying that no one could tell, no one could really tell unless they knew, about the boys not hearing.

Sarah wanted to cry to these kindly women that the simple orders the boys obeyed by reading her lips were not a miracle. If she could ever hear in their long-practiced robot voices a question that had to do with feelings and not facts, and answer it in words that rose beyond the daily, tangible things done or not done, *that* would be a miracle.

Her neighbors didn't know that they themselves confided to one another from a universe of hopes, a world they wanted half lost in the world that was; how often they spoke pitting inflection against meaning to soften it, harden it, make a joke of it, curse by it, bless by it. They didn't realize how they wrapped the bare words of love in gentle humor or wild insults that the loved ones knew were ways of keeping the secret of love between the speaker and the hearer. Mothers lovingly called their children crow-bait, mouse-meat, devils. They predicted dark ends for them, and the children heard the secrets beneath the words, heard them and smiled and knew, and let the love said-unsaid caress their souls. With her own bitter knowledge Sarah could only thank them for well-meaning and return to silence.

Standing on the back porch now, Sarah heard the wind in the poplars and she sighed. It was getting on to noon. Warm air was beginning to ripple the fields. Matthew would be ready for lunch soon, but she wished she could stand out under the warm sky forever and listen to birds stitching sounds into the endless silence. She found herself thinking about Abel again, and the bride. She wondered what Janice would be like. Abel had gone all the way to Chicago to be trained in drafting. He had met her there, in the school. Sarah was afraid of a girl like that. They had been married quickly, without family or friends or toasts or gifts or questions. It hinted at some kind of secret shame. It frightened her. That kind of girl was independent and she might be scornful of a dowdy mother-in-law. And the house was still a mess.

From down the road, dust was rising. Matthew must have seen it too. He came over the rise and toward the house walking faster than usual. He'd want to slick his hair down and wash up to meet the stranger his son had become. She ran inside and bundled up the unsorted laundry, ran upstairs and pulled a comb through her hair, put on a crooked dab of lipstick, banged her shin, took off her apron and saw a spot on her dress, put the apron on again and shouted a curse to all the disorder she suddenly saw around her.

Now the car was crunching up the thin gravel of the driveway. She heard Matthew downstairs washing up, not realizing that the bride and groom were already at the house. Protect your own, she thought, and ran down to tell him. Together they went to the door and opened it, hoping that at least Abel's familiar face would comfort them.

They didn't recognize him at first, and he didn't see them. He and the tiny bride might have been alone in the world. He was walking around to open the door for her, helping her out, bringing her up the path to the house, and all the time their fingers and hands moved and spun meanings at which they smiled and laughed; they were talking somehow, painting thoughts in the air so fast with their fingers that Sarah couldn't see where one began and the other ended. She stared. The school people had always told her that such finger-talk set the deaf apart. It was abnormal; it made freaks of them. . . . How soon Abel had accepted someone else's strangeness and bad ways. She felt so dizzy she thought she was going to fall, and she was more bitterly jealous than she had ever been before.

The little bride stopped before them appealingly and in her dead, deaf-rote voice, said, "Ah-am pliizd to meet'ou." Sarah put out her hand dumbly and it was taken and the girl's eyes shone. Matthew smiled, and this time the girl spoke and waved her hands in time to her words, and then gave Matthew her hand. So Abel had told that girl about Matthew's deafness. It had never been a secret, but Sarah felt somehow betrayed.

They had lunch, saw the farm, the other boys came home from their summer school and met Janice. Sarah put out cake and tea and showed Abel and Janice up to the room she had made ready for them, and all the time the two of them went on with love-talk in their fingers; the jokes and secrets knitted silently between them, fears told and calmed, hopes spoken and echoed in the silence of a kitchen where twenty-five years of silence had imprisoned her. Always they would stop and pull themselves back to their good manners, speaking or writing polite questions and answers for the family; but in a moment or two, the talk would flag, the urgent hunger would over-come them and they would fight it, resolutely turning their eyes to Sarah's mouth. Then the signs would creep into their fingers, and the joy of talk into their faces, and they would fall before the conquering need of their communion.

Sarah's friend Luita came the next day, in the afternoon. They sat over tea with the kitchen window open for the cool breeze and Sarah was relieved and grateful to hold to a familiar thing now that her life had suddenly become so strange to her. Luita hadn't changed at all, thank God—not the hand that waved her tea cool or the high giggle that broke into generous laughter.

"She's darling!" Luita said after Janice had been introduced, and, thankfully, had left them. Sarah didn't want to talk about her, so she agreed without enthusiasm.

Luita only smiled back. "Sarah, you'll never pass for pleased with a face like that."

"It's just—just her ways," Sarah said. "She never even wrote to us before the wedding, and now she comes in and—and changes everything. I'll be honest, Luita, I didn't want Abel to marry someone who was deaf. What did we train him for, all those special classes? . . . *not* to marry another deaf person. And she hangs on him like a wood tick all day. . ." She didn't mention the signs. She couldn't.

Luita said, "It's just somebody new in the house, that's all. She's important to you, but a stranger. Addie Purkhard felt the same way and you know what a lovely girl Velma turned out to be. It just took time. . . . She's going to have a baby, did she tell you?"

"Baby? Who?" Sarah cried, feeling cold and terrified.

"Why, *Velma*. A baby due about a month after my Dolores'."

It had never occurred to Sarah that Janice and Abel could have a baby. She wanted to stop thinking about it and she looked back at Luita whose eyes were glow-ing with something joyful that had to be said. Luita hadn't been able to see beyond it to the anguish of her friend.

Luita said, "You know, Sarah, things haven't been so good between Sam and me. . . ." She cleared her throat. "You know how stubborn he is. The last few weeks, it's been like a whole new start for us. I came over to tell you about it because I'm so happy, and I had to share it with you."

She looked away shyly, and Sarah pulled herself together and leaned forward, putting her hand on her friend's arm. "I'm so happy for you. What happened?"

"It started about three weeks ago—a night that neither of us could get to sleep. We hadn't been arguing; there was just that awful coldness, as if we'd both been frozen stiff. One of us started talking—just lying there in the dark. I don't even know who started, but pretty soon we were telling each other the most secret things—things we never could have said in the light. He finally told me that Dolores having a baby makes him feel old and scared. He's afraid of it, Sarah, and I never knew it, and it ex-plains why he hates to go over and see them, and why he argues with Ken all the time. Right there beside me he told me so many things I'd forgotten or misunder-stood. In the dark it's like thinking out loud—like being alone and yet together at the same time. I love him so and I came so close to forgetting it. . . ."

Sarah lay in bed and thought about Luita and Sam sharing their secrets in the dark. Maybe even now they were talking in their flower-papered upstairs room, moving against the engulfing seas of silence as if in little boats, finding each other and touching and then looking out in awe at the vastness all around them where they might have rowed alone and mute forever. She wondered if Janice and Abel fingered those signs in the dark on each other's body. She began to cry. There was that freedom, at least; other wives had to strangle their weeping.

When she was cried out, she lay in bed and counted all the good things she had: children, possessions, acres of land, respect of neighbors, the years of certainty and success. Then she conjured the little bride, and saw her standing in front of Abel's old car as she had at first—with nothing; all her virtues still unproven, all her fears still forming, and her bed in another woman's house. Against the new gold ring on the bride's finger, Sarah threw all the substance of her years to weigh for her. The balance went with the bride. It wasn't fair! The balance went with the bride because she had put that communion in the scales as well, and all the thoughts that must have been given and taken between them. It outweighed Sarah's twenty-five years of muteness; outweighed the house and barn and well-tended land, and the sleeping family keeping their silent thoughts.

The days went by. Sarah tortured herself with elaborate courtesy to Janice and politeness to the accomplice son, but she couldn't guard her own envy from herself and she found fault wherever she looked. Now the silence of her house was throbbing with her anger. Every morning Janice would come and ask to help, but Sarah was too restless to teach her, so Janice would sit for a while waiting and then get up and go outside to look for Abel. Then Sarah would decide to make coleslaw and sit with the chopping bowl in her lap, smashing the chopper against the wood with a vindictive joy that she alone could hear the sounds she was making, that she alone knew how savage they were and how satisfying.

At church she would see the younger boys all clean and handsome, Matthew greeting friends, Janice demure and fragile, and Abel proud and loving, and she would feel a terrible guilt for her unreasonable anger; but back from town afterwards, and after Sunday dinner, she noticed as never before how disheveled the boys looked, how ugly their hollow voices sounded. Had Matthew always been so patient and unruffled? He was like one of his own stock, an animal, a dumb animal.

Janice kept asking to help and Sarah kept saying their wasn't time to teach her. She was amazed when Matthew, who was very fussy about his fruit, suggested to her that Janice might be able to take care of the grapes and, later, work in the orchard.

"I haven't time to teach her!"

"Ah owill teeech Ja-nuss," Abel said, and they left right after dinner in too much of a hurry.

Matthew stopped Sarah when she was clearing the table and asked why she didn't like Janice. Now it was Sarah's turn to be silent, and when Matthew insisted, Sarah finally turned on him. "You don't understand," she shouted. "You don't understand a thing!" And she saw on his face the same look of confusion she had seen that day in Mama's fussy front room when she had suddenly begun to cry and could not stop. She turned away with the plates, but suddenly his hand shot out and he struck them to the floor, and the voice he couldn't hear or control rose to an awful cry, "Ah ahm dehf! Ah ahm dehf!" Then he went out, slamming the door without the satisfaction of its sound.

If a leaf fell or a stalk sprouted in the grape arbor, Janice told it over like a set of prayers. One night at supper, Sarah saw the younger boys framing those dumb-signs of hers, and she took them outside and slapped their hands. "*We* don't do that!" she shouted at them, and to Janice later she said, "Those . . . signs you make—I know they must have taught you to do that, but out here . . . well, it isn't our way."

Janice looked back at her in a confusion for which there were no words.   55

It was no use raging at Janice. Before she had come there had never been any-thing for Sarah to be angry about. . . . What did they all expect of her? Wasn't it enough that she was left out of a world that heard and laughed without being humiliated by the love-madness they made with their hands? It was like watching them undressing.

The wind cannot be caught. Poplars may sift it, a rising bird can breast it, but it will pass by and no one can stop it. She saw the boys coming home at a dead run now, and they couldn't keep their hands from taking letters, words, and pictures from the fingers of the lovers. If they saw an eagle, caught a fish, or got scolded, they ran to their brother or his wife, and Sarah had to stand in the background and demand to be told.

One day Matthew came up to her and smiled and said, "Look." He put out his two index fingers and hooked the right down on the left, then the left down gently on the right. "Fwren," he said, "Ja-nuss say, fwren."

To Sarah there was something obscene about all those gestures, and she said, "I don't like people waving their hands around like monkeys in a zoo!" She said it very clearly so that he couldn't mistake it.

He shook his head violently and gestured as he spoke. "Mouth eat; mouth kiss,   60 mouth tawk! Fin-ger wohk; fin-ger tawk. E-ah" (and he grabbed his ear, violently), "e-ah dehf. *Mihn*," (and he rapped his head, violently, as if turning a terrible impa-tience against himself so as to spare her) "*mihn not* dehf!"

Later she went to the barn after something and she ran into Lindsay and Franklin Delano standing guilty, and when she caught them in her eye as she turned, she saw their hands framing signs. They didn't come into the house until it was nearly dark. Was their hunger for those signs so great that only darkness could bring them home? They weren't bad boys, the kind who would do a thing just because you told them not to. Did their days have a hunger too, or was it only the spell of the lovers, honey-honeying to shut out a world of moving mouths and silence?

At supper she looked around the table and was reassured. It could have been any farm family sitting there, respectable and quiet. A glance from the father was all that was needed to keep order or summon another helping. Their eyes were lowered, their faces composed. The hands were quiet. She smiled and went to the kitchen to fix the shortcake she had made as a surprise.

When she came back, they did not notice her immediately. They were all busy talking. Janice was telling them something and they all had their mouths ridiculously pursed with the word. Janice smiled in assent and each one showed her his sign and she smiled at each one and nodded, and the signers turned to one another in their joy, accepting and begging acceptance. Then they saw Sarah standing there; the hands came down, the faces faded.

She took the dinner plates away and brought in the dessert things, and when she went back to the kitchen for the cake, she began to cry. It was beyond envy now; it was too late for measuring or weighing. She had lost. In the country of the blind, Mama used to say, the one-eyed man is king. Having been a citizen of such a country, she knew better. In the country of the deaf, the hearing man is lonely. Into that country a girl had come who, with a wave of her hand, had given the deaf ears for one an-other, and had made Sarah the deaf one.

Sarah stood, staring at her cake and feeling for that moment the profundity of the silence which she had once tried to match by stuffing cotton in her ears. Every-one she loved was in the other room, talking, sharing, standing before the awful, im-personal heaven and the unhearing earth with pictures of his thoughts, and she was the deaf one now. It wasn't "any farm family," silent in its strength. It was a yearning family, silent in its hunger, and a demure little bride had shown them all how deep the hunger was. She had shown Sarah that her youth had been sold into silence. She was too old to change now.

An anger rose in her as she stared at the cake. Why should they be free to move and gesture and look different while she was kept in bondage to their silence? Then she remembered Matthew's mute notes, his pride in Abel's training, his face when he had cried, "I am deaf!" over and over. She had actually fought that terrible yearning, that hunger they all must have had for their own words. If they could all speak some-how, what would the boys tell her?

She knew what she wanted to tell them. That the wind sounds through the poplar trees, and people have a hard time speaking to one another even if they aren't deaf. Luita and Sam had to have a night to hide their faces while they spoke. It sud-denly occurred to her that if Matthew made one of those signs with his hands and she could learn that sign, she could put her hands against his in the darkness, and read the meaning—that if she learned those signs she could hear him. . . .

She dried her eyes hurriedly and took in the cake. They saw her and the hands stopped, drooping lifelessly again; the faces waited mutely. Silence. It was a silence she could no longer bear. She looked from face to face. What was behind those eyes she loved? Didn't everyone's world go deeper than chores and bread and sleep?

"I want to talk to you," she said. "I want to talk, to know what you think." She put her hands out before her, offering them.

Six pairs of eyes watched her.

Janice said, "Mo-ther."

Eyes snapped away to Janice; thumb was under lip: the Sign.

Sarah followed them. "Wife," she said, showing her ring.

"Wife," Janice echoed, thumb under lip to the clasp of hands.

Sarah said, "I love. . . ."

Janice showed her and she followed hesitantly and then turned to Matthew to give and to be received in that sign.

QUESTIONS

1. Characterize Sarah. What do we learn about her character from the way she cares for her surroundings and tends to her tasks?

2. What kinds of detail about the appearance and circumstances of the farm ap-pear in the story? Why are these details included?

3. Why does Greenberg not disclose right away that Matthew is deaf? Why does she withhold the same detail about Abel? How does Sarah respond when she learns that Abel is deaf?

4. What attitudes toward deafness and communication does Janice, with her mas-tery of sign language, bring out in Sarah? To what degree may her attitudes be considered a crisis? How does Sarah respond to the crisis? Why?

CYNTHIA OZICK (b. 1928)

Ozick is a native of the Bronx, and she lives in the New York City area. An important writer on Jewish-American themes, she has published two novels, Trust *and* The Cannibal Galaxy, *three short-story collections,* The Pagan Rabbi, Bloodshed, *and* Leviathan; *and frequent essays and reviews. Her 1990 novella "Puttermesser Paired" was the first story featured in* Prize Stories 1992: The O. Henry Awards. *"The Shawl," first published in* The New Yorker *in 1980, was republished in* The Shawl *in 1983, with a companion story describing the heroine's experiences in the United States after surviving the Nazi death camp.*

The Shawl ————————————————————————1980

Stella, cold, cold the coldness of hell. How they walked on the roads together, Rosa with Magda curled up between sore breasts, Magda wound up in the shawl. Sometimes Stella carried Magda. But she was jealous of Magda. A thin girl of fourteen, too small, with thin breasts of her own, Stella wanted to be wrapped in a shawl, hidden away, asleep, rocked by the march, a baby, a round infant in arms. Magda took Rosa's nipple, and Rosa never stopped walking, a walking cradle. There was not enough milk; sometimes Magda sucked air; then she screamed. Stella was ravenous. Her knees were tumors on sticks, her elbows chicken bones.

Rosa did not feel hunger; she felt light, not like someone walking but like someone in a faint, in trance, arrested in a fit, someone who is already a floating angel, alert and seeing everything, but in the air, not there, not touching the road. As if teetering on the tips of her fingernails. She looked into Magda's face through a gap in the shawl: a squirrel in a nest, safe, no one could reach her inside the little house of the shawl's windings. The face, very round, a pocket mirror of a face: but it was not Rosa's bleak complexion, dark like cholera, it was another kind of face altogether, eyes blue as air, smooth feathers of hair nearly as yellow as the Star sewn into Rosa's coat. You could think she was one of *their* babies.

Rosa, floating, dreamed of giving Magda away in one of the villages. She could leave the line for a minute and push Magda into the hands of any woman on the side of the road. But if she moved out of line they might shoot. And even if she fled the line for half a second and pushed the shawl-bundle at a stranger, would the woman take it? She might be surprised, or afraid; she might drop the shawl, and Magda would fall out and strike her head and die. The little round head. Such a good child, she gave up screaming, and sucked now only for the taste of the drying nipple itself. The neat grip of the tiny gums. One mite of a tooth tip sticking up in the bottom gum, how shining, an elfin tombstone of white marble gleaming there. Without complaining, Magda relinquished Rosa's teats, first the left, then the right; both were cracked, not a sniff of milk. The duct crevice extinct, a dead volcano, blind eye, chill hole, so Magda took the corner of the shawl and milked it instead. She sucked and sucked, flooding the threads with wetness. The shawl's good flavor, milk of linen.

It was a magic shawl, it could nourish an infant for three days and three nights. Magda did not die, she stayed alive, although very quiet. A peculiar smell, of cinnamon and almonds, lifted out of her mouth. She held her eyes open every moment, forgetting how to blink or nap, and Rosa and sometimes Stella studied their blueness. On the road they raised one burden of a leg after another and studied Magda's face. "Aryan," Stella said, in a voice grown as thin as a string; and Rosa thought how Stella gazed at Magda like a young cannibal. And the time that Stella said "Aryan," it sounded to Rosa as if Stella had really said "Let us devour her."

But Magda lived to walk. She lived that long, but she did not walk very well, partly because she was only fifteen months old, and partly because the spindles of her legs could not hold up her fat belly. It was fat with air, full and round. Rosa gave almost all her food to Magda, Stella gave nothing; Stella was ravenous, a growing child herself, but not growing much. Stella did not menstruate. Rosa did not menstruate. Rosa was ravenous, but also not; she learned from Magda how to drink the taste of a finger in one's mouth. They were in a place without pity, all pity was annihilated in Rosa, she looked at Stella's bones without pity. She was sure that Stella was waiting for Magda to die so she could put her teeth into the little thighs.

Rosa knew Magda was going to die very soon; she should have been dead already, but she had been buried away deep inside the magic shawl, mistaken there for the shivering mound of Rosa's breasts; Rosa clung to the shawl as if it covered only herself. No one took it away from her. Magda was mute. She never cried. Rosa hid her in the barracks, under the shawl, but she knew that one day someone would inform; or one day someone, not even Stella, would steal Magda to eat her. When Magda began to walk Rosa knew that Magda was going to die very soon, something would happen. She was afraid to fall asleep; she slept with the weight of her thigh on Magda's body; she was afraid she would smother Magda under her thigh. The weight of Rosa was becoming less and less; Rosa and Stella were slowly turning into air.

Magda was quiet, but her eyes were horribly alive, like blue tigers. She watched. Sometimes she laughed—it seemed a laugh, but how could it be? Magda had never seen anyone laugh. Still, Magda laughed at her shawl when the wind blew its corners, the bad wind with pieces of black in it, that made Stella's and Rosa's eyes tear. Magda's eyes were always clear and tearless. She watched like a tiger. She guarded her shawl. No one could touch it; only Rosa could touch it. Stella was not allowed. The shawl was Magda's own baby, her pet, her little sister. She tangled herself up in it and sucked on one of the corners when she wanted to be very still.

Then Stella took the shawl away and made Magda die.

Afterward Stella said: "I was cold."

And afterward she was always cold, always. The cold went into her heart: Rosa saw that Stella's heart was cold. Magda flopped onward with her little pencil legs scribbling this way and that, in search of the shawl; the pencils faltered at the barracks opening, where the light began. Rosa saw and pursued. But already Magda was in the square outside the barracks, in the jolly light. It was the roll-call arena. Every morning Rosa had to conceal Magda under the shawl against a wall of the barracks and go out and stand in the arena with Stella and hundreds of others, sometimes for hours, and Magda, deserted, was quiet under the shawl, sucking on her corner. Every day Magda was silent, and so she did not die. Rosa saw that today Magda was going to die, and at the same time a fearful joy ran into Rosa's two palms, her fingers were on fire, she was astonished, febrile: Magda, in the sunlight, swaying on her pencil legs, was howling. Ever since the drying up of Rosa's nipples, ever since Magda's last scream on the road, Magda had been devoid of any syllable; Magda was a mute. Rosa believed that something had gone wrong with her vocal cords, with her windpipe, with the cave of her larynx; Magda was defective, without a voice; perhaps she was deaf; there might be something amiss with her intelligence; Magda was dumb. Even the laugh that came when the ash-stippled wind made a clown out of Magda's shawl was only the air-blown showing of her teeth. Even when the lice, head lice and body lice, crazed her so that she became as wild as one of the big rats that plundered the barracks at daybreak looking for carrion, she rubbed and scratched and kicked and bit and rolled without a whimper. But now Magda's mouth was spilling a long viscous rope of clamor.

"Maaaa—"

It was the first noise Magda had ever sent out from her throat since the drying up of Rosa's nipples.

"Maaaa . . . aaa!"

Again! Magda was wavering in the perilous sunlight of the arena, scrabbling on such pitiful little bent shins. Rosa saw. She saw that Magda was grieving for the loss of her shawl, she saw that Magda was going to die. A tide of commands hammered in Rosa's nipples: Fetch, get, bring! But she did not know which to go after first, Magda or the shawl. If she jumped out into the arena to snatch Magda up, the howling would not stop, because Magda would still not have the shawl; but if she ran back into the barracks to find the shawl, and if she found it, and if she came after Magda holding it and shaking it, then she would get Magda back, Magda would put the shawl in her mouth and turn dumb again.

Rosa entered the dark. It was easy to discover the shawl. Stella was heaped under it, asleep in her thin bones. Rosa tore the shawl free and flew—she could fly, she was only air—into the arena. The sunheat murmured of another life, of butterflies in summer. The light was placid, mellow. On the other side of the steel fence, far away, there were green meadows speckled with dandelions and deep-colored violets; beyond them, even farther, innocent tiger lilies, tall, lifting their orange bonnets. In the barracks they spoke of "flowers," of "rain": excrement, thick turd-braids, and the slow stinking maroon waterfall that slunk down from the upper bunks, the stink mixed with a bitter fatty floating smoke that greased Rosa's skin. She stood for an instant at the margin of the arena. Sometimes the electricity inside the fence would seem to hum; even Stella said it was only an imagining, but Rosa heard real sounds in the wire: grainy sad voices. The farther she was from the fence, the more clearly the voices crowded at her. The lamenting voices strummed so convincingly, so passionately, it was impossible to suspect them of being phantoms. The voices told her to hold up the shawl, high; the voices told her to shake it, to whip with it, to unfurl it like a flag. Rosa lifted, shook, whipped, unfurled. Far off, very far, Magda leaned across her air-fed belly, reaching out with the rods of her arms. She was high up, elevated, riding someone's shoulder. But the shoulder that carried Magda was not coming toward Rosa and the shawl, it was drifting away, the speck of Magda was moving more and more into the smoky distance. Above the shoulder a helmet glinted. The light tapped the helmet and sparkled it into a goblet. Below the helmet a black body like a domino and a pair of black boots hurled themselves in the direction of the electrified fence. The electric voices began to chatter wildly. "Maa-maa, maaamaaa," they all hummed together. How far Magda was from Rosa now, across the whole square, past a dozen barracks, all the way on the other side! She was no bigger than a moth.

All at once Magda was swimming through the air. The whole of Magda traveled through loftiness. She looked like a butterfly touching a silver vine. And the moment Magda's feathered round head and her pencil legs and balloonish belly and zigzag arms splashed against the fence, the steel voices went mad in their growling, urging

15

Rosa to run and run to the spot where Magda had fallen from her flight against the electrified fence; but of course Rosa did not obey them. She only stood, because if she ran they would shoot, and if she tried to pick up the sticks of Magda's body they would shoot, and if she let the wolf's screech ascending now through the ladder of her skeleton break out, they would shoot; so she took Magda's shawl and filled her own mouth with it, stuffed it in and stuffed it in, until she was swallowing up the wolf's screech and tasting the cinnamon and almond depth of Magda's saliva; and Rosa drank Magda's shawl until it dried.

QUESTIONS

1. Describe how Ozick presents the setting. Why do you not receive a clear picture of how things look? Why does Ozick present the details as she does?

2. In paragraph 15, what is on the other side of the fence? Explain Ozick's description here. Why does Ozick include these details so close to the story's end?

3. What character is the center of interest in "The Shawl"? Why is she being treated as she is? What are her impressions of the conditions and circumstances around her? What are her responses to her hunger and deprivation?

4. Explain the function of the more unpleasant and brutal details. What do you need to know about the circumstances of the story to respond to these details?

EDGAR ALLAN POE (1809–1849)

During his lifetime Poe experienced much pain and difficulty. He was born in Boston and educated in Virginia and England. When still a boy he was alienated from his guardian (from whom he took the name "Allan"), and began a lifelong struggle against poverty, alcohol addiction, and physical and psychological illness. To make a living, he worked at various editorships and produced a steady stream of poems, essays, and stories. "The Masque of the Red Death," for example, was one of his contributions in 1842 to Graham's Magazine, *of which he was then the literary editor. Though he was constantly productive, he did not gain much fame beyond the praise heaped upon his poem "The Raven." His death in 1849, which has been attributed to alcoholism, was more likely the final blow of a severe neurological illness. As a belated recognition of his stature, he was selected to the Hall of Fame of American Authors in 1986.*

The Masque of the Red Death _____ 1842

The "Red Death" had long devastated the country. No pestilence had ever been so fatal, or so hideous. Blood was its Avatar° and its seal—the redness and the horror of

Avatar: model, incarnation, manifestation.

blood. There were sharp pains, and sudden dizziness, and then profuse bleeding at the pores, with dissolution. The scarlet stains upon the body and especially upon the face of the victim, were the pest ban which shut him out from the aid and from the sympathy of his fellow-men. And the whole seizure, progress, and termination of the disease, were the incidents of half an hour.

But the Prince Prospero° was happy and dauntless and sagacious. When his dominions were half depopulated, he summoned to his presence a thousand hale and light-hearted friends from among the knights and dames of his court, and with these retired to the deep seclusion of one of his castellated abbeys. This was an extensive and magnificent structure, the creation of the prince's own eccentric yet august taste. A strong and lofty wall girdled it in. This wall had gates of iron. The courtiers, having entered, brought furnaces and massy hammers and welded the bolts. They resolved to leave means neither of ingress nor egress to the sudden impulses of despair or of frenzy from within. The abbey was amply provisioned. With such precautions the courtiers might bid defiance to contagion. The external world could take care of itself. In the meantime it was folly to grieve, or to think. The prince had provided all the appliances of pleasure. There were buffoons, there were improvisatori, there were ballet-dancers, there were musicians, there was Beauty, there was wine. All these and security were within. Without was the "Red Death."

It was toward the close of the fifth or sixth month of his seclusion, and while the pestilence raged most furiously abroad, that the Prince Prospero entertained his thousand friends at a masked ball of the most unusual magnificence.

It was a voluptuous scene, that masquerade. But first let me tell of the rooms in which it was held. There were seven—an imperial suite. In many palaces, however, such suites form a long and straight vista, while the folding doors slide back nearly to the walls on either hand, so that the view of the whole extent is scarcely impeded. Here the case was very different; as might have been expected from the duke's love of the *bizarre*. The apartments were so irregularly disposed that the vision embraced but little more than one at a time. There was a sharp turn at every twenty or thirty yards, and at each turn a novel effect. To the right and left, in the middle of each wall, a tall and narrow Gothic window looked out upon a closed corridor which pursued the windings of the suite. These windows were of stained glass whose color varied in accordance with the prevailing hue of the decorations of the chamber into which it opened. That at the eastern extremity was hung, for example, in blue—and vividly blue were its windows. The second chamber was purple in its ornaments and tapestries, and here the panes were purple. The third was green throughout, and so were the casements. The fourth was furnished and lighted with orange—the fifth with white—the sixth with violet. The seventh apartment was closely shrouded in black velvet tapestries that hung all over the ceiling and down the walls, falling in heavy folds upon a carpet of the same material and hue. But in this chamber only, the color of the windows failed to correspond with the decorations. The panes here were scarlet—a deep blood color. Now in no one of the seven apartments was there any lamp or candelabrum, amid the profusion of golden ornaments that lay scattered to and fro or depended from the roof. There was no light of any kind emanating from lamp or candle within the suite of chambers. But in the corridors that followed the suite, there stood, opposite to each window, a heavy tripod, bearing a brazier of fire, that pro-

---

Prospero: that is, "prosperous." In Shakespeare's play *The Tempest*, the principal character is Prospero.

jected its rays through the tinted glass and so glaringly illumined the room. And thus were produced a multitude of gaudy and fantastic appearances. But in the western or black chamber the effect of the fire-light that streamed upon the dark hangings through the blood-tinted panes was ghastly in the extreme, and produced so wild a look upon the countenances of those who entered, that there were few of the company bold enough to set foot within its precincts at all.

It was in this apartment, also, that there stood against the western wall, a gigantic clock of ebony. Its pendulum swung to and fro with a dull, heavy, monotonous clang; and when the minute-hand made the circuit of the face, and the hour was to be stricken, there came from the brazen lungs of the clock a sound which was clear and loud and deep and exceedingly musical, but of so peculiar a note and emphasis that, at each lapse of an hour, the musicians of the orchestra were constrained to pause, momentarily, in their performance, to hearken to the sound; and thus the waltzers perforce ceased their evolutions; and there was a brief disconcert of the whole gay company; and, while the chimes of the clock yet rang, it was observed that the giddiest grew pale, and the more aged and sedate passed their hands over their brows as if in confused revery or meditation. But when the echoes had fully ceased, a light laughter at once pervaded the assembly; the musicians looked at each other and smiled as if at their own nervousness and folly, and made whispering vows, each to the other, that the next chiming of the clock should produce in them no similar emotion; and then, after the lapse of sixty minutes (which embrace three thousand and six hundred seconds of the Time that flies), there came yet another chiming of the clock, and then were the same disconcert and tremulousness and meditation as before.

But, in spite of these things, it was a gay and magnificent revel. The tastes of the duke were peculiar. He had a fine eye for colors and effects. He disregarded the *decora*° of mere fashion. His plans were bold and fiery, and his conceptions glowed with barbaric lustre. There are some who would have thought him mad. His followers felt that he was not. It was necessary to hear and see and touch him to be *sure* that he was not.

He had directed, in great part, the movable embellishments of the seven chambers, upon occasion of this great fête,° and it was his own guiding taste which had given character to the masqueraders. Be sure they were grotesque. There were much glare and glitter and piquancy and phantasm—much of what has been since seen in "Hernani."° There were arabesque figures with unsuited limbs and appointments. There were delirious fancies such as the madman fashions. There were much of the beautiful, much of the wanton, much of the *bizarre*, something of the terrible, and not a little of that which might have excited disgust. To and fro in the seven chambers there stalked, in fact, a multitude of dreams. And these—the dreams—writhed in and about, taking hue from the rooms, and causing the wild music of the orchestra to seem as the echo of their steps. And, anon, there strikes the ebony clock which stands in the hall of the velvet. And then, for a moment, all is still, and all is silent save the voice of the clock. The dreams are stiff-frozen as they stand. But the echoes of the chime die away—they have endured but an instant—and a light, half-subdued laughter floats after them as they depart. And now again the music swells, and the dreams live, and writhe to and fro more merrily than ever, taking hue from the many-tinted

decora: schemes, patterns.
fête: party, revel.
Hernani: tragedy by Victor Hugo (1802–1885), featuring elaborate scenes and costumes.

windows through which stream the rays from the tripods. But to the chamber which lies most westwardly of the seven there are now none of the maskers who venture; for the night is waning away; and there flows a ruddier light through the blood-colored panes; and the blackness of the sable drapery appalls; and to him whose foot falls upon the sable carpet, there comes from the near clock of ebony a muffled peal more solemnly emphatic than any which reaches *their* ears who indulge in the more remote gaieties of the other apartments.

But these other apartments were densely crowded, and in them beat feverishly the heart of life. And the revel went whirlingly on, until at length there commenced the sounding of midnight upon the clock. And then the music ceased, as I have told; and the evolutions of the waltzers were quieted; and there was an uneasy cessation of all things as before. But now there were twelve strokes to be sounded by the bell of the clock; and thus it happened, perhaps that more of thought crept, with more of time, into the meditations of the thoughtful among those who revelled. And thus, too, it happened, perhaps, that before the last echoes of the last chime had utterly sunk into silence, there were many individuals in the crowd who had found leisure to become aware of the presence of a masked figure which had arrested the attention of no single individual before. And the rumor of this new presence having spread itself whisperingly around, there arose at length from the whole company a buzz, or murmur, expressive of disapprobation and surprise—then, finally, of terror, of horror, and of disgust.

In an assembly of phantasms such as I have painted, it may well be supposed that no ordinary appearance could have excited such sensation. In truth the masquerade license of the night was nearly unlimited; but the figure in question had out-Heroded Herod,° and gone beyond the bounds of even the prince's indefinite decorum. There are chords in the hearts of the most reckless which cannot be touched without emotion. Even with the utterly lost, to whom life and death are equally jests, there are matters of which no jest can be made. The whole company, indeed, seemed now deeply to feel that in the costume and bearing of the stranger neither wit nor propriety existed. The figure was tall and gaunt, and shrouded from head to foot in the habiliments of the grave. The mask which concealed the visage was made so nearly to resemble the countenance of a stiffened corpse that the closest scrutiny must have had difficulty in detecting the cheat. And yet all this might have been endured, if not approved, by the mad revellers around. But the mummer had gone so far as to assume the type of the Red Death. His vesture was dabbled in *blood*—and his broad brow, with all the features of the face, was besprinkled with the scarlet horror.

When the eyes of Prince Prospero fell upon this spectral image (which, with a slow and solemn movement, as if more fully to sustain its *rôle*, stalked to and fro among the waltzers) he was seen to be convulsed, in the first moment with a strong shudder either of terror or distaste; but, in the next, his brow reddened with rage. 10

"Who dares"—he demanded hoarsely of the courtiers who stood near him—"who dares insult us with this blasphemous mockery? Seize him and unmask him—that we may know whom we have to hang, at sunrise, from the battlements!"

It was in the eastern or blue chamber in which stood the Prince Prospero as he uttered these words. They rang throughout the seven rooms loudly and clearly, for

---

out-Heroded Herod: quoted from Shakespeare's *Hamlet.* Act III, scene 2, line 13, in reference to extreme overacting.

the prince was a bold and robust man, and the music had become hushed at the waving of his hand.

It was in the blue room where stood the prince, with a group of pale courtiers by his side. At first, as he spoke, there was a slight rushing movement of this group in the direction of the intruder, who, at the moment was also near at hand, and now, with deliberate and stately step, made closer approach to the speaker. But from a certain nameless awe with which the mad assumptions of the mummer had inspired the whole party, there were found none who put forth hand to seize him; so that, unimpeded, he passed within a yard of the prince's person; and, while the vast assembly, as if with one impulse, shrank from the centres of the rooms to the walls, he made his way uninterruptedly, but with the same solemn and measured step which had distinguished him from the first, through the blue chamber to the purple—through the purple to the green—through the green to the orange—through this again to the white—and even thence to the violet, ere a decided movement had been made to arrest him. It was then, however, that the Prince Prospero, maddening with rage and the shame of his own momentary cowardice, rushed hurriedly through the six chambers, while none followed him on account of a deadly terror that had seized upon all. He bore aloft a drawn dagger, and had approached, in rapid impetuosity, to within three or four feet of the retreating figure, when the latter, having attained the extremity of the velvet apartment, turned suddenly and confronted his pursuer. There was a sharp cry—and the dagger dropped gleaming upon the sable carpet, upon which, instantly afterward, fell prostrate in death the Prince Prospero. Then, summoning the wild courage of despair, a throng of the revellers at once threw themselves into the black apartment, and, seizing the mummer, whose tall figure stood erect and motionless within the shadow of the ebony clock, gasped in unutterable horror at finding the grave cerements and corpse-like mask, which they handled with so violent a rudeness, untenanted by any tangible form.

And now was acknowledged the presence of the Red Death. He had come like a thief in the night.° And one by one dropped the revellers in the blood-bedewed halls of their revel, and died each in the despairing posture of his fall. And the life of the ebony clock went out with that of the last of the gay. And the flames of the tripods expired. And Darkness and Decay and the Red Death held illimitable dominion over all.

QUESTIONS

1. What is happening throughout the country in this story? What does the Prince's reaction to these events tell us about him?

2. How do the details of number, color, and lighting help create the atmosphere and mood of the story?

3. Why do the color and window of the last room disturb the revellers? To what extent does this last room reflect the plot and ideas of the story?

4. What single object is located in this last room? How is this object described? What effect does its sound have on the revellers? What do you think Poe is suggesting by this object and its effects?

thief in the night: 2 Peter 3:10.

5. How are the nobles dressed for the masquerade? Why is the "masked figure" re-markable? How does Prospero react to him?

WRITING ABOUT SETTING

In preparing to write about setting, determine the number and importance of locations, artifacts, and customs.

Questions for Discovering Ideas

*   How extensive are the visual descriptions? Does the author provide such vivid and carefully arranged detail about surroundings that you could draw a map or plan? Or is the scenery vague and difficult to imagine?

*   What connections, if any, are apparent between locations and characters? Do the locations bring characters together, separate them, facilitate their privacy, make intimacy and conversation difficult?

*   How fully are objects described? How vital are they to the action? How important are they in the development of the plot? How are they connected to the mental states of the characters?

*   How important to plot and character are shapes, colors, times of day, clouds, storms, light and sun, seasons of the year, and conditions of vegetation?

*   Are the characters poor, moderately well off, or rich? How does their economic condition affect their actions and attitudes? How does their economic lot deter-mine what happens to them?

*   What cultural, religious, and political conditions are assumed in the story? How do the characters accept and adjust to these conditions? How do the conditions affect the characters' judgments and actions?

*   What is the state of houses, furniture, and objects (e.g., new and polished, old and worn)? What connections can you find between this condition and the out-look and behavior of the characters?

*   How important are sounds, or silences? To what degree is music, or other sound, important in the development of character and action?

*   Do characters respect or mistreat the environment? If there is an environmental connection, how central is it to the story?

*   What conclusions do you think the author expects you to draw as a result of the neighborhood, culture, and larger world of the story?

Strategies for Organizing Ideas

Following are five possible approaches to essays on setting. Choose the one that seems most appropriate, bearing in mind that some works invite one approach rather than others. As you develop your essay, however, you may find it necessary to introduce one or more of the other approaches. What-ever approach you use, be sure to consider setting not as an end in itself, but rather as illustration and evidence.

1. *Setting and Action.* Explore the importance of setting in the story's actions. How extensively is the setting described? Are locations essential or incidental to the actions? Does the setting serve as part of the action (e.g., places of flight or concealment; public places where people meet openly, or hidden places where they meet privately; natural or environmental conditions; seasonal conditions such as searing heat or numbing cold; customs and conventions)? Do any objects cause inspiration, difficulty, or conflict (for example, a shawl, a rundown house, a recording, a walking stick, a pretty necklace, a coin, a costume, a toy windmill, a dead bird)? How directly do these objects influence the action?

2. *Setting and Organization.* How is the setting connected to the various parts of the work? Does it undergo any changes as the action develops? Why are some parts of the setting more important than others? Is the setting used as a structural frame or enclosure for the story? How do objects, such as money or property, affect the motivation of the characters? How do descriptions made at the start become important in the action later on?

3. *Setting and Character.* (For examples of this approach, see Chapter 1, pp. 24 and 35.) Analyze the degree to which setting influences and interacts with character. Are the characters happy or unhappy where they live? Do they get into discussions or arguments about their home environments? Do they want to stay or leave? Do the economic, philosophical, religious, or ethnic aspects of the setting make the characters undergo changes? What jobs do the characters perform because of their ways of life? What freedoms or restraints do these jobs cause? How does the setting influence their decisions, transportation, speech habits, eating habits, attitudes about love and honor, and general behavior?

4. *Setting and Atmosphere.* To what extent does the setting contribute to moods? Does the setting go beyond the minimum needed for action or character? Are descriptive words used to paint verbal pictures, to evoke moods through references to colors, shapes, sounds, smells, or tastes? Does the setting establish a mood, say, of joy or hopelessness, plenty or scarcity? Do events happen in daylight or at night? Do the movements and locations of the characters suggest permanence or impermanence (like footsteps on a stairway, or wooden bars to keep windows from falling out)? Are things warm and pleasant, or cold and harsh? What connection do you find between the atmosphere and the author's thoughts about existence?

5. *Setting and Other Aspects.* Does setting reinforce the story's meaning? Does it establish irony about the circumstances and ideas in the story? If you choose this approach, consult the earlier sections of this chapter, "Setting and Statement" and "Setting and Irony." If you write about the symbolic implications of a setting, consult the discussions of symbolism in Chapter 9.

To conclude your essay, you may summarize your major points or write about related aspects of setting that you have not considered. Thus, if your essay treats the relationship of setting and action, your conclusion could mention connections of the setting with character or atmosphere. You might also point out whether your central idea about setting also applies to other major aspects of the story.

SAMPLE ESSAY

Poe's Use of Interior Setting to Augment the Eeriness of "The Masque of the Red Death"°

[1] In "The Masque of the Red Death," Poe uses many details of setting to create an eerie atmosphere.* The story is about the foolishness and impossibility of trying to evade death. Poe's Prince Prospero is the example of this idea. He believes that he can lock himself away in his castle, with a thousand followers, and avoid the plague—the red death—raging outside. At the end, however, Death invades the castle in person and destroys all the people. Poe uses interior setting to underscore this irony, and also to make Prospero's pride seem pointless and insane. The prevailing eerie mood is brought out through Poe's use of graphic description, geographical direction, evocative color, and sepulchral sound.[†]

[2] The height of Poe's graphic description is the story's extensive fourth paragraph, where he describes Prince Prospero's bizarre suite of seven rooms. These rooms have different colors, each one suggesting differing moods, from subdued, to garish, to somber. The blue room is in the east, and, moving westward in an order of varying depressiveness, the next six rooms are purple, green, orange, white, violet, and finally black. The moods are determined by the narrator's explanation that each room is lighted by a "brazier of fire" throwing light through a stained glass window which provokes awe by casting a glaring, grisly light.

[3] These rooms are not only vividly described, but they are spatially arranged to complement the certainty of death. The direction of east to west suggests a movement away from life. One might observe that the blue room, in the east, is on the side of the rising sun—an optimistic idea of blue skies and new beginnings of new days. On the other hand the westernmost room, the black one, is the direction of the setting sun and the end of the day at midnight, when Death takes over. If one doubts that Poe intended this geographical direction to have meaning, it is important to note that Prospero's charge against the ghostly figure of the Red Death takes him directly from east to west—from blue to black, from life to death—on his insane rush toward doom.

[4] The most weird and garish room is the black one, on which Poe devotes the most evocative description. The room is hung with black velvet tapestries, but its darkness is made flamboyant by the scarlet, "deep blood" light (Poe avoids the more neutral word "red" here). The narrator states that the room is "ghastly in the extreme" and that it produces a look of wildness (¶ 4). Visually, this room evokes feelings of wildness, evil, and an almost ghoulish delight in blood. It is a sinister room, designed not to relax but to disturb and distress.

° For the text of this story, see pp 254–58.
* Central idea.
[†] Thesis sentence.

[5]

To these ominous locations, Poe adds the eeriness of sepulchral sounds by including a "gigantic clock of ebony" in the black room. He devotes an entire paragraph (the fifth) to this weird clock, and this paragraph is therefore the focal point of the story's setting. Poe's words hint that the clock is vaguely alive. It is not placed or set against the west wall, but is standing there (Poe's word is "stood"), as though living, and its massive pendulum is in constant, "monotonous" motion (like the beating of a ghostly heart?). Poe's implication is that the clock represents death, for every hour the "clang" from its "brazen lungs" chillingly ends another period of life. Poe's narrator points out that the clock's musical but eerie sounds stop all revelry and create a distressed silence among the merrymakers (Poe uses the word "disconcert" twice in the paragraph to describe the clock's effect). This use of sound, having its source in this mysteriously living clock, is designed to make readers as uneasy, unsettled, and anxious as Prospero's companions.

[6]

Thus Poe's interior setting is both descriptive and evocative. The major action takes place in the rooms—the costume party attended by all Prospero's friends, except the one uninvited guest, the Red Death himself, who instantly kills all the party-goers. Prospero's last movement takes him through all the rooms, in a ritual passage from morning to midnight, from life to death. In this way, Poe uses his setting to show the folly of trying to escape death, and also to suggest that the attempt is not only foolish but also bizarre and insane. The events of the story, the sustained mood, the consistent idea, are all tied together by Poe's masterly control of setting.

Commentary on the Essay

Because it treats the relationship of setting to mood or atmosphere, this essay illustrates the fourth approach described on p. 260. The essay considers those aspects of setting needed for the story, and then stresses how Poe's descriptions build the eerie mood, the irony of the major character's pretensions, and the folly of his pride. The thesis sentence announces four topics for further development.

In the body, paragraph 2 describes the physical layout of Prospero's suite of rooms, and it also points out the eerie suggestiveness of Poe's descriptions of color and light. Paragraph 3 treats Poe's geographical arrangement of the rooms, suggesting that this arrangement complements the story's movement from life to death.

Paragraphs 4 and 5 treat the last and most sinister of the rooms. Paragraph 4 stresses the mood brought out by the colors black and scarlet or "deep blood." Paragraph 5, because it deals with the clock, on which Poe lavishes great detail, is the high point of the essay's body. Throughout the paragraph, the topic idea is that the clock, because of its seemingly living connection with the malign world of death, is Poe's major means of achieving an atmosphere complementary to the eerie action.

The conclusion summarizes the central idea, stressing once again that Poe goes beyond simple description to heighten the eerie, macabre atmosphere of his story.

WRITING TOPICS

1. How do Dr. Jenkins and the Musician respond to the setting in "The Portable Phonograph"? How do they adjust to physical conditions? In light of this story, together with other details of your choosing, what conclusions can you draw about the aftereffects of warfare on character?

2. Choose a story included in this chapter and, first, rewrite a page or two, taking the characters out of their setting and placing them in the setting of another story, or in an entirely new setting. Then, write an essay dealing with these questions: How were your characters affected by their new settings? Did you make them change slowly or rapidly? Why? As a result of your rewriting, what can you conclude about the uses of setting in fiction?

3. Write a short narrative for possible inclusion in a longer story (which you may also wish to write for the assignment), using option *a* and/or *b*, below.

    a. Relate a natural setting or type of day to a mood—for example, a nice day to happiness and satisfaction; or a cold, cloudy, rainy day to sadness. Or create irony by relating the nice day to sadness, or the terrible day to happiness.

    b. Indicate how an object or circumstance becomes the cause of conflict or reconciliation (such as the books and records in "The Portable Phonograph," the shawl in "The Shawl," the sign language in "And Sarah Laughed," or the chest in "The Worker in Sandalwood" [Ch. 7]).

4. Compare and contrast how details of setting are used to establish the qualities and traits of the following characters: Mrs. Johnson of "Everyday Use," Miss Brill of "Miss Brill," Sarah of "And Sarah Laughed," Meda Roth of "Meneseteung," and Stella of "The Shawl." As one of your bases of comparison, introduce the ways in which Boucher and Hopper use details in their paintings (pp. 232 and 233).

Style: The Words That Tell the Story

Style, derived from the Latin word *stilus* (a writing instrument), means the way writers assemble words to tell the story, develop the argument, dramatize the play, or compose the poem. Although style is often distinguished from content, it is wiser not to make this separation, for style is best considered as the choice of words in the *service* of content. The written expression of a fictional action or scene, in other words, cannot be separated from the action or scene itself.

Style is also individual, because all authors put words together uniquely to fit the specific conditions in specific works. We may therefore speak of the style of Ernest Hemingway, for example, and of Mark Twain, even though both writers always adapt words to situations. Thus an author may have a distinct style for narrative and descriptive passages, but a very different style for dialogue. For a visual comparison of styles, look again at the paintings by Boucher and Hopper in Chapter 6 (pp. 232 and 233). While the painters treat the same subject—a female figure—the *styles* are different: Boucher's style achieves a beautiful, flattering image of his aristocratic subject, while Hopper invests his more ordinary subject with an impression of emptiness and bleakness. Thus, different styles convey different outlooks on life. Writers, too, vary manner to suit various purposes. Therefore, in judging style the important criterion is its *adaptability*. The more appropriately the words fit the situation, the better the style. Jonathan Swift defined style as the right words in the right places. We may add to this definition that style is also the right words at the right time and in the right circumstances.

DICTION: CHOICE OF WORDS

Diction refers to a writer's selection of words. The selection should be accurate and explicit, so that all actions, scenes, and ideas are clear. If a passage is effective, if it conveys an ideal well or gets at the essence of an action vividly and powerfully, we may confidently say that the words are right. For example, a passage describing action should emphasize active verbs, whereas a description of a place should emphasize nouns and adjectives that provide locations, relationships, colors, and shapes. An explanatory or reflective passage should include words that convey thoughts, states of mind and emotion, and various conditions of human relationships.

Formal, Neutral, and Informal Diction

One aspect of word choice is the degree of formality. There are three levels of diction: **formal** or *high*, **neutral** or *middle*, and **informal** or *low*. *Formal* or *high* diction consists of standard and also "elegant" words (frequently polysyllabic), the retention of correct word order, and the absence of contractions. The sentence "It is I," for example, is formal. The following sentences from Poe's "The Masque of the Red Death" use formal language:

> They resolved to leave means neither of ingress nor egress to the sudden impulses of despair or frenzy from within. The abbey was amply provisioned. With such precautions the courtiers might bid defiance to contagion.

Note here the words *ingress, egress, amply provisioned, bid defiance*, and *contagion*. Though the sentences are brief and simple, and all the words are accurate and apt, the italicized words are more "elegant" than those most of us normally use. Therefore these words may be considered as formal or high diction.

Neutral or *middle* diction is ordinary, everyday, but still standard vocabulary, shunning longer words but using contractions when necessary. The sentence "It's me" is an example of what many people say in preference to the more formal "It is I" when identifying themselves on the telephone. The following passage from Alice Munro's "The Found Boat" illustrates middle, neutral diction.

> What surprised them in the second place was that when the boys did actually see what boat was meant, this old flood-smashed wreck held up in the branches, they did not understand that they had been fooled, that a joke had been played on them. They did not show a moment's disappointment, but seemed as pleased at the discovery as if the boat had been whole and new. They were already barefoot, because they had been wading in the water to get lumber, and they waded in here without a stop, surrounding the boat and appraising it and paying no attention even of an insulting kind of Eva and Carol who bobbed up and down on their log. Eva and Carol had to call to them.

The words of this passage are ordinary and easy. They are centered directly on the subject and do not draw attention to themselves. Even the longer words, like *surprised, disappointment, surrounding, appraising*, and *insulting*, are not beyond the level of conversation, although *appraising* and *surrounding* would also be in place in a more formal passage. Neutral style words are like clear window glass, while high style words are more decorative, like stained glass.

Informal or *low* diction may range from *colloquial*—the language of relaxed, common activities—to the level of *substandard* or *slang* expressions. A person speaking to a close friend uses diction that would not be appropriate in public and formal situations, and even in some social situations. Low style language is thus appropriate for dialogue in stories, depending on who is speaking, and for stories told in the first-person point of view as though the speaker is talking directly to sympathetic and relaxed close friends. In Updike's "A & P," Sammy's first sentence illustrates the informal, low style:

> In walks these three girls in nothing but bathing suits.

Note the idiomatic and ungrammatical "In walks," a singular verb followed by a plural subject. Note also the colloquial use of "these" as a demonstrative adjective with no antecedent.

Specific-General and Concrete-Abstract Language

Another aspect of language is its degree of explicitness. **Specific** refers to words that bring to mind images from the real world. "My dog Woofie is barking" is specific. **General** statements refer to broad classes, such as "All people like pets" and "Dogs make good pets." There is an ascending order of generality from (1) very specific, to (2) less specific, to (3) general, as though the words themselves climb a stairway. Thus *peach* is a specific fruit. *Fruit* is specific but more general because it may also include apples, oranges, and all other fruits. *Dessert* is a still more general word, which can include all sweets, including fruits and peaches, and also other confections, like ice cream. *Food* is more general yet, for the word includes everything eaten by living creatures. If you report that you are having "food" for dinner, you are facetiously general, but if you say that the main course is a charcoal-broiled tenderloin steak with peaches for dessert, you are seriously specific.

While *specific–general* refers to categories, *concrete–abstract* refers to qualities or conditions. **Concrete** words describe qualities of immediate perception. If you say "Ice cream is cold," the word *cold* is concrete because it describes a condition that you may feel, just as you may taste ice cream's *sweetness* and feel its *creamy* texture. **Abstract** words refer to broader, less palpable qualities; they may therefore apply to many separate things. If we describe ice cream as *good*, we are abstract, because *good* is far removed from ice cream itself and conveys no descriptive information about it. A vast number of things may be *good*, just as they may be *bad*, *fine*, "*cool*," *excellent*, and so on.

Usually, narrative and descriptive writing features specific and concrete words. We can easily visualize passages containing words about specific actions, scenes, and objects, for with more specificity and concreteness there is less ambiguity. Because exactness and vividness are goals of most fiction, specific and concrete words are the writer's basic tools, and general and abstract words are used only sparingly, if at all.

The point, however, is not that abstract and general words have no place at all, but rather that *words should be appropriate in the context*. Good writers control style to match their purposes. Observe, for example, Hemingway's diction in "Soldier's Home." This story concerns a young veteran who has just returned from World War I and is having difficulty adjusting to life back home. Hemingway, by combining specific and abstract language to convey this situation, appropriately fits style to subject. In paragraph 6, for example, he uses abstract terms to describe the mental state of Krebs, the young veteran. We read that Krebs feels "nausea in regard to experience that is the result of untruth or exaggeration," that he goes into the "easy pose of the old soldier" when he meets another veteran, and that he "lost everything" during his time abroad. Because the words are mainly abstract and general, it is not possible to determine the precise details about Krebs's dissatisfaction.

By contrast, Hemingway's description of Krebs's typical daily activities is quite specific: getting out of bed, walking to the library, eating lunch, reading on the front porch, and drifting down to the local pool hall. These details enable us to conclude that Krebs's activities are repetitive and essentially meaningless. The two paragraphs therefore complement each other, with the specificity of paragraph 7 clarifying the abstraction of paragraph 6. In short, Hemingway skillfully combines abstract and specific words to build his portrait of a young man who is caught between two worlds—those of the war and the life at home—and because of changing circumstances has no place in either.

Denotation and Connotation

Another way to understand style is to study the author's management of *denotation* and *connotation*. **Denotation** refers to what a word means, and **connotation** to what the word suggests. For example, if a person in a social situation behaves in ways that are *friendly, warm, polite,* or *cordial,* these words all suggest slight differences in behavior because they have different connotations. Similarly, both *cat* and *kitten* are close to each other denotatively, but *kitten* connotes more playfulness and cuteness than *cat*. Consider the connotations of words describing physical appearance. It is one thing to call a person *thin*, for example, but another to use the words *skinny* , *gaunt,* or *skeletal,* and still something else to say *trim, fit, slim,* or *slender.*

Through the careful choice of words, not only for denotation but also for connotation, authors create unique effects even though they might be describing similar or even identical situations. Let us look briefly at Eudora Welty's description of Phoenix's walk through the woods in "A Worn Path":

> Her eyes were blue with age. Her skin had a pattern all its own of numberless branching wrinkles and as though a whole little tree stood in the middle of her forehead, but a golden color ran underneath, and the two knobs of her cheeks

were illumined by a yellow burning under the dark. Under the rag her hair came down on her neck in the frailest of ringlets, still black, and with an odor like copper. (paragraph 2)

The description skillfully conveys a compelling note of admiration. Specifically, the words *golden color* and *illumined* would be appropriate in the description of delicate and lovely medieval book paintings; *frailest of ringlets, still black* suggests girlishness and personal care, despite Phoenix's advancing age and weakness. Comparably, in "A & P," Sammy's words describing the "queen" (paragraphs 2–4, pp. 63–64) suggest his admiration of both her sexual beauty and also her grace. Shirley Jackson's less full description of Tessie Hutchinson in "The Lottery" (paragraph 8, p. 197) reduces Tessie to no more than an average woman of the village. The meager details are that she has a "sweater thrown over her shoulders" and that she "dried her hands on her apron." All these descriptive examples demonstrate the ways in which connotation may complement an author's descriptive intentions.

RHETORIC

Rhetoric refers to the art of persuasive writing and, more broadly, to the general art of writing. There are several ways to study the rhetorical qualities of a passage. Some relatively easy approaches are (a) counting various elements in a passage and (b) analyzing the types of sentences.

Counting

Counting various elements is a quick and easy way to begin the study of style. The number of words in a sentence; the number of verbs, adjectives, prepositions, and adverbs in a passage; or the number of syllables in relation to the total number of words—can provide valuable clues about the style, especially if the count is related to other aspects of the passage. For illustration, let us say that Author A uses words mainly of 1 or 2 syllables, while author B includes many words of 3, 4, and 5 syllables. Going further, let us say that A uses an average of 12 words per sentence and that B uses 35. It would be fair to conclude that Author A is brief, and Author B is more expansive. This is not to say that Author A's passage would be easier or superior, however, for a long string of short sentences with short words might seem choppy and tiresome. Remember that conclusions based on a count will provide tendencies of a particular author rather than absolutes.

Sentence Types

You can also study the rhetorical qualities of a passage by determining the sorts of sentences it contains. Let us review the basic sentence types:

1. **Simple sentences** contain one subject and one verb, together with modifiers and complements. They are short, and are most appropriate for actions and declarations. Often they are idiomatic, particularly in dialogue.

> *Example:* It was at a banquet in London in honor of one of the two or three conspicuously illustrious English military names of this generation. (Twain)

2. **Compound sentences** contain two simple sentences joined by a conjunction (*and, but, for, or, nor,* or *yet*) and a comma, or by a semicolon without a conjunction. Frequently, compound sentences are formed by three or four simple sentences joined by conjunctions.

> *Example:* Later he felt the need to talk but no one wanted to hear about it. (Hemingway)

3. **Complex sentences** contain a main clause and a subordinate clause. Because of the subordinate clause, the complex sentence is suitable for describing cause-and-effect relationships in narrative, and also for analysis and reflection.

> *Example:* It was the Wawanash River, which every spring overflowed its banks. (Munro)

4. **Compound-complex sentences** contain two main clauses and a subordinate clause. In practice many authors produce sentences that contain a number of main and subordinate clauses .

> *Example:* Sometimes he was silent for the rest of the evening; and if he spoke, it was usually to hint some criticism of her household arrangements, suggest some change in the domestic administration, to ask, a little nervously, if she didn't think Joyce's nursery governess was rather young and flighty, or if she herself always saw to it that Peter—whose throat was delicate—was properly wrapped up when he went to school. (Wharton)

Parallelism

To create interest, authors often rely on **parallelism,** the repetition of the same grammatical form (nouns, verbs, phrases, clauses) to balance expressions, conserve words, and build climaxes. Here, for example, is another sentence by Poe, from "The Black Cat":

> I grew, day by day, more moody, more irritable, more regardless of the feelings of others.

Arrangements like this are called *parallel* because they can be laid out graphically, according to parts of speech, in parallel lines, as in the following (with the adverbial phrase "day to day" left out):

I grew $\begin{cases} \text{more moody,} \\ \text{more irritable,} \\ \text{more regardless of the feelings of others} \end{cases}$

Poe's sentence increases in the severity of psychological depression, from personal to social. Such an ascending order marks a deliberate attempt at climax, unlike the parallelism in the following sentence from the concluding paragraph of Clark's "The Portable Phonograph" (p. 241):

$$\text{Then quickly}^{1} \text{ and quietly}^{2}, \text{ looking at the piece of canvas frequently,}$$

he slipped the records into the case,^{1} snapped the lid shut,^{2}
and carried the phonograph to his couch.^{3}

Here are two parallel adverbs at the beginning, both ending in *-ly*, and three past tense verbs ending in *-ed*, all of which have direct objects. The order here is time. Although the sentence is short, Clark uses parallelism to pack in a great deal of action.

You may also see parallel arrangements in individual sentences within a paragraph. In the following passage from Alice Munro's "The Found Boat," for example, there are a number of identically formed sentences which sum up the exhilaration of young people dashing naked to swim in a river. There are seven parallel clauses containing *they* followed by active verbs, which are underlined here:

> Nobody said a word this time, they all bent and stripped themselves. Eva, naked first, started running across the field, and then all the others ran, all five of them running bare through the knee-high hot grass, running towards the river. Not caring now about being caught but in fact leaping and yelling to call attention to themselves, if there was anybody to hear or see. They felt as if they were going to jump off a cliff and fly. They felt that something was happening to them different from anything that had happened before, and it had to do with the boat, the water, the sunlight, the dark ruined station, and each other. They thought of each other now hardly as names or people, but as echoing shrieks, reflections, all bold and white and loud and scandalous, and as fast as arrows. They went running without a break into the cold water and when it came almost to the tops of their legs they fell on it and swam. It stopped their noise. Silence, amazement, came over them in a rush. They dipped and floated and separated, sleek as mink.

CHIASMUS OR ANTIMETABOLE. A favorite parallel device of many writers is **chiasmus** or **antimetabole**. The pattern is *A B B A*, which can be arranged graphically in the form of the Greek letter *chi*:

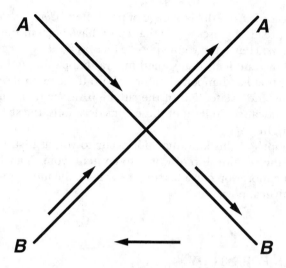

The following sentence from Twain's "Luck" shows the pattern:

A   B   B   A

I drilled him and crammed him, and crammed him and drilled him.

You may not often encounter such easily detected patterns, but you should always be alert to effective arrangements. You need not use a technically correct name, as long as you focus on what you think is especially noteworthy.

STYLE IN GENERAL

If a story is good, you probably do not notice its style, for clear expressions and easy reading are marks of a writer's success. By studying style, however, you can discover and appreciate the author's achievement. The action described in a particular passage, the relationship of the passage to the entire work, the level of the diction, the vividness of the descriptions—all these can enter into an assessment of the passage.

In the paragraph from "The Found Boat" on page 270 for example, Munro's stylistic mastery can be perceived beyond the parallelism that we noted. The passage could be considered the climax of the story, which is, among other things, about emerging sexuality. In an almost ritualistic way, the paragraph describes young people running impetuously toward a river and diving in—an action that may be construed as sexually symbolic. Note that after the first two sentences describing action, Munro's narrator shifts the focus with four sentences of omniscient analysis describing the young people's feelings. If her intention had been to create searching psychological scrutiny, she might have selected words from the language of psychology (*libido, urge, sublimation,* and so on). Instead, she uses words that could have been in the vocabularies of the characters. Hence the young people feel "as if they were going to jump off a cliff and fly" and feel "that something was happening to them different from anything that had happened before." With these neutral words, the passage focuses on the excitement of the situation rather than on hidden psychological significance. In light of these considerations, the style of the paragraph is just right.

Observations of this kind may not occur to you at first, but as long as you focus on the relationship of words to content, your analysis of style will be fruitful. The more you consider stories for style, the more you will discover your own analytical power.

STORIES FOR STUDY

ERNEST HEMINGWAY (1899-1961)

Hemingway was born in Illinois. During World War I he served in the Ambulance Corps in France, where he was wounded. In the 1920s he published The Sun Also Rises *(1926) and* A Farewell to Arms *(1929), and the resulting critical fame made him a major literary celebrity. He developed a sparse style in keeping with the elemental, stark lives of many of the characters he depicted. "Soldier's Home," from the collection* In Our Time *(1925), typifies that pared, annealed style. Notice the ambiguity and irony of the title. It may mean either "The soldier is home," or "The home of the soldier," but, ironically, the soldier's home no longer seems to be home.*

Soldier's Home ——————————————————————— *1925*

Krebs went to the war from a Methodist college in Kansas. There is a picture which shows him among his fraternity brothers, all of them wearing exactly the same height and style collar. He enlisted in the Marines in 1917 and did not return to the United States until the second division returned from the Rhine in the summer of 1919.

There is a picture which shows him on the Rhine with two German girls and another corporal. Krebs and the corporal look too big for their uniforms. The German girls are not beautiful. The Rhine does not show in the picture.

By the time Krebs returned to his home town in Oklahoma the greeting of heroes was over. He came back much too late. The men from the town who had been drafted had all been welcomed elaborately on their return. There had been a great deal of hysteria. Now the reaction had set in. People seemed to think it was rather ridiculous for Krebs to be getting back so late, years after the war was over.

"Will you come down to breakfast, Harold?" his mother said.

"As soon as I get my clothes on," Krebs said.   25

His mother went out of the room and he could hear her frying something downstairs while he washed, shaved and dressed to go down into the dining-room for breakfast. While he was eating breakfast his sister brought in the mail.

"Well, Hare," she said. "You old sleepy-head. What do you ever get up for?"

Krebs looked at her. He liked her. She was his best sister.

"Have you got the paper?" he asked.

She handed him *The Kansas City Star* and he shucked off its brown wrapper and   30
opened it to the sporting page. He folded *The Star* open and propped it against the water pitcher with his cereal dish to steady it, so he could read while he ate.

"Harold," his mother stood in the kitchen doorway, "Harold, please don't muss up the paper. You father can't read his *Star* if it's been mussed."

"I won't muss it," Krebs said.

His sister sat down at the table and watched him while he read.

"We're playing indoor° over at school this afternoon," she said. "I'm going to pitch."

"Good," said Krebs. "How's the old wing?"   35

"I can pitch better than lots of the boys. I tell them all you taught me. The other girls aren't much good."

"Yeah?" said Krebs.

"I tell them all you're my beau. Aren't you my beau, Hare?"

"You bet."

"Couldn't your brother really be your beau just because he's your brother?"   40

"I don't know."

"Sure you know. Couldn't you be my beau, Hare, if I was old enough and if you wanted to?"

"Sure. You're my girl now."

"Am I really your girl?"

"Sure."

"Do you love me?"   45

"Uh, huh."

"Will you love me always?"

"Sure."

"Will you come over and watch me play indoor?"   50

"Maybe."

"Aw, Hare, you don't love me. If you loved me, you'd want to come over and watch me play indoor."

Krebs's mother came into the dining-room from the kitchen. She carried a plate with two fried eggs and some crisp bacon on it and a plate of buckwheat cakes.

"You run along, Helen," she said. "I want to talk to Harold."

She put eggs and bacon down in front of him and brought in a jug of maple   55
syrup for the buckwheat cakes. Then she sat down across the table from Krebs.

"I wish you'd put down the paper a minute. Harold," she said.

Krebs took down the paper and folded it.

"Have you decided what you are going to do yet, Harold?" his mother said, taking off her glasses.

indoor: that is, a softball game.

"No," said Krebs.

"Don't you think it's about time?" His mother did not say this in a mean way. She seemed worried.

"I hadn't thought about it," Krebs said.

"God has some work for every one to do," his mother said. "There can be no idle hands in His Kingdom."

"I'm not in His Kingdom," Krebs said.

"We are all of us in His Kingdom."

Krebs felt embarrassed and resentful as always.

"I've worried about you so much, Harold," his mother went on. "I know the temptations you must have been exposed to. I know how weak men are. I know what your own dear grandfather, my own father, told us about the Civil War and I have prayed for you. I pray for you all day long, Harold."

Krebs looked at the bacon fat hardening on his plate.

"Your father is worried, too," his mother went on. "He thinks you have lost your ambition, that you haven't got a definite aim in life. Charley Simmons, who is just your age, has a good job and is going to be married. The boys are all settling down; they're all determined to get somewhere; you can see that boys like Charley Simmons are on their way to being really a credit to the community."

Krebs said nothing.

"Don't look that way, Harold," his mother said. "You know we love you and I want to tell you for your own good how matters stand. Your father does not want to hamper your freedom. He thinks you should be allowed to drive the car. If you want to take some of the nice girls out riding with you, we are only too pleased. We want you to enjoy yourself. But you are going to have to settle down to work, Harold. Your father doesn't care what you start in at. All work is honorable as he says. But you've got to make a start at something. He asked me to speak to you this morning and then you can stop in and see him at his office."

"Is that all?" Krebs said.

"Yes. Don't you love your mother, dear boy?"

"No," Krebs said.

His mother looked at him across the table. Her eyes were shiny. She started crying.

"I don't love anybody," Krebs said.

It wasn't any good. He couldn't tell her, he couldn't make her see it. It was silly to have said it. He had only hurt her. He went over and took hold of her arm. She was crying with her head in her hands.

"I didn't mean it," he said. "I was just angry at something. I didn't mean I didn't love you."

His mother went on crying. Krebs put his arm on her shoulder.

"Can't you believe me, mother?"

His mother shook her head.

"Please, please, mother. Please believe me."

"All right," his mother said chokily. She looked up at him. "I believe you, Harold."

Krebs kissed her hair. She put her face up to him.

"I'm your mother," she said. "I held you next to my heart when you were a tiny baby."

Krebs felt sick and vaguely nauseated.

"I know, Mummy," he said. "I'll try and be a good boy for you."

"Would you kneel and pray with me, Harold?" his mother asked.

They knelt down beside the dining-room table and Krebs's mother prayed.

"Now, you pray, Harold," she said.

"I can't," Krebs said.   90

"Try, Harold."

"I can't."

"Do you want me to pray for you?"

"Yes."

So his mother prayed for him and then they stood up and Krebs kissed his   95
mother and went out of the house. He had tried so to keep his life from being complicated. Still, none of it had touched him. He had felt sorry for his mother and she
had made him lie. He would go to Kansas City and get a job and she would feel all
right about it. There would be one more scene maybe before he got away. He would
not go down to his father's office. He would miss that one. He wanted his life to go
smoothly. It had just gotten going that way. Well, that was all over now, anyway. He
would go over to the schoolyard and watch Helen play indoor baseball.

QUESTIONS

1. Even though Hemingway is often praised for his specific writing, there are a
    number of vague passages in this story. Why does Hemingway include them? By
    what stylistic means does he control the vagueness?

2. Analyze Hemingway's sentences. What relationship is there between the things
    he describes and the length and complexity of his sentences?

3. Analyze Hemingway's descriptive style. What is the level of his diction? What
    words does he use for things and actions? How vivid are his descriptions?

4. Describe Harold Krebs. How do we learn about him? What does his relationship
    with his sister show about him? How does he change in the story?

ALICE MUNRO (b. 1931)

For a brief biography of Munro, please see Chapter 5, p. 210.

The Found Boat _____ 1974

At the end of Bell Street, McKay Street, Mayo Street, there was the Flood. It was the
Wawanash River, which every spring overflowed its banks. Some springs, say one in
every five, it covered the roads on that side of town and washed over the fields, creating a shallow choppy lake. Light reflected off the water made everything bright and
cold, as it is in a lakeside town, and woke or revived in people certain vague hopes of
disaster. Mostly during the late afternoon and early evening, there were people straggling out to look at it, and discuss whether it was still rising, and whether this time it
might invade the town. In general, those under fifteen and over sixty-five were most
certain that it would.

Eva and Carol rode out on their bicycles. They left the road—it was the end of Mayo Street, past any houses—and rode right into a field, over a wire fence entirely flattened by the weight of the winter's snow. They coasted a little way before the long grass stopped them, then left their bicycles lying down and went to the water.

"We have to find a log and ride on it," Eva said.

"Jesus, we'll freeze our legs off."

"Jesus, we'll freeze our legs off!" said one of the boys who were there too at the water's edge. He spoke in a sour whine, the way boys imitated girls although it was nothing like the way girls talked. These boys—there were three of them—were all in the same class as Eva and Carol at school and were known to them by name (their names being Frank, Bud and Clayton), but Eva and Carol, who had seen and recognized them from the road, had not spoken to them or looked at them or, even yet, given any sign of knowing they were there. The boys seemed to be trying to make a raft, from lumber they had salvaged from the water.

Eva and Carol took off their shoes and socks and waded in. The water was so cold it sent pain up their legs, like blue electric sparks shooting through their veins, but they went on, pulling their skirts high, tight behind and bunched so they could hold them in front.

"Look at the fat-assed ducks in wading."

"Fat-assed fucks."

Eva and Carol, of course, gave no sign of hearing this. They laid hold of a log and climbed on, taking a couple of boards floating in the water for paddles. There were always things floating around in the Flood—branches, fence-rails, logs, road signs, old lumber; sometimes boilers, washtubs, pots and pans, or even a car seat or stuffed chair, as if somewhere the Flood had got into a dump.

They paddled away from shore, heading out into the cold lake. The water was perfectly clear, they could see the brown grass swimming along the bottom. Suppose it was the sea, thought Eva. She thought of drowned cities and countries. Atlantis. Suppose they were riding in a Viking boat—Viking boats on the Atlantic were more frail and narrow than this log on the Flood—and they had miles of clear sea beneath them, then a spired city, intact as a jewel irretrievable on the ocean floor.

"This is a Viking boat," she said. "I am the carving on the front." She stuck her chest out and stretched her neck, trying to make a curve, and she made a face, putting out her tongue. Then she turned and for the first time took notice of the boys.

"Hey, you sucks!" she yelled at them. "You'd be scared to come out here, this water is ten feet deep!"

"Liar," they answered without interest, and she was.

They steered the log around a row of trees, avoiding floating barbed wire, and got into a little bay created by a natural hollow of the land. Where the bay was now, there would be a pond full of frogs later in the spring, and by the middle of summer there would be no water visible at all, just a low tangle of reeds and bushes, green, to show that mud was still wet around their roots. Larger bushes, willows, grew around the steep bank of this pond and were still partly out of the water. Eva and Carol let the log ride in. They saw a place where something was caught.

It was a boat, or part of one. An old rowboat with most of one side ripped out, the board that had been the seat just dangling. It was pushed up among the branches, lying on what would have been its side, if it had a side, the prow caught high.

Their idea came to them without consultation, at the same time:

"You guys! Hey, you guys!"

"We found you a boat!"

"Stop building your stupid raft and come and look at the boat!"

What surprised them in the first place was that the boys really did come, scrambling overland, half running, half sliding down the bank, wanting to see.

"Hey, where?"

"Where is it. I don't see no boat."

What surprised them in the second place was that when the boys did actually see what boat was meant, this old flood-smashed wreck held up in the branches, they did not understand that they had been fooled, that a joke had been played on them. They did not show a moment's disappointment, but seemed as pleased at the discovery as if the boat had been whole and new. They were already barefoot, because they had been wading in the water to get lumber, and they waded in here without a stop, surrounding the boat and appraising it and paying no attention even of an insulting kind to Eva and Carol who bobbed up and down on their log. Eva and Carol had to call to them.

"How do you think you're going to get it off?"

"It won't float anyway."

"What makes you think it will float?"

"It'll sink. Glub-blub-blub, you'll all be drownded."

The boys did not answer, because they were too busy walking around the boat, pulling at it in a testing way to see how it could be got off with the least possible damage. Frank, who was the most literate, talkative and inept of the three, began referring to the boat as *she*, an affectation which Eva and Carol acknowledged with fish-mouths of contempt.

"She's caught two places. You got to be careful not to tear a hole in her bottom. She's heavier than you'd think."

It was Clayton who climbed up and freed the boat, and Bud, a tall fat boy, who got the weight of it on his back to turn it into the water so that they could half float, half carry it to shore. All this took some time. Eva and Carol abandoned their log and waded out of the water. They walked overland to get their shoes and socks and bicycles. They did not need to come back this way but they came. They stood at the top of the hill, leaning on their bicycles. They did not go on home, but they did not sit down and frankly watch, either. They stood more or less facing each other, but glancing down at the water and at the boys struggling with the boat, as if they had just halted for a moment out of curiosity, and staying longer than they intended, to see what came of this unpromising project.

About nine o'clock, or when it was nearly dark—dark to people inside the houses, but not quite dark outside—they all returned to town, going along Mayo Street in a sort of procession. Frank and Bud and Clayton came carrying the boat, upside-down, and Eva and Carol walked behind, wheeling their bicycles. The boys' heads were almost hidden in the darkness of the overturned boat, with its smell of soaked wood, cold swampy water. The girls could look ahead and see the street lights in their tin reflectors, a necklace of lights climbing Mayo Street, reaching all the way up to the standpipe. They turned onto Burns Street heading for Clayton's house, the nearest house belonging to any of them. This was not the way home for Eva or for Carol either, but they followed along. The boys were perhaps too busy carrying the boat to tell them to go away. Some younger children were still out playing, playing hopscotch on the sidewalk though they could hardly see. At this time of year the bare sidewalk was still such a novelty and delight. These children cleared out of the way and watched

20

25

30

the boat go by with unwilling respect; they shouted questions after it, wanting to know where it came from and what was going to be done with it. No one answered them. Eva and Carol as well as the boys refused to answer or even look at them.

The five of them entered Clayton's yard. The boys shifted weight, as if they were going to put the boat down.

"You better take it round to the back where nobody can see it," Carol said. That was the first thing any of them had said since they came into town.

The boys said nothing but went on, following a mud path between Clayton's house and a leaning board fence. They let the boat down in the back yard.

"It's a stolen boat, you know," said Eva, mainly for the effect. "It must've belonged to somebody. You stole it."

"You was the ones who stole it then," Bud said, short of breath. "It was you seen it first."

"It was you took it."

"It was all of us then. If one of us gets in trouble then all of us does."

"Are you going to tell anybody on them?" said Carol as she and Eva rode home, along the streets which were dark between the lights now and potholed from winter.

"It's up to you, I won't if you won't."

"I won't if you won't."

They rode in silence, relinquishing something, but not discontented.

The board fence in Clayton's back yard had every so often a post which supported it, or tried to, and it was on these posts that Eva and Carol spent several evenings sitting, jauntily but not very comfortably. Or else they just leaned against the fence while the boys worked on the boat. During the first couple of evenings neighborhood children attracted by the sound of hammering tried to get into the yard to see what was going on, but Eva and Carol blocked their way.

"Who said you could come in here?"

"Just us can come in this yard."

These evenings were getting longer, the air milder. Skipping was starting on the sidewalks. Further along the street there was a row of hard maples that had been tapped. Children drank the sap as fast as it could drip into the buckets. The old man and woman who owned the trees, and who hoped to make syrup, came running out of the house making noises as if they were trying to scare away crows. Finally, every spring, the old man would come out on his porch and fire his shotgun into the air, and then the thieving would stop.

None of those working on the boat bothered about stealing sap, though all had done so last year.

The lumber to repair the boat was picked up here and there, along back lanes. At this time of year things were lying around—old boards and branches, sodden mitts, spoons flung out with the dishwater, lids of pudding pots that had been set in the snow to cool, all the debris that can sift through and survive winter. The tools came from Clayton's cellar—left over, presumably, from the time when his father was alive—and though they had nobody to advise them the boys seemed to figure out more or less the manner in which boats are built, or rebuilt. Frank was the one who showed up with diagrams from books and *Popular Mechanics* magazines. Clayton looked at these diagrams and listened to Frank read the instructions and then went ahead and decided in his own way what was to be done. Bud was best at sawing. Eva and Carol watched everything from the fence and offered criticism and thought up names. The names for the boat that they thought of were: Water Lily, Sea Horse,

Flood Queen, and Caro-Eve, after them because they had found it. The boys did not say which, if any, of these names they found satisfactory.

The boat had to be tarred. Clayton heated up a pot of tar on the kitchen stove and brought it out and painted slowly, his thorough way, sitting astride the overturned boat. The other boys were sawing a board to make a new seat. As Clayton worked, the tar cooled and thickened so that finally he could not move the brush any more. He turned to Eva and held out the pot and said, "You can go in and heat this on the stove."

Eva took the pot and went up the back steps. The kitchen seemed black after outside, but it must be light enough to see in, because there was Clayton's mother standing at the ironing board, ironing. She did that for a living, took in wash and ironing.   50

"Please may I put the tar pot on the stove?" said Eva, who had been brought up to talk politely to parents, even wash-and-iron ladies, and who for some reason especially wanted to make a good impression on Clayton's mother.

"You'll have to poke up the fire then," said Clayton's mother, as if she doubted whether Eva would know how to do that. But Eva could see now, and she picked up the lid with the stove-lifter, and took the poker and poked up a flame. She stirred the tar as it softened. She felt privileged. Then and later. Before she went to sleep a picture of Clayton came to her mind; she saw him sitting astride the boat, tar-painting, with such concentration, delicacy, absorption. She thought of him speaking to her, out of his isolation, in such an ordinary peaceful taking-for-granted voice.

On the twenty-fourth of May, a school holiday in the middle of the week, the boat was carried out of town, a long way now, off the road over fields and fences that had been repaired, to where the river flowed between its normal banks. Eva and Carol, as well as the boys, took turns carrying it. It was launched in the water from a cow-trampled spot between willow bushes that were fresh out in leaf. The boys went first. They yelled with triumph when the boat did float, when it rode amazingly down the river current. The boat was painted black, and green inside, with yellow seats, and a strip of yellow all the way around the outside. There was no name on it, after all. The boys could not imagine that it needed any name to keep it separate from the other boats in the world.

Eva and Carol ran along the bank, carrying bags full of peanut butter-and-jam sandwiches, pickles, bananas, chocolate cake, potato chips, graham crackers stuck together with corn syrup and five bottles of pop to be cooled in the river water. The bottles bumped against their legs. They yelled for a turn.

"If they don't let us they're bastards," Carol said, and they yelled together. "We found it! We found it!"   55

The boys did not answer, but after a while they brought the boat in, and Carol and Eva came crashing, panting down the bank.

"Does it leak?"

"It don't leak yet."

"We forgot a bailing can," wailed Carol, but nevertheless she got in, with Eva, and Frank pushed them off, crying. "Here's to a Watery Grave!"

And the thing about being in a boat was that it was not solidly bobbing, like a   60
log, but was cupped in the water, so that riding in it was not like being on something in the water, but like being in the water itself. Soon they were all going out in the boat in mixed-up turns, two boys and a girl, two girls and a boy, a girl and a boy, until things were so confused it was impossible to tell whose turn came next, and nobody

cared anyway. They went down the river—those who weren't riding, running along the bank to keep up. They passed under two bridges, one iron, one cement. Once they saw a big carp just resting, it seemed to smile at them, in the bridge-shaded water. They did not know how far they had gone on the river, but things had changed—the water had got shallower, and the land flatter. Across an open field they saw a building that looked like a house, abandoned. They dragged the boat up on the bank and tied it and set out across the field.

"That's the old station," Frank said. "That's Pedder Station." The others had heard this name but he was the one who knew, because his father was the station agent in town. He said that this was a station on a branch line that had been torn up, and that there had been a sawmill here, but a long time ago.

Inside the station it was dark, cool. All the windows were broken. Glass lay in shards and in fairly big pieces on the floor. They walked around finding the larger pieces of glass and tramping on them, smashing them, it was like cracking ice on puddles. Some partitions were still in place, you could see where the ticket window had been. There was a bench lying on its side. People had been here, it looked as if people came here all the time, though it was so far from anywhere. Beer bottles and pop bottles were lying around, also cigarette packages, gum and candy wrappers, the paper from a loaf of bread. The walls were covered with dim and fresh pencil and chalk writings and carved with knives.

I LOVE RONNIE COLES

I WANT TO FUCK

KILROY WAS HERE

RONNIE COLES IS AN ASS-HOLE

WHAT ARE YOU DOING HERE?

WAITING FOR A TRAIN

DAWNA MARY-LOU BARBARA JOANNE

It was exciting to be inside this large, dark, empty place, with the loud noise of breaking glass and their voices ringing back from the underside of the roof. They tipped the old beer bottles against their mouths. That reminded them that they were hungry and thirsty and they cleared a place in the middle of the floor and sat down and ate the lunch. They drank the pop just as it was, lukewarm. They ate everything there was and licked the smears of peanut butter and jam off the bread-paper in which the sandwiches had been wrapped.

They played Truth or Dare.

"I dare you to write on the wall, I am a Stupid Ass, and sign your name."

"Tell the truth—what is the worst lie you ever told?"

"Did you ever wet the bed?"

"Did you ever dream you were walking down the street without any clothes on?"

"I dare you to go outside and pee on the railway sign."

It was Frank who had to do that. They could not see him, even his back, but they knew he did it, they heard the hissing sound of his pee. They all sat still, amazed, unable to think of what the next dare would be.

"I dare everybody," said Frank from the doorway. "I dare—Everybody."

"What?"

"Take off all our clothes."

Eva and Carol screamed.

"Anybody who won't do it has to walk—has to *crawl*—around this floor on their hands and knees."

They were all quiet, till Eva said, almost complacently, "What first?"

"Shoes and socks."

"Then we have to go outside, there's too much glass here."

They pulled off their shoes and socks in the doorway, in the sudden blinding sun. The field before them was bright as water. They ran across where the tracks used to go.

"That's enough, that's enough," said Carol. "Watch out for thistles!"   80

"Tops! Everybody take off their tops!"

"I won't! We won't, will we, Eva?"

But Eva was whirling round and round in the sun where the track used to be. "I don't care, I don't care! Truth or Dare! Truth or Dare!"

She unbuttoned her blouse as she whirled, as if she didn't know what her hand was doing, she flung it off.

Carol took off hers. "I wouldn't have done it, if you hadn't!"   85

"Bottoms!"

Nobody said a word this time, they all bent and stripped themselves. Eva, naked first, started running across the field, and then all the others ran, all five of them running bare through the knee-high hot grass, running towards the river. Not caring now about being caught but in fact leaping and yelling to call attention to themselves, if there was anybody to hear or see. They felt as if they were going to jump off a cliff and fly. They felt that something was happening to them different from anything that had happened before, and it had to do with the boat, the water, the sunlight, the dark ruined station, and each other. They thought of each other now hardly as names or people, but as echoing shrieks, reflections, all bold and white and loud and scandalous, and as fast as arrows. They went running without a break into the cold water and when it came almost to the tops of their legs they fell on it and swam. It stopped their noise. Silence, amazement, came over them in a rush. They dipped and floated and separated, sleek as mink.

Eva stood up in the water her hair dripping, water running down her face. She was waist deep. She stood on smooth stones, her feet fairly wide apart, water flowing between her legs. About a yard away from her Clayton also stood up, and they were blinking the water out of their eyes, looking at each other. Eva did not turn or try to hide; she was quivering from the cold of the water, but also with pride, shame, boldness, and exhilaration.

Clayton shook his head violently, as if he wanted to bang something out of it, then bent over and took a mouthful of river water. He stood up with his cheeks full and made a tight hole of his mouth and shot the water at her as if it was coming out of a hose, hitting her exactly, first one breast and then the other. Water from his mouth ran down her body. He hooted to see it, a loud self-conscious sound that nobody would have expected, from him. The others looked up from wherever they were in the water and closed in to see.

Eva crouched down and slid into the water, letting her head go right under. She   90 swam, and when she let her head out, downstream, Carol was coming after her and the boys were already on the bank, already running into the grass, showing their skinny backs, their white, flat buttocks. They were laughing and saying things to each other but she couldn't hear, for the water in her ears.

"What did he do?" said Carol.

"Nothing."

They crept in to shore. "Let's stay in the bushes till they go," said Eva. "I hate them anyway. I really do. Don't you hate them?"

"Sure," said Carol, and they waited, not very long, until they heard the boys still noisy and excited coming down to the place a bit upriver where they had left the boat. They heard them jump in and start rowing.

"They've got all the hard part, going back," said Eva, hugging herself and shivering violently. "Who cares? Anyway. It never was our boat."

"What if they tell?" said Carol.

"We'll say it's all a lie."

Eva hadn't thought of this solution until she said it, but as soon as she did she felt almost light-hearted again. The ease and scornfulness of it did make them both giggle, and slapping themselves and splashing out of the water they set about developing one of those fits of laughter in which, as soon as one showed signs of exhaustion, the other would snort and start up again, and they would make helpless—soon genuinely helpless—faces at each other and bend over and grab themselves as if they had the worst pain.

QUESTIONS

1.   Consider the details used in passages of description in the story. What kinds of details are included?

2.   What is the level of diction in the dialogue of the story? From the dialogue, what do you learn about the various speakers?

3.   Study paragraph 10. What does the paragraph tell you about Eva as a limited-point-of-view center of interest? How?

4.   Consider the last paragraph in the story as a paragraph of action. What verbs are used and how well do they help you visualize and imagine the sounds of the scene? What is the effect of the verb "snort"?

5.   From the lifestyle and artifacts mentioned, what do you learn about the time of the events and the economic level of the town? What is the effect of the facts that it is early springtime, that the water is still cold, but that in May the water is swimmable? What are the implications for summer?

MARK TWAIN (1835–1910)

Mark Twain (born Samuel Clemens) is one of the literary "giants" of the nineteenth century. Largely because of his use of colloquial and regional English in Huckleberry Finn, *he was acknowledged by Ernest Hemingway as the originator of American literature. He was born in Missouri, and spent much of his youth as a Mississippi River pilot, Confederate soldier, journalist, and miner. In 1863 he adopted "Mark Twain" as his nom de plume. His most famous works are* Tom Sawyer *(1876) and* Huckleberry Finn *(1884–1885). "Luck" is a brief story (Twain calls it a "sketch") illustrating Twain's art of comic debunking, a characteristic that he also shows in works such as* The Innocents Abroad *(1868) and "Fenimore Cooper's Literary Offenses."*

Luck[1] _____*1891*

It was at a banquet in London in honor of one of the two or three conspicuously illustrious English military names of this generation. For reasons which will presently
appear, I will withhold his real name and titles and call him Lieutenant-General Lord
Arthur Scoresby, Y.C., K.C.B., etc., etc. What a fascination there is in a renowned
name! There sat the man, in actual flesh, whom I had heard of so many thousands of
times since that day, thirty years before, when his name shot suddenly to the zenith
from a Crimean battlefield,° to remain forever celebrated. It was food and drink to
me to look, and look, and look at that demi-god; scanning, searching, noting: the
quietness, the reserve, the noble gravity of his countenance; the simple honesty that
expressed itself all over him; the sweet unconsciousness of his greatness—unconsciousness of the hundreds of admiring eyes fastened upon him, unconsciousness of
the deep, loving, sincere worship welling out of the breasts of those people and flowing toward him.

The clergyman at my left was an old acquaintance of mine—clergyman now,
but had spent the first half of his life in the camp and field and as an instructor in the
military school at Woolwich. Just at the moment I have been talking about a veiled
and singular light glimmered in his eyes and he leaned down and muttered confidentially to me—indicating the hero of the banquet with a gesture:

"Privately—he's an absolute fool."

This verdict was a great surprise to me. If its subject had been Napoleon, or
Socrates, or Solomon, my astonishment could not have been greater. Two things I was
well aware of: that the Reverend was a man of strict veracity and that his judgment of
men was good. Therefore I knew, beyond doubt or question, that the world was mistaken about this hero: he *was* a fool. So I meant to find out, at a convenient moment,
how the Reverend, all solitary and alone, had discovered the secret.

Some days later the opportunity came, and this is what the Reverend told me: 5

About forty years ago I was an instructor in the military academy at Woolwich.
I was present in one of the sections when young Scoresby underwent his preliminary
examination. I was touched to the quick with pity, for the rest of the class answered
up brightly and handsomely, while he—why, dear me, he didn't know *anything*, so to
speak. He was evidently good, and sweet, and lovable, and guileless; and so it was exceedingly painful to see him stand there, as serene as a graven image, and deliver himself of answers which were veritably miraculous for stupidity and ignorance. All the
compassion in me was aroused in his behalf. I said to myself, when he comes to be examined again he will be flung over, of course; so it will be simply a harmless act of
charity to ease his fall as much as I can. I took him aside and found that he knew a little of Caesar's history; and as he didn't know anything else, I went to work and drilled
him like a galley-slave on a certain line of stock questions concerning Caesar which I
knew would be used. If you'll believe me, he went through with flying colors on examination day! He went through on that purely superficial "cram," and got compliments too, while others, who knew a thousand times more than he, got plucked. By
some strangely lucky accident—an accident not likely to happen twice in a century—
he was asked no question outside of the narrow limits of his drill.

[1] This is not a fancy sketch. I got it from a clergyman who was an instructor at Woolwich
forty years ago, and who vouched for its truth. [Twain's note.]

Crimean battlefield: In the Crimean War (1853–1856), England was one of the allies that
fought against Russia.

It was stupefying. Well, all through his course I stood by him, with something of the sentiment which a mother feels for a crippled child; and he always saved himself—just by miracle, apparently.

Now, of course, the thing that would expose him and kill him at last was mathematics. I resolved to make his death as easy as I could; so I drilled him and crammed him, and crammed him and drilled him, just on the line of questions which the examiners would be most likely to use, and then launched him on his fate. Well, sir, try to conceive of the result: to my consternation, he took the first prize! And with it he got a perfect ovation in the way of compliments.

Sleep? There was no more sleep for me for a week. My conscience tortured me day and night. What I had done I had done purely through charity, and only to ease the poor youth's fall. I never had dreamed of any such preposterous results as the thing that had happened. I felt as guilty and miserable as Frankenstein. Here was a wooden-head whom I had put in the way of glittering promotions and prodigious responsibilities, and but one thing could happen: he and his responsibilities would all go to ruin together at the first opportunity.

The Crimean War had just broken out. Of course there had to be a war, I said to myself. We couldn't have peace and give this donkey a chance to die before he is found out. I waited for the earthquake. It came. And it made me reel when it did come. He was actually gazetted to a captaincy in a marching regiment! Better men grow old and gray in the service before they climb to a sublimity like that. And who could ever have foreseen that they would go and put such a load of responsibility on such green and inadequate shoulders? I could just barely have stood it if they had made him a cornet; but a captain—think of it! I thought my hair would turn white.

Consider what I did—I who so loved repose and inaction. I said to myself, I am responsible to the country for this, and I must go along with him and protect the country against him as far as I can. So I took my poor little capital that I had saved up through years of work and grinding economy, and went with a sigh and bought a cornetcy in his regiment, and away we went to the field.

And there—oh, dear, it was awful. Blunders?—why he never did anything *but* blunder. But, you see, nobody was in the fellow's secret. Everybody had him focused wrong, and necessarily misinterpreted his performance every time. Consequently they took his idiotic blunders for inspirations of genius. They did, honestly! His mildest blunders were enough to make a man in his right mind cry; and they did make me cry—and rage and rave, too, privately. And the thing that kept me always in a sweat of apprehension was the fact that every fresh blunder he made increased the luster of his reputation! I kept saying to myself, he'll get so high that when discovery does finally come it will be like the sun falling out of the sky.

He went right along, up from grade to grade, over the dead bodies of his superiors, until at last, in the hottest moment of the battle of———down went our colonel, and my heart jumped into my mouth, for Scoresby was next in rank! Now for it, said I: we'll all land in Sheol in ten minutes, sure.

The battle was awfully hot; the allies were steadily giving way all over the field. Our regiment occupied a position that was vital; a blunder now must be destruction. At this crucial moment, what does this immortal fool do but detach the regiment from its place and order a charge over a neighboring hill where there wasn't a suggestion of an enemy! "There you go!" I said to myself; "this *is* the end at last."

And away we did go, and were over the shoulder of the hill before the insane movement could be discovered and stopped. And what did we find? An entire and unsuspected Russian army in reserve! And what happened? We were eaten up? That is necessarily what would have happened in ninety-nine cases out of a hundred. But no; those Russians argued that no single regiment would come browsing around there at such a time. It must be the entire English army, and that the sly Russian game was detected and blocked, so they turned tail, and away they went, pell-mell, over the hill and down into the field, in wild confusion, and we after them; they themselves broke the solid Russian center in the field, and tore through, and in no time there was the most tremendous rout you ever saw, and the defeat of the allies was turned into a sweeping and splendid victory! Marshall Canrobert looked on, dizzy with astonishment, admiration, and delight; and sent right off for Scoresby, and hugged him, and decorated him on the field in presence of all the armies!

And what was Scoresby's blunder that time? Merely the mistaking his right hand for his left—that was all. An order had come to him to fall back and support our right; and, instead, he fell *forward* and went over the hill to the left. But the name he won that day as a marvelous military genius filled the world with his glory, and that glory will never fade while history books last.

He is just as good and sweet and lovable and unpretending as a man can be, but he doesn't know enough to come in when it rains. Now that is absolutely true. He is the supremest ass in the universe; and until half an hour ago nobody knew it but himself and me. He has been pursued, day by day and year by year, by a most phenomenal astonishing luckiness. He has been a shining soldier in all our wars for a generation; he has littered his whole military life with blunders, and yet has never committed one that didn't make him a knight or a baronet or a lord or something. Look at his breast; why, he is just clothed in domestic and foreign decorations. Well, sir, every one of them is the record of some shouting stupidity or other; and, taken together, they are proof that the very best thing in all this world that can befall a man is to be born lucky. I say again, as I said at the banquet, Scoresby's an absolute fool.

QUESTIONS

1. Describe Twain's style as a writer of narrative prose. What kinds of detail does he present? Does he give you enough detail about the battle during the Crimean War, for example, to justify an assertion that he describes action vividly? Or does he confine his detail to illuminate the life of Scoresby?

2. What elements in the story are amusing? How does the development of humor depend on Twain's arrangement of words?

3. Study the first paragraph. What does Twain intend after the "look, and look, and look" phrase? Why do you think he begins the story with such a description, that might even be called heroic? Contrast this paragraph with paragraph 12, where the word "blunder" is repeated.

4. Who begins the story? Who finally tells it? How does the second narrator learn about Scoresby? How does he summarize Scoresby's career?

WRITING ABOUT STYLE

In prewriting, consider the selected passage in the context of the entire story. If you can answer questions such as the following, you will readily assemble materials for your essay on the style of a passage from a story.

Questions for Discovering Ideas

- Use a dictionary to discover the meaning of any words you do not immediately know. Are there any unusual words? Any especially difficult or uncommon words? Do any of the words distract you as you read?

- Are the words the most common ones that might be used? Can you think of more difficult ones? Easier ones? More accurate ones? How many words are particularly short (one or two syllables)? How many are long (three syllables and more)?

- How varied are the sentence lengths? Do you find mostly short sentences (five to twenty words) or mostly long ones (twenty-one and longer), or is there a mixture of long and short sentences? What relationships do you find between the nature of the material and the lengths of the sentences?

- Are the sentences simple, compound, or complex? What is the connection between sentence types and topical material? What variations do you discover within sentences at the beginning, middle, and end of the story?

- Can you easily bring to life the situations described by the words? If you find it easy, or hard, to what degree does your success or difficulty stem out of the level of diction?

- For passages describing *action,* how vivid are the words? How do they help you picture the action? How do they hold your attention?

- For passages describing *exterior or interior scenery,* how specific are the words? How much detail does the writer provide? Should there be more or fewer words? How spatial are the descriptions of scenery? How many words are devoted to colors, shapes, sizes, and so on?

- For passages of *dialogue,* what does the level of speech indicate about the characters doing the talking? How do a person's speeches help to establish her or his character? What use does the speaker make of either formal or informal diction? How much slang do you find? To what degree do the characters seem to be thinking about the level of their language?

- What words belong only to particular occupations or ways of life (e.g., foreign words, specialized or technical words referring to things like horses, airplanes, flowers, medicine, psychology, and so on)? What use do speakers make of contractions?

- Are there any noteworthy rhetorical devices? Are there any sentences that are *periodic* as opposed to *loose?* What effect is gained by this sentence or sentences? What other rhetorical devices have you discovered? How are they used? What is their effect?

Strategies for Organizing Ideas

To describe and evaluate the style of the passage, first consider the style in relationship to the story. For example, suppose the speaker has just returned home after a long and painful journey, or has just finished a race with a close competitor, or is recalling an event of the long-distant past, or is anticipating future happiness or frustration. Keep such conditions in mind throughout your analysis.

To focus your essay, you should either try to single out one aspect of style or to discuss everything, depending on the length of the assignment. Be sure to treat topics like *levels of diction*, categories like *specific-general* or *concrete-abstract*, the degree of *simplicity* or *complexity*, *length*, *numbers* of words, and *denotation-connotation*. In discussing rhetorical aspects, go as far as you can with the terminology at your command. For example, at a minimum, you should be able to consider simple-compound-complex for sentence types, and parallelism for rhetorical devices. If you can draw attention to the elements in a parallel structure by using grammatical terms, do so. If you are able to detect the ways in which the sentences are kept simple or made complex, describe these ways. Be sure to use examples from the passage to illustrate your point.

Your essay should reflect your awareness of style at your own stage of development as a reader. Later, when you have gained sharper perceptions and a wider descriptive vocabulary, you will be able to write more detailed and expert analyses.

In your conclusion, try to evaluate the author's style. To what extent has your analysis increased or reinforced your appreciation of the author's technique? Does the passage take on any added importance as a result of your study? Is there anything elsewhere in the work comparable to the content, words, or ideas that you have discussed in the passage?

Numbers for Easy Reference

Include a copy of your passage at the beginning of your essay, as in the example. For your reader's convenience, number the sentences in the passage, and use these numbers when you refer to them.

SAMPLE ESSAY

Mark Twain's Blending of Style and Purpose in Paragraphs 14 and 15 of "Luck"°

[14] [1] The battle was awfully hot; the allies were steadily giving way all over the field. [2] Our regiment occupied a position that was vital; a blunder now must be destruction. [3] At this crucial moment, what does this immortal fool do but detach the regiment from its place and order a charge over a neighboring hill where there wasn't a suggestion of an enemy! [4] "There you go!" I said to myself; "this is the end at last."

[15] [5] And away we did go, and were over the shoulder of the hill before the insane movement could be discovered and stopped. [6] And what did we find? [7] An entire and unsuspected Russian army in reserve! [8] And what happened? [9] We were eaten up? [10] That is necessarily what would have happened in ninety-nine cases out of a hundred. [11]

° For the text of this story, see pp. 285–87.

But no; those Russians argued that no single regiment would come browsing around there at such a time. [12] It must be the entire English army, and that the sly Russian game was detected and blocked; so they turned tail, and away they went, pell-mell, over the hill and down into the field, in wild confusion, and we after them; they themselves broke the solid Russian center in the field, and tore through, and in no time there was the most tremendous rout you ever saw, and the defeat of the allies was turned into a sweeping and splendid victory! [13] Marshall Canrobert looked on, dizzy with astonishment, admiration, and delight; and sent right off for Scoresby, and hugged him, and decorated him on the field in presence of all the armies!

[1]   Appearing close to the end of "Luck," these two paragraphs are important in Twain's satiric design to puncture the bubble of Scoresby, the widely recognized and decorated British hero who is nothing more than a lucky boob. In the story, the paragraphs come as a climax. By presenting a brief account of a decisive battle in the Crimean War, in which Scoresby's regiment is decisive, they bring out his stupidity and luck to the highest degree. Though the passages are narrative, the mark of Twain's style is to underscore how the hero's blundering foolishness is always saved by luck.* In every respect— description, word level, use of general and abstract diction, grammatical patterns, and the narrator's involvement—the passage embodies Twain's satiric and comic goal.†

[2]   The descriptions in the paragraphs are directed toward the idiocy of the main character. In fact, the descriptions are not about the battle at all. The military matter presented in the thirteen sentences is that the allies are giving way, that Scoresby orders a charge, and that the Russians turn tail and dash away. There is no report of clashing soldiers and dying men and horses—beyond the claim that the Russians themselves "tore through" their own ranks— and there are no vivid words, beyond these, describing the circumstances of victory. Indeed, the descriptions are minimal, containing just enough to describe Scoresby's lucky blunder, but no more. The paragraphs would be unsuccessful as an account of a battle, but as part of this story they superbly serve Twain's satiric goal.

[3]   In keeping with the exposé, Twain uses a middle, or neutral, level of diction. The words are not unusual or difficult. What could be more ordinary, for example, than words like battle, awfully, steadily, occupied, discovered, stopped, argued, and victory? One may grant that splendid, astonishment, pell-mell, immortal, and crucial are not common in everyday speech, but in this context they are appropriate, for they fall within the vocabulary of responses to battle. Because of their aptness, they enable the reader to focus on the subject and on the narrator's expressions of humor, and in this respect they fit into the middle level of diction.

[4]   Not only is the level neutral, but many words are general and abstract, in accord with the intention of debunking Scoresby. The "allies were steadily

---

* Central idea.
† Thesis sentence.

giving way," for example, and the "movement" of many individuals is described as "insane." These broad words are fitting for groups and mass actions, but not for specific individuals. When the Russians conclude from Scoresby's senseless charge that their "game" is "detected," they turn "tail" and run "pell-mell," dashing in such "wild confusion" that there is "the most tremendous rout you ever saw," resulting in "sweeping and splendid victory"—all general and abstract words. Even the "hero," Scoresby, is not detailed anywhere as a specific leader and fighter; it is as though he is less significant than the gigantic forces of stupidity he unleashes. The last sentence of the paragraphs, the thirteenth, continues in this mode with the abstract but worshipful responses of the commander, Marshall Canrobert; he is "dizzy with astonishment, admiration, and delight." These abstract words reflect the public renown of Scoresby, which we, as the narrator's listeners, know to be untrue. Both general and abstract words thus jell perfectly with Twain's debunking humor.

[5]   Grammatically, as well, there is great emphasis on the contrast between Scoresby's stupidity and his success. Twain's first two sentences are neatly balanced with contrasting ideas: Sentence 1 tells us that the battle is "hot" (part 1) and that the allies are losing (part 2). Sentence 2 tells us that the regiment is important (part 1) and that a mistake would be disastrous (part 2). But as the battle descends into the sweeping chaos caused by the charge of Scoresby's regiment, the grammar takes on the same chaotic pattern. Sentence 12, containing all the battle details, is eighty-one words long. It is broken up by semi-colons and commas into a variety of separate statements and structures describing the panic of retreat and the splendidness of victory. In other words, the sentence has the same wildness, sweep, and madness of the events being described—a blending of grammar and subject.

[6]   The major quality of Twain's style, however, is the narrator's amused and scornful language. His words frame the suspense and anticlimax of the battle, as is shown in the first paragraph (sentences 1–4). He tells us (sentence 3) that the "immortal fool" orders a mistaken charge. His lamenting prediction, "this is the end at last" (sentence 4), is designed for full dramatic and suspenseful effect. The narrator's involvement is also shown by his simply phrased questions just before he tells about the results of the charge: "And what did we find?" "And what happened?" "We were eaten up?" His attitude is most amusingly shown by the word "browsing" (sentence 11) which suggests grazing animals, not charging armies. This word emphasizes the dimwittedness of Scoresby's command to attack. Throughout the paragraphs, the speaker thus lends his own wry insights to the language. The skill, naturally, belongs to Twain.

[7]   In all respects, the passage is a model of the right use of words in the right places. If the writing were about an actual military combat, it would be poor. But because it is part of a comic exposé of a fortunate fool, it is hard to imagine better language of description. Twain's speaker gives us what we need to know: namely that Scoresby has a Midas touch in everything he does, no matter how potentially disastrous. The sentences are clear and direct, and convey the facts about Scoresby that show his imbecility. Even the longest and most confused sentence, the twelfth, is appropriate to the confusion that

Scoresby converts to triumph. <u>For these reasons, the paragraphs are examples of accurate, purposeful narrative prose.</u>

Commentary on the Essay

This essay shows how separate stylistic topics may be unified. Important in this objective are the transitions from paragraph to paragraph, such as "not only . . . but," "in keeping with the exposé," "as well," and "in all respects." These transition phrases enable the reader to move easily from one topic to the next.

The beginning of the essay demonstrates the importance of relating the passage being studied to the work as a whole. Because the central idea is connected to Twain's debunking objective, the point is made that style and satiric intention are merged and integrated.

In the body, paragraph 2 treats the absence of specifically descriptive words, explaining this lack by reference to the satiric subject. Paragraph 3 treats the neutral diction, making the point that this language is appropriate because it permits a direct focus on the asinine blunders of the major character. Twain's use of general and abstract language is treated in paragraph 4, which makes the point that this language is appropriate because the story exposes the emptyheadedness of Scoresby. Paragraph 5, which addresses the grammar of the passage, indicates that the movement from balance to chaos complements the chaos of the battle. Paragraph 6, the last of the body, is the high point of the discussion; it asserts that the most important aspect of the writing is the narrative speaker, whose ideas and words permit Twain to keep the narrative brief while emphasizing his hero's blundering stupidity. Paragraph 7, the conclusion, is a tribute to Twain's style, emphasizing again how his satiric objective governs word choices.

WRITING TOPICS

1. Write an essay on the differences in style between the two narrators in "Luck." What purpose do the two narrators serve?

2. Write an essay that answers the following questions: To what degree are the narrative and descriptive styles of "Soldier's Home" appropriate to the nature of the story? What would be the effect on the story if Hemingway had used the style of Faulkner in "Barn Burning" (Chapter 4), or Updike in "A & P" (Chapter 2), or Whitecloud in "Blue Winds Dancing" (Chapter 3)?

3. Stories like "The Found Boat" and "The Blue Hotel" are characterized by full descriptions, so that the reader needs to imagine few details. How appropriate would similarly full descriptions be in stories like "Soldier's Home" and "Luck"?

4. Write two brief character sketches, or a description of an action, to be included in a longer story. Make the first favorable, and the second negative. Analyze your word choices in the contrasting accounts: What kinds of words do you select, and on what principles do you select them? What kinds of words might you

select if you wanted to create a neutral account? On the basis of your answers, what can you conclude about the development of a fiction writer's style?

5. "The Found Boat" and "The Yellow Wallpaper" (for the last story, see Chapter 12) feature the psychological makeup of their major characters (see also Chapter 4 and Appendix D). Write an essay considering the nature and effectiveness of the psychological portraiture in these stories.

8

Tone: The Expression of Attitude in Fiction

Tone refers to the methods by which writers and speakers reveal attitudes or feelings. It is an aspect of all spoken and written statements—from earnest declarations of love, requests to pass a dish at dinner, letters from students asking parents for money, to official government notices threatening penalties if fines are not paid. Because tone is often equated with *attitude*, it is important to realize that tone refers not so much to attitudes themselves but instead to those techniques and modes of presentation that reveal or create attitudes.

As a literary concept, *tone* is adapted from the phrase *tone of voice* in speech. Tone of voice reflects attitudes toward an object or situation, and also toward listeners. Let us suppose that Mary has a difficult assignment, on which she expects to work all day. Things go well, and she finishes quickly. She happily tells her friend Anne, "I'm so pleased. I needed only two hours for that." Then she decides to buy tickets for a popular play, and must wait through a long and slow line. After getting her tickets, she tells the people at the end of the line, "I'm so pleased. I needed only two hours for that." The sentences are exactly the same, but by changing her emphasis and vocal inflection, Mary indicates her disgust and impatience with her long wait, and also shows her sympathy with the people still in line. By controlling the *tone* of her statements, in other words, Mary conveys attitudes of satisfaction at one time, and indignation and also sympathy at another.

Tone and the expression of attitude are vital components of all forms of communication. In Whistler's painting *The White Girl*, for example (p. 295), the young woman dressed in white seems at first to be loveliness personified. But certain features of the painting indicate a greater complexity: The girl is standing on a rug of wolf's fur (the animal's expression makes it seem alive), some of her flowers have fallen and the ones she holds are wilted, and she appears detached, gazing vacantly into space. These details

The White Girl (Symphony in White, No. 1), 1862, James McNeill Whistler, National Gallery of Art, Washington, DC, Harris Whittlemore Collection.

reveal that Whistler's attitude toward his beautiful subject is somewhat negative, with a degree of irony.

As the example about Mary indicates, an attitude itself may be summarized with a word or phrase (satisfaction, indignation; love, contempt; deference, command; and so on), but the study of tone examines those aspects of situation, language, action, and background that *bring out* the attitude. In

Poe's "The Masque of the Red Death," for example, Prince Prospero declares outrage at the intruder costumed as the Red Death. His words indicate anger and intimidation:

> "Who dares"—he demanded hoarsely of the courtiers who stood near him— "who dares insult us with this blasphemous mockery? Seize him and unmask him—that we may know whom we have to hang, at sunrise, from the battlements!" (paragraph 11)

Prospero's commands show that he is judge, jury, and executioner, from whom there is no appeal. In contrast, at the end of "A Worn Path," the attendant offers Phoenix "a few pennies," but Phoenix wants more. Being a recipient of charity, but also being an independent sort, Phoenix makes her request indirectly (paragraph 99):

> "Five pennies is a nickel," said Phoenix stiffly.

This request is less imperious than Prince Prospero's, but it is nevertheless demanding. Although Phoenix is not a literary master, she is a master of tone in this conversational situation.

TONE AND ATTITUDES

ATTITUDE TOWARD THE MATERIAL. By reading a story carefully, we may deduce the author's attitude or attitudes toward the subject matter. In "The Story of an Hour," for example, Kate Chopin sympathetically portrays a young wife's secret wishes for freedom, just as she also humorously reveals the unwitting smugness that often pervades men's relationships with women. In "The Hammon and the Beans," Parédes shows revulsion against the effects of poverty, and pity for the dead young girl who might have been saved with proper health care. Williams in "Taking Care" reveals deep admiration for the character. "Rape Fantasies" reveals Atwood's amused affection for the major character. All these stories exhibit various types of irony, which is one of the most significant aspects of authorial tone (see pp. 299–301).

ATTITUDE TOWARD READERS. Authors recognize that readers participate in the creative act, and that all elements of a story—word choice, characterization, allusions, levels of reality—must take readers' responses into account (note the discussion of "Reader Response" criticism in Appendix D). When Hawthorne's woodland guide in "Young Goodman Brown" refers to King Philip's War, for example (p. 332), Hawthorne assumes that his readers know that this war was inhumanly greedy and cruel. By not explaining this part of history, he indicates respect for the knowledge of his readers, and he also assumes their agreement with his interpretation.

Authors always make such considerations about readers, by implicitly complimenting them on their knowledge and also by satisfying their curiosity and desire to be interested, stimulated, and pleased. Updike in "A & P" (p. 63) assumes that readers understand his use of Sammy's diction to reveal Sammy as a perceptive and independent but insecure young man. In "Soldier's Home," Hemingway assumes that readers may connect Krebs's discontent with the viciousness and frustration of the trench warfare of World War I. Such authorial consideration for readers is a vital aspect of tone.

OTHER DOMINANT ATTITUDES. Beyond general authorial tone, there are many internal and dramatically rendered expressions of attitude. For example, in Collier's "The Chaser" (see the sample essay, p. 319), Alan's farewell is "Thank you again. . . . Goodbye." This courteous and ordinary speech suggests that Alan is still uncomplicated and unsophisticated. In contrast, however, the old man responds with the words "Au revoir," a French phrase meaning "until we meet again." Although this is a common salutation, in the context it indicates the old man's cynicism, for he is predicting that there will be a future meeting in which Alan's purpose will be sinister rather than idealistic. Thus, these two ordinary statements of farewell have ominous implications.

In addition, as characters interact, their tone dramatically shows their judgments about other characters and situations. The brusque young woman in Mansfield's "Miss Brill" (p. 202) compares Miss Brill's fur muff to a "fried whiting," an insult that she makes sure Miss Brill herself hears (paragraph 14). Her speech indicates contempt, indifference, and cruelty. A complicated control of tone occurs in Glaspell's "A Jury of Her Peers," where the two major characters, Mrs. Hale and Mrs. Peters, decide to cover up incriminating evidence about Minnie Wright. When Mrs. Peters agrees to this obstruction of justice, however, she speaks not about illegality, but rather about the possible embarrassment of the action:

> "My!" she began, in a high, false voice, "it's a good thing the men couldn't hear us! Getting all stirred up over a little thing like a—dead canary." She hurried over that. "As if that could have anything to do with—with— My, wouldn't they *laugh*?" (paragraph 267)

Notice that her words reveal her knowledge that men scoff at feminine concerns, like Minnie's quilting knots, and therefore she openly anticipates the men's amusement. But the reader knows that she is joining Mrs. Hale in covering up the evidence about Minnie.

TONE AND HUMOR

A major aspect of tone is the communication of humor. Everyone likes to laugh, and shared laughter is part of good human relationships. But not everyone can explain or convey humor. Laughter resists close analysis; it is unplanned, personal, idiosyncratic, and usually unpredictable. Nonetheless, there are a number of common elements:

1. *An object to laugh at.* There must be something to laugh at—a person, thing, situation, custom, a habit of speech or dialect, or arrangement of words.

2. *Incongruity.* People normally know what to expect under given conditions, and anything contrary to these expectations is *incongruous* and may therefore generate laughter. When the temperature is 100°F, for example, you expect people to dress lightly. But if you see a person dressed in a heavy overcoat, a warm hat, a muffler, and large gloves, who is waving his arms and stamping his feet to keep warm, this person violates your expectations. Because his garments and behavior are *inappropriate* or *incongruous,* you would probably find him amusing. A student in a language class once wrote about a *"congregation* of verbs" and also about parts of speech as "nouns, verbs, and *proverbs."* The student meant the *conjugation* of verbs, of course, and also (maybe) either *adverbs* or *pronouns,* but somehow his understanding slipped and he created humorous incongruities. Such inadvertent verbal errors are called **malapropisms,** after Mrs. Malaprop, a character in Sheridan's eighteenth-century play *The Rivals.* In the literary creation of malapropisms, the tone is directed against the speaker, for the amusement of both readers and author alike.

3. *Safety and/or good will.* Seeing a person slip on a banana peel and hurtle through the air may cause laughter, but only if we ourselves are not that person, for laughter depends on insulation from danger and pain. In humorous situations that involve physical abuse—falling down stairs or being hit in the face by cream pies—the abuse never harms the participants. The incongruity of such situations causes laughter, while the immunity from pain and injury prevents grave or even horrified responses. Good will enters into humor in romantic comedy or in any other work where we are drawn into general sympathy with the major figures, such as Rosie and Vlashkin in Paley's "Goodbye and Good Luck" (p. 531). As the author leads the characters toward recognizing their love, our involvement produces happiness, smiles, and even sympathetic laughter.

4. *Unfamiliarity, newness, uniqueness, spontaneity.* Laughter depends on seeing something new or unique, or on experiencing something familiar in a new light. Because laughter is prompted by flashes of insight, or sudden revelations, it is always spontaneous, even when readers already know what they are laughing at. Indeed, the task of the comic writer is to develop ordinary materials to that point when spontaneity frees readers to laugh. Thus you can read and re-read O'Connor's "First Confession" (p. 520) and laugh each time because, even though you know what happens, the story shapes your acceptance of how reconciliation penetrates a wall of anger and guilt. Young Jackie's experience is and always will be comic because it is so spontaneous and incongruous.

TONE AND IRONY

The capacity to have more than one attitude toward someone or something is a uniquely human trait. We know that people are not perfect, but we love a number of them anyway. Therefore we speak to them not only with love and praise, but also with banter and criticism. On occasion, you may have given mildly insulting greeting cards to your loved ones, not to affront them but to amuse them. As you share smiles and laughs, you also remind them of your affection.

The word **irony** describes such contradictory statements or situations. Irony is natural to human beings, who are aware of life's ambiguities and complexities. It develops from the realization that life does not always measure up to promise, that friends and loved ones are sometimes angry and bitter toward each other, that the universe contains incomprehensible mysteries, that the social and political structure is often oppressive rather than liberating, that doubt exists even in the certainty of knowledge and faith, and that human character is built through chagrin, regret, and pain as much as through emulation and praise. In expressing an idea ironically, writers pay the greatest compliment to their reading audience, for they assume that readers have sufficient intelligence and skill to discover the real meaning of quizzical or ambiguous statements and situations.

VERBAL IRONY. Irony can be *verbal, situational,* or *dramatic.* In **verbal irony** one thing is said and the opposite is meant. In the example at the opening of this chapter, Mary's ironic expression of pleasure after her two-hour wait for tickets really means that she is disgusted. There are important types of verbal irony. In **understatement** the surface expression does not fully describe the importance of a situation, and therefore makes its point by implication. For example, in Collier's "The Chaser," the old man says "nothing I sell has effects which could be precisely described as ordinary" (¶ 5). In the context of the story, it becomes clear that the old man is dealing in things that are absolutely extraordinary. His observation, because it leaves so much unsaid, is ironic.

By contrast, in **overstatement** or **hyperbole**, the words are far in excess of the situation, and readers or listeners therefore understand that the true meaning is considerably less than what is said. An example is the priest's exaggerated dialogue with Jackie in "First Confession" (p. 524, ¶'s 38–50). Though the priest makes incongruously hyperbolic comments on Jackie's plans for slaughtering his grandmother, readers automatically know he means no such thing. The gulf between what is said and what is meant creates smiles and chuckles.

Often verbal irony is ambiguous, having double meaning or **double-entendre.** Midway through "Young Goodman Brown," for example, the woodland guide leaves Brown alone while stating, "when you feel like moving again, there is my staff to help you along" (¶ 40). The word "staff" is ambiguous, for it refers to the staff that resembles a serpent (¶ 13). The word therefore suggests that the devilish guide is leaving Brown not only with a real staff, but also with the spirit of evil (unlike the divine "staff" of Psalm 23 that gives comfort). Ambiguity of course may be used in relation to any topic. Quite often *double-entendre* is used in statements about sexuality, usually for the amusement of listeners or readers.

SITUATIONAL IRONY. **Situational irony,** or **irony of situation,** refers to the chasm between what we hope for or expect and what actually happens. It is pessimistic because it emphasizes that human beings usually have little or no control over their lives or anything else. The forces of opposition may be psychological, social, cultural, political, or environmental. In Atwood's "Rape Fantasies," for example, the narrator Estelle states her inability to understand why men cannot be satisfied by human relationships with women rather than rapacious ones. Though "Rape Fantasies" is not a sociological document, Estelle's uneasiness underscores the irony of the political and social conditions that produce rape. Although situational irony often involves disaster, it need not always do so. For example, a happier occurrence of situational irony is in Chekhov's *The Bear,* for the two characters shift from anger to love as they fall into the grips of emotions that are "bigger than both of them."

COSMIC IRONY. A special kind of situational irony that emphasizes the pessimistic and fatalistic side of life is **cosmic irony,** or **irony of fate.** By the standard of cosmic irony, the universe is indifferent to individuals, who are subject to blind chance, accident, uncontrollable emotions, perpetual misfortune, and misery. Even if things temporarily go well, people's lives end badly, and their best efforts do not rescue them or make them happy. A story illustrating cosmic irony is "The Hammon and the Beans" by Parédes. Among the impoverished Mexican-American families living near the border in Texas, the little girl Chonita dies without a chance to fulfill her potential for a productive, happy life. Her death is no more than a minor statistic—an insignificant part of a gigantic pattern of social and political neglect. Her situation is cosmically ironic, for the implication of "The Hammon and the Beans" is that human beings are caught in a web of adverse circumstances from which there is no escape.

DRAMATIC IRONY. Like cosmic irony, **dramatic irony** is a special kind of situational irony. It happens when a character either lacks information about a situation or else misjudges it, while readers (and often some of the other characters) see everything completely and correctly. The model of dramatic irony is found in Sophocles' play *Oedipus the King* (included in Chapter 27), in which everyone—other characters and readers alike—knows the truth long before Oedipus knows it. Writers of fiction also make abundant use of dramatic irony. For instance, the doctors in "The Story of an Hour" do not know Louise's true responses to the reports about her husband's death, but we readers do, and therefore we see the foolishness and vanity of their judgments. Similarly, in "The Chaser," Alan speaks rapturously about his sweetheart, but the old man and the readers know that one day his enthusiasm will wither and fester.

STORIES FOR STUDY

MARGARET ATWOOD (b. 1939)

Atwood is one of Canada's premier writers, having published many books of poetry, a number of novels and stories, and much criticism. In addition, she is editor of The Oxford Book of Canadian Verse *(1982). One of her most widely recognized works is the anti-utopian novel* The Handmaid's Tale *(1986), which describes a futuristic nightmare society of fear and repression for women. This story was adapted as a movie in 1990. The stories in a recent collection,* Wilderness Tips *(1992), reflect regret and diminished hopes, unlike the more comic topics of her story "Rape Fantasies" and her poem "Siren Song." Her most recent novel is* The Robber Bride *(1993).*

Rape Fantasies ――――――――――――――――――――――――――――――――――*1977*

The way they're going on about it in the magazines you'd think it was just invented, and not only that but it's something terrific, like a vaccine for cancer. They put it in capital letters on the front cover, and inside they have these questionnaires like the ones they used to have about whether you were a good enough wife or an endomorph or an ectomorph, remember that? with the scoring upside down on page 73, and then these numbered do-it-yourself dealies, you know? RAPE, TEN THINGS TO DO ABOUT IT, like it was ten new hairdos or something. I mean, what's so new about it?

So at work they all have to talk about it because no matter what magazine you open, there it is, staring you right between the eyes, and they're beginning to have it on the television, too. Personally I'd prefer a June Allyson° movie anytime but they don't make them any more and they don't even have them that much on the Late Show. For instance, day before yesterday, that would be Wednesday, thank god it's Friday as they say, we were sitting around in the women's lunch room—the *lunch* room, I mean you'd think you could get some peace and quiet in there—and Chrissy closes up the magazine she's been reading and says, "How about it, girls, do you have rape fantasies?"

June Allyson: actress (b. 1917) known for her bright smile and scratchy voice. She specialized in "sweet" movie and musical roles, 1943–1959, and still appears regularly in TV commercials.

The four of us were having our game of bridge the way we always do, and I had a bare twelve points counting the singleton with not that much of a bid in anything. So I said one club, hoping Sondra would remember about the one club convention, because the time before when I used that she thought I really meant clubs and she bid us up to three, and all I had was four little ones with nothing higher than a six, and we went down two and on top of that we were vulnerable. She is not the world's best bridge player. I mean, neither am I but there's a limit.

Darlene passed but the damage was done, Sondra's head went round like it was on ball bearings and she said, "*What* fantasies?"

"Rape fantasies," Chrissy said. She's a receptionist and she looks like one; she's pretty but cool as a cucumber, like she's been painted all over with nail polish, if you know what I mean. Varnished. "It says here all women have rape fantasies."

"For Chrissake, I'm eating an egg sandwich," I said, "and I bid one club and Darlene passed."

"You mean, like some guy jumping you in an alley or something," Sondra said. She was eating her lunch, we all eat our lunches during the game, and she bit into a piece of that celery she always brings and started to chew away on it with this thoughtful expression in her eyes and I knew we might as well pack it in as far as the game was concerned.

"Yeah, sort of like that," Chrissy said. She was blushing a little, you could see it even under her makeup.

"I don't think you should go out alone at night," Darlene said, "you put yourself in a position," and I may have been mistaken but she was looking at me. She's the oldest, she's forty-one though you wouldn't know it and neither does she, but I looked it up in the employees' file. I like to guess a person's age and then look it up to see if I'm right. I let myself have an extra pack of cigarettes if I am, though I'm trying to cut down. I figure it's harmless as long as you don't tell. I mean, not everyone has access to that file, it's more or less confidential. But it's all right if I tell you, I don't expect you'll ever meet her, though you never know, it's a small world. Anyway.

"For *heaven's* sake, it's only *Toronto,*" Greta said. She worked in Detroit for three years and she never lets you forget it, it's like she thinks she's a war hero or something, we should all admire her just for the fact that she's still walking this earth, though she was really living in Windsor° the whole time, she just worked in Detroit. Which for me doesn't really count. It's where you sleep, right?

"Well, do you?" Chrissy said. She was obviously trying to tell us about hers but she wasn't about to go first, she's cautious, that one.

"I certainly don't," Darlene said, and she wrinkled up her nose, like this, and I had to laugh. "I think it's disgusting." She's divorced, I read that in the file too, she never talks about it. It must've been years ago anyway. She got up and went over to the coffee machine and turned her back on us as though she wasn't going to have anything more to do with it.

"Well," Greta said. I could see it was going to be between her and Chrissy. They're both blondes, I don't mean that in a bitchy way but they do try to outdress each other. Greta would like to get out of Filing, she'd like to be a receptionist too so she could meet more people. You don't meet much of anyone in Filing except other people in Filing. Me, I don't mind it so much, I have outside interests.

Windsor: city south of Detroit, noted as the only place where any portion of Canada is south of the United States.

"Well," Greta said, "I sometimes think about, you know my apartment? It's got this little balcony, I like to sit out there in the summer and I have a few plants out there. I never bother that much about locking the door to the balcony, it's one of those sliding glass ones, I'm on the eighteenth floor for heaven's sake, I've got a good view of the lake and the CN Tower and all. But I'm sitting around one night in my housecoat, watching TV with my shoes off, you know how you do, and I see this guy's feet, coming down past the window, and the next thing you know he's standing on the balcony, he's let himself down by a rope with a hook on the end of it from the floor above, that's the nineteenth, and before I can even get up off the chesterfield he's inside the apartment. He's all dressed in black with black gloves on"—I knew right away what show she got the black gloves off because I saw the same one—"and then he, well, you know."

"You know what?" Chrissy said, but Greta said, "And afterwards he tells me that   15
he goes all over the outside of the apartment building like that, from one floor to another, with his rope and his hook . . . and then he goes out to the balcony and tosses his rope, and he climbs up it and disappears."

"Just like Tarzan," I said, but nobody laughed.

"Is that all?" Chrissy said. "Don't you ever think about, well, I think about being in the bathtub, with no clothes on . . ."

"So who takes a bath in their clothes?" I said, you have to admit it's stupid when you come to think of it, but she just went on, ". . . with lots of bubbles, what I use is Vitabath, it's more expensive but it's so relaxing, and my hair pinned up, and the door opens and this fellow's standing there. . . ."

"How'd he get in?" Greta said.

"Oh, I don't know, through a window or something. Well, I can't very well get   20
out of the bathtub, the bathroom's too small and besides he's blocking the doorway, so I just *lie* there, and he starts to very slowly take his own clothes off, and then he gets into the bathtub with me."

"Don't you scream or anything?" said Darlene. She'd come back with her cup of coffee, she was getting really interested. "I'd scream like bloody murder."

"Who'd hear me?" Chrissy said. "Besides, all the articles say it's better not to resist, that way you don't get hurt."

"Anyway you might get bubbles up your nose," I said, "from the deep breathing," and I swear all four of them looked at me like I was in bad taste, like I'd insulted the Virgin Mary or something. I mean, I don't see what's wrong with a little joke now and then. Life's too short, right?

"Listen," I said, "those aren't *rape* fantasies. I mean, you aren't getting *raped*, it's just some guy you haven't met formally who happens to be more attractive than Derek Cummins"—he's the Assistant Manager, he wears elevator shoes or at any rate they have these thick soles and he has this funny way of talking, we call him Derek Duck—"and you have a good time. Rape is when they've got a knife or something and you don't want to."

"So what about you, Estelle," Chrissy said, she was miffed because I laughed at   25
her fantasy, she thought I was putting her down. Sondra was miffed too, by this time she'd finished her celery and she wanted to tell about hers, but she hadn't got in fast enough.

"All right, let me tell you one," I said. "I'm walking down this dark street at night and this fellow comes up and grabs my arm. Now it so happens that I have a plastic lemon in my purse, you know how it always says you should carry a plastic lemon in your purse? I don't really do it, I tried it once but the darn thing leaked all over my chequebook, but in this fantasy I have one, and I say to him, "You're intending to rape me, right?" and he nods, so I open my purse to get the plastic lemon, and I can't find it! My purse is full of all this junk, Kleenex and cigarettes and my change purse and my lipstick and my driver's licence, you know the kind of stuff: so I ask him to hold out his hands, like this, and I pile all this junk into them and down at the bottom there's the plastic lemon, and I can't get the top off. So I hand it to him and he's very obliging, he twists the top off and hands it back to me, and I squirt him in the eye."

I hope you don't think that's too vicious. Come to think of it, it is a bit mean, especially when he was so polite and all.

"*That's* your rape fantasy?" Chrissy says, "I don't believe it."

"She's a card," Darlene says, she and I are the ones that've been here the longest and she never will forget the time I got drunk at the office party and insisted I was going to dance under the table instead of on top of it, I did a sort of Cossack number° but then I hit my head on the bottom of the table—actually it was a desk—when I went to get up, and I knocked myself out cold. She's decided that's the mark of an original mind and she tells everyone new about it and I'm not sure that's fair. Though I did do it.

"I'm being totally honest," I say. I always am and they know it. There's no point in being anything else, is the way I look at it, and sooner or later the truth will out so you might as well not waste the time, right? "You should hear the one about the Easy-Off Cleaner."

But that was the end of the lunch hour, with one bridge game shot to hell, and the next day we spent most of the time arguing over whether to start a new game or play out the hands we had left over from the day before, so Sondra never did get a chance to tell about her rape fantasy.

It started me thinking though, about my own rape fantasies. Maybe I'm abnormal or something, I mean I have fantasies about handsome strangers coming in through the window too, like Mr. Clean, I wish one would, please god somebody without flat feet and big sweat marks on his shirt, and over five feet five, believe me being tall is a handicap though it's getting better, tall guys are starting to like someone whose nose reaches higher than their belly button. But if you're being totally honest you can't count those as rape fantasies. In a real rape fantasy, what you should feel is this anxiety, like when you think about your apartment building catching on fire and whether you should use the elevator or the stairs or maybe just stick your head under a wet towel, and you try to remember everything you've read about what to do but you can't decide.

For instance, I'm walking along this dark street at night and this short, ugly fellow comes up and grabs my arm, and not only is he ugly, you know, with a sort of puffy nothing face, like those fellows you have to talk to in the bank when your account's overdrawn—of course I don't mean they're all like that—but he's absolutely covered in pimples. So he gets me pinned against the wall, he's short but he's heavy, and he starts to undo himself and the zipper gets stuck. I mean, one of the most significant moments in a girl's life, it's almost like getting married or having a baby or something, and he sticks the zipper.

So I say, kind of disgusted, "Oh for Chrissake," and he starts to cry. He tells me

---

Cossack number: a Ukrainian folk dance movement performed in a squatting position, with much hand clapping.

he's never been able to get anything right in his entire life, and this is the last straw, he's going to go jump off a bridge.

"Look," I say, I feel so sorry for him, in my rape fantasies I always end up feel- 35 ing sorry for the guy, I mean there has to be something *wrong* with them, if it was Clint Eastwood° it'd be different but worse luck it never is. I was the kind of little girl who buried dead robins, know what I mean? It used to drive my mother nuts, she didn't like me touching them, because of the germs I guess. So I say, "Listen, I know how you feel. You really should do something about those pimples, if you got rid of them you'd be quite good looking, honest; then you wouldn't have to go around doing stuff like this. I had them myself once," I say, to comfort him, but in fact I did, and it ends up I give him the name of my old dermatologist, the one I had in high school, that was back in Leamington,° except I used to go to St. Catharine's for the dermatologist. I'm telling you, I was really lonely when I first came here; I thought it was going to be such a big adventure and all, but it's a lot harder to meet people in a city. But I guess it's different for a guy.

Or I'm lying in bed with this terrible cold, my face is all swollen up, my eyes are red and my nose is dripping like a leaky tap, and this fellow comes in through the window and *he* has a terrible cold too, it's a new kind of flu that's been going around. So he says, "I'b goig do rabe you"—I hope you don't mind me holding my nose like this but that's the way I imagine it—and he lets out this terrific sneeze, which slows him down a bit, also I'm no object of beauty myself, you'd have to be some kind of pervert to want to rape someone with a cold like mine, it'd be like raping a bottle of LePages mucilage the way my nose is running. He's looking wildly around the room, and I realize it's because he doesn't have a piece of Kleenex! "Id's ride here," I say, and I pass him the Kleenex, god knows why he even bothered to get out of bed, you'd think if you were going to go around climbing in windows you'd wait till you were healthier, right? I mean, that takes a certain amount of energy. So I ask him why doesn't he let me fix him a NeoCitran and scotch, that's what I always take, you still have the cold but you don't feel it, so I do and we end up watching the Late Show together. I mean, they aren't all sex maniacs, the rest of the time they must lead a normal life. I figure they enjoy watching the Late Show just like anybody else.

I do have a scarier one though . . . where the fellow says he's hearing angel voices that're telling him he's got to kill me, you know, you read about things like that all the time in the papers. In this one I'm not in the apartment where I live now, I'm back in my mother's house in Leamington and the fellow's been hiding in the cellar, he grabs my arm when I go downstairs to get a jar of jam and he's got hold of the axe too, out of the garage, that one is really scary. I mean, what do you say to a nut like that?

So I start to shake but after a minute I get control of myself and I say, is he sure the angel voices have got the right person, because I hear the same angel voices and they've been telling me for some time that I'm going to give birth to the reincarnation of St. Anne who in turn has the Virgin Mary and right after that comes Jesus Christ and the end of the world, and he wouldn't want to interfere with that, would he? So he gets confused and listens some more, and then he asks for a sign and I show him my vaccination mark, you can see it's sort of an odd-shaped one, it got infected

---

Clint Eastwood: born 1930, star of many tough-guy detective and western movies; most famous as "Dirty Harry" (1971).
Leamington: in Ontario on the north shore of Lake Erie, southeast of Windsor.

because I scratched the top off, and that does it, he apologizes and climbs out the coal chute° again, which is how he got in in the first place, and I say to myself there's some advantage in having been brought up a Catholic even though I haven't been to church since they changed the service into English,° it just isn't the same, you might as well be a Protestant. I must write to Mother and tell her to nail up that coal chute, it always has bothered me. Funny, I couldn't tell you at all what this man looks like but I know exactly what kind of shoes he's wearing, because that's the last I see of him, his shoes going up the coal chute, and they're the old-fashioned kind that lace up the ankles, even though he's a young fellow. That's strange, isn't it?

Let me tell you though I really sweat until I see him safely out of there and I go upstairs right away and make myself a cup of tea. I don't think about that one much. My mother always said you shouldn't dwell on unpleasant things and I generally agree with that, I mean, dwelling on them doesn't make them go away. Though not dwelling on them doesn't make them go away either, when you come to think of it.

Sometimes I have these short ones where the fellow grabs my arm but I'm really a Kung-Fu° expert, can you believe it, in real life I'm sure it would just be a conk on the head and that's that, like getting your tonsils out, you'd wake up and it would be all over except for the sore places, and you'd be lucky if your neck wasn't broken or something, I could never even hit the volleyball in gym and a volleyball is fairly large, you know?—and I just go *zap* with my fingers into his eyes and that's it, he falls over, or I flip him against a wall or something. But I could never really stick my fingers in anyone's eyes, could you? It would feel like hot jello and I don't even like cold jello, just thinking about it gives me the creeps. I feel a bit guilty about that one, I mean how would you like walking around knowing someone's been blinded for life because of you?

But maybe it's different for a guy.

The most touching one I have is when the fellow grabs my arm and I say, sad and kind of dignified, "You'd be raping a corpse." That pulls him up short and I explain that I've just found out I have leukaemia and the doctors have only given me a few months to live. That's why I'm out pacing the streets alone at night, I need to think, you know, come to terms with myself. I don't really have leukaemia but in the fantasy I do, I guess I chose that particular disease because a girl in my grade four class died of it, the whole class sent her flowers when she was in the hospital. I didn't understand then that she was going to die and I wanted to have leukaemia too so I could get flowers. Kids are funny, aren't they? Well, it turns out that he has leukaemia himself, and *he* only has a few months to live, that's why he's going around raping people, he's very bitter because he's so young and his life is being taken from him before he's really lived it. So we walk along gently under the street lights, it's spring and sort of misty, and we end up going for coffee, we're happy we've found the only other person in the world who can understand what we're going through, it's almost like fate, and after a while we just sort of look at each other and our hands touch, and he comes

---

    coal chute: trough for delivering coal from a truck into a basement coal bin. Estelle's remark indicates that the chute was not fastened over the opening to the bin, thus permitting an illegal entry.

    into English: In accord with the Second Vatican Council (1962–1965), the Latin Mass was replaced by vernacular languages in the late 1960s.

    Kung-Fu: elaborate self-defense system developed in China, similar to Karate.

back with me and moves into my apartment and we spend our last months together before we die, we just sort of don't wake up in the morning, though I've never decided which one of us gets to die first. If it's him I have to go on and fantasize about the funeral, if it's me I don't have to worry about that, so it just about depends on how tired I am at the time. You may not believe this but sometimes I even start crying. I cry at the end of movies, even the ones that aren't all that sad, so I guess it's the same thing. My mother's like that too.

The funny thing about these fantasies is that the man is always someone I don't know, and the statistics in the magazines, well, most of them anyway, they say it's often someone you do know, at least a little bit, like your boss or something—I mean, it wouldn't be *my* boss, he's over sixty and I'm sure he couldn't rape his way out of a paper bag, poor old thing, but it might be someone like Derek Duck, in his elevator shoes, perish the thought—or someone you just met, who invites you up for a drink, it's getting so you can hardly be sociable any more, and how are you supposed to meet people if you can't trust them even that basic amount? You can't spend your whole life in the Filing Department or cooped up in your own apartment with all the doors and windows locked and the shades down. I'm not what you would call a drinker but I like to go out now and then for a drink or two in a nice place, even if I am by myself, I'm with Women's Lib on that even though I can't agree with a lot of the other things they say. Like here for instance, the waiters all know me and if anyone, you know, bothers me . . . I don't know why I'm telling you all this, except I think it helps you get to know a person, especially at first, hearing some of the things they think about. At work they call me the office worry wart, but it isn't so much like worrying, it's more like figuring out what you should do in an emergency, like I said before.

Anyway, another thing about it is that there's a lot of conversation, in fact I spend most of my time, in the fantasy that is, wondering what I'm going to say and what he's going to say, I think it would be better if you could get a conversation going. Like, how could a fellow do that to a person he's just had a long conversation with, once you let them know you're human, you have a life too, I don't see how they could go ahead with it, right? I mean, I know it happens but I just don't understand it, that's the part I really don't understand.

QUESTIONS

1. What elements of the various rape fantasies are comic? How is the comedy brought out (e.g., through subject matter, circumstances of description, attitudes and understanding of the characters, comments by the narrator)?

2. What do the various fantasies of Estelle have in common, and what do they show about her? How does Atwood control the tone so as to keep Estelle from considering rape as a problem in psychology or criminology?

3. Describe the story's tone. How does tone affect your perception of Estelle?

4. Consider the tone of the very last paragraph. What is Atwood's apparent attitude toward the subject? How is it tempered by her attitude toward Estelle?

5. Studies point out that rape is an act of violence. What do the women in the story do to deflect the seriousness of the potential violence involved?

KATE CHOPIN (1851–1904)

Born in St. Louis, Chopin lived in Louisiana from the time of her marriage until 1882. After her husband's death she returned to St. Louis and began to write. She published two collections of stories based on the life she had known back in Louisiana: Bayou Folk *(1894) and* A Night in Acadie *(1897). However, she became best known for her major novel,* The Awakening *(1899), which aroused negative reactions because it mentioned taboo subjects like adultery and miscegenation. Indeed, the critical disapproval was so intense that Chopin did not publish further works after that time, even though she was at the height of her literary power and lived five years after the controversy.*

The Story of an Hour _____ *1894*

Knowing that Mrs. Mallard was afflicted with a heart trouble, great care was taken to break to her as gently as possible the news of her husband's death.

It was her sister Josephine who told her, in broken sentences: veiled hints that revealed in half concealing. Her husband's friend Richards was there, too, near her. It was he who had been in the newspaper office when intelligence of the railroad disaster was received, with Brently Mallard's name leading the list of "killed." He had only taken the time to assure himself of its truth by a second telegram, and had hastened to forestall any less careful, less tender friend in bearing the sad message.

She did not hear the story as many women have heard the same, with a paralyzed inability to accept its significance. She wept at once, with sudden, wild abandonment, in her sister's arms. When the storm of grief had spent itself she went away to her room alone. She would have no one follow her.

There stood, facing the open window, a comfortable, roomy armchair. Into this she sank, pressed down by a physical exhaustion that haunted her body and seemed to reach into her soul.

She could see in the open square before her house the tops of trees that were all aquiver with the new spring life. The delicious breath of rain was in the air. In the street below a peddler was crying his wares. The notes of a distant song which some one was singing reached her faintly, and countless sparrows were twittering in the eaves.

There were patches of blue sky showing here and there through the clouds that had met and piled one above the other in the west facing her window.

She sat with her head thrown back upon the cushion of the chair, quite motionless, except when a sob came up into her throat and shook her, as a child who has cried itself to sleep continues to sob in its dreams.

She was young, with a fair, calm face, whose lines bespoke repression and even a certain strength. But now there was a dull stare in her eyes, whose gaze was fixed away off yonder on one of those patches of blue sky. It was not a glance of reflection, but rather indicated a suspension of intelligent thought.

There was something coming to her and she was waiting for it, fearfully. What was it? She did not know; it was too subtle and elusive to name. But she felt it, creeping out of the sky, reaching toward her through the sounds, the scents, the color that filled the air.

Now her bosom rose and fell tumultuously. She was beginning to recognize this   10
thing that was approaching to possess her, and she was striving to beat it back with her will—as powerless as her two white slender hands would have been.

When she abandoned herself a little whispered word escaped her slightly parted lips. She said it over and over under her breath: "free, free, free!" The vacant stare and the look of terror that had followed it went from her eyes. They stayed keen and bright. Her pulses beat fast, and the coursing blood warmed and relaxed every inch of her body.

She did not stop to ask if it were or were not a monstrous joy that held her. A clear and exalted perception enabled her to dismiss the suggestion as trivial.

She knew that she would weep again when she saw the kind, tender hands folded in death; the face that had never looked save with love upon her, fixed and gray and dead. But she saw beyond that bitter moment a long procession of years to come that would belong to her absolutely. And she opened and spread her arms out to them in welcome.

There would be no one to live for during those coming years; she would live for herself. There would be no powerful will bending hers in that blind persistence with which men and women believe they have a right to impose a private will upon a fellow-creature. A kind intention or a cruel intention made the act seem no less a crime as she looked upon it in that brief moment of illumination.

And yet she had loved him—sometimes. Often she had not. What did it matter!   15
What could love, the unsolved mystery, count for in face of this possession of self-assertion which she suddenly recognized as the strongest impulse of her being!

"Free! Body and soul free!" she kept whispering.

Josephine was kneeling before the closed door with her lips to the keyhole, imploring for admission. "Louise, open the door! I beg; open the door—you will make yourself ill. What are you doing, Louise? For heaven's sake open the door."

"Go away. I am not making myself ill." No; she was drinking in a very elixir of life through that open window.

Her fancy was running riot along those days ahead of her. Spring days, and summer days, and all sorts of days that would be her own. She breathed a quick prayer that life might be long. It was only yesterday she had thought with a shudder that life might be long.

She arose at length and opened the door to her sister's importunities. There   20
was a feverish triumph in her eyes, and she carried herself unwittingly like a goddess of Victory. She clasped her sister's waist, and together they descended the stairs. Richards stood waiting for them at the bottom.

Some one was opening the front door with a latchkey. It was Brently Mallard who entered, a little travel-stained, composedly carrying his grip-sack and umbrella. He had been far from the scene of accident, and did not even know there had been one. He stood amazed at Josephine's piercing cry: at Richards' quick motion to screen him from the view of his wife.

But Richards was too late.

When the doctors came they said she had died of heart disease—of joy that kills.

QUESTIONS

1. What do we learn about Louise's husband? How has he justified her responses? How are your judgments about him controlled by the context of the story?
2. Analyze the tone of paragraph 5. How is the imagery here (and in the following paragraphs) appropriate for her developing mood?
3. What is the apparent attitude of the narrator toward the institution of marriage, and what elements of tone make this apparent?
4. What do Louise's sister and Richards have in common? How do their attitudes contribute to the irony of the story?
5. Consider the tone of the last paragraph. What judgment is being made about how men view their importance to women?

JOHN COLLIER (1901–1980)

Collier was born in England but lived and wrote in America. He produced a number of novels, such as Full Circle *(1933) and* Defy the Foul Fiend *(1934), but he became best known for his sardonic and macabre but finely crafted stories, of which "The Chaser" is a representative example. The 1951 collection* Fancies and Goodnights *includes a number of his best stories.*

The Chaser ————————————————————— *1940*

Alan Austen, as nervous as a kitten, went up certain dark and creaky stairs in the neighborhood of Pell Street, and peered about for a long time on the dim landing before he found the name he wanted written obscurely on one of the doors.

He pushed open this door, as he had been told to do, and found himself in a tiny room, which contained no furniture but a plain kitchen table, a rocking-chair, and an ordinary chair. On one of the dirty buff-coloured walls were a couple of shelves, containing in all perhaps a dozen bottles and jars.

An old man sat in the rocking-chair, reading a newspaper. Alan, without a word, handed him the card he had been given. "Sit down, Mr. Austen," said the old man very politely. "I am glad to make your acquaintance."

"Is it true," asked Alan, "that you have a certain mixture that has—er—quite extraordinary effects?"

"My dear sir," replied the old man, "my stock in trade is not very large—I don't deal in laxatives and teething mixtures—but such as it is, it is varied. I think nothing I sell has effects which could be precisely described as ordinary."

"Well, the fact is . . ." began Alan.

"Here, for example," interrupted the old man, reaching for a bottle from the shelf. "Here is a liquid as colourless as water, almost tasteless, quite imperceptible in coffee, wine, or any other beverage. It is also imperceptible to any known method of autopsy."

"Do you mean it is a poison?" cried Alan, very much horrified.

"Call it a glove-cleaner if you like," said the old man indifferently. "Maybe it will clean gloves. I have never tried. One might call it a life-cleaner. Lives need cleaning sometimes."

"I want nothing of that sort," said Alan.   10

"Probably it is just as well," said the old man. "Do you know the price of this? For one teaspoonful, which is sufficient, I ask five thousand dollars. Never less. Not a penny less."

"I hope all your mixtures are not as expensive," said Alan apprehensively.

"Oh dear, no," said the old man. "It would be no good charging that sort of price for a love potion, for example. Young people who need a love potion very seldom have five thousand dollars. Otherwise they would not need a love potion."

"I am glad to hear that," said Alan.

"I look at it like this," said the old man. "Please a customer with one article, and   15
he will come back when he needs another. Even if it *is* more costly. He will save up for it, if necessary."

"So," said Alan, "you really do sell love potions?"

"If I did not sell love potions," said the old man, reaching for another bottle, "I should not have mentioned the other matter to you. It is only when one is in a position to oblige that one can afford to be so confidential."

"And these potions," said Alan. "They are not just—just—er—"

"Oh, no," said the old man. "Their effects are permanent, and extended far beyond the mere casual impulse. But they include it. Oh, yes, they include it. Bountifully, insistently. Everlastingly."

"Dear me!" said Alan, attempting a look of scientific detachment. "How very in-   20
teresting!"

"But consider the spiritual side," said the old man.

"I do, indeed," said Alan.

"For indifference,' said the old man, "they substitute devotion. For scorn, adoration. Give one tiny measure of this to the young lady—its flavour is imperceptible in orange juice, soup, or cocktails—and however gay and giddy she is, she will change altogether. She will want nothing but solitude and you."

"I can hardly believe it," said Alan. "She is so fond of parties."

"She will not like them any more," said the old man. "She will be afraid of the   25
pretty girls you may meet."

"She will actually be jealous?" cried Alan in a rapture. "Of me?"

"Yes, she will want to be everything to you."

"She is, already. Only she doesn't care about it."

"She will, when she has taken this. She will care intensely. You will be her sole interest in life."

"Wonderful!" cried Alan.   30

"She will want to know all you do," said the old man. "All that has happened to you during the day. Every word of it. She will want to know what you are thinking about, why you smile suddenly, why you are looking sad."

"That is love!" cried Alan.

"Yes," said the old man. "How carefully she will look after you! She will never allow you to be tired, to sit in a draught, to neglect your food. If you are an hour late, she will be terrified. She will think you are killed, or that some siren has caught you."

"I can hardly imagine Diana like that!" cried Alan, overwhelmed with joy.

"You will not have to use your imagination," said the old man. "And, by the way,   35 since there are always sirens, if by any chance you *should*, later on, slip a little, you need not worry. She will forgive you, in the end. She will be terribly hurt, of course, but she will forgive you—in the end."

"That will not happen," said Alan fervently.

"Of course not," said the old man. "But, it if did, you need not worry. She would never divorce you. Oh, no! And, of course, she will never give you the least, the very least, grounds for—uneasiness."

"And how much," said Alan, "is this wonderful mixture?"

"It is not as dear," said the old man, "as the glove-cleaner, or life-cleaner, as I sometimes call it. No. That is five thousand dollars, never a penny less. One has to be older than you are, to indulge in that sort of thing. One has to save up for it."

"But the love potion?" said Alan.

"Oh, that," said the old man, opening the drawer in the kitchen table, and taking out a tiny, rather dirty-looking phial. "That is just a dollar."

"I can't tell you how grateful I am," said Alan, watching him fill it.

"I like to oblige," said the old man. "Then customers come back, later in life, when they are better off, and want more expensive things. Here you are. You will find it very effective."

"Thank you again," said Alan. "Good-bye."

"Au revoir," said the old man.

QUESTIONS

1. Summarize the plot of this story. What are the qualities of the poison that the old man tells Austen about? What are the powers of the love potion? What is the connection between the love potion and the so-called glove cleaner?

2. Are the two characters static or dynamic? Round or flat? To what extent does their characterization focus the story and control the tone?

3. How is the setting of the story described? How does this description contribute to the mood of the story and the characterization of the old man?

4. How do the words of the story control the tone and attitude? What words help us form an attitude toward Alan Austen? Toward the old man?

5. To what extent is the story ironic? What do we and the old man know that Alan Austen doesn't?

6. What point does this story make about love? Youth? Desire? How can the story be taken as a commentary about the need for love relationships that preserve individuality as well as romantic commitment?

AMÉRICO PARÉDES (b. 1915)

Parédes is a Mexican-American storyteller, essayist, and poet, closely identified with the plight of Mexican-Americans living in Texas, his native state. He studied at the University of Texas, receiving his Ph.D. in 1956, and also taught there. He edited the Journal of American Folklore, *and was a co-editor of* Mexican-American Authors. *Among his honors was a Guggenheim fellowship. "The Hammon and the Beans" was first published in* The Texas Observer *in 1963. His poem "Guitarreros" appeared in* The Southwest Review *in 1964.*

The Hammon and the Beans —————————————————————— *1963*

Once we lived in one of my grandfather's houses near Fort Jones.° It was just a block from the parade grounds, a big frame house painted a dirty yellow. My mother hated it, especially because of the pigeons that cooed all day about the eaves. They had fleas, she said. But it was a quiet neighborhood at least, too far from the center of town for automobiles and too near for musical, night-roaming drunks.

At this time Jonesville-on-the-Grande was not the thriving little city that it is today. We told off our days by the routine on the post. At six sharp the flag was raised on the parade grounds to the cackling of the bugles, and a field piece thundered out a salute. The sound of the shot bounced away through the morning mist until its echoes worked their way into every corner of town. Jonesville-on-the-Grande woke to the cannon's roar, as if to battle, and the day began.

At eight the whistle from the post laundry sent us children off to school. The whole town stopped for lunch with the noon whistle, and after lunch everybody went back to work when the post laundry said that it was one o'clock, except for those who could afford to be old-fashioned and took the siesta. The post was the town's clock, you might have said, or like some insistent elder person who was always there to tell you it was time.

At six the flag came down, and we went to watch through the high wire fence that divided the post from the town. Sometimes we joined in the ceremony, standing at salute until the sound of the cannon made us jump. That must have been when we had just studied about George Washington in school, or recited "The Song of Marion's Men"° about Marion the Fox and the British cavalry that chased him up and down the broad Santee. But at other times we stuck out our tongues and jeered at the soldiers. Perhaps the night before we had hung at the edges of a group of old men and listened to tales about Aniceto Pizaña and the "border troubles,"° as the local paper still called them when it referred to them gingerly in passing.

It was because of the border troubles, ten years or so before, that the soldiers   5
had come back to old Fort Jones. But we did not hate them for that; we admired them even, at least sometimes. But when we were thinking about the border troubles instead of Marion the Fox we hooted them and the flag they were lowering, which for the moment was theirs alone, just as we would have jeered an opposing ball team, in a friendly sort of way. On these occasions even Chonita would join in the mockery, though she usually ran home at the stroke of six. But whether we taunted or saluted, the distant men in khaki uniforms went about their motions without noticing us at all.

The last word from the post came in the night when a distant bugle blew. At nine it was all right because all the lights were on. But sometimes I heard it at eleven

Fort Jones: The setting of Fort Jones and Jonesville-on-the-Grande in Texas is fictional. The story takes place in the mid-1920s, one of the most turbulent periods of Mexican history and only a few years after the deaths of two of the greatest heroes of the Mexican revolution— Pancho Villa (1877–1923) and Emiliano Zapata (ca. 1879–1919).

"Song of Marion's Men": A poem by William Cullen Bryant (1794–1878) about Colonel Francis Marion (ca. 1732–1795), who was a leader of irregular guerrilla forces in South Carolina during the Revolutionary War. Because of his hit-and-run tactics, involving his hiding in the swamps near the "broad Santee" river in South Carolina, Marion was nicknamed the "Swamp Fox."

border troubles: The most serious border incidents occurred in 1916, when Pancho Villa was responsible for deaths of Americans on both sides of the border. He made repeated raids into New Mexico and Texas.

when everything was dark and still, and it made me feel that I was all alone in the world. I would even doubt that I was me, and that put me in such a fright that I felt like yelling out just to make sure I was really there. But next morning the sun shone and life began all over again. With its whistles and cannon shots and bugles blowing. And so we lived, we and the post, side by side with the wire fence in between.

The wandering soldiers whom the bugle called home at night did not wander in our neighborhood, and none of us ever went into Fort Jones. None except Chonita. Every evening when the flag came down she would leave off playing and go down towards what was known as the "lower" gate of the post, the one that opened not on Main Street but against the poorest part of town. She went into the grounds and to the mess halls and pressed her nose against the screens and watched the soldiers eat. They sat at long tables calling to each other through food-stuffed mouths.

"Hey bud, pass the coffee!"

"Give me the ham!"

"Yeah, give me the beans!"

After the soldiers were through the cooks came out and scolded Chonita, and then they gave her packages with things to eat.

Chonita's mother did our washing, in gratefulness—as my mother put it—for the use of a vacant lot of my grandfather's which was a couple of blocks down the street. On the lot was an old one-room shack which had been a shed long ago, and this Chonita's father had patched up with flattened-out pieces of tin. He was a laborer. Ever since the end of the border troubles there had been a development boom in the Valley, and Chonita's father was getting his share of the good times. Clearing brush and building irrigation ditches he sometimes pulled down as much as six dollars a week. He drank a good deal of it up, it was true. But corn was just a few cents a bushel in those days. He was the breadwinner, you might say, while Chonita furnished the luxuries.

Chonita was a poet too. I had just moved into the neighborhood when a boy came up to me and said, "Come on! Let's go hear Chonita make a speech."

She was already on top of the alley fence when we got there, a scrawny little girl of about nine, her bare dirty feet clinging to the fence almost like hands. A dozen other kids were there below her, waiting. Some were boys I knew at school; five or six were her younger brothers and sisters.

"Speech! Speech!" they all cried. "Let Chonita make a speech! Talk in English, Chonita!"

They were grinning and nudging each other except for her brothers and sisters, who looked up at her with proud serious faces. She gazed out beyond us all with a grand, distant air and then she spoke.

"Give me the hammon and the beans!" she yelled. "Give me the hammon and the beans!"

She leaped off the fence and everybody cheered and told her how good it was and how she could talk English better than the teachers at the grammar school.

I thought it was a pretty poor joke. Every evening almost, they would make her get up on the fence and yell, "Give me the hammon and the beans!" And everybody would cheer and make her think she was talking English. As for me, I would wait there until she got it over with so we could play at something else. I wondered how long it would be before they got tired of it all. I never did find out because just about that time I got the chills and fever, and when I got up and around Chonita wasn't there anymore.

In later years I thought of her a lot, especially during the thirties when I was   20
growing up. Those years would have been just made for her. Many's the time I have
seen her in my mind's eyes, in the picket lines demanding not bread, not cake, but
the hammon and the beans. But it didn't work out that way.

One night Doctor Zapata came into our kitchen through the back door. He set
his bag on the table and said to my father, who had opened the door for him, "Well,
she is dead."

My father flinched. "What was it?" he asked.

The doctor had gone to the window and he stood with his back to us, looking
out toward the light of Fort Jones. "Pneumonia, flu, malnutrition, worms, the evil
eye," he said without turning around. "What the hell difference does it make?"

"I wish I had known how sick she was," my father said in a very mild tone. "Not
that it's really my affair, but I wish I had."

The doctor snorted and shook his head.   25

My mother came in and I asked her who was dead. She told me. It made me
feel strange but I did not cry. My mother put her arm around my shoulders. "She is
in Heaven now," she said. "She is happy."

I shrugged her arm away and sat down in one of the kitchen chairs.

"They're like animals," the doctor was saying. He turned round suddenly and
his eyes glistened in the light. "Do you know what that brute of a father was doing
when I left? He was laughing! Drinking and laughing with his friends."

"There's no telling what the poor man feels," my mother said.

My father made a deprecatory gesture. "It wasn't his daughter anyway."   30

"No?" the doctor said. He sounded interested.

"This is the woman's second husband," my father explained. "First one died before the girl was born, shot and hanged from a mesquite limb. He was working too
close to the tracks the day the Olmito train was derailed."

"You know what?" the doctor said. "In classical times they did things better.
Take Troy, for instance. After they stormed the city they grabbed the babies by the
heels and dashed them against the wall. That was more humane."

My father smiled. "You sound very radical. You sound just like your relative
down there in Morelos."°

"No relative of mine," the doctor said. "I'm a conservative, the son of a conser-   35
vative, and you know that I wouldn't be here except for that little detail."

"Habit," my father said. "Pure habit, pure tradition. You're a radical at heart."

"It depends on how you define radicalism," the doctor answered. "People tend
to use words too loosely. A dentist could be called a radical, I suppose. He pulls up
things by the roots."

My father chuckled.

"Any bandit in Mexico nowadays can give himself a political label," the doctor
went on, "and that makes him respectable. He's a leader of the people."

"Take Villa, now—" my father began.   40

"Villa was a different type of man," the doctor broke in.

"I don't see any difference."

The doctor came over to the table and sat down. "Now look at it this way," he
began, his finger in front of my father's face. My father threw back his head and
laughed.

Morelos: the home state of Zapata.

"You'd better go to bed and rest," my mother told me. "You're not completely well, you know."

So I went to bed, but I didn't go to sleep, not right away. I lay there for a long time while behind my darkened eyelids Emiliano Zapata's cavalry charged down to the broad Santee, where there were grave men with hoary hairs.° I was still awake at eleven when the cold voice of the bugle went gliding in and out of the dark like something that couldn't find its way back to wherever it had been. I thought of Chonita in Heaven, and I saw her in her torn and dirty dress, with a pair of bright wings attached, flying round and round like a butterfly shouting, "Give me the hammon and the beans!"

Then I cried. And whether it was the bugle, or whether it was Chonita or what, to this day I do not know. But cry I did, and I felt much better after that.

QUESTIONS

1. How does Parédes establish the setting of the story? What is the significance of the fort? Of the "dirty yellow" paint? Of the vacant lot and the shack?

2. Is Chonita round or flat? To what extent does the author make her symbolic and representative?

3. What is the tone of the story (some possibilities: ironic, cynical, resigned, bitter, resentful)? What techniques does Parédes use to control the tone?

4. How does Doctor Zapata's attitude toward Chonita's death, and the words he uses to announce it, help to control the tone?

5. How does the tale of Chonita's brief life and her death fit into the political, social, and broadly human framework of the story?

6. Describe the irony of the situation in which the Mexican-American children are taught United States history, but learn nothing about the political movements represented by Villa and Zapata.

7. Near the end of Bryant's "Song of Marion's Men," the following four lines appear:

> And lovely ladies greet our band [i.e., of soldiers]
> With kindliest welcoming,
> And smiles like those of summer,
> And tears like those of spring.
> —lines 53–56

Contrast these lines with the narrator's vision of Chonita in heaven.

Grave men with hoary hairs: Cf. lines 49–52 of Bryant's "Song of Marion's Men:"

> Grave Men there are by broad Santee,
> Grave men with hoary hairs;
> Their hearts are all with Marion,
> For Marion are their prayers.

WRITING ABOUT TONE

Begin with a careful reading, noting those elements of the story that convey attitudes. Consider whether the story genuinely creates the attitudes it is designed to evoke. In Collier's "The Chaser," for example, does the old man seem sufficiently real to create credibility about what he says? Does the story adequately distinguish between true love and possessive love, and is it therefore predictable in its view of what will eventually happen to Alan? Depending on the story, your devising and answering such questions can help you understand the degree of an author's control over tone. Similar questions apply when you study internal qualities such as style and characterization.

Questions for Discovering Ideas

- How strongly do you respond to the story? What attitudes can you identify and characterize? What elements in the story elicit your concern? indignation? fearfulness? anguish? amusement? affirmation?

- What causes you to sympathize or not to sympathize with the characters? What makes their actions admirable or understandable (or deplorable)?

- What does the dialogue suggest about the author's attitudes toward the characters? How does it influence your attitudes? What qualities of diction permit and encourage your responses?

- To what degree, if any, does the story supersede any previous ideas you might have had about the same or similar subject matter? What do you think effected any changes in your attitude?

- What role does the narrator/speaker play in your attitudes toward the story material? Does the speaker seem intelligent/stupid? Friendly/unfriendly? Sane/insane? Idealistic/pragmatic?

- In an amusing or comic story, what elements of plot, character, and diction are particularly comic? How strongly do you respond to humor-producing situations? Why?

- What ironies do you find in the story (verbal, situational, cosmic)? How is the irony connected to philosophies of marriage, family, society, politics, religion, or morality?

- To what extent are the characters controlled by forces like fate, social or racial discrimination, limitations of intelligence, economic and political inequality, and limited opportunity?

- Do any words seem unusual or noteworthy, such as dialect, polysyllabic words, foreign words or phrases that the author assumes you know, or especially connotative or emotive words? What do these words suggest about the author's apparent assumptions about the readers?

Strategies for Organizing Ideas

Your goal is to show how the author establishes the dominant moods of the story—e.g., the cynicism of "The Chaser" or the comedy of "Rape Fantasies." Some possibilities are the use or misuse of language, the exposé of a pretentious speaker, the use of exact and specific descriptions, the isolation of a major character, the failure of plans, or continued naiveté in a disillusioned world. Some of the things you could address are these:

1. *Audience, Situation, and Characters.* Is any person or group directly addressed by the speaker? What attitude is expressed (love, respect, condescension, confidentiality, confidence, etc.)? What is the basic situation in the story? Do you find irony? If so, what kind is it? What does the irony show (optimism or pessimism, for example)? How is the situation controlled to shape your responses? That is, can actions, situations, or characters be seen as expressions of attitude, or as embodiments of certain favorable or unfavorable ideas or positions? What is the nature of the speaker or persona? Why does the speaker speak exactly as he or she does? How is the speaker's character manipulated to show apparent authorial attitude and to elicit reader response? Does the story promote respect, admiration, dislike, or other feelings about character or situation? How?

2. *Descriptions, diction.* Your concern here is not to analyze descriptions or diction for themselves alone, but to relate these matters to attitude. *For descriptions:* To what degree do descriptions of natural scenery and conditions (snowstorms, cold, rain, ice, intense sunlight) convey an attitude that complements or opposes the circumstances of the characters? Are there any systematic references to colors, sounds, or noises that collectively reflect an attitude? *For diction:* Do connotative meanings of words control response in any way? To what degree does the diction require readers to have a large or technical vocabulary? Do speech patterns or the use of dialect evoke attitudes about speakers or their condition of life? Are speech patterns normal and standard, or slang or substandard? What is the effect of these patterns? Are there unusual or particularly noteworthy expressions? If so, what attitudes do these show? Does the author use verbal irony? To what effect?

3. *Humor.* Is the story funny? How funny, how intense? How is the humor achieved? Does the humor develop out of incongruous situations or language, or both? Is there an underlying basis of attack in the humor, or are the objects of laughter still respected or even loved despite having humor directed against them?

4. *Ideas.* Are any ideas advocated, defended mildly, or attacked? How does the author clarify his or her attitude toward these ideas—directly, by statement, or indirectly, through understatement, overstatement, or a character's speeches? In what ways does the story assume a common ground of assent between author and reader? That is, what common assumptions do you find about religious views, political ideas, moral and behavioral standards, and so on? Is it easy to give assent (temporary or permanent) to these ideas, or is any concession needed by the reader to approach the story? (For example, a major subject of "First Confession" [p. 520] is the proper preparation for a child taking first confession in the Catholic faith. Not everyone can relate to this action, but even a skeptical reader might find common ground

in the psychological situation of the story, or in the desire to learn as much as possible about human beings.)

5. *Unique characteristics of the story.* Each story has unique properties that contribute to the tone. Thus, Collier's "The Chaser" is developed almost entirely through the dialogue between Alan and the old man. The tone of the story is therefore illustrated by the attitudes and interests of each character, almost as though the story is a drama. In Glaspell's "A Jury of Her Peers" there is a role reversal in which the two women prove to be better detectives than their husbands, who are searching the farmhouse. Without these women, we would have no story; the author invites us to perceive the irony of this fact. In other stories there might be some recurring word or phrase that seems special. For example, Mark Twain in "Luck" (p. 285) develops a passage centering on the word *blunder,* and thereby makes his attitude clear about the boob hero, Scoresby (paragraph 12).

In the conclusion, first summarize your main points, and then go on to redefinitions, explanations, or afterthoughts, together with ideas reinforcing earlier points. You might also mention some other major aspect of the story's tone that you did not develop in the body.

SAMPLE ESSAY

The Situational and Verbal Irony of Collier's "The Chaser"[°]

[1] John Collier's "The Chaser" is based on the situational irony of the unreal hope of youth as opposed to the extreme disillusion of age and experience. Collier builds the brief story almost entirely in dialogue between a young man, Alan Austen, who is deeply in love and wants to possess his sweetheart entirely, and an unnamed old man who believes in a life free of romantic encumbrances. The situation reflects disillusionment so completely that the story may seem cynical.[*] This attitude is made plain by the circumstances of the two main characters, the sales method of the old man, and his use of double meaning.[†]

[2] The circumstances of the two men establish the story's dominant cynicism. Alan, the young man full of illusions and unreal expectations, has come to the old man to buy a love potion so that his sweetheart, Diana, will love him with slavelike adoration. Collier makes clear that the old man, a seller of magic brews, has seen many young men in the grips of romantic desire before, and he therefore knows that their possessive love will eventually bore and anger them. He knows, because he has already seen these disillusioned customers return to buy the "chaser," which is a deadly, untraceable poison, so that they could kill the women whom they previously desired. Thus Collier creates the ironic situation of the story—the beginning of an inevitable process in which Alan, like other young men before him, is made to appear so unrealistic and

[°] For the text of this story, see pp. 310–12.
[*] Central idea.
[†] Thesis sentence.

self-defeating that his enthusiastic passion will someday change into hate and murderousness. The tone of the story could hardly be more cynical and pessimistic.

[3] The sales method used by the old man reveals his cynical understanding of men like Alan. Collier makes clear that the old man knows why Alan has come. Thus, before showing his love potion, the old man describes the untraceable poison. His ultimate aim is to sell the expensive poison, and he is using the love potion as inexpensive "bait," or what retailers call a "loss leader." By this means Collier shows the old man's art of manipulation, for even though Alan is horrified by the poison, the seed has been planted in his mind. He will always know, when his love for Diana is lost, that he has the choice of "cleaning" his life, as the old man reminds him. This unscrupulous sales method effectively corrupts Alan in advance. Such a calculation on the old man's part is grimly cynical.

Supporting the cynicism of the old man's sales technique is his use of double meaning. His concluding words, "Au revoir" (i.e., "until I see you again"), for example, mean that he expects a future meeting when Alan will return to buy the poison to kill Diana. His speech acknowledging Alan's gratitude shows the same double edge. He says,

[4]   I like to oblige. . . . Then customers come back, later in life, when they are better off, and want more expensive things. (¶ 43)

Clearly the "expensive" thing he is talking about is the poison, the "chaser." Through such speeches of double meaning, the old man is calmly and politely, but cynically, telling Alan that his love for Diana will not last and that it will eventually irritate him to the point where he will want to get rid of her.

[5] Before "The Chaser" is dismissed as hopelessly cynical, however, it must be said that the only possible result of Alan's idea of love would be just such cynicism. The old man's descriptions of the total enslavement of Diana that Alan has dreamed about would leave no breathing room for either Alan or Diana. This sort of love would exclude everything else in life, and would soon be suffocating rather than pleasing. It would be normal to wish freedom from such psychological imprisonment, even if the prison is of one's own making. Under these conditions, the cynical tone of "The Chaser" suggests that the desire to be totally possessing and possessed—to "want nothing but solitude" and the loved one—can lead only to disaster for both man and woman. The old man's cynicism and the young man's desire thus point toward an ideal of love that permits interchange, individuality, and understanding. Even though this better ideal is not described anywhere in the story, it is compatible with Collier's situational irony. Thus, cynical as the story unquestionably is, it does not exclude an idealism of tolerant and more human love.

Commentary on the Essay

This essay presents one way to describe a story's presentation of pessimism and cynicism while not assenting to that story's negative situational irony. Therefore the essay illustrates how a consideration of tone can aid the development of objective literary judgment.

The introductory paragraph indicates that the aspect of tone to be discussed is the ironic situation—youthful but unrealistic hope in the context of aged cynicism. The thesis sentence indicates that the body of the essay will deal with (1) this situation and how it is related to (2) the sales method of a major character—the old man—and (3) his speeches containing double meaning.

The second paragraph establishes the situational irony by describing the desires of Alan Austen and the cynical attitude of the old man. In the third paragraph the topic is the sinister manipulation of Austen as a result of the old man's skillful and subtle salesmanship. By stressing that the old man plants the seeds of corruption in Austen, this paragraph continues the topic of the cynical tone which is the thematic basis of the essay. The subject of the fourth paragraph, the last in the body, is Collier's use of double meaning in the speeches of the old man to emphasize that Austen will someday want to kill his wife.

The concluding paragraph is a reflective one. In view of the cynicism of the story, this paragraph suggests that a more realistic and optimistic attitude about love is possible—a view that while not perceivable in the story is also not incompatible with it.

WRITING TOPICS

1. Write an essay comparing and contrasting attitudes toward the following female characters: Louise Mallard in "The Story of an Hour," Mathilde in "The Necklace," Diana in "The Chaser," and Phoenix in "A Worn Path." How does the presentation control your understanding of them? What particular details of tone would become important in a feminist approach to these works (See Appendix D, pp. 1655–56)?

2. Consider a short story in which the narrator is the central character (for example, "A & P," "First Confession," "Everyday Use," "Before the Firing Squad," "Blue Winds Dancing," "I Stand Here Ironing"). Write an essay showing how the language of the narrator affects your attitudes toward him or her (that is, your sympathy for the narrator, your interest in the narrative, your feelings toward the other characters and what they do). Be sure to emphasize the relationship between their language and your responses.

3. In "Rape Fantasies," describe the attitude of the narrator, Estelle, toward sexual molestation. How does her character influence the tone of the story (e.g., treating the subject of rape in an amusing, uncomprehending, or serious manner)?

4. Assume that you are writing a story involving, for example, a student, a supervisor, or a politician. Write a fragment treating your character with dramatic irony; that is, your character thinks he or she knows all the details about a situation, but really does not (e.g., a woman declares her interest in a man without realizing that he is engaged to another woman, or the supervisor expresses distrust in a person who is one of the best workers in the firm). What action, words, and situations do you choose to make your irony clear?

9

Symbolism and Allegory:
Keys to Extended Meaning

Symbolism and *allegory* are modes that expand meaning. Although they are literary, they are based in the fact that people associate important qualities of their existence with particular objects, places, or occurrences—either through experience or reading. One person might remember a rowboat ride when he made a vital realization about his moral being. Another person might associate her belief in freedom with catching a large fish and then letting it go. Still another person might connect a friendly word of advice with a major career decision. The significance of details like these can be meaningful not just at the time they occur, but throughout an entire lifetime. Merely speaking about them or bringing them to mind unlocks all their meanings, implications, and consequences. It is as though the reference alone can be the same as pages upon pages of explanation and analysis.

It is from this principle that both symbolism and allegory are derived. By highlighting details as *symbols*, and stories or parts of stories as *allegories*, writers can expand meaning while keeping their works within reasonable lengths.

SYMBOLISM

The words **symbol** and **symbolism** are derived from the Greek word meaning "to throw together" (*syn*, together, and *ballein*, to throw). A symbol creates a direct meaningful equation between (1) a specific object, scene, character, or action and (2) ideas, values, persons, or ways of life. In effect, a symbol is a *substitute* for the elements being signified, much as the flag stands for the ideals of the nation.

In painting and sculpture, symbols are easily recognized, for to tell a story visually, the artist must make every object count. In the anonymous fresco *Hercules and the Infant Telephus* from ancient Herculaneum, for exam-

Hercules and the Infant Telephus. A Roman fresco from Herculaneum,
copy of a lost Greek original. National Archeological Museum, Naples.

ple, the painter has depicted a crucial event in the life of the mythical hero
Hercules—the choice he had to make early in his life between pleasure or
toil. By symbolically turning his head away from the seated figure representing Pleasure, Hercules is rejecting the life of ease that she symbolizes. Instead, his life will be one of work, hardship, battle, victory, and glory, as symbolized by the lion, the eagle, and the sheaf of arrows. The image of his child,
Telephus, whom he later abandons and who is being suckled by a donkey,
symbolizes Hercules' insensitivity, verging on cruelty, that became a part of
his single-minded existence as a warrior and hero.

In stories, symbols are verbal descriptions—of persons, objects, places,
actions, and situations. Each symbol has its own objective identity, and may
function at an ordinary level. Therefore there is often a close topical relationship between the symbol and its meaning or meanings, but the symbol

may also have no apparent connection. What is important is that symbols extend beyond their immediate identity and point toward additional levels of meaning.

Something is a symbol when it consistently refers beyond itself to a significant idea, emotion, or quality. There are two types of symbols—*universal* and *contextual*.

Cultural Symbols

Many symbols are *generally* or *universally* recognized, and are therefore **cultural** (also called **universal**). They embody ideas and emotions that writers and readers share as heirs of the same historical and cultural tradition. When using these symbols, a writer assumes that readers already know what they represent. For example, the ancient mythological character Sisyphus is a widely recognized symbol. In the ancient Greek mythological underworld, Sisyphus is forever doomed to roll a large boulder up a high hill. Just as he gets it to the top, it rolls down, and then he is fated to roll it up again—and again—and again—because the rock always rolls back. The plight of Sisyphus is a symbol of the human condition: In spite of constant struggle, a person rarely if ever completes anything. Work must always be done over and over from day to day and from generation to generation, and the same problems confront humanity throughout all time. Because of such fruitless effort, life seems to have little or no meaning. Nevertheless, there is hope. People who confront their tasks, as Sisyphus does, stay involved and active, and even if they are only temporarily successful, their work makes their lives meaningful. A writer referring to Sisyphus would expect us to understand that this ancient mythological figure symbolizes these conditions.

Similarly, ordinary water, because living creatures could not live without it, is recognized as a universal symbol of life. It has this meaning in the ceremony of baptism, and it can convey this meaning and dimension in a variety of literary contexts. Thus, a spouting fountain may symbolize optimism (as upwelling, bubbling life) while a stagnant pool may symbolize the pollution and diminution of life. Water is also a universal symbol of sexuality, and its condition or state may symbolize various romantic relationships. For instance, stories in which lovers meet near a turbulent stream, a roaring waterfall, a wide river, a stormy sea, a muddy puddle, or a calm lake are symbolically representing love relationships that range from uncertainty to serenity.

Contextual Symbols

Objects and descriptions that are not universal symbols can be symbols *only if they are made so within individual works.* These are **contextual, private,** or **authorial** symbols. Unlike universal symbols, these gain symbolic meaning within their *context.* For example, the standing clock in Poe's "The Masque of the Red Death" (p. 256) symbolizes not only the passage of time but also the sinister forces of death. Similarly, Elisa's chrysanthemums in Steinbeck's

"The Chrysanthemums" seem at first nothing more than prized flowers. As the story progresses, however, they gain symbolic significance. The traveling tinsmith's apparent interest in them is the wedge he uses to get a small mending job from Elisa. Her description of the care needed in planting and tending them suggests that they signify her kindness, love, orderliness, femininity, and motherliness.

Like Poe's clock then, Steinbeck's chrysanthemums are a major *contextual* symbol. But there is no carryover: In other stories, a clock or flowers are not symbolic unless they are deliberately given symbolic meaning in these stories. Further, if they are symbolic, they may represent very different qualities than in the Poe and Steinbeck stories.

Determining What Is Symbolic

In determining whether a particular object, action, or character is a symbol, you need to judge the importance the author gives to it. If the element is prominent, and also maintains a constancy of meaning, you may justify interpreting it as a symbol. For example, Miss Brill's furpiece in Mansfield's "Miss Brill" (p. 202) is shabby and moth-eaten. It has no value. But because Mansfield makes it especially important at both the beginning and ending of the story, it contextually symbolizes Miss Brill's poverty and isolation. At the end of Welty's "A Worn Path" (p. 113), Phoenix, the major character, plans to spend all her money for a toy windmill for her sick grandson. Readers will note that the windmill is small and fragile, like her life and that of her grandson, but that Phoenix wants to give the boy a little pleasure despite their poverty and hopelessness. For these reasons the windmill is a contextual or authorial symbol of her strong character, generous nature, and pathetic existence.

ALLEGORY

An **allegory** is like a symbol because it transfers and broadens meaning. The term is derived from the Greek word *allegorein,* which means "to speak so as to imply other than what is said." Allegory, however, is more sustained than symbolism. An allegory is to a symbol as a motion picture is to a still picture. In form, an allegory is a complete and self-sufficient narrative, but it also signifies another series of events or conditions. While some stories are allegories from beginning to end, many stories that are not allegories may nevertheless contain brief sections or episodes that are *allegorical.*

The Use of Allegory

Allegories and the allegorical method are more than literary exercises. Without question, readers and listeners learn and memorize stories more easily than moral lessons, and therefore allegory is a favorite method of teaching morality. In addition, thought and expression have not always been free. The threat of censorship and the danger of reprisal have sometimes caused authors to express their views indirectly in the form of allegory rather than to write directly and risk political reprisal or accusations of libel. Hence, the double meaning of many allegories is based in both need and reality.

In studying a story for allegory, determine whether all or part of your work may have an extended, allegorical meaning. The continuing popularity of George Lucas's film *Star Wars* and its sequels, for example, is attributable at least partly to its being an allegory about the conflict between good and evil. Obi Wan Kenobi (intelligence) enlists the aid of Luke Skywalker (heroism, boldness), and instructs him in "the force" (moral or religious faith). Thus armed and guided, Skywalker opposes the powers of Darth Vader (evil) to rescue the Princess Leia (purity and goodness) with the aid of the latest spaceships and weaponry (technology). The story is an exciting adventure film, accompanied by dramatic music, and ingenious visual and sound effects. With the obvious allegorical overtones, however, it stands for any person's quest for self-fulfillment.

To apply a part of the allegory more specifically, consider that for a time the evil Vader imprisons Skywalker, and that Skywalker must exert all his skill and strength to get free and to overcome Vader. In the allegorical application of the episode, this temporary imprisonment signifies those moments of doubt, discouragement, and depression that people experience while trying to better themselves through education, work, self-improvement, friendship, marriage, and so on.

Almost from the beginning of recorded literature, similar heroic deeds have been represented in allegorical forms. From ancient Greece, the allegorical hero Jason sails the Argo to distant lands to gain the Golden Fleece (those who take risks are rewarded). From Anglo-Saxon England, the hero Beowulf saves the kingdom by killing Grendel and his monstrous mother (victory comes to those who rely on the forces of good). From seventeenth-century England, Bunyan's *The Pilgrim's Progress* tells how the hero Christian overcomes difficulties and temptations while traveling from this world to the next (belief, perseverance, and resistance to temptation save the faithful). As long as the parallel connections are close and consistent, like those mentioned here, an allegorical interpretation is valid.

FABLE, PARABLE, AND MYTH

Closely related to symbolism and allegory in the ability to extend and expand meaning are three additional forms—*fable, parable,* and *myth.*

FABLE. The **fable** (from Latin *fabula,* a story or narration) is an old and popular form. It is usually short, and often features animals with human traits (which are called **beast fables**), to which writers and editors attach "morals" or explanations. Aesop (sixth century B.C.) was supposedly a slave who composed fables in ancient Greece. His fable of "The Fox and the Grapes," for example, signifies the trait of belittling things we cannot have. More recent contributions to the fable tradition are Walt Disney's "Mickey Mouse" and Walt Kelly's "Pogo." The adjective *fabulous* refers to the collective body of fables of all sorts, even though the word is often used as a vague term of approval.

PARABLE. The **parable** (from Greek *paraballein, to set aside*) is a short, simple allegory with a moral or religious bent. Parables are most often associated with Jesus, who used them to embody unique religious insights and truths. His parables of the Good Samaritan and the Prodigal Son, for example, are interpreted to show God's love, concern, understanding, and forgiveness.

MYTH. A **myth** (from Greek *muthos*, a story) is either a narrative story or narrative protagonist, like the myths of Sisyphus, Oedipus, or Atalanta, that is associated with the religion, philosophy, and collective psychology of various societies or cultures. Myths embody and codify the social and cultural values of the civilization in which they are composed. Unfortunately, the words *myth* and *mythical* are sometimes used to mean "fanciful" or "untrue." Such disparagement reflects a limited understanding, for in fact, the truths of mythology are not to be found literally in the stories themselves, but rather in their symbolic or allegorical interpretations.

ALLUSION IN SYMBOLISM AND ALLEGORY

Universal or cultural symbols and allegories often allude to other works from our cultural heritage, such as the Bible, ancient history and literature, and works of the British and American traditions. Sometimes understanding a story may require knowledge of politics and current events.

If the meaning of a symbol is not immediately clear to you, you will need a dictionary or other reference work. The scope of your college dictionary will surprise you. If you cannot find an entry there, however, try one of the major encyclopedias, or ask your reference librarian, who can direct you to shelves loaded with helpful books. A few excellent guides are *The Oxford Companion to Classical Literature* (ed. M. C. Howatson), *The Oxford Companion to English Literature* (ed. Margaret Drabble), William Rose Benet's *The Reader's Encyclopedia.*, Timothy Gantz's *Early Greek Myth: A Guide to Literary and Artistic Sources*, and Richmond Y. Hathorn's *Greek Mythology*. Useful aids in finding biblical references are *Cruden's Complete Concordance*, which in various editions has been used since 1737, or *Strong's Exhaustive Concordance*, which is fuller and more up to date. These concordances list all the major words used in the Bible, so you can easily locate the chapter and verse of any and all biblical passages. If you still have trouble after using sources like these, see your instructor.

STORIES FOR STUDY

AESOP (ca. 6th c. B.C.)

Not much is known about the ancient fabulist Aesop. According to tradition, he was a freed slave who lived from ca. 620 to 560 B.C. Aristotle claimed that he had been a public defender, but there is no other evidence that he existed at all. In fact, versions of some of the fables were known a millennium before his time. Aesop might therefore be considered as much a collector as a creator of fables.

The Fox and the Grapes ———————————————————— *(ca. 6th c. B.C.)*

A hungry Fox came into a vineyard where there hung delicious clusters of ripe Grapes, his mouth watered to be at them; but they were nailed up to a trellis so high, that with all his springing and leaping he could not reach a single bunch. At last, growing tired and disappointed, "Let who will take them!" says he "they are but green and sour; so I'll e'en let them alone."

QUESTIONS

1. How much do you learn about the characteristics of the fox? How are these characteristics related to the moral or message of the fable?
2. What is the conflict in the fable? What is the resolution?
3. In your own words, explain the meaning of the fable. Is the "sour grape" explanation a satisfactory excuse, or is it a rationalization for failure?
4. From your reading of "The Fox and the Grapes," explain the characteristics of the fable as a type of literature.

THE MYTH OF ATALANTA

The story of Atalanta is an anonymous myth that was known throughout both the ancient Greek and Roman worlds. Because communication in ancient times was uncertain, there were variations in some of the details of the story, such as the names of Atalanta's father and her suitors. However, there was general agreement about the details of her story, which was told by many different writers, such as Apollodorus, Aelian, and Pacuvius. The best-known ancient text of the story appears in Ovid's Metamorphoses. *The story included here is slightly adapted from the brief but comprehensive version by Richmond Y. Hathorn* (Greek Mythology, *1977).*

Atalanta _____ *(5th–1st c. B.C.)*

There was once a man from Arcadia, in southern Greece, who hoped very much for a son, and when his wife gave birth to a daughter, he abandoned the child in the woods. A she-bear that lived there suckled the baby, until some hunters chanced on the child and reared it, calling it Atalanta [i.e., "the invincible one"]. Atalanta grew up to be a true daughter of the wilderness, an incomparable hunter, being instructed by the Goddess of the Hunt, Artemis, herself. Atalanta was a runner who could out-race any man, and a skillful wrestler, on one occasion defeating the hero Peleus at Pelias' funeral games. She tried also to go on the expedition with the Argonauts to re-cover the Golden Fleece, but she was turned away by Jason, who was afraid of the trou-ble a beautiful young woman might cause in a crew of young men.

Then Atalanta took part in the hunting of the Calydonian Boar, falling in love with the Calydonian Prince Meleager and being loved in return. But as this love brought about Meleager's death and as Atalanta was already inclined toward celibacy because of her allegiance to Artemis, she resolved on leading a solitary manless life henceforth, especially because the oracle at Delphi warned her that marriage would cause her whole nature to be changed. So when she gave birth to Meleager's child on her way back from Calydon to Arcadia, she kept it a secret and exposed the baby boy on Mount Parthenion. This child, called Parthenopaeus, was found by the same shep-herds who had found and reared Telephus (the son of Hercules and the Princess Auge), and he grew up to be Telephus' companion in early adventures. Eventually Parthenopaeus met his death in the war of the Seven against Thebes.

Meanwhile Atalanta had returned to her old hunting haunts, fighting off at-tacks of satyrs and discouraging the proposals of mortal men by stipulating that each suitor should compete with her in a race, in which she would be armed with a spear. The condition was that if she overtook her opponent she might stab him to death. And in this way she had disposed of three suitors, cutting off their heads and display-ing them beside the racecourse.

There was a young Arcadian named Milanion, who hated women as much as Atalanta hated men, and who was as fond of the chase as she was. He encountered Atalanta frequently during his hunts, and imperceptibly he fell in love with her. More and more he put himself in her way, until he was faithfully following her around, car-rying her hunting-nets and enduring her endless disdain. Once when a centaur, Hy-laeus, whom Atalanta had rejected, attacked her in anger, Milanion intervened, re-ceiving the blows of the centaur's club and even being wounded by one of the centaur's arrows while protecting Atalanta with his body. Atalanta killed the man-beast, and then nursed the injured Milanion back to health, her feeling for him grow-ing warmer all the while.

Still there was no way of winning Atalanta short of defeating her in the footrace; so in spite of all her discouragements Milanion challenged her. But before the day of the race he prayed to Aphrodite, the Goddess of Love, for aid, and the Goddess plucked three golden apples from the Garden of the Hesperides and instructed him in their use. When the race had begun and Atalanta was drawing near, Milanion dropped one golden apple and the young woman stopped to pick it up. Again she drew near, and again he dropped an apple, the Goddess causing them to weigh heav-ily in Atalanta's bosom. So when the third apple was dropped and picked up, Milan-ion was able to reach the goal unscathed and to claim Atalanta as his bride.

5

But in the flush of his victory and her willing defeat they both forgot to give thanks to Aphrodite. The Goddess punished them by inflicting a rage of lust on both of them, so that they lost all control of themselves. Passing by a sanctuary of Cybele, the Great Mother of Gods, they fell immediately to lovemaking in the holy grotto near the holy temple. They behaved with such abandon that the very statues averted their eyes. The Great Mother was incensed and thought of killing them at once, but instead she changed Milanion into a Lion and Atalanta into a lioness and made them the team that draws her chariot.

QUESTIONS

1. What abilities does Atalanta have? How does she try to preserve her independence?

2. Why does Atalanta vow to shun men? What causes her to change her mind? What finally happens to her?

3. Consider the symbolic significance of Atalanta's name, the golden apples, the chopping off of the heads of slow-running suitors, the father's abandonment of Atalanta, the exposure of the infant Parthenopaeus, the battle with the centaur, the way in which Atalanta loses the race, and the lovemaking in the holy grotto of the Great Mother of Gods.

NATHANIEL HAWTHORNE (1804–1864)

Hawthorne, a friend and associate of the fourteenth president of the United States, Franklin Pierce, is one of the great American writers of the nineteenth century. His most famous work is The Scarlet Letter *(1850), the sale of which gave him a degree of independence. During the administration of President Pierce (1853–1857), Hawthorne served as American Consul in Liverpool, England, and this opportunity enabled him to travel extensively in Europe. Throughout his writing there runs a conflict between freedom and conventionality, with those choosing freedom sometimes suffering from the guilt that their choice brings. "Young Goodman Brown," which is one of the early stories that he included in* Twice-Told Tales *(1837, 1842), embodies this conflict.*

Young Goodman Brown _____ *1835*

Young Goodman Brown came forth at sunset, into the street of Salem village,° but put his head back, after crossing the threshold, to exchange a parting kiss with his young wife. And Faith, as the wife was aptly named, thrust her own pretty head into the

---

Salem village: in Massachusetts, about fifteen miles north of Boston. The time of the story is the late seventeenth or early eighteenth century.

street, letting the wind play with the pink ribbons of her cap, while she called to Goodman Brown.

"Dearest heart," whispered she, softly and rather sadly, when her lips were close to his ear, "prithee, put off your journey until sunrise, and sleep in your own bed tonight. A lone woman is troubled with such dreams and such thoughts, that she's afeared of herself, sometimes. Pray, tarry with me this night, dear husband, of all nights in the year!"

"My love and my Faith," replied young Goodman Brown, "of all nights in the year, this one night must I tarry away from thee. My journey, as thou callest it, forth and back again, must needs be done 'twixt now and sunrise. What, my sweet, pretty wife, dost thou doubt me already, and we but three months married!"

"Then God bless you!" said Faith with the pink ribbons, "and may you find all well, when you come back."

"Amen!" cried Goodman Brown. "Say thy prayers, dear Faith, and go to bed at 5 dusk, and no harm will come to thee."

So they parted; and the young man pursued his way, until, being about to turn the corner by the meeting-house, he looked back and saw the head of Faith still peeping after him, with a melancholy air, in spite of her pink ribbons.

"Poor little Faith!" thought he, for his heart smote him. "What a wretch am I, to leave her on such an errand! She talks of dreams, too. Methought, as she spoke, there was trouble in her face, as if a dream had warned her what work is to be done to-night. But no, no! 't would kill her to think it. Well; she's a blessed angel on earth; and after this one night, I'll cling to her skirts and follow her to Heaven."

With this excellent resolve for the future, Goodman Brown felt himself justified in making more haste on his present evil purpose. He had taken a dreary road, darkened by all the gloomiest trees of the forest, which barely stood aside to let the narrow path creep through, and closed immediately behind. It was all as lonely as could be; and there is this peculiarity in such a solitude, that the traveller knows not who may be concealed by the innumerable trunks and the thick boughs overhead; so that, with lonely footsteps, he may yet be passing through an unseen multitude.

"There may be a devilish Indian behind every tree," said Goodman Brown to himself; and he glanced fearfully behind him, as he added, "What if the devil himself should be at my very elbow!"

His head being turned back, he passed a crook of the road, and looking for- 10 ward again, beheld the figure of a man, in grave and decent attire, seated at the foot of an old tree. He arose at Goodman Brown's approach, and walked onward, side by side with him.

"You are late, Goodman Brown," said he. "The clock of the Old South° was striking, as I came through Boston; and that is full fifteen minutes agone."

"Faith kept me back awhile," replied the young man, with a tremor in his voice, caused by the sudden appearance of his companion, though not wholly unexpected.

It was now deep dusk in the forest, and deepest in that part of it where these two were journeying. As nearly as could be discerned, the second traveller was about fifty years old, apparently in the same rank of life as Goodman Brown, and bearing a considerable resemblance to him, though perhaps more in expression than features. Still, they might have been taken for father and son. And yet, though the elder person was as simply clad as the younger, and as simple in manner too, he had an inde-

Old South: The Old South Church, in Boston, is still there.

scribable air of one who knew the world, and would not have felt abashed at the governor's dinner-table, or in King William's° court, were it possible that his affairs should call him thither. But the only thing about him that could be fixed upon as remarkable, was his staff, which bore the likeness of a great black snake, so curiously wrought, that it might almost be seen to twist and wriggle itself like a living serpent. This, of course, must have been an ocular deception, assisted by the uncertain light.

"Come, Goodman Brown!" cried his fellow-traveller, "this is a dull pace for the beginning of a journey. Take my staff, if you are so soon weary."

"Friend," said the other, exchanging his slow pace for a full stop, "having kept covenant by meeting thee here, it is my purpose now to return whence I came. I have scruples, touching the matter thou wot'st of."°

"Sayest thou so?" replied he of the serpent, smiling apart. "Let us walk on, nevertheless, reasoning as we go, and if I convince thee not, thou shalt turn back. We are but a little way in the forest, yet."

"Too far, too far!" exclaimed the goodman, unconsciously resuming his walk. "My father never went into the woods on such an errand, nor his father before him. We have been a race of honest men and good Christians, since the days of the martyrs.° And shall I be the first of the name of Brown that ever took this path and kept—"

"Such company, thou wouldst say," observed the elder person, interrupting his pause. "Well said, Goodman Brown! I have been as well acquainted with your family as ever a one among the Puritans; and that's no trifle to say. I helped your grandfather, the constable, when he lashed the Quaker woman so smartly through the streets of Salem. And it was I that brought your father a pitch-pine knot, kindled at my own hearth, to set fire to an Indian village, in King Philip's war.° They were my good friends, both; and many a pleasant walk have we had along this path, and returned merrily after midnight. I would fain be friends with you, for their sake."

"If it be as thou sayest," replied Goodman Brown, "I marvel they never spoke of these matters. Or, verily, I marvel not, seeing that the least rumor of the sort would have driven them from New England. We are a people of prayer, and good works to boot, and abide no such wickedness."

"Wickedness or not," said the traveller with twisted staff, "I have a very general acquaintance here in New England. The deacons of many a church have drunk the communion wine with me; the selectmen, of divers towns, make me their chairman; and a majority of the Great and General Court are firm supporters of my interest. The governor and I, too—but these are state secrets."

"Can this be so!" cried Goodman Brown, with a stare of amazement at his undisturbed companion. "Howbeit, I have nothing to do with the governor and council; they have their own ways, and are no rule for a simple husbandman like me. But, were I to go on with thee, how should I meet the eye of that good old man, our minister,

King William: William III was king of England from 1688 to 1701. William IV was King from 1830 to 1837.

Thou wot'st: You know.

days of the martyrs: the martyrdoms of Protestants in England during the reign of Queen Mary (1553–1558).

King Philip's war: This war (1675–1676), infamous for the atrocities committed by the New England settlers, resulted in the suppression of Indian tribal life, and prepared the way for unlimited settlement of New England by European immigrants. "Philip" was the English name of Chief Metacomet of the Wampanoag tribe.

at Salem village? Oh, his voice would make me tremble, both Sabbath-day and lecture-day!"

Thus far, the elder traveller had listened with due gravity, but now burst into a fit of irrepressible mirth, shaking himself so violently, that his snakelike staff actually seemed to wriggle in sympathy.

"Ha! ha! ha!" shouted he, again and again; then composing himself, "Well, go on, Goodman Brown, go on; but, prithee, don't kill me with laughing!"

"Well, then, to end the matter at once," said Goodman Brown, considerably nettled, "there is my wife, Faith. It would break her dear little heart; and I'd rather break my own!"

"Nay, if that be the case," answered the other, "e'en go thy ways, Goodman Brown. I would not, for twenty old women like the one hobbling before us, that Faith should come to any harm."   25

As he spoke, he pointed his staff at a female figure on the path, in whom Goodman Brown recognized a very pious and exemplary dame, who had taught him his catechism in youth, and was still his moral and spiritual adviser, jointly with the minister and Deacon Gookin.

"A marvel, truly, that Goody° Cloyse should be so far in the wilderness, at nightfall!" said he. "But, with your leave, friend, I shall take a cut through the woods, until we have left this Christian woman behind. Being a stranger to you, she might ask whom I was consorting with, and whither I was going."

"Be it so," said his fellow-traveller. "Betake you to the woods, and let me keep the path."

Accordingly, the young man turned aside, but took care to watch his companion, who advanced softly along the road, until he had come within a staff's length of the old dame. She, meanwhile, was making the best of her way, with singular speed for so aged a woman, and mumbling some indistinct words, a prayer, doubtless, as she went. The traveller put forth his staff, and touched her withered neck with what seemed the serpent's tail.

"The devil!" screamed the pious old lady.   30

"Then Goody Cloyse knows her old friend?" observed the traveller, confronting her, and leaning on his writhing stick.

"Ah, forsooth, and is it your worship, indeed?" cried the good dame. "Yea, truly is it, and in the very image of my old gossip,° Goodman Brown, the grandfather of the silly fellow that now is. But, would your worship believe it? My broomstick hath strangely disappeared, stolen, as I suspect, by that unhanged witch, Goody Cory,° and that, too, when I was all anointed with the juice of smallage and cinquefoil and wolf's-bane—"°

"Mingled with fine wheat and the fat of a new-born babe," said the shape of old Goodman Brown.

"Ah, your worship knows the recipe," cried the old lady, cackling aloud. "So, as I was saying, being all ready for the meeting, and no horse to ride on, I made up my

---

Goody: shortened form of "goodwife," a respectful name for a married woman of low rank. A "Goody Cloyse" was one of the women sentenced to execution by Hawthorne's great grandfather, Judge John Hathorne.
  gossip: from "good sib" or "good relative."
  Goody Cory: name of a woman who was also sent to execution by Judge Hathorne.
  smallage and cinquefoil and wolf's-bane: plants commonly used by witches in making ointments.

mind to foot it; for they tell me there is a nice young man to be taken into communion to-night. But now your good worship will lend me your arm, and we shall be
there in a twinkling."

"That can hardly be," answered her friend. "I will not spare you my arm, Goody
Cloyse, but here is my staff, if you will."

So saying, he threw it down at her feet, where, perhaps, it assumed life, being
one of the rods which its owner had formerly lent to the Egyptian Magi.° Of this fact,
however, Goodman Brown could not take cognizance. He had cast up his eyes in astonishment, and looking down again, beheld neither Goody Cloyse nor the serpen-
tine staff, but his fellow-traveller alone, who waited for him as calmly as if nothing had
happened.

"That old woman taught me my catechism!" said the young man; and there was
a world of meaning in this simple comment.

They continued to walk onward, while the elder traveller exhorted his companion to make good speed and persevere in the path, discoursing so aptly, that his
arguments seemed rather to spring up in the bosom of his auditor, than to be suggested by himself. As they went he plucked a branch of maple, to serve for a walking-
stick, and began to strip it of the twigs and little boughs, which were wet with evening
dew. The moment his fingers touched them, they became strangely withered and
dried up, as with a week's sunshine. Thus the pair proceeded, at a good free pace, until suddenly, in a gloomy hollow of the road, Goodman Brown sat himself down on
the stump of a tree, and refused to go any farther.

"Friend," said he, stubbornly, "my mind is made up. Not another step will I
budge on this errand. What if a wretched old woman do choose to go to the devil,
when I thought she was going to Heaven! Is that any reason why I should quit my dear
Faith, and go after her?"

"You will think better of this by and by," said his acquaintance, composedly. "Sit
here and rest yourself a while; and when you feel like moving again, there is my staff
to help you along."

Without more words, he threw his companion the maple stick, and was as
speedily out of sight as if he had vanished into the deepening gloom. The young man
sat a few moments by the roadside, applauding himself greatly, and thinking with how
clear a conscience he should meet the minister, in his morning walk, nor shrink from
the eye of good old Deacon Gookin. And what calm sleep would be his, that very
night, which was to have been spent so wickedly, but purely and sweetly now, in the
arms of Faith! Amidst these pleasant and praiseworthy meditations, Goodman Brown
heard the tramp of horses along the road, and deemed it advisable to conceal himself within the verge of the forest, conscious of the guilty purpose that had brought
him thither, though now so happily turned from it.

On came the hoof-tramps and the voices of the riders, two grave old voices, conversing soberly as they drew near. These mingled sounds appeared to pass along the
road, within a few yards of the young man's hiding-place; but owing, doubtless, to the
depth of the gloom, at that particular spot, neither the travellers nor their steeds were
visible. Though their figures brushed the small boughs by the wayside, it could not be
seen that they intercepted, even for a moment, the faint gleam from the strip of
bright sky, athwart which they must have passed. Goodman Brown alternately
crouched and stood on tiptoe, pulling aside the branches, and thrusting forth his
head as far as he durst, without discerning so much as a shadow. It vexed him the

lent to the Egyptian Magi: See Exodus 7:10–12.

more, because he could have sworn, were such a thing possible, that he recognized the voices of the minister and Deacon Gookin, jogging° along quietly, as they were wont to do, when bound to some ordination or ecclesiastical council. While yet within hearing, one of the riders stopped to pluck a switch.

"Of the two, reverend Sir," said the voice like the deacon's, "I had rather miss an ordination dinner than to-night's meeting. They tell me that some of our community are to be here from Falmouth and beyond, and others from Connecticut and Rhode Island; besides several of the Indian powwows,° who, after their fashion, know almost as much deviltry as the best of us. Moreover, there is a goodly young woman to be taken into communion."

"Mighty well, Deacon Gookin!" replied the solemn old tones of the minister. "Spur up, or we shall be late. Nothing can be done, you know, until I get on the ground."

The hoofs clattered again, and the voices, talking so strangely in the empty air, passed on through the forest, where no church had ever been gathered, nor solitary Christian prayed. Whither, then, could these holy men be journeying, so deep into the heathen wilderness? Young Goodman Brown caught hold of a tree, for support, being ready to sink down on the ground, faint and over-burthened with the heavy sickness of his heart. He looked up to the sky, doubting whether there really was a Heaven above him. Yet, there was the blue arch, and the stars brightening in it.   45

"With Heaven above, and Faith below, I will yet stand firm against the devil!" cried Goodman Brown.

While he still gazed upward, into the deep arch of the firmament, and had lifted his hands to pray, a cloud, though no wind was stirring, hurried across the zenith, and hid the brightening stars. The blue sky was still visible, except directly overhead, where this black mass of cloud was sweeping swiftly northward. Aloft in the air, as if from the depths of the cloud, came a confused and doubtful sound of voices. Once, the listener fancied that he could distinguish the accents of town's people of his own, men and women, both pious and ungodly, many of whom he had met at the communion-table, and had seen others rioting at the tavern. The next moment, so indistinct were the sounds, he doubted whether he had heard aught but the murmur of the old forest, whispering without a wind. Then came a stronger swell of those familiar tones, heard daily in the sunshine, at Salem village, but never, until now, from a cloud at night. There was one voice, of a young woman, uttering lamentations, yet with an uncertain sorrow, and entreating for some favor, which, perhaps, it would grieve her to obtain. And all the unseen multitude, both saints and sinners, seemed to encourage her onward.

"Faith!" shouted Goodman Brown, in a voice of agony and desperation; and the echoes of the forest mocked him, crying—"Faith! Faith!" as if bewildered wretches were seeking her, all through the wilderness.

The cry of grief, rage, and terror was yet piercing the night, when the unhappy husband held his breath for a response. There was a scream, drowned immediately in a louder murmur of voices fading into far-off laughter, as the dark cloud swept away, leaving the clear and silent sky above Goodman Brown. But something fluttered lightly down through the air, and caught on the branch of a tree. The young man seized it and beheld a pink ribbon.

jogging: riding a horse at a slow trot.
powwow: a Narragansett Indian word describing a ritual ceremony of dancing, incantation, and magic.

"My Faith is gone!" cried he, after one stupefied moment. "There is no good on earth, and sin is but a name. Come, devil! for to thee is this world given."

And maddened with despair, so that he laughed loud and long, did Goodman Brown grasp his staff and set forth again, at such a rate, that he seemed to fly along the forest path, rather than to walk or run. The road grew wilder and drearier, and more faintly traced, and vanished at length, leaving him in the heart of the dark wilderness, still rushing onward, with the instinct that guides mortal man to evil. The whole forest was peopled with frightful sounds; the creaking of the trees, the howling of wild beasts, and the yell of Indians; while, sometimes, the wind tolled like a distant church bell, and sometimes gave a broad roar around the traveller, as if all Nature were laughing him to scorn. But he was himself the chief horror of the scene, and shrank not from its other horrors.

"Ha! ha! ha!" roared Goodman Brown, when the wind laughed at him. "Let us hear which will laugh loudest! Think not to frighten me with your deviltry! Come witch, come wizard, come Indian powwow, come devil himself! and here comes Goodman Brown. You may as well fear him as he fear you!"

In truth, all through the haunted forest, there could be nothing more frightful than the figure of Goodman Brown. On he flew, among the black pines, brandishing his staff with frenzied gestures, now giving vent to an inspiration of horrid blasphemy, and now shouting forth such laughter, as set all the echoes of the forest laughing like demons around him. The fiend in his own shape is less hideous than when he rages in the breast of man. Thus sped the demoniac on his course, until, quivering among the trees, he saw a red light before him, as when the felled trunks and branches of a clearing have been set on fire, and throw up their lurid blaze against the sky, at the hour of midnight. He paused, in a lull of the tempest that had driven him onward, and heard the swell of what seemed a hymn, rolling solemnly from a distance, with the weight of many voices. He knew the tune. It was a familiar one in the choir of the village meeting-house. The verse died heavily away, and was lengthened by a chorus, not of human voices, but of all the sounds of the benighted wilderness, pealing in awful harmony together. Goodman Brown cried out; and his cry was lost to his own ear, by its unison with the cry of the desert.

In the interval of silence, he stole forward, until the light glared full upon his eyes. At one extremity of an open space, hemmed in by the dark wall of the forest, arose a rock, bearing some rude, natural resemblance either to an altar or a pulpit, and surrounded by four blazing pines, their tops aflame, their stems untouched, like candles at an evening meeting. The mass of foliage, that had overgrown the summit of the rock, was all on fire, blazing high into the night, and fitfully illuminating the whole field. Each pendent twig and leafy festoon was in a blaze. As the red light arose and fell, a numerous congregation alternately shone forth, then disappeared in shadow, and again grew, as it were, out of the darkness, peopling the heart of the solitary woods at once.

"A grave and dark-clad company!" quoth Goodman Brown.

In truth, they were such. Among them, quivering to-and-fro, between gloom and splendor, appeared faces that would be seen, next day, at the council-board of the province, and others which, Sabbath after Sabbath, looked devoutly heavenward, and benignantly over the crowded pews, from the holiest pulpits in the land. Some affirm that the lady of the governor was there. At least, there were high dames well known to her, and wives of honored husbands, and widows a great multitude, and ancient maidens, all of excellent repute, and fair young girls, who trembled lest their mothers should espy them. Either the sudden gleams of light, flashing over the obscure field, bedazzled Goodman Brown, or he recognized a score of the church members of Salem village, famous for their especial sanctity. Good old Deacon Gookin had arrived, and waited at the skirts of that venerable saint, his reverend pastor. But, irreverently consorting with these grave, reputable, and pious people, these elders of the church, these chaste dames and dewy virgins, there were men of dissolute lives and women of spotted fame, wretches given over to all mean and filthy vice, and suspected even of horrid crimes. It was strange to see, that the good shrank not from the wicked, nor were the sinners abashed by the saints. Scattered, also, among their pale-faced enemies, were the Indian priests, or powwows, who had often scared their native forest with more hideous incantations than any known to English witchcraft.

"But, where is Faith?" thought Goodman Brown; and, as hope came into his heart, he trembled.

Another verse of the hymn arose, a slow and mournful strain, such as the pious love, but joined to words which expressed all that our nature can conceive of sin, and darkly hinted at far more. Unfathomable to mere mortals is the lore of fiends. Verse after verse was sung, and still the chorus of the desert swelled between, like the deepest tone of a mighty organ. And, with the final peal of that dreadful anthem, there came a sound, as if the roaring wind, the rushing streams, the howling beasts, and every other voice of the unconverted wilderness were mingling and according with the voice of guilty man, in homage to the prince of all. The four blazing pines threw up a loftier flame, and obscurely discovered shapes and visages of horror on the smoke-wreaths, above the impious assembly. At the same moment, the fire on the rock shot redly forth, and formed a glowing arch above its base, where now appeared a figure. With reverence be it spoken, the apparition bore no slight similitude, both in garb and manner, to some grave divine of the New England churches.

"Bring forth the converts!" cried a voice, that echoed through the field and rolled into the forest.

At the word, Goodman Brown stepped forth from the shadow of the trees, and approached the congregation, with whom he felt a loathful brotherhood, by the sympathy of all that was wicked in his heart. He could have well-nigh sworn, that the shape of his own dead father beckoned him to advance, looking downward from a smoke-wreath, while a woman, with dim features of despair, threw out her hand to warn him back. Was it his mother? But he had no power to retreat one step, nor to resist, even in thought, when the minister and good old Deacon Gookin seized his arms, and led him to the blazing rock. Thither came also the slender form of a veiled female, led between Goody Cloyse, that pious teacher of the catechism, and Martha Carrier, who had received the devil's promise to be queen of hell. A rampant hag was she! And there stood the proselytes, beneath the canopy of fire.

"Welcome, my children," said the dark figure, "to the communion of your race! Ye have found, thus young, your nature and your destiny. My children, look behind you!"

They turned; and flashing forth, as it were, in a sheet of flame, the fiend-worshippers were seen; the smile of welcome gleamed darkly on every visage.

"There," resumed the sable form, "are all whom ye have reverenced from youth. Ye deemed them holier than yourselves, and shrank from your own sin, contrasting it with their lives of righteousness and prayerful aspirations heavenward. Yet, here are they all, in my worshipping assembly! This night it shall be granted you to know their secret deeds; how hoary-bearded elders of the church have whispered wanton words

60

to the young maids of their households; how many a woman, eager for widow's weeds, has given her husband a drink at bedtime, and let him sleep his last sleep in her bosom; how beardless youths have made haste to inherit their father's wealth; and how fair damsels—blush not, sweet ones!—have dug little graves in the garden, and bidden me, the sole guest, to an infant's funeral. By the sympathy of your human hearts for sin, ye shall scent out all the places—whether in church, bed-chamber, street, field, or forest—where crime has been committed, and shall exult to behold the whole earth one stain of guilt, one mighty blood-spot. Far more than this! It shall be yours to penetrate, in every bosom, the deep mystery of sin, the fountain of all wicked arts, and which inexhaustibly supplies more evil impulses than human power—than my power, at its utmost!—can make manifest in deeds. And now, my children, look upon each other."

They did so; and, by the blaze of the hell-kindled torches, the wretched man beheld his Faith, and the wife her husband, trembling before that unhallowed altar.

"Lo! there ye stand, my children," said the figure, in a deep and solemn tone, almost sad, with its despairing awfulness, as if his once angelic nature° could yet mourn for our miserable race. "Depending upon one another's hearts, ye had still hoped that virtue were not all a dream! Now are ye undeceived!—Evil is the nature of mankind. Evil must be your only happiness. Welcome, again, my children, to the communion of your race!"

"Welcome!" repeated the fiend-worshippers, in one cry of despair and triumph.

And there they stood, the only pair, as it seemed, who were yet hesitating on the verge of wickedness, in this dark world. A basin was hollowed, naturally, in the rock. Did it contain water, reddened by the lurid light? or was it blood? or, perchance, a liquid flame? Herein did the Shape of Evil dip his hand, and prepare to lay the mark of baptism upon their foreheads, that they might be partakers of the mystery of sin, more conscious of the secret guilt of others, both in deed and thought, than they could now be of their own. The husband cast one look at his pale wife, and Faith at him. What polluted wretches would the next glance show them to each other, shuddering alike at what they disclosed and what they saw!

"Faith! Faith!" cried the husband. "Look up to Heaven, and resist the Wicked One!"

Whether Faith obeyed, he knew not. Hardly had he spoken, when he found himself amid calm night and solitude, listening to a roar of the wind, which died heavily away through the forest. He staggered against the rock, and felt it chill and damp, while a hanging twig, that had been all on fire, besprinkled his cheek with the coldest dew.

The next morning, young Goodman Brown came slowly into the street of Salem village staring around him like a bewildered man. The good old minister was taking a walk along the grave-yard, to get an appetite for breakfast and meditate his sermon, and bestowed a blessing, as he passed, on Goodman Brown. He shrank from the venerable saint, as if to avoid an anathema. Old Deacon Gookin was at domestic worship, and the holy words of his prayer were heard through the open window. "What God doth the wizard pray to?" quoth Goodman Brown. Goody Cloyse, that excellent old

---

once angelic nature: Lucifer ("light bearer"), another name for the Devil, led the traditional revolt of the angels, and was thrown into hell as his punishment. See Isaiah 14:12–15.

Christian, stood in the early sunshine, at her own lattice, catechising a little girl, who had brought her a pint of morning's milk. Goodman Brown snatched away the child, as from the grasp of the fiend himself. Turning the corner by the meetinghouse, he spied the head of Faith, with the pink ribbons, gazing anxiously forth, and bursting into such joy at the sight of him that she skipt along the street, and almost kissed her husband before the whole village. But Goodman Brown looked sternly and sadly into her face, and passed on without a greeting.

Had Goodman Brown fallen asleep in the forest, and only dreamed a wild dream of a witch-meeting?

Be it so, if you will. But, alas! it was a dream of evil omen for young Goodman Brown. A stern, a sad, a darkly meditative, a distrustful, if not a desperate man did he become, from the night of that fearful dream. On the Sabbath day, when the congregation were singing a holy psalm, he could not listen, because an anthem of sin rushed loudly upon his ear, and drowned all the blessed strain. When the minister spoke from the pulpit, with power and fervid eloquence, and with his hand on the open Bible, of the sacred truths of our religion, and of saint-like lives and triumphant deaths, and of future bliss or misery unutterable, then did Goodman Brown turn pale, dreading lest the roof should thunder down upon the gray blasphemer and his hearers. Often, awaking suddenly at midnight, he shrank from the bosom of Faith, and at morning or eventide, when the family knelt down in prayer, he scowled, and muttered to himself, and gazed sternly at his wife, and turned away. And when he had lived long, and was borne to his grave, a hoary corpse, followed by Faith, an aged woman, and children and grandchildren, a goodly procession, besides neighbors not a few, they carved no hopeful verse upon his tombstone; for his dying hour was gloom.

QUESTIONS

1. Near the end of the story the narrator asks the following: "Had Goodman Brown fallen asleep in the forest, and only dreamed a wild dream of a witch-meeting?" What is the answer? If Goodman Brown's visions come out of his own dreams (mind, subconscious), what do they tell us about him?

2. Is Goodman Brown round or flat? To what extent is he a symbolic "everyman" or representative of humankind?

3. Consider Hawthorne's use of symbolism, such as sunset and night, the walking stick, the witches' sabbath, the marriage to Faith, and the vague shadows amid the darkness, together with other symbols that you may find.

4. What details establish the two settings? What characterizes Salem? The woods? Why might we be justified in seeing the forest as a symbolic setting?

5. To what extent are the people, objects, and events in Goodman Brown's adventure invested with enough *consistent* symbolic resonance to justify calling his episode in the woods an allegory? Consider Brown's wife, Faith, as an allegorical figure. What do you make of Brown's statements that "I'll cling to her skirts and follow her to Heaven" (paragraph 7) and "Faith kept me back awhile" (paragraph 12). In this same light, consider the other characters Brown meets in the forest, the sunset, the walk into the forest, and the staff "which bore the likeness of a great black snake."

ST. LUKE (First Century A.D.)

Although little is known about St. Luke, evidence in Colossians, Philemon, and II Timothy indicates that a man named Luke was the "beloved physician" and traveling companion of the Apostle Paul, who journeyed in the Mediterranean area during the middle of the first century A.D. Scholars indicate that Luke built his gospel from the Gospel of St. Mark and also from written sources known as "Q," some of which were also used by St. Matthew. Luke also relied on other sources that were available only to him. In addition to his gospel, Luke is also accepted as the author of the Acts of the Apostles.

The Parable of the Prodigal Son (Luke 15: 11–32) _____ *(ca. A.D. 90)*

11 And he [Jesus] said, A certain man had two sons:

12 And the younger of them said to *his* father, Father, give me the portion of goods that falleth *to me*. And he divided unto them *his* living.°

13 And not many days after the younger son gathered all together, and took his journey into a far country,° and there wasted his substance with riotous living.

14 And when he had spent all, there arose a mighty famine in that land; and he began to be in want.

15 And he went and joined himself to a citizen of that country; and he sent him into his fields to feed swine.°

16 And he would fain have filled his belly with the husks° that the swine did eat: and no man gave unto him.

17 And when he came to himself, he said, How many hired servants of my father's have bread enough and to spare, and I perish with hunger!

18 I will arise and go to my father, and will say unto him, Father, I have sinned against heaven, and before thee.

19 And am no more worthy to be called thy son: make me as one of thy hired servants.

20 And he arose, and came to his father. But when he was yet a great way off, his father saw him, and had compassion, and ran, and fell on his neck, and kissed him.

21 And the son said unto him, Father, I have sinned against heaven, and in thy sight, and am no more worthy to be called thy son.

22 But the father said to his servants, Bring forth the best robe, and put *it* on him; and put a ring on his hand, and shoes on *his* feet:

23 And bring hither the fatted calf,° and kill *it*; and let us eat, and be merry:

24 For this my son was dead, and is alive again; he was lost, and is found. And they began to be merry.

25 Now his elder son was in the field: and as he came and drew nigh to the house, he heard music and dancing.

26 And he called one of the servants, and asked what these things meant.

27 And he said unto him, Thy brother is come; and thy father hath killed the fatted calf, because he hath received him safe and sound.

> *divided . . . his living:* one-third of the father's estate; the son had to renounce all further claim.
> *far country:* countries of the Jewish dispersal, or *diaspora*, in the areas bordering the Mediterranean Sea.
> *feed swine:* In Jewish custom, pigs were unclean.
> *husks:* pods of the carob tree, the eating of which was thought to be penitential.
> *fatted calf:* grain-fed calf.

28 And he was angry, and would not go in: therefore came his father out, and intreated him.

29 And he answering said to *his* father, Lo, these many years do I serve thee, neither transgressed I at any time thy commandment: and yet thou never gavest me a kid, that I might make merry with my friends:

30 But as soon as this thy son was come, which hath devoured thy living with harlots, thou hast killed for him the fatted calf.

31 And he said unto him, Son, thou art ever with me, and all that I have is thine.

32 It was meet° that we should make merry, and be glad: for this thy brother was dead, and is alive again: and was lost, and is found.

QUESTIONS

1. Describe the character of the Prodigal Son. Is he flat or round, representative or individual? Why is it necessary that the character be considered representatively, even though he has individual characteristics?

2. What is the plot? What is the antagonism against which the Prodigal Son contends? Why is it necessary that the brother resent the brother's return?

3. What is the resolution of the parable? Why is there no "they lived happily ever after" ending?

4. Using verse numbers, analyze the structure of the parable. What determines your division of the parts? Do these parts coincide with the development of the plot? Describe the relationship of plot to structure in the parable.

5. What is the point of view here? How does the emphasis shift with verse 22?

6. On the basis of the fact that there are many characteristics here of many stories you have read, write a description of the parable as a type of literature.

meet: appropriate.

MARJORIE PICKTHALL (1883–1922)

Pickthall was born in England, but lived enough of her life in Canada to justify her being considered as a Canadian author. She wrote two novels. Her poems were published posthumously in 1937. Her stories were collected and published in one volume a year after her death.

The Worker in Sandalwood _____ *1923*

I like to think of this as a true story, but you who read may please yourselves, siding either with the curé,° who says Hyacinthe dreamed it all, and did the carving himself in his sleep, or with Madame. I am sure that Hyacinthe thinks it true, and so does Madame, but then she has the cabinet, with the little birds and the lilies carved at the

curé: parish priest.

corners. Monsieur le curé shrugs his patient shoulders; but then he is tainted with the infidelities of cities, good man, having been three times to Montreal, and once, in an electric car, to Saint Anne. He and Madame still talk it over whenever they meet, though it happened so many years ago, and each leaves the other forever unconvinced. Meanwhile the dust gathers in the infinite fine lines of the little birds' feathers, and softens the lily stamens where Madame's duster may not go; and the wood, ageing, takes on a golden gleam as of immemorial sunsets: that pale red wood, heavy with the scent of the ancient East; the wood that Hyacinthe loved.

It was the only wood of that kind which had ever been seen in Terminaison.° Pierre L'Oreillard brought it into the workshop one morning; a small heavy bundle wrapped in sacking, and then in burlap, and then in fine soft cloths. He laid it on a pile of shavings, and unwrapped it carefully and a dim sweetness filled the dark shed and hung heavily in the thin winter sunbeams.

Pierre L'Oreillard rubbed the wood respectfully with his knobby fingers. "It is sandalwood," he explained to Hyacinthe, pride of knowledge making him expansive; "a most precious wood° that grows in warm countries, thou great goblin. Smell it, *imbécile*. It is sweeter than cedar. It is to make a cabinet for the old Madame at the big house. Thy great hands shall smooth the wood, *nigaud*,° and I—I, Pierre the cabinetmaker, shall render it beautiful." Then he went out, locking the door behind him.

When he was gone, Hyacinthe laid down his plane, blew on his stiff fingers, and shambled slowly over to the wood. He was a great clumsy boy of fourteen, dark-faced, very slow of speech, dull-eyed and uncared for. He was clumsy because it is impossible to move gracefully when you are growing very big and fast on quite insufficient food. He was dull-eyed because all eyes met his unlovingly; uncared for, because none knew the beauty of his soul. But his heavy young hands could carve simple things, like flowers and birds and beasts, to perfection, as the curé pointed out. Simon has a tobacco-jar, carved with pine-cones and squirrels, and the curé has a pipe whose bowl is the bloom of a moccasin-flower, that I have seen. But it is all very long ago. And facts, in these lonely villages, easily become transfigured, touched upon their gray with a golden gleam.

"Thy hands shall smooth the wood, *nigaud*, and I shall render it beautiful," said Pierre L'Oreillard, and went off to drink brandy at the Cinq Chateaux.

Hyacinthe knew that the making of the cabinet would fall to him, as most of the other work did. He also touched the strange sweet wood, and at last laid his cheek against it, while the fragrance caught his breath. "How it is beautiful," said Hyacinthe, and for a moment his eyes glowed and he was happy. Then the light passed, and with bent head he shuffled back to his bench through a foam of white shavings curling almost to his knees.

"Madame perhaps will want the cabinet next week, for that is Christmas," said Hyacinthe, and fell to work harder than ever, though it was so cold in the shed that his breath hung like a little silver cloud and the steel stung his hands. There was a tiny window to his right, through which, when it was clear of frost, one looked on Terminaison, and that was cheerful and made one whistle. But to the left, through the chink of the ill-fitting door, there was nothing but the forest and the road dying away in it, and the trees moving heavily under the snow. Yet, from there came all Hyacinthe's

Terminaison: (literally, the "ending") a town imagined as a part of French Canada.
a most precious wood: Sandalwood is still rare and precious: it is grown mainly in India and yields to exquisite detail in carving and decoration.
nigaud: simpleton.

dumb dreams and slow reluctant fancies, which he sometimes found himself able to tell—in wood, not in words.

Brandy was good at the Cinq Chateaux, and Pierre L'Oreillard gave Hyacinthe plenty of directions, but no further help with the cabinet.

"That is to be finished for Madame on the festival, *gros escargot!*"° said he, cuffing Hyacinthe's ears furiously, "finished, and with a prettiness about the corners, hearest thou, *ourson?*° I suffer from a delicacy of the constitution and a little feebleness in the legs on these days, so that I cannot handle the tools. I must leave this work to thee, *gâcheur.*° See it is done properly, and stand up and touch a hand to thy cap when I address thee, *orvet,*° great slow-worm."

"Yes, monsieur," said Hyacinthe, wearily.

It is hard, when you do all the work, to be cuffed into the bargain, and fourteen is not very old. He went to work on the cabinet with slow, exquisite skill, but on the eve of Noel, he was still at work, and the cabinet unfinished. It meant a thrashing from Pierre if the morrow came and found it still unfinished, and Pierre's thrashings were cruel. But it was growing into a thing of perfection under his slow hands, and Hyacinthe would not hurry over it.

"Then work on it all night, and show it to me all completed in the morning, or thy bones shall mourn thy idleness," said Pierre with a flicker of his little eyes. And he shut Hyacinthe into the workshop with a smoky lamp, his tools, and the sandalwood cabinet.

It was nothing unusual. The boy had often been left before to finish a piece of work overnight while Pierre went off to his brandies. But this was Christmas Eve, and he was very tired. The cold crept into the shed until the scent of the sandalwood could not make him dream himself warm, and the roof cracked sullenly in the forest. There came upon Hyacinthe one of those awful, hopeless despairs that children know. It seemed to be a living presence that caught up his soul and crushed it in black hands. "In all the world, nothing!" said he, staring at the dull flame; "no place, no heart, no love! O kind God, is there a place, a love for me in another world?"

I cannot endure to think of Hyacinthe, poor lad, shut up despairing in the workshop with his loneliness, his cold, and his hunger, on the eve of Christmas. He was but an overgrown, unhappy child, and for unhappy children no aid, at this season, seems too divine for faith. So Madame says, and she is very old and very wise. Hyacinthe even looked at the chisel in his hand, and thought that by a touch of that he might lose it all, all, and be at peace, somewhere not far from God; only it was forbidden. Then came the tears, and great sobs that sickened and deafened him, so that he scarcely heard the gentle rattling of the latch.

At least, I suppose it came then, but it may have been later. The story is all so vague here, so confused with fancies that have spoiled the first simplicity. I think that Hyacinthe must have gone to the door, opening it upon the still woods and the frosty stars, and the lad who stood outside must have said: "I see you are working late, comrade. May I come in?" or something like it.

Hyacinthe brushed his ragged sleeve across his eyes, and opened the door wider with a little nod to the other to enter. Those little lonely villages strung along the

10

15

gros escargot: big snail.
ourson: bear cub.
gâcheur: bungler, spoiler.
orvet: blind worm, slow worm.

great river see strange wayfarers adrift inland from the sea. Hyacinthe said to himself that surely here was such a one.

Afterwards he told the curé that for a moment he had been bewildered. Dully blinking into the stranger's eyes, he lost for a flash the first impression of youth and received one of some incredible age or sadness. But this also passed and he knew that the wanderer's eyes were only quiet, very quiet, like the little pools in the wood where the wild does went to drink. As he turned within the door, smiling at Hyacinthe and shaking some snow from his fur cap, he did not seem more than sixteen or so.

"It is very cold outside," he said. "There is a big oak tree on the edge of the fields that has split in the frost and frightened all the little squirrels asleep there. Next year it will make an even better home for them. And see what I found close by!" He opened his fingers, and showed Hyacinthe a little sparrow lying unruffled in his palm.

"*Pauvrette!*"° said the dull Hyacinthe. "*Pauvrette!* Is it then dead?" He touched it with a gentle forefinger.

"No," answered the strange boy, "it is not dead. We'll put it here among the shavings, not far from the lamp, and it will be well by morning."°

He smiled at Hyacinthe again, and the shambling lad felt dimly as if the scent of sandalwood had deepened, and the lamp-flame burned clearer. But the stranger's eyes were only quiet, quiet.

"Have you come far?" asked Hyacinthe. "It is a bad season for travelling, and the wolves are out in the woods."

"A long way," said the other; "a long, long way. I heard a child cry. . . ."

"There is no child here," answered Hyacinthe, shaking his head. "Monsieur L'Oreillard is not fond of children, he says they cost too much money. But if you have come far, you must be cold and hungry, and I have no food or fire. At the Cinq Chateaux you will find both!"

The stranger looked at him again with those quiet eyes, and Hyacinthe fancied his face was familiar. "I will stay here," he said, "you are very late at work and you are unhappy."

"Why, as to that," answered Hyacinthe, rubbing again at his cheeks and ashamed of his tears, "most of us are sad at one time or another, the good God knows. Stay here and welcome if it pleases you, and you may take a share of my bed, though it is no more than a pile of balsam boughs and an old blanket, in the loft. But I must work at this cabinet, for the drawer must be finished and the handles put on and these corners carved, all by the holy morning; or my wages will be paid with a stick."

"You have a hard master," put in the other boy, "if he would pay you with blows upon the feast of Noel."

"He is hard enough," said Hyacinthe; "but once he gave me a dinner of sausages and white wine, and once, in the summer, melons. If my eyes will stay open, I will finish this by morning, but indeed I am sleepy. Stay with me an hour or so, comrade, and talk to me of your wanderings, so that the time may pass more quickly."

"I will tell you of the country where I was a child," answered the stranger.

And while Hyacinthe worked, he told—of sunshine and dust; of the shadows of vine-leaves on the flat white walls of a house; of rosy doves on the flat roof; of the flowers that come in the spring, crimson and blue, and the white cyclamen in the shadow of the rocks; of the olive, the myrtle and almond; until Hyacinthe's slow fingers ceased working, and his sleepy eyes blinked wonderingly.

Pauvrette: poor little thing.
. . . by morning: See Psalms 84:4.

"See what you have done, comrade," he said at last; "you have told of such pretty things that I have done no work for an hour. And now the cabinet will never be finished, and I shall be beaten."

"Let me help you," smiled the other; "I also was bred a carpenter."°

At first Hyacinthe would not, fearing to trust the sweet wood out of his own hands, but at length he allowed the stranger to fit in one of the little drawers, and so deftly was the work done, that Hyacinthe pounded his fists on the bench in admiration. "You have a pretty knack," he cried; "it seemed as if you did but hold the drawer in your hands a moment, and hey! ho! it jumped into its place!"

"Let me fit in the other little drawers, while you go and rest a while," said the wanderer. So Hyacinthe curled up among the shavings, and the stranger fell to work upon the little cabinet of sandalwood.

Here begins what the curé will have it is a dream within a dream. Sweetest of dreams was ever dreamed, if that is so. Sometimes I am forced to think with him, but again I see as clearly as with old Madame's eyes, that have not seen the earthly light for twenty years, and with her and Hyacinthe, I say "Credo."°

Hyacinthe said that he lay upon the shavings in the sweetness of the sandalwood, and was very tired. He thought of the country where the stranger had been a boy; of the flowers on the hills; of the laughing leaves of aspen, and poplar; of the golden flowering anise and the golden sun upon the dusty roads, until he was warm. All the time through these pictures, as through a painted veil, he was aware of that other boy with the quiet eyes, at work upon the cabinet, smoothing, fitting, polishing. "He does better work than I," thought Hyacinthe, but he was not jealous. And again he thought, "It is growing towards morning. In a little while I will get up and help him." But he did not, for the dream of warmth and the smell of the sandalwood held him in a sweet drowse. Also he said that he thought the stranger was singing as he worked, for there seemed to be a sense of some music in the shed, though he could not tell whether it came from the other boy's lips, or from the shabby old tools as he used them, or from the stars. "The stars are much paler," thought Hyacinthe, "and soon it will be morning, and the corners are not carved yet. I must get up and help this kind one in a little moment. Only I am so tired, and the music and the sweetness seem to wrap me and fold me close, so that I may not move."

He lay without moving, and behind the forest there shone a pale glow of some indescribable colour that was neither green nor blue, while in Terminaison the church bells began to ring. "Day will soon be here!" thought Hyacinthe, immovable in that deep dream of his, "and with day will come Monsieur L'Oreillard and his stick. I must get up and help, for even yet the corners are not carved."

But he did not get up. Instead, he saw the stranger look at him again, smiling as if he loved him, and lay his brown finger lightly upon the four empty corners of the cabinet. And Hyacinthe saw the little squares of reddish wood ripple and heave and break, as little clouds when the wind goes through the sky. And out of them thrust forth little birds, and after them the lilies, for a moment living, but even while Hyacinthe looked, growing hard and reddish-brown and settling back into the sweet wood. Then the stranger smiled again, and laid all the tools neatly in order, and, opening the door quietly, went away into the woods.

Hyacinthe lay still among the shavings for a long time, and then he crept slowly

. . . *bred a carpenter:* See Matthew 13:55.
Credo: "I believe," the opening words of the *Credo* section of the traditional Mass ("Credo in unum Deum . . ." ("I believe in one God . . .").

35

to the door. The sun, not yet risen, set its first beams upon the delicate mist of frost afloat beneath the trees, and so all the world was aflame with spendid gold. Far away down the road a dim figure seemed to move amid the glory, but the flow and the splendour were such that Hyacinthe was blinded. His breath came sharply as the glow beat in great waves on the wretched shed; on the foam of shavings; on the cabinet with the little birds and the lilies carved at the corners.

He was too pure of heart° to feel afraid. But, "Blessed be the Lord," whispered Hyacinthe, clasping his slow hands, "for He hath visited and redeemed His people.° But who will believe?"

Then the sun of Christ's day rose gloriously, and the little sparrow came from his nest among the shavings and shook his wings to the light.°

QUESTIONS

1.   What point of view is employed in the story? Who is the narrator? To what extent does the narrator know more than we might expect? Why does the narrator repeat that the events happened "very long ago"?

2.   Describe Hyacinthe. How does he deal with his life? How does he react to L'Oreillard's treatment? Why does the "strange child" appear to him?

3.   Why does the narrator stress the quality of Hyacinthe's work? Why does the narrator stress that Hyacinthe dreamed the events? To what extent do these points of emphasis keep the story from becoming too fantastic or sentimentalized?

4.   To what extent does the setting work symbolically to establish mood and tone? Consider the time of year, the specific night, the description of the shed in which Hyacinthe works, the forest, and the animals noted throughout.

5.   Consider the symbolism associated with the "quiet" stranger: his homeland, his training as a carpenter, the sparrow he revives, the heightening of the lamp-flame, and the warming of the workshop.

6.   Would you consider this story an allegory, a myth, a fable, a parable, or simply symbolic? Explain your answer.

JOHN STEINBECK (1902–1968)

Steinbeck was born in Monterey, California, and for a time attended Stanford University. In the 1920s while working at jobs such as surveying, picking fruit, and hatching trout, he began his writing career. A number of stories and novels preceded his best-known novel, The Grapes of Wrath (1939), for which he was awarded the Pulitzer Prize in 1940. He received the Nobel Prize for Literature in 1962. His fiction, often set in rural areas, features a realistic and pessimistic view of life. A number of his novels have been made into films, the best known of which is The Grapes of Wrath. His home in Monterey is open to the visiting public.

pure of heart: See Matthew 5:8.
His people: See Luke 1:68.
wings to the light: See Malachi 4:2.

The Chrysanthemums _____*1937*

The high grey-flannel fog of winter closed off the Salinas Valley° from the sky and from all the rest of the world. On every side it sat like a lid on the mountains and made of the great valley a closed pot. On the broad, level land floor the gang plows bit deep and left the black earth shining like metal where the shares had cut. On the foothill ranches across the Salinas River, the yellow stubble fields seemed to be bathed in pale cold sunshine, but there was no sunshine in the valley now in December. The thick willow scrub along the river flamed with sharp and positive yellow leaves.

It was a time of quiet and of waiting. The air was cold and tender. A light wind blew up from the southwest so that the farmers were mildly hopeful of a good rain before long; but fog and rain do not go together.

Across the river, on Henry Allen's foothill ranch there was little work to be done, for the hay was cut and stored and the orchards were plowed up to receive the rain deeply when it should come. The cattle on the higher slopes were becoming shaggy and rough-coated.

Elisa Allen, working in her flower garden, looked down across the yard and saw Henry, her husband, talking to two men in business suits. The three of them stood by the tractor shed, each man with one foot on the side of the little Fordson.° They smoked cigarettes and studied the machines as they talked.

Elisa watched them for a moment and then went back to her work. She was   5
thirty-five. Her face was lean and strong and her eyes were as clear as water. Her figure looked blocked and heavy in her gardening costume, a man's black hat pulled low down over her eyes, clodhopper shoes, a figured print dress almost completely covered by a big corduroy apron with four big pockets to hold the snips, the trowel and scratcher, the seeds and the knife she worked with. She wore heavy leather gloves to protect her hands while she worked.

She was cutting down the old year's chrysanthemum stalks with a pair of short and powerful scissors. She looked down toward the men by the tractor shed now and then. Her face was eager and mature and handsome; even her work with the scissors was over-eager, over-powerful. The chrysanthemum stems seemed too small and easy for her energy.

She brushed a cloud of hair out of her eyes with the back of her glove, and left a smudge of earth on the cheek in doing it. Behind her stood the neat white farm house with red geraniums close-banked around it as high as the windows. It was a hard-swept looking little house, with hard-polished windows, and a clean mud-mat on the front steps.

Elisa cast another glance toward the tractor shed. The strangers were getting into their Ford coupe. She took off a glove and put her strong fingers down into the forest of new green chrysanthemum sprouts that were growing around the old roots. She spread the leaves and looked down among the close-growing stems. No aphids were there, no sowbugs or snails or cutworms. Her terrier fingers destroyed such pests before they could get started.

Elisa started at the sound of her husband's voice. He had come near quietly, and he leaned over the wire fence that protected her flower garden from cattle and dogs and chickens.

Salinas Valley: in Monterey County, California, about 50 miles south of San José. Steinbeck was born in Salinas, and his home there is open to the public.
Fordson: a tractor manufactured by: the Ford Motor Company, with large rear steel-lugged wheels.

"At it again," he said. "You've got a strong new crop coming."

Elisa straightened her back and pulled on the gardening glove again. "Yes. They'll be strong this coming year." In her tone and on her face there was a little smugness.

"You've got a gift with things," Henry observed. "Some of those yellow chrysanthemums you had this year were ten inches across. I wish you'd work out in the orchard and raise some apples that big."

Her eyes sharpened. "Maybe I could do it, too. I've a gift with things, all right. My mother had it. She could stick anything in the ground and make it grow. She said it was having planters' hands that knew how to do it."

"Well, it sure works with flowers," he said.

"Henry, who were those men you were talking to?"

"Why, sure, that's what I came to tell you. They were from the Western Meat Company. I sold those thirty head of three-year-old steers. Got nearly my own price, too."

"Good," she said. "Good for you."

"And I thought," he continued, "I thought how it's Saturday afternoon, and we might go to Salinas for dinner at a restaurant, and then to a picture show—to celebrate, you see."

"Good," she repeated. "Oh, yes. That will be good."

Henry put on his joking tone. "There's fights tonight. How'd you like to go to the fights?"

"Oh, no," she said breathlessly. "No, I wouldn't like fights."

"Just fooling, Elisa. We'll go to a movie. Let's see. It's two now. I'm going to take Scotty and bring down those steers from the hill. It'll take us maybe two hours. We'll go in town about five and have dinner at the Cominos Hotel. Like that?"

"Of course I'll like it. It's good to eat away from home."

"All right, then. I'll go get up a couple of horses."

She said, "I'll have plenty of time to transplant some of these sets, I guess."

She heard her husband calling Scotty down by the barn. And a little later she saw the two men ride up the pale yellow hillside in search of the steers.

There was a little square sandy bed kept for rooting the chrysanthemums. With her trowel she turned the soil over and over, and smoothed it and patted it firm. Then she dug ten parallel trenches to receive the sets. Back at the chrysanthemum bed she pulled out the little crisp shoots, trimmed off the leaves of each one with her scissors and laid it on a small orderly pile.

A squeak of wheels and plod of hoofs came from the road. Elisa looked up. The country road ran along the dense bank of willows and cottonwoods that bordered the river, and up this road came a curious vehicle, curiously drawn. It was an old spring-wagon, with a round canvas top on it like the cover of a prairie schooner. It was drawn by an old bay horse and a little grey-and-white burro. A big stubble-bearded man sat between the cover flaps and drove the crawling team. Underneath the wagon, between the hind wheels, a lean and rangy mongrel dog walked sedately. Words were painted on the canvas in clumsy, crooked letters. "Pots, pans, knives, sisors, lawn mores. Fixed." Two rows of articles and the triumphantly definitive "Fixed" below. The black paint had run down in little sharp points beneath each letter.

Elisa, squatting on the ground, watched to see the crazy, loose-jointed wagon pass by. But it didn't pass. It turned into the farm road in front of her house, crooked old wheels skirling and squeaking. The rangy dog darted from between the wheels and ran ahead. Instantly the two ranch shepherds flew out at him. Then all three stopped, and with stiff and quivering tails, with taut straight legs, with ambassadorial dignity, they slowly circled, sniffing daintily. The caravan pulled up to Elisa's wire fence and stopped. Now the newcomer dog, feeling outnumbered, lowered his tail and retired under the wagon with raised hackles and bared teeth.

The man on the wagon seat called out. "That's a bad dog in a fight when he gets started." 30

Elisa laughed. "I see he is. How soon does he generally get started?"

The man caught up her laughter and echoed it heartily. "Sometimes not for weeks and weeks," he said. He climbed stiffly down, over the wheel. The horse and the donkey dropped like unwatered flowers.

Elisa saw that he was a very big man. Although his hair and beard were greying, he did not look old. His worn black suit was wrinkled and spotted with grease. The laughter had disappeared from his face and eyes the moment his laughing voice ceased. His eyes were dark and they were full of the brooding that gets in the eyes of teamsters and of sailors. The calloused hands he rested on the wire fence were cracked, and every crack was a black line. He took off his battered hat.

"I'm off my general road, ma'am," he said. "Does this dirt road cut over across the river to the Los Angeles highway?"

Elisa stood up and shoved the thick scissors in her apron pocket. "Well, yes, it 35 does, but it winds around and then fords the river. I don't think your team could pull through the sand."

He replied with some asperity, "It might surprise you what them beasts can pull through."

"When they get started?" she asked.

He smiled for a second. "Yes. When they get started."

"Well," said Elisa, "I think you'll save time if you go back to the Salinas road and pick up the highway there."

He drew a big finger down the chicken wire and made it sing. "I ain't in any 40 hurry, ma'am. I go from Seattle to San Diego and back every year. Takes all my time. About six months each way. I aim to follow nice weather."

Elisa took off her gloves and stuffed them in the apron pocket with the scissors. She touched the under edge of her man's hat, searching for fugitive hairs. "That sounds like a nice kind of a way to live," she said.

He leaned confidentially over the fence. "Maybe you noticed the writing on my wagon. I mend pots and sharpen knives and scissors. You got any of them things to do?"

"Oh, no," she said quickly. "Nothing like that." Her eyes hardened with resistance.

"Scissors is the worst thing," he explained. "Most people just ruin scissors trying to sharpen 'em, but I know how. I got a special tool. It's a little bobbit kind of thing, and patented. But it sure does the trick."

"No. My scissors are all sharp." 45

"All right, then. Take a pot," he continued earnestly, "a bent pot, or a pot with a hole. I can make it like new so you don't have to buy no new ones. That's a saving for you."

"No," she said shortly. "I tell you I have nothing like that for you to do."

His face fell to an exaggerated sadness. His voice took on a whining undertone. "I ain't had a thing to do today. Maybe I won't have no supper tonight. You see I'm off my regular road. I know folks on the highway clear from Seattle to San Diego. They save their things for me to sharpen up because they know I do it so good and save them money."

"I'm sorry," Elisa said irritably. "I haven't anything for you to do."

His eyes left her face and fell to searching the ground. They roamed about until they came to the chrysanthemum bed where she had been working. "What's them plants, ma'am?"

The irritation and resistance melted from Elisa's face. "Oh, those are chrysanthemums, giant whites and yellows. I raise them every year, bigger than anybody around here."

"Kind of a long-stemmed flower? Looks like a quick puff of colored smoke?" he asked.

"That's it. What a nice way to describe them."

"They smell kind of nasty till you get used to them," he said.

"It's a good bitter smell," she retorted, "not nasty at all."

He changed his tone quickly. "I like the smell myself."

"I had ten-inch blooms this year," she said.

The man leaned farther over the fence. "Look. I know a lady down the road a piece, has got the nicest garden you ever seen. Got nearly every kind of flower but no chrysantheums. Last time I was mending a copper-bottom washtub for her (that's a hard job but I do it good), she said to me, 'If you ever run acrost some nice chrysantheums I wish you'd try to get me a few seeds.' That's what she told me."

Elisa's eyes grew alert and eager. "She couldn't have known much about chrysanthemums. You can raise them from seed, but it's much easier to root the little sprouts you see there."

"Oh," he said. "I s'pose I can't take none to her, then."

"Why yes you can," Elisa cried. "I can put some in damp sand, and you can carry them right along with you. They'll take root in the pot if you keep them damp. And then she can transplant them."

"She'd sure like to have some, ma'am. You say they're nice ones?"

"Beautiful," she said. "Oh, beautiful." Her eyes shone. She tore off the battered hat and shook out her dark pretty hair. "I'll put them in a flower pot, and you can take them right with you. Come into the yard."

While the man came through the picket gate Elisa ran excitedly along the geranium-bordered path to the back of the house. And she returned carrying a big red flower pot. The gloves were forgotten now. She kneeled on the ground by the starting bed and dug up the sandy soil with her fingers and scooped it into the bright new flower pot. Then she picked up the little pile of shoots she had prepared. With her strong fingers she pressed them into the sand and tamped around them with her knuckles. The man stood over her. "I'll tell you what to do," she said. "You remember so you can tell the lady."

"Yes, I'll try to remember."

"Well, look. These will take root in about a month. Then she must set them out, about a foot apart in good rich earth like this, see?" She lifted a handful of dark soil for him to look at. "They'll grow fast and tall. Now remember this. In July tell her to cut them down, about eight inches from the ground."

"Before they bloom?" he asked.

"Yes, before they bloom." Her face was tight with eagerness. "They'll grow right up again. About the last of September the buds will start."

She stopped and seemed perplexed. "It's the budding that takes the most care," she said hesitantly. "I don't know how to tell you." She looked deep into his eyes, searchingly. Her mouth opened a little, and she seemed to be listening. "I'll try to tell you," she said. "Did you ever hear of planting hands?"

"Can't say I have, ma'am." 70

"Well, I can only tell you what it feels like. It's when you're picking off the buds you don't want. Everything goes right down into your fingertips. You watch your fingers work. They do it themselves. You can feel how it is. They pick and pick the buds. They never make a mistake. They're with the plant. Do you see? Your fingers and the plant. You can feel that, right up your arm. They know. They never make a mistake. You can feel it. When you're like that you can't do anything wrong. Do you see that? Can you understand that?"

She was kneeling on the ground looking up at him. Her breast swelled passionately.

The man's eyes narrowed. He looked away self-consciously. "Maybe I know," he said. "Sometimes in the night in the wagon there—"

Elisa's voice grew husky. She broke in on him. "I've never lived as you do, but I know what you mean. When the night is dark—why, the stars are sharp-pointed, and there's quiet. Why, you rise up and up! Every pointed star gets driven into your body. It's like that. Hot and sharp and—lovely."

Kneeling there, her hand went out toward his legs in the greasy black trousers. 75 Her hesitant fingers almost touched the cloth. Then her hand dropped to the ground. She crouched low like a fawning dog.

He said, "It's nice, just like you say. Only when you don't have no dinner, it ain't."

She stood up then, very straight, and her face was ashamed. She held the flower pot out to him and placed it gently in his arms. "Here. Put it in your wagon, on the seat, where you can watch it. Maybe I can find something for you to do."

At the back of the house she dug in the can pile and found two old and battered aluminum saucepans. She carried them back and gave them to him. "Here, maybe you can fix these."

His manner changed. He became professional. "Good as new I can fix them." At the back of his wagon he set a little anvil, and out of an oily tool box dug a small machine hammer. Elisa came through the gate to watch him while he pounded out the dents in the kettles. His mouth grew sure and knowing. At a difficult part of the work he sucked his under-lip.

"You sleep right in the wagon?" Elisa asked. 80

"Right in the wagon, ma'am. Rain or shine. I'm dry as a cow in there."

"It must be nice," she said. "It must be very nice. I wish women could do such things."

"It ain't the right kind of a life for a woman."

Her upper lip raised a little, showing her teeth. "How do you know? How can you tell?" she said.

"I don't know ma'am," he protested. "Of course I don't know. Now here's your 85 kettles, done. You don't have to buy no new ones."

"How much?"

"Oh, fifty cents'll do. I keep my prices down and my work good. That's why I have all them satisfied customers up and down the highway."

Elisa brought him a fifty-cent piece from the house and dropped it in his hand.

"You might be surprised to have a rival some time. I can sharpen scissors, too. And I can beat the dents out of little pots. I could show you what a woman might do."

He put his hammer back in the oily box and shoved the little anvil out of sight. "It would be a lonely life for a woman, ma'am, and a scarey life, too, with animals creeping under the wagon all night." He climbed over the single-tree, steadying himself with a hand on the burro's white rump. He settled himself in the seat, picked up the lines. "Thank you kindly, ma'am," he said. "I'll do like you told me; I'll go back and catch the Salinas road."

"Mind," she called, "if you're long in getting there, keep the sand damp."

"Sand, ma'am? . . . Sand? Oh, sure. You mean round the chrysantheums. Sure I will." He clucked his tongue. The beasts leaned luxuriously into their collars. The mongrel dog took his place between the back wheels. The wagon turned and crawled out the entrance road and back the way it had come, along the river.

Elisa stood in front of her wire fence watching the slow progress of the caravan. Her shoulders were straight, her head thrown back, her eyes half-closed, so that the scene came vaguely into them. Her lips moved silently, forming the words "Good-bye—good-bye." Then she whispered, "That's a bright direction. There's a glowing there." The sound of her whisper startled her. She shook herself free and looked about to see whether anyone had been listening. Only the dogs had heard. They lifted their heads toward her from their sleeping in the dust, and then stretched out their chins and settled asleep again. Elisa turned and ran hurriedly into the house.

In the kitchen she reached behind the stove and felt the water tank. It was full of hot water from the noonday cooking. In the bathroom she tore off her soiled clothes and flung them into the corner. And then she scrubbed herself with a little block of pumice, legs and thighs, loins and chest and arms, until her skin was scratched and red. When she had dried herself she stood in front of a mirror in her bedroom and looked at her body. She tightened her stomach and threw out her chest. She turned and looked over her shoulder at her back.

After a while she began to dress, slowly. She put on her newest under-clothing and her nicest stockings and the dress which was the symbol of her prettiness. She worked carefully on her hair, pencilled her eyebrows and rouged her lips.

Before she was finished she heard the little thunder of hoofs and the shouts of Henry and his helper as they drove the red steers into the corral. She heard the gate bang shut and set herself for Henry's arrival.

His step sounded on the porch. He entered the house calling "Elisa, where are you?"

"In my room, dressing. I'm not ready. There's hot water for your bath. Hurry up. It's getting late."

When she heard him splashing in the tub, Elisa laid his dark suit on the bed, and shirt and socks and tie beside it. She stood his polished shoes on the floor beside the bed. Then she went to the porch and sat primly and stiffly down. She looked toward the river road where the willow-line was still yellow with frosted leaves so that under the high grey fog they seemed a thin band of sunshine. This was the only color in the grey afternoon. She sat unmoving for a long time. Her eyes blinked rarely.

Henry came banging out of the door, shoving his tie inside his vest as he came. Elisa stiffened and her face grew tight. Henry stopped short and looked at her. "Why—why, Elisa. You look so nice!"

"Nice? You think I look nice? What do you mean by 'nice'?"

Henry blundered on. "I don't know. I mean you look different, strong and happy."

"I am strong? Yes, strong. What do you mean 'strong'?"

He looked bewildered. "You're playing some kind of a game," he said helplessly. "It's a kind of a play. You look strong enough to break a calf over your knee, happy enough to eat it like watermelon."

For a second she lost her rigidity. "Henry! Don't talk like that. You didn't know what you said." She grew complete again. "I'm strong," she boasted. "I never knew before how strong."

Henry looked down toward the tractor shed, and when he brought his eyes back to her, they were his own again. "I'll get out the car. You can put on your coat while I'm starting." 105

Elisa went into the house. She heard him drive to the gate and idle down his motor, and then she took a long time to put on her hat. She pulled it here and pressed it there. When Henry turned the motor off she slipped into her coat and went out.

The little roadster bounced along on the dirt road by the river, raising the birds and driving the rabbits into the brush. Two cranes flapped heavily over the willow-line and dropped into the river-bed.

Far ahead on the road Elisa saw a dark speck. She knew.

She tried not to look as they passed it, but her eyes would not obey. She whispered to herself sadly. "He might have thrown them off the road. That wouldn't have been much trouble, not very much. But he kept the pot," she explained. "He had to keep the pot. That's why he couldn't get them off the road."

The roadster turned a bend and she saw the caravan ahead. She swung full around toward her husband so she could not see the little covered wagon and the mismatched team as the car passed them. 110

In a moment it was over. The thing was done. She did not look back. She said loudly, to be heard above the motor, "It will be good, tonight, a good dinner."

"Now you're changed again," Henry complained. He took one hand from the wheel and patted her knee. "I ought to take you in to dinner oftener. It would be good for both of us. We get so heavy out on the ranch."

"Henry," she asked, "could we have wine at dinner?"

"Sure we could. Say! That will be fine."

She was silent for a little while; then she said, "Henry, at those prize fights, do the men hurt each other very much?" 115

"Sometimes a little, not often. Why?"

"Well, I've read how they break noses, and blood runs down their chests. I've read how the fighting gloves get heavy and soggy with blood."

He looked around at her. "What's the matter, Elisa? I didn't know you read things like that." He brought the car to a stop, then turned to the right over the Salinas River bridge.

"Do any women ever go to the fights?" she asked.

"Oh, sure, some. What's the matter, Elisa? Do you want to go? I don't think you'd like it, but I'll take you if you really want to go." 120

She relaxed limply in the seat. "Oh, no. No. I don't want to go. I'm sure I don't." Her face was turned away from him. "It will be enough if we can have wine. It will be plenty." She turned up her coat collar so he could not see that she was crying weakly—like an old woman.

QUESTIONS

1. What point of view is used in the story? What are the advantages of this point of view?
2. Consider the symbolism of the setting in this story with respect to the Salinas Valley, the time of year, and the description of the Allen house. What do these things tell us about Elisa Allen and her world?
3. To what extent is Steinbeck's description of Elisa in paragraphs 5 and 6 symbolic? What is she wearing? What do her clothes hide or suppress?
4. What do the chrysanthemums symbolize for Elisa? What do they symbolize *about* her? What role do these flowers play in her life?
5. How does Elisa's character or sense of self change during the episode in which she washes and dresses for dinner? To what extent is this washing-dressing episode symbolic? How would you explain the symbolism?
6. Consider the symbolic impact of Elisa's seeing the chrysanthemum sprouts at the roadside. What does her reaction tell us about her values?

WRITING ABOUT SYMBOLISM OR ALLEGORY

To discover possible parallels that determine the presence of symbolism or allegory, consider the following questions:

Questions for Discovering Ideas

A. SYMBOLISM

• What cultural or universal symbols can you discover in names, objects, places, situations, or actions in the story (e.g., "Faith" and the walking stick in "Young Goodman Brown," "Abner" in "Barn Burning," the miraculous artistry in "A Worker in Sandalwood," the woods in either "Young Goodman Brown" or A Worn Path").

• What contextual symbolism can be found in the story? What makes you think it is symbolic? What is being symbolized? How definite or direct is the symbolism? How systematically is it used? How necessary to the story is it? To what degree does it strengthen the story? How strongly does the story stand on its own without the reading for symbolism?

• Is it possible to make parallel lists that show how qualities of a particular symbol match the qualities of a character or action? (Here is such a list for the toy windmill in Welty's "A Worn Path"):

QUALITIES OF THE WINDMILL	COMPARABLE QUALITIES IN PHOENIX AND HER LIFE
1. Cheap	1. Poor, but she gives all she has for the windmill
2. Breakable	2. Old, and not far from death
3. A gift	3. Generous
4. Not practical	4. Needs relief from reality and practicality
5. Colorful	5. Needs something new and cheerful

B. ALLEGORY

- How clearly does the author point you toward an allegorical reading (i.e., through names and allusions, consistency of narrative, literary context)?
- How consistent is the allegorical application? Does the entire work, or only a part, embody the allegory? On what basis do you draw these conclusions?
- How complete is the allegorical reading? How might the allegory yield to a diagram such as the one included here, which shows how characters, actions, objects, or ideas correspond to an allegorical meaning?

Star Wars	Luke Skywalker	Obi Wan Kenobi	Darth Vader	Princess Leia	Capture	Escape, and defeat of Vader
Allegorical Application to Morality and Faith	Forces of good	Education and faith	Forces of evil	Object to be saved, ideals to be rescued and restored	Doubt, spiritual negligence	Restoration of faith
Allegorical Application to Personal and General Concerns	Individual in pursuit of goals	The means by which goals may be reached	Obstacles to be overcome	Occupation, happiness, goals	Temporary failure, depression, discouragement, disappointment	Success

C. OTHER FORMS

- What enables you to identify the story as a parable or fable? What "lesson" or "moral" is either clearly stated or implicit?
- What mythological identification is established in the story? What do you find in the story (names, situations, etc.) that enables you to determine its mythological significance? How is the myth to be understood? What symbolic value does the myth have? What current and timeless application does it have?

Strategies for Organizing Ideas

Relate the central idea of your essay to the meaning of the major symbols or allegorical thrust of the story. An idea about "Young Goodman Brown," for example, is that fanaticism darkens and limits the human soul. An early incident in the story provides symbolic support for this idea. Specifically, when Goodman Brown enters the woods, he resolves "to stand firm against the devil," and he then looks up "to heaven above." As he looks, a "black mass of cloud" appears to hide the "brightening stars." Within the limits of our central idea, the cloud may be seen as a symbol, just like the widening path or the night walk itself. Look for ways to make solid connections like this in your symbolic ascriptions.

Also, your essay will need to include justifications for your symbols or allegorical parallels. In "The Masque of the Red Death," for example, Prince Prospero's seemingly impregnable "castellated abbey" is a line of defense against the plague. But the Red Death in a human shape easily invades the castle and conquers Prospero and his ill-fated guests. If you treat the abbey as a symbol, it is important to apply it to measures that people take (medicine, escapist activity, etc.) to keep death distant and remote. In the same way, in treating the allegorical elements in "Young Goodman Brown," you need to establish a comprehensive statement such as the following: People lose ideals and forsake principles not because they are evil, but because they misunderstand the people around them.

There are a number of other strategies for discussing symbolism and allegory. You might use one exclusively, or a combination. If you want to write about symbolism, you might consider the following:

1. *The meaning of a major symbol.* Identify the symbol and what it stands for. Then answer questions such as: Is the symbol cultural or contextual? How do you decide? How do you derive your interpretation of the symbolic meaning? What is the extent of the meaning? Does the symbol undergo modification or new applications if it reappears? How does the symbol affect your understanding of the total story? Does the symbol bring out any ironies? How does the symbol add strength and depth to the story?

2. *The development and relationship of symbols.* For two or more symbols, consider issues such as: How do the symbols connect with each other (like night and the cloud in "Young Goodman Brown" as symbols of a darkening mind)? What additional meanings do the symbols provide? Are they complementary, contradictory, or ironic (the windmill and the medicine in "A Worn Path," for example, are ironic because the windmill suggests cheer while the medicine suggests hopelessness)? Do the symbols control the form of the story? How? (For example, in "The Worker in Sandalwood" the concluding episode begins in doubt during the night of Christmas Eve and ends in success on the morning of Christmas Day. By contrast, the conclusion of Joyce's "Araby" begins in anticipation during the day and ends in disillusionment at night.) May these contrasting times be viewed symbolically in relationship to the development of the two stories? Other issues are whether the symbols fit naturally or artificially into the context of the story, or whether and how the writer's symbols create unique qualities or excellences.

If you write about allegory, you might use one of the following approaches:

1. *The application and meaning of the allegory.* What is the subject of the story (allegory, fable, parable, myth)? How may it be more generally applied to ideas or to qualities of human character, not only of its own time but of our own? What other versions of the story do you know, if any? Does it illustrate, either closely or loosely, particular philosophies or religious views? If so, what are these? How do you know?

2. *The consistency of the allegory.* Is the allegory used consistently throughout the story, or is it intermittent? Explain and illustrate this use. Would it be correct to call your story *allegorical* rather than an *allegory*? Can you determine how parts of the story are introduced for their allegorical importance? Examples are the natural obstacles in the woods in Welty's "A Worn Path,"

which are allegorical equivalents of life's difficulties; and the entertainment scene in "The Masque of the Red Death," which corresponds to the ways by which people try to avoid the realities of disease and death.

In concluding you might summarize main points, describe general impressions, explain the impact of the symbolic or allegorical methods, indicate personal responses, or suggest further lines of thought and application. You might also assess the quality and appropriateness of the symbolism or allegory (such as the opening of "Young Goodman Brown" being in darkness, with the closing in gloom).

SAMPLE ESSAY

Allegory and Symbolism in Hawthorne's "Young Goodman Brown"°

[1]　　It is hard to read beyond the third paragraph of Nathaniel Hawthorne's "Young Goodman Brown" without realizing the story's allegory and symbolism. The opening at first seems realistic. Goodman Brown, a young Puritan, leaves his home in colonial Salem to take an overnight trip. His wife's name, "Faith," however, suggests a symbolic reading, and as soon as Brown goes into the forest, his ordinary walk changes into an allegorical trip into evil. The idea that Hawthorne shows by this trip is that rigid belief destroys even the best human qualities.* He develops this thought in the allegory and in many symbols, particularly the sunset, the walking stick, and the path.†

[2]　　The allegory is about how people develop destructive ideas. Most of the story is dreamlike and unreal, and the ideas that Brown gains are also unreal. At the weird "witch meeting," he concludes that everyone he knows is sinful, and he then permits mistrust and loathing to distort his previous love for his wife and neighbors. As a result, he becomes harsh and gloomy for the rest of his life. The location of the story in colonial Salem indicates that Hawthorne's allegorical target is the zealous pursuit of religious principles which dwell on sinfulness rather than love. However, modern readers may also apply the allegory to the ways in which people uncritically accept *any* ideal (most often political loyalties or racial or national prejudices), and thereby reject the integrity and rights of others. If people like Brown apply a rigid standard, they can condemn anyone, particularly if they never try to understand those they condemn. In this way, Hawthorne's allegory applies to any narrow-minded acceptance of ideals or systems that exclude the importance of love, understanding, and tolerance.

[3]　　Hawthorne's attack on such dehumanizing belief is found not just in the allegory, but also in his many symbols. For example, the seventh word in the story, "sunset," may be taken as a symbol. In reality, sunset merely indicates

° See p. 330 for this story.
* Central idea.
† Thesis sentence.

the end of day. Coming at the beginning of the story, however, it suggests that Goodman Brown is beginning his long night of hatred, his spiritual death. For him the night will never end because his final days are shrouded in "gloom" (¶ 72).

The next symbol, the guide's walking stick or staff, suggests the arbitrariness of the standard by which Brown judges his neighbors. Hawthorne's description indicates the symbolic nature of this staff:

[4]

. . . the only thing about him [the guide] that could be fixed upon as remarkable, was his staff, which bore the likeness of a great black snake, so curiously wrought, that it might almost be seen to twist and wriggle itself like a living serpent. This, of course, must have been an ocular deception, assisted by the uncertain light. (¶ 13)

The serpent symbolically suggests Satan, who in Genesis (3:1–7) is the originator of all evil, but the phrase "ocular deception" creates an interesting and realistic ambiguity about the symbol. Since the perception of the snake may depend on nothing more than the "uncertain" light, the staff may be less symbolic of evil than of the tendency to find evil where it does not exist (and could the uncertain light symbolize the uncertainty of human understanding?).

[5]

In the same vein, the path through the forest is a major symbol of the destructive mental confusion that overcomes Brown. As he walks, the path grows "wilder and drearier, and more faintly traced," and "at length" it vanishes (¶ 50). This is like the Biblical description of the "broad" way that leads "to Destruction" (Matthew 7:13). As a symbol, the path shows that most human acts are bad, while a small number, like the "narrow" way to life (Matthew 7:14), are good. Goodman Brown's path is at first clear, as though sin is at first unique and unusual. Soon, however, it is so indistinct that he can see only sin wherever he turns. The symbol suggests that, when people follow evil, their moral vision becomes blurred and they soon fall prey to "the instinct that guides mortal man to evil" (paragraph 50).

[6]

Through Hawthorne's allegory and symbols, "Young Goodman Brown" presents the paradox of how noble beliefs can backfire. Goodman Brown dies in gloom because he believes that his wrong vision is true. This form of evil is the hardest to stop, because wrongdoers who are convinced of their own goodness are beyond reach. In view of such self-righteous evil, whether cloaked in the apparent virtues of Puritanism or of some other blindly rigorous doctrine (political as well as religious), Hawthorne writes that "the fiend in his own shape is less hideous than when he rages in the breast of man" (¶ 53). Young Goodman Brown thus is the central symbol of the story. He is one of those who think they walk in light but who really create their own darkness.

Commentary on the Essay

The introduction justifies the treatment of allegory and symbolism on the grounds that Hawthorne early in the story invites such a reading. The central idea relates Hawthorne's method to the idea that rigid belief destroys the best human qualities. The thesis sentence outlines two major areas of discussion: (1) allegory, and (2) symbolism.

Paragraph 2 considers the allegory as a criticism of rigid Puritan morality. The major thread running through each of the major parts of the paragraph is the hurtful effect of monomaniacal views like those of Brown. Paragraphs 3, 4, and 5 deal with three major symbols: sunset, the staff, and the path. The aim of this discussion is to show how the symbols apply to Hawthorne's attack on unquestioning belief. Throughout these three paragraphs the central idea—the relationship of rigidity to destructiveness—is stressed. Hawthorne's allusions to both the Old and New Testaments are pointed out in paragraphs 4 and 5. The last paragraph builds to the conclusion that Brown symbolizes the idea that the primary cause of evil is the inability to separate reality from unreality.

If you write exclusively about allegory, use paragraph 2 of the sample essay as a guide either for a single paragraph or, as expanded, for an entire essay. If the allegory of "Young Goodman Brown," for example, were to be expanded, additional topics might be Brown's gullibility, the meaning of faith and the requirements for maintaining it, and the causes for preferring to think evil rather than good of other people. Such points are sufficiently important to sustain an entire essay on the topic of allegory.

WRITING TOPICS

1. Write an essay on the allegorical method of *The Prodigal Son* and of other allegories included in the Gospel According to St. Luke, such as *The Bridegroom* (5:34–35), *The Garments and the Wineskins* (5:36–39), *The Sower* (8:4–15), *The Good Samaritan* (10:25–37), *The Ox in the Well* (14:5–6), *The Watering of Animals on the Sabbath* (13:15–17), *The Rich Fool* (12:16–21), *Lazarus* (16:19–31), *The Widow and the Judge* (18:1–8), and *The Pharisee and the Publican* (18:9–14).

2. Compare and contrast the symbolism in Steinbeck's "The Chrysanthemums" and Munro's "The Found Boat" (p. 277). To what degree do the stories rely on contextual symbols? On universal symbols? On the basis of your comparison, what is the case for asserting that realism and fantasy are directly related to the nature of the symbolism employed by the writer?

3. On the basis of "The Parable of the Prodigal Son" and "A Worker in Sandalwood," why do you think religious stories and parables rely heavily on symbolism and allegory?

4. Consider the story of Atalanta, first, as a myth about male dominance in man/woman relationships, and, second, as a myth about the obstacles to a woman's freedom and independence. You may wish to make your essay one of comparison and contrast (Appendix B).

5. Write a brief story using a widely recognized cultural symbol such as the flag (patriotism, love of country, a certain type of politics), water (life, sexuality, regeneration), the population explosion (the end of life on earth). By arranging actions and dialogue, make clear the issues conveyed by your symbol, and also try to resolve the conflicts that the symbol might raise among your characters.

6. Write a brief story in which you develop your own *contextual symbol.* You might, for example, demonstrate how holding a job brings out character strengths that are not at first apparent, or how neglecting to care for the inside or outside of a house indicates a character's decline. The principle is to take something that may at first seem normal and ordinary, and then to make that thing symbolic as your story progresses.

10
Idea or Theme: TheMeaning and the Message in Fiction

The word **idea** refers to the result or results of general and abstract thinking. Synonymous words are *concept, thought, opinion,* and *principle.* In literary study the consideration of ideas relates to *meaning, interpretation, explanation,* and *significance.* Though ideas are usually extensive and complex, separate ideas may be named by a single word, such as *justice, right, good, love, piety, causation,* and, not unsurprisingly, *idea* itself.

IDEAS AND ASSERTIONS

Although a single word may name an idea, it does not operate as an idea until it is put into a sentence or assertion. In other words, an idea needs a subject and a predicate before we can use it as a basis of understanding. It is important to recognize that an assertion of an idea is not the same as an ordinary sentence, such as "It's a nice day." This observation may be true (depending on the weather), but it cannot be called an *idea.* Rather, an idea should indicate *thought* about the day's quality, such as "A nice day requires blue sky and a warm sun." Because this sentence deals with an assertion about "nice," it lends itself to the consideration of the idea of a nice day.

In studying literature, always phrase ideas as assertions. For example, you might claim that an idea in Lawrence's "The Horse Dealer's Daughter" is "love," but it would be difficult to write anything more unless you make an assertion such as, "This story demonstrates the idea that love is irresistible and irrational." This assertion would lead you to explain the unlikely love that suddenly bursts out in the story. Similarly, for Eudora Welty's "A Worn Path" you might make the following assertion: "Phoenix embodies the idea that caring for others gives no reward but the continuation of the duty itself."

Although we have noted only one idea in these stories, there are usually many separate ideas. When one of the ideas seems to be the major one,

Guernica, Pablo Picasso, ARS Centro de Arta Reina Sofia, Madrid, Spain, Giraudon/Art Resource, NY.

it is called the **theme**. In practice, the words *theme* and *major idea* or *central idea* are the same.

IDEAS AND VALUES

Stories embody **values** along with ideas. This means that ideas are presented along with the expression or implication that certain conditions and standards should be—or should not be—highly valued. For example, the *idea of justice* may be considered abstractly and broadly, as Plato does in his *Republic* when developing his concept of a just government. In comparison, justice is also a subject of Ernest J. Gaines in "The Sky Is Gray," but Gaines is not abstract and speculative, like Plato. Rather he is personal. Gaines's idea is that human beings are equal regardless of race, and he asserts the need for equal treatment by showing that the boy narrator has needs, difficulties, discomforts, and pains that are the same as those of all human beings, regardless of race. In short, to talk about Gaines's idea is also to talk about his values.

A graphic connection of ideas and values may be seen in Picasso's massive painting *Guernica* (see p. 362). The painting superbly illustrates the agony of Guernica, the Spanish town bombed by Nazi planes in 1937. The agonized horse and the screaming man, the disembodied head and arms, the mother holding her dead infant—all convey the idea that war is the supreme, unspeakable crime against humanity. Picasso's condemnation of war and the man responsible for the slaughter at Guernica, Francisco Franco, is also clear. That Picasso wanted his values to be understood is confirmed by his instruction that the painting was not to be displayed in Spain until after Generalissimo Franco was dead.

THE PLACE OF IDEAS IN LITERATURE

Because writers of fiction are usually not systematic philosophers, it would be a mistake to go "message hunting" as though their stories contained nothing but ideas. Indeed, there is great benefit and pleasure to be derived from savoring a story, from being taken up in the developing pattern of conflict and interest, from following its implications and suggestions, and from listening to the sounds of its words—to name only a few of the reasons for which literature is treasured.

Nevertheless, ideas are vital to understanding and appreciation, for writers have ideas and want to communicate them. For example, in "The Horse Dealer's Daughter" Lawrence directs sympathy at the sudden emergence of love between two unlikely characters. This love is unusual, and the story is therefore effective, but the story is also provocative because it raises the idea that love pushes aside other decisions that people make. Gaines in "The Sky Is Gray" describes the extraordinary difficulty and pain experienced by a young child and his mother when trying to keep a dental appointment, but the story embodies *ideas* about the need for equality, the strength of human character, and the beauty of human kindness.

Distinguishing between Ideas and Actions

As you analyze stories for ideas, it is important to avoid the trap of confusing ideas and actions. Such a trap is contained in the following sentence about Updike's "A & P": "The major character, Sammy, quits his job to protest the way his boss mistreats the girls." This sentence successfully describes the story's major action, but it does not express an *idea* that connects characters and events, and for this reason it obstructs understanding. The necessary connections might be achieved with sentences like these: "'A & P' illustrates the idea that making a protest also makes life hard," or "'A & P' demonstrates that individual rights are more important than arbitrary regulations." A study based on these connecting formulations could be focused on ideas, and would not be sidetracked into doing no more than retelling Updike's story.

Distinguishing between Ideas and Situations

You should also distinguish between ideas and situations. For example, in Joyce's "Araby," the narrator describes his frustration and embarrassment at the "Araby" Bazaar in Dublin. This is a *situation,* but it is not the *idea* brought out by the situation. Joyce's idea here is rather that immature love causes unreal dreams and hopes that produce disappointment and self-reproach. If you are able to distinguish a story's various situations from the writer's major idea or ideas, as we have done here, you will be able to focus on ideas and therefore sharpen your own thinking.

HOW TO FIND IDEAS

Ideas are not as obvious as characters or setting. To determine an idea, you need to consider the meaning of what you read, and then develop explanatory and comprehensive assertions. Your assertions need not be the same as those that others might make. People notice different things, and individual formulations vary. In Joyce's "Araby," for example, an initial expression of some of the story's ideas might take any of the following forms: (1) The force of sexual attraction is strong and begins early in life. (2) The attraction leads some individuals to the idealization of the loved one. (3) Sexual feelings are private and may therefore cause embarrassment and shame. Although any one of these choices could be a basic idea for studying "Araby," they all have in common the narrator's idealization of his friend's sister. In discovering ideas, you should follow a similar process—making a number of formulations for an idea, and then selecting one for further development.

As you read, be alert to the different ways that authors use to convey ideas. One author might prefer an indirect way through a character's speeches, while another may prefer direct statement. In practice, authors may employ any or all the following methods.

Direct Statements by the Authorial Voice

Although writers of fiction mainly render action, dialogue, and situation, they sometimes state ideas to guide us and deepen our understanding. Authorial ideas are usually brief but are nevertheless crucial. In the second paragraph of "The Necklace," for example (p. 3), Maupassant's authorial voice presents the idea that women have only charm and beauty to get on in the world. Ironically, however, Maupassant uses the story to show that for the major character Mathilde, nothing is effective, for her charm cannot prevent disaster. Poe, in "The Masque of the Red Death," asserts a key idea that "there are matters of which no jest can be made" (p. 257, paragraph 9). This idea is expressed as authorial commentary just as the Red Death has invaded the party, and it demonstrates the futility of Prospero's attempts to overcome death.

Direct Statements by the First-Person Speaker

First-person narrators or speakers frequently express ideas along with their depiction of actions and situations. (See also Chapter 5) Because they are part of a dramatic presentation, the ideas may be right or wrong, well-considered or thoughtless, or brilliant or half-baked, depending on the speaker. The narrator of Atwood's "Rape Fantasies," for example (p. 301), is not noteworthy for her intelligence, yet she voices penetrating ideas about the relationships of men and women. In Zabytko's "Home Soil" (p. 405), the narrator considers the idea that war always causes regret and guilt, no matter when it is fought or who fights in it. A somewhat half-baked speaker, but yet an interesting one, is Sammy, the narrator of Updike's "A & P," who seems engulfed in intellectual commonplaces, particularly in his insinuation about the intelligence of women (paragraph 2). In his defense, however, Sammy *acts* upon the worthy idea that people generally have the right to dress any way they please.

Dramatic Statements Made by Characters

In many stories, characters express their own views, which may be right or wrong, admirable or contemptible. When you consider such dramatic speeches, you must do considerable interpreting and evaluating yourself. For example, Old Man Warner in "The Lottery" (p. 195) states that the lottery is valuable even though we learn from the narrator that the beliefs underlying it have long been forgotten. Because Warner is a zealous and noisy person, however, his words show that outdated ideas continue to do harm even when there is strong reason to throw them out and get new ones. The unnamed young man in the dentist's office in "The Sky Is Gray" speaks in contradictions, but when he amplifies them we learn a number of his ideas about the failure of America to live up to its professed principles of equality.

Figurative Language

Usually figurative language is considered an exclusive property of poetry, but it also abounds in fiction. In Joyce's "Araby," for example, the narrator uses a beautiful figure of speech to describe his youthful admiration for his friend's sister. He says that his body "was like a harp and her words and gestures were like fingers running upon the wires." Another notable figure occurs at the opening of Mansfield's "Miss Brill," when the narrator likens a sunny day to gold and white wine—a lovely comparison conveying the idea that the world is a place of beauty and happiness, but an idea which contrasts ironically with the indifference and cruelty that Miss Brill experiences.

Characters Who Stand for Ideas

Characters and their actions may often be equated with certain ideas and values. The power of Mathilde's story, for example, causes her to stand for the idea that unrealizable dreams may invade and damage the real world. Two diverse or opposed characters may embody contrasting ideas, as with Sammy and Lengel of Updike's "A & P," who stand for opposing views about rights of expression.

In effect, characters who stand for ideas may assume symbolic status, as in Hawthorne's "Young Goodman Brown," where the protagonist symbolizes the alienation accompanying zealousness, or in "The Shawl," where the small child Magda embodies the vulnerability and helplessness of human beings in the face of dehumanizing state brutality. Such characters may be equated directly with particular ideas, and to talk about them is a shorthand way of talking about the ideas.

The Story Itself as It Represents Ideas

One of the most important ways in which authors express ideas is to interlock them within all parts and aspects of the work. The art of painting is instructive here, for a painting may be taken in with a single view, which comprehends all the aspects of color, form, action, and expression that may also be considered separately. Thus, the broken and distorted figures in Picasso's *Guernica* (p. 362), which can be viewed together, all emphasize the idea that war creates horror and suffering for both human beings and beasts.

Comparably, when a story is considered in its totality, various the various ous parts collectively may embody a major idea. In "The Sky Is Gray," for example, Gaines makes objective the idea that the urgency of ending racial barriers overrides the historical reasons for their existence. Although he does not use these exact words, the story powerfully embodies this idea. The conclusion of "Blue Winds Dancing" drives the point home that human beings will not accept anything new when they truly believe that their own way of life is of equal or superior value. Most stories represent ideas in a similar way. Even "escape literature," which ostensibly enables readers to forget their immediate concerns, contains conflicts between good and evil, love and hate, good spies and bad, earthlings and aliens, and so on. Thereby, such stories *do* embody ideas, even though their avowed intention is not to make readers think but rather to help them forget.

 STORIES FOR STUDY

ERNEST J. GAINES (b. 1933)

> *A native of Louisiana, Gaines has spent much of his life in San Francisco. Since 1964, when he published* Catherine Carmier, *he has written a number of novels chronicling the lives of southern blacks, the best known of which is* The Autobiography of Miss Jane Pittman *(1971). His most recent novel is* A Lesson Before Dying, *which was published in 1993. "The Sky Is Gray" is selected from his 1968 collection of stories,* Bloodlines.

The Sky Is Gray ————————————————————————————— *1968*

1

Go'n be coming in a few minutes. Coming round that bend down there full speed. And I'm go'n get out my handkerchief and wave it down, and we go'n get on it and go.

I keep on looking for it, but Mama don't look that way no more. She's looking down the road where we just come from. It's a long old road, and far 's you can see you don't see nothing but gravel. You got dry weeds on both sides, and you got trees on both sides, and fences on both sides, too. And you got cows in the pastures and they standing close together. And when we was coming out here to catch the bus I seen the smoke coming out of the cows's noses.

I look at my mama and I know what she's thinking. I been with Mama so much, just me and her, I know what she's thinking all the time. Right now it's home—Auntie and them. She's thinking if they got enough wood—if she left enough there to keep them warm till we get back. She's thinking if it go'n rain and if any of them go'n have to go out in the rain. She's thinking 'bout the hog—if he go'n get out, and if Ty and Val be able to get him back in. She always worry like that when she leaves the house. She don't worry too much if she leave me there with the smaller ones, 'cause she know I'm go'n look after them and look after Auntie and everything else. I'm the oldest and she say I'm the man.

I look at my mama and I love my mama. She's wearing that black coat and that black hat and she's looking sad. I love my mama and I want put my arm round her and tell her. But I'm not supposed to do that. She say that's weakness and that's crybaby stuff, and she don't want no crybaby round her. She don't want you to be scared, either. 'Cause Ty's scared of ghosts and she's always whipping him. I'm scared of the dark, too, but I make 'tend I ain't. I make 'tend I ain't 'cause I'm the oldest, and I got to set a good sample for the rest. I can't ever be scared and I can't ever cry. And that's why I never said nothing 'bout my teeth. It's been hurting me and hurting me close to a month now, but I never said it. I didn't say it 'cause I didn't want act like a crybaby, and 'cause I know we didn't have enough money to go have it pulled. But, Lord, it been hurting me. And look like it wouldn't start till at night when you was trying to get yourself little sleep. Then soon 's you shut your eyes—ummm-ummm, Lord, look like it go right down to your heartstring.

"Hurting, hanh?" Ty'd say.

I'd shake my head, but I wouldn't open my mouth for nothing. You open your mouth and let that wind in, and it almost kill you.

I'd just lay there and listen to them snore. Ty there, right 'side me, and Auntie and Val over by the fireplace. Val younger than me and Ty, and he sleeps with Auntie. Mama sleeps round the other side with Louis and Walker.

I'd just lay there and listen to them, and listen to that wind out there, and listen to that fire in the fireplace. Sometimes it'd stop long enough to let me get little rest. Sometimes it just hurt, hurt, hurt. Lord, have mercy.

2

Auntie knowed it was hurting me. I didn't tell nobody but Ty, 'cause we buddies and he ain't go'n tell nobody. But some kind of way Auntie found out. When she asked me, I told her no, nothing was wrong. But she knowed it all the time. She told me to mash up a piece of aspirin and wrap it in some cotton and jugg it down in that hole. I did it, but it didn't do no good. It stopped for a little while, and started right back again. Auntie wanted to tell Mama, but I told her, "Uh-uh." 'Cause I knowed we didn't have any money, and it just was go'n make her mad again. So Auntie told Monsieur Bayonne, and Monsieur Bayonne came over to the house and told me to kneel down 'side him on the fireplace. He put his finger in his mouth and made the Sign of the Cross on my jaw. The tip of Monsieur Bayonne's finger is some hard, 'cause he's always playing on that guitar. If we sit outside at night we can always hear Monsieur Bayonne playing on his guitar. Sometimes we leave him out there playing on the guitar.

Monsieur Bayonne made the Sign of the Cross over and over on my jaw, but that didn't do no good. Even when he prayed and told me to pray some, too, that tooth still hurt me.

"How you feeling?" he say.

"Same," I say.

He kept on praying and making the Sign of the Cross and I kept on praying, too.

"Still hurting?" he say.

"Yes, sir."

Monsieur Bayonne mashed harder and harder on my jaw. He mashed so hard he almost pushed me over on Ty. But then he stopped.

"What kind of prayers you praying, boy?" he say.

"Baptist," I say.

"Well, I'll be—no wonder that tooth still killing him. I'm going one way and he pulling the other. Boy, don't you know any Catholic prayers?"

"I know 'Hail Mary,'" I say.   20

"Then you better start saying it."

"Yes, sir."

He started mashing on my jaw again, and I could hear him praying at the same time. And, sure enough, after while it stopped hurting me.

Me and Ty went outside where Monsieur Bayonne's two hounds was and we started playing with them. "Let's go hunting," Ty say. "All right," I say; and we went on back in the pasture. Soon the hounds got on a trail, and me and Ty followed them all 'cross the pasture and then back in the woods, too. And then they cornered this little old rabbit and killed him, and me and Ty made them get back, and we picked up the rabbit and started on back home. But my tooth had started hurting me again. It was hurting me plenty now, but I wouldn't tell Monsieur Bayonne. That night I did-n't sleep a bit, and first thing in the morning Auntie told me to go back and let Mon-sieur Bayonne pray over me some more. Monsieur Bayonne was in his kitchen mak-ing coffee when I got there. Soon 's he seen me he knowed what was wrong.

"All right, kneel down there 'side that stove," he say. "And this time make sure   25
you pray Catholic. I don't know nothing 'bout that Baptist, and I don't want know nothing 'bout him."

3

Last night Mama say, "Tomorrow we going to town."

"It ain't hurting me no more," I say. "I can eat anything on it."

"Tomorrow we going to town," she say.

And after she finished eating, she got up and went to bed. She always go to bed early now. 'Fore Daddy went in the Army,° she used to stay up late. All of us sitting out on the gallery or round the fire. But now, look like soon 's she finish eating she go to bed.

This morning when I woke up, her and Auntie was standing 'fore the fireplace.   30
She say: "Enough to get there and back. Dollar and a half to have it pulled. Twenty-five for me to go, twenty-five for him. Twenty-five for me to come back, twenty-five for him. Fifty cents left. Guess I get little piece of salt meat with that."

"Sure can use it," Auntie say. "White beans and no salt meat ain't white beans."

"I do the best I can," Mama say.

They was quiet after that, and I made 'tend I was still asleep.

"James, hit the floor," Auntie say.

I still made 'tend I was asleep. I didn't want them to know I was listening.   35

"All right," Auntie say, shaking me by the shoulder. "Come on. Today's the day."

I pushed the cover down to get out, and Ty grabbed it and pulled it back.

"You, too, Ty," Auntie say.

"I ain't getting no teef pulled," Ty say.

"Don't mean it ain't time to get up," Auntie say. "Hit it, Ty."   40

Ty got up grumbling.

Daddy went in the Army: The time of: story is about 1942, early in World War II, when mil-lions of men were being drafted into: armed services.

"James, you hurry up and get in your clothes and eat your food," Auntie say. "What time y'all coming back?" she say to Mama.

"That 'leven o'clock bus," Mama say. "Got to get back in that field this evening."

"Get a move on you, James," Auntie say.

I went in the kitchen and washed my face, then I ate my breakfast. I was having bread and syrup. The bread was warm and hard and tasted good. And I tried to make it last a long time.

Ty came back there grumbling and mad at me.

"Got to get up," he say. "I ain't having no teefes pulled. What I got to be getting up for?"

Ty poured some syrup in his pan and got a piece of bread. He didn't wash his hands, neither his face, and I could see that white stuff in his eyes.

"You the one getting your teef pulled," he say. "What I got to get up for. I bet if I was getting a teef pulled, you wouldn't be getting up. Shucks; syrup again. I'm getting tired of this old syrup. Syrup, syrup, syrup. I'm go'n take with the sugar diabetes. I want me some bacon sometime."

"Go out in the field and work and you can have your bacon," Auntie say. She stood in the middle door looking at Ty. "You better be glad you got syrup. Some people ain't got that—hard's time is."

"Shucks," Ty say. "How can I be strong."

"I don't know too much 'bout your strength," Auntie say; "but I know where you go'n be hot at, you keep that grumbling up. James, get a move on you; your mama waiting."

I ate my last piece of bread and went in the front room. Mama was standing 'fore the fireplace warming her hands. I put on my coat and my cap, and we left the house.

4

I look down there again, but it still ain't coming. I almost say, "It ain't coming yet," but I keep my mouth shut. 'Cause that's something else she don't like. She don't like for you to say something just for nothing. She can see it ain't coming. I can see it ain't coming, so why say it ain't coming. I don't say it, I turn and look at the river that's back of us. It's so cold the smoke's just raising up from the water. I see a bunch of pool-doos not too far out—just on the other side of the lilies. I'm wondering if you can eat pool-doos.° I ain't too sure, 'cause I ain't never ate none. But I done ate owls and blackbirds, and I done ate redbirds,° too. I didn't want kill the redbirds, but she made me kill them. They had two of them back there. One in my trap, one in Ty's trap. Me and Ty was go'n play with them and let them go, but she made me kill them 'cause we needed the food.

"I can't," I say. "I can't."

"Here," she say. "Take it."

"I can't," I say. "I can't. I can't kill him, Mama, please."

"Here," she say. "Take this fork, James."

---

pool-doos: Pool-doo is a local Louisiana pronunciation of: French *poule d'eau,* or "bird of water." It refers to a marsh hen, or bird of the rail family—most likely the American Coot.
redbirds: cardinals.

"Please, Mama, I can't kill him," I say.

I could tell she was go'n hit me. I jerked back, but I didn't jerk back soon   60
enough.

"Take it," she say.

I took it and reached in for him, but he kept on hopping to the back.

"I can't, Mama," I say. The water just kept on running down my face. "I can't,"
I say.

"Get him out of there," she say.

I reached in for him and he kept on hopping to the back. Then I reached in   65
farther, and he pecked me on the hand.

"I can't, Mama," I say.

She slapped me again.

I reached in again, but he kept on hopping out my way. Then he hopped to one
side and I reached there. The fork got him on the leg and I heard his leg pop. I pulled
my hand out 'cause I had hurt him.

"Give it here," she say, and jerked the fork out my hand.

She reached in and got the little bird right in the neck. I heard the fork go in   70
his neck, and I heard it go in the ground. She brought him out and helt him right in
front of me.

"That's one," she say. She shook him off and gived me the fork. "Get the other
one."

"I can't, Mama," I say, "I'll do anything, but don't make me do that."

She went to the corner of the fence and broke the biggest switch over there she
could find. I knelt 'side the trap, crying.

"Get him out of there," she say.

"I can't, Mama."   75

She started hitting me 'cross the back. I went down on the ground, crying.

"Get him," she say.

"Octavia?" Auntie say.

'Cause she had come out of the house and she was standing by the tree looking
at us.

"Get him out of there," Mama say.   80

"Octavia," Auntie say, "explain to him. Explain to him. Just don't beat him. Explain to him."

But she hit me and hit me and hit me.

I'm still young—I ain't no more than eight; but I know now; I know why I had
to do it. (They was so little, though. They was so little. I 'member how I picked the
feathers off them and cleaned them and helt them over the fire. Then we all ate them.
Ain't had but a little bitty piece each, but we all had a little bitty piece, and everybody
just looked at me 'cause they was so proud.) Suppose she had to go away? That's why
I had to do it. Suppose she had to go away like Daddy went away? Then who was go'n
look after us? They had to be somebody left to carry on. I didn't know it then, but I
know it now. Auntie and Monsieur Bayonne talked to me and made me see.

5

Time I see it I get out my handkerchief and start waving. It's still 'way down
there, but I keep waving anyhow. Then it come up and stop and me and Mama get

on. Mama tell me go sit in the back while she pay. I do like she say, and the people look at me. When I pass the little sign that say "White" and "Colored," I start looking for a seat. I just see one of them back there, but I don't take it, 'cause I want my mama to sit down herself. She comes in the back and sit down, and I lean on the seat. They got seats in the front, but I know I can't sit there, 'cause I have to sit back of the sign. Anyhow, I don't want sit there if my mama go'n sit back here.

They got a lady sitting 'side my mama and she looks at me and smiles little bit. I smile back, but I don't open my mouth, 'cause the wind'll get in and make that tooth ache. The lady take out a pack of gum and reach me a slice, but I shake my head. The lady just can't understand why a little boy'll turn down gum, and she reach me a slice again. This time I point to my jaw. The lady understands and smiles little bit, and I smile little bit, but I don't open my mouth, though.

They got a girl sitting 'cross from me. She got on a red overcoat and her hair's plaited in one big plait. First, I make 'tend I don't see her over there, but then I start looking at her little bit. She make 'tend she don't see me, either, but I catch her looking that way. She got a cold, and every now and then she h'ist that little handkerchief to her nose. She ought to blow it, but she don't. Must think she's too much a lady or something.

Every time she h'ist that little handkerchief, the lady 'side her say something in her ear. She shakes her head and lays her hands in her lap again. Then I catch her kind of looking where I'm at. I smile at her little bit. But think she'll smile back? Uh-uh. She just turn up her little old nose and turn her head. Well, I show her both of us can turn us head. I turn mine too and look out at the river.

The river is gray. The sky is gray. They have pool-doos on the water. The water is wavy, and the pool-doos go up and down. The bus go round a turn, and you got plenty trees hiding the river. Then the bus go round another turn, and I can see the river again.

I look toward the front where all the white people sitting. Then I look at that little old gal again. I don't look right at her, 'cause I don't want all them people to know I love her. I just look at her little bit, like I'm looking out that window over there. But she knows I'm looking that way, and she kind of look at me, too. The lady sitting 'side her catch her this time, and she leans over and says something in her ear.

"I don't love him nothing," that little old gal says out loud.

Everybody back there hear her mouth, and all of them look at us and laugh.

"I don't love you, either," I say. "So you don't have to turn up your nose, Miss."

"You the one looking," she say.

"I wasn't looking at you," I say. "I was looking out that window, there."

"Out that window, my foot," she say. "I seen you. Everytime I turned round you was looking at me."

"You must of been looking yourself if you seen me all them times," I say.

"Shucks," she say, "I got me all kind of boyfriends."

"I got girlfriends, too," I say.

"Well, I just don't want you getting your hopes up," she say.

I don't say no more to that little old gal 'cause I don't want have to bust her in the mouth. I lean on the seat where Mama sitting, and I don't even look that way no more. When we get to Bayonne, she jugg her little old tongue out at me. I make 'tend I'm go'n hit her, and she duck down 'side her mama. And all the people laugh at us again.

6

Me and Mama get off and start walking in town. Bayonne is a little bitty town. Baton Rouge is a hundred times bigger than Bayonne. I went to Baton Rouge once— me, Ty, Mama, and Daddy. But that was 'way back yonder, 'fore Daddy went in the Army. I wonder when we go'n see him again. I wonder when. Look like he ain't ever coming back home. . . . Even the pavement all cracked in Bayonne. Got grass shooting right out the sidewalk. Got weeds in the ditch, too; just like they got at home.

It's some cold in Bayonne. Look like it's colder than it is home. The wind blows in my face, and I feel that stuff running down my nose. I sniff. Mama says use that handkerchief. I blow my nose and put it back.

We pass a school and I see them white children playing in the yard. Big old red school, and them children just running and playing. Then we pass a café, and I see a bunch of people in there eating. I wish I was in there 'cause I'm cold. Mama tells me keep my eyes in front where they belong.

We pass stores that's got dummies, and we pass another café, and then we pass a shoe shop, and that bald-head man in there fixing on a shoe. I look at him and I butt into that white lady, and Mama jerks me in front and tells me stay there.

We come up to the courthouse, and I see the flag waving there. This flag ain't   105 like the one we got at school. This one here ain't got but a handful of stars.° One at school got a big pile of stars—one for every state. We pass it and we turn and there it is—the dentist office. Me and Mama go in, and they got people sitting everywhere you look. They even got a little boy in there younger than me.

Me and Mama sit on that bench, and a white lady come in there and ask me what my name is. Mama tells her and the white lady goes on back. Then I hear somebody hollering in there. Soon 's that little boy hear him hollering, he starts hollering, too. His mama pats him and pats him, trying to make him hush up, but he ain't thinking 'bout his mama.

The man that was hollering in there comes out holding his jaw. He is a big old man and he's wearing overalls and a jumper.

"Got it, hanh?" another man asks him.

The man shakes his head—don't want open his mouth.

"Man, I thought they was killing you in there," the other man says. "Hollering   110 like a pig under a gate."

The man don't say nothing. He just heads for the door, and the other man follows him.

"John Lee," the white lady says. "John Lee Williams."

The little boy juggs his head down in his mama's lap and holler more now. His mama tells him go with the nurse, but he ain't thinking 'bout his mama. His mama tells him again, but he don't even hear her. His mama picks him up and takes him in there, and even when the white lady shuts the door I can still hear little old John Lee.

"I often wonder why the Lord let a child like that suffer," a lady says to my mama. The lady's sitting right in front of us on another bench. She's got on a white dress and a black sweater. She must be a nurse or something herself, I reckon.

"Not us to question," a man says.   115

"Sometimes I don't know if we shouldn't," the lady says.

handful of stars: The Confederate flag contains thirteen stars. At the time of the story, the American flag had forty-eight.

"I know definitely we shouldn't," the man says. The man looks like a preacher. He's big and fat and he's got on a black suit. He's got a gold chain, too.

"Why?" the lady says.

"Why anything?" the preacher says.

"Yes," the lady says. "Why anything?"

"Not us to question," the preacher says.

The lady looks at the preacher a little while and looks at Mama again.

"And look like it's the poor who suffers the most," she says. "I don't understand it."

"Best not to even try," the preacher says. "He works in mysterious ways—wonders to perform."°

Right then little John Lee bust out hollering, and everybody turn they head to listen.

"He's not a good dentist," the lady says. "Dr. Robillard is much better. But more expensive. That's why most of the colored come here. The white people go to Dr. Robillard. Y'all from Bayonne?"

"Down the river," my mama says. And that's all she go'n say, 'cause she don't talk much. But the lady keeps on looking at her, and so she says, "Near Morgan."

"I see," the lady says.

7

"That's the trouble with the black people in this country today," somebody else says. This one here's sitting on the same side me and Mama's sitting, and he is kind of sitting in front of that preacher. He looks like a teacher or somebody that goes to college. He's got on a suit, and he's got a book that he's been reading. "We don't question is exactly our problem," he says. "We should question and question and question—question everything."

The preacher just looks at him a long time. He done put a toothpick or something in his mouth, and he just keeps on turning it and turning it. You can see he don't like that boy with that book.

"Maybe you can explain what you mean," he says.

"I said what I meant," the boy says. "Question everything. Every stripe, every star, every word spoken. Everything."

"It 'pears to me that this young lady and I was talking 'bout God, young man," the preacher says.

"Question Him, too," the boys says.

"Wait," the preacher says. "Wait now."

"You heard me right," the boy says. "His existence as well as everything else. Everything."

The preacher just looks across the room at the boy. You can see he's getting madder and madder. But mad or no mad, the boy ain't thinking 'bout him. He looks at that preacher just 's hard 's the preacher looks at him.

"Is this what they coming to?" the preacher says. "Is this what we educating them for?"

"You're not educating me," the boy says. "I wash dishes at night so that I can go to school in the day. So even the words you spoke need questioning."

He works . . . perform: an allusion to the well-known hymn "God moves in a mysterious way / His wonders to perform," by William Cowper (1731–1800).

The preacher just looks at him and shakes his head.   140

"When I come in this room and seen you there with your book, I said to myself, 'There's an intelligent man.' How wrong a person can be."

"Show me one reason to believe in the existence of a God," the boy says.

"My heart tells me," the preacher says.

"'My heart tells me,'" the boys says. "'My heart tells me.' Sure, 'My heart tells me.' And as long as you listen to what your heart tells you, you will have only what the white man gives you and nothing more. Me, I don't listen to my heart. The purpose of the heart is to pump blood throughout the body, and nothing else."

"Who's your paw, boy?" the preacher says.   145

"Why?"

"Who is he?"

"He's dead."

"And you mom?"

"She's in Charity Hospital with pneumonia. Half killed herself, working for   150 nothing."

"And 'cause he's dead and she's sick, you mad at the world?"

"I'm not mad at the world. I'm questioning the world. I'm questioning it with cold logic, sir. What do words like Freedom, Liberty, God, White, Colored mean? I want to know. That's why *you* are sending us to school, to read and to ask questions. And because we ask these questions, you call us mad. No sir, it is not us who are mad."

"You keep saying 'us'?"

"'Us.' Yes—us. I'm not alone."

The preacher just shakes his head. Then he looks at everybody in the room—   155 everybody. Some of the people look down at the floor, keep from looking at him. I kind of look 'way myself, but soon 's I know he done turn his head, I look that way again.

"I'm sorry for you," he says to the boy.

"Why?" the boy says. "Why not be sorry for yourself? Why are you so much better off than I am? Why aren't you sorry for these other people in here? Why not be sorry for the lady who had to drag her child into the dentist office? Why not be sorry for the lady sitting on that bench over there? Be sorry for them. Not for me. Some way or the other I'm going to make it."

"No, I'm sorry for you," the preacher says.

"Of course, of course," the boy says, nodding his head. "You're sorry for me because I rock that pillar you're leaning on."

"You can't ever rock the pillar I'm leaning on, young man. It's stronger than   160 anything man can ever do."

"You believe in God because a man told you to believe in God," the boy says. "A white man told you to believe in God. And why? To keep you ignorant so he can keep his feet on your neck."

"So now we the ignorant?" the preacher says.

"Yes," the boy says. "Yes." And he opens his book again.

The preacher just looks at him sitting there. The boy done forgot all about him. Everybody else make 'tend they done forgot the squabble, too.

Then I see that preacher getting up real slow. Preacher's a great big old man   165 and he got to brace himself to get up. He comes over where the boy is sitting.

He just stands there a little while looking down at him, but the boy don't raise his head.

"Get up, boy," preacher says.

The boy looks up at him, then he shuts his book real slow and stands up. Preacher just hauls back and hit him in the face. The boy falls back 'gainst the wall, but he straightens himself up and looks right back at that preacher.

"You forgot the other cheek," he says.°

The preacher hauls back and hit him again on the other side. But this time the boy braces himself and don't fall.

"That hasn't changed a thing," he says.

The preacher just looks at the boy. The preacher's breathing real hard like he just run up a big hill. The boy sits down and opens his book again.

"I feel sorry for you," the preacher says. "I never felt so sorry for a man before."

The boy makes 'tend he don't even hear that preacher. He keeps on reading his book. The preacher goes back and gets his hat off the chair.

"Excuse me," he says to us. "I'll come back some other time. Y'all, please excuse me."

And he looks at the boy and goes out the room. The boy h'ist his hand up to his mouth one time to wipe 'way some blood. All the rest of the time he keeps on reading. And nobody else in there say a word.

8

Little John Lee and his mama come out the dentist office, and the nurse calls somebody else in. Then little bit later they come out, and the nurse calls another name. But fast 's she calls somebody in there, somebody else comes in the place where we sitting, and the room stays full.

The people coming in now, all of them wearing big coats. One of them says something 'bout sleeting, another one says he hope not. Another one says he think it ain't nothing but rain. 'Cause, he says, rain can get awful cold this time of year.

All round the room they talking. Some of them talking to people right by them, some of them talking to people clear 'cross the room, some of them talking to anybody'll listen. It's a little bitty room, no bigger than us kitchen, and I can see everybody in there. The little old room's full of smoke, 'cause you got two old men smoking pipes over by that side door. I think I feel my tooth thumping me some, and I hold my breath and wait. I wait and wait, but it don't thump me no more. Thank God for that.

I feel like going to sleep, and I lean back 'gainst the wall. But I'm scared to go to sleep. Scared 'cause the nurse might call my name and I won't hear her. And Mama might go to sleep, too, and she'll be mad if neither one of us heard the nurse.

I look up at Mama. I love my mama. I love my mama. And when cotton come I'm go'n get her a new coat. And I ain't go'n get a black one, either. I think I'm go'n get her a red one.

"They got some books over there," I say. "Want read one of them?"

Mama looks at the books, but she don't answer me.

"You got yourself a little man there," the lady says.

Mama don't say nothing to the lady, but she must've smiled, 'cause I seen the lady smiling back. The lady looks at me a little while, like she's feeling sorry for me.

"You sure got that preacher out here in a hurry," she says to that boy.

other cheek: Matthew 5:39.

The boy looks up at her and looks in his book again. When I grow up I want be just like him. I want clothes like that and I want keep a book with me, too.

"You really don't believe in God?" the lady says.

"No," he says.

"But why?" the lady says.

"Because the wind is pink," he says.   190

"What?" the lady says.

The boy don't answer her no more. He just reads in his book.

"Talking 'bout the wind is pink," that old lady says. She's sitting on the same bench with the boy and she's trying to look in his face. The boy makes 'tend the old lady ain't even there. He just keeps on reading. "Wind is pink," she says again. "Eh, Lord, what children go'n be saying next?"

The lady 'cross from us bust out laughing.

"That's a good one," she says. "The wind is pink. Yes sir, that's a good one."   195

"Don't you believe the wind is pink?" the boy says. He keeps his head down in the book.

"Course I believe it, honey," the lady says. "Course I do." She looks at us and winks her eye. "And what color is grass, honey?"

"Grass? Grass is black."

She bust out laughing again. The boy looks at her.

"Don't you believe grass is black?" he says.   200

The lady quits her laughing and looks at him. Everybody else looking at him, too. The place quiet, quiet.

"Grass is green, honey," the lady says. "It was green yesterday, it's green today, and it's go'n be green tomorrow."

"How do you know it's green?"

"I know because I know."

"You don't know it's green," the boy says. "You believe it's green because some-   205
one told you it was green. If someone had told you it was black you'd believe it was black."

"It's green," the lady says. "I know green when I see green."

"Prove it's green," the boy says.

"Sure, now," the lady says. "Don't tell me it's coming to that."

"It's coming to just that," the boy says. "Words mean nothing. One means no more than the other."

"That's what it all coming to?" that old lady says. That old lady got on a turban   210
and she got on two sweaters. She got a green sweater under a black sweater. I can see the green sweater 'cause some of the buttons on the other sweater's missing.

"Yes, ma'am," the boy says. "Words mean nothing. Action is the only thing. Doing. That's the only thing."

"Other words, you want the Lord to come down here and show Hisself to you?" she says.

"Exactly, ma'am," he says.

"You don't mean that, I'm sure?" she says.

"I do, ma'am," he says.   215

"Done, Jesus," the old lady says, shaking her head.

"I didn't go 'long with that preacher at first," the other lady says; "but now—I don't know. When a person say the grass is black, he's either a lunatic or something's wrong."

"Prove to me that it's green," the boy says.

"It's green because the people say it's green."

"Those same people say we're citizens of these United States," the boy says.

"I think I'm a citizen," the lady says.

"Citizens have certain rights," the boy says. "Name me one right that you have. One right, granted by the Constitution, that you can exercise in Bayonne."

The lady don't answer him. She just looks at him like she don't know what he's talking 'bout. I know I don't.

"Things changing," she says.

"Things are changing because some black men have begun to think with their brains and not their hearts," the boy says.

"You trying to say these people don't believe in God?"

"I'm sure some of them do. Maybe most of them do. But they don't believe that God is going to touch these white people's hearts and change things tomorrow. Things change through action. By no other way."

Everybody sit quiet and look at the boy. Nobody says a thing. Then the lady 'cross the room from me and Mama just shakes her head.

"Let's hope that not all your generation feel the same way you do," she says.

"Think what you please, it doesn't matter," the boy says. "But it will be men who listen to their heads and not their hearts who will see that your children have a better chance than you had."

"Let's hope they ain't all like you, though," the old lady says. "Done forgot the heart absolutely."

"Yes ma'am, I hope they aren't all like me," the boy says. "Unfortunately, I was born too late to believe in your God. Let's hope that the ones who come after will have your faith—if not in your God, then in something else, something definitely that they can lean on. I haven't anything. For me, the wind is pink, the grass is black."

9

The nurse comes in the room where we all sitting and waiting and says the doctor won't take no more patients till one o'clock this evening.° My mama jumps up off the bench and goes up to the white lady.

"Nurse, I have to go back in the field this evening," she says.

"The doctor is treating his last patient now," the nurse says. "One o'clock this evening."

"Can I at least speak to the doctor?" my mama asks.

"I'm his nurse," the lady says.

"My little boy's sick," my mama says. "Right now his tooth almost killing him."

The nurse looks at me. She's trying to make up her mind if to let me come in. I look at her real pitiful. The tooth ain't hurting me at all, but Mama say it is, so I make 'tend for her sake.

"This evening," the nurse says, and goes on back in the office.

"Don't feel 'jected, honey," the lady says to Mama. "I been round them a long time—they take you when they want to. If you was white, that's something else; but we the wrong color."

Mama don't say nothing to the lady, and me and her go outside and stand 'gainst the wall. It's cold out there. I can feel that wind going through my coat. Some

---

evening: local dialect for *afternoon.*

of the other people come out of the room and go up the street. Me and Mama stand there a little while and we start walking. I don't know where we going. When we come to the other street we just stand there.

"You don't have to make water, do you?" Mama says.

"No, ma'am," I say.

We go on up the street. Walking real slow. I can tell Mama don't know where 245 she's going. When we come to a store we stand there and look at the dummies. I look at a little boy wearing a brown overcoat. He's got on brown shoes, too. I look at my old shoes and look at his'n again. You wait till summer, I say.

Me and Mama walk away. We come up to another store and we stop and look at them dummies, too. Then we go on again. We pass a café where the white people in there eating. Mama tells me keep my eyes in front where they belong, but I can't help from seeing them people eat. My stomach starts to growling 'cause I'm hungry. When I see people eating, I get hungry; when I see a coat, I get cold.

A man whistles at my mama when we go by a filling station. She makes 'tend she don't even see him. I look back and I feel like hitting him in the mouth. If I was bigger, I say; if I was bigger, you'd see.

We keep on going. I'm getting colder and colder, but I don't say nothing. I feel that stuff running down my nose and I sniff.

"That rag," Mama says.

I get it out and wipe my nose. I'm getting cold all over now—my face, my hands, 250 my feet, everything. We pass another little café, but this'n for white people, too, and we can't go in there, either. So we just walk. I'm so cold now I'm 'bout ready to say it. If I knowed where we was going I wouldn't be so cold, but I don't know where we going. We go, we go, we go. We walk clean out of Bayonne. Then we cross the street and we come back. Same thing I seen when I got off the bus this morning. Same old trees, same old walk, same old weeds, same old cracked pave—same old everything.

I sniff again.

"That rag," Mama says.

I wipe my nose real fast and jugg that handkerchief back in my pocket 'fore my hand gets too cold. I raise my head and I can see David's hardware store. When we come up to it, we go in. I don't know why, but I'm glad.

It's warm in there. It's so warm in there you don't ever want to leave. I look for the heater, and I see it over by them barrels. Three white men standing round the heater talking in Creole.° One of them comes over to see what my mama want.

"Got any axe handles?" she says. 255

Me, Mama and the white man start to the back, but Mama stops me when we come up to the heater. She and the white man go on. I hold my hands over the heater and look at them. They go all the way to the back, and I see the white man pointing to the axe handles 'gainst the wall. Mama takes one of them and shakes it like she's trying to figure how much it weighs. Then she rubs her hand over it from one end to the other end. She turns it over and looks at the other side, then she shakes it again, and shakes her head and puts it back. She gets another one and she does it just like she did the first one, then she shakes her head. Then she gets a brown one and do it that, too. But she don't like this one, either. Then she gets another one, but 'fore she shakes it or anything, she looks at me. Look like she's trying to say something to me, but I don't know what it is. All I know is I done got warm now and I'm feeling right smart better. Mama shakes this axe handle just like she did the others, and shakes her

---

Creole: the French Cajun dialect in Louisiana.

head and says something to the white man. The white man just looks at his pile of axe handles, and when Mama pass him to come to the front, the white man just scratch his head and follows her. She tells me come on and we go on out and start walking again.

We walk and walk, and no time at all I'm cold again. Look like I'm colder now 'cause I can still remember how good it was back there. My stomach growls and I suck it in to keep Mama from hearing it. She's walking right 'side me, and it growls so loud you can hear it a mile. But Mama don't say a word.

10

When we come up to the courthouse, I look at the clock. It's got quarter to twelve. Mean we got another hour and a quarter to be out here in the cold. We go and stand 'side a building. Something hits my cap and I look up at the sky. Sleet's falling.

I look at Mama standing there. I want stand close 'side her, but she don't like that. She say that's crybaby stuff. She say you got to stand for yourself, by yourself.

"Let's go back to that office," she says.

We cross the street. When we get to the dentist office I try to open the door, but I can't. I twist and twist, but I can't. Mama pushes me to the side and she twist the knob, but she can't open the door, either. She turns 'way from the door. I look at her, but I don't move and I don't say nothing. I done seen her like this before and I'm scared of her.

"You hungry?" she says. She says it like she's mad at me, like I'm the cause of everything.

"No, ma'am," I say.

"You want eat and walk back, or you rather don't eat and ride?"

"I ain't hungry," I say.

I ain't just hungry, but I'm cold, too. I'm so hungry and cold I want to cry. And look like I'm getting colder and colder. My feet done got numb. I try to work my toes, but I don't even feel them. Look like I'm go'n die. Look like I'm go'n stand right here and freeze to death. I think 'bout home. I think 'bout Val and Auntie and Ty and Louis and Walker. It's 'bout twelve o'clock and I know they eating dinner now. I can hear Ty making jokes. He done forgot 'bout getting up early this morning and right now he's probably making jokes. Always trying to make somebody laugh. I wish I was right there listening to him. Give anything in the world if I was home round the fire.

"Come on," Mama says.

We start walking again. My feet so numb I can't hardly feel them. We turn the corner and go on back up the street. The clock on the courthouse starts hitting for twelve.

The sleet's coming down plenty now. They hit the pave and bounce like rice. Oh, Lord; oh, Lord, I pray. Don't let me die, don't let me die, don't let me die, Lord.

11

Now I know where we going. We going back of town where the colored people eat. I don't care if I don't eat. I been hungry before. I can stand it. But I can't stand the cold.

I can see we go'n have a long walk. It's 'bout a mile down there. But I don't mind. I know when I get there I'm go'n warm myself. I think I can hold out. My hands numb in my pockets and my feet numb, too, but if I keep moving I can hold out. Just don't stop no more, that's all.

The sky's gray. The sleet keeps on falling. Falling like rain now—plenty, plenty. You can hear it hitting the pave. You can see it bouncing. Sometimes it bounces two times 'fore it settles.

We keep on going. We don't say nothing. We just keep on going, keep on going.

I wonder what Mama's thinking. I hope she ain't mad at me. When summer come I'm go'n pick plenty cotton and get her a coat. I'm go'n get her a red one.

I hope they'd make it summer all the time. I'd be glad if it was summer all the time—but it ain't. We got to have winter, too. Lord, I hate the winter. I guess everybody hate the winter.   275

I don't sniff this time. I get out my handkerchief and wipe my nose. My hand's so cold I can hardly hold the handkerchief.

I think we getting close, but we ain't there yet. I wonder where everybody is. Can't see a soul but us. Look like we the only two people moving round today. Must be too cold for the rest of the people to move round in.

I can hear my teeth. I hope they don't knock together too hard and make that bad one hurt. Lord, that's all I need, for that bad one to start off.

I hear a church bell somewhere. But today ain't Sunday. They must be ringing for a funeral or something.

I wonder what they doing at home. They must be eating. Monsieur Bayonne   280
might be there with his guitar. One day Ty played with Monsieur Bayonne's guitar and broke one of the strings. Monsieur Bayonne was some mad with Ty. He say Ty wasn't go'n ever 'mount to nothing. Ty can go just like Monsieur Bayonne when he ain't there. Ty can make everybody laugh when he starts to mocking Monsieur Bayonne.

I used to like to be with Mama and Daddy. We used to be happy. But they took him in the Army. Now, nobody happy no more.... I be glad when Daddy comes home.

Monsieur Bayonne say it wasn't fair for them to take Daddy and give Mama nothing and give us nothing. Auntie say, "Shhh, Etienne. Don't let them hear you talk like that." Monsieur Bayonne say, "It's God truth. What they giving his children? They have to walk three and a half miles to school hot or cold. That's anything to give for a paw? She's got to work in the field rain or shine just to make ends meet. That's anything to give for a husband?" Auntie say, "Shhh, Etienne, shhh." "Yes, you right," Monsieur Bayonne say. "Best don't say it in front of them now. But one day they go'n find out. One day." "Yes, I suppose so," Auntie say. "Then what, Rose Mary?" Monsieur Bayonne say. "I don't know, Etienne," Auntie say. "All we can do is us job, and leave everything else in His hand . . ."

We getting closer, now. We getting closer. I can even see the railroad tracks.

We cross the tracks, and now I see the café. Just to get in there, I say. Just to get in there. Already I'm starting to feel little better.

12

We go in. Ahh, it's good. I look for the heater; there 'gainst the wall. One of   285
them little brown ones. I just stand there and hold my hands over it. I can't open my hands too wide 'cause they almost froze.

Mama's standing right 'side me. She done unbuttoned her coat. Smoke rises out of the coat, and the coat smells like a wet dog.

I move to the side so Mama can have more room. She opens out her hands and rubs them together. I rub mine together, too, 'cause this keeps them from hurting. If you let them warm too fast, they hurt you sure. But if you let them warm just little bit at a time, and you keep rubbing them, they be all right every time.

They got just two more people in the café. A lady back of the counter, and a man on this side the counter. They been watching us even since we come in.

Mama gets out the handkerchief and count up the money. Both of us know how much money she's got there. Three dollars. No, she ain't got three dollars, 'cause she had to pay us way up here. She ain't got but two dollars and a half left. Dollar and a half to get my tooth pulled, and fifty cents for us to go back on, and fifty cents worth of salt meat.

She stirs the money round with her finger. Most of the money is change 'cause   2c
I can hear it rubbing together. She stirs it and stirs it. Then she looks at the door. It's still sleeting. I can hear it hitting 'gainst the wall like rice.

"I ain't hungry, Mama," I say.

"Got to pay them something for they heat," she says.

She takes a quarter out the handkerchief and ties the handkerchief up again. She looks over her shoulder at the people, but she still don't move. I hope she don't spend the money. I don't want her spending it on me. I'm hungry, I'm almost starving I'm so hungry, but I don't want her spending the money on me.

She flips the quarter over like she's thinking. She's must be thinking 'bout us walking back home. Lord, I sure don't want walk home. If I thought it'd do any good to say something, I'd say it. But Mama makes up her own mind 'bout things.

She turns 'way from the heater right fast, like she better hurry up and spend the   2?
quarter 'fore she change her mind. I watch her go toward the counter. The man and the lady look at her, too. She tells the lady something and the lady walks away. The man keeps on looking at her. Her back's turned to the man, and she don't even know he's standing there.

The lady puts some cakes and a glass of milk on the counter. Then she pours a cup of coffee and sets it 'side the other stuff. Mama pays her for the things and comes on back where I'm standing. She tells me sit down at the table 'gainst the wall.

The milk and the cake's for me; the coffee's for Mama. I eat slow and I look at her. She's looking outside at the sleet. She's looking real sad. I say to myself, I'm go'n make all this up one day. You see, one day, I'm go'n make all this up. I want say it now; I want tell her how I feel right now; but Mama don't like for us to talk like that.

"I can't eat all this," I say.

They ain't got but just three little old cakes there. I'm so hungry right now, the Lord knows I can eat a hundred times three, but I want my mama to have one.

Mama don't even look my way. She knows I'm hungry, she knows I want it. I let   3
it stay there a little while, then I get it and eat it. I eat just on my front teeth, though, 'cause if cake touch that back tooth I know what'll happen. Thank God it ain't hurt me at all today.

After I finish eating I see the man go to the juke box. He drops a nickel in it, then he just stand there a little while looking at the record. Mama tells me keep my eyes in front where they belong. I turn my head like she say, but then I hear the man coming toward us.

"Dance, pretty?" he says.

Mama gets up to dance with him. But 'fore you know it, she done grabbed the little man in the collar and done heaved him 'side the wall. He hit the wall so hard he stop the juke box from playing.

"Some pimp," the lady back of the counter says. "Some pimp."

The little man jumps up off the floor and starts toward my mama. 'Fore you know it, Mama done sprung open her knife and she's waiting for him.   305

"Come on," she says. "Come on. I'll gut you from your neighbo° to your throat. Come on."

I go up to the little man to hit him, but Mama makes me come and stand 'side her. The little man looks at me and Mama and goes on back to the counter.

"Some pimp," the lady back of the counter says. "Some pimp." She starts laughing and pointing at the little man. "Yes sir, you a pimp, all right. Yes sirree."

13

"Fasten that coat, let's go," Mama says.

"You don't have to leave," the lady says.   310

Mama don't answer the lady, and we right out in the cold again. I'm warm right now—my hands, my ears, my feet—but I know this ain't go'n last too long. It done sleet so much now you got ice everywhere you look.

We cross the railroad tracks, and soon's we do, I get cold. That wind goes through this little old coat like it ain't even there. I got on a shirt and a sweater under the coat, but that wind don't pay them no mind. I look up and I can see we got a long way to go. I wonder if we go'n make it 'fore I get too cold.

We cross over to walk on the sidewalk. They got just one sidewalk back here, and it's over there.

After we go just a little piece, I smell bread cooking. I look, then I see a baker shop. When we get closer, I can smell it more better. I shut my eyes and make 'tend I'm eating. But I keep them shut too long and I butt up 'gainst a telephone post. Mama grabs me and see if I'm hurt. I ain't bleeding or nothing and she turns me loose.

I can feel I'm getting colder and colder, and I look up to see how far we still   315
got to go. Uptown is 'way up yonder. A half mile more, I reckon. I try to think of something. They say think and you won't get cold. I think of that poem, "Annabel Lee."° I ain't been to school in so long—this bad weather—I reckon they done passed "Annabel Lee" by now. But passed it or not, I'm sure Miss Walker go'n make me recite it when I get there. That woman don't never forget nothing. I ain't never seen nobody like that in my life.

I'm still getting cold. "Annabel Lee" or no "Annabel Lee," I'm still getting cold. But I can see we getting closer. We getting there gradually.

Soon 's we turn the corner, I see a little old white lady up in front of us. She's the only lady on the street. She's all in black and she's got a long black rag over her head.

"Stop," she says.

Me and Mama stop and look at her. She must be crazy to be out in all this bad weather. Ain't got but a few other people out there, and all of them's men.

"Y'all done ate?" she says.   320

neighbo: navel.
"Annabel Lee": poem (1849) by Edgar Allan Poe (1809–1849).

"Just finish," Mama says.

"Y'all must be cold then?" she says.

"We headed for the dentist," Mama says. "We'll warm up when we get there."

"What dentist?" the old lady says. "Mr. Bassett?"

"Yes, ma'am," Mama says.

"Come on in," the old lady says. "I'll telephone him and tell him y'all coming."

Me and Mama follow the old lady in the store. It's a little bitty store, and it don't have much in there. The old lady takes off her head rag and folds it up.

"Helena?" somebody calls from the back.

"Yes, Alnest?" the old lady says.

"Did you see them?"

"They're here. Standing beside me."

"Good. Now you can stay inside."

The old lady looks at Mama. Mama's waiting to hear what she brought us in here for. I'm waiting for that, too.

"I saw y'all each time you went by," she says. "I came out to catch you, but you were gone."

"We went back of town," Mama says.

"Did you eat?"

"Yes, ma'am."

The old lady looks at Mama a long time, like she's thinking Mama might be just saying that. Mama looks right back at her. The old lady looks at me to see what I have to say. I don't say nothing. I sure ain't going 'gainst my mama.

"There's food in the kitchen," she says to Mama. "I've been keeping it warm."

Mama turns right around and starts for the door.

"Just a minute," the old lady says. Mama stops. "The boy'll have to work for it. It isn't free."

"We don't take no handout," Mama says.

"I'm not handing out anything," the old lady says. "I need my garbage moved to the front. Ernest has a bad cold and can't go out there."

"James'll move it for you," Mama says.

"Not unless you eat," the old lady says. "I'm old, but I have my pride, too, you know."

Mama can see that she ain't go'n beat this old lady down, so she just shakes her head.

"All right," the old lady says. "Come into the kitchen."

She leads the way with that rag in her hand. The kitchen is a little bitty little old thing, too. The table and the stove just 'bout fill it up. They got a little room to the side. Somebody in there laying 'cross the bed—'cause I can see one of his feet. Must be the person she was talking to: Ernest or Alnest—something like that.

"Sit down," the old lady says to Mama. "Not you," she says to me. "You have to move the cans."

"Helena?" the man says in the other room.

"Yes, Alnest?" the old lady says.

"Are you going out there again?"

"I must show the boy where the garbage is, Alnest," the old lady says.

"Keep that shawl over your head," the old man says.

"You don't have to remind me, Alnest. Come, boy," the old lady says.

We go out in the yard. Little old back yard ain't no bigger than the store or the kitchen. But it can sleet here just like it can sleet in any big back yard. And 'fore you know it, I'm trembling.

"There," the old lady says, pointing to the cans. I pick up one of the cans and set it right back down. The can's so light, I'm go'n see what's inside of it.

"Here," the old lady says. "Leave that can alone."

I look back at her standing there in the door. She's got that black rag wrapped round her shoulders, and she's pointing one of her little old fingers at me.

"Pick it up and carry it to the front," she says. I go by her with the can, and she's   360
looking at me all the time. I'm sure the can's empty. I'm sure she could've carried it herself—maybe both of them at the same time. "Set it on the sidewalk by the door and come back for the other one," she says.

I go and come back, and Mama looks at me when I pass her. I get the other can and take it to the front. It don't feel a bit heavier than that first one. I tell myself I ain't go'n be nobody's fool, and I'm go'n look inside this can to see just what I been hauling. First, I look up the street, then down the street. Nobody coming. Then I look over my shoulder toward the door. That little old lady done slipped up there quiet 's mouse, watching me again. Look like she knowed what I was go'n do.

"Ehh, Lord," she says. "Children, children. Come in here, boy, and go wash your hands."

I follow her in the kitchen. She points toward the bathroom, and I go in there and wash up. Little bitty old bathroom, but it's clean, clean. I don't use any of her towels; I wipe my hands on my pants legs.

When I come back in the kitchen, the old lady done dished up the food. Rice, gravy, meat—and she even got some lettuce and tomato in a saucer. She even got a glass of milk and a piece of cake there, too. It looks so good, I almost start eating 'fore I say my blessing.

"Helena?" the old man says.   365

"Yes, Alnest?"

"Are they eating?"

"Yes," she says.

"Good," he says. "Now you'll stay inside."

The old lady goes in there where he is and I can hear them talking. I look at   370
Mama. She's eating slow like she's thinking. I wonder what's the matter now. I reckon she's thinking 'bout home.

The old lady comes back in the kitchen.

"I talked to Dr. Bassett's nurse," she says. "Dr. Bassett will take you as soon as you get there."

"Thank you, ma'am," Mama says.

"Perfectly all right," the old lady says. "Which one is it?"

Mama nods toward me. The old lady looks at me real sad. I look sad, too.   375

"You're not afraid, are you?" she says.

"No, ma'am," I say.

"That's a good boy," the old lady says. "Nothing to be afraid of. Dr. Bassett will not hurt you."

When me and Mama get through eating, we thank the old lady again.

"Helena, are they leaving?" the old man says.   380

"Yes, Alnest."

"Tell them I say good-bye."

"They can hear you, Alnest."

"Good-bye both mother and son," the old man says. "And may God be with you."

Me and Mama tell the old man good-bye, and we follow the old lady in the front room. Mama opens the door to go out, but she stops and comes back in the store.

"You sell salt meat?" she says.

"Yes."

"Give me two bits worth."

"That isn't very much salt meat," the old lady says.

"That's all I have," Mama says.

The old lady goes back of the counter and cuts a big piece off the chunk. Then she wraps it up and puts it in a paper bag.

"Two bits," she says.

"That looks like awful lot of meat for a quarter," Mama says.

"Two bits," the old lady says. "I've been selling salt meat behind this counter twenty-five years. I think I know what I'm doing."

"You got a scale there," Mama says.

"What?" the old lady says.

"Weigh it," Mama says.

"What?" the old lady says. "Are you telling me how to run my business?"

"Thanks very much for the food," Mama says.

"Just a minute," the old lady says.

"James," Mama says to me. I move toward the door.

"Just one minute, I said," the old lady says.

Me and Mama stop again and look at her. The old lady takes the meat out of the bag and unwraps it and cuts 'bout half of it off. Then she wraps it up again and juggs it back in the bag and gives the bag to Mama. Mama lays the quarter on the counter.

"Your kindness will never be forgotten," she says. "James," she says to me.

We go out, and the old lady comes to the door to look at us. After we go a little piece I look back, and she's still there watching us.

The sleet's coming down heavy, heavy now, and I turn up my coat collar to keep my neck warm. My mama tells me turn it right back down.

"You not a bum," she says. "You a man."

QUESTIONS

1. What does Gaines establish by using the eight-year-old boy, James, as the narrator who tells the story in the present tense and in his own dialect?

2. Why does James describe the family's need to kill and eat the small birds?

3. What is the major action in the story? What is the result of James and his mother Octavia taking the trip to the dentist? What is gained by the delays, which require the boy and his mother to wait in the office and then to walk out into the cold and sleet?

4. What is the significance of the discussions of suffering occasioned by the protesting child in the dentist's office? What ideas does the young man present (section 7)? When the minister hits him and reproaches him, what is demonstrated about the old and new ideas professed by African-Americans?

5. What values are represented by the elderly couple in the store? Why doesn't the

woman phone Dr. Robillard, the "better" but "more expensive" dentist? Why doesn't Octavia accept the portion of salt meat the woman first offers her? What causes the woman to cut the salt meat in half?

JAMES JOYCE (1882–1941)

Joyce, one of the greatest twentieth-century Irish writers, was born in Ireland and received a vigorous and thorough education there. He left Ireland in 1902, and spent most of the rest of his life in Switzerland and France. His best known works are Dubliners *(1914),* A Portrait of the Artist as a Young Man *(1914–1915),* Ulysses *(1922), and* Finnegans Wake *(1939). Much of his work has been called "fictionalized autobiography," a quality shown in "Araby," which is selected from* Dublin-ers. *As a young child, Joyce had lived on North Richmond Street, just like the narrator of the story. The bazaar which the narrator attends actually did take place in Dublin, from May 14 to 19, 1894, when Joyce was the same age as the narrator. It was called "Araby in Dublin," and was advertised as a "Grand Oriental Fete."*

Araby ————————————————————————1914

North Richmond Street,° being blind,° was a quiet street except at the hour when the Christian Brothers' School set the boys free. An uninhabited house of two storeys stood at the blind end, detached from its neighbours in a square ground. The other houses of the street, conscious of decent lives within them, gazed at one another with brown imperturbable faces.

The former tenant of our house, a priest, had died in the back drawing room. Air, musty from having long been enclosed, hung in all the rooms, and the waste room behind the kitchen was littered with old useless papers. Among these I found a few paper-covered books, the pages of which were curled and damp: *The Abbott,* by Walter Scott, *The Devout Communicant*° and *The Memoirs of Vidocq.°* I liked the last best because its leaves were yellow. The wild garden behind the house contained a central apple-tree and a few straggling bushes under one of which I found the late tenant's rusty bicycle-pump. He had been a very charitable priest; in his will he had left all his money to institutions and the furniture of his house to his sister.

When the short days of winter came dusk fell before we had well eaten our dinners. When we met in the street the houses had grown sombre. The space of sky above us was the colour of ever-changing violet and towards it the lamps of the street lifted their feeble lanterns. The cold air stung us and we played till our bodies glowed. Our shouts echoed in the silent street. The career of our play brought us through the dark

North Richmond Street: Name of a real street in Dublin on which Joyce lived as a boy.
blind: dead-end street.
The Devout Communicant: a book of meditations by Pacificus Baker, published 1873.
The Memoirs of Vidocq: published 1829, the story of François Vidocq, a Parisian chief of detectives.

muddy lanes behind the houses where we ran the gauntlet of the rough tribes from the cottages, to the back doors of the dark dripping gardens where odours arose from the ashpits, to the dark odorous stables where a coachman smoothed and combed the horse or shook music from the buckled harness. When we returned to the street light from the kitchen windows had filled the areas. If my uncle was seen turning the corner we hid in the shadow until we had seen him safely housed. Or if Mangan's sister came out on the doorstep to call her brother in to his tea we watched her from our shadow peer up and down the street. We waited to see whether she would remain or go in and, if she remained, we left our shadow and walked up to Mangan's steps resignedly. She was waiting for us, her figure defined by the light from the half-opened door. Her brother always teased her before he obeyed and I stood by the railings looking at her. Her dress swung as she moved her body and the soft rope of her hair tossed from side to side.

Every morning I lay on the floor in the front parlor watching her door. The blind was pulled down within an inch of the sash so that I could not be seen. When she came out on the doorstep my heart leaped. I ran to the hall, seized my books and followed her. I kept her brown figure always in my eye and, when we came near the point at which our ways diverged, I quickened my pace and passed her. This happened morning after morning. I had never spoken to her, except for a few casual words, and yet her name was like a summons to all my foolish blood.

Her image accompanied me even in places the most hostile to romance. On Saturday evenings when my aunt went marketing I had to go to carry some of the parcels. We walked through the flaring street, jostled by drunken men and bargaining women, amid the curses of labourers, the shrill litanies of shop-boys who stood on guard by the barrels of pigs' cheeks, the nasal chanting of street singers, who sang a *come-all-you* about O'Donovan Rossa,° or a ballad about the troubles in our native land. These noises converged in a single sensation of life for me: I imagined that I bore my chalice safely through the throng of foes. Her name sprang to my lips at moments in strange prayers and praises which I myself did not understand. My eyes were often full of tears (I could not tell why) and at times a flood from my heart seemed to pour itself out into my bosom. I thought little of the future. I did not know whether I would ever speak to her or not or, if I spoke to her, how I could tell her of my confused adoration. But my body was like a harp and her words and gestures were like fingers running upon the wires.

One evening I went into the back drawing-room in which the priest had died. It was a dark rainy evening and there was no sound in the house. Through one of the broken panes I heard the rain impinge upon the earth, the fine incessant needles of water playing in the sodden beds. Some distant lamp or lighted window gleamed below me. I was thankful that I could see so little. All my senses seemed to desire to veil themselves and, feeling that I was about to slip from them, I pressed the palms of my hands together until they trembled, murmuring: *O love! O love!* many times.

At last she spoke to me. When she addressed the first words to me I was so confused that I did not know what to answer. She asked me was I going to *Araby.*° I forget whether I answered yes or no. It would be a splendid bazaar, she said; she would love to go.

O'Donovan Rossa: popular ballad about Jeremiah O'Donovan (1831–1915), a leader in the movement to free Ireland from English control.
Araby: The bazaar held in Dublin from May 14–19, 1894.

—And why can't you? I asked.

While she spoke she turned a silver bracelet round and round her wrist. She could not go, she said, because there would be a retreat° that week in her convent. Her brother and two other boys were fighting for their caps and I was alone at the railings. She held one of the spikes, bowing her head towards me. The light from the lamp opposite our door caught the white curve of her neck, lit up her hair that rested there and, falling, lit up the hand upon the railing. It fell over one side of her dress and caught the white border of a petticoat, just visible as she stood at ease.

—It's well for you, she said.

—If I go, I said, I will bring you something.

What innumerable follies laid waste my waking and sleeping thoughts after that evening! I wished to annihilate the tedious intervening days. I chafed against the work of school. At night in my bedroom and by day in the classroom her image came between me and the page I strove to read. The syllables of the word *Araby* were called to me through the silence in which my soul luxuriated and cast an Eastern enchantment over me. I asked for leave to go to the bazaar on Saturday night. My aunt was surprised and hoped it was not some Freemason° affair. I answered few questions in class. I watched my master's face pass from amiability to sternness; he hoped I was not beginning to idle. I could not call my wandering thoughts together. I had hardly any patience with the serious work of life which, now that it stood between me and my desire, seemed to me child's play, ugly monotonous child's play.

On Saturday morning I reminded my uncle that I wished to go to the bazaar in the evening. He was fussing at the hall-stand, looking for the hatbrush, and answered me curtly:

—Yes, boy, I know.

As he was in the hall I could not go into the front parlour and lie at the window. I left the house in bad humour and walked slowly towards the school. The air was pitilessly raw and already my heart misgave me.

When I came home to dinner my uncle had not yet been home. Still, it was early. I sat staring at the clock for some time and, when its ticking began to irritate me, I left the room. I mounted the staircase and gained the upper part of the house. The high cold empty gloomy rooms liberated me and I went from room to room singing. From the front window I saw my companions playing below in the street. Their cries reached me weakened and indistinct and, leaning my forehead against the cool glass, I looked over at the dark house where she lived. I may have stood there for an hour, seeing nothing but the brown-clad figure cast by my imagination, touched discreetly by the lamplight at the curved neck, at the hand upon the railing and at the border below the dress.

When I came downstairs again I found Mrs. Mercer sitting at the fire. She was an old garrulous woman, a pawnbroker's widow, who collected used stamps for some pious purpose. I had to endure the gossip of the tea-table. The meal was prolonged beyond an hour and still my uncle did not come. Mrs Mercer stood up to go: she was sorry she couldn't wait any longer, but it was after eight o'clock and she did not like to be out late, as the night air was bad for her. When she had gone I began to walk up and down the room, clenching my fists. My aunt said:

—I'm afraid you may put off your bazaar for this night of Our Lord.

retreat: a special time set aside for concentrated religious instruction, discussion, and prayer.

Freemason: and therefore Protestant.

At nine o'clock I heard my uncle's latchkey in the halldoor. I heard him talking to himself and heard the hall-stand rocking when it had received the weight of his overcoat. I could interpret these signs. When he was midway through his dinner I asked him to give me the money to go to the bazaar. He had forgotten.

—The people are in bed and after their first sleep now, he said.

I did not smile. My aunt said to him energetically:

—Can't you give him the money and let him go? You've kept him late enough as it is.

My uncle said he was very sorry he had forgotten. He said he believed in the old saying: *All work and no play makes Jack a dull boy.* He asked me where I was going and, when I had told him a second time he asked me did I know *The Arab's Farewell to his Steed.*° When I left the kitchen he was about to recite the opening lines of the piece to my aunt.

I held a florin° tightly in my hand as I strode down Buckingham Street towards the station. The sight of the streets thronged with buyers and glaring with gas recalled to me the purpose of my journey. I took my seat in a third-class carriage of a deserted train. After an intolerable delay the train moved out of the station slowly. It crept onward among ruinous houses and over the twinkling river. At Westland Row Station a crowd of people pressed to the carriage doors; but the porters moved them back, saying that it was a special train for the bazaar. I remained alone in the bare carriage. In a few minutes the train drew up beside an improvised wooden platform. I passed out on to the road and saw by the lighted dial of a clock that it was ten minutes to ten. In front of me was a large building which displayed the magical name.

I could not find any sixpenny entrance and, fearing that the bazaar would be closed, I passed in quickly through a turnstile, handing a shilling to a weary-looking man. I found myself in a big hall girdled at half its height by a gallery. Nearly all the stalls were closed and the greater part of the hall was in darkness. I recognized a silence like that which pervades a church after a service. I walked into the centre of the bazaar timidly. A few people were gathered about the stalls which were still open. Before a curtain, over which the words *Café Chantant* were written in coloured lamps, two men were counting money on a salver. I listened to the fall of the coins.

Remembering with difficulty why I had come I went over to one of the stalls and examined porcelain vases and flowered tea-sets. At the door of the stall a young lady was talking and laughing with two young gentlemen. I remarked their English accents and listened vaguely to their conversation.

—O, I never said such a thing!

—O, but you did!

—O, but I didn't!

—Didn't she say that?

—Yes I heard her.

—O, there's a . . . fib!

Observing me the young lady came over and asked me did I wish to buy anything. The tone in her voice was not encouraging; she seemed to have spoken to me out of a sense of duty. I looked humbly at the great jars that stood like eastern guards at either side of the dark entrance to the stall and murmured:

The Arab's Farewell to his Steed: poem by Caroline Norton (1808–1877).

florin: a two-shilling coin in the 1890s (when the story takes place), worth perhaps ten dollars in today's money.

—No, thank you.

The young lady changed the position of one of the vases and went back to the   35
two young men. They began to talk of the same subject. Once or twice the young lady
glanced at me over her shoulder.

I lingered before her stall, though I knew my stay was useless, to make my interest in her wares seem the more real. Then I turned away slowly and walked down
the middle of the bazaar. I allowed the two pennies to fall against the sixpence in my
pocket. I heard a voice call from one end of the gallery that the light was out. The upper part of the hall was now completely dark.

Gazing up into the darkness I saw myself as a creature driven and derided by
vanity; and my eyes burned with anguish and anger.

QUESTIONS

1. Describe what you consider to be the story's major idea.

2. How might the bazaar, "Araby," be considered symbolically in the story? To
   what extent does this symbol embody the story's central idea?

3. Consider the attitude of the speaker toward his home as indicated in the first
   paragraph. Why do you think the speaker uses the word *blind* to describe the
   dead-end street? What relationship exists between the speaker's pain at the end
   of the story to the ideas in the first paragraph?

4. Who is the narrator? About how old is he at the time of the story? About how
   old when he tells the story? What effect is produced by this difference in age between narrator-as-character and narrator-as-storyteller?

D. H. LAWRENCE (1885–1930)

*Lawrence was born in an English mining community, but
received a sufficient education to enable him to become a
teacher and writer. He fictionalized the early years of his
life in the novel* Sons and Lovers *(1913). His most controversial work,* Lady Chatterley's Lover, *was printed
privately in Italy in 1928, but was not published in an
uncut version in the United States until the 1960s. He
shocked his contemporaries because of his emphasis on the
importance of sexuality, an idea that is central to "The
Horse Dealer's Daughter." He was afflicted with tuberculosis, and lived in a number of warm, sunny places, including Italy, New Zealand, and New Mexico, in an attempt to restore his health. Nevertheless, his illness claimed him in 1930, when he was only
forty-five years old.*

The Horse Dealer's Daughter _____ 1922

"Well, Mabel, and what are you going to do with yourself?" asked Joe, with foolish flippancy. He felt quite safe himself. Without listening for an answer, he turned aside, worked a grain of tobacco to the tip of his tongue, and spat it out. He did not care about anything, since he felt safe himself.

The three brothers and the sister sat round the desolate breakfast table, attempting some sort of desultory consultation. The morning's post had given the final tap to the family fortunes, and all was over. The dreary dining-room itself, with its heavy mahogany furniture, looked as it were waiting to be done away with.

But the consultation amounted to nothing. There was a strange air of ineffectuality about the three men, as they sprawled at table, smoking and reflecting vaguely on their own condition. The girl was alone, a rather short, sullen-looking young woman of twenty-seven. She did not share the same life as her brothers. She would have been good-looking, save for the impassive fixity of her face, "bulldog," as her brothers called it.

There was a confused tramping of horses' feet outside. The three men all sprawled round in their chairs to watch. Beyond the dark holly-bushes that separated the strip of lawn from the high-road, they could see a cavalcade of shire horses swinging out of their own yard, being taken for exercise. This was the last time. These were the last horses that would go through their hands. The young men watched with critical, callous look. They were all frightened at the collapse of their lives, and the sense of disaster in which they were involved left them no inner freedom.

Yet they were three fine, well-set fellows enough. Joe, the eldest, was a man of thirty-three, broad and handsome in a hot, flushed way. His face was red, he twisted his black moustache over a thick finger, his eyes were shallow and restless. He had a sensual way of uncovering his teeth when he laughed, and his bearing was stupid. Now he watched the horses with a glazed look of helplessness in his eyes, a certain stupor of downfall.

The great draught-horses swung past. They were tied head to tail, four of them, and they heaved along to where a lane branched off from the highroad, planting their great hoofs floutingly in the fine black mud, swinging their great rounded haunches sumptuously, and trotting a few sudden steps as they were led into the lane, round the corner. Every movement showed a massive, slumbrous strength, and a stupidity which held them in subjection. The groom at the head looked back, jerking the leading rope. And the cavalcade moved out of sight up the lane, the tail of the last horse, bobbed up tight and stiff, held out taut from the swinging great haunches as they rocked behind the hedges in a motionlike sleep.

Joe watched with glazed hopeless eyes. The horses were almost like his own body to him. He felt he was done for now. Luckily, he was engaged to a woman as old as himself, and therefore her father, who was steward of a neighbouring estate, would provide him with a job. He would marry and go into harness. His life was over, he would be a subject animal now.

He turned uneasily aside, the retreating steps of the horses echoing in his ears. Then, with foolish restlessness, he reached for the scraps of bacon-rind from the plates, and making a faint whistling sound, flung them to the terrier that lay against the fender. He watched the dog swallow them, and waited till the creature looked into his eyes. Then a faint grin came on his face, and in a high, foolish voice he said:

"You won't get much more bacon, shall you, you little b———?"

The dog faintly and dismally wagged its tail, then lowered its haunches, circled round, and lay down again.

sang-froid: unconcern (literally, cold blood).

There was another helpless silence at the table. Joe sprawled uneasily in his seat, not willing to go till the family conclave was dissolved. Fred Henry, the second brother, was erect, clean-limbed, alert. He had watched the passing of the horses with more *sang-froid*.° If he was an animal, like Joe, he was an animal which controls, not one which is controlled. He was master of any horse, and he carried himself with a well-tempered air of mastery. But he was not master of the situations of life. He pushed his coarse brown moustache upwards, off his lip, and glanced irritably at his sister, who sat impassive and inscrutable.

"You'll go and stop with Lucy for a bit, shan't you?" he asked. The girl did not answer.

"I don't see what else you can do," persisted Fred Henry.

"Go as a skivvy,"° Joe interpolated laconically.

The girl did not move a muscle.   15

"If I was her, I should go in for training for a nurse," said Malcolm, the youngest of them all. He was the baby of the family, a young man of twenty-two, with a fresh, jaunty *museau*.°

But Mabel did not take any notice of him. They had talked at her and round her for so many years, that she hardly heard them at all.

The marble clock on the mantel-piece softly chimed the half-hour, the dog rose uneasily from the hearthrug and looked at the party at the breakfast table. But still they sat on in ineffectual conclave.

"Oh, all right," said Joe suddenly, *à propos* of nothing. "I'll get a move on."

He pushed back his chair, straddled his knees with a downward jerk, to get   20
them free, in horsey fashion, and went to the fire. Still he did not go out of the room; he was curious to know what the others would do or say. He began to charge his pipe, looking down at the dog and saying, in a high, affected voice:

"Going wi' me? Going wi' me are ter? Tha'rt goin' further than tha counts on just now, dost hear?"

The dog faintly wagged its tail, the man stuck out his jaw and covered his pipe with his hands, and puffed intently, losing himself in the tobacco, looking down all the while at the dog, with an absent brown eye. The dog looked up at him in mournful distrust. Joe stood with his knees stuck out, in real horsey fashion.

"Have you had a letter from Lucy?" Fred Henry asked of his sister.

"Last week," came the neutral reply.

"And what does she say?"   25

There was no answer.

"Does she *ask* you to go and stop there?" persisted Fred Henry.

"She says I can if I like."

"Well, then, you'd better. Tell her you'll come on Monday."

This was received in silence.   30

"That's what you'll do then, is it?" said Fred Henry, in some exasperation.

But she made no answer. There was a silence of futility and irritation in the room. Malcolm grinned fatuously.

"You'll have to make up your mind between now and next Wednesday," said Joe loudly, "or else find yourself lodgings on the kerbstone."

The face of the young woman darkened, but she sat on immutable.

skivvy: British slang for housemaid.
museau: French for nose, snout.

"Here's Jack Fergusson!" exclaimed Malcolm, who was looking aimlessly out of the window.

"Where?" exclaimed Joe, loudly.

"Just gone past."

"Coming in?"

Malcolm craned his neck to see the gate.

"Yes," he said.

There was a silence. Mabel sat on like one condemned, at the head of the table. Then a whistle was heard from the kitchen. The dog got up and barked sharply. Joe opened the door and shouted:

"Come on."

After a moment, a young man entered. He was muffled up in overcoat and a purple woolen scarf, and his tweed cap, which he did not remove, was pulled down on his head. He was of medium height, his face was rather long and pale, his eyes looked tired.

"Hello, Jack! Well, Jack!" exclaimed Malcolm and Joe. Fred Henry merely said "Jack!"

"What's doing?" asked the newcomer, evidently addressing Fred Henry.

"Same. We've got to be out by Wednesday—Got a cold?"

"I have—got it bad, too."

"Why don't you stop in?"

"*Me* stop in? When I can't stand on my legs, perhaps I shall have a chance." The young man spoke huskily. He had a slight Scotch accent.

"It's a knock-out, isn't it," said Joe boisterously, "if a doctor goes round croaking with a cold. Looks bad for the patients, doesn't it?"

The young doctor looked at him slowly.

"Anything the matter with *you*, then?" he asked, sarcastically.

"Not as I know of. Damn your eyes, I hope not. Why?"

"I thought you were very concerned about the patients, wondered if you might be one yourself."

"Damn it, no, I've never been patient to no flaming doctor, and hope I never shall be," returned Joe.

At this point Mabel rose from the table, and they all seemed to become aware of her existence. She began putting the dishes together. The young doctor looked at her, but did not address her. He had not greeted her. She went out of the room with the tray, her face impassive and unchanged.

"When are you off then, all of you?" asked the doctor.

"I'm catching the eleven-forty," replied Malcolm. "Are you goin' down wi' th' trap,° Joe?"

"Yes, I've told you I'm going down wi' th' trap, haven't I?"

"We'd better be getting her in then.—So long, Jack, if I don't see you before I go," said Malcolm, shaking hands.

He went out, followed by Joe, who seemed to have his tail between his legs.

"Well, this is the devil's own," exclaimed the doctor, when he was left alone with Fred Henry. "Going before Wednesday, are you?"

"That's the orders," replied the other.

"Where, to Northampton?"

trap: small wagon.

"That's it."   65
"The devil!" exclaimed Fergusson, with quiet chagrin.
And there was silence between the two.
"All settled up, are you?" asked Fergusson.
"About."
There was another pause.   70
"Well, I shall miss yer, Freddy boy," said the young doctor.
"And I shall miss thee, Jack," returned the other.
"Miss you like hell," mused the doctor.
Fred Henry turned aside. There was nothing to say. Mabel came in again, to fin-
ish clearing the table.
"What are *you* going to do then, Miss Pervin?" asked Fergusson. "Going to your   75
sister's, are you?"
Mabel looked at him with her steady, dangerous eyes, that always made him un-
comfortable, unsettling his superficial ease.
"No," she said.
"Well, what in the name of fortune *are* you going to do? Say what you *mean* to
do," cried Fred Henry, with futile intensity.
But she only averted her head, and continued her work. She folded the white
table-cloth, and put on the chenille cloth.
"The sulkiest bitch that ever trod!" muttered her brother.   80
But she finished her task with perfectly impassive face, the young doctor watch-
ing her interestedly all the while. Then she went out.
Fred Henry stared after her, clenching his lips, his blue eyes fixing in sharp an-
tagonism, as he made a grimace of sour exasperation.
"You could bray her into bits, and that's all you'd get out of her," he said, in a
small, narrowed tone.
The doctor smiled faintly.
"What's she *going* to do then?" he asked.   85
"Strike me if *I* know!" returned the other.
There was a pause. Then the doctor stirred.
"I'll be seeing you to-night, shall I?" he said to his friend.
"Ay—where's it to be? Are we going over to Jessdale?"
"I don't know. I've got such a cold on me. I'll come round to the Moon and   90
Stars, anyway."
"Let Lizzie and May miss their night for once, eh?"
"That's it—if I feel as I do now."
"All's one—"
The two young men went through the passage and down to the back door to-
gether. The house was large, but it was servantless now, and desolate. At the back was
a small bricked house-yard, and beyond that a big square, gravelled fine and red, and
having stables on two sides. Sloping, dank, winter-dark fields stretched away on the
open sides.
But the stables were empty. Joseph Pervin, the father of the family, had been a   95
man of no education, who had become a fairly large horse dealer. The stables had
been full of horses, there was a great turmoil and come-and-go of horses and of dealers and grooms. Then the kitchen was full of servants. But of late things had declined.
The old man had married a second time, to retrieve his fortunes. Now he was dead
and everything was gone to the dogs, there was nothing but debt and threatening.

For months, Mabel had been servantless in the big house, keeping the home together in penury for her ineffectual brothers. She had kept house for ten years. But previously, it was with unstinted means. Then, however brutal and coarse everything was, the sense of money had kept her proud, confident. The men might be foul-mouthed, the women in the kitchen might have bad reputations, her brothers might have illegitimate children. But so long as there was money, the girl felt herself established, and brutally proud, reserved.

No company came to the house, save dealers and coarse men. Mabel had no associates of her own sex, after her sister went away. But she did not mind. She went regularly to church, she attended to her father. And she lived in the memory of her mother, who had died when she was fourteen, and whom she had loved. She had loved her father, too, in a different way, depending upon him, and feeling secure in him, until at the age of fifty-four he married again. And then she had set hard against him. Now he had died and left them all hopelessly in debt.

She had suffered badly during the period of poverty. Nothing, however, could shake the curious sullen, animal pride that dominated each member of the family. Now, for Mabel, the end had come. Still she would not cast about her. She would follow her own way just the same. She would always hold the keys of her own situation. Mindless and persistent, she endured from day to day. Why should she think? Why should she answer anybody? It was enough that this was the end, and there was no way out. She need not pass any more darkly along the main street of the small town, avoiding every eye. She need not demean herself any more, going into the shops and buying the cheapest food. This was at an end. She thought of nobody, not even of herself. Mindless and persistent, she seemed in a sort of ecstasy to be coming nearer to her fulfilment, her own glorification, approaching her dead mother, who was glorified.°

In the afternoon she took a little bag, with shears and sponge and a small scrubbing brush, and went out. It was a grey, wintry day, with saddened, dark-green fields and an atmosphere blackened by the smoke of foundries not far off. She went quickly, darkly along the causeway, heeding nobody, through the town to the churchyard.

There she always felt secure, as if no one could see her, although as a matter of fact she was exposed to the stare of everyone who passed along under the churchyard wall. Nevertheless, once under the shadow of the great looming church, among the graves, she felt immune from the world, reserved within the thick churchyard wall as in another country.

Carefully she clipped the grass from the grave, and arranged the pinky-white, small chrysanthemums in the tin cross. When this was done, she took an empty jar from a neighbouring grave, brought water, and carefully, most scrupulously sponged the marble headstone and the coping-stone.

It gave her sincere satisfaction to do this. She felt in immediate contact with the world of her mother. She took minute pains, went through the park in a state bordering on pure happiness, as if in performing this task she came into a subtle, intimate connection with her mother. For the life she followed here in the world was far less real than the world of death she inherited from her mother.

The doctor's house was just by the church. Fergusson, being a mere hired assistant, was slave to the countryside. As he hurried now to attend to the outpatients in

who was glorified: See Romans 8:17,30.

the surgery, glancing across the graveyard with his quick eye, he saw the girl at her task at the grave. She seemed so intent and remote, it was like looking into another world. Some mystical element was touched in him. He slowed down as he walked, watching her as if spell-bound.

She lifted her eyes, feeling him looking. Their eyes met. And each looked again at once, each feeling, in some way, found out by the other. He lifted his cap and passed on down the road. There remained distinct in his consciousness, like a vision, the memory of her face, lifted from the tombstone in the churchyard, and looking at him with slow, large, portentous eyes. It *was* portentous, her face. It seemed to mesmerise him. There was a heavy power in her eyes which laid hold of his whole being, as if he had drunk some powerful drug. He had been feeling weak and done before. Now the life came back into him, he felt delivered from his own fretted, daily self.

He finished his duties at the surgery as quickly as might be, hastily filling up the bottles of the waiting people with cheap drugs. Then, in perpetual haste, he set off again to visit several cases in another part of his round, before teatime. At all times he preferred to walk, if he could, but particularly when he was not well. He fancied the motion restored him.

The afternoon was falling. It was grey, deadened, and wintry, with a slow, moist, heavy coldness sinking in and deadening all the faculties. But why should he think or notice? He hastily climbed the hill and turned across the dark-green fields, following the black cinder-track. In the distance, across a shallow dip in the country, the small town was clustered like smouldering ash, a tower, a spire, a heap of low, raw, extinct houses. And on the nearest fringe of the town, sloping into the dip, was Oldmeadow, the Pervins' house. He could see the stables and the outbuildings distinctly, as they lay towards him on the slope. Well, he would not go there many more times! Another resource would be lost to him, another place gone: the only company he cared for in the alien, ugly little town he was losing. Nothing but work, drudgery, constant hastening from dwelling to dwelling among the colliers and the iron-workers. It wore him out, but at the same time he had a craving for it. It was a stimulant to him to be in the homes of the working people, moving as it were through the innermost body of their life. His nerves were excited and gratified. He could come so near, into the very lives of the rough, inarticulate, powerfully emotional men and women. He grumbled, he said he hated the hellish hole. But as a matter of fact it excited him, the contact with the rough, strongly-feeling people was a stimulant applied direct to his nerves.

Below Oldmeadow, in the green, shallow, soddened hollow of fields, lay a square, deep pond. Roving across the landscape, the doctor's quick eye detected a figure in black passing through the gate of the field, down towards the pond. He looked again. It would be Mabel Pervin. His mind suddenly became alive and attentive.

Why was she going down there? He pulled up on the path on the slope above, and stood staring. He could just make sure of the small black figure moving in the hollow of the failing day. He seemed to see her in the midst of such obscurity, that he was like a clairvoyant, seeing rather with the mind's eye than with ordinary sight. Yet he could see her positively enough, whilst he kept his eye attentive. He felt, if he looked away from her, in the thick, ugly falling dusk, he would lose her altogether.

He followed her minutely as she moved, direct and intent, like something transmitted rather than stirring in voluntary activity, straight down the field towards the pond. There she stood on the bank for a moment. She never raised her head. Then she waded slowly into the water.

105

He stood motionless as the small black figure walked slowly and deliberately towards the centre of the pond, very slowly, gradually moving deeper into the motionless water, and still moving forward as the water got up to her breast. Then he could see her no more in the dusk of the dead afternoon.

"There!" he exclaimed. "Would you believe it?"

And he hastened straight down, running over the wet, soddened fields, pushing through the hedges, down into the depression of callous wintry obscurity. It took him several minutes to come to the pond. He stood on the bank, breathing heavily. He could see nothing. His eyes seemed to penetrate the dead water. Yes, perhaps that was the dark shadow of her black clothing beneath the surface of the water.

He slowly ventured into the pond. The bottom was deep, soft clay, he sank in, and the water clasped dead cold round his legs. As he stirred he could smell the cold, rotten clay that fouled up into the water. It was objectionable in his lungs. Still, repelled and yet not heeding, he moved deeper into the pond. The cold water rose over his thighs, over his loins, upon his abdomen. The lower part of his body was all sunk in the hideous cold element. And the bottom was so deeply soft and uncertain, he was afraid of pitching with his mouth underneath. He could not swim, and was afraid.

He crouched a little, spreading his hands under the water and moving them round, trying to feel for her. The dead cold pond swayed upon his chest. He moved again, a little deeper, and again, with his hands underneath, he felt all around under the water. And he touched her clothing. But it evaded his fingers. He made a desperate effort to grasp it.

And so doing he lost his balance and went under, horribly, suffocating in the foul earthy water, struggling madly for a few moments. At last, after what seemed an eternity, he got his footing, rose again into the air and looked around. He gasped, and knew he was in the world. Then he looked at the water. She had risen near him. He grasped her clothing, and drawing her nearer, turned to take his way to land again.

He went very slowly, carefully, absorbed in the slow progress. He rose higher, climbing out of the pond. The water was not only about his legs; he was thankful, full of relief to be out of the clutches of the pond. He lifted her and staggered on to the bank, out of the horror of wet, grey clay.

He laid her down on the bank. She was quite unconscious and running with water. He made the water come from her mouth, he worked to restore her. He did not have to work very long before he could feel the breathing begin again in her; she was breathing naturally. He worked a little longer. He could feel her live beneath his hands; she was coming back. He wiped her face, wrapped her in his overcoat, looked round into the dim, dark-grey world, then lifted her and staggered down the bank and across the fields.

It seemed an unthinkably long way, and his burden so heavy he felt he would never get to the house. But at last he was in the stable-yard, and then in the house-yard. He opened the door and went into the house. In the kitchen he laid her down on the hearthrug, and called. The house was empty. But the fire was burning in the grate.

Then again he kneeled to attend to her. She was breathing regularly, her eyes were wide open as if conscious, but there seemed something missing in her look. She was conscious in herself, but unconscious of her surroundings.

He ran upstairs, took blankets from a bed, and put them before the fire to warm. Then he removed her saturated, earthy-smelling clothing, rubbed her dry with a towel, and wrapped her naked in the blankets. Then he went into the dining-room, to look for spirits. There was a little whiskey. He drank a gulp himself, and put some into her mouth.

The effect was instantaneous. She looked full into his face, as if she had been seeing him for some time, and yet had only just become conscious of him.

"Dr. Fergusson?" she said.

"What?" he answered.

He was divesting himself of his coat, intending to find some dry clothing upstairs. He could not bear the smell of the dead, clayey water, and he was mortally afraid for his own health.

"What did I do?" she asked.   125

"Walked into the pond," he replied. He had begun to shudder like one sick, and could hardly attend to her. Her eyes remained full on him, he seemed to be going dark in his mind, looking back at her helplessly. The shuddering became quieter in him, his life came back in him, dark and unknowing, but strong again.

"Was I out of my mind?" she asked, while her eyes were fixed on him all the time.

"Maybe, for the moment," he replied. He felt quiet, because his strength had come back. The strange fretful strain had left him.

"Am I out of my mind now?" she asked.

"Are you?" he reflected a moment. "No," he answered truthfully, "I don't see   130
that you are." He turned his face aside. He was afraid, now, because he felt dazed, and felt dimly that her power was stronger than his, in this issue. And she continued to look at him fixedly all the time. "Can you tell me where I shall find some dry things to put on?" he asked.

"Did you dive into the pond for me?" she asked.

"No," he answered. "I walked in. But I went in overhead as well."

There was silence for a moment. He hesitated. He very much wanted to go upstairs to get into dry clothing. But there was another desire in him. And she seemed to hold him. His will seemed to have gone to sleep, and left him, standing there slack before her. But he felt warm inside himself. He did not shudder at all, though his clothes were sodden on him.

"Why did you?" she asked.

"Because I didn't want you to do such a foolish thing," he said.   135

"It wasn't foolish," she said, still gazing at him as she lay on the floor, with a sofa cushion under her head. "It was the right thing to do. *I* knew best, then."

"I'll go and shift these wet things," he said. But still he had not the power to move out of her presence, until she sent him. It was as if she had the life of his body in her hands, and he could not extricate himself. Or perhaps he did not want to.

Suddenly she sat up. Then she became aware of her own immediate condition. She felt the blankets about her, she knew her own limbs. For a moment it seemed as if her reason were going. She looked round, with wild eye, as if seeking something. He stood still with fear. She saw her clothing lying scattered.

"Who undressed me?" she asked, her eyes resting full and inevitable on his face.

"I did," he replied, "to bring you round."   140

For some moments she sat and gazed at him awfully, her lips parted.

"Do you love me then?" she asked.

He only stood and stared at her, fascinated. His soul seemed to melt.

She shuffled forward on her knees, and put her arms round him, round his legs, as he stood there, pressing her breasts against his knees and thighs, clutching him with strange, convulsive certainty, pressing his thighs against her, drawing him to her face, her throat, as she looked up at him with flaring, humble eyes of transfiguration, triumphant in first possession.

"You love me," she murmured, in strange transport, yearning and triumphant and confident. "You love me. I know you love me, I know."

And she was passionately kissing his knees, through the wet clothing, passionately and indiscriminately kissing his knees, his legs, as if unaware of everything.

He looked down at the tangled wet hair, the wild, bare, animal shoulders. He was amazed, bewildered, and afraid. He had never thought of loving her. He had never wanted to love her. When he rescued her and restored her, he was a doctor, and she was a patient. He had had no single personal thought of her. Nay, this introduction of the personal element was very distasteful to him, a violation of his professional honour. It was horrible to have her there embracing his knees. It was horrible. He revolted from it, violently. And yet—and yet—he had not the power to break away.

She looked at him again, with the same supplication of powerful love, and that same transcendent, frightening light of triumph. In view of the delicate flame which seemed to come from her face like a light, he was powerless. And yet he had never intended to love her. He had never intended. And something stubborn in him could not give way.

"You love me," she repeated, in a murmur of deep, rhapsodic assurance. "You love me."

Her hands were drawing him, drawing him down to her. He was afraid, even a little horrified. For he had, really, no intention of loving her. Yet her hands were drawing him towards her. He put out his hand quickly to steady himself, and grasped her bare shoulder. A flame seemed to burn the hand that grasped her soft shoulder. He had no intention of loving her: his whole will was against his yielding. It was horrible— And yet wonderful was the touch of her shoulder, beautiful the shining of her face. Was she perhaps mad? He had a horror of yielding to her. Yet something in him ached also.

He had been staring away at the door, away from her. But his hand remained on her shoulder. She had gone suddenly very still. He looked down at her. Her eyes were now wide with fear, with doubt, the light was dying from her face, a shadow of terrible greyness was returning. He could not bear the touch of her eyes' question upon him, and the look of death behind the question.

With an inward groan he gave way, and let his heart yield towards her. A sudden gentle smile came on his face. And her eyes, which never left his face, slowly, slowly filled with tears. He watched the strange water rise in her eyes, like some slow fountain coming up. And his heart seemed to burn and melt away in his breast.

He could not bear to look at her any more. He dropped on his knees and caught her head with his arms and pressed her face against his throat. She was very still. His heart, which seemed to have broken, was burning with a kind of agony in his breast. And he felt her slow, hot tears wetting his throat. But he could not move.

He felt the hot tears wet his neck and the hollows of his neck, and he remained motionless, suspended through one of man's eternities. Only now it had become indispensable to him to have her face pressed close to him; he could never let her go again. He could never let her head go away from the close clutch of his arm. He wanted to remain like that for ever, with his heart hurting him in a pain that was also life to him. Without knowing, he was looking down on her damp, soft brown hair.

Then, as it were suddenly, he smelt the horrid stagnant smell of the water. And at the same moment she drew away from him and looked at him. Her eyes were wistful and unfathomable. He was afraid of them, and he fell to kissing her, not knowing what he was doing. He wanted here eyes not to have that terrible, wistful, unfathomable look.

When she turned her face to him again, a faint delicate flush was glowing, and there was again dawning that terrible shining of joy in her eyes, which really terrified him, and yet which he now wanted to see, because he feared the look of doubt still more.

"You love me?" she said, rather faltering.

"Yes." The word cost him a painful effort. Not because it wasn't true. But because it was too newly true, the *saying* seemed to tear open again his newly-torn heart. And he hardly wanted it to be true, even now.

She lifted her face to him, and he bent forward and kissed her on the mouth gently, with the one kiss that is an eternal pledge. And as he kissed her his heart strained again in his breast. He never intended to love her. But now it was over. He had crossed over the gulf to her, and all that he had left behind had shrivelled and become void.

After the kiss, her eyes again slowly filled with tears. She sat still, away from him,   160
with her face drooped aside, and her hands folded in her lap. The tears fell very slowly. There was complete silence. He too sat there motionless and silent on the hearthrug. The strange pain of his heart that was broken seemed to consume him. That he should love her? That this was love! That he should be ripped open in this way!—Him, a doctor!—How they would all jeer if they knew!—It was agony to him to think they might know.

In the curious naked pain of the thought he looked again to her. She was sitting there drooped into a muse. He saw a tear fall, and his heart flared hot. He saw for the first time that one of her shoulders was quite uncovered, one arm bare, he could see one of her small breasts; dimly, because it had become almost dark in the room.

"Why are you crying?" he asked, in an altered voice.

She looked up at him, and behind her tears the consciousness of her situation for the first time brought a dark look of shame to her eyes.

"I'm not crying, really," she said, watching him half frightened.

He reached his hand, and softly closed it on her bare arm.   165

"I love you! I love you!" he said in a soft, low vibrating voice, unlike himself.

She shrank, and dropped her head. The soft, penetrating grip of his hand on her arm distressed her. She looked up at him.

"I want to go," she said. "I want to go and get you some dry things."

"Why?" he said. "I'm all right."

"But I want to go," she said. "And I want you to change your things."   170

He released her arm, and she wrapped herself in the blanket, looking at him rather frightened. And still she did not rise.

"Kiss me," she said wistfully.

He kissed her, but briefly, half in anger.

Then, after a second, she rose nervously, all mixed up in the blanket. He watched her in her confusion, as she tried to extricate herself and wrap herself up so that she could walk. He watched her relentlessly, as she knew.

And as she went, the blanket trailing, and as he saw a glimpse of her feet and   175
her white leg, he tried to remember her as she was when he had wrapped her in the blanket. But then he didn't want to remember, because she had been nothing to him

then, and his nature revolted from remembering her as she was when she was nothing to him.

A tumbling muffled noise from within the dark house startled him. Then he heard her voice:—"There are clothes." He rose and went to the foot of the stairs, and gathered up the garments she had thrown down. Then he came back to the fire, to rub himself down and dress. He grinned at his own appearance, when he had finished.

The fire was sinking, so he put on coal. The house was now quite dark, save for the light of a street-lamp that shone in faintly from beyond the holly trees. He lit the gas with matches he found on the mantel-piece. Then he emptied the pockets of his own clothes, and threw all his wet things in a heap into the scullery. After which he gathered up her sodden clothes, gently, and put them in a separate heap on the copper-top in the scullery.

It was six o'clock on the clock. His own watch had stopped. He ought to be back to the surgery. He waited, and still she did not come down. So he went to the foot of the stairs and called:

"I shall have to go."

Almost immediately he heard her coming down. She had on her best dress of black voile, and her hair was tidy, but still damp. She looked at him—and in spite of herself, smiled.

"I don't like you in those clothes," she said.

"Do I look a sight?" he answered.

They were shy of one another.

"I'll make you some tea," she said.

"No, I must go."

"Must you?" And she looked at him again with the wide, strained, doubtful eyes. And again, from the pain of his breast, he knew how he loved her. He went and bent to kiss her, gently, passionately, with his heart's painful kiss.

"And my hair smells so horrible," she murmured in distraction. "And I'm so awful, I'm so awful! Oh, no, I'm too awful." And she broke into bitter, heartbroken sobbing. "You can't want to love me, I'm horrible."

"Don't be silly, don't be silly," he said, trying to comfort her, kissing her, holding her in his arms. "I want you, I want to marry you, we're going to be married, quickly, quickly—to-morrow if I can."

But she only sobbed terribly, and cried.

"I feel awful. I feel awful. I feel I'm horrible to you."

"No, I want you, I want you," was all he answered blindly, with that terrible intonation which frightened her almost more than her horror lest he should *not* want her.

QUESTIONS

1. What idea is Lawrence illustrating by the breakup of the Pervin household?

2. What does the comparison of Joe Pervin and the draft horses mean with regard specifically to Joe, and generally to people without love?

3. What kind of person is Mabel? How do her brothers treat her? How does she feel about her brothers? What dilemma does she face as the story begins?

4. What effect does Mabel have on Fergusson as he watches her in her home, in

the churchyard, and at the pond? What does this effect contribute to Lawrence's ideas about love?

5. What do Mabel and Fergusson realize as he revives and warms her? How do their responses signify their growth as characters?

6. Why does the narrator tell us at the story's end that Fergusson "had no intention of loving" Mabel? What idea does this repeated assertion convey?

7. In this story, there is an extensive exploration of the ambiguous feelings of both Fergusson and Mabel after they realize their love. Why does Lawrence explore these feelings so extensively?

IRENE ZABYTKO (b. 1954)

Zabytko was born in Chicago's Ukrainian neighborhood, and did her undergraduate and graduate study at Vermont College. A proficient speaker of Ukrainian, she has lived in Ukraine and taught English Language courses there. She is a past winner of the PEN Syndicated Fiction Project, and has held fellowships at the Helene Wurlitzer Foundation, the Hambidge Center, and the Virginia Center for the Creative Arts and Sciences. She is the founder / publisher of OdessaPressa Productions. Her fiction has appeared in Catholic Girls *(1992) and* Earth Tones *(1994). Recently she published* Don't Call Me Fluffy: Radical Feline Poetry, *poems "written" by her cat. She has also been heard on "The Sound of Writing" program of National Public Radio. Currently she is completing a novel based on the Chernobyl nuclear accident.*

Home Soil _____ *1992*

I watch my son crack his knuckles, oblivious to the somber sounds of the Old Slavonic hymns the choir behind us is singing.

We are in the church where Bohdan, my son, was baptized nineteen years ago. It is Sunday. The pungent smell of frankincense permeates the darkened atmosphere of this cathedral. Soft sun rays illuminate the stained-glass windows. I sit near the one that shows Jesus on the cross looking down on some unidentifiable Apostles who are kneeling beneath His nailed feet. In the background, a tiny desperate Judas swings from a rope, the thirty pieces of silver thrown on the ground.

There is plenty of room in my pew, but my son chooses not to sit with me. I see him staring at the round carapace of a ceiling, stoic icons staring directly back at him. For the remainder of the Mass, he lightly drums his nervous fingers on top of the cover of *My Divine Friend*, the Americanized prayer book of the Ukrainian service. He took bongo lessons before he graduated high school, and learned the basic rolls from off a record, "Let's Swing with Bongos." I think it was supposed to make him popular with the girls at parties. I also think he joined the army because he wanted the virile image men in uniforms have that the bongos never delivered. When he returned from Nam, he mentioned after one of our many conversational silences that he lost the bongos, and the record is cracked, with the pieces buried somewhere deep inside the duffel bag he still hasn't unpacked.

Bohdan, my son, who calls himself Bob, has been back for three weeks. He looks so "American" in his green tailored uniform: his spit-shined vinyl dress shoes tap against the red-cushioned kneelers. It was his idea to go to church with me. He has not been anywhere since he came home. He won't even visit my garden.

Luba, my daughter, warned me he would be moody. She works for the Voice of America and saw him when he landed from Nam in San Francisco. "Just don't worry, *tato*,"° she said to me on the telephone. "He's acting weird. Culture shock."

"Explain what you mean."

"Just, you know, strange." For a disc jockey, and a bilingual one at that, she is so inarticulate. She plays American jazz and tapes concerts for broadcasts for her anonymous compatriots in Ukraine. That's what she was doing when she was in San Francisco, taping some jazz concert. Pure American music for the huddled gold-toothed youths who risk their *komsomol* privileges and maybe their lives listening to these clandestine broadcasts and to my daughter's sweet voice. She will never be able to visit our relatives back there because American security won't allow it, and she would lose her job. But it doesn't matter. After my wife died, I have not bothered to keep up with anyone there, and I don't care if they have forgotten all about me. It's just as well.

I noticed how much my son resembled my wife when I first saw him again at the airport. He was alone, near the baggage claim ramp. He was taller than ever, and his golden hair was bleached white from the jungle sun. He inherited his mother's high cheekbones, but he lost his baby fat, causing his cheeks to jut out from his lean face as sharp as the arrowheads he used to scavenge for when he was a kid.

We hugged briefly. I felt his medals pinch through my thin shirt. "You look good, son," I lied. I avoided his eyes and concentrated on a pin shaped like an open parachute that he wore over his heart.

"Hi, *tato*," he murmured. We spoke briefly about his flight home from San Francisco, how he'd seen Luba. We stood apart, unlike the other soldiers with their families who were hugging and crying on each other's shoulders in a euphoric delirium.

He grabbed his duffle bag from the revolving ramp and I walked behind him to see if he limped or showed any signs of pain. He showed nothing.

"Want to drive?" I asked, handing him the keys to my new Plymouth.

"Nah," he said. He looked around at the cars crowding the parking lot, and I thought he seemed afraid. "I don't remember how the streets go anymore."

An usher in his best borscht-red polyester suit waits for me to drop some money into the basket. It is old Pan Medved, toothless except for the prominent gold ones he flashes at me as he pokes me with his basket.

"*Nu*, give," he whispers hoarsely, but loud enough for a well-dressed woman with lacquered hair who sits in front of me to turn around and stare in mute accusation.

I take out the gray and white snakeskin wallet Bohdan brought back for me, and transfer out a ten dollar bill. I want the woman to see it before it disappears into the basket. She smiles at me and nods.

---

tato: "Father" or "Dad."

Women always smile at me like that. Especially after they see my money and find out that I own a restaurant in the neighborhood. None of the Ukies° go there; they don't eat fries and burgers much. But the "jackees"—the Americans—do when they're sick of eating in the cafeteria at the plastics factory. My English is pretty good for a D.P., and no one has threatened to bomb my business because they accuse me of being a no-god bohunk commie. Not yet anyway.

But the women are always impressed. I usually end up with the emigrés—some of them Ukrainians. The Polish women are the greediest for gawdy trinkets and for a man to give them money so that they can return to their husbands and children in Warsaw. I like them the best anyway because they laugh more than the other women I see, and they know how to have a good time.

Bohdan knows nothing about my lecherous life. I told the women to stay clear after my son arrived. He is so lost with women. I think he was a virgin when he joined the army, but I'm sure he isn't now. I can't ask him.

After mass ends, I lose Bohdan in the tight clusters of people leaving their pews   20
and genuflecting toward the iconostasis. He waits for me by the holy water font. It looks like a regular porcelain water fountain but without a spout. There is a sponge in the basin that is moistened with the holy water blessed by the priests here. Bohdan stands towering over the font, dabs his fingers into the sponge, but doesn't cross himself the way he was taught to do as a boy.

"What's the matter?" I ask in English. I hope he will talk to me if I speak to him in his language.

But Bohdan ignores me and watches an elderly woman gingerly entering the door of the confessional. "What she got to say? Why is she going in there?"

"Everyone has sins."

"Yeah, but who forgives?"

"God forgives," I say. I regret it because it makes me feel like a hypocrite when-   25
ever I parrot words I still find difficult to believe.

We walk together in the neighborhood; graffiti visible in the alley-ways despite the well-trimmed lawns with flowers and "bathtub" statues of the Blessed Mary smiling benevolently at us as we pass by the small bungalows. I could afford to move out of here, out of Chicago and into some nearby cushy suburb, Skokie or something. But what for? Some smart Jewish lawyer or doctor would be my next door neighbor and find out that I'm a Ukie and complain to me about how his grandmother was raped by Petliura.° I've heard it before. Anyway, I like where I am. I bought a three-flat apartment building after my wife died and I live in one of the apartments rent-free. I can walk to my business, and see the past—old women in babushkas sweeping the sidewalks in front of their cherished gardens; men in Italian-made venetian-slat sandals and woolen socks rushing to a chess match at the Soyuiez, a local meeting place where the D.P.s sit for hours rehashing the war over beers and chess.

Bohdan walks like a soldier. Not exactly a march, but a stiff gait that a good posture in a rigid uniform demands. He looks masculine, but tired and worn. Two pimples are sprouting above his lip where a faint moustache is starting.

"Want a cigarette?" I ask. Soldiers like to smoke. During the forties, I smoked

Ukies: Ukranian Americans.
Petliura: Simeon Petliura (1879–1926), an anti-Bolshevik Ukrainian leader who was accused of responsibility for Jewish pogroms during World War I. When his forces were defeated by the Russians he went into exile in Paris, where he was ultimately assassinated by a Jewish nationalist.

that horrible cheap tobacco, *mahorka*. I watch my son puff heavily on the cigarette I've given him, with his eyes partially closed, delicately cupping his hands to protect it from the wind. In my life, I have seen so many soldiers in that exact pose; they all look the same. When their faces are contorted from sucking the cigarette, there is an unmistakable shadow of vulnerability and fear of living. That gesture and stance are more eloquent than the blood and guts war stories men spew over their beers.

Pan° Medved, the battered gold-toothed relic in the church, has that look. Pan Holewski, one of my tenants, has it too. I would have known it even if he never openly displayed his old underground soldier's cap that sits on a bookshelf in the living room between small Ukrainian and American flags. I see it every time I collect the rent.

I wish Bohdan could tell me what happened to him in Vietnam. What did he do? What was done to him? Maybe now isn't the time to tell me. He may never tell me. I never told anyone either.

I was exactly his age when I became a soldier. At nineteen, I was a student at the university in L'vov, which the Poles occupied. I was going to be a poet, to study poetry and write it, but the war broke out, and my family could not live on the romantic epics I tried to publish, so I was paid very well by the Nazis to write propaganda pamphlets. "Freedom for Ukrainians" I wrote—"Freedom for our people. Fight the Poles and Russians alongside our German brothers" and other such dreck. I even wrote light verse that glorified Hitler as the protector of the free Ukrainian nation that the Germans promised us. My writing was as naïve as my political ideas.

My new career began in a butcher shop, commandeered after the Polish owner was arrested and shot. I set my battered Underwood typewriter atop an oily wooden table where crescents of chicken feathers still clung between the cracks. Meat hooks that once held huge sides of pork hung naked in a back room, and creaked ominously like a deserted gallows whenever anyone slammed the front door. Every shred of meat had been stolen by looters after the Germans came into the city. Even the little bell that shopkeepers kept at the entrance was taken. But I was very comfortable in my surroundings. I thought only about how I was to play a part in a historical destiny that my valiant words would help bring about. That delusion lasted only about a week or so until three burly Nazis came in. "*Schnell!*" they said to me, pushing me out of my chair and pointing to the windows where I saw crowds chaotically swarming about. Before I could question the soldiers, one of them shoved a gun into my hands and pushed me out into the streets. I felt so bewildered until the moment I pointed my rifle at a man who was about—I thought—to hit me with a club of some sort. Suddenly, I felt such an intense charge of power, more so than I had ever felt writing some of my best poems. I was no longer dealing with abstract words and ideas for a mythological cause; I was responsible for life and death.

I enjoyed that power, until it seeped into my veins and poisoned my soul. It was only an instant, a brief interlude, a matter of hours until that transformation occurred. I still replay that scene in my mind almost forty years after it happened, no matter what I am doing, or who I am with.

I think she was a village girl. Probably a Jew, because on that particular day, the Jews were the ones chosen to be rounded up and sent away in cattle cars. Her hair was golden red, short and wavy as was the style, and her neck was awash in freckles. It was a crowded station in the center of the town, not far from the butcher shop. There

Pan: A term of respect for adult males, the equivalent of *Mr.*

were Germans shouting and women crying and church bells ringing. I stood with that German regulation rifle I hardly knew how to handle, frozen because I was too light-headed and excited. I too began to yell at people and held the rifle against my chest, and I was very much aware of how everyone responded to my authority.

Then, this girl appeared in my direct line of vision. Her back was straight, her   35
shoulders tensed; she stopped in the middle of all the chaos. Simply stopped. I ran up and pushed her. I pushed her hard, she almost fell. I kept pushing her, feeling the thin material of her cheap wool jacket against my chapped eager hand; her thin muscles forced forward by my shoves. Once, twice, until she toppled into the open door of a train and fell toward a heap of other people moving deeper into the tiny confines of the stinking cattle car. She never turned around.

I should have shot her. I should have spared her from whatever she had to go through. I doubt she survived. I should have tried to find out what her name was, so I could track down her relatives and confess to them. At least in that way, they could have spat at me in justice and I would have finally received the absolution I will probably never find in this life.

* * *

I don't die. Instead, I go to the garden. It is Sunday evening. I am weeding the crop of beets and cabbages I planted in the patch in my backyard. The sun is lower, a breeze kicks up around me, but my forehead sweats. I breathe in the thick deep earth smells as the dirt crumbles and rotates against the blade of my hoe. I should destroy the honeysuckle vine that is slowly choking my plants, but the scent is so sweet, and its intoxicating perfume reminds me of a woman's gentleness.

I hoe for a while, but not for long, because out of the corner of my eye, I see Bohdan sitting on the grass tearing the firm green blades with his clenched hands. He is still wearing his uniform, all except the jacket, tie, and cap. He sits with his legs apart, his head down, ignoring the black flies that nip at his ears.

I wipe my face with a bright red bandana, which I brought with me to tie up the stalks of my drooping sunflowers. "Bohdan," I say to my son. "Why don't we go into the house and have a beer. I can finish this another time." I look at the orange sun. "It's humid and there's too many flies—means rain will be coming."

My son is quietly crying to himself.   40

"*Tato,* I didn't know anything," he cries out. "You know, I just wanted to jump out from planes with my parachute. I just wanted to fly . . ."

"I should have stopped you," I say more to myself than to him. Bohdan lets me stroke the thin spikes of his army regulation crew-cut which is soft and warm and I am afraid of how easily my hand can crush his skull.

I rock him in my arms the way I saw his mother embrace him when he was afraid to sleep alone.

There is not much more I can do right now except to hold him. I will hold him until he pulls away.

QUESTIONS

1. Where does the narrator live now, and what does he do? What do you learn about his past? What event remains fixed in his memory? Why?

2. What ideas about the exercise of power during warfare are brought out by the

narrator's speaking of "the absolution I will probably never find in this life" (paragraph 36)?

3. Why is the narrator's son Bohdan in tears (paragraph 40)? How are Bohdan's experiences parallel with the narrator's? What ideas underlie this paralleling of experience?

4. What is the significance of the narrator's saying "I am afraid of how easily my hand can crush his skull" (paragraph 42)?

WRITING ABOUT MEANING IN FICTION

Most likely you will write about a major idea or theme, but you may also get interested in one of your story's other ideas. As you begin brainstorming and developing your first drafts, consider questions like the following:

Questions for Discovering Ideas

- How do you discover ideas in the story? Through action? Character depiction? Scenes? Particularly effective language? How compelling are the ideas? Could the story be appreciated without reference to any ideas at all?
- Is the idea asserted directly, indirectly, dramatically, ironically? Does any one method predominate? Why?
- Which characters in their own right represent ideas? What ideas are brought out by what these characters do?
- To what do the ideas pertain? Individuals and their emotional and private lives? Social concerns? Social justice? Political justice? Economic justice? The condition of religion?
- Are the ideas limited to members of the groups represented by the characters (age, social group, race, nationality, personal status)? Or are they applicable to general conditions of life? Explain.
- If characters express ideas, how effective are they? How intelligent and well-considered do the ideas seem? How germane to the story are the ideas? How germane to more general conditions?
- With children, young adults, or the old, how can their circumstances reveal an idea?
- How pervasive in the story is the idea (throughout for a major idea, intermittently, or just once for a secondary idea)?
- How balanced are the ideas? If a particular idea is strongly presented, what conditions and qualifications are also presented (if any). What contradictory ideas are presented?
- What value or values are embodied in the idea? Of what importance are the values to the story's meaning?

Strategies for Organizing Ideas

Remember that in well-written stories (also poems or plays), narrative and dramatic elements are introduced only as they have a bearing on the idea. In this sense, the idea is like a key in music, or like a continuous thread tying together actions, characters, statements, symbols, and dialogue. As readers, we can trace such threads throughout the entire fabric of the work.

As you write about ideas, you may find yourself relying most heavily on the direct statements of the authorial voice, or on a combination of these and your interpretation of characters and action. Or you might focus exclusively on a first-person speaker and use his or her ideas to develop your analysis. Always make clear the sources of your details and distinguish the sources from your own commentary.

Establish patterns like these:

1. In "The Horse Dealer's Daughter," the anonymous narrator describes the reservations that Mabel and Dr. Fergusson have about their newly found love. This description shows Lawrence's idea that love not only creates the excitement of commitment, but also brings out reservations about the possible loss of control over one's life. (Here the first sentence refers to *a statement by the story's narrator.* The second sentence interprets this statement.)

2. Near the end of "A Jury of Her Peers," the county attorney draws attention to the "strange way" in which John Wright was strangled. Because both women would know, upon seeing the rope used in the murder, that the knot was a type used in quilting (a familiar occupation of rural women), this language vividly shows Glaspell's idea that the interests and knowledge of men and women are widely separated. (Here the source of the detail in the first sentence is *a character's dramatic statement.* The second sentence is interpretive.)

3. The speaker in "Araby" states that the boys from the Christian Brothers School, when school lets out, are like inmates just released from prison. This reference to both religious and secular confinement, coming early in the story, complements Joyce's idea that individuals become imprisoned in their own experience, including the occasional chagrin and embarrassment of childhood. (Here the first sentence *locates the source as the first-person narrator,* while the second is interpretive.)

4. In O'Connor's "First Confession," the priest's tolerant, good-humored treatment of Jackie, as contrasted with the harsh, intimidating treatment by the others, shows the idea that religious incentive is best implanted by kindness and understanding, not by fear. (Here the idea, expressed as a single sentence, is derived from a consideration of *the work as a whole.*)

Locating sources in this way keeps the lines of your conclusions clear, helping your reader follow and verify your arguments.

In your essay, your general goal is to describe an idea and show its importance in the story. Each separate work will invite its own approach, but here are a number of strategies you might use to organize your essay.

1. *Analyzing the idea as it applies to character.* Example: "Minnie Wright embodies the idea that living with cruelty and insensitivity leads to alienation, unhappiness, despair, and maybe to violence."

2. *Showing how actions bring out the idea.* Example: "That Mabel and Dr. Fergusson fall in love rather than go their separate ways indicates Lawrence's idea that love literally rescues human lives."

3. *Showing how dialogue and separate speeches bring out the idea.* Example: "The priest's responses to Jackie's confession embody the idea that kindness and understanding are the best means to encourage religious commitment."

4. *Showing how the story's structure is determined by the idea.* Example: "The idea that horror may exist in ordinary things leads to a structure in which Jackson introduces seemingly commonplace people, builds suspense about an impending misfortune, and develops a conclusion of mob destructiveness."

5. *Treating variations or differing manifestations of the idea.* Example: "The idea that zealousness leads to destruction is shown in Brown's nightmarish distortion of reality, his rejection of others, and his dying gloom."

6. *Dealing with a combination of these (together with any other significant aspect).* Example: "The idea in Araby' that devotion is complex and contradictory is shown in the narrator's romantic mission as a carrier of parcels, his outcries to love in the back room of his house, and his self-reproach and shame at the story's end." (Here the idea is traced through speech and action.)

Your conclusion might begin with a summary, together with your evaluation of the validity or force of the idea. If you have been convinced by the author's ideas, you might say that the author has expressed the idea forcefully and convincingly, or else you might show the relevance of the idea to current conditions. If you are not persuaded by the idea, you should not only state your disagreement but should also demonstrate the idea's shortcomings or limitations. If you wish to mention a related idea, whether in the story you have studied or in some other story, you might introduce that here, but be sure to stress the connections.

SAMPLE ESSAY

The Idea in D. H. Lawrence's "The Horse Dealer's Daughter" that Human Destiny is to Love°

[1] There are many ideas in "The Horse Dealer's Daughter" about the love between men and women. The story suggests that love is uncontrollable, and also that love must have a physical basis. It also suggests that love transforms life into something new, that love gives security, that only love gives meaning to life, and that love is not only something to live for but something to be feared. The idea that takes in all these is that loving is an essential part of human nature and that it is human destiny to love.* This idea is embodied negatively in characters who are without love, and positively in characters who find love.†

° See p. 391 for this story.
* Central idea.
† Thesis sentence.

In the first part of the story, loveless characters are negative and incomplete. Their lack of love causes them to be sullen, argumentative, and even cruel. Their lives are similar to those of the draught horses on the Pervin farm, who move with a "massive, slumberous strength, and a stupidity which [holds] them in subjection" (¶ 6). The idea is brought across with force, for the story implies that time is running out on people in this condition, and unless they find love they are doomed to misery. And the love they find must be real, for the underlying theme is that anything short of that is an evasion and will hasten their doom. Joe, the eldest of the Pervin brothers, is the major example of what can happen without love, for even though he is planning to marry, he is doing so without love. His motives are thus destroying him. As the narrator says, in emphasizing the story's major idea, Joe's "life was over, he would be a subject animal" like the horses (¶ 7).

[2]

The idea that life is impossible without love is exemplified most fully in Mabel Pervin, the "horse dealer's daughter." Just as her father's death is breaking up the way of life she knew with her brothers, so is it forcing her toward drastic action. She assumes that the loss of, first, her mother and, now, her father has deprived her of all love. Therefore her attempt to drown herself, which she undertakes quickly after attending to her mother's grave, demonstrates the idea that a life without love, and with no constructive purpose, is a kind of death.

[3]

Rather than ending life, however, the mucky pond illustrates the idea that love begins life. Dr. Jack Fergusson, who rescues Mabel, is her destiny, despite the fact that the two have never thought about loving each other before. Jack has been introduced as an amiable but rudderless person. His common cold, which is mentioned when he first appears, is compatible with the idea that the soul without love is sick. When Jack leaves the Pervin house, his route is aimless, and his seeing Mabel go into the water is only accidental. His heroic entry into the pond is unplanned, but it also is a first step in establishing a new direction for both his life and Mabel's. The rescue thus underscores the idea that once love is found, it restores life.

[4]

But love is also complex, and when it comes it creates unforeseen problems—certainly an idea that is compatible with human destiny. As Lawrence shows his characters finding each other, he shows that love brings out new and strange emotions, and it upsets the habits and attitudes of a lifetime. Indeed, there is a strong element of fear in love; it changes life so completely that no one can ever be the same after experiencing it. We see this kind of fearful change in Jack. The narrator tells us that Jack "had no intention of loving" Mabel, but that destiny drives him into this state. The final paragraph of the story indicates the mixture of desire and terror that love and change can produce:

[5]

> "No, I want you, I want you," was all he answered, blindly, with that terrible intonation which frightened her almost more than the horror lest he should *not* want her. (¶ 191)

Thus, the story forcefully drives home the point that the human destiny that drives people toward love is both exhilarating and fearsome at the same time. This realistic presentation of human emotions raises Lawrence's treatment of his idea above the popular and romantic conception of love. Love creates problems as great as those it solves, but it also builds a platform of emotional strength from which these new problems can be attacked. This strength can be achieved only when men and women know love, because only then, in keeping with Lawrence's idea, are they living life as it was destined to be lived. The problems facing them then are the real ones that men and women should face, since such problems are a natural result of destiny. By contrast, men and women without love, like those at the beginning of the story, have never reached fulfillment. Consequently, they face problems that are irrelevant to life as it should be lived. The entire story of Mabel and Jack is an illustration of the idea that it is the destiny of men and women to love.

[6]

Commentary on the Essay

This essay follows the sixth strategy (p. 410) by showing how separate components from the story exhibit the idea's pervasiveness. Throughout, citations of actions, speeches, circumstances, and narrator's observations are used as evidence for the various conclusions. Transitions between paragraphs are effected by phrases like "The idea that . . ." (3), "however" (4), "But" (5), and "This" (6) all of which emphasize the continuity of the topic.

The introductory paragraph first illustrates a number of ideas about love that the story suggests, and then produces a comprehensive statement of the theme which is made the central idea. This assertion is developed as it applies (1) to characters without love and (2) to those who find it. In the body of the essay, paragraphs 2 and 3 emphasize the emptiness of the lives of characters without love. The relationship of these two paragraphs to the main idea is that if the characters are not living in accord with human destiny, they are cut off from life. Thus Joe is dismissed in the story as a "subject animal," and Mabel, his sister, attempts suicide. These details are brought out in support of the essay's central idea. Paragraphs 4 and 5 treat the positive aspects of the main idea, focusing on the renewing effect of love on both Mabel and Jack, but also on the complexity of their emotional responses to their newly realized love. The last paragraph evaluates the idea or theme of the story, and concludes that it is realistic and well balanced.

WRITING TOPICS

1. On the basis of ideas, write an essay criticizing a story in this anthology which you dislike or to which you are indifferent. You might consult the section in Chapter 1 on "Likes and Dislikes" (pp. 37–44) to get ideas about how to proceed. Explain how your responses are conditioned by your own beliefs and values, and be sure that your criticism is based accurately in the story.

2. Consider "The Sky Is Gray" as an example of the idea of economic determinism (see also Appendix D, p. 1656–57). That is, to what degree are the circumstances and traits of the characters, particularly James, controlled and limited primarily by their economic status? According to the idea, how likely is it that the characters can ever rise above their circumstances?

3. Compare two stories containing similar themes (examples: "Goodbye and Good Luck" and "The Horse Dealer's Daughter"; "Home Soil" and "Soldier's Home"; "The Shawl" and "The Portable Phonograph"; "Barn Burning" and "The Found Boat"; "The Story of an Hour" and "The Yellow Wallpaper"). For help in developing your essay, consult Appendix B on the technique of comparison-contrast.

4. Select an idea that particularly interests you, and write a story showing how characters may or may not live up to the idea. If you have difficulty getting started, try one of these possible ideas:

   a. Interest and enthusiasm are hard to maintain for long.

   b. People always want more than they have or need.

   c. The concerns of adults are different from those of children.

   d. It is awkward to confront another person about a grievance.

   e. Making a decision is hard because it requires a complete change in life's directions.

11

A Career in Fiction: A Collection of Stories by Edith Wharton

LIFE AND CAREER

By birth, Edith Wharton (Edith Newbold Jones, 1862–1937) was a member of the American social élite. She spent her "babyhood" with her parents in Europe, becoming proficient in French, German, and Italian. When the family returned to the United States, she spent many hours in the library of their New York home, reading her father's collection of five to six hundred books. She wrote that she had "free access" to "poetry & history," but, curiously, was prohibited from reading novels without permission. She quickly assimilated what she called the "realm of words," and came to regard it as her "own native country." By age ten she began writing, particularly enjoying the writing of sermons. Her mother was pleased to have a budding author in the family, and paid to have a collection of Edith's juvenile poems published privately.

A young woman of Edith's class was expected to marry a man firmly established within the social structure, and then to spend a life of leisurely visits and international travel. Accordingly, when the time came, she entertained a number of suitors. Her favorite was Walter Berry, a man of intelligence and taste who eventually became an international lawyer, and who remained friends with her throughout his life. Although she probably loved him, no marriage ensued. Instead, in 1885 she married Edward ("Teddy") Wharton, a Bostonian whose chief qualities seem to have been that he loved small dogs (she adored small dogs, and there are many photographs of her and her dogs) and moved in the same social circle as the Jones family. The couple lived in Rhode Island and New York, and for a number of years they enjoyed the estate home, "The Mount," that they built near Lenox, Massachusetts.

Early in the marriage, Wharton began developing her literary career. A number of stories and fledgling novels were followed by one of her best novels, *House of Mirth* (1905), and by this time she had become widely recognized

Edith Wharton (Bettmann).

as a writer of considerable power. While she was growing as a writer, however, her marriage with Teddy was coming apart. In 1913, after Teddy had embezzled a large amount of her money, she sued him for divorce on the grounds of adultery, even though divorce at that time was unusual enough to raise questions about her reputation—a subject that she explored in a number of her works.

After divorce she went to live in France, where she spent most of the rest of her life—summers at a villa near Paris (the "Pavillon Colombe") and winters at a chateau on the French Riviera. When World War I broke out in 1914, she threw herself into the war effort, touring the front to determine the needs of soldiers, and establishing rescue organizations for refugees. For this effort, which cost her much time and wealth, she was made a Chevalier of the Legion of Honor by the French government in 1916. After the war she resumed her writing, receiving a Pulitzer Prize for *The Age of Innocence* in 1921, and a Gold Medal for "special Distinction in Literature" from the American Academy of Arts and Letters in 1929. Weakened by a stroke, she died in 1937, and was buried in the Cimetière des Gonards, near Versailles.

Literary Works

While Wharton's birth placed her among the American social élite, her achievement ranked her among one of America's major writers and enabled her to cultivate the friendship of leading figures like Henry James, Bernard

Berenson, and André Gide. Throughout her career she wrote many novels, both long and short, along with books on gardening, travel, and architecture. But she never stopped writing short stories. Her earliest significant work was a story, and her last work, published posthumously, was also a story. Her completed stories total eighty-six, a considerable output.

In her critical work about stories, "Telling a Short Story," Wharton tells us that the special aim of the short-story writer is to create "situations" from which to drive "a shaft . . . straight into the heart of experience." This observation suggests a major difference between the story and the novel: The novel should emphasize character development and change, whereas the story should aim at achieving a powerful effect. Despite this theory, however, Wharton was too good a writer not to create entire lives for her short-story characters and to render their reactions and feelings as they cope with experience. Therefore, her stories regularly render the development of individuals—particularly women—under the pressure of situations and the need to make decisions. Nowhere is this quality better shown than in *The Age of Innocence*, which reached the best-seller lists in 1993 because of the successful movie starring Michelle Pfeiffer, Daniel Day Lewis, and Winona Ryder.

Wharton's best stories reveal the frustrations and the emotional subtleties of male-female relationships, and the ironic contrasts between outer appearance and inner reality that these relationships force on people. She exploits such a contrast in "The Muse's Tragedy," one of her earliest stories (1899). At the very end of "Roman Fever," one of her last stories (1934), she reveals how the lifelong amiability of two middle-aged women is tinged with previously unvoiced jealousy and resentment. Wharton also successfully uncovers the amusing aspects of male–female relationships. For example, "The Other Two" (1904), which her biographer and editor R. W. B. Lewis calls "very likely the best story Mrs. Wharton ever wrote," is a subtly comic treatment of embarrassments following divorce.

In addition, Wharton admired ghost stories, and wrote a substantial number of them. To her, a good ghost story was no mere "treatise on the sources of the supernatural." It was, rather, a work producing the chill and shudder evoked by "the peculiar category of the eerie." Therefore, instead of dealing with the macabre, her ghost stories explore the borders between conscious and unconscious levels of reality—with, admittedly, an emphasis on the sinister and the destructive. Usually her ghosts reflect characteristics of individuals within the story, as in "The Eyes" (1910) and "The Triumph of Night" (1914). The ghost story included here, "Pomegranate Seed" (1931), is representative, for it dramatizes—but never explains—how the everyday world that we do see clutches the "eerie" world that we don't see. Thematically, the story parallels the conclusion of *The Age of Innocence*, in which the dead past is so strong that it continues to shape the living present.

Wharton lived to be seventy-five, and wrote professionally for forty or more of those years. Even during World War I, when she was preoccupied with her relief work, she produced a novella in 1916, *Summer* (also produced as a film), which demonstrated her continued commitment to her craft as a writer. In the area of life she explores in her fiction—that inner emotional world stemming out of close personal relationships—she is a master. To read her stories is to be convinced that hers was indeed the kind of "first-rate mind" that could "perceive the differences underneath" the surfaces of life that Walter Berry described to her in the days of their courtship. Few writers have created so sensitive a portrayal of human feelings.

Bibliographic Sources

Wharton's autobiographical writings, *A Backward Glance* and *Life and I*, are included in *Edith Wharton: Novellas and Other Writings* (1990), edited by Cynthia Griffin Wolff. The definitive edition of her stories is *The Collected Short Stories of Edith Wharton* (two volumes, 1968), edited by R. W. B. Lewis. These volumes also contain a comprehensive introduction and a useful classification of the stories. The standard biography, *Edith Wharton: A Biography* (1975), is also by Lewis. Wharton's letters are collected in *The Letters of Edith Wharton* (1988), edited by R. W. B. Lewis and Nancy Lewis. The index to the letters provides a key to Wharton's own comments about her various works. A convenient collection of twenty stories is *The Muse's Tragedy and Other Stories by Edith Wharton* (1990), edited by Candace Waid. Significant criticism may be found in Blake Nevius, *Edith Wharton: A Study of Her Fiction* (1953); *Edith Wharton: A Collection of Critical Essays* (1962), edited by Irving Howe; Cynthia Griffin Wolff, *A Feast of Words: The Triumph of Edith Wharton* (1977); Geoffrey Walton, *Edith Wharton, A Critical Interpretation* (1982); Wendy Gimbel, *Edith Wharton: Orphancy and Survival* (1984); Judith Fryer, *Felicitous space: The Imaginative Structures of Edith Wharton and Willa Cather* (1986); Josephine Donovan, *After the Fall: The Demeter-Persephone Myth in Wharton, Cather, and Glasgow* (1989); Susan Goodman, *Wharton's Women: Friends and Rivals* (1990); and Mary E. Papke, *Verging on the Abyss: The Social Fiction of Kate Chopin and Edith Wharton* (1990).

WRITING TOPICS

1. Wharton's idea that the past continues to hold power over the present.
2. Wharton's use of irony.
3. Wharton's views of the relationship of men and women.
4. The social background of the stories (customs of travel, work, husband-wife behavior, work habits).
5. The persistence of innocence within the fabric of experience.
6. Wharton's creation of reality (houses, jobs, social position, personal relationships, etc.).
7. Wharton's use of dramatic dialogue and indirect discourse.
8. Wharton's treatment of women, in their relationships with men and their connection with the world at large.

9. Wharton's use of allusions and symbols. These may be both real (e.g., the Roman Forum, the pouring of coffee, mysterious letters on tables, geographical and topographic locations, etc.) and artificial (the myth of Persephone, literary reputations, works of art, etc.).

The Muse's Tragedy _____1899

I

Danyers afterwards liked to fancy that he had recognized Mrs. Anerton at once; but that, of course, was absurd, since he had seen no portrait of her—she affected a strict anonymity, refusing even her photograph to the most privileged—and from Mrs. Memorall, whom he revered and cultivated as her friend, he had extracted but the one impressionist phrase: "Oh, well, she's like one of those old prints where the lines have the value of color."

He was almost certain, at all events, that he had been thinking of Mrs. Anerton as he sat over his breakfast in the empty hotel restaurant, and that, looking up on the approach of the lady who seated herself at the table near the window, he had said to himself, *"That might be she."*

Ever since his Harvard days—he was still young enough to think of them as immensely remote—Danyers had dreamed of Mrs. Anerton, the Silvia of Vincent Rendle's immortal sonnet cycle, the Mrs. A. of the *Life and Letters*. Her name was enshrined in some of the noblest English verse of the nineteenth century—and of all past or future centuries, as Danyers, from the standpoint of a maturer judgment, still believed. The first reading of certain poems—of the *Antinous*, the *Pia Tolomei*, the *Sonnets to Silvia*—had been epochs in Danyers' growth, and the verse seemed to gain in mellowness, in amplitude, in meaning as one brought to its interpretation more experience of life, a finer emotional sense. When, in his boyhood, he had felt only the perfect, the almost austere beauty of form, the subtle interplay of vowel sounds, the rush and fullness of lyric emotion, he now thrilled to the close-packed significance of each line, the allusiveness of each word—his imagination lured hither and thither on fresh trails of thought, and perpetually spurred by the sense that, beyond what he had already discovered, more marvelous regions lay waiting to be explored. Danyers had written, at college, the prize essay on Rendle's poetry (it chanced to be the moment of the great man's death); he had fashioned the fugitive verse of his own Storm and Stress period on the forms which Rendle had first given to English meter, and when two years later the *Life and Letters* appeared, and the Silvia of the sonnets took substance as Mrs. A., he had included in his worship of Rendle the woman who had inspired not only such divine verse but such playful, tender, incomparable prose.

Danyers never forgot the day when Mrs. Memorall happened to mention that she knew Mrs. Anerton. He had known Mrs. Memorall for a year or more, and had somewhat contemptuously classified her as the kind of woman who runs cheap excursions to celebrities; when one afternoon she remarked, as she put a second lump of sugar in his tea:

"Is it right this time? You're almost as particular as Mary Anerton."

"Mary Anerton?"

"Yes, I never *can* remember how she likes her tea. Either it's lemon *with* sugar, or lemon without sugar, or cream without either, and whichever it is must be put into the cup before the tea is poured in; and if one hasn't remembered, one must begin all over again. I suppose it was Vincent Rendle's way of taking his tea and has become a sacred rite."

"Do you *know* Mrs. Anerton?" cried Danyers, disturbed by this careless familiarity with the habits of his divinity.

"'And did I once see Shelley plain?' Mercy, yes! She and I were at school together—she's an American, you know. We were at a *pension* near Tours for nearly a year; then she went back to New York, and I didn't see her again till after her marriage. She and Anerton spent a winter in Rome while my husband was attached to our Legation there, and she used to be with us a great deal." Mrs. Memorall smiled reminiscently. "It was *the* winter."

"The winter they first met?"

"Precisely—but unluckily I left Rome just before the meeting took place. Wasn't it too bad? I might have been in the *Life and Letters*. You know he mentions that stupid Madame Vodki, at whose house he first saw her."

"And did you see much of her after that?"

"Not during Rendle's life. You know she has lived in Europe almost entirely, and though I used to see her off and on when I went abroad, she was always so engrossed, so preoccupied, that one felt one wasn't wanted. The fact is, she cared only about his friends—she separated herself gradually from all her own people. Now, of course, it's different; she's desperately lonely; she's taken to writing to me now and then; and last year, when she heard I was going abroad, she asked me to meet her in Venice, and I spent a week with her there."

"And Rendle?"

Mrs. Memorall smiled and shook her head. "Oh, I never was allowed a peep at *him*; none of her old friends met him, except by accident. Ill-natured people say that was the reason she kept him so long. If one happened in while he was there, he was hustled into Anerton's study, and the husband mounted guard till the inopportune visitor had departed. Anerton, you know, was really much more ridiculous about it than his wife. Mary was too clever to lose her head, or at least to show she'd lost it—but Anerton couldn't conceal his pride in the conquest. I've seen Mary shiver when he spoke of Rendle as *our poet*. Rendle always had to have a certain seat at the dinner table, away from the draft and not too near the fire, and a box of cigars that no one else was allowed to touch, and a writing table of his own in Mary's sitting room—and Anerton was always telling one of the great man's idiosyncrasies: how he never would cut the ends of his cigars, though Anerton himself had given him a gold cutter set with a star sapphire, and how untidy his writing table was, and how the housemaid had orders always to bring the wastepaper basket to her mistress before emptying it, lest some immortal verse should be thrown into the dustbin."

"The Anertons never separated, did they?"

"Separated? Bless you, no. He never would have left Rendle! And besides, he was very fond of his wife."

"And she?"

"Oh, she saw he was the kind of man who was fated to make himself ridiculous, and she never interfered with his natural tendencies."

From Mrs. Memorall, Danyers further learned that Mrs. Anerton, whose husband had died some years before her poet, now divided her life between Rome, where she had a small apartment, and England, where she occasionally went to stay with those of her friends who had been Rendle's. She had been engaged, for some time

10

15

20

after his death, in editing some juvenilia which he had bequeathed to her care; but that task being accomplished, she had been left without definite occupation, and Mrs. Memorall, on the occasion of their last meeting, had found her listless and out of spirits.

"She misses him too much—her life is too empty. I told her so—I told her she ought to marry."

"Oh!"

"Why not, pray? she's a young woman still—what many people would call young," Mrs. Memorall interjected, with a parenthetic glance at the mirror. "Why not accept the inevitable and begin over again? All the King's horses and all the King's men won't bring Rendle to life—and besides, she didn't marry *him* when she had the chance."

Danyers winced slightly at this rude fingering of his idol. Was it possible that Mrs. Memorall did not see what an anticlimax such a marriage would have been? Fancy Rendle "making an honest woman" of Silvia; for so society would have viewed it! How such a reparation would have vulgarized their past—it would have been like "restoring" a masterpiece; and how exquisite must have been the perceptions of the woman who, in defiance of appearances, and perhaps of her own secret inclination, chose to go down to posterity as Silvia rather than as Mrs. Vincent Rendle!

Mrs. Memorall, from this day forth, acquired an interest in Danyers' eyes. She was like a volume of unindexed and discursive memoirs, through which he patiently plodded in the hope of finding embedded amid layers of dusty twaddle some precious allusion to the subject of his thought. When, some months later, he brought out his first slim volume, in which the remodeled college essay on Rendle figured among a dozen somewhat overstudied "appreciations," he offered a copy to Mrs. Memorall; who surprised him, the next time they met, with the announcement that she had sent the book to Mrs. Anerton.

Mrs. Anerton in due time wrote to thank her friend. Danyers was privileged to read the few lines in which, in terms that suggested the habit of "acknowledging" similar tributes, she spoke of the author's "feeling and insight," and was "so glad of the opportunity," etc. He went away disappointed, without clearly knowing what else he had expected.

The following spring, when he went abroad, Mrs. Memorall offered him letters to everybody, from the Archbishop of Canterbury to Louise Michel. She did not include Mrs. Anerton, however, and Danyers knew, from a previous conversation, that Silvia objected to people who "brought letters." He knew also that she traveled during the summer, and was unlikely to return to Rome before the term of his holiday should be reached, and the hope of meeting her was not included among his anticipations.

The lady whose entrance broke upon his solitary repast in the restaurant of the Hotel Villa d'Este had seated herself in such a way that her profile was detached against the window, and thus viewed, her domed forehead, small arched nose, and fastidious lip suggested a silhouette of Marie Antoinette. In the lady's dress and movements—in the very turn of her wrist as she poured out her coffee—Danyers thought he detected the same fastidiousness, the same air of tacitly excluding the obvious and unexceptional. Here was a woman who had been much bored and keenly interested. The waiter brought her a *Secolo*, and as she bent above it Danyers noticed that the hair rolled back from her forehead was turning gray; but her figure was straight and slender, and she had the invaluable gift of a girlish back.

The rush of Anglo-Saxon travel had not set toward the lakes, and with the exception of an Italian family or two, and a hump-backed youth with an *abbé*, Danyers and the lady had the marble halls of the Villa d'Este to themselves.

When he returned from his morning ramble among the hills he saw her sitting   30
at one of the little tables at the edge of the lake. She was writing, and a heap of books and newspapers lay on the table at her side. That evening they met again in the garden. He had strolled out to smoke a last cigarette before dinner, and under the black vaulting of ilexes, near the steps leading down to the boat landing, he found her leaning on the parapet above the lake. At the sound of his approach she turned and looked at him. She had thrown a black lace scarf over her head, and in this somber setting her face seemed thin and unhappy. He remembered afterwards that her eyes, as they met his, expressed not so much sorrow as profound discontent.

To his surprise she stepped toward him with a detaining gesture.

"Mr. Lewis Danyers, I believe?"

He bowed.

"I am Mrs. Anerton. I saw your name on the visitors' list and wished to thank you for an essay on Mr. Rendle's poetry—or rather to tell you how much I appreciated it. The book was sent to me last winter by Mrs. Memorall."

She spoke in even melancholy tones, as though the habit of perfunctory utter-   35
ance had robbed her voice of more spontaneous accents; but her smile was charming.

They sat down on a stone bench under the ilexes, and she told him how much pleasure his essay had given her. She thought it the best in the book—she was sure he had put more of himself into it than into any other; was she not right in conjecturing that he had been very deeply influenced by Mr. Rendle's poetry? *Pour comprendre il faut aimer*,° and it seemed to her that, in some ways, he had penetrated the poet's inner meaning more completely than any other critic. There were certain problems, of course, that he had left untouched; certain aspects of that many-sided mind that he had perhaps failed to seize—

"But then you are young," she concluded gently, "and one could not wish you, as yet, the experience that a fuller understanding would imply."

II

She stayed a month at Villa d'Este, and Danyers was with her daily. She showed an unaffected pleasure in his society; a pleasure so obviously founded on their common veneration of Rendle, that the young man could enjoy it without fear of fatuity. At first he was merely one more grain of frankincense on the altar of her insatiable divinity; but gradually a more personal note crept into their intercourse. If she still liked him only because he appreciated Rendle, she at least perceptibly distinguished him from the herd of Rendle's appreciators.

Her attitude toward the great man's memory struck Danyers as perfect. She neither proclaimed nor disavowed her identity. She was frankly Silvia to those who knew and cared; but there was no trace of the Egeria in her pose. She spoke often of Rendle's books, but seldom of himself; there was no posthumous conjugality, no use of the possessive tense, in her abounding reminiscences. Of the master's intellectual life, of his habits of thought and work, she never wearied of talking. She knew the his-

Pour comprendre il faut aimer: To understand one must love.

tory of each poem; by what scene or episode each image had been evoked; how many times the words in a certain line had been transposed; how long a certain adjective had been sought, and what had at last suggested it; she could even explain that one impenetrable line, the torment of critics, the joy of detractors, the last line of *The Old Odysseus.*

Danyers felt that in talking of these things she was no mere echo of Rendle's thought. If her identity had appeared to be merged in his it was because they thought alike, not because he had thought for her. Posterity is apt to regard the women whom poets have sung as chance pegs on which they hung their garlands; but Mrs. Anerton's mind was like some fertile garden wherein, inevitably, Rendle's imagination had rooted itself and flowered. Danyers began to see how many threads of his complex mental tissue the poet had owed to the blending of her temperament with his; in a certain sense Silvia had herself created the *Sonnets to Silvia.*

To be the custodian of Rendle's inner self, the door, as it were, to the sanctuary, had at first seemed to Danyers so comprehensive a privilege that he had the sense, as his friendship with Mrs. Anerton advanced, of forcing his way into a life already crowded. What room was there, among such towering memories, for so small an actuality as his? Quite suddenly, after this, he discovered that Mrs. Memorall knew better: his fortunate friend was bored as well as lonely.

"You have had more than any other woman!" he had exclaimed to her one day: and her smile flashed a derisive light on his blunder. Fool that he was, not to have seen that she had not had enough! That she was young still—do years count?—tender, human, a woman; that the living have need of the living.

After that, when they climbed the alleys of the hanging park, resting in one of the little ruined temples, or watching, through a ripple of foliage, the remote blue flash of the lake, they did not always talk of Rendle or of literature. She encouraged Danyers to speak of himself; to confide his ambitions to her; she asked him the questions which are the wise woman's substitute for advice.

"You must write," she said, administering the most exquisite flattery that human lips could give.

Of course he meant to write—why not do something great in his turn? His best, at lest; with the resolve, at the outset, that his best should be *the* best. Nothing less seemed possible with that mandate in his ears. How she had divined him; lifted and disentangled his groping ambitions; laid the awakening touch on his spirit with her creative *Let there be light!*

It was his last day with her, and he was feeling very hopeless and happy.

"You ought to write a book about *him,*" she went on gently.

Danyers started; he was beginning to dislike Rendle's way of walking in unannounced.

"You ought to do it," she insisted. "A complete interpretation—a summing up of his style, his purpose, his theory of life and art. No one else could do it as well."

He sat looking at her perplexedly. Suddenly—dared he guess?

"I couldn't do it without you," he faltered.

"I could help you—I would help you, of course."

They sat silent, both looking at the lake.

It was agreed, when they parted, that he should rejoin her six weeks later in Venice. There they were to talk about the book.

III

Lago d'Iseo, August 14th

When I said good-bye to you yesterday I promised to come back to Venice in a week: 55
I was to give you your answer then. I was not honest in saying that; I didn't mean to
go back to Venice or to see you again. I was running away from you—and I mean to
keep on running! If *you* won't, *I* must. Somebody must save you from marrying a disappointed woman of—well, you say years don't count, and why should they, after all,
since you are not to marry me?

That is what I dare not go back to say. *You are not to marry me.* We have had our
month together in Venice (such a good month, was it not?) and now you are to go
home and write a book—any book but the one we—didn't talk of!—and I am to stay
here, attitudinizing among my memories like a sort of female Tithonus. The dreariness of this enforced immortality!

But you shall know the truth. I care for you, or at least for your love, enough to
owe you that.

You thought it was because Vincent Rendle had loved me that there was so little hope for you. I had had what I wanted to the full; wasn't that what you said? It is
just when a man begins to think he understands a woman that he may be sure he
doesn't! It is because Vincent Rendle *didn't love me* that there is no hope for you. I
never had what I wanted, and never, never, never will I stoop to wanting anything else.

Do you begin to understand? It was all a sham then, you say? No, it was all real
as far as it went. You are young—you haven't learned, as you will later, the thousand
imperceptible signs by which one gropes one's way through the labyrinth of human
nature; but didn't it strike you, sometimes, that I never told you any foolish little anecdotes about him? His trick, for instance, of twirling a paper knife round and round
between his thumb and forefinger while he talked; his mania for saving the backs of
notes; his greediness for wild strawberries, the little pungent Alpine ones; his childish
delight in acrobats and jugglers; his way of always calling me *you—dear you*, every letter began—I never told you a word of all that, did I? Do you suppose I could have
helped telling you, if he had loved me? These little things would have been mine,
then, a part of my life—of our life—they would have slipped out in spite of me (it's
only your unhappy woman who is always reticent and dignified). But there never was
any "our life"; it was always "our lives" to the end. . . .

If you knew what a relief it is to tell someone at last, you would bear with me,   60
you would let me hurt you! I shall never be quite so lonely again, now that someone
knows.

Let me begin at the beginning. When I first met Vincent Rendle I was not
twenty-five. That was twenty years ago. From that time until his death, five years ago,
we were fast friends. He gave me fifteen years, perhaps the best fifteen years, of his
life. The world, as you know, thinks that his greatest poems were written during those
years; I am supposed to have "inspired" them, and in a sense I did. From the first, the
intellectual sympathy between us was almost complete; my mind must have been to
him (I fancy) like some perfectly tuned instrument on which he was never tired of
playing. Someone told me of his once saying of me that I "always understood"; it is
the only praise I ever heard of his giving me. I don't even know if he thought me
pretty, though I hardly think my appearance could have been disagreeable to him, for
he hated to be with ugly people. At all events he fell into the way of spending more

and more of his time with me. He liked our house; our ways suited him. He was nervous, irritable; people bored him and yet he disliked solitude. He took sanctuary with us. When we traveled he went with us; in the winter he took rooms near us in Rome. In England or on the continent he was always with us for a good part of the year. In small ways I was able to help him in his work; he grew dependent on me. When we were apart he wrote to me continually—he liked to have me share in all he was doing or thinking; he was impatient for my criticism of every new book that interested him; I was a part of his intellectual life. The pity of it was that I wanted to be something more. I was a young woman and I was in love with him—not because he was Vincent Rendle, but just because he was himself!

People began to talk, of course—I was Vincent Rendle's Mrs. Anerton; when the *Sonnets to Silvia* appeared, it was whispered that I was Silvia. Wherever he went, I was invited; people made up to me in the hope of getting to know him; when I was in London my doorbell never stopped ringing. Elderly peeresses, aspiring hostesses, lovesick girls and struggling authors overwhelmed me with their assiduities. I hugged my success, for I knew what it meant—they thought that Rendle was in love with me! Do you know, at times, they almost made me think so too? Oh, there was no phase of folly I didn't go through. You can't imagine the excuses a woman will invent for a man's not telling her that he loves her—pitiable arguments that she would see through at a glance if any other woman used them! But all the while, deep down, I knew he had never cared. I should have known it if he had made love to me every day of his life. I could never guess whether he knew what people said about us—he listened so little to what people said; and cared still less, when he heard. He was always quite honest and straightforward with me; he treated me as one man treats another; and yet at times I felt he *must* see that with me it was different. If he did see, he made no sign. Perhaps he never noticed—I am sure he never meant to be cruel. He had never made love to me; it was no fault of his if I wanted more than he could give me. The *Sonnets to Silvia*, you say? But what are they? A cosmic philosophy, not a love poem; addressed to Woman, not to a woman!

But then, the letters? Ah, the letters! Well, I'll make a clean breast of it. You have noticed the breaks in the letters here and there, just as they seem to be on the point of growing a little—warmer? The critics, you may remember, praised the editor for his commendable delicacy and good taste (so rare in these days!) in omitting from the correspondence all personal allusions, all those *détails intimes* which should be kept sacred from the public gaze. They referred, of course, to the asterisks in the letters to Mrs. A. Those letters I myself prepared for publication; that is to say, I copied them out for the editor, and every now and then I put in a line of asterisks to make it appear that something had been left out. You understand? The asterisks were a sham—*there was nothing to leave out.*

No one but a woman could understand what I went through during those years—the moments of revolt, when I felt I must break away from it all, fling the truth in his face and never see him again; the inevitable reaction, when not to see him seemed the one unendurable thing, and I trembled lest a look or word of mine should disturb the poise of our friendship; the silly days when I hugged the delusion that he *must* love me, since everybody thought he did; the long periods of numbness, when I didn't seem to care whether he loved me or not. Between these wretched days came others when our intellectual accord was so perfect that I forgot everything else in the joy of feeling myself lifted up on the wings of his thought. Sometimes, then, the heavens seemed to be opened.

All this time he was so dear a friend! He had the genius of friendship, and he spent it all on me. Yes, you were right when you said that I have had more than any other woman. *Il faut de l'adresse pour aimer,*° Pascal says; and I was so quiet, so cheerful, so frankly affectionate with him, that in all those years I am almost sure I never bored him. Could I have hoped as much if he had loved me?

You mustn't think of him, though, as having been tied to my skirts. He came and went as he pleased, and so did his fancies. There was a girl once (I am telling you everything), a lovely being who called his poetry "deep" and gave him *Lucile* on his birthday. He followed her to Switzerland one summer, and all the time that he was dangling after her (a little too conspicuously, I always thought, for a Great Man), he was writing to *me* about his theory of vowel combinations—or was it his experiments in English hexameter? The letters were dated from the very places where I knew they went and sat by waterfalls together and he thought out adjectives for her hair. He talked to me about it quite frankly afterwards. She was perfectly beautiful and it had been a pure delight to watch her; but she *would* talk, and her mind, he said, was "all elbows." And yet, the next year, when her marriage was announced, he went away alone, quite suddenly . . . and it was just afterwards that he published *Love's Viaticum.* Men are queer!

After my husband died—I am putting things crudely, you see—I had a return of hope. It was because he loved me, I argued, that he had never spoken; because he had always hoped some day to make me his wife; because he wanted to spare me the "reproach." Rubbish! I knew well enough, in my heart of hearts, that my one chance lay in the force of habit. He had grown used to me; he was no longer young; he dreaded new people and new ways; *il avait pris son pli.*° Would it not be easier to marry me?

I don't believe he ever thought of it. He wrote me what people call "a beautiful letter"; he was kind, considerate, decently commiserating; then, after a few weeks, he slipped into his old way of coming in every afternoon, and our interminable talks began again just where they had left off. I heard later that people thought I had shown "such good taste" in not marrying him.

So we jogged on for five years longer. Perhaps they were the best years, for I had given up hoping. Then he died.

After his death—this is curious—there came to me a kind of mirage of love. All the books and articles written about him, all the reviews of the *Life*, were full of discreet allusions to Silvia. I became again the Mrs. Anerton of the glorious days. Sentimental girls and dear lads like you turned pink when somebody whispered, "That was Silvia you were talking to." Idiots begged for my autograph—publishers urged me to write my reminiscences of him—critics consulted me about the reading of doubtful lines. And I knew that, to all these people, I was the woman Vincent Rendle had loved.

After a while that fire went out too and I was left alone with my past. Alone— quite alone; for he had never really been with me. The intellectual union counted for nothing now. It had been soul to soul, but never hand in hand, and there were no little things to remember him by.

Il faut de l'adresse pour aimer: To love one must have skill.
il avait pris son pli: he was set in his ways.

Then there set in a kind of Arctic winter. I crawled into myself as into a snow hut. I hated my solitude and yet dreaded anyone who disturbed it. That phase, of course, passed like the others. I took up life again, and began to read the papers and consider the cut of my gowns. But here was one question that I could not be rid of, that haunted me night and day. Why had he never loved me? Why had I been so much to him, and no more? Was I so ugly, so essentially unlovable, that though a man might cherish me as his mind's comrade, he could not care for me as a woman? I can't tell you how that question tortured me. It became an obsession.

My poor friend, do you begin to see? I had to find out what some other man thought of me. Don't be too hard on me! Listen first—consider. When I first met Vincent Rendle I was a young woman, who had married early and led the quietest kind of life; I had had no "experiences." From the hour of our first meeting to the day of his death I never looked at any other man, and never noticed whether any other man looked at me. When he died, five years ago, I knew the extent of my powers no more than a baby. Was it too late to find out? Should I never know *why*?

Forgive me—forgive me. You are so young; it will be an episode, a mere "document," to you so soon! And, besides, it wasn't as deliberate, as cold-blooded as these disjointed lines have made it appear. I didn't plan it, like a woman in a book. Life is so much more complex than any rendering of it can be. I liked you from the first—I was drawn to you (you must have seen that)—I wanted you to like me; it was not a mere psychological experiment. And yet in a sense it was that, too—I must be honest. I had to have an answer to that question; it was a ghost that had to be laid.

At first I was afraid—oh, so much afraid—that you cared for me only because I was Silvia, that you loved me because you thought Rendle had loved me. I began to think there was no escaping my destiny.

How happy I was when I discovered that you were growing jealous of my past; that you actually hated Rendle! My heart beat like a girl's when you told me you meant to follow me to Venice.

After our parting at Villa d'Este my old doubts reasserted themselves. What did I know of your feeling for me, after all? Were you capable of analyzing it yourself? Was it not likely to be two-thirds vanity and curiosity, and one-third literary sentimentality? You might easily fancy that you cared for Mary Anerton when you were really in love with Silvia—the heart is such a hypocrite! Or you might be more calculating than I had supposed. Perhaps it was you who had been flattering *my* vanity in the hope (the pardonable hope!) of turning me, after a decent interval, into a pretty little essay with a margin.

When you arrived in Venice and we met again—do you remember the music on the lagoon, that evening, from my balcony?—I was so afraid you would begin to talk about the book—the book, you remember, was your ostensible reason for coming. You never spoke of it, and I soon saw your one fear was *I* might do so—might remind you of your object in being with me. Then I knew you cared for me! yes, at that moment really cared! We never mentioned the book once, did we, during that month in Venice?

I have read my letter over; and now I wish that I had said this to you instead of writing it. I could have felt my way then, watching your face and seeing if you understood. But, no, I could not go back to Venice; and I could not tell you (though I tried) while we were there together. I couldn't spoil that month—my one month. It was so good, for once in my life, to get away from literature.

You will be angry with me at first—but, alas! not for long. What I have done would have been cruel if I had been a younger woman; as it is, the experiment will hurt no one but myself. And it will hurt me horribly (as much as, in your first anger, you may perhaps wish), because it has shown me, for the first time, all that I have missed.

QUESTIONS

1. Describe the circumstances of Rendle and Mrs. Anerton—the poet and "Sylvia." How convincing is Wharton's portrayal of these circumstances? How does Danyers get involved in the situation?
2. What sort of person is Mrs. Anerton? Why does she praise Rendle? Why is she critical of him? Why does she say that men are strange?
3. How do Danyers's attitudes toward Mrs. Anerton change?
4. How much time takes place in the story? What happens between sections 2 and 3?
5. Explain why Wharton changes the point of view in section 3. How do you react to the change? Why?
6. Why is the Story named "The Muse's Tragedy"?

The Other Two _____ *1904*

I

Waythorn, on the drawing-room hearth, waited for his wife to come down to dinner.

It was their first night under his own roof, and he was surprised at his thrill of boyish agitation. He was not so old, to be sure—his glass gave him little more than the five-and-thirty years to which his wife confessed—but he had fancied himself already in the temperate zone; yet here he was listening for her step with a tender sense of all it symbolized, with some old trail of verse about the garlanded nuptial doorposts floating through his enjoyment of the pleasant room and the good dinner just beyond it.

They had been hastily recalled from their honeymoon by the illness of Lily Haskett, the child of Mrs. Waythorn's first marriage. The little girl, at Waythorn's desire, had been transferred to his house on the day of her mother's wedding, and the doctor, on their arrival, broke the news that she was ill with typhoid, but declared that all the symptoms were favorable. Lily could show twelve years of unblemished health, and the case promised to be a light one. The nurse spoke as reassuringly, and after a moment of alarm Mrs. Waythorn had adjusted herself to the situation. She was very fond of Lily—her affection for the child had perhaps been her decisive charm in Waythorn's eyes—but she had the perfectly balanced nerves which her little girl had inherited, and no woman ever wasted less tissue in unproductive worry. Waythorn was therefore quite prepared to see her come in presently, a little late because of a last look at Lily, but as serene and well-appointed as if her good-night kiss had been laid on the brow of health. Her composure was restful to him; it acted as ballast to his somewhat unstable sensibilities. As he pictured her bending over the child's bed he thought how soothing her presence must be in illness: her very step would prognosticate recovery.

His own life had been a gray one, from temperament rather than circumstance, and he had been drawn to her by the unperturbed gaiety which kept her fresh and elastic at an age when most women's activities are growing either slack or febrile. He knew what was said about her; for, popular as she was, there had always been a faint undercurrent of detraction. When she had appeared in New York, nine or ten years earlier, as the pretty Mrs. Haskett whom Gus Varick had unearthed somewhere—was it in Pittsburg or Utica—society, while promptly accepting her, had reserved the right to cast a doubt on its own indiscrimination. Inquiry, however, established her undoubted connection with a socially reigning family, and explained her recent divorce as the natural result of a runaway match at seventeen; and as nothing was known of Mr. Haskett it was easy to believe the worst of him.

Alice Haskett's remarriage with Gus Varick was a passport to the set whose recognition she coveted, and for a few years the Varicks were the most popular couple in town. Unfortunately the alliance was brief and stormy, and this time the husband had his champions. Still, even Varick's staunchest supporters admitted that he was not meant for matrimony, and Mrs. Varick's grievances were of a nature to bear the inspection of the New York courts. A New York divorce is in itself a diploma of virtue, and in the semiwidowhood of this second separation Mrs. Varick took on an air of sanctity, and was allowed to confide her wrongs to some of the most scrupulous ears in town. But when it was known that she was to marry Waythorn there was a momentary reaction. Her best friends would have preferred to see her remain in the role of the injured wife, which was as becoming to her as crepe to a rosy complexion. True, a decent time had elapsed, and it was not even suggested that Waythorn had supplanted his predecessor. People shook their heads over him, however, and one grudging friend, to whom he affirmed that he took the step with his eyes open, replied oracularly: "Yes—and with your ears shut."

Waythorn could afford to smile at these innuendoes. In the Wall Street phrase, he had "discounted" them. He knew that society has not yet adapted itself to the consequences of divorce, and that till the adaptation takes place every woman who uses the freedom the law accords her must be her own social justification. Waythorn had an amused confidence in his wife's ability to justify herself. His expectations were fulfilled, and before the wedding took place Alice Varick's group had rallied openly to her support. She took it all imperturbably: she had a way of surmounting obstacles without seeming to be aware of them, and Waythorn looked back with wonder at the trivialities over which he had worn his nerves thin. He had the sense of having found refuge in a richer, warmer nature than his own, and his satisfaction, at the moment, was humorously summed up in the thought that his wife, when she had done all she could for Lily, would not be ashamed to come down and enjoy a good dinner.

The anticipation of such enjoyment was not, however, the sentiment expressed by Mrs. Waythorn's charming face when she presently joined him. Though she had put on her most engaging tea gown she had neglected to assume the smile that went with it, and Waythorn thought he had never seen her look so nearly worried.

"What is it?" he asked. "Is anything wrong with Lily?"

"No; I've just been in and she's still sleeping." Mrs. Waythorn hesitated. "But something tiresome has happened."

He had taken her two hands, and now perceived that he was crushing a paper between them.

"This letter?"

"Yes—Mr. Haskett has written—I mean his lawyer has written."

Waythorn felt himself flush uncomfortably. He dropped his wife's hands.

"What about?"

"About seeing Lily. You know the courts—"   15
"Yes, yes," he interrupted nervously.

Nothing was known about Haskett in New York. He was vaguely supposed to have remained in the outer darkness from which his wife had been rescued, and Waythorn was one of the few who were aware that he had given up his business in Utica and followed her to New York in order to be near his little girl. In the days of his wooing, Waythorn had often met Lily on the doorstep, rosy and smiling, on her way "to see papa."

"I am so sorry," Mrs. Waythorn murmured.

He roused himself. "What does he want?"   20
"He wants to see her. You know she goes to him once a week."
"Well—he doesn't expect her to go to him now, does he?"
"No—he has heard of her illness; but he expects to come here."
"Here?"

Mrs. Waythorn reddened under his gaze. They looked away from each other.   25
"I'm afraid he has the right . . . You'll see. . . . " She made a proffer of the letter.

Waythorn moved away with a gesture of refusal. He stood staring about the softly-lighted room, which a moment before had seemed so full of bridal intimacy.

"I'm so sorry," she repeated. "If Lily could have been moved—"
"That's out of the question," he returned impatiently.
"I suppose so."   30

Her lip was beginning to tremble, and he felt himself a brute.

"He must come, of course," he said. "When is—his day?"
"I'm afraid—tomorrow."
"Very well. Send a note in the morning."

The butler entered to announce dinner.   35

Waythorn turned to his wife. "Come—you must be tired. It's beastly, but try to forget about it," he said, drawing her hand through his arm.

"You're so good, dear. I'll try," she whispered back.

Her face cleared at once, and as she looked at him across the flowers, between the rosy candleshades, he saw her lips waver back into a smile.

"How pretty everything is!" she sighed luxuriously.

He turned to the butler. "The champagne at once, please. Mrs. Waythorn is tired."

In a moment or two their eyes met above the sparkling glasses. Her own were quite clear and untroubled: he saw that she had obeyed his injunction and forgotten.

II

Waythorn, the next morning, went downtown earlier than usual. Haskett was not likely to come till the afternoon, but the instinct of flight drove him forth. He meant to stay away all day—he had thoughts of dining at his club. As his door closed behind him he reflected that before he opened it again it would have admitted another man who had as much right to enter it as himself, and the thought filled him with a physical repugnance.

He caught the "elevated" at the employees' hour, and found himself crushed between two layers of pendulous humanity. At Eighth Street the man facing him wriggled out, and another took his place. Waythorn glanced up and saw that it was Gus

Varick. The men were so close together that it was impossible to ignore the smile of recognition on Varick's handsome overblown face. And after all—why not? They had always been on good terms, and Varick had been divorced before Waythorn's attentions to his wife began. The two exchanged a word on the perennial grievance of the congested trains, and when a seat at their side was miraculously left empty the instinct of self-preservation made Waythorn slip into it after Varick.

The latter drew the stout man's breath of relief. "Lord—I was beginning to feel like a pressed flower." He leaned back, looking unconcernedly at Waythorn. "Sorry to hear that Sellers is knocked out again."

"Sellers?" echoed Waythorn, starting at his partner's name.

Varick looked surprised. "You didn't know he was laid up with the gout?"

"No. I've been away—I only got back last night." Waythorn felt himself reddening in anticipation of the other's smile.

"Ah—yes; to be sure. And Sellers' attack came on two days ago. I'm afraid he's pretty bad. Very awkward for me, as it happens, because he was just putting through a rather important thing for me."

"Ah?" Waythorn wondered vaguely since when Varick had been dealing in "important things." Hitherto he had dabbled only in the shallow pools of speculation, with which Waythorn's office did not usually concern itself.

It occurred to him that Varick might be talking at random, to relieve the strain of their propinquity. That strain was becoming momentarily more apparent to Waythorn, and when, at Cortlandt Street, he caught sight of an acquaintance and had a sudden vision of the picture he and Varick must present to an initiated eye, he jumped up with a muttered excuse.

"I hope you'll find Sellers better," said Varick civilly, and he stammered back: "If I can be of any use to you—" and let the departing crowd sweep him to the platform.

At his office he heard that Sellers was in fact ill with the gout, and would probably not be able to leave the house for some weeks.

"I'm sorry it should have happened so, Mr. Waythorn," the senior clerk said with affable significance. "Mr. Sellers was very much upset at the idea of giving you such a lot of extra work just now."

"Oh, that's no matter," said Waythorn hastily. He secretly welcomed the pressure of additional business, and was glad to think that, when the day's work was over, he would have to call at his partner's on the way home.

He was late for luncheon, and turned in at the nearest restaurant instead of going to his club. The place was full, and the waiter hurried him to the back of the room to capture the only vacant table. In the cloud of cigar smoke Waythorn did not at once distinguish his neighbors: but presently, looking about him, he saw Varick seated a few feet off. This time, luckily, they were too far apart for conversation, and Varick, who faced another way, had probably not even seen him; but there was an irony in their renewed nearness.

Varick was said to be fond of good living, and as Waythorn sat dispatching his hurried luncheon he looked across half enviously at the other's leisurely degustation of his meal. When Waythorn first saw him he had been helping himself with critical deliberation to a bit of Camembert at the ideal point of liquefaction, and now, the cheese removed, he was just pouring his *café double* from its little two-storied earthen pot. He poured slowly, his ruddy profile bent over the task, and one beringed white hand steadying the lid of the coffeepot; then he stretched his other hand to the decanter of cognac at his elbow, filled a liqueur glass, took a tentative sip, and poured the brandy into his coffee cup.

Waythorn watched him in a kind of fascination. What was he thinking of—only of the flavor of the coffee and the liqueur? Had the morning's meeting left no more trace in his thoughts than on his face? Had his wife so completely passed out of his life that even this odd encounter with her present husband, within a week after her remarriage, was no more than an incident in his day? And as Waythorn mused, another idea struck him: had Haskett ever met Varick as Varick and he had just met? The recollection of Haskett perturbed him, and he rose and left the restaurant, taking a circuitous way out to escape the placid irony of Varick's nod.

It was after seven when Waythorn reached home. He thought the footman who opened the door looked at him oddly.

"How is Miss Lily?" he asked in haste.

"Doing very well, sir. A gentleman—"

"Tell Barlow to put off dinner for half an hour," Waythorn cut him off, hurrying upstairs.

He went straight to his room and dressed without seeing his wife. When he reached the drawing room she was there, fresh and radiant. Lily's day had been good; the doctor was not coming back that evening.

At dinner Waythorn told her of Sellers' illness and of the resulting complications. She listened sympathetically, adjuring him not to let himself be overworked, and asking vague feminine questions about the routine of the office. Then she gave him the chronicle of Lily's day; quoted the nurse and doctor, and told him who had called to inquire. He had never seen her more serene and unruffled. It struck him, with a curious pang, that she was very happy in being with him, so happy that she found a childish pleasure in rehearsing the trivial incidents of her day.

After dinner they went to the library, and the servant put the coffee and liqueurs on a low table before her and left the room. She looked singularly soft and girlish in her rosy-pale dress, against the dark leather of one of his bachelor armchairs. A day earlier the contrast would have charmed him.

He turned away now, choosing a cigar with affected deliberation.

"Did Haskett come?" he asked, with his back to her.

"Oh, yes—he came."

"You didn't see him, of course?"

She hesitated a moment. "I let the nurse see him."

That was all. There was nothing more to ask. He swung round toward her, applying a match to his cigar. Well, the thing was over for a week, at any rate. He would try not to think of it. She looked up at him, at trifle rosier than usual, with a smile in her eyes.

"Ready for your coffee, dear?"

He leaned against the mantelpiece, watching her as she lifted the coffeepot. The lamplight struck a gleam from her bracelets and tipped her soft hair with brightness. How light and slender she was, and how each gesture flowed into the next! She seemed a creature all compact of harmonies. As the thought of Haskett receded, Waythorn felt himself yielding again to the joy of possessorship. They were his, those white hands with their flitting motions, his the light haze of hair, the lips and eyes. . . .

She sat down the coffeepot, and reaching for the decanter of cognac, measured off a liqueur glass and poured it into his cup.

Waythorn uttered a sudden exclamation.

"What is the matter?" she said, startled.

"Nothing: only—I don't take cognac in my coffee."

"Oh, how stupid of me," she cried.

Their eyes met, and she blushed a sudden agonized red.

III

Ten days later, Mr. Sellers, still housebound, asked Waythorn to call on his way downtown.

The senior partner, with his swaddled foot propped up by the fire, greeted his associate with an air of embarrassment.

"I'm sorry, my dear fellow; I've got to ask you to do an awkward thing for me."

Waythorn waited, and the other went on, after a pause apparently given to the arrangement of his phrases: "The fact is, when I was knocked out I had just gone into a rather complicated piece of business for—Gus Varick."

"Well?" said Waythorn, with an attempt to put him at his ease.

"Well—it's this way: Varick came to me the day before my attack. He had evidently had an inside tip from somebody, and had made about a hundred thousand. He came to me for advice, and I suggested his going in with Vanderlyn."

"Oh, the deuce!" Waythorn exclaimed. He saw in a flash what had happened. The investment was an alluring one, but required negotiation. He listened quietly while Sellers put the case before him, and, the statement ended, he said: "You think I ought to see Varick?"

"I'm afraid I can't as yet. The doctor is obdurate. And this thing can't wait. I hate to ask you, but no one else in the office knows the ins and outs of it."

Waythorn stood silent. He did not care a farthing for the success of Varick's venture, but the honor of the office was to be considered, and he could hardly refuse to oblige his partner.

"Very well," he said, "I'll do it."

That afternoon, apprised by telephone, Varick called at the office. Waythorn, waiting in his private room, wondered what the others thought of it. The newspapers, at the time of Mrs. Waythorn's marriage, had acquainted their readers with every detail of her previous matrimonial ventures, and Waythorn could fancy the clerks smiling behind Varick's back as he was ushered in.

Varick bore himself admirably. He was easy without being undignified, and Waythorn was conscious of cutting a much less impressive figure. Varick had no experience of business, and the talk prolonged itself for nearly an hour while Waythorn set forth with scrupulous precision the details of the proposed transaction.

"I'm awfully obliged to you," Varick said as he rose. "The fact is I'm not used to having much money to look after, and I don't want to make an ass of myself—" He smiled, and Waythorn could not help noticing that there was something pleasant about his smile. "It feels uncommonly queer to have enough cash to pay one's bills. I'd have sold my soul for it a few years ago!"

Waythorn winced at the allusion. He had heard it rumored that a lack of funds had been one of the determining causes of the Varick separation, but it did not occur to him that Varick's words were intentional. It seemed more likely that the desire to keep clear of embarrassing topics had fatally drawn him into one. Waythorn did not wish to be outdone in civility.

"We'll do the best we can for you," he said. "I think this is a good thing you're in."

"Oh, I'm sure it's immense. It's awfully good of you—" Varick broke off, embarrassed. "I suppose the thing's settled now—but if—"

"If anything happens before Sellers is about, I'll see you again," said Waythorn quietly. He was glad, in the end, to appear the more self-possessed of the two.

The course of Lily's illness ran smooth, and as the days passed Waythorn grew used to the idea of Haskett's weekly visit. The first time the day came round, he stayed out late, and questioned his wife as to the visit on his return. She replied at once that Haskett had merely seen the nurse downstairs, as the doctor did not wish anyone in the child's sickroom till after the crisis.   95

The following week Waythorn was again conscious of the recurrence of the day, but had forgotten it by the time he came home to dinner. The crisis of the disease came a few days later, with a rapid decline of fever, and the little girl was pronounced out of danger. In the rejoicing which ensued the thought of Haskett passed out of Waythorn's mind, and one afternoon, letting himself into the house with a latchkey, he went straight to his library without noticing a shabby hat and umbrella in the hall.

In the library he found a small effaced-looking man with a thinnish gray beard sitting on the edge of a chair. The stranger might have been a piano tuner, or one of those mysteriously efficient persons who are summoned in emergencies to adjust some detail of the domestic machinery. He blinked at Waythorn through a pair of gold-rimmed spectacles and said mildly: "Mr. Waythorn, I presume? I am Lily's father."

Waythorn flushed. "Oh—" he stammered uncomfortably. He broke off, disliking to appear rude. Inwardly he was trying to adjust the actual Haskett to the image of him projected by his wife's reminiscences. Waythorn had been allowed to infer that Alice's first husband was a brute.

"I am sorry to intr.de," said Haskett, with his over-the-counter politeness.

"Don't mention it," returned Waythorn, collecting himself. "I suppose the nurse has been told?"

"I presume so. I can wait," said Haskett. He had a resigned way of speaking, as though life had worn down his natural powers of resistance.   100

Waythorn stood on the threshold, nervously pulling off his gloves.

"I'm sorry you've been detained. I will send for the nurse," he said; and as he opened the door he added with an effort: "I'm glad we can give you a good report of Lily." He winced as the *we* slipped out, but Haskett seemed not to notice it.

"Thank you, Mr. Waythorn. It's been an anxious time for me."

"Ah, well, that's past. Soon she'll be able to go to you." Waythorn nodded and passed out.

In his own room he flung himself down with a groan. He hated the womanish sensibility which made him suffer so acutely from the grotesque chances of life. He had known when he married that his wife's former husbands were both living, and that amid the multiplied contacts of modern existence there were a thousand chances to one that he would run against one or the other, yet he found himself as much disturbed by his brief encounter with Haskett as though the law had not obligingly removed all difficulties in the way of their meeting.   105

Waythorn sprang up and began to pace the room nervously. He had not suffered half as much from his two meetings with Varick. It was Haskett's presence in his own house that made the situation so intolerable. He stood still, hearing steps in the passage.

"This way, please," he heard the nurse say. Haskett was being taken upstairs, then: not a corner of the house but was open to him. Waythorn dropped into another chair, staring vaguely ahead of him. On his dressing table stood a photograph of Alice, taken when he had first known her. She was Alice Varick then—how fine and exquisite he had thought her! Those were Varick's pearls about her neck. At Waythorn's instance they had been returned before her marriage. Had Haskett ever given her any trinkets—and what had become of them, Waythorn wondered? He realized suddenly that he knew very little of Haskett's past or present situation; but from the man's appearance and manner of speech he could reconstruct with curious precision the surroundings of Alice's first marriage. And it startled him to think that she had, in the background of her life, a phase of existence so different from anything with which he had connected her. Varick, whatever his faults, was a gentleman, in the conventional, traditional sense of the term: the sense which at that moment seemed, oddly enough, to have most meaning to Waythorn. He and Varick had the same social habits, spoke the same language, understood the same allusions. But this other man . . . it was grotesquely uppermost in Waythorn's mind that Haskett had worn a made-up tie attached with an elastic. Why should that ridiculous detail symbolize the whole man? Waythorn was exasperated by his own paltriness, but the fact of the tie expanded, forced itself on him, became as it were the key to Alice's past. He could see her, as Mrs. Haskett, sitting in a "front parlor" furnished in plush, with a pianola, and copy of *Ben Hur* on the center table. He could see her going to the theater with Haskett—or perhaps even to a "Church Sociable"—she in a "picture hat" and Haskett in a black frock coat, a little creased, with the made-up tie on an elastic. On the way home they would stop and look at the illuminated shop windows, lingering over the photographs of New York actresses. On Sunday afternoons Haskett would take her for a walk, pushing Lily ahead of them in a white enameled perambulator, and Waythorn had a vision of the people they would stop and talk to. He could fancy how pretty Alice must have looked, in a dress adroitly constructed from the hints of a New York fashion paper, and how she must have looked down on the other women, chafing at her life, and secretly feeling that she belonged in a bigger place.

For the moment his foremost thought was one of wonder at the way in which she had shed the phase of existence which her marriage with Haskett implied. It was as if her whole aspect, every gesture, every inflection, every allusion, were a studied negation of that period of her life. If she had denied being married to Haskett she could hardly have stood more convicted of duplicity than in this obliteration of the self which had been his wife.

Waythorn started up, checking himself in the analysis of her motives. What right had he to create a fantastic effigy of her and then pass judgment on it? She had spoken vaguely of her first marriage as unhappy, had hinted, with becoming reticence, that Haskett had wrought havoc among her young illusions. . . . It was a pity for Waythorn's peace of mind that Haskett's very inoffensiveness shed a new light on the nature of those illusions. A man would rather think that his wife has been brutalized by her first husband than that the process has been reversed.

IV

"Mr. Waythorn, I didn't like that french governess of Lily's."

Haskett, subdued and apologetic, stood before Waythorn in the library, revolving his shabby hat in his hand.

Waythorn, surprised in his armchair over the evening paper, stared back perplexedly at his visitor.

"You'll excuse my asking to see you," Haskett continued. "But this is my last visit, and I thought if I could have a word with you it would be a better way than writing to Mrs. Waythorn's lawyer."

Waythorn rose uneasily. He did not like the French governess either; but that was irrelevant. 115

"I am not so sure of that," he returned stiffly; "but since you wish it I will give your message to—my wife." He always hesitated over the possessive pronoun in addressing Haskett.

The latter sighed. "I don't know as that will help much. She didn't like it when I spoke to her."

Waythorn turned red. "When did you see her?" he asked.

"Not since the first day I came to see Lily—right after she was taken sick. I remarked to her then that I didn't like the governess."

Waythorn made no answer. He remembered distinctly that, after that first visit, 120 he had asked his wife if she had seen Haskett. She had lied to him then, but she had respected his wishes since; and the incident cast a curious light on her character. He was sure she would not have seen Haskett that first day if she had divined that Waythorn would object, and the fact that she did not divine it was almost as disagreeable to the latter as the discovery that she had lied to him.

"I don't like the woman," Haskett was repeating with mild persistency. "She ain't straight, Mr. Waythorn—she'll teach the child to be underhand. I've noticed a change in Lily—she's too anxious to please—and she don't always tell the truth. She used to be the straightest child, Mr. Waythorn—" He broke off, his voice a little thick. "Not but what I want her to have a stylish education," he ended.

Waythorn was touched. "I'm sorry, Mr. Haskett; but frankly, I don't quite see what I can do."

Haskett hesitated. Then he laid his hat on the table, and advanced to the hearthrug, on which Waythorn was standing. There was nothing aggressive in his manner, but he had the solemnity of a timid man resolved on a decisive measure.

"There's just one thing you can do, Mr. Waythorn," he said. "You can remind Mrs. Waythorn that, by the decree of the courts, I am entitled to have a voice in Lily's bringing-up." He paused, and went on more deprecatingly: "I'm not the kind to talk about enforcing my rights, Mr. Waythorn. I don't know as I think a man is entitled to rights he hasn't known how to hold on to; but this business of the child is different. I've never let go there—and I never meant to."

The scene left Waythorn deeply shaken. Shamefacedly, in indirect ways, he had 125 been finding out about Haskett; and all that he had learned was favorable. The little man, in order to be near his daughter, had sold out his share in a profitable business in Utica, and accepted a modest clerkship in a New York manufacturing house. He boarded in a shabby street and had few acquaintances. His passion for Lily filled his life. Waythorn felt that this exploration of Haskett was like groping about with a dark lantern in his wife's past; but he saw now that there were recesses his lantern had not explored. He had never inquired into the exact circumstances of his wife's first matrimonial rupture. On the surface all had been fair. It was she who had obtained the divorce, and the court had given her the child. But Waythorn knew how many ambiguities such a verdict might cover. The mere fact that Haskett retained a right over his daughter implied an unsuspected compromise. Waythorn was an idealist. He always refused to recognize unpleasant contingencies till he found himself confronted with them, and then he saw them followed by a spectral train of consequences. His next days were thus haunted, and he determined to try to lay the ghosts by conjuring them up in his wife's presence.

When he repeated Haskett's request a flame of anger passed over her face; but she subdued it instantly and spoke with a slight quiver of outraged motherhood.

"It is very ungentlemanly of him," she said.

The word grated on Waythorn. "That is neither here nor there. It's a bare question of rights."

She murmured: "It's not as if he could ever be a help to Lily—"

Waythorn flushed. This was even less to his taste. "The question is," he repeated, "what authority has he over her?"

She looked downward, twisting herself a little in her seat. "I am willing to see him—I thought you objected," she faltered.

In a flash he understood that she knew the extent of Haskett's claims. Perhaps it was not the first time she had resisted them.

"My objecting has nothing to do with it," he said coldly; "if Haskett has a right to be consulted you must consult him."

She burst into tears, and he saw that she expected him to regard her as a victim.

Haskett did not abuse his rights. Waythorn had felt miserably sure that he would not. But the governess was dismissed, and from time to time the little man demanded an interview with Alice. After the first outburst she accepted the situation with her usual adaptability. Haskett had once reminded Waythorn of the piano tuner, and Mrs. Waythorn, after a month or two, appeared to class him with that domestic familiar. Waythorn could not but respect the father's tenacity. At first he had tried to cultivate the suspicion that Haskett might be "up" to something, that he had an object in securing a foothold in the house. But in his heart Waythorn was sure of Haskett's single-mindedness; he even guessed in the latter a mild contempt for such advantages as his relation with the Waythorns might offer. Haskett's sincerity of purpose made him invulnerable, and his successor had to accept him as a lien on the property.

Mr. Sellers was sent to Europe to recover from his gout, and Varick's affairs hung on Waythorn's hands. The negotiations were prolonged and complicated; they necessitated frequent conferences between the two men, and the interests of the firm forbade Waythorn's suggesting that his client should transfer his business to another office.

Varick appeared well in the transaction. In moments of relaxation his coarse streak appeared, and Waythorn dreaded his geniality; but in the office he was concise and clearheaded, with a flattering deference to Waythorn's judgment. Their business relations being so affably established, it would have been absurd for the two men to ignore each other in society. The first time they met in a drawing room, Varick took up their intercourse in the same easy key, and his hostess' grateful glance obliged Waythorn to respond to it. After that they ran across each other frequently, and one evening at a ball Waythorn, wandering through the remoter rooms, came upon Varick seated beside his wife. She colored a little, and faltered in what she was saying; but Varick nodded to Waythorn without rising, and the latter strolled on.

In the carriage, on the way home, he broke out nervously: "I didn't know you spoke to Varick."

Her voice trembled a little. "It's the first time—he happened to be standing near me; I didn't know what to do. It's so awkward, meeting everywhere—and he said you had been very kind about some business."

"That's different," said Waythorn.   140

She paused a moment. "I'll do just as you wish," she returned pliantly. "I thought it would be less awkward to speak to him when we meet."

Her pliancy was beginning to sicken him. Had she really no will of her own—no theory about her relation to these men? She had accepted Haskett—did she mean to accept Varick? It was "less awkward," as she had said, and her instinct was to evade difficulties or to circumvent them. With sudden vividness Waythorn saw how the instinct had developed. She was "as easy as an old shoe"—a shoe that too many feet had worn. Her elasticity was the result of tension in too many different directions. Alice Haskett—Alice Varick—Alice Waythorn—she had been each in turn, and had left hanging to each name a little of her privacy, a little of her personality, a little of the inmost self where the unknown god abides.

"Yes—it's better to speak to Varick," said Waythorn wearily.

V

The winter wore on, and society took advantage of the Waythorns' acceptance of Varick. Harassed hostesses were grateful to them for bridging over a social difficulty, and Mrs. Waythorn was held up as a miracle of good taste. Some experimental spirits could not resist the diversion of throwing Varick and his former wife together, and there were those who thought he found a zest in the propinquity. But Mrs. Waythorn's conduct remained irreproachable. She neither avoided Varick nor sought him out. Even Waythorn could not but admit that she had discovered the solution of the newest social problem.

He had married her without giving much thought to that problem. He had fan-   145
cied that a woman can shed her past like a man. But now he saw that Alice was bound to hers both by the circumstances which forced her into continued relation with it, and by the traces it had left on her nature. With grim irony Waythorn compared himself to a member of a syndicate. He held so many shares in his wife's personality and his predecessors were his partners in the business. If there had been any element of passion in the transaction he would have felt less deteriorated by it. The fact that Alice took her change of husbands like a change of weather reduced the situation to mediocrity. He could have forgiven her for blunders, for excesses; for resisting Haskett, for yielding to Varick; for anything but her acquiescence and her tact. She reminded him of a juggler tossing knives; but the knives were blunt and she knew they would never cut her.

And then, gradually, habit formed a protecting surface for his sensibilities. If he paid for each day's comfort with the small change of his illusions, he grew daily to value the comfort more and set less store upon the coin. He had drifted into a dulling propinquity with Haskett and Varick and he took refuge in the cheap revenge of satirizing the situation. He even began to reckon up the advantages which accrued from it, to ask himself if it were not better to own a third of a wife who knew how to make a man happy than a whole one who had lacked opportunity to acquire the art. For it *was* an art, and made up, like all others, of concessions, eliminations and embellishments; of lights judiciously thrown and shadows skillfully softened. His wife knew exactly how to manage the lights, and he knew exactly to what training she owed her skill. He even tried to trace the source of his obligations, to discriminate between the influences which had combined to produce his domestic happiness; he perceived that Haskett's commonness had made Alice worship good breeding, while Varick's liberal construction of the marriage bond had taught her to value the conjugal virtues; so that he was directly indebted to his predecessors for the devotion which made his life easy if not inspiring.

From this phase he passed into that of complete acceptance. He ceased to satirize himself because time dulled the irony of the situation and the joke lost its humor with its sting. Even the sight of Haskett's hat on the hall table had ceased to touch the springs of epigram. The hat was often seen there now, for it had been decided that it was better for Lily's father to visit her than for the little girl to go to his boarding-house. Waythorn, having acquiesced in this arrangement, had been surprised to find how little difference it made. Haskett was never obtrusive, and the few visitors who met him on the stairs were unaware of his identity. Waythorn did not know how often he saw Alice, but with himself Haskett was seldom in contact.

One afternoon, however, he learned on entering that Lily's father was waiting to see him. In the library he found Haskett occupying a chair in his usual provisional way. Waythorn always felt grateful to him for not leaning back.

"I hope you'll excuse me, Mr. Waythorn," he said rising. "I wanted to see Mrs. Waythorn about Lily, and your man asked me to wait here till she came in."

"Of course," said Waythorn, remembering that a sudden leak had that morning given over the drawing room to the plumbers.

He opened his cigar case and held it out to his visitor, and Haskett's acceptance seemed to mark a fresh stage in their intercourse. The spring evening was chilly, and Waythorn invited his guest to draw up his chair to the fire. He meant to find an excuse to leave Haskett in a moment; but he was tired and cold, and after all the little man no longer jarred on him.

The two were enclosed in the intimacy of their blended cigar smoke when the door opened and Varick walked into the room. Waythorn rose abruptly. It was the first time that Varick had come to the house, and the surprise of seeing him, combined with the singular inopportuneness of his arrival, gave a new edge to Waythorn's blunted sensibilities. He stared at his visitor without speaking.

Varick seemed too preoccupied to notice his host's embarrassment.

"My dear fellow," he exclaimed in his most expansive tone, "I must apologize for tumbling in on you in this way, but I was too late to catch you downtown, and so I thought—"

He stopped short, catching sight of Haskett, and his sanguine color deepened to a flush which spread vividly under his scant blond hair. But in a moment he recovered himself and nodded slightly. Haskett returned the bow in silence, and Waythorn was still groping for speech when the footman came in carrying a tea table.

The intrusion offered a welcome vent to Waythorn's nerves. "What the deuce are you bringing this here for?" he said sharply.

"I beg your pardon, sir, but the plumbers are still in the drawing room, and Mrs. Waythorn said she would have tea in the library." The footman's perfectly respectful tone implied a reflection on Waythorn's reasonableness.

"Oh, very well," said the latter resignedly, and the footman proceeded to open the folding tea table and set out its complicated appointments. While this interminable process continued the three men stood motionless, watching it with a fascinated stare, till Waythorn, to break the silence, said to Varick, "Won't you have a cigar?"

He held out the case he had just tendered to Haskett, and Varick helped himself with a smile. Waythorn looked about for a match, and finding none, proffered a light from his own cigar. Haskett, in the background, held his ground mildly, examining his cigar tip now and then, and stepping forward at the right moment to knock its ashes into the fire.

The footman at last withdrew, and Varick immediately began: "If I could just say half a word to you about this business—" 160

"Certainly," stammered Waythorn; "in the dining room—"

But as he placed his hand on the door it opened from without, and his wife appeared on the threshold.

She came in fresh and smiling, in her street dress and hat, shedding a fragrance from the boa which she loosened in advancing.

"Shall we have tea in here, dear?" she began; and then she caught sight of Varick. Her smile deepened, veiling a slight tremor of surprise.

"Why, how do you do?" she said with a distinct note of pleasure. 165

As she shook hands with Varick she saw Haskett standing behind him. Her smile faded for a moment, but she recalled it quickly, with a scarcely perceptible side glance at Waythorn.

"How do you do, Mr. Haskett?" she said, and shook hands with him a shade less cordially.

The three men stood awkwardly before her, till Varick, always the most self-possessed, dashed into an explanatory phrase.

"We—I had to see Waythorn a moment on business," he stammered, brick-red from chin to nape.

Haskett stepped forward with his air of mild obstinacy. "I am sorry to intrude; 170 but you appointed five o'clock—" he directed his resigned glance to the timepiece on the mantel.

She swept aside their embarrassment with a charming gesture of hospitality.

"I'm so sorry—I'm always late; but the afternoon was so lovely." She stood drawing off her gloves, propitiatory and graceful, diffusing about her a sense of ease and familiarity in which the situation lost its grotesqueness. "But before talking business," she added brightly, "I'm sure everyone wants a cup of tea."

She dropped into her low chair by the tea table, and the two visitors, as if drawn by her smile, advanced to receive the cups she held out.

She glanced about for Waythorn, and he took the third cup with a laugh.

QUESTIONS

1. Describe the story's tone. How does Wharton develop the comic possibilities of the relationships between Alice and the three men?

2. Why does Waythorn grow to accept the "other two"? Why does he connect his own happiness to the other men?

3. What is the difference between Alice's description of the other two and Waythorn's own experience with them?

4. Why does Wharton limit the point of view to Waythorn, while preserving dramatic objectivity about both Alice and the other two?

Pomegranate Seed° ————————————————————————*1931*

I

Charlotte Ashby paused on her doorstep. Dark had descended on the brilliancy of the March afternoon, and the grinding rasping street life of the city was at its highest. She turned her back on it, standing for a moment in the old-fashioned, marble-flagged vestibule before she inserted her key in the lock. The sash curtains drawn across the panes of the inner door softened the light within to a warm blur through which no details showed. It was the hour when, in the first months of her marriage to Kenneth Ashby, she had most liked to return to that quiet house in a street long since deserted by business and fashion. The contrast between the soulless roar of New York, its devouring blaze of lights, the oppression of its congested traffic, congested houses, lives, minds and this veiled sanctuary she called home, always stirred her profoundly. In the very heart of the hurricane she had found her tiny islet—or thought she had. And now, in the last months, everything was changed, and she always wavered on the doorstep and had to force herself to enter.

While she stood there she called up the scene within: the hall hung with old prints, the ladderlike stairs, and on the left her husband's long shabby library, full of books and pipes and worn armchairs inviting to meditation. How she had loved that room! Then, upstairs, her own drawing-room, in which, since the death of Kenneth's first wife, neither furniture nor hangings had been changed, because there had never been money enough, but which Charlotte had made her own by moving furniture about and adding more books, another lamp, a table for the new reviews. Even on the occasion of her only visit to the first Mrs. Ashby—a distant, self-centered woman, whom she had known very slightly—she had looked about her with an innocent envy, feeling it to be exactly the drawing-room she would have liked for herself; and now for more than a year it had been hers to deal with as she chose—the room to which she hastened back at dusk on winter days, where she sat reading by the fire, or answering notes at the pleasant roomy desk, or going over her stepchildren's copy books, till she heard her husband's step.

Sometimes friends dropped in; sometimes—oftener—she was alone; and she liked that best, since it was another way of being with Kenneth, thinking over what he had said when they parted in the morning, imagining what he would say when he sprang up the stairs, found her by herself and caught her to him.

Now, instead of this, she thought of one thing only—the letter she might or might not find on the hall table. Until she had made sure whether or not it was there, her mind had no room for anything else. The letter was always the same—a square grayish envelope with "Kenneth Ashby, Esquire," written on it in bold but faint characters. From the first it had struck Charlotte as peculiar that anyone who wrote such a firm hand should trace the letters so lightly; the address was always written as though there were not enough ink in the pen, or the writer's wrist were too weak to bear upon it. Another curious thing was that, in spite of its masculine curves, the writing was so visibly feminine. Some hands are sexless, some masculine, at first glance; the writing

Pomegranate Seed: Wharton explained this title in a letter of January 31, 1931, to her editor, Rutger B. Jewett: "When Persephone left the under-world to re-visit her mother, Demeter, her husband, Hades, lord of the infernal regions, gave her a pomegranate seed to eat, because he knew that if he did so she would never be able to remain among the living, but would be drawn back to the company of the dead."

on the gray envelope, for all its strength and assurance, was without doubt a woman's. The envelope never bore anything but the recipient's name; no stamp, no address. The letter was presumably delivered by hand—but by whose? No doubt it was slipped into the letter box, whence the parlour maid, when she closed the shutters and lit the lights, probably extracted it. At any rate, it was always in the evening, after dark, that Charlotte saw it lying there. She thought of the letter in the singular, as "it," because, though there had been several since her marriage—seven, to be exact—they were so alike in appearance that they had become merged in one another in her mind, become one letter, become "it."

The first had come the day after their return from their honeymoon—a jour-   5
ney prolonged to the West Indies, from which they had returned to New York after an absence of more than two months. Re-entering the house with her husband, late on that first evening—they had dined at his mother's—she had seen, alone on the hall table, the gray envelope. Her eye fell on it before Kenneth's, and her first thought was: "Why, I've seen that writing before"; but where she could not recall. The memory was just definite enough for her to identify the script whenever it looked up at her faintly from the same pale envelope; but on that first day she would have thought no more of the letter if, when her husband's glance lit on it, she had not chanced to be looking at him. It all happened in a flash—his seeing the letter, putting out his hand for it, raising it to his short-sighted eyes to decipher the faint writing, and then abruptly withdrawing the arm he had slipped through Charlotte's, and moving away to the hanging light, his back turned to her. She had waited—waited for a sound, an exclamation; waited for him to open the letter; but he had slipped it into his pocket without a word and followed her into the library. And there they sat down by the fire and lit their cigarettes, and he had remained silent, his head thrown back broodingly against the armchair, his eyes fixed on the hearth, and presently had passed his hand over his forehead and said: "Wasn't it unusually hot at my mother's tonight? I've got a splitting head. Mind if I take myself off to bed?"

That was the first time. Since then Charlotte had never been present when he had received the letter. It usually came before he got home from his office, and she had to go upstairs and leave it lying there. But even if she had not seen it, she would have known it had come by the change in his face when he joined her—which, on those evenings, he seldom did before they met for dinner. Evidently, whatever the letter contained, he wanted to be by himself to deal with it; and when he reappeared he looked years older, looked emptied of life and courage, and hardly conscious of her presence. Sometimes he was silent for the rest of the evening; and if he spoke, it was usually to hint some criticism of her household arrangements, suggest some change in the domestic administration, to ask, a little nervously, if she didn't think Joyce's nursery governess was rather young and flighty, or if she herself always saw to it that Peter—whose throat was delicate—was properly wrapped up when he went to school. At such times Charlotte would remember the friendly warnings she had received when she became engaged to Kenneth Ashby: "Marrying a heartbroken widower! Isn't that rather risky? You know Elsie Ashby absolutely dominated him"; and how she had jokingly replied: "He may be glad of a little liberty for a change." And in this respect she had been right. She had needed no one to tell her, during the first months, that her husband was perfectly happy with her. When they came back from their protracted honeymoon the same friends said: "What have you done to Kenneth? He looks twenty years younger"; and this time she answered with careless joy: "I suppose I've got him out of his groove."

But what she noticed after the gray letters began to come was not so much his nervous tentative fault-finding—which always seemed to be uttered against his will— as the look in his eyes when he joined her after receiving one of the letters. The look was not unloving, not even indifferent; it was the look of a man who had been so far away from ordinary events that when he returns to familiar things they seem strange. She minded that more than the fault-finding.

Though she had been sure from the first that the handwriting on the gray envelope was a woman's, it was long before she associated the mysterious letters with any sentimental secret. She was too sure of her husband's love, too confident of filling his life, for such an idea to occur to her. It seemed far more likely that the letters—which certainly did not appear to cause him any sentimental pleasure—were addressed to the busy lawyer than to the private person. Probably they were from some tiresome client—women, he had often told her, were nearly always tiresome as clients—who did not want her letters opened by his secretary and therefore had them carried to his house. Yes; but in that case the unknown female must be unusually troublesome, judging from the effect her letters produced. Then again, though his professional discretion was exemplary, it was odd that he had never uttered an impatient comment, never remarked to Charlotte, in a moment of expansion, that there was a nuisance of a woman who kept badgering him about a case that had gone against her. He had made more than one semi-confidence of the kind—of course without giving names or details; but concerning this mysterious correspondent his lips were sealed.

There was another possibility: what is euphemistically called an "old entanglement." Charlotte Ashby was a sophisticated woman. She had few illusions about the intricacies of the human heart; she knew that there were often old entanglements. But when she had married Kenneth Ashby, her friends, instead of hinting at such a possibility, had said: "You've got your work cut out for you. Marrying a Don Juan is a sinecure to it. Kenneth's never looked at another woman since he first saw Elsie Corder. During all the years of their marriage he was more like an unhappy lover than a comfortably contented husband. He'll never let you move an armchair or change the place of a lamp; and whatever you venture to do, he'll mentally compare with what Elsie would have done in your place."

Except for an occasional nervous mistrust as to her ability to manage the children—a mistrust gradually dispelled by her good humor and the children's obvious fondness for her—none of these forebodings had come true. The desolate widower, of whom his nearest friends said that only his absorbing professional interests had kept him from suicide after his first wife's death, had fallen in love, two years later, with Charlotte Gorse, and after an impetuous wooing had married her and carried her off on a tropical honeymoon. And ever since he had been as tender and loverlike as during those first radiant weeks. Before asking her to marry him he had spoken to her frankly of his great love for his first wife and his despair after her sudden death; but even then he had assumed no stricken attitude, or implied that life offered no possibility of renewal. He had been perfectly simple and natural, and had confessed to Charlotte that from the beginning he had hoped the future held new gifts for him. And when, after their marriage, they returned to the house where his twelve years with his first wife had been spent, he had told Charlotte at once that he was sorry he couldn't afford to do the place over for her, but that he knew every woman had her own views about furniture and all sorts of household arrangements a man would never notice, and had begged her to make any changes she saw fit without bothering to consult him. As a result, she made as few as possible; but his way of beginning their new life in the old setting was so frank and unembarrassed that it put her immediately at her ease, and she was almost sorry to find that the portrait of Elsie Ashby, which used to hang over the desk in his library, had been transferred in their absence to the children's nursery. Knowing herself to be the indirect cause of this banishment, she spoke of it to her husband; but he answered; "Oh, I thought they ought to grow up with her looking down on them." The answer moved Charlotte, and satisfied her; and as time went by she had to confess that she felt more at home in her house, more at ease and in confidence with her husband, since that long coldly beautiful face on the library wall no longer followed her with guarded eyes. It was as if Kenneth's love had penetrated to the secret she hardly acknowledged to her own heart—her passionate need to feel herself the sovereign even of his past.

With all this stored-up happiness to sustain her, it was curious that she had lately found herself yielding to a nervous apprehension. But there the apprehension was; and on this particular afternoon—perhaps because she was more tired than usual, or because of the trouble of finding a new cook or, for some other ridiculously trivial reason, moral or physical—she found herself unable to react against the feeling. Latchkey in hand, she looked back down the silent street to the whirl and illumination of the great thoroughfare beyond, and up at the sky already aflare with the city's nocturnal life. "Outside there," she thought, "sky-scrapers, advertisements, telephones, wireless, airplanes, movies, motors, and all the rest of the twentieth century; and on the other side of the door something I can't explain, can't relate to them. Something as old as the world, as mysterious as life. . . . Nonsense! What am I worrying about? There hasn't been a letter for three months now—not since the day we came back from the country after Christmas. . . . Queer that they always seem to come after our holidays! . . . Why should I imagine there's going to be one tonight!"

No reason why, but that was the worst of it—one of the worsts!—that there were days when she would stand there cold and shivering with the premonition of something inexplicable, intolerable, to be faced on the other side of the curtained panes; and when she opened the door and went in, there would be nothing; and on other days when she felt the same premonitory chill, it was justified by the sight of the gray envelope. So that ever since the last had come she had taken to feeling cold and premonitory every evening, because she never opened the door without thinking the letter might be there.

Well, she'd had enough of it; that was certain. She couldn't go on like that. If her husband turned white and had a headache on the days when the letter came, he seemed to recover afterward; but she couldn't. With her the strain had become chronic, and the reason was not far to seek. Her husband knew from whom the letter came and what was in it; he was prepared beforehand for whatever he had to deal with, and master of the situation, however bad; whereas she was shut out in the dark with her conjectures.

"I can't stand it! I can't stand it another day!" she exclaimed aloud, as she put her key in the lock. She turned the key and went in; and there, on the table, lay the letter.

II

She was almost glad of the sight. It seemed to justify everything, to put a seal of definiteness on the whole blurred business. A letter for her husband; a letter from a woman—no doubt another vulgar case of "old entanglement." What a fool she had

15

been ever to doubt it, to rack her brains for less obvious explanations! She took up the envelope with a steady contemptuous hand, looked closely at the faint letters, held it against the light and just discerned the outline of the folded sheet within. She knew that now she would have no peace till she found out what was written on that sheet.

Her husband had not come in; he seldom got back from his office before half-past six or seven, and it was not yet six. She would have time to take the letter up to the drawing-room, hold it over the teakettle which at that hour always simmered by the fire in expectation of her return, solve the mystery and replace the letter where she had found it. No one would be the wiser, and her gnawing uncertainty would be over. The alternative, of course, was to question her husband; but to do that seemed even more difficult. She weighed the letter between thumb and finger, looked at it again under the light, started up the stairs with the envelope—and came down again and laid it on the table.

"No, I evidently can't," she said, disappointed.

What should she do, then? She couldn't go up alone to that warm welcoming room, pour out her tea, look over her correspondence, glance at a book or review—not with that letter lying below and the knowledge that in a little while her husband would come in, open it and turn into the library alone, as he always did on the days when the gray envelope came.

Suddenly she decided. She would wait in the library and see for herself; see what happened between him ad the letter when they thought themselves unobserved. She wondered the idea had never occurred to her before. By leaving the door ajar, and sitting in the corner behind it, she could watch him unseen. . . . Well, then, she would watch him! She drew a chair into the corner, sat down, her eyes on the crack, and waited.

As far as she could remember, it was the first time she had ever tried to surprise another person's secret, but she was conscious of no compunction. She simply felt as if she were fighting her way through a stifling fog that she must at all costs get out of.

At length she heard Kenneth's latchkey and jumped up. The impulse to rush out and meet him had nearly made her forget why she was there; but she remembered in time and sat down again. From her post she covered the whole range of his movements—saw him enter the hall, draw the key from the door and take off his hat and overcoat. Then he turned to throw his gloves on the hall table, and at that moment he saw the envelope. The light was full on his face, and what Charlotte first noted there was a look of surprise. Evidently he had not expected the letter—had not thought of the possibility of its being there that day. But though he had not expected it, now that he saw it he knew well enough what it contained. He did not open it immediately, but stood motionless, the color slowly ebbing from his face. Apparently he could not make up his mind to touch it; but at length he put out his hand, opened the envelope, and moved with it to the light. In doing so he turned his back on Charlotte, and she saw only his bent head and slightly stooping shoulders. Apparently all the writing was on one page, for he did not turn the sheet but continued to stare at it for so long that he must have reread it a dozen times—or so it seemed to the woman breathlessly watching him. At length she saw him move; he raised the letter still closer to his eyes, as though he had not fully deciphered it. Then he lowered his head, and she saw his lips touch the sheet.

"Kenneth!" she exclaimed, and went out into the hall.

The letter clutched in his hand, her husband turned and looked at her. "Where were you?" he said, in a low bewildered voice, like a man waked out of his sleep.

"In the library, waiting for you." She tried to steady her voice: "What's the matter! What's in that letter? You look ghastly."

Her agitation seemed to calm him, and he instantly put the envelope into his pocket with a slight laugh. "Ghastly? I'm sorry. I've had a hard day in the office—one or two complicated cases. I look dog-tired, I suppose." 25

"You didn't look tired when you came in. It was only when you opened that letter—"

He had followed her into the library, and they stood gazing at each other. Charlotte noticed how quickly he had regained his self-control; his profession had trained him to rapid mastery of face and voice. She saw at once that she would be at a disadvantage in any attempt to surprise his secret, but at the same moment she lost all desire to maneuvre, to trick him into betraying anything he wanted to conceal. Her wish was still to penetrate the mystery, but only that she might help him to bear the burden it implied. "Even if it *is* another woman," she thought.

"Kenneth," she said, her heart beating excitedly, "I waited here on purpose to see you come in. I wanted to watch you while you opened that letter."

His face, which had paled, turned to dark red; then it paled again. "That letter? Why especially that letter?"

"Because I've noticed that whenever one of those letters comes it seems to have such a strange effect on you." 30

A line of anger she had never seen before came out between his eyes, and she said to herself: "The upper part of his face is too narrow; this is the first time I ever noticed it."

She heard him continue, in the cool and faintly ironic tone of the prosecuting lawyer making a point: "Ah; so you're in the habit of watching people open their letters when they don't know you're there?"

"Not in the habit. I never did such a thing before. But I had to find out what she writes to you, at regular intervals, in those gray envelopes."

He weighed this for a moment; then: "The intervals have not been regular," he said.

"Oh, I daresay you've kept a better account of the dates than I have," she retorted, her magnanimity vanishing at his tone. "All I know is that every time that woman writes to you—" 35

"Why do you assume it's a woman?"

"It's a woman's writing. Do you deny it?"

He smiled. "No, I don't deny it. I asked only because the writing is generally supposed to look more like a man's."

Charlotte passed this over impatiently. "And this woman—what does she write to you about?"

Again he seemed to consider a moment. "About business." 40

"Legal business?"

"In a way, yes. Business in general."

"You look after her affairs for her?"

"Yes."

"You've looked after them for a long time?"

"Yes. A very long time." 45

"Kenneth, dearest, won't you tell me who she is?"

"No. I can't." He paused and brought out, as if with a certain hesitation: "Professional secrecy."

The blood rushed from Charlotte's heart to her temples. "Don't say that—don't!"

"Why not?"

"Because I saw you kiss the letter."

The effect of the words was so disconcerting that she instantly repented having spoken them. Her husband, who had submitted to her cross-questioning with a sort of contemptuous composure, as though he were humouring an unreasonable child, turned on her a face of terror and distress. For a minute he seemed unable to speak; then, collecting himself with an effort, he stammered out: "The writing is very faint; you must have seen me holding the letter close to my eyes to try to decipher it."

"No; I saw you kissing it." He was silent. "Didn't I see you kissing it?"

He sank back into indifference. "Perhaps."

"Kenneth! You stand there and say that—to me?"

"What possible difference can it make to you? The letter is on business, as I told you. Do you suppose I'd lie about it? The writer is a very old friend whom I haven't seen for a long time."

"Men don't kiss business letters, even from women who are very old friends, unless they have been their lovers, and still regret them."

He shrugged his shoulders slightly and turned away, as if he considered the discussion at an end and were faintly disgusted at the turn it had taken.

"Kenneth!" Charlotte moved toward him and caught hold of his arm.

He paused with a look of weariness and laid his hand over hers. "Won't you believe me?" he asked gently.

"How can I? I've watched these letters come to you—for months now they've been coming. Ever since we came back from the West Indies—one of them greeted me the very day we arrived. And after each one of them I see their mysterious effect on you, I see you disturbed, unhappy, as if someone were trying to estrange you from me."

"No, dear; not that. Never!"

She drew back and looked at him with passionate entreaty. "Well, then, prove it to me, darling. It's so easy!"

He forced a smile. "It's not easy to prove anything to a woman who's once taken an idea into her head."

"You've only got to show me the letter."

His hand slipped from hers and he drew back and shook his head.

"You won't?"

"I can't."

"Then the woman who wrote it is your mistress."

"No, dear. No."

"Not now, perhaps. I suppose she's trying to get you back, and you're struggling, out of pity for me. My poor Kenneth!"

"I swear to you she never was my mistress."

Charlotte felt the tears rushing to her eyes. "Ah, that's worse, then—that's hopeless! The prudent ones are the kind that keep their hold on a man. We all know that." She lifted her hands and hid her face in them.

Her husband remained silent; he offered neither consolation nor denial, and at length, wiping away her tears, she raised her eyes almost timidly to his.

"Kenneth, think! We've been married such a short time. Imagine what you're making me suffer. You say you can't show me this letter. You refuse even to explain it." 75

"I've told you the letter is on business. I will swear to that too."

"A man will swear to anything to screen a woman. If you want me to believe you, at least tell me her name. If you'll do that, I promise you I won't ask to see the letter."

There was a long interval of suspense, during which she felt her heart beating against her ribs in quick admonitory knocks, as if warning her of the danger she was incurring.

"I can't," he said at length.

"Not even her name?" 80

"No."

"You can't tell me anything more?"

"No."

Again a pause; this time they seemed both to have reached the end of their arguments and to be helplessly facing each other across a baffling waste of incomprehension.

Charlotte stood breathing rapidly, her hands against her breast. She felt as if she had won a hard race and missed the goal. She had meant to move her husband and had succeeded only in irritating him; and this error of reckoning seemed to change him into a stranger, a mysterious incomprehensible being whom no argument or entreaty of hers could reach. The curious thing was that she was aware in him of no hostility or even impatience, but only of a remoteness, an inaccessibility, far more difficult to overcome. She felt herself excluded, ignored, blotted out of his life. But after a moment or two, looking at him more calmly, she saw that he was suffering as much as she was. His distant guarded face was drawn with pain; the coming of the gray envelope, though it always cast a shadow, had never marked him as deeply as this discussion with his wife.

Charlotte took heart; perhaps, after all, she had not spent her last shaft. She 85 drew nearer and once more laid her hand on his arm. "Poor Kenneth! If you knew how sorry I am for you—"

She thought he winced slightly at this expression of sympathy, but he took her hand and pressed it.

"I can think of nothing worse than to be incapable of loving long," she continued; "to feel the beauty of a great love and to be too unstable to bear its burden."

He turned on her a look of wistful reproach. "Oh, don't say that of me. Unstable!"

She felt herself at last on the right tack, and her voice trembled with excitement 90 as she went on: "Then what about me and this other woman? Haven't you already forgotten Elsie twice within a year?"

She seldom pronounced his first wife's name; it did not come naturally to her tongue. She flung it out now as if she were flinging some dangerous explosive into the open space between them, and drew back a step, waiting to hear the mine go off.

Her husband did not move; his expression grew sadder, but showed no resentment. "I have never forgotten Elsie," he said.

Charlotte could not repress a faint laugh. "Then, you poor dear, between the three of us—"

"There are not—" he began; and then broke off and put his hand to his forehead.

"Not what?"

"I'm sorry; I don't believe I know what I'm saying. I've got a blinding headache." He looked wan and furrowed enough for the statement to be true, but she was exasperated by his evasion.

"Ah, yes; the gray-envelope headache!"

She saw the surprise in his eyes. "I'd forgotten how closely I've been watched," he said coldly. "If you'll excuse me, I think I'll go up and try an hour in the dark, to see if I can rid [myself] of this neuralgia."

She wavered; then she said, with desperate resolution: "I'm sorry your head aches. But before you go I want to say that sooner or later this question must be settled between us. Someone is trying to separate us, and I don't care what it costs me to find out who it is." She looked him steadily in the eyes. "If it costs me your love, I don't care! If I can't have your confidence I don't want anything from you."

He still looked at her wistfully. "Give me time."

"Time for what? It's only a word to say."

"Time to show you that you haven't lost my love or my confidence."

"Well, I'm waiting."

He turned toward the door, and then glanced back hesitatingly. "Oh, do wait, my love," he said, and went out of the room.

She heard his tired step on the stairs and the closing of his bedroom door above. Then she dropped into a chair and buried her face in her folded arms. Her first movement was one of compunction; she seemed to herself to have been hard, unhuman, unimaginative. "Think of telling him that I didn't care if my insistence cost me his love! The lying rubbish!" She started up to follow him and unsay the meaningless words. But she was checked by a reflection. He had had his way, after all; he had eluded all attacks on his secret, and now he was shut up alone in his room, reading that other woman's letter.

III

She was still reflecting on this when the surprised parlor-maid came in and found her. No, Charlotte said, she wasn't going to dress for dinner; Mr. Ashby didn't want to dine. He was very tired and had gone up to his room to rest; later she would have something brought on a tray to the drawing-room. She mounted the stairs to her bedroom. Her dinner dress was lying on the bed, and at the sight the quiet routine of her daily life took hold of her and she began to feel as if the strange talk she had just had with her husband must have taken place in another world, between two beings who were not Charlotte Gorse and Kenneth Ashby, but phantoms projected by her fevered imagination. She recalled the year since her marriage—her husband's constant devotion; his persistent, almost too insistent tenderness; the feeling he had given her at times of being too eagerly dependent on her, too searchingly close to her, as if there were not air enough between her soul and his. It seemed preposterous, as she recalled all this, that a few moments ago she should have been accusing him of an intrigue with another woman! But, then, what—

Again she was moved by the impulse to go up to him, beg his pardon and try to laugh away the misunderstanding. But she was restrained by the fear of forcing herself upon his privacy. He was troubled and unhappy, oppressed by some grief or fear; and he had shown her that he wanted to fight out his battle alone. It would be wiser, as well as more generous, to respect his wish. Only, how strange, how unbearable, to be there, in the next room to his, and feel herself at the other end of the world! In her nervous agitation she almost regretted not having had the courage to open the letter and put it back on the hall table before he came in. At least she would have known what his secret was, and the bogy might have been laid. For she was beginning now to think of the mystery as something conscious, malevolent: a secret persecution before which he quailed, yet from which he could not free himself. Once or twice in his evasive eyes she thought she had detected a desire for help, an impulse of confession, instantly restrained and suppressed. It was as if he felt she could have helped him if she had known, and yet had been unable to tell her!

There flashed through her mind the idea of going to his mother. She was very fond of old Mrs. Ashby, a firm-fleshed clear-eyed old lady, with an astringent bluntness of speech which responded to the forthright and simple in Charlotte's own nature. There had been a tacit bond between them ever since the day when Mrs. Ashby senior, coming to lunch for the first time with her new daughter-in-law, had been received by Charlotte downstairs in the library, and glancing up at the empty wall above her son's desk, had remarked laconically: "Elsie gone, eh?" adding, at Charlotte's murmured explanation: "Nonsense. Don't have her back. Two's company." Charlotte, at this reading of her thoughts, could hardly refrain from exchanging a smile of complicity with her mother-in-law; and it seemed to her now that Mrs. Ashby's almost uncanny directness might pierce to the core of this new mystery. But here again she hesitated, for the idea almost suggested a betrayal. What right had she to call in any one, even so close a relation, to surprise a secret which her husband was trying to keep from her? "Perhaps, by and by, he'll talk to his mother of his own accord," she thought, and then ended: "But what does it matter? He and I must settle it between us."

She was still brooding over the problem when there was a knock on the door and her husband came in. He was dressed for dinner and seemed surprised to see her sitting there, with her evening dress lying unheeded on the bed.

"Aren't you coming down?"   110

"I thought you were not well and had gone to bed," she faltered.

He forced a smile. "I'm not particularly well, but we'd better go down." His face, though still drawn, looked calmer than when he had fled upstairs an hour earlier.

"There it is; he knows what's in the letter and has fought his battle out again, whatever it is," she reflected, "while I'm still in darkness." She rang and gave a hurried order that dinner should be served as soon as possible—just a short meal, whatever could be got ready quickly, as both she and Mr. Ashby were rather tired and not very hungry.

Dinner was announced, and they sat down to it. At first neither seemed able to find a word to say; then Ashby began to make conversation with an assumption of ease that was more oppressive than his silence. "How tired he is! How terribly overtired!" Charlotte said to herself, pursuing her own thoughts while he rambled on about municipal politics, aviation, an exhibition of modern French painting, the health of an old aunt and the installing of the automatic telephone. "Good heavens, how tired he is!"

When they dined alone they usually went into the library after dinner, and   115

Charlotte curled herself up on the divan with her knitting while he settled down in his armchair under the lamp and lit a pipe. But this evening, by tacit agreement, they avoided the room in which their strange talk had taken place, and went up to Charlotte's drawing-room.

They sat down near the fire, and Charlotte said: "Your pipe?" after he had put down his hardly tasted coffee.

He shook his head. "No, not tonight."

"You must go to bed early; you look terribly tired. I'm sure they overwork you at the office."

"I suppose we all overwork at times."

She rose and stood before him with sudden resolution. "Well, I'm not going to have you use up your strength slaving in that way. It's absurd. I can see you're ill." She bent over him and laid her hand on his forehead. "My poor old Kenneth. Prepare to be taken away soon on a long holiday."

He looked up at her, startled. "A holiday?"

"Certainly. Didn't you know I was going to carry you off at Easter? We're going to start in a fortnight on a month's voyage to somewhere or other. On any one of the big cruising steamers." She paused and bent closer, touching his forehead with her lips. "I'm tired, too, Kenneth."

He seemed to pay no heed to her last words, but sat, his hands on his knees, his head drawn back a little from her caress, and looked up at her with a stare of apprehension. "Again? My dear, we can't; I can't possibly go away."

"I don't know why you say 'again,' Kenneth; we haven't taken a real holiday this year."

"At Christmas we spent a week with the children in the country."

"Yes, but this time I mean away from the children, from servants, from the house. From everything that's familiar and fatiguing. Your mother will love to have Joyce and Peter with her."

He frowned and slowly shook his head. "No, dear; I can't leave them with my mother."

"Why, Kenneth, how absurd; she adores them. You didn't hesitate to leave them with her for over two months when we went to the West Indies."

He drew a deep breath and stood up uneasily. "That was different."

"Different? Why?"

"I mean, at that time I didn't realize"—He broke off as if to choose his words and then went on: "My mother adores the children, as you say. But she isn't always very judicious. Grandmothers always spoil children. And she sometimes talks before them without thinking." He turned to his wife with an almost pitiful gesture of entreaty. "Don't ask me to, dear."

Charlotte mused. It was true that the elder Mrs. Ashby had a fearless tongue, but she was the last woman in the world to say or hint anything before her grandchildren at which the most scrupulous parent could take offense. Charlotte looked at her husband in perplexity.

"I don't understand."

He continued to turn on her the same troubled and entreating gaze. "Don't try to," he muttered.

"Not try to?"

"Not now—not yet." He put up his hands and pressed them against his temples.

"Can't you see that there's no use in insisting? I can't go away, no matter how much I might want to."

Charlotte still scrutinized him gravely. "The question is, *do* you want to?"

He returned her gaze for a moment; then his lips began to tremble, and he said, hardly above his breath: "I want—anything you want."

"And yet—"

"Don't ask me. I can't leave—I can't!"

"You mean that you can't go away out of reach of those letters!"

Her husband had been standing before her in an uneasy half-hesitating attitude; now he turned abruptly away and walked once or twice up and down the length of the room, his head bent, his eyes fixed on the carpet.

Charlotte felt her resentfulness rising with her fears. "It's that," she persisted. "Why not admit it? You can't live without them."

He continued his troubled pacing of the room; then he stopped short, dropped into a chair and covered his face with his hands. From the shaking of his shoulders, Charlotte saw that he was weeping. She had never seen a man cry, except her father after her mother's death, when she was a little girl; and she remembered still how the sight had frightened her. She was frightened now; she felt that her husband was being dragged away from her into some mysterious bondage, and that she must use up her last atom of strength in the struggle for his freedom, and for hers.

"Kenneth—Kenneth!" she pleaded, kneeling down beside him. "Won't you listen to me? Won't you try to see what I'm suffering? I'm not unreasonable, darling; really not. I don't suppose I should ever have noticed the letters if it hadn't been for their effect on you. It's not my way to pry into other people's affairs; and even if the effect had been different—yes, yes; listen to me—if I'd seen that the letters made you happy, that you were watching eagerly for them, counting the days between their coming, that you wanted them, that they gave you something I haven't known how to give—why, Kenneth, I don't say I shouldn't have suffered from that, too; but it would have been in a different way, and I should have had the courage to hide what I felt, and the hope that some day you'd come to feel about me as you did about the writer of the letters. But what I can't bear is to see how you dread them, how they make you suffer, and yet how you can't live without them and won't go away lest you should miss one during your absence. Or perhaps," she added, her voice breaking into a cry of accusation—"perhaps it's because she's actually forbidden you to leave. Kenneth, you must answer me! Is that the reason? Is it because she's forbidden you that you won't go away with me?"

She continued to kneel at his side, and raising her hands, she drew his gently down. She was ashamed of her persistence, ashamed of uncovering that baffled disordered face, yet resolved that no such scruples should arrest her. His eyes were lowered, the muscles of his face quivered; she was making him suffer even more than she suffered herself. Yet this no longer restrained her.

"Kenneth, is it that? She won't let us go away together?"

Still he did not speak or turn his eyes to her; and a sense of defeat swept over her. After all, she thought, the struggle was a losing one. "You needn't answer. I see I'm right," she said.

Suddenly, as she rose, he turned and drew her down again. His hands caught hers and pressed them so tightly that she felt her rings cutting into her flesh. There was something frightened, convulsive in his hold; it was the clutch of a man who felt himself slipping over a precipice. He was staring up at her now as if salvation lay in the face she bent above him. "Of course we'll go away together. We'll go wherever you want," he said in a low confused voice; and putting his arm about her, he drew her close and pressed his lips on hers.

IV

Charlotte had said to herself: "I shall sleep tonight," but instead she sat before her fire into the small hours, listening for any sound that came from her husband's room. But he, at any rate, seemed to be resting after the tumult of the evening. Once or twice she stole to the door and in the faint light that came in from the street through his open window she saw him stretched out in heavy sleep—the sleep of weakness and exhaustion. "He's ill," she thought—"he's undoubtedly ill. And it's not overwork; it's this mysterious persecution."

She drew a breath of relief. She had fought through the weary fight and the victory was hers—at least for the moment. If only they could have started at once—started for anywhere! She knew it would be useless to ask him to leave before the holidays; and meanwhile the secret influence—as to which she was still so completely in the dark—would continue to work against her, and she would have to renew the struggle day after day till they started on their journey. But after that everything would be different. If once she could get her husband away under other skies, and all to herself, she never doubted her power to release him from the evil spell he was under. Lulled to quiet by the thought, she too slept at last.

When she woke, it was long past her usual hour, and she sat up in bed surprised and vexed at having overslept herself. She always liked to be down to share her husband's breakfast by the library fire; but a glance at the clock made it clear that he must have started long since for his office. To make sure, she jumped out of bed and went into his room; but it was empty. No doubt he had looked in or on her before leaving, seen that she still slept, and gone downstairs without disturbing her; and their relations were sufficiently loverlike for her to regret having missed their morning hour.

She rang and asked if Mr. Ashby had already gone. Yes, nearly an hour ago, the maid said. He had given orders that Mrs. Ashby should not be waked and that the children should not come to her till she sent for them. . . . Yes, he had gone up to the nursery himself to give the order. All this sounded usual enough; and Charlotte hardly knew why she asked: "And did Mr. Ashby leave no other message?"

Yes, the maid said, he did; she was so sorry she'd forgotten. He'd told her, just as he was leaving, to say to Mrs. Ashby that he was going to see about their passages, and would she please be ready to sail tomorrow?

Charlotte echoed the woman's "Tomorrow," and sat staring at her incredulously. "Tomorrow—you're sure he said to sail tomorrow?"

"Oh, ever so sure, ma'am. I don't know how I could have forgotten to mention it."

"Well, it doesn't matter. Draw my bath, please." Charlotte sprang up, dashed through her dressing, and caught herself singing at her image in the glass as she sat brushing her hair. It made her feel young again to have scored such a victory. The other woman vanished to a speck on the horizon, as this one, who ruled the foreground, smiled back at the reflection of her lips and eyes. He loved her, then—he loved her as passionately as ever. He had divined what she had suffered, had understood that their happiness depended on their getting away at once, and finding each other again after yesterday's desperate groping in the fog. The nature of the influence that had come between them did not much matter to Charlotte now; she had faced the phantom and dispelled it. "Courage—that's the secret! If only people who are in love weren't always so afraid of risking their happiness by looking it in the eyes." As she brushed back her light abundant hair it waved electrically above her head, like the palms of victory. Ah, well, some women knew how to manage men, and some didn't—and only the fair—she gaily paraphrased—deserved the brave! Certainly she was looking very pretty.

The morning danced along like a cockleshell on a bright sea—such a sea as they would soon be speeding over. She ordered a particularly good dinner, saw the children off to their classes, had her trunks brought down, consulted with the maid about getting out summer clothes—for of course they would be heading for heat and sunshine—and wondered if she oughtn't to take Kenneth's flannel suits out of camphor. "But how absurd," she reflected, "that I don't yet know where we're going!" She looked at the clock, saw that it was close on noon, and decided to call him up at his office. There was a slight delay; then she heard his secretary's voice saying that Mr. Ashby had looked in for a moment early, and left again almost immediately. . . . Oh, very well; Charlotte would ring up later. How soon was he likely to be back? The secretary answered that she couldn't tell; all they knew in the office was that when he left he had said he was in a hurry because he had to go out of town.

Out of town! Charlotte hung up the receiver and sat blankly gazing into new darkness. Why had he gone out of town? And where had he gone? And of all days, why should he have chosen the eve of their suddenly planned departure? She felt a faint shiver of apprehension. Of course he had gone to see that woman—no doubt to get her permission to leave. He was as completely in bondage as that; and Charlotte had been fatuous enough to see the palms of victory on her forehead. She burst into a laugh and, walking across the room, sat down again before her mirror. What a different face she saw! The smile on her pale lips seemed to mock the rosy vision of the other Charlotte. But gradually her color crept back. After all, she had a right to claim the victory, since her husband was doing what she wanted, not what the other woman exacted of him. It was natural enough, in view of his abrupt decision to leave the next day, that he should have arrangements to make, business matters to wind up; it was not even necessary to suppose that his mysterious trip was a visit to the writer of the letters. He might simply have gone to see a client who lived out of town. Of course they would not tell Charlotte at the office; the secretary had hesitated before imparting even such meager information as the fact of Mr. Ashby's absence. Meanwhile she would go on with her joyful preparations, content to learn later in the day to what particular island of the blest she was to be carried.

The hours wore on, or rather were swept forward on a rush of eager prepara- 160 tions. At last the entrance of the maid who came to draw the curtains roused Charlotte from her labors, and she saw to her surprise that the clock marked five. And she did not yet know where they were going the next day! She rang up her husband's office and was told that Mr. Ashby had not been there since the early morning. She asked for his partner, but the partner could add nothing to her information, for he himself, his suburban train having been behind time, had reached the office after Ashby had come and gone. Charlotte stood perplexed; then she decided to telephone to her mother-in-law. Of course Kenneth, on the eve of a month's absence, must have gone to see his mother. The mere fact that the children—in spite of his vague objections—would certainly have to be left with old Mrs. Ashby, made it obvious that he would have all sorts of matters to decide with her. At another time Charlotte might have felt a little hurt at being excluded from their conference, but nothing mattered now but that she had won the day, that her husband was still hers and not another woman's. Gaily she called up Mrs. Ashby, heard her friendly voice, and began: "Well, did Kenneth's news surprise you? What do you think of our elopement?"

Almost instantly, before Mrs. Ashby could answer, Charlotte knew what her reply would be. Mrs. Ashby had not seen her son, she had had no word from him and did not know what her daughter-in-law meant. Charlotte stood silent in the intensity of her surprise. "But then, where *has* he been?" she thought. Then, recovering herself, she explained their sudden decision to Mrs. Ashby, and in doing so, gradually regained her own self-confidence, her conviction that nothing could ever again come between Kenneth and herself. Mrs. Ashby took the news calmly and approvingly. She, too, had thought that Kenneth looked worried and overtired, and she agreed with her daughter-in-law that in such cases change was the surest remedy. "I'm always so glad when he gets away. Elsie hated travelling; she was always finding pretexts to prevent his going anywhere. With you, thank goodness, it's different." Nor was Mrs. Ashby surprised at his not having had time to let her know of his departure. He must have been in a rush from the moment the decision was taken; but no doubt he'd drop in before dinner. Five minutes' talk was really all they needed. "I hope you'll gradually cure Kenneth of his mania for going over and over a question that could be settled in a dozen words. He never used to be like that, and if he carried the habit into his professional work he'd soon lose all his clients. . . . Yes, do come in for a minute, dear, if you have time; no doubt he'll turn up while you're here." The tonic ring of Mrs. Ashby's voice echoed on reassuringly in the silent room while Charlotte continued her preparations.

Toward seven the telephone rang, and she darted to it. Now she would know! But it was only from the conscientious secretary, to say that Mr. Ashby hadn't been back, or sent any word, and before the office closed she thought she ought to let Mrs. Ashby know. "Oh, that's all right. Thanks a lot!" Charlotte called out cheerfully, and hung up the receiver with a trembling hand. But perhaps by this time, she reflected, he was at his mother's. She shut her drawers and cupboards, put on her hat and coat and called up to the nursery that she was going out for a minute to see the children's grandmother.

Mrs. Ashby lived near by, and during her brief walk through the cold spring dusk Charlotte imagined that every advancing figure was her husband's. But she did not meet him on the way, and when she entered the house she found her mother-in-law alone. Kenneth had neither telephoned nor come. Old Mrs. Ashby sat by her bright fire, her knitting needles flashing steadily through her active old hands, and her mere bodily presence gave reassurance to Charlotte. Yes, it was certainly odd that Kenneth had gone off for the whole day without letting any of them know; but, after all, it was to be expected. A busy lawyer held so many threads in his hands that any sudden change of plan would oblige him to make all sorts of unforeseen arrangements and adjustments. He might have gone to see some client in the suburbs and been detained there; his mother remembered his telling her that he had charge of the legal business of a queer old recluse somewhere in New Jersey, who was immensely rich but too mean to have a telephone. Very likely Kenneth had been stranded there.

But Charlotte felt her nervousness gaining on her. When Mrs. Ashby asked her at what hour they were sailing the next day and she had to say she didn't know—that Kenneth had simply sent her word he was going to take their passages—the uttering of the words again brought home to her the strangeness of the situation. Even Mrs. Ashby conceded that it was odd; but she immediately added that it only showed what a rush he was in.

"But, mother, it's nearly eight o'clock! He must realize that I've got to know when we're starting tomorrow."

"Oh, the boat probably doesn't sail till evening. Sometimes they have to wait till midnight for the tide. Kenneth's probably counting on that. After all, he has a level head."

Charlotte stood up. "It's not that. Something has happened to him."

Mrs. Ashby took off her spectacles and rolled up her knitting. "If you begin to let yourself imagine things—"

"Aren't you in the least anxious?"

"I never am till I have to be. I wish you'd ring for dinner, my dear. You'll stay and dine? He's sure to drop in here on his way home."

Charlotte called up her own house. No, the maid said, Mr. Ashby hadn't come in and hadn't telephoned. She would tell him as soon as he came that Mrs. Ashby was dining at his mother's. Charlotte followed her mother-in-law into the dining-room and sat with parched throat before her empty plate, while Mrs. Ashby dealt calmly and efficiently with a short but carefully prepared repast. "You'd better eat something, child, or you'll be as bad as Kenneth. . . . Yes, a little more asparagus, please, Jane."

She insisted on Charlotte's drinking a glass of sherry and nibbling a bit of toast; then they returned to the drawing-room, where the fire had been made up, and the cushions in Mrs. Ashby's armchair shaken out and smoothed. How safe and familiar it all looked; and out there, somewhere in the uncertainty and mystery of the night, lurked the answer to the two women's conjectures, like an indistinguishable figure prowling on the threshold.

At last Charlotte got up and said: "I'd better go back. At this hour Kenneth will certainly go straight home."

Mrs. Ashby smiled indulgently. "It's not very late, my dear. It doesn't take two sparrows long to dine."

"It's after nine." Charlotte bent down to kiss her. "The fact is, I can't keep still."

Mrs. Ashby pushed aside her work and rested her two hands on the arms of her chair. "I'm going with you," she said, helping herself up.

Charlotte protested that it was too late, that it was not necessary, that she would call up as soon as Kenneth came in, but Mrs. Ashby had already rung for her maid. She was slightly lame, and stood resting on her stick while her wraps were brought. "If Mr. Kenneth turns up, tell him he'll find me at his own house," she instructed the maid as the two women got into the taxi which had been summoned. During the short drive Charlotte gave thanks that she was not returning home alone. There was something warm and substantial in the mere fact of Mrs. Ashby's nearness, something that corresponded with the clearness of her eyes and the texture of her fresh firm complexion. As the taxi drew up she laid her hand encouragingly on Charlotte's. "You'll see; there'll be a message."

The door opened at Charlotte's ring and the two entered. Charlotte's heart beat excitedly; the stimulus of her mother-in-law's confidence was beginning to flow through her veins.

"You'll see—you'll see," Mrs. Ashby repeated.

The maid who opened the door said no, Mr. Ashby had not come in, and there had been no message from him.

"You're sure the telephone's not out of order?" his mother suggested; and the maid said, well, it certainly wasn't half an hour ago; but she'd just go and ring up to make sure. She disappeared, and Charlotte turned to take off her hat and cloak. As she did so her eyes lit on the hall table, and there lay a gray envelope, her husband's name faintly traced on it. "Oh!" she cried out, suddenly aware that for the first time in months she had entered her house without wondering if one of the gray letters would be there.

"What is it, my dear?" Mrs. Ashby asked with a glance of surprise.

Charlotte did not answer. She took up the envelope and stood staring at it as if she could force her gaze to penetrate to what was within. Then an idea occurred to her. She turned and held out the envelope to her mother-in-law.

"Do you know that writing?" she asked.

Mrs. Ashby took the letter. She had to feel with her other hand for her eye-glasses, and when she had adjusted them she lifted the envelope to the light. "Why!" she exclaimed; and then stopped. Charlotte noticed that the letter shook in her usually firm hand. "But this is addressed to Kenneth," Mrs. Ashby said at length, in a low voice. Her tone seemed to imply that she felt her daughter-in-law's question to be slightly indiscreet.

"Yes, but no matter," Charlotte spoke with sudden decision. "I want to know—do you know the writing?"

Mrs. Ashby handed back the letter. "No," she said distinctly.

The two women had turned into the library. Charlotte switched on the electric light and shut the door. She still held the envelope in her hand.

"I'm going to open it," she announced.

She caught her mother-in-law' startled glance. "But, dearest—a letter not addressed to you? My dear, you can't!"

"As if I cared about that—now!" She continued to look intently at Mrs. Ashby. "This letter may tell me where Kenneth is."

Mrs. Ashby's glossy bloom was effaced by a quick pallor; her firm cheeks seemed to shrink and wither. "Why should it? What makes you believe— It can't possibly—"

Charlotte held her eyes steadily on that altered face. "Ah, then you *do* know the writing?" she flashed back.

"Know the writing? How should I? With all my son's correspondents. . . . What I do know is—" Mrs. Ashby broke off and looked at her daughter-in-law entreatingly, almost timidly.

Charlotte caught her by the wrist. "Mother! What do you know? Tell me! You must!"

"That I don't believe any good ever came of a woman's opening her husband's letters behind his back."

The words sounded to Charlotte's irritated ears as flat as a phrase culled from a book of moral axioms. She laughed impatiently and dropped her mother-in-law's wrist. "Is that all? No good can come of this letter, opened or unopened. I know that well enough. But whatever ill comes, I mean to find out what's in it." Her hands had been trembling as they held the envelope, but now they grew firm, and her voice also. She still gazed intently at Mrs. Ashby. "This is the ninth letter addressed in the same hand that has come for Kenneth since we've been married. Always these same gray envelopes. I've kept count of them because after each one he has been like a man who has had some dreadful shock. It takes him hours to shake off their effect. I've told him so. I've told him I must know from whom they come, because I can see they're killing him. He won't answer my questions; he says he can't tell me anything about the letters; but last night he promised to go away with me—to get away from them."

Mrs. Ashby, with shaking steps, had gone to one of the armchairs and sat down in it, her head drooping forward on her breast. "Ah," she murmured.

"So now you understand—"

"Did he tell you it was to get away from them?"   200

"He said, to get away—to get away. He was sobbing so that he could hardly speak. But I told him I knew that was why."

"And what did he say?"

"He took me in his arms and said he'd go wherever I wanted."

"Ah, thank God!" said Mrs. Ashby. There was a silence, during which she continued to sit with bowed head, and eyes averted from her daughter-in-law. At last she looked up and spoke. "Are you sure there have been as many as nine?"

"Perfectly. This is the ninth. I've kept count."   205

"And he has absolutely refused to explain?"

"Absolutely."

Mrs. Ashby spoke through pale contracted lips. "When did they begin to come? Do you remember?"

Charlotte laughed again. "Remember? The first one came the night we got back from our honeymoon."

"All that time?" Mrs. Ashby lifted her head and spoke with sudden energy.   210
"Then— Yes, open it."

The words were so unexpected that Charlotte felt the blood in her temples, and her hands began to tremble again. She tried to slip her finger under the flap of the envelope, but it was so tightly stuck that she had to hunt on her husband's writing table for his ivory letter-opener. As she pushed about the familiar objects his own hands had so lately touched, they sent through her the icy chill emanating from the little personal effects of someone newly dead. In the deep silence of the room the tearing of the paper as she slit the envelope sounded like a human cry. She drew out the sheet and carried it to the lamp.

"Well?" Mrs. Ashby asked below her breath.

Charlotte did not move or answer. She was bending over the page with wrinkled brows, holding it nearer and nearer to the light. Her sight must be blurred, or else dazzled by the reflection of the lamplight on the smooth surface of the paper, for, strain her eyes as she would, she could discern only a few faint strokes, so faint and faltering as to be nearly undecipherable.

"I can't make it out," she said.

"What do you mean, dear?"   215

"The writing's too indistinct. . . . Wait."

She went back to the table and, sitting down close to Kenneth's reading lamp, slipped the letter under a magnifying glass. All this time she was aware that her mother-in-law was watching her intently.

"Well?" Mrs. Ashby breathed.

"Well, it's no clearer. I can't read it."

"You mean the paper is an absolute blank?"

"No, not quite. There is writing on it. I can make out something like 'mine'—oh, and 'come.' It might be 'come.'"

Mrs. Ashby stood up abruptly. Her face was even paler than before. She advanced to the table and, resting her two hands on it, drew a deep breath. "Let me see," she said, as if forcing herself to a hateful effort.

Charlotte felt the contagion of her whiteness. "She knows," she thought. She pushed the letter across the table. Her mother-in-law lowered her head over it in silence, but without touching it with her pale wrinkled hands.

Charlotte stood watching her as she herself, when she had tried to read the letter, had been watched by Mrs. Ashby. The latter fumbled for her glasses, held them to her eyes, and bent still closer to the outspread page, in order, as it seemed, to avoid touching it. The light of the lamp fell directly on her old face, and Charlotte reflected what depths of the unknown may lurk under the clearest and most candid lineaments. She had never seen her mother-in-law's features express any but simple and sound emotions—cordiality, amusement, a kindly sympathy; now and again a flash of wholesome anger. Now they seemed to wear a look of fear and hatred, of incredulous dismay and almost cringing defiance. It was as if the spirits warring within her had distorted her face to their own likeness. At length she raised her head. "I can't—I can't," she said in a voice of childish distress.

"You can't make it out either?"

She shook her head, and Charlotte saw two tears roll down her cheeks.

"Familiar as the writing is to you?" Charlotte insisted with twitching lips.

Mrs. Ashby did not take up the challenge. "I can make out nothing—nothing."

"But you do know the writing?"

Mrs. Ashby lifted her head timidly; her anxious eyes stole with a glance of apprehension around the quiet familiar room. "How can I tell? I was startled at first. . . ."

"Startled by the resemblance?"

"Well, I thought—"

"You'd better say it out, mother! You knew at once it was *her* writing?"

"Oh, wait, my dear—wait."

"Wait for what?"

Mrs. Ashby looked up; her eyes, travelling slowly past Charlotte, were lifted to the blank wall behind her son's writing table.

Charlotte, following the glance, burst into a shrill laugh of accusation. "I needn't wait any longer! You've answered me now! You're looking straight at the wall where her picture used to hang!"

Mrs. Ashby lifted her hand with a murmur of warning. "Sh-h."

"Oh, you needn't imagine that anything can ever frighten me again!" Charlotte cried.

Her mother-in-law still leaned against the table. Her lips moved plaintively. "But we're going mad—we're both going mad. We both know such things are impossible."

Her daughter-in-law looked at her with a pitying stare. "I've known for a long time now that everything was possible."

"Even this?"

"Yes, exactly this."

"But this letter—after all, there's nothing in this letter—"

"Perhaps there would be to him. How can I tell? I remember his saying to me once that if you were used to a handwriting the faintest stroke of it became legible. Now I see what he meant. He *was* used to it."

"But the few strokes that I can make out are so pale. No one could possibly read that letter."

Charlotte laughed again. "I suppose everything's pale about a ghost," she said stridently.

"Oh, my child—my child—don't say it!"

"Why shouldn't I say it, when even the bare walls cry it out? What difference does it make if her letters are illegible to you and me? If even you can see her face on that blank wall, why shouldn't he read her writing on this blank paper? Don't you see that she's everywhere in this house, and the closer to him because to everyone else she's become invisible?" Charlotte dropped into a chair and covered her face with her hands. A turmoil of sobbing shook her from head to foot. At length a touch on her shoulder made her look up, and she saw her mother-in-law bending over her. Mrs. Ashby's face seemed to have grown still smaller and more wasted, but it had resumed its usual quiet look. Through all her tossing anguish, Charlotte felt the impact of that resolute spirit.

"Tomorrow—tomorrow. You'll see. There'll be some explanation tomorrow." 250

Charlotte cut her short. "An explanation? Who's going to give it, I wonder?"

Mrs. Ashby drew back and straightened herself heroically. "Kenneth himself will," she cried out in a strong voice. Charlotte said nothing, and the old woman went on: "But meanwhile we must act; we must notify the police. Now, without a moment's delay. We must do everything—everything."

Charlotte stood up slowly and stiffly; her joints felt as cramped as an old woman's. "Exactly as if we thought it could do any good to do anything?"

Resolutely Mrs. Ashby cried: "Yes!" and Charlotte went up to the telephone and unhooked the receiver.

QUESTIONS

1. What does the title mean? How does the title determine the story's events?
2. How do the similes contribute to the ghostliness of "Pomegranate Seed"?
3. Why does Wharton not explain the origin of the letters? Would the story be superior if the origin had been explained?
4. How does the ghost plot depend on the character traits of Charlotte and Kenneth?
5. How may "Pomegranate Seed" be read symbolically and allegorically?

Roman Fever _____*1934*

I

From the table at which they had been lunching two American ladies of ripe but well-cared-for middle age moved across the lofty terrace of the Roman restaurant and, leaning on its parapet, looked first at each other, and then down on the outspread glories of the Palatine and the Forum, with the same expression of vague but benevolent approval.

As they leaned there a girlish voice echoed up gaily from the stairs leading to the court below. "Well, come along, then," it cried, not to them but to an invisible companion, "and let's leave the young things to their knitting" and a voice as fresh laughed back: "Oh, look here, Babs, not actually *knitting*—" "Well, I mean figuratively," rejoined the first. "After all, we haven't left our poor parents much else to do . . . " and at that point the turn of the stairs engulfed the dialogue.

The two ladies looked at each other again, this time with a tinge of smiling embarrassment, and the smaller and paler one shook her head and colored-slightly.

"Barbara!" she murmured, sending an unheard rebuke after the mocking voice in the stairway.

The other lady, who was fuller, and higher in color, with a small determined nose supported by vigorous black eyebrows, gave a good-humored laugh. "That's what our daughters think of us!"

Her companion replied by a deprecating gesture. "Not of us individually. We must remember that. It's just the collective modern idea of Mothers. And you see—" Half guiltily she drew from her handsomely mounted black hand-bag a twist of crimson silk run through by two fine knitting needles. "One never knows," she murmured. "The new system has certainly given us a good deal of time to kill; and sometimes I get tired just looking—even at this." Her gesture was now addressed to the stupendous scene at their feet.

The dark lady laughed again, and they both relapsed upon the view, contemplating it in silence, with a sort of diffused serenity which might have been borrowed from the spring effulgence of the Roman skies. The luncheon-hour was long past, and the two had their end of the vast terrace to themselves. At its opposite extremity a few groups, detained by a lingering look at the outspread city, were gathering up guidebooks and fumbling for tips. The last of them scattered, and the two ladies were alone on the air-washed height.

''Well, I don't see why we shouldn't just stay here," said Mrs. Slade, the lady of the high color and energetic brows. Two derelict basket-chairs stood near, and she pushed them into the angle of the parapet, and settled herself in one, her gaze upon the Palatine. "After all, it's still the most beautiful view in the world."

"It always will be, to me," assented her friend Mrs. Ansley, with so slight a stress on the "me" that Mrs. Slade, though she noticed it, wondered if it were not merely accidental, like the random underlinings of old-fashioned letter-writers.

"Grace Ansley was always old-fashioned," she thought; and added aloud, with a retrospective smile: "It's a view we've both been familiar with for a good many years. When we first met here we were younger than our girls are now. You remember?"

"Oh, yes, I remember," murmured Mrs. Ansley, with the same undefinable stress— "There's that head-waiter wondering," she interpolated. She was evidently far less sure than her companion of herself and of her rights in the world.

"I'll cure him of wondering," said Mrs. Slade, stretching her hand toward a bag as discreetly opulent-looking as Mrs. Ansley's. Signing to the head-waiter, she explained that she and her friend were old lovers of Rome, and would like to spend the end of the afternoon looking down on the view—that is, if it did not disturb the service? The head-waiter, bowing over her gratuity, assured her that the ladies were most welcome, and would be still more so if they would condescend to remain for dinner. A full moon night, they would remember. . . .

Mrs. Slade's black brows drew together, as though references to the moon were out-of-place and even unwelcome. But she smiled away her frown as the head-waiter retreated. "Well, why not? We might do worse. There's no knowing, I suppose, when the girls will be back. Do you even know back from *where?* I don't!"

Mrs. Ansley again colored slightly. "I think those young Italian aviators we met at the Embassy invited them to fly to Tarquinia for tea. I suppose they'll want to wait and fly back by moonlight."

"Moonlight—moonlight! What a part it still plays. Do you suppose they're as   15
sentimental as we were?"

"I've come to the conclusion that I don't in the least know what they are," said Mrs. Ansley. "And perhaps we didn't know much more about each other."

"No, perhaps we didn't."

Her friend gave her a shy glance. "I never should have supposed you were sentimental, Alida."

"Well, perhaps I wasn't." Mrs. Slade drew her lids together in retrospect; and for a few moments the two ladies, who had been intimate since childhood, reflected how little they knew each other. Each one, of course, had a label ready to attach to the other's name; Mrs. Delphin Slade, for instance, would have told herself, or any one who asked her, that Mrs. Horace Ansley, twenty-five years ago, had been exquisitely lovely—no, you wouldn't believe it, would you? . . . though, of course, still charming, distinguished. . . . Well, as a girl she had been exquisite; far more beautiful than her daughter Barbara, though certainly Babs, according to the new standards at any rate, was more effective—had more *edge,* as they say. Funny where she got it, with those two nullities as parents. Yes; Horace Ansley was—well, just the duplicate of his wife. Museum specimens of old New York. Good-looking, irreproachable, exemplary. Mrs. Slade and Mrs. Ansley had lived opposite each other—actually as well as figuratively—for years. When the drawing-room curtains in No. 20 East 73rd Street were renewed, No. 23, across the way, was always aware of it. And of all the movings, buyings, travels, anniversaries, illnesses—the tame chronicle of an estimable pair. Little of it escaped Mrs. Slade. But she had grown bored with it by the time her husband made his big *coup* in Wall Street, and when they bought in upper Park Avenue had already begun to think: "I'd rather live opposite a speak-easy for a change; at least one might see it raided." The idea of seeing Grace raided was so amusing that (before the move) she launched it at a woman's lunch. It made a hit, and went the rounds—she sometimes wondered if it had crossed the street, and reached Mrs. Ansley. She hoped not, but didn't much mind. Those were the days when respectability was at a discount, and it did the irreproachable no harm to laugh at them a little.

A few years later, and not many months apart, both ladies lost their husbands.   20
There was an appropriate exchange of wreaths and condolences, and a brief renewal of intimacy in the half-shadow of their mourning; and now, after another interval, they had run across each other in Rome, at the same hotel, each of them the modest appendage of a salient daughter. The similarity of their lot had again drawn them together, lending itself to mild jokes, and the mutual confession that, if in old days it must have been tiring to "keep up" with daughters, it was now, at times, a little dull not to.

No doubt, Mrs. Slade reflected, she felt her unemployment more than poor Grace ever would. It was a big drop from being the wife of Delphin Slade to being his widow. She had always regarded herself (with a certain conjugal pride) as his equal in social gifts, as contributing her full share to the making of the exceptional couple they were: but the difference after his death was irremediable. As the wife of the famous corporation lawyer, always with an international case or two on hand, every day brought its exciting and unexpected obligation: the impromptu entertaining of eminent colleagues from abroad, the hurried dashes on legal business to London, Paris or Rome, where the entertaining was so handsomely reciprocated; the amusement of hearing in her wake: "What that handsome woman with the good clothes and the eyes is Mrs. Slade—*the* Slade's wife? Really? Generally the wives of celebrities are such frumps."

Yes; being *the* Slade's widow was a dullish business after that. In living up to such a husband all her faculties had been engaged; now she had only her daughter to live up to, for the son who seemed to have inherited his father's gifts had died suddenly in boyhood. She had fought through that agony because her husband was there, to be helped and to help; now, after the father's death, the thought of the boy had become unbearable. There was nothing left but to mother her daughter; and dear Jenny was such a perfect daughter that she needed no excessive mothering. "Now with Babs Ansley I don't know that I *should* be so quiet," Mrs. Slade sometimes half-enviously reflected; but Jenny, who was younger than her brilliant friend, was that rare accident, an extremely pretty girl who somehow made youth and prettiness seem as safe as their absence. It was all perplexing—and to Mrs. Slade a little boring. She wished that Jenny would fall in love—with the wrong man, even; that she might have to be watched, outmaneuvred, rescued. And instead, it was Jenny who watched her mother, kept her out of draughts, made sure that she had taken her tonic. . . .

Mrs. Ansley was much less articulate than her friend, and her mental portrait of Mrs. Slade was slighter, and drawn with fainter touches. "Alida Slade's awfully brilliant; but not as brilliant as she thinks," would have summed it up; though she would have added, for the enlightenment of strangers, that Mrs. Slade had been an extremely dashing girl; much more so than her daughter, who was pretty, of course, and clever in a way, but had none of her mother's—well, "vividness," some one had once called it. Mrs. Ansley would take up current words like this, and cite them in quotation marks, as unheard-of audacities. No: Jenny was not like her mother. Sometimes Mrs. Ansley thought Alida Slade was disappointed; on the whole she had had a sad life. Full of failures and mistakes; Mrs. Ansley had always been rather sorry for her. . . .

So these two ladies visualized each other, each through the wrong end of her little telescope.

II

For a long time they continued to sit side by side without speaking. It seemed as though, to both, there was a relief in laying down their somewhat futile activities in the presence of the vast Memento Mori which faced them. Mrs. Slade sat quite still, her eyes fixed on the golden slope of the Palace of the Caesars, and after a while Mrs. Ansley ceased to fidget with her bag, and she too sank into meditation. Like many intimate friends, the two ladies had never before had occasion to be silent together, and Mrs. Ansley was slightly embarrassed by what seemed, after so many years, a new stage in their intimacy, and one with which she did not yet know how to deal.

Suddenly the air was full of that deep clangor of bells which periodically covers Rome with a roof of silver. Mrs. Slade glanced at her wristwatch. "Five o'clock already," she said, as though surprised.

Mrs. Ansley suggested interrogatively: "There's bridge at the Embassy at five."

For a long time Mrs. Slade did not answer. She appeared to be lost in contemplation, and Mrs. Ansley thought the remark had escaped her. But after a while she said, as if speaking out of a dream: "Bridge, did you say? Not unless you want to.... But I don't think I will, you know."

"Oh, no," Mrs. Ansley hastened to assure her. "I don't care to at all. It's so lovely here; and so full of old memories, as you say." She settled herself in her chair, and almost furtively drew forth her knitting. Mrs. Slade took sideway note of this activity, but her own beautifully cared-for hands remained motionless on her knee.

"I was just thinking," she said slowly, "what different things Rome stands for to each generation of travelers. To our grandmothers, Roman fever; to our mothers, sentimental danger—how we used to be guarded!—to our daughters, no more dangers than the middle of Main Street. They don't know it—but how much they're missing!"

The long golden light was beginning to pale, and Mrs. Ansley lifted her knitting   30
a little closer to her eyes. "Yes; how we were guarded!"

"I always used to think," Mrs. Slade continued, "that our mothers had a much more difficult job than our grandmothers. When Roman fever stalked the streets it must have been comparatively easy to gather in the girls at the danger hour; but when you and I were young, with such beauty calling us, and the spice of disobedience thrown in, and no worse risk than catching cold during the cool hour after sunset, the mothers used to be put to it to keep us in—didn't they?"

She turned again toward Mrs. Ansley, but the latter had reached a delicate point in her knitting. "One, two, three—slip two; yes, they must have been," she assented, without looking up.

Mrs. Slade's eyes rested on her with a deepened attention. "She can knit—in the face of *this*! How like her...."

Mrs. Slade leaned back, brooding, her eyes ranging from the ruins which faced her to the long green hollow of the Forum, the fading glow of the church fronts beyond it, and the outlying immensity of the Colosseum. Suddenly she thought: "It's all very well to say that our girls have done away with sentiment and moonlight. But if Babs Ansley isn't out to catch that young aviator—the one who's a Marchese—then I don't know anything. And Jenny has no chance beside her. I know that too. I wonder if that's why Grace Ansley likes the two girls to go everywhere together? My poor Jenny as a foil—!" Mrs. Slade gave a hardly audible laugh, and at the sound Mrs. Ansley dropped her knitting.

"Yes—?"   35

"I—oh, nothing. I was only thinking how your Babs carries everything before her. That Campolieri boy is one of the best matches in Rome. Don't look so innocent, my dear—you know he is. And I was wondering, ever so respectfully, you understand ... wondering how two such exemplary characters as you and Horace had managed to produce anything quite so dynamic." Mrs. slade laughed again, with a touch of asperity.

Mrs. Ansley's hands lay inert across her needles. She looked straight out at the great accumulated wreckage of passion and splendor at her feet. But her small profile was almost expressionless. At length she said: "I think you overrate Babs, my dear."

Mrs. Slade's tone grew easier. "No; I don't. I appreciate her. And perhaps envy you. Oh, my girl's perfect; if I were a chronic invalid I'd—well, I think I'd rather be in Jenny's hands. There must be times ... but there! I always wanted a brilliant daughter ... and never quite understood why I got an angel instead."

Mrs. Ansley echoed her laugh in a faint murmur. "Babs is an angel too."

"Of course—of course! But she's got rainbow wings. Well, they're wandering by the sea with their young men; and here we sit . . . and it all brings back the past a little too acutely."

Mrs. Ansley had resumed her knitting. One might almost have imagined (if one had known her less well, Mrs. Slade reflected) that, for her also, too many memories rose from the lengthening shadows of those august ruins. But no; she was simply absorbed in her work. What was there for her to worry about? She knew that Babs would almost certainly come back engaged to the extremely eligible Campolieri. "And she'll sell the New York house, and settle down near them in Rome, and never be in their way . . . she's much too tactful. But she'll have an excellent cook, and just the right people in for bridge and cocktails . . . and a perfectly peaceful old age among her grandchildren."

Mrs. Slade broke off this prophetic flight with a recoil of self-disgust. There was no one of whom she had less right to think unkindly than of Grace Ansley. Would she never cure herself of envying her? Perhaps she had begun too long ago.

She stood up and leaned against the parapet, filling her troubled eyes with the tranquilizing magic of the hour. But instead of tranquilizing her the sight seemed to increase her exasperation. Her gaze turned toward the Colosseum. Already its golden flank was drowned in purple shadow, and above it the sky curved crystal clear, without light or color. It was the moment when afternoon and evening hang balanced in mid-heaven.

Mrs. Slade turned back and laid her hand on her friend's arm. The gesture was so abrupt that Mrs. Ansley looked up, startled.

"The sun's set. You're not afraid, my dear?"

"Afraid—?"

"Of Roman fever or pneumonia? I remember how ill you were that winter. As a girl you had a very delicate throat, hadn't you?"

"Oh, we're all right up here. Down below, in the Forum, it does get deathly cold, all of a sudden . . . but not here."

"Ah, of course you know because you had to be so careful." Mrs. Slade turned back to the parapet. She thought: "I must make one more effort not to hate her." Aloud she said: "Whenever I look at the Forum from up here I remember that story about a great-aunt of yours, wasn't she? A dreadfully wicked great-aunt?"

"Oh yes; Great-aunt Harriet. The one who was supposed to have sent her young sister out to the Forum after sunset to gather a night-blooming flower for her album. All our great-aunts and grandmothers used to have albums of dried flowers."

Mrs. Slade nodded. "But she really sent her because they were in love with the same man—"

"Well, that was the family tradition. They said Aunt Harriet confessed it years afterward. At any rate, the poor little sister caught the fever and died. Mother used to frighten us with the story when we were children."

"And you frightened *me* with it, that winter when you and I were here as girls. The winter I was engaged to Delphin."

Mrs. Ansley gave a faint laugh. "Oh, did I? Really frightened you? I don't believe you're easily frightened."

"Not often; but I was then. I was easily frightened because I was too happy. I wonder if you know what that means?"

"I—yes. . . . " Mrs. Ansley faltered.

"Well, I suppose that was why the story of your wicked aunt made such an impression on me. And I thought: "There's no more Roman fever, but the Forum is deathly cold after sunset—especially after a hot day. And the Colosseum's even colder and damper.'"

"The Colosseum—?"

"Yes. It wasn't easy to get in, after the gates were locked for the night. Far from easy. Still, in those days it could be managed; it was managed, often. Lovers met there who couldn't meet elsewhere. You knew that?"

"I—I daresay. I don't remember."   60

"You don't remember? You don't remember going to visit some ruins or other one evening, just after dark, and catching a bad chill? You were supposed to have gone to see the moon rise. People always said that expedition was what caused your illness."

There was a moment's silence; then Mrs. Ansley rejoined: "Did they? It was all so long ago."

"Yes. And you got well again—so it didn't matter. But I suppose it struck your friends—the reason given for your illness, I mean—because everybody knew you were so prudent on account of your throat, and your mother took such care of you. . . . You *had* been out late sight-seeing, hadn't you, that night?"

"Perhaps I had. The most prudent girls aren't always prudent. What made you think of it now?"

Mrs. Slade seemed to have no answer ready. But after a moment she broke out: 65
"Because I simply can't bear it any longer—!"

Mrs. Ansley lifted her head quickly. Her eyes were wide and very pale. "Can't bear what?"

"Why—your not knowing that I've always known why you went."

"Why I went—?"

"Yes. You think I'm bluffing, don't you? Well, you went to meet the man I was engaged to—and I can repeat every word of the letter that took you there."

While Mrs. Slade spoke Mrs. Ansley had risen unsteadily to her feet. Her bag,   70
her knitting and gloves, slid in a panic-stricken heap to the ground. She looked at Mrs. Slade as though she were looking at a ghost.

"No, no—don't," she faltered out.

"Why not? Listen, if you don't believe me. 'My one darling, things can't go on like this. I must see you alone. Come to the Colosseum immediately after dark tomorrow. There will be somebody to let you in. No one whom you need fear will suspect'—but perhaps you've forgotten what the letter said?"

Mrs. Ansley met the challenge with an unexpected composure. Steadying herself against the chair she looked at her friend, and replied: "No; I know it by heart too."

"And the signature? 'Only *your* D. S.' Was that it? I'm right, am I? That was the letter that took you out that evening after dark?"

Mrs. Ansley was still looking at her. It seemed to Mrs. Slade that a slow struggle   75
was going on behind the voluntarily controlled mask of her small quiet face. "I shouldn't have thought she had herself so well in hand," Mrs. Slade reflected, almost resentfully. But at this moment Mrs. Ansley spoke, "I don't know how you knew. I burnt that letter at once."

"Yes; you would, naturally—you're so prudent!" The sneer was open now. "And if you burnt the letter you're wondering how on earth I know what was in it. That's it, isn't it?"

Mrs. Slade waited, but Mrs. Ansley did not speak.

"Well, my dear, I know what was in that letter because I wrote it!"

"You wrote it?"

"Yes."

The two women stood for a minute staring at each other in the last golden light. Then Mrs. Ansley dropped back into her chair. "Oh," she murmured, and covered her face with her hands.

Mrs. Slade waited nervously for another word or movement. None came, and at length she broke out: "I horrify you."

Mrs. Ansley's hands dropped to her knee. The face they uncovered was streaked with tears. "I wasn't thinking of you. I was thinking—it was the only letter I ever had from him!"

"And I wrote it. Yes; I wrote it! But I was the girl he was engaged to. Did you happen to remember that?"

Mrs. Ansley's head drooped again. "I'm not trying to excuse myself.... I remembered.... "

"And still you went?"

"Still I went."

Mrs. Slade stood looking down on the small bowed figure at her side. The flame of her wrath had already sunk, and she wondered why she had ever thought there would be any satisfaction in inflicting so purposeless a wound on her friend. But she had to justify herself.

"You do understand? I'd found out—and I hated you, hated you. I knew you were in love with Delphin—and I was afraid; afraid of you, of your quiet ways, your sweetness . . . your . . . well, I wanted you out of the way, that's all. Just for a few weeks; just till I was sure of him. So in a blind fury I wrote that letter.... I don't know why I'm telling you now."

"I suppose," said Mrs. Ansley slowly, "it's because you've always gone on hating me."

"Perhaps. Or because I wanted to get the whole thing off my mind." She paused. "I'm glad you destroyed the letter. Of course I never thought you'd die."

Mrs. Ansley relapsed into silence, and Mrs. Slade, leaning above her, was conscious of a strange sense of isolation, of being cut off from the warm current of human communion. "You think me a monster!"

"I don't know.... It was the only letter I had, and you say he didn't write it?"

"Ah, how you care for him still!"

"I cared for that memory," said Mrs. Ansley.

Mrs. Slade continued to look down on her. She seemed physically reduced by the blow—as if, when she got up, the wind might scatter her like a puff of dust. Mrs. Slade's jealousy suddenly leapt up again at the sight. All these years the woman had been living on that letter. How she must have loved him, to treasure the mere memory of its ashes! The letter of the man her friend was engaged to. Wasn't it she who was the monster?

"You tried your best to get him away from me, didn't you? But you failed; and I kept him. That's all."

"Yes. That's all."

"I wish now I hadn't told you. I'd no idea you'd feel about it as you do; I thought you'd be amused. It all happened so long ago, as you say; and you must do me the justice to remember that I had no reason to think you'd ever taken it seriously. How could I, when you were married to Horace Ansley two months afterward? As soon as you could get out of bed your mother rushed you off to Florence and married you. People were rather surprised—they wondered at its being done so quickly; but I thought I knew. I had an idea you did it out of *pique*—to be able to say you'd got ahead of Delphin and me. Girls have such silly reasons for doing the most serious things. And your marrying so soon convinced me that you'd never really cared."

"Yes. I suppose it would," Mrs. Ansley assented.   100

The clear heaven overhead was emptied of all its gold. Dusk spread over it, abruptly darkening the Seven Hills. Here and there lights began to twinkle through the foliage at their feet. Steps were coming and going on the deserted terrace—waiters looking out of the doorway at the head of the stairs, then reappearing with trays and napkins and flasks of wine. Tables were moved, chairs straightened. A feeble string of electric lights flickered out. Some vases of faded flowers were carried away, and brought back replenished. A stout lady in a dust-coat suddenly appeared, asking in broken Italian if any one had seen the elastic band which held together her tattered Baedeker. She poked with her stick under the table at which she had lunched, the waiters assisting.

The corner where Mrs. Slade and Mrs. Ansley sat was still shadowy and deserted. For a long time neither of them spoke. At length Mrs. Slade began again: "I suppose I did it as a sort of joke—"

"A joke?"

"Well, girls are ferocious sometimes, you know. Girls in love especially. And I remember laughing to myself all that evening at the idea that you were waiting around there in the dark, dodging out of sight, listening for every sound, trying to get in—Of course I was upset when I heard you were so ill afterward."

Mrs. Ansley had not moved for a long time. But now she turned slowly toward her companion. "But I didn't wait. He'd arranged everything. He was there. We were let in at once," she said.

Mrs. Slade sprang up from her leaning position. "Delphin there? They let you   105
in?—Ah, now you're lying!" she burst out with violence.

Mrs. Ansley's voice grew clearer, and full of surprise. "But of course he was there. Naturally he came—"

"Came? How did he know he'd find you there? You must be raving!"

Mrs. Ansley hesitated, as though reflecting. "But I answered the letter. I told him I'd be there. So he came."

Mrs. Slade flung her hands up to her face. "Oh, God—you answered! I never thought of your answering. . . ."

"It's odd you never thought of it, if you wrote the letter."   110

"Yes. I was blind with rage."

Mrs. Ansley rose, and drew her fur scarf about her. "It is cold here. We'd better go. . . . I'm sorry for you," she said as she clasped the fur about her throat.

The unexpected words sent a pang through Mrs. Slade. "Yes; we'd better go." She gathered up her bag and cloak. "I don't know why you should be sorry for me," she muttered.

Mrs. Ansley stood looking away from her toward the dusky secret mass of the Colosseum. "Well—because I didn't have to wait that night."

Mrs. Slade gave an unquiet laugh. "Yes; I was beaten there. But I oughtn't to be-   115 grudge it to you, I suppose. At the end of all these years. After all, I had everything; I had him for twenty-five years. And you had nothing but that one letter that he didn't write."

Mrs. Ansley was again silent. At length she turned toward the door of the terrace. She took a step, and turned back, facing her companion.

"I had Barbara," she said, and began to move ahead of Mrs. Slade toward the stairway.

QUESTIONS

1. What is Roman fever in the story? How has it influenced the lives of the two women, Alida and Grace? Why is its influence still continuing at the time of the story?

2. Describe the two women. How does their conversation constitute a development of their characters and their relationship?

3. Explain how Wharton plants clues throughout the story to establish the situation between Alida and Grace. To what degree is the final speech a surprise?

12

Additional Stories

TONI CADE BAMBARA (b. 1939)

Bambara (an African tribal name that Toni Cade appropriated from an old manuscript) was brought up in Harlem and Bedford Stuyvesant in New York City. She received a B.A. from Queens College and an M.A. from The City College of New York, and for a time she worked as a social worker. In her fiction she treats the subjects of the Black and also the female experience. She avoids using the material for political purposes, however, even though the subjects could easily fall within the political realm. Instead, she deals with her characters on the human level, trying to offer her readers "nourishment." "Raymond's Run," which is reprinted here, illustrates this aim, with its uplifting conclusion that coincides with the growth not only of the major character, the narrator, but also of her principal antagonist.

Raymond's Run _____*1970*

I don't have much work to do around the house like some girls. My mother does that. And I don't have to earn my pocket money by hustling; George runs errands for the big boys and sells Christmas cards. And anything else that's got to get done, my father does. All I have to do in life is mind my brother Raymond, which is enough.

Sometimes I slip and say my little brother Raymond. But as any fool can see he's much bigger and he's older too. But a lot of people call him my little brother cause he needs looking after cause he's not quite right. And a lot of smart mouths got lots to say about that too, especially when George was minding him. But now, if anybody has anything to say to Raymond, anything to say about his big head, they have to come by me. And I don't play the dozens° or believe in standing around with somebody in

_____

the dozens: children's game in which the participants chant insults at each other.

my face doing a lot of talking. I much rather just knock you down and take my chances even if I am a little girl with skinny arms and a squeaky voice, which is how I got the name Squeaky. And if things get too rough, I run. And as anybody can tell you, I'm the fastest thing on two feet.

There is no track meet that I don't win the first-place medal. I used to win the twenty-yard dash when I was a little kid in kindergarten. Nowadays, it's the fifty-yard dash. And tomorrow I'm subject to run the quarter-meter relay all by myself and come in first, second, and third. The big kids call me Mercury° cause I'm the swiftest thing in the neighborhood. Everybody knows that—except two people who know better, my father and me. He can beat me to Amsterdam Avenue° with me having a two-fire-hydrant head start and him running with his hands in his pockets and whistling. But that's private information. Cause can you imagine some thirty-five-year-old man stuffing himself into PAL shorts to race little kids?° So as far as everyone's concerned, I'm the fastest and that goes for Gretchen, too, who has put out the tale that she is going to win the first-place medal this year. Ridiculous. In the second place, she's got short legs. In the third place, she's got freckles. In the first place, no one can beat me and that's all there is to it.

I'm standing on the corner admiring the weather and about to take a stroll down Broadway so I can practice my breathing exercises, and I've got Raymond walking on the inside close to the buildings, cause he's subject to fits of fantasy and starts thinking he's a circus performer and that the curb is a tightrope strung high in the air. And sometimes after a rain he likes to step down off his tightrope right into the gutter and slosh around getting his shoes and cuffs wet. Then I get hit when I get home. Or sometimes if you don't watch him he'll dash across traffic to the island in the middle of Broadway and give the pigeons a fit. Then I have to go behind him apologizing to all the old people sitting around trying to get some sun and getting all upset with the pigeons fluttering around them, scattering their newspapers and upsetting the wax paper lunches in their laps. So I keep Raymond on the inside of me, and he plays like he's driving a stagecoach which is O.K. by me so long as he doesn't run me over or interrupt my breathing exercises, which I have to do on account of I'm serious about my running, and I don't care who knows it.

Now some people like to act like things come easy to them, won't let on that they practice. Not me. I'll high-prance down 34th Street like a rodeo pony to keep my knees strong even if it does get my mother uptight so that she walks ahead like she's not with me, don't know me, is all by herself on a shopping trip, and I am somebody else's crazy child. Now you take Cynthia Procter for instance. She's just the opposite. If there's a test tomorrow, she'll say something like, "Oh, I guess I'll play handball this afternoon and watch television tonight," just to let you know she ain't thinking about the test. Or like last week when she won the spelling bee for the millionth time, "A good thing you got 'receive,' Squeaky, cause I would have got it wrong. I completely forgot about the spelling bee." And she'll clutch the lace on her blouse like it was a narrow escape. Oh, brother. But of course when I pass her house on my early morning trots around the block, she is practicing the scales on the piano over and over and over and over. Then in music class she always lets herself get bumped around so she falls accidently on purpose onto the piano stool and is so surprised to find herself sit-

Mercury: ancient Roman god of travel, portrayed with winged sandals to show his speed.
Amsterdam Avenue: a principal thoroughfare in Harlem.
PAL . . . little kids: reference to children's racing events sponsored by the Police Athletic League.

ting there that she decides just for fun to try out the ole keys. And what do you know—Chopin's waltzes just spring out of her fingertips and she's the most surprised thing in the world. A regular prodigy. I could kill people like that. I stay up all night studying the words for the spelling bee. And you can see me any time of day practicing running. I never walk if I can trot, and shame on Raymond if he can't keep up. But of course he does, cause if he hangs back someone's liable to walk up to him and get smart, or take his allowance from him, or ask him where he got that great big pumpkin head. People are so stupid sometimes.

So I'm strolling down Broadway breathing out and breathing in on counts of seven, which is my lucky number, and here comes Gretchen and her sidekicks: Mary Louise, who used to be a friend of mine when she first moved to Harlem from Baltimore and got beat up by everybody till I took up for her on account of her mother and my mother used to sing in the same choir when they were young girls, but people ain't grateful, so now she hangs out with the new girl Gretchen and talks about me like a dog; and Rosie, who is as fat as I am skinny and has a big mouth where Raymond is concerned and is too stupid to know that there is not a big deal of difference between herself and Raymond and that she can't afford to throw stones. So they are steady coming up Broadway and I see right away that it's going to be one of those Dodge City scenes° cause the street ain't that big and they're close to the buildings just as we are. First I think I'll step into the candy store and look over the new comics and let them pass. But that's chicken and I've got a reputation to consider. So then I think I'll just walk straight on through them or even over them if necessary. But as they get to me, they slow down. I'm ready to fight, cause like I said I don't feature a whole lot of chitchat, I much prefer to just knock you down right from the jump and save everybody a lotta precious time.

"You signing up for the May Day races?" smiles Mary Louise, only it's not a smile at all. A dumb question like that doesn't deserve an answer. Besides, there's just me and Gretchen standing there really, so no use wasting my breath talking to shadows.

"I don't think you're going to win this time," says Rosie, trying to signify with her hands on her hips all salty, completely forgetting that I have whupped her behind many times for less salt than that.

"I always win cause I'm the best," I say straight at Gretchen who is, as far as I'm concerned, the only one talking in this ventriloquist-dummy routine. Gretchen smiles, but it's not a smile, and I'm thinking that girls never really smile at each other because they don't know how and don't want to know how and there's probably no one to teach us how, cause grownup girls don't know either. Then they all look at Raymond who has just brought his mule team to a standstill. And they're about to see what trouble they can get into through him.

"What grade you in now, Raymond?"   10

"You got anything to say to my brother, you say it to me, Mary Louise Williams of Raggedy Town, Baltimore."

"What are you, his mother?" sasses Rosie.

"That's right, Fatso. And the next word out of anybody and I'll be *their* mother too." So they just stand there and Gretchen shifts from one leg to the other and so do they. Then Gretchen puts her hands on her hips and is about to say something with her freckle-face self but doesn't. Then she walks around me looking me up and down

---

Dodge City scenes: The location of "Gunsmoke," a popular TV Western serial, was Dodge City. The opening of the show focused on the protagonist and another man in a showdown gunfight.

but keeps walking up Broadway, and her sidekicks follow her. So me and Raymond smile at each other and he says, "Giddyap" to his team and I continue with my breathing exercises, strolling down Broadway toward the ice man on 145th with not a care in the world cause I am Miss Quicksilver herself.

I take my time getting to the park on May Day because the track meet is the last thing on the program. The biggest thing on the program is the Maypole dancing, which I can do without, thank you, even if my mother thinks it's a shame I don't take part and act like a girl for a change. You'd think my mother'd be grateful not to have to make me a white organdy dress with a big satin sash and buy me new white baby-doll shoes that can't be taken out of the box till the big day. You'd think she'd be glad her daughter ain't out there prancing around a Maypole getting the new clothes all dirty and sweaty and trying to act like a fairy or a flower or whatever you're supposed to be when you should be trying to be yourself, whatever that is, which is, as far as I am concerned, a poor black girl who really can't afford to buy shoes and a new dress you only wear once a lifetime cause it won't fit next year.

I was once a strawberry in a Hansel and Gretel pageant when I was in nursery school and didn't have no better sense than to dance on tiptoe with my arms in a circle over my head doing umbrella steps and being a perfect fool just so my mother and father could come dressed up and clap. You'd think they'd know better than to encourage that kind of nonsense. I am not a strawberry. I do not dance on my toes. I run. That is what I am all about. So I always come late to the May Day program, just in time to get my number pinned on and lay in the grass till they announce the fifty-yard dash.

I put Raymond in the little swings, which is a tight squeeze this year and will be impossible next year. Then I look around for Mr. Pearson, who pins the numbers on. I'm really looking for Gretchen if you want to know the truth, but she's not around. The park is jam-packed. Parents in hats and corsages and breastpocket handkerchiefs peeking up. Kids in white dresses and light blue suits. The parkees unfolding chairs and chasing the rowdy kids from Lenox as if they had no right to be there. The big guys with their caps on backwards, leaning against the fence swirling the basketballs on the tips of their fingers, waiting for all these crazy people to clear out the park so they can play. Most of the kids in my class are carrying bass drums and glockenspiels and flutes. You'd think they'd put in a few bongos or something for real like that.

Then here comes Mr. Pearson with his clipboard and his cards and pencils and whistles and safety pins and fifty million other things he's always dropping all over the place with his clumsy self. He sticks out in a crowd because he's on stilts. We used to call him Jack and the Beanstalk to get him mad. But I'm the only one that can out-run him and get away, and I'm too grown for that silliness now.

"Well, Squeaky," he says, checking my name off the list and handing me number seven and two pins. And I'm thinking he's got no right to call me Squeaky, if I can't call him Beanstalk.

"Hazel Elizabeth Deborah Parker," I correct him and tell him to write it down on his board.

"Well, Hazel Elizabeth Deborah Parker, going to give someone else a break this year?" I squint at him real hard to see if he is seriously thinking I should lose the race on purpose just to give someone else a break. "Only six girls running this time," he continues, shaking his head sadly like it's my fault all of New York didn't turn out in sneakers. "That new girl should give you a run for your money." He looks around the park for Gretchen like a periscope in a submarine movie. "Wouldn't it be a nice gesture if you were . . . to ahhh . . ."

I give him such a look he couldn't finish putting that idea into words. Grownups got a lot of nerve sometimes. I pin number seven to myself and stomp away, I'm so burnt. And I go straight for the track and stretch out on the grass while the band winds up with "Oh, the Monkey Wrapped His Tail Around the Flagpole,"° which my teacher calls by some other name. The man on the loudspeaker is calling everyone over to the track and I'm on my back looking at the sky, trying to pretend I'm in the country, but I can't, because even grass in the city feels hard as sidewalk, and there's just no pretending you are anywhere but in a "concrete jungle" as my grandfather says.

The twenty-yard dash takes all of two minutes cause most of the little kids don't know no better than to run off the track or run the wrong way or run smack into the fence and fall down and cry. One little kid, though, has got the good sense to run straight for the white ribbon up ahead so he wins. Then the second-graders line up for the thirty-yard dash and I don't even bother to turn my head to watch cause Raphael Perez always wins. He wins before he even begins by psyching the runners, telling them they're going to trip on their shoelaces and fall on their faces or lose their shorts or something, which he doesn't really have to do since he is very fast, almost as fast as I am. After that is the forty-yard dash which I use to run when I was in first grade. Raymond is hollering from the swings cause he knows I'm about to do my thing cause the man on the loudspeaker has just announced the fifty-yard dash, although he might just as well be giving a recipe for angel food cake cause you can hardly make out what he's saying for the static. I get up and slip off my sweat pants and then I see Gretchen standing at the starting line, kicking her legs out like a pro. Then as I get into place I see that ole Raymond is on line on the other side of the fence, bending down with his fingers on the ground just like he knew what he was doing. I was going to yell at him but then I didn't. It burns up your energy to holler.

Every time, just before I take off in a race, I always feel like I'm in a dream, the kind of dream you have when you're sick with fever and feel all hot and weightless. I dream I'm flying over a sandy beach in the early morning sun, kissing the leaves of the trees as I fly by. And there's always the smell of apples, just like in the country when I was little and used to think I was a choo-choo train, running through the fields of corn and chugging up the hill to the orchard. And all the time I'm dreaming this, I get lighter and lighter until I'm flying over the beach again, getting blown through the sky like a feather that weighs nothing at all. But once I spread my fingers in the dirt and crouch over the Get on Your Mark, the dream goes and I am solid again and am telling myself, Squeaky you must win, you must win, you are the fastest thing in the world, you can even beat your father up Amsterdam if you really try. And then I feel my weight coming back just behind my knees then down to my feet then into the earth and the pistol shot explodes in my blood and I am off and weightless again, flying past the other runners, my arms pumping up and down and the whole world is quiet except for the crunch as I zoom over the gravel in the track. I glance to my left and there is no one. To the right, a blurred Gretchen, who's got her chin jutting out as if it would win the race all by itself. And on the other side of the fence is Raymond

---

Oh . . . Flagpole: the first line of obscene lyrics to Sousa's "Washington Post" march.

with his arms down to his side and the palms tucked up behind him, running in his very own style, and it's the first time I ever saw that and I almost stop to watch my brother Raymond on his first run. But the white ribbon is bouncing toward me and I tear past it, racing into the distance till my feet with a mind of their own start digging up footfuls of dirt and brake me short. Then all the kids standing on the side pile on me, banging me on the back and slapping my head with their May Day programs, for I have won again and everybody on 151st Street can walk tall for another year.

"In first place . . ." the man on the loudspeaker is clear as a bell now, but then he pauses and the loudspeaker starts to whine. Then static. And I lean down to catch my breath and here comes Gretchen walking back, for she's overshot the finish line too, huffing and puffing with her hands on her hips taking it slow, breathing in steady time like a real pro and I sort of like her a little for the first time. "In first place . . ." and then three or four voices get all mixed up on the loudspeaker and I dig my sneaker into the grass and stare at Gretchen who's staring back, we both wondering just who did win. I can hear old Beanstalk arguing with the man on the loudspeaker and then a few others running their mouths about what the stopwatches say. Then I hear Raymond yanking at the fence to call me and I wave to shush him, but he keeps rattling the fence like a gorilla in a cage like in them gorilla movies, but then like a dancer or something he starts climbing up nice and easy but very fast. And it occurs to me, watching how smoothly he climbs hand over hand and remembering how he looked running with his arms down to his side and with the wind pulling his mouth back and his teeth showing and all, it occurred to me that Raymond would make a very fine runner. Doesn't he always keep up with me on my trots? And he surely knows how to breathe in counts of seven cause he's always doing it at the dinner table, which drives my brother George up the wall. And I'm smiling to beat the band cause if I've lost this race, or if me and Gretchen tied, or even if I've won, I can always retire as a runner and begin a whole new career as a coach with Raymond as my champion. After all, with a little more study I can beat Cynthia and her phony self at the spelling bee. And if I bugged my mother, I could get piano lessons and become a star. And I have a big rep as the baddest thing around. And I've got a roomful of ribbons and medals and awards. But what has Raymond got to call his own?

So I stand there with my new plans, laughing out loud by this time as Raymond jumps down from the fence and runs over with his teeth showing and his arms down to the side, which no one before him has quite mastered as a running style, and by the time he comes over I'm jumping up and down so glad to see him—my brother Raymond, a great runner in the family tradition. But of course everyone thinks I'm jumping up and down because the men on the loudspeaker have finally gotten themselves together and compared notes and are announcing "In first place—Miss Hazel Elizabeth Deborah Parker." (Dig that.) "In second place—Miss Gretchen P. Lewis." And I look at Gretchen wondering what the "P" stands for. And I smile. Cause she's good, no doubt about it. Maybe she'd like to help me coach Raymond; she obviously is serious about running, as any fool can see. And she nods to congratulate me and then she smiles. And I smile. We stand there with this big smile of respect between us. It's about as real a smile as girls can do for each other, considering we don't practice real smiling every day, you know, cause maybe we too busy being flowers or fairies or strawberries instead of something honest and worthy of respect . . . you know . . . like being people.

STEPHEN DIXON (b. 1936)

Dixon was born in New York and attended The City College of New York, receiving his Bachelor's degree in 1958. He has received the O. Henry Award and the Pushcart Prize, among his other distinctions. Early in 1992, his novel Frog *was under consideration for the PEN/Faulkner Award for Fiction. His first collections of stories were* No Relief *(1976) and* Quite Contrary *(1979). "All Gone" (1990) is somewhat like the novel* Too Late *(1978), in which the protagonist, Art, goes in search of his lost woman friend, Donna. His search reveals the city as a bizarre and dangerous place, reminiscent of the dangers that Eliot faces on the subway platform in "All Gone."*

All Gone _____1990

He says goodbye, we kiss at the door, he rings for the elevator, I say "I'll call you when I find out about the tickets," he says "Anytime, as I'll be in all day working on that book jacket I'm behind on," waves to me as the elevator door opens and I shut the door.

I find out about the tickets and call him and he doesn't answer. Maybe he hasn't gotten home yet, though he usually does in half an hour. But it's Saturday and the subway's always much slower on weekends, and I call him half an hour later and he doesn't answer.

He could have got home and I missed him because he right away might have gone out to buy some necessary art supply or something, and I call him an hour later and he doesn't answer. I do warm-ups, go out and run my three miles along the river, come back and shower and call him and he doesn't answer. I dial him every half hour after that for the next three hours and then call Operator and she checks and says his phone's in working order.

I call his landlord and say "This is Maria Pierce, Eliot Schulter's good friend for about the last half-year—you know me. Anyway, could you do me a real big favor and knock on his door? I know it's an inconvenience but he's only one flight up and you see, he should be home and doesn't answer and I've been phoning and phoning him and am getting worried. I'll call you back in fifteen minutes. If he's in and for his own reasons didn't want to answer the phone or it actually is out of order, could you have him call me at home?" 5

I call the landlord back in fifteen minutes and he says "I did what you said and he didn't answer. That would've been enough for me. But you got me worried also, so I went downstairs for his duplicate keys and opened his door just a ways and yelled in for him and then walked in and he wasn't there, though his place looked okay."

"Excuse me, I just thought of something. Was his night light on?"

"You mean the little small-watt-bulb lamp on his fireplace mantel?"

"That's the one. He always keeps it on at night to keep away burglars who like to jump in from his terrace."

"What burglars jumping in from where? He was never robbed that I know."

"The tenant before him said she was. Was it on?"

"That's different. Yes. I thought he'd forgotten about the light, so I shut if off. I was thinking about his electricity cost, but you think I did wrong?"

"No. It only means he never got home. Thanks."

I call every half hour after that till around six, when he usually comes to my apartment. But he never comes here without our first talking on the phone during the afternoon about all sorts of things: how our work's going, what the mail brought, what we might have for dinner that evening and do later and if there's anything he can pick up on the way here and so on. The concert's at eight and I still have to pick up the tickets from my friend who's giving them to me and can't go herself because her baby's sick and her husband won't go without her. I call her and say "I don't see how we can make the concert. Eliot's not here, hasn't called, doesn't answer his phone and from what his landlord said, I doubt he ever got home after he left me this morning."

"Does he have any relatives or close friends in the city for you to call?"

"No, he would have gone to his apartment directly—I know him. He had important work to finish, and the only close person other than myself to him is his mother in Seattle."

"Maybe he did get home but got a very sudden call to drop everything and fly out to her, so he didn't have the time to phone you, or when he did, your line was busy."

"No, we're close enough that he'd know it would worry me. He'd have called from the airport, someplace."

"Your line still could have been busy all the times you were trying to get him. But I'm sure everything's okay, and don't worry about the tickets. Expensive as they are, I'll put them down as a total loss. Though if you are still so worried about him, phone the police in his neighborhood or even his mother in Seattle."

"Not his mother. There's no reason and I'd just worry her and Eliot would get angry at me. But the police is a good idea."

I call the police station in his precinct. The officer who answers says "We've nothing on a Mr. Schulter. But being that you say he left your apartment this morning, phone your precinct station," and she gives me the number. I call it and the officer on duty says "Something did come in today about someone of his name—let me think."

"Oh no."

"Hey, take it easy. It could be nothing. I'm only remembering that I saw an earlier bulletin, but what it was went right past me. What's your relationship to him before I start searching for it?"

"His closest friend. We're really very very close and his nearest relative is three thousand miles from here."

"Well, I don't see it in front of me. I'll locate it, though don't get excited when I'm away. It could be nothing. I might even be wrong. It was probably more like a Mr. Fullter or Schulton I read about, but not him. Want me to phone you back?"

"I'll wait, thanks."

"Let me take your number anyway, just in case I get lost."

He goes, comes back in a minute. "Now take it easy. It's very serious. He had no I.D. on him other than this artist society card with only his signature on it, which we were checking into, so we're grateful you called."

"Please, what is it?"

"According to this elderly witness, he was supposedly thrown on the subway tracks this morning and killed."

I scream, break down, hang up, pound the telephone table with my fists, the officer calls back and says "If you could please revive yourself, Miss, we'd like you to come to the police station here and then, if you could by the end of the night sometime, to the morgue to identify your friend." 30

I say no, I could never go to the morgue, but then go with my best friend. She stays outside the body room when I go in, look and say "That's him." Later I call Eliot's mother and the next day her brother comes to the city and takes care of the arrangements to have Eliot flown to Seattle and his apartment closed down and most of his belongings sold or given away or put on the street. The uncle asks if I'd like to attend the funeral, but doesn't mention anything about providing air fare or where I would stay. Since I don't have much money saved and also think I'll be out of place there and maybe even looked down upon by his family I've never seen, I stay here and arrange on that same funeral day a small ceremony in the basement of a local church, where I and several of our friends and his employers speak about Eliot and read aloud excerpts of his letters to a couple of us and listen to parts of my opera records he most liked to play and for a minute bow our heads, hold hands and pray.

According to that elderly witness, Eliot was waiting for a train on the downtown platform of my stop when he saw a young man speaking abusively to a girl of about fifteen. When the girl continued to ignore him, he made several obscene gestures and said he was going to throw her to the platform and force her to do all sorts of sordid things to him and if he couldn't get her to do them there because people were watching, then in the men's room upstairs. The girl was frightened and started to walk away. The young man grabbed her wrist, started to twist it, stopped and said he would rip her arm off if she gave him a hard time, but didn't let go. There were a few people on the platform. Nobody said anything or tried to help her and in fact all of them except Eliot and this elderly man eventually moved to the other end of the platform or at least away from what was going on. Then Eliot went over to the young man, who was still holding the girl by her wrist, and very politely asked him to let her alone. Something like "Excuse me, I don't like to interfere in anyone's problems. But if this young lady doesn't want to be bothered by you, then I would really think you'd let her go."

"Listen, I know her, so mind your business," the young man said and she said to Eliot "No he don't." Then out of nowhere a friend of the young man ran down the subway stairs and said to him "What's this chump doing, horning in on your act?" The elderly man got up from a bench and started for the upstairs to get help. "You stay right here, grandpa," the first young man said, "or you'll get thrown on your back too." The elderly man stopped. Eliot said to the young men "Please, nobody should be getting thrown on their backs. And I hate to get myself any more involved in this but for your own good you fellows ought to go now or just leave everybody here alone."

"And for your own good," one of the young men said, "you'd be wiser moving your ass out of here."

"I can only move it once I know this girl's out of danger with you two." 35

"She'll be plenty out of danger when you move your ass out of here, now move."

"Believe me, I'd like to, but how can I? Either you leave her completely alone now or I'll have to get the police."

That's when they jumped him, beat him to the ground and, when he continued to fight back with his feet, fists and butting his head, picked him up and threw him on the tracks. He landed on his head and cracked his skull and something like a blood clot suddenly shot through to the brain, a doctor later said. The girl had already run away. The young men ran the opposite way. The elderly man shouted at Eliot to get up, then at people to jump down to the tracks to help Eliot up, then ran in the direction the young men went to the token booth upstairs and told the attendant inside that an unconscious man was lying on the tracks and for her to do something quick to prevent a train from running over him. She phoned from the booth. He ran back to the platform and all the way to the other end of it yelling to the people around him "Stop the train. Man on the tracks, stop the local train." When the downtown local entered the station a minute later, he and most of the people along the platform screamed and waved the motorman to stop the train because someone was on the tracks. The train came to a complete stop ten feet from Eliot. A lot of the passengers were thrown to the floor and the next few days a number of them sued the city for the dizzy spells and sprained fingers and ripped clothes they said they got from the sudden train stop and also for the days and weeks they'd have to miss from their jobs because of their injuries. Anyway, according to that same doctor who examined Eliot at the hospital, he was dead a second or two after his head hit the train rail.

For a week after the funeral I go into my own special kind of mourning: seeing nobody, never leaving the apartment or answering phone calls, eating little and drinking too much, but mostly just sleeping or watching television while crying and lying in bed. Then I turn the television off, answer every phone call, run along the river for twice as many miles than I usually do, go out for a big restaurant dinner with a friend and return to my job.

The Saturday morning after the next Saturday after that I sit on the bench near the place on the subway platform where Eliot was thrown off. I stay there from eight to around one, on the lookout for the two young men. I figure they live in the neighborhood and maybe every Saturday have a job or something to go to downtown and after a few weeks they'll think everything's forgotten about them and their crime and they can go safely back to their old routines, like riding the subway to work at the station nearest their homes. The descriptions I have of them are the ones the elderly witness gave. He said he was a portrait painter or used to be and so he was absolutely exact about their height, age, looks, mannerisms and hair color and style and clothes. He also made detailed drawings of the men for the police, which I have copies of from the newspaper, and which so far haven't done the police any good in finding them.

What I'm really looking out for besides those descriptions are two young men who will try and pick up or seriously annoy or molest a teen-age girl on the platform or do that to any reasonably young woman, including me. If I see them and I'm sure it's them I'll summon a transit policeman to arrest them and if there's none around then I'll follow the young men, though discreetly, till I see a policeman. And if they try and molest or terrorize me on the bench and no policeman's around, I'll scream at the top of my lungs till someone comes and steps in, and hopefully a policeman. But I just want those two young men caught, that's all, and am willing to risk myself a little for it, and though there's probably not much chance of it happening, I still want to give it a good try.

I do this every Saturday morning for months. I see occasional violence on the platform, like a man slapping his woman friend in the face or a mother hitting her infant real hard, but nothing like two or even one man of any description close to those young men terrorizing or molesting a woman or girl or even trying to pick one up. I do see men, both old and young, and a few who look no more than nine years old or ten, leer at women plenty as if they'd like to pick them up or molest them. Some men, after staring at a woman from a distance, then walk near to her when the train comes just to follow her through the same door into the car. But that's as far as it goes on the platform. Maybe when they both get in the car and especially when it's crowded, something worse happens. I know that a few times a year when I ride the subway, a pull or poke from a man has happened to me.

A few times a man has come over to the bench and once even a woman who looked manly and tried to talk to me, but I brushed them off with silence or a remark. Then one morning a man walks over when I'm alone on the bench and nobody else is around. I'm not worried, since he has a nice face and is decently dressed and I've seen him before here waiting for the train and all it seems he wants now is to sit down. He's a big man, so I move over a few inches to the far end of the bench to give him more room.

"No," he says, "I don't want to sit—I'm just curious. I've seen you in this exact place almost every Saturday for the last couple of months and never once saw you get on the train. Would it be too rude—"

"Yes."

"All right. I won't ask it. I'm sorry." 45

"No, go on, ask it. What is it you want to know? Why I sit here? Well I've been here every Saturday for more than three months straight, if you're so curious to know, and why you don't see me get on the car is none of your business, okay?"

"Sure," he says, not really offended or embarrassed. "I asked for and got it and should be satisfied. Excuse me," and he walks away and stands near the edge of the platform, never turning around to me. When the local comes, he gets on it.

Maybe I shouldn't have been that sharp with him, but I don't like to be spoken to by men I don't know, especially in subways.

Next Saturday around the same time he comes downstairs again and stops by 50 my bench.

"Hello," he says.

I don't say anything and look the other way.

"Still none of my business why you sit here every Saturday like this?"

I continue to look the other way.

"I should take a hint, right?" 55

"Do you think that's funny?"

"No."

"Then what do you want me to do, call a policeman?"

"Of course not. I'm sorry and I am being stupid."

"Look, I wouldn't call a policeman. You seem okay. You want to be friendly or 60 so it seems. You're curious besides, which is good. But to me it is solely my business and not yours why I am here and don't want to talk to you and so forth and I don't know why you'd want to persist in it."

"I understand," and he walks away, stays with his back to me and gets on the train when it comes.

Next Saturday he walks down the stairs and stays near the platform edge about ten feet away reading a book. Then he turns to me and seems just about to say something and I don't know what I'm going to say in return, if anything, because he does seem polite and nice and intelligent and I actually looked forward a little to seeing and speaking civilly to him, when the train comes. He waves to me and gets on it. I lift my hand to wave back but quickly put it down. Why start?

Next Saturday he runs down the stairs to catch the train that's pulling in. He doesn't even look at me this time, so in a rush is he to get on the car. He gets past the doors just before they close and has his back to me when the train leaves. He must be late for someplace.

The next Saturday he comes down the stairs and walks over to me with two containers of coffee or tea while the train's pulling in. He keeps walking to me while the train doors open, close, and the train goes. I look at the advertisement clock. He's about fifteen minutes earlier than usual.

"How do you like your coffee if I can ask, black or regular? Or maybe you don't want any from me, if you do drink coffee, which would of course be all right too."

"Regular, but I don't want any, thanks."

"Come on, take it, it's not toxic and I can drink my coffee any old way. And it'll perk you up, not that you need perking up and certainly not from me," and he gives me a container. "Sugar?" and I say "Really, this is—" and he says "Come on: sugar?" and I nod and he pulls out of his jacket pocket a couple of sugar packets and a stirring stick. "I just took these on the way out of the shop without waiting for a bag, don't ask me why. The stick's probably a bit dirty, do you mind?" and I shake my head and wipe the stick though there's nothing on it. "Mind if I sit and have my coffee also?" and I say "Go ahead. It's not my bench and all that and I'd be afraid to think what you'd pull out of your pocket if I said no—probably your own bench and cocktail table," and he says "Don't be silly," and sits.

He starts talking about the bench, how the same oak one has been here for at least thirty years because that's how long he's lived in the neighborhood, then about the coffee, that it's good though always from the shop upstairs a little bitter, then why he happens to see me every Saturday: that he's recently divorced and has a child by that marriage who he goes to in Brooklyn once a week to spend the whole day with. He seems even nicer and more intelligent than I thought and comfortable to be with and for the first time I think he's maybe even goodlooking when before I thought his ears stuck out too far and he had too thin a mouth and small a nose. He dresses well anyway and has a nice profile and his hair's stylish and neat and his face shaven clean which I like and no excessive jewelry or neck chain which I don't and in his other jacket pocket are a paperback and small ribbon-wrapped package, the last I guess a present for his little girl.

His train comes and when the doors open I say "Shouldn't you get on it?" and he says "I'll take the next one if you don't mind," and I say "I don't think it's up to me to decide," and he hunches his shoulders and gives me that expression "Well I don't know what to say," and the train goes and when it's quiet again he continues the conversation, now about what I think of something that happened in Africa yesterday which he read in the paper today. I tell him I didn't read it and that maybe when I do read my paper it won't be the same as his and so might not have that news story and he says "What paper you read?" and I tell him and he says "Same one—front page, left-hand column," and I say "Anyway, on Saturdays I don't, and for my own reasons, have time for the newspaper till I get home later and really also don't have the time to just sit here and talk," and he says "Of course, of course," but seriously, as if he believes me, and we're silent for a while, drinking our coffees and looking at the tracks.

We hear another train coming and I say "I think you better get on this one," and he says "Okay. It's been great and I hope I haven't been too much of a nuisance," and I say "You really haven't at all," and he says "Mind if I ask your name?" and I say "Your train," and he yells to the people going into the subway car "Hold the door," and gets up and says to me "Mine's Vaughn," and shakes my hand and says "Next week," and runs to the train with his container and he's not past the door a second when the man who kept it open for him lets it close.

I picture him on his way to Brooklyn, reading his book, later in Prospect Park with his daughter as he said they would do if the good weather holds up and in an indoor ice-skating rink if it doesn't, and then go back to my lookout. People spit and throw trash on the tracks, a drunk or crazy man urinates on the platform, a boy defaces the tile wall with a marker pen and tells me to go shoot myself when I very politely suggest he stop, there's almost a fight between a man trying to get off the train and the one blocking his way who's trying to get on, which I doubt would have happened if both sides of the double door had opened, but again no sign of my two young men.

Vaughn's not there the next Saturday and the Saturday after that and the third Saturday he's not there I begin thinking that I'm thinking more about him than I do of anybody or thing and spending more time looking at the staircase and around the platform for him than I do for those young men. I've gradually lost interest in finding them and over the last four months my chances have gotten worse and worse that I'll even recognize them if they ever do come down here and as far as their repeating that harassing-the-girl incident at this particular station, well forget it, and I leave the station at noon instead of around my usual two and decide that was my last Saturday there.

A month later I meet Vaughn coming out of a supermarket when I'm going in. He's pulling a shopping cart filled with clean laundry at the bottom and two big grocery bags on top. It's Saturday, we're both dressed in T-shirts and shorts for the warm weather now, and I stop him by saying "Vaughn, how are you?" He looks at me as if he doesn't remember me. "Maybe because you can't place me anywhere else but on a subway bench. Maria Pierce. From the subway station over there."

"That's right. Suddenly your face was familiar, but you never gave me your name. What's been happening?" and I say "Nothing much I guess," and he says "You don't wait in subway stations anymore for whatever you were waiting for those days?" and I say "How would you know? You stopped coming yourself there and to tell you the truth I was sort of looking forward to a continuation of that nice chat we last had."

"Oh, let me tell you what went wrong. My ex-wife, giving me a day's notice, changed jobs and locations and took my daughter to Boston with her. I could have fought it, but don't like arguments. I only get to see her when I get up there, which hasn't happened yet, and maybe for August if I want."   75

"That's too bad. I remember how devoted you were."

"I don't know it's so bad. I'm beginning to enjoy my freedom every Saturday, as much as I miss my kid. But I got to go. Ice cream in the bag will soon be melting," and he says goodbye and goes.

If I knew his last name I might look him up in the phone book and call him and say something like "Since we live in the same neighborhood, would you care to have a cup of coffee one of these days? I owe you one and I'll even, if you're still curious, let you in on my big secret why I every Saturday for months waited at our favorite subway station." Then I think no, even if I did have his phone number. I gave him on the street a couple of openings to make overtures about seeing me again and he didn't take them because he didn't want to or whatever his reasons but certainly not because of his melting ice cream.

Several weeks later I read in the newspaper that those two young men got caught. They were in the Eighth Street subway station and tried to molest a police-woman dressed like an artist with even a sketchbook and drawing pen, and two plain-clothesmen were waiting nearby. The police connected them up with Eliot's death. The two men later admitted to being on my subway platform that day but said they only started a fight with him because he tried to stop one of them from making a date with a girl the young man once knew. They said they told Eliot to mind his business, he refused, so they wrestled him to the ground and then said he could get up if he didn't make any more trouble. Eliot said okay, got up and immediately swung at them, missed, lost his footing and before either of them could grab him away, fell to the tracks. They got scared and ran to the street. They don't know the girl's last name or where she lives except that it's somewhere in the Bronx.

I buy all the newspapers that day and the next. One of them has a photo of the young men sticking their middle fingers up to the news photographers. They don't look anything like the young men I was on the lookout for, so either the witness's de-scription of them or the printing of the photograph was bad, because I don't see how they could have physically changed so much in just a few months.

I continue to read the papers for weeks after that, hoping to find something about the young men going to trial, but don't. Then a month later a co-worker of mine who knew about Eliot and me says she saw on the television last night that the young men were allowed to plead guilty to a lesser charge of negligent manslaughter or something and got off with a jail term of from one to three years. "It seems the el-derly man, that main witness to Eliot's murder, died of a fatal disease a while ago and the young woman witness could never be found. As for molesting the policewoman, that charge was dropped, though the news reporter never said why."

ANDRE DUBUS (b. 1936)

Dubus was born in Louisiana and received degrees from McNeese State College and the Uni-versity of Iowa. He taught at Bradford College in Massachusetts before he was hit by an au-tomobile and became disabled. He sets many of his stories in the area northwest of Boston, where he lives. Many of the stories in Selected Stories *(1988), which includes "The Curse," deal with the darker side of human existence. In "They Now Live in Texas," for ex-ample, a woman awaits her own demons after seeing a horror ghost movie on her VCR. In "Townies," a purposeless young man kills his girlfriend, and then waits serenely for the po-lice to arrive. Dubus has achieved wide recognition. Among his honors are a Guggenheim fellowship and, more recently, a MacArthur fellowship.*

The Curse _____ 1988

Mitchell Hayes was forty-nine years old, but when the cops left him in the bar with Bob, the manager, he felt much older. He did not know what it was like to be very old, a shrunken and wrinkled man, but he assumed it was like this: fatigue beyond reliev-ing by rest, by sleep. He also was not a small man: his weight moved up and down in the hundred and seventies and he was five feet, ten inches tall. But now his body seemed short and thin. Both stood at one end of the bar; he was a large blackhaired man, and there was nothing in front of him but an ash tray he was using. He looked at Mitchell at the cash register and said: "Forget it. You heard what Smitty said."

Mitchell looked away, at the front door. He had put the chairs upside down on the table. He looked from the door past Bob to the empty space of floor at the rear; sometimes people danced there, to the jukebox. Opposite Bob, on the wall behind the bar, was a telephone; Mitchell looked at it. He had told Smitty there were five guys and when he moved to the phone one of them stepped around the corner of the bar and shoved him: one hand against Mitchell's chest, and it pushed him backward; he nearly fell. That was when they were getting rough with her at the bar. When they took her to the floor Mitchell looked once at her sounds, then looked down at the duckboard he stood on, or at the belly or chest of a young man in front of him.

He knew they were not drunk. They had been drinking before they came to his place, a loud popping of motorcycles outside, then walking into the empty bar, young and sunburned and carrying helmets and wearing thick leather jackets in August. They stood in front of Mitchell and drank drafts. When he took their first order he thought they were on drugs and later, watching them, he was certain. They were not relaxed, in the way of most drinkers near closing time. Their eyes were quick, alert as wary animals, and they spoke loudly, with passion, but their passion was strange and disturbing, because they were only chatting, bantering. Mitchell knew nothing of the effects of drugs, so could not guess what was in their blood. He feared and hated drugs because of his work and because he was the stepfather of teenagers: a boy and a girl. He gave last call and served them and leaned against the counter behind him.

Then the door opened and the girl walked in from the night, a girl he had never seen, and she crossed the floor toward Mitchell. He stepped forward to tell her she had missed last call, but before he spoke she asked for change for the cigarette machine. She was young, he guessed nineteen to twenty-one, and deeply tanned and had dark hair. She was sober and wore jeans and a dark blue tee shirt. He gave her the quarters but she was standing between two of the men and she did not get to the machine.

When it was over and she lay crying on the cleared circle of floor, he left the bar and picked up the jeans and tee shirt beside her and crouched and handed them to her. She did not look at him. She lay the clothes across her breasts and what Mitchell thought of now as her wound. He left her and dialed 911, then Bob's number. He woke up Bob. Then he picked up her sneakers from the floor and placed them beside her and squatted near her face, her crying. He wanted to speak to her and touch her, hold a hand or press her brow, but he could not. 5

The cruiser was there quickly, the siren coming east from town, then slowing and deepening as the car stopped outside. He was glad Smitty was one of them; he had gone to high school with Smitty. The other was Dave, and Mitchell knew him because it was a small town. When they saw the girl Dave went out to the cruiser to call for an ambulance, and when he came back he said two other cruisers had those scumbags and were taking them in. The girl was still crying and could not talk to Smitty and Dave. She was crying when a man and woman lifted her onto a stretcher and rolled her out the door and she vanished forever in a siren.

Bob came in while Smitty and Dave were sitting at the bar drinking coffee and Smitty was writing his report; Mitchell stood behind the bar. Bob sat next to Dave as Mitchell said: "I could have stopped them, Smitty."

"That's our job," Smitty said. "You want to be in the hospital now?"

Mitchell did not answer. When Smitty and Dave left, he got a glass of Coke from the cobra and had a cigarette with Bob. They did not talk. Then Mitchell washed his glass and Bob's cup and they left, turning off the lights. Outside Mitchell locked the front door, feeling the sudden night air after almost ten hours of air conditioning. When he had come to work the day had been very hot, and now he thought it would not have happened in winter. They had stopped for a beer on their way somewhere from the beach; he had heard them say that. But the beach was not the reason. He did not know the reason, but he knew it would not have happened in winter. The night was cool and now he could smell trees. He turned and looked at the road in front of the bar. Bob stood beside him on the small porch.

"If the regulars had been here," Bob said.

He turned and with his hand resting on the wooden rail he walked down the ramp to the ground. At his car he stopped and looked over its roof at Mitchell.

"You take it easy," he said.

Mitchell nodded. When Bob got in his car and left, he went down the ramp and drove home to his house on a street that he thought was neither good nor bad. The houses were small and there were old large houses used now as apartments for families. Most of the people had work, most of the mothers cared for their children, and most of the children were clean and looked like they lived in homes, not caves like some he saw in town. He worried about the older kids, one group of them anyway. They were idle. When he was a boy in a town farther up the Merrimack River, he and his friends committed every mischievous act he could recall on afternoons and nights when they were idle. His stepchildren were not part of that group. They had friends from the high school. The front porch light was on for him and one in the kitchen at the rear of the house. He went in the front door and switched off the porch light and walked through the living and dining rooms to the kitchen. He got a can of beer from the refrigerator, turned out the light, and sat at the table. When he could see, he took a cigarette from Susan's pack in front of him.

Down the hall he heard Susan move on the bed then get up and he hoped it wasn't for the bathroom but for him. He had met her eight years ago when he had given up on ever marrying and having kids, then one night she came into the bar with two of her girl friends from work. She made six dollars an hour going to homes of invalids, mostly what she called her little old ladies, and bathing them. She got the house from her marriage, and child support the guy paid for a few months till he left town and went south. She came barefoot down the hall and stood in the kitchen doorway and said: "Are you all right?"

"No."

She sat across from him, and he told her. Very soon she held his hand. She was good. He knew if he had fought all five of them and was lying in pieces in a hospital bed she would tell him he had done the right thing, as she was telling him now. He liked her strong hand on his. It was a professional hand and he wanted from her something he had never wanted before: to lie in bed while she bathed him. When they went to bed he did not think he would be able to sleep, but she kneeled beside him and massaged his shoulders and rubbed his temples and pressed her hands on his forehead. He woke to the voices of Marty and Joyce in the kitchen. They had summer jobs, and always when they woke him he went back to sleep till noon, but now he got up and dressed and went to the kitchen door. Susan was at the stove, her back to him, and Marty and Joyce were talking and smoking. He said good morning, and stepped into the room.

"What are you doing up?" Joyce said.

She was a pretty girl with her mother's wide cheekbones and Marty was a tall good-looking boy, and Mitchell felt as old as he had before he slept. Susan was watching him. Then she poured him a cup of coffee and put it at his place and he sat. Marty said: "You getting up for the day?"

"Something happened last night. At the bar." They tried to conceal their excitement, but he saw it in their eyes. "I should have stopped it. I think I *could* have stopped it. That's the point. There were these five guys. They were on motorcycles but they weren't bikers. Just punks. They came in late, when everybody else had gone home. It was a slow night anyway. Everybody was at the beach."

"They rob you?" Marty said.   20

"No. A girl came in. Young. Nice looking. You know: just a girl, minding her business."

They nodded, and their eyes were apprehensive.

"She wanted cigarette change, that's all. Those guys were on dope. Coke or something. You know: they were flying in place."

"Did they rape her?" Joyce said.

"Yes, honey."   25

"The *fuckers.*"

Susan opened her mouth then closed it and Joyce reached quickly for Susan's pack of cigarettes. Mitchell held his lighter for her and said: "When they started getting rough with her at the bar I went for the phone. One of them stopped me. He shoved me, that's all. I should have hit him with a bottle."

Marty reached over the table with his big hand and held Mitchell's shoulder.

"No, Mitch. Five guys that mean. And coked up or whatever. No way. You wouldn't be here this morning."

"I don't know. There was always a guy with me. But just one guy, taking turns."   30

"Great," Joyce said. Marty's hand was on Mitchell's left shoulder; she put hers on his right hand.

"They took her to the hospital," he said. "The guys are in jail."

"They are?" Joyce said.

"I called the cops. When they left."

"You'll be a good witness," Joyce said.   35

He looked at her proud face.

"At the trial," she said.

The day was hot but that night most of the regulars came to the bar. Some of the younger ones came on motorcycles. They were a good crowd: they all worked, except the retired ones and no one ever bothered the women, not even the young ones with their summer tans. Everyone talked about it: some had read the newspaper story, some had heard the story in town, and they wanted to hear it from Mitchell. He told it as often as they asked but he did not finish it because he was working hard and could not stay with any group of customers long enough.

He watched their faces. Not one of them, even the women, looked at him as if he had not cared enough for the girl, or was a coward. Many of them even appeared sympathetic, making him feel for moments that he was a survivor of something horrible, and when that feeling left him he was ashamed. He felt tired and old, making drinks and change, moving and talking up and down the bar. At the stool at the far end Bob drank coffee and whenever Mitchell looked at him he smiled or nodded and once raised his right fist, with the thumb up.

Reggie was drinking too much. He did that two or three times a month and   40

Mitchell had to shut him off and Reggie always took it humbly. He was a big gentle man with a long brown beard. But tonight shutting off Reggie demanded from Mitchell an act of will, and when the eleven o'clock news came on the television and Reggie ordered another shot and a draft, Mitchell pretended not to hear him. He served the customers at the other end of the bar, where Bob was. He could hear Reggie calling: Hey Mitch; shot and a draft, Mitch. Mitchell was close to Bob now. Bob said softly: "He's had enough."

Mitchell nodded and went to Reggie, leaned closer to him so he could speak quietly, and said: "Sorry, Reggie. Time for coffee. I don't want you dead out there."

Reggie blinked at him.

"Okay, Mitch." He pulled some bills from his pocket and put them on the bar. Mitchell glanced at them and saw at least a ten dollar tip. When he rang up Reggie's tab the change was sixteen dollars and fifty cents, and he dropped the coins and shoved the bills into the beer mug beside the cash register. The mug was full of bills, as it was on most nights, and he kept his hand in there, pressing Reggie's into the others, and saw the sunburned young men holding her down on the floor and one kneeling between her legs, spread and held, and he heard their cheering voices and her screaming and groaning and finally weeping and weeping and weeping, until she was the siren crying then fading into the night. From the floor behind him, far across the room, he felt her pain and terror and grief, then her curse upon him. The curse moved into his back and spread down and up his spine, into his stomach and legs and arms and shoulders until he quivered with it. He wished he were alone so he could kneel to receive it.

GABRIEL GARCÍA MÁRQUEZ (b. 1928)

One of South America's major writers, García Márquez is a native of Colombia, but since 1950 has lived outside his homeland. Early in his career he created a mythical town, Macondo, for his fiction, and began exploiting a vein of realism and fancy known as magic realism. *This characteristic is strongly evident in his novel,* One Hundred Years of Solitude *and also in "A Very Old Man with Enormous Wings." Among his most recent works are* Love in the Time of Cholera *(1988),* Strange Pilgrims *(1993, twelve stories), and* The Handsomest Drowned Man *(1994). He was awarded the Nobel Prize for Literature in 1982.*

A Very Old Man with Enormous Wings _____ *1971*

Translated by Gregory Rabassa

A TALE FOR CHILDREN

On the third day of rain they had killed so many crabs inside the house that Pelayo had to cross his drenched courtyard and throw them into the sea, because the newborn child had a temperature all night and they thought it was due to the stench. The world had been sad since Tuesday. Sea and sky were a single ash-gray thing and the sands of the beach, which on March nights glimmered like powdered light, had become a stew of mud and rotten shellfish. The light was so weak at noon that when Pelayo was coming back to the house after throwing away the crabs, it was hard for him to see what it was that was moving and groaning in the rear of the courtyard. He had to go very close to see that it was an old man, a very old man, lying face down in the mud, who, in spite of his tremendous efforts, couldn't get up, impeded by his enormous wings.

Frightened by that nightmare, Pelayo ran to get Elisenda, his wife, who was putting compresses on the sick child, and he took her to the rear of the courtyard. They both looked at the fallen body with mute stupor. He was dressed like a rag-picker. There were only a few faded hairs left on his bald skull and very few teeth in his mouth, and his pitiful condition of a drenched great-grandfather had taken away any sense of grandeur he might have had. His huge buzzard wings, dirty and half-plucked, were forever entangled in the mud. They looked at him so long and so closely that Pelayo and Elisenda very soon overcame their surprise and in the end found him familiar. Then they dared speak to him, and he answered in an incomprehensible dialect with a strong sailor's voice. That was how they skipped over the inconvenience of the wings and quite intelligently concluded that he was a lonely castaway from some foreign ship wrecked by the storm. And yet, they called in a neighbor woman who knew everything about life and death to see him, and all she needed was one look to show them their mistake.

"He's an angel," she told them. "He must have been coming for the child, but the poor fellow is so old that the rain knocked him down."

On the following day everyone knew that a flesh-and-blood angel was held captive in Pelayo's house. Against the judgment of the wise neighbor woman, for whom angels in those times were the fugitive survivors of a celestial conspiracy, they did not have the heart to club him to death. Pelayo watched over him all afternoon from the kitchen, armed with his bailiff's club, and before going to bed he dragged him out of the mud and locked him up with the hens in the wire chicken coop. In the middle of the night, when the rain stopped, Pelayo and Elisenda were still killing crabs. A short time afterward the child woke up without a fever and with a desire to eat. Then they felt magnanimous and decided to put the angel on a raft with fresh water and provisions for three days and leave him to his fate on the high seas. But when they went out into the courtyard with the first light of dawn, they found the whole neighborhood in front of the chicken coop having fun with the angel, without the slightest reverence, tossing him things to eat through the openings in the wire as if he weren't a supernatural creature but a circus animal.

Father Gonzaga arrived before seven o'clock, alarmed at the strange news. By that time onlookers less frivolous than those at dawn had already arrived and they were making all kinds of conjectures concerning the captive's future. The simplest among them thought that he should be named mayor of the world. Others of sterner mind felt that he should be promoted to the rank of five-star general in order to win all wars. Some visionaries hoped that he could be put to stud in order to implant on earth a race of winged wise men who could take charge of the universe. But Father Gonzaga, before becoming a priest, had been a robust woodcutter. Standing by the wire, he reviewed his catechism in an instant and asked them to open the door so that he could take a close look at that pitiful man who looked more like a huge decrepit hen among the fascinated chickens. He was lying in a corner drying his open wings in the sunlight among the fruit peels and breakfast leftovers that the early risers had

5

thrown him. Alien to the impertinences of the world, he only lifted his antiquarian eyes and murmured something in his dialect when Father Gonzaga went into the chicken coop and said good morning to him in Latin. The parish priest had his first suspicion of an imposter when he saw that he did not understand the language of God or know how to greet His ministers. Then he noticed that seen close up he was much too human: he had an unbearable smell of the outdoors, the back side of his wings was strewn with parasites and his main feathers had been mistreated by terrestrial winds, and nothing about him measured up to the proud dignity of angels. Then he came out of the chicken coop and in a brief sermon warned the curious against the risks of being ingenuous. He reminded them that the devil had the bad habit of making use of carnival tricks in order to confuse the unwary.° He argued that if wings were not the essential element in determining the difference between a hawk and an airplane, they were even less so in the recognition of angels. Nevertheless, he promised to write a letter to his bishop so that the latter would write to his primate so that the latter would write to the Supreme Pontiff° in order to get the final verdict from the highest courts.

His prudence fell on sterile hearts. The news of the captive angel spread with such rapidity that after a few hours the courtyard had the bustle of a marketplace and they had to call in troops with fixed bayonets to disperse the mob that was about to knock the house down. Elisenda, her spine all twisted from sweeping up so much marketplace trash, then got the idea of fencing in the yard and charging five cents admission to see the angel.

The curious came from far away. A traveling carnival arrived with a flying acrobat who buzzed over the crowd several times, but no one paid any attention to him because his wings were not those of an angel but, rather, those of a sidereal bat. The most unfortunate invalids on earth came in search of health: a poor woman who since childhood had been counting her heartbeats and had run out of numbers; a Portuguese man who couldn't sleep because the noise of the stars disturbed him; a sleepwalker who got up at night to undo the things he had done while awake; and many others with less serious ailments. In the midst of that shipwreck disorder that made the earth tremble, Pelayo and Elisenda were happy with fatigue, for in less than a week they had crammed their rooms with money and the line of pilgrims waiting their turn to enter still reached beyond the horizon.

The angel was the only one who took no part in his own act. He spent his time trying to get comfortable in his borrowed nest, befuddled by the hellish heat of the oil lamps and sacramental candles that had been placed along the wire. At first they tried to make him eat some mothballs, which, according to the wisdom of the wise neighbor woman, were the food prescribed for angels. But he turned them down, just as he turned down the papal lunches that the penitents brought him, and they never found out whether it was because he was an angel or because he was an old man that in the end he ate nothing but eggplant mush. His only supernatural virtue seemed to be patience. Especially during the first days, when the hens pecked at him, searching for the stellar parasites that proliferated in his wings, and the cripples pulled out feathers to touch their defective parts with, and even the most merciful threw stones at him, trying to get him to rise so they could see him standing. The only time they

---

He . . . the unwary: See *Hamlet*, Act II, scene 2, lines 573–578, for a further explanation of this power of the devil.
Supreme Pontiff: the Pope in Rome.

succeeded in arousing him was when they burned his side with an iron for branding steers, for he had been motionless for so many hours that they thought he was dead. He awoke with a start, ranting in his hermetic language and with tears in his eyes, and he flapped his wings a couple of times, which brought on a whirlwind of chicken dung and lunar dust and a gale of panic that did not seem to be of this world. Although many thought that his reaction had been one not of rage but of pain, from then on they were careful not to annoy him, because the majority understood that his passivity was not that of a hero taking his ease but that of a cataclysm in repose.

Father Gonzaga held back the crowd's frivolity with formulas of maidservant inspiration while awaiting the arrival of a final judgment on the nature of the captive. But the mail from Rome showed no sense of urgency. They spent their time finding out if the prisoner had a navel, if his dialect had any connection with Aramaic, how many times he could fit on the head of a pin, or whether he wasn't just a Norwegian with wings. Those meager letters might have come and gone until the end of time if a providential event had not put an end to the priest's tribulations.

It so happened that during those days, among so many other carnival attractions, there arrived in town the traveling show of the woman who had been changed into a spider for having disobeyed her parents. The admission to see her was not only less than the admission to see the angel, but people were permitted to ask her all manner of questions about her absurd state and to examine her up and down so that no one would ever doubt the truth of her horror. She was a frightful tarantula the size of a ram and with the head of a sad maiden. What was most heart-rending, however, was not her outlandish shape but the sincere affliction with which she recounted the details of her misfortune. While still practically a child she had sneaked out of her parents' house to go to a dance, and while she was coming back through the woods after having danced all night without permission, a fearful thunderclap rent the sky in two and through the crack came the lightning bolt of brimstone that changed her into a spider. Her only nourishment came from the meatballs that charitable souls chose to toss into her mouth. A spectacle like that, full of so much human truth and with such a fearful lesson, was bound to defeat without even trying that of a haughty angel who scarcely deigned to look at mortals. Besides, the few miracles attributed to the angel showed a certain mental disorder, like the blind man who didn't recover his sight but grew three new teeth, or the paralytic who didn't get to walk but almost won the lottery, and the leper whose sores sprouted sunflowers. Those consolation miracles, which were more like mocking fun, had already ruined the angel's reputation when the woman who had been changed into a spider finally crushed him completely. That was how Father Gonzaga was cured forever of his insomnia and Pelayo's courtyard went back to being as empty as during the time it had rained for three days and crabs walked through the bedrooms.

The owners of the house had no reason to lament. With the money they saved they built a two-story mansion with balconies and gardens and high netting so that crabs wouldn't get in during the winter, and with iron bars on the windows so that angels wouldn't get in. Pelayo also set up a rabbit warren close to town and gave up his job as bailiff for good, and Elisenda bought some satin pumps with high heels and many dresses of iridescent silk, the kind worn on Sunday by the most desirable women in those times. The chicken coop was the only thing that didn't receive any attention. If they washed it down with creolin° and burned tears of myrrh° inside it every so of-

creolin: creosote-based disinfectant.
myrrh: fragrant plant resin used in making incense and perfume.

ten, it was not in homage to the angel but to drive away the dungheap stench that still hung everywhere like a ghost and was turning the new house into an old one. At first, when the child learned to walk, they were careful that he not get too close to the chicken coop. But then they began to lose their fears and got used to the smell, and before the child got his second teeth he'd gone inside the chicken coop to play, where the wires were falling apart. The angel was no less standoffish with him than with other mortals, but he tolerated the most ingenious infamies with the patience of a dog who had no illusions. They both came down with chicken pox at the same time. The doctor who took care of the child couldn't resist the temptation to listen to the angel's heart, and he found so much whistling in the heart and so many sounds in his kidneys that it seemed impossible for him to be alive. What surprised him most, however, was the logic of his wings. They seemed so natural on that completely human organism that he couldn't understand why other men didn't have them too.

When the child began school it had been some time since the sun and rain had caused the collapse of the chicken coop. The angel went dragging himself about here and there like a stray dying man. They would drive him out of the bedroom with a broom and a moment later find him in the kitchen. He seemed to be in so many places at the same time that they grew to think that he'd been duplicated, that he was reproducing himself all through the house, and the exasperated and unhinged Elisenda shouted that it was awful living in that hell full of angels. He could scarcely eat and his antiquarian eyes had also become so foggy that he went about bumping into posts. All he had left were the bare cannulae° of his last feathers. Pelayo threw a blanket over him and extended him the charity of letting him sleep in the shed, and only then did they notice that he had a temperature at night, and was delirious with the tongue twisters of an old Norwegian. That was one of the few times they became alarmed, for they thought he was going to die and not even the wise neighbor woman had been able to tell them what to do with dead angels.

And yet he not only survived his worst winter, but seemed improved with the first sunny days. He remained motionless for several days in the farthest corner of the courtyard, where no one would see him, and at the beginning of December some large, stiff feathers began to grow on his wings, the feathers of a scarecrow, which looked more like another misfortune of decrepitude. But he must have known the reason for those changes, for he was quite careful that no one should notice them, that no one should hear the sea chanteys that he sometimes sang under the stars. One morning Elisenda was cutting some bunches of onions for lunch when a wind that seemed to come from the high seas blew into the kitchen. Then she went to the window and caught the angel in his first attempts at flight. They were so clumsy that his fingernails opened a furrow in the vegetable patch and he was on the point of knocking the shed down with the ungainly flapping that slipped on the light and couldn't get a grip on the air. But he did manage to gain altitude. Elisenda let out a sigh of relief, for herself and for him, when she saw him pass over the last houses, holding himself up in some way with the risky flapping of a senile vulture. She kept watching him even when she was through cutting the onions and she kept on watching until it was no longer possible for her to see him, because then he was no longer an annoyance in her life but an imaginary dot on the horizon of the sea.

---

cannulae: hollow central stems of feathers.

CHARLOTTE PERKINS GILMAN (1860–1938)

Born in 1860, Gilman did not begin writing seriously until after the birth of her daughter in the 1880s, which was followed by her "nervous breakdown." Attempting to establish her own independence, she left her husband in 1890 and went to California, where she launched what was to become a distinguished career as an advocate for women's rights. For many decades she lectured and wrote extensively, her touchstone work being Women and Economics *(1898), in which she championed the need for women's financial independence. Among her many writings were* Concerning Children *(1900),* Human Work *(1904), and* His Religion and Hers *(1923). In the 1930s she became incurably ill, and with death facing her, she took her own life in 1938.*

The Yellow Wallpaper° ———————————————*1892*

It is very seldom that mere ordinary people like John and myself secure ancestral halls for the summer.

A colonial mansion, a hereditary estate, I would say a haunted house and reach the height of romantic felicity—but that would be asking too much of fate!

Still I will proudly declare that there is something queer about it.

Else, why should it be let so cheaply? And why have stood so long untenanted?

John laughs at me, of course, but one expects that.   5

John is practical in the extreme. He has no patience with faith, an intense horror of superstition, and he scoffs openly at any talk of things not to be felt and seen and put down in figures.

John is a physician, and *perhaps*—(I would not say it to a living soul, of course, but this is dead paper and a great relief to my mind)—*perhaps* that is one reason I do not get well faster.

You see, he does not believe I am sick! And what can one do?

If a physician of high standing, and one's own husband, assures friends and relatives that there is really nothing the matter with one but temporary nervous depression—a slight hysterical tendency—what is one to do?

My brother is also a physician, and also of high standing, and he says the same   10
thing.

So I take phosphates or phosphites—whichever it is—and tonics, and air and exercise, and journeys, and am absolutely forbidden to "work" until I am well again.

Personally, I disagree with their ideas.

Personally, I believe that congenial work, with excitement and change, would do me good.

But what is one to do?

I did write for a while in spite of them; but it *does* exhaust me a good deal—hav-   15
ing to be so sly about it, or else meet with heavy opposition.

The Yellow Wallpaper: The story is based on the "rest cure" developed after the Civil War by the famous Philadelphia physician S. Weir Mitchell (1829–1914); see paragraph 83. The Mitchell treatment required confining the patient to a hospital, hotel, or some other remote residence. Once isolated, the patient was to have complete bed rest, increased food intake, iron supplements, exercise, and sometimes massage and electric shock therapy. Gilman had experienced Mitchell's "cure," and sent a copy of this story to him as criticism. After receiving the story Mitchell modified his methods.

I sometimes fancy that in my condition, if I had less opposition and more society and stimulus—but John says the very worst thing I can do is to think about my condition, and I confess it always makes me feel bad.

So I will let it alone and talk about the house.

The most beautiful place! It is quite alone, standing well back from the road, quite three miles from the village. It makes me think of English places that you read about, for there are hedges and walls and gates that lock, and lots of separate little houses for the gardeners and people.

There is a *delicious* garden! I never saw such a garden—large and shady, full of box-bordered paths, and lined with long grape-covered arbors with seats under them.

There were greenhouses, but they are all broken now.

There was some legal trouble, I believe, something about the heirs and co-heirs; anyhow, the place has been empty for years.

That spoils my ghostliness, I am afraid, but I don't care—there is something strange about the house—I can feel it.

I even said so to John one moonlight evening, but he said what I felt was a draught, and shut the window.

I get unreasonably angry with John sometimes. I'm sure I never used to be so sensitive. I think it is due to this nervous condition.

But John says if I feel so I shall neglect proper self-control; so I take pains to control myself—before him, at least, and that makes me very tired.

I don't like our room a bit. I wanted one downstairs that opened onto the piazza and had roses all over the window, and such pretty old-fashioned chintz hangings! But John would not hear of it.

He said there was only one window and not room for two beds, and no near room for him if he took another.

He is very careful and loving, and hardly lets me stir without special direction.

I have a schedule prescription for each hour in the day; he takes all care from me, and so I feel basely ungrateful not to value it more.

He said he came here solely on my account, that I was to have perfect rest and all the air I could get. "Your exercise depends on your strength, my dear," said he, "and your food somewhat on your appetite; but air you can absorb all the time." So we took the nursery at the top of the house.

It is a big, airy room, the whole floor nearly, with windows that look all ways, and air and sunshine galore. It was nursery first, and then playroom and gymnasium, I should judge, for the windows are barred for little children, and there are rings and things in the walls.

The paint and paper look as if a boys' school had used it. It is stripped off—the paper—in great patches all around the head of my bed, about as far as I can reach, and in a great place on the other side of the room low down. I never saw a worse paper in my life. One of those sprawling, flamboyant patterns committing every artistic sin.

It is dull enough to confuse the eye in following, pronounced enough constantly to irritate and provoke study, and when you follow the lame uncertain curves for a little distance they suddenly commit suicide—plunge off at outrageous angles, destroy themselves in unheard-of contradictions.

The color is repellent, almost revolting: a smouldering unclean yellow, strangely faded by the slow-turning sunlight. It is a dull yet lurid orange in some places, a sickly sulphur tint in others.

No wonder the children hated it! I should hate it myself if I had to live in this room long. 35

There comes John, and I must put this away—he hates to have me write a word.

We have been here two weeks, and I haven't felt like writing before, since that first day.

I am sitting by the window now, up in this atrocious nursery, and there is nothing to hinder my writing as much as I please, save lack of strength.

John is away all day, and even some nights when his cases are serious.

I am glad my case is not serious! 40

But these nervous troubles are dreadfully depressing.

John does not know how much I really suffer. He knows there is no reason to suffer, and that satisfies him.

Of course it is only nervousness. It does weigh on me so not to do my duty in any way!

I meant to be such a help to John, such a real rest and comfort, and here I am a comparative burden already!

Nobody would believe what an effort it is to do what little I am able—to dress 45 and entertain, and order things.

It is fortunate Mary is so good with the baby. Such a dear baby!

And yet I *cannot* be with him, it makes me so nervous.

I suppose John never was nervous in his life. He laughs at me so about this wallpaper!

At first he meant to repaper the room, but afterward he said that I was letting it get the better of me, and that nothing was worse for a nervous patient than to give way to such fancies.

He said that after the wallpaper was changed it would be the heavy bedstead, 50 and then the barred windows, and then that gate at the head of the stairs, and so on.

"You know the place is doing you good," he said, "and really, dear, I don't care to renovate the house just for a three months' rental."

"Then do let us go downstairs," I said. "There are such pretty rooms there."

Then he took me in his arms and called me a blessed little goose, and said he would go down cellar, if I wished, and have it whitewashed into the bargain.

But he is right enough about the beds and windows and things.

It is as airy and comfortable a room as anyone need wish, and, of course, I 55 would not be so silly as to make him uncomfortable just for a whim.

I'm really getting quite fond of the big room, all but that horrid paper.

Out of one window I can see the garden—those mysterious deep-shaded arbors, the riotous old-fashioned flowers, and bushes and gnarly trees.

Out of another I get a lovely view of the bay and a little private wharf belonging to the estate. There is a beautiful shaded lane that runs down there from the house. I always fancy I see people walking in these numerous paths and arbors, but John has cautioned me not to give way to fancy in the least. He says that with my imaginative power and habit of story-making, a nervous weakness like mine is sure to lead to all manner of excited fancies, and that I ought to use my will and good sense to check the tendency. So I try.

I think sometimes that if I were only well enough to write a little it would relieve the press of ideas and rest me.

But I find I get pretty tired when I try. 60

It is so discouraging not to have any advice and companionship about my work. When I get really well, John says we will ask Cousin Henry and Julia down for a long visit; but he says he would as soon put fireworks in my pillow-case as to let me have those stimulating people about now.

I wish I could get well faster.

But I must not think about that. This paper looks to me as if it *knew* what a vicious influence it had!

There is a recurrent spot where the pattern lolls like a broken neck and two bulbous eyes stare at you upside down.

I get positively angry with the impertinence of it and the everlastingness. Up and down and sideways they crawl, and those absurd unblinking eyes are everywhere. There is one place where two breadths didn't match, and the eyes go all up and down the line, one a little higher than the other.

I never saw so much expression in an inanimate thing before, and we all know how much expression they have! I used to lie awake as a child and get more entertainment and terror out of blank walls and plain furniture than most children could find in a toy-store.

I remember what a kindly wink the knobs of our big old bureau used to have, and there was one chair that always seemed like a strong friend.

I used to feel that if any of the other things looked too fierce I could always hop into that chair and be safe.

The furniture in this room is no worse than inharmonious, however, for we had to bring it all from downstairs. I suppose when this was used as a playroom they had to take the nursery things out, and no wonder! I never saw such ravages as the children have made here.

The wallpaper, as I said before, is torn off in spots, and it sticketh closer than a brother°—they must have had perseverance as well as hatred.

Then the floor is scratched and gouged and splintered, the plaster itself is dug out here and there, and this great heavy bed, which is all we found in the room, looks as if it had been through the wars.

But I don't mind it a bit—only the paper.

There comes John's sister. Such a dear girl as she is, and so careful of me! I must not let her find me writing.

She is a perfect and enthusiastic housekeeper, and hopes for no better profession. I verily believe she thinks it is the writing which made me sick!

But I can write when she is out, and see her a long way off from these windows.

There is one that commands the road, a lovely shaded winding road, and one that just looks off over the country. A lovely country, too, full of great elms and velvet meadows.

This wallpaper has a kind of sub-pattern in a different shade, a particularly irritating one, for you can only see it in certain lights, and not clearly then.

But in the places where it isn't faded and where the sun is just so—I can see a strange, provoking, formless sort of figure that seems to skulk about behind that silly and conspicuous front design.

There's sister on the stairs!

---

sticketh closer than a brother: Proverbs 18:24.

Well, the Fourth of July is over! The people are all gone, and I am tired out. 80
John thought it might do me good to see a little company, so we just had Mother and
Nellie and the children down for a week.

Of course I didn't do a thing. Jennie sees to everything now.

But it tired me all the same.

John says if I don't pick up faster he shall send me to Weir Mitchell° in the fall.

But I don't want to go there at all. I had a friend who was in his hands once,
and she says he is just like John and my brother, only more so!

Besides, it is such an undertaking to go so far. 85

I don't feel as if it was worthwhile to turn my hand over for anything, and I'm
getting dreadfully fretful and querulous.

I cry at nothing, and cry most of the time.

Of course I don't when John is here, or anybody else, but when I am alone.

And I am alone a good deal just now. John is kept in town very often by serious
cases, and Jennie is good and lets me alone when I want her to.

So I walk a little in the garden or down that lovely lane, sit on the porch under 90
the roses, and lie down up here a good deal.

I'm getting really fond of the room in spite of the wallpaper. Perhaps *because* of
the wallpaper.

It dwells in my mind so!

I lie here on this great immovable bed—it is nailed down, I believe—and follow
that pattern about by the hour. It is as good as gymnastics, I assure you. I start, we'll
say, at the bottom, down in the corner over there where it has not been touched, and
I determine for the thousandth time that I *will* follow that pointless pattern to some
sort of a conclusion.

I know a little of the principle of design, and I know this thing was not arranged
on any laws of radiation, or alternation, or repetition, or symmetry, or anything else
that I ever heard of.

It is repeated, of course, by the breadths, but not otherwise. 95

Looked at in one way, each breadth stands alone; the bloated curves and flourishes—a kind of "debased Romanesque" with delirium tremens go waddling up and
down in isolated columns of fatuity.

But, on the other hand, they connect diagonally, and the sprawling outlines run
off in great slanting waves of optic horror, like a lot of wallowing sea-weeds in full
chase.

The whole thing goes horizontally, too, at least it seems so, and I exhaust myself trying to distinguish the order of its going in that direction.

They have used a horizontal breadth for a frieze, and that adds wonderfully to
the confusion.

There is one end of the room where it is almost intact, and there, when the 100
crosslights fade and the low sun shines directly upon it, I can almost fancy radiation
after all—the interminable grotesque seems to form around a common center and
rush off in headlong plunges of equal distraction.

It makes me tired to follow it. I will take a nap, I guess.

I don't know why I should write this.

Weir Mitchell: See note on page 491.

I don't want to.

I don't feel able.

And I know John would think it absurd. But I *must* say what I feel and think in some way—it is such a relief!

But the effort is getting to be greater than the relief.

Half the time now I am awfully lazy, and lie down ever so much. John says I mustn't lose my strength, and has me take cod liver oil and lots of tonics and things, to say nothing of ale and wine and rare meat.

Dear John! He loves me very dearly, and hates to have me sick. I tried to have a real earnest reasonable talk with him the other day, and tell him how I wish he would let me go and make a visit to Cousin Henry and Julia.

But he said I wasn't able to go, nor able to stand it after I got there; and I did not make out a very good case for myself, for I was crying before I had finished.

It is getting to be a great effort for me to think straight. Just this nervous weakness, I suppose.

And dear John gathered me up in his arms, and just carried me upstairs and laid me on the bed, and sat by me and read to me till it tired my head.

He said I was his darling and his comfort and all he had, and that I must take care of myself for his sake, and keep well.

He says no one but myself can help me out of it, that I must use my will and self-control and not let any silly fancies run away with me.

There's one comfort—the baby is well and happy, and does not have to occupy this nursery with the horrid wallpaper.

If we had not used it, that blessed child would have! What a fortunate escape! Why, I wouldn't have a child of mine, an impressionable little thing, live in such a room for worlds.

I never thought of it before, but it is lucky that John kept me here after all; I can stand it so much easier than a baby, you see.

Of course I never mention it to them any more—I am too wise—but I keep watch for it all the same.

There are things in that wallpaper that nobody knows about but me, or ever will.

Behind that outside pattern the dim shapes get clearer every day.

It is always the same shape, only very numerous.

And it is like a woman stooping down and creeping about behind that pattern. I don't like it a bit. I wonder—I begin to think—I wish John would take me away from here!

It is so hard to talk with John about my case, because he is so wise, and because he loves me so.

But I tried it last night.

It was moonlight. The moon shines in all around just as the sun does.

I hate to see it sometimes, it creeps so slowly, and always comes in by one window or another.

John was asleep and I hated to waken him, so I kept still and watched the moonlight on that undulating wallpaper till I felt creepy.

The faint figure behind seemed to shake the pattern, just as if she wanted to get out.

I got up softly and went to feel and see if the paper *did* move, and when I came back John was awake.

"What is it, little girl?" he said. "Don't go walking about like that—you'll get cold."

I thought it was a good time to talk, so I told him that I really was not gaining   130
here, and that I wished he would take me away.

"Why, darling!" said he. "Our lease will be up in three weeks, and I can't see how to leave before.

"The repairs are not done at home, and I cannot possibly leave town just now. Of course, if you were in any danger, I could and would, but you really are better, dear, whether you can see it or not. I am a doctor, dear, and I know. You are gaining flesh and color, your appetite is better, I feel really much easier about you."

"I don't weigh a bit more," said I, "nor as much; and my appetite may be better in the evening when you are here but it is worse in the morning when you are away!"

"Bless her little heart!" said he with a big hug. "She shall be as sick as she pleases! But now let's improve the shining hours by going to sleep, and talk about it in the morning!"

"And you won't go away?" I asked gloomily.   135

"Why, how can I, dear? It is only three weeks more and then we will take a nice little trip of a few days while Jennie is getting the house ready. Really, dear, you are better!"

"Better in body perhaps—" I began, and stopped short, for he sat up straight and looked at me with such a stern, reproachful look that I could not say another word.

"My darling," said he, "I beg of you, for my sake and for our child's sake, as well as for your own, that you will never for one instant let that idea enter your mind! There is nothing so dangerous, so fascinating, to a temperament like yours. It is a false and foolish fancy. Can you not trust me as a physician when I tell you so?"

So of course I said no more on that score, and we went to sleep before long. He thought I was asleep first, but I wasn't, and lay there for hours trying to decide whether that front pattern and the back pattern really did move together or separately.

On a pattern like this, by daylight, there is a lack of sequence, a defiance of law,   140
that is a constant irritant to a normal mind.

The color is hideous enough, and unreliable enough, and infuriating enough, but the pattern is torturing.

You think you have mastered it, but just as you get well under way in following, it turns a back-somersault and there you are. It slaps you in the face, knocks you down, and tramples upon you. It is like a bad dream.

The outside pattern is a florid arabesque, reminding one of a fungus. If you can imagine a toadstool in joints, an interminable string of toadstools, budding and sprouting in endless convolutions—why, that is something like it.

That is, sometimes!

There is one marked peculiarity about this paper, a thing nobody seems to no-   145
tice but myself, and that is that it changes as the light changes.

When the sun shoots in through the east window—I always watch for that first long, straight ray—it changes so quickly than I never can quite believe it.

That is why I watch it always.

By moonlight—the moon shines in all night when there is a moon—I wouldn't know it was the same paper.

At night in any kind of light, in twilight, candlelight, lamplight, and worst of all by moonlight, it becomes bars! The outside pattern, I mean, and the woman behind it is as plain as can be.

I didn't realize for a long time what the thing was that showed behind, that dim sub-pattern, but now I am quite sure it is a woman.

By daylight she is subdued, quiet. I fancy it is the pattern that keeps her so still. It is so puzzling. It keeps me quiet by the hour.

I lie down ever so much now. John says it is good for me, and to sleep all I can.

Indeed he started the habit by making me lie down for an hour after each meal.

It is a very bad habit, I am convinced, for you see, I don't sleep.

And that cultivates deceit, for I don't tell them I'm awake—oh, no!

The fact is I am getting a little afraid of John.

He seems very queer sometimes, and even Jennie has an inexplicable look.

It strikes me occasionally, just as a scientific hypothesis, that perhaps it is the paper!

I have watched John when he did not know I was looking, and come into the room suddenly on the most innocent excuses, and I've caught him several times *looking at the paper*! And Jennie too. I caught Jennie with her hand on it once.

She didn't know I was in the room, and when I asked her in a quiet, a very quiet voice, with the most restrained manner possible, what she was doing with the paper, she turned around as if she had been caught stealing, and looked quite angry—asked me why I should frighten her so!

Then she said that the paper stained everything it touched, that she had found yellow smooches on all my clothes and John's and she wished we would be more careful!

Did not that sound innocent? But I know she was studying that pattern, and I am determined that nobody shall find it out but myself.

Life is very much more exciting now than it used to be. You see, I have something more to expect, to look forward to, to watch. I really do eat better, and am more quiet than I was.

John is so pleased to see me improve! He laughed a little the other day, and said I seemed to be flourishing in spite of my wallpaper.

I turned it off with a laugh. I had no intention of telling him it was *because* of the wallpaper—he would make fun of me. He might even want to take me away.

I don't want to leave now until I have found it out. There is a week more, and I think that will be enough.

I'm feeling so much better!

I don't sleep much at night, for it is so interesting to watch developments; but I sleep a good deal during the daytime.

In the daytime it is tiresome and perplexing.

There are always new shoots on the fungus, and new shades of yellow all over it. I cannot keep count of them, though I have tried conscientiously.

It is the strangest yellow, that wallpaper! It makes me think of all the yellow things I ever saw—not beautiful ones like buttercups, but old, foul, bad yellow things.

But there is something else about that paper—the smell! I noticed it the moment we came into the room, but with so much air and sun it was not bad. Now we have had a week of fog and rain, and whether the windows are open or not, the smell is here.

It creeps all over the house.

I find it hovering in the dining-room, skulking in the parlor, hiding in the hall, lying in wait for me on the stairs.

It gets into my hair.   175

Even when I go to ride, if I turn my head suddenly and surprise it—there is that smell!

Such a peculiar odor, too! I have spent hours in trying to analyze it, to find what it smelled like.

It is not bad—at first—and very gentle, but quite the subtlest, most enduring odor I ever met.

In this damp weather it is awful. I wake up in the night and find it hanging over me.

It used to disturb me at first. I thought seriously of burning the house—to reach   180
the smell.

But now I am used to it. The only thing I can think of that it is like is the *color* of the paper! A yellow smell.

There is a very funny mark on this wall, low down, near the mopboard. A streak that runs round the room. I goes behind every piece of furniture, except the bed, a long, straight, even *smooch*, as if it had been rubbed over and over.

I wonder how it was done and who did it, and what they did it for. Round and round and round—round and round and round—it makes me dizzy!

I really have discovered something at last.

Through watching so much at night, when it changes so, I have finally found   185
out.

The front pattern *does* move—and no wonder! The woman behind shakes it!

Sometimes I think there are a great many women behind, and sometimes only one, and she crawls around fast, and her crawling shakes it all over.

Then in the very bright spots she keeps still, and in the very shady spots she just takes hold of the bars and shakes them hard.

And she is all the time trying to climb through. But nobody could climb through that pattern—it strangles so; I think that is why it has so many heads.

They get through and then the pattern strangles them off and turns them up-   190
side down, and makes their eyes white!

If those heads were covered or taken off it would not be half so bad.

I think that woman gets out in the daytime!

And I'll tell you why—privately—I've seen her!

I can see her out of every one of my windows!

It is the same woman, I know, for she is always creeping, and most women do   195
not creep by daylight.

I see her in that long shaded lane, creeping up and down. I see her in those dark grape arbors, creeping all around the garden.

I see her on that long road under the trees, creeping along, and when a carriage comes she hides under the blackberry vines.

I don't blame her a bit. It must be very humiliating to be caught creeping by daylight!

I always lock the door when I creep by daylight. I can't do it at night, for I know John would suspect something at once.

And John is so queer now that I don't want to irritate him. I wish he would take another room! Besides, I don't want anybody to get that woman out at night but myself.

I often wonder if I could see her out of all the windows at once.

But, turn as fast as I can, I can only see out of one at a time.

And though I always see her, she *may* be able to creep faster than I can turn! I have watched her sometimes away off in the open country, creeping as fast as a cloud shadow in a wind.

If only that top pattern could be gotten off from the under one! I mean to try it, little by little.

I have found out another funny thing, but I shan't tell it this time! It does not do to trust people too much.

There are only two more days to get this paper off, and I believe John is beginning to notice. I don't like the look in his eyes.

And I heard him ask Jennie a lot of professional questions about me. She had a very good report to give.

She said I slept a good deal in the daytime.

John knows I don't sleep very well at night, for all I'm so quiet!

He asked me all sorts of questions, too, and pretended to be very loving and kind.

As if I couldn't see through him!

Still, I don't wonder he acts so, sleeping under this paper for three months.

It only interests me, but I feel sure John and Jennie are affected by it.

Hurrah! This is the last day, but it is enough. John is to stay in town over night, and won't be out until this evening.

Jennie wanted to sleep with me—the sly thing; but I told her I should undoubtedly rest better for a night all alone.

That was clever, for really I wasn't alone a bit! As soon as it was moonlight and that poor thing began to crawl and shake the pattern, I got up and ran to help her.

I pulled and she shook. I shook and she pulled, and before morning we had peeled off yards of that paper.

A strip about as high as my head and half around the room.

And then when the sun came and that awful pattern began to laugh at me, I declared I would finish it today!

We go away tomorrow, and they are moving all my furniture down again to leave things as they were before.

Jennie looked at the wall in amazement, but I told her merrily that I did it out of pure spite at the vicious thing.

She laughed and said she wouldn't mind doing it herself, but I must not get tired.

How she betrayed herself that time!

But I am here, and no person touches this paper but Me—not *alive*!

She tried to get me out of the room—it was too patent! But I said it was so quiet and empty and clean now that I believed I would lie down again and sleep all I could, and not to wake me even for dinner—I would call when I woke.

So now she is gone, and the servants are gone, and the things are gone, and there is nothing left but that great bedstead nailed down, with the canvas mattress we found on it.

We shall sleep downstairs tonight, and take the boat home tomorrow.

I quite enjoy the room, now it is bare again.

How those children did tear about here!

This bedstead is fairly gnawed!   230

But I must get to work.

I have locked the door and thrown the key down into the front path.

I don't want to go out, and I don't want to have anybody come in, till John comes.

I want to astonish him.

I've got a rope up here that even Jennie did not find. If that woman does get   235
out, and tries to get away, I can tie her!

But I forgot I could not reach far without anything to stand on!

This bed will *not* move!

I tried to lift and push it until I was lame, and then I got so angry I bit off a little piece at one corner—but it hurt my teeth.

Then I peeled off all the paper I could reach standing on the floor. It sticks horribly and the pattern just enjoys it! All those strangled heads and bulbous eyes and waddling fungus growths just shriek with derision!

I am getting angry enough to do something desperate. To jump out of the win-   240
dow would be admirable exercise, but the bars are too strong even to try.

Besides I wouldn't do it. Of course not. I know well enough that a step like that is improper and might be misconstrued.

I don't like to *look* out of the windows even—there are so many of those creeping women, and they creep so fast.

I wonder if they all came out of that wallpaper as I did?

But I am securely fastened now by my well-hidden rope—you don't get *me* out   245
in the road there!

I suppose I shall have to get back behind the pattern when it comes night, and that is hard!

It is so pleasant to be out in this great room and creep around as I please!

I don't want to go outside. I won't, even if Jennie asks me to.

For outside you have to creep on the ground, and everything is green instead of yellow.

But here I can creep smoothly on the floor, and my shoulder just fits in that long smooch around the wall, so I cannot lose my way.

Why, there's John at the door!   250

It is no use, young man, you can't open it!

How he does call and pound!

Now he's crying to Jennie for an axe.

It would be a shame to break down that beautiful door!

"John, dear!" said I in the gentlest voice. "The key is down by the front steps,   255
under a plantain leaf!"

That silenced him for a few moments.

Then he said, very quietly indeed, "Open the door, my darling!"

"I can't," said I. "The key is down by the front door under a plantain leaf!" And then I said it again, several times, very gently and slowly, and said it so often that he had to go and see, and he got it of course, and came in. He stopped short by the door.

"What is the matter?" he cried. "For God's sake, what are you doing!"

I kept on creeping just the same, but I looked at him over my shoulder.   260

"I've got out at last," said I, "in spite of you and Jane. And I've pulled off most of the paper, so you can't put me back!"

Now why should that man have fainted? But he did, and right across my path by the wall, so that I had to creep over him every time!

DORIS LESSING (b. 1919)

Doris Lessing—née Taylor—was born in Persia, and at the age of five went with her family to Southern Rhodesia, where she grew up. She took a number of non-literary jobs after leaving school when she was fifteen, and in 1949 she went to England to take up the writer's craft. Her best-known novel is The Golden Notebook *(1962), and she has written many stories and novels since then. "The Old Chief Mshlanga" is from* That Was the Old Chief's Country *(1951), a part of her African stories, and it reflects her early career as a writer.*

The Old Chief Mshlanga —————————————————————*1951*

They were good, the years of ranging the bush over her father's farm which, like every white farm, was largely unused, broken only occasionally by small patches of cultivation. In between, nothing but trees, the long sparse grass, thorn and cactus and gully, grass and outcrop and thorn. And a jutting piece of rock which had been thrust up from the warm soil of Africa unimaginable eras of time ago, washed into hollows and whorls by sun and wind that had travelled so many thousands of miles of space and bush, would hold the weight of a small girl whose eyes were sightless for anything but a pale willowed river, a pale gleaming castle—a small girl singing: "Out flew the web and floated wide, the mirror cracked from side to side . . ."

Pushing her way through the green aisles of the mealie° stalks, the leaves arching like cathedrals veined with sunlight far overhead, with the packed red earth underfoot, a fine lace of red starred witchweed would summon up a black bent figure croaking premonitions: the Northern witch, bred of cold Northern forests, would stand before her among the mealie fields, and it was the mealie fields that faded and fled, leaving her among the gnarled roots of an oak, snow falling thick and soft and white, the woodcutter's fire glowing red welcome through crowding tree trunks.

A white child, opening its eyes curiously on a sun-suffused landscape, a gaunt and violent landscape, might be supposed to accept it as her own, to take the msasa trees and the thorn trees as familiars, to feel her blood running free and responsive to the swing of the seasons.

This child could not see a msasa tree, or the thorn, for what they were. Her books held tales of alien fairies, her rivers ran slow and peaceful, and she knew the shape of the leaves of an ash or an oak, the names of the little creatures that lived in

mealie: a word for corn in Southern Africa.

English streams, when the words "the veld"° meant strangeness, though she could remember nothing else.

Because of this, for many years, it was the veld that seemed unreal; the sun was   5
a foreign sun, and the wind spoke a strange language.

The black people on the farm were as remote as the trees and the rocks. They were an amorphous black mass, mingling and thinning and massing like tadpoles, faceless, who existed merely to serve, to say "Yes, Baas,"° take their money and go. They changed season by season, moving from one farm to the next, according to their outlandish needs, which one did not have to understand, coming from perhaps hundreds of miles North or East, passing on after a few months—where? Perhaps even as far away as the fabled gold mines of Johannesburg, where the pay was so much better than the few shillings a month and the double handful of mealie meal twice a day which they earned in that part of Africa.

The child was taught to take them for granted: the servants in the house would come running a hundred yards to pick up a book if she dropped it. She was called "Nkosikaas"—Chieftainess, even by the black children her own age.

Later, when the farm grew too small to hold her curiosity, she carried a gun in the crook of her arm and wandered miles a day, from vlei° to vlei, from *kopje* to *kopje,*° accompanied by two dogs: the dogs and the gun were an armour against fear. Because of them she never felt fear.

If a native came into sight along the kaffir° paths half a mile away, the dogs would flush him up a tree as if he were a bird. If he expostulated (in his uncouth language which was by itself ridiculous) that was cheek. If one was in a good mood, it could be a matter for laughter. Otherwise one passed on, hardly glancing at the angry man in the tree.

On the rare occasions when white children met together they could amuse   10
themselves by hailing a passing native in order to make a buffoon of him; they could set the dogs on him and watch him run; they could tease a small black child as if he were a puppy—save that they would not throw stones and sticks at a dog without a sense of guilt.

Later still, certain questions presented themselves in the child's mind: and because the answers were not easy to accept, they were silenced by an even greater arrogance of manner.

It was even impossible to think of the black people who worked about the house as friends, for if she talked to one of them, her mother would come running anxiously: "Come away; you mustn't talk to natives."

It was this instilled consciousness of danger, of something unpleasant, that made it easy to laugh out loud, crudely, if a servant made a mistake in his English or if he failed to understand an order—there is a certain kind of laughter that is fear, afraid of itself.

One evening, when I was about fourteen, I was walking down the side of a mealie field that had been newly ploughed, so that the great red clods showed fresh

---

veld: also *veldt,* a vast, open grass-covered area used for grazing.
Baas: boss.
vlei: a slough or pond (valley).
kopje: a small hill covered with vegetation and rocks. Usually pronounced "copy."
kaffir: pejorative word for the various Bantu peoples and their languages.

and tumbling to the vlei beyond, like a choppy red sea; it was that hushed and listening hour, when the birds send long sad calls from tree to tree, and all the colours of earth and sky and leaf are deep and golden. I had my rifle in the curve of my arm, and the dogs were at my heels.

In front of me, perhaps a couple of hundred yards away, a group of three Africans came into sight around the side of a big antheap. I whistled the dogs close in to my skirts and let the gun swing in my hand, and advanced, waiting for them to move aside, off the path, in respect for my passing. But they came on steadily, and the dogs looked up at me for the command to chase. I was angry. It was "cheek" for a native not to stand off a path, the moment he caught sight of you.

In front walked an old man, stooping his weight on to a stick, his hair grizzled white, a dark red blanket slung over his shoulders like a cloak. Behind him came two young men, carrying bundles of pots, assegais, hatchets.

The group was not a usual one. They were not natives seeking work. These had an air of dignity, of quietly following their own purpose. It was the dignity that checked my tongue. I walked quietly on, talking softly to the growling dogs, till I was ten paces away. Then the old man stopped, drawing his blanket close.

"Morning, Nkosikaas," he said, using the customary greeting for any time of the day.

"Good morning," I said. "Where are you going?" My voice was a little truculent.

The old man spoke in his own language, then one of the young men stepped forward politely and said in careful English: "My Chief travels to see his brothers beyond the river."

A Chief! I thought, understanding the pride that made the old man stand before me like an equal—more than an equal, for he showed courtesy, and I showed none.

The old man spoke again, wearing dignity like an inherited garment, still standing ten paces off, flanked by his entourage, not looking at me (that would have been rude) but directing his eyes somewhere over my head at the trees.

"You are the little Nkosikaas from the farm of Baas Jordan?"

"That's right," I said.

"Perhaps your father does not remember," said the interpreter for the old man, "but there was an affair with some goats. I remember seeing you when you were . . ." The young man held his hand at knee level and smiled.

We all smiled.

"What is your name?" I asked.

"This is Chief Mshlanga," said the young man.

"I will tell my father that I met you," I said.

The old man said: "My greetings to your father, little Nkosikaas."

"Good morning," I said politely, finding the politeness difficult, from lack of use.

"Morning, little Nkosikaas," said the old man, and stood aside to let me pass.

I went by, my gun hanging awkwardly, the dogs sniffing and growling, cheated of their favorite game of chasing natives like animals.

Not long afterwards I read in an old explorer's book the phrase: "Chief Mshlanga's country." It went like this: "Our destination was Chief Mshlanga's country, to the north of the river; and it was our desire to ask his permission to prospect for gold in his territory."

The phrase "ask his permission" was so extraordinary to a white child, brought up to consider all natives as things to use, that it revived those questions, which could not be suppressed: they fermented slowly in my mind.

On another occasion one of those old prospectors who still move over Africa looking for neglected reefs, with their hammers and tents, and pans for sifting gold from crushed rock, came to the farm and, in talking of the old days, used that phrase again: "This was the Old Chief's country," he said. "It stretched from those mountains over there way back to the river, hundreds of miles of country." That was his name for our district: "The Old Chief's Country"; he did not use our name for it—a new phrase which held no implication of usurped ownership.

As I read more books about the time when this part of Africa was opened up, not much more than fifty years before, I found Old Chief Mshlanga had been a famous man, known to all the explorers and prospectors. But then he had been young: or maybe it was his father or uncle they spoke of—I never found out.

During that year I met him several times in the part of the farm that was traversed by natives moving over the country. I learned that the path up the side of the big red field where the birds sang was the recognized highway for migrants. Perhaps I even haunted it in the hope of meeting him: being greeted by him, the exchange of courtesies, seemed to answer the questions that troubled me.

Soon I carried a gun in a different spirit; I used it for shooting food and not to give me confidence. And now the dogs learned better manners. When I saw a native approaching, we offered and took greetings; and slowly that other landscape in my mind faded, and my feet struck directly on the African soil, and I saw the shapes of tree and hill clearly, and the black people moved back, as it were, out of my life: it was as if I stood aside to watch a low intimate dance of landscape and men, a very old dance, whose steps I could not learn.

But I thought: this is my heritage, too; I was bred here; it is my country as well as the black man's country; and there is plenty of room for all of us, without elbowing each other off the pavements and roads.   40

It seemed it was only necessary to let free that respect I felt when I was talking with old Chief Mshlanga, to let both black and white people meet gently, with tolerance for each other's differences: it seemed quite easy.

Then, one day, something new happened. Working in our house as servants were always three natives: cook, houseboy, garden boy. They used to change as the farm natives changed: staying for a few months then moving on to a new job, or back home to their kraals.° They were thought of as "good" or "bad" natives; which meant: how did they behave as servants? Were they lazy, efficient, obedient, or disrespectful? If the family felt good-humoured, the phrase was: "What can you expect from raw black savages?" If we were angry, we said: "These damned niggers, we would be much better off without them."

One day, a white policeman was on his rounds of the district, and he said laughingly: "Did you know you have an important man in your kitchen?"

"What!" exclaimed my mother sharply. "What do you mean?"

"A Chief's son." The policeman seemed amused. "He'll boss the tribe when the   45 old man dies."

"He'd better not put on a Chief's son act with me," said my mother.

When the policeman left, we looked with different eyes at our cook: he was a good worker, but he drank too much at week-ends—that was how we knew him.

He was a tall youth, with very black skin, like black polished metal, his tightly-

kraals: fenced-in native villages.

growing black hair parted white man's fashion at one side, with a metal comb from the store stuck into it; very polite, very distant, very quick to obey an order. Now that it had been pointed out, we said: "Of course, you can see. Blood always tells."

My mother became strict with him now she knew about his birth and prospects. Sometimes, when she lost her temper, she would say: "You aren't the Chief yet, you know." And he would answer her very quietly, his eyes on the ground: "Yes, Nkosikaas."

One afternoon he asked for a whole day off, instead of the customary half-day, to go home next Sunday.

"How can you go home in one day?"

"It will take me half an hour on my bicycle," he explained.

I watched the direction he took; and the next day I went off to look for this kraal; I understood he must be Chief Mshlanga's successor: there was no other kraal near enough our farm.

Beyond our boundaries on that side the country was new to me. I followed unfamiliar paths past *kopjes* that till now had been part of the jagged horizon, hazed with distance. This was Government land, which had never been cultivated by white men; at first I could not understand why it was that it appeared, in merely crossing the boundary, I had entered a completely fresh type of landscape. It was a wide green valley, where a small river sparkled, and vivid water-birds darted over the rushes. The grass was thick and soft to my calves, the trees stood tall and shapely.

I was used to our farm, whose hundreds of acres of harsh eroded soil bore trees that had been cut for the mine furnaces and had grown thin and twisted, where the cattle had dragged the grass flat, leaving innumerable criss-crossing trails that deepened each season into gullies, under the force of the rains.

This country had been left untouched, save for prospectors whose picks had struck a few sparks from the surface of the rocks as they wandered by; and for migrant natives whose passing had left, perhaps, a charred patch on the trunk of a tree where their evening fire had nestled.

It was very silent: a hot morning with pigeons cooing throatily, the midday shadows lying dense and thick with clear yellow spaces of sunlight between and in all that wide green park-like valley, not a human soul but myself.

I was listening to the quick regular tapping of a woodpecker when slowly a chill feeling seemed to grow up from the small of my back to my shoulders, in a constricting spasm like a shudder, and at the roots of my hair a tingling sensation began and ran down over the surface of my flesh, leaving me goosefleshed and cold, though I was damp with sweat. Fever? I thought; then uneasily, turned to look over my shoulder; and realized suddenly that this was fear. It was extraordinary, even humiliating. It was a new fear. For all the years I had walked by myself over this country I had never known a moment's uneasiness; in the beginning because I had been supported by a gun and the dogs, then because I had learnt an easy friendliness for the Africans I might encounter.

I had read of this feeling, how the bigness and silence of Africa, under the ancient sun, grows dense and takes shape in the mind, till even the birds seem to call menacingly, and a deadly spirit comes out of the trees and the rocks. You move warily, as if your very passing disturbs something old and evil, something dark and big and angry that might suddenly rear and strike from behind. You look at groves of entwined trees, and picture the animals that might be lurking there; you look at the river running slowly, dropping from level to level through the vlei, spreading into pools where at night the bucks come to drink, and the crocodiles rise and drag them by their soft noses into underwater caves. Fear possessed me. I found I was turning round and round, because of that shapeless menace behind me that might reach out and take me; I kept glancing at the files of *kopjes* which, seen from a different angle, seemed to change with every step so that even known landmarks, like a big mountain that had sentinelled my world since I first became conscious of it, showed an unfamiliar sunlit valley among its foothills. I did not know where I was. I was lost. Panic seized me. I found I was spinning round and round, staring anxiously at this tree and that, peering up at the sun which appeared to have moved into an eastern slant, shedding the sad yellow light of sunset. Hours must have passed! I looked at my watch and found that this state of meaningless terror had lasted perhaps ten minutes.

The point was that it was meaningless. I was not ten miles from home: I had only to take my way back along the valley to find myself at the fence; away among the foothills of the *kopjes* gleamed the roof of a neighbor's house, and a couple of hours' walking would reach it. This was the sort of fear that contracts the flesh of a dog at night and sets him howling at the full moon. It had nothing to do with what I thought or felt; and I was more disturbed by the fact that I could become its victim than of the physical sensation itself: I walked steadily on, quietened, in a divided mind, watching my own pricking nerves and apprehensive glances from side to side with a disgusted amusement. Deliberately I set myself to think of this village I was seeking, and what I should do when I entered it—if I could find it, which was doubtful, since I was walking aimlessly and it might be anywhere in the hundreds of thousands of acres of bush that stretched about me. With my mind on that village, I realized that a new sensation was added to the fear: loneliness. Now such a terror of isolation invaded me that I could hardly walk; and if it were not that I came over the crest of a small rise and saw a village below me, I should have turned and gone home. It was a cluster of thatched huts in a clearing among trees. There were neat patches of mealies and pumpkins and millet, and cattle grazed under some trees at a distance. Fowls scratched among the huts, dogs lay sleeping on the grass, and goats friezed a *kopje* that jutted up beyond a tributary of the river lying like an enclosing arm round the village.

As I came close I saw the huts were lovingly decorated with patterns of yellow and red and ochre mud on the walls; and the thatch was tied in place with plaits of straw.

This was not at all like our farm compound, a dirty and neglected place, a temporary home for migrants who had no roots in it.

And now I did not know what to do next. I called a small black boy, who was sitting on a lot playing a stringed gourd, quite naked except for the strings of blue beads round his neck, and said: "Tell the Chief I am here." The child stuck his thumb in his mouth and stared shyly back at me.

For minutes I shifted my feet on the edge of what seemed a deserted village, till at last the child scuttled off, and then some women came. They were draped in bright cloths, with brass glinting in their ears and on their arms. They also stared, silently; then turned to chatter among themselves.

I said again: "Can I see Chief Mshlanga?" I saw they caught the name: they did not understand what I wanted. I did not understand myself.

At last I walked through them and came past the huts and saw a clearing under a big shady tree, where a dozen old men sat cross-legged on the ground, talking. Chief Mshlanga was leaning back against the tree, holding a gourd in his hand, from which he had been drinking. When he saw me, not a muscle of his face moved, and I could see he was not pleased: perhaps he was afflicted with my own shyness, due to being unable to find the right forms of courtesy for the occasion. To meet me, on our own farm, was one thing; but I should not have come here. What had I expected? I could not join them socially: the thing was unheard of. Bad enough that I, a white girl, should be walking the veld alone as a white man might: and in this part of the bush where only Government officials had the right to move.

Again I stood, smiling foolishly, while behind me stood the groups of brightly clad, chattering women, their faces alert with curiosity and interest, and in front of me sat the old men, with old lined faces, their eyes guarded, aloof. It was a village of ancients and children and women. Even the two young men who kneeled beside the Chief were not those I had seen with him previously: the young men were all away working on the white men's farms and mines, and the Chief must depend on relatives who were temporarily on holiday for his attendants.

"The small white Nkosikaas is far from home," remarked the old man at last.

"Yes," I agreed, "it is far." I wanted to say: "I have come to pay you a friendly visit, Chief Mshlanga." I could not say it. I might now be feeling an urgent helpless desire to get to know these men and women as people, to be accepted by them as a friend, but the truth was I had set out in a spirit of curiosity: I had wanted to see the village that one day our cook, the reserved and obedient young man who got drunk on Sundays, would one day rule over.

"The child of Nkosi Jordan is welcome," said Chief Mshlanga.

"Thank you," I said, and could think of nothing more to say. There was a silence, while the flies rose and began to buzz around my head: and the wind shook a little in the thick green tree that spread its branches over the old men.

"Good morning," I said at last. "I have to return now to my home."

"Morning, little Nkosikaas," said Chief Mshlanga.

I walked away from the indifferent village, over the rise past the staring amber-eyed goats, down through the tall stately trees into the great rich green valley where the river meandered and the pigeons cooed tales of plenty and the woodpecker tapped softly.

The fear was gone; the loneliness had set into stiff-necked stoicism; there was now a queer hostility in the landscape, a cold, hard, sullen indomitability that walked with me, as strong as a wall, as intangible as smoke; it seemed to say to me: you walk here as a destroyer. I went slowly homewards, with an empty heart: I had learned that if one cannot call a country to heel like a dog, neither can one dismiss the past with a smile in an easy gush of feeling, saying: I could not help it, I am also a victim.

I only saw Chief Mshlanga once again.

One night my father's big red land was trampled down by small sharp hooves, and it was discovered that the culprits were goats from Chief Mshlanga's kraal. This had happened once before, years ago.

My father confiscated all the goats. Then he sent a message to the old Chief that if he wanted them he would have to pay for the damage.

He arrived at our house at the time of sunset one evening, looking very old and bent now, walking stiffly under his regally draped blanket, leaning on a big stick. My father sat himself down in his big chair below the steps of the house; the old man squatted carefully on the ground before him, flanked by his two young men.

The palaver was long and painful, because of the bad English of the young man who interpreted, and because my father could not speak dialect, but only kitchen kaffir.

From my father's point of view, at least two hundred pounds' worth of damage had been done to the crop. He knew he could not get the money from the old man. He felt he was entitled to keep the goats. As for the old Chief, he kept repeating angrily: "Twenty goats! My people cannot lose twenty goats! We are not rich; like the Nkosi Jordan, to lose twenty goats at once."

My father did not think of himself as rich, but rather as very poor. He spoke quickly and angrily in return, saying that the damage done meant a great deal to him, and that he was entitled to the goats.

At last it grew so heated that the cook, the Chief's son, was called from the kitchen to be interpreter, and now my father spoke fluently in English, and our cook translated rapidly so that the old man could understand how very angry my father was. The young man spoke without emotion, in a mechanical way, his eyes lowered, but showing how he felt his position by a hostile uncomfortable set of the shoulders.

It was now in the late sunset, the sky a welter of colours, the birds singing their last songs, and the cattle, lowing peacefully, moving past us towards their sheds for the night. It was the hour when Africa is most beautiful; and here was this pathetic, ugly scene, doing no one any good.

At last my father stated finally: "I'm not going to argue about it. I am keeping the goats."   85

The old Chief flashed back in his own language: "That means that my people will go hungry when the dry season comes."

"Go to the police, then," said my father, and looked triumphant.

There was, of course, no more to be said.

The old man sat silent, his head bent, his hands dangling helplessly over his withered knees. Then he rose, the young men helping him, and he stood facing my father. He spoke once again, very stiffly; and turned away and went home to his village.

"What did he say?" asked my father of the young man, who laughed uncomfortably and would not meet his eyes.

"What did he say?" insisted my father.

Our cook stood straight and silent, his brows knotted together. Then he spoke.   90
"My father says: All this land, this land you call yours, is his land, and belongs to our people."

Having made this statement, he walked off into the bush after his father, and we did not see him again.

Our next cook was a migrant from Nyasaland, with no expectations of greatness.

Next time the policeman came on his rounds he was told this story. He remarked: "That kraal has no right to be there; it should have been moved long ago. I   95
don't know why no one has done anything about it. I'll have a chat with the Native Commissioner next week. I'm going over for tennis on Sunday, anyway."

Some time later we heard that Chief Mshlanga and his people had been moved two hundred miles east, to a proper Native Reserve; the Government land was going to be opened up for white settlement soon.

I went to see the village again, about a year afterwards. There was nothing there. Mounds of red mud, where the huts had been, had long swathes of rotting thatch over them, veined with the red galleries of the white ants. The pumpkin vines rioted everywhere, over the bushes, up the lower branches of trees so that the great golden balls rolled underfoot and dangled overhead: it was a festival of pumpkins. The bushes were crowding up, the new grass sprang vivid green.

The settler lucky enough to be allotted the lush warm valley (if he chose to cultivate this particular section) would find, suddenly, in the middle of a mealie field, the plants were growing fifteen feet tall, the weight of the cobs dragging at the stalks, and wonder what unsuspected vein of richness he had struck.

FLANNERY O'CONNOR (1925–1964)

Mary Flannery O'Connor, a Georgia native, graduated from the Women's College of Georgia and received a Master of Fine Arts from the University of Iowa in 1947. During the last ten years of her life, she suffered from lupus, a degenerative disease which rendered her an invalid. Despite her illness, she wrote extensively, publishing two novels and many short stories. Her first collection was A Good Man Is Hard to Find, *in 1955. A posthumous collection,* Everything That Rises Must Converge, *was published in 1965, and* Complete Stories *appeared in 1971. Her works combine flat realism with grotesque situations; violence is encountered without apparent reason or preparation. Quite often her characters appear to be odd, eccentric, bizarre, and gratuitously cruel.*

A Good Man Is Hard to Find _____1953

The grandmother didn't want to go to Florida. She wanted to visit some of her connections in east Tennessee and she was seizing at every chance to change Bailey's mind. Bailey was the son she lived with, her only son. He was sitting on the edge of his chair at the table, bent over the orange sports section of the *Journal.* "Now look here, Bailey," she said, "see here, read this," and she stood with one hand on her thin hip and the other rattling the newspaper at his bald head. "Here this fellow that calls himself The Misfit is aloose from the Federal Pen and headed toward Florida and you read here what it says he did to these people. Just you read it. I wouldn't take my children in any direction with a criminal like that aloose in it. I couldn't answer to my conscience if I did."

Bailey didn't look up from his reading so she wheeled around then and faced the children's mother, a young woman in slacks, whose face was as broad and innocent as a cabbage and was tied round with a green head-kerchief that had two points on the top like rabbit's ears. She was sitting on the sofa, feeding the baby his apricots out of a jar. "The children have been to Florida before," the old lady said. "You all ought to take them somewhere else for a change so they would see different parts of the world and be broad. They never have been to east Tennessee."

The children's mother didn't seem to hear her but the eight-year-old boy, John Wesley, a stocky child with glasses, said, "If you don't want to go to Florida, why dontcha stay at home?" He and the little girl, June Star, were reading the funny papers on the floor.

"She wouldn't stay at home to be queen for a day," June Star said without raising her yellow head.

"Yes and what would you do if this fellow, The Misfit, caught you?" the grandmother asked.

"I'd smack his face," John Wesley said.

"She wouldn't stay at home for a million bucks," June Star said. "Afraid she'd miss something. She has to go everywhere we go."

"All right, Miss," the grandmother said. "Just remember that the next time you want me to curl your hair."

June Star said her hair was naturally curly.

The next morning the grandmother was the first one in the car, ready to go. 10
She had her big black valise that looked like the head of a hippopotamus in one corner, and underneath it she was hiding a basket with Pitty Sing, the cat, in it. She didn't intend for the cat to be left alone in the house for three days because he would miss her too much and she was afraid he might brush against one of the gas burners and accidentally asphyxiate himself. Her son, Bailey, didn't like to arrive at a motel with a cat.

She sat in the middle of the back seat with John Wesley and June Star on either side of her. Bailey and the children's mother and the baby sat in the front and they left Atlanta at eight forty-five with the mileage on the car at 55890. The grandmother wrote this down because she thought it would be interesting to say how many miles they had been when they got back. It took them twenty minutes to reach the outskirts of the city.

The old lady settled herself comfortably, removing her white cotton gloves and putting them up with her purse on the shelf in front of the back window. The children's mother still had on slacks and still had her head tied up in a green kerchief, but the grandmother had on a navy blue straw sailor hat with a bunch of white violets on the brim and a navy blue dress with a small white dot in the print. Her collar and cuffs were white organdy trimmed with lace and at her neckline she had pinned a purple spray of cloth violets containing a sachet. In case of an accident, anyone seeing her dead on the highway would know at once that she was a lady.

She said she thought it was going to be a good day for driving, neither too hot nor too cold, and she cautioned Bailey that the speed limit was fifty-five miles an hour and that the patrolmen hid themselves behind billboards and small clumps of trees and sped out after you before you had a chance to slow down. She pointed out interesting details of the scenery: Stone Mountain; the blue granite that in some places came up to both sides of the highway; the brilliant red clay banks slightly streaked with purple; and the various crops that made rows of green lacework on the ground. The trees were full of silver-white sunlight and the meanest of them sparkled. The children were reading comic magazines and their mother had gone back to sleep.

"Let's go through Georgia fast so we won't have to look at it much," John Wesley said.

"If I were a little boy," said the grandmother, "I wouldn't talk about my native 15
state that way. Tennessee has the mountains and Georgia has the hills."

"Tennessee is just a hillbilly dumping ground," John Wesley said, "and Georgia is a lousy state too."

"You said it," June Star said.

"In my time," said the grandmother, folding her thin veined fingers, "children were more respectful of their native states and their parents and everything else. People did right then. Oh look at the cute little pickaninny!" she said and pointed to a Negro child standing in the door of a shack. "Wouldn't that make a picture, now?" she asked and they all turned and looked at the little Negro out of the back window. He waved.

"He didn't have any britches on," June said.

"He probably didn't have any," the grandmother explained. "Little niggers in the country don't have things like we do. If I could paint, I'd paint that picture," she said.

The children exchanged comic books.

The grandmother offered to hold the baby and the children's mother passed him over the front seat to her. She set him on her knee and bounced him and told him about the things they were passing. She rolled her eyes and screwed up her mouth and stuck her leathery thin face into his smooth bland one. Occasionally he gave her a faraway smile. They passed a large cotton field with five or six graves fenced in the middle of it, like a small island. "Look at the graveyard!" the grandmother said, pointing it out. "That was the old family burying ground. That belonged to the plantation."

"Where's the plantation?" John Wesley asked.

"Gone With the Wind," said the grandmother. "Ha. Ha."

When the children finished all the comic books they had brought, they opened the lunch and ate it. The grandmother ate a peanut butter sandwich and an olive and would not let the children throw the box and the paper napkins out the window. When there was nothing else to do they played a game by choosing a cloud and making the other two guess what shape it suggested. John Wesley took one the shape of a cow and June Star guessed a cow and John Wesley said, no, an automobile, and June Star said he didn't play fair, and they began to slap each other over the grandmother.

The grandmother said she would tell them a story if they would keep quiet. When she told a story, she rolled her eyes and waved her head and was very dramatic. She said once when she was a maiden lady she had been courted by a Mr. Edgar Atkins Teagarden from Jasper, Georgia. She said he was a very good-looking man and a gentleman and that he brought her a watermelon every Saturday afternoon with his initials cut in it, E. A. T. Well, one Saturday, she said, Mr. Teagarden brought the watermelon and there was nobody at home and he left it on the front porch and returned in his buggy to Jasper, but she never got the watermelon, she said, because a nigger boy ate it when he saw the initials, E. A. T.! This story tickled John Wesley's funny bone and he giggled and giggled but June Star didn't think it was any good. She said she wouldn't marry a man that just brought her a watermelon on Saturday. The grandmother said she would have done well to marry Mr. Teagarden because he was a gentleman and had bought Coca-Cola stock when it first came out and that he had died only a few years ago, a very wealthy man.

They stopped at The Tower for barbecued sandwiches. The Tower was a part stucco and part wood filling station and dance hall set in a clearing outside of Timothy. A fat man named Red Sammy Butts ran it and there were signs stuck here and there on the building and for miles up and down the highway saying, TRY RED SAMMY'S FAMOUS BARBECUE. NONE LIKE FAMOUS RED SAMMY'S! RED SAM! THE FAT BOY WITH THE HAPPY LAUGH. A VETERAN! SAMMY'S YOUR MAN!

Red Sammy was lying on the bare ground outside The Tower with his head under a truck while a gray monkey about a foot high, chained to a small chinaberry tree, chattered nearby. The monkey sprang back into the tree and got on the highest limb as soon as he saw the children jump out of the car and run toward him.

Inside, The Tower was a long dark room with a counter at one end and tables at the other and dancing space in the middle. They all sat down at a broad table next to the nickelodeon and Red Sam's wife, a tall burnt-brown woman with hair and eyes lighter than her skin, came and took their order. The children's mother put a dime in the machine and played "The Tennessee Waltz," and the grandmother said the tune always made her want to dance. She asked Bailey if he would like to dance but he only glared at her. He didn't have a naturally sunny disposition like she did and trips made him nervous. The grandmother's brown eyes were very bright. She swayed her head from side to side and pretended she was dancing in her chair. June Star said play something she could tap to so the children's mother put in another dime and played a fast number and June Star stepped out onto the dance floor and did her tap routine.

"Ain't she cute?" Red Sam's wife said, leaning over the counter. "Would you like to come be my little girl?" 30

"No I certainly wouldn't," June Star said. "I wouldn't live in a broken-down place like this for a million bucks!" and she ran back to the table.

"Ain't she cute?" the woman repeated, stretching her mouth politely.

"Aren't you ashamed?" hissed her grandmother.

Red Sam came in and told his wife to quit lounging on the counter and hurry with these people's order. His khaki trousers reached just to his hip bones and his stomach hung over them like a sack of meal swaying under his shirt. He came over and sat down at a table nearby and let out a combination sigh and yodel. "You can't win," he said. "You can't win," and he wiped his sweating red face with a gray handkerchief. "These days you don't know who to trust," he said. "Ain't that the truth?"

"People are certainly not nice like they used to be," said the grandmother. 35

"Two fellers come in here last week," Red Sammy said, "driving a Chrysler. It was a old beat-up car but it was a good one and these boys looked all right to me. Said they worked at the mill and you know I let them fellers charge the gas they bought? Now why did I do that?"

"Because you're a good man!" the grandmother said at once.

"Yes'm, I suppose so," Red Sam said as if he were struck with the answer.

His wife brought the orders, carrying the five plates all at once without a tray, two in each hand and one balanced on her arm. "It isn't a soul in this green world of God's that you can trust," she said. "And I don't count anybody out of that, not nobody," she repeated, looking at Red Sammy.

"Did you read about that criminal, The Misfit, that's escaped?" asked the grandmother. 40

"I wouldn't be a bit surprised if he didn't attack this place right here," said the woman. "If he hears about it being here, I wouldn't be none surprised to see him. If he hears it's two cent in the cash register, I wouldn't be a tall surprised if he . . ."

"That'll do," Red Sam said. "Go bring these people their Co'Colas," and the woman went off to get the rest of the order.

"A good man is hard to find," Red Sammy said. "Everything is getting terrible. I remember the day you could go off and leave your screen door unlatched. Not no more."

He and the grandmother discussed better times. The old lady said that in her opinion Europe was entirely to blame for the way things were now. She said the way Europe acted you would think we were made of money and Red Sam said it was no use talking about it, she was exactly right. The children ran outside into the white sunlight and looked at the monkey in the lacy chinaberry tree. He was busy catching fleas on himself and biting each one carefully between his teeth as if it were a delicacy.

They drove off again into the hot afternoon. The grandmother took cat naps 45 and woke up every few minutes with her own snoring. Outside of Toombsboro she woke up and recalled an old plantation that she had visited in this neighborhood once when she was a young lady. She said the house had six white columns across the front and that there was an avenue of oaks leading up to it and two little wooden trellis arbors on either side in front where you sat down with your suitor after a stroll in the garden. She recalled exactly which road to turn off to get to it. She knew that Bailey would not be willing to lose any time looking at an old house, but the more she talked about it, the more she wanted to see it once again and find out if the little twin arbors were still standing. "There was a secret panel in this house," she said craftily, not telling the truth but wishing that she were, "and the story went that all the family silver was hidden in it when Sherman° came through but it was never found . . ."

"Hey!" John Wesley said, "Let's go see it! We'll find it! We'll poke all the woodwork and find it! Who lives there? Where do you turn off at? Hey Pop, can't we turn off there?"

"We never have seen a house with a secret panel!" June Star shrieked. "Let's go to the house with the secret panel! Hey, Pop, can't we go see the house with the secret panel!"

"It's not far from here, I know," the grandmother said. "It wouldn't take over twenty minutes."

Bailey was looking straight ahead. His jaw was as rigid as a horseshoe. "No," he said.

The children began to yell and scream that they wanted to see the house with the secret panel. John Wesley kicked the back of the front seat and June Star hung over her mother's shoulder and whined desperately into her ear that they never had any fun even on their vacation, and that they could never do what THEY wanted to do. The baby began to scream and John Wesley kicked the back of the seat so hard that his father could feel the blows in his kidney.

"All right!" he shouted, and drew the car to a stop at the side of the road. "Will you all shut up? Will you all just shut up for one second? If you don't shut up, we won't go anywhere."

"It would be very educational for them," the grandmother murmured.

"All right," Bailey said, "but get this: this is the only time we're going to stop for anything like this. This is the one and only time."

"The dirt road that you have to turn down is about a mile back," the grandmother directed. "I marked it when we passed."

"A dirt road," Bailey groaned.

After they had turned around and were headed toward the dirt road, the grandmother recalled other points about the house, the beautiful glass over the front doorway and the candle-lamp in the hall. John Wesley said that the secret panel was probably in the fireplace.

"You can't go inside this house," Bailey said. "You don't know who lives there."

"While you all talk to the people in front, I'll run around behind and get in a window," John Wesley suggested.

"We'll all stay in the car," his mother said.

They turned onto the dirt road and the car raced roughly along in swirl of pink dust. The grandmother recalled the times when there were no paved roads and thirty miles was a day's journey. The dirt road was hilly and there were sudden washes in it

Sherman: William Tecumseh Sherman (1820–1891), Union general during the Civil War.

and sharp curves on dangerous embankments. All at once they would be on a hill, looking down over the blue tops of trees for miles around, then the next minute, they would be in a red depression with the dust-coated trees looking down on them.

"This place had better turn up in a minute," Bailey said, "or I'm going to turn around."

The road looked as if no one had traveled on it in months.

"It's not much farther," the grandmother said and just as she said it, a horrible thought came to her. The thought was so embarrassing that she turned red in the face and her eyes dilated and her feet jumped up, upsetting her valise in the corner. The instant the valise moved, the newspaper top she had over the basket under it rose with a snarl and Pitty Sing, the cat, sprang onto Bailey's shoulder.

The children were thrown to the floor and their mother, clutching the baby, was thrown out the door onto the ground; the old lady was thrown into the front seat. The car turned over once and landed right-side-up in a gulch on the side of the road. Bailey remained in the driver's seat with the cat—gray-striped with a broad white face and an orange nose—clinging to his neck like a caterpillar.

As soon as the children saw they could move their arms and legs, they scrambled out of the car, shouting, "We've had an ACCIDENT!" The grandmother was curled up under the dashboard, hoping she was injured so that Bailey's wrath would not come down on her all at once. The horrible thought she had had before the accident was that the house she had remembered so vividly was not in Georgia but in Tennessee.   65

Bailey removed the cat from his neck with both hands and flung it out the window against the side of a pine tree. Then he got out of the car and started looking for the children's mother. She was sitting against the side of the red gutted ditch, holding the screaming baby, but she only had a cut down her face and a broken shoulder. "We've had an ACCIDENT!" the children screamed in a frenzy of delight.

"But nobody's killed," June Star said with disappointment as the grandmother limped out of the car, her hat still pinned to her head but the broken front brim standing up at a jaunty angle and the violet spray hanging off the side. They all sat down in the ditch, except the children, to recover from the shock. They were all shaking.

"Maybe a car will come along," said the children's mother hoarsely.

"I believe I have injured an organ," said the grandmother, pressing her side, but no one answered her. Bailey's teeth were clattering. He had on a yellow sport shirt with bright blue parrots designed in it and his face was as yellow as the shirt. The grandmother decided that she would not mention that the house was in Tennessee.

The road was about ten feet above and they could see only the tops of the trees   70
on the other side of it. Behind the ditch they were sitting in there were more woods, tall and dark and deep. In a few minutes they saw a car some distance away on top of a hill, coming slowly as if the occupants were watching them. The grandmother stood up and waved both arms dramatically to attract their attention. The car continued to come on slowly, disappeared around a bend and appeared again, moving even slower, on top of the hill they had gone over. It was a big black battered hearse-like automobile. There were three men in it.

It came to a stop just over them and for some minutes, the driver looked down with a steady expressionless gaze to where they were sitting, and didn't speak. Then he turned his head and muttered something to the other two and they got out. One was a fat boy in black trousers and a red sweat shirt with a silver stallion embossed on the front of it. He moved around on the right side of them and stood staring, his mouth partly open in a kind of loose grin. The other had on khaki pants and a blue striped coat and a gray hat pulled down very low, hiding most of his face. He came around slowly on the left side. Neither spoke.

The driver got out of the car and stood by the side of it, looking down at them. He was an older man than the other two. His hair was just beginning to gray and he wore silver-rimmed spectacles that gave him a scholarly look. He had a long creased face and didn't have on any shirt or undershirt. He had on blue jeans that were too tight for him and was holding a black hat and a gun. The two boys also had guns.

"We've had an ACCIDENT!" the children screamed.

The grandmother had the peculiar feeling that the bespectacled man was someone she knew. His face was as familiar to her as if she had known him all her life but she could not recall who he was. He moved away from the car and began to come down the embankment, placing his feet carefully so that he wouldn't slip. He had on tan and white shoes and no socks, and his ankles were red and thin. "Good afternoon," he said. "I see you all had a little spill."

"We turned over twice!" said the grandmother.

"Oncet," he corrected. "We seen it happen. Try their car and see will it run, Hiram," he said quietly to the boy with the gray hat.

"What you got that gun for?" John Wesley asked, "Whatcha gonna do with that gun?"

"Lady," the man said to the children's mother, "would you mind calling them children to sit down by you? Children make me nervous. I want all you all to set down right together there where you're at."

"What are you telling us what to do for?" June Star asked.

Behind them the line of woods gaped like a dark open mouth. "Come here," said their mother.

"Look here now," Bailey began suddenly, "we're in a predicament! We're in . . ."

The grandmother shrieked. She scrambled to her feet and stood staring. "You're The Misfit!" she said. "I recognized you at once."

"Yes'm" the man said, smiling slightly as if he were pleased in spite of him-self to be known, "but it would have been better for all of you, lady, if you hadn't reckernized me."

Bailey turned his head sharply and said something to his mother that shocked even the children. The old lady began to cry and The Misfit reddened.

"Lady," he said, "don't you get upset: Sometimes a man says things he don't mean. I don't reckon he meant to talk to you thataway."

"You wouldn't shoot a lady, would you?" the grandmother said and removed a clean handkerchief from her cuff and began to slap at her eyes with it.

The Misfit pointed the toe of his shoe into the ground and made a little hole and then covered it up again. "I would hate to have to," he said.

"Listen," the grandmother almost screamed, "I know you're a good man. You don't look a bit like you have common blood. I know you must come from nice people!"

"Yes mam," he said, "finest people in the world." When he smiled he showed a row of strong white teeth. "God never made a finer woman than my mother and my daddy's heart was pure gold," he said. The boy with the red sweat shirt had come around behind them and was standing with his gun at his hip. The Misfit squatted down on the ground. "Watch them children, Bobby Lee," he said. "You know they make me nervous." He looked at the six of them huddled together in front of him and he seemed to be embarrassed as if he couldn't think if anything to say. "Ain't a cloud in the sky," he remarked, looking up at it. "Don't see no sun but don't see no cloud neither."

"Yes, it's a beautiful day," said the grandmother. "Listen," she said, "you shouldn't call yourself The Misfit because I know you're a good man at heart. I can just look at you and tell."   90

"Hush!" Bailey yelled. "Hush! Everybody shut up and let me handle this!" He was squatting in the position of a runner about to sprint forward but he didn't move.

"I pre-chate that, lady," The Misfit said and drew a little circle in the ground with the butt of his gun.

"It'll take a half a hour to fix this here car," Hiram called, looking over the raised hood of it.

"Well, first you and Bobby Lee get him and that little boy to step over yonder with you," The Misfit said, pointing to Bailey and John Wesley. "The boys want to ask you something," he said to Bailey. "Would you mind stepping back in them woods there with them?"

"Listen," Bailey began, "we're in a terrible predicament. Nobody realizes what this is," and his voice cracked. His eyes were as blue and intense as the parrots in his shirt and he remained perfectly still.   95

The grandmother reached up to adjust her hat brim as if she were going to the woods with him but it came off in her hand. She stood staring at it and after a second she let it fall to the ground. Hiram pulled Bailey up by the arm as if he were assisting an old man. John Wesley caught hold of his father's hand and Bobby Lee followed. They went off toward the woods and just as they reached the dark edge, Bailey turned and supporting himself against a gray naked pine trunk, he shouted, "I'll be back in a minute, Mamma, wait on me!"

"Come back this instant!" his mother shrilled but they all disappeared into the woods.

"Bailey Boy!" the grandmother called in a tragic voice but she found she was looking at The Misfit squatting on the ground in front of her. "I just know you're a good man," she said desperately. "You're not a bit common!"

"Nome, I ain't a good man," The Misfit said after a second as if he had considered her statement carefully, "but I ain't the worst in the world neither. My daddy said I was different breed of dog from my brothers and sisters. 'You know,' Daddy said, 'it's some that can live their whole life out without asking about it and it's others has to know why it is, and this boy is one of the latters. He's going to be into everything!'" He put on his black hat and looked up suddenly and then away deep into the woods as if he were embarrassed again. "I'm sorry I don't have on a shirt before you ladies," he said, hunching his shoulders slightly. "We buried our clothes that we had on when we escaped and we're just making do until we can get better. We borrowed these from some folks we met," he explained.

"That's perfectly all right," the grandmother said. "Maybe Bailey has an extra shirt in his suitcase."   100

"I'll look and see terrectly," the Misfit said.

"Where are they taking him?" the children's mother screamed.

"Daddy was a card himself," the Misfit said. "You couldn't put anything over on him. He never got in trouble with the Authorities though. Just had the knack of handling them."

"You could be honest too if you'd only try," said the grandmother. "Think how wonderful it would be to settle down and live a comfortable life and not have to think about somebody chasing you all the time."

The Misfit kept scratching in the ground with the butt of his gun as if he were thinking about it. "Yes'm, somebody is always after you," he murmured.

The grandmother noticed how thin his shoulder blades were just behind his hat because she was standing up looking down on him. "Do you ever pray?" she asked.

He shook his head. All she saw was the black hat wiggle between his shoulder blades. "Nome," he said.

There was a pistol shot from the woods, followed closely by another. Then silence. The old lady's head jerked around. She could hear the wind move through the tree tops like a long satisfied insuck of breath. "Bailey Boy!" she called.

"I was a gospel singer for a while," The Misfit said. "I been most everything. Been in the arm service, both land and sea, at home and abroad, been twict married, been an undertaker, been with the railroads, plowed Mother Earth, been in a tornado, seen a man burnt alive oncet," and he looked up at the children's mother and the little girl who were sitting close together, their faces white and their eyes glassy; "I even seen a woman flogged," he said.

"Pray, pray," the grandmother began, "pray, pray . . ."

"I never was a bad boy that I remember of," The Misfit said in an almost dreamy voice, "but somewheres along the line I done something wrong and got sent to the penitentiary. I was buried alive," and he looked up and held her attention to him by a steady stare.

"That's when you should have started to pray," she said. "What did you do to get sent to the penitentiary that first time?"

"Turn to the right, it was a wall," The Misfit said, looking up again at the cloudless sky. "Turn to the left, it was a wall. Look up it was a ceiling, look down it was a floor. I forgot what I done, lady. I set there and set there, trying to remember what it was I done and I ain't recalled it to this day. Oncet in a while, I would think it was coming to me, but it never come."

"Maybe they put you in by mistake," the old lady said vaguely.

"Nome," he said. "It wasn't no mistake. They had the papers on me."

"You must have stolen something," she said.

The Misfit sneered slightly. "Nobody had nothing I wanted," he said. "It was a head-doctor at the penitentiary said what I had done was kill my daddy but I know that for a lie. My daddy died in nineteen ought nineteen of the epidemic flu and I never had a thing to do with it. He was buried in the Mount Hopewell Baptist churchyard and you can go there and see for yourself."

"If you would pray," the old lady said, "Jesus would help you."

"That's right," The Misfit said.

"Well then, why don't you pray?" she asked trembling with delight suddenly.

"I don't want no hep," he said. "I'm doing all right by myself."

Bobby Lee and Hiram came ambling back from the woods. Bobby Lee was dragging a yellow shirt with bright blue parrots in it.

"Throw me that shirt, Bobby Lee," The Misfit said. The shirt came flying at him and landed on his shoulder and he put it on. The grandmother couldn't name what the shirt reminded her of. "No, lady," The Misfit said while he was buttoning it up. "I found out the crime don't matter. You can do one thing or you can do another, kill a man or take a tire off his car, because sooner or later you're going to forget what it was you done and just be punished for it."

The children's mother had begun to make heaving noises as if she couldn't get her breath. "Lady," he asked, "would you and that little girl like to step off yonder with Bobby Lee and Hiram and join your husband?"

"Yes, thank you," the mother said faintly. Her left arm dangled helplessly and 125 she was holding the baby, who had gone to sleep, in the other. "Hep that lady up, Hiram," The Misfit said as she struggled to climb out of the ditch, "and Bobby Lee, you hold onto that little girl's hand."

"I don't want to hold hands with him," June Star said. "He reminds me of a pig."

The fat boy blushed and laughed and caught her by the arm and pulled her off into the woods after Hiram and her mother.

Alone with The Misfit, the grandmother found that she had lost her voice. There was not a cloud in the sky nor any sun. There was nothing around her but woods. She wanted to tell him that he must pray. She opened and closed her mouth several times before anything came out. Finally she found herself saying, "Jesus, Jesus," meaning Jesus will help you, but the way she was saying it, it sounded as if she might be cursing.

"Yes'm," The Misfit said as if he agreed. "Jesus thown everything off balance. It was the same case with Him as with me except He hadn't committed any crime and they could prove I had committed one because they had the papers on me. Of course," he said, "they never shown me any papers. That's why I sign myself now. I said long ago, you get you a signature and sign everything you do and keep a copy of it. Then you'll know what you done and you can hold up the crime to the punishment and see do they match and in the end you'll have something to prove you ain't been treated right. I call myself The Misfit," he said, "because I can't make what all I done wrong fit what all I gone through in punishment."

There was a piercing scream from the woods, followed closely by a pistol report. 130 "Does it seem right to you, lady, that one is punished a heap and another ain't punished at all?"

"Jesus!" the old lady cried. "You've got good blood! I know you wouldn't shoot a lady! I know you come from nice people! Pray! Jesus, you ought not to shoot a lady: I'll give you all the money I've got!"

"Lady," The Misfit said, looking beyond her far into the woods, "there never was a body that give the undertaker a tip."

There were two more pistol reports and the grandmother raised her head like a parched old turkey hen crying for water and called, "Bailey Boy, Bailey Boy!" as if her heart would break.

"Jesus was the only One that ever raised the dead," The Misfit continued, "and He shouldn't have done it. He thown everything off balance. If He did what He said then it's nothing for you to do but thow away everything and follow Him, and if He didn't, then it's nothing for you to do but enjoy the few minutes you got left the best way you can—by killing somebody or burning down his house or doing some other meanness to him. No pleasure but meanness," he said and his voice had become almost a snarl.

"Maybe He didn't raise the dead," the old lady mumbled, not knowing what she 135 was saying and feeling so dizzy that she sank down in the ditch with her legs twisted under her.

"I wasn't there so I can't say He didn't." The Misfit said, "I wisht I had of been there," he said, hitting the ground with his fist. "It ain't right I wasn't there because if I had of been there I would of known. Listen lady," he said in a high voice, "if I had of been there I would of known and I wouldn't be like I am now." His voice seemed about to crack and the grandmother's head cleared for an instant. She saw the man's face twisted close to her own as if he were going to cry and she murmured, "Why you're one of my babies. You're one of my own children!" She reached out and touched him on the shoulder. The Misfit sprang back as if a snake had bitten him and shot her three times through the chest. Then he put his gun down on the ground and took off his glasses and began to clean them.

Hiram and Bobby Lee returned from the woods and stood over the ditch, looking down at the grandmother who half sat and half lay in a puddle of blood with her legs crossed under her like a child's and her face smiling up at the cloudless sky.

Without his glasses, The Misfit's eyes were red-rimmed and pale and defenseless-looking. "Take her off and thow her where you thown the others," he said, picking up the cat that was rubbing itself against his leg.

"She was a talker, wasn't she?" Bobby Lee said, sliding down the ditch with a yodel.

"She would of been a good woman," The Misfit said, "if it had been somebody there to shoot her every minute of her life."

"Some fun!" Bobby Lee said.

"Shut up, Bobby Lee," The Misfit said. "It's no real pleasure in life."

FRANK O'CONNOR (1903–1966)

Frank O'Connor, the nom de plume *of Michael O'Donovan, was an only child of poor parents in County Cork, Ireland. He began writing when young, and for a time he was a director of Ireland's national theater. His output as a writer was considerable, with sixty-seven stories appearing in the posthumous* Collected Stories *of 1981. A meticulous writer, he was constantly revising his work. "First Confession," for example, went through a number of stages before the final version included here.*

First Confession _____ *1951*

All the trouble began when my grandfather died and my grandmother—my father's mother—came to live with us. Relations in the one house are a strain at the best of times, but, to make matters worse, my grandmother was a real old countrywoman and quite unsuited to the life in town. She had a fat, wrinkled old face, and, to Mother's great indignation, went round the house in bare feet—the boots had her crippled, she said. For dinner she had a jug of porter° and a pot of potatoes with—sometimes— a bit of salt fish, and she poured out the potatoes on the table and ate them slowly, with great relish, using her fingers by way of a fork.

porter: a dark-brown beer.

Now, girls are supposed to be fastidious, but I was the one who suffered most from this. Nora, my sister, just sucked up to the old woman for the penny she got every Friday out of the old-age pension, a thing I could not do. I was too honest, that was my trouble; and when I was playing with Bill Connell, the sergeant-major's son, and saw my grandmother steering up the path with the jug of porter sticking out from beneath her shawl I was mortified. I made excuses not to let him come into the house, because I could never be sure what she would be up to when we went in.

When Mother was at work and my grandmother made the dinner I wouldn't touch it. Nora once tried to make me, but I hid under the table from her and took the bread-knife with me for protection. Nora let on to be very indignant (she wasn't, of course, but she knew Mother saw through her, so she sided with Gran) and came after me. I lashed out at her with the bread-knife, and after that she left me alone. I stayed there till Mother came in from work and made my dinner, but when Father came in later Nora said in a shocked voice: "Oh, Dadda, do you know what Jackie did at dinnertime?" Then, of course, it all came out; Father gave me a flaking; Mother interfered, and for days after that he didn't speak to me and Mother barely spoke to Nora. And all because of that old woman! God knows, I was heart-scalded.

Then, to crown my misfortune, I had to make my first confession and communion. It was an old woman called Ryan who prepared us for these. She was about the one age with Gran; she was well-to-do, lived in a big house on Montenotte, wore a black cloak and bonnet, and came every day to school at three o'clock when we should have been going home, and talked to us of hell. She may have mentioned the other place as well, but that could only have been by accident, for hell had the first place in her heart.

She lit a candle, took out a new half-crown, and offered it to the first boy who would hold one finger—only one finger!—in the flame for five minutes by the school clock. Being always very ambitious I was tempted to volunteer, but I thought it might look greedy. Then she asked were we afraid of holding one finger—only one finger!—in a little candle flame for five minutes and not afraid of burning all over in roasting hot furnaces for all eternity. "All eternity! Just think of that! A whole lifetime goes by and it's nothing, not even a drop in the ocean of your sufferings." The woman was really interesting about hell, but my attention was all fixed on the half-crown. At the end of the lesson she put it back in her purse. It was a great disappointment; a religious woman like that, you wouldn't think she'd bother about a thing like a half-crown.

Another day she said she knew a priest who woke one night to find a fellow he didn't recognize leaning over the end of his bed. The priest was a bit frightened—naturally enough—but he asked the fellow what he wanted, and the fellow said in a deep, husky voice that he wanted to go to confession. The priest said it was an awkward time and wouldn't it do in the morning, but the fellow said that last time he went to confession, there was one sin he kept back, being ashamed to mention it, and now it was always on his mind. Then the priest knew it was a bad case, because the fellow was after making a bad confession and committing a mortal sin. He got up to dress, and just then the cock crew in the yard outside, and—lo and behold!—when the priest looked round there was no sign of the fellow, only a smell of burning timber, and when the priest looked at his bed didn't he see the print of two hands burned in it? That was because the fellow had made a bad confession. This story made a shocking impression on me.

But the worst of all was when she showed us how to examine our conscience.

Did we take the name of the Lord, our God, in vain? Did we honour our father and our mother? (I asked her did this include grandmothers and she said it did.) Did we love our neighbours as ourselves? Did we covet our neighbour's goods? (I thought of the way I felt about the penny that Nora got every Friday.) I decided that, between one thing and another, I must have broken the whole ten commandments, all on account of that old woman, and so far as I could see, so long as she remained in the house I had no hope of ever doing anything else.

I was scared to death of confession. The day the whole class went I let on to have a toothache, hoping my absence wouldn't be noticed; but at three o'clock, just as I was feeling safe, along comes a chap with a message from Mrs. Ryan that I was to go to confession myself on Saturday and be at the chapel for communion with the rest. To make it worse, Mother couldn't come with me and sent Nora instead.

Now, that girl had ways of tormenting me that Mother never knew of. She held my hand as we went down the hill, smiling sadly and saying how sorry she was for me, as if she were bringing me to the hospital for an operation.

"Oh, God help us!" she moaned. "Isn't it a terrible pity you weren't a good boy? Oh, Jackie, my heart bleeds for you! How will you ever think of all your sins? Don't forget you have to tell him about the time you kicked Gran on the shin."

"Lemme go!" I said, trying to drag myself free of her. "I don't want to go to confession at all."

"But sure, you'll have to go to confession, Jackie," she replied in the same regretful tone. "Sure, if you didn't the parish priest would be up to the house, looking for you. 'Tisn't, God knows, that I'm not sorry for you. Do you remember the time you tried to kill me with the bread-knife under the table? And the language you used to me? I don't know what he'll do with you at all, Jackie. He might have to send you up to the bishop."

I remember thinking bitterly that she didn't know the half of what I had to tell—if I told it. I knew I couldn't tell it, and understood perfectly why the fellow in Mrs. Ryan's story made a bad confession; it seemed to me a great shame that people wouldn't stop criticizing him. I remember that steep hill down to the church, and the sunlit hillsides beyond the valley of the river, which I saw in the gaps between the houses like Adam's last glimpse of Paradise.°

Then, when she had manœuvered me down the long flight of steps to the chapel yard, Nora suddenly changed her tone. She became the raging malicious devil she really was.

"There you are!" she said with a yelp of triumph, hurling me through the church door. "And I hope he'll give you the penitential psalms, you dirty little caffler."

I knew then I was lost, given up to eternal justice. The door with the coloured-glass panels swung shut behind me, the sunlight went out and gave place to deep shadow, and the wind whistled outside so that the silence within seemed to crackle like ice under my feet. Nora sat in front of me by the confession box. There were a couple of old women ahead of her, and then a miserable-looking poor devil came and wedged me in at the other side, so that I couldn't escape even if I had the courage. He joined his hands and rolled his eyes in the direction of the roof, muttering aspirations in an anguished tone, and I wondered had he a grandmother too. Only a grandmother could account for a fellow behaving in that heartbroken way, but he was better off than I, for he at least could go and confess his sins; while I would make a

Adam's last glimpse of Paradise: Genesis 3:23–24.

bad confession and then die in the night and be continually coming back and burning people's furniture.

Nora's turn came, and I heard the sound of something slamming, and then her voice as if butter wouldn't melt in her mouth, and then another slam, and out she came. God, the hypocrisy of women! Her eyes were lowered, her head was bowed, and her hands were joined very low down on her stomach, and she walked up the aisle to the side altar looking like a saint. You never saw such an exhibition of devotion, and I remembered the devilish malice with which she had tormented me all the way from our door, and wondered were all religious people like that, really. It was my turn now. With the fear of damnation in my soul I went in, and the confessional door closed of itself behind me.

It was pitch-dark and I couldn't see priest or anything else. Then I really began to be frightened. In the darkness it was a matter between God and me, and He had all the odds. He knew what my intentions were before I even started; I had no chance. All I had ever been told about confession got mixed up in my mind, and I knelt to one wall and said: "Bless me, father, for I have sinned; this is my first confession." I waited for a few minutes, but nothing happened, so I tried it on the other wall. Nothing happened there either. He had me spotted all right.

It must have been then that I noticed the shelf at about one height with my head. It was really a place for grown-up people to rest their elbows, but in my distracted state I thought it was probably the place you were supposed to kneel. Of course, it was on the high side and not very deep, but I was always good at climbing and managed to get up all right. Staying up was the trouble. There was room only for my knees, and nothing you could get a grip on but a sort of wooden moulding a bit above it. I held on to the moulding and repeated the words a little louder, and this time something happened all right. A slide was slammed back; a little light entered the box, and a man's voice said: "Who's there?"

"'Tis me, father," I said for fear he mightn't see me and go away again. I couldn't see him at all. The place the voice came from was under the moulding, about level with my knees, so I took a good grip of the moulding and swung myself down till I saw the astonished face of a young priest looking up at me. He had to put his head on one side to see me, and I had to put mine on one side to see him, so we were more or less talking to one another upside-down. It struck me as a queer way of hearing confessions, but I didn't feel it my place to criticize.

"Bless me, father, for I have sinned; this is my first confession," I rattled off all in one breath, and swung myself down the least shade more to make it easier for him.

"What are you doing up there?" he shouted in an angry voice, and the strain the politeness was putting on my hold of the moulding, and the shock of being addressed in such an uncivil tone, were too much for me. I lost my grip, tumbled, and hit the door an unmerciful wallop before I found myself flat on my back in the middle of the aisle. The people who had been waiting stood up with their mouths open. The priest opened the door of the middle box and came out, pushing his biretta back from his forehead; he looked something terrible. Then Nora came scampering down the aisle.

"Oh, you dirty little caffler!" she said. "I might have known you'd do it. I might have known you'd disgrace me. I can't leave you out of my sight for one minute."

Before I could even get to my feet to defend myself she bent down and gave me a clip across the ear. This reminded me that I was so stunned I had even forgotten to cry, so that people might think I wasn't hurt at all, when in fact I was probably maimed for life. I gave a roar out of me.

20

"What's all this about?" the priest hissed, getting angrier than ever and pushing Nora off me. "How dare you hit the child like that, you little vixen?"

"But I can't do my penance with him, father," Nora cried, cocking an outraged eye up to him.

"Well, go and do it, or I'll give you some more to do," he said, giving me a hand up. "Was it coming to confession you were, my poor man?" he asked me.

"'Twas, father," said I with a sob.

"Oh," he said respectfully, "a big hefty fellow like you must have terrible sins. Is this your first?"

"'Tis, father," said I.

"Worse and worse," he said gloomily. "The crimes of a lifetime. I don't know will I get rid of you at all today. You'd better wait now till I'm finished with these old ones. You can see by the looks of them they haven't much to tell."

"I will, father," I said with something approaching joy.

The relief of it was really enormous. Nora stuck out her tongue at me from behind his back, but I couldn't even be bothered retorting. I knew from the very moment that man opened his mouth that he was intelligent above the ordinary. When I had time to think, I saw how right I was. It only stood to reason that a fellow confessing after seven years would have more to tell than people that went every week. The crimes of a lifetime, exactly as he said. It was only what he expected, and the rest was the cackle of old women and girls with their talk of hell, the bishop, and the penitential psalms. That was all they knew. I started to make my examination of conscience, and barring the one bad business of my grandmother it didn't seem so bad.

The next time, the priest steered me into the confession box himself and left the shutter back the way I could see him get in and sit down at the further side of the grille from me.

"Well, now," he said, "what do they call you?"

"Jackie, father," said I.

"And what's a-trouble to you, Jackie?"

"Father," I said, feeling I might as well get it over while I had him in good humour, "I had it all arranged to kill my grandmother."

He seemed a bit shaken by that, all right, because he said nothing for quite a while.

"My goodness," he said at last, "that'd be a shocking thing to do. What put that into your head?"

"Father," I said, feeling very sorry for myself, "she's an awful woman."

"Is she?" he asked. "What way is she awful?"

"She takes porter, father," I said, knowing well from the way Mother talked of it that this was a mortal sin, and hoping it would make the priest take a more favourable view of my case.

"Oh, my!" he said, and I could see he was impressed.

"And snuff, father," said I.

"That's a bad case, sure enough, Jackie," he said.

"And she goes round in her bare feet, father," I went on in a rush of self-pity, "and she knows I don't like her, and she gives pennies to Nora and none to me, and my da sides with her and flakes me, and one night I was so heartscalded I made up my mind I'd have to kill her."

"And what would you do with the body?" he asked with great interest.

"I was thinking I could chop that up and carry it away in a barrow I have," I said.

"Begor, Jackie," he said, "do you know you're a terrible child?"   50

"I know, father," I said, for I was just thinking the same thing myself. "I tried to kill Nora too with a bread-knife under the table, only I missed her."

"Is that the little girl that was beating you just now?" he asked.

"'Tis, father."

"Someone will go for her with a bread-knife one day, and he won't miss her," he said rather cryptically. "You must have great courage. Between ourselves, there's a lot of people I'd like to do the same to but I'd never have the nerve. Hanging is an awful death."

"Is it, father?" I asked with the deepest interest—I was always very keen on hang-   55
ing. "Did you ever see a fellow hanged?"

"Dozens of them," he said solemnly. "And they all died roaring."

"Jay!" I said.

"Oh, a horrible death!" he said with great satisfaction. "Lots of fellows I saw killed their grandmothers too, but they all said 'twas never worth it."

He had me there for a full ten minutes talking, and then walked out the chapel yard with me. I was genuinely sorry to part with him, because he was the most enter-taining character I'd ever met in the religious line. Outside, after the shadow of the church, the sunlight was like the roaring of waves on a beach; it dazzled me; and when the frozen silence melted and I heard the screech of trams on the road my heart soared. I knew now I wouldn't die in the night and come back, leaving marks on my mother's furniture. It would be a great worry to her, and the poor soul had enough.

Nora was sitting on the railing, waiting for me, and she put on a very sour puss   60
when she saw the priest with me. She was made jealous because a priest had never come out of the church with her.

"Well," she asked coldly, after he left me, "what did he give you?"

"Three Hail Marys," I said.

"Three Hail Marys," she repeated incredulously. "You mustn't have told him anything."

"I told him everything," I said confidently.

"About Gran and all?"   65

"About Gran and all."

(All she wanted was to be able to go home and say I'd made a bad confession.)

"Did you tell him you went for me with the bread-knife?" she asked with a frown.

"I did to be sure."

"And he only gave you three Hail Marys?"   70

"That's all."

She slowly got down from the railing with a baffled air. Clearly, this was beyond her. As we mounted the steps back to the main road she looked at me suspiciously.

"What are you sucking?" she asked.

"Bullseyes."

"Was it the priest gave them to you?"   75

"'Twas."

"Lord God," she wailed bitterly, "some people have all the luck! 'Tis no advan-tage to anybody trying to be good. I might just as well be a sinner like you."

TILLIE OLSEN (b. 1913)

Olsen was born in Nebraska in 1913. After working in domestic service, she married in 1936 and eventually had four daughters. When she took up writing, she worked meticulously, taking almost forty years to publish her first novel Yonnondio. *She is noted as an advocate of feminism and minorities and has lectured frequently at colleges and universities. In her relatively small number of stories she has often fictionalized her own experiences. If one judges "I Stand Here Ironing" as a reflection of Olsen's own background, for example, the story is visualized as happening in about 1951, when Emily is 19 and the mother is 38.*

I Stand Here Ironing ————————————————————— 1953–1954

I stand here ironing, and what you asked me moves tormented back and forth with the iron.

"I wish you would manage the time to come in and talk with me about your daughter. I'm sure you can help me understand her. She's a youngster who needs help and whom I'm deeply interested in helping."

"Who needs help." . . . Even if I came, what good would it do? You think because I am her mother I have a key, or that in some way you could use me as a key? She has lived for nineteen years. There is all that life that has happened outside of me, beyond me.

And when is there time to remember, to sift, to weigh, to estimate, to total? I will start and there will be an interruption and I will have to gather it all together again. Or I will become engulfed with all I did or did not do, with what should have been and what cannot be helped.

She was a beautiful baby. The first and only one of our five that was beautiful at birth. You do not guess how new and uneasy her tenancy in her now-loveliness. You did not know her all those years she was thought homely, or see her poring over her baby pictures, making me tell her over and over how beautiful she had been—and would be, I would tell her—and was now, to the seeing eye. But the seeing eyes were few or nonexistent. Including mine.

I nursed her. They feel that's important nowadays. I nursed all the children, but with her, with all the fierce rigidity of first motherhood, I did like the books then said. Though her cries battered me to trembling and my breasts ached with swollenness, I waited till the clock decreed.

Why do I put that first? I do not even know if it matters, or if it explains anything.

She was a beautiful baby. She blew shining bubbles of sound. She loved motion, loved light, loved color and music and textures. She would lie on the floor in her blue overalls patting the surface so hard in ecstasy her hands and feet would blur. She was a miracle to me, but when she was eight months old I had to leave her daytimes with the woman downstairs to whom she was no miracle at all, for I worked or looked for work and for Emily's father, who "could no longer endure" (he wrote in his good-bye note) "sharing want with us."

I was nineteen. It was the pre-relief, pre-WPA world of the depression. I would start running as soon as I got off the streetcar, running up the stairs, the place smelling sour, and awake or asleep to startle awake, when she saw me she would break into a clogged weeping that could not be comforted, a weeping I can hear yet.

After a while I found a job hashing at night so I could be with her days, and it was better. But it came to where I had to bring her to his family and leave her.   10

It took a long time to raise the money for her fare back. Then she got chicken pox and I had to wait longer. When she finally came, I hardly knew her, walking quick and nervous like her father, looking like her father, thin, and dressed in a shoddy red that yellowed her skin and glared at the pockmarks. All the baby loveliness gone.

She was two. Old enough for nursery school they said, and I did not know then what I know now—the fatigue of the long day, and the lacerations of group life in the kinds of nurseries that are only parking places for children.

Except that it would have made no difference if I had known. It was the only place there was. It was the only way we could be together, the only way I could hold a job.

And even without knowing, I knew. I knew the teacher that was evil because all these years it has curdled into my memory, the little boy hunched in the corner, her rasp, "why aren't you outside, because Alvin hits you? that's no reason, go out, scaredy." I knew Emily hated it even if she did not clutch and implore "don't go Mommy" like the other children, mornings.

She always had a reason why we should stay home. Momma, you look sick.   15
Momma, I feel sick. Momma, the teachers aren't there today, they're sick. Momma, we can't go, there was a fire there last night. Momma, it's a holiday today, no school, they told me.

But never a direct protest, never rebellion. I think of our others in their three-, four-year-oldness—the explosions, the tempers, the denunciations, the demands—and I feel suddenly ill. I put the iron down. What in me demanded that goodness in her? And what was the cost, the cost to her of such goodness?

The old man living in the back once said in his gentle way: "You should smile at Emily more when you look at her." What *was* in my face when I looked at her? I loved her. There were all the acts of love.

It was only with the others I remembered what he said, and it was the face of joy, and not of care or tightness or worry I turned to them—too late for Emily. She does not smile easily, let alone almost always as her brothers and sisters do. Her face is closed and sombre, but when she wants, how fluid. You must have seen it in her pantomimes, you spoke of her rare gift for comedy on the stage that rouses a laughter out of the audience so dear they applaud and applaud and do not want to let her go.

Where does it come from, that comedy? There was none of it in her when she came back to me that second time, after I had had to send her away again. She had a new daddy now to learn to love, and I think perhaps it was a better time.

Except when we left her alone nights, telling ourselves she was old enough.   20

"Can't you go some other time, Mommy, like tomorrow?" she would ask. "Will it be just a little while you'll be gone? Do you promise?"

The time we came back, the front door open, the clock on the floor in the hall. She rigid awake. "It wasn't just a little while. I didn't cry. Three times I called you, just three times, and then I ran downstairs to open the door so you could come faster. The clock talked loud. I threw it away, it scared me what it talked."

She said the clock talked loud again that night I went to the hospital to have Susan. She was delirious with the fever that comes before red measles, but she was fully conscious all the week I was gone and the week after we were home when she could not come near the new baby or me.

She did not get well. She stayed skeleton thin, not wanting to eat, and night after night she had nightmares. She would call for me, and I would rouse from exhaustion to sleepily call back: "You're all right, darling, go to sleep, it's just a dream," and if she still called, in a sterner voice, "now go to sleep, Emily, there's nothing to hurt you." Twice, only twice, when I had to get up for Susan anyhow, I went in to sit with her.

Now when it is too late (as if she would let me hold and comfort her like I do the others) I get up and go to her at once at her moan or restless stirring. "Are you awake, Emily? Can I get you something?" And the answer is always the same: "No, I'm all right, go back to sleep, Mother."

They persuaded me at the clinic to send her away to a convalescent home in the country where "she can have the kind of food and care you can't manage for her, and you'll be free to concentrate on the new baby." They still send children to that place. I see pictures on the society page of sleek young women planning affairs to raise money for it, or dancing at the affairs, or decorating Easter eggs or filling Christmas stockings for the children.

They never have a picture of the children so I do not know if the girls still wear those gigantic red bows and the ravaged looks on the every other Sunday when parents can come to visit "unless otherwise notified"—as we were notified the first six weeks.

Oh it is a handsome place, green lawns and tall trees and fluted flower beds. High up on the balconies of each cottage the children stand, the girls in their red bows and white dresses, the boys in white suits and giant red ties. The parents stand below shrieking up to be heard and the children shriek down to be heard, and between them the invisible wall "Not To Be Contaminated by Parental Germs or Physical Affection."

There was a tiny girl who always stood hand in hand with Emily. Her parents never came. One visit she was gone. "They moved her to Rose Cottage" Emily shouted in explanation. "They don't like you to love anybody here."

She wrote once a week, the labored writing of a seven-year-old. "I am fine. How is the baby. If I write my leter nicly I will have a star. Love." There never was a star. We wrote every other day, letters she could never hold or keep but only hear read—once. "We simply do not have room for children to keep any personal possessions," they patiently explained when we pieced one Sunday's shrieking together to plead how much it would mean to Emily, who loved so to keep things, to be allowed to keep her letters and cards.

Each visit she looked frailer. "She isn't eating," they told us.

(They had runny eggs for breakfast or mush with lumps, Emily said later, I'd hold it in my mouth and not swallow. Nothing ever tasted good, just when they had chicken.)

It took us eight months to get her released home, and only the fact that she gained back so little of her seven lost pounds convinced the social worker.

I used to try to hold and love her after she came back, but her body would stay stiff, and after a while she'd push away. She ate little. Food sickened her, and I think much of life too. Oh she had physical lightness and brightness, twinkling by on skates, bouncing like a ball up and down up and down over the jump rope, skimming over the hill; but these were momentary.

She fretted about her appearance, thin and dark and foreign-looking at a time   35
when every little girl was supposed to look or thought she should look a chubby blonde replica of Shirley Temple. The doorbell sometimes rang for her, but no one seemed to come and play in the house or be a best friend. Maybe because we moved so much.

There was a boy she loved painfully through two school semesters. Months later she told me how she had taken pennies from my purse to buy him candy. "Licorice was his favorite and I brought him some every day, but he still liked Jennifer better'n me. Why, Mommy?" The kind of question for which there is no answer.

School was a worry to her. She was not glib or quick in a world where glibness and quickness were easily confused with ability to learn. To her overworked and exasperated teachers she was an overconscientious "slow learner" who kept trying to catch up and was absent entirely too often.

I let her be absent, though sometimes the illness was imaginary. How different from my now-strictness about attendance with the others. I wasn't working. We had a new baby, I was home anyhow. Sometimes, after Susan grew old enough, I would keep her home from school, too, to have them all together.

Mostly Emily had asthma, and her breathing, harsh and labored, would fill the house with a curiously tranquil sound. I would bring the two old dresser mirrors and her boxes of collections to her bed. She would select beads and single earrings, bottle tops and shells, dried flowers and pebbles, old postcards and scraps, all sorts of oddments; then she and Susan would play Kingdom, setting up landscapes and furniture, peopling them with action.

Those were the only times of peaceful companionship between her and Susan.   40
I have edged away from it, that poisonous feeling between them, that terrible balancing of hurts and needs I had to do between the two, and did so badly, those earlier years.

Oh there are conflicts between the others too, each one human, needing, demanding, hurting, taking—but only between Emily and Susan, no, Emily toward Susan that corroding resentment. It seems so obvious on the surface, yet it is not obvious. Susan, the second child, Susan, golden- and curly-haired and chubby, quick and articulate and assured, everything in appearance and manner Emily was not; Susan, not able to resist Emily's precious things, losing or sometimes clumsily breaking them; Susan telling jokes and riddles to company for applause while Emily sat silent (to say to me later; that was *my* riddle, Mother, I told it to Susan); Susan, who for all the five years' difference in age was just a year behind Emily in developing physically.

I am glad for that slow physical development that widened the difference between her and her contemporaries, though she suffered over it. She was too vulnerable for that terrible world of youthful competition, of preening and parading, of constant measuring of yourself against every other, of envy, "If I had that copper hair," "If I had that skin. . . ." She tormented herself enough about not looking like the others, there was enough of the unsureness, the having to be conscious of words before you speak, the constant caring—what are they thinking of me? without having it all magnified by the merciless physical drives.

Ronnie is calling. He is wet and I change him. It is rare there is such a cry now. That time of motherhood is almost behind me when the ear is not one's own but must always be racked and listening for the child cry, the child call. We sit for a while and I hold him, looking out over the city spread in charcoal with its soft aisles of light, "*Shoogily*," he breathes and curls closer. I carry him back to bed, asleep. *Shoogily.* A funny word, a family word, inherited from Emily, invented by her to say: *comfort.*

In this and other ways she leaves her seal, I say aloud. And startle at my saying it. What do I mean? What did I start to gather together, to try and make coherent? I was at the terrible, growing years. War years. I do not remember them well. I was working, there were four smaller ones now, there was not time for her. She had to help be a mother, a housekeeper, and shopper. She had to set her seal. Mornings of crisis and near hysteria trying to get lunches packed, hair combed, coats and shoes found, everyone to school or Child Care on time, the baby ready for transportation. And always the paper scribbled on by a smaller one, the book looked at by Susan then mislaid, the homework not done. Running out to that huge school where she was one, she was lost, she was a drop; suffering over the unpreparedness, stammering and unsure in her classes.

There was so little time left at night after the kids were bedded down. She would struggle over books, always eating (it was in those years she developed her enormous appetite that is legendary in our family) and I would be ironing, or preparing food for the next day, or writing V-mail to Bill, or tending the baby. Sometimes, to make me laugh, or out of her despair, she would imitate happenings or types at school.

I think I said once: "Why don't you do something like this in the school amateur show?" One morning she phoned me at work, hardly understandable through the weeping: "Mother, I did it. I won, I won; they gave me first prize; they clapped and clapped and wouldn't let me go."

Now suddenly she was Somebody, and as imprisoned in her difference as she had been in anonymity.

She began to be asked to perform at other high schools, even in colleges, then at city and statewide affairs. The first one we went to, I only recognized her that first moment when thin, shy, she almost drowned herself into the curtains. Then: Was this Emily? The control, the command, the convulsing and deadly clowning, the spell, then the roaring, stamping audience, unwilling to let this rare and precious laughter out of their lives.

Afterwards: You ought to do something about her with a gift like that—but without money or knowing how, what does one do? We have left it all to her, and the gift has as often eddied inside, clogged and clotted, as been used and growing.

She is coming. She runs up the stairs two at a time with her light graceful step, and I know she is happy tonight. Whatever it was that occasioned your call did not happen today.

"Aren't you ever going to finish the ironing, Mother? Whistler painted his mother in a rocker. I'd have to paint mine standing over an ironing board." This is one of her communicative nights and she tells me everything and nothing as she fixes herself a plate of food out of the icebox.

She is so lovely. Why did you want me to come in at all? Why were you concerned? She will find her way.

She starts up the stairs to bed. "Don't get me up with the rest in the morning." "But I thought you were having midterms." "Oh, those," she comes back in, kisses me, and says quite lightly, "in a couple of years when we'll all be atom-dead they won't matter a bit."

She has said it before. She *believes* it. But because I have been dredging the past, and all that compounds a human being is so heavy and meaningful in me, I cannot endure it tonight.

I will never total it all. I will never come in to say: She was a child seldom smiled at. Her father left me before she was a year old. I had to work her first six years when there was work, or I sent her home and to his relatives. There were years she had care she hated. She was dark and thin and foreign-looking in a world where the prestige went to blondeness and curly hair and dimples, she was slow where glibness was prized. She was a child of anxious, not proud, love. We were poor and could not afford for her the soil of easy growth. I was a young mother, I was a distracted mother. There were the other children pushing up, demanding. Her younger sister seemed all that she was not. There were years she did not want me to touch her. She kept too much in herself, her life was such she had to keep too much in herself. My wisdom came too late. She has much to her and probably little will come of it. She is a child of her age, of depression, of war, of fear.

Let her be. So all that is in her will not bloom—but in how many does it? There is still enough left to live by. Only help her to know—help make it so there is cause for her to know—that she is more than this dress on the ironing board, helpless before the iron.

GRACE PALEY (b. 1922)

Grace (Goodside) Paley was born in the Bronx, and was educated at Hunter College in New York at a time when it was a women's college. She has taught at Sarah Lawrence College, and has written many stories, publishing notably in magazines such as the Atlantic, Esquire, *and the* Sarah Lawrence Journal. *Three of her story collections are* Little Disturbances of Man *(1959),* Enormous Changes at the Last Minute *(1974), and* Later the Same Day *(1985). In 1992 she published her* New and Collected Poems. *She has earned a solid reputation for her insight, boldness, and meticulous craftsmanship. In 1986 she was awarded the Edith Wharton Citation of Merit from the New York State Writers Institute. In 1988 she was recognized as the first "New York State Writer." "Goodbye and Good Luck" is taken from* Little Disturbances of Man.

Goodbye and Good Luck _____ *1959*

I was popular in certain circles, says Aunt Rose. I wasn't no thinner then, only more stationary in the flesh. In time to come, Lillie, don't be surprised—change is a fact of God. From this no one is excused. Only a person like your mama stands on one foot, she don't notice how big her behind is getting and sings in the canary's ear for thirty years. Who's listening? Papa's in the shop. You and Seymour, thinking about yourself. So she waits in a spotless kitchen for a kind word and thinks—poor Rosie. . . .

Poor Rosie! If there was more life in my little sister, she would know my heart is a regular college of feelings and there is such information between my corset and me that her whole married life is a kindergarten.

Nowadays you could find me any time in a hotel, uptown or downtown. Who needs an apartment to live like a maid with a dustrag in the hand, sneezing? I'm in very good with the bus boys, it's more interesting than home, all kinds of people, everybody with a reason.

And my reason, Lillie, is a long time ago I said to the forelady, "Missus, if I can't sit by the window, I can't sit." "If you can't sit, girlie," she says politely, "go stand on the street corner." And that's how I got unemployed in novelty wear.

For my next job I answered an ad which said: "Refined young lady, medium salary, cultural organization." I went by trolley to the address, the Russian Art Theater of Second Avenue where they played only the best Yiddish plays. They needed a ticket seller, someone like me, who likes the public but is very sharp on crooks. The man who interviewed me was the manager, a certain type.

Immediately he said: "Rosie Lieber, you surely got a build on you!"

"It takes all kinds, Mr. Krimberg."

"Don't misunderstand me, little girl," he said. "I appreciate, I appreciate. A young lady lacking fore and aft, her blood is so busy warming the toes and the finger tips, it don't have time to circulate where it's most required."

Everybody likes kindness. I said to him: "Only don't be fresh, Mr. Krimberg, and we'll make a good bargain."

We did: Nine dollars a week, a glass of tea every night, a free ticket once a week for Mama, and I could go watch rehearsals any time I wanted.

My first nine dollars was in the grocer's hands ready to move on already, when Krimberg said to me, "Rosie, here's a great gentleman, a member of this remarkable theater, wants to meet you, impressed no doubt by your big brown eyes."

And who was it, Lillie? Listen to me before my very eyes was Volodya Vlashkin, called by the people of those days the Valentino of Second Avenue. I took one look, and I said to myself: Where did a Jewish boy grow up so big? "Just outside Kiev," he told me.

How? "My mama nursed me till I was six. I was the only boy in the village to have such health."

"My goodness, Vlashkin, six years old! She must have had shredded wheat there, not breasts, poor woman."

"My mother was beautiful," he said. "She had eyes like stars."

He had such a way of expressing himself, it brought tears.

To Krimberg, Vlashkin said after this introduction: "Who is responsible for hiding this wonderful young person in a cage?"

"That is where the ticket seller sells."

"So, David, go in there and sell tickets for a half hour. I have something in mind in regards to the future of this girl and this company. Go, David, be a good boy. And you, Miss Lieber, please, I suggest Feinberg's for a glass of tea. The rehearsals are long. I enjoy a quiet interlude with a friendly person."

So he took me there, Feinberg's, then around the corner, a place so full of Hungarians, it was deafening. In the back room was a table of honor for him. On the tablecloth embroidered by the lady of the house was "Here Vlashkin Eats." We finished one glass of tea in quietness, out of thirst, when I finally made up my mind what to say.

"Mr. Vlashkin, I saw you a couple weeks ago, even before I started working here, in *The Sea Gull*. Believe me, if I was that girl, I wouldn't look even for a minute on the young bourgeois fellow. He could fall out of the play altogether. How Chekhov could put him in the same play as you, I can't understand."

"You liked me?" he asked, taking my hand and kindly patting it. "Well, well, young people still like me . . . so, and you like the theater too? Good. And you, Rose, you know you have such a nice hand, so warm to the touch, such a fine skin, tell me, why do you wear a scarf around your neck? You only hide your young, young throat. These are not olden times, my child, to live in shame."

"Who's ashamed?" I said, taking off the kerchief, but my hand right away went to the kerchief's place, because the truth is, it really was olden times, and I was still of a nature to melt with shame.

"Have some more tea, my dear."

"No, thank you, I am a samovar already."   25

"Dorfmann!" he hollered like a king. "Bring this child a seltzer with fresh ice!"

In weeks to follow I had the privilege to know him better and better as a person—also the opportunity to see him in his profession. The time was autumn; the theater full of coming and going. Rehearsing without end. After *The Sea Gull* flopped *The Salesman from Istanbul* played, a great success.

Here the ladies went crazy. On the opening night, in the middle of the first scene, one missus—a widow or her husband worked too long hours—began to clap and sing out, "Oi, oi, Vlashkin." Soon there was such a tumult, the actors had to stop acting. Vlashkin stepped forward. Only not Vlashkin to the eyes . . . a younger man with pitch-black hair, lively on restless feet, his mouth clever. A half a century later at the end of the play he came out again, a gray philosopher, a student of life from only reading books, his hands as smooth as silk. . . . I cried to think who I was—nothing—and such a man could look at me with interest.

Then I got a small raise, due to he kindly put in a good word for me, and also for fifty cents a night I was given the pleasure together with cousins, in-laws, and plain stage-struck kids to be part of a crowd scene and to see like he saw every single night the hundreds of pale faces waiting for his feelings to make them laugh or bend down their heads in sorrow.

The sad day came, I kissed my mama goodbye. Vlashkin helped me to get a rea-   30
sonable room near the theater to be more free. Also my outstanding friend would have a place to recline away from the noise of the dressing rooms. She cried and she cried. "This is a different way of living, Mama," I said. "Besides I am driven by love."

"You! You, a nothing, a rotten hole in a piece of cheese, are you telling me what is life?" she screamed.

Very insulted, I went away from her. But I am good-natured—you know fat people are like that—kind, and I thought to myself, poor Mama . . . it is true she got more of an idea of life than me. She married who she didn't like, a sick man, his spirit already swallowed up by God. He never washed. He had an unhappy smell. His teeth fell out, his hair disappeared, he got smaller, shriveled up little by little, till goodbye and good luck he was gone and only came to Mama's mind when she went to the mailbox under the stairs to get the electric bill. In memory of him and out of respect for mankind, I decided to live for love.

Don't laugh, you ignorant girl.

Do you think it was easy for me? I had to give Mama a little something. Ruthie was saving up together with your papa for linens, a couple knives and forks. In the morning I had to do piecework if I wanted to keep by myself. So I made flowers. Before lunch time every day a whole garden grew on my table.

This was my independence, Lillie dear, blooming, but it didn't have no roots   35
and its face was paper.

Meanwhile Krimberg went after me too. No doubt observing the success of Vlashkin, he thought, "Aha, open sesame . . ." Others in the company similar. After me in those years were the following: Krimberg I mentioned. Carl Zimmer, played innocent young fellows with a wig. Charlie Peel, a Christian who fell in the soup by accident, a creator of beautiful sets. "Color is his middle name," says Vlashkin, always to the point.

I put this in to show you your fat old aunt was not crazy out of loneliness. In those noisy years I had friends among interesting people who admired me for reasons of youth and that I was a first-class listener.

The actresses—Raisele, Marya, Esther Leopold—were only interested in tomorrow. After them was the rich men, producers, the whole garment center; their past is a pincushion, future the eye of a needle.

Finally the day came, I no longer could keep my tact in my mouth. I said: "Vlashkin, I hear by carrier pigeon you have a wife, children, the whole combination."

"True, I don't tell stories. I make no pretense."

"That isn't the question. What is this lady like? It hurts me to ask, but tell me, Vlashkin . . . a man's life is something I don't clearly see."

"Little girl, I have told you a hundred times, this small room is the convent of my troubled spirit. Here I come to your innocent shelter to refresh myself in the midst of an agonized life."

"Ach, Vlashkin, serious, serious, who is this lady?"

"Rosie, she is a fine woman of the middle classes, a good mother to my children, three in number, girls all, a good cook, in her youth handsome, now no longer young. You see, could I be more frank? I entrust you, dear, with my soul."

It was some few months later at the New Year's ball of the Russian Artists Club, I met Mrs. Vlashkin, a woman with black hair in a low bun, straight and too proud. She sat at a small table speaking in a deep voice to whoever stopped a moment to converse. Her Yiddish was perfect, each word cut like a special jewel. I looked at her. She noticed me like she notices everybody, cold like Christmas morning. Then she got tired. Vlashkin called a taxi and I never saw her again. Poor woman, she did not know I was on the same stage with her. The poison I was to her role, she did not know.

Later on that night in front of my door I said to Vlashkin, "No more. This isn't for me. I am sick from it all. I am no home breaker."

"Girlie," he said, "don't be foolish."

"No, no, goodbye, good luck," I said. "I am sincere."

So I went and stayed with Mama for a week's vacation and cleaned up all the closets and scrubbed the walls till the paint came off. She was very grateful, all the same her hard life made her say. "Now we see the end. If you live like a bum, you are finally a lunatic."

After this few days I came back to my life. When we met, me and Vlashkin, we said only hello and goodbye, and then for a few sad years, with the head we nodded as if to say, "Yes, yes, I know who you are."

Meanwhile in the field was a whole new strategy. Your mama and your grandmama brought around—boys. Your own father had a brother, you never even seen him. Ruben. A serious fellow, his idealism was his hat and his coat, "Rosie, I offer you a big new free happy unusual life." How? "With me, we will raise up the sands of Palestine to make a nation. That is the land of tomorrow for us Jews." "Ha-ha, Ruben, I'll go tomorrow then." "Rosie!" says Ruben. "We need strong women like you, mothers and farmers." "You don't fool me, Ruben, what you need is dray horses. But for that you need more money." "I don't like your attitude, Rose." "In that case, go and multiply. Goodbye."

Another fellow: Yonkel Gurstein, a regular sport, dressed to kill, with such an excitable nature. In those days—it looks to me like yesterday—the youngest girls wore undergarments like Battle Creek, Michigan. To him it was a matter of seconds. Where did he practice, a Jewish boy? Nowadays I suppose it is easier, Lillie? My goodness, I ain't asking you nothing—touchy, touchy. . . .

Well, by now you must know yourself, honey whatever you do, life don't stop. It only sits a minute and dreams a dream.

While I was saying to all these silly youngsters "no, no, no," Vlashkin went to Europe and toured a few seasons . . . Moscow, Prague, London, even Berlin—already a pessimistic place. When he came back he wrote a book, you could get from the library even today, *The Jewish Actor Abroad*. If someday you're interested enough in my lonesome years, you could read it. You could absorb a flavor of the man from the book. No, no, I am not mentioned. After all, who am I?

When the book came out I stopped him in the street to say congratulations. But 55
I am not a liar, so I pointed out, too, the egotism of many parts—even the critics said something along such lines.

"Talk is cheap," Vlashkin answered me. "But who are the critics? Tell me, do they create? Not to mention," he continues, "there is a line in Shakespeare in one of the plays from the great history of England. It says, 'Self-loving is not so vile a sin, my liege, as self-neglecting.'° This idea also appears in modern times in the moralistic followers of Freud. . . . Rosie, are you listening? You asked a question. By the way, you look very well. How come no wedding ring?"

I walked away from this conversation in tears. But this talking in the street opened the happy road up for more discussions. In regard to many things. . . . For instance, the management—very narrow-minded—wouldn't give him any more certain young men's parts. Fools. What youngest man knew enough about life to be as young as him?

"Rosie, Rosie," he said to me one day, "I see by the clock on your rosy, rosy face you must be thirty."

"The hands are slow, Vlashkin. On a week before Thursday I was thirty-four."

"Is that so? Rosie, I worry about you. It has been on my mind to talk to you. You 60
are losing your time. Do you understand it? A woman should not lose her time."

"Oi, Vlashkin, if you are my friend, what is time?"

For this he had no answer, only looked at me surprised. We went instead, full of interest but not with our former speed, up to my new place on Ninety-fourth Street. The same pictures on the wall, all of Vlashkin, only now everything painted red and black, which was stylish, and new upholstery.

A few years ago there was a book by another member of that fine company, an actress, the one that learned English very good and went uptown—Marya Kavkaz, in which she says certain things regarding Vlashkin. Such as, he was her lover for eleven years, she's not ashamed to write this down. Without respect for him, his wife and children, or even others who also may have feelings in the matter. Now, Lillie, don't be surprised. This is called a fact of life. An actor's soul must be like a diamond. The more faces it got the more shining is his name. Honey, you will no doubt love and marry one man and have a couple kids and be happy forever till you die tired. More

self-loving . . . self-neglecting: Henry V, 2.4. 74–75.

than that, a person like us don't have to know. But a great artist like Volodya Vlashkin . . . in order to make a job on the stage, he's got to practice. I understand it now, to him life is like a rehearsal.

Myself, when I saw him in *The Father-in-law*—an older man in love with a darling young girl, his son's wife, played by Raisele Maisel—I cried. What he said to this girl, how he whispered such sweetness, how all his hot feelings were on his face . . . Lillie, all this experience he had with me. The very words were the same. You can image how proud I was.

So the story creeps to an end.

I noticed it first on my mother's face, the rotten handwriting of time, scribbled up and down her cheeks, across her forehead back and forth—a child could read— it said, old, old, old. But it troubled my heart most to see these realities scratched on Vlashkin's wonderful expression.

First the company fell apart. The theater ended. Esther Leopold died from being very aged. Krimberg had a heart attack. Marya went to Broadway. Also Raisele changed her name to Roslyn and was a big comical hit in the movies. Vlashkin himself, no place to go, retired. It said in the paper, "an actor without peer, he will write his memoirs and spend his last years in the bosom of his family among his thriving grandchildren, the apple of his wife's doting eye."

This is journalism.

We made for him a great dinner of honor. At this dinner I said to him, for the last time, I thought, "Goodbye, dear friend, topic of my life, now we part." And to myself I said further: Finished. This is your lonesome bed. A lady what they call fat and fifty. You made it personally. From this lonesome bed you will finally fall to a bed not so lonesome, only crowded with a million bones.

And now comes? Lillie, guess.

Last week, washing my underwear in the basin, I get a buzz on the phone. "Excuse me, is this the Rose Lieber formerly connected with the Russian Art Theater?"

"It is."

"Well, well, how do you do, Rose? This is Vlashkin."

"Vlashkin! Volodya Vlashkin?"

"In fact. How are you, Rose?"

"Living, Vlashkin, thank you."

"You are all right? Really, Rose? Your health is good? You are working?"

"My health, considering the weight it must carry, is first-class. I am back for some years now where I started, in novelty wear."

"Very interesting."

"Listen, Vlashkin, tell me the truth, what's on your mind?"

"My mind? Rosie, I am looking up an old friend, an old warmhearted companion of more joyful days. My circumstances, by the way, are changed. I am retired, as you know. Also I am a free man."

"What? What do you mean?"

"Mrs. Vlashkin is divorcing me."

"What come over her? Did you start drinking or something from melancholy?"

"She is divorcing me for adultery."

"But, Vlashkin, you should excuse me, don't be insulted, but you got maybe seventeen, eighteen years on me, and even me, all this nonsense—this daydreams and nightmares—is mostly for the pleasure of conversation alone."

"I pointed all this out to her. My dear, I said, my time is past, my blood is as dry as my bones. The truth is, Rose, she isn't accustomed to have a man around all day, reading out loud from the papers the interesting events of our time, waiting for breakfast, waiting for lunch. So all day she gets madder and madder. By nighttime a furious old lady gives me my supper. She has information from the last fifty years to pepper my soup. Surely there was a Judas in that theater, saying every day, 'Vlashkin, Vlashkin, Vlashkin . . .' and while my heart was circulating with his smiles he was on the wire passing the dope to my wife."

"Such a foolish end, Volodya, to such a lively story. What is your plans?"

"First, could I ask you for dinner and the theater—uptown, of course? After this . . . we are old friends. I have money to burn. What your heart desires. Others are like grass, the north wind of time has cut out their heart. Of you, Rosie, I recreate only kindness. What a woman should be to a man, you were to me. Do you think, Rosie, a couple of old pals like us could have a few good times among the material things of this world?" 90

My answer, Lillie, in a minute was altogether. "Yes, yes, come up," I said. "Ask the room by the switchboard, let us talk."

So he came that night and every night in the week, we talked of his long life. Even at the end of time, a fascinating man. And like men are, too, till time's end, trying to get away in one piece.

"Listen, Rosie," he explains the other day. "I was married to my wife, do you realize, nearly half a century. What good was it? Look at the bitterness. The more I think of it, the more I think we would be fools to marry."

"Volodya Vlashkin," I told him straight, "when I was young I warmed your cold back many a night, no questions asked. You admit it, I didn't make no demands. I was softhearted. I didn't want to be called Rosie Lieber, a breaker up of homes. But now, Vlashkin, you are a free man. How could you ask me to go with you on trains to stay in strange hotels, among Americans, not your wife? Be ashamed."

So now, darling Lillie, tell this story to your mama from your young mouth. She don't listen to a word from me. She only screams, "I'll faint, I'll faint," Tell her after all I'll have a husband, which, as everybody knows, a woman should have at least one before the end of the story. 95

My goodness, I am already late. Give me a kiss. After all, I watched you grow from a plain seed. So give me a couple wishes on my wedding day. A long and happy life. Many years of love. Hug Mama, tell her from Aunt Rose, goodbye and good luck.

KATHERINE ANNE PORTER (1894–1980)

Porter, whose birth name was Callie Russell, was born into poverty in a log cabin in Texas. With little formal schooling, she was largely self-taught. It is to her enduring credit that she advanced herself so highly that she lectured at a number of distinguished colleges and universities. She first began publishing in small journals, and established her reputation with her early collections Flowering Judas *(1930) and* Pale Horse, Pale Rider *(1939). Her major novel,* Ship of Fools, *appeared in 1962. For her Collected Stories of 1965, she was awarded the Pulitzer Prize for Fiction and also the National Book Award .*

The Jilting of Granny Weatherall ———————————————————————*1930*

She flicked her wrist neatly out of Doctor Harry's pudgy careful fingers and pulled the sheet up to her chin. The brat ought to be in knee breeches. Doctoring around the country with spectacles on his nose! "Get along now, take your schoolbooks and go. There's nothing wrong with me."

Doctor Harry spread a warm paw like a cushion on her forehead where the forked green vein danced and made her eyelids twitch. "Now, now, be a good girl, and we'll have you up in no time."

"That's no way to speak to a woman nearly eighty years old just because she's down. I'd have you respect your elders, young man."

"Well, Missy, excuse me." Doctor Harry patted her cheek. "But I've got to warn you, haven't I? You're a marvel, but you must be careful or you're going to be good and sorry."

"Don't tell me what I'm going to be. I'm on my feet now, morally speaking. It's Cornelia. I had to go to bed to get rid of her."

Her bones felt loose, and floated around in her skin, and Doctor Harry floated like a balloon around the foot of the bed. He floated and pulled down his waistcoat and swung his glasses on a cord. "Well, stay where you are, it certainly can't hurt you."

"Get along and doctor your sick." said Granny Weatherall. "Leave a well woman alone. I'll call for you when I want you. . . . Where were you forty years ago when I pulled through milk-leg and double pneumonia? You weren't even born. Don't let Cornelia lead you on." she shouted, because Doctor Harry appeared to float up to the ceiling and out. "I pay my own bills, and I don't throw my money away on nonsense!"

She meant to wave good-by, but it was too much trouble. Her eyes closed of themselves, it was like a dark curtain drawn around the bed. The pillow rose and floated under her, pleasant as a hammock in a light wind. She listened to the leaves rustling outside the window. No, somebody was swishing newspapers: no, Cornelia and Doctor Harry were whispering together. She leaped broad awake, thinking they whispered in her ear.

"She was never like this, *never* like this!" "Well, what can we expect?" "Yes, eighty years old. . . ."

Well, and what if she was? She still had ears. It was like Cornelia to whisper around doors. She always kept things secret in such a public way. She was always being tactful and kind. Cornelia was dutiful; that was the trouble with her. Dutiful and good: "So good and dutiful," said Granny, "that I'd like to spank her." She saw herself spanking Cornelia and making a fine job of it.

"What'd you say, Mother?"

Granny felt her face tying up in hard knots.

"Can't a body think, I'd like to know?"

"I thought you might want something."

"I do. I want a lot of things. First off, go away and don't whisper."

She lay and drowsed, hoping in her sleep that the children would keep out and let her rest a minute. It had been a long day. Not that she was tired. It was always pleasant to snatch a minute now and then. There was always so much to be done, let me see: tomorrow.

Tomorrow was far away and there was nothing to trouble about. Things were finished somehow when the time came; thank God there was always a little margin over for peace: then a person could spread out the plan of life and tuck in the edges orderly. It was good to have everything clean and folded away, with the hair brushes and tonic bottles sitting straight on the white embroidered linen: the day started without fuss and the pantry shelves laid out with rows of jelly glasses and brown jugs and white stone-china jars with blue whirligigs and words painted on them: coffee, tea, sugar, ginger, cinnamon, allspice: and the bronze clock with the lion on top nicely dusted off. The dust that lion could collect in twenty-four hours! The box in the attic with all those letters tied up, well she'd have to go through that tomorrow. All those letters—George's letters and John's letters and her letters to them both—lying around for the children to find afterwards made her uneasy. Yes, that would be tomorrow's business. No use to let them know how silly she had been once.

While she was rummaging around she found death in her mind and it felt clammy and unfamiliar. She had spent so much time preparing for death there was no need for bringing it up again. Let it take care of itself now. When she was sixty she had felt very old, finished, and went around making farewell trips to see her children and grandchildren, with a secret in her mind: This is the very last of your mother, children! Then she made her will and came down with a long fever. That was all just a notion like a lot of other things, but it was lucky too, for she had once for all got over the idea of dying for a long time. Now she couldn't be worried. She hoped she had better sense now. Her father had lived to be one hundred and two years old and had drunk a noggin of strong hot toddy on his last birthday. He told the reporters it was his daily habit, and he owed his long life to that. He had made quite a scandal and was very pleased about it. She believed she'd just plague Cornelia a little.

"Cornelia! Cornelia!" No footsteps, but a sudden hand on her cheek. "Bless you, where have you been?"

"Here, mother."

"Well, Cornelia, I want a noggin of hot toddy."   20

"Are you cold, darling?"

"I'm chilly, Cornelia. Lying in bed stops the circulation. I must have told you that a thousand times."

Well, she could just hear Cornelia telling her husband that Mother was getting childish and they'd have to humor her. The thing that most annoyed her was that Cornelia thought she was deaf, dumb, and blind. Little hasty glances and tiny gestures tossed around her and over her head saying. "Don't cross her, let her have her way, she's eighty years old," and she sitting there as if she lived in a thin glass cage. Sometimes Granny almost made up her mind to pack up and move back to her own house where nobody could remind her every minute that she was old. Wait, wait, Cornelia, till your own children whisper behind your back!

In her day she had kept a better house and had got more work done. She   25
wasn't too old yet for Lydia to be driving eighty miles for advice when one of the children jumped the track, and Jimmy still dropped in and talked things over: "Now, Mammy, you've a good business head, I want to know what you think of this? . . ." Old Cornelia couldn't change the furniture around without asking. Little things, little things! They had been so sweet when they were little. Granny wished the old days were back again with the children young and everything to be done over. It had been a hard pull, but not too much for her. When she thought of all the food she had cooked, and all the clothes she had cut and sewed, and all the gardens she had made—well, the children showed it. There they were, made out of her, and they couldn't get away from that. Sometimes she wanted to see John again and point to them and say, Well, I didn't do so badly, did I? But that would have to wait. That was

for tomorrow. She used to think of him as a man, but now all the children were older than their father, and he would be a child beside her if she saw him now. It seemed strange and there was something wrong in the idea. Why, he couldn't possibly recognize her. She had fenced in a hundred acres once, digging the post holes herself and clamping the wires with just a negro boy to help. That changed a woman. John would be looking for a young woman with the peaked Spanish comb in her hair and the painted fan. Digging post holes changed a woman. Riding country roads in the winter when women had their babies was another thing: sitting up nights with sick horses and sick negroes and sick children and hardly ever losing one. John, I hardly ever lost one of them! John would see that in a minute, that would be something he could understand, she wouldn't have to explain anything!

It made her feel like rolling up her sleeves and putting the whole place to rights again. No matter if Cornelia was determined to be everywhere at once, there were a great many things left undone on this place. She would start tomorrow and do them. It was good to be strong enough for everything, even if all you made melted and changed and slipped under your hands, so that by the time you finished you almost forgot what you were working for. What was it I set out to do? she asked herself intently, but she could not remember. A fog rose over the valley, she saw it marching across the creek swallowing the trees and moving up the hill like an army of ghosts. Soon it would be at the near edge of the orchard, and then it was time to go in and light the lamps. Come in children, don't stay out in the night air.

Lighting the lamps had been beautiful. The children huddled up to her and breathed like little calves waiting at the bars in the twilight. Their eyes followed the match and watched the flame rise and settle in a blue curve, then they moved away from her. The lamp was lit, they didn't have to be scared and hang on to mother any more. Never, never, never more. God, for all my life I thank Thee. Without Thee, my God, I could never have done it. Hail, Mary, full of grace.

I want you to pick all the fruit this year and see that nothing is wasted. There's always someone who can use it. Don't let good things rot for want of using. You waste life when you waste good food. Don't let things get lost. It's bitter to lose things. Now, don't let me get to thinking, not when I am tired and taking a little nap before supper. . . .

The pillow rose about her shoulders and pressed against her heart and the memory was being squeezed out of it: oh, push down the pillow, somebody: it would smother her if she tried to hold it. Such a fresh breeze blowing and such a green day with no threats in it. But he had not come, just the same. What does a woman do when she has put on the white veil and set out the white cake for a man and he doesn't come? She tried to remember. No, I swear he never harmed me but in that. He never harmed me but in that . . . and what if he did? There was the day, the day, but a whirl of dark smoke rose and covered it, crept up and over into the bright field where everything was planted so carefully in orderly rows. That was hell, she knew hell when she saw it. For sixty years she had prayed against remembering him and against losing her soul in the deep pit of hell, and now the two things were mingled in one and the thought of him was a smoky cloud from hell that moved and crept in her head when she had just got rid of Doctor Harry and was trying to rest a minute. Wounded vanity, Ellen, said a sharp voice in the top of her mind. Don't let your wounded vanity get the upper hand of you. Plenty of girls get jilted. You were jilted, weren't you. Then stand up to it. Her eyelids wavered and let in streamers of blue-gray light like tissue paper over her eyes. She must get up and pull the shades down or she'd never sleep.

She was in bed again and the shades were not down. How could that happen? Better turn over, hide from the light, sleeping in the light gave you nightmares. "Mother, how do you feel now?" and a stinging wetness on her forehead. But I don't like having my face washed in cold water!

Hapsy? George? Lydia? Jimmy? No, Cornelia, and her features were swollen and full of little puddles. "They're coming, darling, they'll all be here soon." Go wash your face, child, you look funny.

Instead of obeying, Cornelia knelt down and put her head on the pillow. She seemed to be talking but there was no sound. "Well, are you tongue-tied? Whose birthday is it? Are you going to give a party?"

Cornelia's mouth moved urgently in strange shapes. "Don't do that, you bother me, daughter."

"Oh, no, Mother, Oh, no. . . "

Nonsense. It was strange about children. They disputed your every word. "No what, Cornelia?"

"Here's Doctor Harry."

"I won't see that boy again. He just left five minutes ago."

"That was this morning, Mother. It's night now. Here's the nurse."

"This is Doctor Harry, Mrs. Weatherall. I never saw you look so young and happy!"

"Ah, I'll never be young again—but I'd be happy if they'd let me lie in peace and get rested."

She thought she spoke up loudly, but no one answered. A warm weight on her forehead, a warm bracelet on her wrist, and a breeze went on whispering, trying to tell her something. A shuffle of leaves in the everlasting hand of God. He blew on them and they danced and rattled. "Mother, don't mind, we're going to give you a little hypodermic." "Look here, daughter, how do ants get in this bed? I saw sugar ants yesterday." Did you send for Hapsy too?

It was Hapsy she really wanted. She had to go a long way back through a great many rooms to find Hapsy standing with a baby on her arm. She seemed to herself to be Hapsy also, and the baby on Hapsy's arm was Hapsy and himself and herself, all at once, and there was no surprise in the meeting. Then Hapsy melted from within and turned flimsy as gray gauze and the baby was a gauzy shadow, and Hapsy came up close and said, "I thought you'd never come," and looked at her very searchingly and said, "You haven't changed a bit!" They leaned forward to kiss, when Cornelia began whispering from a long way off, "Oh, is there anything you want to tell me? Is there anything I can do for you?"

Yes, she had changed her mind after sixty years and she would like to see George. I want you to find George. Find him and be sure to tell him I forgot him. I want him to know I had my husband just the same and my children and my house like any other woman. A good house too and a good husband that I loved and fine children out of him. Better than I hoped for even. Tell him I was given back everything he took away and more. Oh, no, oh, God, no, there was something else besides the house and the man and the children. Oh, surely they were not all? What was it? Something not given back. . . . Her breath crowded down under her ribs and grew into a monstrous frightening shape with cutting edges; it bored up into her head, and the agony was unbelievable: Yes, John, get the doctor now, no more talk, my time has come.

When this one was born it should be the last. The last. It should have been born

30

35

40

first, for it was the one she had truly wanted. Everything came in good time. Nothing left out, left over. She was strong, in three days she would be as well as ever. Better. A woman needed milk in her to have her full health.

"Mother, do you hear me?"

"I've been telling you—"

"Mother, Father Connolly's here."

"I went to Holy Communion only last week. Tell him I'm not so sinful as all that."

"Father just wants to speak to you."

He could speak as much as he pleased. It was like him to drop in and inquire about her soul as if it were a teething baby, and then stay on for a cup of tea and a round of cards and gossip. He always had a funny story of some sort, usually about an Irishman who made his little mistakes and confessed them, and the point lay in some absurd thing he would blurt out in the confessional showing his struggles between native piety and original sin. Granny felt easy about her soul. Cornelia, where are your manners? Give Father Connolly a chair. She had her secret comfortable understanding with a few favorite saints who cleared a straight road to God for her. All as surely signed and sealed as the papers for the new Forty Acres. Forever . . . heirs and assigns forever. Since the day the wedding cake was not cut, but thrown out and wasted. The whole bottom dropped out of the world, and there she was blind and sweating with nothing under her feet and the walls falling away. His hand had caught her under the breast, she had not fallen, there was the freshly polished floor with the green rug on it, just as before. He had cursed like a sailor's parrot and said. "I'll kill him for you." Don't lay a hand on him, for my sake leave something to God. "Now, Ellen, you must believe what I tell you. . . ."

So there was nothing, nothing to worry about any more, except sometimes in the night one of the children screamed in a nightmare, and they both hustled out shaking and hunting for the matches and calling, "There, wait a minute, here we are!" John, get the doctor now. Hapsy's time has come. But there was Hapsy standing by the bed in a white cap. "Cornelia, tell Hapsy to take off her cap. I can't see her plain."

Her eyes opened very wide and the room stood out like a picture she had seen somewhere. Dark colors with the shadow rising towards the ceiling in long angles. The tall black dresser gleamed with nothing on it but John's picture, enlarged from a little one, with John's eyes very black when they should have been blue. You never saw him, so how do you know how he looked? But the man insisted the copy was perfect, it was very rich and handsome. For a picture, yes, but it's not my husband. The table by the bed had a linen cover and a candle and a crucifix. The light was blue from Cornelia's silk lampshades. No sort of light at all, just frippery. You had to live forty years with kerosene lamps to appreciate honest electricity. She felt very strong and she saw Doctor Harry with a rosy nimbus around him.

"You look like a saint, Doctor Harry, and I vow that's as near as you'll ever come to it."

"She's saying something."

"I heard you, Cornelia. What's all this carrying-on?"

"Father Connolly's saying—"

Cornelia's voice staggered and bumped like a cart in a bad road. It rounded corners and turned back again and arrived nowhere. Granny stepped up in the cart very lightly and reached for the reins, but a man sat beside her and she knew him by his hands, driving the cart. She did not look in his face, for she knew without seeing, but looked instead down the road where the trees leaned over and bowed to each other and a thousand birds were singing a Mass. She felt like singing too, but she put her hand in the bosom of her dress and pulled out a rosary, and Father Connolly murmured Latin in a very solemn voice and tickled her feet. My God, will you stop that nonsense? I'm a married woman. What if he did run away and leave me to face the priest by myself? I found another a whole world better. I wouldn't have exchanged my husband for anybody except St. Michael himself, and you may tell him that for me with a thank you in the bargain.

Light flashed on her closed eyelids, and a deep roaring shook her. Cornelia, is that lightning? I hear thunder. There's going to be a storm. Close all the windows. Call the children in. . . "Mother, here we are, all of us." "Is that you, Hapsy?" "Oh, no, I'm Lydia. We drove as fast as we could." Their faces drifted above her, drifted away. The rosary fell out of her hands and Lydia put it back. Jimmy tried to help, their hands fumbled together, and Granny closed two fingers around Jimmy's thumb. Beads wouldn't do, it must be something alive. She was so amazed her thoughts ran round and round. So, my dear Lord, this is my death and I wasn't even thinking about it. My children have come to see me die. But I can't, it's not time. Oh, I always hated surprises. I wanted to give Cornelia the amethyst set—Cornelia, you're to have the amethyst set, but Hapsy's to wear it when she wants, and, Doctor Harry, do shut up. Nobody sent for you. Oh, my dear Lord, do wait a minute. I meant to do something about the Forty Acres, Jimmy doesn't need it and Lydia will later on with that worthless husband of hers. I meant to finish the altar cloth and send six bottles of wine to Sister Borgia for her dyspepsia. I want to send six bottles of wine to Sister Borgia, Father Connolly, now don't let me forget.

Cornelia's voice made short turns and tilted over and crashed. "Oh, Mother, oh, Mother, oh, Mother. . . ."

"I'm not going, Cornelia. I'm taken by surprise. I can't go."

You'll see Hapsy again. What about her? "I thought you'd never come." Granny made a long journey outward, looking for Hapsy. What if I don't find her? What then? Her heart sank down and down, there was no bottom to death, she couldn't come to the end of it. The blue light from Cornelia's lampshade drew into a tiny point in the center of her brain, it flickered and winked like an eye, quietly it fluttered and dwindled. Granny lay curled down within herself, amazed and watchful, staring at the point of light that was herself; her body was now only a deeper mass of shadow in an endless darkness and this darkness would curl around the light and swallow it up. God, give a sign!

For the second time there was no sign. Again no bridegroom and the priest in the house. She could not remember any other sorrow because this grief wiped them all away. Oh, no, there's nothing more cruel than this—I'll never forgive it. She stretched herself with a deep breath and blew out the light.

60

POETRY

Pieter Brueghel the Elder, Landscape with the Fall of Icarus, Musees Royaux des Beaux-Arts, Brussels, Scala/Art Resources, NY.

13

Meeting Poetry: An Overview

Poetry and **poem** describe a wide variety of spoken and written forms, styles, and patterns, and also a wide variety of subjects. Because of the variety, it is not possible to make a single, comprehensive definition. The origin of the word is the Greek word *poiema*; that is, "something made or fashioned [in words]"—a meaning that applies to both poetry and to poems. Naturally, a **poet** was, and is, a person who writes or speaks poems. Rather than trying to understand poetry by defining it, we believe the best way to understand it is to read it, learn it, experience it, and enjoy it. As your understanding of poetry deepens, you will develop your own ideas and definitions.

We begin with a poem based in the life of students and teachers alike:

BILLY COLLINS   (b. 1941)

Schoolsville ——————————————————————— *1985*

Glancing over my shoulder at the past,
I realize the number of students I have taught
is enough to populate a small town.

I can see it nestled in a paper landscape,
chalk dust flurrying down in winter,   5
nights dark as a blackboard.

The population ages but never graduates.
On hot afternoons they sweat the final in the park
and when it's cold they shiver around stoves
reading disorganized essays out loud.   10
A bell rings on the hour and everybody zigzags
in the streets with their books.

I forgot all their last names first and their
first names last in alphabetical order.
But the boy who always had his hand up
is an alderman and owns the haberdashery.
The girl who signed her papers in lipstick
leans against the drugstore, smoking,
brushing her hair like a machine.

Their grades are sewn into their clothes
like references to Hawthorne.°   i.e., *The Scarlet Letter*
The A's stroll along with other A's.
The D's honk whenever they pass another D.

All the creative writing students recline
on the courthouse lawn and play the lute.
Wherever they go, they form a big circle.

Needless to say, I am the mayor.
I live in the white colonial at Maple and Main.
I rarely leave the house. The car deflates
in the driveway. Vines twirl around the porchswing.

Once in a while a student knocks on the door
with a term paper fifteen years late
or a question about Yeats or double-spacing.
And sometimes one will appear in a window pane
to watch me lecturing the wall paper,
quizzing the chandelier, reprimanding the air.

QUESTIONS

1. What recognizable school experiences does the poem mention? Why is "Schools-ville" the title?
2. Describe the speaker. How does he indicate affection for students?
3. What details indicate that the poem is fantasy and not reality? To what degree is the poem humorous?
4. Compare the details of this poem with those in Roethke's "Dolor" (p. 620). What similarities do you find in the choice and appropriateness of detail? What differences?
5. Each poem you read may help you understand, and therefore define, poetry. How might this poem help you begin making a definition?

"Schoolsville" reveals much about poetry. The topic material is drawn from school or college life. The references are introduced not to tell a story, but to make assertions. The connecting element in the poem is therefore the fanciful and comic but also affectionate ideas the speaker makes about how school life somehow always remains the same. The poem's details are sharply observed and recorded, such as the chalk dust flurrying down like snow, the girl who signs her name in lipstick, and the students forming a circle when they meet. The poem is arranged in lines, but does not follow measured rhythmical patterns, nor does it rhyme. The most important thing about it is that, as it engages us and amuses us, it also rings of truth. Once we have read and followed the poem, we will not forget it, and it will echo in our minds as time passes. Like all good poetry, in short, this poem is alive, and if we read it sensitively it will become a part of us.

THE NATURE OF POETRY

"Schoolsville" is unique; it is at once serious and original, and it is also amusing. There is no other poem like it. Indeed, all good poems are unique, and because this is so we cannot formulate a single definition of poetry to account for all poems. Nevertheless, we can offer a number of descriptive statements about poetry that may be helpful. To begin with, poems are imaginative works expressed in words that are used with the utmost compression, force, and economy. Unlike prose, which is expansive and exhaustive, most poems are brief but also comprehensive, offering us high points of thought, feeling, reflection, and resolution. Poems may take just about any coherent and developed shape, from a line of a single word to lines of twenty, thirty, or more words, and these lines may be organized into any number of repeating or nonrepeating patterns. Some poems may make us think, give us new and unexpected insights, and generally instruct us. Other poems may arouse our emotions, surprise us, amuse us, and inspire us. Ideally, reading and understanding poetry should prompt us to reexamine, reinforce, and reshape our ideas, our attitudes, our feelings, and our lives.

POETRY OF THE ENGLISH LANGUAGE

Today, most nations with their own languages have their own literatures, including poetry, with their own unique characteristics and histories. In this anthology, however, we are concerned primarily with poetry in our own language by American, British, and Canadian poets.

The earliest poems in English date back to late in the period of *Old English* (A.D. 450–1100). Many of these early English poems reflect the influence of Christianity. Indeed, the most famous poem, the epic *Beowulf,* was probably interpreted as a Christian allegory even though it concerns the secular themes of adventure, courage, and war. Ever since the *Middle English* period (A.D. 1100–1500), poets have written about many other subjects, although religious themes have remained important. Today, we may find poetry on virtually all topics, ranging from sexuality, love, society, individuality, warfare, strong drink, government and politics, worship, and music, to special and unusual topics like fishing, computers, exotic birds, and car crashes.

In short, poetry is alive and flourishing. People read it aloud in front of audiences, friends, and families; others read it silently in private. A poem set to music and sung aloud is exceedingly powerful. Francis Scott Key's "The Star-Spangled Banner," for example, which he wrote about events in a battle in the War of 1812, is a poem that has become our national anthem. More recently, musical groups like The Beatles and U2, along with the singer Bruce Springsteen, have given poetic expression to ideas that huge masses of people have taken to heart. Ever since the 1960's, people devoted to civil rights have been unified and strengthened by the simple poetic lyrics of "We shall overcome," not only in the United States but throughout the world. The strength and vitality of poetry could be similarly documented time and time again.

HOW POETRY WORKS

With poetry, as with any other literary form, the more effort we put into understanding, the greater will be our reward. Poems are often about subjects that we have never experienced directly. We have never met the poet, never had his or her exact experiences, and never thought about things in exactly the same way. To recapture the experience of the poem, we need to understand the language, ideas, attitudes, and frames of reference that will make the poem come alive. Consider the following poem by an American poet:

RANDALL JARRELL   (1914–1965)

The Death of the Ball Turret Gunner ———————————— *1945*

From my mother's sleep I fell into the State
And I hunched in its belly till my wet fur froze.
Six miles from earth, loosed from its dream of life,
I woke to black flak and the nightmare fighters.
When I died they washed me out of the turret with a hose.

To understand and experience this poem, we need to know a number of details: The topic is the violent death of a gunner on a World War II bomber, imagined as being told by the dead gunner himself. The poet, Jarrell, tells us in a note that "a ball turret was a Plexiglas sphere set into the belly of a B-17 or B-24 [both large, four-engine, high-altitude, precision-bombing aircraft] and inhabited by two .50-calibre machine guns and one man, a short small man. When this gunner tracked with his machine guns a fighter attacking his bomber from below, he revolved with the turret; hunched upside-down in his little sphere, he looked like a fetus in the womb. The fighters that attacked him were armed with cannon firing exploding shells. The hose was a steam hose." We add that *Flak* (an acronym from the German word for anti-aircraft gun, *FLiegerAbwehrKanone*) describes the high-altitude explosions of anti-air-craft shells fired from the ground.

This explanation helps us understand and experience Jarrell's poem, which dramatizes the grisly reality of aerial warfare. The opening comparison draws a parallel between a fetus in a mother's womb and the gunner in the belly of a plane. Thus the "wet fur" in line 2, a reference to the collar of a flight jacket, also suggests fetal hair. Expanding the metaphor, the poet suggests that the gunner typifies young men who are killed in war before they ever have a chance to live. The nature of the gunner's death is callous and horrible, highlighted by the closing image of his splattered remains—all traces of his former identity ("me")—being washed "out of the turret with a hose." Although the poem makes no direct moral statement, it is obvious that Jarrell sees war as mindless, cruel, indifferent, and wasteful.

HOW TO READ A POEM

Carefully, thoughtfully, and sympathetically. These words sum up the best approach to reading poetry. The economy and compression of poetry mean that every part of the poem must carry some of the impact and meaning, and thus every part repays careful attention. Try to interact with the poem. Do not expect the poem (or the poet) to do all the work. The poem contributes its language, imagery, rhythms, ideas, and all the other aspects that make it poetry, but you, the reader, will need to open your mind to the poem's impact.

There is no single technique for reading, absorbing, and appreciating poetry. In Chapter 1 we offer a number of guidelines for studying any work of literature (pp. 11–18). In addition to these, read each poem more than once and keep in mind the following objectives:

1. *Read straight through to get a general sense of the poem.* In this first reading, do not stop to puzzle out hard passages or obscure words; just read through from beginning to end.

2. *Try to understand the poem's meaning and organization.* As you read and reread the poem, study the following:

a.   **THE TITLE.** The title is almost always informative. The title "Death of the Ball Turret Gunner" indicates both subject and circumstances. The title of Robert Frost's "Stopping by Woods on a Snowy Evening" establishes the poem's setting and situation.

b.   **THE SPEAKER.** Poems are dramatic, having points of view just like prose fiction. First-person speakers talk from the "inside" because they are directly involved in the action (like the speakers in "Schoolsville" and "The Death of the Ball Turret Gunner"). Other speakers are "outside" observers, like the third-person limited and omniscient points of view, as in "Sir Patrick Spens"(see especially Chapter 5, pp. 184–85).

c.   **THE MEANINGS OF ALL WORDS, WHETHER FAMILIAR OR UNFAMILIAR.** The words in many poems are immediately clear, as with "Schoolsville," but other poems may contain unfamiliar words and references that need looking up. You will need to consult dictionaries, encyclopedias, and other sources, until you gain a fairly clear grasp of the poem's content. If you have difficulty even after using your sources, be sure to ask your instructor.

d.   **THE POEM'S SETTING AND SITUATION.** Some poems establish their settings and circumstances vividly. "Stopping by Woods on a Snowy Evening," for example, describes an evening scene in which the speaker stops his sleigh by a woods so that he may watch snow falling amid the trees. Although not all poems are so clear, you should learn as much as you can about setting and situation in every poem you read.

e.   **THE POEM'S BASIC FORM AND DEVELOPMENT.** Some poems, like "Sir Patrick Spens," are narratives; others, like Northrup's "Ogichidag," are personal statements; still others may be speeches to another person. The poems may be laid out in a sonnet form, or may develop in two-line sequences (couplets). They may contain stanzas, each of which is unified by a particular action or thought. Try to determine the form and to trace the way in which the poem unfolds, part by part.

f.   **THE POEM'S SUBJECT AND THEME.** The **subject** indicates the general or specific topic, while the **theme** refers to the idea or ideas that the poem explores. Jarrell's poem announces its subject in the title. However, you must usually infer the theme. In this poem it is about the sickening ugliness of war, the poignancy of untimely death, the callousness of the living toward the dead, and the suddenness with which war forces young people to face cruelty and horror.

3. *Read the poem aloud, sounding each word clearly.* Although this step may seem unnecessary, reading aloud will enable you to judge the effect of sound, rhythm, and rhyme. If you read "Death of the Ball Turret Gunner" aloud, for example, you will notice the impact of rhyming *froze* with *hose* and the suggestion of the percussive sounds of cannon fire in the repeated and rhyming *l*, *a*, and *k* sounds of *black flak* (for further discussion of sounds in poetry, see Chapter 19).

4. *Prepare a paraphrase of the poem, and make an explication of the ideas and themes.* A paraphrase (discussed later in this chapter) is a restatement of the poem in your own words which helps crystallize your understanding (see also Chapter 2, pp. 81–87). An explication, which is both explanation and interpretation, goes beyond paraphrase to consider significance—either of brief passages or of the entire poem.

STUDYING POETRY

Let us now look in detail at a poem, in this case one that tells a story. It was composed orally as a song sometime during the late Middle Ages or early Renaissance, when most people got information about the outside world from strolling balladeers who sang the news to them (there were no newspapers, and besides, few people could read). It tells a story that is probably true, or at least based on a real event.

ANONYMOUS

Sir Patrick Spens ———————————————— *Fifteenth century*

The king sits in Dumferline° town,
  Drinking the blood-red wine:
"O where will I get a good sailor
  To sail this ship of mine?"

Up and spoke an eldern° knight   *old, elderly*   5
  Sat° at the king's right knee: *who sat*
"Sir Patrick Spens is the best sailor
  That sails upon the sea."

The king has written a braid° letter   *large, commanding*
  And signed it wi° his hand,   *with*   10
And sent it to Sir Patrick Spens,
  Was° walking on the sand.   *who was*

The first line that Sir Patrick read,
  A loud laugh laughèd he;
The next line that Sir Patrick read,
  A tear blinded his eye.   15

"O who is this has° done this deed,   *who has*
  This ill deed done to me,
To send me out this time o'° the year,   *of*
  To sail upon the sea?   20

"Make haste, make haste, my merry men all,
  Our good ship sails the morn."°   *in the morning*
"O say not so, my master dear,
  For I fear a deadly storm.

Late late yestere'en° I saw the new moon   *yesterday evening*   25
  With the old moon in her arm,
And I fear, I fear, my dear master,
  That we will come to harm."

O our Scots nobles were right loath
  To wet their cork-heeled shoon,°   *shoes*   30
But long ere a'° the play were played   *all*
  Their hats they swam aboon.°   *about (in the water)*

O long, long may their ladies sit
  Wi' their fans into their hand,
Or e'er they see Sir Patrick Spens
  Come sailing to the land.   35

O long, long may the ladies stand,
  Wi' their gold combs in their hair,
Waiting for their own dear lords,
  For they'll see them no more.   40

Half o'er, half o'er to Aberdour°
  It's fifty fathom deep,
And there lies good Sir Patrick Spens,
  Wi' the Scots lords at his feet.

SIR PATRICK SPENS. 1 *Dumferline:* a town on the Firth of Forth, in Scotland.   41 *Aberdour:* Aberdeen, on the east coast of Scotland on the North Sea, about eighty miles north of Dumferline.

    "Sir Patrick Spens" is a **narrative ballad**. A narrative tells a story, and the term *ballad* defines the poem's shape or form. The first two stanzas set up the situation: The king needs a sailor to undertake a vital mission, and an old knight—one of the king's close advisers—suggests the appointment of Sir Patrick Spens. We know that this knight is a powerful adviser since he sits "at the king's right knee."
    The rest of the poem focuses on the feelings and eventual death of Sir Patrick and his men. The third stanza provides a transition from the king to Sir Patrick. The king writes a letter ordering Sir Patrick to sea, and Sir Patrick reads it. On reading the first line, Sir Patrick laughs—maybe because the king begins by flattering him, or maybe because Sir Patrick at first believes that an order to go to sea at an obvious time of danger is nothing more than a grim joke. But when he reads the next line and realizes that the order is real, he foresees disaster. Our sense of impending calamity is increased when we learn that Sir Patrick's crew is also frightened (lines 23–28).
    The shipwreck, described in stanza 8, is presented with ironic understatement. There is no description of the storm or of the crew's panic, nor does the speaker describe the masts splitting or the ship sinking under the waves. Although these horrors are omitted, the floating hats are grim evidence of destruction and death. The remainder of the poem continues in this vein of understatement. In stanzas 9 and 10 the focus shifts back to the land, and to the ladies who will wait a "long, long" time (forever) for Sir Patrick and his men to return. The poem ends with a vision of Sir Patrick and the "Scots lords" lying "fifty fathom deep."
    On first reflection, "Sir Patrick Spens" tells a sad tale without complications. The subject seems to describe no more than Sir Patrick's unfortunate drowning, along with his crew and the Scots noblemen. One might therefore claim that the poem does not have a clear theme. Even the understated irony of the floating hats and the waiting ladies is straightforward and unambiguous.
    However, you might consider what the poem suggests about the contradictions and conflicts between authority and individuals. Sir Patrick knows the danger, yet he still obeys the king. In addition, there is a suggestion in lines 5 and 32 of political infighting. The "eldern knight" is in effect responsible for dooming the ship. Moreover, the "play" being "played" suggests that a political game is taking place over and beyond the grim game of the men caught in the deadly storm (if Sir Patrick knows the danger, would not the knight

also know it, and would this knight not also know the consequences of choosing Sir Patrick?). These political motives are not spelled out, but are implied.
Thus the poem is not only a sad tale, but is also a poignant dramatization of
how power operates, of how a loyal person responds to a tragic dilemma, and
of the pitiful consequences of that response.

In reading poetry, then, let the poem be your guide. Get all the words,
try to understand dramatic situations, follow the emotional cues the poet gives
you, and try to explain everything that is happening. If you find implications
that you believe are important (as with the political overtones of "Sir Patrick
Spens") use specific details from the poem to support your observations. Resist the temptation to "uncover" unusual or far-fetched elements in the poem
(as a student once did by claiming that Frost's "Stopping by Woods on a Snowy
Evening" is a celebration of Santa Claus, stopping on Christmas Eve for a
brief rest before carrying out his mission to deliver presents throughout the
world). Draw only those conclusions that the poem itself will support.

 POEMS FOR STUDY

EMILY DICKINSON   (1830–1886)

Because I Could Not Stop for Death ———————— *1890 (ca. 1863)*

Because I could not stop for Death–
He kindly stopped for me–
The Carriage held but just Ourselves–
And Immortality.

We slowly drove–He knew no haste   5
And I had put away
My labor and my leisure too,
For His Civility–

We passed the School, where Children strove
At Recess–in the Ring–   10
We passed the Fields of Gazing Grain–
We passed the Setting Sun–

Or rather–He passed Us–
The Dews drew quivering and chill–
For only Gossamer,° my Gown–   *thin fabric*   15
My Tippet°–only Tulle°–   *cape, scarf; thin silk*

We passed before a House that seemed
A Swelling of the Ground–
The Roof was scarcely visible–
The Cornice–in the Ground–   20

Since then–'tis Centuries–and yet
Feels shorter than the Day
I first surmised the Horses' Heads
Were toward Eternity–

QUESTIONS

1. Who is the speaker and what is she like? Why couldn't she stop for death? What perspective does her present position give the poem?

2. In what unusual ways does the poem characterize death?

3. What does the carriage represent? Where is it headed? Who are the riders? What is meant by the things the carriage passes?

4. What is represented by the house in line 17? Why does the poet use the word *house* in preference to some other word?

ROBERT FROST (1874–1963)

Stopping By Woods on a Snowy Evening _____ *1923*

Whose woods these are I think I know.
His house is in the village though;
He will not see me stopping here
To watch his woods fill up with snow.

My little horse must think it queer
To stop without a farmhouse near
Between the woods and frozen lake
The darkest evening of the year.

He gives his harness bells a shake
To ask if there is some mistake.
The only other sound's the sweep
Of easy wind and downy flake.

The woods are lovely, dark and deep,
But I have promises to keep,
And miles to go before I sleep,
And miles to go before I sleep.

QUESTIONS

1. What do we learn about the speaker? Where is he? What is he doing?

2. What is the setting (place, weather, time) of this poem?

3. Why does the speaker want to watch the "woods fill up with snow"?

4. What evidence suggests that the speaker is embarrassed or self-conscious about stopping? Consider the words *though* in line 2 and *must* in line 5.
5. The last stanza offers two alternative attitudes and courses of action. What are they? Which does the speaker choose?
6. To what extent do the sound and rhyme of this poem contribute to its impact? Note especially the *s* sounds in line 11 and the *w* sounds in line 12.

THOMAS HARDY   (1840–1928)

The Man He Killed —————————————————————— *1902*

"Had he and I but met
  By some old ancient inn,
We should have sat us down to wet
  Right many a nipperkin!°   *half-pint cup*

"But ranged as infantry,   5
  And staring face to face,
I shot at him as he at me,
  And killed him in his place.

"I shot him dead because—
  Because he was my foe.   10
Just so: my foe of course he was;
  That's clear enough; although

"He thought he'd 'list,° perhaps,   *enlist*
  Off-hand like—just as I—
Was out of work—had sold his traps°—   *possessions*   15
  No other reason why.

"Yes; quaint and curious war is!
  You shoot a fellow down
You'd treat if met where any bar is,
  Or help to half-a-crown."°   20

THE MAN HE KILLED.   20 *half a crown*: today about 40 cents, but at the time, the equivalent of $10 or $20.

QUESTIONS

1. Who and what is the speaker? What do you learn about him from his language?
2. What situation and event is the speaker recalling and relating?
3. What is the effect produced by repeating the word *because* in lines 9 and 10 and using the word *although* in line 12?
4. What is the speaker's attitude toward his "foe" and toward what he has done?

5. What point, if any, does this poem make about war? How are this poem and Jarrell's "The Death of the Ball Turret Gunner" similar and different?

A. E. HOUSMAN   (1859–1936)

Loveliest of Trees, the Cherry Now ————————————————*1896*

Loveliest of trees, the cherry now
Is hung with bloom along the bough,
And stands about the woodland ride°   path
Wearing white for Eastertide.

Now, of my threescore years and ten,
Twenty will not come again,
And take from seventy springs a score,
It only leaves me fifty more.

And since to look at things in bloom
Fifty springs are little room,
About the woodland I will go
To see the cherry hung with snow.

QUESTIONS

1. How old is the speaker? How can you tell? Why does he assume he will live seventy years ("threescore years and ten")?

2. How would you describe the speaker's perception or sense of time? What is the effect of the words *only* (line 8) and *little* (line 10)?

3. What ideas about time, beauty, and life does this poem explore? What does it suggest about the way we should live?

LOUIS MACNEICE (1907–1963)

Snow ————————————————————— *1935*

The room was suddenly rich and the great bay-window was
Spawning snow and pink roses against it
Soundlessly collateral and incompatible:
World is suddener than we fancy it.

World is crazier and more of it than we think,
Incorrigibly plural. I peel and portion
A tangerine and spit the pips and feel
The drunkenness of things being various.

And the fire flames with a bubbling sound for world
Is more spiteful and gay than one supposes—
On the tongue on the eyes on the ears in the palms of one's hands—
There is more than glass between the snow and the huge roses.

10

QUESTIONS

1. Where is the speaker at the time of the poem? What is the contrast between the roses and the snow? Why is this contrast important?

2. What words describe snow in lines 1–3? What words in lines 4, 5, 6, 8, 10 describe the world generally? Why does the speaker choose these words rather than more descriptive ones?

3. What does the last line suggest?

4. What similarities and differences do you find between "Snow" and Frost's "Stopping by Woods on a Snowy Evening"?

JIM NORTHRUP (b. 1943)

Ogichidag° ———————————————————————— *(1993)*

I was born in war, WW Two.
Listened as the old men told stories
of getting gassed in the trenches, WW One.
Saw my uncles come back from
Guadalcanal, North Africa,   5
and the Battle of the Bulge.
Memorized the war stories
my cousins told of Korea.
Felt the fear in their voices.
Finally it was my turn,   10
my brothers too.
Joined the marines in time
for the Cuban Missile Crisis.
Heard the crack of rifles
in the rice paddies south of Da Nang.   15
Watched my friends die there
then tasted the bitterness of
the only war America ever lost.
My son is now a warrior.
Will I listen to his war stories   20
or cry into his open grave?

OGICHIDAG: The title is the Ojibway word for warriors.

QUESTIONS

1. What battles are mentioned in the poem, and over what period of time do these battles extend?
2. How does the speaker state that he learned about the battles? Why is this method of gaining knowledge important? What experience has the speaker had with war?
3. Why does the speaker finish the poem by referring to his son? In relationship to the poem's structure, why is the concluding question important?

WILLIAM SHAKESPEARE (1564–1616)

Sonnet 55:
Not Marble, Nor the Gilded Monuments _____ *1609*

Not marble, nor the gilded monuments
Of princes, shall outlive this powerful rhyme;
But you shall shine more bright in these contents
Than unswept stone, besmeared with sluttish time.
When wasteful war shall statues overturn,
And broils root out the work of masonry,
Nor° Mars his° sword nor war's quick fire shall burn   *Neither; Mars's*
The living record of your memory.
'Gainst death and all-oblivious enmity
Shall you pace forth; your praise shall still find room
Even in the eyes of all posterity
That wear this world out to the ending doom.°   *Judgment day*
So, till the judgment that yourself arise,
You live in this, and dwell in lovers' eyes.

QUESTIONS

1. Who is the speaker of the poem, and who is being addressed?
2. What powers of destruction does the speaker mention? What, according to the speaker, will survive these powers?
3. What does "the living record of your memory" (line 8) mean?
4. What is the poem's subject? Theme?

JAMES WRIGHT (1927–1980)

Two Hangovers _____ *1963*

NUMBER ONE
I slouch in bed.
Beyond the streaked trees of my window,
All groves are bare.

Locusts and poplars change to unmarried women   5
Sorting slate from anthracite
Between railroad ties:
The yellow-bearded winter of the depression
Is still alive somewhere, an old man
Counting his collection of bottle caps   10
In a tarpaper shack under the cold trees
Of my grave.

I still feel half drunk,
And all those old women beyond my window
Are hunching toward the graveyard.   15

Drunk, mumbling Hungarian,
The sun staggers in,
And his big stupid face pitches
Into the stove.
For two hours I have been dreaming   20
Of green butterflies searching for diamonds

In coal seams;
And children chasing each other for a game
Through the hills of fresh graves.
But the sun has come home drunk from the sea,   25
And a sparrow outside
Sings of the Hanna Coal Co. and the dead moon.
The filaments of cold light bulbs tremble
In music like delicate birds.
Ah, turn it off.   30

NUMBER TWO: I TRY TO WAKEN AND GREET THE WORLD ONCE AGAIN
In a pine tree,
A few yards away from my window sill,
A brilliant blue jay is springing up and down, up and down,
On a branch.   35
I laugh, as I see him abandon himself
To entire delight, for he knows as well as I do
That the branch will not break.

QUESTIONS

1. What do we learn about the speaker in hangover "Number One"? What is his
    physical condition? Where is he? What is he trying to do?

2. How does the speaker's condition affect the way he views the trees outside his
    window? The world? His own life?

3. Do you think the sun really "staggers in" and falls "into the stove"? What does
    the sun stand for in "Number One"?

4. Find all the images of death and desolation that you can in "Number One."
    Why do you suppose these images are so dominant?

5. Why is hangover "Number Two" so much shorter than "Number One"?

6. How does the speaker's mood and perspective change from "Number One" to "Number Two"? How do you account for this shift?

WRITING A PARAPHRASE OF A POEM

Paraphrasing is especially useful in the study of poetry. It fixes both the general shape and the details of a poem in your mind, and also reveals the poetic devices at work. A comparison of the original poem with the paraphrase highlights the techniques and the language that make the poem effective.

To paraphrase a poem, rewrite it in prose, in your own words. Decide what details to include—an amount that you determine partly by the length of the poem and partly by the total length of your paraphrase. When you deal with lyrics, sonnets, and other short poems, you may include all the details, and thus your paraphrase may be as long as the work, or longer. Paraphrases of long poems, however, will be shorter than the originals because some details must be summarized briefly while others may be cut out entirely.

It is vital to make your paraphrase accurate, and also to use *only your own words.* To make sure that your words are all your own, read through the poem several times. Then, put the poem out of sight and write your paraphrase. Once you've finished, check yourself both for accuracy and vocabulary. If you find that you've borrowed too many of the poem's words, choose other words that mean the same, or else use quotation marks to set off the original words (but do not overuse quotations).

Above all, remain faithful to the poem, but *avoid drawing conclusions and making unnecessary explanations.* It would be wrong in a paraphrase of "The Death of the Ball Turret Gunner," for example, to state that "this poem makes a forceful argument against the brutal and wasteful deaths caused by war." This assertion states the poem's *theme,* but it *does not* describe the poem's actual *content.*

Organizing your Paraphrase

The organization of your paraphrase should reflect the poem's form or development. Include material in the order in which it occurs. With short poems, organize your paraphrase to reflect the poem's development line by line or stanza by stanza. In paraphrasing Shakespeare's "Not Marble, nor the Gilded Monuments," for example, you should deal with each quatrain in sequence and then consider the final couplet. With longer poems, look for natural divisions like groups of related stanzas, verse paragraphs, or other possible organizational units. In every situation, the poem's shape should determine the form of your paraphrase.

FIRST SAMPLE ESSAY

A Paraphrase of Thomas Hardy's "The Man He Killed"

[1] If the man I killed had met me in an inn, we would have sat down together and had many drinks. Because we belonged to armies of warring foot soldiers lined up on a battlefield, however, we shot at each other, and my shot killed him.

[2] The reason I killed him, I think, was that he and I were enemies--just that. But as I think of it, I realize that he had enlisted in just the way I did. Perhaps he did it on a whim, or perhaps he had lost his job and sold everything he owned. There was no other reason to enlist.

[3] Being at war is unusual and strange. Instead of buying a man a drink, or helping him out with half a crown, you have to kill him.

Commentary on the Essay

Because Hardy's poem is short, the paraphrase attempts to include all its details. The organization closely follows the poem's development. Paragraph 1, for example, restates the contents of the first two stanzas. Paragraph 2 restates stanzas three and four. Finally, the last paragraph paraphrases the last stanza. This stanza has a separate paragraph because it contains the reflections made by the poem's "I" speaker. It concludes the paraphrase just as the last stanza concludes the poem.

Notice that the sample essay does not (a) abstract details from the poem, such as "The dead man might have become a good friend in peacetime" for stanza 5, or (b) extend details, such as "We would have gotten acquainted, had drinks together, told many stories, and done quite a bit of laughing" for stanza 1 (even though both stanzas suggest these details). Although the paragraph reflects the poem's strong anti-war sentiments, an interpretive sentence like "By his very directness, the narrator brings out the senselessness and brutality of warfare" would be out of place. What is needed is a short restatement of the poem to demonstrate the essay-writer's understanding of the poem's content, and no more.

WRITING AN EXPLICATION OF A POEM

Explication goes beyond the assimilation required for a paraphrase, and thus provides you with the opportunity to show your understanding. There is no need, however, to explain everything in the poem. A complete, or total, explication would theoretically require you to explain the meaning and implications of each word and every line—a technique that obviously would be exhaustive (and exhausting). It would also be self-defeating, for explicating everything would prohibit you from using your judgment and deciding what is important.

A more manageable and desirable technique is therefore the **general explication**, which devotes attention to the meaning of individual parts in relationship to the entire work, as in the previous discussion of "Sir Patrick Spens" (p. 554). You might think of a *general explication* as your explanation or "reading," of the poem. Because it does not require you to go into exhaustive detail, you will need to be selective and to consider only those details which are significant in themselves and vital to your own thematic development.

Questions for Discovering Ideas

- What does the title contribute to the reader's understanding?
- Who is speaking? Where is the speaker when the poem is happening?
- What is the situation? What has happened in the past, or what is happening in the present, that has brought about the speech?
- What difficult, special, or unusual words does the poem contain? What references need explaining? How does an explanation assist in the understanding of the poem?
- How does the poem develop? Is it a personal statement? Is it a story?
- What is the main idea of the poem? What details make possible the formulation of the main idea?

Strategies for Organizing Ideas

Your general explication demonstrates your ability (a) to follow the essential details of the poem (the same as in a paraphrase), (b) to understand the issues and the meaning the poem reveals, (c) to explain some of the relationships of content to technique, and (d) to note and discuss especially important or unique aspects of the poem.

In your introduction, use your central idea to express a general view of the poem, which your essay will bear out. The discussion of "Sir Patrick Spens" above suggests some possible central ideas, namely that (1) the poem highlights a conflict between self preservation and obedience to authority, and (2) innocent people may be caught in political infighting. In the sample essay explicating Hardy's "The Man He Killed," the central idea is that war is senseless.

In the body of your essay, first explain the poem's content—not a paraphrase, but a description of the poem's major organizing elements. Hence, if the speaker of the poem is "inside" the poem as a first-person involved "I," you do not need to reproduce this voice yourself in your description, as with the sample essay paraphrasing "The Man He Killed." Instead, *describe* the poem in your own words, with whatever brief introductory phrases you find necessary, as in the second paragraph of the following sample essay.

Next, explicate the poem in relationship to your central idea. *You* choose *your own* order of discussion, depending on your topics. You should, however, keep stressing your central idea with each new topic. Thus, you may wish to follow your description by discussing the poem's meaning, or even by presenting two or more possible interpretations. You might also wish to refer to significant techniques. For example, in "Sir Patrick Spens" a noteworthy technique is the unintroduced quotations (i.e., quotations appearing without any "he said" or "quoth he" phrases) as the ballad writer's means of dramatizing the commands and responses of Sir Patrick and his doomed crew.

You might also introduce special topics, like the crewman who explains that there will be bad luck because the new moon has "the old moon in her arm" (line 26). Such a reference to superstition might include the explanation of the crewman's assumptions, the relationship of his uneasiness to the remainder of the poem, and also how the ballad writer keeps the narrative brief. In short, discuss those aspects of meaning and technique that bear upon your central idea.

In your conclusion, you may repeat your major idea to reinforce your essay's thematic structure. Because your essay is a general explication, there will be parts of the poem that you will not have discussed. You might therefore mention what might be gained from an exhaustive discussion of various parts of the poem (do not, however, begin to exhaust any subject in the conclusion of an essay). The last stanza of Hardy's "The Man He Killed," for example, contains the words "quaint and curious" in reference to war. These words are unusual, particularly because the speaker might have chosen "hateful," "senseless," "destructive," or other similarly descriptive words. Why did Hardy have his speaker make such a choice? With brief attention to such a problem, you may conclude.

SECOND SAMPLE ESSAY

An Explication of Hardy's "The Man He Killed"°

[1]   Thomas Hardy's "The Man He Killed" exposes the senselessness of war.* It does this through a silent contrast between the needs of ordinary people, as represented by a young man--the speaker--who has killed an enemy soldier in battle, and the anti-human and unnatural deaths of war. Of major note in this contrast are the speaker's circumstances, his language, his sense of identity with the dead man, and his concerns and wishes.†

[2]   The speaker begins by contrasting the circumstances of warfare with those of peace. He does not identify himself, but his speech reveals that he is an ordinary sort--a person, one of "the people"--who enjoys drinking in a bar and who prefers friendship and helpfulness to violence. If he and the man he killed had met in an inn, he says, they would have shared many drinks, but because they met on a battlefield they shot at each other, and he killed the other man. The speaker tries to justify the killing, but can produce no stronger rea-

° For this poem, see p. 557.
* Central idea.
† Thesis sentence.

son than that the dead man was his "foe." Once he states this reason, he again thinks of the similarities between himself and the dead man, and then concludes that warfare is "quaint and curious" (line 17) because one is forced to kill a person he would have befriended if they had met during a time of peace.

[3]
    To make the irony of warfare clear, the poem uses easy, colloquial language to bring out the speaker's ordinary qualities. His manner of speech is conversational, as in "We should have sat us down" (line 3), and "'list" (for "enlist," line 13), and his use of "you" in the last stanza. Also, his word choices, shown in words like "nipperkin," "traps," and "fellow" (lines 4, 15, and 18), are common and informal. This language is important, because it establishes that the speaker is an ordinary man who has been thrown into an unnatural role because of war.

[4]
    As another means of stressing the grim stupidity of war, the poem makes clear that the two men--the live soldier who killed and the dead soldier who was killed--were so alike that they could have been brothers or even twins. They had similar ways of life, similar economic troubles, similar wishes to help other people, and similar motives in doing things like enlisting in the army. Symbolically, at least, the "man he killed" is the speaker himself, and hence the killing is a form of suicide. The poem thus raises the question of why two people who are almost identical should be shoved into opposing battle lines in order to try killing each other. This question is rhetorical, for the obvious answer is that there is no good reason at all.

[5]
    Because the speaker (and also, very likely, the dead man) is shown as a person embodying the virtues of friendliness and helpfulness, Hardy's poem is a strong disapproval of war. Clearly, political reasons for violence as policy are irrelevant to the characters and concerns of the men who fight. They, like the speaker, would prefer to follow their own needs rather than distant and nameless political leaders. The failure of complex but irrelevant political explanations is brought out most clearly in the third stanza, in which the speaker tries to give a reason for shooting the other man. Hardy's use of punctuation--the dashes--stresses the fact that the speaker has no commitment to the cause he served when killing. Thus the speaker stops at the word "because--" and gropes for a good reason (line 9). Not being articulate, he can say only "Because he was my foe. / Just so: my foe of course he was; / That's clear enough" (lines 10–12). These short bursts of words indicate that he cannot explain things to himself or to anyone else except in the most obvious and trite terms, and in apparent embarrassment he inserts "of course" as a way of emphasizing hostility even though he felt none toward the man he killed.

[6]
    A reading thus shows the power of the poem's dramatic argument. Hardy does not establish closely detailed reasons against war as a policy, but rather dramatizes the idea that all political arguments are unimportant in view of the central and glaring brutality of war--killing. Hardy's speaker is not able to express deep feelings; rather he is confused because he is an average sort who wants only to live and let live and to enjoy a drink in a bar with friends. But this very commonness stresses the point that everyone is victimized by war--both those who die and those who kill. The poem is a powerful argument for peace and reconciliation.

Commentary on the Essay

This explication begins by stating a central idea about "The Man He Killed," and then indicates the topics to follow that will develop the idea. Although nowhere does the speaker state that war is senseless, the essay takes the position that the poem embodies this idea. A more detailed examination of the poem's themes might develop the idea by contrasting the ways in which individuals are caught up in social and political forces, or the contrast between individuality and the state. In this essay, however, the simple statement of the idea is enough.

Paragraph 2 describes the major details of the poem, with guiding words like "the speaker begins," "he says," and "he again thinks." Thus the paragraph goes over the poem, like a paraphrase, but explains how things occur, as is appropriate for an explication. Paragraph 3 is devoted to the speaker's words and idioms, with the idea that his conversational manner is part of the poem's contrasting method of argument. If the stylistic analysis were to be more detailed, this topic could be more fully developed as an aspect of Hardy's implied argument against war.

Paragraph 4 extends paragraph 3 inasmuch as it points out the similarities of the speaker and the man he killed. If the situation were reversed, in other words, the dead man might say exactly the same things about the present speaker. This affinity underscores the suicidal nature of war. Paragraph 5 treats the style of the poem's fourth stanza. In this context, the treatment is brief. The last paragraph reiterates the main idea, and concludes with a tribute to the poem as an argument.

The entire essay, therefore, represents a reading and explanation of the poem's high points. It stresses a particular interpretation and briefly shows how various aspects of the poem bear it out.

WRITING TOPICS

1. Skim the titles of poems listed in the table of contents of this book. Judging by the subjects of these poems, describe and discuss the possible range of subject matter for poetry. What topics seem most suitable? Why? Do any topics seem to be ruled out? Why? What additional subject matter would you suggest as possible topics for poems?

2. How accurate is the often-articulated proposition that poetry is a particularly compressed form of expression? To support your position, you might refer to poems such as "The Man He Killed," "Snow," and "Stopping by Woods on a Snowy Evening."

3. Consider the subject of war as brought out in "The Death of the Ball Turret Gunner," "The Man He Killed," and "Ogichidag." What ideas are common to the poems? What ideas are distinct and unique? On the basis of your comparison, consider the use of poetry as a vehicle for the expression of moral and political ideas.

4. Write two poems of your own about your future plans. In one, assume that the world is stable, and will go on forever. In the other, assume the news that a large asteroid is out of orbit and is hurtling toward earth at great speed, and that a collision, expected in six months, will bring untold destruction and perhaps even end life on earth. After composing your poems, write a brief explanation of how and why they differ in terms of language, references, attitudes toward friends, family, country, religion, and so on.

5. Consult the brief section on the "Reader Response" approach to literary criticism in Appendix D. Then write an essay about your responses to one poem, or a number of poems, in this chapter. Assume that your own experiences are valuable guides for your judgment. In the poems that you have read, what has had a bearing on your experiences? What in your own experiences has given you insights into the poems? Try to avoid being anecdotal; instead, try to find a relationship between your experiences and the poetry.

14

Characters and Setting: Who, What, Where, and When in Poetry

Poets, like other writers, bring their works alive through the interactions of fictional characters who experience love and hatred, pleasure and pain, and most of the other conditions and situations of life. Just as in fiction, poetic characters are defined by what they say, what they do, and how they react, and also by what other characters say about them. Not all poetry is narrative, however; hence we will study character in poems in relation to someone or something else—such as the interactions of speakers with listeners or with the reader, the inner conflicts of a speaker discussing the state of his or her spirit, and conditions such as love, hate, acceptance, disagreement, emulation, decision making, and action that are brought out in personal, social, and political life.

In addition, we will examine the *setting* of a poem as one of the major means of measuring character (see also Chapter 6). Poetic protagonists, like those in stories, are necessarily influenced by their possessions, the places they inhabit, and the times in which they live. Poems therefore abound with references to events and situations, and also to objects such as beaches, forests, battlefields, graveyards, teaspoons, melons, museums, and paintings. In fiction, however, we consider setting in a number of different ways, whereas in poetry we focus on the interactions of character with object, place, and time. The period that people have spent in a relationship, their relative wealth or poverty, their social and economic circumstances—all have a bearing on their characters.

CHARACTERS IN POETRY

The Speaker or Persona

The most significant character in poetry is the *speaker*, also called the *persona* (plural *personae*, a term that comes from the Etruscan-Latin word meaning "mask"). In prose fiction, we also use "speaker" and "persona," but we often prefer the word *narrator* because of the obvious role of storyteller. This distinction emphasizes the personal and psychological importance of poetic speakers. Sometimes the speaker is a distinct character, with individual traits and well-imagined circumstances, as with the speakers in "My Last Duchess," "Wellfleet Sabbath," and "The Passionate Shepherd to His Love." In Emily Dickinson's "Because I Could Not Stop for Death," for example (p. 555), the speaker is unique, for she states that she has been dead for hundreds of years and is now looking back from eternity to the moment of her death.

Not all poetic speakers have separate identities, for some embody a position or stance that the poet selects to present detail or advance an argument. The poet is thus the undeniable speaker, but the voice we hear may be considered as a brief dramatization of the poet's personality or need. John Donne in his Holy Sonnets adopts such a stance—a suppliant or penitent praying for divine favor (pp. 615 and 874–75). In these sonnets it is clear that Donne is not creating a separate dramatic character in deep religious anguish, but is expressing many of his own hopes and fears.

Expectedly, poets use many sorts of speakers to voice their poems. In this anthology, for example, there are poems spoken by kings and dukes, husbands and wives, lovers and killers, shepherds and secretaries, believers and non-believers, adults and children, and almost every other kind of person you can imagine. In addition, you meet speakers who are mythological heroes and heroines, skeletons, ordinary persons, machines, philosophers, lovers, former slaves, and ghosts. In fact, speakers do not have to be human; they can be animals, clouds, buildings, computers, or whatever the poet's imagination may create.

INSIDE SPEAKERS.   It is important to discover whether the poetic speaker is *inside* or *outside* the poem. In other words, what **point of view** does the poet use? (Point of view in fiction is the subject of Chapter 5.) The speaker is *inside* the poem if the point of view is first person. Here is such a poem, written by an unknown poet:

Western Wind, When Will Thou Blow? ——————————— *Fifteenth century?*

Western wind, when will thou blow?
The small rain down can rain?
Christ, if my love were in my arms,
And I in my bed again.

In this poem the "my" and "I" pronouns indicate that the speaker is *inside* the poem speaking in the first person, wishing for warm spring rains and the renewal of life and love that is signaled by spring.

OUTSIDE SPEAKERS.   The speaker is outside the poem, however, if the third person is used. In such poems, the speaker is not involved with the action; he or she simply describes what is happening to others, as with this anonymous Scots ballad:

Bonny George Campbell ———————————————— *Late Sixteenth Century*

High upon Highlands
   And low upon Tay,°
Bonny George Campbell
   Rode out on a day.

But toom° came his saddle,   *empty*   5
   All bloody to see,
Oh, home came his good horse,
   But never came he.

Down came his old mother,
   Greeting full sair°   *weeping full sore*   10
And down came his bonny wife,
   Wringing her hair.

Saddled, and bridled,
   And booted rode he;
And home came his good horse,   15
   But never came he.

"My meadow lies green,
   And my corn is unshorn,°   *grain is not harvested*
My barn is to build°   *yet to be built*
   And my babe is unborn."   20

Saddled, and bridled,
   And booted rode he;
Toom home came the saddle,
   But never came he.

BONNY GEORGE CAMPBELL   2 *Tay:* Loch Tay, a lake in Perth County, in central Scotland, about sixty miles north of Glasgow.

QUESTIONS

1. What can you deduce about the character, social status, way of life, and feelings of the three persons mentioned in the poem?
2. Why must you infer the exact nature of what happened to Bonny George Campbell?
3. Who is the speaker of the fifth stanza? What effect has Campbell's absence had on this speaker?

In this ballad the speaker limits his or her perspective to the people left behind, who loved Campbell. They do not know his fate beyond what they learn from the bloody saddle—nor do we—because the speaker does not tell us. However, the speaker does describe the effects upon Campbell's mother and wife, even quoting the wife's lamentation because Campbell's death has deprived her of husband and breadwinner. By avoiding entering the poem as an "I," the speaker maintains objectivity and lets the details speak for themselves.

OTHER INFORMATION ABOUT SPEAKERS.   There is a great deal more to learn about poetic speakers. An obvious place to begin is the title. Take, for example, Marlowe's "The Passionate Shepherd to His Love" (p. 587), which reveals that the speaker is a shepherd and that he is passionately in love.

We can also learn from the speaker's diction. For example, in Housman's "Loveliest of Trees" (p. 558), the speaker reveals that he is twenty years old, that he doesn't think his remaining fifty years (assuming a lifetime of seventy years, the Biblical life expectancy) will give him enough time to experience and observe life fully, that he enjoys the flowering of spring, that he knows enough about Church rituals to claim that the whiteness of cherry blossoms coincides with the liturgical color of white for Easter, and that he is meditative and somber rather than extroverted and hilarious. All this is quite a bit of information from so short a poem.

If we look at all poems with the same care, we will discover many other details. Grammatical forms and word levels may define the speaker's social class or educational level. Similarly, the selection of topics may indicate the speaker's emotional state, self-esteem, knowledge, attitudes, habits, hobbies, and much more.

The Listener

The second type of character in poetry is the **listener**—a person, not the reader, whom a speaker addresses directly and who is therefore "inside" the poem. Occasionally we find poems in the form of a **dialogue** between two persons, so that the characters are *both* speakers and listeners, as in Hardy's "The Workbox" (p. 683). Whatever the form, the speaker-listener relationship creates drama and tension. In effect, we as readers are an audience, hearing either conversational exchanges or one-way conversations. The speakers of course identify themselves with the "I" pronoun, and address their listeners with the pronouns "thou-thy-thee" and "you-your-yours."

In some poems the listener is passive, merely hearing the speaker's words without response, as in Marlowe's "The Passionate Shepherd to His Love" and Raleigh's "The Nymph's Reply to the Shepherd" (included in this chapter's Poems for Study). In a variation of this situation, the listener may not be present, but may instead be the speaker's intended recipient. In this case the speaker is like a letter writer and the listener is the "addressee." Such a listener is the "thou-thee-thine" of Ben Jonson's well-known "Drink to Me, Only, with Thine Eyes":

BEN JONSON   (1573–1637)

Drink to Me, Only, with Thine Eyes ———————————————— *1616*

Drink to me, only, with thine eyes,
  And I will pledge° with mine;   *drink a toast*
Or leave a kiss but in the cup,
  And I'll not look for wine.
The thirst that from the soul doth rise   5
  Doth ask a drink divine:
But might I of Jove's nectar° sup
  I would not change° for thine.   *exchange it [i.e., nectar]*

I sent thee, late, a rosy wreath,
  Not so much honoring thee,   10
As giving it a hope, that there
  It could not withered be.
But thou thereon did'st only breathe,
  And sent'st it back to me:
Since when° it grows, and smells, I swear,   *that time, then*   15
  Not of itself, but thee.

DRINK TO ME, ONLY, WITH THINE EYES.   7 *Jove's nectar:* Jove, or Jupiter, was the principal
Roman god. Nectar (a word meaning "overcoming death") was the drink of the gods; a human
being who drank it would become immortal.

QUESTIONS

1. Who is the speaker? What do you learn about him, his knowledge, his wit, and
   his concern for the listener?
2. What has the speaker sent to the listener? What did she do, and why is he still
   writing to her?
3. How may the poem be seen as an attempt to "top" the listener's disdain? Explain why the speaker seems just as interested in showing his wittiness as in complimenting the listener.

This poem demonstrates that the listener has not been passive; she has
returned the speaker's gift, and thus has spurned him. Therefore the poem
may be seen at least partly as the speaker's attempt, by demonstrating his wit,
to ingratiate himself once again with the listener. In similar poems involving
a speaker and a silent listener, we should be prepared to consider both the
dramatic situation and the listener's stated and implied responses.

A related but distinct type of situation involving a listener is the **dramatic
monologue**, in which the speaker talks directly to an on-the-spot listener whose
reactions may directly affect the course of the poem. Browning's "My Last
Duchess" is such a poem (p. 578), in which the speaker, the Duke, addresses

the "you" listener who has been given the task of arranging financial terms about the dowry to be given by the "Count" when the Duke marries the Count's daughter.

Ultimately, we as readers are the listeners of all poems. In this capacity we are the poet's uninvolved, outside audience. Sometimes, however, the poet may address us directly in our role as readers, as in this brief dedicatory poem that Ben Jonson uses to begin his book of epigrams published in 1616:

To the Reader _____ *1616*

Pray thee, take care, that tak'st my book in hand,
To read it well: that is, to understand.

In this couplet Jonson establishes intimacy with us by using the second-person singular pronoun "thee." Though we are clearly *outside* the poem, Jonson invites us *inside* by asking us to read well and understand all his forthcoming poems. As much as a poet can, he therefore closes the distance that sometimes exists between poem and reader.

Only rarely do poets address us directly, as Jonson does. For this reason it is important to determine what is meant when a poet uses the "you" pronoun. Often the "you" may refer to the speaker himself or herself, and not to listeners or to us as readers (see also Chapter 5, p. 184). The speaker of Hardy's "The Man He Killed," for example, uses such a conversational *you* as a reference to himself and to people generally (p. 557). Similarly, Richard Hugo's "Degrees of Gray in Philipsburg" (p. 585) begins "You might come here Sunday on a whim." The *you* in this poem is neither the reader nor an inside listener. Rather it is an oblique or indirect way for the speaker to talk about himself. Most of the time, in other words, we are not so much listeners as spectators. In poems like Hardy's "The Workbox" and Browning's "My Last Duchess," we are almost literally an audience, whereas in a poem like Housman's "Loveliest of Trees," we are outside listeners, eavesdropping as the speaker meditates on time, death, and beauty.

Participants, Major and Minor

Because poetry is dramatic, it often involves a third type of character—major or minor participants. We learn about these characters from appearance, speech, action, and reaction. In "Sir Patrick Spens" (p. 553), for example, we learn from Sir Patrick's outcry that he is distressed, but from his action that he is obedient. In "Channel Firing," we learn that the ages-old skeletons are sorry that they sacrificed personal enjoyment when they were alive because their stringent living did nothing to improve the lot of humankind.

Most poetic speakers are reliable reporters about the actions and characters of the major and minor participants. For example, the speaker of "Sir

Patrick Spens" is honest and straightforward, and his assessment of Sir Patrick is reliable. But we should also be aware that poetic speakers may have interests beyond those of reportorial accuracy, as in all fiction. In Hardy's "The Workbox" the speaker is a suspicious husband whose ironic words declare his suspicion. A speaker who uses descriptive language for distortion and intimidation is the Duke in "My Last Duchess." This poem makes clear that the Duke is a monstrous liar and that we must look beyond his distortions to learn the character of the Duchess and the nature of his life.

Not all participants, of course, are human. Poets frequently include descriptions of the animal kingdom, such as swimmers (sharks, large game fish), flyers (e.g., orioles, nightingales), and walkers and runners (e.g., bears, deer, lambs, and tigers). Although some of these animals are given character traits (as with the horse in Frost's "Stopping by Woods on a Snowy Evening" and the boobies in Tate's "The Blue Booby"), they are mainly pictorial or symbolic.

SETTING AND CHARACTER IN POETRY

The people in poetry do not exist in a vacuum. When they speak, and act, they reflect the time, place, thought, social conventions, and general circumstances of their lives. Love poetry, for example, is not about desire alone, but rather about love within the possible ranges provided by culture and environment. Religion, economic circumstances, leisure, and the condition of the natural world may all enter into a lover's pronouncements. Thus, the speaker of "The Passionate Shepherd to His Love" (p. 587) daydreams about spending time in open nature with his love, sharing the songs of birds and the sights of "valleys, groves, hills, and fields." Here the setting of an Arcadian dream world—without work, want, or illness—reinforces his desire. In contrast, the speaker of Hardy's "The Walk" (p. 583) speaks about Nature when his beloved is infirm and can no longer share the view of the "hilltop tree / By the gated ways" that the two enjoyed when the world was young and beautiful for them both. Although both poems are about love, one ignores the reality of age and ill health, while the other confronts it.

Poetic settings also include political, philosophical, and religious thoughts, as in Gray's "Elegy Written in a Country Churchyard" (p. 579). Here the approaching "darkness" causes the speaker to think of the "rude forefathers of the hamlet" in their churchyard graves. This thought leads him to speculate about how death cuts off those who are talented and potentially great. The interaction here is complex, interweaving character and history with natural and cultural situations and images. A poem similarly connecting character and setting is Wordsworth's "Tintern Abbey" Lines. This poem, based on the relationship of the past, present, and future of the speaker to the natural scenes he describes, is a model of how poetic setting and character may be fused.

It is no exaggeration to say that setting interacts with character in endless numbers of ways. Thus the Duke's display of valuable art in "My Last

Duchess" forms a setting which exposes his greed and cruelty. In "London" (p. 577), Blake introduces bleak sights and anguished sounds that evoke a response of repulsion and rejection. As the representation of a philosophical judgment, the setting of Arnold's "Dover Beach" (below) demonstrates changeability and impermanence. The speaker's solution is to establish personal fidelity as a fixture against change, dissolution, and brutality. To greater or lesser degrees, most poems offer similar connections of setting and character.

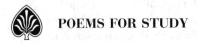

POEMS FOR STUDY

MATTHEW ARNOLD   (1822–1888)

Dover Beach _____ *1867 (1849)*

The sea is calm tonight.
The tide is full, the moon lies fair
Upon the straits—on the French coast the light
Gleams and is gone; the cliffs of England stand,
Glimmering and vast, out in the tranquil bay.
Come to the window, sweet is the night air!
Only, from the long line of spray
Where the sea meets the moon-blanched land,
Listen! you hear the grating roar
Of pebbles which the waves draw back, and fling,
At their return, up the high strand,
Begin, and cease, and then again begin,
With tremulous cadence slow, and bring
The eternal note of sadness in.

Sophocles long ago
Heard it on the Aegean, and it brought
Into his mind the turbid ebb and flow
Of human misery; we
Find also in the sound a thought,
Hearing it by this distant northern sea.

The Sea of Faith
Was once, too, at the full, and round earth's shore
Lay like the folds of a bright girdle furled.
But now I only hear
Its melancholy, long, withdrawing roar,
Retreating, to the breath
Of the night wind, down the vast edges drear
And naked shingles° of the world.   *beaches*

Ah, love, let us be true
To one another! for the world, which seems   30
To lie before us like a land of dreams,
So various, so beautiful, so new,
Hath really neither joy, nor love, nor light,
Nor certitude, nor peace, nor help for pain;
And we are here as on a darkling plain   35
Swept with confused alarms of struggle and flight,
Where ignorant armies clash by night.

QUESTIONS

1. What words and details establish the setting?
2. Where are the speaker and listener? What can they see? Hear?
3. What sort of movement may be topographically traced in the first six lines of the poem, so that the scene finally focuses on the speaker and the listener?
4. What is meant by comparing the English Channel to the Aegean Sea, and relating the Aegean surf to the thought of Sophocles?
5. What faith remains after the loss of religious faith? Defend the claim that the faith is the speaker's commitment to personal fidelity rather than love.

WILLIAM BLAKE   (1757–1827)

London ——————————————————————————— *1794*

I wander thro' each charter'd° street,
Near where the charter'd Thames does flow,
And mark in every face I meet
Marks of weakness, marks of woe.

In every cry of every Man,   5
In every Infant's cry of fear,
In every voice, in every ban,°   *public pronouncement*
The mind-forg'd manacles I hear.

How the Chimney-sweeper's cry
Every blackning Church appalls;°   10
And the hapless Soldier's sigh
Runs in blood down Palace walls.

But most thro' midnight streets I hear
How the youthful Harlot's curse
Blasts the new-born Infant's tear,   15
And blights with plagues the Marriage hearse.

LONDON.   1 *charter'd:* privileged, licensed, authorized.   10 *appalls:* weakens, makes pale, shocks.

QUESTIONS

1. What does London represent to the speaker? How do the persons who live there contribute to the poem's ideas about the state of humanity?
2. What sounds does the speaker mention as a part of the London scene? Characterize these sounds in relation to the poem's main idea.
3. Because of the tension in the poem between civilized activity (as represented in the chartering of the street and the river) and free human impulses, explain how the poem might be considered revolutionary.
4. The poem appeared in *Songs of Experience*, published in 1794. Explain the appropriateness of Blake's including the poem in a collection so named.

ROBERT BROWNING   (1812–1889)

My Last Duchess° _____ 1842

FERRARA

That's my last Duchess painted on the wall,
Looking as if she were alive. I call
That piece a wonder, now: Frà Pandolf's° hands
Worked busily a day, and there she stands.
Will't please you sit and look at her? I said
"Frà Pandolf" by design, for never read
Strangers like you that pictured countenance,
The depth and passion of its earnest glance,
But to myself they turned (since none puts by
The curtain I have drawn for you, but I)
And seemed as they would ask me, if they durst,°   *dared*
How such a glance came there; so, not the first
Are you to turn and ask thus. Sir, 'twas not
Her husband's presence only, called that spot
Of joy into the Duchess' cheek: perhaps
Frà Pandolf chanced to say "Her mantle laps
Over my lady's wrist too much," or "Paint
Must never hope to reproduce the faint
Half-flush that dies along her throat": such stuff
Was courtesy, she thought, and cause enough
For calling up that spot of joy. She had
A heart—how shall I say?—too soon made glad,
Too easily impressed; she liked whate'er
She looked on, and her looks went everywhere.
Sir, 'twas all one! My favor at her breast,
The dropping of the daylight in the West,

MY LAST DUCHESS.   The poem is based on incidents in the life of Alfonso II, Duke of Ferrara, whose first wife died in 1561. Some claimed she was poisoned. The Duke negotiated his second marriage to the daughter of the Count of Tyrol through an agent.   3 *Frà Pandolf:* an imaginary painter who is also a monk.

The bough of cherries some officious fool
Broke in the orchard for her, the white mule
She rode with round the terrace—all and each
Would draw from her alike the approving speech,   30
Or blush, at least. She thanked men—good! but thanked
Somehow—I know not how—as if she ranked
My gift of a nine-hundred-years-old name
With anybody's gift. Who'd stoop to blame
This sort of trifling? Even had you skill   35
In speech—(which I have not)—to make your will
Quite clear to such a one, and say, "Just this
Or that in you disgusts me; here you miss,
Or there exceed the mark"—and if she let
Herself be lessoned so, nor plainly set   40
Her wits to yours, forsooth, and made excuse
—E'en then would be some stooping; and I choose
Never to stoop. Oh sir, she smiled, no doubt,
Whene'er I passed her; but who passed without
Much the same smile? This grew; I gave commands;   45
Then all smiles stopped together. There she stands
As if alive. Will't please you rise? We'll meet
The company below, then. I repeat,
The Count your master's known munificence
Is ample warrant that no just pretense   50
Of mine for dowry will be disallowed;
Though his fair daughter's self, as I avowed
At starting, is my object. Nay, we'll go
Together down, sir. Notice Neptune,° though,
Taming a sea horse, thought a rarity,   55
Which Claus of Innsbruck° cast in bronze for me!

54 *Neptune:* Roman god of the sea.   56 *Claus of Innsbruck:* an imaginary sculptor.

QUESTIONS

1. Describe the speaker. What does he do? What is he like? What does he want?
2. Who is the listener? What is the relationship between speaker and listener?
3. What sort of life does the speaker offer the listener?
4. What is the speaker's understanding of reality?

THOMAS GRAY   (1716–1771)

Elegy Written in a Country Churchyard _____ *1751*

The curfew tolls the knell of parting day,
    The lowing herd wind slowly o'er the lea,
The ploughman homeward plods his weary way,
    And leaves the world to darkness and to me.

Now fades the glimm'ring landscape on the sight,
  And all the air a solemn stillness holds,
Save where the beetle wheels his droning flight,
  And drowsy tinklings lull the distant folds;

Save that from yonder ivy-mantled tower
  The moping owl does to the moon complain
Of such as wand'ring near her secret bower
  Molest her ancient solitary reign.

Beneath those rugged elms, that yew-tree's shade,
  Where heaves the turf in many a mold'ring heap,
Each in his narrow cell forever laid,
  The rude forefathers of the hamlet sleep.

The breezy call of incense-breathing morn,
  The swallow twitt'ring from the straw-built shed,
The cock's shrill clarion, or the echoing horn,°   *hunting horn*
  No more shall rouse them from their lowly bed.

For them no more the blazing hearth shall burn,
  Or busy housewife ply her evening care;
No children run to lisp their sire's return,
  Or climb his knees the envied kiss to share.

Oft did the harvest to their sickle yield,
  Their furrow oft the stubborn glebe° has broke;   *church land*
How jocund did they drive their team afield!
  How bowed the woods beneath their sturdy stroke!

Let not Ambition mock their useful toil
  Their homely joys, and destiny obscure;
Nor Grandeur hear with a disdainful smile
  The short and simple annals of the poor.

The boast of heraldry, the pomp of power,
  And all that beauty, all that wealth e'er gave,
Awaits alike th'inevitable hour.
  The paths of glory lead but to the grave.

Nor you, ye proud, impute to these the fault,
  If mem'ry o'er their tomb no trophies raise,
Where through the long-drawn aisle and fretted vault
  The pealing anthem swells the note of praise.

Can storied urn or animated bust
  Back to its mansion call the fleeting breath?
Can Honor's voice provoke the silent dust,
  Or Flatt'ry soothe the dull cold ear of death?

Perhaps in this neglected spot is laid
  Some heart once pregnant with celestial fire;

Hands that the rod of empire might have swayed,
　　Or waked to ecstasy the living lyre.

But Knowledge to their eyes her ample page
　　Rich with the spoils of time did ne'er unroll;　　　　　　　　50
Chill Penury repressed their noble rage,
　　And froze the genial current of the soul.

Full many a gem of purest ray serene,
　　The dark unfathomed caves of ocean bear;
Full many a flower is born to blush unseen,　　　　　　　　55
　　And waste its sweetness on the desert air.

Some village Hampden,° that with dauntless breast
　　The little tyrant of his fields withstood;
Some mute inglorious Milton here may rest,
　　Some Cromwell guiltless of his country's blood.　　　　　　　　60

Th'applause of list'ning senates to command,
　　The threats of pain and ruin to despise,
To scatter plenty o'er a smiling land,
　　And read their hist'ry in a nation's eyes.

Their lot forbade: nor circumscribed alone　　　　　　　　65
　　Their growing virtues, but their crimes confined;
Forbade to wade through slaughter to a throne,
　　And shut the gates of mercy on mankind,

The struggling pangs of conscious truth to hide,
　　To quench the blushes of ingenuous shame,　　　　　　　　70
Or heap the shrine of luxury and pride
　　With incense kindled at the Muse's flame.

Far from the madding° crowd's ignoble strife,　　　　　　　*raving*
　　Their sober wishes never learned to stray;
Along the cool sequestered vale of life　　　　　　　　75
　　They kept the noiseless tenor of their way.

Yet ev'n these bones from insult to protect
　　Some frail memorial still erected nigh,
With uncouth° rhymes and shapeless sculpture decked,　　　*uneducated, unsophisticated*
　　Implores the passing tribute of a sigh.　　　　　　　　80

Their names, their years, spelt by th'unlettered Muse,
　　The place of fame and elegy supply;
And many a holy text around she strews,
　　That teach the rustic moralist to die.

ELEGY WRITTEN IN A COUNTRY CHURCHYARD.　57 *Hampden:* John Hampden (1594–1643), English statesman who defended the rights of the people against King Charles I and who died in the English Civil War of 1642–1646.

For who to dumb forgetfulness a prey,
   This pleasing anxious being e'er resigned,
Left the warm precincts of the cheerful day,
   Nor cast one longing ling'ring look behind?

On some fond breast the parting soul relies,
   Some pious drops the closing eye requires;
Ev'n from the tomb the voice of Nature cries,
   Ev'n in our ashes live their wonted fires.

For thee, who mindful of th'unhonored dead
   Dost in these lines their artless tale relate;
If chance, by lonely contemplation led,
   Some kindred spirit shall inquire thy fate.

Haply some hoary-headed swain may say,
   "Oft have we seen him at the peep of dawn
Brushing with hasty steps the dews away
   To meet the sun upon the upland lawn.

"There, at the foot of yonder nodding beech
   That wreathes its old fantastic° roots so high,   *natural, following nature*
His listless length at noontide would he stretch
   And pore upon the brook that babbles by.

"Hard by yon wood, now smiling as in scorn,
   Mutt'ring his wayward fancies he would rove,
Now drooping, woeful wan, like one forlorn,
   Or crazed with care, or crossed in hopeless love.

"One morn I missed him on the 'customed hill,
   Along the heath and near his fav'rite tree;
Another came; nor yet beside the rill,
   Nor up the lawn, nor at the wood was he;

"The next with dirges due in sad array
   Slow through the church-way path we saw him borne.
Approach and read (for thou canst read) the lay,
   Graved on the stone beneath yon aged thorn."

THE EPITAPH

Here rests his head upon the lap of earth
   A youth to fortune and to fame unknown;
Fair Science frowned not on his humble birth,
   And Melancholy marked him for her own.

Large was his bounty, and his soul sincere,
   Heav'n did a recompense as largely send:
He gave to mis'ry all he had, a tear:
   He gain'd from Heav'n ('twas all he wished) a friend.

No farther seek his merits to disclose,   125
  Or draw his frailties from their dread abode,
(There they alike in trembling hope repose)
  The bosom of his Father and his God.

QUESTIONS

1. What is the time of day of the speaker's meditation? What is happening in nature
    as the poem opens? Whom is the speaker addressing?

2. Who are the people buried in the church graveyard? What point does Gray make
    about the contributions they might have made if they had not died?

3. How does Gray's use of sights and sounds complement the poem's mood?

4. Who is "thee" (line 93)? What happens to him? Why is he included in the poem?

THOMAS HARDY   (1840–1928)

The Walk _____ *1913*

You did not walk with me
Of late to the hilltop tree
    By the gated ways,
    As in earlier days;
    You were weak and lame,   5
  So you never came,
And I went alone, and I did not mind,
Not thinking of you as left behind.

  I walked up there today
  Just in the former way;   10
    Surveyed around
    The familiar ground
    By myself again:
    What difference, then?
Only that underlying sense   15
Of the look of a room on returning thence.

QUESTIONS

1. What relationship does the speaker have to the person being addressed?

2. Why did the speaker's companion not walk to the hilltop tree? Does the speaker
    admit to being in solitude even though the most recent walk was done alone?
    How does his conclusion reveal his character?

3. Consider the final two lines. What impression do they convey about the location
    where the couple used to walk?

THOMAS HARDY   (1840–1928)

Channel Firing ——————————————————————————————— *1914*

That night your great guns, unawares,
Shook all our coffins° as we lay,
And broke the chancel window-squares,
We thought it was the Judgment Day

And sat upright. While drearisome
Arose the howl of wakened hounds:
The mouse let fall the altar-crumb,
The worms drew back into the mounds,

The glebe° cow drooled. Till God called, "No;
It's gunnery practice out at sea
Just as before you went below;
The world is as it used to be:

"All nations striving strong to make
Red war yet redder. Mad as hatters
They do no more for Christés sake
Than you who are helpless in such matters.

"That this is not the judgment hour
For some of them's a blessed thing,
For if it were they'd have to scour
Hell's floor for so much threatening. . . .

"Ha, ha. It will be warmer when
I blow the trumpet (if indeed
I ever do; for you are men,
And rest eternal sorely need)."

So down we lay again. "I wonder,
Will the world ever saner be,"
Said one, "than when He sent us under
In our indifferent century!"

And many a skeleton shook his head.
"Instead of preaching forty year,"
My neighbor Parson Thirdly said,
"I wish I had stuck to pipes and beer."

Again the guns disturbed the hour,
Roaring their readiness to avenge,
As far inland as Stourton Tower.°
And Camelot,° and starlit Stonehenge.°

CHANNEL FIRING.   2 *coffins:* It has been common practice in England for hundreds of years to bury people in the floors or basements of churches.   9 *glebe:* a parcel of land adjoining and belonging to a church. Cows were grazed there to keep the grass short.   35 *Stourton Tower:* tower commemorating King Alfred the Great's defeat of the Danes in A.D. 879.   36 *Camelot:* legendary seat of King Arthur's court.   *Stonehenge:* group of standing stones on Salisbury Plain, probably built as a place of worship before 1000 B.C.

QUESTIONS

1. Who is the speaker in this poem? What is the setting? The situation?
2. To whom does the *your* in line 1 refer? The *our* in line 2?
3. What has awakened the speaker and his companions? What mistake have they made?
4. What three other voices are heard in the poem? How are their traits revealed?
5. What ideas about war and the nature of humanity does this poem explore?

RICHARD HUGO   (1923–1982)

Degrees of Gray in Philipsburg ———————————————— *1973*

You might come here Sunday on a whim.
Say your life broke down. The last good kiss
you had was years ago. You walk these streets
laid out by the insane, past hotels
that didn't last, bars that did, the tortured try   5
of local drivers to accelerate their lives.
Only churches are kept up. The jail
turned 70 this year. The only prisoner
is always in, not knowing what he's done.

The principal supporting business now   10
is rage. Hatred of the various grays
the mountain sends, hatred of the mill,
The Silver Bill repeal, the best liked girls
who leave each year for Butte. One good
restaurant and bars can't wipe the boredom out.   15
The 1907 boom, eight going silver mines,
a dance floor built on springs—
all memory resolves itself in gaze,
in panoramic green you know the cattle eat
on two stacks high above the town,   20
two dead kilns, the huge mill in collapse
for fifty years that won't fall finally down.

Isn't this your life? That ancient kiss
still burning out your eyes? Isn't this defeat
so accurate, the church bell simply seems   25
a pure announcement: ring and no one comes?
Don't empty houses ring? Are magnesium
and scorn sufficient to support a town,
not just Philipsburg, but towns
of towering blondes, good jazz and booze   30
the world will never let you have
until the town you came from dies inside?

Say no to yourself. The old man, twenty
when the jail was built, still laughs
although his lips collapse. Someday soon,
he says, I'll go to sleep and not wake up.
You tell him no. You're talking to yourself.
The car that brought you here still runs.
The money you buy lunch with,
no matter where it's mined, is silver
and the girl who serves your food
is slender and her red hair lights the wall.

QUESTIONS

1. How does the speaker characterize Philipsburg? What was the past like there? Why has so much changed? Who is the "you" addressed in line 1?

2. What is life like in the town now? What is the principal supporting business?

3. What does the speaker think should characterize a living, as opposed to a dead, town? What does his thought tell you about his character?

4. How can this poem be seen as a philosophic reflection on the ability of human beings to endure and adjust even though new circumstances change previous ways of life?

C. DAY LEWIS   (1904–1972)

Song _____ 1935

Come, live with me and be my love,
And we will all the pleasures prove
Of peace and plenty, bed and board,
That chance employment may afford.

I'll handle dainties on the docks
And thou shalt read of summer frocks:
At evening by the sour canals
We'll hope to hear some madrigals.

Care on thy maiden brow shall put
A wreath of wrinkles, and thy foot
Be shod with pain: not silken dress
But toil shall tire thy loveliness.

Hunger shall make thy modest zone
And cheat fond death of all but bone—
If these delights thy mind may move,
Then live with me and be my love.

QUESTIONS

1. What is the connection and contrast between this poem and Marlowe's "Passionate Shepherd to His Love"?
2. To what other poems in this chapter is this poem related? How?
3. Who is the speaker in this poem? The listener?
4. What is the effect of words like *chance employment* (line 4), *read* (line 6), and *hope* (line 8)?

CHRISTOPHER MARLOWE   (1564–1593)

The Passionate Shepherd to His Love _____ *1599*

Come live with me and be my love,	
And we will all the pleasures prove°	*test*
That valleys, groves, hills, and fields,	
Woods, or steepy mountain yields.	

And we will sit upon the rocks,   5
Seeing the shepherds feed their flocks,
By shallow rivers to whose falls
Melodious birds sing madrigals.

And I will make thee beds of roses
And a thousand fragrant posies,   10
A cap of flowers, and a kirtle°   *long dress*
Embroidered all with leaves of myrtle;

A gown made of the finest wool
Which from our pretty lambs we pull;
Fair lined slippers for the cold,   15
With buckles of the purest gold;

A belt of straw and ivy buds,
With coral clasps and amber studs;
And if these pleasures may thee move,
Come live with me, and be my love.   20

The shepherds' swains° shall dance and sing   *lovers*
For thy delight each May morning:
If these delights thy mind may move,
Then live with me and be my love.

QUESTIONS

1. Describe the speaker. What does he do? What is he like? What does he want?
2. Who is the listener? What is the relationship between speaker and listener?
3. What sort of life does the speaker offer the listener?
4. What is the speaker's understanding of reality?

JAMES MERRILL   (b. 1926)

Laboratory Poem ———————————————————————— *1958*

Charles used to watch Naomi, taking heart
And a steel saw, open up turtles, live.
While she swore they felt nothing, he would gag
At blood, at the blind twitching, even after
The murky dawn of entrails cleared, revealing
Contours he knew, egg-yellows like lamps paling.

Well then. She carried off the beating heart
To the kymograph° and rigged it there, a rag
In fitful wind, now made to strain, now stopped
By her solutions tonic or malign°
Alternately in which it would be steeped.
What the heart bore, she noted on a chart.

For work did not stop only with the heart.
He thought of certain human hearts, their climb
Through violence into exquisite disciplines
Of which, as it now appeared, they all expired.
Soon she would fetch another and start over,
Easy in the presence of her lover.

LABORATORY POEM.   8 *kymograph:* an instrument that measures pulsations or variations of
pressure and records them on a revolving scroll of paper.   10 *tonic or malign:* healthful or poisonous, virtuous or evil.

QUESTIONS

1. What can you determine about the speaker here? Is he or she *inside* or *outside*
   the poem? Engaged in the action or detached?

2. Who are the two characters in the poem? What are they like? What is their relationship? What are they doing?

3. Which character's thoughts does the speaker relate? What are they? What does
   this character conclude about science? Human endeavor?

4. What is the setting of the poem? The situation? The event described? What aspects of human existence does the poem explore?

MARGE PIERCY   (b. 1934)

Wellfleet° sabbath ———————————————————————— *1988*

The hawk eye of the sun slowly shuts.
The breast of the bay is softly feathered
dove grey. The sky is barred like the sand
when the tide trickles out.

The great doors of the sabbath are swinging   5
open over the ocean, loosing the moon
floating up slow distorted vast, a copper
balloon just sailing free.

The wind slides over the waves, patting
them with its giant hand, and the sea   10
stretches its muscles in the deep,
purrs and rolls over.

The sweet beeswax candles flicker
and sigh, standing between the phlox
and the roast chicken. The wine shines   15
its red lantern of joy.

Here on this piney sandspit, the Shekinah°
comes on the short strong wings of the seaside
sparrow raising her song and bringing
down the fresh clean night.   20

WELLFLEET SABBATH.   Title *Wellfleet:* A seaside town close to the northern tip of Cape Cod, Massachusetts.   17 *Shekinah:* In the Jewish faith, a visible sign or manifestation of divinity.

QUESTIONS

1. Who is the speaker? Where is she? What is the special occasion? Who, if anyone, is being addressed?
2. What attributes do the speaker's descriptions confer upon the exterior natural world? How do these attributes, together with the interior scene, contribute to the speaker's apparent mood?
3. Who, if anyone, is being addressed? What is the reader's relationship to the poem?

SIR WALTER RALEIGH   (1552–1618)

The Nymph's Reply to the Shepherd _____ *1600*

If all the world and love were young,
And truth in every shepherd's tongue,
These pretty pleasures might me move
To live with thee and be thy love.

Time drives the flocks from field to fold°   *fenced field*   5
When rivers rage and rocks grow cold,
And Philomel° becometh dumb;   *the nightingale*
The rest complains of cares to come.

The flowers do fade, and wanton fields
To wayward winter reckoning yields;   10
A honey tongue, a heart of gall,
Is fancy's spring, but sorrow's fall.

Thy gowns, thy shoes, thy beds of roses,
Thy cap, thy kirtle,° and thy posies°   *long dress; flowers and poems*
Soon break, soon wither, soon forgotten—
In folly ripe, in reason rotten.

Thy belt of straw and ivy buds,
Thy coral clasps and amber studs,
All these in me no means can move
To come to thee and be thy love.

But could youth last and love still° breed,   *always*
Had joys no date nor age no need,
Then these delights my mind might move
To live with thee and be thy love.

QUESTIONS

1. Who is the speaker? What do we learn about the speaker? Who is the listener?
2. How are the ideas of love and the world in this poem different from those in Marlowe's poem?
3. To what extent is this poem a parody (an imitation that makes fun) of Marlowe's poem? To what extent is it a refutation of Marlowe's poem?
4. Determine the steps of the speaker's logical argument in this poem.

CHRISTINA ROSSETTI (1830–1894)

A Christmas Carol _____ 1872

In the bleak mid-winter
    Frosty wind made moan,
Earth stood hard as iron,
    Water like a stone;
Snow had fallen, snow on snow,
    Snow on snow,
In the bleak mid-winter
    Long ago.

Our God, Heaven cannot hold Him
    Nor earth sustain;
Heaven and earth shall flee away
    When He comes to reign:
In the bleak mid-winter
    A stable-place sufficed°   *see Luke 2:7*
The Lord God Almighty
    Jesus Christ.

Enough for Him whom cherubim
  Worship night and day,
A breastful of milk
  And a mangerful of hay;   20
Enough for Him whom angels
  Fall down before,
The ox and ass and camel
  Which adore.

Angels and archangels   25
  May have gathered there,
Cherubim and seraphim
  Throng'd the air,
But only His mother
  In her maiden bliss   30
Worshipped the Beloved
  With a kiss.

What can I give Him,
  Poor as I am?
If I were a shepherd°   see Luke 2:8–20 35
  I would bring a lamb,
If I were a wise man°   see Matthew 2:1–12
  I would do my part,—
Yet what I can I give Him,
  Give my heart.   40

QUESTIONS

1. Why does Rossetti stress the bitterness and bleakness of the winter setting in this poem?
2. Why does the speaker stress the simplicity of the birthplace of "The Lord God Almighty"? What is the origin and tradition of this setting?
3. How does the fourth stanza prepare you for the speaker's description of her own condition in stanza five?
4. How are the objects considered as gifts by the speaker a part of the setting traditionally associated with the birth of Jesus? How does the speaker's gift reveal her character and condition?

JANE SHORE   (b. 1947)

A Letter Sent to Summer _____ (1977)

Oh summer if you would only come
with your big baskets of flowers,
dropping by like an old friend
just passing through the neighborhood!

If you came to my door disguised
as a thirsty biblical angel
I'd buy all your hairbrushes and magazines!
I'd be more hospitable
than any ancient king.

I'd personally carry your luggage in,
Your monsoons. Your squadrons of bugs,
Your plums and lovely melons.
Let the rose let out its long long sigh
And Desire return to the hapless rabbit.

This request is also in my own behalf.
Inside my head it is always snowing,
even when I sleep. When I wake up,
and still you have not arrived,
I curl back into my blizzard of linens.

Not like winter's buckets of whitewash.
Please wallpaper my bedroom
with leafy vegetables and farms.
If you knocked right now,
I would not interfere.
Start near the window.
Start right here.

QUESTIONS

1. Describe the speaker. What do you learn about her and how she is responding
    to the time of year?
2. Describe what summer means to the speaker. What attributes does she give to
    summer? What contrasts are brought out by references to "bugs" and "mon-
    soons" in addition to "plums" and the "rose"?
3. What does the phrase "always snowing" contribute to your understanding of the
    speaker's yearning for summer?

MAURA STANTON   (b. 1946)

Childhood _____ *1984*

I used to lie on my back, imagining
A reverse house on the ceiling of my house
Where I could walk around in empty rooms
All by myself. There was no furniture
Up there, only a glass globe on the floor.
And knee-high barriers at every door.
The low silled windows opened on blue air.
Nothing hung in the closet; even the kitchen
Seemed immaculate, a place for thought.
I liked to walk across the swirling plaster
Into the parts of the house I couldn't see.

The hum from the other house, now my ceiling,
Reached me only faintly. I'd look up
To find my brothers watching old cartoons,
Or my mother vacuuming the ugly carpet.   15
I'd stare amazed at unmade beds, the clutter,
Shoes, half-dressed dolls, the telephone,
Then return dizzily to my perfect floorplan
Where I never spoke or listened to anyone.

I must have turned down the wrong hall,   20
Or opened a door that locked shut behind me,
For I live on the ceiling now, not the floor.
This is my house, room after empty room.
How do I ever get back to the real house
Where my sisters spill milk, my father calls,   25
And I am at the table, eating cereal?
I fill my white rooms with furniture,
Hang curtains over the piercing blue outside.
I lie on my back. I strive to look down,
This ceiling is higher than it used to be,   30
The floor so far away I can't determine
Which room I'm in, which year, which life.

QUESTIONS

1. How do the first four lines introduce the poem? To what degree is the situation normal? Unusual? Humorous?

2. How accurate is the imaginative explanation of details about the ceiling? About the rooms of the house?

3. How does line 20 constitute a shift in the poem? What purpose is served by these final thirteen lines?

4. Characterize the speaker. How does she explain what has happened to her? In relationship to her opening sentence, explain the last four lines.

WILLIAM WORDSWORTH   (1770–1850)

Lines Composed a Few Miles Above Tintern Abbey on Revisiting the Banks of the Wye During a Tour, June 13, 1798° ——————— *1798*

Five years have past; five summers, with the length
Of five long winters! and again I hear
These waters, rolling from their mountain-springs

LINES COMPOSED ABOVE TINTERN ABBEY.   Wordsworth first visited the valley of the Wye in southwest England in August 1793 at age twenty-three. On this second visit he was accompanied by his sister Dorothy (the "friend" in line 115).

With a soft inland murmur.—Once again
Do I behold these steep and lofty cliffs,
That on a wild secluded scene impress
Thoughts of more deep seclusion, and connect
The landscape with the quiet of the sky.
The day is come when I again repose
Here, under this dark sycamore, and view
These plots of cottage-ground, these orchard-tufts,
Which at this season, with their unripe fruits,
Are clad in one green hue, and lose themselves
'Mid groves and copses. Once again I see
These hedge-rows, hardly hedge-rows, little lines
Of sportive wood run wild; these pastoral farms,
Green to the very door; and wreaths of smoke
Sent up, in silence, from among the trees!
With some uncertain notice, as might seem
Of vagrant dwellers in the houseless woods,
Or of some Hermit's cave, where by his fire
The Hermit sits alone.
                              These beauteous forms,
Through a long absence, have not been to me
As is a landscape to a blind man's eye:
But oft, in lonely rooms, and 'mid the din
Of towns and cities, I have owed to them
In hours of weariness, sensations sweet,
Felt in the blood, and felt along the heart;
And passing even into my purer mind,
With tranquil restoration:—feelings too
Of unremembered pleasure: such, perhaps,
As have no slight or trivial influence
On that best portion of a good man's life,
His little, nameless, unremembered acts
Of kindness and of love. Nor less, I trust,
To them I may have owed another gift,
Of aspect more sublime; that blessed mood,
In which the burden of the mystery,
In which the heavy and the weary weight
Of all this unintelligible world,
Is lightened:—that serene and blessed mood,
In which the affections gently lead us on,—
Until, the breath of this corporeal frame
And even the motion of our human blood
Almost suspended, we are laid asleep
In body, and become a living soul:
While with an eye made quiet by the power
Of harmony, and the deep power of joy,
We see into the life of things.
                              If this
Be but a vain belief, yet, oh!—how oft—

In darkness and amid the many shapes
Of joyless daylight; when the fretful stir
Unprofitable, and the fever of the world,
Have hung upon the beatings of my heart—
How oft, in spirit, have I turned to thee,   55
O sylvan Wye! thou wanderer thro' the woods,
How often has my spirit turned to thee!
    And now, with gleams of half extinguished thought,
With many recognitions dim and faint,
And somewhat of a sad perplexity,   60
The picture of the mind revives again:
While here I stand, not only with the sense
Of present pleasure, but with pleasing thoughts
That in this moment there is life and food
For future years. And so I dare to hope,   65
Though changed, no doubt, from what I was when first
I came among these hills; when like a roe
I bounded o'er the mountains, by the sides
Of the deep rivers, and the lonely streams,
Wherever nature led: more like a man   70
Flying from something that he dreads, than one
Who sought the thing he loved. For nature then
(The coarser pleasures of my boyish days,
And their glad animal movements all gone by)
To me was all in all.—I cannot paint   75
What then I was. The sounding cataract
Haunted me like a passion: the tall rock,
The mountain, and the deep and gloomy wood,
Their colours, and their forms, were then to me
An appetite; a feeling and a love,   80
That had no need of a remoter charm,
By thought supplied, nor any interest
Unborrowed from the eye.—That time is past,
And all its aching joys are now no more,
And all its dizzy raptures. Not for this   85
Faint I, nor mourn nor murmur; other gifts
Have followed; for such loss, I would believe,
Abundant recompense. For I have learned
To look on nature, not as in the hour
Of thoughtless youth; but hearing oftentimes   90
The still, sad music of humanity,
Nor harsh nor grating, though of ample power
To chasten and subdue. And I have felt
A presence that disturbs me with the joy
Of elevated thoughts; a sense sublime   95
Of something far more deeply interfused,
Whose dwelling is the light of setting suns,
And the round ocean, and the living air,
And the blue sky, and in the mind of man;

A motion and a spirit, that impels
All thinking things, all objects of all thought,
And rolls through all things. Therefore am I still
A lover of the meadows and the woods,
And mountains; and of all that we behold
From this green earth; of all the mighty world
Of eye, and ear,—both what they half create,
And what perceive; well pleased to recognize
In nature and the language of the sense,
The anchor of my purest thoughts, the nurse,
The guide, the guardian of my heart, and soul
Of all my moral being.
                         Nor perchance,
If I were not thus taught, should I the more
Suffer my genial spirits to decay:
For thou art with me here upon the banks
Of this fair river; thou my dearest Friend,
My dear, dear Friend; and in thy voice I catch
The language of my former heart, and read
My former pleasures in the shooting lights
Of thy wild eyes. Oh! yet a little while
May I behold in thee what I was once,
My dear, dear Sister! and this prayer I make,
Knowing that Nature never did betray
The heart that loved her; 'tis her privilege,
Through all the years of this our life, to lead
From joy to joy: for she can so inform
The mind that is within us, so impress
With quietness and beauty, and so feed
With lofty thoughts, that neither evil tongues,
Rash judgments, nor the sneers of selfish men,
Nor greetings where no kindness is, nor all
The dreary intercourse of daily life,
Shall e'er prevail against us, or disturb
Our cheerful faith that all which we behold
Is full of blessings. Therefore let the moon
Shine on thee in thy solitary walk;
And let the misty mountain-winds be free
To blow against thee: and, in after years,
When these wild ecstasies shall be matured
Into a sober pleasure; when thy mind
Shall be a mansion for all lovely forms,
Thy memory be as a dwelling-place
For all sweet sounds and harmonies; oh! then,
If solitude, or fear, or pain, or grief,
Should be thy portion, with what healing thoughts
Of tender joy wilt thou remember me,
And these my exhortations! Nor, perchance—
If I should be where I no more can hear

Thy voice, nor catch from thy wild eyes these gleams
Of past existence—wilt thou then forget   155
That on the banks of this delightful stream
We stood together; and that I, so long
A worshipper of Nature, hither came
Unwearied in that service: rather say
With warmer love—oh! with far deeper zeal
Of holier love. Nor wilt thou then forget,
That after many wanderings, many years
Of absence, these steep woods and lofty cliffs,
And this green pastoral landscape, were to me
More dear, both for themselves and for thy sake!

QUESTIONS

1. What is the opening scene? How much time has elapsed since the speaker viewed
    the scene? What has it meant to him in the past?
2. To the speaker, what is the relationship between remembered scenes and the de-
    velopment of moral behavior?
3. What effect does the speaker consider that this present experience will have on
    him in future years?
4. In lines 93–111, how successful is the speaker in making concrete his ideas about
    the moral forces he perceives along with his vision of the natural scenes?
5. What is the power that the speaker attributes to Nature? Characterize the "cheer-
    ful faith" described in lines 133–134

JAMES WRIGHT   (1927–1980)

A Blessing ———————————————————————————————— *1963*

Just off the highway to Rochester, Minnesota,
Twilight bounds softly forth on the grass.
And the eyes of those two Indian ponies
Darken with kindness.
They have come gladly out of the willows   5
To welcome my friend and me.
We step over the barbed wire into the pasture
Where they have been grazing all day, alone.
They ripple tensely, they can hardly contain their happiness
That we have come.   10
They bow shyly as wet swans. They love each other.
There is no loneliness like theirs.
At home once more,
They begin munching the young tufts of spring in the darkness.
I would like to hold the slenderer one in my arms,   15
For she has walked over to me

And nuzzled my left hand.
She is black and white,
Her mane falls wild on her forehead,
And the light breeze moves me to caress her long ear   15
That is delicate as the skin over a girl's wrist.
Suddenly I realize
That if I stepped out of my body I would break
Into blossom.

QUESTIONS

1. What has happened just before the poem opens? Account for the poet's use of the present tense in his descriptions.
2. Is the setting specific or general? What happens as the poem progresses?
3. What realization overtakes the speaker? How does this realization constitute a "blessing," and what does it show about his character?
4. To what degree is it necessary for the poet to include all the detail of the first twenty-one lines before the realization of the last three?

WRITING ABOUT CHARACTER AND SETTING IN POETRY

Writing about character and setting involves many of the same considerations whether you deal with prose fiction or poetry. You might therefore review the material on character presented in Chapter 4. However, there are some important differences between the two writing tasks. One of these is the way you find out about characters. In prose fiction, you can usually judge a character by the details about his or her actions, words, thoughts, appearance, and opinions. In poetry, the speaker is less likely to provide full details. Consequently, many conclusions must be inferred from the speaker's suggestions and hints.

Another difference between fiction and poetry concerns the types of character. Fiction presents a broad range of writing options: You may write about the protagonist, the antagonist, the narrator, or any of the incidental characters. In poetry you are usually limited to the speaker or to one of the characters described by the speaker (although you may sometimes be able to discuss the listener, too). In writing about Browning's "My Last Duchess," for example, you learn enough about both the Duke and the Duchess to write about either.

In planning and prewriting, you should find out as much as you can about the characters and their relationship to their situations; that is, to the action, emotion, ideas, setting, and other characters. Answering the following questions will help you to focus your ideas:

Questions for Discovering Ideas

ABOUT THE SPEAKER

- Who is the speaker? What is he or she doing? What has already occurred? What does he or she say about himself or herself? About others?
- How reliable is the speaker as an observer and reporter? What knowledge enables the speaker to make judgments and opinions?
- What do the speaker's word choices reveal about his or her education and social standing? How does the language reveal his or her assumptions?
- What tone of voice is suggested in the speaker's presentation?
- How deeply is the speaker involved with the action of the poem? What connection does she or he make with the other characters? With the poem's actions?

ABOUT OTHER CHARACTERS

- How vividly does the poem describe action, appearance, emotions, responses, and ideas? How strong a picture do you get of any other character (characters)?
- How does each significant character respond to the surroundings presented in the poem?
- What is the character trying to gain or learn?
- How is the character affected by others, and how do others respond to her or him?
- What degree of control does the character exert, and what does his or her effort tell you?
- How does the character speak and behave, and what do you learn from these words and actions?

Strategies for Organizing Ideas

When you write about a single character, formulate a central idea that focuses on his or her personality or status. If you are writing about the Duke in "My Last Duchess," for example, your idea might be that he is arrogant, cruel, greedy, and power-mad. In writing about Sir Patrick Spens, your idea would likely be about his self-sacrificing fidelity to the King. If the topic is a set of characters, the central idea should express some relationship or commonality among them. Thus the grieving characters in "Bonny George Campbell" show their love for Campbell, and the characters in "London" illustrate the withering effects of discriminatory religion and laws.

Consider organizing your essay along the lines of one of the following approaches:

1. *Character as revealed by action.* Often the speaker describes himself or herself as a major character or major mover. What does the action reveal about him or her? In Shore's "A Letter Sent to Summer," the speaker indicates that she would be willing to buy "hairbrushes and magazines" from summer. What does this proposed action demonstrate? In Gray's "Elegy Written in a Country

Churchyard," the speaker enters the churchyard at sunset, and his action causes him to think of life, glory, fame, fortune, and religious dedication. What do his speculations and conclusions reveal about his character?

In a parallel way, the speaker of Wordsworth's "Tintern Abbey" Lines has returned to a scene visited five years before. His thoughts deal with his actions as a child and as an adult, prompting him to connect Nature with the development of his own identity. In the light of this spectrum of action, what conclusions might we make about his character?

2. *Character as revealed by interaction.* Poems based in a dramatic situation yield best to this treatment. "My Last Duchess" is a fine example, as are Hardy's "Channel Firing" and Jonson's "Drink to Me, Only, with Thine Eyes." The situation in Hardy's "The Walk" is that the speaker is talking directly to an infirm listener. What does the speaker's attitude toward the listener reveal about his character? In this and other poems, what do you learn about relationships and how they have affected the poetic characters?

3. *Character as revealed by circumstance or setting.* The essay based on the interrelationship of character and setting presupposes that time, place, artifact, money, family, culture, and history influence character and motivation, and also that individual and collective traits are developed as people try to control their surroundings. For instance, the speaker of Wright's "A Blessing" describes the thrill of looking at a roadside pasture, and at the end of the poem he feels as though he is about to "break / Into blossom." What enables him to reach this happy conclusion? Why does he feel safe rather than frightened? Why does he believe in the benevolence of the two ponies, and, in turn, why do the ponies treat him with affection? What aspects of character enable him to step over the barbed wire without fear, and to believe that the experience is really a "blessing"? Would such an experience have been possible at a more suspicious, less civilized time, when people stepping uninvited onto property might have been considered intruders and peppered with buckshot? In short, how has setting in the broadest sense entered into the speaker's character?

In dealing with the interrelationship of character and external situation, you might be able to organize the body of your essay by relying on certain aspects of the setting. Thus you might select the details about time in past, present, and future as presented in Wordsworth's "Tintern Abbey" lines. Similarly, the details about the roaring surf and the dim lights in Arnold's "Dover Beach" would provide thematic links for a discussion of the speaker's sense of alienation, loss, and dedication. In such ways, you may use aspects of setting not only as topics to shed light on character but also to guide and shape your essay.

Whatever strategy you choose, remember that your organization will finally be determined by your poem. Each poem suggests its own avenues of exploration, directing your thought and organization.

In your conclusion you might summarize your major points about the character or characters, or you might tie your conclusions into an assessment of the poem as a whole. Thus, you might briefly discuss the connection between character and character, character and environment, character and death, character and greed, character and love, and so on, and deal with these topics generally as you write your final sentences.

SAMPLE ESSAY

The Character of the Duke in Browning's "My Last Duchess"°

[1]   In this dramatic monologue, Browning skillfully develops the character of his speaker, who holds the high position of Duke of Ferrara (in Italy) during the sixteenth century, a period of aristocratic absolutism. Because the Duke is at the top of the aristocracy, he exerts absolute control, whether for good or for bad. Browning's Duke is bad; not only is he bad, but he is totally evil.* He reveals his evil nature in his one-way conversation with the listener, who is an envoy of a less powerful aristocrat, the Count, whose daughter the Duke is going to marry. The Duke's evil character is brought out by his indulgence in power, his intimidation of others, his manipulation of his dead wife, and his general contempt for others.†

[2]   The Duke's indulgence in power, the basis of his evil, is apparent in his use of indirect speech. On the surface, Browning makes him seem intelligent, civilized, and friendly. The Duke begins speaking by pointing out to his listener the beauty of a painting of his "last Duchess," but his entire speech--comprising the entire poem--reveals the horror of his self-indulgence. His indirect but threatening description of how he treated the Duchess shows that he delights in evil. When he says "I gave commands; / Then all smiles stopped together" (lines 45–46), he is actually bragging. He is coldly horrible, the more so because he masks his evil with quiet words and a love of good art.

[3]   Another horrible quality is the way the Duke intimidates people. Although at first it seems that he is doing no more than telling about his dead wife, it is clear at the poem's end that he has been intimidating both his listener and also the Count, the listener's master. The last nine lines (48–56), indicate that his monologue should have been a dialogue, in which he should have negotiated the terms for the dowry he is to receive from the Count. The fact that he has talked only about how he got rid of his "last Duchess" shows his arrogance. Thus, there is no mention of dowry until lines 48–53, when the Duke states that he will make a "just pretense" for a dowry which of course the Count will honor (for "just pretense," read a demand for all the Count's money and land). In addition, the Duke's commands, "Will't please you rise? We'll meet / The company below then," indicate that the negotiation that never began is now over, and that the envoy is totally in his power. This is intimidation, and the character who intimidates by describing one of his own death sentences is ruthless and inhuman.

°For this poem, see p. 578.
*Central idea.
†Thesis sentence.

The Duke's evil nature is also brought out in his description of the Duchess. If we look through his words at what the Duchess was really like, we conclude that she was even-tempered and pleasant to all--the soul of graciousness and courtesy. In fact, it would be hard to say that she was anything but perfect. But the Duke, rather than indicating pleasure with her, states that she was ungrateful because she was not submissive. He complains that the smile she gave to others was the same as the smile she gave to him (it probably was not; we may conclude that her smile to him probably covered fear):

[4]
> O sir, she smiled, no doubt,
> Whene'er I passed her; but who passed without
> Much the same smile? (lines 43–45)

These lines show that the Duke is a manipulator of the worst sort and that the poor Duchess was in an impossible situation. Very likely he would have complained also if she had smiled only at him and not at others--thereby leaving herself open to the Duke's perverted judgment that she did not show the graciousness toward others that he expected from his wife. No matter how good she was, there was no way for her to have pleased him. He would have manipulated her into an unfavorable position that would have justified his giving the "commands" to remove her.

[5]
Perhaps the worst of this monster's traits is the contempt he shows for people by thinking of them not as human beings but rather as things. Most notable is the way he thinks of the Duchess; he calls her painting a "piece" (line 3) to hang on a wall, looking "as if she were alive" (line 2). He does not even name her, or recognize her humanity by calling her "the late Duchess," and he speaks about the bronze statue of Neptune "taming a sea horse" (line 55) as being equal to her (it is worth noting that the subject of this statue is domination). This same contempt for people is shown in his claim that his interest in the Count's daughter is the "fair daughter's self" (line 52), while the rest of the poem makes clear that he wants only wealth and power out of the marriage. Oddly, also, he seems to think of himself less as a person than as a "nine-hundred-years-old name" (line 33), and it is this intangible distinction that he prizes above his own humanity. In other words, he views even himself with contempt.

[6]
Browning's Duke, then, is a person with absolute power but without the kindness and understanding to use it for anyone but himself. His complaints about the dead Duchess are meaningless, for they are no more than pretexts for cruel self-indulgence. He is at the top of the aristocratic power structure, and therefore he is able to do what he wants without reprisal. People must defer to him and obey him, but only because he makes everyone afraid. His intimidation, his manipulation, his lust for power--all govern him, and leave him unable to look at human beings as anything more than pawns in his game for control. He is an example of the saying that absolute power corrupts absolutely, and his character is therefore a frightening portrait of evil.

Commentary on the Essay

Because the subject of the discussion, the Duke, is the speaker, the essay is based partially on details presented by him, but it is also partially based on interpretations. The principal subject matter is the interaction of the Duke and the subject of the poem—the "last Duchess"—in addition to his interaction with the listener, who is a representative of an inferior aristocrat, and whom he therefore treats with contempt. Elements of setting are also introduced to illuminate the Duke's character: his works of art, his absolute power, his pride in his name and title, and his wealth. The essay thus demonstrates how character may be analyzed with reference (a) to interactions between persons and persons, and also (b) to connection of persons with environment.

The central idea is that the Duke is evil. This point is made in the first paragraph, with sufficient accompanying detail to explain that the Duke's position enables him to exercise absolute power. Paragraph 2 discloses that indulgence in power is one of the Duke's primary evil traits, while paragraphs 3, 4, and 5 bring out traits of intimidation, manipulation, and contempt. The final paragraph, 6, summarizes but also asserts that the Duke's justifications for killing his wife are meaningless in the light of his greed and lust for power.

As the essay develops, transitions are effected by phrases such as "another," "worst," "also," and "then." The assertions in the essay are supported by references to specific details from the poem, quotations from the poem (with line numbers noted), and interpretations of details.

WRITING TOPICS

1. Write an essay comparing the speakers of the various "Passionate Shepherd" poems (by Marlowe, Raleigh, and Lewis). How are the speakers alike, and how are they different? How do their words and references indicate their characters? How do the speakers influence your judgments of the poems in which they appear?

2. Write an essay discussing the relationships between location, thought, and character as asserted in the poems by Shore, Blake, Arnold, and Wordsworth (or poems in other chapters). What importance do place and time have on the opportunity for life and the development of character? How do responses to time, historical period, and place influence ideas about how to live?

3. Write a short poem, biographical or autobiographical, showing how a certain time, place, or experience has shaped a present quality of character and/or a certain decision about life, friendships, and goals.

4. Consider "Wellfleet Sabbath," "Elegy Written in a Country Churchyard," "A Christmas Carol," "The Tintern Abbey Lines," and "A Blessing" as poems embodying a type or types of religious experience. What common or similar circumstances occasion the religious reflections in the poems? What common ideas and conclusions do the poems express? What philosophical or sectarian differences do you find? On the basis of your study, explain typical patterns of religious experience. (For ideas about how to approach this topic, you may wish to consult Appendix B and also the section entitled "Archetypal Criticism" in Appendix D.)

15

Words: The Building Blocks of Poetry

Words are the recognized and accepted *signifiers* of thoughts, objects, and actions. They are also the building blocks of both poetry and prose, but poetry is unique because by its nature it uses words with the utmost economy. The words of poetry create rhythm, rhyme, meter, and form. They define the speaker, the characters, the setting, and the situation. They also carry the ideas and the emotions. For this reason, each poet searches for perfect and indispensable words, words that convey all the compressed meanings, overtones, and emotions that each poem requires, and also the words that look right and sound right.

Life—and poetry—might be simpler (but less interesting) if there were an exact one-to-one correspondence between words and the objects or ideas they signify. Such close correspondence exists in artificial language systems like chemical equations and computer languages. This identical correlation, however, is not characteristic of English or any other language. Instead, words have the independent and glorious habit of acquiring a vast array of different meanings.

Even if we have not thought much about language, most of us recognize that words are sometimes ambiguous, and much literature is built on ambiguity. For instance, in Shakespeare's *Romeo and Juliet*, when Mercutio says "Seek for me tomorrow and you shall find me a grave man," the joke works because *grave* has two separate meanings, both of which come into play. In reading poetry, we recognize that poets rejoice in this shifting and elusive but also rich nature of language.

CHOICE OF DICTION: SPECIFIC AND CONCRETE VS. GENERAL AND ABSTRACT

Because poets are always trying to use only the words that are exactly right, they constantly make both conscious and subconscious decisions about diction. One of the major categories of their choice is diction that is either *specific* and *concrete*, or *general* and *abstract.*

Specific language refers to objects or conditions that can be perceived or imagined, while **general language** signifies broad classes of persons, objects, and phenomena. **Concrete diction** describes conditions or qualities that are exact and particular, while **abstract** diction refers to qualities that are rarefied and theoretical. In practice, poems using specific and concrete words tend to be visual, familiar, and compelling. By contrast, poems using general and abstract words tend to be detached and cerebral, frequently dealing with universal questions or emotions.

These distinctions become clear when we compare Housman's "Loveliest of Trees" (p. 558) and Richard Eberhart's "The Fury of Aerial Bombardment" (p. 616). Many of the terms and images that Housman uses, such as "three score years and ten" and "Cherry . . . hung with bloom," are specific and concrete; they evoke exact time and clear visualization. By contrast, Eberhart's terms, such as "infinite spaces" and "eternal truth," are general and abstract. It is hard to envision them with clarity and exactness. This contrast, which by no means implies that Housman is superior to Eberhart, reflects differences in word choices for different objectives.

Most poets employ mixtures of words in these categories because in many poems they draw general observations and abstract conclusions from specific situations and concrete responses. They therefore interweave their words to fit their situations and ideas, as in Theodore Roethke's "Dolor" (p. 620), which uses specific and concrete words to define a series of abstract emotional states.

LEVELS OF DICTION

Like ordinary speakers and writers of prose, poets choose words from the category of the three levels of diction: *high or formal, middle or neutral,* and *low or informal.*

High or Formal Diction

High or **formal diction** is elevated and elaborate; it follows the rules of syntax exactly, and avoids idioms, colloquialisms, contractions, and slang. Beyond "correctness," formal language is characterized by complex words and a lofty tone. Graves uses formal diction in "The Naked and the Nude" (p. 611) when the speaker asserts that the terms in the title are "By lexicographers construed / As synonyms that should express / The same deficiency of dress." These Latinate words stiffen and generalize the passage. We find *lexicographers* instead of *dictionary writers, construed* (from Latin) instead of *thought* (native English), *express* (from Latin) instead of *say* or *show* (native English), and *deficiency* (Latin) instead of *lack* (English).

Middle or Neutral Diction

Middle or **neutral diction** maintains the correct language and word order of formal diction but avoids elaborate words and elevated tone. For example, Emily Dickinson's "Because I Could Not Stop for Death" (p. 555) is almost entirely in middle diction.

Low or Informal Diction

Low or **informal diction** is the language of everyday use; it is relaxed and conversational. Poems using informal diction often include common and simple words, idiomatic expressions, slang, and contractions. Informal diction may be seen in Thomas Hardy's "The Man He Killed" (p. 557), where the speaker uses words and phrases like "many a nipperkin," "He thought he'd 'list,'" and "off-hand like." In general, formal diction uses longer words of French, Latin, and Greek derivation, while informal diction uses words of native English, most of which are short (together with many short words that were originally taken from French, such as *use, common, delight, tender,* and *trace*). A good college-level dictionary includes etymologies, so that as an exercise you might trace the origins of a number of words in a poem.

SPECIAL TYPES OF DICTION

Depending on their poetic subjects and purposes, poets (and writers of prose) may wish to introduce four special types of diction into their poems: *idiom, dialect, slang,* and *jargon.*

Idiom

The words *idiom* and *idioms* refer to words and phrases that are common and acceptable in a given level of language, even though they might, upon analysis, seem peculiar. Standard idioms are so ingrained into our language that we hardly notice them. Poems automatically reflect these idioms. Thus, for example, a poet may "think *of*" an idea, speak of "living *in*" a house, talk of "going *out* to play," or describe a woman "lovely *as* chandeliers." Poets hardly have choices about such idioms as long as they are using standard English. Real choice occurs when poets select idioms that are unusual or even ungrammatical, as in phrases like "we was happy," "had he and I but met," and "except that You than He." Idioms of this sort enable poets to achieve levels of ordinary and colloquial diction, depending on their purposes.

Dialect

Dialect refers to the words and pronunciation of a particular region or group. In addition to "general American," we can recognize many common dialects such as Brooklynese, American Black English, Yiddish English, Texan,

DECORUM

A vital concept in literature is **decorum**; that is, that words and subjects should be exactly appropriate—high or formal words for serious subjects, and low or informal words for low subjects and comedy. In Shakespeare's *A Midsummer Night's Dream,* for example, the nobles generally speak in poetry while the "mechanicals" speak in prose. When the nobility are relaxed and in the forest, however, they drop into prose. It is decorum that governs Shakespeare's choices of language.

In the eighteenth century, many writers tried to give the English language the dignity of ancient Latin, which was the international language of discourse. They therefore believed that only formal diction was appropriate for poetry. Common life and colloquial language were excluded except in drama and popular ballads. These rules of decorum made it necessary to use standard and elevated language rather than common words and phrases. The development of scientific terminology during the eighteenth century also influenced the choice of language. In the scientific mode, poets of the time used genus-species phrases like "lowing herd" for cattle (Gray) and "finny prey" for fish (Pope). In this formal and scientific vein, Thomas Gray observed the dependence of color on light in the line "cheerful fields resume their green attire" from the "Sonnet on the Death of Richard West" (p. 617).

Alexander Pope, one of the greatest eighteenth-century poets, maintained these rules of decorum—and made fun of them at the same time—in his mock-epic poem *The Rape of the Lock,* and more fully in a mock-critical work entitled *The Art of Sinking in Poetry.* In *The Rape of the Lock,* for example, he refers to a scissors as a "glittering forfex." Similarly, in the following couplet he elevates the simple act of pouring coffee:

From silver spouts the grateful liquors glide,
While China's earth receives the smoking tide.

In our own day the topics and language of people of all classes, with a special stress on common folk, have become a feature of poetry. Poets have continued to follow rules of decorum, however, inasmuch as the use of colloquial diction and even slang is a necessary consequence of popular subject matter.

Southern, and Scottish English. Dialect is concerned with whether we refer to a *pail* (general American) or a *bucket* (southern), or sit down on a *sofa* (eastern) or a *couch* (general American) or *davenport* (midwestern), and drink *soda* (eastern), *pop* (midwestern), *soda pop* (a confused midwesterner living in the east, or a confused easterner living in the midwest), or *tonic* (Bostonian). The anonymous "Bonny George Campbell" (p. 571) and Burns's "Green Grow the Rashes, O" (p. 613) illustrate the poetic use of dialect.

Slang

Slang refers to informal and sub-standard vocabulary and idiom. It is made up of spontaneous words and phrases that may exist for a time and then vanish. Recently, for example, the word "bad" has been slang for "good." Slang has a way of persisting, as may be seen in the many phrases that Americans have developed to describe dying, such as "kick the bucket," "croak," "be wasted," "be disappeared," and "be offed." A non-native speaker of English would have difficulty understanding that a person who "kicked the bucket" or was "offed" had actually died.

Even when slang is widely accepted, it usually goes no farther than colloquial or conversational levels. If it is introduced into a standard context it will mar and jar, as in Larkin's "Next, Please" (p. 850), where the speaker describes the female statue at the bow of a ship as "a figurehead with golden tits." Because the poem is designed to expose the fatuousness of unreal hopes, the slang word creates a clashing, deflating effect that underscores this intention.

Jargon

Jargon refers to words and idioms developed by a particular group of people to fit their special needs. Without some kind of initiation (including intensive study), people not in the group cannot understand the jargon. Usually such groups are specific professions or trades, such as lawyers, plumbers, astronauts, doctors, and football players. Although jargon at its worst befuddles rather than informs, it is interesting when it becomes part of mainstream English or is used in literature. Poets may introduce jargon for special effects. For example, Paul Zimmer, in "The Day Zimmer Lost Religion" (p. 1012), wryly uses the phrase "ready for him now," a boxing expression that describes a fighter in top condition. Linda Pastan uses "gives me an A" and "I'm dropping out," both phrases from school life, to create comic effects in "Marks" (p. 974). Poems in this chapter employing jargon are Henry Reed's "Naming of Parts" and Richard Eberhart's "The Fury of Aerial Bombardment." Both poems use technical terms about firearms to establish the authenticity of their references and therefore to reinforce their judgments about warfare.

SYNTAX

Syntax refers to word order and sentence structure. Normal English word order is firmly fixed in a *subject-verb-object* sequence. At the simplest level, we say "A dog (*subject*) bites (*verb*) a man (*object*)." This order is so central to our communication that any change significantly affects meaning: "A dog bites a man" is not the same as "A man bites a dog."

Much of the time, poets follow normal word order. In "The Lamb," for example, Blake creates a simple, easy order in keeping with the poem's purpose of presenting a childlike praise of God. Many modern poets like James Wright go out of their way to create ordinary, everyday syntax, on the theory that a poem's sentence structures should not get in the way of the reader's perceptions.

Yet, just as good poets always explore the limits of ideas, so also do they sometimes explore the many possibilities of syntax. In Donne's "Holy Sonnet

14," for example (p. 615), line 7 is "Reason, Your viceroy in me, me should defend." In prose, this sentence would read "Reason, which is Your viceroy in me, should defend me." But note that Donne drops out the "which is," thus making an appositive instead of a relative clause. In the predicate, he places the direct object *me* before and not after the verb. The resulting emphasis on the pronoun *me* is appropriate to the personal-divine relationship that is the topic of the sonnet. The alteration also meets the demand of the poem's rhyme scheme. A set of particularly noteworthy syntactic variations occurs in Roethke's "Dolor" (p. 620). The poet uses an irregular and idiosyncratic combination of direct objects, prepositional phrases, and appositives to create ambiguity and uncertainty that reflects the poem's meaning—that school and office routines produce aimlessness and depression.

In addition to these techniques used by Blake, Wright, Donne, and Roethke, there are many other ways in which poets shape word order to create emphasis. Rhetoric, for example, has an important influence on sentence structures. A fundamental and easily recognized device is **parallelism**, the duplication of forms and word order (see also pp. 269–70). The simplest form of parallelism is the **repetition** of the same words and phrases, to be seen in Blake's "The Lamb." Through the use of the same *forms* of *different* words, parallelism produces lines or portions of lines that impress our minds strongly, as in this passage from Robinson's "Richard Cory," in which there are four parallel past-tense verbs (italicized here):

> So on we *worked*, and *waited* for the light,
> And *went* without the meat, and *cursed* the bread;

The final two lines of this poem demonstrate how parallelism may embody **antithesis**—a contrasting situation or idea that effects the strength of surprise and climax:

> And Richard Cory, one calm summer night,
> *Went* home and *put* a bullet through his head.

A major quality of parallelism is the packing of words (the *economy* and *compression* of poetry), for by using a parallel structure the poet makes a single word or phrase function a number of times, with no need for repetition. The opening verb phrase in Roethke's "Dolor," though used once, controls six parallel direct objects. At the end of Donne's "Holy Sonnet 14," parallelism permits Donne to omit the italicized words added and bracketed in the last line:

> ... for I,
> Except You enthrall me, never shall be free,
> Nor *[shall I]* ever *[be]* chaste, except° You ravish me.   unless

Note also that parallelism and antithesis make possible the unique A-B-B-A ordering of these two lines, with the pattern *enthrall* (verb)-*free* (adjective)-*chaste* (adjective)-*ravish* (verb). This pattern, called **chiasmus** or **antimetabole**, is a common means by which poets create emphasis (see also p. 270).

DENOTATION AND CONNOTATION

The control over denotation and connotation (also discussed in Chapter 7) is so important in poetry that it has been called the very soul of the poet's art. **Denotation** refers to the standard dictionary meaning of a word. It indicates conventional correspondences between a sign (the word) and an object or idea. We might expect denotation to be fairly straightforward. However, most English words have multiple denotations. The word *house,* for example, can refer to a *building,* a *family,* a *chamber of congress,* a *theater,* a *theater audience,* a *sorority* or *fraternity,* an *astrological classification,* and a *brothel.* Although context usually makes the denotation of *house* more specific, the various meanings confer a built-in ambiguity to this simple word.

Denotation presents problems because with the passing of time new meanings emerge and old ones are shed. In poems written in the eighteenth century and earlier, there are many words that have changed so completely that a modern dictionary is not much help. In Andrew Marvell's "To His Coy Mistress," for example, the speaker asserts that his *"vegetable* love should grow / Vaster than empires, and more slow." At first, some readers may imagine that *vegetable* refers to something like a giant, loving cabbage. When we turn to a current dictionary, we discover that *vegetable* is an adjective meaning "plant-like," but *plantlike love* does not get us much beyond *vegetable love.* A reference to the *Oxford English Dictionary (OED),* however, tells us that *vegetable* was used as an adjective in the seventeenth century to mean "living or growing like a plant." Thus we find out that *vegetable love* means love that grows slowly but steadily larger.

Connotation refers to the emotional, psychological, or social overtones that words carry beyond their denotations. According to the dictionary, for example, the words *childish* and *childlike* denote the state of being like a child. Nevertheless, they connote or imply different sets of characteristics. *Childish* suggests a person who is bratty, stubborn, immature, silly, and petulant, whereas *childlike* describes a person who is innocent, charming, and unaffected. These different meanings are based entirely on connotation, for the denotations make little distinction.

We constantly encounter the manipulation of connotation. Advertising, for example, depends on the skillful management of connotation. This manipulation may be as simple as calling a *used* car *pre-owned* to avoid the negative connotations of *used.* On the other hand, the manipulation may be as sophisticated as the current use of the words *lite* or *light* to describe foods and drinks. In all such products, *lite* means dietetic, low-calorie, or even weak. The distinction—and the selling point—is found in connotation. Imagine how difficult it would be to sell a drink called "dietetic beer" or "weak beer." *Light* and *lite,* however, carry none of the negative connotations. Instead, *lite* suggests a product that is pleasant, sparkling, bright, and healthy.

Poets always try to make individual words carry as many appropriate and effective denotations and connotations as possible. Put another way, poets use *packed* or *loaded* words that carry a broad range of meaning and association. With this in mind, read the following poem by Robert Graves:

ROBERT GRAVES (1895–1985)

The Naked and the Nude ——————————————————— *1957*

For me, the naked and the nude
(By lexicographers° construed
As synonyms that should express
The same deficiency of dress
Or shelter) stand as wide apart   5
As love from lies, or truth from art.

Lovers without reproach will gaze
On bodies naked and ablaze;
The Hippocratic° eye will see
In nakedness, anatomy;   10
And naked shines the Goddess when
She mounts her lion among men.

The nude are bold, the nude are sly
To hold each treasonable eye.
While draping by a showman's trick   15
Their dishabille° in rhetoric,
They grin a mock-religious grin
Of scorn at those of naked skin.

The naked, therefore, who compete
Against the nude may know defeat;   20
Yet when they both together tread
The briary pastures of the dead,
By Gorgons° with long whips pursued,
How naked go the sometime nude!

THE NAKED AND THE NUDE.   2 *lexicographers:* writers of dictionaries.   9 *Hippocratic:* medical; the adjective derives from Hippocrates (ca. 460–377 B.C.), the ancient Greek who is considered the "father of medicine."   16 *dishabille:* being carelessly or partly dressed.   23 *Gorgons:* mythological female monsters with snakes for hair.

QUESTIONS

1. How does the speaker explain the denotations and connotations of *naked* and *nude* in the first stanza? What is indicated by the fact that the word *naked* is derived from Old English *nacod* while *nude* comes from Latin *nudus*?
2. What examples of "the naked" and "the nude" do the second and third stanzas provide? What do the examples have in common?

3. How do the connotations of words like *sly, draping, dishabille, rhetoric,* and *grin* contribute to the poem's ideas about "the nude"?
4. What does "briary pastures of the dead" mean in line 22?

This poem explores the connotative distinctions between the title words, *naked* and *nude,* which share a common denotation. The title also suggests that the poem is about human customs, for if the speaker were considering the words alone, he would say *naked* and *nude* instead of "*the* naked and *the* nude." The speaker's use of *the* signifies a double focus on both language and human perspectives. In the first five lines the poem establishes that the two key words should be "synonyms that should express / The same deficiency of dress" (lines 2–4). By introducing elevated and complex words such as *lexicographers* and *construed,* however, Graves implies that the connection between "the naked" and "the nude" is highly sophisticated and artificial.

In the rest of the poem, Graves develops this distinction, linking the word *naked* to virtues of love, truth, innocence, and honesty, while connecting *nude* to artifice, hypocrisy, and deceit. At the end, he visualizes a classical underworld in which all pretentiousness will disappear, and the nude will lose their sophistication and become merged with the naked. The implication is that artifice will disappear in the face of eternal reality. A thorough study of the words in the poem bears out the consistency of Graves's idea, not only about the two title words, but also about the accumulated layers of history, usage, and philosophy that weigh upon human life and thought.

 POEMS FOR STUDY

WILLIAM BLAKE   (1757–1827)

The Lamb _____ *1789*

Little Lamb, who made thee?
Dost thou know who made thee?
Gave thee life & bid thee feed,
By the stream & o'er the mead;
Gave thee clothing of delight,
Softest clothing wooly bright;
Gave thee such a tender voice,
Making all the vales rejoice!
    Little Lamb who made thee?
    Dost thou know who made thee?

Little Lamb I'll tell thee,
Little Lamb I'll tell thee!

He is called by thy name,
For he calls himself a Lamb:
He is meek & he is mild,   15
He became a little child:
I a child & thou a lamb,
We are callèd by his name.
　　Little Lamb God bless thee.
　　Little Lamb God bless thee.   20

QUESTIONS

1. Who or what is the speaker in this poem? The listener? How are they related?
2. What is the effect of repetition in the poem?
3. How would you characterize the diction in this poem? High, middle, or low? Abstract or concrete? How is it consistent with the speaker?
4. What are the connotations of *softest, bright, tender, meek,* and *mild?* What do these words imply about the Creator?
5. Describe the characteristics of God imagined in this poem. Contrast the image here with the image of God in Donne's "Batter My Heart."

ROBERT BURNS   (1756–1796)

Green Grow the Rashes, O ——————————————————— *1787*

1

There's naught but care on ev'ry han',°   *hand*
　In every hour that passes, O;
What signifies the life o'° man   *of*
　An' 'twere na° for the lasses, O?   *if it were not*
Chorus:
Green grow the rashes,° O;   *rushes*   5
Green grow the rashes, O;
The sweetest hours that e'er I spend
　Are spent among the lasses, O!

2

The war'ly° race may riches chase,   *worldly*
　An' riches still may fly them, O;   10
An' tho' at last they catch them fast,
　Their hearts can ne'er enjoy them, O.
Chorus.

3

But gie me a cannie° hour at e'en,°   *give me a happy; evening*
　My arms about my dearie, O,
An' war'ly cares an' war'ly men   15
　May a' gae tapsalteerie,° O!   *all go topsy-turvy*
Chorus.

4

For you sae douce° ye sneer at this,   *so sober, so straight laced*
　Ye're naught but senseless asses, O:
The wisest man the warl' e'er° saw,   *world ever*
　He dearly loved the lasses, O.
Chorus.

5

Auld Nature swears the lovely dears
　Her noblest work she classes, O;
Her prentice han'° she tried on man,   *apprentice hand*
　An' then she made the lasses, O.
Chorus.

QUESTIONS

1.　Who is the speaker? What is he like? What is his highest value? How seriously do
　　you take his pronouncements?

2.　How does the speaker justify his feelings? How does he compare his interests with
　　those of other people?

3.　What is the speaker's explanation of the origins of men and women? How might
　　this explanation have been received in 1787, the year of publication, when most
　　people accepted the creation story as told in Genesis?

LEWIS CARROLL　　(1832–1898)

Jabberwocky° _____ *1871*

'Twas brillig, and the slithy toves
　Did gyre and gimble in the wabe;
All mimsy were the borogoves,
　And the mome raths outgrabe.

"Beware the Jabberwock, my son!
　The jaws that bite, the claws that catch!
Beware the Jubjub bird, and shun
　The frumious Bandersnatch!"

He took his vorpal sword in hand;
　Long time the manxome foe he sought—
So rested he by the Tumtum tree,
　And stood awhile in thought.

And, as in uffish thought he stood,
　The Jabberwock, with eyes of flame,
Came whiffling through the tulgey wood,
　And burbled as it came!

One, two! One, two! And through and through
  The vorpal blade went snicker-snack!
He left it dead, and with its head
  He went galumphing back.   20

"And hast thou slain the Jabberwock?
  Come to my arms, my beamish boy!
O frabjous day! Callooh! Callay!"
  He chortled in his joy.

'Twas brillig, and the slithy toves   25
  Did gyre and gimble in the wabe;
All mimsy were the borogoves,
  And the mome raths outgrabe.

JABBERWOCKY. The poem, which appears in the first chapter of *Through the Looking Glass,* is full of nonsense words that Carroll made up with the sound (rather than the sense) in mind. Alice admits that the poem makes some sense even though she does not know the words: "It seems very pretty . . . but it's rather hard to understand! . . . Somehow it seems to fill my head with ideas—only I don't exactly know what they are!"

QUESTIONS

1. Summarize in your own words the story that this poem tells.
2. Humpty Dumpty begins to explain or explicate this poem for Alice in Chapter 6 of *Through the Looking Glass.* He explains that " 'brillig' means four o'clock in the afternoon—the time when you begin *broiling* things for dinner." He also explains that " 'slithy' means 'lithe' and 'slimy.' 'Lithe' is the same as 'active.' You see it's like a portmanteau—there are two meanings packed into one word." Go through the poem and determine what combinations of words are packed into these portmanteau words. *Brillig,* for example, might be seen as a combination of *broiling, brilliant,* and *light.*

JOHN DONNE   (1572–1631)

Holy Sonnet 14: Batter My Heart, Three-Personed God ————— *1633*

Batter my heart, three-personed God; for You
As yet but knock, breathe, shine, and seek to mend;
That I may rise and stand, o'erthrow me, and bend
Your force to break, blow, burn and make me new.
I, like an usurped° town, to another due,   *stolen* 5
Labor to admit You, but Oh, to no end;
Reason, Your viceroy in me, me should defend,
But is captived, and proves weak or untrue.
Yet dearly I love You, and would be loved fain,°   *gladly*
But am betrothed unto Your enemy.   10
Divorce me, untie or break that knot again;

Take me to You, imprison me, for I,
Except You enthrall me, never shall be free,
Nor ever chaste, except you ravish me.

QUESTIONS

1. What kind of God is suggested by the words *batter, knock, overthrow,* and *break?* What does "three-personed God" mean?
2. With which person of God might the verbs *knock* and *break* be associated? The verbs *breathe* and *blow?* The verbs *shine* and *burn?*
3. What is the effect of the altered word order at the ends of lines 7 and 9?
4. Explain the words *enthrall* (line 13) and *ravish* (line 14) to resolve the apparent paradox or contradiction in the last two lines.

RICHARD EBERHART   (b. 1904)

The Fury of Aerial Bombardment ———————————————— *1947*

You would think the fury of aerial bombardment
Would rouse God to relent; the infinite spaces
Are still silent. He looks on shock-pried faces.
History, even, does not know what is meant.

You would feel that after so many centuries
God would give man to repent; yet he can kill
As Cain could, but with multitudinous will,
No farther advanced than in his ancient furies.

Was man made stupid to see his own stupidity?
Is God by definition indifferent, beyond us all?
Is the eternal truth man's fighting soul
Wherein the Beast ravens in its own avidity?

Of Van Wettering I speak, and Averill,
Names on a list, whose faces I do not recall
But they are gone to early death, who late in school
Distinguished the belt feed lever from the belt holding pawl.

QUESTIONS

1. Who or what is the speaker in this poem? What does the last stanza tell you about him? (Eberhart was a gunnery instructor during World War II.)
2. What type and level of diction predominate in lines 1–12? What observations about God are made in these lines? Compare the image of God presented here with the one found in Donne's "Batter My Heart, Three-Personed God" and Blake's "The Lamb." What similarities or differences do you find?

3. How does the level and type of diction change in the last stanza? What is the effect of these changes? How is jargon used here?

4. Compare this poem with Thomas Hardy's "Channel Firing" (p. 584). How are the ideas in the poems similar?

THOMAS GRAY (1716–1771)

Sonnet on the Death of Richard West —————————————— *(1742) 1775*

In vain to me the smiling mornings shine,
  And redd'ning Phoebus° lifts his golden fire;
The birds in vain their amorous descant° join,   *love songs*
  Or cheerful fields resume their green attire:°
These ears, alas! for other notes repine;   5
  A different object do these eyes require.
My lonely anguish melts no heart but mine,
  And in my breast the imperfect joys expire.
Yet morning smiles the busy race to cheer,
  And new-born pleasure brings to happier men;   10
The fields to all their wonted tribute bear;°
  To warm their little loves the birds complain:°
I fruitless mourn to him that cannot hear,
  And weep the more because I weep in vain.

SONNET ON THE DEATH OF RICHARD WEST   2 *Phoebus:* Apollo, the Sun God   4 *resume their green attire:* During the darkness of night, the "cheerful fields" have no color, but in the light of the morning sun they become green again.   11 *The fields . . . bear:* The fields contribute their customary harvest to benefit all creation.   12 *complain:* sing love songs

QUESTIONS

1. What is the poem's subject, the speaker or the dead friend? How effective is the poem as a lament or dirge?

2. Describe the poem's level of diction. Why does the speaker use phrases like *smiling mornings* (line 1), *redd'ning Phoebus* (2), *golden fire* (2), *resume their green attire* (4), and *notes* (5)? How common are these phrases? What is their effect?

3. Consider the syntax in lines 5, 6, 9, 10, 11, and 12. What is unusual about the word order in these lines? What is the effect of this word order?

4. In the 1800 *Preface* to *Lyrical Ballads*, William Wordsworth printed this poem. He italicized lines 6–8 and 13 and 14, and wrote, "It will easily be perceived, that the only part of this Sonnet which is of any value is the lines printed in Italics; it is equally obvious, that . . . the language of these lines does in no respect differ from that of prose." What does Wordsworth's criticism mean? To what degree is it justified?

MAXINE KUMIN   (b. 1925)

Hello, Hello Henry ————————————————— *1982*

My neighbor in the country, Henry Manley,
with a washpot warming on his woodstove,
with a heifer and two goats and yearly chickens,
has outlasted Stalin, Roosevelt and Churchill
but something's stirring in him in his dotage.

Last fall he dug a hole and moved his privy
and a year ago in April reamed his well out.
When the county sent a truck and poles and cable,
his daddy ran the linemen off with birdshot
and swore he'd die by oil lamp, and did.

Now you tell me that all yesterday in Boston
you set your city phone at mine, and had it ringing
inside a dead apartment for three hours
room after empty room, to keep yours busy.
I hear it in my head, that ranting summons.

That must have been about the time that Henry
walked up two miles, shy as a girl come calling,
to tell me he has a phone now, 264, ring two.
It rang one time last week—wrong number.
He'd be pleased if one day I would think to call him.

Hello, hello Henry? Is that you?

QUESTIONS

1. What is the poem's level of diction? What does this level contribute to your response to the poem?
2. What words in this poem are appropriate for a country location? What do the words show about Henry Manley, and about the conditions on his farm?
3. Who is the speaker? What does the selection of words indicate about the speaker's character and state of mind?
4. How does the listener enter into the poem's action in the third stanza? What is the meaning of the listener's action?

HENRY REED   (1914–1986)

Naming of Parts ————————————————— *1946*

To-day we have naming of parts. Yesterday,
We had daily cleaning. And to-morrow morning,
We shall have what to do after firing. But to-day,
To-day we have naming of parts. Japonica

Glistens like coral in all of the neighboring gardens,   5
    And to-day we have naming of parts.

This is the lower sling swivel. And this
Is the upper sling swivel, whose use you will see,
When you are given your slings. And this is the piling swivel,
Which in your case you have not got. The branches   10
Hold in the gardens their silent, eloquent gestures,
    Which in our case we have not got.

This is the safety-catch, which is always released
With an easy flick of the thumb. And please do not let me
See anyone using his finger. You can do it quite easy   15
If you have any strength in your thumb. The blossoms
Are fragile and motionless, never letting anyone see
    Any of them using their finger.

And this you can see is the bolt. The purpose of this
Is to open the breech, as you see. We can slide it   20
Rapidly backwards and forwards: we call this
Easing the spring. And rapidly backwards and forwards
The early bees are assaulting and fumbling the flowers:
    They call it easing the Spring.

They call it easing the Spring: it is perfectly easy   25
If you have any strength in your thumb: like the bolt,
And the breech, and the cocking-piece, and the point of balance,
Which in our case we have not got; and the almond-blossom
Silent in all of the gardens and the bees going backwards and forwards,
    For to-day we have naming of parts.   30

QUESTIONS

1. There may be two speakers in this poem, or one speaker repeating the words of another and adding his own thoughts. What two voices do you hear?
2. What is the setting? The situation? How do these affect the speaker?
3. How and why is jargon used in the poem? With what set of "parts" is the jargon initially associated? How does this change?
4. How are phrases like "easing the spring" (lines 22, 24, 25) and "point of balance" (27) used ambiguously? What is the effect of repetition?

EDWIN ARLINGTON ROBINSON (1869–1935)

Richard Cory _____ *1897*

Whenever Richard Cory went down town,
We people on the pavement looked at him:
He was a gentleman from sole to crown,
Clean favored, and imperially slim.

And he was always quietly arrayed,
And he was always human when he talked;
But still he fluttered pulses when he said,
'Good-morning,' and he glittered when he walked.

And he was rich—yes, richer than a king—
And admirably schooled in every grace:
In fine, we thought that he was everything
To make us wish that we were in his place.

So on we worked, and waited for the light,
And went without the meat, and cursed the bread;
And Richard Cory, one calm summer night,
Went home and put a bullet through his head.

QUESTIONS

1. What is the effect of using *down town, pavement, meat,* and *bread* in connection with the people who admire Richard Cory?
2. What are the connotations and implications of the name *Richard Cory?* Of the word *gentleman?*
3. Why does the poet use "sole to crown" instead of "head to toe" and "imperially slim" instead of "very thin" to describe Cory?
4. What effect does repetition produce in this poem? Consider especially the six lines that begin with "And."
5. What positive characteristic does Richard Cory possess (at least from the perspective of the speaker) besides wealth?

THEODORE ROETHKE   (1907–1963)

Dolor _____ *1943*

I have known the inexorable sadness of pencils,
Neat in their boxes, dolor of pad and paper-weight,
All the misery of manila folders and mucilage,
Desolation in immaculate public places,
Lonely reception room, lavatory, switchboard,
The unalterable pathos of basin and pitcher,
Ritual of multigraph, paper-clip, comma,
Endless duplication of lives and objects.
And I have seen dust from the walls of institutions,
Finer than flour, alive, more dangerous than silica,
Sift, almost invisible, through long afternoons of tedium,
Dropping a fine film on nails and delicate eyebrows,
Glazing the pale hair, the duplicate grey standard faces.

QUESTIONS

1. What does *dolor* mean? What words objectify the concept?
2. Why does "Dolor" not contain the fourteen lines usual in a sonnet?

3. What institutions, conditions, and places does the speaker associate with "dolor"? What do these have in common?
4. Describe the relationships of sentence structures and lines in "Dolor."

WALLACE STEVENS   (1879–1955)

Disillusionment of Ten O'Clock ———————————————— *1923*

The houses are haunted
By white night-gowns.
None are green,
Or purple with green rings,
Or green with yellow rings,   5
Or yellow with blue rings.
None of them are strange,
With socks of lace
And beaded ceintures.°   *belts*
People are not going   10
To dream of baboons and periwinkles.
Only, here and there, an old sailor,
Drunk and asleep in his boots,
Catches tigers
In red weather.   15

QUESTIONS

1. Is the "Ten O'Clock" here morning or night? How can you tell?
2. What do "haunted" and "white night-gowns" suggest about the people who live in the houses? What do the negative images in lines 3–9 suggest?
3. To whom are these people contrasted in lines 12–15?
4. What are the connotations of "socks with lace" and "beaded ceintures"? With which character in the poem would you associate these things?
5. What is the effect of using words and images like *baboons, periwinkles, tigers,* and *red weather* in lines 11–15? Who will dream of these things?
6. Explain the term *disillusionment* and explore its relation to the point that this poem makes about dreams, images, and imagination.

MARK STRAND   (b. 1934)

Eating Poetry ——————————————————————— *1968*

Ink runs from the corners of my mouth.
There is no happiness like mine.
I have been eating poetry.

The librarian does not believe what she sees.
Her eyes are sad
and she walks with her hands in her dress.

The poems are gone.
The light is dim.
The dogs are on the basement stairs and coming up.

Their eyeballs roll,
their blond legs burn like brush.
The poor librarian begins to stamp her feet and weep.

She does not understand.
When I get on my knees and lick her hand,
She screams.

I am a new man.
I snarl at her and bark.
I romp with joy in the bookish dark.

QUESTIONS

1. In the first three lines, which words tell you that the poem is not to be taken literally?
2. What is the serious topic of the poem? What words indicate that the poem has a serious intent?
3. What is the comic topic? Which words tell you that the poem's action is comic?

WRITING ABOUT DICTION AND SYNTAX IN POETRY

Study your poem carefully, line by line, to gain a general sense of its meaning. Try to establish how diction and syntax may be connected to elements such as tone, character, and idea. As you develop your ideas, look for effective and consistent patterns of word choice, connotation, repetition, or syntactic patterns that help create and reinforce the conclusions you have already reached about the poem. Ask questions like the following:

Questions for Discovering Ideas

- Who is the speaker? What is the speaker's profession or way of life? How does the speaker's background affect his or her power of observation? How does the background affect his or her level of speech?
- Who is the listener? How does the listener affect what the speaker says?
- What other characters are in the poem? How are their actions described? How accurate and fair do you think these descriptions are?
- Is the level of diction in the poem elevated, neutral, or informal, and how does this level affect your perception of the speaker, subject, and main idea or ideas?

- What patterns of diction or syntax do you discover in the poem? (Example: words related to situation, action, setting, particular characters.) How ordinary or unusual are these words? Which, if any, are unusual enough to warrant further examination?

- Does the poem contain many "loaded" or connotative words in connection with any single element like setting, speaker, or theme?

- Does the poem contain a large number of general and abstract or specific and concrete words? What is the effect of these choices?

- Does the poem contain dialect? colloquialisms? jargon? If so, how does this special diction shape your response to the poem?

- What is the nature of the poem's syntax? Is there any unusual word order? What seems to be the purpose or effect of syntactic variations?

- Has the poet used any striking patterns of sentence structure such as parallelism or repetition? If so, what is the effect?

Strategies for Organizing Ideas

When you narrow your examination to one or two specific areas of diction or syntax, list important words, phrases, and sentences, and investigate the full range of meaning and effect that the examples produce. Begin grouping examples that work in similar ways or produce similar effects. Eventually you may be able to develop the related examples as potential units or sections for your essay.

Your central idea should emerge from your investigation of the specific diction or syntax that you find most fruitful and interesting. Since diction and syntax contribute to the poem's impact and meaning, try to connect your thesis and examples to your other conclusions. If you are writing about Stevens's "Disillusionment of Ten O'Clock," for example, your central idea might assert that Stevens uses words describing colors (i.e., white, green, purple, yellow, blue, red) to contrast life's visual reality with the psychological "disillusionment" of the "houses," "People," and "old sailor." Such a formulation makes a clear connection between diction and meaning.

There are many different ways to organize your material. If you choose to deal with only one aspect of diction, such as connotative words, you might treat these in the order in which they appear in the poem. When you deal with two or three different aspects of diction and syntax, however, you might devote a series of paragraphs to related examples of multiple denotation, then connotation, and finally jargon (assuming the presence of jargon in the poem). In such an instance, your organization would be controlled by the types of material under consideration rather than by the order in which the words occur.

Alternatively, you might deal with the impact of diction or syntax on a series of other elements, such as character, setting, or situation. Such an essay would focus on a single type of lexical or syntactic device as it relates to these different elements in sequence. Thus, you might use sequential paragraphs to discuss the link between connotation and character, then setting, and finally situation. Whatever organization you select, keep in mind that each poem will suggest its own avenues of exploration and strategies of organization.

In your conclusion summarize your ideas about the impact of the poem's diction or syntax. You might also consider the larger implications of your ideas in connection with the thoughts and emotions evoked by your reading.

SAMPLE ESSAY

Diction and Character in Robinson's "Richard Cory"°

[1]   In "Richard Corey," Edwin Arlington Robinson dramatizes the observation that nothing can ensure happiness. He explores this idea by focusing on a central character--Richard Cory--who apparently has everything: wealth, status, dignity, taste, and respect. Cory's suicide, however, reveals that these qualities do not necessarily bestow happiness. By creating a gulf between Cory and the people of the town who admire and envy him, Robinson sets us up for the surprising suicide described in the last two lines. The distinction is produced through the words that Robinson uses to demean the general populace and elevate the central character.* The speaker and his or her fellow townspeople are associated with words that connote their common lot, while Richard Cory is described in terms of nobility and privilege.†

[2]   For the most part, the poem focuses on Richard Cory as perceived by the townspeople, who wish that they "were in his place" (line 12). Robinson skillfully employs words about these common folk to suggest their poverty and low status. In the first line, for example, the speaker places himself or herself and these other people "down town." The phrase refers to a central business district, but here it also carries the negative connotation of the word down. The word implies that Cory's journey to town seems to be a descent, and that the people constantly live in this "down" condition. A similar instance of connotative diction is pavement (line 2), which can mean "sidewalk," but can also mean "street" or "roadbed." The net effect of the word pavement rather than sidewalk is to place the "people" even lower than Richard Cory--literally on the street.

[3]   In contrast to these few words suggesting the people's lowness, the poem contains many words that connote Cory's elevation. Many words and phrases suggest nobility or royalty. These implications begin with the title of the poem and the name "Richard Cory." That the word rich is contained within Richard implies Cory's wealth and privilege. It is also the name of a number of English kings, most notably Richard the Lion Hearted ("*Richard Coeur de Lion*"). The name Cory is equally connotative. It clearly suggests the "coeur" of the famous king, and it also reminds us of core, the central or innermost part

° See p. 619 for this poem.
* Central idea.
† Thesis sentence.

of anything. The name thus points toward Cory's singular position and significance. Through sound, <u>Cory</u> also suggests the English word <u>court</u>--that is, a place for kings and courtiers. The name "Richard Cory" thus begins an association through sound and implication that links the central character to kingship and elegance.

[4]

<u>There are other similar words in the poem's first stanza.</u> The speaker describes Richard Cory as "a gentleman from sole to crown" (line 3). <u>Gentleman</u> refers to a civilized and well-mannered individual, but it originally also meant "highborn" or "noble." The phrase "from sole to crown" means "from head to toe," but it connotes a great deal more. <u>Sole</u> means both "the bottom of a shoe or foot" and "alone" or "singular." Thus, the word suggests Cory's isolation and separation from the common folk. The word is also a pun (and homophone) on <u>soul</u>, implying that Cory's gentility is inward as well as outward. The final touch is the word <u>crown</u>. In context, the term denotes the top of the head, but its aristocratic and royal connotations are self-evident.

[5]

<u>The speaker also describes Cory as "clean favored" and "imperially slim"</u> (line 4). The word <u>imperially</u>, like <u>crown</u>, makes an explicit connection between Cory and emperors. "Clean favored," instead of the more common <u>good-looking</u>, connotes crisp and untouched features. More to the point, the term <u>favored</u> also means "preferred," "elevated," "honored," and "privileged." "Imperially slim," instead of <u>thin</u>, is equally connotative of wealth and status. While both terms denote the same physical condition, <u>slim</u> denotes elegance, wealth, and choice, whereas <u>thin</u> suggests poverty and necessity.

[6]

<u>Although this type of diction is mostly in the first stanza, Robinson sustains the link between Cory and royalty by using similar terms in the rest of the poem.</u> In the stanza two, for example, he uses "quietly arrayed" and "glittered." Both carry elevated and imperial connotations. <u>Arrayed</u> means "dressed," but it is also a word in the King James Bible that suggests elegant and heavenly clothing (see Matthew 6:29; Acts 12:21, Revelation 7:13). <u>Quietly</u> also suggests solitude and introversion. <u>Glittered</u> complements <u>quietly</u>; it connotes richness of dress and manner, suggesting that the man himself is golden. In the third stanza, the deliberate cliché "richer than a king" again clearly links Richard Cory to royalty. The speaker also notes that Cory was "schooled in every grace" (line 10). The phrase means that Cory was trained in manners and social niceties, but <u>grace</u> connotes privilege and nobility ("Your Grace") and also the idea of heavenly love and forgiveness ("God's Grace").

[7]

<u>It is clear, then, that Robinson uses the effects of connotation to lower the common folk and elevate the central character.</u> The words linked to the speaker and the other townspeople have demeaning and negative implications. At the same time, the poet uses words and phrases about Cory that connote royalty and privilege. This careful manipulation of diction widens the gulf between Cory and the town. It also heightens our sense that Cory has aristocratic looks, manners, taste, and breeding. The network of associations built through this skillful diction makes the poem's ending powerfully shocking, and reinforces the poem's idea that appearance, wealth, and high status cannot ensure happiness.

Commentary on the Essay

This essay deals with Robinson's use of connotative words to elevate the central character and demean the townspeople. The opening paragraph makes a general assertion about the poem's theme, connects character to this assertion, and argues that Robinson manipulates diction to make his distinctions.

The body of the essay, in five paragraphs, deals with the effects of a number of examples of word choice. The examples of connotative words are arranged to reflect partly the characters they define and partly the order in which they appear in the poem. Thus, paragraph 2 discusses the common people and the speaker in connection with two highly connotative terms: *down town* and *pavement*.

The next four paragraphs (3–6) focus on Richard Cory and words or phrases that suggest royalty and privilege. The examples or diction examined here are taken up in the order in which they appear in the poem. Thus, paragraph 3 considers Cory's name, and the fourth explores the effects of *gentleman* and *sole to crown*. Paragraphs 5 and 6 continue this process, examining instances of diction that sustain the association between Cory and nobility. Taken together, the four paragraphs devoted to this central character illustrate Robinson's consistent manipulation of diction both to ennoble and isolate Cory.

The conclusion reasserts that Robinson's diction not only contributes to Cory's isolation, but also adds to the impact of his mysterious suicide. In this way, the words and phrases examined in the essay are linked to the poem's exploration of ideas about the human condition.

WRITING TOPICS

1. Using the poems of Jarrell (p. 550), Owen (pp. 630, 681), and Reed and Eberhart in this chapter, study the words that these poets use to indicate weapons and actions of warfare. In an essay, consider these questions: What shared details make the poems similar? What separate details make them different? How do word choices assist the poets in making their points about war as action, tragedy, and horror?

2. Write an essay considering the sound qualities of the invented words in "Jabberwocky." Some obvious choices are *brillig, frumious, vorpal,* and *manxome,* but you are free to choose any or all of them. What is the relationship between the sound and apparent meaning of these words? What effect do the surrounding normal words and normal word order have upon the special words? How does Carroll succeed in creating a narrative "structure" even though the key words are, on the surface, nonsense?

3. Write a short poem describing a violent crime and commenting on it. Then, assume that you are the "perpetrator" of the crime, and write another poem on the same topic. Even though you describe the same situation, how do your words differ, and why have you made these different choices? Explain the other different word choices you have made. You might also discuss words that you considered using but rejected.

16

Imagery: The Poem's Link to the Senses

In literature, **imagery** refers to words that trigger your imagination to recall and recombine **images**—memories or mental pictures of sights, sounds, tastes, smells, sensations of touch, and motions. The process is active, and even vigorous, for when words or descriptions produce images, you are using your personal experiences with life and language to help you understand the poems you are reading. In effect, you are re-creating the work *in your own way* through the controlled stimulation produced by the poet's words. Imagery is therefore one of the strongest modes of literary expression because it provides a channel to your active imagination, and along this channel, poets, like all writers, bring their works directly to you and into your consciousness.

For example, reading the word "lake" may bring to your mind your literal memory of a particular lake. Your mental picture—or image—may be a distant view of calm waters reflecting blue sky, a nearby view of gentle waves rippled by the wind, a view of the lake bottom from a boat, or an overhead view of a sandy and sunlit shoreline. Similarly, the words *rose, apple, hot dog, malted milk,* and *pizza* all cause you to recollect these objects, and, in addition, may cause you to recall their smells and tastes. Active and graphic words like *row, swim,* and *dive* stimulate you to picture moving images of someone performing these actions.

RESPONSES AND THE WRITER'S USE OF DETAIL

In studying imagery we try to comprehend and explain our imaginative reconstruction of the pictures and impressions evoked by the work's images. We let the poet's words simmer and percolate in our minds. To get our imaginations stirring, we might follow Coleridge in this description from "Kubla Khan" (lines 37–41):

A damsel with a dulcimer
In a vision once I saw:
It was an Abyssinian maid,
And on her dulcimer she played,
Singing of Mount Abora.

We do not read about the color of the young woman's clothing, or anything else about her appearance except that she is playing a stringed instrument, a dulcimer, and that she is singing a song about a mountain in a foreign, remote land. But Coleridge's image is enough. From it we can imagine a vivid, exotic picture of a young woman from a distant land singing, together with the loveliness of her song (even though we never hear it or understand it). The image lives.

IMAGERY, IDEAS, AND ATTITUDES

Images do more than elicit impressions. By the *authenticating* effects of the vision and perceptions underlying them, they give you new ways of seeing the world or strengthen your old ways of seeing it. Langston Hughes, in "Theme for English B," for example (p. 691), develops the idea that human beings are equal. Rather than stating the idea directly, he uses a number of images of everyday, ordinary activities that his speaker shares in common with most human beings (line 21):

I like to eat, sleep, drink, and be in love.

These literal action images form an equalizing link that is not only true, but unarguable. Such uses of imagery are one of the strongest means by which literature reinforces ideas.

In addition, as you form mental pictures from a poet's images, you also respond with appropriate attitudes and feelings. Thus the phrase "beside a lake, beneath the trees," from Wordsworth's poem "Daffodils," prompts both the visualization of a wooded lakeshore and also the related pleasantness of outdoor relaxation and happiness (p. 858). A contrasting visualization is to be found in Herkomer's painting *Hard Times,* where all the images—the tired faces, the heavy load, the tools, the bleak road, the leafless trees—point toward the harsh life of the worker and his family, causing a response of sadness and sympathy (p. 629). Similar negative imagery is used by Jonathan Swift in the poem "Description of the Morning," which triggers unpleasant responses by offering images of street hawkers, thieves, bill collectors, and hesitant schoolboys (p. 730). By such a use of imagery, artists and poets not only create sensory vividness, but also influence and control the attitudes of their readers.

CLASSIFICATION OF IMAGERY

SIGHT.   Sight is the most significant of our senses, for it is the key to our remembrance of other impressions. Therefore, the most frequently occur-

Hard Times, Sir Hubert von Herkomet, Manchester City Art Gallery, The Bridgeman Art Library/Art Resource, NY.

ring literary imagery is to things we can visualize either exactly or approximately—**visual images**. In "Cargoes" (the subject of the sample essay, pp. 646–47), Masefield asks us to re-create mental pictures or images of ocean-going merchant vessels from three periods of human history:

JOHN MASEFIELD   (1878–1967)

Cargoes —————————————————————————— *1902*

Quinquereme° of Nineveh° from distant Ophir,°
Rowing home to haven in sunny Palestine,
With a cargo of ivory,
And apes and peacocks,°
Sandalwood, cedarwood,° and sweet white wine.   5

Stately Spanish galleon coming from the Isthmus,°
Dipping through the Tropics by the palm-green shores,

CARGOES.   1 *quinquereme:* the largest of the ancient ships. It was powered by three tiers of oars, and was named "quinquereme" because five men operated each vertical oar station. The top two oars were each taken by two men, while one man alone took the bottom oar.   1 *Nineveh:* capital of ancient Assyria, an "exceeding great city" (Jonah 3:3).   1 *Ophir:* Ophir probably was in Africa, and was known for its gold (I Kings 10:22; I Chron. 29:4). Masefield echoes some of the Biblical verses in his first stanza.   4 *apes and peacocks:* I Kings 10:22, and II Chron. 9:21. 5 *cedarwood:* I Kings 9:11.   6 *Isthmus:* the Isthmus of Panama.

With a cargo of diamonds,
Emeralds, amethysts,
Topazes, and cinnamon, and gold moidores.°

Dirty British coaster with a salt-caked smoke-stack,
Butting through the Channel in the mad March days,
With a cargo of Tyne coal,°
Road-rails, pig-lead,
Firewood, iron-ware, and cheap tin trays.

10 *moidores:* Coins in use in Portugal and Brazil during the exploration of the new world.   13
Tyne coal: Newcastle upon Tyne, a coal-producing city in northern England.

QUESTIONS

1. Consider the images of life during three periods of history: Ancient Israel at the time of Solomon (ca. 950 B.C.), sixteenth-century Spain, and modern England. What do these images tell you about Masefield's interpretation of modern commercial life?
2. To what senses do most of the images refer (e.g., sight, taste, etc.)?
3. The poem contains no complete sentences. Why do you think that Masefield included only verbals ("rowing," "dipping," "butting") to begin the second line of each stanza, rather than finite verbs?
4. As historical reality, the quinquereme was likely rowed by slaves, and the Spanish galleon likely carried riches stolen from Central American natives. How might these unpleasant details affect the impressions otherwise achieved in the first two stanzas?

Masefield's images in "Cargoes" are vivid as they stand, and need no further amplification. In order to reconstruct them imaginatively, we do not need ever to have seen the ancient Biblical lands or waters, or ever to have seen or handled the cheap commodities on a modern merchantship. We have seen enough in our lives both in reality and in pictures to *imagine* places and objects like these, and hence Masefield is successful in implanting his visual images into our minds.

SOUND.   **Auditory images** trigger our experiences with sound. For such images, let us consider Wilfred Owen's "Anthem for Doomed Youth."

WILFRED OWEN   (1893–1918)

Anthem for Doomed Youth —————————————————— *1920*

What passing-bells° for these who die as cattle?
Only the monstrous anger of the guns.
Only the stuttering rifles' rapid rattle

ANTHEM FOR DOOMED YOUTH.   1 *passing-bells:* church bells that are tolled at the entry of a funeral cortège into the church cemetery.

Can patter out their hasty orisons.° *prayers*
No mockeries for them from prayers or bells, 5
Nor any voice of mourning save the choirs—
The shrill, demented choirs of wailing shells;
And bugles calling for them from sad shires.°

What candles may be held to speed them all?
Not in the hands of boys, but in their eyes 10
Shall shine the holy glimmers of good-byes.
The pallor of girls' brows shall be their pall;
Their flowers the tenderness of patient minds,
And each slow dusk a drawing-down of blinds.

8 *shires:* British counties.

QUESTIONS

1. What type of imagery predominates in the first eight lines? How does the imagery change in the last six lines?
2. Contrast the images of death at home and death on the battlefield. How does this contrast affect your experience and understanding of the poem?
3. Consider these images: *holy glimmers of good-byes, pallor of girls' brows, patient minds, drawing-down of blinds.* What relationship do the people imagined in these images have to the doomed youth?

In asking what "passing-bells" may be tolled for "those who die as cattle," Owen's speaker is referring to the traditional tolling of a parish church bell to announce the burial of a parishioner. Such a ceremony suggests a period of peace and order, when there is time to pay respect to the dead. But the poem then points out that the only sound for those who have fallen in battle is the "rapid rattle" of "stuttering" rifles—in other words, not the solemn, dignified sounds of peace, but the horrifying noises of war. Owen's auditory images evoke corresponding sounds in our imaginations, and help us experience the poem and hate the uncivilized depravity of war.

SMELL, TASTE, AND TOUCH. In addition to sight and sound, you will also find images from the other senses. An **olfactory image** refers to smell, a **gustatory image** to taste, and a **tactile image** to touch. A great deal of love poetry, for example, includes *olfactory images* about the fragrances of flowers. As a twist on this common olfactory imagery, Shakespeare's speaker in Sonnet 130, "My Mistress' Eyes," candidly admits that the breath of his woman friend is not the same as the scent of roses (lines 7–8).

Images derived from and referring to taste—*gustatory images*—are also common, though less frequent than those to sight and sound. In lines 5 and 10 of Masefield's "Cargoes," for example, there are references to "sweet white wine" and "cinnamon." Although the poem refers to these commodities as cargoes, the words themselves also register in our minds as gustatory images because they appeal to our sense of taste.

Tactile images of touch and texture are not as common because touch is difficult to render except in terms of effects. The speaker of Lowell's "Patterns," for example (p. 963), uses tactile imagery when imagining a never-to-happen embrace with her fiancé who we learn has been killed in war. Her imagery records the effect of the embrace ("bruised"), while her internalized feelings are expressed in metaphors ("aching, melting"):

> And the buttons of his waistcoat bruised my body as he clasped me
> Aching, melting, unafraid. (lines 51–52)

Tactile images are not uncommon in love poetry, where references to touch and feeling are natural, as in Rukeyser's "Looking at Each Other" (p. 666) and in Lowell's "Patterns." But usually love poetry deals with yearning and hope (as in Keats's "Bright Star," p. 654) rather than sexual fulfillment.

IMAGES OF MOTION AND ACTIVITY.   References to movement are also images. Images of general motion are **kinetic** (remember that *motion pictures* are also called "cinema"), while the term **kinesthetic** is applied to human or animal movement. Imagery of motion is closely related to visual images, for motion is most often seen. Masefield's British coaster, for example, is a visual image, but when it goes "Butting through the channel," the motion makes it also kinetic. When Hardy's corpses sit upright at the beginning of "Channel Firing" (p. 584), the image is kinesthetic, as is the action of Amy Lowell's speaker walking in the garden after hearing about her fiancé's death. Both types may be seen at the conclusion of the following poem, Elizabeth Bishop's "The Fish":

ELIZABETH BISHOP   (1911–1979)

The Fish ⸻⸻⸻⸻⸻⸻⸻⸻⸻⸻⸻⸻ *1946*

I caught a tremendous fish
and held him beside the boat
half out of water, with my hook
fast in a corner of his mouth.
He didn't fight
He hadn't fought at all.
He hung a grunting weight,
battered and venerable
and homely. Here and there
his brown skin hung in strips
like ancient wallpaper,
and its pattern of darker brown
was like wallpaper:
shapes like full-blown roses
stained and lost through age.

He was speckled with barnacles,
fine rosettes of lime,
and infested
with tiny white sea-lice,
and underneath two or three   20
rags of green weed hung down.
While his gills were breathing in
the terrible oxygen
—the frightening gills,
fresh and crisp with blood,   25
that can cut so badly—
I thought of the coarse white flesh
packed in like feathers,
the big bones and the little bones,
the dramatic reds and blacks   30
of his shiny entrails,
and the pink swim-bladder
like a big peony.
I looked into his eyes
which were far larger than mine   35
but shallower, and yellowed,
the irises backed and packed
with tarnished tinfoil
seen through the lenses
of old scratched isinglass.   40
They shifted a little, but not
to return my stare.
—It was more like the tipping
of an object toward the light.
I admired his sullen face,   45
the mechanism of his jaw,
and then I saw
that from his lower lip
—if you could call it a lip—
grim, wet, and weaponlike,   50
hung five old pieces of fish-line,
or four and a wire leader
with the swivel still attached,
with all their five big hooks
grown firmly in his mouth.   55
A green line, frayed at the end
where he broke it, two heavier lines,
and a fine black thread
still crimped from the strain and snap
when it broke and he got away.   60
Like medals with their ribbons
frayed and wavering,
a five-haired beard of wisdom
trailing from his aching jaw.

I stared and stared
and victory filled up
the little rented boat,
from the pool of bilge
where oil had spread a rainbow
around the rusted engine
to the bailer rusted orange,
the sun-cracked thwarts,
the oarlocks on their strings,
the gunnels—until everything
was rainbow, rainbow, rainbow!
And I let the fish go.

QUESTIONS

1. Describe the poem's images of action. What is unusual about them?
2. What impression does the fish make upon the speaker? Is the fish beautiful? ugly? Why is the fish described in such detail?
3. What do the "five old pieces of fish line" indicate?
4. How is the rainbow formed around the boat's engine? What does the rainbow mean to the speaker?
5. What right does the speaker have to keep the fish? Why does she choose to relinquish this right?

The kinetic images at the end of "The Fish" are those of victory filling the board (difficult to visualize) and the oil spreading to make a rainbow (easier to visualize). The kinesthetic images are readily imagined—the speaker's staring, observing, and letting the fish go—and they are vivid and real. The final gesture is the necessary outcome of the observed contrast between the deteriorating artifacts of human beings and the natural world of the fish, and it is a vivid expression of the right of the natural world to exist without human intervention. In short, Bishop's kinetic and kinesthetic images are designed to objectivize the need for freedom not only for human beings but for all the earth and animated Nature.

The range of objects or activities that poets employ as imagery is both vast and unpredictable. Indeed, an important quality about imagery is its very unpredictability. At a first reading of "The Pulley," by George Herbert, for example, you might be hard put to explain the connection between the title and the poem itself.

GEORGE HERBERT   (1593–1633)

The Pulley ————————————————————— *1633*

When God at first made man,
Having a glass of blessings standing by,

"Let us," said he, "pour on him all we can.
Let the world's riches, which dispersed lie,
  Contract into a span."°   5

So strength first made a way;
Then beauty flowed, then wisdom, honor, pleasure.
  When almost all was out, God made a stay,
Perceiving that, alone of all his treasure,
  Rest° in the bottom lay.   10

"For if I should," said he,
"Bestow this jewel also on my creature,
  He would adore my gifts instead of me.
And rest in Nature, not the God of Nature;
  So both should losers be.   15

"Yet let him keep the rest,
But keep them with repining restlessness.
  Let him be rich and weary, that at least,
If goodness lead him not, yet weariness
  May toss him to my breast."   20

THE PULLEY.   4 *span:* that is, within the control of human beings.   10 *rest:* (1) repose, security; (2) all that remains.

QUESTIONS

1. Describe the dramatic scene of the poem. Who is doing what?
2. What are the particular "blessings" that God confers on humanity, according to the speaker? Why should these be considered as blessings?
3. Consider the image of the pulley as the means, or device (through "repining restlessness"), by which God compels people to become worshipful.
4. Analyze and discuss the meaning of the images signified by the words *rest, pour, flowed,* and *toss.*

The connection between title and poem becomes clear if we recall that pulleys, because they increase mechanical advantage, may enable large and heavily resistant objects to be moved easily by only a small force. Herbert's image of the pulley assumes that the resistant object is the human race. People, according to Herbert's speaker, have been blessed with so much that they can easily neglect God. But God nevertheless has mechanical advantage because human beings are never satisfied with all their blessings. God uses *restlessness* to pull people away from their worldly preoccupations and "toss" them to the divine breast in worship and adoration. Although this mechanical image at first seems unusual and far-fetched, Herbert makes it seem natural and inevitable. Indeed, once we finish reading "The Pulley," the image no longer seems unusual or far-fetched at all, because it so aptly illustrates the connection between human behavior and divine power. Herbert has chosen and developed his image in a masterly way.

The areas from which kinetic and kinesthetic imagery may be derived are almost too varied to describe. Occupations, trades, professions, businesses, recreational activities—all these might furnish images. One poet introduces references from gardening, another from money and banking, another from modern real estate developments, another from life in the jungle. The freshness, newness, and surprise of literature result from the many and varied areas from which poets draw their images.

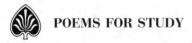 POEMS FOR STUDY

WILLIAM BLAKE   (1757–1827)

The Tyger° ————————————————————————— *1794*

Tyger! Tyger! burning bright
In the forests of the night,
What immortal hand or eye
Could frame thy fearful symmetry?

In what distant deeps or skies
Burnt the fire of thine eyes?
On what wings dare he aspire?
What the hand, dare seize the fire?

And what shoulder, & what art,
Could twist the sinews of thy heart?
And when thy heart began to beat,
What dread hand? & what dread feet?

What the hammer? what the chain?
In what furnace was thy brain?
What the anvil? what dread grasp
Dare its deadly terrors clasp?

When the stars threw down their spears,
And water'd heaven with their tears,
Did he smile his work to see?
Did he who made the Lamb make thee?

Tyger! Tyger! burning bright
In the forests of the night,
What immortal hand or eye
Dare frame thy fearful symmetry?

THE TYGER.   The title refers not only to a tiger, but to any large, wild, ferocious cat.

QUESTIONS

1. What do the associations of the image of "burning" suggest? Why is the burning done at night rather than day? What does night suggest?
2. Describe the kinesthetic images of lines 4–20. What ideas is Blake's speaker representing by these images? What attributes does the speaker suggest may belong to the blacksmith-type initiator of these actions?
3. Line 20 presents the kinesthetic image of a creator. What is implied about the mixture of good and evil in the world? What answer does the poem offer? Why does Blake phrase this line as a question rather than an assertion?
4. Stanza six repeats stanza one with only one change of imagery of action. Contrast these stanzas, stressing the difference between *could* (line 4) and *dare* (24).

SAMUEL TAYLOR COLERIDGE   (1772–1834)

Kubla Khan ——————————————————— *1816*

In Xanadu did Kubla Khan
A stately pleasure dome decree:
Where Alph,° the sacred river, ran
Through caverns measureless to man
   Down to a sunless sea.   5
So twice five miles of fertile ground
With walls and towers were girdled round:
And there were gardens bright with sinuous rills,
Where blossomed many an incense-bearing tree;
And here were forest ancient as the hills,   10
Enfolding sunny spots of greenery.

But oh! that deep romantic chasm which slanted
Down the green hill athwart a cedarn cover!
A savage place! as holy and enchanted
As e'er beneath a waning moon was haunted   15
By woman wailing for her demon lover!
And from this chasm, with ceaseless turmoil seething,
As if this earth in fast thick pants were breathing,
A mighty fountain momently was forced:
Amid whose swift half-intermitted burst   20
Huge fragments vaulted like rebounding hail,
Or chaffy grain beneath the thresher's flail:
And 'mid these dancing rocks at once and ever
It flung up momently the sacred river.
Five miles meandering with a mazy motion   25
Through wood and dale the sacred river ran,

KUBLA KHAN.   3 *Alph:* possibly a reference to the river Alpheus in Greece, as described by the ancient writers Virgil and Pausanias.

Then reached the caverns measureless to man,
And sank in tumult to a lifeless ocean:
And 'mid this tumult Kubla heard from far
Ancestral voices prophesying war!
   The shadow of the dome of pleasure
   Floated midway on the waves;
   Where was heard the mingled measure
   From the fountain and the caves.
It was a miracle of rare device,
A sunny pleasure dome with caves of ice!

   A damsel with a dulcimer
   In a vision once I saw:
   It was an Abyssinian maid,
   And on her dulcimer she played
   Singing of Mount Abora.°
Could I revive within me
Her symphony and song,
To such a deep delight 'twould win me,
That with music loud and long,
I would build that dome in air,
That sunny dome! those caves of ice!
And all who heard should see them there,
And all should cry, Beware! Beware!
His flashing eyes, his floating hair!
Weave a circle round him thrice,
And close your eyes with holy dread,
For he on honeydew hath fed,
And drunk the milk of Paradise.

41 *Mount Abora:* a mountain of Coleridge's imagination. But see John Milton's *Paradise Lost*, IV, lines 268–284.

QUESTIONS

1. How many of the poem's images might be sketched or visualized? Which ones would be panoramic landscapes? Which might be close-ups?

2. What is the effect of auditory images such as "wailing," "fast thick pants," "tumult," "ancestral voices prophesying war," and "mingled measure"?

3. When Coleridge was writing this poem, he was recalling it from a dream. At line 54 he was interrupted, and when he resumed he could write no more. How might an argument be made that the poem is finished?

4. How do lines 35–36 establish the pleasure dome as a place of mysterious oddity? What is the effect of the words *miracle* and *rare*? The effect of combining the images "sunny" with "caves of ice"?

5. Why does the speaker yearn for the power of the singing Abyssinian maid? What kinesthetic images end the poem? How are these images important in the speaker's desire to reconstruct the vision of the pleasure dome?

RICHARD CRASHAW   (1613–1649)

On Our Crucified Lord, Naked and Bloody ———————— *1646*

Th' have° left Thee naked,° Lord, O that they had;   *they have*
This garment too I would they had denied.
Thee with Thyself they have too richly clad,
Opening the purple° wardrobe of Thy side.°
    O never could be found garments too good   5
    For Thee to wear, but these, of Thine own blood.

ON OUR CRUCIFIED LORD, NAKED AND BLOODY.   1 *naked:* See Mark 15:24.   3–4
Thee . . . side: John 20:34.   4 *purple:* Mark 15:17.

QUESTIONS

1. Explain the contradiction and irony in the poem. Why does clothing made by human beings seem unworthy of being draped upon the crucified Lord?
2. What is meant by "this garment" in line 2? What is the relationship between this phrase and "Thee with Thyself" in line 3?
3. Does the emphasis on the blood of Christ in this poem seem appropriate or inappropriate for a devotional poem?

H. D. (HILDA DOOLITTLE)   (1886–1961)

Heat ——————————————— *1916*

O wind, rend open the heat,
cut apart the heat,
rend it to tatters.

Fruit cannot drop
through this thick air—   5
fruit cannot fall into heat
that presses up and blunts
the points of pears
and rounds of grapes.

Cut the heat—   10
plough through it,
turning it on either side
of your path.

QUESTIONS

1. What is the meaning of the images of rending and cutting?
2. In 4–9, is it true that fruit cannot fall? If not, what is the meaning of the image that heat may blunt the points of pears and rounds of grapes?

3. Discuss the image of a plough as a cutter and separator of heat.

4. In light of the images, what impression of heat does the poet express?

T. S. ELIOT   (1888–1965)

Preludes _____ *1910*

I

The winter evening settles down
With smell of steaks in passageways.
Six o'clock.
The burnt-out ends of smoky days.
And now a gusty shower wraps
The grimy scraps
Of withered leaves about your feet
And newspapers from vacant lots;
The showers beat
On broken blinds and chimney-pots,
And at the corner of the street
A lonely cab-horse steams and stamps.
And then the lighting of the lamps.

II

The morning comes to consciousness
Of faint stale smells of beer
From the sawdust-trampled street
With all its muddy feet that press
To early coffee-stands.
With the other masquerades
That time resumes,
One thinks of all the hands
That are raising dingy shades
In a thousand furnished rooms.

III

You tossed a blanket from the bed,
You lay upon your back, and waited;
You dozed, and watched the night revealing
The thousand sordid images
Of which your soul was constituted;
They flickered against the ceiling.
And when all the world came back
And the light crept up between the shutters
And you heard the sparrows in the gutters,
You had such a vision of the street,
As the street hardly understands;

Sitting along the bed's edge, where   35
You curled the papers from your hair,
Or clasped the yellow soles of feet
In the palms of both soiled hands.

        IV

His soul stretched tight across the skies
That fade behind a city block,   40
Or trampled by insistent feet
At four and five and six o'clock;
And short square fingers stuffing pipes,
And evening newspapers, and eyes
Assured of certain certainties,   45
The conscience of a blackened street
Impatient to assume the world.

  I am moved by fancies that are curled
Around these images, and cling:
The notion of some infinitely gentle   50
Infinitely suffering thing.

  Wipe your hand across your mouth, and laugh;
The worlds revolve like ancient women
Gathering fuel in vacant lots.

QUESTIONS

1. From what locations are the images in stanza one derived? How do the images shift in the second stanza? What is the connection between the images in stanza two and stanza three?

2. Who is the "you" in stanza three? What images are associated with this listener?

3. Who is the "His" of stanza four? How do the images develop in this stanza? What is meant particularly in the images of lines 46–47?

4. What is the nature of the bodily imagery in the poem? The urban imagery? What impressions do these images cause?

5. In lines 48–51, what does the speaker conclude? How do the last two unnumbered stanzas constitute a contrast of attitude?

GERARD MANLEY HOPKINS   (1844–1889)

Spring ———————————————————————— *1877*

Nothing is so beautiful as Spring—
  When weeds, in wheels, shoot long and lovely and lush;
  Thrush's eggs look little low heavens, and thrush

Through the echoing timber does so rinse and wring
The ear, it strikes like lightnings to hear him sing;
   The glassy peartree leaves and blooms, they brush
   The descending blue; that blue is all in a rush
With richness; the racing lambs too have fair their fling.

What is all this juice and all this joy?
   A strain of the earth's sweet being in the beginning
In Eden garden.—Have, get, before it cloy,
   Before it cloud, Christ, lord, and sour with sinning,
Innocent mind and Mayday in girl and boy,
   Most, O maid's child, thy choice and worthy the winning.

QUESTIONS

1. What images does the speaker mention as support for his first line, "Nothing is so beautiful as Spring"? Are these images those that you would normally expect? To what degree do they seem to be new or unusual?

2. What images of motion and activity do you find in the poem? Are these mainly static or dynamic? What do these suggest about the speaker's view of spring?

3. What is the relationship between "Eden garden" in line 11 and the scene described in lines 1–8? To what extent are spring and "innocent mind and Mayday" a glimpse of the Garden of Eden?

4. Christ is mentioned in lines 12 and 14 (as "maid's child"). Do these references seal the poem off from readers who are not Christian? Why or why not?

EZRA POUND   (1885–1972)

In a Station of the Metro° _____ *1916*

The apparition of these faces in the crowd;
Petals on a wet, black bough.

IN A STATION OF THE METRO.   *Metro:* the Paris subway.

QUESTIONS

1. Is the image of the wet, black bough happy or sad? If the petals were on a tree in the sunlight, what would be the effect?

2. What is the meaning of the image suggested by *apparition*? Does it suggest a positive or negative view of human life?

3. This poem contains only two lines. Is it proper to consider it as a poem nevertheless? If it is not a poem, what is it?

WILLIAM SHAKESPEARE   (1564–1616)

Sonnet 130: My Mistress' Eyes Are Nothing Like the Sun ——————— *1609*

My mistress'° eyes are nothing like the sun;	*woman friend*
Coral is far more red than her lips' red;	
If snow be white, why then her breasts are dun;	
If hairs be wires, black wires grow on her head.	
I have seen roses damasked,° red and white,	*set in an elaborate bouquet* 5
But no such roses see I in her cheeks;	
And in some perfumes is there more delight	
Than in the breath that from my mistress reeks.	
I love to hear her speak, yet well I know	
That music hath a far more pleasing sound;	10
I grant I never saw a goddess go;	
My mistress, when she walks, treads on the ground.	
And yet, by heaven, I think my love as rare	
As any she belied with false compare.	

QUESTIONS

1. To what does the speaker negatively compare his mistress's eyes? Lips? Breasts? Hair? Cheeks? Breath? Voice? Walk? What kinds of images are created in these negative comparisons?

2. What conventional images does this poem ridicule? What sort of poem is Shakespeare mocking by using the negative images in lines 1–12?

3. In the light of the last two lines, do you think the speaker intends the images as insults? If not as insults, how should they be taken?

4. Are most of the images auditory, olfactory, visual, or kinesthetic? Explain.

5. What point does this poem make about love poetry? About human relationships? How does the imagery contribute to the development of both points?

DAVID WOJAHN   (b. 1953)

"It's Only Rock and Roll But I Like It":
The Fall of Saigon ———————————————————— *1975*

The guttural stammer of the chopper blades
Raising arabesques of dust, tearing leaves
From the orange trees lining the Embassy compound:
One chopper left, and a CBS cameraman leans
From inside its door, exploiting the artful   5
Mayhem. Somewhere a radio blares the Stones,
"I like it, like it, yes indeed. . . ." Carts full
Of files blaze in the yard. Flak-jacketed marines
Gunpoint the crowd away. The overloaded chopper strains

And blunders from the roof. An ice-cream-suited
Saigonese drops his briefcase; both hands
Now cling to the airborne skis. The camera gets
It all: the marine leaning out the copter bay,
His fists beating time. Then the hands giving way.

QUESTIONS

1. What actions take place in this poem? Why does the Saigonese "cling to the air-
    borne skis"? What happens to him?
2. Describe the poem's images of sound. How many such images does the poem
    contain? What is their effect? What images of sight do you find? What other types
    of images?
3. Contrast the poem's title with its content.
4. Cumulatively, what is the relationship of the poem's images to the phrase "art-
    ful / Mayhem" in lines 5 and 6 and also to the poem's judgment about the Amer-
    ican presence in Vietnam?

WRITING ABOUT IMAGERY

Questions for Discovering Ideas

In preparing to write you should develop a set of thoughtful notes, dealing with issues such as the following:

*   What type or types of images prevail in the work? Visual (shapes, colors)? auditory
    (sounds)? olfactory (smells)? tactile (touch and texture)? gustatory (taste)? kinetic
    or kinesthetic (motion)? Or is the imagery a combination of these?
*   To what degree do the images reflect (a) the poet's actual observation or (b) the
    poet's reading and knowledge of fields like science or history?
*   How well do the images stand out? How vivid are they? How is this vividness
    achieved?
*   Within a group of images, say visual or auditory, do the images pertain to one
    location or area rather than another (e.g., natural scenes rather than interiors,
    snowy scenes rather than grassy ones; loud and harsh sounds rather than quiet
    and civilized ones)?
*   What explanation is needed for the images? (Images might be derived from the
    Classics or the Bible, the Revolutionary War or World War II, the behaviors of
    four-footed creatures or birds, and so on.)
*   What effect do the poem's circumstances (e.g., conditions of brightness or dark-
    ness, warmth or cold, etc.) have upon the images and your responses to them?
    What poetic purpose is served by your responses?
*   How well are the images integrated within the poem's argument or development?

Answering questions like these should provide you with a sizable body of ready-
made material that you can convert directly to the body of your essay.

Strategies for Organizing Ideas

Connect a brief overview of the poem to your plan for the body of your essay, such as that the writer uses images to strengthen ideas about war, character, love, and so on, or that the writer relies predominantly on images of sight, sound, and action. You might choose to deal exclusively with one of the following aspects, or, equally likely, you may combine your approaches, as you wish.

1. *Images Suggesting Ideas and/or Moods.* Such an essay should emphasize the results of the imagery. What ideas or moods are evoked by the images? (The auditory images beginning "Anthem for Doomed Youth," for example, all point toward a condemnation of war's brutal cruelty. The visual images of "Preludes" all point toward a loss of principle and vitality in modern urban life.) Do the images promote approval or disapproval? Cheerfulness? Melancholy? Are the images drab, exciting, vivid? How? Why? Are they conducive to humor, or surprise? How does the writer achieve these effects? Are the images consistent, or are they ambiguous? (For example, the images in Masefield's "Cargoes" indicate first approval and then disapproval, with no ambiguity. By contrast, Shakespeare's images in "My Mistress' Eyes" might be construed as insults, but in context, they may be seen as compliments.)

2. *The Types of Images.* Here the emphasis is on the categories of images themselves. Is there a predominance of a particular type of image (e.g., visual or auditory images), or is there a blending? Is there a bunching of types at particular points in the poem or story? If so, why? Is there any shifting as the work develops (as, for example, in Owen's "Anthem for Doomed Youth," where the auditory images first evoke loudness and harshness, but later bring out quietness and sorrow)? Are the images appropriate, granting the nature and apparent intent of the work? Do they assist in making the ideas seem convincing? If there seems to be any inappropriateness, what is its effect?

3. *Systems of Images.* Here the emphasis should be on the areas from which the images are drawn. This is another way of considering the appropriateness of the imagery. Is there a pattern of similar or consistent images, such as darkness and dinginess (Eliot's "Preludes") or color and activity (Hopkins's "Spring")? Do all the images adhere consistently to a particular frame of reference, such as a sunlit garden (Lowell's "Patterns"), an extensive recreational forest and garden (Coleridge's "Kubla Khan" [p. 637]), dreary urban scenes (Eliot's "Preludes"), a church graveyard (Hardy's "Channel Firing" [p. 584]), or a darkened forest (Blake's "The Tyger")? What is unusual or unique about the set of images? What unexpected or new responses do they produce?

Your conclusion, in addition to recapitulating your major points, is the place for additional insights. It would not be proper to go too far in new directions here, but you might briefly take up one or more of the ideas that you have not developed in the body. In short, what have you learned from your study of imagery in your poem?

SAMPLE ESSAY

The Images of Masefield's "Cargoes"°

[1] In the three-stanza poem "Cargoes," John Masefield develops imagery to create a negative impression of modern commercial life.* There is a contrast between the first two stanzas and the third, with the first two idealizing the romantic, distant past and the third demeaning the modern, gritty, grimy present. Masefield's images are thus both positive and lush, on the one hand, and negative and stark, on the other.†

The most evocative and pleasant images in the poem are in the first stanza. The speaker asks that we imagine a "Quinquereme of Nineveh from distant Ophir" (line 1), an ocean-going, many-oared vessel loaded with treasure for the Biblical King Solomon. As Masefield identifies the cargo, the visual images are rich and romantic (lines 3–5):

[2]
> With a cargo of ivory,
> And apes and peacocks,
> Sandalwood, cedarwood, and sweet white wine.

Ivory suggests richness, which is augmented by the exotic "apes and peacocks" in all their exciting strangeness. The "sandalwood, cedarwood, and sweet white wine" evoke pungent smells and tastes. The "sunny" light of ancient Palestine (line 2) not only illuminates the imaginative scene (visual), but invites readers to imagine the sun's warming touch (tactile). The references to animals and birds also suggest the sounds that these creatures would make (auditory). Thus, in this lush first stanza, images derived from all the senses are introduced to create impressions of a glorious past.

[3] Almost equally lush are the images of the second stanza, which completes the poem's first part. Here the visual imagery evokes the royal splendor of a tall-masted, full-sailed galleon (line 6) at the height of Spain's commercial power in the sixteenth century. The galleon's cargo suggests great wealth, with sparkling diamonds and amethysts, and Portugese "gold moidores" gleaming in open chests (line 10). With cinnamon in the second stanza's bill of lading (line 10), Masefield includes the image of a pleasant-tasting spice.

[4] The negative imagery of the third stanza is in stark contrast to the first two stanzas. Here the poem draws the visual image of a modern "Dirty British coaster" (line 11) to focus on the griminess and suffocation of modern civilization. This spray-swept ship is loaded with materials that pollute the earth with noise and smoke. The smoke-stack of the coaster (line 11) and the firewood it is carrying suggest choking smog. The Tyne Coal (line 13) and road rails (line 14) suggest the noise and smoke of puffing railroad engines. As if this were not enough, the "pig-lead" (line 14) to be used in various industrial processes indicates not just more unpleasantness, but also something more poisonous

---

° For this poem, see p. 629.
* Central idea.
† Thesis sentence.

and deadly. In contrast to the lush and stately imagery of the first two stanzas, the images in the third stanza invite the conclusion that people now, when the "Dirty British coaster" butts through the English Channel, are surrounded and threatened by visual, olfactory, and auditory pollution.

The poem thus establishes a romantic past and ugly present through images of sight, smell, and sound. The images of motion also emphasize this view: In stanzas one and two the quinquereme is "rowing" and the galleon is "dipping." These kinetic images suggest dignity and lightness. The British coaster, however, is "butting," an image indicating bull-like hostility and stupid force. These, together with all the other images, focus the poem's negative views of modern life. The facts that existence for both the ancient Palestinians and the Renaissance Spaniards included slavery (of those men rowing the quinquereme) and piracy (by those Spanish "explorers" who robbed and killed the natives of the isthmus) should probably not be emphasized as a protest against Masefield's otherwise valid contrasts in images. His final commentary may hence be thought of as the banging of his "cheap tin trays" (line 15), which makes a percussive climax of the oppressive images filling too large a portion of modern lives.

[5]

Commentary on the Essay

The method illustrated in this sample essay is the first strategy (p. 645), using images to develop ideas and moods. All the examples—derived directly from the poem—emphasize the qualities of Masefield's images. This method permits the introduction of imagery drawn from all the senses in order to demonstrate Masefield's ideas about the past and the present. Other approaches might have concentrated exclusively on Masefield's visual images, or upon his images drawn from trade and commerce. Because Masefield uses auditory and gustatory images, but does not develop them extensively, sound or taste might be appropriately devoted to short, paragraph-length essays.

The introductory paragraph of the essay presents the central idea that Masefield uses his images climactically to lead to his negative view of modern commercialism. The thesis sentence indicates that the topics to be developed are those of [1] lushness, and [2] starkness.

Paragraphs two and three form a unit stressing the lushness and exoticism of stanza one and the wealth and colorfulness of stanza two. In particular, paragraph 2 uses words like *lush, evocative, rich, exotic, pungent,* and *romantic* to characterize the pleasing mental pictures the images invoke. Although the paragraph indicates enthusiastic responses to the images, however, it does not go beyond the limits of the images themselves.

Paragraph four stresses the contrast of Masefield's images in stanza three with those of stanzas one and two. To this end the paragraph illustrates the imaginative reconstruction needed to develop an understanding of this contrast. The unpleasantness, annoyance, and even the danger of the cargoes mentioned in stanza three are therefore emphasized as the qualities evoked by the images.

The last paragraph demonstrates that the imagery of motion—not much stressed in the poem—is in agreement with the rest of Masefield's imagery. As a demonstration of the need for fair, impartial judgment, the conclusion introduces the possible objection that Masefield's imagistic portraits may be slanted because they include not a full but rather a partial view of their respective historical periods. Thus the concluding paragraph adds balance to the analysis illustrated in paragraphs 2, 3, and 4.

WRITING TOPICS

1. Compare the images of home in "Anthem for Doomed Youth" and Alan Seeger's "I Have a Rendezvous with Death" (p. 982). Describe the differing effects of the images. How are the images used? How effectively do these images aid in the development of the attitudes toward war expressed in each poem? How is your reading of the poems affected by the knowledge that both Owen and Seeger were killed in war?

2. Based on the poems in this chapter by Crashaw, Blake, Coleridge, H. D., and Hopkins, write an essay discussing the poetic use of images drawn from the natural world. What sorts of references do the poets make? What attitudes do they express about the details they select? What is the relationship between the images and religious views? What judgments about God and nature do the poets show by their images?

3. Considering the imagery of Eliot's "Preludes," write an essay explaining the power of imagery. As you develop your thoughts, be sure to consider the dramatic nature of Eliot's images, and to account for the impressions and ideas that they create. You may also wish to introduce references to images from other poems that are relevant to your points.

4. Write a poem describing one of these:
   a. Athletes who have just completed an exhausting run.
   b. Children getting out of school for the day.
   c. Your recollection of having been lost as a child.
   d. The antics of your dog, cat, horse, or other pet.
   e. A particularly good meal you ate recently.
   f. The best concert you ever attended.
   g. Driving to work/school on a rainy/snowy day.

   Then, write an analysis of the images you selected for your poem, and explain your choices. What details stand out in your mind? What do you recall best—sight, smell, sound, action? What is the relationship between your images and the ideas you express in your poem?

5. Study the reproduction of Herkomer's painting *Hard Times* (p. 629). Then write an essay comparing and contrasting the artistic techniques with Hopkins's poem "Spring" (p. 641) and Pound's "In a Station of the Metro" (p. 642), along with other poems that you may wish to include. What similarities and differences do you find in subject matter, treatment, arrangement, and general idea? On the basis of your comparison, what relationships do you perceive between poetic and painterly technique?

17

Rhetorical Figures: A Source of Depth and Range in Poetry

Figurative Language refers to expressions that conform to regularized arrangements of words and thought. These patterns, called **rhetorical figures** or **rhetorical devices**, are the tools that help make literary works effective, persuasive, and forceful.

The two most important figures are *metaphor* and *simile*. Others are *paradox, anaphora, apostrophe, personification, synecdoche* and *metonymy, synæsthesia, pun* (or *paronomasia*), *overstatement*, and *understatement*. All these figures are modes of comparison, and they may be expressed in single words, phrases, clauses, and entire structures. The use of figures enables poets to extend and deepen their range of subject matter just as symbolism does. Indeed, the words *metaphor* and *metaphorical* are often broadly applied to most rhetorical figures, including symbols.

METAPHOR AND SIMILE

A **metaphor** (a "carrying out a change") describes something as though it actually were something else, thereby enhancing understanding and insight. One of Shakespeare's best-known metaphors is "All the world's a stage, / And all the men and women merely players," in which Shakespeare's character Jacques (from *As You Like It*, II.7) explains human life in terms of stage life. It is important to recognize that the comparison, as a metaphor, does not state that the world is *like* a stage, but that it literally *is* a stage.

While a metaphor merges identities in this way, a **simile** (the "showing of similarity or oneness") utilizes *similarity* to carry out the explanation. A simile is distinguishable from a metaphor because it is introduced by "like" with nouns and "as" (also "as if" and "as though") with clauses. Campion's sentence "Her brows like bended bows do stand," from the poem "Cherry Ripe" (p. 926), points out that the young woman being described puts down offenders with frowns as though she were shooting them with arrows. Because the simile is introduced by "like," the emphasis of the figure is on the *similarity* of her eyebrows to bows (and arrows), not on the *identification* of the two.

Imagery, Metaphor, and Simile

In Chapter 16, we saw how imagery stimulates the imagination and recalls memories (*images*) of sights, sounds, tastes, smells, sensations of touch, and motions. Metaphors and similes go beyond such literal imagery to introduce perceptions and comparisons that may be unusual, unpredictable, and surprising. They connect the thing or things to be communicated—such as qualities of love or the excitement of unexpected discovery—with a new insight that is made objective through the comparison of a simile or the equation of a metaphor. For example, in "A Valediction: Forbidding Mourning," Donne's speaker points out that a trip away from a loved one is not really a separation, but is rather a thinning out, like the hammering of gold into gold foil. How many people have ever perceived such a metaphorical connection—between the malleability of metal and the constancy of lovers? But is it not true that the metaphor emphasizes the bond between two lovers, and also that gold shows how valuable the bond is? Such a figure extends knowledge and awareness by introducing perceptions that otherwise would not come to light. First and foremost, then, the use of metaphors and similes is one of the ways in which great literature leads us to see the world in fresh and original ways.

For example, to communicate a character's joy and excitement, the sentence "She was happy" is accurate but not interesting or effective. A more vivid way of saying the same thing is to use an image of an action, such as, "She jumped for joy." This image gives us a literal picture of an action demonstrating happiness. But an even better way of communicating a happy state is the following simile: "She felt as if she had just inherited fifty million tax-free dollars." Because readers easily understand the excitement, disbelief, exhilaration, and joy that such an event would bring, they also understand—and feel—the character's happiness. It is the *simile* that evokes this perception, for no simple description could help a reader comprehend the same degree of emotion.

As a poetic example, let us refer to Keats's "On First Looking into Chapman's Homer," which Keats wrote soon after reading the translation of Homer's *Iliad* and *Odyssey* by the Renaissance poet George Chapman. Keats's main idea is that Chapman not only translated Homer's words but also transmitted his greatness.

JOHN KEATS   (1795–1821)

On First Looking into Chapman's Homer _____ *1816*

Much have I travell'd in the realms of gold,
   And many goodly states and kingdoms seen:
   Round many western islands have I been

Which bards in fealty to Apollo° hold.
Oft of one wide expanse had I been told   5
  That deep-brow'd Homer ruled as his demesne;°
  Yet did I never breathe its pure serene°
Till I heard Chapman speak out loud and bold:
Then felt I like some watcher of the skies
  When a new planet swims into his ken;°   10
Or like stout Cortez° when with eagle eyes
  He star'd at the Pacific—and all his men
Look'd at each other with a wild surmise—
  Silent, upon a peak in Darien.

ON FIRST LOOKING INTO CHAPMAN'S HOMER. George Chapman (c. 1560–1634) published his translations of Homer's *Iliad* in 1612 and *Odyssey* in 1614–15.   4 *bards . . . Apollo:* writers who are sworn subjects of Apollo, the Greek god of light, music, poetry, prophecy, and the sun.   6 *demesne:* realm, estate.   7 *serene:* a clear expanse of air; also grandeur, clarity; rulers were also sometimes called "serene majesty."   10 *ken:* field of sight.   11 *Cortez:* Hernando Cortez (1485–1547), a Spanish general and the conqueror of Mexico. Keats confuses him with Vasco de Balboa (c. 1475–1519), the first European to see the Pacific Ocean (in 1510) from Darien, an old name for the Isthmus of Panama).

QUESTIONS

1. What is being discovered in this poem? To what extent is this process of discovery a universal experience?

2. Explain the metaphor of land and travel that Keats develops in lines 1–6. Be careful to consider the words *realms, states, kingdoms, islands, expanse,* and *demesne.*

3 How successfully does Keats convey excitement through the similes in lines 9–10 and 11–14? Create a simile of your own to express a feeling about discovery. How does yours compare with Keats's?

4. Describe the metaphor of *swims* in line 10. What might have been the impact if Keats had used words such as *drifts, floats, flows,* or *wanders?*

To illustrate the power of metaphorical language, we may first briefly paraphrase the sonnet's content:

> I have enjoyed much art and read much European literature, and have been told that Homer is the best writer of all. However, because I do not know Greek, I could not really appreciate his works until I discovered them in Chapman's translation. To me, this experience was exciting and awe-inspiring.

If all Keats had written were a paragraph like this one, we would pay no attention to it, for it carries no sense of excitement or stimulation at all. The third sentence, for example, is informative but not interesting. But the last six lines of the sonnet as Keats wrote them contain two memorable similes ("like some watcher" and "like stout Cortez"). They stand out, and demand a special effort of imagination. When we mull them over, we might suppose that we actually *are* astronomers just discovering a new planet, and that we actually *are* the first explorers to see the Pacific Ocean. As we imagine ourselves in these roles, we can understand the amazement, wonder, excitement, exhilaration, anticipation, joy, and feeling of accomplishment that would accompany such discoveries. If we imagine these feelings, then Keats has unlocked experiences that the relatively unpromising title does not suggest. He has given us something new. He has enlarged us.

Tenor and Vehicle

To describe the relationship between a writer's ideas and the metaphors and similes chosen to objectify them, two useful terms have been coined by I. A. Richards (in *The Philosophy of Rhetoric*). First is the **tenor**, which is the totality of ideas and attitudes not only of the literary speaker but also of the author. Second is the **vehicle**, or the details that carry the tenor. The vehicle of the fifty-million dollars simile is the description of the inheritance, while the tenor is joy. Similarly, the tenor of the similes in the last six lines of Keats's sonnet is awe and wonder; the vehicle is the reference to astronomical and geographical discovery.

Characteristics of Metaphorical Language

It would be difficult to find any piece of good writing that does not use metaphors and similes. Such language is most vital, however, in imaginative writing, particularly poetry, where it compresses thought, promotes understanding, and shapes response.

As we saw in Chapter 16, images are embodied in words or descriptions. For example, the word *rose* alone may evoke an image of roses. But the word is not a metaphor or simile until its associations are used in an equative or comparative way, as in "A Red, Red Rose" by Robert Burns.

ROBERT BURNS   (1759–1796)

A Red, Red Rose ———————————————————————— *1796*

O my Luve's like a red, red rose,
  That's newly sprung in June:
O my Luve's like the melodie
  That's sweetly play'd in tune.

As fair art thou, my bonnie lass,
  So deep in luve am I;
And I will luve thee still, my Dear,
  Till a'° the seas gang° dry.   *all; go*

Till a' the seas gang dry, my Dear,
  And the rocks melt wi'° the sun: *with*
And I will luve thee still, my Dear,
  While the sands o'° life shall run.   *of*

And fare thee weel, my only Luve!
  And fare thee weel, awhile!
And I will come again, my Luve,   15
  Tho' it were ten thousand mile!

QUESTIONS

1. In light of the character and background of the speaker, do the two opening similes seem common or unusual? If they are just ordinary, does that fact diminish their value? How and why?
2. Describe the shift of listener envisioned after the first stanza. How are the last three stanzas related to the first?
3. Consider the metaphors concerning time and travel. How do the metaphors assist you in comprehending the speaker's character?

In the first stanza the speaker is telling us about his romantic enthusiasm. *We* know that such a lover could pay compliments forever, but *the poet* knows that too many compliments would bore us. For this reason the similes keep us interested but also keep the poem brief. The simile of the rose, for example, brings to mind many possible associations and feelings: After winter's drab leaflessness, springtime's lush growth creates new life; one of the loveliest and most fragrant flowers is the rose. The associations of roses are therefore beauty, color, love, the end of dreariness, and the seasonal renewal of the earth's fertility. Once we have expanded the simile in this way, we have come close to comprehending the speaker's enthusiasm, and we have done so without wading through an endless number of compliments.

This development of Burns's simile may seem at first like a great deal more than Burns intended; indeed, it uses many more words in prose than he uses in verse. However, it reflects the power of metaphorical language: Once it unlocks our minds, we may then give our thoughts free rein as we consider the full ramifications of metaphors, that equal, and similes, that compare.

OTHER RHETORICAL FIGURES

Paradox

A **paradox** is a device in which an apparent contradiction reveals an unexpected truth. The wit of the figure is that the contradiction is not a contradiction at all. The second line of Sir Thomas Wyatt's sonnet "I Find No Peace," for example (p. 670), shows two paradoxes. One contrasts fear and hope, the other fire and ice: "I fear and hope; I burn and freeze like ice." These paradoxes reflect the contradictory states of people in love—wanting love ("hope," "burn"), but also being uncertain and unsure about the relationship ("fear," "freeze"). The paradoxes thus highlight the truth that love is a complex emotion.

Anaphora

Anaphora (to carry again or repeat) is the repetition of the same word or phrase throughout a work or a section of a work. The effect is to lend weight and emphasis. In "The Bells," for example, Poe repeats the word *bells* many times, both for emphasis and also to suggest tolling bells. In Blake's "The Tyger," the interrogative word *what* is used five times to emphasize the mystery of evil:

> *What* the hammer? *what* the chain?
> In *what* furnace was thy brain?
> *What* the anvil? *what* dread grasp
> Dare its deadly terrors clasp?

Anaphora is the most obvious feature of Rukeyser's "Looking at Each Other," where the word *yes* begins each of the poem's twenty-five lines.

Apostrophe

In an **apostrophe** (a turning away, or redirection of attention) a speaker addresses a real or imagined listener who is not present. It is like a public speech, with readers as audience. Apostrophe enables the speaker to develop ideas that might arise naturally on a public occasion, as in Wordsworth's sonnet "London, 1802," which is addressed to the long dead English poet Milton. In Keats's sonnet "Bright Star," the speaker addresses a distant and inanimate star, yet through apostrophe he proceeds as though the star has human understanding and divine power.

JOHN KEATS (1795–1822)

Bright Star ————————————————————— *1838 (1819)*

Bright star! would I were steadfast as thou art—
  Not in lone splendor hung aloft the night,
And watching, with eternal lids apart,
  Like Nature's patient, sleepless eremite,°   *hermit*
The moving waters at their priestlike task
  Of pure ablution round earth's human shores,
Or gazing on the new soft-fallen mask
  Of snow upon the mountains and the moors;
No—yet still steadfast, still unchangeable,
  Pillowed upon my fair love's ripening breast,
To feel forever its soft fall and swell,
  Awake forever in a sweet unrest,
    Still, still to hear her tender-taken breath,
    And so live ever—or else swoon to death.

QUESTIONS

1. With what topic is the speaker concerned in this sonnet? How does he compare himself with the distant star?

2. What qualities does the speaker attribute specifically to the star? What sort of role does he seem to assign to it? In light of this role, and the qualities needed to serve in it, how might the star be compared to a divine and benign presence?

3. In light of the stress made on the words "forever" and "ever" in lines 11–14, how appropriate is the choice of the star as the subject of the apostrophe in the poem?

In this sonnet the speaker addresses the star as though it is a person or god, an object of adoration, and the poem is therefore like a petitional prayer. The star is idealized with qualities that the speaker wishes to establish in himself, namely steadfastness, eternal watchfulness, and fidelity. The point of the apostrophe is thus to dramatize the speaker's yearning, and to stress the permanence of space and eternity as contrasted with earthly impermanence.

Personification

A close neighbor of apostrophe is **personification**—the attribution of human characteristics to either non-human objects or abstractions. Poets introduce personification to explore relationships to environment, ideals, and inner lives. In "Bright Star," as we have just seen, Keats personifies the star addressed by the speaker. Shakespeare, in Sonnet 146, "Poor Soul, the Center of My Sinful Earth" (p. 986), personifies his own soul so that he can deal with earthly versus heavenly concerns. Other major examples of personification are Keats's "To Autumn" and "Ode on a Grecian Urn," and Shelley's "Ode to the West Wind" (pp. 661, 848, 776).

Synecdoche and Metonymy

These figures are close in purpose and effect. **Synecdoche** ("taking one thing out of another") is a device in which a part stands for the whole, or a whole for a part, like the expression "All hands aboard" to signify that a ship's crew should return to ship. **Metonymy** (a "transfer of name") substitutes one thing for another with which it is closely identified, as when "the White House" signifies the policies and activities of the President. The purpose of both devices is the creation of new insights and ideas, just like metaphors and similes.

Synecdoche may be seen in Keats's "To Autumn," where the gourd and hazel shells in lines 7–8, which are single instances of ripe produce, stand for the entire autumnal harvest. In Wordsworth's "London, 1802" (p. 669), the phrase "thy heart" (line 13) is a synecdoche in which a part—the heart—refers to the complete person. Metonymy may be seen in Keats's "To Autumn" (again), when the "granary floor," the place where grain is stored, bears the transferred meaning of the entire harvest stored there. In "Exit, Pursued by a Bear" (p. 664), Ogden Nash metonymically uses brand names, the names of artists, and the names of cities to mean objects, artworks, and places.

Synæsthesia

In **synæsthesia** (the bringing together of feelings) a poet describes one feeling or perception with words that are usually used for a totally different or even opposite feeling or perception, as in darkness that is visible, a thought that is green, or a soul that may clap its hands. Keats makes great use of synæsthesia, as, for example, in the "Ode to a Nightingale" (p. 770), where a plot of ground is *melodious*, a draught of wine tastes of "Dance, and Provençal song, and sunburnt mirth," and beaded bubbles of wine *wink* at the brim of a glass.

Pun, or Paronomasia

Another transferring figure is the **pun** (a point or a puncture), or **paronomasia** (something beside a name). A pun is a word play which reveals that words with different meanings have similar or even identical sounds. Because puns can be outrageous, and often require a little bit of thinking, people often groan when they hear them (even while they enjoy them). Also, because puns often seem to play only with sound, they have not always enjoyed critical acclaim, but good puns may always be relished because they work with sounds to *reveal* ideas. John Gay, for example, utilizes clever and complex puns in the following song, sung by the gang of thieves in *The Beggar's Opera* (1728), a play which, incidentally, marked the beginning of the musical comedy tradition:

JOHN GAY   (1685–1732)

Let Us Take the Road ———————————————— *1728*

Let us take the road.
  Hark! I hear the sound of coaches!
  The hour of attack approaches,
To your arms, brave boys, and load.
    See the ball I hold! [*holding up a bullet*]
  Let the chymists° toil like asses,   *alchemists*
  Our fire their fire surpasses,
    And turns all our lead to gold.

QUESTIONS

1. What traits are shown by the singers of this poem? Why do they not seem frightening, despite their "profession" of theft?
2. Describe the puns in the poem. What kind of knowledge is needed to explain them fully? How many puns are there? How are they connected? Why do the puns seem particularly witty and also outrageous?

Here *fire, lead,* and *gold* are puns. *Lead* was the "base" or "low" metal that the medieval alchemists ("chymists") tried to transform into *gold,* using the heat from their *fires.* The puns develop because the gang of cutthroats singing the song is about to go out to rob people riding in horse-drawn coaches. Hence their "lead" is in the form of bullets, which will be transformed into the "gold" coins they steal. Their "fire" is not the alchemists' fire, but rather the fire of pistols. Through these puns, Gay's villains charm us by their wit, even though in real life they would scare us to death.

Overstatement and Understatement

Two important devices creating emphasis are **overstatement,** or **hyperbole,** and **understatement.** Overstatement, also called the *overreacher,* is exaggeration for effect. In "London, 1802," for example (p. 669), Wordsworth declares that England is a "fen of stagnant waters." That is, the country and its people make up collectively a stinking, smelly, polluted marsh, a muddy dump. What Wordsworth establishes by this overstatement is his judgment that England in 1802 needed a writer to unite the people around noble moral and political ideas, just as Milton had once done.

In contrast with overstatement, *understatement* is the deliberate underplaying or undervaluing of a thing for purposes of emphasis. One of the most famous poetic understatements is in Andrew Marvell's "To His Coy Mistress" (p. 852):

> The grave's a fine and private place,
> But none, I think, do there embrace.

Here the understatement grimly emphasizes the eternity of death by contrasting the permanent privacy of the grave with the temporary privacy of a trysting place sought by lovers. Another ironic use of understatement is in lines 17–20 of Ogden Nash's "Exit, Pursued by a Bear," where the speaker indicates that the "lion and the lizard" cannot hear "heavenly harmonies." In this figure Nash emphasizes that the people have been killed who once inhabited the rooms where such melodies were played, and therefore he emphasizes the ignorance and horror of war.

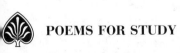 **POEMS FOR STUDY**

ELIZABETH BISHOP   (1911–1979)

Rain Towards Morning ———————————————————— *1947*

The great light cage has broken up in the air,
freeing, I think, about a million birds
whose wild ascending shadows will not be back,

and all the wires come falling down.
No cage, no frightening birds; the rain
is brightening now. The face is pale
that tried the puzzle of their prison
and solved it with an unexpected kiss,
whose freckled unsuspected hands alit.

QUESTIONS

1. What sort of personal situation is being described in the poem? How much does the poet allow you to learn about the situation? Do you discover enough to determine the general pattern of what is happening?

2. Describe the effect of the overstatement in lines 1–4. In light of the "kiss," which is more powerful: understatement or overstatement?

3. What is the meaning of the "great light cage" in lines 1–4? What is the "puzzle" of the birds' prison in line 7?

4. How can the "face" of line 6 and the "kiss" in line 8 be explained, through the figure of synecdoche, to have "hands" in line 9? What do these figures suggest about the nature of the experience being described?

5. Explain the paradox of how rain can be brightening (line 6).

JOHN DONNE   (1572–1631)

A Valediction: Forbidding Mourning ————————————————— *1633*

As virtuous men pass mildly away,
　And whisper to their souls to go,
Whilst some of their sad friends do say
　The breath goes now, and some say, No;

So let us melt, and make no noise,
　No tear-floods, nor sigh-tempests move,
'Twere profanation of our joys
　To tell the laity° our love.

Moving of th'earth° brings harm and fears,　　　　　　　　　　　　　　　*earthquakes*
　Men reckon what it did and meant:
But trepidation° of the spheres,
　Though greater far, is innocent.

A VALEDICTION: FORBIDDING MOURNING.　　7, 8 *profanation . . . laity:* as though the lovers are priests of love, whose love is a mystery.　　11 *trepidation:* Before Sir Isaac Newton explained the precession of the equinoxes, it was assumed that the positions of heavenly bodies should be constant and perfectly circular. The clearly observable irregularities (caused by the slow wobbling of the earth's axis) were explained by the concept of *trepidation,* or a trembling or oscillation that occurred in the outermost of the spheres surrounding the earth.

Dull sublunary lovers' love
  (Whose soul is sense°) cannot admit
Absence, because it doth remove   15
  Those things which elemented it.

But we by a love so much refined
  That our selves know not what it is,
Inter-assured of the mind,
  Care less, eyes, lips, and hands to miss.   20

Our two souls therefore, which are one,
  Though I must go, endure not yet
A breach, but an expansion
  Like gold to airy thinness beat.°

If they be two, they are two so   25
  As stiff twin compasses° are two;
Thy soul, the fixt foot, makes no show
  To move, but doth, if th'other do.

And though it in the center sit,
  Yet when the other far doth roam,   30
It leans and harkens after it,
  And grows erect, as that comes home.

Such wilt thou be to me, who must
  Like th'other foot, obliquely run;
Thy firmness draws my circle just,°   35
  And makes me end where I begun.

14 *soul is sense:* lovers whose attraction is totally physical.   24 *gold to airy thinness beat:* a reference to the malleability of gold.   26 *compasses:* a compass used for drawing circles.   35 *just:* perfectly round.

QUESTIONS

1. What is the situation envisioned as the occasion for the poem? Who is talking to whom? What is their relationship?

2. What is the intention of the first two stanzas? What is the effect of the phrases "tear-floods" and "sigh-tempests"?

3. Describe the effect of the opening simile about men on their deathbeds.

4. What is the metaphor of stanza three (lines 9–12)? In what sense might the "trepidation of the spheres" be less harmful than the parting of the lovers?

5. In lines 13–20 there is a comparison making the love of the speaker and his sweetheart superior to the love of average lovers. What is the basis for the speaker's claim?

6. What is the comparison begun by the word *refined* in line 17 and continued by the simile in line 24?

T. S. ELIOT   (1888–1965)

Eyes That Last I Saw in Tears _____ *1924*

Eyes that last I saw in tears
Through division
Here in death's dream kingdom
The golden vision reappears
I see the eyes but not the tears
This is my affliction

This is my affliction
Eyes I shall not see again
Eyes of decision
Eyes I shall not see unless
At the door of death's other kingdom
Where, as in this,
The eyes outlast a little while
A little while outlast the tears
And hold us in derision.

QUESTIONS

1. What do *eyes* and *tears* signify as a synecdoche and as a metonymy?
2. What is the cause of the tears (line 2)? What is meant by the eyes outlasting the tears (lines 13, 14)? Why should the eyes "hold us in derision"? In line 9 the eyes are "of decision." What does this synecdoche mean?
3. Explain the paradox of the speaker's declaration in line 5 that he sees the eyes but not the tears. Why does he say that this is his "affliction"?
4. Why might the entire poem be considered a paradox? What happened in life? What does the speaker look forward to in death?
5. What is the distinction in the poem between "death's dream kingdom" and "death's other kingdom"?

LANGSTON HUGHES   (1902–1967)

Harlem _____ *1951*

What happens to a dream deferred?

Does it dry up
like a raisin in the sun?
Or fester like a sore—
And then run?
Does it stink like rotten meat?
Or crust and sugar over—
like a syrupy sweet?

Maybe it just sags
like a heavy load.   10

Or does it explode?

QUESTIONS

1. In the light of the black experience with the "American Dream," what do you
    think is meant by the phrase "dream deferred"?
2. Explain the structure of the poem in terms of the speaker's questions and
    answers. How is the structure here similar to the one in Blake's "The Tyger"
    (p. 636)?
3. Explain the similes in lines 3, 4, 6, 8, and 10. Why are these apt comparisons?
    What sorts of human actions are implied in these figures?
4. What is the meaning of the metaphor in line 11? Why do you think Hughes shifted
    from similes to a metaphor in this line?

JOHN KEATS (1795–1821)

To Autumn ———————————————————————— *1820 (1819)*

Season of mists and mellow fruitfulness!
   Close bosom-friend of the maturing sun;
Conspiring with him how to load and bless
   With fruit the vines that round the thatch-eaves run;
To bend with apples the mossed cottage-trees,   5
   And fill all fruit with ripeness to the core;
     To swell the gourd, and plump the hazel shells
With a sweet kernel; to set budding more,
   And still more, later flowers for the bees,
   Until they think warm days will never cease,   10
     For Summer has o'erbrimmed their clammy cells.

Who hath not seen thee oft amid thy store?
   Sometimes whoever seeks abroad may find
Thee sitting careless on a granary floor,
   Thy hair soft-lifted by the winnowing wind,   15
Or on a half-reaped furrow sound asleep,
   Drowsed with the fume of poppies, while thy hook
     Spares the next swath and all its twinèd flowers;
And sometimes like a gleaner thou dost keep
   Steady thy laden head across a brook;   20
   Or by a cider-press, with patient look,
     Thou watchest the last oozings hours by hours.

Where are the songs of Spring? Ay, where are they?
   Think not of them, thou hast thy music too,—

While barrèd clouds bloom the soft-dying day,
    And touch the stubble-plains with rosy hue;
Then in a wailful choir the small gnats mourn
    Among the river sallows, borne aloft
        Or sinking as the light wind lives or dies;
And full-grown lambs loud bleat from hilly bourn;
    Hedge-crickets sing; and now with treble soft
    The redbreast whistles from a garden-croft;
        And gathering swallows twitter in the skies.

QUESTIONS

1. How is personification used in the first stanza? How does it change in the second? What is the effect of such personification?

2. How does Keats structure the poem to accord with his apostrophe to autumn? That is, in what ways may the stanzas be distinguished by the type of discourse addressed to the season?

3. Analyze Keats's metonymy in stanza one and synecdoche in stanza two. What effects does he achieve with these devices?

4. How, through the use of images, does Keats develop his idea that autumn is a season of "mellow fruitfulness"?

HENRY KING   (1592–1669)

Sic Vita° _____ *1657*

Like to the falling of a star,
Or as the flights of eagles are,
Or like the fresh spring's gaudy hue,
Or silver drops of morning dew,
Or like a wind that chafes the flood,
Or bubbles which on water stood:
Even such is man, whose borrowed light
Is straight called in, and paid to night.
    The wind blows out, the bubble dies;
    The spring entombed in autumn lies:
    The dew dries up, the star is shot;
    The flight is past, and man forgot.

SIC VITA.   (Latin): Such is life.

QUESTIONS

1. How many similes do you find in lines 1–6? Describe the range of references; that is, from what sources are the similes derived? What do all these similes (and references) have in common?

2. Explain the two metaphors in lines 7–8. (One is brought out by the words *borrowed, called in,* and *paid*; the other by *light* and *night*.)

3. Explain the continuation in lines 9–12 of the similes in 1–6. Do you think that these last four lines are essential, or might the poem have been successfully concluded with line 8? Explain.

4. What point does this poem make about humanity? In what ways do the similes in the poem help explore these ideas and bring them to life?

JUDITH MINTY   (b. 1937)

Conjoined _____ *1981*

a marriage poem

The onion in my cupboard, a monster, actually
two joined under one transparent skin:
each half-round, then flat and deformed
where it pressed and grew against the other.

An accident, like the two-headed calf rooted   5
in one body, fighting to suck at its mother's teats;
or like those other freaks, Chang and Eng,° twins
joined at the chest by skin and muscle, doomed
to live, even make love, together for sixty years.

Do you feel the skin that binds us   10
together as we move, heavy in this house?
To sever the muscle could free one,
but might kill the other. Ah, but men
don't slice onions in the kitchen, seldom see
what is invisible. We cannot escape each other.   15

CONJOINED.   7 *Chang and Eng:* born in 1811, the original and most famous Siamese twins. Although they were never separated, they nevertheless fathered twenty-two children. They died in 1874.

QUESTIONS

1. What are the two things—the "us" and "we" of lines 10 and 11—that are conjoined? Since this is "a marriage poem," might they be the man and the woman? Why might they also be considered as the body and soul of the speaker; or the desire to be married and subordinated, on the one hand, and to be free and in control of destiny, on the other?

2. Explore the metaphor of the onion and the similes of the two-headed calf and the Siamese twins. Why do you think the poet introduces the words *monster, accident,* and *freaks* into these figures in lines 1, 5, and 7? In what sense do you believe that these words are applicable to the nature and plight of women?

3. Is it true that *all* "men / don't slice onions in the kitchen, seldom see / what is invisible"? Explain.

OGDEN NASH   (1902–1970)

Exit, Pursued by a Bear ————————————————————————— *1954*

Chipmunk chewing the Chippendale,°
Mice on the Meissen° shelf,
Pigeon stains on the Aubusson,°
Spider lace on the delf.°

Squirrel climbing the Sheraton,°
Skunk on the Duncan Phyfe,°
Silverfish in the Gobelins°
And the calfbound volumes of *Life.*

Pocks on the pink Picasso,
Dust on the four Cézannes,
Kit on the keys of the Steinway,
Cat on the Louis Quinze.°

Rings on the Adam° mantel
From a thousand bygone thirsts,
Mold on the Henry Millers°
And the Ronald Firbank° firsts.

The lion and the lizard°
No heavenly harmonies hear
From the high-fidelity speaker
Concealed behind the Vermeer.

Jamshid° squats in a cavern
Screened by a waterfall,
Catered by Heinz and Campbell,
And awaits the fireball.

EXIT, PURSUED BY A BEAR.   The title is a stage direction in Shakespeare's *The Winter's Tale* (Act III, scene 3, 58). The character is torn apart by the bear. When this poem was first published, the atomic bomb had existed for nine years, and the hydrogen bomb for two. In late 1953, Russia, which is sometimes symbolized by a bear, announced that it possessed the hydrogen bomb. 1 *Chippendale:* ornate furniture made by Thomas Chippendale (1718–1779).   2 *Meissen:* expensive chinaware made in Meissen, Germany. Also called "Dresden China."   3 *Aubusson:* carpet imported from France.   4 *delf:* expensive pottery made in Delft, The Netherlands.   5 *Sheraton:* furniture made by Thomas Sheraton (1751–1806).   6 *Duncan Phyfe:* furniture made by Duncan Phyfe (1768–1854), a Scotsman who came to America in 1783.   7 *Gobelins:* rare and exquisitely crafted tapestries made by Gobelin of Paris.   12 *Louis Quinze:* furniture made in France during the reign of Louis XV (1710–1774).   13 *Adam:* Robert Adam (1728–1792) was one of the most famous English architects.   15 *Henry Miller:* American author (1891–1980). 16 *Ronald Firbank:* Arthur Ainsley Ronald Firbank (1886–1926), British author.   17 *The lion and the lizard:* See Edward Fitzgerald's (1809–1883) version of *The Rubáiyát of Omar Khayyám,* stanza eighteen, particularly in reference to Nash's last stanza.   21 *Jamshid:* a reference to the legendary Persian hero Jamshid, who found a cup containing the elixir of life and lived for 700 years. At one point in the story Jamshid remained hidden for a hundred years. Note also the reference to Fitzgerald's *Rubáiyát,* stanza eighteen.

QUESTIONS

1. In relationship to the serious subject matter of the poem, what is the effect of the title? What is the possible pun on the word *bear*?
2. What location is the speaker describing? How is metonymy used to suggest the wealth of the collections of household items and art? What sort of lifestyle is suggested by the metonymy?
3. Why is it that animals rather than people are living with the expensive artifacts? Judging from line 14, how long has this situation existed?
4. How might the situation presented in the poem be considered as a paradox?

MARGE PIERCY   (b. 1934)

A Work of Artifice ————————————————— *1973*

The bonsai tree
in the attractive pot
could have grown eighty feet tall
on the side of a mountain
till split by lightning.   5
But a gardener
carefully pruned it.
It is nine inches high.
Every day as he
whittles back the branches   10
the gardener croons,
It is your nature
to be small and cozy
domestic and weak;
how lucky, little tree,   15
to have a pot to grow in.
With living creatures
one must begin very early
to dwarf their growth:
the bound feet,   20
the crippled brain,
the hair in curlers,
the hands you
love to touch.

QUESTIONS

1. What is a bonsai tree? In what ways is it an apt metaphor for women? The tree "could have grown eighty feet tall." What would be the comparable growth and development of a woman?

2. What do you make of the gardener's song (lines 12–16)? If the bonsai tree were able to respond, would it accept the gardener's consolation? What conclusions about women's lives are implied by the metaphor of the tree?

3. How does the poem shift at line 17? To what extent do the next images (lines 20–24) embody women's lives? How are the images metaphorical?

SYLVIA PLATH   (1932–1963)

Metaphors ———————————————————————— *1960*

I'm a riddle in nine syllables,
An elephant, a ponderous house,
A melon strolling on two tendrils.
O red fruit, ivory, fine timbers!
This loaf's big with its yeasty rising.
Money's new-minted in this fat purse.
I'm a means, a stage, a cow in calf.
I've eaten a bag of green apples,
Boarded the train there's no getting off.

QUESTIONS

1. What evidence can you find in the poem that the speaker is a woman?

2. The speaker calls herself a "riddle in nine syllables." What is the answer to the riddle? Why nine syllables (as opposed to eight or ten)? In what sense is the poem also a riddle? How are the answers to both riddles related?

3. Which of the metaphors do you find amusing, shocking, or demeaning? What do these suggest about the speaker's attitude toward herself?

4. What aspect of the speaker's condition is captured in the "bag of green apples" metaphor (line 8)? What two meanings are suggested by the *stage* metaphor (line 7)? Why is the *train* metaphor (line 9) appropriate to the speaker's condition and the results of that condition?

MURIEL RUKEYSER   (b. 1913)

Looking at Each Other ———————————————————— *1978*

Yes, we were looking at each other
Yes, we knew each other very well
Yes, we had made love with each other many times
Yes, we had heard music together
Yes, we had gone to the sea together
Yes, we had cooked and eaten together
Yes, we had laughed often day and night

Yes, we fought violence and knew violence
Yes, we hated the inner and outer oppression
Yes, that day we were looking at each other   10
Yes, we saw the sunlight pouring down
Yes, the corner of the table was between us
Yes, bread and flowers were on the table
Yes, our eyes saw each other's eyes
Yes, our mouths saw each other's mouth   15
Yes, our breasts saw each other's breasts
Yes, our bodies entire saw each other
Yes, it was beginning in each
Yes, it threw waves across our lives
Yes, the pulses were becoming very strong   20
Yes, the beating became very delicate
Yes, the calling   the arousal
Yes, the arriving   the coming
Yes, there it was for both entire
Yes, we were looking at each other   25

QUESTIONS

1. What is the dramatic situation of the poem? What sort of listener is the speaker addressing?

2. Describe the rhetorical device at work here. How many different words are being repeated?

3. What is the effect of the repetitions? What is their relationship to the emotions and experiences that the speaker is describing?

WILLIAM SHAKESPEARE   (1564–1616)

Sonnet 30: When to the Sessions of Sweet Silent Thought ——————— *1609*

When to the sessions° of sweet silent thought   *holding of court*
I summon° up remembrance of things past,
I sigh the lack of many a thing I sought,
And with old woes new wail my dear time's waste:°
Then can I drown an eye (un-used to flow)   5
For precious friends hid in death's dateless° night,   *endless*
And weep afresh love's long since canceled° woe,   *paid in full*
And moan th'expense° of many a vanished sight.   *cost, loss*
Then can I grieve at grievances foregone,
And heavily° from woe to woe tell° o'er   *sadly; count*   10
The sad account of fore-bemoanèd moan,

SONNET 30.   2 *summon*: to issue a summons to appear at a legal hearing.   4 *old woes . . . waste:* revive old sorrows about lost opportunities and express sorrow for them again.

Which I new pay, as if not paid before.
   But if the while I think on thee (dear friend)
   All losses are restored, and sorrows end.

QUESTIONS

1. Explain the metaphor of "sessions" and "summon" in lines 1–2. Where are the
    sessions being held? What is a *summons* for remembrance?
2. What is the metaphor brought out by the word *canceled* in line 7? In what sense
    might a "woe" of love be canceled? Explain the metaphor of *expense* in line 8.
3. What type of transaction does Shakespeare refer to in the metaphor of lines
    9–12? What understanding does the metaphor provide about the sadness and
    regret that a person feels about past mistakes and sorrows?
4. What role does the speaker assign to the "dear friend" of line 13 in relation to
    the metaphors of the poem?

DIANE WAKOSKI   (b. 1937)

Inside Out _____ *1965*

I walk the purple carpet into your eye,
carrying the silver butter server,
but a truck rumbles by,
      leaving its black tire prints on my foot,
and old images—
      the sound of banging screen doors on hot afternoons
      and a fly buzzing over Kool-Aid spilled on the sink—
flicker, as reflections on the metal surface.

Come in, you said,
inside your paintings, inside the blood factory, inside the
old songs that line your hands, inside
eyes that change like a snowflake every second,

inside spinach leaves holding that one piece of gravel,

inside the whiskers of a cat,

inside your old hat, and most of all inside your mouth where you
grind the pigments with your teeth, painting
with a broken bottle on the floor, and painting
with an ostrich feather on the moon that rolls out of my mouth.

You cannot let me walk inside you too long
inside the veins where my small feet touch
bottom.

You must reach inside and pull me
like a silver bullet°
from your arm.

INSIDE OUT.   23 *silver bullet:* According to legend, silver bullets were used to kill vampires. The Lone Ranger, of the radio and television series popular in the 1940s and 1950s, always used silver bullets as a trademark of his pursuit of justice.

QUESTIONS

1. What "inside out" details of the listener's anatomy does the speaker mention? What do you think is meant by the poem's title?
2. Consider details of the eye and the veins as synecdoche, and the paintings and the old hat as metonymy. In the determination of the poem's characterization of the "you" inside the poem, what do these details stand for?
3. Consider the truck's black tire prints on the speaker's foot (lines 3–4) as an instance of synesthesia, that is, the application of one set of sensuous references to another sense. What might this figure mean? Do the same for the mouth with the ground pigments (lines 15–16), the ostrich feather and the rolling moon (line 18), and the walk inside the veins (lines 19–20).
4. What is meant by lines 19–24? Why, after the establishment of so personal and intimate a relationship, might the speaker express the reservations that are contained here? How might these lines be interpreted as a reflection upon the paradoxical nature of the love relationship generally?
5. Describe the paradox of the purple carpet and the silver butter server.

WILLIAM WORDSWORTH   (1770–1850)

London, 1802 ————————————————————— *1807 (1802)*

Milton! thou should'st be living at this hour:	
England hath need of thee: she is a fen°	*bog, marsh*
Of stagnant waters: altar, sword, and pen,	
Fireside, the heroic wealth of hall and bower,	
Have forfeited their ancient English dower°	*widow's inheritance* 5
Of inward happiness. We are selfish men;	
Oh! raise us up, return to us again;	
And give us manners,° virtue, freedom, power.	
Thy soul was like a star, and dwelt apart:	
Thou hadst a voice whose sound was like the sea:	10
Pure as the naked heavens, majestic, free,	
So didst thou travel on life's common way,	
In cheerful godliness; and yet thy heart	
The lowliest duties on herself did lay.	

LONDON, 1802.   8 *manners:* customs, moral modes of social and political conduct.

QUESTIONS

1. What is the effect of Wordworth's apostrophe to Milton? What elements of Milton's career as a writer does Wordsworth emphasize?
2. In lines 3 and 4, the device of metonymy is used. How does Wordsworth judge the respective institutions represented by the details?
3. Consider the use of overstatement, or hyperbole, from lines 2–6. What effect does Wordsworth achieve by using the device as extensively as he does here?
4. What effect does Wordsworth make through his use of overstatement in his praise of Milton in lines 9–14? What does he mean by the metonymic references to *soul* (line 9) and *heart* (line 13)?

SIR THOMAS WYATT   (1503–1542)

I Find No Peace _____ *1557*

I find no peace, and all my war is done,
   I fear and hope, I burn and freeze like ice;
   I fly above the wind yet can I not arise;
   And naught I have and all the world I season.
That looseth nor locketh holdeth me in prison,°
   And holdeth me not, yet I can scape° nowise;   *escape*
   Nor letteth me live nor die at my devise,°   *choice*
   And yet of death it giveth none occasion.
Without eyen° I see, and without tongue I plain;°   *eyes*
   I desire to perish, and yet I ask health;
   I love another, and thus I hate myself;
I feed me in sorrow, and laugh in all my pain.
   Likewise displeaseth me both death and life°
   And my delight is causer of this strife.

I FIND NO PEACE.   5 *that . . . prison:* that is, "that which neither lets me go nor contains me holds me in prison." At the time of Wyatt, *-eth* was used for the third person singular present tense.   9 *plain:* express desires about love.   13 *likewise . . . life:* literally, "it is displeasing to me, in the same way, both death and life." That is "both death and life are equally distasteful to me."

QUESTIONS

1. What situation is the speaker reflecting upon? What metaphors and similes express his feelings? How successful are these figures?
2. How many paradoxes are in the poem? What is their cumulative effect? What is the topic of the paradoxes in lines 1–4? In lines 5–8? Why does the speaker declare that hating himself is a consequence of loving another? Why is it ironic that his "delight" is the "causer of this strife"?
3. To what extent do you think the paradoxes express the feelings of a person in love, particularly because in the sixteenth century, the free and unchaperoned meetings of lovers were not easily arranged?

WRITING ABOUT RHETORICAL FIGURES

Begin by determining the use, line by line, of metaphors, similes, or other rhetorical figures. Obviously, similes are the easiest figures to recognize, because they introduce comparisons with the words "like" or "as." Metaphors may be recognized because the topics are discussed not as themselves but as other topics. If the poems speak of falling leaves or law courts, for example, but the subjects are memory or increasing age, you are looking at metaphors. Similarly, if the poet is addressing an absent person, or a natural object, or if you find clear double meanings in words, you may have apostrophe, personification, or puns.

Questions for Discovering Ideas

• What figures does the work contain? Where do they occur? Under what circumstances? How extensive are they?

• How do you recognize them? Are they signaled by a single word, like "bows" in Campion's "Cherry Ripe," or are they more extensively detailed, as in Shakespeare's "When to the Sessions of Sweet Silent Thought"?

• How vivid are the figures? How obvious? How unusual? What kind of effort is needed to understand them in context?

• Structurally, how are the figures developed? How do they rise out of the situation? To what degree are the figures integrated into the poem's development of ideas? How do they relate to other aspects of the poem?

• Is one type of figure used in a particular section while another predominates in another? Why?

• If you have discovered a number of figures, what relationships can you find among them (such as the judicial and financial connections in Shakespeare's Sonnet 30)?

• How do they broaden, deepen, or otherwise assist in making the ideas in the poem forceful?

• In short, how appropriate and meaningful are the figures in the poem? What effect do the figures have on the poem's tone? On your understanding and appreciation of the poem?

Strategies for Organizing Ideas

For this essay, two types of compositions are possible. One is a full-scale essay. The other, because some rhetorical figures may occupy only a small part of the poem, is a single paragraph. Let us consider the single paragraph first.

1. *A paragraph.* For a single paragraph you need only one topic, such as the opening paradox and metonymy that begin Eliot's "Eyes That Last I Saw in Tears" (p. 660). The goal is to deal with the single figure and its relationship to the poem's main idea. Thus the essay should describe the figure and discuss its meaning and implications. It is important to begin with a compre-

hensive topic sentence, such as one that explains the cleverness of the puns in Gay's "Let Us Take the Road" (p. 656), or the use of synæsthesia in Keats's "Ode to a Nightingale" (p. 770).

2. *A full-length essay.* One type of essay might examine just one figure, if the figure is pervasive enough in the poem to justify a full treatment. Most often, the poet's use of metaphors and similes is suitable for extensive discussion. The second type of essay might explore the meaning and effect of two or more figures, with the various parts of the body of the essay being taken up with each figure. The unity of this second kind of essay is achieved by the linking of a series of two or three different rhetorical devices to a single idea or emotion.

In the introduction, relate the quality of the figures to the general nature of the work. Thus, metaphors and similes of suffering might be appropriate to a religious, redemptive work, while those of sunshine and cheer might be right for a romantic one. If there is any discrepancy between the metaphorical language and the topic, you could consider that contrast as a possible central idea, for it would clearly indicate the writer's ironic perspective. Suppose that the topic of the poem is love, but the figures put you in mind of darkness and cold: What would the writer be saying about the quality of love? You should also try to justify any claims that you make about the figures. For example, one of the similes in Coleridge's "Kubla Khan" compares the sounds of a "mighty fountain" to the breathing of the earth in "fast thick pants." How is this simile to be taken? As a reference to the animality of the earth? As a suggestion that the fountain, and the earth, are dangerous? Or simply as a comparison suggesting immense, forceful noise? How do you explain your answer or answers? Your introduction is the place to establish ideas and justifications of this sort.

The following approaches for discussing rhetorical figures are not mutually exclusive, and you may combine them as you wish. Most likely, your essay will bring in most of the following classifications.

a. *Interpret the meaning and effect of the figures.* Here you explain how the figures enable you to make an interpretation. In stanza two of "A Valediction: Forbidding Mourning," for example, the following metaphor equates love with the structure of the church:

> 'Twere profanation of our joys
> To tell the laity our love.

Here Donne emphasizes the private, mystical relationship of two lovers, drawing the metaphor from the religious tradition whereby any explanation of religious mysteries is considered a desecration. This interpretive approach is a direct one, requiring that metaphors, similes, or other figures be expanded and interpreted, including the explanation of necessary references and allusions.

b. *Analyze the frames of reference, and their appropriateness to the subject matter.* Here you classify and locate the sources and types of the references, and determine the appropriateness of these to the poem's subject matter. Ask questions similar to those you might ask in a study of imagery: Does the writer refer extensively to nature, science, warfare, politics, business, reading (e.g., Shakespeare's metaphor equating personal reverie with courtroom proceedings)? How appropriate is the metaphor? Does it seem right in the poem's development? How?

c. *Focus on the interests and sensibilities of the poet.* In a way this approach is like the second one, but the emphasis here is on what the selectivity of the writer might show about his or her vision and interests. You might begin by listing the figures in the poem and then determining the sources, just as you would do in discussing the sources of images generally. But then you should raise questions like the following: Does the writer use figures derived from one sense rather than another (i.e., sight, hearing, taste, smell, touch)? Does he or she record color, brightness, shadow, shape, depth, height, number, size, slowness, speed, emptiness, fullness, richness, drabness? Has the writer relied on the associations of figures of sense? Do metaphors and similes referring to green plants and trees, to red roses, or to rich fabrics, for example, suggest that life is full and beautiful, or do references to touch suggest amorous warmth? This approach is designed to help you to draw whatever conclusions you can about the author's—or the speaker's—taste or sensibility.

d. *Examine the effect of one figure on the other figures and ideas of the poem.* The assumption of this approach is that each literary work is unified and organically whole, so that each part is closely related and inseparable from everything else. Usually it is best to pick a figure that occurs at the beginning of the poem and then determine how this figure influences your perception of the rest of the poem. Your aim is to consider the relationship of part to parts, and part to whole. The beginning of Donne's "A Valediction: Forbidding Mourning," for example, contains a simile comparing the parting of the speaker and his listener to the quiet dying of "virtuous men." What is the effect of this comparison upon the rest of the poem? To help you in approaching such a question, you might substitute a totally different detail, such as, here, the violent death of a condemned criminal, or the slaughter of a domestic animal, rather than the deaths of "virtuous men." Such suppositions, which would clearly be out of place and inappropriate, may help you to understand and then explain the poet's rhetorical figures.

In your conclusion, summarize your main points, describe your general impressions, try to describe the impact of the figures, indicate your personal responses, or show what might further be done along the lines you have been developing. If you know other works by the same writer, or other works by other writers who use comparable or contrasting figures, you might explain the relationship of the other work or works to your present analysis.

FIRST SAMPLE ESSAY: A PARAGRAPH

Wordsworth's Use of Overstatement in "London, 1802"°

Through overstatement in "London, 1802," William Wordsworth emphasizes his tribute to Milton as a master of idealistic thought. The speaker's claim that England is "a fen / Of stagnant waters" (lines 2–3) is overstated, just as the implication that people ("we") in England have no "manners, virtue, freedom, [or] power" (line 8). With the overstatements, however, Wordsworth implies that the nation's well-being depends on the constant flow of creative thoughts by persons of great ideas. Because Milton was clearly the greatest of these, in the view of Wordsworth's speaker, the overstatements stress the need for leadership. Milton is the model, and the overstated criticism lays the foundation in the real political and moral world for the rebirth of another Milton. Thus, through overstatement, Wordsworth emphasizes Milton's importance, and in this way pays tribute to him.

Commentary on the Paragraph

This sample illustrates how a single rhetorical figure can be the subject of a short paragraph, in this case Wordsworth's use of overstatement in "London, 1802." Although most often the figure will be prominent, as this one is, prominence is not a requirement. In addition, there is no need to write an excessively long paragraph. The goal here is not to describe all the details of Wordsworth's overstatement, but to show how the figure affects his tribute to Milton. For this reason the paragraph shows the need for clear and direct support of the major point.

SECOND SAMPLE ESSAY

A Study of Shakespeare's Metaphors in Sonnet 30[*]

[1]   In this sonnet Shakespeare's speaker stresses the sadness and regret of remembered experience, but he states that a person with these feelings may be cheered by the thought of a friend. His metaphors, cleverly used, create new and fresh ways of seeing personal life in this perspective.[†] He presents metaphors drawn from the public and business world of law courts, money, and banking or money-handling.[‡]
         The courtroom metaphor of the first four lines shows that memories of

---

° See p. 669 for this poem.
* See p. 667 for this poem.
† Central idea.
‡ Thesis sentence.

[2] past experience are constantly present and influential. Like a judge commanding defendants to appear in court, the speaker "summon[s]" his memory of "things past" to appear on trial before him. This metaphor suggests that people are their own judges and that their ideals and morals are like laws by which they measure themselves. The speaker finds himself guilty of wasting his time in the past. Removing himself, however, from the strict punishment that a real judge might require, he does not condemn himself for his "dear time's waste," but instead laments it (line 4). The metaphor is thus used to indicate that a person's consciousness is made up just as much of self doubt and reproach as by more positive qualities.

[3] With the closely related reference of money in the next group of four lines, Shakespeare shows that living is a lifelong investment and is valuable for this reason. According to the money metaphor, living requires the spending of emotions and commitment to others. When friends move away and loved ones die, it is as though this expenditure has been lost. Thus, the speaker's dead friends are "precious" because he invested time and love in them, and the "sights" that have "vanished" from his eyes make him "moan" because he went to great "expense" for them (line 8).

[4] Like the money metaphor, the metaphor of banking or money-handling in the next four lines emphasizes that memory is a bank in which life's experiences are deposited. The full emotions surrounding experience are recorded there, and may be withdrawn in moments of "sweet silent thought" just as a depositor may withdraw money. Thus the speaker states that he counts out the sad parts of his experience--his woe--just as a merchant or banker counts money: "And heavily from woe to woe _tell_ o'er" (line 10). Because strong emotions still accompany his memories of past mistakes, the metaphor extends to borrowing and the payment of interest. The speaker thus says that he pays again with "new" woe the accounts that he had already paid with old woe. The metaphor suggests that the past is so much a part of the present that a person never stops feeling pain and regret.

[5] The legal, financial, and money-handling metaphors combine in the last two lines to show how a healthy present life may overcome past regrets. The "dear friend" being addressed in these lines has the resources (financial) to settle all the emotional judgments that the speaker as a self-judge has made against himself (legal). It is as though the friend is a rich patron who rescues him from emotional bankruptcy (legal and financial) and the possible doom resulting from the potential sentence of emotional misery and depression (legal).

[6] In these metaphors, therefore, Shakespeare's references are drawn from everyday public and business actions, but his use of them is creative and unusual. In particular, the idea of line 8 ("And moan th'expense of many a vanished sight") stresses that people spend much emotional energy on others. Without such personal commitment, one cannot have precious friends and loved ones. In keeping with this metaphor of money and investment, one could measure life not in months or years, but in the spending of emotion and involvement in personal relationships. Shakespeare, by inviting readers to explore the values brought out by his metaphors, gives new insights into the nature and value of life.

Commentary on the Essay

This essay treats the three classes of metaphors that Shakespeare introduces in Sonnet 30. It thus illustrates the second approach (p. 673). But the aim of the discussion is not to explore the extent and nature of the comparison between the metaphors and the personal situations described in the sonnet. Instead the goal is to explain how the metaphors develop Shakespeare's meaning. This method therefore also illustrates the first approach (p. 672).

In addition to providing a brief description of the sonnet, the introduction brings out the central idea and the thesis sentence. Paragraph 2 deals with the meaning of Shakespeare's courtroom metaphor. His money metaphor is explained in paragraph 3. Paragraph 4 considers the banking, or money-handling figure. The fifth paragraph shows how Shakespeare's last two lines bring together the three strands of metaphor. The conclusion comments generally on the creativity of Shakespeare's metaphors, and it also amplifies the way in which the money metaphor leads toward an increased understanding of life.

Throughout the essay, transitions are brought about by the linking words in the topic sentences. In paragraph 3, for example, the words "closely related" and "next group" move the reader from paragraph 2 to the new content. In paragraph 4, the words effecting the transition are "like the money metaphor" and "the next four lines." The opening sentence of paragraph 5 refers collectively to the subjects of paragraphs 2, 3, and 4, thereby focusing them on the new topic of paragraph 5.

WRITING TOPICS

1. Study the simile of the "stiff twin compasses" in Donne's "A Valediction: Forbidding Mourning." Using such a compass, or a drawing of one, write an essay that demonstrates the accuracy of Donne's descriptions. What light does the simile shed on the relationship of two lovers? How does it emphasize any or all of these aspects of love: closeness, immediacy, extent, importance, duration, intensity?

2. Consider some of the metaphors and similes in the poems included in this chapter. Write an essay that answers the following questions. How effective are the figures you select? (Examples: the bonsai tree [Piercy], the Siamese twins [Minty], the explosive [Hughes], the session of court [Shakespeare].) What insights do the figures provide within the contexts of their respective poems? How appropriate are they? Might they be expanded more fully, and if they were, what would be the effect?

3. Consider some of the other rhetorical figures in the poems of this chapter. Write an essay describing the importance of figures in creating emphasis and in extending and deepening the ideas of poetry. A few topics might be:

Paradox in Wyatt's "I Find No Peace"

The Simile of the Compass in Donne's "Valediction"

Metaphor in Minty's "Conjoined," Piercy's "A Work of Artifice," or Wakoski's "Inside Out"

Anaphora in Rukeyser's "Yes, We Were Looking at Each Other," Wakoski's "Inside Out," or King's "Sic Vita"

Similes in King's "Sic Vita" or Hughes's "Harlem"

Personification in Wordsworth or Keats

Metonymy in Keats's "To Autumn" or Nash's "Exit, Pursued by a Bear"

4. Write a poem in which you create a governing metaphor or simile. An example might be: My girl/boyfriend is like (a) an opening flower, (b) a difficult book, (c) an insoluble mathematical problem, (d) a bill that cannot be paid, (e) a slow-moving chess game. Another example: Teaching a person how to do a particular job is like (a) shoveling heavy snow, (b) climbing a mountain during a landslide, (c) having someone force you underwater when you're gasping for breath. When you finish, describe the relationship between your comparison and the development and structure of your poem.

18

Tone: The Creation
of Attitude in Poetry

Tone (see also Chapter 8), a term describing the shaping of attitudes in poetry, comes from the phrase *tone of voice*. Each poet's choice of words governs
the reader's responses, as do the participants and situations in the poem. In
addition, the poet shapes responses through denotation and connotation, seriousness or humor, irony, metaphors, similes, understatement, overstatement, and other rhetorical figures. Of major importance is the poem's narrator or speaker. How much self-awareness does the speaker show? What is
his or her background? What relationship does the speaker establish with listeners and readers? What does he or she assume about the readers and about
their knowledge? How do these assumptions affect the ideas and the diction?

To compare poetic and artistic tone, see Leger's painting "The City" (p.
679). A viewer's response to the painting depends on the relationships of the
various shapes to Leger's arrangement and color. The painting's figures,
signs, stairs, and pole are all common in modern cities. By cutting them up
or leaving them partially hidden, Leger creates an atmosphere suggesting
that today's urban life is truncated, sinister, and even threatening.

The same control is necessary in poetry. The sentences must be just
long enough to achieve the poet's intended effect—no shorter and no
longer. If a conversational style is established, formal words must be avoided.
Conversely, in a formal style there should be no slang, no rollicking rhythms,
no frivolous rhymes. In all the features that contribute to a poem's tone, consistency is primary. If anything falls short, the poem sinks, and the poet fails.

TONE, CHOICE, AND RESPONSE

Remember that a major objective of poets is to inform, enrich, inspire, and
generally affect readers. Poets may begin their poems with a brief idea, a
vague feeling, or a fleeting impression. Then, in the light of their developing
design, they *choose* what to say—the form of their material and the words and

Fernand Leger (1881–1955), The City, 1919. Oil on canvas, 90¾″ × 117¼″ (Philadelphia Museum of Art: A.E. Gallatin Collection)

phrases to express their ideas. The poem "Theme for English B," by Langston Hughes (the topic of the sample essay) illustrates this process in almost outline form. Hughes's speaker lays out many interests that he shares with his intended reader, his English teacher. In this way Hughes enables all readers to accept his ideas of human equality.

In the long run, readers might not accept all the ideas in any poem, but the successful poem will have gained the reader's agreement—at least for a time—because the poet's control over tone will have been right. Each poem attempts to evoke *total* responses, which lapses in tone might destroy. Let us look at a poem in which the tone misses, and misses badly.

CORNELIUS WHUR   (1782–1853)

The First-Rate Wife ————————————————————— *1837*

This brief effusion I indite,
  And my vast wishes send,
That thou mayst be directed right,
And have ere long within thy sight
  A most *enchanting* friend!   5

The *maiden* should have *lovely face,*
  And be of *genteel mien;*
If not, within thy dwelling place,
There may be vestige of disgrace,
  Not much admired—when seen.

Nor will thy dearest be complete
  Without *domestic* care;
If otherwise, howe'er discreet,
Thine eyes will very often meet
  What none desire to share!

And further still—thy future *dear,*
  Should have some *mental* ray;
If not, thou mayest drop a tear,
Because no *real sense* is there
  To charm life's dreary day!

QUESTIONS

1. What kind of person is the poem's speaker? The listener? What is the situation? What requirements does the speaker create for the "first-rate wife"?
2. Describe the poem's tone. How does the speaker's character influence the tone? In light of the tone, to what degree may the poem be considered insulting?
3. How might lines 14 and 15 be interpreted as a possible threat if the woman as a wife does not take care of the house?

    In this poem the speaker explains his requirements for a "first-rate wife." From his tone, he clearly regards getting married as little more than hiring a pretty housekeeper. In the phrase "some *mental* ray," for example, the word *some* does not mean "a great deal," but is more like "*at least* some," as though nothing more could be expected of a woman. Even allowing for the fact that the poem was written in the nineteenth century and represents a benighted view of women and marriage, "The First-Rate Wife" offends most readers. Do you wonder why you've never heard of Cornelius Whur before?

TONE AND THE NEED FOR CONTROL

"The First-Rate Wife" demonstrates that it is essential for the poet to be in control over all facets of the poem. The speaker must be aware of his or her situation, and should not, like Whur's speaker, demonstrate any smugness or insensitivity, unless the poet is deliberately revealing the shortcomings of the speaker by dramatizing them for the reader's amusement, as E. E. Cummings does in the poem "Next to of course God" (p. 929). In a poem with well-controlled tone, details and situations should be factually correct; observations should be both logical and fair, within the poem's structure, and also comprehensive and generally applicable. The following poem illustrates a masterly control over tone:

WILFRED OWEN   (1893–1918)

Dulce et Decorum Est° _____ *1920*

Bent double, like old beggars under sacks,
Knock-kneed, coughing like hags, we cursed through sludge,
Till on the haunting flares we turned our backs
And towards our distant rest began to trudge.
Men marched asleep. Many had lost their boots   5
But limped on, blood-shod. All went lame; all blind;
Drunk with fatigue; deaf even to the hoots
Of tired, outstripped Five-Nines° that dropped behind.

Gas!° GAS! Quick, boys!—An ecstasy of fumbling,
Fitting the clumsy helmets° just in time;   10
But someone still was yelling out and stumbling
And flound'ring like a man in fire or lime . . .
Dim, through the misty panes and thick green° light,
As under a green sea, I saw him drowning.

In all my dreams, before my helpless sight,   15
He plunges at me, guttering, choking, drowning.

If in some smothering dreams you too could pace
Behind the wagon that we flung him in.
And watch the white eyes writhing in his face,
His hanging face, like a devil's sick of sin;   20
If you could hear, at every jolt, the blood
Come gargling from the froth-corrupted lungs,
Obscene as cancer, bitter as the cud
Of vile, incurable sores on innocent tongues.—
My friend, you would not tell with such high zest   25
To children ardent for some desperate glory,
The old Lie: Dulce et decorum est
Pro patria mori.

DULCE ET DECORUM EST. The Latin title comes from Horace's *Odes*, Book 3, line 13: *Dulce et decorum est pro patria mori* ("It is sweet and honorable to die [while fighting] for [one's] country"). 8 *Five-Nines.* Artillery shells that made a hooting sound just before landing.   9 *Gas:* Chlorine gas was used as an anti-personnel weapon in 1915 by the Germans at Ypres, in Belgium.   10 *helmets:* Soldiers carried gas masks as normal battle equipment.   13 *thick green.* The chlorine gas used in gas attacks has a greenish-yellow color.

QUESTIONS

1.   What is the scene described in lines 1–8? What expressions does the speaker use to indicate his attitude toward the conditions?

2. What does the title of the poem mean? What attitude or conviction does it embody?
3. Does the speaker really mean "my friend" in line 25? In what tone of voice might this phrase be spoken?
4. What is the tonal relationship between the patriotic fervor of the Latin phrase and the images of the poem? How does the tonal contrast create the dominant tone of the poem?

The tone of "Dulce et Decorum Est" never once lapses. The poet intends the description to evoke a response of horror, for he contrasts the strategic goals of warfare with the speaker's up-close experience of terror in battle. The speaker's language skillfully emphasizes first the dreariness and fatigue of warfare (with words like *sludge, trudge, lame*, and *blind*) and second the agony of violent death from chlorine (embodied in the participles *guttering, choking, drowning, smothering*, and *writhing*). With these details established, the concluding attack against the "glory" of war is difficult to refute, even if warfare is undertaken to defend or preserve one's country. Although the details about the agonized death may distress or discomfort a sensitive reader, they are not designed to do that alone, but instead are integral to the poem's argument. Ultimately, it is the contrast between the high ideals of the Latin phrase and the ugliness of battlefield death that creates the dominant tone of the poem. The Latin phrase treats war and death in the abstract; the poem makes images of battle and death vividly real. The resultant tone is that of controlled bitterness and irony.

TONE AND COMMON GROUNDS OF ASSENT

This is not to say that all those reading the poem will deny that war is ever necessary. The issues of politics and warfare are far too complex for that. But the poem does show another important aspect of tone—namely, the degree to which the poet judges and tries to control responses through the establishment of a *common ground of assent.* An appeal to a bond of commonly held interests, concerns, and assumptions is essential if a poet is to maintain an effective tone. Owen, for example, does not create arguments against the necessity of a just war. Instead, he bases the poem upon realistic details about the writhing, spastic death suffered by the speaker's comrade, and he appeals to emotions that everyone, pacifist and militarist alike, would commonly feel—horror at the contemplation of violent death. Even assuming a widely divergent audience, in other words, the *tone* of the poem is successful because it is based on commonly acknowledged facts and commonly felt emotions. Knowing a poem like this one, even advocates of a strong military would need to defend their ideas on the grounds of *prevention* of just such needless, ugly deaths. Owen wisely and carefully considers the responses of his readers, and regulates speaker, situation, detail, and argument in order to make the poem acceptable for the broadest possible spectrum of opinion.

TONE AND IRONY

Irony is a mode of indirection, a means of making a point by emphasizing a discrepancy or opposite (see also pp. 299–301). Thus Owen uses the title "Dulce et Decorum Est" to emphasize that death in warfare is not fitting and noble, but rather demeaning and horrible. The title ironically reminds us of eloquent holiday speeches at the tombs of unknown soldiers, but as we have seen, it also reminds us of the reality of the agonized death of Owen's soldier. As an aspect of tone, therefore, irony is a powerful way of conveying attitudes, for it draws your attention to at least two ways of seeing a situation, enabling you not only to *understand* but also to *feel.*

Situational Irony

Poetry shares with fiction and drama the various kinds of ironies that poets believe may afflict human life. "The Workbox," by Thomas Hardy, illustrates a skillful manipulation of irony:

THOMAS HARDY   (1840–1928)

The Workbox ————————————————————— *1914*

"See, here's the workbox, little wife,
  That I made of polished oak."
He was a joiner,° of village° life;   *cabinetmaker*
  She came of borough° folk.

He holds the present up to her   5
  As with a smile she nears
And answers to the profferer,
  "'Twill last all my sewing years!"

"I warrant it will. And longer too.
  'Tis a scantling° that I got   10
Off poor John Wayward's coffin, who
  Died of they knew not what.

"The shingled pattern that seems to cease
  Against your box's rim
Continues right on in the piece   15
  That's underground with him.

THE WORKBOX.   4,5 *village, borough:* A village was small and rustic; a borough was larger and more sophisticated.   10 *scantling:* a small, leftover piece of wood.

"And while I worked it made me think
    Of timber's varied doom:
One inch where people eat and drink,
    The next inch in a tomb.

"But why do you look so white, my dear,
    And turn aside your face?
You knew not that good lad, I fear,
    Though he came from your native place?"

"How could I know that good young man,
    Though he came from my native town,
When he must have left far earlier than
    I was a woman grown?"

"Ah, no. I should have understood!
    It shocked you that I gave
To you one end of a piece of wood
    Whose other is in a grave?"

"Don't, dear, despise my intellect.
    Mere accidental things
Of that sort never have effect
    On my imaginings."

Yet still her lips were limp and wan,
    Her face still held aside,
As if she had known not only John,
    But known of what he died.

QUESTIONS

1. Who does most of the speaking here? What does the speaker's tone show about the characters of the man and the wife? What does the tone indicate about the poet's attitude toward them?

2. What do lines 21–40 indicate about the wife's knowledge of John and about her earlier relationship with him? Why does she deny such knowledge? What does the last stanza show about her? Why is John's death kept a mystery?

3. In lines 17–20, what irony is suggested by the fact that the wood was used both for John's coffin and the workbox?

4. Why is the husband's irony more complex than he realizes? What do his words and actions show about his character?

5. The narrator, or poet, speaks only in lines 3–7 and 37–40. How much of his explanation is essential? How much shows his attitude? How might the poem have been more effectively concluded?

"The Workbox" is a little domestic drama of deception, cruelty, and sadness. The complex details are evidence of situational irony; that is, an awareness that human beings do not control themselves but are rather controlled by powerful forces—in this case by both death and earlier feelings and commitments. Beyond this irony evolving out of the domestic scene, Hardy also emphasizes symbolically the direct connection that death has with the living. As a result of the husband's gift made of the wood with which he has also made a coffin for the dead man, the wife will never escape being reminded of this man. Within the life imagined in the poem, she will have to live with regret and the endless need to deny her true emotions.

Dramatic Irony

In addition to situational irony, the wife's deception reveals that the husband is in a situation of **dramatic irony**. The character understands one set of circumstances while the readers understand, in greater perspective, something completely different. In this poem, the husband does not know that the wife is not being truthful or open about her earlier relationship with the dead man. The tone of "The Workbox" suggests that the husband may be suspicious, however. By emphasizing the wood, he is apparently trying to draw her out. But he does not actually *know* the true circumstances, and hence he is unsure of his wife's attitude toward him. Because of this mixture of dramatic and situational irony, Hardy has created a poem of great complexity.

Verbal Irony

Poetry often contains **verbal irony**; that is, ambiguous language. "she being Brand / -new" by E. E. Cummings (p. 688) is filled with double meanings that develop from the terms used for the breaking in of a new car. Indeed, the entire poem is a virtuoso piece of *double entendre*. Another example of verbal irony may be seen in Roethke's "My Papa's Waltz" (p. 697), in which the speaker uses the name of this orderly, stately dance to describe his childhood memories of his father's whirling him around the kitchen in wild, boisterous drunkenness.

TONE AND SATIRE

Satire, an important genre in the study of tone, is designed to expose human follies and vices. In method, a satiric poem may be bitter and vituperative, but often it employs humor and irony, on the grounds that anger turns readers away while a comic tone more easily wins agreement. The speaker of a satiric poem either may attack folly and vice *directly*, or may dramatically *embody* the folly or vice, and thus serve as an illustration of the subject of satire. An example of the first type is the following short poem by Alexander Pope, in which the speaker directly attacks a listener who has claimed to be a poet, but whom the speaker considers a fool. The speaker cleverly uses insult as the tone of attack:

ALEXANDER POPE   (1688–1744)

Epigram from the French ———————————————————————— *1732*

Sir, I admit your general rule
That every poet is a fool:
But you yourself may serve to show it,
That every fool is not a poet.

QUESTIONS

1. What has the listener said before the poem begins? How does the speaker build on the listener's previous comment?
2. Considering this poem as a brief satire, describe the nature of satiric attack and the corresponding tone of attack.
3. Look at the pattern *poet, fool, fool, poet*. What kind of rhetorical figure is this (see p. 271)? What does the pattern contribute to the poem's effectiveness?

An example of the second type of satiric poem is another of Pope's epigrams, in which the speaker is an actual embodiment of the subject being attacked:

ALEXANDER POPE   (1688–1744)

Epigram. Engraved on the Collar of a Dog
which I gave to His Royal Highness ———————————————— *1738 (1737)*

I am his Highness' dog at Kew:°   *a royal palace near London*
Pray tell me sir, whose dog are you?

QUESTIONS

1. Who or what is the specific subject of the satiric attack?
2. What is the attitude of this poem toward class pretensions?

Here the speaker is the King's dog, and the listener an unknown dog. Pope's satire is directed not against canines, however, but against human pretentiousness based on class. The first line ridicules those who claim derived, not earned, status. The second implies an unwillingness to recognize the listener until the question of rank is resolved. Pope, by using the dog as a speaker, reduces such snobbishness to an absurdity. A similar satiric poem attacking pretentiousness is "next to of course God" by E. E. Cummings (p. 929), where the speaker voices a set of patriotic platitudes, and in doing so illustrates Cummings's satiric point that such claims are usually empty headed. Satiric tone may thus range widely, sometimes being objective, comic, and distant;

sometimes deeply concerned and scornful; and sometimes dramatic, ingenuous, and revelatory. Always, however, the satiric mode aims toward confrontation and exposé.

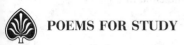 **POEMS FOR STUDY**

ANNE BRADSTREET (1612–1672)

The Author to Her Book ————————————————————— *1678*

Thou ill-formed offspring of my feeble brain,
Who after birth did'st by my side remain,
Till snatched from thence by friends, less wise than true,
Who thee abroad exposed to public view;
Made thee in rags, halting, to the press to trudge,   5
Where errors were not lessened, all may judge.
At thy return my blushing was not small,
My rambling brat° (in print) should mother call;
I cast thee by as one unfit for light,
Thy visage was so irksome in my sight;   10
Yet being mine own, at length affection would
Thy blemishes amend, if so I could:
I washed thy face, but more defects I saw,
And rubbing off a spot, still made a flaw.
I stretched thy joints to make thee even feet,°   *regular poetic meter* 15
Yet still thou run'st more hobbling than is meet;
In better dress to trim thee was my mind,
But nought save homespun cloth, in the house I find.
In this array, 'mongst vulgars may'st thou roam;
In critics hands beware thou dost not come;   20
And take thy way where yet thou art not known.
If for thy Father asked, say thou had'st none;
And for thy Mother, she alas is poor,
Which caused her thus to send thee out of door.

THE AUTHOR TO HER BOOK.   8 *brat:* The word here emphasizes the insignificance rather than the unpleasant aspects of a child.

QUESTIONS

1. What is the tone of the speaker's references to those friends who "exposed" her book to "public view" (that is, circulated it without her consent)? How does this tone indicate her ambiguous feelings about them?

2. How does the speaker excuse the fact that she is issuing her book of poetry on her own initiative? How does the tone produce humor? How does the tone of the concluding metaphor encourage you to smile, or even to laugh?

3. What attitude toward herself does the speaker express? How do you react to this attitude? How do you think you are expected by the poet to react?

4. What is the tone of the extended metaphor of the child in lines 11–18?

LUCILLE CLIFTON (b. 1936)

homage to my hips _____ *1987*

these hips are big hips
they need space to
move around in.
they don't fit into little
petty places. these hips
are free hips.
they don't like to be held back.
these hips have never been enslaved.
they go where they want to go.
they do what they want to do.
these hips are mighty hips.
these hips are magic hips.
i have known them
to put a spell on a man and
spin him like a top!

QUESTIONS

1. What is unusual about the subject matter? Considering that some people are embarrassed to mention their hips, what attitudes does the speaker express here?

2. How do the words "enslaved," "want to go," "want to do," "mighty," and "spell" define the poem's ideas about the relationship between mentality and physicality?

3. To what degree is this a comic poem? What about the subject and the diction makes the poem funny?

e. e. cummings (1894–1962)

she being Brand / -new _____ *1926*

she being Brand

-new;and you
know consequently a
little stiff i was
careful of her and(having

thoroughly oiled the universal
joint tested my gas felt of
her radiator made sure her springs were O.
K.)i went right to it flooded-the-carburetor cranked her

up,slipped the   10
clutch(and then somehow got into reverse she
kicked what
the hell)next
minute i was back in neutral tried and

again slo-wly;bare,ly nudg. ing(my   15

lev-er Right-
oh and her gears being in

A 1 shape passed
from low through
second-in-to-high like   20
greasedlightning) just as we turned the corner of Divinity

avenue i touched the accelerator and give

her the juice,good

                (it
was the first ride and believe i we was   25
happy to see how nice she acted right up to
the last minute coming back down by the Public
Gardens i slammed on
the

internalexpanding   30
&
externalcontracting
brakes Bothatonce and

brought allofher tremB
-ling   35
to a:dead.

stand-
;Still)

QUESTIONS

1. How extensive is the verbal irony, the double entendre, in this poem? This poem
    is considered comic. Do you agree? Why or why not?
2. How do the spacing and alignment affect your reading of the poem? How does
    the unexpected and sometimes absent punctuation—such as in line 15, "again
    slo-wly;bare,ly nudg. ing(my"—contribute to the humor?

3. Can this poem in any respect be called off-color or bawdy? How might you refute such charges in light of the tone the speaker uses to equate a first sexual experience with the breaking in of a new car?

ANNE FINCH   (1661–1720)

To the Nightingale ———————————————————— *1713*

Exert thy voice, sweet harbinger° of spring!   *forerunner, herald*
   This moment is thy time to sing,
   This moment I attend to praise,
And set my numbers to thy lays.°   *ballads*
   Free as thine shall be my song
   As thy music, short or long.
Poets, wild as thee, were born,
   Pleasing best when unconfined,
   When to please is least designed,
Soothing but their cares to rest;
   Cares do still their thoughts molest,
   And still the unhappy poet's breast,
Like thine, when best he sings, is placed against a thorn.°
   She begins. Let all be still!
    Muse, thy promise now fulfil!
   Sweet, oh sweet! still sweeter yet!
   Can thy words such accents fit,
   Canst thou syllables refine,
   Melt a sense that shall retain
   Still some spirit of the brain,
Till with sounds like these it join?
     'Twill not be! then change thy note,
    Let division° shake thy throat.
Hark! division now she tries,
Yet as far the Muse outflies.
    Cease then, prithee, cease thy tune!
    Trifler, wilt thou sing till June?
Till thy business all lies waste,
And the time of building's past?
    Thus we poets that have speech,
Unlike what thy forests teach,
   If a fluent vein be shown
   That's transcendent to our own,
Criticize, reform, or preach,
Or censure what we cannot reach.

TO THE NIGHTINGALE.   13 *thorn:* a reference to the (untrue) legend that nightingales sing most sweetly only when they are in pain because of thorns.   23 *division:* in music, the rapid singing of many notes.

QUESTIONS

1. What is the tone of the speaker's description of the nightingale? Is the tone consistent or mixed? How do you know?

2. For what reasons does the speaker admire the song of the bird? Describe the tone of the speaker's description of the bird's song as noted from lines 14–25. Why does the speaker censure the bird in lines 26–29? What attitude toward the speaker does the poet intend by the tone of these lines?

3. What is the tone of the connection the speaker makes between the song of the nightingale and the works of poets? What ideas does the speaker derive from this connection about the future of poetic creativity?

4. In lines 11–13 what is the tone of the speaker's metaphor of the thorn? How does the tone reveal the speaker's attitude toward herself?

5. What is the purpose of lines 30–35? What does the tone of these lines show about the speaker's attitude toward herself?

LANGSTON HUGHES   (1902–1967)

Theme for English B ——————————————————————— *1959*

The instructor said,

  Go home and write
  a page tonight.
  And let that page come out of you—
  Then, it will be true.   5

I wonder if it's that simple?

I am twenty-two, colored, born in Winston-Salem.
I went to school there, then Durham, then here
to this college on the hill above Harlem.°
I am the only colored student in my class.   10
The steps from the hill lead down to Harlem,
through a park, then I cross St. Nicholas,
Eighth Avenue, Seventh, and I come to the Y,
the Harlem Branch Y, where I take the elevator
up to my room, sit down, and write this page: 15

It's not easy to know what is true for you or me
at twenty-two, my age. But I guess I'm what
I feel and see and hear. Harlem, I hear you:
hear you, hear me—we two—you, me talk on this page.
(I hear New York, too.) Me—who?   20

THEME FOR ENGLISH B.   9 *college . . . Harlem:* a reference to Columbia University in the Columbia Heights section of New York City. The other streets and buildings mentioned in lines 11–14 refer to specific places in the same vicinity.

Well, I like to eat, sleep, drink, and be in love.
I like to work, read, learn, and understand life.
I like a pipe for a Christmas present,
or records—Bessie,° bop,° or Bach.°

I guess being colored doesn't make me not like
the same things other folks like who are other races.
So will my page be colored that I write?
Being me, it will not be white.
But it will be
a part of you, instructor.
You are white—
yet a part of me, as I am a part of you.
That's American.

Sometimes perhaps you don't want to be a part of me.
Nor do I often want to be a part of you.
But we are, that's true!
As I learn from you,
I guess you learn from me—
although you're older—and white—
and somewhat more free.

This is my page for English B.

24 *Bessie:* Bessie Smith (ca. 1898–1937), American jazz singer, famed as the "Empress of the Blues."   *bop:* a type of popular music which was in vogue in the 1940s through the 1960s. *Bach:* Johann Sebastian Bach (1685–1750), German composer, considered the master of the baroque style of music.

QUESTIONS

1. What is the tone of the speaker's self-assessment? What does the tone indicate about his feelings toward the situation in the class and at the Y?
2. What tone is implicit in the fact that the speaker, in response to a theme assignment, has composed a poem rather than a prose essay?
3. What is the tone of lines 21–24, where the speaker indicates his likes? In what way may the characteristics brought out in these lines serve as an argument for social and political equality?
4. How does the tone in lines 27–40, particularly lines 34–36, prevent the statements of the speaker from becoming overly assertive or strident?

X. J. KENNEDY   (b. 1929)

John while swimming in the ocean ———————————————— *1986*

John while swimming in the ocean
Rubbed sharks' backs with suntan lotion.
Now those sharks have skin of bronze
In their bellies—namely, John's.

QUESTIONS

1. What is the "action" of the poem? Why is it ludicrous?
2. What do the rhymes contribute to the poem's comic tone?
3. Describe the poem's attitude toward beach and ocean culture.

ARTHUR O'SHAUGHNESSY   (1844–1881)

A Love Symphony ——————————————————————— *1881*

Along the garden° ways just now   *a green area*
  I heard the flowers speak;
The white rose told me of your brow,
  The red rose of your cheek;
The lily of your bended head,   5
  The bindweed of your hair;
Each looked its loveliest and said
  You were more fair.

I went into the wood anon,°   *later, soon after*
  And heard the wild birds sing   10
How sweet you were; they warbled on,
  Piped, trilled the self-same thing,
Thrush, blackbird, linnet, without pause
  The burden did repeat,
And still began again because   15
  You were more sweet.

And then I went down to the sea,
  And heard it murmuring too,
Part of an ancient mystery,
  All made of me and you.   20
How many a thousand years ago
  I loved, and you were sweet—
Longer I could not stay, and so
  I fled back to your feet.

QUESTIONS

1. What is the "symphony" of love? What is the tone of the speaker's descriptions of the symphony as coming from flowers, birds, and the sea?
2. What is the tone of the phrase "ancient mystery / All made of me and you" (lines 19–20)? Compare this use of the idea of religious mysteriousness and love with the use in John Donne's "The Canonization" (p. 871) and Browning's "How Do I Love Thee" (p. 923). What common attitudes about love do these three poems contain? What differences?
3. What tone is expressed about the loved one in lines 23–24? In the light of his tone in describing her qualities, what sort of relationship is he celebrating?

ALEXANDER POPE   (1685–1744)

From *Epilogue to the Satires, Dialogue I* ——————————————— *1738*

Lines 137–172

Virtue may choose the high or low degree,
'Tis just alike to Virtue, and to me;
Dwell in a monk, or light upon a king,
She's still the same, beloved, contented thing.
Vice is undone, if she forgets her birth,
And stoops from angels to the dregs of earth:
But 'tis the Fall degrades her to a whore;
Let Greatness own her, and she's mean no more:°
Her birth, her beauty, crowds and courts confess,°
Chaste matrons praise her, and grave bishops bless:
In golden chains the willing world she draws,
And hers the gospel is, and hers the laws:
Mounts the tribunal, lifts her scarlet head,
And sees pale Virtue carted° in her stead!
Lo! at the wheels of her triumphal car,°   *carriage*
Old England's genius, rough with many a scar,
Dragged in the dust! his arms hang idly round,
His flag inverted trails along the ground!°
Our youth, all liveried o'er with foreign gold,
Before her dance; behind her crawl the old!
See thronging millions to the pagod° run,
And offer country, parent, wife, or son!
Hear her black trumpet through the land proclaim,
That "not to be corrupted is the shame."
In soldier, churchman, patriot, man in power,
'Tis avarice all, ambition is no more!
See, all our nobles begging to be slaves!
See all our fools aspiring to be knaves!
The wit of cheats, the courage of a whore,
Are what ten thousand envy and adore.
All, all look up, with reverential awe,
On crimes that scape,° or triumph o'er the law: *escape*
While truth, worth, wisdom, daily they decry—

EPILOGUE TO THE SATIRES, DIALOGUE I.   144 *mean no more*: i.e., if the rich and powerful follow vice, vice is no longer low, but fashionable.   145 *Her birth . . . confess*: i.e., Under the
dictates of fashion, both crowds and courts claim that Vice is both high-born and beautiful.
150 *carted*: It was an eighteenth-century punishment to display prostitutes in a cart; in addition,
condemned criminals were carried in a cart from prison to Tyburn, in London, where they were
hanged.   152–4 *Old England's genius . . . along the ground*: i.e., the spirit of England is humiliated by being tied to Vice's triumphal carriage and then dragged along the ground. The idea is
that corrupt politicians have sacrificed England's defensive power for their own gain.   157
pagod: i.e., a pagoda, a symbol of how many people have forsaken their own religion and adopted
foreign religions.

"Nothing is sacred now but villainy."   170
   Yet may this verse (if such a verse remain)
Show there was one who held it in disdain.

QUESTIONS

1. The entire poem is in the form of a dialogue, in which these concluding lines
    are identified as being spoken by "P" (Pope). Should readers therefore take these
    lines as an expression of Pope's own ideas? In your answer, pay special attention
    to the final couplet.

2. Explain this poem as social satire. What is attacked? What evidence does the
    speaker advance to support his case that society has deserted virtue and religion?

3. Describe the poem's tone. What specific charges does the speaker make against
    the prevailing social-political structure?

4. How timely is the poem? To what degree might such charges be advanced in our
    society today?

SALVATORE QUASÍMODO (1901–1968)

Auschwitz°   *1983*

translated by Jack Bevan

Far from the Vistula,° along the northern plain,
love, in a death-camp there at Auschwitz:
on the pole's rust and tangled fencing, rain
funeral cold.
No tree, no birds in the grey air   5
or above our thought, but limp
pain that memory leaves
to its silence without irony or anger.
You ask no elegies or idylls: only
the meaning of our destiny, you, here,   10
hurt by the mind's war,
uncertain at the clear
presence of life. For life is here
in every No that seems a certainty:
here we shall hear the angel weep, the monster, hear   15
our future time

AUSCHWITZ. *Auschwitz* is the German name for the town of Oswiecim in southern Poland,
site of the most notorious of the German concentration-extermination camps in World War II.
There were two major camps—Auschwitz itself, a former Polish army camp, and nearby Birke-
nau, which contained many temporary barracks for worker-prisoners, together with gas chambers and crematoria for the extermination of hundreds of thousands of victims.   1 *Vistula*:
The Vistula River rises in the northern Carpathian Mountains, south of Auschwitz.

beating the hereafter that is here, forever
in motion, not an image
of dreams, of possible pity.
Here are the myths, the metamorphoses.
Lacking the name of symbols or a god,
they are history, earth places,
they are Auschwitz, love. How suddenly
the dear forms of Alpheus and Arethusa°
changed into shadow-smoke!

Out of that hell hung with a white
inscription "work will make you free"°
there came the endless smoke
of many thousand women thrust at dawn
out of the kennels up to the firing-wall,
or, screaming for mercy to water, choked,
their skeleton mouths under the jets of gas.
You, soldier, will find them in your annals
taking the forms of animals and rivers,
or are you too, now, ash of Auschwitz,
medal of silence?
Long tresses in glass urns can still be seen
bound up with charms, and an infinity
of ghostly little shoes and shawls of Jews:°
relics of a time of wisdom,
of man whose knowledge takes the shape of arms,
they are the myths, our metamorphoses.

Over the plains where love and sorrow
and pity rotted, there in the rain
a No inside us beat;
a No to death that died at Auschwitz
never from the pit of ashes
to show itself again.

24 *Alpheus and Arethusa:* A river and fountain in Greece. In ancient mythology, Alpheus, who loved Arethusa, was transformed into the river (bearing his name) to be united with Arethusa, who was transformed into the fountain (bearing her name).   27 *work will make you free:* A translation of the large metal sign *Arbeit macht frei*, which crested the main gate of Auschwitz and is still on display there. A copy of the sign is displayed in the Holocaust Museum in Washington, D. C. 37–39 *Long tresses . . . shawls of Jews:* Today the barracks at Auschwitz house permanent displays that include the hair, shoes, eyeglasses, luggage, and clothing of thousands of the victims.

QUESTIONS

1. Compare the tone of the first ten lines with that of the last six. What differences do you notice? How does the idea of the last three lines answer the question posed in lines 9 and 10?

2. Even though the speaker is referring to the deadliest of all the camps, what does he mean by the lines *For life is here / in every No that seems a certainty?*

3. In line 20 the speaker mentions ancient myths about metamorphoses or transformations. What type of metamorphosis is linked to the death camps in lines
   25–43? What attitudes are brought out by this linkage?

THEODORE ROETHKE (1907–1963)

My Papa's Waltz ——————————————————— 1942

The whiskey on your breath
Could make a small boy dizzy;
But I hung on like death:
Such waltzing was not easy.

We romped until the pans   5
Slid from the kitchen shelf;
My mother's countenance
Could not unfrown itself.

The hand that held my wrist
Was battered on one knuckle;   10
At every step you missed
My right ear scraped a buckle.

You beat time on my head
With a palm caked hard by dirt,
Then waltzed me off to bed   15
Still clinging to your shirt.

QUESTIONS

1. What is the tone of the speaker's opening description of his father? What is the
   tone of the phrases "like death" and "such waltzing"?
2. What is the "waltz" the speaker describes? What is the tone of his words describing it in lines 5–15?
3. What does the reference to his "mother's countenance" contribute to the tone?
   What situation is suggested by the selection of the word "unfrown"?
4. What does the tone of the physical descriptions of the father contribute to your
   understanding of the speaker's attitude toward his childhood experiences as his
   father's dancing partner?

WRITING ABOUT TONE IN POETRY

Be careful to note those elements of the work that touch particularly on attitudes or authorial consideration. Thus, for example, you may be studying
Hughes's "Theme For English B," where it is necessary to consider the force

of the poet's claim for equality. How serious is the claim? Does the speaker's apparent matter-of-factness make him seem less than enthusiastic? Or does this tone indicate that equality is so fundamental a right that its realization should be an everyday part of life? Devising and answering such questions can help you understand the degree to which authors show control of tone.

Similar questions apply when you study internal qualities such as style and characterization.

Questions for Discovering Ideas

- What kind of character is the speaker? Is he or she intelligent, observant, friendly, idealistic, realistic, trustworthy? How do you believe that you are supposed to respond to the speaker's characteristics?

- Do all the speeches seem right for the speaker and situation? Are all descriptions appropriate, all actions believable?

- If the work is comic, at what is the comedy directed? At situations? At characters? At the speaker himself or herself? What is the apparent attitude of the poem toward the comic objects?

- Does the writer ask you to (a) sympathize with those in misfortune, (b) rejoice with those who have found happiness, (c) lament the human condition, (d) become angry against unfairness and inequality, (e) admire examples of noble human behavior, (f) have another appropriate emotional response?

- Do any words seem unusual or especially noteworthy, such as dialect, polysyllabic words, foreign words or phrases that the author assumes you know, or especially connotative words? What is the effect of such words on the poem's tone?

Strategies for Organizing Ideas

The goal of your essay is to examine all aspects bearing on the tone. Some of the things to cover might be these:

1. *The Audience, Situation, and Characters.* Is any person or group directly addressed by the speaker? What attitude is expressed (love, respect, condescension, confidentiality, confidence, etc.)? What is the basic situation in the work? What is the nature of the speaker or persona? What is the relationship of the speaker to the material? What is the speaker's authority? Does the speaker give you the whole truth? Is he or she trying to withhold anything? Why? How is the speaker's character manipulated to show apparent authorial attitude and to stimulate responses? Do you find any of the various sorts of irony? If so, what does the irony show (optimism or pessimism, for example)? How is the situation controlled to shape your responses? That is, can actions, situations, or characters be seen as expressions of attitude, or as embodiments of certain favorable or unfavorable ideas or positions? How does the work promote respect, admiration, dislike, or other feelings about character or situation?

2. *Descriptions, diction.* Your concern here is to relate style to attitude. Are there any systematic references, such as to colors, sounds, noises, natural

scenes, and so on, that collectively reflect an attitude? Do connotative meanings of words control response in any way? Is any special knowledge of references or unusual words expected of readers? What is the extent of this knowledge? Do speech or dialect patterns indicate attitudes about speakers or their condition of life? Are speech patterns normal and standard, or slang or substandard? What is the effect of these patterns? Are there unusual or particularly noteworthy expressions? If so, what attitudes do these show? Does the author use verbal irony? To what effect?

3. *Humor.* Is the work funny? How funny, how intense? How is the humor achieved? Does the humor develop out of incongruous situations or language, or both? Is there an underlying basis of attack in the humor, or are the objects of laughter still respected or even loved despite having humor directed against them?

4. *Ideas.* Ideas may be advocated, defended mildly, or attacked. Which is present in the work you have been studying? How does the author make his or her attitude clear—directly, by statement, or indirectly, through understatement, overstatement, or the language of a character? In what ways does the work assume a common ground of assent between author and reader? That is, are there apparently common assumptions about religious views, political ideas, moral and behavioral standards, and so on? Are these common ideas readily acceptable, or is any concession needed by the reader to approach the work? (For example, a major subject of "Dover Beach" is that absolute belief in the truth of Christianity has been lost. This subject may not be important to everyone, but even an irreligious reader, or a follower of another faith, may find common ground in the poem's psychological situation, or in the desire to learn as much as possible about so important a phenomenon of modern Western society.)

5. *Unique characteristics.* Each work has unique properties that contribute to the tone. Anne Bradstreet, for example, in "The Author to Her Book," introduces the metaphor of her work being like an unwanted child that she is sending out into the world. Her apology hence introduces a tone of amused but sincere self-effacement that the reader must consider. Theodore Roethke's "My Papa's Waltz" is a brief narrative in which the speaker's feelings about memories of his childhood participation in his father's boisterously drunken behavior must be inferred from understatement like "waltz." Hardy's "Channel Firing" develops from the comic idea that the firing of guns at sea is so loud it could awaken the dead. Be alert for such special circumstances in your poem, and as you plan and develop your essay, take them into account.

Your conclusion may summarize your main points, and from there go on to any needed definitions, explanations, or afterthoughts, together with ideas reinforcing earlier points. If you have changed your mind, or have made new realizations, briefly explain these. Finally, you might mention some other major aspect of the work's tone that you did not develop in the body.

SAMPLE ESSAY

The Tone of Confidence in "Theme for English B" by Langston Hughes°

[1] "Theme for English B" grows from the situational irony of racial differences as seen by the speaker, an African-American college student. This situation might easily produce bitterness, anger, outrage, or vengefulness. However, the poem contains none of these. It is not angry or indignant; it is not an appeal for revenge or revolution. It is rather a declaration of personal independence and individuality. The tone is one of objectivity, daring, occasional playfulness, but above all, confidence.* These attitudes are made plain in the speaker's situation, the ideas, the poetic form, the diction, and the expressions.†

[2] Hughes's poetic treatment is objective, factual, and personal, not emotional or political. The poem contains a number of factual details: The speaker is black in an otherwise all-white College English class. He has come from North Carolina, and is now living alone at the Harlem YMCA, away from family and roots. He is also, at 22, an older student. All this is evidence of disadvantage, yet the speaker does no more than present the facts objectively, without comment.

[3] Hughes's thoughts about equality--the idea underlying the poem--are presented in the same objective, cool manner. The speaker writes to his instructor as an equal, not as an inferior. His idea is that all people are the same, regardless of race or background. In defining himself, therefore, he does not deal in abstractions, but emphasizes that he, like everyone else, has ordinary likes and needs, and that his abilities and activities are like those of everyone else. By causing the speaker to avoid emotionalism and controversy, Hughes makes counter-arguments difficult if not impossible.

[4] The argument for equality is carried out even in Hughes's actual use of the poetic form. The title here is the key, for it does not promise the most exciting of topics. Normally, in fact, one would expect nothing much more than a short prose theme in response to an English assignment, but a poem is unexpected and therefore daring and original, particularly one like this that touches on the topic of equality and identity. The wit, originality, and skill of the speaker's use of the form itself demonstrate the self-confidence and self-sufficiency that underlie the theoretical claim for equality.

[5] Hughes's diction is also in keeping with the poem's confidence and daring. Almost all the words are short and simple--of no more than one or two syllables--showing the speaker's confidence in the truth and power of his ideas. This high proportion of short words reflects a conscious attempt to keep the diction clear and direct. A result is that Hughes avoids any possible ambiguities, as the following words show:

Well, I like to eat, sleep, drink, and be in love.
I like to work, read, learn, and understand life.

° For this poem, see p. 691.
* Central idea.
† Thesis sentence.

> I like a pipe for a Christmas present,
> or records--Bessie, bop, or Bach. (lines 21–24)

With the exception of what it means to "understand life," these words are free of emotional overtones. They reflect the speaker's confident belief that equality should replace inequality and prejudice.

A number of the speaker's phrases and expressions also show this same confidence. Although most of the language is simple and descriptive, it is also playful and ironic. In lines 18–20 there seems to be a deliberate use of confusing language to bring about a verbal merging of the identities of the speaker, the instructor, Harlem, and the greater New York area:

> Harlem, I hear you:
> hear you, hear me--we two--you, me talk on this page.
> (I hear New York, too.) Me--who? (lines 18–20)

[6]

One may also find a certain whimsicality in the way in which the speaker treats the irony of the black-white situation:

> So will my page be colored that I write? (line 27)

Underlying this last expression is an awareness that, despite the claim that people are equal and are tied to each other by common humanity, there are also strong differences among individuals. The speaker is confidently asserting grounds for independence as well as equality.

[7]

Thus, an examination of "Theme for English B" reveals vitality and confidence. The poem is a statement of trust and an almost open challenge on the personal level to the unachieved ideal of equality. Hughes makes this point through the deliberate simplicity of the speaker's words and descriptions. Yet the poem is not without irony, particularly at the end, where the speaker mentions that the instructor is "somewhat more free" than he is. "Theme for English B" is complex and engaging. It shows the speaker's confidence through objectivity, daring, and playfulness.

Commentary on the Essay

Because this essay embodies a number of approaches by which tone may be studied in any work (situation, common ground, diction, special characteristics), it is typical of many essays that use a combined, eclectic approach. The central idea is that the dominant attitude in "Theme for English B" is the speaker's confidence, and that this confidence is shown in the similar but separable attitudes of objectivity, daring, and playfulness.

Paragraph 2 deals with situational irony in relation to the social and political circumstance of racial discrimination (see approach 1, p. 698). Paragraph 3 considers the objectivity with which Hughes considers the idea of equality (approach 4).

Paragraph 4 shows how a topic that might ordinarily be taken for granted, in this case the basic form or genre of expression, can be seen as a unique feature of tone (approach 5). The paragraph contrasts the *expected* student response (no more than a brief prose essay) with the *actual* response (the poem itself, with its interesting twists and turns). Since the primary tone of the poem is that of self-confidence, which is the unspoken basis for the speaker's assertion of independence and equality, the paragraph stresses that the form itself embodies this attitude.

Paragraphs 5 and 6 consider how Hughes's word choices exhibit his attempts at clarity, objectivity, playfulness, and confidence (approach 2). The attention given in these paragraphs to Hughes's simple, direct diction is justified by its importance in the poem's tone.

The concluding paragraph stresses again the attitude of confidence in the poem, and also notes additional attitudes of trust, challenge, irony, daring, and playfulness.

WRITING TOPICS

1. Consider "A Love Symphony," "homage to my hips," "she being Brand/ -new," "The Workbox," and "The First-Rate Wife" as poems about love. What similarities do you find? That is, do the poets state that love creates joy, satisfaction, distress, embarrassment, trouble? How does the tone of each of the poems enable you to draw your conclusions? What differences do you find in the ways the poets either control or do not control tone?

2. Consider these same poems from a feminist viewpoint (see Appendix D). What importance and value do the poems give to women? How do they view women's actions? Generally, what praise or blame do the poems deserve because of their treatment of women?

3. Consider the tone of "My Papa's Waltz." Some readers have concluded that the speaker is expressing fond memories of his childhood experiences with his father. Others believe that the speaker is ambiguous about the father, and that he blocks out remembered pain as he describes the amusing boisterousness in the kitchen. On the basis of the poem's tone, how should the poem be interpreted?

4. Write a poem about a person or occasion that has made you either glad or angry. Try to create the same feelings in your reader, but create these feelings through your rendering of situation and your choices of the right words. (Possible topics: a social injustice, an unfair grade, a compliment you have received on a task well done, the landing of a good job, the winning of a game, a rise in the price of gasoline, a good book or movie, and so on.)

5. What judgments about modern city life do you think that Leger conveys in his painting *The City* (p. 679)? If the tone of paintings may be considered as similar to poetic tone, in what ways is *The City* comparable to the presentation of detail in Blake's "London" (p. 575), Eliot's "Preludes" (p. 640), Swift's "A Description of the Morning" (p. 730), and Sandburg's "Chicago" (p. 981)—together with any other poems you wish to include?

6. Quasímodo's "Auschwitz" concerns one of the twentieth century's central evils, about which people have expressed anger, horror, indignation, outrage, disgust, hatred, and vengefulness. To what degree do you find these attitudes in Quasímodo's poem? Do these attitudes, or others, govern the poem's tone?

19

Prosody: Sound, Rhythm, and Rhyme in Poetry

Prosody (*the pronunciation of a song or poem*) is the general word describing the study of poetic sounds and rhythms. Common alternative words are **metrics, versification, mechanics of verse**, and the **music of poetry**. Most readers, when reading poetry aloud, interpret the lines and develop an appropriate speed and expressiveness of delivery—a proper *rhythm*. Indeed, some people think that rhythm and sound are the *music* of poetry because they are like musical rhythms and tempos. Like music, poetry often requires a regular beat. The tempo and loudness may vary freely, however, and a reader may stop at any time to repeat the sounds and to think about the words and ideas.

It is important to recognize that poets, being especially attuned to language, blend words and ideas together so that "the sound" becomes "an echo to the sense" (Pope). Readers may therefore accept as a rule that *prosodic technique cannot be separated from a poem's content*. For this reason, the study of prosody aims at determining how poets have controlled their words so that the sound of a poem complements its expression of emotions and ideas.

IMPORTANT DEFINITIONS FOR STUDYING PROSODY

To study prosody you need a few basic linguistic facts. Individual sounds in combination make up syllables and words, and separate words in combination make up lines of poetry. Syllables and words are made up of **segments**, or individually meaningful sounds (*segmental phonemes*). In the word *top* there are three segments: *t, o,* and *p*. When you hear these three sounds in order, you recognize the word "top." It takes three alphabetical letters—*t, o,* and *p*—to spell (*graph*) "top," because each letter is identical with a segment. Sometimes, however, it takes more than one letter to spell a segment. For example, in the word *enough* there are four segments (*ē, n, ŭ, f*) although six letters are required for the correct spelling: *e, n, ou,* and *gh.* The last two segments (*u* and *f*) require two letters each (two letters forming one segment are called a *digraph*). In the word *through* there are three segments but *seven* letters. To be correctly spelled in this word, the *oo* segment must have four letters (*ough*). Note, however, that in the word *flute* the *oo* segment requires only one letter, *u.* When we study the effects of various segments in relationship to the poetic rhythm, we deal with **sound**; usually our concern is with prosodic devices such as **alliteration, assonance,** and **rhyme.**

When segments are meaningfully combined, they make up syllables and words. A **syllable**, in both prose and poetry, consists of a single meaningful strand of sound such as the article *a* in "*a* table," *lin* in "*lin*en," and *flounce* in "the little girls *flounce* into the room." (The article *a*, which is both a syllable and a word, has only one segment; *lin*, the first syllable of a two-syllable word [*lin* never occurs alone; it is always used in combinations such as *lingerie* and *linoleum*], contains three segments; *flounce* is a word of one syllable consisting of six segments: *f, l, ow, n, t,* and *s*). The understanding of what constitutes syllables is important because the rhythm of most poetry is determined by the measured relationship of heavily stressed to less heavily stressed syllables.

SOUND AND SPELLING

It is important—vital—to distinguish between spelling, or graphics, and pronunciation, or phonetics. Not all English sounds are spelled and pronounced in the same way, as with *top.* Thus the letter *s* has three very different sounds in the words *sweet, sugar,* and *flows: s, sh* (as in "sharp") and *z.* On the other hand, the words *shape, ocean, nation, sure, fissure, Eschscholtzia,* and *machine* use different letters or combinations of letters to spell the same *sh* sound.

Vowel sounds may also be spelled in different ways. The *e* sound, for example, can be spelled *i* in *machine, ee* in *speed, ea* in *eat, e* in *even,* and *y* in *funny,* yet the vowel sounds in *eat, break,* and *bear* are not the same even though they are spelled the same. Remember this: With both consonants and vowel sounds, *do not confuse spellings with sounds.*

RHYTHM

Rhythm in speech is a combination of vocal speeds, rises and falls, starts and stops, vigor and slackness, and relaxation and tension. In ordinary speech and in prose, rhythm is not as important as the flow of ideas. In poetry, rhythm is significant because poetry is so emotionally charged, compact, and intense. Poets invite us to change speeds while reading—to slow down and linger over some words and sounds, and to pass rapidly over others. They also invite us to give more-than-ordinary vocal stress or emphasis to certain syllables, and less stress to others. The more intense syllables are called **heavy stress** syllables, and

VOWEL AND CONSONANT SOUNDS

Studying the nature of vocal production can take, and has taken, entire careers. A brief reference to the production of sound, however, is still in order, for without introductory knowledge you will have difficulty determining segments and their effects.

Vowel sounds result from vibrations resonating in the space between the tongue and the top of the mouth. As our tongues go up or down, or forward or backward, or as they curl or flatten out, and as our lips move synchronously with our tongues, we form our vowel sounds. Some vowel sounds are "long," such as ē (flee), ā (stay), ō (open), and o͞o (food). Others are "short," such as ĭ (fĭt), ŭ (fŭn) and ĕ (sĕt). Some vowels are called "front" (e.g., see, play) and some are called "back" (knowing, moon). Some are rounded (hope, hoop), and more are unrounded (green, swim).

Many of our English vowel sounds are pronounced as a *schwa*, or minimal sound, despite their spellings (e.g., the e in "the boy"). Thus, "about," "stages," "rapid," "nation," and "circus" contain the vowels a, e, i, o, and u, but all the italicized letters make the same *schwa* sounds, which in pronunciation receive a light stress.

There are three **diphthongs**—that is, sounds that begin with one vowel sound and move to another vowel sound, namely i (fly), ou (house), and oi (foil).

Consonant sounds are classified into three major groups. (1) *Stop sounds,* also called *plosives,* are percussive and abrupt. They are made by the momentary stoppage and release of breath either when the lips touch each other or when the tongue touches the teeth or palate. The stops are p, b, t, d, k, and g.

(2) *Continuant sounds* are smooth and flowing. They are produced by the steady release of the breath in conjunction with various positions of the tongue in relation to the lips, teeth, and palate, as in n, ng, l, r, th (thorn), th (the), f, v, s, z, sh (sharp), and zh (pleasure); or with the touching of the lower lip and upper teeth for the sounds f and v; or with the touching of both lips for the sound m. Two special sounds called *affricates* begin with the stops t and d, and then become the continuants sh and zh (as in chew and judge).

(3) *Semivowel sounds* are midway between vowels and consonants, but are more like consonants than vowels. These have in common that they move from an originating sound and then move to another vowel sound. They are w (wagon, win, weather), y (yes, young, union), and h (hope, heap).

Consonant sounds are either *voiced*; that is, produced with the vibration of the vocal chords (e.g., b, d, g, v, z, zh), or *voiceless*, produced by the breath alone, as a whisper (e.g., p, t, k, f, s, sh). Among the semivowels, w and y are voiced, but h is unvoiced.

---

it is the heavy stresses that determine the **accent** or **beat** of a poetic line. The less intense syllables receive **light stress.** In traditional verse, poets select patterns called **feet,** which consist of a regularized relationship of heavy stresses to light stresses.

Rhythm and Scansion

To study the patterns of versification in any poem, you **scan** the poem. The act of scanning—**scansion**—enables you to discover how the poem establishes a prevailing metrical pattern, and also how and why there are variations in the pattern.

RECORDING STRESSES OR BEATS.   In scansion, it is important to use a commonly recognized notational system to record stresses or accents. A *heavy* or *primary* stress (also called an **accented syllable**) is commonly indicated by a prime mark or acute accent (´). A *light* stress (also called an **unaccented syllable**) is indicated by a bowl-like half circle called a **breve** (˘), or sometimes by a raised circle or degree sign (°). To separate one foot from another, a **virgule** or slash (/) is used. Thus, the following line, from Coleridge's "The Rime of the Ancient Mariner," is schematized formally in this way:

$$\text{Wa - ter, / wa - ter, / ev - ery where,}$$

Here the virgules show that the line contains two two-syllable feet followed by a three-syllable foot.

RECORDING THE METER OR MEASURE.   Another important part of scansion is the determination of a poem's **meter,** or the number of feet in its lines. Lines containing five feet are **pentameter,** four are **tetrameter,** three are **trimeter,** two are **dimeter**, and one is **monometer.** (To these may be added the less common line lengths **hexameter,** a six-foot line, **heptameter** or **the septenary,** seven feet, and **octameter,** eight feet.) In terms of accent or beat, a trimeter line has three beats (heavy stresses), a pentameter line five beats, and so on.

Metrical Feet

Equipped with this knowledge, you are ready to scan poems and determine the rhythmical patterns of feet. The most important ones, the specific names of which are derived from Greek poetry, are the two-syllable foot, the three syllable foot, and the one-syllable (or imperfect) foot.

THE TWO-SYLLABLE FOOT.   (a) **The Iamb.** The most important two-syllable foot in English is the **iamb**, which contains a light stress followed by a heavy stress:

$$\text{the winds}$$

The iamb is the most common foot in English poetry because it most nearly duplicates natural speech while also elevating speech to poetry. It is the most versatile of English poetic feet, and it is capable of great variation. Even within the same line, iambic feet may vary in intensity, so that they may support or undergird the shades of meaning designed by the poet. For example, in this line of iambic pentameter from Wordsworth ("The World is Too Much with Us"), each foot is unique:

$$\text{The winds / that will / be howl- / ing at / all hours.}$$

Even though *will* and *at* receive the heavy stress in their individual iambic feet, they are not as strongly emphasized as *winds, howl-,* and *hours* (indeed, they are also less strong than *all,* which is in the light-stress position in the concluding iamb). Such variability, approximating the stresses and rhythms of actual speech, makes the iamb suitable for both serious or light verse, and it therefore helps poets focus attention on ideas and emotions. If they use it with skill, it never becomes monotonous, for it does not distract readers by drawing attention to its own rhythm.

   (b) The Trochee. The trochee consists of a heavy accent followed by a light:

$$\acute{\text{flow}} - \breve{\text{er}}$$

Rhythmically, most English words are trochaic, as may be seen in the words *water, snowfall, author, willow, morning, early, follow, singing, window,* and *something.* A major exception is seen in two-syllable words beginning with prefixes, such as *sublime, because,* and *impel.* Another exception is found in two-syllable words that are borrowed from another language but are still pronounced as in the original language, as with *machine, technique, garage,* and *chemise,* all of which are French importations. To see the strength of the trochaic tendency in English, French words borrowed six hundred or more years ago have lost their original iambic structure and have become trochaic, as with *language, very, nation,* and *cherry.*

   Because trochaic rhythm has often been called *falling, dying, light,* or *anti-climactic,* while iambic rhythm is *rising, elevating, serious,* and *climactic,* poets have preferred the iambic foot. They therefore have arranged various placements of two syllable words, using single syllable words and a variety of other means, so that the heavy-stress syllable is at the end of the foot, as in Shakespeare's

$$\text{his ben̆d - / ĭng síck - /lĕ's cóm - / păss cóme/,}$$

in which three successive trochaic words are arranged to match the iambic meter.

   (c) The Spondee. The **spondee**—also called a **hovering accent**—consists of two successive, equally heavy accents, as in *men's eyes* in Shakespeare's line:

$$\text{Whĕn, ín / dĭs -gráce / wĭth for - / tŭne ănd / men's eyes.}$$

The spondee is mainly a substitute foot in English verse because successive spondees usually become iambs or trochees. An entire poem written in spondees would be unlikely within traditional metrical patterns and ordinary English syntax (but see Gwendolyn Brooks's poem "We Real Cool," p. 718). As a substitute, however, the spondee creates emphasis. The usual way to indicate the spondaic foot is to link the two syllables together with chevronlike marks ( ), like this:

men's eyes

(d) The Pyrrhic. The **pyrrhic** consists of two unstressed syllables (even though one of them may be in a normally stressed position), as in *on their* in Pope's line:

Now sleep - / ing flocks / on their / soft fleec - /es lie.

The pyrrhic is made up of weakly accented words such as prepositions (e.g., *on, to*) and articles (*the, a*). Like the spondee, it is usually substituted for an iamb or trochee, and therefore a complete poem cannot be in pyrrhics. As a substitute foot, however, the pyrrhic acts as a rhythmic catapult to move the reader swiftly to the next heavy-stress syllable, and therefore it undergirds the ideas conveyed by more important words.

THE THREE-SYLLABLE FOOT.   **(a) The Anapæst.** The anapæst consists of two light accents followed by a heavy accent:

by the dawn's / ear-ly light.   (Key)

(b) The Dactyl. A heavy stress followed by two lights:

green as our / hope in it, / white as our/ faith in it.   (Swinburne)

THE IMPERFECT FOOT.   The imperfect foot consists of a single syllable (´) by itself, or (˘) by itself. This foot is a variant or substitute occurring in a poem in which one of the major feet forms the metrical pattern. The second line of Key's "The Star-Spangled Banner," for example, is anapæstic, but it contains an imperfect foot at the end:

What so proud -/ly we hailed/at the twi-/light's last gleam-/ing.

Other Rhythmic Devices

ACCENTUAL, STRONG-STRESS, AND "SPRUNG" RHYTHMS.   Accentual or strong-stress lines are historically derived from the poetry of Old English (see pp. 549–50). At that time, each line was divided in two, with two major stresses, also alliterated, occurring in each half. In the nineteenth century, Gerard Manley Hopkins (1844–1889) developed what he called "sprung" rhythm, a rhythm in which the major stresses would be released or "sprung" from the

SPECIAL METERS

In many poems you will find meters other than those described above. Poets like Browning, Tennyson, Poe, and Swinburne introduce special or unusual meters. Other poets manipulate pauses or **caesurae** (discussed later) to create the effects of unusual meters. For these reasons, you should know about metrical feet such as the following:

1. AMPHIBRACH. A light, heavy, and light:

Ah fĕed mĕ / ănd fíll mĕ / wĭth plĕas - sŭre (Swinburne).

2. AMPHIMACER OR CRETIC. A heavy, light, and heavy:

Lóve ĭs bést (Browning).

3. BACCHIUS OR BACCHIC. A light stress followed by two heavy stresses:

Sŏme láte lárk / [sĭng -ĭng] (Henley).

4. DIPODIC MEASURE, OR SYZYGY. Dipodic measure (literally, "two feet" combining to make one) develops in longer lines when a poet submerges two regular feet under a stronger beat, so that a "galloping" or "rollicking" rhythm results. The following line from Masefield's "Cargoes," for example, may be scanned as trochaic hexameter, with the concluding foot being an iamb:

Quín-que / reme ŏf / Nín-e- / veh frŏm / dís-tănt / Ō-phir.

In reading, however, a stronger beat is superimposed, which makes one foot out of two—dipodic measure or syzygy:

Quínquĕrĕme ŏf / Nínĕvĕh frŏm / dístănt Ōphir

line. The method is complex, but one characteristic is the juxtaposing of one-syllable stressed words, as in this line from "Pied Beauty":

Wíth swíft, slów; swéet, soúr; ădázzlĕ, dím;

Here a number of elements combine to create six major stresses. Many of Hopkins's lines combine alliteration and strong stresses in this way to create the same effect of heavy emphasis.

A parallel instance of strongly stressed lines may be seen in "We Real Cool" by Gwendolyn Brooks (p. 718). In this poem the effect is achieved by the exclusive use of monosyllabic stressed words combined with internal rhyme, repetition, and alliteration.

THE CAESURA, OR PAUSE.   Whenever we speak, we run our words to-gether rapidly, without pause. We do, however, stop briefly and almost unno-ticeably between significant units or phrases. These significant units, both grammatically and rhythmically, are **cadence groups**. In poetry that empha-sizes a regular meter, the cadence groups operate just as they do in prose to make the ideas intelligible. Although we are following the poetic rhythm, we also pause briefly at the ends of phrases, and make longer pauses at the ends of sentences. In scansion, the name of these pauses, which linguists call *junc-tures*, is **caesura** (plural **caesurae**). When scanning a line, we note a caesura with two diagonal lines or virgules (//), so that the caesura may be distin-guished from the single virgule separating feet. Sometimes the caesura coin-cides with the end of a foot, as at the end of the second iamb in this line by William Blake ("To Mrs. Anna Flaxman"):

With hands / di- vine // he mov'd / the gen - / tle Sod. /

The caesura, however, may fall within a foot, and there may be more than one in a line, as within the second and third iambs in this line by Ben Jonson:

Thou art / not, //Pens - / hurst, // built / to en - / vious show./

When a caesura ends a line, usually marked by a comma, semicolon, or period, that line is **end-stopped**, as in this line which opens Keats's "Endymion":

A thing / of beau - / ty // is / a joy / for - ev -er. //

If a line has no punctuation at the end and runs over to the next line, it is called run-on. A term also used to indicate run-on lines is *enjambement*. The follow-ing passage, a continuation of the line from Keats, contains three run-on lines:

Its loveliness increases; // it will never
Pass into nothingness; // but still will keep
A bower quiet for us, // and a sleep
Full of sweet dreams, // . . .

FORMAL SUBSTITUTION.   Most regular poems follow a formal pattern that may be analyzed according to the feet we have been describing here. For interest and emphasis, however (and also perhaps because of the natural rhythms of English speech), poets may **substitute** other feet for the regular feet of the poem. For example, the following line is from the "January" Eclogue of Edmund Spenser's *Shepherd's Calendar*. Although the pattern of the poem is iambic pentameter (i.e., five iambs per line), Spenser includes two substitute feet in the line:

All in /a sun - / shine day, /as did / be - fall./

In the first foot, *All in* is a trochee, and *shine day* is a spondee. These are *formal substitutions*; that is, Spenser uses separate, formally structured feet in place of the normal iambic feet. The effect is to move rapidly from "All" to "sunshine day" in order to allow the reader to delight in the sound of the words and also to savor the idea of unexpectedly nice weather during the middle of winter.

RHETORICAL SUBSTITUTION. By manipulating the caesura, poets may achieve the effects that are provided by formal substitution. If the pauses are placed within feet, they may cause us actually to *hear* trochees, amphibrachs, and other variant feet even though the line may scan regularly in the established meter. This type of *de facto* variation is **rhetorical substitution**. A noteworthy example in an iambic pentameter line is this one from Pope's Essay on Man:

His ac-/tions', // pas-/sions', // be-/ing's, // use/and end.

The theory of this type of line is that there be a caesura after the fourth syllable, but in this one Pope has made three, each producing a strong pause. The line is regularly iambic, but the effect is different in actual reading or speaking. Because of the caesurae after the third, fifth, and seventh syllables, the rhythm produces an amphibrach, a trochee, another trochee, and an amphimacer, thus:

His ac-/tions', // pas-/sions', // be-/ing's, // use/and end.

AMPHIBRACH	TROCHEE	TROCHEE	AMPHIMACER

The spoken substitutions produced by the caesurae in this regular line produce the effect of substitution and therefore tension and interest.

When studying rhythm, your main concern in noting substitutions is to determine the formal metrical pattern, and then to analyze the formal and rhetorical variations on this pattern and their principal techniques and effects. Always try to show how these variations have enabled the poet to get points across and to achieve emphasis.

SEGMENTAL POETIC DEVICES

Once you have completed your analysis of rhythms, you may go on to consider the segmental poetic devices in the poem. Usually these devices are used to create emphasis, but sometimes in context they may echo or imitate actions and objects. The segmental devices most common in poetry are *assonance, alliteration, onomatopoeia,* and *euphony and cacophony.*

Assonance

Assonance is the repetition of identical vowel sounds in different words—for example, the short *i* in "sw*i*ft Cam*i*lla sk*i*ms." It is a strong means of emphasis, as in the following line, where the *u* sound connects the two words *lull* and *slumber,* and the short *i* connects *him, in,* and *his*:

> And more, to lull him in his slumber soft.   (Spenser)

In some cases, poets may use assonance elaborately, as in the first line of Pope's An Essay on Criticism:

> 'Tis hard to say, if greater want of skill.

Here the line is framed and balanced with the short $\breve{i}$ in *'Tis, if,* and *skill.* The *ä* in h*a*rd and *want* forms another, internal frame, and the *ā* in s*a*y and *greater* creates still another frame. Such a balanced use of vowels is unusual, however, for in most lines assonance occurs simply as a means of highlighting important words, without such elaborate patterning.

Alliteration

Like assonance, **alliteration** is a means of highlighting ideas by words containing the same **consonant** sound—for example, the repeated *m* in Spenser's "Mixed with a *m*urmuring wind," or the s sound in Waller's praise of Cromwell, "Your never-failing sword made war to cease," which emphasizes the connection between the words "sword" and "cease."

There are two kinds of alliteration. Most commonly, alliteration is regarded as the repetition of identical consonant sounds that begin syllables in close patterns—for example, in Pope's lines "La*b*orious, heavy, *b*usy, *b*old, and *b*lind," and "While *p*ensive *p*oets *p*ainful vigils keep." Used judiciously, alliteration gives strength to ideas by emphasizing key words, but too much *c*an *c*ause *c*omic and *c*atastrophic *c*onsequences. The second form of alliteration occurs when a poet repeats identical or similar consonant sounds that do not begin syllables but nevertheless create a pattern—for example, the z segment in the line "In the*s*e places freezing breeze*s* easily cau*s*e sneeze*s*," or the *b, m,* and *p* segments (all of which are made *bilabially*; that is, with both lips) in "The *m*iserably *mumb*ling and *mo*mentously *mur*muring *b*eggar *pro*pels *p*egs and *p*e*bb*les in the *bub*bling *p*ool." Such clearly designed patterns are hard to overlook.

Onomatopoeia

Onomatopoeia is a blend of consonant and vowel sounds designed to *imitate* or *suggest* a situation or action. It is made possible in poetry because many English words are **echoic** in origin; that is, they are verbal echoes of the actions they describe, such as *buzz, bump, slap,* and so on. Poe used such words to create onomatopoeia in "The Bells," where through the combined use of assonance and alliteration he imitates the kinds of bells he celebrates. Thus, wedding bells sound softly with "m*o*lten g*o*lden n*o*tes" (*ō*), while alarm bells "*cl*ang and *cl*ash and roar" (*kl*). David Wagoner includes imitative words like *tweedledy, thump,* and *wheeze* to suggest the sounds of the music produced by the protagonist of his "March for a One-Man Band."

Euphony and Cacophony

Words describing smooth or jarring sounds, particularly those resulting from consonants, are **euphony** and **cacophony.** Euphony ("good sound") refers to words containing consonants that permit an easy and smooth flow of spoken sound. Although there is no rule that some consonants are inherently more pleasant than others, students of poetry often cite sounds like *m, n, ng, l, v,* and *z,* together with *w* and *y,* as being especially easy on the ears. The opposite of euphony is cacophony ("bad sound"), in which percussive and choppy sounds make for vigorous and noisy pronunciation, as in tongue-twisters like "black bug's blood" and "shuffling shellfish fashioned by a selfish sushi chef." Obviously, unintentional cacophony is a mark of imperfect control. When a poet deliberately creates it for effect, however, as in Tennyson's line "The bare black cliff clang'd round him," Pope's "The hoarse, rough verse should like the torrent roar," and Coleridge's "Huge fragments vaulted like rebounding hail, / Or chaffy grain beneath the thresher's flail," cacophony is a mark of poetic skill. Although poets generally aim at easily flowing, euphonious lines, cacophony does have a place, always depending on the poet's intention and subject matter.

RHYME

Rhyme refers to words containing identical final syllables. One type of rhyme involves words with identical concluding vowel sounds, or assonance, as in *day, weigh, grey, bouquet, fiancé,* and *matinee.* A second type of rhyme is created by assonance combined with identical consonant sounds, as in *ache, bake, break,* and *opaque,* or *turn, yearn, fern, spurn,* and *adjourn,* or *apple* and *dapple,* or *slippery* and *frippery.* Rhymes like these, because their rhyming sounds are identical, are called **exact rhymes.** It is important to note that rhymes result from *sound* rather than spelling; words do not have to be spelled the same way or look alike to rhyme. All the words rhyming with *day*, for example, are spelled differently, but because they all contain the same $\bar{a}$ sound, they rhyme.

The Nature and Function of Rhyme

Rhyme, above all, gives delight. It also strengthens a poem's psychological impact. Through its network of similar sounds that echo and resonate in our minds, it promotes memory by clinching feelings and ideas. It has been an important aspect of poetry for hundreds of years, and, although many poets have not used it, and other poets have shunned it because they find it restrictive and artificial, it is closely connected with how well given poems move us or leave us flat.

Most often, rhymes are placed at the ends of lines. Two successive lines may rhyme, for example, and rhymes may appear in alternating lines. It is also possible to introduce rhyming words at intervals of four, five, or more lines. A problem, however, is that if rhyming sounds are too far away from each other, they lose their immediacy and therefore their effectiveness.

Poets who are skillful and original rhymers are able to create fresh, unusual, and surprising turns of thought. We may therefore judge poets on their use of rhyme. Often poets become quite creative rhymers, putting together words like "bent 'em" and "Tarentum" or "masterly" and "dastardly." Some rhymers, whom a sixteenth-century critic called a "rakehelly route of ragged rhymers," are satisfied with easy rhymes, or **cliché rhymes**, like *trees* and *breeze* (a rhyme that Pope criticized in 1711). But good rhymes and good poets go together, in creative cooperation. The seventeenth-century poet Dryden, who wrote volumes of rhyming couplets, acknowledged that the need to find rhyming words inspired ideas that he had not anticipated. In this sense, rhyme has been—and still is—a vital element of poetic creativity.

There are few restrictions on English rhymes. Poets may rhyme nouns with other nouns, or with verbs and adjectives, or with any other rhyming word, regardless of part of speech. Of course, exact rhymes are to be preferred, but the shortage of exact rhymes in English has enabled poets to be creative, rhyming words that almost rhyme but don't exactly (**slant rhyme**) or words that look alike but sound different (**eye rhyme**). Some poets use the same words to complete a rhyming pattern (**identical rhyme**), although this repetition eliminates some of the surprise and interest that good rhymes should produce.

Rhyme and Meter

HEAVY-STRESS RHYME.   The effects of rhyme are closely connected with those of rhythm and meter. Rhymes that are produced with one-syllable words—like *moon, June, tune,* and *soon*—or with multisyllabic words in which the accent falls on the last syllable—like *combine, decline, supine,* and *refine*—are called **heavy-stress rhyme, accented rhyme**, or **rising rhyme**. In general, rising rhyme lends itself to serious effects. The accenting of heavy-stress rhyme appears in the opening lines of Robert Frost's "Stopping by Woods on a Snowy Evening" (p. 556):

Whose woods / these are / I think / I know
His house / is in / the vil - / lage though.

Here, the rhyming sounds are produced by one-syllable words—*know* and *though*—that occur in the final heavy-stress positions of the lines.

TROCHAIC AND DACTYLIC RHYME.   Rhymes using words of two or more syllables in which the heavy stress falls on any syllable other than the last are called *trochaic*, or *double rhyme* for rhymes of two syllables, and *dactylic*, or *triple rhyme* for rhymes of three syllables. Less technically, these types of rhymes are also called **falling**, or **dying rhymes**; this is probably because the intensity of pronunciation decreases on the light accent or accents following the heavy accent.

In general, **trochaic** or **double rhymes** are appropriate to light, amusing, and satiric poetry, as may be seen in lines 2 and 4 of the first stanza of "Miniver Cheevy" by Edwin Arlington Robinson:

> Miniver Cheevy, child of scorn
> Grew lean while he assailed the *seasons*;
> He wept that he was ever born,
> And he had *reasons*.

In this poem the effect of the double rhyme is humorous, thus helping to make Miniver Cheevy seem ridiculous and pathetic.

Double rhymes can also be a means of emphasizing or underscoring irony or anticlimax in serious poems, as in *A-flying* and *dying* in the first stanza of Herrick's "To the Virgins, to Make Much of Time":

> Gather ye rosebuds while ye may,
> Old time is still a-flying;
> And this same flower that smiles today
> Tomorrow will be dying.

Herrick uses falling rhymes in the second and fourth lines of every stanza of this poem. The result is a poignant contrast between pleasures of everyday life and the eternal truths of mortality.

Dactylic or **triple rhyme** is often light or humorous because it tends to divert attention from the subject to the words, as in these lines from Browning's "The Pied Piper of Hamelin" (italics added):

> Small feet were *pattering*, wooden shoes *clattering*,
> Little hands clapping and little tongues *chattering*.
> And, like fowls in a farm-yard where barley is *scattering*,

Here, the ending words *clattering, chattering,* and *scattering* are all instances of triple rhyme. The poem indeed does make a serious point (about the failure to keep a pledge), but in this stanza, which deals with the children following the Pied Piper, the triple rhyme is appropriate to the sounds of running children.

Variations in Rhyme

INTERNAL RHYME.   As the stanza from Browning shows, the fourth word in the first line, *pattering*, rhymes with the line-ending rhymes. This is an example of **internal rhyme**—the presence of a rhyming word within a line of verse. It is not a common variation, but you should be alert for it, and make note of it when it occurs.

INEXACT RHYME.   Writers of English poetry have often felt limited in selecting rhymes because our language is short in exactly rhyming words. Italian, by contrast, in which most words end in vowel sounds, offers virtually endless rhyming possibilities. A tradition has therefore grown in English that words may be rhymed even though they are not exact.

Rhymes may often be created out of words with similar but not identical sounds. In most of these instances, either the vowel segments are different while the consonants are the same, or vice versa. This type of rhyme is variously called **slant rhyme, near rhyme, half rhyme, off rhyme, analyzed rhyme**, or **suspended rhyme**. In employing slant rhyme, a poet can pair *bleak* with *broke* or *could* with *solitude*. Emily Dickinson uses slant rhyme extensively in "To Hear an Oriole Sing"; in the second stanza of the poem she rhymes *Bird, unheard*, and *Crowd. Bird* and *unheard* make up an exact rhyme, but the vowel and consonant shift in *Crowd* produces a slant rhyme.

Another common variation is **eye rhyme** or **sight rhyme**. In eye rhyme, the sounds to be eye-rhymed are *identical in spelling* but *different in pronunciation*. Entire words may be eye-rhymed, so that *wind* (verb) may be joined to *wind* (noun), and *cóntest* (noun) may be used with *contést* (verb). In most eye rhymes, however, it is only the relevant parts of words that must be spelled identically. Thus, *stove* may pair with *prove* and *above*, and *bough* may match *cough, dough, enough,* and *through*, despite all the differing pronunciations. The following lines contain eye rhyme:

> Although his claim was not to praise but bury,
> His speech for Caesar roused the crowd to fury.

The different pronunciations of *bury* and *fury* make clear the contrast between exact rhyme and eye rhyme. In exact rhyme identical sound is crucial; spelling is usually the same but may be different as long as the sounds remain identical. In eye rhyme, the eye-rhyming patterns must be spelled identically but the sounds must be different.

ADDITIONAL VARIATIONS. Poets sometimes may use **identical rhyme** (noted earlier); that is, the same words in rhyming positions, such as *veil* and *veil*, or *stone* and *stone*. **Vowel rhyme** is the use of any vowels in rhyming positions, as in *day* and *sky*, or *key* and *play*.

Rhyme Schemes

A **rhyme scheme** refers to a poem's pattern of rhyming sounds, which are indicated by alphabetical letters. The first rhyming sounds, such as *love* and *dove*, for example, are marked with an *a*. A poem's first rhyming line receives an *a*, and each new rhyming sound is assigned the next letter. Thus, a pattern of lines ending with the words *love, moon, thicket; dove, June, picket;* and *above, croon,* and *wicket* may be schematized as *a b c; a b c; a b c.*

To formulate a rhyme scheme or pattern, you include the meter and the number of feet in each line as well as the letters indicating rhymes. Here is such a formulation:

Iambic pentameter: a b a b, c d c d, e f e f

This scheme shows that all the lines in the poem are iambic, with five feet in each. Commas separating the units indicate a stanzaic pattern of three 4-line units, or **quatrains**, with the rhymes falling on the first and third, and the second and fourth, lines of each quatrain.

Should the number of feet in the lines of a poem or **stanza** vary, you show this fact by using a number in front of each letter:

Iambic: 4a 3b 4a 3b 5a 5a 4b

This formulation shows an intricate pattern of rhymes and line-lengths in a stanza of seven lines. The first, third, fifth, and sixth lines rhyme, and vary from four to five feet. The second, fourth, and seventh lines also rhyme, and vary from three to four feet.

The absence of a rhyme sound is indicated by an *x*. Thus, you formulate the rhyme scheme of **ballad measure** like this:

Iambic: 4x 3a 4x 3a

The formulation shows that the quatrain alternates iambic tetrameter with trimeter. In this ballad quatrain, only lines 2 and 4 rhyme; there is no end rhyme in lines 1 and 3.

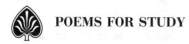

POEMS FOR STUDY

GWENDOLYN BROOKS   (b. 1917)

We Real Cool ——————————————————————————— *1959*

The Pool Players.
Seven at the Golden Shovel.

We real cool. We
Left school. We

Lurk late. We
Strike straight. We

Sing sin. We
Thin gin. We

Jazz June. We
Die soon.

QUESTIONS

1. What is the major idea of the poem? Who is the speaker? How is the last sentence a climax? How is this sentence consistent with the declarations in lines 1–7? How is the poet's attitude made clear?

2. Describe the patterning of stresses in the poem. Explain the absence of light stresses. What method is employed to achieve the constant strong stresses?

EMILY DICKINSON   (1830–1886)

To Hear an Oriole Sing ———————————————— *1891 (ca. 1862)*

To hear an Oriole sing
May be a common thing–
Or only a divine.

It is not of the Bird
Who sings the same, unheard,
As unto Crowd–

The Fashion of the Ear
Attireth that it hear
In Dun, or fair–

So whether it be Rune,
Or whether it be none
Is of within.

The "Tune is in the Tree–"
The Skeptic–showeth me–
"No Sir! In Thee!"   15

QUESTIONS

1. What can you deduce about the speaker? The listener? Who speaks in line 13?
    To whom is line 15 addressed?

2. Formulate the rhyme scheme of this poem. How does it help subdivide the poem
    into cohesive units of thought? To what extent does it unify the poem?

3. Locate all the slant rhymes in this poem. What effect do these have on your read-
    ing and perception? How is the rhyme here like the oriole's song?

4. To what degree does rhyme reinforce meaning? Note especially the rhyme words
    in the final stanza.

T. S. ELIOT   (1888–1965)

Macavity: The Mystery Cat —————————————————— *1939*

Macavity's a Mystery Cat: he's called the Hidden Paw—
For he's the master criminal who can defy the Law.
He's the bafflement of Scotland Yard, the Flying Squad's despair:
For when they reach the scene of the crime—*Macavity's not there!*

Macavity, Macavity, there's no one like Macavity,   5
He's broken every human law, he breaks the law of gravity.
His powers of levitation would make a fakir stare,
And when you reach the scene of crime—*Macavity's not there!*
You may seek him in the basement, you may look up in the air—
But I tell you once and once again, *Macavity's not there!*   10

Macavity's a ginger cat, he's very tall and thin;
You would know him if you saw him, for his eyes are sunken in.
His brow is deeply lined with thought, his head is highly domed;
His coat is dusty from neglect, his whiskers are uncombed.
He sways his head from side to side, with movements like a snake;   15
And when you think he's half asleep, he's always wide awake.

Macavity, Macavity, there's no one like Macavity,
For he's a fiend in feline shape, a monster of depravity.
You may meet him in a by-street, you may see him in the square—
But when a crime's discovered, then *Macavity's not there!*   20

He's outwardly respectable. (They say he cheats at cards.)
And his footprints are not found in any file of Scotland Yard's.
And when the larder's looted, or the jewel-case is rifled,

Or when the milk is missing, or another Peke's been stifled,°
Or the greenhouse glass is broken, and the trellis past repair—
Ay, there's the wonder of the thing! *Macavity's not there!*

And when the Foreign Office find a Treaty's gone astray,
Or the Admiralty lose some plans and drawings by the way,
There may be a scrap of paper in the hall or on the stair—
But it's useless to investigate—*Macavity's not there!*
And when the loss has been disclosed, the Secret Service say:
"It *must* have been Macavity!"—but he's a mile away.
You'll be sure to find him resting, or a-licking of his thumbs,
Or engaging in doing complicated long division sums.

Macavity, Macavity, there's no one like Macavity,
There never was a Cat of such deceitfulness and suavity.
He always has an alibi, and one or two to spare:
At whatever time the deed took place—MACAVITY WASN'T THERE!
And they say that all the Cats whose wicked deeds are widely known
(I might mention Mungojerrie, I might mention Griddlebone)
Are nothing more than agents for the Cat who all the time
Just controls their operations: the Napoleon of Crime!

MACAVITY: THE MYSTERY CAT.   24 *Peke's been stifled:* A Pekinese dog (a small animal, with silky hair) has been found dead.

QUESTIONS

1. What are some of Macavity's major "crimes" as a master criminal and "mystery cat"? How, if the "crimes" had been attributed to a human being, would they be grievous wrongs? Since they are attributed to a cat, how do they add to the comic qualities of the poem?

2. What is the basic metrical foot of the poem? How many feet are contained in each of the lines? What is the norm?

3. Once you begin reading and getting into the lines, what new kind of pattern emerges? How many major stresses appear in each line? In light of the nature of the poem, how is the dipodic rhythm appropriate?

JAMES EMANUEL   (b. 1921)

The Negro ——————————————————————————— *1968*

Never saw him.
Never can.
Hypothetical,
Haunting man:

Eyes a-saucer,
Yessir bossir,

Dice a-clicking.
Razor flicking.

The-ness froze him
In a dance.   10
A-ness never
Had a chance.

QUESTIONS

1. What are the attributes of the black man in lines 1–4, 5 and 6, and 7 and 8? What attitude does the poem convey about the plight of the man?

2. What is the meaning of *The-ness* and *A-ness* in the third stanza?

3. What metrical foot is dominant? Why do you think the poet chose this foot in preference to a foot having a rising rhythm, such as the iamb?

ISABELLA GARDNER   (1915–1981)

At a Summer Hotel _____ *1979*

I am here with my bountiful womanful child
to be soothed by the sea not roused by these roses roving wild.
My girl is gold in the sun and bold in the dazzling water,
She drowses on the blond sand and in the daisy fields my daughter
dreams. Uneasy in the drafty shade I rock on the veranda   5
reminded of Europa Persephone Miranda.°

AT A SUMMER HOTEL. 6 *Europa Persephone Miranda:* Europa was a princess in Greek mythology who attracted the attention of Zeus, the king of the gods. He took the form of a bull and carried her over the sea to Crete. She bore him three sons. Persephone, in Greek mythology, was the daughter of Zeus and Demeter, the goddess of fertility. She attracted the attention of Hades, the god of the underworld, who forcibly carried her off and married her. Miranda is an innocent young woman in Shakespeare's play *The Tempest* who was exiled on an island for twelve years with her father, Prospero. One of his servants, the beastlike Caliban, attempted to rape her.

QUESTIONS

1. Why is the speaker "uneasy" (line 5)? How do the references to Europa, Persephone, and Miranda help define this uneasiness?

2. To what extent do alliteration and repetition unify the lines and make the sound echo sense? Note especially the *b* and *ful* sounds in line 1, the *s* and *r* sounds in line 2, and the *d* and *dr* sounds in lines 4–5.

3. What is the effect of internal rhyme in this poem?

4. What kind of rhyme (rising or falling, exact or slant) is in lines 1–2? To what extent does this rhyme highlight the poem's central idea? What rhyme is in lines 3–6? How does this rhyme affect the poem's tone and impact?

ROBERT HERRICK   (1591–1674)

Upon Julia's Voice ——————————————————————— *1648*

So smooth, so sweet, so silv'ry is thy voice,
As, could they hear, the damned would make no noise,
But listen to thee (walking in thy chamber)
Melting melodious words, to lutes of amber.

QUESTIONS

1. How do the words *silv'ry* and *amber* contribute to the praise of Julia's voice? How powerful does the speaker claim her voice is?
2. What is the "joke" of the poem? How can the praise of Julia's voice be interpreted as general praise for Julia herself?
3. How and where is alliteration used in the poem? Which of the alliterative sounds best complement the words praising the sweetness of Julia's voice?

GERARD MANLEY HOPKINS   (1844–1889)

God's Grandeur ——————————————————————— *1877*

The world is charged with the grandeur of God.
　It will flame out, like shining from shook foil;
　It gathers to a greatness, like the ooze of oil
Crushed. Why do men then now not reck his rod?°
Generations have trod, have trod, have trod;
　And all is seared with trade; bleared, smeared with toil;
　And wears man's smudge and shares man's smell: the soil
Is bare now, nor can foot feel, being shod.
And for all this, nature is never spent;
　There lives the dearest freshness deep down things;
And though the last lights off the black West went
　Oh, morning, at the brown brink eastward, springs—
Because the Holy Ghost over the bent
　World broods with warm breast and with ah! bright wings.

GOD'S GRANDEUR.   4 *reck his rod:* God as king holds a scepter, making official laws through scriptures which people ("men") disobey.

QUESTIONS

1. What is the contrast between the assertions in lines 1–4 and 5–8? How do lines 9–14 develop out of this contrast?
2. Analyze Hopkins's use of alliteration. What alliterative patterns occur? How do these affect meter and emphasis? On the basis of your analysis, describe "sprung rhythm" as used by Hopkins.
3. What instances of assonance, repetitions, and internal rhyme do you find?

BARBARA HOWES   (b. 1914)

Death of a Vermont Farm Woman ———————————— *1954*

Is it time now to go away?
July is nearly over; hay
Fattens the barn, the herds are strong,
Our old fields prosper; these long
Green evenings will keep death at bay.   5

Last winter lingered; it was May
Before a flowering lilac spray
Barred cold for ever. I was wrong.
    Is it time now?

Six decades vanished in a day!   10
I bore four sons: one lives; they
Were all good men; three dying young
Was hard on us. I have looked long
For these hills to show me where peace lay.
    Is it time now?   15

QUESTIONS

1. What does this poem suggest about the life of "A Vermont Farm Woman"? About the lives of many women?
2. How many different rhyme sounds are used in this poem? What is the effect of using so few?
3. To what extent does rhyme divide the poem into coherent units of thought and tie the whole poem together?
4. Normally, repetition of the same rhyming word is judged to be a flaw in poetry. To what extent is that the case in this poem?

LANGSTON HUGHES   (1902–1967)

Let America Be America Again ———————————— *1936*

Let America be America again.
Let it be the dream it used to be.
Let it be the pioneer on the plain
Seeking a home where he himself is free.

(America never was America to me.)   5

Let America be the dream the dreamers dreamed—
Let it be that great strong land of love
Where never kings connive nor tyrants scheme
That any man be crushed by one above.

(It never was America to me.)   10

O, let my land be a land where Liberty
Is crowned with no false patriotic wreath,
But opportunity is real, and life is free,
Equality is in the air we breathe.

(There's never been equality for me,
Nor freedom in this "homeland of the free.")

Say who are you that mumbles in the dark?
And who are you that draws your veil across the stars?
I am the poor white, fooled and pushed apart,
I am the Negro bearing slavery's scars.
I am the red man driven from the land,
I am the immigrant clutching the hope I seek—
And finding only the same old stupid plan
Of dog eat dog, of mighty crush the weak.

I am the young man, full of strength and hope,
Tangled in that ancient endless chain
Of profit, power, gain, of grab the land!
Of grab the gold! Of grab the ways of satisfying need!
Of work the men! Of take the pay!
Of owning everything for one's own greed!

I am the farmer, bondsman to the soil.
I am the worker sold to the machine.
I am the Negro, servant to you all.
I am the people, worried, hungry, mean—
Hungry yet today despite the dream.
Beaten yet today—O, Pioneers!
I am the man who never got ahead,
The poorest worker bartered through the years.

Yet I'm the one who dreamt our basic dream
In the Old World while still a serf of kings,
Who dreamt a dream so strong, so brave, so true,
That even yet its mighty daring sings
In every brick and stone, in every furrow turned
That's made America the land it has become.
O, I'm the man who sailed those early seas
In search of what I meant to be my home—
For I'm the one who left dark Ireland's shore,
And Poland's plain, and England's grassy lea,
And torn from Black Africa's strand I came
To build a "homeland of the free."
The free?

A dream—
Still beckoning to me!

O, let America be America again—
The land that never has been yet—   55
And yet must be—
The land where *every* man is free.
The land that's mine—
The poor man's, Indian's, Negro's, ME—
Who made America,   60
Whose sweat and blood, whose faith and pain,
Whose hand at the foundry, whose plow in the rain,
Must bring back our mighty dream again.

Sure, call me any ugly name you choose—
The steel of freedom does not stain.   65
From those who live like leeches on the people's lives,
We must take back our land again,
America!

O, yes,
I say it plain,   70
America never was America to me,
And yet I swear this oath—
America will be!
An ever-living seed,
Its dream   75
Lies deep in the heart of me.

We, the people, must redeem
Our land, the mines, the plants, the rivers,
The mountains and the endless plain—
All, all the stretch of these great green states—   80
And make America again!

QUESTIONS

1. In light of the poet's ideas, what is the effect of the changing stanzaic patterns? After the opening, fairly regular quatrains, why do the groupings become irregular?

2. What is the effect of the refrains in lines 5, 10, and 15–16? Why does the poet stop using the refrain after the third quatrain and not bring it out again until line 71?

3. Describe the use of alliteration. In phrases like "pushed apart" and "slavery's scars," together with other phrases, how does the alliteration emphasize the poet's ideas?

4. Describe the use of assonance, rhyme, and slant rhyme. What is gained by the slant rhymes?

EDGAR ALLAN POE   (1809–1849)

The Bells ———————————————————————— *1849*

I

Hear the sledges with the bells—
　　Silver bells!
What a world of merriment their melody foretells!
How they tinkle, tinkle, tinkle,
　　In the icy air of night!
While the stars that oversprinkle
All the heavens, seem to twinkle
　　With a crystalline delight;
　　　Keeping time, time, time,
　　　In a sort of Runic rhyme,
To the tintinnabulation that so musically wells
　　　From the bells, bells, bells, bells,
　　　　Bells, bells, bells—
From the jingling and the tinkling of the bells.

II

Hear the mellow wedding bells—
　　Golden bells!
What a world of happiness their harmony foretells!
　　Through the balmy air of night
　　How they ring out their delight!—
　　　From the molten-golden notes,
　　　And all in tune,
　　What a liquid ditty floats
To the turtle-dove that listens, while she gloats
　　　On the moon!
　　Oh, from out the sounding cells,
What a gush of euphony voluminously wells!
　　　How is swells!
　　　How it dwells
　　On the Future!—how it tells
　　Of the rapture that impels
　To the swinging and the ringing
　　Of the bells, bells, bells—
Of the bells, bells, bells, bells,
　　　Bells, bells, bells—
To the rhyming and the chiming of the bells!

III

Hear the loud alarum bells—
　　Brazen bells!
What a tale of terror, now, their turbulency tells!
　　In the startled ear of night
　　How they scream out their affright!

Too much horrified to speak,
They can only shriek, shriek,
      Out of tune,
In a clamorous appealing to the mercy of the fire,
In a mad expostulation with the deaf and frantic fire,   45
      Leaping higher, higher, higher,
      With a desperate desire,
      And a resolute endeavor
      Now—now to sit, or never,
By the side of the pale-faced moon,   50
      Oh, the bells, bells, bells!
      What a tale their terror tells
         Of Despair!
      How they clang, and clash, and roar!
      What a horror they outpour   55
On the bosom of the palpitating air!
      Yet the ear, it fully knows,
         By the twanging
         And the clanging,
      How the danger ebbs and flows;   60
   Yet the ear distinctly tells,
         In the jangling
         And the wrangling,
   How the danger sinks and swells,
By the sinking or the swelling in the anger of the bells—   65
         Of the bells,—
   Of the bells, bells, bells, bells,
         Bells, bells, bells—
In the clamor and the clangor of the bells!

            IV
Hear the tolling of the bells—   70
         Iron bells!
What a world of solemn thought their monody compels!
   In the silence of the night,
   How we shiver with affright
At the melancholy menace of their tone!   75
   For every sound that floats
   From the rust within their throats
         Is a groan.
      And the people—ah, the people—
      They that dwell up in the steeple,   80
         All alone,
   And who tolling, tolling, tolling,
      In that muffled monotone,
   Feel a glory in so rolling
      On the human heart a stone—   85
   They are neither man nor woman—

They are neither brute nor human—
    They are Ghouls:—
And their king it is who tolls:—
And he rolls, rolls, rolls,
        Rolls
    A paean from the bells!
And his merry bosom swells
    With the paean of the bells!
And he dances, and he yells;
Keeping time, time, time,
In a sort of Runic rhyme,
        To the paean of the bells—
    Of the bells:
Keeping time, time, time,
In a sort of Runic rhyme,
        To the throbbing of the bells—
    Of the bells, bells, bells—
        To the sobbing of the bells;
Keeping time, time, time,
    As he knells, knells, knells,
In a happy Runic rhyme,
        To the rolling of the bells—
    Of the bells, bells, bells:—
        To the tolling of the bells—
Of the bells, bells, bells, bells,
        Bells, bells, bells—
To the moaning and the groaning of the bells.

QUESTIONS

1. What kinds of bells does Poe extol in each of the stanzas? What metals and images does he associate with each type of bell? How appropriate are these? Why do you think the stanzas become progressively longer?

2. What segmental sounds does Poe utilize as imitative of the various bells? What differences in vowels are observable between the silver sledge bells, for example, and the brass ("brazen") alarum bells? Between the vowels describing the iron bells and the golden bells?

3. What is the effect of the repetition of the word *bells* throughout? What onomatopoeic effect is created by these repetitions?

4. Describe the pattern of rhymes in this poem.

EDWIN ARLINGTON ROBINSON   (1869–1935)

Miniver Cheevy _____ *1910*

Miniver Cheevy, child of scorn,
    Grew lean while he assailed the seasons;

He wept that he was ever born,
    And he had reasons.

Miniver loved the days of old   5
    When swords were bright and steeds were prancing;
The vision of a warrior bold
    Would set him dancing.

Miniver sighed for what was not,
    And dreamed, and rested from his labors;   10
He dreamed of Thebes° and Camelot,°
    And Priam's° neighbors.

Miniver mourned the ripe renown
    That made so many a name so fragrant;
He mourned Romance, now on the town,   15
    And Art, a vagrant.

Miniver loved the Medici,°
    Albeit he had never seen one;
He would have sinned incessantly
    Could he have been one.   20

Miniver cursed the commonplace
    And eyed a khaki suit with loathing;
He missed the medieval grace
    Of iron clothing.

Miniver scorned the gold he sought,   25
    But sore annoyed was he without it;
Miniver thought, and thought, and thought,
    And thought about it.

Miniver Cheevy, born too late,
    Scratched his head and kept on thinking;   30
Miniver coughed, and called it fate,
    And kept on drinking.

MINIVER CHEEVY.   11 *Thebes:* a city in Greece prominent in Greek legend and mythology in connection with Cadmus and Oedipus.   *Camelot:* legendary seat of the Round Table and capital of Britain during the reign of King Arthur.   12 *Priam's:* Priam was the king of Troy during the Trojan War.   17 *Medici:* wealthy Italian family that ruled Florence from the fifteenth to the eighteenth century. During the Renaissance, Lorenzo de'Medici was an important patron of the arts.

QUESTIONS

1. What is the speaker's attitude toward the central character? How does rhyme help define this attitude?

2. How does repetition reinforce the image of the central character and the speaker's attitude? Consider the beginning of each stanza and lines 27–28.

3. What rhyme predominates in lines 2 and 4 of each stanza? How does this rhyme help make sound echo sense?

WILLIAM SHAKESPEARE   (1564–1616)

Sonnet 73: That Time of Year Thou Mayst in Me Behold ——————— *1609*

That time of year thou mayst in me behold
When yellow leaves, or none, or few, do hang
Upon those boughs which shake against the cold,
Bare ruined choirs,° where late the sweet birds sang.
In me thou see'st the twilight of such day
As after sunset fadeth in the west;
Which by and by black night doth take away,
Death's second self,° that seals up all in rest.
In me thou see'st the glowing of such fire,
That on the ashes of his° youth doth lie,   *its*
As the death-bed whereon it must expire,
Consumed with that which it was nourished by,°
   This thou perceivest, which makes thy love more strong,
   To love that well which thou must leave ere long.

SONNET 73.   4 *choirs:* the part of a church just in front of the altar.   8 *Death's . . . self;* That is, night is a mirror image of death inasmuch as it brings the sleep of rest just as death brings the sleep of actual death.   12 *Consumed . . . by:* That is, the ashes of the fuel burned at the fire's height now prevent the fire from continuing, and in fact extinguish it.

QUESTIONS

1. Describe the content of lines 1–4, 5–8, and 9–12. What connects these three sections? How does the concluding couplet relate to the first twelve lines?

2. Analyze the iambic pentameter of the poem. Consider the spondees in lines 2 (*do hang*), 4 (*bare ru-* and *birds sang*), 5 (*such day*), 7 (*black night*), 8 (*death's sec-*), 9 (*such fire*), 10 (*doth lie*), 11 (*death-bed*), 13 (*more strong*), and 14 (*ere long*). What is the effect of these substitutions on the poem's ideas?

3. How does the enjambement of lines 1–3 and 5–6 permit these lines to seem to conclude *as lines* even though grammatically they carry over to form sentences?

4. In lines 2, 5, 6, and 9, where does Shakespeare place the caesurae? What relationship is there between the rhythms produced by these caesurae and the content of lines 1–12? In lines 13 and 14, how do the rising stressed caesurae relate to the content?

JONATHAN SWIFT   (1667–1745)

A Description of the Morning ——————————————————————— *1709*

Now hardly here and there a hackney-coach
Appearing, showed the ruddy morn's approach.
Now Betty from her master's bed had flown.
And softly stole to discompose her own.
The slip-shod 'prentice from his master's door

Had pared the dirt, and sprinkled round the floor.
Now Moll had whirled her mop with dextrous airs,
Prepared to scrub the entry and the stairs.
The youth with broomy stumps began to trace
The kennel's edge,° where wheels had worn the place.   10
The small-coal man° was heard with cadence deep,   *charcoal seller*
Till drowned in shriller notes of chimney-sweep.
Duns° at his lordship's gate began to meet;   *bill collectors*
And brickdust Moll had screamed through half the street.
The turnkey° now his flock returning sees,   15
Duly let out a-nights to steal for fees.
The watchful bailiffs take their silent stands,
And schoolboys lag° with satchels in their hands.

A DESCRIPTION OF THE MORNING.   10 *kennel's edge:* that is, the edge of the gutter. Swift
annotated this line "To find old Nails."   15 *turnkey:* an entrepreneur, operating a jail for profit,
who allowed prisoners to go free at night so that they might bring him a night's booty to pay for
the necessities provided them in jail.   18 *schoolboys lag:* cf. Shakespeare's *As You Like It*, Act II,
scene 7, lines 145–147.

QUESTIONS

1. What antiheroic images of life in London are presented in this poem? What atti-
    tude is shown toward "his lordship"?
2. Analyze the poem for alliterative patterns. What is their effect?
3. Make the same kind of analysis for assonance. How many different assonantal
    patterns are there? What is their effect?
4. Iambic rhyming couplets are often called "heroic." How does Swift's choice of
    this form affect the subject matter of the poem?

ALFRED, LORD TENNYSON   (1809–1892)

From *Idylls of the King: The Passing of Arthur*
Lines 344–393 ——————————————————— *1869 (1842)*

But, as he walked, King Arthur panted hard,
Like one that feels a nightmare on his bed   345
When all the house is mute. So sighed the King,
Muttering and murmuring at his ear, "Quick, quick!
I fear it is too late, and I shall die."
But the other swiftly strode from ridge to ridge,
Clothed with his breath, and looking, as he walked,   350
Larger than human on the frozen hills.
He heard the deep behind him, and a cry
Before. His own thought drove him like a goad.
Dry clashed his harness in the icy caves
And barren chasms, and all to left and right   355

The bare black cliff clanged round him, as he based
His feet on juts of slippery crag that rang
Sharp-smitten with the dint of armèd heels—
And on a sudden, lo! the level lake,
And the long glories of the winter moon.

   Then saw they how there hove a dusky barge,
Dark as a funeral scarf from stem to stern,
Beneath them; and descending they were ware°   *aware*
That all the decks were dense with stately forms,
Black-stoled, black-hooded, like a dream—by these
Three Queens with crowns of gold: and from them rose
A cry that shivered to the tingling stars,
And, as it were one voice, an agony
Of lamentation, like a wind that shrills
All night in a waste land, where no one comes,
Or hath come, since the making of the world.

   Then murmured Arthur, "Place me in the barge."
So to the barge they came. There those three Queens
Put forth their hands, and took the King, and wept.
But she, that rose the tallest of them all
And fairest, laid his head upon her lap,
And loosed the shattered casque,° and chafed his hands,   *helmet*
And called him by his name, complaining loud,
And dropping bitter tears against a brow
Striped with dark blood: for all his face was white
And colorless, and like the withered moon
Smote by the fresh beam of the springing east;
And all his greaves and cuisses° dashed with drops   *pieces of armor*
Of onset;° and the light and lustrous curls—   *blood*
That made his forehead like a rising sun
High from the dais-throne—were parched with dust:
Or, clotted into points and hanging loose,
Mixed with the knightly growth that fringed his lips.
So like a shattered column lay the King:
Not like that Arthur who, with lance in rest,
From spur to plume a star of tournament,
Shot through the lists at Camelot, and charged
Before the eyes of ladies and of kings.

QUESTIONS

1. How does Tennyson develop the mood of depression and loss associated with the dying of Arthur? What is the effect of the concluding simile?
2. Analyze the patterns of assonance and alliteration in the passage. What patterns are developed most extensively? What effects are thus achieved?
3. Describe Tennyson's use of onomatopoeia in lines 349–360, 369–371, and 380–383. What segments contribute to this effect?

FRANCIS THOMPSON   (1859–1907)

To a Snowflake ————————————————————————— *1897*

What heart could have thought you?
Past our devisal
(O filigree petal!)
Fashioned so purely,
Fragilely, surely,   5
From what Paradisal
Imagineless metal,
Too costly for cost?
Who hammered you, wrought you
From argentine° vapour?—   *silver*   10
"God was my shaper.
Passing surmisal,
He hammered, He wrought me.
From curled silver vapour,
To lust of His mind:—   15
Thou could'st not have thought me!
So purely, so palely,
Tinily, surely,
Mightily, frailly,
Insculped and embossed,   20
With His hammer of wind,
And His graver of frost."

QUESTIONS

1. The poem is in dimeter (lines consisting of two feet). Why is this short line appropriate to the subject?
2. What is the prevailing metrical pattern? How is this meter appropriate for the subject of a snowflake? Would iambs have been more or less appropriate? What variations on the predominant foot can you find? Why do you think the poet made the last three lines conclude with stressed syllables?
3. Why are some of the rhymes placed on heavy stressed syllables even though most of the rhymes are linked with falling or trochaic rhythms?
4. Compare this poem with Blake's "The Lamb" (p. 612) and "The Tyger" (p. 636). To which of the two Blake poems is "To a Snowflake" more similar? Why? In what ways is Thompson's poem different from those of Blake?

DAVID WAGONER   (b. 1926)

March for a One-Man Band ———————————————————— *1983*

He's *a boom a blat* in the uniform
Of an army *tweedledy* band *a toot*

Complete with medals *a honk* cornet
Against *a thump* one side of his lips
And the other stuck with *a sloop a tweet*
A whistle *a crash* on top of *a crash*
A helmet *a crash* a cymbal a drum
At his *bumbledy* knee and a *rimshot* flag
A *click* he stands at attention *a wheeze*
And plays the Irrational Anthem *bang.*

QUESTIONS

1. What attitude does the speaker convey about the one-man band? Why is the Anthem "Irrational" rather than "National"?

2. Describe the onomatopoeic effect of the italicized percussive words. What is the purpose of the rhythms that these words cause?

3. What ambiguity is suggested by the "bang" of line 10? How does this ambiguity make the poem seem more than simply an entertaining display of sounds?

WRITING ABOUT PROSODY

Because studying prosody requires a good deal of specific detail and description, it is best to limit your study to a short poem or to a short passage from a long poem. A sonnet, a stanza of a lyric poem, or fragment from a long poem will usually be sufficient. If you choose a fragment, it should be self-contained, such as an entire speech or short episode or scene (as in the example from Tennyson chosen for the sample essay on pp. 737–43).

The analysis of even a short poem, however, can grow long because of the need to describe word positions and stresses, and also to determine the various effects. For this reason you do not have to exhaust your topic. Try to make your discussion representative of the prosody of your poem or passage.

Your first reading in preparation for your essay should be for comprehension. On second and third readings, make notes of sounds, accents, and rhymes by reading the poem aloud. To perceive sounds, one student helped herself by reading aloud in an exaggerated way in front of a mirror. If you have privacy, or are not self-conscious, you might do the same. Let yourself go a bit. As you dramatize your reading (maybe even in front of fellow students), you will find that heightened levels of reading also accompany the poet's expression of important ideas. Mark these spots for later analysis, so that you will be able to make strong assertions about the relationship of sound to sense.

In planning, it is vital to prepare study sheets, so that your observations will be correct, for if your factual analysis is wrong, your writing will also be wrong. Experience has shown that it is best to make four triple-spaced copies of the poem or passage (with photocopy or, if necessary, carbon paper). These will be for the separate analysis of rhythm, assonance, alliteration, and rhyme. If you have been assigned just one of these, of course, only one copy will be necessary. Leave spaces between syllables and words for marking out the various feet of the poem. Ultimately, this duplication of the passage, with your markings, should be included as a first page, as in the sample essays. Carry out your study of the passage in the following way.

Strategies for Discovering Ideas

- Number each line of the passage, regardless of length, beginning with *1*, so that you may use these numbers as location references in your essay.
- Determine the formal pattern of feet, using the short acute accent or stress mark for heavily stressed syllables (´), and the breve for unaccented or lightly stressed syllables (˘). Use chevrons to mark spondees (/\ ).
- Indicate the separate feet by a diagonal slash or virgule (/). Indicate caesurae and end-of-line pauses by double virgules (//).
- Use colored pencils to underline, circle, make boxes, or otherwise mark the formal and rhetorical substitutions that you discover. Because such substitutions may occur throughout the poem, develop a numbering system for each type (e.g., 1 = spondee, 7 = trochee, etc., as in the sample worksheet, p. 738). Provide a key to your numbers at the bottom of the page.
- Do the same for alliteration, assonance, onomatopoeia, and rhyme. It has proved particularly effective to draw lines to connect the repeating sounds, for these effects will be close together in the poem, and your connections will dramatize this closeness. The use of a separate color for each separate effect is helpful, for different colors make prosodic distinctions stand out clearly.
- Use your worksheets as a reference for your reader's benefit. In writing your essay, however, you make your examples specific by including brief illustrative quotations, as in the examples (i.e., words, phrases, and entire lines, with proper marks and accents). Do not rely on line numbers alone.

Once you have analyzed the various effects in your poem, and you have recorded these on your worksheets and in your notes, you will be ready to formulate a central idea and organization. The focus of your essay should reflect the most significant features of prosody in relationship to some other element of the poem, such as speaker, tone, or ideas. Thus, in planning an essay about Eliot's "Macavity," you might argue that the dipodic rhythm contributes to the humor of the poem, and makes the "Napoleon of Crime" seem comic.

Strategies for Organizing Ideas

Depending on your assignment, you might wish to discuss all aspects of rhythm or sound, or perhaps just one, such as the poet's use of regular meter, a particular substitution, alliteration, or assonance. It would be possible, for example, to devote an entire essay to (1) regular meter, (2) one particular variation in meter, such as the anapæst or spondee, (3) the caesura, (4) assonance, (5) alliteration, (6) onomatopoeia, or (7) rhyme. For brevity, we here treat rhythm and segments together in one essay, and rhyme in a separate essay.

After a brief description of the poem (such as that it is a sonnet, a two-stanza lyric, a dipodic burlesque poem, and so on) establish the scope of your essay. Your central idea will outline the thought you wish to carry out through your prosodic analysis, such as that regularity of meter is consistent with a happy, firm vision of love or life, or that frequent spondees emphasize the solidity of the speaker's wish to love, or that particular sounds echo some of the poem's actions.

1. *Rhythm.* Establish the formal metrical pattern. What is the dominant metrical foot and line length? Are some lines shorter than the pattern? What relationship do the variable lengths have with the subject matter? If the poem is a lyric, or a sonnet, are important words and syllables successfully placed in stressed positions in order to achieve emphasis? Try to relate line lengths to exposition, development of ideas, and rising or falling emotions. It is also important to look for either repeating or varying metrical patterns as the subject matter reaches peaks or climaxes. Generally, deal with the relationship between the formal rhythmical pattern and the poet's ideas and attitudes.

When noting substitutions, analyze the formal variations and the principal effects of these. If you concentrate on only one substitution, describe any apparent pattern in its use; that is, its locations, recurrences, and effects on meaning.

For caesurae, treat the effectiveness of the poet's control. Can you see any pattern of use? Are the pauses regular or random? Describe noticeable principles of placement, such as (1) the creation of rhythmical similarities in various parts of the poem, (2) the development of particular rhetorical effects, or (3) the creation of interest through rhythmical variety. Do the caesurae lead to important ideas and attitudes? Are the lines all end-stopped, or do you discover enjambement? How do these rhythmical characteristics aid in descriptions and in the expressions of ideas?

2. *Segmental Effects.* Here you might be discussing, collectively or separately, the use and effects of assonance, alliteration, onomatopoeia, and cacophony and euphony. Be sure to establish that the instances you choose have really occurred systematically enough within the poem to form a pattern. Illustrate sounds by including relevant words within parentheses. You might make separate paragraphs on alliteration, assonance, and any other seemingly important pattern. Also, because space is always at a premium, you might concentrate on only one noteworthy effect, like a certain pattern of assonance, rather than on everything. Throughout your discussion, always keep foremost the relationship between content and sound.

Note: To make illustrations clear, underline all sounds to which you are calling attention. If you use an entire word to illustrate a sound, underline only the sound and not the entire word, but put the word within quotation marks (for example, The poet uses a t ["tip," "top," and "terrific"]). When you refer to entire words containing particular segments, however, underline these words (for example, "The poet uses a t in tip, top, and terrific").

3. *Rhyme.* This essay should describe the major features of the poem's rhymes, specifically the scheme and variants, the lengths and rhythms of the rhyming words, and noteworthy segmental characteristics. In discussing the grammar of the rhymes, note the various kinds of words (i.e., verbs, nouns, etc.) that are used for rhymes: Are they all the same? Does one form predominate? Is there variety? Can you determine the grammatical positions of the rhyming words? How may these characteristics be related to the idea or theme of the poem?

You might also discuss the qualities of the rhyming words. Are the words specific? Concrete? Abstract? Are there any striking rhymes? Any surprises? Any rhymes that are particularly clever and witty? Do any rhymes give unique comparisons or contrasts? How?

Generally, note rhyming effects that are unique or particularly striking. Without becoming overly subtle or farfetched, you can arrive at valid and interesting conclusions. Do any sounds in the rhyming words appear in patterns of assonance or alliteration elsewhere in the poem? Do the rhymes enter into any onomatopoeic effects? Broadly, what aspects of rhyme are uniquely effective because they blend so fully with the poem's thought and mood?

In your conclusion, try to develop a short evaluation of the poet's prosodic performance. If we accept the premise that poetry is designed not only to stimulate emotions, but also to provide information and transfer attitudes, to what degree do the prosodic techniques of your poem contribute to these goals? Without going into excessive detail (and writing another essay), what more can you say here? What has been the value of your study to your understanding and appreciating the poem? If you think your analysis has helped you to develop new awareness of the poet's craft, it would be appropriate to state what you have learned.

FIRST SAMPLE ESSAY

A Study of Tennyson's Rhythm and Segments in "The Passing of Arthur," 349–360

*Note: For illustration, this essay analyzes a passage from Tennyson's "The Passing of Arthur," which is part of **Idylls of the King**. Containing 469 lines, "The Passing of Arthur" describes the last battle and death of Arthur, legendary king of early Britain. After the fight, in which Arthur has been mortally wounded by the traitor Mordred, only Arthur and his follower Sir Bedivere remain alive. Arthur commands Bedivere to throw the royal sword Excalibur into the lake from which Arthur had originally received it. After great hesitation and some false claims, Bedivere does throw the sword into the lake, and a hand rises out of the water to catch it. Bedivere then carries Arthur to the lake shore, where the dying king is taken aboard a mysterious funeral barge. In the passage selected for discussion (lines 349–360), Tennyson describes Bedivere carrying Arthur down the hills and cliffs from the battlefield to the lake below.*

1. RHYTHMICAL ANALYSIS

But the o- / ther swift- / ly strode / / from ridge / to ridge, / /   1

Clothed with / his breath, / / and look- / ing, / / as / he walk'd, / /   2

Lar-ger / than hu- / man / / on / the fro- / zen hills. / /   3

He heard / the deep / be-hind / him, / / and / a cry   4

Be-fore. / / His own / thought drove / him / / like / a goad. / /   5

Dry clash'd / his har- / ness / / in / the i / cy caves   6

And bar- ren / chasms, / / and all / to left / and right   7

The bare / black cliff / clang'd round / him, / / as / he based   8

His feet / on juts / of slip- / pe-ry crag / / that rang   9

Sharp- smit- / ten / / with / the / dint / of ar- / med heels— / /   10

And on / a sud- / den, / / lo! / / the lev- / el lake, / /   11

And the / long glor- / ies / / of / the win- / ter moon. / /   12

---

1 = Anapaest, or effect of anapaest.   4 = Effect of imperfect foot.
2 = Amphibrach, or the effect   5 = Pyrrhic.
   of amphibrach.   6 = Trochee, or the effect
3 = Spondee.   of trochee.

2. ALLITERATION

But the other (s) wiftly (s) trode from ridge to ridge,   1

Clothed with his breath, and looking, as (h) e walked,   2

Larger than (h) uman on the frozen (h) ills.   3

(H) e (h) eard the deep be (h) ind (h) im, and a cry   4

Before. (H) is own thought drove him like a goad.   5

Dry (c) lashed (h) is (h) arness in the icy (c) aves   6

And (b) arren (ch) asms, and all to left and right   7

The (b) are (b) (l) ack (c) (l) iff (c) (l) anged round him, as he (b) ased   8

His feet on juts of s (l) ippery (c) rag that rang   9

Sharp-smitten with the dint of armed heels—   10

And on a sudden, (l) o! the (l) evel (l) ake,   11

And the (l) ong g (l) ories of the winter moon.   12

ⵯⵯⵯⵯⵯ = s   ——————— = b

----------- = h   ‿‿‿‿‿‿ = l as second consonant sound in words

············ = k   —·——·——·— = l

3. ASSONANCE

But the other sw ⓘ ftly str ⓞ de from r ⓘ dge to r ⓘ dge,   1

Cl ⓞ thed w ⓘ th h ⓘ s breath, and looking, as he walked,   2

Larger than human on the fr ⓞ zen hills.   3

He heard the deep beh ⓘ nd him, and a cr ⓨ   4

Before. His ⓞ̄w̄ n thought dr ⓞ ve him l ⓘ ke a g ⓞ̄a̅ d.   5

Dr ⓨ clashed his harness in the ⓘ cy caves   6

And barren ch ⓐ sms, and all to left and r ⓘ ght   7

The bare bl ⓐ ck cliff cl ⓐ nged round him, as he based   8

H ⓘ s feet on juts of sl ⓘ ppery cr ⓐ g that r ⓐ ng   9

Sh ⓐ̄r̅ p-sm ⓘ tten w ⓘ th the d ⓘ nt of ⓐ̄r̅ med heels—   10

And on a sudden, lo, the level lake,   11

And the long glories of the winter moon!   12

——————— = ō*   •—·—·—·—·= ä

----------- = ī   〰〰〰〰 = ĭ

• • • • • • • • • = a

*Pronunciation symbols as in *Webster's New World Dictionary,* 2nd ed.

[1]
In these 12 lines, Tennyson describes the ordeal of Sir Bedivere as he carries King Arthur, who is dying, from the mountainous heights, where he was wounded, down to the lake, where he will be sent to his final rest. Tennyson emphasizes the bleakness and hostility of this ghostly and deserted landscape. The metrical pattern he uses is unrhymed iambic pentameter--blank verse--which is suitable for descriptions of actions and scenes. Appropriately, the verse augments the natural descriptions and echoes first Bedivere's tenseness and then his relaxation.* Tennyson's control enables a true blending of sound and sense, as may be seen in his use of rhythm and in his manipulation of segmental devices, including onomatopoeia.†

[2]
Tennyson controls his meter to emphasize exertions and moods. In line 1 the meter is regular, except for an anapæst in the first foot. This regularity may be interpreted as emphasizing the swiftness and surefootedness of Bedivere. But he is about to undergo a severe test, and the rhythm quickly becomes irregular, as though to strain the pentameter verse in illustration of Bedivere's exertions. Tennyson therefore uses variations to highlight key words. For example, he uses the effect of anapæsts in a number of lines. In line 2 he emphasizes the chill air and Bedivere's vitality in the following way:

Clothed with / his breath.//

The image is one of being surrounded by one's own breath that vaporizes on hitting the cold air, and the rhythmical variation--a trochaic substitution in the first foot--enables the voice to build up to the word breath, a most effective internal climax.

[3]
Tennyson uses the same kind of rhythmical effect in line 3. He emphasizes the frozen hills by creating a caesura in the middle of the third foot, and then by making the heavy stress of the third foot fall on the preposition on, which with the creates the effect of an anapæst consisting of two unstressed syllables leading up to the first, stressed, syllable of frozen. The effect is that the voice builds up to the word and thus emphasizes the extreme conditions in which Bedivere is walking:

// on / the fro - / zen hills.//

Tennyson uses this rhythmical effect twelve times in the passage. It is one of his major means of rhetorical emphasis.

[4]
Tennyson's most effective metrical variation is the spondee, which appears in lines 5, 6, 8, (twice), 10, and 12. These substitutions, occurring mainly in the section describing how Bedivere forces his way down the frozen hills, permits the descriptive lines to ring out, as in:

The bare / black cliff / clanged round /

and

Dry clashed / his har - / ness

---

* Central idea.
† Thesis sentence.

These substitutions are so strong that they are almost literally like the actual sounds of Bedivere's exertions. In addition to this use of the spondee as a sound effect, a remarkable use of the spondee for psychological effect occurs in line 5. Here, the stresses internalize Bedivere's mental anguish, reaching a climax on the word drove:

His own / thought drove / him //

There is other substitution, too, both formal and rhetorical, and the tension these variations create keeps the responsive reader aware of Bedivere's tasks. One type of variation is the appearance of amphibrachic rhythm, which is produced in lines 2, 3, 4, 6, 7, and 11. The effect is achieved by a pattern which complements the rhetorical anapæsts. A caesura in the middle of a foot leaves the three preceding syllables as a light, heavy, and light, the rhythmical form of the amphibrach. In line 2, for example, it appears thus:

[5]

// and look - / ing //

In line 6 it takes this form:

/ his har - / ness //

Still another related variation is that of the apparently imperfect feet in lines 5, 8, 11, and 12. These imperfect feet are produced by a caesura, which isolates the syllable, as him is in line 8:

[6]

The bare / black cliff / clanged round / him. //

In line 11 the syllable (on the word lo!) is surrounded by two caesurae, and is therefore thrust into a position of great stress:

And on / a sud - / den // lo! // the lev - /el lake

Other, less significant substitutions are the trochees in lines 3 and 7, and the pyrrhic in line 12. All the described variations suggest the energy that Bedivere expends during his heroic action.

Many of the variations are produced by Tennyson's sentence structure, which results in a free placement of the caesurae and in a free use of end-stopping and enjambement. Four of the first five lines are end-stopped (two by commas, two by periods). Bedivere is exerting himself during these lines and he is making short tests to gather strength. His dangerous descent is described during the next four lines, and none of these lines is end-stopped. Bedivere is disturbed (being goaded by "his own thought"), but he must keep going, and the free sentence structure and free metrical variation underscore his physical and mental difficulties. But in the last two lines, when he has reached the lake, the lines "relax" with falling caesurae exactly at the fifth syllable. In other words,

[7]

the sentence structure of the last two lines is regular, an effect suggesting the return to order and beauty after the previous, rugged chaos.

[8] This rhythmical virtuosity is accompanied by a similarly brilliant control over segmental devices. Alliteration is the most obvious, permitting Tennyson to tie key words and their signifying actions together, as in the s's in swiftly strode in line 1, or the b's in barren, bare, black, and based in lines 7 and 8. Other notable examples are the aspirated h's in lines 2–6 (he, human, hills, heard, behind, him, his, harness); the k's in lines 6–9 (clashed, caves, chasms, cliff, clanged, crag); and the l's in lines 11 and 12 (lo, level, lake, long, glories). One might compare these l's with the l's in the more anguished context of lines 8 and 9, where the sounds appear as the second segment in the heavy, ringing words there (black, cliff, clanged, slippery). The sounds are the same, and the emphasis is similar, but the effects are different.

[9] Assonance is also present throughout the passage. In the first five lines, for example, the ō appears in six words. The first three ō's are in descriptive or metaphoric words (strō de, clō thed, frō zen), while the last three are in words describing Bedivere's pain and anguish (ō wn, drō ve, g ō ad). The ō therefore ties the physical to the psychological. Other patterns of assonance are the ă in lines 7, 8, and 9 (chăsms, clăng'd, blăck, crăg, răng), the ä of line 10 (shärp, ärmed), the ī of lines 4–7 (behī nd, crȳ , lī ke, drȳ , rī ght), and the short ĭ of lines 1 and 2, and 9 and 10 (swĭftly, rĭdge, wĭth, hĭs, slĭppery, smĭtten, wĭth, dĭnt). One might remark also that in the last two lines, which describe the level lake and the moon, Tennyson introduces a number of relaxed ō and ōō and similar vowel sounds:

And on a sudden, lo! the level lake,

And the long glories of the winter moon.

[10] The last two lines are, in fact, onomatopoeic, since the liquid l sounds suggest the gentle lapping of waves on a lake shore. There are other examples of onomatopoeia, too. In line 2 Tennyson describes Bedivere in the cold air as being "Clothed with his breath," and in the following five lines Tennyson employs many words with the aspirate h (e.g., his harness). In the context, these sounds enable readers to see and hear sights and sounds just like those of Bedivere as he carries his royal burden. Similarly, the explosive stops b and k, and d, and t in lines 6–10 imitate the sounds of Sir Bedivere's feet on the "juts of slippery crag."

[11] This short passage is filled with many examples of poetic excellence. Tennyson's sounds and rhythms actually speak along with the meaning. They emphasize the grandeur of Arthur and his faithful follower, and for one brief moment they bear out the magic that Tennyson associated with the fading past.

Commentary on the Essay

This essay presents a full treatment of the prosody of the passage from Tennyson. Paragraphs 2 through 7 deal with the relationship of the rhythm to the content. Note that prosody is not discussed in isolation, but as it augments Tennyson's descriptions of action and scenes. Thus, paragraph 4 refers to the use of the spondee as a substitute foot to reinforce ideas. Also in this paragraph, there is a short comparison of alternative ways of saying what Tennyson says so well. While such a speculative comparison should not be attempted often, it is effective here in bringing out the quality of Tennyson's use of the spondee as a means of emphasis.

Paragraphs 8 and 9 present a discussion of the alliteration and assonance of the passage, and paragraph 10 considers onomatopoeia.

Of greatest importance for the clarity of the essay, there are many supporting examples, spaced, centered and accurately marked, and numbered by line. In any essay about prosody, readers are likely to be unsure of the validity of the writer's observation unless such examples are provided and are located within the poem.

SECOND SAMPLE ESSAY

The Rhymes in Christina Rossetti's "Echo"

1   Come to me in the silence of the *night*,   (n)   5a

2   Come in the speaking silence of a *dream*;   (n)   5b

3   Come with soft rounded cheeks and eyes as *bright*   (adj)   5a

4   As sunlight on a *stream*;   (n)   3b

5   Come back in *tears*,   (n)   2c

6   O memory, hope, love of finished *years*.   (n)   5c

7   O *dream* how *sweet*, too *sweet*, too bitter *sweet*,   (adj)   5d

8   Whose wakening should have been in *paradise*,   (n)   5e

9   Where souls brimful of love abide and *meet*,   (v)   5d

10   Where thirsty longing *eyes*   (n)   3e

11   Watch the slow *door*   (n)   2f

adv
12 That opening, letting in, lets out no *more.*   5f

v
13 Yet *come* to me in *dreams,* that I may *live*   5g

n
14   My very life again though cold in *death*;   5h

v
15 *Come* back to me in *dreams,* that I may *give*   5g

n
16   Pulse for pulse, *breath* for *breath*:   3h

adv
17   Speak *low,* lean *low,*   2i

adj
18 As *long ago,* my love, how *long ago.*   5i

[1]   In the three-stanza lyric poem "Echo," Christina Rossetti uses rhyme as a way of saying that one might regain in dreams a love that is lost in reality.* As the dream of love is to the real love, so is an echo to an original sound. From this comparison comes the title of the poem and also Rossetti's unique use of rhyme. Aspects of her rhyme are the lyric pattern, the forms and qualities of the rhyming words, and the special use of repetition.†

[2]   The rhyme pattern is simple, and, like rhyme generally, it may be thought of as a pattern of echoes. Each stanza contains four lines of alternating rhymes concluded by a couplet, as follows: 5a, 5b, 5a, 3b, 2c, 5c (lambic). There are nine separate rhymes throughout the poem, three in each stanza. Only two words are used for each rhyme; no rhyme is used twice. Of the eighteen rhyming words, sixteen--almost all--are of one syllable. The remaining two words consist of two and three syllables. With such a great number of single-syllable words, the rhymes are all rising ones, on the accented halves of iambic feet, and the end-of-line emphasis is on simple words.

[3]   The grammatical forms and positions of the rhyming words lend support to the inward, introspective subject matter. Although there is variety, more than half the rhyming words are nouns. There are ten in all, and eight are placed as the objects of prepositions. Such enclosure helps the speaker emphasize her yearning to relive her love within dreams. Also, the repeated verb "come" in stanzas one and three is in the form of commands to the absent lover. A careful study shows that most of the verbal energy in the stanzas is in the first parts of the lines, leaving the rhymes to occur in elements modifying the verbs, as in these lines:

Come to me in the silence of the *night*; (1)

Yet come to me in dreams, that I may *live* (13)

My very life again though cold in *death*; (14)

* Central idea.
† Thesis sentence.

Most of the other rhymes are also in such internalized positions. The free rhyming verbs occur in subordinate clauses, and the nouns that are not the objects of prepositions are the subject (10) and object (11) of the same subordinate clause.

[4] The qualities of the rhyming words are also consistent with the poem's emphasis on the speaker's internal life. Most of the words are impressionistic. Even the concrete words--*stream, tears, eyes, door,* and *breath*--reflect the speaker's mental condition rather than describe reality. In this regard, the rhyming words of 1 and 3 are effective. These are *night* and *bright*, which contrast the bleakness of the speaker's condition, on the one hand, with the vitality of her inner life, on the other. Another effective contrast is in 14 and 16, where *death* and *breath* are rhymed. This rhyme may be taken to illustrate the sad fact that even though the speaker's love is past, it can yet live in present memory just as an echo continues to sound.

[5] It is in emphasizing how memory echoes experience that Rossetti creates the special use of rhyming words. There is an ingenious but not obtrusive repetition of a number of words--echoes. The major echoing word is of course the verb *come,* which appears six times at the beginnings of lines in stanzas 1 and 3. But rhyming words, stressing as they do the ends of lines, are also repeated systematically. The most notable is *dream,* the rhyming word in 2. Rossetti repeats the word in 7 and uses the plural in 13 and 15. In 7 the rhyming word *sweet* is the third use of the word, a climax of "how *sweet,* too *sweet,* too bitter *sweet.*" Concluding the poem, Rossetti repeats *breath* (16), *low* (17), and the phrase *long ago* (18). This special use of repetition justifies the title "Echo," and it also stresses the major idea that it is only in one's memory that past experience has reality, even if dreams are no more than echoes.

[6] Thus rhyme is not just ornamental in "Echo," but integral. The skill of Rossetti here is the same as in her half-serious, half-mocking poem "Eve," even though the two poems are totally different. In "Eve," she uses very plain rhyming words together with comically intended double rhymes. In "Echo," her subject might be called fanciful and maybe even morbid, but the easiness of the rhyming words, like the diction of the poem generally, keeps the focus on regret and yearning rather than self-indulgence. As in all rhyming poems, Rossetti's rhymes emphasize the conclusions of her lines. The rhymes go beyond this effect, however, because of the internal repetition--echoes--of the rhyming words. "Echo" is a poem in which rhyme is inseparable from meaning.

Commentary on the Essay

Throughout the essay, illustrative words are italicized, and numbers are used to indicate the lines from which the illustrations are drawn. The introductory paragraph asserts that rhyme is important in Rossetti's poem. It also attempts to explain the title, "Echo." The thesis sentence indicates the four topics to be developed in the body.

Paragraph 2 deals with the mechanical, mathematical aspects of the poem's rhyme. The high number of monosyllabic rhyming words is used to explain the rising, heavy-stress rhyme.

The third paragraph treats the grammar of the rhymes. For example, an analysis and count reveal that there are ten rhyming nouns and three rhyming verbs. The verb of command "come" is mentioned to show that most of the rhyming words exist within groups modifying this word, and three lines from the poem illustrate this fact. The grammatical analysis is related to the internalized nature of the subject of the poem.

Paragraph 4 emphasizes the impressionistic nature of the rhyming words and also points out two instances in which rhymes stress the contrast between real life and the speaker's introspective life.

Paragraph 5 deals with repetitions within the poem of five rhyming words. This repetition is seen as a pattern of echoes, in keeping with the title of the poem.

In the concluding paragraph, the rhymes in "Echo" are compared briefly with those in "Eve," another poem by Christina Rossetti. The conclusion is that Rossetti is a skilled rhymer because she uses rhyme appropriately in both poems. At the end of the essay the central idea is reiterated.

WRITING TOPICS

1. For Shakespeare's Sonnet 73, analyze the ways in which Shakespeare creates his iambics. That is, what is the relationship of lightly accented syllables to the heavily accented ones? Where does Shakespeare use articles (*the*), pronouns (*thus, his*), prepositions (*upon, against, of*), relative clause markers (*which, that*) and adverb clause markers (*as, when*) in relation to syllables of heavy stress? Determine the number and placement of one-syllable words and two-syllable words in the sonnet. On the basis of this study, how would you characterize Shakespeare's control of the iambic foot?

2. Compare the sounds used in Poe's "The Bells" with those of Wagoner's "March for a One-Man Band." What effects are achieved by each poet? What is the relationship in each poem between sound and content? Which poem do you prefer on the basis of sound? Why?

3. The poems "Barbara Allan," "Miniver Cheevy," and "At a Summer Hotel" all utilize falling, or trochaic, rhyme. What is the effect of this rhyming pattern in the three poems? How do the poems achieve seriousness, despite the fact that trochaic rhyme is often used generally to complement humorous and light verse?

4. Try writing a limerick. If you are at a loss for a topic, use one of the following lines to begin:

> There once was a man in a rowboat.
> Two happy friends tried to study.
> A fellow walked into a bar.

Once you have finished, use the same topic and detail for a poem in iambics. Describe the differences and challenges you encounter because of the differences between the rollicking form of the limerick and the more steady pace of the iambics. How do you handle the different demands of the form? What can you say about the iambic foot as a result of this experience?

5. Try writing a few short poems using comic rhymes. An example of what might be done is the following set of lines in which an anonymous poet was finding rhymes for the Irish town of Tipperary:

The stubborn muse he could not vary,
For still the lines would run contrary
Whene'er he thought on Tipperary.

Some words for rhyming: *bookcase, Schenectady, computer, seven, Chanhassen, grammar,* and so on. If you find trouble with exact rhymes, see what you can do with slant rhymes and eye rhymes. The idea is to use your ingenuity. Have fun.

20

Form: The Shape of the Poem

Poetry is tightly compressed and highly rhythmical language, and it always exists under self-imposed restrictions, or conventions, many of which are examined in Chapter 19. The goal of poets has been not only to *say* something important and moving, but also to say it with intelligence, wit, insight, and skill. Poets have therefore traditionally exercised their verbal powers within a variety of clearly recognizable shapes or forms—**closed form poetry**. Since the middle of the nineteenth century, however, many poets have rejected the more obvious conventions, thereby producing poems which follow patterns of thought and emotion that appear to be spontaneous and free—**open form poetry**. Bear in mind that these terms refer to the structure and technique of the poems, not to content or ideas.

CLOSED-FORM POETRY

Closed-form poetry is written in specific and traditional patterns of lines produced through *rhyme, meter, line length,* and *line groupings.* In the closed form, the **stanza** is the poetic analogue of the paragraph. It consist of a number of lines connected by subject or theme, and often grouped or separated both topically and visually. Examples of closed form that have been used for hundreds of years and that are recognizable because of their structure are *ballads, sonnets, couplets, blank verse, limericks, hymns, odes,* and *lyrics.*

The Building Blocks of Closed-Form Poetry

The basic building block of closed-form poetry is the single line of verse. Various numbers of lines may be grouped together through rhyme to form *stanzas* or *sections* of poems which in turn are assembled to create the many *traditional closed forms.*

BLANK VERSE. One of the most common types of English poetry is blank verse, or *unrhymed iambic pentameter* (see p. 706). Shakespeare's plays use blank verse extensively, and Milton's long epic, *Paradise Lost,* uses it exclusively. An example of Shakespeare's blank verse is this speech from the first act of *Hamlet,* where the prince tells his mother that his sorrow over his father's death is real and not superficial:

Seems, madam? nay it is. I know not "seems."
'Tis not alone my inky cloak good mother,
Nor customary suits of solemn black,
Nor windy suspiration of forced breath,
No, nor the fruitful river of the eye,°   *tears*
Nor the dejected havior° of the visage,°   *appearance; face*
Together with all forms, moods, shapes of grief,
That can denote me truly: these indeed seem,
For they are actions, that a man might play,
But I have that within which passes show,
These but the trappings and the suits of woe.

(Act I, scene 2, lines 76-86)

While these lines are linked together to make up the entire speech, each one creates an identifiable unit of thought and grammatical coherence. (The rhyming lines mark the conclusion, not a new form.) In the footsteps of Shakespeare, poets of English have used blank verse again and again, for without forsaking its poetic identity as a closed form, it closely resembles normal speech.

THE COUPLET. The basic two-line poetic form is the **couplet**. The two lines usually rhyme, and usually are of the same length, although English translations of Biblical poetry contain couplets unified by parallel ideas and assertions, not by meter and rhyme. Some couplets are extremely short; even monometric lines like "Some play / All day" comprise a couplet. However, couplets are most often in iambic pentameter and iambic tetrameter. The following couplet by John Dryden (1631-1700), which he included in *Absalom and Achitophel* (1682), is justly considered one of the most memorable of his many fine couplets:

Great Wits are sure to Madness near allied;
And thin Partitions do their Bounds divide.

Ever since the fourteenth century, when Chaucer used them, couplets have been a regular feature of English poetry. In the seventeenth and eighteenth centuries, the five-stress couplet was considered particularly appropriate for epic, or heroic, poetry. For this reason it is often called a **heroic couplet**. Also because the period is considered the "neo-classic" age of literature, the form is also called the **neo-classic couplet**. It was used with consummate skill by Dryden, and also by Alexander Pope (1685-1744).

Usually, the heroic couplet expresses a complete idea, and is grammatically self-sufficient. It thrives on the rhetorical strategies of **parallelism** and **antithesis**. Look, for example, at these lines from "The Rape of the Lock," Pope's great mock-epic poem:

> Here *Britain's* Statesmen oft the Fall foredoom
> Of Foreign Tyrants, and of Nymphs at home;
> Here Thou, Great *Anna*! whom three Realms obey,
> Dost sometimes Counsel take—and sometimes *Tea*.

These lines describe activities at Hampton Court, the royal palace and residence of Queen Anne (reigned 1701–1714). Notice that the first couplet allows Pope to link *"Britain's* Statesmen" with two related but antithetical events: the fall of nations and the fall of young women. Similarly, the second heroic couplet allows for the parallel and comic linking of royal meetings of state (*counsel*) and tea time (in the early eighteenth century, *tea* was pronounced "tay"). The example thus demonstrates how the heroic couplet may place contrasting actions and situations in amusing and ironic parallels.

THE TERCET OR TRIPLET. A three-line stanza is called a **tercet** or **triplet**. Tercets may be written in any uniform line length or meter, and most commonly contain three rhymes (*a a a, b b b,* and so on), which in effect creates short stanzaic units. The following poem is written in iambic tetrameter triplets.

ALFRED, LORD TENNYSON (1809–1892)

The Eagle _____ *1851*

He clasps the crag with crooked hands;
Close to the sun in lonely lands,
Ring'd with the azure world, he stands.

The wrinkled sea beneath him crawls;
He watches from his mountain walls,
And like a thunderbolt he falls.

5

The lines are of even length, with the rhyming sounds being repeated three times in each stanza. In the first tercet we view the eagle, as though at a distance. In the second, the perspective shifts, and we see through the eagle's eyes and follow his actions. In this tercet the verbs are active: the sea "crawls" and the eagle "falls." While the two tercets and the shift in perspective divide the poem, alliteration pulls things back together. This is especially true of the *k* sound in *clasps, crag, crooked, close,* and *crawls,* and the *w* sound in *with, world, watches,* and *walls.*

There are two important variations on the tercet pattern, each requiring a high degree of ingenuity and control. The first tercet variation is **terza rima**, in which stanzas are interlocked through a pattern that requires the center termination in one tercet to be rhymed twice in the next, as follows: *a b a, b c b, c d c, d e d,* and so on. You can see an example of terza rima in Shelley's "Ode to the West Wind" (p. 776).

The most complex variation of the tercet pattern is the **villanelle**, in which every triplet in the poem is rhymed *a b a,* and the first and third lines of the first tercet are repeated alternately in subsequent stanzas as a refrain, and also are used as the concluding lines (for examples, see Thomas's "Do Not Go Gentle Into That Good Night," p. 781, and Roethke's "The Waking," p. 979).

THE QUATRAIN.   The most common and adaptable stanzaic building block in English and American poetry is the four-line **quatrain**. This stanza has been popular for hundreds of years and has lent itself to a great many variations. Like couplets and triplets, quatrains may be written in any line length and meter; even the line lengths *within* a quatrain may vary. The determining factor is always the rhyme scheme, and even that can vary significantly, given the demands of the form and the desires of the poet. Quatrains may be rhymed *a a a a,* but they can also be rhymed *a b a b, a b b a, a a b a,* or even *a b c b.* All these variations are determined, at least in part, by the larger patterns or forms in which quatrains are used. Quatrains are basic components of many traditional closed forms, most notably ballads and sonnets.

Common Types of Closed-Form Poetry

Over the centuries English and American poetry has evolved or appropriated many traditional closed forms, all of them determined by combinations of meter, rhyme scheme, line length, and stanza form, and embodying couplets, tercets, and quatrains. The following are the more common traditional forms.

THE ITALIAN, OR PETRARCHAN SONNET.   The **sonnet** is one of the most durable and popular traditional forms. All sonnets are fourteen lines long. Initially, they were an Italian poetic form (*sonnetto* means "little song") popularized by Petrarch (1304–1374), who wrote long collections or *cycles* of sonnets. The form and style of Petrarch's sonnets were adapted to English poetry in the early sixteenth century, and with variations have been used ever since. The **Italian** or **Petrarchan sonnet** is in iambic pentameter and is composed of two quatrains and two tercets. The first eight lines are the **octave** (an eight-line unit of thought) and the last six form the **sestet**.

The rhyme scheme of the octave is usually fixed in an *a b b a, a b b a* pattern. The sestet offers a number of different rhyming possibilities, including *c d c, c d c* and *c d e, c d e*. In terms of structure and meaning, the octave presents a problem or situation, and the sestet offers a resolution. As a result, there is often a clear shift or turn in thought from the octave to the sestet, as in Milton's "When I Consider How My Light Is Spent" (p. 773).

THE ENGLISH, OR SHAKESPEAREAN SONNET.   Named after its most famous practitioner, the **Shakespearean**, or **English Sonnet** is written in iambic pentameter and has the following rhyme scheme: *a b a b, c d c d, e f e f, g g.* Shakespeare recognized that there are fewer rhyming words in English than in Italian, and hence he based his form on seven rhymes rather than the five of the Italian sonnet. As indicated by the rhyme scheme, the Shakespearean sonnet contains three quatrains and a concluding couplet. The pattern of thought therefore shifts from the octave-sestet organization of the Italian sonnet to a four-part argument on a single thought or emotion. Each quatrain usually contains a separate development of the sonnet's central idea, with the couplet providing a conclusion, climax, and resolution. Shakespeare's Sonnet 116, "Let Me Not to the Marriage of True Minds" (p. 757), is an example of the English sonnet.

THE BALLAD.   The **ballad**, which originated in folk literature, is the oldest continuously used closed form in English poetry. A ballad consists of a long series of quatrains in which lines of iambic tetrameter alternate with iambic trimeter. Normally, only the second and fourth lines of each stanza rhyme, and so the rhyme scheme is *x a x a, x b x b, x c x c,* and so on. The ballad of tradition was a lengthy narrative, designed for singing, like the anonymous ballads "Sir Patrick Spens" (p. 553) and "Barbara Allan" (p. 912). Often a single tune was used over and over again by later balladeers, and many of the tunes have survived to the present day (e.g., "Barbara Allan," "Lord Randal," and "Greensleeves").

COMMON MEASURE OR HYMNAL STANZA.   **Common measure** is similar to the ballad stanza. It shares with the ballad the alternation of four-beat and three-beat iambic lines, but adds a second rhyme to each quatrain: *a b a b, c d c d,* and so on. As with the ballad, the building block of common measure is the quatrain. The measure is often used in hymns, so it is sometimes called the **hymnal stanza**. Many of Emily Dickinson's poems, including "Because I Could Not Stop for Death" (p. 555), are written in common measure.

THE SONG OR LYRIC.   The **song**, or **lyric** is a free stanzaic form that was originally designed to be sung to a repeating melody. The structure and rhyme scheme of the first stanza are therefore duplicated in all subsequent stanzas. Next to the ballad, it is one of the oldest traditional closed poetic forms. The individual stanzas of a lyric may be built from any combination of single lines, couplets, triplets, and quatrains. The line lengths may shift, and a great deal of metrical variation is common.

There is theoretically no limit to the number of stanzas in a lyric, although there are usually no more than five or six. We can find a great deal of variation in the structure. A. E. Housman's "Loveliest of Trees" (p. 558), for example, is a lyric made up of three quatrains containing two couplets each. It is in iambic tetrameter, and rhymes *a a b b*. The second and third stanza repeat the same pattern. Christina Rossetti's "Echo" (p. 744) is also a lyric, but its structure is different from that of Housman's poem. Here, the structural formulation of each stanza is iambic: *5a 5b 5a 3b 2c 5c*. Lyrics can have very complex and ingenious stanzaic structures. John Donne's "The Canonization" (p. 871), for instance, contains five stanzas that reflect the following pattern: *Iambic: 5a 4b 5b 5a 4c 4c 4c 4a 3a*. The nine-line stanza contains three different rhymes and three different line lengths. Nevertheless, the same intricate pattern is repeated in each of the five stanzas.

THE ODE.   The **ode** is a more complex stanzaic form than the lyric, with varying line lengths and intricate rhyme schemes. Some odes have repeating patterns, while others offer no duplication, and introduce a new structure in each stanza. Although some odes were intended for music, most do not fit repeating melodies. There is no set form for the ode. Poets have developed their own structure according to their needs. John Keats's great odes were particularly congenial to his ideas, as in the "Ode to a Nightingale" (p. 770), which consists of ten stanzas in iambic pentameter with the repeating form *a b a b c d e 3c d e*.

THE HAIKU.   The **haiku** originated in Japan, where it has been a favorite genre for hundreds of years. In its original form, the haiku imposed strict rules on the writer: The poem must be only three lines long and have a total of seventeen syllables in a pattern of *five, seven*, and *five* syllables per line. The traditional subject matter was nature and the seasons. Today English-language poets have treated many different subjects in haiku, and have also taken liberties with the syllabic count. Because of the rigid pattern, haiku poetry must aim for objectivity, simplicity, and clarity, and should be judged by these standards. The following anonymous haiku illustrates some of these qualities.

Spun in high, dark clouds

Spun in high, dark clouds,
Snow forms vast webs of white flakes
And drifts lightly down.

In the tradition of haiku, the subject of this poem is derived from nature. The poem's metaphor equates gathering snow with the webs of spiders or silkworms. To supply a degree of tension, the lines contrast "high" with "down," and "dark" with "white." Because of the enforced brevity of the form, the diction is simple and, except for the word *forms*, is of English derivation (*form* is a word derived from French). In addition, the words are mainly monosyllabic, and the poem therefore crowds sixteen words to fulfill the seventeen-syllable requirement. Most English haiku similarly emphasize one-syllable words.

Other Closed-Form Types

EPIGRAMS AND EPITAPHS.   Many other closed forms have enjoyed long popularity. One of these, the **epigram**, is a short and witty poem that usually makes a humorous or satiric point. Epigrams are two to four lines long and are often written in couplets. The form was developed by the Roman poet Martial (A.D. 40–102) and is still popular. Humorous **epitaphs**, lines composed to mark the death of someone, can also be epigrams. The following epitaph-epigram was written to commemorate John Hewet and Sara Drew, who were killed by lightning on July 31, 1718, while helping bring in the harvest. It is followed by an epigram by Coleridge.

ALEXANDER POPE (1688–1744)

Epitaph on the Stanton-Harcourt Lovers ——————————————— *1718*

Here lie two poor Lovers, who had the mishap,
Though very chaste people, to die of a Clap.

SAMUEL TAYLOR COLERIDGE (1772–1834)

What Is an Epigram? ——————————————————————— *1802*

What is an epigram? a dwarfish whole,
Its body brevity, and wit its soul.

THE LIMERICK.   Another popular type is the **limerick**. Like the epigram, the limerick is usually comic, the humor often being reinforced by double or falling rhymes (see pp. 715–16). Most limericks today are sexual and bawdy. We do not know who invented the limerick, but it was popularized by Edward Lear (1812–1888), an English artist and humorist. Limericks are always five lines long and the dominant foot is the *anapaest* ($\smile\smile{'}$). The structure of most limericks may thus be described as *anapaestic, with variations: 3a 3a 2b 2b 3a*. Here are a few anonymous limericks:

A diner while dining at Crewe,
Found a rather large mouse in his stew.
   Said the waiter, "Don't shout
   And wave it about,
Or the rest will be wanting one too."

There once was a man from Tarentum
Who gnashed his false teeth till he bent 'em.
   When asked the cost
   Of what he had lost,
He said, "I can't say, for I rent 'em."

THE CLERIHEW.   Humorous closed forms continue to be devised by enterprising writers. Although none has become as popular as the limerick, they illustrate both the pleasures and the agonies of working within closed forms. The **clerihew**, invented in the late nineteenth century by Edmund Clerihew Bentley (1875–1956), is related to the epigram. Clerihews are usually composed of two couplets and focus on a well-known person, who is named in the first line. Here are two clerihews, both written by Bentley and published in 1937:

George the Third
Ought never to have occurred.
One can only wonder
At so grotesque a blunder.

Alfred, Lord Tennyson
Lived upon venison:
Not cheap, I fear,
Because venison's deer.

QUESTIONS

1. Describe the common tone and structure of these poems.
2. Write several clerihews about contemporary figures and share them with your class. Try to maintain the tone and style of Bentley's work.

THE DOUBLE DACTYL.   As a final illustration of humorous closed form, we offer the **double dactyl**, devised in the 1960s by Anthony Hecht and John Hollander. The form is related to the epigram, limerick, and clerihew, and has rules that govern the meter, line length, and specific content of lines 1, 2, and 6 or 7. Here is an example.

ANTHONY HECHT (b. 1923)

Nominalism ———————————————————— *1967*

Higgledy-piggledy
Juliet Capulet

Cherished the tenderest
Thoughts of a rose:

"What's in a name?" said she,   5
Etymologically,
"Save that all Montagues
Stink in God's nose."

QUESTIONS

1. What form does line 1 take? What requirement governs line 2? Lines 6 or 7?
2. What is the rhyme? The meter? What change occurs in lines 4 and 8?
3. Try writing a few double dactyls, maintaining the tone and spirit of the example. You will probably have the most trouble with line 2, 6, or 7, but keep at it.

Closed Form and Meaning

Although traditional closed forms seem restrictive to many contemporary poets, they provide a framework within which a poet can express ideas, attitudes, and feelings. The poet's challenge is to take an existing framework and breathe new life into it by arranging images, emotions, and ideas. A skillful poet uses the demands of a closed form to his or her own ends. With this in mind, let us look at the way a specific closed form may be employed to shape thoughts and emotions.

WILLIAM SHAKESPEARE (1564–1616)

Sonnet 116: Let Me Not to the Marriage of True Minds ———————— 1609

Let me not to the marriage of true minds
Admit impediments.° Love is not love
Which alters when it alteration finds,
Or bends with the remover to remove:
Oh, no! it is an ever-fixéd mark,   5
That looks on tempests and is never shaken;
It is the star to every wandering bark,
Whose worth's unknown, although his height° be taken   *altitude*
Love's not Time's fool,° though rosy lips and cheeks   *slave*
Within his° bending sickle's compass come;   *Time's*   10
Love alters not with his brief hours and weeks,
But bears it out even to the edge of doom.°   *The Last Judgment*
If this be error and upon me proved,
I never writ, nor no man ever loved.

SONNET 116.   2 *impediments:* a reference to "The Order of Solemnization of Matrimony" in the Anglican *Book of Common Prayer:* "I require that if either of you know of any impediment why ye may not be lawfully joined together in Matrimony, ye do now confess it."

QUESTIONS

1. Describe the restrictions of this closed form. How is the poem's argument structured by the form?
2. What is the poem's meter? Rhyme scheme? Structure?
3. Describe the varying ideas about love explored in the three quatrains.
4. What does the concluding couplet contribute to the poem's argument about love?

We immediately recognize that this poem is a Shakespearean sonnet. It is in iambic pentameter and contains three quatrains and a concluding couplet, rhyming *a b a b, c d c d, e f e f, g g*. The topic is that real love is a "marriage of true minds." The sonnet puts forward the idea that such love exists independently of earthly time and change.

Shakespeare's sonnet form provides the organization for the poem's argument, with each quatrain advancing a new perspective on the central thought. The first quatrain presents the sonnet's *thesis* that true and permanent love is based on the "marriage of true minds," and it stresses that this love cannot be altered by outside forces. The second quatrain illustrates the permanence of true love by introducing a nautical and navigational metaphor. The third quatrain stresses that true love lasts beyond life, "even to the edge of doom"; that is, until the Day of Judgment. The final couplet presents evidence designed to support the truth and validity of the poem's development.

Shakespeare brings out his ideas brilliantly within the space of the closed form. This is not to say either that he exhausts his topic, or that he wants to. The ideas of the third quatrain, for example, about how love transcends time, could be greatly expanded. A philosophical analysis of the topic would need to deal extensively with Platonic ideas about reality—whether it exists in *particulars* or *universals*. Such a discussion would require many pages and chapters.

But that is not Shakespeare's interest. Within the framework of a quatrain he strongly asserts that human love has the power to exceed mortal restrictions. Similarly, the poem's very last line, if it became the topic of a prose inquiry, might require the introduction of evidence about the poet's own writing, and also about many examples of human love. But the two lines are enough here, within the restrictions of the poem, and more would be superfluous. One might add that most readers find Shakespeare's poem interesting and vital, while extensive philosophical discourses often drop into laps as readers fall asleep.

The closed poetic form therefore may be viewed as a natural function of characteristic poetic compression. No matter what form a poet chooses—couplet, sonnet, song, ballad, ode—that form imposes restrictions, and it therefore challenges and shapes the poet's thought. The poet of the closed form shares with all writers the need to make ideas seem logical and well-supported, but the challenge of the form is to make all this happen *within the form itself.* The thought must be developed clearly and also fully, and there should be no lingering doubts once the poem is completed. The words must seem absolutely right, as though they were the easiest and most natural ones on earth that could be selected. All this means that when we look at good poems in the closed form, we may be sure that they represent the ultimate degree of poetic thought, discipline, and skill.

OPEN-FORM POETRY

Open-form poetry avoids traditional patterns of organization and does not rely on meter, rhyme, line length, or stanzas to produce order. Poetry of this type was once termed **free verse** (from the French *vers libre*) to signify its liberation from regular metrical rules and its adoption of the rhythms of spoken language. That term is somewhat misleading, however. Open-form poetry has indeed shaken off the traditional poetic demands, but it is not therefore disorganized or chaotic. Open-form poets have instead sought new ways to arrange words and lines, new ways to express thoughts and feelings, and new ways to order poetic experience.

The Building Blocks of Open-Form Poetry

Poets of the open form attempt to fuse form and content by stressing speechlike rhythms, creating a natural and easy-flowing word order, altering and varying line lengths according to the importance of ideas, and creating emphasis through the control of shorter and longer pauses. They often isolate individual words and/or phrases into single lines, freely emphasize their ideas through the manipulation of spaces separating words and sentences, and sometimes even break up individual words to highlight their importance. They may even write poems that look exactly like prose and that are printed in paragraphs instead of stanzas or lines. These **prose poems** rely on the cadences of language and the progression of images to convey the poetic experience.

Open Form and Meaning

We can see an early instance of open-form poetry in Walt Whitman's "Reconciliation." It was written as part of *Drum Taps*, a collection of 53 poems about the poet's reactions to Civil War battles in Virginia.

WALT WHITMAN (1819–1892)

Reconciliation ——————————————————————————— *1865, 1881*

Word over all, beautiful as the sky,
Beautiful that war and all its deeds of carnage must in time be utterly lost,
That the hands of the sisters Death and Night incessantly softly wash again,

and ever again, this soil'd world;
For my enemy is dead, a man divine as myself is dead,
I look where he lies white-faced and still in the coffin—I draw near,
Bend down and touch lightly with my lips the white face in the coffin.

QUESTIONS

1. How do individual lines, varying line lengths, punctuation, pauses, and cadences create rhythm and organize the images and ideas in this poem?
2. How does alliteration, assonance, and the repetition of words unify the poem and reinforce its content?
3. What is the "word" referred to in line 1? What does the speaker find "beautiful" about this "word" and the passage of time?
4. What instances of personification can you find? What do these personified figures do? What does the speaker do in lines 5–6? Why does he do this?

Whitman's "Reconciliation" shows the power of open-form poetry. There is no dominant meter, rhyme scheme, or stanza pattern. Instead, the poet uses individual lines and varying line lengths to organize and emphasize the images, ideas, and emotions. He also uses repetition, alliteration, and assonance to make internal line connections.

Without going into every aspect of the poem, one may note the unifying elements in the first few lines. The *word over all* (i.e., reconciliation, peace) is linked to the second line by the repetition of the words *beautiful* and *all*, while *beautiful* is grammatically complemented by the clauses "that . . . lost" (line 2) and "That . . . world" (line 3). The reconciling word is thus connected to the image of the two personified figures, Death and Night, who "wash" war and carnage (bloodshed) out of "this soil'd world."

In the third line, unity and emphasis are created through the repetition of *again* and the alliteration on the *ly* sound of *incessantly* and *softly*, the *s* sound in *hands, sisters, incessantly, softly,* and *soil'd,* and the *d* sound in *hands, Death, soil'd,* and *World.* One may also note the unifying assonance patterns of *ĭ* in *its, in, sisters, incessantly,* and *this,* and *ī* in *sky, time,* and *Night.* The pauses, or junctures, of the line create remarkable internal rhythms that coincide with the thought: *That the hands // of the sisters // Death and Night // incessantly // softly // wash again // and ever again // this soil'd world.*

This selective analysis demonstrates that open-form poetry creates its own unity. While some of the unifying elements, such as alliteration and assonance, are also a property of closed-form poetry, many are unique to poetry of the open form, such as the repetitions, the reliance on grammatical structures, and the careful control of rhythms. The concept of the open form is that the topic itself shapes the number of lines, the line lengths, and the physical appearance on the page. Unity is there—development is there—but the open form demands that there be as many shapes and forms as there are topics.

VISUAL POETRY

In **visual poetry** poets emphasize not only the idea and emotion of their subject, but also fashion the poem into a recognizable shape on the page. Some visual poetry seeks to strike a balance between the pleasures of seeing and those of hearing. Other visual poetry, however, abandons sound completely and invests all its impact in our perception of the visual image or picture.

Visual poetry is not a recent development. The Chinese have been producing it for thousands of years, and there are surviving examples from ancient Greece. In the seventeenth century, traditional English poets were manipulating the lines of their poems to represent wings, altars, squares, triangles, stars, and the like. This type of poetry, also called **shaped verse**, was often more ingenious than significant. Exceptional poets, however, produced shaped verse in which the visual image and the meaning strikingly echo each other.

After World War II, picture poems experienced a revival when visual poetry reentered the literary landscape with the birth of a new movement called **concrete poetry**. Poets in this tradition focus their attention almost completely on the medium from which the poem is created. In the case of printed work, this means that the writers pay far more attention to the visual arrangement of letters, words, lines, and white spaces than they do to content. Concrete poetry represents a fusion of writing with painting or graphic design, and the emphasis is on the visual. Form is both the means and the end of creation.

Form and Meaning in Visual Concrete Poetry

In reading visual and concrete poetry, you should seek correspondences between the image and the words. In your consideration, include the shape of the poem, the connotations of this shape, the varying line lengths, the placement of individual words and phrases, and the use of space. A superb example of seventeenth-century visual poetry is George Herbert's "Easter Wings," a religious poem that offers two different pictures, both of which are relevant to the content.

GEORGE HERBERT (1593-1633)

Easter Wings ———————————————————————— *1633*

Lord, who createdst man in wealth and store,°   *abundance*
  Though foolishly he lost the same,
    Decaying more and more
      Till he became
        Most poor: 5
        With thee
        O let me rise
      As larks, harmoniously,

And sing this day thy victories:
Then shall the fall° further the flight in me.

My tender age in sorrow did I begin:
  And still with sicknesses and shame
    Thou didst so punish sin,
      That I became
        Most thin.
        With thee
      Let me combine,
    And feel this day thy victory;°
  For, if I imp° my wing on thine,
Affliction shall advance the flight in me.

EASTER WINGS.   10 *fall:* the Biblical account of how sin and death were introduced as a punishment for humankind after Adam and Eve disobeyed God. See also line 2.   18 *victory:* I Corinthians 15:54-57.   19 *imp:* to repair a falcon's wing or tail by grafting on feathers.

QUESTIONS

1. What does the poem look like when viewed straight on? When viewed sideways, with the left side at the top? How do these two images echo and emphasize the poem's content?

2. How does the typographical arrangement echo the sense? In lines 5 and 15, for example, how are typography, shape, and meaning fused?

3. What do lines 1-5 tell you about humanity's spiritual history, according to Herbert? What do lines 11-15 tell you about the speaker's spiritual state? How are these parallel?

This poem is an admission of sin and a prayer for redemption. It compares humanity's loss of Eden ("wealth and store") to the speaker's spiritual state as a petitioner seeking salvation. When viewed straight on, each stanza resembles an altar. Sideways, the poem resembles two pairs of angel's wings. The images are thus linked with the title of the poem, and they connote prayer, contrition, grace, and angelic salvation.

The correspondence between shape and meaning goes even further. Herbert reinforces the ideas in various lines by the careful manipulation of line lengths. Thus, in discussing humanity's spiritual history, the original "wealth and store" of Eden are described in the poem's longest (widest) line. As the fall from grace is described, the lines get progressively shorter (narrower), until humanity's fallen state is reached in the narrowest line, "most poor" (line 5). This same pattern is repeated in lines 11–15 to portray the sinful state that has left the speaker spiritually "most thin." In the second half of each stanza, this pattern is reversed, and the lines gradually expand, echoing the speaker's prayers for grace and salvation. Thus, the full lengths of lines 10 and 20 reflect the original states of grace, described in lines 1 and 11, and the glorious wealth of redemption.

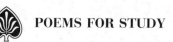

POEMS FOR STUDY

e.e. cummings   (1874–1963)

Buffalo Bill's Defunct° _____ *1923*

Buffalo Bill's
defunct
  who used to
  ride a watersmooth-silver
      stallion   5
and break onetwothreefourfive pigeonsjustlikethat
            Jesus
he was a handsome man
      and what i want to know is
how do you like your blueeyed boy   10
Mister Death

BUFFALO BILL'S DEFUNCT.   The poem has no title; it is usually referred to as "Portrait" or by its first two lines. Buffalo Bill (William F. Cody, 1846–1917) was an American plainsman, hunter, army scout, sharpshooter, and showman whose Wild West show began touring the world in 1883; he became a symbol of the Wild West.

QUESTIONS

1. What is the effect of devoting a whole line to *Buffalo Bill's* (line 1), *defunct* (line 2), *stallion* (line 5), *Jesus* (line 7), and *Mister Death* (line 11)? How does this technique reflect and emphasize the content of the poem?

2. How does the typographical arrangement of line 6 contribute to the fusion of sound and sense? What other examples of this technique do you find?

3. Explain the denotations and connotations of *defunct*. What would be lost (or gained) by using the term *dead* or *deceased* instead?

4. To what extent is this poem a "portrait" of Buffalo Bill? What do we learn about him? Is the portrait respectful, mocking, or something in between?

JOHN DRYDEN   (1631–1700)

To the Memory of Mr. Oldham° _____ *1684*

Farewell, too little and too lately known,
Whom I began to think and call my own:
For sure our souls were near allied, and thine
Cast in the same poetic mold with mine.

TO THE MEMORY OF MR. OLDHAM.   John Oldham (1653–1683) was a young poet whom Dryden admired.

One common note on either lyre did strike,
And knaves and fools we both abhorred alike.
To the same goal did both our studies drive;
The last set out the soonest did arrive.
Thus Nisus° fell upon the slipp'ry place,
While his young friend performed and won the race.
O early ripe! to thy abundant store
What could advancing age have added more?
It might (what nature never gives the young)
Have taught the numbers of thy native tongue.
But satire needs not those, and wit will shine
Through the harsh cadence of a rugged line;
A noble error, and but seldom made,
When poets are by too much force betrayed.
Thy gen'rous fruits, though gathered ere their prime,
Still showed a quickness; and maturing time
But mellows what we write to the dull sweets of rhyme.
Once more, hail and farewell;° farewell, thou young.
But ah too short, Marcellus° of our tongue;
Thy brows with ivy and with laurels° bound;
But fate and gloomy night encompass thee around.

9 *Nisus:* a character in Vergil's *Aeneid* who slipped in a pool of blood while running a race, thus allowing his best friend to win.   22 *hail and farewell:* an echo of the Latin phrase "ave atque vale" spoken by gladiators about to fight.   23 *Marcellus:* a Roman general who was adopted by the Emperor Augustus as his successor but died at the age of twenty.   24 *laurels:* a plant sacred to Apollo, the Greek god of poetry; the traditional prize given to poets is a wreath of laurel.

QUESTIONS

1. What is the meter of this poem? Rhyme scheme? Closed form? How does the form control the tempo? Why is this tempo appropriate?

2. What does the speaker reveal about himself in lines 1–10? About Oldham? About his relationship with Oldham? What did the two have in common?

3. What is the effect of Dryden's frequent classical allusions? What pairs of rhyming words most effectively clinch ideas?

ROBERT FROST   (1874–1963)

Desert Places ———————————————————————— *1936*

Snow falling and night falling fast, oh, fast
In a field I looked into going past,
And the ground almost covered smooth in snow,
But a few weeds and stubble showing last.

The woods around it have it—it is theirs.
All animals are smothered in their lairs.

I am too absent-spirited to count;
The loneliness includes me unawares.

And lonely as it is that loneliness
Will be more lonely ere it will be less—   10
A blanker whiteness of benighted snow
With no expression, nothing to express.

They cannot scare me with their empty spaces
Between stars—on stars where no human race is.
I have it in me so much nearer home   15
To scare myself with my own desert places.

QUESTIONS

1. What is the meter? The rhyme scheme? The form?

2. What setting and situation are established in lines 1–4? What does the snow affect here? What does it affect in lines 5–8? In lines 9–12?

3. What different kinds of "desert places" is this poem about? Which kind is the most important? Most frightening?

4. How does the type of rhyme (rising or falling) change in the last stanza? How does this change affect the tone and impact of the poem?

5. How does the stanzaic pattern of this poem organize the progression of the speaker's thoughts, feelings, and conclusions?

ALLEN GINSBERG   (b. 1926)

A Supermarket in California ———————————————— *1955*

What thoughts I have of you tonight, Walt Whitman,° for
I walked down the sidestreets under the trees with a headache
self-conscious looking at the full moon.
    In my hungry fatigue, and shopping for images, I went
into the neon fruit supermarket, dreaming of your enumera-   5
tions!°
    What peaches and what penumbras! Whole families
shopping at night! Aisles full of husbands! Wives in the
avocados, babies in the tomatoes!—and you, Garcia Lorca,° what
were you doing down by the watermelons?   10

    I saw you, Walt Whitman, childless, lonely old grubber,
poking among the meats in the refrigerator and eyeing the
grocery boys.

A SUPERMARKET IN CALIFORNIA.   1 *Walt Whitman:* American poet (1819–1892) who experimented with open forms and significantly influenced the development of twentieth-century poetry.   5 *enumerations:* Many of Whitman's poems contain long lists.   9 *Garcia Lorca:* Spanish surrealist poet and playwright (1896–1936) whose later poetry became progressively more like prose.

I heard you asking questions of each: Who killed the pork
chops? What price bananas? Are you my Angel?
I wandered in and out of the brilliant stacks of cans
following you, and followed in my imagination by the store
detective.
We strode down the open corridors together in our solitary
fancy tasting artichokes, possessing every frozen delicacy, and
never passing the cashier.

Where are we going, Walt Whitman? The doors close in
an hour. Which way does your beard point tonight?
(I touch your book and dream of our odyssey in the supermarket
and feel absurd.)
Will we walk all night through solitary streets? The trees
add shade to shade, lights out in the houses, we'll both be
lonely.

Will we stroll dreaming of the lost America of love past blue
automobiles in driveways, home to our silent cottage?
Ah, dear father, graybeard, lonely old courage-teacher,
what America did you have when Charon° quit poling his ferry
and you got out on a smoking bank and stood watching the
boat disappear on the black waters of Lethe?°

32 *Charon:* boatman in Greek mythology who ferried the souls of the dead across the river Styx
into Hades, the underworld.   34 *Lethe:* the river of forgetfulness in Hades. The dead drank
from this river and forgot their former lives.

QUESTIONS

1. Where is the speaker? What is he doing? What is his condition?
2. What effect is produced by placing Whitman and Lorca in the market?
3. To what extent do we find Whitman-like enumerations in this work? What is the
    effect of such enumerations?
4. Why is this a poem? What poetic devices are employed here? To what extent
    might it make more sense to consider this prose rather than poetry?

NIKKI GIOVANNI   (b. 1943)

Nikki-Rosa —————————————————————————— *1968*

childhood remembrances are always a drag
if you're Black
you always remember things like living in Woodlawn°
with no inside toilet
and if you become famous or something

NIKKI-ROSA.   3 *Woodlawn:* a predominantly black suburb of Cincinnati, Ohio.

they never talk about how happy you were to have your mother
all to yourself and
how good the water felt when you got your bath from one of those
big tubs that folk in chicago barbecue in
and somehow when you talk about home   10
it never gets across how much you
understood their feelings
as the whole family attended meetings about Hollydale
and even though you remember
your biographers never understand   15
your father's pain as he sells his stock
and another dream goes
and though you're poor it isn't poverty that
concerns you
and though they fought a lot   20
it isn't your father's drinking that makes any difference
but only that everybody is together and you
and your sister have happy birthdays and very good christmasses
and I really hope no white person ever has cause to write about me
because they never understand Black love is Black wealth and they'll   25
probably talk about my hard childhood and never understand that
all the while I was quite happy

QUESTIONS

1. To what extent do individual lines, caesurae, and cadences create a rhythm and reinforce the sense of this poem?

2. What points does the speaker make about childhood in general, the childhoods of blacks, and his or her own childhood?

3. What ideas about the ways in which whites understand or misunderstand blacks does this poem explore?

GEORGE HERBERT (1593–1633)

Virtue° _____ *1633*

Sweet day, so cool, so calm, so bright,
The bridal of the earth and sky:
The dew shall weep thy fall tonight;
    For thou must die.

Sweet rose, whose hue, angry° and brave,°   *red; splendid* 5
Bids the rash gazer wipe his eye:
Thy root is ever in its grave,
    And thou must die.

VIRTUE.   The title can allude to (*a*) divine Power operating both outside and inside an individual; (*b*) a characteristic quality or property; (*c*) conformity to divine and moral laws.   *6* rash: eager or sympathetic.

Sweet spring, full of sweet days and roses,
A box where sweets° compacted lie: *perfumes*
My music shows ye have your closes,°
      And all must die.

Only a sweet and virtuous soul,
Like seasoned timber, never gives;°
But though the whole world turn to coal,°
      Then chiefly lives.

11 *closes:* A *close* is the conclusion of a musical composition.   14 *never gives:* i.e., never gives in,
never deteriorates and collapses (like rotted timber).   15 *turn to coal:* the burned-out residue
of the earth and universe after the universal fire on Judgment Day.

QUESTIONS

1. What is the rhyme scheme of this poem? The meter? The form?
2. What points does the speaker make about the day, the rose, spring, and the "sweet and virtuous soul"?

WILLIAM HEYEN   (b. 1940)

Mantle ————————————————————————————— *1980*

      Mantle ran so hard, they said,
      he tore his legs to pieces.
      What is this but spirit?

52 homers in '56, the triple crown.
I was a high school junior, batting
      fourth behind him in a dream.

I prayed for him to quit, before
his lifetime dropped below .300.
But he didn't, and it did.

He makes Brylcreem commercials now,
models with open mouths draped around him
      as they never were in Commerce, Oklahoma,

      where the sandy-haired, wide-shouldered boy
      stood up against his barn,
            lefty for an hour (Ruth, Gehrig),

            then righty (DiMaggio),
         as his father winged them in,
            and the future blew toward him,

               now a fastball, now a slow
               curve hanging
               like a model's smile.

QUESTIONS

1. Describe the shape of the poem, being careful to study the last stanza. Why is this shape appropriate for a famous baseball player?

2. How does the poet use Mantle as a symbol in this poem?

3. Who are Ruth, Gehrig, and DiMaggio? In what ways are they like Mantle?

JOHN HOLLANDER   (b. 1929)

Swan and Shadow ———————————————————— *1969*

                    Dusk
                  Above the
              water hang the
                        loud
                         flies   5
                    Here
                  O so
                  gray
                  then
                  What   A pale signal will appear   10
                  When   Soon before its shadow fades
                  Where   Here in this pool of opened eye
                  In us   No Upon us As at the very edges
                    of where we take shape in the dark air
                      this object bares its image awakening   15
                        ripples of recognition that will
                          brush darkness up into light
even after this bird this hour both drift by atop the perfect sad instant now
                        already passing out of sight
                      toward yet-untroubled reflection   20
                    this image bears its object darkening
                  into memorial shades Scattered bits of
                  light   No of water Or something across
                  water   Breaking up No Being regathered
                  soon   Yet by then a swan will have   25
                  gone   Yes out of mind into what
                    vast
                    pale
                    hush
                    of a   30
                      place
                      past
              sudden dark as
                if a swan
                sang   35

QUESTIONS

1. How effectively and consistenly does the shape image reinforce the meaning?
2. What specific words, phrases, and lines are emphasized by the typographical arrangement? To what extent does this effect give added impact to the poem?
3. How well does the structure echo the verbal images of the poem?
4. Do you find John Hollander's experiment with shaped verse as successful as George Herbert's in "Easter Wings" (p. 761)? If so, demonstrate how it succeeds. If not, explain why.

JOHN KEATS   (1795–1821)

Ode to a Nightingale ———————————————————————— *1819*

1

My heart aches, and a drowsy numbness pains
  My sense, as though of hemlock° I had drunk,   *a poisonous herb*
Or emptied some dull opiate to the drains
  One minute past, and Lethe-wards° had sunk:
'Tis not through envy of thy happy lot,
    But being too happy in thine happiness,—
      That thou, light-winged Dryad° of the trees,
        In some melodious plot
    Of beechen green, and shadows numberless,
      Singest of summer in full-throated ease.

2

O, for a draught of vintage! that hath been
  Cool'd a long age in the deep-delved earth,
Tasting of Flora° and the country green,
  Dance, and Provençal song, and sunburnt mirth!
O for a beaker full of the warm South,
  Full of the true, the blushful Hippocrene,°
    With beaded bubbles winking at the brim,
      And purple-stainèd mouth;
  That I might drink, and leave the world unseen,
    And with thee fade away into the forest dim:

3

Fade far away, dissolve, and quite forget
  What thou among the leaves hast never known,
The weariness, the fever, and the fret

ODE TO A NIGHTINGALE.   4 *Lethe-wards*: toward the river of forgetfulness in Hades, the underworld of Greek mythology.   7 *Dryad*: in Greek mythology, a semidivine tree spirit.   13 *Flora*: the Roman goddess of flowers.   16 *Hippocrene*: the fountain of the Muses on Mt. Helicon in Greek mythology; the phrase thus refers to both the waters of poetic inspiration and a cup of wine.

Here, where men sit and hear each other groan;
Where palsy shakes a few, sad, last gray hairs,   25
  Where youth grows pale, and spectre-thin, and dies;
    Where but to think is to be full of sorrow
      And leaden-eyed despairs,
  Where Beauty cannot keep her lustrous eyes,
    Or new Love pine at them beyond to-morrow.   30

4

Away! away! for I will fly to thee,
  Not charioted by Bacchus° and his pards,°   *leopards*
But on the viewless wings of Poesy,°   *poetry*
  Though the dull brain perplexes and retards:
Already with thee! tender is the night,   35
  And haply the Queen-Moon is on her throne,
    Cluster'd around by all her starry Fays;°   *fairies*
      But here there is no light,
  Save what from heaven is with the breezes blown
  Through verdurous glooms and winding mossy ways.   40

5

I cannot see what flowers are at my feet,
  Nor what soft incense hangs upon the boughs,
But, in embalmed° darkness, guess each sweet   *fragrant*
  Wherewith the seasonable month endows
The grass, the thicket, and the fruit-tree wild;   45
  White hawthorn, and the pastoral eglantine;°   *honeysuckle*
    Fast fading violets cover'd up in leaves;
      And mid-May's eldest child,
  The coming musk-rose, full of dewy wine,
    The murmurous haunt of flies on summer eves.   50

6

Darkling° I listen; and, for many a time   *in the dark*
  I have been half in love with easeful Death,
Call'd him soft names in many a musèd rhyme,
  To take into the air my quiet breath;
Now more than ever seems it rich to die,   55
  To cease upon the midnight with no pain,
    While thou art pouring forth thy soul abroad
      In such an ecstasy!
  Still wouldst thou sing, and I have ears in vain—
    To thy high requiem become a sod.   60

7

Thou wast not born for death, immortal Bird!
  No hungry generations tread thee down;
The voice I hear this passing night was heard

---

32 *Bacchus*: the Greek god of wine. See p. 1070.

In ancient days by emperor and clown:
Perhaps the self-same song that found a path
  Through the sad heart of Ruth,° when, sick for home,
    She stood in tears amid the alien corn;°   *wheat, grain*
      The same that oft-times hath
  Charm'd magic casements, opening on the foam
    Of perilous seas, in faery lands forlorn.

8

Forlorn! the very word is like a bell
 To toll me back from thee to my sole self!
Adieu! the fancy° cannot cheat so well   *imagination*
  As she is fam'd to do, deceiving elf.
Adieu! adieu! thy plaintive anthem fades
  Past the near meadows, over the still stream,
    Up the hill-side; and now 'tis buried deep
      In the next valley-glades:
  Was it a vision, or a waking dream?
  Fled is that music:—Do I wake or sleep?

66 *Ruth:* the widow of Boaz in the biblical Book of Ruth.

QUESTIONS

1. Formulate the structure (meter of each line and rhyme scheme) of the stanzas. What traditional form is employed here?

2. What is the speaker's mental and emotional state in stanza 1? What similes are employed to describe this condition?

3. What does the speaker want in stanza 2? Whom does he want to join? Why? From what aspects of the world (stanza 3) does he want to escape?

4. How do the speaker's mood and perspective change in stanza 4? How does he achieve this transition? What characterizes the world that the speaker enters in stanza 5? What senses are employed to describe this world?

5. What does the speaker establish about the nightingale's song in the seventh stanza? What does the song come to symbolize?

CLAUDE MCKAY (1890–1948)

In Bondage ———————————————————————— *1922*

I would be wandering in distant fields
Where man, and bird, and beast, lives leisurely,
And the old earth is kind, and ever yields
Her goodly gifts to all her children free;
Where life is fairer, lighter, less demanding,
And boys and girls have time and space for play
Before they come to years of understanding—

Somewhere I would be singing, far away.
For life is greater than the thousand wars
Men wage for it in their insatiate lust,   10
And will remain like the eternal stars,
When all that shines to-day is drift and dust.

But I am bound with you in your mean graves,
O black men, simple slaves of ruthless slaves.

QUESTIONS

1. What is the meter of this poem? The rhyme scheme? The form? To what extent does the form organize the speaker's thoughts?

2. Lines 1–8 present a conditional (rather than actual) situation that the speaker desires. What word signals this nature? What is the speaker's wish?

3. What point does the speaker make about life in lines 9–12?

4. How does the couplet undermine the rest of the poem? What single word conveys this reversal? How effectively do the rhymes clinch the poem's meaning? What is the speaker telling us about the lives of African Americans?

JOHN MILTON   (1608–1674)

When I Consider How My Light Is Spent° _____ *1655*

When I consider how my light is spent
  Ere half my days, in this dark world and wide,
  And that one talent° which is death to hide,
  Lodged with me useless, though my soul more bent
To serve therewith my Maker, and present   5
  My true account, lest he returning chide;
  "Doth God exact day-labor, light denied?"
  I fondly° ask; but Patience to prevent°   *foolishly; forestall*
That murmur, soon replies, "God doth not need
  Either man's work or his own gifts; who best   10
  Bear his mild yoke, they serve him best. His state
Is kingly. Thousands at his bidding speed
  And post o'er land and ocean without rest;
  They also serve who only stand and wait."

WHEN I CONSIDER HOW MY LIGHT IS SPENT.   Milton began to go blind in the late 1640s and was completely blind by 1651.   3 *talent:* both a skill and a reference to the talents discussed in the parable in Matthew 25:14–30.

QUESTIONS

1. What is the meter of this poem? The rhyme scheme? The closed form?

2. To what extent do the two major divisions of this form organize the poem's ideas?

3. What problem is raised in the octave? What are the speaker's complaints? Who is the speaker in the sestet? How are the earlier conflicts resolved?

4. Explore the word *talent* and relate its various meanings to the poem as a whole.

EDWIN MORGAN   (b. 1920)

The Computer's First Christmas Card ————————————— *1968*

```
jollymerry
hollyberry
jollyberry
merryholly
happyjolly
jollyjelly
jellybelly
bellymerry
hollyheppy
jollyMolly
marryJerry
merryHarry
hoppyBarry
heppyJarry
boppyheppy
berryjorry
jorryjolly
moppyjelly
Mollymerry
Jerryjolly
bellyboppy
jorryhoppy
hollymoppy
Barrymerry
Jarryhappy
happyboppy
boppyjolly
jollymerry
merrymerry
merrymerry
merryChris
ammerryasa
Chrismerry
asMERRYCHR
YSANTHEMUM
```

QUESTIONS

1. To what extent is the effect of this work visual? What aspects or devices link it to a computer?

2. The writer (or computer) has generated some interesting word variations and
    images. What is the logic of the movement from line to line?

3. How successful is this work in conveying ideas or images of Christmas? How far
    away from Christmas does "the computer" wander? What do you make of the fact
    that the work ends "asMERRYCHR / YSANTHEMUM"?

4. Why might you consider this a poem?

DUDLEY RANDALL   (b. 1914)

Ballad of Birmingham° ————————————————————— *1966*

(On the bombing of a church in Birmingham, Alabama, 1963)

"Mother dear, may I go downtown
Instead of out to play,
And march the streets of Birmingham
In a Freedom March today?"

"No, baby, no, you may not go,   5
For the dogs are fierce and wild,
And clubs and hoses, guns and jails
Aren't good for a little child."

"But, mother, I won't be alone.
Other children will go with me,   10
And march the streets of Birmingham
To make our country free."

"No, baby, no, you may not go,
For I fear those guns will fire.
But you may go to church instead   15
And sing in the children's choir."

She has combed and brushed her night-dark hair,
And bathed rose petal sweet,
And drawn white gloves on her small brown hands,
And white shoes on her feet.   20

The mother smiled to know her child
Was in the sacred place,
But that smile was the last smile
To come upon her face.

For when she heard the explosion,   25
Her eyes grew wet and wild.
She raced through the streets of Birmingham
Calling for her child.

BALLAD OF BIRMINGHAM.   Four black children were killed when the 16th Street Baptist
Church in Birmingham, Alabama, was bombed in 1963. A man was finally indicted for the murders in 1977 and convicted in 1982.

She clawed through bits of glass and brick,
Then lifted out a shoe
"Oh, here's the shoe my baby wore,
But, baby, where are you?"

QUESTIONS

1. Formulate the structure (meter, rhyme scheme, stanza form) of this poem. What traditional closed form is employed here?
2. Who is the speaker in stanzas 1 and 3? In stanzas 2 and 4? How are quotation and repetition employed to create tension?
3. What ironies do you find in the mother's assumptions? In the poem as a whole? In the society pictured in the poem?
4. Compare the poem to "Sir Patrick Spens" (p. 553) and to "Barbara Allan" (p. 913). How are the structures of all three alike? To what extent do all three deal with the same type of subject matter?

PERCY BYSSHE SHELLEY   (1792–1822)

Ode to the West Wind ————————————————————— *1820*

I

O wild West Wind, thou breath of Autumn's being,
Thou, from whose unseen presence the leaves dead
Are driven, like ghosts from an enchanter fleeing,

Yellow, and black, and pale, and hectic° red,
Pestilence-stricken multitudes: O Thou,
Who chariotest to their dark wintry bed

The winged seeds, where they lie cold and low,
Each like a corpse within its grave, until
Thine azure sister of the Spring° shall blow

Her clarion o'er the dreaming earth, and fill
(Driving sweet buds like flocks to feed in air)
With living hues and odours plain and hill:

Wild Spirit, which art moving everywhere;
Destroyer and Preserver; hear, O hear!

II

Thou on whose stream, 'mid the steep sky's commotion,
Loose clouds like Earth's decaying leaves are shed,
Shook from the tangled boughs of Heaven and Ocean,

ODE TO THE WEST WIND.   4 *hectic:* a tubercular fever that produces flushed cheeks.   9
Spring: the wind that will blow in the spring.

Angels of rain and lightning: there are spread
On the blue surface of thine aery surge,
Like the bright hair uplifted from the head   20

Of some fierce Maenad,° even from the dim verge
Of the horizon to the zenith's height,
The locks of the approaching storm. Thou Dirge

Of the dying year, to which this closing night
Will be the dome of a vast sepulchre,   25
Vaulted with all thy congregated might

Of vapours,° from whose solid atmosphere   *clouds*
Black rain and fire and hail will burst: O hear!

III
Thou who didst waken from his summer dreams
The blue Mediterranean, where he lay,   30
Lulled by the coil of his crystalline streams,

Beside a pumice isle in Baiae's bay,°
And saw in sleep old palaces and towers
Quivering within the wave's intenser day,

All overgrown with azure moss and flowers   35
So sweet, the sense faints picturing them! Thou
For whose path the Atlantic's level powers

Cleave themselves into chasms, while far below
The sea-blooms and the oozy woods which wear
The sapless foliage of the ocean, know   40

Thy voice, and suddenly grow grey with fear,
And tremble and despoil themselves: O hear!

IV
If I were a dead leaf thou mightest bear;
If I were a swift cloud to fly with thee;
A wave to pant beneath thy power, and share   45

The impulse of thy strength, only less free
Than thou, O Uncontrollable! If even
I were as in my boyhood, and could be

The comrade of thy wanderings over Heaven,
As then, when to outstrip thy skiey speed   50
Scarce seemed a vision; I would ne'er have striven

As thus with thee in prayer in my sore need,
Oh! lift me as a wave, a leaf, a cloud!
I fall upon thorns of life! I bleed!

A heavy weight of hours has chained and bowed   55
One too like thee: tameless, and swift, and proud.

21 *Maenad*: a frenzied female worshipper of Dionysus, the god of wine and fertility in Greek mythology.   32 *Baiae's bay*: a bay of the Mediterranean Sea west of Naples, famous for the elaborate villas built on the shore by Roman emperors.

V

Make me thy lyre,° even as the forest is:
What if my leaves are falling like its own!
The tumult of thy mighty harmonies

Will take from both a deep, autumnal tone,
Sweet though in sadness. Be thou, Spirit fierce,
My spirit! Be thou me, impetuous one!

Drive my dead thoughts over the universe
Like withered leaves to quicken a new birth!
And, by the incantation of this verse,

Scatter, as from an unextinguished hearth
Ashes and sparks, my words among mankind!
Be through my lips to unawakened Earth

The trumpet of a prophecy! O Wind,
If Winter comes, can Spring be far behind?

57 *Lyre:* an Aeolian harp, a musical device which is sounded by the wind blowing across strings.

QUESTIONS

1. Formulate the structure (meter of each line and rhyme scheme) of the stanzas. What two traditional closed forms are combined in this poem?
2. How many times (and where) is the *e* rhyme of the first stanza repeated as a rhyme sound throughout the poem? What is the effect of this repetition?
3. What aspect of the natural world does the wind affect in the first section of the poem? The second section? The third?
4. What does the speaker assert (in section 4) that time has done to him? What does he want from the West Wind? What does he want to become?
5. To what extent are the speaker's thoughts and feelings organized by the poem's five sections? What is the logical progression from section to section?
6. What does the West Wind symbolize? Compare this poem to Keats's "Ode to a Nightingale." How are the nightingale's song and the West Wind related to each other as symbols?

PERCY BYSSHE SHELLEY   (1792–1822)

Ozymandias ————————————————————————— *1818*

I met a traveller from an antique land,
Who said—"Two vast and trunkless legs of stone
Stand in the desert. . . . Near them, on the sand,
Half sunk, a shattered visage lies, whose frown,
And wrinkled lip, and sneer of cold command,
Tell that its sculptor well those passions read
Which yet survive, stamped on these lifeless things,
The hand that mocked them, and the heart that fed;
And on the pedestal, these words appear;

'My name is Ozymandias, King of Kings,   10
Look on my Works, ye Mighty, and despair!'
Nothing beside remains. Round the decay
Of that colossal Wreck, boundless and bare
The lone and level sands stretch far away."

QUESTIONS

1. What is the meter of this poem? The rhyme scheme? What traditional closed
    form is modified here? How do the modifications affect the poem?
2. To what extent are content and meaning shaped by the closed form? What is
    described in the octave? In the sestet?
3. Characterize Ozymandias (thought to be Ramses II, Pharoah of Egypt, who died
    in 1225 B.C.) from the way he is portrayed in this poem.

MARY ELLEN SOLT (b. 1920)

Forsythia _____ *1966*

QUESTIONS

1. Is this a poem or is it rather what is called in art a "wordwork"? What does this work tell you about forsythia?

2. When this work was originally published, it was printed over a square of yellow. What additional visual effect might have been produced by this color?

3. What is the meaning of the dots and dashes between each letter of "FORSYTHIA"? What is the link between this device and the word "TELEGRAM"?

MAY SWENSON   (1919–1989)

Women ———————————————————————————— *1968*

Women	Or they
should be	should be
pedestals	little horses
moving	those wooden
pedestals	sweet
moving	oldfashioned
to the	painted
motions	rocking
of men	horses

the gladdest things in the toyroom

The	feelingly
pegs	and then
of their	unfeelingly
ears	To be
so familiar	joyfully
and dear	ridden
to the trusting	rockingly
fists	ridden until
To be chafed	the restored

egos dismount and the legs stride away

Immobile	willing
sweetlipped	to be set
sturdy	into motion
and smiling	Women
women	should be
should always	pedestals
be waiting	to men

QUESTIONS

1. Is this poem an instance of closed form, open form, or visual poetry? In what different ways or sequences can it be read? How do the different sequences change the meaning?

2. How well does the image of the poem reinforce its meaning? Would the effect be different if the columns of words were straight instead of undulating?

3. To what extent do repetition and alliteration help to organize the poem and underscore its sense? Note especially *w, m, f, r,* and *s* sounds.

4. What does this poem *say* that women should be? Does it mean what it says? How are men characterized? In what way is this poem ironic?

DYLAN THOMAS   (1914–1953)

Do Not Go Gentle Into That Good Night ————————————— *1951*

Do not go gentle into that good night,
Old age should burn and rave at close of day;
Rage, rage against the dying of the light.

Though wise men at their end know dark is right,
Because their words had forked no lightning they   5
Do not go gentle into that good night.

Good men, the last wave by, crying how bright
Their frail deeds might have danced in a green bay,
Rage, rage against the dying of the light.

Wild men who caught and sang the sun in flight,   10
And learn, too late, they grieved it on its way,
Do not go gentle into that good night.

Grave men, near death, who see with blinding sight
Blind eyes could blaze like meteors and be gay,
Rage, rage against the dying of the light.   15

And you, my father, there on the sad height,
Curse, bless, me now with your fierce tears, I pray.
Do not go gentle into that good night.
Rage, rage against the dying of the light.

QUESTIONS

1. This poem is written in a traditional closed form called the **villanelle,** which was developed in France during the Middle Ages. A villanelle may be nineteen lines long. There are additional rules governing the length and structure of stanzas, the rhyme scheme, and the repetition of complete lines. Try to formulate these rules. To look at another example, see Roethke's "The Waking" (p. 979).

2. What do you conclude about the speaker, listener, and situation here?

3. What four different kinds of men does the speaker discuss in lines 4–15? What do they have in common?

4. What puns and connotative words can you find in this poem? Consider the *good* of "good night" and the word *grave* (line 13).

JEAN TOOMER   (1894–1967)

Reapers ———————————————————————— *1923*

Black reapers with the sound of steel on stones
Are sharpening scythes. I see them place the hones
In their hip-pockets as a thing that's done,
And start their silent swinging, one by one.
Black horses drive a mower through the weeds,
And there, a field rat, startled, squealing bleeds,
His belly close to ground. I see the blade,
Blood-stained, continue cutting weeds and shade.

QUESTIONS

1. What is the poem's meter? The rhyme scheme? The form? What is the difference
    between Toomer's use of the form and Dryden's?
2. How do the images of this poem relate to each other? How does the image of
    the bleeding field rat and the "blood-stained" blade heighten the impact?
3. How does alliteration unify this poem and make sound echo sense? Note espe-
    cially the *s* and *b* sounds, and the phrase *silent swinging.*

WILLIAM CARLOS WILLIAMS   (1883–1963)

The Dance ———————————————————————— *1944*

In Breughel's° great picture, The Kermess,
the dancers go round, they go round and
around, the squeal and the blare and the
tweedle of bagpipes, a bugle and fiddles
tipping their bellies (round as the thick-
sided glasses whose wash they impound)
their hips and their bellies off balance
to turn them. Kicking and rolling about
the Fair Grounds, swinging their butts, those
shanks must be sound to bear up under such
rollicking measures, prance as the dance
in Breughel's great picture, The Kermess.

THE DANCE.   1 *Breughel's:* Pieter Breughel (ca. 1525–1569), a Flemish painter. *The Kermess*
shows peasants dancing in celebration of the anniversary of the founding of a church (*church mass*).

QUESTIONS

1. What effect is produced by repeating the first line as the last line?
2. How do repetition, alliteration, assonance, onomatopoeia, and internal rhyme
    affect the tempo, feeling, and meaning of the poem? How do the numerous par-
    ticiples (like *tipping, kicking, rolling*) make sound echo sense?

The Peasant Dance by Pieter Brueghel the Elder, Kunsthistorisches Museum, Vienna, Foto Marburg/Art Resource, NY

3. What words are capitalized? What effect is produced by omitting the capital letters at the beginning of each line? How does this typographical choice reinforce the sound and the sense of the poem?

4. Most of the lines of this poem are run-on rather than end-stopped, and many of them end with fairly weak words such as *and, the, about,* and *such.* What effect is produced through these techniques?

5. How successful is Williams in making the words and sentence rhythms echo the visual rhythms in Breughel's painting? Why is this open form more appropriate to the images of the poem than any closed form could be?

WRITING ABOUT FORM IN POETRY

Essays about form in poetry should demonstrate a relationship between the structure and content of the poem you have selected. Do not discuss form or shape in isolation, for then your essay would be no more than a detailed description. As with essays about meter, sound, and rhyme, composition follows a double process of discovery, in which you investigate both sense and form.

The first thing to do in prewriting is to examine the poem's main ideas. Consider the various elements that contribute to the poem's impact and effectiveness: the speaker, listener, setting, situation, diction, imagery, and rhetorical devices. Once you understand these, it will be easier to establish a connection between form and content.

It will be helpful to prepare a worksheet much like the ones for writing about prosody (pp. 738, 739, 740). In this case the worksheet will highlight structural elements. For closed forms, these will include the rhyme scheme, meter, line lengths, and stanzaic pattern. They may also include significant words and phrases linking stanzas together. The worksheet for an open-form poem should indicate variables such as rhythm and phrases, pauses and enjambements, significant words that are isolated or emphasized through typography, and patterns of repeated sounds, words, phrases, and images.

Questions for Discovering Ideas

CLOSED FORM

- What is the predominant meter? Line length? Rhyme scheme? To what extent do these establish and/or reinforce the form?
- What is the form of each stanza or unit? What building blocks does the poet use? How many stanzas or divisions does the poem contain? How does the poem establish a pattern? How is the pattern repeated?
- What is the form of the poem (e.g., a ballad or sonnet)? In what ways is the poem traditional, and what variations does it introduce? What is the effect of the variations?
- How effectively does the structure create or reinforce the poem's internal logic? What topical, logical, or thematic progressions can unite the various parts of the poem?
- To what extent does the form organize the images of the poem? Are key images developed within single units or stanzas? Do images recur in several units?
- To what extent does the form organize and bring out the ideas or emotions of the poem?

OPEN FORM

- What does the poem look like on the page? What is the relationship of its shape to its meaning?
- How does the poet use variable line lengths, spaces, punctuation, capitalization, and the like to shape the poem? How do these variables contribute to the poem's sense and impact?
- What rhythms are built into the poem through language or typography? How are these relevant to the poem's content?
- What is the poem's progression of ideas, images, and/or emotions? How is the logic created and what does it contribute?
- How does form or typography isolate or group, and thus emphasize, various words and phrases? What is the effect of such emphasis?
- What patterns do you discover of words and sounds? To what degree do the patterns create order and structure? How are they related to the sense of the poem?

Strategies for Organizing Ideas

In developing your central idea, it is not enough simply to assert that form organizes and underscores meaning. You should explain *how* this occurs. If you are planning an essay on Shakespeare's Sonnet 116, "Let Me Not to the Marriage of True Minds," for example, you might argue that form controls meaning. Such an assertion, while true, is not an adequate central idea. A better formulation might be this: "The sonnet form organizes the speaker's thoughts into a three-part argument in which each quatrain examines a different aspect of love's permanence, and the couplet provides a conclusion."

Sometimes the formulation of a central idea involves a two-step connection between form and content. In planning an essay on Williams's "The Dance," for instance, you might decide that meaning is most effectively reinforced and echoed through rhythm. Hence, you would focus on the ways in which form creates rhythm, and your central idea would link form to rhythm and meaning. Above all, make sure that the evidence you are developing is clearly relevant to your main idea. If you find that your examples are leading you into digressions, you should rethink the essay and make revisions to bring your digressions into your main line of thought.

Your introduction may contain some general remarks about the poem, but it should focus on the connection between form and substance. It should include your statement about the ways in which structure and content interact together, with a brief listing of the specific topics that you will be discussing.

Early in one of your paragraphs, it is important to describe the formal characteristics of your poem, using schemes and numbers. With closed forms, this paragraph will detail such standard features as the traditional form, meter, rhyme scheme, stanzaic structure, and number of stanzas. With open-form poetry, the paragraph should focus on the most striking and significant features of the verse. The problem of this sort of paragraph is to present the essential information while preserving the central idea of your essay. Most likely, you can succeed if you relate the form to the poem's development of ideas.

The order in which you deal with your topics is entirely up to you. It may be that you have uncovered a good deal of information about a technical feature such as alliteration, or rhyme, or you may wish to stress the ways in which words or types of phrases and clauses form a developing pattern of ideas. Always, be sure that your references to form are integrated with a discussion of the poem's content. Remember that you are not making a paraphrase or a general explication of the poem, but rather that you are demonstrating how the poet has used the form—either an open or a closed one—in the service of meaning.

The conclusion of your essay might contain any additional observations about shape or structure that seem relevant. It should also include a summation of your argument. Here, as in all essays about literature, you should make sure that you reach an actual conclusion rather than simply a stopping point.

SAMPLE ESSAY

Form and Meaning in Herbert's "Virtue"°

[1]
George Herbert's devotional four-stanza poem "Virtue" (1633) contrasts the mortality of worldly things with the immortality of the "virtuous soul." This is not an uncommon topic in religious poetry and hymns, and there is nothing particularly unusual about this contrast. What is unusual, however, is the simplicity and directness of Herbert's expressions, and the way in which he integrates his ideas within the confinement of his stanzaic song pattern. Each part of the poem organizes the images logically and underscores the supremacy of life over death."* Through control over line and stanza groupings, rhyme scheme, and repeated sounds and words, Herbert's stanzas create a structural and visual distinction between the "sweet" soul and the rest of creation.†

[2]
Herbert's control over lines within the stanzas is particularly strong. Each stanza follows the same basic a b a b rhyme scheme. Since some rhyme sounds and words are repeated throughout the first three stanzas, however, the structure of the poem may be formulated as 4a 4b 4a 2b, 4c 4b 4c 2b, 4d 4b 4d 2b, 4e 4f 4e 2f. Each stanza thus contains three lines of iambic tetrameter with a final line of iambic dimeter—an unusual pattern that creates a unique emphasis. In the first three stanzas, the dimeter lines repeat the phrase "must die," while in the last stanza the contrast is made on the words "Then chiefly lives." These rhythms require a sensitive reading, and they powerfully underscore Herbert's idea that death is conquered by eternal life.

[3]
Like individual lines, Herbert's stanzaic structure provides the poem's pattern of organization and logic. The first stanza focuses on the image of the "Sweet day," comparing the day to "The bridal of the earth and sky" (line 2) and asserting that the day inevitably "must die." Similarly, the second stanza focuses on the image of a "Sweet rose," and asserts that it too "must die." The third stanza shifts to the image of "Sweet spring." Here the poet blends the images of the first two stanzas into the third by noting that the "Sweet spring" is "full of sweet days and roses" (line 9). The stanza concludes with the summarizing claim that "all must die." In this way, the third stanza is the climax of Herbert's imagery of beauty and mortality. The last stanza introduces a new image—"a sweet and virtuous soul"—and an assertion which is the opposite of the ideas expressed in the previous three. Although the day, the rose, and the spring "must die," the soul "never" deteriorates, but "chiefly lives" even though "the whole world turn to coal" (line 15). With its key image of the "virtuous soul," this last stanza marks the logical conclusion of Herbert's argument. The pattern of organization of the lyric form allows this key image of the one thing that lives to be separated structurally from the images of things that die.

[4]
This structural organization of images and ideas is repeated and reinforced by other techniques that Herbert employs within the poem's form. The rhyme scheme, for example, links the first three stanzas while isolating the

° See p. 767 for this poem.
* Central idea.
† Thesis sentence.

fourth. That the b rhyme is repeated at the ends of the second and fourth lines of each of the first three stanzas makes these stanzas into a complete unit. The fourth stanza, however is different, both in content and in rhyme. The stanza introduces the concept of immortality, and it also introduces entirely new rhymes, replacing the b rhyme with an f rhyme. Thus the rhyme scheme, by sound alone, parallels the poem's imagery and logic.

[5] As a complement to the rhyming sounds, the poem also demonstrates organizing patterns of assonance. Most notable is the o͞o sound, which is repeated throughout the first three stanzas in the words cool, dew, whose, hue, root, and music. In Herbert's time, the sound was also prominent in the word thou, so that in the first three stanzas the o͞o, which is not unlike a moan (certainly appropriate to things that die), is repeated eight times. In the last stanza there is a stress on the ō sound, in only, soul, though, whole, and coal. While oh may also be a moan, in this context it is more like an exclamation, in keeping with the triumph contained in the final line.

[6] Herbert's repetition of key words and phrases also distinguishes the first three stanzas from the last stanza. Each of the first three stanzas begins with sweet and ends with must die. These repetitions stress both the beauty and the mortality of worldly things. In the last stanza, however, this repetition is abandoned, just as the stress on immortality transcends mortality. The sweet that begins each of the first three stanzas is replaced by Only (line 13). Similarly, must die is replaced with chiefly lives. Both substitutions separate this final stanza from the three previous stanzas. More important, the shift in the verbal pattern emphasizes the conceptual transition from death to the virtuous soul's immortality.

[7] It is therefore clear that the lyric form of Herbert's "Virtue" provides an organizational pattern for the poem's images and ideas. At the same time, the pattern of stanzas and the rhyme scheme allows the poet to draw a valid structural distinction between the corruptible world and the immortal soul. The closed form of this poem is not arbitrary or incidental; it is an integral way of asserting the singularity of the key image, the "sweet and virtuous soul."

Commentary on the Essay

The introductory paragraph establishes the groundwork of the essay—the treatment of form in relationship to content. The main idea is that each part of the poem represents a complete blending of image, logic, and meaning.

Paragraph 2 , the first in the body, demonstrates how the poem's schematic formulation is integrated into Herbert's contrast of death and life. In this respect the paragraph demonstrates how a formal enumeration may be integrated within an essay's thematic development.

The focus of paragraph 3 is the organization of both images and ideas from stanza to stanza. Paragraph 4 begins with a transitional sentence that repeats part of the essay's central idea and, at the same time, connects it to paragraph 3. In the same way, paragraph 4 is closely tied to both paragraphs 1 and 3. The main topic here, the rhyme scheme of "Virtue," is introduced in the second sentence, which asserts that it also reinforces the division between mortality and immortality. On much the same topic, paragraph 5, which introduces Herbert's use of assonance, may be seen as integral in the poem's blending of form and content.

Paragraph 6 takes up the last structural element mentioned in the introduction—the repetition of key words and phrases. The paragraph asserts that repeated words and phrases underscore the poem's division between mortality and immortality.

Paragraph 7, the conclusion, provides a brief overview and summation of the essay's argument. In addition, it concludes that form in "Virtue" is neither arbitrary nor incidental, but rather an integral part of the poem's meaning.

WRITING TOPICS

1. Describe the use of the ode form as exemplified by Shelley's "Ode to the West Wind" and Keats's "Ode to a Nightingale." What patterns of regularity do you find? What differences do you find in the form and content of the poems? How do you account for these differences?

2. How do Cummings, Thomas, Randall, and Dryden use different forms to consider the subject of death (in "Buffalo Bill's defunct," "Do not Go Gentle," "Ballad of Birmingham," and "To the memory of Mr. Oldham")? What differences in form and treatment do you find? What similarities do you find, despite these differences?

3. Write a visual poem, and explain the principles on which you develop your lines. Here are some possible topics (just to get you started): a "boom box," a duck, a beer bottle, a sweater, a snow shovel, a skunk. After finishing your poem, write a short essay that considers these questions: What are the strengths and limitations of the visual form, according to your experience? Does the form help make you serious or comic? Does it encourage any particularly creative language or development of ideas?

4. Write a haiku. Be sure to fit your poem to the 5–7–5 pattern of syllables. What challenges and problems do you encounter in this form? Once you have completed your haiku (which, to be traditional, should be on a topic concerned with nature), try to cut the number of syllables to 4–5–4. Explain how you establish the first haiku pattern, and also explain how you go about cutting the total number of syllables. Be sure to explain what kinds of words you use (length, choice of diction, etc.).

5. Consider the structural arrangement and shaping of the following works: Brueghel's painting *La Kermesse* (p. 783), Hollander's "Swan and Shadow" (p. 769), Wagoner's "March for a One-Man Band" (p. 733), Ginsberg's "A Supermarket in California" (p. 765), and Williams's "The Dance" (p. 782). How do painter and poets utilize topic, arrangement, shape, and space to draw attention to their main ideas? How does Hollander's "Swan and Shadow" blend poetic and artistic techniques? (You may consider other poems, and/or stories, in your discussion.)

21

Symbolism and Allusion: Windows to a Wide Expanse of Meaning

Symbolism refers to the use of symbols in works of art. As we have noted in Chapter 9, a **symbol** has meaning in and of itself, but it also stands for something else, like the flag for the country or the school song for the school. Symbols occur in stories as well as in poems, but poetry relies more heavily on symbolism because it is more concise and because it comprises more forms than fiction, which is always based in a narrative structure.

Words are symbols, for they stand for various objects without actually being those objects. When we say *horse*, for example, or *tree*, these words are not horses or trees, but are only symbols of horses and trees. They direct our minds to real horses and real trees in the real world that we have seen and can therefore easily imagine. In literature, however, symbolism implies a special relationship that extends beyond our ordinary understanding of words, descriptions, and arguments.

SYMBOLISM AND MEANING IN POETRY

Symbolism goes beyond the close referral of word to thing; it is more like a window through which one can get a glimpse at the extensive world outside. Because poetry is compact, its descriptions and portrayals of experience are brief. Symbolism is therefore one of its primary characteristics. It is a shorthand way of referring to extensive ideas or attitudes that otherwise would be impossible to state in the brief format of poetry. Thus William Butler Yeats, who believed that the city of Constantinople, or Byzantium, represented a pinnacle of human civilization, used the city as a symbol of human achievement in peace, politics, and particularly art and literature. His poem "Sailing to Byzantium" (p. 1011) does not expand upon the full meaning and interpretation of this idea, for it would take a long history and a detailed analysis of Byzantine art and literature to do that. But the poem does use Byzantium as a symbol of excellence—a standard by which Yeats measures what he thought was the declining state of twentieth-century civilization. In short, the use of symbols is a means of encapsulating or crystallizing information—a means of saying a great deal within a short space.

Symbolism in Operation

Symbolism expands meaning beyond the normal connotation of words. For example, at the time of William Blake (1757–1827), the word *tiger* meant both a large, wild cat and also the specific animal we know today as a tiger. The word's connotation therefore links it with wildness and predation. As a symbol in "The Tyger," however, Blake uses the animal as a stand-in for the negativism and evil in the world—the savage, wild forces that prompt human beings to evil actions. Thus the tiger as a symbol is more meaningful than either the denotation or the connotation of the word would indicate. A visual comparison may be made with Goya's painting "The Colossus", in which the

Francisco de Goya, *The Colossus.* (Museo del Prado, Madrid, Spain)

giant pugilistic figure above the tiny figures in the landscape suggests the combination of anger, defiance, and ruthlessness that are unleashed in warfare.

CULTURAL OR UNIVERSAL SYMBOLS.   In poetry, some symbols possess a ready-made, clearly agreed upon meaning. These are **cultural** or **universal symbols** (also described in Chapter 9). Many such symbols, like the tiger, are drawn directly from nature. Springtime and morning are universal symbols signifying beginnings, growth, hope, optimism, and love. A reference to spring is normal and appropriate in a love poem. If the topic were death, however, the symbol of spring would still be appropriate as the basis of ironic observations about the untimeliness with which death claims its victims.

Cultural symbols are drawn from history and custom. Many Judeo-Christian religious symbols, for example, have been taken up by poets. References to the lamb, Eden, Egyptian bondage, shepherds, exile, the temple, blood, water, bread, the cross, and wine—all Jewish and/or Christian symbols—appear over and over again in poetry of the English language. Sometimes these symbols occur in purely devotional poems. At other times they may be contrasted with symbols of warfare and corruption to show how extensively people neglect their moral and religious obligations.

CONTEXTUAL, PRIVATE, OR AUTHORIAL SYMBOLS.   Symbols that are not widely or universally recognized are termed **contextual**, **private**, or **authorial symbols** (also discussed in Chapter 9). Some of these have a natural relationship with the objects and ideas being symbolized. Snow, for example, is cold and white, and when it falls it covers everything. A poet can thus exploit this quality and make snow a symbol. At the beginning of the long poem "The Waste Land," for example, T. S. Eliot ironically uses snow to symbolize a retreat from life, an intellectual and moral hibernation. Another poem utilizing snow as a symbol linking the living and the dead both literally and figuratively is the following one:

VIRGINIA SCOTT   (b. 1938)

Snow _____*1977*

A doe stands at the roadside,
spirit of those who have lived here
and passed known through our memory.
The doe stands at the edge of the icy road,
then darts back into the woods.   5

Snow falling,
mother-spirit hovering,
white on the drops in the road and fields,
light from the windows
of the old house   10
brightening the snow.

Presences: mother,
grandmother,
here in their place
at the foot of *ben lomond,*
green trees black in the hemlock night.

The doe stands at the edge of the icy road,
then darts back into the woods.

Golden Grove, New Brunswick, Canada
January 5, 1977

QUESTIONS

1. How is snow described in the poem? How and where is it seen? As a symbol, what does it signify in relationship to the doe, the memory of persons, the mother-spirit, the old house, the light, the presences, the mountains, and the trees?

2. Explain the structural purpose for which the doe is mentioned three times in the poem, with lines 17 and 18 repeating 4 and 5. As a symbol, what might the doe signify?

3. What are the relationships described in the poem between memory of the past and existence in the present? What does the symbolism contribute to your understanding of these relationships?

This poem describes a real circumstance at a real place at a real time; the poet has even provided an actual location and date, just as we do when writing a letter. We may therefore presume that the snow was real snow, falling at a time in the evening when lights had been put on in the nearby house. This detail by itself would be sufficient as a realistic image. But as Scott develops the poem, the snow symbolizes the link between the speaker's memory of the past and perception of the present. The reality of the moment is suffused with the memory of the people—mother, / grandmother"—who "lived here." The poet is meditating on the idea that individuals, though they may often be alone like the speaker, are never alone as long as they have a vivid memory of the past. Just as the snow covers the scene, the past and present are always connected.

At the poem's conclusion, the doe darting into the woods suggests a linking of the present with the future (i.e., as long as there are woods, there will be does darting into them). Both the snow and the deer are private and contextual symbols, for they are established and developed within the poem, and do not possess symbolic value elsewhere. Through the symbolism, therefore, the poet has converted a private moment into an idea of general significance.

Similarly, references to other ordinary materials may be symbolic if the poet emphasizes them sufficiently. Keats's "La Belle Dame Sans Merci," for example (p. 806), opens and closes with the image of withered sedge, or grass. What might seem like an appropriate detail therefore becomes symbolic of the loss and bewilderment felt by people when the persons they love seem to be unreal, faithless, and destructive rather than genuine, loyal, and supportive.

The Integration of Symbols into Poetry

Poets may integrate symbols into their poems through the use of single words, the introduction of various actions, the description of settings, the development of characters and character traits, and the control of situations.

SINGLE WORDS.   With general and universal symbols, a single word is often sufficient, as with references to the lamb, shepherd, cross, blood, bread, and wine, or to summer and winter, or to drought and flood, morning and night, heat and shade, storm and calm, or feast and famine. The nightingale is an example of how a single word may become instantly symbolic. Because the bird has such a beautiful song, it frequently symbolizes natural, unspoiled beauty as contrasted with the contrived attempts by human beings to create beauty. Keats refers to the bird in this way in his "Ode to a Nightingale," and he compares the virtually eternal beauty of this singer with his own mortality.

Anne Finch, in her poem "To the Nightingale" (p. 690), makes a similar comparison between the poet and the bird, stating (lines 11-12): "the unhappy poet's breast, / Like thine, when best he sings, is placed against a thorn." Here the symbol emphasizes the claim that poetic expression originates in the deep pain and feeling of poets. By contrast, T. S. Eliot uses the less idealistic aspects of the bird in "Sweeney Among the Nightingales." Here Eliot refers to the song not as a symbol of beauty, but rather as a backdrop for the horrible murder of the ancient king Agamemnon. The only contribution the nightingales make as a symbol is their droppings—a staining, dirtying commentary on human affairs. Eliot's example notwithstanding, however, poets usually emphasize the lovelier aspects of the bird as a symbol.

ACTIONS.   Not only words but also actions may be presented as symbols. In Scott's "Snow," as we have just observed, the doe darting into the darkening woods symbolizes both the renewal and the mystery of life. In Thomas Hardy's "In Time of 'The Breaking of Nations'" (p. 801), the action of the man plowing a field symbolizes the continued life and vitality of the folk, the people, despite political and military changes that are constantly raging in the world.

SETTINGS.   Sometimes, a setting or natural scene may be symbolic. For example, Randall Jarrell's brief poem "The Death of the Ball Turret Gunner" (p. 550) unites the ball turret of a World War II high-altitude bomber with a mother's womb, symbolically indicating that war and brutal death are the human lot from the very beginning of life. Similarly, the "elfin grot" (grotto) of the "lady in the meads" in Keats's "La Belle Dame Sans Merci" is an unreal and magical, womblike location symbolizing both the allure and the disappointment that sometimes characterize sexual attraction.

CHARACTERS.   Poets also devise characters or people as symbols representing ideas or values. In E. E. Cummings's "in just," for example, the balloonman is such a figure (p. 797). Although the balloonman is not fully visualized, Cummings includes enough detail about him to indicate that he symbolizes the primitive vitality, joy, and sexuality that is calling the children out of childhood. The fairy child of "La Belle Dame Sans Merci" is a symbol of the mystery of love. The figures in Hardy's "In Time of 'The Breaking of Nations'" are symbolic of the poet's faith in the power of unimportant people to endure even though "Dynasties pass."

SITUATIONS.   Situations, circumstances, and conditions can also be used symbolically. Jarrell's ball turret gunner, vulnerable and helpless six miles in the air, symbolizes the condition of humankind in the age of fear and anxiety, under the threat of global war and technological annihilation. E. E. Cummings, in "she being Brand / -new," cleverly uses the situation of the speaker's breaking in a new automobile as the symbol of another kind of encounter involving the speaker.

The Qualities of Symbols

Just as symbols may be expressed in these various ways, the meanings of symbols may be placed on a continuum of qualities from good to bad, high to low, favorable to unfavorable. For example, Cummings's old balloonman of "in just-" is on the positive end, symbolizing the irresistible and joyful call of growth and sexuality. Outright horror is suggested by the symbol of the rough beast slouching towards Bethlehem in Yeats's "The Second Coming" (p. 810). While the beast shares the same birthplace with Jesus, the commonality is ironic because the beast represents the extremes of anger, hatred, and brutality that in Yeats's judgment are dominant in twentieth-century politics.

ALLUSION AND MEANING IN POETRY

Just as symbolism enriches meaning, so also does **allusion**. Also discussed in Chapter 9, *allusion* is the adaptation and assimilation of (a) unacknowledged brief quotations from other works and (b) references to historical events and any aspect of human culture—art, music, literature, and so on. It is a means of recognizing both the literary tradition and the broader cultural environment of which the poem is a part. In addition it assumes a common bond of knowledge between the poet and the reader. On the one hand, allusion compliments the past, and on the other it salutes the reader who is able to recognize it and find new meaning in it in its new context.

Allusions may be seen in no more than a single word, provided that the word is unusual enough or associative enough to bear the weight of the reference. Virginia Scott's "Snow," for example, speaks of "green trees black in the hemlock night." *Hemlock*, of course, refers to a type of evergreen tree observed by the speaker, but hemlock was also the poison drunk by Socrates when he was executed by the ancient Athenians. Just about any reference to hemlock calls to mind the death of Socrates and also the idea that death is oblivion and the common end of all life. At the beginning of "Ode to a Nightingale" (p. 770), Keats's speaker describes a numbness that might come "As though of hemlock . . . [he] had drunk." Here the allusion is placed in the context of a wish to be connected and united to the universal spirit not of oblivion but of creative power.

Allusions may also be longer, consisting of extensive phrases or also of descriptions or situations. When these are made, they add their own interest and power before the poet moves on to other ideas. Line 6 of Scott's "Snow," for example, is simply "Snow falling." This phrase is descriptive and accurate, but it also is a direct quotation from the first line of Robert Frost's poem "Desert Places" (p. 764). The contexts are of course different. Frost's line introduces the topic of the speaker's fear of bleakness, unconcern, coldness—his "desert places"—while in "Snow," as we stated earlier, Scott is referring to the continuity of the past and the present. There is bleakness and isolation in Scott's scene, but her old house also throws light on the snow, and the dead are fondly recalled because their spirit and memory are as alive as the doe who darts back into the woods. By making the allusion, Scott actually emphasizes the difference between her idea and Frost's.

The Sources of Allusions

Allusions may be drawn from just about any area of life, history, and art. Sometimes symbols are allusions as well as symbols. In "The Second Coming," Yeats's "lion body and the head of a man" is a descriptive allusion to the Sphinx, which was an ancient mythical monster that destroyed those who could not solve its riddle. As Yeats uses the description he is referring to the monstrous aspects of the figure as a means of focusing on both the horror and mystery, the brutality and coldness, that often infest human political institutions.

As works become well known, they become a source of allusions for subsequent writers. One of Robert Frost's most famous lines, for example, is the conclusion of "Stopping by Woods on a Snowy Evening": "And miles to go before I sleep." This line is so often quoted that it has become a metaphor for having a task to complete and responsibilities to fulfill. Isabella Gardner alludes to the line in her "Collage of Echoes," a poem which is deliberately built out of allusions. Interestingly, Frost's line itself alludes to a line in Keats's sonnet "Keen Fitful Gusts," where Keats says "The stars are very cold about the sky, / And I have many miles on foot to fare." Any allusion to Frost is therefore also an indirect allusion to Keats's lines.

The Original Context of Allusions

If an allusion is made to a literary work, it carries with it the entire context of the work from which it is drawn. Perhaps the richest storehouses of such ready-made stories and quotations are the King James version of The Bible and the plays of Shakespeare. In "Ode to a Nightingale," Keats alludes to the Biblical story of Ruth who, he says, was "sick with tears amid the alien corn." This allusion is particularly rich, because Ruth became the mother of Jesse. According to the Gospel of Matthew it was from the line of Jesse that King David was born, and it was from the house of David that Jesus was born. Thus Keats's nightingale is not only a symbol of natural beauty, but through this Biblical allusion it becomes symbolic of regeneration and redemption, much in keeping with Keats's assertion that the bird is "not born for death." In Yeats's "The Second Coming," the reference to the "blood-dimmed tide" suggests Macbeth's soliloquy in the second act of Shakespeare's *Macbeth*. Macbeth, after murdering Duncan, asks if there is enough water in Neptune's ocean to wash the blood from his hands. His immediate, guilt-ridden response is that Duncan's blood on his hands will instead stain the ocean, turning the green of the water to red. This image of crime being bloody enough to stain the ocean's water is thus the reference of Yeats's "blood-dimmed tide," for Yeats's authorial speaker is just as concerned about the global implications of evil as is Shakespeare's Macbeth.

Allusions are an important means by which poets broaden the context and deepen the meaning of their poems. The issues a poet raises in a new poem, in other words, are not important only there, but are linked through allusion to issues raised earlier by other thinkers, or brought out by previous events, places, or persons. With connections made through allusions, poets clarify their own ideas. Allusion is hence not literary "theft," but is rather a means of enrichment.

STUDYING FOR SYMBOLS AND ALLUSIONS

As you study poetry for its symbols and allusions, it is important to realize that these devices do not come ready marked with special notice and fanfare. A decision to call a feature of the poem *symbolic* is based on qualities within the poem: Perhaps a major item of importance is introduced at a climactic part of the poem, or a description has something noteworthy or unusual about it, such as the connection between "stony silence" and the "rough beast" in Yeats's "The Second Coming." When such a connection occurs, the element may no longer be taken just literally, but should be read as a symbol.

Even after you have found a hint such as this, however, you will have to discover its symbolic value. For instance, in the context of Yeats's "The Second Coming," the phrase "rough beast" might refer to the person or persons hinted at in traditional interpretations of the New Testament as the "anti-Christ." In a secular frame of reference, the associations of blankness and pitilessness suggest brutality and suppression. Still further, however, if the twentieth century were not a period in which millions of people have been persecuted and exterminated in military and secret police operations, even these associations might make the "rough beast" quizzical but not necessarily symbolic. But because of the rightness of the application, together with the traditional Biblical associations, the figure clearly should be construed as a symbol of heartless persecution and brutality.

As you can see, the interpretation of a symbol requires that you identify and objectivize the person, object, situation, or action. If the element can be seen as general and representative—characteristic of the condition of a large number of human beings—it assumes symbolic significance. As a rule, the more ideas that you can associate with the element, the more likely it is to be a symbol.

As for allusions, the identification of an allusion is often quite simple. Either a word, situation, or phrase is an allusion or it is not, and hence the matter is easily settled once a source is located. The problem comes in determining how the allusion affects the context of the poem you are reading. Thus we understand that in the poem "Snow," Virginia Scott alludes to Robert Frost's "Desert Places" by borrowing Frost's phrase "Snow falling." Once this allusion is established, its purpose must still be discovered. Thus the allusion might mean that the situation in "Snow" is the same as in Frost's poem, namely that the authorial speaker is making observations about interior blankness—the "desert places" of the mind, or soul. On the other hand, the poet may be using the allusion in a new sense, and this indeed seems to be the case. Whereas Frost uses the falling snow to suggest coldness of spirit, Scott uses it, more warmly, to connect the natural scene to the memory of family. In other words, once the presence of an allusion is established, the challenge of reading and understanding still continues.

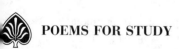 **POEMS FOR STUDY**

e. e. cummings   (1894–1962)

In Just- ──────────────────────────────── *1923*

in Just-
spring   when the world is mud-
luscious the little
lame balloonman

whistles   far   and wee   5

and eddieandbill come
running from marbles and
piracies and it's
spring

when the world is puddle-wonderful

the queer
old balloonman whistles
far   and   wee
and bettyandisbel come dancing

from hop-scotch and jump-rope and
it's
spring
and
    the
        goat-footed°

balloonMan   whistles
far
and
wee

IN JUST-.   20 *goat-footed:* The mythological Greek god Pan, a free-spirited and lascivious god who presides over fields, forests, and herds, was portrayed with the body of a man and the legs of a goat.

QUESTIONS

1. Explain the following as symbols: spring, mud-luscious, marbles, puddle-wonderful, hop-scotch. What does the whistle of the balloonman symbolize?

2. In what way is the balloonman symbolic?

3. Besides the balloonman, there are four other characters in the poem. Who are they? Why does Cummings run their names together? What impulses do these characters represent symbolically?

4. Read the poem aloud. Taking into account the spacing and alignment, how does the physical arrangement on the page influence your perception?

T. S. ELIOT   (1888–1965)

Sweeney Among the Nightingales° ————————————————————*1918*

ὤμοι πέπληγμαι καιρίαν πληγὴν ἔσω.

Apeneck Sweeney spreads his knees
Letting his arms hang down to laugh,
The zebra strips along his jaw
Swelling to maculate° giraffe.   *dirty, stained*   5

The circles of the stormy moon
Slide westward toward the River Plate,°
Death and the Raven° drift above
And Sweeney guards the hornèd gate.°

Gloomy Orion° and the Dog°   10
Are veiled; and hushed the shrunken seas;
The person in the Spanish cape
Tries to sit on Sweeney's knees

Slips and pulls the tablecloth
Overturns a coffee-cup,   15
Reorganized upon the floor
She yawns and draws a stocking up;

The silent man in mocha brown°   *Sweeney*
Sprawls at the window sill and gapes;
The waiter brings in oranges
Bananas figs and hothouse grapes;   20

The silent vertebrate in brown°   *Sweeney*
Contracts and concentrates, withdraws;
Rachel *née* Rabinovitch
Tears at the grapes with murderous paws;

SWEENEY AMONG THE NIGHTINGALES.   Eliot wrote two other works featuring Sweeney. These are "Sweeney Erect" (a poem) and *Sweeney Agonistes* (a drama). The character represents the grosser aspects of modern human beings. In the play, Sweeney says "Birth, and copulation, and death. / That's all, that's all, that's all." Sweeney is also the name of a hero of Irish legend and folklore.   The Greek epigraph below the title is from Aeschylus, *Agamemnon*, line 1348, and may be translated "Alas I am struck with a mortal blow within." This is the off-stage cry of Agamemnon when he is being murdered.   6 *River Plate:* The River Plate, or Rio de la Plata, is the large estuary extending from the Atlantic Ocean to Buenos Aires. It separates Argentina and Uruguay.   7 *Raven:* a bird of ill omen; also the constellation Corvus.   8 *hornèd gate:* one of the two gates of the underworld, according to Virgil, *Aeneid*, book 6:1192–1193. The usual guardian of the gates was the three-headed dog, Cerberus.   9 *Orion:* a mythological Greek giant and hunter. Because of a misunderstanding, he was killed by Artemis, the Goddess of the Moon and of the Hunt. Orion is also one of the most prominent winter constellations.   *Dog:* Orion's dog. The "dog star," Sirius, is in the constellation Canis Major, east of Orion, and it is the brightest star in the sky.

She and the lady in the cape
Are suspect, thought to be in league;
Therefore the man with heavy eyes
Declines the gambit, shows fatigue,

Leaves the room and reappears
Outside the window, leaning in,
Branches of wistaria
Circumscribe a golden grin;

The host with someone indistinct°
Converses at the door apart,
The nightingales are singing near
The Convent of the Sacred Heart,

And sang within the bloody° wood
When Agamemnon cried aloud,
And let their liquid siftings fall
To stain the stiff dishonored shroud.

33 *someone indistinct:* a murderer, corresponding to Aegisthus, the murderer of Agamemnon.
37 *bloody:* A pun: (1) covered with blood; (2) a vulgar word in British slang.

QUESTIONS

1. What does Sweeney represent as a symbol? Why does the poet use as the epigraph the passage from Aeschylus in which Agamemnon cries out in the pain of death? Why do you think the speaker describes Sweeney as "apeneck" (line 1) and as a "vertebrate in brown" (line 21)?

2. Why does Eliot include references to constellations? Consider also the geography (i.e., South America, Greece, the underworld). What is the effect of this broad set of references upon the symbolic meaning of the central incidents involving Agamemnon and Sweeney?

3. In stanza 2, how might the references to the moon, westward, the raven, and hornèd gate be considered as symbols? What do these symbols represent?

4. How does the speaker describe "Rachel *née* Rabinovitch"? Knowing that Sweeney is the name of a hero of Irish folklore, what do you make of Eliot's selection of that name for his antihero?

5. What are the host and the "indistinct" man conferring about? What is going to happen to Sweeney?

6. What do nightingales usually symbolize? What do they represent here? How may this use of the nightingales be considered as ironic?

ISABELLA GARDNER   (1915–1981)

Collage of Echoes _____ *1979*

I have no promises to keep
Nor miles to go before I sleep,°
For miles of years I have made promises
and (mostly) kept them.
    It's time I slept.   5
Now I lay me down to sleep°
With no promises to keep.
    My sleaves are ravelled°
    I have travelled.°

COLLAGE OF ECHOES.   2 *miles to go before I sleep:* see Robert Frost, "Stopping by Woods on
a Snowy Evening" (p. 556), lines 13–16.   6 *Now I lay me down to sleep:* from the child's prayer:
Now I lay me down to sleep; / I pray the Lord my soul to keep. / If I should die before I wake, /
I pray the Lord my soul to take.   8 *My sleaves are ravelled:* See *Macbeth,* Act II, scene 2, line 37:
"Sleep that knits up the ravelled sleave of care."   9 *I have travelled:* See Keats, "On First Look-
ing into Chapman's Homer" (p. 650).

QUESTIONS

1. Given the allusions in the poem, what do you conclude about the speaker's judgment of the reader's knowledge of literature?
2. How reliant is "Collage of Echoes" upon the contexts being echoed? How do the
   echoes assist in enabling enjoyment and appreciation of the poem?
3. In relation to the speaker's character as demonstrated in the poem, consider the
   phrases "(mostly) kept them," "With no promises to keep," and "My sleaves are
   ravelled." What do they show about the speaker's self-assessment? In what way
   might these phrases be considered comic?

THOMAS HARDY   (1840–1928)

In Time of "The Breaking of Nations"° _____ *1916 (1915)*

Only a man harrowing clods
    In a slow silent walk,
With an old horse that stumbles and nods
    Half asleep as they stalk.

Only thin smoke without flame   5
    From the heaps of couch grass:°   *quack grass*
Yet this will go onward the same
    Though Dynasties pass.

IN TIME OF "THE BREAKING OF NATIONS."   See Jeremiah 51:20, "with you I break nations
in pieces."

Yonder a maid and her wight°   *fellow*
    Come whispering by;
War's annals will fade into night
    Ere their story die.

QUESTIONS

1. What does Hardy symbolize by the man, horse, smoke, and couple? How realistic and vivid are these symbols? Are they universal or contextual?

2. How does Hardy show that the phrase "breaking of nations" is to be taken symbolically? What meaning is gained by the biblical allusion of this phrase?

3. Contrast the structure of stanza 1 with that of stanzas 2 and 3. How does the form of stanzas 2 and 3 enable Hardy to emphasize the main idea?

4. How does the speaker show his evaluation of the life of the common people? You might consider that at the time (1915), World War I was raging in Europe.

GEORGE HERBERT   (1593–1633)

The Collar° —————————————————————————— *1633*

I struck the board, and cry'd, "No more;
        I will abroad!
What? shall I ever sigh and pine?
My lines and life are free; free as the road,
    Loose as the wind, as large as store,
        Shall I be still in suit?°
Have I no harvest but a thorn°
To let me blood, and not restore
What I have lost with cordial fruit?
            Sure there was wine
    Before my sighs did dry it: there was corn
        Before my tears did drown it.
    Is the year only lost to me?
        Have I no bays° to crown it?
No flowers, no garlands gay? all blasted?
            All wasted?
    Not so, my heart: but there is fruit,
            And thou hast hands.
    Recover all thy sigh-blown age
On double pleasures: leave thy cold dispute
Of what is fit, and not; forsake thy cage;
            Thy rope of sands,

THE COLLAR.   *collar:* (a) the collar worn by a member of the clergy; (b) the collar of the harness of a draft animal such as a horse; (c) a restraint placed on prisoners; (d) a pun on *choler* (yellow bile), a bodily substance that was thought to cause quick rages.   6 *in suit:* waiting upon a person of power to gain favor or position.   7 *thorn:* See Mark 15:17.   14 *bays:* laurel crowns to signify victory and honor.

Which petty thoughts have made, and made to thee
   Good cable, to enforce and draw,
      And be thy law,   25
While thou didst wink and wouldst not see.
      Away; take heed:
      I will abroad.
Call in thy death's head there: tie up thy fears.
      He that forbears   30
   To suit° and serve his need,   *follow*
   Deserves his load."
But as I rav'd and grew more fierce and wild
      At every word,
Me thought I heard one calling, "Child:"   35
   And I replied, "*My Lord.*"

QUESTIONS

1. What is the opening situation? Why is the speaker angry? Against what role in life is he complaining?

2. In light of the many possible meanings of *collar* (see note), explain the title as a symbol in the poem.

3. Explain the symbolism of the thorn (line 7), blood (line 8), wine (line 10), bays (line 14), flowers and garlands (line 15), cage (line 21), rope of sands (line 22), death's head (line 29), and the dialogue in lines 35 and 36.

JOSEPHINE JACOBSEN   (b. 1908)

Tears —————————————————————— *1981*

Tears leave no mark on the soil
or pavement; certainly not in sand
or in any known rain forest;
never a mark on stone.
One would think that no one in Persepolis°   5
or Ur° ever wept.

You would assume that, like Alice,°
we would all be swimming, buffeted
in a tide of tears.
But they disappear. Their heat goes.   10
Yet the globe is salt
with that savor.°

TEARS.   5, 6 *Persepolis . . . Ur:* Persepolis was the capital city of ancient Persia (now Iran). Ur, on the Persian Gulf, was the capital city of the ancient Sumerian Empire. Today, both cities survive only in ruins. The Hebrew patriarch Abraham traveled from "Ur of the Chaldees" to settle in the land of Canaan, the "promised land."   7 *Alice:* In Lewis Carroll's *Alice in Wonderland* (Ch. 2), Alice sheds tears, and then is reduced in size and almost drowns in her own teardrops. 11–12 *Yet . . . savor:* Matthew 5:13.

The animals want no part in this.
The hare both screams and weeps
at her death, one poet says.
The stag, at death, rolls round drops
down his muzzle; but he is in
Shakespeare's forest.°

These cases are mythically rare.
No, it is the human being who persistently
weeps; in some countries, openly, in others, not.
Children who, even when frightened, weep most hopefully;
women, licensed weepers.°
Men, in secret, or childishly; or nobly.

Could tears not make a sea of their mass?
It could be salt and wild enough;
it could rouse storms and sink ships,
erode, erode its shores:
tears of rage, of love, of torture,
of loss. Of loss.

Must we see the future
in order to weep? Or the past?
Is that why the animals
refuse to shed tears?
But what of the present, the tears of the present?
The awful relief, like breath

after strangling? The generosity
of the verb "to shed"?
They are a classless possession
yet are not found in the museum
of even our greatest city.
Sometimes what was human, turns
into an animal, dry-eyed.

14–18 *The hare . . . forest:* In the poem *Autumn* by James Thomson (1700–1748), lines 401–457, a cruel hunt of the hare and the stag is described. It is the stag who sheds "big round tears" and "groans in anguish" when dying. Jacobsen's allusion to Shakespeare—to whom Thomson is also alluding—is *As You Like It,* Act II, scene i, lines 29–43.   23 *licensed weepers:* In certain countries, such as Greece, women are hired to weep and cry aloud at funerals.

QUESTIONS

1. What does the poem's major symbol, tears, mean? What significance does the poem attribute to tears? Why are tears sometimes disregarded?

2. How does the poem apply the symbol to various cultures and conditions?

3. How do tears differentiate human beings from animals? What is the symbolic value of this difference? In light of the contrast, what is the meaning of the last two lines?

4. Explain the poem's use of allusions (i.e., Persepolis, Ur, the New Testament, *Alice in Wonderland,* professional mourners, Shakespeare).

ROBINSON JEFFERS   (1887–1962)

The Purse-Seine _____ *1937*

1
Our sardine fishermen work at night in the dark of the moon; daylight or
   moonlight
They could not tell where to spread the net, unable to see the phosphorescence
   of the shoals of fish.
They work northward from Monterey, coasting Santa Cruz; off New Year's Point
   or off Pigeon Point
The look-out man will see some lakes of milk-color light on the seas's night-purple;
   he points, and the helmsman
Turns the dark prow, the motorboat circles the gleaming shoal and drifts out   5
   her seine-net. They close the circle
And purse the bottom of the net, then with great labor haul it in.

2
                              I cannot tell you
How beautiful the scene is, and a little terrible, then, when the crowded fish
Know they are caught, and wildly beat from one wall to the other of their closing
   destiny the phosphorescent
Water to a pool of flame, each beautiful slender body sheeted with flame, like a   10
   live rocket
A comet's tail wake of clear yellow flame; while outside the narrowing
Floats and cordage of the net great sea-lions come up to watch, sighing in the
   dark; the vast walls of night
Stand erect to the stars.

3
                        Lately I was looking from a night mountain-top
On a wide city, the colored splendor, galaxies of light: how could I help but recall   15
   the seine-net
Gathering the luminous fish? I cannot tell you how beautiful the city appeared,
   and a little terrible.
I thought, We have geared the machines and locked all together into
   interdependence; we have built the great cities; now
There is no escape. We have gathered vast populations incapable of free survival,
   insulated
From the strong earth, each person in himself helpless, on all dependent. The
   circle is closed, and the net
Is being hauled in. They hardly feel the cords drawing, yet they shine already.   20
   The inevitable mass-disasters
Will not come in our time nor in our children's, but we and our children
Must watch the net draw narrower, government take all powers—or revolution,
   and the new government
Take more than all, add to kept bodies kept souls—or anarchy, the mass-disasters.

4
These things are Progress;
Do you marvel our verse is troubled or frowning, while it keeps its reason? Or it
lets go, lets the mood flow
In the manner of the recent young men into mere hysteria, splintered gleams,
crackled laughter. But they are quite wrong.
There is no reason for amazement: surely one always knew that cultures decay,
and life's end is death.

QUESTIONS

1. Describe how the purse-seine is used to haul in the sardines. What is the speaker's reaction to the scene as described in stanza 2?

2. How does the speaker explain that the purse-seine is a symbol? What does it symbolize? What do the sardines symbolize?

3. Compare the ideas of Jeffers with those of Yeats in "The Second Coming." Are the ideas of Jeffers more or less methodical?

4. Is the statement at the end to be taken as a fact or as a resigned acceptance of that fact? Does the poem offer any solution to the problem?

5. How may the sea lions of line 12, and their sighs, be construed as a symbol?

JOHN KEATS   (1795–1821)

La Belle Dame Sans Merci: A Ballad° ————————————— *1820 (1819)*

1
O what can ail thee, knight at arms,
  Alone and palely loitering?
The sedge has wither'd from the lake,
  And no birds sing.

2
O what can ail thee, knight at arms,
  So haggard and so woe-begone?
The squirrel's granary is full,
  And the harvest's done.

3
I see a lily on thy brow
  With anguish moist and fever dew,
And on thy cheeks a fading rose
  Fast withereth too.

LA BELLE DAME SANS MERCI: French for "The beautiful lady without pity" (that is, "The heartless woman"). "La Belle Dame Sans Merci" is the title of a medieval poem by Alain Chartier; Keats's poem bears no other relationship to the medieval poem, which was thought at the time to have been by Chaucer.

4

I met a lady in the meads,°   *meadows*
    Full beautiful, a fairy's child;
Her hair was long, her foot was light,   15
    And her eyes were wild.

5

I made a garland for her head,
    And bracelets too, and fragrant zone;°   *belt*
She look'd at me as she did love,
    And made sweet moan.   20

6

I set her on my pacing steed,
    And nothing else saw all day long,
For sidelong would she bend, and sing
    A fairy's song.

7

She found me roots of relish° sweet,   *magical potion*   25
    And honey wild, and manna° dew,   *see Exodus 16:14–36*
And sure in language strange she said—
    I love thee true.

8

She took me to her elfin grot,°   *grotto*
    And there she wept, and sigh'd full sore,   30
And there I shut her wild wild eyes
    With kisses four.

9

And there she lullèd me asleep,
    And there I dream'd—Ah! woe betide!
The latest° dream I ever dream'd   *last*   35
    On the cold hill's side.

10

I saw pale kings, and princes too,
    Pale warriors, death pale were they all;
They cried—"La belle dame sans merci
    Hath thee in thrall!"°   *slavery*   40

11

I saw their starv'd lips in the gloam
    With horrid warning gapèd wide,
And I awoke and found me here
    On the cold hill's side.

12

And this is why I sojourn here,   45
    Alone and palely loitering,
Though the sedge is wither'd from the lake,
    And no birds sing.

QUESTIONS

1. Who is the speaker of stanzas 1–3? Who speaks after that?
2. In light of the dreamlike content of the poem, how can the knight's experience be viewed as symbolic? What is being symbolized?
3. Consider *relish* (line 25), *honey* (line 26), and *manna* (line 26) as symbols. Are they realistic or mythical? What does the allusion to manna signify? What is symbolized by the "pale kings, and princes too" and "Pale warriors"?
4. Consider the poem's setting as symbols of the knight's state of mind.

X. J. KENNEDY   (b. 1929)

Old Men Pitching Horseshoes ———————————————— *1985*

Back in a yard where ringers groove a ditch,
These four in shirtsleeves congregate to pitch
Dirt-burnished iron. With appraising eye,
One sizes up a peg, hoists and lets fly—
A clang resounds as though a smith had struck
Fire from a forge. His first blow, out of luck,
Rattles in circles. Hitching up his face,
He swings, and weight once more inhabits space,
Tumbles as gently as a new-laid egg.
Extended iron arms surround their peg
Like one come home to greet a long-lost brother.
Shouts from one outpost. Mutters from the other.

Now changing sides, each withered pitcher moves
As his considered dignity behooves
Down the worn path of earth where August flies
And sheaves of air in warm distortions rise.
To stand ground, fling, kick dust with all the force
Of shoes still hammered to a living horse.

QUESTIONS

1. How does the poet indicate that the pitching of horseshoes is symbolic? As symbols, why are old men chosen rather than young men?
2. Discuss the effects of the words *congregate, outpost, withered, sheaves, kick dust,* and *force.* What do these words contribute to the poem's symbolism?
3. Compare the topic of this poem with the concluding lines of T. S. Eliot's "Preludes" (p. 640), especially the last two lines. How is the symbolism of these poems similar? Different?

CAROL MUSKE   (b. 1945)

Real Estate _____*1981*

You think you earned this space on earth,
but look at the gold face of the teen-age
pharaoh,° smug as a Shriner, in his box

with no diploma, a plot flashy enough
for Manhattan.° Early death, then what.   5
a task dragging a sofa into the grave,
a couple of floor lamps, the alarm set

for another century. Someday we'll heed
the testament of that paid escort watching
himself in all the ballroom mirrors: slide   10

with each slide of the old trombone,
be good to the bald, press up against
the ugly duck-like.° Time is never old,

never lies. What a past you'd have
if you'd only admit to it: the real estate   15
your family dabbled in for generations,
the vacant lots° developed like the clan

overbite—through years of sudden
foreclosure. Who knows what it costs?
First you stand for the national anthem,   20

then you start waltzing around without
strings, reminding yourself of yourself,
expecting to live in that big city
against daddy's admonition: buy land°

get some roots down under those spike   25
heels, let the river bow and scrape as
it enters the big front door of your property.

REAL ESTATE.   3 *teen-age pharaoh:* Tutankhamen, the Egyptian "boy king" of the fourteenth
century B.C. The discovery of his tomb in 1922, when hundreds of precious household objects
were found with the sarcophagus, showed the lavishness of Egyptian royal burials. The mummy
of King Tut was covered with a mask of gold and colored metals.   5 *Manhattan:* In 1981 a large
number of treasures from Tutankhamen's tomb were displayed at the Metropolitan Museum of
Art in Manhattan.   13 *ugly duck-like:* "The Ugly Duckling" is a children's story by Hans Christian
Andersen.   17 *vacant lots:* See T. S. Eliot, "Preludes," concluding lines.   24 *buy land:* See
Robert Frost's poem "Build Soil" (1932).

QUESTIONS

1. Who is speaking? Who is being addressed? What sort of person is the speaker?
    What does she think of old age? Of sex? What advice does she offer?

2. What does "the teen-age pharaoh" symbolize? Why does the poet mention modern objects that might be found in a comparable tomb of a person of the twentieth century? What might these things symbolize?

3. What does the "paid escort" (line 9) symbolize? What does the "old trombone" symbolize? What does the choice of these symbolize about the traditional role of women with regard to men? What attitude is conveyed by this choice?

4. Consider the ambiguity of lines 25–27. What might "roots" and "property" signify as the means of causing the "river" to "bow and scrape"? Why is it difficult to understand these lines without symbolic explanations?

5. Consider the allusion in line 24 to Robert Frost's "Build Soil" (1932). Frost delivered his poem at Columbia University just before the party conventions of 1932. The United States was in its worst economic depression. Frost spoke about agriculture, world politics, and the need for developing the nation's resources. In comparison, what does Muske achieve by the allusion?

WILLIAM BUTLER YEATS   (1865–1939)

The Second Coming°   *1920 (1919)*

Turning and turning in the widening gyre°
The falcon cannot hear the falconer;
Things fall apart; the center cannot hold;
Mere anarchy is loosed upon the world,
The blood-dimmed tide° is loosed, and everywhere
The ceremony of innocence is drowned;
The best lack all conviction, while the worst
Are full of passionate intensity.

Surely some revelation is at hand;
Surely the Second Coming is at hand.
The Second Coming! Hardly are those words out
When a vast image out of *Spiritus Mundi*°
Troubles my sight; somewhere in sands of the desert
A shape with lion body and the head of a man,°
A gaze blank and pitiless as the sun,
Is moving its slow thighs, while all about it
Reel shadows of the indignant desert birds.
The darkness drops again; but now I know
That twenty centuries of stony sleep
Were vexed to nightmare by a rocking cradle,
And what rough beast, its hour come round at last,
Slouches towards Bethlehem to be born?

THE SECOND COMING. The phrase "second coming" has been traditionally used to refer to expectations of the return of Jesus for the salvation of believers, as described in the New Testament. The prophecies foretold that Christ's return would be preceded by famine, epidemics, wars between nations, and general civil disturbance. Yeats believed that human history could be measured in cycles of approximately 2,000 years (see line 19, "twenty centuries"). According to this system, the birth of Jesus ended the Greco-Roman cycle and in 1919, when Yeats wrote "The

Second Coming," it appeared to him that the Christian period was ending and a new era was about to take its place. The New Testament expectation was that Jesus would reappear. Yeats, by contrast, holds that the disruptions of the twentieth century were preceding a takeover by the forces of evil.   1 *gyre:* a radiating spiral, cone, or vortex. Yeats used the intersecting of two of these shapes as a visual symbol of his cyclic theory. As one gyre spiraled and widened out, to become dissipated, one period of history would end; at the same time a new gyre, closer to the center, would begin and spiral in a reverse direction to the starting point of the old gyre. A drawing of this plan looks like this:

The falcon of line 2 is at the broadest, centrifugal point of one gyre, symbolically illustrating the end of a cycle. The "indignant desert birds" of line 17 "reel" in a tighter circle, symbolizing the beginning of the new age in the new gyre.   5 *blood-dimmed tide:* quotation from Shakespeare's *Macbeth,* Act II, scene 2, lines 60–63.   12 *Spiritus Mundi:* literally, the spirit of the world, a collective human consciousness that furnished writers and thinkers with a common fund of images and symbols. Yeats referred to this collective repository as "a great memory passing on from generation to generation."   14 *lion body and the head of a man:* that is, the Sphinx, which in ancient Egypt symbolized the pharaoh as a spirit of the sun. Because of this pre-Christian origin, the reincarnation of a sphinx could therefore represent qualities associated in New Testament books like Revelation (11, 13, 17), Mark (13:14–20), and 2 Thessalonians (2:1–12) with a monstrous, super-human, satanic figure. For a picture of the Sphinx, see p. 827.

QUESTIONS

1. Consider the following as symbols: the gyre, the falcon, the "blood-dimmed tide," the ceremony of innocence, the "worst" who are "full of passionate intensity." What ideas and values do these symbolize in the poem?

2. Why does Yeats capitalize the phrase "Second Coming"? To what does this phrase refer? Explain the irony of Yeats's use of the phrase in this poem.

3. Contrast the symbols of the falcon of line 2 and the desert birds of line 17. Considering that these are realistically presented, how does the realism contribute to their identity as symbols?

4. What is symbolized by the sphinx being revealed as a "rough beast"? What is the significance of the beast's going "to Bethlehem to be born"?

WRITING ABOUT SYMBOLISM AND ALLUSION IN POETRY

As you read your poem, take notes and make all the observations you can about the presence of symbols or allusions or both. Explanatory notes will help you establish basic information, but you also need to explain meanings and create interpretations in your own words. Use a dictionary for understanding words or phrases that require further study. For allusions, you might check out original sources to determine original contexts. Try to determine the ways in which your poem is similar to, or different from, the original work or source, and then determine the purpose served by the allusion.

Questions for Discovering Ideas

CULTURAL SYMBOLS

- What symbols that you can characterize as cultural or universal can you discover in names, objects, places, situations, or actions in the poem (e.g., nightingales, hemlock, a thorn, two lovers, Bethlehem)?
- How are these symbols used? What do they mean, both specifically, in the poem, and universally, in a broader context? What would the poem be like without the symbolic meaning?

CONTEXTUAL SYMBOLS

- What contextual symbols can you locate in the poem (e.g., withered sedge, a spiraling gyre, a doe running into a woods)? How are these symbols used specifically in the poem? What would the poem be like if the contextual symbol were not taken to be symbolic?
- What causes you to conclude that the symbols are truly symbolic? What is being symbolized? What do the symbols mean? How definite or direct is the symbolism?
- Is the symbolism used systematically throughout the poem, or is it used only once? How does the symbolism affect the ideas or emotions expressed in the poem?

ALLUSIONS

- Granted your knowledge of literature, science, geography, television, the Bible, film, popular culture, and other fields of knowledge, what kinds of allusion are you likely to recognize immediately?
- Do you find any references that fit into any of these or other categories? What do these allusions mean in their original context? What do they mean in the context of the poem?
- Do you see any possible allusions that you are not sure about? What help do you find in the explanatory notes in the text you are using? Consult a dictionary or other reference work (ask your reference librarian) to discover the nature of these allusions.

Strategies for Organizing Ideas

Begin with a brief description of the poem and of the symbolism or allusions in it. A symbol might be central to the poem, or an allusion might be introduced at a particularly important point. Your central idea might take you in a number of directions, such as that the symbolism is based on objects like flowers and natural scenes, or that it stems out of an action or set of actions, or that it is developed from an initial situation. Or, the symbols may be universal, or they may be contextual. Or, they may be applicable particularly to personal life, or political or social life. Allusions may emphasize the differences between your poem and the work or event being alluded to, or they may highlight the circumstances of your poem. Also, you might make a point that the symbols and/or allusions make your poem seem optimistic, or pessimistic, and so on.

Some possible approaches for your essay, which may be combined as need arises, are these:

THE MEANING OF SYMBOLS OR ALLUSIONS.   This approach is the most natural one to take for an essay on symbolism or allusion. If you have discovered a symbol or symbols, or allusions, explain the meaning as best you can. In effect, you are writing about the poem's ideas as they are developed through the various symbols and allusions. Thus you will need to answer questions like these: What is the poem's major idea? How do you know that your interpretation is valid? How do the poem's symbols and allusions contribute to your interpretation? How pervasive, how applicable, are these devices? If you have discovered many symbols and allusions, which ones predominate? What do they mean? Why are some more important than others? What connects them with each other and with the poem's main idea? How are you able to make conclusions about all this?

THE EFFECT OF SYMBOLS OR ALLUSIONS ON THE POEM'S FORM.   Here the goal is to determine how symbolism or allusion is related to the poetic structure. Where does the symbol occur in the poem? If it is early, how do the following parts relate to the ideas of the symbol? What logical or chronological function does the symbol serve in the poem's development? Is the symbol repeated, and if so, to what effect? If the symbol is introduced later, has it been anticipated earlier? How do you know? Can the symbol be considered climactic? What might the structure of the poem have been like if the symbolism had not been used? (Answering this question can help you judge how the symbol influences the poem's structure.) Many of these same questions might also be applied to an allusion or allusions. In addition, for an allusion, it is important to compare the contexts of your work and the original to determine how the poet has used the allusion as a part of your poem's form or structure.

THE RELATIONSHIP BETWEEN THE LITERAL AND THE SYMBOLIC.   The object here is to describe the literal nature of the symbols, and then to determine their appropriateness to the poem's context. If the symbol is part of a narrative, what is its literal function? If the symbol is a person, object, or setting, what physical aspects are described? Are colors included? Shapes? Sizes? Sounds? In the light of this description, how applicable is the symbol to the ideas it embodies? How appropriate is the literal condition to the symbolic? The answers to questions like these should lead not so much to a detailed account of the meaning of the symbols, but rather to an account of their appropriateness to the topics and ideas of the poem.

THE IMPLICATIONS AND RESONANCES OF SYMBOLS AND ALLUSIONS.   This type of essay is more personal than the others, for it is devoted to the suggestions and associations—the "implications and resonances"—that the poem's symbols and allusions bring out. The object of the essay is to describe your own process or chain of thinking that the poem sets in motion. You are therefore free to move in your own direction as long as you base your discussion in the symbols and allusions you find in the poem. If the poet is speaking in general terms about the end of an era, for example, as with the symbol of the rough beast in Yeats's "The Second Coming" and the giant fishnets in Jeffers's "The Purse Seine," then you could apply these symbols to your own thinking. It is not easy to summon the knowledge and authority to contradict the work of any poet, but if you can point out shortcomings in the thought of the symbols or allusions, you should do so.

Your conclusion might contain a summary of your main points. If your poem is particularly rich in symbols or allusions, you might also briefly consider some of the elements that you have not considered fully in the body, and try to tie these together with those you have already discussed. It would also be appropriate to introduce any responses or new ideas you developed as a result of your study.

SAMPLE ESSAY

Symbolism and Allusion in Yeats's "The Second Coming"°

[1]   William Butler Yeats's "The Second Coming" is a prophetical poem that lays out reasons for being scared about the future. The poem's symbolism and allusiveness combine traditional materials from ancient history and literature together with Yeats's own visual scheme designed to explain the rise and fall of civilizations. These devices are arranged to explain both the disruption of our present but old culture, and also the installation of a fearsome new one.* To make his prophecies clear, Yeats describes major symbols and allusions separately, and combines them as a reflection of horror.†

[2]   Yeats's first symbol, the gyre, or rather two gyres interconnecting, is pervasive in the poem, for it indicates the cyclical nature of political changes. Flying outward at the widest point of the gyre—symbolizing our present era—a falcon is used by Yeats to introduce the idea that "the center cannot hold." The "desert birds," hovering around the "lion body and the head of a man" (the sphinx-like figure) show a tighter circle in a second gyre, symbolizing a new stage of human existence. Thus the widening symbolic gyre in line 1 is interpenetrating with the narrowing gyre pointing at the "rough beast." This blending and intersecting show that new things blend into old things, while separating from them at the same time. The spatial and geometrical symbolism thus illustrates that the order of the past is breaking up, while the future order is about to take the shape of the past—but at its worst, not at its best.

Embodying this horror-to-be, the second major symbol is the sphinx-like creature moving its slow thighs in the sands of the desert. The attributes of the

---

° For this poem, see p. 810
* Central idea.
† Thesis sentence.

creature—a monster, really—are blankness and pitilessness. Yeats describes it as a "rough beast," with the "indignant desert birds," perhaps vultures, flying in circles above it. This description of the symbol emphasizes the brutal nature

[3] of the new age. Yeats wrote the poem in 1919, right after the conclusion of World War I, which had seen particularly mindless and vicious trench warfare. The disruption of life caused by this war was a disturbing indicator that the new period would be one of political repression and heartless brutality.

It is this forthcoming brutality that makes ironic the poem's major allusion—the "second coming." Yeats alludes to the second coming in the poem's title, and also in lines 9 and 10:

> Surely some revelation is at hand;
> Surely the Second Coming is at hand.

The allusion is to the usual understanding of New Testament prophecies about

[4] the return of Christ at the end of historical time, when the Kingdom will come on earth. In the Bible, war and rumors of war are claimed as being the signs indicating that the return, or "second coming," is near. Thus far, both the Biblical signs and the observations of Yeats coincide. The twist, however, is that Yeats is suggesting in the allusion that after the breakup of the present age, the new age will be marked not by God's Kingdom but by the "rough beast." Because Yeats describes the beast as a sphinx, his model is the kind of despotism known in ancient Egypt, when power was held absolutely by the pharaoh, and when few people were granted any freedom or civil rights.

A unique aspect of Yeats's symbolism and allusiveness is that he fuses the two together. The "ceremony of innocence," for example (line 6), refers to the ritual of communion and also to its symbolic value of regeneration. By indicating that it is being drowned, he doubles the impact of his assertion that tradition is being lost and brutalized. The Spiritus Mundi is an abstract allusion to

[5] a common human bond of images and characteristics, but because of the image of brutality it produces, as a symbol it demonstrates that horror is a normal condition of human life. In addition, the "blood-dimmed tide" is an allusion to Shakespeare's Macbeth, who symbolically has stained the ocean red with King Duncan's blood. The "blood-dimmed tide" therefore both allusively and symbolically indicates the global importance of the forthcoming age of evil.

"The Second Coming" is therefore rich in symbols that are both traditional and also personal with Yeats, but there are additional symbols and allusions. The most easily visualized of these is the falcon out of control, flying higher and higher and farther away from the falconer, to symbolize the anarchy that Yeats mentions in line 4 as being "loosed" in the world. An example

[6] of a symbol being used ironically is the reference to Bethlehem where, according to Matthew and Luke, Jesus, the "Prince of Peace," was born. In "The Second Coming," Yeats asserts that the new birth will not lead to peace, but instead will bring about a future age of repression and brutality. The poem thus offers a complex and disturbing fabric of symbol and allusion.

Commentary on the Essay

This essay combines the topics of symbolism and allusion, and illustrates how each may be treated. The introduction briefly characterizes the poem and asserts that the arguments are made through the use of symbols and allusions. The central idea is about the replacement of the old by the new, and the thesis sentence lists two major symbols and allusions to be discussed in the body. Paragraph 2 describes the shape of the symbol, thus illustrating method 2 as just described, and also explains it, illustrating method 1. Paragraph 3 considers the "rough beast" as a symbol of emerging brutality. Paragraph 4 treats the title's allusion to New Testament prophetic tradition, showing that Yeats makes his point by reversing the outcome that tradition had predicted. Paragraph 5 demonstrates the complexity of Yeats's poem by stressing how he fuses symbolism and allusion as a common topic. The sixth and last paragraph summarizes and characterizes the body briefly, and proceeds to illustrate the richness of "The Second Coming" with brief reference to additional symbols and allusions.

WRITING TOPICS

1. Analyze the ways in which Keats, Herbert, and Jeffers use symbols to convey the fact and idea of capture and thralldom ("La Belle Dame Sans Merci," "The Collar," and "The Purse-Seine"). What major symbols do the three poets use? How appropriate is each symbol in its respective poem? How do the poets use the symbols to focus on the problems they present in their poems?

2. Describe the differences in the ways in which E. E. Cummings, T. S. Eliot, and W. B. Yeats use allusions in "In Just-," "Sweeney Among the Nightingales," and "The Second Coming." How possible is it to understand these poems without an explanation of the allusions? How extensive should explanations be? To what extent does the allusiveness make the poems difficult? Challenging? Interesting? Enriching?

3. Write a poem in which you develop a major symbol, as Jeffers does in "The Purse-Seine" and Kennedy does in "Old Men Pitching Horseshoes." Some symbols you might consider are these:

    Atomic waste, or nuclear weapons.

    Foreign-made cars.

    A superstar athlete.

    A computer.

    A dog staring out a window as the children leave for school.

    Now, write an essay describing the process of your creation. How do you begin? How much detail is necessary? How many conclusions do you need to bring out about your symbol? When do you think you have said enough? Too much? How do you know?

4. Write a poem in which you make your own allusions to your own experiences, such as school, an activity, a team, a book, a movie character, or a recent artistic or political event. What assumptions do you make about your reader when you bring out your allusions? How do you make the allusion (i.e., by a quotation, a name, a title, an indirect reference)? How does your allusion deepen your meaning? How does your allusion increase your own power of expression?

Myth: Systems of Symbolic Allusion in Poetry

Our word *myth* is derived from the Greek word *muthos,* meaning a story, narrative, or plot. Primarily, a **myth** is a story that deals with the relationships of gods to humanity (the *myths* of Oedipus or Odysseus), or with battles among heroes (the *myths* of Hercules or Achilles). A myth may also be a set of beliefs or assumptions among societies. **Mythology** refers collectively to all the stories and beliefs, either of a group (*Greek Mythology*) or of a number of groups (*Mythology of the Ancient Near East*). A system of beliefs and religious or historical doctrine is a **mythos** (the *Islamic Mythos,* or the *Buddhist Mythos*).

MYTHOLOGY AS AN EXPLANATION OF HOW THINGS ARE

Throughout the ages, people have developed myths because they want to know who they are, where they have been, where they are going, how the world got the way it is, and whether anyone up there cares. Mythical stories and characters do exactly that. They comprise narrative systems that explain the history, culture, religion, and collective psychology of individual societies and civilizations, and that satisfy our human need to understand and humanize conditions that are otherwise mysterious and frightening.

Although many myths originated in primitive times, they still provide a wealth of material and allusion in literature and art. The world around us seems more rich, awesome, and divine when we know that many events, places, creatures, trees, and flowers are important in the beautiful stories and legends that we have inherited from the past.

Myth, Science, and Belief

Myth and science overlap, since both attempt to provide explanations for the universe. At the beginning of civilization, almost all the vital questions were answered by myths, such as those about gods, the creation of the earth and humanity, lightning and thunder, earthquakes and volcanoes, sexuality, birth, good, evil, and death.

As Western civilization became progressively more educated and sophisticated, particularly after the time of Copernicus (1473-1543), scientific discoveries replaced myths as the means of explaining the "how's" of life and existence. Thus we understand today that lightning and thunder are produced by the friction of electrically charged clouds being buffeted in high winds, not by the great and powerful gods Zeus and Thor hurling lightning bolts from the sky. Wherever there are volcanic eruptions, we know that the cause is molten lava deep within the earth's crust being vented violently through fissures in the volcanoes.

Even though myths are not scientific, they should not be dismissed. While we know an immense amount scientifically about *how* things happen, we do not really know *why* they happen. For instance, although cosmogonists tell us a great deal about the early stages of the universe and the development of galaxies, stars, the solar system, and our earth, they do not even approach answering the imponderable religious and philosophical questions about causes that are explained by myths.

The Power of Symbolic Mythical Truth

Even when science provides illumination, myths are still important because they are ingrained into our very thought patterns. For example, we *know* with scientific certainty that we have day when we are turned into the sun's direct light, and that we have night when we are turned away from the sun and are in the earth's shadow. Nevertheless, we continue to use the words "the sun rises" and "the sun sets" to explain day and night, as though we still believed the mythical story about a flat earth with the sun turning about it. Such mythically originated language is inseparable from our minds. Even the belief that science and technology can solve all earthly problems may be seen as a myth. Human beings, in short, are **mythopoeic**—that is, not only do we live with myths, but we habitually create them.

It is therefore important to realize that myths express truth symbolically even if mythical heroes and stories themselves are scientifically or historically inadmissible. The truths are not to be found in the actual lore itself but rather in what they show about our earthly existence. Thus, when we read about the problems of the ancient Theban king Oedipus, we may safely assume that the specific details of his life (if he actually ever did live) did not happen just as Sophocles dramatizes them in *Oedipus the King*. But we find in the play a powerful rendering of how human beings make mistakes and how they must pay for them. In short, the truth of the Oedipus myth is psychological, not literal and historical.

Myth as Concept and Perspective

We may broaden our consideration by adding that myths also imply a special perspective about how people see their place and purpose in the world. This kind of myth may be constructive and generative. Thus, at one time most North Americans accepted the myth that Nature was limitless and wild, and

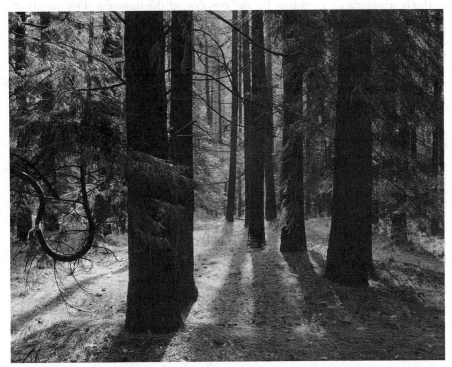

Ansel Adams, "Forest Floor," Yosemite Valley. (Photograph by Ansel Adams. Copyright © 1994 by the Trustees of the Ansel Adams Publishing Rights Trust. All rights reserved.)

in need of being conquered. With this concept in mind, settlers moved into every available corner of the land—to build, farm, create industries, and establish new ways of life. Without such an inspiring myth, people would have stayed put, and the nation would never have achieved its current prominence.

This is not to say that all myths are positive; indeed, some myths may be destructive. Thus, the once-positive myth of limitless and inexhaustible Nature has led us into the massive problems we face today with environmental exploitation and degradation. A new attitude is in the process of coming into existence—that the earth is no longer inimical, in need of taming, but is beautiful, tender, and fragile, in need of conservation. The Ansel Adams photograph "Forest Floor, Yosemite Valley" is a visual embodiment of this attitude. While the reasons for the changing attitude are largely scientific, the attitude itself marks a new *mythos*—that of a caring relationship for Nature, with all the consequent approaches to preserving wild animals, the land, and natural resources.

Mythological Themes or Motifs

Since myths address our human need to know, it is not surprising to find that many civilizations, separated by time and space, have parallel myths, such as the many stories accounting for the creation of the universe. The details of these myths are different, but the *patterns* are similar inasmuch as they all posit both an original time and action of creation, and a creator god or gods who also take part in human history. The principal god is perceived as a shaper, a modeler, a divine artisan, who has fashioned the orderly systems we find in the world, such as life, daylight, ecological dependence, tides, warmth, fertility, harvests, morality, and social stability.

One of the most crucial of all myths involves sin, disobedience, and evil, which are usually blamed for winter, natural calamities, and death. A corollary of the myth is that a god-hero or goddess-heroine must undergo a sacrifice to atone for sin and to ensure the renewed vitality of spring. In *The Golden Bough*, a massive collection and analysis of mythic stories, Sir James Frazer (1854–1941) compares a series of mythical death-renewal motifs. Among such sacrificed and reborn gods are Thammuz (Babylonia), Attis (Phrygia), Osiris (Egypt), and Adonis, Dionysus, and Persephone (Greece). Again, the specific myths take different forms, but they reflect the same mysteries, fears, and hopes.

Scholars and anthropologists like Frazer were among the first to observe the interrelationships among myths produced by diverse cultures. The Swiss psychoanalyst Carl Gustav Jung (1875–1961) offered an explanation for this duplication. He noticed that images, characters, and events similar to those in literature, mythology, and religion also occurred in the dreams of his patients. He termed these recurring images **archetypes** (from the Greek word meaning "model" or "first mold") and developed a theory that all human beings share in a universal or collective unconscious mind. Even if Jung's theory is ignored, the fact remains that types of mythic creatures such as dragons and centaurs, archetypal mother-daughter and father-son stories, and narratives involving sacrifices, heroic quests, and trips to the underworld recur throughout various mythologies and pervade our literature.[1]

MYTHOLOGY AND LITERATURE

When writing was invented, the first written works recorded mythologies that already existed. The early Greek poet Homer, for example (perhaps a mythical figure himself), told about the mythical gods and heroes of the Trojan war. Homer did not actually write (tradition says he was blind), but other writers recorded and transmitted his epics. The Latin writer Ovid (43 B.C.-17 A.D.) received a large body of mythology and wrote poetic stories based on it. The result of this assimilation of myth into poetry was a combination of literature and religion that served the double purpose of teaching and entertaining. In this way, poets throughout antiquity used mythology as a mine for ideas, images, and symbols.

Although almost two thousand years have passed since Ovid lived, writers

---

[1] See also Appendix D, pp. 1659–60, for a further discussion of archetypes.

and artists still rely on mythology. In every generation since the earliest Anglo-Saxon poems and legends, poets of English have retold and updated mythological stories. Indeed, many of the poems in this chapter are from the twentieth century. Modern poetry utilizing mythology, however, is no longer designed to reinforce the dominant religion. Instead, it uses mythology to link past and present, to dramatize important concerns, and to symbolize universal patterns of thought.

Most western poets who use mythological material in their verse turn to long-standing bodies of myth, particularly those of Greco-Roman, Norse-Teutonic, and Judeo-Christian origin. These systems of mythology are **universal** or **public**, since they are part of a vast common heritage. Like universal symbols, they make up a reservoir of material that all writers are free to employ.

Mythological References in Poetry

When poets make references to a myth, as in poems like Tennyson's "Ulysses" and Parker's "Penelope," both of which refer to the myth of Odysseus (Ulysses), they assume that readers already understand something about the stories and characters. With these poems, readers are expected to know enough of Homer's *Odyssey* to recall that this hero fought in the Trojan War for ten years, and then was forced to spend ten years returning home. In other words, during most of his reign as king of Ithaca he was a warrior and adventurer—an absentee ruler—but at the same time his queen, Penelope, stayed at home.

While you may often have enough background in mythology to understand all the poet's references, you may sometimes need to fill in or reinforce your knowledge. A good place to start is a dictionary or general encyclopedia, where you will find brief identifications of mythic figures and a key to further reading. Eventually you will want access to more detailed information. Excellent books that retell the stories of Greco-Roman mythology are Richmond Hathorn's *Greek Mythology*, M. C. Howatson's *The Oxford Companion to Classical Literature*, and Timothy Gantz's *Early Greek Myth*. Bulfinch's *The Age of Fable* and Edith Hamilton's *Mythology* are respected traditional books. There are also many classical dictionaries, such as the *Oxford Classical Dictionary*, that are immensely useful. John Keats learned much of his mythology from Lemprière's *Classical Dictionary*. Many libraries have this book on their reference shelves, and your use of it will both give you information and impress you with a sense of historical scholarship. Not all allusions are classical. Should you want to understand allusions to the myths of Paul Bunyan and Johnny Appleseed, for example, you would want a collection of American folk tales. References to *Odin, Thor, the Valkyries*, or *Asgard* should lead you to a collection of Norse-Teutonic mythology.

Studying Mythology in Poetry

We are now ready to look at a poem that is built upon a myth. The poem is by William Butler Yeats, and it draws on Greco-Roman mythology.

WILLIAM BUTLER YEATS   (1865–1939)

Leda and the Swan _____ *1924 (1923)*

A sudden blow: the great wings beating still
Above the staggering girl, her thighs caressed
By the dark webs, her nape caught in his bill,
He holds her helpless breast upon his breast.

How can those terrified vague fingers push
The feathered glory from her loosening thighs?
And how can body, laid in that white rush,
But feel the strange heart beating where it lies?

A shudder in the loins engenders there
The broken wall, the burning roof and tower
And Agamemnon dead.
                Being so caught up,
So mastered by the brute blood of the air,
Did she put on his knowledge with his power
Before the indifferent beak could let her drop?

QUESTIONS

1. What mythic event does the poem retell? Who was Leda? The swan? Who were Leda's children? What events are alluded to in lines 10 and 11?
2. How is Leda described? What words suggest her helplessness? What phrases suggest the swan's mystery and divinity?
3. What question is raised in the last two lines? To what extent does the poem provide an answer to this question?

Yeats's sonnet focuses on a specific event of ancient Greek mythology: Zeus, king of the gods, having taken the form of a swan, raped Leda, a Spartan queen. According to the myth, this violent event was a starting point not only of Greek civilization, but also of humanity's angers and troubles. One of the children born of the rape was Helen of Troy, whose abduction by Paris precipitated the Trojan War. Yeats's phrase "the broken wall, the burning roof and tower" refers to the destruction of Troy. Another child was Clytemnestra, married to Agamemnon, king of Mycenae and leader of the allied Greek forces. Because Agamemnon had sacrificed their daughter Iphigeneia as a part of the war effort, Clytemnestra vowed revenge and had him murdered when he returned home from the Trojan War. (See also Eliot's "Sweeney Among the Nightingales," p. 799.)

After a graphic recounting of the swan's attack on Leda, and a brief reference to the sack of Troy and Agamemnon's death, Yeats's concluding lines raise a central issue stemming from the myth. While Leda took on some of Zeus's divine power with the rape (through the process of childbearing), the poem asks whether she also "put on" some of his divine knowledge—whether she acquired Zeus's foreknowledge of the fall of Troy, the murder of Agamemnon, and, by extension, the subsequent events in history. Of course, the question is rhetorical and the answer is negative.

If all the poem did were to question the ancient myth in this way, it would be of limited interest for modern readers. But it does more than that; it directs our attention to concerns of today. Thus, we may conclude from Yeats's use of the myth that human beings, like Leda, do not have preknowledge, but have only their own culture, experience, and intelligence as their guides. If divine beings exist, they have no interest in human affairs, but are rather uninvolved and "indifferent" (line 14). By extension the myth suggests that the burden of civilization is on human beings themselves, and that if knowledge and power are ever to be combined for constructive goals, that blending must be a human achievement.

Yeats thus employs mythic material in this sonnet to raise a searching question about the nature of existence, knowledge, and power. The historical process is embodied in the rape, the children born out of it, and their troubles. As the central figure of the myth, Leda is the focal point of circumstances and concerns that have extended from the distant past to the present, and that will likely extend into the future.

Because most myths similarly embody recurring issues, they have great value for modern readers. Muriel Rukeyser's "Myth," for example, uses the ancient myth about Oedipus to shed light amusingly on misperceptions about male-female relationships. Edward Field's "Icarus" (one of a number of Icarus poems we include here) uses the ancient Icarus myth to decry the impact of modern society upon individuals. In these and in other poems based in mythology, you may look for such original ways in which poets receive something old and make it new. Myths do not belong only to the past, but are alive and well in the present.

 POEMS FOR STUDY

MARGARET ATWOOD   (b. 1939)

Siren Song————————————————————————— *1974*

This is the one song everyone
would like to learn: the song
that is irresistible:

the song that forces men
to leap overboard in squadrons   5
even though they see the beached skulls

the song nobody knows
because anyone who has heard it
is dead, and the others can't remember.

Shall I tell you the secret
and if I do, will you get me
out of this bird suit?

I don't enjoy it here
squatting on this island
looking picturesque and mythical

with these two feathery maniacs,
I don't enjoy singing
this trio, fatal and valuable.

I will tell the secret to you,
to you, only to you.
Come closer. This song

is a cry for help: Help me!
Only you, only you can,
you are unique

at last, Alas
it is a boring song
but it works every time.

QUESTIONS

1. Who were the sirens in Greek mythology? What effect did their song have?

2. Who is the speaker in this poem? What is the effect of her colloquial diction? What does she tell you about her song?

3. Who is the "you" referred to in lines 10–24? What does the speaker say about her life? What "works every time"? To what extent is the conclusion amusing?

OLGA BROUMAS   (b. 1949)

Circe _____ *1977*

The Charm

The fire bites, the fire bites.   Bites
to the little death.   Bites

till she comes to nothing.   Bites
on her own sweet tongue. She goes on.   Biting.

The Anticipation

They tell me a woman waits, motionless
till she's wooed.   I wait

spiderlike, effortless as they weave
even my web for me, tying the cord in knots   10

with their courting hands. Such power
over them.   And the spell

their own.   Who could release them?   Who
would untie the cord

with a cloven hoof?   15

The Bite

What I wear in the morning pleases
me: green shirt, skirt of wine.   I am wrapped

in myself as the smell of night
wraps round my sleep when I sleep   20

outside.   By the time
I get to the corner

bar, corner store, corner construction
site, I become divine.   I turn

men into swine.   Leave   25
them behind me whistling, grunting, wild.

QUESTIONS

1. Who was Circe? What powers did she have?
2. Who or what is the speaker in this poem? What is the connection between the speaker and Circe? Why is the poem entitled "Circe"?
3. What do Circe and the speaker symbolize in the poem? What is the source of Circe's power in the myth and the poem? What does this power symbolize?
4. What is the "fire" (lines 1–5)? Who are "they" (lines 6–15)? What is the effect of "spiderlike" (line 9) and "courting hands" (line 11)? What is "the spell" (line 12)? What is the significance of "a cloven hoof" (line 15)?
5. What is the speaker's attitude toward herself in lines 16–26? What happens to her in these lines? What happens to the men she encounters?

W. S. MERWIN   (b. 1927)

Odysseus _____ *1960*

Always the setting forth was the same,
Same sea, same dangers waiting for him
As though he had got nowhere but older.
Behind him on the receding shore

The identical reproaches, and somewhere
Out before him, the unravelling patience
He was wedded to. There were the islands
Each with its woman and twining welcome
To be navigated, and one to call "home."
The knowledge of all that he betrayed
Grew till it was the same whether he stayed
Or went. Therefore he went. And what wonder
If sometimes he could not remember
Which was the one who wished on his departure
Perils that he could never sail through,
And which, improbable, remote, and true,
Was the one he kept sailing home to?

QUESTIONS

1. What aspects of the Odysseus myth are evoked in this poem? What point does the poem make about Odysseus's experiences?
2. To what extent is Odysseus symbolic of a specific kind of life and attitude toward life? How does our knowledge of Odysseus contribute to the impact and meaning of the poem?
3. Compare this poem with Parker's "Penelope." How is the same mythic material used toward different ends in these poems?
4. Compare this poem with Tennyson's "Ulysses." Explain how and why the same mythic figure can be used to convey such different ideas.

DOROTHY PARKER   (1893–1967)

Penelope _____ *1936*

In the pathway of the sun,
In the footsteps of the breeze,
Where the world and sky are one,
He shall ride the silver seas,
He shall cut the glittering wave.
I shall sit at home, and rock;
Rise, to heed a neighbor's knock;
Brew my tea, and snip my thread;
Bleach the linen for my bed.
They will call him brave.

QUESTIONS

1. How does the speaker describe her life? How is her life different from that of the male figure described in lines 1–5?
2. To what extent is Penelope a symbol? What does she symbolize? How does our knowledge of the myth deepen our response to this symbolism?

MURIEL RUKEYSER   (b. 1913)

Myth ——————————————————————————————— *1978*

Long afterward, Oedipus, old and blinded, walked the
roads.   He smelled a familiar smell.   It was
the Sphinx.°   Oedipus said, "I want to ask one question.
Why didn't I recognize my mother?"   "You gave the
wrong answer," said the Sphinx.   "But that was what   5
made everything possible," said Oedipus.   "No," she said.
"When I asked, What walks on four legs in the morning,
two at noon, and three in the evening, you answered,
Man.   You didn't say anything about woman."
"When you say Man," said Oedipus, "you include women   10
too. Everyone knows that."   She said, "That's what
you think."

MYTH.   3 *Sphinx:* The photograph below shows the Sphinx at Gîza in Egypt.

QUESTIONS

1. Who was Oedipus? The Sphinx? According to this poem, what was wrong with
    Oedipus's answer to the Riddle of the Sphinx?
2. What elements and techniques in this work allow you to consider it a poem?
3. What two myths and meanings of *myth* are embodied in the title?
4. To what extent does the poem's colloquial language revitalize the mythic ma-
    terial?

The great sphinx at Gîza, Egypt. (Foto Marburg/Art Resource)

ALFRED, LORD TENNYSON   (1809–1892)

Ulysses _____ *1842 (1833)*

It little profits that an idle king,
By this still hearth, among these barren crags,
Matched with an aged wife, I mete and dole
Unequal laws° unto a savage race,   *rewards and punishments*
That hoard, and sleep, and feed, and know not me.

I cannot rest from travel; I will drink
Life to the lees.° All times I have enjoyed   *dregs*
Greatly, have suffered greatly, both with those
That loved me, and alone; on shore, and when
Through scudding drifts the rainy Hyades°
Vexed the dim sea. I am become a name;
For always roaming with a hungry heart
Much have I seen and known—cities of men
And manners, climates, councils, governments,
Myself not least, but honored of them all—
And drunk delight of battle with my peers,
Far on the ringing plains of windy Troy.
I am a part of all that I have met;
Yet all experience is an arch wherethrough
Gleams that untraveled world whose margin fades
Forever and forever when I move.
How dull it is to pause, to make an end,
To rust unburnished, not to shine in use!
As though to breathe were life! Life piled on life
Were all too little, and of one to me
Little remains; but every hour is saved
From that eternal silence, something more,
A bringer of new things; and vile it were
For some three suns to store and hoard myself,
And this gray spirit yearning in desire
To follow knowledge like a sinking star,
Beyond the utmost bound of human thought.

This is my son, mine own Telemachus,
To whom I leave the scepter and the isle—°
Well-loved of me, discerning to fulfill
This labor, by slow prudence to make mild
A rugged people, and through soft degrees

ULYSSES.   10 *Hyades:* nymphs who were placed among the stars by Zeus, the king of the gods. The name means "rain," and the rising of the stars was thought to precede a storm.   34 *isle:* Ithaca, the island realm ruled by Odysseus.

Subdue them to the useful and the good.
Most blameless is he, centered in the sphere
Of common duties, decent not to fail   40
In offices of tenderness, and pay
Meet° adoration to my household gods,   *appropriate*
When I am gone. He works his work, I mine.

   There lies the port; the vessel puffs her sail;
There gloom the dark, broad seas. My mariners,   45
Souls that have toiled, and wrought, and thought with me—
That ever with a frolic welcome took
The thunder and the sunshine, and opposed
Free hearts, free foreheads—you and I are old;
Old age hath yet his honor and his toil.   50
Death closes all; but something ere the end,
Some work of noble note, may yet be done,
Not unbecoming men that strove with Gods.
The lights begin to twinkle from the rocks;
The long day wanes; the slow moon climbs; the deep   55
Moans round with many voices. Come, my friends,
'Tis not too late to seek a newer world.
Push off, and sitting well in order smite
The sounding furrows; for my purpose holds
To sail beyond the sunset, and the baths   60
Of all the western stars, until I die.
It may be that the gulfs will wash us down;
It may be we shall touch the Happy Isles,°
And see the great Achilles,° whom we knew.

Though much is taken, much abides; and though   65
We are not now that strength which in old days
Moved earth and heaven, that which we are, we are—
One equal temper of heroic hearts,
Made weak by time and fate, but strong in will
To strive, to seek, to find, and not to yield.   70

---

63 *Happy Isles:* the Elysian Fields, dwelling place of mortals who have been made immortal by the
gods.   64 *Achilles:* Greek hero of the Trojan War who killed Hector and was, in turn, killed by
Paris.

QUESTIONS

1. Who is the speaker of the poem? What is his attitude toward his life in Ithaca?
What key phrases and adjectives in lines 1–5 establish this attitude?

2. Who is Telemachus? What is the speaker's attitude toward him? How are the
speaker and Telemachus different?

3. What aspects of Ulysses are emphasized in this poem? To what extent does he
become symbolic? What does he symbolize?

POEMS ABOUT ICARUS

The next five poems, written between 1933 and 1963, all draw on the same mythic material—the story of the death of Icarus. According to Greek myth, Icarus was the son of Daedalus, an inventor and craftsman who was employed by Minos, the king of Crete, to design and build a labyrinth in which the king wanted to imprison the Minotaur, a monster that was half man and half bull. With Daedalus's help, Theseus killed the Minotaur and freed Athens from its annual tribute of sacrificial youths. As punishment for helping Theseus, Minos imprisoned Daedalus and Icarus in a tower. He also posted guards permanently on all roads and at the seaport to prevent escape. Daedalus realized that he and Icarus could escape only by air, so he fashioned two pairs of wings made of feathers and wax. As father and son were about to fly away from Crete and imprisonment, Daedalus warned Icarus not to fly too near the sun, because the heat would melt the wax and destroy the wings. In the glory of flight, however, Icarus forgot his father's warnings and began to soar higher and higher toward the sun. He continued to mount upward, despite his father's passionate cries, until the wax melted and the wings fell apart; he plunged into the sea and drowned.

Although the next five poems all feature Icarus as the central mythic figure, the focus and the symbolic resonance is different in each. Each poet went to the common storehouse of Greek mythology, selected the story and the figure of Icarus, and shaped these materials according to his or her own poetic goals. Thus, Icarus is used in various ways to illustrate and symbolize ideas about pride, daring, suffering, creativity, idealism, society, and the tedium of daily life. Each of the "Icarus" poems offers its own meaning, impact, and poetic experience. Taken together, however, the group of poems illustrates the way myth can be used for very different effects in various poetic contexts. As you study these poems, try to answer the following questions.

1.   What is Icarus's symbolic meaning or value in the myth? What qualities or characteristics does Icarus represent in mythology?

2.   On what aspects of the Icarus myth does each poet focus? Some possibilities include character, action, motivation, emotion, death, suffering, or the implications of the action.

3.   To what extent does the allusion to Icarus contribute symbolic resonance and meaning to each poem? In what ways is the poetic effect of the mythic allusion different in each?

4.   How do such poetic elements as diction, meter, rhyme, tone, and form help to reshape the myth and the figure of Icarus in each poem?

5.   What themes or ideas are explored in each poem? Explain the connection between the Icarus myth and the meaning of each poem.

STEPHEN SPENDER (b. 1909)

Icarus ———————————————————————————— *1933*

He will watch the hawk with an indifferent eye
  Or pitifully;
Nor on those eagles that so feared him, now
  Will strain his brow;
Weapons men use, stone, sling and strong-thewed bow   5
  He will not know.

This aristocrat, superb of all instinct,
  With death close linked
Had paced the enormous cloud, almost had won
  War on the sun;   10
Till now, like Icarus mid-ocean-drowned,
  Hands, wings, are found.

W. H. AUDEN (1907–1973)

Musée des Beaux Arts° ———————————————————— *1940*

About suffering they were never wrong,
The Old Masters: how well they understood
Its human position; how it takes place
While someone else is eating or opening a window or just walking dully along;
How, when the aged are reverently, passionately waiting   5
For the miraculous birth, there always must be
Children who did not specially want it to happen, skating
On a pond at the edge of the wood:
They never forgot
That even the dreadful martyrdom must run its course   10
Anyhow in a corner, some untidy spot
Where the dogs go on with their doggy life and the torturer's horse
Scratches its innocent behind on a tree.
In Brueghel's° *Icarus*, for instance: how everything turns away
Quite leisurely from the disaster; the ploughman may   15
Have heard the splash, the forsaken cry,
But for him it was not an important failure; the sun shone

MUSÉE DES BEAUX ARTS: "Museum of Fine Arts."   14 *Brueghel:* Pieter Brueghel or Breughel (ca. 1525–1569) was a Flemish painter whose subjects include the Nativity ("the miraculous birth"), the Crucifixion ("the dreadful martyrdom"), and the fall of Icarus. His *Landscape with the Fall of Icarus* is reproduced in color opposite page 547. See pp. 782 and 832 for two other poems based on the work of Brueghel.

As it had to on the white legs disappearing into the green
Water; and the expensive delicate ship that must have seen
Something amazing, a boy falling out of the sky,
Had somewhere to get to and sailed calmly on.

ANNE SEXTON   (1928–1974)

*To a Friend Whose Work Has Come to Triumph°*_____*1962*

Consider Icarus, pasting those sticky wings on,
testing that strange little tug at his shoulder blade,
and think of that first flawless moment over the lawn
of the labyrinth. Think of the difference it made!
There below are the trees, as awkward as camels;
and here are the shocked starlings pumping past
and think of innocent Icarus who is doing quite well:
larger than a sail, over the fog and the blast
of the plushy ocean, he goes. Admire his wings!
Feel the fire at his neck and see how casually
he glances up and is caught, wondrously tunneling
into that hot eye. Who cares that he fell back to the sea?
See him acclaiming the sun and come plunging down
while his sensible daddy goes straight into town.

TO A FRIEND WHOSE WORK HAS COME TO TRIUMPH.   The title alludes to and reverses
the title of a poem by William Butler Yeats, "To a Friend Whose Work Has Come to Nothing"
(1914).

WILLIAM CARLOS WILLIAMS   (1883–1963)

Landscape with the Fall of Icarus   *1962*

According to Brueghel°
when Icarus fell
it was spring

a farmer was ploughing
his field
the whole pageantry

LANDSCAPE WITH THE FALL OF ICARUS.   1 *Brueghel:* See the note for line

of the year was
awake tingling
near

the edge of the sea   10
concerned
with itself

sweating in the sun
that melted
the wings' wax   15

unsignificantly
off the coast
there was

a splash quite unnoticed
this was   20
Icarus drowning

14 in Auden's "Musée des Beaux Arts," p. 831.

EDWARD FIELD   (b. 1924)

Icarus _____ *1963*

Only the feathers floating around the hat
Showed that anything more spectacular had occurred
Than the usual drowning. The police preferred to ignore
The confusing aspects of the case,
And the witnesses ran off to a gang war.   5
So the report filed and forgotten in the archives read simply
"Drowned," but it was wrong: Icarus
Had swum away, coming at last to the city
Where he rented a house and tended the garden.

"That nice Mr. Hicks" the neighbors called him,   10
Never dreaming that the gray, respectable suit
Concealed arms that had controlled huge wings
Nor that those sad, defeated eyes had once
Compelled the sun. And had he told them
They would have answered with a shocked, uncomprehending stare.   15
No, he could not disturb their neat front yards;
Yet all his books insisted that this was a horrible mistake:
What was he doing aging in a suburb?
Can the genius of the hero fall
To the middling stature of the merely talented?   20

And nightly Icarus probes his wound
And daily in his workshop, curtains carefully drawn,
Constructs small wings and tries to fly
To the lighting fixture on the ceiling:
Fails every time and hates himself for trying.

He had thought himself a hero, had acted heroically,
And dreamt of his fall, the tragic fall of the hero;
But now rides commuter trains,
Serves on various committees,
And wishes he had drowned.

WRITING ABOUT MYTH IN POETRY

An essay on myth in poetry will normally connect the mythic material in a poem to some other consideration, such as speaker, character, action, tone, setting, situation, imagery, form, and meaning. This suggests a two-part exploration of the poem, one concerned with its general sense, and the other with the ways in which myth shapes and controls that sense.

As you reexamine the poem, look for the ways in which myth enriches the poem and focuses its meaning. The following questions should help:

Questions for Discovering Ideas

- To what extent does the title identify the mythic content of the poem and thus provide a key for understanding?
- How much of the poem's action, setting, and situation are borrowed from mythology? What is the significance of the action in the myth? What does this action symbolize? How does the poet reshape the action and its significance?
- To what extent does our understanding of the myth explain the poem's speaker, characters, situations, and ideas? What characters, including the speaker, are drawn from mythology?
- In what ways are these characters symbolic? What aspects of this symbolism are carried into the poem? How does the poem either maintain or change the symbolism?
- How do the various formal elements of the poem, such as diction, rhyme, meter, and form, reshape the mythic material and affect the meaning and impact of the myth?
- Do specific words and phrases, for instance, undercut or reinforce the ideas and implications that we find in the myth itself?
- Does the rhyme (if any) lead us to deal with the mythic content seriously or humorously?
- Does the tone of the poem support or undercut the implications of the myth?
- Generally, how does the mythic content help develop and clarify the poem?

Strategies for Organizing Ideas

As with most other essays, the main challenge in writing about myths is developing a focus or central idea. If, for example, you find that the poem retells a myth in order to make a point about history or society, you should fashion your central idea to reflect that connection. Similarly, if the poem employs a mythical speaker or character to convey ideas about war or heroism, your essay will focus on the linkage among myth, character, and those ideas.

When you formulate a central idea, draft it as a complete sentence that conveys the full scope of your ideas. It is not enough merely to assert that a given poem contains a great deal of mythic material. If you are writing about Yeats's "Leda and the Swan," for example, you might be tempted to form a central idea that argues that "William Butler Yeats's 'Leda and the Swan' retells the myth of Leda's rape by Zeus and the consequences of that event." That sentence does not tell the reader anything about the *way* the Leda myth works in the poem. Nor does it provide a basis for moving beyond summary and paraphrase. A more effective formulation would be the following: "In Yeats's 'Leda and the Swan,' the myth of Leda's rape by Zeus and the consequences of that rape illustrate the process of history and question the connection between knowledge and power." This sentence points to a specific connection between mythological content and the poem's effect, and it gives a clear direction to the essay.

In your introductory paragraph or paragraphs, you should briefly summarize the significant parts of your poem's mythical elements, together with any noteworthy details about the poem's form or circumstances of composition. Your aim should be to focus on the poem (and the mythic material within the poem) rather than on the myth itself. Thus, you should link the mythical elements with other aspects of the poem, and make assertions about the effects of this connection.

You can employ various strategies to organize the body of your essay. (1) You might decide to echo the organization of the poem, and shape the central paragraphs so as to reflect the poem's line-by-line or stanza-by-stanza logic. (2) Alternatively, you might choose an organization based on a series of different mythic elements or figures. If a poem alludes to Odysseus, his wife Penelope, and his son Telemachus, for instance, you might devote paragraphs to the way each figure shapes the poem's impact and meaning. (3) As a third option, you might use the relevant elements of poetry as the focal points of organization. Thus, if you argue that diction, rhyme, and tone shape the mythological material to produce significant effects, you would deal with each element in turn.

To bring your essay to a convincing and assertive close, you might summarize your major points. At the same time, you might draw your reader's attention to the significance of your observations and to any further implications of the ways in which the myth is integrated into the poem you have considered.

SAMPLE ESSAY

Myth and Meaning in Dorothy Parker's "Penelope"°

[1]   Dorothy Parker's short lyric poem "Penelope" uses mythic allusion and symbolism to criticize conventional ideas about the roles of women and men. Her speaker is the mythic figure Penelope, the wife of King Odysseus of the ancient realm of Ithaca. Not only is Penelope the speaker, but she is also the poem's major figure. Parker uses her to assert that society has consistently misjudged and undervalued women's lives.* Her assertions are brought out through the poem's title, its mythic resonance, its diction, and its view of the representative lives of both Odysseus and Penelope.†

[2]   The key to the poem's use of myth is the title, "Penelope." As the only place where the poem's mythological speaker is named, the title alludes to Homer's The Odyssey, which tells that Penelope waits at home in Ithaca for twenty years while her husband adventures in the Trojan War and struggles to return home despite the enmity of the Sea God, Poseidon. Penelope's seemingly interminable wait is filled with trouble. Her palace is occupied by boorish suitors who assume that Odysseus is dead and that his kingship is vacant. They therefore demand that Penelope choose a new husband. Only Penelope and Telemachus, her son, cling to the hope that Odysseus is still alive. She keeps the arrogant suitors at bay by promising to marry one of them after she finishes weaving a shroud for Odysseus's father. To delay this event, she works at the loom by day and unravels the work by night.

[3]   Although the title refers directly to Penelope, the poem itself also deals with Odysseus. Lines 1-5 evoke the King's adventures in the phrases "He shall ride the silver seas" (line 4) and "He shall cut the glittering wave" (line 5). Because Odysseus is not identified by name, but only by the pronoun "he," readers might see this male figure as a symbol of all men who leave home to pursue adventure. The adjectives silver and glittering connote splendor and glory, while the verbs ride and cut suggest resoluteness and boldness. In addition, the phrases "pathway of the sun" (line 1) and "footsteps of the breeze" (line 2) add romance and mystery. In the same lines, however, one may perceive a subtle undercutting of the heroic figure. The phrase "ride the silver seas," for example, suggests that some of the Homeric lines are clichés. The implication is that an overglorified image of active heroes like Odysseus is both exaggerated and inaccurate.

[4]   Just as this language has general implications for men, the language about Penelope is significant for women. In lines 6-9 she, as the speaker, contrasts her restricted life with the freedom of males. Here we find no adjectives at all; the woman's existence is thus rendered drab and tedious. In addition, the verbs represent passive and domestic activities: sit, rock, rise, brew, snip, and bleach. These last two verbs are especially effective. The phrase "snip my thread" (line 8) is the only allusion to Penelope's unhappy existence. It refers to her daring deception of the suitors through her nightly unraveling of the

° See p. 826 for this poem.
* Central idea.
† Thesis sentence.

shroud. At the same time, <u>snip</u> is contrasted with the verb <u>cut</u> used earlier in the poem. While the words are synonyms, their connotations are different, for <u>cut</u> implies a degree of violence while <u>snip</u> suggests careful and delicate activity. <u>Bleach</u> is equally connotative; although it refers directly to "the linen for my bed," it is consistent with the view that Penelope's life is faded and colorless.

[5]
The poem's final line ironically clarifies Penelope's attitude toward the different roles of men and women. Penelope asserts that "They will call him brave." They refers to society, to the world at large, and to generations of readers who have admired Odysseus in Homer's <u>Iliad</u> and <u>Odyssey</u>. The meter of the line--a concluding spondee--places a great emphasis on the word <u>him</u>, thus demonstrating the speaker's realization, and the poet's assertion, that society ignores or dismisses the quiet bravery of women. In myth and in life, the woman's role demands just as much courage and conviction as the man's.

[6]
"Penelope" thus employs mythic figures and events to criticize the historical perception of the roles of men and women. Odysseus, the mythical and typical male, is presented as a heroic figure, but he too is human, and his adventures are tinged with overdramatization. Parker's point is not to demean him, however, but rather to emphasize that women, too, have their own heroism. Biology and destiny may have traditionally confined women to stay at home, weave tapestries, and "make cookies," while men are granted the freedom to find adventure in far off lands. But waiting at home while meeting domestic challenges takes courage too. Penelope and Odysseus lived at a time of the old ways, but if Parker's poem is understood properly, it is time for new ways to begin. Penelope is right to express annoyance and irony when considering the judgment of history. Our knowledge of her courageous survival in Ithaca during the absence of Odysseus adds significantly to the truth and depth of her feelings.

Commentary on the Essay

This essay's major rhetorical purpose is to show how the poet uses the Penelope-Odysseus myth to shed new light on conventional attitudes about men and women. As a guide for your own writing aims, therefore, the essay illustrates how the mythological material may lead to ideas for development.

The body of the essay follows the organization of the poem itself. Thus, paragraph 2 focuses on the title, paragraph 3 on lines 1–5, paragraph 4 on lines 6–9, and paragraph 5 on the last line. Each of the paragraphs also advances a specific aspect of the essay's central idea. In paragraph 2 Penelope is identified, and the relevant mythic material is reviewed. Logically, the information in this paragraph is essential for the remainder of the essay.

In paragraph 3, the title and its mythic importance introduce Odysseus and the symbol of the heroic male. Here, the point is that Parker's diction undercuts the active male image while seeming to glorify it. The first sentence of paragraph 4 provides a transition from Odysseus and heroic males to Penelope and the perceived passiveness of women. Again, the essay explores the way diction and mythic allusion in the poem demonstrate that there is more to the lives of women than usually is claimed. Paragraph 5 looks at the poem's final line in relation to the contrasted lives of "heroic" men and "passive" women. Here, the essay shows how tone and meter reveal the speaker's attitude toward these contrasting lives and society's misperception of them.

The conclusion goes quickly over the essay's basic points, and it emphasizes how the poem, with its ancient myth, brings new light to a traditional problem. The result is that the conclusion is a brief personal essay that considers the poem's ideas and their current importance.

WRITING TOPICS

1. In the poems "Ulysses," "Penelope," "Odysseus," "Siren Song," and "Circe," the poets evoke the same myth but for different purposes. What are these purposes? What views do you find about adventure, domesticity, and sexuality? What attitudes toward figures in the myth (Odysseus, Penelope, the Siren, Circe) do the poets bring out? How does word choice, selection of detail, and point of view influence each poet's conclusions?

2. The myth of Icarus is used by Spender, Auden, Sexton, Williams, and Field. Basing your conclusions on two or more of their poems in this group, what similarities and differences can you describe? How do the poets present the myth? How do they use the myth to create unusual or surprising endings, and to comment on contemporary but also permanent attitudes about life and the sufferings of others?

3. What point does Muriel Rukuyser's "Myth" make about both men and women and their attitudes toward each other? How does our knowledge of the Oedipus myth (Sophocles' play *Oedipus the King* is included in the Drama section) help clarify these aspects of the poem? In what respects is the poem contemporary?

4. Select a story from among the many myths, traditions, and historical events that are a part of our heritage: e.g., Oedipus, Jason, Romulus and Remus, Antigone, Sisyphus, the fight between God and Satan, the Captivity in Egypt and the Exodus, the Babylonian Captivity, Robin Hood, Beaver stealing fire from the Pines (Nez Percé legend), Paul Bunyan, Davy Crockett, the Amistad event, the Forty-Niners, the Lone Ranger, the log cabin, the Roughriders, etc. Write a poem based on the story, and try to present your own view about its importance, timeliness, intelligence, and truth. What kinds of detail do you select? How do you give the figures mythic status? How do you make your own attitudes apparent by your arrangement of detail and your word choice?

23

Theme: Idea, Motif, and Meaning in Poetry

Poetry, like music, is a unique form of thinking. As readers we may therefore determine many poetic ideas, both for their external importance and also for their internal thematic and unifying significance. Words that are concerned with the ways in which poetry expresses ideas are *idea, theme, motif,* and *meaning* (see also Chapter 10). These words are often used interchangeably, and their shades of difference are not easily distinguished. By **idea** we mean a *concept, principle, scheme, method, idealization,* or *archetype.* An idea may yield to extensive description and definition, such as the *idea of goodness,* the *idea of time,* and so on. When we use the word **theme** we refer to an idea, image, principle, or **motif** that, like a melody in music, is *embodied and developed* within a literary work.

POETRY AND MEANING

Going up the scale from idea, theme, and motif, we arrive at **meaning**, the word referring comprehensively to the ideas expressed within the poem—the poem's *sense* or *message.* For example, we might say that one of the meanings of Wordsworth's "Daffodils" is that close contact with Nature provides energy for the mind and spirit. Wordsworth introduces this idea by describing his impressions at the sight of daffodils in bloom. At the end of the poem he underscores the idea by pointing out how the remembered vision gives him spiritual comfort and joy:

> For oft, when on my couch I lie
> In vacant or in pensive mood,
> They flash upon that inward eye
> Which is the bliss of solitude;
> And then my heart with pleasure fills,
> And dances with the daffodils.
>
> (lines 19-24)

In this way, Wordsworth develops his theme, or motif, by drawing general conclusions about his specific experience.

But even when we try to describe a meaning in this way, it is important to recognize the limitations of our effort. Our sentences are no more than our sentences. They demonstrate our perception and comprehension, but only the poem itself contains its *entire* meaning. We know that individual poems are made up of separate parts, that each part has its own meaning, that the various parts together make up the whole, and that the poem is an artifact intricately connected to the poet's mind, the circumstances of composition, and the historical period of the poem's origin. Thus, as we continue to ask and try to answer questions about what we read—as the best way to comprehend individual poems—we recognize that our understanding may fall short of our efforts to understand.

A major problem of comprehension lies in the nature of poetry itself as a *time art*. It takes time for a poem to unfold, and we cannot hold the entire poem in our minds all at once. When we read a poem, the content of the early lines recedes in our minds as we encounter new words, images, ideas, symbols, sounds, and rhythms. Although it is clear that meaning in a poem develops, it is hard to maintain that we achieve both a comprehensive and instantaneous understanding of the meaning.

Our own time frame and stage of life also influence the impact that poems have on us. Individual parts may seem to shift in meaning, depending on our circumstances and responses. Lines that we read today may not impress us much, whereas at a later time these same lines may burst upon us with great meaning and power. President Eisenhower once introduced a new legislative proposal by quoting the following couplet from "An Essay on Criticism" by Alexander Pope:

> Be not the *first* by whom the *New* are try'd,
> Nor yet the *last* to lay the *Old* aside.

Everyone who studies Pope's poem reads these lines, which refer to the need for discrimination about new critical approaches. But the President, or someone on his staff, thought the lines provided a meaningful justification for new proposals to address the nation's needs. Here we have a clear example of how meaning may emerge as a result of time and circumstance.

But even after we complete our analysis and derive what we consider to be a poem's meanings, the poem is independent; it always maintains its own distinct identity and integrity. A dancer was once asked why she danced. Her response was that if she could explain her reasons in words, she would not need to dance. The meaning of poetry is like that. No matter how well we follow a poem's intricate threads of theme or motif, or how comprehensively we determine the meaning of individual parts, the poem is still out there—dancing. We see it and try to understand it, but it evidences techniques and meaning that elude our total grasp and comprehension. This is what leads Archibald MacLeish, in his poem "Ars Poetica," to claim that "A poem should not mean / But be."

THE SUBJECT OF A POEM AND ITS EXPRESSION OF IDEAS

To determine the meaning or theme of poems, we employ the basic elements we have been working with throughout this book, beginning with **subject**. Subjects are often general, and may include such broad categories as love, death, war, art, youth, age, work, and nature. Thomas Hardy's "Channel Firing" (p. 584) and Wilfred Owen's "Dulce et Decorum Est" (p. 681), for example, share the same subject—war.

But the subject of a poem is only the beginning of our comprehension, for subjects alone are static. To move us, poems must take us somewhere. In prose, ideas are established directly and openly. For example, a major point in our Declaration of Independence, written in prose, is that human beings have the unalienable rights of life, liberty, and the pursuit of happiness. In poetry, however, points are made dramatically and indirectly. Even if we grant that many poems may have no *overt* intention to express ideas (poems are not newspaper articles, or sermons), it is nevertheless true that poems contain ideas about their subjects.

Thus, Hardy's "Channel Firing" and Owen's "Dulce et Decorum Est" are both powerful and dramatic poems. They share the common subject of war, and they also share a common thread of hostility toward war as a human institution. But in addition, both poems may be read as strong statements of ideas. Hardy's poem asserts that war is a perpetual condition of human life, and that despite the perversity of war it will likely continue to threaten all the positive and noble achievements that humanity has created. Owen's poem, briefly dramatizing the death of a soldier in a wartime gas attack, asserts that war is obscene, and that ideas about war's nobility are unreal and untrue. Both poems, in short, contain clear ideas.

Moreover, no matter what the subject, poems achieve much of their impact through the strength of their ideas. Andrew Marvell's "To His Coy Mistress" and Robert Herrick's "To the Virgins, to Make Much of Time," for example, both concern the subject of love within the context of passing time. But while Herrick's poem argues that the pressure of eventual death should lead people toward delight in marriage, Marvell's poem asserts that this same pressure should lead toward the full but desperate pursuit of pleasures through the "iron gates of life." These ideas, like those of Hardy and Owen, are not frivolous expressions of idle poetic moments, but are deeply felt ideas that people should know, think about, and apply or not apply, as they wish, to their own lives.

Strategies for Dealing with Meaning

So that we may approach comprehension of poetic meaning, we need to consider a poem's ideas together with its intellectual and emotional impact. In effect, meaning involves us in a transfer of experience from the poet's mind to our own. It is no exaggeration to claim that the structure and development of a poem also produce a corresponding development of thoughts, reactions, considerations, and emotions in readers. To get at meaning, then, is to get at all the ways in which poetry brings these effects about.

An initial understanding of meaning can therefore be gained by a close, sentence-by-sentence reading. But for most poems the meaning emerges as a result of comprehending not only the direct statements but also the results of the poet's technique. In the various chapters of this book we have studied many of these elements of technique separately: speaker; character, setting and action; diction; imagery and rhetorical figures; tone; rhythm, meter, sound, and rhyme; structure and form; and symbol and allusion, together with others.

SPEAKER. The identity and circumstances of the speaker significantly affect a poem's meaning. It is essential for us to understand, for example, that the speaker of Hardy's "Channel Firing" is a skeleton who has been wakened in his grave by the noise of "great guns" at sea, and that the speaker in Sharon Olds's "35/10" is a mother brushing her daughter's hair. The attitudes and ironies so essential to the meanings of these poems would not be clear if we did not know who these speakers are and what they are doing at the "time" of the poems. Similarly, it is important to determine whether a speaker is trustworthy. Thus in Browning's "My Last Duchess" the speaker presents himself as a friendly and intelligent man of integrity, but his words betray him as intimidating, cold, cruel, and heartless. In short, each poem produces its own unique speaker, whose circumstances have a vital bearing on the content and meaning of the poem.

CHARACTER, SETTING, AND ACTION. The characters, settings, and actions in a poem do much to shape the meaning. A poem that is set in a graveyard and that refers to gunnery practice at sea ("Channel Firing") conveys a different meaning from one that tells about a walk through the woodland in spring (Housman's "Loveliest of Trees") or that tells about a mother brushing her daughter's hair at bedtime (Olds's "35/10"). Even if all three poems dealt with the common subject of death, their radically different contexts and actions produce a new perspective, a different emotional response, a new experience, and a different meaning.

DICTION. The words of a poem—denotation, connotation, diction, and syntax—all shape a poem's total meaning and emotional impact. In Robert

Herrick's "To the Virgins, to Make Much of Time," for example, the speaker advises virgins to gather "rosebuds," which could easily be interpreted as an invitation to promiscuous sexuality. However, the poem concludes on the advice to "go marry," and thereby it places the urgency of sex in a context of socially and religiously approved behavior. By contrast, in Ben Jonson's "To Celia," the speaker urges "sports of love" and "love's fruit," but provides no additional context. Thus "To Celia" primarily advises seduction, while "To the Virgins" provides happy but mature advice about life, even though both poems similarly belong to the "seize the day" or "carpe diem" tradition of love poetry.

IMAGERY AND RHETORICAL FIGURES. Imagery, metaphor, simile, and other devices of language make abstract ideas and situations concrete and immediate. We have stressed how Keats creates a sense of excitement through his simile of the "watcher of the skies" in "On First Looking into Chapman's Homer" (p. 650). Beyond such uses, a poet may use imagery and metaphorical language to reinforce or to negate what appears to be the speaker's major thrust. In Owen's "Dulce et Decorum Est," for example, soldiers are described as "Bent double, like old beggars under sacks." The simile is consistent with the rest of the poem; it defines the speaker's dislike of the drudgery and difficulty of war, and it shapes the poem's ultimate point that war is humiliating, dehumanizing, and horrible. In contrast, the first part of Dorothy Parker's "Penelope" (p. 826) contains clichéd images that undercut the heroic ideal. The poem thereby emphasizes the negative truth that heroes, while pursuing their goals, may also be self-centered and neglectful.

TONE. The tone of a poem has a significant effect on the expression of ideas. In Arthur O'Shaughnessy's "A Love Symphony," for example (p. 693), the speaker's admiration for the listener is clear, unambiguous, and unreserved, as indicated by phrases like "You were more sweet." There is no question about the content of this poem. Tone may sometimes create ambiguity, however, or it may even work against the stated purpose of the speaker, as in the Duke's mentioning the marriage settlement in "My Last Duchess." The Duke speaks of the Count's "known munificence" as justification for his "just" claims, while we conclude that the Duke will make confiscatory demands. Through irony, therefore, Browning shows that the Duke is an inhuman monster. Irony is also present in Marvell's "To His Coy Mistress," in which the *carpe diem* mode is colored by the speaker's many details about death and eternity. In short, although the ostensible purpose of Marvell's speaker is persuasion and seduction, the tone makes the poem not happy and loving but rather somber and desperate.

RHYTHM, METER, SOUND, AND RHYME. Devices like rhythm, alliteration, assonance, and onomatopoeia shape meaning significantly in tandem with other elements. Rhythm and meter may throw particularly important words into strong positions of emphasis, and therefore they may shape our perception of the importance of particular ideas. The last line of Parker's "Penelope," for example, is "They will call him brave." The meter literally demands that "him" be accented, thus underscoring the powerful irony of this line, and of the poem. Similarly, meaning can be refined through the skillful use of alliteration, assonance, and the repetition of identical or similar sounds. In Pope's line, "The sound must seem an echo to the sense," for example, the alliteration of the *s* sound connected the key words "sound," "seem," and "sense." The words are important in themselves, but they are made more emphatic, in the context, by Pope's linking them by sound. Rhyme may be employed to clinch ideas, regulate the tone, and thus shape meaning. In fact, rhyme is the best single poetic technique for helping people's memories. The falling or double rhymes in Herrick's "To the Virgins," for example, lighten the poem's tone and thus augment and qualify Herrick's message.

STRUCTURE AND FORM.   Form can provide a method for ordering and shaping a poem's theme and meaning. The coherent units or stanzas of a closed form often reflect specific steps in the poem's expression of meaning. Such is the case in Spenser's *Amoretti* 75, "One Day I Wrote Her Name upon the Strand." In this poem the formal divisions of the sonnet reflect a logical pattern that moves from an action to a reaction and finally to an explanation.

SYMBOL AND ALLUSION.   Poets employ symbol and allusion as a shorthand way of conveying complex ideas and a great deal of information as quickly and economically as possible. In "To the Virgins," for example, two symbols—rosebuds and flowers—point beyond themselves to human sexuality, marriage and families, and full engagement with life. The symbols thus carry much of the poem's impact and message. Allusion can be equally important. In "To His Coy Mistress" we find geographic and biblical allusions that are crucial in shaping the meaning of the first part of the poem's argument.

Admittedly, the eight areas discussed above form a large number of variables to consider as you work toward an understanding of a poem's central idea and meaning. Keep in mind, however, that this is an outside number of approaches, and that as you study you will probably focus not on all but rather on just a few. In addition, you will eventually be able to evaluate the impact of many of these elements on meaning rather quickly. Indeed, experienced readers of poetry do much of this step-by-step analysis almost unconsciously and simultaneously as they read. The point to remember about analyzing poetic meaning is that all elements of poetry—statements and techniques—are available, and you can introduce any element that is relevant to assist you in developing your comprehension.

POEMS FOR STUDY

DONALD HALL (b. 1928)

Whip-poor-will ——————————————————————— *1981*

As the last light
of June withdraws
the whip-poor-will sings   5
his clear brief notes
by the darkening house, then
rises abruptly from sandy
ground, a brown bird
in the near-night, soaring   10
over shed and woodshed
to far dark fields. When
he returns at dawn,
in my sleep I hear
his three syllables make   15
a man's name, who slept
fifty years in this bed
and ploughed these fields:
Wes-ley-Wells °. . .*Wes-*
ley-Wells . . .   20
      It is good
to wake early in high
summer with work to do,
and look out the window
at a ghost bird lifting away   25
to drowse all morning
in his grassy hut.

WHIP-POOR-WILL   17 *Wes-ley-Wells:* the name of the poet's grandfather.

QUESTIONS

1. What is a whippoorwill? How does its song figure into the poem's development? Why does the speaker stress that he hears the name *Wesley Wells* not when waking but when asleep?

2. Who was Wesley Wells? What connection is established between him and the home and life of the speaker?

3. Why is so much attention given to the flying and singing habits of the bird?

4. How comparable is this poem to Keats's "Ode to a Nightingale" (p. 770)? How do birds and their songs serve to bring out major ideas in both poems?

ROBERT HERRICK   (1591–1674)

To the Virgins, to Make Much of Time ————————————— *1648*

Gather ye rosebuds while ye may,
  Old time is still a-flying;
And this same flower that smiles today
  Tomorrow will be dying.

The glorious lamp of heaven, the sun,
  The higher he's a-getting,
The sooner will his race be run,
  And nearer he's to setting.

That age is best which is the first,
  When youth and blood are warmer;
But being spent, the worse, and worst
  Times still succeed the former.

Then be not coy, but use your time,
  And, while ye may, go marry;
For, having lost but once your prime,
  You may forever tarry.

QUESTIONS

1. What does the title of this poem tell us? What can we deduce about the speaker? To whom is the poem addressed?
2. What point does this poem make about time? Life? Love?
3. How does symbolism help shape the message and meaning of the poem? Consider especially "rosebuds," "flower," and "the sun."
4. How do rhyme and tone help create and focus the meaning of this poem?
5. This type of poem is called *carpe diem* (Latin for "seize the day" or "enjoy the present"). Compare this poem with Jonson's "To Celia" and Marvell's "To His Coy Mistress," which are also *carpe diem* poems. How are the tone and message of this poem similar to and different from those in the poems by Jonson and Marvell?

BEN JONSON   (1572–1632)

To Celia° ——————————————————————————— *1606*

Come my Celia, let us prove,°   *try*
While we may, the sports of love;
Time will not be ours forever;
He at length our good will sever.

TO CELIA.   The poem is from Jonson's play *Volpone;* it is spoken by Volpone (the name means "the fox") to Celia, a married woman whom he is trying to seduce.

Spend not then his gifts in vain.   5
Suns that set may rise again;
But if once we lose this light,
'Tis with us perpetual night.
Why should we defer our joys?
Fame° and rumor are but toys.   *reputation*   10
Cannot we delude the eyes
Of a few poor household spies,
Or his° easier ears beguile,   *Celia's husband*
So removed by our wile?
'Tis no sin love's fruit to steal;   15
But the sweet theft to reveal,
To be taken, to be seen,
These have crimes accounted been.

QUESTIONS

1. What is the speaker like? What is his attitude toward time? Love? Celia?
2. What is personified in lines 3–5? What power does this force have?
3. How is the idea of "seizing the day" relevant to the first eight lines of this poem?
4. How does the speaker's argument change in the last ten lines? What assertions does the poem make about time, love, reputation, and crime?
5. What is the tone of the poem? How does it affect the meaning?

DONALD JUSTICE   (b. 1925)

On the Death of Friends in Childhood _____ 1960

We shall not ever meet them bearded in heaven,
Nor sunning themselves among the bald of hell;
If anywhere, in the deserted schoolyard at twilight,
Forming a ring, perhaps, or joining hands
In games whose very names we have forgotten,   5
Come, memory, let us seek them there in the shadows.

QUESTIONS

1. What is the subject of this poem: the living, or the dead? How accurate is the title as a guide to subject and theme?
2. What point (if any) does this poem make about death? Time? Memory? The living?
3. How do imagery, diction, rhetoric and tone contribute to the total meaning of
   this poem? Consider phrases like "bearded in heaven" and "sunning themselves
   among the bald of hell." What is personified in the last line?

JOHN KEATS   (1795–1821)

Ode on a Grecian Urn _____ *1820 (1819)*

1

Thou still unravish'd bride of quietness,
  Thou foster-child of silence and slow time,
Sylvan historian, who canst thus express
A flowery tale more sweetly than our rhyme:
What leaf-fring'd legend° haunts about thy shape   *border and tale*
  Of deities or mortals, or of both,
    In Tempe° or the dales of Arcady?°
  What men or gods are these? What maidens loth?
What mad pursuit? What struggle to escape?
    What pipes and timbrels? What wild ecstasy?

2

Heard melodies are sweet, but those unheard
  Are sweeter; therefore, ye soft pipes, play on;
Not to the sensual ear, but, more endear'd,
  Pipe to the spirit ditties of no tone:
Fair youth, beneath the trees, thou canst not leave
  Thy song, nor ever can those trees be bare;
    Bold lover, never, never canst thou kiss,
Though winning near the goal—yet, do not grieve;
  She cannot fade, though thou hast not thy bliss,
For ever wilt thou love, and she be fair!

3

Ah, happy, happy boughs! that cannot shed
  Your leaves, nor ever bid the spring adieu;
And, happy melodist, unwearied,
  For ever piping songs for ever new;
More happy love! more happy, happy love!
  For ever warm and still to be enjoy'd,
    For ever panting, and for ever young;
All breathing human passion far above,
  That leaves a heart high-sorrowful and cloy'd,
    A burning forehead, and a parching tongue.

4

Who are these coming to the sacrifice?
  To what green altar, O mysterious priest,
Lead'st thou that heifer lowing at the skies,
  And all her silken flanks with garlands drest?
What little town by river or sea shore,

ODE ON A GRECIAN URN.   The imaginary Grecian urn to which the poem is addressed combines design motifs from many different existing urns. This imaginary one is decorated with a border of leaves and trees, men (or gods) chasing women, a young musician sitting under a tree, lovers, and a priest and congregation leading a heifer to sacrifice.   7 *Tempe:* a beautiful rustic valley in Greece.   *Arcady:* refers to the valleys of Arcadia, a state in ancient Greece known for its beauty and peacefulness.

The Krater of Thanagra. Fourth century B.C., showing a wedding procession and musicians. National Museum, Athens. (Archivi Alinari/Art Resource)

Or mountain-built° with peaceful citadel,	*built on a mountain*
Is emptied of this folk, this pious morn?	
And, little town, thy streets for evermore	
Will silent be; and not a soul to tell	
Why thou art desolate, can e'er return.	40

5

O Attic shape! Fair attitude! with brede°	*braid, pattern*
Of marble men and maidens overwrought,°	*ornamented*
With forest branches and the trodden weed;	
Thou, silent form, dost tease us out of thought	
As doth eternity: Cold Pastoral!	45
When old age shall this generation waste,	
Thou shalt remain, in midst of other woe	
Than ours, a friend to man, to whom thou say'st,	
"Beauty is truth, truth beauty,"—that is all	
Ye know on earth, and all ye need to know.	50

QUESTIONS

1. What is the dramatic situation? What does the speaker see and do?
2. What does the speaker call the urn in the first stanza? What is suggested in these lines about the urn's relationship to time and change? To poetry?
3. What are "unheard melodies" (line 11) and "ditties of no tone" (line 14)? Why are these "sweeter" than songs heard by "the sensual ear" (line 13)? What central contrast is created through this comparison?
4. What do the trees, the musician, and the lovers have in common? How are they all related to the real world of time and change?

PHILIP LARKIN　(1922–1985)

Next, Please ———————————————————————————— *1955*

Always too eager for the future, we
Pick up bad habits of expectancy.
Something is always approaching; every day
Till then we say,

Watching from a bluff the tiny, clear,
Sparkling armada of promises draw near.
How slow they are! And how much time they waste,
Refusing to make haste!

Yet still they leave us holding wretched stalks
Of disappointment, for, though nothing balks
Each big approach, leaning with brasswork prinked,°　　　　　　*adorned*
Each rope distinct,

Flagged, and the figurehead with golden tits
Arching our way, it never anchors; it's
No sooner present than it turns to past.
Right to the last

We think each one will heave to and unload
All good into our lives, all we are owed
For waiting so devoutly and so long.
But we are wrong:

Only one ship is seeking us, a black-
Sailed unfamiliar, towing at her back
A huge and birdless silence. In her wake
No waters breed or break.

QUESTIONS

1. What is the subject of the poem? The theme? What point does it make about time, expectation, human nature, and the way we live our lives?
2. What cliché does the extended metaphor that begins in the second stanza ironi-

cally revitalize and reverse? How does this metaphor make the total meaning of the poem clearer and more palpable?

3. How do meter, rhyme, and diction help create meaning? Consider, for example, the metrical variation in the fourth line of each stanza, rhyming pairs such as *waste-haste* and *wake-break*, or words such as *bluff* and *armada*.

4. Compare this poem to the three *carpe diem* poems in this chapter including Marvell's "To His Coy Mistress". To what extent is "Next, Please" a *carpe diem* poem?

ARCHIBALD MACLEISH   (1892–1982)

Ars Poetica ————————————————————————*1926*

A poem should be palpable and mute
As a globed fruit,

Dumb
As old medallions to the thumb,

Silent as the sleeve-worn stone   5
Of casement ledges where the moss has grown—

A poem should be wordless
As the flight of birds
          *   *   *

A poem should be motionless in time
As the moon climbs.   10

Leaving, as the moon releases
Twig by twig the night-entangled trees,

Leaving, as the moon behind the winter leaves,
Memory by memory the mind—

A poem should be motionless in time   15
As the moon climbs.
          *   *   *

A poem should be equal to:
Not true.

For all the history of grief
An empty doorway and a maple leaf   20

For love
The leaning grasses and two lights above the sea—

A poem should not mean
But be.

QUESTIONS

1. What do lines 1–8 assert about a poem? How do the similes make this assertion clear and concrete?

2. How do you resolve the paradoxes that a poem may be both "mute" and "dumb," and also "silent" and "wordless"?

3. How do symbolism and simile clarify the claims about poetry in lines 9-16? How can something be "motionless" and also "climb"?

4. What does the third section (lines 17–24) state about a poem? Why are the symbols of grief and love included here?

5. To what extent does "Ars Poetica" illustrate its own definition of poetry?

ANDREW MARVELL   (1621–1678)

To His Coy Mistress _____ *1681*

Had we but world enough, and time,
This coyness, lady, were no crime.
We would sit down, and think which way
To walk, and pass our long love's day.

Thou by the Indian Ganges° side
Shouldst rubies find; I by the tide
Of Humber° would complain. I would
Love you ten years before the flood,°   *Noah's flood*
And you should, if you please, refuse
Till the conversion of the Jews.°
My vegetable love should grow
Vaster than empires and more slow;
An hundred years should go to praise
Thine eyes, and on thy forehead gaze;
Two hundred to adore each breast,
But thirty thousand to the rest;
An age at least to every part,
And the last age should show your heart.
For, lady, you deserve this state,
Nor would I love at lower rate.
  But at my back I always hear
Time's wingéd chariot hurrying near;
And yonder all before us lie
Deserts of vast eternity.
Thy beauty shall no more be found,
Nor, in thy marble vault, shall sound
My echoing song; then worms shall try
That long-preserved virginity,
And your quaint honor turn to dust,
And into ashes all my lust:

TO HIS COY MISTRESS.   5 *Ganges:* a large river that runs across most of India.   7 *Humber:* a small river that runs through the north of England to the North Sea.   10 *Jews:* Traditionally, this conversion is supposed to occur just before the Last Judgment.

The grave's a fine and private place,
But none, I think, do there embrace.
  Now therefore, while the youthful hue
Sits on thy skin like morning dew,
And while thy willing soul transpires
At every pore with instant fires,
Now let us sport us while we may,   35
And now, like amorous birds of prey,
Rather at once our time devour
Than languish in his slow-chapped° power.   *slow-jawed*
Let us roll all our strength and all
Our sweetness up into one ball,   40
And tear our pleasures with rough strife
Thorough° the iron gates of life: *through*
Thus, though we cannot make our sun
Stand still, yet we will make him run.

                                                                45

QUESTIONS

1. In lines 1 through 20 the speaker sets up a hypothetical situation and the first part of a pseudo-logical proof: If *A* then *B*. What specific words indicate the logic of this section? What hypothetical situation is established?
2. How do geographic and biblical allusions affect our sense of time and place?
3. In lines 21 through 32 the speaker refutes the hypothetical condition set up in the first twenty lines. What word indicates that this is a refutation? How does imagery help create and reinforce meaning here?
4. The last part of the poem (lines 33–46) presents the speaker's "logical" conclusion. What words indicate that this is a conclusion? What is the conclusion?

MARIANNE MOORE   (1887–1982)

Poetry ° _____ *1921*

I, too, dislike it: there are things that are important beyond all this fiddle.
  Reading it, however, with a perfect contempt for it, one discovers in
  it after all, a place for the genuine.
    Hands that can grasp, eyes
    that can dilate, hair that can rise
      if it must, these things are important not because a

high-sounding interpretation can be put upon them but because they are
  useful. When they become so derivative as to become unintelligible,
    the same thing may be said for all of us, that we
      do not admire what   10

POETRY. In the most recent edition of her *Collected Poems*, Moore deleted everything in this poem following "genuine" in line 3.

we cannot understand: the bat
    holding on upside down or in quest of something to

eat, elephants pushing, a wild horse taking a roll, a tireless wolf under
    a tree, the immovable critic twitching his skin like a horse that feels a
        flea, the base-
    ball fan, the statistician—
        nor is it valid
            to discriminate against 'business documents and

school-books';° all these phenomena are important. One must make a distinction
    however: when dragged into prominence by half poets, the result is not poetry,
    nor till the poets among us can be
        'literalists of
        the imagination'°—above
            insolence and triviality and can present

for inspection, 'imaginary gardens with real toads in them', shall we have
    it. In the meantime, if you demand on the one hand,
    the raw material of poetry in
        all its rawness and
        that which is on the other hand
            genuine, you are interested in poetry.

18–19 '*business . . . school-books*': The phrase is quoted from the Russian novelist, Leo Tolstoy (1828–1910). Moore's original note cites a passage in Tolstoy's *Diaries* (1917) in which he discusses the difference between prose and poetry: "Where the boundary between prose and poetry lies, I shall never be able to understand. . . . Poetry is verse: prose is not verse. Or else poetry is everything with the exception of business documents and school books."   22–23 *literalists of the imagination:* Moore's original note refers to W. B. Yeats's discussion of William Blake in *Ideas of Good and Evil* (1903), where Yeats observes that Blake was "a too literal realist of imagination."

QUESTIONS

1. What is the tone of this poem? How do words like *fiddle* (line 1) and *perfect contempt* (line 2) affect the tone and meaning?
2. What is the subject of this poem? The theme?
3. How does the speaker modify his or her initial assertion about poetry? What can poetry provide? What is its value? How should we experience it?
4. What is meant by poems "we cannot understand" (line 11)? How does imagery clarify the assertion about incomprehensible things?

SHARON OLDS   (b. 1942)

35/10 _____ *1984*

Brushing out my daughter's dark
silken hair before the mirror
I see the grey gleaming on my head,

the silver-haired servant behind her. Why is it 5
just as we begin to go
they begin to arrive, the fold in my neck
clarifying as the fine bones of her
hips sharpen? As my skin shows
its dry pitting, she opens like a small 10
pale flower on the tip of a cactus;
as my last chances to bear a child
are falling through my body, the duds among them,
her full purse of eggs, round and
firm as hard-boiled yolks, is about 15
to snap its clasp. I brush her tangled
fragrant hair at bedtime. It's an old
story—the oldest we have on our planet—
the story of replacement.

QUESTIONS

1. Who is the speaker in this poem? What is she doing? What is the setting?

2. How does the speaker contrast her own state of being to her daughter's stage of life? How are images, metaphors, and similes used to clarify this contrast? How does this contrast help convey the poem's meaning?

3. What point does this poem make about life and nature? To what extent does the last sentence clarify (or overclarify) the poem's theme?

LINDA PASTAN (b. 1932)

Ethics _____ *1980*

In ethics class so many years ago
our teacher asked this question every fall:
if there were a fire in a museum
which would you save, a Rembrandt painting
or an old woman who hadn't many 5
years left anyhow? Restless on hard chairs
caring little for pictures or old age
we'd opt one year for life, the next for art
and always half-heartedly. Sometimes
the woman borrowed my grandmother's face 10
leaving her usual kitchen to wander
some drafty, half-imagined museum.
One year, feeling clever, I replied
why not let the woman decide herself?
Linda, the teacher would report, eschews 15
the burdens of responsibility.
This fall in a real museum I stand
before a real Rembrandt, old woman,

or nearly so, myself. The colors
within this frame are darker than autumn,
darker even than winter—the browns of earth,
though earth's most radiant elements burn
through the canvas. I know now that woman
and painting and season are almost one
and all beyond saving by children.

QUESTIONS

1. What can we surmise about the speaker in this poem? How does this knowledge contribute to our understanding of theme?

2. What are the two settings, situations, and actions presented here? How are they related? How much time has passed between them? How does the contrast between them help create meaning?

3. How has the passage of time changed the speaker's attitudes? What does she now realize about "woman / and painting and season" (lines 23–24)? About children?

4. What is the subject of this poem? The theme? What point does it make about art, life, time, and values?

EDMUND SPENSER   (1552–1599)

Amoretti 75: One Day I Wrote Her Name upon the Strand _____ 1595

One day I wrote her name upon the strand,°	*beach*
But came the waves and washèd it away:	
Again I wrote it with a second hand,	
But came the tide and made my pains his prey.	
"Vain man," said she, "that doest in vain assay,	
A mortal thing so to immortalize,	
For I myself shall like to this decay,	
And eek° my name be wiped out likewise."	*also, indeed*
"Not so," quod° I, "let baser things devise,	*said*
To die in dust, but you shall live by fame:	
My verse your virtues rare shall eternize,	
And in the heavens write your glorious name.	
Where whenas death shall all the world subdue,	
Our love shall live, and later life renew."	

QUESTIONS

1. What action is described in the first quatrain? What point does the speaker's mistress make about this action in the second quatrain?

2. What is the subject of this poem? What is its theme?

3. How do rhyme, meter, and form contribute to the poem's meaning?

JUDITH VIORST (b. 1931)

*True Love** _____ *1968*

It's true love because
I put on eyeliner and a concerto and make pungent observations
   about the great issues of the day
Even when there's no one here but him,
And because
I do not resent watching the Green Bay Packers   5
Even though I am philosophically opposed to football,
And because
When he is late for dinner and I know he must be either having
   an affair or lying dead in the middle of the street,
I always hope he's dead.

It's true love because   10
If he said quit drinking martinis but I kept drinking them and
   the next morning I couldn't get out of bed,
He wouldn't tell me he told me,
And because
He is willing to wear unironed undershorts
Out of respect for the fact that I am philosophically   15
   opposed to ironing,
And because
If his mother was drowning and I was drowning and he had to
   choose one of us to save,
He says he'd save me.

It's true love because
When he went to San Francisco on business while I had to stay   20
   home with the painters and the exterminator and the baby
   who was getting the chicken pox,
He understood why I hated him,
And because
When I said that playing the stock market was juvenile and
   irresponsible and then the stock I wouldn't let him buy
   went up twenty-six points,
I understood why he hated me,
And because   25
Despite cigarette cough, tooth decay, acid indigestion, dandruff,
   and other features of married life that tend to dampen the
   fires of passion,
We still feel something
We can call
True love.

TRUE LOVE Compare the title with this line in Shakespeare's *A Midsummer Night's Dream:* "The course of true love never did run smooth" (Act I. scene i, line132).

QUESTIONS

1. What does the poet mean by "true love"?

2. What situations described here are anti-romantic? What importance do they have in the speaker's idea of the wife-husband relationship?

3. What comic situations and statements does the poem contain? How do these elements contribute to the poem's tone and meaning?

4. Explain why lines 2, 8, 11, 17, 20, 23, and 26 are the poem's longest lines. In what ways is the meaning of these lines contrasted with the meaning of the shorter lines?

WILLIAM WORDSWORTH (1770-1850)

Daffodils (I Wandered Lonely as a Cloud) _____ *1807 (1804)*

I wandered lonely as a cloud
That floats on high o'er vales and hills,
When all at once I saw a crowd,
A host, of golden daffodils;
Beside the lake, beneath the trees,
Fluttering and dancing in the breeze.

Continuous as the stars that shine
And twinkle on the milky way,
They stretched in never-ending line
Along the margin of a bay:
Ten thousand saw I at a glance,
Tossing their heads in sprightly dance.

The waves beside them danced; but they
Out-did the sparkling waves in glee:
A poet could not but be gay,
In such a jocund° company: *cheerful, merry*
I gazed—and gazed—but little thought
What wealth the show to me had brought:

For oft, when on my couch I lie
In vacant or in pensive mood,
They flash upon that inward eye
Which is the bliss of solitude;
And then my heart with pleasure fills,
And dances with the daffodils.

Wordsworths' note: "Written at Town-end, Grasmere Daffodils grew and still grow on the margin of Ullswater, and probably may be seen to this day as beautiful in the month of March, nodding their golden heads beside the dancing and foaming waves." Wordsworth also pointed out that lines 21 and 22, the "best lines," were by his wife, Mary.

QUESTIONS

1. Describe the occasion that prompts the poem. Why does the speaker specify that he was alone?
2. What is the significance of the verbs and verbals describing the flowers? What idea about Nature is suggested by these words?
3. How has the scene affected the speaker? In what way? For how long? What general conclusion about human beings and Nature does the speaker draw, and invite us to draw?

WRITING ABOUT THEME AND MEANING IN POETRY

The prewriting process for this essay includes reading and rereading, developing your initial ideas about the poem, testing those ideas against the poem itself, formulating a tentative central idea for your essay, and organizing your observations into coherent units. Always keep foremost that your essay should connect the poem's theme and meaning to other poetic elements, such as speaker, imagery, metaphor, symbol, or tone.

Questions for Discovering Ideas

• What does the title of the poem tell you about subject and meaning?
• What do you learn about the speaker? How does the speaker shape and communicate theme?
• How do the other characters in the poem (if any) affect theme and meaning?
• What impact do setting, situation, and action have on theme?
• How do diction, imagery, metaphor, simile, and other rhetorical devices affect the ideas? How are multiple denotations and connotations employed? To what extent are special types of diction or word order used?
• Describe the tone of the poem. What effect does the tone have on the theme?
• What role do rhythm, meter, sound, and rhyme play in shaping and emphasizing important words and ideas?
• How does the poem's form shape its theme? What effect does the form have on your response?
• How do symbol, allusion, or myth contribute to the poem's theme and impact?

You will find poems for which all these questions are relevant, for some poets employ every element and device in the poetic repertory to create meaning and impact. Other poems touch on only a few of these areas. Be sure to look for major elements that have the most profound impact on the poem's theme and on your ability to consider the poem both as an emotional and intellectual experience.

Strategies for Organizing Ideas

Be careful to distinguish between *subject* and *theme*. In planning to write about Larkin's "Next, Please," for example, you might write the following:

"Larkin's 'Next, Please' makes a clear assertion about human habits of expectation." This sentence describes the poem's *subject*, and might even be a good beginning sentence for your essay. It is not, however, a good central idea because it tells the reader nothing about the poem's theme or meaning. A better central idea might be, "Larkin's 'Next, Please' exposes the futility of ignoring the present while hoping for a better future." This sentence summarizes the theme of the poem and makes a strong statement on which to build an effective essay.

Next, focus on the relationship between your idea and the ways in which the poem creates meaning. Use the information you gain from answering the "Questions for Discovering Ideas." Thus, if you find that a poem's theme is established through symbol and allusion, you should make this connection by relating meaning to these elements. Such a plan might be: (1) theme, (2) theme and symbol, and (3) theme and allusion. Or it might be that the poet's meaning is made plain through a dominant image or metaphor. You might then plan to develop the idea part by part, and show how the metaphor develops it, or you might want to stress the metaphor itself as it grows and develops as support for the poem's idea, as in the sample essay.

Before bringing out your central idea, make any specific points that are relevant to the poem and your essay. If your poem is about life at the front in World War I, for example, or if the speaker is a lover speaking to a sweetheart, it is important to make these basic facts clear.

As you organize and develop your paragraphs, keep in mind the following structural patterns. They will be useful for almost all the poems you encounter:

1. The poem may convey meaning through direct statement. In such a case you might organize your essay to reflect the line-by-line or sentence-by-sentence structure of the poem itself.

2. You might find that the *logic* of the speaker's argument most effectively creates meaning. To follow such a pattern of logic, for example, would be useful in an essay about the meaning of Andrew Marvell's "To His Coy Mistress."

3. The poet's use of a *single element*, such as a metaphor or simile, or a set of consistent references (such as explorers, bankers, darkness, rain), might bring out the poem's meaning. Your organization might reflect how the element works and develops in the poem.

4. Finally, it might be that a number of *different poetic elements* (e.g., rhythm, rhyme, metaphor, level of language, imagery, and so on) work together to shape theme and impact. The structure of an essay dealing with such elements can be based on a sequential discussion of each element as it contributes to meaning.

Please note that these four structural patterns can be modified and combined. To accommodate the specific poem you are considering, you should always be ready to adjust whatever plan you choose.

In your conclusion, you might pull all the strands of the essay together, and reaffirm the connection between the poem's method and meaning. This is most conveniently done through a summary of your major points. The conclusion is also the place where you can consider additional aspects of the poem's theme and impact. The ideas and experiences created when you read a poem often suggest additional ideas. Similarly, you might want to consider the extent to which your own circumstances (such as age, sex, race, or religion) help determine the meaning and impact that the poem has for you.

SAMPLE ESSAY

Metaphor and Meaning in Larkin's "Next, Please"°

[1]   Philip Larkin's "Next, Please" exposes the futility of ignoring the present while hoping for a better future.* The idea is borne out in the poem's contrast between the slowness of hope and fulfillment and the certainty of disappointment and death. The theme is conveyed through the extended metaphor that begins in the second stanza; within this metaphor, diction and meter reinforce the meaning of the poem and the human experience that it defines.†

[2]   The poem announces its subject and begins to develop its theme through the title and the direct statements of the first stanza. The title refers to the desire to hope and look ahead. It suggests that we are never satisfied with what we have, but always expect happiness "just around the corner." These implications are brought into focus in the first stanza, where the speaker notes that we are "Always too eager for the future" and that "we / Pick up bad habits of expectancy" (lines 1-2). Our habitual hope for the future is captured in the speaker's observation that "every day / Till then we say" (lines 3-4). By using the pronouns we (and us) here and throughout, the speaker generalizes: It is not just he or she alone, but all human beings who habitually indulge in wishful thinking.

[3]   Beginning in the second stanza, the poem asserts that these "bad habits of expectancy" leave us disappointed. This point is made through an extended metaphor based on a hidden cliché, which may be expressed either as "Someday my ship will come in," or "Someday I'll win out over everything." This cliché, which Larkin expresses originally as a "Sparkling armada of promises," embodies the vain dream that we will eventually get everything we want or deserve. Larkin's metaphor suggests that these hopes are mostly doomed.

[4]   He begins developing the metaphor's meaning by making it dramatic. We as readers are "Watching from a bluff" at not just one hope, but at a whole fleet of hopeful promises. Right at the beginning, however, Larkin's diction directs our attention to the vanity of hope. A bluff of course is a hill, but it is also an attempt to mislead or deceive through false confidence. Armada is similarly loaded because it evokes the memory of the Spanish Armada that sailed against England in 1588 and was destroyed by bad planning, storms,

---

° See p. 850 for this poem.
* Central idea.
† Thesis sentence.

and failure in battle. The clear prediction of wreckage is thus built into the metaphor.

The metaphor makes the poem's meaning vivid and immediate through a wealth of detail. We notice that the "armada of promises" moves very slowly: "How slow they are! And how much time they waste, / Refusing to make haste" (lines 7-8). The metaphor is extended, with more and more details, such as the shining "brasswork," "Each rope distinct," the flag, and "the figurehead with golden tits / Arching our way" (lines 11-14). The metaphor suggests through these details that our dreams enable us to visualize the shapes that success can take. Even as our promises draw closer, their elusiveness is also established: "Yet still they leave us holding wretched stalks / Of disappointment" (lines 9-10). This image--within the metaphor--leaves us standing on the "bluff" with wilted flowers representing our unrealized hopes.

[5]

This disappointment is brought into explicit focus as the "armada" metaphor continues in the fourth stanza. We see that the fleet "never anchors" because it is "No sooner present than it turns to past" (line 14-15). Most of these words carry double meanings. It, for example, refers to both the ships and time. Turns to indicates both a change of course and the inevitable transformation of the present into the past. Similarly, present and past signify both the physical status of the ships and the movement of time. The metaphor thus conveys the experience of disappointment both in terms of the "armada of promises" and the time we waste waiting for a reward that never comes.

[6]

Larkin's last two stanzas conclude the armada metaphor and expand on the theme of disappointment. The speaker observes that we always expect one of our ships to "heave to" and deliver "All good into our lives" (line 18). The stanza's last line, however, completely undercuts all hope. Here, we sense the impact of a metrical technique that Larkin has employed throughout. The poem is mostly in iambic pentameter, but the fourth line of each stanza is cut short to two or three feet. This metrical falling-off parallels the diminishing of hope. Like the "armada" and the future, each stanza fails to deliver what we expect. The force of this device strikes us at the close of the fifth stanza, where the final two-beat line bleakly tells us, "But we are wrong" (line 20).

[7]

In the sixth stanza, Larkin makes absolutely clear his ironic contrast between hope and disappointment. Although we seek the ships of expectation, which never come, there is "one ship" that "is seeking us" (line 21). It is not a ship full of good things; instead, it is a "black- / Sailed unfamiliar" ship "towing at her back / A huge and birdless silence" (lines 22-23). This is the only ship that is sure to come--the ship of death.

[8]

"Next, Please" thus tells us that passive hope is vain. The poem lets us experience this meaning through an extended metaphor, in which an "armada of promises" seems to be coming close, but then leaves without unloading anything and without winning any battles for us. The meaning of the poem becomes our movement through the metaphor, and our experience of the metaphor is disappointment and a vision of death. At the same time, however, the poem is not totally bleak and hopeless. It implies that we should live in and for the present, making the most of what we have. To this extent, "Next, Please" is a carpe diem poem, suggesting that we should "seize" today, which is real, rather than waste our time in unreal expectation.

[9]

Commentary on the Essay

The essay illustrates the need to combine and adjust strategies of organization in dealing with a specific poem. It combines a focus on a specific poetic element (metaphor) with secondary interest in two other elements (diction and meter). The essay thus represents a modification and combination of organizational strategies 3 and 4, on page 860. Paragraph 2 deals primarily with the subject of the poem; it grows directly out of the first two sentences of the introduction. This discussion is essential because it provides the foundation for the essay's subsequent treatment of theme and meaning.

Paragraphs 3 through 8 grow out of the last two sentences of the introduction; they treat the connection between metaphor and meaning, and they take up the secondary subjects of diction and meter. Paragraph 3 provides transition from subject to theme, introduces the dominant metaphor, and explains the hidden cliché (or clichés) on which the metaphor is based. Paragraph 4 examines the way that the "armada" metaphor creates a palpable experience and how the poem's diction lessens the promise of the experience.

Paragraph 5 sustains the focus on the link between metaphor and meaning through attention to the details that the speaker mentions in the second, third, and fourth stanzas of the poem. Again, the first sentence connects this paragraph to both the introduction and the previous paragraph. Similarly, the concluding sentence leads into paragraph 6, which takes up the next stage of the extended metaphor and the articulation of disappointment. This focus on the end of the metaphor and on the experience of disappointment is continued in paragraph 7, which explores the impact of the poem's meter. The poem's last stanza is discussed in paragraph 8 which, like the stanza, emphasizes the contrast between the uncertainty of hope and the certainty brought by the black-sailed ship.

The concluding paragraph briefly considers the implications of the poem's meaning, offers a second and implied theme for the poem, and connects "Next, Please" to the long-standing *carpe diem* poetic tradition. The value of this paragraph as an example is that it is more than a summary, leaving the reader with new thoughts.

WRITING TOPICS

1. Compare two or all of the following poems: Jonson's "To Celia," Herrick's "To the Virgins" (and also "Corinna's Going A-Maying," in Chapter 25), and Marvell's "To His Coy Mistress" as *carpe diem* poems. How well does each poem express the central idea of the *carpe diem* tradition? What are the similarities and differences of the tone and ideas? How accurate is it to say that these poems are not about seduction but rather about life and values?

2. On the basis of ideas about age, change, and the loss of time and life, compare Pastan's "Ethics," Olds's "35/10," Wordsworth's "Daffodils," and Justice's "On the Death of Friends in Childhood." How do the ideas of the poems merge, even

though they are about different subjects? Which of the poems do you prefer? Why?

3. Keats's line "Beauty is truth, truth beauty" from his "Ode on a Grecian Urn" has generated considerable discussion. What do you think it means? How does the material in the poem support Keats's idea? Would the idea be tenable if it had come early in the poem rather than late? Why?

4. Write your own poem in which you stress a particular idea. You might write about a friend or acquaintance who has: endured an illness, performed an important service, admitted a mistake or failure, or succeeded in a task. Other possible topics are: a social, religious, or political issue; or some aspect of education, work, or community life. When you finish, explain how you go about making the situation clear to your reader, and how you use the situation to bring out your ideas. Do not neglect the title as one of the means of expressing ideas.

Three Poetic Careers: John Donne, Emily Dickinson, and Robert Frost

In Chapters 13 to 23 we have considered poetry in terms of its elements and effects. In this chapter we examine collections of poems by three major poets: John Donne (1572–1631), Emily Dickinson (1830–1886), and Robert Frost (1874–1963). Donne, one of the most important English poets during the reigns of Elizabeth I and James I, is the major seventeenth-century metaphysical poet. Dickinson and Frost are both American poets and New Englanders. Dickinson is one of the most prominent poetic voices of the nineteenth-century, and Frost is recognized as a poetic giant of the twentieth century. Although the poems included here cannot encompass their entire poetic careers, they do provide an opportunity to consider a substantial representative body of their work. We have chosen poems that illustrate the central concerns and major characteristics of each poet.

JOHN DONNE

John Donne (1572–1631)was born into a Roman Catholic family in 1572, during the reign of Queen Elizabeth I. She had been queen for only fourteen years, having been crowned after the death of her sister, Queen Mary I ("Bloody Mary"). Elizabeth's Anglican subjects did their utmost to keep Catholics out of power in order to prevent a return of the earlier Catholic persecutions of Protestants. Religious divisiveness therefore had a significant impact on Donne during his formative years. Although he attended both Oxford and Cambridge between 1584 and 1590, his Catholicism barred him from receiving degrees.

    In 1591 Donne moved to London and enrolled at Lincoln's Inn, where he studied science, philosophy, law, languages, and literature. Eventually he

William Marshall, *Portrait of John Donne,* engraving 1591. © The Board of Trustees of the Victoria & Albert Museum. Art Resource

was to work these subjects (and more) into his poetry. During the ensuing years he acquired a reputation as a wit and a ladies' man. He wrote many love poems and satires, and circulated them privately in manuscript. Although the manuscripts were widely read and frequently copied, the poems were not published. Except for a few poems issued in 1610–1612, almost all of Donne's poetry remained unpublished during his lifetime.

In 1592 Donne converted to Anglicanism, the English state religion, and began his rise in aristocratic circles. In 1598 he became private secretary to Sir Thomas Egerton, the Lord Keeper. He was on the verge of a brilliant political career when he eloped in December, 1601 with his employer's sixteen-year-old niece, Anne More. At this time, a clandestine marriage was a major offense. Egerton had Donne jailed and dismissed from court, and barred his further employment in government service. Donne's response is recorded: "John Donne, Anne Donne, undone." Fortunately, the marriage was recognized in April, 1602, and Donne was released from prison. The next thirteen years, however, were not good ones. Donne eked out a meager living at various jobs, and during this time he and his wife had twelve children, five of whom died. He desperately petitioned for royal favor, and of course he was writing poems. The King, James I (reigned 1603–1625), was sympathetic, but he did not help, believing that Donne's proper place was as a priest in the Anglican Church.

Under this pressure, Donne finally gave in, and in 1615 he took holy orders. After receiving a Doctorate in Divinity in 1616, he began his meteoric rise in the Anglican Church. His wife Anne died in 1617, and she therefore never knew his time of greatest success. In 1621 he was appointed Dean of St. Paul's Cathedral in London, the most fashionable church in seventeenth-century England (but not the building that exists today). He became famous as a preacher—over 130 of his sermons were published—and the nobility and gentry flocked to his services as long as good health permitted him to preach. Ironically, he previewed his own funeral sermon before the new King (Charles I) on February 25, 1631, and supposedly wrote his last poem ("Hymn to God My God, in My Sickness") eight days before he died in May, 1631.

Poetic Characteristics

Traditionally, scholars have claimed that Donne had two poetic careers—love poet and satirist in his youth, and religious poet after he became an Anglican priest in 1615. Such a clear division cannot be maintained, however, since Donne wrote a great deal of religious verse before 1615 and very little poetry at all after that. It is true that his poetry falls into two broad categories—love poetry and religious poetry—but there is no evidence that he was not writing them simultaneously.

Donne's poems are commonly termed *metaphysical,* a word used to describe verse that is intellectual, complex, subtle, and elaborate. The label was first assigned to Donne by the poet-critic John Dryden (1631–1700), who asserted in *A Discourse Concerning the Original and Progress of Satire* (1693) that Donne's love poetry "affects the metaphysics" and "perplexes the minds of the fair sex with nice [i.e., subtle] speculations of philosophy, when he should engage their hearts, and entertain them with the softnesses of love." Samuel Johnson, in his *Life of Cowley* (1779–1781), first applied the word *metaphysical* both to Donne and the metaphysical "school" of poetry.

Donne is, above all, a provocative and daring poet. His poems are marked by dramatic situations, a conversational style, abrupt beginnings, rapid shifts in tone, rigorous logic, sharp puns, and puzzling paradoxes. In his imagery he ranges freely to include the words and concepts of fields of learning such as alchemy, metallurgy, law, theology, philosophy, economics, astronomy, and geography. Without question, Donne's poetry represents not only a departure from the poetry of the sixteenth century, but also a revolution.

His most famous and most notable feature is the so-called **metaphysical conceit.** A *conceit* is an elaborate metaphor, and a *metaphysical conceit* is an extended metaphor that links two apparently unrelated topics in an unusual and surprising conjunction of ideas, such as that lovers are joined together like the two legs of a compass, or that death and salvation are identical in the same sense that east and west meet on a map of the world. As a body of poetic achievement, Donne's poems illustrate *wit,* the ability to advance complex arguments through the ingenious use of logic, analogies, scientific references, and wide-ranging allusions.

The characteristic poetic forms for Donne's love poetry and religious verse include the lyric and the sonnet. The stanzaic structure of the lyrics is intricately inventive, with varying line lengths and complex rhyme schemes. There is so much variation that many of his accents and rhythms seem irregular. Indeed, Ben Jonson, a fellow poet and dramatist, stated in conversation that Donne, "for not keeping of accent, deserved hanging." If we consider, however, that many of the poems were intended as musical texts, much of the irregularity becomes unimportant.

Poetic Subjects

Donne's love poetry, written mostly between 1590 and 1615, established what we now call the "metaphysical style." That is, the poems are ingenious, and they overflow with images and allusions. They clearly state that passion and love are overpowering and mysterious, and cannot be explained any more satisfactorily than the divine mysteries of the universe. The poems also state that true love creates a psychologically separate, complete, and independent world for lovers, with properties and dimensions that transcend the everyday world. In this intimate and enclosed world, lovers need nothing else but their own love.

Critics have often observed that there is much religion in Donne's love poetry, and much love in his religious poetry. Like the love poetry, the religious poetry is witty, passionate, devotional, and intellectual. In the religious poetry, however, the object of love is God, not woman, and the poet-speaker emphasizes his personal anguish, self doubt, and powerlessness before God while placing his entire trust and hope in Divine acceptance. Thus, in the *Holy Sonnets*, Donne uses the Italian sonnet, traditionally associated with love, to consider human sin and divine grace. In these poems Donne often introduces the techniques of religious meditation, focusing at first on a specific time or event and then considering the meaning of that event in connection with his own spiritual state. In "At the Round Earth's Imagined Corners," for example, Donne begins with a vivid meditation on the moment of the Last Judgment. The *Hymns*, like the Holy Sonnets, maintain the metaphysical style. The "Hymn to God the Father," for instance, plays repeatedly with a pun on Donne's name. Similarly, the "Hymn to God My God, In My Sickness," Donne's last poem, is full of puns, paradoxes, difficult reasoning, and inventive metaphors.

Bibliographic Sources

Donne's poetry, widely circulated in manuscript during his lifetime, was published in many editions during the thirty years after his death, but it fell into neglect during the latter half of the seventeenth century. Alexander Pope (1685–1744) "versified" Donne's satires for his eighteenth-century audience, but ignored the songs and sonnets. Although an awareness of Donne's work grew in the late 1800s, two events in the twentieth century dramatically rekindled interest in him. One was the publication of Sir Herbert Grierson's complete edition of *The Poems of John Donne* in 1912 and the other was T. S. Eliot's spirited defense of Donne and metaphysical poetry in "The Metaphysical Poets" in 1921 (reprinted in 1960 in his *Selected Essays*). More recent editions of Donne's work include Helen Gardner's editions of *The Divine Poems* (1952) and *The Elegies and the Songs and Sonnets* (1965). A newly available selected edition is Arthur L. Clements's Norton Critical Edition, *John Donne's Poetry* (1992). The Twayne English Authors Series includes a biography by Frank Warnke, *John Donne* (1987).

Significant critical discussions of Donne's work may be found in Joan Bennett, *Five Metaphysical Poets*, 3rd ed. (1964); Helen White, *The Metaphysical Poets* (1936); Louis L. Martz, *The Poetry of Meditation* (1954); J. B. Leishman, *The Monarch of Wit* (5th ed., 1962); Helen Gardner, ed., *John Donne: A Collection of Critical Essays* (1962); Richard E. Hughes, *The Progress of the Soul* (1968); Murray Roston, *The Soul of Wit: A Study of John Donne* (1974); John Carey, *John Donne: Life, Mind, and Art* (1981); and George Parfitt, *John Donne: A Literary Life* (1989). Harold Bloom has edited *John Donne and the Seventeenth-Century Metaphysical Poets* (1986), a collection of essays on Donne and other metaphysicals.

POEMS BY JOHN DONNE

The Good Morrow ————————————————————— *1633*

I wonder, by my troth, what thou and I
Did, till we loved! Were we not weaned till then,
But sucked on country pleasures, childishly?
Or snorted we in the seven sleepers' den?°
T'was so; But this, all pleasures fancies be.   5
If ever any beauty I did see,
Which I desired, and got, t'was but a dream of thee.

And now good morrow to our waking souls,
Which watch not one another out of fear;
For love all love of other sights controls,°   10
And makes one little room an everywhere.

THE GOOD MORROW.   4 *seven sleepers' den:* a reference to the miraculous legend of the Seven Sleepers of Ephesus, in Asia Minor. Seven young nobles fled Ephesus to avoid religious persecution by the Emperor Decius (ca A.D. 250). They took refuge in a cave and were sealed inside. They then slept for either 230 or 309 years, and they emerged praising God. After they died, their remains were taken to St. Victor's Church in Marseilles, France, where they were encrypted.   10 *For love . . . controls:* i.e., Love is so powerful that it eliminates fear and makes everything in the world worthy of love.

Let sea-discoverers to new worlds have gone,
Let maps to other, worlds on worlds have shown,°
Let us possess one world; each hath one, and is one.

My face in thine eye, thine in mine appears,°
And true plain hearts do in the faces rest;
Where can we find two better hemispheres
Without sharp North, without declining West?
Whatever dies was not mixed equally;
If our two loves be one, or thou and I
Love so alike, that none do slacken, none can die.°

13, 14 *Let sea-discoverers . . . shown:* i.e., Let sea-explorers discover new worlds, and let maps show
other new worlds to other discoverers.   15 *My face . . . appears:* Each face is reflected in the
pupils of the other lover's eyes.   19–21 *Whatever . . . can die:* Scholastic philosophy argued that
elements which are united in perfect balance will never change or decay; hence, such a mixture
cannot die. Donne's analogy suggests—humorously—that the love of the lovers is too pure to
die, and that they may therefore go on making love forever.

Song (Go, and Catch a Falling Star) —————————————— *1633*

Go, and catch a falling star,
    Get with child a mandrake root,°
Tell me where all past years are,
    Or who cleft the Devil's foot,
Teach me to hear mermaids singing,
Or to keep off envy's stinging,
        And find
        What wind
Serves to advance an honest mind.

If thou beest born to strange sights,
    Things invisible to see,
Ride ten thousand days and nights
    Till age snow white hairs on thee,
Thou, when thou return'st, wilt tell me
All strange wonders that befell thee
        And swear
        Nowhere
Lives a woman true, and fair.

If thou findst one, let me know,
    Such a Pilgrimage were sweet;
Yet do not, I would not go,
    Though at next door we might meet;
Though she were true when you met her,

SONG.   2 *mandrake root:* The mandrake, or mandragora, is a European narcotic herb once considered an aphrodisiac because the two-pronged root was thought to resemble a woman's torso
and legs.

And last till you write your letter,
  Yet she   25
   Will be
False, ere I come, to two, or three.

The Sun Rising ——————————————————— *1633*

  Busy old fool, unruly sun,
   Why dost thou thus,
Through windows and through curtains call on us?
Must to thy motions lovers' seasons run?
   Saucy pedantic wretch, go chide   5
   Late school boys and sour prentices,°   *apprentices*
To tell court huntsmen that the King will ride,
Call country ants to harvest offices;°   *duties*
Love, all alike, no season knows nor clime,
Nor hours, days, months, which are the rags of time.   10

  Thy beams, so reverend and strong
   Why shouldst thou think?
I could eclipse and clod them with a wink,
But that I would not lose her sight so long;
   If her eyes have not blinded thine,   15
   Look, and tomorrow late, tell me,
  Whether both the Indias of spice and mine°
Be where thou leftst them, or lie here with me.
Ask for those kings whom thou saw'st yesterday,
And thou shalt hear, All here in one bed lay.   20

  She is all states, and all princes, I,
   Nothing else is.
Princes do but play us; compared to this,
All honor's mimic, all wealth alchemy.°   *counterfeit*
   Thou, sun, art half as happy as we,   25
   In that the world's contracted thus;
  Thine age asks ease, and since thy duties be
  To warm the world, that's done in warming us.
Shine here to us, and thou art everywhere;
This bed thy center° is, these walls, thy sphere.   30

THE SUN RISING.   17 *Indias of spice and mine:* the India of "spice" is East India or the East Indies;
the India of "mine" or gold is the West Indies.   30 *center:* the central point of the sun's orbit.

The Canonization ——————————————————— *1633*

For God's sake hold your tongue,° and let me love,
  Or chide my palsy, or my gout,

THE CANONIZATION.   1 *your tongue:* "Your" refers to either the public world in general or
a specific but unheard critic who attacks the speaker's love.

My five gray hairs, or ruined fortune, flout,
  With wealth your state, your mind with arts improve,
    Take you a course,° get you a place,°
    Observe His Honor, or His Grace,
Or the King's real, or his stamped face°
  Contemplate,—what you will, approve,°   *test, try*
  So you will let me love.

Alas, alas, who's injured by my love?
  What merchant's ships have my sighs drowned?
Who says my tears have overflowed his ground?
  When did my colds a forward spring remove?
    When did the heats which my veins fill
    Add one more to the plaguy bill?°
Soldiers find wars, and lawyers find out still
  Litigious men, which quarrels move,
  Though she and I do love.

Call us what you will, we are made such by love;
  Call her one, me another fly,
We're tapers too, and at our own cost die,°
  And we in us find the eagle and the dove.°
    The phoenix riddle° hath more wit
    By us,—we two being one, are it.
So, to one neutral thing both sexes fit.
  We die and rise the same, and prove
  Mysterious by this love.

We can die by it, if not live by love,
  And if unfit for tombs and hearse
Our legend be, it will be fit for verse;
  And if no piece of chronicle we prove,
    We'll build in sonnets pretty rooms;
    As well a well-wrought urn becomes°   *befits, suits*
The greatest ashes, as half-acre tombs,
  And by these hymns, all shall approve°
  Us canonized for love:

---

5 *course:* a course of action.   *place:* office or position, probably at court.   7 *stamped face:* the king's portrait on coins.   15 *plaguy bill:* a weekly list of people who have died from the plague. 20–21 *fly . . . die:* Both flies and candles are symbols of the brevity of life. Since the word *die* was a common euphemism in the seventeenth century for sexual orgasm, the line suggests that each sex act shortens the lovers' lives.   22 *eagle and the dove:* proverbial symbols of male strength and female mildness.   23 *phoenix riddle:* the riddle of the phoenix's perpetuation; the phoenix is a mythological Arabian bird—only one exists at a time—that lives for a thousand years and then burns itself to ashes on a funeral pyre. A new phoenix then miraculously rises from the ashes of the old. The phoenix thus symbolizes immortality, death, and resurrection, and the rekindling of sexual desire.   35 *hymns . . . approve:* The hymns refer to the speaker's poetry and this poem in particular. The idea is that succeeding generations will confirm ("approve") the sainthood of the lovers in a new religion of love because of this poem.

And thus invoke us: "You whom reverend love
   Made one another's hermitage;
You, to whom love was peace, that now is rage;
   Who did the whole world's soul contract, and drove
     Into the glasses of your eyes   40
     (So made such mirrors, and such spies,
That they did all to you epitomize)
   Countries, towns, courts: Beg from above
   A pattern of your love!"°

37–45 "*You . . . love*": These lines are spoken by lovers in succeeding generations who are praying to the lover-saints that the speaker and his beloved have become. Hence, *You* (line 37) refers to the speaker and his mistress.

A Fever _____ *1633*

Oh do not die, for I shall hate
   All women so, when thou art gone,
That thee I shall not celebrate,°   *mourn*
   When I remember, thou wast one.

But yet thou canst not die, I know;   5
   To leave this world behind, is death;
But when thou from this world wilt go,
   The whole world vapours° with thy breath.   *evaporates*

Or if, when thou, the world's soul, goest,
   It stay, 'tis but thy carcass then;   10
The fairest woman, but thy ghost,
   But corrupt worms, the worthiest men.

O wrangling schools,° that search what fire
   Shall burn this world, had none the wit
Unto this knowledge to aspire,   15
   That this her fever might be it?

And yet she cannot waste by this,
   Nor long bear this torturing wrong,
For much corruption needful is,
   To fuel such a fever long.°   *for long* 20

These burning fits but meteors be,
   Whose matter in thee is soon spent:
Thy beauty, and all parts which are thee,
   Are unchangeable firmament.°

Yet 'twas of my mind, seizing thee,   25
   Though it in thee cannot persever:°   *persist*
For I had rather owner be
   Of thee one hour, than all else ever.

A FEVER. 13 *wrangling schools:* competing sects of pagan and Christian philosophy that debated what sort of fire would ultimately destroy the world. 24 *firmament:* the vault of heaven and the stars.

The Flea ———————————————————————————— *1633*

Mark° but this flea, and mark in this,   *note, look at*
How little that which thou deniest me is;
It sucked me first, and now sucks thee,
And in this flea our two bloods mingled be;
Thou know'st that this cannot be said°   *called*
A sin, nor shame, nor loss of maidenhead,
   Yet this enjoys before it woo,°   *marry*
   And pampered swells with one blood made of two,°
   And this, alas, is more than we would do.

Oh stay, three lives in one flea spare,
Where we almost, yea more than married, are.
This flea is you and I, and this
Our marriage bed and marriage temple is;
Though parents grudge, and you,° w'are met,
And cloister'd in these living walls of jet,
   Though use° make you apt to kill me   *custom*
   Let not to that, self-murder added be,
   And sacrilege, three sins in killing three.

Cruel and sudden, hast thou since
Purpled thy nail, in blood of innocence?°
Wherein could this flea guilty be,
Except in that drop which it sucked from thee?
Yet thou triumph'st, and say'st that thou
Find'st not thy self nor me the weaker now;
   'Tis true, then learn how false fears be;
   Just so much honor, when thou yield'st to me,
   Will waste, as this flea's death took life from thee.

THE FLEA.   8 *two:* The flea has bitten both the speaker and the lady and thus mingles their blood; the image also suggests pregnancy.   14 *you:* You [the lady] also "grudge" or resent the idea of premarital sex.   20 *innocence:* a possible allusion to Herod's slaughter of the innocents (Matthew 2:16).

Holy Sonnet 6: This Is My Play's Last Scene ——————————— *1633*

This is my play's last scene; here heavens appoint
My pilgrimage's last mile; and my race
Idly, yet quickly run, hath this last pace,
My span's last inch, my minute's last point,
And gluttonous Death will instantly unjoint
My body, and soul, and I shall sleep a space,
But my ever-waking part° shall see that face,   *the soul*
Whose fear already shakes my every joint.
Then, as my soul, t'heaven her first seat, takes flight,
And earth-borne body, in the earth shall dwell,

So, fall my sins, that all may have their right,
To where they are bred, and would press me, to hell.
Impute me righteous, thus purged of evil,
For thus I leave the world, the flesh, and devil.

Holy Sonnet 7: At the Round Earth's Imagined Corners —————— *1633*

At the round earth's imagined corners, blow
Your trumpets, angels,° and arise, arise
From death, you numberless infinities
Of souls, and to your scattered bodies go,
All whom the flood did, and fire shall o'erthrow,   5
All whom war, dearth, age, agues, tyrannies,
Despair, law, chance, hath slain, and you whose eyes
Shall behold God, and never taste death's woe.°
But let them sleep, Lord, and me mourn a space,
For, if above all these, my sins abound,   10
'Tis late to ask abundance of Thy grace,
When we are there. Here on this lowly ground,
Teach me how to repent; for that's as good
As if Thou hadst sealed my pardon with Thy blood.

AT THE ROUND EARTH'S IMAGINED CORNERS.   1–2 *At . . . angels:* The lines combine the
image of the angels or winds drawn at the four corners of old maps with an allusion to the four
angels mentioned in Revelations 7:1.   7–8 *you whose eyes . . . woe:* a reference to those people
who are still living on the day of the Last Judgment and thus move directly from life to judgment without experiencing death.

Holy Sonnet 10: Death Be Not Proud ————————————— *1633*

Death, be not proud, though some have callèd thee
Mighty and dreadful, for thou art not so;
For those whom thou think'st thou dost overthrow
Die not, poor Death, nor yet canst thou kill me.
From rest and sleep, which but thy pictures° be,   *imitations*   5
Much pleasure; then from thee much more must flow,
And soonest our best men with thee do go,
Rest of their bones, and soul's delivery.
Thou art slave to fate, chance, kings, and desperate men,
And dost with poison, war, and sickness dwell,   10
And poppy° or charms can make us sleep as well   *opium*
And better than thy stroke; why swell'st° thou then?   *puff up with pride*
One short sleep past, we wake eternally°   *on Judgment Day*
And death shall be no more; Death, thou shalt die.

A Hymn to God the Father ———————————————— 1633 (1623?)

Wilt Thou forgive that sin where I begun,
  Which is my sin, though it were done before?
Wilt Thou forgive those sins through which I run,
  And do them still, though still I do deplore?
    When Thou hast done, Thou hast not done,
      For I have more.

Wilt Thou forgive that sin by which I won
  Others to sin and made my sin their door?
Wilt Thou forgive that sin which I did shun
  A year or two, but wallowed in a score?
    When Thou hast done, Thou hast not done,
      For I have more.

I have a sin of fear, that when I have spun
  My last thread, I shall perish on the shore;
Swear by Thy Self, that at my death Thy sun
  Shall shine as it shines now and heretofore;
    And, having done that, Thou hast done,
      I have no more.

Hymn to God My God, in My Sickness ———————————— 1633 (1631)

Since I am coming to that Holy Room,°
  Where, with Thy choir of saints for evermore,
I shall be made thy music; as I come
  I tune the instrument here at the door,
  And what I must do then, think here before.

Whilst my physicians by their love are grown
  Cosmographers, and I their map, who lie
Flat on this bed, that by them may be shown
  That this is my southwest discovery
  Per fretum febris,° by these straits to die,

I joy, that in these straits,° I see my West;°
  For, though their currents yield return to none,
What shall my West hurt me? As West and East°
  In all flat maps (and I am one) are one,
  So death doth touch the Resurrection.

Is the Pacific Sea my home? Or are
  The Eastern riches? Is Jerusalem?

HYMN TO GOD.   1 *Holy Room:* See John 14:2–7.   10 *Per fretum febris:* through the channel of a fever.   11 *straits:* a pun meaning (a) a channel, and (b) difficulties.   11–13 *West . . . East:* The setting sun in the west represents death; the rising sun in the east, the Resurrection.

Anyan,° and Magellan,° and Gibraltar,°
    All straits, and none but straits, are ways to them,
    Whether where Japhet dwelt, or Cham, or Sem.°   20

We think that Paradise and Calvary
    Christ's cross, and Adam's tree, stood in one place;
Look, Lord, and find both Adams met in me;
    As the first Adam's sweat surrounds my face,
    May the last Adam's blood° my soul embrace.   25

So, in his purple wrapped,° receive me, Lord,
    By these his thorns give me his other crown;
And as to others' souls I preached thy word,
    Be this my text, my sermon to mine own,
    Therefore that He may raise, the Lord throws down.   30

18 *Anyan:* Anyang, a city in central China, noted for "Eastern riches."   18 *Magellan:* the Straits of Magellan at the tip of South America, considered the entry-way to the lucrative Eastern trade.   18 *Gibraltar:* the Strait of Gibraltar, the entrance to the Mediterranean.   20 *Japhet, Cham, Sem:* the three sons of Noah. Japhet's descendants were dispersed into many areas of the ancient Near East. The descendants of Cham (also Ham) were the Hamites, principally Egyptians. Sem was the patriarch of the Semitic people, including Jews.   25 *last Adam's blood:* the blood of Christ, who is named in I Cor. 15:45 as the "last Adam." See also Romans 5:12–21 and I Cor. 15: 20–28, 46–49.   26 *in his purple wrapped:* i.e. wrapped in Christ's blood-drenched linen that remained in the tomb after the Resurrection. Purple, or red, is the royal color.

EMILY DICKINSON

Emily Elizabeth Dickinson (1830–1886) was born and raised in Amherst, Massachusetts, which in the nineteenth century was a small and tradition-bound town. Dominating the Dickinson family was Emily's father, Edward, a lawyer and also a rigorous Calvinist whose concept of life was stern religious observance and obedience to God's laws as expressed in the Bible and lyricized in the Protestant hymnal. Emily spent three years at school—two at Amherst Academy and one at the South Hadley Seminary for Women (now Mount Holyoke College). After returning from school, she spent the rest of her life in the family home in Amherst. The only existing photograph of her shows her as a girl of about seventeen.

    After 1862 Dickinson became a virtual recluse. She habitually wore only white, and was rarely seen by visitors at the Dickinson household. Thomas Higginson, who came to see her in 1870, wrote that she had a uniquely irritating capacity to drain his "nerve power," and he was therefore glad he did not live near her. Aside from such fleeting glances, there is little direct evidence about her appearance and activities during her last twenty-five years. All one can say is that her external daily life was uneventful and dull. Her inner life, however, was anything but dull, for her poetry attests to a woman of lively personality, bright wit, deep sensitivity, and acute powers of observation.

Emily Dickinson (Culver Pictures, Inc.)

Because of the paucity of precise biographical information about Dickinson, we do not know the connections between the events in her life and her poems. She never married or had a love affair that we know about, but she wrote poems about love and the psychology of personal relationships. Some critics have concluded that this choice of subject may reflect her feelings about the three men whom she knew best as an adult. The first of these was Benjamin Newton, a law student whom she met in 1848 and who undertook to guide her reading. This guidance was cut short, however, because Newton married, moved away, and died of tuberculosis in 1856. Scholars have assumed that Newton is one of the two persons referred to in Dickinson's "I Never Lost as Much But Twice," which she wrote in about 1858.

The second man important to Dickinson was the Reverend Charles Wadsworth, a Philadelphia minister. She met him in 1854 and regarded him as an intellectual adviser. He was married, and there is no evidence of any romantic involvement whatever between the two. But he was the person whom she called her "dearest earthly friend," and her poetic activity was extraordinary during the time she knew and corresponded with him. A number of the poems of this period focus directly on love, marriage, and emotional relationships. "Wild Nights—Wild Nights!" (ca. 1861), for example, illustrates the poet's concept of Edenic sexuality. "I Cannot Live with You" (ca. 1862), poignantly expresses the impossibility of a relationship between the speaker and the "you" being addressed, ending on the finality of "that White Sustenance— / Despair." We can only imagine Dickinson's anguish when Wadsworth went west in 1862 to accept a ministerial call from a church in San Francisco. The two never saw each other again.

After Wadsworth departed, Dickinson became even more reclusive, but she began corresponding with Thomas Higginson, a literary critic who had written an article encouraging young writers. Dickinson enclosed some of her poetry and asked if her verses "breathed" enough to warrant publication. She may have viewed Higginson as another mentor, but she soon discovered that his literary judgments were no more than conventional. Ironically, Higginson became one of the first editors of her work after her death in 1886.

Poetic Characteristics

Dickinson began writing poetry in her early twenties, her first efforts being occasional poems and valentines. She was not really serious about poetry until around 1858, but after that her poetic output exploded. She wrote many of her poems on sheets of paper and others on scraps, preserving all these in packets and bundles which she concealed from the members of her household and which were not discovered until after her death. In addition, she wrote many letters, often embodying brief poems, some only two lines long. These short poems, which have only recently been separately published, bring the total count of her poems close to 2,275. During her most productive years, between 1862 and 1865, she wrote 760 of the poems that are traditionally recognized. This astounding number is hard to account for. One possible explanation is that her energy was spurred by her sadness over the departure of Reverend Wadsworth. Equally plausible and more likely is that she had matured as an observer, thinker, and poet.

Dickinson's verse is emotional and passionate but at the same time economical. Often her style is elliptical and obscure, producing a rapid interplay of thoughts and images. Her diction is mainly neutral, although she occasionally uses words from the formal level and intersperses many poems with references from her reading. Her sentences are frequently broken by interjections and sentence fragments. She uses these grammatical irregularities deliberately, just as she employs capital letters to emphasize words. In addition, she indulges in eccentricities of punctuation: Because her poems are mostly private monologues, she usually ignores periods and commas, and adopts the dash and the exclamation point to mark rhythm and vocal modulations. To suggest special expressiveness, she often uses dashes of differing lengths, although most printed texts obscure this subtlety.

The poetic forms that Dickinson most often uses are common measure and the ballad stanza (see p. 753). Her earliest poetic experiences would have been with the quatrain form, which abounds in the Protestant hymnal, the major poetic text of her youth. She is no metronomic follower of the form, however, for she achieves great flexibility and originality by shortening many lines, varying many of the meters, and freely inserting mid-line *caesurae.* She uses rhyme with great skill, preferring exact rhymes but also using slant rhymes, eye rhymes, vowel rhymes, and repeated-word rhymes (*identical rhyme*). Although these irregularities confounded Dickinson's first editors, they have since been recognized as important and effective elements of her poetic craft.

Poetic Subjects

The outward occasions inspiring Dickinson's poems are often clear and specific. The world she lived in was small—she found her subjects in the life of house, yard, garden, and village. A crawling worm is the topic of one of her poems, as are butterflies, a singing oriole, and a vibrating hummingbird. She even wrote a poem about the railroad locomotives servicing Amherst.

Death was a regular visitor in her town, and Dickinson's concerns with the possibilities of immortality led her to consider funerals, the eternal silence of death, the hope and expectation of eternal life, the littleness of human beings, and the difficulties of comprehending God. Along with reverence, however, one also finds a wry religious maturity. If going to church on Sunday was expected of the dutiful Christian, she writes a poem explaining why she prefers staying home. Although the Civil War battles were distant, some of her poems reflect about the brutalities of that conflict.

Most of her inspiration, however, rose not from external but from internal concerns. Dickinson is primarily a personal, contemplative, confessional poet, and it is difficult to avoid concluding that she herself is her own principal poetic speaker. Many of her poems start with no more than a single word or concept that seems to have arisen from her own interior monologue (great pain, a word, a haunted mind, winter light entering a room), but we can only guess what situations may have prompted her poetic responses. The conclusion of "I Died for Beauty," for example, is poignantly, crushingly sad, but biography is silent about the causes of the sadness, and it is useless to speculate about so powerful a poem. What we know about Dickinson is that her inquiring and restless mind was the source of her compulsive poetic strength, and that she wrote many poems expressing the vital personal feelings and psychological insights that rose out of her thoughts about the nature of life, love, death, and God.

Bibliographic Sources

Only seven of Dickinson's poems were published during her lifetime—anonymously, without her consent, and in obscure periodicals. She may have rejected further publication because of editors' tendencies to normalize her sentence structures and punctuation, or else because of Thomas Higginson's discouraging advice. In any event, her poems were only for her own eyes, except for those she included in her letters.

After she died, her sister Lavinia was astonished when she found the many bundles and boxes of poems. Lavinia recognized the significance of this work and eventually turned much of it over to Higginson and Mabel L. Todd for editing and publication. They published three volumes of Dickinson's verse (in 1890, 1891, and 1896), each containing about 100 poems. In these editions, the editors eliminated slant rhymes, smoothed out the meter, revised those metaphors that struck them as outrageous, and regularized the punctuation. In short, they removed the poetry from Dickinson's poems.

The well-intended but destructive editorial adjustments remained intact until 1955, when the Harvard University Press published Thomas H. Johnson's three-volume edition containing 1775 poems. Johnson went back to the manuscripts to establish the original texts (with variants), and his edition of these poems is definitive. Johnson published a single-volume edition of the poems in 1961, and also a paperback selection entitled *Final Harvest: Emily Dickinson's Poems* (1961). The poems that Dickinson embodied in her letters, which we have already mentioned, have been edited by William Shurr, with Anna Dunlap and Emily Shurr. This work, containing 498 poems, has been published as *New Poems of Emily Dickinson* (1993).

Important biographical and critical studies of Dickinson include Charles R. Anderson, *Emily Dickinson's Poetry* (1960); Ruth Miller, *The Poetry of Emily Dickinson* (1968); Richard B. Sewall, *The Life of Emily Dickinson* (1974); Joanne F. Diehl, *Dickinson and the Romantic Imagination* (1981); David Porter, *Dickinson, the Modern Idiom* (1981); Barbara Antonina Mossberg, *Emily Dickinson: When a Writer Is a Daughter* (1982); Susan Juhasz, *The Undiscovered Continent: Emily Dickinson and the Space of the Mind* (1983); E. Miller Budick, *Emily Dickinson and the Life of Language: A Study in Symbolic Poetics* (1985); Sharon Leder and Andrea Abbott, *The Language of Exclusion* (1987); Joanne Dobson, *Dickinson and the Strategies of Reticence* (1989); Paula Bennett, *Emily Dickinson: Woman Poet* (1990); and Martha Smith, *Rowing in Eden: Rereading Emily Dickinson* (1992). One of the hour-long programs in the PBS "Voices and Visions" series (1987) features her work.

POEMS BY EMILY DICKINSON

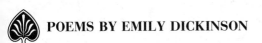

I Never Lost as Much But Twice ———————————————— *1890 (ca. 1858)*

I never lost as much but twice,
And that was in the sod.
Twice have I stood a beggar
Before the door of God!

Angels–twice descending   5
Reimbursed my store–
Burglar! Banker–Father!
I am poor once more!

Success Is Counted Sweetest _____*1878, 1890 (ca. 1859)*

Success is counted sweetest
By those who ne'er succeed.
To comprehend a nectar
Requires sorest need.

Not one of all the purple Host
Who took the Flag today
Can tell the definition
So clear of Victory

As he defeated–dying–
On whose forbidden ear
The distant strains of triumph
Burst agonized and clear!

"Faith" Is a Fine Invention _____*1891 (ca. 1860)*

"Faith" is a fine invention
When Gentlemen can *see*–
But *Microscopes* are prudent
In an Emergency.

I Taste a Liquor Never Brewed _____*1861, 1891 (ca. 1860)*

I taste a liquor never brewed–
From Tankards scooped in Pearl–
Not all the Frankfort Berries°   *grapes*
Yield such an Alcohol!

Inebriate of Air–am I–
And Debauchee of Dew–
Reeling–thro endless summer days–
From inns of Molten Blue–

When "Landlords" turn the drunken Bee
Out of the Foxglove's door–
When Butterflies–renounce their "drams"–
I shall but drink the more!

Till Seraphs swing their snowy Hats–
And Saints–to windows run–
To see the little Tippler
From Manzanilla° come!

I TASTE A LIQUOR NEVER BREWED   16 *Manzanilla:* a pale sherry from Spain. Dickinson
may also have been thinking of Manzanillo, a Cuban city often associated with rum.

Safe in Their Alabaster Chambers———————————— *1862, 1890 (1861)*

Safe in their Alabaster Chambers–
Untouched by Morning–
And untouched by Noon–
Lie the meek members of the Resurrection–
Rafter of Satin–and Roof of Stone!   5

Grand go the Years–in the Crescent–above them–
Worlds scoop their Arcs–
And Firmaments–row–
Diadems–drop–and Doges°–surrender–
Soundless as dots–on a Disc of Snow–   10

SAFE IN THEIR ALABASTER CHAMBERS.   9 *Doges:* Renaissance rulers of the Italian city-states
of Venice and Genoa.

Wild Nights–Wild Nights!———————————————— *1890 (ca. 1861)*

Wild Nights–Wild Nights!
Were I with thee
Wild Nights should be
Our luxury!

Futile–the Winds–   5
To a Heart in port–
Done with the Compass–
Done with the Chart!

Rowing in Eden–
Ah, the Sea!   10
Might I but moor–Tonight–
In Thee!

There's a Certain Slant of Light———————————— *1890 (ca. 1861)*

There's a certain Slant of light,
Winter Afternoons–
That oppresses, like the Heft
Of Cathedral Tunes–

Heavenly Hurt, it gives us–   5
We can find no scar,
But internal difference,
Where the Meanings, are–

None may teach it–Any–
'Tis the Seal Despair–   10
An imperial affliction
Sent us of the Air–

When it comes, the Landscape listens–
Shadows–hold their breath–
When it goes, 'tis like the Distance
On the look of Death–

The Soul Selects Her Own Society _____1890 (ca. 1862)

The Soul selects her own Society–
Then–shuts the Door–
To her divine Majority–
Present no more–

Unmoved–she notes the Chariots–pausing–
At her low Gate–
Unmoved–an Emperor be kneeling
Upon her Mat–

I've known her–from an ample nation–
Choose One–
Then–close the Valves of her attention–
Like Stone–

Some Keep the Sabbath Going to Church _____1864 (ca. 1862)

Some keep the Sabbath going to Church–
I keep it, staying at Home–
With a Bobolink for a Chorister–
And an Orchard, for a Dome–

Some keep the Sabbath in Surplice–
I just wear my Wings–
And instead of tolling the Bell, for Church,
Our little Sexton–sings.

God preaches, a noted Clergyman–
And the sermon is never long,
So instead of getting to Heaven, at last–
I'm going, all along.

After Great Pain, a Formal Feeling Comes _____1929 (ca. 1862)

After great pain, a formal feeling comes–
The Nerves sit ceremonious, like Tombs–
The stiff Heart questions was it He, that bore,
And Yesterday, or Centuries before?

The Feet, mechanical, go round–
Of Ground, or Air, or Ought°–   *anything, nothing*

A Wooden way
Regardless grown,
A Quartz contentment, like a stone—

This is the Hour of Lead—   10
Remembered, if outlived,
As Freezing persons, recollect the Snow—
First—Chill—then Stupor—then the letting go—

Much Madness Is Divinest Sense————————— *1890 (ca. 1862)*

Much Madness is divinest Sense—
To a discerning Eye—
Much Sense—the starkest Madness—
'Tis the Majority
In this, as All, prevail—   5
Assent—and you are sane—
Demur—you're straightway dangerous—
And handled with a Chain—

I Heard a Fly Buzz—When I Died————————— *1896 (ca. 1862)*

I heard a Fly buzz—when I died—
The Stillness in the Room
Was like the Stillness in the Air—
Between the Heaves of Storm—

The Eyes around—had wrung them dry—   5
And Breaths were gathering firm
For that last Onset—when the King
Be witnessed—in the Room—

I willed my Keepsakes—Signed away
What portion of me be   10
Assignable—and then it was
There interposed a Fly—

With Blue—uncertain stumbling Buzz—
Between the light—and me—
And then the Windows failed—and then   15
I could not see to see—

I Like to See It Lap the Miles————————— *1891 (ca. 1862)*

I like to see it lap the Miles—
And lick the Valleys up—
And stop to feed itself at Tanks—
And then—prodigious step

Around a Pile of Mountains–
And supercilious peer
In Shanties–by the sides of Roads–
And then a Quarry pare

To fit its sides
And crawl between
Complaining all the while
In horrid–hooting stanza–
Then chase itself down Hill–

And neigh like Boanerges°–
Then–prompter than a Star
Stop–docile and omnipotent
At its own stable door–

I LIKE TO SEE IT LAP THE MILES.   14 *Boanerges:* a surname meaning "the sons of thunder"
that appears in Mark 3:17.

I Cannot Live with You ————————————————————*1890 (ca. 1862)*

I cannot live with You–
It would be Life–
And Life is over there–
Behind the Shelf

The Sexton keeps the Key to–
Putting up
Our Life–His Porcelain–
Like a Cup–

Discarded of the Housewife–
Quaint–or Broke–
A newer Sevres° pleases–   *a fine French porcelain*
Old Ones crack–

I could not die–with You–
For One must wait
To shut the Other's Gaze down–
You–could not–

And I–Could I stand by
And see You–freeze–
Without my Right of Frost–
Death's privilege?

Nor could I rise–with You–
Because Your Face
Would put out Jesus'–
That New Grace

Glow plain–and foreign   25
On my homesick Eye–
Except that You than He
Shone closer by–

They'd judge Us–How–
For You–served Heaven–You know,   30
Or sought to–
I could not–

Because You saturated Sight–
And I had no more Eyes
For sordid excellence   35
As Paradise

And were You lost, I would be–
Though My Name
Rang loudest
On the Heavenly fame–   40

And were You–saved–
And I–condemned to be
Where You were not–
That self–were Hell to Me–

So We must meet apart–   45
You there–I–here–
With just the Door ajar
That Oceans are–and Prayer–
And that White Sustenance–
Despair–   50

One Need Not Be a Chamber–To Be Haunted _____ *1891 (ca. 1863)*

One need not be a Chamber–to be Haunted–
One need not be a House–
The Brain has Corridors–surpassing
Material Place–

Far safer, of a Midnight Meeting   5
External Ghost
Than its interior Confronting–
That Cooler Host.

Far safer, through an Abbey gallop,
The Stones a'chase–   10
Than Unarmed, one's a'self encounter–
In lonesome Place–

Ourself behind ourself, concealed–
Should startle most–

Assassin hid in our Apartment
Be Horror's least.

The Body–borrows a Revolver–
He bolts the Door–
O'erlooking a superior spectre–
Or More–

The Bustle in a House —————————————————1890 *(ca. 1866)*

The Bustle in a House
The Morning after Death
Is solemnest of industries
Enacted upon Earth–

The Sweeping up the Heart
And putting Love away
We shall not want to use again
Until Eternity.

My Triumph Lasted Till the Drums ————————1935 *(ca. 1872)*

My Triumph lasted till the Drums
Had left the Dead alone
And then I dropped my Victory
And chastened stole along
To where the finished Faces
Conclusion turned on me
And then I hated Glory
And wished myself were They.
What is to be is best descried
When it has also been–
Could Prospect taste of Retrospect
The tyrannies of Men
Were Tenderer–diviner
The Transitive toward.
A Bayonet's contrition
Is nothing to the Dead.

The Heart Is the Capital of the Mind ————————1929 *(ca. 1876)*

The Heart is the Capital of the Mind–
The Mind is a single State–
The Heart and the Mind together make
A single Continent–

One–is the Population–
Numerous enough–   5
This ecstatic Nation
Seek–it is Yourself.

My Life Closed Twice Before Its Close ————————— *1896*

My life closed twice before its close;
It yet remains to see
If Immortality unveil
A third event to me,

So huge, so hopeless to conceive   5
As these that twice befel.
Parting is all we know of heaven,
And all we need of hell.

A Word Made Flesh Is Seldom ———————— *1955 (date of writing unknown)*

A Word made Flesh is seldom
And tremblingly partook
Nor then perhaps reported
But have I not mistook
Each one of us has tasted   5
With ecstasies of stealth
The very food debated
To our specific strength–

A Word that breathes distinctly
Has not the power to die   10
Cohesive as the Spirit
It may expire if He–
"Made Flesh and dwelt among us"
Could condescension be
Like this consent of Language   15
This loved Philology.

A WORD MADE FLESH   13 *"Made Flesh and dwelt among us"*: John I:14

I Never Felt at Home–Below– ————————— *1929 (ca. 1862)*

I never felt at Home–Below–
And in the Handsome Skies
I shall not feel at Home–I know–
I don't like Paradise–

Because it's Sunday–all the time–
And Recess–never comes–
And Eden'll be so lonesome
Bright Wednesday Afternoons–

If God could make a visit–
Or ever took a Nap–
So not to see us–but they say
Himself–a Telescope

Perennial beholds us–
Myself would run away
From Him–and Holy Ghost–and All–
But there's the "Judgment Day"!

I Died for Beauty–but Was Scarce —————————— 1890 (*ca. 1862*)

I died for Beauty–but was scarce
Adjusted in the tomb
When One who died for Truth, was lain
In an adjoining Room–

He questioned softly "Why I failed"?
"For Beauty", I replied–
"And I–for Truth–Themself are One–
We Brethren, are", He said–

And so, as Kinsmen, met a Night–
We talked between the Rooms–
Until the Moss had reached our lips–
And covered up–our names–

I'm Nobody! Who Are You? —————————— 1891 (*ca. 1861*)

I'm Nobody! Who are you?
Are you–Nobody–Too?
Then there's a pair of us?
Don't tell! they'd advertise–you know!

How dreary–to be–Somebody!
How public–like a Frog–
To tell one's name–the livelong June–
To an admiring Bog!

This World Is Not Conclusion —————————— 1896 (*ca. 1862*)

This World is not Conclusion.
A Species stands beyond–

Invisible, as Music–
But positive, as Sound–
It beckons, and it baffles–   5
Philosophy–don't know–
And through a Riddle, at the last–
Sagacity, must go–
To guess it, puzzles scholars–
To gain it, Men have borne   10
Contempt of Generations
And Crucifixion, shown–
Faith slips–and laughs, and rallies–
Blushes, if any see–
Plucks at a twig of Evidence–   15
And asks a Vane, the way–
Much Gesture, from the Pulpit–
Strong Hallelujahs roll–
Narcotics cannot still the Tooth
That nibbles at the soul–   20

ROBERT FROST

Robert Lee Frost (1874–1963) published his first book of poems, *A Boy's Will*, in England in 1913. At this time he was virtually unknown in the United States. Ezra Pound wrote that "it is a sinister thing that so American ... a talent ... should have to be exported before it can find due encouragement and recognition." Time, of course, made Frost the most visible and admired American poet of his day. He eventually received over twenty honorary degrees and four Pulitzer Prizes. Although there was no officially recognized national poet until the 1980s, with the establishment of the annual poet laureateships, he came as close as possible to being America's official poet when he read "The Gift Outright" at the inauguration of President John F. Kennedy in 1961. His collected poetic works continue to earn him that recognition.

Although he presented himself as the quintessential New Englander in person and in his poetry, he was born in San Francisco on March 26, 1874. His father had moved the family west so that he could take a job with the *San Francisco Bulletin*. When his father died in 1885, Frost's mother brought the family back to Lawrence, Massachusetts, where Frost attended high school, studied classics, and began writing poetry. He graduated in 1892 as co-valedictorian with Elinor White, whom he married in 1895. After high school he attended Dartmouth College for seven weeks and then turned to newspaper work and teaching school. He continued to write poetry, little of which was published. Two years after his marriage, he began attending classes at Harvard (1897–1899), but he left without a degree.

In 1900 Frost's grandfather gave him a farm in Derry, New Hampshire,

Robert Frost (Herbert H. Lamson Library, Plymouth State College, Plymouth, New Hampshire)

and for the next twelve years he farmed, wrote poetry which was mostly ignored, and taught English at Pinkerton Academy. Then in 1912 he sold the farm to devote himself to writing and moved to England, where he met a number of emerging and established poets, including Ezra Pound and William Butler Yeats. His first two books of poetry, *A Boy's Will* (1913) and *North of Boston* (1914), were well received in England, and when they were published in the United States in 1915, Frost finally began to receive recognition at home.

That same year Frost and his family returned to the United States and took up residence on a farm near Franconia, New Hampshire. More books of poetry and greater acclaim followed quickly. In 1916 he published *Mountain Interval,* a book containing "The Road Not Taken," "Birches," and "Out, Out—." He also became poet-in-residence at Amherst College, a relationship that would continue sporadically for much of his life.

More books of poetry and more recognition followed throughout Frost's life. In 1923 he published *Selected Poems* and *New Hampshire.* The latter book, for which he won a Pulitzer Prize, contains some of his best-known work: "Stopping by Woods on a Snowy Evening," "Fire and Ice," and "Nothing Gold Can Stay." These were followed by *West-Running Brook* (1928), *Collected Poems* (1930), *A Further Range* (1936), *A Witness Tree* (1942), *Steeple Bush* (1947), *Complete Poems* (1949), *Aforesaid* (1954), and *In the Clearing* (1962).

Poetic Characteristics

Early in his career and throughout his long public experience as a speaker and lecturer, Frost cultivated his persona as a philosophical, wry, and wise country poet. This is the friendly, almost avuncular voice we usually hear, the one that expresses knowledge and concern for the land, history, and human nature. Even with this point of view, however, there are complicated undertones of wit and irony. There is also what Randall Jarrell called "The Other Frost," the often agonized and troubled spirit whose voice is heard in poems like "Acquainted with the Night" and "Fire and Ice."

Regardless of the voice we hear, Frost's poetic style is consistent. His diction is informal, plain, and conversational, and his phrases are simple and direct. More often than not, he uses and refines the natural speech patterns and rhythms of New England, polishing the language that people actually speak, and fashioning it into a compact and terse poetic texture.

Structurally, Frost's poems typically move in a smooth, uninterrupted flow from an event or an object, through a metaphor, to an idea. Within this pattern, he usually describes a complete event rather than a single vision. The heart of the process is the image or metaphor. Frost's metaphors are sparse and careful; they are brought sharply into focus and skillfully interwoven within each poem. Frost himself saw metaphors as the beginning of the process. In *Education by Poetry* (1931) he wrote that "poetry begins in trivial metaphors, pretty metaphors, 'grace' metaphors, and goes on to the profoundest thinking that we have. Poetry provides the one permissible way of saying one thing and meaning another."

Frost preferred traditional poetic forms and rhythms, and he was so disapproving of free verse that he once asserted that writing it was like playing tennis without a net. We therefore find conventional rhyme schemes and clear meters (with traditional metrical substitutions) in much of his work, together with closed forms such as couplets, sonnets (with interesting varying rhyme patterns), terza rima (see p. 752), quatrains, stanzas, and blank verse.

Poetic Subjects

Frost's poems are usually based in rural, everyday life. Poems are occasioned by flowers, stone fences, woodcutting, picking apples, sleigh riding, falling leaves, rain, snow, birch trees, insects, birds, hired men, and children, to name just a few of the topics. However, the Frostian poetic structure always moves from such subjects toward philosophical generalizations about life and death, survival and responsibility, and nature and humanity.

One of Frost's major appeals is that his poems are easily accessible. They are by no means simplistic, however, but run deep, as may be seen in poems like "The Road Not Taken" and "Misgiving." They also may be complex and ambiguous. In "Mending Wall," for example, the philosophies of the speaker and his fence-repairing neighbor are well presented and contrasted. Readers often conclude that the speaker's wish to remove barriers is the major idea, but the neighbor's argument for maintaining them is equally strong. In "Desert Places" we are presented with a chilling view of the infinite desert within the human mind. In "Acquainted with the Night," Frost's sophisticated urban speaker tells us of the night of the city and also presents hints about the dark night of the soul.

Bibliographic Sources

The standard edition of Frost's work is The *Poetry of Robert Frost* (1969), edited by Edward Connery Lathem. During his later years, Frost was much in demand as a speaker, and he was the first American poet to appear frequently before the television camera. Twelve of his lectures are published in Reginald Cook, *Robert Frost, A Living Voice* (1974). The standard biography is by Lawrence Thompson, in three volumes: *Robert Frost: The Early Years* (1966), *The Years of Triumph* (1970), and *The Later Years* (1977). The last volume was completed after Thompson's death by R. H. Winnick. Useful criticism of the poetry includes George Nitchie, *Human Values in the Poetry of Robert Frost* (1960); Reuben Brower, *The Poetry of Robert Frost* (1963); J. F. Lynan, *The Pastoral Art of Robert Frost* (1964); Philip L. Gerber, *Robert Frost* (1966); John Kemp, *Robert Frost and New England* (1979), Richard Wakefield, *Robert Frost and the Opposing Light* (1985); James Potter, *A Robert Frost Handbook* (1980); Harold Bloom, ed., *Robert Frost* (a collection of critical essays published in 1986); and George Monteiro, *Robert Frost and the New England Renaissance* (1988). One of the PBS "Voices and Visions" series (1987) features his work.

POEMS BY ROBERT FROST

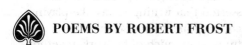

The Tuft of Flowers _____1906

I went to turn the grass once after one
Who mowed it in the dew before the sun.

The dew was gone that made his blade so keen
Before I came to view the leveled scene.

I looked for him behind an isle of trees;
I listened for his whetstone on the breeze.

But he had gone his way, the grass all mown,
And I must be, as he had been,–alone,

'As all must be,' I said within my heart,
'Whether they work together or apart.'

But as I said it, swift there passed me by
On noiseless wing a bewildered butterfly,

Seeking with memories grown dim o'er night
Some resting flower of yesterday's delight.

And once I marked his flight go round and round,   15
As where some flower lay withering on the ground.

And then he flew as far as eye could see,
And then on tremulous wing came back to me.

I thought of questions that have no reply,
And would have turned to toss the grass to dry;   20

But he turned first, and led my eye to look
At a tall tuft of flowers beside a brook,

A leaping tongue of bloom the scythe had spared
Beside a reedy brook the scythe had bared.

The mower in the dew had loved them thus,   25
By leaving them to flourish, not for us,

Nor yet to draw one thought of ours to him,
But from sheer morning gladness at the brim.

The butterfly and I had lit upon,
Nevertheless, a message from the dawn,   30

That made me hear the wakening birds around,
And hear his long scythe whispering to the ground,

And feel a spirit kindred to my own;
So that henceforth I worked no more alone;

But glad with him, I worked as with his aid,   35
And weary, sought at noon with him the shade;

And dreaming, as it were, held brotherly speech
With one whose thought I had not hoped to reach.

'Men work together,' I told him from the heart,
'Whether they work together or apart.'   40

A Line-Storm Song ——————————————— *1913*

The line-storm clouds fly tattered and swift.
    The road is forlorn all day,
Where a myriad snowy quartz stones lift,
    And the hoof-prints vanish away.
The roadside flowers, too wet for the bee,   5
    Expend their bloom in vain.
Come over the hills and far with me,
    And be my love in the rain.

The birds have less to say for themselves
    In the wood-world's torn despair   10

Than now these numberless years the elves,
  Although they are no less there:
All song of the woods is crushed like some
  Wild, easily shattered rose.
Come, be my love in the wet woods, come,
  Where the boughs rain when it blows.

There is the gale to urge behind
  And bruit our singing down,
And the shallow waters aflutter with wind
  From which to gather your gown.
What matter if we go clear to the west,
  And come not through dry-shod?
For wilding brooch shall wet your breast
  The rain-fresh goldenrod.

Oh, never this whelming east wind swells
  But it seems like the sea's return
To the ancient lands where it left the shells
  Before the age of the fern;
And it seems like the time when after doubt
  Our love came back amain.
Oh, come forth into the storm and rout
  And be my love in the rain.

Mending Wall ————————————————————*1914*

Something there is that doesn't love a wall,
That sends the frozen-ground-swell under it,
And spills the upper boulders in the sun;
And makes gaps even two can pass abreast.
The work of hunters is another thing:
I have come after them and made repair
Where they have left not one stone on a stone,
But they would have the rabbit out of hiding,
To please the yelping dogs. The gaps I mean,
No one has seen them made or heard them made,
But at spring mending-time we find them there.
I let my neighbor know beyond the hill;
And on a day we meet to walk the line
And set the wall between us once again.
We keep the wall between us as we go.
To each the boulders that have fallen to each.
And some are loaves and some so nearly balls
We have to use a spell to make them balance:
'Stay where you are until our backs are turned!'
We wear our fingers rough with handling them.
Oh, just another kind of outdoor game,
One on a side. It comes to little more:

There where it is we do not need the wall:
He is all pine and I am apple orchard.
My apple trees will never get across   25
And eat the cones under his pines, I tell him.
He only says, 'Good fences make good neighbors.'
Spring is the mischief in me, and I wonder
If I could put a notion in his head:
'*Why* do they make good neighbors? Isn't it   30
Where there are cows? But here there are no cows.
Before I built a wall I'd ask to know
What I was walling in or walling out,
And to whom I was like to give offense.
Something there is that doesn't love a wall,   35
That wants it down.' I could say 'Elves' to him,
But it's not elves exactly, and I'd rather
He said it for himself. I see him there
Bringing a stone grasped firmly by the top
In each hand, like an old-stone savage armed.   40
He moves in darkness as it seems to me,
Not of woods only and the shade of trees.
He will not go behind his father's saying,
And he likes having thought of it so well
He says again, 'Good fences make good neighbors.'   45

Birches ———————————————————————— *1915*

When I see birches bend to left and right
Across the lines of straighter darker trees,
I like to think some boy's been swinging them.
But swinging doesn't bend them down to stay
As ice-storms do. Often you must have seen them   5
Loaded with ice a sunny winter morning
After a rain. They click upon themselves
As the breeze rises, and turn many-colored
As the stir cracks and crazes their enamel.
Soon the sun's warmth makes them shed crystal shells   10
Shattering and avalanching on the snow-crust–
Such heaps of broken glass to sweep away
You'd think the inner dome of heaven had fallen.
They are dragged to the withered bracken by the load,
And they seem not to break; though once they are bowed   15
So low for long, they never right themselves:
You may see their trunks arching in the woods
Years afterwards, trailing their leaves on the ground
Like girls on hands and knees that throw their hair
Before them over their heads to dry in the sun.   20
But I was going to say when Truth broke in
With all her matter-of-fact about the ice-storm

I should prefer to have some boy bend them
As he went out and in to fetch the cows–
Some boy too far from town to learn baseball,
Whose only play was what he found himself,
Summer or winter, and could play alone.
One by one he subdued his father's trees
By riding them down over and over again
Until he took the stiffness out of them,
And not one but hung limp, not one was left
For him to conquer. He learned all there was
To learn about not launching out too soon
And so not carrying the tree away
Clear to the ground. He always kept his poise
To the top branches, climbing carefully
With the same pains you use to fill a cup
Up to the brim, and even above the brim.
Then he flung outward, feet first, with a swish,
Kicking his way down through the air to the ground.
So was I once myself a swinger of birches.
And so I dream of going back to be.
It's when I'm weary of considerations,
And life is too much like a pathless wood
Where your face burns and tickles with the cobwebs
Broken across it, and one eye is weeping
From a twig's having lashed across it open.
I'd like to get away from earth awhile
And then come back to it and begin over.
May no fate willfully misunderstand me
And half grant what I wish and snatch me away
Not to return. Earth's the right place for love:
I don't know where it's likely to go better.
I'd like to go by climbing a birch tree,
And climb black branches up a snow-white trunk
Toward Heaven, till the tree could bear no more,
But dipped its top and set me down again.
That would be good both going and coming back.
One could do worse than be a swinger of birches.

The Road Not Taken ———————————————————— *1915*

Two roads diverged in a yellow wood,
And sorry I could not travel both
And be one traveler, long I stood
And looked down one as far as I could
To where it bent in the undergrowth;

Then took the other, as just as fair,
And having perhaps the better claim,

Because it was grassy and wanted wear;
Though as for that the passing there
Had worn them really about the same,   10
And both that morning equally lay
In leaves no step had trodden black.
Oh, I kept the first for another day!
Yet knowing how way leads on to way,
I doubted if I should ever come back.   15

I shall be telling this with a sigh
Somewhere ages and ages hence:
Two roads diverged in a wood, and I–
I took the one less traveled by,
And that has made all the difference.   20

'Out, Out—' ——————————————————— *1916*

The buzz saw snarled and rattled in the yard
And made dust and dropped stove-length sticks of wood,
Sweet-scented stuff when the breeze drew across it.
And from there those that lifted eyes could count
Five mountain ranges one behind the other   5
Under the sunset far into Vermont.
And the saw snarled and rattled, snarled and rattled,
As it ran light, or had to bear a load.
And nothing happened: day was all but done.
Call it a day, I wish they might have said   10
To please the boy by giving him the half hour
That a boy counts so much when saved from work.
His sister stood beside them in her apron
To tell them 'Supper.' At the word, the saw,
As if to prove saws knew what supper meant,   15
Leaped out at the boy's hand, or seemed to leap–
He must have given the hand. However it was,
Neither refused the meeting. But the hand!
The boy's first outcry was rueful laugh,
As he swung toward them holding up the hand   20
Half in appeal, but half as if to keep
The life from spilling. Then the boy saw all–
Since he was old enough to know, big boy
Doing a man's work, though a child at heart–
He saw all spoiled. 'Don't let him cut my hand off–   25
The doctor, when he comes. Don't let him, sister!'
So. But the hand was gone already.
The doctor put him in the dark of ether.
He lay and puffed his lips out with his breath.
And then–the watcher at his pulse took fright.

No one believed. They listened at his heart.
Little–less–nothing!–and that ended it.
No more to build on there. And they, since they
Were not the one dead, turned to their affairs.

The Oven Bird _____ *1916*

There is a singer everyone has heard,
Loud, a mid-summer and a mid-wood bird,
Who makes the solid tree trunks sound again.
He says that leaves are old and that for flowers
Mid-summer is to spring as one to ten.
He says the early petal-fall is past
When pear and cherry bloom went down in showers
On sunny days a moment overcast;
And comes that other fall we name the fall.
He says the highway dust is over all.
The bird would cease and be as other birds
But that he knows in singing not to sing.
The question that he frames in all but words
Is what to make of a diminished thing.

Fire and Ice _____ *1920*

Some say the world will end in fire,
Some say in ice.
From what I've tasted of desire
I hold with those who favor fire.
But if it had to perish twice,
I think I know enough of hate
To say that for destruction ice
Is also great
And would suffice.

Nothing Gold Can Stay _____ *1923*

Nature's first green is gold,
Her hardest hue to hold.
Her early leaf's a flower;
But only so an hour.
Then leaf subsides to leaf.
So Eden sank to grief,
So dawn goes down to day.
Nothing gold can stay.

Misgiving ———————————————————————— *1923*

All crying, 'We will go with you, O Wind!'
The foliage follow him, leaf and stem;
But a sleep oppresses them as they go,
And they end by bidding him stay with them.

Since ever they flung abroad in spring   5
The leaves had promised themselves this flight,
Who now would fain seek sheltering wall,
Or thicket, or hollow place for the night.

And now they answer his summoning blast
With an ever vaguer and vaguer stir,   10
Or at utmost a little reluctant whirl
That drops them no further than where they were.

I only hope that when I am free
As they are free to go in quest
Of the knowledge beyond the bounds of life   15
It may not seem better to me to rest.

Acquainted with the Night ——————————————— *1928*

I have been one acquainted with the night.
I have walked out in rain—and back in rain.
I have outwalked the furthest city light.

I have looked down the saddest city lane.
I have passed by the watchman on his beat   5
And dropped my eyes, unwilling to explain.

I have stood still and stopped the sound of feet
When far away an interrupted cry
Came over houses from another street,

But not to call me back or say good-by;   10
And further still at an unearthly height,
One luminary clock against the sky

Proclaimed the time was neither wrong nor right.
I have been one acquainted with the night.

Design ——————————————————————————— *1936*

I found a dimpled spider, fat and white,
On a white heal-all,° holding up a moth

———————————————————————————————
DESIGN.   2 *heal-all:* a flower, usually blue, thought to have healing powers.

Like a white piece of rigid satin cloth—
Assorted characters of death and blight
Mixed ready to begin the morning right,
Like the ingredients of a witches' broth—
A snow-drop spider, a flower like a froth,
And dead wings carried like a paper kite.

What had that flower to do with being white,
The wayside blue and innocent heal-all?
What brought the kindred spider to that height,
Then steered the white moth thither in the night?
What but design of darkness to appall?—
If design govern in a thing so small.

The Strong Are Saying Nothing ——————————————————1937

The soil now gets a rumpling soft and damp,
And small regard to the future of any weed.
The final flat of the hoe's approval stamp
Is reserved for the bed of a few selected seed.

There is seldom more than a man to a harrowed piece.
Men work alone, their lots plowed far apart,
One stringing a chain of seed in an open crease,
And another stumbling after a halting cart.

To the fresh and black of the squares of early mold
The leafless bloom of a plum is fresh and white;
Though there's more than a doubt if the weather is not too cold
For the bees to come and serve its beauty aright.

Wind goes from farm to farm in wave on wave,
But carries no cry of what is hoped to be.
There may be little or much beyond the grave,
But the strong are saying nothing until they see.

A Considerable Speck ——————————————————1942

(Microscopic)

A speck that would have been beneath my sight
On any but a paper sheet so white
Set off across what I had written there.
And I had idly poised my pen in air
To stop it with a period of ink
When something strange about it made me think.
This was no dust speck by my breathing blown,
But unmistakably a living mite
With inclinations it could call its own.

It paused as with suspicion of my pen,   5
And then came racing wildly on again
To where my manuscript was not yet dry;
Then paused again and either drank or smelt—
With loathing, for again it turned to fly.
Plainly with an intelligence I dealt.   10
It seemed too tiny to have room for feet,
Yet must have had a set of them complete
To express how much it didn't want to die.
It ran with terror and with cunning crept.
It faltered: I could see it hesitate;   15
Then in the middle of the open sheet
Cower down in desperation to accept
Whatever I accorded it of fate.
I have none of the tenderer-than-thou
Collectivistic regimenting love   20
With which the modern world is being swept
But this poor microscopic item now!
Since it was nothing I knew evil of
I let it lie there till I hope it slept.
I have a mind myself and recognize   25
Mind when I meet with it in any guise.
No one can know how glad I am to find
On any sheet the least display of mind.

WRITING ABOUT A POET'S WORK

It is difficult to write an effective essay on a poet's entire career based on a
small selection of verse. It is both possible and reasonable, however, to write
about a limited number of poems by a single poet. There are three approaches
to this type of essay: biographical, developmental, and comparative.

The *biographical essay* is perhaps the least productive; it seeks to relate poems to specific events or stages in a poet's life. Thus, you might attempt an
essay that connects specific events in Emily Dickinson's life with specific poems; this type of essay requires extensive biographical research.

The *developmental essay* traces the growth of a single image, concept, or
technique throughout a poet's career. Such an essay presupposes both development and the ability to look at a poet's work in the order in which it was
written. An essay of this type might focus, for example, on Frost's use of snow
imagery or Dickinson's employment of slant rhyme. In either case, the objective is to use examples to establish that, over the poet's creative life, the image, concept, or technique grew, changed, or developed.

The *comparative essay* is the easiest to formulate and the most common,
since it neither assumes development nor requires biographical research (see
Appendix B for an additional discussion of comparison as a strategy). Like the

developmental essay, the comparative essay focuses on a specific element, image, idea, or technique in a poet's work; however, the goal is to assert *continuity* or *commonality* rather than development, and to use each work to clarify the others. Thus, such an essay will usually argue that a poet uses the same devices or addresses the same concerns in a similar way in a number of poems to establish related ideas or emotions. Such an essay might deal with snow imagery in Frost, biblical allusions in Donne, or death and eternal life in Dickinson.

Almost any essay dealing with a number of poems by the same author will focus on a specific element of the poems rather than attempt a wholesale treatment. You might choose to work with speaker, setting and situation, diction, imagery, tone, rhythm, rhyme and form, symbol, allusion, or theme. The choice, of course, is never arbitrary; you should look for an element or technique that strikes you as especially significant and effective.

Prewriting strategies for either a developmental or comparative essay include selecting a poet, an approach, and a focus. These choices are not always easy, but some investigation of the works at hand will usually help you narrow the options. As you plan the essay, remember that your aim is to discover development or commonality.

Questions for Discovering Ideas

- Are the speakers in the poems similar or related to each other? Does the speaker remain constant throughout the poems, develop gradually, or change radically from poem to poem? To what extent do the speakers share a common tone or attitude? Do tone and attitude remain constant, or do they change?

- Do the poems have common or similar settings or situations? Are these established vividly and quickly, or left undeveloped? To what extent do setting and situation produce similar effects in a number of poems by the same author?

- Can you find common threads of diction, imagery, metaphor, simile, symbol, or allusion in a number of poems by the same author? Are these common devices always used the same way and to the same effect, or do the method and impact change?

- Does the poet's use of the elements of form—rhythm, rhyme, meter, stanza—remain constant or develop? Does form consistently reinforce meaning? Does the connection between form and content remain consistent or become less or more effective?

- In a significant number of poems, how does the poet deal with the same subject or convey similar ideas? How do the poet's attitudes toward this subject and treatment of the idea remain constant or change? To what extent can you see logical connection or development among the poems in question?

These questions cover a broad range of topics. In actual practice, however, the poems at hand will usually direct you quickly to specific areas of consideration. As you answer the relevant questions, the focus for your essay should emerge.

Once you have chosen a poet, isolated an area of interest, and selected a series of poems, you can shape a central idea. As usual, this is probably the most difficult step in the prewriting process. Discovering an area of commonality or development is only half the battle; you must go on to assert a central fact about this common thread. It is not enough, for example, to argue in an essay that "we find the idea of death in three of Emily Dickinson's poems" or that "snow imagery recurs in a number of Robert Frost's poems." Rather, you must link the common thread to an assertion about its effect, impact, or significance. Thus, you might formulate a tentative thesis that argues that "death is presented in a number of Emily Dickinson's poems as the natural and welcome end to a life of toil" or that "the common image of snow in many of Robert Frost's poems grows progressively more grim and ironic throughout his career." Notice that both these formulations identify an area of commonality *and* make an assertion about that area. The first thesis would produce a comparative essay, the second a developmental one.

Having formulated a tentative central idea, go back through the poet's work and reexamine those poems that offer support and illustration. Look for aspects of specific poems that will eventually form the body of the essay. During this stage you may need to revise or refocus the thesis several times to solidify the connection between your central idea and the supporting details.

Strategies for Organizing Ideas

The introductory paragraph should indicate, at least indirectly, the type of approach. After reading the first paragraph, a reader should be able to tell if the essay is biographical, developmental, or comparative. The introduction should also specify which poems will be examined to support the central idea of the essay.

The organization of the essay is determined almost completely by the strategy outlined in the introduction. A biographical essay would be organized around crucial events in the poet's life and key poems that reflect those events. A developmental essay would consider a number of the author's poems in chronological order, based on approximate or exact dates of composition. A comparative essay, on the other hand, might take up one topic at a time in almost any order, and introduce references to various poems as they are relevant to the major idea.

To support and illustrate your introductory assertions, and to keep your essay within reasonable bounds, you will normally work with no more than three to five poems. An effective organizational strategy is to divide your topic, and then to begin by dealing with poems in order, stanza by stanza or unit by unit, focusing on each of your divisions. Although your first topic might be a single poem, as you develop your essay you will be able to connect the later poems to the earlier ones through increasing elements for comparison and contrast. Be especially careful to provide clear transitions between your treatments of each poem and to tie each separate discussion back into the central idea and the introductory paragraph so that your essay does not break down into three or four disjointed discussions.

The conclusion should pull together all the strands of your argument and provide an overview. At the same time, you might relate your argument to a broader consideration of the poet's work. Thus, an essay on the speaker in three of Frost's poems might conclude by connecting the narrative voice to the dominant tones or moods of some of Frost's other poems.

SAMPLE ESSAY

Images of Expanding and Contracting Space in John Donne's Love Poetry°

[1]
John Donne's love poetry has extended images and metaphors that emphasize the mystery and the power of love. Images expanding or contracting space help to create a private and separate world for lovers and to demonstrate the power of love.* We can see this skillful and effective use of spatial imagery in "The Good Morrow," "The Sun Rising," and "The Flea."†

[2]
"The Good Morrow," a three-stanza lyric spoken by a lover to his mistress, contains spatial images that illustrate both the expansion and the contraction of space to include a private world of love. The central image in the poem is the world or the globe; this image is skillfully manipulated to demonstrate love's power. In the second stanza the speaker introduces the image by asserting that "love all love of other sights controls, / And makes one little room an everywhere" (lines 10–11). This image suggests that love is powerful enough to expand "one little room" into an entire world containing everything the lovers need. In the rest of the stanza, the self-sustaining world image is even more explicit:

> Let sea-discoverers to new worlds have gone.
> Let maps to other, worlds on worlds have shown,
> Let us possess one world; each hath one, and is one.
>
> (lines 12–14)

The movement of the spatial imagery is complex but consistent. These lines make a clear distinction between the public world of "sea-discoverers" or "maps" and the private world of the lovers. The speaker asserts that the lovers "possess" their own world; each lover is a world and "hath" the other lover-world. More to the point, the movement here is inward and progressively contracting, from the actual globe to maps and finally to the lovers as little worlds.

[3]
The contraction of the world and space—the movement inward—is continued in the third stanza with the image of reflected faces: "My face in thine eye, thine in mine appears, / And true plain hearts do in the faces rest" (lines 15–16). At first, this image of reflected faces and hearts seems to depart from the spatial imagery of the second stanza. The connection, however, is established when we realize that eyes are spheres or globes, and that the

---

° See "The Good Morrow" (p. 869), "The Sun Rising" (p. 871), and "The Flea" (p. 874).
* Central idea.
† Thesis sentence.

reflection occurs on the outward half or "hemisphere" of the eyes. This witty contraction of worlds to eyes is brought home in the next two lines: "Where can we find two better hemispheres / Without sharp North, without declining West?" (lines 17–18). Here, the image finally contracts to a single world or globe, and the lovers become that world. Thus, the poem simultaneously contracts global space to the physical presence of the lovers and expands their "little room" into a total cosmos.

We find a similar manipulation of spatial imagery in "The Sun Rising," another three-stanza lyric spoken by a lover. This time the poem is spoken to the sun, which like an unwelcome intruder is announcing the day and thus calling the lovers away from their night together. In stanza one the speaker establishes the distinction between the lovers and the drowsy outside world—the "school boys," "sour prentices," "huntsmen," and "country ants." The second stanza, as in "The Good Morrow," returns to images of expanding and contracting space that define love as self-sufficient and all-encompassing. Here the speaker tells the sun:

[4]
> Look, and tomorrow late, tell me,
> Whether both the Indias of spice and mine
> Be where thou leftst them, or lie here with me.
> Ask for those kings whom thou saw'st yesterday,
> And thou shalt hear, All here in one bed lay.
>
> (lines 16–20)

In this instance, the image contracts space, pulling most of the world into the bed and into the lovers themselves. The lady becomes both the East Indies of spices and the West Indies of gold. Similarly, the speaker becomes all the kings of the earth.

[5]
This imagery of spatial contraction becomes far more vivid in the last stanza of "The Sun Rising," when the speaker asserts that "She is all states, and all princes, I, / Nothing else is" (lines 21–22). The woman thus becomes the world and the speaker the ruler of "all states." The spatial contraction, pulling "all states" into bed with the speaker, underscores the irrelevance of the world at large and the importance of the lovers as a self-contained world, just as the image of both lovers being entire worlds is stressed in "The Good Morrow." The imagery in both poems becomes delightful. In "The Sun Rising" the speaker cites the advantage to the sun of the spacial contraction, since warming the two lovers will take less energy now that they are joined into one world. Similarly, in "The Good Morrow" the advantage is that the new world of the lovers is free of harsh winters and cruel death ("sharp North, . . . declining West," line 18). Again in "The Sun Rising," the concluding two lines assert that the lovers on their bed become not only the world but also the center of the solar system: "Shine here to us, and thou art everywhere; / This bed thy center is, these walls, thy sphere" (lines 29–30). The movement of the image in this poem, as in "The Good Morrow," is thus both contracting and expanding. In this way, the spatial imagery creates a mixed serious and comic tone even while delineating the immense power of love.

[6]
Although "The Flea" is a different type of poem than either "The Good Morrow" or "The Sun Rising," similar images of spatial manipulation emphasize the singularity and power of love. Unlike the other two lyrics, "The

Flea" is a song of seduction spoken by an eager lover to an unwilling lady. Again, however, space expands and contracts to create a private (and in this case amusing) world for the lovers. Reduced to its basic logic, the poem almost flippantly asserts that the loss of virginity is no more significant than a flea bite. The master image of the poem is that the blood of both the eager lover and resistant lady is "mingled" in the flea. Indeed, the first stanza is given over to the image of the flea biting each lover and swelling "with one blood made of two" (line 8).

The speaker does not begin to manipulate spatial imagery until the second stanza of "The Flea," where images of expanding and contracting space become both amusing and bizarre. Working from the premise established in the first stanza, that the flea contains both the speaker's and the lady's blood, the flea suddenly becomes all three beings: "Oh stay, three lives in one flea spare, / Where we almost, yea more than married, are" (lines 10–11). In terms of the dramatic situation, the lady is about to kill the flea; the speaker argues that they are married within the flea since their bloods are "mingled." This sets up one of Donne's most outrageous spatial images:

[7]
This flea is you and I, and this
Our marriage bed and marriage temple is;
Though parents grudge, and you, w'are met,
And cloister'd in these living walls of jet.

(lines 12–15)

This manipulation of space and place is obviously witty and bizarre, but it is also consistent with the images of expanding and contracting space that occur in "The Good Morrow" and "The Sun Rising." Here the lovers contract—or the flea expands—until it has become both a "marriage bed and marriage temple." At the end of the passage we see that the image and the outrageous logic create the lovers' private world; they are "met / And cloister'd" within the black sides of the flea.

[8]
In each of these poems, images of space are thus manipulated to demonstrate the power of love and the private world of the lovers. In all three instances, extended metaphors establish the power of love (or desire) to contract the whole world into one bed or to expand a little room (or even a little flea) into "an everywhere." Such imagery is consistent with the attitude toward love expressed throughout Donne's songs and sonnets; love and passion are private, powerful, and mysterious. The use of images of expanding and contracting space is one of the many ways in which Donne emphasizes the miracle of love.

Commentary on the Essay

This comparative essay deals with a common thread of Donne's imagery in the three selected poems: Images of expanding and contracting space demonstrate both the private world of lovers and the power of love.

Unifying the essay is the structure: Each separate unit (paragraphs 2,3; 4,5; 6,7) is tied to the central idea announced in the introductory paragraph. In addition, the topic sentences in paragraphs 4 and 6 establish transition from poem to poem (and discussion to discussion) by using transitional words such as *similar, another,* and *although.* Additionally, there is a cumulative development of comparison and contrast. Although the first unit is devoted almost exclusively to the development of the large world-small world imagery in "The Good Morrow," the later units introduce elements from the other poems for comparison. These strategies help to connect the essay's various parts.

The conclusion (paragraph 8) restates the central idea of the essay and summarizes the major point illustrated in the three poems. In addition, it relates these observations about spatial imagery to the broader context of Donne's love poetry. Thus, the essay ends as it begins, with a general assertion about Donne's songs and sonnets.

WRITING TOPICS

Donne

1. Religious themes and ideas in Donne's love poems.
2. Romantic themes and ideas in Donne's religious poems.
3. The metaphysical conceit: Donne's use of metaphor and simile.
4. Donne's poetic diction and its level and quality in the love poems or religious poems.
5. What did Dryden mean by claiming that Donne's poetry is perplexing because he introduces metaphysics into it?
6. Donne's poetic techniques: stanzas, rhymes, rhythms, assonance, onomatopoeia, etc.

Dickinson

1. Dickinson's characteristic brevity and the expression of her ideas.
2. Dickinson's use of personal but not totally disclosed subject matter.
3. Dickinson's use of images: sources, types, meanings.
4. Dickinson's ideas about (1) death, (2) religion, (3) personal pain.
5. Dickinson's humor and irony.
6. Dickinson's poems as they appear on the page: the relationship of meaning to lines, stanzas, capitalization, and punctuation.

Frost

1. Frost as a poet of ideas. His vision of the way things are or should be.
2. The nature of Frost's topics and images, and his use of them for observation, narration, and metaphor.
3. The speaker of Frost's poems: character, experiences, recollections, and reflections.
4. Characteristic structure of Frost's poems: observation, narration, and generalization.
5. Frost's poetic diction: level and style, and relationship to topic.
6. Poetic forms in Frost: rhythm, meter, rhyme, and line and stanza patterns.

25

Additional Poems

LEONARD ADAMÉ   (b. 1947)

My Grandmother Would Rock Quietly and Hum ——————— *1973*

in her house
she would rock quietly and hum
until her swelled hands
calmed

in summer
she wore thick stockings
sweaters
and grey braids

(when "el cheque" came
we went to Payless°   *a grocery store*
and I laughed greedily
when given a quarter)

mornings,
sunlight barely lit
the kitchen
and where
there were shadows
it was not cold

she quietly rolled
flour tortillas—
the "papas"°   *potatoes*
cracking in hot lard
would wake me

she had lost her teeth
and when we ate

she had bread
soaked in "café"°   *coffee*

always her eyes
were clear
and she could see   30
as I cannot yet see—
through her eyes
she gave me herself

she would sit
and talk   35
of her girlhood—
of things strange to me:
    México
    epidemics
    relatives shot   40
    her father's hopes
    of this country—
how they sank
with cement dust
to his insides   45

now
when I go
to the old house
the worn spots
by the stove   50
echo of her shuffling
and
México
still hangs in her
fading   55
calendar pictures

A. R. AMMONS   (b. 1926)

80-Proof————————————————————————— *1975*

A fifth of me's me:
the rest's chaser:
35 lbs.'s
my true self: but
chuck 10 lbs. or so for bones,   5
what's left's
steaks & chops &
chicken fat,
two-over-easy & cream-on-the-side:
strip off a sheath of hide,   10

strip out nerves & veins
& permeable membranes,
what's left's a greasy spot:
the question's
whether
to retain
the shallow stain
or go 100% spiritual
and fifth by fifth
achieve a whole,
highly transcendental.

MAYA ANGELOU (b. 1928)

My Arkansas —————————————————————*1978*

There is a deep brooding
in Arkansas.
Old crimes like moss pend
from poplar trees.
The sullen earth
is much too
red for comfort.

Sunrise seems to hesitate
and in that second
lose its
incandescent aim, and
dusk no more shadows
than the noon.
The past is brighter yet.

Old hates and
ante-bellum° lace, are rent
but not discarded.
Today is yet to come
in Arkansas.
It writhes. It writhes in awful
waves of brooding.

MY ARKANSAS.   16 *ante-bellum:* before the U.S. Civil War (1861–1865).

ANONYMOUS

Barbara Allan ————————————————————*Sixteenth century*

It was in and about the Martinmas° time,   *November 11*
  When the green leaves were a-fallin',

That Sir John Graeme in the West Country
    Fell in love with Barbara Allan.

He sent his man down through the town   5
    To the place where she was dwellin':
"O haste and come to my master dear,
    Gin° ye be Barbara Allan."   *if*

O slowly, slowly rose she up,
    To the place where he was lyin',   10
And when she drew the curtain by:
    "Young man, I think you're dyin'."

"O it's I'm sick, and very, very sick,
    And 'tis all for Barbara Allan."
"O the better for me ye shall never be,   15
    Though your heart's blood were a-spillin'."

"O dinna ye mind,° young man," said she,   *don't you recall*
    "When ye the cups were fillin',
That ye made the healths° go round and round,   *toasts*
    And slighted Barbara Allan?"   20

He turned his face unto the wall,
    And death with him was dealin':
"Adieu, adieu,° my dear friends all,   *farewell*
    And be kind to Barbara Allan."

And slowly, slowly, rose she up,   25
    And slowly, slowly left him;
And sighing said she could not stay,
    Since death of life had reft° him.   *bereft, taken from*

She had not gone a mile but twa,°   *two*
    When she heard the dead-bell knellin',   30
And every jow° that the dead-bell ga'ed°   *stroke; made*
    It cried, "Woe to Barbara Allan!"

"O mother, mother, make my bed,
    O make it soft and narrow:
Since my love died for me today,   35
    I'll die for him tomorrow."

ANONYMOUS

Lord Randal ————————————————— Sixteenth century

"Oh, where have you been, Lord Randal, my son?
Oh, where have you been, my handsome young man?"
"Oh, I've been to the wildwood; mother, make my bed soon,
I'm weary of hunting and I fain° would lie down."   *gladly*

"And whom did you meet there, Lord Randal, my son?
And whom did you meet there, my handsome young man?"
"Oh, I met with my true love; mother, make my bed soon,
I'm weary of hunting and I fain would lie down."

"What got you for supper, Lord Randal, my son?
What got you for supper, my handsome young man?"
"I got eels boiled in broth; mother, make my bed soon,
I'm weary of hunting and I fain would lie down."

"And who got your leavings, Lord Randal, my son?
And who got your leavings, my handsome young man?"
"I gave them to my dogs; mother, make my bed soon,
I'm weary of hunting and I fain would lie down."

"And what did your dogs do, Lord Randal, my son?
And what did your dogs do, my handsome young man?"
"Oh, they stretched out and died; mother, make my bed soon,
I'm weary of hunting and I fain would lie down."

"Oh, I fear you are poisoned, Lord Randal, my son,
Oh, I fear you are poisoned, my handsome young man."
"Oh, yes, I am poisoned; mother, make my bed soon,
For I'm sick at my heart and I fain would lie down."

"What will you leave your mother, Lord Randal, my son?
What will you leave your mother, my handsome young man?"
"My house and my lands; mother, make my bed soon,
For I'm sick at my heart and I fain would lie down."

"What will you leave your sister, Lord Randal, my son?
What will you leave your sister, my handsome young man?"
"My gold and my silver; mother, make my bed soon,
For I'm sick at my heart and I fain would lie down."

"What will you leave your brother, Lord Randal, my son?
What will you leave your brother, my handsome young man?"
"My horse and my saddle; mother, make my bed soon,
For I'm sick at my heart and I fain would lie down."

"What will you leave your true-love, Lord Randal, my son?
What will you leave your true-love, my handsome young man?"
"A halter to hang her; mother, make my bed soon,
For I'm sick at my heart and I want to lie down."

ANONYMOUS

The Three Ravens _____ *Sixteenth century*

There were three ravens sat on a tree,
  Down a down, hay down, hay down,

There were three ravens sat on a tree,
  With a down,
There were three ravens sat on a tree,   5
They were as black as they might be,
  With a down, derry, derry, derry, down, down.°

The one of them said to his mate,
"Where shall we our breakfast take?

"Down in yonder green field   10
There lies a knight slain under his shield.

"His hounds they lie down at his feet,
So well they can their master keep.

"His hawks they fly so eagerly,°   *fiercely*
There's no fowl° dare him come nigh. "   *bird*   15

Down there comes a fallow° doe,   *light brown*
As great with young as she might go,°   *walk*

She lifted up his bloody head,
And kissed his wounds that were so red.

She got him up upon her back,   20
And carried him to earthen lake.°   *pit*

She buried him before the prime,°   *morning prayer service*
She was dead herself ere evensong time.°
God send every gentleman
Such hawks, such hounds, and such a lemman.°   *mistress*   25

THE THREE RAVENS.   7 *down:* In singing this ballad, the first line of each stanza is repeated
three times and the refrain is repeated as in stanza 1.   23 *evensong time:* the time for the evening
prayer service.

MARGARET ATWOOD (b. 1939)

Variation on the Word Sleep————————————— *(1981)*

I would like to watch you sleeping,
which may not happen.
I would like to watch you,
sleeping. I would like to sleep
with you, to enter   5
your sleep as its smooth dark wave
slides over my head

and walk with you through that lucent
wavering forest of bluegreen leaves
with its watery sun & three moons   10
towards the cave where you must descend,
towards your worst fear

I would like to give you the silver
branch, the small white flower, the one
word that will protect you
from the grief at the center
of your dream, from the grief
at the center. I would like to follow
you up the long stairway
again & become
the boat that would row you back
carefully, a flame
in two cupped hands
to where your body lies
beside me, and you enter
it as easily as breathing in

I would like to be the air
that inhabits you for a moment
only. I would like to be that unnoticed
& that necessary.

W. H. AUDEN   (1907–1973)

The Unknown Citizen ———————————————————— *1940*

(To JS/07/M/378
This Marble Monument
Is Erected by the State)

He was found by the Bureau of Statistics to be
One against whom there was no official complaint,
And all the reports on his conduct agree
That, in the modern sense of an old-fashioned word, he was a saint,
For in everything he did he served the Greater Community.

Except for the War till the day he retired
He worked in a factory and never got fired,
But satisfied his employers, Fudge Motors Inc.
Yet he wasn't a scab° or odd in his views.   *strikebreaker*
For his Union reports that he paid his dues,
(Our report on his Union shows it was sound)
And our Social Psychology workers found
That he was popular with his mates° and liked a drink.   *co-workers*
The Press are convinced that he bought a paper every day
And that his reactions to advertisements were normal in every way.
Policies taken out in his name prove that he was fully insured,
And his Health-card shows he was once in hospital but left it cured.
Both Producers Research and High-Grade Living declare
He was fully sensible to the advantages of the Installment Plan

And had everything necessary to the Modern Man,   25
A phonograph, a radio, a car and a frigidaire.
Our reseachers into Public Opinion are content
That he held the proper opinions for the time of year;
When there was peace, he was for peace; when there was war, he went.
He was married and added five children to the population,   30
Which our Eugenist says was the right number for a parent of his generation,
And our teachers report that he never interfered with their education.
Was he free? Was he happy? The question is absurd:
Had anything been wrong, we should certainly have heard.

IMAMU AMIRI BARAKA (LEROI JONES)   (b. 1934)

Ka 'Ba ———————————————————————————————— *1969*

A closed window looks down
on a dirty courtyard, and black people
call across or scream across or walk across
defying physics in the stream of their will

Our world is full of sound   5
Our world is more lovely than anyone's
tho we suffer, and kill each other
and sometimes fail to walk the air

We are beautiful people
with african imaginations   10
full of masks and dances and swelling chants
with african eyes, and noses, and arms,
though we sprawl in grey chains in a place
full of winters, when what we want is sun.

We have been captured,   15
brothers. And we labor
to make our getaway, into
the ancient image, into a new

correspondence with ourselves
and our black family. We need magic   20
now we need the spells, to raise up
return, destroy, and create. What will be

the sacred words?

MARVIN BELL   (b. 1937)

Things We Dreamt We Died For ——————————————————— *1969*

Flags of all sorts.
The literary life.

Each time we dreamt we'd done
the gentlemanly thing,
covering our causes
in closets full of bones
to remove ourselves forever
from dearest possibilities,
the old weapons re-injured us,
the old armies conscripted us,
and we gave in to getting even,
a little less like us
if a lot less like others.
Many, thus, gained fame
in the way of great plunderers,
retiring to the university
to cultivate grand plunder-gardens
in the service of literature,
the young and no more wars.
Their continuing tributes
make them our greatest saviours,
whose many fortunes are followed
by the many who have not one.

EARLE BIRNEY   (b. 1904)

Can. Lit.° ———————————————————— *1962*

(or them able leave her ever)

since we'd always sky about
when we had eagles they flew out
leaving no shadow bigger than wren's
to trouble even our broodiest hens
too busy bridging loneliness
to be alone
we hacked in railway ties
what Emily° etched in bone

we French & English never lost
our civil war
endure it still
a bloody civil bore

the wounded sirened off
no Whitman° wanted
it's only by our lack of ghosts
we're haunted

CAN LIT.   The title is an abbreviation for "Canadian Literature."   8 Emily: Emily Dickinson
(1830–1886), American poet (see pp. 877–81).   14 Whitman: Walt Whitman (1819–1892),
American poet.

WILLIAM BLAKE   (1757–1827)

The Sick Rose _____ *1794*

O Rose thou art sick.
The invisible worm
That flies in the night,
In the howling storm:

Has found out thy bed   5
Of crimson joy:
And his dark secret love
Does thy life destroy.

WILLIAM BLAKE   (1757–1827)

Ah Sun-flower _____ *1794*

Ah Sun-flower! weary of time,
Who countest the steps of the Sun,
Seeking after that sweet golden clime
Where the traveller's journey is done;

Where the Youth pined away with desire,   5
And the pale Virgin shrouded in snow,
Arise from their graves and aspire,
Where my Sun-flower wishes to go.

LOUISE BOGAN   (1879–1970)

Women _____ *1923*

Women have no wilderness in them,
They are provident instead,
Content in the tight hot cell of their hearts
To eat dusty bread.

They do not see cattle cropping red winter grass,   5
They do not hear
Snow water going down under culverts
Shallow and clear.

They wait, when they should turn to journeys,
They stiffen, when they should bend.   10
They use against themselves that benevolence
To which no man is friend.

They cannot think of so many crops to a field
Or of clean wood cleft by an axe.
Their love is an eager meaninglessness
Too tense, or too lax.

They hear in every whisper that speaks to them
A shout and a cry.
As like as not, when they take life over their door-sills
They should let it go by.

ARNA BONTEMPS   (1902–1973)

A Black Man Talks of Reaping —————————————————— *1940*

I have sown beside all waters in my day.
I planted deep, within my heart the fear
that wind or fowl would take the grain away.
I planted safe against this stark, lean year.

I scattered seed enough to plant the land
in rows from Canada to Mexico
but for my reaping only what the hand
can hold at once is all that I can show.

Yet what I sowed and what the orchard yields
my brother's sons are gathering stalk and root;
small wonder then my children glean in fields
they have not sown, and feed on bitter fruit.

ANNE BRADSTREET   (1612–1672)

To My Dear and Loving Husband —————————————— *1678*

If ever two were one, then surely we.
If ever man were loved by wife, then thee;
If ever wife was happy in a man,
Compare with me ye women if you can.
I prize thy love more than whole mines of gold,
Or all the riches that the East doth hold.
My love is such that rivers cannot quench,
Nor ought but love from thee give recompense.
Thy love is such I can no way repay;
The heavens reward thee manifold, I pray.
Then while we live, in love let's so persever,
That when we live no more we may live ever.

ROBERT BRIDGES   (1844–1930)

Nightingales ———————————————————— *1893*

   Beautiful must be the mountains whence ye come,
And bright in the fruitful valleys the streams, wherefrom
      Ye learn your song:
Where are those starry woods? O might I wander there,
   Among the flowers, which in that heavenly air   5
      Bloom the year long!

   Nay, barren are those mountains and spent the streams:
Our song is the voice of desire, that haunts our dreams,
      A throe of the heart,
Whose pining visions dim, forbidden hopes profound,   10
   No dying cadence nor long sigh can sound,
      For all our art.

   Alone, aloud in the raptured ear of men
We pour our dark nocturnal secret; and then,
      As night is withdrawn   15
From these sweet-springing meads° and bursting boughs of May.   *meadows*
   Dream, while the innumerable choir of day
      Welcome the dawn.

JOSEPH BRODSKY   (b. 1940)

In Memory of My Father: Australia ———————————— *1990*

You arose—I dreamt so last night—and left for
Australia. The voice, with a triple echo,
ebbed and flowed, complaining about climate,
grime, that the deal with the flat is stymied,
pity it's not downtown, though near the ocean,   5
no elevator but the bathtub's indeed an option,
ankles keep swelling. "Looks like I've lost my slippers"
came through rapt yet clear via satellite.
And at once the receiver burst into howling "*Adelaida! Adelaida!*"—
into rattling and crackling, as if a shutter,   10
ripped off its hinges, were pounding the wall with inhuman power.

Still, better this than the silky powder
canned by the crematorium, than the voucher—
better these snatches of voice, this patchwork
monologue of a recluse trying to play a genie   15

for the first time since you formed a cloud above a chimney.

GWENDOLYN BROOKS   (b. 1917)

Primer for Blacks _____ *1980*

Blackness
is a title,
is a preoccupation,
is a commitment Blacks
are to comprehend—
and in which you are
to perceive your Glory.

The conscious shout
of all that is white is
"It's Great to be white."
The conscious shout
of the slack in Black is
"It's Great to be white."
Thus all that is white
has white strength and yours.

The word Black
has geographic power,
pulls everybody in:
Blacks here—
Blacks there—
Blacks wherever they may be.
And remember, you Blacks, what they told you—
remember your Education:
"one Drop—one Drop
maketh a brand new Black."
        Oh mighty Drop.
——And because they have given us kindly
so many more of our people

Blackness
stretches over the land.
Blackness—
the Black of it,
the rust-red of it,
the milk and cream of it,
the tan and yellow-tan of it,
the deep-brown middle-brown high-brown of it,
the "olive" and ochre of it—
Blackness
marches on.

The huge, the pungent object of our prime out-ride
is to Comprehend,

to salute and to Love the fact that we are Black,
which *is* our "ultimate Reality,"
which is the lone ground
from which our meaningful metamorphosis,   45
from which our prosperous staccato,
group of individual, can rise.

Self-shriveled Blacks.
Begin with gaunt and marvelous concession:
YOU are our costume and our fundamental bone.   50

All of you—
You COLORED ones,
you NEGRO ones,
those of you who proudly cry
"I'm half INDian"—   55
those of you who proudly screech
"I'VE got the blood of George WASHington in
MY veins"—

ALL of you—
you proper Blacks,   60
you half-Blacks,
you wish-I-weren't Blacks,
Niggeroes and Niggerenes.

You.

ELIZABETH BARRETT BROWNING   (1806–1861)

Sonnets from the Portuguese: Number 43 _____ *1850*

How do I love thee? Let me count the ways.
I love thee to the depth and breadth and height
My soul can reach, when feeling out of sight
For the ends of Being and ideal Grace.
I love thee to the level of every day's   5
Most quiet need, by sun and candelight.
I love thee freely, as men strive for Right;
I love thee purely, as they turn from Praise.
I love thee with the passion put to use
In my old griefs, and with my childhood's faith.   10
I love thee with a love I seemed to lose
With my lost saints,—I love thee with the breath,
Smiles, tears, of all my life!—and, if God choose,
I shall but love thee better after death.

ROBERT BROWNING   (1812–1889)

Soliloquy of the Spanish Cloister ————————————————— *1842*

1

Gr-r-r—there go, my heart's abhorrence!
    Water your damned flowerpots, do!
If hate killed men, Brother Lawrence,
    God's blood, would not mine kill you!
What? your myrtle bush wants trimming?
    Oh, that rose has prior claims—
Needs its leaden vase filled brimming?
    Hell dry you up with its flames!

2

At the meal we sit together:
    Salve tibi!° I must hear   *Hail to thee!*
Wise talk of the kind of weather,
    Sort of season, time of year:
Not a plenteous cork crop: scarcely
    Dare we hope oak-galls, I doubt:
What's the Latin name for "parsley"?
    What's the Greek name for Swine's Snout?

3

Whew! We'll have our platter burnished,
    Laid with care on our own shelf!
With a fire-new spoon we're furnished,
    And a goblet for ourself,
Rinsed like something sacrificial
    Ere 'tis fit to touch our chaps°   *jaws*
Marked with L. for our initial!
    (He-he! There his lily snaps!)

4

Saint, forsooth! While brown Dolores
    Squats outside the Convent bank
With Sanchicha, telling stories,
    Steeping tresses in the tank,
Blue-black, lustrous, thick like horsehairs,
    —Can't I see his dead eye glow,
Bright as 'twere a Barbary corsair's?°   *pirate's*
    (That is, if he'd let it show!)

5

When he finishes refection,°   *dinner*
    Knife and fork he never lays

Cross-wise, to my recollection,   35
    As do I, in Jesu's praise.
I the Trinity illustrate,
    Drinking watered orange-pulp—
In three sips the Arian° frustrate;   *Anti-Trinitarian (a heretic)*
    While he drains his at one gulp.   40

6

Oh, those melons? If he's able
    We're to have a feast! so nice!
One goes to the Abbot's table,
    All of us get each a slice.
How go on your flowers? None double?   45
    Not one fruit-sort can you spy?
Strange!—And I, too, at such trouble,
Keep them close-nipped on the sly!

7

There's a great text in Galatians,°   *perhaps 3:10 or 5:19–21*
    Once you trip on it, entails   50
Twenty-nine distinct damnations,
    One sure, if another fails:
If I trip him just a-dying,
    Sure of heaven as sure can be,
Spin him round and send him flying   55
    Off to hell, a Manichee?°   *heretic*

8

Or, my scrofulous° French novel   *pornographic*
    On gray paper with blunt type!
Simply glance at it, you grovel
    Hand and foot in Belial's° gripe: *the Devil*   60
If I double down its pages
    At the woeful sixteenth print,
When he gathers his greengages,
    Ope a sieve and slip it in't?

9

Or, there's Satan!—one might venture   65
    Pledge one's soul to him, yet leave
Such a flaw in the indenture°   *contract*
    As he'd miss till, past retrieve,
Blasted lay that rose-acacia
    We're so proud of! *Hy, Zy, Hine* . . .   70
'St, there's Vespers! *Plena gratiâ*°   *full of grace*
    Ave, Virgo!° Gr-r-r—you swine!   *Hail Virgin*

GEORGE GORDON, LORD BYRON   (1788–1824)

The Destruction of Sennacherib° _____ *1815*

The Assyrian came down like the wolf on the fold,
And his cohorts were gleaming in purple and gold;
And the sheen of their spears was like stars on the sea,
When the blue wave rolls nightly on deep Galilee.

Like the leaves of the forest when summer is green,
That host with their banners at sunset were seen:
Like the leaves of the forest when autumn hath blown,
That host on the morrow lay withered and strown.

For the Angel of Death spread his wings on the blast,
And breathed in the face of the foe as he passed;
And the eyes of the sleepers waxed deadly and chill,
And their hearts but once heaved—and for ever grew still!

And there lay the steed with his nostril all wide,
But through it there rolled not the breath of his pride;
And the foam of his gasping lay white on the turf,
And cold as the spray of the rock-beating surf.

And there lay the rider distorted and pale,
With the dew on his brow, and the rust on his mail;
And the tents were all silent, the banners alone,
The lances unlifted, the trumpet unblown.

And the widows of Ashur° are loud in their wail,
And the idols are broke in the temple of Baal;°
And the might of the Gentile, unsmote by the sword,
Hath melted like snow in the glance of the Lord!

THE DESTRUTION OF SENNACHERIB.   Sennacherib was king of the ancient Near Eastern empire of Assyria from 705 to 681 B.C. He laid seige to Jerusalem in about 702 B.C., even though
King Hezekiah had already rendered tribute to Assyria. According to 2 Kings 19:35–36, a miracle occurred to save the besieged Hebrews: "the angel of the Lord went out and smote . . .
[185,000 Assyrian soldiers]; and when they [the Hebrews] arose early in the morning, behold,
they [the Assyrians] were all dead corpses."   21 *Ashur:* the land of the Assyrians.   22 *Baal:*
a god who supposedly controlled weather and storms.

THOMAS CAMPION   (1567–1620)

Cherry Ripe _____ *1617*

There is a garden in her face,
Where roses and white lilies grow;
A heavenly paradise is that place,

Wherein all pleasant fruits do flow.
There cherries grow, which none may buy   5
Till "Cherry ripe" themselves do cry.

Those cherries fairly do enclose
Of orient pearl a double row;
Which when her lovely laughter shows,
They look like rosebuds filled with snow.   10
Yet them nor peer nor prince can buy
Till "Cherry ripe" themselves do cry.

Her eyes like angels watch them still;
Her brows like bended bows do stand,
Threatening with piercing frowns to kill   15
All that attempt, with eye or hand,
Those sacred cherries to come nigh
Till "Cherry ripe" themselves do cry.

LUCILLE CLIFTON   (b. 1936)

this morning
(for the girls of eastern high school) _____ *1987*

this morning
this morning
       i met myself

coming in

a bright   5
jungle girl
shining
quick as a snake
a tall
tree girl a   10
me girl

       i met myself
this morning
coming in

and all day   15
i have been
a black bell
ringing
i survive

      survive   20

survive

LUCILLE CLIFTON   (b. 1936)

the poet ———————————————————————— *1987*

i beg my bones to be good but
they keep clicking music and
i spin in the center of myself
a foolish frightful woman
moving my skin against the wind and
tap dancing for my life.

STEPHEN CRANE   (1871–1900)

Do Not Weep, Maiden, for War Is Kind ——————— *1896, 1899 (1895)*

Do not weep, maiden, for war is kind.
Because your lover threw wild hands toward the sky
And the affrighted steed ran on alone,
Do not weep.
War is kind.

    Hoarse, booming drums of the regiment
    Little souls who thirst for fight,
    These men were born to drill and die
    The unexplained glory flies above them
    Great is the battle-god, great, and his kingdom—
    A field where a thousand corpses lie.

Do not weep, babe, for war is kind.
Because your father tumbled in the yellow trenches,
Raged at his breast, gulped and died,
Do not weep.
War is kind.

    Swift, blazing flag of the regiment
    Eagle with crest of red and gold,
    These men were born to drill and die
    Point for them the virtue of slaughter
    Make plain to them the excellence of killing
    And a field where a thousand corpses lie.

Mother whose head hung humble as a button
On the bright splendid shroud of your son,
Do not weep.
War is kind.

COUNTEE CULLEN   (1903–1946)

Yet Do I Marvel ————————————————————— *1925*

I doubt not God is good, well-meaning, kind,
And did He stoop to quibble could tell why
The little buried mole continues blind,
Why flesh that mirrors Him must some day die.
Make plain the reason tortured Tantalus°   5
Is baited by the fickle fruit, declare
If merely brute caprice dooms Sisyphus°
To struggle up a never-ending stair.
Inscrutable His ways are, and immune
To catechism by a mind too strewn   10
With petty cares to slightly understand
What awful brain compels His awful hand.
Yet do I marvel at this curious thing:
To make a poet black, and bid him sing!

YET I DO MARVEL.   5 *Tantalus:* a figure in Greek mythology condemned to eternal hunger and thirst. He stood in Hades chin deep in water with a fruit-laden branch just above his head, but could never eat or drink.   7 *Sisyphus:* a figure in Greek mythology condemned to eternally useless labor. He was fated to roll a huge boulder up a hill in the underworld, but each time he neared the top, the stone slipped and he had to begin anew. See also p. 324.

e. e. cummings   (1894–1962)

next to of course god america i ————————————————— *1926*

"next to of course god america i
love you land of the pilgrims' and so forth oh
say can you see by the dawn's early my
country 'tis of centuries come and go
and are no more what of it we should worry
in every language even deafanddumb   5
thy sons acclaim your glorious name by gorry
by jingo by gee by gosh by gum
why talk of beauty what could be more beautiful than these heroic happy dead
who rushed like lions to the roaring slaughter   10
they did not stop to think they died instead
then shall the voice of liberty be mute?"

He spoke. And drank rapidly a glass of water

e. e. cummings   (1894–1962)

if there are any heavens _____ *1931*

if there are any heavens my mother will(all by herself)have
one.   It will not be a pansy heaven nor
a fragile heaven of lilies-of-the-valley but
it will be a heaven of blackred roses

my father will be(deep like a rose
tall like a rose)

standing near my

swaying over her
(silent)
with eyes which are really petals and see

nothing with the face of a poet really which
is a flower and not a face with
hands
which whisper
This is my beloved my

                    (suddenly in sunlight

he will bow,

& the whole garden will bow)

JAMES DICKEY   (b. 1923)

The Performance _____ *1967*

The last time I saw Donald Armstrong
He was staggering oddly off into the sun,
Going down, off the Philippine Islands.
I let my shovel fall, and put that hand
Above my eyes, and moved some way to one side
That his body might pass through the sun,

And I saw how well he was not
Standing there on his hands,
On his spindle-shanked forearms balanced,
Unbalanced, with his big feet looming and waving
In the great, untrustworthy air
He flew in each night, when it darkened.

Dust fanned in scraped puffs from the earth
Between his arms, and blood turned his face inside out,

To demonstrate its suppleness   15
Of veins, as he perfected his role.
Next day, he toppled his head off
On an island beach to the south,

And the enemy's two-handed sword
Did not fall from anyone's hands   20
At that miraculous sight,
As the head rolled over upon
Its wide-eyed face, and fell
Into the inadequate grave

He had dug for himself, under pressure.   25
Yet I put my flat hand to my eyebrows
Months later, to see him again
In the sun, when I learned how he died,
And imagined him, there,
Come, judged, before his small captors,   30

Doing all his lean tricks to amaze them—
The back somersault, the kip-up—
And at last, the stand on his hands,
Perfect, with his feet together,
His head down, evenly breathing,   35
As the sun poured up from the sea

And the headsmen broke down
In a blaze of tears, in that light
Of the thin, long human frame
Upside down in its own strange joy,   40
And, if some other one had not told him,
Would have cut off the feet

Instead of the head,
And if Armstrong had not presently risen
In kingly, round-shouldered attendance,   45
And then knelt down in himself
Beside his hacked, glittering grave, having done
All things in this life that he could.

JAMES DICKEY   (b. 1923)

Kudzu _____ *1964*

Japan invades. Far Eastern vines
Run from the clay banks they are

Supposed to keep from eroding,
Up telephone poles,

Which rear, half out of leafage,
As though they would shriek,
Like things smothered by their own
Green, mindless, unkillable ghosts.
In Georgia, the legend says
That you must close your windows

At night to keep it out of the house.
The glass is tinged with green, even so,

As the tendrils crawl over the fields.
The night the kudzu has
Your pasture, you sleep like the dead.
Silence has grown Oriental
And you cannot step upon ground:
Your leg plunges somewhere
It should not, it never should be,
Disappears, and waits to be struck

Anywhere between sole and kneecap:
For when the kudzu comes,

The snakes do, and weave themselves
Among its lengthening vines,
Their spade heads resting on leaves,
Growing also, in earthly power
And the huge circumstance of concealment.
One by one the cows stumble in,
Drooling a hot green froth,
And die, seeing the wood of their stalls

Strain to break into leaf.
In your closed house, with the vine

Tapping your window like lightning,
You remember what tactics to use.
In the wrong yellow fog-light of dawn
You herd them in, the hogs,
Head down in their hairy fat,
The meaty troops, to the pasture.
The leaves of the kudzu quake
With the serpents' fear, inside

The meadow ringed with men
Holding sticks, on the country roads.

The hogs disappear in the leaves.
The sound is intense, subhuman,
Nearly human with purposive rage.
There is no terror
Sound from the snakes.

No one can see the desperate, futile
Striking under the leaf heads.
Now and then, the flash of a long   50

Living vine, a cold belly,
Leaps up, torn apart, then falls

Under the tussling surface.
You have won, and wait for frost,
When, at the merest touch   55
Of cold, the kudzu turns
Black, withers inward and dies,
Leaving a mass of brown strings
Like the wires of a gigantic switchboard.
You open your windows,   60

With the lightning restored to the sky
And no leaves rising to bury
You alive inside your frail house,
And you think, in the opened cold,
Of the surface of things and its terrors,   65
And of the mistaken, mortal
Arrogance of the snakes

JAMES DICKEY   (b. 1923)

The Lifeguard ——————————————————— *1962*

In a stable of boats I lie still,
From all sleeping children hidden.
The leap of a fish from its shadow
Makes the whole lake instantly tremble.
With my foot on the water, I feel   5
The moon outside

Take on the utmost of its power.
I rise and go out through the boats.
I set my broad sole upon silver,
On the skin of the sky, on the moonlight,   10
Stepping outward from earth onto water
In quest of the miracle

This village of children believed
That I could perform as I dived
For one who had sunk from my sight.   15
I saw his cropped haircut go under.
I leapt, and my steep body flashed
Once, in the sun.

Dark drew all the light from my eyes.
Like a man who explores his death
By the pull of his slow-moving shoulders,
I hung head down in the cold,
Wide-eyed, contained, and alone
Among the weeds,

And my fingertips turned into stone
From clutching immovable blackness.
Time after time I leapt upward
Exploding in breath, and fell back
From the change in the children's faces
At my defeat.

Beneath them I swam to the boathouse
With only my life in my arms
To wait for the lake to shine back
At the risen moon with such power
That my steps on the light of the ripples
Might be sustained.

Beneath me is nothing but brightness
Like the ghost of a snowfield in summer.
As I moved toward the center of the lake,
Which is also the center of the moon,
I am thinking of how I may be
The saviour of one

Who has already died in my care.
The dark trees fade from around me.
The moon's dust hovers together.
I call softly out, and the child's
Voice answers through blinding water.
Patiently, slowly,

He rises, dilating to break
The surface of stone with his forehead.
He is one I do not remember
Having ever seen in his life.
The ground I stand on is trembling
Upon his smile.

I wash the black mud from my hands.
On a light given off by the grave
I kneel in the quick of the moon
At the heart of a distant forest
And hold in my arms a child
Of water, water, water.

H. D. (HILDA DOOLITTLE)   (1886–1961)

Pear Tree —————————————————————————— *1916*

Silver dust
lifted from the earth,
higher than my arms reach,
you have mounted,
O silver,   5
higher than my arms reach
you front us with great mass;
no flower ever opened
so staunch a white leaf,
no flower ever parted silver   10
from such rare silver;

O white pear,
your flower-tufts
thick on the branch
bring summer and ripe fruits   15
in their purple hearts.

RITA DOVE   (b. 1952)

Ö° —————————————————————————————— *1980*

Shape the lips to an *o*, say *a*.
That's *island.*

One word of Swedish has changed the whole neighborhood.
When I look up, the yellow house on the corner
is a galleon stranded in flowers. Around it
the wind. Even the high roar of a leaf-mulcher   5
could be the horn-blast from a ship
as it skirts the misted shoals.

We don't need much more to keep things going.
Families complete themselves
and refuse to budge from the present,   10
the present extends its glass forehead to sea
(backyard breezes, scattered cardinals)

and if, one evening, the house on the corner
took off over the marshland,
neither I nor my neighbor   15
would be amazed. Sometimes

Ö: the Swedish word for "island," pronounced as explained in lines 1 and 2.

a word is found so right it trembles
at the slightest explanation.
You start out with one thing, end
up with another, and nothing's
like it used to be, not even the future.

MICHAEL DRAYTON   (1563–1631)

Since There's No Help ————————————————*1619*

Since there's no help, come let us kiss and part;
Nay, I have done, you get no more of me,
And I am glad, yea glad with all my heart
That thus so cleanly I myself can free;
Shake hands forever, cancel all our vows,
And when we meet at any time again,
Be it not seen in either of our brows
That we one jot of former love retain.
Now at the last gasp of love's latest breath,
When, his pulse failing, passion speechless lies,
When faith is kneeling by his bed of death,
And innocence is closing up his eyes;
Now if thou wouldst, when all have given him over,
From death to life thou mightst him yet recover.

PAUL LAURENCE DUNBAR   (1872–1906)

Sympathy ————————————————*1895*

I know what the caged bird feels, alas!
When the sun is bright on the upland slopes;
When the wind stirs soft through the springing grass
And the river flows like a stream of glass;
When the first bird sings and the first bud opes,
And the faint perfume from its chalice steals—
I know what the caged bird feels!

I know why the caged bird beats his wing
Till its blood is red on the cruel bars;
For he must fly back to his perch and cling
When he fain would be on the bough a-swing;
And a pain still throbs in the old, old scars
And they pulse again with a keener sting—
I know why he beats his wing!

I know why the caged bird sings, ah me,
When his wing is bruised and his bosom sore,

When he beats his bars and would be free;
It is not a carol of joy or glee,
But a prayer that he sends from his heart's deep core,
But a plea, that upward to Heaven he flings—   20
I know why the caged bird sings!

RICHARD EBERHART   (b. 1904)

The Groundhog _____ *1936*

In June, amid the golden fields,
I saw a groundhog lying dead.
Dead lay he; my senses shook,
And mind outshot our naked frailty.
There lowly in the vigorous summer   5
His form began its senseless change,
And made my senses waver dim
Seeing nature ferocious in him.
Inspecting close his maggots' might
And seething cauldron of his being,   10
Half with loathing, half with a strange love,
I poked him with an angry stick.
The fever arose, became a flame
And Vigour circumscribed the skies,
Immense energy in the sun,   15
And through my frame a sunless trembling.
My stick had done nor good nor harm.
Then stood I silent in the day
Watching the object, as before;
And kept my reverence for knowledge   20
Trying for control, to be still,
To quell the passion of the blood;
Until I had bent down on my knees
Praying for joy in the sight of decay.
And so I left; and I returned   25
In Autumn strict of eye, to see
The sap gone out of the groundhog,
But the bony sodden hulk remained.
But the year had lost its meaning,
And in intellectual chains   30
I lost both love and loathing,
Mured up in the wall of wisdom.
Another summer took the fields again
Massive and burning, full of life,
But when I chanced upon the spot   35
There was only a little hair left,

And bones bleaching in the sunlight
Beautiful as architecture;
I watched them like a geometer,
And cut a walking stick from a birch.
It has been three years, now.
There is no sign of the groundhog.
I stood there in the whirling summer,
My hand capped a withered heart,
And thought of China and of Greece,
Of Alexander° in his tent;
Of Montaigne° in his tower,
Of Saint Theresa° in her wild lament.

THE GROUNDHOG.   46 *Alexander:* Alexander the Great (356–323 B.C.) king of Macedonia and conquerer of virtually the entire civilized world.   47 *Montaigne:* Michel de Montaigne (1553–1592), French essayist and commentator on human nature and society.   48 *Saint Theresa:* Theresa de Avila (1515–1582), Spanish religious mystic, writer, and founder of a religious order.

T. S. ELIOT   (1888–1965)

The Love Song of J. Alfred Prufrock° ————————————— *1915 (1910–1911)*

S'io credesse che mia risposta fosse
A persona che mai tornasse al mondo,
Questa fiamma staria senza piu scosse.
Ma perciocche giammai di questo fondo
Non torno vivo alcun, s'i'odo il vero,
Senza tema d'infamia ti rispondo.°

Let us go then, you and I
When the evening is spread out against the sky
Like a patient etherized upon a table;
Let us go, through certain half-deserted streets,
The muttering retreats
Of restless nights in one-night cheap hotels
And sawdust restaurants with oyster shells;
Streets that follow like a tedious argument
Of insidious intent
To lead you to an overwhelming question . . .

THE LOVE SONG OF J. ALFRED PRUFROCK.   The poem is a monologue spoken by Prufrock; the name is invented but suggests a businessman.   EPIGRAPH: The Italian epigraph is quoted from Dante's *Inferno* (Canto 27, lines 61–66) and is spoken by a man who relates his evil deeds to Dante because he assumes that Dante will never return to the world: "If I believed that my response were made to a person who would ever revisit the world, this flame would stand motionless. But since none has ever returned from this depth alive, if I hear the truth, I answer you without fear of infamy."

Oh, do not ask, "What is it?"
Let us go and make our visit.

In the room the women come and go
Talking of Michelangelo.°

The yellow fog that rubs its back upon the windowpanes,   15
The yellow smoke that rubs its muzzle on the windowpanes
Licked its tongue into the corners of the evening,
Lingered upon the pools that stand in drains,
Let fall upon its back the soot that falls from chimneys,
Slipped by the terrace, made a sudden leap,   20
And seeing that it was a soft October night,
Curled once about the house, and fell asleep.

And indeed there will be time
For the yellow smoke that slides along the street,
Rubbing its back upon the windowpanes;   25
There will be time, there will be time°
To prepare a face to meet the faces that you meet;
There will be time to murder and create,
And time for all the works and days° of hands
That lift and drop a question on your plate;   30
Time for you and time for me,
And time yet for a hundred indecisions,
And for a hundred visions and revisions,
Before the taking of a toast and tea.

In the room the women come and go   35
Talking of Michelangelo.

And indeed there will be time
To wonder, "Do I dare?" and, "Do I dare?"
Time to turn back and descend the stair,
With a bald spot in the middle of my hair—   40
(They will say: "How his hair is growing thin!")
My morning coat, my collar mounting firmly to the chin,
My necktie rich and modest, but asserted by a simple pin—
(They will say: "But how his arms and legs are thin!")
Do I dare   45
Disturb the universe?
In a minute there is time
For decisions and revisions which a minute will reverse.

For I have known them all already, known them all—
Have known the evenings, mornings, afternoons,   50

14 *Michelangelo:* one of the greatest Italian Renaissance painters and sculptors (1475–1564). The
name suggests that the women are cultured, or at least pretending to be so.   26 *time:* a possible allusion to Andrew Marvell's "To His Coy Mistress" (p. 852).   29 *works and days:* the title of
a poem about farming by the Greek poet Hesiod. Here the phrase ironically refers to social gestures.

I have measured out my life with coffee spoons;
I know the voices dying with a dying fall°
Beneath the music from a farther room.
   So how should I presume?

And I have known the eyes already, known them all—
The eyes that fix you in a formulated phrase,
And when I am formulated, sprawling on a pin,
When I am pinned and wriggling on the wall,
Then how should I begin
To spit out all the butt-ends of my days and ways?
And how should I presume?

And I have known the arms already, known them all—
Arms that are braceleted and white and bare
(But in the lamplight, downed with light brown hair!)
Is it perfume from a dress
That makes me so digress?
Arms that lie along a table, or wrap about a shawl.
   And should I then presume?
   And how should I begin?

Shall I say, I have gone at dusk through narrow streets
And watched the smoke that rises from the pipes
Of lonely men in shirt-sleeves, leaning out of windows? . . .

I should have been a pair of ragged claws
Scuttling across the floors of silent seas.

And the afternoon, the evening, sleeps so peacefully!
Smoothed by long fingers,
Asleep . . . tired . . . or it malingers,°
Stretched on the floor, here beside you and me.
Should I, after tea and cakes and ices,
Have the strength to force the moment to its crisis?
But though I have wept and fasted, wept and prayed,
Though I have seen my head (grown slightly bald) brought in upon a platter,°
I am no prophet—and here's no great matter;
I have seen the moment of my greatness flicker,
And I have seen the eternal Footman hold my coat, and snicker,
And in short, I was afraid.

And would it have been worth it, after all,
After the cups, the marmalade, the tea,
Among the porcelain, among some talk of you and me,
Would it have been worth while,

---

52 *dying fall:* an allusion to a speech by Orsino in Shakespeare's *Twelfth Night* (Act I, scene 1, line 4).   77 *malingers:* pretends to be ill.   82 *platter:* as was the head of John the Baptist; see Mark 6:17–28 and Matthew 14:3–11.

To have bitten off the matter with a smile,
To have squeezed the universe into a ball°
To roll it toward some overwhelming question,
To say: "I am Lazarus,° come from the dead,
Come back to tell you all, I shall tell you all"—   95
If one, setting a pillow by her head,
    Should say: "That is not what I meant at all.
    That is not it, at all."

And would it have been worth it, after all,
Would it have been worth while,   100
After the sunsets and the dooryards and the sprinkled streets,
After the novels, after the teacups, after the skirts that trail along the floor—
And this, and so much more?—
It is impossible to say just what I mean!
But as if a magic lantern threw the nerves in patterns on a screen: 105
Would it have been worth while
If one, setting a pillow or throwing off a shawl,
And turning toward the window, should say:
    "That is not it at all,
    That is not what I meant, at all."   110

No! I am not Prince Hamlet,° nor was meant to be;
Am an attendant lord, one that will do
To swell a progress,° start a scene or two,
Advise the prince; no doubt, an easy tool,
Deferential, glad to be of use,   115
Politic, cautious, and meticulous;
Full of high sentence,° but a bit obtuse;
At times, indeed, almost ridiculous—
Almost, at times, the Fool.

I grow old . . . I grow old . . .   120
I shall wear the bottoms of my trousers rolled.°

Shall I part my hair behind? Do I dare to eat a peach?
I shall wear white flannel trousers, and walk upon the beach.
I have heard the mermaids singing, each to each.

I do not think that they will sing to me.   125

I have seen them riding seaward on the waves
Combing the white hair of the waves blown back
When the wind blows the water white and black.

We have lingered in the chambers of the sea
By sea-girls wreathed with seaweed red and brown   130
Till human voices wake us, and we drown.

---

92 *ball:* another allusion to Marvell's "Coy Mistress."   94 *Lazarus:* See John 11:1–44.   111
Prince Hamlet: the hero of Shakespeare's play *Hamlet.*   113 *swell a progress:* enlarge a royal procession.   117 *sentence:* ideals, opinions, sentiment.   121 *rolled:* a possible reference to cuffs,
which were becoming fashionable in 1910.

JOHN ENGELS   (b. 1931)

Naming the Animals —————————————————————— *1981*

Since spring I've seen two deer,
one lashed to a fender. The other fed
in a clearing on the back slope
of Bean Hill, his big rack° still   *antlers*
in velvet. The shot buck bled,

its tongue frozen
to the rusty hood.
But the other, in its simpler stance,
felt merely the delicate itch
of antler skin.

And three does, mildly alert,
cocked ears toward where I watched from
in the hemlocks. I saw, of course,
five deer; but I
count only what by plain necessity of death

or feeding is oblivious to me,
does not watch back.

MARI EVANS   (b. 1923)

I Am a Black Woman —————————————————————— *1970*

I am a black woman
the music of my song
some sweet arpeggio of tears
is written in a minor key
and I
can be heard humming in the night
Can be heard
    humming
in the night

I saw my mate leap screaming to the sea
and I/with these hands/cupped the lifebreath
from my issue in the canebrake
I lost Nat's swinging body° in a rain of tears

and heard my son scream all the way from Anzio°
for Peace he never knew. . . . I

I AM A BLACK WOMAN.   13 *Nat's swinging body:* Nat Turner was hanged in 1831 for leading
a slave revolt in Southampton, Virginia.   14 *Anzio:* seacoast town in Italy, the scene of fierce
fighting between the Allies and the Germans in 1943 during World War II.

learned Da Nang° and Pork Chop Hill°
in anguish
Now my nostrils know the gas
and these trigger tire/d fingers
seek the softness in my warrior's beard   20

I
am a black woman
tall as a cypress
strong
beyond all definition still   25
defying place
and time
and circumstance
  assailed
    impervious   30
      indestructible

Look
  on me and be
renewed

16 *Da Nang:* major American military base in South Vietnam, frequently attacked during the Vietnam War.   *Pork Chop Hill:* site of a bloody battle between U.N. and Communist forces during the Korean War (1950–1953).

CAROLYN FORCHÉ (b. 1950)

Because One Is Always Forgotten _____ *1981*

IN MEMORIAM, JOSÉ RUDOLFO VIERA
1939–1981: EL SALVADOR

When Viera was buried we knew it had come to an end,
his coffin rocking into the ground like a boat or a cradle.

I could take my heart, he said, and give it to a *campesino*°   *peasant*   5
and he would cut it up and give it back:

you can't eat heart in those four dark
chambers where a man can be kept years.

A boy soldier in the bone-hot sun works his knife
to peel the face from a dead man   10

and hang it from the branch of a tree
flowering with such faces.

The heart is the toughest part of the body.
Tenderness is in the hands.

DAN GEORGAKAS   (b. 1938)

Hiroshima Crewman ————————————————————————*1969*

Somewhere in California
his body humbled by a hair shirt,
a vow of silence on his lips,
a Hiroshima crewman tries to find a life.
If he should ever choose to break his peace,
he might speak of death by fire
no Nazi ordered; he might tell how
war produces many brands of
Auschwitz soap and Dachau lampshade.

NIKKI GIOVANNI   (b. 1943)

Woman ————————————————————————————*1978*

she wanted to be a blade
of grass amid the fields
but he wouldn't agree
to be the dandelion

she wanted to be a robin singing
through the leaves
but he refused to be
her tree

she spun herself into a web
    and looking for a place to rest
turned to him
but he stood straight
declining to be her corner

she tried to be a book
but he wouldn't read
she turned herself into a bulb
but he wouldn't let her grow

she decided to become
a woman
and though he still refused
to be a man
she decided it was all
right

MARILYN HACKER   (b. 1942)

Sonnet Ending with a Film Subtitle —————————————— *1979*

For Judith Landry

Life has its nauseating ironies:
The good die young, as often has been shown;
Chaste spouses catch Venereal Disease;
And feminists sit by the telephone.
Last night was rather bleak, tonight is starker.   5
I may stare at the wall till half-past-one.
My friends are all convinced Dorothy Parker
Lives, but is not well, in Marylebone.°   *a district in London*
I wish that I could imitate my betters
And fortify my rhetoric with guns.   10
Some day we women all will break our fetters
And raise our daughters to be Lesbians.
(I wonder if the bastard kept my letters?)
Here follow untranslatable French puns.

JOHN HAINES   (b. 1936)

Little Cosmic Dust Poem ————————————————— *1985*

Out of the debris of dying stars,
this rain of particles
that waters the waste with brightness;
the sea-wave of atoms hurrying home,
collapse of the giant,   5
unstable guest who cannot stay;

the sun's heart reddens and expands,
his mighty aspiration is lasting,
as the shell of his substance
one day will be white with frost.   10

In the radiant field of Orion°
great hordes of stars are forming,
just as we see every night,
fiery and faithful to the end.

Out of the cold and fleeing dust   15
that is never and always,
the silence and waste to come—

LITTLE COSMIC DUST POEM.   11 *Orion:* a prominent winter constellation. Recent observations have led scientists to conclude that stars are being formed in the nebulous area in the
"sword" of the constellation.

this arm, this hand,
my voice, your face, this love.

DONALD HALL   (b. 1928)

Scenic View _____ *1981*

Every year the mountains
get paler and more distant—
trees less green, rock piles
disappearing—as emulsion
from a billion Kodaks
sucks color out.
In fifteen years
Monadnock and Kearsarge,
the Green Mountains
and the White, will turn
invisible, all
tint removed
atom by atom to albums
in Medford and Greenwich,
while over the valleys
the still intractable granite
rears with unseeable peaks
fatal to airplanes.

DANIEL HALPERN   (b. 1945)

Snapshot of Hue _____ *1982*

For Robert Stone

They are riding bicycles on the other side
of the Perfume River.

A few months ago the bridges were down
and there was no one on the streets.

There were the telling piles on corners,
debris that contained a little of everything.

There was nothing not under cover—
even the sky remained impenetrable

day after day. And if you were seen
on the riverbank you were knocked down.

It is clear today. The litter in the streets
has been swept away. It couldn't have been

that bad, one of us said, the river barely moving,
the bicycles barely moving, the sun posted above.

DANIEL HALPERN   (b. 1945)

Summer in the Middle Class————————————————— *1991*

All over America
it's suddenly
mid-July
We're chasing
our sons around   5
the yard
with balls and sticks
We are lumbering
because we are overweight
and a little older   10
being survivors
of the baby boom
making good the legacy
At sundown
a million barbecues ignite   15
as if from a single match
Webers
Crestlines
international hibachis
and the sad slabs of meat   20
begin to emerge
from their various marinades
the tables get set
and the mosquitoes awaken
for the evening meal   25

When they have finished
what is rightfully theirs
the children are removed
from the tables
and the adults open   30
another bottle or can of beer
The evenings are special
this time of year
the heat finally bearable
the coals a coolish grey   35
dying into themselves
It's what happens in unison

that makes America America
the lights going off
the fluorescent show
of t.v. coming on
and then
the total darkness

H. S. (SAM) HAMOD   (b. 1936)

Leaves _____ *1973*

(for Sally)

Tonight, Sally and I are making stuffed
grapeleaves, we get out a package, it's
drying out, I've been saving it in the freezer, it's
one of the last things my father ever picked in this
life—they're over five years old
and up to now
we just kept finding packages of them in the
freezer, as if he were still picking them
somewhere packing them
carefully to send to us
making sure they didn't break into pieces.
                    ***
"To my Dar Garnchildn
Davd and Lura
from Thr Jido"
twisted on tablet paper
between the lines
in this English lettering
hard for him even to print,
I keep this small torn record,
this piece of paper stays in the upstairs storage,
one of the few pieces of American
my father ever wrote. We find his Arabic letters
all over the place, even in the files we find
letters to him in English, one I found from Charles Atlas
telling him, in 1932,
"Of course, Mr. Hamod, you too can build
your muscles like mine . . ."
                    ***
Last week my mother told me, when I was
asking why I became a poet, "But don't you remember,
your father made up poems, don't you remember him
singing in the car as we drove—those were poems."
Even now, at night, I sometimes
get out the Arabic grammar book
though it seems so late.

FRANCES E. W. HARPER (1825–1911)

She's Free! ——————————————————— *1854*

How say that by law we may torture and chase
A woman whose crime is the hue of her face?—
With her step on the ice, and her arm on her child,
The danger was fearful, the pathway was wild. . . .
But she's free! yes, free from the land where the slave,   5
From the hand of oppression, must rest in the grave;
Where bondage and blood, where scourges and chains,
Have placed on our banner indelible stains. . . .

The bloodhounds have miss'd the scent of her way,
The hunter is rifled and foiled of his prey,   10
The cursing of men and clanking of chains
Make sounds of strange discord on Liberty's plains. . . .
Oh! poverty, danger and death she can brave,
For the child of her love is no longer a slave.

MICHAEL S. HARPER (b. 1938)

Called ——————————————————————— *1975*

Digging the grave
through black dirt,
gravel and rocks
that will hold her down,
we speak of her heat   5
which has driven her out
over the highway
in her first year.

A fly glides from her mouth
as we take her four legs,   10
and the great white neck
muddled at the lakeside
bends gracefully into the arc
of her tongue, colorless, now,
and we set her in the bed   15
of earth and rock
which will hold her as the sun
sets over her shoulders.

You had spoken of her brother,
100 lbs or more,   20
and her slight frame
from the diet of chain

she had broken;
on her back
as the spade cools her brow
with black dirt, rocks,
sand, white tongue,
what pups does she hold
that are seeds unspayed
in her broken body;
what does her brother say
to the seed gone out over
the prairie, on the hunt
of the unreturned:
and what do we say
to the master of the dog dead,
heat, highway, this bed
on the shoulder
of the road west
where her brother called, calls

ROBERT HAYDEN   (b. 1913–1980)

Those Winter Sundays _____ *1962*

Sundays too my father got up early
and put his clothes on in the blueblack cold,
then with cracked hands that ached
from labor in the weekday weather made
banked fires blaze. No one ever thanked him.
I'd wake and hear the cold splintering, breaking,
When the rooms were warm, he'd call,
and slowly I would rise and dress,
fearing the chronic angers of that house,

Speaking indifferently to him,
who had driven out the cold
and polished my good shoes as well.
What did I know, what did I know
of love's austere and lonely offices?

SEAMUS HEANEY   (b. 1939)

Valediction _____ *1966*

Lady with the frilled blouse
And simple tartan skirt,

Since you have left the house
Its emptiness has hurt
All thought. In your presence   5
Time rode easy, anchored
On a smile; but absence
Rocked love's balance, unmoored
The days. They buck and bound
Across the calendar   10
Pitched from the quiet sound
Of your flower-tender
Voice. Need breaks on my strand;
You've gone, I am at sea.
Until you resume command   15
Self is in mutiny.

GEORGE HERBERT   (1593–1633)

Love (III) ° ——————————————————————————— *1633*

Love bade me welcome: yet my soul drew back,
    Guilty of dust and sin.
But quick-eyed Love, observing me grow slack
    From my first entrance in,
Drew nearer to me, sweetly questioning   5
    If I lacked° anything.

"A guest," I answered, "worthy to be here":
    Love said, "You shall be he."
"I, the unkind, ungrateful? Ah, my dear,
    I cannot look on thee."   10
Love took my hand, and smiling did reply,
    "Who made the eyes but I?"

"Truth, Lord; but I have marred them; let my shame
    Go where it doth deserve."
"And know you not," says Love, "who bore the blame?"   15
    "My dear, then I will serve."
"You must sit down," says Love, "and taste my meat."°
    So I did sit and eat.

LOVE (III).   cf. I John 4:8: "He that loveth not knoweth not God; for God is love."   6 *lacked:*
wanted; the phrase is a standard question asked by innkeepers.   17 *and taste my meat:* Job 12:11:
"Doth not the ear try words? and the mouth taste his meat?" Here, *meat* refers simply to food in
general.   17–18 *You must sit down . . . eat:* Luke 13:37: "Blessed are those servants, whom the
Lord when he cometh shall find watching: verily I say unto you, that he shall gird himself, and
make them to sit down to meat, and will come forth and serve them."

ROBERT HERRICK   (1591–1674)

Corinna's Going A-Maying ————————————————————*1648*

Get up! get up for shame! the blooming morn
Upon her wings presents the god unshorn°   *Apollo, god of the sun*
  See how Aurora° throws her fair   *Roman goddess of dawn*
  Fresh-quilted colors through the air:
  Get up, sweet slug-a-bed, and see
  The dew bespangling herb and tree.
Each flower has wept and bowed toward the east
Above an hour since, yet you not dressed;
  Nay, not so much as out of bed?
  When all the birds have matins° said,   *morning prayers*
  And sung their thankful hymns, 'tis sin,
  Nay, profanation to keep in,
Whenas a thousand virgins on this day
Spring, sooner than the lark, to fetch in May.°   *May Day*

Rise, and put on your foliage, and be seen
To come forth, like the springtime, fresh and green,
  And sweet as Flora.° Take no care   *Roman goddess of flowers*
  For jewels for your gown or hair;
  Fear not; the leaves will strew
  Gems in abundance upon you;
Besides, the childhood of the days has kept,
Against you come, some orient° pearls unwept;   *eastern*
  Come and receive them while the light
  Hangs on the dew-locks of the night,
  And Titan° on the eastern hill   *the sun*
  Retires himself, or else stands still
Till you come forth. Wash, dress, be brief in praying:
Few beads° are best when once we go a-Maying.   *prayers, rosaries*

Come, my Corinna, come; and, coming, mark°   *note*
How each field turns° a street, each street a park   *turns into*
  Made green and trimmed with trees: see how
  Devotion gives each house a bough
  Or branch: each porch, each door ere this,
  An ark, a tabernacle is,
Made up of whitethorn neatly interwove,
As if here were those cooler shades of love.
  Can such delights be in the street
  And open fields, and we not see 't?
  Come, we'll abroad; and let's obey
  The proclamation made for May,
And sin no more, as we have done, by staying;
But, my Corinna, come, let's go a-Maying.

There's not a budding boy or girl this day
But is got up and gone to bring in May;
  A deal° of youth, ere this, is come   *great many*   45
  Back, and with whitethorn laden home.
  Some have dispatched their cakes and cream
  Before that we have left to dream;
And some have wept, and wooed, and plighted troth,
And chose their priest, ere we can cast off sloth.   50
  Many a green-gown° has been given,   *green with grass stains*
  Many a kiss, both odd and even;
  Many a glance, too, has been sent
  From out the eye, love's firmament;
Many a jest told of the keys betraying   55
This night, and locks picked; yet we're not a-Maying.

Come, let us go while we are in our prime,
And take the harmless folly of the time.
  We shall grow old apace, and die
  Before we know our liberty.   60
  Our life is short, and our days run
  As fast away as does the sun;
And, as a vapor or a drop of rain
Once lost, can ne'er be found again;
  So when or you or I are made   65
  A fable, song, or fluting shade,
  All love; all liking, all delight
  Lies drowned with us in endless night.
Then while time serves, and we are but decaying,
Come, my Corinna, come, let's go a-Maying.   70

WILLIAM HEYEN   (b. 1940)

The Hair: Jacob Korman's Story ——————————— *1980*

Ten Kilometers from Warsaw,
I arrived in Rembertow where
hundreds of Jews had lived
until the wheel turned: *Judenrein*.   *cleansed; rid of Jews*

You think they let themselves be taken?
They would not fill the trucks.   5
Men were shot trying to pull guns
from the guards' hands.

and hands of dead women
clutched hair, hair of SS guards
blood-patched hair everywhere,   10
a *velt mit hor,* a field of hair.

ROBERTA HILL   (b. 1947)

Dream of Rebirth ———————————————————— *1970*

We stand on the edge of wounds, hugging canned meat,
waiting for owls to come grind
nightsmell in our ears. Over fields,
darkness has been rumbling. Crows gather.
Our luxuries are hatred. Grief. Worn-out hands
carry the pale remains of forgotten murders.
If I could only lull or change this slow hunger,
this midnight swollen four hundred years.

Groping within us are cries yet unheard.
We are born with cobwebs in our mouths
bleeding with prophecies.
Yet within this interior, a spirit kindles
moonlight glittering deep into the sea.
These seeds take root in the hush
of dusk. Songs, a thin echo, heal the salted marsh,
and yield visions untrembling in our grip.

GERARD MANLEY HOPKINS   (1844–1889)

The Windhover° ———————————————————— *1918 (1877)*

To Christ Our Lord

I caught this morning morning's minion,° king-   *darling*
    dom of daylight's dauphin,° dapple-dawn-drawn Falcon, in his riding
    Of the rolling level underneath him steady air, and striding
High there, how he rung upon the rein of a wimpling wing
In his ecstasy! then off, off forth on swing,
    As a skate's heel sweeps smooth on a bow-bend: the hurl and gliding
    Rebuffed the big wind. My heart in hiding
Stirred for a bird,—the achieve of, the mastery of the thing!

Brute beauty and valour and act, oh, air, pride, plume, here
    Buckle!° AND the fire that breaks from thee then, a billion   *join*
Times told lovelier, more dangerous. O my chevalier!°   *knight*
    No wonder of it: shéer plód makes plough down sillion°
Shine, and blue-beak embers, ah my dear,
    Fall, gall themselves, and gash gold-vermilion.

THE WINDHOVER: The poem's title refers to a kestrel—or falcon—that glides or hovers in
the wind.   2 *dauphin:* prince, heir to the throne of France.   12 *sillion:* the ridge of earth between two plowed furrows in a field.

GERARD MANLEY HOPKINS (1844–1889)

Pied Beauty —————————————————————————— *(1918) 1877*

Glory be to God for dappled things—
   For skies of couple-colour as a brinded cow;
      For rose-moles all in stipple upon trout that swim;
Fresh-firecoal chestnut-falls;° finches' wings;
   Landscape plotted and pieced°—fold,° fallow,° and plough;   5
      And áll trádes, their gear and tackle and trim.

All things counter,° original, spare,° strange;
   Whatever is fickle, freckled (who knows how?)
      With swift, slow; sweet, sour; adazzle, dim;
He fathers-forth whose beauty is past change: 10
Praise him.

PIED BEAUTY.   4 *Chestnut-falls:* the meat of a roasted chestnut.   5 *pieced:* divided into fields
of different colors, depending on the crops or use.   *fold:* an enclosed field for animals. *fallow:*
a plowed but unplanted field.   7 *counter:* opposed, as in contrasting patterns.   *spare:* rare.

JULIA WARD HOWE (1819–1910)

Battle Hymn of the Republic ——————————————————— *1862*

Mine eyes have seen the glory of the coming of the Lord;
He is trampling out the vintage where the grapes of wrath are stored:
He hath loosed the fateful lightning of His terrible swift sword;
   His truth is marching on!
     Glory! glory! hallelujah!   5
     Glory! glory! hallelujah!
     Glory! glory! hallelujah!
      Our God is marching on!

I have seen Him in the watch-fire of a hundred circling camps,
They have builded Him an altar in the evening dews and damps;   10
I can read His righteous sentence by the dim and flaring lamps;
   His day is marching on!
     Glory! etc.

I have read a fiery gospel writ in burnished rows of steel:
"As ye deal with my contemners so with you my grace shall deal!"   15
Let the Hero born of woman crush the serpent with his heel,
   Since God is marching on!
     Glory! etc.

He has sounded forth the trumpet that shall never call retreat;
He is sifting out the hearts of men before His judgment seat;   20
Oh! be swift, my soul, to answer Him, be jubilant, my feet!
   Our God is marching on!
     Glory! etc.

In the beauty of the lilies Christ was born across the sea,
With a glory in his bosom that transfigures you and me;
As he died to make men holy, let us die to make men free.
    While God is marching on!
        Glory! etc.

LANGSTON HUGHES   (1902–1967)

Negro ————————————————————————————————*1958*

I am a Negro:
    Black as the night is black,
    Black like the depths of my Africa.

I've been a slave:
    Caesar told me to keep his door-steps clean.
    I brushed the boots of Washington.

I've been a worker:
    Under my hand the pyramids arose.
    I made mortar for the Woolworth Building.

I've been a singer:
    All the way from Africa to Georgia
    I carried my sorrow songs.
    I made ragtime.

I've been a victim:
    The Belgians cut off my hands in the Congo.
    They lynch me still in Mississippi.

I am a Negro:
    Black as the night is black,
    Black like the depths of my Africa.

ROBINSON JEFFERS   (1887–1962)

The Answer ————————————————————————————————*1937*

Then what is the answer?—Not to be deluded by dreams.
To know that great civilizations have broken down into violence, and their tyrants
    come, many times before.
When open violence appears, to avoid it with honor or choose the least ugly faction;
    these evils are essential.
To keep one's own integrity, be merciful and uncorrupted and not wish for evil;
    and not be duped
By dreams of universal justice or happiness. These dreams will not be fulfilled.

To know this, and know that however ugly the parts appear the whole remains beautiful. A severed hand
Is an ugly thing, and man dissevered from the earth and stars and his history . . . for contemplation or in fact . . .

Often appears atrociously ugly. Integrity is wholeness, the greatest beauty is
Organic wholeness, the wholeness of life and things, the divine beauty of the universe. Love that, not man
Apart from that, or else you will share man's pitiful confusions, or drown in despair when his days darken.   10

MARY NOËL KERNAN   (b. 1923)

Majdanek _____ *1993*

Where dandelions sprout
   through the tall grass
     and birds cry out,   5
I skirted the barbed-wire fence
   to pluck a pebble from the
     cobbled road
     at Majdanek;

Breathed deep the fresh, sun-   10
   drenched air
after the attic-musty smell of
   wooden barracks
beneath watchtowers shaped
   like windmills gone awry.
                                                                                      15
Green grass, sweet lilacs, and
   poplar trees
   flank meadows marked
   for massacre.

Beyond them, a huge cup-like   20
   monument stands
   with Polish words carved
     deep in stone:
"Our fate is a warning to you."

MAJDANEK. A Nazi extermination camp in southeastern Poland, near Lublin. It is now a memorial, containing a number of preserved wooden barracks, a gas chamber, and a crematorium. The monument described in stanza 4 covers the piled ashes of hundreds of thousands of victims.

CAROLYN KIZER (b. 1925)

Night Sounds ——————————————————————————*1984*

imitated from the Chinese

The moonlight on my bed keeps me awake;
Living alone now, aware of the voices of evening,
A child weeping at nightmares, the faint love-cries of a woman,
Everything tinged by terror or nostalgia.

No heavy, impassive back to nudge with one foot
While coaxing, "Wake up and hold me,"
When the moon's creamy beauty is transformed
Into a map of impersonal desolation.

But, restless in this mock dawn of moonlight
That so chills the spirit, I alter our history:
You were never able to lie quite peacefully at my side,
Not the night through. Always withholding something.

Awake before morning, restless and uneasy,
Trying not to disturb me, you would leave my bed
While I lay there rigidly, feigning sleep.
Still—the night was nearly over, the light not as cold
As a full cup of moonlight.

And there were the lovely times when, to the skies' cold *No*
You cried to me, *Yes!* Impaled me with affirmation.
Now when I call out in fear, not in love, there is no answer.
Nothing speaks in the dark but the distant voices,
A child with the moon on his face, a dog's hollow cadence.

ETHERIDGE KNIGHT (1931–1991)

Haiku° ——————————————————————————*1968*

1

Eastern guard tower
glints in sunset; convicts rest
like lizards on rocks.

2

The piano man
is sitting at 3 am
his songs drop like plum.

HAIKU. The haiku is a Japanese lyric verse form consisting of three lines that total seventeen syllables, divided 5-7-5. See the discussion on p. 754.

3

Morning sun slants cell.
Drunks stagger like cripple flies
On the Jailhouse floor.

4

To write a blues song   10
is to regiment riots
and pluck gems from graves.

5

A bare pecan tree
slips a pencil shadow down
a moonlit snow slope.   15

6

The falling snow flakes
Can not blunt the hard aches nor
Match the steel stillness.

7

Under moon shadows
A tall boy flashes knife and   20
Slices star bright ice.

8

In the August grass
Struck by the last rays of sun
The cracked teacup screams.

9

Making jazz swing in   25
Seventeen syllables AIN'T
No square poet's job.

MAXINE KUMIN   (b. 1925)

Woodchucks ————————————————————————— *1972*

Gassing the woodchucks didn't turn out right.
The knockout bomb from the Feed and Grain Exchange
was featured as merciful, quick at the bone
and the case we had against them was airtight,
both exits shoehorned shut with puddingstone,   5
but they had a sub-sub-basement out of range.

Next morning they turned up again, no worse
for the cyanide than we for our cigarettes

and state-store Scotch, all of us up to scratch.
They brought down the marigolds as a matter of course
and then took over the vegetable patch
nipping the broccoli shoots, beheading the carrots.

The food from our mouths, I said, righteously thrilling
to the feel of the .22, the bullet's neat noses.
I, a lapsed pacifist fallen from grace
puffed with Darwinian pieties° for killing,
now drew a bead on the littlest woodchuck's face.
He died down in the everbearing roses.

Ten minutes later I dropped the mother. She
flipflopped in the air and fell, her needle teeth
still hooked in a leaf of early Swiss chard.
Another baby next. O one-two-three
the murderer inside me rose up hard,
the hawkeye killer came on stage forthwith.

There's one chuck left. Old wily fellow, he keeps
me cocked and ready day after day after day.
All night I hunt his humped-up form. I dream
I sight along the barrel in my sleep.
If only they'd all consented to die unseen
gassed underground the quiet Nazi way.°

WOODCHUCKS.   16 *Darwinian pieties:* Charles Darwin (1809–1892) was a British naturalist
who formulated the theory of evolution; the piety is "survival of the fittest."   30 *gassed . . . way:*
a reference to the extermination of millions of people in gas chambers by the Nazis during World
War II.

JOANNE KYGER   (b. 1934)

Destruction _____ *1980*

First of all do you remember the way a bear goes through
a cabin when nobody is home? He goes through
the front door. I mean he really goes *through* it. Then
he takes the cupboard off the wall and eats a can of lard.

He eats all the apples, limes, dates, bottled decaffeinated
coffee, and 35 pounds of granola. The asparagus soup cans
fall to the floor. Yum! He chomps up Norwegian crackers
stashed for the winter. And the bouillon, salt, pepper,
paprika, garlic, onions, potatoes.

                    He rips the Green Tara
poster from the wall. Tries the Coleman Mustard, spills
the ink, tracks in the flour. Goes up stairs and takes

a shit. Rips open the water bed, eats the incense and
drinks the perfume. Knocks over the Japanese tansu   15
and the Persian miniature of a man on horseback watching
a woman bathing.

      Knocks *Shelter, Whole Earth Catalogue,*
Planet Drum, Northern Mists, Truck Tracks, and
Women's Sports into the oozing water bed mess.

           He goes   20
down stairs and out the back wall. He keeps on going
for a long way and finds a good cave to sleep it all off.
Luckily he ate the whole medicine cabinet, including stash
of LSD, Peyote, Psilocybin, Amanita, Benzedrine, Valium
and aspirin.

IRVING LAYTON   (b. 1912)

Rhine Boat Trip° ————————————————————— *1977*

The castles on the Rhine
are all haunted
by the ghosts of Jewish mothers
looking for their ghostly children

And the clusters of grapes   5
in the sloping vineyards
are myriads of blinded eyes
staring at the blind sun

The tireless Lorelei°
can never comb from their hair   10
the crimson beards
of murdered rabbis

However sweetly they sing
one hears only
the low wailing of cattle-cars°   15
moving invisibly across the land

RHINE BOAT TRIP: The title refers to the Rhine River, which flows through Germany. 9
Lorelei: legendary seductive nymphs who lived in the cliffs overlooking the Rhine, and whose
singing lured sailors to shipwreck. 15 *cattle-cars:* railroad cars designed to transport cattle but
used by the Nazis to transport Jews from the cities of Europe to extermination camps.

ALAN P. LIGHTMAN   (b. 1948)

In Computers ———————————————————— *1982 (1981)*

In the magnets of computers will
  be stored

Blend of sunset over wheat
  fields.
Low thunder of gazelle.
Light, sweet wind on high
  ground.
Vacuum stillness spreading from
  a thick snowfall.

Men will sit in rooms
upon the smooth, scrubbed earth
or stand in tunnels on the moon
and instruct themselves in how it
  was.
Nothing will be lost.
Nothing will be lost.

AUDRE LORDE (b. 1934)

Every Traveler Has One Vermont Poem ———————————— *(1986)*

Spikes of lavender aster under Route 91
hide a longing or confession
"I remember when air was invisible"
from Chamberlin Hill down to Lord's Creek
tree mosses point the way home.

Two nights of frost
and already the hills are turning
curved green against the astonished morning
sneeze-weed and ox-eye daisies
nor caring   I am a stranger
making a living choice.

Tanned boys I do not know
on their first proud harvest
wave from their father's tractor
one smiles as we drive past
the other hollers
nigger
into cropped and fragrant air.

RICHARD LOVELACE (1618–1657)

To Lucasta, Going to the Wars ———————————— *1649*

Tell me not, Sweet, I am unkind
That from the nunnery
Of thy chaste breast and quiet mind,
To war and arms I fly.

True, a new mistress now I chase,
The first foe in the field;
And with a stronger faith embrace   5
A sword, a horse, a shield.

Yet this inconstancy is such
As you too shall adore;
I could not love thee, Dear, so much,
Loved I not honor more.   10

AMY LOWELL   (1874–1925)

Patterns ———————————————————————— *1916*

I walk down the garden paths,
And all the daffodils
Are blowing, and the bright blue squills.
I walk down the patterned garden-paths
In my stiff, brocaded gown.   5
With my powdered hair and jewelled fan,
I too am a rare
Pattern. As I wander down
The garden paths.
My dress is richly figured,   10
And the train
Makes a pink and silver stain
On the gravel, and the thrift
Of the borders.
Just a plate of current fashion   15
Tripping by in high-heeled, ribboned shoes.
Not a softness anywhere about me,
Only whalebone° and brocade.
And I sink on a seat in the shade
Of a lime tree. For my passion   20
Wars against the stiff brocade.
The daffodils and squills
Flutter in the breeze
As they please.
And I weep;   25
For the lime-tree is in blossom
And one small flower has dropped upon my bosom.

And the plashing of waterdrops
In the marble fountain
Comes down the garden-paths.   30
The dripping never stops.

PATTERNS.   18 *whalebone:* Bones from whales were used to make extremely rigid corsets for women.

Underneath my stiffened gown
Is the softness of a woman bathing in a marble basin,
A basin in the midst of hedges grown
So thick, she cannot see her lover hiding,
But she guesses he is near,
And the sliding of the water
Seems the stroking of a dear
Hand upon her.
What is Summer in a fine brocaded gown!
I should like to see it lying in a heap upon the ground.
All the pink and silver crumpled up on the ground.

I would be the pink and silver as I ran along the paths,
And he would stumble after,
Bewildered by my laughter.
I should see the sun flashing from his sword-hilt and buckles on his shoes.
I would choose
To lead him in a maze along the patterned paths,
A bright and laughing maze for my heavy-booted lover.
Till he caught me in the shade,
And the buttons of his waistcoat bruised my body as he clasped me,
Aching, melting, unafraid.
With the shadows of the leaves and the sundrops,
And the plopping of the waterdrops,
All about us in the open afternoon—
I am very like to swoon
With the weight of this brocade,
For the sun sifts through the shade.

Underneath the fallen blossom
In my bosom,
Is a letter I have hid.
It was brought to me this morning by a rider from the Duke.
Madam, we regret to inform you that Lord Hartwell
Died in action Thursday se'nnight.°
As I read it in the white, morning sunlight,
The letters squirmed like snakes.
"Any answer, Madam," said my footman.
"No," I told him.
"See that the messenger takes some refreshment.

No, no answer."
And I walked into the garden,
Up and down the patterned paths,
In my stiff, correct brocade.
The blue and yellow flowers stood up proudly in the sun,
Each one.
I stood upright too,

---

64 *se'nnight:* seven nights, hence a week ago.

Held rigid to the pattern
By the stiffness of my gown.
Up and down I walked.
Up and down.   80

In a month he would have been my husband.
In a month, here, underneath this lime,
We would have broken the pattern;
He for me, and I for him,
He as Colonel, I as Lady,   85
On this shady seat.
He had a whim
That sunlight carried blessing.
And I answered, "It shall be as you have said."
Now he is dead.   90

In Summer and In Winter I shall walk
Up and down
The patterned garden-paths
In my stiff, brocaded gown.
The squills and daffodils   95
Will give peace to pillared roses, and to asters, and to snow.
I shall go
Up and down,
In my gown.
Gorgeously arrayed,   100
Boned and stayed.
And the softness of my body will be guarded from embrace
By each button, hook, and lace.
For the man who should loose me is dead,
Fighting with the Duke in Flanders,°   105
In a pattern called a war.
Christ! What are patterns for?

105 *Flanders:* a place of frequent warfare in Belgium. The speaker's clothing (lines 5, 6) suggests
the time of the Duke of Marlborough's Flanders campaigns of 1702–1710. The Battle of Water-
loo (1815) was also fought nearby under the Duke of Wellington. During World War I, fierce
fighting against the Germans occurred in Flanders in 1914 and 1915, with great loss of life.

CYNTHIA MACDONALD   (b. 1928)

A Critical Age ———————————————————————————*1991*

So that's what it's like to stand helpless at the phone,
Glasses cracked in snowflake patterns, and Information telling you
The vital numbers are unlisted. So that's what it's like

To realize you will never know what goes on behind
Closed door, the grunts and creaking prying through the cracks,
Realize you can only know what you yourself already know.
So that's what it's like to lie helpless feeling stars of pain in
Your left side, the side you abandoned though they warned you.
So that's what it's like to win those prizes you once believed
Would provide the necessary ballast, and realize Moses
Had to find the tablets, could not tell water from stone
Within himself. Within himself, he seized on what he could,
Conviction somehow there long enough to part the sea, the waves
Of doubt. So that's what it's like to see a clear path ahead for
A moment and to know that certainty for long is like convict labor.
So that's what it's like to become weightier, as if it would keep you
Where you need to be, would provide the necessary provender.
So that's what it's like to become lighter, translucent
As a metaphor of air, to hear the music of the spheres: forte/piano,
Piano/forte—Mozart, as if on the spinet in the next room,
The windows open to those fields of particular color.
So that's what it's like, like nothing really, beyond compare.

HEATHER McHUGH   (b. 1948)

Lines _____ *1981*

Some are waiting, some can't wait.
The stores are full of necessities.

The sun dies down, the graveyard
grows, the subway is a wind
instrument with so many stops, but
even the underground comes
to an end, and all those flights
of fancy birds settle for one
telephone wire, the one on which

just now, the man in utterly
unheard-of love has caught
the word goodbye. He puts
the receiver back in the cradle
and stands. Outside his window
an old man with a hearing-aid walks
without aim, happy just to be alive.

CLAUDE McKAY   (1890–1948)

The White City ——————————————————————— *1922*

I will not toy with it nor bend an inch.
Deep in the secret chambers of my heart
I muse my life-long hate, and without flinch
I bear it nobly as I live my part.
My being would be a skeleton, a shell,   5
If this dark Passion that fills my every mood,
And makes my heaven in the white world's hell,
Did not forever feed me vital blood.
I see the mighty city through a mist—
The strident trains that speed the goaded mass,   10
The poles and spires and towers vapor-kissed,
The fortressed port through which the great ships pass,
The tides, the wharves, the dens I contemplate,
Are sweet like wanton loves because I hate.

EDNA ST. VINCENT MILLAY   (1892–1950)

What Lips My Lips Have Kissed, and Where, and Why ————————— *1923*

What lips my lips have kissed, and where, and why,
I have forgotten, and what arms have lain
Under my head till morning; but the rain
Is full of ghosts tonight, that tap and sigh
Upon the glass and listen for reply,   5
And in my heart there stirs a quiet pain
For unremembered lads that not again
Will turn to me at midnight with a cry.
Thus in the winter stands the lonely tree,
Nor knows what birds have vanished one by one,   10
Yet knows it boughs more silent than before:
I cannot say what loves have come and gone,
I only know that summer sang in me
A little while, that in me sings no more.

VASSAR MILLER   (b. 1924)

Loneliness ——————————————————————————— *1963*

So deep is this silence
that the insects, the birds,
the talk of the neighbors in the distance,

the whir of the traffic, the music
are only its voices
and do not contradict it.

So deep is this crying
that the silence, the hush,
the quiet, the stillness, the not speaking,
the never hearing a word
are only the surge
of its innumerable waters.

This silence, this crying,
O my God, is my country
with Yours the sole footstep besides my own.
Save me amid its landscapes
so terrible, strange
I am almost in love with them!

JOHN MILTON   (1608–1674)

O Nightingale! _____ *1630*

O Nightingale, that on yon bloomy Spray
   Warbl'st at eve, when all the Woods are still,
   Thou with fresh hope the Lover's heart dost fill,
   While the jolly hours lead on propitious *May*
Thy liquid notes that close the eye of Day,
   First heard before the shallow Cuckoo's bill,
   Portend success in love; O, if *Jove's* will
   Have linkt that amorous power to thy soft lay,
Now timely sing, ere the rude Bird of Hate
   Foretell my hopeless doom in some Grove nigh:
   As thou from year to year hast sung too late
For my relief; yet hadst no reason why.
   Whether the Muse, or Love call thee his mate,
   Both them I serve, and of their train am I.

THOMAS MOORE   (1779–1852)

Believe Me, If All Those Endearing Young Charms _____ *1834*

Believe me, if all those endearing young charms,
   Which I gaze on so fondly to-day,
Were to change by tomorrow, and fleet° in my arms,   *vanish*
   Like fairy gifts fading away!

Thou wouldst still be adored, as this moment thou art,   5
   Let thy loveliness fade as it will,
And around the dear ruin each wish of my heart
   Would entwine itself verdantly still.

It is not while beauty and youth are thine own,
   And thy cheeks unprofaned by a tear,   10
That the fervor and faith of a soul may be known,
   To which time will but make thee more dear!
Oh the heart that has truly loved never forgets,
   But as truly loves on to the close,
As the sunflower turns to her god when he sets   15
   The same look which she turned when he rose!

OGDEN NASH   (1902–1971)

Very Like a Whale° ———————————————————— *1934*

One thing that literature would be greatly the better for
Would be a more restricted employment by authors of simile and metaphor.
Authors of all races, be they Greeks, Romans, Teutons or Celts,
Can't seem just to say that anything is the thing it is but have to go out of their
   way to say that it is like something else.   5
What does it mean when we are told
That the Assyrian came down like a wolf on the fold?
In the first place, George Gordon Byron° had had enough experience
To know that it probably wasn't just one Assyrian, it was a lot of Assyrians.
However, as too many arguments are apt to induce apoplexy and thus hinder
   longevity,
We'll let it pass as one Assyrian for the sake of brevity.   10
Now then, this particular Assyrian; the one whose cohorts were gleaming in purple
   and gold,
Just what does the poet mean when he says he came down like a wolf on the
   fold?
In heaven and earth more than is dreamed of in our philosophy there are a great
   many things,
But I don't imagine that among them there is a wolf with purple and gold cohorts
   or purple and gold anythings.
No, no, Lord Byron, before I'll believe that this Assyrian was actually like a wolf   15
   I must have some kind of proof;
Did he run on all fours and did he have a hairy tail and a big red mouth and big
   white teeth and did he say Woof woof woof?
Frankly I think it very unlikely, and all you were entitled to say, at the very most,
Was that the Assyrian cohorts came down like a lot of Assyrian cohorts about to
   destroy the Hebrew host.

VERY LIKE A WHALE: See *Hamlet*, Act III, scene 2, line 358.   *7 George Gordon Byron:* See Byron, "The Destruction of Sennacherib," (p. 926), which Nash is satirizing in this poem.

But that wasn't fancy enough for Lord Byron, oh dear me no, he had to invent a
　lot of figures of speech and then interpolate them.
With the result that whenever you mention Old Testament soldiers to people they
　say Oh yes, they're the ones that a lot of wolves dressed up in gold and purple
　ate them.
That's the kind of thing that's being done all the time by poets, from Homer to
　Tennyson;
They're always comparing ladies to lilies° and veal to venison.
How about the man who wrote,
Her little feet stole in and out like mice beneath her petticoat?°
Wouldn't anybody but a poet think twice
Before stating that his girl's feet were mice?
Then they always say things like that after a winter storm
The snow is a white blanket. Oh it is, is it, all right then, you sleep under a six-
　inch blanket of snow and I'll sleep under a half-inch blanket of unpoetical
　blanket material and we'll see which one keeps warm.
And after that maybe you'll begin to comprehend dimly
What I meant by too much metaphor and simile.

22 *ladies:* See Campion, "Cherry Ripe," stanza 1, and also Burns, "A Red, Red Rose."   24 *little
feet . . . petticoat:* In Sir John Suckling's, "A Ballad upon a Wedding" (1641), the following lines
appear: "Her feet beneath her petticoat/Like little mice stole in and out." Also in a poem by
Robert Herrick complimenting the feet of Susanna Southwell (1648), he wrote: "Her pretty
feet/Like snails did creep."

HOWARD NEMEROV   (1920–1991)

Life Cycle of Common Man —————————————————————————*1960*

Roughly figured, this man of moderate habits,
This average consumer of the middle class,
Consumed in the course of his average life span
Just under half a million cigarettes,
Four thousand fifths of gin and about
A quarter as much vermouth; he drank
Maybe a hundred thousand cups of coffee,
And counting his parents' share it cost
Something like half a million dollars
To put him through life. How many beasts
Died to provide him with meat, belt and shoes
Cannot be certainly said.

　　　　　　　But anyhow,
It is in this way that a man travels through time,
Leaving behind him a lengthening trail
Of empty bottles and bones, of broken shoes,
Frayed collars and worn out or outgrown
Diapers and dinnerjackets, silk ties and slickers.

Given the energy and security thus achieved,
He did . . . ? What? The usual things, of course,

The eating, dreaming, drinking and begetting,
And he worked for the money which was to pay
For the eating, et cetera, which were necessary
If he were to go on working for the money, et cetera,
But chiefly he talked. As the bottles and bones   25
Accumulated behind him, the words proceeded
Steadily from the front of his face as he
Advanced into the silence and made it verbal.
Who can tally the tale of his words? A lifetime
Would barely suffice for their repetition;   30
If you merely printed all his commas the result
Would be a very large volume, and the number of times
He said "thank you" or "very little sugar, please,"
Would stagger the imagination. There were also
Witticisms, platitudes, and statements beginning   35
"It seems to me" or "As I always say."
Consider the courage in all that, and behold the man
Walking into deep silence, with the ectoplastic
Cartoon's balloon of speech proceeding
Steadily out of the front of his face, the words   40
Borne along on the breath which is his spirit
Telling the numberless tale of his untold Word
Which makes the world his apple, and forces him to eat.

JIM NORTHRUP   (b. 1943)

wahbegan° _____ *1993*

Didja ever hear a sound
smell something
taste something
that brought you back
to Vietnam, instantly?   5
Didja ever wonder
when it would end?
It ended for my brother.
He died in the war
but didn't fall down   10
for fifteen tortured years.
His flashbacks are over,
another casualty whose name
will never be on the Wall.
Some can find peace   15
only in death.
The sound of his
family crying hurt.

WAHBEGAN.   The title is an Ojibway name.

The smell of the flowers
didn't comfort us.
The bitter taste
in my mouth
still sours me.
How about a memorial
for those who made it
through the war
but still died
before their time?

NAOMI SHIHAB NYE (b. 1952)

Where Children Live ——————————————————————*1982*

Homes where children live exude a pleasant rumpledness,
like a bed made by a child, or a yard littered with balloons.

To be a child again one would need to shed details
till the heart found itself dressed in the coat with a hood.
Now the heart has taken on gloves and mufflers,
the heart never goes outside to find something to "do."
And the house takes on a new face, dignified.
No lost shoes blooming under bushes.
No chipped trucks in the drive.
Grown-ups like swings, leafy plants, slow-motion back and forth.
While the yard of a child is strewn with the corpses
of bottle-rockets and whistles,
anything whizzing and spectacular, brilliantly short-lived.

Trees in children's yards speak in clearer tongues.
Ants have more hope. Squirrels dance as well as hide.
The fence has a reason to be there, so children can go in and out.
Even when the children are at school, the yards glow
with the leftovers of their affection,
the roots of the tiniest grasses curl toward one another
like secret smiles.

FRANK O'HARA (1926–1966)

Poem ——————————————————————————*1952*

The eager note on my door said "Call me,
call when you get in!" so I quickly threw
a few tangerines into my overnight bag,
straightened my eyelids and shoulders, and

headed straight for the door. It was autumn   5
by the time I got around the corner, oh all
unwilling to be either pertinent or bemused, but
the leaves were brighter than grass on the sidewalk!

Funny, I thought, that the lights are on this late
and the hall door open; still up at this hour, a   10
champion jai-alai player like himself? Oh fie!
for shame! What a host, so zealous! And he was

there in the hall, flat on a sheet of blood that
ran down the stairs. I did appreciate it. There are few
hosts who so thoroughly prepare to greet a guest   15
only casually invited, and that several months ago.

SIMON ORTIZ   (b. 1941)

*A Story of How a Wall Stands*_____ *1976*

At Aacqu there is a wall almost 400 years old which
supports hundreds of tons of dirt and bones—it's a
graveyard built on a steep incline—and it looks like
it's about to fall down the incline but will not for a long time.

My father, who works with stone,
says, "That's just the part you see,
the stones which seem to be
just packed in on the outside,"
and with his hands put the stone and mud   5
in place. "Underneath
what looks like loose stone,
there is stone woven together."
He ties one hand over the other,
fitting like the bones of his hands   10
and fingers. "That's what is
holding it together."

"It is built that carefully,"
he says, "the mud mixed
to a certain texture," patiently   15
"with the fingers," worked
in the palm of his hand. "So that
placed between the stones, they hold
together for a long, long time."

He tells me those things,   20
the story of them worked
with his fingers, in the palm
of his hands, working the stone

and the mud until they become
the wall that stands a long, long time.

DOROTHY PARKER   (1893–1967)

Résumé ———————————————————————————*1936*

Razors pain you;
Rivers are damp;
Acids stain you;
And drugs cause cramp.
Guns aren't lawful;
Nooses give;
Gas smells awful;
You might as well live.

LINDA PASTAN   (b. 1932)

Marks ———————————————————————————*1978*

My husband gives me an A
for last night's supper,
an incomplete for my ironing,
a B plus in bed.
My son says I am average,
an average mother, but if
I put my mind to it
I could improve.
My daughter believes
in Pass/Fail and tells me
I pass. Wait 'til they learn
I'm dropping out.

MARGE PIERCY   (b. 1936)

The Secretary Chant ———————————————————*1973*

My hips are a desk.
From my ears hang
chains of paper clips.
Rubber bands form my hair.
My breasts are wells of mimeograph ink.
My feet bear casters.
Buzz. Click.

My head is a badly organized file.
My head is a switchboard
where crossed lines crackle.   10
Press my fingers
and in my eyes appear
credit and debit.
Zing. Tinkle.
My navel is a reject button.   15
From my mouth issue canceled reams.
Swollen, heavy, rectangular
I am about to be delivered
of a baby
Xerox machine.   20
File me under W
because I wonce
was
a woman.

MARGE PIERCY   (b. 1936)

*Will We Work Together?*_____ *1980*

You wake in the early grey
morning in bed alone and curse
me, that I am only
sometimes there. But when
I am with you, I light   5
up the corners, I am bright
as a fireplace roaring
with love, every bone in my back
and my fingers is singing
like a tea kettle on the boil.   10
My heart wags me, a big dog
with a bigger tail. I am
a new coin printed with
your face. My body wears
sore before I can express   15
on yours the smallest part
of what moves me. Words
shred and splinter.
I want to make with you
some bold new thing   20
to stand in the marketplace,
the statue of a goddess
laughing, armed and wearing
flowers and feathers. Like sheep
of whose hair is made   25

blankets and coats, I want
to force from this fierce sturdy
rampant love some useful thing.

SYLVIA PLATH   (1932–1963)

Last Words ———————————————————————————*1971 (1961)*

I do not want a plain box, I want a sarcophagus
With tigery stripes, and a face on it
Round as the moon, to stare up.
I want to be looking at them when they° come
Picking among the dumb minerals, the roots,
I see them already—the pale, star-distance faces.
Now they are nothing, they are not even babies.
I imagine them without fathers or mothers, like the first gods.
They will wonder if I was important.
I should sugar and preserve my days like fruit!
My mirror is clouding over—
A few more breaths, and it will reflect nothing at all.
The flowers and the faces whiten to a sheet.

I do not trust the spirit. It escapes like steam
In dreams, through mouth-hole or eye-hole. I can't stop it.
One day it won't come back. Things aren't like that.
They stay, their little particular lusters
Warmed by much handling. They almost purr.
When the soles of my feet grow cold,
The blue eye of my turquoise will comfort me.
Let me have my copper cooking pots, let my rouge pots
Bloom about me like night flowers, with a good smell.
They will roll me up in bandages, they will store my heart
Under my feet in a neat parcel.°
I shall hardly know myself. It will be dark,
And the shine of these small things sweeter than the face of Ishtar.°

LAST WORDS.   4 *they:* possibly archeologists exploring the speaker's tomb or stone coffin ("sar-cophagus").   19–24 *When . . . parcel:* The objects and procedures here refer to the household goods normally entombed with a body in ancient Egypt and to the preparation of a mummy. 27 *Ishtar:* Ancient Babylonian goddess of fertility, love, and war.

SYLVIA PLATH   (1932–1963)

Mirror ———————————————————————————*1965 (1961)*

I am silver and exact. I have no preconceptions.
Whatever I see I swallow immediately

Just as it is, unmisted by love or dislike.
I am not cruel, only truthful—
The eye of a little god, four-cornered.   5
Most of the time I meditate on the opposite wall.
It is pink, with speckles. I have looked at it so long
I think it is a part of my heart. But it flickers.
Faces and darkness separate us over and over.

Now I am a lake. A woman bends over me,   10
Searching my reaches for what she really is.
Then she turns to those liars, the candles or the moon.
I see her back, and reflect it faithfully.
She rewards me with tears and an agitation of hands.
I am important to her. She comes and goes.   15
Each morning it is her face that replaces the darkness.
In me she has drowned a young girl, and in me an old woman
Rises toward her day after day, like a terrible fish.

KATHA POLLITT   (b. 1949)

Archaeology _____ *1981*

"Our real poems are already in us
and all we can do is dig."
          —*Jonathan Galassi*

You knew the odds on failure from the start,
that morning you first saw, or thought you saw,
beneath the heartstruck plains of a second-rate country
the outline of buried cities. A thousand to one
you'd turn up nothing more than the rubbish heap   5
of a poor Near Eastern backwater:
a few chipped beads,
splinters of glass and pottery, broken tablets
whose secret lore, laboriously deciphered,
would prove to be only a collection of ancient grocery lists.   10
Still, the train moved away from the station without you.

How many lives ago
was that? How many choices?
Now that you've got your bushelful of shards
do you say, *give me back my years*   15
or wrap yourself in the distant
glitter of desert stars,
telling yourself it was foolish after all
to have dreamed of uncovering
some fluent vessel, the bronze head of a god?   20
Pack up your fragments. Let the simoom°   *a desert sandstorm*

flatten the digging site. Now come
the passionate midnights in the museum basement
when out of that random rubble you'll invent
the dusty market smelling of sheep and spices,   2
streets, palmy gardens, courtyards set with wells
to which, in the blue of evening, one by one
come strong veiled women, bearing their perfect jars.

EZRA POUND   (1885–1972)

The River-Merchant's Wife: A Letter° _____ *1926 (1915)*

While my hair was still cut straight across my forehead
I played about the front gate, pulling flowers.
You came by on bamboo stilts, playing horse,
You walked about my seat, playing with blue plums.
And we went on living in the village of Chokan:°
Two small people, without dislike or suspicion.

At fourteen I married My Lord you.
I never laughed, being bashful.
Lowering my head, I looked at the wall.
Called to, a thousand times, I never looked back.   1

At fifteen I stopped scowling,
I desired my dust to be mingled with yours
Forever and forever and forever.
Why should I climb the look out?

At sixteen you departed,   1
You went into far Ku-tō-en,° by the river of swirling eddies,
And you have been gone five months.
The monkeys make sorrowful noise overhead.

You dragged your feet when you went out.
By the gate now, the moss is grown, the different mosses,   2
Too deep to clear them away!
The leaves fall early this autumn, in wind.
The paired butterflies are already yellow with August

Over the grass in the West garden;
They hurt me, I grow older.   2
If you are coming down through the narrows of the river Kiang,
Please let me know beforehand,
And I will come out to meet you
As far as Chō-fū-sa

THE RIVER-MERCHANTS WIFE: A LETTER. Freely translated from the Chinese of Li Po
(701–762).   5 *Chokan:* a suburb of Nanking, China.   16 *Ku-tō-en* an island several hundred
miles up the Kiang River from Nanking.   29 *Chō-fū-sa* a beach near Ku-tō-en

JOHN CROWE RANSOM   (1888–1974)

Bells for John Whiteside's Daughter —————————————— *1924*

There was such speed in her little body,
And such lightness in her footfall,
It is no wonder her brown study
Astonishes us all.

Her wars were bruited in our high window.   5
We looked among orchard trees and beyond
Where she took arms against her shadow,
Or harried unto the pond.

The lazy geese, like a snow cloud
Dripping their snow on the green grass,   10
Tricking and stopping, sleepy and proud,
Who cried in goose, Alas,

For the tireless heart within the little
Lady with rod that made them rise
From their noon apple-dreams and scuttle   15
Goose-fashion under the skies!

But now go the bells, and we are ready,
In one house we are sternly stopped
To say we are vexed at her brown study,
Lying so primly propped.   20

THEODORE ROETHKE   (1908–1963)

The Waking —————————————————————— *1953*

I wake to sleep, and take my waking slow.
I feel my fate in what I cannot fear.
I learn by going where I have to go.

We think by feeling. What is there to know?
I hear my being dance from ear to ear.   5
I wake to sleep, and take my waking slow.

Of those so close beside me, which are you?
God bless the Ground! I shall walk softly there,
And learn by going where I have to go.

Light takes the Tree; but who can tell us how?   10
The lowly worm climbs up a winding stair;
I wake to sleep, and take my waking slow.

Great Nature has another thing to do
To you and me; so take the lively air,
And, lovely, learn by going where to go.   15

This shaking keeps me steady. I should know.
What falls away is always. And is near.
I wake to sleep, and take my waking slow.
I learn by going where I have to go.

LUIS OMAR SALINAS   (b. 1937)

In a Farmhouse ——————————————————————— *1973*

Fifteen miles
out of Robstown
with the Texas sun
fading in the distance
I sit in the bedroom
profoundly,
animated by the day's work
in the cottonfields.

I made two dollars and
thirty cents today
I am eight years old
and I wonder
how the rest of the Mestizos°
do not go hungry
and if one were to die
of hunger
what an odd way
to leave for heaven.

IN A FARMHOUSE.   13 *Mestizos:* persons of mixed Spanish and Amerindian ancestry.

SONIA SANCHEZ   (b. 1934)

right on: white america ——————————————————— *1970*

this country might have
been a pio
   neer land
once.
   but.   there ain't
no mo
      indians   blowing
custer's° mind
         with a different

RIGHT ON: WHITE AMERICA.   8 *custer's:* General George Armstrong Custer (1839–1876) was
killed in his "last stand" at the Little Bighorn in Montana during a battle with Sioux Indians.

image of america.   10
   this country
might have
   needed shoot/
outs/ daily/
   once.   15
    but. there ain't
no mo real/ white/ allamerican
     bad/guys.
just
  u & me.   20
   blk/ and un/armed.
this country might have
been a pion
   eer land. once.
     and it still is.   25
check out
  the falling
gun/shells on our blk/tomorrows.

CARL SANDBURG (1878–1967)

Chicago ———————————————————— *1916*

 Hog Butcher for the World,
 Tool Maker, Stacker of Wheat,
 Player with Railroads and the Nation's Freight Handler;
 Stormy, husky, brawling,
 City of the Big Shoulders: 5

They tell me you are wicked and I believe them, for I have seen your painted
 women under the gas lamps luring the farm boys.
And they tell me you are crooked and I answer: Yes, it is true I have seen the
 gunman kill and go free to kill again.
And they tell me you are brutal and my reply is: On the faces of women and
 children I have seen the marks of wanton hunger.
And having answered so I turn once more to those who sneer at this my city,
 and I give them back the sneer and say to them:
Come and show me another city with lifted head singing so proud to be alive 10
 and coarse and strong and cunning.
Flinging magnetic curses amid the toil of piling job on job, here is a tall bold
 slugger set vivid against the little soft cities;
Fierce as a dog with tongue lapping for action, cunning as a savage pitted against
 the wilderness,
 Bareheaded,
 Shoveling,
 Wrecking,   15

Planning,
Building, breaking, rebuilding,
Under the smoke, dust all over his mouth, laughing with white teeth,
Under the terrible burden of destiny laughing as a young man laughs,
Laughing even as an ignorant fighter laughs who has never lost a battle,
Bragging and laughing that under his wrist is the pulse, and under his ribs the
　　heart of the people,
　　　　Laughing!
Laughing the stormy, husky, brawling laughter of Youth, half-naked, sweating,
　　proud to be Hog Butcher, Tool Maker, Stacker of Wheat, Player with Railroads
　　and Freight Handler to the Nation.

SIEGFRIED SASSOON   (1886–1967)

Dreamers _____ *1918*

Soldiers are citizens of death's grey land,
　　Drawing no dividend from time's to-morrows.
In the great hour of destiny they stand,
　　Each with his feuds, and jealousies, and sorrows.

　　Soldiers are sworn to action; they must win
　　Some flaming, fatal climax with their lives.
Soldiers are dreamers; when the guns begin
　　They think of firelit homes, clean beds, and wives.

I see them in foul dug-outs, gnawed by rats,
　　And in the ruined trenches, lashed with rain,
Dreaming of things they did with balls and bats,
　　And mocked by hopeless longing to regain
Bank-holidays,° and picture shows, and spats,
　　And going to the office in the train.

DREAMERS.　　13 *Bank-holidays:* legal holidays in Great Britain.

ALAN SEEGER   (1886–1916)

I Have a Rendezvous with Death _____ *1916*

I have a rendezvous with Death
At some disputed barricade,
When Spring comes back with rustling shade
And apple blossoms fill the air—
I have a rendezvous with Death
When Spring brings back blue days and fair.

It may be he shall take my hand
And lead me into his dark land
And close my eyes and quench my breath—
It may be I shall pass him still.

I have a rendezvous with Death
On some scarred slope of battered hill,
When Spring comes round again this year
And the first meadow flowers appear.

God knows 'twere better to be deep   15
Pillowed in silk and scented down,
Where Love throbs out in blissful sleep,
Pulse nigh to pulse and breath to breath,
Where hushed awakenings are dear. . . .
But I've a rendezvous with Death   20
At midnight in some flaming town,
When Spring trips north again this year,
And I to my pledged word am true,
I shall not fail that rendezvous.

BRENDA SEROTTE   (b. 1946)

My Mother's Face ————————————————————— *1991*

Dressing for work
I glanced in the mirror
startled to see my mother's face
white, with the mouth turned down
her red frizzled hair   5
wild in all directions.
She turned sideways
to study my dress
standing tiptoe like I do
craning her long neck   10
in a futile attempt to see my feet.
Then without warning, the tears
rolling from the outer corners down
past slightly pitted cheeks
past that inverted smile   15
into the cave of her bosom
which heaved a sigh so forlorn
so weighted with loss
that had I not been standing silent
I would have surely thought it was me.   20

ANNE SEXTON   (1928–1974)

Three Green Windows ———————————————— *1966 (1962)*

Half awake in my Sunday nap
I see three green windows
in three different lights—
one west, one south, one east.

I have forgotten that old friends are dying.
I have forgotten that I grow middle-aged.
At each window such rustlings!
The trees persist, yeasty and sensuous,
as thick as saints.
I see three wet gargoyles covered with birds.
Their skins shine in the sun like leather.

I'm on my bed as light as a sponge.
Soon it will be summer.
She is my mother.
She will tell me a story and keep me asleep
against her plump and fruity skin.
I see leaves—
leaves that are washed and innocent,
leaves that never knew a cellar,
born in their own green blood
like the hands of mermaids.

I do not think of the rusty wagon on the walk.
I pay no attention to the red squirrels
that leap like machines beside the house.
I do not remember the real trunks of the trees
that stand beneath the windows
as bulky as artichokes.
I turn like a giant,
secretly watching, secretly knowing,
secretly naming each elegant sea.

I have misplaced the Van Allen belt,°
the sewers and the drainage,
the urban renewal and the suburban centers.
I have forgotten the names of the literary critics.
I know what I know.
I am the child I was,
living the life that was mine.
I am young and half asleep.
It is a time of water, a time of trees.

THREE GREEN WINDOWS.   31 *Van Allen belt:* radiation belt around the earth, named after
its discoverer, American astrophysicist James A. Van Allen (b. 1914).

WILLIAM SHAKESPEARE   (1564–1616)

Fear No More the Heat o' the Sun° ———————————————— *1623 (ca. 1609)*

Fear no more the heat o' the sun,
  Nor the furious winter's rages;

FEAR NO MORE THE HEAT O' THE SUN. A dirge or lament sung over the supposedly dead
body of Imogen in Act IV of Shakespeare's *Cymbeline.*

Thou thy worldly task hast done,
   Home art gone, and ta'en° thy wages: *taken*
Golden lads and girls all must,   5
   As° chimney-sweepers, come to dust.   *like*

Fear no more the frown o' the great;
   Thou art past the tyrant's stroke;
Care no more to clothe and eat;
   To thee the reed is as the oak;   10
The scepter, learning, physic, must
All follow this, and come to dust.

Fear no more the lightning flash,
   Nor the all-dreaded thunder stone;°
Fear not slander, censure rash;   15
   Thou hast finished joy and moan:°   *sadness*
All lovers young, all lovers must
Consign to thee, and come to dust.

No exorciser harm thee!
Nor no witchcraft charm thee!   20
Ghost unlaid forbear thee!
Nothing ill come near thee!
Quiet consummation have;
And renownéd be thy grave!

14 *thunder stone:* The sound of thunder was believed to be caused by stones falling from the sky.

WILLIAM SHAKESPEARE   (1564–1616)

Sonnet 29: When in Disgrace with Fortune and Men's Eyes _____ *1609*

When, in disgrace with Fortune and men's eyes,
I all alone beweep my outcast state,
And trouble deaf heaven with my bootless° cries,   *futile, useless*
And look upon myself and curse my fate,   5
Wishing me like to one more rich in hope,
Featured like him, like him with friends possessed,
Desiring this man's art and that man's scope,
With what I most enjoy contented least,
Yet in these thoughts myself almost despising;   10
Haply I think on thee, and then my state,
(Like to the lark at break of day arising)
From sullen earth sings hymns at heaven's gate,
For thy sweet love remembered such wealth brings
That then I scorn to change my state with kings.

WILLIAM SHAKESPEARE   (1564–1616)

Sonnet 146: Poor Soul, The Center of My Sinful Earth _____1609

Poor soul, the center of my sinful earth,
Thrall° to these rebel powers that thee array,°   captive
Why dost thou pine within and suffer dearth
Painting thy outward walls so costly gay?
Why so large cost having so short a lease,
Dost thou upon thy fading mansion spend?
Shall worms, inheritors of this excess,
Eat up thy charge? Is this thy body's end?
Then, soul, live thou upon thy servant's loss,°
And let that pine to aggravate thy store;°
Buy terms° divine in selling hours of dross°   periods; refuse
Within be fed, without be rich no more:
So shalt thou feed on Death, that feeds on men,
And Death once dead, there's no more dying then.

POOR SOUL.   2 *array:* surround or dress out, as in a military formation.   9 *thy servant's loss:*
the loss of the body.   10 *let . . . store:* let the body ("that") dwindle ("pine") to increase ("aggravate") the riches ("store") of the soul.

KARL SHAPIRO   (b. 1913)

Auto Wreck _____1941

Its quick soft silver bell beating, beating,
And down the dark one ruby flare
Pulsing out red light like an artery,
The ambulance at top speed floating down
Past beacons and illuminated clocks
Wings in a heavy curve, dips down,
And brakes speed, entering the crowd.
The doors leap open, emptying light;
Stretchers are laid out, the mangled lifted
And stowed into the little hospital.
Then the bell, breaking the hush, tolls once,
And the ambulance with its terrible cargo
Rocking, slightly rocking, moves away,
As the doors, an afterthought, are closed.

We are deranged, walking among the cops
Who sweep glass and are large and composed.
One is still making notes under the light.
One with a bucket douches ponds of blood
Into the street and gutter.

One hangs lanterns on the wrecks that cling,   20
Empty husks of locusts, to iron poles.
Our throats were tight as tourniquets,
Our feet were bound with splints, but now,
Like convalescents intimate and gauche,
We speak through sickly smiles and warn   25
With the stubborn saw of common sense,
The grim joke and the banal resolution.
The traffic moves around with care,
But we remain, touching a wound
That opens to our richest horror.   30
Already old, the question Who shall die?
Becomes unspoken Who is innocent?
For death in war is done by hands;
Suicide has cause and stillbirth, logic;
And cancer, simple as a flower, blooms.   35
But this invites the occult mind,
Cancels our physics with a sneer,
And spatters all we knew of dénouement
Across the expedient and wicked stones.

SIR PHILIP SIDNEY   (1554–1586)

Astrophil and Stella, Number 71———————————— *1591*

Who will in fairest book of Nature know,
How Virtue may best lodged in beauty be,
Let him but learn of Love to read in thee,
Stella, those fair lines, which true goodness show.
There shall he find all vices' overthrow,   5
Not by rude force, but sweetest sovereignty
Of reason, from whose light those night birds fly;
That inward sun in thine eyes shineth so.
And not content to be Perfection's heir
Thyself, dost strive all minds that way to move,   10
Who mark in thee what is in thee most fair.
So while thy beauty draws the heart to love,
As fast thy Virtue bends that love to good:
"But ah," desire still cries, "give me some food."

JON SILKIN   (b. 1930)

Worm————————————————————— *1971*

Look out, they say, for yourself.
The worm doesn't. It is blind

As a sloe; its death by cutting,
Bitter. Its oozed length is ringed,
With parts swollen. Cold and blind
It is graspable, and writhes
In your hot hand; a small snake, unvenomous.
Its seeds furred and moist
It sexes by lying beside another,
In its eking conjunction of seed
Wriggling and worm-like.
Its ganglia are in its head,
And if this is severed
It must grow backwards.
It is lowly, useful, pink. It breaks
Tons of soil, gorging the humus
Its whole length; its shit a fine cast
Coiled in heaps, a burial mound, or like a shell
Made by a dead snail.
It has a life, which is virtuous
As a farmer's, making his own food.
Passionless as a hoe, sometimes, persistent.
Does not want to kill a thing.

LESLIE MARMON SILKO   (b. 1948)

Where Mountain Lion Lay Down with Deer ————————————1974

I climb the black rock mountain
   stepping from day to day
           silently.
I smell the wind for my ancestors
   pale blue leaves
   crushed wild mountain smell.
Returning
   up the gray stone cliff
   where I descended
      a thousand years ago.

Returning to faded black stone
   where mountain lion lay down with deer.
It is better to stay up here
         watching wind's reflection
         in tall yellow flowers.
The old ones who remember me are gone
     the old songs are all forgotten
and the story of my birth.
How I danced in snow-frost moonlight
    distant stars to the end of the Earth,

How I swam away
        in freezing mountain water
        narrow mossy canyon tumbling down
            out of the mountain
                out of the deep canyon stone   25
      down
           the memory
                spilling out
                into the world.

DAVE SMITH (b. 1942)

Bluejays ———————————————————————— *1981*

She tries to call them down,
quicknesses of air.
They bitch and scorn,
they roost away from her.

It isn't that she's brutal.   5
She's just a girl. Worse,
her touch is total.
Her play is dangerous.

Darkly they spit each at each,
from tops of pine and spruce.   10
Her words are shy and sweet,
but it's no use.

Ragged, blue, shrill,
they dart around like boys.
They fear the beautiful   15
but do not fly away.

STEVIE SMITH (1902–1971)

Not Waving But Drowning ————————————————— *1957*

Nobody heard him, the dead man,
But still he lay moaning:
I was much further out than you thought
And not waving but drowning.

Poor chap, he always loved larking   5
And now he's dead
It must have been too cold for him his heart gave way,
They said.

Oh, no no no, it was too cold always
(Still the dead one lay moaning)
I was much too far out all my life
And not waving but drowning.

W. D. SNODGRASS   (b. 1926)

These Trees Stand . . . _____ *1960*

These trees stand very tall under the heavens.
While *they* stand, if I walk, all stars traverse
This steep celestial gulf their branches chart.
Though lovers stand at sixes and at sevens
While civilizations come down with the curse,
Snodgrass is walking through the universe.

I can't make any world go around *your* house.
But note this moon. Recall how the night nurse
Goes ward-rounds, by the mild, reflective art
Of focusing her flashlight on her blouse.
Your name's safe conduct into love or verse;
Snodgrass is walking through the universe.

Your name's absurd, miraculous as sperm
And as decisive. If you can't coerce
One thing outside yourself, why you're the poet!
What irrefrangible atoms whirl, affirm
Their destiny and form Lucinda's skirts!
She can't make up your mind. Soon as you know it,
Your firmament grows touchable and firm.
If all this world runs battlefield or worse,
Come, let us wipe our glasses on our shirts:
Snodgrass is walking through the universe.

CATHY SONG   (b. 1955)

Lost Sister _____ *1983*

1

In China,
even the peasants
named their first daughters
Jade—°
the stone that in the far fields

LOST SISTER.   4 *Jade:* Both the mineral and the name are considered signs of good fortune
and health in China.

could moisten the dry season,
could make men move mountains
for the healing green of the inner hills
glistening like slices of winter melon.
And the daughters were grateful: 10
they never left home.
To move freely was a luxury
stolen from them at birth.
Instead, they gathered patience,
learning to walk in shoes   15
the size of teacups,°
without breaking—
the arc of their movements
as dormant as the rooted willow,
as redundant as the farmyard hens.   20
But they traveled far
in surviving,
learning to stretch the family rice,
to quiet the demons,
the noisy stomachs.   25

2

There is a sister
across the ocean,
who relinquished her name,
diluting jade green
with the blue of the Pacific.   30
Rising with a tide of locusts,
she swarmed with others
to inundate another shore.
In America,
there are many roads   35
and women can stride along with men.

But in another wilderness,
the possibilities,
the loneliness,
can strangulate like jungle vines.   40
The meager provisions and sentiments
of once belonging—
fermented roots, Mah-Jongg° tiles and firecrackers—
set but a flimsy household
in a forest of nightless cities.   45
A giant snake rattles above,
spewing black clouds into your kitchen.

16 *teacups:* Traditionally, girls' feet were bound at the age of seven in China because minuscule feet were considered beautiful and aristocratic. The binding inhibited the natural growth of the feet and made it painful and difficult to walk.   43 *Mah-Jongg:* a Chinese game played with 144 domino-like tiles marked in suits, counters, and dice.

Dough-faced landlords
slip in and out of your keyholes,
making claims you don't understand,
tapping into your communication systems
of laundry lines and restaurant chains.

You find you need China:
your one fragile identification,
a jade link
handcuffed to your wrist.
You remember your mother
who walked for centuries,
footless—
and like her,
you have left no footprints,
but only because
there is an ocean in between,
the unremitting space of your rebellion.

GARY SOTO (b. 1952)

Oranges ————————————————————————*1984*

The first time I walked
With a girl, I was twelve,
Cold, and weighted down
With two oranges in my jacket.
December. Frost cracking
Beneath my steps, my breath
Before me, then gone,
As I walked toward
Her house, the one whose
Porch light burned yellow
Night and day, in any weather.
A dog barked at me, until
She came out pulling
At her gloves, face bright
With rouge. I smiled,
Touched her shoulder, and led
Her down the street, across
A used car lot and a line
Of newly planted trees,
Until we were breathing
Before a drugstore. We
Entered, the tiny bell
Bringing a saleslady
Down a narrow aisle of goods.
I turned to the candies

Tiered like bleachers,
And asked what she wanted—
Light in her eyes, a smile
Starting at the corners
Of her mouth. I fingered   30
A nickel in my pocket,
And when she lifted a chocolate
That cost a dime,
I didn't say anything.
I took the nickel from   35
My pocket, then an orange,
And set them quietly on
The counter. When I looked up,
The lady's eyes met mine,
And held them, knowing   40
Very well what it was all
About.

      Outside,
A few cars hissing past,
Fog hanging like old   45
Coats between the trees.
I took my girl's hand
In mine for two blocks,
Then released it to let
Her unwrap the chocolate.   50
I peeled my orange
That was so bright against
The gray of December
That, from some distance,
Someone might have thought   55
I was making a fire in my hands.

GARY SOTO (b. 1952)

*Kearney Park*_____ *1985*

True Mexicans or not, let's open our shirts
And dance, a spark of heels
Chipping at the dusty cement. The people
Are shiny like the sea, turning
To the clockwork of rancheras,   5
The accordion wheezing, the drum-tap
Of work rising and falling.
Let's dance with our hats in hand.
The sun is behind the trees,
Behind my stutter of awkward steps   10
With a woman who is a brilliant arc of smiles,

An armful of falling water. Her skirt
Opens and closes. My arms
Know no better but to flop
On their own, and we spin, dip
And laugh into each other's faces—
Faces that could be famous
On the coffee table of my abuelita.°   *little grandmother*
But grandma is here, at the park, with a beer
At her feet, clapping
And shouting, "Dance, hijo,° dance!"   *son, child*
Laughing, I bend, slide, and throw up
A great cloud of dust,
Until the girl and I are no more.

EDMUND SPENSER   (1552–1599)

Amoretti° *54: Of This World's Theater in Which We Stay* ———— *1595*

Of this world's theater in which we stay,
My love like the spectator idly sits,
Beholding me that all the pageants° play,   *roles*
Disguising diversly my troubled wits.
Sometimes I joy when glad occasion fits,
And mask in mirth like to a comedy:
Soon after when my joy to sorrow flits,
I wail and make my woes a tragedy.
Yet she, beholding me with constant eye,
Delights not in my mirth nor rues° my smart: *regrets*
But when I laugh, she mocks, and when I cry
She laughs and hardens evermore her heart.
What then can move her? if not mirth nor moan,
She is no woman, but a senseless stone.

AMORETTI 54.   *Amoretti* means "little loves" or "little love songs."

WILLIAM STAFFORD   (1914–1993)

Traveling Through the Dark ———————————— *1960*

Traveling through the dark I found a deer
dead on the edge of the Wilson River road.
It is usually best to roll them into the canyon:
that road is narrow; to swerve might make more dead.

By glow of the tail-light I stumbled back of the car
and stood by the heap, a doe, a recent killing;

she had stiffened already, almost cold.
I dragged her off; she was large in the belly.

My fingers touching her side brought me the reason—
her side was warm; her fawn lay there waiting,   10
alive, still, never to be born.
Beside that mountain road I hesitated.

The car aimed ahead its lowered parking lights;
under the hood purred the steady engine.
I stood in the glare of the warm exhaust turning red;   15
around our group I could hear the wilderness listen.
I thought hard for us all—my only swerving—,
then pushed her over the edge into the river.

GERALD STERN   (b. 1925)

Burying an Animal on the Way to New York _____ *1977*

Don't flinch when you come across a dead animal lying on the road;
you are being shown the secret of life.
Drive slowly over the brown flesh;
you are helping to bury it.
If you are the last mourner there will be no caress   5
at all from the crushed limbs
and you will have to slide over the dark spot imagining
the first suffering all by yourself
Shreds of spirit and little ghost fragments will be spread out
for two miles above the white highway.   10
Slow down with your radio off and your window open
to hear the twittering as you go by.

WALLACE STEVENS   (1879–1955)

The Emperor of Ice-Cream _____ *1923*

Call the roller of big cigars,
The muscular one, and bid him whip
In kitchen cups concupiscent curds.
Let the wenches dawdle in such dress
As they are used to wear, and let the boys   5
Bring flowers in last month's newspapers.
Let be be finale° of seem.
The only emperor is the emperor of ice-cream.

THE EMPEROR OF ICE-CREAM.   7 *finale:* the grand conclusion.

Take from the dresser of deal,°
Lacking the three glass knobs, that sheet
On which she embroidered fantails° once
And spread it so as to cover her face.
If her horny feet protrude, they come
To show how cold she is, and dumb.
Let the lamp affix its beam.
The only emperor is the emperor of ice-cream.

9 *deal:* unfinished pine or fir used to make cheap furniture.   11 *fantails:* fantail pigeons.

MARK STRAND   (b. 1934)

The Remains _____ *1969*

I empty myself of the names of others.
I empty my pockets, I empty my shoes and leave them beside
the road. At night I turn back the clocks; I open the family
album and look at myself as a boy.

What good does it do? The hours have done their job.
I say my own name. I say goodbye.
The words follow each other downwind.
I love my wife but send her away.

My parents rise out of their thrones
into the milky rooms of clouds. How can I sing?
Time tells me what I am. I change and I am the same.
I empty myself of my life and my life remains.

MAY SWENSON   (1919–1989)

Question _____ *1978*

Body my house
my horse my hound
what will I do
when you are fallen

Where will I sleep
How will I ride
What will I hunt

Where can I go
without my mount
all eager and quick
How will I know
in thicket ahead

is danger or treasure
when Body my good
bright dog is dead

How will it be
to lie in the sky
without roof or door
and wind for an eye

With cloud for shift
how will I hide?

15

20

JONATHAN SWIFT   (1667–1745)

A Riddle (The Vowels) ———————————————————— *1746*

We are little airy Creatures,
All of different Voice and Features;
One of us in Glass is set,
One of us you'll find in Jet.
T'other you may see in Tin,
And the fourth a Box within.
If the fifth you shou'd pursue,
It can never fly from you.

5

JAMES TATE   (b. 1943)

The Blue Booby ———————————————————————— *1969*

The blue booby lives
on the bare rocks
of Galápagos°
and fears nothing.
It is a simple life:
they live on fish,
and there are few predators.
Also, the males do not
make fools of themselves
chasing after the young
ladies. Rather,
they gather the blue
objects of the world
and construct from them

5

10

THE BLUE BOOBY.   3 *Galápagos:* islands in the Pacific Ocean on the equator about 600 miles
west of Ecuador where many unique species of animals live.

a nest—an occasional
Gaulois° package,
a string of beads,
a piece of cloth from
a sailor's suit. This
replaces the need for
dazzling plumage;
in fact, in the past
fifty million years
the male has grown
considerably duller,
nor can he sing well.
The female, though,

asks little of him—
the blue satisfies her
completely, has
a magical effect
on her. When she returns
from her day of
gossip and shopping,
she sees he has found her
a new shred of blue foil:
for this she rewards him
with her dark body,
the stars turn slowly
in the blue foil beside them
like the eyes of a mild savior.

16 *Gaulois:* a brand of French cigarettes with a blue package.

ALFRED, LORD TENNYSON   (1809–1892)

Tithonus ——————————————————————— *1860*

The woods decay, the woods decay and fall,
The vapors weep their burthen to the ground,
Man comes and tills the field and lies beneath,
And after many a summer dies the swan.
Me only cruel immortality
Consumes; I wither slowly in thine arms,
Here at the quiet limit of the world,
A white-haired shadow roaming like a dream
The ever-silent spaces of the East,
Far-folded mists, and gleaming halls of morn.
    Alas! for this gray shadow, once a man—
So glorious in his beauty and thy choice,
Who madest him thy chosen, that he seemed

To his great heart none other than a God!
I asked thee, "Give me immortality."   15
Then didst thou grant mine asking with a smile,
Like wealthy men who care not how they give.
But thy strong Hours indignant worked their wills,
And beat me down and marred and wasted me,
And though they could not end me, left me maimed   20
To dwell in presence of immortal youth,
Immortal age beside immortal youth,
And all I was in ashes. Can thy love,
Thy beauty, make amends, though even now,
Close over us, the silver star, thy guide,   25
Shines in those tremulous eyes that fill with tears
To hear me? Let me go; take back thy gift.
Why should a man desire in any way
To vary from the kindly race of men,
Or pass beyond the goal of ordinance   30
Where all should pause, as is most meet for all?
      A soft air fans the cloud apart; there comes
A glimpse of that dark world where I was born.
Once more the old mysterious glimmer steals
From thy pure brows, and from thy shoulders pure,   35
And bosom beating with a heart renewed.
Thy cheek begins to redden through the gloom,
Thy sweet eyes brighten slowly close to mine,
Ere yet they blind the stars, and the wild team
Which love thee, yearning for thy yoke, arise,   40
And shake the darkness from their loosened manes,
And beat the twilight into flakes of fire.
      Lo! ever thus thou growest beautiful
In silence, then before thine answer given
Departest, and thy tears are on my cheek.   45
      Why wilt thou ever scare me with thy tears,
And make me tremble lest a saying learnt,
In days far-off, on that dark earth, be true?
"The Gods themselves cannot recall their gifts."
      Ay me! ay me! with what another heart   50
In days far-off, and with what other eyes
I used to watch—if I be he that watched—
The lucid outline forming round thee; saw
The dim curls kindle into sunny rings;
Changed with thy mystic change, and felt my blood   55
Glow with the glow that slowly crimsoned all
Thy presence and thy portals, while I lay,
Mouth, forehead, eyelids, growing dewy-warm
With kisses balmier than half-opening buds
Of April, and could hear the lips that kissed   60
Whispering I knew not what of wild and sweet,
Like that strange song I heard Apollo sing,

While Ilion like a mist rose into towers.
   Yet hold me not forever in thine East;
How can my nature longer mix with thine?
Coldly thy rose shadows bathe me, cold
Are all thy lights, and cold my wrinkled feet
Upon thy glimmering thresholds, when the steam
Floats up from those dim fields about the homes
Of happy men that have the power to die,
And grassy barrows of the happier dead.
Release me, and restore me to the ground.
Thou seest all things, thou wilt see my grave;
Thou wilt renew thy beauty morn by morn,
I earth in earth forget these empty courts,
And thee returning on thy silver wheels.

DYLAN THOMAS   (1914–1953)

A Refusal to Mourn the Death, by Fire, of a Child in London ————1946

Never until the mankind making
Bird beast and flower
Fathering and all humbling darkness
Tells with silence the last light breaking
And the still hour
Is come of the sea tumbling in harness

And I must enter again the round
Zion of the water bead
And the synagogue of the ear of corn
Shall I let pray the shadow of a sound
Or sow my salt seed
In the least valley of sackcloth to mourn

The majesty and burning of the child's death.
I shall not murder
The mankind of her going with a grave truth
Nor blaspheme down the stations of the breath
With any further
Elegy of innocence and youth.

Deep with the first dead lies London's daughter,
Robed in the long friends,
The grains beyond age, the dark veins of her mother,
Secret by the unmourning water
Of the riding Thames.°
After the first death, there is no other.

A REFUSAL TO MOURN.   23 *Thames:* the River Thames, which flows through London.

CHASE TWICHELL   (b. 1950)

Blurry Cow ————————————————————————————— *1983*

Two cows stand transfixed
by a trough of floating leaves,
facing as if into the camera,
black and white. One stamps
at the hot sting of a deerfly.   5

Seen from the window of a train,
the hoof lifts forever
over hay crosshatched by speed,
and the scales of the haunches
balance. The rest is lost: 10
the head a sudden slur of light,
the dog loping along the tracks
toward a farm yard
where a woman wavers
in her mirage of laundry.   15
A blurry cow, of all things,
strays into the mind's eye,
the afterimage
of this day on earth.

MONA VAN DUYN   (b. 1921)

Advice to a God ————————————————————————— *1971*

Before you leave her, the woman who thought you lavish,
whose body you led to parade without a blush
the touching vulgarity of the *nouveau-riche*,

whose every register your sexual coin   5
crammed full, whose ignorant bush mistook for sunshine
the cold, brazen battering of your rain,

rising, so little spent, strange millionaire
who feels in his loins' pocket clouds of power
gathering again for shower upon golden shower,   10

say to her, since she loves you, "Those as unworldly
as you are fated, and I can afford, to be
may find in Love's bed the perfect economy,

but, in all of his other places, a populace
living in fear of his management, his excess   15
of stingy might and extravagant helplessness.

Turn from him, Danae. I am greater by far,
whose flower reseeds without love for another flower,
whose seas part without loneliness, whose air

brightens or darkens heartlessly. By chance
I have come to you, and a progeny of events,
all that the mind of man calls consequence,

will follow my coming, slaughter and marriage, intrigue,
enchantment, definition of beauty, hag
and hero, a teeming, throwaway catalogue

of the tiniest, riskiest portion of my investment.
Yet pity your great landlord, for if I lent
so much as an ear to you, one loving tenant,

your bankrupt scream as I leave might tempt me to see
all creation in the ungainly, ungodly
throes of your individuality."

TINO VILLANUEVA   (b. 1941)

Day-Long Day ———————————————————— *1972*

Again the drag of pisca,° pisca . . . pisca . . .
Daydreams border on sun-fed hallucinations,
eyes and hands automatically discriminate
whiteness of cotton from field of vision.
Pisca, pisca.
                    "Un Hijo del Sol,"°
                    Genaro Gonzales°

Third-generation timetable.
Sweat day-long dripping into open space;
sun blocks out the sky, suffocates the only breeze.
From el amo desgraciado,° a sentence:

"I wanna bale a day, and the boy here
don't hafta go to school."
*   *   *
In time-binding motion—
a family of sinews and backs,
row-trapped,
zigzagging through summer-long rows
of cotton: Lubbock by way of Wharton.°

DAY-LONG DAY.   EPIGRAPH: *pisca:* picking cotton.   *Un Hijo del Sol:* A Son of the Sun. *Genaro Gonzales:* Hispanic author, born 1949.   4 *el amo desgraciado:* the despicable boss.   11 *Lubbock . . . Wharton:* cities on opposite sides of Texas.

"Está como si escupieran fuego,"° a mother moans
in sweat-patched jeans,
stooping
with unbending dreams.   15
"Estudia para que no seas burro como nosotros,"°
our elders warn, their gloves and cuffs
leaf-stained by seasons.
*   *   *
Bronzed and blurry-eyed by
the blast of degrees,   20
we blend into earth's rotation.
And sweltering toward Saturday, the
day-long day is sunstruck by 6:00 P.M.
One last chug-a-lug from a water jug
old as granddad.   25
Day-long sweat dripping into open space:
Wharton by way of Lubbock.

12 *Está . . . fuego:* "It's as if they are spewing fire."   16 *Estudia . . . nosotros:* "Study so that you will not be a burro like us."

SHELLY WAGNER   (b. ca. 1950)

The Boxes————————————————————— *1991*

When I told the police I couldn't find you,
they began a search that included everything—
even the boxes in the house:
the footlockers of clothes in the attic,
the hamper in the bathroom,   5
and the Chinese lacquered trunk by the sofa.
They made me raise every lid.
I told them you would never stay in a box,
not with all the commotion.
You would have jumped out,   10
found your flashlight
and joined the search.

Poor Thomas, taking these men
who don't know us
through our neighbors' garages   15
where you never played,
hoping they were right
and we were wrong
and he would find you and
snatch you home by the hand   20

so the police cars could
get out of our driveway

and the divers would
get out of our river
because it was certainly
past our bedtime.
We would double-bolt our doors
like always,
say longer prayers than usual
and go to bed. But during the night
I would have sat till morning
beside my sleeping boys.

But that's not what happened.
Thomas is still here, now older.
I still go to his room
when he is sleeping
just to look at him.
I still visit the cemetery,
not as often,
but the urge is the same:
to lie down on the grass,
put my arm around the hump of ground
and tell you, "Get out of this box!
Put a stop to this commotion. Come home.
You should be in bed."

DIANE WAKOSKI   (b. 1937)

The Ring ————————————————————————————————1977

I carry it on my keychain, which itself
is a big brass ring
large enough for my wrist,
holding keys for safe-deposit box,
friends' apartments,
my house, office and faithless car.

I would like to wear it,
the only ornament on my plain body,
but it is a relic,
the husband gone to other wives,
and it could never be a symbol of sharing,
but like the gold it's made of, stands for possession, power,
the security of a throne.

So, on my keyring,
dull from resting in my dark purse,
it hangs, reminding me of failure, of beauty I once had,
of more ancient searches for an enchanted ring.

I understand, now, what that enchantment is, though.
It is being loved.
Or, conversely, loving so much that you feel loved.   20
And the ring hangs there
with my keys,
reminding of failure.

This vain head full of roses,
crystal,   25
bleeding lips,
a voice doomed to listen, forever,
to itself.

ALICE WALKER   (b. 1944)

Revolutionary Petunias ————————————————————— *1972*

Sammy Lou of Rue
sent to his reward
the exact creature who
murdered her husband,
using a cultivator's hoe   5
with verve and skill;
and laughed fit to kill
in disbelief
at the angry, militant
pictures of herself   10
the Sonneteers quickly drew:
not any of them people that
she knew.
A backwoods woman
her house was papered with   15
funeral home calendars and
faces appropriate for a Mississippi
Sunday School. She raised a George,
a Martha, a Jackie and a Kennedy. Also
a John Wesley Junior.°   20
"Always respect the word of God,"
she said on her way to she didn't
know where, except it would be by
electric chair, and she continued
"Don't yall forgit to *water*   25
my purple petunias."

REVOLUTIONARY PETUNIAS.   18–20 *George . . . Junior:* The children are named after George
and Martha Washington, Jackie and John Fitzgerald Kennedy (1917–1963, thirty-fifth U.S. president), and John Wesley (1703–1791), English evangelical preacher who founded Methodism.

EDMUND WALLER   (1606–1687)

Go, Lovely Rose _____ *1645*

Go, lovely rose!
Tell her that wastes her time and me
    That now she knows,
When I resemble° her to thee,   *compare*
How sweet and fair she seems to be.

    Tell her that's young,
And shuns to have her graces spied,
    That hadst thou sprung
In deserts, where no men abide,
Thou must have uncommended died.

    Small is the worth
Of beauty from the light retired;
    Bid her come forth,
Suffer herself to be desired,
And not blush so to be admired.

    Then die! that she
The common fate of all things rare
    May read in thee;
How small a part of time they share
That are so wondrous sweet and fair.

ROBERT PENN WARREN   (1905–1989)

Heart of Autumn _____ *1978*

Wind finds the northwest gap, fall comes.
Today, under gray cloud-scud and over gray
Wind-flicker of forest, in perfect formation, wild geese
Head for a land of warm water, the *boom*, the lead pellet.

Some crumple in air, fall. Some stagger, recover control,
Then take the last glide for a far glint of water. None
Knows what has happened. Now, today, watching
How tirelessly *V* upon *V* arrows the season's logic,

Do I know my own story? At least, they know
When the hour comes for the great wing-beat. Sky-strider,
Star-strider—they rise, and the imperial utterance,
Which cries out for distance, quivers in the wheeling sky.

That much they know, and in their nature know
The path of pathlessness, with all the joy

Of destiny fulfilling its own name.   15
I have known time and distance, but not why I am here.

Path of logic, path of folly, all
The same—and I stand, my face lifted now skyward,
Hearing the high beat, my arms outstretched in the tingling
Process of transformation, and soon tough legs,   20

With folded feet, trail in the sounding vacuum of passage,
And my heart is impacted with a fierce impulse
To unwordable utterance—
Toward sunset, at a great height.

BRUCE WEIGL   (b. 1949)

*Song of Napalm*_____ *1985*

For My Wife

After the storm, after the rain stopped pounding,
We stood in the doorway watching horses
Walk off lazily across the pasture's hill.
We stared through the black screen,
Our vision altered by the distance   5
So I thought I saw a mist
Kicked up around their hooves when they faded
Like cut-out horses
Away from us.
The grass was never more blue in that light, more   10
Scarlet; beyond the pasture
Trees scraped their voices in the wind, branches
Criss-crossed the sky like barbed-wire
But you said they were only branches.

Okay. The storm stopped pounding.   15
I am trying to say this straight: for once
I was sane enough to pause and breathe
Outside my wild plans and after the hard rain
I turned my back on the old curses, I believed
They swung finally away from me . . .   20

But still the branches are wire
And thunder is the pounding mortar,
Still I close my eyes and see the girl
Running from her village, napalm
Stuck to her dress like jelly,   25
Her hands reaching for the no one
Who waits in waves of heat before her.

So I can keep on living,
So I can stay here beside you,
I try to imagine she runs down the road and wings
Beat inside her until she rises
Above the stinking jungle and her pain
Eases, and your pain, and mine.
But the lie swings back again.
The lie works only as long as it takes to speak
And the girl runs only so far
As the napalm allows
Until her burning tendons and crackling
Muscles draw her up
Into that final position
Burning bodies so perfectly assume. Nothing
Can change that; she is burned behind my eyes
And not your good love and not the rain-swept air
And not the jungle green
Pasture unfolding before us can deny it.

PHYLLIS WHEATLEY   (1754–1784)

On Being Brought from Africa to America ———————— *1773*

'Twas mercy brought me from my *Pagan* land,
Taught my benighted soul to understand
That there's a God, that there's a *Saviour* too:
Once I redemption neither sought nor knew.
Some view our sable race with scornful eye,
"Their colour is a diabolic die."
Remember, *Christians, Negroes,* black as *Cain,*
May be refin'd, and join th' angelic train.

RICHARD WILBUR   (b. 1921)

The Sirens ———————————————————— *1950*

I never knew the road
From which the whole earth didn't call away,
With wild birds rounding the hill crowns,
Haling out of the heart an old dismay,
Or the shore somewhere pounding its slow code,
Or low-lighted towns
Seeming to tell me, stay.

Lands I have never seen
And shall not see, loves I will not forget,

All I have missed, or slighted, or foregone   10
Call to me now. And weaken me. And yet
I would not walk a road without a scene.
I listen going on,
The richer for regret.

WILLIAM CARLOS WILLIAMS   (1883–1963)

The Red Wheelbarrow ———————————————————— *1923*

    so much depends
    upon

    a red wheel
    barrow

    glazed with rain   5
    water

    beside the white
    chickens.

WILLIAM WORDSWORTH   (1770–1850)

Lines Written in Early Spring ———————————————— *1798*

I heard a thousand blended notes,
While in a grove I sate° reclined,   *sat*
In that sweet mood when pleasant thoughts
Bring sad thoughts to the mind.

To her fair works did Nature link   5
The human soul that through me ran;
And much it grieved my heart to think
What man has made of man.

Through primrose tufts, in that green bower,
The periwinkle° trailed its wreaths;   10
And 'tis my faith that every flower
Enjoys the air it breathes.

The birds around me hopped and played,
Their thoughts I cannot measure—
But the least motion which they made,   15
It seemed a thrill of pleasure.

LINES WRITTEN IN EARLY SPRING.   10 *periwinkle:* a trailing evergreen plant with blue or
white flowers.

The budding twigs spread out their fan,
To catch the breezy air;
And I must think, do all I can,
That there was pleasure there.

If this belief from heaven be sent,
If such be Nature's holy plan,
Have I not reason to lament
What man has made of man?

WILLIAM WORDSWORTH   (1770–1850)

The Solitary Reaper —————————————————————————— *1807*

Behold her, single in the field,
Yon solitary Highland Lass!
Reaping and singing by herself;
Stop here, or gently pass!

Alone she cuts and binds the grain,
And sings a melancholy strain;
O listen! for the Vale profound
Is overflowing with the sound.

No Nightingale did ever chaunt
More welcome notes to weary bands
Of travelers in some shady haunt,
Among Arabian sands;
A voice so thrilling ne'er was heard
In springtime from the Cuckoo bird,
Breaking the silence of the seas
Among the farthest Hebrides.°

Will no one tell me what she sings?°
Perhaps the plaintive numbers flow
For old, unhappy, far-off things,
And battles long ago;
Or is it some more humble lay,
Familiar matter of today?
Some natural sorrow, loss, or pain,
That has been, and may be again?

Whate'er the theme, the Maiden sang
As if her song could have no ending;
I saw her singing at her work,
And o'er the sickle bending—

THE SOLITARY REAPER.   16 *Hebrides:* a group of islands belonging to and off the west coast
of Scotland.   17 *Will . . . sings:* The speaker does not understand Scots Gaelic, the language
in which the woman sings.

I listened, motionless and still;
And, as I mounted up the hill,   30
The music in my heart I bore,
Long after it was heard no more.

WILLIAM BUTLER YEATS   (1865–1939)

Sailing to Byzantium°————————————————— *1927*

1

That is no country for old men. The young
In one another's arms, birds in the trees
—Those dying generations—at their song,
The salmon-falls, the mackerel-crowded seas,
Fish, flesh, or fowl, commend all summer long   5
Whatever is begotten, born, and dies.
Caught in that sensual music all neglect
Monuments of unaging intellect.

2

An aged man is but a paltry thing.
A tattered coat upon a stick, unless   10
Soul clap its hands and sing, and louder sing
For every tatter in its mortal dress,
Nor is there singing school but studying
Monuments of its own magnificence;
And therefore I have sailed the seas and come   15
To the holy city of Byzantium.

3

O sages standing in God's holy fire
As in the gold mosaic of a wall,
Come from the holy fire, perne in a gyre,°
And be the singing-masters of my soul.   20
Consume my heart away; sick with desire
And fastened to a dying animal
It knows not what it is; and gather me
Into the artifice of eternity.

4

Once out of nature I shall never take   25
My bodily form from any natural thing,
But such a form as Grecian goldsmiths make
Of hammered gold and gold enameling

SAILING TO BYZANTIUM.   In Yeats's private mythology, Byzantium (called Constantinople in Roman times and Istanbul today) symbolizes art, artifice, sophistication, and eternity as opposed to the natural world and physicality.   19 *perne in a gyre:* turning about in a spiral motion. See the diagram on p. 811.

To keep a drowsy Emperor awake;
Or set upon a golden bough to sing
To lords and ladies of Byzantium
Of what is past, or passing, or to come.

PAUL ZIMMER   (b. 1934)

The Day Zimmer Lost Religion ————————————————————————*1973*

The first Sunday I missed Mass on purpose
I waited all day for Christ to climb down
Like a wiry flyweight° from the cross and
Club me on my irreverent teeth, to wade into
My blasphemous gut and drop me like a
Red hot thurible,° the devil roaring in
Reserved seats until he got the hiccups.

It was a long cold way from the old days
When cassocked and surpliced° I mumbled Latin
At the old priest and rang his obscure bell.
A long way from the dirty wind that blew
The soot like venial sins° across the schoolyard
Where God reigned as a threatening,
One-eyed triangle high in the fleecy sky.

The first Sunday I missed Mass on purpose
I waited all day for Christ to climb down
Like the playground bully, the cuts and mice
Upon his face agleam, and pound me
Till my irreligious tongue hung out.
But of course He never came, knowing that
I was grown up and ready for Him now.

THE DAY ZIMMER LOST RELIGION.   3 *flyweight:* a boxer weighing less than 112 pounds.
6 *thurible:* a censer, a container in which incense is burned.   9 *cassocked and surpliced:* wearing
the traditional garb of an altar boy during Mass.   12 *venial sins:* minor inadvertent sins.

DRAMA

Theatre of Dionysus, Athens

26

Drama: An Overview

The word **drama** is derived from the Greek word *dran*, which means "to do" or "to act," and *doing* and *acting* have always been drama's major characteristics. Although the word sometimes refers to a single **play**, it may also refer to a group of plays (*Elizabethan drama*) or to all plays collectively (*world drama*). A person who writes plays is a **dramatist** or a **playwright**. (*Playwright* is a word combining *play* with the word *wright*—a worker or builder).

DRAMA AND PERFORMANCE

The text of a play consists of **dialogue, monologue,** and **stage directions.** *Dialogue* is the conversation of two or more characters. A *monologue* is spoken by a single character who is usually alone on stage. *Stage directions* are the playwright's instructions about vocal expression, "body language," stage appearance, lighting, and similar matters.

Performance: The Life of a Play

Although drama shares many characteristics with fiction and poetry, the most important difference is that plays are written to be presented by actors on a stage before an audience. The actors *perform* the various actions and also *mimic* or *imitate* the emotions of the major characters, in order to create a maximum impact on the audience. It is **performance** that creates the movement, immediacy, and excitement of drama.

ACTORS. Actors bring the characters and the dialogue to life—loving or hating, strutting or cringing, shouting or whispering, laughing or crying, and inspiring or deceiving. Actors give their bodies and emotions to the characters, providing vocal quality and inflection, gestures, and facial expressions.

They move about the stage according to patterns called **blocking**. They also engage in **stage business**—gestures or movements that keep the production active, dynamic, and often funny.

COSTUMES AND MAKEUP. Actors also make the play vivid by wearing **costumes** and using **makeup,** which help the audience understand the time period, occupation, mentality, and social status of the characters. Costumes may be used realistically (a king in rich robes, a salesman in a rumpled business suit) or symbolically (the use of black clothing for a character suffering depression). Makeup usually enhances an actor's facial features, but it also may help fix the illusion of youth or age or emphasize a character's joy or sorrow.

THE DIRECTOR AND PRODUCER. In the theater, all aspects of performance are controlled by the **director**, the person who plans the production in association with the **producer**, who takes responsibility for financing and arranging the physical aspects of the production. The director tells the actors to move, speak, and act in ways that are consistent with his or her vision of the play. When a play calls for special effects, as in Molière's *Love Is the Doctor,* the director and producer work with specialists such as musicians, choreographers, and sound technicians to enhance and enliven the performance.

THE STAGE. Most modern plays are performed on a **proscenium stage** (like a room with one wall missing so that the audience may look in on the action), a **thrust stage** (an acting area that projects into the audience), or a **theater-in-the-round** (an area that is surrounded by the audience). Regardless of the kind of stage, the modern theater is likely to provide **scenery** and **properties** (or **props**), which locate the action in place and time, and which underscore the ideas of the director. The **sets** (the appurtenances for a particular scene) may change a number of times during a performance, as in *Hamlet,* or a single set may be used throughout, as in *Oedipus the King.*

LIGHTING. Today's theater relies heavily on **lighting**. Until the seventeenth century, however, lights were not used in the theater. Before then, plays were performed during the day and under the sky, in inn yards and in courtyard-like theaters like the Globe Theatre, in which many of Shakespeare's plays were first performed. Because open-air performances depended on favorable weather, plays were eventually taken indoors, and theaters then relied on candles, and later gaslight, for lighting effects (yes, some theaters burned down). The development of electric lights in the late nineteenth century revolutionized dramatic productions. For today's performances, producers may use spotlights, filters, dimmers, and other lighting technology to emphasize various parts of the stage, to shape the mood of a scene, and to highlight individual characters. In productions of plays like *The Glass Menagerie* and *Death of a Salesman,* lighting is even used to indicate changes in time or place.

THE AUDIENCE. The **audience** plays a significant role in a theatrical performance. The reactions of spectators to the onstage action provide instant feedback to the actors, and thus continually influence the delivery and pace of the performance. Similarly, the audience, sitting together in a darkened auditorium, offers a communal response to the play. Thus, drama *in the theater* is the most immediate and accessible of the literary arts. There is no intermediary between the audience and the stage action—no narrator, as in prose fiction, and no speaker, as in poetry.

Full-Length Plays and Short Plays

The basic forms of drama are **full-length plays** and **short plays**, just as in fiction the basic forms are novels and short stories. Full-length plays, also sometimes called *regular plays,* may consist of three, four, or five separate acts (*A Doll House, Hamlet*), a long series of separate scenes (*Oedipus the King* and *The Glass Menagerie*), or two long acts (*Death of a Salesman*). Such plays are designed for a full performance of three or more hours (with intermissions); they provide for complete and in-depth development of character, conflict, and idea. Full-length plays containing separate acts, like *A Midsummer Night's Dream*, are also subdivided. These subdivisions, or **scenes**, are not always noted in the text, but often they are given formal scene numbers. Characteristic of scenes are a coherent action, a unified setting, and a fixed group of characters, much like sections and chapters in novels.

Short plays, usually consisting of one act, do not permit extensive development and subdivision. They are not commercially self-sustaining unless two or three of them are put together for an entire evening in the theater. However, one-act plays may be used for studio and classroom performance, or, for that matter, for adaptation as hour- or half-hour performances for film or television. Usually, one-act plays like *Before Breakfast* and *The Bear* flow smoothly from beginning to end without a break. On the other hand, somewhat longer short plays, like *Love Is the Doctor* and *Am I Blue,* may contain formal scene and act divisions. *Love Is the Doctor* is unique because it features **French scenes**, in which a new scene begins each time a character enters or leaves the stage.

TYPES OF DRAMA

In our times we do not even have to go to the theater to have drama at our fingertips. We can find virtually everything on the television screen. Some representative samples are situation comedies, continuous narrative dramas (including soap operas), made-for-TV films, short skits on comedy shows, and many other types. All these various genres ultimately spring from the drama that was developed originally in ancient Greece twenty-five hundred years ago. Although the centuries have produced many variations, the types the Greeks created are still as important today as they were then. They are *tragedy* and *comedy.*[1]

---

[1] Fuller discussions of tragedy and comedy are given in Chapters 27 and 28.

The Development of Tragedy and Comedy

During the sixth century B.C. in ancient Athens, episodes from the lives of the many Grecian religious cult heroes were celebrated in public choral performances of poetry during yearly religious festivals. Drama as we know it, specifically **tragedy**, began when a small number of choral members started to impersonate the heroes and other important figures; impersonation or imitation was the key. The heroes of course were noteworthy for their achievements, but they were not immortal and they suffered death, and they also experienced grief and sorrow. Therefore the dramatizations about them, which were called *tragedies* ("goat songs") by the Greeks, portrayed their tribulations and often even their deaths. It was this pattern of drama that during the fifth century B.C. produced the powerful tragedies that are represented by the surviving plays of Aeschylus, Sophocles, and Euripides. The pattern also led to our common understanding today that tragedy recounts an individual's death or downfall, beginning high and ending low.

Not long afterward, **comedy** became an additional feature of the yearly festivals. Because the ancient Athenians tolerated great freedom of speech, the comedy writers created a boisterous, lewd, and freely critical type of comedy, known as "Old Comedy." In the fourth century B.C., when Athenian power and freedom of speech were in decline, this type of comedy was replaced by "Middle Comedy," a more social, discreet, and international drama, and then by "New Comedy," a type of play featuring the development of plot, situation, and character that has also been called "comedy of manners." New Comedy gave rise to the type of play that dramatizes the regeneration of individuals, beginning in doubt and ending in success.

The two Greek forms (tragedy and comedy) were adopted by the Romans during the periods of the Republic (before 29 B.C.) and the Empire (after 29 B.C.). Although Republican Rome produced writers of note who created comedies, the only significant playwright during the days of the Empire was the tragedian Seneca (4 B.C.–A.D. 65), who wrote "closet dramas"—that is, plays for reading and not performing.

After the breakup of the Roman Empire in the west (Fifth century A.D.), drama was all but forgotten. When it reemerged it had nothing to do with the Greek and Roman dramatic tradition because it took place in the churches. Beginning about the eleventh and twelfth centuries, special short dramatizations took place during Easter and Christmas masses. By the end of the thirteenth century, plays had become too long and complex to be performed as part of religious services. Accordingly, they were moved outdoors, and were performed during the spring or early summer as a part of post-Easter celebrations, particularly *Corpus Christi Day*. These dramatizations, called **Mystery Plays** or **Corpus Christi Plays**, were collections or cycles of plays dramatizing Biblical stories such as Adam and Eve, Cain and Abel, Noah, Abraham and Isaac, Herod, the Shepherds Abiding in the Field, the trial of Jesus, and the Crucifixion and Resurrection. Later, another type of play developed, the **Morality Play**, the objective of which was how to live a Christian life.

By the sixteenth century, drama became liberated from these religious foundations and began rendering the twists and turns of purely human conflicts. It was at this time also that a revival of the culture and drama of ancient Greece and Rome began. Therefore, the performing tradition growing out of the medieval church was combined with the surviving classical tragedies and comedies to create an entirely new drama that quickly reached its highest point in the plays of Shakespeare. In this way, tragedy and comedy, the forms originated by the Greeks, had a new beginning during the Renaissance in Europe.

Other Types of Drama Flowing from Tragedy and Comedy

The new Renaissance drama was by no means a copy of ancient forms, however, even though a number of sixteenth- and seventeenth-century playwrights (including Shakespeare) rewrote or reworked many of the ancient plays. The plays of Renaissance England, and later the plays of the United States, offer a mixture of the forms of tragedy and comedy. For example, Shakespeare's tragedies include witty and humorous scenes, and his comedies often deal with serious and threatening problems. When the patterns and emotions are truly mixed, the play is called a **tragicomedy**, a term first used by the Roman playwright Plautus (254–184 b.c.). In many ways tragicomedy is the dominant form of twentieth-century drama.

Other forms of drama that have evolved from tragedy and comedy include **farce**, **melodrama**, and **social drama**. *Farce*, which was also a strong element in the Greek Old Comedy, is intended to make audiences laugh. Typically, it is crammed full of slapstick stage business and extravagant dialogue, with exaggerated emotions and rapid extremes of action. Chekhov's *The Bear* is a good example of farce, as are the scenes featuring the "mechanicals" in Shakespeare's *A Midsummer Night's Dream*. In *melodrama* the characterizations are exaggerated and the villains are especially villainous. There is, for example, a great element of melodrama in O'Neill's *Before Breakfast,* and Chekhov's Mrs. Popov of *The Bear* begins as a melodramatic character. Melodrama as a pure form brings characters to the brink of ruin, only to be saved by the hero, who always arrives just in time, and with superhuman resources and strength pays the mortgage, saves the business, and rescues the heroine, while the grumbling villain flees the stage saying something like "Curses, foiled again!"

Social drama, sometimes called *problem drama*, evolved in the nineteenth century. This type of play explores social problems and the individual's place in society. The plays can be tragic, comic, or mixed. Examples of social drama are Ibsen's *A Doll House*, Glaspell's *Trifles*, and Miller's *Death of a Salesman*.

Despite all these terms and types, keep in mind that classification is not the goal of reading or seeing plays. It is less important to identify *Am I Blue* as a comedy or *Before Breakfast* as a melodramatic tragedy than it is to understand and share the experiences and ideas that each play offers.

THE BASIC ELEMENTS OF DRAMA

The basic elements of drama are *plot, character, point of view, setting, language, tone, symbolism,* and *theme* or *meaning.* Poetic drama, such as Shakespeare's *Hamlet* and *A Midsummer Night's Dream,* add poetic elements such as *meter* and *rhyme.* All these elements have remained relatively constant throughout the history of drama.

Plot, Action, and Conflict

Plot, in drama as in fiction, is an ordered chain of physical, emotional, or intellectual events that ties the action together (see also Chapter 3). It is a planned sequence of interrelated actions that begins in a state of imbalance, grows out of conflict, reaches a peak of complication, and resolves into some new situation. It is easy to oversimplify the idea of plot in a play. Dramatic plots are often more complicated than a single movement toward a single solution or resolution. Some plays have **double plots**—two different but related lines of action going on at the same time. Other plays offer a **main plot**, together with a **subplot** that comments, either directly or indirectly, on the main plot. In *A Midsummer Night's Dream,* four separate plots are woven together to form a single story.

The mainspring of plot in a play is **conflict**, which can be physical, psychological, social, or all three. It can involve a character's struggle against another person, against the environment, or against himself or herself. Most commonly, the conflict in a play is a combination of these general types. In Albee's *The Sandbox,* for example, Grandma is in conflict with her family, society, and death. Similarly, the hero in *Hamlet* is in conflict with himself, his enemies, and his society—all at the same time. Conflict in drama can be more explicit than in prose fiction because we actually see the clash of wills and characters on stage or on the page.

A classic full-length play, sometimes called a **regular play** (*i.e.,* conforming to *rule*), has a five-stage *plot structure*—exposition, complication, crisis or climax, catastrophe, and resolution. The German critic Gustav Freytag (1816–1895) compares this pattern to a pyramid, in which the rising action (exposition and complication) leads up to the point of crisis or climax and is followed by the falling action (the catastrophe and resolution).

The Freytag Pyramid of Plot Structure

1. Exposition or Introduction
2. Complication and Development
3. Climax or Crisis
4. Falling Action, Catastrophe
5. Resolution or Dénouement

In the first of these stages, the **exposition**, the audience receives essential background information; we are introduced to the characters, the situations, and the conflicts. In *Oedipus the King* this material is conveyed in the prologue. Other playwrights might have several characters discuss the people in the play and the crucial events that have occurred before the beginning of the play's action. In *Hamlet*, for example, the conversations of Barnardo, Marcellus, and Horatio provide critical information. Other plays distribute the information throughout the entire action, as in *Trifles*.

In the second stage, the **complication**, the conflicts grow heated and the plot becomes more involved. As the complication develops, the situation becomes more and more tightly knotted, leading to the most excruciating part of the play—the **crisis** or **climax**—which is the *turning point* or *high point*. In this third stage, the hero or heroine faces an agonizing decision and almost simultaneously chooses a course of action (for better or worse) that determines the outcome.

The pyramid begins its downward slope in stage four, the **catastrophe** (an "overturning"). In the catastrophe (not to be confused with our modern use of the term to mean "disaster"), all the pieces and strands of the plot fall into place. It is often caused by the discovery of certain information or events that have been unknown to most of the characters up to that instant. During the final stage, the **resolution** or **dénouement**, conflicts are resolved, lives are straightened out or ended, loose ends are tied up, and the play ends.

Since the days of Shakespeare, English dramatists have generally been more concerned with *dramatic effect* than with *dramatic form*. As a result, many plays in English do not perfectly follow the regular structure outlined here. The pattern is rather an abstract model, which individual dramatists vary at will. You should therefore be prepared for plays that offer little exposition, have no dénouement, compress the crisis-climax-catastrophe-resolution into a short space, or modify the formal pattern in some other significant way.

Character

A **character** is a person created by the playwright to carry the action, language, ideas, and emotions of the play. Many of the types of characters that populate prose fiction are also found in drama (see Chapter 4). In drama as in fiction, for instance, we find both *round* and *flat* characters. A **round character**, like Shakespeare's Hamlet and Ibsen's Nora, undergoes a change or development as the play progresses. On the other hand, a **flat character**, like Molière's Lisette, is undeveloped, even though she or he may be interesting, vital, and amusing. As in fiction, dramatic characters can also be considered **static**—that is, fixed and unchanging—or **dynamic**—that is, growing and developing.

Because drama, like fiction, depends on conflict, we also find protagonists and antagonists in plays. The **protagonist** is usually the central character in the action. The **antagonist** opposes the protagonist and is often a villain. A classic opposition of this type may be seen in *Hamlet*, in which Prince

Hamlet is the protagonist while his uncle King Claudius is the antagonist. The play develops as Hamlet the protagonist tries first to confirm, and then to punish, the villainy of his uncle the antagonist

There are also characters who set off or highlight the protagonist, and others who are peripheral. The first of these types, the **foil**, is somewhat like the protagonist, but with contrasting qualities. In *Hamlet*, for instance, both Laertes and Fortinbras are foils to Hamlet. The second type, called a **choric figure**, is rooted in the choruses of Greek tragedy, and is usually played by a single character, often a friend or confidant of the protagonist, such as Horatio in *Hamlet*. If this type of character provides commentary about the play's major issues and actions, he or she is called a **raisonneur** (the French word meaning *reasoner*) or **commentator**.

Dramatic characters may be **realistic**, **nonrealistic**, **symbolic**, and **stereotyped** or **stock**. Realistic characters are normally accurate imitations of individualized men and women; they are given backgrounds, personalities, desires, motivations, and thoughts. Nonrealistic characters are usually stripped of such individualizing touches; they are often undeveloped and symbolic. All of the characters in *The Sandbox* are nonrealistic. Symbolic characters represent an idea, a way of life, moral values, or some other abstraction. The two women in *Tea Party* symbolize the agonized loneliness of old age, while Dr. Fillpocket in *Love is the Doctor* symbolizes cynicism, greed, charlatanism, and the misuse of responsibility.

Stereotyped or stock characters have been used in drama (and other types of literature) throughout the ages. In effect they serve as a shortcut in characterization. The general types developed in classical and Renaissance drama are the *bumpkin*, the *braggart*, the *trickster*, the *victim*, the *stubborn father*, the *shrewish wife*, the *lusty youth*, and the *prodigal son*. Modern drama continues these stereotypes, and it has also invented many of its own, such as the *hardboiled detective*, the *loner cowboy*, the *honest policeman*, and the *whore with a heart of gold*.

The major difference between characters in fiction or poetry and characters in drama is the way they are revealed. Playwrights do not have the fiction writer's freedom to describe a character directly. We therefore must listen to the words of characters, watch and interpret their actions, heed what other characters say about them, and observe what other characters do to them.

Point of View and Perspective

Point of view in drama is strikingly different from the comparable element in fiction and poetry (see also Chapter 5). With the exception of works like Tennessee Williams's *The Glass Menagerie*, plays rarely have narrators, and it is difficult for a playwright to sustain a perspective that is exclusively first-person-protagonist or third-person-omniscient. Instead, playwrights employ the **dramatic point of view**, whereby the playwright gives us the objective raw materials—the actions and the words—but arranges them in such a way that we ourselves must draw all the conclusions.

Within these limits, playwrights do have techniques to lead an audience to see things from a specific character's perspective. In O'Neill's *Before Breakfast*, the entire play is a monologue spoken by Mrs. Rowland. Another commonly used device is the **soliloquy**, in which a character reveals his or her thoughts directly to the audience. In plays from the sixteenth- and seventeenth-century, soliloquies are common, and in the twentieth century, soliloquies have again become an important element in experimental and nonrealistic drama. Another device, called the **aside**, allows a character to address brief remarks to the audience—or to another character—which the other characters do not hear.

Setting or Scenery

A play's **scenery** or **setting** is what we first see on the stage, and it brings the written directions to life through backdrops, furnishings, properties, and lighting. The function of scenery is to establish plays in specific places and times and also to determine the level of reality.

Like characters, the setting may be realistic or nonrealistic. A **realistic setting** requires extensive construction and properties, for the object is to create as lifelike a stage as possible. In *Trifles*, for example, the setting is a realistic copy of an early twentieth-century midwestern farm kitchen. A **nonrealistic setting** is nonrepresentational and often symbolic, as in *The Sandbox*, where the scenery consists of a sandbox and a number of chairs. Often such scenery is produced in a **unit set**—a series of platforms, rooms, stairs, and exits that form the locations for all the play's actions, as in *Death of a Salesman*.

Generally, one-act plays rely on a single setting and a short imagined time of action, as with *The Bear*, *Trifles*, *Tea Party*, and *Before Breakfast*. Many full-length plays also confine the action to a single setting and a short time of action, as with Sophocles' *Oedipus the King*, which takes place in less than a day of imagined time before the royal palace in ancient Thebes. Other longer plays may extend imagined time while being set in the same location, as in *The Glass Menagerie*, in which all the action takes place, in a rather long imagined time, in the apartment home of the Wingfields. Some full-length plays change settings frequently just as they also stretch out imagined time. *Hamlet* takes place in a number of different locations, including battlements, a throne room, bed chambers, castle halls, and a graveyard (all these scene changes put great strain on a production committed to realistic scene design).

Diction, Imagery, Style, and Language

Most of what we learn about characters, relationships, and conflict is conveyed through dramatic language (see also Chapter 7). Characters tell us what they think, hope, fear, and desire. Their dialogue may reflect the details of their daily lives or their deepest thoughts about life and death. Their words must fit the circumstances, the time, and the place of the play. Thus it would be as wrong for Miller's Willy Loman to speak in Elizabethan blank verse as it would be for Shakespeare's Hamlet to speak in modern American English.

The words and rhetorical devices of a play delineate character, emotion, and theme, much as they do in fiction and poetry. Dramatists may employ words that have wide-ranging connotations or that acquire many layers of meaning. Such is the case with the words *trifle* and *knot* in Glaspell's play *Trifles*. Similarly, playwrights may have their characters speak in similes or metaphors that contribute significantly to the play's meaning and impact. Again in *Trifles*, one of the characters compares another to a bird, and this simile grows to become one of the play's central symbols.

Dramatists may also employ accents, dialects, idiom, jargon, and cliché to indicate character traits. The characters in *The Sandbox*, for example, speak in clichés that mark their limitations and shortcomings. The Gravedigger in *Hamlet* speaks in an Elizabethan dialect which distinguishes him from the aristocratic persons in the play. Most of the characters in *The Glass Menagerie* speak in dialect, complete with slang expressions, that locates them in the Southern United States.

Tone and Atmosphere

Tone in drama, as in fiction and poetry, signifies the way moods and attitudes are created and presented (See also Chapter 8, pp. 294–321). In plays, tone may be conveyed directly to the spectator through voice and through the stage gestures that accompany dialogue, such as rolling one's eyes, throwing up one's hands, shaking one's head, jumping for joy, and staggering in grief. Even silence can be an effective device for creating tone and mood.

Whereas voice and movement establish tone on the stage, we have no such exacting guides while reading a play. Sometimes a playwright indicates the tone of specific lines through stage directions. In *The Sandbox*, for instance, Albee prefaces many speeches with directions such as *whining, vaguely, impatiently,* and *mocking.* These cues to tone are intended for the actors, but they also help readers. When such directions are lacking, the diction, tempo, imagery, and context all become clues to the tone of specific speeches and whole plays.

Tone may create an atmosphere or mood that dominates a play. Consider the opening scene of *Hamlet*, in which Shakespeare uses tempo and diction to create an atmosphere of fear and apprehension. It is dark and close to midnight, and Francisco, one of the guards, carries a torch:

BARNARDO. Who's there?
FRANCISCO. Nay, answer me. Stand and unfold yourself.
BARNARDO. Long live the king!
FRANCISCO. Barnardo?
BARNARDO. He.

Notice the short lines, the questions, and the choppy and rapid exchange. The tone of the dialogue is anxious and questioning. The exchange thus suggests nervousness, tension, and insecurity. When Hamlet later says that things are bad in Denmark, these opening phrases have established a groundwork that confirms his conclusion.

One of the most common methods employed by playwrights to control the tone of the play is **dramatic irony**. This type of **situational** (as opposed to **verbal**) irony may be created in any circumstance where the audience knows more than the characters in a play or when one or two characters know more than the others. In *Trifles*, one of the male characters mockingly dismisses the women's concerns by noting that "women are used to worrying about such trifles." The line acquires vast dramatic irony as we watch Mrs. Hale and Mrs. Peters achieve understanding through careful attention to the "trifles" that the men ignore.

Symbolism and Allegory

In drama, as in fiction and poetry, the meaning of **symbols** extends beyond the apparent meaning of the symbol itself (see also Chapters 9 and 21). Dramatic symbols, which may be characters, settings, objects, actions, situations, or statements, may be both universal and private. **Cultural** or **universal symbols**—such as crosses, flags, snakes, flowers—are generally understood by the audience or reader regardless of the context in which they appear. In Act V of *Hamlet*, for example, we recognize Yorick's skull as a symbol of death. **Contextual** or **private symbols** develop their impact only within the context of a specific play or even a particular scene. We often don't realize at first that such objects or actions are symbolic; they acquire symbolic meaning only through context and continued action. *The Sandbox*, for instance, opens with a "large child's sandbox with a toy pail and shovel" on stage. Initially, these objects seem to have little significance. As the play goes on, however, we realize that the sandbox symbolizes a lifetime of ease (a beach), advancing senility, the waste products of life, and, finally, death and the grave.

When a play offers consistent and sustained symbols that refer to general human experiences, that play may be read as an **allegory**. Keller's *Tea Party* dramatizes the preparations that two elderly women make for a young newspaperboy who avoids their party. As an allegory, the play deals with the pathos of the old, who live out their lives with lost memories and hopeless expectations. A more cheerful reading may be applied to Chekhov's *The Bear*, which allegorizes the triumph of love, desire, and life over disappointment, renunciation, and death.

Subject and Theme

Although most playwrights do not seek primarily to persuade or propagandize their audience, they do write their plays to dramatize ideas about the human condition (see also Chapters 10 and 23). The aspects of humanity a playwright explores constitute the play's **subject**. Plays may thus be *about* love, religion, hatred, war, ambition, death, envy, or anything else that is part of the human condition.

The ideas that the play dramatizes about its subject make up the play's **theme** or meaning. Thus, a play might explore the idea that love will always find a way or that marriage may be destructive, that pride always leads to disaster, or that grief can be conquered through strength and a commitment to life. The theme is the end result of all the other elements of drama, and for this reason it is often difficult to isolate and identify. Even short plays may have complex themes, as in Molière's *Love Is the Doctor*, which farcically explores the themes that freedom seeks ways out of suppression, that love is one of the most powerfully inventive human emotions, and that deceit is thoroughly infused within the human spirit and may be as strong as life itself.

Full-length plays may contain even more thematic strands. Ibsen creates such complexity in *A Doll House*, where he deals with themes of selfless devotion, egotism, pompousness, hypocrisy, betrayal, and determination. Some plays may even explore contradictory themes, thus further complicating analysis. For instance, the theme of Sophocles' *Oedipus the King* is that human beings cannot escape the destiny ordained for them by the gods, or by the fates, or by fortune. At the same time, however, it also explores the idea that fate is the result of an individual's personality and choices. These are contradictory themes, but no more contradictory, perhaps, than life itself.

HOW TO READ A PLAY

The clear difference between the text of a play and its production might lead you to ask why we bother to read plays. The most obvious answer is that you may never get a chance actually to *see* the performance of a play you want to learn. We also read plays to familiarize ourselves with important literature. Plays are not simply maps to production; they are a significant and valuable part of our literary heritage. Dramas like *Oedipus the King, Hamlet, Death of a Salesman,* and *The Glass Menagerie* have become cultural touchstones of other works of literature, art, film, and television. Finally, we read plays in order to have the time to study and understand them. Only through reading do we have the opportunity to look at the parts that make up the whole, and to determine how they fit together to create a moving and meaningful experience.

Reading a play, as opposed to watching a performance, carries both advantages and disadvantages. The major *disadvantage* is that you lack the immediacy of live theater. You do not hear the whispers of the murderer and the ranting of the madman, or see the strutting of the soldier and the furtive glances of the conspirators. You do not have the splendor of the palace or the shock of an emptied stage, the spotlight that rivets the audience's attention on a single defiant gesture, the blare of trumpets, or the pathos of the beggar's rags.

The major *advantage* of reading is that you may consider each element in the play at length, and may "stage" the play in your own imagination. In the theater, the action rushes by at the director's pace. There is no opportunity to turn back to an interesting scene or to reconsider an important speech. In addition, a performance always represents someone else's interpretation. The director and the actors have already made choices that emphasize certain avenues of exploration and cut off others. Reading a play lets you avoid these drawbacks, provided that you read attentively and with understanding. You may read at your own tempo, turn back and reread a particular speech or scene, or explore those implications or ideas that strike you as interesting.

Try to use the advantages of reading and study to compensate for the disadvantages. You have time and freedom to read carefully, reflect deeply, and follow your thoughts. Rely on your experiences in watching theatrical productions, movies, and television to enhance your reading. Stage the play as fully as you can in the theater of your mind. Become the director, set designer, lighting technician, costume designer, and all the actors. Build whatever mental sets you like, dress your actors as you see fit, and move the characters across the stage of your mind.

Plays for Study

ANTON CHEKHOV, *THE BEAR*

Chekhov was born in Taganrog in southern Russia in 1860, the son of a merchant and grandson of a serf. He entered medical school in Moscow in 1879, graduating in 1884. While studying he also needed to help support the family, and he made money by writing many stories, jokes, and pot-boilers under a variety of pen names, one of which was "The Doctor without Patients." *The Bear* belongs to the end of this early period, ten years before Chekhov's association with the Moscow Arts Theater at the end of the century (see also p. 1426).

Chekhov spoke slightingly of this play, referring to it as a "joke" and also as a "vaudeville"—both words suggesting a farcical work with little form or substance. Nevertheless, *The Bear* was greatly acclaimed and was a financial success, to the author's amazement and delight. Three months after its first performance in 1888, he likened *The Bear* to a "milk cow" because it earned him a constant supply of money.

The Bear is a farce, a dramatic form designed preeminently to evoke laughter, and it therefore contains extravagant language and boisterous and sudden action. But there is also an underlying seriousness that sustains the humor. In their way, both Smirnov and Mrs. Popov have been failures; they could possibly sink into lives of depression and futility, and both are on a very fine wire as the play begins. Chekhov makes clear that Mrs. Popov is filled with resentment at her unfaithful and now dead husband, and also that she is chafing under her self-imposed resolution to lead a life of mourning and self-denial in his memory. Smirnov is having difficulty with creditors, and admits that his relationships with the many women he has known have ended unhappily. He is therefore both cynical and angry.

The climax of the play is the improbable and preposterous challenge that Smirnov offers to Mrs. Popov, resolved by the equally sudden and preposterous outcome. Despite the improbabilities of the play, however, the actions are not impossible because they manifest the true internal needs of the main characters. Chekhov's friend Tolstoy, who criticized some of Chekhov's late plays, laughed heartily at *The Bear*, and countless audiences and readers since then have joined him in laughter.

ANTON CHEKHOV   (1860–1904)

The Bear: A Joke in One Act _____ *1900*

CAST OF CHARACTERS

> Mrs. Popov. *A widow of seven months, Mrs. Popov is small and pretty, with dimples. She is a landowner. At the start of the play, she is pining away in memory of her dead husband.*
> Grigory Stepanovich Smirnov. *Easily angered and loud, Smirnov is older. He is a landowner, too, and a man of substance.*
> Luka. *Luka is Mrs. Popov's footman (a servant whose main tasks were to wait table and attend the carriages, in addition to general duties). He is old enough to feel secure in telling Mrs. Popov what he thinks.*
> Gardener, Coachman, Workmen, *who enter at the end.*

SCENE. *The drawing room of* MRS. POPOV'S *country home.*

[*MRS. POPOV, in deep mourning, does not remove her eyes from a photograph.*]

LUKA.   It isn't right, madam . . . you're only destroying yourself. . . . The chambermaid and the cook have gone off berry picking; every living being is rejoicing; even the cat knows how to be content, walking around the yard catching birds, and you sit in your room all day as if it were a convent, and you don't take pleasure in anything. Yes, really! Almost a year has passed since you've gone out of the house!

MRS. POPOV.   And I shall never go out. . . . What for? My life is already ended. *He* lies in his grave; I have buried myself in these four walls . . . we are both dead.

LUKA.   There you go again! Your husband is dead, that's as it was meant to be, it's the will of God, may he rest in peace. . . . You've done your mourning and that will do. You can't go on weeping and mourning forever. My wife died when her time came, too. . . . Well? I grieved, I wept for a month, and that was enough for her; the old lady wasn't worth a second more. [*Sighs.*] You've forgotten all your neighbors. You don't go anywhere or accept any calls. We live, so to speak, like spiders. We never see the light. The mice have eaten my uniform. It isn't as if there weren't any nice neighbors—the district is full of them . . . there's a regiment stationed at Riblov, such officers—they're like candy—you'll never get your fill of them! And in the barracks, never a Friday goes by without a dance; and, if you please, the military band plays music every day. . . . Yes, madam, my dear lady: you're young, beautiful, in the full bloom of youth—if only you took a little pleasure in life . . . beauty doesn't last forever, you know! In ten years' time, you'll be wanting to wave your fanny in front of the officers—and it will be too late.

MRS. POPOV. [*determined.*] I must ask you never to talk to me like that! You know that when Mr. Popov died, life lost all its salt for me. It may seem to you that I am alive, but that's only conjecture! I vowed to wear mourning to my grave and not to see the light of day. . . . Do you hear me? May his departed spirit see how much I love him. . . . Yes, I know, it's no mystery to you that he was often mean to me, cruel . . . and even unfaithful, but I shall remain true to the grave and show him I know how to love. There, beyond the grave, he will see me as I was before his death. . . .

LUKA. Instead of talking like that, you should be taking a walk in the garden 5 or have Toby or Giant harnessed and go visit some of the neighbors . . .

MRS. POPOV. Ai! [*She weeps.*]

LUKA. Madam! Dear lady! What's the matter with you! Christ be with you!

MRS. POPOV. Oh, how he loved Toby! He always used to ride on him to visit the Korchagins or the Vlasovs. How wonderfully he rode! How graceful he was when he pulled at the reins with all his strength! Do you remember? Toby, Toby! Tell them to give him an extra bag of oats today.

LUKA. Yes, madam.

[*Sound of loud ringing.*]

MRS. POPOV. [*shudders.*] Who's that? Tell them I'm not at home! 10

LUKA. Of course, madam. [*He exits.*]

MRS. POPOV. [*alone. Looks at the photograph.*] You will see, Nicholas, how much I can love and forgive . . . my love will die only when I do, when my poor heart stops beating. [*Laughing through her tears.*] Have you no shame? I'm a good girl, a virtuous little wife. I've locked myself in and I'll be true to you to the grave, and you . . . aren't you ashamed, you chubby cheeks? You deceived me, you made scenes, for weeks on end you left me alone . . .

LUKA. [*enters, alarmed.*] Madam, somebody is asking for you. He wants to see you. . . .

MRS. POPOV. But didn't you tell them that since the death of my husband, I don't see anybody?

LUKA. I did, but he didn't want to listen; he spoke about some very important 15 business.

MRS. POPOV. I am *not at home!*

LUKA. That's what I told him . . . but . . . the devil . . . he cursed and pushed past me right into the room . . . he's in the dining room right now.

MRS. POPOV. [*losing her temper.*] Very well, let him come in . . . such manners!

[*LUKA goes out.*] How difficult these people are! What does he want from me? Why should he disturb my peace? [*Sighs.*] But it's obvious I'll have to go live in a convent. . . . [*Thoughtfully.*] Yes, a convent. . . .

SMIRNOV.   [*enters while speaking to LUKA.*] You idiot, you talk too much. . . . Ass! [*Sees MRS. POPOV and changes to dignified speech.*] Madam, may I introduce myself: retired lieutenant of the artillery and landowner, Grigory Stepanovich Smirnov! I feel the necessity of troubling you about a highly important matter. . . .

MRS. POPOV.   [*refusing her hand.*] What do you want?

SMIRNOV.   Your late husband, whom I had the pleasure of knowing, has remained in my debt for two twelve-hundred-ruble notes. Since I must pay the interest at the agricultural bank tomorrow, I have come to ask you, madam, to pay me the money today.

MRS. POPOV.   One thousand two hundred. . . . And why was my husband in debt to you?

SMIRNOV.   He used to buy oats from me.

MRS. POPOV.   [*sighing, to LUKA.*] So, Luka, don't you forget to tell them to give Toby an extra bag of oats.

[*LUKA goes out.*]

[*To SMIRNOV.*] If Nikolai, my husband, was in debt to you, then it goes without saying that I'll pay; but please excuse me today. I haven't any spare cash. The day after tomorrow, my steward will be back from town and I will give him instructions to pay you what is owed; until then I cannot comply with your wishes. . . . Besides, today is the anniversary—exactly seven months ago my husband died, and I'm in such a mood that I'm not quite disposed to occupy myself with money matters.

SMIRNOV.   And I'm in such a mood that if I don't pay the interest tomorrow, I'll be owing so much that my troubles will drown me. They'll take away my estate!

MRS. POPOV.   You'll receive your money the day after tomorrow.

SMIRNOV.   I don't want the money the day after tomorrow. I want it today.

MRS. POPOV.   You must excuse me. I can't pay you today.

SMIRNOV.   And I can't wait until after tomorrow.

MRS. POPOV.   What can I do, if I don't have it now?

SMIRNOV.   You mean to say you can't pay?

MRS. POPOV.   I can't pay. . . .

SMIRNOV.   Hm! Is that your last word?

MRS. POPOV.   That is my last word.

SMIRNOV.   Positively the last?

MRS. POPOV.   Positively.

SMIRNOV.   Thank you very much. We'll make a note of that. [*Shrugs his shoulders.*] And people want me to be calm and collected! Just now, on the way here, I met a tax officer and he asked me: why are you always so angry, Grigory Stepanovich? Goodness' sake, how can I be anything but angry? I need money desperately . . . I rode out yesterday early in the morning, at daybreak, and went to see all my debtors; and if only one of them had paid his debt . . . I was dog-tired, spent the night God knows where—a Jewish tavern beside a barrel of vodka. . . . Finally I got here, fifty miles from home, hoping to be paid, and you treat me to a "mood." How can I help being angry?

MRS. POPOV.   It seems to me that I clearly said: My steward will return from the country and then you will be paid.

SMIRNOV.   I didn't come to your steward, but to you! What the hell, if you'll pardon the expression, would I do with your steward?

MRS. POPOV.   Excuse me, my dear sir, I am not accustomed to such profane ex-   40
pressions nor to such a tone. I'm not listening to you any more. [*Goes out quickly.*]

SMIRNOV.   [*alone.*] Well, how do you like that? "A mood." . . . "Husband died seven months ago"! Must I pay the interest or mustn't I? I ask you: Must I pay, or must I not? So, your husband's dead, and you're in a mood and all that finicky stuff . . . and your steward's away somewhere; may he drop dead. What do you want me to do? Do you think I can fly away from my creditors in a balloon or something? Or should I run and bash my head against the wall? I go to Gruzdev—and he's not at home; Yaroshevich is hiding, with Kuritsin it's a quarrel to the death and I almost throw him out the window; Mazutov has diarrhea, and this one is in a "mood." Not one of these swine wants to pay me! And all because I'm too nice to them. I'm a sniveling idiot, I'm spineless, I'm an old lady! I'm too delicate with them! So, just you wait! You'll find out what I'm like! I won't let you play around with me, you devils! I'll stay and stick it out until she pays. Rrr! . . . How furious I am today, how furious! I'm shaking inside from rage and I can hardly catch my breath. . . . Damn it! My God, I even feel sick! [*He shouts.*] Hey, you!

LUKA.   [*enters.*] What do you want?

SMIRNOV.   Give me some beer or some water! [*LUKA exits.*] What logic is there in this! A man needs money desperately, it's like a noose around his neck—and she won't pay because, you see, she's not disposed to occupy herself with money matters! . . . That's the logic of a woman! That's why I never did like and do not like to talk to women. I'd rather sit on a keg of gunpowder than talk to a woman. Brr! . . . I even have goose pimples, this broad has put me in such a rage! All I have to do is see one of those spoiled bitches from a distance, and I get so angry it gives me a cramp in the leg. I just want to shout for help.

LUKA.   [*entering with water.*] Madam is sick and won't see anyone.

SMIRNOV.   Get out! [*LUKA goes.*] Sick and won't see anyone! No need to see me   45
. . . I'll stay and sit here until you give me the money. You can stay sick for a week, and I'll stay for a week . . . if you're sick for a year, I'll stay a year. . . . I'll get my own back, dear lady! You can't impress me with your widow's weeds and your dimpled cheeks . . . we know all about those dimples! [*Shouts through the window.*] Semyon, unharness the horses! We're not going away quite yet! I'm staying here! Tell them in the stable to give the horses some oats! You brute, you let the horse on the left side get all tangled up in the reins again! [*Teasing.*] "Never mind" . . . I'll give you a never mind! [*Goes away from the window.*] Shit! The heat is unbearable and nobody pays up. I slept badly last night and on top of everything else this broad in mourning is "in a mood" . . . my head aches . . . [*Drinks, and grimaces.*] Shit! This is water! What I need is a drink! [*Shouts.*] Hey, you!

LUKA.   [*Enters.*] What is it?

SMIRNOV.   Give me a glass of vodka. [*LUKA goes out.*] Oaf! [*Sits down and examines himself.*] Nobody would say I was looking well! Dusty all over, boots dirty, unwashed, unkept, straw on my waistcoat. . . . The dear lady probably took me for a robber. [*Yawns.*] It's not very polite to present myself in a drawing room looking like this; oh well, who cares? . . . I'm not here as a visitor but as a creditor, and there's no official costume for creditors. . . .

LUKA.   [*enters with vodka.*] You're taking liberties, my good man. . . .

SMIRNOV.   [*angrily.*] What?

LUKA.   I . . . nothing . . . I only . . .

SMIRNOV.   Who are you talking to? Shut up!

LUKA.   [*aside.*] The devil sent this leech. An ill wind brought him. . . . [*LUKA goes out.*]

SMIRNOV.   Oh how furious I am! I'm so mad I could crush the whole world into a powder! I even feel faint! [*Shouts.*] Hey, you!

MRS. POPOV.   [*enters, eyes downcast.*] My dear sir, in my solitude, I have long ago grown unaccustomed to the masculine voice and I cannot bear shouting. I must request you not to disturb my peace and quiet!

SMIRNOV.   Pay me my money and I'll go.

MRS. POPOV.   I told you in plain language: I haven't any spare cash now; wait until the day after tomorrow.

SMIRNOV.   And I also told you respectfully, in plain language: I don't need the money the day after tomorrow, but today. If you don't pay me today, then tomorrow I'll have to hang myself.

MRS. POPOV.   But what can I do if I don't have the money? You're so strange!

SMIRNOV.   Then you won't pay me now? No?

MRS. POPOV.   I can't. . . .

SMIRNOV.   In that case, I can stay here and wait until you pay. . . . [*Sits down.*] You'll pay the day after tomorrow? Excellent! In that case I'll stay here until the day after tomorrow. I'll sit here all that time . . . [*Jumps up.*] I ask you: Have I got to pay the interest tomorrow, or not? Or do you think I'm joking?

MRS. POPOV.   My dear sir, I ask you not to shout! This isn't a stable!

SMIRNOV.   I wasn't asking you about a stable but about this: Do I have to pay the interest tomorrow or not?

MRS. POPOV.   You don't know how to behave in the company of a lady!

SMIRNOV.   No, I don't know how to behave in the company of a lady!

MRS. POPOV.   No, you don't! You are an ill-bred, rude man! Respectable people don't talk to a woman like that!

SMIRNOV.   Ach, it's astonishing! How would you like me to talk to you? In French, perhaps? [*Lisps in anger.*] *Madame, je vous prie*° . . . how happy I am that you're not paying me the money. . . . Ah, pardon, I've made you uneasy! Such lovely weather we're having today! And you look so becoming in your mourning dress. [*Bows and scrapes.*]

MRS. POPOV.   That's rude and not very clever!

SMIRNOV.   [*teasing.*] Rude and not very clever! I don't know how to behave in the company of ladies. Madam, in my time I've seen far more women than you've seen sparrows. Three times I've fought duels over women; I've jilted twelve women, nine have jilted me! Yes! There was a time when I played the fool; I became sentimental over women, used honeyed words, fawned on them, bowed and scraped. . . . I loved, suffered, sighed at the moon; I became limp, melted, shivered . . . I loved passionately, madly, every which way, devil take me, I chattered away like a magpie about the emancipation of women, ran through half my fortune as a result of my tender feelings; but now, if you will excuse me, I'm on to your ways! I've had enough! Dark eyes, passionate eyes, ruby lips, dimpled cheeks; the moon, whispers, bated breath—for all that I wouldn't give a good goddamn. Present company excepted, of course, but all women,

Madame, je vous prie. I beg you, Madam.

young and old alike, are affected clowns, gossips, hateful, consummate liars to the marrow of their bones, vain, trivial, ruthless, outrageously illogical, and as far as this is concerned [*taps on his forehead.*], well, excuse my frankness, any sparrow could give pointers to a philosopher in petticoats! Look at one of those romantic creatures: muslin, ethereal demigoddess, a thousand raptures, and you look into her soul—a common crocodile! [*Grips the back of a chair; the chair cracks and breaks.*] But the most revolting part of it all is that this crocodile imagines that she has, above everything, her own privilege, a monopoly on tender feelings. The hell with it—you can hang me upside down by that nail if a woman is capable of loving anything besides a lapdog. All she can do when she's in love is slobber! While the man suffers and sacrifices, all her love is expressed in playing with her skirt and trying to lead him around firmly by the nose. You have the misfortune of being a woman, you know yourself what the na- ture of a woman is like. Tell me honestly: Have you ever in your life seen a woman who is sincere, faithful, and constant? You never have! Only old and ugly ladies are faithful and constant! You're more liable to meet a horned cat or a white woodcock than a faithful woman!

MRS. POPOV.   Pardon me, but in your opinion, who is faithful and constant in   70
love? The man?

SMIRNOV.   Yes, the man!

MRS. POPOV.   The man! [*Malicious laugh.*] Men are faithful and constant in love! That's news! [*Heatedly.*] What right have you to say that? Men are faithful and constant! For that matter, as far as I know, of all the men I have known and now know, my late husband was the best. . . . I loved him passionately, with all my being, as only a young intellectual woman can love; I gave him my youth, my happiness, my life, my fortune; he was my life's breath; I worshipped him as if I were a heathen, and . . . and, what good did it do—this best of men himself deceived me shamelessly at every step of the way. After his death, I found his desk full of love letters; and when he was alive—it's terrible to remember—he used to leave me alone for weeks at a time, and before my eyes he flirted with other women and deceived me. He squandered my money, made a mockery of my feelings . . . and, in spite of all that, I loved him and was true to him . . . and besides, now that he is dead, I am still faithful and constant. I have shut myself up in these four walls forever and I won't remove these widow's weeds until my dying day. . . .

SMIRNOV.   [*laughs contemptuously.*] Widow's weeds! . . . I don't know what you take me for! As if I didn't know why you wear that black outfit and bury yourself in these four walls! Well, well! It's no secret, so romantic! When some fool of a poet passes by this country house, he'll look up at your window and think: "Here lives the mysterious Tamara, who, for the love of her husband, buried herself in these four walls." We know these tricks!

MRS. POPOV.   [*flaring.*] What? How dare you say that to me?

SMIRNOV.   You may have buried yourself alive, but you haven't forgotten to   75
powder yourself!

MRS. POPOV.   How dare you use such expressions with me?

SMIRNOV.   Please don't shout. I'm not your steward! You must allow me to call a spade a spade. I'm not a woman and I'm used to saying what's on my mind! Don't you shout at me!

MRS. POPOV.   I'm not shouting, you are! Please leave me in peace!

SMIRNOV.   Pay me my money and I'll go.

MRS. POPOV.   I won't give you any money!   80

SMIRNOV. Yes, you will.

MRS. POPOV. To spite you, I won't pay you anything. You can leave me in peace!

SMIRNOV. I don't have the pleasure of being either your husband or your fiancé, so please don't make scenes! [*Sits down.*] I don't like it.

MRS. POPOV. [*choking with rage.*] You're sitting down?

SMIRNOV. Yes, I am.

MRS. POPOV. I ask you to get out!

SMIRNOV. Give me my money . . . [*Aside.*] Oh, I'm so furious! Furious!

MRS. POPOV. I don't want to talk to impudent people! Get out of here! [*Pause.*] You're not going? No?

SMIRNOV. No.

MRS. POPOV. No?

SMIRNOV. No!

MRS. POPOV. We'll see about that. [*Rings.*]

[*LUKA enters.*]

Luka, show the gentleman out!

LUKA. [*goes up to SMIRNOV.*] Sir, will you please leave, as you have been asked. You mustn't . . .

SMIRNOV. [*jumping up.*] Shut up! Who do you think you're talking to? I'll make mincemeat out of you!

LUKA. [*his hand to his heart.*] Oh my God! Saints above! [*Falls into chair.*] Oh, I feel ill! I can't catch my breath!

MRS. POPOV. Where's Dasha? Dasha! [*She shouts.*] Dasha! Pelagea! Dasha! [*She rings.*]

LUKA. Oh! They've all gone berry picking . . . there's nobody at home . . . I'm ill! Water!

MRS. POPOV. Will you please get out!

SMIRNOV. Will you please be more polite?

MRS. POPOV. [*clenches her fist and stamps her feet.*] You're nothing but a crude bear! A brute! A monster!

SMIRNOV. What? What did you say?

MRS. POPOV. I said that you were a bear, a monster!

SMIRNOV. [*advancing toward her.*] Excuse me, but what right do you have to insult me?

MRS. POPOV. Yes, I am insulting you . . . so what? Do you think I'm afraid of you?

SMIRNOV. And do you think just because you're one of those romantic creations, that you have the right to insult me with impunity? Yes? I challenge you!

LUKA. Lord in Heaven! Saints above! . . . Water!

SMIRNOV. Pistols!

MRS. POPOV. Do you think just because you have big fists and you can bellow like a bull, that I'm afraid of you? You're such a bully!

SMIRNOV. I challenge you! I'm not going to let anybody insult me, and I don't care if you are a woman, a delicate creature!

MRS. POPOV. [*trying to get a word in edgewise.*] Bear! Bear! Bear!

SMIRNOV. It's about time we got rid of the prejudice that only men must pay for their insults! Devil take it, if women want to be equal, they should behave as equals! Let's fight!

MRS. POPOV.　You want to fight! By all means!

SMIRNOV.　This minute!

MRS. POPOV.　This minute! My husband had some pistols . . . I'll go and get them right away. [*Goes out hurriedly and then returns.*] What pleasure I'll have putting a bullet through that thick head of yours! The hell with you! [*She goes out.*]

SMIRNOV.　I'll shoot her down like a chicken! I'm not a little boy or a senti-　115
mental puppy. I don't care if she is delicate and fragile.

LUKA.　Kind sir! Holy father! [*kneels.*] Have pity on a poor old man and go away from here! You've frightened her to death and now you're going to shoot her?

SMIRNOV.　[*not listening to him.*] If she fights, then it means she believes in equality of rights and emancipation of women. Here the sexes are equal! I'll shoot her like a chicken! But what a woman! [*Imitates her.*] "The hell with you! . . . I'll put a bullet through that thick head of yours! . . ." What a woman! How she blushed, her eyes shone . . . she accepted my challenge! To tell the truth, it was the first time in my life I've seen a woman like that. . . .

LUKA.　Dear sir, please go away! I'll pray to God on your behalf as long as I live!

SMIRNOV.　That's a woman for you! A woman like that I can understand! A real woman! Not a sour-faced nincompoop but fiery, gunpowder! Fireworks! I'm even sorry to have to kill her!

LUKA.　[*weeps.*] Dear sir . . . go away!　120

SMIRNOV.　I positively like her! Positively! Even though she has dimpled cheeks, I like her! I'm almost ready to forget about the debt. . . . My fury has diminished. Wonderful woman!

MRS. POPOV.　[*enters with pistols.*] Here they are, the pistols. Before we fight, you must show me how to fire. . . . I've never had a pistol in my hands before . . .

LUKA.　Oh dear Lord, for pity's sake. . . . I'll go and find the gardener and the coachman. . . . What did we do to deserve such trouble? [*Exit.*]

SMIRNOV.　[*examining the pistols.*] You see, there are several sorts of pistols . . . there are special dueling pistols, the Mortimer with primers. Then there are Smith and Wesson revolvers, triple action with extractors . . . excellent pistols! . . . they cost a minimum of ninety rubles a pair. . . . You must hold the revolver like this . . . [*Aside.*] What eyes, what eyes! A woman to set you on fire!

MRS. POPOV.　Like this?　125

SMIRNOV.　Yes, like this . . . then you cock the pistol . . . take aim . . . put your head back a little . . . stretch your arm out all the way . . . that's right . . . then with this finger press on this little piece of goods . . . and that's all there is to do . . . but the most important thing is not to get excited and aim without hurrying . . . try to keep your arm from shaking.

MRS. POPOV.　Good . . . it's not comfortable to shoot indoors. Let's go into the garden.

SMIRNOV.　Let's go. But I'm giving you advance notice that I'm going to fire into the air.

MRS. POPOV.　That's the last straw! Why?

SMIRNOV.　Why? . . . Why . . . because it's my business, that's why.　130

MRS. POPOV.　Are you afraid? Yes? Aahhh! No, sir. You're not going to get out of it that easily! Be so good as to follow me! I will not rest until I've put a hole through your forehead . . . that forehead I hate so much! Are you afraid?

SMIRNOV.   Yes, I'm afraid.

MRS. POPOV.   You're lying! Why don't you want to fight?

SMIRNOV.   Because . . . because you . . . because I like you.

MRS. POPOV.   [*laughs angrily.*] He likes me! He dares say that he likes me! [*Points to the door.*] Out!

SMIRNOV.   [*loads the revolver in silence, takes cap and goes; at the door, stops for half a minute while they look at each other in silence; then he approaches MRS. POPOV hesitantly.*] Listen. . . . Are you still angry? I'm extremely irritated, but, do you understand me, how can I express it . . . the fact is, that, you see, strictly speaking . . . [*He shouts.*] Is it my fault, really, for liking you? [*Grabs the back of a chair, which cracks and breaks.*] Why the hell do you have such fragile furniture! I like you! Do you understand? I . . . I'm almost in love with you!

MRS. POPOV.   Get away from me—I hate you!

SMIRNOV.   God, what a woman! I've never in my life seen anything like her! I'm lost! I'm done for! I'm caught like a mouse in a trap!

MRS. POPOV.   Stand back or I'll shoot!

SMIRNOV.   Shoot! You could never understand what happiness it would be to die under the gaze of those wonderful eyes, to be shot by a revolver which was held by those little velvet hands. . . . I've gone out of my mind! Think about it and decide right away, because if I leave here, then we'll never see each other again! Decide . . . I'm a nobleman, a respectable gentleman, of good family. I have an income of ten thousand a year. . . . I can put a bullet through a coin tossed in the air . . . I have some fine horses. . . . Will you be my wife?

MRS. POPOV.   [*indignantly brandishes her revolver.*] Let's fight! I challenge you!

SMIRNOV.   I'm out of my mind . . . I don't understand anything . . . [*Shouts.*] Hey, you, water!

MRS. POPOV.   [*shouts.*] Let's fight!

SMIRNOV.   I've gone out of my mind. I'm in love like a boy, like an idiot! [*He grabs her hand, she screams with pain.*] I love you! [*Kneels.*] I love you as I've never loved before! I've jilted twelve women, nine women have jilted me, but I've never loved one of them as I love you. . . . I'm weak, I'm a limp rag. . . . I'm on my knees like a fool, offering you my hand. . . . Shame, shame! I haven't been in love for five years, I vowed I wouldn't; and suddenly I'm in love, like a fish out of water. I'm offering my hand in marriage. Yes or no? You don't want to? You don't need to! [*Gets up and quickly goes to the door.*]

MRS. POPOV.   Wait!

SMIRNOV.   [*stops.*] Well?

MRS. POPOV.   Nothing . . . you can go . . . go away . . . wait. . . . No, get out, get out! I hate you! But—don't go! Oh, if you only knew how furious I am, how angry! [*Throws revolver on table.*] My fingers are swollen from that nasty thing. . . . [*Tears her handkerchief furiously.*] What are you waiting for? Get out!

SMIRNOV.   Farewell!

MRS. POPOV.   Yes, yes, go away! [*Shouts.*] Where are you going? Stop. . . . Oh, go away! Oh, how furious I am! Don't come near me! Don't come near me!

SMIRNOV.   [*approaching her.*] How angry I am with myself! I'm in love like a student. I've been on my knees. . . . It gives me the shivers. [*Rudely.*] I love you! A lot of good it will do me to fall in love with you! Tomorrow I've got to pay the interest, begin the mowing of the hay. [*Puts his arm around her waist.*] I'll never forgive myself for this. . . .

MRS. POPOV. Get away from me! Get your hands away! I . . . hate you! I . . . challenge you!

[*Prolonged kiss, LUKA enters with an ax, the GARDENER with a rake, the COACHMAN with a pitchfork, and WORKMEN with cudgels.*]

LUKA. [*catches sight of the pair kissing.*] Lord in heaven! [*Pause.*]

MRS. POPOV. [*lowering her eyes.*] Luka, tell them in the stable not to give Toby any oats today.

CURTAIN

QUESTIONS

1. What was Mrs. Popov's life like with her late husband? What did she learn about him after his death? How has this knowledge affected her?

2. Who is Smirnov? What is he like, and how do you know? Why does he say what he does about women?

4. Why is Luka important? How do his responses highlight the emotions developing between Smirnov and Mrs. Popov?

5. What causes Mrs. Popov to call Smirnov a bear, a brute, a monster? What is his immediate response?

6. Why is Toby significant? How does he symbolize Mrs. Popov's shifting emotions?

GENERAL QUESTIONS

1. Where did you laugh in the play? Analyze those moments and try to determine the causes of your laughter.

2. From this play, what conclusions can you draw about farce as a dramatic form? Consider the breaking chairs, the shouting, the challenge, the attitude of Smirnov about being shot, the shifting of feelings, etc.

3. How does Chekhov's presentation of Smirnov and Mrs. Popov make their reversal of feelings seem normal and logical, although sudden, unexpected, and surprising?

4. What are the major ideas or themes in *The Bear*? Consider vows made by the living to the dead, the difficulty of keeping resolutions, the nature of powerful emotions, the need to maintain conventions and expectations, etc.

SUSAN GLASPELL, *TRIFLES*

Susan Glaspell, playwright and writer of fiction, grew up in Iowa and moved to the Northeast in her thirties. She helped found the Provincetown Players (Cape Cod, Massachusetts) in 1914, and wrote most of her plays for that company. Much of her work—both plays and short stories—is strongly feminist. It deals with the roles that women play (or are forced to play) in society and with the relationships between men and women. She wrote or co-authored over ten plays for the Provincetown Players, including *Women's Honor* (1918), *Bernice* (1919), *The Inheritors* (1921), and

The Verge (1921). After 1922, however, she gave up the theater and turned almost exclusively to fiction. The one exception was *Alison's House* (1930), a play loosely based on the life and family of Emily Dickinson, for which Glaspell won a Pulitzer Prize.

   Trifles (1916) is Glaspell's best-known play; she wrote it in ten days for the Provincetown Players, and it was produced by them in 1916. For her topic, she was inspired by a murder trial she covered while working as a reporter for a Des Moines newspaper. In 1917 she refashioned the material for the short story "A Jury of Her Peers," which is included in Chapter 4 (pp. 155–69).

   Although *Trifles* concerns a murder investigation, the play is not a murder mystery; the audience and the characters identify the killer almost as soon as the play begins. The action of the play is focused on revealing a motive, and the theme involves the differing capacities of men and women to understand the motive. The men—the County Attorney and the Sheriff—look for signs of violent rage. The women—Mrs. Hale and Mrs. Peters—draw their conclusions from the "trifles" they find in the kitchen. Finally, the women must decide how to judge the killer and what to do with their evidence.

SUSAN GLASPELL   (1882–1948)

Trifles ————————————————————————————*1916*

CAST OF CHARACTERS

> George Henderson, *county attorney*
> Henry Peters, *sheriff*
> Lewis Hale, *a neighboring farmer*
> Mrs. Peters
> Mrs. Hale

SCENE. *The kitchen in the now abandoned farmhouse of JOHN WRIGHT, a gloomy kitchen, and left without having been put in order—unwashed pans under the sink, a loaf of bread outside the bread-box, a dish-towel on the table—other signs of incompleted work. At the rear the outer door opens and the SHERIFF comes in followed by the COUNTY ATTORNEY and HALE. The SHERIFF and HALE are men in middle life, the COUNTY ATTORNEY is a young man; all are much bundled up and go at once to the stove. They are followed by the two women—the SHERIFF's wife first; she is a slight wiry woman, a thin nervous face. MRS. HALE is larger and would ordinarily be called more comfortable looking, but she is disturbed now and looks fearfully about as she enters. The women have come in slowly, and stand close together near the door.*

    COUNTY ATTORNEY. [*Rubbing his hands.*] This feels good. Come up to the fire, ladies.

    MRS. PETERS. [*After taking a step forward.*] I'm not—cold.

    SHERIFF. [*Unbuttoning his overcoat and stepping away from the stove as if to mark the beginning of official business.*] Now, Mr. Hale, before we move things about, you explain to Mr. Henderson just what you saw when you came here yesterday morning.

    COUNTY ATTORNEY. By the way, has anything been moved? Are things just as you left them yesterday?

    SHERIFF. [*Looking about.*] It's just the same. When it dropped below zero last   5 night I thought I'd better send Frank out this morning to make a fire for us—no use getting pneumonia with a big case on, but I told him not to touch anything except the stove—and you know Frank.

    COUNTY ATTORNEY. Somebody should have been left here yesterday.

    SHERIFF. Oh—yesterday. When I had to send Frank to Morris Center for that man who went crazy—I want you to know I had my hands full yesterday. I knew you could get back from Omaha by today and as long as I went over everything here myself—

    COUNTY ATTORNEY. Well, Mr. Hale, tell just what happened when you came here yesterday morning.

    HALE. Harry and I had started to town with a load of potatoes. We came along the road from my place and as I got here I said, "I'm going to see if I can't get John Wright to go in with me on a party telephone." I spoke to Wright about it once before and he put me off, saying folks talked too much anyway, and all he asked was peace and quiet—I guess you know about how much he talked himself; but I thought maybe if I went to the house and talked about it before his wife, though I said to Harry that I didn't know as what his wife wanted made much difference to John—

    COUNTY ATTORNEY. Let's talk about that later, Mr. Hale. I do want to talk   10 about that, but tell now just what happened when you got to the house.

    HALE. I didn't hear or see anything; I knocked at the door, and still it was all quiet inside. I knew they must be up, it was past eight o'clock. So I knocked again, and I thought I heard somebody say, "Come in." I wasn't sure, I'm not sure yet, but I opened the door—this door [*Indicating the door by which the two women are still standing.*] and there in that rocker—[*Pointing to it.*] sat Mrs. Wright.

[*They all look at the rocker.*]

    COUNTY ATTORNEY. What—was she doing?

    HALE. She was rockin' back and forth. She had her apron in her hand and was kind of—pleating it.

    COUNTY ATTORNEY. And how did she—look?

HALE.   Well, she looked queer.

COUNTY ATTORNEY.   How do you mean—queer?

HALE.   Well, as if she didn't know what she was going to do next. And kind of done up.

COUNTY ATTORNEY.   How did she seem to feel about your coming?

HALE.   Why, I don't think she minded—one way or other. She didn't pay much attention. I said, "How do, Mrs. Wright, it's cold, ain't it?" And she said, "Is it?"—and went on kind of pleating at her apron. Well, I was surprised; she didn't ask me to come up to the stove, or to set down, but just sat there, not even looking at me, so I said, "I want to see John." And then she—laughed. I guess you would call it a laugh. I thought of Harry and the team outside, so I said a little sharp: "Can't I see John?" "No," she says, kind o' dull like. "Ain't he home?" says I. "Yes," says she, "he's home." "Then why can't I see him?" I asked her, out of patience. "'Cause he's dead," says she. "*Dead?*" says I. She just nodded her head, not getting a bit excited, but rockin' back and forth. "Why—where is he?" says I, not knowing what to say. She just pointed upstairs—like that. [*himself pointing to the room above.*] I got up, with the idea of going up there. I walked from there to here—then I says, "Why, what did he die of?" "He died of a rope round his neck," says she, and just went on pleatin' at her apron. Well, I went out and called Harry. I thought I might—need help. We went upstairs and there he was lyin'—

COUNTY ATTORNEY.   I think I'd rather have you go into that upstairs, where you can point it all out. Just go on now with the rest of the story.

HALE.   Well, my first thought was to get that rope off. It looked . . . [*Stops, his face twitches.*] . . . but Harry, he went up to him, and he said, "No, he's dead all right, and we'd better not touch anything." So we went back downstairs. She was still sitting that same way. "Has anybody been notified?" I asked. "No," says she, unconcerned. "Who did this, Mrs. Wright?" said Harry. He said it businesslike—and she stopped pleatin' of her apron. "I don't know," she says. "You don't *know?*" says Harry. "No," says she. "Weren't you sleepin' in the bed with him?" says Harry. "Yes," says she, "but I was on the inside." "Somebody slipped a rope round his neck and strangled him and you didn't wake up?" says Harry. "I didn't wake up," she said after him. We must 'a looked as if we didn't see how that could be, for after a minute she said, "I sleep sound." Harry was going to ask her more questions but I said maybe we ought to let her tell her story first to the coroner, or the sheriff, so Harry went fast as he could to Rivers' place, where there's a telephone.

COUNTY ATTORNEY.   And what did Mrs. Wright do when she knew that you had gone for the coroner?

HALE.   She moved from that chair to this one over here [*Pointing to a small chair in the corner.*] and just sat there with her hands held together and looking down. I got a feeling that I ought to make some conversation, so I said I had come in to see if John wanted to put in a telephone, and at that she started to laugh, and then she stopped and looked at me—scared. [*The* COUNTY ATTORNEY, *who has had his notebook out, makes a note.*] I dunno, maybe it wasn't scared. I wouldn't like to say it was. Soon Harry got back, and then Dr. Lloyd came, and you, Mr. Peters, and so I guess that's all I know that you don't.

COUNTY ATTORNEY.   [*Looking around.*] I guess we'll go upstairs first—and then out to the barn and around there. [*To the* SHERIFF.] You're convinced that there was nothing important here—nothing that would point to any motive.

SHERIFF.   Nothing here but kitchen things.

[*The* COUNTY ATTORNEY, *after again looking around the kitchen, opens the door of a cupboard closet. He gets up on a chair and looks on a shelf. Pulls his hand away, sticky.*]

COUNTY ATTORNEY. Here's a nice mess.

[*The women draw nearer.*]

MRS. PETERS. [*To the other woman.*] Oh, her fruit; it did freeze. [*To the* LAWYER.] She worried about that when it turned so cold. She said the fire'd go out and her jars would break.

SHERIFF. Well, can you beat the women! Held for murder and worryin' about her preserves.

COUNTY ATTORNEY. I guess before we're through she may have something more serious than preserves to worry about.

HALE. Well, women are used to worrying over trifles. 30

[*The two women move a little closer together.*]

COUNTY ATTORNEY. [*With the gallantry of a young politician.*] And yet, for all their worries, what would we do without the ladies? [*The women do not unbend. He goes to the sink, takes a dipperful of water from the pail and pouring it into a basin, washes his hands. Starts to wipe them on the roller-towel, turns it for a cleaner place.*] Dirty towels! [*Kicks his foot against the pans under the sink.*] Not much of a housekeeper, would you say, ladies?

MRS. HALE. [*Stiffly.*] There's a great deal of work to be done on a farm.

COUNTY ATTORNEY. To be sure. And yet [*with a little bow to her.*] I know there are some Dickson county farmhouses which do not have such roller towels.

[*He gives it a pull to expose its full length again.*]

MRS. HALE. Those towels get dirty awful quick. Men's hands aren't always as clean as they might be.

COUNTY ATTORNEY. Ah, loyal to your sex, I see. But you and Mrs. Wright were 35 neighbors. I suppose you were friends, too.

MRS. HALE. [*Shaking her head.*] I've not seen much of her of late years. I've not been in this house—it's more than a year.

COUNTY ATTORNEY. And why was that? You didn't like her?

MRS. HALE. I liked her all well enough. Farmers' wives have their hands full, Mr. Henderson. And then—

COUNTY ATTORNEY. Yes—?

MRS. HALE. [*Looking about.*] It never seemed a very cheerful place. 40

COUNTY ATTORNEY. No—it's not cheerful. I shouldn't say she had the home-making instinct.

MRS. HALE. Well, I don't know as Wright had, either.

COUNTY ATTORNEY. You mean that they didn't get on very well?

MRS. HALE. No, I don't mean anything. But I don't think a place'd be any cheerfuller for John Wright's being in it.

COUNTY ATTORNEY. I'd like to talk more of that a little later. I want to get the 45 lay of things upstairs now.

[*He goes to the left, where three steps lead to a stair door.*]

SHERIFF.   I suppose anything Mrs. Peters does'll be all right. She was to take in some clothes for her, you know, and a few little things. We left in such a hurry yesterday.

COUNTY ATTORNEY.   Yes, but I would like to see what you take, Mrs. Peters, and keep an eye out for anything that might be of use to us.

MRS. PETERS.   Yes, Mr. Henderson.

[*The women listen to the men's steps on the stairs, then look about the kitchen.*]

MRS. HALE.   I'd hate to have men coming into my kitchen, snooping around and criticising.

[*She arranges the pans under the sink which the LAWYER had shoved out of place.*]

MRS. PETERS.   Of course it's no more than their duty.

MRS. HALE.   Duty's all right, but I guess that deputy sheriff that came out to make the fire might have got a little of this on. [*Gives the roller towel a pull.*] Wish I'd thought of that sooner. Seems mean to talk about her for not having things slicked up when she had to come away in such a hurry.

MRS. PETERS.   [*Who had gone to a small table in the left rear corner of the room, and lifted one end of a towel that covers a pan.*] She had bread set.

[*Stands still.*]

MRS. HALE.   [*Eyes fixed on a loaf of bread beside the breadbox, which is on a low shelf at the other side of the room. Moves slowly toward it.*] She was going to put this in there. [*Picks up loaf, then abruptly drops it. In a manner of returning to familiar things.*] It's a shame about her fruit. I wonder if it's all gone. [*Gets up on the chair and looks.*] I think there's some here that's all right, Mrs. Peters. Yes—here; [*Holding it toward the window.*] this is cherries, too. [*Looking again.*] I declare I believe that's the only one. [*Gets down, bottle in her hand. Goes to the sink and wipes it off on the outside.*] She'll feel awful bad after all her hard work in the hot weather. I remember the afternoon I put up my cherries last summer.

[*She puts the bottle on the big kitchen table, center of the room. With a sigh, is about to sit down in the rocking-chair. Before she is seated realizes what chair it is; with a slow look at it, steps back. The chair which she has touched rocks back and forth.*]

MRS. PETERS.   Well, I must get those things from the front room closet. [*She goes to the door at the right, but after looking into the other room, steps back.*] You coming with me, Mrs. Hale? You could help me carry them.

[*They go in the other room; reappear, MRS. PETERS carrying a dress and skirt, MRS. HALE following with a pair of shoes.*]

MRS. PETERS.   My, it's cold in there.

[*She puts the clothes on the big table and hurries to the stove.*]

MRS. HALE.   [*Examining the skirt.*] Wright was close. I think maybe that's why she kept so much to herself. She didn't even belong to the Ladies Aid. I suppose she felt she couldn't do her part, and then you don't enjoy things when you feel shabby. She used to wear pretty clothes and be lively, when she was Minnie Foster, one of the town girls singing in the choir. But that—oh, that was thirty years ago. This all you was to take in?

MRS. PETERS.   She said she wanted an apron. Funny thing to want, for there isn't much to get you dirty in jail, goodness knows. But I suppose just to make her feel more natural. She said they was in the top drawer in this cupboard. Yes, here. And then her little shawl that always hung behind the door. [*Opens stair door and looks.*] Yes, here it is.

[*Quickly shuts door leading upstairs.*]

MRS. HALE.   [*Abruptly moving toward her.*] Mrs. Peters?
MRS. PETERS.   Yes, Mrs. Hale?
MRS. HALE.   Do you think she did it?   60
MRS. PETERS.   [*In a frightened voice.*] Oh, I don't know.
MRS. HALE.   Well, I don't think she did. Asking for an apron and her little shawl. Worrying about her fruit.
MRS. PETERS.   [*Starts to speak, glances up, where footsteps are heard in the room above. In a low voice.*] Mr. Peters says it looks bad for her. Mr. Henderson is awful sarcastic in a speech and he'll make fun of her sayin' she didn't wake up.
MRS. HALE.   Well, I guess John Wright didn't wake when they was slipping that rope under his neck.
MRS. PETERS.   No, it's strange. It must have been done awful crafty and still.   65
They say it was such a—funny way to kill a man, rigging it all up like that.
MRS. HALE.   That's just what Mr. Hale said. There was a gun in the house. He says that's what he can't understand.
MRS. PETERS.   Mr. Henderson said coming out that what was needed for the case was a motive; something to show anger, or—sudden feeling.
MRS. HALE.   [*Who is standing by the table.*] Well, I don't see any signs of anger around here. [*She puts her hand on the dish towel which lies on the table, stands looking down at table, one half of which is clean, the other half messy.*] It's wiped to here. [*Makes a move as if to finish work, then turns and looks at loaf of bread outside the breadbox. Drops towel. In that voice of coming back to familiar things.*] Wonder how they are finding things upstairs. I hope she had it a little more red-up° up there. You know, it seems kind of *sneaking.* Locking her up in town and then coming out here and trying to get her own house to turn against her!
MRS. PETERS.   But Mrs. Hale, the law is the law.
MRS. HALE.   I s'pose 'tis. [*Unbuttoning her coat.*] Better loosen up your things,   70
Mrs. Peters. You won't feel them when you go out.

[*MRS. PETERS takes off her fur tippet,° goes to hang it on hook at back of room, stands looking at the under part of the small corner table.*]

MRS. PETERS.   She was piecing a quilt.

[*She brings the large sewing basket and they look at the bright pieces.*]

MRS. HALE.   It's log cabin pattern. Pretty, isn't it? I wonder if she was goin' to quilt it or just knot it?

[*Footsteps have been heard coming down the stairs. The SHERIFF enters followed by HALE and the COUNTY ATTORNEY.*]

---

red-up: neat, arranged in order.   *tippet:* scarf-like garment of fur or wool for the neck and shoulders.

SHERIFF.   They wonder if she was going to quilt it or just knot it!

[*The men laugh; the women look abashed.*]

COUNTY ATTORNEY.   [*Rubbing his hands over the stove.*] Frank's fire didn't do much up there, did it? Well, let's go out to the barn and get that cleared up.

[*The men go outside.*]

MRS. HALE.   [*Resentfully.*] I don't know as there's anything so strange, our-takin' up our time with little things while we're waiting for them to get the evidence. [*She sits down at the big table smoothing out a block with decision.*] I don't see as it's any-thing to laugh about.

MRS. PETERS.   [*Apologetically.*] Of course they've got awful important things on their minds.

[*Pulls up a chair and joins MRS. HALE at the table.*]

MRS. HALE.   [*Examining another block.*] Mrs. Peters, look at this one. Here, this is the one she was working on, and look at the sewing! All the rest of it has been so nice and even. And look at this! It's all over the place! Why, it looks as if she didn't know what she was about!

[*After she has said this they look at each other, then start to glance back at the door. After an in-stant MRS. HALE has pulled at a knot and ripped the sewing.*]

MRS. PETERS.   Oh, what are you doing, Mrs. Hale?

MRS. HALE.   [*Mildly.*] Just pulling out a stitch or two that's not sewed very good. [*Threading a needle.*] Bad sewing always made me fidgety.

MRS. PETERS.   [*Nervously.*] I don't think we ought to touch things.

MRS. HALE.   I'll just finish up this end. [*Suddenly stopping and leaning forward.*] Mrs. Peters?

MRS. PETERS.   Yes, Mrs. Hale?

MRS. HALE.   What do you suppose she was so nervous about?

MRS. PETERS.   Oh—I don't know. I don't know as she was nervous. I sometimes sew awful queer when I'm just tired. [*MRS. HALE starts to say something, looks at MRS. PE-TERS, then goes on sewing.*] Well I must get these things wrapped up. They may be through sooner than we think. [*Putting apron and other things together.*] I wonder where I can find a piece of paper, and string.

MRS. HALE.   In that cupboard, maybe.

MRS. PETERS.   [*Looking in cupboard.*] Why, here's a bird-cage. [*Holds it up.*] Did she have a bird, Mrs. Hale?

MRS. HALE.   Why, I don't know whether she did or not—I've not been here for so long. There was a man around last year selling canaries cheap, but I don't know as she took one; maybe she did. She used to sing real pretty herself.

MRS. PETERS.   [*Glancing around.*] Seems funny to think of a bird here. But she must have had one, or why would she have a cage? I wonder what happened to it?

MRS. HALE.   I s'pose maybe the cat got it.

MRS. PETERS.   No, she didn't have a cat. She's got that feeling some people have about cats—being afraid of them. My cat got in her room and she was real up-set and asked me to take it out.

MRS. HALE.   My sister Bessie was like that. Queer, ain't it?

MRS. PETERS.   [*Examining the cage.*] Why, look at this door. It's broke. One hinge is pulled apart.

MRS. HALE.   [*Looking too.*] Looks as if someone must have been rough with it.

MRS. PETERS.   Why, yes.

[*She brings the cage forward and puts it on the table.*]

MRS. HALE.   I wish if they're going to find any evidence they'd be about it. I   95
don't like this place.

MRS. PETERS.   But I'm awful glad you came with me, Mrs. Hale. It would be
lonesome for me sitting here alone.

MRS. HALE.   It would, wouldn't it? [*Dropping her sewing.*] But I tell you what I
do wish, Mrs. Peters. I wish I had come over sometimes when *she* was here. I—[*Looking around the room.*]—wish I had.

MRS. PETERS.   But of course you were awful busy, Mrs. Hale—your house and
your children.

MRS. HALE.   I could've come. I stayed away because it weren't cheerful—and
that's why I ought to have come. I—I've never liked this place. Maybe because it's
down in a hollow and you don't see the road. I dunno what it is, but it's a lonesome
place and always was. I wish I had come over to see Minnie Foster sometimes. I can
see now—

[*Shakes her head.*]

MRS. PETERS.   Well, you mustn't reproach yourself, Mrs. Hale. Somehow we   100
just don't see how it is with other folks until—something comes up.

MRS. HALE.   Not having children makes less work—but it makes a quiet house,
and Wright out to work all day, and no company when he did come in. Did you know
John Wright, Mrs. Peters?

MRS. PETERS.   Not to know him; I've seen him in town. They say he was a good
man.

MRS. HALE.   Yes—good; he didn't drink, and kept his word as well as most, I
guess, and paid his debts. But he was a hard man, Mrs. Peters. Just to pass the time of
day with him—[*Shivers.*] Like a raw wind that gets to the bone. [*Pauses, her eye falling
on the cage.*] I should think she would 'a wanted a bird. But what do you suppose went
with it?

MRS. PETERS.   I don't know, unless it got sick and died.

[*She reaches over and swings the broken door, swings it again, both women watch it.*]

MRS. HALE.   You weren't raised round here, were you? [*MRS. PETERS shakes her   105
head.*] You didn't know—her?

MRS. PETERS.   Not till they brought her yesterday.

MRS. HALE.   She—come to think of it, she was kind of like a bird herself—real
sweet and pretty, but kind of timid and—fluttery. How—she—did—change. [*Silence;
then as if struck by a happy thought and relieved to get back to everyday things.*] Tell you what,
Mrs. Peters, why don't you take the quilt in with you? It might take up her mind.

MRS. PETERS.   Why, I think that's a real nice idea, Mrs. Hale. There couldn't
possibly be any objection to it, could there? Now, just what would I take? I wonder if
her patches are in here—and her things.

[*They look in the sewing basket.*]

MRS. HALE.   Here's some red. I expect this has got sewing things in it. [*Brings
out a fancy box.*] What a pretty box. Looks like something somebody would give you.

Maybe her scissors are in here. [*Opens box. Suddenly puts her hand to her nose.*] Why—
[*Mrs. Peters bends nearer, then turns her face away.*] There's something wrapped up in
this piece of silk.

MRS. PETERS.   Why, this isn't her scissors.

MRS. HALE.   [*Lifting the silk.*] Oh, Mrs. Peters—it's—

[*Mrs. Peters bends closer.*]

MRS. PETERS.   It's the bird.

MRS. HALE.   [*Jumping up.*] But, Mrs. Peters—look at it! Its neck! Look at its
neck! It's all—other side *to.*

MRS. PETERS.   Somebody—wrung—its—neck.

[*Their eyes meet. A look of growing comprehension, of horror. Steps are heard outside. MRS.
HALE slips box under quilt pieces, and sinks into her chair. Enter SHERIFF and COUNTY AT-
TORNEY. MRS. PETERS rises.*]

COUNTY ATTORNEY.   [*As one turning from serious things to little pleasantries.*] Well,
ladies, have you decided whether she was going to quilt it or knot it?

MRS. PETERS.   We think she was going to—knot it.

COUNTY ATTORNEY.   Well, that's interesting, I'm sure. [*Seeing the bird-cage.*] Has
the bird flown?

MRS. HALE.   [*Putting more quilt pieces over the box.*] We think the—cat got it.

COUNTY ATTORNEY.   [*Preoccupied.*] Is there a cat?

[*Mrs. Hale glances in a quick covert way at MRS. PETERS.*]

MRS. PETERS.   Well, not *now.* They're superstitious, you know. They leave.

COUNTY ATTORNEY.   [*To SHERIFF PETERS, continuing an interrupted conversation.*]
No sign at all of anyone having come from the outside. Their own rope. Now let's go
up again and go over it piece by piece. [*They start upstairs.*] It would have to have been
someone who knew just the—

[*Mrs. Peters sits down. The two women sit there not looking at one another, but as if peering
into something and at the same time holding back. When they talk now it is in the manner of
feeling their way over strange ground, as if afraid of what they are saying, but as if they cannot
help saying it.*]

MRS. HALE.   She liked the bird. She was going to bury it in that pretty box.

MRS. PETERS.   [*In a whisper.*] When I was a girl—my kitten—there was a boy
took a hatchet, and before my eyes—and before I could get there—[*Covers her face an
instant.*] If they hadn't held me back I would have—[*Catches herself, looks upstairs where
steps are heard, falters weakly.*]—hurt him.

MRS. HALE.   [*With a slow look around her.*] I wonder how it would seem never to
have had any children around. [*Pause.*] No, Wright wouldn't like the bird—a thing
that sang. She used to sing. He killed that, too.

MRS. PETERS.   [*Moving uneasily.*] We don't know who killed the bird.

MRS. HALE.   I knew John Wright.

MRS. PETERS.   It was an awful thing was done in this house that night, Mrs.
Hale. Killing a man while he slept, slipping a rope around his neck that choked the
life out of him.

MRS. HALE.   His neck. Choked the life out of him.

[*Her hand goes out and rests on the bird-cage.*]

MRS. PETERS. [*With rising voice.*] We don't know who killed him. We don't know.

MRS. HALE. [*Her own feeling not interrupted.*] If there'd been years and years of nothing, then a bird to sing to you, it would be awful—still, after the bird was still.

MRS. PETERS. [*Something within her speaking.*] I know what stillness is. When we   130
homesteaded in Dakota, and my first baby died—after he was two years old, and me with no other then—

MRS. HALE. [*Moving.*] How soon do you suppose they'll be through, looking for the evidence?

MRS. PETERS. I know what stillness is. [*Pulling herself back.*] The law has got to punish crime, Mrs. Hale.

MRS. HALE. [*Not as if answering that.*] I wish you'd seen Minnie Foster when she wore a white dress with blue ribbons and stood up there in the choir and sang. [*A look around the room.*] Oh, I *wish* I'd come over here once in a while! That was a crime! That was a crime! Who's going to punish that?

MRS. PETERS. [*Looking upstairs.*] We mustn't—take on.

MRS. HALE. I might have known she needed help! I know how things can be—   135
for women. I tell you, it's queer, Mrs. Peters. We live close together and we live far apart. We all go through the same things—it's all just a different kind of the same thing. [*Brushes her eyes, noticing the bottle of fruit, reaches out for it.*] If I was you I wouldn't tell her her fruit was gone. Tell her it *ain't*. Tell her it's all right. Take this in to prove it to her. She—she may never know whether it was broke or not.

MRS. PETERS. [*Takes the bottle, looks about for something to wrap it in; takes petticoat from the clothes brought from the other room, very nervously begins winding this around the bottle. In a false voice.*] My, it's a good thing the men couldn't hear us. Wouldn't they just laugh! Getting all stirred up over a little thing like a—dead canary. As if that could have anything to do with—with—wouldn't they *laugh!*

[*The men are heard coming down stairs.*]

MRS. HALE. [*Under her breath.*] Maybe they would—maybe they wouldn't.

COUNTY ATTORNEY. No, Peters, it's all perfectly clear except a reason for doing it. But you know juries when it comes to women. If there was some definite thing. Something to show—something to make a story about—a thing that would connect up with this strange way of doing it—

[*The women's eyes meet for an instant. Enter HALE from outer door.*]

HALE. Well, I've got the team° around. Pretty cold out there.

COUNTY ATTORNEY. I'm going to stay here a while by myself. [*To the SHERIFF.*]   140
You can send Frank out for me, can't you? I want to go over everything. I'm not satisfied that we can't do better.

SHERIFF. Do you want to see what Mrs. Peters is going to take in?

[*The COUNTY ATTORNEY goes to the table, picks up the apron, laughs.*]

COUNTY ATTORNEY. Oh, I guess they're not very dangerous things the ladies have picked out. [*Moves a few things about, disturbing the quilt pieces which cover the box. Steps back.*] No, Mrs. Peters doesn't need supervising. For that matter, a sheriff's wife is married to the law. Ever think of it that way, Mrs. Peters?

team: team of horses drawing a wagon or sleigh.

MRS. PETERS.   Not—just that way.

SHERIFF.   [*Chuckling.*] Married to the law. [*Moves toward the other room.*] I just want you to come in here a minute, George. We ought to take a look at these windows.

COUNTY ATTORNEY.   [*Scoffingly.*] Oh, windows!   1

SHERIFF.   We'll be right out, Mr. Hale.

[*HALE goes outside. The SHERIFF follows the COUNTY ATTORNEY into the other room. Then MRS. HALE rises, hands tight together, looking intensely at MRS. PETERS, whose eyes make a slow turn, finally meeting MRS. HALE'S. A moment MRS. HALE holds her, then her own eyes point the way to where the box is concealed. Suddenly MRS. PETERS throws back quilt pieces and tries to put the box in the bag she is wearing. It is too big. She opens box, starts to take bird out, cannot touch it, goes to pieces, stands there helpless. Sound of a knob turning in the other room. MRS. HALE snatches the box and puts it in the pocket of her big coat. Enter COUNTY ATTORNEY and SHER-IFF.*]

COUNTY ATTORNEY.   [*Facetiously.*] Well, Henry, at least we found out that she was not going to quilt it. She was going to—what is it you call it, ladies?

MRS. HALE.   [*Her hand against her pocket.*] We call it—knot it, Mr. Henderson.

CURTAIN

QUESTIONS

1. How does the first entrance of the characters establish a distinction between the men and women in the play? What is suggested by the different reactions of the men and women to the frozen preserves?

2. What does Mr. Hale report to the County Attorney in his extended narrative? How observant is he? How accurate?

3. What is needed for a strong legal case against Minnie? What does the Sheriff conclude about the kitchen? What do his conclusions tell you about the men?

4. What are the women's conclusions about the bad sewing? What does Mrs. Hale do about it? At this point, what might she be thinking about the murder?

5. Of what importance are Mrs. Hale's descriptions (a) of Minnie as a young woman and (b) of the Wrights' marriage?

6. What do the women deduce from the broken birdcage and the dead bird? How are these symbolic, and what do they symbolize?

7. How did Minnie Wright murder her husband? What hints lead you to this solution? What information permits the women to make the right inferences about the crime and the method of strangulation?

8. What does Mrs. Hale do with the "trifles" of evidence? Why? How is her reaction to the evidence different from that of Mrs. Peters? What conflict develops between these women? How is it resolved?

9. Why does Mrs. Hale feel guilty about her relationship with Minnie Wright? To what degree does her guilt shape her decisions and actions?

GENERAL QUESTIONS

1. To what does the title of this play refer? How does this irony of the word *trifles* help shape the play's meaning?
2. What are the men like? Are they round characters or flat? How observant are they? What is their attitude toward their jobs? Toward their own importance? Toward the women and "kitchen things"?
3. What is Mrs. Hale like? How observant is she? What is her attitude toward the men and their work, and toward herself?
4. Some critics argue that Minnie is the play's most important character, even though she never appears on stage. Do you agree? Why do you think Glaspell did not make Minnie a speaking character?
5. How is symbolism employed to establish and underscore the play's meaning? Consider especially the birdcage, the dead bird, and the repeated assertion that Mrs. Wright was going to "knot" (tie) rather than "quilt" (sew) the quilt?

BETTY KELLER, *TEA PARTY*

Betty Keller has brought a wide variety of experiences to her work for the theater, including such unlikely jobs as insurance adjuster, farmer, photographer's assistant, and prison matron. She served as a director in many theatrical workshops in Vancouver, British Columbia, and for four years was a principal director with Playhouse Holiday in Vancouver. She taught drama and theater at the Windsor Secondary School in North Vancouver until 1974, the year she published the collection of short plays and sketches from which *Tea Party* is selected. More recently she has published a biography of the Canadian naturalist and writer, Ernest Thompson Seton.

Brief as *Tea Party* is, it illustrates the power of drama to depict character and situation, and to convey emotion. The main characters are two lonely elderly sisters who have outlived their friends and relatives and have no one except the people who occasionally come to their house to perform various services, such as delivering the paper and reading the meters. The sketch presents their plight deftly and succinctly, touching with great tenderness on the pathos of their loneliness.

Tea Party is too short to present difficult choices for the characters, and hence they hardly get the opportunity to go through the responses and changes that are found in full-length plays. Both Alma and Hester are individualized, however, as they carry on a minor controversy about names and dates from their long-vanished past. Beyond this, in Alma's last speech, which ends the dramatic sketch, one might find a hint of the awareness and recognition that we expect of round, developed characters. Even though the paperboy is not a speaking part, his unkindness to the sisters is clearly shown, and in this way Keller dramatizes the poignant situation of persons whom life has passed by. It is difficult to find a play that conveys so much of life and feeling in so short a span of time and action.

BETTY KELLER   (b. 1930)

Tea Party _____*1974*

CHARACTERS

> Alma Evans: *seventy-five years old, small and spare framed. Her clothing is simple but not outdated, her grey hair cut short and neat. She walks with the aid of a cane, although she would not be classed as a cripple.*
>
> Hester Evans: *seventy-nine years old. There is little to distinguish her physically from her sister, except perhaps a face a little more pinched and pain-worn. She sits in a wheelchair; but although her legs may be crippled, her mind certainly is not.*
>
> The Boy: *in his early teens, seen only fleetingly.*

SCENE. *The sitting room of the Evans sisters' home. The door to the street is on the rear wall Upstage Left,° a large window faces the street Upstage Center. On the right wall is the door to the kitchen; on the left, a door to the remainder of the house. Downstage Left is an easy chair, Upstage Right a sofa, Downstage Right a tea trolley. The room is crowded with the knickknacks gathered by its inhabitants in three-quarters of a century of living.*

[*At rise,* ALMA *is positioning* HESTER'S *wheelchair Upstage Left.* ALMA'S *cane is on* HESTER'S *lap.*]

HESTER.   That's it.

[ALMA *takes her cane from* HESTER. *They both survey the room.*]

ALMA.   I think I'll sit on the sofa . . . at the far end.
HESTER.   Yes. That will be cosy. Then he can sit on this end between us.

[ALMA *sits on the Downstage Right end of the sofa. They both study the effect.*]

ALMA.   But then he's too close to the door, Hester!

[HESTER *nods, absorbed in the problem.*]

ALMA.   [*moving to the Upstage Left end of sofa.*] Then I'd better sit here.
HESTER.   But now he's too far away from me, Alma.

[ALMA *stands; both of them study the room again.*]

ALMA.   But if I push the tea trolley in front of you, he'll have to come to you, won't he?

Upstage Left: To visualize stage locations, assume that the stage directions are described from the viewpoint of an actor facing the audience. Thus "Right" is actually to the left of the audience, and "Left" is right. "Downstage" refers to the front of the stage, while "Upstage" is the back. The terms *down* and *up* were established at a time when stages were tilted toward the audience, so that spectators at floor level could have as complete a view as possible of the entire stage.

HESTER.   Oh, all right, Alma. You're sure it's today?

ALMA.   [*pushing the tea trolley laden with cups and napkins, etc. to* HESTER.] The first Thursday of the month.

HESTER.   You haven't forgotten the chocolate biscuits?°   10

ALMA.   No dear, they're on the plate. I'll bring them in with the tea. [*Goes to the window, peering up the street to the Right.*]

HESTER.   And cocoa?

ALMA.   I remembered.

HESTER.   You didn't remember for Charlie's visit.

ALMA.   Charlie drinks tea, Hester. I didn't make cocoa for him because he   15
drinks tea.

HESTER.   Oh. He didn't stay last time anyway.

ALMA.   It was a busy day. . . .

HESTER.   Rushing in and out like that. I was going to tell him about father and the *Bainbridge* . . . and he didn't stay.

ALMA.   What about the *Bainbridge?*

HESTER.   Her maiden voyage out of Liverpool . . . when father was gone three   20
months and we thought he'd gone down with her.

ALMA.   That wasn't the *Bainbridge.*

HESTER.   Yes, it was. It was the *Bainbridge.* I remember standing on the dock in the snow when she finally came in. That was the year I'd begun first form, and I could spell out the letters on her side.

ALMA.   It was her sister ship, the *Heddingham.*

HESTER.   The *Bainbridge.* You were too young to remember. Let's see, the year was . . .

ALMA.   Mother often told the story. It was the *Heddingham* and her engine   25
broke down off Cape Wrath beyond the Hebrides.

HESTER.   It was 1902 and you were just four years old.

ALMA.   The *Heddingham,* and she limped into port on January the fifth.

HESTER.   January the fourth just after nine in the morning, and we stood in the snow and watched the *Bainbridge* nudge the pier, and I cried and the tears froze on my cheeks.

ALMA.   The *Heddingham.*

HESTER.   Alma, mother didn't cry, you know. I don't think she ever cried. My   30
memory of names and places is sharp so that I don't confuse them as some others I could mention, but sometimes I can't remember things like how people reacted. But I remember that day. There were tears frozen on my cheeks but mother didn't cry.

ALMA.   [*nodding.*] She said he didn't offer a word of explanation. Just marched home beside her.

HESTER.   [*smiling.*] He never did say much. . . . Is he coming yet?

ALMA.   No, can't be much longer though. Almost half past four.

HESTER.   Perhaps you'd better bring in the tea. Then it will seem natural.

ALMA.   Yes dear, I know. [*Exits out door Upstage Right.*] Everything's ready.   35

HESTER.   What will you talk about?

ALMA.   [*re-entering with the teapot*] I thought perhaps . . . [*carefully putting down the teapot.*] . . . perhaps brother George!

---

chocolate biscuits: chocolate cookies.

HESTER.   And the torpedo? No, Alma, he's not old enough for that story!

ALMA.   He's old enough to know about courage. I thought I'd show him the medal, too. [*She goes to the window, peers both ways worriedly, then carries on towards the kitchen.*]

HESTER.   Not yet? He's late to-night. You're sure it's today?

ALMA.   He'll come. It's the first Thursday. [*Exit.*]

HESTER.   You have his money?

ALMA.   [*returning with the plate of biscuits.*] I've got a twenty dollar bill, Hester.

HESTER.   Alma!

ALMA.   Well, we haven't used that one on him. It was Dennis, the last one, who always had change. We could get two visits this way, Hester.

HESTER.   Maybe Dennis warned him to carry change for a twenty.

ALMA.   It seemed worth a try. [*Goes to the window again.*] Are you going to tell him about the *Heddingham?*

HESTER.   The *Bainbridge.* Maybe . . . or maybe I'll tell him about the day the Great War ended. Remember, Alma, all the noise, the paper streamers . . .

ALMA.   And father sitting silent in his chair.

HESTER.   It wasn't the same for him with George gone. Is he coming yet?

ALMA.   No dear, maybe he's stopped to talk somewhere. [*looking to the right.*] . . . No . . . no, there he is, on the Davis' porch now!

HESTER.   I'll pour then. You get the cocoa, Alma.

ALMA.   [*going out.*] It's all ready, I just have to add hot water.

HESTER.   Don't forget the marshmallows!

ALMA.   [*reappearing*] Oh, Hester, what if he comes in and just sits down closest to the door? He'll never stay!

HESTER.   You'll have to prod him along. For goodness sakes, Alma, get his cocoa!

[*ALMA disappears.*]

HESTER.   He must be nearly here. He doesn't go to the Leschynskis, and the Blackburns don't get home till after six.

ALMA.   [*returning with the cocoa.*] Here we are! Just in . . .

[*The BOY passes the window. There is a slapping sound as the newspaper lands on the porch.*]

[*ALMA and HESTER look at the door and wait, hoping to hear a knock, but they both know the truth. Finally, ALMA goes to the door, opens it and looks down at the newspaper.*]

ALMA.   He's gone on by.

HESTER.   You must have had the day wrong.

ALMA.   No, he collected at the Davis'.

HESTER.   [*after a long pause.*] He couldn't have forgotten us.

ALMA.   [*still holding the cocoa, she turns from the door.*] He's collecting at the Kerighan's now. [*She closes the door and stands forlornly.*]

HESTER.   Well, don't stand there with that cocoa! You look silly. [*ALMA brings the cocoa to the tea trolley.*] Here's your tea. [*ALMA takes the cup, sits on the Upstage Left end of the sofa. There is a long silence.*]

HESTER.   I think I'll save that story for the meter man.

ALMA.   The *Heddingham?*

HESTER. The *Bainbridge.*

ALMA. [*after a pause.*] They don't read the meters for two more weeks.

SLOW BLACKOUT

QUESTIONS

1. What is the play's major conflict? The minor conflict?

2. Why do the two sisters discuss their seating arrangements for the paperboy? How do we learn that they have made these arrangements before?

3. What does Alma's plan for the twenty-dollar bill show about her? What does the discussion about both the money and the paperboys indicate about their own self-awareness?

4. How does controversy about the names *Bainbridge* and *Heddingham* help you understand the two sisters?

GENERAL QUESTIONS

1. How does Keller's description of the sets aid you in understanding the action? The normal tasks of the women? From the setting of this play, what are your conclusions about the relationship of objects and spatial arrangements to the action and development of drama?

2. Consider the women particularly with regard to their age. In the light of their health and their isolation, how does *Tea Party* present the circumstances of the aged? How can the play be construed as a sociological/political argument, with the elderly as the focus?

EUGENE O'NEILL, *BEFORE BREAKFAST*

Eugene O'Neill is one of America's great playwrights. He wrote more than forty plays, won three Pulitzer Prizes, and received the Nobel Prize for literature in 1936. The son of a well-known actor, in his youth he traveled about the world as a seaman, studied briefly at Princeton and Harvard, and began writing plays in 1912. The first of his plays to be produced, *Bound East for Cardiff,* was acted by the Provincetown Players at the Wharf Theater in Provincetown, Massachusetts, in 1916. O'Neill maintained a close connection with this company for several years, providing them with ten one-act plays between 1916 and 1920. His later (and longer) works include *The Emperor Jones* (1920), *Anna Christie* (1921), *Desire Under the Elms* (1924), *Strange Interlude* (1928), *Mourning Becomes Electra* (1931), and *The Iceman Cometh* (1946). O'Neill also wrote an autobiographical play, *A Long Day's*

Journey Into Night (1936), which at his request was suppressed until after his death. When it was staged on Broadway in 1956, it won him a third Pulitzer Prize in drama, and it was later made into a film starring Katherine Hepburn.

Before Breakfast, though one of O'Neill's earliest plays, shows his characteristic control of conflict, character, setting, and point of view. The play was first staged in December, 1916, by the Provincetown Players at the Playwright's Theater in New York City's Greenwich Village (where Christopher Street, the address of the Rowlands' apartment, is located). The play contains little action, and yet it is charged with conflict. The plot is simple and straightforward—a wife onstage harangues her offstage husband for twenty minutes before breakfast. The conflict between them is longstanding and bitter, and it is resolved in the play's horrifying conclusion.

Above all, *Before Breakfast* illustrates O'Neill's skillful employment of the dramatic point of view. By giving Mrs. Rowland every word spoken onstage, O'Neill causes the audience to understand everything as it is filtered through her petty and selfish mind. Indeed, the play is a bravura piece for a gifted actress. Finally, however, the audience (and the reader) must determine both the validity and the limitations of her perspective.

Setting is equally important in *Before Breakfast.* O'Neill uses the single stage setting, described at length in the opening stage directions, to show the audience (and the reader) a great deal about the characters and their lives. The Rowlands' flat is in Greenwich Village, the location of New York University and a traditional haunt of artists, artisans, poets, novelists, dramatists, actors, singers, and dancers, and it therefore suggests the type of life that Alfred Rowland is seeking to attain. The implications of the setting are confirmed throughout the rest of the play.

EUGENE O'NEILL   (1888–1953)

Before Breakfast _____ *1916*

CHARACTERS

> Mrs. Rowland, *The Wife*
> Mr. Alfred Rowland, *The Husband*

SCENE. *A small room serving both as kitchen and dining room in a flat on Christopher Street, New York City. In the rear, to the right, a door leading to the outer hallway. On the left of the doorway, a sink, and a two-burner gas stove. Over the stove, and extending to the left wall, a wooden closet for dishes, etc. On the left, two windows looking out on a fire escape where several potted plants are dying of neglect. Before the windows, a table covered with oilcloth. Two cane-bottomed chairs are placed by the table. Another stands against the wall to the right of door in rear. In the right wall, rear, a doorway leading into a bedroom. Farther forward, different articles of a man's and a woman's clothing are hung on pegs. A clothes line is strung from the left corner, rear, to the right wall, forward.*

It is about eight-thirty in the morning of a fine, sunshiny day in the early fall.

Mrs. Rowland enters from the bedroom, yawning, her hands still busy putting the finishing touches on a slovenly toilet by sticking hairpins into her hair which is bunched up in a drab-colored mass on top of her round head. She is of medium height and inclined to a shapeless stoutness, accentuated by her formless blue dress, shabby and worn. Her face is characterless, with small regular features and eyes of a nondescript blue. There is a pinched expression about her eyes and nose and her weak, spiteful mouth. She is in her early twenties but looks much older.

She comes to the middle of the room and yawns, stretching her arms to their full length. Her drowsy eyes stare about the room with the irritated look of one to whom a long sleep has not been a long rest. She goes wearily to the clothes hanging on the right and takes an apron from a hook. She ties it about her waist, giving vent to an exasperated "damn" when the knot fails to obey her clumsy fingers. Finally gets it tied and goes slowly to the gas stove and lights one burner. She fills the coffee pot at the sink and sets it over the flame. Then slumps down into a chair by the table and puts a hand over her forehead as if she were suffering from headache. Suddenly her face brightens as though she had remembered something, and she casts a quick glance at the dish closet; then looks sharply at the bedroom door and listens intently for a moment or so.

MRS. ROWLAND.   [*In a low voice.*] Alfred! Alfred! [*There is no answer from the next room and she continues suspiciously in a louder tone.*] You needn't pretend you're asleep. [*There is no reply to this from the bedroom, and, reassured, she gets up from her chair and tiptoes cautiously to the dish closet. She slowly opens one door, taking great care to make no noise, and slides out, from their hiding place behind the dishes, a bottle of Gordon gin and a glass. In doing so she disturbs the top dish, which rattles a little. At this sound she starts guiltily and looks with sulky defiance at the doorway to the next room.*]

[*Her voice trembling.*] Alfred!

[*After a pause, during which she listens for any sound, she takes the glass and pours out a large drink and gulps it down; then hastily returns the bottle and glass to their hiding place. She closes the closet door with the same care as she had opened it, and, heaving a great sigh of relief, sinks down into her chair again. The large dose of alcohol she has taken has an almost immediate effect. Her features become more animated, she seems to gather energy, and she looks at the bedroom door with a hard, vindictive smile on her lips. Her eyes glance quickly about the room and are fixed on a man's coat and vest which hang from a hook at right. She moves stealthily over to the open doorway and stands there, out of sight of anyone inside, listening for any movement.*]

[*Calling in a half-whisper.*] Alfred!

[*Again there is no reply. With a swift movement she takes the coat and vest from the hook and returns with them to her chair. She sits down and takes the various articles out of each pocket but quickly puts them back again. At last, in the inside pocket of the vest, she finds a letter.*]

[*Looking at the handwriting—slowly to herself.*] Hmm! I knew it.

[*She opens the letter and reads it. At first her expression is one of hatred and rage, but as she goes on to the end it changes to one of triumphant malignity. She remains in deep thought for a moment, staring before her, the letter in her hands, a cruel smile on her lips. Then she puts the letter back in the pocket of the vest, and still careful not to awaken the sleeper, hangs the clothes up again on the same hook, and goes to the bedroom door and looks in.*]

[*In a loud, shrill voice.*] Alfred! [*Still louder.*] Alfred! [*There is a muffled, yawning groan from the next room.*] Don't you think it's about time you got up? Do you want to

5

stay in bed all day? [*Turning around and coming back to her chair.*] Not that I've got any doubts about your being lazy enough to stay in bed forever. [*She sits down and looks out of the window, irritably.*] Goodness knows what time it is. We haven't even got any way of telling the time since you pawned your watch like a fool. The last valuable thing we had, and you knew it. It's been nothing but pawn, pawn, pawn, with you—anything to put off getting a job, anything to get out of going to work like a man. [*She taps the floor with her foot nervously, biting her lips.*]

[*After a short pause.*] Alfred! Get up, do you hear me? I want to make that bed before I go out. I'm sick of having this place in a continual muss on your account. [*With a certain vindictive satisfaction.*] Not that we'll be here long unless you manage to get some money some place. Heaven knows I do my part—and more—going out to sew every day while you play the gentleman and loaf around bar rooms with that good-for-nothing lot of artists from the Square.°

[*A short pause during which she plays nervously with a cup and saucer on the table.*]

And where are you going to get money, I'd like to know? The rent's due this week and you know what the landlord is. He won't let us stay a minute over our time. You say you *can't* get a job. That's a lie and you know it. You never even look for one. All you do is moon around all day writing silly poetry and stories that no one will buy—and no wonder they won't. I notice I can always get a position, such as it is; and it's only that which keeps us from starving to death.

[*Gets up and goes over to the stove—looks into the coffee pot to see if the water is boiling; then comes back and sits down again.*]

You'll have to get money to-day some place. I can't do it all, and I won't do it all. You've got to come to your senses. You've got to beg, borrow, or steal it somewheres. [*With a contemptuous laugh.*] But where, I'd like to know? You're too proud to beg, and you've borrowed the limit, and you haven't the nerve to steal.

[*After a pause—getting up angrily.*] Aren't you up yet, for heaven's sake? It's just like you to go to sleep again, or pretend to. [*She goes to the bedroom door and looks in.*] Oh, you are up. Well, it's about time. You needn't look at me like that. Your airs don't fool me a bit any more. I know you too well—better than you think I do—you and your goings-on. [*Turning away from the door—meaningly.*] I know a lot of things, my dear. Never mind what I know, now. I'll tell you before I go, you needn't worry. [*She comes to the middle of the room and stands there, frowning.*]

[*Irritably.*] Hmm! I suppose I might as well get breakfast ready—not that there's anything much to get. [*Questioningly.*] Unless you have some money? [*She pauses for an answer from the next room which does not come.*] Foolish question! [*She gives a short, hard laugh.*] I ought to know you better than that by this time. When you left here in such a huff last night I knew what would happen. You can't be trusted for a second. A nice condition you came home in! The fight we had was only an excuse for you to make a beast of yourself. What was the use pawning your watch if all you wanted with the money was to waste it in buying drink?

[*Goes over to the dish closet and takes out plates, cups, etc., while she is talking.*]

Hurry up! It don't take long to get breakfast these days, thanks to you. All we

---

°*Square:* Washington Square, at the center of Greenwich Village.

got this morning is bread and butter and coffee; and you wouldn't even have that if it wasn't for me sewing my fingers off. [*She slams the loaf of bread on the table with a bang.*]

The bread's stale. I hope you'll like it. *You* don't deserve any better, but I don't see why *I* should suffer.

[*Going over to the stove.*] The coffee'll be ready in a minute, and you needn't expect me to wait for you.

[*Suddenly with great anger.*] What on earth are you doing all this time? [*She goes over to the door and looks in.*] Well, you're *almost* dressed at any rate. I expected to find you back in bed. That'd be just like you. How awful you look this morning! For heaven's sake, shave! You're disgusting! You look like a tramp. No wonder no one will give you a job. I don't blame them—when you don't even look halfway decent. [*She goes to the stove.*] There's plenty of hot water right here. You've got no excuse. [*Gets a bowl and pours some of the water from the coffee pot into it.*] Here.

[*He reaches his hand into the room for it. It is a sensitive hand with slender fingers. It trembles and some of the water spills on the floor.*]

[*Tauntingly.*] Look at your hand tremble! You'd better give up drinking. You 15 can't stand it. It's just your kind that get the D.T.'s. *That would be* the last straw! [*Looking down at the floor.*] Look at the mess you've made of this floor—cigarette butts and ashes all over the place. Why can't you put them on a plate? No, you wouldn't be considerate enough to do that. You never think of me. You don't have to sweep the room and that's all you care about.

[*Takes the broom and commences to sweep viciously, raising a cloud of dust. From the inner room comes the sound of a razor being stropped.*]°

[*Sweeping.*] Hurry up! It must be nearly time for me to go. If I'm late I'm liable to lose my position, and then I couldn't support you any longer. [*As an afterthought she adds sarcastically.*] And then you'd have to go to work or something dreadful like that. [*Sweeping under the table.*] What I want to know is whether you're going to look for a job to-day or not. You know your family won't help us any more. They've had enough of you, too. [*After a moment's silent sweeping.*] I'm about sick of all this life. I've a good notion to go home, if I wasn't too proud to let them know what a failure you've been—you, the millionaire Rowland's only son, the Harvard graduate, the poet, the catch of the town—Huh! [*With bitterness.*] There wouldn't be many of them now envy my catch if they knew the truth. What has our marriage been, I'd like to know? Even before your *millionaire* father died owing every one in the world money, you certainly never wasted any of your time on your wife. I suppose you thought I'd ought to be glad you were *honorable* enough to marry me—after getting me into trouble. You were ashamed of me with your fine friends because my father's only a grocer, that's what you were. At least he's honest, which is more than any one could say about yours. [*She is sweeping steadily toward the door. Leans on her broom for a moment.*]

You hoped every one'd think you'd been forced to marry me, and pity you, didn't you? You didn't hesitate much about telling me you loved me, and making me believe your lies, before it happened, did you? You made me think you didn't want your father to buy me off as he tried to do. I know better now. I haven't lived with you

---

stropped: Alfred is using a leather strap to sharpen a straight razor, the kind barbers still use, with a very sharp steel blade that is hinged to a handle.

all this time for nothing. [*Somberly.*] It's lucky the poor thing was born dead, after all. What a father you'd have been!

[*Is silent, brooding moodily for a moment—then she continues with a sort of savage joy.*]

But I'm not the only one who's got you to thank for being unhappy. There's one other, at least, and *she* can't hope to marry you now. [*She puts her head into the next room.*] How about Helen? [*She starts back from the doorway, half frightened.*]

Don't look at me that way! Yes, I read her letter. What about it? I got a right to. I'm your wife. And I know all there is to know, so don't lie. You needn't stare at me so. You can't bully me with your superior airs any longer. Only for me you'd be going without breakfast this very morning. [*She sets the broom back in the corner—whiningly.*] You never did have any gratitude for what I've done. [*She comes to the stove and puts the coffee into the pot.*] The coffee's ready. I'm not going to wait for you. [*She sits down in her chair again.*]

[*After a pause—puts her hand to her head—fretfully.*] My head aches so this morning. It's a shame I've got to go to work in a stuffy room all day in my condition. And I wouldn't if you were half a man. By rights I ought to be lying on my back instead of you. You know how sick I've been this last year; and yet you object when I take a little something to keep up my spirits. You even didn't want me to take that tonic I got at the drug store. [*With a hard laugh.*] I know you'd be glad to have me dead and out of your way; then you'd be free to run after all these silly girls that think you're such a wonderful, misunderstood person—this Helen and the others. [*There is a sharp exclamation of pain from the next room.*]

[*With satisfaction.*] There! I knew you'd cut yourself. It'll be a lesson to you. You know you oughtn't to be running around nights drinking with your nerves in such an awful shape. [*She goes to the door and looks in.*]

What makes you so pale? What are you staring at yourself in the mirror that way for? For goodness sake, wipe that blood off your face! [*With a shudder.*] It's horrible. [*In relieved tones.*] There, that's better. I never could stand the sight of blood. [*She shrinks back from the door a little.*] You better give up trying and go to a barber shop. Your hand shakes dreadfully. Why do you stare at me like that? [*She turns away from the door.*] Are you still mad at me about that letter? [*Defiantly.*] Well, I had a right to read it. I'm your wife. [*She comes to the chair and sits down again. After a pause.*]

I knew all the time you were running around with someone. Your lame excuses about spending the time at the library didn't fool me. Who is this Helen, anyway? One of those artists? Or does she write poetry, too? Her letter sounds that way. I'll bet she told you your things were the best ever, and you believed her, like a fool. Is she young and pretty? I was young and pretty, too, when you fooled me with your fine, poetic talk; but life with you would soon wear anyone down. What I've been through!

[*Goes over and takes the coffee off the stove.*] Breakfast is ready. [*With a contemptuous glance.*] Breakfast! [*Pours out a cup of coffee for herself and puts the pot on the table.*] Your coffee'll be cold. What are you doing—still shaving, for heaven's sake? You'd better give it up. One of these mornings you'll give yourself a serious cut. [*She cuts off bread and butters it. During the following speeches she eats and sips her coffee.*]

I'll have to run as soon as I've finished eating. One of us has got to work. [*Angrily.*] Are you going to look for a job to-day or aren't you? I should think some of your fine friends would help you, if they really think you're so much. But I guess they just like to hear you talk. [*Sits in silence for a moment.*]

I'm sorry for this Helen, whoever she is. Haven't you got any feelings for other people? What will her family say? I see she mentions them in her letter. What is she going to do—have the child—or go to one of those doctors? That's a nice thing, I must say. Where can she get the money? Is she rich? [*She waits for some answer to this volley of questions.*]

Hmm! You won't tell me anything about her, will you? Much I care. Come to think of it, I'm not so sorry for her after all. She knew what she was doing. She isn't any schoolgirl, like I was, from the looks of her letter. Does she know you're married? Of course, she must. All your friends know about your unhappy marriage. I know they pity you, but they don't know my side of it. They'd talk different if they did.

[*Too busy eating to go on for a second or so.*]

This Helen must be a fine one, if she knew you were married. What does she expect, then? That I'll divorce you and let her marry you? Does she think I'm crazy enough for that—after all you've made me go through? I guess not! And you can't get a divorce from me and you know it. No one can say *I've* ever done anything wrong. [*Drinks the last of her cup of coffee.*]

She deserves to suffer, that's all I can say. I'll tell you what I think; I think your Helen is no better than a common street-walker, that's what I think. [*There is a stifled groan of pain from the next room.*]

Did you cut yourself again? Serves you right. [*Gets up and takes off her apron.*] 30 Well, I've got to run along. [*Peevishly.*] This is a fine life for me to be leading! I won't stand for your loafing any longer. [*Something catches her ear and she pauses and listens intently.*] There! You've overturned the water all over everything. Don't say you haven't. I can hear it dripping on the floor. [*A vague expression of fear comes over her face.*] Alfred! Why don't you answer me?

[*She moves slowly toward the room. There is the noise of a chair being overturned and something crashes heavily to the floor. She stands, trembling with fright.*]

Alfred! Alfred! Answer me! What is it you knocked over? Are you still drunk? [*Unable to stand the tension a second longer she rushes to the door of the bedroom.*]
Alfred!

[*She stands in the doorway looking down at the floor of the inner room, transfixed with horror. Then she shrieks wildly and runs to the other door, unlocks it and frenziedly pulls it open, and runs shrieking madly into the outer hallway.*]

[*The curtain falls.*]

QUESTIONS

1. What does the setting tell you about the Rowlands?
2. How is Mrs. Rowland described in the opening stage directions? How does O'Neill use adjectives to shape your initial response to her? How does the rest of the play sustain or alter this image?
3. How does Mrs. Rowland speak to Alfred? What does she complain about? What does she accuse Alfred of being and doing?
4. What happened during Mrs. Rowland's premarital affair with Alfred? Why didn't she let Alfred's father "buy her off"?

5. Where is the play's crisis? Which character comes to a crisis? What leads you to conclude that the character and play have reached a crisis?

6. Mrs. Rowland precipitates the climax by discussing Alfred's affair. What do we learn about Helen? What pushes Alfred over the edge?

GENERAL QUESTIONS

1. How does the setting define the characters, their relationship, and their life? What details of setting are most significant?

2. Is Mrs. Rowland flat or round? Static or dynamic? Individualized or stereotyped? Why does she have no first name?

3. Why is Alfred Rowland kept off stage (except for his hand) and given no dialogue? How does this affect the play?

4. Alfred is presented from his wife's point of view. How accurate is this portrait? To what degree does Alfred justify his wife's accusations?

5. Why does O'Neill present the history of Alfred's family and his relationship with Mrs. Rowland out of chronological order? What is the effect of this method of presentation?

WRITING ABOUT THE ELEMENTS OF DRAMA

Although some aspects of drama, such as lighting and stage movement, are purely theatrical, drama shares a number of elements with fiction and poetry. The planning and the writing processes for essays about drama are similar to those used for essays on fiction or poetry. Thus, in the following discussion we refer to pages earlier in the text that discuss strategies for writing about specific elements.

As you plan, select a play and an appropriate element or series of elements. It would be inappropriate, for example, to attempt an essay about character development in *The Sandbox* (pp. 1431–36), because this play does not get deeply into the various characters. Be certain to choose elements that are clearly defined.

Once you select the play, choose a focus. This focus, which is your central idea, asserts something about a single element or about the relationship among elements. For example, you might argue that a character is flat, static, nonrealistic, and symbolic of good or evil. Or, to prove relationship among elements, you might claim that a play's meaning is shaped and emphasized through setting and symbolism.

Topics for Discovering Ideas

PLOT, ACTION, CONFLICT. (See also Chapter 3.) In planning an essay on plot or structure, try to demonstrate how actions and conflicts unfold. In addition, link this concern to other dramatic elements, such as tone or theme. In general, this topic breaks down into three areas—conflict, plot, and structure. For conflict, determine what the conflicts are, which one is central, and how it is resolved. What kind of conflict is it? Does it suggest any general behavioral patterns? For plot, determine the separate stages of development. What is the climax? The catastrophe? How are they anticipated or foreshadowed? In examining plot structures and patterns, determine if the play has a subplot or second plot. If so, how is it related to the main plot? Is a significant pattern of action repeated? If so, what is the effect? To what extent do these parallel or repetitive patterns influence theme and meaning? How do they control your responses?

CHARACTERS. (See also Chapter 4.) Focus on a significant figure and formulate a central idea about his or her personality, function, or meaning. Is the character round or flat? Static or dynamic? Individualized or stereotyped? Realistic or nonrealistic? Symbolic? How is the character described in the stage directions? By other characters? By himself or herself? What does he or she do, think, say? What is the character's attitude toward the environment? The action? Other characters? Himself or herself? To what extent does he or she articulate and/or embody key ideas in the play?

POINT OF VIEW AND PERSPECTIVE. (See also Chapter 5.) In many plays, such as *Hamlet, Before Breakfast,* and *The Glass Menagerie,* the playwright presents the action from the perspective of an individual character. The audience therefore sees things as this character sees them, influences them, and is influenced by them. When you deal with this technique, consider how such a perspective affects the play's structure and meaning. Why is this point of view useful or striking? What does it suggest about characters? Theme? To what extent does your reaction to the play correspond with or diverge from this perspective?

Another feature of perspective is that characters may speak directly to the audience, in a *soliloquy,* or indirectly, in a *monologue.* In dealing with these perspectives, consider whether you sympathize with the character doing the speaking. What information does the character convey? What is he or she trying to prove? What is the tone of the speech? What do these devices contribute to your response? Generally, what does the perspective contribute to your understanding of the play?

SETTING, SETS, AND PROPS. (See also Chapter 6.) Normally, you will not write about setting and properties in isolation; such an essay would simply produce a detailed description of the setting(s) and objects. Instead, a discussion of setting in drama should be linked to another element, such as character, mood, or meaning. Such an essay will demonstrate the ways in which setting(s) and objects help establish the time, place, characters, lifestyle, values, or ideas.

When dealing with a single setting, pay close attention to the opening stage directions and any other directions or dialogue that describe the environment or objects. In plays with multiple settings you will normally select one or two for examination. Ask yourself if the setting is realistic or nonrealistic, and to what extent it may be symbolic. What details and objects are specified? What do these tell you about the time, place, characters, way of life, and values? To what extent do they contribute to the play's tone, atmosphere, impact, and meaning?

DICTION, IMAGERY, AND STYLE. (See also Chapters 7 and 15.) As with setting, try to connect the devices of language to some other element such as tone, character, or meaning. Investigate the play's levels of diction and types of dialect, jargon, slang, or clichés. To what extent do these techniques define the characters and support or undercut their ideas? What connotative words or phrases are repeated? Which are spoken at particularly significant moments? What striking or consistent threads of imagery, metaphor, tone, or meaning do you find? How do all these aspects of language shape your reaction?

TONE AND ATMOSPHERE. (See also Chapters 8 and 18.) Try to deal with *how* the tone is established and *what* impact it has on the play's meaning. Seek those devices the playwright employs to control your attitudes toward individual characters, situations, and outcomes. Look for clues in stage directions, diction, imagery, rhetorical devices, tempo, and context. Is tone articulated directly? Or indirectly, through irony? Also try to establish the presence of dramatic irony: To what extent do you (as a reader or spectator) know more than many of the onstage characters?

SYMBOLISM AND ALLEGORY. (See also Chapters 9 and 21.) Try to determine the characters, objects, settings, situations, actions, words or phrases, and/or costumes that seem to be symbolic. What do they symbolize, and how do you know that they are symbolic? Are they universal or contextual? Is the symbolism extensive and consistent enough to form an allegorical system? If so, what are the two levels of meaning addressed by the allegory? To what extent does the symbolism or allegory shape the play's meaning and your responses to it?

THEME. (See also Chapters 10 and 23.) The questions and areas of concern listed above should help you in discussing theme. Try to connect theme with various other aspects of the play such as character, conflict, action, setting, language, or symbolism. What key ideas does the play explore, and what aspects of the play convey these ideas most emphatically? In dealing with each topic and question, isolate the elements and devices that have the strongest impact on meaning.

REFERRING TO PLAYS AND PARTS OF PLAYS

Underline (or *italicize*) the titles of plays, as you would for a printed book. In referring to speeches, assume that your reader may have a text different from yours. Therefore provide the information necessary for finding the exact location, regardless of text.

In the body of the essay: For a play with act, scene, and line or speech numbers, refer to *act* (roman numeral), *scene* (Arabic numeral), and *line* or *speech* number (Arabic numeral). For clarity, spell out these words. Examples are Act II. scene 3. line 24, or Act IV. scene 1. speech 4).

In direct quotations, however, including **block quotations** (set apart from your own writing), include the numbers in parentheses following the quotation. Examples are III.1.33 (when no word precedes the last number, it is ordinarily understood to refer to a line), or V.3, speech 4 (for clarity, it is best to spell out that you are referring to a speech number).

When a play is divided into acts but not scenes, or if the play contains only one act, spell out the details completely. Thus, a play like *Death of a Salesman*, which contains two acts and an epilogue, may be referred to as Act I, speech 348, or Epilogue, speech 5, both in your text and in block quotations. If the play contains only numbered scenes, like *The Glass Menagerie* spell things out similarly, such as Scene I, speech 29. When referring to a one-act play like *The Bear*, use the speech or line number, such as Speech 265.

STAGE DIRECTIONS. If you refer to a stage direction, use the line or speech number immediately preceding the direction, and abbreviate "stage direction" as *S.D.*, as in Scene I, speech 16, S.D. Your reader will then know that you are referring to the stage direction following speech 16 in Scene 1. If there are stage directions at the very opening of the play, before the speeches begin (as in *The Glass Menagerie* and *Before Breakfast*), use a *zero* and then a decimal point followed by an Arabic numeral to refer to the paragraph of directions. Thus 0.3, S.D. refers to the third paragraph of directions at the play's beginning.

PREFACES, SCENE DIRECTIONS, AND CASTS OF CHARACTERS. In referring to introductions and prefaces, such as the "Production Notes" of *The Glass Menagerie*, use the title and then the paragraph number. Example: In the "Production Notes," Williams describes *The Glass Menagerie* as a "memory play" (paragraph 1).

For scene directions at the beginning of acts or scenes, the most certain way is to spell out the circumstances, such as "The scene directions for Hughes's *Mulatto* describe the depressingly shabby living room of Colonel Norwood, the plantation owner.

For the cast of characters, the same principle applies: Spell out what you mean, such as "the cast of characters," "the *Characters* list," or "the Dramatis Personae."

The important thing about referring to parts of plays is that you be clear and exact. The guidance offered here will cover most situations, but complications and exceptions will occur. When they do, always ask for your instructor's advice.

Strategies for Organizing Ideas

For an essay on drama, you might choose from a number of strategies. If you are writing about loneliness and frustration in Keller's *Tea Party*, for example, you might select a number of objects or occurrences as the launching point for your discussion. Some of these might be the tea trolley and the sofa, or the bringing in of the cocoa and the paperboy's rapid movement past the window. In discussing the crimes of Claudius in *Hamlet*, you might choose (1) the testimony of the Ghost to Hamlet, (2) Claudius's reaction to the players' scene, (3) his speech as he is praying, and (4) his poisoning of the cup, to show how these actions convincingly establish his villainy. For such essays, you might devote separate paragraphs to each element, or you might use two or more paragraphs for each element as you further develop your ideas.

Similar strategies may be found for every possible type of essay on drama. In dealing with character in Glaspell's *Trifles*, for example, you might claim that a number of symbolic props help establish and reinforce the character of Minnie Wright or the ideas about marriage conveyed in the play. You might then use separate paragraphs to discuss these related symbols, such as Minnie's clothes, her dead canary, and her unfinished quilt. Similarly, in writing about language in plays like Chekhov's *The Bear* or Albee's *The Sandbox*, you would establish how the particular play connects qualities of speech to revelations about topics such as character and idea. Thus, *The Sandbox* makes extensive use of clichés, repetition, and connotative words, all of which are related to the traits of the characters. In *The Bear*, Smirnov's constant use of exclamations, shouts, and profanity establish his irascibility, at least until closely before the play's end. Similarly, each play and topic will offer a variety of logical, clear, and convincing methods.

SAMPLE ESSAY

O'Neill's Use of Negative Descriptions and Stage Directions in Before Breakfast° as a Means of Revealing Character

[1]   In the one-act play Before Breakfast, Eugene O'Neill dramatizes the suicidal crisis and climax of a worsening husband-wife relationship. The story is clear. Mrs. Rowland, when still a young girl, was naive and opportunistic. She seduced and then married Alfred Rowland, who was the heir of his father's millions. Her resulting pregnancy ended in stillbirth. As if this were not enough, Alfred's father died not a millionaire, but a pauper. During the years of these disappointments, Mrs. Rowland has lost whatever pleasantness she once possessed, and has descended into a state of personal neglect, alcoholism,

° See p. 1054 for this play.

and selfishness.* To bring out these traits early in the play, O'Neill relies on negative descriptions and stage directions.†

[2] The descriptions of Mrs. Rowland's personal neglect emphasize her loss of self-esteem. The directions indicate that she has allowed her figure to become a "shapeless stoutness," and that she has piled her hair into a "drab-colored mass." This neglect of her physical person is capped off, according to O'Neill's description, by her blue dress, which is "shabby and worn" and "formless" (0.1, S.D.). Clearly, the shabbiness and excessive wear may result from poverty, and thus show little about her character, but the formlessness of the dress indicates a characteristic lack of concern about appearance, also shown by her stoutness and her hair. This slovenliness shows how she wants to appear in public, because she is dressed and ready to go to work for the day. O'Neill's negative descriptions thus define her lack of self-respect.

Similarly uncomplimentary, O'Neill's directions about her sneakiness reveal her dependence on alcohol. A serious sign of distress, even though it might also be funny on stage, is the direction indicating that she takes out a bottle of gin, which she keeps hidden in a "dish closet" (speech 1 S.D). With this stage direction O'Neill symbolizes the weakest trait of the secret drinker, which he also shows in the direction that Mrs. Rowland brightens up once she has taken a stiff jolt of gin:

[3] The large dose of alcohol she has taken has an almost immediate effect. Her features become more animated, she seems to gather energy, and she looks at the bedroom with a hard, vindictive smile on her lips. (speech 1, S.D.)

It is safe to assume that these stage directions, on the morning of the play's action, would also have applied to her behavior on many previous mornings. In short, O'Neill is telling us that Mrs. Rowland is a secret alcoholic.

[4] The furtiveness of her drinking also shows up in her search of Alfred's clothing, which also shows her selfishness and bitterness. When she methodically empties his pockets, and uncovers the letter that we soon learn is from his mistress, the stage directions show that she unhesitatingly reads the letter. Then O'Neill directs the actress to form "a cruel smile on her lips" as she thinks about what to do with this new information (speech 3, S.D.). As with the drinking, we see Mrs. Rowland rifling through Alfred's things only this once, but the action suggests that this secretive prying is a regular feature of her life. However, it is her discovery on <u>this</u> morning—before breakfast—which is the key to the action, because her extensive monologue against her husband, which constitutes most of the play, allows her to vent all her hatred by reproaching him about his lack of work, his neglect of her, the time he spends with friends, and his love affair.

[5] While O'Neill uses these stage directions and descriptions to convey Mrs. Rowland's unpleasantness, he provides balance in her speeches and additional actions. He makes her a master of harangue, but there is nothing either in the directions or in her speeches to indicate that she wants to drive Alfred to suicide. Indeed, her horror at his suicide is genuine—just as it con-

* Central idea.
† Thesis sentence.

cludes the play with an incredible shock. On the positive side, her speeches show that despite her alcoholism and anger she is actually functioning in the outside world—as a seamstress—and that it is she who provides the meager money on which the couple is living (speech 5). In addition, she is working despite the fact that she has been feeling ill for a period of time (speech 19). She also has enough concern for Alfred to bring him hot water for shaving (speech 13, S.D.).

[6] It is clear that O'Neill wants us to conclude that if Mrs. Rowland were a supportive person, Alfred might not be the nervous alcoholic who cuts his throat in the bathroom. However, the play does not make clear that he ever could have been better, even with the maximum support of a perfect wife. Certainly, Mrs. Rowland is not supportive. The stage directions and speeches show that she is limited by her weakness and bitterness. With such defects of character, she has unquestionably never given Alfred any support at all, and probably never could. Everything that O'Neill tells us about her indicates that she is petty and selfish, and that she originally married Alfred expecting to receive and not to give.

[7] As things stand at the beginning of the play, then, Alfred is at the brink of despair, and Mrs. Rowland's bitter and reproachful speeches drive him to self-destruction. Despite all the malice that O'Neill attributes to her character through the stage descriptions and directions, however, it is not possible to say that she is the sole cause of Alfred's suicide. O'Neill shows that Mrs. Rowland is an unpleasant, spiteful, and messy whiner, but it is not possible to reach any conclusions beyond this characterization.

Commentary on the Essay

This essay is designed to show how specifically dramatic conventions (italicized in this commentary) may be considered in reference to the analysis of character. Although the essay refers briefly to Mrs. Rowland's speeches, it stresses those descriptions and directions that O'Neill designs specifically for the actress performing the role. The essay thus indicates one way to discuss a play, as distinguished from a story or poem.

The introductory paragraph contains enough of the story about Mrs. Rowland and her husband to make sense of the subsequent material about the stage directions and descriptions. Throughout the essay, paragraph transitions are effected by words such as *similarly, also, while,* and *then.*

Paragraph 2, the first of the body, deals with O'Neill's *directions* concerning Mrs. Rowland's *slovenly appearance* and *personal care.* As distinguished from her personal appearance, paragraphs 3 and 4 are concerned with *directions about her behavior*—first her drinking and then her search of Alfred's clothing. Paragraph 5 briefly attempts to consider how O'Neill uses Mrs. Rowland's *speeches and other actions* to balance the totally negative portrait he builds up through the negative stage directions.

Paragraphs 6 and 7 jointly close the essay. Paragraph 6 considers how the *stage directions* lead no further than the conclusion that the Rowlands' marriage is a terrible one. Paragraph 7 continues the argument of paragraph 6, with the additional thought that O'Neill's *directions* do not justify concluding that Mrs. Rowland's spiteful character is the cause of her husband's suicide.

WRITING TOPICS

1. *Tea Party* might be considered a sentimental work, on the grounds that the two elderly characters are presented to evoke sympathy and anguish, not to resemble the life of real persons. Write an essay defending the play against this judgment, being sure to make references to Keller's characterizations and her development of character.

2. *The Bear* is one of Chekhov's most popular plays. Read another Chekhov play (for example, *The Cherry Orchard, The Seagull, Three Sisters, Uncle Vanya*) and compare it to *The Bear* (characters with characters, dialogue with dialogue, situations with situations, and so on). In light of your comparison, write an essay in which you explain and justify the continued popularity of *The Bear.*

3. *Before Breakfast* is set in an apartment in Greenwich Village in lower Manhattan around 1916. It was performed in Greenwich Village in December 1916. Write an essay that deals with the following questions:

    a. What do you make of this convergence of settings—artistic and realistic?

    b. What could O'Neill assume about his original audience's reaction to the setting?

4. Write an essay that considers the following questions: Is Glaspell's *Trifles* about crime? Rural life? Marriage? The roles of rural and frontier women? The way men regard women? The way in which anger that is bottled up must eventually explode? Write an essay detailing your response, using specific details from the play to support your argument. To what degree is the situation in the play realistic? If it were to be presented as a play about a similar murder in the 1980s and 1990s (there have been a number of them), what freedom would the women have to explore the kitchen?

5. Read the story "A Jury of Her Peers" (Chapter 4, p. 155), which Glaspell wrote a year after *Trifles.* Write an essay describing the differences you find between the story and the play (for example, the openings of the two works, the descriptions of the women's reactions, the amounts of detail used in the play and in the story). Using your findings, contrast the characteristics of drama and of fiction.

6. Write an essay on one of the following topics. Before you begin writing, consult Appendix D for a description of how to proceed:

    a. A feminist analysis of *Trifles.*

    b. A psychological consideration of Mrs. Rowland in *Before Breakfast.*

    c. A close formal (new critical) analysis of one of Smirnov's early speeches in *The Bear.*

    d. The two sisters as archetypal old people in *Tea Party.*

7. On the basis of the plays included in this chapter, write an essay dealing with the characteristics of the dramatic form. Consider topics like dialogue, monologue, soliloquy, action, vocal ranges, staging, comparative lengths of plays, pauses in speech, stage directions, laughter, seriousness, and the means by which the dramatists engage the audience in characters and situations.

27

Tragedy: Affirmation Through Loss

THE ORIGINS OF TRAGEDY

Tragedy is commonly thought to be about the death or misfortune of a major character. The four infamous "D's" summarize this view: *deterioration, downfall, disaster,* and *death.* In addition, there is a consensus that tragedy is the most "elevated" literary form; that is, tragedy, above all literary genres, connects human beings to religion and the cosmos. For the most part, these views are correct,[1] but in light of them it is puzzling that in ancient classical Greek the word *tragedy (tragodia)* originally meant "a goat song." It is natural to ask how so high a literary genre could ever have been linked with lowly goats.

Tragedy in Ancient Athens

Although tragedy flourished in ancient Athens during the height of Athenian political and economic power in the fifth century B.C., it originated a century earlier, when the city was growing but still minor. The exact details of the origin are uncertain, but by the end of the sixth century the performance of tragedies had become a vital part of one of the most important Athenian religious festivals.

THE CHORUSES. The relationship of tragedy to goats is therefore open to conjecture. One strong hypothesis is that the form grew out of cere-

---

[1] Although the tragic protagonist often dies at the play's end, the extant Athenian tragedies do not follow this pattern rigidly. It is true that the major figures experience difficulty and suffering, and sometimes death, but often they escape punishment, and may even receive divine pardon.

monials danced and sung by organized choruses ("dancing groups") at the sacrificing of a goat. Another is that tragic performances began as a literary-choral competition with a goat as a prize. A persuasive recent argument is that the word *tragedy* was derived from the pejorative word *tragoidoi*, or "billy-goat singers," which was applied to the young men who made up the choruses. Indeed, at first tragedy was not called *tragodia* (tragedy) but rather *tragoidoi*, as though the chorus members were more important than the literary form. Apparently the reasoning was that the men were like young goats because they lacked knowledge and discipline. To prepare them for their future military and governing duties, the expanding city state required them to undergo intensive military training, which stressed cooperation, coordination, and precision. The best ones at close-order drill were recruited for the choruses, and during rehearsal and performance they were excused from their military obligations. Until they completed their training, however, they were still like young goats.[2]

TRAGEDY AND RELIGIOUS FESTIVALS. The choruses performed at a number of outdoor religious festivals celebrated each year by the Athenians. The festivals, which were established during the sixth century, B.C., honored Dionysus, the God of the earth, fertility, vegetation, peasants, peace, poetry, music, and happiness. He was also the God of vines and vineyards—the giver of wine, the transformer of personality, and the liberator of human beings from care and grief. The most significant of the Dionysiac festivals were (1) the *Lenaia* and (2) the *Great*, or *City Dionysia*. The Lenaia, held for two days in *Gamelion*, the month of weddings (January), was mainly for local residents because the Athenian port was closed and people were cooped up in town. In contrast, the City Dionysia was a week-long event in *Elaphebolion*, the month of stags (March–April), right after the spring equinox. The port was then open, and crowds from neighboring areas surged into town to worship, to attend the various ceremonies, and to spend their money among local businesses.

TRAGEDY AND THE GREEK HEROES. Tragedy developed as a part of the City Dionysia. The ancient scientist, philosopher, and critic Aristotle (384–322 B.C.) claimed that the first tragedies sprang out of a choral form called a **dithyramb** that was performed at the festivals. Some said that the dithyrambs were songs of praise inspired by the legendary "double-birth" of

---

[2] For this argument, see John J. Winkler, "The Ephebes' Song: *Tragodia* and *Polis*," in John J. Winkler and Froma I. Zeitlin, eds., *Nothing to Do with Dionysos? Athenian Drama in Its Social Context* (Princeton: Princeton U. P., 1990), pp. 20–62. For a discussion of the military nature of the ancient Greek city-state, see Paul Rahe, "The Martial Republics of Classical Greece," *The Wilson Quarterly*, Vol. 17, No. 1 (Winter, 1993): 58–70.

Dionysus.[3] According to Aristotle, the first tragedies were "mere improvisation" associated with the dithyrambs (*Poetics* IV.12, p. 19). If that is so, then the form that became tragedy soon went its own way. Writers began focusing on myths about the heroes and demigods who had "lived" in the prehistoric period between the vanished age of bronze and the living age of iron. These stories told about individual adventures and achievements, including distant explorations and epic battles, principally the Trojan War. Beyond the exploits of these heroic figures, the early tragedies explored their conflicts, their relationships to the gods, and, often, their deaths. In the fourth century B.C., Aristotle called the myths the "received legends" that by his time were the "usual subjects of tragedy" (*Poetics* IX.7, p. 37).

The legendary heroes—many of whom were worshipped in cults—were kings, queens, princes, and princesses. They were therefore "highly renowned and prosperous" (*Poetics* XII.3, p. 45), and possessed the integrity and honor consistent with their elevated stations. However, although they were great, they were not "eminently good and just," for they demonstrated a full range of negative emotions, such as jealousy, anger, rage, humiliation, indignation, regret, and shame. Their destructive actions included deceit, subterfuge, lying, betrayal, revenge, murder, suicide, patricide, infanticide, and mutilation. In fact, a common critical judgment is that the heroes created their own troubles because of their dominating **hubris** (insolence, contemptuous violence), or pride. As a result of these complexities, the writers of tragedy dealt seriously with philosophical and religious issues in an attempt to find meaning in the conflicts and misfortunes that rend even the greatest lives.

THE BEGINNING OF ACTING IN TRAGEDIES. Because the surviving Athenian tragedies are dominated by acting parts, some modern readers think of the chorus parts as interludes or even interruptions. The tragedies were not always this way, however, for in the beginning there were no actors, but only choruses. The process that led to the dominance of actors seems clear: At some point, a member of the company was given lines to introduce and also to link the choral speeches. Because of this special function, the new speaker was soon separated and distinguished from the chorus. The word that the Athenians gave to this speaker—*hypocrites* (hih-POCK-rih-tayss)—became the Greek word for *actor.*

[3] S. H. Butcher, *Aristotle's Theory of Poetry and Fine Art,* 4th ed. (New York: Dover, 1951), p. 19 (VI.12). All parenthetical references to Aristotle are from this edition. The word *dithyrambos* was one of the many attributive names for Dionysus. It was conjectured to have been derived from *dis* (two) and *thyra* (door), referring to the myth that Zeus removed Dionysus from the womb of his mother, Semele, and placed the fetus within his thigh. When Zeus removed Dionysus, the god had "come through the door" of birth twice. This derivation has been denied by some modern scholars. For a description of the origin of comedy during the festivals for Dionysus, see pp. 1316–18.

The next essential step was impersonation, or the taking of a role. The *hypocrites* began imitating a hero, and the chorus began imitating groups such as townspeople, worshippers, youths, or elders. Once such role-playing had occurred, genuine drama had begun. According to tradition, the first actor—and therefore the acknowledged founder of the acting profession—was the writer and choral leader Thespis, in about 536–533 B.C.

SUMMARY. Tragedy is a genre that evolved unpredictably "by slow degrees" (*Poetics*, IV.12, p. 19), developing new elements as they became appropriate. It is particularly important to stress that *tragedy originated as a form for choruses, not for actors.* Even after actors became dominant, the chorus was important enough for Aristotle to state that "the chorus should be regarded as one of the actors" (XVIII. 7, p. 69). In addition, the characteristic tragic emphasis on misfortune occurred *not* because of an original theoretical design, but rather because of the *reality of suffering* in the lives of the heroic subjects.

The Ancient Competitions in Tragedy

After Thespis had set the pattern of action between actor and chorus, tragedy writing as a competition within the City Dionysia became institutionalized.

THE TRAGIC DRAMATISTS AND THEIR WORK. Early each summer, a number of dramatists vied for the honor of having their plays performed at the City Dionysia. They wrote three tragedies (a **trilogy**) together with a **satyr** play (a boisterous burlesque play), and submitted the four works to one of the city magistrates. The three best submissions were approved for the next festival, to be held eight months later. On the last day, after the performances had been given, the magistrate awarded a prize to the best of the three playwrights. The winner was given no money, but instead received a crown of ivy and the glory of triumph.

THE THREE GREAT ATHENIAN TRAGEDIANS. To gain such honor during the approximately 250 years when the competitions were held, many writers wrote many hundreds, probably thousands, of plays. Most of these have long since vanished (there were only a few copies of each play, all written on perishable rolls of papyrus), along with the names of most of the hopeful entrants. A small number of works by the three best tragic playwrights, however, have survived. These are (1) Aeschylus (525/4–456 B.C.), who added a second actor; (2) Sophocles (ca. 500/494–406/5 B.C.), who added a third actor, created scene design, and increased the members of the chorus from twelve to fifteen; and (3) Euripides (485/4–406 B.C.).

The combined output of these three playwrights was about 305 plays, of which approximately 230 were tragedies (the other 75 were satyr plays). All these plays might have vanished, too, except that some of them were considered too important to lose. After about A.D. 200, seven tragedies by Aeschylus, seven by Sophocles, and ten by Euripides were selected by scholars at Byzantium (Constantinople) to illustrate classical Greek language and literature. Because these anthologized plays were teaching texts, they were copied and recopied many times, and they have therefore survived to the present day. In addition, a manuscript containing nine more plays by Euripides was discovered late in the medieval period, bringing his total to nineteen. Therefore, of all the hundreds and hundreds of plays written by the ancient Greek tragic playwrights, only thirty-three complete plays still exist.

ARISTOTLE AND THE NATURE OF TRAGEDY

Aristotle was the giant of ancient criticism. Not only did he attend many tragic performances, but he also read many plays that he had never seen performed. His major critical work, *The Poetics*, is based on this first-hand experience, and in addition it also reflects his own powerful judgment. Interestingly, he uses Sophocles' *Oedipus the King*, the first play in this chapter, as the basis for many of his conclusions.

Aristotle's Theory of Tragedy

His famous definition of tragedy appears in the sixth chapter of *The Poetics*. It is that tragedy is "an imitation of an action that is serious, complete, and of a certain magnitude; in language embellished with each kind of artistic ornament; . . . in the form of action, not of narrative; through pity and fear effecting the proper purgation of these emotions" (VI. 2, p. 23). A consideration of the main parts of this definition will help you read and respond to tragedies.

ACTION. First is the observation that a tragedy is the imitation of a single **action** and not a narration or epic. By *action* Aristotle means a concentrated, self-contained, non-digressive dramatic portrayal of a real or lifelike series of events. Thus, in *Oedipus the King*, the action develops from Oedipus's determination, as King of Thebes, to free his city from the pollution that is destroying it. (Similarly, in Shakespeare's *Hamlet* the action and the final resolution grow out of Hamlet's promise to avenge his father's murder.)

PLOT (MUTHOS). Aristotle describes three major elements of *muthos*, or **plot**, that govern the development of the tragic action. First is the "**reversal** of the situation" (*peripeteia*) from apparent good to bad, or a "change [usually also a surprise] by which the action veers round to its opposite," as in *Oedipus the King*, where the outcome is the opposite of what Oedipus intends and expects (XI.1, p. 41). Second is "a change from ignorance to knowledge," which Aristotle calls *anagnorisis* or **recognition** (XI. 2, p. 41). Again in *Oedipus the King*, the final action is Oedipus's recognition of the terrible truth, no matter how he tries to resist it. In the best and most powerful tragedies, according to Aristotle, the reversal and the recognition occur simultaneously.

Aristotle describes the third part of plot as a "scene of suffering," which he defines as "a destructive or painful action, such as death on the stage, bodily agony, wounds, and the like" (XI. 6. p. 43). He stresses that the destructive or painful action (not exclusively death) should be caused by "those who are near or dear to one another" (XIV. 4, pp. 49–50). That is, violence should occur within a royal household or family rather than against a hostile foe. The resulting suffering is especially horrifying because the trust, love, and protectiveness that one hopes for in a family is replaced by treachery, hate, and mayhem.

Aristotle's concept of recognition is of great importance because it is an affirmative signal in the midst of negative events. Ideally, upon recognizing the real truth, the protagonist acknowledges errors and accepts responsibility. Without such positive recognition, we would have works that are no more than horrifying, sad, or pathetic. With the affirmative recognition, however, we have tragedy—the dramatic form which illustrates human integrity even in the lowest depths of adversity.

SERIOUSNESS, COMPLETENESS, AND ARTISTIC BALANCE. Of comparable importance with the elements of plot is Aristotle's assertion that a tragedy is "serious, complete, and of a certain magnitude." The term *serious*, or elevated, concerns the play's tone and level of life, in contrast with the boisterousness and ribaldry of Athenian comedies. While comedy makes people seem worse than they are, tragedy, more seriously, shows them as better (II. 4, p.13). Seriousness is also a consequence of the political and cosmological dimensions of the issues in which the heroic characters are engaged. By *complete*, or whole, Aristotle means that the tragedy must be shaped and perfected to be logical and finished. Everything, whether beginning, middle, or end, must be so perfectly placed that changing or removing any part would spoil the entirety (VII. 2,3, p. 31). By stating that a tragedy should be of a "certain" or proportional *magnitude*, Aristotle refers to a perfected limitation in length and subject matter. The play should be short enough to "be easily embraced by the memory, " and long enough to "admit of a change . . . from good fortune to bad" (VII. 6, p. 33). In other words, everything is artistically balanced; nothing superfluous is included, and nothing essential is omitted.

CATHARSIS, OR PURGATION. The most difficult and uncertain part of Aristotle's definition is his claim that tragedy, by arousing pity and fear (*eleos* and *phobos*), brings about a "proper **purgation**," or purification (catharsis) of these emotions. He uses the word *catharsis* only once in *The Poetics*, though he often uses the combination "pity and fear," but the concept of catharsis is essential to tragedy. At a basic psychological level, catharsis may be understood as a sympathetic release of emotions. One of Aristotle's predecessors, the philosopher Gorgias (ca. 483–ca 385 B.C.), has left us a similar description of this effect:

> There comes over the audience of poetry [*i.e.*, tragedy] a fearful horror and tearful pity and doleful yearning. By means of the discourse their spirit feels a personal emotion on account of the good and bad fortune of others.[4]

This concept implies that tragedy may improve mental well-being. If people have no way to express their feelings legitimately, they may build up real and imagined grievances that lead to frustration and anger. But the performance of a tragedy brings about sympathy for the characters, whose suffering and danger evoke pity and fear (accompanied by responses like shock, horror, and anxiety). When watching a tragedy, then, people's concerns are directed not *inwardly*, at their own problems, but rather *outwardly*, at those of the tragic characters. Psychologically, such an emotional purgation is one of tragedy's major humanizing and civilizing effects.

In addition, catharsis has overtones of religious purification, and tragedy was a key feature of the Dionysiac celebrations for this reason. It has been said that the subject matter of tragedies has "nothing to do with Dionysus," but the fact is that the City Dionysia in ancient Athens was not only a week-long celebration but was also a period of purification. To the ancient Athenians, the emotional purgation accompanying a tragic performance permitted individuals to become receptive to divine power. In this way the tragic catharsis led toward the spiritual purification that was also sought in the ecstatic and orgiastic worship of Dionysus as the *liberating* god. Indeed, just attending a tragic performance was considered a religiously purifying experience.

THE TRAGIC HERO. Further on in *The Poetics*, Aristotle explains the artistry necessary to bring about proper tragic responses. His idea is that the misfortunes of the noble protagonist should be caused not by "vice" or "depravity" but rather by "error" or "frailty" (XIII. 3, p. 45). Aristotle's word for such shortcomings is *hamartia*, which is often translated as **tragic flaw** (in the New Testament *hamartia* is usually translated as *sin*). Thus we, as normally imperfect human beings, identify with a tragic protagonist who is also imperfect. We could not sympathize with a criminal protagonist, for then the downfall would cause not pity but satisfaction. Nor could we sympathize with the downfall of a saint (one who is "preeminently good and just"), which would produce anger and indignation rather than unmixed pity. An ideal tragedy, therefore, is fine-tuned to control our responses exactly, producing horror or

---

[4] Gorgias's *Encomium of Helen*, cited in Oliver Elton, *Greek Tragedy in Action* (Berkeley: U. of California Press, 1979), p. 168.

fear because of the protagonist's suffering, and pity because the suffering far exceeds what the protagonist deserves.

Later Tragedy and Aristotle

Because Aristotle has been so dominant in the history of philosophy and literature, his views in *The Poetics* may be adapted in the analysis of later tragedies. For example, although Shakespeare and his Renaissance English contemporaries sometimes relied on recorded history for subjects, they were still dealing with "received legends" from the past. Also, even though the tragic milieu changed—the disorganized pantheon of arbitrary and sometimes cranky Greek gods gave way to the more formal Christian theology—writers still attempted to make their tragedies serious, complete, and artistically balanced. In addition, human concerns have remained constant although tragic protagonists have been seemingly reduced in stature. In the eighteenth century the development of **domestic tragedy** featured characters from the middle class, and later tragedians included members of the working class. Arthur Miller's name *Loman* for the protagonist of *Death of a Salesman*, for example ("low man"), emphasizes that modern human beings occupy a niche far below the heroes and demi-gods of ancient Greece.

IRONY IN TRAGEDY

Implicit in the excessiveness of tragic suffering is the idea that the universe is mysterious and often unfair, and that unseen but powerful forces—like fate, fortune, circumstances, and the gods—directly intervene in human life. The ancient Athenians believed that the gods give rewards or punishments to suit their own purposes, which mortals can neither prevent nor understand. In *Prometheus Bound* by Aeschylus, for example, the god Hephaestus binds Prometheus to a rock in the Scythian Mountains as punishment for having given fire and technology to humankind. (A good deed produces suffering.) Conversely, in *Medea* Euripides shows that the god Apollo permits Medea to escape after killing her own children. (An evil deed produces reward.)

Situational Irony

These examples illustrate the pervasiveness of situational irony in tragedy. Characters try to act reasonably, but consistent with Aristotle's idea of *reversal*, their actions do not produce the expected results, and often, no matter what they do, things come out badly. Oedipus, for example, brings suffering on himself just when he succeeds—and *because* he succeeds—in rescuing his city. One of the most powerful situational ironies is brought about by recognition. Ironically, self-knowledge and understanding never occur until calamity is already certain. Such irony is not confined to ancient tragedies. In *Death of a Salesman*, Arthur Miller shows that misfortune results not from divine power but rather from economic circumstances. Shakespeare's tragic hero, Hamlet, speaks about the "divinity that shapes our ends," thus expressing the unpredictability of hopes, plans, and achievements.

Dramatic Irony

It is from a perspective of something like "divinity" that we as readers or spectators perceive the action of tragedies. We are like the gods because we always know more than the characters. Such dramatic irony permits us, for example, to know that Oedipus, in defensive rage, killed his real father, and that Claudius deliberately murdered his brother, the elder King Hamlet— long before the tragic heroes in either play learn the truth.

THE TRAGIC DILEMMA These ironies are related to what is called the **tragic dilemma**—a situation that forces the tragic protagonist to make one of two equally difficult choices. Thus, Oedipus cannot shirk his duty as King of Thebes because that would be ruinous. He therefore tries to eliminate his city's pollution, but that also is ruinous. Similarly, Hamlet must either become a murderous avenger, contrary to his own good nature, or avoid the entire situation and retreat into ineffectiveness or suicide, which he considers cowardly. In other words, the tragic dilemma seemingly permits freedom of will, but powerful forces baffle even the most reasonable intentions.

THE ANCIENT ATHENIAN AUDIENCE AND THEATER

Athenians of the fifth century—all free males, for slaves and women were not citizens—took their theater seriously. Indeed, many of them, when young, had taken active parts in the parades and presentations during the festivals. There was a charge, but poorer people received a subsidy for their admittance. Rich Athenians, as a duty to the state, underwrote the costs of the productions—except for the three professional actors who were paid by the government. Each wealthy man, for his contribution, was known as a *choregus* or choral sponsor. To gain public recognition, the choregus sometimes performed as the leader of the chorus.

The Origin of Theater in the Athenian Marketplace

In the beginning, tragic performances were given specially designated space in the Athenian *agora*, or marketplace. In the center of the performing area was an altar dedicated to Dionysus, around which the choruses danced and chanted. Wooden risers were set up for the spectators.

The Athenian Theater of Dionysus

By early in the fifth century, a half-circular outdoor theater (*theatron*, or place for seeing) was created out of the hill at the southern base of the

Acropolis in the area sacred to Dionysus. All later performances of tragedies were held at this **Theater of Dionysus**, which had an estimated capacity of as many as 14,000 people. Originally, most spectators sat on the ground, but eventually wooden and then stone benches were constructed, with more elegant seating for the dignitaries in front. Although the Theater was outdoors, the acoustics were sufficiently good to permit audiences to hear everything that the actors and the choruses said and sang.

Centered at the base of the hill—the focus of attention—was a round area modeled on the one that had been used in the agora. This was the *orchestra* or dancing place, and was about sixty-five feet in diameter. It was here that each chorus sang its odes and performed its dance movements to the rhythm of a double-piped flute, an instrument that was also used to mark the step in military drill. In the center was a permanent altar.

Behind the *orchestra* there was a building for actors, costumes, and props called the ***skene*** (*tent*), from which is derived our modern word *scene*. Originally a hut or tent, the *skene* was later made of wood and then stone, and it was decorated to provide backdrops for the various plays. In the center a double door for entrances and exits opened out to the *orchestra*. Through this door a large platform could be rolled out to show interior scenes. Some theater historians argue that there was a wooden platform (*proskenion* or proscenium) in front of the *skene* to elevate the actors and set them off from the chorus. There was no curtain; indeed, there was no need for a curtain and no structure that could have held one.

Ancient theater at Epidauros, Greece. (Gian Berto Vanni/Art Resource)

The roof of the *skene* was sometimes used as a place of action (as in Aeschylus's *Agamemnon*). A *mechane* (*may-kahn-ay*) or crane was also located there so that actors playing gods could be swung up, down, and around as a mark of divine power. It was this crane that eventually gave rise to the Latin phrase ***deus ex machina*** (a god out of the machine), which refers to an artificial and/or illogical action or device introduced at a play's end to bring otherwise impossible conflicts to a satisfactory solution.

The performing space for the actors was mainly in front of the *skene*. The space for the chorus was the entire *orchestra*. The chorus entered the *orchestra*—and left it at the end of the play—along the aisles between the retaining wall of the hillside seats and the front of the *skene*. Each of these lateral walkways was known as a *parados* (way in), the name also given to the chorus's entering scene. The actors often used the *skene* for entries and exits, but they were also free to use either of the walkways.

In the centuries after it was built, the Theater of Dionysus was remodeled and restored a number of times. When Aeschylus's trilogy *The Oresteia* was performed in 458 B.C., for example, there had been a recent renovation. In Roman times the Theater was allowed to go into ruins. Today its broken remains give only a small idea of its ancient importance (see the color plate on p. 1014). By contrast, the Theater of Epidaurus, which even in antiquity was considered the best of the Greek theaters, has been preserved in excellent condition (see the photograph, p. 1078).

TRAGIC ACTORS AND THEIR COSTUMES

For the three competing playwrights who had been "given a chorus" by the archon to stage their works during the City Dionysia (and later during the Lenaia) the task was to plan, choreograph, and direct the productions, usually with the aid of professionals. By performance time, the dramatists would already have spent many months in preparing the three assigned actors and fifteen choristers. They also would have directed rehearsals for a small number of auxiliary chorus members and other silent extra roles such as servants and soldiers.

Costumes

All these participants needed costumes. The chorus members were lightly clad, for ease of movement, and were apparently barefoot when they performed their formations. The main actors wore the identifying costumes of tragedy, namely sleeved robes, boots, and masks. Their robes were heavily decorated and embroidered. Their calf-high leather boots, called *kothornoi* or **buskins**, were like the elegant boots worn by the patron god Dionysus in painting and statuary. During the following centuries, the buskins became elevator shoes which made the tragic actors taller, in keeping with their heroic stature.

Masks

A vital aspect of ancient tragic costuming was the use of conventional-ized masks that were made up of linen and plaster. As many as twenty-eight different types of masks were available for the tragic productions. Each mask portrayed a separate facial type and expression (e.g., king, queen, young woman, old man, etc.). The choristers wore identical masks for their group roles. Apparently the masks covered the entire head, containing a high hair-dress and, when necessary, a beard.

The masks, along with costume changes, gave the actors great versatil-ity. Each actor could take a number of different roles simply by entering the *skene*, changing mask and costume, and reentering as a new character. Thus, in *Oedipus the King* a single actor could represent the seer Tiresias and later reappear as the Messenger. Technically, the masks even made it possible for two actors, or even all three, to perform as the same character in separate parts of the play, if such a need arose.

PERFORMANCE AND THE FORMAL ORGANIZATION OF GREEK TRAGEDY

On the days of performance, the competing playwrights staged their plays from morning to afternoon, the tragedies first, and then the satyr plays. Be-cause plays were performed with only a minimum of scenery and props, dramatists used their dialogue to establish the times and locations of the dra-matic action. Each tragedy was produced in the order of the formally desig-nated sections that are marked in the printed texts. It is therefore possible to describe the production of a play in terms of these structural divisions.

The first scene was the **prologue**, which contained the exposition. There was considerable variety in the performance of the prologue. Some-times it was given by a single actor, speaking as either a mortal or a god. In *Oedipus the King*, Sophocles used all three actors for the prologue (Oedipus, the Priest, and Creon), speaking to themselves and also to the extras acting as the Theban populace.

The next unit was the *parados*, or the entry of the chorus into the *or-chestra*, where they remained until the end of the play. The chorus chanted and sang, and also danced or moved rhythmically in a number of stanzaic *strophes* (turns), *antistrophes* (counterturns), and *epodes* (units following the songs) to prepare the audience for the action to come. The dance move-ments, to the rhythm of the flute, were done in straight-line formations of five or three, but we do not know if the chorus stopped or continued moving when delivering their lines. After the *parados* was finished, the choristers knelt or sat at attention, in this way focusing on the following action and, when necessary, responding as a group.

With the chorus as a model audience, the drama itself consisted of four full sections or acting units. The major part of each section was the **episode**.

Each episode featured the actors, who presented both action and speech, including swift one-line interchanges known as **stichomythy**.

When the episode ended, the actors withdrew.[5] The following second part of the acting section was called a ***stasimon*** (plural *stasima*), performed by the chorus exclusively in the *orchestra*. Like the *parados*, the *stasima* required dance movements, along with the chanting and singing of strophes, antistrophes, and epodes. The topics concerned the play's developing action, although over time the *stasima* became more general and therefore less integral to the play.

When the last of the four episode-*stasimon* sections had been completed, the ***exodos*** was the final section. It contained the resolution of the drama, the exit of the actors, and the last pronouncements, dance movements, and exit of the chorus.

Classical Athenian tragedies of the fifth century B.C. substantially followed this pattern. We know little about tragic structure before Aeschylus, Sophocles' older contemporary. Aristotle, however, states that Aeschylus lengthened the episodes, thus emphasizing the actors and minimizing the chorus (IV.13, p. 19). Sophocles made the chorus even less important. Euripides, Sophocles's younger contemporary, concentrated almost entirely on the episodes, making the chorus almost incidental. In later centuries, dramatists dropped the choral sections completely, thereby creating the five-act structure adopted by the Romans and later by Shakespeare and his contemporaries.

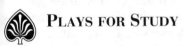

PLAYS FOR STUDY

SOPHOCLES, *OEDIPUS THE KING*

Sophocles was born between 500 and 494 B.C. into an affluent Athenian family. He began acting and singing early, and served as a choral leader in the celebrations for the defeat of the Persians at Marathon in 480 B.C. In 468 he was victorious with the first play he submitted for competition, *Triptolemos*. He wrote at least 122 more plays, approximately 90 of them tragedies, and he won the prize 24 times, a record. He was also an active citizen. He was twice elected general of his tribe. In addition, he served as a priest in the cult of Asclepius, the God of Healing. Because of his dramatic and

[5] For example, at the end of the first episode, Oedipus goes into the *skene*—the palace—while a servant leads Tiresias off along the *parados*, thus indicating that he is leaving Thebes entirely.

public achievements, he was venerated during his lifetime. After his death in 406–405 B.C., a cult was established in his honor.

When *Oedipus the King* was first performed between 430 and 425 B.C., most of the audience would have known the general outlines of the story: the antagonism of the gods Hephaestus and Hera toward Cadmus of Thebes (of whom Oedipus was a descendant); the prophecy that the Theban King Laius would be killed by his own son; the exposure of the new-born Oedipus on a mountainside; his rescue by a well-meaning shepherd; his youth spent as the adopted son of Queen Merope and King Polybus of Corinth; his trip to Delphi to learn his origins; his impetuous murder of Laius (a stranger to him); his solution of the Sphinx's riddle; his ascension as King of Thebes and his marriage to Queen Jocasta, his mother; his reign as King; the plague that afflicted Thebes; his attempts at restoration; and Jocasta's suicide when the truth of Oedipus's past is revealed.

Although these details were commonly known, there was disagreement about the outcome of Oedipus's life. One version told that he remarried, had four children with his new wife, reigned long and successfully, died in battle, and was finally worshipped as a hero. Sophocles, however, dramatizes a version—either a current one or one which he created himself—that tells of Oedipus's self-imposed punishment.

As we have said, Aristotle prized *Oedipus the King* so highly that he used it to illustrate many of his principles of tragedy. Of particular interest is that the play embodies the so-called three **unities**, which are implicit in *The Poetics* although Aristotle does not stress them. Sophocles creates *unity of place* by using the front of the royal palace of Thebes as the location for the entire action. He creates *unity of action* by dramatizing only those activities leading to Oedipus's recognition about the true polluter of the city. Finally, he creates *unity of time* because the stage or action time coincides with the real-life time. In fact, the play's time is considerably shorter than the "single revolution of the sun" (*sic*) that Aristotle recommends as the proper period for a complete tragic action (V. 4, p. 23). Above all, *Oedipus the King* meets Aristotle's requirements for one of the very best plays because of the skill with which Sophocles makes Oedipus's recognition of his guilt coincide exactly with the disastrous reversal of his fortunes (XI. 2, p. 41).

SOPHOCLES   (ca. 496–406 B.C.)

Oedipus the King ————————————————————— *ca. 430* B.C.

Translated by Thomas Gould

CHARACTERS

> Oedipus,° *The King of Thebes*
> Priest of Zeus, *Leader of the Suppliants*

Oedipus: The name means "swollen foot." It refers to the mutilation of Oedipus's feet done by his father, Laius, before the infant was sent to Mount Cithaeron to be put to death by exposure.

Creon, *Oedipus's Brother-in-law*
Chorus, *a Group of Theban Elders*
Choragos, *Spokesman of the Chorus*
Tiresias, *a blind Seer or Prophet*
Jocasta, *The Queen of Thebes*
Messenger, *from Corinth, once a Shepherd*
Herdsman, *once a Servant of Laius*
Second Messenger, *a Servant of Oedipus*

MUTES

Suppliants, *Thebans seeking Oedipus's help*
Attendants, *for the Royal Family*
Servants, *to lead Tiresias and Oedipus*
Antigone, *Daughter of Oedipus and Jocasta*
Ismene, *Daughter of Oedipus and Jocasta*

[*The action takes place during the day in front of the royal palace in Thebes. There are two altars (left and right) on the Proscenium and several steps leading down to the Orchestra. As the play opens, Thebans of various ages who have come to beg Oedipus for help are sitting on these steps and in part of the Orchestra. These suppliants are holding branches of laurel or olive which have strips of wool° wrapped around them. Oedipus enters from the palace (the central door of the Skene).*]

PROLOGUE

OEDIPUS.   My children, ancient Cadmus'° newest care,
    why have you hurried to those seats, your boughs
    wound with the emblems of the suppliant?
    The city is weighed down with fragrant smoke,
    with hymns to the Healer° and the cries of mourners.   5
    I thought it wrong, my sons, to hear your words
    through emissaries, and have come out myself,
    I, Oedipus, a name that all men know.

[*OEDIPUS addresses the PRIEST.*]

Old man—for it is fitting that you speak
    for all—what is your mood as you entreat me,   10
    fear or trust? You may be confident
    that I'll do anything. How hard of heart
    if an appeal like this did not rouse my pity!
PRIEST.   You, Oedipus, who hold the power here,
    you see our several ages, we who sit   15
    before your altars—some not strong enough
    to take long flight, some heavy in old age,
    the priests, as I of Zeus,° and from our youths
    a chosen band. The rest sit with their windings

Stage direction: *wool:* Branches wrapped with wool are traditional symbols of prayer or supplication.
Cadmus: Oedipus's great great grandfather (although he does not know this) and the founder of
Thebes.   5 *Healer:* Apollo, god of prophecy, light, healing, justice, purification, and destruction.
18 *Zeus:* father and king of the gods.

in the markets, at the twin shrines of Pallas,°
and the prophetic embers of Ismēnos.°
Our city, as you see yourself, is tossed
too much, and can no longer lift its head
above the troughs of billows red with death.
It dies in the fruitful flowers of the soil,
it dies in its pastured herds, and in its women's
barren pangs. And the fire-bearing god°
has swooped upon the city, hateful plague,
and he has left the house of Cadmus empty.
Black Hades° is made rich with moans and weeping.
Not judging you an equal of the gods,
do I and the children sit here at your hearth,
but as the first of men, in troubled times
and in encounters with divinities.
You came to Cadmus' city and unbound
the tax we had to pay to the harsh singer,°
did it without a helpful word from us,
with no instruction; with a god's assistance
you raised up our life, so we believe.
Again now Oedipus, our greatest power,
we plead with you, as suppliants, all of us,
to find us strength, whether from a god's response,
or learned in some way from another man.
I know that the experienced among men
give counsels that will prosper best of all.
Noblest of men, lift up our land again!
Think also of yourself; since now the land
calls you its Savior for your zeal of old,
oh let us never look back at your rule
as men helped up only to fall again!
Do not stumble! Put our land on firm feet!
The bird of omen was auspicious then,
when you brought that luck; be that same man again!
The power is yours; if you will rule our country,
rule over men, not in an empty land.
A towered city or a ship is nothing
if desolate and no man lives within.

20 *Pallas:* Athena, goddess of wisdom, arts, crafts, and war.   21 *Ismēnos:* a reference to the temple of Apollo near the river Ismēnos in Thebes. Prophecies were made here by "reading" the ashes of the altar fires.   27 *fire-bearing god:* contagious fever viewed as a god.   30 *Black Hades:* refers to both the underworld, where the spirits of the dead go, and the god of the underworld.   36 *harsh singer:* the Sphinx, a monster with a woman's head, a lion's body, and wings. The "tax" that Oedipus freed Thebes from was the destruction of all the young men who failed to solve the Sphinx's riddle and were subsequently devoured. The Sphinx always asked the same riddle: "What goes on four legs in the morning, two legs at noon, and three legs in the evening, and yet is weakest when supported by the largest number of feet?" Oedipus discovered the correct answer—man, who crawls in infancy, walks in his prime, and uses a stick in old age—and thus ended the Sphinx's reign of terror. The Sphinx destroyed herself when Oedipus answered the riddle. Oedipus's reward for freeing Thebes of the Sphinx was the throne and the hand of the recently widowed Jocasta. (A photograph of a Sphinx built in ancient Egypt appears on p. 827.)

OEDIPUS.   Pitiable children, oh I know, I know
   the yearnings that have brought you. Yes, I know
   that you are sick. And yet, though you are sick,   60
   there is not one of you so sick as I.
   For your affliction comes to each alone,
   for him and no one else, but my soul mourns
   for me and for you, too, and for the city.
   You do not waken me as from a sleep,   65
   for I have wept, bitterly and long,
   tried many paths in the wanderings of thought,
   and the single cure I found by careful search
   I've acted on: I sent Menoeceus' son,
   Creon, brother of my wife, to the Pythian   70
   halls of Phoebus,° so that I might learn
   what I must do or say to save this city.
   Already, when I think what day this is,
   I wonder anxiously what he is doing.
   Too long, more than is right, he's been away.   75
   But when he comes, then I shall be a traitor
   if I do not do all that the god reveals.
PRIEST.   Welcome words! But look, those men have signaled
   that it is Creon who is now approaching!
OEDIPUS.   Lord Apollo! May he bring Savior Luck,   80
   a Luck as brilliant as his eyes are now!
PRIEST.   His news is happy, it appears. He comes,
   forehead crowned with thickly berried laurel.°
OEDIPUS.   We'll know, for he is near enough to hear us.

[*Enter* CREON *along one of the Parados.*]

   Lord, brother in marriage, son of Menoeceus!   85
   What is the god's pronouncement that you bring?
CREON.   It's good. For even troubles, if they chance
   to turn out well, I always count as lucky.
OEDIPUS.   But what was the response? You seem to say
   I'm not to fear—but not to take heart either.   90
CREON.   If you will hear me with these men present,
   I'm ready to report—or go inside.

[*CREON moves up the steps toward the palace.*]

OEDIPUS.   Speak out to all! The grief that burdens me
   concerns these men more than it does my life.
CREON.   Then I shall tell you what I heard from the god.   95
   The task Lord Phoebus sets for us is clear:
   drive out pollution sheltered in our land,
   and do not shelter what is incurable.
OEDIPUS.   What is our trouble? How shall we cleanse ourselves?

70–71 *Pythian . . . Phoebus:* the temple of Phoebus Apollo's oracle or prophet at Delphi.
83 *laurel:* Creon is wearing a garland of laurel leaves, sacred to Apollo.

CREON.   We must banish or murder to free ourselves   1
   from a murder that blows storms through the city.
OEDIPUS.   What man's bad luck does he accuse in this?
CREON.   My Lord, a king named Laius ruled our land
   before you came to steer the city straight.
OEDIPUS.   I know. So I was told—I never saw him.   1
CREON.   Since he was murdered, you must raise your hand
   against the men who killed him with their hands.
OEDIPUS.   Where are they now? And how can we ever find
   the track of ancient guilt now hard to read?
CREON.   In our own land, he said. What we pursue,   1
   that can be caught; but not what we neglect.
OEDIPUS.   Was Laius home, or in the countryside—
   or was he murdered in some foreign land?
CREON.   He left to see a sacred rite, he said;
   He left, but never came home from his journey.   1
OEDIPUS.   Did none of his party see it and report—
   someone we might profitably question?
CREON.   They were all killed but one, who fled in fear,
   and he could tell us only one clear fact.
OEDIPUS.   What fact? One thing could lead us on to more   1!
   if we could get a small start on our hope.
CREON.   He said that bandits chanced on them and killed him—
   with the force of many hands, not one alone.
OEDIPUS.   How could a bandit dare so great an act—
   unless this was a plot paid off from here!   1!
CREON.   We thought of that, but when Laius was killed,
   we had no one to help us in our troubles.
OEDIPUS.   It was your very kingship that was killed!
   What kind of trouble blocked you from a search?
CREON.   The subtle-singing Sphinx asked us to turn   1!
   from the obscure to what lay at our feet.
OEDIPUS.   Then I shall begin again and make it plain.
   It was quite worthy of Phoebus, and worthy of you,
   to turn our thoughts back to the murdered man,
   and right that you should see me join the battle   1!
   for justice to our land and to the god.
   Not on behalf of any distant kinships,
   it's for myself I will dispel this stain.
   Whoever murdered him may also wish
   to punish me—and with the selfsame hand.   14
   In helping him I also serve myself.
   Now quickly, children: up from the altar steps,
   and raise the branches of the suppliant!
   Let someone go and summon Cadmus' people:
   say I'll do anything.

   [*Exit an* ATTENDANT *along one of the Parados.*]

            Our luck will prosper   14
   if the god is with us, or we have already fallen.

PRIEST.   Rise, my children; that for which we came,
 he has himself proclaimed he will accomplish.
 May Phoebus, who announced this, also come
 as Savior and reliever from the plague.   150

[*Exit OEDIPUS and CREON into the Palace. The PRIEST and the SUPPLIANTS exit left
 and right along the Parados. After a brief pause, the CHORUS (including the
     CHOKAGOS) enters the Orchestra from the Parados.*]

PARADOS

Strophe 1°

CHORUS.   Voice from Zeus,° sweetly spoken, what are you
 that have arrived from golden
 Pytho° to our shining
 Thebes? I am on the rack, terror
  shakes my soul.   155
 Delian Healer,° summoned by "iē!"
 I await in holy dread what obligation, something new
 or something back once more with the revolving years,
  you'll bring about for me.
 Oh tell me, child of golden Hope,   160
  deathless Response!

Antistrophe 1°

I appeal to you first, daughter of Zeus,
  deathless Athena,
  and to your sister who protects this land,
  Artemis,° whose famous throne is the whole circle 165
  of the marketplace,
and Phoebus, who shoots from afar: iō!
 Three-fold defenders against death, appear!
 If ever in the past, to stop blind ruin
  sent against the city,   170
you banished utterly the fires of suffering,
  come now again!

Strophe 2

Ah! Ah! Unnumbered are the miseries
I bear. The plague claims all
our comrades. Nor has thought found yet a spear   175
by which a man shall be protected. What our glorious

151,162 *Strophe, Antistrophe:* These stanzaic units refer to movements, counter-movements, and
gestures that the Chorus performed while singing or chanting in the orchestra. See p. 1080.
151 *Voice from Zeus:* a reference to Apollo's prophecy. Zeus taught Apollo how to prophesy.
153 *Pytho:* Delphi. 156 *Delian Healer:* Apollo. 165 *Artemis:* goddess of virginity, childbirth,
and hunting.

earth gives birth to does not grow. Without a birth
from cries of labor
    do the women rise.
One person after another
    you may see, like flying birds,
faster than indomitable fire, sped
to the shore of the god that is the sunset.°

Antistrophe 2

And with their deaths unnumbered dies the city.
Her children lie unpitied on the ground,
spreading death, unmourned.
Meanwhile young wives, and gray-haired mothers with them,
on the shores of the altars, from this side and that,
suppliants from mournful trouble,
    cry out their grief.
A hymn to the Healer shines,
    the flute a mourner's voice.
Against which, golden goddess, daughter of Zeus,
    send lovely Strength.

Strophe 3

Cause raging Ares°—who,
    armed now with no shield of bronze,
burns me, coming on amid loud cries—
to turn his back and run from my land,
with a fair wind behind, to the great
    hall of Amphitritē,°
or to the anchorage that welcomes no one,
Thrace's troubled sea!
If night lets something get away at last,
    it comes by day.
Fire-bearing god . . . . . .
    you who dispense the might of lightning,
Zeus! Father! Destroy him with your thunderbolt!

[*Enter* OEDIPUS *from the palace.*]

Antistrophe 3

Lycēan Lord!° From your looped
    bowstring, twisted gold,
I wish indomitable missiles might be scattered
and stand forward, our protectors; also fire-bearing
radiance of Artemis, with which
    she darts across the Lycian mountains.
I call the god whose head is bound in gold,

---

183 *god . . . sunset:* Hades, god of the underworld.   195 *Ares:* god of war and destruction.
200 *Amphitritē:* the Atlantic Ocean.   208 *Lycēan Lord:* Apollo.

with whom this country shares its name,   215
Bacchus,° wine-flushed, summoned by "euoi!,"
     Maenads' comrade,
to approach ablaze
     with gleaming . . . . . .
pine, opposed to that god-hated god.   220

Episode 1

OEDIPUS.   I hear your prayer. Submit to what I say
and to the labors that the plague demands
and you'll get help and a relief from evils.
I'll make the proclamation, though a stranger
to the report and to the deed. Alone,   225
had I no key, I would soon lose the track.
Since it was only later that I joined you,
to all the sons of Cadmus I say this:
whoever has clear knowledge of the man
who murdered Laius, son of Labdacus,   230
I command him to reveal it all to me—
nor fear if, to remove the charge, he must
accuse himself: his fate will not be cruel—
he will depart unstumbling into exile.
But if you know another, or a stranger,   235
to be the one whose hand is guilty, speak:
I shall reward you and remember you.
But if you keep your peace because of fear,
and shield yourself or kin from my command,
hear you what I shall do in that event: 240
I charge all in this land where I have throne
and power, shut out that man—no matter who—
both from your shelter and all spoken words,
nor in your prayers or sacrifices make
him partner, nor allot him lustral° water.   245
All men shall drive him from their homes: for he
is the pollution that the god-sent Pythian
response has only now revealed to me.
In this way I ally myself in war
with the divinity and the deceased.°   250
And this curse, too, against the one who did it,
whether alone in secrecy, or with others:
may he wear out his life unblest and evil!
I pray this, too: if he is at my hearth
and in my home, and I have knowledge of him,   255
may the curse pronounced on others come to me.
All this I lay to you to execute,
for my sake, for the god's, and for this land

216 *Bacchus:* Dionysus, god of fertility and wine.   245 *lustral:* purifying.   250 *the deceased:*
Laius.

now ruined, barren, abandoned by the gods.
Even if no god had driven you to it,
you ought not to have left this stain uncleansed,
the murdered man a nobleman, a king!
You should have looked! But now, since, as it happens,
It's I who have the power that he had once,
and have his bed, and a wife who shares our seed,
and common bond had we had common children
(had not his hope of offspring had back luck—
but as it happened, luck lunged at his head);
because of this, as if for my own father,
I'll fight for him, I'll leave no means untried,
to catch the one who did it with his hand,
for the son of Labdacus, of Polydōrus,
of Cadmus before him, and of Agēnor.°
This prayer against all those who disobey:
the gods send out no harvest from their soil,
nor children from their wives. Oh, let them die
victims of this plague, or of something worse.
Yet for the rest of us, people of Cadmus,
we the obedient, may Justice, our ally,
and all the gods, be always on our side!

CHORAGOS.   I speak because I feel the grip of your curse:
the killer is not I. Nor can I point
to him. The one who set us to this search,
Phoebus, should also name the guilty man.

OEDIPUS.   Quite right, but to compel unwilling gods—
no man has ever had that kind of power.

CHORAGOS.   May I suggest to you a second way?

OEDIPUS.   A second or a third—pass over nothing!

CHORAGOS.   I know of no one who sees more of what
Lord Phoebus sees than Lord Tiresias.
My Lord, one might learn brilliantly from him.

OEDIPUS.   Nor is this something I have been slow to do.
At Creon's word I sent an escort—twice now!
I am astonished that he has not come.

CHORAGOS.   The old account is useless. It told us nothing.

OEDIPUS.   But tell it to me. I'll scrutinize all stories.

CHORAGOS.   He is said to have been killed by travelers.

OEDIPUS.   I have heard, but the one who did it no one sees.

CHORAGOS.   If there is any fear in him at all,
he won't stay here once he has heard that curse.

OEDIPUS.   He won't fear words: he had no fear when he did it.

[*Enter* TIRESIAS *from the right, led by a* SERVANT *and two of Oedipus's* ATTENDANTS.]

CHORAGOS.   Look there! There is the man who will convict him!
It's the god's prophet they are leading here,
one gifted with the truth as no one else.

272–73 *son . . . Agēnor:* refers to Laius by citing his genealogy.

OEDIPUS.   Tiresias, master of all omens—   305
    public and secret, in the sky and on the earth—
    your mind, if not your eyes, sees how the city
    lives with a plague, against which Thebes can find
    no Saviour or protector, Lord, but you.
    For Phoebus, as the attendants surely told you,   310
    returned this answer to us: liberation
    from the disease would never come unless
    we learned without a doubt who murdered Laius—
    put them to death, or sent them into exile.
    Do not begrudge us what you may learn from birds   315
    or any other prophet's path you know!
    Care for yourself, the city, care for me,
    care for the whole pollution of the dead!
    We're in your hands. To do all that he can
    to help another is man's noblest labor.   320
TIRESIAS.   How terrible to understand and get
    no profit from the knowledge! I knew this,
    but I forgot, or I had never come.
OEDIPUS.   What's this? You've come with very little zeal.
TIRESIAS.   Let me go home! If you will listen to me,   325
    You will endure your troubles better—and I mine.
OEDIPUS.   A strange request, not very kind to the land
    that cared for you—to hold back this oracle!
TIRESIAS.   I see your understanding comes to you
    inopportunely. So that won't happen to me . . .   330
OEDIPUS.   Oh, by the gods, if you understand about this,
    don't turn away! We're on our knees to you.
TIRESIAS.   None of you understands! I'll never bring
    my grief to light—I will not speak of yours.
OEDIPUS.   You know and won't declare it! Is your purpose   335
    to betray us and to destroy this land?
TIRESIAS.   I will grieve neither of us. Stop this futile
    cross-examination. I'll tell you nothing!
OEDIPUS.   Nothing? You vile traitor! You could provoke
    a stone to anger! You still refuse to tell?   340
    Can nothing soften you, nothing convince you?
TIRESIAS.   You blamed anger in me—you haven't seen.
    Can nothing soften you, nothing convince you?
OEDIPUS.   Who wouldn't fill with anger, listening
    to words like yours which now disgrace this city?   345
TIRESIAS.   It will come, even if my silence hides it.
OEDIPUS.   If it will come, then why won't you declare it?
TIRESIAS.   I'd rather say no more. Now if you wish,
    respond to that with all your fiercest anger!
OEDIPUS.   Now I am angry enough to come right out   350
    with this conjecture: you, I think, helped plot
    the deed; you did it—even if your hand
    cannot have struck the blow. If you could see,
    I should have said the deed was yours alone.

TIRESIAS.   Is that right! Then I charge you to abide   3
    by the decree you have announced: from this day
    say no word to either these or me,
    for you are the vile polluter of this land!
OEDIPUS.   Aren't you appalled to let a charge like that
    come bounding forth? How will you get away?   3
TIRESIAS.   You cannot catch me. I have the strength of truth.
OEDIPUS.   Who taught you this? Not your prophetic craft!
TIRESIAS.   You did. You made me say it. I didn't want to.
OEDIPUS.   Say what? Repeat it so I'll understand.
TIRESIAS.   I made no sense? Or are you trying me?   3
OEDIPUS.   No sense I understood. Say it again!
TIRESIAS.   I say you are the murderer you seek.
OEDIPUS.   Again that horror! You'll wish you hadn't said that.
TIRESIAS.   Shall I say more, and raise your anger higher?
OEDIPUS.   Anything you like! Your words are powerless.   3
TIRESIAS.   You live, unknowing, with those nearest to you
    in the greatest shame. You do not see the evil.
OEDIPUS.   You won't go on like that and never pay!
TIRESIAS.   I can if there is any strength in truth.
OEDIPUS.   In truth, but not in you! You have no strength,   3
    blind in your ears, your reason, and your eyes.
TIRESIAS.   Unhappy man! Those jeers you hurl at me
    before long all these men will hurl at you.
OEDIPUS.   You are the child of endless night; it's not
    for me or anyone who sees to hurt you.   3
TIRESIAS.   It's not my fate to be struck down by you.
    Apollo is enough. That's his concern.
OEDIPUS.   Are these inventions Creon's or your own?
TIRESIAS.   No, your affliction is yourself, not Creon.
OEDIPUS.   Oh success!—in wealth, kingship, artistry,   3
    in any life that wins much admiration—
    the envious ill will stored up for you!
    to get at my command, a gift I did not
    seek, which the city put into my hands,
    my loyal Creon, colleague from the start,   3
    longs to sneak up in secret and dethrone me.
    So he's suborned this fortuneteller—schemer!
    deceitful beggar-priest!—who has good eyes
    for gains alone, though in his craft he's blind.
    Where were your prophet's powers ever proved?   3
    Why, when the dog who chanted verse° was here,
    did you not speak and liberate this city?
    Her riddle wasn't for a man chancing by
    to interpret; prophetic art was needed,
    but you had none, it seems—learned from birds   4
    or from a god. I came along, yes I,
    Oedipus the ignorant, and stopped her—

396 *dog . . . verse:* the Sphinx.

by using thought, not augury from birds.
And it is I whom you may wish to banish,
so you'll be close to the Creontian throne.   405

You—and the plot's concocter—will drive out
pollution to your grief: you look quite old
or you would be the victim of that plot!

CHORAGOS.   It seems to us that this man's words were said
in anger, Oedipus, and yours as well.   410
Insight, not angry words, is what we need,
the best solution to the god's response.

TIRESIAS.   You are the king, and yet I am your equal
in my right to speak. In that I too am Lord,
for I belong to Loxias,° not you.   415
I am not Creon's man. He's nothing to me.
Hear this, since you have thrown my blindness at me:
Your eyes can't see the evil to which you've come,
nor where you live, nor who is in your house.
Do you know your parents? Now knowing, you are   420
their enemy, in the underworld and here.
A mother's and a father's double-lashing
terrible-footed curse will soon drive you out.
Now you can see, then you will stare into darkness.
What place will not be harbor to your cry,   425
or what Cithaeron° not reverberate
when you have heard the bride-song in your palace
to which you sailed? Fair wind to evil harbor!
Nor do you see how many other woes
will level you to yourself and to your children.   430
So, at my message, and at Creon, too,
splatter muck! There will never be a man
ground into wretchedness as you will be.

OEDIPUS.   Am I to listen to such things from him!
May you be damned! Get out of here at once!   435
Go! Leave my palace! Turn around and go!

[*TIRESIAS begins to move away from OEDIPUS.*]

TIRESIAS.   I wouldn't have come had you not sent for me.
OEDIPUS.   I did not know you'd talk stupidity,
or I wouldn't have rushed to bring you to my house.
TIRESIAS.   Stupid I seem to you, yet to your parents   440
who gave you natural birth I seemed quite shrewd.
OEDIPUS.   Who? Wait! Who is the one who gave me birth?
TIRESIAS.   This day will give you birth,° and ruin too.
OEDIPUS.   What murky, riddling things you always say!
TIRESIAS.   Don't you surpass us all at finding out?   445
OEDIPUS.   You sneer at what you'll find has brought me greatness.

---

415 *Loxias:* Apollo.   426 *Cithaeron:* reference to the mountain on which Oedipus was to be
exposed as an infant.   443 *give you birth:* that is, identify your parents.

TIRESIAS.   And that's the very luck that ruined you.
OEDIPUS.   I wouldn't care, just so I saved the city.
TIRESIAS.   In that case I shall go. Boy, lead the way!
OEDIPUS.   Yes, let him lead you off. Here, underfoot,
   you irk me. Gone, you'll cause no further pain.
TIRESIAS.   I'll go when I have said what I was sent for.
   Your face won't scare me. You can't ruin me.
   I say to you, the man whom you have looked for
   as you pronounced your curses, your decrees
   on the bloody death of Laius—he is here!
   A seeming stranger, he shall be shown to be
   a Theban born, though he'll take no delight
   in that solution. Blind, who once could see,
   a beggar who was rich, through foreign lands
   he'll go and point before him with a stick.
   To his beloved children, he'll be shown
   a father who is also brother; to the one
   who bore him, son and husband; to his father,
   his seed-fellow and killer. Go in
   and think this out; and if you find I've lied,
   say then I have no prophet's understanding!

[*Exit* TIRESIAS, *led by a* SERVANT. OEDIPUS *exits into the palace with his* ATTENDANTS.]

STASIMON 1

Strophe 1

CHORUS.   Who is the man of whom the inspired
      rock of Delphi° said
  he has committed the unspeakable
    with blood-stained hands?
  Time for him to ply a foot
  mightier than those of the horses
    of the storm in his escape;
  upon him mounts and plunges the weaponed
  son of Zeus,° with fire and thunderbolts,
  and in his train the dreaded goddesses
  of Death, who never miss.

Antistrophe 1

  The message has just blazed,
    gleaming from the snows
  of Mount Parnassus: we must track
    everywhere the unseen man.
  He wanders, hidden by wild
  forests, up through caves
    and rocks, like a bull,

469 *rock of Delphi:* Apollo's oracle at Delphi.   476 *son of Zeus:* Apollo

anxious, with an anxious foot, forlorn.
He puts away from him the mantic° words come from earth's
navel,° at its center, yet these live
forever and still hover round him.

Strophe 2

Terribly he troubles me,   490
    the skilled interpreter of birds!°
I can't assent, nor speak against him.
    Both paths are closed to me.
I hover on the wings of doubt,
    not seeing what is here nor what's to come.   495
What quarrel started in the house of Labdacus°
or in the house of Polybus,°
    either ever in the past
    or now, I never
heard, so that . . . with this fact for my touchstone   500
I could attack the public
    fame of Oedipus, by the side of the Labdaceans
an ally, against the dark assassination.

Antistrophe 2

No, Zeus and Apollo
    understand and know things   505
mortal; but that another man
    can do more as a prophet than I can—
for that there is no certain test,
    though, skill to skill,
one man might overtake another.   510
No, never, not until
    I see the charges proved,
when someone blames him shall I nod assent.
For once, as we all saw, the winged maiden° came
against him: he was seen then to be skilled,   515
    proved, by that touchstone, dear to the people. So,
never will my mind convict him of the evil.

EPISODE 2

[*Enter* CREON *from the right door of the skene and speaks to the* CHORUS.]
CREON. Citizens, I hear that a fearful charge
    is made against me by King Oedipus!
    I had to come. If, in this crisis,   520
    he thinks that he has suffered injury

---

487 *mantic:* prophetic.   487–88 *earth's navel:* Delphi.   491 *interpreter of birds:* Tiresias. The
Chorus is troubled by his accusations.   496 *house of Labdacus:* the line of Laius.   497 *Polybus:*
Oedipus's foster father.   514 *winged maiden:* the Sphinx.

from anything that I have said or done,
I have no appetite for a long life—
bearing a blame like that! It's no slight blow
the punishment I'd take from what he said: 5
it's the ultimate hurt to be called traitor
by the city, by you, by my own people!
CHORAGOS.   The thing that forced that accusation out
could have been anger, not the power of thought.
CREON.   But who persuaded him that thoughts of mine   5
had led the prophet into telling lies?
CHORAGOS.   I do not know the thought behind his words.
CREON.   But did he look straight at you? Was his mind right
when he said that I was guilty of this charge?
CHORAGOS.   I have no eyes to see what rulers do.   5
But here he comes himself out of the house.

[*Enter OEDIPUS from the palace.*]

OEDIPUS.   What? You here? And can you really have
the face and daring to approach my house
when you're exposed as its master's murderer
and caught, too, as the robber of my kingship?   5
Did you see cowardice in me, by the gods,
or foolishness, when you began this plot?
Did you suppose that I would not detect
your stealthy moves, or that I'd not fight back?
It's your attempt that's folly, isn't it—   5
tracking without followers or connections,
kingship which is caught with wealth and numbers?
CREON.   Now wait! Give me as long to answer back!
Judge me for yourself when you have heard me!
OEDIPUS.   You're eloquent, but I'd be slow to learn   5
from you, now that I've seen your malice toward me.
CREON.   That I deny. Hear what I have to say.
OEDIPUS.   Don't you deny it! You are the traitor here!
CREON.   If you consider mindless willfulness
a prized possession, you are not thinking sense.   5
OEDIPUS.   If you think you can wrong a relative
and get off free, you are not thinking sense.
CREON.   Perfectly just, I won't say no. And yet
what is this injury you say I did you?
OEDIPUS.   Did you persuade me, yes or no, to send   5
someone to bring that solemn prophet here?
CREON.   And I still hold to the advice I gave.
OEDIPUS.   How many years ago did your King Laius . . .
CREON.   Laius! Do what? Now I don't understand.
OEDIPUS.   Vanish—victim of a murderous violence?   5
CREON.   That is a long count back into the past.
OEDIPUS.   Well, was this seer then practicing his art?

CREON.   Yes, skilled and honored just as he is today.
OEDIPUS.   Did he, back then, ever refer to me?
CREON.   He did not do so in my presence ever.   570
OEDIPUS.   You did inquire into the murder then.
CREON.   We had to, surely, though we discovered nothing.
OEDIPUS.   But the "skilled" one did not say this then? Why not?
CREON.   I never talk when I am ignorant.
OEDIPUS.   But you're not ignorant of your own part.   575
CREON.   What do you mean? I'll tell you if I know.
OEDIPUS.   Just this: if he had not conferred with you
    he'd not have told about my murdering Laius.
CREON.   If he said that, you are the one who knows.
    But now it's fair that you should answer me.   580
OEDIPUS.   Ask on! You won't convict me as the killer.
CREON.   Well then, answer. My sister is your wife?
OEDIPUS.   Now there's a statement that I can't deny.
CREON.   You two have equal power in this country?
OEDIPUS.   She gets from me whatever she desires.   585
CREON.   And I'm a third? The three of us are equals?
OEDIPUS.   That's where you're treacherous to your kinship!
CREON.   But think about this rationally, as I do.
    First look at this: do you think anyone
    prefers the anxieties of being king   590
    to untroubled sleep—if he has equal power?
    I'm not the kind of man who falls in love
    with kingship. I am content with a king's power.
    And so would any man who's wise and prudent.
    I get all things from you, with no distress;   595
    as king I would have onerous duties, too.
    How could the kingship bring me more delight
    than this untroubled power and influence?
    I'm not misguided yet to such a point
    that profitable honors aren't enough.   600
    As it is, all wish me well and all salute;
    those begging you for something have me summoned,
    for their success depends on that alone.
    Why should I lose all this to become king?
    A prudent mind is never traitorous.   605
    Treason's a thought I'm not enamored of;
    nor could I join a man who acted so.
    In proof of this, first go yourself to Pytho°
    and ask if I brought back the true response.
    Then, if you find I plotted with that portent   610
    reader,° don't have me put to death by your vote
    only—I'll vote myself for my conviction.

---

608 *Pytho:* Delphi.   610–11 *portent reader:* Apollo's oracle or prophet.

Don't let an unsupported thought convict me!
It's not right mindlessly to take the bad
for good or to suppose the good are traitors.   6▶
Rejecting a relation who is loyal
is like rejecting life, our greatest love.
In time you'll know securely without stumbling,
for time alone can prove a just man just,
though you can know a bad man in a day.   6▶
CHORAGOS.   Well said, to one who's anxious not to fall.
Swift thinkers, Lord, are never safe from stumbling.
OEDIPUS.   But when a swift and secret plotter moves
against me, I must make swift counterplot.
If I lie quiet and await his move,   6▶
he'll have achieved his aims and I'll have missed.
CREON.   You surely cannot mean you want me exiled!
OEDIPUS.   Not exiled, no. Your death is what I want!
CREON.   If you would first define what envy is . . .
OEDIPUS.   Are you still stubborn! Still disobedient?   6▶
CREON.   I see you cannot think!
OEDIPUS.   For me I can.
CREON.   You should for me as well!
OEDIPUS.   But you're a traitor!
CREON.   What if you're wrong?
OEDIPUS.   Authority must be maintained.
CREON.   Not if the ruler's evil.
OEDIPUS.   Hear that, Thebes!
CREON.   It is my city too, not yours alone!   6▶
CHORAGOS.   Please don't, my Lords! Ah, just in time, I see
Jocasta there, coming from the palace.
With her help you must settle your quarrel.

[*Enter* JOCASTA *from the Palace.*]

JOCASTA.   Wretched men! What has provoked this ill-
advised dispute? Have you no sense of shame,   6▶
with Thebes so sick, to stir up private troubles?
Now go inside! And Creon, you go home!
Don't make a general anguish out of nothing!
CREON.   My sister, Oedipus your husband here
sees fit to do one of two hideous things: 6▶
to have me banished from the land—or killed!
OEDIPUS.   That's right: I caught him, Lady, plotting harm
against my person—with a malignant science.
CREON.   May my life fail, may I die cursed, if I
did any of the things you said I did!   6▶
JOCASTA.   Believe his words, for the god's sake, Oedipus,
in deference above all to his oath
to the gods. Also for me, and for these men!

KOMMOS°

Strophe 1

CHORUS.   Consent, with will and mind,
 my king, I beg of you!   655
OEDIPUS.   What do you wish me to surrender?
CHORUS.   Show deference to him who was not feeble in time past
 and is now great in the power of his oath!
OEDIPUS.   Do you know what you're asking?
CHORUS.   Yes.
OEDIPUS.   Tell me then.
CHORUS.   Never to cast into dishonored guilt, with an unproved   660
 assumption, a kinsman who has bound himself by curse.
OEDIPUS.   Now you must understand, when you ask this,
 you ask my death or banishment from the land.

Strophe 2

CHORUS.   No, by the god who is the foremost of all gods,
 the Sun! No! Godless,   665
  friendless, whatever death is worst of all,
 let that be my destruction, if this
  thought ever moved me!
 But my ill-fated soul
  this dying land   670
 wears out—the more if to these older troubles
 she adds new troubles from the two of you!
OEDIPUS.   Then let him go, though it must mean my death,
 or else disgrace and exile from the land.
 My pity is moved by your words, not by his—   675
 he'll only have my hate, wherever he goes.
CREON.   You're sullen as you yield; you'll be depressed
 when you've passed through this anger. Natures like yours
 are hardest on themselves. That's as it should be.
OEDIPUS.   Then won't you go and let me be?
CREON.   I'll go.   680
 Though you're unreasonable, they know I'm righteous.

                [*Exit* CREON.]

Antistrophe 1

CHORUS.   Why are you waiting, Lady?
 Conduct him back into the palace!
JOCASTA.   I will, when I have heard what chanced.   685

Kommos: a dirge or lament sung by the Chorus and one or more of the chief characters.

CHORUS.   Conjectures—words alone, and nothing based on thought.
    But even an injustice can devour a man.
JOCASTA.   Did the words come from both sides?
CHORUS.   Yes.
JOCASTA. What was said?
CHORUS.   To me it seems enough! enough! the land already troubled,   69
    that this should rest where it has stopped.
OEDIPUS.   See what you've come to in your honest thought,
    in seeking to relax and blunt my heart?

Antistrophe 2

CHORUS.   I have not said this only once, my Lord.
    That I had lost my sanity,   69
        without a path in thinking—
    be sure this would be clear
        if I put you away
    who, when my cherished land
        wandered crazed   7(
    with suffering, brought her back on course.
    Now, too, be a lucky helmsman!
JOCASTA.   Please, for the god's sake, Lord, explain to me
    the reason why you have conceived this wrath?
OEDIPUS.   I honor you, not them,° and I'll explain   7(
    to you how Creon has conspired against me.
JOCASTA.   All right, if that will explain how the quarrel started.
OEDIPUS.   He says I am the murderer of Laius!
JOCASTA.   Did he claim knowledge or that someone told him?
OEDIPUS.   Here's what he did: he sent that vicious seer   7▶
    so he could keep his own mouth innocent.
JOCASTA.   Ah then, absolve yourself of what he charges!
    Listen to this and you'll agree, no mortal
    is ever given skill in prophecy.
    I'll prove this quickly with one incident.   7▶
    It was foretold to Laius—I shall not say
    by Phoebus himself, but by his ministers—
    that when his fate arrived he would be killed
    by a son who would be born to him and me.
    And yet, so it is told, foreign robbers   72
    murdered him, at a place where three roads meet.
    As for the child I bore him, not three days passed
    before he yoked the ball-joints of its feet,°
    then cast it, by others' hands, on a trackless mountain.
    That time Apollo did not make our child   72
    a patricide, or bring about what Laius
    feared, that he be killed by his own son.

---

705 *them:* the Chorus.   723 *ball-joints of its feet:* the ankles.

That's how prophetic words determined things!
Forget them. The things a god must track
he will himself painlessly reveal.   730
OEDIPUS.   Just now, as I was listening to you, Lady,
what a profound distraction seized my mind!
JOCASTA.   What made you turn around so anxiously?
OEDIPUS.   I thought you said that Laius was attacked
and butchered at a place where three roads meet.   735
JOCASTA.   That is the story, and it is told so still.
OEDIPUS.   Where is the place where this was done to him?
JOCASTA.   The land's called Phocis, where a two-forked road
comes in from Delphi and from Daulia.
OEDIPUS.   And how much time has passed since these events?   740
JOCASTA.   Just prior to your presentation here
as king this news was published to the city.
OEDIPUS.   Oh, Zeus, what have you willed to do to me?
JOCASTA.   Oedipus, what makes your heart so heavy?
OEDIPUS.   No, tell me first of Laius' appearance,   745
what peak of youthful vigor he had reached.
JOCASTA.   A tall man, showing his first growth of white.
He had a figure not unlike your own.
OEDIPUS.   Alas! It seems that in my ignorance
I laid those fearful curses on myself.   750
JOCASTA.   What is it, Lord? I flinch to see your face.
OEDIPUS.   I'm dreadfully afraid the prophet sees.
But I'll know better with one more detail.
JOCASTA.   I'm frightened too. But ask: I'll answer you.
OEDIPUS.   Was his retinue small, or did he travel   755
with a great troop, as would befit a prince?
JOCASTA.   There were just five in all, one a herald.
There was a carriage, too, bearing Laius.
OEDIPUS.   Alas! Now I see it! But who was it,
Lady, who told you what you know about this?   760
JOCASTA.   A servant who alone was saved unharmed.
OEDIPUS.   By chance, could he be now in the palace?
JOCASTA.   No, he is not. When he returned and saw
you had the power of the murdered Laius,
he touched my hand and begged me formally   765
to send him to the fields and to the pastures,
so he'd be out of sight, far from the city.
I did. Although a slave, he well deserved
to win this favor, and indeed far more.
OEDIPUS.   Let's have him called back in immediately.   770
JOCASTA.   That can be done, but why do you desire it?
OEDIPUS.   I fear, Lady, I have already said
too much. That's why I wish to see him now.
JOCASTA.   Then he shall come; but it is right somehow
that I, too, Lord, should know what troubles you.   775
OEDIPUS.   I've gone so deep into the things I feared

I'll tell you everything. Who has a right
greater than yours, while I cross through this chance?
Polybus of Corinth was my father,
my mother was the Dorian Meropē.   7
I was first citizen, until this chance
attacked me—striking enough, to be sure,
but not worth all the gravity I gave it.
This: at a feast a man who'd drunk too much
denied, at the wine, I was my father's son.   7
I was depressed and all that day I barely
held it in. Next day I put the question
to my mother and father. They were enraged
at the man who'd let this fiction fly at me.
I was much cheered by them. And yet it kept   7
grinding into me. His words kept coming back.
Without my mother's or my father's knowledge
I went to Pytho. But Phoebus sent me away
dishonoring my demand. Instead, other
wretched horrors he flashed forth in speech.   7
He said that I would be my mother's lover,
show offspring to mankind they could not look at,
and be his murderer whose seed I am.°
When I heard this, and ever since, I gauged
the way to Corinth by the stars alone,   8
running to a place where I would never see
the disgrace in the oracle's words come true.
But I soon came to the exact location
where, as you tell of it, the king was killed.
Lady, here is the truth. As I went on,   8
when I was just approaching those three roads,
a herald and a man like him you spoke of
came on, riding a carriage drawn by colts.
Both the man out front and the old man himself°
tried violently to force me off the road.   8
The driver, when he tried to push me off,
I struck in anger. The old man saw this, watched
me approach, then leaned out and lunged down
with twin prongs° at the middle of my head!
He got more than he gave. Abruptly—struck   8
once by the staff in this my hand—he tumbled
out, head first, from the middle of the carriage.
And then I killed them all. But if there is
a kinship between Laius and this stranger,
who is more wretched than the man you see?   8
Who was there born more hated by the gods?

---

798 *be . . . am:* that is, murder my father.   809 *old man himself:* Laius.   813–14 *lunged . . .
prongs:* Laius strikes Oedipus with a two-pronged horse goad or whip.

For neither citizen nor foreigner
may take me in his home or speak to me.
No, they must drive me off. And it is I
who have pronounced these curses on myself!   825
I stain the dead man's bed with these my hands,
by which he died. Is not my nature vile?
Unclean?—if I am banished and even
in exile I may not see my own parents,
or set foot in my homeland, or else be yoked   830
in marriage to my mother, and kill my father,
Polybus, who raised me and gave me birth?
If someone judged a cruel divinity
did this to me, would he not speak the truth?
You pure and awful gods, may I not ever   835
see that day, may I be swept away
from men before I see so great and so
calamitous a stain fixed on my person!
CHORAGOS.   These things seem fearful to us, Lord, and yet,
    until you hear it from the witness, keep hope!   840
OEDIPUS.   That is the single hope that's left to me,
    to wait for him, that herdsman—until he comes.
JOCASTA.   When he appears, what are you eager for?
OEDIPUS.   Just this: if his account agrees with yours
    then I shall have escaped this misery.   845
JOCASTA.   But what was it that struck you in my story?
OEDIPUS.   You said he spoke of robbers as the ones
    who killed him. Now: if he continues still
    to speak of many, then I could not have killed him.
    One man and many men just do not jibe.   850
    But if he says one belted man, the doubt
    is gone. The balance tips toward me. I did it.
JOCASTA.   No! He told it as I told you. Be certain.
    He can't reject that and reverse himself.
    The city heard these things, not I alone.   855
    But even if he swerves from what he said,
    he'll never show that Laius' murder, Lord,
    occurred just as predicted. For Loxias
    expressly said my son was doomed to kill him.
    The boy—poor boy—he never had a chance   860
    to cut him down, for he was cut down first.
    Never again, just for some oracle
    will I shoot frightened glances right and left.
OEDIPUS.   That's full of sense. Nonetheless, send a man
    to bring that farm hand here. Will you do it?   865
JOCASTA.   I'll send one right away. But let's go in.
    Would I do anything against your wishes?

[*Exit OEDIPUS and JOCASTA through the central door into the palace.*]

STASIMON 2

Strophe 1

CHORUS.   May there accompany me
    the fate to keep a reverential purity in what I say,
    in all I do, for which the laws have been set forth   8ʳ
    and walk on high, born to traverse the brightest,
    highest upper air; Olympus° only
    is their father, nor was it
    mortal nature
    that fathered them, and never will   8ʳ
    oblivion lull them into sleep;
    the god in them is great and never ages.

Antistrophe 1

    The will to violate, seed of the tyrant,
    if it has drunk mindlessly of wealth and power,
    without a sense of time or true advantage,   8ª
    mounts to a peak, then
    plunges to an abrupt . . . destiny,
    where the useful foot
    is of no use. But the kind
    of struggling that is good for the city   8ª
    I ask the god never to abolish.
    The god is my protector: never will I give that up.

Strophe 2

    But if a man proceeds disdainfully
        in deeds of hand or word
    and has no fear of Justice   8ª
        or reverence for shrines of the divinities
    (may a bad fate catch him
        for his luckless wantonness!),
    if he'll not gain what he gains with justice
    and deny himself what is unholy,   8ⁱ
    or if he clings, in foolishness, to the untouchable
    (what man, finally, in such an action, will have strength
    enough to fend off passion's arrows from his soul?),
    if, I say, this kind of
        deed is held in honor—   9(
    why should I join the sacred dance?

Antistrophe 2

    No longer shall I visit and revere
        Earth's navel,° the untouchable,

---

872 *Olympus:* Mount Olympus, home of the gods, treated as a god.   903 *Earth's navel:* Delphi.

nor visit Abae's° temple,
  or Olympia,°   905
if the prophecies are not matched by events
  for all the world to point to.
No, you who hold the power, if you are rightly called
Zeus the king of all, let this matter not escape you
and your ever-deathless rule,   910
for the prophecies to Laius fade . . .
and men already disregard them;
nor is Apollo anywhere
  glorified with honors.
Religion slips away.   915

EPISODE 3

[*Enter JOCASTA from the palace carrying a branch wound with wool and a jar of incense. She is attended by two women.*]

JOCASTA.   Lords of the realm, the thought has come to me
  to visit shrines of the divinities
  with suppliant's branch in hand and fragrant smoke.
  For Oedipus excites his soul too much
  with alarms of all kinds. He will not judge   920
  the present by the past, like a man of sense.
  He's at the mercy of all terror-mongers.

[*JOCASTA approaches the altar on the right and kneels.*]

  Since I can do no good by counseling,
  Apollo the Lycēan!—you are the closest—
  I come a suppliant, with these my vows,   925
  for a cleansing that will not pollute him.
  For when we see him shaken we are all
  afraid, like people looking at their helmsman.

[*Enter a MESSENGER along one of the Parados. He sees JOCASTA at the altar and then addresses the CHORUS.*]

MESSENGER.   I would be pleased if you would help me, stranger.
  Where is the palace of King Oedipus?   930
  Or tell me where he is himself, if you know.
CHORUS.   This is his house, stranger. He is within.
  This is his wife and mother of his children.
MESSENGER.   May she and her family find prosperity,
  if, as you say, her marriage is fulfilled.   935
JOCASTA.   You also, stranger, for you deserve as much
  for your gracious words. But tell me why you've come.
  What do you wish? Or what have you to tell us?

---

904 *Abae:* a town in Phocis where there was another oracle of Apollo.   905 *Olympia:* site of the oracle of Zeus.

MESSENGER.   Good news, my Lady, both for your house and
   husband.
JOCASTA.   What is your news? And who has sent you to us?   94
MESSENGER.   I come from Corinth. When you have heard my
   news
   you will rejoice, I'm sure—and grieve perhaps.
JOCASTA.   What is it? How can it have this double power?
MESSENGER.   They will establish him their king, so say
   the people of the land of Isthmia.°   94
JOCASTA.   But is old Polybus not still in power?
MESSENGER.   He's not, for death has clasped him in the tomb.
JOCASTA.   What's this? Has Oedipus' father died?
MESSENGER.   If I have lied then I deserve to die.
JOCASTA.   Attendant! Go quickly to your master,   95
   and tell him this.

                          [*Exit an* ATTENDANT *into the palace.*]

                 Oracles of the gods!
   Where are you now? The man whom Oedipus
   fled long ago, for fear that he should kill him—
   he's been destroyed by chance and not by him!

[*Enter* OEDIPUS *from the palace.*]

OEDIPUS.   Darling Jocasta, my beloved wife,   95
   Why have you called me from the palace?
JOCASTA.   First hear what this man has to say. Then see
   what the god's grave oracle has come to now!
OEDIPUS.   Where is he from? What is this news he brings me?
JOCASTA.   From Corinth. He brings news about your father: 96
   that Polybus is no more! that he is dead!
OEDIPUS.   What's this, old man? I want to hear you say it.
MESSENGER.   If this is what must first be clarified,
   please be assured that he is dead and gone.
OEDIPUS.   By treachery or by the touch of sickness?   96
MESSENGER.   Light pressures tip agéd frames into their sleep.
OEDIPUS.   You mean the poor man died of some disease.
MESSENGER.   And of the length of years that he had tallied.
OEDIPUS.   Aha! Then why should we look to Pytho's vapors,°
   or to the birds that scream above our heads?°   97
   If we could really take those things for guides,
   I would have killed my father. But he's dead!
   He is beneath the earth, and here am I,
   who never touched a spear. Unless he died
   of longing for me and I "killed" him that way!   97
   No, in this case, Polybus, by dying, took
   the worthless oracle to Hades with him.

945 *land of Isthmia:* Corinth, which was on an isthmus.   969 *Pytho's vapors:* the prophecies of
the oracle at Delphi.   970 *birds . . . heads:* the prophecies derived from interpreting the flights
of birds.

JOCASTA.   And wasn't I telling you that just now?
OEDIPUS.   You were indeed. I was misled by fear.
JOCASTA.   You should not care about this anymore.   980
OEDIPUS.   I must care. I must stay clear of my mother's bed.
JOCASTA.   What's there for man to fear? The realm of chance
      prevails. True foresight isn't possible.
      His life is best who lives without a plan.
      This marriage with your mother—don't fear it.   985
      How many times have men in dreams, too, slept
      with their own mothers! Those who believe such things
      mean nothing endure their lives most easily.
OEDIPUS.   A fine, bold speech, and you are right, perhaps,
      except that my mother is still living,   990
      so I must fear her, however well you argue.
JOCASTA.   And yet your father's tomb is a great eye.
OEDIPUS.   Illuminating, yes. But I still fear the living.
MESSENGER.   Who is the woman who inspires this fear?
OEDIPUS.   Meropē, Polybus' wife, old man.   995
MESSENGER.   And what is there about her that alarms you?
OEDIPUS.   An oracle, god-sent and fearful, stranger.
MESSENGER.   Is it permitted that another know?
OEDIPUS.   It is. Loxias once said to me
      I must have intercourse with my own mother   1000
      and take my father's blood with these my hands.
      So I have long lived far away from Corinth.
      This has indeed brought much good luck, and yet,
      to see one's parents' eyes is happiest.
MESSENGER.   Was it for this that you have lived in exile?   1005
OEDIPUS.   So I'd not be my father's killer, sir.
MESSENGER.   Had I not better free you from this fear,
      my Lord? That's why I came—to do you service.
OEDIPUS.   Indeed, what a reward you'd get for that!
MESSENGER.   Indeed, this is the main point of my trip,   1010
      to be rewarded when you get back home.
OEDIPUS.   I'll never rejoin the givers of my seed!°
MESSENGER.   My son, clearly you don't know what you're doing.
OEDIPUS.   But how is that, old man? For the gods' sake, tell me!
MESSENGER.   If it's because of them you won't go home.   1015
OEDIPUS.   I fear that Phoebus will have told the truth.
MESSENGER.   Pollution from the ones who gave you seed?
OEDIPUS.   That is the thing, old man, I always fear.
MESSENGER.   Your fear is groundless. Understand that.
OEDIPUS.   Groundless? Not if I was born their son.   1020
MESSENGER.   But Polybus is not related to you.
OEDIPUS.   Do you mean Polybus was not my father?
MESSENGER.   No more than I. We're both the same to you.
OEDIPUS.   Same? One who begot me and one who didn't?

1012 *givers of my seed:* that is, my parents. Oedipus still thinks Meropē and Polybus are his parents.

MESSENGER.   He didn't beget you any more than I did.   10!

OEDIPUS.   But then, why did he say I was his son?

MESSENGER.   He got you as a gift from my own hands.

OEDIPUS.   He loved me so, though from another's hands?

MESSENGER.   His former childlessness persuaded him.

OEDIPUS.   But had you bought me, or begotten me?   10!

MESSENGER.   Found you. In the forest hallows of Cithaeron.

OEDIPUS.   What were you doing traveling in that region?

MESSENGER.   I was in charge of flocks which grazed those mountains.

OEDIPUS.   A wanderer who worked the flocks for hire?

MESSENGER.   Ah, but that day I was your savior, son.   10!

OEDIPUS.   From what? What was my trouble when you took me?

MESSENGER.   The ball-joints of your feet might testify.

OEDIPUS.   What's that? What makes you name that ancient trouble?

MESSENGER.   Your feet were pierced and I am your rescuer.

OEDIPUS.   A fearful rebuke those tokens left for me!   10·

MESSENGER.   That was the chance that names you who you are.

OEDIPUS.   By the gods, did my mother or my father do this?

MESSENGER.   That I don't know. He might who gave you to me.

OEDIPUS.   From someone else? You didn't chance on me?

MESSENGER.   Another shepherd handed you to me.   10·

OEDIPUS.   Who was he? Do you know? Will you explain!

MESSENGER.   They called him one of the men of—was it Laius?

OEDIPUS.   The one who once was king here long ago?

MESSENGER.   That is the one! The man was shepherd to him.

OEDIPUS.   And is he still alive so I can see him?   10!

MESSENGER.   But you who live here ought to know that best.

OEDIPUS.   Does any one of you now present know
        about the shepherd whom this man has named?
        Have you seen him in town or in the fields? Speak out!
        The time has come for the discovery!   10!

CHORAGOS.   The man he speaks of, I believe, is the same
        as the field hand you have already asked to see.
        But it's Jocasta who would know this best.

OEDIPUS.   Lady, do you remember the man we just
        now sent for—is that the man he speaks of?   10(

JOCASTA.   What? The man he spoke of? Pay no attention!
        His words are not worth thinking about. It's nothing.

OEDIPUS.   With clues like this within my grasp, give up?
        Fail to solve the mystery of my birth?

JOCASTA.   For the love of the gods, and if you love your life,   10(
        give up this search! My sickness is enough.

OEDIPUS.   Come! Though my mothers for three generations
        were in slavery, you'd not be lowborn!

JOCASTA.   No, listen to me! Please! Don't do this thing!

OEDIPUS.   I will not listen; I will search out the truth.   10;

JOCASTA.   My thinking is for you—it would be best.

OEDIPUS.   This "best" of yours is starting to annoy me.

JOCASTA.   Doomed man! Never find out who you are!

OEDIPUS.   Will someone go and bring that shepherd here?
    Leave her to glory in her wealthy birth! 1075
JOCASTA.   Man of misery! No other name
    shall I address you by, ever again.

        [*Exit JOCASTA into the palace after a long pause.*]

CHORAGOS.   Why has your lady left, Oedipus,
    hurled by a savage grief? I am afraid
    disaster will come bursting from this silence. 1080
OEDIPUS.   Let it burst forth! However low this seed
    of mine may be, yet I desire to see it.
    She, perhaps—she has a woman's pride—
    is mortified by my base origins.
    But I who count myself the child of Chance, 1085
    the giver of good, shall never know dishonor.
    She is my mother,° and the months my brothers
    who first marked out my lowness, then my greatness.
    I shall not prove untrue to such a nature
    by giving up the search for my own birth. 1090

STASIMON 3

Strophe

CHORUS.   If I have mantic power
    and excellence in thought,
    by Olympus,
        you shall not, Cithaeron, at tomorrow's
    full moon, 1095
    fail to hear us celebrate you as the countryman
    of Oedipus, his nurse and mother,
    or fail to be the subject of our dance,
        since you have given pleasure
    to our king. 1100
    Phoebus, whom we summon by "iē!,"
    may this be pleasing to you!

Antistrophe

    Who was your mother, son?
    which of the long-lived nymphs
    after lying with Pan,° 1105
        the mountain roaming . . . Or was it a bride
    of Loxias?°

1087 *She . . . mother:* Chance is my mother.   1105 *Pan:* god of shepherds and woodlands, half
man and half goat.   1107 *Loxias:* Apollo.

For dear to him are all the upland pastures.
Or was it Mount Cyllēnē's lord,°
or the Bacchic god,°   11
        dweller of the mountain peaks,
who received you as a joyous find
from one of the nymphs of Helicon,
the favorite sharers of his sport?

EPISODE 4

OEDIPUS.   If someone like myself, who never met him,   11
    may calculate—elders, I think I see
    the very herdsman we've been waiting for.
    His many years would fit that man's age,
    and those who bring him on, if I am right,
    are my own men. And yet, in real knowledge,   11
    you can outstrip me, surely: you've seen him.

[*Enter the old* HERDSMAN *escorted by two of Oedipus's* ATTENDANTS. *At first, the* HERDSMAN
will not look at OEDIPUS.]

CHORAGOS.   I know him, yes, a man of the house of Laius,
    a trusty herdsman if he ever had one.
OEDIPUS.   I ask you first, the stranger come from Corinth:
    is this the man you spoke of?
MESSENGER.   That's he you see.   11
OEDIPUS.   Then you, old man. First look at me! Now answer:
    did you belong to Laius' household once?
HERDSMAN.   I did. Not a purchased slave but raised in the palace.
OEDIPUS.   How have you spent your life? What is your work?
HERDSMAN.   Most of my life now I have tended sheep.   11
OEDIPUS.   Where is the usual place you stay with them?
HERDSMAN.   On Mount Cithaeron. Or in that district.
OEDIPUS.   Do you recall observing this man there?
HERDSMAN.   Doing what? Which is the man you mean?
OEDIPUS.   This man right here. Have you had dealings with him?   11
HERDSMAN.   I can't say right away. I don't remember.
MESSENGER.   No wonder, master. I'll bring clear memory
    to his ignorance. I'm absolutely sure
    he can recall it, the district was Cithaeron,
    he with a double flock, and I, with one,
    lived close to him, for three entire seasons,   11
    six months long, from spring right to Arcturus.°
    Then for the winter I'd drive mine to my fold,
    and he'd drive his to Laius' pen again.
    Did any of the things I say take place?   11
HERDSMAN.   You speak the truth, though it's from long ago.

1109 *Mount Cyllēnē's lord:* Hermes, messenger of the gods.   1110 *Bacchic god:* Dionysus.
1142 *from spring right to Arcturus:* That is, from spring to early fall, when the summer star Arcturus (in the constellation Boötes) is no longer visible in the early evening sky. It does not rise
at night again until the following spring.

MESSENGER.   Do you remember giving me, back then,
    a boy I was to care for as my own?
HERDSMAN.   What are you saying? Why do you ask me that?
MESSENGER.   There, sir, is the man who was that boy!   1150
HERDSMAN.   Damn you! Shut your mouth! Keep your silence!
OEDIPUS.   Stop! Don't you rebuke his words.
    Your words ask for rebuke far more than his.
HERDSMAN.   But what have I done wrong, most royal master?
OEDIPUS.   Not telling of the boy of whom he asked.   1155
HERDSMAN.   He's ignorant and blundering toward ruin.
OEDIPUS.   Tell it willingly—or under torture.
HERDSMAN.   Oh god! Don't—I am old—don't torture me!
OEDIPUS.   Here! Someone put his hands behind his back!
HERDSMAN.   But why? What else would you find out, poor man?   1160
OEDIPUS.   Did you give him the child he asks about?
HERDSMAN.   I did. I wish that I had died that day!
OEDIPUS.   You'll come to that if you don't speak the truth.
HERDSMAN.   It's if I speak that I shall be destroyed.
OEDIPUS.   I think this fellow struggles for delay.   1165
HERDSMAN.   No, no! I said already that I gave him.
OEDIPUS.   From your own home, or got from someone else?
HERDSMAN.   Not from my own. I got him from another.
OEDIPUS.   Which of these citizens? What sort of house?
HERDSMAN.   Don't—by the gods!—don't, master, ask me more!   1170
OEDIPUS.   It means your death if I must ask again.
HERDSMAN.   One of the children of the house of Laius.
OEDIPUS.   A slave—or born into the family?
HERDSMAN.   I have come to the dreaded thing, and I shall say it.
OEDIPUS.   And I to hearing it, but hear I must.   1175
HERDSMAN.   He was reported to have been—his son.
    Your lady in the house could tell you best.
OEDIPUS.   Because she gave him to you?
HERDSMAN.   Yes, my lord.
OEDIPUS.   What was her purpose?
HERDSMAN.   I was to kill the boy.
OEDIPUS.   The child she bore?
HERDSMAN.   She dreaded prophecies.   1180
OEDIPUS.   What were they?
HERDSMAN.   The word was that he'd kill his parents.
OEDIPUS.   Then why did you give him up to this old man?
HERDSMAN.   In pity, master—so he would take him home,
    to another land. But what he did was save him
    for this supreme disaster. If you are the one   1185
    he speaks of—know your evil birth and fate!
OEDIPUS.   Ah! All of it was destined to be true!
    Oh light, now may I look my last upon you,
    shown monstrous in my birth, in marriage monstrous,
    a murderer monstrous in those I killed.   1190

[*Exit* OEDIPUS, *running into the palace.*]

STASIMON 4

Strophe 1

CHORUS. Oh generations of mortal men,
    while you are living, I will
        appraise your lives at zero!
What man
comes closer to seizing lasting blessedness
than merely to seize its semblance,
and after living in this semblance, to plunge?
With your example before us,
with your destiny, yours,
        suffering Oedipus, no mortal
can I judge fortunate.

Antistrophe 1

For he,° outranging everybody,
shot his arrow° and became the lord
    of wide prosperity and blessedness,
oh Zeus, after destroying
the virgin with the crooked talons,°
singer of oracles; and against death,
in my land, he arose a tower of defense.
From which time you were called my king
and granted privileges supreme—in mighty
Thebes the ruling lord.

Strophe 2

But now—whose story is more sorrowful than yours?
Who is more intimate with fierce calamities,
with labors, now that your life is altered?
Alas, my Oedipus, whom all men know:
one great harbor°—
one alone sufficed for you,
as son and father,
when you tumbled,° plowman° of the woman's chamber.
How, how could your paternal
        furrows, wretched man,
endure you silently so long.

Antistrophe 2

Time, all-seeing, surprised you living an unwilled life
and sits from of old in judgment on the marriage, not a marriage,

1202 *he:* Oedipus.   1203 *shot his arrow:* took his chances; made a guess at the Sphinx's riddle. 1206 *virgin . . . talons:* the Sphinx.   1216 *one great harbor:* metaphorical allusion to Jocasta's body.   1219 *tumbled:* were born and had sex.   *plowman:* Plowing is used here as a sexual metaphor.

where the begetter is the begot as well.   1225
Ah, son of Laius . . . ,
would that—oh, would that
I had never seen you!
I wail, my scream climbing beyond itself
from my whole power of voice. To say it straight: 1230
  from you I got new breath—
but I also lulled my eye to sleep.°

EXODOS

[Enter the SECOND MESSENGER from the palace.]

SECOND MESSENGER.   You who are first among the citizens,
  what deeds you are about to hear and see!
  What grief you'll carry, if, true to your birth,   1235
  you still respect the house of Labdacus!
  Neither the Ister nor the Phasis river
  could purify this house, such suffering
  does it conceal, or soon must bring to light—
  willed this time, not unwilled. Griefs hurt worst   1240
  which we perceive to be self-chosen ones.
CHORAGOS.   They were sufficient, the things we knew before,
  to make us grieve. What can you add to those?
SECOND MESSENGER.   The thing that's quickest said and quickest heard:
  our own, our royal one, Jocasta's dead.   1245
CHORAGOS.   Unhappy queen! What was responsible?
SECOND MESSENGER.   Herself. The bitterest of these events
  is not for you, you were not there to see,
  but yet, exactly as I can recall it,
  you'll hear what happened to that wretched lady.   1250
  She came in anger through the outer hall,
  and then she ran straight to her marriage bed,
  tearing her hair with the fingers of both hands.
  Then, slamming shut the doors when she was in,
  she called to Laius, dead so many years,   1255
  remembering the ancient seed which caused
  his death, leaving the mother to the son
  to breed again an ill-born progeny.
  She mourned the bed where she, alas, bred double—
  husband by husband, children by her child.   1260
  From this point on I don't know how she died,
  for Oedipus then burst in with a cry,
  and did not let us watch her final evil.
  Our eyes were fixed on him. Wildly he ran
  to each of us, asking for his spear   1265

1232 *I . . . sleep:* I failed to see the corruption you brought.

and for his wife—no wife: where he might find
the double mother-field, his and his children's.
He raved, and some divinity then showed him—
for none of us did so who stood close by.
With a dreadful shout—as if some guide were leading—   12
he lunged through the double doors; he bent the hollow
bolts from the sockets, burst into the room,
and there we saw her, hanging from above,
entangled in some twisted hanging strands.
He saw, was stricken, and with a wild roar   12
ripped down the dangling noose. When she, poor woman,
lay on the ground, there came a fearful sight:
he snatched the pins of worked gold from her dress,
with which her clothes were fastened: these he raised
and struck into the ball-joints of his eyes.°   12
He shouted that they would no longer see
the evils he had suffered or had done,
see in the dark those he should not have seen,
and know no more those he once sought to know.
While chanting this, not once but many times   12
he raised his hand and struck into his eyes.
Blood from his wounded eyes poured down his chin,
not freed in moistening drops, but all at once
a stormy rain of black blood burst like hail.
These evils, coupling them, making them one,   12
have broken loose upon both man and wife.
The old prosperity that they had once
was true prosperity, and yet today,
mourning, ruin, death, disgrace, and every
evil you could name—not one is absent.   12
CHORAGOS.   Has he allowed himself some peace from all this grief?
SECOND MESSENGER.   He shouts that someone slide the bolts and show
to all the Cadmeians the patricide,
his mother's—I can't say it, it's unholy—
so he can cast himself out of the land,   13
not stay and curse his house by his own curse.
He lacks the strength, though, and he needs a guide,
for his is a sickness that's too great to bear.
Now you yourself will see: the bolts of the doors
are opening. You are about to see   13
a vision even one who hates must pity.

[*Enter the blinded* OEDIPUS *from the palace, led in by a household* SERVANT.]

CHORAGOS.   This suffering sends terror through men's eyes,
    terrible beyond any suffering
    my eyes have touched. Oh man of pain,

1280 *ball-joints of his eyes:* his eyeballs. Oedipus blinds himself in both eyes at the same time.

what madness reached you? Which god from far off,   1310
  surpassing in range his longest spring,
    struck hard against your god-abandoned fate?
  Oh man of pain,
  I cannot look upon you—though there's so much
  I would ask you, so much to hear,   1315
  so much that holds my eyes—
    so awesome the convulsions you send through me.
OEDIPUS.   Ah! Ah! I am a man of misery.
  Where am I carried? Pity me! Where
  is my voice scattered abroad on wings?   1320
    Divinity, where has your lunge transported me?
CHORAGOS.   To something horrible, not to be heard or seen.

KOMMOS

Strophe 1

OEDIPUS.   Oh, my cloud
  of darkness, abominable, unspeakable as it attacks me,
  not to be turned away, brought by an evil wind!   1325
  Alas!
  Again alas! Both enter me at once:
  the sting of the prongs,° the memory of evils!
CHORUS.   I do not marvel that in these afflictions
  you carry double griefs and double evils.   1330

Antistrophe 1

OEDIPUS.   Ah, friend,
  so you at least are there, resolute servant!
  Still with a heart to care for me, the blind man.
  Oh! Oh!
  I know that you are there. I recognize   1335
  even inside my darkness, that voice of yours.
CHORUS.   Doer of horror, how did you bear to quench
  your vision? What divinity raised your hand?

Strophe 2

OEDIPUS.   It was Apollo there, Apollo, friends,
  who brought my sorrows, vile sorrows to their perfection,   1340
    these evils that were done to me.
  But the one who struck them with his hand,
    that one was none but I, in wretchedness.

1328 *prongs:* refers to both the whip that Laius used and the two gold pins Oedipus used to blind
himself.

For why was I to see
when nothing I could see would bring me joy?   13

CHORUS.   Yes, that is how it was.

OEDIPUS.   What could I see, indeed,
or what enjoy—what greeting
is there I could hear with pleasure, friends?
Conduct me out of the land   13
       as quickly as you can!
Conduct me out, my friends,
    the man utterly ruined,
supremely cursed,
    the man who is by gods   13
the most detested of all men!

CHORUS.   Wretched in disaster and in knowledge:
oh, I could wish you'd never come to know!

Antistrophe 2

OEDIPUS.   May he be destroyed, whoever freed the savage shackles
from my feet when I'd been sent to the wild pasture,   13
      whoever rescued me from murder
and became my savior—
    a bitter gift:
if I had died then,
I'd not have been such grief to self and kin.   13

CHORUS.   I also would have had it so.

OEDIPUS.   I'd not have returned to be my father's
murderer; I'd not be called by men
my mother's bridegroom.
Now I'm without a god,   13
    child of a polluted parent,
fellow progenitor with him
    who gave me birth in misery.
If there's an evil that
    surpasses evils, that   13
has fallen to the lot of Oedipus.

CHORAGOS.   How can I say that you have counseled well?
Better not to be than live a blind man.

OEDIPUS.   That this was not the best thing I could do—
don't tell me that, or advise me any more!   13
Should I descend to Hades and endure
to see my father with these eyes? Or see
my poor unhappy mother? For I have done,
to both of these, things too great for hanging.
Or is the sight of children to be yearned for,   13
to see new shoots that sprouted as these did?
Never, never with these eyes of mine!
Nor city, nor tower, nor holy images
of the divinities! For I, all-wretched,

most nobly raised—as no one else in Thebes—   1390
deprived myself of these when I ordained
that all expel the impious one—god-shown
to be polluted, and the dead king's son!°
Once I exposed this great stain upon me,
could I have looked on these with steady eyes?   1395
No! No! And if there were a way to block
the source of hearing in my ears, I'd gladly
have locked up my pitiable body,
so I'd be blind and deaf. Evils shut out—
that way my mind could live in sweetness.   1400
Alas, Cithaeron,° why did you receive me?
Or when you had me, not killed me instantly?
I'd not have had to show my birth to mankind.
Polybus, Corinth, halls—ancestral,
they told me—how beautiful was your ward,   1405
a scar that held back festering disease!
Evil my nature, evil my origin.
You, three roads, and you, secret ravine,
you oak grove, narrow place of those three paths
that drank my blood° from these my hands, from him   1410
who fathered me, do you remember still
the things I did to you? When I'd come here,
what I then did once more? Oh marriages! Marriages!
You gave us life and when you'd planted us
you sent the same seed up, and then revealed   1415
fathers, brothers, sons, and kinsman's blood,
and brides, and wives, and mothers, all the most
atrocious things that happen to mankind!
One should not name what never should have been.
Somewhere out there, then, quickly, by the gods,   1420
cover me up, or murder me, or throw me
to the ocean where you will never see me more!

[*OEDIPUS moves toward the* CHORUS *and they back away from him.*]

Come! Don't shrink to touch this wretched man!
Believe me, do not be frightened! I alone
of all mankind can carry these afflictions.   1425

[*Enter CREON from the palace with ATTENDANTS.*]

CHORAGOS.   Tell Creon what you wish for. Just when we need him
he's here. He can act, he can advise you.
He's now the land's sole guardian in your place.
OEDIPUS.   Ah! Are there words that I can speak to him?
What ground for trust can I present? It's proved   1430
that I was false to him in everything.

1391–1393 *I . . . son:* Oedipus refers to his own curse against the murderer as well as his sins of
patricide and incest.   1401 *Cithaeron:* the mountain on which the infant Oedipus was supposed to be exposed.   1410 *my blood:* that is, the blood of my father, Laius.

CREON. I have not come to mock you, Oedipus,
    nor to reproach you for your former falseness.
    You men, if you have no respect for sons
    of mortals, let your awe for the all-feeding   14
    flames of lordly Hēlius° prevent
    your showing unconcealed so great a stain,
    abhorred by earth and sacred rain and light.
    Escort him quickly back into the house!
    If blood kin only see and hear their own   14
    afflictions, we'll have no impious defilement.
OEDIPUS. By the gods, you've freed me from one terrible fear,
    so nobly meeting my unworthiness:
    grant me something—not for me; for you!
CREON. What do you want that you should beg me so?   14
OEDIPUS. To drive me from the land at once, to a place
    where there will be no man to speak to me!
CREON. I would have done just that—had I not wished
    to ask first of the god what I should do.
OEDIPUS. His answer was revealed in full—that I,   14
    the patricide, unholy, be destroyed.
CREON. He said that, but our need is so extreme,
    it's best to have sure knowledge what must be done.
OEDIPUS. You'll ask about a wretched man like me?
CREON. Is it not time you put your trust in the god?   14
OEDIPUS. But I bid you as well, and shall entreat you.
    Give her who is within what burial
    you will—you'll give your own her proper rites;
    but me—do not condemn my fathers' land
    to have me dwelling here while I'm alive,   14
    but let me live on mountains—on Cithaeron
    famed as mine, for my mother and my father,
    while they yet lived, made it my destined tomb,
    and I'll be killed by those who wished my ruin!
    And yet I know: no sickness will destroy me,   14
    nothing will: I'd never have been saved
    when left to die unless for some dread evil.
    Then let my fate continue where it will!
    As for my children, Creon, take no pains
    for my sons—they're men and they will never lack   14
    the means to live, wherever they may be—
    but my two wretched, pitiable girls,
    who never ate but at my table, never
    were without me—everything that I
    would touch, they'd always have a share of it—   14
    please care for them! Above all, let me touch
    them with my hands and weep aloud my woes!
    Please, my Lord!

1436 *Hēlius:* the sun.

Please, noble heart! Touching with my hands,
I'd think I held them as when I could see.   1480

[*Enter* ANTIGONE *and* ISMENE *from the palace with* ATTENDANTS.]

What's this?
Oh gods! Do I hear, somewhere, my two dear ones
sobbing? Has Creon really pitied me
and sent to me my dearest ones, my children?
Is that it?   1485
CREON.   Yes, I prepared this for you, for I knew
you'd feel this joy, as you have always done.
OEDIPUS.   Good fortune, then, and, for your care, be guarded
far better by divinity than I was!
Where are you, children? Come to me! Come here   1490
to these my hands, hands of your brother, hands
of him who gave you seed, hands that made
these once bright eyes to see now in this fashion.

[OEDIPUS *embraces his daughters.*]

He, children, seeing nothing, knowing nothing,
he fathered you where his own seed was plowed.   1495
I weep for you as well, though I can't see you,
imagining your bitter life to come,
the life you will be forced by men to live.
What gatherings of townsmen will you join,
what festivals, without returning home   1500
in tears instead of watching holy rites?
And when you've reached the time for marrying,
where, children, is the man who'll run the risk
of taking on himself the infamy
that will wound you as it did my parents?   1505
What evil is not here? Your father killed
his father, plowed the one who gave him birth,
and from the place where he was sown, from there
he got you, from the place he too was born.
These are the wounds: then who will marry you?   1510
No man, my children. No, it's clear that you
must wither in dry barrenness, unmarried.

[OEDIPUS *addresses* CREON.]

Son of Menoeceus! You are the only father
left to them—we two who gave them seed
are both destroyed: watch that they don't become   1515
poor, wanderers, unmarried—they are your kin.
Let not my ruin be their ruin, too!
No, pity them! You see how young they are,
bereft of everyone, except for you.
Consent, kind heart, and touch me with your hand!   1520

[CREON *grasps* OEDIPUS'S *right hand.*]

You, children, if you had reached an age of sense,
I would have counseled much. Now, pray you may live
always where it's allowed, finding a life
better than his was, who gave you seed.

CREON.   Stop this now. Quiet your weeping. Move away, into the house.   15

OEDIPUS.   Bitter words, but I obey them.

CREON.   There's an end to all things.

OEDIPUS.   I have first this request.

CREON.   I will hear it.

OEDIPUS.   Banish me from my homeland.

CREON.   You must ask that of the god.

OEDIPUS.   But I am the gods' most hated man!

CREON.   Then you will soon get what you
want.

OEDIPUS.   Do you consent?

CREON.   I never promise when, as now, I'm ignorant.   15

OEDIPUS.   Then lead me in.

CREON.   Come. But let your hold fall from your children.

OEDIPUS.   Do not take them from me, ever!

CREON.   Do not wish to keep all of the
power. You had power, but that power did not follow you through life.

[*Oedipus's daughters are taken from him and led into the palace by* ATTENDANTS. OEDIPUS *is
led into the palace by a* SERVANT. CREON *and the other* ATTENDANTS *follow. Only the* CHORUS
remains.]

CHORUS.   People of Thebes, my country, see: here is that Oedipus—
he who "knew" the famous riddle, and attained the highest power,   15
whom all citizens admired, even envying his luck!
See the billows of wild troubles which he has entered now!
Here is the truth of each man's life: we must wait, and see his end,
scrutinize his dying day, and refuse to call him happy
till he has crossed the border of his life without pain.   15

[*Exit the* CHORUS *along each of the Parados.*]

QUESTIONS

Prologue and Parados

1. What is the situation in Thebes as the play begins? Why does Oedipus want to find Laius's murderer?

Episode 1 and Stasimon 1

2. How does Oedipus react to Tiresias's refusal to speak? How is this reaction characteristic of Oedipus? What other instances of this sort of behavior can you find in Oedipus's story?

3. When Tiresias does speak, he answers the central question of the play and tells the truth. Why doesn't Oedipus recognize this as the truth?

Episode 2 and Stasimon 2

4. What does Oedipus accuse Creon of doing? How does Creon defend himself? Do you find Creon's defense convincing? Why?

5. What is Jocasta's attitude toward oracles and prophecy? Why does she have this attitude? How does it contrast with the attitude of the chorus?

6. At what point in the play does Oedipus begin to suspect that he killed Laius? What details make him begin to suspect himself?

Episode 3 and Stasimon 3

7. What news does the messenger from Corinth bring? Why does this news seem to be good at first? How is this situation reversed?

Episode 4 and Stasimon 4

8. What do you make of the coincidence that the same herdsman (1) saved the infant Oedipus from death, (2) was with Laius at the place where three roads meet and was the lone survivor of the attack, and (3) will now be the agent to destroy Oedipus?

9. What moral does the chorus see in Oedipus's life?

Exodos

10. Why does Oedipus blind himself? What is the significance of the instruments that he uses to blind himself?

11. Who or what does Oedipus blame for his tragic life and destruction?

GENERAL QUESTIONS

1. In *Oedipus*, the peripeteia, anagnorisis, and catastrophe all occur at the same moment. When is this moment? Who is most severely affected by it?

2. Sophocles tells the events of Oedipus's life out of chronological order. Put all the events of his life in chronological order and consider how you might dramatize them. Why does Sophocles's ordering of these events produce an effective play?

3. Each episode of the play introduces new conflicts: Oedipus against the plague, against Tiresias, against Creon. What is the central conflict of the play? Why is it central?

4. All the violent acts of this play—the suicide of Jocasta and the blinding of Oedipus—occur offstage and are reported rather than shown. What are the advantages and disadvantages of dealing with violence this way?

5. Discuss the use of coincidences in the play. How do you react to them? Do they seem convincing or forced, given the plot of the play?

6. Explore the ways in which Sophocles employs dramatic irony, with reference to three specific examples.

7. Consider that *Oedipus* is a tragedy of both the individual and the state. What do you think will happen to Thebes after Oedipus is exiled?

8. Discuss the functions of the chorus and the Choragos. What do the choral odes contribute to the play?

9. Early in the play Oedipus begins a search for a murderer. How does the object of his search change as the play progresses? Why does it change?

THE REBIRTH AND DEVELOPMENT OF DRAMA IN THE CENTURIES BEFORE SHAKESPEARE

As we have seen, drama fell into decline for hundreds of years after the fall of the Roman Empire in the West (see p. 1018). There were no public theaters, no patrons able to support public performances, no popular audiences with the money to pay for admission, no practicing dramatists, and no official permission by secular and religious authorities—in short, there was no drama.

Medieval Religious Drama

During the tenth century, however, drama reemerged. Dramatic **tropes** (short musical interludes performed in conjunction with the Mass) developed in the churches; and because of the churches, a full-blown religious drama flowered in the fourteenth century.

CORPUS CHRISTI PLAYS. This new drama was made possible by the development of the religious celebration of *Corpus Christi Day*, a day celebrating the Doctrine of Transubstantiation (the miraculous change of consecrated bread and wine into the body and blood of Jesus). The Day of Corpus Christi (meaning "the body of Christ") was a movable feast that was (and is) observed on a Thursday sixty days after Easter.

When it began, Corpus Christi Day featured local processions devoted to the worship of the Eucharist, and in this way it brought religious celebration out of the church and into the streets. Because the feast occurred at the end of the liturgical year, it coincided with the beginning of good weather. The winter and spring rains abated, the ground got dry (or drier), short trips from country villages to nearby towns became possible, and people could spend an entire day outside and still be comfortable.

THE CRAFT GUILDS, OR MYSTERIES. The second influence on the drama was the development of medieval trade or craft guilds. The members, or masters, of these guilds, or "mysteries," controlled the prices and general conditions governing their work. Naturally, the guildsmen wanted to boost the prestige of their towns, along with their own wealth and power, and they therefore welcomed an annual religious celebration that would attract potential customers.

THE DRAMATIZATION OF BIBLICAL STORIES. The key for the development of drama was that the guilds took on the tasks of sponsoring and managing the dramatization of Biblical tales and religious traditions at the time of the Corpus Christi celebrations. It is vital to recognize that in the Middle Ages the Bible, with its accompanying church interpretations and traditions, was accepted not only as absolute religious truth about God's revelation to humankind, but also as absolute historical truth. The idea was that everything that had ever occurred in human history—as chronicled in the Bible—led up to or developed out of the real and continued presence of Christ as the Savior of all humankind. Therefore the major stories in the Bible were considered essential for practicing Christians.

But most people at the time were illiterate and could not read the Bible. The only Biblical texts they knew were derived from passages read during church services. Some of the gaps in Biblical knowledge were filled by the stories brilliantly depicted in stained glass windows, and also by the sculptures that decorated both the interiors and exteriors of the churches. The dramatization of religious stories during the Corpus Christi Feasts thus became a major method of Biblical and theological instruction. The goal of the authors was to create a complete sequence or **cycle** of plays dramatizing the divine history of the world from the Creation to the Day of Judgment.

THE CORPUS CHRISTI CYCLES, OR MYSTERY PLAYS. As the Corpus Christi celebrations grew in importance, forty or more towns, mainly in the north and east of England, but also in Scotland and Ireland, developed their own unique cycles of **Corpus Christi Plays** or **Mystery Plays**. The plays ceased to be simply a part of the procession of the Eucharist, and instead became a highlight of town life in the early summer. Often the performances, which were held outdoors, took place not only on the Thursday of the Corpus Christi Feast, but also on both Friday and Saturday, thus creating an extensive religious and secular celebration. By the fifteenth century, a large number of separate cycles existed.

THE ACTORS OF THE CYCLES. Although there were no professional acting companies like the one of which Shakespeare became a member in the late sixteenth century, the annual staging of the mystery plays would have required large numbers of actors. In one of the existing cycles, for example (Wakefield), there are 243 separate speaking parts. Other towns would have had similar and even greater needs. Obviously, the leading roles would have been taken by a regular cadre of local actors who were paid for their services. These actors would each have taken a major role, and some of them might also have assumed a number of other important roles. Augmenting the leading actors were many minor actors, who might also have performed multiple roles. In this way, the total number of performers needed for the entire cycle would have been reduced, but the number was still quite large.

Other Religious Dramas

In the course of time, additional types of religious drama were developed. One of these was the **miracle play**, a devotional dramatization of the lives of saints. In addition, the **morality play** was developed as a genre instructing the faithful in the proper way to lead a devotional life. The most famous of these, in about 1500, was *Everyman*, which even today retains a good deal of interest and power.

RENAISSANCE DRAMA AND SHAKESPEARE'S THEATER

In the early part of the English Renaissance, then, there was a flourishing native tradition of theater. The bridge from religious drama to the drama of the Renaissance was created in a number of ways. Of great importance was the growth of traveling dramatic companies, who performed their plays in local inn yards—square or quadrangular spaces surrounded by the rooms of the inn. In addition, plays were performed at court, in the great rooms of aristocratic houses, in the law courts, and at universities.

Aside from the performing tradition, the immediate influence on the creation of a new drama was the development of a taste for dramatic topics drawn from nonreligious sources. The earliest of such plays in the sixteenth century was the so-called **Tudor interlude**, named after the monarchs of the Tudor family who ruled England from 1485 to 1603. *Interlude* is a misnomer, for the plays were often quite long, one of them lasting an entire day. The interludes, supported by the nobility, were short tragedies, comedies, or historical plays that were performed by both professional actors and students. They sometimes featured abstract and allegorical characters and provided opportunities for both music and farcical action.

After the middle of the sixteenth century the revival of ancient drama and culture came increasingly to the fore. The dominating influence was the Roman dramatist Seneca (4 B.C.–A.D. 65), eight of whose tragedies, derived from the Greek tragedy, had survived from antiquity. A vital quality of the Senecan tragedies was that they were bloody, and thus they gave a classical precedent for the revenge and murder that were to be featured in the Elizabethan drama. Seneca became important not so much because he had written great works but rather because he had written in Latin. He could therefore be readily understood by a generation of new dramatists whose education had primarily been in Roman history, culture, and literature.

Elizabethan Dramatists and Shakespeare

The first group of these Elizabethan playwrights included Christopher Marlowe, Thomas Kyd, Robert Greene, George Peele, Thomas Lodge, and John Lyly. These were the men whose plays William Shakespeare watched and acted in when he first arrived in London from Stratford-upon-Avon early in the 1590s. By 1594 Shakespeare had joined the Lord Chamberlain's Men, the most popular of the London acting companies. He rose swiftly as both an actor and dramatist, and by 1599 he had become an active partner with the Lord Chamberlain's Men in a venture to construct a new theater, the Globe, within a stone's throw of the earlier theater, the Rose. It was at the Globe that Shakespeare's greatest plays were first produced, including *Hamlet.*

Shakespeare's Theater, the Globe (1599–1612)

Compared with the massive Greek outdoor theaters, the Globe was relatively small. Some theater historians have calculated that it held as many as two or three thousand spectators, although this estimate seems excessive, for half of that number would have been an extremely large audience.

THE SIZE AND SHAPE OF THE GLOBE. Recent archaeological excavations of the site of the Globe show that it was a twenty- or twenty-four-sided building. For practical purposes it was round—as it is shown in a contemporary drawing—and its outer diameter was approximately 100 feet. From above, it would have resembled a ring, or, as Shakespeare called the type in *Henry V,* a "wooden O." Its central yard was open to the sky, a detail that it had appropriated from the confined areas of the inns. The stage, covered by a roof, was built thirty feet into the yard at the building's south side.

ACTING AREAS. This thrust stage was close to five feet high—lower in front (*downstage*) and higher in back (*upstage*). The area below the stage was called the "hell." At center stage there was a trapdoor to the *hell,* which was used for the entrances and exits of devils, monsters, and ghosts. Downstage there were two columns holding up the protective roof. Called the *heavens,* the ceiling of the roof was decorated, and the roof itself also contained a hut where machinery was kept to lower and raise actors taking the roles of witches, fairies, and deities. Behind the upstage area, which could have been curtained off for interior scenes, there was a *tiring house* and storage area where actors changed their costumes and waited for their cues. Two or three doors opened out from the tiring house to the stage. On the second level above the stage was a gallery used for spectators, musicians, and actors (as in the balcony scene in Shakespeare's *Romeo and Juliet*).

PLACES FOR THE AUDIENCE. The admission price permitted spectators into the ground area. Those who remained there stood during the entire performance and crowded as close as they could to the stage. These people were patronizingly called the *groundlings.* For additional charges, spectators could sit in one of the three seating levels within the roofed galleries (part of the "O"). Those who could afford it paid still another charge for seats directly on the stage—a custom that continued in English theaters until the time of the actor-manager David Garrick in the middle of the eighteenth century.

A reconstruction of the stage of the Globe Theatre, drawn by Theo Crosby. From Andrew Gurr et al. *The Design of the Globe* (Coventry, England: The International Shakespeare Globe Centre, 1993), Figure 36.

PRODUCTION AND STAGE CONVENTIONS. Just as in the Athenian theater, there was no artificial lighting, and performances therefore took place in the afternoon. The plays were performed rapidly, without intermissions or indications of act and scene changes except for occasional rhymed couplets. With no curtain and no scenery, shifts in scene were indicated by the exits and entrances of the actors. This type of scene division produced swift changes in time and place, and made for great fluidity and fast pacing.

The conditions of performance and the physical shape of the theater produced a number of theatrical conventions. The two columns supporting the stage roof, for example, were versatile. Sometimes they represented trees or the sides of buildings, and conventionally they were used as places of concealment and eavesdropping. Time, place, and circumstances of weather were established through dialogue, as in the first scene of *Hamlet* when Horatio speaks of "the morn, in russet mantle clad" (line 166), or in *As You Like It*, when Rosalind says "this is the forest of Arden" (Act II. scene 4, line 15).

The Globe's relatively small size and its thrusting stage made for intimate performances. There was little separation between the audience and the actors, unlike the orchestra in Greek theaters that widened the distance between the people and the actors, and also unlike the proscenium and curtain that are used in most theaters today. Consequently, there was much interaction between actors and spectators. The closeness of spectators to the stage led to two unique stage conventions. One of these, the **aside**, permits a character to make brief remarks directly to the audience or to another character without the rest of the characters hearing the words. In the other, the **soliloquy**, a character alone on stage speaks his or her thoughts or plans directly to the audience. For example, in Hamlet's second soliloquy, he criticizes his emotional detachment from his father's murder and explains how he plans to test Claudius's guilt (Act II. scene 2, lines 524–580). We should realize that actors using these conventions spoke directly to members of the audience who were sitting next to the action. These people almost literally became additional members of the cast.

ACTING CONVENTIONS AND COSTUMES. The actors in Shakespeare's day were legally bound to the company of which they were members. Without the protection of the company, they were considered as "rogues and vagabonds." They were exclusively male, with adolescent boys performing the women's roles because women were excluded from the stage. The actors used no masks. Instead, they developed conventional expressions and gestures that would seem to us, today, excessively stylized. The acting conventions sometimes seemed excessive to Shakespeare, too, as is indicated by Hamlet's instructions to the traveling actors. He tells them not to "saw the air too much with your hand" and not to "tear a passion to tatters, to very rags" (Act III. scene 2, lines 4, 8).

The actors wore elaborate costumes to demonstrate the nature and status of the characters. Thus kings always wore robes and crowns, and carried orbs and scepters. Fools (a type of comic and ironic commentator) wore multicolored or *motley* costumes, and clowns and "mechanicals" wore the common clothing of their humble classes. Ragged clothing indicated a reduction in circumstances, as in *King Lear,* and Ophelia's description of Hamlet's disordered clothing in the second act of *Hamlet* indicates the Prince's disturbed mental condition (Act II. scene 1, lines 74–82). Whenever characters took on a disguise, as in *As You Like It,* this disguise was impenetrable to the other characters.

CURRENT RECONSTRUCTION OF THE GLOBE. Shakespeare's Globe burned in 1612, and the rebuilt Globe was torn down by the Puritans under Oliver Cromwell in 1644. Since that time the site has been occupied by tenements, breweries, other buildings, and a road. In the late 1980s, however, archaeological excavations took place at the sites of both the Globe and the nearby Rose theaters, and the subsequent discoveries are providing exciting new information about theaters and theater-going in Shakespeare's day. A reconstruction of the Globe is now under way near the original location, which cannot be used because it is preempted by a vital street leading to Southwark Bridge. Visitors to London will soon be able to attend performances of Shakespeare's plays in this new theater under conditions almost identical to those that Shakespeare's acting company knew (see the drawing of the proposed reconstruction of the Globe stage, p. 1126).

WILLIAM SHAKESPEARE, *HAMLET*

Shakespeare was born in 1564 in Stratford-upon-Avon, in the western part of England. He attended the Stratford grammar school, married in 1582, and had three children. He left his family and moved to London sometime between 1585 and 1592. During this period he became a professional actor, and began writing plays and poems. Because the London theaters were closed during the plague years 1592 to 1594, he apparently worked at other jobs, about which we know nothing. By 1595, however, he was recognized as a major writer of comedies and tragedies. He soon became a member of the Lord Chamberlain's Men, the leading theatrical company, and, as we have seen, he became a shareholder in the new Globe Theater in 1599. Because he realized good returns from the business venture and also from his plays, he became moderately wealthy. He stopped writing for the stage in 1611, having written a total of thirty-seven plays, of which eleven were tragedies. He spent his retirement years in Stratford. He died in 1616, and he is buried beside the altar of Stratford's Trinity Church, beneath a bust and an inscribed gravestone.

When the Lord Chamberlain's Men first staged *Hamlet* in 1600 or 1601 at the Globe Theater, it was not the first time that the story had been dramatized on the London stage. There is evidence that a play based on the Hamlet story, now lost, had been performed before 1589. Therefore, at least some of the theatergoers might have known the story.

Even if none of them knew it, however, they would have known the tradition of **revenge tragedy.** The Elizabethans had been introduced to the drama of vengeance through the English translations of Seneca's tragedies during the 1570s and early 1580s. Another important precedent was Thomas Kyd's *Spanish Tragedy* (ca. 1587), which was the first English play in the revenge tradition and which contained a hero who committed suicide. The genre featured a number of conventions. The major ones were a ghost who calls for vengeance and a revenger who pretends to be insane at least part of the time. Above all, the tradition required that the revenger would also die, no matter how good the person or how just the cause.

Although Elizabethan audiences were prepared for *Hamlet* by the revenge formula, they could have anticipated neither a protagonist of Hamlet's likeableness and complexity nor a play of such profundity. The earlier revengers were flat characters with a single fixation on getting even through personal vengeance. Hamlet, however, is acutely aware of the political and moral corruption of the Danish court, and he reflects on the fallen state of humanity. Undergoing despair and guilt, he even contemplates suicide. He learns from his experiences and meditations, discovering that he must look beyond reason and philosophy for ways of coping with the world. He also develops patience and learns to trust in Providence, the "divinity that shapes our ends" (Act V, scene 2, line 10).

The play itself demonstrates the far-reaching effects of evil, which branches inexorably outward from Claudius's initial act of murder. The evil ultimately ensnares innocent and guilty alike. Hamlet, the avenger, becomes the direct and indirect cause of deaths, and as a result, he also becomes an object of revenge. By the play's end, all the major figures are dead: Polonius, Ophelia, Rosencrantz, Guildenstern, Gertrude, Claudius, Laertes, and, finally, Hamlet himself. The play's crowning irony is that Hamlet does not complete his vengeance because of the murder of his father, King Hamlet, but rather kills Claudius immediately upon learning that the king has murdered Gertrude, his mother.

In the centuries since Shakespeare wrote *Hamlet*, the play has remained among the most popular, most moving, and most effective plays in the world. It has been translated into scores of languages. All the major actors from Shakespeare's day to ours—including Richard Burbage, the first Hamlet, and Mel Gibson, the most recent—have starred in the role. Beyond the play's stage popularity, *Hamlet* has become one of the central documents of western civilization. Somehow, we all know about Hamlet, and we know passages like "to be or not to be," "the play's the thing," and "The undiscovered country, from whose bourn / No traveler returns" even if we have never read the play or seen a live or filmed performance. These facts testify to Shakespeare's consummate skill as a poet and playwright.

WILLIAM SHAKESPEARE   (1564–1616)

The Tragedy of Hamlet, Prince of Denmark _____ *ca. 1600*

Edited by Alice Griffin°

CHARACTERS

Claudius, *King of Denmark*
Hamlet, *Son to the former, and nephew to the present King*
Polonius, *Lord Chamberlain*
Horatio, *Friend to Hamlet*
Laertes, *Son to Polonius*
Valtemand ⎫
Cornelius ⎪
Rosencrantz ⎬ *Courtiers*
Guildenstern ⎪
Osric ⎭

Professor Griffin's text for *Hamlet* was the Second Quarto (edition) published in 1604, with modifications based on the First Folio, published in 1623. Stage directions in those editions are printed here without brackets; added stage directions are printed within brackets. We have edited Griffin's notes for this text.

A Gentleman
A Priest
Marcellus ⎫
Barnardo ⎭ *Officers*
Francisco, *a Soldier*
Reynaldo, *Servant to Polonius*
Players
Two Clowns, *gravediggers*
Fortinbras, *Prince of Norway*
A Norwegian Captain
English Ambassadors
Gertrude, *Queen of Denmark, mother to Hamlet*
Ophelia, *Daughter to Polonius*
Ghost of Hamlet's Father
Lords, Ladies, Officers, Soldiers, Sailors, Messengers, Attendants

[*Scene: Elsinore*]

ACT 1

Scene 1. [*A platform on the battlements of the castle*]

Enter Barnardo and Francisco, two Sentinels

BARNARDO. Who's there?
FRANCISCO. Nay, answer me. Stand and unfold° yourself.
BARNARDO. Long live the king.
FRANCISCO. Barnardo?
BARNARDO. He.
FRANCISCO. You come most carefully upon your hour.
BARNARDO. 'Tis now struck twelve, get thee to bed Francisco.
FRANCISCO. For this relief much thanks, 'tis bitter cold,
    And I am sick at heart.
BARNARDO. Have you had quiet guard?
FRANCISCO.   Not a mouse stirring.
BARNARDO. Well, good night:
    If you do meet Horatio and Marcellus,
    The rivals° of my watch, bid them make haste.

Enter Horatio and Marcellus.

FRANCISCO. I think I hear them. Stand ho, who is there?
HORATIO. Friends to this ground.
MARCELLUS.   And liegemen° to the Dane.°
FRANCISCO. Give you good night.
MARCELLUS.   O, farewell honest soldier,
    Who hath relieved you?

---

2 *unfold:* reveal.   13 *rivals:* partners.   15 *liegemen:* subjects.   *Dane:* King of Denmark.

FRANCISCO.   Barnardo hath my place;
  Give you good night.   *Exit FRANCISCO*
MARCELLUS.   Holla, Barnardo!
BARNARDO.   Say,
  What, is Horatio there?
HORATIO.   A piece of him.
BARNARDO.   Welcome Horatio, welcome good Marcellus.   20
HORATIO.   What, has this thing appeared again tonight?
BARNARDO.   I have seen nothing.
MARCELLUS.   Horatio says 'tis but our fantasy,°
  And will not let belief take hold of him,
  Touching this dreaded sight twice seen of us,   25
  Therefore I have entreated him along
  With us to watch the minutes of this night,
  That if again this apparition come,
  He may approve° our eyes and speak to it.
HORATIO.   Tush, tush, 'twill not appear.
BARNARDO.   Sit down awhile,   30
  And let us once again assail your ears,
  That are so fortified against our story,
  What we have two nights seen.
HORATIO.   Well, sit we down,
  And let us hear Barnardo speak of this.   35
BARNARDO.   Last night of all,
  When yon same star that's westward from the pole°
  Had made his course t'illume that part of heaven
  Where now it burns, Marcellus and myself,
  The bell then beating one—

Enter GHOST.

MARCELLUS.   Peace, break thee off, look where it comes again.   40
BARNARDO.   In the same figure like the king that's dead.
MARCELLUS.   Thou art a scholar, speak to it Horatio.
BARNARDO.   Looks a' not like the king? mark it Horatio.
HORATIO.   Most like, it harrows me with fear and wonder.
BARNARDO.   It would be spoke to.
MARCELLUS.   Question it Horatio.   45
HORATIO.   What art thou that usurp'st° this time of night,
  Together with that fair and warlike form,
  In which the majesty of buried Denmark°
  Did sometimes° march? by heaven I charge thee speak.
MARCELLUS.   It is offended.
BARNARDO.   See, it stalks away.   50
HORATIO.   Stay, speak, speak, I charge thee speak.   *Exit GHOST.*
MARCELLUS.   'Tis gone and will not answer.

---

23 *fantasy:* imagination.   29 *approve:* prove reliable.   36 *pole:* North Star.   46 *usurp'st:*
wrongfully occupy (both the time and the shape of the dead king).   48 *buried Denmark:* the
buried King of Denmark.   49 *sometimes:* formerly.

BARNARDO.   How now Horatio, you tremble and look pale,
    Is not this something more than fantasy?
    What think you on't?   5
HORATIO.   Before my God I might not this believe,
    Without the sensible and true avouch°
    Of mine own eyes.
MARCELLUS.   Is it not like the king?
HORATIO.   As thou art to thyself.
    Such was the very armour he had on,   6
    When he the ambitious Norway° combated:
    So frowned he once, when in an angry parle°
    He smote the sledded Polacks° on the ice.
    'Tis strange.
MARCELLUS.   Thus twice before, and jump° at this dead hour,   6
    With martial stalk hath he gone by our watch.
HORATIO.   In what particular thought to work, I know not,
    But in the gross and scope° of mine opinion,
    This bodes some strange eruption to our state.
MARCELLUS.   Good now sit down, and tell me he that knows,   7
    Why this same strict and most observant watch
    So nightly toils the subject° of the land,
    And why such daily cast of brazen cannon
    And foreign mart,° for implements of war,
    Why such impress° of shipwrights, whose sore° task   7
    Does not divide the Sunday from the week,
    What might be toward° that this sweaty haste
    Doth make the night joint-labourer with the day,
    Who is't that can inform me?
HORATIO.   That can I.
    At least the whisper goes so; our last king,   8
    Whose image even but now appeared to us,
    Was as you know by Fortinbras of Norway,
    Thereto pricked on by a most emulate° pride,
    Dared to the combat; in which our valiant Hamlet
    (For so this side of our known world esteemed him)   8
    Did slay this Fortinbras, who by a sealed compact,°
    Well ratified by law and heraldy,°
    Did forfeit (with his life) all those his lands
    Which he stood seized° of, to the conqueror:
    Against the which a moiety competent°   9
    Was gagèd° by our King, which had returned
    To the inheritance of Fortinbras,
    Had he been vanquisher; as by the same co-mart,°

57 *Sensible . . . avouch:* assurance of the truth of the senses.   61 *Norway:* King of Norway.
62 *parle:* parley, verbal battle.   63 *sledded Polacks:* Poles on sleds.   65 *jump:* just.   68 *gross and scope:* general view.   72 *toils the subject:* makes the subjects toil.   74 *mart:* trade.
75 *impress:* conscription.   *sore:* difficult.   77 *toward:* forthcoming.   83 *emulate:* rivaling.
86 *compact:* treaty.   87 *law and heraldy:* heraldic law regulating combats.   89 *seized:* possessed.   90 *moiety competent:* equal amount.   91 *gagèd:* pledged.   93 *co-mart:* joint bargain.

And carriage of the article designed,°
His fell to Hamlet; now sir, young Fortinbras,   95
Of unimprovèd mettle° hot and full,
Hath in the skirts° of Norway here and there
Sharked up° a list of lawless resolutes°
For food and diet to some enterprise
That hath a stomach° in't, which is no other,   100
As it doth well appear unto our state,
But to recover of us by strong hand
And terms compulsatory, those foresaid lands
So by his father lost; and this I take it,
Is the main motive of our preparations,   105
The source of this our watch, and the chief head°
Of this post-haste and romage° in the land.
BARNARDO.   I think it be no other, but e'en so;
  Well may it sort° that this portentous figure
  Comes armèd through our watch so like the king   110
  That was and is the question of these wars.
HORATIO.   A mote it is to trouble the mind's eye:
  In the most high and palmy° state of Rome,
  A little ere the mightest Julius fell,
  The graves stood tenantless, and the sheeted dead   115
  Did squeak and gibber in the Roman streets,
  As stars with trains of fire,° and dews of blood,
  Disasters° in the sun; and the moist star,°
  Upon whose influence Neptune's empire stands,
  Was sick almost to doomsday with eclipse.   120
  And even the like precurse° of feared events,
  As harbingers preceding still° the fates
  And prologue to the omen° coming on,
  Have heaven and earth together demonstrated
  Unto our climatures° and countrymen.   125

Enter GHOST.

  But soft, behold, lo where it comes again.
  I'll cross° it though it blast me: *Spreads his arms.*
                              stay illusion,
  If thou hast any sound or use of voice,
  Speak to me.
  If there be any good thing to be done   130
  That may to thee do ease, and grace° to me,

---

94 *carriage . . . designed:* intent of the treaty drawn up.   96 *unimprovèd mettle:* untested (1)
metal (2) spirit.   97 *skirts:* outskirts.   98 *Sharked up:* gathered up indiscriminately (as a
shark preys).   *lawless resolutes:* determined outlaws.   100 *stomach:* show of courage.
106 *head:* fountainhead.   107 *romage:* bustle (rummage).   109 *sort:* turn out.   113 *palmy:*
triumphant.   117 *stars . . . fire:* meteors.   118 *Disasters:* unfavorable portents.   *moist star:*
moon.   121 *precurse:* portent.   122 *still:* always.   123 *omen:* disaster.   125 *climatures:*
regions.   127 *cross:* (1) cross its path (2) spread my arms to make a cross of my body (to ward
against evil).   131 *grace:* (1) honor (2) blessedness.

Speak to me.
If thou art privy° to thy country's fate
Which happily° foreknowing may avoid,
O speak: 13
Or if thou hast uphoarded in thy life
Extorted treasure in the womb of earth,
For which they say you spirits oft walk in death,

The cock crows.

Speak of it, stay and speak. Stop it Marcellus.
MARCELLUS.   Shall I strike at it with my partisan?°   14
HORATIO.   Do, if it will not stand
BARNARDO.   'Tis here.
HORATIO.   'Tis here.
MARCELLUS.   'Tis gone.   *Exit GHOST.*
We do it wrong being so majestical,
To offer it the show of violence,
For it is as the air, invulnerable,   14
And our vain blows malicious mockery.°
BARNARDO.   It was about to speak when the cock crew.°
HORATIO.   And then it started like a guilty thing,
Upon a fearful summons; I have heard,
The cock that is the trumpet to the morn,
Doth with his lofty and shrill-sounding throat   15
Awake the god of day, and at his warning
Whether in sea or fire, in earth or air,°
Th'extravagant and erring° spirit hies°
To his confine, and of the truth herein   15
This present object made probation.°
MARCELLUS.   It faded on the crowing of the cock.
Some say that ever 'gainst° that season comes
Wherein our Saviour's birth is celebrated
This bird of dawning singeth all night long,   16
And then they say no spirit dare stir abroad,
The nights are wholesome,° then no planets strike,°
No fairy takes,° nor witch hath power to charm,
So hallowed, and so gracious is that time.
HORATIO.   So have I heard and do in part believe it.   16
But look, the morn in russet° mantle clad
Walks o'er the dew of yon high eastward hill:
Break we our watch up and by my advice
Let us impart what we have seen tonight
Unto young Hamlet, for upon my life   17

---

133 *art privy:* know secretly of.   134 *happily:* perhaps.   140 *partisan:* spear.   146 *malicious mockery:* mockery because they only imitate harm.   147 *cock crew:* (traditional signal for ghosts to return to their confines).   153 *sea . . . air:* the four elements (inhabited by spirits, each indigenous to a particular element).   154 *extravagant and erring:* going beyond its bounds (vagrant) and wandering.   *hies:* hastens.   156 *made probation:* gave proof.   158 *'gainst:* just before.   162 *wholesome:* healthy (night air was considered unhealthy).   *strike:* exert evil influence   163 *takes:* bewitches.   166 *russet:* reddish.

This spirit dumb to us, will speak to him:
Do you consent we shall acquaint him with it,
As needful in our loves,° fitting our duty?
MARCELLUS.   Let's do't I pray, and I this morning know
Where we shall find him most convenient.   *Exeunt.°*   175

Scene 2. *[A room of state in the castle]*

Flourish.° Enter CLAUDIUS *King of Denmark,* GERTRUDE *the Queen,* [*members of the*] *Council:*
as POLONIUS; *and his son* LAERTES, HAMLET, [VALTEMAND *and* CORNELIUS] *cum aliis.°*
KING.   Though yet of Hamlet our dear brother's death
        The memory be green, and that it us befitted
        To bear our hearts in grief, and our whole kingdom
        To be contracted in one brow of woe,
        Yet so far hath discretion fought with nature,°   5
        That we° with wisest sorrow think on him
        Together with remembrance of ourselves:°
        Therefore our sometime° sister,° now our queen,
        Th'imperial jointress° to this warlike state,
        Have we as 'twere with a defeated joy,   10
        With an auspicious, and a dropping eye,°
        With mirth in funeral, and with dirge in marriage,
        In equal scale weighing delight and dole,
        Taken to wife: nor have we herein barred
        Your better wisdoms,° which have freely gone   15
        With this affair along—for all, our thanks.
        Now follows that you know, young Fortinbras,
        Holding a weak supposal of our worth,°
        Or thinking by our late dear brother's death
        Our state to be disjoint and out of frame,°   20
        Colleaguèd° with this dream of his advantage,°
        He hath not failed to pester us with message
        Importing the surrender of those lands
        Lost by his father, with all bands° of law,
        To our most valiant brother—so much for him: 25
        Now for ourself, and for this time of meeting,
        Thus much the business is. We have here writ
        To Norway, uncle of young Fortinbras—
        Who impotent and bed-rid scarcely hears
        Of this his nephew's purpose—to suppress   30
        His further gait° herein, in that the levies,

---

173 *needful ... loves:* urged by our friendship.   175 stage direction: *Exeunt:* all exit.   stage
direction: *Flourish:* fanfare of trumpets.   *cum aliis:* with others.   5 *nature:* natural impulse
(of grief).   6 *we:* royal plural. The King speaks not only for himself, but for his entire
government.   7 *remembrance of ourselves:* reminder of our duties.   8 *sometime:* former.
sister: sister-in-law.   9 *jointress:* widow who inherits the estate.   11 *auspicious ... eye:* one eye
happy, the other tearful.   14–15 *barred ... wisdoms:* failed to seek and abide by your good
advice.   18 *weak ... worth:* low opinion of my ability in office.   20 *out of frame:* tottering.
21 *Colleaguèd:* supported.   *advantage:* superiority.   24 *bands:* bonds.   31 *gait:* progress.

The lists, and full proportions are all made
Out of his subject:° and we here dispatch
You good Cornelius, and you Valtemand,
For bearers of this greeting to old Norway,   3
Giving to you no further personal power
To business with the king, more than the scope
Of these delated° articles allow:
Farewell, and let your haste commend your duty.°
CORNELIUS, VALTEMAND.   In that, and all things, will we show our duty.   4
KING.   We doubt it nothing, heartily farewell.

Exeunt VALTEMAND and CORNELIUS.

And now Laertes what's the news with you?
You told us of some suit, what is't Laertes?
You cannot speak of reason to the Dane
And lose your voice;° what wouldst thou beg Laertes,   4
That shall not be my offer, not thy asking?°
The head is not more native° to the heart,
The hand more instrumental to the mouth,
Than is the throne of Denmark to thy father.
What wouldst thou have Laertes?
LAERTES.   My dread lord,   5
Your leave and favour° to return to France,
From whence, though willingly I came to Denmark,
To show my duty in your coronation,
Yet now I must confess, that duty done,
My thoughts and wishes bend again toward France,   5
And bow them to your gracious leave and pardon.°
KING.   Have you your father's leave? What says Polonius?
POLONIUS.   He hath my lord wrung from me my slow leave
By laboursome petition, and at last
Upon his will I sealed my hard consent.°   6
I do beseech you give him leave to go.
KING.   Take thy fair hour Laertes, time be thine,
And thy best graces spend it at thy will.
But now my cousin° Hamlet, and my son—
HAMLET.   [*Aside.*] A little more than kin,° and less than kind.°   6
KING.   How is it that the clouds still hang on you?
HAMLET.   Not so my lord, I am too much in the sun.°

31–33 *levies . . . subject:* Taxes, conscriptions, and supplies are all obtained from his subjects.
38 *delated:* accusing.   39 *haste . . . duty:* prompt departure signify your respect.   45 *lose your
voice:* speak in vain.   46 *offer . . . asking:* grant even before requested.   47 *native:* related.
51 *leave and favour:* kind permission.   56 *pardon:* allowance.   60 *Upon . . . consent:* (1) At his
request, I gave my grudging consent. (2) On the soft sealing wax of his (legal) will, I stamped
my approval.   64 *cousin:* kinsman (used for relatives outside the immediate family).
65 *more than kin:* too much of a kinsman, being both uncle and stepfather.   *less than kind:* (1)
unkind because of being a kin (proverbial) and taking the throne from the former king's son
(2) unnatural (as it was considered incest to marry the wife of one's dead brother).   67 *in the
sun:* (1) in presence of the king (often associated metaphorically with the sun) (2) proverbial:
"out of heaven's blessing into the warm sun" (3) of a "son."

QUEEN.   Good Hamlet cast they nighted colour° off
　　And let thine eye look like a friend on Denmark,°
　　Do not for ever with they vailèd° lids   70
　　Seek for thy noble father in the dust,
　　Thou know'st 'tis common, all that lives must die,
　　Passing through nature to eternity.
HAMLET.   Ay madam, it is common.°
QUEEN.   If it be,   75
　　Why seems it so particular with thee?
HAMLET.   Seems, madam? nay it is, I know not "seems."
　　'Tis not alone my inky cloak good mother,
　　Nor customary suits of solemn black,
　　Nor windy suspiration of forced breath,   80
　　No, nor the fruitful river in the eye,°
　　Nor the dejected haviour° of the visage,
　　Together with all forms, moods, shapes of grief,
　　That can denote me truly: these indeed seem,
　　For they are actions that a man might play,°
　　But I have that within which passes show,   85
　　These but the trappings and the suits of woe.°
KING.   'Tis sweet and commendable in your nature Hamlet,
　　To give these mourning duties to your father:
　　But you must know your father lost a father,
　　That father lost, lost his, and the survivor bound   90
　　In filial obligation for some term
　　To do obsequious sorrow:° but to persever
　　In obstinate condolement,° is a course
　　Of impious stubbornness, 'tis unmanly grief,
　　It shows a will most incorrect to heaven,   95
　　A heart unfortified, a mind impatient,
　　An understanding simple and unschooled:
　　For what we know must be, and is as common
　　As any the most vulgar thing to sense,°
　　Why should we in our peevish opposition   100
　　Take it to heart? Fie, 'tis a fault to heaven,
　　A fault against the dead, a fault to nature,
　　To reason most absurd, whose common theme
　　Is death of fathers, and who still° hath cried
　　From the first corse,° till he that died today,   105
　　"This must be so." We pray you throw to earth
　　This unprevailing° woe, and think of us
　　As of a father, for let the world take note

68 *nighted colour:* black.   69 *Denmark:* the King of Denmark.   70 *vailèd:* downcast.
74 *common:* (1) general (2) vulgar.   79–80 *windy . . . eye:* (hyperbole used to describe
exaggerated sighs and tears).   81 *haviour:* behavior.   84 *play:* act.   86 *trappings . . . woe:*
outward, superficial costumes of mourning.   92 *do obsequious sorrow:* express sorrow
befitting obsequies or funerals.   93 *condolement:* grief.   99 *As any . . . sense:* as the most
ordinary thing the senses can perceive.   104 *still:* always.   105 *corse:* corpse (of Abel, also,
ironically, the first fratricide).   107 *unprevailing:* useless.

You are the most immediate° to our throne,
And with no less nobility of love   11●
Than that which dearest father bears his son,
Do I impart toward you. For your intent
In going back to school in Wittenberg,
It is most retrograde° to our desire,
And we beseech you, bend you° to remain   11
Here in the cheer and comfort of our eye,
Our chiefest courtier, cousin, and our son.
QUEEN.   Let not thy mother lose her prayers Hamlet,
I pray thee stay with us, go not to Wittenberg.
HAMLET.   I shall in all my best obey you madam.   12
KING.   Why 'tis a loving and a fair reply,
Be as ourself in Denmark. Madam come,
This gentle and unforced accord of Hamlet
Sits smiling to my heart, in grace whereof,
No jocund health that Denmark drinks today,   12●
But the great cannon to the clouds shall tell,
And the king's rouse° the heaven shall bruit° again,
Re-speaking earthly thunder; come away.

                                  Flourish, Exeunt all but HAMLET.

HAMLET.   O that this too too sullied° flesh would melt,
Thaw and resolve itself into a dew,   13●
Or that the Everlasting had not fixed
His canon° 'gainst self-slaughter. O God, God,
How weary, stale, flat, and unprofitable
Seems to me all the uses of this world!
Fie on't, ah fie, 'tis an unweeded garden   13
That grows to seed, things rank° and gross in nature
Possess it merely.° That it should come to this,
But two months dead, nay not so much, not two,
So excellent a king, that was to this
Hyperion° to a satyr,° so loving to my mother,   14●
That he might not beteem° the winds of heaven
Visit her face too roughly—heaven and earth,
Must I remember? why, she would hang on him
As if increase of appetite had grown
By what it fed on,° and yet within a month—   14.
Let me not think on't: Frailty, thy name is woman—
A little month or ere those shoes were old
With which she followed my poor father's body

---

109 *most immediate:* next in succession (though Danish kings were elected by the council, an Elizabethan audience might feel that Hamlet, not Claudius, should be king).   114 *retrograde:* movement (of planets) in a reverse direction.   115 *beseech . . . you:* hope you will be inclined. 127 *rouse:* toast that empties the wine cup.   *bruit:* sound.   129 *sullied:* tainted. 132 *canon:* divine edict.   136 *rank:* (1) luxuriant, excessive (2) bad-smelling.   137 *merely:* entirely.   140 *Hyperion:* god of the sun.   *satyr:* part-goat, part-man woodland deity (noted for lust).   141 *beteem:* allow.   144–145 *As if . . . on:* as if the more she fed, the more her appetite increased.

Like Niobe° all tears, why she, even she—
O God, a beast that wants° discourse of reason   150
Would have mourned longer—married with my uncle,
My father's brother, but no more like my father
Than I to Hercules: within a month,
Ere yet the salt of most unrighteous° tears
Had left the flushing° in her gallèd° eyes,   155
She married. O most wicked speed, to post°
With such dexterity to incestuous° sheets:
It is not, nor it cannot come to good,
But break my heart, for I must hold my tongue.

Enter HORATIO, MARCELLUS *and* BARNARDO.

HORATIO.   Hail to your lordship.
HAMLET.   I am glad to see you well;   160
    Horatio, or I do forget my self.
HORATIO.   The same my lord, and your poor servant ever.
HAMLET.   Sir my good friend, I'll change° that name with you:
    And what make you from Wittenberg, Horatio?
    Marcellus.   165
MARCELLUS.   My good lord.
HAMLET.   I am very glad to see you: good even, sir.
    But what in faith make you from Wittenberg?
HORATIO.   A truant disposition, good my lord.
HAMLET.   I would not hear your enemy say so,   170
    Nor shall you do mine ear that violence
    To make it truster of your own report
    Against yourself. I know you are no truant,
    But what is your affair in Elsinore?
    We'll teach you to drink deep ere you depart.   175
HORATIO.   My Lord, I came to see your father's funeral.
HAMLET.   I prithee do not mock me, fellow student,
    I think it was to see my mother's wedding.
HORATIO.   Indeed my lord it followed hard upon.
HAMLET.   Thrift, thrift, Horatio, the funeral baked meats°   180
    Did coldly° furnish forth the marriage tables.
    Would I had met my dearest° foe in heaven
    Or ever I had seen that day Horatio.
    My father, methinks I see my father.
HORATIO.   Where my lord?
HAMLET.   In my mind's eye Horatio.   185
HORATIO.   I saw him once, a' was a goodly° king.
HAMLET.   A' was a man, take him for all in all,
    I shall not look upon his like again.

---

149 *Niobe:* (who boasted of her children before Leto and was punished by their destruction; Zeus changed the weeping mother to a stone dropping continual tears).   150 *wants:* lacks. 154 *unrighteous:* (because untrue).   155 *flushing:* redness.   *gallèd:* rubbed sore. 156 *post:* rush.   157 *incestuous:* (the church forbade marriage to one's brother's widow). 163 *change:* exchange (and be called your friend).   180 *funeral baked meats:* food prepared for the funeral.   181 *coldly:* when cold.   182 *dearest:* direst.   186 *goodly:* handsome.

HORATIO.   My lord, I think I saw him yesternight.

HAMLET.   Saw? Who?   190

HORATIO.   My lord, the king your father.

HAMLET.   The king my father?

HORATIO.   Season your admiration° for a while
    With an attent ear till I may deliver
    Upon the witness of these gentlemen
    This marvel to you.

HAMLET.   For God's love let me hear!   195

HORATIO.   Two nights together had these gentlemen,
    Marcellus and Barnardo, on their watch
    In the dead waste and middle of the night,
    Been thus encountered. A figure like your father
    Armed at point exactly, cap-a-pe,°   200
    Appears before them, and with solemn march,
    Goes slow and stately by them; thrice he walked
    By their oppressed° and fear-surprisèd eyes
    Within his truncheon's° length, whilst they distilled°
    Almost to jelly with the act of fear,   205
    Stand dumb and speak not to him; this to me
    In dreadful secrecy° impart they did,
    And I with them the third night kept the watch,
    Where as they had delivered, both in time,
    Form of the thing, each word made true and good,   210
    The apparition comes: I knew your father,
    These hands are not more like.

HAMLET.   But where was this?

MARCELLUS.   My lord upon the platform where we watch.

HAMLET.   Did you not speak to it?

HORATIO.   My lord I did,
    But answer made it none, yet once methought   215
    It lifted up it° head, and did address
    Itself to motion° like as it would speak:
    But even then the morning cock crew loud,
    And at the sound it shrunk in haste away
    And vanished from our sight.

HAMLET.   'Tis very strange.   220

HORATIO.   As I do live my honoured lord 'tis true,
    And we did think it writ down in our duty
    To let you know of it.

HAMLET.   Indeed indeed sirs, but this troubles me.
    Hold you the watch tonight?

ALL.   We do my lord.   225

HAMLET.   Armed say you?

ALL.   Armed my lord.

---

192 *Season your admiration:* control your wonder.   200 *at point . . . cap-a-pe:* in every detail,
head to foot.   203 *oppressed:* overcome by horror.   204 *truncheon:* staff (of office).
distilled: dissolved.   207 *in dreadful secrecy:* as a dread secret.   216 *it:* its.   216–217 *address
. . . motion:* start to move.

HAMLET.   From top to toe?
ALL.   My lord from head to foot.
HAMLET.   Then saw you not his face.
HORATIO.   O yes my lord, he wore his beaver° up.   230
HAMLET.   What, looked he frowningly?
HORATIO.   A countenance more in sorrow than in anger.
HAMLET.   Pale, or red?
HORATIO.   Nay, very pale.
HAMLET.   And fixed his eyes upon you?
HORATIO.   Most constantly.
HAMLET.   I would I had been there.   235
HORATIO.   It would have much amazed you.
HAMLET.   Very like, very like, stayed it long?
HORATIO.   While one with moderate haste might tell° a hundred.
MARCELLUS, BARNARDO.   Longer, longer.
HORATIO.   Not when I saw't.
HAMLET.   His beard was grizzled,° no?   240
HORATIO.   It was as I have seen it in his life,
     A sable silvered.°
HAMLET.   I will watch tonight;
     Perchance 'twill walk again.
HORATIO.   I warr'nt it will.
HAMLET.   If it assume my noble father's person,
     I'll speak to it though hell itself should gape   245
     And bid me hold my peace;° I pray you all
     If you have hitherto concealed this sight
     Let it be tenable° in your silence still,
     And whatsoever else shall hap tonight,
     Give it an understanding but no tongue.   250
     I will requite your loves, so fare you well:
     Upon the platform 'twixt eleven and twelve
     I'll visit you.
ALL.   Our duty to your honour.
HAMLET.   Your loves, as mine to you:° farewell.   *Exeunt.*
     My father's spirit (in arms) all is not well,   255
     I doubt° some foul play, would the night were come;
     Till then sit still my soul, foul deeds will rise,
     Though all the earth o'erwhelm them, to men's eyes.   *Exit.*

Scene 3. [*Polonius's chambers*]

Enter LAERTES *and* OPHELIA *his sister.*

LAERTES.   My necessaries are embarked, farewell,
     And sister, as the winds give benefit

---

230 *beaver:* visor.   238 *tell:* count.   240 *grizzled:* grey.   242 *A sable silvered:* black flecked with grey.   245–246 *though hell . . . peace:* despite the risk of hell (for speaking to a demon) warning me to be silent.   248 *tenable:* held, kept.   254 *Your loves . . . you:* offer your friendship (rather than duty) in exchange for mine.   256 *doubt:* fear.

And convoy° is assistant, do not sleep
But let me hear from you.
OPHELIA.   Do you doubt that?
LAERTES.   For Hamlet, and the trifling of his favour,
        Hold it a fashion, and a toy in blood,°
        A violet in the youth of primy nature,°
        Forward,° not permanent, sweet, not lasting,
        The perfume and suppliance of° a minute,
        No more.
OPHELIA.   No more but so?
LAERTES.   Think it no more.
        For nature crescent° does not grow alone
        In thews and bulk,° but as this temple waxes°
        The inward service of the mind and soul
        Grows wide withal.° Perhaps he loves you now,
        And now no soil nor cautel° doth besmirch
        The virtue of his will:° but you must fear,
        His greatness weighed,° his will is not his own,
        For he himself is subject to his birth:
        He may not as unvalued persons° do,
        Carve° for himself, for on his choice depends
        The sanctity and health of this whole state,
        And therefore must his choice be circumscribed
        Unto the voice and yielding° of that body
        Whereof he is the head. Then if he says he loves you,
        It fits your wisdom so far to believe it
        As he in his particular act and place
        May give his saying deed,° which is no further
        Than the main voice of Denmark goes withal.
        Then weigh what loss your honour may sustain
        If with too credent° ear you list° his songs,
        Or lose your heart, or your chaste treasure open
        To his unmast'red importunity.°
        Fear it Ophelia, fear it my dear sister,
        And keep you in the rear of your affection,
        Out of the shot and danger of desire.
        The chariest° maid is prodigal enough
        If she unmask her beauty to the moon.
        Virtue itself 'scapes not calumnious strokes.
        The canker galls the infants° of the spring

---

3 *convoy:* conveyance.   6 *toy in blood:* whim of the passions.   7 *youth of primy nature:* early
spring.   8 *Forward:* premature.   9 *suppliance of:* supplying diversion for.   11 *nature
crescent:* man as he grows.   12 *thews and bulk:* sinews and body.   *temple waxes:* body grows
(1 Cor. 6:19).   14 *withal:* at the same time.   15 *cautel:* deceit.   16 *will:* desire.
17 *weighed:* considered.   19 *unvalued persons:* common people.   20 *Carve:* choose (as does
the one who carves the food).   23 *voice and yielding:* approving vote.   26–27 *in his . . . deed:*
limited by personal responsibilities and rank, may perform what he promises.   30 *credent:*
credulous.   *list:* listen to.   31–32 *your chaste . . . importunity:* lose your virginity to his
uncontrolled persistence.   36 *chariest:* most cautious.   39 *canker . . . infants:* cankerworm or
caterpillar harms the young plants.

Too oft before their buttons° be disclosed,   40
And in the morn and liquid dew of youth
Contagious blastments° are most imminent.
Be wary then, best safety lies in fear,
Youth to itself rebels,° though none else near.
OPHELIA.   I shall the effect° of this good lesson keep   45
As watchman to my heart: but good my brother,
Do not as some ungracious° pastors do,
Show me the steep and thorny way to heaven,
Whiles like a puffed and reckless libertine
Himself the primrose path of dalliance treads,   50
And recks not his own rede.°

Enter POLONIUS.

LAERTES.   O fear me not,°
I stay too long, but here my father comes:
A double blessing is a double grace,
Occasion smiles upon a second leave.°
POLONIUS.   Yet here Laertes? aboard, aboard for shame,   55
The wind sits in the shoulder of your sail,
And you are stayed for: there, my blessing with thee,
And these few precepts in thy memory
Look thou character.° Give thy thoughts no tongue,
Nor any unproportioned thought his act: 60
Be thou familiar, but by no means vulgar:°
Those friends thou hast, and their adoption tried,°
Grapple them unto thy soul with hoops of steel,
But do not dull° thy palm with entertainment
Of each new-hatched unfledged° comrade. Beware   65
Of entrance to a quarrel, but being in,
Bear't that th'opposèd may beware of thee.
Give every man thy ear, but few thy voice:
Take each man's censure,° but reserve thy judgment.
Costly thy habit° as thy purse can buy,   70
But not expressed in fancy;° rich, not gaudy,
For the apparel oft proclaims the man,
And they in France of the best rank and station,
Are of a most select and generous chief° in that:
Neither a borrower nor a lender be,   75
For loan oft loses both itself and friend,
And borrowing dulls the edge of husbandry;°
This above all, to thine own self be true
And it must follow as the night the day,

40 *buttons:* buds.   42 *blastments:* blights.   44 *to itself rebels:* lusts by nature.   45 *effect:* moral.   47 *ungracious:* lacking God's grace.   51 *recks . . . rede:* does not follow his own advice.   *fear me not:* Don't worry about me.   54 *Occasion . . . leave:* opportunity favors a second leave-taking.   59 *character:* write, impress, imprint.   61 *vulgar:* indiscriminately friendly.   62 *adoption tried:* loyalty proved.   64 *dull:* get callouses on.   65 *new-hatched, unfledged:* new and untested.   69 *censure:* opinion.   70 *habit:* clothing.   71 *expressed in fancy:* so fantastic as to be ridiculous.   74 *select . . . chief:* judicious and noble eminence. 77 *husbandry:* thrift.

Thou canst not then be false to any man.
Farewell, my blessing season° this in thee.   8

LAERTES.   Most humbly do I take my leave my lord.

POLONIUS.   The time invites you, go, your servants tend.°

LAERTES.   Farewell Ophelia, and remember well
   What I have said to you.

OPHELIA.   'Tis in my memory locked,   8
   And you yourself shall keep the key of it.

LAERTES.   Farewell.   *Exit* LAERTES.

POLONIUS.   What is't Ophelia he hath said to you?

OPHELIA.   So please you, something touching the Lord Hamlet.

POLONIUS.   Marry,° well bethought: 9
   'Tis told me he hath very oft of late
   Given private time to you, and you yourself
   Have of your audience been most free and bounteous.
   If it be so, as so 'tis put on me,
   And that in way of caution, I must tell you,   9
   You do not understand yourself so clearly
   As it behooves my daughter, and your honour.
   What is between you? give me up the truth.

OPHELIA.   He hath my lord of late made many tenders°
   Of his affection to me.   10

POLONIUS.   Affection, puh, you speak like a green girl
   Unsifted° in such perilous circumstance.
   Do you believe his tenders as you call them?

OPHELIA.   I do not know my lord what I should think.

POLONIUS.   Marry, I will teach you; think yourself a baby   10
   That you have ta'en these tenders° for true pay
   Which are not sterling.° Tender yourself more dearly,°
   Or (not to crack the wind of the poor phrase,
   Running it thus°) you'll tender me a fool.°

OPHELIA.   My lord he hath importuned me with love   11
   In honourable fashion.

POLONIUS.   Ay, fashion you may call it, go to, go to.

OPHELIA.   And hath given countenance° to his speech, my lord,
   With almost all the holy vows of heaven.

POLONIUS.   Ay, springes° to catch woodcocks.° I do know   11
   When the blood burns, how prodigal the soul
   Lends the tongue vows: these blazes daughter,
   Giving more light than heat, extinct in both,
   Even in their promise, as it is a-making,°

---

81 *season:* bring to maturity.   83 *tend:* attend, wait.   90 *Marry:* (a mild oath, from "By the
Virgin Mary").   99 *tenders:* offers (see lines 106–109).   102 *Unsifted:* untested.
106 *tenders:* offers (of money).   107 *sterling:* genuine (currency).   *Tender . . . dearly:* hold
yourself at a higher value.   108–109 *crack . . . thus:* make the phrase lose its breath.
109 *tender . . . fool:* (1) make me look foolish (2) present me with a baby.   113 *countenance:*
confirmation.   115 *springes:* snares.   *woodcocks:* snipelike birds (believed to be stupid and
therefore easily trapped).   118–119 *extinct . . . a-making:* losing both appearance, because of
brevity, and substance, because of broken promises.

You must not take for fire. From this time   120
Be something scanter of your maiden presence,
Set your entreatments at a higher rate
Than a command to parle;° for Lord Hamlet,
Believe so much in him that he is young,
And with a larger tether may he walk   125
Than may be given you: in few° Ophelia,
Do not believe his vows, for they are brokers°
Not of that dye which their investments° show,
But mere implorators° of unholy suits,
Breathing° like sanctified and pious bonds,°   130
The better to beguile. This is for all,
I would not in plain terms from this time forth
Have you so slander any moment leisure
As to give words or talk with the Lord Hamlet.
Look to't I charge you, come your ways.°   135
OPHELIA.   I shall obey, my lord.   [*Exeunt.*]

Scene 4. [*The platform on the battlements*]

Enter HAMLET, HORATIO *and* MARCELLUS.

HAMLET.   The air bites shrewdly,° it is very cold.
HORATIO.   It is a nipping and an eager° air.
HAMLET.   What hour now?
HORATIO.   I think it lacks of twelve.
MARCELLUS.   No, it is struck.
HORATIO.   Indeed? I heard it not: it then draws near the season,°   5
     Wherein the spirit held his wont to walk.

A flourish of trumpets, and two pieces [of ordnance] go off.

     What does this mean my lord?
HAMLET.   The king doth wake° tonight and takes his rouse,°
     Keeps wassail° and the swagg'ring up-spring° reels:
     And as he drains his draughts of Rhenish° down,   10
     The kettle-drum and trumpet thus bray out
     The triumph of his pledge.°
HORATIO.   Is it a custom?
HAMLET.   Ay marry is't,
     But to my mind, though I am native here
     And to the manner born,° it is a custom   15

122–123 *Set . . . parle:* Don't rush to negotiate a surrender as soon as the besieger asks for a
discussion of terms.   126 *few:* short.   127 *brokers:* (1) business agents (2) procurers.
128 *investments:* (1) business ventures (2) clothing.   129 *implorators:* solicitors.   130 *Breathing:* speaking softly.   *bonds:* pledges.   135 *come your ways:* come along.   1 *shrewdly:*
piercingly.   2 *eager:* sharp.   5 *season:* time, period.   8 *wake:* stay awake.   *rouse:* drinks
that empty the cup.   9 *Keeps wassail:* holds drinking bouts.   *up-spring:* a vigorous German
dance.   10 *Rhenish:* Rhine wine.   12 *triumph . . . pledge:* victory of emptying the cup with
one draught.   15 *to . . . born:* accustomed to the practice since birth.

More honoured in the breach than the observance.°
This heavy-headed revel east and west
Makes us traduced and taxed of° other nations:
They clepe° us drunkards, and with swinish phrase
Soil our addition,° and indeed it takes
From our achievements, though performed at height,°
The pith and marrow of our attribute.°
So oft it chances in particular men,
That for some vicious mole of nature° in them,
As in their birth, wherein they are not guilty
(Since nature cannot choose his origin),
By the o'ergrowth of some complexion,°
Oft breaking down the pales° and forts of reason,
Or by some habit, that too much o'er-leavens°
The form of plausive° manners—that these men,
Carrying I say the stamp of one defect,
Being nature's livery,° or fortune's star,°
His virtues else be they as pure as grace,
As infinite as man may undergo,
Shall in the general censure° take corruption
From that particular fault: the dram of evil
Doth all the noble substance of a doubt,
To his own scandal.°

Enter GHOST.

HORATIO.   Look my lord, it comes.
HAMLET.   Angels and ministers of grace defend us:
Be thou a spirit of health, or goblin damned,°
Bring with thee airs from heaven, or blasts from hell,
Be thy intents wicked, or charitable,
Thou com'st in such a questionable° shape,
That I will speak to thee. I'll call thee Hamlet,
King, father, royal Dane. O answer me,
Let me not burst in ignorance, but tell
Why thy canonized° bones hearsèd° in death
Have burst their cerements°? why the sepulchre,
Wherein we saw thee quietly interred
Hath oped his ponderous and marble jaws,

---

16 *More . . . observance:* better to break than to observe.   18 *traduced and taxed of:* defamed and taken to task by.   19 *clepe:* call.   19–20 *with swinish . . . addition:* blemish our reputation by comparing us to swine.   21 *at height:* to the maximum.   22 *attribute:* reputation.   24 *mole of nature:* natural blemish.   27 *o'er growth . . . complexion:* overbalance of one of the body's four humors or fluids believed to determine temperament.   28 *pales:* defensive enclosures.   29 *too much o'er-leavens:* excessively modifies (like too much leaven in bread).   30 *plausive:* pleasing.   32 *nature's livery:* marked by nature.   *fortune's star:* destined by chance.   35 *general censure:* public opinion.   36–38 *the dram . . . scandal:* the minute quantity of evil casts doubt upon his noble nature, to his shame.   40 *spirit . . . damned:* true ghost or demon from hell.   43 *questionable:* question-raising.   47 *canonized:* buried in accordance with church edict.   *hearsèd:* entombed.   48 *cerements:* waxed cloth wrappings.

To cast thee up again? What may this mean
That thou, dead corse, again in complete steel
Revisits thus the glimpses of the moon,
Making night hideous, and we fools of nature°
So horridly to shake our disposition   55
With thoughts beyond the reaches of our souls,
Say why is this? wherefore? what should we do?   *GHOST beckons HAMLET.*
HORATIO.   It beckons you to go away with it,
  As if it some impartment did desire°
  To you alone.
MARCELLUS.   Look with what courteous action   60
  It waves you to a more removèd ground,
  But do not go with it.
HORATIO.   No, by no means.
HAMLET.   It will not speak, then I will follow it.
HORATIO.   Do not my lord.
HAMLET.   Why what should be the fear?
  I do not set my life at a pin's fee,°   65
  And for my soul, what can it do to that
  Being a thing immortal as itself;
  It waves me forth again, I'll follow it.
HORATIO.   What if it tempt you toward the flood my lord,
  Or to the dreadful summit of the cliff   70
  That beetles o'er° his base into the sea,
  And there assume some other horrible form
  Which might deprive your sovereignty of reason,°
  And draw you into madness? think of it,
  The very place puts toys of desperation,°   75
  Without more motive, into every brain
  That looks so many fathoms to the sea
  And hears it roar beneath.
HAMLET.   It waves me still:
  Go on, I'll follow thee.
MARCELLUS.   You shall not go my lord.
HAMLET.   Hold off your hands.   80
HORATIO.   Be ruled, you shall not go.
HAMLET.   My fate cries out,
  And makes each petty artire° in this body
  As hardy as the Nemean lion's° nerve;°
  Still am I called, unhand me gentlemen,
  By heaven I'll make a ghost of him that lets° me: 85
  I say away; go on, I'll follow thee.   *Exeunt GHOST and HAMLET.*
HORATIO.   He waxes desperate° with imagination.

---

54 *fools of nature:* mocked by our natural limitations when faced with the supernatural.
59 *some . . . desire:* desired to impart something.   65 *fee:* value. 71 *beetles o'er:*
overhangs.   73 *deprive . . . reason:* dethrone your reason from its sovereignty.   75 *toys of des-*
peration: desperate whims.   82 *artire:* ligament.   83 *Nemean lion:* (killed by Hercules as one
of his twelve labors).   *nerve:* sinew.   85 *lets:* prevents.   87 *waxes desperate:* grows frantic.

MARCELLUS.   Let's follow, 'tis not fit thus to obey him.
HORATIO.   Have after—to what issue will this come?
MARCELLUS.   Something is rotten in the state of Denmark.
HORATIO.   Heaven will direct it.
MARCELLUS.   Nay, let's follow him.   *Exeunt.*

Scene 5. [Another part of the platform]

Enter GHOST *and* HAMLET.

HAMLET.   Whither wilt thou lead me? Speak, I'll go no further.
GHOST.   Mark me.
HAMLET.   I will.
GHOST.   My hour is almost come
    When I to sulphurous and tormenting flames
    Must render up myself.
HAMLET.   Alas poor ghost.
GHOST.   Pity me not, but lend thy serious hearing
    To what I shall unfold.
HAMLET.   Speak, I am bound° to hear.
GHOST.   So art thou to revenge, when thou shalt hear.
HAMLET.   What?
GHOST.   I am thy father's spirit,
    Doomed for a certain term to walk the night,
    And for the day confined to fast in fires,
    Till the foul crimes done in my days of nature°
    Are burnt and purged away: but that I am forbid
    To tell the secrets of my prison-house,
    I could a tale unfold whose lightest word
    Would harrow up thy soul, freeze thy young blood,
    Make thy two eyes like stars start from their spheres,°
    Thy knotted and combinèd locks to part,
    And each particular hair to stand an° end,
    Like quills upon the fretful porpentine:°
    But this eternal blazon° must not be
    To ears of flesh and blood; list, list, O list:
    If though didst ever thy dear father love—
HAMLET.   O God!
GHOST.   Revenge his foul and most unnatural murder.
HAMLET.   Murder?
GHOST.   Murder most foul, as in the best it is,
    But this most foul, strange and unnatural.
HAMLET.   Haste me to know't, that I with wings as swift
    As meditation or the thoughts of love,
    May sweep to my revenge.

---

6 *bound:* obliged by duty.   12 *crimes . . . nature:* sins committed during my life on earth.
17 *spheres:* (1) orbits (according to Ptolemy, each planet was confined to a sphere revolving
around the earth) (2) sockets.   19 *an:* on.   20 *fretful porpentine:* angry porcupine.
21 *eternal blazon:* revelation about eternity.

GHOST.   I find thee apt,°
  And duller shouldst thou be than the fat° weed
  That rots itself in ease on Lethe wharf,°
  Wouldst thou not stir in this; now Hamlet hear,
  'Tis given out, that sleeping in my orchard,°   35
  A serpent stung me, so the whole ear of Denmark
  Is by a forgèd process° of my death
  Rankly abused:° but know thou noble youth,
  The serpent that did sting thy father's life
  Now wears his crown.
HAMLET.   O my prophetic soul!   40
  My uncle?
GHOST. Ay, that incestuous, that adulterate° beast,
  With witchcraft of his wit, with traitorous gifts,
  O wicked wit and gifts, that have the power
  So to seduce; won to his shameful lust   45
  The will of my most seeming-virtuous queen;
  O Hamlet, what a falling-off was there,
  From me whose love was of that dignity
  That it went hand in hand, even with the vow
  I made to her in marriage, and to decline   50
  Upon° a wretch whose natural gifts were poor
  To° those of mine;
  But virtue, as it never will be moved,
  Though lewdness court it in a shape of heaven,°
  So lust, though to a radiant angle linked,   55
  Will sate itself in a celestial bed
  And prey on garbage.
  But soft, methinks I scent the morning air,
  Brief let me be; sleeping within my orchard,
  My custom always of the afternoon,   60
  Upon my secure° hour thy uncle stole
  With juice of cursèd hebona° in a vial,
  And in the porches of my ears did pour
  The leperous° distilment, whose effect
  Holds such an enmity with blood of man,   65
  That swift as quicksilver it courses through
  The natural gates and alleys of the body,
  And with a sudden vigour it doth posset°
  And curd, like eager° droppings into milk,
  The thin and wholesome° blood; so did it mine,   70
  And a most instant tetter° barked about°
  Most lazar°-like with vile and loathsome crust

31 *apt:* ready.   32 *fat:* slimy.   33 *Lethe wharf:* the banks of Lethe (river in Hades from which spirits drank to forget their past lives).   35 *orchard:* garden.   37 *process:* account. 38 *abused:* deceived.   42 *adulterate:* adulterous.   50–51 *decline Upon:* descend to.   52 *To:* compared to.   54 *shape of heaven:* angelic appearance.   61 *secure:* unsuspecting. 62 *hebona:* poisonous sap of the ebony or henbane.   64 *leperous:* leprosy-causing.   68 *posset:* curdle.   69 *eager:* sour.   70 *wholesome:* healthy.   71 *tetter:* skin eruption.   *barked about:* covered (like bark on a tree).   72 *lazar:* leper.

All my smooth body.
Thus was I sleeping by a brother's hand,
Of life, of crown, of queen at once dispatched,
Cut off even in the blossoms of my sin,
Unhouseled, disappointed, unaneled,°
No reck'ning° made, but sent to my account°
With all my imperfections on my head;
O horrible, O horrible, most horrible!
If thou hast nature in thee bear it not,
Let not the royal bed of Denmark be
A couch for luxury° and damnèd incest.
But howsoever thou pursues this act,
Taint not thy mind, nor let thy soul contrive
Against thy mother aught;° leave her to heaven,
And to those thorns that in her bosom lodge
To prick and sting her. Fare thee well at once,
The glow-worm shows the matin° to be near
And 'gins to pale this uneffectual fire:°
Adieu, adieu, adieu, remember me.   *Exit.*

HAMLET.   O all you host of heaven! O earth! what else?
And shall I couple° hell? O fie! Hold, hold my heart,
And you my sinews, grow not instant old,
But bear me stiffly up; remember thee?
Ay thou poor ghost, whiles memory holds a seat
In this distracted globe.° Remember thee?
Yea, from the table° of my memory
I'll wipe away all trivial fond° records,
All saws of books,° all forms, all pressures° past
That youth and observation copied there,
And thy commandment all alone shall live
Within the book and volume of my brain,
Unmixed with baser matter, yes by heaven:
O most pernicious woman!
O villain, villain, smiling damnèd villain!
My tables,° meet° it is I set it down
That one may smile, and smile, and be a villain,
At least I am sure it may be so in Denmark.
So uncle, there you are: now to my word,°
It is 'Adieu, adieu, remember me.'
I have sworn't.

Enter HORATIO and MARCELLUS.

77 *Unhouseled . . . unaneled:* without final sacrament, unprepared (without confession) and lacking extreme unction (anointing).   78 *reck'ning:* (1) accounting (2) payment of my bill (3) confession and absolution.   *account:* judgment.   83 *luxury:* lust.   86 *aught:* anything. 89 *matin:* dawn.   90 *'gins . . . fire:* his light becomes ineffective, made pale by day. 93 *couple:* engage in a contest against.   97 *distracted globe:* (his head).   98 *table:* tablet, "table-book."   99 *fond:* foolish.   100 *saws of books:* maxims (sayings) copied from books. *forms, pressures:* ideas, impressions.   107 *tables:* See note for line 98.   *meet:* fitting. 110 *word:* motto (to guide my actions).

HORATIO.   My lord, my lord!
MARCELLUS.   Lord Hamlet!
HORATIO.   Heaven secure° him.
HAMLET.   So be it.
MARCELLUS.   Illo, ho, ho, my lord!   115
HAMLET.   Hillo, ho, ho, boy, come° bird, come.
MARCELLUS.   How is't my noble lord?
HORATIO.   What news my lord?
HAMLET.   O, wonderful!
HORATIO.   Good my lord, tell it.
HAMLET.   No, you will reveal it.
HORATIO.   Not I my lord, by heaven.
MARCELLUS.   Nor I my lord.   120
HAMLET.   How say you then, would heart of man once think it?
    But you'll be secret?
BOTH.   Ay, by heaven, my lord.
HAMLET.   There's ne'er a villain dwelling in all Denmark
    But he's an arrant° knave.
HORATIO.   There needs no ghost my lord, come from the grave   125
    To tell us this.
HAMLET.   Why right, you are in the right,
    And so without more circumstance° at all
    I hold it fit that we shake hands and part,
    You, as your business and desire shall point you,
    For every man hath business and desire   130
    Such as it is, and for my own poor part,
    Look you, I will go pray.
HORATIO.   These are but wild and whirling words my lord.
HAMLET.   I am sorry they offend you, heartily,
    Yes faith, heartily.
HORATIO.   There's no offence my lord.   135
HAMLET.   Yes by Saint Patrick, but there is Horatio,
    And much offence too: touching this vision here,
    It is an honest° ghost, that let me tell you:
    For your desire to know what is between us,
    O'ermaster't as you may. And now good friends,   140
    As you are friends, scholars, and soldiers,
    Give me one poor request.
HORATIO.   What is't, my lord? we will.
HAMLET.   Never make known what you have seen tonight.
BOTH.   My lord we will not.
HAMLET.   Nay, but swear't.
HORATIO.   In faith   145
    My lord, not I.
MARCELLUS.   Nor I my lord, in faith.

---

113 *secure:* protect.   116 *Hillo . . . come:* falconer's cry with which Hamlet replies to their calls.
124 *arrant:* thoroughgoing.   127 *circumstance:* ceremony.   138 *honest:* true (not a devil in disguise).

HAMLET.   Upon my sword.

MARCELLUS.   We have sworn my lord already.

HAMLET.   Indeed, upon my sword,° indeed.

GHOST.   Swear.   *Ghost cries under the stage.*

HAMLET.   Ha, ha, boy, say'st thou so, art thou there, truepenny°?   1.
Come on, you hear this fellow in the cellarage,
Consent to swear.

HORATIO.   Propose the oath my lord.

HAMLET.   Never to speak of this that you have seen.
Swear by my sword.

GHOST.   [*Beneath.*] Swear.   1.

HAMLET.   Hic et ubique?° then we'll shift our ground:
Come hither gentlemen,
And lay your hands again upon my sword,
Swear by my sword
Never to speak of this that you have heard.   1.

GHOST.   [*Beneath.*] Swear by his sword.

HAMLET.   Well said old mole, canst work i'th' earth so fast?
A worthy pioner°—once more remove,° good friends.

HORATIO.   O day and night, but this is wondrous strange.

HAMLET.   And therefore as a stranger give it welcome.   1.
There are more things in heaven and earth Horatio,
Than are dreamt of in your philosophy.
But come,
Here as before, never so help you mercy,
How strange or odd some'er I bear myself,   1.
(As I perchance hereafter shall think meet
To put an antic disposition on°)
That you at such times seeing me, never shall
With arms encumbered° thus, or this head-shake,
Or by pronouncing of some doubtful phrase,   1.
As "Well, well, we know," or "We could and if we would,"
Or "If we list° to speak," or "There be and if they might,"
Or such ambiguous giving out, to note
That you know aught of me; this do swear,
So grace and mercy at your need help you.   1.

GHOST. [*Beneath.*] Swear.   [*They swear.*]

HAMLET.   Rest, rest, perturbed spirit: so gentlemen,
With all my love I do commend me to you,°
And what so poor a man as Hamlet is,
May do t'express his love and friending to you   1.
God willing shall not lack: let us go in together,
And still° your fingers on your lips I pray.
The time is out of joint: O cursèd spite,

---

148 *sword:* (the cross-shaped hilt).   150 *truepenny:* old pal.   156 *Hic et ubique:* here and
everywhere.   163 *pioner:* digger (army trencher).   *remove:* move elsewhere.   172 *put . . .
on:* assume a mad or grotesque behavior.   174 *encumbered:* folded.   177 *list:* please.
183 *commend . . . you:* put myself in your hands.   187 *still:* always.

That ever I was born to set it right.
Nay come, let's go together.   *Exeunt.*   190

ACT 2

Scene 1. *[Polonius's chambers]*

Enter old POLONIUS *with his man* REYNALDO.

POLONIUS.   Give him this money, and these notes Reynaldo.
REYNALDO.   I will my lord.
POLONIUS.   You shall do marvellous° wisely, good Reynaldo,
Before you visit him, to make inquire
Of his behaviour.
REYNALDO.   My lord, I did intend it.   5
POLONIUS.   Marry, well said, very well said; look you sir,
Inquire me first what Danskers° are in Paris,
And how, and who, what means, and where they keep,°
What company, at what expense, and finding
By this encompassment° and drift of question   10
That they do know my son, come you more nearer
Than your particular demands° will touch it,
Take you as 'twere some distant knowledge of him,
As thus, "I know his father, and his friends,
And in part him"—do you mark this, Reynaldo?   15
REYNALDO.   Ay, very well my lord.
POLONIUS.   'And in part him, but,' you may say, 'not well,
But if't be he I mean, he's very wild,
Addicted so and so;' and there put on him
What forgeries° you please, marry none so rank°   20
As may dishonour him, take heed of that,
But sir, such wanton, wild, and usual slips,
As are companions noted and most known
To youth and liberty.
REYNALDO.   As gaming my lord.
POLONIUS.   Ay, or drinking, fencing, swearing,   25
Quarrelling, drabbing°—you may go so far.
REYNALDO.   My lord, that would dishonour him.
POLONIUS.   Faith no, as you may season it in the charge.°
You must not put another scandal on him,
That he is open to incontinency,°   30
That's not my meaning, but breathe his faults so quaintly°
That they may seem the taints of° liberty,

---

3 *marvellous:* wonderfully.   7 *danskers:* Danes.   8 *keep:* lodge.   10 *encompassment:* roundabout way.   12 *particular demands:* specific questions.   20 *forgeries:* inventions.   *rank:*
excessive.   26 *drabbing:* whoring.   28 *season . . . charge:* temper the charge as you make it.
30 *incontinency:* uncontrolled lechery.   31 *quaintly:* delicately.   32 *taints of:* blemishes due
to.

The flash and outbreak of a fiery mind,
A savageness in unreclaimèd blood,°
Of general assault.°
REYNALDO.   But my good lord—
POLONIUS.   Wherefore° should you do this?
REYNALDO.   Ay my lord,
  I would know that.
POLONIUS.   Marry sir, here's my drift,
  And I believe it is a fetch of warrant:°
  You laying these slight sullies on my son,
  As 'twere a thing a little soiled i'th' working,°
  Mark you, your party in converse, him you would sound,
  Having ever seen° in the prenominate crimes°
  The youth you breathe of guilty, be assured
  He closes with you in this consequence,°
  "Good sir," or so, or "friend," or "gentleman,"
  According to the phrase, or the addition°
  Of man and country.
REYNALDO.   Very good my lord.
POLONIUS.   And then sir, does a'° this, a' does, what was I
    about to say?
  By the mass I was about to say something,
  Where did I leave?
REYNALDO.   At "closes in the consequence,"
  At "friend, or so, and gentleman."
POLONIUS.   At "closes in the consequence," ay marry,
  He closes thus, "I know the gentleman,
  I saw him yesterday, or th'other day,
  Or then, or then, with such or such, and as you say,
  There was a' gaming, there o'ertook in's rouse,°
  There falling out at tennis," or perchance
  "I saw him enter such a house of sale,"
  Videlicet,° a brothel, or so forth. See you now,
  Your bait of falsehood takes this carp of truth,
  And thus do we of wisdom, and of reach,°
  With windlasses,° and with assays of bias,°
  By indirections find directions out:
  So by my former lecture and advice
  Shall you my son; you have me, have you not?
REYNALDO.   My lord I have.
POLONIUS.   God bye ye, fare ye well.
REYNALDO.   Good my lord.

---

34 *unreclaimèd blood:* unbridled passion.   35 *general assault:* attacking all (young men).
36 *Wherefore:* why.   38 *fetch of warrant:* trick guaranteed to succeed.   40 *working:* handling.
42 *Having ever seen:* if he has ever seen.   *prenominate crimes:* aforenamed sins.   44 *closes . . .
consequence:* comes to terms with you as follows.   46 *addition:* title, form of address.
48 *'a:* he.   56 *o'ertook in's rouse:* overcome by drunkenness.   59 *Videlicet:* namely.
61 *reach:* far-reaching knowledge.   62 *windlasses:* roundabout approaches.   *assays of bias:*
indirect attempts.

POLONIUS. Observe his inclination in yourself.°
REYNALDO. I shall my lord.
POLONIUS. And let him ply° his music.
REYNALDO.   Well my lord.   70
POLONIUS. Farewell.

                                                    Exit REYNALDO.

Enter OPHELIA.

                        How now Ophelia, what's the matter?
OPHELIA. O my lord, my lord, I have been so affrighted.
POLONIUS. With what, i'th'name of God?
OPHELIA. My lord, as I was sewing in my closet,°
    Lord Hamlet with his doublet all unbraced,°   75
    No hat upon his head, his stockings fouled,
    Ungart'red, and down-gyvèd° to his ankle,
    Pale as his shirt, his knees knocking each other,
    And with a look so piteous in purport°
    As if he had been loosèd out of hell   80
    To speak of horrors, he comes before me.
POLONIUS. Mad for thy love?
OPHELIA.   My lord I do not know,
    But truly I do fear it.
POLONIUS.   What said he?
OPHELIA. He took me by the wrist, and held me hard,
    Then goes he to the length of all his arm,°   85
    And with his other hand thus o'er his brow,
    He falls to such perusal of my face
    As° a' would draw it; long stayed he so,
    At last, a little shaking of mine arm,
    And thrice his head thus waving up and down,   90
    He raised a sigh so piteous and profound
    As it did seem to shatter all his bulk,°
    And end his being; that done, he lets me go,
    And with his head over his shoulder turned
    He seemed to find his way without his eyes,   95
    For out adoors he went without their helps,
    And to the last bended their light on me.
POLONIUS. Come, go with me, I will go seek the king,
    This is the very ecstasy° of love,
    Whose violent property fordoes itself,°   100
    And leads the will to desperate undertakings
    As oft as any passion under heaven
    That does afflict our natures: I am sorry.
    What, have you given him any hard words of late?

---

68 *in yourself:* personally.   70 *ply:* practice.   74 *closet:* private room.   75 *doublet all un-*
braced: jacket all unfastened.   77 *down-gyvèd:* down around his ankles (like prisoners' fetters
or gyves).   79 *purport:* expression.   85 *goes . . . arm:* holds me at arm's length.   88 *As:* as
if.   92 *bulk:* body.   99 *ecstasy:* madness.   100 *Whose . . . itself:* that, by its violent nature,
destroys the lover.

OPHELIA.   No my good lord, but as you did command   1(
    I did repel his letters, and denied
    His access to me.
POLONIUS.   That hath made him mad.
    I am sorry that with better heed and judgment
    I had not quoted° him. I feared he did but trifle
    And meant to wrack° thee, but beshrew my jealousy:°   1
    By heaven it is as proper to our age
    To cast beyond ourselves in our opinions,°
    As it is common for the younger sort
    To lack discretion; come, go we to the king,
    This must be known, which being kept close, might move   1
    More grief to hide, than hate to utter love.°   [*Exeunt.*]

Scene 2. [A room in the Castle]

Flourish. Enter KING *and* QUEEN, ROSENCRANTZ *and* GUILDENSTERN, *cum aliis.*

KING.   Welcome dear Rosencrantz and Guildenstern.
    Moreover° that we much did long to see you,
    The need we have to use you did provoke
    Our hasty sending. Something have you heard
    Of Hamlet's transformation—so call it.
    Sith° nor th'exterior nor the inward man
    Resembles that it was. What it should be,
    More than his father's death, that thus hath put him
    So much from th'understanding of himself,
    I cannot dream of: I entreat you both,   1
    That being of so young days° brought up with him,
    And sith so neighboured to his youth and haviour,
    That you vouchsafe your rest° here in our court
    Some little time, so by your companies
    To draw him on to pleasures, and to gather   1
    So much as from occasion you may glean,
    Whether aught to us unknown afflicts him thus,
    That opened° lies within our remedy.
QUEEN.   Good gentlemen, he hath much talked of you,
    And sure I am, two men there are not living   2
    To whom he more adheres. If it will please you
    To show us so much gentry° and good will,
    As to expend your time with us awhile,
    For the supply and profit of our hope,
    Your visitation shall receive such thanks   2
    As fits a king's remembrance.

---

109 *quoted:* observed.   110 *wrack:* ruin.   *beshrew my jealousy:* curse my suspicion.
111–112 *proper . . . opinions:* natural for old people to read more into something than is actually
there.   115–116 *being kept . . . love:* if kept secret, might cause more grief than if we risked the
king's displeasure.   2 *Moreover:* in addition to the fact.   6 *Sith:* since.   11 *of . . . days:*
from your early days.   13 *vouchsafe your rest:* agree to stay.   18 *Opened:* discovered.
22 *gentry:* courtesy.

ROSENCRANTZ.   Both your majesties
  Might by the sovereign power you have of us,
  Put your dread pleasures more into command
  Than to entreaty.
GUILDENSTERN.   But we both obey,
  And here give up ourselves in the full bent,°   30
  To lay our service freely at your feet
  To be commanded.
KING.   Thanks Rosencrantz, and gentle Guildenstern.
QUEEN.   Thanks Guildenstern, and gentle Rosencrantz.
  And I beseech you instantly to visit   35
  My too much changèd son. Go some of you
  And bring these gentlemen where Hamlet is.
GUILDENSTERN.   Heavens make our presence and our practices°
  Pleasant and helpful to him.
QUEEN.   Ay, amen.

                    Exeunt ROSENCRANTZ *and* GUILDENSTERN.

Enter POLONIUS.

POLONIUS.   Th'ambassadors from Norway my good lord,   40
  Are joyfully returned.
KING.   Thou still° hast been the father of good news.
POLONIUS.   Have I, my lord? Assure you, my good liege,
  I hold my duty as I hold my soul,
  Both to my God and to my gracious king;   45
  And I do think, or else this brain of mine
  Hunts not the trail of policy° so sure
  As it hath used to do, that I have found
  The very cause of Hamlet's lunacy.
KING.   O speak of that, that do I long to hear.   50
POLONIUS.   Give first admittance to th' ambassadors,
  My news shall be the fruit° to that great feast.
KING.   Thyself do grace to them, and bring them in.   [*Exit* POLONIUS.]
  He tells me my dear Gertrude, he hath found
  The head and source of all your son's distemper.   55
QUEEN.   I doubt° it is no other but the main,
  His father's death and our o'erhasty marriage.
KING.   Well, we shall sift him.

Enter POLONIUS, VALTEMAND, *and* CORNELIUS.

                    Welcome, my good friends.
  Say Valtemand, what from our brother Norway?
VALTEMAND.   Most fair return of greetings and desires;   60
  Upon our first,° he sent out to suppress
  His nephew's levies, which to him appeared

30 *in the full bent:* to the utmost (in archery, bending the bow).   38 *practices:* (1) actions (2)
plots.   42 *still:* always.   47 *policy:* (1) politics (2) plots.   52 *fruit:* dessert.   56 *doubt:*
suspect.   61 *first:* first presentation.

To be a preparation 'gainst the Polack,
But better looked into, he truly found
It was against your highness, whereat grieved
That so his sickness, age, and impotence
Was falsely borne in hand,° sends out arrests
On Fortinbras, which he in brief obeys,
Receives rebuke from Norway, and in fine,°
Makes vow before his uncle never more
To give th'assay° of arms against your majesty:
Whereon old Norway, overcome with joy,
Gives him threescore thousand crowns in annual fee,
And his commission to employ those soldiers
So levied (as before) against the Polack,
With an entreaty herein further shown,
That it might please you to give quiet pass°
Through your dominions for this enterprise,
On such regards of safety and allowance
As therein are set down.   *[Giving a paper.]*
KING.   It likes° us well,
And at our more considered time,° we'll read,
Answer, and think upon this business:
Meantime, we thank you for your well-took labour,
Go to your rest, at night we'll feast together.
Most welcome home.   *Exeunt AMBASSADORS.*
POLONIUS   This business is well ended.
My liege and madam, to expostulate°
What majesty should be, what duty is,
Why day is day, night night, and time is time.
Were nothing but to waste night, day, and time.
Therefore since brevity is the soul of wit,°
And tediousness the limbs and outward flourishes,°
I will be brief. Your noble son is mad:
Mad call I it, for to define true madness,
What is't but to be nothing else but mad?
But let that go.
QUEEN.   More matter, with less art.
POLONIUS.   Madam, I swear I use no art at all:
That he is mad 'tis true: 'tis true, 'tis pity,
And pity 'tis 'tis true: a foolish figure,°
But farewell it, for I will use no art.
Mad let us grant him then, and now remains
That we find out the cause of this effect,
Or rather say, the cause of this defect,

---

67 *borne in hand:* deceived.   69 *fine:* finishing.   71 *assay:* test.   77 *pass:* passage.   80
likes: pleases.   81 *at . . . time:* when time is available for consideration.   86 *expostulate:*
discuss.   90 *wit:* understanding.   91 *tediousness . . . flourishes:* embellishments and flourishes cause tedium.   98 *figure:* rhetorical figure.

For this effect defective comes by cause:
Thus it remains, and the remainder thus.
Perpend.°   105
I have a daughter, have while she is mine,
Who in her duty and obedience, mark,
Hath given me this, now gather and surmise.
[*Reads.*] "To the celestial, and my soul's idol, the most
beautified° Ophelia,"—   110
That's an ill phrase, a vile phrase, "beautified" is a vile
phrase, but you shall hear. Thus: [*Reads.*]
        "In her excellent white bosom, these," &c.—
QUEEN.   Came this from Hamlet to her?
POLONIUS.   Good madam stay awhile, I will be faithful.   [*Reads.*]   115
        "Doubt thou the stars are fire,
            Doubt that the sun doth move,°
        Doubt° truth to be a liar,
            But never doubt I love.
O dear Ophelia, I am ill at these numbers, I have not   120
art to reckon° my groans, but that I love thee best, O
most best, believe it. Adieu.
        Thine evermore, most dear lady, whilst
            this machine° is to° him, Hamlet."
This in obedience hath my daughter shown me,   125
And more above hath his solicitings,
As they fell out by time, by means, and place,
All given to mine ear.
KING.   But how hath she
        Received his love?
POLONIUS.   What do you think of me?
KING.   As of a man faithful and honourable.   130
POLONIUS.   I would fain prove so. But what might you think
        When I had seen this hot love on the wing,
        As I perceived it (I must tell you that)
        Before my daughter told me, what might you,
        Or my dear majesty your queen here think,   135
        If I had played the desk or table-book,°
        Or given my heart a winking° mute and dumb,
        Or looked upon this love with idle° sight,
        What might you think? No, I went round to work,
        And my young mistress this I did bespeak,   140
        "Lord Hamlet is a prince out of thy star,°
        This must not be:" and then I prescripts° gave her

---

105 *Perpend:* consider.   110 *beautified:* beautiful.   117 *move:* (as it was believed to do, around
the earth).   118 *Doubt:* suspect.   121 *reckon:* express in meter.   124 *machine:* body.
to: attached to.   136 *played . . . book:* kept it concealed as in a desk or personal
notebook.   137 *given . . . winking:* had my heart shut its eyes to the matter.   138 *idle:*
unseeing.   141 *out . . . star:* out of your sphere (above you in station).   142 *prescripts:*
orders.

That she should lock herself from his resort,°
Admit no messengers, receive no tokens:
Which done, she took the fruits of my advice,   14
And he repellèd, a short tale to make,
Fell into a sadness, then into a fast,
Thence to a watch,° thence into a weakness,
Thence to a lightness,° and by this declension,
Into the madness wherein now he raves,   15
And all we mourn for.

KING.   Do you think 'tis this?
QUEEN.   It may be very like.
POLONIUS.   Hath there been such a time, I would fain know that,
That I have positively said "'Tis so,"
When it proved otherwise?
KING.   Not that I know.   15
POLONIUS.   Take this, from this, if this be otherwise;

[*Points to his head and shoulder.*]

If circumstances lead me, I will find
Where truth is hid, though it were hid indeed
Within the center.
KING.   How may we try° it further?
POLONIUS.   You know sometimes he walks four hours together   16
Here in the lobby.
QUEEN.   So he does indeed.
POLONIUS.   At such a time, I'll loose° my daughter to him.
Be you and I behind an arras° then,
Mark the encounter: if he love her not,
And be not from his reason fall'n thereon,   16
Let me be no assistant for a state,°
But keep a farm and carters.
KING.   We will try it.

Enter HAMLET reading on a book.

QUEEN.   But look where sadly the poor wretch comes reading.
POLONIUS.   Away, I do beseech you both away,
I'll board him presently,° O give me leave.   *Exeunt KING and QUEEN.*   17
How does my good Lord Hamlet?
HAMLET.   Well, God-a-mercy.
POLONIUS.   Do you know me, my lord?
HAMLET.   Excellent well, you are a fishmonger.°   17
POLONIUS.   Not I my lord.
HAMLET.   Then I would you were so honest a man.
POLONIUS.   Honest, my lord?

---

143 *resort:* company.   148 *watch:* sleeplessness.   149 *lightness:* lightheadedness.   159 *try:*
test.   162 *loose:* (1) release (2) turn loose.   163 *arras:* hanging tapestry.   166 *assistant
. . . state:* state official.   170 *board him presently:* approach him immediately.   174 *fishmonger:*
(1) fish dealer (2) pimp.

HAMLET.   Ay sir, to be honest as this world goes, is to be one
man picked out of ten thousand.
POLONIUS.   That's very true, my lord.   180
HAMLET.   For if the sun breed maggots° in a dead dog, being a good
kissing carrion°—have you a daughter?
POLONIUS.   I have my lord.
HAMLET.   Let her not walk i'th'sun:° conception° is a blessing, but as
your daughter may conceive, friend look to'it.   185
POLONIUS.   [*Aside.*] How say you by that? Still harping on my daughter,
yet he knew me not at first, a' said I was a fishmonger.
A' is far gone, far gone, and truly in my youth, I suffered
much extremity for love, very near this. I'll speak to him
again. What do you read my lord?   190
HAMLET.   Words, words, words.
POLONIUS.   What is the matter my lord?
HAMLET.   Between who?
POLONIUS.   I mean the matter° that you read, my lord.
HAMLET.   Slanders sir; for the satirical rogue says here, that old men   195
have grey beards, that their faces are wrinkled, their eyes
purging thick amber and plum-tree gum,° and that they
have a plentiful lack of wit, together with most weak
hams. All which sir, though I most powerfully and
potently believe, yet I hold it not honesty° to have it thus set   200
down, for yourself sir shall grow old as I am: if like a crab
you could go backward.
POLONIUS.   [*Aside.*] Though this be madness, yet there is method
in't.
Will you walk out of the air° my lord?   205
HAMLET.   Into my grave.
POLONIUS.   [*Aside.*] Indeed that's out of the air; how pregnant°
sometimes his replies are, a happiness° that often
madness hits on, which reason and sanity could not so
prosperously° be delivered of. I will leave him, and   210
suddenly contrive the means of meeting between him
and my daughter. My honourable lord, I will most
humbly take leave of you.
HAMLET.   You cannot sir take from me anything that I will more
willingly part withal: except my life, except my life,   215
except my life.
POLONIUS.   Fare you well my lord.
HAMLET.   These tedious old fools.

---

181 *breed maggots:* (in the belief that the rays of the sun caused maggots to breed in dead flesh).
182 *kissing carrion:* piece of flesh for kissing.   184 *Let . . . sun:* (1) (proverbial: "out of God's
blessing, into the warm sun") (2) because the sun is a breeder (3) don't let her go near me
(with a pun on "sun" and "son"). *conception:* (1) understanding (2) pregnancy.   194 *matter:*
(1) content (Polonius's meaning) (2) cause of a quarrel (Hamlet's interpretation).
197–198 *purging . . . gum:* exuding a viscous yellowish discharge.   200 *honesty:* decency.
205 *out . . . air:* (in the belief that fresh air was bad for the sick).   207 *pregnant:* full of meaning.   208 *happiness:* aptness.   210 *prosperously:* successfully.

Enter ROSENCRANTZ *and* GUILDENSTERN.

POLONIUS.   You go to seek the Lord Hamlet, there he is.

ROSENCRANTZ.   [*To Polonius.*] God save you sir.   [*Exit* POLONIUS.]   2

GUILDENSTERN.   My honoured lord.

ROSENCRANTZ.   My most dear lord.

HAMLET.   My excellent good friends, how dost thou Guildenstern?
      Ah Rosencrantz, good lads, how do you both?

ROSENCRANTZ.   As the indifferent° children of the earth.   2

GUILDENSTERN.   Happy, in that we are not over-happy:
      On Fortune's cap we are not the very button.°

HAMLET.   Nor the soles of her shoe?

ROSENCRANTZ.   Neither my lord.

HAMLET.   Then you live about her waist, or in the middle of her   2.
      favours?

GUILDENSTERN.   Faith, her privates° we.

HAMLET.   In the secret parts of Fortune? O most true, she is a
      strumpet.° What news?

ROSENCRANTZ.   None my lord, but that the world's grown honest.   2

HAMLET.   Then is doomsday near: but your news is not true. Let me
      question more in particular: what have you my good
      friends, deserved at the hands of Fortune, that she sends
      you to prison hither?

GUILDENSTERN.   Prison, my lord?

HAMLET.   Denmark's a prison.   24

ROSENCRANTZ.   Then is the world one.

HAMLET.   A goodly one, in which there are many confines, wards,°
      and dungeons; Denmark being one o'th'worst.

ROSENCRANTZ.   We think not so my lord.   24

HAMLET.   Why then 'tis none to you; for there is nothing either good
      or bad, but thinking makes it so: to me it is a prison.

ROSENCRANTZ.   Why then your ambition makes it one: 'tis too narrow for
      your mind.

HAMLET.   O God, I could be bounded in a nutshell, and count   25
      myself a king of infinite space; were it not that I have bad
      dreams.

GUILDENSTERN.   Which dreams indeed are ambition: for the very substance
      of the ambitious, is merely the shadow of a dream.

HAMLET.   A dream itself is but a shadow.   25

ROSENCRANTZ.   Truly, and I hold ambition of so airy and light a quality,
      that it is but a shadow's shadow.

HAMLET.   Then are our beggars bodies, and our monarchs and
      outstretched heroes the beggars' shadows:° shall we to th'
      court? for by my fay,° I cannot reason.   26

225 *indifferent:* ordinary.   227 *on Fortune's . . . button:* we are not at the height of our fortunes.
232 *privates:* (1) intimate friends (2) private parts.   234 *strumpet:* inconstant woman, giving
favor to many.   243 *wards:* cells.   258–259 *Then are . . . shadows:* then beggars are the true
substance and ambitious kings and heroes the elongated shadows of beggars' bodies (for only a
real substance can cast a shadow).   260 *fay:* faith.

BOTH.   We'll wait upon° you.

HAMLET.   No such matter. I will not sort° you with the rest of my
    servants: for to speak to you like an honest man, I am most
    dreadfully attended. But in the beaten way of friendship,
    what make you at Elsinore?   265

ROSENCRANTZ.   To visit you my lord, no other occasion.

HAMLET.   Beggar that I am, I am even poor in thanks, but I thank
    you, and sure dear friends, my thanks are too dear a
    halfpenny:° were you not sent for? is it your own inclining?
    is it a free° visitation? come, come, deal justly with me,   270
    come, come, nay speak.

GUILDENSTERN.   What should we say my lord?

HAMLET.   Anything but to th'purpose: you were sent for, and there
    is a kind of confession in your looks, which your modesties
    have not craft enough to colour: I know the good king and   275
    queen have sent for you.

ROSENCRANTZ.   To what end my lord?

HAMLET.   That you must teach me: but let me conjure° you, by the
    rights of our fellowship, by the consonancy of our youth,°
    by the obligation of our ever-preserved love, and by what   280
    more dear a better proposer can charge you withal,° be
    even and direct with me whether you were sent for or no.

ROSENCRANTZ.   [*Aside to Guildenstern.*] What say you?

HAMLET.   Nay then, I have an eye of° you: If you love me,
    hold not off.   285

GUILDENSTERN.   My lord, we were sent for.

HAMLET.   I will tell you why, so shall my anticipation prevent° your
    discovery,° and your secrecy to the king and queen moult
    no feather.° I have of late, but wherefore I know not, lost all
    my mirth, forgone all custom of exercises: and indeed it   290
    goes so heavily with my disposition, that this goodly
    frame the earth, seems to me a sterile promontory, this
    most excellent canopy the air, look you, this brave°
    o'erhanging firmament, this majestical roof fretted° with
    golden fire,° why it appeareth nothing to me but a foul and   295
    pestilent congregation of vapours.° What a piece of work is
    a man! How noble in reason, how infinite in faculties,° in
    form and moving, how express° and admirable in action,
    how like an angel in apprehension, how like a god: the
    beauty of the world; the paragon of animals; and yet to   300
    me, what is this quintessence of dust? Man delights not
    me, no, nor woman neither, though by your smiling, you
    seem to say so.

261 *wait upon:* attend.   262 *sort:* class.   268–269 *too dear a halfpenny:* worth not even a halfpenny (as I have no influence).   270 *free:* voluntary.   278 *conjure:* appeal to.   279 *conso-
nancy . . . youth:* agreement in our ages.   281 *withal:* with.   284 *of:* on.   287 *prevent:* forestall.   288 *discovery:* disclosure.   288–289 *moult no feather:* change in no way.   293 *brave:*
splendid.   294 *fretted:* ornamented with fretwork.   295 *golden fire:* stars.   296 *pestilent . . .
vapours:* (clouds were believed to carry contagion).   297 *faculties:* physical powers.   298 *express:* well framed.

ROSENCRANTZ.   My lord, there was no such stuff in my thoughts.

HAMLET.   Why did ye laugh then, when I said 'man delights not me'?   30

ROSENCRANTZ.   To think, my lord, if you delight not in man, what lenten
    entertainment° the players shall receive from you: we coted°
    them on the way, and hither are they coming to offer you
    service.

HAMLET.   He that plays the king shall be welcome, his majesty shall   31
    have tribute of me, the adventurous knight° shall use his
    foil and target,° the lover shall not sigh gratis,° the humorous
    man° shall end his part in peace,° the clown shall make
    those laugh whose lungs are tickle o'th'sere,° and the lady   31
    shall say her mind freely: or the blank verse shall halt° for't.
    What players are they?

ROSENCRANTZ.   Even those you were wont to take such delight in, the
    tragedians of the city.

HAMLET.   How chances it they travel? Their residence° both in
    reputation and profit was better both ways.   32

ROSENCRANTZ.   I think their inhibition comes by the means of the late
    innovation.°

HAMLET.   Do they hold the same estimation they did when I was in
    the city; are they so followed?

ROSENCRANTZ.   No indeed are they not.   32

HAMLET.   How comes it? Do they grow rusty?

ROSENCRANTZ.   Nay, their endeavour keeps in the wonted pace; but there
    is sir an aery° of children, like eyases,° that cry out on the
    top of question,° and are most tyrannically° clapped for't:
    these are now the fashion, and so berattle° the common   330
    stages° (so they call them) that many wearing rapiers° are
    afraid of goose-quills,° and dare scarce come thither.

HAMLET.   What, are they children? Who maintains 'em? How are
    they escoted°? Will they pursue the quality no longer than
    they can sing°? Will they not say afterwards if they should   33
    grow themselves to common players (as it is most like, if

---

306–307 *lenten entertainment:* meager treatment.   307 *coted:* passed.   311 *adventurous knight:*
knight errant (a popular stage character).   312 *foil and target:* sword blunted for stage
fighting, and small shield.   312 *gratis:* (without applause).   312–313 *humorous man:*
eccentric character with a dominant trait, caused by an excess of one of the four humors, or
bodily fluids.   313 *in peace:* without interruption.   314 *tickle o'th'sere:* attuned to respond to
laughter, as the finely adjusted gunlock responds to the touch of the trigger (fr. hunting).
315 *halt:* limp (if she adds her own opinions and spoils the meter).   319 *residence:* i.e., in a
city theatre.   321–322 *inhibition . . . innovation:* i.e., they were forced out of town by a more
popular theatrical fashion. The following speeches allude to the "War of the Theatres"
(1601–1602) between the child and adult acting companies.   328 *aery:* nest.   *eyases:* young
hawks.   328–329 *that cry . . . question:* whose shrill voices can be heard above all others.
329 *tyrannically:* strongly.   330 *berattle:* berate.   330–331 *common stages:* public playhouses
(the children's companies performed in private theatres).   331 *wearing rapiers:* (worn by
gentlemen).   332 *goose-quills:* pens (of satirical dramatists who wrote for the children).
334 *escoted:* supported.   334–335 *pursue . . . sing:* continue acting only until their voices
change.

their means are not better) their writers do them wrong, to
make them exclaim against their own succession°?

ROSENCRANTZ. Faith, there has been much to-do on both sides: and the
nation holds it no sin to tarre° them to controversy. There 340
was for a while, no money bid for argument,° unless the
poet and the player went to cuffs in the question.°

HAMLET. Is't possible?

GUILDENSTERN. O there has been much throwing about of brains.

HAMLET. Do the boys carry it away°? 345

ROSENCRANTZ. Ay, that they do my lord, Hercules and his load too.°

HAMLET. It is not very strange, for my uncle is king of Denmark,
and those that would make mows° at him while my father
lived, give twenty, forty, fifty, a hundred ducats apiece
for his picture in little.° 'Sblood,° there is something in this 350
more than natural, if philosophy° could find it out.

A flourish for the Players.

GUILDENSTERN. There are the players.

HAMLET. Gentlemen, you are welcome to Elsinore: your hands,
come then, th'appurtenance° of welcome is fashion and
ceremony; let me comply with you in this garb,° lest my 355
extent° to the players, which I tell you must show fairly
outwards, should more appear like entertainment than
yours.° You are welcome: but my uncle-father, and aunt-
mother, are deceived.

GUILDENSTERN. In what my dear lord? 360

HAMLET. I am but mad north-north-west; when the wind is southerly,
I know a hawk from a handsaw.°

Enter POLONIUS.

POLONIUS. Well be with you, gentlemen.

HAMLET. Hark you Guildenstern, and you too, at each ear a hearer:
that great baby you see there is not yet out of his swaddling 365
clouts.°

ROSENCRANTZ. Happily° he is the second time come to them, for they say
an old man is twice a child.

HAMLET. I will prophesy, he comes to tell me of the players, mark

---

338 *succession:* inheritance. 340 *tarre:* provoke. 341 *bid for argument:* paid for the plot of a
proposed play. 342 *went . . . question:* came to blows on the subject. 345 *carry it away:*
carry off the prize. 346 *Hercules . . . too:* (Shakespeare's own company at the Globe Theatre,
whose sign was Hercules carrying the globe of the world). 348 *mows:* mouths, grimaces.
350 *little:* a miniature. *'Sblood:* by God's blood. 351 *philosophy:* science. 354 *appurte-
nance:* accessory. 355 *comply . . . garb:* observe the formalities with you in this style.
356 *extent:* i.e., of welcome. 357–358 *should . . . yours:* should appear more hospitable than
yours. 362 *I know . . . handsaw:* I can tell the difference between two things that are unlike
("hawk" = (1) bird of prey (2) mattock, pickaxe; "handsaw" = (1) hernshaw or heron bird (2)
small saw). 365–366 *swaddling clouts:* strips of cloth binding a newborn baby.
367 *Happily:* perhaps.

it.—You say right sir, a Monday morning, 'twas then   37
indeed.

POLONIUS.   My lord, I have news to tell you.

HAMLET.   My lord, I have news to tell you. When Roscius° was an
actor in Rome—

POLONIUS.   The actors are come hither, my lord.   37

HAMLET.   Buz, buz.°

POLONIUS.   Upon my honour.

HAMLET.   Then came each actor on his ass—

POLONIUS.   The best actors in the world, either for tragedy, comedy,
history, pastoral, pastoral-comical, historical-pastoral,   38
tragical-historical, tragical-comical-historical-pastoral,
scene individable,° or poem unlimited.° Seneca cannot be
too heavy, nor Plautus° too light for the law of writ, and the
liberty:° these are the only men.

HAMLET.   O Jephthah,° judge of Israel, what a treasure hadst thou.   38

POLONIUS.   What a treasure had he, my lord?

HAMLET.   Why
'One fair daughter and no more,
      The which he lovèd passing° well.'

POLONIUS.   [*Aside.*] Still on my daughter.   39

HAMLET.   Am I not i'th' right, old Jephthah?

POLONIUS.   If you call me Jephthah my lord, I have a daughter that I
love passing well.

HAMLET.   Nay, that follows not.

POLONIUS.   What follows then, my lord?   39

HAMLET.   Why
"As by lot, God wot,"
and then you know
"It came to pass, as most like° it was:"
the first row° of the pious chanson will show you more, for   40
look where my abridgement° comes.

Enter four or five PLAYERS.

You are welcome masters, welcome all. I am glad to see
thee well: welcome, good friends. O my old friend, why
thy face is valanced° since I saw thee last, com'st thou to
beard me in Denmark? What, my young lady° and   40
mistress? by'r lady, your ladyship is nearer to heaven than
when I saw you last, by the altitude of a chopine.° Pray
God your voice, like a piece of uncurrent° gold, be not

373 *Roscius:* famous Roman actor.   376 *Buz, buz:* (contemptuous).   382 *scene individable:* play observing the unities (time, place, action).   *poem unlimited:* play ignoring the unities. 382–383 *Seneca, Plautus:* Roman writers of tragedy and comedy, respectively.   383–384 *law . . . liberty:* "rules" regarding the unities and those exercising freedom from the unities. 385 *Jephthah:* (who was forced to sacrifice his only daughter because of a rash promise: Judges 11:29–39).   389 *passing:* surpassingly.   399 *like:* likely.   400 *row:* stanza. 401 *abridgement:* (the players who will cut short my song).   404 *valanced:* fringed with a beard. 405 *lady:* boy playing women's role.   407 *chopine:* thick-soled shoe.   408 *uncurrent:* not legal tender.

cracked within the ring.° Masters, you are all welcome:
we'll e'en to't like French falconers, fly at any thing we see:°   410
we'll have a speech straight. Come give us a taste of your
quality: come, a passionate speech.

I. PLAYER.   What speech, my good lord?

HAMLET.   I heard thee speak me a speech once, but it was never
acted, or if it was, not above once, for the play I remember   415
pleased not the million, 'twas caviary to the general,° but it
was (as I received it, and others, whose judgments in such
matters cried in the top of mine°) an excellent play, well
digested in the scenes, set down with as much modesty as
cunning.° I remember one said there were no sallets° in the   420
lines, to make the matter savoury, nor no matter in the
phrase that might indict the author of° affection, but called
it an honest method, as wholesome as sweet, and by very
much more handsome than fine:° one speech in't I chiefly
loved, 'twas Aeneas' tale to Dido, and thereabout of it   425
especially where he speaks of Priam's slaughter.° If it live in
your memory begin at this line, let me see, let me see:
    "The rugged Pyrrhus,° like th'Hyrcanian beast"°—
'tis not so: it begins with Pyrrhus—
    "The rugged Pyrrhus, he whose sable° arms,   430
Black as his purpose, did the night resemble
When he lay couched in th'ominous horse,°
Hath now this dread and black complexion smeared
With heraldy more dismal: head to foot
Now is he total gules,° horridly tricked°   435
With blood of fathers, mothers, daughters, sons,
Baked and impasted° with the parching° streets,
That lend a tyrannous and damnèd light
To their lord's murder. Roasted in wrath and fire,
And thus o'er-sizèd° with coagulate gore,   440
With eyes like carbuncles,° the hellish Pyrrhus
Old grandsire Priam seeks;"
So proceed you.

POLONIUS.   'Fore God, my lord, well spoken, with good accent and
good discretion.°   445

I. PLAYER.   "Anon he finds him,
Striking too short at Greeks, his antique° sword,

---

409 *ring:* (1) ring enclosing the design on a gold coin (to crack it within the ring [to steal the
gold] made it "uncurrent") (2) sound.   410 *fly . . . see:* undertake any difficulty.
416 *caviary . . . general:* like caviar, too rich for the general public.   418 *cried . . . mine:* spoke
with more authority than mine.   419–420 *modesty as cunning:* moderation as skill.
420 *sallets:* spicy bits.   422 *indict . . . of:* charge . . . with.   424 *handsome than fine:* dignified
than finely wrought.   426 *Priam's slaughter:* the murder of the King of Troy (as told in the
Aeneid).   428 *Pyrrhus:* son of Achilles.   *Hyrcanian beast:* tiger noted for fierceness.
430 *sable:* black.   432 *horse:* the hollow wooden horse used by the Greeks to enter Troy.
435 *gules:* red.   *horridly tricked:* horribly decorated.   437 *impasted:* coagulated.   *parching:*
(because the city was on fire).   440 *o'er-sizèd:* covered over.   441 *carbuncles:* red gems.
445 *discretion:* interpretation.   447 *antique:* ancient.

Rebellious to his arm, lies where it falls,
Repugnant to command;° unequal matched,
Pyrrhus at Priam drives, in rage strikes wide,   45
But with the whiff and wind of his fell° sword,
Th'unnerved father falls: then senseless Ilium,°
Seeming to feel this blow, with flaming top
Stoops to his base; and with a hideous crash
Takes prisoner Pyrrhus' ear. For lo, his sword   45
Which was declining on the milky head
Of reverend Priam, seemed i'th'air to stick;
So as a painted° tyrant Pyrrhus stood,
And like a neutral to his will and matter,°
Did nothing: 46
But as we often see, against° some storm,
A silence in the heavens, the rack° stand still,
The bold winds speechless, and the orb° below
As hush as death, anon the dreadful thunder
Doth rend the region, so after Pyrrhus' pause,   46
A rousèd vengeance sets him new awork,
And never did the Cyclops'° hammers fall
On Mars's armour, forged for proof eterne,°
With less remorse than Pyrrhus' bleeding sword
Now falls on Priam.   47
Out, out, thou strumpet Fortune: all you gods,
In general synod° take away her power,
Break all the spokes and fellies from her wheel,°
And bowl the round nave° down the hill of heaven
As low as to the fiends."°   47
POLONIUS.   This is too long.
HAMLET.   It shall to the barber's with your beard; prithee say on: he's
    for a jig, or a tale of bawdry, or he sleeps. Say on, come to
    Hecuba.
I. PLAYER.   "But who, ah woe, had seen the mobled° queen—"   48
HAMLET.   "The mobled queen"?
POLONIUS.   That's good, "mobled queen" is good.
I. PLAYER.   "Run barefoot up and down, threat'ning the flames
    With bissom rheum,° a clout° upon that head
    Where late the diadem stood, and for a robe,   48
    About her lank and all o'er-teemèd° loins,
    A blanket in the alarm of fear caught up—
    Who this had seen, with tongue in venom steeped,

---

449 *Repugnant to command:* refusing to obey its commander.   451 *fell:* savage.   452 *senseless Ilium:* unfeeling Troy.   458 *painted:* pictured.   459 *like . . . matter:* unmoved by either his purpose or its achievement.   461 *against:* before.   462 *rack:* clouds.   463 *orb:* earth. 467 *Cyclops:* workmen of Vulcan, armorer of the gods.   468 *for proof eterne:* to be eternally invincible.   472 *synod:* assembly.   473 *fellies . . . wheel:* curved pieces of the rim of the wheel that fortune turns, representing a man's fortunes.   474 *nave:* hub.   475 *fiends:* i.e., of hell. 480 *mobled:* muffled in a scarf.   484 *bissom rheum:* binding tears.   *clout:* cloth. 486 *o'erteemed:* worn out by excessive childbearing.

'Gainst Fortune's state° would treason have pronounced;
But if the gods themselves did see her then,   490
When she saw Pyrrhus make malicious sport
In mincing with his sword her husband's limbs,
The instant burst of clamour that she made,
Unless things mortal move them not at all,
Would have made milch° the burning eyes of heaven,   495
And passion in the gods."

POLONIUS.   Look whe'r° he has not turned° his colour, and has tears in's
    eyes, prithee no more.

HAMLET.   'Tis well, I'll have thee speak out the rest of this soon.
    Good my lord, will you see the players well bestowed;° do   500
    you hear, let them be well used, for they are the abstract°
    and brief chronicles° of the time; after your death you were
    better have a bad epitaph than their ill report while you
    live.

POLONIUS.   My lord, I will use them according to their desert.°   505

HAMLET.   God's bodkin° man, much better. Use every man after° his
    desert, and who shall 'scape whipping? Use them after
    you own honour and dignity: the less they deserve, the
    more merit is in your bounty. Take them in.

POLONIUS.   Come sirs.   *Exeunt POLONIUS and PLAYERS.*   510

HAMLET.   Follow him friends, we'll hear a play tomorrow; [*Stops the
    First Player.*] dost thou hear me, old friend, can you play
    The Murder of Gonzago?

I. PLAYER   Ay my lord.

HAMLET.   We'll ha't tomorrow night. You could for a need° study a   515
    speech of some dozen or sixteen lines, which I would set
    down and insert in't, could you not?

I. PLAYER.   Ay my lord.

HAMLET.   Very well, follow that lord, and look you mock him not.

                                            [*Exit FIRST PLAYER.*]

[*To Rosencrantz and Guildenstern.*] My good friends, I'll   520
    leave you till night, you are welcome to Elsinore.

ROSENCRANTZ.   Good my lord.   [*Exeunt ROSENCRANTZ and GUILDENSTERN.*]

HAMLET.   Ay so, God bye to you, now I am alone.
    O what a rogue and peasant slave am I.
    Is it not monstrous that this player here,   525
    But in a fiction, in a dream of passion,°
    Could force his soul so to his own conceit°
    That from her working all his visage wanned,°
    Tears in his eyes, distraction in his aspect,
    A broken voice, and his whole function° suiting   530

---

489 *state:* reign.   495 *milch:* milky, moist.   497 *whe'r:* whether.   *turned:* changed.
500 *bestowed:* lodged.   501 *abstract:* summary (noun).   502 *brief chronicles:* history in brief.
505 *desert:* merit.   506 *God's bodkin:* God's little body, the communion wafer (an oath).
after: according to.   515 *for a need:* if necessary.   526 *dream of passion:* portrayal of emotion.
527 *conceit:* imagination.   528 *wanned:* grew pale.   530 *function:* bearing.

With forms° to his conceit; and all for nothing,
For Hecuba!
What's Hecuba to him, or he to Hecuba,
That he should weep for her? what would he do,
Had he the motive and the cue for passion   5
That I have? he would drown the stage with tears,
And cleave the general ear° with horrid speech,
Make mad the guilty and appal the free,°
Confound° the ignorant, and amaze indeed
The very faculties of eyes and ears; yet I,   54
A dull and muddy-mettled° rascal, peak°
Like John-a-dreams,° unpregnant of° my cause,
And can say nothing; no, not for a king,
Upon whose property and most dear life,
A damned defeat was made: am I a coward?   54
Who calls me villain, breaks my pate° across,
Plucks off my beard° and blows it in my face,
Tweaks me by the nose, gives me the lie i'th'throat
As deep as to the lungs,° who does me this?
Ha, 'swounds,° I should take it; for it cannot be   55
But I am pigeon-livered,° and lack gall
To make oppression bitter, or ere this
I should ha' fatted all the region kites°
With this slave's offal: bloody, bawdy villain,
Remorseless, treacherous, lecherous, kindless° villain!   55
O vengeance!
Why what an ass am I, this is most brave,°
That I, the son of a dear father murdered,
Prompted to my revenge by heaven and hell,
Must like a whore unpack my heart with words,   56
And fall a-cursing like a very drab,°
A scullion,° fie upon't, foh.
About, my brains; hum, I have heard,
That guilty creatures sitting at a play,
Have by the very cunning of the scene   56
Been struck so to the soul, that presently°
They have proclaimed their malefactions:
For murder, though it have no tongue, will speak
With most miraculous organ: I'll have these players
Play something like the murder of my father   57
Before mine uncle, I'll observe his looks,
I'll tent° him to the quick, if a' do blench°

---

531 *With forms:* in appearance.   537 *general ear:* ears of all in the audience.   538 *free:* innocent.   539 *Confound:* confuse.   541 *muddy-mettled:* dull-spirited.   *peak:* pine, mope.
542 *John-a-dreams:* a daydreaming fellow.   *unpregnant of:* unstirred by.   546 *pate:* head.
547 *Plucks . . . beard:* (a way of giving insult).   548–549 *gives . . . lungs:* insults me by calling me
a liar of the worst kind (the lungs being deeper than the throat).   550 *'swounds:* God's
wounds.   551 *pigeon-livered:* meek and uncourageous.   553 *region kites:* vultures of the upper
air.   555 *kindless:* unnatural.   557 *brave:* fine.   561 *drab:* whore.   562 *scullion:* kitchen
wench.   566 *presently:* immediately.   572 *tent:* probe.   *blench:* flinch.

I know my course. The spirit that I have seen
May be a devil, and the devil hath power
T'assume a pleasing shape, yea, and perhaps   575
Out of my weakness, and my melancholy,
As he is very potent with such spirits,
Abuses me to damn me; I'll have grounds
More relative than this: the play's the thing
Wherein I'll catch the conscience of the king.   *Exit.*

[ACT 3]

Scene 1. *[A room in the castle]*

Enter KING, QUEEN, POLONIUS, OPHELIA, ROSENCRANTZ, GUILDENSTERN, *and* LORDS.

KING. And can you by no drift of conference°
    Get from him why he puts on this confusion,°
    Grating so harshly all his days of quiet
    With turbulent and dangerous lunacy?
ROSENCRANTZ. He does confess he feels himself distracted,   5
    But from what cause, a' will by no means speak.
GUILDENSTERN. Nor do we find him forward to be sounded,°
    But with a crafty madness keeps aloof
    When we would bring him on to some confession
    Of his true state.
QUEEN.   Did he receive you well?   10
ROSENCRANTZ. Most like a gentleman.
GUILDENSTERN. But with much forcing of his disposition.°
ROSENCRANTZ. Niggard of question,° but of our demands
    Most free in his reply.
QUEEN.   Did you assay° him
    To any pastime?   15
ROSENCRANTZ. Madam, it so fell out that certain players
    We o'er-raught° on the way: of these we told him,
    And there did seem in him a kind of joy
    To hear of it: they are here about the court,
    And as I think, they have already order   20
    This night to play before him.
POLONIUS. 'Tis most true,
    And he beseeched me to entreat your majesties
    To hear and see the matter.°
KING. With all my heart, and it doth much content me
    To hear him so inclined.   25

---

1 *drift of conference:* turn of conversation.   2 *puts . . . confusion:* seems so distracted ("puts on" indicates the king's private suspicion that Hamlet is playing mad).   7 *forward . . . sounded:* disposed to be sounded out.   12 *forcing . . . disposition:* forcing himself to be so.   13 *Niggard of question:* unwilling to talk.   14 *assay:* tempt.   17 *o'er-raught:* overtook.   23 *matter:* i.e., of the play.

Good gentlemen, give him a further edge,°
And drive his purpose into these delights.
ROSENCRANTZ.   We shall my lord.   *Exeunt* ROSENCRANTZ *and* GUILDENSTERN.
KING.   Sweet Gertrude, leave us too,
For we have closely° sent for Hamlet hither,
That he, as 'twere by accident, may here
Affront° Ophelia;
Her father and myself, lawful espials,°
Will so bestow° ourselves, that seeing unseen,
We may of their encounter frankly° judge,
And gather by him as he is behaved,
If't be th'affliction of his love or no
That thus he suffers for.
QUEEN.   I shall obey you.
And for your part Ophelia, I do wish
That your good beauties be the happy cause
Of Hamlet's wildness, so shall I hope your virtues
Will bring him to his wonted° way again,
To both your honours.
OPHELIA.   Madam, I wish it may.   [*Exit* QUEEN.]
POLONIUS.   Ophelia, walk you here—Gracious,° so please you,
We will bestow ourselves—read on this book,°
That show of such an exercise° may colour°
Your loneliness; we are oft to blame in this,
'Tis too much proved,° that with devotion's visage
And pious action, we do sugar o'er
The devil himself.
KING.   [*Aside.*] O 'tis too true,°
How smart a lash that speech doth give my conscience.
The harlot's cheek, beautied with plast'ring art,
Is not more ugly to° the thing that helps it,
Than is my deed to my most painted word:°
O heavy burden!
POLONIUS.   I hear him coming, let's withdraw my lord.   *Exeunt.*

Enter HAMLET.

HAMLET.   To be, or not to be, that is the question,
Whether 'tis nobler in the mind° to suffer
The slings and arrows of outrageous fortune,
Or to take arms against a sea of troubles,
And by opposing, end them: to die, to sleep,

---

26 *give . . . edge:* encourage his keen interest.   29 *closely:* secretly.   31 *Affront:* meet face to face with.   32 *espials:* spies.   33, 44 *bestow:* place.   34 *frankly:* freely.   41 *wonted:* customary.   43 *Gracious:* i.e., Your Grace.   44 *book:* (of prayer).   45 *exercise:* religious exercise.   *colour:* make plausible.   47 *'Tis . . . proved:* it is all too apparent.   49 *'tis too true:* (the king's first indication that he is guilty).   52 *to:* compared to.   51–53 *harlot's cheek . . . word:* just as the harlot's cheek is even uglier by contrast to the makeup that tries to beautify it, so my deed is uglier by contrast to the hypocritical words under which I hide it. 57 *nobler in the mind:* best, according to "sovereign" reason.

No more; and by a sleep, to say we end
The heart-ache, and the thousand natural shocks
That flesh is heir to; 'tis a consummation
Devoutly to be wished. To die, to sleep,
To sleep, perchance to dream, ay there's the rub,°   65
For in that sleep of death what dreams may come
When we have shuffled off this mortal coil°
Must give us pause—there's the respect°
That makes calamity of so long life:°
For who would bear the whips and scorns of time,   70
Th'oppressor's wrong, the proud man's contumely,°
The pangs of disprized love, the law's delay,°
The insolence of office,° and the spurns
That patient merit of th'unworthy takes,
When he himself might his quietus° make   75
With a bare bodkin;° who would fardels° bear,
To grunt and sweat under a weary life,
But that the dread of something after death,
The undiscovered° country, from whose bourn°
No traveller returns, puzzles the will,   80
And makes us rather bear those ills we have,
Than fly to others that we know not of.
Thus conscience does make cowards of us all,
And thus the native hue° of resolution
Is sicklied o'er with the pale cast of thought,   85
And enterprises of great pitch° and moment,°
With this regard° their currents turn awry,°
And lose the name of action. Soft you now,
The fair Ophelia—Nymph, in thy orisons°
Be all my sins remembered.
OPHELIA.   Good my lord,   90
    How does your honour for this many a day°?
HAMLET.   I humbly thank you: well, well, well.
OPHELIA.   My lord, I have remembrances of yours
    That I have longèd long to re-deliver,
    I pray you now receive them.
HAMLET.   No, not I,   95
    I never gave you aught.
OPHELIA.   My honoured lord, you know right well you did,
    And with them words of so sweet breath° composed
    As made the things more rich: their perfume lost,

---

65 *rub:* obstacle.   67 *mortal coil:* (1) turmoil of mortal life (2) coil of flesh encircling the body.
68 *respect:* consideration.   69 *makes calamity of so long life:* makes living long a calamity.
71 *contumely:* contempt.   72 *law's delay:* longevity of lawsuits.   73 *office:* officials.
75 *quietus:* settlement of his debt.   76 *bare bodkin:* mere dagger.   *fardels:* burdens.
79 *undiscovered:* unknown, unexplored.   *bourn:* boundary.   84 *native hue:* natural
complexion.   86 *pitch:* height, excellence.   *moment:* importance.   87 *regard:*
consideration.   *their currents turn awry:* change their course.   89 *orisons:* prayers (referring
to her prayer book).   91 *this . . . day:* all these days.   98 *breath:* speech.

Take these again, for to the noble mind   1⬤
Rich gifts wax° poor when givers prove unkind.
There my lord.

HAMLET.   Ha, ha, are you honest°?

OPHELIA.   My lord.

HAMLET.   Are you fair°?   1⬤

OPHELIA.   What means your lordship?

HAMLET.   That if you be honest and fair, your honesty should admit
no discourse to your beauty.°

OPHELIA.   Could beauty my lord, have better commerce than with
honesty?   1⬤

HAMLET.   Ay truly, for the power of beauty will sooner transform
honesty° from what it is to a bawd,° than the force of
honesty can translate beauty into his likeness. This was
sometime° a paradox, but now the time gives it proof. I did
love you once.   1⬤

OPHELIA.   Indeed my lord, you made me believe so.

HAMLET.   You should not have believed me, for virtue cannot so
inoculate our old stock, but we shall relish of it.° I loved
you not.

OPHELIA.   I was the more deceived.   12⬤

HAMLET.   Get thee to a nunnery,° why wouldst thou be a breeder of
sinners? I am myself indifferent honest,° but yet I could
accuse me of such things, that it were better my mother
had not borne me: I am very proud, revengeful, ambitious,
with more offences at my beck,° than I have thoughts   12⬤
to put them in, imagination to give them shape, or time to
act them in: what should such fellows as I do, crawling
between earth and heaven? we are arrant° knaves all,
believe none of us, go thy ways to a nunnery. Where's
your father?   13⬤

OPHELIA.   At home my lord.

HAMLET.   Let the doors be shut upon him, that he may play the fool
no where but in's own house. Farewell.

OPHELIA.   O help him, you sweet heavens.

HAMLET.   If thou dost marry, I'll give thee this plague° for thy dowry: 13⬤
be thou as chaste as ice, as pure as snow, thou shalt not
escape calumny; get thee to a nunnery, go, farewell. Or if
thou wilt needs marry, marry a fool, for wise men know
well enough what monsters° you make of them: to a nunnery
go, and quickly too, farewell.   14⬤

---

101 *wax:* grow.   103 *honest:* (1) chaste (2) truthful.   105 *fair:* (1) beautiful (2) honorable.
107–108 *admit . . . beauty:* (1) not allow communication with your beauty (2) not allow your
beauty to be used as a trap (Hamlet may have overheard the Polonius–Claudius plot or spotted
their movement behind the arras).   112 *honesty:* chastity.   *bawd:* procurer, pimp.
114 *sometime:* once.   118 *inoculate . . . it:* change our sinful nature (as a tree is grafted to
improve it) but we will keep our old taste (as will the fruit of the grafted tree).   121 *nunnery:*
(1) cloister (2) slang for "brothel" (cf. "bawd" above).   122 *indifferent honest:* reasonably
virtuous.   125 *beck:* beckoning.   128 *arrant:* absolute.   135 *plague:* curse.
139 *monsters:* horned cuckolds (men whose wives were unfaithful).

OPHELIA.   O heavenly powers, restore him.

HAMLET.   I have heard of your paintings too, well enough. God hath
given you one face, and you make yourselves another: you
jig,° you amble, and you lisp,° you nick-name God's
creatures, and make your wantonness your ignorance;° go to,   145
I'll no more on't, it hath made me mad. I say we will have
no moe° marriage. Those that are married already, all but
one shall live, the rest shall keep as they are: to a nunnery,
go.   *Exit HAMLET.*

OPHELIA.   O what a noble mind is here o'erthrown!   150
The courtier's, soldier's, scholar's, eye, tongue, sword,
Th'expectancy and rose° of the fair state,
The glass° of fashion, and the mould of form,°
Th'observed of all observers, quite quite down,
And I of ladies most deject and wretched,   155
That sucked the honey of his music vows,
Now see that noble and most sovereign° reason
Like sweet bells jangled, out of tune and harsh,
That unmatched form and feature° of blown° youth
Blasted with ecstasy.° O woe is me,   160
T'have seen what I have seen, see what I see.

Enter KING and POLONIUS.

KING.   Love? his affections° do not that way tend,
Nor what he spake, though it lacked form a little,
Was not like madness. There's something in his soul
O'er which his melancholy sits on brood,   165
And I do doubt,° the hatch and the disclose°
Will be some danger; which for to prevent,
I have in quick determination
Thus set it down: he shall with speed to England,
For the demand of our neglected° tribute: 170
Haply° the seas, and countries different,
With variable° objects, shall expel
This something°-settled matter in his heart,
Whereon his brains still beating puts him thus
From fashion of himself.° What think you on't?   175

POLONIUS.   It shall do well. But yet do I believe
The origin and commencement of his grief
Sprung from neglected° love. How now Ophelia?
You need not tell us what Lord Hamlet said,

---

144 *jig:* walk in a mincing way.   *lisp:* put on affected speech.   145 *make your . . . ignorance:*
excuse your caprices as being due to ignorance.   147 *moe:* more.   152 *expectancy and rose:*
fair hope.   153 *glass:* mirror.   *mould of form:* model of manners.   157 *sovereign:* (because
it should rule).   159 *feature:* external appearance.   159 *blown:* flowering.   160 *Blasted
with ecstasy:* blighted by madness.   162 *affections:* emotions, afflictions.   166 *doubt:* fear.
165–166 *on brood . . . hatch . . . disclose:* (metaphor of a hen sitting on eggs).   170 *neglected:*
(being unpaid).   171 *Haply:* perhaps.   172 *variable:* varied.   173 *something-:* somewhat-.
175 *fashion of himself:* his usual self.   178 *neglected:* unrequited.

We heard it all. My lord, do as you please,
But if you hold it fit, after the play,
Let his queen-mother all alone entreat him
To show his grief, let her be round° with him,
And I'll be placed (so please you) in the ear
Of° all their conference. If she find° him not,
To England send him: or confine him where
Your wisdom best shall think.

KING.   It shall be so,
Madness in great ones must not unwatched go.   *Exeunt.*

Scene 2. *[A hall in the castle]*

Enter HAMLET *and three of the* PLAYERS.

HAMLET.   Speak the speech° I pray you as I pronounced it to you,
trippingly on the tongue, but if you mouth it° as many of
your players do, I had as lief the town-crier spoke my
lines. Nor do not saw the air too much with your hand
thus, but use all gently, for in the very torrent, tempest,
and as I may say, whirlwind of your passion, you must
acquire and beget° a temperance that may give it smoothness.
O it offends me to the soul, to hear a robustious°
periwig-pated° fellow tear a passion to tatters, to very rags,
to split the ears of the groundlings,° who for the most part
are capable of° nothing but inexplicable dumb shows° and
noise: I would have such a fellow whipped for o'erdoing
Termagant:° it out-herods Herod,° pray you avoid it.

I. PLAYER.   I warrant you honour.

HAMLET.   Be not too tame neither, but let your own discretion be
your tutor, suit the action to the word, the word to the
action, with this special observance, that you o'erstep not
the modesty° of nature: for any thing so o'erdone, is from°
the purpose of playing, whose end both at the first, and
now, was and is, to hold as 'twere the mirror up to nature,
to show virtue her own feature, scorn° her own image, and
the very age and body of the time his form and pressure.°
Now this overdone, or come tardy off,° though it make the
unskilful° laugh, cannot but make the judicious grieve, the
censure of the which one,° must in your allowance°

---

183 *round:* direct.   184–185 *in the ear Of:* so as to overhear.   185 *find:* find out.   1 *the*
speech: i.e., that Hamlet has inserted.   2 *mouth it:* deliver it slowly and overdramatically.
7 *acquire and beget:* achieve for yourself and instill in other actors.   8 *robustious:* boisterous.
9 *periwig-pated:* wig-wearing.   10 *groundlings:* audience who paid least and stood on the ground
floor.   11 *capable of:* able to understand.   *dumb shows:* pantomimed synopses of the action
to follow (as below).   13 *Termagant:* violent, ranting character in the guild or mystery plays.
out-herods Herod: outdoes even Herod, King of Judea (who commanded the slaughter of the innocents and who was a ranting tyrant in the mystery plays).   18 *modesty:* moderation.   *from:*
away from.   21 *scorn:* that which should be scorned.   22 *age . . . pressure:* shape of the times
in its accurate impression.   23 *come tardy off:* understated, underdone.   24 *unskilful:*
unsophisticated.   25 *one:* the judicious.   *allowance:* estimation.

o'erweigh a whole theatre of others. O there be players
that I have seen play, and heard others praise, and that
highly (not to speak it profanely) that neither having
th'accent of Christians, nor the gait of Christian, pagan,
nor man, have so strutted and bellowed, that I have   30
thought some of nature's journeymen° had made men, and
not made them well, they imitated humanity so
abominably.

I. PLAYER.   I hope we have reformed that indifferently° with us, sir.

HAMLET.   O reform it altogether, and let those that play your clowns   35
speak no more than is set down for them,° for there be of
them that will themselves laugh, to set on some quantity
of barren° spectators to laugh too, though in the meantime,
some necessary question° of the play be then to be considered:
that's villainous, and shows a most pitiful ambition   40
in the fool that uses it. Go make you ready.   *Exeunt* PLAYERS.

Enter POLONIUS, ROSENCRANTZ, *and* GUILDENSTERN.

How now my lord, will the king hear this piece of work?

POLONIUS.   And the queen too, and that presently.

HAMLET.   Bid the players make haste.   *Exit* POLONIUS.
Will you two help to hasten them?   45

ROSENCRANTZ.   Ay my lord.   *Exeunt they two.*

HAMLET.   What ho, Horatio!

Enter HORATIO.

HORATIO.   Here sweet lord, at your service.

HAMLET.   Horatio, thou art e'en as just° a man
As e'er my conversation coped withal.°   50

HORATIO.   O my dear lord.

HAMLET.   Nay, do not think I flatter,
For what advancement may I hope from thee,
That no revenue hast but thy good spirits
To feed and clothe thee? Why should the poor be flattered?
No, let the candied° tongue lick° absurd pomp,   55
And crook the pregnant° hinges of the knee
Where thrift may follow fawning.° Dost thou hear,
Since my dear soul was mistress of her choice,
And could of men distinguish her election,°
Sh'hath sealed° thee for herself, for thou hast been   60
As one in suff'ring all that suffers nothing,
A man that Fortune's buffets° and rewards
Hast ta'en with equal thanks; and blest are those

---

31 *journeymen:* artisans working for others and not yet masters of their trades.   34 *indifferently:*
reasonably well.   36 *speak no more . . . them:* stick to their lines.   38 *barren:* witless.
39 *question:* dialogue.   49 *just:* well balanced.   50 *coped withal:* had to do with.
55–57 *candied . . . fawning:* (metaphor of a dog licking and fawning for candy).   55 *candied:*
flattering.   *lick:* pay court to.   56–57 *crook . . . fawning:* obsequiously kneel when personal
profit may ensue.   56 *pregnant:* quick in motion.   59 *election:* choice.   60 *sealed:*
confirmed.   62 *buffets:* blows.

Whose blood° and judgment are so well co-mingled,
That they are not a pipe for Fortune's finger
To sound what stop° she please:° give me that man
That is not passion's slave, and I will wear him
In my heart's core, ay in my heart of heart,
As I do thee. Something too much of this.
There is a play tonight before the king,
One scene of it comes near the circumstance
Which I have told thee of my father's death.
I prithee when thou seest that act afoot,
Even with the very comment° of thy soul
Observe my uncle: if his occulted° guilt
Do not itself unkennel° in one speech,
It is a damnèd ghost° that we have seen,
And my imaginations are as foul
As Vulcan's stithy;° give him heedful note,
For I mine eyes will rivet to his face,
And after we will both our judgments join
In censure of his seeming.°
HORATIO.   Well my lord,
If a' steal aught the whilst this play is playing,
And 'scape detecting, I will pay° the theft.   *Sound a flourish.*
HAMLET.   They are coming to the play. I must be idle,°
Get you a place.

Enter Trumpets and Kettledrums, KING, QUEEN, POLONIUS, OPHELIA, ROSENCRANTZ, GUILD-
ENSTERN, *and other* LORDS *attendant, with his* GUARD *carrying torches. Danish March.*

KING.   How fares° our cousin Hamlet?
HAMLET.   Excellent i'faith, of the chameleon's dish: I eat the air,°
   promise-crammed, you cannot feed capons so.°
KING.   I have nothing with° this answer Hamlet, these words are
   not mine.°
HAMLET.   No, nor mine now. [*To Polonius.*] My lord, you played
   once i'th'university you say?
POLONIUS.   That did I my lord, and was accounted a good actor.
HAMLET.   What did you enact?
POLONIUS.   I did enact Julius Caesar, I was killed i'th'Capitol, Brutus
   killed me.
HAMLET.   It was a brute part of him to kill so capital a calf there. Be
   the players ready?

64 *blood:* passions.   66 *sound . . . please:* play whatever tune she likes.   *stop:* finger hole in
wind instrument for varying the sound.   74 *very comment:* acutest observation.   75 *occulted:*
hidden.   76 *unkennel:* force from hiding.   77 *damnèd ghost:* devil (not the ghost of my
father).   79 *Vulcan's stithy:* the forge of the blacksmith of the gods.   82 *censure . . . seeming:*
(1) judgment of his appearance (2) disapproval of his pretending.   84 *pay:* i.e., for.   85 *be
idle:* act mad.   87 *fares:* does, but Hamlet takes it to mean "eats" or "dines."   88 *eat the air:*
the chamelion supposedly ate air, but Hamlet also puns on "heir."   89 *you cannot . . . so:*
(1) even a capon cannot feed on air and your promises (2) like a capon stuffed with food
before being killed, I am stuffed (fed up) with your promises.   90 *nothing with:* nothing to do
with.   91 *not mine:* not in answer to my question.

ROSENCRANTZ. Ay my lord, they stay upon your patience.°   100
QUEEN. Come hither my dear Hamlet, sit by me.
HAMLET. No, good mother, here's metal more attractive.°
POLONIUS. [*To the King.*] O ho, do you mark that?
HAMLET. Lady, shall I lie in your lap?
OPHELIA. No my lord.   105
HAMLET. I mean, my head upon your lap?
OPHELIA. Ay my lord.
HAMLET. Do you think I meant country° matters?
OPHELIA. I think nothing my lord.
HAMLET. That's a fair thought to lie between maids' legs.   110
OPHELIA. What is, my lord?
HAMLET. Nothing.
OPHELIA. You are merry my lord.
HAMLET. Who, I?
OPHELIA. Ay my lord.   115
HAMLET. O God, your only jig-maker: what should a man do but be
     merry, for look you how cheerfully my mother looks, and
     my father died within's two hours.
OPHELIA. Nay, 'tis twice two months my lord.
HAMLET. So long? Nay then let the devil wear black, for I'll have a   120
     suit of sables;° O heavens, die two months ago, and not
     forgotten yet? Then there's hope a great man's memory
     may outlive his life half a year, but by'r lady° a' must build
     churches then, or else shall a' suffer not thinking on,° with
     the hobby-horse,° whose epitaph is "For O, for O, the   125
     hobby-horse is forgot."

*The trumpets sound. The Dumb Show° follows. Enter a King and a Queen, very lovingly,
the Queen embracing him, and he her. She kneels and makes show of protestation unto him. He
takes him up, and declines his head upon her neck. He lies him down upon a bank of flowers;
she seeing him asleep leaves him: anon comes in another man, takes off his crown, kisses it, pours
poison in the sleeper's ears, and leaves him: the Queen returns, finds the King dead, and makes
passionate action. The poisoner with some three or four mutes° comes in again, seeming to condole with her. The dead body is carried away. The poisoner wooes the Queen with gifts: she seems
harsh and unwilling awhile, but in the end accepts his love.
Exeunt.*

OPHELIA. What means this, my lord?
HAMLET. Marry, this is miching mallecho,° it means mischief.
OPHELIA. Belike this show imports the argument° of the play.

Enter PROLOGUE.

100 *stay . . . patience:* await your permission.   102 *metal more attractive:* (1) iron more magnetic
(2) stuff ("mettle") more beautiful.   108 *country:* rustic, sexual (with a pun on a slang word
for the female sexual organ).   121 *sables:* (1) rich fur (2) black mourning garb.
123 *by'r lady:* by Our Lady (the Virgin Mary).   124 *not thinking on:* being forgotten.
125 *hobby-horse:* (1) character in the May games (2) slang for "prostitute."   126 stage direction: *Dumb Show:* pantomimed synopsis of the action to follow.   126 stage direction: *mutes:* actors without speaking parts.   128 *miching mallecho:* skulking mischief.   129 *imports the argument:* signifies the plot.

HAMLET.   We shall know by this fellow: the players cannot keep
   counsel,° they'll tell all.   1

OPHELIA.   Will a' tell us what this show meant?

HAMLET.   Ay, or any show that you will show him. Be not you
   ashamed to show, he'll not shame to tell you what it
   means.   1.

OPHELIA.   You are naught,° you are naught, I'll mark the play.

PROLOGUE.   For us and for our tragedy,
      Here stooping to your clemency,
      We beg your hearing patiently.   [*Exit.*]

HAMLET.   Is this a prologue, or the posy° of a ring?   1

OPHELIA.   'Tis brief, my lord.

HAMLET.   As woman's love.

Enter Player KING *and* QUEEN.

PLAYER KING.   Full thirty times hath Phoebus' cart° gone round
      Neptune's salt wash,° and Tellus' orbèd ground,°
      And thirty dozen moons with borrowed sheen   1
      About the world have times twelve thirties been,
      Since love our hearts, and Hymen° did our hands
      Unite commutual,° in most sacred bands.

PLAYER QUEEN.   So many journeys may the sun and moon
      Make us again count o'er ere love be done,   1
      But woe is me, you are so sick of late,
      So far from cheer, and from your former state,
      That I distrust you:° yet though I distrust,
      Discomfort you, my lord, it nothing must.
      For women fear too much, even as they love,   1
      And women's fear and love hold quantity,°
      In neither aught, or in extremity:°
      Now what my love is, proof° hath made you know,
      And as my love is sized, my fear is so.
      Where love is great, the littlest doubts are fear,   1
      Where little fears grow great, great love grows there.

PLAYER KING.   Faith, I must leave thee love, and shortly too,
      My operant° powers their functions leave° to do,
      And thou shalt live in this fair world behind,
      Honoured, beloved, and haply° one as kind   1
      For husband shalt thou—

PLAYER QUEEN.   O confound the rest:
      Such love must needs be treason in my breast.
      In second husband let me be accurst,
      None wed the second, but who killed the first.

---

131 *counsel:* a secret.   136 *naught:* naughty, lewd.   140 *posy:* motto (engraved in a ring).
143 *Phoebus' cart:* chariot of the sun.   144 *wash:* sea.   *Tellus'* . . . *ground:* the earth (Tellus
was a Roman earth goddess).   147 *Hymen:* Roman god of marriage.   148 *commutual:* mutually.   153 *distrust you:* am worried about you.   156 *quantity:* proportion.   157 *In neither*
. . . *extremity:* their love and fear are either absent or excessive.   158 *proof:* experience.
163 *operant:* vital.   *leave:* cease.   165 *haply:* perhaps.

HAMLET.   [*Aside.*] That's wormwood,° wormwood.   170
PLAYER QUEEN.   The instances° that second marriage move°
   Are base respects of thrift,° but none of love.
   A second time I kill my husband dead,
   When second husband kisses me in bed.
PLAYER KING.   I do believe you think what now you speak,   175
   But what we do determine, oft we break:
   Purpose is but the slave to memory,
   Of violent birth but poor validity:°
   Which now like fruit unripe sticks on the tree,
   But fall unshaken when they mellow be.   180
   Most necessary 'tis that we forget
   To pay ourselves what to ourselves is debt:°
   What to ourselves in passion we propose,
   The passion ending, doth the purpose lose.
   The violence of either grief or joy   185
   Their own enactures° with themselves destroy:
   Where joy most revels, grief doth most lament;
   Grief joys, joy grieves, on slender accident.
   This world is not for aye,° nor 'tis not strange
   That even our loves should with our fortunes change: 190
   For 'tis a question left us yet to prove,
   Whether love lead fortune, or else fortune love.°
   The great man down, you mark his favourite flies,
   The poor advanced, makes friends of enemies:
   And hitherto doth love on fortune tend,   195
   For who not needs, shall never lack a friend,
   And who in want a hollow friend doth try,
   Directly seasons him° his enemy.
   But orderly to end where I begun,
   Our wills and fates do so contrary run,   200
   That our devices still° are overthrown,
   Our thoughts are ours, their ends none of our own.
   So think thou wilt no second husband wed,
   But die thy thoughts when thy first lord is dead.
PLAYER QUEEN.   Nor earth to me give food, nor heaven light,   205
   Sport and repose lock from me day and night,
   To desperation turn my trust and hope,
   An anchor's° cheer in prison be my scope,
   Each opposite that blanks° the face of joy,
   Meet what I would have well, and it destroy,   210
   Both here and hence° pursue me lasting strife,
   If once a widow, ever I be wife.

---

170 *wormwood:* bitter (like the herb).   171 *instances:* causes.   *move:* motivate.   172 *respects of thrift:* consideration of profit.   178 *validity:* strength.   181–182 *Most . . . debt:* we are easy creditors to ourselves and forget our former promises (debts).   186 *enactures:* fulfillments. 189 *aye:* ever.   192 *fortune love:* fortune lead love.   198 *seasons him:* causes him to become. 201 *devices still:* plans always.   208 *anchor's:* hermit's.   209 *opposite that blanks:* contrary event that pales.   211 *here and hence:* in this world and the next.

HAMLET.   If she should break it now.

PLAYER KING.   'Tis deeply sworn: sweet, leave me here awhile,
　　My spirits grow dull, and fain° I would beguile   21
　　The tedious day with sleep.   *Sleeps.*

PLAYER QUEEN.　　　　　　Sleep rock thy brain.
　　And never come mischance between us twain.   *Exit.*

HAMLET.   Madam, how like you this play?

QUEEN.   The lady doth protest too much methinks.

HAMLET.   O but she'll keep her word.   22

KING.   Have you heard the argument°? Is there no offence in't?

HAMLET.   No, no, they do but jest, poison in jest, no offence
　　i'th'world.

KING.   What do you call the play?

HAMLET.   The Mouse-trap. Marry, how? Tropically:° this play is the   22
　　image of a murder done in Vienna: Gonzago is the duke's
　　name, his wife Baptista, you shall see anon, 'tis a knavish
　　piece of work, but what of that? Your majesty, and we
　　that have free° souls, it touches us not: let the galled jade
　　winch,° our withers are unwrung.°   22

Enter LUCIANUS.

　　This is one Lucianus, nephew to the king.

OPHELIA.   You are as good as a chorus,° my lord.

HAMLET.   I could interpret between you and your love, if I could see
　　the puppets dallying.

OPHELIA.   You are keen my lord, you are keen.°   23

HAMLET.   It would cost you a groaning to take off mine edge.

OPHELIA.   Still better and worse.°

HAMLET.   So you mistake° your husbands. Begin, murderer. Pox,°
　　leave thy damnable faces° and begin. Come, the croaking
　　raven doth bellow for revenge.   24

LUCIANUS.   Thoughts black, hands apt, drugs fit, and time agreeing,
　　Confederate season, else no creature seeing,°
　　Thou mixture rank, of midnight weeds collected,
　　With Hecate's° ban° thrice blasted, thrice infected,
　　Thy natural magic, and dire property,   24
　　On wholesome° life usurps immediately.   *Pours the poison in his ears.*

HAMLET.   A' poisons him i'th'garden for's estate, his name's Gonzago,
　　the story is extant, and written in very choice
　　Italian, you shall see anon how the murderer gets the love
　　of Gonzago's wife.   25

OPHELIA.   The king rises.

HAMLET.   What, frighted with false fire°?

215 *fain:* gladly.　　221 *argument:* plot.　　225 *Tropically:* figuratively.　　229 *free:* innocent.
229–230 *galled jade winch:* chafed old horse wince (from its sores).　　230 *withers are unwrung:*
(1) shoulders are unchafed (2) consciences are clear.　　232 *chorus:* actor who introduced the
action.　　235 *keen:* (1) sharp (Ophelia's meaning) (2) sexually excited (Hamlet's
interpretation).　　237 *better and worse:* better wit but a worse meaning, with a pun on "better"
and "bitter."　　238 *mistake:* mis-take.　　*Pox:* a plague on it.　　239 *faces:* exaggerated facial
expressions.　　242 *Confederate . . . seeing:* no one seeing me except time, my confederate.
244 *Hecate:* goddess of witchcraft.　　*ban:* evil spell.　　246 *wholesome:* healthy.　　252 *false fire:*
discharge of blanks (not gunpowder).

QUEEN.   How fares my lord?
POLONIUS.   Give o'er the play.
KING.   Give me some light. Away!   255
ALL.   Lights, lights, lights!   *Exeunt all but* HAMLET *and* HORATIO.
HAMLET.   Why, let the stricken deer go weep,
      The hart ungallèd° play,°
   For some must watch while some must sleep,
      Thus runs the world away.   260
  Would not this° sir, and a forest of feathers,° if the rest of my
  fortunes turn Turk with° me, with two Provincial roses° on
  my razed° shoes, get me a fellowship° in a cry° of players?
HORATIO.   Half a share.°
HAMLET.   A whole one, I.   265
  For thou dost know, O Damon° dear,
    This realm dismantled was
  Of Jove° himself, and now reigns here
    A very very—pajock.°
HORATIO.   You might have rhymed.°   270
HAMLET.   O good Horatio, I'll take the ghost's word for a thousand
  pound. Didst perceive?
HORATIO.   Very well my lord.
HAMLET.   Upon the talk of the poisoning?
HORATIO.   I did very well note him.   275

Enter ROSENCRANTZ *and* GUILDENSTERN.

HAMLET.   Ah ha, come, some music. Come, the recorders.°
  For if the king like not the comedy,
  Why then belike he likes it not, perdy.°
  Come, some music.
GUILDENSTERN.   Good my lord, vouchsafe me a word with you.   280
HAMLET.   Sir, a whole history.
GUILDENSTERN.   The king, sir—
HAMLET.   Ay sir, what of him?
GUILDENSTERN.   Is in his retirement, marvellous distempered.
HAMLET.   With drink sir?   285
GUILDENSTERN.   No my lord, with choler.°
HAMLET.   Your wisdom should show itself more richer to signify
  this to the doctor: for, for me to put him to his purgation,°
  would perhaps plunge him into more choler.
GUILDENSTERN.   Good my lord, put your discourse into some frame,° and   290
  start not so wildly from my affair.

257–258 *deer . . . play:* (the belief that a wounded deer wept, abandoned by the others).
258 *ungallèd:* unhurt.   261 *this:* i.e., sample (of my theatrical talent).   *feathers:* plumes
(worn by actors).   262 *turn Turk with:* cruelly turn against.   *Provincial roses:* rosettes named
for Provins, France.   263 *razed:* slashed, decorated with cutouts.   *fellowship:* partnership.
cry: pack, troupe.   264 *share:* divisions of profits among members of a theatrical production
company.   266 *Damon:* legendary ideal friend to Pythias.   268 *Jove:* (Hamlet's father).
269 *pajock:* peacock (associated with lechery).   270 *rhymed:* (used "ass" instead of "pajock").
276 *recorders:* soft-toned woodwind instruments, similar to flutes.   278 *perdy:* by God (*par dieu*).
286 *choler:* anger.   288 *purgation:* (1) purging of excessive bile (2) judicial investigations (3)
purgatory.   290 *frame:* order.

HAMLET.   I am tame sir, pronounce.

GUILDENSTERN.   The queen your mother, in most great affliction of spirit,
hath sent me to you.

HAMLET.   You are welcome.

GUILDENSTERN.   Nay good my lord, this courtesy is not of the right breed.°
If it shall please you to make me a wholesome° answer, I
will do your mother's commandment: if not, your pardon°
and my return shall be the end of my business.

HAMLET.   Sir I cannot.

ROSENCRANTZ.   What, my lord?

HAMLET.   Make you a wholesome answer: my wit's diseased. But
sir, such answer as I can make, you shall command, or
rather as you say, my mother: therefore no more, but to
the matter. My mother you say.

ROSENCRANTZ.   Then thus she says, your behaviour hath struck her into
amazement and admiration.°

HAMLET.   O wonderful son that can so 'stonish a mother. But is there
no sequel at the heels of this mother's admiration? Impart.

ROSENCRANTZ.   She desires to speak with you in her closet°
ere you go to bed.

HAMLET.   We shall obey, were she ten times our mother. Have you
any further trade with us?

ROSENCRANTZ.   My lord, you once did love me.

HAMLET.   And do still, by these pickers and stealers.°

ROSENCRANTZ.   Good my lord, what is your cause of distemper? You do
surely bar the door upon your own liberty, if you deny
your griefs to your friend.°

HAMLET.   Sir, I lack advancement.

ROSENCRANTZ.   How can that be, when you have the voice° of the king
himself for your succession in Denmark?

HAMLET.   Ay sir, but 'while the grass grows'°—the proverb is
something musty.°

Enter the PLAYERS with recorders.

O the recorders, let me see one. To withdraw° with you,
why do you go about to recover the wind of me,° as if you
would drive me into a toil°?

GUILDENSTERN.   O my lord, if my duty be too bold, my love is too
unmannerly.°

HAMLET.   I do not well understand that. Will you play
upon this pipe°?

---

296 *breed:* (1) species (2) manners.   297 *wholesome:* reasonable.   298 *pardon:* permission to
depart.   307 *admiration:* wonder.   310 *closet:* private room, bedroom.   315 *pickers and
stealers:* hands (from the prayer, "Keep my hands from picking and stealing").   317–318 *deny
. . . friend:* refuse to let your friend know the cause of your suffering.   320 *voice:* vote.
322 *while . . . grows:* (the proverb ends: "the horse starves").   323 *something musty:* somewhat
too old and trite (to finish).   324 *withdraw:* speak privately.   325 *recover . . . me:* drive me
toward the wind, as with a prey, to avoid its scenting the hunter.   326 *toil:* snare.
327–328 *is too unmannerly:* makes me forget my good manners.   330 *pipe:* recorder.

GUILDENSTERN.   My lord I cannot.

HAMLET.   I pray you.

GUILDENSTERN.   Believe me. I cannot.

HAMLET.   I do beseech you.

GUILDENSTERN.   I know no touch of it° my lord.   335

HAMLET.   It is as easy as lying; govern these ventages° with your
    fingers and thumb, give it breath with your mouth, and it
    will discourse most eloquent music. Look you, these are
    the stops.

GUILDENSTERN.   But these cannot I command to any utt'rance of harmony,   340
    I have not the skill.

HAMLET.   Why look you now how unworthy a thing you make of
    me: you would play upon me, you would seem to know
    my stops, you would pluck out the heart of my mystery,
    you would sound me from my lowest note to the top of my   345
    compass:° and there is much music, excellent voice in this
    little organ,° yet cannot you make it speak. 'Sblood, do you
    think I am easier to be played on than a pipe? Call me what
    instrument you will, though you can fret° me, you cannot
    play upon me.   350

Enter POLONIUS.

    God bless you sir.

POLONIUS.   My lord, the queen would speak with you, and presently.

HAMLET.   Do you see yonder cloud that's almost in shape of a camel?

POLONIUS.   By th'mass and 'tis, like a camel indeed.

HAMLET.   Methinks it is like a weasel.   355

POLONIUS.   It is backed like a weasel.

HAMLET.   Or like a whale?

POLONIUS.   Very like a whale.

HAMLET.   Then I will come to my mother by and by.°
    [*Aside.*] They fool me to the top of my bent.°   360
    I will come by and by.

POLONIUS.   I will say so.   *Exit.*

HAMLET.   "By and by" is easily said.
    Leave me, friends.   [*Exeunt all but HAMLET.*]
    'Tis now the very witching time of night.   365
    When churchyards yawn,° and hell itself breathes out
    Contagion° to this world: now could I drink hot blood,
    And do such bitter business as the day
    Would quake to look on: soft, now to my mother—
    O heart, lose not thy nature,° let not ever   370
    The soul of Nero° enter this firm bosom,
    Let me be cruel, not unnatural.

---

335 *know . . . it:* have no skill at fingering it.   336 *ventages:* holes, stops.   346 *compass:* range.
347 *organ:* musical instrument.   349 *fret:* (1) irritate (2) play an instrument that has "frets" or
bars to guide the fingering.   359 *by and by:* very soon.   360 *fool me . . . bent:* force me to play
the fool to my utmost.   366 *churchyards yawn:* graves open.   367 *Contagion:* (1) evil
(2) diseases.   370 *nature:* natural affection.   371 *Nero:* (who killed his mother).

I will speak daggers to her, but use none:
My tongue and soul in this be hypocrites,°
How in my words somever she be shent,°   37
To give them seals,° never my soul consent.   *Exit.*

Scene 3. *[A room in the castle]*

Enter KING, ROSENCRANTZ, *and* GUILDENSTERN.

KING. I like him not, nor stands it safe with us
    To let his madness range. Therefore prepare you,
    I your commission will forthwith dispatch,°
    And he to England shall along with you:
    The terms of our estate° may not endure
    Hazard so near's° as doth hourly grow
    Out of his brows.°
GUILDENSTERN.   We will ourselves provide:°
    Most holy and religious fear it is
    To keep those many many bodies safe
    That live and feed upon your majesty.   1
ROSENCRANTZ.   The single and peculiar° life is bound
    With all the strength and armour of the mind
    To keep itself from noyance,° but much more
    That spirit, upon whose weal° depends and rests
    The lives of many; the cess° of majesty   1
    Dies not alone, but like a gulf° doth draw
    What's near it, with it. O 'tis a massy wheel
    Fixed on the summit of the highest mount,
    To whose huge spokes, ten thousand lesser things
    Are mortised° and adjoined, which when it falls,   2
    Each small annexment, petty consequence,
    Attends° the boist'rous ruin. Never alone
    Did the king sigh, but with a general groan.
KING.   Arm° you I pray you, to this speedy voyage,
    For we will fetters put about this fear,   2
    Which now goes too free-footed.
ROSENCRANTZ.   We will haste us.

                    Exeunt [ROSENCRANTZ *and* GUILDENSTERN.]

Enter POLONIUS.

POLONIUS.   My lord, he's going to his mother's closet:
    Behind the arras I'll convey myself
    To hear the process.° I'll warrant she'll tax him home,

374 *My tongue . . . hypocrites:* I will speak cruelly but intend no harm.   375 *shent:* chastised.
376 *give them seals:* confirm them with action (as a legal "deed" is confirmed with a "seal").
3 *forthwith dispatch:* immediately have prepared.   5 *terms . . . estate:* circumstances of my royal
office.   6 *near's:* near us.   7 *brows:* effronteries.   *provide:* prepare.   11 *peculiar:*
individual.   13 *noyance:* harm.   14 *weal:* well-being.   15 *cess:* cessation, death.
16 *gulf:* whirlpool.   20 *mortised:* securely fitted.   22 *Attends:* accompanies.   24 *Arm:* prepare.   29 *the process:* what proceeds.

And as you said, and wisely was it said, 30
'Tis meet° that some more audience than a mother,
Since nature makes them partial, should o'erhear
The speech of vantage;° fare you well my liege,°
I'll call upon you ere you go to bed,
And tell you what I know.
KING.   Thanks, dear my lord.   *Exit [POLONIUS.]* 35
O my offence is rank, it smells to heaven,
It hath the primal eldest curse° upon't,
A brother's murder. Pray can I not,
Though inclination be as sharp as will:°
My stronger guilt defeats my strong intent, 40
And like a man to double business bound,
I stand in pause where I shall first begin,
And both neglect; what if this cursèd hand
Were thicker than itself with brother's blood,
Is there not rain enough in the sweet heavens 45
To wash it white as snow? Whereto serves mercy
But to confront the visage of offence°?
And what's in prayer but this two-fold force,
To be forestallèd° ere we come to fall,
Or pardoned being down? Then I'll look up, 50
My fault is past. But O what form of prayer
Can serve my turn? "Forgive me my foul murder":
That cannot be, since I am still possessed
Of those effects° for which I did the murder:
My crown, mine own ambition, and my queen. 55
May one be pardoned and retain th'offence?
In the corrupted currents of this world,
Offence's gilded hand may shove by justice,
And oft 'tis seen the wicked prize itself
Buys out the law;° but 'tis not so above, 60
There is no shuffling,° there the action lies
In his true nature,° and we ourselves compelled
Even to the teeth and forehead of our faults°
To give in evidence. What then? What rests°?
Try what repentance can. What can it not? 65
Yet what can it, when one can not repent?
O wretched state? O bosom black as death!
O limèd soul, that struggling to be free,
Art more engaged;° help, angels, make assay:°

31 *meet*: fitting.   33 *of vantage*: from an advantageous position.   *liege*: lord.
37 *primal . . . curse*: curse of Cain.   39 *inclination . . . will*: my desire to pray is as strong as my
determination to do so.   47 *confront . . . offence*: plead in man's behalf against sin (at the Last
Judgment).   49 *forestallèd*: prevented.   54 *effects*: results.   59–60 *wicked . . . law*: fruits of
the crime bribe the judge.   61 *shuffling*: evasion.   61–62 *action . . . nature*: (1) deed is seen
in its true nature (2) legal action is sustained according to the truth.   63 *to the teeth . . . faults*:
meeting our sins face to face.   64 *rests*: remains.   68–69 *limèd . . . engaged*: like a bird
caught in lime (a sticky substance spread on twigs as a snare), the soul in its struggle to clear itself only becomes more entangled.   69 *make assay*: I'll make an attempt.

Bow stubborn knees, and heart with strings of steel,
Be soft as sinews of the new-born babe,
All may be well.   [*He kneels.*]

Enter HAMLET.

HAMLET.   Now might I do it pat,° now a' is a-praying,
    And now I'll do't, [*Draws his sword.*] and so a' goes to heaven,
    And so am I revenged: that would be scanned:°
    A villain kills my father, and for that,
    I his sole son, do this same villain send
    To heaven.
    Why, this is hire and salary, not revenge.
    A' took my father grossly,° full of bread,°
    With all his crimes° broad blown,° as flush° as May,
    And how his audit° stands who knows save heaven,
    But in our circumstance and course of thought,
    'Tis heavy° with him: and am I then revenged
    To take him in the purging of his soul,
    when he is fit and seasoned° for his passage?
    No.   [*Sheathes his sword.*]
    Up sword, and know thou a more horrid hent,°
    When he is drunk asleep, or in his rage,
    Or in th'incestuous pleasure of his bed,
    At game, a-swearing, or about some act
    That has no relish° of salvation in't,
    Then trip him that his heels may kick at heaven,
    And that his soul may be as damned and black
    As hell whereto it goes; my mother stays,
    This physic° but prolongs thy sickly days.   *Exit.*
KING. [*Rises.*]   My words fly up, my thoughts remain below,
    Words without thoughts never to heaven go.   *Exit.*

Scene 4. [*The queen's closet*]

Enter QUEEN *and* POLONIUS.

POLONIUS.   A' will come straight, look you lay home° to him,
    Tell him his pranks have been too broad° to bear with,
    And that your grace hath screened and stood between
    Much heat° and him. I'll silence me° even here:
    Pray you be round with him.

---

73 *pat:* opportunely.   75 *would be scanned:* needs closer examination.   80 *grossly:* unpuri-
fied (by final rites).   *bread:* self-indulgence.   81 *crimes:* sins.   *broad blown:* in full flower.
flush: lusty.   82 *audit:* account.   84 *heavy:* grievous.   86 *seasoned:* ready (prepared).
88 *horrid hent:* horrible opportunity ("hint") for seizure ("hent") by me.   92 *relish:* taste.
96 *physic:* (1) medicine (2) purgation of your soul by prayer.   1 *lay home:* thrust home; speak
sharply.   2 *broad:* unrestrained.   4 *heat:* anger.   *silence me:* hide in silence.

HAMLET. [*Within.*]   Mother, mother, mother.
QUEEN.   I'll war'nt you,
  Fear me not. Withdraw, I hear him coming. [*POLONIUS hides behind the arras.*]

Enter HAMLET.

HAMLET.   Now mother, what's the matter?
QUEEN.   Hamlet, thou hast thy father much offended.
HAMLET.   Mother, you have my father much offended.   10
QUEEN.   Come, come, you answer with an idle° tongue.
HAMLET.   Go, go, you question with a wicked tongue.
QUEEN.   Why, how now Hamlet?
HAMLET.   What's the matter now?
QUEEN.   Have you forgot me?
HAMLET.   No by the rood,° not so,
  You are the queen, your husband's brother's wife,   15
  And would it were not so, you are my mother.
QUEEN.   Nay, then I'll set those to you that can speak.°
HAMLET.   Come, come, and sit you down, you shall not budge,
  You go not till I set you up a glass°
  Where you may see the inmost part of you.   20
QUEEN.   What wilt thou do? Thou wilt not murder me?
  Help, help, ho!
POLONIUS. [*Behind the arras.*]   What ho! help, help, help!
HAMLET.   How now, a rat? dead for a ducat,° dead.

                                   Kills POLONIUS [through the arras.]

POLONIUS.   O I am slain!
QUEEN.   O me, what hast thou done?
HAMLET.   Nay I know not,   25
  Is it the king?
QUEEN.   O what a rash and bloody deed is this!
HAMLET.   A bloody deed, almost as bad, good mother,
  As kill a king, and marry with his brother.
QUEEN.   As kill a king?
HAMLET.   Ay lady, it was my word.   30
  [*To Polonius.*] Thou wretched, rash, intruding fool, farewell,
  I took thee for thy better,° take thy fortune,
  Thou find'st to be too busy is some danger.
  [*To the Queen.*] Leave wringing of your hands, peace, sit you down,
  And let me wring your heart, for so I shall   35
  If it be made of penetrable stuff,
  If damnèd custom° have not brazed° it so,
  That it be proof° and bulwark against sense.°
QUEEN.   What have I done, that thou dar'st wag thy tongue
  In noise so rude against me?

---

11 *idle:* foolish.   14 *rood:* cross.   17 *speak:* i.e., to you as you should be spoken to.
19 *glass:* looking glass.   23 *for a ducat:* I wager a ducat (an Italian gold coin).   32 *thy better:*
the king.   37 *custom:* habit.   *brazed:* brass-plated (brazened).   38 *proof:* armor.
sense: sensibility.

HAMLET.   Such an act   40
    That blurs the grace and blush of modesty,
    Calls virtue hypocrite, takes off the rose°
    From the fair forehead of an innocent love
    And sets a blister there,° makes marriage vows
    As false as dicers' oaths, O such a deed,   45
    As from the body of contraction° plucks
    The very soul, and sweet religion makes
    A rhapsody° of words; heaven's face does glow,°
    Yea this solidity and compound mass°
    With heated visage, as against the doom,°   50
    Is thought-sick at the act.
QUEEN.   Ay me, what act,
    That roars so loud, and thunders in the index°?
HAMLET.   Look here upon this picture, and on this,
    The counterfeit presentment° of two brothers:
    See what a grace was seated on this brow,   55
    Hyperion's° curls, the front° of Jove himself,
    An eye like Mars, to threaten and command,
    A station° like the herald Mercury,
    New-lighted on a heaven-kissing hill,
    A combination and a form indeed,   60
    Where every god did seem to set his seal
    To give the world assurance of a man.
    This was your husband. Look you now what follows.
    Here is your husband, like a mildewed ear,°
    Blasting° his wholesome brother. Have you eyes?   65
    Could you on this fair mountain leave to feed,°
    And batten° on this moor? Ha! Have you eyes?
    You cannot call it love, for at your age
    The hey-day in the blood° is tame, it's humble,
    And waits upon the judgment, and what judgment   70
    Would step from this to this? Sense° sure you have
    Else could you not have motion,° but sure that sense
    Is apoplexed,° for madness would not err,
    Nor sense to ecstasy was ne'er so thralled°
    But it reserved some quantity of choice   75
    To serve in such a difference.° What devil was't
    That thus hath cozened you at hoodman-blind°?

42 *rose:* (symbol of perfection and innocence).   44 *blister there:* (whores were punished by being branded on the forehead).   46 *body of contraction:* marriage contract.   48 *rhapsody:* (meaningless) mixture.   *glow:* blush.   49 *solidity . . . mass:* solid earth, compounded of the four elements.   50 *against the doom:* expecting Judgment Day.   52 *index:* (1) table of contents (2) prologue.   54 *counterfeit presentment:* painted likeness.   56 *Hyperion:* Greek sun god.   *front:* forehead.   58 *station:* bearing.   64 *ear:* i.e., of grain.   65 *Blasting:* blighting.   66 *leave to feed:* leave off feeding.   67 *batten:* gorge yourself.   69 *hey-day in the blood:* youthful passion.   71 *Sense:* perception by the senses.   72 *motion:* impulse.   73 *apoplexed:* paralyzed.   74 *sense . . . thralled:* sensibility was never so enslaved by madness.   76 *in . . . difference:* where the difference was so great.   77 *cozened . . . blind:* cheated you at blindman's bluff.

Eyes without feeling, feeling without sight,
Ears without hands or eyes, smelling sans all,°
Or but a sickly part of one true sense   80
Could not so mope:° O shame, where is thy blush?
Rebellious hell,
If thou canst mutine in a matron's bones,
To flaming youth let virtue be as wax
And melt in her own fire. Proclaim no shame   85
When the compulsive° ardour gives the charge,°
Since frost itself as actively doth burn,
And reason panders will.°
QUEEN.   O Hamlet, speak no more,
Thou turn'st my eyes into my very soul,
And there I see such black and grainèd° spots   90
As will not leave their tinct.°
HAMLET.   Nay, but to live
In the rank sweat of an enseamèd° bed,
Stewed in corruption, honeying, and making love
Over the nasty sty.
QUEEN.   O speak to me no more,
These words like daggers enter in mine ears,   95
No more, sweet Hamlet.
HAMLET.   A murderer and a villain,
A slave that is not twentieth part the tithe°
Of your precedent lord, a vice° of kings,
A cutpurse° of the empire and the rule,
That from a shelf the precious diadem stole   100
And put it in his pocket.
QUEEN.   No more.
HAMLET.   A king of shreds and patches—

Enter the GHOST *in his night-gown.*°

Save me and hover o'er me with your wings,
You heavenly guards. What would your gracious figure?
QUEEN.   Alas, he's mad.   105
HAMLET.   Do you not come your tardy son to chide,
That lapsed in time and passion° lets go by
Th'important acting of your dread command?
O say!
GHOST.   Do not forget: this visitation   110
Is but to whet thy almost blunted purpose.
But look, amazement on thy mother sits,
O step between her and her fighting soul,

79 *sans all:* without the other senses.   81 *so mope:* be so dull.   86 *compulsive:* compelling.
gives the charge: attacks.   88 *panders will:* pimps for lust.   90 *grainèd:* dyed in grain,
unfading.   91 *leave their tinct:* lose their color.   92 *enseamèd:* greasy.   97 *tithe:* one-tenth
part.   98 *vice:* buffoon (like the character of Vice in the morality plays).   99 *cutpurse:* pick-
pocket.   102.1 stage direction: *night-gown:* dressing gown.   107 *lapsed . . . passion:* having
let time elapse and passion cool.

    Conceit° in weakest bodies strongest works,
    Speak to her Hamlet.
HAMLET.   How is it with you lady?   11
QUEEN.   Alas, how is't with you,
    That you do bend your eye on vacancy,°
    And with th'incorporal° air do hold discourse?
    Forth at your eyes your spirits° wildly peep,
    And as the sleeping soldiers in th'alarm,   12
    Your bedded° hairs, like life in excrements,°
    Start up and stand an° end. O gentle son,
    Upon the heat and flame of thy distemper
    sprinkle cool patience. Whereon do you look?
HAMLET.   On him, on him, look you how pale he glares,
    His form and cause conjoined, preaching to stones,
    Would make them capable.° Do not look upon me,
    Lest with this piteous action you convert
    My stern effects,° then what I have to do
    Will want° true colour,° tears perchance for blood.   13
QUEEN.   To whom do you speak this?
HAMLET.   Do you see nothing there?
QUEEN.   Nothing at all, yet all that is I see.
HAMLET.   Nor did you nothing hear?
QUEEN.   No, nothing but ourselves.
HAMLET.   Why look you there, look how it steals away,
    My father in his habit as he lived,°   13
    Look where he goes, even now out at the portal.   *Exit* [*GHOST.*]
QUEEN.   This is the very coinage of your brain,
    This bodiless creation ecstasy
    Is very cunning in.°
HAMLET.   Ecstasy?
    My pulse as yours doth temperately keep time,   14
    And makes as healthful music. It is not madness
    That I have uttered; bring me to the test
    And I the matter will re-word, which madness
    Would gambol° from. Mother, for love of grace,
    Lay not that flattering unction° to your soul,   14
    That not your trespass but my madness speaks,
    It will but skin and film the ulcerous place,
    Whiles rank corruption mining° all within,
    Infects unseen. Confess yourself to heaven,
    Repent what's past, avoid what is to come,   15
    And do not spread the compost° on the weeds

---

114 *Conceit:* imagination.   117 *vacancy:* (she cannot see the ghost).   118 *incorporal:*
bodiless.   119 *spirits:* vital forces.   121 *bedded:* lying flat.   *excrements:* outgrowths (of the
body).   122 *an:* on.   127 *capable:* i.e., of feeling pity.   128–129 *convert . . . effects:*
transform my outward signs of sternness.   130 *want:* lack.   *colour:* (1) complexion
(2) motivation.   135 *habit . . . lived:* clothing he wore when alive.
138–139 *bodiless . . . cunning in:* madness (ecstasy) is very skillful in causing an affected person
to hallucinate.   144 *gambol:* leap.   145 *unction:* salve.   148 *mining:* undermining.
151 *compost:* manure.

To make them ranker. Forgive me this my virtue,°
For in the fatness° of these pursy° times
Virtue itself of vice must pardon beg,
Yea curb and woo° for leave to do him° good.   155
QUEEN.   O Hamlet, thou hast cleft my heart in twain.
HAMLET.   O throw away the worser part of it,
    And live the purer with the other half.
    Good night, but go not to my uncle's bed,
    Assume° a virtue if you have it not.   160
    That monster custom, who all sense doth eat
    Of habits evil,° is angel yet in this,
    That to the use° of actions fair and good,
    He likewise gives a frock or livery
    That aptly° is put on. Refrain tonight,   165
    And that shall lend a kind of easiness
    To the next abstinence, the next more easy:
    For use° almost can change the stamp° of nature,
    And either . . . the° devil, or throw him out
    With wondrous potency: once more good night,   170
    And when you are desirous to be blessed,
    I'll blessing beg of you. For this same lord,°
    I do repent; but heaven hath pleased it so
    To punish me with this, and this with me,
    That I must be their scourge and minister.°   175
    I will bestow° him and will answer well°
    The death I gave him; so again good night.
    I must be cruel only to be kind;
    This bad begins, and worse remains behind.°
    One word more, good lady.
QUEEN.   What shall I do?   180
HAMLET.   Not this by no means that I bid you do:
    Let the bloat° king tempt you again to bed,
    Pinch wanton on your cheek, call you his mouse,
    And let him for a pair of reechy° kisses,
    Or paddling in your neck with his damned fingers,   185
    Make you to ravel° all this matter out
    That I essentially am not in madness,
    But mad in craft. 'Twere good you let him know,
    For who that's but a queen, fair, sober, wise,
    Would from a paddock, from a bat, a gib,°   190

---

152 *virtue:* sermon on virtue.   153 *fatness:* grossness.   *pursy:* flabby.   155 *curb and woo:*
bow and plead.   *him:* vice.   160 *Assume:* put on the guise of.   161–162 *all sense . . . evil:*
confuses the sense of right and wrong in a habitué.   163 *use:* habit.   165 *aptly:* readily.
168 *use:* habit.   *stamp:* form.   169 *either . . . the:* (word omitted, for which "tame," "curls,"
and "quell" have been suggested).   172 *lord:* Polonius.   175 *their . . . minister:* heaven's
punishment and agent of retribution.   176 *bestow:* stow away.   *answer well:* assume full
responsibility for.   179 *bad . . . behind:* is a bad beginning to a worse end to come.   182 *bloat:*
bloated with dissipation.   184 *reechy:* filthy.   186 *ravel:* unravel.   190 *paddock, bat, gib:*
toad, bat, tomcat ("familiars" or demons in animal shape that attend on witches).

Such dear concernings hide? who would do so?
No, in despite of sense and secrecy,
Unpeg the basket on the house's top,
Let the birds fly, and like the famous ape,
To try conclusions° in the basket creep,   19
And break your own neck down.°
QUEEN.   Be thou assured, if words be made of breath,
And breath of life, I have no life to breathe
What thou hast said to me.
HAMLET.   I must to England, you know that.
QUEEN.   Alack,   20
I had forgot: 'tis so concluded on.
HAMLET.   There's letters sealed, and my two school-fellows,
Whom I will trust as I will adders fanged,
They bear the mandate, they must sweep my way
And marshal me to knavery:° let it work,   20
For 'tis the sport to have the enginer°
Hoist with his own petar,° and't shall go hard
But I will delve one yard below their mines,
And blow them at the moon: O 'tis most sweet
When in one line two crafts directly meet.°   21
This man shall set me packing,°
I'll lug the guts into the neighbour room;
Mother good night indeed. This counsellor
Is now most still, most secret, and most grave,
Who was in life a foolish prating knave.   21
Come sir, to draw toward an end with you.
Good night mother.   *Exit HAMLET tugging in POLONIUS.*

[ACT 4]

Scene 1. *[A room in the castle]*

Enter KING and QUEEN with ROSENCRANTZ and GUILDENSTERN.

KING.   There's matter in these sighs, these profound heaves,
You must translate, 'tis fit we understand them.
Where is your son?
QUEEN.   Bestow this place on us° a little while.

Exeunt ROSENCRANTZ and GUILDENSTERN.

Ah mine own lord, what have I seen tonight!

193–196 *Unpeg . . . down:* (the story refers to an ape that climbs to the top of a house and opens a basket of birds; when the birds fly away, the ape crawls into the basket, tries to fly, and breaks his neck. The point is that if she gives away Hamlet's secret, she harms herself).
195 *try conclusions:* experiment.   204–205 *sweep . . . knavery:* (like the marshal who went before a royal procession, clearing the way, so Rosencrantz and Guildenstern clear Hamlet's path to some unknown evil).   206 *enginer:* maker of war engines.   207 *Hoist . . . petar:* blown up by his own bomb.   210 *in one . . . meet:* the digger of the mine and the digger of the countermine meet halfway in their tunnels.   211 *packing:* (1) i.e., my bags (2) rushing away (3) plotting.   4 *Bestow . . . us:* leave us.

KING.   What, Gertrude? How does Hamlet?

QUEEN.   Mad as the sea and wind when both contend
　　　Which is the mightier, in his lawless fit,
　　　Behind the arras hearing something stir,
　　　Whips out his rapier, cries "A rat, a rat,"　　　　　　　　　　10
　　　And in this brainish apprehension° kills
　　　The unseen good old man.

KING.　　　　　　　　　　　　O heavy deed!
　　　It had been so with us° had we been there:
　　　His liberty is full of threats to all,
　　　To you yourself, to us, to every one.　　　　　　　　　　　15
　　　Alas, how shall this bloody deed be answered?
　　　It will be laid to us,° whose providence°
　　　Should have kept short,° restrained, and out of haunt°
　　　This mad young man; but so much was our love,
　　　We would not understand what was most fit,　　　　　　　20
　　　But like the owner of a foul disease,
　　　To keep it from divulging,° let it feed
　　　Even on the pith of life: where is he gone?

QUEEN.   To draw apart the body he hath killed,
　　　O'er whom his very madness, like some ore　　　　　　　25
　　　Among a mineral of metals base,°
　　　Shows itself pure: a' weeps for what is done.

KING.   O Gertrude, come away:
　　　The sun no sooner shall the mountains touch,
　　　But we will ship him hence and this vile deed　　　　　　30
　　　We must with all our majesty and skill
　　　Both countenance° and excuse. Ho Guildenstern!

Enter ROSENCRANTZ and GUILDENSTERN.

　　　Friends both, go join you with some further aid;
　　　Hamlet in madness hath Polonius slain,
　　　And from his mother's closet hath he dragged him.　　　35
　　　Go seek him out, speak fair, and bring the body
　　　Into the chapel; I pray you haste in this.　　　*Exeunt Gent[lemen.]*
　　　Come Gertrude, we'll call up our wisest friends,
　　　And let them know both what we mean to do
　　　And what's untimely done: [so haply slander,]　　　　　40
　　　Whose whisper o'er the world's diameter,
　　　As level° as the cannon to his blank°
　　　Transports his° poisoned shot, may miss our name,
　　　And hit the woundless° air. O come away,
　　　My soul is full of discord and dismay.　　　*Exeunt.*　　45

---

11 *brainish apprehension:* insane delusion.　　13 *us:* me (royal plural).　　17 *laid to us:* blamed
on me.　　*providence:* foresight.　　18 *short:* tethered by a short leash.　　*out of haunt:* away
from others.　　22 *divulging:* being divulged.　　25–26 *ore . . . base:* pure ore (such as gold) in
a mine of base metal.　　32 *countenance:* defend.　　42 *As level:* with a straight aim.　　*blank:*
while bull's-eye at the target's center.　　43 *his:* slander's.　　44 *woundless:* invulnerable.

Scene 2. *[Another room in the castle]*

Enter HAMLET.

HAMLET. Safely stowed.
　　Gentlemen within: Hamlet, Lord Hamlet!
　　But soft, what noise, who calls on Hamlet?
　　O here they come.

Enter ROSENCRANTZ *and* GUILDENSTERN.

ROSENCRANTZ. What have you done my lord with the dead body?
HAMLET. Compounded it with dust whereto 'tis kin.
ROSENCRANTZ. Tell us where 'tis that we may take it thence,
　　And bear it to the chapel.
HAMLET. Do not believe it.
ROSENCRANTZ. Believe what?
HAMLET. That I can keep your counsel° and not mine own.° Besides,   1
　　to be demanded of° a sponge, what replication° should be
　　made by the son of a king?
ROSENCRANTZ. Take you me for a sponge, my lord?
HAMLET. Ay sir, that soaks up the king's countenance,° his rewards,
　　his authorities. But such officers do the king best service in   1
　　the end; he keeps them like an apple in the corner of his
　　jaw, first mouthed to be last swallowed: when he needs
　　what you have gleaned, it is but squeezing you, and
　　sponge, you shall be dry again.
ROSENCRANTZ. I understand you not my lord.   2
HAMLET. I am glad of it: a knavish speech sleeps in° a foolish ear.
ROSENCRANTZ. My lord, you must tell us where the body is, and go with
　　us to the king.
HAMLET. The body is with the king, but the king° is not with the
　　body. The king is a thing—   2
GUILDENSTERN. A thing my lord?
HAMLET. Of nothing, bring me to him. Hide fox, and all after.°   *Exeunt.*

[Scene 3. Another room in the castle.]

Enter KING *and two or three.*

KING. I have sent to seek him, and to find the body:
　　How dangerous is it that this man goes loose,
　　Yet must not we put the strong law on him,
　　He's loved of the distracted multitude,°
　　Who like not in° their judgment, but their eyes,
　　And where 'tis so, th'offender's scourge° is weighed
　　But never the offence: to bear all° smooth and even,

10 *counsel:* (1) advice (2) secret.　　*keep . . . own:* follow your advice and not keep my own
secret.　　11 *demanded of:* questioned by.　　*replication:* reply to a charge.　　14 *countenance:*
favor.　　21 *sleeps in:* means nothing to.　　24 *king . . . king:* Hamlet's father . . . Claudius.
27 *Hide fox . . . after:* (cry in a children's game, like hide-and-seek).　　4 *distracted multitude:*
confused mob.　　5 *in:* according to.　　6 *scourge:* punishment.　　7 *bear all:* carry out
everything.

This sudden sending him away must seem
Deliberate pause:° diseases desperate grown,
By desperate appliance° are relieved, 10
Or not at all.

Enter ROSENCRANTZ and all the rest.

                How now, what hath befallen?
ROSENCRANTZ.   Where the dead body is bestowed my lord,
    We cannot get from him.
KING.   But where is he?
ROSENCRANTZ.   Without, my lord, guarded,° to know your pleasure.
KING.   Bring him before us.
ROSENCRANTZ.   Ho, bring in the lord. 15

Enter HAMLET (guarded) and GUILDENSTERN.

KING.   Now Hamlet, where's Polonius?
HAMLET.   At supper.
KING.   At supper? where?
HAMLET.   Not where he eats, but where a' is eaten: a certain
    convocation of politic° worms are e'en° at him. Your worm is your 20
    only emperor for diet, we fat all creatures else to fat us,
    and we fat ourselves for maggots. Your fat king and your
    lean beggar is but variable service,° two dishes but to one
    table, that's the end.
KING.   Alas, alas. 25
HAMLET.   A man may fish with the worm that hath eat of a king, and
    eat of the fish that hath fed of that worm.
KING.   What dost thou mean by this?
HAMLET.   Nothing but to show you how a king may go a progress°
    through the guts of a beggar. 30
KING.   Where is Polonius?
HAMLET.   In heaven, send thither to see. If your messenger find him
    not there, seek him i'th'other place yourself: but if indeed
    you find him not within this month, you shall nose him as
    you go up the stairs into the lobby. 35
KING.   [*To Attendants.*] Go seek him there.
HAMLET.   A' will stay till you come.   [*Exeunt.*]
KING.   Hamlet, this deed, for thine especial safety—
    Which we do tender,° as we dearly grieve
    For that which thou hast done—must send thee hence 40
    With fiery quickness. Therefore prepare thyself,
    The bark is ready, and the wind at help,°
    Th'associates tend,° and every thing is bent
    For England.

---

9 *Deliberate pause:* considered delay.   10 *appliance:* remedy.   14 *guarded:* (Hamlet is under
guard until he boards the ship).   20 *politic:* (1) statesmanlike (2) crafty.   *e'en:* even now.
23 *variable service:* different types of food.   29 *go a progress:* make a splendid royal journey from
one part of the country to another.   39 *tender:* cherish.   42 *at help:* helpful.   43 *tend:*
wait.

HAMLET.   For England.
KING.   Ay Hamlet.
HAMLET.   Good.
KING.   So is it if thou knew'st our purposes.
HAMLET.   I see a cherub° that sees them: but come, for England.
    Farewell dear mother.
KING.   Thy loving father, Hamlet.
HAMLET.   My mother: father and mother is man and wife, man and
    wife is one flesh, and so my mother: come, for England.   *Exit.*   5
KING.   [*To ROSENCRANTZ and GUILDENSTERN.*]
    Follow him at foot,° tempt him with speed aboard,
    Delay it not, I'll have him hence tonight.
    Away, for every thing is sealed and done
    That else leans on° th'affair, pray you make haste.   [*Exeunt.*]
    And England,° if my love thou hold'st at aught°—   5
    As my great power thereof may give thee sense,
    Since yet thy cicatrice° looks raw and red
    After the Danish sword, and thy free awe
    Pays homage° to us—thou mayst not coldly set°
    Our sovereign process,° which imports at full   6
    By letters congruing° to that effect,
    The present° death of Hamlet. Do it England,
    For like the hectic° in my blood he rages,
    And thou must cure me; till I know 'tis done,
    Howe'er my haps,° my joys were ne'er begun.   *Exit.*   6

Scene 4. [*A plain in Denmark*]

Enter FORTINBRAS with his army over the stage.

FORTINBRAS.   Go captain, from me greet the Danish king,
    Tell him that by his license, Fortinbras
    Craves the conveyance° of a promised march
    Over his kingdom. You know the rendezvous:
    If that his majesty would aught with us,
    We shall express our duty in his eye,°
    And let him know so.
CAPTAIN.   I will do't, my lord.
FORTINBRAS.   Go softly° on.   *Exit.*

Enter HAMLET, ROSENCRANTZ, [GUILDENSTERN,] etc.

HAMLET.   Good sir whose powers° are these?
CAPTAIN.   They are of Norway sir.
HAMLET.   How purposed sir I pray you?

46 *cherub:* (considered the watchmen of heaven).   51 *at foot:* at his heels.   54 *leans on:*
relates to.   55 *England:* King of England.   *my love . . . aught:* you place any value on my
favor.   57 *cicatrice:* scar.   58–59 *free . . . homage:* awe which you, though free, still show by
paying homage.   59 *coldly set:* lightly estimate.   60 *process:* command.   61 *congruing:*
agreeing.   62 *present:* immediate.   63 *hectic:* fever.   65 *haps:* fortunes.   3 *conveyance
of:* escort for.   6 *in his eye:* face to face.   8 *softly:* slowly.   9 *powers:* troops.

CAPTAIN. Against some part of Poland.
HAMLET. Who commands them sir?
CAPTAIN. The nephew to old Norway, Fortinbras.
HAMLET. Goes it against the main° of Poland sir,   15
   Or for some frontier?
CAPTAIN. Truly to speak, and with no addition,
   We go to gain a little patch of ground
   That hath in it no profit but the name.°
   To pay five ducats, five, I would not farm it;   20
   Nor will it yield to Norway or the Pole
   A ranker° rate, should it be sold in fee.°
HAMLET. Why then the Polack never will defend it.
CAPTAIN. Yes, it is already garrisoned.
HAMLET. Two thousand souls, and twenty thousand ducats   25
   Will not debate the question of° this straw:°
   This is th'imposthume of much wealth and peace,°
   That inward breaks, and shows no cause without
   Why the man dies. I humbly thank you sir.
CAPTAIN. God bye you sir.   [*Exit.*]
ROSENCRANTZ.   Will't please you go my lord?   30
HAMLET. I'll be with you straight, go a little before.

                              [*Exeunt all but* HAMLET.]

   How all occasions do inform against me,
   And spur my dull revenge. What is a man
   If his chief good and market° of his time
   Be but to sleep and feed? a beast, no more: 35
   Sure he that made us with such large discourse,°
   Looking before and after,° gave us not
   That capability and god-like reason
   To fust° in us unused. Now whether it be
   Bestial oblivion,° or some craven° scruple   40
   Of thinking too precisely on th'event°—
   A thought which quartered hath but one part wisdom,
   And ever three parts coward—I do not know
   Why yet I live to say "This thing's to do,"
   Sith I have cause, and will, and strength, and means   45
   To do't; examples gross° as earth exhort me:
   Witness this army of such mass and charge,°
   Led by a delicate and tender° prince,
   Whose spirit with divine ambition puffed,

---

15 *main:* body.   19 *name:* glory.   22 *ranker:* higher (as annual interest on the total).
in fee: outright.   26 *debate . . . of:* settle the dispute over.   *straw:* triviality.
27 *imposthume . . . peace:* swelling discontent (inner abscess) resulting from too much wealth and
peace.   34 *market:* profit.   36 *discourse:* power of reasoning.   37 *Looking . . . after:* seeing
causes and effects.   39 *fust:* grow moldy.   40 *Bestial oblivion:* forgetfulness, as a beast forgets
its parents.   *craven:* cowardly.   41 *event:* outcome.   46 *gross:* obvious.
47 *charge:* expense.   48 *delicate and tender:* gentle and young.

Makes mouths° at the invisible event,°
Exposing what is mortal, and unsure,
To all that fortune, death, and danger dare,
Even for an egg-shell. Rightly to be great,
Is not to stir without great argument,
But greatly to find quarrel in a straw
When honour's at the stake.° How stand I then
That have a father killed, a mother stained,
Excitements° of my reason, and my blood,
And let all sleep, while to my shame I see
The imminent death of twenty thousand men,
That for a fantasy and trick° of fame
Go to their graves like beds, fight for a plot
Whereon the numbers cannot try the cause,°
Which is not tomb enough and continent°
To hide the slain. O from this time forth,
My thoughts be bloody, or be nothing worth.   *Exit.*

Scene 5. [*A room in the castle*]

Enter QUEEN, HORATIO *and a* GENTLEMAN.

QUEEN.   I will not speak with her.
GENTLEMAN.   She is importunate, indeed distract,°
   Her mood will needs be° pitied.
QUEEN.   What would she have?
GENTLEMAN.   She speaks much of her father, says she hears
   There's tricks i'th'world, and hems,° and beats her heart,
   Spurns enviously at straws,° speaks things in doubt°
   That carry but half sense: her speech is nothing,
   Yet the unshapèd use of it doth move
   The hearers to collection;° they aim° at it,
   And botch° the words up fit to their own thoughts,
   Which as her winks, and nods, and gestures yield them,
   Indeed would make one think there might be thought,
   Though nothing sure, yet much unhappily.
HORATIO.   'Twere good she were spoken with, for she may strew
   Dangerous conjectures in ill-breeding minds.
QUEEN.   Let her come in.   *Exit* GENTLEMAN.
   [*Aside.*] To my sick soul, as sin's true nature is,°
   Each toy° seems prologue to some great amiss,°

---

50 *mouths:* faces.   *event:* outcome.   53–56 *Rightly . . . stake:* the truly great do not fight without just cause ("argument"), but it is nobly ("greatly") done to fight even for a trifle if honor is at stake.   58 *Excitements:* incentives.   61 *fantasy and trick:* illusion and trifle.
63 *Whereon . . . cause:* too small to accommodate all the troops fighting for it.   64 *continent:* container.   2 *distract:* insane.   3 *will needs be:* needs to be.   5 *hems:* coughs.   6 *Spurns . . . straws:* reacts maliciously to trifles.   *in doubt:* ambiguous.   9 *collection:* inference. *aim:* guess.   10 *botch:* patch.   17 *as sin's . . . is:* as is natural for the guilty.   18 *toy:* trifle. *amiss:* disaster.

So full of artless jealousy° is guilt,
It spills itself, in fearing to be spilt.   20

Enter OPHELIA, distracted.°

OPHELIA.   Where is the beauteous majesty of Denmark?
QUEEN.   How now Ophelia?
OPHELIA.   [*Sings.*] How should I your true love know
                From another one?
                By his cockle hat and staff,°   25
                And his sandal shoon.°
QUEEN.   Alas sweet lady, what imports this song?
OPHELIA.   Say you? nay, pray you mark.
        [*Sings.*] He is dead and gone, lady,
                He is dead and gone,   30
                At his head a grass-green turf,
                At his heels a stone.
    O ho.
QUEEN.   Nay but Ophelia—
OPHELIA   Pray you mark.
    [*Sings.*] White his shroud as the mountain snow—

Enter KING.

QUEEN.   Alas, look here my lord.   35
OPHELIA.   [*Sings.*] Larded° all with sweet flowers,
           Which bewept to the ground did not go,
           With true-love showers.
KING.   How do you, pretty lady?
OPHELIA.   Well, God 'ild° you. They say the owl was a baker's   40
daughter.° Lord, we know what we are, but know not what
we may be. God be at your table.°
KING   Conceit° upon her father.
OPHELIA.   Pray you let's have no words of this, but when they ask
you what it means, say you this: 45

    [*Sings.*] Tomorrow is Saint Valentine's day,

        All in the morning betime,°
      And I a maid at your window
        To be your Valentine.
      Then up he rose, and donned his clo'es,   50
        And dupped° the chamber door,
      Let in the maid, that out a maid,
        Never departed more.

19 *artless jealousy:* uncontrollable suspicion.   20 stage direction: *distracted:* insane.   25 *cockle hat and staff:* (marks of the pilgrim, the cockle shell symbolizing his journey to the shrine of St. James; the pilgrim was a common metaphor for the lover).   26 *shoon:* shoes.   36 *Larded:* trimmed.   40 *God 'ild:* God yield (reward).   40–41 *owl . . . daughter:* (in a medieval legend, a baker's daughter was turned into an owl because she gave Jesus short weight on a loaf of bread).   42 *God . . . table:* (a blessing at dinner).   43 *Conceit:* thinking.   47 *betime:* early (because the first woman a man saw on Valentine's Day would be his true love).   51 *dupped:* opened.

KING.   Pretty Ophelia.

OPHELIA.   Indeed, la, without an oath I'll make an end on't.   55

> [*Sings.*] By Gis° and by Saint Charity,
>   Alack and fie for shame,
>   Young men will do't, if they come to't,
>   By Cock° they are to blame.
>   Quoth she, Before you tumbled me,   60
>   You promised me to wed.

(He answers)

>   So would I ha' done, by yonder sun,
>   An° thou hadst not come to my bed.

KING.   How long hath she been thus?   65

OPHELIA.   I hope all will be well. We must be patient, but I cannot
choose but weep to think they would lay him i'th'cold
ground. My brother shall know of it, and so I thank you
for your good counsel. Come, my coach: good night
ladies, good night. Sweet ladies, good night, good night.   [*Exit* OPHELIA.]   70

KING.   Follow her close, give her good watch I pray you.   [*Exit* HORATIO.]
O this is the poison of deep grief, it springs
All from her father's death, and now behold:
O Gertrude, Gertrude,
When sorrows come, they come not single spies,   75
But in battalions: first her father slain,
Next, your son gone, and he most violent author
Of his own just remove, the people muddied,°
Thick and unwholesome in their thoughts and whispers
For good Polonius' death: and we have done but greenly°   80
In hugger-mugger° to inter him: poor Ophelia
Divided from herself and her fair judgment,
Without the which we are pictures or mere beasts,
Last, and as much containing° as all these,
Her brother is in secret come from France,   85
Feeds on his wonder,° keeps himself in clouds,°
And wants not buzzers° to infect his ear
With pestilent speeches of his father's death,
Wherein necessity, of matter beggared,
Will nothing stick our person to arraign°   90
In ear and ear:° O my dear Gertrude, this
Like to a murdering-piece° in many places
Gives me superfluous death.   *A noise within.*

---

56 *Gis:* contraction of "Jesus."   59 *Cock:* (vulgarization of "God" in oaths).   64 *An:* if.
78 *muddied:* stirred up.   80 *done but greenly:* acted like amateurs.   81 *hugger-mugger:* secret
haste.   84 *containing:* i.e., cause for sorrow.   86 *Feeds . . . wonder:* sustains himself by
wondering about his father's death.   *clouds:* gloom, obscurity.   87 *wants not buzzers:* lacks
not whispering gossips.   89–90 *Wherein . . . arraign:* in which the tellers, lacking facts, will not
hesitate to accuse me.   91 *In ear and ear:* whispering from one ear to another.
92 *murdering-piece:* small cannon shooting shrapnel, to inflict numerous wounds.

QUEEN.   Alack, what noise is this?
KING.   Attend!   *Enter a MESSENGER.*
   Where are my Switzers°? Let them guard the door.   95
   What is the matter?
MESSENGER.   Save yourself, my lord.
   The ocean, overpeering of his list,°
   Eats not the flats° with more impiteous haste
   Than young Laertes in a riotous head°
   O'erbears your officers: the rabble call him lord,   100
   And as the world were now but to begin,
   Antiquity forgot, custom not known,
   The ratifiers and props of every word,
   They cry "Choose we, Laertes shall be king!"
   Caps, hands, and tongues applaud it to the clouds,   105
   "Laertes shall be king, Laertes king!"   *A noise within.*
QUEEN.   How cheerfully on the false trail they cry.
   O this is counter,° you false Danish dogs.
KING.   The doors are broke.

Enter LAERTES with others.

LAERTES.   Where is this king? Sirs, stand you all without.°   110
DANES.   No, let's come in.
LAERTES.   I pray you give me leave.°
DANES.   We will, we will.   [*They retire.*]
LAERTES.   I thank you, keep the door. O thou vile king,
   Give me my father.
QUEEN.   Calmly, good Laertes.
LAERTES.   That drop of blood that's calm proclaims me bastard,   115
   Cries cuckold° to my father, brands° the harlot
   Even here between the chaste unsmirchèd brows
   Of my true mother.
KING.   What is the cause Laertes,
   That thy rebellion looks so giant-like?
   Let him go Gertrude, do not fear° our person,   120
   There's such divinity° doth hedge a king,
   That treason can but peep to° what it would,
   Acts little of his° will. Tell me Laertes,
   Why thou art this incensed. Let him go Gertrude.
   Speak man.   125
LAERTES.   Where is my father?
KING.   Dead.
QUEEN.   But not by him.

---

95 *Switzers:* Swiss guards.   97 *overpeering . . . list:* rising above its usual limits.   98 *flats:*
lowlands.   99 *head:* armed force.   108 *counter:* following the scent backward.
110 *without:* outside.   111 *leave:* i.e., to enter alone.   116 *cuckold:* betrayed husband.
brands: (so harlots were punished).   120 *fear:* i.e., for.   121 *divinity:* divine protection.
122 *peep to:* strain to see.   123 *his:* treason's.

KING.   Let him demand his fill.
LAERTES.   How came he dead? I'll not be juggled with.
      To hell allegiance, vows to the blackest devil,
      Conscience and grace, to the profoundest pit.   135
      I dare damnation: to this point I stand,
      That both the worlds I give to negligence,°
      Let come what comes, only I'll be revenged
      Most throughly for my father.
KING.   Who shall stay you?
LAERTES.   My will, not all the world's:°   135
      And for my means, I'll husband° them so well,
      They shall go far with little.
KING.   Good Laertes,
      If you desire to know the certainty
      Of your dear father, is't writ in your revenge
      That swoopstake,° you will draw both friend and foe,   140
      Winner and loser?
LAERTES.   None but his enemies.
KING.   Will you know them then?
LAERTES.   To his good friends thus wide I'll ope my arms,
      And like the kind life-rend'ring pelican,°
      Repast them with my blood.
KING.   Why now you speak   14
      Like a good child, and a true gentleman.
      That I am guiltless of your father's death,
      And am most sensibly° in grief for it,
      It shall as level° to your judgment 'pear
      As day does to your eye.   15

      [*A noise within.*]

      [*Crowd shouts.*] Let her come in.
LAERTES.   How now, what noise is that?

Enter OPHELIA.

      O heat, dry up my brains, tears seven time salt,
      Burn out the sense and virtue° of mine eye!
      By heaven, thy madness shall be paid with weight,°
      Till our scale turn the beam,° O rose of May,   15
      Dear maid, kind sister, sweet Ophelia:
      O heavens, is't possible a young maid's wits
      Should be as mortal as an old man's life?

---

132 *both . . . negligence:* I care nothing for this world or the next.   135 *world's:* i.e., will.
136 *husband:* economize.   140 *swoopstake:* sweeping in all the stakes in a game, both of winner and loser.   144 *pelican:* (the mother pelican was believed to nourish her young with
blood pecked from her own breast).   148 *sensibly:* feelingly.   149 *level:* plain.   153 *sense
and virtue:* feeling and power.   154 *with weight:* with equal weight.   155 *turn the beam:* out-
weigh the other side.

Nature is fine in love, and where 'tis fine,
It sends some previous instance of itself 160
after the thing it loves.°
OPHELIA. [*Sings.*] They bore him barefaced on the bier,
        Hey non nonny, nonny, hey nonny:
        And in his grave rained many a tear—
       Fare you well my dove. 165
LAERTES. Hadst thou thy wits, and didst persuade revenge,
It could not move thus.
OPHELIA. You must sing "adown adown," and you call him adown-a.
O how the wheel becomes it.° It is the false steward that
stole his master's daughter. 170
LAERTES. This nothing's more than matter.°
OPHELIA. There's rosemary,° that's for remembrance, pray you love
remember: and there is pansies, that's for thoughts.
LAERTES. A document° in madness, thoughts and remembrance
fitted.° 175
OPHELIA. There's fennel for you, and columbines.° There's rue° for
you, and here's some for me, we may call it herb of grace°
o'Sundays: O, you must wear your rue with a difference.°
There's a daisy,° I would give you some violets,° but they
withered all when my father died: they say a' made a good 180
end;
       [*Sings.*] For bonny sweet Robin is all my joy.
LAERTES. Thought and affliction, passion, hell itself,
She turns to favour and to prettiness.
OPHELIA. [*Sings.*] And will a' not come again, 185
        And will a' not come again?
        No, no, he is dead,
        Go to thy death-bed,
        He never will come again.
        His beard was as white as snow, 190
        All flaxen was his poll,°
        He is gone, he is gone,
        And we cast away moan,
        God ha' mercy on his soul.
And of all Christian souls, I pray God. God bye you. 195

                                    Exit OPHELIA.

159–161 *Nature . . . loves:* filial love that is so refined and pure sends some precious token (her wits) after the beloved dead.　　169 *wheel becomes it:* refrain ("adown") suits the subject (Polonius's fall).　　171 *more than matter:* more eloquent than sane speech.　　172 *There's rosemary:* (given to Laertes; she may be distributing imaginary or real flowers).　　174 *document:* lesson.　　*thoughts . . . fitted:* thoughts of revenge matched with remembrance of Polonius. 176 *fennel, columbines:* (given to the king, symbolizing flattery and ingratitude).　　*rue:* (given to the queen, symbolizing sorrow or repentance).　　177 *herb of grace:* (because it symbolizes repentance).　　178 *with a difference:* for a different reason (Ophelia's is for sorrow and the queen's for repentance).　　179 *daisy:* (symbolizing dissembling).　　*violets:* (symbolizing faithfulness).　　191 *flaxen . . . poll:* white was his head.

LAERTES.   Do you see this, O God?
KING.   Laertes, I must commune with your grief,
　　Or you deny me right: go but apart,
　　Make choice of whom your wisest friends you will,
　　And they shall hear and judge 'twixt you and me;　　　　　　　　20
　　If by direct or by collateral° hand
　　They find us touched,° we will our kingdom give,
　　Our crown, our life, and all that we call ours
　　To you in satisfaction; but if not,
　　Be you content to lend your patience to us,　　　　　　　　　　20
　　And we shall jointly labour with your soul
　　To give it due content.
LAERTES.　　　　　　　　Let this be so.
　　His means of death, his obscure funeral,
　　No trophy,° sword, nor hatchment° o'er his bones,
　　No noble rite, nor formal ostentation,°　　　　　　　　　　　21
　　Cry° to be heard as 'twere from heaven to earth,
　　That I must call't in question.
KING.　　　　　　　　So you shall,
　　And where th'offence is, let the great axe fall.
　　I pray you go with me.　　　　　　　　　　　　　　[*Exeunt.*]

Scene 6. [*Another room in the castle*]

Enter HORATIO and others.
HORATIO.   What are they that would speak with me?
GENTLEMAN.   Seafaring men sir, they say they have letters for you.
HORATIO.   Let them come in.　　　　　　　　[*Exit ATTENDANT.*]
　　I do not know from what part of the world
　　I should be greeted, if not from Lord Hamlet.

Enter SAILORS.

SAILOR.   God bless you sir.
HORATIO.   Let him bless thee too.
SAILOR.   A' shall sir, an't please him. There's a letter for you sir, it
　　came from th'ambassador that was bound for England, if
　　your name be Horatio, as I am let to know it is.　　　　　　　1(
HORATIO.   [*Reads the letter.*] "Horatio, when thou shalt have
　　overlooked° this, give these fellows some means to the king,
　　they have letters for him. Ere we were two days old at sea,
　　a pirate of very warlike appointment° gave us chase.
　　Finding ourselves too slow of sail, we put on a compelled　　　1
　　valour, and in the grapple° I boarded them. On the instant
　　they got clear of our ship, so I alone became their prisoner.
　　They have dealt with me like thieves of mercy,° but they

201 *collateral:* indirect.　　202 *touched:* tainted with guilt.　　209 *trophy:* memorial.
hatchment: tablet displaying coat of arms.　　210 *ostentation:* ceremony.　　211 *Cry:* cry out.
12 *overlooked:* read over.　　14 *appointment:* equipment.　　16 *in the grapple:* when the pirate
ship hooked onto ours.　　18 *of mercy:* merciful.

knew what they did. I am to do a good turn for them. Let
the king have the letters I have sent, and repair° thou to me   20
with as much speed as thou wouldst fly death. I have
words to speak in thine ear will make thee dumb, yet are
they much too light for the bore° of the matter. These good
fellows will bring thee where I am. Rosencrantz and
Guildenstern hold their course for England. Of them I   25
have much to tell thee. Farewell.
        He that thou knowest thine, Hamlet."
Come, I will give you way° for these your letters,
And do't the speedier that you may direct me
To him from whom you brought them.   *Exeunt.*   30

Scene 7. *[Another room in the castle]*

Enter KING *and* LAERTES.

KING. Now must your conscience my acquittance seal,°
        And you must put me in your heart for friend,
        Sith you have heard and with a knowing ear,
        That he which hath your noble father slain
        Pursued my life.
LAERTES.   It well appears: but tell me   5
        Why you proceeded not against these feats
        So crimeful and so capital in nature,
        As by your safety, greatness, wisdom, all things else,
        You mainly were stirred up.°
KING.   O for two special reasons,
        Which may to you perhaps seem much unsinewed,°   10
        But yet to me they're strong. The queen his mother
        Lives almost by his looks, and for myself,
        My virtue or my plague, be it either which,
        She's so conjunctive° to my life and soul,
        That as the star moves not but in his sphere,°   15
        I could not but by her. The other motive,
        Why to a public count° I might not go,
        Is the great love the general gender° bear him,
        Who dipping all his faults in their affection,
        Would like the spring that turneth wood to stone,°   20
        Convert his gyves to graces,° so that my arrows,
        Too slightly timbered° for so loud a wind,
        Would have reverted to my bow again,
        And not where I had aimed them.

20 *repair:* come.   23 *bore:* size, caliber.   28 *way:* access (to the king).   1 *my acquittance
seal:* confirm my acquittal.   9 *mainly . . . up:* were strongly urged.   10 *much unsinewed:* very
weak.   14 *conjunctive:* closely allied.   15 *in his sphere:* (referring to the Ptolemaic belief that
each planet, fixed in its own sphere, revolved around the earth).   17 *count:* accounting.
18 *general gender:* common people.   20 *the spring . . . stone:* (the baths of King's Newnham in
Warwickshire were described as being able to turn wood into stone because of their high
concentrations of lime).   21 *Convert . . . graces:* regard his fetters (had he been imprisoned)
as honors.   22 *slightly timbered:* light-shafted.

LAERTES.   And so have I a noble father lost,
  A sister driven into desperate terms,°
  Whose worth, if praises may go back° again,
  Stood challenger on mount of all the age
  For her perfections.° But my revenge will come.
KING.   Break not your sleeps for that, you must not think
  That we are made of stuff so flat and dull,
  That we can let our beard be shook with danger,
  And think it pastime. You shortly shall hear more,
  I loved your father, and we love ourself,
  And that I hope will teach you to imagine—

Enter a MESSENGER with letters.

  How now. What news?
MESSENGER.   Letters my lord, from Hamlet.
  These to your majesty, this to the queen.
KING.   From Hamlet? Who brought them?
MESSENGER.   Sailors my lord they say, I saw them not:
  They were given me by Claudio, he received them
  Of him that brought them.
KING.   Laertes you shall hear them:
  Leave us.   *Exit [MESSENGER]*
  [*Reads*] "High and mighty, you shall know I am set naked° on
  your kingdom. Tomorrow shall I beg leave to see your kingly
  eyes, when I shall, first asking your pardon° thereunto,
  recount the occasion of my sudden and more strange return
                                        Hamlet."
  What should this mean? Are all the rest come back?
  Or is it some abuse,° and no such thing?
LAERTES.   Know you the hand?
KING.   'Tis Hamlet's character.° "Naked,"
  And in a postscript here he says "alone."
  Can you devise° me?
LAERTES.   I am lost in it my lord, but let him come,
  It warms the very sickness in my heart
  That I shall live and tell him to his teeth,
  "Thus didest thou."
KING.   If it be so Laertes—
  As how should it be so? how otherwise?—
  Will you be ruled by me?
LAERTES.   Ay my lord,
  So you will not o'errule me to a peace.
KING.   To thine own peace: if he be now returned,
  As checking at° his voyage, and that he means

---

26 *desperate terms:* madness.   27 *go back:* i.e., before her madness.   28–29 *challenger . . . perfections:* like a challenger on horseback, ready to defend against the world her claim to perfection.   43 *naked:* without resources.   45 *pardon:* permission.   49 *abuse:* deception.   50 *character:* handwriting.   52 *devise me:* explain it.   61 *checking at:* altering the course of (when the falcon forsakes one quarry for another).

No more to undertake it, I will work him
To an exploit, now ripe in my device,°
Under the which he shall not choose but fall:
And for his death no wind of blame shall breathe,   65
But even his mother shall uncharge the practice,°
And call it accident.

LAERTES.   My lord, I will be ruled,
The rather if you could devise it so
That I might be the organ.°

KING.   It falls right.
You have been talked of since your travel much,   70
And that in Hamlet's hearing, for a quality
Wherein they say you shine: your sum of parts°
Did not together pluck such envy from him
As did that one, and that in my regard
Of the unworthiest siege.°

LAERTES.   What part is that my lord?   75

KING.   A very riband° in the cap of youth,
Yet needful too, for youth no less becomes°
The light and careless livery° that it wears,
Than settled age his sables° and his weeds°
Importing health and graveness; two months since,°   80
Here was a gentleman of Normandy—
I have seen myself, and served against the French,
And they can° well on horseback—but this gallant
Had witchcraft in't, he grew unto his seat,
And to such wondrous doing brought his horse,   85
As had he been incorpsed and demi-natured°
With the brave beast. So far he topped my thought,
That I in forgery of° shapes and tricks
Come short of what he did.

LAERTES.   A Norman was't?

KING.   A Norman.   90

LAERTES.   Upon my life, Lamord.

KING.   The very same.

LAERTES.   I know him well, he is the brooch° indeed
And gem of all the nation.

KING.   He made confession° of you,
And gave you such a masterly report   95
For art and exercise in your defence,
And for your rapier most especial,
That he cried out 'twould be a sight indeed

---

63 *ripe in my device:* already planned by me.   66 *uncharge the practice:* acquit the plot (of
treachery).   69 *organ:* instrument.   72 *your sum of parts:* all your accomplishments.
75 *siege:* rank.   76 *riband:* decoration.   77 *becomes:* befits.   78 *livery:* clothing (denoting
rank or occupation).   79 *sables:* fur-trimmed gowns.   *weeds:* garments.   80 *since:* ago.
83 *can:* can do.   86 *incorpsed . . . natured:* made into one body, sharing half its nature.
88 *in forgery of:* imagining.   92 *brooch:* ornament.   94 *confession:* report.

If one could match you; the scrimers° of their nation
He swore had neither motion, guard, nor eye,   10
If you opposed them; sir this report of his
Did Hamlet so envenom° with his envy,
That he could nothing do but wish and beg
Your sudden coming o'er to play with him.
Now out of this—

LAERTES.   What out of this, my lord?   10
KING.   Laertes, was your father dear to you?
    Or are you like the painting of a sorrow,
    A face without a heart?

LAERTES.   Why ask you this?
KING.   Not that I think you did not love your father,
    But that I know love is begun by time,
    And that I see in passages of proof,°   11
    Time qualifies° the spark and fire of it:
    There lives within the very flame of love
    A kind of wick or snuff that will abate it,°
    And nothing is at a like goodness still,°   11
    For goodness growing to a plurisy,°
    Dies in his own too-much. That we would do
    We should do when we would: for this "would"° changes,
    And hath abatements and delays as many
    As there are tongues, are hands, are accidents,   12
    And then this "should"° is like a spendthrift sigh,
    That hurts by easing;° but to the quick° of th'ulcer:
    Hamlet comes back, what would you undertake
    To show yourself in deed your father's son
    More than in words?

LAERTES.   To cut his throat i'th'church.   12
KING.   No place indeed should murder sanctuarize,°
    Revenge should have no bounds: but good Laertes,
    Will you do this, keep close within your chamber:
    Hamlet returned shall know you are come home,
    We'll put on° those shall praise your excellence,   13
    And set a double varnish on the fame
    The Frenchman gave you, bring you in fine° together,
    And wager on your heads; he being remiss,°
    Most generous, and free from all contriving,
    Will not peruse the foils, so that with ease,   13
    Or with a little shuffling, you may choose

---

99 *scrimers:* fencers.   102 *envenom:* poison.   111 *passages of proof:* examples drawn from
experience.   112 *qualifies:* weakens.   114 *snuff . . . it:* charred end of the wick that will
diminish the flame.   115 *still:* always.   116 *plurisy:* excess.   118 *"would":* will to act.
121 *"should":* reminder of one's duty.   121–122 *spendthrift . . . easing:* A sigh which, though
giving temporary relief, wastes life, as each sigh draws a drop of blood away from the heart (a
common Elizabethan belief).   122 *quick:* most sensitive spot.   126 *murder sanctuarize:* give
sanctuary to murder.   130 *put on:* incite.   132 *in fine:* finally.   133 *remiss:* easy-going.

A sword unbated,° and in a pass of practice°
Requite him for your father.
LAERTES.   I will do't,
    And for the purpose, I'll anoint my sword.
    I bought an unction° of a mountebank°   140
    So mortal,° that but dip a knife in it,
    Where it draws blood, no cataplasm° so rare,
    Collected from all simples° that have virtue°
    Under the moon,° can save the thing from death
    That is but scratched withal: I'll touch my point   145
    With this contagion, that if I gall° him slightly,
    It may be death.
KING.   Let's further think of this,
    Weigh what convenience both of time and means
    May fit us to our shape;° if this should fail,
    And that our drift° look through° our bad performance,   150
    'Twere better not assayed; therefore this project
    Should have a back or second that might hold
    If this did blast in proof;° soft, let me see,
    We'll make a solemn wager on your cunnings°—
    I ha't: 155
    When in your motion you are hot and dry,
    As make your bouts more violent to that end,
    And that he calls for drink, I'll have prepared him
    A chalice for the nonce,° whereon but sipping,
    If he by chance escape your venomed stuck,°   160
    Our purpose may hold there; but stay, what noise?

Enter QUEEN.

    How, sweet queen?
QUEEN.   One woe doth tread upon another's heel,
    So fast they follow; your sister's drowned, Laertes.
LAERTES.   Drowned! O where?   165
QUEEN.   There is a willow grows aslant a brook,
    That shows his hoar° leaves in the glassy stream,
    There with fantastic garlands did she make
    Of crow-flowers,° nettles, daisies, and long purples,°
    That liberal° shepherds give a grosser name,   170
    But our cold° maids do dead men's fingers call them.
    There on the pendent boughs her coronet weeds°

---

137 *unbated:* not blunted (the edges and points were blunted for fencing).   *pass of practice:*
(1) match for exercise (2) treacherous thrust.   140 *unction:* ointment.   *mountebank:* quack
doctor, medicine man.   141 *mortal:* deadly.   142 *cataplasm:* poultice.   143 *simples:*
herbs.   *virtue:* power (of healing).   144 *Under the moon:* (when herbs were supposed to be
collected to be most effective).   146 *gall:* scratch.   149 *shape:* plan.   150 *drift:* aim.
look through: be exposed by.   153 *blast in proof:* fail when tested (as a bursting cannon).
154 *cunnings:* skills.   159 *nonce:* occasion.   160 *stuck:* thrust.   167 *hoar:* grey (on the
underside).   169 *crow-flowers:* buttercups.   *long purples:* spikelike early orchid.
170 *liberal:* libertine.   171 *cold:* chaste.   172 *coronet weeds:* garland of weeds.

Clamb'ring to hang, an envious sliver° broke,
When down her weedy trophies and herself
Fell in the weeping brook: her clothes spread wide,   1͗
And mermaid-like awhile they bore her up,
Which time she chanted snatches of old tunes,
As one incapable of° her own distress,
Or like a creature native and indued
Unto° that element: but long it could not be   18
Till that her garments, heavy with their drink,
Pulled the poor wretch from her melodious lay
To muddy death.

LAERTES.   Alas, then she is drowned?

QUEEN.   Drowned, drowned.

LAERTES.   Too much of water hast thou, poor Ophelia,   18
And therefore I forbid my tears; but yet
It is our trick, nature her custom holds,
Let shame say what it will; when these° are gone,
The woman will be out.° Adieu my lord,
I have a speech o' fire that fain would blaze,   1ς
But that this folly douts it.°   *Exit.*

KING.   Let's follow, Gertrude,
How much I had to do to calm his rage;
Now fear I this will give it start again,
Therefore let's follow.   *Exeunt.*

[ACT 5]

Scene 1. *[A churchyard]*

Enter two CLOWNS.°

1. CLOWN.   Is she to be buried in Christian burial,° when she wilfully
   seeks her own salvation?°

2. CLOWN.   I tell thee she is, therefore make her grave straight.° The
   crowner hath sat on her,° and finds it Christian burial.

1. CLOWN.   How can that be, unless she drowned herself in her own
   defence?°

2. CLOWN.   Why, 'tis found so.

1. CLOWN.   It must be "se offendendo,"° it cannot be else: for here lies
   the point: if I drown myself wittingly, it argues an act,

---

173 *envious sliver:* malicious branch   178 *incapable of:* unable to understand.
179–180 *indued Unto:* endowed by nature to exist in.   188 *these:* i.e., tears.   189 *woman . . .
out:* womanly habits will be out of me.   191 *folly douts it:* tears put it out.   0.2 Stage
direction: *clowns:* rustics.   1 *Christian burial:* consecrated ground within a churchyard (where
suicides were not allowed burial).   2 *salvation:* i.e., "damnation." The gravediggers make a
number of such "mistakes," later termed "malapropisms."   3 *straight:* straightaway, at once.
4 *crowner . . . her:* coroner has ruled on her case.   5–6 *her own defence:* (as self-defense justifies
homicide, so may it justify suicide).   8 *"se offendendo":* (he means *"se defendendo,"* in
self-defense).

and an act hath three branches, it is to act, to do, and to   10
perform; argal,° she drowned herself wittingly.

2. CLOWN.   Nay, but hear you, goodman delver.

1. CLOWN.   Give me leave: here lies the water, good. Here stands the
man, good. If the man go to this water and drown himself,
it is, will he nill he,° he goes, mark you that. But if the   15
water come to him, and drown him, he drowns not
himself. Argal, he that is not guilty of his own death, shortens not his own
life.

2. CLOWN.   But is this law?

1. CLOWN.   Ay marry is't, crowner's quest° law.   20

2. CLOWN.   Will you ha' the truth on't? If this had not been a
gentlewoman, she would have been buried out o'Christian
burial.

1. CLOWN.   Why there thou say'st, and the more pity that great folk
should have countenance° in this world to drown or hang   25
themselves more than their even-Christen.° Come, my
spade; there is no ancient gentlemen but gardeners,
ditchers and grave-makers; they hold up Adam's profession.

2. CLOWN.   Was he a gentleman?

1. CLOWN.   A' was the first that ever bore arms.°   30

2. CLOWN.   Why, he had none.

1. CLOWN.   What, art a heathen? How dost thou understand the
Scripture? The Scripture says Adam digged; could he dig
without arms? I'll put another question to thee; if thou
answerest me not to the purpose, confess thyself—   35

2. CLOWN.   Go to.

1. CLOWN.   What is he that builds stronger than either the mason, the
shipwright, or the carpenter?

2. CLOWN.   The gallows-maker, for that frame outlives a thousand
tenants.   40

1. CLOWN.   I like thy wit well in good faith, the gallows does well, but
how does it well? It does well to those that do ill. Now
thou dost ill to say the gallows is built stronger than the
church. Argal, the gallows may do well to thee.° To't
again, come.   45

2. CLOWN.   'Who builds stronger than a mason, a shipwright, or a
carpenter?'

1. CLOWN.   Ay, tell me that, and unyoke.°

2. CLOWN.   Marry, now I can tell.

1. CLOWN.   To't.   50

2. CLOWN.   Mass,° I cannot tell.

1. CLOWN.   Cudgel thy brains no more about it, for your dull ass will
not mend his pace with beating, and when you are asked
this question next, say "a grave-maker:" the houses he

---

11 *argal:* (corruption of "ergo" = therefore).   15 *will he nill he:* will he or will he not (willy
nilly).   20 *quest:* inquest.   25 *countenance:* privilege.   26 *even-Christen:* fellow Christian.
30 *arms:* (with a pun on "coat of arms").   44 *to thee:* i.e., by hanging you.   48 *unyoke:*
unharness (your wits, after this exertion).   51 *Mass:* by the mass.

makes last till doomsday. Go get thee to Yaughan,° and
fetch me a stoup° of liquor.   [*Exit 2. CLOWN.*]

Enter HAMLET and HORATIO afar off.

1. CLOWN.   (*Sings.*) In youth when I did love, did love,
                         Methought it was very sweet,
                    To contract oh the time for a° my behove,°
                    O methought there a was nothing a meet.°
HAMLET.   Has this fellow no feeling of his business, that a'sings in
    grave-making?
HORATIO.   Custom hath made it in him a property of easiness.°
HAMLET.   'Tis e'en so, the hand of little employment hath the
    daintier sense.°
1. CLOWN.   (*Sings.*) But age with his stealing steps
                    Hath clawed me in his clutch,
                    And hath shipped me intil° the land,
                    As if I had never been such.   [*Throws up a skull.*]
HAMLET.   That skull had a tongue in it, and could sing once: how the
    knave jowls° it to the ground, as if 'twere Cain's jaw-bone,°
    that did the first murder. This might be the pate of a
    politician, which this ass now o'erreaches;° one that
    would circumvent° God, might it not?
HORATIO.   It might my lord.
HAMLET.   Or of a courtier, which could say "Good morrow sweet
    lord, how dost thou good lord?" This might be my lord
    such-a-one, that praised my lord such-a-one's horse, when
    a'meant to beg it, might it not?
HORATIO.   It might my lord.
HAMLET.   Why e'en so, and now my Lady Worm's, chopless,° and
    knocked about the mazzard° with a sexton's spade; here's
    fine revolution an° we had the trick° to see't. Did these
    bones cost no more the breeding, but to play at loggets°
    with them? Mine ache to think on't.
1. CLOWN.   (*Sings.*) A pick-axe and a spade, a spade,
                    For and a shrouding sheet,
                    O a pit of clay for to be made
                    For such a guest is meet.°   [*Throws up another skull.*]
HAMLET.   There's another: why may not that be the skull of a
    lawyer? Where be his quiddities° now, his quillets,° his
    cases, his tenures,° and his tricks? Why does he suffer this
    rude knave now to knock him about the sconce° with a

---

55 *Yaughan:* probably a local innkeeper.   56 *stoup:* stein, drinking mug.   59 *oh, a:* (he
grunts as he works).   *behove:* benefit.   60 *meet:* suitable.   63 *Custom . . . easiness:* being
accustomed to it has made him indifferent.   65 *daintier sense:* finer sensibility (being
uncalloused).   68 *intil:* into.   71 *jowls:* casts (with obvious pun).   *Cain's jaw-bone:* the
jawbone of an ass with which Cain murdered Abel.   73 *o'erreaches:* (1) reaches over (2) gets
the better of.   74 *would circumvent:* tried to outwit.   81 *chopless:* lacking the lower jaw.
82 *mazzard:* head.   83 *an:* if.   *trick:* knack.   84 *loggets:* game in which small pieces of
wood were thrown at fixed stakes.   89 *meet:* fitting.   91 *quiddities:* subtle definition.
quillets: minute distinctions.   92 *tenures:* property holdings.   93 *sconce:* head.

dirty shovel, and will not tell him of his action of battery?
Hum, this fellow might be in's time a great buyer of land, 95
with his statutes,° his recognizances,° his fines,° his double
vouchers,° his recoveries:° is this the fine° of his fines, and
the recovery° of his recoveries, to have his fine pate full of
fine dirt? Will his vouchers vouch him no more of his
purchases, and double ones too, than the length and 100
breadth of a pair of indentures?° The very conveyances° of
his lands will scarcely lie in this box,° and must th'inheritor°
himself have no more, ha?

HORATIO.   Not a jot more my lord.

HAMLET.   Is not parchment made of sheep-skins? 105

HORATIO.   Ay my lord, and of calves'-skins too.

HAMLET.   They are sheep and calves which seek out assurance° in
that. I will speak to this fellow. Whose grave's this, sirrah?

1. CLOWN.   Mine sir:
            [*Sings.*] O a pit of clay for to be made 110
            For such a guest is meet.

HAMLET.   I think it be thine indeed, for thou liest in't.

1. CLOWN.   You lie out on't° sir, and therefore 'tis not yours; for my
part I do not lie in't, and yet it is mine.

HAMLET.   Thous dost lie in't, to be in't and say it is thine: 'tis for the 115
dead, not for the quick,° therefore thou liest.

1. CLOWN.   'Tis a quick lie sir, 'twill away again from me to you.

HAMLET.   What man dost thou dig it for?

1. CLOWN.   For no man sir.

HAMLET.   What woman then? 120

1. CLOWN.   For none neither.

HAMLET.   Who is to be buried in't?

1. CLOWN.   One that was a woman sir, but rest her soul she's dead.

HAMLET.   How absolute° the knave is, we must speak by the card,° or
equivocation° will undo us. By the lord, Horatio, this 125
three years I have took note of it, the age is grown so
picked,° that the toe of the peasant comes so near the heel of
the courtier, he galls his kibe.° How long hast thou been
grave-maker?

1. CLOWN.   Of all the days i'th'year I came to't that day that our last 130
king Hamlet overcame Fortinbras.

HAMLET.   How long is that since?

1. CLOWN.   Cannot you tell that? Every fool can tell that. It was the very
day that young Hamlet was born: he that is mad and
sent into England. 135

---

96 *statutes:* mortgages.   *recognizances:* promissory bonds.   96–97 *fines, recoveries:* legal
processes for transferring real estate.   97 *vouchers:* persons who vouched for a title to real
estate.   *fine:* end.   98 *recovery:* attainment.   100–101 *length . . . indentures:* contracts in
duplicate, which spread out, would just cover his grave.   101 *conveyances:* deeds.   102 *box:*
the grave.   *inheritor:* owner.   107 *assurance:* (1) security (2) transfer of land.   113 *on:* of.
116 *quick:* living.   124 *absolute:* precise.   *by the card:* exactly to the point (card on which
compass points are marked).   125 *equivocation:* ambiguity.   127 *picked:* fastidious ("picky").
128 *galls his kibe:* chafes the sore on the courtier's heel.

HAMLET.   Ay marry, why was he sent into England?

1. CLOWN.   Why because a' was mad: a' shall recover his wits there, or
 if a' do not, 'tis no great matter there.

HAMLET.   Why?

1. CLOWN.   'Twill not be seen in him there, there the men are as mad   14
 as he.

HAMLET.   How came he mad?

1. CLOWN.   Very strangely they say.

HAMLET.   How strangely?

1. CLOWN.   Faith, e'en with losing his wits.   14

HAMLET.   Upon what ground?

1. CLOWN.   Why here in Denmark: I have been sexton here man and
 boy thirty years.

HAMLET.   How long will a man lie i'ith'earth ere he rot?

1. CLOWN.   Faith, if a' be not rotten before a' die, as we have many   15
 pocky° corses nowadays that will scarce hold the laying in,
 a' will last you some eight year, or nine year. A tanner will
 last you nine year.

HAMLET.   Why he more than another?

1. CLOWN.   Why sir, his hide is so tanned with his trade, that a' will   15
 keep out water a great while; and your water is a sore°
 decayer of your whoreson dead body. Here's a skull now:
 this skull hath lain you i'th'earth three-and-twenty years.

HAMLET.   Whose was it?

1. CLOWN.   A whoreson mad fellow's it was, whose do you think it   16
 was?

HAMLET.   Nay, I know not.

1. CLOWN.   A pestilence on him for a mad rogue, a' poured a flagon of
 Rhenish° on my head once; this same skull sir, was sir,
 Yorick's skull, the king's jester.   16

HAMLET.   This?

1. CLOWN.   E'en that.

HAMLET.   Let me see. [*Takes the skull.*] Alas poor Yorick, I knew him
 Horatio, a fellow of infinite jest, of most excellent fancy,°
 he hath borne me on his back a thousand times: and now   17
 how abhorred in my imagination it is: my gorge rises at it.
 Here hung those lips that I have kissed I know not how
 oft. Where be your gibes now? your gambols, your songs,
 your flashes of merriment, that were wont to set the table
 on a roar?° not one now to mock your own grinning? quite   17
 chop-fallen?° Now get you to my lady's chamber, and tell
 her, let her paint an inch thick, to this favour° she must
 come. Make her laugh at that. Prithee Horatio, tell me one
 thing.

HORATIO.   What's that, my lord?   18

---

151 *pocky:* rotten (with venereal disease).   156 *sore:* grievous.   164 *Rhenish:* Rhine wine.
169 *fancy:* imagination.   175 *on a roar:* roaring with laughter.   176 *chop-fallen:* (a) lacking
a lower jaw (2) dejected, "down in the mouth."   177 *favour:* appearance.

HAMLET.   Dost thou think Alexander looked o' this fashion
    i'th'earth?
HORATIO.   E'en so.
HAMLET.   And smelt so? pah.   [*Puts down the skull.*]
HORATIO.   E'en so my lord.   185
HAMLET.   To what base uses we may return, Horatio. Why may not
    imagination trace the noble dust of Alexander, til a'find it
    stopping a bung-hole?°
HORATIO.   'Twere to consider too curiously,° to consider so.
HAMLET.   No faith, not a jot, but to follow him thither with modesty°   190
    enough, and likelihood to lead it; as thus: Alexander died,
    Alexander was buried, Alexander returneth to dust, the
    dust is earth, of earth we make loam,° and why of that loam
    whereto he was converted, might they not stop a
    beer-barrel?   195
      Imperious Caesar, dead and turned to clay,
      Might stop a hole to keep the wind away.
      O that that earth which kept the world in awe,
      Should patch a wall t'expel the winter's flaw.°
    But soft, but soft awhile, here comes the king,   200
    The queen, the courtiers.

Enter KING, QUEEN, LAERTES, *[Doctor of Divinity], and a coffin, with Lords attendant.*

               Who is this they follow?
    And with such maimèd° rites? This doth betoken
    The corse they follow did with desp'rate hand
    Fordo it° own life; 'twas of some estate.°
    Couch° we awhile, and mark.   [*They retire.*]   205
HAMLET.   That is Laertes,
    A very noble youth: mark.
LAERTES.   What ceremony else?
DOCTOR.   Her obsequies have been as far enlarged
    As we have warranty: her death was doubtful,°   210
    And but that great command o'ersways the order,
    She should in ground unsanctified have lodged
    Til the last trumpet: for charitable prayers,
    Shards,° flints and pebbles should be thrown on her:
    Yet here she is allowed her virgin crants,°   215
    Her maiden strewments,° and the bringing home
    Of° bell and burial.
LAERTES.   Must there no more be done?
DOCTOR.   No more be done:
    We should profane the service of the dead,
    To sing sage requiem° and such rest to her   220
    As to peace-parted souls.

188 *bung-hole:* hole in a cask.   189 *curiously:* minutely.   190 *modesty:* moderation.
193 *loam:* a clay mixture used as plaster.   199 *flaw:* windy gusts.   202 *maimèd:* abbreviated.
204 *Fordo it:* destroy its.   *estate:* social rank.   205 *Couch:* hide.   210 *doubtful:* suspicious.
214 *Shards:* bits of broken pottery.   215 *crants:* garland.   216 *strewments:* flowers strewn on
the grave.   216–217 *bringing home Of:* laying to rest with.   220 *sage requiem:* solemn dirge.

LAERTES.   Lay her i'th'earth,
 And from her fair and unpolluted flesh
 May violets spring: I tell thee churlish priest,
 A minist'ring angel shall my sister be,
 When thou liest howling.
HAMLET.   What, the fair Ophelia?   2?
QUEEN.   [*Scattering flowers.*] Sweets to the sweet, farewell.
 I hoped thou shouldst have been my Hamlet's wife:
 I thought thy bride-bed to have decked, sweet maid,
 And not have strewed thy grave.
LAERTES.   O treble woe
 Fall ten times treble on that cursèd head   2?
 Whose wicked deed thy most ingenious sense°
 Deprived thee of. Hold off the earth awhile,
 Till I have caught her once more in mine arms;   *Leaps in the grave.*
 Now pile your dust upon the quick° and dead,
 Till of this flat a mountain you have made   2.
 T'o'ertop old Pelion,° or the skyish head
 Of blue Olympus.
HAMLET.   [*Comes forward.*] What is he whose grief
 Bears such an emphasis? whose phrase of sorrow
 Conjures the wand'ring stars,° and makes them stand
 Like wonder-wounded hearers? This is I,   2
 Hamlet the Dane.   HAMLET *leaps in after* LAERTES.
LAERTES.   [*Grapples with him.*] The devil take thy soul.
HAMLET.   Thou pray'st not well,
 I prithee take thy fingers from my throat,
 For though I am not splenitive° and rash,
 Yet have I in me something dangerous,   2
 Which let thy wiseness fear; hold off thy hand.
KING.   Pluck them asunder.
QUEEN.   Hamlet, Hamlet!
ALL.   Gentlemen!
HORATIO.   Good my lord, be quiet.

                    [*Attendants part them, and they come out of the grave.*]

HAMLET.   Why, I will fight with him upon this theme
 Until my eyelids will no longer wag.   2
QUEEN.   O my son, what theme?
HAMLET.   I loved Ophelia, forty thousand brothers
 Could not with all their quantity of love
 Make up my sum. What wilt thou do for her?
KING.   O he is mad, Laertes.   2
QUEEN.   For love of God, forbear° him.

---

231 *sense:* mind.   234 *quick:* live.   236 *Pelion:* mountain (on which the Titans placed Mt.
Ossa, to scale Mt. Olympus and reach the gods).   239 *Conjures . . . stars:* casts a spell over the
planets.   244 *spenitive:* quick-tempered (anger was thought to originate in the spleen).
256 *forbear:* be patient with.

HAMLET.   'Swounds,° show me what thou't do:
    Woo't° weep? woo't fight? woo't fast? woo't tear thyself?
    Woo't drink up eisel?° eat a crocodile?°
    I'll do't. Dost thou come here to whine?   260
    To outface me with leaping in her grave?
    Be buried quick with her, and so will I.
    And if thou prate of mountains, let them throw
    Millions of acres on us, till our ground,
    Singeing his pate against the burning zone,°   265
    Make Ossa° like a wart. Nay, an thou'lt mouth,
    I'll rant as well as thou.
QUEEN.   This is mere° madness,
    And thus awhile the fit will work on him:
    Anon as patient as the female dove
    When that her golden couplets° are disclosed,   270
    His silence will sit drooping.
HAMLET.   Hear you sir,
    What is the reason that you use me thus?
    I loved you ever; but it is no matter.
    Let Hercules himself do what he may,
    The cat will mew, and dog will have his day.   *Exit HAMLET.* 275
KING.   I pray thee good Horatio, wait upon him.   [*HORATIO* follows.]
    [*Aside to Laertes.*] Strengthen your patience in our last night's speech,
    We'll put the matter to the present push°—
    Good Gertrude, set some watch over your son—
    This grave shall have a living monument:°   280
    An hour of quiet shortly shall we see,
    Till then, in patience our proceeding be.   *Exeunt.*

Scene 2. *[A hall in the castle]*

Enter HAMLET and HORATIO.
HAMLET.   So much for this sir, now shall you see the other;
    You do remember all the circumstance.
HORATIO.   Remember it my lord!
HAMLET.   Sir, in my heart there was a kind of fighting
    That would not let me sleep; methought I lay   5
    Worse than the mutines in the bilboes.° Rashly—
    And praised be rashness for it: let us know,
    Our indiscretion sometimes serves us well
    When our deep plots do pall,° and that should learn us
    There's a divinity that shapes our ends,   10
    Rough-hew them how we will—

---

257 *'Swounds:* corruption of "God's wounds."   258 *Woo't:* wilt thou.   259 *eisel:* vinegar
(thought to reduce anger and encourage melancholy).   *crocodile:* (associated with
hypocritical tears).   265 *burning zone:* sun's sphere.   266 *Ossa:* (see above, line 236 n.).
267 *mere:* absolute.   270 *golden couplets:* fuzzy yellow twin fledglings.   278 *present push:*
immediate test.   280 *living monument:* (1) lasting tombstone (2) living sacrifice (Hamlet) to
memorialize it.   6 *mutines . . . bilboes:* mutineers in shackles.   9 *pall:* fail.

HORATIO.   That is most certain.

HAMLET.   Up from my cabin,
My sea-gown° scarfed about me, in the dark
Groped I to find out them, had my desire,
Fingered° their packet, and in fine° withdrew
To mine own room again, making so bold,
My fears forgetting manners, to unseal
Their grand commission; where I found, Horatio—
Ah royal knavery—an exact command,
Larded° with many several sorts of reasons,
Importing Denmark's health, and England's too,
With ho, such bugs and goblins in my life,°
That on the supervise,° no leisure bated,°
No, not to stay° the grinding of the axe,
My head should be struck off.

HORATIO.   Is't possible?

HAMLET.   Here's the commission, read it at more leisure.
But wilt thou hear now how I did proceed?

HORATIO.   I beseech you.

HAMLET.   Being thus be-netted round with villainies,
Ere I could make a prologue to my brains,
They had begun the play.° I sat me down,
Devised a new commission, wrote it fair°—
I once did hold it, as our statists° do,
A baseness° to write fair, and laboured much
How to forget that learning, but sir now
It did me yeoman's° service: wilt thou know
Th'effect of what I wrote?

HORATIO.   Ay, good my lord.

HAMLET.   An earnest conjuration° from the king,
As England was his faithful tributary,
As love between them like the palm might flourish,
As peace should still her wheaten garland wear
And stand a comma° 'tween their amities,
And many such like "as'es"° of great charge,°
That on the view and know of these contents,
Without debatement further, more or less,
He should those bearers put to sudden death,
Not shriving° time allowed.

---

13 *sea-gown:* short-sleeved knee-length gown worn by seamen.   15 *Fingered:* got my fingers on.
in fine: to finish.   20 *Larded:* embellished.   22 *bugs . . . life:* imaginary evils attributed to me,
like imaginary goblins ("bugs") meant to frighten children.   23 *supervise:* looking over (the
commission).   *leisure bated:* delay excepted.   24 *stay:* await.   30–31 *Ere . . . play:* Before I
could outline the action in my mind, my brains started to play their part.   32 *wrote it fair:*
wrote a finished (neat) copy, a "fair copy."   33 *statists:* statesmen.   34 *baseness:* mark of
humble status.   36 *yeoman's:* (in the sense of "faithful").   38 *conjuration:* entreaty (he parodies the rhetoric of such documents).   42 *comma:* connection.   43 *as'es:* (1) the "as"
clauses in the commission (2) asses.   *charge:* (1) weight (in the clauses) (2) burdens (on the
asses).   47 *shriving:* confession and absolution.

HORATIO.   How was this sealed?
HAMLET.   Why even in that was heaven ordinant,°
   I had my father's signet° in my purse,
   Which was the model° of that Danish seal: 50
   Folded the writ up in the form of th'other,
   Subscribed° it, gave't th'impression,° placed it safely,
   The changeling° never known: now the next day
   Was our sea-fight, and what to this was sequent
   Thou knowest already.   55
HORATIO.   So Guildenstern and Rosencrantz go to't.
HAMLET.   Why man, they did make love to this employment,°
   They are not near my conscience, their defeat
   Does by their own insinuation° grow:
   'Tis dangerous when the baser nature comes   60
   Between the pass° and fell° incensed points
   Of mighty opposites.
HORATIO.   Why, what a king is this!
HAMLET.   Does it not, think thee, stand me now upon°—
   He that hath killed my king, and whored my mother,
   Popped in between th'election° and my hopes,   65
   Thrown out his angle° for my proper° life,
   And with such cozenage°—is't not perfect conscience
   To quit° him with this arm? And is't not to be damned,
   To let this canker of our nature° come
   In further evil?   70
HORATIO.   It must be shortly known to him from England
   What is the issue of the business there.
HAMLET.   It will be short, the interim is mine,
   And a man's life's no more than to say "One."°
   But I am very sorry good Horatio,   75
   That to Laertes I forgot myself;
   For by the image of my cause, I see
   The portraiture of his;° I'll court his favours:
   But sure the bravery° of his grief did put me
   Into a towering passion.
HORATIO.   Peace, who comes here?   80

Enter young OSRIC.

OSRIC.   Your lordship is right welcome back to Denmark.
HAMLET.   I humbly thank you sir. [*Aside to Horatio.*] Dost know this
   water-fly?

---

48 *was heaven ordinant:* it was divinely ordained.   49 *signet:* seal.   50 *model:* replica.
52 *Subscribed:* signed.   *impression:* i.e., of the seal.   53 *changeling:* substitute (baby imp left
when an infant was spirited away).   57 *did . . . employment:* asked for it.   59 *insinuation:*
intrusion.   61 *pass:* thrust.   *fell:* fierce.   63 *stand . . . upon:* become incumbent upon me
now.   65 *election:* (the Danish king was so chosen).   66 *angle:* fishing hook.   *proper:* very
own.   67 *cozenage:* deception.   68 *quit:* repay, requite.   69 *canker of our nature:* cancer of
humanity.   74 *to say "One":* to score one hit in fencing.   77–78 *by the image . . . his:* in the
depiction of my situation, I see the reflection of his.   79 *bravery:* ostentation.

HORATIO.   No my good lord.

HAMLET.   Thy state is the more gracious,° for 'tis a vice to know him: 8
   he hath much land, and fertile: let a beast be lord of beasts,
   and his crib shall stand at the king's mess;° 'tis a chough,°
   but as I say, spacious in the possession of dirt.

OSRIC.   Sweet lord, if your lordship were at leisure, I should
   impart a thing to you from his majesty.   9

HAMLET.   I will receive it sir, with all diligence of spirit; put your
   bonnet° to his right use, 'tis for the head.

OSRIC.   I thank your lordship, it is very hot.

HAMLET.   No, believe me, 'tis very cold, the wind is northerly.

OSRIC.   It is indifferent° cold my lord indeed.   9

HAMLET.   But yet methinks it is very sultry and hot for my
   complexion.°

OSRIC.   Exceedingly, my lord, it is very sultry, as 'twere, I cannot
   tell how: but my lord, his majesty bade me signify to you
   that a' has laid a great wager on your head. Sir, this is the   10
   matter—

HAMLET.   [*Moves him to put on his hat.*] I beseech you remember—

OSRIC.   Nay good my lord, for mine ease,° in good faith. Sir, here
   is newly come to court Laertes, believe me, an absolute
   gentleman, full of most excellent differences,° of very soft   10
   society, and great showing: indeed to speak feelingly of
   him, he is the card° or calendar of gentry: for you shall find
   in him the continent of what part a gentleman would see.°

HAMLET.   Sir, his definement° suffers no perdition° in you, though I
   know to divide him inventorially would dozy°   11
   th'arithmetic of memory, and yet but yaw neither, in
   respect of his quick sail,° but in the verity of extolment,° I
   take him to be a soul of great article,° and his infusion° of
   such dearth and rareness, as to make true diction of him,
   his semblable° is his mirror, and who else would trace° him,
   his umbrage,° nothing more.°   11

OSRIC.   Your lordship speaks most infallibly of him.

HAMLET.   The concernancy° sir? why do we wrap the gentleman in
   our more rawer breath?°

---

85 *gracious:* favorable.   86–87 *let a beast . . . mess:* An ass who owns enough property can eat
with the king.   87 *chough:* chattering bird, jackdaw.   92 *bonnet:* hat.   95 *indifferent:*
reasonably.   97 *complexion:* temperament.   103 *for mine ease:* for my own comfort.
105 *differences:* accomplishments.   107 *card:* shipman's compass card.   108 *continent . . . see:*
(continuing the marine metaphor) (1) geographical continent (2) all the qualities a
gentleman would look for.   109–116 *Sir . . . more:* (Hamlet outdoes Osric in affected speech).
109 *definement:* description.   *perdition:* loss.   110 *dozy:* dizzy.   111–112 *yaw . . . sail:* (1)
moving in an unsteady course (as another boat would do, trying to catch up with Laertes' "quick
sail") (2) staggering to one trying to list his accomplishments.   112 *in . . . extolment:* to praise
him truthfully.   113 *article:* scope.   *infusion:* essence.   114–116 *as to make . . . more:* to
describe him truly I would have to employ his mirror to depict his only equal—himself, and who
would follow him is only a shadow.   115 *semblable:* equal.   *trace:* (1) describe (2) follow.
116 *umbrage:* shadow.   118 *concernancy:* relevance.   119 *rawer breath:* crude speech.

OSRIC.   Sir?   120
HORATIO.   Is't not possible to understand in another tongue?° You
    will do't sir, really.
HAMLET.   What imports the nomination° of this gentleman?
OSRIC.   Of Laertes?
HORATIO.   His purse is empty already, all's golden words are spent.   125
HAMLET.   Of him, sir.
OSRIC.   I know you are not ignorant—
HAMLET.   I would you did sir, yet in faith if you did, it would not
    much approve me.° Well, sir.
OSRIC.   You are not ignorant of what excellence Laertes is—   130
HAMLET.   I dare not confess that, lest I should compare with him in
    excellence, but to know a man well were to know himself.°
OSRIC.   I mean sir for his weapon, but in the imputation° laid on
    him by them in his meed,° he's unfellowed.°
HAMLET.   What's his weapon?   135
OSRIC.   Rapier and dagger.
HAMLET.   That's two of his weapons—but well.
OSRIC.   The king sir, hath wagered with him six Barbary horses,
    against which he has impawned,° as I take it, six French
    rapiers and poniards,° with their assigns,° as girdle, hangers,°   140
    and so. Three of the carriages° in faith are very dear to
    fancy,° very responsive to the hilts, most delicate carriages,
    and of very liberal conceit.°
HAMLET.   What call you the carriages?
HORATIO.   I knew you must be edified by the margent° ere you had   145
    done.
OSRIC.   The carriages sir, are the hangers.
HAMLET.   The phrase would be more germane to the matter, if we
    could carry a cannon by our sides: I would it might be
    hangers till then, but on: six Barbary horses against six   150
    French swords, their assigns, and three liberal-conceited
    carriages—that's the French bet against the Danish. Why
    is this all "impawned" as you call it?
OSRIC.   The king sir, hath laid sir, that in a dozen passes between
    yourself and him, he shall not exceed you three hits°; he   155
    hath laid on twelve for nine, and it would come to
    immediate trial, if your lordship would vouchsafe the
    answer.°

---

121 *Is't not . . . tongue:* Cannot Osric understand his own way of speaking when used by another?
123 *nomination:* naming.   128–129 *if you did . . . me:* If you found me to be "not ignorant," it
would prove little (as you are no judge of ignorance).   132 *to know . . . himself:* to know a man
well, one must first know oneself.   133 *imputation:* repute.   134 *meed:* worth.   *unfellowed:*
unequaled.   139 *impawned:* staked.   140 *poniards:* daggers.   *assigns:* accessories.
girdle, hangers: belt, straps attached thereto, from which swords were hung.   141 *carriages:*
hangers.   141–142 *dear to fancy:* rare in design.   143 *liberal conceit:* elaborate conception.
145 *margent:* marginal note.   154–155 *laid . . . three hits:* wagered that in twelve bouts Laertes
must win three more than Hamlet.   158 *answer:* acceptance of the challenge (Hamlet
interprets as "reply").

HAMLET.   How if I answer no?

OSRIC.   I mean my lord, the opposition of your person in trial.

HAMLET.   Sir, I will walk here in the hall; if it please his majesty, it is
the breathing time° of day with me; let the foils be brought,
the gentleman willing, and the king hold his purpose, I
will win for him an I can, if not, I will gain nothing but my
shame and the odd hits.

OSRIC.   Shall I re-deliver you° e'en so?

HAMLET.   To this effect sir, after what flourish your nature will.°

OSRIC.   I commend° my duty to your lordship.

HAMLET.   Yours, yours.   [*Exit* OSRIC.]
He does well to commend it himself, there are no tongues
else for's turn.°

HORATIO.   This lapwing° runs away with the shell on his head.

HAMLET.   A' did comply° sir, with his dug° before a' sucked it: thus
has he—and many more of the same bevy that I know the
drossy° age dotes on—only got the tune of the time, and
out of an habit of encounter,° a kind of yeasty collection,°
which carries them through and through the most fond
and winnowed° opinions; and do but blow them to their
trial, and bubbles are out.°

Enter a LORD.

LORD.   My lord, his majesty commended him to you by young
Osric, who brings back to him that you attend him in
the hall. He sends to know if your pleasure hold to play
with Laertes, or that you will take longer time.

HAMLET.   I am constant to my purposes, they follow the king's
pleasure, if his fitness speaks,° mine is ready: now or
whensoever, provided I be so able as now.

LORD.   The king, and queen, and all are coming down.

HAMLET.   In happy time.

LORD.   The queen desires you to use some gentle entertainment°
to Laertes, before you fall to play.

HAMLET.   She well instructs me.   [*Exit* LORD.]

HORATIO.   You will lose this wager, my lord.

HAMLET.   I do not think so, since we went into France, I have been in
continual practice, I shall win at the odds; but thou
wouldst not think how ill all's here about my heart: but it
is no matter.

HORATIO.   Nay good my lord—

163 *breathing time:* exercise period.   166 *re-deliver you:* take back your answer.
167 *after . . . will:* embellished as you wish.   168 *commend:* offer (Hamlet interprets as "praise").
170–171 *no tongues . . . turn:* no others who would.   172 *lapwing:* (reported to be so precocious
that it ran as soon as hatched).   173 *comply:* observe the formalities of
courtesy.   *dug:* mother's breast.   175 *drossy:* frivolous.   176 *habit of encounter:* habitual
association (with others as frivolous).   *yeasty collection:* frothy assortment of phrases.
177–178 *fond and winnowed:* trivial and considered.   178–179 *blow . . . out:* blow on them to
test them and they are gone.   185 *his fitness speaks:* it agrees with his convenience.
189 *gentle entertainment:* friendly treatment.

HAMLET.   It is but a foolery, but it is such a kind of gaingiving° as
    would perhaps trouble a woman.
HORATIO.   If your mind dislike any thing, obey it. I will forestall their   200
    repair° hither, and say you are not fit.
HAMLET.   Not a whit, we defy augury;° there is a special providence
    in the fall of a sparrow.° If it be now, 'tis not to come:
    if it be not to come, it will be now; if it be not now,
    yet it will come—the readiness is all. Since no man has   205
    aught of what he leaves, what is't to leave betimes?° let
    be.

A table prepared. Trumpets, Drums, and officers with cushions. Enter KING, QUEEN, *and all
the state,* [OSRIC], *foils daggers, and* LAERTES.

KING.   Come Hamlet, come and take this hand from me.
    [*Puts Laertes' hand into Hamlet's.*]
HAMLET.   Give me your pardon sir, I have done you wrong,
    But pardon't as you are a gentleman.   210
    This presence knows, and you must needs have heard,
    How I am punished with a sore distraction.°
    What I have done
    That might your nature, honour, and exception°
    Roughly awake, I here proclaim was madness: 215
    Was't Hamlet wronged Laertes? never Hamlet.
    If Hamlet from himself be ta'en away,
    And when he's not himself, does wrong Laertes,
    Then Hamlet does it not, Hamlet denies it:
    Who does it then? his madness. If't be so,   220
    Hamlet is of the faction that is wronged,
    His madness is poor Hamlet's enemy.
    Sir, in this audience,
    Let my disclaiming from a purposed evil,
    Free me so far in your most generous thoughts,   225
    That I have shot my arrow o'er the house
    And hurt my brother.°
LAERTES.   I am satisfied in nature,
    Whose motive in this case should stir me most
    To my revenge, but in my terms of honour
    I stand aloof, and will no reconcilement,   230
    Till by some elder masters of known honour
    I have a voice and precedent° of peace
    To keep my name ungored:° but till that time,

---

198 *gaingiving:* misgiving.   201 *repair:* coming.   202 *augury:* omens.
202–203 *special . . . sparrow:* ("Are not two sparrows sold for a farthing? and one of them shall
not fall on the ground without your Father": Matthew 10:29).   206 *betimes:* early (before one's
time).   212 *sore distraction:* grievous madness.   214 *exception:* disapproval.
226–227 *That I have . . . brother:* (that it was accidental).   232 *voice and precedent:* opinion based
on precedent.   233 *name ungored:* reputation uninjured. Laertes says that he cannot accept
Hamlet's apology formally until he is assured that his acceptance will not harm his honor or
damage his reputation.

I do receive your offered love, like love,
And will not wrong it.

HAMLET.   I embrace it freely,   23
And will this brother's wager frankly° play.
Give us the foils: come on.

LAERTES.   Come, one for me.

HAMLET.   I'll be your foil° Laertes, in mine ignorance
Your skill shall like a star i'th' darkest night
Stick fiery off° indeed.   24

LAERTES.   You mock me sir.

HAMLET. No, by this hand.

KING.   Give them the foils young Osric. Cousin° Hamlet,
You know the wager.

HAMLET.   Very well my lord.
Your grace has laid the odds o'th'weaker side.

KING.   I do not fear it, I have seen you both,   24
But since he is bettered,° we have therefore odds.

LAERTES.   This is too heavy: let me see another.°

HAMLET.   This likes° me well, these foils have all a° length?

OSRIC.   Ay my good lord.   *Prepare to play.*

KING.   Set me the stoups° of wine upon that table: 25
If Hamlet give the first or second hit,
Or quit in answer of° the third exchange,
Let all the battlements their ordnance fire.
The king shall drink to Hamlet's better breath,
And in the cup an union° shall he throw,   25
Richer than that which four successive kings
In Denmark's crown have worn: give me the cups,
And let the kettle° to the trumpet speak,
The trumpet to the cannoneer without,
The cannons to the heavens, the heaven to earth,   26
"Now the king drinks to Hamlet." Come begin.
And you the judges bear a wary eye.   *Trumpets the while.*

HAMLET.   Come on sir.

LAERTES.   Come my lord.   *They play.*

HAMLET.   One.

LAERTES.   No.

HAMLET.   Judgment.

OSRIC.   A hit, a very palpable hit.

Flourish. Drum, trumpets and shot. A piece° goes off.

---

236 *frankly:* freely.   238 *foil:* (1) the blunted sword with which they fence (2) leaf of metal set
under a jewel to make it shine more brilliantly.   240 *Stick fiery off:* show in shining contrast.
242 *Cousin:* kinsman.   246 *bettered:* either (a) judged to be better, or (b) better trained.
247 *another:* (the unbated and poisoned sword).   248 *likes:* pleases.   *all a:* all the same.
250 *stoups:* goblets.   252 *quit in answer of:* score a draw in.   255 *union:* large pearl.
258 *kettle:* kettledrum.   264.1 stage direction: *piece:* i.e., a cannon.

LAERTES.   Well, again.

KING.   Stay, give me drink. Hamlet, this pearl is thine.   265
   Here's to thy health: give him the cup.

HAMLET.   I'll play this bout first, set it by a while.
   Come.   [*They play.*]
             Another hit. What say you?

LAERTES.   A touch, a touch, I do confess't.

KING.   Our son shall win.

QUEEN.   He's fat° and scant of breath.   270
   Here Hamlet, take my napkin,° rub thy brows.   [*She takes HAMLET'S cup.*]
   The queen carouses° to thy fortune, Hamlet.

HAMLET.   Good madam.

KING.   Gertrude, do not drink.

QUEEN.   I will my lord, I pray you pardon me.

KING.   [*Aside.*] It is the poisoned cup, it is too late.   275

HAMLET.   I dare not drink yet madam: by and by.

QUEEN.   Come, let me wipe thy face.

LAERTES.   [*To the King.*] My lord, I'll hit him now.

KING.   I do not think't.

LAERTES.   [*Aside.*] And yet 'tis almost 'gainst my conscience.

HAMLET.   Come for the third Laertes, you do but dally,   280
   I pray you pass° with your best violence,
   I am afeard you make a wanton of me.°

LAERTES.   Say you so? Come on.   *Play.*

OSRIC.   Nothing neither way   [*They break off.*]

LAERTES.   Have at you now.°   [*Wounds Hamlet.*]

                              In scuffling they change rapiers.

KING.   Part them, they are incensed.   285

HAMLET.   Nay, come again.   [*The QUEEN falls.*]

OSRIC.   Look to the queen there, ho!

                              [*HAMLET wounds LAERTES.*]

HORATIO.   They bleed on both side. How is it, my lord?

OSRIC.   How is't, Laertes?

LAERTES.   Why as a woodcock° to my own springe,° Osric,
   I am justly killed with mine own treachery.   290

HAMLET.   How does the queen?

KING.   She sounds° to see them bleed.

QUEEN.   No, no, the drink, the drink, O my dear Hamlet,
   The drink, the drink, I am poisoned.   [*Dies.*]

270 *fat:* sweating (sweat was thought to be melted body fat).   271 *napkin:* handkerchief.
272 *carouses:* drinks.   281 *pass:* thrust.   282 *make a wanton of me:* are indulging me like a
spoiled child.   285 *Have . . . now:* (the bout is over when Laertes attacks Hamlet and catches
him off guard).   289 *woodcock:* snipe-like bird (believed to be foolish and therefore easily
trapped).   *springe:* trap.   291 *sounds:* swoons.

HAMLET.   O villainy! ho! let the door be locked,
　　Treachery, seek it out!   2⁹

LAERTES.   It is here Hamlet. Hamlet, thou art slain,
　　No medicine in the world can do thee good,
　　In thee there is not half an hour of life,
　　The treacherous instrument is in thy hand,
　　Unbated° and envenomed. The foul practice°   30
　　Hath turned itself on me, lo, here I lie
　　Never to rise again: thy mother's poisoned:
　　I can no more: the king, the king's to blame.

HAMLET.   The point envenomed too:
　　Then venom, to thy work.   *Hurts the* KING.   30

ALL.   Treason! treason!

KING.   O yet defend me friends, I am but hurt.°

HAMLET.   Here, thou incestuous, murderous, damnèd Dane,
　　Drink off this potion: is thy union here?
　　Follow my mother.   *King dies.*   31

LAERTES.   He is justly served,
　　It is a poison tempered° by himself:
　　Exchange forgiveness with me, noble Hamlet,
　　Mine and my father's death come not upon thee,°
　　Nor thine on me.   *Dies.*

HAMLET.   Heaven make thee free° of it, I follow thee.   31
　　I am dead, Horatio; wretched queen, adieu.
　　You that look pale, and tremble at this chance,
　　That are but mutes,° or audience to this act,
　　Had I but time, as this fell sergeant° Death
　　Is strict in his arrest, O I could tell you—   32
　　But let it be; Horatio, I am dead,
　　Thou livest, report me and my cause aright
　　To the unsatisfied.°

HORATIO.   Never believe it;
　　I am more an antique Roman° than a Dane:
　　Here's yet some liquor left.

HAMLET.   As thou'rt a man,   32
　　Give me the cup, let go, by heaven I'll ha't.
　　O God, Horatio, what a wounded name,
　　Things standing thus unknown, shall live behind me.
　　If thou didst ever hold me in thy heart,
　　Absènt thee from felicity awhile,   33
　　And in this harsh world draw thy breath in pain
　　To tell my story.   *A march afar off, and shot within.*
　　　　　　　What warlike noise is this?

OSRIC.   Young Fortinbras with conquest come from Poland,

---

300 *Unbated:* not blunted.   *practice:* plot.   307 *but hurt:* only wounded.   311 *tempered:*
mixed.   313 *come . . . thee:* are not to be blamed on you.   315 *free:* guiltless.   318 *mutes:*
actors without speaking parts.   319 *fell sergeant:* cruel sheriff's officer.   323 *unsatisfied:* uninformed.   324 *antique Roman:* ancient Roman (who considered suicide honorable).

To th'ambassadors of England gives
This warlike volley.
HAMLET.   O I die Horatio,   335
The potent poison quite o'er-crows° my spirit,
I cannot live to hear the news from England,
But I do prophesy th'election° lights
On Fortinbras, he has my dying voice,°
So tell him, with th'occurrents more and less°   340
Which have solicited°—the rest is silence.   *Dies.*
HORATIO.   Now cracks a noble heart: good night sweet prince,
And flights of angels sing thee to thy rest.
Why does the drum come hither?

Enter FORTINBRAS *and English Ambassadors, with drum, colours, and attendants.*

FORTINBRAS.   Where is this sight?
HORATIO.   What is it you would see?   345
If aught of woe, or wonder, cease your search.
FORTINBRAS.   This quarry cries on havoc.° O proud death,
What feast is toward° in thine eternal cell,
That thou so many princes at a shot
So bloodily hast struck?   350
AMBASSADOR.   The sight is dismal,
And our affairs from England come too late;
The ears° are senseless that should give us hearing,
To tell him his commandment is fulfilled,
That Rosencrantz and Guildenstern are dead:
Where should we have our thanks?
HORATIO.   Not from his mouth,   355
Had it th'ability of life to thank you;
He never gave commandment for their death;
But since so jump° upon this bloody question,
You from the Polack wars, and you from England
Are here arrived, give order that these bodies   360
High on a stage be placèd to the view,
And let me speak to th'yet unknowing world
How these things came about; so shall you hear
Of carnal, bloody and unnatural acts,
Of accidental judgments, casual° slaughters,   365
Of deaths put on° by cunning and forced cause,°
And in this upshot, purposes mistook,
Fall'n on th'inventors' heads:° all this can I
Truly deliver.

---

336 *o'er-crows:* overpowers, conquers.   338 *election:* (for king of Denmark).   339 *voice:* vote.
340 *occurrents more and less:* events great and small.   341 *solicited:* incited me.
347 *quarry . . . havoc:* heap of dead bodies proclaims slaughter done here.   348 *toward:* in
preparation.   352 *ears:* (of Claudius).   358 *jump:* opportunely.   365 *casual:*
unpremeditated.   366 *put on:* prompted by.   *forced cause:* being forced to act in
self-defense.   367–368 *purposes . . . heads:* plots gone wrong and destroying their inventors.

FORTINBRAS.   Let us haste to hear it,
And call the noblest to the audience.   37
For me, with sorrow I embrace my fortune;
I have some rights of memory° in this kingdom,
Which now to claim my vantage° doth invite me.
HORATIO.   Of that I shall have also cause to speak,
And from his mouth whose voice will draw on more:°   37
But let this same° be presently performed,
Even while men's minds are wild,° lest more mischance
On° plots and errors happen.
FORTINBRAS.   Let four captains
Bear Hamlet like a soldier to the stage,
For he was likely, had he been put on,°   38
To have proved most royal; and for his passage,°
The soldiers' music and the rite of war
Speak loudly for him:
Take up the bodies, such a sight as this,
Becomes the field, but here shows much amiss.   38
Go bid the soldiers shoot.

> *Exeunt marching: after the which a peal of ordnance are shot off.*

372 *of memory:* remembered.   373 *vantage:* advantageous position.   375 *draw on more:*
influence more (votes).   376 *this same:* this telling of the story.   377 *wild:* upset.
378 *On:* on top of.   380 *put on:* i.e., put on the throne.   381 *passage:* i.e., to the next world.

QUESTIONS

Act I

1. Discuss the various ways in which the first scene of *Hamlet* shows you that something is wrong in Denmark.
2. What impression does Claudius make in scene 2? Is he a rational man? A good administrator? A competent ruler? A loving husband and uncle?
3. What does Hamlet reveal about his own mental state in his first soliloquy?
4. What attitude toward Ophelia's relationship with Hamlet do Laertes and Polonius share? What do they want Ophelia to do? Why?
5. What does the ghost tell Hamlet? What does the ghost want Hamlet to do and not to do? Why does Hamlet need proof that the ghost's words are true?

Act II

6. What does Polonius think is the cause of Hamlet's madness? What do Polonius's diagnosis and his handling of the situation show us about him?
7. What does Hamlet accuse himself of in the soliloquy that begins "O what a rogue and peasant slave am I" (Act II, scene 2, lines 524–580)? To what extent is his self-accusation justified?

Act III

8. How do you react to Hamlet's treatment of Ophelia in the first scene of Act III? What evidence might indicate that Hamlet knows that Claudius and Polonius are watching and listening to everything that occurs?

9. Hamlet sets up the performance of "The Murder of Gonzago"—the play-within-a-play—to test Claudius's guilt. What is the relationship between the events of this play-within-a-play and the events of *Hamlet?*

10. How does Claudius react to "The Murder of Gonzago"? What does this reaction tell Hamlet? Why do you suppose Claudius did not react to the dumb show presented at the beginning of the play-within-a-play?

11. What is Hamlet's reason for not killing Claudius at prayer?

12. How does Hamlet treat his mother during their confrontation in her closet? Is Hamlet's behavior overly nasty or justified? Why does the ghost reappear during this confrontation?

13. What crimes or sins does Hamlet accuse Gertrude of committing?

Act IV

14. Do you think Laertes's desire to avenge his father's murder is any more or less justified than Hamlet's desire?

15. How does Claudius plan to use Laertes's desire for revenge to manipulate him? To what extent does Laertes unwittingly allow himself to be used by Claudius?

Act V

16. The conversation between the two clowns (grave-diggers) and between Hamlet and the first clown is seen as comic relief—a humorous episode designed to ease tension. Why is comic relief appropriate at this point?

17. How does this scene of comic relief reflect and broaden the play's themes?

18. Why does Hamlet describe Osric as a "water-fly"? How does Shakespeare use Osric's language and behavior to characterize him?

19. Discuss the lessons that Hamlet tells Horatio he has learned about life. How does this understanding change Hamlet? Why is it ironic?

20. How is Gertrude killed? Hamlet? Laertes? Claudius? Why does Hamlet insist that Horatio not commit suicide?

GENERAL QUESTIONS

1. Describe the character of Claudius. Do you consider him purely evil or merely a flawed human? Why? To what degree can you justify calling this play "The Tragedy of Claudius, King of Denmark"?

2. Characterize Horatio. Why does Hamlet admire and trust him? How is he different from Polonius or Rosencrantz and Guildenstern?

3. Describe Rosencrantz and Guildenstern. Are they round or flat? How does Claudius use them? Why do they cooperate with Claudius? How does Hamlet arrange their deaths? To what extent can this action be justified?

4. Evaluate Polonius's character. Is he a wise counselor? A fool? Sincere? Self-serving? Hypocritical? What are his motives? How is he like Rosencrantz and Guildenstern? How is his death like their deaths?

5. *Hamlet* is full of conflicts that oppose people to other people, to society, and to themselves. List all the conflicts you can find in the play. Decide which of these is the central conflict, and explain your choice.

6. What is the crisis of *Hamlet?* When does it occur? Whom does it affect? What is the catastrophe? The resolution?

7. In Act IV, Claudius notes that "sorrows come . . . in battalions." By the end of the play these sorrows include the deaths of Polonius, Rosencrantz, Guildenstern, Ophelia, Laertes, Gertrude, Claudius, and Hamlet. To what degree can Claudius be held responsible for all the sorrows of the play? Which sorrows are primarily Hamlet's responsibility?

8. Is *Hamlet* a tragedy of the state as well as a tragedy of the individual? In what condition is Denmark at the beginning of the play? Is the condition of Denmark better or worse at the end?

THE THEATER OF ARTHUR MILLER

When we shift to the twentieth-century theater of Arthur Miller, we abandon the masks of the Greek theater and the soliloquies of the Elizabethan stage for drama that mixes realism and nonrealism (this genre is examined in Chapter 29). By **realistic drama**, we mean plays that present an image of the world as we know it. This world is populated by salespeople, workers,

Stage set for Death of a Salesman. (Billy Rose Theater Collection; The New York Public Library at Lincoln Center; Astor, Lenox and Tilden Foundation)

bankers, housewives, lawyers, and thieves instead of kings, revengers, and soothsayers. In addition, these plays are spoken in the colloquial language of our own lives instead of in choric odes or blank verse.

With the nineteenth-century movement into realism, the drama required both a theater and a stage that could accommodate plays reflecting middle-class lives and values. Thus, the theater became the darkened auditorium in which we sit in rows and face a proscenium arch and a vast curtain that separate us from the acting areas. When the curtain rises, we often see a room resembling one we might live in or visit. This **box set** signals an attempt to make settings look as much like the real world as possible.

Today, stage settings have been embellished with the full range of sound and lighting effects made possible by modern technology. This technological revolution has been especially significant in the area of lighting, which is managed by a switchboard (now computerized) that can be programmed to control hundreds or even thousands of lights in any combination and intensity. Lighting can establish times, places, moods, atmospheres, and effects. It can also divide the stage or a unit set into different acting areas simply through the illumination of one section and the darkening of the rest. As a result, lighting has become an element of set design, especially when the dramatist uses a *scrim*, which permits great variety in the portrayal of scenes and great rapidity in scene changes.

In addition, recent theater designers have abandoned the proscenium stage and experimented with stages inspired by theaters of the past. Thus, the shape of the ancient Greek amphitheaters (with the seats rising from the stage in an expanding half circle) is reflected in theaters like Tyrone Guthrie (Minneapolis) and Shakespeare Festival (Ashland, Oregon). As with many other modern theaters, these theaters also feature a **thrust** stage modeled on the Elizabethan theaters. Such experimentation is evident in *Death of a Salesman*, which calls for an extended **apron** stage while also varying the box set to show rooms inside the Loman house.

ARTHUR MILLER, *DEATH OF A SALESMAN*

Arthur Miller is one of the dominant modern American playwrights. He was born in New York in 1915 and was educated at the University of Michigan, where he won a prize for a play he had written as an undergraduate. After graduation he wrote with the Federal Theater Project, and when that was shut down by the government he wrote radio plays for a time. During World War II he wrote an account of military training and also a novel. It was then also that he wrote *The Man Who Had All the Luck*, which met little success on Broadway in

1944. After the war he quickly catapulted into fame as a dramatist with *All My Sons* (1947), *Death of a Salesman* (1949), *An Enemy of the People* (1951, an adaptation of Ibsen's play), *The Crucible* (1953), and *A View from the Bridge* (1955). Many of these combine his interests in family relationships and social issues. For instance, *All My Sons* explores the relationship between Joe Keller, an industrialist and war profiteer who had allowed damaged engines to be installed in U.S. military aircraft, and his son Chris, an army pilot returning home from World War II. The play also investigates Joe Keller's guilt and his emerging realization that the airmen who died because of his defective engines were "all my sons." Such thematic concerns reveal the extent to which Miller was influenced by Ibsen (see p. 1463).

Miller's later work includes the screenplay *The Misfits* (1961), the last film in which his wife, Marilyn Monroe, starred, and the plays *After the Fall* (1964), *Incident at Vichy* (1964), *The Price* (1968), *Fame* (1970), *The Reason Why* (1972), *The Creation of the World and Other Business* (1972), *The Archbishop's Ceiling* (1976), *The American Clock* (1980), *Playing for Time* (1985), *I Can't Remember Anything* (1987), *Clara* (1987), a filmscript entitled *Everybody Wins* (1990), and *Broken Glass* (1994).

Death of a Salesman, which opened on Broadway on February 10, 1949, is similar to both *Oedipus the King* and the traditional *well-made play* (see p. 1465). Miller's play dramatizes the end of a much longer story. The stage action in the present (in Acts I and II) covers about twenty-four hours, from Monday evening to Tuesday evening. The story, however, goes back as far as Willy Loman's childhood, and his memories of past events constantly impose themselves on the present. Additionally, at least one of the central conflicts stems from a secret known only to Willy and his son Biff, but which is withheld from the rest of the characters and from us for most of the play. The secret, however, is not the linchpin of the drama, as it would be in a "well-made" play.

In writing a tragedy about the struggle and failure of Willy Loman, Miller effectively redefines the nature of the tragic protagonist. In a *New York Times* essay published shortly after the Broadway opening, Miller argues that "the common man is as apt a subject for tragedy in its highest sense as kings were."[6] He asserts that tragedy springs from the individual's quest for a proper place in the world and from his or her readiness "to lay down . . . life, if need be, to secure one thing—. . . [a] sense of personal dignity." Willy is certainly flawed. He is self-deluded, deceitful, unfaithful, and weak. But Miller links his protagonist's defects with this quest for dignity: "the flaw or crack in the character is really nothing . . . but his inherent unwillingness to remain passive in the face of what he conceives to be a challenge to his dignity, his image of his rightful status."

Death of a Salesman is developed around the character of Willy Loman. At first, Miller wanted to call the play "The Inside of His Head," and his ini-

---

[6] "Tragedy and the Common Man," *The New York Times*, February 27, 1949, sec. 2, p. 1.

tial vision was of "an enormous face the height of the proscenium arch that would appear and open up, and we would see the inside of a man's head."[7] The play contains two types of time and action: real and remembered. Present events are enacted and described realistically. Such action, however, often triggers Willy's memory of the past. Sometimes, past events occur simultaneously with present action; thus, in Act I Willy speaks with his dead brother (whom he is remembering) while at the same time he plays cards with Charley. At other times, past events take over the play completely, although Willy still continues to exist in the present. Willy's past is always with him—as he remembers it or reconstructs it—shaping the way he reacts to the present.

Like the acting of past events, the setting of *Death of a Salesman* is symbolic and nonrealistic (see p. 1426). It is designed to allow fluid transitions between present and past, between current action and memory. The Loman house is a framework with three rooms (or acting areas) on three levels: the kitchen, the sons' bedroom, and Willy's bedroom. The forestage and apron are used for all scenes away from the house and for "memory" scenes. In the present, the house is hemmed in by apartment houses and lit with an "angry glow of orange," thus suggesting that Willy's present existence is urbanized and claustrophobic. When memory takes over, however, the apartment houses disappear (a technique of lighting), and the orange glow gives way to pastoral colors and the shadows of leaves—the setting of dreams.

Death of a Salesman is very much about dreams, illusions, and self-deception. Dreams pervade Willy's thoughts, conversation, family, and house. The central dream (and illusion) is the American dream of success and wealth through the merchandizing of the self. This dream is recapitulated in a series of smaller dreams (illusions, lies) that Willy and his sons build out of thin air. Throughout the play, these dreams are destroyed when confronted with reality. Willy's dream of a "New York city job" and a salary, for example, collides with reality in his disastrous encounter with his younger and unsympathetic boss. Only Linda escapes the tyranny of dreams. While she serves and supports Willy completely, she remains firmly planted in the reality of house payments, insurance premiums, and her husband's need for dignity and "attention" as his world falls apart.

At the end of the play, we are left with a number of questions about the degree to which Willy recognizes and understands the corruption and the illusory nature of the American dream, his own dreams, and his self-image. He does understand that he has run out of lies and has nothing left to sell. He also understands—according to Miller—his alienation from true values:

> Had Willy been unaware of his separation from values that endure he would have died contentedly while polishing his car. . . . But he was agonized by his

---

[7] Arthur Miller, "Introduction to the Collected Plays," *Arthur Miller's Collected Plays* (New York: Viking, 1957), p. 23.

awareness of being in a false position, so constantly haunted by the hollowness of all he had placed his faith in, so aware, in short, that he must somehow be filled with his spirit or fly apart, that he staked his life on the ultimate assertion.[8]

Yet at the end of the play, Willy is still in the grip of delusions of glory for Biff and for himself. He imagines that his insurance money will make Biff "magnificent." Similarly, he dreams that his funeral will be massive. Both visions are delusions, for Biff has already abandoned the business world, and the funeral is attended by only five people. In the *Requiem* scene, Biff states that Willy's dreams were illusory: "He had all the wrong dreams. All, all wrong" (speech 16). Only Happy remains trapped in selfishness and his own petty version of Willy's dream: "He had a good dream. It's the only dream you can have—to come out number-one man" (speech 25)

ARTHUR MILLER   (b. 1915)

Death of a Salesman _____ *1949*

CHARACTERS

Willy Loman
Linda, *his wife*
Biff ⎱
Happy ⎰ *his sons*
Uncle Ben
Charley
Bernard
The Woman
Howard Wagner
Jenny
Stanley
Miss Forsythe
Letta

    The action takes place in WILLY LOMAN's *house and yard and in various places he visits in the New York and Boston of today.*

ACT 1

A melody is heard, played upon a flute. It is small and fine, telling of grass and trees and the horizon. The curtain rises.

[8] *Ibid.*, pp. 34–35.

Before us is the Salesman's house. We are aware of towering, angular shapes behind it, surrounding it on all sides. Only the blue light of the sky falls upon the house and forestage; the surrounding area shows an angry glow of orange. As more light appears, we see a solid vault of apartment houses around the small, fragile-seeming home. An air of the dream clings to the place, a dream rising out of reality. The kitchen at center seems actual enough, for there is a kitchen table with three chairs, and a refrigerator. But no other fixtures are seen. At the back of the kitchen there is a draped entrance, which leads to the living-room. To the right of the kitchen, on a level raised two feet, is a bedroom furnished only with a brass bedstead and a straight chair. On a shelf over the bed a silver athletic trophy stands. A window opens onto the apartment house at the side.

Behind the kitchen, on a level raised six and a half feet, is the boys' bedroom, at present barely visible. Two beds are dimly seen, and at the back of the room a dormer window. (This bedroom is above the unseen living-room.) At the left a stairway curves up to it from the kitchen.

The entire setting is wholly or, in some places, partially transparent. The roof-line of the house is one-dimensional; under and over it we see the apartment buildings. Before the house lies an apron, curving beyond the forestage into the orchestra. This forward area serves as the back yard as well as the locale of all WILLY's imaginings and of his city scenes. Whenever the action is in the present the actors observe the imaginary wall-lines, entering the house only through its door at the left. But in the scenes of the past these boundaries are broken, and characters enter or leave a room by stepping "through" a wall onto the forestage.

[From the right, WILLY LOMAN, The Salesman, enters, carrying two large sample cases. The flute plays on. He hears but is not aware of it. He is past sixty years of age, dressed quietly. Even as he crosses the stage to the doorway of the house, his exhaustion is apparent. He unlocks the door, comes into the kitchen, and thankfully lets his burden down, feeling the soreness of his palms. A word-sigh escapes his lips—it might be "Oh, boy, oh, boy." He closes the door, then carries his cases out into the living-room, through the draped kitchen doorway.]

[LINDA, his wife, has stirred in her bed at the right. She gets out and puts on a robe, listening. Most often jovial, she has developed an iron repression of her exceptions to WILLY's behavior— she more than loves him, she admires him, as though his mercurial nature, his temper, his massive dreams and little cruelties, served her only as sharp reminders of the turbulent longings within him, longings which she shares but lacks the temperament to utter and follow to their end.]

LINDA.   [*hearing WILLY outside the bedroom, calls with some trepidation*] Willy!

WILLY.   It's all right. I came back.

LINDA.   Why? What happened? [*slight pause*] Did something happen, Willy?

WILLY.   No, nothing happened.

LINDA.   You didn't smash the car, did you?   5

WILLY.   [*with casual irritation*] I said nothing happened. Didn't you hear me?

LINDA.   Don't you feel well?

WILLY.   I'm tired to the death. [*The flute has faded away. He sits on the bed beside her, a little numb.*] I couldn't make it. I just couldn't make it, Linda.

LINDA.   [*very carefully, delicately*] Where were you all day? You look terrible.

WILLY.   I got as far as a little above Yonkers.° I stopped for a cup of coffee.   10
Maybe it was the coffee.

Yonkers: Yonkers is immediately north of New York City, touching the city limits of the Bronx. Because Willy lives in Brooklyn, to the south, he got no more than thirty or thirty-five miles from home.

LINDA.   What?

WILLY.   [*after a pause*] I suddenly couldn't drive any more. The car kept going off onto the shoulder, y'know?

LINDA.   [*helpfully*] Oh. Maybe it was the steering again. I don't think Angelo knows the Studebaker.

WILLY.   No, it's me, it's me. Suddenly I realize I'm goin' sixty miles an hour and I don't remember the last five minutes. I'm—I can't seem to—keep my mind to it.

LINDA.   Maybe it's your glasses. You never went for your new glasses.

WILLY.   No, I see everything. I came back ten miles an hour. It took me nearly four hours from Yonkers.

LINDA.   [*resigned*] Well, you'll just have to take a rest, Willy, you can't continue this way.

WILLY.   I just got back from Florida.

LINDA.   But you didn't rest your mind. Your mind is overactive, and the mind is what counts, dear.

WILLY.   I'll start out in the morning. Maybe I'll feel better in the morning. [*She is taking off his shoes.*] These goddam arch supports are killing me.

LINDA.   Take an aspirin. Should I get you an aspirin? It'll soothe you.

WILLY.   [*with wonder*] I was driving along, you understand? And I was fine. I was even observing the scenery. You can imagine, me looking at scenery, on the road every week of my life. But it's so beautiful up there, Linda, the trees are so thick, and the sun is warm. I opened the windshield and just let the warm air bathe over me. And then all of a sudden I'm goin' off the road! I'm tellin' ya, I absolutely forgot I was driving. If I'd've gone the other way over the white line I might've killed somebody. So I went on again—and five minutes later I'm dreamin' again, and I nearly—[*He presses two fingers against his eyes.*] I have such thoughts, I have such strange thoughts.

LINDA.   Willy, dear. Talk to them again. There's no reason why you can't work in New York.

WILLY.   They don't need me in New York. I'm the New England man. I'm vital in New England.

LINDA.   But you're sixty years old. They can't expect you to keep traveling every week.

WILLY.   I'll have to send a wire to Portland. I'm supposed to see Brown and Morrison tomorrow morning at ten o'clock to show the line. Goddammit, I could sell them! [*He starts putting on his jacket.*]

LINDA.   [*taking the jacket from him*] Why don't you go down to the place tomorrow and tell Howard you've simply got to work in New York? You're too accommodating, dear.

WILLY.   If old man Wagner was alive I'd a been in charge of New York now! That man was a prince, he was a masterful man. But that boy of his, that Howard, he don't appreciate. When I went north the first time, the Wagner Company didn't know where New England was!

LINDA.   Why don't you tell those things to Howard, dear?

WILLY.   [*encouraged*] I will, I definitely will. Is there any cheese?

LINDA.   I'll make you a sandwich.

WILLY.   No, go to sleep. I'll take some milk. I'll be up right away. The boys in?

LINDA.   They're sleeping. Happy took Biff on a date tonight.

WILLY.   [*interested*] That so?

LINDA.   It was so nice to see them shaving together, one behind the other, in the bathroom. And going out together. You notice? The whole house smells of shaving lotion.

WILLY.   Figure it out. Work a lifetime to pay off a house. You finally own it, and there's nobody to live in it.

LINDA.   Well, dear, life is a casting off. It's always that way.

WILLY.   No, no, some people—some people accomplish something. Did Biff say anything after I went this morning?

LINDA.   You shouldn't have criticized him, Willy, especially after he just got off the train. You mustn't lose your temper with him.

WILLY.   When the hell did I lose my temper? I simply asked him if he was making any money. Is that a criticism?

LINDA.   But, dear, how could he make any money?

WILLY.   [*worried and angered*] There's such an undercurrent in him. He became a moody man. Did he apologize when I left this morning?

LINDA.   He was crestfallen, Willy. You know how he admires you. I think if he finds himself, then you'll both be happier and not fight any more.

WILLY.   How can he find himself on a farm? Is that a life? A farmhand? In the beginning, when he was young, I thought, well, a young man, it's good for him to tramp around, take a lot of different jobs. But it's more than ten years now and he has yet to make thirty-five dollars a week!

LINDA.   He's finding himself, Willy.

WILLY.   Not finding yourself at the age of thirty-four is a disgrace!

LINDA.   Shh!

WILLY.   The trouble is he's lazy, goddammit!

LINDA.   Willy, please!

WILLY.   Biff is a lazy bum!

LINDA.   They're sleeping. Get something to eat. Go on down.

WILLY.   Why did he come home? I would like to know what brought him home.

LINDA.   I don't know. I think he's still lost, Willy. I think he's very lost.

WILLY.   Biff Loman is lost. In the greatest country in the world a young man with such—personal attractiveness, gets lost. And such a hard worker. There's one thing about Biff—he's not lazy.

LINDA.   Never.

WILLY.   [*with pity and resolve*] I'll see him in the morning; I'll have a nice talk with him. I'll get him a job selling. He could be big in no time. My God! Remember how they used to follow him around in high school? When he smiled at one of them their faces lit up. When he walked down the street . . . [*He loses himself in reminiscences.*]

LINDA.   [*trying to bring him out of it*] Willy, dear, I got a new kind of American-type cheese today. It's whipped.

WILLY.   Why do you get American when I like Swiss?

LINDA.   I just thought you'd like a change—

WILLY.   I don't want a change! I want Swiss cheese. Why am I always being contradicted?

LINDA.   [*with a covering laugh*] I thought it would be a surprise.

WILLY.   Why don't you open a window in here, for God's sake?

LINDA.   [*with infinite patience*] They're all open dear.

WILLY.   The way they boxed us in here. Bricks and windows, windows and bricks.

LINDA.   We should've bought the land next door.

WILLY.   The street is lined with cars. There's not a breath of fresh air in the neighborhood. The grass don't grow any more, you can't raise a carrot in the back yard. They should've had a law against apartment houses. Remember those two beautiful elm trees out there? When I and Biff hung the swing between them?

LINDA.   Yeah, like being a million miles from the city.

WILLY.   They should've arrested the builder for cutting those down. They massacred the neighborhood. [*lost*] More and more I think of those days, Linda. This time of year it was lilac and wisteria. And then the peonies would come out, and the daffodils. What fragrance in this room!

LINDA.   Well, after all, people had to move somewhere.

WILLY.   No, there's more people now.

LINDA.   I don't think there's more people. I think—

WILLY.   There's more people! That's what's ruining this country! Population is getting out of control. The competition is maddening! Smell the stink from that apartment house! And another one on the other side . . . How can they whip cheese?

[*On* WILLY'S *last line,* BIFF *and* HAPPY *raise themselves up in their beds, listening.*]

LINDA.   Go down, try it. And be quiet.

WILLY.   [*turning to* LINDA, *guiltily*] You're not worried about me, are you, sweetheart?

BIFF.   What's the matter?

HAPPY.   Listen!

LINDA.   You've got too much on the ball to worry about.

WILLY.   You're my foundation and my support, Linda.

LINDA.   Just try to relax, dear. You make mountains out of molehills.

WILLY.   I won't fight with him any more. If he wants to go back to Texas, let him go.

LINDA.   He'll find his way.

WILLY.   Sure. Certain men just don't get started till later in life. Like Thomas Edison, I think. Or B. F. Goodrich.° One of them was deaf. [*He starts for the bedroom doorway.*] I'll put my money on Biff.

LINDA.   And Willy—if it's warm Sunday we'll drive in the country. And we'll open the windshield, and take lunch.

WILLY.   No, the windshields don't open on the new cars.

LINDA.   But you opened it today.

WILLY.   Me? I didn't. [*He stops.*] Now isn't that peculiar! Isn't that a remarkable— [*He breaks off in amazement and fright as the flute is heard distantly.*]

LINDA.   What, darling?

WILLY.   That is the most remarkable thing.

Thomas Edison, B. F. Goodrich: Thomas A. Edison (1847–1931) was an American inventor who developed the electric light and the phonograph. Benjamin Franklin Goodrich (1841–1888) founded the B. F. Goodrich Rubber and Tire Company. It was Edison who suffered from deafness.

LINDA. What, dear?

WILLY. I was thinking of the Chevvy. [*slight pause*] Nineteen twenty-eight   90
. . . when I had that red Chevvy— [*Breaks off.*] That funny? I coulda sworn I was driving that Chevvy today.

LINDA. Well, that's nothing. Something must've reminded you.

WILLY. Remarkable. Ts. Remember those days? The way Biff used to simonize
that car? The dealer refused to believe there was eighty thousand miles on it. [*He
shakes his head.*] Heh! [*to Linda*] Close your eyes, I'll be right up. [*He walks out of the
bedroom.*]

HAPPY. [*to BIFF*] Jesus, maybe he smashed up the car again!

LINDA. [*calling after WILLY*] Be careful on the stairs, dear! The cheese is on the
middle shelf! [*She turns, goes over to the bed, takes his jacket, and goes out of the bedroom.*]

[*Light has risen on the boys' room. Unseen, WILLY is heard talking to himself, "Eighty thousand
miles," and a little laugh. BIFF gets out of bed, comes downstage a bit, and stands attentively.
BIFF is two years older than his brother HAPPY, well built, but in these days bears a worn air and
seems less self-assured. He has succeeded less, and his dreams are stronger and less acceptable
than HAPPY's. HAPPY is tall, powerfully made. Sexuality is like a visible color on him, or a scent
that many women have discovered. He, like his brother, is lost, but in a different way, for he has
never allowed himself to turn his face toward defeat and is thus more confused and hard-skinned,
although seemingly more content.*]

HAPPY. [*getting out of bed*] He's going to get his license taken away if he   95
keeps that up. I'm getting nervous about him, y'know, Biff?

BIFF. His eyes are going.

HAPPY. No, I've driven with him. He sees all right. He just doesn't keep his
mind on it. I drove into the city with him last week. He stops at a green light and then
it turns red and he goes. [*He laughs.*]

BIFF. Maybe he's color-blind.

HAPPY. Pop? Why he's got the finest eye for color in the business. You know
that.

BIFF. [*sitting down on his bed*] I'm going to sleep.   100

HAPPY. You're not still sour on Dad, are you, Biff?

BIFF. He's all right, I guess.

WILLY. [*underneath them, in the living-room*] Yes, sir, eighty thousand miles—
eighty-two thousand!

BIFF. You smoking?

HAPPY. [*holding out a pack of cigarettes*] Want one?   105

BIFF. [*taking a cigarette*] I can never sleep when I smell it.

WILLY. What a simonizing job, heh!

HAPPY. [*with deep sentiment*] Funny, Biff y'know? Us sleeping in here again?
The old beds. [*He pats his bed affectionately.*] All the talk that went across those two
beds, huh? Our whole lives.

BIFF. Yeah. Lotta dreams and plans.

HAPPY. [*with a deep and masculine laugh*] About five hundred women would like   110
to know what was said in this room.

[*They share a soft laugh.*]

BIFF. Remember that big Betsy something—what the hell was her name—over
on Bushwick Avenue?

HAPPY. [*combing his hair*] With the collie dog!

BIFF. That's the one. I got you in there, remember?

HAPPY. Yeah, that was my first time—I think. Boy, there was a pig! [*They laugh, almost crudely.*] You taught me everything I know about women. Don't forget that.

BIFF. I bet you forgot how bashful you used to be. Especially with girls.

HAPPY. Oh, I still am, Biff.

BIFF. Oh, go on.

HAPPY. I just control it, that's all. I think I got less bashful and you got more so. What happened, Biff? Where's the old humor, the old confidence? [*He shakes BIFF's knee. BIFF gets up and moves restlessly about the room.*] What's the matter?

BIFF. Why does Dad mock me all the time?

HAPPY. He's not mocking you, he—

BIFF. Everything I say there's a twist of mockery on his face. I can't get near him.

HAPPY. He just wants you to make good, that's all. I wanted to talk to you about Dad for a long time, Biff. Something's—happening to him. He—talks to himself.

BIFF. I noticed that this morning. But he always mumbled.

HAPPY. But not so noticeable. It got so embarrassing I sent him to Florida. And you know something? Most of the time he's talking to you.

BIFF. What's he say about me?

HAPPY. I can't make it out.

BIFF. What's he say about me?

HAPPY. I think the fact that you're not settled, that you're still kind of up in the air . . .

BIFF. There's one or two other things depressing him, Happy.

HAPPY. What do you mean?

BIFF. Never mind. Just don't lay it all to me.

HAPPY. But I think if you just got started—I mean—is there any future for you out there?

BIFF. I tell ya, Hap, I don't know what the future is. I don't know—what I'm supposed to want.

HAPPY. What do you mean?

BIFF. Well, I spent six or seven years after high school trying to work myself up. Shipping clerk, salesman, business of one kind or another. And it's a measly manner of existence. To get on that subway on the hot mornings in summer. To devote your whole life to keeping stock, or making phone calls, or selling or buying. To suffer fifty weeks of the year for the sake of a two-week vacation, when all you really desire is to be outdoors, with your shirt off. And always to have to get ahead of the next fella. And still—that's how you build a future.

HAPPY. Well, you really enjoy it on a farm? Are you content out there?

BIFF. [*with rising agitation*] Hap, I've had twenty or thirty different kinds of jobs since I left home before the war, and it always turns out the same. I just realized it lately. In Nebraska when I herded cattle, and the Dakotas, and Arizona, and now in Texas. It's why I came home now, I guess, because I realized it. This farm I work on, it's spring there now, see? And they've got about fifteen new colts. There's nothing more inspiring or—beautiful than the sight of a mare and a new colt. And it's cool there now, see? Texas is cool now, and it's spring. And whenever spring comes to where I am, I suddenly get the feeling, my God, I'm not gettin' anywhere! What the hell am I doing, playing around with horses, twenty-eight dollars a week! I'm thirty-four years old, I oughta be makin' my future. That's when I come running home. And now, I get here, and I don't know what to do with myself. [*after a pause*] I've always made a point of not wasting my life, and everytime I come back here I know that all I've done is to waste my life.

HAPPY.   You're a poet, you know that, Biff? You're a—you're an idealist!

BIFF.   No, I'm mixed up very bad. Maybe I oughta get married. Maybe I oughta get stuck into something. Maybe that's my trouble. I'm like a boy. I'm not married, I'm not in business, I just—I'm like a boy. Are you content, Hap? You're a success, aren't you? Are you content?

HAPPY.   Hell, no!   140

BIFF.   Why? You're making money, aren't you?

HAPPY.   [*moving about with energy, expressiveness*] All I can do now is wait for the merchandise manager to die. And suppose I get to be merchandise manager? He's a good friend of mine, and he just built a terrific estate on Long Island. And he lived there about two months and sold it, and now he's building another one. He can't enjoy it once it's finished. And I know that's just what I would do. I don't know what the hell I'm workin' for. Sometimes I sit in my apartment—all alone. And I think of the rent I'm paying. And it's crazy. But then, it's what I always wanted. My own apartment, a car, and plenty of women. And still, goddammit, I'm lonely.

BIFF.   [*with enthusiasm*] Listen, why don't you come out West with me?

HAPPY.   You and I, heh?

BIFF.   Sure, maybe we could buy a ranch. Raise cattle, use our muscles. Men   145
built like we are should be working out in the open.

HAPPY.   [*avidly*] The Loman Brothers, heh?

BIFF.   [*with vast affection*] Sure, we'd be known all over the counties!

HAPPY.   [*enthralled*] That's what I dream about, Biff. Sometimes I want to just rip my clothes off in the middle of the store and outbox that goddam merchandise manager. I mean I can outbox, outrun, and outlift anybody in that store, and I have to take orders from those common, petty sons-of-bitches till I can't stand it any more.

BIFF.   I'm tellin' you, kid, if you were with me I'd be happy out there.

HAPPY.   [*enthused*] See, Biff, everybody around me is so false that I'm   150
constantly lowering my ideals . . .

BIFF.   Baby, together we'd stand up for one another, we'd have someone to trust.

HAPPY.   If I were around you—

BIFF.   Hap, the trouble is we weren't brought up to grub for money. I don't know how to do it.

HAPPY.   Neither can I!

BIFF.   Then let's go!   155

HAPPY.   The only thing is—what can you make out there?

BIFF.   But look at your friend. Builds an estate and then hasn't the peace of mind to live in it.

HAPPY.   Yeah, but when he walks into the store the waves part in front of him. That's fifty-two thousand dollars a year coming through the revolving door, and I got more in my pinky finger than he's got in his head.

BIFF.   Yeah, but you just said—

HAPPY.   I gotta show some of those pompous, self-important executives over   160
there that Hap Loman can make the grade. I want to walk into the store the way he

walks in. Then I'll go with you, Biff. We'll be together yet, I swear. But take those two we had tonight. Now weren't they gorgeous creatures?

BIFF.   Yeah, yeah, most gorgeous I've had in years.

HAPPY.   I get that any time I want, Biff. Whenever I feel disgusted. The only trouble is, it gets like bowling or something. I just keep knockin' them over and it doesn't mean anything. You still run around a lot?

BIFF.   Naa. I'd like to find a girl—steady, somebody with substance.

HAPPY.   That's what I long for.

BIFF.   Go on! You'd never come home.

HAPPY.   I would! Somebody with character, with resistance! Like Mom, y'know? You're gonna call me a bastard when I tell you this. That girl Charlotte I was with tonight is engaged to be married in five weeks. [*He tries on his new hat.*]

BIFF.   No kiddin'!

HAPPY.   Sure, the guy's in line for the vice-presidency of the store. I don't know what gets into me, maybe I just have an overdeveloped sense of competition or something, but I went and ruined her, and furthermore I can't get rid of her. And he's the third executive I've done that to. Isn't that a crummy characteristic? And to top it all, I go to their weddings! [*Indignantly, but laughing*] Like I'm not supposed to take bribes. Manufacturers offer me a hundred-dollar bill now and then to throw an order their way. You know how honest I am, but it's like this girl, see. I hate myself for it. Because I don't want the girl, and, still, I take it and—I love it!

BIFF.   Let's go to sleep.

HAPPY.   I guess we didn't settle anything, heh?

BIFF.   I just got one idea that I think I'm going to try.

HAPPY.   What's that?

BIFF.   Remember Bill Oliver?

HAPPY.   Sure, Oliver is very big now. You want to work for him again?

BIFF.   No, but when I quit he said something to me. He put his arm on my shoulder and he said, "Biff, if you ever need anything, come to me."

HAPPY.   I remember that. That sounds good.

BIFF.   I think I'll go to see him. If I could get ten thousand or even seven or eight thousand dollars I could buy a beautiful ranch.

HAPPY.   I bet he'd back you. 'Cause he thought highly of you, Biff. I mean, they all do. You're well liked, Biff. That's why I say to come back here, and we both have the apartment. And I'm tellin' you, Biff, any babe you want . . .

BIFF.   No, with a ranch I could do the work I like and still be something. I just wonder though. I wonder if Oliver still thinks I stole that carton of basketballs.

HAPPY.   Oh, he probably forgot that long ago. It's almost ten years. You're too sensitive. Anyway, he didn't really fire you.

BIFF.   Well, I think he was going to. I think that's why I quit. I was never sure whether he knew or not. I know he thought the world of me, though. I was the only one he'd let lock up the place.

WILLY.   [*below*] You gonna wash the engine, Biff?

HAPPY.   Shh!

[*BIFF looks at HAPPY, who is gazing down, listening. WILLY is mumbling in the parlor.*]

HAPPY.   You hear that?

[*They listen. WILLY laughs warmly.*]

BIFF.   [*growing angry*] Doesn't he know Mom can hear that?   185
WILLY.   Don't get your sweater dirty, Biff!

[*A look of pain crosses BIFF's face.*]

HAPPY.   Isn't that terrible! Don't leave again, will you? You'll find a job here. You gotta stick around. I don't know what to do about him, it's getting embarrassing.
WILLY.   What a simonizing job!
BIFF.   Mom's hearing that!
WILLY.   No kiddin', Biff, you got a date? Wonderful!   190
HAPPY.   Go on to sleep. But talk to him in the morning, will you?
BIFF.   [*reluctantly getting into bed*] With her in the house. Brother!
HAPPY.   [*getting into bed*] I wish you'd have a good talk with him.

[*The light on their room begins to fade.*]

BIFF.   [*to himself in bed*] That selfish, stupid . . .
HAPPY.   Sh . . . Sleep, Biff.   195

[*Their light is out. Well before they have finished speaking, WILLY's form is dimly seen below in the darkened kitchen. He opens the refrigerator, searches in there, and takes out a bottle of milk. The apartment houses are fading out, and the entire house and surroundings become covered with leaves. Music insinuates itself as the leaves appear.*]

WILLY.   Just wanna be careful with those girls, Biff, that's all. Don't make any promises. No promises of any kind. Because a girl, y'know, they always believe what you tell 'em, and you're very young, Biff, you're too young to be talking seriously to girls.

[*Light rises on the kitchen. WILLY, talking, shuts the refrigerator door and comes downstage to the kitchen table. He pours milk into a glass. He is totally immersed in himself, smiling faintly.*]

WILLY.   Too young entirely, Biff. You want to watch your schooling first. Then when you're all set, there'll be plenty of girls for a boy like you. [*He smiles broadly at a kitchen chair.*] That so? The girls pay for you? [*He laughs.*] Boy, you must really be makin' a hit.

[*WILLY is gradually addressing—physically—a point offstage, speaking through the wall of the kitchen, and his voice has been rising in volume to that of a normal conversation.*]

WILLY.   I been wondering why you polish the car so careful. Ha! Don't leave the hubcaps, boys. Get the chamois to the hubcaps. Happy, use newspaper on the windows, it's the easiest thing. Show him how to do it, Biff! You see, Happy? Pad it up, use it like a pad. That's it, that's it, good work. You're doin' all right, Hap. [*He pauses, then nods in approbation for a few seconds, then looks upward.*] Biff, first thing we gotta do when we get time is clip that big branch over the house. Afraid it's gonna fall in a storm and hit the roof. Tell you what. We get a rope and sling her around, and then we climb up there with a couple of saws and take her down. Soon as you finish the car, boys, I wanna see ya. I got a surprise for you, boys.
BIFF.   [*offstage*] Whatta ya got, Dad?
WILLY.   No, you finish first. Never leave a job till you're finished—remember   200
that. [*looking toward the "big trees"*] Biff, up in Albany I saw a beautiful hammock. I think I'll buy it next trip, and we'll hang it right between those two elms. Wouldn't that be something? Just swingin' there under those branches. Boy, that would be . . .

[*YOUNG BIFF and YOUNG HAPPY appear from the direction WILLY was addressing. HAPPY carries rags and a pail of water. BIFF, wearing a sweater with a block "S," carries a football.*]

BIFF.   [*pointing in the direction of the car offstage*] How's that, Pop, professional?
WILLY.   Terrific. Terrific job, boys. Good work, Biff.
HAPPY.   Where's the surprise, Pop?
WILLY.   In the back seat of the car.
HAPPY.   Boy! [*He runs off.*]
BIFF.   What is it, Dad? Tell me, what'd you buy?
WILLY.   [*laughing, cuffs him*] Never mind, something I want you to have.
BIFF.   [*turns and starts off*] What is it, Hap?
HAPPY.   [*offstage*] It's a punching bag!
BIFF.   Oh, Pop!
WILLY.   It's got Gene Tunney's° signature on it!

[*HAPPY runs onstage with a punching bag.*]

BIFF.   Gee, how'd you know we wanted a punching bag?
WILLY.   Well, it's the finest thing for the timing.
HAPPY.   [*lies down on his back and pedals with his feet*] I'm losing weight, you notice, Pop?
WILLY.   [*to HAPPY*] Jumping rope is good too.
BIFF.   Did you see the new football I got?
WILLY.   [*examining the ball*] Where'd you get a new ball?
BIFF.   The coach told me to practice my passing.
WILLY.   That so? And he gave you the ball, heh?
BIFF.   Well, I borrowed it from the locker room. [*He laughs confidentially.*]
WILLY.   [*laughing with him at the theft*] I want you to return that.
HAPPY.   I told you he wouldn't like it!
BIFF.   [*angrily*] Well, I'm bringing it back!
WILLY.   [*stopping the incipient argument, to HAPPY*] Sure, he's gotta practice with a regulation ball, doesn't he? [*to BIFF*] Coach'll probably congratulate you on your initiative!
BIFF.   Oh, he keeps congratulating my initiative all the time, Pop.
WILLY.   That's because he likes you. If somebody else took that ball there'd be an uproar. So what's the report, boys, what's the report?
BIFF.   Where'd you go this time, Dad? Gee we were lonesome for you.
WILLY.   [*pleased, puts an arm around each boy and they come down to the apron*] Lonesome, heh?
BIFF.   Missed you every minute.
WILLY.   Don't say? Tell you a secret, boys. Don't breathe it to a soul. Someday I'll have my own business, and I'll never have to leave home any more.
HAPPY.   Like Uncle Charley, heh?
WILLY.   Bigger than Uncle Charley! Because Charley is not—liked. He's liked, but he's not—well liked.
BIFF.   Where'd you go this time, Dad?
WILLY.   Well, I got on the road, and I went north to Providence. Met the Mayor.

Gene Tunney: James Joseph Tunney, a boxer who won the heavyweight championship from Jack Dempsey in 1926 and retired undefeated in 1928.

BIFF.   The Mayor of Providence!   235

WILLY.   He was sitting in the hotel lobby.

BIFF.   What'd he say?

WILLY.   He said, "Morning!" And I said, "You got a fine city here, Mayor." And then he had coffee with me. And then I went to Waterbury. Waterbury is a fine city. Big clock city, the famous Waterbury clock. Sold a nice bill there. And then Boston— Boston is the cradle of the Revolution. A fine city. And a couple of other towns in Mass., and on to Portland and Bangor and straight home!

BIFF.   Gee, I'd love to go with you sometime, Dad.

WILLY.   Soon as summer comes.   240

HAPPY.   Promise?

WILLY.   You and Hap and I, and I'll show you all the towns. America is full of beautiful towns and fine, upstanding people. And they know me, boys, they know me up and down New England. The finest people. And when I bring you fellas up, there'll be open sesame for all of us, 'cause one thing, boys: I have friends. I can park my car in any street in New England, and the cops protect it like their own. This summer, heh?

BIFF and HAPPY.   [*together*] Yeah! You bet!

WILLY.   We'll take our bathing suits.

HAPPY.   We'll carry your bags, Pop!   245

WILLY.   Oh, won't that be something! Me comin' into the Boston stores with you boys carryin' my bags. What a sensation!

[*BIFF is prancing around, practicing passing the ball.*]

WILLY.   You nervous, Biff, about the game?

BIFF.   Not if you're gonna be there.

WILLY.   What do they say about you in school, now that they made you captain?

HAPPY.   There's a crowd of girls behind him everytime the classes change.   250

BIFF.   [*taking WILLY's hand*] This Saturday, Pop, this Saturday—just for you, I'm going to break through for a touchdown.

HAPPY.   You're supposed to pass.

BIFF.   I'm takin' one play for Pop. You watch me, Pop, and when I take off my helmet, that means I'm breakin' out. Then you watch me crash through that line!

WILLY.   [*kisses BIFF*] Oh, wait'll I tell this in Boston!

[*BERNARD enters in knickers. He is younger than BIFF, earnest and loyal, a worried boy.*]

BERNARD.   Biff, where are you? You're supposed to study with me today.   255

WILLY.   Hey, looka Bernard. What're you lookin' so anemic about, Bernard?

BERNARD.   He's gotta study, Uncle Willy. He's got Regents° next week.

HAPPY.   [*tauntingly, spinning BERNARD around*] Let's box, Bernard!

BERNARD.   Biff! [*He gets away from HAPPY.*] Listen, Biff, I heard Mr. Birnbaum say that if you don't start studyin' math he's gonna flunk you, and you won't graduate. I heard him!

Regents: A statewide high school proficiency examination administered in New York State.

WILLY.   You better study with him, Biff. Go ahead now.   2·

BERNARD.   I heard him!

BIFF.   Oh, Pop, you didn't see my sneakers! [*He holds up a foot for WILLY to look at.*]

WILLY.   Hey, that's a beautiful job of printing!

BERNARD.   [*wiping his glasses*] Just because he printed University of Virginia on his sneakers doesn't mean they've got to graduate him, Uncle Willy!

WILLY.   [*angrily*] What're you talking about? With scholarships to three uni-   2·
versities they're gonna flunk him?

BERNARD.   But I heard Mr. Birnbaum say—

WILLY.   Don't be a pest, Bernard! [*to his boys*] What an anemic!

BERNARD.   Okay, I'm waiting for you in my house, Biff.

[*BERNARD goes off. The LOMANS laugh.*]

WILLY.   Bernard is not well liked, is he?

BIFF.   He's liked, but he's not well liked.   2

HAPPY.   That's right, Pop.

WILLY.   That's just what I mean. Bernard can get the best marks in school, y'understand, but when he gets out in the business world, y'understand, you are go-ing to be five times ahead of him. That's why I thank Almighty God you're both built like Adonises. Because the man who makes an appearance in the business world, the man who creates personal interest, is the man who gets ahead. Be liked and you will never want. You take me, for instance. I never have to wait in line to see a buyer. "Willy Loman is here!" That's all they have to know, and I go right through.

BIFF.   Did you knock them dead, Pop?

WILLY.   Knocked 'em cold in Providence, slaughtered 'em in Boston.

HAPPY.   [*on his back, pedaling again*] I'm losing weight, you notice, Pop?   2

[*LINDA enters, as of old, a ribbon in her hair, carrying a basket of washing.*]

LINDA.   [*with youthful energy*] Hello, dear!

WILLY.   Sweetheart!

LINDA.   How'd the Chevvy run?

WILLY.   Chevrolet, Linda, is the greatest car ever built. [*to the boys*] Since when do you let your mother carry wash up the stairs?

BIFF.   Grab hold there, boy!   2·

HAPPY.   Where to, Mom?

LINDA.   Hang them up on the line. And you better go down to your friends, Biff. The cellar is full of boys. They don't know what to do with themselves.

BIFF.   Ah, when Pop comes home they can wait!

WILLY.   [*laughs appreciatively*] You better go down and tell them what to do, Biff.

BIFF.   I think I'll have them sweep out the furnace room.   2·

WILLY.   Good work, Biff.

BIFF.   [*goes through wall-line of kitchen to doorway at back and calls down*] Fellas! Everybody sweep out the furnace room! I'll be right down!

VOICES.   All right! Okay, Biff.

BIFF.   George and Sam and Frank, come out back! We're hangin' up the wash! Come on, Hap, on the double! [*He and HAPPY carry out the basket.*]

LINDA.   The way they obey him!   2·

WILLY. Well, that's training, the training. I'm tellin' you, I was sellin' thousands and thousands, but I had to come home.

LINDA. Oh, the whole block'll be at that game. Did you sell anything?

WILLY. I did five hundred gross in Providence and seven hundred gross in Boston.

LINDA. No! Wait a minute, I've got a pencil. [*She pulls pencil and paper out of her apron pocket.*] That makes your commission . . . Two hundred—my God! Two hundred and twelve dollars!

WILLY. Well, I didn't figure it yet, but . . .   295

LINDA. How much did you do?

WILLY. Well, I—I did—about a hundred and eighty gross in Providence. Well, no—it came to—roughly two hundred gross on the whole trip.

LINDA. [*without hesitation*] Two hundred gross. That's . . . [*She figures.*]

WILLY. The trouble was that three of the stores were half closed for inventory in Boston. Otherwise I woulda broke records.

LINDA. Well, it makes seventy dollars and some pennies. That's very good.   300

WILLY. What do we owe?

LINDA. Well, on the first there's sixteen dollars on the refrigerator—

WILLY. Why sixteen?

LINDA. Well, the fan belt broke, so it was a dollar eighty.

WILLY. But it's brand new.   305

LINDA. Well, the man said that's the way it is. Till they work themselves in, y'know.

[*They move through the wall-line into the kitchen.*]

WILLY. I hope we didn't get stuck on that machine.

LINDA. They got the biggest ads of any of them!

WILLY. I know, it's a fine machine. What else?

LINDA. Well, there's nine-sixty for the washing machine. And for the vacuum   310
cleaner there's three and a half due on the fifteenth. Then the roof, you got twenty-one dollars remaining.

WILLY. It don't leak, does it?

LINDA. No, they did a wonderful job. Then you owe Frank for the carburetor.

WILLY. I'm not going to pay that man! That goddam Chevrolet, they ought to prohibit the manufacture of that car!

LINDA. Well, you owe him three and a half. And odds and ends, comes to around a hundred and twenty dollars by the fifteenth.

WILLY. A hundred and twenty dollars! My God, if business don't pick up   315
I don't know what I'm gonna do!

LINDA. Well, next week you'll do better.

WILLY. Oh, I'll knock 'em dead next week. I'll go to Hartford. I'm very well liked in Hartford. You know, the trouble is, Linda, people don't seem to take to me.

[*They move onto the forestage.*]

LINDA. Oh, don't be foolish.

WILLY. I know it when I walk in. They seem to laugh at me.

LINDA. Why? Why would they laugh at you? Don't talk that way, Willy.   320

[*WILLY moves to the edge of the stage. LINDA goes into the kitchen and starts to darn stockings.*]

WILLY.   I don't know the reason for it, but they just pass me by. I'm not noticed.

LINDA.   But you're doing wonderful, dear. You're making seventy to a hundred dollars a week.

WILLY.   But I gotta be at it ten, twelve hours a day. Other men—I don't know—they do it easier. I don't know why—I can't stop myself—I talk too much. A man oughta come in with a few words. One thing about Charley. He's a man of few words, and they respect him.

LINDA.   You don't talk too much, you're just lively.

WILLY.   [*smiling*] Well, I figure, what the hell, life is short, a couple of jokes.   3: [*to himself*] I joke too much! [*The smile goes.*]

LINDA.   Why? You're—

WILLY.   I'm fat. I'm very—foolish to look at, Linda. I didn't tell you, but Christmas time I happened to be calling on F. H. Stewarts, and a salesman I know, as I was going in to see the buyer I heard him say something about—walrus. And I—I cracked him right across the face. I won't take that. I simply will not take that. But they do laugh at me. I know that.

LINDA.   Darling . . .

WILLY.   I gotta overcome it. I know I gotta overcome it. I'm not dressing to advantage, maybe.

LINDA.   Willy, darling, you're the handsomest man in the world—   3:

WILLY.   Oh, no, Linda.

LINDA.   To me you are. [*slight pause*] The handsomest.

[*From the darkness is heard the laughter of a woman. WILLY doesn't turn to it, but it continues through LINDA's lines.*]

LINDA.   And the boys, Willy. Few men are idolized by their children the way you are.

[*Music is heard as behind a scrim, to the left of the house, THE WOMAN, dimly seen, is dressing.*]

WILLY.   [*with great feeling*] You're the best there is, Linda, you're a pal, you know that? On the road—on the road I want to grab you sometimes and just kiss the life outa you.

[*The laughter is loud now, and he moves into a brightening area at the left, where THE WOMAN has come from behind the scrim and is standing, putting on her hat, looking into a "mirror" and laughing.*]

WILLY.   Cause I get so lonely—especially when business is bad and there's   3: nobody to talk to. I get the feeling that I'll never sell anything again, that I won't make a living for you, or a business, a business for the boys. [*He talks through THE WOMAN's subsiding laughter; THE WOMAN primps at the "mirror."*] There's so much I want to make for—

THE WOMAN.   Me? You didn't make me, Willy. I picked you.

WILLY.   [*pleased*] You picked me?

THE WOMAN.   [*who is quite proper-looking, WILLY's age*] I did. I've been sitting at that desk watching all the salesmen go by, day in, day out. But you've got such a sense of humor, and we do have such a good time together, don't we?

WILLY. Sure, sure. [*He takes her in his arms.*] Why do you have to go now?

THE WOMAN. It's two o'clock . . . 340

WILLY. No, come on in! [*He pulls her.*]

THE WOMAN. . . . my sisters'll be scandalized. When'll you be back?

WILLY. Oh, two weeks about. Will you come up again?

THE WOMAN. Sure thing. You do make me laugh. It's good for me. [*She squeezes his arm, kisses him.*] And I think you're a wonderful man.

WILLY. You picked me, heh? 345

THE WOMAN. Sure. Because you're so sweet. And such a kidder.

WILLY. Well, I'll see you next time I'm in Boston.

THE WOMAN. I'll put you right through to the buyers.

WILLY. [*slapping her bottom*] Right. Well, bottoms up!

THE WOMAN. [*slaps him gently and laughs*] You just kill me, Willy. [*He suddenly* 350 *grabs her and kisses her roughly.*] You kill me. And thanks for the stockings. I love a lot of stockings. Well, good night.

WILLY. Good night. And keep your pores open!

THE WOMAN. Oh, Willy!

[*THE WOMAN bursts out laughing, and LINDA's laughter blends in. THE WOMAN disappears into the dark. Now the area at the kitchen table brightens. LINDA is sitting where she was at the kitchen table, but now is mending a pair of her silk stockings.*]

LINDA. You are, Willy. The handsomest man. You've got no reason to feel that—

WILLY. [*coming out of THE WOMAN's dimming area and going over to LINDA*] I'll make it all up to you, Linda, I'll—

LINDA. There's nothing to make up, dear. You're doing fine, better than— 355

WILLY. [*noticing her mending*] What's that?

LINDA. Just mending my stockings. They're so expensive—

WILLY. [*angrily, taking them from her*] I won't have you mending stockings in this house! Now throw them out!

[*LINDA puts the stockings in her pocket.*]

BERNARD. [*entering on the run*] Where is he? If he doesn't study!

WILLY. [*moving to the forestage, with great agitation*] You'll give him the an- 360 swers!

BERNARD I do, but I can't on a Regents! That's a state exam! They're liable to arrest me!

WILLY. Where is he? I'll whip him, I'll whip him!

LINDA. And he'd better give back that football, Willy, it's not nice.

WILLY. Biff! Where is he? Why is he taking everything?

LINDA. He's too rough with the girls, Willy. All the mothers are afraid of 365 him!

WILLY. I'll whip him!

BERNARD. He's driving the car without a license!

[*THE WOMAN's laugh is heard.*]

WILLY. Shut up!

LINDA. All the mothers—

WILLY. Shut up!

BERNARD. [*backing quietly away and out*] Mr. Birnbaum says he's stuck up.

WILLY. Get outa here!

BERNARD. If he doesn't buckle down he'll flunk math! [*He goes off.*]

LINDA. He's right, Willy, you've gotta—

WILLY. [*exploding at her*] There's nothing the matter with him! You want him to be a worm like Bernard? He's got spirit, personality . . .

[*As he speaks,* LINDA, *almost in tears, exits into the living-room.* WILLY *is alone in the kitchen, wilting and staring. The leaves are gone. It is night again, and the apartment houses look down from behind.*]

WILLY. Loaded with it. Loaded! What is he stealing? He's giving it back, isn't he? Why is he stealing? What did I tell him? I never in my life told him anything but decent things.

[HAPPY *in pajamas has come down the stairs;* WILLY *suddenly becomes aware of* HAPPY's *presence.*]

HAPPY. Let's go now, come on.

WILLY. [*sitting down at the kitchen table*] Huh! Why did she have to wax the floors herself? Everytime she waxes the floors she keels over. She knows that!

HAPPY. Shh! Take it easy. What brought you back tonight?

WILLY. I got an awful scare. Nearly hit a kid in Yonkers. God! Why didn't I go to Alaska with my brother Ben that time! Ben! That man was a genius, that man was success incarnate! What a mistake! He begged me to go.

HAPPY. Well, there's no use in—

WILLY. You guys! There was a man started with the clothes on his back and ended up with diamond mines!

HAPPY. Boy, someday I'd like to know how he did it.

WILLY. What's the mystery? The man knew what he wanted and went out and got it! Walked into a jungle, and comes out, the age of twenty-one, and he's rich! The world is an oyster, but you don't crack it open on a mattress!

HAPPY. Pop, I told you I'm gonna retire you for life.

WILLY. You'll retire me for life on seventy goddam dollars a week? And your women and your car and your apartment, and you'll retire me for life! Christ's sake, I couldn't get past Yonkers today! Where are you guys, where are you? The woods are burning! I can't drive a car!

[CHARLEY *has appeared in the doorway. He is a large man, slow of speech, laconic, immovable. In all he says, despite what he says, there is pity, and now, trepidation. He has a robe over pajamas, slippers on his feet. He enters the kitchen.*]

CHARLEY. Everything all right?

HAPPY. Yeah, Charley, everything's . . .

WILLY. What's the matter?

CHARLEY. I heard some noise. I thought something happened. Can't we do something about the walls? You sneeze in here, and in my house hats blow off.

HAPPY. Let's go to bed, Dad. Come on.

[CHARLEY *signals to* HAPPY *to go.*]

WILLY. You go ahead, I'm not tired at the moment.

HAPPY. [*to WILLY*] Take it easy, huh? [*He exits.*]

WILLY. What're you doin' up?

CHARLEY. [*sitting down at the kitchen table opposite WILLY*] Couldn't sleep good.   395
I had a heartburn.

WILLY. Well, you don't know how to eat.

CHARLEY. I eat with my mouth.

WILLY. No, you're ignorant. You gotta know about vitamins and things like
that.

CHARLEY. Come on, let's shoot. Tire you out a little.

WILLY. [*hesitantly*] All right. You got cards?   400

CHARLEY. [*taking a deck from his pocket*] Yeah, I got them. Someplace. What is it
with those vitamins?

WILLY. [*dealing*] They build up your bones. Chemistry.

CHARLEY. Yeah, but there's no bones in a heartburn.

WILLY. What are you talkin' about? Do you know the first thing about it?

CHARLEY. Don't get insulted.   405

WILLY. Don't talk about something you don't know anything about.

[*They are playing. Pause.*]

CHARLEY. What're you doin' home?

WILLY. A little trouble with the car.

CHARLEY. Oh. [*Pause*] I'd like to take a trip to California.

WILLY. Don't say.   410

CHARLEY. You want a job?

WILLY. I got a job, I told you that. [*after a slight pause*] What the hell are you
offering me a job for?

CHARLEY. Don't get insulted.

WILLY. Don't insult me.

CHARLEY. I don't see no sense in it. You don't have to go on this way.   415

WILLY. I got a good job. [*slight pause*] What do you keep comin' in for?

CHARLEY. You want me to go?

WILLY. [*after a pause, withering*] I can't understand it. He's going back to Texas
again. What the hell is that?

CHARLEY. Let him go.

WILLY. I got nothin' to give him, Charley, I'm clean, I'm clean.   420

CHARLEY. He won't starve. None a them starve. Forget about him.

WILLY. Then what have I got to remember?

CHARLEY. You take it too hard. To hell with it. When a deposit bottle is broken you don't get your nickel back.

WILLY. That's easy enough for you to say.

CHARLEY. That ain't easy for me to say.   425

WILLY. Did you see the ceiling I put up in the living-room?

CHARLEY. Yeah, that's a piece of work. To put up a ceiling is a mystery to me.
How do you do it?

WILLY. What's the difference?

CHARLEY. Well, talk about it.

WILLY. You gonna put up a ceiling?   430

CHARLEY. How could I put up a ceiling?

WILLY. Then what the hell are you bothering me for?

CHARLEY. You're insulted again.

WILLY. A man who can't handle tools is not a man. You're disgusting.

CHARLEY. Don't call me disgusting, Willy.   45

[*UNCLE BEN, carrying a valise and an umbrella, enters the forestage from around the right corner of the house. He is a stolid man, in his sixties, with a mustache and an authoritative air. He is utterly certain of his destiny, and there is an aura of far places about him. He enters exactly as WILLY speaks.*]

WILLY. I'm getting awfully tired, Ben.

[*BEN's music is heard. BEN looks around at everything.*]

CHARLEY. Good, keep playing; you'll sleep better. Did you call me Ben?

[*BEN looks at his watch.*]

WILLY. That's funny. For a second there you reminded me of my brother Ben.

BEN. I only have a few minutes. [*He strolls, inspecting the place. WILLY and CHARLEY continue playing.*]

CHARLEY. You never heard from him again, heh? Since that time?   4

WILLY. Didn't Linda tell you? Couple of weeks ago we got a letter from his wife in Africa. He died.

CHARLEY. That so.

BEN. [*chuckling*] So this is Brooklyn, eh?

CHARLEY. Maybe you're in for some of his money.

WILLY. Naa, he had seven sons. There's just one opportunity I had with   4
that man . . .

BEN. I must make a train, William. There are several properties I'm looking at in Alaska.

WILLY. Sure, sure! If I'd gone with him to Alaska that time, everything would've been totally different.

CHARLEY. Go on, you'd froze to death up there.

WILLY. What're you talking about?

BEN. Opportunity is tremendous in Alaska, William. Surprised you're not   4
up there

WILLY. Sure, tremendous.

CHARLEY. Heh?

WILLY. There was the only man I ever met who knew the answers.

CHARLEY. Who?

BEN. How are you all?   4

WILLY. [*taking a pot, smiling*] Fine, fine.

CHARLEY. Pretty sharp tonight.

BEN. Is Mother living with you?

WILLY. No, she died a long time ago.

CHARLEY. Who?   4

BEN. That's too bad. Fine specimen of a lady, Mother.

WILLY. [*to CHARLEY*] Heh?

BEN. I'd hoped to see the old girl.

CHARLEY. Who died?

BEN. Heard anything from Father, have you?   465

WILLY. [*unnerved*] What do you mean, who died?

CHARLEY. [*taking a pot*] What're you talkin' about?

BEN. [*looking at his watch*] William, it's half-past eight!

WILLY. [*As though to dispel his confusion he angrily stops* CHARLEY'S *hand.*] That's my build!

CHARLEY. I put the ace—   470

WILLY. If you don't know how to play the game I'm not gonna throw my money away on you!

CHARLEY. [*rising*] It was my ace, for God's sake!

WILLY. I'm through, I'm through!

BEN. When did Mother die?

WILLY. Long ago. Since the beginning you never knew how to play cards.   475

CHARLEY. [*picks up the cards and goes to the door*] All right! Next time I'll bring a deck with five aces.

WILLY. I don't play that kind of game!

CHARLEY. [*turning to him*] You ought to be ashamed of yourself!

WILLY. Yeah?

CHARLEY. Yeah! [*He goes out.*]   480

WILLY. [*slamming the door after him*] Ignoramus!

BEN. [*as* WILLY *comes toward him through the wall-line of the kitchen*] So you're William.

WILLY. [*shaking* BEN'S *hand*] Ben! I've been waiting for you so long! What's the answer? How did you do it?

BEN. Oh, there's a story in that.

[LINDA *enters the forestage, as of old, carrying the wash basket.*]

LINDA. Is this Ben?   485

BEN. [*gallantly*] How do you do, my dear.

LINDA. Where've you been all these years? Willy's always wondered why you—

WILLY. [*pulling* BEN *away from her impatiently*] Where is Dad? Didn't you follow him? How did you get started?

BEN. Well, I don't know how much you remember.

WILLY. Well, I was just a baby, of course, only three or four years old—   490

BEN. Three years and eleven months.

WILLY. What a memory, Ben!

BEN. I have many enterprises, William, and I have never kept books.

WILLY. I remember I was sitting under the wagon in—was it Nebraska?

BEN. It was South Dakota, and I gave you a bunch of wild flowers.   495

WILLY. I remember you walking away down some open road.

BEN. [*laughing*] I was going to find Father in Alaska.

WILLY. Where is he?

BEN. At that age I had a very faulty view of geography, William. I discovered after a few days that I was heading due south, so instead of Alaska, I ended up in Africa.

LINDA. Africa!   500

WILLY. The Gold Coast!

BEN. Principally diamond mines.

LINDA. Diamond mines!

BEN.   Yes, my dear. But I've only a few minutes—

WILLY.   No! Boys! Boys! [*YOUNG BIFF and HAPPY appear.*] Listen to this. This   5o
is your Uncle Ben, a great man! Tell my boys, Ben!

BEN.   Why, boys, when I was seventeen I walked into the jungle, and when I
was twenty-one I walked out. [*He laughs.*] And by God I was rich.

WILLY.   [*to the boys*] You see what I been talking about? The greatest things can
happen!

BEN.   [*glancing at his watch*] I have an appointment in Ketchikan Tuesday week.

WILLY.   No, Ben. Please tell about Dad. I want my boys to hear. I want them to
know the kind of stock they spring from. All I remember is a man with a big beard,
and I was in Mamma's lap, sitting around a fire, and some kind of high music.

BEN.   His flute. He played the flute.   5o

WILLY.   Sure, the flute, that's right!

[*New music is heard, a high, rollicking tune.*]

BEN.   Father was a very great and a very wild-hearted man. We would start in
Boston, and he'd toss the whole family into the wagon, and then he'd drive the team
right across the country; through Ohio, and Indiana, Michigan, Illinois, and all the
Western states. And we'd stop in the towns and sell the flutes that he'd made on the
way. Great inventor, Father. With one gadget he made more in a week than a man
like you could make in a lifetime.

WILLY.   That's just the way I'm bringing them up, Ben—rugged, well liked, all-
around.

BEN.   Yeah? [*to BIFF*] Hit that, boy—hard as you can. [*He pounds his stomach.*]

BIFF.   Oh, no, sir!   5o

BEN.   [*taking boxing stance*] Come on, get to me! [*He laughs.*]

BIFF.   Okay! [*He cocks his fists and starts in.*]

WILLY.   Go to it, Biff! Go ahead, show him!

LINDA.   [*to WILLY*] Why must he fight, dear?

BEN.   [*sparring with BIFF*] Good boy! Good boy!   5o

WILLY.   How's that, Ben, heh?

HAPPY.   Give him the left, Biff!

LINDA.   Why are you fighting?

BEN.   Good boy! [*suddenly comes in, trips BIFF, and stands over him, the point of his
umbrella poised over BIFF's eye.*]

LINDA.   Look out, Biff!   5o

BIFF.   Gee!

BEN.   [*patting BIFF's knee*] Never fight fair with a stranger, boy. You'll never get
out of the jungle that way. [*taking LINDA's hand and bowing*] It was an honor and a pleasure to meet you, Linda.

LINDA.   [*withdrawing her hand coldly, frightened*] Have a nice—trip.

BEN.   [*to WILLY*] And good luck with your—what do you do?

WILLY.   Selling.   5

BEN.   Yes. Well . . . [*He raises his hand in farewell to all.*]

WILLY.   No, Ben, I don't want you to think . . . [*He takes BEN's arm to show him.*]
It's Brooklyn, I know, but we hunt too.

BEN.   Really, now.

WILLY.   Oh, sure, there's snakes and rabbits and—that's why I moved out here.
Why, Biff can fell any one of these trees in no time! Boys! Go right over to where

they're building the apartment house and get some sand. We're gonna rebuild the entire front stoop right now! Watch this, Ben!

BIFF. Yes, sir! On the double, Hap!   535

HAPPY. [*as he and BIFF run off*] I lost weight, Pop, you notice?

[*CHARLEY enters in knickers, even before the boys are gone.*]

CHARLEY. Listen, if they steal any more from that building the watchman'll put the cops on them!

LINDA. [*to WILLY*] Don't let Biff . . .

[*BEN laughs lustily.*]

WILLY. You shoulda seen the lumber they brought home last week. At least a dozen six-by-tens worth all kinds a money.

CHARLEY. Listen, if that watchman—   540

WILLY. I gave them hell, understand. But I got a couple of fearless characters there.

CHARLEY. Willy, the jails are full of fearless characters.

BEN. [*clapping WILLY on the back, with a laugh at CHARLEY*] And the stock exchange, friend!

WILLY. [*joining in BEN's laughter*] Where are the rest of your pants?

CHARLEY. My wife bought them.   545

WILLY. Now all you need is a golf club and you can go upstairs and go to sleep. [*to BEN*] Great athlete! Between him and his son Bernard they can't hammer a nail!

BERNARD. [*rushing in*] The watchman's chasing Biff!

WILLY. [*angrily*] Shut up! He's not stealing anything!

LINDA. [*alarmed, hurrying off left*] Where is he? Biff, dear! [*She exits.*]

WILLY. [*moving toward the left, away from BEN*] There's nothing wrong. What's   550
the matter with you?

BEN. Nervy boy. Good!

WILLY. [*laughing*] Oh, nerves of iron, that Biff!

CHARLEY. Don't know what it is. My New England man comes back and he's bleedin', they murdered him up there.

WILLY. It's contacts, Charley, I got important contacts!

CHARLEY. [*sarcastically*] Glad to hear it, Willy. Come in later, we'll shoot a   555
little casino. I'll take some of your Portland money. [*He laughs at WILLY and exits.*]

WILLY. [*turning to BEN*] Business is bad, it's murderous. But not for me, of course.

BEN. I'll stop by on my way back to Africa.

WILLY. [*longingly.*] Can't you stay a few days? You're just what I need, Ben, because I—I have a fine position here, but I—well, Dad left when I was such a baby and I never had a chance to talk to him and I still feel—kind of temporary about myself.

BEN. I'll be late for my train.

[*They are at opposite ends of the stage.*]

WILLY. Ben, my boys—can't we talk? They'd go into the jaws of hell for   560
me, see, but I—

BEN. William, you're being first-rate with your boys. Outstanding, manly chaps!

WILLY. [*hanging on to his words*] Oh, Ben, that's good to hear! Because sometimes I'm afraid that I'm not teaching them the right kind of—Ben, how should I teach them?

BEN. [*giving great weight to each word, and with a certain vicious audacity*] William, when I walked into the jungle, I was seventeen. When I walked out I was twenty-one. And, by God, I was rich! [*He goes off into darkness around the right corner of the house.*]

WILLY. . . . was rich! That's just the spirit I want to imbue them with! To walk into a jungle! I was right! I was right! I was right!

[*BEN is gone, but WILLY is still speaking to him as LINDA, in her nightgown and robe, enters the kitchen, glances around for WILLY, then goes to the door of the house, looks out and sees him. Comes down to his left. He looks at her.*]

LINDA. Willy, dear? Willy?   5

WILLY. I was right!

LINDA. Did you have some cheese? [*He can't answer.*] It's very late, darling. Come to bed, heh?

WILLY. [*looking straight up*] Gotta break your neck to see a star in this yard.

LINDA. You coming in?

WILLY. Whatever happened to that diamond watch fob? Remember? When   5 Ben came from Africa that time? Didn't he give me a watch fob with a diamond in it?

LINDA. You pawned it, dear. Twelve, thirteen years ago. For Biff's radio correspondence course.

WILLY. Gee, that was a beautiful thing. I'll take a walk.

LINDA. But you're in your slippers.

WILLY. [*starting to go around the house at the left*] I was right! I was! [*Half to LINDA, as he goes, shaking his head*] What a man! There was a man worth talking to. I was right!   5

LINDA. [*calling after WILLY*] But in your slippers, Willy!

[*WILLY is almost gone when BIFF, in his pajamas, comes down the stairs and enters the kitchen.*]

BIFF. What is he doing out there?

LINDA. Sh!

BIFF. God Almighty, Mom, how long has he been doing this?

LINDA. Don't, he'll hear you.   5

BIFF. What the hell is the matter with him?

LINDA. It'll pass by morning.

BIFF. Shouldn't we do anything?

LINDA. Oh, my dear, you should do a lot of things, but there's nothing to do, so go to sleep.

[*HAPPY comes down the stairs and sits on the steps.*]

HAPPY. I never heard him so loud, Mom.   5

LINDA. Well, come around more often; you'll hear him. [*She sits down at the table and mends the lining of WILLY's jacket.*]

BIFF. Why didn't you ever write me about this, Mom?

LINDA. How would I write to you? For over three months you had no address.

BIFF. I was on the move. But you know I thought of you all the time. You know that, don't you, pal?

LINDA.   I know, dear, I know. But he likes to have a letter. Just to know that there's still a possibility for better things.

BIFF.   He's not like this all the time, is he?   590

LINDA.   It's when you come home he's always the worst.

BIFF.   When I come home?

LINDA.   When you write you're coming, he's all smiles, and talks about the future, and—he's just wonderful. And then the closer you seem to come, the more shaky he gets, and then, by the time you get here, he's arguing, and he seems angry at you. I think it's just that maybe he can't bring himself to—to open up to you. Why are you so hateful to each other? Why is that?

BIFF.   [*evasively*] I'm not hateful, Mom.

LINDA.   But you no sooner come in the door than you're fighting!   595

BIFF.   I don't know why. I mean to change. I'm tryin', Mom, you understand?

LINDA.   Are you home to stay now?

BIFF.   I don't know. I want to look around, see what's doin'.

LINDA.   Biff, you can't look around all your life, can you?

BIFF.   I just can't take hold, Mom. I can't take hold of some kind of a life.   600

LINDA.   Biff, a man is not a bird, to come and go with the springtime.

BIFF.   Your hair . . . [*He touches her hair.*] Your hair got so gray.

LINDA.   Oh, it's been gray since you were in high school. I just stopped dyeing it, that's all.

BIFF.   Dye it again, will ya? I don't want my pal looking old. [*He smiles.*]

LINDA.   You're such a boy! You think you can go away for a year and . . .   605
You've got to get it into your head now that one day you'll knock on this door and there'll be strange people here—

BIFF.   What are you talking about? You're not even sixty, Mom.

LINDA.   But what about your father?

BIFF.   [*lamely*] Well, I meant him, too.

HAPPY.   He admires Pop.

LINDA.   Biff, dear, if you don't have any feeling for him, then you can't have   610
any feeling for me.

BIFF.   Sure I can, Mom.

LINDA.   No. You can't just come to see me, because I love him. [*with a threat, but only a threat, of tears*] He's the dearest man in the world to me, and I won't have anyone making him feel unwanted and low and blue. You've got to make up your mind now, darling, there's no leeway any more. Either he's your father and you pay him that respect, or else you're not to come here. I know he's not easy to get along with—nobody knows that better than me—but . . .

WILLY.   [*from the left, with a laugh*] Hey, hey, Biffo!

BIFF.   [*starting to go out after WILLY*] What the hell is the matter with him? [*HAPPY stops him.*]

LINDA.   Don't—don't go near him!   615

BIFF.   Stop making excuses for him! He always, always wiped the floor with you. Never had an ounce of respect for you.

HAPPY.   He's always had respect for—

BIFF.   What the hell do you know about it?

HAPPY.   [*surlily*] Just don't call him crazy!

BIFF.   He's got no character—Charley wouldn't do this. Not in his own   620
house—spewing out that vomit from his mind.

HAPPY.   Charley never had to cope with what he's got to.

BIFF.   People are worse off than Willy Loman. Believe me, I've seen them!

LINDA.   Then make Charley your father, Biff. You can't do that, can you? I don't say he's a great man. Willy Loman never made a lot of money. His name was never in the paper. He's not the finest character that ever lived. But he's a human being, and a terrible thing is happening to him. So attention must be paid. He's not to be allowed to fall into his grave like an old dog. Attention, attention must be finally paid to such a person. You called him crazy—

BIFF.   I didn't mean—

LINDA.   No, a lot of people think he's lost his—balance. But you don't have   6⁹
to be very smart to know what his trouble is. The man is exhausted.

HAPPY.   Sure!

LINDA.   A small man can be just as exhausted as a great man. He works for a company thirty-six years this March, opens up unheard-of-territories to their trademark, and now in his old age they take his salary away.

HAPPY.   [*indignantly*] I didn't know that, Mom.

LINDA.   You never asked, my dear! Now that you get your spending money someplace else you don't trouble your mind with him.

HAPPY.   But I gave you money last—   6⁹

LINDA.   Christmas time, fifty dollars! To fix the hot water it cost ninety-seven fifty! For five weeks he's been on straight commission,° like a beginner, an unknown!

BIFF.   Those ungrateful bastards!

LINDA.   Are they any worse than his sons? When he brought them business, when he was young, they were glad to see him. But now his old friends, the old buyers that loved him so and always found some order to hand him in a pinch—they're all dead, retired. He used to be able to make six, seven calls a day in Boston. Now he takes his valises out of the car and puts them back and takes them out again and he's exhausted. Instead of walking he talks now. He drives seven hundred miles, and when he gets there no one knows him any more, no one welcomes him. And what goes through a man's mind, driving seven hundred miles home without having earned a cent? Why shouldn't he talk to himself? Why? When he has to go to Charley and borrow fifty dollars a week and pretend to me that it's his pay? How long can that go on? How long? You see what I'm sitting here and waiting for? And you tell me he has no character? The man who never worked a day but for your benefit? When does he get the medal for that? Is this his reward—to turn around at the age of sixty-three and find his sons, who he loved better than his life, one a philandering bum—

HAPPY.   Mom!

LINDA.   That's all you are, my baby! [*To BIFF*] And you! What happened to   6⁹
the love you had for him? You were such pals! How you used to talk to him on the phone every night! How lonely he was till he could come home to you!

BIFF.   All right, Mom. I'll live here in my room, and I'll get a job. I'll keep away from him, that's all.

LINDA.   No, Biff. You can't stay here and fight all the time.

BIFF.   He threw me out of this house, remember that.

LINDA.   Why did he do that? I never knew why.

---

straight commission: refers to the fact that Willy is receiving no salary, only a commission (percentage) on the sales he makes.

BIFF.   Because I know he's a fake and he doesn't like anybody around who   640
knows!

LINDA.   Why a fake? In what way? What do you mean?

BIFF.   Just don't lay it all at my feet. It's between me and him—that's all I have
to say. I'll chip in from now on. He'll settle for half my pay check. He'll be all right.
I'm going to bed. [*He starts for the stairs.*]

LINDA.   He won't be all right.

BIFF.   [*turning on the stairs, furiously*] I hate this city and I'll stay here. Now what
do you want?

LINDA.   He's dying, Biff.   645

[*HAPPY turns quickly to her, shocked.*]

BIFF.   [*after a pause*] Why is he dying?

LINDA.   He's been trying to kill himself.

BIFF.   [*with great horror*] How?

LINDA.   I live from day to day.

BIFF.   What're you talking about?   650

LINDA.   Remember I wrote you that he smashed up the car again? In February?

BIFF.   Well?

LINDA.   The insurance inspector came. He said that they have evidence. That
all these accidents in the last year—weren't—weren't—accidents.

HAPPY.   How can they tell that? That's a lie.

LINDA.   It seems there's a woman . . . [*She takes a breath as*]   655

BIFF.   [*sharply but contained*] What woman?

LINDA.   [*simultaneously*] . . . and this woman . . .

LINDA.   What?

BIFF.   Nothing. Go ahead.

LINDA.   What did you say?   660

BIFF.   Nothing. I just said what woman?

HAPPY.   What about her?

LINDA.   Well, it seems she was walking down the road and saw his car. She says
that he wasn't driving fast at all, and that he didn't skid. She says he came to that little bridge, and then deliberately smashed into the railing, and it was only the shal-
lowness of the water that saved him.

BIFF.   Oh, no, he probably just fell asleep again.

LINDA.   I don't think he fell asleep.   665

BIFF.   Why not?

LINDA.   Last month . . . [*with great difficulty*] Oh, boys, it's so hard to say a thing
like this! He's just a big stupid man to you, but I tell you there's more good in him
than in many other people. [*She chokes, wipes her eyes.*] I was looking for a fuse. The
lights blew out, and I went down the cellar. And behind the fuse box—it happened
to fall out—was a length of rubber pipe—just short.

HAPPY.   No kidding?

LINDA.   There's a little attachment on the end of it. I knew right away. And
sure enough, on the bottom of the water heater there's a new little nipple on the gas
pipe.

HAPPY.   [*angrily*] That—jerk.   667

BIFF.   Did you have it taken off?

LINDA.   I'm—I'm ashamed to. How can I mention it to him? Every day I go down and take away that little rubber pipe. But, when he comes home, I put it back where it was. How can I insult him that way? I don't know what to do. I live from day to day, boys. I tell you, I know every thought in his mind. It sounds so old-fashioned and silly, but I tell you he put his whole life into you and you've turned your backs on him. [*She is bent over in the chair, weeping, her face in her hands.*] Biff, I swear to God! Biff, his life is in your hands!

HAPPY.   [*to* BIFF] How do you like that damned fool!

BIFF.   [*kissing her*] All right, pal, all right. It's all settled now. I've been remiss. I know that, Mom. But now I'll stay, and I swear to you, I'll apply myself. [*kneeling in front of her, in a fever of self-reproach*] It's just—you see, Mom, I don't fit in business. Not that I won't try. I'll try, and I'll make good.

HAPPY.   Sure you will. The trouble with you in business was you never tried to please people.

BIFF.   I know, I—

HAPPY.   Like when you worked for Harrison's. Bob Harrison said you were tops, and then you go and do some damn fool thing like whistling whole songs in the elevator like a comedian.

BIFF.   [*against* HAPPY] So what? I like to whistle sometimes.

HAPPY.   You don't raise a guy to a responsible job who whistles in the elevator!

LINDA.   Well, don't argue about it now.

HAPPY.   Like when you'd go off and swim in the middle of the day instead of taking the line around.

BIFF.   [*his resentment rising*] Well, don't you run off? You take off sometimes, don't you? On a nice summer day?

HAPPY.   Yeah, but I cover myself!

LINDA.   Boys!

HAPPY.   If I'm going to take a fade the boss can call any number where I'm supposed to be and they'll swear to him that I just left. I'll tell you something that I hate to say, Biff, but in the business world some of them think you're crazy.

BIFF.   [*angered*] Screw the business world!

HAPPY.   All right, screw it! Great, but cover yourself!

LINDA.   Hap, Hap!

BIFF.   I don't care what they think! They've laughed at Dad for years, and you know why? Because we don't belong in this nuthouse of a city! We should be mixing cement on some open plain, or—or carpenters. A carpenter is allowed to whistle!

[*WILLY walks in from the entrance of the house, at left.*]

WILLY.   Even your grandfather was better than a carpenter. [*pause. They watch him.*] You never grew up. Bernard does not whistle in the elevator, I assure you.

BIFF.   [*as though to laugh* WILLY *out of it*] Yeah, but you do, Pop.

WILLY.   I never in my life whistled in an elevator! And who in the business world thinks I'm crazy?

BIFF.   I didn't mean it like that, Pop. Now don't make a whole thing out of it, will ya?

WILLY.   Go back to the West! Be a carpenter, a cowboy, enjoy yourself!

LINDA.   Willy, he was just saying—

WILLY.   I heard what he said!

HAPPY.   [*trying to quiet* WILLY] Hey, Pop, come on now . . .

WILLY. [*continuing over HAPPY's line*] They laugh at me, heh? Go to Filene's, go to the Hub, go to Slattery's,° Boston. Call out the name Willy Loman and see what happens! Big shot!

BIFF. All right, Pop.

WILLY. Big!   700

BIFF. All right!

WILLY. Why do you always insult me?

BIFF. I didn't say a word. [*to LINDA*] Did I say a word?

LINDA. He didn't say anything, Willy.

WILLY. [*going to the doorway of the living room*] All right, good night, good   705
night.

LINDA. Willy, dear, he just decided . . .

WILLY. [*to BIFF*] If you get tired hanging around tomorrow, paint the ceiling I put up in the living-room.

BIFF. I'm leaving early tomorrow.

HAPPY. He's going to see Bill Oliver, Pop.

WILLY. [*interestedly*] Oliver? For what?   710

BIFF. [*with reserve, but trying, trying*] He always said he'd stake me. I'd like to go into business, so maybe I can take him up on it.

LINDA. Isn't that wonderful?

WILLY. Don't interrupt. What's wonderful about it? There's fifty men in the City of New York who'd stake him. [*to BIFF*] Sporting goods?

BIFF. I guess so. I know something about it and—

WILLY. He knows something about it! You know sporting goods better than   715
Spalding, for God's sake! How much is he giving you?

BIFF. I don't know. I didn't even see him yet, but—

WILLY. Then what're you talkin' about?

BIFF. [*getting angry*] Well, all I said was I'm gonna see him, that's all!

WILLY. [*turning away*] Ah, you're counting your chickens again.

BIFF. [*starting left for the stairs*] Oh, Jesus, I'm going to sleep!   720

WILLY. [*calling after him*] Don't curse in this house!

BIFF. [*turning*] Since when did you get so clean?

HAPPY. [*trying to stop them*] Wait a . . .

WILLY. Don't use that language to me! I won't have it!

HAPPY. [*grabbing BIFF, shouts*] Wait a minute! I got an idea. I got a feasible   725
idea. Come here, Biff, let's talk this over now, let's talk some sense here. When I was down in Florida last time, I thought of a great idea to sell sporting goods. It just came back to me. You and I, Biff—we have a line, the Loman Line. We train a couple of weeks, and put on a couple of exhibitions, see?

WILLY. That's an idea!

HAPPY. Wait! We form two basketball teams, see? Two waterpolo teams. We play each other. It's a million dollars' worth of publicity. Two brothers, see? The Loman Brothers. Displays in the Royal Palms—all the hotels. And banners over the ring and the basketball court: "Loman Brothers." Baby, we could sell sporting goods!

WILLY. That is a one-million-dollar idea!

LINDA. Marvelous!

BIFF. I'm in great shape as far as that's concerned.   730

Filene's, the Hub, Slattery's: department stores in New England.

HAPPY. And the beauty of it is, Biff, it wouldn't be like a business. We'd be out playin' ball again . . .

BIFF. [*enthused*] Yeah, that's . . .

WILLY. Million-dollar . . .

HAPPY. And you wouldn't get fed up with it, Biff. It'd be the family again. There'd be the old honor, and comradeship, and if you wanted to go off for a swim or somethin'—well, you'd do it! Without some smart cooky gettin' up ahead of you!

WILLY. Lick the world! You guys together could absolutely lick the civilized world.   73

BIFF. I'll see Oliver tomorrow. Hap, if we could work that out . . .

LINDA. Maybe things are beginning to—

WILLY. [*wildly enthused, to* LINDA] Stop interrupting! [*to* BIFF] But don't wear sport jacket and slacks when you see Oliver.

BIFF. No, I'll—

WILLY. A business suit, and talk as little as possible, and don't crack any   74 jokes.

BIFF. He did like me. Always liked me.

LINDA. He loved you!

WILLY. [*to* LINDA] Will you stop! [*to* BIFF] Walk in very serious. You are not applying for a boy's job. Money is to pass. Be quiet, fine, and serious. Everybody likes a kidder, but nobody lends him money.

HAPPY. I'll try to get some myself, Biff. I'm sure I can.

WILLY. I see great things for you kids. I think your troubles are over. But   74 remember, start big and you'll end big. Ask for fifteen. How much you gonna ask for?

BIFF. Gee, I don't know—

WILLY. And don't say "Gee." "Gee" is a boy's word. A man walking in for fifteen thousand dollars does not say "Gee!"

BIFF. Ten, I think, would be top though.

WILLY. Don't be so modest. You always started too low. Walk in with a big laugh. Don't look worried. Start off with a couple of your good stories to lighten things up. It's not what you say, it's how you say it—because personality always wins the day.

LINDA. Oliver always thought the highest of him—   75

WILLY. Will you let me talk?

BIFF. Don't yell at her, Pop, will ya?

WILLY. [*angrily*] I was talking, wasn't I?

BIFF. I don't like you yelling at her all the time, and I'm tellin' you, that's all.

WILLY. What're you, takin' over this house?   75

LINDA. Willy—

WILLY. [*turning on her*] Don't take his side all the time, godammit!

BIFF. [*furiously*] Stop yelling at her!

WILLY. [*suddenly pulling on his cheek, beaten down, guilt ridden*] Give my best to Bill Oliver—he may remember me.

[*He exits through the living-room doorway.*]

LINDA. [*her voice subdued*] What'd you have to start that for? [BIFF *turns*   76 *away.*] You see how sweet he was as soon as you talked hopefully? [*She goes over to* BIFF.] Come up and say good night to him. Don't let him go to bed that way.

HAPPY. Come on, Biff, let's buck him up.

LINDA.   Please, dear. Just say good night. It takes so little to make him happy. Come. [*She goes through the living-room doorway, calling upstairs from within the living-room.*] Your pajamas are hanging in the bathroom, Willy!

HAPPY.   [*looking toward where LINDA went out*] What a woman! They broke the mold when they made her. You know that, Biff?

BIFF.   He's off salary. My God, working on commission!   765

HAPPY.   Well, let's face it: he's no hot-shot selling man. Except that sometimes, you have to admit, he's a sweet personality.

BIFF.   [*deciding*] Lend me ten bucks, will ya? I want to buy some new ties.

HAPPY.   I'll take you to a place I know. Beautiful stuff. Wear one of my striped shirts tomorrow.

BIFF.   She got gray. Mom got awful old. Gee, I'm gonna go in to Oliver tomorrow and knock him for a—

HAPPY.   Come on up. Tell that to Dad. Let's give him a whirl. Come on.   770

BIFF.   [*steamed up*] You know, with ten thousand bucks, boy!

HAPPY.   [*as they go into the living-room*] That's the talk, Biff, that's the first time I've heard the old confidence out of you! [*from within the living-room, fading off*] You're gonna live with me, kid, and any babe you want just say the word . . . [*The last lines are hardly heard. They are mounting the stairs to their parents' bedroom.*]

LINDA.   [*entering her bedroom and addressing WILLY, who is in the bathroom. She is straightening the bed for him.*] Can you do anything about the shower? It drips.

WILLY.   [*from the bathroom*] All of a sudden everything falls to pieces! Goddam plumbing, oughta be sued, those people. I hardly finished putting it in and the thing . . . [*His words rumble off.*]

LINDA.   I'm just wondering if Oliver will remember him. You think he might?

WILLY.   [*coming out of the bathroom in his pajamas*] Remember him? What's   775 the matter with you, you crazy? If he'd've stayed with Oliver he'd be on top by now! Wait'll Oliver gets a look at him. You don't know the average caliber any more. The average young man today—[*He is getting into bed*]—is got a caliber of zero. Greatest thing in the world for him was to bum around.

[*BIFF and HAPPY enter the bedroom. Slight pause.*]

WILLY.   [*stops short, looking at BIFF*] Glad to hear it, boy.

HAPPY.   He wanted to say good night to you, sport.

WILLY.   [*to BIFF*] Yeah. Knock him dead, boy. What'd you want to tell me?

BIFF.   Just take it easy, Pop. Good night. [*He turns to go.*]

WILLY.   [*unable to resist*] And if anything falls off the desk while you're   780 talking to him—like a package or something—don't you pick it up. They have office boys for that.

LINDA.   I'll make a big breakfast—

WILLY.   Will you let me finish? [*to BIFF*] Tell him you were in the business in the West. Not farm work.

BIFF.   All right, Dad.

LINDA.   I think everything—

WILLY.   [*going right through her speech*] And don't undersell yourself. No less   785 than fifteen thousand dollars.

BIFF.   [*unable to bear him*] Okay. Good night, Mom. [*He starts moving.*]

WILLY.   Because you got a greatness in you, Biff, remember that. You got all kinds a greatness . . . [*He lies back, exhausted.*]

[*BIFF walks out.*]

LINDA. [*calling after BIFF*] Sleep well, darling!
HAPPY. I'm gonna get married, Mom. I wanted to tell you.
LINDA. Go to sleep, dear.   79●
HAPPY. [*going*] I just wanted to tell you.
WILLY. Keep up the good work. [*HAPPY exits.*] God . . . remember that Ebbets
Field° game? The championship of the city?
LINDA. Just rest. Should I sing to you?
WILLY. Yeah. Sing to me. [*LINDA hums a soft lullaby.*] When that team came
out—he was the tallest, remember?
LINDA. Oh, yes. And in gold.   79

[*BIFF enters the darkened kitchen, takes a cigarette, and leaves the house. He comes downstage
into a golden pool of light. He smokes, staring at the night.*]

WILLY. Like a young god. Hercules—something like that. And the sun, the
sun all around him. Remember how he waved to me? Right up from the field, with
the representatives of three colleges standing by? And the buyers I brought, and the
cheers when he came out—Loman, Loman, Loman! God Almighty, he'll be great yet.
A star like that, magnificent, can never really fade away!

[*The light on WILLY is fading. The gas heater begins to glow through the kitchen wall, near the
stairs, a blue flame beneath red coils.*]

LINDA. [*timidly*] Willy dear, what has he got against you?
WILLY. I'm so tired. Don't talk any more.

[*BIFF slowly returns to the kitchen. He stops, stares toward the heater.*]

LINDA. Will you ask Howard to let you work in New York?
WILLY. First thing in the morning. Everything'll be all right.   80●

[*BIFF reaches behind the heater and draws out a length of rubber tubing. He is horrified and
turns his head toward WILLY'S room, still dimly lit, from which the strains of LINDA'S desperate
but monotonous humming rise.*]

WILLY. [*staring through the window into the moonlight*] Gee, look at the moon
moving between the buildings!

[*BIFF wraps the tubing around his hand and quickly goes up the stairs.*]

ACT 2

[*Music is heard, gay and bright. The curtain rises as the music fades away. WILLY, in shirt
sleeves, is sitting at the kitchen table, sipping coffee, his hat in his lap. LINDA is filling his cup
when she can.*]

Ebbets Field: the baseball stadium of the Brooklyn Dodgers before they moved to Los Angeles in
1958. Biff had played there in a city championship football game. See II.210 (p. 1275).

WILLY.   Wonderful coffee. Meal in itself.

LINDA.   Can I make you some eggs?

WILLY.   No. Take a breath.

LINDA.   You look so rested, dear.

WILLY.   I slept like a dead one. First time in months. Imagine, sleeping till ten   5
on a Tuesday morning. Boys left nice and early, heh?

LINDA.   They were out of here by eight o'clock.

WILLY.   Good work!

LINDA.   It was so thrilling to see them leaving together. I can't get over the
shaving lotion in this house!

WILLY.   [*smiling*] Mmm—

LINDA.   Biff was very changed this morning. His whole attitude seemed to   10
be hopeful. He couldn't wait to get downtown to see Oliver.

WILLY.   He's heading for a change. There's no question, there simply are certain men that take longer to get—solidified. How did he dress?

LINDA.   His blue suit. He's so handsome in that suit. He could be a—anything
in that suit!

[*WILLY gets up from the table. LINDA holds his jacket for him.*]

WILLY.   There's no question, no question at all. Gee, on the way home tonight
I'd like to buy some seeds.

LINDA.   [*laughing*] That'd be wonderful. But not enough sun gets back there.
Nothing'll grow any more.

WILLY.   You wait, kid, before it's all over we're gonna get a little place out   15
in the country, and I'll raise some vegetables, a couple of chickens . . .

LINDA.   You'll do it yet, dear.

[*WILLY walks out of his jacket, LINDA follows him.*]

WILLY.   And they'll get married, and come for a weekend. I'd build a little
guest house. 'Cause I got so many fine tools, all I'd need would be a little lumber and
some peace of mind.

LINDA.   [*joyfully*] I sewed the lining . . .

WILLY.   I could build two guest houses, so they'd both come. Did he decide
how much he's going to ask Oliver for?

LINDA.   [*getting him into the jacket*] He didn't mention it, but I imagine ten   20
or fifteen thousand. You going to talk to Howard today?

WILLY.   Yeah. I'll put it to him straight and simple. He'll just have to take me
off the road.

LINDA.   And Willy, don't forget to ask for a little advance, because we've got
the insurance premium. It's the grace period now.

WILLY.   That's a hundred . . . ?

LINDA.   A hundred and eight, sixty-eight. Because we're a little short again.

WILLY.   Why are we short?   25

LINDA.   Well, you had the motor job on the car . . .

WILLY.   That goddam Studebaker!

LINDA.   And you got one more payment on the refrigerator . . .

WILLY.   But it just broke again!

LINDA.   Well, it's old, dear.   30

WILLY.   I told you we should've bought a well-advertised machine. Charley bought a General Electric and it's twenty years old and it's still good, that son-of-a-bitch.

LINDA.   But, Willy—

WILLY.   Whoever heard of a Hastings refrigerator? Once in my life I would like to own something outright before it's broken! I'm always in a race with the junkyard! I just finished paying for the car and it's on its last legs. The refrigerator consumes belts like a goddam maniac. They time those things. They time them so when you finally paid for them, they're used up.

LINDA.   [*buttoning up his jacket as he unbuttons it*] All told, about two hundred dollars would carry us, dear. But that includes the last payment on the mortgage. After this payment, Willy, the house belongs to us.

WILLY.   It's twenty-five years!

LINDA.   Biff was nine years old when we bought it.

WILLY.   Well, that's a great thing. To weather a twenty-five year mortgage is—

LINDA.   It's an accomplishment.

WILLY.   All the cement, the lumber, the reconstruction I put in this house! There ain't a crack to be found in it any more.

LINDA.   Well, it served its purpose.

WILLY.   What purpose? Some stranger'll come along, move in, and that's that. If only Biff would take this house, and raise a family . . . [*He starts to go.*] Good-by, I'm late.

LINDA.   [*suddenly remembering*] Oh, I forgot! You're supposed to meet them for dinner.

WILLY.   Me?

LINDA.   At Frank's Chop House on Forty-eighth near Sixth Avenue.

WILLY.   Is that so! How about you?

LINDA.   No, just the three of you. They're gonna blow you to a big meal!

WILLY.   Don't say! Who thought of that?

LINDA.   Biff came to me this morning, Willy, and he said, "Tell Dad, we want to blow him to a big meal." Be there six o'clock. You and your two boys are going to have dinner.

WILLY.   Gee whiz! That's really somethin'. I'm gonna knock Howard for a loop, kid. I'll get an advance, and I'll come home with a New York job. Goddammit, now I'm gonna do it!

LINDA.   Oh, that's the spirit, Willy!

WILLY.   I will never get behind a wheel the rest of my life!

LINDA.   It's changing, Willy, I can feel it changing!

WILLY.   Beyond a question. G'by, I'm late. [*He starts to go again.*]

LINDA.   [*calling after him as she runs to the kitchen table for a handkerchief*] You got your glasses?

WILLY.   [*feels for them, then comes back in*] Yeah, yeah, got my glasses.

LINDA.   [*giving him the handkerchief*] And a handkerchief.

WILLY.   Yeah, handkerchief.

LINDA.   And your saccharine?

WILLY.   Yeah, my saccharine.

LINDA.   Be careful on the subway stairs.

[*She kisses him, and a silk stocking is seen hanging from her hand. WILLY notices it.*]

WILLY.   Will you stop mending stockings? At least while I'm in the house. It gets me nervous. I can't tell you. Please.

[*LINDA hides the stocking in her hand as she follows WILLY across the forestage in front of the house.*]

LINDA. Remember, Frank's Chop House.

WILLY. [*passing the apron*] Maybe beets would grow out there.

LINDA. [*laughing*] But you tried so many times.

WILLY. Yeah. Well, don't work hard today. [*He disappears around the right   65
corner of the house.*]

LINDA. Be careful!

[*As WILLY vanishes, LINDA waves to him. Suddenly the phone rings. She runs across the stage and into the kitchen and lifts it.*]

LINDA. Hello? Oh, Biff! I'm so glad you called, I just . . . Yes, sure, I just told him. Yes, he'll be there for dinner at six o'clock, I didn't forget. Listen, I was just dying to tell you. You know that little rubber pipe I told you about? That he connected to the gas heater? I finally decided to go down the cellar this morning and take it away and destroy it. But it's gone! Imagine? He took it away himself, it isn't there! [*She listens.*] When? Oh, then you took it. Oh—nothing, it's just that I'd hoped he'd taken it away himself. Oh, I'm not worried, darling, because this morning he left in such high spirits, it was like the old days! I'm not afraid any more. Did Mr. Oliver see you? . . . Well, you wait there then. And make a nice impression on him, darling. Just don't perspire too much before you see him. And have a nice time with Dad. He may have big news too! . . . That's right, a New York job. And be sweet to him tonight, dear. Be loving to him. Because he's only a little boat looking for a harbor. [*She is trembling with sorrow and joy.*] Oh, that's wonderful, Biff, you'll save his life. Thanks, darling. Just put your arm around him when he comes into the restaurant. Give him a smile. That's the boy . . . Good-by, dear . . . You got your comb? . . . That's fine. Good-by, Biff dear.

[*In the middle of her speech, HOWARD WAGNER, thirty-six, wheels in a small typewriter table on which is a wire-recording machine and proceeds to plug it in. This is on the left forestage. Light slowly fades on LINDA as it rises on HOWARD. HOWARD is intent on threading the machine and only glances over his shoulder as WILLY appears.*]

WILLY. Pst! Pst!

HOWARD. Hello, Willy, come in.

WILLY. Like to have a little talk with you, Howard.   70

HOWARD. Sorry to keep you waiting. I'll be with you in a minute.

WILLY. What's that, Howard?

HOWARD. Didn't you ever see one of these? Wire recorder.

WILLY. Oh. Can we talk a minute?

HOWARD. Records things. Just got delivery yesterday. Been driving me   75
crazy, the most terrific machine I ever saw in my life. I was up all night with it.

WILLY. What do you do with it?

HOWARD. I bought it for dictation, but you can do anything with it. Listen to this. I had it home last night. Listen to what I picked up. The first one is my daughter. Get this. [*He flicks the switch and "Roll out the Barrel" is heard being whistled.*] Listen to that kid whistle.

WILLY. That is lifelike, isn't it?

HOWARD. Seven years old. Get that tone.

WILLY. Ts, ts. Like to ask a little favor if you . . .   80

[*The whistling breaks off, and the voice of* HOWARD'S DAUGHTER *is heard.*]

HIS DAUGHTER.   "Now you, Daddy."

HOWARD.   She's crazy for me! [*Again the same song is whistled.*] That's me! Ha! [*He winks.*]

WILLY.   You're very good!

[*The whistling breaks off again. The machine runs silent for a moment.*]

HOWARD.   Sh! Get this now, this is my son.

HIS SON.   "The capital of Alabama is Montgomery; the capital of Arizona is Phoenix; the capital of Arkansas is Little Rock; the capital of California is Sacramento . . ." [*and on, and on*]

HOWARD.   [*holding up five fingers*] Five years old, Willy!

WILLY.   He'll make an announcer some day!

HIS SON.   [*continuing*] "The capital . . ."

HOWARD.   Get that—alphabetical order! [*The machine breaks off suddenly.*] Wait a minute. The maid kicked the plug out.

WILLY.   It certainly is a—

HOWARD.   Sh, for God's sake!

HIS SON.   "It's nine o'clock, Bulova watch time. So I have to go to sleep."

WILLY.   That really is—

HOWARD.   Wait a minute! The next is my wife.

[*They wait.*]

HOWARD'S VOICE.   "Go on, say something." [*pause*] "Well, you gonna talk?"

HIS WIFE.   "I can't think of anything."

HOWARD'S VOICE.   "Well, talk—it's turning."

HIS WIFE.   [*shyly, beaten*] "Hello." [*Silence*] "Oh, Howard, I can't talk into this. . ."

HOWARD.   [*snapping the machine off*] That was my wife.

WILLY.   That is a wonderful machine. Can we—

HOWARD.   I tell you, Willy, I'm gonna take my camera, and my bandsaw, and all my hobbies, and out they go. This is the most fascinating relaxation I ever found.

WILLY.   I think I'll get one myself.

HOWARD.   Sure, they're only a hundred and a half. You can't do without it. Supposing you wanna hear Jack Benny,° see? But you can't be at home at that hour. So you tell the maid to turn the radio on when Jack Benny comes on, and this automatically goes on with the radio . . .

WILLY.   And when you come home you . . .

HOWARD.   You can come home twelve o'clock, one o'clock, any time you like, and you get yourself a Coke and sit yourself down, throw the switch, and there's Jack Benny's program in the middle of the night!

WILLY.   I'm definitely going to get one. Because lots of time I'm on the road, and I think to myself, what I must be missing on the radio!

HOWARD.   Don't you have a radio in the car?

WILLY.   Well, yeah, but who ever thinks of turning it on?

Jack Benny: (1894–1974), vaudeville, radio, television and movie comedian.

HOWARD.   Say, aren't you supposed to be in Boston?

WILLY.   That's what I want to talk to you about, Howard. You got a minute?   110

[*He draws a chair in from the wing.*]

HOWARD.   What happened? What're you doing here?

WILLY.   Well . . .

HOWARD.   You didn't crack up again, did you?

WILLY.   Oh, no. No . . .

HOWARD.   Geez, you had me worried there for a minute. What's the trouble?   115

WILLY.   Well, tell you the truth, Howard, I've come to the decision that I'd rather not travel any more.

HOWARD.   Not travel! Well, what'll you do?

WILLY.   Remember, Christmas time, when you had the party here? You said you'd try to think of some spot for me here in town.

HOWARD.   With us?

WILLY.   Well, sure.   120

HOWARD.   Oh, yeah, yeah. I remember. Well, I couldn't think of anything for you, Willy.

WILLY.   I tell ya, Howard. The kids are all grown up, y'know. I don't need much any more. If I could take home—well, sixty-five dollars a week, I could swing it.

HOWARD.   Yeah, but Willy, see I—

WILLY.   I tell ya why, Howard. Speaking frankly and between the two of us, y'know—I'm just a little tired.

HOWARD.   Oh, I could understand that, Willy. But you're a road man, Willy,   125
and we do a road business. We've only got a half-dozen salesmen on the floor here.

WILLY.   God knows, Howard, I never asked a favor of any man. But I was with the firm when your father used to carry you up here in his arms.

HOWARD.   I know that, Willy, but—

WILLY.   Your father came to me the day you were born and asked me what I thought of the name of Howard, may he rest in peace.

HOWARD.   I appreciate that, Willy, but there just is no spot here for you. If I had a spot I'd slam you right in, but I just don't have a single solitary spot.

[*He looks for his lighter. WILLY has picked it up and gives it to him. Pause.*]

WILLY.   [*with increasing anger*] Howard, all I need to set my table is fifty   130
dollars a week.

HOWARD.   But where am I going to put you, kid?

WILLY.   Look, it isn't a question of whether I can sell merchandise, is it?

HOWARD.   No, but it's a business, kid, and everybody's gotta pull his own weight.

WILLY.   [*desperately*] Just let me tell you a story, Howard—

HOWARD.   'Cause you gotta admit, business is business.   135

WILLY.   [*angrily*] Business in definitely business, but just listen for a minute. You don't understand this. When I was a boy—eighteen, nineteen—I was already on the road. And there was a question in my mind as to whether selling had a future for me. Because in those days I had a yearning to go to Alaska. See, there were three gold strikes in one month in Alaska, and I felt like going out. Just for the ride, you might say.

HOWARD. [*barely interested*] Don't say.

WILLY. Oh, yeah, my father lived many years in Alaska. He was an adventurous man. We've got quite a little streak of self-reliance in our family. I thought I'd go out with my older brother and try to locate him, and maybe settle in the North with the old man. And I was almost decided to go, when I met a salesman in the Parker House.° His name was Dave Singleman. And he was eighty-four years old, and he'd drummed merchandise in thirty-one states. And old Dave, he'd go up to his room, y'understand, put on his green velvet slippers—I'll never forget—and pick up his phone and call the buyers, and without ever leaving his room, at the age of eighty-four, he made his living. And when I saw that, I realized that selling was the greatest career a man could want. 'Cause what could be more satisfying than to be able to go, at the age of eighty-four, into twenty or thirty different cities, and pick up a phone, and be remembered and loved and helped by so many different people? Do you know? when he died—and by the way he died the death of a salesman, in his green velvet slippers in the smoker of the New York, New Haven and Hartford, going into Boston—when he died, hundreds of salesmen and buyers were at his funeral. Things were sad on a lotta trains for months after that. [*He stands up. HOWARD has not looked at him.*] In those days there was personality in it, Howard. There was respect, and comradeship, and gratitude in it. Today, it's all cut and dried, and there's no chance for bringing friendship to bear—or personality. You see what I mean? They don't know me any more.

HOWARD. [*moving away, to the right*] That's just the thing, Willy.

WILLY. If I had forty dollars a week—that's all I'd need. Forty dollars, Howard.

14

HOWARD. Kid, I can't take blood from a stone, I—

WILLY. [*desperation is on him now*] Howard, the year Al Smith° was nominated, your father came to me and—

HOWARD. [*starting to go off*] I've got to see some people, kid.

WILLY. [*stopping him*] I'm talking about your father! There were promises made across this desk! You mustn't tell me you've got people to see—I put thirty-four years into this firm, Howard, and now I can't pay my insurance! You can't eat the orange and throw the peel away—a man is not a piece of fruit! [*after a pause*] Now pay attention. Your father—in 1928 I had a big year. I averaged a hundred and seventy dollars a week in commissions.

HOWARD. [*impatiently*] Now, Willy, you never averaged—

14

WILLY. [*banging his hand on the desk*] I averaged a hundred and seventy dollars a week in the year of 1928! And your father came to me—or rather, I was in the office here—it was right over this desk—and he put his hand on my shoulder—

HOWARD. [*getting up*] You'll have to excuse me, Willy, I gotta see some people. Pull yourself together. [*going out*] I'll be back in a little while.

[*On HOWARD's exit, the light on his chair grows very bright and strange.*]

WILLY. Pull myself together! What the hell did I say to him? My God, I was yelling at him! How could I! [*WILLY breaks off, staring at the light, which occupies the chair,*

Parker House: a hotel in Boston.
Al Smith: Alfred E. Smith was governor of New York State (1919–1921, 1923–1929) and the Democratic presidential candidate defeated by Herbert Hoover in 1928.

animating it. He approaches this chair, standing across the desk from it.] Frank, Frank, don't you remember what you told me that time? How you put your hand on my shoulder, and Frank . . . [*He leans on the desk and as he speaks the dead man's name he accidentally switches on the recorder, and instantly*]

HOWARD'S SON.   ". . . of New York is Albany. The capital of Ohio is Cincinnati, the capital of Rhode Island is . . ." [*The recitation continues.*]

WILLY.   [*leaping away with fright, shouting*] Ha! Howard! Howard! Howard!   150

HOWARD.   [*rushing in*] What happened?

WILLY.   [*pointing at the machine, which continues nasally, childishly, with the capital cities*] Shut it off! Shut it off!

HOWARD.   [*pulling the plug out*] Look, Willy . . .

WILLY.   [*pressing his hands to his eyes*] I gotta get myself some coffee. I'll get some coffee . . .

[*WILLY starts to walk out. HOWARD stops him.*]

HOWARD.   [*rolling up the cord*] Willy, look . . .   155

WILLY.   I'll go to Boston.

HOWARD.   Willy, you can't go to Boston for us.

WILLY.   Why can't I go?

HOWARD.   I don't want you to represent us. I've been meaning to tell you for a long time now.

WILLY.   Howard, are you firing me?

HOWARD.   I think you need a good long rest, Willy.   160

WILLY.   Howard—

HOWARD.   And when you feel better, come back, and we'll see if we can work something out.

WILLY.   But I gotta earn money, Howard. I'm in no position to—

HOWARD.   Where are your sons? Why don't your sons give you a hand?   165

WILLY.   They're working on a very big deal.

HOWARD.   This is no time for false pride, Willy. You go to your sons and you tell them that you're tired. You've got two great boys, haven't you?

WILLY.   Oh, no question, no question, but in the meantime . . .

HOWARD.   Then that's that, heh?

WILLY.   All right, I'll go to Boston tomorrow.   170

HOWARD.   No, no.

WILLY.   I can't throw myself on my sons. I'm not a cripple!

HOWARD.   Look, kid, I'm busy this morning.

WILLY.   [*grasping HOWARD's arm*] Howard, you've got to let me go to Boston!

HOWARD.   [*hard, keeping himself under control*] I've got a line of people to see   175
this morning. Sit down, take five minutes, and pull yourself together, and then go home, will ya? I need the office, Willy. [*He starts to go, turns, remembering the recorder, starts to push off the table holding the recorder.*] Oh, yeah. Whenever you can this week, stop by and drop off the samples. You'll feel better, Willy, and then come back and we'll talk. Pull yourself together, kid, there's people outside.

[*HOWARD exits, pushing the table off left. WILLY stares into space, exhausted. Now the music is heard—BEN's music—first distantly, then closer. As WILLY speaks, BEN enters from the right. He carries valise and umbrella.*]

WILLY.   Oh, Ben, how did you do it? What is the answer? Did you wind up the Alaska deal already?

BEN.   Doesn't take much time if you know what you're doing. Just a short business trip. Boarding ship in an hour. Wanted to say good-by.

WILLY.   Ben, I've got to talk to you.

BEN.   [*glancing at his watch*] Haven't much time, William.

WILLY.   [*crossing the apron to BEN*] Ben, nothing's working out. I don't know what to do.

BEN.   Now, look here, William. I've bought timberland in Alaska and I need a man to look after things for me.

WILLY.   God, timberland! Me and my boys in those grand outdoors!

BEN.   You've a new continent at your doorstep, William. Get out of these cities, they're full of talk and time payments and courts of law. Screw on your fists and you can fight for a fortune up there.

WILLY.   Yes, yes! Linda, Linda!

[*LINDA enters as of old, with the wash.*]

LINDA.   Oh, you're back?

BEN.   I haven't much time.

WILLY.   No, wait! Linda, he's got a proposition for me in Alaska.

LINDA.   But you've got—[*to BEN*] He's got a beautiful job here.

WILLY.   But in Alaska, kid, I could—

LINDA.   You're doing well enough, Willy!

BEN.   [*to LINDA*] Enough for what, my dear?

LINDA.   [*frightened of BEN and angry at him*] Don't say those things to him! Enough to be happy right here, right now. [*to WILLY, while BEN laughs*] Why must everybody conquer the world? You're well liked, and the boys love you, and someday—[*to BEN*]—why old man Wagner told him just the other day that if he keeps it up he'll be a member of the firm, didn't he, Willy?

WILLY.   Sure, sure. I am building something with this firm, Ben, and if a man is building something he must be on the right track, mustn't he?

BEN.   What are you building? Lay your hand on it. Where is it?

WILLY.   [*hesitantly*] That's true, Linda, there's nothing.

LINDA.   Why? [*to BEN*] There's a man eighty-four years old—

WILLY.   That's right, Ben, that's right. When I look at that man I say, what is there to worry about?

BEN.   Bah!

WILLY.   It's true, Ben. All he has to do is go into any city, pick up the phone, and he's making his living and you know why?

BEN.   [*picking up his valise*] I've got to go.

WILLY.   [*holding BEN back*] Look at this boy!

[*BIFF, in his high school sweater, enters carrying suitcase. HAPPY carries BIFF'S shoulder guards, gold helmet, and football pants.*]

WILLY.   Without a penny to his name, three great universities are begging for him, and from there the sky's the limit, because it's not what you do, Ben. It's who you know and the smile on your face! It's contacts, Ben, contacts! The whole wealth of Alaska passes over the lunch table at the Commodore Hotel,° and that's the won-

Commodore Hotel: a large hotel in New York City.

der, the wonder of this country, that a man can end with diamonds here on the basis of being liked! [*He turns to* BIFF] And that's why when you get out on that field today it's important. Because thousands of people will be rooting for you and loving you. [*to* BEN, *who has again begun to leave*] And Ben! when he walks into a business office his name will sound out like a bell and all the doors will open to him! I've seen it, Ben, I've seen it a thousand times! You can't feel it with your hand like timber, but it's there!

BEN.   Good-by, William.

WILLY.   Ben, am I right? Don't you think I'm right? I value your advice.

BEN.   There's a new continent at your doorstep, William. You could walk   205
out rich. Rich! [*He is gone.*]

WILLY.   We'll do it here, Ben! You hear me? We're gonna do it here!

[*YOUNG BERNARD rushes in. The gay music of the Boys is heard.*]

BERNARD.   Oh, gee, I was afraid you left already!

WILLY.   Why? What time is it?

BERNARD.   It's half-past one!

WILLY.   Well, come on, everybody! Ebbets Field next stop! Where's the   210
pennants? [*He rushes through the wall-line of the kitchen and out into the dining-room.*]

LINDA.   [*to* BIFF] Did you pack fresh underwear?

BIFF.   [*who has been limbering up*] I want to go!

BERNARD.   Biff, I'm carrying your helmet, ain't I?

HAPPY.   No, I'm carrying the helmet.

BERNARD.   Oh, Biff, you promised me.   215

HAPPY.   I'm carrying the helmet.

BERNARD.   How am I going to get in the locker room?

LINDA.   Let him carry the shoulder guards. [*She puts her coat and hat on in the kitchen.*]

BERNARD.   Can I, Biff? 'Cause I told everybody I'm going to be in the locker room.

HAPPY.   In Ebbets Field it's the clubhouse.   220

BERNARD.   I meant the clubhouse. Biff!

HAPPY.   Biff!

BIFF.   [*grandly, after a slight pause.*] Let him carry the shoulder guards.

HAPPY.   [*as he gives* BERNARD *the shoulder guards*] Stay close to us now.

[*WILLY rushes in with the pennants.*]

WILLY.   [*handing them out*] Everybody wave when Biff comes out on the field.   225

[*HAPPY and BERNARD run off.*] You set now, boy?

[*The music has died away.*]

BIFF.   Ready to go, Pop. Every muscle is ready.

WILLY.   [*at the edge of the apron*] You realize what this means?

BIFF.   That's right, Pop.

WILLY.   [*feeling* BIFF's *muscles*] You're comin' home this afternoon captain of the All-Scholastic Championship Team of the City of New York.

BIFF.   I got it, Pop. And remember, pal, when I take off my helmet, that touch-   230
down is for you.

WILLY. Let's go! [*He is starting out, with his arm around* BIFF, *when* CHARLEY *enters, as of old, in knickers.*] I got no room for you, Charley.

CHARLEY. Room? For what?

WILLY. In the car.

CHARLEY. You goin' for a ride? I wanted to shoot some casino.

WILLY. [*furiously*] Casino! [*incredulously*] Don't you realize what today is?

LINDA. Oh, he knows, Willy. He's just kidding you.

WILLY. That's nothing to kid about!

CHARLEY. No, Linda, what's goin' on?

LINDA. He's playing in Ebbets Field.

CHARLEY. Baseball in this weather?

WILLY. Don't talk to him. Come on, come on! [*He is pushing them out.*]

CHARLEY. Wait a minute, didn't you hear the news?

WILLY. What?

CHARLEY. Don't you listen to the radio? Ebbets Field just blew up.

WILLY. You go to hell! [CHARLEY *laughs. Pushing them out.*] Come on, come on! We're late.

CHARLEY. [*as they go*] Knock a homer, Biff, knock a homer!

WILLY. [*the last to leave, turning to* CHARLEY] I don't think that was funny, Charley. This is the greatest day of his life.

CHARLEY. Willy, when are you going to grow up?

WILLY. Yeah, heh? When this game is over, Charley, you'll be laughing out the other side of your face. They'll be calling him another Red Grange.° Twenty-five thousand a year.

CHARLEY. [*kidding*] Is that so?

WILLY. Yeah, that's so.

CHARLEY. Well, then, I'm sorry, Willy. But tell me something.

WILLY. What?

CHARLEY. Who is Red Grange?

WILLY. Put up your hands. Goddam you, put up your hands!

[CHARLEY, *chuckling, shakes his head and walks away, around the left corner of the stage.* WILLY *follows him. The music rises to a mocking frenzy.*]

WILLY. Who the hell do you think you are, better than everybody else? You don't know everything, you big, ignorant, stupid. . . . Put up your hands!

[*Light rises, on the right side of the forestage, on a small table in the reception room of* CHARLEY'S *office. Traffic sounds are heard.* BERNARD, *now mature, sits whistling to himself. A pair of tennis rackets and an overnight bag are on the floor beside him.*]

WILLY. [*offstage*] What are you walking away for? Don't walk away! If you're going to say something say it to my face! I know you laugh at me behind my back. You'll laugh out of the other side of your goddam face after this game. Touchdown! Touchdown! Eighty thousand people! Touchdown. Right between the goal posts.

[BERNARD *is a quiet, earnest, but self-assured young man.* WILLY'S *voice is coming from right upstage now.* BERNARD *lowers his feet off the table and listens.* JENNY, *his father's secretary, enters.*]

Red Grange: Harold Edward Grange (1903–1991), all-America halfback (1923–1925) at the University of Illinois.

JENNY. [*distressed*] Say, Bernard, will you go out in the hall?

BERNARD. What is that noise? Who is it?

JENNY. Mr. Loman. He just got off the elevator.   260

BERNARD. [*getting up*] Who's he arguing with?

JENNY. Nobody. There's nobody with him. I can't deal with him any more, and your father gets all upset everytime he comes. I've got a lot of typing to do, and your father's waiting to sign it. Will you see him?

WILLY. [*entering*] Touchdown! Touch—[*He sees* JENNY.] Jenny, Jenny, good to see you. How're ya? Workin'? Or still honest?

JENNY. Fine. How've you been feeling?

WILLY. Not much any more, Jenny. Ha, ha! [*He is surprised to see the rackets.*]   265

BERNARD. Hello, Uncle Willy.

WILLY. [*almost shocked*] Bernard! Well, look who's here! [*He comes quickly, guiltily, to* BERNARD *and warmly shakes his hand.*]

BERNARD. How are you? Good to see you.

WILLY. What are you doing here?

BERNARD. Oh, just stopped off to see Pop. Get off my feet till my train   270
leaves. I'm going to Washington in a few minutes.

WILLY. Is he in?

BERNARD. Yes, he's in his office with the accountants. Sit down.

WILLY. [*sitting down*] What're you going to do in Washington?

BERNARD. Oh, just a case I've got there, Willy.

WILLY. That so? [*Indicating the rackets*] You going to play tennis there?   275

BERNARD. I'm staying with a friend who's got a court.

WILLY. Don't say. His own tennis court. Must be fine people, I bet.

BERNARD. They are, very nice. Dad tells me Biff's in town.

WILLY. [*with a big smile*] Yeah, Biff's in. Working on a very big deal, Bernard.

BERNARD. What's Biff doing?   280

WILLY. Well, he's been doing very big things in the West. But he decided to establish himself here. Very big. We're having dinner. Did I hear your wife had a boy?

BERNARD. That's right. Our second.

WILLY. Two boys! What do you know!

BERNARD. What kind of a deal has Biff got?

WILLY. Well, Bill Oliver—very big sporting-goods man—he wants Biff very   285
badly. Called him in from the West. Long distance, carte blanche, special deliveries.
Your friends have their own private tennis court?

BERNARD. You still with the old firm, Willy?

WILLY. [*after a pause*] I'm—I'm overjoyed to see how you made the grade, Bernard, overjoyed. It's an encouraging thing to see a young man really—really—Looks very good for Biff—very—[*He breaks off, then*] Bernard— [*He is so full of emotion, he breaks off again.*]

BERNARD. What is it, Willy?

WILLY. [*small and alone*] What—what's the secret?

BERNARD. What secret?   290

WILLY. How—how did you? Why didn't he ever catch on?

BERNARD. I wouldn't know that, Willy.

WILLY. [*confidentially, desperately*] You were his friend, his boyhood friend. There's something I don't understand about it. His life ended after that Ebbets Field game. From the age of seventeen nothing good ever happened to him.

BERNARD.   He never trained himself for anything.

WILLY.   But he did, he did. After high school he took so many correspondence courses. Radio mechanics; television; God knows what, and never made the
slightest mark.

BERNARD.   [*taking off his glasses*] Willy, do you want to talk candidly?

WILLY.   [*rising, faces BERNARD*] I regard you as a very brilliant man, Bernard. I
value your advice.

BERNARD.   Oh, the hell with the advice, Willy. I couldn't advise you. There's
just one thing I've always wanted to ask you. When he was supposed to graduate, and
the math teacher flunked him—

WILLY.   Oh, that son-of-a-bitch ruined his life.

BERNARD.   Yeah, but, Willy, all he had to do was go to summer school and
make up that subject.

WILLY.   That's right, that's right.

BERNARD.   Did you tell him not to go to summer school?

WILLY.   Me? I begged him to go. I ordered him to go!

BERNARD.   Then why wouldn't he go?

WILLY.   Why? Why! Bernard, that question has been trailing me like a ghost
for the last fifteen years. He flunked the subject, and laid down and died like a hammer hit him!

BERNARD.   Take it easy, kid.

WILLY.   Let me talk to you—I got nobody to talk to. Bernard, Bernard, was it
my fault? Y'see? It keeps going around in my mind, maybe I did something to him. I
got nothing to give him.

BERNARD.   Don't take it so hard.

WILLY.   Why did he lay down? What is the story there? You were his friend!

BERNARD.   Willy, I remember, it was June, and our grades came out. And
he'd flunked math.

WILLY.   That son-of-a-bitch!

BERNARD.   No, it wasn't right then. Biff just got very angry, I remember, and
he was ready to enroll in summer school.

WILLY.   [*surprised*] He was?

BERNARD.   He wasn't beaten by it at all. But then, Willy, he disappeared from
the block for almost a month. And I got the idea that he'd gone up to New England
to see you. Did he have a talk with you then?

[*WILLY stares in silence.*]

BERNARD.   Willy?

WILLY.   [*with a strong edge of resentment in his voice*] Yeah, he came to Boston.
What about it?

BERNARD.   Well, just that when he came back—I'll never forget this, it always
mystifies me. Because I'd thought so well of Biff, even though he'd always taken advantage of me. I loved him, Willy, y'know? And he came back after that month and
took his sneakers—remember the sneakers with "University of Virginia" printed on
them? He was so proud of those, wore them every day. And he took them down in the
cellar, and burned them up in the furnace. We had a fist fight. It lasted at least half
an hour. Just the two of us, punching each other down the cellar, and crying right
through it. I've often thought of how strange it was that I knew he'd given up his life.
What happened in Boston, Willy?

[*WILLY looks at him as at an intruder.*]

BERNARD.   I just bring it up because you asked me.

WILLY.   [*angrily*] Nothing. What do you mean, "What happened?" What's that got to do with anything?

BERNARD.   Well, don't get sore.   320

WILLY.   What are you trying to do, blame it on me? If a boy lays down is that my fault?

BERNARD.   Now, Willy, don't get—

WILLY.   Well, don't—don't talk to me that way! What does that mean, "What happened?"

[*CHARLEY enters. He is in his vest, and he carries a bottle of bourbon.*]

CHARLEY.   Hey, you're going to miss that train. [*He waves the bottle.*]

BERNARD.   Yeah, I'm going. [*He takes the bottle.*] Thanks, Pop. [*He picks up   325
his rackets and bag.*] Good-by, Willy, and don't worry about it. You know, "If at first you don't succeed . . ."

WILLY.   Yes, I believe in that.

BERNARD.   But sometimes, Willy, it's better for a man just to walk away.

WILLY.   Walk away?

BERNARD.   That's right.

WILLY.   But if you can't walk away?   330

BERNARD.   [*after a slight pause*] I guess that's when it's tough. [*extending his
hand*] Good-by, Willy.

WILLY.   [*shaking BERNARD'S hand*] Good-by, boy.

CHARLEY.   [*an arm on BERNARD'S shoulder*] How do you like this kid? Gonna argue a case in front of the Supreme Court.

BERNARD.   [*protesting*] Pop!

WILLY.   [*genuinely shocked, pained, and happy*] No! The Supreme Court!   335

BERNARD.   I gotta run. 'By, Dad!

CHARLEY.   Knock 'em dead, Bernard!

[*BERNARD goes off.*]

WILLY.   [*as CHARLEY takes out his wallet*] The Supreme Court! And he didn't even mention it!

CHARLEY.   [*counting out money on the desk*] He don't have to—he's gonna do it.

WILLY.   And you never told him what to do, did you? You never took any   340
interest in him.

CHARLEY.   My salvation is that I never took any interest in anything. There's some money—fifty dollars. I got an accountant inside.

WILLY.   Charley, look . . . [*with difficulty*] I got my insurance to pay. If you can manage it—I need a hundred and ten dollars.

[*CHARLEY doesn't reply for a moment; merely stops moving.*]

WILLY.   I'd draw it from my bank but Linda would know, and I . . .

CHARLEY.   Sit down, Willy.

WILLY.   [*moving toward the chair*] I'm keeping an account of everything,   345
remember. I'll pay every penny back. [*He sits.*]

CHARLEY.   Now listen to me, Willy . . .

WILLY.   I want you to know I appreciate . . .

CHARLEY.   [*sitting down on the table*] Willy, what're you doin'? What the hell is goin' on in your head?

WILLY.   Why? I'm simply . . .

CHARLEY.   I offered you a job. You can make fifty dollars a week. And I won't send you on the road.

WILLY.   I've got a job.

CHARLEY.   Without pay? What kind of job is a job without pay? [*He rises.*] Now, look, kid, enough is enough. I'm no genius but I know when I'm being insulted.

WILLY.   Insulted!

CHARLEY.   Why don't you want to work for me?

WILLY.   What's the matter with you? I've got a job.

CHARLEY.   Then what're you walkin' in here every week for?

WILLY.   [*getting up*] Well, if you don't want me to walk in here—

CHARLEY.   I am offering you a job.

WILLY.   I don't want your goddam job!

CHARLEY.   When the hell are you going to grow up?

WILLY.   [*furiously*] You big ignoramus, if you say that to me again I'll rap you one! I don't care how big you are! [*He's ready to fight.*]

[*Pause.*]

CHARLEY.   [*kindly, going to him*] How much do you need, Willy?

WILLY.   Charley, I'm strapped. I'm strapped. I don't know what to do. I was just fired.

CHARLEY.   Howard fired you?

WILLY.   That snotnose. Imagine that? I named him. I named him Howard.

CHARLEY.   Willy, when're you gonna realize that them things don't mean anything? You named him Howard, but you can't sell that. The only thing you got in this world is what you can sell. And the funny thing is that you're a salesman, and you don't know that.

WILLY.   I've tried to think otherwise, I guess. I always felt that if a man was impressive, and well liked, that nothing—

CHARLEY.   Why must everybody like you? Who liked J. P. Morgan?° Was he impressive? In a Turkish bath he'd look like a butcher. But with his pockets on he was very well liked. Now listen, Willy, I know you don't like me, and nobody can say I'm in love with you, but I'll give you a job because—just for the hell of it, put it that way. Now what do you say?

WILLY.   I—I just can't work for you, Charley.

CHARLEY.   What're you, jealous of me?

WILLY.   I can't work for you, that's all, don't ask me why.

CHARLEY.   [*angered, takes out more bills*] You been jealous of me all your life, you damned fool! Here, pay your insurance. [*He puts the money in* WILLY'S *hand.*]

WILLY.   I'm keeping strict accounts.

CHARLEY.   I've got some work to do. Take care of yourself. And pay your insurance.

J. P. Morgan: John Pierpont Morgan (1837–1913) was the founder of U.S. Steel and the head of a gigantic family fortune that was enlarged by his son, John Pierpont Morgan (1867–1943). Charley is probably referring to the son.

WILLY. [*moving to the right*] Funny, y'know? After all the highways, and the   375
trains, and the appointments, and the years, you end up worth more dead than alive.

CHARLEY. Willy, nobody's worth nothin' dead. [*after a slight pause*] Did you
hear what I said?

[*WILLY stands still, dreaming.*]

CHARLEY. Willy!

WILLY. Apologize to Bernard for me when you see him. I didn't mean to argue with him. He's a fine boy. They're all fine boys, and they'll end up big—all of
them. Someday they'll all play tennis together. Wish me luck, Charley. He saw Bill
Oliver today.

CHARLEY. Good luck.

WILLY. [*on the verge of tears*] Charley, you're the only friend I got. Isn't   380
that a remarkable thing? [*He goes out.*]

CHARLEY. Jesus!

[*CHARLEY stares after him a moment and follows. All light blacks out. Suddenly raucous music
is heard, and a red glow rises behind the screen at right. STANLEY, a young waiter, appears, carrying a table, followed by HAPPY, who is carrying two chairs.*]

STANLEY. [*putting the table down*] That's all right, Mr. Loman. I can handle it
myself. [*He turns and takes the chairs from HAPPY and places them at the table.*]

HAPPY. [*glancing around.*] Oh, this is better.

STANLEY. Sure, in the front there you're in the middle of all kinds a noise.
Whenever you got a party, Mr. Loman, you just tell me and I'll put you back here.
Y' know, there's a lotta people they don't like it private, because when they go out
they like to see a lotta action around them because they're sick and tired to stay in the
house by theirself. But I know you, you ain't from Hackensack.° You know what I
mean?

HAPPY. [*sitting down*] So how's it coming, Stanley?   385

STANLEY. Ah, it's a dog's life. I only wish during the war they'd a took me in
the Army. I coulda been dead by now.

HAPPY. My brother's back, Stanley.

STANLEY. Oh, he come back, heh? From the Far West.

HAPPY. Yeah, big cattle man, my brother, so treat him right. And my father's
coming too.

STANLEY. Oh, your father too!   390

HAPPY. You got a couple of nice lobsters?

STANLEY. Hundred per cent, big.

HAPPY. I want them with claws.

STANLEY. Don't worry. I don't give you no mice. [*HAPPY laughs.*] How about
some wine? It'll put a head on the meal.

HAPPY. No. You remember, Stanley, that recipe I brought you from   395
overseas? With the champagne in it?

STANLEY. Oh, yeah, sure. I still got it tacked up yet in the kitchen. But that'll
have to cost a buck apiece anyways.

HAPPY. That's all right.

Hackensack: a city in northeastern New Jersey; Stanley uses the name as a reference to unsophisticated visitors to New York City.

STANLEY. What'd you, hit a number or somethin'?

HAPPY. No, it's a little celebration. My brother is—I think he pulled off a big deal today. I think we're going into business together.

STANLEY. Great! That's the best for you. Because a family business, you know what I mean?—that's the best.

HAPPY. That's what I think.

STANLEY. 'Cause what's the difference? Somebody steals? It's in the family. Know what I mean? [*sotto voce*°] Like this bartender here. The boss is goin' crazy what kinda leak he's got in the cash register. You put it in but it don't come out.

HAPPY. [*raising his head*] Sh!

STANLEY. What?

HAPPY. You notice I wasn't lookin' right or left, was I?

STANLEY. No.

HAPPY. And my eyes are closed.

STANLEY. So what's the—?

HAPPY. Strudel's comin'.

STANLEY. [*catching on, looks around*] Ah, no, there's no—

[*He breaks off as a furred, lavishly dressed GIRL enters and sits at the next table. Both follow her with their eyes.*]

STANLEY. Geez, how'd ya know?

HAPPY. I got radar or something. [*staring directly at her profile*] Oooooooo . . . Stanley.

STANLEY. I think that's for you, Mr. Loman.

HAPPY. Look at that mouth. Oh God. And the binoculars.

STANLEY. Geez, you got a life, Mr. Loman.

HAPPY. Wait on her.

STANLEY. [*going to the GIRL's table*] Would you like a menu, ma'am?

GIRL. I'm expecting someone, but I'd like a—

HAPPY. Why don't you bring her—excuse me, miss, do you mind? I sell champagne, and I'd like you to try my brand. Bring her a champagne, Stanley.

GIRL. That's awfully nice of you.

HAPPY. Don't mention it. It's all company money. [*He laughs.*]

GIRL. That's a charming product to be selling, isn't it?

HAPPY. Oh, gets to be like everything else. Selling is selling, y'know.

GIRL. I suppose.

HAPPY. You don't happen to sell, do you?

GIRL. No, I don't sell.

HAPPY. Would you object to a compliment from a stranger? You ought to be on a magazine cover.

GIRL. [*looking at him a little archly*] I have been.

[*STANLEY comes in with a glass of champagne.*]

HAPPY. What'd I say before, Stanley? You see? She's a cover girl.

STANLEY. Oh, I could see, I could see.

HAPPY. [*to the GIRL*] What magazine?

---

sotto voce: spoken in an undertone or "stage" whisper.

GIRL.   Oh, a lot of them. [*She takes the drink.*] Thank you.

HAPPY.   You know what they say in France, don't you? "Champagne is the drink of the complexion"—Hya, Biff!

[*BIFF has entered and sits with HAPPY.*]

BIFF.   Hello, kid. Sorry I'm late.

HAPPY.   I just got here. Uh, Miss—?   435

GIRL.   Forsythe.

HAPPY.   Miss Forsythe, this is my brother.

BIFF.   Is Dad here?

HAPPY.   His name if Biff. You might've heard of him. Great football player.

GIRL.   Really? What team?   440

HAPPY.   Are you familiar with football?

GIRL.   No. I'm afraid I'm not.

HAPPY.   Biff is quarterback with the New York Giants.

GIRL.   Well, that is nice, isn't it? [*She drinks.*]

HAPPY.   Good health.   445

GIRL.   I'm happy to meet you.

HAPPY.   That's my name. Hap. It's really Harold, but at West Point they called me Happy.

GIRL.   [*now really impressed*] Oh, I see. How do you do? [*She turns her profile.*]

BIFF.   Isn't Dad coming?

HAPPY.   You want her?   450

BIFF.   Oh, I could never make that.

HAPPY.   I remember the time that idea would never come into your head. Where's the old confidence, Biff?

BIFF.   I just saw Oliver—

HAPPY.   Wait a minute. I've got to see that old confidence again. Do you want her? She's on call.

BIFF.   Oh, no. [*He turns to look at the GIRL.*]   455

HAPPY.   I'm telling you. Watch this. [*turning to the GIRL*] Honey? [*She turns to him.*] Are you busy?

GIRL.   Well, I am . . . but I could make a phone call.

HAPPY.   Do that, will you, honey? And see if you can get a friend. We'll be here for a while. Biff is one of the greatest football players in the country.

GIRL.   [*standing up*] Well, I'm certainly happy to meet you.

HAPPY.   Come back soon.   460

GIRL.   I'll try.

HAPPY.   Don't try, honey, try hard.

[*The GIRL exits. STANLEY follows, shaking his head in bewildered admiration.*]

HAPPY.   Isn't that a shame now? A beautiful girl like that? That's why I can't get married. There's not a good woman in a thousand. New York is loaded with them, kid!

BIFF.   Hap, look—

HAPPY.   I told you she was on call!   465

BIFF.   [*strangely unnerved*] Cut it out, will ya? I want to say something to you.

HAPPY.   Did you see Oliver?

BIFF. I saw him all right. Now look, I want to tell Dad a couple of things and I want you to help me.

HAPPY. What? Is he going to back you?

BIFF. Are you crazy? You're out of your goddam head, you know that?

HAPPY. Why? What happened?

BIFF. [*breathlessly*] I did a terrible thing today, Hap. It's been the strangest day I ever went through. I'm all numb, I swear.

HAPPY. You mean he wouldn't see you?

BIFF. Well, I waited six hours for him, see? All day. Kept sending my name in. Even tried to date his secretary so she'd get me to him, but no soap.

HAPPY. Because you're not showin' the old confidence, Biff. He remembered you, didn't he?

BIFF. [*stopping HAPPY with a gesture*] Finally, about five o'clock, he comes out. Didn't remember who I was or anything. I felt like such an idiot, Hap.

HAPPY. Did you tell him my Florida idea?

BIFF. He walked away. I saw him for one minute. I got so mad I could've torn the walls down! How the hell did I ever get the idea I was a salesman there? I even believed myself that I'd been a salesman for him! And then he gave me one look and— I realized what a ridiculous lie my whole life has been! We've been talking in a dream for fifteen years. I was a shipping clerk.

HAPPY. What'd you do?

BIFF. [*with great tension and wonder*] Well, he left, see. And the secretary went out. I was all alone in the waiting-room. I don't know what came over me, Hap. The next thing I know I'm in his office—paneled walls, everything. I can't explain it. I—Hap, I took his fountain pen.

HAPPY. Geez, did he catch you?

BIFF. I ran out. I ran down all eleven flights. I ran and ran and ran.

HAPPY. That was an awful dumb—what'd you do that for?

BIFF. [*agonized*] I don't know, I just—wanted to take something. I don't know. You gotta help me, Hap, I'm gonna tell Pop.

HAPPY. You crazy? What for?

BIFF. Hap, he's got to understand that I'm not the man somebody lends that kind of money to. He thinks I've been spiting him all these years and it's eating him up.

HAPPY. That's just it. You tell him something nice.

BIFF. I can't.

HAPPY. Say you got a lunch date with Oliver tomorrow.

BIFF. So what do I do tomorrow?

HAPPY. You leave the house tomorrow and come back at night and say Oliver is thinking it over. And he thinks it over for a couple of weeks, and gradually it fades away and nobody's the worse.

BIFF. But it'll go on forever!

HAPPY. Dad is never so happy as when he's looking forward to something!

[*WILLY enters.*]

HAPPY. Hello, scout!

WILLY. Gee, I haven't been here in years!

[*STANLEY has followed WILLY in and sets a chair for him. STANLEY starts off but HAPPY stops him.*]

HAPPY.   Stanley!

[*STANLEY stands by, waiting for an order.*]

BIFF.   [*going to WILLY with guilt, as to an invalid*] Sit down, Pop. You want a drink?

WILLY.   Sure, I don't mind.

BIFF.   Let's get a load on.

WILLY.   You look worried.   500

BIFF.   N-no. [*to STANLEY*] Scotch all around. Make it doubles.

STANLEY.   Doubles, right. [*He goes.*]

WILLY.   You had a couple already, didn't you?

BIFF.   Just a couple, yeah.

WILLY.   Well, what happened, boy? [*nodding affirmatively, with a smile*] Every-   505
thing go all right?

BIFF.   [*takes a breath, then reaches out and grasps WILLY's hand*] Pal . . . [*He is smiling bravely, and WILLY is smiling too.*] I had an experience today.

HAPPY.   Terrific, Pop.

WILLY.   That so? What happened?

BIFF.   [*high, slightly alcoholic, above the earth*] I'm going to tell you everything
from first to last. It's been a strange day. [*Silence. He looks around, composes himself as best
he can, but his breath keeps breaking the rhythm of his voice.*] I had to wait quite a while for
him, and—

WILLY.   Oliver?   510

BIFF.   Yeah, Oliver. All day, as a matter of cold fact. And a lot of—instances—
facts, Pop, facts about my life came back to me. Who was it, Pop? Who ever said I was
a salesman with Oliver?

WILLY.   Well, you were.

BIFF.   No, Dad, I was a shipping clerk.

WILLY.   But you were practically—

BIFF.   [*with determination*] Dad, I don't know who said it first, but I was never   515
a salesman for Bill Oliver.

WILLY.   What're you talking about?

BIFF.   Let's hold on to the facts tonight, Pop. We're not going to get anywhere
bullin' around. I was a shipping clerk.

WILLY.   [*angrily*] All right, now listen to me—

BIFF.   Why don't you let me finish?

WILLY.   I'm not interested in stories about the past or any crap of that kind   520
because the woods are burning, boys, you understand? There's a big blaze going on
all around. I was fired today.

BIFF.   [*shocked*] How could you be?

WILLY.   I was fired, and I'm looking for a little good news to tell your mother,
because the woman has waited and the woman has suffered. The gist of it is that I
haven't got a story left in my head, Biff. So don't give me a lecture about facts and aspects. I am not interested. Now what've you got to say to me?

[*STANLEY enters with three drinks. They wait until he leaves.*]

WILLY.   Did you see Oliver?

BIFF.   Jesus, Dad!

WILLY. You mean you didn't go up there?

HAPPY. Sure he went up there.

BIFF. I did. I—saw him. How could they fire you?

WILLY. [*on the edge of his chair*] What kind of a welcome did he give you?

BIFF. He won't even let you work on commission?

WILLY. I'm out! [*driving*] So tell me, he gave you a warm welcome?

HAPPY. Sure, Pop, sure!

BIFF. [*driven*] Well, it was kind of—

WILLY. I was wondering if he'd remember you. [*to HAPPY*] Imagine, man doesn't see him for ten, twelve years and gives him that kind of a welcome!

HAPPY. Damn right!

BIFF. [*trying to return to the offensive*] Pop, look—

WILLY. You know why he remembered you, don't you? Because you impressed him in those days.

BIFF. Let's talk quietly and get this down to the facts, huh?

WILLY. [*as though BIFF had been interrupting*] Well, what happened? It's great news, Biff. Did he take you into his office or'd you talk in the waiting-room?

BIFF. Well, he came in, see, and—

WILLY. [*with a big smile*] What'd he say? Betcha he threw his arm around you.

BIFF. Well, he kinda—

WILLY. He's a fine man. [*to HAPPY*] Very hard man to see, y'know.

HAPPY. [*agreeing*] Oh, I know.

WILLY. [*to BIFF*] Is that where you had the drinks?

BIFF. Yeah, he gave me a couple of—no, no!

HAPPY. [*cutting in*] He told him my Florida idea.

WILLY. Don't interrupt. [*to BIFF*] How'd he react to the Florida idea?

BIFF. Dad, will you give me a minute to explain?

WILLY. I've been waiting for you to explain since I sat down here! What happened? He took you into his office and what?

BIFF. Well—I talked. And—and he listened, see.

WILLY. Famous for the way he listens, y'know. What was his answer?

BIFF. His answer was—[*He breaks off, suddenly angry.*] Dad, you're not letting me tell you what I want to tell you!

WILLY. [*accusing, angered*] You didn't see him, did you?

BIFF. I did see him!

WILLY. What'd you insult him or something? You insulted him, didn't you?

BIFF. Listen, will you let me out of it, will you just let me out of it!

HAPPY. What the hell!

WILLY. Tell me what happened!

BIFF. [*to HAPPY*] I can't talk to him!

[*A single trumpet note jars the ear. The light of green leaves stains the house, which holds the air of night and a dream. YOUNG BERNARD enters and knocks on the door of the house.*]

YOUNG BERNARD. [*frantically*] Mrs. Loman, Mrs. Loman!

HAPPY. Tell him what happened!

BIFF. [*to HAPPY*] Shut up and leave me alone!

WILLY. No, no! You had to go and flunk math!

BIFF. What math? What're you talking about?

[*THE WOMAN laughs, off left.*]

MISS FORSYTHE.   I guess we might as well. This is Letta.   635

THE WOMAN.   Willy, are you going to wake up?

BIFF.   [*ignoring WILLY*] How're ya, miss, sit down. What do you drink?

MISS FORSYTHE.   Letta might not be able to stay long.

LETTA.   I gotta get up very early tomorrow. I got jury duty. I'm so excited! Were you fellows ever on a jury?

BIFF.   No, but I been in front of them! [*The girls laugh.*] This is my father.   640

LETTA.   Isn't he cute? Sit down with us, Pop.

HAPPY.   Sit him down, Biff!

BIFF.   [*going to him*] Come on, slugger, drink us under the table. To hell with it! Come on, sit down, pal.

[*On BIFF's last insistence, WILLY is about to sit.*]

THE WOMAN.   [*now urgently*] Willy, are you going to answer the door!

[*THE WOMAN's call pulls WILLY back. He starts right, befuddled.*]

BIFF.   Hey, where are you going?   645

WILLY.   Open the door.

BIFF.   The door?

WILLY.   The washroom . . . the door . . . where's the door?

BIFF.   [*leading WILLY to the left*] Just go straight down.

[*WILLY moves left.*]

THE WOMAN.   Willy, Willy, are you going to get up, get up, get up, get   650
up?

[*WILLY exits left.*]

LETTA.   I think it's sweet you bring your daddy along.

MISS FORSYTHE.   Oh, he isn't really your father!

BIFF.   [*at left, turning to her resentfully*] Miss Forsythe, you've just seen a prince walk by. A fine, troubled prince. A hard-working, unappreciated prince. A pal, you understand? A good companion. Always for his boys.

LETTA.   That's so sweet.

HAPPY.   Well, girls, what's the program? We're wasting time. Come on, Biff.   655
Gather round. Where would you like to go?

BIFF.   Why don't you do something for him?

HAPPY.   Me!

BIFF.   Don't you give a damn for him, Hap?

HAPPY.   What're you talking about? I'm the one who—

BIFF.   I sense it, you don't give a good goddam about him. [*He takes the rolled-*   660
up hose from his pocket and puts it on the table in front of HAPPY.] Look what I found in the cellar, for Christ's sake. How can you bear to let it go on?

HAPPY.   Me? Who goes away? Who runs off and—

BIFF.   Yeah, but he doesn't mean anything to you. You could help him—I can't! Don't you understand what I'm talking about? He's going to kill himself, don't you know that?

HAPPY.   Don't I know it! Me!

BIFF.   Hap, help him! Jesus . . . help him . . . Help me, help me, I can't bear to look at his face! [*Ready to weep, he hurries out, up right.*]

HAPPY.   [*staring after him*] Where are you going?

MISS FORSYTHE.   What's he so mad about?

HAPPY.   Come on, girls, we'll catch up with him.

MISS FORSYTHE.   [*as HAPPY pushes her out*] Say, I don't like that temper of his!

HAPPY.   He's just a little overstrung, he'll be all right!

WILLY.   [*off left, as THE WOMAN laughs*] Don't answer! Don't answer!

LETTA.   Don't you want to tell your father—

HAPPY.   No, that's not my father. He's just a guy. Come on, we'll catch Biff, and, honey, we're going to paint this town! Stanley, where's the check! Hey, Stanley!

[*They exit. STANLEY looks toward left.*]

STANLEY.   [*calling to HAPPY indignantly*] Mr. Loman! Mr. Loman!

[*STANLEY picks up a chair and follows them off. Knocking is heard off left. THE WOMAN enters, laughing. WILLY follows her. She is in a black slip; he is buttoning his shirt. Raw, sensuous music accompanies their speech.*]

WILLY.   Will you stop laughing? Will you stop?

THE WOMAN.   Aren't you going to answer the door? He'll wake the whole hotel.

WILLY.   I'm not expecting anybody.

THE WOMAN.   Whyn't you have another drink, honey, and stop being so damn self-centered?

WILLY.   I'm so lonely.

THE WOMAN.   You know you ruined me, Willy? From now on, whenever you come to the office, I'll see that you go right through to the buyers. No waiting at my desk any more, Willy. You ruined me.

WILLY.   That's nice of you to say that.

THE WOMAN.   Gee, you are self-centered! Why so sad? You are the saddest, self-centeredest soul I ever did see-saw. [*She laughs. He kisses her.*] Come on inside, drummer boy. It's silly to be dressing in the middle of the night. [*As knocking is heard*] Aren't you going to answer the door?

WILLY.   They're knocking on the wrong door.

THE WOMAN.   But I felt the knocking! And he heard us talking in here. Maybe the hotel's on fire!

WILLY.   [*his terror rising*] It's a mistake.

THE WOMAN.   Then tell him to go away!

WILLY.   There's nobody there.

THE WOMAN.   It's getting on my nerves, Willy. There's somebody standing out there and it's getting on my nerves!

WILLY.   [*pushing her away from him*] All right, stay in the bathroom here, and don't come out. I think there's a law in Massachusetts about it, so don't come out. It may be that new room clerk. He looked very mean. So don't come out. It's a mistake, there's no fire.

[*The knocking is heard again. He takes a few steps away from her, and she vanishes into the wing. The light follows him, and now he is facing YOUNG BIFF, who carries a suitcase. BIFF steps toward him. The music is gone.*]

BIFF.   Why didn't you answer?

WILLY.   Biff! What are you doing in Boston?   690

BIFF.   Why didn't you answer? I've been knocking for five minutes, I called you on the phone—

WILLY.   I just heard you. I was in the bathroom and had the door shut. Did anything happen home?

BIFF.   Dad—I let you down.

WILLY.   What do you mean?

BIFF.   Dad . . .   695

WILLY.   Biffo, what's this about? [*putting his arm around* BIFF] Come on, let's go downstairs and get you a malted.

BIFF.   Dad, I flunked math.

WILLY.   Not for the term?

BIFF.   The term. I haven't got enough credits to graduate.

WILLY.   You mean to say Bernard wouldn't give you the answers?   700

BIFF.   He did, he tried, but I only got a sixty-one.

WILLY.   And they wouldn't give you four points?

BIFF.   Birnbaum refused absolutely. I begged him, Pop, but he won't give me those points. You gotta talk to him before they close the school. Because if he saw the kind of man you are, and you just talked to him in your way, I'm sure he'd come through for me. The class came right before practice, see, and I didn't go enough. Would you talk to him? He'd like you, Pop. You know the way you could talk.

WILLY.   You're on. We'll drive right back.

BIFF.   Oh, Dad, good work! I'm sure he'll change it for you!   705

WILLY.   Go downstairs and tell the clerk I'm checkin' out. Go right down.

BIFF.   Yes, sir! See, the reason he hates me, Pop—one day he was late for class so I got up at the blackboard and imitated him. I crossed my eyes and talked with a lithp.

WILLY.   [*laughing*] You did? The kids like it?

BIFF.   They nearly died laughing!

WILLY.   Yeah? What'd you do?   710

BIFF.   The thquare root of thixty twee is . . . [*WILLY bursts out laughing;* BIFF *joins him.*] And in the middle of it he walked in!

[*WILLY laughs and* THE WOMAN *joins in offstage.*]

WILLY.   [*without hesitation*] Hurry downstairs and—

BIFF.   Somebody in there?

WILLY.   No, that was next door.

[*THE WOMAN laughs offstage.*]

BIFF.   Somebody got in your bathroom!   715

WILLY.   No, it's the next room, there's a party—

THE WOMAN.   [*enters, laughing. She lisps this.*] Can I come in? There's something in the bathtub, Willy, and it's moving!

[*WILLY looks at* BIFF, *who is staring open-mouthed and horrified at* THE WOMAN.]

WILLY.   Ah—you better go back to your room. They must be finished painting by now. They're painting her room so I let her take a shower here. Go back, go back . . . [*He pushes her.*]

THE WOMAN. [*resisting*] But I've got to get dressed, Willy, I can't—

WILLY. Get out of here! Go back, go back . . . [*suddenly striving for the ordinary*] This is Miss Francis, Biff, she's a buyer. They're painting her room. Go back, Miss Francis, go back . . .

THE WOMAN. But my clothes, I can't go out naked in the hall!

WILLY. [*pushing her offstage*] Get outa here! Go back, go back!

[*BIFF slowly sits down on his suitcase as the argument continues offstage.*]

THE WOMAN. Where's my stockings? You promised me stockings, Willy!

WILLY. I have no stockings here!

THE WOMAN. You had two boxes of size nine sheers for me, and I want them!

WILLY. Here, for God's sake, will you get outa here!

THE WOMAN. [*enters holding a box of stockings*] I just hope there's nobody in the hall. That's all I hope. [*To BIFF*] Are you football or baseball?

BIFF. Football.

THE WOMAN. [*angry, humiliated*] That's me too. G'night. [*she snatches her clothes from WILLY, and walks out.*]

WILLY. [*after a pause*] Well, better get going. I want to get to the school first thing in the morning. Get my suits out of the closet. I'll get my valise. [*BIFF doesn't move.*] What's the matter? [*BIFF remains motionless, tears falling*] She's a buyer. Buys for J. H. Simmons. She lives down the hall—they're painting. You don't imagine—[*He breaks off. After a pause*] Now listen, pal, she's just a buyer. She sees merchandise in her room and they have to keep it looking just so . . . [*Pause. Assuming command*] All right, get my suits. [*BIFF doesn't move.*] Now stop crying and do as I say. I gave you an order. Biff, I gave you an order! Is that what you do when I give you an order? How dare you cry! [*putting his arm around BIFF*] Now look, Biff, when you grow up you'll understand about these things. You mustn't—you mustn't overemphasize a thing like this. I'll see Birnbaum first thing in the morning.

BIFF. Never mind.

WILLY. [*getting down beside BIFF*] Never mind! He's going to give you those points. I'll see to it.

BIFF. He wouldn't listen to you.

WILLY. He certainly will listen to me. You need those points for the U. of Virginia.

BIFF. I'm not going there.

WILLY. Heh? If I can't get him to change that mark you'll make it up in summer school. You've got all summer to—

BIFF. [*his weeping breaking from him*] Dad . . .

WILLY. [*infected by it*] Oh, my boy . . .

BIFF. Dad . . .

WILLY. She's nothing to me, Biff. I was lonely, I was terribly lonely.

BIFF. You—you gave her Mama's stockings! [*His tears break through and he rises to go.*]

WILLY. [*grabbing for BIFF*] I gave you an order!

BIFF. Don't touch me, you—liar!

WILLY. Apologize for that!

BIFF. You fake! You phony little fake! [*Overcome, he turns quickly and weeping fully goes out with his suitcase. WILLY is left on the floor on his knees.*]

WILLY. I gave you an order! Biff, come back here or I'll beat you! Come back here! I'll whip you!

[*STANLEY comes quickly in from the right and stands in front of WILLY.*]

WILLY. [*shouts at STANLEY*] I gave you an order . . .

STANLEY. Hey, let's pick it up, pick it up, Mr. Loman. [*He helps WILLY to his feet.*] Your boys left with the chippies. They said they'll see you home.

[*A SECOND WAITER watches some distance away.*]

WILLY. But we were supposed to have dinner together.

[*Music is heard, WILLY's theme.*]

STANLEY. Can you make it?   750

WILLY. I'll—sure, I can make it. [*suddenly concerned about his clothes*] Do I—I look all right?

STANLEY. Sure, you look all right. [*He flicks a speck off WILLY's lapel.*]

WILLY. Here—here's a dollar.

STANLEY. Oh, your son paid me. It's all right.

WILLY. [*putting it in STANLEY's hand*] No, take it. You're a good boy.   755

STANLEY. Oh, no, you don't have to . . .

WILLY. Here—here's some more, I don't need it any more. [*after a slight pause*] Tell me—is there a seed store in the neighborhood?

STANLEY. Seeds? You mean like to plant?

[*As WILLY turns, STANLEY slips the money back into his jacket pocket.*]

WILLY. Yes. Carrots, peas . . .

STANLEY. Well, there's hardware stores on Sixth Avenue, but it may be   760
too late now.

WILLY. [*anxiously*] Oh, I'd better hurry. I've got to get some seeds. [*He starts off to the right.*] I've got to get some seeds, right away. Nothing's planted. I don't have a thing in the ground.

[*WILLY hurries out as the light goes down. STANLEY moves over to the right after him, watches him off. The other waiter has been staring at WILLY.*]

STANLEY. [*to the WAITER*] Well, whatta you looking at?

[*The WAITER picks up the chairs and moves off right. STANLEY takes the table and follows him. The light fades on this area. There is a long pause, the sound of the flute coming over. The light gradually rises on the kitchen, which is empty. HAPPY appears at the door of the house, followed by BIFF. HAPPY is carrying a large bunch of long-stemmed roses. He enters the kitchen, looks around for LINDA. Not seeing her, he turns to BIFF, who is just outside the house door, and makes a gesture with his hands, indicating "Not here, I guess." He looks into the living-room and freezes. Inside, LINDA, unseen, is seated, WILLY's coat on her lap. She rises ominously and quietly and moves toward HAPPY, who backs up into the kitchen, afraid.*]

HAPPY. Hey, what're you doing up? [*LINDA says nothing but moves toward him implacably.*] Where's Pop? [*He keeps backing to the right, and now LINDA is in full view in the doorway to the living-room.*] Is he sleeping?

LINDA. Where were you?

HAPPY. [*trying to laugh it off*] We met two girls, Mom, very fine types. Here,   7ϵ
we brought you some flowers. [*offering them to her*] Put them in your room, Ma.

[*She knocks them to the floor at BIFF's feet. He has now come inside and closed the door behind
him. She stares at BIFF, silent.*]

HAPPY.   Now what'd you do that for? Mom, I want you to have some flowers—
LINDA.   [*cutting HAPPY off, violently to BIFF*] Don't you care whether he lives or
dies?
HAPPY.   [*going to the stairs*] Come upstairs, Biff.
BIFF.   [*with a flare of disgust, to HAPPY*] Go away from me! [*to LINDA*] What do
you mean, lives or dies? Nobody's dying around here, pal.
LINDA.   Get out of my sight! Get out of here!   7ϡ
BIFF.   I wanna see the boss.
LINDA.   You're not going near him!
BIFF.   Where is he? [*He moves into the living-room and LINDA follows.*]
LINDA.   [*shouting after BIFF*] You invite him for dinner. He looks forward to it
all day—[*BIFF appears in his parents' bedroom, looks around, and exits.*]—and then you
desert him there. There's no stranger you'd do that to!
HAPPY.   Why? He had a swell time with us. Listen, when I—[*LINDA comes back*   77
into the kitchen.]—desert him I hope I don't outlive the day!
LINDA.   Get out of here!
HAPPY.   Now look, Mom . . .
LINDA.   Did you have to go to women tonight? You and your lousy rotten
whores!

[*BIFF re-enters the kitchen.*]

HAPPY.   Mom, all we did was follow Biff around trying to cheer him up! [*to*
BIFF] Boy, what a night you gave me!
LINDA.   Get out of here, both of you, and don't come back! I don't want   78
you tormenting him any more. Go on now, get your things together! [*to BIFF*] You can
sleep in his apartment. [*She starts to pick up the flowers and stops herself.*] Pick up this
stuff, I'm not your maid any more. Pick it up, you bum, you!

[*HAPPY turns his back to her in refusal. BIFF slowly moves over and gets down on his knees, picking up the flowers.*]

LINDA.   You're a pair of animals! Not one, not another living soul would have
had the cruelty to walk out on that man in a restaurant!
BIFF.   [*not looking at her*] Is that what he said?
LINDA.   He didn't have to say anything. He was so humiliated he nearly limped
when he came in.
HAPPY.   But, Mom, he had a great time with us—
BIFF.   [*cutting him off violently*] Shut up!   78

[*Without another word, HAPPY goes upstairs.*]

LINDA.   You! You didn't even go in to see if he was all right!
BIFF.   [*still on the floor in front of LINDA, the flowers in his hand; with self-loathing*]
No. Didn't. Didn't do a damned thing. How do you like that, heh? Left him babbling
in a toilet.

LINDA. You louse. You . . .

BIFF. Now you hit it on the nose! [*He gets up, throws the flowers in the wastebasket.*] The scum of the earth, and you're looking at him!

LINDA. Get out of here!   790

BIFF. I gotta talk to the boss, Mom. Where is he?

LINDA. You're not going near him. Get out of this house!

BIFF. [*with absolute assurance, determination*] No. We're gonna have an abrupt conversation, him and me.

LINDA. You're not talking to him!

[*Hammering is heard from outside the house, off right. BIFF turns toward the noise.*]

LINDA. [*suddenly pleading*] Will you please leave him alone?   795

BIFF. What's he doing out there?

LINDA. He's planting the garden!

BIFF. [*quietly*] Now? Oh, my God!

[*BIFF moves outside, LINDA following. The light dies down on them and comes up on the center of the apron as WILLY walks into it. He is carrying a flashlight, a hoe, and a handful of seed packets. He raps the top of the hoe sharply to fix it firmly, and then moves to the left, measuring off the distance with his foot. He holds the flashlight to look at the seed packets, reading off the instructions. He is in the blue of night.*]

WILLY. Carrots . . . quarter-inch apart. Rows . . . one-foot rows. [*He measures it off.*] One foot. [*He puts down a package and measures off.*] Beets. [*He puts down another package and measures again.*] Lettuce. [*He reads the package, puts it down.*] One foot—[*He breaks off as BEN appears at the right and moves slowly down to him.*] What a proposition, ts, ts. Terrific, terrific. 'Cause she's suffered, Ben, the woman has suffered. You understand me? A man can't go out the way he came in, Ben, a man has got to add up to something. You can't, you can't—[*BEN moves toward him as though to interrupt.*] You gotta consider, now. Don't answer so quick. Remember, it's a guaranteed twenty-thousand-dollar proposition. Now look, Ben, I want you to go through the ins and outs of this thing with me. I've got nobody to talk to, Ben, and the woman has suffered, you hear me?

BEN. [*standing still, considering*] What's the proposition?   800

WILLY. It's twenty thousand dollars on the barrelhead. Guaranteed, gilt-edged, you understand?

BEN. You don't want to make a fool of yourself. They might not honor the policy.

WILLY. How can they dare refuse? Didn't I work like a coolie to meet every premium on the nose? And now they don't pay off? Impossible!

BEN. It's called a cowardly thing, William.

WILLY. Why? Does it take more guts to stand here the rest of my life   805
ringing up a zero?

BEN. [*yielding*] That's a point, William. [*He moves, thinking, turns.*] And twenty thousand—that *is* something one can feel with the hand, it is there.

WILLY. [*now assured, with rising power*] Oh, Ben, that's the whole beauty of it! I see it like a diamond, shining in the dark, hard and rough, that I can pick up and touch in my hand. Not like—like an appointment! This would not be another damned-fool appointment, Ben, and it changes all the aspects. Because he thinks I'm nothing, see, and so he spites me. But the funeral—[*straightening up*] Ben, that funeral will be massive! They'll come from Maine, Massachusetts, Vermont, New Hampshire! All the old-timers with the strange license plates—that boy will be thunderstruck, Ben, because he never realized—I am known! Rhode Island, New York, New Jersey—I am known, Ben, and he'll see it with his eyes once and for all. He'll see what I am, Ben! He's in for a shock, that boy!

BEN. [*coming down to the edge of the garden*] He'll call you a coward.

WILLY. [*suddenly fearful*] No, that would be terrible.

BEN. Yes. And a damned fool.

WILLY. No, no, he mustn't, I won't have that! [*He is broken and desperate.*]

BEN. He'll hate you, William.

[*The gay music of the Boys is heard.*]

WILLY. Oh, Ben, how do we get back to all the great times? Used to be so full of light, and comradeship, the sleigh-riding in winter, and the ruddiness on his cheeks. And always some kind of good news coming up, always something nice coming up ahead. And never even let me carry the valises in the house, and simonizing, simonizing that little red car! Why, why can't I give him something and not have him hate me?

BEN. Let me think about it. [*He glances at his watch.*] I still have a little time. Remarkable proposition, but you've got to be sure you're not making a fool of yourself.

[*BEN drifts upstage and goes out of sight. BIFF comes down from the left.*]

WILLY. [*suddenly conscious of BIFF, turns and looks up at him, then begins picking up the packages of seeds in confusion*] Where the hell is that seed? [*Indignantly*] You can't see nothing out here! They boxed in the whole goddam neighborhood!

BIFF. There are people all around here. Don't you realize that?

WILLY. I'm busy. Don't bother me.

BIFF. [*taking the hoe from WILLY*] I'm saying good-by to you, Pop. [*WILLY looks at him, silent, unable to move.*] I'm not coming back any more.

WILLY. You're not going to see Oliver tomorrow?

BIFF. I've got no appointment, Dad.

WILLY. He put his arm around you, and you've got no appointment?

BIFF. Pop, get this now, will you? Everytime I've left it's been a fight that sent me out of here. Today I realized something about myself and I tried to explain it to you and I—I think I'm just not smart enough to make any sense out of it for you. To hell with whose fault it is or anything like that. [*He takes WILLY's arm.*] Let's just wrap it up, heh? Come on in, we'll tell Mom. [*He gently tries to pull WILLY to left.*]

WILLY. [*frozen, immobile, with guilt in his voice*] No, I don't want to see her.

BIFF. Come on! [*He pulls again, and WILLY tries to pull away.*]

WILLY. [*highly nervous*] No, no, I don't want to see her.

BIFF. [*tries to look into WILLY's face, as if to find the answer there*] Why don't you want to see her?

WILLY. [*more harshly now*] Don't bother me, will you?

BIFF. What do you mean, you don't want to see her? You don't want them calling you yellow, do you? This isn't your fault; it's me, I'm a bum. Now come inside! [*WILLY strains to get away.*] Did you hear what I said to you?

[*WILLY pulls away and quickly goes by himself into the house. BIFF follows.*]

LINDA.   [*to WILLY*] Did you plant, dear?

BIFF.   [*at the door, to LINDA*] All right, we had it out. I'm going and I'm not   830
writing any more.

LINDA.   [*going to WILLY in the kitchen*] I think that's the best way, dear. 'Cause
there's no use drawing it out, you'll just never get along.

[*WILLY doesn't respond.*]

BIFF.   People ask where I am and what I'm doing, you don't know, and you
don't care. That way it'll be off your mind and you can start brightening up again. All
right? That clears it, doesn't it? [*WILLY is silent, and BIFF goes to him.*] You gonna wish
me luck, scout? [*He extends his hand.*] What do you say?

LINDA.   Shake his hand, Willy.

WILLY.   [*turning to her, seething with hurt*] There's no necessity to mention the
pen at all, y'know.

BIFF.   [*gently*] I've got no appointment, Dad.   835

WILLY.   [*erupting fiercely*] He put his arm around . . . ?

BIFF.   Dad, you're never going to see what I am, so what's the use of arguing?
If I strike oil I'll send you a check. Meantime forget I'm alive.

WILLY.   [*to LINDA*] Spite, see?

BIFF.   Shake hands, Dad.

WILLY.   Not my hand.   840

BIFF.   I was hoping not to go this way.

WILLY.   Well, this is the way you're going. Good-by.

[*BIFF looks at him a moment, then turns sharply and goes to the stairs.*]

WILLY.   [*stops him with*] May you rot in hell if you leave this house!

BIFF.   [*turning*] Exactly what is it that you want from me?

WILLY.   I want you to know, on the train, in the mountains, in the valleys,   845
wherever you go, that you cut down your life for spite!

BIFF.   No, no.

WILLY.   Spite, spite, is the word of your undoing! And when you're down and
out, remember what did it. When you're rotting somewhere beside the railroad
tracks, remember, and don't you dare blame it on me!

BIFF.   I'm not blaming it on you!

WILLY.   I won't take the rap for this, you hear?

[*HAPPY comes down the stairs and stands on the bottom step, watching.*]

BIFF.   That's just what I'm telling you!   850

WILLY.   [*sinking into a chair at the table, with full accusation*] You're trying to put
a knife in me—don't think I don't know what you're doing!

BIFF.   All right, phony! Then let's lay it on the line. [*He whips the rubber tube out
of his pocket and puts it on the table.*]

HAPPY.   You crazy—

LINDA.   Biff! [*She moves to grab the hose, but BIFF holds it down with his hand.*]

BIFF.   Leave it here! Don't move it!   855

WILLY.   [*not looking at it*] What is that?

BIFF.   You know goddam well what that is.

WILLY.   [*caged, wanting to escape*] I never saw that.

BIFF. You saw it. The mice didn't bring it into the cellar! What is this supposed to do, make a hero out of you? This supposed to make me sorry for you?

WILLY. Never heard of it.

BIFF. There'll be no pity for you, you hear it? No pity!

WILLY. [*to* LINDA] You hear the spite!

BIFF. No, you're going to hear the truth—what you are and what I am!

LINDA. Stop it!

WILLY. Spite!

HAPPY. [*coming down toward* BIFF] You cut it now!

BIFF. [*to* HAPPY] The man don't know who we are! The man is gonna know! [*to* WILLY] We never told the truth for ten minutes in this house!

HAPPY. We always told the truth!

BIFF. [*turning on him*] You big blow, are you the assistant buyer? You're one of the two assistants to the assistant, aren't you?

HAPPY. Well, I'm practically—

BIFF. You're practically full of it! We all are! And I'm through with it. [*to* WILLY] Now hear this, Willy, this is me.

WILLY. I know you!

BIFF. You know why I had no address for three months? I stole a suit in Kansas City and I was in jail. [*to* LINDA, *who is sobbing*] Stop crying. I'm through with it.

[LINDA *turns from them, her hands covering her face.*]

WILLY. I suppose that's my fault!

BIFF. I stole myself out of every good job since high school!

WILLY. And whose fault is that?

BIFF. And I never got anywhere because you blew me so full of hot air I could never stand taking orders from anybody! That's whose fault it is!

WILLY. I hear that!

LINDA. Don't, Biff!

BIFF. It's goddam time you heard that! I had to be boss big shot in two weeks, and I'm through with it!

WILLY. Then hang yourself! For spite, hang yourself!

BIFF. No! Nobody's hanging himself, Willy! I ran down eleven flights with a pen in my hand today. And suddenly I stopped, you hear me? And in the middle of that office building, do you hear this? I stopped in the middle of that building and I saw—the sky. I saw the things that I love in this world. The work and the food and time to sit and smoke. And I looked at the pen and said to myself, what the hell am I grabbing this for? Why am I trying to become what I don't want to be? What am I doing in an office, making a contemptuous, begging fool of myself, when all I want is out there, waiting for me the minute I say I know who I am! Why can't I say that, Willy?

[*He tries to make* WILLY *face him, but* WILLY *pulls away and moves to the left.*]

WILLY. [*with hatred, threateningly.*] The door of your life is wide open!

BIFF. Pop! I'm a dime a dozen, and so are you!

WILLY. [*turning on him now in an uncontrolled outburst*] I am not a dime a dozen! I am Willy Loman, and you are Biff Loman!

[BIFF *starts for* WILLY, *but is blocked by* HAPPY. *In his fury,* BIFF *seems on the verge of attacking his father.*]

BIFF.   I am not a leader of men, Willy, and neither are you. You were never any-thing but a hard-working drummer who landed in the ash can like all the rest of them! I'm one dollar an hour, Willy! I tried seven states and couldn't raise it. A buck an hour! Do you gather my meaning? I'm not bringing home any prizes any more, and you're going to stop waiting for me to bring them home!

WILLY.   [*directly to* BIFF] You vengeful, spiteful mut!

[BIFF *breaks from* HAPPY. WILLY, *in fright, starts up the stairs.* BIFF *grabs him.*]

BIFF.   [*at the peak of his fury*] Pop I'm nothing! I'm nothing, Pop. Can't you un-derstand that? There's no spite in it any more. I'm just what I am, that's all.

[BIFF's *fury has spent itself, and he breaks down, sobbing, holding on to* WILLY, *who dumbly fumbles for* BIFF's *face.*]

WILLY.   [*astonished*] What're you doing? What're you doing? [*to* LINDA] Why is he crying?

BIFF.   [*crying, broken*] Will you let me go, for Christ's sake? Will you take   890
that phony dream and burn it before something happens? [*Struggling to contain him-self, he pulls away and moves to the stairs.*] I'll go in the morning. Put him—put him to bed. [*Exhausted,* BIFF *moves up the stairs to his room.*]

WILLY.   [*after a long pause, astonished, elevated*] Isn't that—isn't that remarkable? Biff—he likes me!

LINDA.   He loves you, Willy!

HAPPY.   [*deeply moved*] Always did, Pop.

WILLY.   Oh, Biff! [*staring wildly*] He cried! Cried to me. [*He is choking with his love, and now cries out his promise.*] That boy—that boy is going to be magnificent!

[BEN *appears in the light just outside the kitchen.*]

BEN.   Yes, outstanding, with twenty thousand behind him.   895

LINDA.   [*sensing the racing of his mind, fearfully, carefully*] Now come to bed, Willy. It's all settled now.

WILLY.   [*finding it difficult not to rush out of the house*] Yes, we'll sleep. Come on. Go to sleep, Hap.

BEN.   And it does take a great kind of a man to crack the jungle.

[*In accents of dread,* BEN's *idyllic music starts up.*]

HAPPY.   [*his arm around* LINDA] I'm getting married, Pop, don't forget it. I'm changing everything. I'm gonna run that department before the year is up. You'll see, Mom. [*He kisses her.*]

BEN.   The jungle is dark but full of diamonds, Willy.   900

[WILLY *turns, moves, listening to* BEN.]

LINDA.   Be good. You're both good boys, just act that way, that's all.

HAPPY.   'Night, Pop. [*He goes upstairs.*]

LINDA.   [*to* WILLY] Come, dear.

BEN.   [*with greater force*] One must go in to fetch a diamond out.

WILLY.   [*to* LINDA, *as he moves slowly along the edge of the kitchen, toward the*   905
door] I just want to get settled down, Linda. Let me sit alone for a little.

LINDA.   [*almost uttering her fear*] I want you upstairs.

WILLY. [*taking her in his arms*] In a few minutes, Linda. I couldn't sleep right now. Go on, you look awful tired. [*He kisses her.*]

BEN. Not like an appointment at all. A diamond is rough and hard to the touch.

WILLY. Go on now. I'll be right up.

LINDA. I think this is the only way, Willy.   91

WILLY. Sure, it's the best thing.

BEN. Best thing!

WILLY. The only way. Everything is gonna be—go on, kid, get to bed. You look so tired.

LINDA. Come right up.

WILLY. Two minutes.   91

[*LINDA goes into the living-room, then reappears in her bedroom. WILLY moves just outside the kitchen door.*]

WILLY. Loves me. [*wonderingly*] Always loved me. Isn't that a remarkable thing? Ben, he'll worship me for it!

BEN. [*with promise*] It's dark there, but full of diamonds.

WILLY. Can you imagine that magnificence with twenty thousand dollars in his pocket?

LINDA. [*calling from her room*] Willy! Come up!

WILLY. [*calling into the kitchen*] Yes! Yes. Coming! It's very smart, you realize   92
that, don't you, sweetheart? Even Ben sees it. I gotta go, baby. 'By! 'By! [*going over to BEN, almost dancing*] Imagine? When the mail comes he'll be ahead of Bernard again!

BEN. A perfect proposition all around.

WILLY. Did you see how he cried to me? Oh, if I could kiss him, Ben!

BEN. Time, William, time!

WILLY. Oh, Ben, I always knew one way or another we were gonna make it, Biff and I!

BEN. [*looking at his watch*] The boat. We'll be late. [*He moves slowly off into   92
the darkness.*]

WILLY. [*elegiacally, turning to the house*] Now when you kick off, boy, I want a seventy-yard boot, and get right down the field under the ball, and when you hit, hit low and hit hard, because it's important, boy. [*He swings around and faces the audience.*] There's all kinds of important people in the stands, and the first thing you know . . . [*suddenly realizing he is alone*] Ben! Ben, where do I . . . ? [*He makes a sudden movement of search.*] Ben, how do I . . . ?

LINDA. [*calling*] Willy, you coming up?

WILLY. [*uttering a gasp of fear, whirling about as if to quiet her*] Sh! [*He turns around as if to find his way; sounds, faces, voices, seem to be swarming in upon him and he flicks at them, crying*] Sh! Sh! [*Suddenly music, faint and high, stops him. It rises in intensity, almost to an unbearable scream. He goes up and down on his toes, and rushes off around the house.*] Shhh!

LINDA. Willy?

[*There is no answer. LINDA waits. BIFF gets up off his bed. He is still in his clothes. HAPPY sits up. BIFF stands listening.*]

LINDA. [*with real fear*] Willy, answer me! Willy!   930

[*There is the sound of a car starting and moving away at full speed.*]

LINDA.   No!
BIFF.   [*rushing down the stairs*] Pop!

[*As the car speeds off, the music crashes down in a frenzy of sound, which becomes the soft pulsation of a single cello string. BIFF slowly returns to his bedroom. He and HAPPY gravely don their jackets. LINDA slowly walks out of her room. The music has developed into a dead march. The leaves of day are appearing over everything. CHARLEY and BERNARD somberly dressed, appear and knock on the kitchen door. BIFF and HAPPY slowly descend the stairs to the kitchen as CHARLEY and BERNARD enter. All stop a moment when LINDA, in clothes of mourning, bearing a little bunch of roses, comes through the draped doorway into the kitchen. She goes to CHARLEY and takes his arm. Now all move toward the audience, through the wall-line of the kitchen. At the limit of the apron, LINDA lays down the flowers, kneels, and sits back on her heels. All stare down at the grave.*]

REQUIEM

CHARLEY.   It's getting dark, Linda.

[*LINDA doesn't react. She stares at the grave.*]

BIFF.   How about it, Mom? Better get some rest, heh? They'll be closing the gate soon.

[*LINDA makes no move. Pause.*]

HAPPY.   [*deeply angered*] He had no right to do that. There was no necessity for it. We would've helped him.
CHARLEY.   [*grunting*] Hmmm.
BIFF.   Come along, Mom.   5
LINDA.   Why didn't anybody come?
CHARLEY.   It was a very nice funeral.
LINDA.   But where are all the people he knew? Maybe they blame him.
CHARLEY.   Naa. It's a rough world, Linda. They wouldn't blame him.
LINDA.   I can't understand it. At this time especially. First time in thirty-   10
five years we were just about free and clear. He only needed a little salary. He was even finished with the dentist.
CHARLEY.   No man only needs a little salary.
LINDA.   I can't understand it.
BIFF.   There were a lot of nice days. When he'd come home from a trip; or on Sundays, making the stoop; finishing the cellar; putting on the new porch; when he built the extra bathroom; and put up the garage. You know something, Charley, there's more of him in that front stoop than in all the sales he ever made.
CHARLEY.   Yeah. He was a happy man with a batch of cement.
LINDA.   He was so wonderful with his hands.   15
BIFF.   He had all the wrong dreams. All, all, wrong.
HAPPY.   [*almost ready to fight BIFF*] Don't say that!
BIFF.   He never knew who he was.
CHARLEY.   [*stopping HAPPY's movement and reply. To BIFF*] Nobody dast blame this

man. You don't understand. Willy was a salesman. And for a salesman, there is no rock bottom to the life. He don't put a bolt to a nut, he don't tell you the law or give you medicine. He's a man way out there in the blue, riding on a smile and a shoeshine. And when they start not smiling back—that's an earthquake. And then you get yourself a couple of spots on your hat, and you're finished. Nobody dast blame this man. A salesman is got to dream, boy. It comes with the territory.

BIFF.   Charley, the man didn't know who he was.

HAPPY.   [*infuriated*] Don't say that!

BIFF.   Why don't you come with me, Happy?

HAPPY.   I'm not licked that easily. I'm staying right in this city, and I'm gonna beat this racket! [*He looks at BIFF, his chin set.*] The Loman Brothers!

BIFF.   I know who I am, kid.

HAPPY.   All right, boy. I'm gonna show you and everybody else that Willy Loman did not die in vain. He had a good dream. It's the only dream you can have— to come out number-one man. He fought it out here, and this is where I'm gonna win it for him.

BIFF.   [*with a hopeless glance at HAPPY, bends toward his mother*] Let's go, Mom.

LINDA.   I'll be with you in a minute. Go on, Charley. [*He hesitates.*] I want to, just for a minute. I never had a chance to say good-by.

[*CHARLEY moves away, followed by HAPPY. BIFF remains a slight distance up and left of LINDA. She sits there, summoning herself. The flute begins, not far away, playing behind her speech.*]

LINDA.   Forgive me, dear. I can't cry. I don't know what it is, but I can't cry. I don't understand it. Why did you ever do that? Help me, Willy, I can't cry. It seems to me that you're just on another trip. I keep expecting you. Willy, dear, I can't cry. Why did you do it? I search and search and I search, and I can't understand it, Willy. I made the last payment on the house today. Today, dear. And there'll be nobody home. [*A sob rises in her throat.*] We're free and clear. [*sobbing more fully, released*] We're free. [*BIFF comes slowly toward her.*] We're free . . . We're free . . .

[*BIFF lifts her to her feet and moves out up right with her in his arms. LINDA sobs quietly. BERNARD and CHARLEY come together and follow them, followed by HAPPY. Only the music of the flute is left on the darkening stage as over the house the hard towers of the apartment buildings rise into sharp focus, and*

The curtain falls.]

QUESTIONS

Act I

1. What do you learn about Willy from the first stage direction?
2. What instances of stealing are in the play? Why do Biff and Happy steal? Where did they learn about stealing? How is stealing related to salesmanship?
3. In Act I Willy claims that "I never in my life told him [Biff] anything but decent things." Is this assertion true? What does it show you about Willy?

Act II and Requiem

4. What does Willy's difficulty with machines—especially his car, the refrigerator, and Howard's wire recorder—suggest about him? To what extent are these machines symbolic?

5. When Willy sees Bernard in Charley's office, he asks, "What—what's the secret?" What secret is he asking about? Does such a secret exist?

6. In Act II Willy buys seeds and tries to plant a garden at night. Why is Willy so disturbed that "nothing's planted" and "I don't have a thing in the ground"? What do this garden and having "things in the ground" mean to Willy?

7. In Act II, speech 267, Biff claims that "we never told the truth for ten minutes in this house!" What does he mean? To what extent is he right?

8. Linda's last line in the play—"We're free . . . we're free"—seems to refer to the house mortgage. In what other ways, however, might you take it?

GENERAL QUESTIONS

1. How does Miller use lighting, the set, blocking, and music to differentiate between action in the present and "memory" action?

2. The stage directions are full of information that cannot be played. In describing Happy, for example, Miller notes that "sexuality is like a color on him." What is the function of such stage directions?

3. How is Willy's suicide foreshadowed throughout the play? To what extent does this foreshadowing create tension?

4. Which characters are "real" and which are "hallucinations" that spring from Willy's memory? What are the major differences between these two groups?

5. Which characters are symbolic and what do they symbolize?

6. Describe the character of Willy Loman. What are his good qualities? In what ways does he have heroic stature? What are his bad qualities? To what extent is his "fall" the result of his flaws, and to what extent is it caused by circumstances beyond his control?

7. How is the relationship between Charley and Bernard different from the one between Willy and his sons? Why is this difference important?

8. Discuss Linda's character and role. In what ways is she supportive of Willy? In what ways does she encourage his deceptions and self-delusions?

9. What sort of person is Happy? What has he inherited from Willy? How is he a debasement of Willy? To what degree is he successful or happy?

10. Willy claims that success in business is based not on "what you do" but on "who you know and the smile on your face! It's contacts. . . . a man can end up with diamonds on the basis of being well liked." How does the play support or reject this assertion?

11. Most of Willy's memories—Ben's visit, Boston, the football game—are from 1928. Why does Willy's memory return to 1928? Why is the contrast between 1928 and the present significant for Willy and for the play as a whole?

WRITING ABOUT TRAGEDY

As you plan and write an essay about tragedy, keep in mind all the elements of drama. A full discussion of traditional approaches to these elements—plot, character, point of view, setting, language, tone, symbol, and theme—can be found in Chapter 26. Review this material before you begin your essay.

Although the basic elements remain consistent in tragedy, the form requires a few special considerations. In planning and writing about plot and conflict, you can explore in detail the crisis/climax—that point at which the downfall becomes inevitable. Similarly, you should consider the degree to which the conflicts shape or accelerate the tragic action. With character, pay special attention to the tragic protagonist and the major antagonists. What is the connection between the protagonist's strengths and weaknesses? To what extent does the protagonist bring on or cooperate with his or her own destruction? What key characteristics and behavior patterns ensure both the protagonist's heroic stature and fall? In dealing with tone, consider the degree to which the play is ironic. Do you know more about what is going on than the protagonist? Than most of the characters? If so, how does this knowledge affect the play's impact and meaning?

All the traditional elements of drama, along with the special considerations noted above, can provide fruitful essays about tragic drama. Here, however, we introduce two new ways of writing about literature: an examination of a problem and a close reading of a passage. Both of these approaches have universal application. They can be employed to write about prose fiction, poetry, or any type of dramatic literature. Our discussion will naturally focus on tragedy—specifically *Hamlet*—and the plays in which problem solving and close reading can generate effective essays about tragic drama.

AN ESSAY ABOUT A PROBLEM

A **problem** is any question that you cannot answer easily and correctly about a body of material that you know. The question, "Who is the major character in *Hamlet*?" is not a problem, because the obvious answer is Hamlet.

Let us, however, ask another question: "Why is it *correct* to say that Hamlet is the major character?" This question is not as easy as the first, and for this reason it is a problem. It requires that we think about our answer, even though we do not need to search very far. Hamlet is the title character. He is involved in most of the actions of the play. He is so much the center of our liking and concern that his death causes sadness and regret. To "solve" this problem has required a set of responses, all of which provide answers to the question "why?"

More complex, however, and more typical of most problems, are questions like these: "Why does Hamlet talk of suicide in his first soliloquy?" "Why does he treat Ophelia so coarsely in the 'nunnery' scene?" "Why does he delay in avenging his father's death?" Essays on a problem are normally concerned with such questions, because they require a good deal of thought, together with a number of interpretations knitted together into a whole essay. More broadly, dealing with problems is one of the major tasks of the intellectual, scientific, social, and political disciplines. Being able to advance and then explain solutions is therefore one of the most important techniques that you can acquire.

Strategies for developing an essay about a problem

Your first purpose is to convince your reader that your solution is a good one. This you do by making sound conclusions from supporting evidence. In nonscientific subjects like literature you rarely find absolute proofs, so your conclusions will not be *proved* in the way you prove triangles congruent in geometry. But your organization, your use of facts from the text, your interpretations, and your application of general or specific knowledge should all make your conclusions convincing. Thus your basic strategy is *persuasion*.

STRATEGY 1: DEMONSTRATE THAT CONDITIONS FOR A SOLUTION ARE FULFILLED. This type of development is the most basic in writing—namely, illustration. You first explain that certain conditions need to exist for your solution to be plausible. Your central idea—really a brief answer to the question—is that the conditions do indeed exist. Your development is to show how the conditions may be found in the work.

Suppose that you are writing on the problem of why Hamlet delays revenge against Claudius. Suppose also that you make the point that Hamlet delays because he is never sure that Claudius is guilty. This is your "solution" to the problem. In your essay you support your answer by showing the flimsiness of the information Hamlet receives about the crime (i.e., the two visits from the Ghost and Claudius's distress at the play within the play). Once you have "attacked" these sources of data on the grounds that they are unreliable, you have succeeded because your solution is consistent with the details of the play.

STRATEGY 2: ANALYZE WORDS IN THE PHRASING OF THE PROBLEM. Your object in this approach is to clarify important words in the statement of the problem, and then to decide how applicable they are. This kind of attention to words, in fact, might give you enough material for all or part of your essay. Thus, an essay on the problem of Hamlet's delay might focus in part on a treatment of the word *delay*: What, really, does *delay* mean? For Hamlet, is there a difference between delay that is reasonable and delay that is unreasonable? Does Hamlet delay unreasonably? Is his delay the result of a psychological fault? Would speedy revenge be more or less reasonable than the delay? By the time you have answered such pointed questions, you will also have sufficient material for your full essay.

STRATEGY 3: REFER TO LITERARY CONVENTIONS OR EXPECTATIONS. With this strategy, the argument is to establish that the problem can be solved by reference to the literary mode or conventions of a work, or to the work's own self-limitations. In other words, what appears to be a problem is really no more than a normal characteristic. A problem about the artificiality of the choruses in *Oedipus the King*, for example, might be resolved by reference to the fact that choruses were a normal feature of Greek drama. In a similar manner, the knowledge that delay is a convention of all revenge tragedy might provide a key to the problem of Hamlet's apparent procrastination. Similarly, a question about the differing functions of Tom in *The Glass Menagerie* (pp. 1519–68) can be explained by the free use that Tennessee Williams makes of nonrealistic stage conventions.

STRATEGY 4: ARGUE AGAINST POSSIBLE OBJECTIONS. With this strategy, you raise your own objections and then argue against them. Called **procatalepsis** or **anticipation**, this approach helps you sharpen your arguments, because *anticipating* and dealing with objections forces you to make analyses and use facts that you might otherwise overlook. Although procatalepsis may be used point by point throughout your essay, you may find it most useful at the end.

The situation to imagine is that someone is raising objections to your solution to the problem. It is then your task to show that the objections (1) are not accurate or valid, (2) are not strong or convincing, or (3) are based on unusual rather than usual conditions (on an exception and not the rule). Here are some examples of these approaches. The objections raised are italicized, so that you can easily distinguish them from the answers.

a. The objection is not accurate or valid. Here you reject the objection by showing that either the interpretation or the conclusions are wrong and also by emphasizing that the evidence supports your solution:

> Although Hamlet's delay is reasonable, *the claim might be made that his duty is to kill Claudius in revenge immediately after the Ghost's accusations.* This claim is not persuasive because it assumes that Hamlet knows everything the audience knows. The audience accepts the Ghost's word that Claudius is guilty, but Hamlet has no certain reasons to believe the Ghost. Would it not seem insane for Hamlet to kill Claudius, who reigns legally, and then to claim he did it because of the Ghost's words? The argument for speedy revenge is not good because it is based on an incorrect view of Hamlet's situation.

b. The objection is not strong or convincing. Here you *concede* that the objection has some truth or validity, but you then try to show that it is weak and that your own solution is stronger:

> One might claim that Claudius's distress at the play within the play is evidence for his guilt and that therefore Hamlet should carry out his revenge right away. This argument has merit, and Hamlet's speech after Claudius has fled the scene

("I'll take the Ghost's word for a thousand pound") shows that the "conscience of the king" has been caught. But the king's guilty behavior is not a strong cause for killing him. Hamlet could justifiably ask for an investigation of his father's death on these grounds, but he could not justify a revenge killing. Claudius could not be convicted in any court on the testimony that he was disturbed at seeing the "Murder of Gonzago." Even after the play within the play, the reasons for delay are stronger than for action.

c. The objection is based on unusual rather than usual conditions. Here you reject the objection on the grounds that it could be valid only if normal conditions were suspended. The objection depends on an exception, not a rule:

> The case for quick action is simple: *Hamlet should kill Claudius right after seeing the Ghost (I.3), or else after seeing the King's reaction to the stage murder of Gonzago (III.2) or else after seeing the Ghost again (III.4).* Redress under these circumstances, goes the argument, must be both personal and extra-legal. This argument wrongly assumes that due process does not exist in the Denmark of Hamlet and Claudius. Nothing in the play indicates that the Danes, even though they carouse a bit, do not value legality and the rules of evidence. Thus Hamlet cannot rush out to kill Claudius, because he knows that the King has not had anything close to due process. The argument for quick action is poor because it rests on an exception being made from civilized law.

Remember that writing an essay on a problem requires you to argue a position: Either there is a solution or there is not. To develop your position requires that you show the steps to your conclusion. Your general thematic form is thus (1) to describe the conditions that need to be met for the solution you propose, and then (2) to demonstrate that these conditions exist. If you assert that there is no solution, then your form would be the same for the first part, but your second part—the development—would show that these conditions have *not* been met.

In developing your response, use one or more of the strategies described in this chapter. These are, again, (1) to demonstrate that conditions for a solution are fulfilled, (2) to analyze the words in the phrasing of the problem, (3) to refer to literary expectations or limitations, and (4) to argue against possible objections. You might combine these. Thus, if we assume that your argument is that Hamlet's delay is reasonable, you might first consider the word *delay* (strategy 2). Then you might use strategy 1 to explain the reasons for Hamlet's delay. Finally, to answer objections to your argument, you might show that he acts promptly when he believes he is justified (strategy 4). Whatever your topic, the important thing is to use the method or methods that best help you make a good argument for your solution.

In your conclusion, try to affirm the validity of your solution in view of the supporting evidence. You might do this by reemphasizing your strongest points, or you might simply present a brief summary. Or you might think of your argument as still continuing and thus use the strategy of procatalepsis to raise and answer possible objections to your solution, as in the last paragraph of the sample essay.

SAMPLE ESSAY

The Problem of Hamlet's Apparent Delay°

[1]
For hundreds of years, readers and spectators of Shakespeare's <u>Hamlet</u> have been puzzled by the prince's apparent failure to kill Claudius quickly. Early in the play, the Ghost calls on his son to "Revenge his foul and most unnatural murder" (Act I. scene 5, line 25). Hamlet, however, delays his vengeance until the end of the play. Why does he not act sooner? <u>The answer is that there is no unjustified delay and that in fact Hamlet acts as quickly as possible.</u>* This becomes evident when we examine the conventions of revenge tragedy, the actual "call to revenge," and the steps that Hamlet takes to achieve vengeance.†

[2]
<u>Revenge tragedy conventionally requires that vengeance be delayed until the closing moments of the play.</u> Given this limitation, Shakespeare must justify the wide gap of time between the call to revenge in Act I and the killing of Claudius in Act V. We find such justification in the unreliability of the ghost's initial accusation, Hamlet's need for additional evidence, and the events that occur after this evidence is obtained.

[3]
The Ghost's accusations and demands are straightforward: he accuses his brother of murdering him and he calls on his son for vengeance. <u>Shakespeare is careful, however, to establish that this testimony may be doubtful.</u> Horatio questions the Ghost's truthfulness and motives, and he warns Hamlet that the spirit might "assume some other horrid form / Which might deprive your sovereignty of reason, / And draw you into madness" (Act I. scene 4, lines 72–74). Hamlet himself expresses doubt about the ghost:

> The spirit that I have seen
> may be a devil, and the devil hath power
> T'assume a pleasing shape, yea, and perhaps
> Out of my weakness, and my melancholy,
> As he is very potent with such spirits,
> Abuses me to damn me; I'll have grounds
> More relative than this. (II.2.573–579)

The prince thus cannot act simply on the unsupported word of the ghost; he needs more evidence.

[4]
<u>There is no delay at this point in the play, because Hamlet quickly begins developing a plan of action.</u> Immediately after speaking with the ghost, he decides to cover himself under an "antic disposition" while he gathers information. He swears his companions to silence and warns them not to react knowingly if he should seem to behave strangely or insanely (Act I. scene 5, lines 169–179). His idea is that this pose will make him less suspect and make others less careful.

<u>Once Hamlet has begun his plan, he takes advantage of every opportunity to carry out his vengeance.</u> When the players come to Elsinore, he adroitly

---

° See p. 1130 for this play.
* Central idea.
† Thesis sentence.

plans to test Claudius by making him publicly view a play, *The Mousetrap*, which shows a murder just like Claudius's murder of Hamlet's father. Hamlet states that Claudius's appearance will give him the clue he needs to confirm the Ghost's information:

> I'll observe his looks,
> I'll tent him to the quick, if a' do blench
> I know my course.   (II.2, 571–573)

[5] Once the king breaks up the performance in great agitation, which Hamlet correctly interprets as an admission of guilt, Hamlet declares confidence in the Ghost ("I'll take the ghost's word for a thousand pound" [Act III. scene 2, lines 271–272]). Moreover, he is psychologically ready to act against the king, for he asserts that he could "drink hot blood, / And do such bitter business as the day / Would quake to look on" (Act III. scene 2, lines 367–369). Without doubt, Hamlet is only a prayer away from stabbing Claudius, for when he sees the king kneeling, his opportunity has merged with his desire and also with his promise to the Ghost. He tells the audience, "Now might I do it pat, now a' is a-praying, / And now I'll do't" (Act III. scene 3, lines 73–74).

But he does not "do't," and for this reason he is open to the claim that he cannot act. Again, however, Shakespeare carefully justifies this hesitation. The prince does not want to send Claudius's soul to heaven by killing him at prayer. Rather, he wants the revenge to match Claudius's treacherous murder of old King Hamlet, who died without the chance to pray and repent:

> Up sword, and know thou a more horrid hent,
> When he is drunk asleep, or in his rage,
> Or in th'incestuous pleasure of his bed,
[6] At game, a-swearing, or about some act
> That has no relish of salvation in't,
> Then trip him that his heels may kick at heaven,
> And that his soul may be as damned and black
> As hell whereto it goes. (III.3.88–95)

This deferral is in keeping with the code of personal blood vengeance, whereby the revenge must match or exceed the original crime. There is no question of Hamlet's incapacity to act, because his putting up his sword is totally reasonable and justifiable.

From this point on, Hamlet acts or reacts to every situation as the opportunity presents itself. After he kills Polonius, Claudius initiates a counterplot to send Hamlet off to England and execution. Clearly, Hamlet's chances to kill the king are thus reduced to zero. It is not until Act V that Hamlet gets back to Denmark, after having decisively thwarted Claudius's murderous instructions by turning them against Rosencrantz and Guildenstern. He makes it clear to Horatio, however, that he will take the earliest opportunity, and that "the readiness is all" (Act V. scene 2, line 205). Once the rigged fencing match is under
[7] way, the opportunity finally comes. Claudius, Hamlet learns, has not only killed his father, but has poisoned his mother, and he himself is about to die from Laertes's poisoned sword. Upon such certain information, Hamlet immediately kills Claudius. When the revenge is complete, the Ghost, who began the cry for vengeance, is nowhere to be heard or seen, and four bodies lie on the stage.

[8] Thus, we see that the problem of Hamlet's delay—and the vengeance does take four acts to carry out—is really not a problem. The prince acts in accordance with the code of revenge as quickly as circumstances permit. Although the text of the play supports this solution, critics might still argue that procrastination is an issue because Hamlet twice accuses himself of delay. This objection does not take into consideration that Hamlet's perception of time and action is distorted by his eagerness for vengeance. From Hamlet's subjective point of view, any break in activity is delay. From our objective viewpoint, however, delay is not a true issue.

Commentary on the Essay

The structure of the essay illustrates strategy 1 (p. 1305). The second paragraph, however, makes brief use of strategy 3 in its reference to the conventions of revenge tragedy. In both paragraphs 6 and 8, the argument is carried on by use of *procatalepsis*, or strategy 4, whereby a counter argument is raised and then answered.

The introductory paragraph raises the problem of Hamlet's apparent delay and offers a brief statement of the solution (the central idea). This plan is developed in paragraphs 2–7 in exactly the same order in which the issues are raised in the introduction. Paragraph 2 deals with the conventions of revenge tragedy, and paragraph 3 takes up the issue of the Ghost's reliability. Paragraphs 4 and 5 deal with Hamlet's attempts to corroborate the ghost's accusations, and paragraphs 6 and 7 consider the subsequent action. Note that each paragraph in the argument grows naturally out of the one that precedes it just as all the paragraphs are linked to the introductory paragraph.

The concluding paragraph asserts that the original problem is solved; the paragraph then summarizes the steps of the solution. It also continues the argument by raising and then dealing with a possible objection.

AN ESSAY ON A CLOSE READING
OF A PASSAGE

An essay on a close reading is a detailed study of a passage of prose or verse that may be part of a longer work—in this chapter, a play—or it may be an entire short poem. The close-reading essay is specific because it focuses on the selected passage. It is also general because you do not consider only a single topic (such as *character*, *setting*, or *theme*), but rather deal with *all* the elements to be found in the passage. If the passage describes a person, for example, you must discuss character, but your emphasis should be on what the passage itself brings out about the character. *The passage dictates the content of your essay.*

Focus on the general meaning and impact of the passage. Who speaks it? What is it about? What does it tell you about the speaker or the world of the play? Once these questions are answered, write notes that you can use later in paragraphs. Try to reach specific and focused conclusions: Does the passage (1) describe a scene, (2) develop a character, (3) present an action, (4) reveal a character's thoughts, (5) advance an argument, or (6) introduce an idea? What is the thematic content? How does the passage relate to earlier and later parts of the whole text? (To deal with this question, you may assume that your reader is familiar with the entire work.)

Strategies for Organizing Ideas

FOR AN EARLY PASSAGE. If the passage is early in the play, you may conclude that the author is setting things in motion (exposition, complication). Thus, you should determine how themes, characterizations, and arguments in the passage are related to later developments. Always assume that everything is there for a purpose, and then find that purpose.

FOR A LATER, MIDPOINT PASSAGE. In a passage at the play's midpoint, a character's fortunes may take either an expected or an unexpected turn. If the change is unexpected, you should explain how the passage focuses the various themes or ideas and then propels them toward the forthcoming crisis/climax (the turning point or high point). It may be that the work features surprises, and the passage thus acquires a different meaning on second reading. Or it may be that the speaker has one set of assumptions while the readers have others, and that the passage marks the speaker's increasing self-awareness. Any part of any work is part of a whole, and it is therefore your task to determine the extent to which the passage (a) builds on what has happened previously, and (b) prepares the way for the outcome.

FOR A CONCLUDING PASSAGE. A passage at or near the play's end is designed to solve problems or to be a focal point or climax for all the cumulative situations and ideas. You will thus need to show how the passage brings together all details, ideas, and themes. What is happening? Is any action described in the passage a major action, or a step leading to the major action? Has everything in the passage been prepared for earlier, or are there any surprises?

When you prepare your essay, begin by quoting the entire passage just as it appears in the text. It is also helpful to number the lines for easy reference. Because the close-reading essay is concerned with details, you might have a problem developing a thematic structure. You can overcome this difficulty if you begin to work with either a generalization about the passage or a thesis based on the relationship of the passage to the work. Suppose, for example, that the passage is factually descriptive or that it introduces a major character or raises a major idea. Any one of these observations may serve as a thesis.

Develop the body of the essay according to what you find in the passage. For a passage of character description, analyze what is disclosed about the character, together with your analysis of what bearing this information has on the play as a whole. For a passage presenting an idea or ideas, analyze the idea and, also, demonstrate how the idea is important for the rest of the work. In short, your aim in this kind of essay is double: first, discuss the passage itself, and, second, show how the passage functions within the entire play.

To conclude, stress the important details of your analysis. In addition, you may want to deal with secondary issues that arise in the passage but do not merit full consideration. The passage may contain specific phrases or underlying assumptions that you have not considered in the body of your essay. The conclusion is the place to mention these matters, without developing them fully.

SAMPLE ESSAY

Appearance and Reality: A Close Reading of <u>Hamlet</u>, I.ii.76–86°

> 76 Seems, madam? nay it is. I know not "seems."
> 77 'Tis not alone my inky cloak good mother,
> 78 Nor customary suits of solemn black,
> 79 Nor windy suspiration of forced breath,
> 80 No, nor the fruitful river of the eye,
> 81 Nor the dejected havior of the visage,
> 82 Together with all forms, moods, shapes of grief,
> 83 That can denote me truly: these indeed seem,
> 84 For they are actions, that a man might play,
> 85 But I have that within which passes show,
> 86 These but the trappings and the suits of woe.

[1] Hamlet speaks these lines during his first appearance in Act I. Gertrude—his mother—has just tried to convince him that death is "common" to all humanity and that he "seems" to be spinning out his grief over his father's death. Hamlet's speech grows out of Gertrude's word "seems." <u>In this way, Shakespeare introduces one of the play's central ideas that there is a difference between appearance and reality.</u>˙ <u>This concept is stated directly, is then amplified, and shows up repeatedly throughout the play in both character and action.</u>†

[2] The discrepancy between appearance and reality is introduced in Hamlet's first line: "Seems, madam? nay, it is." In this disarmingly simple statement, Hamlet opposes things that seem to be and those that actually exist.

˙ See p. 1130 for this play.
˙ Central idea.
† Thesis sentence.

This opposition of illusion or appearance ("seems") and reality ("is") becomes the cornerstone of his words.

[3]

Hamlet expands on the contrast in lines 77–86 with reference to the outward trappings of mourning. In an almost scholarly way (he has just come home from school), he lists five of the traditional signs of grief: an "inky cloak" (77); "suits of solemn black" (78); sighs, or the "windy suspiration of forced breath" (79); tears, or "the fruitful river of the eye" (80); and sad looks, or "the dejected [be]havior of the visage" (81). Having listed these items, Hamlet identifies them in three separate lines as the outward displays of mourning. First, he calls them the "forms, moods, shapes of grief" (82). In line 84 he also notes that "they are actions that a man might play." And in line 86 he labels this list as "the trappings [costumes] and the suits of woe." These three lines thus show that the five signs of grief are all outward shows. His contrast is especially emphasized in the words forms, shapes, play, and trappings. His speech is capped off logically by his contrast of all the appearances of grief with his own real and internal feelings: "I have that within which [sur]passes show" (line 85). Again, we have the direct contrast between appearance ("show") and reality ("that within").

[4]

This contrast is a vital idea in the entire play, for it shows up repeatedly in both character and situation. Claudius, for example, appears to be a loving uncle, a good king, and a reasonable man, but we know that he is actually a murderer and a usurper. Rosencrantz and Guildenstern are Hamlet's school chums, but they easily succumb to Claudius's wiles, and they then become spies. Such discrepancies are also apparent in actions. For example, in Act III, Claudius appears to be praying. In his brief soliloquy, however, he admits that he cannot be contrite, but rather he is "still possessed / Of those effects for which I did the murder" (III.iii.53–54). Similarly, the duel between Hamlet and Laertes seems to be a straightforward fencing match but is actually a complicated trap by which Claudius plans to kill Hamlet by either sword or poison, or both.

[5]

Hamlet's speech therefore shows his wit in responding to his mother, and it also shows his scholarly nature in his assertions contrasting superficial grief with his own deep grief. The contrast obviously governs his own view of reality, and it also puts forward one of the play's most important issues. It is, after all, the difference between appearance and reality that permits Claudius to reign even though he is a murderer, and it is the difficulty of distinguishing between appearance and reality that Hamlet encounters when trying to carry out the Ghost's cry for revenge. Generally, also, the difference is a cause of the confusion, and also the evil, that exists in the personal, social, and political world. Because characters and events in *Hamlet* are rarely what they appear to be, the passage thus provides a key to Shakespeare's profound tragedy.

Commentary on the Essay

This essay deals with one of Shakespeare's major themes in *Hamlet*: the difference between appearance and reality and the effects of these differences.

The body takes up the specific details in Hamlet's speech, and then shows how these details are developed throughout the play. Paragraph 2 deals with Hamlet's first statement of the idea, and paragraph 3 discusses how he applies the concept to the expression of grief. Paragraph 4 demonstrates the relationship of the idea to character and situation elsewhere in the text. The conclusion brings the arguments of the essay together, stressing that the contrast is important to our understanding of Hamlet's character, the play's major ideas, Hamlet's task of revenge, and, generally, the world at large.

WRITING TOPICS

1. Much has been made of the contrast in *Oedipus the King* between seeing and blindness. Write an essay which considers this contrast as it is related to the character of Oedipus. How are blindness and seeing reversed, with regard to his understanding about the curse on the city, his attempts to ferret out the guilty ones, his awakening perceptions of his own responsibility and guilt, and his self-blinding? How may Tiresias be compared and contrasted with Oedipus?

2. Develop an argument for one of these assertions:

    a. Oedipus's fall is the result of fate, predestination, and the gods, and would happen despite his character.

    b. Oedipus's fall is the result only of his character, and has nothing to do with fate or the gods.

3. Write an essay considering the degree to which Gertrude and Ophelia in *Hamlet* justify Hamlet's assertion, "Frailty, thy name is woman" (Act I. scene 2, line 146). Questions you might take into account concern the status of these women, their power to exert their own individuality and to make their own decisions, Gertrude as a royal queen and Ophelia as an aristocratic daughter, their ability to undergo the pain of being bereaved, Hamlet's own feelings about the death of his father, and so on. To what degree should the issues about these women be subjected to a feminist critical analysis? (See Appendix D, p. 1655.)

4. Hamlet, Laertes, and Fortinbras are all young men whose fathers have been killed and who set out to avenge these deaths. Their courses of action, however, are different. In an essay, consider these three as typical or archetypal sons. What characteristics do they share? What, in turn, makes them individual and distinct? Compare and contrast how each character deals with his father's death. Which approach seems most reasonable to you? Most emotional? Most effective? For additional directions, consult Appendix D (p. 1659).

5. *Death of a Salesman* was successfully produced in the People's Republic of China in 1983, and was revived on Broadway in 1984, not to mention the successful Lee J. Cobb and Dustin Hoffman television productions of the 1950's and 1980's. How do you account for the continuing interest in the play from the time it was first produced until the present moment, in contemporary America and in other cultures?

6. Write an essay discussing the ways in which *Death of a Salesman* comments on American life and values. What specific shortcomings of American life—social,

economic, political, and personal—does Miller expose and attack? In what ways does Willy Loman represent these shortcomings, but, conversely, how may he be seen as an innocent victim? To what degree might Willy's death be seen as a redemption, and therefore as a defense of American life?

7. Considering *Oedipus the King, Hamlet,* and *Death of a Salesman,* write an essay defining and explaining tragedy. Include references to the nature of the tragic protagonists, the situations they face, their solutions to their problems, their responses to the consequences of their actions, and their worthiness of character. Be sure to compare and contrast the actions and speeches of the characters in the plays as evidence.

28

Comedy: Restoring the Balance

Comedy is the fraternal, not the identical, twin of tragedy. While the mask of tragedy frowns, the mask of comedy smiles. Tragedy moves toward despair or death; comedy toward success, happiness, and marriage. The words of tragedy are elevated and heroic. The words of comedy may be elevated too, but often they are common or colloquial, and although they may be witty, they are often witless and bawdy. Despite these differences, there are also similarities that show the common birth. Many comedies are filled with tragic potential, and many tragedies contain potentially comic plots. Indeed, tragedy may be seen as an abortive or incomplete comedy in which affairs go wrong, and comedy may be considered a tragedy in which the truth is discovered (or covered up), the hero saves the day, the villain confesses in time to avert disaster, and equilibrium and balance are restored.

THE ORIGINS OF COMEDY

In the *Poetics*, Aristotle admits that little is known about the origin of comedy because at first the form was not taken seriously (V. 2, p. 21). He does say, however, that comedy, like tragedy, developed from "improvisation" (IV.12, p. 19). The improvising apparently happened during the religious festivals at Athens, the most important of which was the Great, or City Dionysia, held in worship of the god Dionysus in March–April every year.[1] While tragedy grew out of performances of "dithyrambs," or choric songs, comedy branched out from "phallic songs," or wildly bacchanalian celebrations. The word *comedy* is consistent with this explanation, for as "a *komos* song" its Greek meaning is a "song of revels" or "songs sung by merrymakers." During parades or proces-

---

[1] For a more detailed discussion of the festivals, see Chapter 27, pp. 1070–71.

sions, the merrymakers expressed their joy boisterously, carried giant phalluses, traded bawdy remarks with spectators, and lampooned public persons.

Comedy Competitions

Aristotle states that it was "late" when comic performances were separated from the phallic songs (V. 2, p. 21); that is, comedy followed tragedy by many years. The earliest certain date for the existence of comedy is 486 B.C., when a state-sponsored comedy competition was held during the City Dionysia and was won by a writer named Chionides. Although these earliest comedies apparently consisted of little more than loosely connected lampoons, they were highly enough regarded to justify regular competitions. In the festivals, the comedies were scheduled on each day, after the tragedies and satyr plays were completed.

According to Aristotle, the first writer to transform comedy by creating a thematic plot development was Crates, who won the first of his three prizes in about the mid fifth century (V. 3, p. 21). It was at this time that comedies became popular enough to justify an additional state comedy competition, which was instituted in about 440 B.C. during the *Lenaia*, the Dionysian festival that the Athenians held in January. For the remainder of the century, writers of comedy as well as tragedy tried to win prizes for their new plays at both the City Dionysia and the Lenaia.

GREEK OLD COMEDY. The fifth-century comedies, called **Old Comedy** or **Old Attic Comedy**, followed intricate structural patterns and displayed complex poetic conventions. Nevertheless, they bore the marks of their origins in the bacchanalian *komos* processions. The actors (three or four men) and the chorus (twenty four) each displayed an exaggerated leather phallus, dressed in distortingly padded costumes, and wore a character-defining mask. The role of the chorus usually dictated the comedy's title (e.g., *The Frogs, The Wasps*). Customarily, the plot was fantastic and impossible, and the dialogue was farcical and bawdy. In the tradition of satires and tirades associated with the phallic songs and with early comedy, the comic dramatists freely lashed public persons (usually but not always without legal reprisal).

Although the most successful comedy writer of the fifth century B.C. was Magnes (flourished 475–450 B.C.), who won eleven times, the only writer whose works survive is Aristophanes (450/445–385 B.C.), who won four times. His work constitutes our principal first-hand knowledge of Greek Old Comedy. He wrote at least thirty-two comedies. Fortunately, eleven are still intact. There are also surviving fragments of some of his other plays. His plots and actions are outrageous, his characters are funny, and his language is satirical, bawdy, and biting.

MIDDLE COMEDY. Aristophanes lived into the next period of Greek comedy, which is called **Middle Comedy**. Except for his plays *Ecclesiazusae* (ca.

391 B.C.)and *Plutus* (388 B.C.), which presaged Middle Comedy, all the Middle Comedy plays are lost, although there are many extant fragments. Middle Comedy eliminated some of the complex patterns of Old Comedy, and the topics became less Athenian and more international. Political criticism was abandoned, and character types like the braggart soldier were introduced. The role of the chorus was lessened or eliminated (as with tragedy), and the exaggerated costumes were eliminated.

NEW COMEDY. By the end of the fourth century, B.C., Middle Comedy was replaced by **New Comedy**. The most important of the New Comedy dramatists was Menander (342–ca. 291 B.C.), who was heralded in ancient times as the greatest comic writer of them all. Everyone knows quotations from Menander, such as "calling a spade a spade" and "the gods first make mad those they intend to destroy." St. Paul quotes him in I Corinthians 15: 33 ("Bad company ruins good morals."), but after the fifth century A.D., Menander's plays were lost. In the last hundred years, however, many Menandrian manuscripts have been discovered, mostly in the sands of Egypt. We now have an entire comedy of his, the *Dyscolus* (*The Grouch*), and almost complete versions of a number of other plays, together with numerous fragments and passages. In total, the titles of close to one hundred of his plays are known. His comedies are romantic rather than satirical, and employ stock characters such as young lovers, stubborn fathers, clever slaves, and long-separated relatives.

Roman Comedy

After the time of Menander, Greek power failed in the Mediterranean area and was replaced by the might of Rome. In the third century B.C. Roman comedy began and flourished, largely through the translation and adaptation of Greek New Comedies. The significant writers were Plautus (ca. 250–184 B.C.), with twenty surviving comedies, and Terence (193 or 183–159 B.C.), whose six comedies still exist. Briefly, the comedies of Plautus are brisk, while those of Terence are more restrained. The central issue in most of the Roman comedies is the overcoming of a **blocking agent**, or obstruction to true love, which could be almost anyone or anything—a rival lover, an angry father, a family feud, an old law, a previously arranged marriage, or differences in social class. The pattern of action, traditionally called the **plot of intrigue**, stems from the subterfuges that young lovers undertake to overcome the blocking agent, so that the outcome frequently heralds the victory of youth over age and the passing of control from one generation to the next.

Comedy from Roman Times to the Renaissance

By the time the Empire was established in 29 B.C., the writing of comedy had virtually stopped because Roman dramatic creativeness had been preempted by pantomime entertainments and public spectacles, principally gladiatorial combat. Comedy thus accompanied tragedy into 1500 years of obscurity—a period when the Empire grew and fell, the dark ages descended, and the medieval period flourished. Although many comic and farcical scenes were included in the medieval mystery cycles in late medieval times,[2] comedy as a form was not reestablished until the Renaissance.

Once comedy was introduced it grew rapidly. By 1500 the six plays of Terence were achieving recognition, followed by the twenty surviving plays of Plautus. When English dramatists began writing comedies, they followed Roman conventions. The English plays of the mid-sixteenth century contained five acts, and they observed the unities of time, place, and action, thus following the rules and justifying the claim that they were "regular." Character types from the Roman comedies became preeminent, such as the intriguing couple, the fussing father, and the bragging soldier. Soon, more specifically English types appeared, anticipating the roisterers in Shakespeare's *Henry IV* plays and the "mechanicals" in *A Midsummer Night's Dream.* By the end of the sixteenth century, when Shakespeare had completed many of his comedies, English comedy was in full bloom. It has commonly been observed that the comedy was Latin in structure but English in character.

When the sixteenth century began, the chief obstacle to a wide public assimilation of drama had been the absence of institutionalized theaters. London authorities maintained that playgoing was a sinful public nuisance, and they permitted no theaters. When theaters were built, therefore, they had to be located outside the London city limits. For example, the Rose and the Globe theaters, where Shakespeare saw his plays produced from the mid 1590s to 1611, were built in Southwark. We should realize that most people in Shakespeare's audiences had gotten to the theater by walking over London Bridge or by being ferried across the river, and they returned home the same way.

COMIC PATTERNS, CHARACTERS, AND LANGUAGE

Dictionaries sometimes give *funny* as a synonym for *comic,* but the two terms are not the same. Words like "funny," "amusing," or "humorous" define our emotional conditioning to incidents, and our reactions always depend on context. We usually think it is funny to see an actor in a slapstick routine being struck with a paddle, whereas if we leave the theater and see a person being beaten with a similar object, such as a baseball bat, we are repelled and horrified. The *context* makes the difference.

---

[2] For a description of the medieval *Mystery* or *Corpus Christi* Plays, see pp. 1122–23.

The Comic Pattern

Comic, the adjective derived from *comedy*, describes the pattern or context which conditions our responses. *Comic* means that a literary work or set of situations conforms to the patterns and characteristics of comedy. Within these patterns, we are conditioned to perceive most dialogue and action— even serious problems and dangerous situations—as being amusing and funny. At heart, therefore, comedy and the term *comic* suggest a pattern of action, including funny situations and language, that we perceive as solvable and correctable. The pattern grows out of character or situation, and it leads to a resolution that satisfies us.

COMIC PROBLEMS. The problems with which comedies begin may be individual or social. They may involve thwarted love, eccentric behavior, corruption in high places, or a combination of other difficulties. As the comedies move from exposition to complication, the problems usually get much worse. In comedy, complication is often fueled by confusion, misunderstanding, mistakes in identity, errors in judgment, excessive or unreasonable behavior, and coincidences that stretch our credulity.

THE COMIC CLIMAX. The climax of a comedy occurs when these confusions reach a peak, misunderstanding is dominant, pressure is at a high point, choices must be made, and solutions must be found. The climax—the changing or turning point—frequently introduces a sudden revelation in which a key fact, identity, or event is explained to characters and audience at the same time.

THE COMIC CATASTROPHE. In most comedies, the events of the catastrophe resolve the initial problems and allow for the comic resolution, which involves setting things right at every level of action. Individual lives are thereby straightened out, people at odds with each other are reconciled, new families are formed through marriages, and a healthy social order is reestablished.

COMIC EDUCATION AND CHANGE. Two key features of the comic pattern are *education* and *change*. In many comedies at least some of the characters learn something about themselves, their society, or the way to love and live. Their education makes it possible for them to improve, and, by implication, for the world also to improve. In other comedies, however, particularly those which touch on major social and political problems, the *audience* is educated, and the playwright hopes that change will occur in the world as well as on the stage.

Comic Characters

Characters in comedy are far more limited than in tragedy because comedies usually deal with representative types or groups rather than with individuals of heroic stature. In comedy, we rarely find characters with the depth or individuality of Hamlet or Oedipus. Instead, comedy gives us stock characters who represent classes, types, and generations. In Shakespeare's *A Midsummer Night's Dream*, for instance, most of the characters are representative and stock figures. Egeus is a conventional indignant father. Similarly, Hermia and Lysander (along with Helena and Demetrius) are typical young lovers.

Comic Language

As in other types of literature, comic dramatists use language to delineate character, to establish tone and mood, and to express ideas and feelings. In comedy, however, language is also one of the most important vehicles for humor. Some comedies are characterized by elegant and witty language, others by puns and bawdy jokes.

Characters in comedy tend either to be masters of language or to be mastered by it. Those who are skillful with language, such as Lisette in *Love Is the Doctor*, can use a witty phrase like a knife to satirize their foes and friends alike. Those who are unskilled with language, like Bottom in *A Midsummer Night's Dream*, bungle through a speech with their misuse of words and inadvertent puns. Both types of characters are amusing; we smile a knowing smile with the wits and laugh out loud at the bunglers.

TYPES OF COMEDY

Differences in comic style, content, and intent that have evolved over the centuries make it possible to divide comedy into various types. The broadest of these divisions, based on both style and content, separates all comic literature into *high comedy* and *low comedy*.

High Comedy

Ideally, high comedy (a term coined by George Meredith in 1877 in *The Idea of Comedy*) is witty, graceful, and sophisticated. The complications and problems grow out of character rather than situation, and the appeal is to the intellect.

ROMANTIC COMEDY. One of the major kinds of high comedy is **romantic comedy**, which views action and character from the standpoint of earnest young lovers like Hermia and Lysander in *A Midsummer Night's Dream*. Ultimately derived from Roman comedy, this kind of play is built on a plot of intrigue featuring lovers who try to overcome opposition (like Egeus) to achieve a successful union. The aim of such plays is amusement and entertainment rather than ridicule and reform. Although vice and folly may be exposed in romantic comedy, especially in the antagonists blocking the young lovers, the dominant impulse is toleration and amused indulgence.

COMEDY OF MANNERS. Related to romantic comedy is the **comedy of manners**, an important type from the seventeenth century to our own times. The comedy of manners examines and satirizes attitudes and customs in the light of high intellectual and moral standards. The dialogue is witty and sophisticated, with characters who are often measured according to their linguistic and intellectual powers. The love plots are serious and real, even though they share with romantic lovers the need to intrigue to overcome blocking forces. The reality and seriousness in some of the manners comedies written in Restoration England (1660–1700), in fact, are so great that one might consider them not only as plays of manners but also of social and personal problems.

SATIRIC COMEDY. Midway between high and low comedy is **satiric comedy**, which is designed to ridicule vices and follies. The playwright of satiric comedy assumes the perspective of a rational and moderate observer measuring human life against a moderate norm, which may be represented by high and serious characters. The audience is invited to share this viewpoint as they, along with the dramatist, heap scorn upon the vicious and laugh loudly at the eccentric and the foolish.

Low Comedy

In low comedy emphasis is on funny remarks and outrageous circumstances, and complications develop from situation and plot rather than from character. Plays of this type are by definition full of physical humor and stage business—a character rounds his forefinger and thumb to imitate a wall, through which other characters speak; an irascible man constantly breaks furniture; a character disguised as a doctor takes a father's pulse to determine his daughter's condition.

FARCE. The quintessential type of low comedy is **farce** (a word derived from the Latin word *farsus,* meaning "stuffed"). A farce is an outlandish physical comedy overflowing with silly characters, improbable happenings, wild clowning, extravagant language, and bawdy jokes.

COMMEDIA DELL'ARTE. A unique kind of farce is the ***commedia dell'arte***, which developed among traveling companies in Italy and France in the sixteenth and seventeenth centuries. The broadly humorous characters recurred from play to play, and always had their own names and characteristics. The action usually involved a plot of intrigue. The lovers were the *Inamorato* and *Inamorata* (like Clitander and Lucinda in *Love Is the Doctor*), who were aided by the Inamorata's clever servant, the *Soubrette* (like Lisette) to overcome *Pantaloon*, the old man (like Sganarelle). The servant characters were *Harlequin* (who was invisible) and *Columbine* (his sweetheart, also invisible), who were joined in highjinks by Pierrot (a clown lover) and *Scaramouche* (the soldier). There were also other stock characters, most of whom were derived from Greek New Comedy by way of Roman comedy, and these have, in turn, become constant features of much subsequent comedy.

SLAPSTICK. With characters of low comedy, of course, there is much tomfoolery and improvisation—the major qualities of the extreme form of farce, **slapstick,** which is named after the double paddles ("slap sticks") that made loud cracking noises when actors in the *commedia dell'arte* used them to whack each other. Slapstick depends heavily on exaggerated poses and facial expressions. In slapstick there is constant onstage business with objects like paddles, pies, pails, paint, paste, or toilet paper, along with wild and improbable actions like squirming, hiding, tripping, stumbling, tumbling, falling, and flopping.

Other Kinds of Comedy

Other types of modern and contemporary comedy include **ironic comedy, realistic comedy,** and **comedy of the absurd.** All of these usually shun the happy endings of traditional comedy. In many of them, the blocking agents are successful and the protagonists are defeated. Often, the initial problem—either a realistic or an absurdist dilemma—remains unresolved. Such comedies, which began to appear in the late nineteenth century, illustrate the complexities and absurdities of modern life and the funny but futile efforts that people make when coming to grips with existence.

Many of the types of comedy just discussed still flourish. Romantic comedies, comedies of manners, farces, and slapstick may be found on innumerable stages and movie screens. They revolve about a central situation, which might be quite ordinary (Will Art Smith get along with a visiting lodge member? Will Sue get accepted by schoolmates at her new school? Will Jim get a date for the prom?). Such situations find their ways into the many *sitcoms* (*situation comedies*) that occupy prime-time television programs.

In view of the various kinds of comedies, it is most important to recognize that comedy is rarely a pure and discrete form. High comedies might include crude physical humor, especially with characters to be disapproved. Low comedies may sometimes contain wit and elegance. Satiric comedies might deal with successful young lovers. Romantic comedies may mock the vices and follies of weird and eccentric characters. Farce and slapstick may contain satire on social values and conventions.

WILLIAM SHAKESPEARE, *A MIDSUMMER NIGHT'S DREAM*

A Midsummer Night's Dream was written early in Shakespeare's career, in 1594 or 1595.[3] It is a romantic comedy dramatizing the idea that "the course of

---

[3] See also Chapter 27, where Shakespeare's theater and his career as a dramatist are described.

true love never did run smooth." This central line of action, which owes much to Roman comedy, involves blocked love, a journey of circumvention and education that takes the lovers from the world of laws and problems into an imaginary world of chaos and transformations, and an ultimate victory back in the world of daylight and order.

The subject of *A Midsummer Night's Dream* is love. Shakespeare skillfully interweaves this topic in the play's four separate plots, four groups of characters, and four styles of language. Each plot explores the nature of love, the madness of irrational love, and the harmony needed for regenerative love.

In the *overplot*—the action that establishes the time for the play—the relationship is between the rulers, Theseus and Hippolyta, who have undergone a change from irrational war to rational peace. As such, they represent the dynastic continuity of the state, the order of the daylight world of Athens, and the rigor of the law. These characters are the rulers, and they speak predominantly in blank verse (unrhymed iambic pentameter; see p. 750).

The two connected *middle plots* concern the adventures of the four lovers and the actions of Oberon and Titania. The four lovers, embodying the most passionate and insistent phase of love, are from the middle class, and they speak mainly in rhymed couplets (see p. 750). During their long night in the woods of illusion fashioned by Oberon and his servant, Puck, their adventures drive them toward rationality, and they recognize and accept the need for faithfulness and constancy.

The parallel middle love plot involves the conflicts between Oberon and Titania, the king and queen of the fairies, because of their infatuations for a "changeling" child. To cure Titania's infatuation, Oberon humbles her, and she then reacknowledges his superiority—the proper attitude of a wife according to Elizabethan males. Oberon and Titania, of course, are supernatural forces. Although they and the other fairies speak in both blank verse and rhymed couplets, the fairies are the only singing characters, and also the only characters to speak in iambic tetrameter.

The examination of love in the *subplot* occurs partly in Titania's relationship with Bottom—the most hilarious instance of love madness in the play—and partly in the play-within-the-play about Pyramus and Thisby. This absurd and funny tragedy echoes the central plot of *A Midsummer Night's Dream* and demonstrates, again, the pitfalls and unpredictability of love. It also emphasizes the happy and harmonious marriages and rapprochements that occur in both the overplot and the middle plots.

While *A Midsummer Night's Dream* is chiefly about love, it is equally concerned with the complicated relationship of perception, imagination, passion, art, and illusion. In Act V Theseus asserts that "The lunatic, the lover, and the poet" are alike because they all try to make reality conform with their own imaginations and desires (scene i, lines 7–22). It would seem that chaos would therefore be the normal state, but, as Hippolyta concludes in response to Theseus, order and certainty somehow prevail, "howsoever" extraordinary and almost miraculous this result may seem (lines 23–27). The movement of the play is governed by these ideas, which, along with the brilliant language and comic actions, are directly attributable to the genius of Shakespeare.

WILLIAM SHAKESPEARE   (1564–1616)

A Midsummer Night's Dream ———————————— *1600 (ca. 1594)*

Edited by Alice Griffin°

[*THE NAMES OF THE ACTORS*

Theseus, *Duke of Athens*
Egeus, *father of Hermia*
Lysander, *beloved of Hermia*
Demetrius, *in love with Hermia, favoured by Egeus*
Philostrate, *Master of the Revels to Theseus*
Peter Quince, *a carpenter* (*Prologue*)*
Nick Bottom, *a weaver* (*Pyramus*)*
Francis Flute, *a bellows-mender* (*Thisby*)*
Tom Snout, *a tinker* (*Wall*)*
Snug, *a joiner* (*Lion*)*
Robin Starveling, *a tailor* (*Moonshine*)*
Hippolyta, *Queen of the Amazons, betrothed to Theseus*
Hermia, *daughter of Egeus, in love with Lysander*
Helena, *in love with Demetrius*
Oberon, *King of the Fairies*
Titania, *Queen of the Fairies*
Puck, *or* Robin Goodfellow
Peaseblossom ⎫
Cobweb   ⎬ *Fairies*
Moth   ⎪
Mustardseed ⎭

Other Fairies attending Oberon and Titania. Attendants on Theseus and Hippolyta.

Scene: *Athens, and a wood nearby*

ACT 1

[Scene 1. Athens. The palace of Theseus]

Enter THESEUS, HIPPOLYTA,° [PHILOSTRATE,] *with others.*

THESEUS.   Now fair Hippolyta, our nuptial hour
   Draws on apace: four happy days bring in

Professor Griffin's text for *A Midsummer Night's Dream* is the First Quarto (edition) published in 1600, with modifications based on the Quarto edition of 1619 and the First Folio, published in 1623. Stage directions in those editions are printed here without brackets; added stage directions are printed within brackets. We have edited Griffin's notes for this text.
*Characters played in the interlude.   0.3 Stage direction: *Theseus, Hippolyta:* In Greek legend, Theseus captured the Amazon Queen Hippolyta and brought her to Athens where they were married.

Another moon: but O, methinks how slow
This old moon wanes! she lingers° my desires,
Like to a stepdame or a dowager,°
Long withering out° a young man's revenue.
HIPPOLYTA.   Four days will quickly steep themselves in night:
Four nights will quickly dream away the time:
And then the moon, like to a silver bow
New-bent in heaven, shall behold the night   1
Of our solemnities.
THESEUS.   Go Philostrate,
Stir up the Athenian youth to merriments,
Awake the pert° and nimble spirit of mirth,
Turn melancholy forth to funerals:
The pale companion° is not for our pomp.   [*Exit PHILOSTRATE.*]   1
Hippolyta, I wooed thee with my sword,
And won thy love doing thee injuries;
But I will wed thee in another key,
With pomp, with triumph,° and with revelling.

Enter EGEUS and his daughter HERMIA, LYSANDER and DEMETRIUS.

EGEUS.   Happy be Theseus, our renownèd duke.   2
THESEUS.   Thanks good Egeus:° what's the news with thee?
EGEUS.   Full of vexation come I, with complaint
Against my child, my daughter Hermia.
Stand forth Demetrius. My noble lord,
This man hath my consent to marry her.   2
Stand forth Lysander. And my gracious duke,
This man hath bewitched the bosom of my child.
Thou, thou Lysander, thou hast given her rhymes,
And interchanged love tokens with my child:
Thou hast by moonlight at her window sung,   3
With feigning voice, verses of feigning° love,
And stol'n the impression of her fantasy°
With bracelets of thy hair, rings, gauds,° conceits,°
Knacks,° trifles, nosegays, sweetmeats—messengers
Of strong prevailment in unhardened youth.   3
With cunning hast thou filched my daughter's heart,
Turned her obedience, which is due to me,
To stubborn harshness. And my gracious duke,
Be it so° she will not here before your grace
Consent to marry with Demetrius,   4
I beg the ancient privilege of Athens:
As she is mine, I may dispose of her:

---

4 *lingers:* delays the fulfillment of.   5 *dowager:* a widow supported by her dead husband's heirs.
6 *withering out:* (1) depleting (2) growing withered.   13 *pert:* lively.   15 *companion:* fellow
(contemptuous).   19 *triumph:* public festival.   21 *Egeus:* (trisyllabic).   31 *feigning:* (1)
deceptive (2) desirous ("faining").   32 *stol'n . . . fantasy:* stealthily imprinted your image upon
her fancy.   33 *gauds:* trinkets.   *conceits:* either (a) love poetry, or (b) love tokens.   34
Knacks: knick-knacks.   39 *Be it so:* if it be that.

Which shall be, either to this gentleman,
Or to her death, according to our law
Immediately° provided in that case.   45
THESEUS.   What say you, Hermia? Be advised, fair maid.
To you your father should be as a god:
One that composed your beauties: yea and one
To whom you are but as a form in wax
By him imprinted, and within his power   50
To leave the figure, or disfigure it:
Demetrius is a worthy gentleman.
HERMIA.   So is Lysander.
THESEUS   In himself he is:
But in this kind, wanting your father's voice,°
The other must be held the worthier.   55
HERMIA.   I would my father looked but with my eyes.
THESEUS.   Rather your eyes must with his judgment look.
HERMIA.   I do entreat your grace to pardon me.
I know not by what power I am made bold,
Nor how it may concern my modesty,   60
In such a presence, here to plead my thoughts:
But I beseech your grace that I may know
The worst that may befall me in this case,
If I refuse to wed Demetrius.
THESEUS.   Either to die the death, or to abjure   65
For ever the society of men.
Therefore fair Hermia, question your desires,
Know of your youth,° examine well your blood,°
Whether, if you yield not to your father's choice,
You can endure the livery° of a nun,   70
For aye° to be in shady cloister mewed,°
To live a barren sister all your life,
Chanting faint hymns to the cold fruitless moon.°
Thrice blessèd they that master so their blood,
To undergo such maiden pilgrimage: 75
But earthlier happy° is the rose distilled,°
Than that which, withering on the virgin thorn,
Grows, lives, and dies, in single blessedness.
HERMIA.   So will I grow, so live, so die my lord,
Ere I will yield my virgin patent° up   80
Unto his lordship, whose unwishèd yoke
My soul consents not to give sovereignty.
THESEUS.   Take time to pause, and by the next moon,
The sealing day betwixt my love and me,
For everlasting bond of fellowship,   85

---

45 *Immediately:* precisely.   54 *in . . . voice:* in this respect, lacking your father's approval.
68 *Know . . . youth:* ask yourself as a young person.   68 *blood:* passions.   70 *livery:* habit.
71 *aye:* ever.   *mewed:* shut up.   73 *moon:* (the moon goddess Diana represented unmarried
chastity).   76 *earthlier happy:* more happy on earth.   *distilled:* i.e., into perfume (thus its
essence is passed on, as to a child).   80 *patent:* privilege.

Upon that day either prepare to die
For disobedience to your father's will,
Or else to wed Demetrius, as he would,
Or on Diana's altar to protest°
For aye, austerity and single life.   9

DEMETRIUS.   Relent, sweet Hermia, and Lysander, yield
    Thy crazèd° title to my certain right.

LYSANDER.   You have her father's love, Demetrius:
    Let me have Hermia's: do you marry him.

EGEUS.   Scornful Lysander, true, he hath my love: 9
    And what is mine, my love shall render him.
    And she is mine, and all my right of her
    I do estate° unto Demetrius.

LYSANDER.   I am, my lord, as well derived° as he,
    As well possessed:° my love is more than his: 10
    My fortunes every way as fairly ranked
    (If not with vantage) as° Demetrius':
    And, which is more than all these boasts can be,
    I am beloved of beauteous Hermia.
    Why should not I then prosecute my right?   10
    Demetrius, I'll avouch it to his head,°
    Made love to Nedar's daughter, Helena,
    And won her soul: and she, sweet lady, dotes,
    Devoutly dotes, dotes in idolatry,
    Upon this spotted° and inconstant man.   11

THESEUS.   I must confess that I have heard so much,
    And with Demetrius thought to have spoke thereof:
    But being over-full of self-affairs,
    My mind did lose it. But Demetrius come,
    And come Egeus, you shall go with me: 11
    I have some private schooling for you both.
    For you fair Hermia, look you arm yourself,
    To fit your fancies to your father's will;
    Or else the law of Athens yields you up
    (Which by no means we may extenuate)   12
    To death or to a vow of single life.
    Come my Hippolyta, what cheer my love?
    Demetrius and Egeus, go along:
    I must employ you in some business
    Against° our nuptial, and confer with you   12
    Of something nearly° that concerns yourselves.

EGEUS.   With duty and desire we follow you.

Exeunt.° Manent° LYSANDER and HERMIA.

---

89 *protest:* vow.   92 *crazèd:* flawed.   98 *estate:* transfer.   99 *well derived:* well born.
100 *well possessed:* wealthy.   102 *with vantage, as:* better, than.   106 *avouch . . . head:* prove it
to his face.   110 *spotted:* stained (by betrayal of Helena).   125 *Against:* in preparation for.
126 *nearly:* closely.   127 stage direction: *Exeunt:* they exit.   *Manent:* they remain.

LYSANDER.   How now my love? Why is your cheek so pale?
How chance the roses there do fade so fast?
HERMIA.   Belike° for want of rain, which I could well   130
Beteem° them from the tempest of my eyes,
LYSANDER.   Ay me, for aught that I could ever read,
Could ever hear by tale or history,
The course of true love never did run smooth;
But either it was different in blood—   135
HERMIA.   O cross! too high° to be enthralled to low.°
LYSANDER.   Or else misgraffèd° in respect of years—
HERMIA.   O spite! too old to be engaged to young.
LYSANDER.   Or else it stood upon the choice of friends—
HERMIA.   O hell! to choose love by another's eyes.   140
LYSANDER.   Or if there were a sympathy in choice,
War, death, or sickness did lay siege to it;
Making it momentany° as a sound,
Swift as a shadow, short as any dream,
Brief as the lightning in the collied° night,   145
That, in a spleen,° unfolds both heaven and earth;
And ere a man hath power to say "Behold,"
The jaws of darkness do devour it up:
So quick bright things come to confusion.
  HERMIA.   If then true lovers have been ever crossed,°   150
It stands as an edict in destiny:
Then let us teach our trial patience,°
Because it is a customary cross,
As due to love as thoughts and dreams and sighs,
Wishes and tears; poor Fancy's° followers.   155
LYSANDER.   A good persuasion: therefore hear me, Hermia:
I have a widow aunt, a dowager,
Of great revenue, and she hath no child:
From Athens is her house remote seven leagues,
And she respects° me as her only son: 160
There gentle Hermia, may I marry thee,
And to that place the sharp Athenian law
Cannot pursue us. If thou lov'st me then,
Steal forth thy father's house tomorrow night:
And in the wood, a league without the town,   165
Where I did meet thee once with Helena
To do observance to a morn of May,°
There will I stay° for thee.
HERMIA.   My good Lysander,
I swear to thee, by Cupid's strongest bow,

---

130 *Belike:* likely.   131 *Beteem:* (1) pour out on (2) allow.   136 *high:* highborn.   *enthralled to low:* made a slave to one of low birth.   137 *misgraffèd:* badly joined.   143 *momentany:* momentary.   145 *collied:* black as coal.   146 *in a spleen:* impulsively, in a sudden outburst. 150 *ever crossed:* evermore thwarted.   152 *teach . . . patience:* teach ourselves to be patient. 155 *Fancy:* love (sometimes infatuation).   160 *respects:* regards.   167 *do . . . May:* celebrate May Day.   168 *stay:* wait.

By his best arrow, with the golden head,°   170
By the simplicity of Venus' doves,
By that which knitteth souls and prospers loves,
And by that fire which burned the Carthage queen,
When the false Troyan° under sail was seen,
By all the vows that ever men have broke,   175
(In number more than ever women spoke)
In that same place thou has appointed me,
Tomorrow truly will I meet with thee.

LYSANDER.   Keep promise love: look, here comes Helena.

Enter HELENA.

HERMIA.   God speed fair Helena: whither away?   180
HELENA.   Call you me fair? That fair again unsay.
  Demetrius loves your fair:° O happy fair!
  Your eyes are lodestars,° and your tongue's sweet air°
  More tuneable than lark to shepherd's ear,
  When wheat is green, when hawthorn buds appear.   185
  Sickness is catching: O were favour° so,
  Yours would I catch, fair Hermia, ere I go,
  My ear should catch your voice,° my eye your eye,°
  My tongue should catch your tongue's sweet melody.
  Were the world mine, Demetrius being bated,°   190
  The rest I'd give to be to you translated.°
  O teach me how you look, and with what art
  You sway the motion of Demetrius' heart.
HERMIA.   I frown upon him; yet he loves me still.
HELENA.   O that your frowns would teach my smiles such skill.   195
HERMIA.   I give him curses; yet he gives me love.
HELENA.   O that my prayers could such affection move.
HERMIA.   The more I hate, the more he follows me.
HELENA.   The more I love, the more he hateth me.
HERMIA.   His folly, Helena, is no fault of mine.   200
HELENA.   None but your beauty; would that fault were mine.
HERMIA.   Take comfort: he no more shall see my face:
  Lysander and myself will fly this place.
  Before the time I did Lysander see,
  Seemed Athens as a paradise to me: 205
  O then, what graces in my love do dwell,
  That he hath turned a heaven unto a hell!
LYSANDER.   Helen, to you our minds we will unfold:
  Tomorrow night, when Phoebe° doth behold
  Her silver visage in the wat'ry glass,°   210

---

170 *golden head:* (The arrow with the gold head causes love).   173–174 *Carthage Queen . . . false Troyan:* Dido, who burned herself to death on a funeral pyre when Trojan Aeneas deserted her. 182 *your fair:* i.e., beauty.   183 *lodestars:* guiding stars.   *air:* music. 186 *favour:* appearance.   188 *My ear . . . voice:* my ear should catch the tone of your voice. *my eye your eye:* my eye should catch the way you glance.   190 *bated:* subtracted, excepted. 191 *translated:* transformed.   209 *Phoebe:* Diana, the moon.   210 *wat'ry glass:* mirror of the water.

Decking with liquid pearl the bladed grass
(A time that lovers' flights doth still° conceal)
Through Athens gates have we devised to steal.
HERMIA.   And in the wood, where often you and I
   Upon faint primrose beds were wont to lie,   215
   Emptying our bosoms of their counsel° sweet,
   There my Lysander and myself shall meet,
   And thence from Athens turn away our eyes,
   To see new friends and stranger companies.°
   Farewell, sweet playfellow: pray thou for us: 220
   And good luck grant thee thy Demetrius.
   Keep word Lysander: we must starve our sight
   From lovers' food,° till morrow deep midnight.
LYSANDER.   I will my Hermia.   *Exit HERMIA.*
              Helena adieu:
   As you on him, Demetrius dote on you.°   *Exit LYSANDER.*   225
HELENA.   How happy some, o'er other some, can be!
   Through Athens I am thought as fair as she.
   But what of that? Demetrius thinks not so:
   He will not know what all but he do know.
   And as he errs, doting on Hermia's eyes,   230
   So I, admiring of his qualities.
   Things base and vile, holding no quantity.°
   Love can transpose to form and dignity.
   Love looks not with the eyes, but with the mind:
   And therefore is winged Cupid painted blind.   235
   Nor hath Love's mind of any judgment taste:
   Wings, and no eyes, figure° unheedy haste.
   And therefore is Love said to be a child:
   Because in choice he is so oft beguiled.
   As waggish boys in game themselves forswear: 240
   So the boy Love is perjured everywhere.
   For ere Demetrius looked on Hermia's eyne,°
   He hailed down oaths that he was only mine.
   And when this hail some heat from Hermia felt,
   So he dissolved, and show'rs of oaths did melt.   245
   I will go tell him of fair Hermia's flight:
   Then to the wood will he tomorrow night
   Pursue her: and for this intelligence,°
   If I have thanks, it is a dear expense:°
   But herein mean I to enrich my pain,   250
   To have his sight° thither and back again.   *Exit.*

---

212 *still:* always.   216 *counsel:* secrets.   219 *stranger companies:* the companionship of
strangers.   223 *lovers' food:* the sight of the loved one.   225 *As . . . you:* As you dote on
Demetrius, so may Demetrius also dote on you.   232 *holding no quantity:* out of proportion.
237 *figure:* symbolize.   242 *eyne:* eyes.   248 *intelligence:* information.   249 *dear expense:*
costly outlay (on Demetrius' part).   250–251 *But . . . sight:* but I will be rewarded just by the
sight of him.

[Scene 2. Quince's house]

Enter QUINCE *the Carpenter; and* SNUG *the Joiner; and* BOTTOM *the Weaver; and* FLUTE *the Bellows-mender; and* SNOUT *the Tinker; and* STARVELING *the Tailor.*°

QUINCE.   Is all our company here?

BOTTOM.   You were the best to call them generally,° man by man,
    according to the scrip.

QUINCE.   Here is the scroll of every man's name which is thought
    fit, through all Athens, to play in our interlude° before
    the duke and the duchess, on his wedding-day at night.

BOTTOM.   First good Peter Quince, say what the play treats on,
    then read the names of the actors: and so grow to a point.

QUINCE.   Marry,° our play is "The most lamentable comedy, and
    most cruel death of Pyramus and Thisby."

BOTTOM.   A very good piece of work I assure you, and a merry. Now
    good Peter Quince, call forth your actors by the scroll.
    Masters, spread yourselves.

QUINCE.   Answer as I call you. Nick Bottom the weaver?

BOTTOM.   Ready: name what part I am for, and proceed.

QUINCE.   You, Nick Bottom, are set down for Pyramus.

BOTTOM.   What is Pyramus? A lover, or a tyrant?

QUINCE.   A lover that kills himself, most gallant, for love.

BOTTOM.   That will ask some tears in the true performing of it. If I
    do it, let the audience look to their eyes: I will move
    storms: I will condole° in some measure. To the rest—
    yet my chief humour° is for a tyrant. I could play Ercles°
    rarely, or a part to tear a cat in, to make all split.°
        The raging rocks
        And shivering shocks,
        Shall break the locks
          Of prison gates,
        And Phibbus' car°
        Shall shine from far,
        And make and mar
          The foolish Fates.
    This was lofty. Now name the rest of the players. This is
    Ercles' vein, a tyrant's vein: a lover is more condoling.

QUINCE.   Francis Flute, the bellows-mender?

FLUTE.   Here Peter Quince.

QUINCE.   Flute, you must take Thisby on you.

FLUTE.   What is Thisby? A wand'ring knight?

0.2 Stage direction: the low characters' names describe their work: *Quince:* quoins, wooden
wedges used in building.   *Snug:* fitting snugly, suiting a joiner of furniture.
Bottom: bobbin or core on which yarn is wound.   *Flute:* mender of fluted church organs and
bellows.   *Snout:* spout (of the kettles he mends).   *Starveling:* (tailors being traditionally
thin).   2 *generally:* Bottom often uses the wrong word; here he means the opposite: "severally,
one-by-one."   5 *interlude:* short play.   9 *Marry:* indeed (mild oath, corruption of "by the
Virgin Mary").   21 *condole:* lament.   22 *humour:* inclination.   *Ercles:* Hercules (typified
by ranting).   23 *tear . . . split:* (terms for ranting and raging on the stage).
28 *Phibbus' car:* Phoebus Apollo's chariot.

QUINCE.   It is the lady that Pyramus must love.

FLUTE.   Nay faith, let not me play a woman: I have a beard
coming.   40

QUINCE.   That's all one:° you shall play it in a mask, and you may
speak as small° as you will.

BOTTOM.   And° I may hide my face, let me play Thisby too: I'll speak
in a monstrous little voice; "Thisne, Thisne," "Ah
Pyramus, my lover dear, thy Thisby dear, and lady   45
dear."

QUINCE.   No, no, you must play Pyramus: and Flute, you Thisby.

BOTTOM.   Well, proceed.

QUINCE.   Robin Starveling, the tailor?

STARVELING.   Here Peter Quince.   50

QUINCE.   Robin Starveling, you must play Thisby's mother. Tom
Snout, the tinker?

SNOUT.   Here Peter Quince.

QUINCE.   You, Pyramus' father; myself, Thisby's father; Snug the
joiner, you the lion's part: and I hope here is a play   55
fitted.°

SNUG.   Have you the lion's part written? Pray you, if it be, give
it me: for I am slow of study.

QUINCE.   You may do it extempore: for it is nothing but roaring.

BOTTOM.   Let me play the lion too. I will roar, that° I will do any   60
man's heart good to hear me. I will roar, that I will make
the duke say "Let him roar again: let him roar again."

QUINCE.   And you should do it too terribly, you would fright the
duchess and the ladies, that they would shriek: and
that were enough to hang us all.   65

ALL.   That would hang us, every mother's son.

BOTTOM.   I grant you, friends, if you should fright the ladies out of
their wits, they would have no more discretion but to
hang us: but I will aggravate° my voice so, that I will roar
you as gently as any sucking dove: I will roar you and   70
'twere° any nightingale.

QUINCE.   You can play no part but Pyramus: for Pyramus is a
sweet-faced man; a proper° man as one shall see in a
summer's day; a most lovely gentleman-like man: therefore
you must needs play Pyramus.   75

BOTTOM.   Well: I will undertake it. What beard were I best to play
it in?

QUINCE.   Why, what you will.

BOTTOM.   I will discharge it in either your straw-colour beard, your
orange-tawny beard, your purple-in-grain° beard, or your   80
French-crown-colour° beard, your perfit yellow.

---

41 *That's all one:* never mind.   42 *small:* softly.   43 *And:* if.   56 *fitted:* cast.   60 *that:* so
that.   69 *aggravate:* (he means "moderate").   70–71 *and 'twere:* as if it were.
73 *proper:* handsome.   80 *purple-in-grain:* dyed permanently purple.   81 *French-crown-colour:*
golden, like French crowns (gold coins).

QUINCE.   Some of your French crowns° have no hair at all; and
then you will play barefaced. But masters here are your
parts, and I am to entreat you, request you, and desire
you, to con° them by tomorrow night: and meet me in the   8
palace wood, a mile without the town, by moonlight;
there will we rehearse: for if we meet in the city, we
shall be dogged with company, and our devices° known.
In the meantime, I will draw a bill of properties,° such
as our play wants. I pray you fail me not.   9

BOTTOM.   We will meet, and there we may rehearse most obscenely°
and courageously. Take pain, be perfit: adieu.

QUINCE.   At the duke's oak we meet.

BOTTOM.   Enough: hold, or cut bow-strings.°   *Exeunt.*

ACT 2

[Scene 1. A wood near Athens]

Enter a FAIRY at one door, and ROBIN GOODFELLOW [Puck] at another.

PUCK.   How now spirit, whither wander you?

FAIRY.   Over hill, over dale,
    Thorough bush, thorough brier,
Over park, over pale,°
    Thorough flood, thorough fire:
I do wander everywhere,
Swifter than the moon's sphere:
And I serve the Fairy Queen,
To dew ° her orbs° upon the green.
The cowslips° tall her pensioners° be,   1
In their gold coats, spots you see:
Those be rubies, fairy favours:°
In those freckles live their savours.°
I must go seek some dewdrops here,
And hang a pearl in every cowslip's ear.   1
Farewell thou lob° of spirits: I'll be gone,
Our queen and all her elves come here anon.

PUCK.   The king doth keep his revels here tonight.
Take heed the queen come not within his sight.
For Oberon is passing fell° and wrath,   2
Because that she, as her attendant, hath
A lovely boy, stol'n from an Indian king:

---

82 *French crowns:* bald heads believed to be caused by syphilis, the "French" disease.
85 *con:* learn by heart.   88 *devices:* plans.   89 *bill of properties:* list of stage props.
91 *obscenely:* (he may mean "fittingly," or "obscurely").   94 *hold, or cut bow-strings:* (meaning uncertain, but equivalent to "fish, or cut bait").   4 *pale:* enclosure.   9 *dew:* bedew.   *orbs:*
fairy rings (circles of high grass).   10 *cowslips:* primroses.   *pensioners:* royal bodyguards.
12 *favours:* gifts.   13 *savours:* perfumes.   16 *lob:* lout, lubber.   20 *passing fell:* surpassingly
fierce.

She never had so sweet a changeling.°
And jealous Oberon would have the child
Knight of his train, to trace° the forests wild.   25
But she, perforce,° withholds the lovèd boy,
Crowns him with flowers, and makes him all her joy.
And now, they never meet in grove or green,
By fountain clear, or spangled starlight sheen,
But they do square,° that all their elves for fear   30
Creep into acorn cups, and hide them there.

FAIRY.   Either I mistake your shape and making quite,
Or else you are that shrewd and knavish sprite
Called Robin Goodfellow. Are not you he
That frights the maidens of the villagery,   35
Skim milk,° and sometimes labour in the quern,°
And bootless° make the breathless housewife churn,
And sometime make the drink to bear no barm,°
Mislead night-wanderers, laughing at their harm?
Those that Hobgoblin call you, and sweet Puck,   40
You do their work, and they shall have good luck.
Are not you he?

PUCK.   Thou speakest aright;
I am that merry wanderer of the night.
I jest to Oberon, and make him smile,
When I a fat and bean-fed horse beguile,   45
Neighing in likeness of a filly foal;
And sometime lurk I in a gossip's° bowl,
In very likeness of a roasted crab,°
And when she drinks, against her lips I bob,
And on her withered dewlap° pour the ale.   50
The wisest aunt, telling the saddest tale,
Sometime for three-foot stool mistaketh me:
Then slip I from her bum, down topples she,
And "tailor"° cries, and falls into a cough;
And then the whole quire° hold their hips and laugh,   55
And waxen° in their mirth, and neeze,° and swear
A merrier hour was never wasted° there.
But room° fairy: here comes Oberon.

FAIRY.   And here, my mistress. Would that he were gone.

---

23 *changeling:* creature exchanged by fairies for a stolen baby (among the fairies, the stolen child).   25 *trace:* traverse.   26 *perforce:* by force.   30 *square:* quarrel.   36 *Skim milk:* steals the cream off the milk.   *quern:* handmill for grinding grain.   37 *bootless:* without result.   38 *barm:* foamy head (therefore the drink was flat).   47 *gossip's:* old woman's.
48 *crab:* crabapple (often put into ale).   50 *dewlap:* loose skin hanging about the throat.
54 *"tailor":* (variously explained: perhaps the squatting position of the tailor, or "tailard"—one with a tail).   55 *quire:* choir, group.   56 *waxen:* increase.   *neeze:* sneeze.
57 *wasted:* spent.   58 *room:* make room.

Enter [*OBERON*] the KING OF FAIRIES, *at one door with his* TRAIN, *and the* QUEEN [*TITANIA*], *at another, with hers.*

OBERON.   Ill met by moonlight, proud Titania.   6[

QUEEN.   What, jealous Oberon? Fairy, skip hence.
   I have forsworn his bed and company.

OBERON.   Tarry, rash wanton.° Am not I thy lord?

QUEEN.   Then I must be thy lady: but I know
   When thou hast stol'n away from fairyland,   6[
   And in the shape of Corin° sat all day,
   Playing on pipes of corn,° and versing love
   To amorous Phillida.° Why art thou here
   Come from the farthest steep of India?
   But that, forsooth, the bouncing Amazon,°   7[
   Your buskined° mistress and your warrior love,
   To Theseus must be wedded; and you come,
   To give their bed joy and prosperity.

OBERON.   How canst thou thus, for shame, Titania,
   Glance at my credit with° Hippolyta,   7[
   Knowing I know thy love to Theseus?
   Didst thou not lead him through the glimmering night,
   From Perigenia, whom he ravishèd?
   And make him with fair Aegles break his faith,
   With Ariadne, and Antiopa°?   8[

QUEEN.   These are the forgeries of jealousy:
   And never, since the middle summer's spring,°
   Met we on hill, in dale, forest, or mead,
   By pavèd° fountain, or by rushy brook,
   Or in the beachèd margent° of the sea,   8[
   To dance our ringlets to the whistling wind,
   But with thy brawls thou hast disturbed our sport.
   Therefore the winds, piping to us in vain,
   As in revenge, have sucked up from the sea
   Contagious° fogs: which falling in the land,   9[
   Hath every pelting° river made so proud,
   That they have overborne their continents.°
   The ox hath therefore stretched his yoke in vain,
   The ploughman lost his sweat, and the green corn°
   Hath rotted, ere his youth attained a beard:°   9[
   The fold° stands empty in the drownèd field,

---

63 *Tarry, rash wanton:* wait, headstrong one.   66–68 *Corin, Phillida:* (traditional names in pastoral literature for a shepherd and his loved one, respectively).   67 *corn:* wheat straws.
70 *Amazon:* Hippolyta.   71 *buskined:* wearing boots.   75 *Glance . . . credit with:* hint at my favors from.   78–80 *Perigenia . . . Antiopa:* women that Theseus supposedly loved and deserted.
82 *middle . . . spring:* beginning of midsummer.   84 *pavèd:* with a pebbly bottom.
85 *margent:* margin, shore.   88–117 *Therefore . . . original:* (the disturbance in nature reflects the discord between Oberon and Titania).   90 *Contagious:* spreading pestilence.
91 *pelting:* paltry.   92 *overborne their continents:* overflown the banks which contain them.
94 *corn:* grain.   95 *beard:* the tassels on ripened grain.   96 *fold:* enclosure for livestock.

And crows are fatted with the murrion° flock.
The nine men's morris° is filled up with mud:
And the quaint mazes° in the wanton green,°
For lack of tread, are undistinguishable.   100
The human mortals want° their winter here,
No night is now with hymn or carol blest;
Therefore the moon, the governess of floods,
Pale in her anger, washes all the air,
That rheumatic diseases do abound.   105
And thorough this distemperature,° we see
The seasons alter: hoary-headed frosts
Fall in the fresh lap of the crimson rose,
And on old Hiems'° thin and icy crown,
An odorous chaplet° of sweet summer buds   110
Is, as in mockery, set. The spring, the summer,
The childing° autumn, angry winter change
Their wonted liveries:° and the mazèd° world,
By their increase, now knows not which is which:
And this same progeny of evils comes   115
From our debate, from our dissension:
We are their parents and original.
OBERON.   Do you amend it then: it lies in you.
Why should Titania cross her Oberon?
I do but beg a little changeling boy,   120
To be my henchman.°
QUEEN.   Set your heart at rest.
The fairy land buys not the child of me.
His mother was a vot'ress° of my order:
And in the spicèd Indian air, by night,
Full often hath she gossiped by my side.   125
And sat with me on Neptune's yellow sands,
Marking th' embarkèd traders° on the flood:
When we have laughed to see the sails conceive,
And grow big-bellied with the wanton° wind:
Which she, with pretty and with swimming gait,   130
Following (her womb then rich with my young squire)
Would imitate, and sail upon the land,
To fetch me trifles, and return again,
As from a voyage, rich with merchandise.
But she, being mortal, of that boy did die,   135
And for her sake, do I rear up her boy:
And for her sake, I will not part with him.

---

97 *murrion:* dead from murrain, a cattle disease.   98 *nine men's morris:* game played on squares
cut in the grass on which stones or disks are moved.   99 *quaint mazes:* intricate paths.
wanton green: luxuriant grass.   101 *want:* lack.   106 *distemperature:* upset in nature.
109 *Hiems:* god of winter.   110 *odorous chaplet:* sweet-smelling wreath.   112 *childing:* fruitful.
113 *wonted liveries:* accustomed dress.   *mazèd:* amazed.   121 *henchman:* attendant.
123 *vot'ress:* vowed and devoted follower.   127 *traders:* merchant ships.
129 *wanton:* sportive.

OBERON.   How long within this wood intend you stay?

QUEEN.   Perchance till after Theseus' wedding day.
    If you will patiently dance in our round,°   14
    And see our moonlight revels, go with us:
    If not, shun me, and I will spare° your haunts.

OBERON.   Give me that boy, and I will go with thee.

QUEEN.   Not for thy fairy kingdom. Fairies away
    We shall chide downright, if I longer stay.   14

Exeunt [TITANIA and her TRAIN.]

OBERON.   Well, go thy way. Thou shalt not from this grove,
    Till I torment thee for this injury.
    My gentle Puck come hither: thou rememb'rest,
    Since° once I sat upon a promontory,
    And heard a mermaid, on a dolphin's back,
    Uttering such dulcet and harmonious breath,   15
    That the rude° sea grew civil° at her song,
    And certain stars shot madly from their spheres,
    To hear the sea-maid's music.

PUCK.   I remember.

OBERON.   That very time, I saw (but thou couldst not)   15
    Flying between the cold moon and the earth,
    Cupid, all armed: a certain aim he took
    At a fair Vestal,° thronèd by the west,
    And loosed his love-shaft smartly from his bow,
    As it should pierce a hundred thousand hearts: 16
    But I might see young Cupid's fiery shaft
    Quenched in the chaste beams of the wat'ry moon:
    And the imperial vot'ress° passèd on,
    In maiden meditation, fancy-free.°
    Yet marked I where the bolt° of Cupid fell.   16
    It fell upon a little western flower;
    Before, milk-white; now purple with love's wound,
    And maidens call it love-in-idleness.°
    Fetch me that flow'r: the herb I showed thee once.
    The juice of it, on sleeping eyelids laid,   17
    Will make or man or woman madly dote
    Upon the next live creature that it sees.
    Fetch me this herb, and be thou here again
    Ere the leviathan° can swim a league.

PUCK.   I'll put a girdle round about the earth,   17
    In forty minutes.   *[Exit.]*

OBERON.   Having once this juice,
    I'll watch Titania when she is asleep,

---

140 *round:* round dance.   142 *spare:* shun.   149 *Since:* when.   152 *rude:* rough.
civil: calm.   158 *Vestal:* virgin, probable reference to Queen Elizabeth.   162 *imperial vot'ress:*
royal devotee (Queen Elizabeth) of Diana.   164 *fancy-free:* free from love.   165 *bolt:* arrow.
168 *love-in-idleness:* pansy.   174 *leviathan:* whale.

And drop the liquor of it in her eyes:
The next thing then she waking looks upon,
(Be it on lion, bear, or wolf, or bull,   180
On meddling monkey, or on busy° ape)
She shall pursue it, with the soul of love.
And ere I take this charm from off her sight
(As I can take it with another herb)
I'll make her render up her page to me.   185
But who comes here? I am invisible,
And I will overhear their conference.

Enter DEMETRIUS, HELENA following him.

DEMETRIUS. I love thee not: therefore pursue me not.
     Where is Lysander and fair Hermia?
     The one I'll slay: the other slayeth me.   190
     Thou told'st me they were stol'n unto this wood:
     And here am I, and wood° within this wood:
     Because I cannot meet my Hermia.
     Hence, get thee gone, and follow me no more.
HELENA. You draw me, you hard-hearted adamant:°   195
     But yet you draw not iron, for my heart
     Is true as steel. Leave you your power to draw,
     And I shall have no power to follow you.
DEMETRIUS. Do I entice you? Do I speak you fair°?
     Or rather do I not in plainest truth   200
     Tell you I do not, nor I cannot love you?
HELENA. And even for that, do I love you the more:
     I am your spaniel: and Demetrius,
     The more you beat me, I will fawn on you.
     Use me but as your spaniel: spurn me, strike me,   205
     Neglect me, lose me: only give me leave,
     Unworthy as I am, to follow you.
     What worser place can I beg in your love
     (And yet a place of high respect with me)
     Than to be usèd as you use your dog.   210
DEMETRIUS. Tempt not too much the hatred of my spirit,
     For I am sick, when I do look on thee.
HELENA. And I am sick, when I look not on you.
DEMETRIUS. You do impeach° your modesty too much,
     To leave the city and commit yourself   215
     Into the hands of one that loves you not,
     To trust the opportunity of night,
     And the ill counsel of a desert° place,
     With the rich worth of your virginity.
HELENA. Your virtue is my privilege:° for that°   220

---

181 *busy:* mischievous.   192 *wood:* crazy.   195 *adamant:* (1) magnet (2) impenetrably hard
lodestone.   199 *you fair:* to you in a kindly way.   214 *impeach:* discredit.   218 *desert:* deserted.   220 *Your . . . privilege:* your attraction is my excuse (for coming).   *for that:* because.

It is not night, when I do see your face,
Therefore I think I am not in the night.
Nor doth this wood lack worlds of company,
For you, in my respect,° are all the world.
Then how can it be said I am alone,   22
When all the world is here to look on me?
DEMETRIUS.   I'll run from thee and hide me in the brakes,°
And leave thee to the mercy of wild beasts.
HELENA.   The wildest hath not such a heart as you.
Run when you will: the story shall be changed;   29
Apollo flies, and Daphne° holds the chase:
The dove pursues the griffin:° the mild hind°
Makes speed to catch the tiger. Bootless° speed,
When cowardice pursues, and valour flies.
DEMETRIUS.   I will not stay° thy questions. Let me go: 23
Or if thou follow me, do not believe
But I shall do thee mischief in the wood.   [*Exit DEMETRIUS.*]
HELENA.   Ay, in the temple, in the town, the field,
You do me mischief. Fie Demetrius,
Your wrongs do set a scandal on my sex: 24
We cannot fight for love, as men may do:
We should be wooed, and were not made to woo.
I'll follow thee and make a heaven of hell,
To die upon the hand I love so well.   *Exit.*
OBERON.   Fare thee well nymph. Ere he do leave this grove,   24
Thou shalt fly him, and he shall seek thy love.

Enter PUCK.

Hast thou the flower there? Welcome wanderer.
PUCK.   Ay, there it is.
OBERON.   I pray thee give it me.
I know a bank where the wild thyme blows,
Where oxlips and the nodding violet grows,   25
Quite over-canopied with luscious woodbine,
With sweet musk-roses, and with eglantine:
There sleeps Titania, sometime of the night,
Lulled in these flowers, with dances and delight:
And there the snake throws° her enamelled skin,   25
Weed° wide enough to wrap a fairy in.
And with the juice of this, I'll streak her eyes,
And make her full of hateful fantasies.
Take thou some of it, and seek through this grove:
A sweet Athenian lady is in love   26
With a disdainful youth: anoint his eyes.
But do it when the next thing he espies

224 *respect:* regard.   227 *brakes:* thickets.   231 *Apollo . . . Daphne:* (in Ovid, Apollo pursues
Daphne, who turns into a laurel tree).   232 *griffin:* legendary beast with the head of an eagle
and the body of a lion.   *hind:* doe.   233 *Bootless:* useless.   235 *stay:* wait for.
255 *throws:* casts off.   256 *weed:* garment.

May be the lady. Thou shalt know the man
By the Athenian garments he hath on.
Effect it with some care, that he may prove   265
More fond° on her, than she upon her love:
And look thou meet me ere the first cock crow.

PUCK.   Fear not my lord: your servant shall do so.   *Exeunt.*

[Scene 2. Another part of the wood]

Enter TITANIA Queen of Fairies with her train.

QUEEN.   Come, now a roundel° and a fairy song:
   Then, for the third part of a minute, hence—
   Some to kill cankers in the musk-rose buds,
   Some war with reremice° for their leathren wings,
   To make my small elves coats, and some keep back   5
   The clamorous owl, that nightly hoots and wonders
   At our quaint° spirits. Sing me now asleep:
   Then to your offices,° and let me rest.

Fairies sing.

   You spotted snakes with double° tongue,
      Thorny hedgehogs be not seen,   10
   Newts and blind-worms° do no wrong,
      Come not near our Fairy Queen.

   Philomele,° with melody,
      Sing in our sweet lullaby,
   Lulla, lulla, lullaby, lulla, lulla, lullaby.   15
      Never harm,
      Nor spell, nor charm,
   Come our lovely lady nigh.
   So good night, with lullaby.

1. FAIRY.   Weaving spiders come not here: 20
   Hence you long-legged spinners, hence:
   Beetles black approach not near:
   Worm nor snail do no offence.
   Philomele, with melody, &c.   *She sleeps.*

2. FAIRY.   Hence away: now all is well: 25
   One aloof stand sentinel.   [*Exeunt fairies.*]

Enter OBERON [and applies the flower juice to TITANIA'S eyelids.]

OBERON.   What thou seest, when thou dost wake,
   Do it for thy true love take:
   Love and languish for his sake.
   Be it ounce,° or cat, or bear,   30

---

266 *fond:* doting, madly in love.   1 *roundel:* dance in a ring.   4 *reremice:* bats.
7 *quaint:* dainty.   8 *offices:* duties.   9 *double:* forked.   11 *blind-worms:* legless lizards.
13 *Philomele:* the nightingale.   30 *ounce:* lynx.

Pard,° or boar with bristled hair,
In thy eye that shall appear,
When thou wak'st, it is thy dear:
Wake when some vile thing is near.   [*Exit.*]

Enter LYSANDER *and* HERMIA.

LYSANDER.   Fair love, you faint with wand'ring in the wood:
   And to speak troth° I have forgot our way.
   We'll rest us Hermia, if you think it good,
   And tarry for the comfort of the day.
HERMIA.   Be't so Lysander: find you out a bed:
   For I upon this bank will rest my head.
LYSANDER.   One turf shall serve as pillow for us both,
   One heart, one bed, two bosoms, and one troth.°
HERMIA.   Nay good Lysander: for my sake, my dear,
   Lie further off yet; do not lie so near.
LYSANDER.   O take the sense, sweet, of my innocence:°
   Love takes the meaning in love's conference.°
   I mean that my heart unto yours is knit,
   So that but one heart we can make of it:
   Two bosoms interchainèd with an oath,
   So then two bosoms and a single troth.
   Then by your side no bed-room me deny:
   For lying so, Hermia, I do not lie.
HERMIA.   Lysander riddles very prettily.
   Now much beshrew° my manners and my pride,
   If Hermia meant to say Lysander lied.
   But gentle friend, for love and courtesy,
   Lie further off, in human modesty:
   Such separation as may well be said
   Becomes a virtuous bachelor and a maid,
   So far be distant, and good night sweet friend:
   Thy love ne'er alter till thy sweet life end.
LYSANDER.   Amen, amen, to that fair prayer say I,
   And then end life, when I end loyalty.
   Here is my bed: sleep give thee all his rest.
HERMIA.   With half that wish, the wisher's eyes be pressed.°

                                             They sleep.

Enter PUCK.

PUCK.   Through the forest have I gone,
   But Athenian found I none,
   On whose eyes I might approve°

31 *Pard:* leopard.   36 *troth:* truth.   42 *troth:* true love.   45 *take . . . innocence:* understand the innocence of my remark.   68 *approve:* test.   46 *Love . . . conference:* love enables lovers to understand each other when they converse.   54 *beshrew:* curse.   65 *pressed:* i.e., by sleep.   68 *approve:* test

This flower's force in stirring love.

Night and silence. Who is here?   70

Weeds° of Athens he doth wear:

This is he (my master said)

Despisèd the Athenian maid:

And here the maiden, sleeping sound,

On the dank and dirty ground.   75

Pretty soul, she durst not lie

Near this lack-love, this kill-courtesy.

Churl, upon thy eyes I throw

All the power this charm doth owe:°

When thou wak'st, let love forbid   80

Sleep his seat on thy eyelid.°

So awake when I am gone:

For I must now to Oberon.   *Exit.*

Enter DEMETRIUS and HELENA running.

HELENA.   Stay, thou kill me, sweet Demetrius.

DEMETRIUS.   I charge thee hence, and do not haunt me thus.   85

HELENA.   O, wilt thou darkling° leave me? Do not so.

DEMETRIUS.   Stay on thy peril: I alone will go.   *Exit DEMETRIUS.*

HELENA.   O, I am out of breath in this fond° chase:

    The more my prayer, the lesser is my grace.°

    Happy is Hermia, wheresoe'er she lies: 90

    For she hath blessèd and attractive eyes.

    How came her eyes so bright? Not with salt tears:

    If so, my eyes are oft'ner washed than hers.

    No, no: I am as ugly as a bear:

    For beasts that meet me run away for fear.   95

    Therefore no marvel, though Demetrius

    Do as a monster, fly my presence thus.

    What wicked and dissembling glass° of mine,

    Made me compare with Hermia's sphery eyne°!

    But who is here? Lysander, on the ground?   100

    Dead, or asleep? I see no blood, no wound.

    Lysander, if you live, good sir awake.

LYSANDER.   [*Wakes.*] And run through fire, I will for thy sweet sake.

    Transparent° Helena, nature shows art,

    That through thy bosom, makes me see thy heart.   105

    Where is Demetrius? O how fit a word

    Is that vile name to perish on my sword!

HELENA.   Do not say so, Lysander, say not so.

    What though he love your Hermia? Lord, what though?

    Yet Hermia still loves you: then be content.   110

LYSANDER.   Content with Hermia? No: I do repent

---

71 *Weeds:* garments.   79 *owe:* own.   80–81 *forbid . . . eyelid:* make you sleepless (with love).
86 *darkling:* in the dark.   88 *fond:* foolishly doting.   89 *my grace:* favor shown to me.
98 *glass:* looking glass.   99 *sphery eyne:* starry eyes.   104 *Transparent:* radiant.

The tedious minutes I with her have spent.
Not Hermia, but Helena I love.
Who will not change a raven for a dove?
The will of man is by his reason swayed:°   1⟫
And reason says you are the worthier maid.
Things growing are not ripe until their season:
So I, being young, till now ripe° not to reason.
And touching now the point° of human skill,°
Reason becomes the marshal to my will,   1⟫
And leads me to your eyes; where I o'erlook
Love's stories, written in love's richest book.

HELENA.   Wherefore° was I to this keen mockery born?
When at your hands did I deserve this scorn?
Is't not enough, is't not enough, young man,   1⟫
That I did never, no, nor never can,
Deserve a sweet look from Demetrius' eye,
But you must flout° my insufficiency?
Good troth you do me wrong, good sooth you do,
In such disdainful manner me to woo.   1⟫
But fare you well: perforce I must confess,
I thought you lord of more true gentleness.°
O, that a lady, of one man refused,
Should of another, therefore be abused!   *Exit.*

LYSANDER.   She sees not Hermia. Hermia, sleep thou there,   1⟫
And never mayst thou come Lysander near.
For, as a surfeit of the sweetest things
The deepest loathing to the stomach brings:
Or as the heresies that men do leave,
Are hated most of those they did deceive: 14⟫
So thou, my surfeit and my heresy,
Of all be hated; but the most, of me:
And all my powers, address your love and might,
To honour Helen, and to be her knight.   *Exit.*

HERMIA.   [*Wakes.*] Help me Lysander, help me: do thy best   14⟫
To pluck this crawling serpent from my breast.
Ay me, for pity. What a dream was here?
Lysander, look how I do quake with fear.
Methought a serpent eat my heart away,
And you sat smiling at his cruel prey.°   1⟫
Lysander: what, removed? Lysander, lord!
What, out of hearing, gone? No sound, no word?
Alack, where are you? Speak, and if you hear:
Speak, of° all loves. I swoon almost with fear.
No? Then I well perceive you are not nigh: 15⟫
Either death, or you, I'll find immediately.   *Exit.*

---

115 *swayed:* ruled.   118 *ripe:* mature.   119 *point:* peak.   *skill:* knowledge.
123 *Wherefore:* why.   128 *flout:* mock.   132 *lord . . . gentleness:* more of a gentleman.
150 *prey:* preying.   154 *of:* for the sake of.

ACT 3

[Scene 1. The wood]

Enter the CLOWNS [*QUINCE, SNUG, BOTTOM, FLUTE, SNOUT, and STARVELING.*]

BOTTOM.   Are we all met?

QUINCE.   Pat, pat: and here's a marvellous convenient place for
our rehearsal. This green plot shall be our stage, this
hawthorn brake° our tiring-house,° and we will do it in
action, as we will do it before the duke.   5

BOTTOM.   Peter Quince?

QUINCE.   What sayest thou, bully° Bottom?

BOTTOM.   There are things in this Comedy of Pyramus and Thisby
that will never please. First, Pyramus must draw a sword
to kill himself; which the ladies cannot abide. How   10
answer you that?

SNOUT.   By'r lakin,° a parlous° fear.

STARVELING.   I believe we must leave the killing out, when all is done.

BOTTOM.   Not a whit: I have a device to make all well. Write me
a prologue, and let the prologue seem to say, we will   15
do no harm with our swords, and that Pyramus is not
killed indeed: and for the more better assurance, tell
them that I Pyramus am not Pyramus, but Bottom the
weaver: this will put them out of fear.

QUINCE.   Well, we will have such a prologue, and it shall be   20
written in eight and six.°

BOTTOM.   No, make it two more: let it be written in eight and
eight.

SNOUT.   Will not the ladies be afeared of the lion?

STARVELING.   I fear it, I promise you.   25

BOTTOM.   Masters, you ought to consider with yourselves, to bring
in (God shield us) a lion among ladies, is a most dreadful
thing. For there is not a more fearful wild-fowl than
your lion living: and we ought to look to't.

SNOUT.   Therefore another prologue must tell he is not a lion.   30

BOTTOM.   Nay, you must name his name, and half his face must be
seen through the lion's neck, and he himself must speak
through, saying thus, or to the same defect:° "Ladies,"
or "Fair ladies—I would wish you," or "I would request
you," or "I would entreat you, not to fear,   35
not to tremble: my life for yours. If you think I come
hither as a lion, it were pity of my life. No, I am no
such thing: I am a man as other men are." And there

---

4 *brake:* thicket.   *tiring-house:* dressing room.   7 *bully:* "old pal."   12 *By'r lakin:* mild oath,
"by Our Lady."   *parlous:* awful, perilous.   21 *eight and six:* alternate lines of eight and six syllables (the ballad meter).   33 *defect:* (he means "effect").

indeed let him name his name, and tell them plainly he
is Snug the joiner.

QUINCE.   Well, it shall be so, but there is two hard things: that is,
to bring the moonlight into a chamber: for you know,
Pyramus and Thisby meet by moonlight.

SNOUT.   Doth the moon shine that night we play our play?

BOTTOM.   A calendar, a calendar: look in the almanac: find out
moonshine, find out moonshine.

QUINCE.   Yes, it doth shine that night.

BOTTOM.   Why then may you leave a casement of the great
chamber window, where we play, open; and the moon may
shine in at the casement.

QUINCE.   Ay, or else one must come in with a bush of thorns° and
a lantern, and say he comes to disfigure,° or to present,
the person of Moonshine. Then, there is another thing;
we must have a wall in the great chamber: for Pyramus
and Thisby, says the story, did talk through the chink
of a wall.

SNOUT.   You can never bring in a wall. What say you, Bottom?

BOTTOM.   Some man or other must present wall: and let him have
some plaster, or some loam, or some rough-cast° about
him, to signify wall; and let him hold his fingers thus:
and through that cranny, shall Pyramus and Thisby whisper.

QUINCE.   If that may be, then all is well. Come, sit down every
mother's son, and rehearse your parts. Pyramus, you
begin: when you have spoken your speech, enter into that
brake, and so every one according to his cue.

Enter PUCK.

PUCK.   What hempen homespuns° have we swagg'ring here,
So near the cradle of the Fairy Queen?
What, a play toward°? I'll be an auditor,
An actor too perhaps, if I see cause.

QUINCE.   Speak Pyramus. Thisby stand forth.

PYRAMUS.   Thisby, the flowers of odious savours sweet—

QUINCE.   "Odorous, odorous."

PYRAMUS.   —odours savours sweet,
So hath thy breath, my dearest Thisby dear.
But hark, a voice: stay thou but here awhile,
And by and by I will to thee appear.   *Exit PYRAMUS.*

PUCK.   A stranger Pyramus than e'er played here.   *[Exit.]*

THISBY.   Must I speak now?

QUINCE.   Ay marry must you. For you must understand he goes
but to see a noise that he heard, and is to come again.

---

51 *bush of thorns:* bundle of firewood (the man in the moon was supposed to have been placed
there as a punishment for gathering wood on Sundays).   52 *disfigure:* (he means "figure,"
symbolize).   59 *rough-cast:* coarse plaster of lime and gravel.   66 *hempen homespuns:*
wearers of clothing spun at home from hemp.   68 *toward:* in preparation.

THISBY.   Most radiant Pyramus, most lily-white of hue,
    Of colour like the red rose, on triumphant brier,
    Most brisky juvenal,° and eke most lovely Jew,°
       As true as truest horse, that yet would never tire,
    I'll meet thee Pyramus, at Ninny's tomb.   85
QUINCE.   "Ninus' tomb,"° man: why, you must not speak that yet.
    That you answer to Pyramus. You speak all your part
    at once, cues and all. Pyramus, enter; your cue is past:
    it is "never tire."
THISBY.   O—As true as truest horse, that yet would never tire.   90

Enter PYRAMUS with the ass-head [followed by PUCK].

PYRAMUS.   If I were fair, Thisby, I were only thine.
QUINCE.   O monstrous! O strange! We are haunted. Pray masters,
    fly masters. Help!   *The clowns all exeunt.*
PUCK.   I'll follow you: I'll lead you about a round,°
    Through bog, through bush, through brake, through brier.   95
    Sometime a horse I'll be, sometime a hound,
       A hog, a headless bear, sometime a fire,
    And neigh, and bark, and grunt, and roar, and burn,
    Like horse, hound, hog, bear, fire, at every turn.   *Exit.*
BOTTOM.   Why do they run away? This is a knavery of them to   100
    make me afeared.

Enter SNOUT.

SNOUT.   O Bottom, thou art changed. What do I see on thee?
BOTTOM.   What do you see? You see an ass-head of your own, do
    you?   *[Exit SNOUT.]*

Enter QUINCE.

QUINCE.   Bless thee Bottom, bless thee. Thou art translated.°   *Exit.*   105
BOTTOM.   I see their knavery. This is to make an ass of me, to
    fright me if they could: but I will not stir from this
    place, do what they can. I will walk up and down here,
    and will sing that they shall hear I am not afraid.
       [*Sings.*] The woosel° cock, so black of hue,   110
              With orange tawny bill,
              The throstle,° with his note so true,
              The wren, with little quill.°
TITANIA.   What angel wakes me from my flow'ry bed?
BOTTOM.   [*Sings.*] The finch, the sparrow, and the lark,   115
            The plain-song° cuckoo gray:
            Whose note full many a man doth mark,
            And dares not answer, nay.

83 *brisky juvenal:* lively youth.   *Jew:* diminutive of either "juvenal" or "jewel."
86 *Ninus' tomb:* (tomb of the founder of Nineveh, and meeting place of the lovers in Ovid's version of the Pyramus story).   94 *about a round:* in circles, like a round dance (round about).
105 *translated:* transformed.   110 *woosel:* ousel, blackbird.   112 *throstle:* thrush.
113 *quill:* piping note.   116 *plain-song:* sounding a simple unvaried note.

For indeed, who would set his wit to° so foolish a bird?
Who would give a bird the lie,° though he cry "cuckoo"°   12
    never so°?
TITANIA.   I pray thee, gentle mortal, sing again.
    Mine ear is much enamoured of thy note:
    So is mine eye enthrallèd to thy shape,
    And thy fair virtue's force (perforce°) doth move me,   12
    On the first view to say, to swear, I love thee.
BOTTOM.   Methinks mistress, you should have little reason for
    that. And yet, to say the truth, reason and love keep
    little company together now-a-days. The more the pity,
    That some honest neighbours will not make them friends.   1£
    Nay, I can gleek° upon occasion.
TITANIA.   Thou art as wise as thou art beautiful.
BOTTOM.   Not so neither: but if I had wit enough to get out of
    this wood, I have enough to serve mine own turn.
TITANIA.   Out of this wood do not desire to go: 1£
    Thou shalt remain here, whether thou wilt or no.
    I am a spirit of no common rate:°
    The summer still doth tend upon my state,°
    And I do love thee: therefore go with me.
    I'll give thee fairies to attend on thee: 14
    And they shall fetch thee jewels from the deep,
    And sing, while thou on pressèd flowers dost sleep:
    And I will purge thy mortal grossness so,
    That thou shalt like an airy spirit go.
    Peaseblossom, Cobweb, Moth,° and Mustardseed!   14

Enter four FAIRIES.

PEASEBLOSSOM.   Ready.
COBWEB.   And I.
MOTH.   And I.
MUSTARDSEED.   And I.
ALL.   Where shall we go?
TITANIA.   Be kind and courteous to this gentleman,
    Hop in his walks and gambol° in his eyes,
    Feed him with apricocks° and dewberries,°   1£
    With purple grapes, green figs, and mulberries.
    The honey-bags steal from the humblebees,°
    And for night-tapers, crop° their waxen thighs,
    And light them at the fiery glow-worm's eyes,

---

119 *set . . . to:* match his wit against.   120 *Who . . . lie:* who could call a bird a liar. *"cuckoo":* (which sounded like "cuckold" = a deceived husband).   121 *never so:* i.e., often.   125 *perforce:* by force.   131 *gleek:* joke satirically.   137 *rate:* rank, value   138 *still . . . state:* always serves as an attendant in my royal train.   145 *Moth:* mote (so pronounced), tiny speck. 149 *gambol in:* caper before.   150 *apricocks:* apricots.   *dewberries:* blackberries.   152 *humblebees:* bumblebees.   153 *crop:* clip.

To have my love to bed and to arise: 155
And pluck the wings from painted butterflies,
To fan the moonbeams from his sleeping eyes.
Nod to him elves, and do him courtesies.
PEASEBLOSSOM.   Hail, mortal.
COBWEB.   Hail.   160
MOTH.   Hail.
MUSTARDSEED.   Hail.
BOTTOM.   I cry your worships mercy,° heartily: I beseech your
    worship's name.
COBWEB.   Cobweb.   165
BOTTOM.   I shall desire you of more acquaintance, good Master
    Cobweb: if I cut my finger,° I shall make bold with you.
    Your name, honest gentleman?
PEASEBLOSSOM.   Peaseblossom.
BOTTOM.   I pray you commend me° to Mistress Squash,° your mother,   170
    and to Master Peascod,° your father. Good Master Peaseblossom,
    I shall desire you of more acquaintance, too.
    Your name I beseech you sir?
MUSTARDSEED.   Mustardseed.
BOTTOM.   Good Master Mustardseed, I know your patience well.   175
    That same cowardly giant-like ox beef hath devoured
    many a gentleman of your house. I promise you, your
    kindred hath made my eyes water ere now. I desire you
    of more acquaintance, good Master Mustardseed.
TITANIA.   Come wait upon him: lead him to my bower.   180
        The moon methinks looks with a wat'ry eye:
        And when she weeps, weeps every little flower,
        Lamenting some enforcèd° chastity.
        Tie up my lover's tongue, bring him silently.   *Exeunt.*

[Scene 2. *Another part of the wood*]

Enter [OBERON,] *King of Fairies, solus.*°

OBERON.   I wonder if Titania be awaked;
        Then what it was that next came in her eye,
        Which she must dote on in extremity.

Enter PUCK.

        Here comes my messenger. How now, mad spirit?
        What night-rule° now about this haunted grove?   5
PUCK.   My mistress with a monster is in love.
        Near to her close and consecrated bower,

---

163 *I . . . mercy:* I respectfully beg your pardons.   167 *cut my finger:* (cobwebs were used to stop
bleeding).   170 *commend me:* offer my respects.   *Squash:* unripe peapod.
171 *Peascod:* ripe peapod.   183 *enforcèd:* violated.   Stage direction: *solus:* alone.
5 *night-rule:* diversion ("misrule") in the night.

While she was in her dull° and sleeping hour,
A crew of patches,° rude mechanicals,°
That work for bread upon Athenian stalls,°   1
Were met together to rehearse a play,
Intended for great Theseus' nuptial day:
The shallowest thickskin of that barren sort,°
Who Pyramus presented in their sport,
Forsook his scene and entered in a brake: 1
When I did him at this advantage take,
An ass's nole° I fixèd on his head.
Anon° his Thisby must be answerèd,
And forth my mimic° comes. When they him spy,
As wild geese, that the creeping fowler° eye,   2
Or russet-pated choughs,° many in sort,°
Rising and cawing at the gun's report,
Sever themselves and madly sweep the sky,
So at his sight away his fellows fly:
And at our stamp, here o'er and o'er one falls: 2
He murder cries, and help from Athens calls.
Their sense thus weak, lost with their fears thus strong,
Made senseless things begin to do them wrong.
For briers and thorns at their apparel snatch:
Some° sleeves, some hats; from yielders, all things catch.°   3
I led them on in this distracted° fear,
And left sweet Pyramus translated there:
When in that moment (so it came to pass)
Titania waked, and straightway loved an ass.

OBERON.   This falls out better than I could devise.   3
    But has thou yet latched° the Athenian's eyes
    With the love-juice, as I did bid thee do?
PUCK.   I took him sleeping (that is finished too)
    And the Athenian woman by his side;
    That when he waked, of force° she must be eyed.   4

Enter DEMETRIUS and HERMIA.

OBERON.   Stand close:° this is the same Athenian.
PUCK.   This is the woman: but not this the man.
DEMETRIUS.   O why rebuke you him that loves you so?
    Lay breath so bitter on your bitter foe.
HERMIA.   Now I but chide: but I should use thee worse,   4
    For thou, I fear, hast given me cause to curse.
    If thou hast slain Lysander in his sleep,

8 *dull:* drowsy.   9 *patches:* fools.   *mechanicals:* workers.   10 *stalls:* shops.   13 *barren sort:* stupid crew.   17 *nole:* head, noodle.   18 *Anon:* presently.   19 *mimic:* actor.
20 *fowler:* hunter of fowl.   21 *russet-pated choughs:* grey-headed jackdaws.   *sort:* a flock.
30 *Some:* ie., snatch.   *from yielders . . . catch:* (everything joins in to harm the weak).
31 *distracted:* maddened.   36 *latched:* moistened.   40 *of force:* by necessity.
41 *close:* hidden.

Being o'er shoes in blood, plunge in the deep,
And kill me too.
The sun was not so true unto the day,   50
As he to me. Would he have stolen away
From sleeping Hermia? I'll believe as soon
This whole° earth may be bored,° and that the moon
May through the center creep, and so displease
Her brother's noontide with th' Antipodes.°   55
It cannot be but thou hast murdered him.
So should a murderer look; so dead,° so grim.
DEMETRIUS.   So should the murdered look, and so should I,
Pierced through the heart with your stern cruelty.
Yet you, the murderer, look as bright, as clear,   60
As yonder Venus in her glimmering sphere.°
HERMIA.   What's this to my Lysander? Where is he?
Ah good Demetrius, wilt thou give him me?
DEMETRIUS.   I had rather give his carcass to my hounds.
HERMIA.   Out dog, out cur! Thou driv'st me past the bounds   65
Of maiden's patience. Hast thou slain him then?
Henceforth be never numbered among men.
O, once tell true: tell true, even for my sake:
Durst thou have looked upon him, being awake?
And hast thou killed him sleeping? O brave touch°!   70
Could not a worm,° an adder, do so much?
An adder did it: for with doubler tongue°
Than thine, thou serpent, never adder stung.
DEMETRIUS.   You spend your passion on a misprised mood:°
I am not guilty of Lysander's blood: 75
Nor is he dead, for aught that I can tell.
HERMIA.   I pray thee, tell me then that he is well.
DEMETRIUS.   And if I could, what should I get therefore?
HERMIA.   A privilege never to see me more:
And from thy hated presence part I so: 80
See me no more, whether he be dead or no.   *Exit.*
DEMETRIUS.   There is no following her in this fierce vein.
Here therefore for a while I will remain.
So sorrow's heaviness doth heavier grow
For debt that bankrout sleep doth sorrow owe:°   85
Which now in some slight measure it will pay,
If for his tender° here I make some stay.°   *Lie down.*
OBERON.   What hast thou done? Thou hast mistaken quite,

---

53 *whole:* solid.   *be bored:* have a hole bored through it.   55 *Her brother's . . . Antipodes:* the
noon of her brother sun, by appearing among the Antipodes (the people on the other side of
the earth).   57 *dead:* deadly.   61 *sphere:* (in the Ptolemaic system, each planet moved in its
own sphere around the earth).   70 *brave touch:* splendid stroke (ironic).   71 *worm:* snake.
72 *doubler tongue:* (1) tongue more forked (2) more deceitful speech.   74 *on . . . mood:* in
mistaken anger.   85 *For debt . . . owe:* because sleep cannot pay the debt of repose he owes the
man who is kept awake by sorrow.   87 *tender:* offer.   *stay:* pause.

And laid the love-juice on some true-love's sight.
Of thy misprision° must perforce° ensue   90
Some true love turned, and not a false turned true.
PUCK.   Then fate o'errules, that one man holding troth,
     A million fail, confounding° oath on oath.°
OBERON.   About the wood, go swifter than the wind,
     And Helena of Athens look thou find.   95
     All fancy-sick° she is, and pale of cheer,°
     With sighs of love, that costs the fresh blood dear.
     By some illusion see thou bring her here:
     I'll charm his eyes against she do appear.°
PUCK.   I go, I go, look how I go.   100
     Swifter than arrow from the Tartar's bow.°   *Exit.*
OBERON.   Flower of this purple dye,
          Hit with Cupid's archery,
          Sink in apple of his eye:
          When his love he doth espy,   105
          Let her shine as gloriously
          As the Venus of the sky.
          When thou wak'st, if she be by,
          Beg of her for remedy.

Enter PUCK.

PUCK.   Captain of our fairy band,
          Helena is here at hand,
          And the youth, mistook by me,
          Pleading for a lover's fee.°
          Shall we their fond pageant° see?
          Lord, what fools these mortals be!   110
OBERON.   Stand aside. The noise they make
          Will cause Demetrius to awake.
PUCK.   Then will two at once woo one:
          That must needs be sport alone.°
          And those things do best please me   120
          That befall prepost'rously.

Enter LYSANDER *and* HELENA.

LYSANDER.   Why should you think that I should woo in scorn?
          Scorn and derision never come in tears.
          Look when I vow, I weep: and vows so born,
          In their nativity all truth appears.°   125
          How can these things in me seem scorn to you,
          Bearing the badge° of faith to prove them true?

90 *misprision:* mistake.   *perforce:* of necessity.   93 *confounding:* destroying.   *oath on oath:*
one oath after another.   96 *fancy-sick:* lovesick.   *cheer:* face.   99 *against ... appear:* in
preparation for her appearance.   101 *Tartar's bow:* (the Tartars, who used powerful Oriental
bows, were famed as archers).   113 *fee:* reward.   114 *fond pageant:* foolish spectacle.
119 *alone:* unique.   124–125 *vows ... appears:* vows born in weeping must be true ones.
127 *badge:* (1) outward signs (2) family crest.

HELENA.   You do advance your cunning more and more.
      When truth kills truth,° O devilish-holy fray!
      These vows are Hermia's. Will you give her o'er?   130
      Weigh oath with oath, and you will nothing weigh.
      Your vows to her and me, put in two scales,
      Will even weigh: and both as light as tales.
Lysander.   I had no judgment, when to her I swore.
HELENA.   Nor none, in my mind, now you give her o'er.   135
LYSANDER.   Demetrius loves her: and he loves not you.
DEMETRIUS.   (*Awakes.*) O Helen, goddess, nymph, perfect, divine,
      To what, my love, shall I compare thine eyne!
      Crystal is muddy. O, how ripe in show,
      Thy lips, those kissing cherries, tempting grow!   140
      That pure congealèd white, high Taurus'° snow,
      Fanned with the eastern wind, turns to a crow,
      When thou hold'st up thy hand. O let me kiss
      This princess of pure white,° this seal of bliss.
HELENA.   O spite! O hell! I see you all are bent   145
      To set against me, for your merriment.
      If you were civil,° and knew courtesy,
      You would not do me thus much injury.
      Can you not hate me, as I know you do,
      But you must join in souls° to mock me too?   150
      If you were men, as men you are in show,
      You would not use a gentle lady so;
      To vow, and swear, and superpraise my parts,°
      When I am sure you hate me with your hearts.
      You both are rivals, and love Hermia: 155
      And now both rivals, to mock Helena.
      A trim° exploit, a manly enterprise,
      To conjure tears up in a poor maid's eyes
      With your derision. None of noble sort
      Would so offend a virgin, and extort°   160
      A poor soul's patience, all to make you sport.
LYSANDER.   You are unkind, Demetrius: be not so.
      For you love Hermia: this you know I know.
      And here, with all good will, with all my heart,
      In Hermia's love I yield you up my part: 165
      And yours of Helena to be bequeath,
      Whom I do love, and will do to my death.
HELENA.   Never did mockers waste more idle breath.
DEMETRIUS.   Lysander, keep thy Hermia: I will none.°
      If e'er I loved her, all that love is gone.   170
      My heart to her but as guest-wise sojourned:°

---

129 *truth kills truth:* former true love is killed by vows of present true love.   141 *Taurus:*
mountain range in Asia Minor.   144 *princess . . . white:* sovereign example of whiteness (her
hand).   147 *civil:* well behaved.   150 *join in souls:* agree in spirit.   153 *parts:* qualities.
157 *trim:* fine (ironic).   160 *extort:* wring.   169 *none:* have none of her.
171 *to her . . . sojourned:* visited her only as a guest.

And now to Helen is it home returned,
There to remain.
LYSANDER.   Helen, it is not so.
DEMETRIUS.   Disparage not the faith thou dost not know,
    Lest to thy peril thou aby it dear.°   175
    Look where thy love comes: yonder is thy dear.

Enter HERMIA.

HERMIA.   Dark night, that from the eye his function takes,
    The ear more quick of apprehension makes.
    Wherein it doth impair the seeing sense,
    It pays the hearing double recompense.   180
    Thou art not by mine eye, Lysander, found:
    Mine ear, I thank it, brought me to thy sound.
    But why unkindly didst thou leave me so?
LYSANDER.   Why should he stay, whom love doth press to go?
HERMIA.   What love could press Lysander from my side?   185
LYSANDER.   Lysander's love, that would not let him bide—
    Fair Helena: who more engilds the night
    Than all your fiery oes and eyes of light.°
    Why seek'st thou me? Could not this make thee know,
    The hate I bare thee made me leave thee so?   190
HERMIA.   You speak not as you think: it cannot be.
HELENA.   Lo: She is one of this confederacy.
    Now I perceive they have conjoined all three,
    To fashion this false sport in spite of° me.
    Injurious° Hermia, most ungrateful maid,   195
    Have you conspired, have you with these contrived
    To bait° me with this foul derision?
    Is all the counsel° that we two have shared,
    The sisters' vows, the hours that we have spent,
    When we have chid the hasty-footed time   200
    For parting us; O, is all forgot?
    All schooldays' friendship, childhood innocence?
    We Hermia, like two artificial° gods,
    Have with our needles created both one flower,
    Both on one sampler,° sitting on one cushion,   205
    Both warbling of one song, both in one key;
    As if our hands, our sides, voices, and minds
    Had been incorporate.° So we grew together,
    Like to a double cherry, seeming parted,
    But yet an union in partition,   210
    Two lovely berries moulded on one stem:
    So with two seeming bodies, but one heart,
    Two of the first, like coats in heraldry,

175 *aby it dear:* buy it at a high price.   188 *oes . . . light:* stars.   194 *in spite of:* to spite.
195 *Injurious:* insulting.   197 *bait:* attack.   198 *counsel:* secrets.   203 *artificial:* skilled in
art.   205 *sampler:* work of embroidery.   208 *incorporate:* in one body.

Due but to one, and crownèd with one crest.°
And will you rent° our ancient love asunder,   215
To join with men in scorning your poor friend?
It is not friendly, 'tis not maidenly.
Our sex, as well as I, may chide you for it;
Though I alone do feel the injury.
HERMIA.   I am amazèd at your passionate words: 220
I scorn you not. It seems that you scorn me.
HELENA.   Have you not set Lysander, as in scorn,
To follow me, and praise my eyes and face?
And made your other love, Demetrius
(Who even but now did spurn° me with his foot)   225
To call me goddess, nymph, divine, and rare,
Precious, celestial? Wherefore speaks he this
To her he hates? And wherefore doth Lysander
Deny your love, so rich within his soul,
And tender° me (forsooth) affection,   230
But by your setting on, by your consent?
What though I be not so in grace° as you,
So hung upon with love, so fortunate,
But miserable most, to love unloved?
This you should pity, rather than despise.   235
HERMIA.   I understand not what you mean by this.
HELENA.   Ay, do. Persèver, counterfeit sad° looks:
Make mouths upon° me when I turn my back:
Wink each at other, hold the sweet jest up.
This sport well carried, shall be chronicled.°   240
If you have any pity, grace, or manners,
You would not make me such an argument.°
But fare ye well: 'tis partly my own fault:
Which death or absence soon shall remedy.
LYSANDER.   Stay, gentle Helena: hear my excuse,   245
My love, my life, my soul, fair Helena.
HELENA.   O excellent!
HERMIA.   Sweet, do not scorn her so.
DEMETRIUS.   If she cannot entreat,° I can compel.
LYSANDER.   Thou canst compel no more than she entreat.
Thy threats have no more strength than her weak prayers.   250
Helen, I love thee, by my life I do:
I swear by that which I will lose for thee,
To prove° him false that says I love thee not.
DEMETRIUS.   I say I love thee more than he can do.
LYSANDER.   If thou say so, withdraw, and prove° it too.   255

213–214 *Two . . . crest:* (the two bodies being) like double coats of arms joined under one crest
(with one heart).   215 *rent:* rend, tear.   225 *spurn:* kick.   230 *tender:* offer.
232 *in grace:* favored.   237 *sad:* serious.   238 *mouths upon:* faces at.   240 *chronicled:* written down in the history books.   242 *argument:* subject (of your mockery).
248 *entreat:* sway you by entreaty.   253, 255 *prove:* i.e., by a duel.

DEMETRIUS.   Quick, Come.
HERMIA.   Lysander, whereto tends all this?
LYSANDER.   Away, you Ethiope.°
DEMETRIUS.   No, no, sir,
   Seem to break loose: take on as you would follow;
   But yet come not.° You are a tame man, go.
LYSANDER.   Hang off,° thou cat, thou burr: vile thing, let loose;   260
   Or I will shake thee from me like a serpent.
HERMIA.   Why are you grown so rude? What change is this,
   Sweet love?
LYSANDER.   Thy love? Out, tawny Tartar, out: 270
   Out, loathèd med'cine: O hated potion, hence!
HERMIA.   Do you not jest?
HELENA.   Yes sooth: and so do you.   265
LYSANDER.   Demetrius, I will keep my word° with thee.
DEMETRIUS.   I would I had your bond.° For I perceive
   A weak bond holds you. I'll not trust your word.
LYSANDER.   What? Should I hurt her, strike her, kill her dead?
   Although I hate her, I'll not harm her so.   270
HERMIA.   What? Can you do me greater harm than hate?
   Hate me, wherefore°? O me, what news,° my love?
   Am not I Hermia? Are not you Lysander?
   I am as fair now, as I was erewhile.°
   Since night, you loved me; yet since night, you left me.   275
   Why then, you left me—O, the gods forbid—
   In earnest, shall I say?
LYSANDER   Ay, by my life:
   And never did desire to see thee more.
   Therefore be out of hope, of question, of doubt:
   Be certain: nothing truer: 'tis no jest   280
   That I do hate thee, and love Helena.
HERMIA.   O me, you juggler,° you canker blossom,°
   You thief of love: what, have you come by night,
   And stol'n my love's heart from him?
HELENA.   Fine, i' faith.
   Have you no modesty, no maiden shame,   285
   No touch of bashfulness? What, will you tear
   Impatient answers from my gentle tongue?
   Fie, fie, you counterfeit, you puppet,° you.
HERMIA.   Puppet? Why so—ay, that way goes the game.
   Now I perceive that she hath made compare   290
   Between our statures, she hath urged her height,

---

257 *Ethiope:* (because she is a brunette).   258–259 *Seem . . . not:* You only seem to break loose
from Hermia and pretend to follow me to a duel, but you actually hold back.
260 *Hang off:* let go.   266 *keep my word:* i.e., to duel.   267 *bond:* written agreement.
272 *wherefore:* why.   *what news:* what's the matter.   274 *erewhile:* a short while ago.
282 *juggler:* deceiver.   *canker blossom:* worm that causes canker in blossoms.
288 *puppet:* (Hermia is short and Helena tall).

And with her personage, her tall personage,
Her height (forsooth) she hath prevailed with him.
And are you grown so high in his esteem,
Because I am so dwarfish and so low?   295
How low am I, thou painted maypole? Speak:
How low am I? I am not yet so low,
But that my nails can reach unto thine eyes.
HELENA.   I pray you, though you mock me, gentlemen,
Let her not hurt me. I was never curst:°   300
I have no gift at all in shrewishness:
I am a right maid for my cowardice:°
Let her not strike me. You perhaps may think,
Because she is something lower than myself,
That I can match her.
HERMIA.   Lower? Hark again.   305
HELENA.   Good Hermia, do not be so bitter with me,
I evermore did love you Hermia.
Did ever keep your counsels, never wronged you;
Save that in love unto Demetrius,
I told him of your stealth unto this wood.   310
He followed you: for love I followed him.
But he hath chid me hence, and threatened me
To strike me, spurn me, nay to kill me too;
And now, so° you will let me quiet go,
To Athens will I bear my folly back,   315
And follow you no further. Let me go.
You see how simple and how fond° I am.
HERMIA.   Why, get you gone. Who is't that hinders you?
HELENA.   A foolish heart, that I leave here behind.
HERMIA.   What, with Lysander?
HELENA.   With Demetrius.   320
LYSANDER.   Be not afraid: she shall not harm thee Helena.
DEMETRIUS.   No sir: she shall not, though you take her part.
HELENA.   O when she's angry, she is keen and shrewd.°
She was a vixen when she went to school:
And though she be but little, she is fierce.   325
HERMIA.   "Little" again? Nothing but "low" and "little"?
Why will you suffer her to flout° me thus?
Let me come to her.
LYSANDER.   Get you gone, you dwarf;
You minimus,° of hind'ring knot-grass° made;   330
You bead, you acorn.
DEMETRIUS.   You are too officious
In her behalf that scorns your services.
Let her alone: speak not of Helena,

---

300 *curst:* bad-tempered.   302 *right . . . cowardice:* true woman in being cowardly.   314 *so:* if.
317 *fond:* foolish.   323 *keen and shrewd:* sharp and malicious.   327 *flout:* mock.
329 *minimus:* smallest of creatures.   *knot-grass:* weed believed to stunt the growth if eaten.

Take not her part. For if thou dost intend°
Never so little show of love to her,
Thou shalt aby it.°
LYSANDER.   Now she holds me not: 3.
Now follow, if thou dar'st, to try whose right,
Of thine or mine, is most in Helena.°
DEMETRIUS.   Follow? Nay, I'll go with thee, cheek by jowl.

Exeunt LYSANDER *and* DEMETRIUS.

HERMIA.   You, mistress, all this coil is long of° you.
Nay, go not back.
HELENA.   I will not trust you, I,   34
Nor longer stay in your curst company
Your hands than mine are quicker for a fray:
My legs are longer though, to run away.   *[Exit.]*
HERMIA.   I am amazed,° and know not what to say.   *Exit.*
OBERON.   This is thy negligence: still thou mistak'st,   34
Or else commit'st thy knaveries wilfully.
PUCK.   Believe me, king of shadows, I mistook.
Did not you tell me I should know the man
By the Athenian garments he had on?
And so far blameless proves my enterprise,   35
That I have 'nointed an Athenian's eyes:
And so far am I glad it so did sort,°
As this their jangling I esteem a sport.
OBERON.   Thou seest these lovers seek a place to fight;
Hie therefore Robin, overcast the night,   35.
The starry welkin° cover thou anon
With drooping fog as black as Acheron,°
And lead these testy° rivals so astray,
As° one come not within another's way.
Like to Lysander sometime frame thy tongue: 36(
Then stir Demetrius up with bitter wrong:°
And sometime rail thou like Demetrius:
And from each other look thou lead them thus;
Till o'er their brows death-counterfeiting sleep
With leaden legs and batty wings doth creep: 36.
Then crush this herb into Lysander's eye;
Whose liquor hath this virtuous° property,
To take from thence all error with his might,
And make his eyeballs roll with wonted° sight.
When they next wake, all this derision°   37(

333 *intend:* extend.   335 *aby it:* buy it dearly.   336–337 *try . . . Helena:* prove by fighting which of us has most right to Helena.   339 *coil is long of:* turmoil is because of.
344 *amazed:* confused.   352 *sort:* turn out.   356 *welkin:* sky.   357 *Acheron:* one of the four rivers in the underworld.   358 *testy:* irritable.   359 *As:* so that.   361 *wrong:* insult.
367 *virtuous:* potent.   369 *wonted:* (previously) accustomed.   370 *derision:* laughable interlude.

Shall seem a dream, and fruitless vision,
And back to Athens shall the lovers wend,
With league whose date° till death shall never end.
Whiles I in this affair do thee employ,
I'll to my queen and beg her Indian boy: 375
And then I will her charmèd eye release
From monster's view, and all things shall be peace.

PUCK.   My fairy lord, this must be done with haste,
For night's swift dragons cut the clouds full fast:
And yonder shines Aurora's harbinger,°   380
At whose approach, ghosts wand'ring here and there,
Troop home to churchyards: damnèd spirits all,
That in crossways° and floods° have burial,
Already to their wormy beds are gone:
For fear lest day should look their shames upon,   385
They wilfully themselves exile from light,
And must for aye consort° with black-browed night.

OBERON.   But we are spirits of another sort.
I with the morning's love have oft made sport,°
And like a forester, the groves may tread   390
Even till the eastern gate all fiery red,
Opening on Neptune, with fair blessèd beams,
Turns into yellow gold his salt green streams.
But notwithstanding, haste, make no delay:
We may effect this business yet ere day.   [*Exit.*]   395

PUCK.   Up and down, up and down,
    I will lead them up and down.
    I am feared in field and town.
    Goblin, lead them up and down.
    Here comes one.   400

Enter LYSANDER.

LYSANDER.   Where art thou, proud Demetrius? Speak thou now.
PUCK.   Here villain, drawn° and ready. Where art thou?
LYSANDER.   I will be with thee straight.
PUCK.   Follow me then
    To plainer° ground.   [*Exit LYSANDER.*]

Enter DEMETRIUS.

DEMETRIUS.   Lysander, speak again.
    Thou runaway, thou coward, art thou fled?   405
    Speak: in some bush? Where dost thou hide thy head?

---

373 *date:* term.   380 *Aurora's harbinger:* the morning star heralding Aurora, the dawn.
383 *crossways:* crossroads, where suicides were buried.   *floods:* those who drowned.
387 *aye consort:* ever associate.   389 *morning's . . . sport:* hunted with Cephalus (beloved of
Aurora and himself devoted to his wife Procris, whom he killed by accident; "sport"
also = "amorous dalliance," and "love" = Aurora's love for Oberon).   402 *drawn:* with sword
drawn.   404 *plainer:* more level.

PUCK.   Thou coward, art thou bragging to the stars,
　　　Telling the bushes that thou look'st for wars,
　　　And wilt not come? Come recreant,° come thou child,
　　　I'll whip thee with a rod. He is defiled
　　　That draws a sword on thee.   41
DEMETRIUS.   Yea, art thou there?
PUCK.   Follow my voice: we'll try no manhood° here.   *Exeunt.*

[*Enter LYSANDER.*]

LYSANDER.   He goes before me and still dares me on:
　　　When I come where he calls, then he is gone
　　　The villain is much lighter-heeled than I;   41
　　　I followed fast: but faster he did fly,
　　　That fallen am I in dark uneven way,
　　　And here will rest me. (*Lie down.*) Come thou gentle day,
　　　For if but once thou show me thy grey light.
　　　I'll find Demetrius and revenge this spite.   [*Sleeps.*] 42

Enter PUCK and DEMETRIUS.

PUCK.   Ho, ho, ho! Coward, why com'st thou not?
DEMETRIUS.   Abide° me, if thou dar'st, for well I wot°
　　　Thou run'st before me, shifting every place,
　　　And dar'st not stand, nor look me in the face.
　　　Where art thou now?
PUCK.   Come hither: I am here.   42
DEMETRIUS.   Nay then thou mock'st me. Thou shalt buy this dear,°
　　　If ever I thy face by daylight see.
　　　Now go thy way. Faintness constraineth me
　　　To measure out my length on this cold bed.
　　　By day's approach look to be visited.   [*Lies down and sleeps.*] 43

Enter HELENA.

HELENA.   O weary night, O long and tedious night,
　　　Abate° thy hours; shine comforts° from the east,
　　　That I may back to Athens by daylight,
　　　From these that my poor company detest:
　　　And sleep, that sometimes shuts up sorrow's eye.   43
　　　Steal me awhile from mine own company.   *Sleeps.*
PUCK.   Yet but three? Come one more,
　　　Two of both kinds makes up four.
　　　Here she comes, curst° and sad.
　　　Cupid is a knavish lad,   44
　　　Thus to make poor females mad.

---

409 *recreant:* oath-breaker, coward.   412 *try no manhood:* test no valor.   422 *Abide:* wait for.
wot: know.   426 *buy this dear:* pay dearly for this.   432 *Abate:* shorten.   *shine comforts:* may
comforts shine.   439 *curst:* cross.

Enter HERMIA.

HERMIA.   Never so weary, never so in woe,
      Bedabbled with the dew, and torn with briers:
      I can no further crawl, no further go:
        My legs can keep no pace with my desires.   445
      Here will I rest me till the break of day.
      Heavens shield Lysander, if they mean a fray.   *[Lies down and sleeps.]*
PUCK.   On the ground,
      Sleep sound:
      I'll apply   450
      To your eye,
Gentle lover, remedy.   *[Squeezes the love-juice on* LYSANDER'S *eyelids.]*
      When thou wak'st,
      Thou tak'st
      True delight   455
      In the sight
Of thy former lady's eye:
And the country proverb known,
That every man should take his own,
In your waking shall be shown.   460
      Jack shall have Jill:
      Naught shall go ill:
The man shall have his mare again, and all shall be well.

          [Exit PUCK. *The lovers remain asleep on stage.]*

ACT 4

[Scene 1. The wood]

Enter [TITANIA] QUEEN OF FAIRIES, *and* [BOTTOM THE] CLOWN, *and* FAIRIES, *and the* KING
[OBERON] *behind them* [*unseen*].

TITANIA.   Come sit thee down upon this flow'ry bed,
      While I thy amiable° cheeks do coy,°
      And stick musk-roses in thy sleek smooth head,
      And kiss thy fair large ears, my gentle joy.
BOTTOM.   Where's Peaseblossom?   5
PEASEBLOSSOM.   Ready.
BOTTOM.   Scratch my head, Peaseblossom. Where's Mounsieur
    Cobweb?
COBWEB.   Ready.
BOTTOM.   Mounsieur Cobweb, good mounsieur, get you your weapons   10
    in your hand, and kill me a red-hipped humblebee on

---

2 *amiable:* lovely.   *coy:* caress.

the top of a thistle: and good mounsieur, bring me the
honey-bag. Do not fret yourself too much in the action,
mounsieur: and good mounsieur have a care the honey-
bag break not, I would be loath to have you overflowen   1
with a honey bag, signior. Where's Mounsieur
Mustardseed?

MUSTARDSEED.   Ready.

BOTTOM.   Give me your neaf,° Mounsieur Mustardseed. Pray you
leave your curtsy,° good mounsieur.   2

MUSTARDSEED.   What's your will?

BOTTOM.   Nothing, good mounsieur, but to help Cavalery° Cobweb
to scratch. I must to the barber's mounsieur, for
methinks I am marvellous hairy about the face. And I am
such a tender ass, if my hair do but tickle me, I must   2
scratch.

TITANIA.   What, will thou hear some music, my sweet love?

BOTTOM.   I have a reasonable good ear in music. Let's have the tongs°
and the bones.°

TITANIA.   Or say, sweet love, what thou desirest to eat.   3

BOTTOM.   Truly, a peck of provender. I could munch your good
dry oats. Methinks I have a great desire to a bottle° of hay.
Good hay, sweet hay, hath no fellow.

TITANIA.   I have a venturous fairy that shall seek
The squirrel's hoard, and fetch thee new nuts.   3

BOTTOM.   I had rather have a handful or two of dried pease. But
I pray you, let none of your people stir me: I have an
exposition of° sleep come upon me.

TITANIA.   Sleep thou, and I will wind thee in my arms.
Fairies, be gone, and be all ways° away.   [*Exeunt FAIRIES.*] 4
So doth the woodbine the sweet honeysuckle
Gently entwist: the female ivy so
Enrings the barky fingers of the elm.
O how I love thee! how I dote on thee!   [*They sleep.*]

Enter ROBIN GOODFELLOW [PUCK.]

OBERON.   [*Advances.*] Welcome good Robin. Seest thou this sweet sight? 4
Her dotage now I do begin to pity.
For meeting her of late behind the wood,
Seeking sweet favours° for this hateful fool,
I did upbraid her and fall out with her.
For she his hairy temples then had rounded   5
With coronet of fresh and fragrant flowers
And that same dew which sometime° on the buds

---

19 *neaf:* fist.   20 *leave your curtsy:* either (a) stop bowing, or (b) replace your hat.
22 *Cavalery:* (he means "cavalier").   29 *tongs:* crude music made by striking tongs with a piece
of metal.   *bones:* pieces of bone held between the fingers and clapped together rhythmically.
32 *bottle:* bundle.   38 *exposition of:* (he means "disposition to").   40 *all ways:* in every
direction.   48 *favours:* bouquets as love tokens.   52 *sometime:* formerly.

Was wont to° swell like round and orient° pearls,
Stood now within the pretty flowerets' eyes,
Like tears that did their own disgrace bewail.   55
When I had at my pleasure taunted her,
And she in mild terms begged my patience,
I then did ask of her her changeling child:
Which straight she gave me, and her fairy sent
To bear him to my bower in fairy land.   60
And now I have the boy, I will undo
This hateful imperfection of her eyes.
And gentle Puck, take this transformèd scalp
From off the head of this Athenian swain;
That he awaking when the other do,   65
May all to Athens back again repair,°
And think no more of this night's accidents,°
But as the fierce vexation of a dream.
But first I will release the Fairy Queen.
   Be as thou wast wont to be: 70
   See, as thou wast wont to see.
   Dian's bud o'er Cupid's flower°
   Hath such force and blessèd power.
Now my Titania, wake you, my sweet queen.
TITANIA.   My Oberon, what visions have I seen!   75
Methought I was enamoured of an ass.
OBERON.   There lies your love.
TITANIA.   How came these things to pass?
  O, how mine eyes do loathe his visage now!
OBERON.   Silence awhile Robin, take off this head:
Titania, music call, and strike more dead   80
Than common sleep of all these five the sense.°
TITANIA.   Music, ho music! such as charmeth sleep.
PUCK.   Now, when thou wak'st, with thine own fools' eyes peep.
OBERON.   Sound music: *Music still.*°
          come my queen, take hands with me,
And rock the ground whereon these sleepers be.   *[Dance.]*   85
Now thou and I are new in amity,
And will tomorrow midnight solemnly
Dance in Duke Theseus' house triumphantly,°
And bless it to all fair prosperity.
There shall the pairs of faithful lovers be   90
Wedded, with Theseus, all in jollity.
PUCK.   Fairy King, attend and mark:
    I do hear the morning lark.

---

53 *Was wont to:* used to.   *orient:* (where the most beautiful pearls came from).
66 *repair:* return.   67 *accidents:* incidents.   72 *Dian's bud . . . flower:* (Diana's bud counter-
acts the effects of love-in-idleness, the pansy).   80–81 *strike . . . sense:* Make these five (the
lovers and Bottom) sleep more soundly.   84.1 stage direction: *still:* continuously.
88 *triumphantly:* in celebration.

OBERON.   Then my queen, in silence sad,°
　　　　Trip we after the night's shade:
　　　　We the globe can compass soon,
　　　　Swifter than the wand'ring moon.
TITANIA.   Come my lord, and in our flight,
　　　　Tell me how it came this night,
　　　　That I sleeping here was found,
　　　　With these mortals on the ground.   1(

Exeunt.

Wind° horns. Enter THESEUS, HIPPOLYTA, EGEUS *and all his train.*

THESEUS.   Go one of you, find out the forester:
　　　　For now our observation° is performed.
　　　　And since we have the vaward° of the day,
　　　　My love shall hear the music of my hounds.
　　　　Uncouple° in the western valley, let them go: 10
　　　　Dispatch I say, and find the forester.   [*Exit an* ATTENDANT.]
　　　　We will, fair queen, up to the mountain's top,
　　　　And mark the musical confusion
　　　　Of hounds and echo in conjunction.   11
HIPPOLYTA.   I was with Hercules and Cadmus° once,
　　　　When in a wood of Crete they bayed the bear,°
　　　　With hounds of Sparta:° never did I hear
　　　　Such gallant chiding. For besides the groves,
　　　　The skies, the fountains, every region near   11
　　　　Seemed all one mutual cry. I never heard
　　　　So musical a discord, such sweet thunder.
THESEUS.   My hounds are bred out of the Spartan kind:
　　　　So flewed, so sanded:° and their heads are hung
　　　　With ears that sweep away the morning dew,   12
　　　　Crook-kneed, and dewlapped° like Thessalian bulls:
　　　　Slow in pursuit; but matched in mouth like bells,
　　　　Each under each.° A cry° more tuneable
　　　　Was never holloa'd to, nor cheered with horn,
　　　　In Crete, in Sparta, nor in Thessaly.   12£
　　　　Judge when you hear. But soft.° What nymphs are these?
EGEUS.   My lord, this is my daughter here asleep,
　　　　And this Lysander, this Demetrius is,
　　　　This Helena, old Nedar's Helena.
　　　　I wonder of their being here together.   13(
THESEUS.   No doubt they rose up early to observe
　　　　The rite of May: and hearing our intent,
　　　　Came here in grace° of our solemnity.

---

94 *sad:* serious.   101.1 stage direction: *wind:* blow, sound.   103 *observation:* observance of
the May Day rites.   104 *vaward:* vanguard, earliest part.   106 *Uncouple:* unleash (the dogs).
111 *Cadmus:* mythical builder of Thebes.   112 *bayed the bear:* brought the bear to bay, to its last
stand.   113 *hounds of Sparta:* (a breed famous for their swiftness and quick scent).
119 *flewed, so sanded:* with hanging cheeks, so sand-colored.   121 *dewlapped:* with skin hanging
from the chin.   122–23 *matched . . . each:* with each voice matched for harmony with the next
in pitch, like bells in a chime.   123 *cry:* pack of dogs.   126 *soft:* wait.   133 *grace:* honor.

But speak Egeus, is not this the day
That Hermia should give answer of her choice?   135
EGEUS.   It is, my lord.
THESEUS.   Go bid the huntsmen wake them with their horns.

Shout within: wind horns. They all start up.

Good morrow, friends. Saint Valentine is past.
Begin these wood-birds but to couple now?°
LYSANDER.   Pardon, my lord.   [*They kneel.*]
THESEUS.   I pray you all, stand up.   140
I know you two are rival enemies.
How comes this gentle concord in the world,
That hatred is so far from jealousy,°
To sleep by hate° and fear no enmity?
LYSANDER.   My lord, I shall reply amazedly,   145
Half sleep, half waking. But as yet, I swear,
I cannot truly say how I came here.
But as I think—for truly would I speak,
And now I do bethink me, so it is—
I came with Hermia hither. Our intent   150
Was to be gone from Athens, where we might,
Without° the peril of the Athenian law—
EGEUS.   Enough, enough, my lord: you have enough.
I beg the law, the law upon his head:
They would have stol'n away, they would, Demetrius,   155
Thereby to have defeated you and me:
You of your wife, and me of my consent:
Of my consent that she should be your wife.
DEMETRIUS.   My lord, fair Helen told me of their stealth,
Of this their purpose hither, to this wood,   160
And I in fury hither followed them;
Fair Helena in fancy° following me.
But my good lord, I wot not by what power
(But by some power it is) my love to Hermia,
Melted as the snow, seems to me now   165
As the remembrance of an idle gaud,°
Which in my childhood I did dote upon:
And all the faith, the virtue of my heart,
The object and the pleasure of mine eye,
Is only Helena. To her, my lord,   170
Was I betrothed ere I saw Hermia:
But like a sickness,° did I loathe this food.
But as in health, come° to my natural taste,
Now I do wish it, love it, long for it.
And will for evermore be true to it.   175

138–139 *Saint . . . now:* (birds traditionally chose their mates on St. Valentine's Day).
143 *jealousy:* suspicion.   144 *hate:* one it hates.   152 *Without:* beyond.   162 *in fancy:* out
of doting love.   166 *idle gaud:* trifling toy.   172 *sickness:* sick person.   173 *come:* i.e., back.

THESEUS.   Fair lovers, you are fortunately met.
  Of this discourse we more will hear anon.
  Egeus, I will overbear your will:
  For in the temple, by and by,° with us,
  These couples shall eternally be knit.
  And for the morning now is something worn,°
  Our purposed hunting shall be set aside.
  Away with us to Athens. Three and three,
  We'll hold a feast in great solemnity.
  Come Hippolyta.

Exeunt DUKE [HIPPOLYTA, EGEUS] and LORDS.

DEMETRIUS.   These things seem small and undistinguishable,
  Like far-off mountains turnèd into clouds.
HERMIA.   Methinks I see these things with parted° eye,
  When everything seems double.
HELENA.   So methinks:
  And I have found Demetrius, like a jewel,
  Mine own, and not mine own.°
DEMETRIUS.   Are you sure
  That we are awake? It seems to me,
  That yet we sleep, we dream. Do not you think
  The duke was here, and bid us follow him?
HERMIA.   Yea, and my father.
HELENA.   And Hippolyta.
LYSANDER.   And he did bid us follow to the temple.
DEMETRIUS.   Why then, we are awake: let's follow him,
  And by the way let us recount our dreams.   *Exeunt Lovers.*
BOTTOM.   (*Wakes.*) When my cue comes, call me, and I will answer.
  My next is "Most fair Pyramus." Hey ho. Peter Quince?
  Flute the bellows-mender? Snout the tinker? Starveling?
  God's my life! Stol'n hence, and left me asleep? I have
  had a most rare vision. I have had a dream, past the wit
  of man to say what dream it was. Man is but an ass, if he
  go about° to expound this dream. Methought I was—
  there is no man can tell what. Methought I was, and
  methought I had—but man is but a patched fool,° if he
  will offer to say what methought I had. The eye of man
  hath not heard, the ear of man hath not seen, man's hand is
  not able to taste, his tongue to conceive, nor his
  heart to report, what my dream was. I will get Peter
  Quince to write a ballad of this dream: it shall be called
  Bottom's Dream; because it hath no bottom: and I
  will sing it in the latter end of our play, before the duke.

---

179 *by and by:* immediately.   181 *something worn:* somewhat worn on.   188 *parted:* divided
(each eye seeing a separate image).   190–191 *like . . . own:* like a person who finds a jewel: the
finder is the owner, but insecurely so.   205 *go about:* attempt.   207 *patched fool:* fool dressed
in motley.

Peradventure, to make it the more gracious, I shall sing   215
it at her° death.   *Exit.*

[Scene 2. Athens, Quince's house]

Enter QUINCE, FLUTE, SNOUT, and STARVELING.

QUINCE.   Have you sent to Bottom's house? Is he come home yet?
STARVELING.   He cannot be heard of. Out of doubt he is transported.°
FLUTE.   If he come not, then the play is marred. It goes not forward,
    doth it?
QUINCE.   It is not possible. You have not a man in all Athens able   5
    to discharge° Pyramus but he.
FLUTE.   No, he hath simply the best wit of any handicraft man in Athens.
QUINCE.   Yea, and the best person too, and he is a very paramour
    for a sweet voice.
FLUTE.   You must say "paragon." A paramour is (God bless us)   10
    a thing of naught.°

Enter SNUG THE JOINER.

SNUG.   Masters, the duke is coming from the temple, and there
    is two or three lords and ladies more married. If our
    sport had gone forward, we had all been made men.°
FLUTE.   O sweet bully Bottom. Thus hath he lost sixpence a day°   15
    during his life: he could not have 'scaped sixpence a day.
    And the duke had not given him sixpence a day for playing
    Pyramus, I'll be hanged. He would have deserved it.
    Sixpence a day in Pyramus, or nothing.

Enter BOTTOM.

BOTTOM.   Where are these lads? Where are these hearts?   20
QUINCE.   Bottom! O most courageous° day! O most happy hour!
BOTTOM.   Masters, I am to discourse wonders: but ask me not what.
    For if I tell you, I am not true Athenian. I will tell you
    everything, right as it fell out.
QUINCE.   Let us hear, sweet Bottom.   25
BOTTOM.   Not a word of me. All that I will tell you is, that the
    duke hath dined. Get your apparel together, good
    strings to your beards, new ribbands to your pumps, meet
    presently° at the palace, every man look o'er his part: for
    the short and the long is, our play is preferred.° In any   30
    case, let Thisby have clean linen: and let not him that
    plays the lion pare his nails, for they shall hang out for
    the lion's claws. And most dear actors, eat no onions nor
    garlic, for we are to utter sweet breath: and I do not

---

216 *her:* Thisby's.   2 *transported:* carried away (by spirits).   6 *discharge:* portray.
11 *of naught:* wicked, naughty.   14 *made men:* men made rich.   15 *sixpence a day:* i.e., as a
pension   .21 *courageous:* (he may mean "auspicious").   29 *presently:* immediately.
30 *preferred:* recommended (for presentation).

doubt but to hear them say it is a sweet comedy. No more
words: away, go away.   *Exeunt.*

ACT 5

[Scene 1. The palace of Theseus]

Enter THESEUS, HIPPOLYTA, and PHILOSTRATE, and his LORDS.

HIPPOLYTA.   'Tis strange, my Theseus, that these lovers speak of.
THESEUS.   More strange than true. I never may believe
    These antick° fables, nor these fairy toys.°
    Lovers and madmen have such seething brains,
    Such shaping fantasies,° that apprehend
    More than cool reason ever comprehends.
    The lunatic, the lover, and the poet,
    Are of imagination all compact.°
    One sees more devils than vast hell can hold:
    That is the madman. The lover, all as frantic,   1
    Sees Helen's beauty in a brow of Egypt.°
    The poet's eye, in a fine frenzy rolling,
    Doth glance from heaven to earth, from earth to heaven.
    And as imagination bodies forth
    The forms of things unknown, the poet's pen   1
    Turns them to shapes, and gives to airy nothing,
    A local habitation and a name.
    Such tricks hath strong imagination,
    That if it would but apprehend some joy,
    It comprehends° some bringer of that joy.   2
    Or in the night, imagining some fear,
    How easy is a bush supposed a bear.
HIPPOLYTA.   But all the story of the night told over,
    And all their minds transfigured so together,
    More witnesseth than fancy's images,°   2
    And grows to something of great constancy:°
    But howsoever, strange and admirable.°

Enter LOVERS: LYSANDER, DEMETRIUS, HERMIA, and HELENA.

THESEUS.   Here come the lovers, full of joy and mirth.
    Joy, gentle friends, joy and fresh days of love
    Accompany your hearts.

---

3 *antick:* fantastic.   *fairy toys:* trivial fairy stories.   5 *fantasies:* imaginations.
8 *of . . . compact:* totally composed of imagination.   11 *a brow of Egypt:* the swarthy face of a
gypsy (believed to come from Egypt).   20 *comprehends:* includes.   25 *More . . . images:*
testifies that it is more than just imagination.   26 *constancy:* certainty.   27 *admirable:* to be
wondered at.   30 *More:* even more (joy and love).

LYSANDER.   More° than to us   30
    Wait in your royal walks, your board, your bed.
THESEUS.   Come now, what masques,° what dances shall we have,
    To wear away this long age of three hours
    Between our after-supper° and bed-time?
    Where is our usual manager of mirth?   35
    What revels are in hand? Is there no play,
    To ease the anguish of a torturing hour?
    Call Philostrate.
PHILOSTRATE.   Here, mighty Theseus.
THESEUS.   Say, what abridgment° have you for this evening?
    What masque,° what music? How shall we beguile   40
    The lazy time, if not with some delight?
PHILOSTRATE.   There is a brief° how many sports are ripe:°
    Make choice of which your highness will see first.

[*Gives a paper.*]

THESEUS.   "The battle with the Centaurs, to be sung
    By an Athenian eunuch to the harp."   45
    We'll none of that. That have I told my love
    In glory of my kinsman Hercules.
    "The riot of the tipsy Bacchanals,
    Tearing the Thracian singer in their rage."°
    That is an old device: and it was played   50
    When I from Thebes came last a conqueror.
    "The thrice three Muses mourning for the death
    Of Learning, late deceased in beggary."
    That is some satire keen and critical,
    Not sorting with° a nuptial ceremony.   55
    "A tedious brief scene of young Pyramus
    And his love Thisby; very tragical mirth."
    Merry and tragical? Tedious and brief?
    That is hot ice and wondrous strange snow.
    How shall we find the concord of this discord?   60
PHILOSTRATE.   A play there is, my lord, some ten words long,
    Which is as brief as I have known a play:
    But by ten words, my lord, it is too long,
    Which makes it tedious: for in all the play
    There is not one word apt, one player fitted.°   65
    And tragical, my noble lord, it is:
    For Pyramus therein doth kill himself.
    Which when I saw rehearsed, I must confess,
    Made mine eyes water; but more merry tears
    The passion of loud laughter never shed.   70

32, 40 *masques:* lavish courtly entertainments combining song and dance.   34 *after-supper:* late
supper.   39 *abridgment:* either (a) diversion to make the hours seem shorter or (b) short
entertainment.   42 *brief:* list.   *ripe:* ready.   48–49 *riot . . . rage:* (The singer Orpheus of
Thrace was torn limb from limb by the Maenads, frenzied female priests of Bacchus).
55 *sorting with:* befitting.   65 *fitted:* (well) cast.

THESEUS.   What are they that do play it?
PHILOSTRATE.   Hard-handed men, that work in Athens here,
    Which never laboured in their minds till now:
    And now have toiled their unbreathed° memories
    With this same play, against° your nuptial.
THESEUS.   And we will hear it.
PHILOSTRATE.   No, my noble lord,
    It is not for you. I have heard it over,
    And it is nothing, nothing in the world;
    Unless you can find sport in their intents,
    Extremely stretched and conned° with cruel pain.
    To do your service.
THESEUS.   I will hear that play.
    For never anything can be amiss,
    When simpleness and duty tender° it.
    Go bring them in, and take your places, ladies.   [*Exit PHILOSTRATE.*]
HIPPOLYTA.   I love not to see wretchedness o'ercharged,°
    And duty in his service perishing.
THESEUS.   Why, gentle sweet, you shall see no such thing.
HIPPOLYTA.   He says they can do nothing in this kind.°
THESEUS.   The kinder we, to give them thanks for nothing.
    Our sport shall be to take what they mistake.
    And what poor duty cannot do, noble respect
    Takes it in might, not merit.°
    Where I have come, great clerks° have purposèd
    To greet me with premeditated welcomes;
    Where I have seen them shiver and look pale,
    Make periods in the midst of sentences,
    Throttle° their practised accent in their fears,
    And in conclusion dumbly have broke off,
    Not paying me a welcome. Trust me, sweet,
    Out of this silence yet I picked a welcome: 1(
    And in the modesty of fearful duty°
    I read as much as from the rattling tongue
    Of saucy and audacious eloquence.
    Love, therefore, and tongue-tied simplicity,
    In° least, speak most, to my capacity.°   1(

[*Enter PHILOSTRATE.*]

PHILOSTRATE.   So please your grace, the Prologue is addressed.°
THESEUS.   Let him approach.

---

74 *unbreathed:* unpracticed, unexercised.   75 *against:* in preparation for.   80 *stretched and conned:* strained and memorized.   83 *tender:* offer.   85 *wretchedness o'ercharged:* poor fellows taxing themselves too much.   88 *in this kind:* of this sort.   91–92 *noble . . . merit:* a noble nature considers the sincerity of effort rather than the skill of execution.   93 *clerks:* scholars.   97 *Throttle:* choke on.   101 *fearful duty:* subjects whose devotions gave them stage fright.   105 *In:* i.e., saying.   *capacity:* way of thinking.   106 *addressed:* ready.

Flourish trumpets. Enter the PROLOGUE [QUINCE].

PROLOGUE.   If we offend, it is with our good will,
      That you should think, we come not to offend,
    But with good will. To show our simple skill,   110
      That is the true beginning of our end.
    Consider then, we come but in despite.°
      We do not come, as minding to content you,
    Our true intent is. All for your delight,
      We are not here. That you should here repent you,   115
    The actors are at hand: and by their show,
      You shall know all, that you are like to know.°
THESEUS.   This fellow doth not stand upon points.°
LYSANDER.   He hath rid his prologue like a rough colt: he knows
    not the stop.° A good moral my lord: it is not enough   120
    to speak; but to speak true.
HIPPOLYTA.   Indeed he hath played on his prologue like a child on a
    recorder:° a sound, but not in government.°
THESUS.   His speech was like a tangled chain: nothing impaired, but
    all disordered. Who is next?   125

Enter PYRAMUS and THISBY, WALL, MOONSHINE, and LION.

PROLOGUE.   Gentles, perchance you wonder at this show,
      But wonder on, till truth make all things plain.
    This man is Pyramus, if you would know:
      This beauteous lady, Thisby is certain.
    This man, with lime and rough-cast,° doth present   130
      Wall, that vile wall which did these lovers sunder:
    And through Wall's chink, poor souls, they are content
      To whisper. At the which, let no man wonder.
    This man, with lantern, dog, and bush of thorn,
      Presenteth Moonshine. For if you will know,   135
    By moonshine did these lovers think no scorn
      To meet at Ninus' tomb, there, there to woo:
    This grisly beast (which Lion hight° by name)
    The trusty Thisby, coming first by night,
    Did scare away, or rather did affright: 140
    And as she fled, her mantle she did fall:°
      Which Lion vile with bloody mouth did stain.
    Anon comes Pyramus, sweet youth and tall,°
      And finds his trusty Thisby's mantle slain:
    Whereat, with blade, with bloody blameful blade,   145
      He bravely broached° his boiling bloody breast.

108–117 *If . . . know:* (Quince's blunders in punctuation exactly reverse the meaning).
112 *despite:* malice.   181 *stand upon points:* (1) pay attention to punctuation (2) bother about
the niceties (of expression).   120 *stop:* (1) halt (2) period.   123 *recorder:* flutelike wind
instrument.   *in government:* well managed.   130 *rough-cast:* rough plaster made of lime and
gravel.   138 *hight:* is called.   141 *fall:* let fall.   143 *tall:* brave.   146 *broached:* opened
(Shakespeare parodies the overuse of alliteration in the earlier bombastic Elizabethan plays).

And Thisby, tarrying in mulberry shade,
  His dagger drew, and died. For all the rest,
Let Lion, Moonshine, Wall, and lovers twain.
At large° discourse, while here they do remain.   150
THESEUS.   I wonder if the lion be to speak.
DEMETRIUS.   No wonder, my lord: one lion may, when many asses do.

*Exeunt [*PROLOGUE, PYRAMUS,*] LION, THISBY, MOONSHINE.*

WALL.   In this same interlude° it doth befall
  That I, one Snout by name, present a wall:
  And such a wall, as I would have you think,   155
  That had in it a crannied hole or chink:
  Through which the lovers, Pyramus and Thisby,
  Did whisper often, very secretly.
  This loam, this rough-cast, and this stone doth show
  That I am that same wall: the truth is so.   160
  And this the cranny is, right and sinister,°
  Through which the fearful lovers are to whisper.
THESEUS.   Would you desire lime and hair to speak better?
DEMETRIUS.   It is the wittiest° partition° that ever I heard discourse,
  my lord.   165

Enter PYRAMUS.

THESEUS.   Pyramus draws near the wall: silence.
PYRAMUS.   O grim-looked night, O night with hue so black,
    O night, which ever art when day is not:
  O night, O night, alack, alack, alack,
    I fear my Thisby's promise is forgot.   170
  And thou O wall, O sweet, O lovely wall,
    That stand'st between her father's ground and mine,
  Thou wall, O wall, O sweet and lovely wall,
    Show me thy chink, to blink through with mine eyne.°

                                    [*WALL holds up his fingers.*]

  Thanks, courteous wall. Jove shield thee well for this.   175
    But what see I? No Thisby do I see.
  O wicked wall, through whom I see no bliss,
    Cursed by thy stones for thus deceiving me.
THESEUS.   The wall methinks being sensible,° should curse again.°
PYRAMUS.   No in truth sir, he should not. "Deceiving me" is   180
  Thisby's cue: she is to enter now, and I am to spy her
  through the wall. You shall see it will fall pat° as I told you:
  yonder she comes.

Enter THISBY.

---

150 *At large:* in full.   153 *interlude:* short play.   161 *right and sinister:* from right to left (he
probably uses the fingers of his right and left hands to form the cranny).   164 *wittiest:* most
intelligent.   *partition:* (1) wall (2) section of a learned book or speech.   174 *eyne:* eyes.
179 *sensible:* capable of feelings and perception.   *again:* back.   182 *pat:* exactly.

THISBY.   O wall, full often hast thou heard my moans,
        For parting my fair Pyramus and me.   185
        My cherry lips have often kissed thy stones;
        Thy stones with lime and hair knit up in thee.
PYRAMUS.   I see a voice: now will I to the chink,
        To spy and I can hear my Thisby's face.
        Thisby?   190
THISBY.   My love thou art, my love I think.
PYRAMUS.   Think what thou wilt, I am thy lover's grace:
        And, like Limander,° am I trusty still.
THISBY.   And I like Helen,° till the Fates me kill.
PYRAMUS.   Not Shafalus to Procrus,° was so true.   195
THISBY.   As Shafalus to Procrus, I to you.
PYRAMUS.   O kiss me through the hole of this vile wall.
THISBY.   I kiss the wall's hole, not your lips at all.
PYRAMUS.   Wilt thou at Ninny's° tomb meet me straightway?
THISBY.   Tide° life, tide death, I come without delay.   200

                          [*Exeunt* PYRAMUS *and* THISBY.]

WALL.   Thus have I, Wall, my part dischargèd so;
        And being done, thus Wall away doth go.   *Exit.*
THESEUS.   Now is the mural° down between the two neighbours.
DEMETRIUS.   No remedy my lord, when walls are so wilful to hear
        without warning.°   205
HIPPOLYTA.   This is the silliest stuff that ever I heard.
THESEUS.   The best in this kind are but shadows:° and the worst are
        no worse, if imagination amend them.
HIPPOLYTA.   It must be your imagination then, and not theirs.
THESEUS.   If we imagine no worse of them than they of themselves,   210
        they may pass for excellent men. Here come two noble
        beasts in, a man and a lion.

Enter LION *and* MOONSHINE.

LION.   You ladies, you, whose gentle hearts do fear
        The smallest monstrous mouse that creeps on floor,
        May now perchance both quake and tremble here.   215
        When lion rough in wildest rage doth roar.
        Then know that I, as Snug the joiner am
        A lion fell,° nor else no lion's dam:°
        For if I should as lion come in strife
        Into this place, 'twere pity on my life.   220
THESEUS.   A very gentle beast, and of a good conscience.
DEMETRIUS.   The very best at a beast,° my lord, that e'er I saw.

---

193 *Limander:* (he means "Leander").   194 *Helen:* (he means "Hero").   195 *Shafalus to Procrus:* (he means "Cephalus" and "Procis" [see Act III, scene 2, 389 n.]).   199 *Ninny:* fool (he means "Ninus").   200 *Tide:* come, betide.   203 *mural:* wall.   205 *without warning:* either (a) without warning the parents or (b) unexpectedly.   207 *in . . . shadows:* of this sort are only plays (or only actors).   218 *fell:* fierce.   *nor . . . dam:* and not a lioness. 222 *best, beast:* (pronounced similarly).

LYSANDER.   This lion is a very fox for his valour.

THESEUS.   True: and a goose for his discretion.

DEMETRIUS.   Not so my lord: for his valour cannot carry his discretion, and the fox carries the goose.   22

THESEUS.   His discretion, I am sure, cannot carry his valour: for the goose carries not the fox. It is well: leave it to his discretion, and let us listen to the moon.

MOONSHINE.   This lanthorn° doth the hornèd moon present—   23

DEMETRIUS.   He should have worn the horns on his head.°

THESEUS.   He is no crescent, and his horns are invisible within the circumference.

MOONSHINE.   This lanthorn doth the hornèd moon present, Myself, the man i' th' moon do seem to be.   23

THESEUS.   This is the greatest error of all the rest; the man should be put into the lanthorn. How is it else the man i' th' moon?

DEMETRIUS.   He dares not come there for the candle; for you see, it is already in snuff.°   24

HIPPOLYTA.   I am aweary of this moon. Would he would change.

THESEUS.   It appears, by his small light of discretion, that he is in the wane: but yet in courtesy, in all reason, we must stay° the time.

LYSANDER.   Proceed, Moon.   24

MOONSHINE.   All that I have to say, is to tell you that the lanthorn is the moon, I the man i' th' moon, this thornbush my thornbush, and this dog my dog.

DEMETRIUS.   Why, all these should be in the lanthorn: for all these are in the moon. But silence: here comes Thisby.   25

Enter THISBY.

THISBY.   This is old Ninny's tomb. Where is my love?

LION.   Oh!   *The LION roars. THISBY runs off.*

DEMETRIUS.   Well roared, Lion.

THESEUS.   Well run, Thisby.

HIPPOLYTA.   Well shone, Moon. Truly, the moon shines with a good grace.   25

[*The LION shakes THISBY's mantle.*]

THESEUS.   Well moused,° Lion.

DEMETRIUS.   And then came Pyramus.

Enter PYRAMUS. [Exit LION.]

LYSANDER.   And so the lion vanished.

PYRAMUS.   Sweet moon, I thank thee for thy sunny beams,   26

---

230 *lanthorn:* lantern (once made of horn).   230–231 *hornèd . . . head:* (referring to the cuckold or deceived husband, who supposedly grew horns).   240 *in snuff:* (1) in need of snuffing (having a long, burnt-out wick or snuff) (2) in a temper.   243 *stay:* await.
257 *moused:* shaken, as a cat shakes a mouse.

I thank thee, moon, for shining now so bright.
For by thy gracious, golden, glittering gleams,
    I trust to take of truest Thisby sight.
        But stay: O spite!
        But mark, poor knight,   265
        What dreadful dole° is here?
            Eyes, do you see!
            How can it be!
        O dainty duck, O dear!
            Thy mantle good,   270
            What, stained with blood?
        Approach, ye Furies° fell:
            O Fates!° come, come:
            Cut thread and thrum.°
        Quail,° crush, conclude, and quell.°   275

THESEUS.   This passion, and the death of a dear friend, would go
    near to make a man look sad.
HIPPOLYTA.   Beshrew° my heart, but I pity the man.
PYRAMUS.   O wherefore Nature, didst thou lions frame?
        Since lion vile hath here deflowered my dear.   280
    Which is—no, no—which was the fairest dame
        That lived, that loved, that liked, that looked with cheer.
        Come tears, confound:
        Out sword, and wound
        The pap° of Pyramus: 285
            Ay, that left pap,
            Where heart doth hop.   [*Stabs himself.*]
        Thus die, I, thus, thus, thus.
            Now am I dead,
            Now am I fled,   290
        My soul is in the sky.
            Tongue lose thy light,
            Moon° take thy flight,   [*Exit MOONSHINE.*]
            Now die, die, die, die, die.   [*Dies.*]
DEMETRIUS.   No die,° but an ace° for him. For he is but one.   295
LYSANDER.   Less than an ace, man. For he is dead, he is nothing.
THESEUS.   With the help of a surgeon, he might yet recover, and
    prove an ass.
HIPPOLYTA.   How chance Moonshine is gone before Thisby comes
    back and finds her lover?   300

Enter THISBY.

THESEUS.   She will find him by starlight. Here she comes, and her
    passion ends the play.

266 *dole:* grief.   272 *Furies:* classical spirits of the underworld who avenged murder.
273 *Fates:* three sisters who spun the thread of human destiny, which at will was cut with a shears.
274 *thrum:* fringelike end of the warp in weaving.   275 *Quail:* subdue.   *quell:* kill.
278 *Beshrew:* curse (meant lightly).   285 *pap:* breast.   292–293 *Tongue . . . Moon:* (he
reverses the two subjects).   295 *die:* (singular of "dice").   *ace:* a throw of one at dice.

HIPPOLYTA.   Methinks she should not use a long one for such a
    Pyramus: I hope she will be brief.

DEMETRIUS.   A mote will turn the balance, which Pyramus, which   30
    Thisby, is the better: he for a man, God warr'nt° us;
    she for a woman, God bless us.

LYSANDER.   She hath spied him already with those sweet eyes.

DEMETRIUS.   And thus she means,° videlicet°—

THISBY.   Asleep my love?   31
                What, dead, my dove?
            O Pyramus, arise,
                Speak, speak. Quite dumb?
                Dead, dead? A tomb
            Must cover thy sweet eyes.   31
                These lily lips,
                This cherry nose,
            These yellow cowslip° cheeks,
                Are gone, are gone:
                Lovers, make moan: 32
            His eyes were green as leeks.
                O Sisters Three,°
                Come, come to me,
            With hands as pale as milk,
                Lay them in gore,   32
                Since you have shore
            With shears his thread of silk.
                Tongue, not a word:
                Come trusty sword,
            Come blade, my breast imbrue   [*Stabs herself.*]   33
                And farewell friends:
                Thus Thisby ends:
            Adieu, adieu, adieu.   [*Dies.*]

THESEUS.   Moonshine and Lion are left to bury the dead.

DEMETRIUS.   Ay, and Wall too.   33

BOTTOM.   [*Starts up*] No, I assure you, the wall is down that parted
    their fathers. Will it please you to see the Epilogue, or
    to hear a Bergomask° dance between two of our company?

THESEUS.   No epilogue, I pray you; for your play needs no excuse.
    Never excuse: for when the players are all dead, there   34
    need none to be blamed. Marry, if he that writ it had
    played Pyramus and hanged himself in Thisby's garter,
    it would have been a fine tragedy: and so it is truly, and
    very notably discharged. But come, your Bergomask:
    let your Epilogue alone.   [*A dance.*]   34
    The iron tongue° of midnight hath told° twelve.

---

306 *warr'nt:* warrant, protect.   309 *means:* laments.   *videlicet:* namely.   318 *cowslip:* yellow
primrose.   322 *Sisters Three:* the Fates.   330 *imbrue:* stain with gore.   338 *Bergomask:*
exaggerated country dance.   346 *iron tongue:* i.e., of the bell.   *told:* counted, tolled.

Lovers, to bed, 'tis almost fairy time.°
I fear we shall outsleep the coming morn,
As much as we this night have overwatched.
This palpable gross° play hath well beguiled   350
The heavy gait of night. Sweet friends, to bed.
A fortnight hold we this solemnity,
In nightly revels, and new jollity.   *Exeunt.*

Enter PUCK [*with a broom*].

PUCK.   Now the hungry lion roars,
            And the wolf behowls the moon;   355
        Whilst the heavy° ploughman snores,
            All with weary task fordone.°
        Now the wasted brands° do glow,
        Whilst the screech-owl, screeching loud,
            Puts the wretch that lies in woe°   360
        In remembrance of a shroud.
            Now it is the time of night,
        That the graves, all gaping wide,
            Every one lets forth his sprite,°
        In the church-way paths to glide.   365
            And we fairies, that do run
        By the triple Hecate's° team,°
            From the presence of the sun,
        Following darkness like a dream,
            Now are frolic:° not a mouse   370
        Shall disturb this hallowed house.
        I am sent with broom before,
            To sweep the dust° behind° the door.

Enter KING *and* QUEEN OF FAIRIES, *with all their train.*

OBERON.   Through the house give glimmering light,
            By the dead and drowsy fire,   375
        Every elf and fairy sprite,
            Hop as light as bird from brier,
        And this ditty after me,
            Sing, and dance it trippingly.
TITANIA.   First rehearse your song by rote,   380
        To each word a warbling note.
        Hand in hand, with fairy grace,
        Will we sing and bless this place.   [*Song and dance.*]
OBERON.   Now, until the break of day,
        Through this house each fairy stray.   385

---

347 *fairy time*: (from midnight to daybreak).   350 *palpable gross*: obvious and crude.
356 *heavy*: sleepy.   357 *fordone*: worn out, "done in."   358 *wasted brands*: burnt logs.
360 *wretch . . . woe*: sick person.   364 *sprite*: spirit, ghost.   367 *triple Hecate*: the moon
goddess, identified as Cynthia in heaven, Diana on earth, and Hecate in hell.   *team*: dragons
that pull the chariot of the night moon.   370 *frolic*: frolicsome.   373 *To sweep the dust*: (Puck
often helped with household chores).   *behind*: from behind.

To the best bride-bed will we,
Which by us shall blessèd be:
And the issue° there create,°
Ever shall be fortunate:
So shall all the couples three   3•
Ever true in loving be:
And the blots of Nature's hand°
Shall not in their issue° stand.
Never mole, harelip, nor scar,
Nor mark prodigious,° such as are   3•
Despisèd in nativity,
Shall upon their children be.
With this field-dew consecrate.
Every fairy take his gait,°
And each several° chamber bless,   4(
Through this palace, with sweet peace;
And the owner of its blest,
Ever shall in safety rest.
Trip away: make no stay: *Exeunt [all but* PUCK].
Meet me all by break of day.   4•
PUCK.   If we shadows have offended,
Think but this, and all is mended,
That you have but slumbered here,
While these visions did appear.
And this weak and idle° theme,   41
No more yielding but° a dream,
Gentles, do not reprehend.
If you pardon, we will mend.°
And as I am an honest Puck,
If we have unearnèd luck,   41
Now to scape the serpent's tongue,°
We will make amends, ere long:
Else the Puck a liar call.
So, good night unto you all.
Give me your hands,° if we be friends;   42
And Robin shall restore amends.°   *[Exit.]*

388, 393 *issue*: children.   388 *create*: created.   392 *blots . . . hand*: birth defects.
395 *mark prodigious*: unnatural birthmark.   399 *take his gait*: proceed.   400 *several*: separate.
410 *idle*: foolish.   411 *No . . . but*: yielding nothing more than.   413|*mend*: improve.
416 *serpent's tongue*: hissing of the audience.   420 *hands*: applause.   421 *restore amends*: do
better in the future.

QUESTIONS

Act I

1. Describe the relationship between Theseus and Hippolyta. What does each of
   them represent? How does Shakespeare show us that they have different attitudes toward their marriage?

2. Characterize Hermia and Lysander. What blocks their relationship? How do they plan to circumvent these obstructions?

3. What are Helena's feelings about herself? About Hermia? About Demetrius? How might you account for her self-image?

4. Why have the mechanicals gathered at Quince's house? How does Shakespeare show us that Bottom is eager, ill-educated, energetic, and funny?

Act II

5. What is Puck's job? What do you find out about his personality, habits, and pastimes in his first conversation?

6. Why are Titania and Oberon fighting with each other, and what are the specific consequences of their conflict?

7. What does Oberon plan to do to Titania? Why? What is "love-in-idleness"? What power does it have? What does it symbolize?

8. Why are Demetrius and Helena in the woods? What does Oberon decide to do to them? What error occurs? What happens to Lysander when Helena awakens him?

Act III

9. How and why does Puck change Bottom? How is this transformation appropriate? What happens when Bottom awakens Titania? Why?

10. What does Oberon decide to do when he realizes that Puck has made a mistake? What is Puck's attitude toward the confusion he has created?

11. What happens when Helena awakens Demetrius? How does this situation reverse the one that began the play? Explain Helena's reaction to the behavior of Demetrius and Lysander.

12. What real dangers (tragic potential) do the lovers face in Act III? How do Oberon and Puck deal with these dangers? What is their plan? How successful is it?

Act IV

13. Why does Oberon cure Titania of her infatuation with Bottom? How does the relationship between Oberon and Titania change? How is this change symbolized? Why is it significant?

14. How are the relationships among the four lovers straightened out? How does each explain his or her feelings? What does Theseus decide about the couples? Why is this significant?

15. What momentous event occurs offstage and is briefly reported in Act IV, scene 2?

Act V

16. Describe Pyramus and Thisby. What blocks their relationship? How do they plan to circumvent these obstructions? What happens to them?

17. What is the significance of the fairy masque (a combination of poetry, music, dance, and drama) that ends the play?

18. What does Puck's epilogue suggest about you as a reader or spectator? How does it reinforce the connections among dreaming, imagination, illusion, and drama?

GENERAL QUESTIONS

1. To what extent are the characters in this play conventional and representative types? What is the effect of Shakespeare's style of characterization?

2. Are any of the characters symbolic? If so, what do they symbolize? How does such symbolism reinforce the themes of the play?

3. How does Shakespeare employ language, imagery, and poetic form to define the characters in this play and differentiate among the various groups of characters?

4. To what extent do the two settings—city and woods—structure the play? Where does exposition occur? Complication and catastrophe? The comic resolution? How complete is the resolution? Why is the round-trip journey from one setting to the other necessary for the lovers? The rulers? The "hempen homespuns"?

5. What are the similarities or parallels in plot and theme between *A Midsummer Night's Dream* and "Pyramus and Thisby"? To what degree are they versions of the same play with different endings? Why do you think Shakespeare included the play-within-the-play in *A Midsummer Night's Dream*?

6. In the first soliloquy of the play, Helena discusses love. What kind of love is she talking about? What are its qualities and characteristics? How far do the relationships in the play bear out her ideas about love?

7. How well do the mechanicals understand the nature of dramatic illusion? What sorts of production problems concern them? How do they solve these?

8. What ideas about drama and the ways in which audiences respond to it does *A Midsummer Night's Dream* explore?

9. Compare the play-within-a-play in *A Midsummer Night's Dream* to the one in Act III of *Hamlet.* How are the internal plays and situations similar? Different? What parallels do you see in the connections between each play-within-a-play and the larger play in which each occurs?

THE THEATER OF MOLIÈRE

The seventeenth century was the golden age of French neoclassical theater (called *neo* or *new* because it marked the reintroduction of Greek and Latin models). The dominant political figure of the age was the "Sun King," Louis XIV, the absolute monarch of France. He and his court—a set of nobles, wits, would-be wits, and ladies- and gentlemen-in-waiting—dictated fashion to the world at large and made Paris the cultural center of Europe.

This ruling class profoundly determined the drama of the age because they were the theater's patrons and protectors. Writers of tragedy, the two most important of whom were Pierre Corneille (1606–1684) and Jean Racine (1639–1699), complimented the understanding and sympathy of the nobility by creating serious poetic dramas for them. More daring and risky was the role of the writers of comedy, who populated the stage with characters derived not so much from the nobility as from the middle classes, often mocking their appearance, customs, and tastes.

The most important of the comic writers, the acknowledged master of comedy, was Molière, the pen name of Jean Baptiste Poquelin. Born in 1622, he received a Jesuit education and took up the study of law at Orléans. His favorite reading, however, was not law, but rather the six surviving comedies of the Roman dramatist Terence.[4] In 1643 he shocked his family by abandoning both the law and his father's prosperous upholstering business and going into the theater, a career that was considered scandalous and sinful. He joined a company of actors called *The Illustrious Theater*, who established themselves in a playhouse, produced a tragedy, and then went bankrupt.

The acting company spent the next thirteen years touring the provinces of France, performing *commedia dell'arte* farces and short comic plays, many of them by Molière. These years gave him his real education in the theater. He soon developed into a superb actor, director, and, more important, writer.

Although the years in the provinces were not easy, the company was achieving recognition. The group returned to Paris in 1658 upon the invitation of King Louis XIV. The king was pleased with Molière's comedies and publicly provided support and protection. He also gave the company the authorization to use the *Théâtre de Petit Bourbon* at Versailles. In 1659, when the *Théâtre* was torn down, Louis provided a royal patent to use the *Palais Royale* in Paris. With the king's support, Molière spent the rest of his career at this theater as an actor, director, manager, and playwright.

Molière's personal life was a great deal more troubled than his professional life. At the age of forty he began an unhappy marriage with Armande Béjart, the twenty-year-old daughter (or sister) of his former mistress Madeleine Béjart (his enemies whispered that Armande was also *his* daughter). He endured constant ill health, but he was a fighter. He performed even on the day he died, collapsing on stage in 1773 when acting the lead role in his *The Imaginary Invalid*, and dying several hours later. Because of his sudden death he was not given last rites, and was denied burial in consecrated ground.

Despite the adversities of his life, his creative output was great. He wrote twenty-nine plays, ranging from broad farce to satirical comedies of manners. He observed the theatrical conventions of his age, and drew his plots from Roman comedy, Italian *commedia dell'arte*, and French farce, all of which schooled him in comic character, tempo, and situation. His inspirations were the manners, morals, and customs of the French gentry and middle class.

He was also innovative as a dramatist. He elevated comedy to the seri-

---

[4] See pp. 1318–19 for a discussion of the Roman dramatists.

Molière in the character of Sganarelle

ousness of tragedy, as in his satiric comedies *The Ridiculous Dilettantes* (*Les Pré-cieuses Ridicules*, 1659), *The Misanthrope* (1666), *The Miser* (1668), and *Tartuffe* (1669). What is new in these serious comedies is Molière's thoughtful and de-tached perspective on vices and follies. His mainspring is character, and mod-eration in all forms of behavior is his norm. From this point of balance, his plots mock and expose religious posturing, personal greed, social snobbery, and professional hypocrisy. In short, whatever is excessive is the subject of his satiric thrusts.

The *Théâtre Royale*, the Paris theater in which most of Molière's plays were produced, was patterned on Italian theater design of the early seven-teenth century—a design which by and large has dominated theater archi-tecture right up to our own day. The building was rectangular, with a prosce-nium stage at one end and seating in the approximate shape of a horseshoe—orchestra and balcony—for as many as 600 spectators at the other end and both sides. Also at the sides were galleries or private boxes. There may have been space in front of the stage for special dances and ballets. A major innovation in design was the use of footlights and large chandeliers, which were essential for indoor performances. Either candles or oil lamps provided the light, and there was a constant need for attentive stagehands and candle snuffers to forestall accidental fires.

The stage scenery could be lavish, but for economy much of it was probably used in the productions of many separate plays. Molière apparently favored sparse sets and only minimal stage properties. The actors and actresses (women were never excluded from the French stage) wore contemporary costumes. This convention made Molière's satires all the more effective. Since his performers were costumed like the social types being pictured and mocked, the comedies became images of the social scenes inhabited by his audiences.

MOLIÈRE, *LOVE IS THE DOCTOR (L'AMOUR MÉDECIN)*

Love Is the Doctor (*L'Amour Médecin*) was first performed in 1665 at the palace of Louis XIV at Versailles, where the king himself sometimes joined Molière's casts to indulge his own acting fantasies and to win applause from his courtiers. The play is typical of Molière's comic farces, relying heavily on pantomime, dance, and music in the *commedia dell'arte* tradition. The incidental music by Jean Baptiste Lully (1632–1687), who provided music for many other Molière plays, has survived and is available on records.

The central character in *Love Is the Doctor*, Sganarelle, appears with the same name in other Molière comedies, also as in the tradition of the *commedia dell'arte*. Usually Sganarelle tries to beat others, but as often as not he is beaten himself, and therefore he is both the cause and the butt of laughter. His function in *Love Is the Doctor* is typical: He is a wealthy businessman and a traditional *pater familias*, with the final word in family matters (like Egeus in *A Midsummer Night's Dream* and Polonius in *Hamlet*). He closely guards his daughter, Lucinda, from suitors to avoid having to pay a massive dowry to a son-in-law who, as he says, might be a perfect stranger.

The plan by Lucinda and her suitor Clitander to marry despite Sganarelle's opposition is an example of the traditional intrigue plot, in which the father (or guardian), acting as blocking agent, chooses another man for the young woman, or, as in *Love Is the Doctor*, tries to prevent marriage entirely.[5] The *soubrette* in the play, who aids and abets the intrigue, is Lisette. Although in some intrigue plots the blocker is reconciled by the fact that the young man is independently rich, that does not happen in this play, for at the end Sganarelle is frustrated and outraged despite the surrounding merriment.

Molière's notable addition to the intrigue plot in *Love Is the Doctor* is his satiric treatment of doctors. Medical practice in the seventeenth century was

---

[5] The origin and nature of intrigue plots are more fully described on pp. 1318 and 1322.

based on the widely held theory that a healthy body contained a harmonious balance of the four bodily fluids or "humors"—blood, yellow bile, black bile, and phlegm. When one of the humors became excessive or "putrid," the imbalance made the patient sick. Illness, including mental illness, could also be caused by the *adust*, or burning, of a particular humor during a high fever. (The understanding of bacterial and viral causes of disease did not develop until two centuries after Molière.) When doctors made a diagnosis based on this system, their treatment was to purge the offending humor and its noxious pressures (as the doctors recommend for Lucinda many times in *Love Is the Doctor*). Depending on the humor, they employed one of four methods of purgation: (1) a lancing or "bleeding," to draw off blood, or "sanguine" (the most common purgation, but the patient, weakened by blood loss, would often die more speedily from the original disease); (2) an emetic, to eliminate yellow bile, or "choler," through vomiting; (3) a laxative, to purge black bile, or "melancholy"; and (4) various irritating (and sometimes poisonous) powders, to eliminate "phlegm" through violent sneezing.

With such principles and treatments, doctors were open targets for satire, and *Love Is the Doctor* holds nothing back. Once Lisette reports Lucinda's illness, the play is invaded by Molière's cadre of funny physicians, who, like their real-life counterparts, were bearded men who dressed in black robes and hats. Molière satirizes his doctors on the grounds of cronyism, indifference to the condition of patients, pompousness, exploitation of gullibility, ignorance and indecision, resistance to innovation, and simple greed.

Despite the severity of his satire, however, Molière also presents the doctors in a comic-farcical light. Both when they are summoned and then paid, for example, they perform dances and pantomimes. Even the blatant self-exposure of Dr. Fillpocket may be construed as the excess one expects of farce, and therefore honest medical practitioners in Molière's day could have claimed that the doctors in *Love Is the Doctor* represented the exception, not the rule.

Although my translation follows Molière's text faithfully, I have taken latitude in a few instances to emphasize his sharp comic intentions. For example, his introduction of the quack elixir "Orviétan" in Act II, scene 6 requires explanation, which I have included as part of the dramatic text in preference to creating an extensive footnote. Because the names of the doctors are not particularly meaningful, I have given them "tag names" that I hope will be readily appreciated by today's readers. Thus Drs. *Tomès, De Fonandrès, Macroton, Bahays,* and *Filerin* are, respectively, *Slicer, De Pits, Gouger, Golfer,* and *Fillpocket.* Generally, the medical recommendations of these doctors cannot be translated into modern terms. Readers will therefore need to rely on the brief description given here about medical practice in Molière's day. Alert readers may notice some anachronisms and inconsistencies, such as "pathological" and "psychosomatic"; these are not inadvertent, but are made in the hope that they are consistent with the comic spirit of Molière.

MOLIÈRE [JEAN BAPTISTE POQUELIN]   (1622–1673)

*Love Is the Doctor*_____ *(1665) 1666*

Translated by Edgar V. Roberts

CHARACTERS

Sganarelle, *a wealthy Parisian merchant, father of* Lucinda
Aminta, *his neighbor*
Lucretia, *his niece*
Mr. Williams, *his friend, a seller of tapestries*
Mr. Josse, *another friend, a jeweller*
Lucinda, *daughter of* Sganarelle, *in love with* Clitander
Lisette, *maid to* Lucinda, *a soubrette*
Champagne, *an assistant to* Sganarelle, *a dancer*
Dr. Slicer [Tomès]
Dr. De Pits [De Fonandrès]
Dr. Gouger [Macroton]   } *doctors*
Dr. Golfer [Bahays]
Dr. Fillpocket [Filerin]
Clitander, *in love with Lucinda*
A Justice
A Mountebank, *a quack, seller of the cure-all "Orviétan"*
Buffoons and Scaramouches, *assistants to the Mountebank*
The Spirit of Comedy
Musicians
Singers
Dancers
Servants, etc.

The action takes place in Paris, in the house and drawing room of SGANARELLE *[and also on a street in Paris].*

ACT I

Scene 1

Enter SGANARELLE, AMINTA, LUCRETIA, MR. WILLIAMS, *and* MR. JOSSE.

SGANARELLE.   Life is strange. I agree with that great classical philosopher who said that those who have wealth also have woe,° and that misery breeds more misery. I've been married only once, and my wife is now dead.

MR. WILLIAMS.   How many wives would you have liked?

SGANARELLE.   Don't mock, Mr. Williams; my loss is great, and I'm still sad when I think about her. I never liked her lifestyle, and we argued a great deal, but Death, as they say, settles everything. She's dead and I'm sorry, but if she were alive we would

---

1 *woe:* Ecclesiastes 2:9–11

still be fighting. Of all the children that Heaven blessed us with, only my daughter has survived, but she is my greatest sorrow because she is sad beyond belief—in a deep depression I can't get her out of. Beyond that, she won't tell me what's wrong. I'm almost beside myself, and I need your good advice. You [*to* LUCRETIA] are my niece. You [*to* AMINTA] are my neighbor. You [*to* MR. WILLIAMS *and* MR. JOSSE] are my friends and equals. What should I do?

MR. JOSSE.   I believe that jewelry is what young women like best, and if I were you I would buy her some nice necklaces, brooches, or rings set with expensive diamonds, rubies, and emeralds.

MR. WILLIAMS.   If I were in your position, I'd get her an elegant tapestry showing a landscape or historical scene. The sight of something like that in her room would pick up both her vision and her spirits.

AMINTA.   If you ask me, I wouldn't do anything of the sort. Rather, I'd get her married off as soon as possible—maybe to the man who, they say, asked you for her hand some time ago.

LUCRETIA.   I don't agree. She's not ready for marriage, and she's not strong enough to bear children. For her, having babies would be a quick way to go six feet under. She's too good for this world, and I think you should send her off to a convent, where she'll be able to do things to suit her special personality.

SGANARELLE.   I appreciate your thoughts, but they seem more to your interests than mine. You are a jeweler, Mr. Josse, and your advice would probably make you a handsome profit. You, Mr. Williams, have a tapestry shop, and I think you're trying to get rid of a little excess inventory. I've heard that your boyfriend, neighbor Aminta, is carrying a torch for my daughter, and you'd therefore like to have her married off and out of circulation. And as for you, my dear niece, you know that I have no plans to consent to a marriage for my daughter—I've got my reasons—but your advice to send her to religious orders suggests that you wouldn't mind becoming the only heir to all my money. So, ladies and gentlemen, your advice is perhaps the best in the world, but, if you please, I want none of it. Please go.

[*They leave, grumbling to themselves.* SGANARELLE *then speaks sarcastically to the audience.*]

There you have modern, up-to-date friends, who give their impersonal advice with no hope of gain whatever.

Act I, Scene 2

He remains. Enter LUCINDA.

SGANARELLE.   [Aside.] That's my daughter taking a walk for exercise. She doesn't see me; she's sighing. Now she's raising her eyes to Heaven. [*To* LUCINDA.] Bless you, Lucinda. What's the matter? Why so sad and sorrowful? Why don't you tell me what's wrong? You can trust your dear old dad, so tell me what's on your mind. Don't worry. Give me a kiss, like a good little girl. [*Aside.*] I can't stand seeing her like this. [*To* LUCINDA.] Do you want me to die with unhappiness because of you? Won't you tell me what's troubling you? Tell me what's wrong and I'll do anything for you, I promise. Just tell me what's making you sad, because I swear on a stack of Bibles that there's nothing I won't do to make you happy. Tell me what you want. Are you jealous of any friends because they seem better dressed? I'll get you clothes that will make theirs seem like rags.—No? Does your room seem bare? I'll let you pick out the best furniture to be found anywhere.—No again? Well, maybe you want to learn music; I'll get you the best piano teacher there is.—Not that either? Maybe you're in love, and would like to be married. [*LUCINDA nods her head in agreement.*]

Act I, Scene 3

They remain. Enter LISETTE.

LISETTE. Sir, you've just been chatting with your daughter. Did she tell you what's wrong?

SGANARELLE. No, she's being bitchy and it's making me mad.

LISETTE. Let me try; I'll sound her out a little.

SGANARELLE. It won't work. Since she's so stubborn, let her alone.

LISETTE. Just let me try. She may be more open with me than you. [*To LU-   5
CINDA. During LISETTE'S speech, which SGANARELLE also overhears, he gets increasingly irritated with his daughter.*] Now, Madam, let us know what's wrong; don't keep on like this and upset everybody. It seems to me that something really mysterious is bothering you, and if you won't tell your father, maybe you'll tell me. Do you want anything from him? You know that he'll spare no expense for you. Do you want him to give you more freedom? More promenades in the park? More presents to tempt your fancy?—No? Maybe you're angry with someone, then.—No? Well then, maybe you have a secret wish to get married, and you'd like your father's consent. [*LUCINDA nods enthusiastically.*]—Ah, that's it; why all the secrecy? Sir, the mystery is solved, and—

SGANARELLE. [*Interrupting her.*] Get away, you ingrate; I won't talk to you any more. Be as stubborn as you like.

LUCINDA. Father, since you want me to tell you—

SGANARELLE. No, I'm finished with you.

LISETTE. Sir, her sadness—

SGANARELLE. She's a hussy, and enjoys hurting me.   10

LUCINDA. Father, I want—

SGANARELLE. Is this the gratitude I get for bringing you up so well?

LISETTE. But, sir—

SGANARELLE. No, I'm so mad I may have a stroke.

LUCINDA. But, Father—   15

SGANARELLE. I no longer have a speck of kindness for you.

LISETTE. But—

SGANARELLE. She's a cheap wench.

LISETTE. But—

SGANARELLE. An ungrateful slut.   20

LISETTE. But—

SGANARELLE. A trollop, who won't tell me what's wrong with her.

LISETTE. It's a husband that she wants!

SGANARELLE. [*Hearing but deliberately ignoring this piece of information.*] I'll turn her out of my house.

LISETTE. A husband!   25

SGANARELLE. I detest her.

LISETTE. [*shouting increasingly more loudly.*] A husband!

SGANARELLE. And I disown her as my daughter.

LISETTE. A husband!

SGANARELLE. No, don't talk to me about it.   30

LISETTE. A husband!

SGANARELLE. Don't talk to me about it.
LISETTE. A husband!
SGANARELLE. Don't talk to me about it.
LISETTE. A husband, a husband, a husband!

[*SGANARELLE stalks off.*]

Act I, Scene 4

LISETTE and LUCINDA remain.

LISETTE. It's really true that none are so deaf as those who refuse to hear.

LUCINDA. [*ironically.*] Well, Lisette, you see how wrong I was to hide my feelings, and how all I had to do was to tell my father about everything I wanted.

LISETTE. My God, he's a hard man. I swear, I'd enjoy playing some kind of trick on him to show him up. But why, Madam, did you hide your wishes from me?

LUCINDA. Alas, what would I have gained? I might just as well have kept the secret for the rest of my life. Do you think I didn't foresee what he would do? I know his temper, and I'm in despair about the refusal he gave to the envoy sent to him to propose marriage to me. I've lost hope.

LISETTE. [*As though recalling a forgotten incident.*] What's this? It's that stranger—who arranged for the proposal, the one for whom you—

LUCINDA. Perhaps it's not right for me to speak so freely, but I confess, if I had the liberty to choose, he's the one I'd want. We've never spoken together; he's never been able to tell me he loves me. But, in all the places where he's seen me, his looks and gestures have indicated such tenderness, and his formal request for my hand has given me such a sense of his honor, that I can't help believing he loves me. No matter; you see how my father's reaction has hardened all this tenderness.

LISETTE. Well, I have to say, I think you shouldn't have kept things secret from me, but I'll still help you. You need to be certain of your determination—

LUCINDA. But what should I do against my father's authority?—And if he won't listen to my hopes—

LISETTE. Come on now, you can't let yourself be led around like a sheep. As long as you don't offend his honor, you can free yourself at least a little from him. What does he want with you? You're of age, and you're not made of stone. I say again I'll help you in this affair. Your interests are mine, and, you'll see, I know a thing or two—But I see your father; let's go in. Leave everything to me.

[*They hurry off.*]

Act I, Scene 5

Enter SGANARELLE.

SGANARELLE. [*Laughing to himself.*] It's sometimes good to seem not to hear things you hear only too well. I was smart to sidestep that declaration of her hopes that I do not mean to satisfy. Is there anything more tyrannical than that custom by which marriage arrangements make paupers out of fathers?—Anything more futile and ridiculous than to spend your life grubbing and grabbing to get rich, and raising a daughter with care and love, only to be robbed of both of them at the hands of a total stranger, a nobody? No, no, I don't give a damn for that custom, and I'll keep my wealth and my daughter to myself.

Act I, Scene 6

He remains. Enter LISETTE.

LISETTE.   [*Pretending not to see* SGANARELLE.]—Oh unhappiness! Oh disgrace! Oh, poor Mr. Sganarelle! Where can I find him?

SGANARELLE.   [*Aside.*] What's all this?

LISETTE.   Oh unhappy father, what will you do when you learn about this?

SGANARELLE.   [*Aside.*] What's going on?

LISETTE.   My poor mistress!   5

SGANARELLE.   [*Aside.*] I'm lost!

LISETTE.   —Oh!

SGANARELLE.   [*Running after* LISETTE.] Lisette!

LISETTE.   [*Pretending not to hear him, but making sure he hears her.*] What a misfortune!

SGANARELLE.   —Lisette!   10

LISETTE.   [*Still pretending.*] What bad luck!

SGANARELLE.   —Lisette!

LISETTE.   [*Pretending yet.*] How ghastly awful!

SGANARELLE.   —Lisette!

LISETTE.   [*Pretending just now to have noticed him.*] Ah, Sir.   15

SGANARELLE.   What's going on? What's wrong?

LISETTE.   Sir, your daughter—

SGANARELLE.   Oh, no!

LISETTE.   Sir, sir, don't cry like that. [*Aside.*] You'll make me laugh if you keep on.

SGANARELLE.   Tell me quickly.   20

LISETTE.   You daughter was hurt by your words and scared by your anger. [*Dramatizing and exaggerating her following descriptions to the utmost.*] She went to her room and, in despair, she opened the window facing the river—

SGANARELLE.   Oh, my God, no!

LISETTE.   Then, raising her head heavenward, she said, "No, it's impossible for me to live with the anger of my father, and since he is disowning me, I want to die!"

SGANARELLE.   She threw herself out?

LISETTE.   No sir. She sorrowfully closed the window, and threw herself on her   25
bed, where she wept bitterly. Suddenly, her face got pale, her eyes rolled in her head, her heart seemed to stop, and she fell into my arms!

SGANARELLE.   Oh, my poor daughter!

LISETTE.   By slapping her face and using smelling salts, I revived her. But she's getting worse, and I don't believe she can last the day.

SGANARELLE.   [*Calling to the offstage servant* CHAMPAGNE.] Champagne! Champagne! Champagne! [*Enter* CHAMPAGNE.] Quickly, go get the doctors, and as many as you can find! There can't be too many for this! Oh, my daughter, my poor daughter!

[*They leave quickly.*]

FIRST ENTR'ACTE

[CHAMPAGNE, *while dancing, knocks on the doors of four doctors, who begin dancing and then ceremoniously enter the house of the patient's father.*]

ACT II

Scene 1

Enter SGANARELLE and LISETTE.

LISETTE.   Why do you need four doctors, Sir? Just one alone is enough to kill you.

SGANARELLE.   Be quiet. Four opinions are better than one.

LISETTE.   Can't your daughter die by herself, without the help of these gentlemen?

SGANARELLE.   Do you mean to say that it's the doctor who causes death, and not the disease?

LISETTE.   Absolutely. I know a man who proved beyond doubt that we should never say, "This person died of a raging fever or a galloping consumption," but rather "That person was killed by the incompetence of two druggists and four doctors."

SGANARELLE.   Stop. You'll offend these gentlemen.

LISETTE.   Lord, Sir, our cat needed no drugs or treatment to recover from that jump she made from the rooftop to the street, and she didn't eat or move a muscle for three days. It's lucky for her there are no cat doctors, or they'd have wiped her out with their mindless purging and bleeding.

SGANARELLE.   Will you please keep your impertinent remarks to yourself? Here they are.

LISETTE.   Watch out. They'll tell you what you already know—that your daughter's sick. Only they'll bamboozle you by saying it in Latin!

Act II, Scene 2

Enter DR. SLICER, DR. GOUGER, DR. DE PITS, and DR. GOLFER.

SGANARELLE.   Welcome, gentlemen!

DR. SLICER.   [*Pompously.*] We have made our diagnosis of your daughter, and she unquestionably has many impurities in her.

SGANARELLE.   My daughter is impure?

DR. SLICER.   You must understand that it is her body that is full of impurities—many corrupt and putrid humors.°

SGANARELLE.   Oh, thank you, I understand.

DR. SLICER.   But, we plan to consult about her.

SGANARELLE.   [*To attending servants.*] Come, bring chairs for the doctors.

LISETTE.   [*To DR. SLICER.*] Doctor, is that you?

SGANARELLE.   How do you know Dr. Slicer?

LISETTE.   From having seen him the other day at the home of a good friend of   1
your niece.

DR. SLICER.   How is her coachman?

LISETTE.   Fabulous; he's dead.

DR. SLICER.   Dead?

LISETTE.   Yes, dead.

DR. SLICER.   That cannot be!   1

LISETTE.   I don't know if it couldn't happen, but I do know that it did.

---

4 *corrupt and putrid humors:* internal illness of body fluids.

DR. SLICER.   And I tell you he can't be dead.

LISETTE.   And I tell you he's dead and buried.

DR. SLICER.   You've made a mistake.

LISETTE.   I saw it with my own eyes.   20

DR. SLICER.   It's impossible. Hippocrates° says that patients don't die of this disease until the end of the second or third week, and he was sick for only six days.

LISETTE.   Let Hippocrates talk all he wants; the coachman is dead.

SGANARELLE.   [*To LISETTE.*] Be quiet, chatterbox; we should leave. [*To the doctors.*] Gentlemen, we will leave you in peace for your consultation. I know it's not customary to pay in advance, but I'll pay you now, before I forget.

[*He pays them, and each one, upon receiving the fee, makes a different show of thanks. SGANARELLE and LISETTE then leave.*]

Act II, Scene 3

DR. SLICER, DR. GOUGER, DR. DE PITS, and DR. GOLFER remain.

DR. DE PITS.   Paris is an incredibly large city, and a good medical practice requires long trips.

DR. SLICER.   I have an excellent mule for that; you won't believe the distances I make him go each day.

DR. DE PITS.   I have a marvelous horse; he never gets tired.

DR. SLICER.   Do you know the ground my mule has covered today? I was near the Arsenal first. Then I went to the suburb of St. Germain, from there to Le Marais, and then to St. Honoré Gate; after that to St. Jacques, to the Richelieu Gate, and finally here. When I leave, I'll go to the Place Royale.

DR. DE PITS.   My horse has gone to all those places today, and in addition I   5
rode him all the way to Ruel so I could see a patient.

DR. SLICER.   By the way, what position do you gentlemen take in the controversy between Doctors Theophrastus and Artemius? This is a matter that's dividing the whole profession.

DR. DE PITS.   I think Artemius is right.

DR. SLICER.   I do too. It's true that his treatment killed the patient, and that the recommendation of Theophrastus was infinitely better, but in the circumstances, Theophrastus was wrong. He should not have ignored the recommendation of Artemius, who was, we must recognize, the senior physician in the case. What do you say about it?

DR. DE PITS.   Proper procedure should always be respected. I think we would be lost without our strict order of authority.

DR. SLICER.   I agree; I'm as severe about this as the devil—unless it's among   10
friends. The other day three of us were consulting with an outside physician about a patient. I stopped the whole business until we proceeded in absolute order. Meanwhile, the people of the house did their best as the illness reached a crisis, but I continued to insist on proper consultative procedure. Before we could end our conference, the patient died—may he rest in peace.

DR. DE PITS.   Insisting on our rights like that is the best way to keep lay people in their place, and show them that we're in control.

---

21 *Hippocrates:* Ancient Greek physician, known as the father of medicine.

DR. SLICER. A dead person is a dead person, and of no importance; but any neglect of standard operating procedures puts our whole profession in a bad light.

Act II, Scene 4

They remain. Enter SGANARELLE.

SGANARELLE. Gentlemen, my daughter's condition is becoming serious. Please tell me at once what you have decided.

DR. SLICER. [*To DR. DE PITS.*] Sir, you speak.

DR. DE PITS. No, Sir, you speak first.

DR. SLICER. Please, Sir, don't be modest.

DR. DE PITS. No, Sir, please, after you.

DR. SLICER. Sir!

DR. DE PITS. Sir!

SGANARELLE. With all respect, gentlemen, forget your ceremony and remember our present urgency.

[*All four doctors now speak together.*]

DR. SLICER. The illness of your daughter—

DR. DE PITS. The judgment of all these gentlemen together—

DR. GOUGER. After our most exhaustive consultation—

DR. GOLFER. To consider the case step by step, we—

SGANARELLE. Gentlemen, please, speak one at a time.

DR. SLICER. Sir, we have reached a diagnosis of your daughter's illness. My opinion is that it stems from a sanguinary superabundance—too much blood, to you. So my recommendation is blood letting; as soon as possible you should let as much blood from her as you can.

DR. DE PITS. My best judgment is that her illness results from a putrefaction of humors, caused by too much repletion. So my advice—listen carefully—is that she be given an emetic.

DR. SLICER. I submit that an emetic will kill her.

DR. DE PITS. And I believe that a bleeding is contra-indicated; it will bring about instant expiration—in other words, death.

DR. SLICER. [*Huffily, to DR. DE PITS.*] You of course are a great authority.

DR. DE PITS. [*Defensively, to DR. SLICER.*] Yes, I am; I'll outshine you in any branch of medical knowledge.

DR. SLICER. Do you recall that your wrongheaded treatment killed a man the other day?

DR. DE PITS. Do you recall that your bungling put a woman in her grave just three days ago?

DR. SLICER. [*To SGANARELLE.*] I've given you my opinion.

DR. DE PITS. [*To SGANARELLE.*] And I've informed you of my professional judgment.

DR. SLICER. If you don't bleed your daughter immediately, she'll be a goner. [*He leaves.*]

DR. DE PITS. And if you do bleed her, she'll die in a quarter of an hour.

[*He leaves.*]

Act II, Scene 5

SGANARELLE, DR. GOUGER, and DR. GOLFER remain.

SGANARELLE.   Which of the two should I believe, and what should I do with such contrary advice? Gentlemen, I ask you to understand my predicament and tell me objectively what you believe would cure my daughter.

DR. GOUGER.   [*He speaks agonizingly slowly, drawing out his syllables and even stressing ordinarily silent letters.*] Sir, in these matters, we must proceed with circumspection, and, as they say, do nothing rashly, because the mistakes that we may make, according to our master, Hippocrates, may have dangerous consequences.

DR. GOLFER.   [*This one speaks at breakneck speed.*] He's right; we must be careful in what we do. This is not a child's game, and when we fail, it's not easy to repair the damage and restore the dead to life: *Experimentum periculosum: in other words, medicine is a perilous experiment that we learn from as we go along.* That's why we must reason carefully, weigh the alternatives, consider individual cases, examine all the possible causes of the illness, and see what remedies we may bring to the patient.

SGANARELLE.   [*Aside.*] One is as slow as a turtle, the other as fast as a jackrabbit.

DR. GOUGER.   [*He is the turtle.*] Therefore, Sir, to get down to the matter, I find   5
that your daughter is sick. She has a chronic sickness which will get worse unless it gets better, for her symptoms indicate a pathological and mordant—that is to say, bad—vapor which penetrates the membranes of the brain. Now this vapor, which is called *atmos* in Greek, is caused by putrid, tenacious, and glutinous humors which are contained in the lower bowel.

DR. GOLFER.   [*He is the jackrabbit.*] And, inasmuch as these humors were engendered there during an extended period, they have turned adust—that is, they have been overcooked, so to speak—and have produced the present pathology of the brain.

DR. GOUGER.   [*Still speaking slowly.*] Therefore, in order that we may draw out, detach, withdraw, expel, and evacuate these said humors, we must recommend an aggressive treatment of purgation. But first, I find, it would not be improper to prescribe anodynes of emollients° and cleansing solutions, together with refreshing medicinal juleps and syrups to be mixed with her herbal tea and her tonic.

DR. GOLFER.   After this, should come purging and bleeding, to be repeated as necessary.

DR. GOUGER.   This does not mean that your daughter won't die after all this, but at least you will have done your best, and may be consoled by the realization that she died in accordance with proper procedures.

DR. GOLFER.   It's much better to die by the rules than to recover in spite of   10
them.

DR. GOUGER.   We are giving you our best professional advice.

DR. GOLFER.   And we have spoken to you as though you were our brother.

SGANARELLE.   [*To DR. GOUGER, drawing out his words.*] I thank you most humbly, Sir. [*To DR. GOLFER, as rapidly as possible.*] To you, Sir, I am infinitely obliged for the care that you have taken.

[*The doctors exit.*]

7 *anodynes of emollients*: soothing lotions.

Act II, Scene 6

SGANARELLE, alone.

SGANARELLE.   Now I'm more uncertain than ever. What can I do? [*He ponders this question for a few moments.*] I've got an idea: I've heard about a medicine that can cure everything, which they make down in Orvieto, Italy. It's a marvelous new elixir called "Orviétan." The advertising says it's cured millions of people. I'll buy some for her. It's got to work.

[*He leaves.*]

Act II, Scene 7

A Street. Enter SGANARELLE and MOUNTEBANK, accompanied by his BUFFOONS and SCARA-MOUCHES.

SGANARELLE.   Hello, Sir. Please give me a bottle of your amazing new drug, Orviétan. How much does it cost?
MOUNTEBANK.   [*Singing.*]

> *Would the gold in the richest of mines*
> *Be enough for this all-curing pill?*
> *By its magic it separates the ill*
> *From more ailments than forests have pines.*
> > *Agues and itches,*
> > *Fevers and twitches,*
> > *Plagues and neuroses,*
> > *Funks and psychoses,*
> > *Measles, congestions,*
> > *Strokes and depressions,*
> > *Organs that fail you,*
> > *All things that ail you—*
> *All can be cured by my Orviétan, my Orviétan,*
> *All can be cured by my Orviétan.*

SGANARELLE.   Sir, I believe that all the gold in the world is not enough to pay you for your medicine. However, here's five hundred for you.
MOUNTEBANK.   [*Singing.*]

> *Sing my praise, for these pills, I surmise—*
> *Such a bargain for such a small cost—*
> *Give new strength to those lives that are tossed*
> *By diseases the heavens devise.*
> > *Agues and itches,*
> > *Fevers and twitches,*
> > *Plagues and neuroses,*
> > *Funks and psychoses,*
> > *Measles, congestions,*
> > *Strokes and depressions,*
> > *Organs that fail you,*
> > *All things that ail you—*

All can be cured by my Orviétan, my Orviétan,
All can be cured by my Orviétan.

[*Exit* SGANARELLE.]

SECOND ENTR'ACTE

A dance by the MOUNTEBANK'S BUFFOONS and SCARAMOUCHES.

ACT III

Scene 1

Enter DR. FILLPOCKET, DR. SLICER, *and* DR. DE PITS.

DR. FILLPOCKET.   Gentlemen, as men of your experience you should be ashamed to have been so imprudent as to quarrel like young blockheads. Don't you see that such open arguments hurt us in the public eye? Isn't it enough that expert critics know all about the controversy and dissension among our authorities and ancient masters, without disclosing our humbug to the world by wrangling in front of spectators? I'm concerned that some members of our profession mismanage their public relations so badly, because lately we've been hurt, and if we're not careful we may ruin ourselves. I have nothing to lose in this, because I've already made my pile. Let it blow, rain, and hail, the dead are dead, and I'm rich enough not to fear the living. But in the long run, our squabbles and disputes don't advance the medical profession. Since Heaven has smiled on us and enabled us to hoodwink the public for centuries, let's not disabuse people by our excesses, but let us go on taking advantage of the gullible—and thereby go on making our bundles. You know we're not the only profession to prey on human vulnerability; it's the major study of half the world's population. Everyone wants to catch people in moments of weakness in order to cash in. Flatterers, for example, benefit from the human need for praise, and so they lay it on with a trowel; some people have made huge fortunes in this way. Alchemists benefit from people's greed by promising mountains of gold to fools stupid enough to invest in their phony technology about making gold out of lead. And people even pour money into those consummate fakers, the psychics, who manipulate the vanity and ambition of their victims by making rosy predictions about the future. But the greatest weakness of humanity is the love of life—yes, our instinct for self-preservation—and we, as doctors, all profit from it, even with our pompous nonsense. We reap gigantic rewards because of the worship and adoration that our profession gains from our patients' fear of death. Let us then preserve the high esteem that human fallibility has given us, and let us, in the eyes of that world of believers out there, agree to take the credit for our cures while we deceive people by convincing them to blame Nature for our blunders. Let's not go about, I say, stupidly destroying the happy continuation of this public misperception which puts bread on our tables; and from the dead, whom we put into the ground, let us raise up our boundless wealth.

DR. SLICER.   [*spellbound.*] You are so right—so very right. But our dispute arose simply from hot blood, which we cannot always control.

DR. FILLPOCKET.   All right, then, gentlemen, put rancor aside, and make your apologies now.

DR. DE PITS.   I agree, if my emetic can be given to our present patient then Dr. Slicer can do as he pleases with the next patient.

DR. FILLPOCKET.   I couldn't say it better myself, and I'm glad to see good sense prevail.

DR. DE PITS.   It's done.

DR. FILLPOCKET.   Shake hands, then. [*DR. DE PITS and DR. SLICER shake hands.*] Goodbye. And next time, be more careful.

[*Exit DR. FILLPOCKET.*]

Act III, Scene 2

DR. DE PITS and DR. SLICER remain. Enter LISETTE.

LISETTE.   Gentlemen, how can you stand there without seeking a way of getting even for the attack that has just been made against the practice of medicine?

DR. SLICER.   What do you mean?

LISETTE.   A brazen fellow has just had the nerve to practice your profession without a licence; he has just wiped out another fellow with a sword clean through the body.

DR. SLICER.   Listen, you can make fun of us now, but some day you'll be sick, and then we'll get you in our clutches.

LISETTE.   When I'm ready, then I'll give you permission to do me in.

[*Exit the doctors.*]

Act III, Scene 3

LISETTE remains. Enter CLITANDER, dressed as a doctor.

CLITANDER.   Well, Lisette, what do you think of my outfit? Do you think I can fool our gentleman with it? Do I look the part of a doctor?

LISETTE.   You look fine, but you're late. It's good that Heaven has made me so good-natured. I can't see two lovers sighing for each other without feeling soft myself, and wishing to satisfy their longing. Hang the consequences, I've sworn to free Lucinda from her tyranny and give her to you. I liked you from the first. I'm an authority when it comes to men, and she couldn't have made a better choice than you. True love requires great risks, and we have devised a scheme that we hope will succeed. Our plans are already moving ahead. The man we're dealing with is not one of your brightest in the world, and if we fail now, we can find a thousand other ways to reach our goal. Wait for me alone over there; I'll be right back to get you.

[*CLITANDER leaves.*]

Act III, Scene 4

LISETTE remains. Enter SGANARELLE.

LISETTE.   Sir, joy, joy!

SGANARELLE.   What's this?

LISETTE.   Rejoice.

SGANARELLE.   What for?

LISETTE.   And again, I say, rejoice!

SGANARELLE.   Tell me what's going on, and then I'll rejoice—maybe.

LISETTE.   No, I want you to rejoice in advance; I want you to sing and dance!

SGANARELLE.   Upon what?

LISETTE.   Upon my word.

SGANARELLE.   Okay, then. [*He sings and dances.*] La lera la la, la lera la. What   10
the devil!

LISETTE.   Sir, your daughter is cured!

SGANARELLE.   My daughter is cured?

LISETTE.   Yes. I am bringing you a doctor, but not just any doctor. He is the
most important doctor on earth, who makes miraculous cures and puts all other doctors to shame.

SGANARELLE.   Where is he?

LISETTE.   I'll have him come in. [*She leaves.*]   15

SGANARELLE.   [*Alone.*] Let's see if this one will do better than the others.

Act III, Scene 5

SGANARELLE remains. Enter LISETTE and CLITANDER in his doctor's robes.

LISETTE.   [*Leading CLITANDER.*] Here he is.

SGANARELLE.   This doctor has only a small growth of beard.

LISETTE.   Science is not measured by a beard, and he did not get his degrees
because of his chin.

SGANARELLE.   Sir, I'm told that you have effective medications for regular
bowel movements.

CLITANDER.   Sir, my remedies are entirely unique. Other doctors use emetics,   5
bleeding, medicines, and enemas, but I cure by words, sounds, letters, signs, and mystical rings.

LISETTE.   What did I tell you?

SGANARELLE.   Here is a great man!

LISETTE.   Sir, since your daughter is up and around, I'll get her over here.

SGANARELLE.   Please do. [*LISETTE leaves.*]

CLITANDER.   [*Taking SGANARELLE's pulse.*] Your daughter is indeed sick.   10

SGANARELLE.   You know that from taking *my* pulse?

CLITANDER.   Yes, because of the sympathetic vibrations passing between father
and daughter.

Act III, Scene 6

SGANARELLE and CLITANDER remain. Enter LUCINDA and LISETTE.

LISETTE.   [*To CLITANDER.*] Here, Sir, take this chair. [*To SGANARELLE.*] Let's go
and leave them together.

SGANARELLE.   Why? I want to stay here.

LISETTE.   Are you kidding? We should go; a doctor has a hundred questions
that it's not right for us to hear.

[*SGANARELLE and LISETTE move to a side of the stage.*]

CLITANDER.   [*Speaking to LUCINDA alone.*] Ah, Madam, I'm so overwhelmed with
joy I hardly know how to begin speaking to you! When I could speak only with my

eyes, I thought I had hundreds of things to say; but now that I have freedom to say what I want, I feel tongue-tied, and my happiness stifles my words.

LUCINDA.   I feel the same thing, and like you I sense movements of joy that catch in my throat and prevent my speaking.

CLITANDER.   Ah, Madam, I would be so happy if you felt everything I feel, and if I could judge your heart by mine! But, Madam, may I believe that you were the one who thought of this happy stratagem that gives me such joy in your presence?

LUCINDA.   If you don't owe me the idea, at least you should know that I approved it eagerly.

SGANARELLE.   [*To LISETTE.*] He seems very close to her.

LISETTE.   [*To SGANARELLE.*] He's a doctor, and he's studying her facial features.

CLITANDER.   [*To LUCINDA.*] Will you be faithful, Madam, in the promises you   1 make to me?

LUCINDA.   And you, will you be firm in your present resolutions?

CLITANDER.   Ah, Madam, until death, and I'll demonstrate my love by what I'm now about to do.

SGANARELLE.   [*To CLITANDER.*] Well, our patient seems to be perking up.

CLITANDER.   That's because I've already tried one of the remedies of my great art on her. The mind has power over the body, and sickness often begins in the mind. My method is therefore to cure the spirit first before treating the body. Accordingly, I have studied her looks, her facial features, and the lines of her two hands; and by the science bestowed on me by Heaven, I have determined that her sickness is psychosomatic—she is sick in spirit. This disease comes entirely from her disordered imagination, which prompts her depraved wish to be married. My view is that there is nothing more extravagant or ridiculous than this wish for marriage.

SGANARELLE.   [*Aside.*] This is indeed a man of skill!   1.

CLITANDER.   And all my life I have had, and will continue to have, an aversion for it.

SGANARELLE.   [*Aside.*] A great physician!

CLITANDER.   But, since it's necessary to flatter the imagination of patients, and because I see schizophrenic tendencies in her, and also because it would be perilous not to treat her quickly, I have taken advantage of her weakness and told her that I came here to ask you for her hand in marriage. When she heard that, her appearance changed for the better, her complexion brightened, and her eyes sparkled. I believe that if you keep her in this error for several days, you will see her recover completely.

SGANARELLE.   There's nothing I want more.

CLITANDER.   Afterwards we'll apply other remedies to cure her of this fantasy   2(entirely.

SGANARELLE.   That will be marvellous! [*To LUCINDA.*] Well, daughter, here is a gentleman who wishes to marry you, and I have told him he has my blessing!

LUCINDA.   Dear me, is this possible?

SGANARELLE.   Yes.

LUCINDA.   I'm not dreaming?

SGANARELLE.   No, you're not dreaming.   25

LUCINDA.   [*To CLITANDER.*] You really want to be my husband?

CLITANDER.   Yes, Madam.

LUCINDA.   And my father consents?

SGANARELLE.   Yes, daughter.

LUCINDA.   If this is true, I couldn't be happier!   30

    CLITANDER.   Don't doubt it, Madam. It is not just today that I began loving you and longing to marry you. I came here only to ask for your hand, and, if you want to know the whole truth exactly as it is, this doctor's costume is nothing more than a false front. I pretended to be a doctor only to come close to you, the more easily to realize my goal of marrying you.

    LUCINDA.   This all shows me the proofs of your tender love. I am deeply moved by them.

    SGANARELLE.   [*Aside.*] Oh, the fool! the fool! the fool!

    LUCINDA.   You approve of this gentleman as my husband, father, and do so willingly?

    SGANARELLE.   Yes. Give me your hand, and you, Sir, give me yours, too, by way   35
of witness.

    CLITANDER.   But, Sir—

    SGANARELLE.   [*Stifling laughter.*] No, no, it's to—it's to ease her mind. Now, join hands. There, it's done.

    CLITANDER.   Accept as a token of my faith this ring that I give you. [*Speaking low, to SGANARELLE.*] It's a special ring to cure her distracted mind.

    LUCINDA.   Let us draw up the contract, so that everything will be complete.

    CLITANDER.   Certainly; I would like that, Madam. [*To SGANARELLE.*] I'll show   40
her the man who writes my prescriptions, and make her believe he's a genuine Justice.

    SGANARELLE.   Excellent!

    CLITANDER.   [*Calling offstage.*] You there, send in the Justice I brought with me!

    LUCINDA.   What, you brought along a Justice?

    CLITANDER.   Yes, Madam.

    LUCINDA.   I'm delighted!   45

    SGANARELLE.   [*Chuckling.*] Oh, the fool! the fool!

Act III, Scene 7

They all remain. Enter the JUSTICE, appropriately robed. CLITANDER whispers to the JUSTICE.

    SGANARELLE.   [*To the JUSTICE.*] Welcome, Sir. I commission you to draft a contract for these two young people. Please begin writing. [*While the JUSTICE is writing, SGANARELLE speaks to LUCINDA.*] This will be a contract to end all contracts. [*To the JUSTICE.*] I give her twenty million upon her marriage. Write that down!

    LUCINDA.   I'm so overwhelmingly grateful to you, father.

    JUSTICE.   [*Giving the contract to SGANARELLE.*] There, it's done; you need only to come and sign.

    SGANARELLE.   How's that for a contract speedily finished?

    CLITANDER.   [*To SGANARELLE.*] At least, Sir—   5

    SGANARELLE.   No, no words of gratitude; say nothing, I beg you. [*Aside to CLITANDER.*] Don't we both know what we're doing? [*To the JUSTICE.*] Come, give him the pen. [*After CLITANDER signs, SGANARELLE gives the pen to LUCINDA.*] Come, come, sign it. Go ahead; I'll sign too. [*He signs.*]

    LUCINDA.   No, no. I want to hold the contract myself.

    SGANARELLE.   All right, take it. [*After she has signed.*] Now, are you happy?

    LUCINDA.   More than you can imagine!

SGANARELLE.   I'm please. I'm very pleased.

CLITANDER.   As for the rest, I not only took the trouble to bring a Justice along, but to celebrate the occasion I brought singers and musicians too. Send them in! These are the people I take with me every day on my rounds; I direct them, with their harmony, to pacify the troubled minds of my patients.

Final Scene

All remain. Enter the SPIRIT OF COMEDY, DANCERS, *and* MUSICIANS.

ALL THREE [*COMEDY, DANCERS, and MUSICIANS*].

If you didn't have music and singing and dancing,
  You'd spend your life with your mind in chains;
For it's we, with our wonderful songs and our prancing,
  Who win the fight against aches and pains.

COMEDY

Do you want to break free,
  In the happiest way,
From the mis'ry and grief
  Of each long day?
    Then sing your song
    The whole day long;
    Throw away your medicine,
    Along with the jar it's in,
    And join our throng
    As we sing along.

ALL THREE

If you didn't have music and singing and dancing,
  You'd spend your life with your mind in chains;
For it's we, with our wonderful songs and our prancing,
  Who win the fight against aches and pains.

[*While they are singing and dancing, and amidst all the Games, Smiles, and Pleasures,* CLITANDER *leads* LUCINDA *away.*]

SGANARELLE.   This is a marvelous way to cure someone! But where is my daughter, and where is the doctor?

LISETTE.   They left—to complete the rest of the marriage ritual.

SGANARELLE.   What are you saying? What—what marriage?

LISETTE.   In truth, Sir, the game has been bagged, and what you thought was a joke turns out to be the absolute truth!

SGANARELLE.   [*The* DANCERS *catch hold of him and bring him into the dance by force.*] What's this? The devil! Let me go! Let me go, I tell you! Still more? A plague on everything!

[*Finis.*]

QUESTIONS

Act I

1. What does the opening scene indicate about Sganarelle's responses to other people? Describe his traits. What do you learn about his economic status? Why is this status important in the plot?
2. Describe the father-daughter relationship that is brought out in Scenes 2 and 3. Why is the relationship made to seem comic and not serious?
3. Why is it important that we learn about a suitor whom Lucinda likes, and that there has been an "envoy" from him seeking to negotiate a marriage?
4. Describe Lisette. Is she flat or round, representative or individualized? Why is she important? What is her relationship with Lucinda?
5. Why does Sganarelle not want his daughter married? What do his reasons disclose about him? What effect does Sganarelle's behavior toward his daughter have on your attitude toward him at the play's conclusion?

Act II

6. Why is Sganarelle dramatized as a person with great faith in doctors? Why is Lisette skeptical about them?
7. Study the dialogue between Lisette and Dr. Slicer (scene 2, paragraphs 8–22). Describe how character and speech here produce laughter.
8. At the end of scene 2 a stage direction describes Sganarelle's payment to the doctors. Explain how pantomime and dance might be used here to augment Molière's satiric presentation of doctors. Be specific.
9. Though scene 3 is supposedly a medical "consultation" about the condition of Lucinda, the conversation has nothing to do with her. What does Molière achieve by introducing the topics the doctors actually discuss?
10. What treatments do the doctors prescribe for Lucinda? Though the doctors are contradictory, in what respects are some of them truthful? Why is their telling the truth comic?
11. Explain Sganarelle's role in the scenes with the doctors. What is the effect of these scenes on his seeking out the Mountebank, and also on his reception of Clitander in the next act when Clitander appears disguised as a doctor?

Act III

12. Why does Dr. Fillpocket make such a long speech? How honest is he? Would he give this speech to anyone but fellow doctors? Is Molière's treatment of the speech comic? Serious? True? Partly true? Untrue?
13. What is the stratagem devised by Lisette and Clitander? How is it related to Sganarelle's already proven faith in doctors and medication?
14. Explain the irony of Clitander's confession to Lucinda and also of Sganarelle's responses beginning in scene 6, and extending to the revelation in the last scene. How does Molière keep the final scene light and comic?
15. How does Sganarelle react to the news that the marriage of Lucinda and

Clitander is real? How is his reaction kept from seeming serious? If you were a director, what might you tell the actor playing Sganarelle to do during the concluding dance? Why?

GENERAL QUESTIONS

1. Who is the protagonist of *Love Is the Doctor*? What conflicts develop? Who and what are the antagonists? Which "side" is triumphant at the end?
2. A traditional topic for laughter is that the "biter gets bitten" and the "tables are turned." To what degree does Molière use this topic in the play? How successful is it as a means of developing humor?
3. The critic Harold C. Knutson has observed that in *Love Is the Doctor* we have "a particularly biting commentary on doctors and doctoring," and that one of the modes of satire is that the doctors "drop the mask and betray their callousness" and "contentiousness," and that their "concern" is not with their patients but rather with rules and formalities (*Moliere: An Archetypal Approach* [Toronto: U. of Toronto Press, 1976], pp. 52–53). Do you agree or disagree with Professor Knutson's observations? Explain in detail.
4. Aside from the medical satire, describe the various doctors as characters. Which of the doctors is the most fully developed? Which are most amusing? Why?

BETH HENLEY, *AM I BLUE*

Brought up in Mississippi, Beth Henley attended Southern Methodist University in Texas, where she wrote *Am I Blue* in her sophomore year. She attended an acting school in Illinois and went to Hollywood to attempt an acting career in the movies. She continued working on plays, however, and it is her writing career that has blossomed. Her most notable achievement to date is her "Southern Gothic" play *Crimes of the Heart*, for which she won the Great American Play contest in 1978 and the Pulitzer Prize in 1981. In addition to completing two other full-length plays, she has
also seen some of her shorter scripts into production. *Crimes of the Heart* was produced as a film in 1986, starring Diane Keaton, Jessica Lange, Sam Shepard, and Sissy Spacek.

Henley's comedic manner develops out of the eccentricity or "kookiness" of her main female characters. The comic pattern of behavior is to do something unusual, but to regard the action as more ordinary than ridiculous. One of the characters in *Crimes of the Heart*, for example, after a failed suicide attempt, explains her action by saying that she has been having a "bad day." A character in another play inadvertently sets a house afire, but the outcome, although disastrous, is fortunate. Ashbe of *Am I Blue* is an early original in this pattern, with her liking for hot Kool-Aid and colored marshmallows, her habit of stealing ashtrays and then donating them to a fellow tenant, and her dabbling in voodoo.

Though *Am I Blue* is an amusing play, it deals with serious problems such as the difficulties of adjustment to adulthood, misconceptions about social roles, unfulfilled dreams, general indecision and purposelessness, and the attempt to develop individuality. The larger political and historical context of the year of the supposed events of the play, 1968, is not mentioned by either of the main characters, but one might locate their difficulties in some of the disturbances of that year: the assassinations of Martin Luther King and Robert Kennedy, the several-year-old and seemingly endless war in Vietnam, and the many antiwar demonstrations and riots, especially during the Democratic presidential convention in Chicago. Henley is particular in dating the action of *Am I Blue* on November 11–12, 1968; in other words, after all these nationally disturbing events had taken place, and also less than a week after the presidential election. One might note the irony that November 11 had before 1954 been called "Armistice Day" (now Veterans Day)—a holiday dedicated to the establishment of peace and stability.

Although Ashbe and John Polk reflect the frustration and disruption of the late 1960s, their lives are their own, seemingly untouched by politics. Ashbe has been left to her own resources at the age of sixteen, with a father who is alcoholic and absent, and a mother who has deserted the home entirely. John Polk is facing a difficult decision about his future. He is also attempting to stay afloat in the swim of fraternity life, and is seeking strength in rum instead of his own character. Nothing earthshaking is claimed for either Ashbe or John Polk at the play's end, but they both develop a degree of recognition, rejecting behaviors imposed by convention, and discovering their own capacities for dignity and friendship.

BETH HENLEY (B. 1952)

Am I Blue°   *(1973) 1982*

CHARACTERS

> John Polk Richards, *seventeen*
> Ashbe Williams, *sixteen*
> Hilda, *a waitress, thirty-five*
> Street People: Barker, Whore, Bum, Clareece

[*SCENE: A bar, the street, the living room of a run-down apartment.*]

[*TIME: Fall 1968.*]

The scene opens on a street in the New Orleans French Quarter on a rainy, blue bourbon night. Various people—a WHORE, BUM, STREET BARKER, CLAREECE—*appear and disappear along the*

First produced in New York City by the Circle Repertory Company.

street. The scene then focuses on a bar where a piano is heard from the back room playing softly and indistinctly "Am I Blue?" The lights go up on JOHN POLK, who sits alone at a table. He is seventeen, a bit overweight and awkward. He wears nice clothes, perhaps a navy sweater with large white monograms. His navy raincoat is slung over an empty chair. While drinking John Polk concentrates on the red and black card that he holds in his hand. As soon as the scene is established, ASHBE enters from the street. She is sixteen, wears a flowered plastic raincoat, a white plastic rain cap, red galoshes, a butterfly barrette, and jeweled cat-eye glasses. She is carrying a bag full of stolen goods. Her hair is very curly. Ashbe makes her way cautiously to John Polk's table. As he sees her coming, he puts the card into his pocket. She sits in the empty chair and pulls his raincoat over her head.

ASHBE.   Excuse me . . . do you mind if I sit here please?

JOHN POLK.   [*Looks up at her—then down into his glass.*] What are you doing hiding under my raincoat? You're getting it all wet.

ASHBE.   Well, I'm very sorry, but after all it is a raincoat. [*He tries to pull off coat.*] It was rude of me I know, but look I just don't want them to recognize me.

JOHN POLK.   [*Looking about.*] Who to recognize you?

ASHBE.   Well, I stole these two ashtrays from the Screw Inn, ya know right down the street. [*She pulls out two glass commercial ashtrays from her white plastic bag.*] Anyway, I'm scared the manager saw me. They'll be after me I'm afraid.

JOHN POLK.   Well, they should be. Look, do you mind giving me back my raincoat? I don't want to be found protecting any thief.

ASHBE.   [*Coming out from under coat.*] Thief—would you call Robin Hood a thief?

JOHN POLK.   Christ.

ASHBE.   [*Back under coat.*] No, you wouldn't. He was valiant—all the time stealing from the rich and giving to the poor.

JOHN POLK.   But your case isn't exactly the same, is it? You're stealing from some crummy little bar and keeping the ashtrays for yourself. Now give me back my coat.

ASHBE.   [*Throws coat at him.*] Sure, take your old coat. I suppose I should have explained—about Miss Marcey. [*Silence.*] Miss Marcey, this cute old lady with a little hump in her back. I always see her in her sun hat and blue print dress. Miss Marcey lives in the apartment building next to ours. I leave all the stolen goods, as gifts on her front steps.

JOHN POLK.   Are you one of those kleptomaniacs? [*He starts checking his wallet.*]

ASHBE.   You mean when people all the time steal and they can't help it?

JOHN POLK.   Yeah.

ASHBE.   Oh, no. I'm not a bit careless. Take my job tonight, my very first night job, if you want to know. Anyway, I've been planning it for two months, trying to decipher which bar most deserved to be stolen from. I finally decided on the Screw Inn. Mainly because of the way they're so mean to Mr. Groves. He works at the magazine rack at Diver's Drugstore and is really very sweet, but he has a drinking problem. I don't think that's fair to be mean to people simply because they have a drinking problem—and, well, anyway, you see I'm not just stealing for personal gain. I mean, I don't even smoke.

JOHN POLK.   Yeah, well, most infants don't, but then again, most infants don't hang around bars.

ASHBE.   I don't see why not, Toulouse Lautrec did.

JOHN POLK.   They'd throw me out.

ASHBE.   Oh, they throw me out too, but I don't accept defeat. [*Slowly moves into him.*] Why it's the very same with my pickpocketing.

[*JOHN POLK sneers, turns away.*]

ASHBE.   It's a very hard act to master. Why every time I've done it, I've been   20
caught.

JOHN POLK.   That's all I need, is to have some slum kid tell me how good it is to steal. Everyone knows it's not.

ASHBE.   [*About his drink.*] That looks good. What is it?

JOHN POLK.   Hey, would you mind leaving me alone—I just wanted to be alone.

ASHBE.   Okay. I'm sorry. How about if I'm quiet?

[*JOHN POLK shrugs. He sips drink, looks around, catches her eye, she smiles and sighs.*]

ASHBE.   I was just looking at your pin. What fraternity are you in?   25
JOHN POLK.   S.A.E.
ASHBE.   Is it a good fraternity?
JOHN POLK.   Sure, it's the greatest.
ASHBE.   I bet you have lots of friends.
JOHN POLK.   Tons.   30
ASHBE.   Are you being serious?
JOHN POLK.   Yes.
ASHBE.   Hmm. Do they have parties and all that?
JOHN POLK.   Yeah, lots of parties, booze, honking horns, it's exactly what you would expect.
ASHBE.   I wouldn't expect anything. Why did you join?   35
JOHN POLK.   I don't know. Well, my brother . . . I guess it was my brother . . . he told me how great it was, how the fraternity was supposed to get you dates, make you study, solve all your problems.
ASHBE.   Gee, does it?
JOHN POLK.   Doesn't help you study.
ASHBE.   How about dates? Do they get you a lot of dates?
JOHN POLK.   Some.   40
ASHBE.   What were the girls like?
JOHN POLK.   I don't know—they were like girls.
ASHBE.   Did you have a good time?
JOHN POLK.   I had a pretty good time.
ASHBE.   Did you make love to any of them?   45
JOHN POLK.   [*To self.*] Oh, Christ . . .
ASHBE.   I'm sorry . . . I just figured that's why you had the appointment with the whore . . . cause you didn't have anyone else . . . to make love to.
JOHN POLK.   How did you know I had the, ah, the appointment?
ASHBE.   I saw you put the red card in your pocket when I came up. Those red cards are pretty familiar around here. The house is only about a block or so away. It's one of the best though, really very plush. Only two murders and a knifing in its whole history. Do you go there often?
JOHN POLK.   Yeah, I like to give myself a treat.   50

ASHBE.   Who do you have?

JOHN POLK.   What do you mean?

ASHBE.   I mean which girl. [*JOHN POLK gazes into his drink.*] Look, I just thought I might know her is all.

JOHN POLK.   Know her, ah, how would you know her?

ASHBE.   Well, some of the girls from my high school go there to work when they get out.

JOHN POLK.   G.G., her name is G.G.

ASHBE.   G.G. . . . Hmm, well, how does she look?

JOHN POLK.   I don't know.

ASHBE.   Oh, you've never been with her before?

JOHN POLK.   No.

ASHBE.   [*Confidentially.*] Are you one of those kinds that likes a lot of variety?

JOHN POLK.   Variety? Sure, I guess I like variety.

ASHBE.   Oh, yes, now I remember.

JOHN POLK.   What?

ASHBE.   G.G., that's just her working name. Her real name is Myrtle Reims, she's Kay Reims' older sister. Kay is in my grade at school.

JOHN POLK.   Myrtle? Her name is Myrtle?

ASHBE.   I never liked the name either.

JOHN POLK.   Myrtle, oh, Christ. Is she pretty?

ASHBE.   [*Matter of fact.*] Pretty, no she's not real pretty.

JOHN POLK.   What does she look like?

ASHBE.   Let's see . . . she's, ah, well, Myrtle had acne and there are a few scars left. It's not bad. I think they sort of give her character. Her hair's red, only I don't think it's really red. It sort of fizzles out all over her head. She's got a pretty good figure . . . big top . . . but the rest of her is kind of skinny.

JOHN POLK.   I wonder if she has a good personality.

ASHBE.   Well, she was a senior when I was a freshman; so I never really knew her. I remember she used to paint her fingernails lots of different colors . . . pink, orange, purple. I don't know, but she kind of scares me. About the only time I ever saw her true personality was around a year ago. I was over at Kay's making a health poster for school. Anyway, Myrtle comes busting in, screaming about how she can't find her spangled bra anywhere. Kay and I just sat on the floor cutting pictures of food out of magazines while she was storming about slamming drawers and swearing. Finally, she found it. It was pretty garish—red with black and gold sequined G's on each cup. That's how I remember the name—G.G.

[*As ASHBE illustrates the placement of the G's she spots HILDA, the waitress, approaching. Ashbe pulls the raincoat over her head and hides on the floor. Hilda enters through the beaded curtains spilling her tray. Hilda is a woman of few words.*]

HILDA.   Shit, damn curtain. Nuther drink?

JOHN POLK.   Mam?

HILDA.   [*Points to drink.*] Vodka coke?

JOHN POLK.   No, thank you. I'm not quite finished yet.

HILDA.   Napkins clean.

[*ASHBE pulls her bag off the table. HILDA looks at ASHBE then to JOHN POLK. She walks around the table, as ASHBE is crawling along the floor to escape. ASHBE runs into HILDA'S toes.*]

ASHBE.   Are those real gold?

HILDA.   You again. Out.   80

ASHBE.   She wants me to leave. Why should a paying customer leave? [*Back to HILDA.*] Now I'll have a mint julip and easy on the mint.

HILDA.   This pre-teen with you?

JOHN POLK.   Well, I . . . No . . . I . . .

HILDA.   I.D.'s.

ASHBE.   Certainly, I always try to cooperate with the management.   85

HILDA.   [*Looking at JOHN POLK'S I.D.*] I.D., 11-12-50. Date: 11-11-68.

JOHN POLK.   Yes, but . . . well, 11-12 is less than two hours away.

HILDA.   Back in two hours.

ASHBE.   I seem to have left my identification in my gold lamé bag.

HILDA.   Well, boo-hoo. [*Motions for ASHBE to leave with a minimum of effort. She*   90
goes back to table.] No tip.

ASHBE.   You didn't tip her?

JOHN POLK.   I figured the drinks were so expensive . . . I just didn't . . .

HILDA.   No tip!

JOHN POLK.   Look, Miss, I'm sorry. [*Going through his pockets.*] Here would you
like a . . . a nickel . . . wait, wait, here's a quarter.

HILDA.   Just move ass, sonny. You too, Barbie.   95

ASHBE.   Ugh, I hate public rudeness. I'm sure I'll refrain from ever coming
here again.

HILDA.   Think I'll go in the back room and cry.

[*ASHBE and JOHN POLK exit. HILDA picks up tray and exits*

through the curtain, tripping again.]

HILDA.   Shit. Damn curtain.

[*ASHBE and JOHN POLK are now standing outside under the awning of the bar.*]

ASHBE.   Gee, I didn't know it was your birthday tomorrow. Happy birthday!
Don't be mad. I thought you were at least twenty or twenty-one, really.

JOHN POLK.   It's o.k. Forget it.   100

[*As they begin walking, various blues are heard coming from the nearby bars.*]

ASHBE.   It's raining.

JOHN POLK.   I know.

ASHBE.   Are you going over to the house now?

JOHN POLK.   No, not till twelve.

ASHBE.   Yeah, the red and black cards—they mean all night. Midnight till   105
morning.

[*At this point a street BARKER beckons the couple into his establishment. Perhaps he is accompanied by a WHORE.*]

BARKER.   Hey mister, bring your baby on in, buy her a few drinks, maybe
tonight ya get lucky.

ASHBE.   Keep walking.

JOHN POLK.   What's wrong with the place?

ASHBE.   The drinks are watery rot gut, and the show girls are boys . . .

BARKER.   Up yours, punk!   110

JOHN POLK. [*Who has now sat down on a street bench.*] Look, just tell me where a cheap bar is. I've got to stay drunk, but I don't have much money left.

ASHBE. Yikes, there aren't too many cheap bars around here, and a lot of them check I.D.'s.

JOHN POLK. Well, do you know of any that don't?

ASHBE. No, not for sure.

JOHN POLK. Oh, God, I need to get drunk.

ASHBE. Aren't you?

JOHN POLK. Some, but I'm losing ground fast.

[*By this time a* BUM *who has been traveling drunkenly down the street falls near the couple and begins throwing up.*]

ASHBE. Oh, I know! You can come to my apartment. It's just down the block. We keep one bottle of rum around. I'll serve you a grand drink, three or four if you like.

JOHN POLK. [*Fretfully.*] No, thanks.

ASHBE. But look, we're getting all wet.

JOHN POLK. Sober too, wet and sober.

ASHBE. Oh, come on! Rain's blurring my glasses.

JOHN POLK. Well, how about your parents? What would they say?

ASHBE. Daddy's out of town and Mama lives in Atlanta; so I'm sure they won't mind. I think we have some cute little marshmallows. [*Pulling on him.*] Won't you really come?

JOHN POLK. You've probably got some gang of muggers waiting to kill me. Oh, all right . . . what the hell, let's go.

ASHBE. Hurrah! Come on. It's this way. [*She starts across the stage, stops, and picks up an old hat.*] Hey, look at this hat. Isn't it something! Here, wear it to keep off the rain.

JOHN POLK. [*Throwing hat back onto street.*] No, thanks, you don't know who's worn it before.

ASHBE. [*Picking hat back up.*] That makes it all the more exciting. Maybe it was a butcher's who slaughtered his wife or a silver pirate with a black bird on his throat. Who do you guess?

JOHN POLK. I don't know. Anyway what's the good of guessing? I mean you'll never really know.

ASHBE. [*Trying the hat on.*] Yeah, probably not.

[*At this point* ASHBE *and* JOHN POLK *reach the front door.*]

ASHBE. Here we are.

[ASHBE *begins fumbling for her key.* CLAREECE, *a teeny-bopper, walks up to* JOHN POLK.]

CLAREECE. Hey, man, got any spare change?

JOHN POLK. [*Looking through his pockets.*] Let me see . . . I . . .

ASHBE. [*Coming up between them, giving* CLAREECE *a shove.*] Beat it, Clareece. He's my company.

CLAREECE. [*Walks away and sneers.*] Oh, shove it, Frizzels.

ASHBE. A lot of jerks live around here. Come on in. [*She opens the door. Lights go up on the living room of a run-down apartment in a run-down apartment house. Besides being merely run-down the room is a malicious pig sty with colors, paper hats, paper dolls, masks, torn up stuffed animals, dead flowers and leaves, dress-up clothes, etc., thrown all about.*] My bones are cold. Do you want a towel to dry off?

JOHN POLK.   Yes, thank you.

ASHBE.   [*She picks up a towel off the floor and tosses it to him.*] Here. [*He begins drying off, as she takes off her rain things; then she begins raking things off the sofa.*] Please do sit down. [*He sits.*] I'm sorry the place is disheveled, but my father's been out of town. I always try to pick up and all before he gets in. Of course, he's pretty used to messes. My mother never was too good at keeping things clean.

JOHN POLK.   When's he coming back?

ASHBE.   Sunday, I believe. Oh, I've been meaning to say . . .   140

JOHN POLK.   What?

ASHBE.   My name's Ashbe Williams.

JOHN POLK.   Ashbe?

ASHBE.   Yeah, Ashbe.

JOHN POLK.   My name's John Polk Richards.   145

ASHBE.   John Polk? They call you John Polk?

JOHN POLK.   It's family.

ASHBE.   [*Putting on socks.*] These are my favorite socks, the red furry ones. Well, here's some books and magazines to look at while I fix you something to drink. What do you want in your rum?

JOHN POLK.   Coke's fine.

ASHBE.   I'll see if we have any. I think I'll take some hot Kool-Aid myself.   150

[*She exits to the kitchen.*]

JOHN POLK.   Hot Kool-Aid?

ASHBE.   It's just Kool-Aid that's been heated, like hot chocolate or hot tea.

JOHN POLK.   Sounds great.

ASHBE.   Well, I'm used to it. You get so much for your dime, it makes it worth your while. I don't buy presweetened, of course, it's better to sugar your own.

JOHN POLK.   I remember once I threw up a lot of grape Kool-Aid when I was a   155
kid. I've hated it ever since. Hey, would you check on the time?

ASHBE.   [*She enters carrying a tray with several bottles of food coloring, a bottle of rum, and a huge glass.*] I'm sorry we don't have Coke. I wonder if rum and Kool-Aid is good? Oh, we don't have a clock either.

[*She pours a large amount of rum into the large glass.*]

JOHN POLK.   I'll just have it with water then.

ASHBE.   [*She finds an almost empty glass of water somewhere in the room and dumps it in with the rum.*] Would you like food coloring in the water? It makes a drink all the more aesthetic. Of course, some people don't care for aesthetics.

JOHN POLK.   No, thank you, just plain water.

ASHBE.   Are you sure? The taste is entirely the same. I put it in all my water.   160

JOHN POLK.   Well . . .

ASHBE.   What color do you want?

JOHN POLK.   I don't know.

ASHBE.   What's your favorite color?

JOHN POLK.   Blue, I guess.   165

[*She puts a few blue drops into the glass. As she has nothing to stir with, she blows into the glass turning the water blue.*]

JOHN POLK. Thanks.

ASHBE. [*Exits. She screams from kitchen.*] Come on, say come on, cat, eat your fresh, good milk.

JOHN POLK. You have a cat?

ASHBE. [*off.*] No.

JOHN POLK. Oh.

ASHBE. [*She enters carrying a tray with a cup of hot Kool-Aid and Cheerios and colored marshmallows.*] Here are some Cheerios and some cute, little, colored marshmallows to eat with your drink.

JOHN POLK. Thanks.

ASHBE. I one time smashed all the big white marshmallows in the plastic bag at the grocery store.

JOHN POLK. Why did you do that?

ASHBE. I was angry. Do you like ceramics?

JOHN POLK. Yes.

ASHBE. My mother makes them. It's sort of her hobby. She is very talented.

JOHN POLK. My mother never does anything. Well, I guess she can shuffle the bridge deck okay.

ASHBE. Actually, my mother is a dancer. She teaches at a school in Atlanta. She's really very talented.

JOHN POLK. [*Indicates ceramics.*] She must be to do all these.

ASHBE. Well, Madeline, my older sister, did the blue one. Madeline gets to live with Mama.

JOHN POLK. And you live with your father.

ASHBE. Yeah, but I get to go visit them sometimes.

JOHN POLK. You do ceramics too?

ASHBE. No, I never learned . . . but I have this great potholder set. [*Gets up to show him.*] See, I make lots of multicolored potholders and send them to Mama and Madeline. I also make paper hats. [*Gets material to show him.*] I guess they're more creative, but making potholders is more relaxing. Here would you like to make a hat?

JOHN POLK. I don't know, I'm a little drunk.

ASHBE. It's not hard a bit. [*Hands him material.*] Just draw a real pretty design on the paper. It really doesn't have to be pretty, just whatever you want.

JOHN POLK. It's kind of you to give my creative drives such freedom.

ASHBE. Ha, ha, ha, I'll work on my potholder set a bit.

JOHN POLK. What time is it? I've really got to check on the time.

ASHBE. I know. I'll call the time operator.

[*She goes to the phone.*]

JOHN POLK. How do you get along without a clock?

ASHBE. Well, I've been late for school a lot. Daddy has a watch. It's 11:03.

JOHN POLK. I've got a while yet. [*Ashbe twirls back to her chair, drops, and sighs.*] Are you a dancer, too?

ASHBE. [*Delighted.*] I can't dance a bit, really. I practice a lot is all, at home in the afternoon. I imagine you go to a lot of dances.

JOHN POLK. Not really, I'm a terrible dancer. I usually get bored or drunk.

ASHBE. You probably drink too much.

JOHN POLK. No, it's just since I've come to college. All you do there is drink more beer and write more papers.

ASHBE.   What are you studying for to be?

JOHN POLK.   I don't know.   200

ASHBE.   Why don't you become a rancher?

JOHN POLK.   Dad wants me to help run his soybean farm.

ASHBE.   Soybean farm. Yikes, that's really something. Where is it?

JOHN POLK.   Well, I live in the Delta, Hollybluff, Mississippi. Anyway, Dad feels I should go to business school first; you know, so I'll become, well, management-minded. Pass the blue.

ASHBE.   Is that what you really want to do?   205

JOHN POLK.   I don't know. It would probably be as good as anything else I could do. Dad makes good money. He can take vacations whenever he wants. Sure it'll be a ball.

ASHBE.   I'd hate to have to be management-minded. [*John Polk shrugs.*] I don't mean to hurt your feelings, but I would really hate to be a management mind. [*She starts walking on her knees, twisting her fists in front of her eyes, and making clicking sounds as a management mind would make.*]

JOHN POLK.   Cut it out. Just forget it. The farm could burn down, and I wouldn't even have to think about it.

ASHBE.   [*After a pause.*] Well, what do you want to talk about?

JOHN POLK.   I don't know.   210

ASHBE.   When was the last dance you went to?

JOHN POLK.   Dances. That's a great subject. Let's see, oh, I don't really remember—it was probably some blind date. God, I hate dates.

ASHBE.   Why?

JOHN POLK.   Well, they always say that they don't want popcorn, and they wind up eating all of yours.

ASHBE.   You mean, you hate dates just because they eat your popcorn? Don't   215
you think that's kind of stingy?

JOHN POLK.   It's the principle of the thing. Why can't they just say, yes, I'd like some popcorn when you ask them. But, no, they're always so damn coy.

ASHBE.   I'd tell my date if I wanted popcorn. I'm not that immature.

JOHN POLK.   Anyway, it's not only the popcorn. It's a lot of little things. I've finished coloring. What do I do now?

ASHBE.   Now you have to fold it. Here . . . like this. [*She explains the process with relish.*] Say, that's really something.

JOHN POLK.   It's kind of funny looking. [*Putting the hat on.*] Yeah, I like it, but   220
you could never wear it anywhere.

ASHBE.   Well, like what anyway?

JOHN POLK.   Huh?

ASHBE.   The things dates do to you that you don't like, the little things.

JOHN POLK.   Oh, well, just the way they wear those false eyelashes and put their hand on your knee when you're trying to parallel park, and keep on giggling and going off to the bathroom with their girl friends. It's obvious they don't want to go out with me. They just want to go out so that they can wear their new clothes and won't have to sit on their ass in the dormitory. They never want to go out with me. I can never even talk to them.

ASHBE.   Well, you can talk to me, and I'm a girl.   225

JOHN POLK.   Well, I'm really kind of drunk, and you're a stranger . . . well, I probably wouldn't be able to talk to you tomorrow. That makes a difference.

ASHBE.   Maybe it does. [*A bit of a pause and then extremely pleased by the idea she says.*] You know we're alike because I don't like dances either.

JOHN POLK.   I thought you said you practiced . . . in the afternoons.

ASHBE.   Well, I like dancing. I just don't like dances. At least not like . . . well, not like the one our school was having tonight . . . they're so corny.

JOHN POLK.   Yeah, most dances are.   2?

ASHBE.   All they serve is potato chips and fruit punch, and then this stupid baby band plays and everybody dances around thinking they're so hot. I frankly wouldn't dance there. I would prefer to wait till I am invited to an exclusive ball. It doesn't really matter which ball, just one where they have huge, golden chandeliers and silver fountains, and serve delicacies of all sorts and bubble blue champagne. I'll arrive in a pink silk cape. [*Laughing.*] I want to dance in pink!

JOHN POLK.   You're mixed up. You're probably one of those people that live in a fantasy world.

ASHBE.   I do not. I accept reality as well as anyone. Anyway, you can talk to me, remember. I know what you mean by the kind of girls it's hard to talk to. There are girls a lot that way in the small clique at my school. Really tacky and mean. They expect everyone to be as stylish as they are, and they won't even speak to you in the hall. I don't mind if they don't speak to me, but I really love the orphans, and it hurts my feelings when they are so mean to them.

JOHN POLK.   What do you mean—they're mean to the "orpheens"? [*Giggles to himself at the wordplay.*]

ASHBE.   Oh, well, they sometimes snicker at the orphans' dresses. The orphans   23■ usually have hand-me-down, drab, ugly dresses. Once Shelly Maxwell wouldn't let Glinda borrow her pencil, even though she had two. It hurt her feelings.

JOHN POLK.   Are you best friends with these orphans?

ASHBE.   I hardly know them at all. They're really shy. I just like them a lot. They're the reason I put spells on the girls in the clique.

JOHN POLK.   Spells, what do you mean, witch spells?

ASHBE.   Witch spells? Not really, mostly just voodoo.

JOHN POLK.   Are you kidding? Do you really do voodoo?   24

ASHBE.   Sure, here I'll show you my doll. [*Goes to get doll, comes back with straw voodoo doll. Her air as she returns is one of frightening mystery.*] I know a lot about the subject. Cora, she used to wash dishes in the Moonlight Cafe, told me all about voodoo. She's a real expert on the subject, went to all the meetings and everything. Once she caused a man's throat to rot away and turn almost totally black. She's moved to Chicago now.

JOHN POLK.   It doesn't really work. Does it?

ASHBE.   Well, not always. The thing about voodoo is that both parties have to believe in it for it to work.

JOHN POLK.   Do the girls in school believe in it?

ASHBE.   Not really, I don't think. That's where my main problem comes in. I   24 have to make the clique believe in it, yet I have to be very subtle. Mainly, I give reports in English class or Speech.

JOHN POLK.   Reports?

ASHBE.   On voodoo.

JOHN POLK.   That's really kind of sick, you know.

ASHBE.   Not really. I don't cast spells that'll do any real harm. Mainly, just the kind of thing to make them think . . . to keep them on their toes. [*Blue-drink intoxication begins to take over and JOHN POLK begins laughing.*] What's so funny?

JOHN POLK.   Nothing. I was just thinking what a mean little person you are.   250

ASHBE.   Mean! I'm not mean a bit.

JOHN POLK.   Yes, you are mean . . . [*Picking up color.*] . . . and green too.

ASHBE.   Green?

JOHN POLK.   Yes, green with envy of those other girls; so you play all those mean little tricks.

ASHBE.   Envious of those other girls, that stupid, close-minded little clique!   255

JOHN POLK.   Green as this marshmallow. [*Eats marshmallow.*]

ASHBE.   You think I want to be in some group . . . a sheep like you? A little sheep like you that does everything when he's supposed to do it!

JOHN POLK.   Me a sheep . . . I do what I want!

ASHBE.   Ha! I've known you for an hour and already I see you for the sheep you are!

JOHN POLK.   Don't take your green meanness out on me.   260

ASHBE.   Not only are you a sheep, you are a NORMAL sheep. Give me back my colors! [*Begins snatching colors away.*]

JOHN POLK.   [*Pushing colors at her.*] Green and mean! Green and mean! Green and mean!

ASHBE.   [*Throwing marshmallows at him.*] That's the reason you're in a fraternity and the reason you're going to manage your mind. And dates . . . you go out on dates merely because it's expected of you even though you have a terrible time. That's the reason you go to the whorehouse to prove you're a normal man. Well, you're much too normal for me.

JOHN POLK.   Infant bitch. You think you're really cute.

ASHBE.   That really wasn't food coloring in your drink, it was poison! [*She   265 laughs, he picks up his coat to go, and she stops throwing marshmallows at him.*] Are you going? I was only kidding. For Christ sake, it wasn't really poison. Come on, don't go. Can't you take a little friendly criticism?

JOHN POLK.   Look, did you have to bother me tonight? I had enough problems without . . .

[*Phone rings. Both look at phone, it rings for the third time. He stands undecided.*]

ASHBE.   Look, wait, we'll make it up. [*She goes to answer phone.*] Hello . . . Daddy. How are you? . . . I'm fine . . . Dad, you sound funny . . . What? . . . Come on, Daddy, you know she's not here. [*Pause.*] Look, I told you I wouldn't call anymore. You've got her number in Atlanta. [*Pause, as she sinks to the floor.*] Why have you started again? . . . Don't say that. I can tell it. I can. Hey, I have to go to bed now, I don't want to talk anymore, okay? [*Hangs up phone, then softly to self.*] Goddamnit.

JOHN POLK.   [*He has heard the conversation and is taking off his coat.*] Hey, Ashbe . . . [*She looks at him blankly, her mind far away.*] You want to talk?

ASHBE.   No. [*Slight pause.*] Why don't you look at my shell collection? I have this special shell collection. [*She shows him collection.*]

JOHN POLK.   They're beautiful, I've never seen colors like this. [*ASHBE is silent,   270 he continues to himself.*] I used to go to Biloxi° a lot when I was a kid . . . One time my brother and I, we camped out on the beach. The sky was purple. I remember it was really purple. We ate pork and beans out of a can. I'd always kinda wanted to do that.

Biloxi: city in southern Mississippi, on the Gulf of Mexico.

Every night for about a week after I got home, I dreamt about these waves foaming over my head and face. It was funny. Did you find these shells or buy them?

ASHBE.   Some I found, some I bought. I've been trying to decipher their meaning. Here, listen, do you hear that?

JOHN POLK.   Yes.

ASHBE.   That's the soul of the sea. [*She listens.*] I'm pretty sure it's the soul of the sea. Just imagine when I decipher the language. I'll know all the secrets of the world.

JOHN POLK.   Yeah, probably you will. [*Looking into the shell.*] You know, you were right.

ASHBE.   What do you mean?   27

JOHN POLK.   About me, you were right. I am a sheep, a normal one. I've been trying to get out of it, but now I'm as big a sheep as ever.

ASHBE.   Oh, it doesn't matter. You're company. It was rude of me to say.

JOHN POLK.   No, because it was true. I really didn't want to go into a fraternity, I didn't even want to go to college, and I sure as hell don't want to go back to Hollybluff and work the soybean farm till I'm eighty.

ASHBE.   I still say you could work on a ranch.

JOHN POLK.   I don't know. I wanted to be a minister or something good, but I   28
don't even know if I believe in God.

ASHBE.   Yeah.

JOHN POLK.   I never used to worry about being a failure. Now I think about it all the time. It's just I need to do something that's . . . fulfilling.

ASHBE.   Fulfilling, yes, I see what you mean. Well, how about college? Isn't it fulfilling? I mean, you take all those wonderful classes, and you have all your very good friends.

JOHN POLK.   Friends, yeah, I have some friends.

ASHBE.   What do you mean?

JOHN POLK.   Nothing . . . well, I do mean something. What the hell, let me try   28
to explain. You see it was my "friends," the fraternity guys that set me up with G.G.,
excuse me, Myrtle, as a gift for my eighteenth birthday.

ASHBE.   You mean, you didn't want the appointment?

JOHN POLK.   No, I didn't want it. Hey, ah, where did my blue drink go?

ASHBE.   [*As she hands him the drink.*] They probably thought you really wanted to go.

JOHN POLK.   Yeah, I'm sure they gave a damn what I wanted. They never even   29
asked me. Hell, I would have told them a handkerchief, a pair of argyle socks, but, no, they have to get me a whore just because it's a cool-ass thing to do. They make me sick. I couldn't even stay at the party they gave. All the sweaty T-shirts, and moron sex stories . . . I just couldn't take it.

ASHBE.   Is that why you were at the Blue Angel so early?

JOHN POLK.   Yeah, I needed to get drunk, but not with them. They're such creeps.

ASHBE.   Gosh, so you really don't want to go to Myrtle's?

JOHN POLK.   No, I guess not.

ASHBE.   Then are you going?   29

JOHN POLK.   [*Pause.*] Yes.

ASHBE.   That's wrong. You shouldn't go just to please them.

JOHN POLK.   Oh, that's not the point anymore, maybe at first it was, but it's not anymore. Now I have go for myself . . . to prove to myself that I'm not afraid.

ASHBE.   Afraid? [*Slowly, as she begins to grasp his meaning.*] You mean, you've
never slept with a girl before?

JOHN POLK.   Well, I've never been in love.   300

ASHBE.   [*In amazement.*] You're a virgin?

JOHN POLK.   Oh, God.

ASHBE.   No, don't feel bad, I am too.

JOHN POLK.   I thought I should be in love . . .

ASHBE.   Well, you're certainly not in love with Myrtle. I mean, you haven't even   305
met her.

JOHN POLK.   I know, but, God, I thought maybe I'd never fall in love. What
then? You should experience everything . . . shouldn't you? Oh, what's it matter,
everything's so screwed.

ASHBE.   Screwed? Yeah, I guess it is. I mean, I always thought it would be fun
to have a lot of friends who gave parties and go to dances all dressed up. Like the
dance tonight . . . it might have been fun.

JOHN POLK.   Well, why didn't you go?

ASHBE.   I don't know. I'm not sure it would have been fun. Anyway, you can't
go . . . alone.

JOHN POLK.   Oh, you need a date?   310

ASHBE.   Yeah, or something.

JOHN POLK.   Say, Ashbe, ya wanna dance here?

ASHBE.   No, I think we'd better discuss your dilemma.

JOHN POLK.   What dilemma?

ASHBE.   Myrtle. It doesn't seem right you should . . .   315

JOHN POLK.   Let's forget Myrtle for now. I've got a while yet. Here have some
more of this blue-moon drink.

ASHBE.   You're only trying to escape through artificial means.

JOHN POLK.   Yeah, you got it. Now come on. Would you like to dance? Hey,
you said you liked to dance.

ASHBE.   You're being ridiculous.

JOHN POLK.   [*Winking at her.*] Dance?   320

ASHBE.   John Polk, I just thought . . .

JOHN POLK.   Hmm?

ASHBE.   How to solve your problem . . .

JOHN POLK.   Well . . .

ASHBE.   Make love to me!   325

JOHN POLK.   What?!

ASHBE.   It all seems logical to me. It would prove you weren't scared, and you
wouldn't be doing it just to impress others.

JOHN POLK.   Look, I . . . I mean, I hardly know you . . .

ASHBE.   But we've talked. It's better this way, really. I won't be so apt to point
out your mistakes.

JOHN POLK.   I'd feel great, stripping a twelve-year-old of her virginity.   330

ASHBE.   I'm sixteen! Anyway, I'd be stripping you of yours just as well. I'll go
put on some Tiger Claw perfume. [*She runs out.*]

JOHN POLK.   Hey, come back! Tiger Claw perfume, Christ.

ASHBE.   [*Entering.*] I think one should have different scents for different
moods.

JOHN POLK.   Hey, stop spraying that! You know I'm not going to . . . well, you'd get neurotic, or pregnant, or some damn thing. Stop spraying, will you!

ASHBE.   Pregnant? You really think I could get pregnant?   33

JOHN POLK.   Sure, it'd be a delightful possibility.

ASHBE.   It really wouldn't be bad. Maybe I would get to go to Tokyo for an abortion. I've never been to the Orient.

JOHN POLK.   Sure getting cut on is always a real treat.

ASHBE.   Anyway, I might just want to have my dear baby. I could move to Atlanta with Mama and Madeline. It'd be wonderful fun. Why I could take him to the supermarket, put him in one of those little baby seats to stroll him about. I'd buy peach baby food and feed it to him with a tiny golden spoon. Why I could take colored pictures of him and send them to you through the mail. Come on . . . [*Starts putting pillows onto the couch.*] Well, I guess you should kiss me for a start. It's only etiquette, everyone begins with it.

JOHN POLK.   I don't think I could even kiss you with a clear conscience. I   34 mean, you're so small with those little cat-eye glasses and curly hair . . . I couldn't even kiss you.

ASHBE.   You couldn't even kiss me? I can't help it if I have to wear glasses. I got the prettiest ones I could find.

JOHN POLK.   Your glasses are fine. Let's forget it, okay?

ASHBE.   I know, my lips are too purple, but if I eat carrots, the dye'll come off and they'll be orange.

JOHN POLK.   I didn't say anything about your lips being too purple.

ASHBE.   Well, what is it? You're just plain chicken, I suppose . . .   34

JOHN POLK.   Sure, right, I'm chicken, totally chicken. Let's forget it. I don't know how, but, somehow, this is probably all my fault.

ASHBE.   You're darn right it's all your fault! I want to have my dear baby or at least get to Japan. I'm so sick of school I could smash every marshmallow in sight! [*She starts smashing.*] Go on to your skinny pimple whore. I hope the skinny whore laughs in your face, which she probably will because you have an easy face to laugh in.

JOHN POLK.   You're absolutely right, she'll probably hoot and howl her damn fizzle red head off. Maybe you can wait outside the door and hear her, give you lots of pleasure, you sadistic, little thief.

ASHBE.   Thief! Was Robin Hood . . . Oh, what's wrong with this world? I just wasn't made for it, is all. I've probably been put in the wrong world, I can see that now.

JOHN POLK.   You're fine in this world.   35

ASHBE.   Sure, everyone just views me as an undesirable lump.

JOHN POLK.   Who?

ASHBE.   You, for one.

JOHN POLK.   [*Pause.*] You mean because I wouldn't make love to you?

ASHBE.   It seems clear to me.   35

JOHN POLK.   But you're wrong, you know.

ASHBE.   [*To self, softly.*] Don't pity me.

JOHN POLK.   The reason I wouldn't wasn't that . . . it's just that . . . well, I like you too much to.

ASHBE.   You like me?

JOHN POLK.   Undesirable lump, Jesus. Your cheeks they're . . . they're . . .   36

ASHBE. My cheeks? They're what?

JOHN POLK. They're rosy.

ASHBE. My cheeks are rosy?

JOHN POLK. Yeah, your cheeks, they're really rosy.

ASHBE. Well, they're natural, you know. Say, would you like to dance? 365

JOHN POLK. Yes.

ASHBE. I'll turn on the radio. [*She turns on radio. Ethel Waters is heard singing "Honey in the Honeycomb." ASHBE begins snapping her fingers.*] Yikes, let's jazz it out.

[*They dance.*]

JOHN POLK. Hey, I'm not good or anything . . .

ASHBE. John Polk.

JOHN POLK. Yeah? 370

ASHBE. Baby, I think you dance fine!

[*They dance on, laughing, saying what they want till end of song. Then a radio announcer comes on and says the 12:00 news will be in five minutes. Billie Holiday, or Terry Pierce, begins singing, "Am I Blue?"*]

JOHN POLK. Dance?

ASHBE. News in five minutes.

JOHN POLK. Yeah.

ASHBE. That means five minutes till midnight. 375

JOHN POLK. Yeah, I know.

ASHBE. Then you're not . . .

JOHN POLK. Ashbe, I've never danced all night. Wouldn't it be something to . . . to dance all night and watch the rats come out of the gutter?

ASHBE. Rats?

JOHN POLK. Don't they come out at night? I hear New Orleans has lots of rats. 380

ASHBE. Yeah, yeah, it's got lots of rats.

JOHN POLK. Then let's dance all night and wait for them to come out.

ASHBE. All right . . . but, but how about our feet?

JOHN POLK. Feet?

ASHBE. They'll hurt. 385

JOHN POLK. Yeah.

ASHBE. [*Smiling.*] Okay, then let's dance.

[*He takes her hand, and they dance as lights black out and the music soars and continues to play.*]

End.

QUESTIONS

1. What do Ashbe's actions at the start tell you about her (such as hiding under the coat, stealing and giving the stolen things away, crawling away from the waitress)? What is disclosed by her speeches?

2. Describe the circumstances of Ashbe and her family. To what degree can her character and behavior be explained by these circumstances?

3. What is Ashbe's intention in her description of G.G., or Myrtle? What does her description tell you about her? What do you learn about her from her description of the only sort of dance she would like to go to (speech 231)?

4. What personal, occupational, and social difficulties is John Polk experiencing? Why is he trying to stay drunk before going to G.G.? What are his reactions to fraternity life and to the family business?

5. Explain the effects of the arguments between Ashbe and John Polk. How does their occasionally taunting each other influence their developing relationship?

6. Why does John Polk not take up Ashbe's invitation to make love? How does this refusal suggest the development of his character? Of Ashbe's character? What may be inferred by their concluding decision to dance the night away?

GENERAL QUESTIONS

1. What is the plot of *Am I Blue?* Who is the protagonist (or protagonists)? Who or what is the antagonist? How is the plot resolved?

2. Describe and analyze the verbal comedy of the play, such as the "two murders and a knifing" (speech 49), Ashbe's description of Myrtle (speeches 71–73), and the inquiry about what to mix with rum (speech 148).

3. What is appealing (or not appealing) about Ashbe and John Polk? To what extent are you to consider them as realistic persons? How might they be seen as symbols, and what might they symbolize?

4. What are the major themes or ideas of the play? To what extent does the comic mode obscure these ideas? To what extent does it bring them out?

5. What is the effect of the setting in the New Orleans French Quarter and the characters to be found there? What is shown about Ashbe and John Polk by their brief interactions with the characters in the bar, especially Hilda, and on the street?

WRITING ABOUT COMEDY

For an essay about comedy, you may choose most of the conventional topics such as *plot, conflict, character, point of view, setting, style, tone, symbolism,* or *theme.* You might choose one of these, or two or more; e.g., how language and action define character, how character and symbol convey meaning, or how setting may influence comic structure.

Planning and prewriting strategies for each of these conventional elements are discussed at some length in Chapter 26 (pp. 1060–64) and in other chapters on prose fiction and poetry. As you develop your essay, you will find it helpful to look at these suggestions.

For the most part, planning and writing about specific features of comedy are much like addressing the same topics in other forms of drama, short stories, and poetry. However, a few areas of consideration—such as plot, character, and language—are especially significant in comic drama, and may be handled in a distinctive fashion.

Questions for Discovering Ideas

PLOT, CONFLICT, STRUCTURE. What problems, adversities, or abnormal situations are in place at the comedy's opening? How is this initial situation complicated? Do the complications spring mainly from character or from situation? If from character, what aspects of behavior or personality create the problems? If from situation, what dilemmas or troubles plague the characters? What kinds of complications dominate—misunderstandings, disagreements, mistakes in identity, situational problems, or emotional entanglements? How important is coincidence?

What problems and complications occur early? Who is the comic protagonist (or protagonists) and what is the protagonist's goal (money, success, marriage, land, freedom)? How is the protagonist blocked (fathers, rivals, laws, customs, his or her own personality)? How threatening is the obstruction? What plans are hatched to overcome the blocking agents? Are the plans sensible or silly? Who initiates and executes the plans? To what extent do plans succeed (or fail)—because of chance and good luck or because of skillful planning and manipulation?

Describe the conflicts. Which conflict is central, and whom do the conflicts involve? Do they result from personality clashes or from situations? To what degree are they related to blocking activities? How does the action reach the crisis, and which characters are involved? What choices, decisions, plans, or conclusions become necessary? What events or revelations (of character, emotion, background) produce the catastrophe, and how do these affect characters, circumstances, and relationships?

In the comic resolution, to what extent are loose ends tied up, lives straightened out, reasonable order restored, and regeneration assured or implied? Is the resolution satisfying? Disturbing? Does it leave you happy or thoughtful, or both? Are you amused by farce, pleased by romance, or disturbed by satire? If there is to be a marriage, whom will it bring together? What will the marriage settle, or whom will it divide? Most important, how can you account for your responses to the resolution and the play as a whole? How do they reflect the general aims of comedy?

CHARACTER. Which characters are realistic, conventional, round, flat, changing, standing still? Who is the protagonist or lover, the antagonist or blocking agent? Who is the choric figure or *raisonneur*, if there is one? Who is the confidant? The foil or foils? From what classes are the characters derived? What class characteristics do you find? Who are the stock or stereotyped characters, and what is their significant to the protagonist? How does the playwright invigorate the characters?

What characters are excessive, eccentric, or irrational? What is the nature of such excesses? To what extent do the excesses define the characters? How do you respond to the excessive or exaggerated characters? Does the comedy provide a "cure" for the excesses? In other words, do the characters learn and change? If so, why and how? If not, why not?

LANGUAGE. Does the language consist of witty turns of phrase, confusions, puns, misunderstandings, or a mixture? Which characters are masters of language and which are mastered by it? Do characters use the same type of language and level of diction consistently? To what extent does language expose a character's self interest or hypocrisy? If the language is witty and sparkling, what devices make it work effectively? If it is garbled and filled with misunderstandings, what types of errors does the playwright put into the characters' mouths? How does the language shape your response to characters, to ideas, and to the play as a whole?

Strategies for Organizing Ideas

To develop a central idea, isolate the feature you wish to explore and consider how it affects the shape and impact of the play. For *A Midsummer Night's Dream,* for example, you might focus on Puck's character and function. You might also develop a link between Puck's conventional role as a tricky servant with his love of mischief and the chaos he creates. Remember that it is difficult to develop essays from sentences like "Puck is a comic character" or "*Love Is the Doctor* contains dramatic satire." A more focused assertion that also reveals your thematic development is necessary, such as "Puck, modeled on the tricky servant of Roman Comedy, causes most of the play's confusion," or "*Love Is the Doctor* satirizes the medical profession on the grounds of ignorance and greed."

Organize your essay by grouping related types of details together (such as observations about characters, actions, direct statements, and specific words), and choose your own order of presentation. In writing about Puck as a tricky servant and creator of chaos, for example, you might present only one kind of detail—such as direct statements by the character—and introduce these not in their order in the play but rather as they contribute to your analysis of Puck's character.

More often than not, your supporting details will represent a variety of types of evidence—dramatic dialogue and action, individual soliloquies, special properties (such as a love potion, or a disguise), or the failure or development of various plans. For example, you might support an assertion about Puck by referring to his reputation, actions, and attitudes as though each of these is equally important. Other possible strategies are to demonstrate how the topics are related according to cause-and-effect, to build the topics from the least to the most significant, and to trace how a common idea or image provides unity. Whatever your method of development, be sure to validate your arguments with supporting details.

A summary of key points will make your conclusion useful and effective. In addition, you may show how your conclusions in the body of the essay bear upon larger aspects of the play's meaning.

SAMPLE ESSAY

Setting as Symbol and Comic Structure in A Midsummer Night's Dream°

[1] Shakespeare's *A Midsummer Night's Dream* might superficially be considered light and inconsequential. The changes of mind undergone by the two sets of lovers, the placing of an ass's head on one of the characters, the presence of unrealistic fairies, the acting of a silly sketch—all seem far from reality and also far-fetched. But the play is real. It dramatizes the accidental and arbitrary origins of love, even though it considers this serious subject in the good-natured medium of comedy.* To bring out both message and merriment, Shakespeare uses two settings—the city of Athens and the nearby forest. The play's comic structure is governed by the movements between the order and the chaos that these two locations represent.†

[2] At the play's beginning, Athens is presented as a world of daylight, rigid order, and strict law. In this setting, Duke Theseus has absolute authority, fathers are always right, and the law permits Egeus to "dispose" of Hermia "either to this gentleman Demetrius, / Or to her death" (Act I. scene 1, lines 43–44). The city is also the place for the exposition and the beginning of complications. Here, we meet the various groups of characters (except the fairies), and learn about the initial problem—namely that the relationship between Hermia and Lysander is blocked by a raging father, a rival suitor, and an old law. To flee and then to overcome these obstructions, Lysander asks Hermia to meet him in the woods. Her agreement begins a journey from Athens to the forest that ultimately includes everyone in the play—the four lovers, Egeus, the city rulers, and the "mechanicals."

[3] The play's second setting, the woods outside Athens, is the kingdom of Oberon and Titania, the king and queen of the fairies. It is a world of darkness, moonlight, chaos, madness, and dreams, a world that symbolizes the power of imagination and passion. The disorder in this world has many sources, including Oberon's jealousy, Titania's infatuation, and Puck's delight in mischief. When the lovers and the mechanicals enter this setting, they also enter this disorder and chaos.

[4] The woods are the setting for complication, crisis, and catastrophe. Confusion dominates the action here. Puck disrupts the mechanicals' rehearsal and transforms Bottom into an ass-headed monster. More important, the passions of the lovers are rearranged several times by Oberon and Puck through the magic of "love-in-idleness," a flower that symbolizes love's irra-

---

° See p. 1325 for this play
* Central idea.
† Thesis sentence.

tional but overwhelming power. Although the first two adjustments of the lovers' feelings are done to help, each has the effect of raising the levels of complication and disorder. Puck gleefully observes that his actions are the cause of the play's confusions:

> those things do best please me
> That befall prepost'rously. (III.ii.120–121)

Puck is right; his first application of love-in-idleness causes Lysander to fall wildly in love with Helena, and his second does the same to Demetrius.

[5]
The crisis and catastrophe of the main plot also occur in the woods. A crisis occurs when the two lovers challenge each other and the women attack each other. At this point, complication is at a peak, and the fairies must develop a plan to resolve the threats. Puck therefore misleads the lovers to end their potential duel, and adjusts their emotions one more time. The catastrophe—the revelation of the newly restored emotions—occurs the next morning at the edge of the woods, in the presence of Egeus, Theseus, and Hippolyta. Thus, it ends the confusing relationships occurring in the forest, and begins the regularity of relationships in the orderly world of city and society.

[6]
Resolution—the marriages and the mechanicals' production of "Pyramus and Thisby"—occurs in the first setting, the city, that represents law and order. But the journey to the second setting has had a significant effect on the urban world both for Theseus and for the lovers. The law has been softened, Egeus overruled, the young lovers allowed to marry as they like, and lives set right. In the end, this second setting has also become the dream world of night and the supernatural, and the fairy dance and blessings closing the play only emphasize the harmony and the regenerative implications of the comic resolutions.

[7]
Setting, symbolism, and comic pattern thus combine in *A Midsummer Night's Dream* to produce an intricately plotted structure. Each element reinforces the others, bringing the play toward completion though time after time there seems to be no way out. The marvel of the play is that the two settings represent, realistically, two opposed states of being, and, dramatically, two distinct stages of comic structure. The journey out of Athens, into the woods, and then back to the city is also a journey from exposition and adversity, through complication, crisis, and catastrophe, to comic resolution.

Commentary on the Essay

This essay deals with three elements of *A Midsummer Night's Dream*: setting, symbol, and comic structure. It demonstrates the way by which a number of different topics may be combined in a single essay. Consequently, the essay is organized to reflect the journey from the city to the woods and then back to the city.

The body of the essay takes up the settings, their symbolic meaning, and the relationship between setting and structure. Paragraph 2 deals with Athens both as a world of law and order and as the setting for exposition and the beginnings of complication. The supporting details include circumstance, actions, and dialogue.

Paragraphs 3–5 deal with the middle of the journey and of the play.

Paragraph 3 discusses the symbolic implications of the forest setting, and paragraphs 4 and 5 take up the connection between the setting and comic structure, specifically complication, crisis, and catastrophe. Again, the supporting details in these paragraphs are a mixture of actions, circumstances, and direct quotations.

Paragraph 6 deals briefly with the return to the city, linking this setting with the play's comic resolution. The concluding paragraph returns to the idea about how *A Midsummer Night's Dream* connects setting, symbol, and comic pattern.

WRITING TOPICS

1. Write an essay describing Shakespeare's comic technique in *A Midsummer Night's Dream*. Consider these questions: Is the basic situation serious? How does Shakespeare keep it comic? How does the boisterousness of the low characters influence your perceptions of the lovers and the courtly characters? Would the play be as interesting without Bottom and his crowd, and without the fairies and their involvement? How does the comic outcome depend on the boisterousness and colorfulness provided by the players and the fairies?

2. Although *Love Is the Doctor* is a comic farce, it deals with serious topic material, namely a father trying to control his daughter's life, the exploitation of gullibility, and an illegal deception. How does Molière treat these topics and yet preserve the play's comic tone?

3. Write an essay which analyzes the relationship of situation to comedy in *Am I Blue*. How do the eccentricity of the characters and the improbability of their circumstances produce amusement? When you finish the play, do you believe that you have been seriously engaged? Just entertained? Explain.

4. Write an essay about the nature of comedy, using *A Midsummer Night's Dream*, *Am I Blue*, and *Love Is the Doctor* as material. Deal with issues like the following: How may comic material be defined? Does the happy outcome of a serious action qualify a play as a comedy, or should no action be serious ? When does a play stop being comic and start being tragic? Are jokes necessary? Is farcical action necessary? Where are the edges between comedy and farce, on the one hand, and comedy and tragedy on the other?

5. Treat the lovers in *A Midsummer Night's Dream* and *Love Is the Doctor* as types or archetypes (see Appendix D). What is their situation? What problems block the fulfillment of their love? How serious are these problems? What actions and ruses do they plan to make things right? How are the pairs of lovers in the two plays similar? Different?

6. Write a comic scene of your own between two people, perhaps between a boy and a girl, as in *Am I Blue*, or between a father and daughter, as in *Love Is the Doctor*, or between a person under a spell and a person in normal touch with reality, as in *A Midsummer Night's Dream*. When you've finished, write a short essay explaining the principles on which you've written your scene, such as the reasons for your choice of material, your use of jokes (if any), straightforward dialogue, anger, outrage, amused responses, and so on.

Realistic and Nonrealistic Drama: Varying the Idea of Drama as Imitation

A major dimension of drama is the relationship to reality that dramatists seek to create. From Aristotle's description of the origin of tragedy, we may conclude that drama was originally considered to be an "imitation of an action"; that is, each play constructs, or "mirrors," a significant lifelike story or complete incident. The circumstances of dramatic presentation force concentration on only actions and dialogue that are integrally related to the story, together with an outcome that is the logical consequence of the conflicts and issues raised in the play. To achieve this concentration, dramatists must introduce restrictions and nonrealistic conventions that aid the presentation of the story. Thus there can be no absolutely realistic drama in the sense of the straightforward duplication of life. The issue is how far drama goes either toward or away from reality.

REALISM AND NONREALISM IN DRAMA

The most important difference between realistic and nonrealistic drama concerns the play's relationships to the world at large, the audience, and the theater. In **realistic drama**, the playwright seeks to create an *illusion* of reality—*verisimilitude*. The situations, problems, characters, dialogue, and other elements are all those that might genuinely exist in the real world. The play, in effect, presents a self-contained action in a self-contained world that professes to imitate reality. Ideally, the illusion of reality is never compromised; the actors never drop out of character; the audience is never addressed; and the play never acknowledges that it is a play.

In **nonrealistic drama**, even the pretense to achieve realism is abandoned, and the goal instead is to present essential features of character and society through techniques that *do not* try to mirror life. Nonrealistic drama employs whatever conventions the playwright finds useful. It can be full of devices that break through the illusion on the stage (or the page) and scream out that the play is a play, a work of art, a stylized imitation of something remotely connected to life.

The Prevalence of Nonrealistic Drama

From ancient Greek tragedy through Victorian melodrama, plays were artificial and conventionalized. The conventions of drama changed from age to age—choruses and masks in Greek tragedy, soliloquies and blank verse in Elizabethan plays, rhymed couplets in French and much English neoclassical drama. Although these conventions were nonrealistic, they were accepted by audiences and readers as normal features of dramatic presentation. The enduring eloquence and power of the nonrealistic tradition may be found in plays like Sophocles' *Oedipus the King,* Shakespeare's *Hamlet,* and Molière's *Love Is the Doctor.*

By the nineteenth century, artificial and romantic drama had come to dominate the stage. These plays featured lavish sets, gorgeous costumes, flamboyant acting, conventionalized plots, and happy endings. The characters were exaggerated and idealized—heroes saving the day, heroines swooning at every opportunity, and villains twirling their mustaches and leering at the audience as they plotted to appropriate the hero's money and steal his sweetheart.

The Development of Realistic Drama

As a reaction against such plays, some nineteenth-century dramatists created plays that presented realistic characters in realistic situations and that explored the real problems of contemporary society. The rebellion began slowly, and most of these writers were Europeans; among them Emile Zola (French), Henrik Ibsen (Norwegian), Maxim Gorki (Russian), and George Bernard Shaw (Irish-English). American realists, who came to this tradition somewhat later than the Europeans, included Eugene O'Neill, Langston Hughes, and Susan Glaspell (pp. 1053, 1437, and 1038).

THE NATURE OF REALISM IN DRAMA. In keeping with the goal of verisimilitude, realistic plays eliminate traditional but artificial dramatic conventions that do not occur in daily life, such as disguises, overheard conversations, asides, soliloquies, and verse. At its best, realistic drama is a close examination of character in conflict. The plots are straightforward and progress chronologically. The characters look, speak, and act as much as possible like real people. The settings are middle-class living rooms, the country houses of the wealthy, the squalid slums of the poor. Usually the plays explore ideas about the nature of humanity in conflict with social customs and prejudices.

REALISM AND THE THEATER. The new realism called for equally new and realistic methods of production and action. Most theaters of the nineteenth century already featured a darkened auditorium, a proscenium arch separating the audience from the players, and a picture-frame stage. The spectators watched the play as though the fourth wall of a room had been removed. The illusion was that the audience was eavesdropping on private conversations and events.

The settings and stage directions for the realistic drama became as detailed and lifelike as possible. When the curtain went up, the audience saw a completely furnished room or office, much like the ones in which they themselves lived or worked. Ibsen's lengthy description of the setting for Acts I and II of *An Enemy of the People* (1882), for example, calls for the elaborate duplication of Norwegian middle-class living and dining rooms of the late nineteenth century (1882), complete with a sofa, a coffee table, a lighted lamp, a ceramic tile heating stove, a dining table at the end of a meal with all the china and utensils still on it, and a platter of roast beef. Lighting and costumes were equally realistic. Lighting was designed to duplicate the natural light at a particular time of day or the lamps burning in a room at night. Similarly, the lavish and beautiful costumes of nineteenth-century melodrama gave way to detailed realism in dress and makeup on the stage.

REALISM AND ACTING. The most radical and permanent change caused by the new realism was in acting styles. In the Victorian theater, actors stood in one place, assumed a conventional stance, and declaimed their lines. In realistic drama the acting became more natural and intimate. Actors began to combine movement with dialogue and to play "within the scene" to each other rather than to the spectators.

These changes were due, in large measure, to Constantin Stanislavski (1863–1938), one of the founders of the Moscow Art Theater (1898) and the inventor of what we now term *method acting*. Stanislavski argued that actors had to build characterizations on a lifelong study of inner truths and motivation. He taught actors to search inwardly, within the depths of their own souls, for the feelings, motivations, and behavior of the characters they portray.

The Rebellion Against Realism: The New Nonrealism

No sooner had realism taken over the stage than a new nonrealistic drama began to emerge as a reaction against realism. Many playwrights in Europe and America decided that realism had gone too far and that the quest for minutely realistic details had sacrificed the essence of drama—character and universal truth. Playwrights began to explore every avenue of anti-realistic drama.

NONREALISTIC DRAMA AND THE THEATER. At the same time, new types of stages and theaters began to appear. The **thrust stage**, from Elizabethan theaters, was reintroduced. It projected into the audience, thus helping to destroy the fourth-wall principle of realistic drama. The **arena stage**, or **theater-in-the-round**, was developed, which also called for new concepts in drama and production.

Playwrights like the Italian Luigi Pirandello (1867–1936) and the German Bertolt Brecht (1898–1956) wrote plays that required only minimal sets or no sets at all. Using this same tradition, Thornton Wilder wrote plays (such as *Our Town*) in which the action occurs on a bare stage, with the backstage area in full view showing brick walls, heating pipes, ropes, pulleys, and other stage appurtenances. Edward Albee's *The Sandbox* is in this tradition, in which the staging reminds us constantly that we are reading or watching a play—an illusion and an imitation—rather than real life.

ELEMENTS OF REALISTIC AND NONREALISTIC DRAMA

THE STORIES. Because realistic plays, like life, unfold chronologically, the *story* (as opposed to the *play*) is usually nearing conclusion when the stage action begins. In Susan Glaspell's *Trifles*, for example, the story comprises incidents from Mrs. Wright's youth, her marital difficulties, and her reaction against her husband. All this, however, is presented in conversation; it all occurred *before* the play begins. Such events from the past have a profound impact on the present action in realistic drama, but the play itself presents only the last part of the story.

In nonrealistic drama, the structure of the plot is more fluid. Action may shift easily from the present to the past with little or no transition. Flashbacks may be mixed with present action, and the entire play may dramatize the past through a present perspective. In Tennessee Williams's *The Glass Menagerie*, recollected past action is revealed through the present memories of the narrator. Similarly, the action in Miller's *Death of a Salesman* constantly shifts between present action, past action, and fantasy.

THE CHARACTERS. The characters in realistic drama are as much as possible like living people. They can be representative, symbolic, or even stock characters, but they must sound and act like actual human beings, with backgrounds, emotions, motivations, and last names as well as first names. There must be reasons for their actions, words, conflicts, and relationships. Most important, they must be consistent. Their responses, decisions, and characteristics must be the same as in real life. Such fidelity to life is apparent in realistic plays like Glaspell's *Trifles* and Hughes's *Mulatto*.

In modern nonrealistic drama, the characters may be nameless figures who have no background or motivation and who drop in and out of character as the playwright desires. Such is the case in Albee's *The Sandbox*, a play that is nonrealistic to an extreme. Characters in nonrealistic drama may assume a number of different roles at different times in the play. In *The Glass Menagerie*, for example, Tom is variously a character in the action, a narrator of the action, and a stage manager. As a character, he interacts with Laura and Amanda, but he also provides ongoing narration directly to the audience, and occasionally he cues the technicians offstage about music and lighting.

These distinctions do not mean that realistic characters are always round and nonrealistic ones always flat. The *way* in which a playwright develops characters, realistically or nonrealistically, does not control the *degree* to which they are developed. Thus, true-to-life characters like Mr. Hale in *Trifles* or Jim O'Connor in *The Glass Menagerie* may be flat. By the same token, nonrealistic characters, like Tom in *The Glass Menagerie* or Willy Loman in *Death of a Salesman*, may have enough depth and scope to be considered fully round.

LANGUAGE. In a realistic play, the language is usually an accurate reproduction of the diction appropriate to the class or group of people portrayed. There is no poetry, no radical shift in style, and no direct address to the reader or speaker. In *Mulatto*, for instance, Cora and her uneducated children consistently use the vernacular speech patterns of African Americans living in the South during the 1930s. Similarly, the characters in Glaspell's *Trifles* sound like Midwest farmers and small-town residents.

Such verisimilitude is not required in nonrealistic drama. Playwrights may employ any linguistic devices that suit their needs. Characters may speak in verse, clichés, or even nonsense sounds. One character may have two or three separate speeds of presentation, as Tom does in *The Glass Menagerie*. Dramatists are free to introduce snippets of poetry or song into the play, and characters may speak directly to the audience, and frequently do. Often the characters may speak as though they are in a dream, or are living through their memories, or are so preoccupied with their concerns that the other characters are incidental to them.

THE STAGE. Such differences in plot, characterization, and language are matched by differences in production techniques. Whereas the staging of a realistic drama must be as true to life as possible, as in *A Doll House*, nonrealistic drama can be staged with few or no realistic effects. Thus, lighting can indicate flashbacks, changes in mood, and shifts of location. Spotlights may illuminate and emphasize objects and characters in ways that never happen in reality. Nonrealistic plays may call for a virtually bare stage, as in *The Sandbox*. Alternatively, the sets may be symbolic and expressive of mood, employing lighting and semitransparent painted cloth (called a *scrim*) to create the simultaneous effect of multiple places or times. Such expressionistic settings are described in the stage directions for both *Death of a Salesman* and *The Glass Menagerie*.

Modern nonrealistic drama tends toward the other extreme. It may introduce music, special sound effects, words or images projected onto a wall or screen, minimalist or expressionistic settings, special lighting effects, action that flows off the stage into the auditorium, and speeches made directly to the spectators or the reader. All these and other devices break the illusion of reality, and demand that we consider the play as an artistic construction.

In this way, nonrealistic drama has moved progressively further away from realism throughout the latter half of the twentieth century. With the development of flexible theaters, in which the seats are removed and acting areas are set up throughout the house, the action of plays has moved offstage and into the space once occupied by the audience.

Paradoxically, as such drama becomes more nonrealistic, the theater itself, as a place for acting and performing, becomes the dominant reality. In the 1960s and 1970s, acting companies like The Living Theater in New York experimented with plays that began onstage, moved into the audience, and ended on the streets outside. Such productions represent the edge of drama. In the mid 1980s, the Old Vic Company in England produced *The Creation*—a series of medieval mystery plays—in which the actors mingled among the spectators, separating only when their parts were called for. Whenever new scenes were introduced, the standing spectators were (literally) swept aside to provide space, so that acting areas were being shaped by the shifting audience. A production popular in many American cities in the 1990s is *Tony n' Tina's Wedding*, which is the staging of a wedding and reception (in two different locations). Because performers and audience interact, particularly at the reception, many members of the audience take on impromptu acting and speaking roles. Every performance is therefore spontaneous and unique. An argument might be made that such one-time performances represent super-realism, but in fact they blur the distinction between drama and the real world to the point where art almost ceases to be art, and all action everywhere—both real life and stage life—seems nothing but performance.

The Spectrum of Realism

To this point we have been speaking as though realistic and nonrealistic drama were always at opposite extremes. Most plays are not purely realistic or nonrealistic. Rather, the terms represent the opposite ends of a spectrum, and most plays fall somewhere between the extremes. Both *Trifles* and *A Doll House*, for example, are highly realistic, yet each modifies its realism through symbolism and selective emphasis. Conversely, *The Sandbox* is extremely nonrealistic, yet the play includes enough realistic elements so that we can understand the correspondence between Albee's art and the real world. Both *Death of a Salesman* and *The Glass Menagerie* fall near the middle of the spectrum; they combine realistic language and characterization with nonrealistic settings, lighting, and structure.

EDWARD ALBEE, *THE SANDBOX*

Edward Albee, the leading American playwright of the 1960s, began life under many personal and educational handicaps. He was an adopted child whose stepmother alienated him and eventually disowned him. As a child he was moved in and out of many schools. Eventually he studied at Trinity College, but left without a degree, and then for a number of years he worked at a variety of odd jobs.

At the urging of Thornton Wilder, however, Albee turned his talent to writing plays, and he has been a constantly productive playwright ever since. His first play was *The Zoo Story* (1958), which was first performed in 1959 in Berlin and published in 1960. This was followed by *The Sandbox* and *The Death of Bessie Smith* (1960), *The American Dream* (1961), and *Who's Afraid of Virginia Woolf* (1962), Albee's best-known play. This play still stands as the pinnacle of his career; it had a highly successful run in New York City and was awarded the "Tony" as best play in 1963. It was made into a successful film in 1966, featuring Richard Burton and Elizabeth Taylor (who won the Academy Award for her performance).

Albee's work after *Who's Afraid of Virginia Woolf* met with mixed reactions. *Tiny Alice* (1964) was viewed as confusing and derivative, but *A Delicate Balance* (1966) and *Seascape* (1975) both won Pulitzer Prizes for drama. Other plays and adaptations have had short lives in the theater. His *The Lady from Dubuque* (1980), survived only twelve performances on Broadway, and the negative reviews of *The Man Who Had Three Arms* forced this play off the Broadway stage in 1983.

Recently, his work has achieved more favorable recognition. In 1993–1994, the Signature Theater Company in New York presented a season-long set of Albee performances. One of them featured *The Sandbox* as one of three one-act "sand plays," the others being *Box* (1968) and *Finding the Sun* (1983). Additionally, two of his other plays, *Three Tall Women* (1991, Pulitzer Prize 1994), and *Fragments* (1994), were performed to acclaim.

Albee claims that his plays are about "closings down"; that is, about how dreams never reach fulfillment, and how happiness—the greatest dream—is never achieved. Many of his plays, including *The Sandbox*, represent such a pessimistic view, a view also predominant in the Theater of the Absurd, a type of drama that evolved in the 1940s and 1950s. Albee has constantly experimented with the Absurdist type of play, which is characterized by a coldly critical examination of the foundations of character and existence, and which strips away conventions of behavior and accidents of personality. Like the Existentialist philosophy on which Absurdist position is based, most plays of the Absurd dramatize the assertion that life is irrational and meaningless. A quality of many Absurdist plays is that language, action, and relationships are theatrical games in which the characters view their own existence as fictional rather than real.

In *The Sandbox*, which was written in 1959 and first performed in New York City in 1960, Albee's characters are Absurdist. They are not individualized women and men, but instead are types. Grandma, the protagonist, is in conflict with her family, society, and death; only the last of these conflicts is resolved at the conclusion. Mommy and Daddy represent Albee's vision of the American family reduced to a bare bones form. He employs all the elements of drama to build meaning and impact into the play. Plot, character, setting, and symbol all convey the judgment that modern lives and values have become drab and meaningless. In addition, Albee has provided his characters with speeches filled with repetition, parallel speech patterns, idioms, connotative words, and clichés, so that they illustrate their own bleak lives in their very own words.

EDWARD ALBEE   (b. 1928)

The Sandbox ————————————————————————— *1960 (1959)*

THE PLAYERS

The Young Man, 25, *a good-looking, well-built boy in a bathing suit*
Mommy, 55, *a well-dressed, imposing woman*
Daddy, 60, *a small man; gray, thin*
Grandma, 86, *a tiny, wizened woman with bright eyes*
The Musician, *no particular age, but young would be nice*

Note: When, in the course of the play, MOMMY *and* DADDY *call each other by these names, there should be no suggestion of regionalism. These names are of empty affection and point up the presenility and vacuity of their characters.*

The Scene: A bare stage, with only the following: Near the footlights, far stage-right, two simple chairs set side by side, facing the audience; near the footlights, far stage-left, a chair facing stage-right with a music stand before it; farther back, and stage-center, slightly elevated and raked, a large child's sandbox with a toy pail and shovel; the background is the sky, which alters from brightest day to deepest night.

At the beginning, it is brightest day; the YOUNG MAN *is alone on stage, to the rear of the sandbox, and to one side. He is doing calisthenics; he does calisthenics until quite at the very end of the play. These calisthenics, employing the arms only, should suggest the beating and fluttering of wings. The* YOUNG MAN *is, after all, the Angel of Death.*

MOMMY *and* DADDY *enter from stage-left,* MOMMY *first.*

MOMMY.   [*Motioning to Daddy*] Well, here we are; this is the beach.
DADDY.   [*Whining*] I'm cold.
MOMMY.   [*Dismissing him with a little laugh*] Don't be silly; it's as warm as toast. Look at that nice young man over there: *he* doesn't think it's cold. [*Waves to the* YOUNG MAN] Hello.
YOUNG MAN.   [*With an endearing smile*] Hi!

MOMMY.   [*Looking about*] This will do perfectly . . . don't you think so, Daddy? There's sand there . . . and the water beyond. What do you think, Daddy?

DADDY.   [*Vaguely*] Whatever you say, Mommy.

MOMMY.   [*With the same little laugh*] Well, of course . . . whatever I say. Then, it's settled, is it?

DADDY.   [*Shrugs*] She's *your* mother, not mine.

MOMMY.   *I* know she's my mother. What do you take me for? [*A pause*] All right, now; let's get on with it. [*She shouts into the wings, stage-left.*] You! Out there! You can come in now.

[*The* MUSICIAN *enters, seats himself in the chair, stage-left, places music on the music stand, is ready to play.* MOMMY *nods approvingly.*]

MOMMY.   Very nice; very nice. Are you ready, Daddy? Let's go get Grandma.

DADDY.   Whatever you say, Mommy.

MOMMY.   [*Leading the way out, stage-left*] Of course, whatever I say. [*To the* MU-SICIAN] You can begin now. [*The* MUSICIAN *begins playing;* MOMMY *and* DADDY *exit; the* MUSICIAN, *all the while playing, nods to the* YOUNG MAN.]

YOUNG MAN.   [*With the same endearing smile*] Hi!

[*After a moment,* MOMMY *and* DADDY *re-enter, carrying* GRANDMA. *She is borne in by their hands under her armpits; she is quite rigid; her legs are drawn up; her feet do not touch the ground; the expression on her ancient face is that of puzzlement and fear.*]

DADDY.   Where do we put her?

MOMMY.   [*The same little laugh*] Wherever I say, of course. Let me see . . . well . . . all right, over there . . . in the sandbox. [*Pause*] Well, what are you waiting for, Daddy? . . . The sandbox!

[*Together they carry* GRANDMA *over to the sandbox and more or less dump her in.*]

GRANDMA.   [*Righting herself to a sitting position; her voice a cross between a baby's laugh and cry*] Ahhhhhh! Graaaaa!

DADDY.   [*Dusting himself*] What do we do now?

MOMMY.   [*To the* MUSICIAN] You can stop now.

[*The* MUSICIAN *stops.*]

[*Back to* DADDY] What do you mean, what do we do now? We go over there and sit down, of course. [*To the* YOUNG MAN] Hello there.

YOUNG MAN.   [*Again smiling*] Hi!

[MOMMY *and* DADDY *move to the chairs, stage-right, and sit down. A pause*]

GRANDMA.   [*Same as before*] Ahhhhhh! Ah-haaaaaa! Graaaaaa!

DADDY.   Do you think . . . do you think she's . . . comfortable?

MOMMY.   [*Impatiently*] How would I know?

DADDY.   [*Pause*] What do we do now?

MOMMY.   [*As if remembering*] We . . . wait. We . . . sit here . . . and we wait . . . that's what we do.

DADDY.   [*After a pause*] Shall we talk to each other?

MOMMY.   [*With that little laugh; picking something off her dress*] Well, *you* can talk, if you want to . . . if you can think of anything to *say* . . . if you can think of anything *new*.

DADDY. [*Thinks*] No . . . I suppose not.

MOMMY. [*With a triumphant laugh*] Of course not!

GRANDMA. [*Banging the toy shovel against the pail*] Haaaaaa! Ah-haaaaaa! 30

MOMMY. [*Out over the audience*] Be quiet, Grandma . . . just be quiet, and wait.

[*GRANDMA throws a shovelful of sand at MOMMY.*]

MOMMY. [*Still out over the audience*] She's throwing sand at me! You stop that,
Grandma; you stop throwing sand at Mommy! [*To DADDY*] She's throwing sand at me.

[*DADDY looks around at GRANDMA, who screams at him.*]

GRANDMA. GRAAAAA!

MOMMY. Don't look at her. Just . . . sit here . . . be very still . . . and wait. [*To
the MUSICIAN*] You . . . uh . . . you go ahead and do whatever it is you do.

[*The MUSICIAN plays.*]

[*MOMMY and DADDY are fixed, staring out beyond the audience. GRANDMA looks at them, looks
at the MUSICIAN, looks at the sandbox, throws down the shovel.*]

GRANDMA. Ah-haaaaaa! Graaaaaa! [*Looks for reaction; gets none. Now . . . directly
to the audience*] Honestly! What a way to treat an old woman! Drag her out of the house
. . . stick her in a car . . . bring her out here from the city . . . dump her in a pile of
sand . . . and leave her here to set. I'm eighty-six years old! I was married when I was
seventeen. To a farmer. He died when I was thirty. [*To the MUSICIAN*] Will you stop
that, please?

[*The MUSICIAN stops playing.*]

I'm a feeble old woman . . . how do you expect anybody to hear me over that peep!
peep! peep! [*To herself*] There's no respect around here. [*To the YOUNG MAN*] There's
no respect around here!

YOUNG MAN. [*Same smile*] Hi! 35

GRANDMA. [*After a pause, a mild double-take, continues, to the audience*] My husband died when I was thirty [*indicates MOMMY*], and I had to raise that big cow over
there all by my lonesome. You can imagine what *that* was like. Lordy! [*To the YOUNG
MAN*] Where'd they get *you*?

YOUNG MAN. Oh . . . I've been around for a while.

GRANDMA. I'll bet you have! Heh, heh, heh. Will you look at you!

YOUNG MAN. [*Flexing his muscles*] Isn't that something? [*Continues his calisthenics*]

GRANDMA. Boy, oh boy; I'll say. Pretty good. 40

YOUNG MAN. [*Sweetly*] I'll say.

GRANDMA. Where ya from?

YOUNG MAN. Southern California.

GRANDMA. [*Nodding*] Figgers; figgers. What's your name, honey?

YOUNG MAN. I don't know. . . . 45

GRANDMA. [*To the audience*] Bright, too!

YOUNG MAN. I mean . . . I mean, they haven't given me one yet . . . the studio . . .

GRANDMA. [*Giving him the once-over*] You don't say . . . you don't say. Well . . .
uh, I've got to talk some more . . . don't you go 'way.

YOUNG MAN. Oh, no.

GRANDMA. [*Turning her attention back to the audience*] Fine; fine. [*Then, once   5 more, back to the* YOUNG MAN] You're . . . you're an actor, hunh?

YOUNG MAN. [*Beaming*] Yes. I am.

GRANDMA. [*To the audience again; shrugs*] I'm smart that way. *Anyhow*, I had to raise . . . *that* over there all by my lonesome; and what's next to her there . . . that's what she married. Rich? I tell you . . . money, money, money. They took me off the *farm* . . . which was real decent of them . . . and they moved me into the big town house with *them* . . . fixed a nice place for me under the stove . . . gave me an army blanket . . . and my own dish . . . my very own dish! So, what have I got to complain about? Nothing, of course. I'm not complaining. [*She looks up at the sky, shouts to some- one off-stage.*] Shouldn't it be getting dark now, dear?

[*The lights dim; night comes on. The* MUSICIAN *begins to play, it becomes deepest night. There are spots on all the players, including the* YOUNG MAN, *who is, of course, continuing his calis- thenics.*]

DADDY. [*Stirring*] It's nighttime.

MOMMY. Shhhh. Be still . . . wait.

DADDY. [*Whining*] It's so hot.   5.

MOMMY. Shhhhhh. Be still . . . wait.

GRANDMA. [*To herself*] That's better. Night. [*To the* MUSICIAN] Honey, do you play all through this part?

[*The* MUSICIAN *nods.*]

Well, keep it nice and soft; that's a good boy.

[*The* MUSICIAN *nods again; plays softly.*]

That's nice.

[*There is an off-stage rumble.*]

DADDY. [*Starting*] What was that?

MOMMY. [*Beginning to weep*] It was nothing.

DADDY. It was . . . it was . . . thunder . . . or a wave breaking . . . or something.   6●

MOMMY. [*Whispering, through her tears*] It was an off-stage rumble . . . and you know what *that* means. . . .

DADDY. I forget. . . .

MOMMY. [*Barely able to talk*] It means the time has come for poor Grandma . . . and I can't bear it!

DADDY. [*Vacantly*] I . . . I suppose you've got to be brave.

GRANDMA. [*Mocking*] That's right, kid; be brave. You'll bear up; you'll get over   6! it.

[*Another off-stage rumble . . . louder*]

MOMMY. Ohhhhhhhhhh . . . poor Grandma . . . poor Grandma. . . .

GRANDMA. [*To* MOMMY] I'm fine! I'm all right! It hasn't happened yet!

[*A violent off-stage rumble. All the lights go out, save the spot on the* YOUNG MAN; *the* MUSI- CIAN *stops playing.*]

MOMMY. Ohhhhhhhhhhh . . . Ohhhhhhhhhh. . . .

[*Silence*]

GRANDMA.   Don't put the lights up yet . . . I'm not ready; I'm not quite ready. [*Silence*] All right, dear . . . I'm about done.

[*The lights come up again, to brightest day; the* MUSICIAN *begins to play.* GRANDMA *is discovered, still in the sandbox, lying on her side, propped up on an elbow, half covered, busily shoveling sand over herself.*]

GRANDMA.   [*Muttering*] I don't know how I'm supposed to do anything with   70
this goddam toy shovel. . . .
DADDY.   Mommy! It's daylight!
MOMMY.   [*Brightly*] So it is! Well! Our long night is over. We must put away our tears, take off our mourning . . . and face the future. It's our duty.
GRANDMA.   [*Still shoveling; mimicking*] . . . take off our mourning . . . face the future. . . . Lordy!

[MOMMY *and* DADDY *rise, stretch.* MOMMY *waves to the* YOUNG MAN.]

YOUNG MAN.   [*With that smile*] Hi!

[GRANDMA *plays dead. (!)* MOMMY *and* DADDY *go over to look at her; she is a little more than half buried in the sand; the toy shovel is in her hands, which are crossed on her breast.*]

MOMMY.   [*Before the sandbox; shaking her head*] Lovely! It's . . . it's hard to be   75
sad . . . she looks . . . so happy. [*With pride and conviction*] It pays to do things well. [*To the* MUSICIAN] All right, you can stop now, if you want to. I mean, stay around for a swim, or something; it's all right with us. [*She sighs heavily.*] Well Daddy . . . off we go.
DADDY.   Brave Mommy!
MOMMY.   Brave Daddy!

[*They exit, stage-left.*]

GRANDMA.   [*After they leave; lying quite still*] It pays to do things well. . . . Boy, oh boy! [*She tries to sit up*] . . . well, kids . . . [*but she finds she can't.*] . . . I . . . I can't get up. I . . . I can't move. . . .

[*The* YOUNG MAN *stops his calisthenics, nods to the* MUSICIAN, *walks over to* GRANDMA, *kneels down by the sandbox.*]

GRANDMA.   I . . . can't move. . . .
YOUNG MAN.   Shhhhh . . . be very still. . . .   80
GRANDMA.   I . . . I can't move. . . .
YOUNG MAN.   Uh . . . ma'am; I . . . I have a line here.
GRANDMA.   Oh, I'm sorry, sweetie; you go right ahead.
YOUNG MAN.   I am . . . uh . . .
GRANDMA.   Take your time, dear.   85
YOUNG MAN.   [*Prepares; delivers the line like a real amateur.*] I am the Angel of Death. I am . . . uh . . . I am come for you.
GRANDMA.   What . . . wha . . . [*Then, with resignation*] . . . ohhh . . . ohhhh, I see.

[*The* YOUNG MAN *bends over, kisses* GRANDMA *gently on the forehead.*]

GRANDMA.   [*Her eyes closed, her hands folded on her breast again, the shovel between her hands, a sweet smile on her face*] Well . . . that was very nice, dear. . . .
YOUNG MAN.   [*Still kneeling*] Shhhhhh . . . be still. . . .
GRANDMA.   What I meant was . . . you did that very well, dear. . . .   90

YOUNG MAN. [*Blushing*] . . . oh . . .

GRANDMA. No; I mean it. You've got that . . . you've got a quality.

YOUNG MAN. [*With his endearing smile*] Oh . . . thank you; thank you very much . . . ma'am.

GRANDMA. [*Slowly; softly—as the* YOUNG MAN *puts his hands on top of* GRANDMA's] You're . . . you're welcome . . . dear.

[*Tableau. The* MUSICIAN *continues to play as the curtain slowly comes down.*]

[*Curtain*]

QUESTIONS

1. Why does Mommy say, "This is the beach"? What are the characters waiting for there?

2. Why does Albee indicate that Daddy is *whining*? What is the effect of Daddy's repetition of "Whatever you say, Mommy"?

3. How does Grandma "speak" to Mommy and Daddy? How does she speak to the audience and the Young Man? How do you account for this difference?

4. Albee identifies the Young Man as the Angel of Death; what else does he symbolize or represent? What is Grandma's attitude toward him? How does he treat her?

5. What does the "off-stage rumble" signify?

6. How do Mommy and Daddy react to Grandma's "death"? How would you characterize their language?

7. How does Grandma react to the comments of Mommy and Daddy about her death? What does Grandma reveal about the way Mommy and Daddy deal with death?

GENERAL QUESTIONS

1. How does the setting, described at the beginning of the play, illustrate the level of realism/non-realism? What props are realistic? Symbolic? What is the realistic/non-realistic effect of speeches such as Mommy's telling the Musician "You can come in now," Grandma's cueing of the lighting technician, and Mommy's reference to an "off-stage rumble"?

2. Are the characters in this play round or flat? Why don't they have names? What does each symbolize?

3. *The Sandbox* is full of repetition; characters repeat words and even whole lines two or three times. What is the effect of this repetition on your understanding of character, meaning, and level of reality?

4. How does Albee employ diction, speech patterns, connotative words, clichés, and tone to shape character and meaning?

5. How many different generations are presented in *The Sandbox*? Which characters represent each generation? To what extent do the different generations illustrate different phases of American history?

LANGSTON HUGHES, *MULATTO*

James Mercer Langston Hughes was born in Missouri in 1902, and raised in Kansas and Ohio. After living for a year in Mexico he attended Columbia University, but left after one year. He received a B.A. from Lincoln University in Pennsylvania in 1929, and when he came to New York he soon became one of the leading figures in the "Harlem Renaissance," an energetic burst of African-American literary creativity which also included Countee Cullen and Claude McKay (see pp. 929 and 967). Over the next 45 years, Hughes was to write in every major literary genre, including translations, regular columns for a weekly newspaper, and reports on the Spanish Civil War. His earliest works were poems, which he published in *The Crisis*, the official journal of the National Association for the Advancement of Colored People. Eventually he published fourteen books of poems and two novels, together with a number of short-story collections and many plays and texts for musical plays.

The Great Depression, which began with the Stock Market crash in 1929, destroyed the economic underpinnings of the Harlem Renaissance. It was during the Depression that Hughes became radicalized. After visiting Haiti and Cuba he attacked what he considered American imperialist interventions in those countries. He then spent a year in Soviet Russia, assisting in the preparation of a film on American race relations. When he returned he published his first collection of stories, *The Ways of White Folks* (1934), in which he fictionalized his disaffection with the condition of both Southern and Northern African Americans. One of the stories included in this collection was "Father and Son," a version of the material that he turned into the two-act play *Mulatto*, which was produced at the Vanderbilt Theater in New York in October, 1935. The play had a run of 373 performances, the record for a Broadway play by an African-American dramatist.

At that time, the growing African-American theater was dominated by two major themes, the first being the customs and problems of Southern blacks. The most pressing problem was of course the cruelty and injustice of lynching. Angelina Grimke's *Rachael* (1920) and James Miller's *Never No More* (1932, Miller was white) openly exposed the practice. Dennis Donaghue's *Legal Murder* (1934) was a condemnation of the false conviction for rape of nine young black men from Scottsboro, Alabama, a topic that Hughes also treated in his early drama *Scottsboro Limited: Four Poems and a Play in Verse* (1932). The second major theme concerned the adjustments that blacks needed to make after they left the South and began living in the North. Frank Wilson's *Meek Mose* was perhaps the most optimistic of these plays, in which dispossessed blacks discover oil on their new property. More typical were Garland Anderson's *Appearances* (1925), about how a black bellhop overcomes false charges of rape, and Wallace Thurman's *Harlem* (1929), about the difficulties of a black family living in Chicago. This theme also dominates Lorraine Hansberry's *A Raisin in the Sun* (1959), the classic drama that marked the coming of age of post-World War II African-American playwrights.

Although Langston Hughes is not considered principally as a dramatist, he wrote plays throughout his career. In addition to the plays already mentioned, he wrote *Little Ham* (1936) and *Soul Gone Home* (1937), a short fantasy play. As the first production for the radical Suitcase Theater, which he founded after returning as a correspondent from the Spanish Civil War, he wrote *Don't You Want To Be Free* (1938). He collaborated with Arna Bontemps in *When the Jack Hollers* (1936), and with Zora Neale Hurston in *Mule Bone* (reissued in 1991). In 1948 he wrote the lyrics for the Kurt Weill and Elmer Rice musical *Street Scene*, perhaps the best known of the plays in which he was involved. In 1951 he produced a libretto, *Just Around the Corner*, and in 1957 he wrote *Simply Heavenly*, a blues-musical play featuring the character Jesse Semple, whom he had created as a character in his weekly columns for the *Chicago Defender*. Although *Simply Heavenly* (which is a musical version of an earlier play, *Simple Takes a Wife*) concludes optimistically, one may find within it the serious theme of frustration resulting from the difficulties that African Americans experience in seeking identity and recognition. Semple says, at one point:

> I'm broke, busted, and disgusted. And just spent mighty near my last nickel for a paper—and there ain't no news in it about colored folks. Unless we commit murder, robbery or rape, or are being chased by a mob, do we get on the front page, or hardly on the back. (Act I. scene 5).

During the last decades of Hughes's life, his interests were in the musical theater, particularly the introduction of gospel-related music and jazz. Three of his major efforts were *Black Nativity* (1961), *The Gospel Glory* (1962), and *Jerico Jim Crow* (1964). His output as a dramatist was indeed great, even if it is overshadowed by his preeminence as a poet and fiction writer.

Hughes's *Mulatto* is one of his plays dealing with life in the South during the 1930s, a time when the system of white control over blacks was virtually absolute. Hughes's first conception of the play, as one dealing with "father and son," is a perennial one. Colonel Tom Norwood and Robert Lewis, his mulatto son, recognize their relationship but also hate and reject each other. In *Mulatto* the realistic cause of conflict is the "color line"—the line which people must step over in order to accept each other as human beings. This is an ideal goal, just as it is also an insurmountable obstacle, granted the society which the play depicts. The lack of ability or will to cross the line governs the pattern of action and also the violent outcome. Colonel Norwood has lived in the same house with Cora Lewis for many years, and they do well together as long as he is not confronted with the issues of his paternity and his control over the plantation. There is no way he can recognize the four "yard blacks" on his plantation as his legitimate children, however, unless he is willing to forsake his identity as a white.

There are many other marks of dramatic realism, particularly the exploitation of black women (described in Act I. speech 61), the front entrance of the Norwood house, Robert's complaints about Miss Gray, and his speeding with the Ford. All of Robert's so-called "uppity" actions would be acceptable among the ruling white society, but because he is black they indicate a state of revolt. In addition, Robert's identity as half-white, half-black—he is called "yellow" by Colonel Tom—leaves him in an anomalous position, for he is not "white" enough to be equal nor "black" enough to be subservient. The reality of his situation leads him to hate both whites and blacks alike, and the sudden eruption of his seething anger leads to his uncontrolled violence.

It is important to note that *Mulatto* reflects the reality of language in the South of the 1930s. Hughes's blacks, except for Robert and Sallie, use Southern black vernacular (called "darky talk" by Hughes). The introduction of such speech in literature was controversial at the time. Many black intellectuals, who had also been a part of the Harlem Renaissance, believed that dialect should be shunned, on the principle that it reinforced negative African-American stereotypes. However, Hughes believed that using the vernacular was above all truthful and realistic, enabling writers to demonstrate that blacks are not stereotypes, that they face human problems just like everyone else, and that they succeed and fail just like everyone else. Moreover, there were precedents for the realistic use of dialect that had been set by Mark Twain in *Tom Sawyer* and *Huckleberry Finn*, both of which were acknowledged classics of American literature.

Mulatto is one of Hughes's most important plays. In 1950 he refashioned it as a libretto, entitled *The Barrier*, which was set to music by the composer Jan Meyerowitz. In addition, the play was translated into Spanish and published in South America in 1954.

LANGSTON HUGHES (1902–1967)

Mulatto ———————————————————————— *1935*

CHARACTERS

Colonel Thomas Norwood. *Plantation owner, a still vigorous man of about sixty, nervous, refined, quick-tempered, and commanding; a widower who is the father of four living mulatto children by his Negro housekeeper.*

Cora Lewis. *A brown woman in her forties who has kept the house and been the mistress of Colonel Norwood for some thirty years.*

William Lewis. *The oldest son of Cora Lewis and the Colonel; a fat, easy-going, soft looking mulatto of twenty-eight; married.*

Sallie Lewis. *The seventeen-year-old daughter, very light with sandy hair and freckles, who could pass for white.*

Robert Lewis [Bert]. *Eighteen, the youngest boy; strong and well-built; a light mulatto with ivory-yellow skin and proud thin features like his father's; as tall as the Colonel, with the same gray-blue eyes, but with curly black hair instead of brown; of a fiery, impetuous temper—immature and willful—resenting his blood and the circumstances of his birth.*

Fred Higgins. *A close friend of Colonel Norwood; a county politician; fat and elderly, conventionally Southern.*

Sam. *An old Negro retainer, a personal servant of the Colonel.*

Billy. *The small son of William Lewis; a chubby brown kid about five.*

Talbot. *The overseer.*

Mose. *An elderly Negro, chauffeur for Mr. Higgins.*

A Storekeeper.

An Undertaker.

Undertaker's Helper. *Voice off-stage only.*

The Mob.

ACT I

TIME.   *An afternoon in early fall.*

THE SETTING.   *The living room of the Big House on a plantation in Georgia. Rear center of the room, a vestibule with double doors leading to the porch; at each side of the doors, a large window with lace curtains and green shades; at left a broad flight of stairs leading to the second floor; near the stairs, downstage, a doorway leading to the dining room and kitchen; opposite at right of stage, a door to the library. The room is furnished in the long out-dated horsehair and walnut style of the nineties; a crystal chandelier, a large old-fashioned rug, a marble-topped table, upholstered chairs. At the right there is a small cabinet. It is a very clean, but somewhat shabby and rather depressing room, dominated by a large oil painting of NORWOOD's wife of his youth on the center wall. The windows are raised. The afternoon sunlight streams in.*

ACTION.   *As the curtain rises, the stage is empty. The door at the right opens and* COLONEL NORWOOD *enters, crossing the stage toward the stairs, his watch in his hand. Looking up, he shouts:*

NORWOOD.   Cora! Oh Cora!

CORA.   [*Heard above*] Yes, sir, Colonel Tom.

NORWOOD.   I want to know if that child of yours means to leave here this afternoon?

CORA.   [*At head of steps now*] Yes, sir, she's goin' directly. I's gettin' her ready now, packin' up an' all. 'Course, she wants to tell you goodbye 'fore she leaves.

NORWOOD.   Well, send her down here. Who's going to drive her to the railroad? The train leaves at three—and it's after two now. You ought to know you can't drive ten miles in no time.

CORA.   [*Above*] Her brother's gonna drive her. Bert. He ought to be back here most any time now with the Ford.

NORWOOD.   [*Stopping on his way back to the library*] Ought to be *back* here? Where's he gone?

CORA. [*Coming downstairs nervously*] Why, he driv in town 'fore noon, Colonel Tom. Said he were lookin' for some tubes or somethin' 'nother by de mornin' mail for de radio he's been riggin' up out in de shed.

NORWOOD. Who gave him permission to be driving off in the middle of the morning? I bought that Ford to be used when I gave orders for it to be used, not . . .

CORA. Yes, sir, Colonel Tom, but . . . 10

NORWOOD. But what? [*Pausing. Then deliberately*] Cora, if you want that hard-headed yellow son of yours to get along around here, he'd better listen to me. He's no more than any other black buck on this plantation—due to work like the rest of 'em. I don't take such a performance from nobody under me—driving off in the middle of the day to town, after I've told him to bend his back in that cotton. How's Talbot going to keep the rest of those darkies working right if that boy's allowed to set that kind of an example? Just because Bert's your son, and I've been damn fool enough to send him off to school for five or six years, he thinks he has a right to privileges, acting as if he owned this place since he's been back here this summer.

CORA. But, Colonel Tom. . .

NORWOOD. Yes, I know what you're going to say. I don't give a damn about him! There's no nigger-child of mine, yours, ours—no darkie—going to disobey me. I put him in that field to work, and he'll stay on this plantation till I get ready to let him go. I'll tell Talbot to use the whip on him, too, if he needs it. If it hadn't been that he's yours, he'd-a had a taste of it the other day. Talbot's a damn good overseer, and no saucy, lazy Nigras stay on this plantation and get away with it. [*To* CORA] Go on back upstairs and see about getting Sallie out of here. Another word from you and I won't send your [*Sarcastically*] pretty little half-white daughter anywhere, either. Schools for darkies! Huh! If you take that boy of yours for an example, they do 'em more harm than good. He's learned nothing in college but impudence, and he'll stay here on this place and work for me awhile before he gets back to any more schools. [*He starts across the room.*]

CORA. Yes, sir, Colonel Tom. [*Hesitating*] But he's just young, sir. And he was mighty broke up when you said last week he couldn't go back to de campus. [*COLONEL NORWOOD turns and looks at* CORA *commandingly. Understanding, she murmurs*] Yes, sir. [*She starts upstairs, but turns back.*] Can't I run and fix you a cool drink, Colonel Tom?

NORWOOD. No, damn you! Sam'll do it. 15

CORA. [*Sweetly*] Go set down in de cool, then, Colonel. 'Taint good for you to be going' on this way in de heat. I'll talk to Robert maself soon's he comes in. He don't mean nothing—just smart and young and kinder careless, Colonel Tom, like ma mother said you used to be when you was eighteen.

NORWOOD. Get on upstairs, Cora. Do I have to speak again? Get on! [*He pulls the cord of the servants' bell.*]

CORA. [*On the steps*] Does you still be in the mind to tell Sallie good-bye?

NORWOOD. Send her down here as I told you. [*Impatiently*] Where's Sam? Send him here first. [*Fuming*] Looks like he takes his time to answer that bell. You colored folks are running the house to suit yourself nowadays.

CORA. [*Coming downstairs again and going toward door under the steps*] I'll get 20
Sam for you.

[CORA *exits left.* NORWOOD *paces nervously across the floor. Goes to the window and looks out down the road. Takes a cigar from his pocket, sits in a chair with it unlighted, scowling. Rises, goes toward servants' bell and rings it again violently as* SAM *enters, out of breath.*]

NORWOOD.   What the hell kind of a tortoise race is this? I suppose you were out in the sun somewhere sleeping?

SAM.   No, sah, Colonel Norwood. Just tryin' to get Miss Sallie's valises down to de yard so's we can put 'em in de Ford, sah.

NORWOOD.   [*Out of patience*] Huh! Darkies waiting on darkies! I can't get service in my own house. Very well. [*Loudly*] Bring me some whiskey and soda, and ice in a glass. Is that damn Frigidaire working right? Or is Livonia still too thickheaded to know how to run it? Any ice cubes in the thing?

SAM.   Yes, sah, Colonel, yes, sah. [*Backing toward door left*] 'Scuse me, please sah, but [*as NORWOOD turns toward library*] Cora say for me to ask you is it all right to bring that big old trunk what you give Sallie down by de front steps. We ain't been able to tote it down them narrer little back steps, sah. Cora, say, can we bring it down de front way through here?

NORWOOD.   No other way? [*SAM shakes his head*] Then pack it on through the back, quick. Don't let me catch you carrying any of Sallie's baggage out of that front door here. You-all'll be wanting to go in and out the front way next. [*Turning away, complaining to himself*] Darkies have been getting mighty fresh in this part of the country since the war. The damn Germans should've ... [*To SAM*] Don't take that trunk out that front door.

SAM.   [*Evilly, in a cunning voice*] I's seen Robert usin' de front door—when you ain't here, and he comes up from de cabin to see his mammy. [*SALLIE, the daughter, appears at the top of the stairs, but hesitates about coming down.*]

NORWOOD.   Oh, you have, have you? Let me catch him and I'll break his young neck for him. [*Yelling at SAM*] Didn't I tell you some whiskey and soda an hour ago?

[*SAM exits left. SALLIE comes shyly down the stairs and approaches her father. She is dressed in a little country-style coat-suit ready for traveling. Her features are Negroid, although her skin is very fair. COLONEL NORWOOD gazes down at her without saying a word as she comes meekly toward him, half-frightened.*]

SALLIE.   I just wanted to tell you goodbye, Colonel Norwood, and thank you for letting me go back to school another year, and for letting me work here in the house all summer where mama is. [*NORWOOD says nothing. The girl continues in a strained voice as if making a speech*] You mighty nice to us colored folks certainly, and mama says you the best white man in Georgia. [*Still NORWOOD says nothing. The girl continues.*] You been mighty nice to your—I mean to us colored children, letting my sister and me go off to school. The principal says I'm doing pretty well and next year I can go to Normal and learn to be a teacher. [*Raising her eyes*] You reckon I can, Colonel Tom?

NORWOOD.   Stand up straight and let me see how you look. [*Backing away*] Hum-m-m! Getting kinder grown, ain't you? Do they teach you in that school to have good manners, and not be afraid of work, *and to respect white folks?*

SALLIE.   Yes, sir, I been taking up cooking and sewing, too.

NORWOOD.   Well, that's good. As I recall it, that school turned your sister out a right smart cook. Cora tells me she's got a good job in some big hotel in Chicago. I'm thinking about you going on up North there with her in a year or two. You're getting too old to be around here, and too womanish. [*He puts his hands on her arms as if feeling her flesh*]

SALLIE.   [*Drawing back slightly*] But I want to live down here with mama. I want to teach school in that there empty school house by the Cross Roads what hasn't had a teacher for five years.

[*SAM has been standing with the door cracked, overhearing the conversation. He enters with the drink and places it on the table, right. NORWOOD sits down, leaving the girl standing, as SAM pours out a drink.*]

NORWOOD.   Don't get that into your head, now. There's been no teacher there for years—and there won't be any teacher there, either. Cotton teaches these pickaninnies enough around here. Some of 'em's too smart as it is. The only reason I did have a teacher there once was to get you young ones o' Cora's educated. I gave you all a chance and I hope you appreciate it. [*He takes a long drink.*] Don't know why I did it. No other white man in these parts ever did it, as I know of. [*To SAM*] Get out of here! [*SAM exits left*] Guess I couldn't stand to see Cora's kids working around here dumb as the rest of these no good darkies—need a dozen of 'em to chop one row of cotton, or to keep a house clean. Or maybe I didn't want Talbot eyeing you gals. [*Taking another drink*] Anyhow, I'm glad you and Bertha turned out right well. Yes, hum-m-m! [*Straightening up*] You know I tried to do something for those brothers of yours, too, but William's stupid as an ox—good for work, though—and that Robert's just an impudent, hardheaded, yellow young fool. I'm gonna break his damn neck for him if he don't watch out. Or else put Talbot on him.

SALLIE.   [*Suddenly frightened*] Please, sir, don't put the overseer on Bert, Colonel Tom. He was the smartest boy at school, Bert was. On the football team, too. Please, sir, Colonel Tom. Let brother work here in the house, or somewhere else where Talbot can't mistreat him. He ain't used . . .

NORWOOD.   [*Rising*] Telling me what to do, heh? [*Staring at her sternly*] I'll use   35 the back of my hand across your face if you don't hush. [*He takes another drink. The noise of a Ford is heard outside.*] That's Bert now, I reckon. He's to take you to the railroad line, and while you're riding with him, you better put some sense into his head. And tell him I want to see him as soon as he gets back here. [*CORA enters left with a bundle and an umbrella. SAM and WILLIAM come downstairs with a big square trunk, and exit hurriedly, left.*]

SALLIE.   Yes, sir, I'll tell him.

CORA.   Colonel Tom, Sallie ain't got much time now. [*To the girl*] Come on, chile. Bert's here. Yo' big brother and Sam and Livonia and everybody's all waiting at de back door to say goodbye. And your baggage is being packed in. [*Noise of another car is heard outside.*] Who else is that there coming up de drive? [*CORA looks out the window.*] Mr. Higgins' car, Colonel Tom. Reckon he's coming to see you . . .Hurry up out o' this front room, Sallie. Here, take these things of your'n [*Hands her the bundle and parasol*] while I opens de door for Mr. Higgins. [*In a whisper*] Hurry up, chile! Get out! [*NORWOOD turns toward the front door as CORA goes to open it*]

SALLIE.   [*Shyly to her father*] Goodbye, Colonel Tom.

NORWOOD.   [*His eyes on the front door, scarcely noticing the departing SALLIE, he motions.*] Yes, yes goodbye! Get on now! [*CORA opens the front door as her daughter exits left.*] Well, well! Howdy do, Fred. Come in, come in! [*CORA holds the outer door of the vestibule wide as FRED HIGGINS enters with rheumatic dignity, supported on the arm of his chauffeur, MOSE, a very black Negro in a slouchy uniform. CORA closes the door and exits left hurriedly, following SALLIE.*]

NORWOOD.   [*Smiling*] How's the rheumatiz today? Women or licker or heat   40 must've made it worse—from the looks of your speed!

HIGGINS   [*Testly, sitting down puffing and blowing in a big chair*] I'm in no mood for fooling, Tom, not now. [*To MOSE*] All right. [*The CHAUFFEUR exits front. HIGGINS continues angrily.*] Norwood, that damned yellow nigger buck of yours that drives that new

Ford tried his best just now to push my car off the road, then got in front of me and blew dust in my face for the last mile coming down to your gate, trying to beat me in here—which he did. Such a deliberate piece of impudence I don't know if I've ever seen out of a nigger before in all the sixty years I've lived in this country. [*The noise of the Ford is head going out the drive, and the cries of the* NEGROES *shouting farewells to* SALLIE. HIGGINS *listens indignantly.*] What kind of crazy coons have you got on your place, anyhow? Sounds like a black Baptist picnic to me. [*Pointing to the window with his cane*] Tom, listen to that.

NORWOOD.   [*Flushing*] I apologize to you, Fred, for each and every one of my darkies. [SAM *enters with more ice and another glass.*] Permit me to offer you a drink. I realize I've got to tighten down here.

HIGGINS.   Mose tells me that was Cora's boy in that Ford—and that young black fool is what I was coming here to talk to you about today. That boy! He's not gonna be around here long—not the way he's acting. The white folks in town'll see to that. Knowing he's one of your yard niggers, Norwood, I thought I ought to come and tell you. The white folks at the Junction aren't intending to put up with him much longer. And I don't know what good the jail would do him once he got in there.

NORWOOD.   [*Tensely*] What do you mean, Fred—jail? Don't I always take care of the folks on my plantation without any help from the Junction's police force? Talbot can do more with an unruly black buck than your marshal.

HIGGINS.   Warn't lookin' at it that way, Tom. I was thinking how weak the   4!
doors to that jail is. They've broke 'em down and lynched four niggers to my memory since it's been built. After what happened this morning, you better keep that yellow young fool out o' town from now on. It might not be safe for him around there—today, or no other time.

NORWOOD.   What the hell? [*Perturbed*] He went in just now to take his sister to the depot. Damn it, I hope no ruffians'll break up my new Ford. What was it, Fred, about this morning?

HIGGINS.   You haven't heard? Why, it's all over town already. He sassed out Miss Gray in the post office over a box of radio tubes that come by mail.

NORWOOD   He did, heh?

HIGGINS.   Seems like the stuff was sent C.O.D. and got here all smashed up, so he wouldn't take it. Paid his money first before he saw the box was broke. Then wanted the money order back. Seems like the post office can't give money orders back—rule against it. Your nigger started to argue, and the girl at the window—Miss Gray—got scared and yelled for some of the mail clerks. They threw Bert out of the office that's all. But that's enough. Lucky nothing more didn't happen. [*Indignantly*] That Bert needs a damn good beating—talking back to a white woman—and I'd like to give it to him myself, the way he kicked the dust up in my eyes all the way down the road coming out here. He was mad, I reckon. That's one yellow buck don't know his place, Tom, and it's your fault he don't—sending 'em off to be educated.

NORWOOD.   Well, by God, I'll show him. I wish I'd have known it before he left   5●
here just now.

HIGGINS.   Well, he's sure got mighty aggravating ways for a buck his color to have. Drives down the main street and don't stop for nobody, white or black. Comes in my store and if he ain't waited on as quick as the white folks are, he walks out and tells the clerk his money's as good as a white man's any day. Said last week standing out on my store front that he wasn't *all* nigger no how; said his name was Norwood—not Lewis, like the rest of his family—and part of your plantation here would be his when you passed out—and all that kind of stuff, boasting to the walleyed coons listening to him.

NORWOOD.   [*Astounded*] Well, I'll be damned!

HIGGINS.   Now, Tom, you know that don't go 'round these parts 'o Georgia, nor nowhere else in the South. A darkie's got to keep in his place down here. Ruinous to other niggers hearing that talk, too. All this postwar propaganda on the radio about freedom and democracy—why the niggers think it's meant for them! And that Eleanor Roosevelt,° she ought to been muzzled. She's driving our niggers crazy—your boy included! Crazy! Talking about civil rights. Ain't been no race trouble in our country for three years—since the Deekin's lynching—but I'm telling you, Norwood, you better see that that buck of yours goes away from here. I'm speaking on the quiet, but I can see ahead. And what happened this morning about them radio tubes wasn't none too good.

NORWOOD.   [*Beside himself with rage*] A black ape! I——I . . .

HIGGINS.   You been too decent to your darkies, Norwood. That's what's the matter with you. And then the whole country suffers from a lot of impudent bucks who take lessons from your crowd. Folks been kicking about that, too. Guess you know it. Maybe that's the reason you didn't get that nomination for committeeman a few years back.

NORWOOD.   Maybe 'tis, Higgins. [*Rising and pacing the room*] God damn niggers! [*Furiously*] Everything turns on niggers, niggers, niggers! No wonder Yankees call this the Black Belt! [*He pours a large drink of whiskey.*]

HIGGINS.   [*Soothingly*] Well, let's change the subject. Hand me my glass, there, too.

NORWOOD.   Pardon me, Fred. [*He puts ice in his friend's glass and passes him the bottle.*]

HIGGINS.   Tom, you get excited too easy for warm weather . . . Don't ever show black folks they got you going, though. I think sometimes that's where you make your mistake. Keep calm, keep calm—and then you command. Best plantation manager I ever had never raised his voice to a nigger—and they were scared to death of him.

NORWOOD.   Have a smoke. [*Pushes cigars toward HIGGINS*]

HIGGINS.   You ought've married again, Tom—brought a white woman out here on this damn place o' yours. A woman could help you run things. Women have soft ways, but they can keep things humming. Nothing but blacks in the house—a man gets soft like niggers are inside. [*Puffing at cigar*] And living with a colored woman! Of course, I know we all have 'em—I didn't know you could make use of a white girl till I was past twenty. Thought too much o' white women for that—but I've given many a yellow gal a baby in my time. [*Long puff at cigar*] But for a man's own house you need a wife, not a black woman.

NORWOOD.   Reckon you're right, Fred, but it's too late to marry again now. [*Shrugging his shoulders*] Let's get off of darkies and women for awhile. How's crops? [*Sitting down*] How's politics going?

HIGGINS.   Well, I guess you know the Republicans is trying to stir up trouble for us in Washington. I wish the South had more men like Bilbo and Rankin° there.

Eleanor Roosevelt: Eleanor Roosevelt [1884–1962], the wife of President Franklin D. Roosevelt, was an outspoken champion of minority causes.

Bilbo, Rankin: Theodore Bilbo [1877–1947], Senator from Mississippi from 1935 to 1947, and John Eliot Rankin [1882–1960], Mississippi Representative to the House from 1921 to 1953, were both noted advocates of white supremacy.

But, say, by the way, Lawyer Hotchkiss wants to see us both about that budget money next week. He's got some real Canadian stuff at his office, in his filing case, too—brought back from his vacation last summer. Taste better'n this old mountain juice we get around here. Not meaning to insult your drinks, Tom, but just remarking. I serve the same as you myself, label and all.

NORWOOD.   [*Laughing*] I'll have you know, sir, that this is prewar licker, sir!

HIGGINS.   Hum-m-m! Well, it's got me feelin' better'n I did when I come in here—whatever it is. [*Puffs at his cigar*] Say, how's your cotton this year?   6

NORWOOD.   Doin' right well, specially down in the south field. Why not drive out that road when you leave and take a look at it? I'll ride down with you. I want to see Talbot, anyhow.

HIGGINS.   Well, let's be starting. I got to be back at the Junction by four o'clock. Promised to let that boy of mine have the car to drive over to Thomasville for a dance tonight.

NORWOOD.   One more shot before we go. [*He pours out drinks.*] The young ones must have their fling, I reckon. When you and I grew up down here it used to be a carriage and the best pair of black horses when you took the ladies out—now it's an automobile. That's a good lookin' new car of yours, too.

HIGGINS.   Right nice.

NORWOOD.   Been thinking about getting a new one myself, but money's been   7 kinder tight this year, and conditions are none too good yet, either. Reckon that's why everybody's so restless. [*He walks toward stairs calling.*] Cora! Oh, Cora! . . . If I didn't have a few thousand put away, I'd feel the pinch myself. [*As CORA appears on the stairs.*] Bring me my glasses up there by the side of my bed . . . Better whistle for Mose, hadn't I, Higgins? He's probably 'round back with some of his women. [*Winking*] You know I got some nice black women in this yard.

HIGGINS.   Oh, no, not Mose. I got my servants trained to stay in their places—right where I want 'em—while they're working for me. Just open the door and tell him to come in here and help me out. [*NORWOOD goes to the door and calls the CHAUFEUR. MOSE enters and assists his master out to the car. CORA appears with the glasses, goes to the vestibule and gets the COLONEL'S hat and cane which she hands him.*]

NORWOOD.   [*To CORA*] I want to see that boy o' yours soon as I get back. That won't be long, either. And tell him to put up that Ford of mine and don't touch it again.

CORA.   Yes, sir, I'll have him waiting here. [*In a whisper*] It's hot weather, Colonel Tom. Too much of this licker makes your heart upset. It ain't good for you, you know. [*NORWOOD pays her no attention as he exits toward the car. The noise of the departing motor is heard. Cora begins to tidy up the room. She takes a glass from a side table. She picks up a doily that was beneath the glass and looks at it long and lovingly. Suddenly she goes to the door left and calls toward the kitchen.*] William, you William! Com'ere, I want to show you something. Make haste, son. [*As CORA goes back toward the table, her eldest son, WILLIAM enters carrying a five-year-old boy.*] Look here at this purty doily yo' sister made this summer while she been here. She done learned all about sewing and making purty things at school. Ain't it nice, son?

WILLIAM   Sho' is. Sallie takes after you, I reckon. She's a smart little crittur, ma. [*Sighs*] De Lawd knows, I was dumb at school. [*To his child*] Get down, Billy, you's too heavy. [*He puts the boy on the floor*] This here sewin's really fine.

BILLY.   [*Running toward the big upholstered chair and jumping up and down on the*   75
spring seat] Gityap! I's a mule driver. Haw! Gee!

CORA.   You Billy, get out of that chair 'fore I skins you alive. Get on into de
kitchen, sah.

BILLY.   I'm playin' horsie, grandma. [*Jumps up in the chair*] Horsie! Horsie!

CORA.   Get! That's de Colonel's favorite chair. If he knows any little darkie's
been jumpin' on it, he raise sand. Get on, now.

BILLY.   Ole Colonel's ma grandpa, ain't he? Ain' he ma white grandpa?

WILLIAM.   [*Snatching the child out of the chair*] Boy, I'm gonna fan your hide if   80
you don't hush!

CORA.   Shs-ss-s! You Billy, hush yo' mouth! Chile, where you hear that? [*To her
son*] Some o' you all been talking too much in front o' this chile. [*To the boy*] Honey,
go on in de kitchen till yo' daddy come. Get a cookie from 'Vonia and set down on
de back porch. [*Little BILLY exits left*]

WILLIAM.   Ma, you know it 'twarn't me told him. Bert's the one been goin' all
over de plantation since he come back from Atlanta remindin' folks right out we's
Colonel Norwood's chilluns.

CORA.   [*Catching her breath*] Huh!

WILLIAM.   He comes down to my shack tellin' Billy and Marybell they got a
white man for grandpa. He's gonna get my chilluns in trouble sho'—like he got himself in trouble when Colonel Tom whipped him.

CORA.   Ten or 'leven years ago, warn't it?   85

WILLIAM.   And Bert's *sho'* in trouble now. Can't go back to that college like he
could-a if he'd-a had any sense. You can't fool with white folks—an de Colonel ain't
never really liked Bert since that there first time he beat him, either.

CORA.   No, he ain't. Leastwise, he ain't understood him. [*Musing sadly in a low
voice*] Time Bert was 'bout seven, warn't it? Just a little bigger'n yo' Billy.

WILLIAM.   Yes.

CORA.   Went runnin' up to Colonel Tom out in de horse stables when de
Colonel was showin' off his horses—I 'members so well—to fine white company from
town. Lawd, that boy's always been foolish! He went runnin' up and grabbed a-holt
de Colonel and yelled right in front o' de white folks' faces, "O, papa, Cora say de dinner's ready, papa!" Ain't never called him papa before, and I don't know where he
got it from. And Colonel Tom knocked him right backwards under de horse's feet.

WILLIAM.   And when de company were gone, he beat that boy unmerciful.   90

CORA.   I thought sho' he were gonna kill ma chile that day. And he were mad
at me, too, for months. Said I was teaching you chilluns who they pappy were. Up till
then Bert had been his favorite little colored child round here.

WILLIAM.   Sho' had.

CORA.   But he never like him no more. That's why he sent him off to school so
soon to stay, winter and summer, all these years. I had to beg and plead to have him
home this summer—but I's sorry now I ever got that boy back here again.

WILLIAM.   He's sho' growed more like de Colonel all de time, ain't he? Bert
thinks he's a real white man hisself now. Look at de first thing he did when he come
home, he ain't seen de Colonel in six years—and Bert sticks out his hand fo' to shake
hands with him!

CORA.   Lawd! That chile!

WILLIAM.   Just like white folks! And de Colonel turns his back and walks off.   95
Can't blame him. He ain't used to such doings from colored folks. God knows what's

got into Bert since he come back. He's acting like a fool—just like he was a boss man round here. Won't even say "Yes, sir" and "No, sir" no more to de white folks. Talbot asked him warn't he gonna work in de field this mornin'. Bert say "No!" and turn and walk away. White man so mad, I could see him nearly foam at de mouth. If he warn't yo' chile, ma, he'd been knocked in de head fo' now.

CORA. You's right.

WILLIAM. And you can't talk to him. I tried to tell him something the other day, but he just laughed at me, and said we's all just scared niggers on this plantation. Says he ain't no nigger, no how. He's a Norwood. He's half-white, and he's gonna act like it. [*In amazement at his brother's daring*] And this is Georgia, too!

CORA. I's scared to death for de boy, William. I don't know what to do. De Colonel says he won't send him off to school no mo'. Says he's mo' sassy and impudent now than any nigger he ever seed. Bert never has been like you was, and de girls, quiet and sensible like you knowed you had to be. [*She sits down*] De Colonel say he's gonna make Bert stay here now and work on this plantation like de rest of his niggers. He's gonna show him what color he is. Like that time when he beat him for callin' him "papa." He say he's gwine to teach him his place and make de boy know where he belongs. Seems like me or you can't show him. Colonel Tom has to take him in hand, or these white folks'll kill him around here and then—oh, My God!

WILLIAM. A nigger's just got to know his place in de South, that's all, ain't he, ma?   100

CORA. Yes, son. That's all, I reckon.

WILLIAM. And ma brother's one damn fool nigger. Don't seems like he knows nothin'. He's gonna ruin us all round here. Makin' it bad for everybody.

CORA. Oh, Lawd, have mercy! [*Beginning to cry*] I don't know what to do. De way he's acting up can't go on. Way he's acting to de Colonel can't last. Somethin's gonna happen to ma chile. I had a bad dream last night, too, and I looked out and seed de moon all red with blood. I seed a path o' living blood across this house, I tell you, in ma sleep. Oh, Lawd, have mercy! [*Sobbing*] Oh, Lawd, help me in ma troubles. [*The noise of the returning Ford is heard outside. CORA looks up, rises, and goes to the window.*] There's de chile now, William. Run out to de back door and tell him I wants to see him. Bring him in here where Sam and Livonia and de rest of 'em won't hear ever'thing we's sayin'. I got to talk to ma boy. He's ma baby boy, and he don't know de way.

[*Exit WILLIAM through the door left. CORA is wiping her eyes and pulling herself together when the front door is flung open with a bang and ROBERT enters.*]

ROBERT. [*Running to his mother and hugging her teasingly*] Hello, ma! Your daughter got off, and I've come back to keep you company in the parlor! Bring out the cookies and lemonade. *Mister* Norwood's here!

CORA. [*Beginning to sob anew*] Take yo' hands off me, boy! Why don't you mind? Why don't you mind me?   105

ROBERT. [*Suddenly serious, backing away*] Why, mamma, what's the matter? Did I scare you? Your eyes are all wet! Has somebody been telling you 'bout this morning?

CORA. [*Not heeding his words*] Why don't you mind me, son? Ain't I told you and told you not to come in that front door, never? [*Suddenly angry*] Will somebody have to beat it into you? What's got wrong with you when you was away at that school? What am I gonna do?

ROBERT.   [*Carelessly*] Oh, I knew that the Colonel wasn't here. I passed him and old man Higgins on the road down by the south patch. He wouldn't even look at me when I waved at him. [*Half playfully*] Anyhow, isn't this my old man's house? Ain't I his son and heir? [*Grandly, strutting around*] Am I not Mr. Norwood, Junior?

CORA.   [*Utterly serious*] I believe you goin' crazy, Bert. I believes you wants to get us all killed or run away or something awful like that. I believes . . . [*WILLIAM enters left*]

WILLIAM.   Where's Bert? He ain't come round back——[*Seeing his brother in the room*] How'd you get in here?   110

ROBERT.   [*Grinning*] Houses have front doors.

WILLIAM.   Oh, usin' de front door like de white folks, heh? You gwine do that once too much.

ROBERT.   Yes, like de white folks. What's a front door for, you rabbit-hearted coon?

WILLIAM.   Rabbit-hearted coon's better'n a dead coon any day.

ROBERT.   I wouldn't say so. Besides you and me's only half-coons, anyhow, big boy. And I'm gonna act like my white half, not my black half. Get me, kid?   115

WILLIAM.   Well, you ain't gonna act like it long here in de middle o' Georgy. And you ain't gonna act like it when de Colonel's around, either.

ROBERT.   Oh, no? My stay down here'll be short and sweet, boy, short and sweet. The old man won't send me away to college no more—so you think I'm gonna stick around and work in the fields? Like fun? I might stay here awhile and teach some o' you darkies to think like men, maybe—till it gets too much for the old Colonel— but no more bowing down to white folks for me—not Robert Norwood.

CORA.   Hush, son!

ROBERT.   Certainly not right on my own old man's plantation—Georgia or no Georgia.

WILLIAM.   [*Scornfully*] I hears you.   120

ROBERT.   *You* can do it if you want to, but I'm ashamed of you. I've been away from here six years. [*Boasting*] I've learned something, seen people in Atlanta, and Richmond, and Washington where the football team went—real colored people who don't have to take off their hats to white folks or let'em go to bed with their sisters— like that young Higgins boy, asking me what night Sallie was comin' to town. A damn cracker! [*To CORA*] 'Scuse me, ma. [*Continuing*] Back here in these woods maybe Sam and Livonia and you and mama and everybody's got their places fixed for 'em, but not me. [*Seriously*] Nobody's gonna fix a place for me. I'm old man Norwood's son. Nobody fixed a place for him. [*Playfully again*] Look at me. I'm a 'fay boy. [*Pretends to shake his hair back*] See these gray eyes? I got the right to everything everybody else has. [*Punching his brother in the belly*], Don't talk to me, old slavery-time Uncle Tom.

WILLIAM.   [*Resentfully*] I ain't playin', boy. [*Pushes younger brother back with some force*] I ain't playin' a-tall.

CORA.   All right, chilluns, stop. Stop! And William, you take Billy and go on home. 'Vonia's got to get supper and she don't like no young-uns under her feet in de kitchen. I wants to talk to Bert in here now 'fore Colonel Tom gets back. [*Exit WILLIAM left. CORA continues to BERT*] Sit down, child, right here a minute and listen.

ROBERT.   [*Sitting down*] All right, ma.

CORA.   Hard as I's worked and begged and humbled maself to get de Colonel to keep you chilluns in school, you comes home wid yo' head full o' stubbornness and yo' mouth full o' sass for me an' de white folks an' everybody. You know can't no col-   125 ored boy here talk like you's been doin' to no white folks, let alone to de Colonel and that old devil of a Talbot. They ain't gonna stand fo' yo' sass. Not only you, but I 'spects we's all gwine to pay fo' it, every colored soul on this place. I was scared to death today fo' yo' sister, Sallie, scared de Colonel warn't gwine to let her go back to school, neither, 'count o' yo' doins, but he did, thank Gawd—and then you come near makin' her miss de train. Did she have time to get her ticket and all?

ROBERT. Sure! Had to drive like sin to get there with her, though. I didn't mean to be late getting back here for her, ma, but I had a little run-in about them radio tubes in town.

CORA. [*Worried*] What's that?

ROBERT. The tubes was smashed when I got 'em, and I had already made out my money order, so the woman in the post office wouldn't give the three dollars back to me. All I did was explain to her that we could send the tubes back—but she got hot because there were two or three white folks waiting behind me to get stamps, I guess. So she yells at me to move on and not give her any of my "educated nigger talk." So I said, "I'm going to finish showing you these tubes before I move on"—and then she screamed and called the mail clerk working in the back, and told him to throw me out. [*Boasting*] He didn't do it by himself, though. Had to call all the white loafers out in the square to get me through that door.

CORA. [*Fearfully*] Lawd have mercy!

ROBERT. Guess if I hadn't-a had the Ford then, they'd've beat me half-to-death, but when I saw how many crackers there was, I jumped in the car and beat it on away. 130

CORA. Thank God for that!

ROBERT. Not even a football man [*Half-boasting*] like me could tackle the whole junction. 'Bout a dozen colored guys standing around, too, and not one of 'em would help me—the dumb jiggaboos! They been telling me ever since I been here, [*Imitating darky talk*] "You can't argue wid whut folks, man. You better stay out o' this Juncton. You must ain't got no sense, nigger! You's a fool" . . . Maybe I am a fool, ma—but I didn't want to come back here nohow.

CORA. I's sorry I sent for you.

ROBERT. Besides you, there ain't nobody in this country but a lot of evil white folks and cowardly niggers. [*Earnstly*] I'm no nigger, anyhow, am I, ma? I'm half-white. The Colonel's my father—the richest man in the county—and I'm not going to take a lot of stuff from nobody if I do have to stay here, not from the old man either. He thinks I ought to be out there in the sun working, with Talbot standing over me like I belonged in the chain gang. Well, he's got another thought coming! [*Stubbornly*] I'm a Norwood—not a field-hand nigger.

CORA. You means you ain't workin' no mo'? 135

ROBERT. [*Flaring*] No, I'm not going to work in the fields. What did he send me away to school for—just to come back here and be his servant, or pick his hills of cotton?

CORA. He sent you away to de school because *I* asked him and begged him, and got down on my knees to him, that's why. [*Quietly*] And now I just wants to make you see some sense, if you can. I knows, honey, you reads in de books and de papers, and you knows a lot more'n I do. But, chile, you's in Georgy—and I don't see how it is you don't know where you's at. This ain't up North—and even up yonder where we hears it's so fine, yo' sister has to pass for white to get along good.

ROBERT. [*Bitterly*] I know it.

CORA.   She ain't workin' in no hotel kitchen like de Colonel thinks. She's in a office typewriting. And Sallie's studyin' de typewriter, too, at de school, but yo' pappy don't know it. I knows we ain't s'posed to study nothin' but cookin' and hard workin' here in Georgy. That's all I ever done, or knowed about. I been workin' on this very place all ma life—even 'fore I come to live in this Big House. When de Colonel's wife died, I come here, and borned you chilluns. And de Colonel's been real good to me in his way. Let you all sleep in this house with me when you was little, and sent you all off to school when you growed up. Ain't no white man in this county done that with his cullud chilluns before, far as I can know. But you—Robert, be awful, awful careful! When de Colonel comes back, in a few minutes, he wants to talk to you. Talk right to him, boy. Talk like you was colored, 'cause you ain't white.

ROBERT.   [*Angrily*] And I'm not black either. Look at me, mama. [*Rising and throwing up his arms*] Don't I look like my father? Ain't I as light as he is? Ain't my eyes gray like his eyes are? [*The noise of a car is heard outside*] Ain't this our house?   140

CORA.   That's him now. [*Agitated*] Hurry, chile, and let's get out of this room. Come on through yonder to the kitchen. [*She starts toward the door left.*] And I'll tell him you're here.

ROBERT.   I don't want to run into the kitchen. Isn't this our house? [*As CORA crosses hurriedly left, ROBERT goes toward the front door*] The Ford is parked out in front, anyway.

CORA.   [*At the door left to the rear of the house*] Robert! Robert! [*As ROBERT nears the front door, COLONEL NORWOOD enters, almost runs into the boy, stops at the threshold and stares unbelievingly at his son. CORA backs up against the door left.*

NORWOOD.   Get out of here! [*He points toward the door to rear of the house where CORA is standing*].

ROBERT.   [*Half-smiling*] Didn't you want to talk to me?   145

NORWOOD.   Get out of here!

ROBERT.   Not that way. [*The COLONEL raises his cane to strike the boy. CORA screams. BERT draws himself up to his full height, taller than the old man and looking very much like him, pale and proud. The man and the boy face each other. NORWOOD does not strike.*]

NORWOOD.   [*In a hoarse whisper*] Get out of here. [*His hand is trembling as he points.*]

CORA.   Robert! Come on, son, come on! Oh, my God, come on. [*Opening the door left*]

ROBERT.   Not that way, ma. [*ROBERT walks proudly out the front door. NORWOOD, in an impotent rage, crosses the room to a small cabinet right, opens it nervously with a key from his pocket, takes out a pistol, and starts toward the front door. CORA overtakes him, seizes his arm, stops him.*]

CORA.   He's our son, Tom. [*She sinks slowly to her knees, holding his body.*]   150
Remember, he's our son.

Curtain

ACT II

Scene 1

TIME.   *After supper. Sunset.*
SETTING.   *The same.*
ACTION.   *As the curtain rises, the stage is empty. Through the windows the late after-*

noon sun makes two bright paths toward the footlights. SAM, *carrying a tray bearing a whiskey bottle and a bowl of ice, enters left and crosses toward the library. He stoops at the door right, listens a moment, knocks, then opens the door and goes in. In a moment* SAM *returns. As he leaves the library, he is heard replying to a request of* NORWOOD's.

SAM.   Yes, sah, Colonel! Sho' will, sah! Right away, sah! Yes, sah, I'll tell him. [*He closes the door and crosses the stage muttering to himself.*] Six o'clock. Most nigh that now. Better tell Cora to get that boy right in here. Can't nobody else do notin' with that fool Bert but Cora. [*He exits left. Can be heard calling*] Cora! You, Cora . . .

[*Again the stage is empty. Off stage, outside, the bark of a dog is heard, the sound of Negroes singing down the road, the cry of a child. The breeze moves the shadows of leaves and tree limbs across the sunlit paths from the windows. The door left opens and* CORA *enters, followed by* ROBERT.]

CORA.   [*Softly to* ROBERT *behind her in the dining room*] It's all right, son. He ain't come out yet, but it's nearly six, and that's when he said he wanted you, but I was afraid maybe you was gonna be late. I sent for you to come up here to de house and eat supper with me in de kitchen. Where'd you eat yo' vittuals at, chile?

ROBERT.   Down at Willie's house, ma. After the old man tried to hit me you still want me to hang around and eat up here?

CORA.   I wanted you to be here on time, honey, that's all. [*She is very nervous.*] I kinder likes to have you eat with me sometimes, too, but you ain't et up here more'n once this summer. But this evenin' I just wanted you to be here when de Colonel sent word for you, 'cause we's done had enough trouble today.

ROBERT.   He's not here on time, himself, is he?

CORA.   He's in de library. Sam couldn't get him to eat no supper tonight, and I ain't seen him a-tall.

ROBERT.   Maybe he wants to see me in the library, then.

CORA.   You know he don't 'low no colored folks in there 'mongst his books and things 'cept Sam. Some o' his white friends goes in there, but none o' us.

ROBERT.   Maybe he wants to see *me* in there, though.

CORA.   Can't you never talk sense, Robert? This ain't no time for foolin' and jokin'. Nearly thirty years in this house and I ain't never been in there myself, not once, 'mongst de Colonel's papers. [*The clock strikes six.*] Stand over yonder and wait till he comes out. I's gwine on upstairs now, so's he can talk to you. And don't aggravate him no mo' for' God's sake. Agree to whatever he say. I's scared fo' you, chile, de way you been actin', and de fool tricks you done today, and de trouble about de post office besides. Don't aggravate him. Fo' yo' sake, honey, 'cause I loves you—and fo' all de po' colored folks on this place what has such a hard time when his humors get on him—agree to whatever he say, will you, Bert?

ROBERT.   All right, ma. [*Voice rising*] But he better not start to hit me again.

CORA.   Shs-ss-s! He'll hear you. He's right in there.

ROBERT.   [*Sullenly*] This was the day I ought to have started back to school—like my sister. I stayed my summer out here, didn't I? Why didn't he keep his promise to me? You said if I came home I could go back to college again.

CORA.   Shs-ss-s! He'll be here now. Don't say nothin', chile, I's done all I could.

ROBERT.   All right, ma.

CORA.   [*Approaching the stairs*] I'll be in ma room, honey, where I can hear you when you goes out. I'll come down to de back door and see you 'fore you goes back to de shack. Don't aggravate him, chile.

[*She ascends the stairs. The boy sits down sullenly, left, and stares at the door opposite from which his father must enter. The clock strikes the quarter after six. The shadows of the window curtains have lengthened on the carpet. The sunshine has deepened to a pale orange, and the light paths grow less distinct across the floor. The boy sits up straight in his chair. He looks at the library door. It opens. NORWOOD enters. He is bent and pale. He looks across the room and sees the boy. Suddenly he straightens up. The old commanding look comes into his face. He strides directly across the room towad his son. The boy, half afraid, half defiant, yet sure of himself, rises. Now that ROBERT is standing, the white man turns, goes back to a chair near the table, right, and seats himself. He takes out a cigar, cuts off the end and lights it, and in a voice of mixed condescension and contempt, he speaks to his son. ROBERT remains standing near the chair.*]

NORWOOD.   I don't want to have to beat you another time as I did when you were a child. The next time I might not be able to control myself. I might kill you if I touched you again. I been runnin' this plantation for thirty-five years, and I never had to beat a Nigra as old as you are. I never had to beat one of Cora's children either—but you. The rest of 'em had sense 'nough to keep out of my sight, and to speak to me like they should . . . I don't have any trouble with my colored folks. Never have trouble. They do what I say, or what Mr. Talbot says, and that's all there is to it. I give 'em a chance. If they turn in crops they get paid. If they're workin' for wages, they get paid. If they want to spend their money on licker, or buy an old car, or fix up their cabins, they can. Do what they choose long as they know their places and it don't hinder their work. And to Cora's young ones I give all the chances any colored folks ever had in these parts. More'n many a white child's had. I sent you all off to school. Let Bertha go on up North when she got grown and educated. Intend to let Sallie do the same. Gave your brother William that house he's living in when he got married, pay him for his work, help him out if he needs it. None of my darkies suffer. Sent you to college. Would have kept on, would have sent you back today, but I don't intend to pay for no darky, or white boy either if I had one, that acts the way you've been acting. And certainly for no black fool. Now I want to know what's wrong with you? I don't usually talk about what I'm going to do with anybody on this place. It's my habit to tell people *what to do*, not discuss it with 'em. But I want to know what's the matter with you—whether you're crazy or not. In that case, you'll have to be locked up. And if you aren't, you'll have to change your ways a damn sight or it won't be safe for you here, and you know it—venting your impudence on white women, parking the car in front of my door, driving like mad through the Junction, and going, everywhere, just as you please. Now, I'm going to let you talk to me, but I want you to talk right.

ROBERT.   [*Still standing*] What do you mean, "talk right?"

NORWOOD.   I mean talk like a nigger should to a white man.

ROBERT.   Oh! But I'm not a nigger, Colonel Tom. I'm your son.   20

NORWOOD.   [*Testily*] You're Cora's boy.

ROBERT.   Women don't have children by themselves.

NORWOOD.   Nigger women don't know the fathers. You're a bastard.

[*ROBERT clenches his fist. NORWOOD turns toward the drawer where the pistol is, takes it out, and lays it on the table. The wind blows the lace curtains at the windows, and sweeps the shadows of falling leaves across the paths of sunlight on the floor.*]

ROBERT.   I've heard that before. I've heard it from Negroes, and I've heard it from white folks. Now I hear it from you. [*Slowly*] You're talking about my mother.

NORWOOD.   I'm talking about Cora, yes. Her children are bastards.   25

ROBERT.   [*Quickly*] And you're their father. [*Angrily*] How come I look like you, if you're not my father?

NORWOOD.   Don't shout at me, boy. I can hear you. [*Half-smiling*] How come your skin is yellow and your elbows rusty? How come they threw you out of the post office today for talking to a white woman? How come you're the crazy young buck you are?

ROBERT.   They had no right to throw me out. I asked for my money back when I saw the broken tubes. Just as you had no right to raise that cane today when I was standing at the door of this house where *you* live, while *I* have to sleep in a shack down the road with the field hands. [*Slowly*] But my mother sleeps with you.

NORWOOD.   You don't like it?

ROBERT.   No, I don't like it.   3•

NORWOOD.   What can you do about it?

ROBERT.   [*After a pause*] I'd like to kill all the white men in the world.

NORWOOD.   [*Starting*] Niggers like you are hung to trees.

ROBERT.   I'm not a nigger.

NORWOOD.   You don't like your own race? [*ROBERT is silent*] Yet you don't like   3•
white folks either?

ROBERT.   [*Defiantly*] You think I ought to?

NORWOOD.   You evidently don't like me.

ROBERT.   [*Boyishly*] I used to like you, when I first knew you were my father, when I was a little kid, before that time you beat me under the feet of your horses. [*Slowly*] I liked you until then.

NORWOOD.   [*A little pleased*] So you did, heh? [*Fingering his pistol*] A pickaninny calling me "papa." I should've broken your young neck for that first time. I should've broken your head for you today, too—since I didn't then.

ROBERT.   [*Laughing scornfully*] You should've broken my head?   4•

NORWOOD.   Should've gotten rid of you before this. But you was Cora's child. I tried to help you. [*Aggrieved*] I treated you decent, schooled you. Paid for it. But tonight you'll get the hell off this place and stay off. Get the hell out of this county. [*Suddenly furious*] Get out of this state. Don't let me lay eyes on you again. Get out of here now. Talbot and the storekeeper are coming up here this evening to talk cotton with me. I'll tell Talbot to *see* that you go. That's all. [*NORWOOD motions toward the door, left.*] Tell Sam to come in here when you go out. Tell him to make a light here.

ROBERT.   [*Impudently*] *Ring* for Sam—I'm not going through the kitchen. [*He starts toward the front door*] I'm not your servant. You're not going to tell me what to do. You're not going to have Talbot run me off the place like a field hand you don't want to use any more.

NORWOOD.   [*Springing between his son and the front door, pistol in hand*] You black bastard! [*ROBERT goes toward him calmly, grasps his father's arm and twists it until the gun falls to the floor. The older man bends backward in startled fury and pain.*] Don't you dare put your . . .

ROBERT.   [*Laughing*] Why don't you shoot, papa? [*Louder*] Why don't you shoot?

NORWOOD.   [*Gasping as he struggles, fighting back*] . . . black . . . hands . . . on . . .   4•
you . . .

ROBERT.   [*Hysterically, as he takes his father by the throat*] Why don't you shoot, papa? [*NORWOOD's hands claw the air helplessly. ROBERT chokes the struggling white man un-*

til his body grows limp] Why don't you shoot! [*Laughing*] Why don't you shoot? Huh? Why?

[*CORA appears at the top of the stairs, hearing the commotion. She screams.*]

CORA.   Oh, my God! [*She rushes down. ROBERT drops the body of his father at her feet in a path of flame from the setting sun. CORA starts and stares in horror.*]

ROBERT.   [*Wildly*] Why didn't he shoot, mama? He didn't want *me* to live. Why didn't he shoot? [*Laughing*] He was the boss. Telling me what to do. Why didn't he shoot, then? He was the white man.

CORA.   [*Falling on the body*] Colonel Tom! Colonel Tom! Tom! Tom! [*Gazes across the corpse at her son*] He's yo' father, Bert.

ROBERT.   He's dead. The white man's dead. My father's dead. [*Laughing*] I'm living.   50

CORA.   Tom! Tom! Tom!

ROBERT.   Niggers are living. He's dead. [*Picks up the pistol*] This is what he wanted to kill me with, but he's dead. I can use it now. Use it on all the white men in the world, because they'll be coming looking for me now. [*Stuffs the pistol into his shirt*] They'll want me now.

CORA.   [*Rising and running toward her boy*] Quick, chile, out that way, [*Pointing toward the front door*] so they won't see you in de kitchen. Make for de swamp, honey. Cross de fields fo' de swamp. Go de crick way. In runnin' water, dogs can't smell no tracks. Hurry, chile!

ROBERT.   Yes, mama. I can go out the front way now, easy. But if I see they gonna get me before I can reach the swamp, I'm coming back here, mama, and [*Proudly*] let them take me out of my father's house—if they can. [*Pats the gun under his shirt*] They're not going to string me up to some roadside tree for the crackers to laugh at.

CORA.   [*Moaning aloud*] Oh, O-o-o! Hurry! Hurry, chile!   55

ROBERT.   I'm going, ma. [*He opens the door. The sunset streams in like a river of blood*]

CORA.   Run, chile!

ROBERT.   Not out of my father's house. [*He exits slowly, tall and straight against the sun.*]

CORA.   Fo' God's sake, hurry, chile! [*Glancing down the road*] Lawd have mercy! There's Talbot and de storekeeper in de drive. They sees my boy! [*Moaning*] They sees ma boy. [*Relieved*] But thank God, they's passin' him! [*CORA backs up against the wall in the vestibule. She stands as if petrified as TALBOT and the STOREKEEPER enter*]

TALBOT.   Hello, Cora. What's the matter with you? Where's that damn fool boy   60
o' your'n goin', coming out the front door like he owned the house? What's the matter with you, woman? Can't you talk? Can't you talk? Where's Norwood? Let's have some light in this dark place. [*He reaches behind the door and turns on the lights. CORA remains backed up against the wall, looking out into the twilight, watching ROBERT as he goes across the field*] Good God, Jim! Look at this! [*The TWO WHITE MEN stop in horror before the sight of NORWOOD's body on the floor.*]

STOREKEEPER.   He's blue in the face. [*Bends over the body*] That nigger we saw walking out the door! [*Rising excitedly*] That nigger bastard of Cora's . . . [*Stooping over the body again*] Why the Colonel's dead!

TALBOT.   That nigger! [*Rushes toward the door*] He's running toward the swamp now . . . We'll get him . . . Telephone town—there, in the library. Telephone the sheriff. Get men, white men, after that nigger.

[*STOREKEEPER rushes into the library. He can be heard talking excitedly on the phone.*]

STOREKEEPER.   Sheriff! Sheriff! Is this the sheriff? I'm calling from Norwood's plantation. That nigger, Bert, has just killed Norwood—and run, headed for the swamp. Notify the gas station at the crossroads! Tell the boys at the sawmill to head him off at the creek. Warn everybody to be on the lookout. Call your deputies! Yes! Spread a dragnet. Get out the dogs. Meanwhile we'll start after him. [*He slams the phone down and comes back into the room.*] Cora, where's Norwood's car? In the barn? [*CORA does not answer.*]

TALBOT.   Talk, you black bitch!

[*She remains silent. TALBOT runs, yelling and talking, out into the yard, followed by the STOREKEEPER. Sounds of excited shouting outside, and the roar of a motor rushing down the drive. In the sky the twilight deepens into early night. CORA stands looking into the darkness.*]

CORA.   My boy can't get to de swamp now. They's telephoned the white folks   6
down that way. So he'll come back home now. Maybe he'll turn into de crick and follow de branch home directly. [*Protectively*] But they shan't get him. I'll make a place for to hide him. I'll make a place upstairs down under de floor, under ma bed. In a minute ma boy'll be runnin' from de white folks with their hounds and their ropes and their guns and everything they uses to kill po' colored folks with. [*Distressed*] Ma boy'll be out there runnin. [*Turning to the body on the floor*] Colonel Tom, you hear me? Our boy, out there runnin'. [*Fiercely*] You said he was ma boy—ma bastard boy. I heard you . . . but he's yours too . . . but yonder in de dark runnin'—runnin' from yo' people, from white people. [*Pleadingly*] Why don't you get up and stop 'em? He's *your* boy. His eyes is gray—like your eyes. He's tall like you's tall. He's proud like you's proud. And he's runnin'—runnin' from po' white trash what ain't worth de little finger o' nobody what's got your blood in 'em, Tom. [*Demandingly*] Why don't you get up from there and stop 'em, Colonel Tom? What's that you say? He ain't your chile? He's ma bastard chile? My yellow bastard chile? [*Proudly*] Yes, he's mine. But don't call him that. Don't you touch him. Don't you put your white hands on him. You's beat him enough, and cussed him enough. Don't you touch him now. He *is* ma boy and no white folks gonna touch him now. That's finished. I'm gonna make a place for him upstairs under ma bed. [*Backs away from the body toward the stairs*] He's ma chile. Don't you come in ma bedroom while he's up there. Don't you come to my bed no mo'. I calls you to help me now, and you just lays there. I calls you for to wake up, and you just lays there. Whenever you called me, in de night, I woke up. When you called for me to love, I always reached out ma arms fo' you. I borned you five chilluns and now one of 'em is out yonder in de dark runnin' from yo' people. Our youngest boy out yonder in de dark runnin'. [*Accusingly*] He's runnin' from you, too. You said he warn't your'n—he's just Cora's po' little yellow bastard. But he *is* your'n, Colonel Tom. [*Sadly*] And he's runnin' from you. You are out yonder in de dark, [*Points toward the door*] runnin' our chile, with de hounds and de gun in yo' hand, and Talbot's followin' 'hind you with a rope to hang Robert with. [*Confidently*] I been sleepin' with you too long, Colonel Tom, not to know that this ain't you layin' down there with yo'

eyes shut on de floor. You can't fool me—you ain't never been so still like this before—you's out yonder runnin' ma boy through de fields in de dark, runnin' ma poor
little helpless Bert through de fields in de dark to lynch him ... Damn you, Colonel
Norwood! [*Backing slowly up the stairs, staring at the rigid body below her*] Damn you,
Thomas Norwood! God damn you!

Curtain

Scene 2

TIME.   *One hour later. Night.*
SETTING.   *The same.*
ACTION.   *As the curtain rises, the* UNDERTAKER *is talking to* SAM *at the outer door. All
through this act the approaching cries of the man hunt are heard.*

UNDERTAKER.   Reckon there won't be no orders to bring his corpse back out
here, Sam. None of us ain't seen Talbot or Mr. Higgins, but I'm sure they'll be having the funeral in town. The coroner told us to bring the body into the Junction. Ain't
nothing' but niggers left out here now.
SAM.   [*Very frightened*] Yes, sah! Yes, sah! You's right, sah! Nothin' but us niggers, sah!
UNDERTAKER.   The Colonel didn't have no relatives far as you know, did he,
Sam?
SAM.   No, sah. Ain't had none. No, sah! You's right, sah!
UNDERTAKER.   Well, you got everything o' his locked up around here, ain't   5
you? Too bad there ain't no white folks about to look after the Colonel's stuff, but
every white man that's able to walk's out with the posse. They'll have that young nig-
ger swingin' before ten.
SAM.   [*Trembling*] Yes, sah, yes, sah! I 'spects so. Yes, sah!
UNDERTAKER.   Say, where's that woman the Colonel's been living with—
where's that black housekeeper, Cora, that murderin's bastard's mother?
SAM.   She here, sah! She's up in her room.
UNDERTAKER.   [*Curiously*] I'd like to see how she looks. Get her down here.
Say, how about a little drink before we start that ride back to town, for me and my
partner out there with the body?
SAM.   Cora got de keys to all de licker, sah!   10
UNDERTAKER.   Well, get her down here then, double quick! [*SAM goes up the
stairs. The* UNDERTAKER *leans in the front doorway talking to his partner outside in the
wagon*] Bad business, a white man having saucy nigger children on his hands, and his
black woman living in his own house.
VOICE OUTSIDE.   Damn right, Charlie.
UNDERTAKER.   Norwood didn't have a gang o' yellow gals, though, like Higgins
and some o' these other big bugs. Just this one bitch far's I know, livin' with him
damn near like a wife. Didn't even have much company out here. And they tell me
ain't been a white woman stayed here overnight since his wife died when I was a baby.
[*SAM'S shuffle is heard on the stairs*] Here comes a drink, I reckon, boy. You needn't get
down off the ambulance. I'll have Sam bring it out there to you. [*SAM descends followed
by* CORA *who comes down the stairs. She says nothing. The* UNDERTAKER *looks up grinning at*
CORA] Well, so you're the Cora that's got these educated nigger children? Hum-m!
Well, I guess you'll see one of 'em swinging full of bullet holes when you wake up in

the morning. They'll probably hang him to that tree down here by the Colonel's gate—'cause they tell me he strutted right out the front gate past that tree after the murder. Or maybe they'll burn him. How'd you like to see him swinging there roasted in the morning when you wake up, girlie?

CORA.   [*Calmly*] Is that all you wanted to say to me?

UNDERTAKER.   Don't get smart! Maybe you think there's nobody to boss you now. We gonna have a little drink before we go. Get out a bottle of rye.

CORA.   I takes ma orders from Colonel Norwood, sir.

UNDERTAKER.   Well, you'll take no more orders from him. He's dead out there in my wagon—so get along and get the bottle.

CORA.   He's out yonder with de mob, not in your wagon.

UNDERTAKER.   I tell you he's in my wagon!

CORA.   He's out there with de mob.

UNDERTAKER.   God damn! [*To his partner outside*] I believe this black woman's gone crazy in here. [*To CORA*] Get the keys out for that licker, and be quick about it! [*CORA does not move. SAM looks from one to the other, frightened.*]

VOICE OUTSIDE.   Aw, to hell with the licker, Charlie. Come on, let's start back to town. We want to get in on some of that excitement, too. They should've found that nigger by now—and I want to see 'em drag him out here.

UNDERTAKER.   All right, Jim. [*To CORA and SAM*] Don't you all go to bed until you see that bonfire. You niggers are getting besides yourselves around Polk County. We'll burn a few more of you if you don't be careful. [*He exits, and the noise of the dead-wagon going down the road is heard.*]

SAM.   Oh, Lawd, hab mercy on me! I prays, Lawd hab mercy! O, ma Lawd, ma Lawd, ma Lawd! Cora, is you a fool? *Is* you a fool? Why didn't you give de mens de licker, riled as these white folks is? In ma old age is I gonna be burnt by de crackers? Lawd, is I sinned? Lawd, what has I done? [*Suddenly stops moaning and becomes schemingly calm*] I don't have to stay here tonight, does I? I done locked up de Colonel's library, and he can't be wantin' nothin'. No, ma Lawd, he won't want nothin' now. He's with Jesus—or with de devil, one. [*To CORA*] I's gwine on away from here. Sam's gwine in town to his chilluns' house, and I ain't gwine by no road either. I gwine through de holler where I don't have to pass no white folks.

CORA.   Yes, Samuel, you go on. De Colonel can get his own drinks when he comes back tonight.

SAM.   [*Bucking his eyes in astonishment at CORA*] Lawd God Jesus!

[*He bolts out of the room as fast as his old legs will carry him. CORA comes down stairs, looks for a long moment out into the darkness, then closes the front door and draws the blinds. She looks down at the spot where the COLONEL's body lay.*]

CORA.   All de colored folks are runnin' from you tonight. Po' Colonel Tom, you too old now to be out with de mob. You got no business goin', but you had to go, I reckon. I 'members that time they hung Luke Jordan, you sent yo' dogs out to hunt him. The next day you killed all de dogs. You were kinder softhearted. Said you didn't like that kind of sport. Told me in bed one night you could hear them dogs howlin' in yo' sleep. But de time they burnt de courthouse when that po' little cullud boy was locked up in it cause they said he hugged a white girl, you was with 'em again. Said you had to go help 'em. Now you's out chasin' ma boy. [*As she stands at the window, she sees a passing figure.*] There goes yo' other woman, Colonel Tom, Livonia is runnin' from you too, now. She would've wanted you last night. Been wantin' you again ever since she got old and fat and you stopped layin' with her and put her in the kitchen to cook. Don't think I don't know, Colonel Tom. Don't think I don't remember them nights when you used to sleep in that cabin down by de spring. I knew 'Vonia was there with you. I ain't no fool, Colonel Tom. But she ain't bore you no chilluns. I'm de one that bore 'em. [*Musing*] White mens, and colored womens, and little bastard chilluns—that's de old way of de South—but it's ending now. Three of your yellow brothers yo' father had by Aunt Sallie Deal—what had to come and do your laundry to make her livin'—you got colored relatives scattered all over this county. Them de ways o' de South—mixtries, mixtries. [*WILLIAM enters left, silently, as his mother talks. She is sitting in a chair now. Without looking up*] Is that you, William?

WILLIAM.   Yes, ma, it's me.

CORA.   Is you runnin' from him, too?

WILLIAM.   [*Hesitatingly*] Well, ma, you see . . . don't you think kinder . . . well,   30
I reckon I ought to take Libby and ma babies on down to de church house with Reverend Martin and them, or else get 'long to town if I can hitch up them mules. They's scared to be out here, my wife and her ma. All de folks done gone from de houses down yonder by de branch, and you can hear de hounds a bayin' off yonder by de swamp, and cars is tearin' up that road, and de white folks is yellin' and hollerin' and carryin' on somethin' terrible over toward de brook. I done told Robert 'bout his foolishness. They's gonna hang him sure. Don't you think you better be comin' with us, ma. That is, do you want to? 'Course we can go by ourselves, and maybe you wants to stay here and take care o' de big house. I don't want to leave you, ma, but I . . . I . . .

CORA.   Yo' brother'll be back, son, then I won't be by myself.

WILLIAM.   [*Bewildered by his mothers sureness*] I thought Bert went . . . I thought he run . . . I thought . . .

CORA.   No, honey. He went, but they ain't gonna get him out there. I sees him comin' back here now, to be with me. I's gwine to guard him 'till he can get away.

WILLIAM.   Then de white folks'll come here, too.

CORA.   Yes, de Colonel'll come back here sure. [*The deep baying of the hounds is*   35
heard at a distance through the night.] Colonel Tom will come after his son.

WILLIAM.   My God, ma! Come with us to town.

CORA.   Go on, William, go on! Don't wait for them to get back. You never was much like neither one o' them—neither de Colonel or Bert—you's mo' like de field hands. Too much o' ma blood in you, I guess. You never liked Bert much, neither, and you always was afraid of de Colonel. Go on, son, and hide yo' wife and her ma and your chilluns. Ain't nothin' gonna hurt you. You never did go against nobody. Neither did I, till tonight. Tried to live right and not hurt a soul, white or colored. [*Addressing space*] I tried to live right, Lord. [*Angrily*] Tried to live right, Lord. [*Throws out her arms resentfully as if to say, "and this is what you give me."*] What's de matter, Lawd, you ain't with me?

[*The hounds are heard howling again.*]

WILLIAM.   I'm gone, ma. [*He exits fearfully as his mother talks.*]

CORA.   [*Bending over the spot on the floor where the COLONEL has lain. She calls.*] Colonel Tom! Colonel Tom! Colonel Tom! Look! Bertha and Sallie and William and Bert, all your chilluns, runnin' from you, and you layin' on de floor there, dead! [*Pointing*] Out yonder with the mob, dead. And when you come home, upstairs in my bed on top of my body, dead. [*Goes to the window, returns, sits down, and begins to speak as if remembering a far-off dream.*] Colonel Thomas Norwood! I'm just poor Cora Lewis, Colonel Norwood. Little black Cora Lewis, Colonel Norwood. I'm just fifteen years old. Thirty years ago, you put your hands on me to feel my breasts, and you say, "You a pretty little piece of flesh, ain't you? Black and sweet, ain't you?" And I lift up ma face, and you pull me to you, and we laid down under the trees that night, and I wonder if your wife'll know when you go back up the road into the big house. And I wonder if my mama'll know it, when I go back to our cabin. Mama said she nursed you when you was a baby, just like she nursed me. And I loved you in the dark, down there under that tree by de gate, afraid of you and proud of you, feelin' your gray eyes lookin' at me in de dark. Then I cried and cried and told ma mother about it, but she didn't take it hard like I thought she'd take it. She said fine white mens like de young Colonel always took good care o' their colored womens. She said it was better than marryin' some black field hand and workin' all your life in de cotton and cane. Better even than havin' a job like ma had, takin' care o' de white chilluns. Takin' care o' you, Colonel Tom. [*As* CORA *speaks the sound of the approaching mob gradually grows louder and louder. Auto horns, the howling of dogs, the far-off shouts of men, full of malignant force and power, increase in volume.*] And I was happy because I liked you, 'cause you was tall and proud, 'cause you said I was sweet to you and called me purty. And when yo' wife died—de Mrs. Norwood [*Scornfully*] that never bore you any chilluns, the pale beautiful Mrs. Norwood that was like a slender pine tree in de winter frost . . . I knowled you wanted me. I was full with child by you then—William, it was—our first boy. And ma mammy said, go up there and keep de house for Colonel Tom, sweep de floors and make de beds, and by and by, you won't have to sweep de floors and make no beds. And what ma mammy said was right. It all come true. Sam and Rusus and 'Vonia and Lucy did de waitin' on you and me, and de washin' and de cleanin' and de cookin'. And all I did was a little sewin' now and then, and a little preservin' in de summer and a little makin' of pies and sweet cakes and things you like to eat on Christmas. And de years went by. And I was always ready for you when you come to me in de night. And we had them chilluns, your chilluns and mine, Tom Norwood, all of 'em! William, born dark like me, dumb like me, and then Baby John what died; then Bertha, white and smart like you; and then Bert with your eyes and your ways and your temper, and mighty nigh your color; then Sallie, nearly white, too, and smart, and purty. But Bert was yo' chile! He was always yo' child . . . Good-looking, and kind, and headstrong, and strange, and stubborn, and proud like you, and de one I could love most 'cause he needed de most lovin'. And he wanted to call you "papa," and I tried to teach him no, but he did it anyhow and [*Sternly*] you beat him, Colonel Thomas Norwood. And he growed up with de beatin' in his heart and your eyes in his head, and your ways, and your pride. And this summer he looked like you that time I first knowed you down by de road under them trees, young and fiery and proud. There was no touchin' Bert, just like there was no touchin' you. I could only love him, like I loved you. I could only love him. But I couldn't talk to him, because he hated you. He had your ways—and you beat him! After you beat that chile, then you died, Colonel Norwood. You died here in this house, and you been living dead a long time. You lived dead. [*Her voice rises above the nearing sounds of the mob.*] And when I said this evenin', "Get up! Why don't you help me?" You'd done been dead a long time—a long time before you laid down on this floor, here, with the breath choked out o' you—and Bert standin' over you living, living, living. That's why you hated him. And you want to kill him. Always, you wanted to kill him. Out there with de hounds and de torches and de cars and de guns, you want to kill ma boy. But you won't kill him! He's comin' home first. He's comin' home to me. He's comin' home! [*Outside the noise is tremendous now, the lights of autos flash on the window curtains, there are shouts and cries.* CORA *sits, tense, in the middle of the room.*] He's comin' home!

A MAN'S VOICE.   [*Outside*] He's somewhere on this lot.   40

ANOTHER VOICE.   Don't shoot, men. We want to get him alive.

VOICE.   Close in on him. He must be in them bushes by the house.

FIRST VOICE.   Porch! Porch! Porch! There he is yonder—running to the door!

[*Suddenly shots are heard. The door bursts open and* ROBERT *enters, firing back into the darkness. The shots are returned by the mob, breaking the windows. Flares, lights, voices, curses, screams.*]

VOICES.   Nigger! Nigger! Nigger! Get the nigger!

[CORA *rushes toward the door and bolts it after her son's entrance.*]

CORA.   [*Leaning against the door*] I was waiting for you, honey. Yo' hiding place   45
is all ready, upstairs, under ma bed, under de floor. I sawed a place there fo' you. They
can't find you there. Hurry—before yo' father comes.

ROBERT.   [*Panting*] No time to hide, ma. They're at the door now. They'll be
coming up the back way, too. [*Sounds of knocking and the breaking of glass*] They'll be
coming in the windows. They'll be coming in everywhere. And only one bullet left,
ma. It's for me.

CORA.   Yes, it's fo' you, chile. Save it. Go upstairs in mama's room. Lay on ma
bed and rest.

ROBERT.   [*Going slowly toward the stairs with the pistol in his hand*] Goodnight, ma.
I'm awful tired of running, ma. They been chasing me for hours.

CORA.   Goodnight, son.

[CORA *follows him to the foot of the steps. The door begins to give at the forcing of the mob. As*
ROBERT *disappears above, it bursts open. A great crowd of white men pour into the room with
guns, ropes, clubs, flashlights, and knives.* CORA *turns on the stairs, facing them quietly.* TAL-
BOT, *the leader of the mob, stops.*]

TALBOT.   Be careful, men. He's armed. [*To* CORA] Where is that yellow bastard   50
of yours—upstairs?

CORA.   Yes, he's going to sleep. Be quiet, you all. Wait. [*She bars the way with outspread arms.*]

TALBOT.   [*Harshly*] Wait, hell! Come on, boys, let's go. [*A single shot is heard upstairs.*] What's that?

CORA.   [*Calmly*] My boy . . . is gone . . . to sleep!

[TALBOT *and some of the men rush up the stairway,* CORA *makes a final gesture of love toward
the room above. Yelling and shouting, through all the doors and windows, a great crowd pours
into the room. The roar of the mob fills the house, the whole night, the whole world. Suddenly*
TALBOT *returns at the top of the steps and a hush falls over the crowd.*]

TALBOT.   Too late, men. We're just a little too late.

[*A sigh of disappointment rises from the mob.* TALBOT *comes down the stairs, walks up to* CORA
*and slaps her once across the face. She does not move. It is as though no human hand can touch
her again.*]

Curtain

QUESTIONS

Act I

1. Throughout the act—and the play—why are the children of Colonel Norwood and Cora referred to as just Cora's children?

2. Why does the Colonel deny permission for Sallie's bags to be carried through the front door?

3. Throughout the act, what do we learn about Robert's attitudes toward his circumstances on the plantation? What do the Colonel and Higgins say about his attitude? Once Robert appears, what does he himself say about his situation?

4. What does the Colonel say about Sallie's ambition to start a nearby school? What does he advise her to do instead?

5. Who is Talbot? What does he represent? Why does he not appear until late in the second act?

6. What does Higgins report about how Robert has behaved in town? What does he tell Colonel Norwood to do about it?

7. As expressed in speech 35, what is Higgins's attitude toward black women? What does this attitude disclose about his character?

8. Describe the effect on both Robert and Colonel Norwood of the childhood incident when Robert called the Colonel "papa."

9. What has the Colonel decided to do about Robert? What are Cora's fears not only for Robert but for others?

Act II. Scene 1.

10. What are the issues in the confrontation between Robert and Colonel Norwood?

11. What is Robert's dilemma (speech 35)? What has the Colonel now determined to do about Robert?

12. What is Robert's response to the Colonel's display of the gun, and his threat to use it?

13. What do Talbot and the storekeeper do once they learn that Colonel Norwood is dead? What chance does Robert have to escape?

14. Why does Cora speak so extensively over the Colonel's body?

Act II. Scene 2.

15. Why are the undertaker and his companion introduced at this point? What are they like

16. According to Cora (speech 27) what was the nature of the old "ways" of the South?

17. What is the purpose of Cora's second extensive monologue (speech 39)?

18. What finally happens to Robert? Why does Talbot slap Cora at the end?

GENERAL QUESTIONS

1. Describe *Mulatto* as a realistic play. Why is it important that the play contain many details about the plantation and the customs of the country?

2. What is the symbolism of the front door? The incident at the post office in town? Driving the Ford fast?

3. Describe Colonel Norwood. What characteristics of a Southern plantation owner does he exhibit? What is shown about him by his having sent Robert and Sallie away to school? What does Cora say about him before and after he is dead?

4. Describe the character of Robert. What are his dominant traits? How politic is he in dealing with his circumstances? To what extent does he bring about his own destruction?

5. Describe Cora. What has her life been like? To what degree has she sacrificed her individuality to stay with Colonel Norwood? How does she try to protect her children? In her two major lengthy speeches, what seems to be happening to her?

6. In light of the historical time when the play was written and produced, could there have been any other outcome?

HENRIK IBSEN, *A DOLL HOUSE*

The Norwegian playwright Henrik Johan Ibsen (1828–1906) is the acknowledged originator—the "father"— of modern drama. He deserves this distinction because of his pioneering selections of realistic and sometime shocking private and public issues. Today there are few restrictions on dramatists except success at the box office, and plays may range freely on almost any subject. If one includes film as drama, there is virtually no limit to the topics that today's playwrights may explore. It is well to stress that dramatists have not always been this free, and that Ibsen was in the forefront of the struggle for free dramatic expression. A brief consideration of some of his major dramatic topics shows his originality and daring: the blinding and crippling effects of congenital syphilis, a woman's renunciation of a traditional protective marriage, suicide, the manipulations of people seeking personal benefits, the sacrifices of pursuing truth, the rejection of a child by a parent, and the abandonment of personal happiness in favor of professional interests.

Ibsen's Life and Early Work

Ibsen's beginnings were inauspicious. He was born in Skien (*shee-en*), Norway, a small town just 70 miles southwest of the capital, Christiana (now Oslo). His parents went bankrupt when he was only seven, and afterwards the family struggled against poverty. At the age of fifteen he was apprenticed to a pharmacist, and seemed headed for a career in this profession even though he hated it. By 1849, however, when he wrote *Catiline*, his first play in verse, it was clear that the theater was to be his life. Largely through the efforts of the famous violinist Ole Bull, a new National Theater had been started in Bergen, and Ibsen was appointed its director. He stayed in Bergen for six years, and then went to Christiana, where for the next five years he tried to fashion a truly Norwegian national theater. His attempts proved fruitless, for the theater went bankrupt in 1862. After his play *The Pretenders* in 1864, he left Norway, and for the next twenty-seven years lived in Germany and Italy in what has been called a "self-imposed" exile.

EARLY DRAMATIC EXPERIENCE. Although this first part of Ibsen's theatrical career was devoted to many practical matters—production, management, directing, and finances—he was also constantly writing. His early plays were in verse and were mainly national and romantic. Circumstances, however, pointed him toward realism. During his early years of struggle in the theater, Europe was undergoing great political and intellectual changes. Ibsen's home country, Norway, was in the throes of releasing itself from the domination of neighboring Sweden and establishing its own territorial and national integrity. In Ibsen's twentieth year, 1848, the "February Uprising" occurred in Paris, resulting in the deposition of the French king and the establishment of a new French republic. This same year also saw the publication of the *Communist Manifesto* of Karl Marx (1818–1883). In 1864, the year when Ibsen left Norway, Marx's first socialist International was held in London. In addition, during the time Ibsen lived in Italy and Germany, both countries were going through the tenuous political evolution into nation states. In short, change was going on everywhere.

Ibsen's Creation of Realistic Problem Plays

Ibsen also was changing and growing as a thinker and dramatist, driven by the idea that a forward and creative drama could bring about deeper and more permanent changes than could be effected by soldiers and politicians. Toward this end he developed the realistic *problem play*. Such a play posited a major personal, social, professional, or political problem, which occasioned the play's dramatic conflicts and tensions. Each problem was timely, topical, and realistic, as were the characters, places, situations, and outcomes. In this vein Ibsen wrote the twelve major prose plays on which his reputation rests: *The Pillars of Society* (1877), *A Doll House* (1879), *Ghosts* (1881), *An Enemy of the People* (1882), *The Wild Duck* (1884), *Rosmersholm* (1886), *The Lady from the Sea* (1888), *Hedda Gabler* (1890), *The Master Builder* (1892), *Little Eyolf* (1894), *John Gabriel Borkman* (1896), and *When We Dead Awaken* (1899).

In these major plays Ibsen dramatizes human beings breaking free from restrictions and inhibitions, and trying to establish their individuality and freedom—freedom of self, inquiry, pursuit of truth, artistic dedication, and, above all, the freedom of love. In attempting to achieve these goals, Ibsen's dramatic characters find internal opposition in self-interest, self-indulgence, and self-denial, and external opposition in the personal and political influences and manipulations of others. Because the plays are designed to be realistic, which also usually involves a certain degree of pessimism, Ibsen's characters fall short of their goals. At best they begin a quest in new directions, as in *A Doll House*, or achieve a respite in their combat, as in *An Enemy of the People*. They always undergo great sacrifice, sometimes losing life itself, as in *Hedda Gabler* and *John Gabriel Borkman*.

ELEMENTS OF REALISM. *A Doll House* (*Et Dukkehjem*, 1879) is representative of Ibsen's major realistic drama. Its scenes are realistic, including appropriate furniture, a piano, a Christmas tree, carpeting, and wall engravings. Its characters are realistically confronting overwhelming personal, marital, and economic problems. Realism extends also to the technique of presentation, particularly the exposition about the root causes of the problems that come to a head in the play itself. As *A Doll House* unfolds, we learn that years earlier, Nora Helmer had extended herself beyond her means to save Torvald from a near-fatal illness. We also learn that there had been an earlier relationship between Krogstad and Christine Linde.

SYMBOLISM. *A Doll House* is representative of Ibsen's realism, but it is also replete with contextual symbolism, like the major plays which came before and after it. At the end of the late play *John Gabriel Borkman*, for example, the major character freezes to death, an occurrence symbolic of what he had done to himself much earlier by denying love. In reference to *A Doll House*, the title itself symbolizes the dependent and dehumanized role of the wife within traditional middle-class marriages. (The Norwegian-Danish word for *doll* [*dukke*] may also mean "puppet" or "marionette.") In addition, the entire nation of Norway (cold, legal, male) is contrasted symbolically with Italy (warm, emotional, female). Ironically, the break in the Helmers' marriage is symbolically aligned with events that occur or have occurred in both locations. Other symbols in *A Doll House* are the Christmas tree, the children's presents, the death of Dr. Rank, and the mailbox.

IBSEN AND THE "WELL-MADE PLAY." The plot and structure of *A Doll House* show Ibsen's use of the conventions of the **well-made play** (*la pièce bien faite*), a form developed and popularized in nineteenth-century France by Eugène Scribe (1791–1861) and Victorien Sardou (1831–1908). Ibsen was familiar with well-made plays, having directed many of them himself at Bergen and Oslo. The typical well-made plot is built on a secret known by the audience and perhaps one or two of the characters. The play thus begins in suspense and offers a pattern of increasing tension produced through exposition and the timely arrivals of new characters and threatening news or props like the disclosure of Nora's earlier financial transactions. In the course of action of the prototypical well-made play, the fortunes of the protagonist go from a low point, through a **peripeteia** or reversal (Aristotle's concept), to a high point, at which the protagonist confronts and defeats the villain.

Although Ibsen makes use of many of the structural elements of the well-made play, he varies and departs from the pattern to suit his realistic purposes. Thus in *A Doll House* his variation is that Nora's confrontation with Krogstad, who is the apparent villain, does not lead to a satisfactory resolution, but precipitates the more significant albeit intractable confrontation with her husband. In *A Doll House,* just as in many other Ibsen plays, there is not a traditionally well-made victorious outcome; rather there are provisional outcomes—adjustments—in keeping with the realistic concept that as life goes on, problems continue.

IBSEN'S TIMELINESS AND DRAMATIC POWER. Ibsen's focus on real-life issues has given his plays continued timeliness and strength. *A Doll House,* for example, is prophetic in its portrayal of the helpless position of married women in the nineteenth century. Most notably, a woman could not borrow funds without a man's co-signature, and Nora had to violate the law to obtain the money to restore her husband's health. The mailbox, to which Torvald has the only key, symbolizes this limitation, and the ultimate disclosure of the box's contents, rather than freeing Nora and Torvald, highlights her dependency. Today's feminism has stressed the issues of female freedom and equality, together with many other issues vital to women, but the need for feminine individuality and independence has never been more originally and forcefully dramatized than in *A Doll House.*

HENRIK IBSEN   (1828–1906)

A Doll House ————————————————————————— *1879*

Translated by R. Farquharson Sharp

CHARACTERS

> Torvald Helmer, *a lawyer and bank manager*
> Nora, *his wife*
> Doctor Rank
> Mrs. Christine Linde
> Nils Krogstad, *a lawyer and bank clerk*
> Ivar, Bob, and Emmy, the Helmers' *three young children*
> Anne, *their nurse*
> Helen, *a housemaid*
> A Porter

> *The action takes place in* HELMER'S *apartment.*

ACT 1

SCENE.—*A room furnished comfortably and tastefully, but not extravagantly. At the back, a door to the right leads to the entrance hall, another to the left leads to* HELMER'S *study.*

Between the doors stands a piano. In the middle of the left-hand wall is a door, and beyond it a window. Near the window are a round table, armchairs and a small sofa. In the right-hand wall, at the farther end, another door; and on the same side, nearer the footlights, a stove, two easy chairs and a rocking-chair; between the stove and the door, a small table. Engravings on the walls; a cabinet with china and other small objects; a small book-case with well-bound books. The floors are carpeted, and a fire burns in the stove. It is winter.

A bell rings in the hall; shortly afterwards the door is heard to open. Enter NORA, *humming a tune and in high spirits. She is in out-door dress and carries a number of parcels; these she lays on the table to the right. She leaves the outer door open after her, and through it is seen a* PORTER *who is carrying a Christmas Tree and a basket, which he gives to the* MAID *who has opened the door.*

NORA Hide the Christmas Tree carefully, Helen. Be sure the children do not see it till this evening, when it is dressed. [*to the* PORTER, *taking out her purse.*] How much?

PORTER. Sixpence.

NORA. There is a shilling. No, keep the change. [*The* PORTER *thanks her, and goes out.* NORA *shuts the door. She is laughing to herself, as she takes off her hat and coat. She takes a packet of macaroons from her pocket and eats one or two; then goes cautiously to her husband's door and listens.*] Yes, he is in.

[*Still humming, she goes to the table on the right.*]

HELMER. [*calls out from his room*] Is that my little lark twittering out there?

NORA. [*busy opening some of the parcels*] Yes, it is!   5

HELMER. Is my little squirrel bustling about?

NORA. Yes!

HELMER. When did my squirrel come home?

NORA. Just now. [*puts the bag of macaroons into her pocket and wipes her mouth.*] Come in here, Torvald, and see what I have bought.

HELMER. Don't disturb me. [*A little later, he opens the door and looks into the room,*   10
pen in hand.] Bought, did you say? All these things? Has my little spendthrift been wasting money again?

NORA. Yes, but, Torvald, this year we really can let ourselves go a little. This is the first Christmas that we have not needed to economise.

HELMER. Still, you know, we can't spend money recklessly.

NORA. Yes, Torvald, we may be a wee bit more reckless now, mayn't we? Just a tiny wee bit! You are going to have a big salary and earn lots and lots of money.

HELMER. Yes, after the New Year; but then it will be a whole quarter before the salary is due.

NORA. Pooh! we can borrow till then.   15

HELMER. Nora! [*goes up to her and takes her playfully by the ear.*] The same little featherhead! Suppose, now, that I borrowed fifty pounds to-day, and you spent it all in the Christmas week, and then on New Year's Eve a slate fell on my head and killed me, and—

NORA. [*putting her hands over his mouth*] Oh! don't say such horrid things.

HELMER. Still, suppose that happened—what then?

NORA. If that were to happen, I don't suppose I should care whether I owed money or not.

HELMER. Yes, but what about the people who had lent it?   20

NORA. They? Who would bother about them? I should not know who they were.

HELMER. That is like a woman! But seriously, Nora, you know what I think about that. No debt, no borrowing. There can be no freedom or beauty about a home life that depends on borrowing and debt. We two have kept bravely on the straight road so far, and we will go on the same way for the short time longer that there need be any struggle.

NORA. [*moving towards the stove*] As you please, Torvald.

HELMER. [*following her*] Come, come, my little skylark must not droop her wings. What is this! Is my little squirrel out of temper? [*taking out his purse.*] Nora, what do you think I have got here?

NORA. [*turning around quickly*] Money!

HELMER. There you are. [*gives her some money*] Do you think I don't know what a lot is wanted for housekeeping at Christmas-time?

NORA. [*counting*] Ten shillings—a pound—two pounds! Thank you, thank you, Torvald; that will keep me going for a long time.

HELMER. Indeed it must.

NORA. Yes, yes, it will. But come here and let me show you what I have bought. And all so cheap! Look, here is a new suit for Ivar, and a sword; and a horse and a trumpet for Bob; and a doll and dolly's bedstead for Emmy—they are very plain, but anyway she will soon break them in pieces. And here are dress-lengths and handkerchiefs for the maids; old Anne ought really to have something better.

HELMER. And what is in this parcel?

NORA. [*crying out*] No, no! you mustn't see that till this evening.

HELMER. Very well. But now tell me, you extravagant little person, what would you like for yourself?

NORA. For myself? Oh, I am sure I don't want anything.

HELMER. Yes, but you must. Tell me something reasonable that you would particularly like to have.

NORA. No, I really can't think of anything—unless, Torvald——

HELMER. Well?

NORA. [*playing with his coat buttons, and without raising her eyes to his*] If you really want to give me something, you might—you might——

HELMER. Well, out with it!

NORA. [*speaking quickly*] You might give me money, Torvald. Only just as much as you can afford; and then one of these days I will buy something with it.

HELMER. But, Nora——

NORA. Oh, do! dear Torvald; please, please do! Then I will wrap it up in beautiful gilt paper and hang it on the Christmas Tree. Wouldn't that be fun?

HELMER. What are little people called that are always wasting money?

NORA. Spendthrifts—I know. Let us do as you suggest, Torvald, and then I shall have time to think what I am most in want of. That is a very sensible plan, isn't it?

HELMER. [*smiling*] Indeed it is—that is to say, if you were really to save out of the money I give you, and then really buy something for yourself. But if you spend it all on the housekeeping and any number of unnecessary things, then I merely have to pay up again.

NORA. Oh but, Torvald——

HELMER. You can't deny it, my dear little Nora. [*puts his arm round her waist*] It's a sweet little spendthrift, but she uses up a deal of money. One would hardly believe how expensive such little persons are!

NORA. It's a shame to say that. I do really save all I can.

HELMER. [*laughing*] That's very true—all you can. But you can't save anything!

NORA. [*smiling quietly and happily*] You haven't any idea how many expenses we skylarks and squirrels have, Torvald.

HELMER. You are an odd little soul. Very like your father. You always find some 50 new way of wheedling money out of me, and, as soon as you have got it, it seems to melt in your hands. You never know where it has gone. Still, one must take you as you are. It is in the blood; for indeed it is true that you can inherit these things, Nora.

NORA. Ah, I wish I had inherited many of papa's qualities.

HELMER. And I would not wish you to be anything but just what you are, my sweet little skylark. But, do you know, it strikes me that you are looking rather—what shall I say—rather uneasy to-day?

NORA. Do I?

HELMER. You do, really. Look straight at me. 55

NORA. [*looks at him*] Well?

HELMER. [*wagging his finger at her*] Hasn't Miss Sweet-Tooth been breaking rules in town to-day?

NORA. No; what makes you think that?

HELMER. Hasn't she paid a visit to the confectioner's?

NORA. No, I assure you, Torvald—— 60

HELMER. Not been nibbling sweets?

NORA. No, certainly not.

HELMER. Not even taken a bite at a macaroon or two?

NORA. No, Torvald, I assure you really——

HELMER. There, there, of course I was only joking. 65

NORA. [*going to the table on the right*] I should not think of going against your wishes.

HELMER. No, I am sure of that! besides, you gave me your word—[*going up to her*] Keep your little Christmas secrets to yourself, my darling. They will all be revealed to-night when the Christmas Tree is lit, no doubt.

NORA. Did you remember to invite Doctor Rank?

HELMER. No. But there is no need; as a matter of course he will come to dinner with us. However, I will ask him when he comes in this morning. I have ordered some good wine. Nora, you can't think how I am looking forward to this evening.

NORA. So am I! And how the children will enjoy themselves, Torvald! 70

HELMER. It is splendid to feel that one has a perfectly safe appointment, and a big enough income. It's delightful to think of, isn't it?

NORA. It's wonderful!

HELMER. Do you remember last Christmas? For a full three weeks beforehand you shut yourself up every evening till long after midnight, making ornaments for the Christmas Tree and all the other fine things that were to be a surprise to us. It was the dullest three weeks I ever spent!

NORA. I didn't find it dull.

HELMER. [*smiling*] But there was precious little result, Nora. 75

NORA. Oh, you shouldn't tease me about that again. How could I help the cat's going in and tearing everything to pieces?

HELMER. Of course you couldn't, poor little girl. You had the best of intentions to please us all, and that's the main thing. But it is a good thing that our hard times are over.

NORA. Yes, it is really wonderful.

HELMER. This time I needn't sit here and be dull all alone, and you needn't ruin your dear eyes and your pretty little hands——

NORA. [*clapping her hands*] No, Torvald, I needn't any longer, need I! It's wonderfully lovely to hear you say so! [*taking his arm*] Now I will tell you how I have been thinking we ought to arrange things, Torvald. As soon as Christmas is over——[*A bell rings in the hall.*] There's the bell. [*She tidies the room a little.*] There's someone at the door. What a nuisance!

HELMER. If it is a caller, remember I am not at home.

MAID. [*in the doorway*] A lady to see you, ma'am—a stranger.

NORA. Ask her to come in.

MAID. [*to HELMER*] The doctor came at the same time, sir.

HELMER. Did he go straight into my room?

MAID. Yes sir.

[*HELMER goes into his room. The MAID ushers in MRS. LINDE, who is in travelling dress, and shuts the door.*]

MRS. LINDE. [*in a dejected and timid voice*] How do you do, Nora?

NORA. [*doubtfully*] How do you do——

MRS. LINDE. You don't recognise me, I suppose.

NORA. No, I don't know—yes, to be sure, I seem to——[*suddenly*] Yes! Christine! Is it really you?

MRS. LINDE. Yes, it is I.

NORA. Christine! To think of my not recognising you! And yet how could I——[*in a gentle voice*] How you have altered, Christine!

MRS. LINDE. Yes, I have indeed. In nine, ten long years——

NORA. Is it so long since we met? I suppose it is. The last eight years have been a happy time for me, I can tell you. And so now you have come into the town, and have taken this long journey in winter—that was plucky of you.

MRS. LINDE. I arrived by steamer this morning.

NORA. To have some fun at Christmas-time, of course. How delightful! We will have such fun together! But take off your things. You are not cold, I hope. [*helps her*] Now we will sit down by the stove, and be cosy. No, take this arm-chair; I will sit here in the rocking-chair. [*takes her hands*] Now you look like your old self again; it was only the first moment——You are a little paler, Christine, and perhaps a little thinner.

MRS. LINDE. And much, much older, Nora.

NORA. Perhaps a little older; very, very little; certainly not much. [*stops suddenly and speaks seriously*] What a thoughtless creature I am, chattering away like this. My poor, dear Christine, do forgive me.

MRS. LINDE. What do you mean, Nora?

NORA. [*gently*] Poor Christine, you are a widow.

MRS. LINDE. Yes; it is three years ago now.

NORA. Yes, I knew; I saw it in the papers. I assure you, Christine, I meant ever so often to write to you at the time, but I always put it off and something always prevented me.

MRS. LINDE. I quite understand, dear.

NORA. It was very bad of me, Christine. Poor thing, how you must have suffered. And he left you nothing?

MRS. LINDE. No.

NORA. And no children? 105

MRS. LINDE. No.

NORA. Nothing at all, then?

MRS. LINDE. Not even any sorrow or grief to live upon.

NORA. [*looking incredulously at her*] But, Christine, is that possible?

MRS. LINDE. [*smiles sadly and strokes her hair*] It sometimes happens, Nora. 110

NORA. So you are quite alone. How dreadfully sad that must be. I have three lovely children. You can't see them just now, for they are out with their nurse. But now you must tell me all about it.

MRS. LINDE. No, no; I want to hear you.

NORA. No, you must begin. I mustn't be selfish to-day; to-day I must only think of your affairs. But there is one thing I must tell you. Do you know we have just had a great piece of good luck?

MRS. LINDE. No, what is it?

NORA. Just fancy, my husband has been made manager of the Bank! 115

MRS. LINDE. Your husband? What good luck!

NORA. Yes, tremendous! A barrister's profession is such an uncertain thing, especially if he won't undertake unsavoury cases; and naturally Torvald has never been willing to do that, and I quite agree with him. You may imagine how pleased we are! He is to take up his work in the Bank at the New Year, and then he will have a big salary and lots of commissions. For the future we can live quite differently—we can do just as we like. I feel so relieved and so happy, Christine! It will be splendid to have heaps of money and not need to have any anxiety, won't it?

MRS. LINDE. Yes, anyhow I think it would be delightful to have what one needs.

NORA. No, not only what one needs, but heaps and heaps of money.

MRS. LINDE. [*smiling*] Nora, Nora haven't you learnt sense yet? In our school- 120 days you were a great spendthrift.

NORA. [*laughing*] Yes, that is what Torvald says now. [*wags her finger at her*] But "Nora, Nora" is not so silly as you think. We have not been in a position for me to waste money. We have both had to work.

MRS. LINDE. You too?

NORA. Yes; odds and ends, needlework, crochet-work, embroidery, and that kind of thing. [*dropping her voice*] And other things as well. You know Torvald left his office when we were married? There was no prospect of promotion there, and he had to try and earn more than before. But during the first year he overworked himself dreadfully. You see, he had to make money every way he could, and he worked early and late; but he couldn't stand it, and fell dreadfully ill, and the doctors said it was necessary for him to go south.

MRS. LINDE. You spent a whole year in Italy didn't you?

NORA. Yes. It was no easy matter to get away, I can tell you. It was just after Ivar 125 was born; but naturally we had to go. It was a wonderfully beautiful journey, and it saved Torvald's life. But it cost a tremendous lot of money, Christine.

MRS. LINDE. So I should think.

NORA. It cost about two hundred and fifty pounds. That's a lot, isn't it?

MRS. LINDE. Yes, and in emergencies like that it is lucky to have the money.

NORA. I ought to tell you that we had it from papa.

MRS. LINDE. Oh, I see. It was just about that time that he died, wasn't it? 130

NORA. Yes; and, just think of it, I couldn't go and nurse him. I was expecting little Ivar's birth every day and I had my poor sick Torvald to look after. My dear, kind father—I never saw him again, Christine. That was the saddest time I have known since our marriage.

MRS. LINDE. I know how fond you were of him. And then you went off to Italy?

NORA. Yes; you see we had money then, and the doctors insisted on our going, so we started a month later.

MRS. LINDE. And your husband came back quite well?

NORA. As sound as a bell!

MRS. LINDE. But—the doctor?

NORA. What doctor?

MRS. LINDE. I thought your maid said the gentleman who arrived here just as I did was the doctor?

NORA. Yes, that was Doctor Rank, but he doesn't come here professionally. He is our greatest friend, and comes in at least once every day. No, Torvald has not had an hour's illness since then, and our children are strong and healthy and so am I. [*jumps up and claps her hands*] Christine! Christine! it's good to be alive and happy!— —But how horrid of me; I am talking of nothing but my own affairs. [*Sits on a stool near her, and rests her arms on her knees*] You mustn't be angry with me. Tell me, is it really true that you did not love your husband? Why did you marry him?

MRS. LINDE. My mother was alive then, and was bedridden and helpless, and I had to provide for my two younger brothers; so I did not think I was justified in refusing his offer.

NORA. No, perhaps you were quite right. He was rich at that time, then?

MRS. LINDE. I believe he was quite well off. But his business was a precarious one; and, when he died, it all went to pieces and there was nothing left.

NORA. And then?——

MRS. LINDE. Well, I had to turn my hand to anything I could find—first a small shop, then a small school, and so on. The last three years have seemed like one long working-day, with no rest. Now it is at an end, Nora. My poor mother needs me no more, for she is gone; and the boys do not need me either; they have got situations and can shift for themselves.

NORA. What a relief you must feel it——

MRS. LINDE. No, indeed; I only feel my life unspeakably empty. No one to live for any more. [*gets up restlessly*] That was why I could not stand the life in my little back-water any longer. I hope it may be easier here to find something which will busy me and occupy my thoughts. If only I could have the good luck to get some regular work—office work of some kind——

NORA. But, Christine, that is so frightfully tiring, and you look tired out now. You had far better go away to some watering-place.

MRS. LINDE. [*walking to the window*] I have no father to give me money for a journey, Nora.

NORA. [*rising*] Oh, don't be angry with me.

MRS. LINDE. [*going up to her*] It is you that must not be angry with me, dear. The worst of a position like mine is that it makes one so bitter. No one to work for, and yet obliged to be always on the look-out for chances. One must live, and so one becomes selfish. When you told me of the happy turn your fortunes have taken—you will hardly believe it—I was delighted not so much on your account as on my own.

NORA. How do you mean?—Oh, I understand. You mean that perhaps Torvald could get you something to do.

MRS. LINDE. Yes, that was what I was thinking of.

NORA. He must, Christine. Just leave it to me; I will broach the subject very cleverly—I will think of something that will please him very much. It will make me so happy to be of some use to you.

MRS. LINDE. How kind you are, Nora, to be so anxious to help me! It is doubly kind in you, for you know so little of the burdens and troubles of life.   155

NORA. I——? I know so little of them?

MRS. LINDE. [*smiling*] My dear! Small household cares and that sort of thing!—You are a child, Nora.

NORA. [*tosses her head and crosses the stage*] You ought not to be so superior.

MRS. LINDE. No?

NORA. You are just like the others. They all think that I am incapable of anything really serious——   160

MRS. LINDE. Come, come——

NORA. —that I have gone through nothing in this world of cares.

MRS. LINDE. But, my dear Nora, you have just told me all your troubles.

NORA. Pooh!—those were trifles. [*lowering her voice*] I have not told you the important thing.

MRS. LINDE. The important thing? What do you mean?   165

NORA. You look down upon me altogether, Christine—but you ought not to. You are proud, aren't you, of having worked so hard and so long for your mother?

MRS. LINDE. Indeed, I don't look down on any one. But it is true that I am both proud and glad to think that I was privileged to make the end of my mother's life almost free from care.

NORA. And you are proud to think of what you have done for your brothers.

MRS. LINDE. I think I have the right to be.

NORA. I think so, too. But now, listen to this; I too have something to be proud of and glad of.   170

MRS. LINDE. I have no doubt you have. But what do you refer to?

NORA. Speak low. Suppose Torvald were to hear! He mustn't on any account—no one in the world must know, Christine, except you.

MRS. LINDE. But what is it?

NORA. Come here. [*pulls her down on the sofa beside her*] Now I will show you that I too have something to be proud and glad of. It was I who saved Torvald's life.

MRS. LINDE. "Saved"? How?   175

NORA. I told you about our trip to Italy. Torvald would never have recovered if he had not gone there——

MRS. LINDE. Yes, but your father gave you the necessary funds.

NORA. [*smiling*] Yes, that is what Torvald and all the others think, but——

MRS. LINDE. But——

NORA. Papa didn't give us a shilling. It was I who procured the money.   180

MR. LINDE. You? All that large sum?

NORA. Two hundred and fifty pounds. What do you think of that?

MRS. LINDE. But, Nora, how could you possibly do it? Did you win a prize in the Lottery?

NORA. [*contemptuously*] In the Lottery? There would have been no credit in that.

MRS. LINDE. But where did you get it from, then?   185

NORA. [*humming and smiling with an air of mystery*] Hm, hm! Aha!

MRS. LINDE. Because you couldn't have borrowed it.

NORA. Couldn't I? Why not?

MRS. LINDE. No, a wife cannot borrow without her husband's consent.

NORA. [*tossing her head*] Oh, if it is a wife who has any head for business—a wife who has the wit to be a little bit clever—— 19●

MRS. LINDE. I don't understand it at all, Nora.

NORA. There is no need you should. I never said I had borrowed the money. I may have got it some other way. [*lies back on the sofa*] Perhaps I got it from some other admirer. When anyone is as attractive as I am——

MRS. LINDE. You are a mad creature.

NORA. Now, you know you're full of curiosity, Christine.

MRS. LINDE. Listen to me, Nora dear. Haven't you been a little bit imprudent? 19.

NORA. [*sits up straight*] Is it imprudent to save your husband's life?

MRS. LINDE. It seems to me imprudent, without his knowledge, to——

NORA. But it was absolutely necessary that he should not know! My goodness, can't you understand that? It was necessary he should have no idea what a dangerous condition he was in. It was to me that the doctors came and said that his life was in danger, and that the only thing to save him was to live in the south. Do you suppose I didn't try, first of all, to get what I wanted as if it were for myself? I told him how much I should love to travel abroad like other young wives; I tried tears and entreaties with him; I told him that he ought to remember the condition I was in, and that he ought to be kind and indulgent to me; I even hinted that he might raise a loan. That nearly made him angry, Christine. He said I was thoughtless, and that it was his duty as my husband not to indulge me in my whims and caprices—as I believe he called them. Very well I thought, you must be saved—and that was how I came to devise a way out of the difficulty——

MRS. LINDE. And did your husband never get to know from your father that the money had not come from him?

NORA. No, never. Papa died just at that time. I had meant to let him into the secret and beg him never to reveal it. But he was so ill then—alas, there never was any need to tell him. 20●

MRS. LINDE. And since then have you never told your secret to your husband?

NORA. Good Heavens, no! How could you think so? A man who has such strong opinions about these things! And besides, how painful and humiliating it would be for Torvald, with his manly independence, to know that he owed me anything! It would upset our mutual relations altogether; our beautiful happy home would no longer be what it is now.

MRS. LINDE. Do you mean never to tell him about it?

NORA. [*meditatively, and with a half smile*] Yes—some day, perhaps, after many years, when I am no longer as nice-looking as I am now. Don't laugh at me! I mean of course, when Torvald is no longer as devoted to me as he is now; when my dancing and dressing-up and reciting have palled on him; then it may be a good thing to have something in reserve——[*breaking off*] What nonsense! That time will never come. Now, what do you think of my great secret, Christine? Do you still think I am of no use? I can tell you, too, that this affair has caused me a lot of worry. It has been by no means easy for me to meet my engagements punctually. I may tell you that there is something that is called, in business, quarterly interest, and another thing called payment in instalments, and it is always so dreadfully difficult to manage them. I have had to save a little here and there, where I could, you understand. I have not been able to put aside much from my housekeeping money, for Torvald must have a good table. I couldn't let my children be shabbily dressed; I have felt obliged to use up all he gave me for them, the sweet little darlings!

MRS. LINDE. So it has all had to come out of your own necessaries of life, poor Nora?

NORA. Of course. Besides, I was the one responsible for it. Whenever Torvald has given me the money for new dresses and such things, I have never spent more than half of it; I have always bought the simplest and cheapest things. Thank Heaven, any clothes look well one me, and so Torvald has never noticed it. But it was often very hard on me, Christine—because it is delightful to be really well dressed, isn't it?

MRS. LINDE. Quite so.

NORA. Well, then I have found other ways of earning money. Last winter I was lucky enough to get a lot of copying to do; so I locked myself up and sat writing every evening until quite late at night. Many a time I was desperately tired; but all the same it was a tremendous pleasure to sit there working and earning money. It was like being a man.

MRS. LINDE. How much have you been able to pay off in that way?

NORA. I can't tell you exactly. You see, it is very difficult to keep an account of a business matter of that kind. I only know that I have paid every penny that I could scrape together. Many a time I was at my wits' end. [*smiles*] Then I used to sit here and imagine that a rich old gentleman had fallen in love with me——

MRS. LINDE. What! Who was it?

NORA. Be quiet!—that he had died; and that when his will was opened it contained, written in big letters, the instruction: "The lovely Mrs. Nora Helmer is to have all I possess paid over to her at once in cash."

MRS. LINDE. But, my dear Nora—who could the man be?

NORA. Good gracious, can't you understand? There was no old gentleman at all; it was only something that I used to sit here and imagine, when I couldn't think of any way of procuring money. But it's all the same now; the tiresome old person can stay where he is, as far as I am concerned; I don't care about him or his will either, for I am free from care now. [*jumps up*] My goodness, it's delightful to think of, Christine! Free from care! To be able to be free from care, quite free from care; to be able to play and romp with the children; to be able to keep the house beautifully and have everything just as Torvald likes it! And, think of it, soon the spring will come and the big blue sky! Perhaps we shall be able to take a little trip—perhaps I shall see the sea again! Oh, it's a wonderful thing to be alive and be happy. [*A bell is heard in the hall.*]

MRS. LINDE. [*rising*] There is the bell; perhaps I had better go.

NORA. No, don't go; no one will come in here; it is sure to be for Torvald.

SERVANT. [*at the hall door*] Excuse me, ma'am—there is a gentleman to see the master, and as the doctor is with him——

NORA. Who is it?

KROGSTAD. [*at the door*] It is I, Mrs. Helmer. [*MRS. LINDE starts, trembles, and turns to the window.*]

NORA. [*takes a step towards him, and speaks in a strained, low voice*] You? What is it? What do you want to see my husband about?

KROGSTAD. Bank business—in a way. I have a small post in the Bank, and I hear your husband is to be our chief now——

NORA. Then it is——

KROGSTAD. Nothing but dry business matters, Mrs. Helmer; absolutely nothing else.

NORA. Be so good as to go into the study, then. [*She bows indifferently to him and shuts the door into the hall; then comes back and makes up the fire in the stove.*]

MRS. LINDE. Nora—who was that man?

NORA. A lawyer, of the name of Krogstad.

MRS. LINDE. Then it really was he.

NORA. Do you know the man?

MRS. LINDE. I used to—many years ago. At one time he was a solicitor's clerk in our town.

NORA. Yes, he was.

MRS. LINDE. He is greatly altered.

NORA. He made a very unhappy marriage.

MRS. LINDE. He is a widower now, isn't he?

NORA. With several children. There now, it is burning up.

[*Shuts the door of the stove and moves the rocking-chair aside.*]

MRS. LINDE. They say he carries on various kinds of business.

NORA. Really! Perhaps he does; I don't know anything about it. But don't let us think of business; it is so tiresome.

DOCTOR RANK. [*comes out of HELMER'S study. Before he shuts the door he calls to him.*] No, my dear fellow, I won't disturb you; I would rather go into your wife for a little while. [*shuts the door and sees MRS. LINDE*] I beg your pardon; I am afraid I am disturbing you too.

NORA. No, not at all. [*introducing him*] Doctor Rank, Mrs. Linde.

RANK. I have often heard Mrs. Linde's name mentioned here. I think I passed you on the stairs when I arrived, Mrs. Linde?

MRS. LINDE. Yes, I go up very slowly; I can't manage stairs well.

RANK. Ah! some slight internal weakness?

MRS. LINDE. No, the fact is I have been overworking myself.

RANK. Nothing more than that? Then I suppose you have come to town to amuse yourself with our entertainments?

MRS. LINDE. I have come to look for work.

RANK. Is that a good cure for overwork?

MRS. LINDE. One must live, Doctor Rank.

RANK. Yes, the general opinion seems to be that it is necessary.

NORA. Look here, Doctor Rank—you know you want to live.

RANK. Certainly. However wretched I may feel, I want to prolong the agony as long as possible. All my patients are like that. And so are those who are morally diseased; one of them, and a bad case too, is at this very moment with Helmer——

MRS. LINDE. [*adly*] Ah!

NORA. Whom do you mean?

RANK. A lawyer of the name of Krogstad, a fellow you don't know at all. He suffers from a diseased moral character, Mrs. Helmer; but even he began talking of its being highly important that he should live.

NORA. Did he? What did he want to speak to Torvald about?

RANK. I have no idea; I only heard that it was something about the Bank.

NORA. I didn't know this—what's his name—Krogstad had anything to do with the Bank.

RANK. Yes, he has some sort of appointment there. [*to MRS. LINDE*] I don't know whether you find also in your part of the world that there are certain people who go zealously snuffing about to smell out moral corruption, and, as soon as they have found some, put the person concerned into some lucrative position where they can keep their eye on him. Healthy natures are left out in the cold.

MRS. LINDE. Still I think the sick are those who most need taking care of.

RANK. [*shrugging his shoulders*] Yes, there you are. That is the sentiment that is turning Society into a sickhouse.

[*NORA, who has been absorbed in her thoughts, breaks out into smothered laughter and claps her hands.*]

RANK. Why do you laugh at that? Have you any notion what Society really is?

NORA. What do I care about tiresome Society? I am laughing at something quite different, something extremely amusing. Tell me, Doctor Rank, are all the people who are employed in the Bank dependent on Torvald now?

RANK. Is that what you find so extremely amusing?   260

NORA. [*smiling and humming*] That's my affair! [*walking about the room*] It's perfectly glorious to think that we have—that Torvald has so much power over so many people. [*takes the packet from her pocket*] Doctor Rank, what do you say to a macaroon?

RANK. What, macaroons? I thought they were forbidden here.

NORA. Yes, but these are some Christine gave me.

MRS. LINDE. What! I?—

NORA. Oh, well, don't be alarmed! You couldn't know that Torvald had forbid-   265
den them. I must tell you that he is afraid they will spoil my teeth. But, bah!—once in a way—— That's so, isn't it, Doctor Rank? By your leave? [*puts a macaroon into his mouth*] You must have one too, Christine. And I shall have one, just a little one—or at most two. [*walking about*] I am tremendously happy. There is just one thing in the world now that I should dearly love to do.

RANK. Well, what is that?

NORA. It's something I should dearly love to say, if Torvald could hear me.

RANK. Well, why can't you say it?

NORA. No, I daren't; it's so shocking.

MRS. LINDE. Shocking?   270

RANK. Well, I should not advise you to say it. Still, with us you might. What is it you would so much like to say if Torvald could hear you?

NORA. I should just love to say—Well, I'm damned!

RANK. Are you mad?

MRS. LINDE. Nora, dear——!

RANK. Say it, here he is!   275

NORA. [*hiding the packet*] Hush! Hush! Hush!

[*HELMER comes out of his room, with his coat over his arm and his hat in his hands.*]

NORA. Well, Torvald dear, have you got rid of him?

HELMER. Yes, he has just gone.

NORA. Let me introduce you—this is Christine, who has come to town.

HELMER. Christine——? Excuse me, but I don't know——   280

NORA. Mrs. Linde, dear; Christine Linde.

HELMER. Of course. A school friend of my wife's, I presume?

MRS. LINDE. Yes, we have known each other since then.

NORA. And just think, she has taken a long journey in order to see you.

HELMER. What do you mean?   285

MRS. LINDE. No, really, I——

NORA. Christine is tremendously clever at book-keeping, and she is frightfully anxious to work under some clever man, so as to perfect herself——

HELMER. Very sensible, Mrs. Linde.

NORA. And when she heard you had been appointed manager of the Bank—the news was telegraphed, you know—she travelled here as quick as she could. Torvald, I am sure you will be able to do something for Christine, for my sake, won't you?

HELMER. Well, it is not altogether impossible. I presume you are a widow, Mrs. Linde?   290

MRS. LINDE. Yes.

HELMER. And have had some experience of book-keeping?

MRS. LINDE. Yes, a fair amount.

HELMER. Ah! well, it's very likely I may be able to find something for you——

NORA. [*clapping her hands*]What did I tell you? What did I tell you?   295

HELMER. You have just come at a fortunate moment, Mrs. Linde.

MRS. LINDE.How am I to thank you?

HELMER. There is no need. [*puts on his coat*] But to-day you must excuse me—

RANK. Wait a minute; I will come with you.

[*Brings his fur coat from the hall and warms it at the fire.*]

NORA. Don't be long away, Torvald dear.

HELMER. About an hour, not more.   300

NORA. Are you going too, Christine?

MRS. LINDE. [*putting on her cloak*] Yes, I must go and look for a room.

HELMER. Oh, well then, we can walk down the street together.

NORA. [*helping her*] What a pity it is we are so short of space here: I am afraid it is impossible for us——   305

MRS. LINDE. Please don't think of it! Good-bye, Nora dear, and many thanks.

NORA. Good-bye for the present. Of course you will come back this evening. And you too, Dr. Rank. What do you say? If you are well enough? Oh, you must be! Wrap yourself up well.

[*They go to the door all talking together. Children's voices are heard on the staircase.*]

NORA. There they are. There they are! [*She runs to open the door. The NURSE comes in with the children.*] Come in! Come in! [*stoops and kisses them*] Oh, you sweet blessings! Look at them, Christine! Aren't they darlings?

RANK. Don't let us stand here in the draught.

HELMER. Come along, Mrs. Linde; the place will only be bearable for a mother now!   310

[*RANK, HELMER and MRS. LINDE go downstairs. The NURSE comes forward with the children; NORA shuts the hall door.*]

NORA. How fresh and well you look! Such red cheeks!—like apples and roses. [*The children all talk at once while she speaks to them.*] Have you had great fun? That's splendid! What, you pulled both Emmy and Bob along on the sledge?—both at once?—that *was* good. You are a clever boy, Ivar. Let me take her for a little, Anne. My sweet little baby doll! [*takes the baby from the MAID and dances it up and down*] Yes, yes, mother will dance with Bob too. What! Have you been snowballing? I wish I had been there too! No, no, I will take their things off, Anne; please let me do it, it is such fun. Go in now, you look half frozen. There is some coffee for you on the stove.

[*The* NURSE *goes into the room on the left.* NORA *takes off the children's things and throws them about, while they all talk to her at once.*]

NORA. Really! Did a big dog run after you? But it didn't bite you? No, dogs don't bite nice little dolly children. You mustn't look at the parcels, Ivar. What are they? Ah, I daresay you would like to know. No, no—it's something nasty! Come, let us have a game! What shall we play at? Hide and Seek? Yes, we'll play Hide and Seek. Bob shall hide first. Must I hide? Very well, I'll hide first.

[*She and the children laugh and shout, and romp in and out of the room; at last* NORA *hides under the table, the children rush in and look for her, but do not see her; they hear her smothered laughter, run to the table, lift up the cloth and find her. Shouts of laughter. She crawls forward and pretends to frighten them. Fresh laughter. Meanwhile there has been a knock at the hall door, but none of them has noticed it. The door is half opened, and* KROGSTAD *appears. He waits a little; the game goes on.*]

KROGSTAD. Excuse me, Mrs. Helmer.

NORA. [*with a stifled cry, turns round and gets up on to her knees*] Ah! what do you want?

KROGSTAD. Excuse me, the outer door was ajar; I suppose someone forgot to   315
shut it.

NORA. [*rising*] My husband is out, Mr. Krogstad.

KROGSTAD. I know that.

NORA. What do you want here, then?

KROGSTAD. A word with you.

NORA. With me?—[*to the children, gently*] Go in to nurse. What? No, the strange   320
man won't do mother any harm. When he has gone we will have another game. [*She takes the children into the room on the left, and shuts the door after them.*] You want to speak to me?

KROGSTAD. Yes, I do.

NORA. To-day? It is not the first of the month yet.

KROGSTAD. No, it is Christmas Eve, and it will depend on yourself what sort of a Christmas you will spend.

NORA. What do you want? To-day it is absolutely impossible for me——

KROGSTAD. We won't talk about that till later on. This is something different. I   325
presume you can give me a moment?

NORA. Yes—yes, I can—although——

KROGSTAD. Good. I was in Olsen's Restaurant and saw your husband going down the street——

NORA. Yes?

KROGSTAD. With a lady.

NORA. What then?   330

KROGSTAD. May I make so bold as to ask if it was a Mrs. Linde?

NORA. It was.

KROGSTAD. Just arrived in town?

NORA. Yes, to-day.

KROGSTAD. She is a great friend of yours, isn't she?   335

NORA. She is. But I don't see——

KROGSTAD. I knew her too, once upon a time.

NORA. I am aware of that.

KROGSTAD. Are you? So you know all about it; I thought as much. Then I can ask you, without beating about the bush—is Mrs. Linde to have an appointment in the Bank?

NORA. What right have you to question me, Mr. Krogstad?—You, one of my hus-   340
band's subordinates! But since you ask, you shall know. Yes, Mrs. Linde *is* to have an appointment. And it was I who pleaded her cause, Mr. Krogstad, let me tell you that.

KROGSTAD. I was right in what I thought, then.

NORA. [*walking up and down the stage*] Sometimes one has a tiny little bit of influence, I should hope. Because one is a woman, it does not necessarily follow that—. When anyone is in a subordinate position, Mr. Krogstad, they should really be careful to avoid offending anyone who—who——

KROGSTAD. Who has influence?

NORA. Exactly.

KROGSTAD. [*changing his tone*] Mrs. Helmer, you will be so good as to use your   345
influence on my behalf.

NORA. What? What do you mean?

KROGSTAD. You will be so kind as to see that I am allowed to keep my subordinate position in the Bank.

NORA. What do you mean by that? Who proposes to take your post away from you?

KROGSTAD. Oh, there is no necessity to keep up the pretence of ignorance. I can quite understand that your friend is not very anxious to expose herself to the chance of rubbing shoulders with me; and I quite understand, too, whom I have to thank for being turned out.

NORA. But I assure you——   350

KROGSTAD. Very likely; but, to come to the point, the time has come when I should advise you to use your influence to prevent that.

NORA. But, Mr. Krogstad, I *have* no influence.

KROGSTAD. Haven't you? I thought you said yourself just now——

NORA. Naturally I did not mean you to put that construction on it. I! What should make you think I have any influence of that kind with my husband?

KROGSTAD. Oh, I have known your husband from our student days. I don't sup-   355
pose he is any more unassailable than other husbands.

NORA. If you speak slightingly of my husband, I shall turn you out of the house.

KROGSTAD. You are bold, Mrs. Helmer.

NORA. I am not afraid of you any longer. As soon as the New Year comes, I shall in a very short time be free of the whole thing.

KROGSTAD. [*controlling himself*] Listen to me, Mrs. Helmer. If necessary, I am prepared to fight for my small post in the Bank as if I were fighting for my life.

NORA. So it seems.   360

KROGSTAD. It is not only for the sake of the money; indeed, that weighs least with me in the matter. There is another reason—well, I may as well tell you. My position is this. I daresay you know, like everybody else, that once, many years ago, I was guilty of an indiscretion.

NORA. I think I have heard something of the kind.

KROGSTAD. The matter never came into court; but every way seemed to be closed to me after that. So I took to the business that you know of. I had to do something; and, honestly, I don't think I've been one of the worst. But now I must cut myself free from all that. My sons are growing up; for their sake I must try and win back as much respect as I can in the town. This post in the Bank was like the first step up for me—and now your husband is going to kick me downstairs again into the mud.

NORA. But you must believe me, Mr. Krogstad; it is not in my power to help you at all.

KROGSTAD. Then it is because you haven't the will; but I have means to compel you. 365

NORA. You don't mean that you will tell my husband that I owe you money?

KROGSTAD. Hm!—suppose I were to tell him?

NORA. It would be perfectly infamous of you. [*Sobbing*] To think of his learning my secret, which has been my joy and pride, in such an ugly, clumsy way—that he should learn it from you! And it would put me in a horribly disagreeable position——

KROGSTAD. Only disagreeable?

NORA. [*impetuously*] Well, do it, then!—and it will be the worse for you. My husband will see for himself what a blackguard you are, and you certainly won't keep your post then. 370

KROGSTAD. I asked you if it was only a disagreeable scene at home that you were afraid of?

NORA. If my husband does get to know of it, of course he will at once pay you what is still owing, and we shall have nothing more to do with you.

KROGSTAD. [*coming a step nearer*] Listen to me, Mrs. Helmer. Either you have a very bad memory or you know very little of business. I shall be obliged to remind you of a few details.

NORA. What do you mean?

KROGSTAD. When your husband was ill, you came to me to borrow two hundred and fifty pounds. 375

NORA. I didn't know any one else to go to.

KROGSTAD. I promised to get you that amount——

NORA. Yes, and you did so.

KROGSTAD. I promised to get you that amount, on certain conditions. Your mind was so taken up with your husband's illness, and you were so anxious to get the money for your journey, that you seem to have paid no attention to the conditions of our bargain. Therefore it will not be amiss if I remind you of them. Now, I promised to get the money on the security of a bond which I drew up.

NORA. Yes, and which I signed. 380

KROGSTAD. Good. But below your signature there were a few lines constituting your father a surety for the money; those lines your father should have signed.

NORA. Should? He did sign them.

KROGSTAD. I had left the date blank; that is to say your father should himself have inserted the date on which he signed the paper. Do you remember that?

NORA. Yes, I think I remember——

KROGSTAD. Then I gave you the bond to send by post to your father. Is that not so? 385

NORA. Yes.

KROGSTAD. And you naturally did so at once, because five or six days afterwards you brought me the bond with your father's signature. And then I gave you the money.

NORA. Well, haven't I been paying it off regularly?

KROGSTAD. Fairly so, yes. But—to come back to the matter in hand—that must have been a very trying time for your, Mrs. Helmer?

NORA. It was, indeed.

KROGSTAD. Your father was very ill, wasn't he?

NORA. He was very near his end.

KROGSTAD. And died soon afterwards?

NORA. Yes.

KROGSTAD. Tell me, Mrs. Helmer, can you by any chance remember what day your father died?—on what day of the month, I mean.

NORA. Papa died on the 29th of September.

KROGSTAD. That is correct; I have ascertained it for myself. And, as that is so, there is a discrepancy [*taking a paper from his pocket*] which I cannot account for.

NORA. What discrepancy? I don't know——

KROGSTAD. The discrepancy consists, Mrs. Helmer, in the fact that your father signed this bond three days after his death.

NORA. What do you mean? I don't understand——

KROGSTAD. Your father died on the 29th of September. But, look here; your father has dated his signature the 2nd of October. It is a discrepancy, isn't it? [*NORA is silent.*] Can you explain it to me? [*NORA is still silent.*] It is a remarkable thing, too, that the words ""2nd of October," as well as the year, are not written in your father's handwriting but in one that I think I know. Well, of course it can be explained; your father may have forgotten to date his signature, and someone else may have dated it haphazard before they knew of his death. There is no harm in that. It all depends on the signature of the name; and *that* is genuine, I suppose, Mrs. Helmer? It was your father himself who signed his name here?

NORA. [*after a short pause, throws her head up and looks defiantly at him*] No, it was not. It was I that wrote papa's name.

KROGSTAD. Are you aware that is a dangerous confession?

NORA. In what way? You shall have your money soon.

KROGSTAD. Let me ask you a question; why did you not send the paper to your father?

NORA. It was impossible; papa was so ill. If I had asked him for his signature, I should have had to tell him what the money was to be used for; and when he was so ill himself I couldn't tell him that my husband's life was in danger—it was impossible.

KROGSTAD. It would have been better for you if you had given up your trip abroad.

NORA. No, that was impossible. That trip was to save my husband's life; I couldn't give that up.

KROGSTAD. But did it never occur to you that you were committing a fraud on me?

NORA. I couldn't take that into account; I didn't trouble myself about you at all. I couldn't bear you, because you put so many heartless difficulties in my way, although you knew what a dangerous condition my husband was in.

KROGSTAD. Mrs. Helmer, you evidently do not realise clearly what it is that you have been guilty of. But I can assure you that my one false step, which lost me all my reputation, was nothing more or nothing worse than what you have done.

NORA. You? Do you ask me to believe that you were brave enough to run a risk to save your wife's life?

KROGSTAD. The law cares nothing about motives.

NORA. Then it must be a very foolish law.

KROGSTAD. Foolish or not, it is the law by which you will be judged, if I produce   415
this paper in court.

NORA. I don't believe it. Is a daughter not to be allowed to spare her dying father anxiety and care? Is a wife not to be allowed to save her husband's life? I don't
know much about law; but I am certain that there must be laws permitting such things
as that. Have you no knowledge of such laws—you who are a lawyer? You must be a
very poor lawyer, Mr. Krogstad.

KROGSTAD. Maybe. But matters of business—such business as you and I have
had together—do you think I don't understand that? Very well. Do as you please. But
let me tell you this—if I lose my position a second time, you shall lose yours with me.

[*He bows, and goes out through the hall.*]

NORA. [*appears buried in thought for a short time, then tosses her head*] Nonsense! Trying to frighten me like that!—I am not so silly as he thinks. [*begins to busy herself putting
the children's things in order*] And yet——? No, it's impossible! I did it for love's sake.

THE CHILDREN. [*in the doorway on the left*] Mother, the stranger man has gone
out through the gate.

NORA. Yes, dears, I know. But, don't tell anyone about the stranger man. Do you   420
hear? Not even papa.

CHILDREN. No, mother; but will you come and play again?

NORA. No, no—not now.

CHILDREN. But, mother, you promised us.

NORA. Yes, but I can't now. Run away in; I have such a lot to do. Run away in,
my sweet little darlings. [*She gets them into the room by degrees and shuts the door on them;
then sits down on the sofa, takes up a piece of needlework and sews a few stitches, but soon stops.*]
No! [*throws down the work, gets up, goes to the hall door and calls out*] Helen! bring the
Tree in. [*goes to the table on the left, opens a drawer, and stops again*] No, no! it is quite impossible!

MAID. [*coming in with the Tree*] Where shall I put it, ma'am?   425

NORA. Here, in the middle of the floor.

MAID. Shall I get you anything else?

NORA. No, thank you. I have all I want.   [*Exit MAID.*]

NORA. [*begins dressing the tree*] A candle here—and flowers here——. The horrible man! It's all nonsense—there's nothing wrong. The Tree shall be splendid! I will
do everything I can think of to please you, Torvald!—I will sing for you, dance for
you—[*HELMER comes in with some papers under his arm*] Oh! are you back already?

HELMER. Yes. Has anyone been here?   430

NORA. Here? No.

HELMER. That is strange. I saw Krogstad going out of the gate.

NORA. Did you? Oh yes, I forgot, Krogstad was here for a moment.

HELMER. Nora, I can see from your manner that he has been here begging you
to say a good word for him.

NORA. Yes.   435

HELMER. And you were to appear to do it of your own accord; you were to conceal from me the fact of his having been here; didn't he beg that of you too?

NORA. Yes, Torvald, but——

HELMER. Nora, Nora, and you would be a party to that sort of thing? To have any talk with a man like that, and give him any sort of promise? And to tell me a lie into the bargain?

NORA. A lie——?

HELMER. Didn't you tell me no one had been here? [*shakes his finger at her*] My little song-bird must never do that again. A song-bird must have a clean beak to chirp with—no false notes! [*puts his arm round her waist*] That is so, isn't it? Yes, I am sure it is. [*lets her go*] We will say no more about it. [*sits down by the stove*] How warm and snug it is here!

[*Turns over his papers.*]

NORA. [*after a short pause, during which she busies herself with the Christmas Tree*] Torvald!

HELMER. Yes.

NORA. I am looking forward tremendously to the fancy dress ball at the Stenborgs' the day after to-morrow.

HELMER. And I am tremendously curious to see what you are going to surprise me with.

NORA. It was very silly of me to want to do that.

HELMER. What do you mean?

NORA. I can't hit upon anything that will do; everything I think of seems so silly and insignificant.

HELMER. Does my little Nora acknowledge that at last?

NORA. [*standing behind his chair with her arms on the back of it*] Are you very busy, Torvald?

HELMER. Well——

NORA. What are all those papers?

HELMER. Bank business.

NORA. Already?

HELMER. I have got authority from the retiring manager to undertake the necessary changes in the staff and in the rearrangement of the work; and I must make use of the Christmas week for that, so as to have everything in order for the new year.

NORA. Then that was why this poor Krogstad——

HELMER. Hm!

NORA. [*leans against the back of his chair and strokes his hair*] If you hadn't been so busy I should have asked you a tremendously big favour, Torvald.

HELMER. What is that? Tell me.

NORA. There is no one has such good taste as you. And I do so want to look nice at the fancy-dress ball. Torvald, couldn't you take me in hand and decide what I shall go as, and what sort of a dress I shall wear?

HELMER. Aha! so my obstinate little woman is obliged to get someone to come to her rescue?

NORA. Yes, Torvald, I can't get along a bit without your help.

HELMER. Very well, I will think it over, we shall manage to hit upon something.

NORA. That *is* nice of you. [*goes to the Christmas Tree. A short pause.*] How pretty the red flowers look——. But, tell me, was it really something very bad that this Krogstad was guilty of?

HELMER. He forged someone's name. Have you any idea what that means?

NORA. Isn't it possible that he was driven to do it by necessity? 465
HELMER. Yes; or, as in so many cases, by imprudence. I am not so heartless as to condemn a man altogether because of a single false step of that kind.
NORA. No you wouldn't, would you, Torvald?
HELMER. Many a man has been able to retrieve his character, if he has openly confessed his fault and taken his punishment.
NORA. Punishment——?
HELMER. But Krogstad did nothing of that sort; he got himself out of it by a cun- 470
ning trick, and that is why he has gone under altogether.
NORA. But do you think it would——?
HELMER. Just think how a guilty man like that has to lie and play the hypocrite with everyone, how he has to wear a mask in the presence of those near and dear to him, even before his own wife and children. And about the children—that is the most terrible part of it all, Nora.
NORA. How?
HELMER. Because such an atmosphere of lies infects and poisons the whole life of a home. Each breath the children take in such a house is full of the germs of evil.
NORA. [*coming nearer him*] Are you sure of that? 475
HELMER. My dear, I have often seen it in the course of my life as a lawyer. Almost everyone who has gone to the bad early in life has had a deceitful mother.
NORA. Why do you only say—mother?
HELMER. It seems most commonly to be the mother's influence, though naturally a bad father's would have the same result. Every lawyer is familiar with the fact. This Krogstad, now, has been persistently poisoning his own children with lies and dissimulation; that is why I say he has lost all moral character. [*holds out his hands to her*] That is why my sweet little Nora must promise me not to plead his cause. Give me your hand on it. Come, come, what is this? Give me your hand. There now, that's settled. I assure you it would be quite impossible for me to work with him; I literally feel physically ill when I am in the company of such people.
NORA. [*takes her hand out of his and goes to the opposite side of the Christmas Tree*] How hot it is in here; and I have such a lot to do.
HELMER. [*getting up and putting his papers in order*] Yes, and I must try and read 480
through some of these before dinner; and I must think about your costume, too. And it is just possible I may have something ready in gold paper to hang up on the Tree. [*Puts his hand on her head.*] My precious little singing-bird!

[*He goes into his room and shuts the door after him.*]

NORA. [*after a pause, whispers*] No, no—it isn't true. It's impossible; it must be impossible.

[*The NURSE opens the door on the left.*]

NURSE. The little ones are begging so hard to be allowed to come in to mamma.
NORA. No, no, no! Don't let them come in to me! You stay with them, Anne.
NURSE. Very well, ma'am.

[*Shuts the door.*]

NORA. [*pale with terror*] Deprave my little children? Poison my home? [*a short* 485
pause. Then she tosses her head.] It's not true. It can't possibly be true.

ACT 2

THE SAME SCENE.—*The Christmas Tree is in the corner by the piano, stripped of its ornaments and with burnt-down candle-ends on its dishevelled branches. NORA's cloak and hat are lying on the sofa. She is alone in the room, walking about uneasily. She stops by the sofa and takes up her cloak.*

NORA. [*drops the cloak*] Someone is coming now! [*goes to the door and listens*] No— it is no one. Of course, no one will come to-day, Christmas Day—nor tomorrow either. But, perhaps—[*opens the door and looks out*] No, nothing in the letter-box; it is quite empty. [*comes forward*] What rubbish! of course he can't be in earnest about it. Such a thing couldn't happen; it is impossible—I have three little children.

[*Enter the NURSE from the room on the left, carrying a big cardboard box.*]

NURSE. At last I have found the box with the fancy dress.

NORA. Thanks; put it on the table.

NURSE. [*doing so*] But it is very much in want of mending.

NORA. I should like to tear it into a hundred thousand pieces.   5

NURSE. What an idea! It can easily be put in order—just a little patience.

NORA. Yes, I will go and get Mrs. Linde to come and help me with it.

NURSE. What, out again? In this horrible weather? You will catch cold, ma'am, and make yourself ill.

NORA. Well, worse than that might happen. How are the children?

NURSE. The poor little souls are playing with their Christmas presents, but——   10

NORA. Do they ask much for me?

NURSE. You see, they are so accustomed to have their mamma with them.

NORA. Yes, but, nurse, I shall not be able to be so much with them now as I was before.

NURSE. Oh well, young children easily get accustomed to anything.

NORA. Do you think so? Do you think they would forget their mother if she went   15
away altogether?

NURSE. Good heavens!—went away altogether?

NORA. Nurse, I want you to tell me something I have often wondered about— how could you have the heart to put your own child out among strangers?

NURSE. I was obliged to, if I wanted to be little Nora's nurse.

NORA. Yes, but how could you be willing to do it?

NURSE. What, when I was going to get such a good place by it? A poor girl who   20
has got into trouble should be glad to. Besides, that wicked man didn't do a single thing for me.

NORA. But I suppose your daughter has quite forgotten you.

NURSE. No, indeed she hasn't. She wrote to me when she was confirmed, and when she was married.

NORA. [*putting her arms round her neck*] Dear old Anne, you were a good mother to me when I was little.

NURSE. Little Nora, poor dear, had no other mother but me.

NORA. And if my little ones had no other mother, I am sure you would——What   25
nonsense I am talking! [*opens the box*] Go in to them. Now I must——. You will see to-morrow how charming I shall look.

NURSE. I am sure there will be no one at the ball so charming as you, ma'am.

[*Goes into the room on the left.*]

NORA. [*begins to unpack the box, but soon pushes it away from her*] If only I dared go out. If only no one would come. If only I could be sure nothing would happen here in the meantime. Stuff and nonsense! No one will come. Only I mustn't think about it. I will brush my muff. What, lovely gloves! Out of my thoughts, out of my thoughts! One, two, three, four, five, six——[*screams.*] Ah! there is someone coming——.

[*Makes a movement towards the door, but stands irresolute.*]

[*Enter* MRS. LINDE *from the hall, where she has taken off her cloak and hat.*]

NORA. Oh, it's you, Christine. There is no one else out there, is there? How good of you to come!

MRS. LINDE. I heard you were up asking for me.

NORA. Yes, I was passing by. As a matter of fact, it is something you could help   30
me with. Let us sit down here on the sofa. Look here. To-morrow evening there is to be a fancy-dress ball at the Stenborgs', who live about us; and Torvald wants me to go as a Neapolitan fisher-girl, and dance the Tarantella that I learnt at Capri.

MRS. LINDE. I see; you are going to keep up the character.

NORA. Yes, Torvald wants me to. Look, here is the dress; Torvald had it made for me there, but now it is all so torn, and I haven't any idea——

MRS. LINDE. We will easily put that right. It is only some of the trimming come unsewn here and there. Needle and thread? Now then, that's all we want.

NORA. It *is* nice of you.

MRS. LINDE. [*sewing*] So you are going to be dressed up to-morrow, Nora. I will   35
tell you what—I shall come in for a moment and see you in your fine feathers. But I have completely forgotten to thank you for a delightful evening yesterday.

NORA. [*gets up, and crosses the stages*] Well I don't think yesterday was a pleasant as usual. You ought to have come to town a little earlier, Christine. Certainly Torvald does understand how to make a house dainty and attractive.

MRS. LINDE. And so do you, it seems to me; you are not your father's daughter for nothing. But tell me, is Doctor Rank always as depressed as he was yesterday?

NORA. No; yesterday it was very noticeable. I must tell you that he suffers from a very dangerous disease. He has consumption of the spine, poor creature. His father was a horrible man who committed all sorts of excesses; and that is why his son was sickly from childhood, do you understand?

MRS. LINDE. [*dropping her sewing*] But, my dearest Nora, how do you know anything about such things?

NORA. [*walking about*] Pooh! When you have three children, you get visits now   40
and then from—from married women, who know something of medical matters, and they talk about one thing and another.

MRS. LINDE. [*goes on sewing. A short silence*] Does Doctor Rank come here every day?

NORA. Every day regularly. He is Torvald's most intimate friend, and a great friend of mine too. He is just like one of the family.

MRS. LINDE. But tell me this—is he perfectly sincere? I mean, isn't he the kind of man that is very anxious to make himself agreeable?

NORA. Not in the least. What makes you think that?

MRS. LINDE. When you introduced him to me yesterday, he declared he had of-   45
ten heard my name mentioned in this house; but afterwards I noticed that your husband hadn't the slightest idea who I was. So how could Doctor Rank——?

NORA. That is quite right, Christine. Torvald is so absurdly fond of me that he wants me absolutely to himself, as he says. At first he used to seem almost jealous if I mentioned any of the dear folk at home, so naturally I gave up doing so. But I often talk about such things with Doctor Rank, because he likes hearing about them.

MRS. LINDE. Listen to me, Nora. You are still very like a child in many things, and I am older than you in many ways and have a little more experience. Let me tell you this—you ought to make an end of it with Doctor Rank.

NORA. What ought I to make an end of?

MRS. LINDE. Of two things, I think. Yesterday you talked some nonsense about a rich admirer who was to leave you money——

NORA. An admirer who doesn't exist, unfortunately! But what then?   50

MRS. LINDE. Is Doctor Rank a man of means?

NORA. Yes, he is.

MRS. LINDE. And has no one to provide for?

NORA. No, no one; but——

MRS. LINDE. And comes here every day?   55

NORA. Yes, I told you so.

MRS. LINDE. But how can this well-bred man be so tactless?

NORA. I don't understand you at all.

MRS. LINDE. Don't prevaricate, Nora. Do you suppose I don't guess who lent you the two hundred and fifty pounds?

NORA. Are you out of your senses? How can you think of such a thing! A friend   60
of ours, who comes here every day! Do you realise what a horribly painful position that would be?

MRS. LINDE. Then is really isn't he?

NORA. No, certainly not. It would never have entered into my head for a moment. Besides, he had no money to lend then; he came into his money afterwards.

MRS. LINDE. Well, I think that was lucky for you, my dear Nora.

NORA. No, it would never have come into my head to ask Doctor Rank. Although I am quite sure that if I had asked him——

MRS. LINDE. But of course you won't.   65

NORA. Of course not. I have no reason to think it could possibly be necessary. But I am quite sure that if I told Doctor Rank——

MRS. LINDE. Behind your husband's back?

NORA. I must make an end of it with the other one, and that will be behind his back too. I *must* make an end of it with him.

MRS. LINDE. Yes, that is what I told you yesterday, but——

NORA. [*walking up and down*] A man can put a thing like that straight much eas-   70
ier than a woman——

MRS. LINDE. One's husband, yes.

NORA. Nonsense! [*standing still*] When you pay off a debt you get your bond back, don't you?

MRS. LINDE. Yes, as a matter of course.

NORA. And can tear it into a hundred thousand pieces, and burn it up— the nasty dirty paper!

MRS. LINDE. [*looks hard at her, lays down her sewing and gets up slowly*] Nora, you   75
are concealing something from me.

NORA. Do I look as if I were?

MRS. LINDE. Something has happened to you since yesterday morning. Nora, what is it?

NORA. [*going nearer to her*] Christine! [*listens*] Hush! there's Torvald come home. Do you mind going in to the children for the present? Torvald can't bear to see dressmaking going on. Let Anne help you.

MRS. LINDE. [*gathering some of the things together*] Certainly—but I am not going away from here till we have had it out with one another.

[*She goes into the room on the left, as HELMER comes in from the hall.*]

NORA. [*going up to HELMER*] I have wanted you so much, Torvald dear.   80

HELMER. Was that the dressmaker?

NORA. No, it was Christine; she is helping me to put my dress in order. You will see I shall look quite smart.

HELMER. Wasn't that a happy thought of mine, now?

NORA. Splendid! But don't you think it is nice of me, too, to do as you wish?

HELMER. Nice?—because you do as your husband wishes? Well, well, you little   85 rogue, I am sure you did not mean it in that way. But I am not going to disturb you; you will want to be trying on your dress, I expect.

NORA. I suppose you are going to work.

HELMER. Yes. [*shows her a bundle of papers*] Look at that. I have just been into the bank.   [*Turns to go into his room.*]

NORA. Torvald.

HELMER. Yes.

NORA. If your little squirrel were to ask you for something very, very prettily——?   90

HELMER. What then?

NORA. Would you do it?

HELMER. I should like to hear what it is, first.

NORA. Your squirrel would run about and do all her tricks if you would be nice, and do what she wants.

HELMER. Speak plainly.   95

NORA. Your skylark would chirp about in every room, with her song rising and falling——

HELMER. Well, my skylark does that anyhow.

NORA. I would play the fairy and dance for you in the moonlight, Torvald.

HELMER. Nora—you surely don't mean that request you made of me this morning?

NORA. [*going near him*] Yes, Torvald, I beg you so earnestly——   100

HELMER. Have you really the courage to open up that question again?

NORA. Yes, dear, you *must* do as I ask; you *must* let Krogstad keep his post in the Bank.

HELMER. My dear Nora, it is his post that I have arranged Mrs. Linde shall have.

NORA. Yes, you have been awfully kind about that; but you could just as well dismiss some other clerk instead of Krogstad.

HELMER. This is simply incredible obstinacy! Because you chose to give him a   105 thoughtless promise that you would speak for him, I am expected to——

NORA. That isn't the reason, Torvald. It is for your own sake. This fellow writes in the most scurrilous newspapers; you have told me so yourself. He can do you an unspeakable amount of harm. I am frightened to death of him——

HELMER. Ah, I understand; it is recollections of the past that scare you.

NORA. What do you mean?

HELMER. Naturally you are thinking of your father.

NORA. Yes—yes, of course. Just recall to your mind what these malicious crea-   110
tures wrote in the papers about papa, and how horribly they slandered him. I believe
they would have procured his dismissal if the Department had not sent you over to inquire into it, and if you had not been so kindly disposed and helpful to him.

HELMER. My little Nora, there is an important difference between your father
and me. Your father's reputation as a public official was not above suspicion. Mine is,
and I hope it will continue to be so, as long as I hold my office.

NORA. You never can tell what mischief these men may contrive. We ought to
be so well off, so snug and happy here in our peaceful home, and have no cares—you
and I and the children, Torvald! That is why I beg you so earnestly——

HELMER. And it is just by interceding for him that you make it impossible
for me to keep him. It is already known at the Bank that I mean to dismiss Krogstad.
Is it to get about now that the new manager has changed his mind at his wife's
bidding——

NORA. And what if it did?

HELMER. Of course!—if only this obstinate little person can get her way! Do you   115
suppose I am going to make myself ridiculous before my whole staff, to let people
think that I am a man to be swayed by all sorts of outside influence? I should very soon
feel the consequences of it, I can tell you! And besides, there is one thing that makes
it quite impossible for me to have Krogstad in the Bank as long as I am manager.

NORA. Whatever is that?

HELMER. His moral failings I might perhaps have overlooked, if necessary——

NORA. Yes, you could—couldn't you?

HELMER. And I hear he is a good worker, too. But I knew him when we were
boys. It was one of those rash friendships that so often prove an incubus in after life.
I may as well tell you plainly, we were once on very intimate terms with one another.
But this tactless fellow lays no restraint on himself when other people are present. On
the contrary, he thinks it gives him the right to adopt a familiar tone with me, and
every minute it is "I say, Helmer, old fellow!" and that sort of thing. I assure you it is
extremely painful for me. He would make my position in the Bank intolerable.

NORA. Torvald, I don't believe you mean that.   120

HELMER. Don't you? Why not?

NORA. Because it is such a narrow-minded way of looking at things.

HELMER. What are you saying? Narrow-minded? Do you think I am narrow-
minded?

NORA. No, just the opposite, dear—and it is exactly for that reason.

HELMER. It's the same thing. You say my point of view is narrow-minded, so I   125
must be so too. Narrow-minded! Very well—I must put an end to this. [*Goes to the halldoor and calls.*] Helen!

NORA. What are you going to do?

HELMER. [*looking among his papers*] Settle it. [*Enter MAID.*] Look here; take this
letter and go downstairs with it at once. Find a messenger and tell him to deliver it,
and be quick. The address is on it, and here is the money.

MAID. Very well, sir.

[*Exits with the letter.*]

HELMER. [*putting his papers together*] Now then, little Miss Obstinate.

NORA. [*breathlessly*] Torvald—what was that letter?   130

HELMER. Krogstad's dismissal.

NORA. Call her back, Torvald! There is still time. Oh Torvald, call her back! Do it for my sake—for your own sake—for the children's sake! Do you hear me, Torvald? Call her back!! You don't know what that letter can bring upon us.

HELMER. It's too late.

NORA. Yes, it's too late.

HELMER. My dear Nora, I can forgive the anxiety you are in, although really it   135 is an insult to me. It is, indeed. Isn't it an insult to think that I should be afraid of a starving quill-driver's vengeance? But I forgive you nevertheless, because it is such eloquent witness to your great love for me. [*takes her in his arms*] And that is as it should be, my own darling Nora. Come what will, you may be sure I shall have both courage and strength if they be needed. You will see I am man enough to take everything upon myself.

NORA. [*in a horror-stricken voice*] What do you mean by that?

HELMER. Everything, I say——

NORA. [*recovering herself*] You will never have to do that.

HELMER. That's right. Well, we will share it, Nora, as man and wife should. That is how it shall be. [*caressing her*] Are you content now? There! there!—not these frightened dove's eyes! The whole thing is only the wildest fancy!—Now, you must go and play through the Tarantella and practise with your tambourine. I shall go into the inner office and shut the door, and I shall hear nothing; you can make as much noise as you please. [*turns back at the door*] And when Rank comes, tell him where he will find me.

[*Nods to her, takes his papers and goes into his room, and shuts the door after him*]

NORA. [*bewildered with anxiety, stands as if rooted to the spot, and whispers*] He is ca-   140 pable of doing it. He will do it. He will do it in spite of everything.—No, not that! Never, never! Anything rather than that! Oh, for some help, some way out of it! [*The door-bell rings.*] Doctor Rank! Anything rather than that—anything, whatever it is!

[*She puts her hands over her face, pulls herself together, goes to the door and opens it. RANK is standing without, hanging up his coat. During the following dialogue it begins to grow dark.*]

NORA. Good-day, Doctor Rank. I knew your ring. But you mustn't go into Torvald now; I think he is busy with something.

RANK. And you?

NORA. [*brings him in and shuts the door after him*] Oh, you know very well I always have time for you.

RANK. Thank you. I shall make use of as much of it as I can.

NORA. What do you mean by that? As much of it as you can?   145

RANK. Well, does that alarm you?

NORA. It was such a strange way of putting it. Is anything likely to happen?

RANK. Nothing but what I have long been prepared for. But I certainly didn't expect it to happen so soon.

NORA. [*gripping him by the arm*] What have you found out? Doctor Rank, you must tell me.

RANK. [*sitting down by the stove*] It is all up with me. And it can't be helped.   150

NORA. [*with a sigh of relief*] Is it about yourself?

RANK. Who else? It is no use lying to one's self. I am the most wretched of all my patients, Mrs. Helmer. Lately I have been taking stock of my internal economy. Bankrupt! Probably within a month I shall lie rotting in the churchyard.

NORA. What an ugly thing to say!

RANK. The thing itself is cursedly ugly, and the worst of it is that I shall have to face so much more that is ugly before that. I shall only make one more examination of myself; when I have done that, I shall know pretty certainly when it will be that the horrors of dissolution will begin. There is something I want to tell you. Helmer's refined nature gives him an unconquerable disgust at everything that is ugly; I won't have him in my sick-room.

NORA. Oh, but, Doctor Rank——   155

RANK. I won't have him there. Not on any account. I bar my door to him. As soon as I am quite certain that the worst has come, I shall send you my card with a black cross on it, and then you will know that the loathsome end has begun.

NORA. You are quite absurd to-day. And I wanted you so much to be in a really good humour.

RANK. With death stalking beside me?—To have to pay this penalty for another man's sin! Is there any justice in that? And in every single family, in one way or another, some such inexorable retribution is being exacted——

NORA. [*putting her hands over her ears*] Rubbish! Do talk of something cheerful.

RANK. Oh, it's a mere laughing matter, the whole thing. My poor innocent   160
spine has to suffer for my father's youthful amusements.

NORA. [*sitting at the table on the left*] I suppose you mean that he was too partial to asparagus and pâté de foie gras, don't you.

RANK. Yes, and to truffles.

NORA. Truffles, yes. And oysters too, I suppose?

RANK. Oysters, of course, that goes without saying.

NORA. And heaps of port and champagne. It is sad that all these nice things   165
should take their revenge on our bones.

RANK. Especially that they should revenge themselves on the unlucky bones of those who have not had the satisfaction of enjoying them.

NORA. Yes, that's the saddest part of it all.

RANK. [*with a searching look at her*] Hm!——

NORA. [*after a short pause*] Why did you smile?

RANK. No, it was you that laughed.   170

NORA. No, it was you that smiled, Doctor Rank!

RANK. [*rising*] You are a greater rascal than I thought.

NORA. I am in a silly mood to-day.

RANK. So it seems.

NORA. [*putting her hands on his shoulders*] Dear, dear Doctor Rank, death   175
mustn't take you away from Torvald and me.

RANK. It is a loss you would easily recover from. Those who are gone are soon forgotten.

NORA. [*looking at him anxiously*] Do you believe that?

RANK. People form new ties, and then——

NORA. Who will form new ties?

RANK. Both you and Helmer, when I am gone. You yourself are already on the   180
high road to it, I think. What did that Mrs. Linde want here last night?

NORA. Oho!—you don't mean to say you are jealous of poor Christine?

RANK. Yes, I am. She will be my successor in this house. When I am done for, this woman will—

NORA. Hush! don't speak so loud. She is in that room.

RANK. To-day again. There, you see.

NORA. She has only come to sew my dress for me. Bless my soul, how unrea-   185
sonable you are! [*sits down on the sofa*] Be nice now, Doctor Rank, and tomorrow you will see how beautifully I shall dance, and you can imagine I am doing it all for you— and for Torvald too, of course. [*takes various things out of the box*] Doctor Rank, come and sit down here, and I will show you something.

RANK. [*sitting down*] What is it?

NORA. Just look at those!

RANK. Silk stockings.

NORA. Flesh-coloured. Aren't they lovely? It is so dark here now, but to-mor-row—. No, no, no! you must only look at the feet. Oh well, you may have leave to look at the legs too.

RANK. Hm!—   190

NORA. Why are you looking so critical? Don't you think they will fit me?

RANK. I have no means of forming an opinion about that.

NORA. [*looks at him for a moment*] For shame! [*hits him lightly on the ear with the stockings*] That's to punish you. [*folds them up again*]

RANK. And what other nice things am I to be allowed to see?

NORA. Not a single thing more, for being so naughty. [*She looks among the things,*   195
humming to herself.]

RANK. [*after a short silence*] When I am sitting here, talking to you as intimately as this, I cannot imagine for a moment what would have become of me if I had never come into this house.

NORA. [*smiling*] I believe you do feel thoroughly at home with us.

RANK. [*in a lower voice, looking straight in front of him*] And to be obliged to leave it all——

NORA. Nonsense, you are not going to leave it.

RANK. [*as before*] And not be able to leave behind one the slightest token of   200
one's gratitude, scarcely even a fleeting regret—nothing but an empty place which the first comer can fill as well as any other.

NORA. And if I asked you now for a—? No!

RANK. For what?

NORA. For a big proof of your friendship——

RANK. Yes, yes!

NORA. I mean a tremendously big favour——   205

RANK. Would you really make me so happy for once?

NORA. Ah, but you don't know what it is yet.

RANK. No—but tell me.

NORA. I really can't, Doctor Rank. It is something out of all reason; it means ad-vice, and help, and a favour——

RANK. The bigger a thing it is the better. I can't conceive what it is you mean.   210
Do tell me. Haven't I your confidence?

NORA. More than anyone else. I know you are my truest and best friend, and so I will tell you what it is. Well, Doctor Rank, it is something you must help me to prevent. You know how devotedly, how inexpressibly deeply Torvald loves me; he would never for a moment hesitate to give his life for me.

RANK. [*leaning towards her*] Nora—do you think he is the only one——?

NORA. [*with a slight start*] The only one——?

RANK. The only one who would gladly give his life for your sake.

NORA. [*sadly*] Is that it?

RANK. I was determined you should know it before I went away, and there will never be a better opportunity than this. Now you know it, Nora. And now you know, too, that you can trust me as you would trust no one else.

NORA. [*rises, deliberately and quietly*] Let me pass.

RANK. [*makes room for her to pass him, but sits still*] Nora!

NORA. [*at the hall door*] Helen, bring in the lamp. [*goes over to the stove*] Dear Doctor Rank, that was really horrid of you.

RANK. To have loved you as much as anyone else does? Was that horrid?

NORA. No, but to go and tell me so. There was really no need——

RANK. What do you mean? Did you know——? [*MAID enters with lamp, puts it down on the table, and goes out.*] Nora—Mrs. Helmer—tell me, had you any idea of this?

NORA. Oh, how do I know whether I had or whether I hadn't? I really can't tell you— To think you could be so clumsy, Doctor Rank! We were getting on so nicely.

RANK. Well, at all events you know now that you can command me, body and soul. So won't you speak out?

NORA. [*looking at him*] After what happened?

RANK. I beg you to let me know what it is.

NORA. I can't tell you anything now.

RANK. Yes, yes. You mustn't punish me in that way. Let me have permission to do for you whatever a man may do.

NORA. You can do nothing for me now. Besides, I really don't need any help at all. You will find that the whole thing is merely fancy on my part. It really is so—of course it is! [*Sits down in the rocking-chair, and looks at him with a smile*] You are a nice sort of man, Doctor Rank!—don't you feel ashamed of yourself, now the lamp has come?

RANK. Not a bit. But perhaps I had better go—for ever?

NORA. No, indeed, you shall not. Of course you must come here just as before. You know very well Torvald can't do without you.

RANK. Yes, but you?

NORA. Oh, I am always tremendously pleased when you come.

RANK. It is just that, that put me on the wrong track. You are a riddle to me. I have often thought that you would almost as soon be in my company as in Helmer's.

NORA. Yes—you see there are some people one loves best, and others whom one would almost always rather have as companions.

RANK. Yes, there is something in that.

NORA. When I was at home, of course I loved papa best. But I always thought it tremendous fun if I could steal down into the maid's room, because they never moralised at all, and talked to each other about such entertaining things.

RANK. I see—it is *their* place I have taken.

NORA. [*jumping up and going to him*] Oh, dear, nice Doctor Rank, I never meant that at all. But surely you can understand that being with Torvald is a little like being with papa——

[*Enter MAID from the hall*]

MAID. If you please, ma'am. [*whispers and hands her a card*]   240
NORA. [*glancing at the card*] Oh! [*puts it in her pocket*]
RANK. Is there anything wrong?
NORA. No, no, not in the least. It is only something—it is my new dress——
RANK. What? Your dress is lying there.
NORA. Oh, yes, that one; but this is another. I ordered it. Torvald mustn't know   245
about it——
RANK. Oho! Then that was the great secret.
NORA. Of course. Just go in to him; he is sitting in the inner room. Keep him
as long as——
RANK. Make your mind easy; I won't let him escape. [*goes into HELMER's room*]
NORA. [*to the MAID*] And he is standing waiting in the kitchen?
MAID. Yes; he came up the back stairs.   250
NORA. But didn't you tell him no one was in?
MAID. Yes, but it was no good.
NORA. He won't go away?
MAID. No; he says he won't until he has seen you, ma'am.
NORA. Well, let him come in—but quietly. Helen, you mustn't say anything   255
about it to anyone. It is a surprise for my husband.
MAID. Yes, ma'am, I quite understand. [*Exit.*]
NORA. This dreadful thing is going to happen! It will happen in spite of me! No,
no, no, it can't happen—it shan't happen!

[*She bolts the door of HELMER's room. The MAID opens the hall door for KROGSTAD and shuts
it after him. He is wearing a fur coat, high boots and a fur cap.*]

NORA. [*advancing towards him*] Speak low—my husband is at home.
KROGSTAD. No matter about that.
NORA. What do you want of me?   260
KROGSTAD. An explanation of something.
NORA. Make haste then. What is it?
KROGSTAD. You know, I suppose, that I have got my dismissal.
NORA. I couldn't prevent it, Mr. Krogstad. I fought as hard as I could on your
side, but it was no good.
KROGSTAD. Does your husband love you so little, then? He knows that what I can   265
expose you to, and yet he ventures——
NORA. How can you suppose that he has any knowledge of the sort?
KROGSTAD. I didn't suppose so at all. It would not be the least like our dear Tor-
vald Helmer to show so much courage—
NORA. Mr. Krogstad, a little respect for my husband, please.
KROGSTAD. Certainly—all the respect he deserves. But since you have kept the
matter so carefully to yourself, I make bold to suppose that you have a little clearer
idea, than you had yesterday, of what it actually is that you have done?
NORA. More than you could ever teach me.   270
KROGSTAD. Yes, such a bad lawyer as I am.
NORA. What is it you want of me?
KROGSTAD. Only to see how you were, Mrs. Helmer. I have been thinking about
you all day long. A mere cashier, a quill-driver, a—well, a man like me—even he has
a little of what is called feeling, you know.
NORA. Show it, then; think of my little children.

KROGSTAD. Have you and your husband thought of mine? But never mind about that. I only wanted to tell you that you need not take this matter too seriously. In the first place there will be no accusation made on my part.

NORA. No, of course not; I was sure of that.

KROGSTAD. The whole thing can be arranged amicably; there is no reason why anyone should know anything about it. It will remain a secret between us three.

NORA. My husband must never get to know anything about it.

KROGSTAD. How will you be able to prevent it? Am I to understand that you can pay the balance that is owing?

NORA. No, not just at present.

KROGSTAD. Or perhaps that you have some expedient for raising the money soon?

NORA. No expedient that I mean to make use of.

KROGSTAD. Well, in any case, it would have been of no use to you now. If you stood there with ever so much money in your hand, I would never part with your bond.

NORA. Tell me what purpose you mean to put it to.

KROGSTAD. I shall only preserve it—keep it in my possession. No one who is not concerned in the matter shall have the slightest hint of it. So that if the thought of it has driven you to any desperate resolution——

NORA. It has.

KROGSTAD. If you had it in your mind to run away from your home——

NORA. I had.

KROGSTAD. Or even something worse——

NORA. How could you know that?

KROGSTAD. Give up the idea.

NORA. How did you know I had thought of *that?*

KROGSTAD. Most of us think of that at first. I did, too—but I hadn't the courage.

NORA. [*faintly*] No more had I.

KROGSTAD. [*in a tone of relief*] No, that's it, isn't it—you hadn't the courage either?

NORA. No, I haven't—I haven't.

KROGSTAD. Besides, it would have been a great piece of folly. Once the first storm at home is over—. I have a letter for your husband in my pocket.

NORA. Telling him everything?

KROGSTAD. In as lenient a manner as I possibly could.

NORA. [*quickly*] He mustn't get the letter. Tear it up. I will find some means of getting money.

KROGSTAD. Excuse me, Mrs. Helmer, but I think I told you just now——

NORA. I am not speaking of what I owe you. Tell me what sum you are asking my husband for, and I will get the money.

KROGSTAD. I am not asking your husband for a penny.

NORA. What do you want, then?

KROGSTAD. I will tell you. I want to rehabilitate myself, Mrs. Helmer; I want to get on; and in that your husband must help me. For the last year and a half I have not had a hand in anything dishonourable, and all that time I have been struggling in most restricted circumstances. I was content to work my way up step by step. Now I am turned out, and I am not going to be satisfied with merely being taken into favour again. I want to get on, I tell you. I want to get into the Bank again, in a higher position. Your husband must make a place for me——

NORA. That he will never do!

KROGSTAD. He will; I know him; he dare not protest. And as soon as I am in there again with him, then you will see! Within a year I shall be the manager's right hand. It will be Nils Krogstad and not Torvald Helmer who manages the Bank.

NORA. That's a thing you will never see!

KROGSTAD. Do you mean that you will——?

NORA. I have courage enough for it now.   310

KROGSTAD. Oh, you can't frighten me. A fine, spoilt lady like you——

NORA. You will see, you will see.

KROGSTAD. Under the ice, perhaps? Down into the cold, coal-black water? And then, in the spring, to float up to the surface, all horrible and unrecognisable, with your hair fallen out——

NORA. You can't frighten me.

KROGSTAD. Nor you me. People don't do such things, Mrs. Helmer. Besides,   315
what use would it be? I should have him completely in my power all the same.

NORA. Afterwards? When I am no longer——

KROGSTAD. Have you forgotten that it is I who have the keeping of your reputation? [*Nora stands speechlessly looking at him.*] Well, now, I have warned you. Do not do anything foolish. When Helmer has had my letter, I shall expect a message from him. And be sure you remember that it is your husband himself who has forced me into such ways as this again. I will never forgive him for that. Good-bye, Mrs. Helmer.

[*Exit through the hall*]

NORA. [*goes to the hall door, opens it slightly and listens*] He is going. He is not putting the letter in the box. Oh no, no! that's impossible! [*opens the door by degrees*] What is that? He is standing outside. He is not going downstairs. Is he hesitating? Can he——

[*A letter drops into the box; then* KROGSTAD's *footsteps are heard, till they die away as he goes downstairs.* NORA *utters a stifled cry and runs across the room to the table by the sofa. A short pause.*]

NORA. In the letter-box. [*steals across to the hall door*] There it lies—Torvald, Torvald, there is no hope for us now!

[*MRS. LINDE comes in from the room on the left, carrying the dress.*]

MRS. LINDE. There, I can't see anything more to mend now. Would you like to   320
try it on——?

NORA. [*in a hoarse whisper*] Christine, come here.

MRS. LINDE. [*throwing the dress down on the sofa*] What is the matter with you? You look so agitated!

NORA. Come here. Do you see that letter? There, look—you can see it through the glass in the letter-box.

MRS. LINDE. Yes, I see it.

NORA. That letter is from Krogstad.   325

MRS. LINDE. Nora—it was Krogstad who lent you the money!

NORA. Yes, and now Torvald will know all about it.

MRS. LINDE. Believe me, Nora, that's the best thing for both of you.

NORA. You don't know all. I forged a name.

MRS. LINDE. Good heavens——!

NORA. I only want to say this to you, Christine—you must be my witness.

MRS. LINDE. Your witness? What do you mean? What am I to—?

NORA. If I should go out of my mind—and it might easily happen——

MRS. LINDE. Nora!

NORA. Or if anything else should happen to me—anything, for instance, that might prevent my being here—

MRS. LINDE. Nora! Nora! you are quite out of your mind.

NORA. And if it should happen that there were someone who wanted to take all the responsibility, all the blame, you understand——

MRS. LINDE. Yes, yes—but how can you suppose—?

NORA. Then you must be my witness, that it is not true, Christine. I am not out of my mind at all; I am in my right senses now, and I tell you no one else has known anything about it; I, and I alone, did the whole thing. Remember that.

MRS. LINDE. I will, indeed. But I don't understand all this.

NORA. How should you understand it? A wonderful thing is going to happen.

MRS. LINDE. A wonderful thing?

NORA. Yes, a wonderful thing!—But it is so terrible, Christine; it *mustn't* happen, not for all the world.

MRS. LINDE. I will go at once and see Krogstad.

NORA. Don't go to him; he will do you some harm.

MRS. LINDE. There was a time when he would gladly do anything for my sake.

NORA. He?

MRS. LINDE. Where does he live?

NORA. How should I know—? Yes [*feeling in her pocket*] here is his card. But the letter, the letter——!

HELMER. [*calls from his room, knocking at the door*] Nora!

NORA. [*cries out anxiously*] Oh, what's that? What do you want?

HELMER. Don't be so frightened. We are not coming in; you have locked the door. Are you trying on your dress?

NORA. Yes, that's it. I look so nice, Torvald.

MRS. LINDE. [*who has read the card*] I see he lives at the corner here.

NORA. Yes, but it's no use. It is hopeless. The letter is lying there in the box.

MRS. LINDE. And your husband keeps the key?

NORA. Yes, always.

MRS. LINDE. Krogstad must ask for his letter back unread, he must find some pretence——

NORA. But it is just at this time that Torvald generally——

MRS. LINDE. You must delay him. Go in to him in the meantime. I will come back as soon as I can.

[*She goes out hurriedly through the hall door.*]

NORA. [*goes to* HELMER's *door, opens it and peeps in*] Torvald!

HELMER. [*from the inner room*] Well? May I venture at last to come into my own room again? Come along, Rank, now you will see— [*halting in the doorway*] But what is this?

NORA. What is what, dear?

HELMER. Rank led me to expect a splendid transformation.

RANK. [*in the doorway*] I understood so, but evidently I was mistaken. 365

NORA. Yes, nobody is to have the chance of admiring me in my dress until tomorrow.

HELMER. But, my dear Nora, you look so worn out. Have you been practising too much?

NORA. No, I have not practised at all.

HELMER. But you will need to—

NORA. Yes, indeed I shall, Torvald. But I can't get on a bit without you to help 370
me; I have absolutely forgotten the whole thing.

HELMER. Oh, we will soon work it up again.

NORA. Yes, help me, Torvald. Promise that you will! I am so nervous about it—all the people—. You must give yourself up to me entirely this evening. Not the tiniest bit of business—you mustn't even take a pen in your hand. Will you promise, Torvald dear?

HELMER. I promise. This evening I will be wholly and absolutely at your service, you helpless little mortal. Ah, by the way, first of all I will just——

[*Goes towards the hall door*]

NORA. What are you going to do there?

HELMER. Only see if any letters have come. 375

NORA. No, no! don't do that, Torvald!

HELMER. Why not?

NORA. Torvald, please don't. There is nothing there.

HELMER. Well, let me look. [*Turns to go to the letter-box.* NORA, *at the piano, plays the first bars of the Tarantella.* HELMER *stops in the doorway.*] Aha!

NORA. I can't dance to-morrow if I don't practise with you. 380

HELMER. [*going up to her*] Are you really so afraid of it, dear.

NORA. Yes, so dreadfully afraid of it. Let me practise at once; there is time now, before we go to dinner. Sit down and play for me, Torvald dear; criticise me, and correct me as you play.

HELMER. With great pleasure, if you wish me to.

[*Sits down at the piano.*]

NORA. [*takes out of the box a tambourine and a long variegated shawl. She hastily drapes the shawl round her. Then she springs to the front of the stage and calls out.*] Now play for me! I am going to dance!

[HELMER *plays and* NORA *dances.* RANK *stands by the piano behind* HELMER *and looks on.*]

HELMER. [*as he plays*] Slower, slower! 385

NORA. I can't do it any other way.

HELMER. Not so violently, Nora!

NORA. This is the way.

HELMER. [*stops playing*] No, no—that is not a bit right.

NORA. [*laughing and swinging the tambourine*] Didn't I tell you so? 390

RANK. Let me play for her.

HELMER. [*getting up*] Yes, do. I can correct her better then.

[*RANK sits down at the piano and plays. NORA dances more and more wildly. HELMER has taken up a position beside the stove, and during her dance gives her frequent instructions. She does not seem to hear him; her hair comes down and falls over her shoulders; she pays no attention to it, but goes on dancing. Enter MRS. LINDE.*]

MRS. LINDE. [*standing as if spell-bound in the doorway*] Oh!——

NORA. [*as she dances*] Such fun, Christine!

HELMER. My dear darling Nora, you are dancing as if your life depended on it.   39

NORA. So it does.

HELMER. Stop, Rank; this is sheer madness. Stop, I tell you! [*RANK stops playing, and NORA suddenly stands still. HELMER goes up to her.*] I could never have believed it. You have forgotten everything I taught you.

NORA. [*throwing away the tambourine*] There, you see.

HELMER. You will want a lot of coaching.

NORA. Yes, you see how much I need it. You must coach me up to the last   40
minute. Promise me that, Torvald!

HELMER. You can depend on me.

NORA. You must not think of anything but me, either to-day or to-morrow; you mustn't open a single letter—not even open the letter-box——

HELMER. Ah, you are still afraid of that fellow——

NORA. Yes, indeed I am.

HELMER. Nora, I can tell from your looks that there is a letter from him lying   40
there.

NORA. I don't know; I think there is; but you must not read anything of that kind now. Nothing horrid must come between us till this is all over.

RANK. [*whispers to HELMER*] You mustn't contradict her.

HELMER. [*taking her in his arms*] The child shall have her way. But to-morrow night, after you have danced——

NORA. Then you will be free.

[*MAID appears in the doorway to the right.*]

MAID. Dinner is served, ma'am.   41

NORA. We will have champagne, Helen.

MAID. Very good, ma'am.   [*Exit.*]

HELMER. Hullo!—are we going to have a banquet?

NORA. Yes, a champagne banquet till the small hours. [*calls out*] And a few macaroons, Helen—lots, just for once!

HELMER. Come, come, don't be so wild and nervous. Be my own little skylark,   41
as you used.

NORA. Yes, dear, I will. But go in now and you too, Doctor Rank. Christine, you must help me to do up my hair.

RANK. [*whispers to HELMER as they go out*] I suppose there is nothing—she is not expecting anything?

HELMER. Far from it, my dear fellow; it is simply nothing more than this childish nervousness I was telling you of.

[*They go into the right-hand room.*]

NORA. Well!

MRS. LINDE. Gone out of town.   42

NORA. I could tell from your face.

MRS. LINDE. He is coming home to-morrow evening. I wrote a note for him.

NORA. You should have let it alone; you must prevent nothing. After all, it is splendid to be waiting for a wonderful thing to happen.

MRS. LINDE. What is it that you are waiting for?

NORA. Oh, you wouldn't understand. Go in to them, I will come in a moment.   425

[*MRS. LINDE goes into the dining-room. NORA stands still for a little while, as if to compose herself. Then she looks at her watch.*] Five o'clock. Seven hours till midnight; and then four-and-twenty hours till the next midnight. Then the Tarantella will be over. Twenty-four and seven? Thirty-one hours to live.

HELMER. [*from the doorway on the right*] Where's my little skylark?

NORA. [*going to him with her arms outstretched*] Here she is!

ACT 3

THE SAME SCENE. *The table has been placed in the middle of the stage, with chairs round it. A lamp is burning on the table. The door into the hall stands open. Dance music is heard in the room above. MRS. LINDE is sitting at the table idly turning over the leaves of a book; she tries to read, but does not seem able to collect her thoughts. Every now and then she listens intently for a sound at the outer door.*

MRS. LINDE. [*looking at her watch*] Not yet—and the time is nearly up. If only he does not—. [*listens again*] Ah, there he is. [*Goes into the hall and opens the outer door carefully. Light footsteps are heard on the stairs. She whispers.*] Come in. There is no one here.

KROGSTAD. [*in the doorway*] I found a note from you at home. What does this mean?

MRS. LINDE. It is absolutely necessary that I should have a talk with you.

KROGSTAD. Really? And is it absolutely necessary that it should be here?

MRS. LINDE. It is impossible where I live; there is no private entrance to my   5
rooms. Come in; we are quite alone. The maid is asleep, and the Helmers are at the dance upstairs.

KROGSTAD. [*coming into the room*] Are the Helmers really at a dance to-night?

MRS. LINDE. Yes, why not?

KROGSTAD. Certainly—why not?

MRS. LINDE. Now, Nils, let us have a talk.

KROGSTAD. Can we two have anything to talk about?   10

MRS. LINDE. We have a great deal to talk about.

KROGSTAD. I shouldn't have thought so.

MRS. LINDE. No, you have never properly understood me.

KROGSTAD. Was there anything else to understand except what was obvious to all the world—a heartless woman jilts a man when a more lucrative chance turns up?

MRS. LINDE. Do you believe I am as absolutely heartless as all that? And do you   15
believe that I did it with a light heart?

KROGSTAD. Didn't you?

MRS. LINDE. Nils, did you really think that?

KROGSTAD. If it were as you say, why did you write to me as you did at the time?

MRS. LINDE. I could do nothing else. As I had to break with you, it was my duty also to put an end to all that you felt for me.

KROGSTAD. [*wringing his hands*] So that was it. and all this—only for the sake of money!

MRS. LINDE. You must not forget that I had a helpless mother and two little brothers. We couldn't wait for you, Nils; your prospects seemed hopeless then.

KROGSTAD. That may be so, but you had no right to throw me over for any one else's sake.

MRS. LINDE. Indeed I don't know. Many a time did I ask myself if I had the right to do it.

KROGSTAD. [*more gently*] When I lost you, it was as if all the solid ground went from under my feet. Look at me now—I am a shipwrecked man clinging to a bit of wreckage.

MRS. LINDE. But help may be near.

KROGSTAD. It *was* near; but then you came and stood in my way.

MRS. LINDE. Unintentionally, Nils. It was only to-day that I learnt it was your place I was going to take in the Bank.

KROGSTAD. I believe you, if you say so. But now that you know it, are you not going to give it up to me?

MRS. LINDE. No, because that would not benefit you in the least.

KROGSTAD. Oh, benefit, benefit—I would have done it whether or no.

MRS. LINDE. I have learnt to act prudently. Life, and hard, bitter necessity have taught me that.

KROGSTAD. And life has taught me not to believe in fine speeches.

MRS. LINDE. Then life has taught you something very reasonable. But deeds you must believe in?

KROGSTAD. What do you mean by that?

MRS. LINDE. You said you were like a shipwrecked man clinging to some wreckage.

KROGSTAD. I had good reason to say so.

MRS. LINDE. Well, I am like a shipwrecked woman clinging to some wreckage—no one to mourn for, no one to care for.

KROGSTAD. It was your own choice.

MRS. LINDE. There was no other choice—then.

KROGSTAD. Well, what now?

MRS. LINDE. Nils, how would it be if we two shipwrecked people could join forces?

KROGSTAD. What are you saying?

MRS. LINDE. Two on the same piece of wreckage would stand a better chance than each on their own.

KROGSTAD. Christine!

MRS. LINDE. What do you suppose brought me to town?

KROGSTAD. Do you mean that you gave me a thought?

MRS. LINDE. I could not endure life without work. All my life, as long as I can remember, I have worked, and it has been my greatest and only pleasure. But now I am quite alone in the world—my life is so dreadfully empty and I feel so forsaken. There is not the least pleasure in working for one's self. Nils, give me someone and something to work for.

KROGSTAD. I don't trust that. It is nothing but a woman's overstrained sense of generosity that prompts you to make such an offer of yourself.

MRS. LINDE. Have you ever noticed anything of the sort in me?

KROGSTAD. Could you really do it? Tell me—do you know all about my past life?   50

MRS. LINDE. Yes.

KROGSTAD. And do you know what they think of me here?

MRS. LINDE. You seemed to me to imply that with me you might have been quite another man.

KROGSTAD. I am certain of it.

MRS. LINDE. Is it too late now?   55

KROGSTAD. Christine, are you saying this deliberately? Yes, I am sure you are. I see it in your face. Have you really the courage, then—?

MRS. LINDE. I want to be a mother to someone, and your children need a mother. We two need each other. Nils, I have faith in your real character—I can dare anything together with you.

KROGSTAD. [*grasps her hands*] Thanks, thanks, Christine! Now I shall find a way to clear myself in the eyes of the world. Ah, but I forgot——

MRS. LINDE. [*listening*] Hush! The Tarantella! Go, go!

KROGSTAD. Why? What is it?   60

MRS. LINDE. Do you hear them up there? When that is over, we may expect them back.

KROGSTAD. Yes, yes—I will go. But it is all no use. Of course you are not aware what steps I have taken in the matter of the Helmers.

MRS. LINDE. Yes. I know all about that.

KROGSTAD. And in spite of that have you the courage to—?

MRS. LINDE. I understand very well to what lengths a man like you might be   65
driven by despair.

KROGSTAD. If I could only undo what I have done!

MRS. LINDE. You can. Your letter is lying in the letter-box now.

KROGSTAD. Are you sure of that?

MRS. LINDE. Quite sure, but——

KROGSTAD. [*with a searching look at her*] Is that what it all means?—that you want   70
to save your friend at any cost? Tell me frankly. Is that it?

MRS. LINDE. Nils, a woman who has once sold herself for another's sake, doesn't do it a second time.

KROGSTAD. I will ask for my letter back.

MRS. LINDE. No, no.

KROGSTAD. Yes, of course I will. I will wait here till Helmer comes; I will tell him he must give me my letter back—that it only concerns my dismissal—that he is not to read it——

MRS. LINDE. No, Nils, you must not recall your letter.   75

KROGSTAD. But, tell me, wasn't it for that very purpose that you asked me to meet you here?

MRS. LINDE. In my first moment of fright, it was. But twenty-four hours have elapsed since then, and in that time I have witnessed incredible things in this house. Helmer must know all about it. This unhappy secret must be disclosed; they must have a complete understanding between them, which is impossible with all this concealment and falsehood going on.

KROGSTAD. Very well, if you will take the responsibility. But there is one thing I can do in any case, and I shall do it at once.

MRS. LINDE. [*listening*] You must be quick and go! The dance is over; we are not safe a moment longer.

KROGSTAD. I will wait for you below.

MRS. LINDE. Yes, do. You must see me back to my door.

KROGSTAD. I have never had such an amazing piece of good fortune in my life.

[*Goes out through the outer door. The door between the room and the hall remains open.*]

MRS. LINDE. [*tidying up the room and laying her hat and cloak ready*] What a difference! what a difference! Someone to work for and live for—a home to bring comfort into. That I will do, indeed. I wish they would be quick and come— [*listens*] Ah, there they are now. I must put on my things.

[*Takes up her hat and cloak. HELMER's and NORA's voices are heard outside; a key is turned, and HELMER brings NORA almost by force into the hall. She is in an Italian costume with a large black shawl round her; he is in evening dress and a black domino which is flying open.*]

NORA. [*hanging back in the doorway, and struggling with him*] No, no, no!—don't take me in. I want to go upstairs again; I don't want to leave so early.

HELMER. But, my dearest Nora——

NORA. Please, Torvald dear—please, *please*—only an hour more.

HELMER. Not a single minute, my sweet Nora. You know that was our agreement. Come along into the room; you are catching cold standing there.

[*He brings her gently into the room, in spite of her resistance.*]

MRS. LINDE. Good evening.

NORA. Christine!

HELMER. You here, so late, Mrs. Linde?

MRS. LINDE. Yes, you must excuse me; I was so anxious to see Nora in her dress.

NORA. Have you been sitting here waiting for me?

MRS. LINDE. Yes, unfortunately I came too late, you had already gone upstairs; and I thought I couldn't go away without having seen you.

HELMER. [*taking off NORA's shawl*] Yes, take a good look at her. I think she is worth looking at. Isn't she charming, Mrs. Linde?

MRS. LINDE. Yes, indeed she is.

HELMER. Doesn't she look remarkably pretty? Everyone thought so at the dance. But she is terribly self-willed, this sweet little person. What are we to do with her? You will hardly believe that I had almost to bring her away by force.

NORA. Torvald, you will repent not having let me stay, even if it were only for half an hour.

HELMER. Listen to her, Mrs. Linde! She had danced her Tarantella, and it had been a tremendous success, as it deserved—although possibly the performance was a trifle too realistic—a little more so, I mean, than was strictly compatible with the limitations of art. But never mind about that! The chief thing is, she had made a success—she had made a tremendous success. Do you think I was going to let her remain there after that, and spoil the effect? No indeed! I took my charming little Capri maiden—my capricious little Capri maiden, I should say—on my arm; took one quick turn round the room; a curtsey on either side, and, as they say in novels, the beautiful apparition disappeared. An exit ought always to be effective, Mrs. Linde; but that is what I cannot make Nora understand. Pooh! this room is hot. [*throws his domino on a chair and opens the door of his room*] Hullo! it's all dark in here. Oh, of course—excuse me——.

[*He goes in and lights some candles.*]

NORA. [*in a hurried and breathless whisper*] Well?

MRS. LINDE. [*in a low voice*] I have had a talk with him.   100

NORA. Yes, and——

MRS. LINDE. Nora, you must tell your husband all about it.

NORA. [*in an expressionless voice*] I knew it.

MRS. LINDE. You have nothing to be afraid of as far as Krogstad is concerned; but you must tell him.

NORA. I won't tell him.   105

MRS. LINDE. Then the letter will.

NORA. Thank you, Christine. Now I know what I must do. Hush——!

HELMER. [*coming in again*] Well, Mrs. Linde, have you admired her?

MRS. LINDE. Yes, and now I will say good-night.

HELMER. What already? Is this yours, this knitting?   110

MRS. LINDE. [*taking it*] Yes, thank you, I had very nearly forgotten it.

HELMER. So you knit?

MRS. LINDE. Of course.

HELMER. Do you know, you ought to embroider.

MRS. LINDE. Really? Why?   115

HELMER. Yes, it's far more becoming. Let me show you. You hold the embroidery thus in your left hand, and use the needle with the right—like this—with a long, easy sweep. Do you see?

MRS. LINDE. Yes, perhaps——

HELMER. But in the case of knitting—that can never be anything but ungraceful; look here—the arms close together, the knitting-needles going up and down—it has a sort of Chinese effect—. That was really excellent champagne they gave us.

MRS. LINDE. Well,—good-night, Nora, and don't be self-willed any more.

HELMER. That's right, Mrs. Linde.   120

MRS. LINDE. Good-night, Mr. Helmer.

HELMER. [*accompanying her to the door*] Good-night, good-night. I hope you will get home all right. I should be very happy to—but you haven't any great distance to go. Good-night, good-night. [*She goes out; he shuts the door after her, and comes in again.*] Ah!—at last we have got rid of her. She is a frightful bore, that woman.

NORA. Aren't you very tired, Torvald?

HELMER. No, not in the least.

NORA. Nor sleepy?   125

HELMER. Not a bit. On the contrary, I feel extraordinarily lively. And you?—you really look both tired and sleepy.

NORA. Yes, I am very tired. I want to go to sleep at once.

HELMER. There, you see it was quite right of me not to let you stay there any longer.

NORA. Everything you do is quite right, Torvald.

HELMER. [*kissing her on the forehead*] Now my little skylark is speaking reasonably.   130
Did you notice what good spirits Rank was in this evening?

NORA. Really? Was he? I didn't speak to him at all.

HELMER. And I very little, but I have not for a long time seen him in such good form. [*looks for a while at her and then goes nearer to her*] It is delightful to be at home by ourselves again, to be all alone with you—you fascinating, charming little darling!

NORA. Don't look at me like that, Torvald.

HELMER. Why shouldn't I look at my dearest treasure?—at all the beauty that is mine, all my very own?

NORA. [*going to the other side of the table*] You mustn't say things like that to me to-night.   13⒤

HELMER. [*following her*] You have still got the Tarantella in your blood, I see. And it makes you more captivating than ever. Listen—the guests are beginning to go now. [*in a lower voice*] Nora—soon the whole house will be quiet.

NORA. Yes, I hope so.

HELMER. Yes, my own darling Nora. Do you know, when I am out at a party with you like this, why I speak so little to you, keep away from you, and only send a stolen glance in your direction now and then?—do you know why I do that? It is because I make believe to myself that we are secretly in love, and you are my secretly promised bride, and that no one suspects there is anything between us.

NORA. Yes, yes—I know very well your thoughts are with me all the time.

HELMER. And when we are leaving, and I am putting the shawl over your beau-   14⒪ tiful young shoulders—on your lovely neck—then I imaging that you are my young bride and that we have just come from the wedding, and I am bringing you for the first time into our home—to be alone with you for the first time—quite alone with my shy little darling! All this evening I have longed for nothing but you. When I watched the seductive figures of the Tarantella, my blood was on fire; I could endure it no longer, and that was why I brought you down so early——

NORA. Go away, Torvald! You must let me go. I won't——

HELMER. What's that? You're joking, my little Nora! You won't—you won't? Am I not your husband—?

[*A knock is heard at the outer door.*]

NORA. [*starting*] Did you hear——?

HELMER. [*going into the hall*] Who is it?

RANK. [*outside*] It is I. May I come in for a moment?   14⒮

HELMER. [*in a fretful whisper*] Oh, what does he want now? [*aloud*] Wait a minute! [*unlocks the door*] Come, that's kind of you not to pass by our door.

RANK. I thought I heard your voice, and felt as if I should like to look in. [*with a swift glance round*] Ah, yes!—these dear familiar rooms. You are very happy and cosy in here, you two.

HELMER. It seems to me that you looked after yourself pretty well upstairs too.

RANK. Excellently. Why shouldn't I? Why shouldn't one enjoy everything in this world?—at any rate as much as one can, and as long as one can. The wine was capital——

HELMER. Especially the champagne.   15⒪

RANK. So you noticed that too? It is almost incredible how much I managed to put away!

NORA. Torvald drank a great deal of champagne tonight, too.

RANK. Did he?

NORA. Yes, and he is always in such good spirits afterwards.

RANK. Well, why should one not enjoy a merry evening after a well-spent day?   15⒮

HELMER. Well spent? I am afraid I can't take credit for that.

RANK. [*clapping him on the back*] But I can, you know!

NORA. Doctor Rank, you must have been occupied with some scientific investigation to-day.

RANK. Exactly.

HELMER. Just listen!—little Nora talking about scientific investigations!   160

NORA. And may I congratulate you on the result?

RANK. Indeed you may.

NORA. Was it favourable, then?

RANK. The best possible, for both doctor and patient—certainty.

NORA. [*quickly and searchingly*] Certainty?   165

RANK. Absolute certainty. So wasn't I entitled to make a merry evening of it after that?

NORA. Yes, you certainly were, Doctor Rank.

HELMER. I think so too, so long as you don't have to pay for it in the morning.

RANK. Oh well, one can't have anything in this life without paying for it.

NORA. Doctor Rank—are you fond of fancy-dress balls?   170

RANK. Yes, if there is a fine lot of pretty costumes.

NORA. Tell me—what shall we two wear at the next?

HELMER. Little featherbrain!—are you thinking of the next already?

RANK. We two? Yes, I can tell you. You shall go as a good fairy——

HELMER. Yes, but what do you suggest as an appropriate costume for that?   175

RANK. Let your wife go dressed just as she is in everyday life.

HELMER. That was really very prettily turned. But can't you tell us what you will be?

RANK. Yes, my dear friend, I have quite made up my mind about that.

HELMER. Well?

RANK. At the next fancy dress ball I shall be invisible.   180

HELMER. That's a good joke!

RANK. There is a big black hat—have you never heard of hats that make you invisible? If you put one on, no one can see you.

HELMER. [*suppressing a smile*] Yes, you are quite right.

RANK. But I am clean forgetting what I came for. Helmer, give me a cigar—one of the dark Havanas.

HELMER. With the greatest pleasure. [*offers him his case*]   185

RANK. [*takes a cigar and cuts off the end*] Thanks.

NORA. [*striking a match*] Let me give you a light.

RANK. Thank you. [*She holds the match for him to light his cigar.*] And now good-bye!

HELMER. Good-bye, good-bye, dear old man!

NORA. Sleep well, Doctor Rank.   190

RANK. Thank you for that wish.

NORA. Wish me the same.

RANK. You? Well, if you want me to sleep well! And thanks for the light.

[*He nods to them both and goes out.*]

HELMER. [*in a subdued voice*] He has drunk more than he ought.

NORA. [*absently*] Maybe. [*HELMER takes a bunch of keys out of his pocket and goes into*   195
the hall.] Torvald! what are you going to do there?

HELMER. Empty the letter-box; it is quite full; there will be no room to put the newspaper in to-morrow morning.

NORA. Are you going to work to-night?

HELMER. You know quite well I'm not. What is this? Some one has been at the lock.

NORA. At the lock—?

HELMER. Yes, someone has. What can it mean? I should never have thought the maid—. Here is a broken hairpin. Nora, it is one of yours.

NORA. [*quickly*] Then it must have been the children—

HELMER. Then you must get them out of those ways. There, at last I have got it open. [*Takes out the contents of the letter-box, and calls to the kitchen.*] Helen!— Helen, put out the light over the front door. [*Goes back into the room and shuts the door into the hall. He holds out his hand full of letters.*] Look at that—look what a heap of them there are. [*turning them over*] What on earth is that?

NORA. [*at the window*] The letter—No! Torvald, no!

HELMER. Two cards—of Rank's.

NORA. Of Doctor Rank's?

HELMER. [*looking at them*] Doctor Rank. They were on the top. He must have put them in when he went out.

NORA. Is there anything written on them?

HELMER. There is a black cross over the name. Look there—what an uncomfortable idea! It looks as if he were announcing his own death.

NORA. It is just what he is doing.

HELMER. What? Do you know anything about it? Has he said anything to you?

NORA. Yes. He told me that when the cards came it would be his leave-taking from us. He means to shut himself up and die.

HELMER. My poor old friend. Certainly I knew we should not have him very long with us. But so soon! And so he hides himself away like a wounded animal.

NORA. If it has to happen, it is best it should be without a word—don't you think so, Torvald?

HELMER. [*walking up and down*] He had so grown into our lives. I can't think of him as having gone out of them. He, with his sufferings and his loneliness, was like a cloudy background to our sunlit happiness. Well, perhaps it is best so. For him, anyway. [*standing still*] And perhaps for us too, Nora. We two are thrown quite upon each other now. [*puts his arms round her*] My darling wife, I don't feel as if I could hold you tight enough. Do you know, Nora, I have often wished that you might be threatened by some great danger, so that I might risk my life's blood, and everything, for your sake.

NORA. [*disengages herself, and says firmly and decidedly*] Now you must read your letters, Torvald.

HELMER. No, no; not to-night. I want to be with you, my darling wife.

NORA. With the thought of your friend's death——

HELMER. You are right, it has affected us both. Something ugly has come between us—the thought of the horrors of death. We must try and rid our minds of that. Until then—we will each go to our own room.

NORA. [*hanging on his neck*] Good-night, Torvald—Good-night!

HELMER. [*kissing her on the forehead*]. Good-night, my little singing-bird. Sleep sound, Nora. Now I will read my letters through.

[*He takes his letters and goes into his room, shutting the door after him.*]

NORA. [*gropes distractedly about, seizes* HELMER's *domino, throws it round her, while she says in quick, hoarse, spasmodic whispers*] Never to see him again. Never! Never! [*puts her shawl over her head*] Never to see my children again either—never again. Never! Never!—Ah! the icy, black water—the unfathomable depths—If only it were over! He has got it now—now he is reading it. Good-by, Torvald and my children!

[*She is about to rush out through the hall, when* HELMER *opens his door hurriedly and stands with an open letter in his hand.*]

HELMER. Nora!

NORA. Ah!——

HELMER. What is this? Do you know what is in this letter?

NORA. Yes, I know. Let me go! Let me get out!   225

HELMER. [*holding her back*] Where are you going?

NORA. [*trying to get free*] You shan't save me, Torvald!

HELMER. [*reeling*] True? Is this true, that I read here? Horrible! No, no—it is impossible that it can be true.

NORA. It is true. I have loved you above everything else in the world.

HELMER. Oh, don't let us have any silly excuses.   230

NORA. [*taking a step towards him*] Torvald——!

HELMER. Miserable creature—what have you done?

NORA. Let me go. You shall not suffer for my sake. You shall not take it upon yourself.

HELMER. No tragedy airs, please. [*locks the hall door*] Here you shall stay and give me an explanation. Do you understand what you have done? Answer me? Do you understand what you have done?

NORA. [*looks steadily at him and says with a growing look of coldness in her face*] Yes,   235
now I am beginning to understand thoroughly.

HELMER. [*walking about the room*] What a horrible awakening! All these eight years—she who was my joy and pride—a hypocrite, a liar—worse, worse—a criminal! The unutterable ugliness of it all! For shame! For shame! [NORA *is silent and looks steadily at him. He stops in front of her.*] I ought to have suspected that something of the sort would happen. I ought to have foreseen it. All your father's want of principle—be silent!—all your father's want of principle has come out in you. No religion, no morality, no sense of duty—. How I am punished for having winked at what he did! I did it for your sake, and this is how you repay me.

NORA. Yes, that's just it.

HELMER. Now you have destroyed all my happiness. You have ruined all my future. It is horrible to think of! I am in the power of an unscrupulous man; he can do what he likes with me, ask anything he likes of me, give me any orders he pleases—I dare not refuse. And I must sink to such miserable depths because of a thoughtless woman!

NORA. When I am out of the way, you will be free.

HELMER. No fine speeches, please. Your father had always plenty of those ready,   240
too. What good would it be to me if you were out of the way, as you say? Not the slightest. He can make the affair known everywhere; and if he does, I may be falsely suspected of having been a party to your criminal action. Very likely people will think I was behind it all—that it was I who prompted you! And I have to thank you for all this—you whom I have cherished during the whole of our married life. Do you understand now what it is you have done for me?

NORA. [*coldly and quietly*] Yes.

HELMER. It is so incredible that I can't take it in. But we must come to some understanding. Take off that shawl. Take it off, I tell you. I must try and appease him some way or another. The matter must be hushed up at any cost. And as for you and me, it must appear as if everything between us were just as before—but naturally only in the eyes of the world. You will still remain in my house, that is a matter of course. But I shall not allow you to bring up the children; I dare not trust them to you. To think that I should be obliged to say so to one whom I have loved so dearly, and whom I still——. No, that is all over. From this moment happiness is not the question; all that concerns us is to save the remains, the fragments, the appearance——

[*A ring is heard at the front-door bell.*]

HELMER. [*with a start*] What is that? So late! Can the worst——? Can he ——? Hide yourself, Nora. Say you are ill.

[*NORA stands motionless. HELMER goes and unlocks the hall door.*]

MAID. [*half-dressed, comes to the door*] A letter for the mistress.

HELMER. Give it to me. [*takes the letter, and shuts the door*] Yes, it is from him. You   245
shall not have it; I will read it myself.

NORA. Yes, read it.

HELMER. [*standing by the lamp*] I scarcely have the courage to do it. It may mean ruin for both of us. No, I must know. [*tears open the letter, runs his eye over a few lines, looks at a paper enclosed and gives a shout of joy*] Nora! [*She looks at him questioningly.*] Nora!—No, I must read it once again——. Yes, it is true! I am saved! Nora, I am saved!

NORA. And I?

HELMER. You too, of course; we are both saved, both you and I. Look, he sends you your bond back. He says he regrets and repents—that a happy change in his life—never mind what he says! We are saved, Nora! No one can do anything to you. Oh, Nora, Nora!—no, first I must destroy these hateful things. Let me see—. [*takes a look at the bond*] No, no, I won't look at it. The whole thing shall be nothing but a bad dream to me. [*tears up the bond and both letters, throws them all into the stove, and watches them burn*] There—now it doesn't exist any longer. He says that since Christmas Eve you——. These must have been three dreadful days for you, Nora.

NORA. I have fought a hard fight these three days.   250

HELMER. And suffered agonies, and seen no way out but——. No, we won't call any of the horrors to mind. We will only shout with joy, and keep saying "It's all over! It's all over!" Listen to me, Nora. You don't seem to realise that it is all over. What is this?—such a cold, set face! My poor little Nora, I quite understand; you don't feel as if you could believe that I have forgiven you. But it is true, Nora, I swear it; I have forgiven you everything. I know that what you did, you did out of love for me.

NORA. That is true.

HELMER. You have loved me as a wife ought to love her husband. Only you had not sufficient knowledge to judge of the means you used. But do you suppose you are any the less dear to me, because you don't understand how to act on your own responsibility? No, no; only lean on me; I will advise you and direct you. I should not be a man if this womanly helplessness did not just give you a double attractiveness in my eyes. You must not think any more about the hard things I said in my first moment of consternation, when I thought everything was going to overwhelm me. I have forgiven you, Nora; I swear to you I have forgiven you.

NORA. Thank you for your forgiveness.

[*She goes out through the door to the right.*]

HELMER. No, don't go——. [*looks in*] What are you doing in there? 255

NORA. [*from within*] Taking off my fancy dress.

HELMER. [*standing at the open door*] Yes, do. Try and calm yourself, and make your mind easy again, my frightened little singing-bird. Be at rest, and feel secure; I have broad wings to shelter you under. [*walks up and down by the door*] How warm and cosy our home is, Nora. Here is shelter for you; here I will protect you like a hunted dove that I have saved from a hawk's claws. I will bring peace to your poor beating heart. It will come, little by little, Nora, believe me. Tomorrow morning you will look upon it all quite differently; soon everything will be just as it was before. Very soon you won't need me to assure you that I have forgiven you; you will yourself feel the certainty that I have done so. Can you suppose I should ever think of such a thing as repudiating you, or even reproaching you? You have no idea what a true man's heart is like, Nora. There is something so indescribably sweet and satisfying, to a man, in the knowledge that he has forgiven his wife—forgiven her freely, and with all his heart. It seems as if that had made her, as it were, doubly his own; he has given her a new life, so to speak; and she has in a way become both wife and child to him. So you shall be for me after this, my little scared, helpless darling. Have no anxiety about anything, Nora; only be frank and open with me, and I will serve as will and conscience both to you——. What is this? Not gone to bed? Have you changed your things?

NORA. [*in everyday dress*] Yes, Torvald, I have changed my things now.

HELMER. But what for?—so late as this.

NORA. I shall not sleep to-night. 260

HELMER. But, my dear Nora——

NORA. [*looking at her watch*] It is not so very late. Sit down here, Torvald. You and I have much to say to one another.

[*She sits down at one side of the table.*]

HELMER. Nora—what is this?—this cold, set face?

NORA. Sit down. it will take some time; I have a lot to talk over with you.

HELMER. [*sits down at the opposite side of the table*] You alarm me, Nora!—and I 265 don't understand you.

NORA. No, that is just it. You don't understand me, and I have never understood you either—before to-night. No, you mustn't interrupt me. You must simply listen to what I say. Torvald, this is a settling of accounts.

HELMER. What do you mean by that?

NORA. [*after a short silence*] Isn't there one thing that strikes you as strange in our sitting here like this?

HELMER. What is that?

NORA. We have been married now eight years. Does it not occur to you that this 270 is the first time we two, you and I, husband and wife, have had a serious conversation?

HELMER. What do you mean by serious?

NORA. In all these eight years—longer than that—from the very beginning of our acquaintance, we have never exchanged a word on any serious subject.

HELMER. Was it likely that I would be continually and for ever telling you about worries that you could not help me to bear?

NORA. I am not speaking about business matters. I say that we have never sat down in earnest together to try and get at the bottom of anything.

HELMER. But, dearest Nora, would it have been any good to you?   2:

NORA. That is just it; you have never understood me. I have been greatly wronged, Torvald—first by papa and then by you.

HELMER. What! By us two—by us two, who have loved you better than anyone else in the world?

NORA. [*shaking her head*] You have never loved me. You have only thought it pleasant to be in love with me.

HELMER. Nora, what do I hear you saying?

NORA. It is perfectly true, Torvald. When I was at home with papa, he told me   28 his opinion about everything, and so I had the same opinions; and if I differed from him I concealed the fact, because he would not have liked it. He called me his doll-child, and he played with me just as I used to play with my dolls. And when I came to live with you——

HELMER. What sort of an expression is that to use about our marriage?

NORA. [*undisturbed*] I mean that I was simply transferred from papa's hands into yours. You arranged everything according to your own taste, and so I got the same tastes as you—or else I pretended to, I am really not quite sure which—I think sometimes the one and sometimes the other. When I look back on it, it seems to me as if I had been living here like a poor woman—just from hand to mouth. I have existed merely to perform tricks for you, Torvald. But you would have it so. You and papa have committed a great sin against me. It is your fault that I have made nothing of my life.

HELMER. How unreasonable and how ungrateful you are, Nora! Have you not been happy here?

NORA. No, I have never been happy. I thought I was, but it has never really been so.

HELMER. Not—not happy!   28

NORA. No, only merry. And you have always been so kind to me. But our home has been nothing but a playroom. I have been your doll-wife, just as at home I was papa's doll-child; and here the children have been my dolls. I thought it great fun when you played with me, just as they thought it great fun when I played with them. That is what our marriage has been, Torvald.

HELMER. There is some truth in what you say—exaggerated and strained as your view of it is. But for the future it shall be different. Playtime shall be over, and lesson-time shall begin.

NORA. Whose lessons? Mine, or the children's?

HELMER. Both yours and the children's, my darling Nora.

NORA. Alas, Torvald, you are not the man to educate me into being a proper   29• wife for you.

HELMER. And you can say that!

NORA. And I—how am I fitted to bring up the children?

HELMER. Nora!

NORA. Didn't you say so yourself a little while ago—that you dare not trust me to bring them up?

HELMER. In a moment of anger! Why do you pay any heed to that?   29:

NORA. Indeed, you were perfectly right. I am not fit for the task. There is another task I must undertake first. I must try and educate myself—you are not the man to help me in that. I must do that for myself. And that is why I am going to leave you now.

HELMER. [*springing up*] What do you say?

NORA. I must stand quite alone, if I am to understand myself and everything about me. It is for that reason that I cannot remain with you any longer.

HELMER. Nora! Nora!

NORA. I am going away from here now, at once. I am sure Christine will take   300
me in for the night——

HELMER. You are out of your mind! I won't allow it! I forbid you!

NORA. It is no use forbidding me anything any longer. I will take with me what belongs to myself. I will take nothing from you, either now or later.

HELMER. What sort of madness is this!

NORA. To-morrow I shall go home—I mean, to my old home. It will be easiest for me to find something to do there.

HELMER. You blind, foolish woman!   305

NORA. I must try and get some sense, Torvald.

HELMER. To desert your home, your husband and your children! And you don't consider what people will say!

NORA. I cannot consider that at all. I only know that it is necessary for me.

HELMER. It's shocking. This is how you would neglect your most sacred duties.

NORA. What do you consider my most sacred duties?   310

HELMER. Do I need to tell you that? Are they not your duties to your husband and your children?

NORA. I have other duties just as sacred.

HELMER. That you have not. What duties could those be?

NORA. Duties to myself.

HELMER. Before all else, you are a wife and a mother.   315

NORA. I don't believe that any longer. I believe that before all else I am a reasonable human being, just as you are—or, at all events, that I must try and become one. I know quite well, Torvald, that most people would think you right, and that views of that kind are to be found in books; but I can no longer content myself with what most people say, or with what is found in books. I must think over things for myself and get to understand them.

HELMER. Can you not understand your place in your own home? Have you not a reliable guide in such matters as that?—have you no religion?

NORA. I am afraid, Torvald, I do not exactly know what religion is.

HELMER. What are you saying?

NORA. I know nothing but what the clergyman said when I went to be con-   320
firmed. He told us that religion was this, and that, and the other. When I am away from all this, and am alone, I will look into that matter too. I will see if what the clergyman said is true, or at all events if it is true for me.

HELMER. This is unheard of in a girl of your age! But if religion cannot lead you aright, let me try and awaken your conscience. I suppose you have some moral sense? Or—answer me—am I to think you have none?

NORA. I assure you, Torvald, that is not an easy question to answer. I really don't know. The thing perplexes me altogether. I only know that you and I look at it in quite a different light. I am learning, too, that the law is quite another thing from what I supposed; but I find it impossible to convince myself that the law is right. According to it a woman has no right to spare her old dying father, or to save her husband's life. I can't believe that.

HELMER. You talk like a child. You don't understand the conditions of the world in which you live.

NORA. No, I don't. But now I am going to try. I am going to see if I can make out who is right, the world or I.

HELMER. You are ill, Nora; you are delirious; I almost think you are out of your mind. 325

NORA. I have never felt my mind so clear and certain as to-night.

HELMER. And is it with a clear and certain mind that you forsake your husband and your children?

NORA. Yes, it is.

HELMER. Then there is only one possible explanation.

NORA. What is that? 330

HELMER. You do not love me any more.

NORA. No, that is just it.

HELMER. Nora!—and you can say that?

NORA. It gives me great pain, Torvald, for you have always been so kind to me, but I cannot help it. I do not love you any more.

HELMER. [*regaining his composure*] Is that a clear and certain conviction too? 335

NORA. Yes, absolutely clear and certain. That is the reason why I will not stay here any longer.

HELMER. And can you tell me what I have done to forfeit your love?

NORA. Yes, indeed I can. It was to-night, when the wonderful thing did not happen; then I saw you were not the man I had thought you.

HELMER. Explain yourself better—I don't understand you.

NORA. I have waited so patiently for eight years; for, goodness knows, I knew 340 very well that wonderful things don't happen every day. Then this horrible misfortune came upon me; and then I felt quite certain that the wonderful thing was going to happen at last. When Krogstad's letter was lying out there, never for a moment did I imagine that you would consent to accept this man's conditions. I was so absolutely certain that you would say to him: Publish the thing to the whole world. And when that was done——

HELMER. Yes, what then?—when I had exposed my wife to shame and disgrace?

NORA. When that was done, I was so absolutely certain, you would come forward and take everything upon yourself, and say: I am the guilty one.

HELMER. Nora——!

NORA. You mean that I would never have accepted such a sacrifice on your part? No, of course not. But what would my assurances have been worth against yours? That was the wonderful thing which I hoped for and feared; and it was to prevent that, that I wanted to kill myself.

HELMER. I would gladly work night and day for you, Nora—bear sorrow and 345 want for your sake. But no man would sacrifice his honour for the one he loves.

NORA. It is a thing hundreds of thousands of women have done.

HELMER. Oh, you think and talk like a heedless child.

NORA. Maybe. But you neither think nor talk like the man I could bind myself to. As soon as your fear was over—and it was not fear for what threatened me, but for what might happen to you—when the whole thing was past, as far as you were concerned it was exactly as if nothing at all had happened. Exactly as before, I was your little skylark, your doll, which you would in future treat with doubly gentle care, because it was so brittle and fragile. [*getting up*] Torvald—it was then it dawned upon me that for eight years I had been living here with a strange man, and had borne him three children——. Oh, I can't bear to think of it! I could tear myself into little bits!

HELMER. [*sadly*] I see, I see. An Abyss has opened between us—there is no denying it. But, Nora, would it not be possible to fill it up?

NORA. As I am now, I am no wife for you.   350

HELMER. I have it in me to become a different man.

NORA. Perhaps—if your doll is taken away from you.

HELMER. But to part!—to part from you! No, no, Nora, I can't understand that idea.

NORA. [*going out to the right*] That makes it all the more certain that it must be done.

[*She comes back with her cloak and hat and a small bag which she puts on a chair by the table.*]

HELMER. Nora, Nora, not now! Wait till to-morrow.   355

NORA. [*putting on her cloak*] I cannot spend the night in a strange man's room.

HELMER. But can't we live here like brother and sister——?

NORA. [*putting on her hat*] You know very well that would not last long. [*puts the shawl round her*] Good-bye, Torvald. I won't see the little ones. I know they are in better hands than mine. As I am now, I can be of no use to them.

HELMER. But some day, Nora—some day?

NORA. How can I tell? I have no idea what is going to become of me.   360

HELMER. But you are my wife, whatever becomes of you.

NORA. Listen, Torvald. I have heard that when a wife deserts her husband's house, as I am doing ow, he is legally freed from all obligations towards her. In any case I set you free from all your obligations. You are not to feel yourself bound in the slightest way, any more than I shall. There must be perfect freedom on both sides. See here is your ring back. Give me mine.

HELMER. That too?

NORA. That too.

HELMER. Here it is.   365

NORA. That's right. Now it is all over. I have put the keys here. The maids know all about everything in the house—better than I do. To-morrow, after I have left her, Christine will come here and pack up my own things that I brought with me from home. I will have them sent after me.

HELMER. All over! All over!—Nora, shall you never think of me again?

NORA. I know I shall often think of you and the children and this house.

HELMER. May I write to you, Nora?

NORA. No—never. You must not do that.   370

HELMER. But at least let me send you——

NORA. Nothing—nothing——

HELMER. Let me help you if you are in want.

NORA. No. I can receive nothing from a stranger.

HELMER. Nora—can I never be anything more than a stranger to you?   375

NORA. [*taking her bag*] Ah, Torvald, the most wonderful thing of all would have to happen.

HELMER. Tell me what that would be!

NORA. Both you and I would have to be so changed that——. Oh, Torvald, I don't believe any longer in wonderful things happening.

HELMER. But I will believe in it. Tell me? So changed that——?

NORA. That our life together would be a real wedlock. Good-bye.

380

[*She goes out through the hall.*]

HELMER. [*sinks down on a chair at the door and buries his face in his hands*] Nora! Nora! [*looks round, and rises*] Empty. She is gone. [*A hope flashes across his mind.*] The most wonderful thing of all——?

[*The sound of a door slamming is heard from below.*]

QUESTIONS

Act I

1. What does the opening stage direction reveal about the Helmer family? About the time of year?

2. Explain the ways Nora and Torvald behave toward each other.

3. What does Torvald's refusal to consider borrowing and debt tell you about him (speech 22)? Where else in the play are these characteristics important?

4. What have the Helmer finances been like in the past? How is their situation about to change?

5. How are Mrs. Linde and Nora alike? Different? Why is it ironic that Nora helps Christine get a job at the bank? How will this affect Krogstad? Nora?

6. How does Ibsen show that Krogstad is a threat when he first appears?

7. Why should Nora's scene with her children in Act I not be cut in production? What does it show about Nora and the household?

8. What is Nora's secret "crime"? What is the explanation and justification for it? At the end of the act, what new problems does she face?

Act II

9. What is symbolized by the stripped Christmas tree?

10. What is implied about Nora's self perceptions when she calls herself "your little squirrel" and "your skylark"?

11. After sending Krogstad's dismissal, Torvald tells Nora that "You will see I am man enough to take everything upon myself" (speech 135). How does this speech conform to Nora's hopes? How is it ironic?

12. Why does Nora flirt with Dr. Rank? How and why does he distress her?

13. Why does Nora dance the Tarantella so wildly?

14. What is the "wonderful thing" that Nora is waiting for?

Act III

15. Explain Christine's past rejection of Krogstad. Why will she accept him now? How will their union differ from the Helmers' marriage?
16. What does Christine decide to do about Krogstad's letter? Why?
17. Explain the reactions of Torvald and Nora to the death of Dr. Rank.
18. Describe Torvald's reaction to Krogstad's first letter. How does Nora respond to Torvald? How do you respond to him? Why?
19. Explain what Nora learns about Torvald, herself, her marriage, and her identity as a woman as a result of Torvald's responses. Why does she decide to leave?

GENERAL QUESTIONS

1. Which elements and aspects of *A Doll House* are most and least realistic? Explain.

2. Consider Ibsen's symbolism, with reference to Dr. Rank, macaroons, the Christmas tree, the presents, the locked mailbox, the dance, Nora's black shawl, her change of clothing in Act III, and the door slam at the play's close.

3. Is Nora a victim of circumstances or a villain who brings about problems? What is Ibsen's view? What is yours? Why?

4. Describe the "role-playing" in the Helmer marriage? Does any evidence suggest that Nora knows she is playing a role? What degree of self-awareness, if any, characterizes Torvald's role-playing?

5. When Nora asks Torvald to restore Krogstad's job, Torvald refuses on the ground that he should not give in to his wife's pressure (Act II. speech 113). Later, he claims that their marriage is destroyed, but that they should keep up the appearance of marital stability (Act III. speech 242). In the light of such statements, describe Torvald's character. What concerns him most about life and marriage?

6. A major theme in the play is that weakness and corruption are passed from generation to generation. Examine this theme in connection with Krogstad and his sons, Nora and her children, Nora and her father, and Dr. Rank.

7. Discuss the ideas about individual growth, marriage, and social convention in the play. How are these ideas developed and related? Which character most closely embodies Ibsen's ideas?

8. Write an essay about any or all of the following questions:

    a. Is *A Doll House* a comedy, a tragedy, or something in between?
    b. How do the play's characters change for the better (or worse)?
    c. How negative, or affirmative, is the conclusion? Why?

TENNESSEE WILLIAMS, *THE GLASS MENAGERIE*

Tennessee Williams (1911-1983) grew up in Mississippi and Missouri, and many of his plays reflect the attitudes and customs that he encountered in his early years. Until he was eight, his family lived in genteel poverty, mostly in Columbus, Mississippi. In 1919 the family moved to a lower-class neighborhood in St. Louis. Williams, who was sickly and bookish, tried to escape from poverty and family conflicts by writing and going to the movies. One of his few companions during those years was his shy and withdrawn sister, Rose.

He began college at the University of Missouri in 1931, but the Depression and family poverty forced him to drop out and go to work in a shoe warehouse. After two years of this work, he suffered a nervous collapse, but finally finished college at the University of Iowa. He then began wandering the country, doing odd jobs, but also writing. His first full-length play, *Battle of Angels*, was produced in 1940 but was unsuccessful. He continued to write, however, and was able to get *The Glass Menagerie* staged in 1945. The critical and popular success of this play was the beginning of many good years in the theater. Along with Arthur Miller, during the 1940s and 1950s he dominated the American stage, going on to write many one-act plays and over fifteen full-length dramas (many of which became successful films), including *A Streetcar Named Desire* (1947, Pulitzer Prize), *The Rose Tattoo* (1951), *Cat on a Hot Tin Roof* (1955, Pulitzer Prize), *Suddenly Last Summer* (1958), and *The Night of the Iguana* (1961).

The Glass Menagerie, written in 1944 and produced to rave reviews in Chicago and New York in 1945, is a highly autobiographical play which explores the family dynamics, delusions, and personalities of the Wingfields. Williams originally developed his ideas for the play in a short story called "Portrait of a Girl in Glass" and then in a screenplay for Metro-Goldwyn-Mayer entitled "The Gentleman Caller." In these, and in *The Glass Menagerie*, Laura Wingfield is modeled after his sister, Rose Williams. The least competent member of the family, she is crippled by her own insecurity and her mother's expectations. At every opportunity, Laura withdraws into a world of glass figurines and old phonograph records left by her father when he abandoned the family. Amanda Wingfield is patterned after Williams's mother. She valiantly tries to hold the family together and provide for Laura's future, but her perspectives are skewed by her romanticized memories of a gracious southern past of plantations, formal dances, and "gentleman callers." Tom, a figure based on the playwright himself, is desperate to escape the trap of his impoverished family. He seeks to emulate the long-missing father and move out of the drab Wingfield apartment into adventure and experience.

The play offers a fascinating mixture of realistic and nonrealistic dramatic techniques. The realistic elements are the characters (excluding Tom when he narrates) and the language. This is especially true of Amanda's language, in which Williams skillfully recreates the diction and cadences characteristic of speakers from Mississippi. As he points out in his production notes and stage directions, the play's structure and staging are nonrealistic. Williams employs various devices nonrealistically, including the narrator, music, lighting, and screen projections, to underscore the emotions of his characters and to explore ideas about family and personality.

One of Williams's most effective nonrealistic techniques in *The Glass Menagerie* is its structure as "a memory play," and therefore its illustration of how a first-person narrator may be used in a drama. The characters and the action are neither real nor in the present. Rather, they represent Tom's memories and feelings about events that occurred approximately five years earlier, when America was in the grips of the Great Depression, when the Spanish Civil War had established fascism in Spain, and when World War II was beginning in Europe. As the narrator, Tom exists at the time of the action (1944), but the events he introduces are occurring in about 1939. When Tom becomes a character in the Wingfield household, he is the Tom of this earlier period, quite distinct from his identity as the present narrator. Thus, the action in the apartment is not strictly a realistic recreation of life. Instead, even though the actions and characters seem realistic, they are exaggerated and reshaped as Tom remembers them and regrets them.

TENNESSEE WILLIAMS (1911–1983)

The Glass Menagerie —————————————— *1945*

THE CHARACTERS

Amanda Wingfield (*the mother*)
A little woman of great but confused vitality clinging frantically to another time and place. Her characterization must be carefully created, not copied from type. She is not paranoiac, but her life is paranoia. There is much to admire in Amanda, and as much to love and pity as there is to laugh at. Certainly she has endurance and a kind of heroism, and though her foolishness makes her unwittingly cruel at times, there is tenderness in her slight person.

Laura Wingfield (*her daughter*)
Amanda, having failed to establish contact with reality, continues to live vitally in her illusions, but Laura's situation is even graver. A childhood illness has left her crippled, one leg slightly shorter than the other, and held in a brace. This defect need not be more than suggested on the stage. Stemming from this, Laura's separation increases till she is like a piece of her own glass collection, too exquisitely fragile to move from the shelf.

Tom Wingfield (*her son*)
And the narrator of the play. A poet with a job in a warehouse. His nature is not remorseless, but to escape from a trap he has to act without pity.

Jim O'Connor (*the gentleman caller*)
A nice, ordinary, young man.

PRODUCTION NOTES

Being a "memory play," *The Glass Menagerie* can be presented with unusual freedom of convention. Because of its considerably delicate or tenuous material, atmospheric touches and subtleties of direction play a particularly important part. Expressionism and all other unconventional techniques in drama have only one valid aim, and that is a closer approach to truth. When a play employs unconventional techniques, it is not, or certainly shouldn't be, trying to escape its responsibility of dealing with reality, or interpreting experience, but is actually or should be attempting to find a closer approach, a more penetrating and vivid expression of things as they are. The straight realistic play with its genuine Frigidaire and authentic ice-cubes, its characters who speak exactly as its audience speaks, corresponds to the academic landscape and has the same virtue of a photographic likeness. Everyone should know nowadays the unimportance of the photographic in art: that truth, life, or reality is an organic thing which the poetic imagination can represent or suggest, in essence, only through transformation, through changing into other forms than those which were merely present in appearance.

These remarks are not meant as a preface only to this particular play. They have to do with a conception of a new, plastic theatre which must take the place of the exhausted theatre of realistic conventions if the theatre is to resume vitality as a part of our culture.

THE SCREEN DEVICE: There is *only one important difference between the original and the acting version of the play* and that is the *omission* in the latter of the device that I tentatively included in my *original* script. This device was the use of a screen on which were projected magic-lantern slides bearing images or titles. I do not regret the omission of this device from the original Broadway production. The extraordinary power of Miss Taylor's° performance made it suitable to have the utmost simplicity in the physical production. But I think it may be interesting to some readers to see how this device was conceived. So I am putting it into the published manuscript. These images and legends, projected from behind, were cast on a section of wall between the front-room and dining-room areas, which should be indistinguishable from the rest when not in use.

The purpose of this will probably be apparent. It is to give accent to certain values in each scene. Each scene contains a particular point (or several) which is structurally the most important. In an episodic play, such as this, the basic structure or narrative line may be obscured from the audience; the effect may seem fragmentary rather than architectural. This may not be the fault of the play so much as a lack of attention in the audience. The legend or image upon the screen will strengthen the effect of what is merely allusion in the writing and allow the primary point to be made more simply and lightly than if the entire responsibility were on the spoken lines. Aside from this structural value, I think the screen will have a definite emotional appeal, less definable but just as important. An imaginative producer or director may invent many other uses for this device than those indicated in the present script. In fact the possibilities of the device seem much larger to me than the instance of this play can possibly utilize.

Miss Taylor's: The role of Amanda was first played by the American actress Laurette Taylor (1884–1946).

THE MUSIC: Another extra-literary accent in this play is provided by the use of music. A single recurring tune, "The Glass Menagerie,"° is used to give emotional emphasis to suitable passages. This tune is like circus music, not when you are on the grounds or in the immediate vicinity of the parade, but when you are at some distance and very likely thinking of something else. It seems under those circumstances to continue almost interminably and it weaves in and out of your preoccupied consciousness; then it is the lightest, most delicate music in the world and perhaps the saddest. It expresses the surface vivacity of life with the underlying strain of immutable and inexpressible sorrow. When you look at a piece of delicately spun glass you think of two things: how beautiful it is and how easily it can be broken. Both of those ideas should be woven into the recurring tune, which dips in and out of the play as if it were carried on a wind that changes. It serves as a thread of connection and allusion between the narrator with his separate point in time and space and the subject of his story. Between each episode it returns as reference to the emotion, nostalgia, which is the first condition of the play. It is primarily Laura's music and therefore comes out most clearly when the play focuses upon her and the lovely fragility of glass which is her image.

THE LIGHTING: The lighting in the play is not realistic. In keeping with the atmosphere of memory, the stage is dim. Shafts of light are focused on selected areas or actors, sometimes in contradistinction to what is the apparent center. For instance, in the quarrel scene between Tom and Amanda, in which Laura has no active part, the clearest pool of light is on her figure. This is also true of the supper scene, when her silent figure on the sofa should remain the visual center. The light upon Laura should be distinct from the others, having a peculiar pristine clarity such as light used in early religious portraits of female saints or madonnas. A certain correspondence to light in religious paintings, such as El Greco's,° where the figures are radiant in atmosphere that is relatively dusky, could be effectively used throughout the play. (It will also permit a more effective use of the screen.) A free, imaginative use of light can be of enormous value in giving a mobile, plastic quality to plays of a more or less static nature.

Tennessee Williams

Scene 1

The Wingfield apartment is in the rear of the building, one of those vast hive-like conglomerations of cellular living-units that flower as warty growths in overcrowded urban centers of lower middle-class population and are symptomatic of the impulse of this largest and fundamentally enslaved section of American society to avoid fluidity and differentiation and to exist and function as one interfused mass of automatism.

The apartment faces an alley and is entered by a fire escape, a structure whose name is a touch of accidental poetic truth, for all of these huge buildings are always burning with the slow and implacable fires of human desperation. The fire escape is part of what we see—that is, the landing of it and steps descending from it.

The scene is memory and is therefore nonrealistic. Memory takes a lot of poetic license. It omits some details; others are exaggerated, according to the emotional value of the articles it

---

"The Glass Menagerie": Original music, including this recurrent theme, was composed for the play by Paul Bowles.   *El Greco:* Greek painter (ca. 1548–1614) who lived in Spain; typical paintings have elongated and distorted figures and extremely vivid foreground lighting set against a murky background.

touches, for memory is seated predominantly in the heart. The interior is therefore rather dim and poetic.

At the rise of the curtain, the audience is faced with the dark, grim rear wall of the Wingfield tenement. This building is flanked on both sides by dark, narrow alleys which run into murky canyons of tangled clotheslines, garbage cans, and the sinister latticework of neighboring fire escapes. It is up and down these side alleys that exterior entrances and exits are made during the play. At the end of TOM's opening commentary, the dark tenement wall slowly becomes transparent° and reveals the interior of the ground-floor Wingfield apartment.

Nearest the audience is the living room, which also serves as a sleeping room for LAURA, the sofa unfolding to make her bed. Just beyond, separated from the living room by a wide arch or second proscenium with transparent faded portieres° (or second curtain), is the dining room. In an old-fashioned whatnot° in the living room are seen scores of transparent glass animals. A blown-up photograph of the father hangs on the wall of the living room, to the left of the archway. It is the face of a very handsome young man in a doughboy's° First World War cap. He is gallantly smiling, ineluctably smiling, as if to say "I will be smiling forever."

Also hanging on the wall, near the photograph, are a typewriter keyboard chart and a Gregg shorthand diagram. An upright typewriter on a small table stands beneath the charts.

The audience hears and sees the opening scene in the dining room through both the transparent fourth wall of the building and the transparent gauze portieres of the dining-room arch. It is during this revealing scene that the fourth wall slowly ascends, out of sight. This transparent exterior wall is not brought down again until the very end of the play, during TOM's final speech.

The narrator is an undisguised convention of the play. He takes whatever license with dramatic convention is convenient to his purposes.

TOM enters, dressed as a merchant sailor, and strolls across to the fire escape. There he stops and lights a cigarette. He addresses the audience.

TOM.   Yes, I have tricks in my pocket, I have things up my sleeve. But I am the opposite of a stage magician. He gives you illusion that has the appearance of truth. I give you truth in the pleasant disguise of illusion.

To begin with, I turn back time. I reverse it to that quaint period, the thirties, when the huge middle class of America was matriculating in a school for the blind. Their eyes had failed them, or they had failed their eyes, and so they were having their fingers pressed forcibly down on the fiery Braille alphabet of a dissolving economy.

In Spain there was revolution. Here there was only shouting and confusion. In Spain there was Guernica.° Here there were disturbances of labor, sometimes pretty violent, in otherwise peaceful cities such as Chicago, Cleveland, Saint Louis . . . This is the social background of the play.

[*Music begins to play.*]

The play is memory. Being a memory play, it is dimly lighted, it is sentimental, it is not realistic. In memory everything seems to happen to music. That explains the fiddle in the wings.

---

transparent: The wall is painted on a scrim, a transparent curtain that is opaque when lit from the front and transparent when lit from behind.   *portieres:* curtains hung in a doorway; in production, these may also be painted on a scrim.   *whatnot:* a small set of shelves for ornaments.   *doughboy:* popular name for an American infantryman during World War I.
Guernica: a Basque town that was destroyed in 1937 by German planes fighting on General Franco's side during the Spanish Civil War. The huge mural *Guernica*, painted by Pablo Picasso, depicts the horror of that bombardment (see p. 362).

I am the narrator of the play, and also a character in it. The other characters are my mother, Amanda, my sister, Laura, and a gentleman caller who appears in the final scenes. He is the most realistic character in the play, being an emissary from a world of reality that we were somehow set apart from. But since I have a poet's weakness for symbols, I am using this character also as a symbol; he is the long-delayed but always expected something that we live for.

There is a fifth character in the play who doesn't appear except in this larger-than-life-size photograph over the mantel. This is our father who left us a long time ago. He was a telephone man who fell in love with long distances; he gave up his job with the telephone company and skipped the light fantastic out of town . . .

The last we heard of him was a picture postcard from Mazatlan, on the Pacific coast of Mexico, containing a message of two words: "Hello—Goodbye!" and no address.

I think the rest of the play will explain itself. . . .

[AMANDA's *voice becomes audible through the portieres.*]

[*Legend on screen:* "Où sont les neiges."°]

TOM *divides the portieres and enters the dining room.* AMANDA *and* LAURA *are seated at a drop-leaf table. Eating is indicated by gestures without food or utensils.* AMANDA *faces the audience.* TOM *and* LAURA *are seated profile. The interior has lit up softly and through the scrim we see* AMANDA *and* LAURA *seated at the table.*]

AMANDA. [*calling*] Tom?

TOM. Yes, Mother.

AMANDA. We can't say grace until you come to the table!

TOM. Coming, Mother. [*He bows slightly and withdraws, reappearing a few mo-* 5 *ments later in his place at the table.*]

AMANDA. [*to her son*] Honey, don't *push* with your *fingers.* If you have to push with something, the thing to push with is a crust of bread. And chew—chew! Animals have secretions in their stomachs which enable them to digest food without mastication, but human beings are supposed to chew their food before they swallow it down. Eat food leisurely, son, and really enjoy it. A well-cooked meal has lots of delicate flavors that have to be held in the mouth for appreciation. So chew your food and give your salivary glands a chance to function!

[TOM *deliberately lays his imaginary fork down and pushes his chair back from the table.*]

TOM. I haven't enjoyed one bite of this dinner because of your constant directions on how to eat it. It's you that make me rush through meals with your hawk-like attention to every bite I take. Sickening—spoils my appetite—all this discussion of—animals' secretion—salivary glands—mastication!

AMANDA. [*lightly*] Temperament like a Metropolitan star.°

[TOM *rises and walks toward the living room.*]

"Où sont les neiges": "Where are the snows (of yesteryear)," refrain from "The Ballade of Dead Ladies" by the French poet François Villon (ca. 1431–1463).   8 *Metropolitan star:* the Metropolitan Opera in New York City; opera stars are traditionally considered to be highly temperamental.

You're not excused from the table.

TOM.   I'm getting a cigarette.

AMANDA.   You smoke too much.   10

[*LAURA rises.*]

LAURA.   I'll bring in the blanc mange.°

[*TOM remains standing with his cigarette by the portieres.*]

AMANDA.   [*rising*] No, sister, no, sister°—you be the lady this time and I'll be the darky.

LAURA.   I'm already up.

AMANDA.   Resume your seat, little sister—I want you to stay fresh and pretty—for gentlemen callers!

LAURA.   [*sitting down*] I'm not expecting any gentlemen callers.   15

AMANDA.   [*crossing out to the kitchenette, airily*] Sometimes they come when they are least expected! Why, I remember one Sunday afternoon in Blue Mountain°—

[*She enters the kitchenette.*]

TOM.   I know what's coming!

LAURA.   Yes. But let her tell it.

TOM.   Again?

LAURA.   She loves to tell it.   20

[*AMANDA returns with a bowl of dessert.*]

AMANDA.   One Sunday afternoon in Blue Mountain—your mother received—*seventeen!*—gentlemen callers! Why, sometimes there weren't chairs enough to accommodate them all. We had to send the nigger over to bring in folding chairs from the parish house.

TOM.   [*remaining at the portieres*] How did you entertain those gentlemen callers?

AMANDA.   I understood the art of conversation!

TOM.   I bet you could talk.

AMANDA.   Girls in those days *knew* how to talk, I can tell you.   25

TOM.   Yes?

[*Image on screen: AMANDA as a girl on a porch, greeting callers.*]

AMANDA.   They knew how to entertain their gentlemen callers. It wasn't enough for a girl to be possessed of a pretty face and a graceful figure—although I wasn't slighted in either respect. She also needed to have a nimble wit and a tongue to meet all occasions.

TOM.   What did you talk about?

---

11 *blanc mange:* a bland molded pudding or custard.   12 *sister:* In the South of Amanda's youth, the oldest daughter in a family was frequently called "sister" by her parents and siblings. 16 *Blue Mountain:* an imaginary town in northwest Mississippi modeled after Clarksville, where Williams spent much of his youth. Blue Mountain (Clarksville) is at the northern edge of the Mississippi Delta, a large fertile plain that supports numerous plantations. This is the recollected world of Amanda's youth—plantations, wealth, black servants, and gentlemen callers who were the sons of cotton planters.

AMANDA.   Things of importance going on in the world! Never anything coarse or common or vulgar.

[*She addresses* TOM *as though he were seated in the vacant chair at the table though he remains by the portieres. He plays this scene as though reading from a script.*°]

My callers were gentleman—all! Among my callers were some of the most prominent young planters of the Mississippi Delta—planters and sons of planters!

[TOM *motions for music and a spot of light on* AMANDA. *Her eyes lift, her face glows, her voice becomes rich and elegiac.*

[*Screen legend*: "Où sont les neiges d'antan?"°]

There was young Champ Laughlin who later became vice-president of the Delta Planters Bank. Hadley Stevenson who was drowned in Moon Lake and left his widow one hundred and fifty thousand in Government bonds. There were the Cutrere brothers, Wesley and Bates. Bates was one of my bright particular beaux! He got in a quarrel with that wild Wainwright boy. They shot it out on the floor of Moon Lake Casino. Bates was shot through the stomach. Died in the ambulance on his way to Memphis. His widow was also well provided-for, came into eight or ten thousand acres, that's all. She married him on the rebound—never loved her—carried my picture on him the night he died! And there was that boy that every girl in the Delta had set her cap for! That beautiful, brilliant young Fitzhugh boy from Greene County!

TOM.   What did he leave his widow?   30

AMANDA.   He never married! Gracious, you talk as though all of my old admirers had turned up their toes to the daisies!

TOM.   Isn't this the first you've mentioned that still survives?

AMANDA.   That Fitzhugh boy went North and made a fortune—came to be known as the Wolf of Wall Street! He had the Midas touch,° whatever he touched turned to gold! And I could have been Mrs. Duncan J. Fitzhugh, mind you! But—I picked your *father!*

LAURA.   [*rising*] Mother, let me clear the table.

AMANDA.   No, dear, you go in front and study your typewriter chart. Or prac-   35
tice your shorthand a little. Stay fresh and pretty!—It's almost time for our gentlemen callers to start arriving. [*She flounces girlishly toward the kitchenette.*] How many do you suppose we're going to entertain this afternoon?

[TOM *throws down the paper and jumps up with a groan.*]

LAURA.   [*alone in the dining room*] I don't believe we're going to receive any, Mother.

AMANDA.   [*reappearing airily*] What? No one?—not one? You must be joking!

[LAURA *nervously echoes her laugh. She slips in a fugitive manner through the half-open portieres and draws them gently behind her. A shaft of very clear light is thrown on her face against the faded tapestry of the curtains. Faintly the music of "The Glass Menagerie" is heard as she continues lightly:*]

29.1 *script*: Here Tom becomes both a character in the play and the stage manager.
29.2 *"Où sont les neiges d'antan?"*: Where are the snows of yesteryear? See p. 1523.
33 *Midas touch*: In Greek mythology, King Midas was given the power to turn everything he touched into gold.

Not one gentleman caller? It can't be true! There must be a flood, there must have been a tornado!

LAURA.   It isn't a flood, it's not a tornado, Mother. I'm just not popular like you were in Blue Mountain. . . .

[*TOM utters another groan.* LAURA *glances at him with a faint, apologetic smile. Her voice catches a little:*]

Mother's afraid I'm going to be an old maid.

[*The scene dims out with the "Glass Menagerie" music.*]

Scene 2

On the dark stage the screen is lighted with the image of blue roses. Gradually LAURA's *figure becomes apparent and the screen goes out. The music subsides.*

LAURA *is seated in the delicate ivory chair at the small clawfoot table. She wears a dress of soft violet material for a kimono—her hair is tied back from her forehead with a ribbon. She is washing and polishing her collection of glass.* AMANDA *appears on the fire escape steps. At the sound of her ascent,* LAURA *catches her breath, thrusts the bowl of ornaments away, and seats herself stiffly before the diagram of the typewriter keyboard as though it held her spellbound. Something has happened to* AMANDA. *It is written in her face as she climbs to the landing: a look that is grim and hopeless and a little absurd. She has on one of those cheap or imitation velvety-looking cloth coats with imitation fur collar. Her hat is five or six years old, one of those dreadful cloche hats that were worn in the late Twenties, and she is clutching an enormous black patent-leather pocketbook with nickel clasps and initials. This is her full-dress outfit, the one she usually wears to the D.A.R.° Before entering she looks through the door. She purses her lips, opens her eyes very wide, rolls them upward and shakes her head. Then she slowly lets herself in the door. Seeing her mother's expression,* LAURA *touches her lips with a nervous gesture.*

LAURA.   Hello, Mother, I was—[*She makes a nervous gesture toward the chart on the wall.* AMANDA *leans against the shut door and stares at* LAURA *with a martyred look.*]

AMANDA.   Deception? Deception? [*She slowly removes her hat and gloves, continuing the sweet suffering stare. She lets the hat and gloves fall on the floor—a bit of acting.*]

LAURA.   [*shakily*] How was the D.A.R. meeting?

[AMANDA *slowly opens her purse and removes a dainty white handkerchief which she shakes out delicately and delicately touches to her lips and nostrils.*]

Didn't you go to the D.A.R. meeting, Mother?

AMANDA.   [*faintly, almost inaudibly*] —No.—No. [*then more forcibly:*] I did not have the strength—to go to the D.A.R. In fact, I did not have the courage! I wanted to find a hole in the ground and hide myself in it forever! [*She crosses slowly to the wall and removes the diagram of the typewriter keyboard. She holds it in front of her for a second, staring at it sweetly and sorrowfully—then bites her lips and tears it in two pieces.*]

LAURA.   [*faintly*] Why did you do that, Mother?

[AMANDA *repeats the same procedure with the chart of the Gregg Alphabet.*]

Why are you—

0.2 *D.A.R.:* Daughters of the American Revolution, a patriotic women's organization (founded in 1890) open only to women whose ancestors aided the American Revolution.

AMANDA.   Why? Why? How old are you, Laura?

LAURA.   Mother, you know my age.

AMANDA.   I thought you were an adult; it seems that I was mistaken. [*She crosses slowly to the sofa and sinks down and stares at* LAURA.]

LAURA.   Please don't stare at me, Mother.

[*AMANDA closes her eyes and lowers her head. There is a ten-second pause.*]

AMANDA.   What are we going to do, what is going to become of us, what is the   10
future?

[*There is another pause.*]

LAURA.   Has something happened, Mother?

[*AMANDA draws a long breath, takes out the handkerchief again, goes through the dabbing process.*]

Mother, has—something happened?

AMANDA.   I'll be all right in a minute, I'm just bewildered—[*She hesitates.*]—by life. . . .

LAURA.   Mother, I wish that you would tell me what's happened!

AMANDA.   As you know, I was supposed to be inducted into my office at the D.A.R. this afternoon.

[*Screen image: A swarm of typewriters.*]

But I stopped off at Rubicam's Business College to speak to your teachers about your having a cold and ask them what progress they thought you were making down there.

LAURA.   Oh. . . .   15

AMANDA.   I went to the typing instructor and introduced myself as your mother. She didn't know who you were.

"Wingfield," she said, "We don't have any such student enrolled at the school!"

I assured her she did, that you had been going to classes since early in January.

"I wonder," she said, "if you could be talking about that terribly shy little girl who dropped out of school after only a few days' attendance?"

"No," I said, "Laura, my daughter, has been going to school every day for the past six weeks!"

"Excuse me," she said. She took the attendance book out and there was your name, unmistakably printed, and all the dates you were absent until they decided that you had dropped out of school.

I still said, "No, there must have been some mistake! There must have been some mix-up in the records!"

And she said, "No—I remember her perfectly now. Her hands shook so that she couldn't hit the right keys! The first time we gave a speed test, she broke down completely—was sick at the stomach and almost had to be carried into the wash room! After that morning she never showed up any more. We phoned the house but never got any answer"—While I was working at Famous-Barr,° I suppose, demonstrating those—

[*She indicates a brassiere with her hands.*]

Oh! I felt so weak I could barely keep on my feet! I had to sit down while they got me

16.8 *Famous-Barr:* a department store in St. Louis.

a glass of water! Fifty dollars' tuition, all of our plans—my hopes and ambitions for you—just gone up the spout, just gone up the spout like that.

[*LAURA draws a long breath and gets awkwardly to her feet. She crosses to the Victrola and winds it up.*°]

What are you doing?

    LAURA.   Oh! [*She releases the handle and returns to her seat.*]

    AMANDA.   Laura, where have you been going when you've gone out pretending that you were going to business college?

    LAURA.   I've just been going out walking.

    AMANDA.   That's not true.

    LAURA.   It is. I just went walking.   20

    AMANDA.   Walking? Walking? In winter? Deliberately courting pneumonia in that light coat? Where did you walk to, Laura?

    LAURA.   All sorts of places—mostly in the park.

    AMANDA.   Even after you'd started catching that cold?

    LAURA.   It was the lesser of two evils, Mother.   25

[*Screen image: Winter scene in a park.*]

I couldn't go back there. I—threw up—on the floor!

    AMANDA.   From half past seven till after five every day you mean to tell me you walked around the park, because you wanted to make me think that you were still going to Rubicam's Business College?

    LAURA.   It wasn't as bad as it sounds. I went inside places to get warmed up.

    AMANDA.   Inside where?

    LAURA.   I went in the art museum and the bird houses at the Zoo. I visited the penguins every day! Sometimes I did without lunch and went to the movies. Lately I've been spending most of my afternoons in the Jewel Box, that big glass house where they raise the tropical flowers.

    AMANDA.   You did all this to deceive me, just for deception? [*LAURA looks*   30 *down.*] Why?

    LAURA.   Mother, when you're disappointed, you get that awful suffering look on your face, like the picture of Jesus' mother in the museum!

    AMANDA.   Hush!

    LAURA.   I couldn't face it.

[*There is a pause. A whisper of strings is heard. Legend on screen: "The Crust of Humility."*]

    AMANDA.   [*hopelessly fingering the huge pocketbook*] So what are we going to do the rest of our lives? Stay home and watch the parades go by? Amuse ourselves with the glass menagerie, darling? Eternally play those worn-out phonograph records your father left as a painful reminder of him? We won't have a business career—we've given that up because it gave us nervous indigestion! [*She laughs wearily.*] What is there left but dependency all our lives? I know so well what becomes of unmarried women who aren't prepared to occupy a position. I've seen such pitiful cases in the South—barely tolerated spinsters living upon the grudging patronage of sister's husband or broth-

---

16.11 *winds it up:* Laura is using a spring-powered (rather than electric) phonograph that has to be rewound frequently.

er's wife!—stuck away in some little mousetrap of a room—encouraged by one in-law to visit another—little birdlike women without any nest—eating the crust of humility all their life!

Is that the future that we've mapped out for ourselves? I swear it's the only alternative I can think of! [*She pauses.*] It isn't a very pleasant alternative, is it? [*She pauses again.*] Of course—some girls *do marry.*

[*LAURA twists her hands nervously.*]

Haven't you ever liked some boy?

LAURA.   Yes. I liked one once. [*She rises.*] I came across his picture a while ago.   35
AMANDA.   [*with some interest*] He gave you his picture?
LAURA.   No, it's in the yearbook.
AMANDA.   [*disappointed*] Oh—a high school boy.

[*Screen image: JIM as the high school hero bearing a silver cup.*]

LAURA.   Yes. His name was Jim. [*She lifts the heavy annual from the claw-foot table.*]
Here he is in *The Pirates of Penzance.*°
AMANDA.   [*absently*] The what?   40
LAURA.   The operetta the senior class put on. He had a wonderful voice and we sat across the aisle from each other Mondays, Wednesdays and Fridays in the Aud. Here he is with the silver cup for debating! See his grin?
AMANDA.   [*absently*] He must have had a jolly disposition.
LAURA.   He used to call me—Blue Roses.

[*Screen image: Blue roses.*]

AMANDA.   Why did he call you such a name as that?
LAURA.   When I had that attack of pleurosis—he asked me what was the mat-   45
ter when I came back. I said pleurosis—he thought that I said Blue Roses! So that's what he always called me after that. Whenever he saw me, he'd holler, "Hello, Blue Roses!" I didn't care for the girl that he went out with. Emily Meisenbach. Emily was the best-dressed girl at Soldan. She never struck me, though, as being sincere . . . It says in the Personal Section—they're engaged. That's—six years ago! They must be married by now.
AMANDA.   Girls that aren't cut out for business careers usually wind up married to some nice man. [*She gets up with a spark of revival.*] Sister, that's what you'll do!

[*LAURA utters a startled, doubtful laugh. She reaches quickly for a piece of glass.*]

LAURA.   But, Mother—
AMANDA.   Yes? [*She goes over to the photograph.*]
LAURA.   [*in a tone of frightened apology*] I'm—crippled!
AMANDA.   Nonsense! Laura, I've told you never, never to use that word.   50
Why, you're not crippled, you just have a little defect—hardly noticeable, even! When people have some slight disadvantage like that, they cultivate other things to make up for it—develop charm—and vivacity—and—*charm!* That's all you have to do! [*She turns again to the photograph.*] One thing your father had *plenty of*—was *charm!*

[*The scene fades out with music.*]

39 *The Pirates of Penzance:* a comic light opera (1879) by W. S. Gilbert and Arthur Sullivan.

Scene 3

[*Legend on screen: "After the fiasco—"*

TOM *speaks from the fire escape landing.*]

TOM. After the fiasco at Rubicam's Business College, the idea of getting a gentleman caller for Laura began to play a more and more important part in Mother's calculations. It became an obsession. Like some archetype of the universal unconscious, the image of the gentleman caller haunted our small apartment. . . .

[*Screen image: A young man at the door of a house with flowers.*]

An evening at home rarely passed without some allusion to this image, this specter, this hope. . . . Even when he wasn't mentioned, his presence hung in Mother's preoccupied look and in my sister's frightened, apologetic manner—hung like a sentence passed upon the Wingfields!

Mother was a woman of action as well as words. She began to take logical steps in the planned direction. Late that winter and in the early spring—realizing that extra money would be needed to properly feather the nest and plume the bird—she conducted a vigorous campaign on the telephone, roping in subscribers to one of those magazines for matrons called *The Homemaker's Companion*, the type of journal that features the serialized sublimations of ladies of letters who think in terms of delicate cuplike breasts, slim, tapering waists, rich, creamy thighs, eyes like wood smoke in autumn, fingers that soothe and caress like strains of music, bodies as powerful as Etruscan sculpture.

[*Screen image: The cover of a glamor magazine.*

AMANDA *enters with the telephone on a long extension cord. She is spotlighted in the dim stage.*]

AMANDA. Ida Scott? This is Amanda Wingfield! We *missed* you at the D.A.R. last Monday! I said to myself: She's probably suffering with that sinus condition! How is that sinus condition?

Horrors! Heaven have mercy!—You're a Christian martyr, yes, that's what you are, a Christian martyr!

Well, I just now happened to notice that your subscription to the *Companion's* about to expire! Yes, it expires with the next issue, honey!—just when that wonderful new serial by Bessie Mae Hopper is getting off to such an exciting start. Oh, honey, it's something that you can't miss! You remember how *Gone with the Wind*° took everybody by storm? You simply couldn't go out if you hadn't read it. All everybody *talked* was Scarlett O'Hara. Well, this is a book that critics already compare to *Gone with the Wind*. It's the *Gone with the Wind* of the post-World-War generation!—What?—Burning?—Oh, honey, don't let them burn, go take a look in the oven and I'll hold the wire! Heavens—I think she's hung up!

[*The scene dims out.*]

[*Legend on screen: "You think I'm in love with Continental Shoemakers?"*]

[*Before the lights come up again, the violent voices of* TOM *and* AMANDA *are heard. They are*

2.3 *Gone with the Wind*: popular novel (1936) by Margaret Mitchell (1900–1949), set in the South before, during, and after the Civil War. Scarlett O'Hara was the heroine.

quarreling behind the portieres. In front of them stands LAURA *with clenched hands and panicky expression. A clear pool of light is on her figure throughout this scene.*]

TOM.   What in Christ's name am I—
AMANDA.   [*shrilly*] Don't you use that—   5
TOM.   —supposed to do!
AMANDA.   —expression! Not in my—
TOM.   Ohhh!
AMANDA.   —presence! Have you gone out of your senses?
TOM.   I have, that's true, *driven* out!
AMANDA.   What is the matter with you, you—big—big—IDIOT!   10
TOM.   Look!—I've got *no thing*, no single thing—
AMANDA.   Lower your voice!
TOM.   —in my life here that I can call my OWN! Everything is—
AMANDA.   Stop that shouting!
TOM.   Yesterday you confiscated my books! You had the nerve to—   15
AMANDA.   I took that horrible novel back to the library—yes! That hideous
book by that insane Mr. Lawrence.°

[*TOM laughs wildly.*]

I cannot control the output of diseased minds or people who cater to them—

[*TOM laughs still more wildly.*]

BUT I WON'T ALLOW SUCH FILTH BROUGHT INTO MY HOUSE! No, no, no, no, no!
TOM.   House, house! Who pays rent on it, who makes a slave of himself to—
AMANDA.   [*fairly screeching*] Don't you DARE to—
TOM.   No, no, *I* mustn't say things! *I've* got to just—
AMANDA.   Let me tell you—   20
TOM.   I don't want to hear any more!

[*He tears the portieres open. The dining-room area is lit with turgid smoky red glow. Now we see* AMANDA; *her hair is in metal curlers and she is wearing a very old bathrobe, much too large for her slight figure, a relic of the faithless Mr. Wingfield. The upright typewriter now stands on the drop-leaf table, along with a wild disarray of manuscripts. The quarrel was probably precipitated by* AMANDA'*s interruption of* TOM'*s creative labor. A chair lies overthrown on the floor. Their gesticulating shadows are cast on the ceiling by the fiery glow.*]

AMANDA.   You *will* hear more, you—
TOM.   No, I won't hear more, I'm going out!
AMANDA.   You come right back in—
TOM.   Out, out, out! Because I'm—   25
AMANDA.   Come back here, Tom Wingfield! I'm not through talking to you!
TOM.   Oh, go—
LAURA.   [*desperately*] —Tom!
AMANDA.   You're going to listen, and no more insolence from you! I'm at the
end of my patience!

[*He comes back toward her.*]

16 *Lawrence:* D. H. Lawrence (1885–1930), English poet and fiction writer, popularly known as
an advocate of passion and sexuality. See "The Horse Dealer's Daughter," p. 391.

TOM.   What do you think I'm at? Aren't I supposed to have any patience to   3
reach the end of, Mother? I know, I know. It seems unimportant to you, what I'm *do-ing*—what I *want* to do—having a little *difference* between them! You don't think that—

AMANDA.   I think you've been doing things that you're ashamed of. That's why you act like this. I don't believe that you go every night to the movies. Nobody goes to the movies night after night. Nobody in their right minds goes to the movies as often as you pretend to. People don't go to the movies at nearly midnight, and movies don't let out at two A.M. Come in stumbling. Muttering to yourself like a maniac! You get three hours' sleep and then go to work. Oh, I can picture the way you're doing down there. Moping, doping, because you're in no condition.

TOM.   [*wildly*] No, I'm in no condition!

AMANDA.   What right have you got to jeopardize your job? Jeopardize the security of us all? How do you think we'd manage if you were—

TOM.   Listen! You think I'm crazy about the *warehouse*? [*He bends fiercely toward her slight figure.*] You think I'm in love with the Continental Shoemakers? You think I want to spend fifty-five *years* down there in that—*celotex interior!* with— *fluorescent— tubes!* Look! I'd rather somebody picked up a crowbar and battered out my brains—than go back mornings! I *go*! Every time you come in yelling that God damn *"Rise and Shine!" "Rise and Shine!"* I say to myself, "How *lucky dead* people are!" But I get up. I *go*! For sixty-five dollars a month I give up all that I dream of doing and being *ever*! And you say self—*self's* all I ever think of. Why, listen, if self is what I thought of, Mother, I'd be where he is—GONE! [*He points to his father's picture.*] As far as the system of transportation reaches! [*He starts past her. She grabs his arm.*] Don't grab at me, Mother!

AMANDA.   Where are you going?   3!

TOM.   I'm going to the *movies*!

AMANDA.   I don't believe that lie!

[*TOM crouches toward her, overtowering her tiny figure. She backs away, gasping.*]

TOM.   I'm going to opium dens! Yes, opium dens, dens of vice and criminals' hangouts, Mother. I've joined the Hogan Gang,° I'm a hired assassin, I carry a tommy gun in a violin case! I run a string of cat houses in the Valley! They call me Killer, Killer Wingfield, I'm leading a double-life, a simple, honest warehouse worker by day, by night a dynamic *czar* of the *underworld, Mother*. I go to gambling casinos, I spin away fortunes on the roulette table! I wear a patch over one eye and a false mustache, sometimes I put on green whiskers. On those occasions they call me—*El Diablo!*° Oh, I could tell you many things to make you sleepless! My enemies plan to dynamite this place. They're going to blow us all sky-high some night! I'll be glad, very happy, and so will you! You'll go up, up on a broomstick, over Blue Mountain with seventeen gentlemen callers! You ugly—babbling old—*witch. . . .*

[*He goes through a series of violent, clumsy movements, seizing his overcoat, lunging to the door, pulling it fiercely open. The women watch him, aghast. His arm catches in the sleeve of the coat as he struggles to pull it on. For a moment he is pinioned by the bulky garment. With an outraged groan he tears the coat off again, splitting the shoulder of it, and hurls it across the room. It strikes against the shelf of LAURA's glass collection, and there is a tinkle of shattering glass. LAURA cries out as if wounded.*]

Music.

38 *Hogan Gang:* one of the major criminal organizations in St. Louis in the 1930s.
El Diablo: the devil.

Screen legend: "The Glass Menagerie."]

LAURA.   [*shrilly*] My glass!—menagerie.... [*She covers her face and turns away.*]

[*But* AMANDA *is still stunned and stupefied by the "ugly witch" so that she barely notices this occurrence. Now she recovers her speech.*]

AMANDA.   [*in an awful voice*] I won't speak to you—until you apologize!   40

[*She crosses through the portieres and draws them together behind her.* TOM *is left with* LAURA. LAURA *clings weakly to the mantel with her face averted.* TOM *stares at her stupidly for a moment. Then he crosses to the shelf. He drops awkwardly on his knees to collect the fallen glass, glancing at* LAURA *as if he would speak but couldn't.*

"The Glass Menagerie" music steals in as the scene dims out.]

Scene 4

The interior of the apartment is dark. There is a faint light in the alley. A deep-voiced bell in a church is tolling the hour of five.

TOM *appears at the top of the alley. After each solemn boom of the bell in the tower, he shakes a little noisemaker or rattle as if to express the tiny spasm of man in contrast to the sustained power and dignity of the Almighty. This and the unsteadiness of his advance make it evident that he has been drinking. As he climbs the few steps to the fire escape landing light steals up inside.* LAURA *appears in the front room in a nightdress. She notices that* TOM's *bed is empty.* TOM *fishes in his pockets for his door key, removing a motley assortment of articles in the search, including a shower of movie ticket stubs and an empty bottle. At last he finds the key, but just as he is about to insert it, it slips from his fingers. He strikes a match and crouches below the door.*

TOM.   [*bitterly*] One crack—and it falls through!

[LAURA *opens the door.*]

LAURA.   Tom! Tom, what are you doing?
TOM.   Looking for a door key.
LAURA.   Where have you been all this time?
TOM.   I have been to the movies.   5
LAURA.   All this time at the movies?
TOM.   There was a very long program. There was a Garbo° picture and a Mickey Mouse and a travelogue and a newsreel and a preview of coming attractions. And there was an organ solo and a collection for the Milk Fund—simultaneously— which ended up in a terrible fight between a fat lady and an usher!
LAURA.   [*innocently*] Did you have to stay through everything?
TOM.   Of course! And, oh I forgot! There was a big stage show! The headliner on this stage show was Malvolio° the Magician. He performed wonderful tricks, many of them, such as pouring water back and forth between pitchers. First it turned to wine and then it turned to beer and then it turned to whisky. I know it was whisky it finally turned into because he needed somebody to come up out of the audience to help him, and I came up—both shows! It was Kentucky Straight Bourbon. A very gen-

7 *Garbo:* Greta Garbo (1905–1990), Swedish star of American silent and early sound films.
9 *Malvolio:* the name, borrowed from a puritanical character in Shakespeare's *Twelfth Night*, means "malevolence" or "ill-will."

erous fellow, he gave souvenirs. [*He pulls from his back pocket a shimmering rainbow-colored scarf.*] He gave me this. This is his magic scarf. You can have it, Laura. You wave it over a canary cage and you get a bowl of goldfish. You wave it over the goldfish bowl and they fly away canaries. . . . But the wonderfullest trick of all was the coffin trick. We nailed him into a coffin and he got out of the coffin without removing one nail. [*He has come inside.*] There is a trick that would come in handy for me—get me out of this two-by-four situation! [*He flops onto the bed and starts removing his shoes.*]

    LAURA.   Tom—shhh!   10

    TOM.   What're you shushing me for?

    LAURA.   You'll wake up Mother.

    TOM.   Goody, goody! Pay 'er back for all those "Rise an' Shines." [*He lies down, groaning.*] You know it don't take much intelligence to get yourself into a nailed-up coffin, Laura. But who in hell ever got himself out of one without removing one nail?

[*As if in answer, the father's grinning photograph lights up. The scene dims out.*]

[*Immediately following, the church bell is heard striking six. At the sixth stroke the alarm clock goes off in* AMANDA*'s room, and after a few moments we hear her calling: "Rise and Shine! Rise and Shine! Laura, go tell your brother to rise and shine!"*]

    TOM.   [*sitting up slowly*] I'll rise—but I won't shine.

[*The light increases.*]

    AMANDA.   Laura, tell your brother his coffee is ready.   15

[LAURA *slips into the front room.*]

    LAURA.   Tom!—It's nearly seven. Don't make Mother nervous.

[*He stares at her stupidly.*]

[*Beseechingly.*] Tom, speak to Mother this morning. Make up with her, apologize, speak to her!

    TOM.   She won't to me. It's her that started not speaking.

    LAURA.   If you just say you're sorry she'll start speaking.

    TOM.   Her not speaking—is that such a tragedy?

    LAURA.   Please—please!   20

    AMANDA.   [*calling from the kitchenette*] Laura, are you going to do what I asked you to do, or do I have to get dressed and go out myself?

    LAURA.   Going, going—soon as I get on my coat!

[*She pulls on a shapeless felt hat with a nervous, jerky movement, pleadingly glancing at* TOM. *She rushes awkwardly for her coat. The coat is one of* AMANDA*'s, inaccurately made-over, the sleeves too short for* LAURA.]

Butter and what else?

    AMANDA.   [*entering from the kitchenette*] Just butter. Tell them to charge it.

    LAURA.   Mother, they make such faces when I do that.

    AMANDA.   Sticks and stones can break our bones, but the expression on   25
Mr. Garfinkel's face won't harm us! Tell your brother his coffee is getting cold.

    LAURA.   [*at the door*] Do what I asked you, will you, will you, Tom?

[*He looks sullenly away.*]

AMANDA.   Laura, go now or just don't go at all!

LAURA.   [*rushing out*] Going—going!

[*A second later she cries out. TOM springs up and crosses to the door. TOM opens the door.*]

TOM.   Laura?

LAURA.   I'm all right. I slipped, but I'm all right.   30

AMANDA.   [*peering anxiously after her*] If anyone breaks a leg on those fire-escape steps, the landlord ought to be sued for every cent he possesses! [*She shuts the door. Now she remembers she isn't speaking to TOM and returns to the other room.*]

[*As TOM comes listlessly for his coffee, she turns her back to him and stands rigidly facing the window on the gloomy gray vault of the areaway. Its light on her face with its aged but childish features is cruelly sharp, satirical as a Daumier print.°*]

The music of "Ave Maria"° is heard softly.

TOM *glances sheepishly but sullenly at her averted figure and slumps at the table. The coffee is scalding hot; he sips it and gasps and spits it back in the cup. At his gasp, AMANDA catches her breath and half turns. Then she catches herself and turns back to the window. TOM blows on his coffee, glancing sidewise at his mother. She clears her throat. TOM clears his. He starts to rise, sinks back down again, scratches his head, clears his throat again. AMANDA coughs. TOM raises his cup in both hands to blow on it, his eyes staring over the rim of it at his mother for several moments. Then he slowly sets the cup down and awkwardly and hesitantly rises from the chair.*]

TOM.   [*hoarsely*] Mother. I—I apologize, Mother.

[*AMANDA draws a quick, shuddering breath. Her face works grotesquely. She breaks into child-like tears.*]

I'm sorry for what I said, for everything that I said, I didn't mean it.

AMANDA.   [*sobbingly*] My devotion has made me a witch and so I make myself hateful to my children!

TOM.   *No, you don't.*

AMANDA.   I worry so much, don't sleep, it makes me nervous!   35

TOM.   [*gently*] I understand that.

AMANDA.   I've had to put up a solitary battle all these years. But you're my right-hand bower!° Don't fall down, don't fail!

TOM.   [*gently*] I try, Mother.

AMANDA.   [*with great enthusiasm*] Try and you will *succeed!* [*The notion makes her breathless.*] Why, you—you're just *full* of natural endowments! Both of my children— they're *unusual* children! Don't you think I know it? I'm so—*proud!* Happy and—feel I've—so much to be thankful for but—promise me one thing, son!

TOM.   What, Mother?   40

AMANDA.   Promise, son, you'll—never be a drunkard!

TOM.   [*turns to her grinning*] I will never be a drunkard, Mother.

AMANDA.   That's what frightened me so, that you'd be drinking! Eat a bowl of Purina!

31.1 *Daumier print:* Honoré Daumier (1808–1879), French painter and engraver whose prints frequently satirized his society.   31.2 *"Ave Maria":* a Roman Catholic prayer to the Virgin Mary; the musical setting called for here is by Franz Schubert (1797–1828).   37 *right-hand bower:* or *rightbower:* the Jack of trump in the card game *500*, the second-highest card (below the joker).

TOM.   Just coffee, Mother.

AMANDA.   Shredded wheat biscuit?

TOM.   No. No, Mother, just coffee.

AMANDA.   You can't put in a day's work on an empty stomach. You've got ten minutes—don't gulp! Drinking too-hot liquids makes cancer of the stomach. . . . Put cream in.

TOM.   No, thank you.

AMANDA.   To cool it.

TOM.   No! No, thank you, I want it black.

AMANDA.   I know, but it's not good for you. We have to do all that we can to build ourselves up. In these trying times we live in, all that we have to cling to is—each other. . . . That's why it's so important to—Tom, I—I sent out your sister so I could discuss something with you. If you hadn't spoken I would have spoken to you. [*She sits down.*]

TOM.   [*gently*] What is it, Mother, that you want to discuss?

AMANDA.   *Laura!*

[*TOM puts his cup down slowly.*]

[*Legend on screen "Laura." Music: "The Glass Menagerie."*]

TOM.   —Oh.—Laura . . .

AMANDA.   [*touching his sleeve*] You know how Laura is. So quiet but—still water runs deep! She notices things and I think she—broods about them.

[*TOM looks up.*]

A few days ago I came in and she was crying.

TOM.   What about?

AMANDA.   You.

TOM.   Me?

AMANDA.   She has an idea that you're not happy here.

TOM.   What gave her that idea?

AMANDA.   What gives her any idea? However, you do act strangely. I—I'm not criticizing, understand *that*! I know your ambitions do not lie in the warehouse, that like everybody in the whole wide world—you've had to—make sacrifices, but—Tom—Tom—life's not easy, it calls for—Spartan endurance! There's so many things in my heart that I cannot describe to you! I've never told you but I—*loved* your father. . . .

TOM.   [*gently*] I know that, Mother.

AMANDA.   And you—when I see you taking after his ways! Staying out late—and—well, you *had* been drinking the night you were in that—terrifying condition! Laura says that you hate the apartment and that you go out nights to get away from it! Is that true, Tom?

TOM.   No. You say there's so much in your heart that you can't describe to me. That's true of me, too. There's so much in my heart that I can't describe to *you!* So let's respect each other's—

AMANDA.   But, why—*why*, Tom—are you always so *restless*? Where do you *go* to, nights?

TOM.   I—go to the movies.

AMANDA.   Why do you go to the movies so much, Tom?

TOM.   I go to the movies because—I like adventure. Adventure is something I don't have much of at work, so I go to the movies.

AMANDA.   But, Tom, you go to the movies *entirely* too *much!*

TOM.   I like a lot of adventure.   70

[*AMANDA looks baffled, then hurt. As the familiar inquisition resumes, TOM becomes hard and impatient again. AMANDA slips back into her querulous attitude toward him.*

Image on screen: A sailing vessel with Jolly Roger.°]

AMANDA.   Most young men find adventure in their careers.

TOM.   Then most young men are not employed in a warehouse.

AMANDA.   The world is full of young men employed in warehouses and offices and factories.

TOM.   Do all of them find adventure in their careers?

AMANDA.   They do or they do without it! Not everybody has a craze for adven-   75
ture.

TOM.   Man is by instinct a lover, a hunter, a fighter, and none of those instincts are given much play at the warehouse!

AMANDA.   Man is by instinct! Don't quote instinct to me! Instinct is something that people have got away from! It belongs to animals! Christian adults don't want it!

TOM.   What do Christian adults want, then, Mother?

AMANDA.   Superior things! Things of the mind and the spirit! Only animals have to satisfy instincts! Surely your aims are somewhat higher than theirs! Than monkeys—pigs—

TOM.   I reckon they're not.   80

AMANDA.   You're joking. However, that isn't what I wanted to discuss.

TOM.   [*rising*] I haven't much time.

AMANDA.   [*pushing his shoulders*] Sit down.

TOM.   You want me to punch in red° at the warehouse, Mother?

AMANDA.   You have five minutes. I want to talk about Laura.   85

[*Screen legend: "Plans and Provisions."*]

TOM.   All right! What about Laura?

AMANDA.   We have to be making some plans and provisions for her. She's older than you, two years, and nothing has happened. She just drifts along doing nothing. It frightens me terribly how she just drifts along.

TOM.   I guess she's the type that people call home girls.

AMANDA.   There's no such type, and if there is, it's a pity! That is unless the home is hers, with a husband!

TOM.   What?   90

AMANDA.   Oh, I can see the handwriting on the wall as plain as I see the nose in front of my face! It's terrifying! More and more you remind me of your father! He was out all hours without explanation! —Then *left! Goodbye!* And me with the bag to hold. I saw that letter you got from the Merchant Marine. I know what you're dreaming of. I'm not standing here blindfolded. [*She pauses.*] Very well, then. Then *do* it! But not till there's somebody to take your place.

TOM.   What do you mean?

70.2 *Jolly Roger:* the traditional flag of a pirate ship—a skull and crossed bones on a field of black.
84 *punch in red:* arrive late for work; the time clock stamps late arrival times in red on the time card.

AMANDA.   I mean that as soon as Laura has got somebody to take care of her, married, a home of her own, independent—why, then you'll be free to go wherever you please, on land, on sea, whichever way the wind blows you! But until that time you've got to look out for your sister. I don't say me because I'm old and don't matter! I say for your sister because she's young and dependent.

I put her in business college—a dismal failure! Frightened her so it made her sick at the stomach. I took her over to the Young People's League at the church. Another fiasco. She spoke to nobody, nobody spoke to her. Now all she does is fool with those pieces of glass and play those worn-out records. What kind of a life is that for a girl to lead?

TOM.   What can I do about it?

AMANDA.   Overcome selfishness! Self, self, self is all that you ever think of!   9⁵

[*TOM springs up and crosses to get his coat. It is ugly and bulky. He pulls on a cap with earmuffs.*]

Where is your muffler? Put your wool muffler on!

[*He snatches it angrily from the closet, tosses it around his neck and pulls both ends tight.*]

Tom! I haven't said what I had in mind to ask you.

TOM.   I'm too late to—

AMANDA.   [*catching his arm—very importunately; then shyly*] Down at the warehouse, aren't there some—nice young men?

TOM.   No!

AMANDA.   There *must* be—*some* . . .

TOM.   Mother— [*He gestures.*]   10⁰

AMANDA.   Find out one that's clean-living—doesn't drink and ask him out for sister!

TOM.   What?

AMANDA.   For *sister*! To *meet*! Get *acquainted*!

TOM.   [*stamping to the door*] Oh, my *go-osh*!

AMANDA.   Will you? [*He opens the door. She says, imploringly:*] Will you?   10⁵

[*He starts down the fire escape.*]

Will you? *Will* you, dear?

TOM.   [*calling back*] Yes!

[*AMANDA closes the door hesitantly and with a troubled but faintly hopeful expression.*

Screen image: The cover of a glamor magazine.

The spotlight picks up AMANDA on the phone.]

AMANDA.   Ella Cartwright? This is Amanda Wingfield! How are you honey? How is that kidney condition?

[*There is a five-second pause.*]

Horrors!

[*There is another pause.*]

You're a Christian martyr, yes, honey, that's what you are, a Christian martyr! Well, I just now happened to notice in my little red book that your subscription to the *Com-*

panion has just run out! I knew that you wouldn't want to miss out on the wonderful serial starting in this new issue. It's by Bessie Mae Hopper, the first thing she's written since *Honeymoon for Three*. Wasn't that a strange and interesting story? Well, this one is even lovelier, I believe. It has a sophisticated, society background. It's all about the horsey set on Long Island!

[*The light fades out.*]

Scene 5

[*Legend on the screen: "Annunciation."*]

Music is heard as the light slowly comes on.

It is early dusk of a spring evening. Supper has just been finished in the Wingfield apartment. AMANDA *and* LAURA, *in light-colored dresses, are removing dishes from the table in the dining room, which is shadowy, their movements formalized almost as a dance or ritual, their moving forms as pale and silent as moths.* TOM, *in white shirt and trousers, rises from the table and crosses toward the fire escape.*]

> AMANDA. [*as he passes her*] Son, will you do me a favor?
> TOM. What?
> AMANDA. Comb your hair! You look so pretty when your hair is combed!

[*TOM slouches on the sofa with the evening paper. Its enormous headline reads: "Franco Triumphs."°*]

> There is only one respect in which I would like you to emulate your father.
> TOM. What respect is that?
> AMANDA. The care he always took of his appearance. He never allowed himself to look untidy.   5

[*He throws down the paper and crosses to the fire escape.*]

> Where are you going?
> TOM. I'm going out to smoke.
> AMANDA. You smoke too much. A pack a day at fifteen cents a pack. How much would that amount to in a month? Thirty times fifteen is how much, Tom? Figure it out and you will be astounded at what you could save. Enough to give you a night-school course in accounting at Washington U.°! Just think what a wonderful thing that would be for you, son!

[*TOM is unmoved by the thought.*]

> TOM. I'd rather smoke. [*He steps out on the landing, letting the screen door slam.*]
> AMANDA. [*sharply*] I know! That's the tragedy of it. . . . [*Alone, she turns to look at her husband's picture.*]

[*Dance music: "The World Is Waiting for the Sunrise!"°*]

> TOM. [*to the audience*] Across the alley from us was the Paradise Dance Hall.   10
> On evenings in spring the windows and doors were open and the music came out-

---

3.1 *"Franco Triumphs"*: Francisco Franco (1892–1975), dictator of Spain from 1939 until his death, was the general of the victorious Falangist armies in the Spanish Civil War (1936–1939).
7 *Washington U*: Washington University, a highly competitive liberal arts school in St. Louis.
9.1 *"The World . . . Sunrise"*: popular song written in 1919 by Eugene Lockhart and Ernest Seitz.

doors. Sometimes the lights were turned out except for a large glass sphere that hung from the ceiling. It would turn slowly about and filter the dusk with delicate rainbow colors. Then the orchestra played a waltz or a tango, something that had a slow and sensuous rhythm. Couples would come outside, to the relative privacy of the alley. You could see them kissing behind ash pits and telephone poles. This was the compensation for lives that passed like mine, without any change or adventure. Adventure and change were imminent in this year. They were waiting around the corner for all these kids. Suspended in the mist over Berchtesgaden,° caught in the folds of Chamberlain's umbrella. In Spain there was Guernica! But here there was only hot swing music and liquor, dance halls, bars, and movies, and sex that hung in the gloom like a chandelier and flooded the world with brief, deceptive rainbows. . . . All the world was waiting for bombardments!

[AMANDA *turns from the picture and comes outside.*]

AMANDA.   [*sighing*] A fire escape landing's a poor excuse for a porch. [*She spreads a newspaper on a step and sits down, gracefully and demurely as if she were settling into a swing on a Mississippi veranda.*] What are you looking at?

TOM.   The moon.

AMANDA.   Is there a moon this evening?

TOM.   It's rising over Garfinkel's Delicatessen.

AMANDA.   So it is! A little silver slipper of a moon. Have you made a wish on it yet?   15

TOM.   Um-hum.

AMANDA.   What did you wish for?

TOM.   That's a secret.

AMANDA.   A secret, huh? Well, I won't tell mine either. I will be just as mysterious as you.

TOM.   I bet I can guess what yours is.   20

AMANDA.   Is my head so transparent?

TOM.   You're not a sphinx.°

AMANDA.   No, I don't have secrets. I'll tell you what I wished for on the moon. Success and happiness for my precious children! I wish for that whenever there's a moon, and when there isn't a moon, I wish for it, too.

TOM.   I thought perhaps you wished for a gentleman caller.

AMANDA.   Why do you say that?   25

TOM.   Don't you remember asking me to fetch one?

AMANDA.   I remember suggesting that it would be nice for your sister if you brought home some nice young man from the warehouse. I think that I've made that suggestion more than once.

TOM.   Yes, you have made it repeatedly.

---

10 *Berchtesgaden . . . Guernica:* The three names mentioned are all foreshadowings of World War II. Berchtesgaden, a resort in the Bavarian Alps, was Adolf Hitler's favorite residence. Neville Chamberlain was the British prime minister who signed the Munich Pact with Hitler in 1938, allowing Nazi Germany to occupy parts of Czechoslovakia. Chamberlain, who always carried an umbrella, declared that he had ensured "peace in our time." The bombardment of Guernica during the Spanish Civil War made the name of the town synonymous with the horrors of war, and especially the killing of civilian women and children. (See pp. 362, 1522.)
22 *sphinx:* a mythological monster with the head of a woman and body of a lion, famous for her riddles. See p. 827.

AMANDA. Well?
TOM. We are going to have one.   30
AMANDA. *What?*
TOM. A gentleman caller!

[*The annunciation is celebrated with music.*

AMANDA *rises.*

Image on screen: A caller with a bouquet.]

AMANDA. You mean you have asked some nice young man to come over?
TOM. Yep. I've asked him to dinner.
AMANDA. You really did?   35
TOM. I did!
AMANDA. You did, and did he—*accept?*
TOM. He did!
AMANDA. Well, well—well, well! That's—lovely!
TOM. I thought that you would be pleased.   40
AMANDA. It's definite then?
TOM. Very definite.
AMANDA. Soon?
TOM. Very soon.
AMANDA. For heaven's sake, stop putting on and tell me some things, will you?   45
TOM. What things do you want me to tell you?
AMANDA. *Naturally* I would like to know when he's *coming!*
TOM. He's coming tomorrow.
AMANDA. *Tomorrow?*
TOM. Yep. Tomorrow.   50
AMANDA. But, Tom!
TOM. Yes, Mother?
AMANDA. Tomorrow gives me no time!
TOM. Time for what?
AMANDA. Preparations! Why didn't you phone me at once, as soon as you   55
asked him, the minute that he accepted? Then, don't you see, I could have been get-
ting ready!
TOM. You don't have to make any fuss.
AMANDA. Oh, Tom, Tom, Tom, of course I have to make a fuss! I want things
nice, not sloppy! Not thrown together. I'll certainly have to do some fast thinking,
won't I?
TOM. I don't see why you have to think at all.
AMANDA. You just don't know. We can't have a gentleman caller in a pigsty!
All my wedding silver has to be polished, the monogrammed table linen ought to be
laundered! The windows have to be washed and fresh curtains put up. And how about
clothes? We have to *wear* something, don't we?
TOM. Mother, this boy is no one to make a fuss over!   60
AMANDA. Do you realize he's the first young man we've introduced to your sis-
ter? It's terrible, disgraceful that poor little sister has never received a single gentle-
man caller! Tom, come inside! [*She opens the screen door.*]
TOM. What for?
AMANDA. I want to ask you some things.

TOM.   If you're going to make such a fuss, I'll call it off, I'll tell him not to come!

AMANDA.   You certainly won't do anything of the kind. Nothing offends people worse than broken engagements. It simply means I'll have to work like a Turk! We won't be brilliant, but we will pass inspection. Come on inside.

[*TOM follows her inside, groaning.*]

Sit down.

TOM.   Any particular place you would like me to sit?

AMANDA.   Thank heavens I've got that new sofa! I'm also making payments on a floor lamp I'll have sent out! And put the chintz covers on, they'll brighten things up! Of course I'd hoped to have these walls re-papered. . . . What is the young man's name?

TOM.   His name is O'Connor.

AMANDA.   That, of course, means fish°—tomorrow is Friday! I'll have that salmon loaf—with Durkee's dressing! What does he do? He works at the warehouse?

TOM.   Of course! How else would I—

AMANDA.   Tom, he—doesn't drink?

TOM.   Why do you ask me that?

AMANDA.   Your father *did*!

TOM.   Don't get started on that!

AMANDA.   He *does* drink, then?

TOM.   Not that I know of!

AMANDA.   Make sure, be certain! The last thing I want for my daughter's a boy who drinks!

TOM.   Aren't you being a little bit premature? Mr. O'Connor has not yet appeared on the scene!

AMANDA.   But will tomorrow. To meet your sister, and what do I know about his character? Nothing! Old maids are better off than wives of drunkards!

TOM.   Oh, my God!

AMANDA.   Be still!

TOM.   [*leaning forward to whisper*] Lots of fellows meet girls whom they don't marry!

AMANDA.   Oh, talk sensibly, Tom—and don't be sarcastic! [*She has gotten a hairbrush.*]

TOM.   What are you doing?

AMANDA.   I'm brushing that cowlick down! [*She attacks his hair with the brush.*] What is this young man's position at the warehouse?

TOM.   [*submitting grimly to the brush and the interrogation*] This young man's position is that of a shipping clerk, Mother.

AMANDA.   Sounds to me like a fairly responsible job, the sort of job *you* would be in if you just had more *get-up.* What is his salary? Have you any idea?

TOM.   I would judge it to be approximately eighty-five dollars a month.

AMANDA.   Well—not princely, but—

TOM.   Twenty more than I make.

AMANDA.   Yes, how well I know! But for a family man, eighty-five dollars a month is not much more than you can just get by on. . . .

---

69 *fish:* Amanda assumes that O'Connor is Catholic. Until the 1960s, Roman Catholics were required by the church to abstain from meat on Fridays.

TOM.   Yes, but Mr. O'Connor is not a family man.

AMANDA.   He might be, mightn't he? Some time in the future?

TOM.   I see. Plans and provisions.

AMANDA.   You are the only young man that I know of who ignores the fact that   95
the future becomes the present, the present the past, and the past turns into everlasting regret if you don't plan for it!

TOM.   I will think that over and see what I can make of it.

AMANDA.   Don't be supercilious with your mother! Tell me some more about
this—what do you call him?

TOM.   James D. O'Connor. The D. is for Delaney.

AMANDA.   Irish on *both* sides! *Gracious!* And he doesn't drink?

TOM.   Shall I call him up and ask him right this minute?   100

AMANDA.   The only way to find out about those things is to make discreet in-
quiries at the proper moment. When I was a girl in Blue Mountain and it was suspected that a young man drank, the girl whose attentions he had been receiving, if
any girl *was*, would sometimes speak to the minister of his church, or rather her
father would if her father was living, and sort of feel him out on the young man's character. That is the way such things are discreetly handled to keep a young woman from
making a tragic mistake!

TOM.   Then how did you happen to make a tragic mistake?

AMANDA.   That innocent look of your father's had everyone fooled! He
smiled—the world was *enchanted*! No girl can do worse than put herself at the mercy of
a handsome appearance! I hope that Mr. O'Connor is not too good-looking.

TOM.   No, he's not too good-looking. He's covered with freckles and hasn't
too much of a nose.

AMANDA.   He's not right-down homely, though?   105

TOM.   Not right-down homely. Just medium homely, I'd say.

AMANDA.   Character's what to look for in a man.

TOM.   That's what I've always said, Mother.

AMANDA.   You've never said anything of the kind and I suspect you would
never give it a thought.

TOM.   Don't be so suspicious of me.   110

AMANDA.   At least I hope he's the type that's up and coming.

TOM.   I think he really goes in for self-improvement.

AMANDA.   What reason have you to think so?

TOM.   He goes to night school.

AMANDA.   [*beaming*] Splendid! What does he do, I mean study?   115

TOM.   Radio engineering and public speaking!

AMANDA.   Then he has visions of being advanced in the world! Any young man
who studies public speaking is aiming to have an executive job some day! And radio
engineering? A thing for the future! Both of these facts are very illuminating. Those
are the sort of things that a mother should know concerning any young man who
comes to call on her daughter. Seriously or—not.

TOM.   One little warning. He doesn't know about Laura. I didn't let on that we
had dark ulterior motives. I just said, why don't you come and have dinner with us?
He said okay and that was the whole conversation.

AMANDA.   I bet it was! You're eloquent as an oyster. However, he'll know about
Laura when he gets here. When he sees how lovely and sweet and pretty she is, he'll
thank his lucky stars he was asked to dinner.

TOM.   Mother, you mustn't expect too much of Laura.   12(

AMANDA.   What do you mean?

TOM.   Laura seems all those things to you and me because she's ours and we love her. We don't even notice she's crippled any more.

AMANDA.   Don't say crippled! You know that I never allow that word to be used!

TOM.   But face facts, Mother. She is and—that's not all—

AMANDA.   What do you mean "not all"?   12F

TOM.   Laura is very different from other girls.

AMANDA.   I think the difference is all to her advantage.

TOM.   Not quite all—in the eyes of others—strangers—she's terribly shy and lives in a world of her own and those things make her seem a little peculiar to people outside the house.

AMANDA.   Don't say peculiar.

TOM.   Face the facts. She is.   13(

[*The dance hall music changes to a tango that has a minor and somewhat ominous tone.*]

AMANDA.   In what way is she peculiar—may I ask?

TOM.   [*gently*] She lives in a world of her own—a world of little glass ornaments, Mother. . . .

[*He gets up. AMANDA remains holding the brush, looking at him, troubled.*]

She plays old phonograph records and—that's about all—[*He glances at himself in the mirror and crosses to the door.*]

AMANDA.   [*sharply*] Where are you going?

TOM.   I'm going to the movies. [*He goes out the screen door.*]

AMANDA.   Not to the movies, every night to the movies! [*She follows quickly to the   135 screen door.*] I don't believe you always go to the movies!

[*He is gone. AMANDA looks worriedly after him for a moment. Then vitality and optimism return and she turns from the door, crossing to the portieres.*]

Laura! Laura!

[*LAURA answers from the kitchenette.*]

LAURA.   Yes, Mother.

AMANDA.   Let those dishes go and come in front!

[*LAURA appears with a dish towel. AMANDA speaks to her gaily.*]

Laura, come here and make a wish on the moon!

[*Screen image: The Moon.*]

LAURA.   [*entering*] Moon—moon?

AMANDA.   A little silver slipper of a moon. Look over your left shoulder, Laura, and make a wish!

[*LAURA looks faintly puzzled as if called out of sleep. AMANDA seizes her shoulders and turns her at an angle by the door.*]

Now! Now, darling, *wish!*

LAURA.   What shall I wish for, Mother?   140
   AMANDA.   [*her voice trembling and her eyes suddenly filling with tears*] Happiness!
Good fortune!

[*The sound of the violin rises and the stage dims out.*]

Scene 6

[*The light comes up on the fire escape landing. Tom is leaning against the grill, smoking. Screen image: The high school hero.*]

TOM.   And so the following evening I brought Jim home to dinner. I had known Jim slightly in high school. In high school Jim was a hero. He had tremendous Irish good nature and vitality with the scrubbed and polished look of white chinaware. He seemed to move in a continual spotlight. He was a star in basketball, captain of the debating club, president of the senior class and the glee club and he sang the male lead in the annual light operas. He was always running or bounding, never just walking. He seemed always at the point of defeating the law of gravity. He was shooting with such velocity through his adolescence that you would logically expect him to arrive at nothing short of the White House by the time he was thirty. But Jim apparently ran into more interference after his graduation from Soldan. His speed had definitely slowed. Six years after he left high school he was holding a job that wasn't much better than mine.

[*Screen image: The Clerk.*]

He was the only one at the warehouse with whom I was on friendly terms. I was valuable to him as someone who could remember his former glory, who had seen him win basketball games and the silver cup in debating. He knew of my secret practice of retiring to a cabinet of the washroom to work on poems when business was slack in the warehouse. He called me Shakespeare. And while the other boys in the warehouse regarded me with suspicious hostility, Jim took a humorous attitude toward me. Gradually his attitude affected the others, their hostility wore off and they also began to smile at me as people smile at an oddly fashioned dog who trots across their path at some distance.
   I knew that Jim and Laura had known each other at Soldan, and I had heard Laura speak admiringly of his voice. I didn't know if Jim remembered her or not. In high school Laura had been as unobtrusive as Jim had been astonishing. If he did remember Laura, it was not as my sister, for when I asked him to dinner, he grinned and said, "You know, Shakespeare, I never thought of you as having folks!"
   He was about to discover that I did. . . .

[*Legend on screen: "The accent of a coming foot."*]

[*The light dims out on Tom and comes up in the Wingfield living room—a delicate lemony light. It is about five on a Friday evening of late spring which comes "scattering poems in the sky."*

AMANDA *has worked like a Turk in preparation for the gentleman caller. The results are astonishing. The new floor lamp with its rose silk shade is in place, a colored paper lantern conceals the broken light fixture in the ceiling, new billowing white curtains are at the windows, chintz covers are on the chairs and sofa, a pair of new sofa pillows make their initial appearance. Open boxes and tissue paper are scattered on the floor.*

LAURA stands in the middle of the room with lifted arms while AMANDA crouches before her, adjusting the hem of a new dress, devout and ritualistic. The dress is colored and designed by memory. The arrangement of LAURA's hair is changed; it is softer and more becoming. A fragile, unearthly prettiness has come out in LAURA: she is like a piece of translucent glass touched by light, given a momentary radiance, not actual, not lasting.]

AMANDA.   [*impatiently*] Why are you trembling?
LAURA.   Mother, you've made me so nervous!
AMANDA.   How have I made you nervous?
LAURA.   By all this fuss! You make it seem so important!
AMANDA.   I don't understand you, Laura. You couldn't be satisfied with just sitting home, and yet whenever I try to arrange something for you, you seem to resist it. [*She gets up.*] Now take a look at yourself. No, wait! Wait just a moment—I have an idea!   5
LAURA.   What is it now?

[*AMANDA produces two powder puffs which she wraps in handkerchiefs and stuffs in LAURA's bosom.*]

LAURA.   Mother, what are you doing?
AMANDA.   They call them "Gay Deceivers"!
LAURA.   I won't wear them!   10
AMANDA.   You will!
LAURA.   Why should I?
AMANDA.   Because, to be painfully honest, your chest is flat.
LAURA.   You make it seem like we were setting a trap.
AMANDA.   All pretty girls are a trap, a pretty trap, and men expect them to be.   15

[*Legend on screen: "A pretty trap."*]

  Now look at yourself, young lady. This is the prettiest you will ever be! [*She stands back to admire LAURA.*] I've got to fix myself now! You're going to be surprised by your mother's appearance!

[*AMANDA crosses through the portieres, humming gaily. LAURA moves slowly to the long mirror and stares solemnly at herself. A wind blows the white curtains inward in a slow, graceful motion and with a faint, sorrowful sighing.*]

AMANDA.   [*from somewhere behind the portieres*] It isn't dark enough yet.

[*LAURA turns slowly before the mirror with a troubled look.*

Legend on screen: "This is my sister: Celebrate her with strings!" Music plays.]

AMANDA.   [*laughing, still not visible*] I'm going to show you something. I'm going to make a spectacular appearance!
LAURA.   What is it, Mother?
AMANDA.   Possess your soul in patience—you will see! Something I've resurrected from that old trunk! Styles haven't changed so terribly much after all.... [*She parts the portieres.*] Now just look at your mother! [*She wears a girlish frock of yellowed voile*

with a blue silk sash. She carries a bunch of jonquils—the legend of her youth is nearly revived. Now she speaks feverishly:] This is the dress in which I led the cotillion. Won the cakewalk twice at Sunset Hill, wore one Spring to the Governor's Ball in Jackson!° See how I sashayed around the ballroom, Laura? [*She raises her skirt and does a mincing step around the room.*] I wore it on Sundays for my gentlemen callers! I had it on the day I met your father. . . . I had malaria fever all that Spring. The change of climate from East Tennessee to the Delta—weakened resistance. I had a little temperature all the time—not enough to be serious—just enough to make me restless and giddy! Invitations poured in—parties all over the Delta! "Stay in bed," said Mother, "you have a fever!"—but I just wouldn't. I took quinine° but kept on going, going! Evenings, dances! Afternoons, long, long rides! Picnics—lovely! So lovely, that country in May— all lacy with dogwood, literally flooded with jonquils! That was the spring I had the craze for jonquils. Jonquils became an absolute obsession. Mother said, "Honey, there's no more room for jonquils." And still I kept on bringing in more jonquils. Whenever, wherever I saw them, I'd say, "Stop! Stop! I see jonquils!" I made the young men help me gather the jonquils! It was a joke, Amanda and her jonquils. Finally there were no more vases to hold them, every available space was filled with jonquils. No vases to hold them? All right, I'll hold them myself! And then I—[*She stops in front of the picture. Music plays.*] met your father! Malaria fever and jonquils and then— this—boy. . . . [*She switches on the rose-colored lamp.*] I hope they get here before it starts to rain. [*She crosses the room and places the jonquils in a bowl on the table.*] I gave your brother a little extra change so he and Mr. O'Connor could take the service car home.

LAURA.   [*with an altered look*] What did you say his name was?   20
AMANDA.   O'Connor.
LAURA.   What is his first name?
AMANDA.   I don't remember. Oh, yes, I do. It was—Jim.

[*LAURA sways slightly and catches hold of a chair.*

Legend on screen: "Not Jim!"]

LAURA.   [*faintly*] Not—Jim!
AMANDA.   Yes, that was it, it was Jim! I've never known a Jim that wasn't nice!   25

[*The music becomes ominous.*]

LAURA.   Are you sure his name is Jim O'Connor?
AMANDA.   Yes. Why?
LAURA.   Is he the one that Tom used to know in high school?
AMANDA.   He didn't say so. I think he just got to know him at the warehouse.
LAURA.   There was a Jim O'Connor we both knew in high school—[*Then, with   30
effort.*] If that is the one that Tom is bringing to dinner—you'll have to excuse me, I won't come to the table.
AMANDA.   What sort of nonsense is this?
LAURA.   You asked me once if I'd ever liked a boy. Don't you remember I showed you this boy's picture?

19 *Jackson:* capital of Mississippi. Amanda refers to the social events of her youth. A cotillion is a formal ball, often given for debutantes. The cakewalk is a strutting dance step.
26 *quinine:* long used as a standard drug to control malaria.

AMANDA.   You mean the boy you showed me in the yearbook?

LAURA.   Yes, that boy.

AMANDA.   Laura, Laura, were you in love with that boy?   3⏐

LAURA.   I don't know, Mother. All I know is I couldn't sit at the table if it was
him!

AMANDA.   It won't be him! It isn't the least bit likely. But whether it is or not,
you will come to the table. You will not be excused.

LAURA.   I'll have to be, Mother.

AMANDA.   I don't intend to humor your silliness, Laura. I've had too much
from you and your brother, both! So just sit down and compose yourself till they
come. Tom has forgotten his key so you'll have to let them in, when they arrive.

LAURA.   [*panicky*] Oh, Mother—*you* answer the door!   4⏐

AMANDA.   [*lightly*] I'll be in the kitchen—busy!

LAURA.   Oh, Mother, please answer the door, don't make me do it!

AMANDA.   [*crossing into the kitchenette*] I've got to fix the dressing for the salmon.
Fuss, fuss—silliness!—over a gentleman caller!

[*The door swings shut, LAURA is left alone.*

Legend on screen: "Terror!"

    *She utters a low moan and turns off the lamp—sits stiffly on the edge of the sofa, knot-
ting her fingers together.*

Legend on screen: "The Opening of a Door!"

    TOM *and* JIM *appear on the fire escape steps and climb to the landing. Hearing their ap-
proach,* LAURA *rises with a panicky gesture. She retreats to the portieres. The doorbell rings.*
LAURA *catches her breath and touches her throat. Low drums sound.*]

AMANDA.   [*calling*] Laura, sweetheart! The door!

[LAURA *stares at it without moving.*]

JIM.   I think we just beat the rain.   45

TOM.   Uh-huh. [*He rings again, nervously.* JIM *whistles and fishes for a cigarette.*]

AMANDA.   [*very, very gaily*] Laura, that is your brother and Mr. O'Connor! Will
you let them in, darling?

[LAURA *crosses toward the kitchenette door.*]

LAURA.   [*breathlessly*] Mother—you go to the door!

[AMANDA *steps out of the kitchenette and stares furiously at* LAURA. *She points imperiously at*
the door.]

LAURA.   Please, please!

AMANDA.   [*in a fierce whisper*] What is the matter with you, you silly thing?   50

LAURA.   [*desperately*] Please, you answer it, *please!*

AMANDA.   I told you I wasn't going to humor you, Laura. Why have you chosen
this moment to lose your mind?

LAURA.   Please, please, please, you go!

AMANDA.   You'll have to go to the door because I can't.

LAURA.   [*despairingly*] I can't either!   55

AMANDA.   *Why?*

LAURA. I'm *sick!*

AMANDA. I'm sick, too—of your nonsense! Why can't you and your brother be normal people? Fantastic whims and behavior!

[*TOM gives a long ring.*]

Preposterous goings on! Can you give me one reason—[*She calls out lyrically.*] Coming! Just one second!—why you should be afraid to open a door? Now you answer it, Laura!

LAURA. Oh, oh, oh . . . [*She returns through the portieres, darts to the Victrola, winds it frantically and turns it on.*]

AMANDA. Laura Wingfield, you march right to that door!   60

LAURA. *Yes—yes, Mother!*

[*A faraway, scratchy rendition of "Dardanella"° softens the air and gives her strength to move through it. She slips to the door and draws it cautiously open. TOM enters with the caller, JIM O'CONNOR.*]

TOM. Laura, this is Jim. Jim, this is my sister, Laura.

JIM. [*stepping inside*] I didn't know that Shakespeare had a sister!

LAURA. [*retreating, stiff and trembling, from the door*] How—how do you do?

JIM. [*heartily, extending his hand*] Okay!   65

[*LAURA touches it hesitantly with hers.*]

JIM. Your hand's *cold*, Laura!

LAURA. Yes, well—I've been playing the Victrola. . . .

JIM. Must have been playing classical music on it! You ought to play a little hot swing music to warm you up!

LAURA. Excuse me—I haven't finished playing the Victrola. . . . [*She turns awkwardly and hurries into the front room. She pauses a second by the Victrola. Then she catches her breath and darts through the portieres like a frightened deer.*]

JIM. [*grinning*] What was the matter?   70

TOM. Oh—with Laura? Laura is—terribly shy.

JIM. Shy, huh? It's unusual to meet a shy girl nowadays. I don't believe you ever mentioned you had a sister.

TOM. Well, now you know. I have one. Here is the *Post Dispatch.*° You want a piece of it?

JIM. Uh-huh.

TOM. What piece? The comics?   75

JIM. Sports! [*He glances at it.*] Ole Dizzy Dean° is on his bad behavior.

TOM. [*uninterested*] Yeah? [*He lights a cigarette and goes over to the fire-escape door.*]

JIM. Where are *you* going?

TOM. I'm going out on the terrace.

JIM. [*going after him*] You know, Shakespeare—I'm going to sell you a bill of   80
goods!

TOM. What goods?

61.1 *"Dardanella":* a popular song and dance tune written in 1919 by Fred Fisher, Felix Bernard, and Johnny S. Black.   73 *Post Dispatch: The St. Louis Post Dispatch*, a newspaper.
76 *Dizzy Dean:* Jerome Herman (or Jay Hanna) Dean (1911–1974), outstanding pitcher with the St. Louis Cardinals (1932–1938).

JIM.   A course I'm taking.

TOM.   Huh?

JIM.   In public speaking! You and me, we're not the warehouse type.

TOM.   Thanks—that's good news. But what has public speaking got to do with   85
it?

JIM.   It fits you for—executive positions!

TOM.   Awww.

JIM.   I tell you it's done a helluva lot for me.

[*Image on screen: Executive at his desk.*]

TOM.   In what respect?

JIM.   In every! Ask yourself what is the difference between you an' me and men   90
in the office down front? Brains?—No!—Ability?—No! Then what? Just one little
thing—

TOM.   What is that one little thing?

JIM.   Primarily it amounts to—social poise! Being able to square up to people
and hold your own on any social level!

AMANDA.   [*from the kitchenette*] Tom?

TOM.   Yes, Mother?

AMANDA.   Is that you and Mr. O'Connor?   95

TOM.   Yes, Mother.

AMANDA.   Well, you just make yourselves comfortable in there.

TOM.   Yes, Mother.

AMANDA.   Ask Mr. O'Connor if he would like to wash his hands.

JIM.   Aw, no—no—thank you—I took care of that at the warehouse. Tom—   100

TOM.   Yes?

JIM.   Mr. Mendoza was speaking to me about you.

TOM.   Favorably?

JIM.   What do you think?

TOM.   Well—   105

JIM.   You're going to be out of a job if you don't wake up.

TOM.   I am waking up—

JIM.   You show no signs.

TOM.   The signs are interior.

[*Image on screen: The sailing vessel with the Jolly Roger again.*]

TOM.   I'm planning to change. [*He leans over the fire escape rail, speaking with*   110
quiet exhilaration. The incandescent marquees and signs of the first-run movie houses light his
face from across the alley. He looks like a voyager.] I'm right at the point of committing myself to a future that doesn't include the warehouse and Mr. Mendoza or even a night-
school course in public speaking.

JIM.   What are you gassing about?

TOM.   I'm tired of the movies.

JIM.   Movies!

TOM.   Yes, movies! Look at them—[*a wave toward the marvels of Grand Avenue*]
All of those glamorous people—having adventures—hogging it all, gobbling the
whole thing up! You know what happens? People go to the *movies* instead of *moving*!
Hollywood characters are supposed to have all the adventures for everybody in America, while everybody in America sits in a dark room and watches them have them! Yes,

until there's a war. That's when adventure becomes available to the masses! *Everyone's* dish, not only Gable's!° Then the people in the dark room come out of the dark room to have some adventures themselves—goody, goody! It's our turn now, to go to the South Sea Island—to make a safari—to be exotic, far-off! But I'm not patient. I don't want to wait till then. I'm tired of the *movies* and I am *about* to *move!*

JIM.   [*incredulously*] Move?   115
TOM.   Yes.
JIM.   When?
TOM.   Soon!
JIM.   Where? Where?

[*The music seems to answer the question, while TOM thinks it over. He searches in his pockets.*]

TOM.   I'm starting to boil inside. I know I seem dreamy, but inside—well, I'm   120
boiling! Whenever I pick up a shoe, I shudder a little thinking how short life is and what I am doing! Whatever that means, I know it doesn't mean shoes—except as something to wear on a traveler's feet! [*He finds what he has been searching for in his pockets and holds out a paper to JIM.*] Look—
JIM.   What?
TOM.   I'm a member.
JIM.   [*reading*] The Union of Merchant Seamen.
TOM.   I paid my dues this month, instead of the light bill.
JIM.   You will regret it when they turn off the lights.   125
TOM.   I won't be here.
JIM.   How about your mother?
TOM.   I'm like my father. The bastard son of a bastard! Did you notice how he's grinning in his picture in there? And he's been absent going on sixteen years!
JIM.   You're just talking, you drip. How does your mother feel about it?
TOM.   Shhh! Here comes Mother! Mother is not acquainted with my plans!   130
AMANDA.   [*coming through the portieres*] Where are you all?
TOM.   On the terrace, Mother.

[*They start inside. She advances to them. TOM is distinctly shocked at her appearance. Even JIM blinks a little. He is making his first contact with the girlish Southern vivacity and in spite of the night-school course in public speaking is somewhat thrown off the beam by the unexpected outlay of social charm. Certain responses are attempted by JIM but are swept aside by AMANDA's gay laughter and chatter. TOM is embarrassed but after the first shock JIM reacts very warmly. He grins and chuckles, is altogether won over.*

Image on screen: AMANDA as a girl.]

AMANDA.   [*coyly smiling, shaking her girlish ringlets*] Well, well, well, so this is Mr. O'Connor. Introductions entirely unnecessary. I've heard so much about you from my boy. I finally said to him, Tom—good gracious!—why don't you bring this paragon to supper? I'd like to meet this nice young man at the warehouse!—instead of just hearing him sing your praises so much! I don't know why my son is so stand-offish—that's not Southern behavior!

Let's sit down and—I think we could stand a little more air in here! Tom, leave the door open. I felt a nice fresh breeze a moment ago. Where has it gone to? Mmm,

114 *Gable:* Clark Gable (1901–1960), popular American screen actor and matinee idol from the 1930s to his death.

so warm already! And not quite summer, even. We're going to burn up when summer really gets started. However, we're having—we're having a very light supper. I think light things are better fo' this time of year. The same as light clothes are. Light clothes an' light food are what warm weather calls fo'. You know our blood gets so thick during th' winter—it takes a while fo' us to *adjust* ourselves!—when the season changes . . . It's come so quick this year. I wasn't prepared. All of sudden—heavens! Already summer! I ran to the trunk an' pulled out this light dress—terribly old! Historical almost! But feels so good—so good an' co-ol, y'know. . . .

TOM.   Mother—

AMANDA.   Yes, honey?   13?

TOM.   How about—supper?

AMANDA.   Honey, you go ask Sister if supper is ready! You know that Sister is in full charge of supper! Tell her you hungry boys are waiting for it. [*To* JIM.] Have you met Laura?

JIM.   She—

AMANDA.   Let you in? Oh, good, you've met already! It's rare for a girl as sweet an' pretty as Laura to be domestic! But Laura is, thank heavens, not only pretty but also very domestic. I'm not at all. I never was a bit. I never could make a thing but angel-food cake. Well, in the South we had so many servants. Gone, gone, gone. All vestige of gracious living! Gone completely! I wasn't prepared for what the future brought me. All of my gentlemen callers were sons of planters and so of course I assumed that I would be married to one and raise my family on a large piece of land with plenty of servants. But man proposes—and woman accepts the proposal! to vary that old, old saying a little but—I married no planter! I married a man who worked for the telephone company! That gallantly smiling gentleman over there! [*She points to the picture.*] A telephone man who—fell in love with long-distance! Now he travels and I don't even know where! But what am I going on for about my—tribulations? Tell me yours—I hope you don't have any! Tom?

TOM.   [*returning*] Yes, Mother?   140?

AMANDA.   Is supper nearly ready?

TOM.   It looks to me like supper is on the table.

AMANDA.   Let me look— [*She rises prettily and looks through the portieres.*] Oh lovely! But where is Sister?

TOM.   Laura is not feeling well and she says that she thinks she'd better not come to the table.

AMANDA.   What? Nonsense! Laura? Oh, Laura!

LAURA.   [*from the kitchenette, faintly*] Yes, Mother.   145

AMANDA.   You really must come to the table. We won't be seated until you come to the table! Come in, Mr. O'Connor. You sit over there and I'll. . . . Laura? Laura Wingfield! You're keeping us waiting, honey! We can't say grace until you come to the table!

[*The kitchenette door is pushed weakly open and* LAURA *comes in. She is obviously quite faint, her lips trembling, her eyes wide and staring. She moves unsteadily toward the table.*

Screen legend: "Terror!"

Outside a summer storm is coming on abruptly. The white curtains billow inward at the windows and there is a sorrowful murmur from the deep blue dusk.

LAURA suddenly stumbles; she catches at a chair with a faint moan.]

TOM. Laura!
AMANDA. Laura!

[There is a clap of thunder.

Screen legend: "Ah!"]

[despairingly] Why, Laura, you *are* ill, darling! Tom, help your sister into the living room, dear! Sit in the living room, Laura—rest on the sofa. Well! *[To JIM as TOM helps his sister to the sofa in the living room.]* Standing over the hot stove made her ill! I told her that it was just too warm this evening, but—

[TOM comes back to the table.]

Is Laura all right now?
TOM. Yes.   150
AMANDA. What is that? Rain? A nice cool rain has come up! *[She gives JIM a frightened look.]* I think we may—have grace—now . . . *[TOM looks at her stupidly.]* Tom, honey—you say grace!
TOM. Oh . . . "For these and all thy mercies—"

[They bow their heads, AMANDA stealing a nervous glance at JIM. In the living room LAURA, stretched on the sofa, clenches her hand to her lips, to hold back a shuddering sob.]

God's Holy Name be praised—

[The scene dims out.]

Scene 7

[It is half an hour later. Dinner is just being finished in the dining room, LAURA is still huddled upon the sofa, her feet drawn under her, her head resting on a pale blue pillow, her eyes wide and mysteriously watchful. The new floor lamp with its shade of rose-colored silk gives a soft, becoming light to her face, bringing out the fragile, unearthly prettiness which usually escapes attention. From outside there is a steady murmur of rain, but it is slackening and soon stops; the air outside becomes pale and luminous as the moon breaks through the clouds. A moment after the curtain rises, the lights in both rooms flicker and go out.]

JIM. Hey, there, Mr. Light Bulb!

[AMANDA laughs nervously.

Legend on screen: "Suspension of a public service."]

AMANDA. Where was Moses when the lights went out? Ha-ha. Do you know the answer to that one, Mr. O'Connor?
JIM. No, Ma'am, what's the answer?
AMANDA. In the dark!

[JIM laughs appreciatively.]

Everybody sit still. I'll light the candles. Isn't it lucky we have them on the table? Where's a match? Which of you gentlemen can provide a match?
JIM. Here.   5

AMANDA.   Thank you, Sir.

JIM.   Not at all, Ma'am!

AMANDA.   [*as she lights the candles*] I guess the fuse has burnt out. Mr. O'Connor, can you tell a burnt-out fuse? I know I can't and Tom is a total loss when it comes to mechanics. [*They rise from the table and go into the kitchenette, from where their voices are heard.*] Oh, be careful you don't bump into something. We don't want our gentleman caller to break his neck. Now wouldn't that be a fine howdy-do?

JIM.   Ha-ha! Where is the fuse-box?

AMANDA.   Right here next to the stove. Can you see anything?

JIM.   Just a minute.

AMANDA.   Isn't electricity a mysterious thing? Wasn't it Benjamin Franklin who tied a key to a kite? We live in such a mysterious universe, don't we? Some people say that science clears up all the mysteries for us. In my opinion it only creates more! Have you found it yet?

JIM.   No, Ma'am. All these fuses look okay to me.

AMANDA.   Tom!

TOM.   Yes, Mother?

AMANDA.   That light bill I gave you several days ago. That one I told you we got the notices about?

[*Legend on screen: "Ha!"*]

TOM.   Oh—yeah.

AMANDA.   You didn't neglect to pay it by any chance?

TOM.   Why, I—

AMANDA.   Didn't! I might have known it!

JIM.   Shakespeare probably wrote a poem on that light bill, Mrs. Wingfield.

AMANDA.   I might have known better than to trust him with it! There's such a high price for negligence in this world!

JIM.   Maybe the poem will win a ten-dollar prize.

AMANDA.   We'll just have to spend the remainder of the evening in the nineteenth century, before Mr. Edison made the Mazda lamp!°

JIM.   Candlelight is my favorite kind of light.

AMANDA.   That shows you're romantic! But that's no excuse for Tom. Well, we got through dinner. Very considerate of them to let us get through dinner before they plunged us into everlasting darkness, wasn't it, Mr. O'Connor?

JIM.   Ha-ha!

AMANDA.   Tom, as a penalty for your carelessness you can help me with the dishes.

JIM.   Let me give you a hand.

AMANDA.   Indeed you will not!

JIM.   I ought to be good for something.

AMANDA.   Good for something? [*Her tone is rhapsodic.*] You? Why, Mr. O'Connor, nobody, *nobody's* given me this much entertainment in years—as you have!

JIM.   Aw, now, Mrs. Wingfield!

AMANDA.   I'm not exaggerating, not one bit! But Sister is all by her lonesome. You go keep her company in the parlor! I'll give you this lovely old candelabrum that used to be on the altar at the Church of the Heavenly Rest. It was melted a little out

24 *Mazda lamp:* Thomas A. Edison (1847–1931) developed the first practical incandescent lamp in 1879.

of shape when the church burnt down. Lightning struck it one spring. Gypsy Jones was holding a revival at the time and he intimated that the church was destroyed because the Episcopalians gave card parties.

JIM.   Ha-ha.   35

AMANDA.   And how about you coaxing Sister to drink a little wine? I think it would be good for her! Can you carry both at once?

JIM.   Sure. I'm Superman!

AMANDA.   Now, Thomas, get into this apron!

[*JIM comes into the dining room, carrying the candelabrum, its candles lighted, in one hand and a glass of wine in the other. The door of the kitchenette swings closed on AMANDA's gay laughter; the flickering light approaches the portieres. LAURA sits up nervously as JIM enters. She can hardly speak from the almost intolerable strain of being alone with a stranger.*]

Screen legend: "I don't suppose you remember me at all!"

At first, before JIM's warmth overcomes her paralyzing shyness, LAURA's voice is thin and breathless, as though she had just run up a steep flight of stairs. JIM's attitude is gently humorous. While the incident is apparently unimportant, it is to LAURA the climax of her secret life.]

JIM.   Hello there, Laura.

LAURA.   [*faintly*] Hello.   40

[*She clears her throat.*]

JIM.   How are you feeling now? Better?

LAURA.   Yes. Yes, thank you.

JIM.   This is for you. A little dandelion wine. [*He extends the glass toward her with extravagant gallantry.*]

LAURA.   Thank you.

JIM.   Drink it—but don't get drunk!   45

[*He laughs heartily. LAURA takes the glass uncertainly; she laughs shyly.*]

Where shall I set the candles?

LAURA.   Oh—oh, anywhere . . .

JIM.   How about here on the floor? Any objections?

LAURA.   No.

JIM.   I'll spread a newspaper under to catch the drippings. I like to sit on the floor. Mind if I do?

LAURA.   Oh, no.   50

JIM.   Give me a pillow?

LAURA.   What?

JIM.   A pillow!

LAURA.   Oh . . . [*She hands him one quickly.*]

JIM.   How about you? Don't you like to sit on the floor?   55

LAURA.   Oh—yes.

JIM.   Why don't you, then?

LAURA.   I—will.

JIM.   Take a pillow!

[*Laura does. She sits on the floor on the other side of the candelabrum. JIM crosses his legs and smiles engagingly at her.*] I can't hardly see you sitting way over there.

LAURA. I can—see you.

JIM. I know, but that's not fair, I'm in the limelight.   6

[*LAURA moves her pillow closer.*]

Good! Now I can see you! Comfortable?

LAURA. Yes.

JIM. So am I. Comfortable as a cow! Will you have some gum?

LAURA. No, thank you.

JIM. I think that I will indulge, with your permission. [*He musingly unwraps a*   6
stick of gum and holds it up.] Think of the fortune made by the guy that invented the
first piece of chewing gum. Amazing, huh? The Wrigley Building° is one of the sights
of Chicago—I saw it when I went up to the Century of Progress.° Did you take in the
Century of Progress?

LAURA. No, I didn't.

JIM. Well, it was quite a wonderful exposition. What impressed me most was
the Hall of Science. Gives you an idea of what the future will be in America, even
more wonderful than the present time is! [*There is a pause. JIM smiles at her.*] Your
brother tells me you're shy. Is that right—Laura?

LAURA. I—don't know.

JIM. I judge you to be an old-fashioned type of girl. Well, I think that's a pretty
good type to be. Hope you don't think I'm being too personal—do you?

LAURA. [*Hastily, out of embarrassment*] I believe I *will* take a piece of gum, if   70
you—don't mind. [*clearing her throat*] Mr. O'Connor, have you—kept up with your
singing?

JIM. Singing? Me?

LAURA. Yes. I remember what a beautiful voice you had.

JIM. When did you hear me sing?

[*LAURA does not answer, and in the long pause which follows a man's voice is heard singing
offstage.*]

VOICE:

> O blow, ye winds, heigh-ho,
> A-roving I will go!
>   I'm off to my love
>   With a boxing glove—
> Ten thousand miles away!

JIM. You say you've heard me sing?   75

LAURA. Oh, Yes! Yes, very often . . . I—don't suppose—you remember me—at
all?

JIM. [*smiling doubtfully*] You know I have an idea I've seen you before. I had
that idea soon as you opened the door. It seemed almost like I was about to remember your name. But the name that I started to call you—wasn't a name! And so I
stopped myself before I said it.

LAURA. Wasn't it—Blue Roses?

JIM. [*springing up, grinning*] Blue Roses! My gosh, yes—Blue Roses! That's what

---

65 *Wrigley Building:* Finished in 1924, this was one of the first skyscrapers in the United States.
66 *Century of Progress:* a world's fair held in Chicago (1933–1934) to celebrate the city's
centennial.

I had on my tongue when you opened the door! Isn't it funny what tricks your memory plays? I didn't connect you with high school somehow or other. But that's where it was; it was high school. I didn't even know you were Shakespeare's sister! Gosh, I'm sorry.

LAURA.   I didn't expect you to. You—barely knew me!   80

JIM.   But we did have a speaking acquaintance, huh?

LAURA.   Yes, we—spoke to each other.

JIM.   When did you recognize me?

LAURA.   Oh, right away!

JIM.   Soon as I came in the door?   85

LAURA.   When I heard your name I thought it was probably you. I knew that Tom used to know you a little in high school. So when you came in the door—well, then I was—sure.

JIM.   Why didn't you *say* something, then?

LAURA.   [*breathlessly*] I didn't know what to say, I was—too surprised!

JIM.   For goodness' sakes! You know, this sure is funny!

LAURA.   Yes! Yes, isn't it, though . . .   90

JIM.   Didn't we have a class in something together?

LAURA.   Yes, we did.

JIM.   What class was that?

LAURA.   It was—singing—chorus!

JIM.   Aw!   95

LAURA.   I sat across the aisle from you in the Aud.

JIM.   Aw!

LAURA.   Mondays, Wednesdays, and Fridays.

JIM.   Now I remember—you always came in late.

LAURA.   Yes, it was so hard for me, getting upstairs. I had that brace on my   100
leg—it clumped so loud!

JIM.   I never heard any clumping.

LAURA.   [*wincing at the recollection*] To me it sounded like—thunder!

JIM.   Well, well, well, I never even noticed.

LAURA.   And everybody was seated before I came in. I had to walk in front of all those people. My seat was in the back row. I had to go clumping all the way up the aisle with everyone watching!

JIM.   You shouldn't have been self-conscious.   105

LAURA.   I know, but I was. It was always such a relief when the singing started.

JIM.   Aw, yes, I've placed you now! I used to call you Blue Roses. How was it that I got started calling you that?

LAURA.   I was out of school a little while with pleurosis. When I came back you asked me what was the matter. I said I had pleurosis—you thought that I said *Blue Roses.* That's what you always called me after that!

JIM.   I hope you didn't mind.

LAURA.   Oh, no—I liked it. You see, I wasn't acquainted with many—peo-   110
ple. . . .

JIM.   As I remember you sort of stuck by yourself.

LAURA.   I—I—never have had much luck at—making friends.

JIM.   I don't see why you wouldn't.

LAURA.   Well, I—started out badly.

JIM.   You mean being—   115

LAURA.   Yes, it sort of—stood between me—
JIM.   You shouldn't have let it!
LAURA.   I know, but it did, and—
JIM.   You were shy with people!
LAURA.   I tried not to be but never could—   120
JIM.   Overcome it?
LAURA.   No, I—I never could!
JIM.   I guess being shy is something you have to work out of kind of gradually.
LAURA.   [*sorrowfully*] Yes—I guess it—
JIM.   Takes time!   125
LAURA.   Yes—

JIM.   People are not so dreadful when you know them. That's what you have to remember! And everybody has problems, not just you, but practically everybody has got some problems. You think of yourself as having the only problems, as being the only one who is disappointed. But just look around you and you will see lots of people as disappointed as you are. For instance, I hoped when I was going to high school that I would be further along at this time, six years later, than I am now. You remember that wonderful write-up I had in *The Torch*?

LAURA.   Yes! [*She rises and crosses to the table.*]
JIM.   It said I was bound to succeed in anything I went into!

[*LAURA returns with the high school yearbook.*]

Holy Jeez! *The Torch!*

[*He accepts it reverently. They smile across the book with mutual wonder. LAURA crouches beside him and they begin to turn the pages. LAURA's shyness is dissolving in his warmth.*]

LAURA.   Here you are in *The Pirates of Penzance!*   130
JIM.   [*wistfully*] I sang the baritone lead in that operetta.
LAURA.   [*raptly*] So—beautifully!
JIM.   [*protesting*] Aw—
LAURA.   Yes, yes—beautifully—beautifully!
JIM.   You heard me?   135
LAURA.   All three times!
JIM.   No!
LAURA.   Yes!
JIM.   All three performances?
LAURA.   [*looking down*] Yes.   140
JIM.   Why?
LAURA.   I—wanted to ask you to—autograph my program. [*She takes the program from the back of the yearbook and shows it to him.*]
JIM.   Why didn't you ask me to?
LAURA.   You were always surrounded by your own friends so much that I never had a chance to.
JIM.   You should have just—   145
LAURA.   Well, I—thought you might think I was—
JIM.   Thought I might think you was—what?
LAURA.   Oh—
JIM.   [*with reflective relish*] I was beleaguered by females in those days.
LAURA.   You were terribly popular!   150

JIM.   Yeah—
LAURA.   You had such a—friendly way—
JIM.   I was spoiled in high school.
LAURA.   Everybody—liked you!
JIM.   Including you?
LAURA.   I—yes, I—did, too— [*She gently closes the book in her lap.*]   155
JIM.   Well, well, well! Give me that program, Laura.

[*She hands it to him. He signs it with a flourish.*]

There you are—better late than never!
     LAURA.   Oh, I—what a—surprise!
     JIM.   My signature isn't worth very much right now. But some day—maybe—it
will increase in value! Being disappointed is one thing and being discouraged is something else. I am disappointed but I am not discouraged. I'm twenty-three years old.
How old are you?
     LAURA.   I'll be twenty-four in June.   160
     JIM.   That's not old age!
     LAURA.   No, but—
     JIM.   You finished high school?
     LAURA.   [*with difficulty*] I didn't go back.
     JIM.   You mean you dropped out?   165
     LAURA.   I made bad grades in my final examinations. [*She rises and replaces the
book and the program on the table. Her voice is strained.*] How is—Emily Meisenbach getting along?
     JIM.   Oh, that kraut-head!
     LAURA.   Why do you call her that?
     JIM.   That's what she was.
     LAURA.   You're not still—going with her?   170
     JIM.   I never see her.
     LAURA.   It was in the "Personal" section that you were—engaged!
     JIM.   I know, but I wasn't impressed by that—propaganda!
     LAURA.   It wasn't—the truth?
     JIM.   Only in Emily's optimistic opinion!   175
     LAURA.   Oh—

[*Legend: "What have you done since high school?"*]

*JIM lights a cigarette and leans indolently back on his elbows smiling at LAURA with a warmth
and charm which lights her inwardly with altar candles. She remains by the table, picks up a
piece from the glass menagerie collection, and turns it in her hands to cover her tumult.*]

     JIM.   [*after several reflective puffs on his cigarette*] What have you done since high
school?

[*She seems not to hear him.*]

Huh?

[*LAURA looks up.*]

I said what have you done since high school, Laura?
     LAURA.   Nothing much.

JIM. You must have been doing something these six long years.

LAURA. Yes.   18◖

JIM. Well, then, such as what?

LAURA. I took a business course at business college—

JIM. How did that work out?

LAURA. Well, not very—well—I had to drop out, it gave me—indigestion—

[*JIM laughs gently.*]

JIM. What are you doing now?   18◖

LAURA. I don't do anything—much. Oh, please don't think I sit around doing nothing! My glass collection takes up a good deal of time. Glass is something you have to take good care of.

JIM. What did you say—about glass?

LAURA. Collection I said—I have one—[*She clears her throat and turns away again, acutely shy.*]

JIM. [*abruptly*] You know what I judge to be the trouble with you? Inferiority complex! Know what that is? That's what they call it when someone low-rates himself! I understand it because I had it too. Although my case was not so aggravated as yours seems to be. I had it until I took up public speaking, developed my voice, and learned that I had an aptitude for science. Before that time I never thought of myself as being outstanding in any way whatsoever! Now I've never made a regular study of it, but I have a friend who says I can analyze people better than doctors that make a profession of it. I don't claim that to be necessarily true, but I can sure guess a person's psychology. Laura! [*He takes out his gum.*] Excuse me, Laura. I always take it out when the flavor is gone. I'll use this scrap of paper to wrap it in. I know how it is to get it stuck on a shoe. [*He wraps the gum in paper and puts it in his pocket.*] Yep—that's what I judge to be your principal trouble. A lack of confidence in yourself as a person. You don't have the proper amount of faith in yourself. I'm basing that fact on a number of your remarks and also on certain observations I've made. For instance that clumping you thought was so awful in high school. You say that you even dreaded to walk into class. You see what you did? You dropped out of school, you gave up an education because of a clump, which as far as I know was practically nonexistent! A little physical defect is what you have. Hardly noticeable even! Magnified thousands of times by imagination! You know what my strong advice to you is? Think of yourself as *superior* in some way!

LAURA. In what way would I think?   190

JIM. Why, man alive, Laura! Just look about you a little. What do you see? A world full of common people! All of 'em born and all of 'em going to die! Which of them has one-tenth of your good points! Or mine! Or anyone else's, as far as that goes—gosh! Everybody excels in some one thing. Some in many! [*He unconsciously glances at himself in the mirror.*] All you've got to do is discover in *what*! Take me, for instance. [*He adjusts his tie at the mirror.*] My interest happens to lie in electro-dynamics. I'm taking a course in radio engineering at night school, Laura, on top of a fairly responsible job at the warehouse. I'm taking that course and studying public speaking.

LAURA. Ohhhh.

JIM. Because I believe in the future of television! [*turning his back to her*] I wish to be ready to go up right along with it. Therefore I'm planning to get in on the ground floor. In fact I've already made the right connections and all that remains is

for the industry itself to get under way! Full steam—[*His eyes are starry.*] *Knowledge*—
Zzzzzp! *Money*—Zzzzzp!—Power! That's the cycle democracy is built on!

[*His attitude is convincingly dynamic.* LAURA *stares at him, even her shyness eclipsed in her absolute wonder. He suddenly grins.*]

I guess you think I think a lot of myself!

LAURA.   No—o-o-o, I—

JIM.   Now how about you? Isn't there something you take more interest in than   195
anything else?

LAURA.   Well, I do—as I said—have my—glass collection—

[*A peal of girlish laughter rings from the kitchenette.*]

JIM.   I'm not right sure I know what you're talking about. What kind of glass is it?

LAURA.   Little articles of it, they're ornaments mostly! Most of them are little
animals made out of glass, the tiniest little animals in the world. Mother calls them a
glass menagerie! Here's an example of one, if you'd like to see it! This one is one of
the oldest. It's nearly thirteen.

[*Music: "The Glass Menagerie."*

He stretches out his hand.]

Oh, be careful—if you breathe, it breaks!

JIM.   I'd better not take it. I'm pretty clumsy with things.

LAURA.   Go, on, I trust you with him! [*She places the piece in his palm.*] There   200
now—you're holding him gently! Hold him over the light, he loves the light! You see
how the light shines through him?

JIM.   It sure does shine!

LAURA.   I shouldn't be partial, but he is my favorite one.

JIM.   What kind of a thing is this one supposed to be?

LAURA.   Haven't you noticed the single horn on his forehead?

JIM.   A unicorn, huh?   205

LAURA.   Mmmm-hmmm!

JIM.   Unicorns—aren't they extinct in the modern world?

LAURA.   I know!

JIM.   Poor little fellow, he must feel sort of lonesome.

LAURA.   [*smiling*] Well, if he does, he doesn't complain about it. He stays on a   210
shelf with some horses that don't have horns and all of them seem to get along nicely
together.

JIM.   How do you know?

LAURA.   [*lightly*] I haven't heard any arguments among them!

JIM.   [*grinning*] No arguments, huh? Well, that's a pretty good sign! Where
shall I set him?

LAURA.   Put him on the table. They all like a change of scenery once in a while!

JIM.   Well, well, well, well—[*He places the glass piece on the table, then raises his arms*   215
and stretches.] Look how big my shadow is when I stretch!

LAURA.   Oh, oh, yes—it stretches across the ceiling!

JIM.   [*crossing to the door*] I think it's stopped raining. [*He opens the fire-escape door*
and the background music changes to a dance tune.] Where does the music come from?

LAURA. From the Paradise Dance Hall across the alley.

JIM. How about cutting the rug a little, Miss Wingfield?

LAURA. Oh, I—

JIM. Or is your program filled up? Let me have a look at it. [*He grasps an imaginary card.*] Why, every dance is taken! I'll just have to scratch some out.

[*Waltz music: "La Golondrina"°*]

Ahh, a waltz! [*He executes some sweeping turns by himself, then holds his arms toward* LAURA.]

LAURA. [*breathlessly*] I—can't dance.

JIM. There you go, that inferiority stuff!

LAURA. I've never danced in my life!

JIM. Come on, try!

LAURA. Oh, but I'd step on you!

JIM. I'm not made out of glass.

LAURA. How—how—how do we start?

JIM. Just leave it to me. You hold your arms out a little.

LAURA. Like this?

JIM. [*taking her in his arms*] A little bit higher. Right. Now don't tighten up, that's the main thing about it—relax.

LAURA. [*laughing breathlessly*] It's hard not to.

JIM. Okay.

LAURA. I'm afraid you can't budge me.

JIM. What do you bet I can't? [*He swings her into motion.*]

LAURA. Goodness, yes, you can!

JIM. Let yourself go, now, Laura, just let yourself go.

LAURA. I'm—

JIM. Come on!

LAURA. —trying!

JIM. Not so stiff—easy does it!

LAURA. I know but I'm—

JIM. Loosen th' backbone! There now, that's a lot better.

LAURA. Am I?

JIM. Lots, lots better! [*He moves her about the room in a clumsy waltz.*]

LAURA. Oh, my!

JIM. Ha-ha!

LAURA. Oh, my goodness!

JIM. Ha-ha-ha!

[*They suddenly bump into the table, and the glass piece on it falls to the floor.* JIM *stops the dance.*]

What did we hit?

LAURA. Table.

JIM. Did something fall off it? I think—

LAURA. Yes.

JIM. I hope that it wasn't the little glass horse with the horn!

LAURA. Yes. [*She stoops to pick it up.*]

220.1 *"La Golondrina":* a popular Mexican song (1883) written by Narciso Seradell (1843–1910).

JIM.   Aw, aw, aw. Is it broken?   255
LAURA.   Now it is just like all the other horses.
JIM.   It's lost its—
LAURA.   Horn! It doesn't matter. Maybe it's a blessing in disguise.
JIM.   You'll never forgive me. I bet that that was your favorite piece of glass.
LAURA.   I don't have favorites much. It's no tragedy, Freckles. Glass breaks so   260
easily. No matter how careful you are. The traffic jars the shelves and things fall off
them.
JIM.   Still I'm awfully sorry that I was the cause.
LAURA.   [*smiling*] I'll just imagine he had an operation. The horn was removed
to make him feel less—freakish!

[*They both laugh.*]

Now he will feel more at home with the other horses, the ones that don't have
horns. . . .
JIM.   Ha-ha, that's very funny! [*Suddenly he is serious.*] I'm glad to see that you
have a sense of humor. You know—you're—well—very different! Surprisingly different from anyone else I know! [*His voice becomes soft and hesitant with a genuine feeling.*]
Do you mind me telling you that?

[*LAURA is abashed beyond speech.*]

I mean it in a nice way—

[*LAURA nods shyly, looking away.*]

You make me feel sort of—I don't know how to put it! I'm usually pretty good at expressing things, but—this is something that I don't know how to say!

[*LAURA touches her throat and clears it—turns the broken unicorn in her hands. His voice becomes softer.*]

Has anyone ever told you that you were pretty?

[*There is a pause, and the music rises slightly. LAURA looks up slowly, with wonder, and shakes
her head.*]

Well, you are! In a very different way from anyone else. And all the nicer because of the difference, too.

[*His voice becomes low and husky. LAURA turns away, nearly faint with the novelty of her emotions.*]

I wish that you were my sister. I'd teach you to have some confidence in yourself. The different people are not like other people, but being different is nothing to
be ashamed of. Because other people are not such wonderful people. They're one
hundred times one thousand. You're one times one! They walk all over the earth. You
just stay here. They're common as—weeds, but—you—well, you're—*Blue Roses*!

[*Image on screen: Blue Roses.*

The music changes.]

LAURA.   But blue is wrong for—roses. . . .
JIM.   It's right for you! You're—pretty!   265

LAURA.   In what respect am I pretty?

JIM.   In all respects—believe me! Your eyes—your hair—are pretty! Your hands are pretty! [*He catches hold of her hand.*] You think I'm making this up because I'm invited to dinner and have to be nice. Oh, I could do that! I could put on an act for you, Laura, and say lots of things without being very sincere. But this time I am. I'm talking to you sincerely. I happened to notice you had this inferiority complex that keeps you from feeling comfortable with people. Somebody needs to build your confidence up and make you proud instead of shy and turning away and—blushing. Somebody— ought to—*kiss* you, Laura!

[*His hand slips slowly up her arm to her shoulder as the music swells tumultuously. He suddenly turns about and kisses her on the lips. When he releases her,* LAURA *sinks on the sofa with a bright, dazed look.* JIM *backs away and fishes in his pocket for a cigarette.*]

Legend on screen: "A souvenir."]

Stumblejohn!

[*He lights the cigarette, avoiding her look. There is a peal of girlish laughter from* AMANDA *in the kitchenette.* LAURA *slowly raises and opens her hand. It still contains the little broken glass animal. She looks at it with a tender, bewildered expression.*]

Stumblejohn! I shouldn't have done that—that was way off the beam. You don't smoke, do you?

[*She looks up, smiling, not hearing the question. He sits beside her rather gingerly. She looks at him speechlessly—waiting. He coughs decorously and moves a little further aside as he considers the situation and senses her feelings, dimly, with perturbation. He speaks gently.*]

Would you—care for a mint?

[*She doesn't seem to hear him but her look grows brighter even.*]

Peppermint? Life Saver? My pocket's a regular drugstore—wherever I go. . . . [*He pops a mint in his mouth. Then he gulps and decides to make a clean breast of it. He speaks slowly and gingerly.*] Laura, you know, if I had a sister like you, I'd do the same thing as Tom. I'd bring out fellows and—introduce her to them. The right type of boys— of a type to—appreciate her. Only—well—he made a mistake about me. Maybe I've got no call to be saying this. That may not have been the idea in having me over. But what if it was? There's nothing wrong about that. The only trouble is that in my case— I'm not in a situation to—do the right thing. I can't take down your number and say I'll phone. I can't call up next week and—ask for a date. I thought I had better explain the situation in case you—misunderstood it and—I hurt your feelings. . . .

[*There is a pause. Slowly, very slowly,* LAURA'*s look changes, her eyes returning slowly from his to the glass figure in her palm.* AMANDA *utters another gay laugh in the kitchenette.*]

LAURA.   [*faintly*] You—won't—call again?

JIM.   No, Laura, I can't. [*He rises from the sofa.*] As I was just explaining, I've— got strings on me, Laura, I've—been going steady! I go out all the time with a girl named Betty. She's a home-girl like you, and Catholic, and Irish, and in a great many ways we—get along fine. I met her last summer on a moonlight boat trip up the river to Alton,° on the *Majestic.* Well—right away from the start it was—love!

69.1 *Alton:* a city in Illinois about twenty miles north of St. Louis on the Mississippi River.

[*Legend: Love!*

LAURA *sways slightly forward and grips the arm of the sofa. He fails to notice, now enrapt in his own comfortable being.*]

Being in love has made a new man of me!

[*Leaning stiffly forward, clutching the arm of the sofa,* LAURA *struggles visibly with her storm. But* JIM *is oblivious; she is a long way off.*]

The power of love is really pretty tremendous! Love is something that—changes the whole world, Laura!

[*The storm abates a little and* LAURA *leans back. He notices her again.*]

It happened that Betty's aunt took sick, she got a wire and had to go to Centralia.° So Tom—when he asked me to dinner—I naturally just accepted the invitation, not knowing that you—that he—that I—[*He stops awkwardly.*] Huh—I'm a stumblejohn!

[*He flops back on the sofa. The holy candles on the altar of* LAURA's *face have been snuffed out. There is a look of almost infinite desolation.* JIM *glances at her uneasily.*]

I wish that you would—say something.

[*She bites her lip which was trembling and then bravely smiles. She opens her hand again on the broken glass figure. Then she gently takes his hand and raises it level with her own. She carefully places the unicorn in the palm of his hand, then pushes his fingers closed upon it.*]

What are you—doing that for? You want me to have him? Laura?

[*She nods.*]

What for?
    LAURA. A—souvenir. . . .   270

[*She rises unsteadily and crouches beside the Victrola to wind it up.*

Legend on screen: "Things have a way of turning out so badly!" *Or image:* "Gentleman caller waving goodbye—gaily."

At this moment AMANDA *rushes brightly back into the living room. She bears a pitcher of fruit punch in an old-fashioned cut-glass pitcher, and a plate of macaroons. The plate has a gold border and poppies painted on it.*]

    AMANDA. Well, well, well! Isn't the air delightful after the shower? I've made you children a little liquid refreshment. [*She turns gaily to* JIM.] Jim, do you know that song about lemonade?
    "Lemonade, lemonade
    Made in the shade and stirred with a spade—
    Good enough for any old maid!"
    JIM. [*uneasily*] Ha-ha! No—I never heard it.
    AMANDA. Why, Laura! You look so serious!
    JIM. We were having a serious conversation.   275
    AMANDA. Good! Now you're better acquainted!

69.8 *Centralia:* a city in Illinois about sixty miles east of St. Louis.

JIM.   [*uncertainly*] Ha-ha! Yes.

AMANDA.   You modern young people are much more serious-minded than my generation. I was so gay as a girl!

JIM.   You haven't changed, Mrs. Wingfield.

AMANDA.   Tonight I'm rejuvenated! The gaiety of the occasion, Mr. O'Connor! [*She tosses her head with a peal of laughter, spilling some lemonade.*] Oooo! I'm baptizing myself!

JIM.   Here—let me—   280

AMANDA.   [*setting the pitcher down*] There now. I discovered we had some maraschino cherries. I dumped them in, juice and all!

JIM.   You shouldn't have gone to that trouble, Mrs. Wingfield.

AMANDA.   Trouble, trouble? Why, it was loads of fun! Didn't you hear me cutting up in the kitchen? I bet your ears were burning! I told Tom how outdone with him I was for keeping you to himself so long a time! He should have brought you over much, much sooner! Well, now that you've found your way, I want you to be a very frequent caller! Not just occasional but all the time. Oh, we're going to have a lot of gay times together! I see them coming! Mmm, just breathe that air! So fresh, and the moon's so pretty! I'll skip back out—I know where my place is when young folks are having a—serious conversation!

JIM.   Oh, don't go out, Mrs. Wingfield. The fact of the matter is I've got to be going.

AMANDA.   Going, now? You're joking! Why, it's only the shank of the evening,° Mr. O'Connor!   285

JIM.   Well, you know how it is.

AMANDA.   You mean you're a young workingman and have to keep workingmen's hours. We'll let you off early tonight. But only on the condition that next time you stay later. What's the best night for you? Isn't Saturday night the best night for you workingmen?

JIM.   I have a couple of time-clocks to punch, Mrs. Wingfield. One at morning, another one at night!

AMANDA.   My, but you *are* ambitious! You work at night, too?

JIM.   No, Ma'am, not work but—Betty!   290

[*He crosses deliberately to pick up his hat. The band at the Paradise Dance Hall goes into a tender waltz.*]

AMANDA.   Betty? Betty? Who's—Betty!

[*There is an ominous cracking sound in the sky.*]

JIM.   Oh, just a girl. The girl I go steady with!

[*He smiles charmingly. The sky falls.*

Legend: "The Sky Falls."]

AMANDA.   [*a long-drawn exhalation*] Ohhh ... Is it a serious romance, Mr. O'Connor?

JIM.   We're going to be married the second Sunday in June.

AMANDA.   Ohhh—how nice! Tom didn't mention that you were engaged to be   295
married.

---

285 *shank of the evening:* still early, the best part of the evening.

JIM. The cat's not out of the bag at the warehouse yet. You know how they are. They call you Romeo and stuff like that. [*He stops at the oval mirror to put on his hat. He carefully shapes the brim and the crown to give a discreetly dashing effect.*] It's been a wonderful evening, Mrs. Wingfield. I guess this is what they mean by Southern hospitality.

AMANDA. It really wasn't anything at all.

JIM. I hope it don't seem like I'm rushing off. But I promised Betty I'd pick her up at the Wabash depot, an' by the time I get my jalopy down there her train'll be in. Some women are pretty upset if you keep 'em waiting.

AMANDA. Yes, I know—the tyranny of women! [*She extends her hand.*] Goodbye, Mr. O'Connor. I wish you luck—and happiness—and success! All three of them, and so does Laura! Don't you, Laura?

LAURA. Yes!   300

JIM. [*taking LAURA's hand*] Goodbye, Laura. I'm certainly going to treasure that souvenir. And don't you forget the good advice I gave you. [*He raises his voice to a cheery shout.*] So long, Shakespeare! Thanks again, ladies. Good night!

[*He grins and ducks jauntily out. Still bravely grimacing, AMANDA closes the door on the gentleman caller. Then she turns back to the room with a puzzled expression. She and LAURA don't dare to face each other. LAURA crouches beside the Victrola to wind it.*]

AMANDA. [*faintly*] Things have a way of turning out so badly. I don't believe that I would play the Victrola. Well, well—well! Our gentleman caller was engaged to be married? [*She raises her voice.*] Tom!

TOM. [*from the kitchenette*] Yes, Mother?

AMANDA. Come in here a minute. I want to tell you something awfully funny.

TOM. [*entering with a macaroon and a glass of the lemonade*] Has the gentleman   305
caller gotten away already?

AMANDA. The gentleman caller has made an early departure. What a wonderful joke you played on us!

TOM. How do you mean?

AMANDA. You didn't mention that he was engaged to be married.

TOM. Jim? Engaged?

AMANDA. That's what he just informed us.   310

TOM. I'll be jiggered! I didn't know about that.

AMANDA. That seems very peculiar.

TOM. What's peculiar about it?

AMANDA. Didn't you call him your best friend down at the warehouse?

TOM. He is, but how did I know?   315

AMANDA. It seems extremely peculiar that you wouldn't know your best friend was going to be married!

TOM. The warehouse is where I work, not where I know things about people!

AMANDA. You don't know things anywhere! You live in a dream; you manufacture illusions!

[*He crosses to the door.*]

Where are you going?

TOM. I'm going to the movies.

AMANDA. That's right, now that you've had us make such fools of ourselves.   320
The effort, the preparations, all the expense! The new floor lamp, the rug, the clothes for Laura! All for what? To entertain some other girl's fiancé! Go to the movies, go!

Don't think about us, a mother deserted, an unmarried sister who's crippled and has no job! Don't let anything interfere with your selfish pleasure! Just go, go, go—to the movies!

TOM.   All right, I will! The more you shout about my selfishness to me the quicker I'll go, and I won't go to the movies!

AMANDA.   Go, then! Go to the moon—you selfish dreamer!

[*TOM smashes his glass on the floor. He plunges out on the fire escape, slamming the door. LAURA screams in fright. The dance-hall music becomes louder. TOM stands on the fire escape, gripping the rail. The moon breaks through the storm clouds, illuminating his face.*

Legend on screen: "And so goodbye. . ."

TOM's closing speech is timed with what is happening inside the house. We see, as though through soundproof glass, that AMANDA appears to be making a comforting speech to LAURA, who is huddled upon the sofa. Now that we cannot hear the mother's speech, her silliness is gone and she has dignity and tragic beauty. LAURA's hair hides her face until, at the end of the speech, she lifts her head to smile at her mother. AMANDA's gestures are slow and graceful, almost dance-like, as she comforts her daughter. At the end of her speech she glances a moment at the father's picture—then withdraws through the portieres. At the close of TOM's speech, LAURA blows out the candles, ending the play.]

TOM.   I didn't go to the moon, I went much further—for time is the longest distance between two places. Not long after that I was fired for writing a poem on the lid of a shoe-box. I left Saint Louis. I descended the steps of this fire escape for a last time and followed, from then on, in my father's footsteps, attempting to find in motion what was lost in space. I traveled around a great deal. The cities swept about me like dead leaves, leaves that were brightly colored but torn away from the branches. I would have stopped, but I was pursued by something. It always came upon me unawares, taking me altogether by surprise. Perhaps it was a familiar bit of music. Perhaps it was only a piece of transparent glass. Perhaps I am walking along a street at night, in some strange city, before I have found companions. I pass the lighted window of a shop where perfume is sold. The window is filled with pieces of colored glass, tiny transparent bottles in delicate colors, like bits of a shattered rainbow. Then all at once my sister touches my shoulder. I turn around and look into her eyes. Oh, Laura, Laura, I tried to leave you behind me, but I am more faithful than I intended to be! I reach for a cigarette, I cross the street, I run into the movies or a bar, I buy a drink, I speak to the nearest stranger—anything that can blow your candles out!

[*LAURA bends over the candles.*]

For nowadays the world is lit by lightning! Blow out your candles, Laura—and so goodbye. . . .

[*She blows the candles out.*]

QUESTIONS

1.   What does the setting described in the opening stage direction tell you about the Wingfields? Consider especially the adjectives and the symbolism of the alley and the fire escape.

2. Who is the "fifth character" in the play and how is his presence established? In what ways is Tom a parallel to this character?

3. What does Amanda reveal about her past in scene 1? How does Williams reveal that Amanda often dwells in the past?

4. What happened to Laura at Rubican's Business College? How can you account for her behavior? What plan of Amanda's did she upset?

5. What new plan for Laura's future does Amanda begin to develop in scene 2? Why is the plan impracticable? Why is the image of Jim introduced here?

6. Summarize the argument between Tom and Amanda in scene 3. What does Amanda assert about Tom? What does he claim about his life? Why is Laura spotlighted throughout the argument?

7. What sort of agreement does Amanda try to reach with Tom about Laura in scene 4?

8. How do Amanda and Laura react to the news of a gentleman caller? Describe Laura's feelings toward Jim during the conversation and the dancing in scene 7. Describe how he changes after the kiss.

9. Explain the symbolism of the unicorn (both whole and broken). Why does Laura give it to Jim as a souvenir?

10. What is Tom's situation at the end? To what degree has he achieved his dreams of escape and adventure?

11. Describe Amanda's and Laura's concluding situations. Why does Laura blow out of the candles? What is the future for these women?

GENERAL QUESTIONS

1. Explain the most striking nonrealistic aspects of the play. What do these contribute to the play's meaning and impact? Which aspect is the most effective? Why?

2. Which characters in the play change significantly? To what extent do the characters succeed or fail? How do they try to escape the realities they face?

3. Consider Tom as character and narrator. Explain why his language changes as he shifts between narrator and character. What does the character dream about and strive for? What does the narrator learn about these dreams and strivings?

4. Explain why Laura cannot deal with reality. What does her glass menagerie symbolize?

5. Williams says that there is much to admire, pity, and laugh at in Amanda. What aspects of her character are admirable? Pitiable? Laughable? Which reaction is dominant for you at the close of the play? Why?

6. Tom calls Jim the play's "most realistic character." In what ways is Jim realistic? How are his dreams and goals more (or less) realistic than Tom's?

7. At the opening, Tom (as narrator) mentions the "social background," and he remarks on it throughout. Discuss how this background relates to the play, especially the events occurring in Europe.

8. Discuss the play's religious allusion and imagery, especially Malvolio the Magician, the "Ave Maria," the "Annunciation," the Paradise Dance Hall, and Laura's candles. How do these references affect the play's level of reality?

WRITING ABOUT REALISTIC AND NONREALISTIC DRAMA

Your essay should take into account the traditional elements of drama—plot, character, language, setting, symbol, and theme. Conventional approaches to these elements are discussed in Chapter 26 (pp. 1020–26), and you may want to review this material. As you plan your essay, your overall concern should be to determine the relative degrees of realism or nonrealism with which the elements are presented and developed. Your discoveries here will enable you to describe the ways in which the play establishes its views and ideas about life and the world. In short, how do conventional aspects of dramatic structure, together with the degree of realism or nonrealism, create a perspective that is the unique property of the play?

Questions for Discovering Ideas

PLOT. Does the play unfold in a chronological order that imitates reality, or does it mix past and present action? Is the action true to life or stylized? Are the conflicts resolved realistically, or does the playwright employ a conventional and perhaps improbable happy (or sad) ending? How does the realistic or nonrealistic development of these aspects affect the play's meaning and impact?

CHARACTER. Are the characters mainly realistic, or symbolic, representative, or stereotyped? Are they round or flat? Are they motivated by lifelike considerations, such as Amanda in *The Glass Menagerie*, who lives only in the past? Or are they motivated by the play's requirements, such as the narrator, who has the artificial role of speaking directly to the audience? Are the characters consistent, or do they drop in and out of character? Is their clothing and makeup (as described in the stage directions) an imitation of real life, or is it theatrical and nonrealistic? Are all the characters developed in the same manner, or are there differences in the degree of realism you find in each? Is one character more or less realistic than any of the others? If so, what impact does this have on the play?

LANGUAGE. Look carefully at the diction, style, and patterns of the dialogue. In realistic drama, what is the nature of the speeches? Is the language colloquial, formal, low? Is it appropriate for the characters? Do the characters speak normally to each other? Do they shout? Whisper? Why? What pattern of consistency can you discover by studying how the characters speak? Within the confines of realistic drama, what normal or realistic variations occur (e.g., a letter is read aloud; a phone conversation occurs; a character is alone onstage and speaks to characters offstage [as in *Before Breakfast*])? What proportion of the dialogue is normal two- or three-way conversation? How much variation occurs, and what kind is it? Why do you think the dramatists have varied the normal dialogue, and how do these variations shape your perception of the play?

In nonrealistic drama, some dialogue will be realistically normal, or appear so, but much of it will be shaped by the play's nonrealistic premise. How do you identify nonrealistic speech? Do you find nonrealistic devices such as verse, song, or unnatural and patterned repetition? Does any character seem to be speaking in different voices? If so, why? Which characters seem to ignore other characters, and speak instead to the air, or to the audience? How extensive is such direct address? Does a single character do most of this talking? If so, what is he or she like? What does the character tell you about himself or herself? About the other characters in the play? The background? Plot? Action? Setting? Staging? How accurate and objective is this character? How does this direct address shape and control your responses?

In sum, how do all aspects of language determine the extent to which the play effectively communicates ideas and emotions to you? As you deal with language, also consider the significance of other aspects of sound indicated in the stage directions, such as sound effects or music.

SETTING. To what degree do the stage directions present the setting as realistic or nonrealistic? Do they call in minute detail for the reproduction of an actual room or place? If less than a fully realistic setting is described, how far does the playwright go in reducing the setting to the bare stage? How much of the physical theater (brick walls, pipes, wires, lights, backstage ropes) does the playwright indicate that he or she wants you to see or imagine? To what extent do you find symbolic, impressionistic, and nonrealistic devices such as transparent walls? How do the stage directions describe lighting? Is the lighting used realistically, to recreate natural illumination, or nonrealistically, to isolate and emphasize specific places, objects, characters, or actions? Most important, how does the setting and its degree of realism (or nonrealism) contribute to the impact and meaning of the play?

SYMBOLISM. Because symbols operate in life as they do in art, there is symbolism both in the realistic plays of Glaspell and Ibsen, and in the relatively nonrealistic dramas of Miller and Williams. Are symbols introduced through realistic or logical techniques, or do they appear illogically and nonrealistically? You can focus your exploration directly on the symbol and its meaning (the locked mailbox in *A Doll House*) or the nonrealistic methods though which it is established (the blue roses in *The Glass Menagerie*).

THEME. What are the important concepts in the play, and how are they conveyed? Be sure to give special consideration to significantly realistic or nonrealistic techniques. In a realistic play like *Trifles* or *Mulatto*, explore the ways in which realism in character, action, and setting contribute to the play's ideas. Conversely, consider how Williams employs a strikingly nonrealistic device, such as the music of the screen projections, to convey and emphasize the themes of *The Glass Menagerie*.

Strategies for Organizing Ideas

Your central idea should show how specifically realistic or nonrealistic elements affect part or all of the play. Try to connect the topic with its effect. For example, begin with sentences such as: (1) "Tom as a nonrealistic narrator and realistic character unifies *The Glass Menagerie* and gives the play a coherent and subjective point of view." (2) In *A Doll House*, Torvald's threats against Nora actually cause her decision to determine her own destiny.

The supporting details may be organized in any way that produces a logical and convincing essay. If you are writing about the ways in which nonrealistic devices emphasize meaning in *The Glass Menagerie*, for example, you might organize your essay around the setting, the lighting, and the screen device. When your essay focuses on only one element, you may organize your supporting details to reflect the order in which they occur in the play.

In your conclusion you might raise larger issues than you have already raised, or make broader connections not only about your topics, but also about the play as a whole. You might also reconsider the significance of the play's general level of realistic or nonrealistic techniques.

SAMPLE ESSAY

Realism and Nonrealism in Tom's Triple Role in *The Glass Menagerie*°

[1] In *The Glass Menagerie*, Tennessee Williams combines realistic and nonrealistic elements to explore the personalities and conflicts of the Wingfield family. One of his most effective nonrealistic elements in the play is his use of Tom in three different roles.* As realistic character within the action, nonrealistic stage manager of the action, and nonrealistic narrator of the entire play, Tom combines three functions that significantly shape our perception of the drama.†

[2] As a realistic character involved in the recollected action of the play, Tom is ensnared by the economic and emotional demands of his family and his job. In the opening description of the characters, Williams describes Tom's plight: "To escape from a trap he [Tom] has to act without pity." In addition, Tom himself dramatically expresses his need to escape from his stifling life at home. He discusses this need with his mother in scene 3, with Laura in scene 4, and, above all, with Jim in scene 6. Here, we see that Tom craves not only escape but also adventure. He tells Jim, "I'm planning a change." And he clearly expresses his desire to move out of the prison house of the family:

> It's our turn now, to go the South Sea Island—to make a safari—to be exotic, far off! But I'm not patient. I don't want to wait till then, I'm tired of the movies and I am about to move! (speech 114)

° See page 1519 for this play.
* Central idea.
† Thesis sentence.

I'm starting to boil inside. I know I seem dreamy, but inside—well, I'm boiling. (speech 120)

These expressions of his need to escape define a major line of the realistic thought and action in The Glass Menagerie.

[3]
Tom's realism as a character is deeply undercut by his momentary role as a stage manager in scene 1. Here, he speaks with Amanda "as though reading from a script." In this same scene, "Tom motions for music and a spot of light on Amanda." Although this device is abandoned, the image of Tom holding an imaginary script and giving cues to the musicians and the lighting technicians breaks any possible illusions that the play is imitating real life. The role as manager emphasizes the fact that The Glass Menagerie is a play designed for the stage and for live actors carrying out conventional stage roles.

[4]
Tom's part in shaping and unifying the play is most apparent in his nonrealistic function as narrator. In this role, he stands aside from the action occurring in the Wingfield apartment, and he also speaks directly to us. He introduces the characters, provides background, and supplies an ongoing retrospective commentary. In addition, he performs the unifying function of personifying the theme of escape and presenting his own subjective perspective. As the past character, the one actually involved in the play's action, he represents a yearning for freedom and adventure. As the present narrator, however, he speaks truths that his character in its past role has not yet learned, and he thus recognizes that escape from the past is impossible. When the play closes, he tells us that he remains trapped (speech 323), and thus he provides a final perspective on the central theme of escape.

[5]
The second striking aspect of Tom's function as narrator concerns his complete control of the play. Because he is the narrator, the action in The Glass Menagerie represents Tom's memories of events, rather than the events themselves. In his first speech, Tom tells us that "The play is memory. Being a memory play, it is dimly lighted, it is sentimental, it is not realistic." Since the events which occur on stage from the past emerge from Tom's memory, it is he who provides an overriding unity and perspective. We see everything through his mind and from his point of view. As a nonrealistic narrator, he holds the stage action together and totally controls our responses.

[6]
Williams thus uses Tom in three distinct ways to create unity and perspective. As a realistic character aching to leave the confines of home, he embodies the theme of escape. As a nonrealistic stage manager, he illustrates the artificiality of the dramatic literary form and stresses the legendary nature of the action. As the play's narrator, he imposes a subjective but coherent control over the action and offers thematic resolution. The nonrealistic aspects of his roles mesh perfectly with other devices that Williams employs nonrealistically, especially the slides, music and lighting.

[7]
Whether realistic or unrealistic, however, The Glass Menagerie is about life—its desires, its dreams, its need for independent action, its disappointments, and its poignancy. If Williams did not dramatize these issues, the technique alone would not make a great play. But he does dramatize them, and as a result the freedom of action and character he achieves through the combination of roles for Tom enables him to achieve a remarkable unity of topic, merging past with present and reality with unreality. Williams's use of Tom,

then, is a major reason for which The Glass Menagerie is a great modern drama.

Commentary on the Essay

This essay shows how Williams's manipulation of Tom creates artistic and thematic unity in *The Glass Menagerie*. The primary focus is on character, but a number of distinct topics are taken up in connection with this element because the essay concerns Tom as a character, stage director, and narrator.

The body of the essay (paragraphs 2–5) takes up these three roles in the order listed in the introduction. Notice that this order does not reflect the sequence in which these roles occur in the play. Rather, they are organized to reflect a progression from the most realistic to the most nonrealistic aspects of Tom's three different functions. Thus, paragraph 2 discusses Tom as a realistic character and connects him to one of the plays central themes—entrapment and the desire to escape. Paragraphs 3, 4, and 5 shift to a consideration of Tom first as stage manager and second as narrator. These paragraphs explain the nonrealistic nature of these roles, and explore the effects of Tom as the nonrealistic figure.

The concluding two paragraphs (6 and 7) provide a review-summary of the three roles that Tom plays and the effects that each produces in connection with theme and unity. In addition, they suggest a connection between the nonrealistic aspects of Tom's roles and the play's great power.

Throughout the body, direct quotation of dialogue or action as indicated in the stage directions is employed as supporting evidence. Quotations are used to validate specific points, and are documented either within parentheses or in the body of discourse itself.

WRITING TOPICS

1. Compare the families of Mommy and Daddy in *The Sandbox*, the Wingfields in *The Glass Menagerie*, the Helmers in *A Doll House*, and Colonel Norwood in *Mulatto*. What concept of family do these plays present? What good and bad effects do the families create? Which type of effect predominates? How realistic is the internal family dissension? How serious? How essential to the various plots? What is unusual or illogical about the dissensions? How? Why?

2. Compare the sets of *The Sandbox* and *The Glass Menagerie*. What elements of realism or nonrealism are common? How? Why? What effects would the sets have on the audience? Why?

3. The screen device described in Williams's Production Notes (see p. 1520) is omitted from most productions of *The Glass Menagerie*. Why? Consider the advantages or disadvantages of referring to this device in the printed text. How do the screen images affect your reading?

4. Describe Hughes's symbolism in *Mulatto*. How does the symbolism bring out the black-white differences in the play? Which locations, objects, and actions are symbolic, and what do they symbolize? In what ways are the symbols realistic? If they were not realistic, would they be successful as symbols?

5. Consider any of the plays in this chapter, using either a feminist or an economic determinist approach (see Appendix D for discussions of these approaches). What elements of realism or nonrealism are relevant to such a discussion?

6. Write two separate versions of a scene of your own. (Some possible topics: a woman confronts her boyfriend upon learning that he has been seeing someone else; a man has an interview with his boss and learns that he must be let go; an army lieutenant tells his platoon that they are about to be attacked; a woman realizes that she is the best salesperson in the firm.) First, aim for total reality, and second, for total unreality. What differences do you think your differing intentions require of you as a practicing dramatist? What different requirements are made on your dialogue, on your action, on your setting, and on your costuming and suggested makeup for your actors? What elements do you think are the most unrealistic in your unrealistic version, and why do you believe you make them so unrealistic? Does the lack of realism, in your judgment, make your scene either more or less dramatic? Write an introductory essay to your two versions explaining these and other principles of your dramatic composition.

30
Film: Drama on the Silver and Color Screens

Film is the word most often used for motion pictures, although other common words are "picture" and (more likely) "movie." It is a specialized type of drama, utilizing, like drama, the techniques of dialogue, monologue, and action. Also like drama, it employs movement and spectacle. For these reasons, film may be studied for aspects such as character, structure, tone, theme, and symbolism. Unlike drama, however, film embodies techniques from photography, film chemistry, sound, and editing. These techniques are so specialized that they require special consideration.

A THUMBNAIL HISTORY OF FILM

Film arose out of technologies developed in the late nineteenth century. The first of these was the creation of a flexible substance—celluloid—that could accept the silver iodide emulsions that in the early years of photography were applied to glass. The other significant inventions were the motion picture camera and projector. Once these were in place, and once producers and directors decided to use the medium for full-length dramas, movies as we know them came into existence.

Although the earliest filmmakers thought of motion pictures as private entertainment, it soon became apparent that the development of large filmmaking studios, national distribution, and a system of local movie theaters could become extremely lucrative. The history of film is hence just as much a history of the film *business* as of the art and development of film dramas and film acting. With the production in 1915 of D. W. Griffith's *Birth of a Nation*, which realized an enormous profit on a small investment, filmmaking became a major industry.

The first motion pictures were black and white and were silent. Producers realized that large profits required easily recognized actors with "big names," and hence the "star system" made national figures out of actors like Mary Pickford, Charlie Chaplin, and Rudolph Valentino. In 1928 the first talking picture, *Lights of New York*, was made. In 1932, with the first technicolor film, *La Cucaracha*, most of the current basic filmmaking tools were in existence.

For a time after the end of World War II, the growth of television inhibited the power of the large studios. Soon, however, many films were developed specifically for television viewing, and popular pictures were released for television use. In the last decade, with the advent of videotape and laser technology, home viewing has become a normal feature of American life. Today, film rental outlets may be found in shopping districts everywhere, with the result that virtually the entire corpus of movies, from the origins to the present, are within the reach of everyone with a VCR and a television set.[1] Early dramatists dreamed of filling their theaters for a number of consecutive performances, thus reaching perhaps several thousand persons. Film writers today, however, reach millions in the first-run movie houses, and many millions more on television re-runs and videocassettes.

STAGE PLAYS AND FILM

While the film we speak about is a form of drama, there are a number of important differences between a film and the stage production of a play. A play may be produced many times, in many different places, with many different people. In bringing a play to life, the producer and director not only employ actors, but also use artists, scene designers, carpenters, painters, lighting technicians, costume-makers, choreographers, and music directors and musicians. Each production is therefore different from every other, because not only the actors, but also the appurtenances of the staging, are unique.

A film, however, because of high production costs, and also because it reaches a mass audience, usually exists in only one version ("remakes" being excepted). Thus Shakespeare's play *Hamlet* has been staged innumerable times since Shakespeare's actors first produced it at the beginning of the seventeenth century. Orson Welles's *Citizen Kane* (1941) is in only one form, however, and, although it was restored and reedited in 1991, it cannot undergo any substantial changes.

As might be expected, then, stage and movie productions are radically different. In a play, actors enter, speak to each other, and remain in front of the audience until they exit. The stage itself limits what can be done. How-

---

[1] In addition, the technology of CD-ROM (*Compact Disk—Read Only Memory*) has recently been introduced. The film *A Hard Day's Night*, starring the Beatles, has been set up as a pilot example of how films may be adapted for CD-ROM on a personal computer. The offering includes the film itself (which may be stopped, moved forward, or moved backward at any point), together with explanations, commentary, the original script, notes on the songs, and other materials. This technology is only in the initial stages for film, but if it is widely adapted and distributed, the implications for film study are overwhelming, particularly if CD-ROM disks can be made available for inexpensive rental, as has happened with videocassettes.

ever, the makers of a film have few such limitations, and the absence of restrictions permits the inclusion of any detail whatever, from a car chase to a scene in the Napoleonic wars. If there is to be a scene on a desert island, the film-maker goes to such an island and presents it in all its reality, complete with beach, palm trees, huts, and authentic natives-turned-actors. Nothing is left to your imagination. If the scene is a distant planet, obviously the film-maker cannot go on location there, but instead creates a working location in the studio, with lighting, props, costumes, and special effects. In addition, modern computerized special effects create scenes that were unimaginable in the past. Film, in short, enables a dramatic production to approach almost complete freedom.

THE AESTHETIC OF FILM

To the degree that film is confined to a screen, it may be compared visually to the art of the painter and the still photographer. It uses the language of visual art. One object in a painting may take on special relationships to others as the artist directs the eyes of the observer. A color used in one part may be balanced with the same color, or its complement, in another part. Painters and photographers may introduce certain colors and details as symbols, and may suggest allegorical interpretations through the inclusion of mythical figures or universally recognized objects. Particular effects may be achieved with the use of the textures of the paint and control over shutter speed, focus, and various techniques of development. The techniques and effects are extensive.

The film-maker is able to utilize most of the resources of the still photographer and many of those of the painter, and may augment these with special effects. Artistically, the most confining aspect of film is the rectangular screen, but aside from that, film is unrestricted. Based in a dramatic text called a "filmscript" or "shooting script," it uses words and their effects, but it also employs the language of visual art, and especially the particular vividness and power of moving pictures. When considering film, then, you should realize that film communicates not only with words, but also by various techniques. The visual presentation is inseparable from the medium of film itself.

TECHNIQUES OF FILM

There are many techniques of film, and a full description and documentation of them can be—and has become—extensive.[2] In evaluating film, how-

---

[2] See, for example, Louis D. Giannetti, *Understanding Movies*, 7th ed. (Englewood Cliffs: Prentice Hall, 1995); Ephraim Katz, *The Film Encyclopedia* (New York: Crowell, 1979; Katz died in 1993, and a new edition will be done by other editors.); James Monaco et al., *The Encyclopedia of Film* (New York: Perigee, 1991); James Monaco, *How to Read a Film*, rev. ed. (New York: Oxford University Press, 1981); Daniel Talbot, ed., *Film: An Anthology* (Berkeley: University of California Press, 1969); and John Wyver, *The Moving Image* (Oxford: Basil Blackwell, 1989).

ever, you need to familiarize yourself only with those aspects of technique that have an immediate bearing on your responses and interpretations.

Editing or Montage

A finished film is not a continuous work, filmed from start to end, but is instead a composite. The putting together of the film is the process of *editing*, or **montage** (assemblage, mounting, construction), which is a cutting and gluing. Depending on the flexibility of the filmscript, the various scenes of the film are planned before shooting begins, but the major task of montage is done in a studio, by special film editors.

If we again compare film with a stage play, we may note that a theatrical production moves continuously, with pauses only for intermissions and scene changes. Your perception of the action is caused by your distance from the stage (perhaps aided by opera glasses or binoculars). Also, even as you move your eyes from one character to another, you still perceive the entire stage. In a film, however, the directors and editors *create* these continuous perceptions for you by piecing together different parts. The editors begin with many "takes" (separately filmed scenes, including many versions of the same scenes). What they select, or mount, will be the film, and we never see the discarded scenes. Thus, it is editing that puts everything together.

MONTAGE AND NARRATIVE CONTINUITY. The first use of montage, already suggested, is narrative continuity. For example, a climb up a steep cliff may be shown at the bottom, middle, and top (with backward slips and falls to show the danger of the climb and to make viewers catch their breaths). All such narrative sequences result from the assembling of individual pieces, each one representing phases of the activity. A classic example of a large number of separate parts forming a narrative unit is the well-known shower murder in Alfred Hitchcock's *Psycho* (1959), where a forty-five second sequence is made up of seventy-eight different shots (e.g., the woman in the shower, the murderer behind the curtain, the attack, the slumping figure, the running water, the dead woman's eye, the bathtub drain, etc.).

EXPLANATION OF CHARACTER AND MOTIVATION. Montage is used in "flashbacks" to explain present, ongoing actions or characteristics, or in illustration of a character's thoughts and memories, or in brief examples from the unremembered past of a character suffering from amnesia. It also supplies direct visual explanation of character. A famous example occurs in Welles's *Citizen Kane* (the subject of the sample essay in this chapter). The concluding scene shows overhead views of Kane's vast collection of statues and mementos. At the very end, the camera focuses on a raging incinerator, into which workmen have thrown his boyhood sled, which bears the brand name "Rosebud" (and which we have fleetingly seen him playing with as a boy). Because "Rosebud" is Kane's last word, which everyone in the film is trying to learn about, this final scene shows that Kane's dying thoughts are about his lost boyhood, before he was taken away from his parents, and that his unhappy life has resulted from his early rejection and personal pain.

DIRECTORIAL COMMENTARY. In addition, montage is used symbolically as commentary, as in an early sequence in Charlie Chaplin's *Modern Times* (1936), which shows a large group of workers rushing to their factory jobs. Immediately following this scene is a view of a large, milling herd of sheep. By this symbolic montage, Chaplin suggests that the men are being herded and dehumanized by modern industry. Thus, montage and editorial statement go hand in hand.

OTHER USES. Montage may also produce other characteristics through camera work, development, and special effects. For example, filmmakers can reverse an action to emphasize its illogicality or ridiculousness. Editing can also speed up action (which makes even the most serious things funny), or slow things down. It can also blend one scene with another, or juxtapose two or more actions in quick succession to show what people may be doing while they are separated. The possibilities for creativity and uniqueness are extensive.

Visual Techniques

THE CAMERA. While editing or montage is a finishing technique, the work of film begins with the camera, which permits great freedom in the presentation of characters and actions. In a film, the visual viewpoint can shift. Thus, a film may begin with a distant shot of the actors—a "longshot"—much like the view of actors on stage. Then the camera can zoom in to give a closeup, or zoom out to present a wide and complete panorama. Usually a speaking actor will be the subject of a closeup, but the camera may also show closeups of other actors who are reacting. You must decide on the effects of closeups and longshots yourself, but it should be plain that the frequent use of either—or of middle-distance photographs—is a means by which film directors control perceptions of their characters and situations.

The camera may also move from character to character, or from character to an object. In this way a film may show a series of reactions to an event. It may also concentrate your attention on a character's attitude, or it may be a visual commentary on his or her actions. If a man and woman are in love, as an example, the camera may shift, either directly or through montage, from the couple to flowers and trees, thus associating their love visually with objects of beauty and growth. Should the flowers be wilted and the trees leafless, however, the visual commentary might be that their love is doomed and hopeless.

The camera may also create unique effects. Slow motion, for example, can focus on a certain aspect of a person's character. The concentrated focus on a child running happily in a meadow (as in *The Color Purple* [1985] by

Steven Spielberg) suggests the joy inherent in such movement. Surprisingly, speed is sometimes indicated by slow motion, which emphasizes strong muscular effort (as in the running scenes in Hugh Hudson's *Chariots of Fire* [1981]).

Many other camera techniques bear on action and character. The focus may be sharp at one point, indistinct at another. Moving a speaking character out of focus may suggest that listeners are bored. Sharp or blurred focus may also show that a character has seen things exactly or inexactly. In action sequences, the camera may be mounted in a moving vehicle to "track" or follow running human beings or horses, speeding bicycles and cars (as in Woody Allen's *Annie Hall*), or moving sailboats, canoes, speedboats, or rowboats. A camera operator on foot may also be the tracker, or the camera may track ground movement from an aircraft. Movement may also be captured by a rotating camera that follows a moving object or character. Then, too, the camera may be fixed while the moving object goes from one side to the other.

LIGHT, SHADOW, AND COLOR. As in the theater, the film-maker uses light, shadow, and color to reinforce ideas and to create realistic and symbolic effects. A scene in sunshine, which brings out colors, and the same scene in rain and clouds or in twilight, all of which mute colors, create different moods. Characters in bright light are presumably open and frank, whereas characters in shadow may be hiding something, particularly in black and white films. Flashing or strobe lights might show a changeable or sinister character or situation.

Colors, of course, have much the same meaning that they have in any other artistic medium. Blue sky and clear light suggest happiness, while greenish light may indicate something ghoulish. A memorable control of color occurs midway through David O. Selznick's *Gone With the Wind* (1939), when Scarlet O'Hara reflects upon the devastation of her plantation home, Tara. She resolves never to be hungry again, and as she speaks she is silhouetted against a darkened orange sky—a background which suggests how totally the way of life she knew as a young woman has been burned away. As in this example, you may expect colors to complement the story of the film. Thus, lovers may wear clothing with the same or complementary colors, while people who are not "right" for each other may wear clashing colors.

Action Techniques

The strength of film is direct action. Actions of all sorts—running, swimming, driving a car, fighting, embracing and kissing, or even just sitting; chases, trick effects, ambushes—all these and more create a sense of immediate reality, and all are tied (or should be) to narrative development. Scenes of action may run on for several minutes, with little or no accompanying dialogue, to carry on the story or to convey ideas about the interests and abilities of the characters.

Closely related to the portrayal of action is the way in which film shows the human body (and animal bodies), together with bodily motion and gesture (or body language). The view or perspective that the film-maker presents is particularly important. A torso shot of a character may stress no more than the content alone of that character's speech. A closeup shot, however, with the character's head filling the screen, may emphasize motives as well as content. The camera may also distort ordinary expectations of reality. With wide-angle lenses and closeups, for example, human subjects may be made to seem bizarre or grotesque, as with the faces in the crowd in Woody Allen's *Stardust Memories* (1980). Sometimes the camera creates other bodily distortions, enlarging certain limbs, for example, as with the forest dweller in Ingmar Bergman's *Virgin Spring* (1959), or throwing into unnatural prominence a scolding mouth or a suspicious eye. If distortion is used, it invites interpretation: The film-maker may be asserting that certain human beings, even supposedly normal ones, are odd, sinister, intimidating, or psychotic.

Sound Techniques

DIALOGUE AND MUSIC. The first business of the sound track is the spoken dialogue, which is "mixed" in editing to be synchronized with the action. There are also many other elements in the sound track. Music, the most important, creates and augments moods. A melody in a major or minor key, or in a slow or fast tempo, may affect our perception of actions. If a character is thinking deeply, muted strings may create a complementary sound. But if the character is going insane, the music may become discordant and percussive.

Sometimes, music gives a film a special identity. In Hudson's *Chariots of Fire*, for example, Vangelis Papathanassiou wrote music that has become separately popular, but which is always identified with the film. In addition, musical accompaniments may directly render dramatic statement, without dialogue. An example occurs in Welles's *Citizen Kane.* Beginning that portion of the narrative derived from the autobiography of a character who is now dead (the scene first focuses on his statue), the musical sound track by Bernard Herrmann quotes the "Dies Irae" theme from the traditional Mass for the Dead. The instrumentation, however, makes the music funny, and we do not grieve but rather smile. Herrmann, incidentally, varies this theme elsewhere in the film, usually for comic effect.

SPECIAL SOUND EFFECTS. Special sound effects may also augment a film's action. The sound of a blow, for example, may be enhanced electronically to cause an impact similar to the force of the blow itself (as in the boxing scenes from the many *Rocky* films). At times some sounds, such as the noises of wailing people, squeaking or slamming doors, marching feet, or moving vehicles, may be filtered through an electronic apparatus to create weird or ghostly effects. Often a character's words may echo rapidly and sickeningly to show dismay or anguish. In a word, sound is a vital part of film.

ORSON WELLES AND HERMAN J. MANKIEWICZ

Shot 71 from the Shooting Script of Citizen Kane

Orson Welles (1915–1985) developed an early interest in the theater. As a youth he traveled extensively, even spending some time in Spain as a bullfighter. In 1937 he co-founded the Mercury Theatre, specializing in hour-long Sunday evening radio dramatizations. In October, 1938, he achieved early immortality by acting in and directing a version of H. G. Wells's *The War of the Worlds*. This production created a near panic in the nation among listeners who did not understand they were hearing a dramatic production, not a real news broadcast about invaders from the planet Mars.

Within a few years Welles, along with Herman J. Mankiewicz, planned a film on a larger-than-life American figure. Their model was the newspaper magnate William Randolph Hearst. Mankiewicz produced a lengthy draft of the script, which was first titled *American*, and then, a little later, *John Citizen, USA*. Welles contributed by changing the plot, rewriting many sections, and editing and shortening much of the original material. It was during this process of rewriting and editing that the title *Citizen Kane* was proposed and accepted. Soon, Welles began production with many of the actors of the Mercury Theatre. Hearst, who quickly learned about the forthcoming film, sought a legal restraint on it, but *Citizen Kane* was successfully completed despite his efforts. The film reached the movie theaters with massive critical acclaim.

In 1958, a poll of international critics listed *Citizen Kane* as one of the twelve best films ever made. Its use of the format similar to *The March of Time* (a popular news feature series that ran regularly as a "selected short subject" in movie theaters), deep-focus camera work, unusual camera angles, contrasts of light and shadow, and its employment of four separate points of view, together with its relentless insights into the major figure—all combined to make it a pioneering work in the history of film. Today, it is one of the touchstones in any discussion of movies, and its continued recognition justifies the claim that Welles was one of the great directors. After *Citizen Kane*, however, Welles encountered personal and financial difficulties with each of his films, and he never again reached the heights of his first attempt.

The scene included here occurs about two-thirds of the way through the film. It is vital because it is a major indicator of Kane's personal decline. At first imbued with ideals for informing and reforming society, Kane (Orson Welles) becomes publisher of a newspaper he has inherited, and he assumes public-minded editorial policies. A high point in his career is his running for governor of the state, but because news of his secret love affair becomes public, he loses the election. The scene occurs right after the loss. His most loyal supporter and co-worker, Jedediah Leland (Joseph Cotten), confronts him and asks for a transfer to Chicago. The unspoken issue in the scene is that both men know that their friendship has been lost not because of the election, but because of Kane's misperceptions of people and his desertion of his earlier ideals.

The scene is taken from the so-called "shooting script," which in film most closely corresponds to a dramatic text, and it is the full version, with copious directions for the actors. A comparison of this "shot," or scene, with the filmed version will show that some of the dialogue has been trimmed for purposes of pacing and speed. The shortening indicates a major characteristic of film (and the production of plays), namely, to reduce speeches to no more than the essentials in order to keep the action moving and hold the audience's attention.

Still from *Citizen Kane* (Bettmann)

ORSON WELLES (1915–1985)
AND HERMAN J. MANKIEWICZ (1897–1953)

Shot 71 of the Shooting Script of Citizen Kane——————————— *(1941)*

RKO Radio Pictures. A Mercury Production. Producer and Director, Orson Welles. Photographer, Gregg Toland, Editor, Robert Wise. Art Director, Van Nest Polglase. Music, Bernard Herrmann. Special Effects, Vernon L. Walker.

Dissolve In

71 Int. Kane's Office—"Inquirer"—Night—1916

KANE looks up from his desk as there is a knock on the door.

KANE.   Come in.

LELAND enters.

KANE.   (*Surprised*) I thought I heard somebody knock.

LELAND.   (*A bit drunk*) I knocked. (*He looks at him defiantly*)

KANE.   (*Trying to laugh it off*) Oh! An official visit of state, eh? (*Waves his hand*) Sit down, Jedediah.

LELAND.   (*Sitting down angrily*) I'm drunk.   5

KANE.   Good! It's high time—

LELAND.   You don't have to be amusing.

KANE.   All right. Tell you what I'll do. I'll get drunk, too.

LELAND.   (*Thinks this over*) No. That wouldn't help. Besides, you never get drunk. (*Pauses*) I want to talk to you—about—about—(*He can't get it out*)

KANE.   (*Looks at him sharply a moment*) If you've got yourself drunk to talk to me   10 about Susan Alexander—I'm not interested.

LELAND.   She's not important. What's much more important—(*He keeps glaring at Kane*)

KANE.   (*As if genuinely surprised*) Oh! (*He gets up*) I frankly didn't think I'd have to listen to that lecture from you. (*Pauses*) I've betrayed the sacred cause of reform, is that it? I've set back the sacred cause of reform in this state twenty years. Don't tell me, Jed, *you*—

Despite his load,° LELAND manages to achieve a dignity about the silent contempt with which he looks at KANE.

KANE.   (*An outburst*) What makes the sacred cause of reform so sacred? Why does the sacred cause of reform have to be exempt from all the other facts of life? Why do the laws of this state have to be executed by a man on a white charger?

LELAND lets the storm ride over his head.

KANE.   (*Cont'd*) (*Calming down*) But, if that's the way they want it—they've made their choice. The people of this state obviously prefer Mr. Rogers to me. (*His lips tighten*) So be it.

LELAND.   You talk about the people as though they belong to you. As long as I   15 can remember you've talked about giving the people their rights as though you could make them a present of liberty—in reward for services rendered. You remember the workingman? You used to write an awful lot about the workingman. Well, he's turning into something called organized labor, and you're not going to like that a bit when you find out it means that he thinks he's entitled to something as his right and not your gift. (*He pauses*) And listen, Charles. When your precious underprivileged really do get together—that's going to add up to something bigger—than your privilege—and then I don't know what you'll do. Sail away to a desert island, probably, and lord it over the monkeys.

Load: i.e., a heavy amount of liquor.

KANE. Don't worry about it too much, Jed. There's sure to be a few of them there to tell me where I'm wrong.

LELAND. You may not always be that lucky. (*Pauses*) Charlie, why can't you get to look at things less personally? Everything doesn't have to be between you and—the personal note doesn't always—

KANE. (*Violently*) The personal note is all there is to it. It's all there ever is to it. It's all there ever is to anything! Stupidity in our government—crookedness—even just complacency and self-satisfaction and an unwillingness to believe that anything done by a certain class of people can be wrong—you can't fight those things impersonally. They're not impersonal crimes against the people. They're being done by actual persons—with actual names and positions and—the right of the American people to their own country is not an academic issue, Jed, that you debate—and then the judges retire to return a verdict—and the winners give a dinner for the losers.

LELAND. You almost convince me, almost. The truth is, Charlie, you just don't care about anything except you. You just want to convince people that you love them so much that they should love you back. Only you want love on your own terms. It's something to be played your way—according to your rules. And if anything goes wrong and you're hurt—then the game stops, and you've got to be soothed and nursed, no matter what else is happening—and no matter who else is hurt!

They look at each other.

KANE. (*Trying to kid him into a better humor*) Hey, Jedediah!

LELAND is not to be seduced.

LELAND. Charlie, I wish you'd let me work on the Chicago paper—you said yourself you were looking for someone to do dramatic criticism there—

KANE. You're more valuable here.

There is silence.

LELAND. Well, Charlie, then I'm afraid there's nothing I can do but to ask you to accept—

KANE. (*Harshly*) All right. You can go to Chicago.

LELAND. Thank you.

There is an awkward pause. KANE *opens a drawer of his desk and takes out a bottle and two glasses.*

KANE. I guess I'd better *try* to get drunk, anyway.

KANE *hands JED a glass, which he makes no move to take.*

KANE. (*Cont'd*) But I warn you, Jedediah, you're not going to like it in Chicago. The wind comes howling in off the lake, and the Lord only knows if they've ever heard of lobster Newburg.

LELAND. Will a week from Saturday be all right?

KANE. (*Wearily*) Anytime you say.

LELAND. Thank you.

KANE *looks at him intently and lifts the glass.*

KANE. A toast, Jedediah—to love on *my* terms. Those are the only terms anybody knows—his own.

Dissolve

QUESTIONS

1. What do you learn about the past and present relationship of Kane and Leland in this scene? What do Leland's speeches indicate about Kane's attitudes toward people? About Kane's shortcomings?

2. Basing your conclusions on this scene, why do you think the film is named *Citizen Kane*, and not something like *The Life of an American Tycoon*, or *The Perils of Wealth*?

3. This scene is one of the revolutionary ones in the film because Welles and Toland (the principal photographer) shot it from floor height, emphasizing the distance from the camera to the heads of the characters. What effect do you think this vantage point has on viewers of the film? If you have seen the film, what do you think the camera angles and the lighting contribute to your perception of the characters?

ARTHUR LAURENTS, A SCENE FROM *THE TURNING POINT*

Arthur Laurents is one of the most successful dramatists and screenplay writers of the postwar period. Among his achievements in film are *The Snake Pit* (1948), *Anastasia* (1956), and *The Way We Were* (1973). His plays *West Side Story* (1957), and *Gypsy* (1959) had successful Broadway runs as musicals, and also became successful films. *The Turning Point* (1977), which Laurents also created as a novel, received the Golden Globe Award, the National Board of Review Best Picture, and the Writers Guild of America Award as the best film of that year.

The Turning Point takes place against the background of ballet and the life of ballerinas. Deedee Rodgers (Shirley Maclaine) and Emma Jacklin (Anne Bancroft) had been close friends when they were beginning dancers with the American Ballet Theater. Deedee married, but before she had a chance to become a star, she became pregnant and had a daughter, Emilia. She left the company and moved to Oklahoma, had two more children and established a successful ballet school with her husband Wayne (Tom Skerrit), also a dancer.

During the following seventeen years, Deedee has believed she could have gained stardom if she had not become a mother. She has also nursed a grudge against Emma for having urged her to have the baby. In this way, Deedee believes, Emma pushed her aside when the two women had competed for the once-in-a-lifetime opportunity to dance in a new ballet, *Anna Karenina*. Emma, who won the role, went on to become famous as the company's *prima ballerina*. However, she has lived her life alone, her principal companions being the three dogs she keeps in her elegant apartment.

As the film opens, the ballet company comes to perform in Oklahoma City. Deedee's first daughter, Emilia (Leslie Browne), is now a promising dancer, and with Emma's help and support she becomes a star with the company during the following summer in New York. The scene included here occurs after a gala performance by the company, in which Emilia has brilliantly performed her first major solo dance, and in which Emma has done a solo from *Anna Karenina*, perhaps for the last time.

At the reception after the gala, Emma makes a show of acknowledging Emilia, a gesture which angers Deedee and leads her to conclude that for a number of months Emma has been trying to gain undue influence over Emilia. Shortly after this, the company's director, Adelaide (Martha Scott) asks Emma to create a new production of Tchaikowsky's *Sleeping Beauty* ballet, but *not* to dance in it. This request hits Emma with full force, for she now recognizes that she is getting old and is about to be pushed aside by dancers who, like Emilia, are young and strong. She rushes out and stops at the nearby bar, where she encounters Deedee. The scene, which is virtually a short play all by itself, then develops, as the long pent-up frustration, apprehension, and guilt of both women emerge.

ARTHUR LAURENTS   (b. 1918)

A Scene from The Turning Point ———————————— *(1977)*

Twentieth Century Fox. Producers, Herbert Ross and Arthur Laurents. Executive Producer, Nora Kaye. Photography, Robert Surtees. Film editor, William Reynolds. Music adapter, John Lanchbery. Director, Herbert Ross.

[SCENE] Interior Bar—Rainbow Room

DEEDEE is alone at the bar, drinking champagne. As EMMA, on her way to the Ladies' room, comes toward her, DEEDEE smiles and does a half-curtsy. EMMA stops and smiles back. Then she tosses her evening bag onto the bar.

EMMA.   (*to the bartender*).   Champagne, please.

Declaration of war accepted. During the following, they both get refills, but they do not guzzle; there is no need for them to get drunk. Emotionally, each is ready to burst anyway. They (and we) are unaware of the bartender and he is unaware of them. For despite the lines, despite what each feels underneath, they are totally charming: two smiling, lovely, delightful friends having a chat.

DEEDEE.   Remember the fairy tales we used to take turns reading to Emilia? Like the one about the two princesses? Every time one opened her mouth, out came diamonds and rubies. Every time the other opened her mouth, out came newts and hoptoads. Newts and hoptoads—(*taps her chest*)—coming out.

EMMA.   One of those little toads has already made an appearance.

DEEDEE.   Really! When?

EMMA.   In my dressing room. When you said I shouldn't have bought Emilia   5
that dress. Twice, you said it. Just before a performance. . . . I danced better tonight
than I have in years.

DEEDEE.   So I heard.

EMMA.   Oh, another little toad! You've kept quite a few bottled up all these years, haven't you?

DEEDEE.   Ohhh—embalmed, really.

EMMA.   I think not. Why don't you let them out? I don't have a performance tomorrow.

DEEDEE looks at her, then accepts the challenge. She puts her glass down on the bar and holds out her hands with her fists clenched.

DEEDEE.   Okay. Pick.   10

EMMA puts her glass down and points to a fist. DEEDEE opens it.

DEEDEE.   Ah, a tiny one. I'd practically forgotten him. (*Looks up now.*) Why'd you make your best pal doubt herself and her hubby, Emma? Why'd you take the chance of lousing up her marriage? Why'd you say: "You better have that baby. It's the only way you can hold on to Wayne." I'm just curious now.

EMMA.   You have a curious memory. but don't we all? As I remember, I said if you had an abortion, you might lose Wayne.

DEEDEE.   Sweet, but inaccurate. I've remembered your exact words for lo, these too many moons. I eventually figured out why you said 'em. Because you also said: "Forget Michael's ballet, there'll be others." You clever little twinkletoes! You knew a ballet like that comes once in a career. You wanted it real bad, so you lied to make sure you got what you wanted.

EMMA.   I've never had to lie to get what I wanted, Deedee. I'm too good.

DEEDEE.   Really?   15

EMMA.   Oh, yes.

DEEDEE.   Well, I suppose if you said "bullshit," you'd say it in French.

Close shot.

EMMA.   If that word came as naturally to me as it does to you, I'd have used it several times by now. In English. I think it's more appropriate that you say it—to yourself. For trying to blame *me* for what you did, for example. The choice was yours. It's much too late to regret it now, Deedee.

DEEDEE.   And the same to you, Emma me darlin'.

EMMA.   I certainly don't regret mine.   20

DEEDEE.   Then why are you trying to become a mother at your age?

EMMA.   Ooh, that's not a little toad. That's a rather large bullfrog. I don't want to be anybody's mother. I think of Emilia as a friend. And one reason I tried to help— stupid me!—I thought it would make you happy if your daughter became what you wanted to be and couldn't be.

DEEDEE.   Meaning you. It's so lovely to be you.

EMMA.   Obviously, you think so.

DEEDEE.   Oh, no no no no no no!   25

EMMA.   No no no no?

DEEDEE.   No; alas. And I doubt if Emilia could become you. Oh, she's as talented. She works as hard. But there's one thing, dearest friend, that you are that she, poor darling, is not.

EMMA.   And what, pray tell, is that?

DEEDEE.   A killer. You'll walk over anybody and still get a good night's sleep. That's what got you where you are, Emma.

*She is smiling adorably. E*MMA *smiles back, finishes her drink, pushes the glass to the bartender, keeps smiling until it is refilled, then picks it up. They are both smiling, almost laughing as* EMMA *looks at her drink, looks at* DEEDEE, *then throws the champagne in* DEEDEE'S *face. A moment. Then* DEEDEE *sets down her glass.*

DEEDEE.   Good girl.   30

She picks up her evening bag and starts out of the bar toward the exit and the elevators. The cool reaction infuriates EMMA. *She puts down her glass and starts after* DEEDEE.

Interior corridor outside Rainbow Room

EMMA *comes through the entrance to the Rainbow Room just as* DEEDEE *steps into an elevator.*

EMMA.   Deedee!

She runs for the elevator and just gets in as the doors are closing.

Interior elevator—Rockefeller Center

EMMA.   I'm sick to death of your jealousy and resentment!
DEEDEE.   So am I.
EMMA.   Then stop blaming your goddamn life on me! You picked it!
DEEDEE.   You did. You took away the choice, you didn't give me the chance to   35
find out if I was good enough.
EMMA.   I can tell you now: you weren't.

The elevator doors open and DEEDEE *strides out,* EMMA *after her.*

Exterior Rockefeller Plaza—Night

EMMA *is fast after* DEEDEE, *their heels clicking on the stone.*

EMMA.   You knew it yourself. That's why you married Wayne!
DEEDEE (*whirls around*).   I loved him!
EMMA.   So much that you said to hell with your career!
DEEDEE.   Yes!   40
EMMA.   And got pregnant to prove you meant it!
DEEDEE.   Yes!
EMMA.   Lie to yourself, not to me. You got married because you knew you were
second-rate; you got pregnant because Wayne was a ballet dancer, and that meant
queer!
DEEDEE.   *He wasn't!*
EMMA.   Still afraid someone will think he is? You were terrified then! You had   45
to *prove* he was a man! *That's* why you had a baby!
DEEDEE.   That's a goddamn lie!
EMMA.   It's the goddamn truth! You saddled him with a baby and blew his career! And now she's grown up and better than you ever were and you're jealous!
DEEDEE.   You're certifiable! You'll use anything for an excuse.
EMMA.   What's that an excuse for?
DEEDEE.   Trying to take away my child!   50
EMMA.   I return the compliment: you're a liar!

DEEDEE.   And you're a user. You have been your whole life! Me, Michael—pretending to love him!—Adelaide and now Emilia!

EMMA.   How Emilia?!

DEEDEE.   "How Emilia." That display five minutes ago: curtsy! Applause! Embrace! For *you*, not her! You were using her so everyone'd say: "Emma's so gracious, Emma's so wonderful!"

EMMA.   Untrue!   55

DEEDEE.   You *are* wonderful! You're amazing! It's incredible how you keep going on. You're over the hill; you know it and *you're* terrified. All you've got are your scrapbooks and your old toe shoes and those stupid, ridiculous dogs! What are you going to fill in with, Emma? Not my daughter. You keep your goddam hands off!

EMMA.   I'm better for her than you are.

DEEDEE.   Like hell!

EMMA.   She came to me because her mother wasn't there. Her mother was too busy screwing her head off!

DEEDEE.   You bitch!   60

She whacks EMMA with her evening bag. For a moment, EMMA is too startled to move. But as DEEDEE lifts her bag again, EMMA blocks it with one hand and with the other whacks DEEDEE with her evening bag. They both go at it: rarely hitting, ducking blows, slamming out blindly with their evening bags.

Exterior Rockefeller Center—Night

There they are, these two ladies in their evening gowns, each making a last pass, a last weak attempt to hit the other, and missing. They are panting, exhausted, and at last, they stop and just stand there, breathing hard.

Close shot—Their breath is coming back. DEEDEE smiles.

DEEDEE.   If there'd been a photographer handy, you'd have a whole new career.

EMMA.   I must look awful.

DEEDEE.   No: beautiful. I don't know how you do it.

EMMA has taken out a mirror and is looking in it.

EMMA.   If I can borrow your comb, I'll show you. Oh, I lost an earring.

DEEDEE (*handing her a comb*).   I'm sorry.   65

EMMA.   I'm not.

DEEDEE.   Really?

EMMA.   Yes.

She returns the comb, and they start walking, looking for the lost earring. The following is very quiet:

DEEDEE.   Jealousy is poison. Makes you a monster.

EMMA.   Well, it does make one unfair. (*Smiles.*) Two.   70

DEEDEE.   Two?

EMMA.   Me, too.

DEEDEE (*a second, then laughs*).   Emma, you made a good joke!

EMMA. Yes, I did. . . . I'm really not so humorless.

DEEDEE. Listen, you got off some really good ones before. Oh, look!   7₅

She picks up the earring and gives it to EMMA.

EMMA. How did it get over here? Thank you.

DEEDEE. You also hit a couple of bull's-eyes before.

EMMA. So did you.

DEEDEE. Sit?

EMMA. Oh, please.   80

They sit on the rim of the fountain.

EMMA. I don't really remember what I said about having the baby. But I do know I would have said anything to make sure I got that ballet. . . . I had to have it, Deedee. I just had to.

DEEDEE. My God. Oh Emma. Emma, I didn't know how much all I wanted was for you to say just that. . . . Let's have a drink!

EMMA. Absolutely!

They get up. EMMA links her arm through DEEDEE's as they start walking.

EMMA. It's good.

DEEDEE. You bet.

EMMA. I'm glad Wayne's coming.   85

DEEDEE. Me, too. . . . How's with Carter?

EMMA. Ça va. . . . *That's* bullshit in French.

DEEDEE laughs and walks toward the street, to a taxi. But EMMA has stopped, turned toward the entrance to the party.

DEEDEE. Not back to the party?

EMMA. I have to.   90

DEEDEE (*nods, understands*). Call me when you wake up.

EMMA. If not before.

They smile—and walk in opposite directions.

QUESTIONS

1. Despite the fact that the two women carry their anger so far as to strike each other, what does the scene show about the nature of friendship? What key admissions do the women make to effect their reconciliation?

2. The film omits the last ten speeches of the script (concluding with "to say just that" in speech 82). Justify eliminating these last speeches.

3. What is the effect of the fact that the locations of this scene move from the interior bar to the exterior plaza? Granted the actions of the two women, why can the scene not be in a single location (as it would necessarily be if written for the theater)? On the basis of your answers, what conclusions can you draw about the comparative freedoms and limitations of film and theater?

4. View the film *The Turning Point*, and compare the details of the script with the final filmed version of the scene. Explain the purpose and nature of the

changes in the film. If you had the freedom of a film director, what other liberties might you take in the performance? Why?

WRITING ABOUT FILM

Obviously the first requirement is to see the film, either in a theater or with videocassette. No matter how you see it, you should go through it at least twice, making notes, because your discussion takes on value the more thoroughly you know the material. Include the names of the script-writer, director, composer, special effects editor, chief photographer, and major actresses and actors. If particular speeches are worth quoting, remember the general circumstances of the quotation, and also, if possible, key words. Take notes on costume and color, or (if the film is in black and white) light and shade. You will need to rely on memory, but if you have videotape, you may easily check important details.

If you have no other instructions, you might decide on usual literary subjects like plot, structure, character, ideas, or setting. Remember, however, to consider not only dialogue and action, but also film techniques.

Questions for Discovering Ideas

Action

- How important is action? Is there much repetition of action, say, in slow motion, or from different angles? Are actors (and animals) viewed closely or distantly? Why?
- What actions are stressed (chases, concealment, gun battles, lovemaking, etc.)? What does the type of action contribute to the film?
- What do closeups show about character and motivation (smiles and laughter, frowns, leers, anxious looks, etc.)?
- What actions indicate seasonal conditions (cold by a character's stamping of feet, warmth by the character's removing a coat or shirt)? What connection do these actions have to the film's general ideas?
- Does the action show any changing of mood, from sadness to happiness, or from indecision to decision?

Cinematographic Techniques

- What notable techniques are used (colors, lighting, etc.)? What is their relationship to the film's characterizations and themes?
- What characterizes the use of the camera (tracking, closeups, distant shots, camera angles, etc.)? How do the camera perspectives reinforce or detract from the film's theme and plot?
- How does the editing (the sequencing of scenes) reinforce or detract from story and theme?
- What scene or scenes best exemplify how the cinematographic techniques interact with the theme, plot, characters, setting, and so on? Why?

Acting

- How well do the actors adapt to the medium of film? How convincing are their performances?
- How well do the actors control their facial expressions and body movement? Are they graceful? Awkward?
- What does their appearance lend to your understanding of their characters?
- Does it seem that the actors are genuinely creating their roles, or just reading through the parts?

Strategies for Organizing Ideas

Any of the organizing strategies discussed in the Drama chapters are equally valid for an essay on a film, except that you will need to consider them in a visual context. For example, if you choose the effects of a character on the plot, you need to develop your argument using the evidence of camera techniques, montage, sound effect, and the like.

When discussing film techniques, be sure to have good notes, so that your supporting details are accurate. A good method is to concentrate on technique in only a few scenes. If you analyze the effects of montage, for example, you may use your stop-action control (for a Videocassette Recorder) to go over the scene a number of times.

In the conclusion of your essay, you might evaluate the effectiveness of the cinematic form to story and idea. Are all the devices of film used in the best possible way? Is anything overdone? Is anything underplayed? Is the film good, bad, or indifferent up to a point, and then does it change? How? Why?

SAMPLE ESSAY

Citizen Kane: Whittling a Giant Down to Size

[1] Citizen Kane (1941) is a superbly crafted film in black and white. The script is by Herman Mankiewicz and Orson Welles, with photography by Gregg Toland, music by Bernard Herrmann, direction and production by Welles, and the leading role by Welles. It is the story of a wealthy and powerful man, Charles Foster Kane, who exemplifies the American Dream of economic self sufficiency, self determination, and self, period. The film does not explore the "greatness" of the hero, however, but rather exposes him as a misguided, unhappy person who tries to buy love and remake reality.* All aspects of the picture—characterization, structure, and technique—are directed to this goal.†

At the film's heart is the deterioration of Kane, the newly deceased newspaper magnate and millionaire. He is not all bad, for he begins well and

* Central idea.
† Thesis sentence.

then goes downward, in a tragic sequence. For example, the view we see of him as a child, being taken away from home, invites sympathy. When we next see him as a young man, he idealistically takes over a daily newspaper, the *Inquirer*. This idealism makes him admirable but also makes his deterioration tragic. As he says to Thatcher in a moment of insight, he could have been a great person if he had not been wealthy. His corruption begins when he tries to alter the world to suit himself, such as his demented attempt to make an opera star out of his second wife, Susan, and his related attempt to shape critical praise for her despite her terrible singing. Even though he builds an opera house for her, and also sponsors many performances, he cannot change reality. This tampering with truth indicates how completely he loses his youthful integrity.

[2]

The structure is progressively arranged to bring out such weaknesses. The film flows out of the opening obituary newsreel, from which we learn that Kane's dying word was the name "Rosebud" (the brand name of his boyhood sled, which is spoken at the beginning by a person [Kane] whose mouth is shown in closeup). The newsreel director, wanting to get the inside story, assigns a reporter named Thompson to learn about "Rosebud." Thompson's search unifies the rest of the film; he goes from place to place and person to person to collect materials and conduct interviews which disclose Kane's increasing strangeness and alienation. At the end, although the camera leaves Thompson to focus on the burning sled, he has been successful in uncovering the story of Kane's deterioration (even though he himself never learns what "Rosebud" means). Both the sled and the reporter therefore tie together the many aspects of the film.

[3]

It is through Thompson's searches that the film presents the flashback accounts of Kane's deterioration. The separate persons being interviewed (including Thatcher's handwritten account) each contribute something different to the narrative because their experiences with Kane have all been unique. As a result of these individual points of view, the story is quite intricate. We learn in the Bernstein section, for example, that Jedediah proudly saves a copy of Kane's declaration about truth in reporting. We do not learn in Jedediah's interview, however, that he, Jedediah, sends the copy back to Kane as an indictment of Kane's betrayal of principle. Rather, it is in *Susan's* account that we learn about the return, even though she herself understands nothing about it. This subtlety, so typical of the film, marks the ways in which the biography of Kane is perceptively revealed.

[4]

Thus, the major importance of these narrating characters is to reveal and reflect Kane's disintegration. Jedediah (Joseph Cotten) is a person of principle who works closely with Kane, but after the lost election he rebels when he understands the falseness of Kane's personal life. He is totally alienated after Kane completes the unfinished attack on Susan's performance. Jedediah's change, or perhaps his assertion of principle, thus reveals Kane's increasing corruption. Susan, Kane's second wife (Dorothy Comingore), is naive, sincere, and warm, but her drinking, her attempted suicide, and her final separation show the harm of Kane's warped visions. Bernstein (Everett Sloane), the first person Thompson interviews, is a solitary figure who is uncritical of Kane, but it is he who first touches the theme about the mystery of Kane's motivations. Bernstein also takes on life when he speaks poignantly of

[5]

his forty-five year memory of the girl in white. Even though this revelation is brief, it suggests layers of feeling and longing.

In addition to these perceptive structural characterizations, Citizen Kane is a masterpiece of film technique. The camera images are sharp, with clear depths of field. In keeping with Kane's disintegration and mysteriousness, the screen is rarely bright. Instead, the film makes strong use of darkness and contrasts, almost to the point at times of blurring distinctions between people.

[6]   Unique in Gregg Toland's camera work are the many shots taken from waist high or below, which distort the bodies of the characters by distancing their heads—suggesting that the characters are preoccupied with their own concerns and oblivious to normal perspectives. Nowhere is this distortion better exemplified than in the scene between Kane and Jedediah in the empty rooms after the lost election, when Jedediah asks permission to leave for Chicago.

As might be expected in a film so dominated by its central figure, the many symbols create strong statements about character. The most obvious is the sled, "Rosebud," the dominating symbol of the need for love and acceptance in childhood. Another notable symbol is glass and, in one scene, ice. In the party scene, two ice statues are in the foreground of the employees of the *Inquirer*. In another scene, a bottle looms large in front of Jedediah, who is drunk. In another, a pill bottle and drinking glass are in front of Susan, who has

[7]   just used them in her suicide attempt. The suggestion of these carefully photographed symbols is that life is brittle and temporary. Particularly symbolic is the bizarre entertainment in the party scene. Because Kane joins the dancing and singing, the action suggests that he is doing no more than taking a role in life, never being himself or knowing himself. Symbols that frame the film are the wire fence and the "No Trespassing" sign at both beginning and end. These symbols suggest that even if we understand a little about Kane, or anyone, there are boundaries we cannot pass, depths we can never reach.

There are also amusing symbols which suggest not only the diminution of Kane, but also of the other characters. An example is Bernstein's high-backed chair, which makes him look like a small child. Similarly, the gigantic fireplace at Xanadu makes both Kane and Susan seem like pigmies—a symbol that great wealth dwarfs and dehumanizes people. Especially comic is Kane's picnic at Xanadu. In going into the country, Kane and his friends do not walk, but ride in a long line of cars—more like a funeral procession than a pic-

[8]   nic—and they stay overnight in a massive tent. Quite funny is the increasing distance between Kane and Emily, his first wife, in the rapid-fire shots that portray their developing separation. Even more comic is the vast distance at Xanadu between Kane and Susan when they discuss their life together. They are so far apart that they must shout to be heard. Amusing as these symbols of diminution and alienation are, however, they are also pathetic, because at first Kane finds closeness with both his wives.

In all respects, Citizen Kane is a masterly film. This is not to say that the characters are likable, or that the amusing parts make it a comedy. Instead, the film pursues truth, suggesting that greatness and wealth cannot give happiness. It is relentless in whittling away at its major figure. Kane is likable at times, and he is enormously generous (as shown when he sends Jedediah

[9] $25,000 in severance pay). But these high moments show the contrasting depths to which Kane falls, with the general point being that people who are

powerful and great may deteriorate even at their height. The goal of the newsreel director at the beginning is to get at the "real story" behind the public man. There is more to any person than a two-hour film can reveal, but within its limits, Citizen Kane gets at the real story, and the real story is both sad and disturbing.

Commentary on the Essay

The major point of the essay is that the film diminishes the major figure, Kane. In this respect the essay illustrates the analysis of *character* (Chapter 4), and it therefore emphasizes how film may be considered as a form of literature. Also shown in the essay are other methods of literary analysis: *structure* (Chapter 3) and *symbolism* (Chapter 9). Of these topics, only the use of symbols, because they are visually presented in the film, is unique to the medium of film as opposed to the medium of words.

Any one of the topics might be developed as a separate essay. There is more than enough about the character of Susan, for example, to sustain a complete essay, and the film's structure could be extensively explored. *Citizen Kane* itself as a repository of film techniques is rich enough for an exhaustive, book-length account.

Because the essay is about a film, the unique aspect of the introductory paragraph is the opening brief description (stressing the medium of black and white), and the credits to the script writers, principal photographer, composer, and director. Unlike works written by a single author, film is a collaborative medium, and therefore it is appropriate to recognize the separate efforts of the principal contributors.

Paragraph 2 begins the body, and carries out a brief analysis of the major character. Paragraphs 3–5 discuss various aspects of the film's structure (the second topic announced in the thesis sentence) as they bear on Kane. In paragraph 3 the unifying importance of the sled and the reporter, Thompson, is explained. Paragraph 4 focuses on the film's use of flashback as a structural technique, while paragraph 5 discusses three of the flashback characters as they either intentionally or unintentionally reveal Kane's flaws.

In paragraphs 6–8, the topic is film technique, the third and last topic of the thesis sentence. Paragraph 6 focuses on light, camera angles, and distortion; paragraph 7 treats visual symbols; paragraph 8 continues the topic of symbols, but extends it to amusing ones.

The final paragraph restates the central idea, and also relates the theme of deterioration to the larger issue of how great wealth and power affect character. Thus, as a conclusion, this paragraph not only presents a summary, but also notes the film's general ideas.

WRITING TOPICS

1. Select a single film technique, such as the use of color, the control of light, or the photographing of action, and write an essay describing how it is used in a

film. For best results, use a videocassette for your study. As much as possible, try to explain how the technique is used throughout the film. Determine constant and contrasting features, the relationship of the technique to the development of story and character, and so on.

2. Write an essay explaining how all the film techniques of a particular scene are employed (i.e., camera angles, closeups or longshots, tracking, on-camera and off-camera speeches, lighting, depth of field, etc.). For your study, you will have to rerun your scene a number of times, trying to notice elements for the first time, and also reinforcing your first observations.

3. Pick out a news story and write a dramatic scene about it. Next, consider how to do it for a film, providing directions for actors and camera people (e.g., "As Character A speaks, his face shows that he is lying; the camera zooms slowly in on his face, with a loss of focus," or, "As Character A speaks, the camera focuses on Character B exchanging looks with Character C."). When you are done, write an explanation of how you designed your directions to bring out details about your story and characters.

Appendix A
Taking Examinations
On Literature

Succeeding on literature examinations is largely a matter of preparation. Preparing means (1) studying the material assigned in conjunction with the comments made in class by your instructor and by fellow students in discussion, (2) developing and reinforcing your own thoughts, (3) anticipating the questions by creating and answering your own practice questions; and (4) understanding the precise function of the test in your education.

First, realize that the test is not designed either to trap you or to hold down your grade. The grade you receive is a reflection of your achievement in the course. If your grades are low, you can improve them by studying coherently and systematically. Those students who can easily do satisfactory work might do superior work if they improve their method of preparation. From whatever level you begin, you can increase your achievement by improving your method of study.

Your instructor has three major concerns in evaluating your tests (assuming literate English): (1) to assess the extent of your command over the subject material of the course ("How good is your retention?"), (2) to assess how well you are able to think about the material ("How well are you educating yourself?"), and (3) to assess how well you respond to a question or deal with an issue.

Many elements go into writing good answers on tests, but this last point, about responsiveness, is the most important. A major cause of low exam grades is that students really do not *answer* the questions asked. Does that seem surprising? The problem is that some students do no more than retell a story or restate an argument, never confronting the issues in the question. This common problem has been treated throughout this book. Therefore, if you are asked, "Why does …," be sure to emphasize the *why*, and use the *does* only to exemplify the *why*. If the question is about organization, focus on that. If a problem has been raised, deal with the problem. In short, always *respond directly* to the question or instruction. Compare the following two answers to the same question:

Question: How does the setting of Jackson's "The Lottery" figure in the development of the story?

A

The setting of Jackson's "The Lottery" is a major element in the development of the story. The scene is laid in the village square, between the bank and the post office. There are many flowers blooming, and the grass is green. A pile of stones is set up in the square. Into this place, just before ten o'clock in the morning, come the villagers to hold their annual lottery. There are 300 of them—children, men, and housewives. In the center of the square the black lottery box is set up on a three-legged stool. This box has been around for years, and looks broken and shabby. The setting requires that the villagers gather around the box, and that the male head representing each village family draw a slip of paper for that family. Once they have all drawn, it is discovered that Bill Hutchinson is the "winner." He is not a lucky winner, however, because his family of five has to draw again individually. Bill's wife Tessie draws the black spot that Bill had drawn for the family. Then all the villagers in the square fall upon her to stone her to death, because that is the fate of the "winner." The setting here is therefore all important in the development of the story.

B

The setting of Jackson's "The Lottery" is a major element in the development of the story. As a setting for all the action, the town square of the unnamed village is large enough to contain all 300 villagers, piles of stones which they can pick up and hurl, and the black box on a three-legged stool. As a setting in time, the entire action takes place within a two-hour period between ten in the morning and 12:00 noon. As a seasonal setting, the date of June 27, specifically mentioned as the day of the action, suggests an anachronistic and mindless but nevertheless cruel early summer ritual. As a setting in character and society, the homey, simple life-style of the people indicates inertia and fallibility, not sophistication and innovativeness. It is *likely* that such people would preserve cruel and meaningless customs without thinking about their horrible effects. In all respects, then, the setting in place, time, season, and culture is all-important in the development of the story.

While column *A* begins well and introduces important details of the story's setting, it does not address the question because it does not show how the details figure into the story's development. On the other hand, column *B* focuses directly on the connection between the setting and the development of "The Lottery." Because of this emphasis, *B* is shorter than *A*. That is, with the focus directly on the issue, there is no need for irrelevant narrative details. Thus, *A* is unresponsive and unnecessarily long, while *B* is responsive and includes details only if they exemplify the major points.

PREPARATION

Your challenge is how best to prepare yourself to have a knowledgeable and ready mind at examination time. If you simply cram facts into your head for the examination in hopes that you will be able to adjust to the questions, you will likely flounder. You need a systematic approach.

Read and Reread

Above all, keep in mind that your preparation should begin as soon as the course begins, not on the night before the exam. Complete each assignment by the date due, for you will understand the classroom discussion only if you know the material (see also the guides for study in Chapter 1, pp. 11–18). Then, about a week before the exam, review each assignment, preferably rereading everything completely. With this preparation, your study on the night before the exam will be fruitful, for it might be viewed as a climax of preparation, not the entire preparation itself.

Construct Your Own Questions: Go on the Attack

To give yourself the masterly preparation you want for an exam, read actively, not passively. Read with a goal, go on the attack by anticipating test conditions—composing and answering your own practice questions. Do not waste time trying to guess the questions you think your instructor might ask. That might happen—and wouldn't you be happy if it did?—but do not turn your study into a game of chance. Instead, arrange the subject matter by asking yourself questions that help you get things straight.

How can you construct your own questions? It is not as hard as you might think. Your instructor may have announced certain topics or ideas to be tested on the exam, and you might develop questions from these. Or you might apply general questions to the specifics of your assignments, as in the following examples:

1. *About a character and the interactions of characters* (see also Chapter 4). What is *A* like? How does *A* grow or change in the work? What does *A* learn, or not learn, that brings about the conclusion? To what degree does *A* represent a type, or an idea? How does *B* influence *A*? Does a change in *C* bring about any corresponding change in *A*?

2. *About technical and structural questions.* These may be broad, covering everything from *point of view* (Chapter 6) to *prosody* (Chapter 18). The best guide here is to study those technical aspects that have been discussed in class, for it is unlikely that you will be asked to go beyond the levels expected in classroom discussion.

3. *About events or situations.* (See also Chapter 3.) What relationship does episode *A* have to situation *B*? Does *C's* thinking about situation *D* have any influence on the outcome of event *E*?

4.   *About a problem* (see also Chapter 27, pp. 1304–10). Why is character *A* or situation *X* this way and not that way? Is the conclusion justified by the ideas and events leading up to it?

Convert Your Notes to Questions

One of the best ways to construct questions is to adapt your classroom notes, for notes are the fullest record you have about your instructor's views. As you work with your notes, refer to passages from the text that were studied by the class or stressed by your instructor. If there is time, memorize as many important phrases or lines as you can; plan to incorporate these into your answers as evidence to support the points you make. Remember that it is useful to work not only with main ideas from your notes, but also with matters such as style, imagery, and organization.

Obviously, you cannot make questions from all your notes, and you will therefore need to select from those that seem most important. As an example, here is a short note from a classroom discussion of *Hamlet*: "In a major respect, a study in how private problems get public, how a court conspiracy may produce disastrous consequences." Notice how you can devise practice questions from this note:

1.   In what ways is *Hamlet* not only about private problems, but also public ones?
2.   Why should the consequences of Claudius's murder of Hamlet's father be considered disastrous?

The principle shown here is that exam questions should never be asked just about *what*, but should rather get into the issues of *why*. Observe that the first question therefore adapts the words *in what ways* to the phrasing of the note. For the second, the word *why* has been adapted. Either question would force pointed study, and neither would ask you merely to describe events. Question 1 would require you to consider the wider political effects of Hamlet's hostility toward Claudius, including his murder of Polonius and the subsequent madness of Ophelia. Question 2, with its emphasis on disaster, would lead you to consider not only the ruination of the hopes and lives of those in the play, but also the importance of Young Fortinbras and the eventual establishment of Norwegian control over Denmark after Claudius and Hamlet are gone. If you spent fifteen or twenty minutes writing practice answers to these questions, you could be confident in taking an examination on the material, for it is likely that you could adapt your answers to any exam question about the personal and political implications of Claudius's murder of his brother.

Work with Questions Even When Time Is Short.

Whatever your subject, spend as much study time as possible making and answering your own questions. Remember also to work with your own remarks and ideas that you will have developed in the journal entries you have made when doing your regular assignments (see Chapter 1, pp. 10–18). Many of these will give you additional ideas for your own questions, which you may practice along with the questions you develop from your notes.

Obviously, with the limited time you have before your examination, you will not be able to create your own questions and answers indefinitely. Even so, do not give up on the question method. If time is too short for full practice answers, write out the main heads, or topics, of an answer. When the press of time (or the need for sleep) no longer permits you to make even such a brief outline answer, keep thinking of questions, and think about the answers on the way to the exam. *Try never to read passively or unresponsively, but always with a creative, question-and-answer goal.* Think of studying as a prewriting experience.

The time you spend in this way will be valuable, for as you practice, you will develop control and therefore confidence. Often those who have difficulty with tests, or claim a phobia about them, engage in *passive* rather than *active* preparation. Test questions compel thought, arrangement, and responsiveness, but a passively prepared student is not ready for this challenge and therefore writes answers that are unresponsive and filled with summary. The grade for such a performance is low, and the student's fear of tests is reinforced. The best way to break such long-standing patterns of fear or uncertainty is active, creative study.

Study with a Classmate

Often the thoughts of another person can help you understand the material to be tested. Find a fellow student with whom you can work comfortably but also productively, for both of you together can help each other individually. In view of the need for steady preparation throughout a course, regular discussions about the material are a good idea. You might also make your joint study systematic by setting aside a specific evening or afternoon for work sessions. Make the effort; working with someone else can be stimulating and rewarding.

TWO BASIC TYPES OF QUESTIONS ABOUT LITERATURE

Generally, you will find two types of questions on literature exams. Keep them in mind as you prepare. The first type is *factual,* or *mainly objective,* and the second is *general, comprehensive, broad,* or *mainly subjective.* In a literature course very few questions are purely objective, except for multiple-choice questions.

Factual Questions

Multiple-Choice Questions. These are mainly factual. In a literature course, your instructor will most likely use them for short quizzes, usually on days when an assignment is due, to make sure that you are keeping up with the reading. Multiple choice items test your knowledge of facts and your in-genuity in perceiving subtleties of phrasing. On a literature exam, however, this type of question is rare.

IDENTIFICATION QUESTIONS. These questions are more interesting and challenging because they require you both to know details and also to develop thoughts about them. This type of question will frequently be used as a check on the depth and scope of your reading. In fact, an entire exam could be composed of only identification questions, each demanding per-haps five minutes to write. Typical examples of what you might be asked to identify are:

1. *A character*. To identify a character, it is necessary to describe briefly the char-acter's position, main activity, and significance. Let us assume that "Prince Pros-pero" is the character to be identified. Our answer should state that he is the prince (position) who invites a thousand followers to his castle to enjoy them-selves while keeping out the plague of the red death in Poe's "The Masque of the Red Death" (main activity). He is the major cause of the action, and he em-bodies the story's theme that pride is vain and that death is inescapable (sig-nificance). Under the category of "significance," of course, you might develop as many ideas as you have time for, but the short example here is a general model for most examinations.

2. *Incidents or situations*. For example: "A woman mourns the death of her hus-band." To identify this incident, first give the location (Mrs. Popov in Chekhov's play *The Bear* or the Widow in "The Widow of Ephesus"), and try to demonstrate its significance in the work. (That is, in *The Bear* Mrs. Popov is mourning the death of her husband, and in the course of the play Chekhov uses her feelings to show amusingly that life with real emotion is stronger than duty to the dead. Very much the same point is made in "The Widow of Ephesus").

3. *Things, places, and dates*. Your instructor may ask you to identify a cavalry charge (Twain's "Luck"), a village square (Jackson's "The Lottery"), or the dates of Mansfield's "Miss Brill" (1920) or Amy Lowell's "Patterns" (1916). For dates, you may be given a leeway of five or ten years. What is important about a date is not so much exactness as historical and intellectual perspective. The date of "Patterns," for example, was the third year of Word War I, and the poem con-sequently reflects a reaction against the protracted and senseless loss of life that war was producing. Thus, to claim "World War I" as the date of the poem would likely be acceptable as an answer, if it happens that you cannot remember the exact date.

4. *Quotations*. You should remember enough of the text to identify a passage taken from it, or at least to make an informed guess. Generally, you should (1) locate the quotation, if you remember it, or else describe the probable location, (2) show the ways in which the quotation is typical of the content and style of the work you have read, and (3) describe the importance of the passage. If you suf-fer a momentary lapse of memory, write a reasoned and careful explanation of your guess. Even if your guess is wrong, the knowledge and cogency of your ex-planation should give you points.

TECHNICAL AND ANALYTICAL QUESTIONS AND PROBLEMS. In a scale of ascending importance, the third and most difficult type of factual question relates to those matters with which this book has been concerned: technique, analysis, and problems. You might be asked to discuss the *setting, images, point of view,* or *important idea* of a work; you might be asked about a *specific problem;* or you might be asked to analyze a poem that may or may not be duplicated for your benefit (if it is not duplicated, woe to students who have not studied their assignments). Questions like these assume that you have technical knowledge, while they also ask you to examine the text within the limitations imposed by the terms.

Obviously, technical questions occur more frequently in advanced courses than in elementary ones, and the questions become more subtle as the courses become more advanced. Instructors of elementary courses may use main-idea or special-problem questions, but will probably not use many of the others unless they state their intentions to do so in advance, or unless technical terms have been studied in class.

Questions of this type are fairly long, perhaps with from fifteen to twenty-five minutes allowed for each. If you have two or more of these questions, try to space your time sensibly; do not devote eighty percent of your time to one question and leave only twenty percent for the rest.

Basis of Judging Factual Questions

IDENTIFICATION QUESTIONS. In all factual questions, your instructor is testing (1) your factual command, and (2) your quickness in relating a part of the whole. Thus, suppose you are identifying the incident "A man kills a canary." It is correct to say that Susan Glaspell's play *Trifles* (pp. 1038–48; see also "A Jury of Her Peers," pp. 155–69) is the location of the incident, that the murdered farmer John Wright was the killer, and that the canary belonged to his wife. Knowledge of these details clearly establishes that you know the facts. But a strong answer must go further. Even in the brief time you have for short answers, you should always connect the facts to (1) major causation in the work, (2) an important idea or ideas, (3) the development of the work, and (4) for a quotation, the style. Time is short and you must be selective, but if you can make your answer move from facts to significance, you will always fashion superior responses. Along these lines, let us look at an answer identifying the action from *Trifles*:

> The action is from Glaspell's *Trifles*. The man who kills the bird is John Wright, and the owner is Mrs. Wright. The killing is important because it is shown as the final indignity in Mrs. Wright's desperate life, and it prompts her to strangle Wright in his sleep. It is thus the cause not only of the murder but also of the investigation bringing the officers and their wives on stage. In fact, the wringing of the bird's neck makes the play possible because it is the wives who discover the dead bird, and this discovery is the means by which Glaspell highlights them as the major characters in the play. Because the husband's brutal

act shows how bleak the life of Mrs. Wright actually was, it dramatizes the lonely plight of women in a male-dominated way of life like that on the Wright farm. The discovery also raises the issue of legality and morality, because the two wives decide to conceal the evidence, therefore protecting Mrs. Wright from conviction and punishment.

Any of the points in this answer could be developed as a separate essay, but the paragraph is successful as a short answer because it goes beyond fact to deal with significance. Clearly, such answers are possible at the time of an exam only if you have devoted considerable thought to the various exam works beforehand. The more thinking and practicing you do before an exam, the better your answers will be. Remember this advice as an axiom: *You cannot write really superior answers if you do not think extensively before the exam.* By studying well beforehand, you will be able to reduce surprise to an absolute minimum.

LONGER FACTUAL QUESTIONS. More extended factual questions also require more thoroughly developed organization. Remember that for these questions your knowledge of essay writing is important, for the quality of your composition will determine a major share of your instructor's evaluation of your answers. It is therefore best to take several minutes to gather your thoughts together before you begin to write, because *a ten-minute planned answer is preferable to a twenty-five minute unplanned answer.* You do not need to write every possible fact on each particular question. Of greater importance is the use to which you put the facts you know and the organization of your answer. Use a sheet of scratch paper to jot down the facts you remember and your ideas about them in relation to the question. Then put them together, phrase a thesis sentence, and use your facts to exemplify and support your thesis.

It is always necessary to begin your answer pointedly, using key words or phrases from the question or direction if possible, so that your answer will have thematic shape. You should never begin an answer with "Because" and then go on from there without referring again to the question. To be most responsive during the short time available for an exam, you should use the question as your guide for your answer. Let us suppose that you have the following question on your test: "How does Glaspell use details in *Trifles* to reveal the character of Mrs. Wright?" The most common way to go astray on such a question, and the easiest thing to do also, is to concentrate on Mrs. Wright's character rather than on how Glaspell uses detail to bring out her character. The word *how* makes a vast difference in the nature of the final answer, and hence a good method on the exam is to duplicate key phrases in the question to ensure that you make your major points clear. Here is an opening sentence that uses the key words and phrases (underlined here) from the question to direct thought and provide focus:

Glaspell <u>uses details</u> of setting, marital relationships, and personal habits <u>to reveal the character of Mrs. Wright</u> as a person of great but unfulfilled potential whom anger has finally overcome.

Because this sentence repeats the key phrases from the question, and also because it promises to show *how* the details are to be focused on the character, it suggests that the answer to follow will be responsive.

General or Comprehensive Questions

General or comprehensive questions are particularly important on final examinations, when your instructor is testing your total comprehension of the course material. Considerable time is usually allowed for answering this type of question, which may be phrased in a number of ways:

1. A *direct question* asking about philosophy, underlying attitudes, main ideas, characteristics of style, backgrounds, and so on. Here are some possible questions in this category:

   "What use do _____, _____, and _____ make of the topic of _____?"
   "Define and characterize the short story as a genre of literature."
   "Explain the use of dialogue by Hawthorne, Welty, and Maupassant."
   "Contrast the technique of point of view as used by _____, _____, and _____."

2. A *"comment" question*, often based on an extensive quotation, borrowed from a critic or written by your instructor for the occasion, about a broad class of writers, a literary movement, or the like. Your instructor may ask you to treat this question broadly (taking in many writers) or else to apply the quotation to a specific writer.

3. A *"suppose" question*, such as "What advice might Mrs. Wright of *Trifles* give the speakers of Lowell's 'Patterns' and Keats's 'Bright Star'?", or "What might the speaker of Rossetti's poem 'Echo' say if she learned that her dead lover was Goodman Brown of Hawthorne's 'Young Goodman Brown'?" Although suppose questions might seem whimsical at first sight, they have a serious design and should prompt original and radical thinking. The first question, for example, should cause a test writer to bring out, from Mrs. Wright's perspective, that the love of both speakers was/is potential, not actual. She would likely sympathize with the speaker's loss in "Patterns," but might also say the lost married life might not have been as totally happy as the speaker assumes. For the speaker of "Bright Star," a male, Mrs. Wright might say that the steadfast love sought by him should also be linked to kindness and toleration as well as passion.

Although "suppose" questions, and answers, are speculative, the need to respond to them requires a detailed consideration of the works involved, and in this respect the suppose question is a salutary means of learning. It is of course difficult to prepare for a suppose question, which you may therefore regard as a test not only of your knowledge, but also of your inventiveness and ingenuity.

Basis of Judging General Questions

When answering broad, general questions, you are dealing with an unstructured situation, and you must not only supply an *answer* but—equally important—you must also create a *structure* within which your answer can have meaning. You might say that you make up your own specific question out of the original general question. If you were asked to "Consider the role of women as seen in Lowell, Mansfield, and Glaspell," for example, you would do well to structure the question by focusing a number of clearly defined topics. A possible way to begin answering such a question might be this:

> Lowell, Mansfield, and Glaspell present a view of female resilience by demonstrating inner control, power of adaptation, and endurance.

With this sort of focus you would be able to proceed point by point, introducing supporting data as you form your answer.

As a general rule, the best method for answering a comprehensive question is comparison-contrast (see also Appendix B, pp. 1609–23). The reason is that in dealing with, say, a general question on Rossetti, Chekhov, and Keats, it is too easy to write *three* separate essays rather than *one*. Thus, you should try to create a topic like "The treatment of real or idealized love" or "The difficulties in male-female relationships," and then develop your answer point by point rather than writer by writer. By creating your answer in this way, you can bring in references to each or all of the writers as they become relevant to your main idea. But if you were to treat each writer separately, your comprehensive answer would lose focus and effectiveness, and it would be needlessly repetitive.

Remember these things, then: In judging your response to a general question, your instructor is interested in seeing: (1) how effectively you perceive and explain the significant issues in the question, (2) how intelligently and clearly you organize your answer, (3) how persuasively you use materials from the work as supporting evidence.

Bear in mind that in answering comprehensive questions, you don't have complete freedom. What you have is the freedom to create your own structure. The underlying idea of the comprehensive, general question is that you possess special knowledge and insights that cannot be discovered by more factual questions. You must therefore formulate your own responses to the material and introduce evidence that reflects your own insights and command of information.

Two final words: Good luck.

Appendix B
Comparison-Contrast and Extended Comparison-Contrast

A comparison-contrast essay is used to compare and contrast different authors; two or more works by the same author; different drafts of the same work; or characters, incidents, techniques, and ideas in the same work or in different works. The virtue of comparison-contrast is that it enables the study of works in perspective. No matter what works you consider together, the method helps you isolate and highlight individual characteristics, for the quickest way to get at the essence of one thing is to compare it with another. Similarities are brought out by comparison; differences, by contrast. In other words, you can enhance your understanding of what a thing *is* by using comparison-contrast to determine what it *is not*.

For example, our understanding of Shakespeare's Sonnet 30, "When to the Sessions of Sweet Silent Thought" (p. 667) may be enhanced if we compare it with Christina Rossetti's poem "Echo" (p. 744). Both poems treat personal recollections of past experiences, told by a speaker to a listener who is not intended to be the reader. Both also refer to persons, now dead, with whom the speakers were closely involved. In addition to these similarities, there are important differences. Shakespeare's speaker numbers the dead persons as friends whom he laments generally, while Rossetti refers specifically to one person with whom the speaker was in love. Rossetti's topic is the sorrow of dead love, the irrevocability of the past, and the present loneliness of the speaker. Shakespeare includes the references to dead friends as a way of accounting for present sorrows, but then his speaker turns to the present, and asserts that thinking about the "dear friend" being addressed enables him to restore past "losses" and end all "sorrows." In Rossetti's poem, there is no reconciliation of past and present, and instead the speaker focuses entirely upon the sadness of the present moment. Though both poems are retrospective, Shakespeare's poem looks toward the present while Rossetti's looks to the past.

GUIDELINES FOR THE COMPARISON-CONTRAST METHOD

This example, although brief, shows how the comparison-contrast method makes it possible to identify leading similarities and distinguishing differences in both works. Frequently you can overcome difficulty with one work by comparing and contrasting it with another work on a comparable subject. A few guidelines will help direct your efforts in writing comparison-contrast essays.

Clarify Your Intention

When planning a comparison-contrast essay, first decide on your goal, for you may use the method in a number of ways. One objective may be *the equal and mutual illumination of two (or more) works.* For example, an essay comparing Welty's "A Worn Path" (p. 112) with Hawthorne's "Young Goodman Brown" (p. 330) might be designed to (1) compare ideas, characters, or methods in these stories equally, without stressing or favoring either. But you might also (2) emphasize "Young Goodman Brown," and therefore you would use "A Worn Path" as material for highlighting Hawthorne's story. Or you could (3) show your liking of one story at the expense of another, or (4) emphasize a method or idea that you think is especially noteworthy or appropriate.

A first task is therefore to decide what to emphasize. The first sample essay (p. 1615) gives "equal time" to both works being considered, without claiming the superiority of either. Unless you want to pursue a different rhetorical goal, This essay is a suitable model for most comparisons.

Find Common Grounds for Comparison

The second stage in prewriting for this essay is to select a common ground for discussion. It is pointless to compare dissimilar things, for the resulting conclusions will not have much value. Instead, find a common ground. Compare like with like: idea with idea, characterization with characterization, imagery with imagery, point of view with point of view, tone with tone, problem with problem. Nothing much can be learned from a comparison of "Welty's view of courage and Chekhov's view of love," but a comparison of "The relationship of love to stability and courage in Chekhov and Welty" suggests common ground, with the promise of important things to be learned through the examination of similarities and differences.

In seeking common ground, you will need to be inventive and creative. For instance, if you compare Maupassant's "The Necklace" and Chekhov's *The Bear,* these two works at first seem dissimilar. Yet a common ground can be found, such as "The treatment of Self-Deceit," "The Effects of Chance on Human Affairs," and "The View of Women," and so on. Although other works may seem even more dissimilar than these, it is usually possible to find a common ground for comparison and contrast. Much of your success with this essay depends on your finding a workable basis—a common denominator—for comparison.

Integrate the Bases of Comparison

Let us assume that you have decided on your rhetorical purpose and on the basis or bases of your comparison. You have done your reading, taken notes, and have a rough idea of what to say. The remaining problem is the treatment of your material. Here are two ways:

A common way is to make your points first about one work and then about the other. Unfortunately, this method makes your paper seem like two separate lumps. ("Work 1" takes up one half of your paper, and "work 2" takes up the other half.) Also, the method involves repetition because you must repeat many points when you treat the second subject.

A better method therefore is to treat the major aspects of your main idea, and to refer to the two (or more) works as they support your arguments. Thus you refer constantly to *both* works, sometimes within the same sentence, and remind your reader of the point of your discussion. There are reasons for the superiority of this method: (1) You do not repeat your points needlessly, for you document them as you raise them. (2) By constantly referring to the two works, you make your points without requiring a reader with a poor memory to reread previous sections.

As a model, here is a paragraph on "Natural References as a Basis of Comparison in Frost's 'Desert Places' and Shakespeare's Sonnet 73 ['That Time of Year Thou Mayest in Me Behold']" (pp. 764 and 730). The virtue of the paragraph is that it uses material from both poems simultaneously (as nearly as the time sequence of sentences allows) as the substance for the development of the ideas:

[1] Both writers link their ideas to events occurring in the natural world. [2] Night as a parallel with death is common to both poems, with Frost speaking about it in his first line, and Shakespeare introducing it in his seventh. [3] Along with night, Frost emphasizes the onset of winter and snow as a time of death and desolation. [4] With this natural description, Frost also symbolically refers to empty, secret, dead places in the inner spirit—crannies of the soul where bleak winter snowfalls correspond to selfishness and indifference to others. [5] By contrast, Shakespeare uses the fall season, with the yellowing and dropping of leaves and also the flying away of birds, to stress the closeness of real death and therefore also the need to love fully during the time remaining. [6] Both poems therefore share a sense of gloom, because both present death as inevitable and final, just like the oncoming season of barrenness and waste. [7] Because Shakespeare's sonnet is addressed to a listener who is also a loved one, however, it is more outgoing than the more introspective poem of Frost. [8] Frost turns the snow, the night, and the emptiness of the universe inwardly in order to show the speaker's inner bleakness, and by extension, the bleakness of many human spirits. [9] Shakespeare instead uses the bleakness of seasons, night, and dying fires to state the need for loving "well." [10] The poems thus use common and similar references for different purposes and effects.

The paragraph links Shakespeare's references to nature with those of Frost. Five sentences speak of both authors together; three speak of Frost alone, and two of Shakespeare alone, but all the sentences are unified topically. This interweaving of references indicates that the writer has learned both poems well enough to think of them at the same time, and it also enables the writing to be more pointed and succinct than if the works were separately treated.

You can learn from this example: If you develop your essay by putting your two subjects constantly together, you will write economically and pointedly (not only for essays, but also for tests). Beyond that, if you digest the material as successfully as this method indicates, you demonstrate that you are fulfilling a major educational goal—the assimilation and *use* of material. Too often, because you learn things separately (in separate works and courses, at separate times), you tend also to compartmentalize them. But instead, you should always try to relate them, to *synthesize* them. Comparison and contrast help in this process of putting together, of seeing things not as fragments but as parts of wholes.

Avoid the "Tennis-Ball" Method

As you make your comparison, do not confuse an interlocking method with a "tennis-ball" method, in which you bounce your subject back and forth constantly and repetitively, almost as though you were hitting observations back and forth over a net. The tennis-ball method is shown in the following example from a comparison of the characters Mathilde (Maupassant's "The Necklace") and Mrs. Popov (Chekhov's *The Bear*):

> Mathilde is a young married woman, while Miss Brill is single and getting older. Mathilde has at least some kind of social life, even though she doesn't have more than one friend, while Miss Brill leads a life of solitude. Mathilde's daydreams are responsible for her misfortune, but the shattering of Miss Brill's is done by someone from the outside. Therefore, Mathilde is made unhappy because of her own shortcomings, but Miss Brill is a helpless victim. In Mathilde's case the focus is on adversity not only causing trouble but also strengthening character. In Miss Brill's case the focus is on the weak getting hurt and becoming weaker.

Imagine the effect of an entire essay written in this boring 1,2—1,2—1,2 order. Aside from the repetition and unvaried patterning of subjects, the tennis-ball method does not permit much illustrative development. You should not feel so constrained that you cannot take two or more sentences to develop a point about one writer or subject before you include comparative references to another. If you remember to interlock the two subjects of comparison, however, as in the paragraph about Frost and Shakespeare, your method will give you the freedom to develop your topics fully.

THE EXTENDED COMPARISON-CONTRAST ESSAY

For a longer essay about a number of works—such as a limited research paper, comprehensive exam questions, and the sort of extended essay required at the end of a semester—comparison-contrast is an essential method. You may wish to compare the works on the basis of elements such as ideas, plot, structure, character, metaphor, point of view, or setting. Because of the larger number of works, however, you will need to modify the way in which you employ the comparison-contrast method. Suppose that you are dealing with not just two works but six, seven, or more. You need first to find a common ground that you may use as your central, unifying idea, just as you do for a comparison of only two works. Once you establish the common ground, you can classify or group your works on the basis of the similarities and differences they exemplify with regard to the topic. The idea is to get two *groups* for comparison, not just two works.

Let us assume that three or four works treat a topic in one way, while two or three do it in another (e.g., either criticism or praise of wealth and trade, or the joys or sorrows of love, or the enthusiasm or disillusionment of youth). In writing about these works, you might treat the topic itself in a straightforward comparison-contrast method, but use details from the works within the groupings as the material which you use for illustration and argument.

To make your essay as specific as possible, it is best to stress only a small number of major works with each of your sub-points. Once you have established these points in detail, there is no need to go into similar detail with all the other works you are studying. Instead, you may refer to the other works briefly, your purpose being to strengthen your points without creating more and more examples. Once you go to another sub-point, you may use different works for illustration, so that by the end of your essay you will have given due attention to each work in your assignment. In this way—by treating many works in small comparative groups—you can keep your essay reasonably brief, for there is no need for unproductive detail.

For illustration, the second sample essay (p. 1618) shows how this grouping may be done. There, six works are included in a general category of how love and service offer guidance and stability. This group is contrasted with another group of four works (including two characters from one of the works in the first group), in which love is shown as an escape or retreat.

Citing References in a Longer Comparison-Contrast Essay

For the longer comparison-contrast essay you may find a problem in making references to many different works. Generally you do not need to repeat full references. For example, if you refer to Phoenix of Welty's "A Worn Path," or to Sammy of Updike's "A & P," you should make the full references only once, and then refer later just to the character, story, or author, according to your needs.

When you quote lines or passages, or when you cite actions or characters in special ways, you should use parenthetical line, speech, or paragraph
references, as in the second sample essay. Be guided by the following principle: If you make a specific reference that you think your reader might want
to examine in more detail, supply the line, speech, or paragraph number. If
you refer to minor details that might easily be unnoticed or forgotten, also
supply the appropriate number.

WRITING COMPARISON-CONTRAST ESSAYS

Narrowing Your Subject

First, narrow and simplify your subject so that you can handle it conveniently. Should your subject be a comparison of Amy Lowell and Wilfred
Owen (as in the first sample essay), pick out one or two of each poet's poems
on the same or a similar topic, and write your essay about these. For the
longer comparison-contrast essay, you will need no more than one work by
each author. Be wary, however, of the limitations of your selection, because
generalizations made from one or two works may not apply to all works of the
same writer.

Once you have found an organizing principle along with the relevant
works, begin to refine and focus the direction of your essay. As you study each
work, note common or contrasting elements, and use these to form your central idea. At the same time, you can select the most illustrative works and classify them according to your topic, such as war (first sample essay) or love (second).

Organizing Your Essay

In your introduction, state the works, authors, characters, or ideas
which you are considering. Then show how you have narrowed the topic.
Your central idea should briefly highlight the principal grounds of comparison and contrast, such as that both works treat a common topic, exhibit a similar idea, use a similar form, develop an identical attitude, and so on, and also
that major or minor differences help make the works unique. You may also
assert that one work is superior to the other, if you wish to make this judgment and defend it.

The body of your essay is governed by the works and your basis of comparison (ideas and essays, depictions of character, uses of setting, qualities of
style, or uses of point of view, and so on). For a comparison-contrast treatment on such a basis, your goal should be to shed light on both (or more) of
the works you are treating. For example, you might examine a number of stories written in the first-person point of view (see Chapter 6). An essay on this
topic might compare the ways each author uses the point of view to achieve
similar or distinct effects. Or you might compare a group of poems that em-

ploy similar images, symbols, or ironic methods. Sometimes, the process can be as simple as identifying female or male protagonists, and comparing the ways in which their characters are developed. Another approach is to compare the *subjects*, as opposed to the *theme*. You might identify works dealing with general subjects like love, death, youth, race, or war. Such groupings provide a basis of excellent comparisons and contrasts.

As you develop the body, remember to keep comparison-contrast foremost. That is, your discussions of point of view, metaphorical language, or whatever should not so much explain these topics as topics, but rather explore similarities and differences about the works you are comparing. If your topic is an idea, for example, you need to explain the idea, but only enough to establish points of similarity or difference. As you develop such an essay, you might illustrate your arguments by referring to related uses of elements like setting, characterization, rhythm or rhyme, symbolism, point of view, or metaphor. When you introduce these new subjects, you will be on target as long as you use them comparatively.

The conclusion of your essay may reflect on other ideas or techniques in the works you have compared, make observations about similar qualities, or summarize briefly the grounds of your comparison. The conclusion of an extended comparison-contrast essay should represent a final synthesis of your materials. In the body of your essay, you may not have referred to all the works in each paragraph. However, in your conclusion you should try to include them all. If your writers belong to any "period" or "school" (information about such topics would require research and the use of correct documentation), you also might show how they relate to these larger movements. References of this sort provide an obvious common ground for comparison and contrast.

FIRST SAMPLE ESSAY (TWO WORKS)

The Treatment of Responses to War in Amy Lowell's "Patterns" and Wilfred Owen's "Anthem for Doomed Youth"°

[1]   <u>"Patterns" and "Anthem for Doomed Youth" are both powerful and unique condemnations of war.</u>* Owen's short poem speaks broadly and generally about the ugliness of war and also about large groups of bereaved people, while Lowell's longer poem focuses upon the personal grief of just one person. In a sense, Lowell's poem begins where Owen's ends, a fact which accounts for both the similarities and differences between the two works. <u>The anti-war themes may be compared on the basis of their subjects, their lengths, their concreteness, and their use of a common major metaphor.</u>†

°For these poems, see pp 963 and 630.
*Central idea.
†Thesis sentence.

"Anthem for Doomed Youth" attacks war more directly than "Patterns." Owen's opening line, "What passing bells for those who die as cattle," suggests that in war human beings are depersonalized before they are slaughtered, like so much meat, while his observations about the "monstrous" guns and the "shrill, demented" shells unambiguously condemn the horrors of war. By contrast, in "Patterns" warfare is far away, on another continent, intruding only when the messenger delivers the letter stating that the speaker's fiancé has been killed (lines 63–64). Similar news governs the last six lines of Owen's poem, quietly describing how those at home respond to the news that their loved ones have died in war. Thus the anti-war focus in "Patterns" is the contrast between the calm, peaceful life of the speaker's garden and the anguish of her responses, while in Owen's poem the stress is more the external horrors of war which bring about the need for ceremonies honoring the dead.

[2]

Another difference, which is surprising, is that Owen's poem is less than one-seventh as long as Lowell's. "Patterns" is an interior monologue or meditation of 107 lines, but it could not be shorter and still be convincing. In the poem the speaker thinks about the present and past, and contemplates the future loneliness to which her intended husband's death has doomed her. Her final outburst, "Christ, what are patterns for?", can make no sense if she does not explain her situation as extensively as she does. On the other hand, "Anthem for Doomed Youth" is brief—a 14-line sonnet—because it is more general and less personal than "Patterns." Although Owen shows great sympathy through his speaker, he treats the sorrows of others distantly, unlike Lowell, who goes right into the mind and spirit of the grieving woman. Owen's use, in his last six lines, of phrases like "tenderness of patient minds" and "drawing down of blinds" is a short but powerful representation of deep grief. He gives no further detail even though thousands of individual stories might be told. In contrast, Lowell tells one of these stories as she focuses on her solitary speaker's lost hopes and dreams. Thus the contrasting lengths of the poems are governed by each poet's treatment of the topic.

[3]

Despite these differences of approach and length, both poems are similarly concrete and real. Owen moves from the real scenes and sounds of far-off battlefields to the homes of the many soldiers who have been killed in battle, while Lowell's scene is a single place—the garden of the estate where the speaker has just received news of her lover's death. Her speaker walks on real gravel along garden paths which contain daffodils, squills, a fountain, and a lime tree. She thinks of her clothing and her ribboned shoes, and also of her fiancé's boots, sword hilts, and buttons. The images in Owen's poem are equally real, but are not associated with individuals as in "Patterns." Thus his images refer to cattle, bells, rifle shots, shells, bugles, candles, and window blinds. While both poems thus reflect reality, Owen's details are more general and public, whereas Lowell's are more personal and intimate.

[4]

Along with this concreteness, the poems share a major metaphor: that cultural patterns both control and frustrate human wishes and hopes. In "Patterns" this metaphor is shown in warfare itself (line 106), which is the supremely destructive political structure, or pattern. Further examples of the metaphor are found in details about clothing (particularly the speaker's stiff, confining gown in lines 5, 18, 21, 73, and 100, but also the lover's military boots in lines 46 and 49); the orderly, formal garden paths in which the

[5] speaker is walking (lines 1, 93); her restraint at hearing about her lover's death; and her courtesy, despite her grief, in ordering refreshment for the messenger (line 69). Within such rigid patterns, her hopes for happiness have vanished, along with the sensuous spontaneity symbolized by her lover's plans to make love with her on a "shady seat" in the garden (lines 85–89). The metaphor of the constricting pattern may also be seen in "Anthem for Doomed Youth," except that in this poem the pattern is the funeral, not love or marriage. Owen's speaker contrasts the calm, peaceful tolling of "passing-bells" (line 1) with the frightening sounds of war represented by the "monstrous anger of the guns," "the rifles' rapid rattle," and "the demented choirs of wailing shells" (lines 2–8). Thus, while Lowell uses the metaphor to reveal the irony of hope and desire being destroyed by war, Owen uses it to reveal the irony of war's nullification of peaceful ceremonies.

[6] Although the poems in these ways share topics and some aspects of treatment, they are distinct and individual. "Patterns" is visual and kinesthetic, whereas "Anthem for Doomed Youth" is strongly auditory. Both poems conclude on powerfully emotional although different notes. Owen's poem dwells on the pathos and sadness that war brings to many unnamed people, while Lowell's expresses the most intimate thoughts of a particular woman in the first agony of sorrow. Although neither poem directly attacks the usual platitudes and justifications for war (the needs to mobilize, to sacrifice, to achieve peace through fighting, and so on), the attack is there by implication, for both poems make their appeal by stressing how war destroys the relationships that make life worth living. For this reason, despite their differences, both "Patterns" and "Anthem for Doomed Youth," are parallel anti-war poems, and both are strong expressions of feeling.

Commentary on the Essay

This example shows how an essay may devote approximately equal attention to the two works being studied. Words stressing the similarity of elements in the two poems are "common," "share," "equally," "parallel," "both" "similar," and "also." Contrasting elements are stressed by words like "while," "whereas," "different," "dissimilar," "contrast," "although," and "except." Transitions from paragraph to paragraph are not different in this type of essay from those in other essays. Thus, "despite," "along with this . . ." and "in these ways," which are used here, could be used anywhere for the same transitional purpose.

The central idea—that the poems mutually condemn war—is brought out in the introductory paragraph, together with the supporting idea that the poems blend into each other because both show responses to news of battle casualties.

Paragraph 2, the first in the body, discusses how each poem brings out its attack on warfare. Paragraph 3 explains the differing lengths of the poems as a function of differences in perspective. Because Owen's sonnet views war and its effects at a distance, it is brief, while Lowell's interior monologue views death intimately, needing more detail and greater length. Paragraph 4, on the topic of concreteness and reality, shows that the two works may receive equal attention without the bouncing of the "tennis-ball" method. Three of the sentences in this paragraph (3, 4, and 6) are devoted exclusively to details in one or the other poem, while sentences 1, 2, 5, and 7 refer to both works, stressing points of broad or specific comparison. The scheme demonstrates that the two works are, in effect, interlocked within the paragraph.

Paragraph 5, the last in the body, considers the similar and dissimilar ways in which the poems treat the common metaphor of cultural patterns.

The final paragraph summarizes the central idea, and it also stresses the ways in which both poems, while similar, are distinct and unique.

SECOND SAMPLE ESSAY (EXTENDED COMPARISON-CONTRAST)

The Complexity of Love and Devoted Service

[1]
On the surface, sexual attraction, love, and devoted duty are simple, and their results should be good. When love works and is in balance, a person loves and devotes attention to someone, or serves a cause with respect and willingness. Such devotion leads to stability and a healthy sense of identity. It is a way of saying "yes." When love and devotion do not work, the effect is extreme unhappiness, a way of saying "no." Love, in short, is not simple. It is complex, and its results are not uniformly good.° This idea can be traced in a comparison of ten works: Shakespeare's Sonnet 116, Keats's "Bright Star," Rossetti's "Echo," Arnold's "Dover Beach," Hardy's "Channel Firing," Owen's "Anthem for Doomed Youth," Chekhov's The Bear, Glaspell's Trifles, Updike's "A & P," and Welty's "A Worn Path."* The complexity in these works is that love and devotion do not operate in a vacuum but rather in the context of personal, philosophical, economic, and national difficulties. The works show that love and devotion may be forces for stability and refuge, but also for harm.†

[2]
Love as an ideal and stabilizing force is a major principle asserted by Shakespeare in Sonnet 116, Keats in the sonnet "Bright Star," and Rossetti in "Echo." All three writers think of love as a constant, and associate it with guidance and illumination. Shakespeare states that love gives lovers strength and stability in a complex world of opposition and difficulty. Such love is like a "star" (obviously the North Star) that guides wandering ships (line 7), and like a "fixed mark" that stands against the shaking of life's tempests (lines 5 and 6). Fixity is also the condition stressed by Keats in "Bright Star," where the speaker contrasts his own apparent instability with his desire to be as steadfast in his loving as the star is in the sky (line 1). Rossetti refers to love as a light in darkness (stanza 1), even though the light, to her speaker, has been snuffed out by the death of her beloved.

°   Central idea.
*   Use the index to locate the texts of these works.
†   Thesis sentence.

[3]   For these three writers, love grows out of the need for stability and guidance, just as it also supplies this need. Love is a simplifying force, but it simplifies primarily because the darkness and the "tempests" complicating life are so strong. Such love is one of the best things that happen to human beings, because it fulfills them and prepares them to face life. Either directly or indirectly, all the writers being considered here are working with this same positive assumption about love.

[4]   The desire to seek identity in love is so strong that it can also cause people to do strange and funny things. The two major characters in Chekhov's short comedy-farce The Bear are examples, as is Sammy of Updike's story "A & P." Sammy watches the three girls in the store with great sexual curiosity, and within minutes after they leave, he quits his job in a gesture that combines sexual adoration, chivalric respect, and his own individuality. A similar quick change is shown by Chekhov's Mrs. Popov and Smirnov, who as The Bear opens are enmeshed in their own confusion. She is devoted to the memory of her dead husband, while he is disillusioned and cynical about women because of mismanaged love affairs. But Chekhov makes them go through hoops for love. As the two argue, insult each other, and reach the point of dueling with real pistols, their need for love overcomes their anger. In their case, as in Sammy's, it is as though the impulse for love and admiration overcomes all the contrary influences, because the common need for a stabilizing base is so strong.

[5]   Either seriously or comically, then, love and love interest are like a rudder, guiding people in powerful and conflicting currents. The results may be sudden and passionate kisses, as with Chekhov's characters, or they may be the establishment of a new condition or ideal, as in Shakespeare, Keats, and Rossetti, and in the decision that Updike's Sammy makes. All these works, however, demonstrate that love shapes lives in ways that go beyond a person's immediate intentions.

[6]   This thought is somewhat like the view presented by Eudora Welty in "A Worn Path." Welty's story describes how love is manifested in loving service, in this respect being not only a guide, but a controlling force. A poor grandmother, Phoenix Jackson, has a hard life in caring for her incurably ill grandson. The walk she takes along the "worn path" to Natchez symbolizes the hardships she endures because of her single-minded love. Her care is the closest thing to pure simplicity that may be found in all the works examined, with the possible exception of the sudden falling in love in Chekhov's play.

[7]   Even Phoenix's devoted service, however, does not solve problems, but rather brings them out. She is not surrounded by the joyless, loveless, violent world described by Hardy in "Channel Firing," Owen in "Anthem for Doomed Youth," and Arnold in "Dover Beach," but her life is nevertheless quite grim. She is poor and ignorant, and her grandson has nowhere to go but down. If she would think only about her own condition, she might be as despairing as Arnold and Hardy. But her strength is her ability either to accept her difficult life or to ignore the grimness of it. With her service as her "star" and "ever-fixed mark," to recall Shakespeare's words in Sonnet 116, she stays cheerful and lives in friendship with the animals and the woods. Her life has meaning and dignity.

Arnold's view of love and devotion under such bad conditions marks a departure from the views of love's power as a guiding and governing force. For Arnold, the public world seems to be so far gone that there is nothing left but personal relationships. Thus love is not so much a guide as a refuge, a condition accepted for sanity and safety. After describing what he considers the worldwide shrinking of the "Sea of Faith" (i.e., the loss of absolute belief in the existence of a personal and caring God), he states:

[8]

Ah, love, let us be true
To one another! for the world, which seems
To lie before us like a land of dreams,
So various, so beautiful, so new,
Hath really neither joy, nor love, nor light,
Nor certitude, nor peace, nor help for pain;
And we are here as on a darkling plain
Swept with confused alarms of struggle and flight
Where ignorant armies clash by night.

—lines 29–37

Here the word true should be underlined, as Shakespeare emphasizes "true minds" and as Welty gives us in Phoenix a portrait of true service. "True" in Arnold's poem involves the creation of a small area of fidelity and certainty in the world of horrible naval gunnery and rattling rifles of "Channel Firing" and "Anthem for Doomed Youth," where there is only madness and death. Love is not so much a guide as a condition of hope, a retreat where truth can still have meaning.

[9]

In practice, perhaps, Arnold's idea of love as a refuge is not different from the view that love is a guide. Once the truthful pledge is made, it is a force for goodness, at least for the lovers making the pledge, just as love creates stability and purpose for Shakespeare, Chekhov, Welty, and Keats. Yet Arnold's view is weaker. It does not come from within, as with the longing of Rossetti's speaker, the gesture of support that Updike's Sammy makes for the rights of the young ladies to wear nothing but bathing suits in a public place, or the abrupt love of Chekhov's major characters. Rather, Arnold's appeal for truth and fidelity results from a philosophical decision to ignore political and philosophical forces, which are beyond control, and to seek meaning and fidelity only in small and private relationships.

[10]

Thus far love and devotion have been considered more or less as ideals, but the ideal is always subject to the reality of human personality. A major idea is hence that the character of a person may turn love sour and damage life. In the set of works being considered here, such destructiveness is brought out best by Susan Glaspell in Trifles (and in the other version of the story, "A Jury of Her Peers"). Ideally, the love of John and Minnie Wright should give them the strength and stability to live satisfactory if not happy lives on their isolated small farm. Instead, John has used his power to suppress Minnie's femininity and love of song. The result is her simmering anger for the thirty years of their life together, resulting in the outburst of her strangling John in his sleep.

[11]   Minnie's anger is not dissimilar to that of Mrs. Popov, whose dead husband Nicolai had been neglectful and unfaithful. John, however, is not unfaithful, but overbearing and cruel, thus justifying Minnie's rage. Mrs. Popov has some of the same rage, but submerges it at the start of The Bear by devoting her life to the role of a grieving (but angry) widow. She of course is more fortunate than Minnie, for fate takes her husband Nicolai while Minnie, in desperation and presumed rage, takes the burden of eliminating her husband herself. Even though neither husband appears in The Bear and Trifles, they both demonstrate the worst possible result of love—its use for personal power rather than for mutual understanding, tenderness, and devoted caring.

[12]   John Wright and Nicolai Popov are minor compared with those unseen, unnamed and distant persons firing the big guns during the "gunnery practice out at sea" of Hardy's "Channel Firing" (line 10) and also those who create "the monstrous anger of the guns" of Owen's "Anthem for Doomed Youth" (line 2). Neither poet treats the gunners as individuals but as an evil collective force made up of persons who, under the sheltering claim of devoted service to country, are "striving strong to make / Red war yet redder" (Hardy, lines 13, 14) and to create great hordes of "these who die as cattle" (Owen, line 1). For them, love of country is a last refuge and not a guide, and it is therefore a misuse of devoted service. In their blind obedience, as Hardy's God says, they are not much better than the dead because they do nothing "for Christés sake" (line 15). They operate the ships and fill the columns of Arnold's "ignorant armies," and, like Wright and Nicolai, they have forsaken the guidance that love should give while they pursue mindless and destructive ends.

[13]   In summary, love and devotion as seen in these various works may be compared with a continuous line formed out of the human need for love and for the stability and guidance that love offers. At one end love is totally good and ideal; at the other it becomes totally bad. Shakespeare, Keats, Rossetti, Welty, Chekhov's Smirnov and Mrs. Popov, and Updike's Sammy are at the end that is good. Still at the good end, but moving toward the center, is Arnold's use of love as a refuge. On the other side of the line are Chekhov's Nicolai Popov and Glaspell's John Wright, while all the way at the bad end are the insensible and invisible gunners in Hardy's "Channel Firing" and Owen's "Anthem for Doomed Youth."

[14]   The difficulty noted in all the works, and a major problem in life, is to keep oneself on the stabilizing, constructive part of the line. Although in his farce Chekhov causes love to win against gigantic odds, he shows the problem most vividly of all the authors studied. Under normal conditions, people like Mrs. Popov and Smirnov would not find love. Instead, they would continue following their destructive and false guides. They would be unhappy and disillusioned, and would continue to spread talk about their own confused ideas (as Smirnov actually does almost right up to his sudden conversion to loving Mrs. Popov). Like the military and naval forces of Arnold and Hardy, they would then wind up at the destructive end of the line.

[15]   Change, death, opposition, confusion, anger, resignation, economic difficulty, illness—these are only some of the forces that attack people as they try to find meaning and stability in love and service as in Sonnet 116, "Bright Star," "Echo," the major characters in The Bear, "A Worn Path," and, to smaller degrees, "A & P" and "Dover Beach." If confusion wins, they are locked into

harmful positions, like the gunners in "Channel Firing" and "Anthem for Doomed Youth" and like Nicolai Popov of <u>The Bear</u> and John Wright of <u>Trifles</u>. Thus love is complicated by circumstances, and is not by itself alone the simple force for good that it should ideally be. <u>The works compared and contrasted here have shown these difficulties and complexities.</u>

Commentary on the Essay

This essay, combining for discussion all three of the genres, is visualized as an assignment at the end of a unit of study. The expectation prompting the assignment is that a fairly large number of literary works can be profitably compared on the basis of a unifying subject, idea, or technique. For this sample, the works—six poems, two stories, and two plays—are compared and contrasted on the common ground or central idea of the complexity of love and service. The essay develops this central idea in three major sections: (1) love as an ideal and guide, in paragraphs 2 to 7; (2) love as a refuge or escape, in paragraphs 8 and 9; and (3) love as an excuse for doing harm, as in paragraphs 10 to 12.

The various works are grouped generally according to these sections. Thus Sonnet 116, "Bright Star," "Echo," *The Bear*, "A & P," and "A Worn Path" are together in the first group—love as an ideal and guide. "Dover Beach" and "Channel Firing" are considered in the second section, but are also introduced for comparison in paragraph 7 as part of a point about the nature of Phoenix's condition in "A Worn Path." Similarly, some of the works in the first group are included as subjects of comparison and contrast in all the sections.

It is obviously impossible to discuss all the works in detail in every paragraph. Thus, in paragraph 2 of this essay, only three works are introduced on the common topic, not all ten, and paragraph 3 consists of a reflection on these three works. Paragraph 4 introduces two works on a slightly different point ("strange and funny things") than that of paragraphs 2 and 3. Paragraph 5 is like the third paragraph because it, too, serves as a point of reflection—this time about all the works considered to that point. The form of comparison and contrast throughout the essay might hence be thought of as one of expansion (when a number of works are introduced) and contraction (when there are just a few).

Paragraph 6 introduces references to just one work, Welty's "A Worn Path," with a brief comparison of only one other work at the end. The seventh paragraph continues the subject of the sixth, and introduces two additional works for comparison.

Paragraph 8 illustrates how almost the entire number of works being studied may be focused on a single topic—here, the use of love as refuge or retreat, with the central work of the paragraph being "Dover Beach." The first sentence contrasts Arnold's view with the common idea in the six works in the first group—that love is a guide. The fifth sentence shows how Arnold is similar in one respect to Shakespeare and Welty, and the sixth sentence shows a similarity of Arnold with Owen and Hardy. The paragraph thus brings together most of the works being studied, either through specific mention or general allusion. Like paragraph 8, paragraph 9 uses Arnold's "Dover Beach" as the key work, with reference to a number of other works for comparison.

The third major section of the essay, consisting of paragraphs 10 to 12, is devoted primarily to four works, although the general ideal of love, as established early in the essay, provides the overall thematic linkage.

The technique of extended comparison-contrast used in this way shows how the various works may be defined and distinguished in relation to the common idea. Paragraph 13, the first in the conclusion, summarizes these distinctions by suggesting a continuous line along which each of the works may be placed. Paragraphs 14 and 15 continue the summary by showing the prominence of complicating difficulties, and, by implication, the importance of love and devoted duty.

Clearly, an extended comparison-contrast essay cannot present a full treatment of each of the works. Indeed, the works are unique, and there are many elements that would not yield to the comparison-contrast method. In "Channel Firing," for example, there are ideas that human beings need eternal rest and eternal life, that God is amused by—or indifferent to—human affairs, that religious service may be futile, and that war itself is the supreme form of cruelty. To introduce the poem into this comparison-contrast structure requires questioning the motives for patriotic duty of the distant gunners. While this consideration forms a link with the other works, it is by no means the major idea in Hardy's poem. So it is with the other works, each of which could be the subject of analysis from a number of separate standpoints. The effect of the comparison of all the works collectively, however, is the enhanced understanding of each of the works separately. To achieve such an understanding and to explain it are the major goals of the extended comparison-contrast method.

Appendix C
Writing and Documenting the Research Essay

Broadly, **research** is the act of systematic investigation, examination, and experimentation. It is the basic tool of intellectual inquiry for anyone engaged in any discipline—physics, chemistry, biology, psychology, anthropology, history, and literature, to name just a few disciplines. With research, our understanding and our civilization grow; without it, they die.

While research is the animating spark of all disciplines, our topic here is **literary research**—the systematic use of primary and secondary sources in studying a literary problem. In doing literary research, you consult not only individual works themselves (*primary sources*), but many other works that shed light on them and interpret them (*secondary sources*). Typical research tasks are to learn important facts about a work and about the period in which it was written; to learn about the lives, careers, and other works of authors; to discover some of the comments and judgments of modern or earlier critics; to learn details that help explain the meaning of works; and to learn about critical and artistic taste.

A certain amount of research is always necessary in any literary essay or assignment. Using a dictionary, for example, is a minimal form of research. More involved research uses an array of resources: encyclopedias, biographies, introductions, critical studies, bibliographies, and histories.

SELECTING A TOPIC

In most instances, your instructor assigns a research essay on a specific topic. Sometimes, however, the choice of a topic is left entirely up to you. In such cases, it is helpful to know the types of research essays you might find most congenial. Here are some possibilities.

1. *A particular work.* You might treat character (for example, "The Character of Bottom in *A Midsummer Night's Dream*," or "The Question of Whether Willie Loman is a Hero or Antihero in *Death of a Salesman*"), or tone, ideas, form, problems, and the like. A research paper on a single work is similar to an essay on the same work, except that the research paper takes into account more views and facts than those you are likely to have without the research.

2. *A particular author.* This essay is about an idea or some facet of style, imagery, setting, or tone of the author, tracing the origins and development of the topic through a number of different stories, poems, or plays. An example is "The Idea of the True Self as Developed by Frost in His Poetry before 1920." This type of essay is suitable if you are writing on a poet whose works are short, though a topic like "Shakespeare's Idea of the Relationships Between Men and Women as Dramatized in *A Midsummer Night's Dream* and *Hamlet*" is also possible.

3. Comparison and contrast (see Appendix B). There are two types:

    a. *An idea or quality common to two or more authors.* Here you show points of similarity or contrast, or else show how one author's work may criticize another's. A possible subject is "The Theme of Ineffectuality in Eliot, Steinbeck, and Williams," or "Hughes's Anti-discrimination Poems in the Context of Twentieth-Century Race Relations." Consult the second sample essay in Appendix B for an example.

    b. *Different critical views of a particular work or body of works.* Sometimes much is to be gained from an examination of differing critical opinions on topics like "The Meaning of Shirley Jackson's 'The Lottery,'" "The Interpretations of Gray's *Elegy*," or "The Question of Hamlet's Hesitation." Such a study would attempt to determine the critical opinion and taste to which a work did or did not appeal, and it might also aim at conclusions about whether the work was in the advance or rear guard of its time.

4. The influence of an idea, author, philosophy, political situation, or artistic movement on specific works of an author or authors. An essay on influences can be specific and to the point, as in "Details of Early Twentieth-Century Mexican-American Culture as Reflected in Parédes's 'The Hammon and the Beans,'" or else it can be more abstract and critical, as in "The Influence of Early Twentieth-Century Oppression of Mexican-Americans on the Narrator of 'The Hammon and the Beans.'"

5. *The origin of a particular work or type of work.* Such an essay might examine an author's biography to discover the germination and development of a work—for example, "'The Old Chief Mshlanga' as an Outgrowth of Lessing's Life in Rhodesia-Zimbabwe." Another way of discovering origins might be to relate a work to a particular type or tradition: "*Hamlet* as Revenge Tragedy," or "*Love Is the Doctor* and Its Origins in the Tradition of the *Commedia dell'Arte*."

If you consider these types, an idea of what to write may come to you. Perhaps you have particularly liked one author, or several authors. If so, you might start to think along the lines of types 1, 2, and 3. If you are interested in influences or in origins, then types 4 or 5 may suit you better.

If you still cannot decide on a topic after rereading the works you have liked, then you should carry your search for a topic into your school library. Look up your author or authors in the card or computer catalogue. Your first goal should be to find a relatively recent book-length critical study published by a university press. Look for a title indicating that the book is a general one dealing with the author's major works rather than just one work. Study those chapters relevant to the work or works you have chosen. Most writers of critical studies describe their purpose and plan in their introductions or first chapters, so begin with the first part of the book. If there is no separate chapter on the primary text, use the index and go to the relevant pages. Reading in this way will give you enough knowledge about the issues and ideas raised by the work to enable you to select a promising topic. Once you make your decision, you are ready to go ahead and develop a working bibliography.

SETTING UP A BIBLIOGRAPHY

The best way to develop a working bibliography of books and articles is to begin with major critical studies of the writer or writers. Again, go to the catalogue and pick out books that have been published by university presses. These books usually contain comprehensive bibliographies. Be careful to read the chapters on your primary work or works and to look for the footnotes or end notes, for often you can save time if you record the names of books and articles listed in these notes. Then refer to the bibliographies included at the ends of the books, and select likely looking titles. Now, look at the dates of publication of the critical books. Let us suppose that you have been looking at three, published in 1963, 1987, and 1992. The chances are that the bibliography in a book published in 1992 will be complete up through about 1990, for the writer will usually have completed the manuscript about two years before the book was published. What you should do then is to gather a bibliography of works published since 1990; you may safely assume that writers of critical works will have done the selecting for you of works published before that time.

Bibliographical Guides

Fortunately for students doing literary research, the Modern Language Association (MLA) of America has been providing a complete bibliography of literary studies for years, not only in English and American literatures, but in the literatures of many foreign languages. The MLA started achieving completeness in the late 1950's, and by 1969 had reached such an advanced state that it divided the bibliography into four parts, which are bound together in library editions. University and college libraries have a set of these bibliographies on open shelves or tables. Recently, the bibliographies have become available on CD-ROM.

There are many other bibliographies useful for students doing literary research, such as the *Essay and General Literature Index,* the *International Index,* and various specific indexes. For most purposes, however, the *MLA International Bibliography* is more than adequate. Remember that as you progress in your reading, the notes and bibliographies in the works you consult also will constitute an unfolding bibliography. For the sample research essay in this chapter, for example, a number of entries were discovered not from the bibliographies, but from the reference lists in critical works.

The *MLA International Bibliography* is conveniently organized by period and author. If your author is Gwendolyn Brooks, for example, look her up under "American Literature V. Twentieth Century," the relevant listing for all twentieth-century American writers. If your author is Shakespeare, refer to "English Literature VI. Renaissance and Elizabethan." You will find most books and articles listed under the author's last name. For special help for students and researchers, the MLA provides an exhaustive topics list that is keyed to the bibliographical entries. Using these topics, you may locate important works that you might miss with only the authors list. In the MLA bibliographies, journal references are abbreviated, but a lengthy list explaining abbreviations appears at the beginning of the volume. Using the MLA bibliographies, begin with the most recent one and then go backward to your stopping point. Be sure to get the complete information, especially volume numbers and years of publication, for each article and book. You are now ready to find your sources and to take notes.

Online Computerized Library Services

Localized and nationwide online reference services are available through most libraries and library systems. You therefore have the possibility of access to the collections of large research libraries, which are of immense value for research. If your own library does not have a book you discover through the online reference service, you can use the Interlibrary Loan Service to acquire the copy you need. Also, many associated libraries, such as state colleges and urban public libraries, have pooled their resources in online systems. If you use the services of a network of county libraries, for example, you may locate works that are not available in your college or local library. Usually, with time, the libraries will accommodate as many of your needs as they can. Librarians are immensely helpful and cooperative.

You may use a personal computer yourself to gain access to the online service of a large library, provided that you have a modem, a telecommunications program, the correct telephone number and other entry information, the ability to follow the program codes, and patience and persistence. Once you gain access, you may ask for books by specific authors, or for books about specific topics. If your topic is *Shakespeare*, for example, you may ask for specific titles of his works or for books about him. A recent request for general critical works about Shakespeare from a large urban university library produced a list of 396 items, including all the pertinent bibliographical information. The same library listed 113 works containing specific material about *Hamlet*. Once you have such materials on your screen, you may select and list only the most likely looking titles—the ones you think will be most useful. Such a list comprises a fairly comprehensive search bibliography, which you may use once you physically enter the library to begin collecting and using materials.

If you gain access to online services, be careful to determine the year when the computerization began. Many libraries have a recent commencement date—like 1973, for example, or 1978. For completeness, therefore, you would need to use the complete catalogue for items published before these years.

TAKING NOTES AND PARAPHRASING MATERIAL

There are many ways of taking notes, but the consensus is that the best method is to use note cards. If you have never used cards before, you might profit from consulting any one of a number of handbooks and special workbooks on research. A lucid and methodical explanation of using cards and taking notes can be found in Glenn Leggett et al., *Prentice-Hall Handbook for Writers,* 10th ed., (Englewood Cliffs: Prentice Hall, 1988). The principal advantage of cards is that they can be classified, numbered, renumbered, shuffled, tried out in one place, rejected, and then used in another place (or thrown away), and arranged in order when you start to write.

Taking Notes

WRITE THE SOURCE ON EACH CARD. As you take notes, write the source of your information on each card. This may seem like a bother, but it is easier than going back to the library to locate the correct source after you have begun your essay. You can save time if you take the complete data on one card—a "master card" for that source—and then make up an abbreviation for your notes. Here is an example, which also includes the location where the reference was originally found (e.g., card catalogue, computer search, bibliography in a book, the *MLA International Bibliography*, etc.). Observe that the author's last name goes first.

Donovan, Josephine, ed. Feminist Literary Criticism: Explorations in Theory. Lexington: The University Press of Kentucky, 1975.	PN 98 .W64 F4

DONOVAN

Card Catalogue, "Women"

If you take many notes from this book, the name "Donovan" will serve as identification. Be sure not to lose your complete master cards because you will need them when you prepare your list of works cited. If possible, record the complete bibliographical data in a computer file.

RECORD THE PAGE NUMBER FOR EACH NOTE. It would be hard to guess how much exasperation has been caused by the failure to record page numbers in notes. Be sure to get the page number down first, *before* you begin to take your note, and, to be doubly sure, write the page number again at the end of your note. If the detail goes from one page to the next in your source, record the exact spot where the page changes, as in this example:

Heilbrun and Stimson, in DONOVAN, pp. 63–64

[63] After the raising of the feminist consciousness it is necessary to develop/ [64] "the growth of moral perception" through anger and the correction of social inequity.

The reason for such care is that you may wish to use only a part of a note you have taken, and when there are two pages you will need to be accurate in locating what goes where.

RECORD ONLY ONE FACT OR OPINION PER CARD. Record only one major element on each card—one quotation, one paraphrase, one observation—*never two or more.* You might be tempted to fill up the entire card with many separate but unrelated details, but such a try at economy often gets you in trouble because you might want to use some of the details in other places. If you have only one entry per card, you will avoid such hassles and also retain the freedom you need.

USE QUOTATION MARKS FOR ALL QUOTED MATERIAL. In taking notes it is extremely important to distinguish copied material from your own words. *Always put quotation marks around every direct quotation you copy verbatim from a source.* Make the quotation marks immediately, before you forget, so that you will always know that the words of your notes within quotation marks are the words of another writer.

Often, as you take a note, you may use some of your own words and some of the words from your source. In cases like this you should be even more cautious. Put quotation marks around *every word* that you take directly from the source, even if your note looks like a picket fence. Later, when you begin writing your paper, your memory of what is yours and not yours will be dim, and if you use another's words in your own essay without proper acknowledgment, you are risking the charge of plagiarism. Most of the time, apparent plagiarism is caused not by deliberate deception but rather by sloppy note taking.

Paraphrasing

When you take notes, it is best to paraphrase the sources. A paraphrase is a restatement in your own words, and because of this it is actually a first step in the writing of the essay. In Chapter 2 (pp. 81–86) this book explains in full how to write a précis or abridgment . If you work on this technique, you will be well prepared to paraphrase for your research paper.

A big problem in paraphrasing is to capture the idea in the source without duplicating the words. The best way is to read and reread the passage you are noting. Turn over the book or journal and write out the idea *in your own words* as accurately as you can. Once you have this note, compare it with the original and make corrections to improve your thought and emphasis. Add a short quotation if you believe it is needed, but be sure to use quotation marks. If your paraphrase is too close to the original, *throw out the note and try again.* This effort is worthwhile because often you can transfer much of your note directly to the appropriate place in your research paper.

To see the problems of paraphrasing, let us look at a paragraph of criticism and then see how a student doing research might take notes on it. The paragraph is by Maynard Mack, from an essay entitled "The World of Hamlet," originally published in *The Yale Review* 41 (1952) and reprinted in *Twentieth Century Interpretations of Hamlet,* ed. David Bevington (Englewood Cliffs: Prentice Hall, 1968), p. 57:

> The powerful sense of mortality in *Hamlet* is conveyed to us, I think, in three ways. First, there is the play's emphasis on human weakness, the instability of human purpose, the subjection of humanity to fortune—all that we might call the aspect of failure in man. Hamlet opens this theme in Act I, when he describes how from that single blemish, perhaps not even the victim's fault, a man's whole character may take corruption. Claudius dwells on it again, to an extent that goes far beyond the needs of the occasion, while engaged in seducing Laertes to step behind the arras of a seemer's world and dispose of Hamlet by a trick. Time qualifies everything, Claudius says, including love, including purpose. As for love—it has a "plurisy" in it and dies of its own too much. As for purpose—"That we would do, We should do when we would, for the 'would' changes. And hath abatements and delays as many As there are tongues, are hands, are accidents; And then this 'should' is like a spendthrift's sigh, That hurts by easing." The player-king, in his long speeches to his queen in the play within the play, sets the matter in a still darker light. She means these protestations of undying love, he knows, but our purposes depend on our memory, and our memory fades fast. Or else, he suggests, we propose something to ourselves in a condition of strong feeling, but then the feeling goes, and with it the resolve. Or else our fortunes change, he adds, and with these our loves: "The great man down, you mark his favorite flies." The subjection of human aims to fortune is a reiterated theme in *Hamlet,* as subsequently in *Lear.* Fortune is the harlot goddess in whose secret parts men like Rosencrantz and Guildenstern live and thrive; the strumpet who threw down Troy and Hecuba and Priam; the outrageous foe whose slings and arrows a man of principle must suffer or seek release in suicide. Horatio suffers them with composure: he is one of the blessed few "Whose blood and judgment are so well co-mingled That they are not a pipe for fortune's finger To sound what stop she please." For Hamlet the task is of a greater difficulty.

Because taking notes forces a shortening of this or any criticism, it also requires you to discriminate, judge, interpret, and select; good note taking is not easy. There are some things to guide you, however, when you go through the many sources you uncover.

THINK OF THE PURPOSE OF YOUR RESEARCH. You may not know exactly what you are "fishing for" when you start to take notes, for you cannot prejudge what your essay will contain. Research is a form of discovery. But soon you will notice subjects and issues that your sources constantly explore. If you can accept one of these as your major topic, or focus of interest, you may use that as your guide in all further note-taking.

For example, suppose you are taking notes on *Hamlet* criticism, and after a certain amount of reading you have decided to focus on "Shakespeare's Tragic Views in *Hamlet*." This decision would prompt you to take a note when you come to Mack's thought about mortality and death in the passage quoted above. In this instance, the following note would suffice:

Mack, in Bevington, 57   Death and
                                                                  Mortality

Mack cites three ways in which *Hamlet* stresses death and mortality.
The first (57) is an emphasis on human shortcomings and
"weakness." Corruption, loss of memory and enthusiasm, bad luck,
misery--all suit the sense of the closeness of death to life. 57

Let us now suppose that you want a fuller note, in the expectation that you need not just the topic but also some of Mack's detail. Such a note might look like this:

Mack, in Bevington, 57   Death and
                                                                  Mortality

The first of Mack's "three ways" in which a "powerful sense of
mortality" is shown in *Hamlet* is the illustration of human "weakness,"
"instability," and helplessness before fate. In support, Mack refers to
Hamlet's early speech on a single fault leading to corruption, also to
Claudius's speech (in the scene persuading Laertes to trick Hamlet).
The player-king also talks about his queen's forgetfulness and
therefore inconstancy by default. As slaves to fortune, Rosencrantz
and Guildenstern are examples. Horatio is not a slave, however.
Hamlet's case is by far the worst of all. 57

In an actual essay, any part of this note would be useful. The words are almost all the note-taker's own, and the few quotations are within quotation marks. Note that Mack, the critic, is properly recognized as the source of the criticism, so that you could adapt the note easily when you are doing your writing. The key here is that your taking of notes should be guided by your developing plan for your essay.

Note taking is part of your thinking and composing process. You may not always know whether you will be able to use each note that you take, and you will always exclude many notes when you write your essay. You will always find, however, that taking notes is easier once you have determined your purpose.

TITLE YOUR NOTES. To help plan and develop the various parts of your essay, write a title for each of your notes, in the upper right corner of the card, as in the examples in this chapter. This practice is a form of outlining. Let us assume that you have chosen to study the importance of the Ghost in the play. As you do research, you discover that there are conflicting views about how the Ghost should be understood. Here is a note about one of the questionable qualities of this character:

Prosser, 133, 134   Negative, Devilish

   [133] When describing his pain and suffering as a dead spirit, the Ghost is not specific but emphasizes the horror. He should, if a good spirit, try to use his suffering to urge repentance and salvation for Hamlet. [134] This emphasis is a sign that he is closer in nature to a devil than to a soul earning its way to redemption.

Notice that the title classifies the topic of the note. If you use such classifications while taking notes, a number of like-titled cards could form the substance of a section in your essay about the negative qualities of the Ghost in *Hamlet*. In addition, once you decide that "Negative, Devilish" is one of the topics you plan to explore, the topic itself will guide you in further study and note-taking.

RECORD YOUR OWN THOUGHTS. As you take your notes, be aware of your own thoughts. Do not let these go, on the chance of remembering them later, but write them down immediately. Often you may notice a detail that your source does not mention, or you may get a hint for an idea that the critic does not develop. Often, too, you may get thoughts which can serve as "bridges" between details in your notes or as introductions or concluding observations. Be sure to title your comment and also to mark it as your own thought. Here is such a note, which is related to the importance of the Ghost in the structure of *Hamlet:*

My Own   Structure

   Shakespeare does a superb job with the Ghost. His characterization shows many qualities of a living human being, and the Ghost is fully integrated in the play's structure.

Observe that some of the ideas and language from this note are used in paragraphs 9 and 10 of the sample research essay (p. 1645).

SORT YOUR CARDS INTO GROUPS. If you have taken your notes well, your essay will have been forming in your mind already. The titles of your cards will suggest areas to be developed as you do your planning and initial drafting. Once you have assembled a stack of note cards derived from a reasonable number of sources (your instructor may have assigned a minimum number), you can sort them into groups according to the topics and titles. For the sample essay, after some shuffling and retitling, the cards were assembled in the following groups:

1. Importance in the action
2. Importance in themes
3. Condition as a spirit
    a. Good signs
    b. Negative, devilish signs
4. Human traits
5. Importance in the structure
6. Effect on other characters

If you look at the major sections of the sample essay, you will see that the topics are closely adapted from these groups of cards. In other words, the arrangement of the cards is an effective means of outlining and organizing a research essay.

ARRANGE THE CARDS IN EACH GROUP. There is still much to do with each group of cards. You cannot use the details as they happen to fall randomly in your stack. You need to decide which notes are relevant. You might also need to retitle some cards and use them elsewhere. Those that remain will have to be arranged in a logical order to be used in the essay.

Once you have your cards in order, you can write whatever comments or transitions are needed to move from detail to detail. Write this material directly on the cards, and be sure to use a different color ink so that you can distinguish later between the original note and what you add now. Here is an example of such a "developed" note card:

Campbell, 127   Negative, Devilish

Shakespeare's Ghost reflects the general uncertainty at the time about how ghosts were to be interpreted.   127

This may be the best way to answer the questions about the Ghost's ambiguous nature. Moreover, Shakespeare may have been trying to be more lifelike than consistent with his Ghost.

By adding such commentary to your note cards, you will facilitate the actual writing of your first draft. In many instances, the note and the comment may be moved directly into the paper with minor adjustments (material from this note and comment appears in paragraph 5 of the sample essay).

BE CREATIVE AND ORIGINAL. This is not to say you can always transfer your notes directly into your essay. The major trap to avoid in a research paper is that your use of sources can become an end in itself and therefore a shortcut for your own thinking and writing. Often, students make the mistake of introducing details the way a master of ceremonies introduces performers in a variety show. This is unfortunate because it is the *student* whose essay will be judged, even though the sources, like the performers, do all the work. Thus, it is important to be creative and original in a research essay, and do your own thinking and writing, even though you are relying heavily on your sources. Here are four ways in which research essays may be original:

1. *Selection.* In each major section of your essay you will include many details from your sources. To be creative you should select different but related details and avoid overlapping or repetition. The essay will be judged on the basis of the thoroughness with which you make your point with different details (which in turn will represent the completeness of your research). Even though you are relying on published materials and cannot be original on that score, your selection can be original because you bring *these* materials together for the first time, and because you emphasize some details and minimize others. Inevitably, your assemblage of details from your sources will be unique and therefore original.

2. *Development.* Your arrangement of your various points is an obvious area of originality: One detail seems naturally to precede another, and certain conclusions stem from certain details. As you present the details, conclusions, and arguments from your sources, you may also add your own original stamp by using supporting details that are different from those in your sources. You may also add your own emphasis to particular points—an emphasis that you do not find in your sources.

Naturally, the words that you use will be original. Your topic sentences, for example, will all be your own. As you introduce details and conclusions, you will need to write "bridges" to get yourself from point to point. These may be introductory remarks or transitions. In other words, as you write, you are not just stringing things out but are actively tying thoughts together in a variety of creative ways. Your success in these efforts will constitute your greatest originality.

3. *Explanation of controversial views.* Closely related to your selection is that in your research you may have found conflicting or differing views on a topic. If you make a point to describe and distinguish these views, and explain the reasons for the differences, you are presenting material originally. To see how differing views may be handled, see paragraphs 4 and 5 of the sample essay.

4. *Creation of your own insights and positions.* There are three possibilities here, all related to how well you have learned the primary texts on which your research in secondary sources is based:

a. *Your own interpretations and ideas.* An important part of taking notes is to make your own points precisely when they occur to you. Often you can expand these as truly original parts of your essay. Your originality does not need to be extensive; it may consist of no more than a single insight. Here is such a card, which was written during the research on the ghost in *Hamlet:*

My Own   introductory

The Ghost is minor in the action but major in the play. He is seen twice in scene 1, but this scene is really all about him. (Also about his appearances before the play opens.) In scene 4 of Act 1 he comes again and leads Hamlet off to scene 5--the biggest for him as an acting and speaking character. He speaks after this only from under the stage, and then a small appearance (but important) in 3.4, and that's all. But he is dominant because he set everything in motion and therefore his presence is felt everywhere in the play.

The originality here is built around the idea of the small role but dominant significance of the Ghost. The discovery is not unusual or startling, but it nevertheless represents original thought about *Hamlet*. When modified and adapted (and put into full sentences with proper punctuation), the material of the card supplies much of the opening paragraph of the sample essay. You can see that the development of a *my own* note card is important for a research essay.

   b. *Gaps in the sources.* As you read your secondary sources you may realize that a certain, obvious conclusion is not made, or that a certain detail is not stressed. Here is an area you can develop on your own. Your conclusion may involve a particular interpretation or major point of comparison, or it may rest on a particularly important but underemphasized word or fact. In the sample essay, for example, the writer discusses the idea that the Ghost's commands to Hamlet make it impossible for him to solve problems through negotiation or research—the ways he might have chosen as prince and student. The commands force him instead into a pattern requiring murder. Most critics observe that Hamlet's life is changed because of the Ghost but have not quite stressed this aspect of the change. Given such a critical "vacuum" (assuming that you cannot read all the articles about some of your topics, where your discovery may already have been published a number of times), it is right to begin filling it with your own insights. A great deal of scholarship is created in this way.

   c. *Disputes with the sources.* Your sources may present certain arguments that you wish to dispute. As you develop your disagreement, you will be arguing originally, for you will be using details in a different way from that of the critic or critics whom you are disputing, and your conclusions will be your own. This area of originality is similar to the laying out of controversial critical views, except that you furnish one of the opposing views yourself. The approach is limited because it is difficult to find many substantive points of interpretation on which there are not already clearly delineated opposing views. Paragraph 5 of the sample research essay shows a small point of disagreement (about whether Shakespeare was concerned with consistency in presenting the Ghost's spirit nature), but one that is nevertheless original.

DOCUMENTING YOUR WORK

It is essential to acknowledge—to *document*—all sources from which you have *quoted or paraphrased* factual and interpretive information. If you do not give due acknowledgment, you run the risk of being challenged for presenting other people's work as your own. This is plagiarism. As the means of documentation, there are many reference systems, some using parenthetical references, and others using footnotes or end notes. Whatever system is used, documentation almost always includes a carefully prepared list of *works cited* or *bibliography*.

We will first discuss the list of works cited, and then review the two major reference systems for use in a research paper: (1) Parenthetical references, preferred by the Modern Language Association (MLA) since 1984, are described in Joseph Gibaldi and Walter S. Achtert, *MLA Handbook for Writers of Research Papers*, 3rd ed., 1988; (2) Footnotes or end notes, recommended by the MLA before 1984, and still widely required.

List of Works Cited (Bibliography)

The key to any reference system is a carefully prepared list of *Works Cited* that is included at the end of the essay. *Works Cited* means exactly that; the list should contain just those books and articles which you have actually *used* in your essay. If, however, your instructor requires that you use footnotes or end notes, you may extend your concluding list to be a complete bibliography of works both cited and also consulted but not actually used. *Always, always, always, follow your instructor's preferences.*

The *Works Cited* list should include the following information, in each entry, in the form indicated:

FOR A BOOK

1. The author's name, last name first, period.
2. Title, underlined, period.
3. City of publication (not state), colon; publisher (easily recognized abbreviations or key words may be used unless they seem awkward or strange; see the *MLA Handbook*, 213–16), comma; date, period.

FOR AN ARTICLE

1. The author's name, last name first, period.
2. Title of article in quotation marks, period.
3. Name of journal or periodical, underlined, followed by volume number in Arabic (*not* Roman) numbers with no punctuation, followed by the year of publication within parentheses, colon. For a daily paper or weekly magazine, omit the parentheses and cite the date in the British style (day, month, year; i.e., 29 Feb. 1988:) followed by a colon. Inclusive page numbers, period (without any preceding "p." or "pp.").

The list of works cited should be arranged alphabetically by author, with unsigned articles being listed by title. Bibliographical lists are begun at the left margin, with subsequent lines being indented, so that the key locating word—usually the author's last name—may be easily seen. The many unpredictable and complex combinations, including ways to describe works of art, musical or other performances, and films, are detailed extensively in the *MLA Handbook* (86–154). Here are two model entries:

BOOK: Alpers, Antony. Katherine Mansfield, A Biography. New York: Knopf, 1953.

ARTICLE: Hankin, Cheryl. "Fantasy and the Sense of an Ending in the Work
                  of Katherine Mansfield." Modern Fiction Studies 24
                  (1978): 465–74.

Parenthetical References to the List of Works Cited

Within the text of the essay, refer parenthetically to the list of works cited. The parenthetical reference system recommended in the *MLA Handbook* (155–77) involves the insertion of the author's last name and the relevant page number or numbers into the body of the essay. If the author's name is mentioned in the discussion, only the page number or numbers are given in parentheses. Here are two examples:

> Pope believed in the idea that the universe is a whole, a totally unified body, which provides a "viable benevolent system for the salvation of everyone who does good" (Kallich 24).

> Martin Kallich draws attention to Pope's belief in the idea that the universe is a whole, a totally unified body, which provides a "viable benevolent system for the salvation of everyone who does good" (24).

For a fuller discussion of the types of in-text references and the format to use, see the *MLA Handbook*, 155–61.

Footnotes and End notes

The most formal system of documentation still widely used is that of *footnotes* (references at the bottom of each page) or *end notes* (references listed numerically at the end of the essay). If your instructor wants you to use one of these formats, do the following: The first time you quote or refer to the source, make a note with the details in this order:

FOR A BOOK

1. The author's name, first name or initials first, comma.
2. The title: underlined for a book, no punctuation. If you are referring to a work (article, story, poem) in a collection, use quotation marks for that, but underline the title of the book. (Use a comma after the title if an editor, translator, or edition follows.)
3. The name of the editor or translator, if relevant. Abbreviate "editor" or "edited by" as *ed.*, "editors" as *eds.* Use *trans.* for "translator" or "translated by."
4. The edition (if indicated), abbreviated thus: *2nd ed., 3rd ed.,* and so on.
5. The publication facts should be given in parentheses, without any preceding or following punctuation, in the following order:
    a. City (but *not* the state) of publication, colon.
    b. Publisher (clear abbreviations are acceptable and desirable), comma.
    c. Year of Publication, comma.

6.   The page number(s), for example, 65, 6–10, 15–19, 295–307, 311–16. If you are referring to longer works, such as novels or longer stories that may have division or chapter numbers, include these number for readers who may be using an edition different from yours.

FOR AN ARTICLE

1.   The author, first name or initials first, comma.
2.   The title of the article, in quotation marks, comma.
3.   The name of the journal, underlined, no punctuation.
4.   The volume number, in Arabic letters, no punctuation.
5.   The year of publication in parentheses, colon. For newspaper and journal articles, omit the parentheses, and include day, month, and year (in the British style), colon.
6.   The page number(s); for example, 65, 6–10, 34–36, 98–102, 345–47.

For later notes to the same work, use the last name of the author as the reference unless you are referring to two or more works by the same author. Thus, if you refer to only one work by, say, Langston Hughes, the name "Hughes" will be enough for all later references. Should you be referring to other works by Hughes, however, you will also need to make a short reference to the specific works to distinguish them, such as "Hughes, 'Mulatto'" and "Hughes, 'Let America Be America.'"

Footnotes are placed at the bottom of each page, and end notes are included in separate page(s) at the end of the essay. The first lines of both footnotes and end notes should be paragraph indented, and continuing lines should be flush with the left margin. Both endnote and footnote numbers are positioned slightly above the line (as superior numbers) like this ([12]). Generally, you may single-space footnotes and end notes, and leave a space between them. Additionally, today's computer programs have specially designed and consecutively numbered footnote formats. These are generally acceptable, but be sure to make the proper agreements with your instructor. For more detailed coverage of footnoting practices, see the *MLA Handbook*, 185–200.

SAMPLE FOOTNOTES. In the examples below, book titles and periodicals, which are usually *italicized* in print, are shown underlined, as they would be in your typewritten or carefully handwritten essay.

[1]James Anderson Winn, John Dryden and His World (New Haven: Yale UP, 1987), 299.

[2]Susan Gubar, "The Birth of the Artist as Heroine: (Re)production, the Kunstlerroman Tradition, and the Fiction of Katherine Mansfield," in The Representation of Women in Fiction, eds. Carolyn G. Heilbrun and Margaret R. Higonnet, Selected Papers from the English Institute, 1981 (Baltimore: Johns Hopkins UP, 1982), 25.

[3]John O'Meara, "Hamlet and the Fortunes of Sorrowful Imagination: A re-examination of the Genesis and Fate of the Ghost," Cahiers Élisabéthains 35 (1989), 21.

[4]Gubar 29.

[5]Winn 55.

[6]O'Meara 17.

As a principle, you do not need to repeat in a note any material you have already mentioned in your own discourse. For example, if you recognize the author and title of your source, then the note should merely give no more than the data about publication. Here is an example:

> In *The Fiction of Katherine Mansfield*, Marvin Magalaner points out that Mansfield was as skillful in the development of epiphanies (that is, the use of highly significant though perhaps unobtrusive actions or statements to reveal the depths of a particular character) as Joyce himself, the "inventor" of the technique.[9]

[9](Carbondale: Southern Illinois UP, 1971) 130.

Other Reference Systems

Other reference systems and style manuals have been adopted by various disciplines (e.g., mathematics, medicine, psychology) to serve their own particular needs. If you receive no instructions from your instructors in other courses, you may adapt the systems described here. If you need to use the documentation methods of other fields, however, use the *MLA Handbook*, 201–202 for guidance about what style manual to select.

Some Final Advice

As long as all you want from a reference is the page number of a quotation or a paraphrase, the parenthetical system described briefly here—and detailed fully in the *MLA Handbook*—is the most suitable and convenient one you can use. It saves your reader the trouble of searching the bottom of the page or of thumbing through pages at the end to find a reference in a long list of notes. However, you may wish to use footnotes or end notes if you need to add more details or refer your readers to other materials that you are not using.

Whatever method you follow, *there is an unchanging need to acknowledge sources properly*. Remember that whenever you begin to write and make references, you might forget a number of specific details about documentation, and you will certainly discover that you have many questions. Be sure then to ask your instructor, who is your final authority.

ORGANIZING YOUR ESSAY

Introduction

For a research essay, the introduction may be expanded beyond the length of that for an ordinary essay because of the need to relate the problem of research to your topic. You may wish to bring in relevant historical or biographical information (see, for example, the introduction of the sample essay). You may also wish to summarize critical opinion or describe critical problems about your topic. The idea is to lead your reader into your topic by providing interesting and significant materials that you have found. Because of the greater length of most research essays, some instructors require a topic outline, which is in effect a brief table of contents. This pattern is observed in the sample essay. *Because the inclusion of an outline is a matter of instructor's choice, be sure you understand whether your instructor requires it.*

Body, Conclusion

For both the body and the conclusion, your development will be governed by your choice of topic. Consult the relevant chapters in this book about what to include for whatever approach or approaches you select (setting, idea, point of view, character, tone, or any other).

In length, the research essay may be anywhere from five to fifteen or more pages. Obviously, an essay on a single work will likely be shorter than one based on several. If you narrow the scope of your topic, as suggested in the approaches described above, you can readily keep your essay within the assigned length. The sample research essay below, for example, illustrates the first approach by being limited to only one character in one play. Were you to write on characters in a number of other plays by Shakespeare (the second approach), you could limit your total number of pages by stressing comparative treatments and by avoiding excessive detail about problems pertaining to only one work.

Although you limit your topic yourself in consultation with your instructor, you may encounter problems because you will be dealing not with one text alone but with many. Naturally the sources will provide you with details and also with many of your ideas. The problem is to handle the many strands without piling on too many details, and also without being led into digressions. It is important therefore to keep your central idea foremost; the constant stressing of your central idea will help you both to select relevant materials and to reject irrelevant ones.

It bears reemphasis that you need to distinguish between *your own work* and the *sources* you are using. Your readers will assume that everything you write is your own unless you indicate otherwise. Therefore, when blending your words with the ideas from sources, be clear about proper acknowledgments. Most commonly, if you are simply presenting details and facts, you can write straightforwardly and let parenthetical references suffice as your authority, as in the following sentence from the sample essay:

> Thus he is most emphatic that Hamlet should not kill her along with Claudius (Fisch 80), and he also voices concern about the reputation and future of Denmark (Gottschalk, "Scanning" 165).

Although the words belong to the writer of the essay, the parenthetical references clearly indicate that the sentence is derived from the two sources.

If you are using an interpretation that is unique to a particular writer, or if you are relying on a significant quotation from your source, you should make your acknowledgment as an essential part of your discussion, as in this sentence:

> A. C. Bradley (126) suggests that these speeches indicate Shakespeare's master touch in the development of the Ghost's character.

Here the idea of the critic is singled out for special acknowledgment. If you indicate your sources in this way, no confusion can possibly arise about how you have used your sources.

SAMPLE RESEARCH ESSAY

The Ghost in Hamlet

OUTLINE

I. INTRODUCTION
    A. THE IMPORTANCE OF THE GHOST IN HAMLET
    B. THE GHOST'S INFLUENCE UPON THE PLAY'S THEMES
II. THE GHOST'S STATUS AS A SPIRIT
III. THE GHOST'S CHARACTER
IV. THE GHOST'S IMPORTANCE IN THE STRUCTURE OF THE PLAY
V. THE GHOST'S EFFECT
VI. CONCLUSION

I. Introduction

A. The Importance of the Ghost in Hamlet

Even though the Ghost of old Hamlet is present in only a few scenes of Hamlet, he is a dominating presence.* He is seen twice in the first scene, and this entire scene itself is about the meaning of these and earlier appearances.

---

* Central idea.

[1]
He enters again in the fourth scene of the first act, when he beckons and leads Hamlet off stage, in this way providing an early illustration of Hamlet's courage (Edgar 257). In the fifth scene of act 1 he finally speaks, to describe how his brother Claudius murdered him and to urge his son, Hamlet, to kill Claudius in retribution. His appeal for revenge causes the rest of the play's action. After some words which he speaks from underground (i.e., under the stage), he does not enter again until the fourth scene of act three, in the Queen's closet or bedroom, when he reveals himself to Hamlet--but not to Gertrude--to reproach the Prince for not having yet killed Claudius. The Ghost is not present at the play's end, but the actions he sets in motion are concluded there, and hence his effect remains dominant.

B. The Ghost's Influence Upon The Play's Themes

[2]
Not only is the Ghost dominant, he is also directly linked to many of the play's themes. Jean Paris observes that Hamlet reveals "an intensification of interior suffering" (85). Hamlet's anguished soliloquies, together with the pain of Ophelia and Laertes (and even that of Claudius himself) may thus be traced to the Ghost. The commands the Ghost makes to Hamlet are direct and urgent, and therefore the Ghost introduces another of the play's major themes--that of responsibility, whether personal, political, or conjugal (McFarland 15). Hamlet of course does not rush right out to kill Claudius, despite the Ghost's urgings, and therefore his hesitation--this great "Sphinx of modern Literature" (Ernest Jones 22)--has become one of the weaknesses cited most frequently about Hamlet's character. The Ghost's scary presence also poses questions about the power of superstition, terror, and fear (Campbell 211). Beyond these, deeply within the psychological realm, the Ghost has been cited as a "confirmation" of the influence of "psychic residues in governing and shaping human life" (McFarland 34), not to mention the significance of the Oedipus Complex in the development of Hamlet's character.

[3]
Because the Ghost is so important, one hardly needs to justify studying him. His importance may be traced in his spirit nature, his influence on the play's structure, and his effect upon Hamlet and therefore indirectly on all the major characters.[†]

II. The Ghost's Status as a Spirit

[4]
The Ghost is an apparition of questionable status. When Hamlet first sees the Ghost he raises a question about whether the vision is "a spirit of health, or goblin damned" (1.4.40). Horatio adds that Hamlet is "desperate with imagination" (1.4.87), thus casting doubt upon the Ghost's reality, even though everyone on stage shares Hamlet's vision. When speaking with Hamlet, the Ghost is vague about his out-of-earth location, complaining that he is suffering hellish fires, but intimating that he will do so only until his earthly sins are purged away. In the meanwhile, he says, he is able to walk the earth for a certain time, presumably only at night (but is his visit in 3.4 made in the daytime?). Surprising at it might seem, this detail about where ghosts spend their time reflects Renaissance controversies about Protestantism and Catholicism.

[†] Thesis sentence.

Showing a ghost of someone long dead who was returning from Purgatory might have been interpreted as a ratification of Catholic doctrine. It was apparently safest for Protestant writers to show a ghost only of a person who was "freshly dead or on the point of death" (O'Meara 15), and leave the precise details vague.

[5] The status and existence of ghosts therefore reflects uncertainties during the Elizabethan period. Lily Campbell offers a number of ways in which Elizabethans dealt with these uncertainties. First, James I of England (when still James VI of Scotland), in writing about departed spirits, emphasized that the Devil himself could choose the shape of loved ones in order to deceive living persons and lead them to damnation. It is this danger that Hamlet specifically describes. Second, as already mentioned, Elizabethan Catholic teaching held it possible for souls in Purgatory to return to earth for a time to communicate with the living. Third, scientifically oriented thinkers interpreted ghostly appearances as a sign of madness or deep melancholia (121), or what O'Meara calls "sorrowful imagination" (19). There were apparently a number of "tests" that might have enabled people to determine whether ghosts were authentic, and not creations of the Devil or products of a sick imagination. Most of these required that the spirit in question be good, comforting, and sweet (Campbell 123).

The Ghost of King Hamlet passes parts of these tests, but fails others. Even though he has redeeming qualities (Campbell 126), he also imposes a duty of revenge on Hamlet, something that no ghost trying to reach Heaven would ever do (Prosser 136; McFarland 36). Although the Ghost describes the pain of a soul in Purgatory, he does so with a desire to horrify, not to urge Hamlet to commit himself to Christian repentance and salvation. Again, his description is an indication that he is closer in nature to the Devil than to a soul earning its way to redemption (Prosser 133–34). Another sign suggesting that the Ghost is a devilish spirit is that he withholds his appearance from Gertrude when he shows himself to Hamlet in 3.4 (Campbell 124; Prosser 200). Ham-[6] let of course creates his own test of the Ghost by getting the traveling actors to perform "The Murder of Gonzago." Once he sees the king's disturbance at the play, he concludes that the Ghost is real, and not just a "figment of his melancholy imagination" (Harrison 883). However, perhaps the best answer to the conflicting signs about the Ghost is provided by Lily Campbell, who suggests that the ambiguity is a reflection of the general uncertainty about ghosts among Shakespeare's contemporaries (127). In other words, there was no unanimity about the nature and purposes of ghosts at the time Shakespeare wrote, and Shakespeare, if he was even concerned about theological issues of ghostly consistency, was reflecting common understanding and attitudes.

III.   The Ghost's Character

Uncertainty aside, the ghost is probably Shakespeare's rendering of what he thought a ghost would be like. He inherited a tradition of noisy, bloodthirsty ghosts from his sources—what Harold Fisch calls a "Senecan ghost" (91). There was also a tradition of the "hungry ghost," spirits who prowled about the earth "searching for the life they were deprived of" (Austin 93). In this tradition, Shakespeare's Ghost is bloodthirsty, although ironically not as

[7] bloodthirsty as Hamlet himself (Gottschalk 166). The Ghost is also surrounded by awe and horror (DeLuca 147), and is frightening, both to the soldiers at the beginning of the play, and also to Hamlet in 3.4 (Charney, Style 167–168). In addition, his speeches are designed to evoke grief, fear, and despair (Prosser 135). This effect also refers to readers and viewers; a famous example is James Boswell's testimony that Dr. Johnson, when young, was "terrified" when he read "the speech of the ghost when alone" (52). It would seem that horror is the main effect that Shakespeare was trying to create with the Ghost.

But the Ghost is not only an imitation of the Senecan ghost. He is real, and well drawn as an individual person (Alexander 30). Indeed, Shakespeare has toned down the Ghost from one in an earlier play, perhaps one of the sources used for Hamlet, which was described by Shakespeare's contemporary Thomas Lodge (1558?–1625). Lodge talked about "ye ghost which cried so miserally [pitifully, sorrowfully] at ye theator . . . Hamlet, reuenge" (sic). The Ghost in Shakespeare's Hamlet is preoccupied with vengeance (Allman 243),

[8] but as a former king he is concerned about his country, and as a former loving husband he is also considerate of Hamlet's mother, Gertrude. Thus he is most emphatic that Hamlet should not kill her along with Claudius (Fisch 80), and he also voices concern about the reputation and future of Denmark (Gottschalk 165). Paul Gottschalk draws attention to this redeeming dimension as an indication that the Ghost is concerned with "restoration" as well as "retaliation" (166), a view not shared by Norman Austin, who calls the Ghost "the spirit of ruin" (105).

Indeed, the Ghost has many qualities of a living human being. For example, he is witty, as Maurice Charney, observes about the following interchange between the Ghost and Hamlet just at the beginning of the revelation speeches in 1.5.6–7:

> HAMLET.   Speak, I am bound to hear.
> GHOST.   So art thou to revenge, when thou shalt hear.

[9] In other words, even though the Ghost may have come "with airs from heaven, or blasts from hell" (1.4.41), he is still mentally alert enough to make a pun out of Hamlet's word "bound" (Charney, Style, 118). To this quickness may be added his shrewd ability to judge his son's character. He knows that Hamlet may neglect duty, and hence his last words in 1.5 are "remember me," and his first words in 3.4 are "Do not forget." A. C. Bradley suggests that these speeches indicate Shakespeare's master touch in the development of the Ghost's character (126).

The Ghost also shows other human traits. He feels strong remorse about his lifelong crimes and "imperfections" for which his sudden death did not give him time to atone. It is this awareness that has made him bitter and vengeful. Also, he has a sense of appropriateness that extends to what he wears. Thus, at the beginning he appears on the parapets dressed in full ar-

[10] mor. This battle uniform is in keeping with the location, and also with his vengeful mission urging Hamlet to kill Claudius (Aldus 54). The armor is in fact intimidating, a means of enforcing the idea that the Ghost in death has become a "spirit of hatred" (Austin 99). By contrast, in the closet scene he wears a dressing gown ("in his habit as he lived," 3.4.135), as though he is prepared for ordinary palace activities of both business and leisure (Charney, Style 26).

IV.   The Ghost's Importance in the Structure of the Play

[11]

Shakespeare's great strength as a dramatist is shown not only in his giving the Ghost such a round, full character, but also in integrating him fully within the play's structure. According to Peter Alexander, the Ghost is "indispensable" in the plot as the source of communication to set things in motion (29). He is also a director and organizer as well as an informer--a figure who keeps the action moving until there is no stopping it (Aldus 100). A careful study of his speeches shows that he is a manipulator, playing upon his son's emotions to make him see that his role is to carry out the necessary revenge. In addition, the Ghost is persistent, because his return to Hamlet in 3.4 to "whet thy almost blunted purpose" (line 111) is the mark of the manager who gets nervous and then intervenes when he sees his directions being neglected by the one entrusted to carry them out.

[12]

The Ghost is also significant as a part of some of the other major structures of the play. During the imagined period when the events at Elsinore are taking place, there is a national mobilization going on in preparation for war against Norway (Alexander 34). This note of future warfare and impending political change reminds the audience that the events being witnessed are politically vital. Indeed, King Hamlet, when alive, had conquered the Norwegian king Fortinbras in single combat. Now, with the Danish state being torn by the internal anguish following Claudius's fratricide, the state lies weak and exposed--an easy prey to the Norwegians. Structurally, the beginning and ending of Hamlet are marked by the fear of war and the political takeover by "Young Fortinbras" of Norway. It is therefore ironic that the Ghost in death is responsible for the fall of the state he so courageously defended in life.

[13]

There is an additional major structure involving the Ghost. Maurice Charney observes that the Ghost is significant in the "symmetrical" poison plots in the play (39). The first of these plots, the poisoning of King Hamlet, is described by the Ghost himself in 1.5. The poisoning of the Player King in 3.2 is a reenactment of the first murder, and it occurs in approximately the middle of the action. The final poisonings--of Gertrude, Laertes, Claudius, and finally Hamlet himself--occurs in 5.2, the play's last scene. These actions have value as a set of symbolic frames which measure the deterioration of the play's major characters.

V.   The Ghost's Effect

[14]

Beyond the Ghost's practical and structural importance in the action, he has profound psychological influence, mainly negative, on the characters. Roy Walker describes him as a "prologue" to the "omen" of Hamlet himself, who is the agent of the "dread purpose" of vengeance (220). Because Hamlet is already suffering depression and melancholia, this murderous mission opens the wounds of his vulnerability (Campbell 127–28). Literally, Hamlet must give up everything he has ever learned, even "the movement of existence itself," so that he may carry out the Ghost's commandment (McFarland 32–33). In an invasive, overpowering manner, Hamlet's melancholy influences his love for Ophelia, his possible friendship with Laertes, and his relationship with his mother (Kott 49; Kirsch 31). No one escapes. The effect is like waves radiating outwardly, with the Ghost at the center as a relentless, destructive force.

[15] These effects occur because, almost literally, Hamlet himself cannot escape (Allman 218). In Act I. scene 5, the Ghost, who has gone underground, follows him and hears his conversations with Horatio and the guards--an obvious symbolic representation of the Ghost's pervasive power. He therefore represents "dimensions of reality" beyond what we see on the stage, a mysterious world "elsewhere" that dominates the very souls of living persons (Charney, "Asides" 127). As a result of this ever-present force, which as far as Hamlet is concerned might become visible at any moment, Hamlet is denied the healing that might normally occur after the death of a parent (Kirsch 26). The steady pressure toward vengeance disrupts any movement to mental health, and creates what Kirsch calls a "pathology of depression" (26) that inhibits Hamlet's actions (Bradley 123), causes his Oedipal preoccupation with the sexuality of his parents (Kirsch 22), and brings about his desire for the oblivion that suicide might bring (Kirsch 27).

[16] It is, finally, this power over his son that gives the Ghost the greatest influence in the play. Once the Ghost has appeared, Hamlet can never be the same. He loses the dignity and composure that he has assumed as his right as a Prince of Denmark and as a student in quest of knowledge (McFarland 38). Rather than attack problems that he might have solved normally and easily with negotiations and research, he must sink into acts of murder. Is it any wonder that he hesitates? What could be more normal than hesitation under such circumstances? Despite all his reflection and hesitation, finally the web of vengeance woven by the Ghost closes in on all those caught in it, and the consequence is that Hamlet becomes not only a murderer, but a victim (Allman 254). There is no solution but the final one--real death, which is the literal conclusion of the symbolic death represented by the Ghost when he first appears on the Elsinore battlements.

VI. Conclusion

[17] The Ghost is real in terms of the play's action and structure. He is seen by the characters on the stage, and when he speaks we hear him. He is made round and full by Shakespeare, and his motivation is direct and clear, even though the signs of his status as a spirit are presented ambiguously. But the Ghost is more. He has been made a Ghost by the greed and envy of Claudius, and in this respect he becomes in the play either a conscious or unwitting agent of the "unseen Fates or forces" of his own doom (Walker 220). What he brings is the unavoidable horror that seems somehow to be just beneath the surface of good, moral people, waiting for the license to reach out and destroy. Once the forces are released, there is no holding them, and the tragedy of Hamlet is that there is no way to win against such odds.

List of Works Cited

Aldus, P. J. Mousetrap: Structure and Meaning in Hamlet. Toronto: U of Toronto P, 1977.

Alexander, Peter. Hamlet: Father and Son. Oxford: Clarendon, 1955.

Allman, Eileen Jorge. Player-King and Adversary. Baton Rouge: Louisiana State UP, 1980.

Austin, Norman. "Hamlet's Hungry Ghost." Shenandoah 37.1 (1987): 78–105.

Boswell, James. Boswell's Life of Johnson. 1952. London: Oxford UP, 1957.

Bradley, A. C. Shakespearean Tragedy. 1904. London: Macmillan, 1950.

Campbell, Lily B. Shakespeare's Tragic Heroes: Slaves of Passion. New York: Barnes & Noble, 1959.

Charney, Maurice. "Asides, Soliloquies, and Offstage Speech in Hamlet." Shakespeare and the Sense of Performance: Essays in the Tradition of Performance Criticism in Honor of Bernard Beckerman, Ed. Marvin and Ruth Thompson. Newark: U of Delaware P, 1989. 116–31.

— Style in Hamlet. Princeton: Princeton UP, 1969.

DeLuca, Diana Macintyre. "The Movements of the Ghost in Hamlet." Shakespeare Quarterly 24 (1973): 147–54.

Edgar, Irving I. Shakespeare, Medicine and Psychiatry. New York, Philosophical Library, 1970.

Fisch, Harold. Hamlet and the Word. New York: Ungar, 1971.

Gottschalk, Paul. "Hamlet and the Scanning of Revenge." Shakespeare Quarterly 24 (1973): 155–70.

Harrison, G. B., ed. Shakespeare: The Complete Works. 1948. New York: Harcourt, 1968.

Jones, Ernest. Hamlet and Oedipus. 1949. New York: Doubleday, 1954.

Kirsch, Arthur. "Hamlet's Grief." ELH 48 (1981): 17–36.

Kott, Jan. Shakespeare Our Contemporary. trans. Boleslaw Taborski. 1967. London: Methuen, 1970.

McFarland, Thomas. Tragic Meanings in Shakespeare. New York: Random House, 1966.

O'Meara, John. "Hamlet and the Fortunes of Sorrowful Imagination: A Re-examination of the Genesis and Fate of the Ghost." Cahiers Élisabéthains 35 (1989): 15–25.

Paris, Jean. Shakespeare. trans. Richard Seaver. New York: Grove, 1960.

Prosser, Eleanor. Hamlet and Revenge. 2nd ed. Stanford: Stanford UP, 1971.

Walker, Roy. "Hamlet: the Opening Scene." Shakespeare: Modern Essays in Criticism. Ed. Leonard F. Dean. New York: Oxford UP, 1961.

Commentary on the Essay

This sample essay illustrates an assignment requiring about twenty sources (there are 22) and about 2500 words. The sources were located through an examination of a library catalogue, the *MLA International Bibliography,* library bookshelves, and the bibliographies in some of the listed books.

They represent the range of materials available in a college library with a selective, not exhaustive, set of holdings. Two of the sources (Austin, O'Meara) were obtained through the Interlibrary Loan Service because they were recent publications and also because their titles suggested that they should not be overlooked.

The writing itself is all derived and developed out of the sources listed; originality is provided by the structure and development of the essay, additional observations not existing in the sources, and transitions. The outline is placed appropriately at the beginning, and it indicates the major divisions to follow. If you are asked for an outline, be sure to ask your instructor if the topics alone are sufficient, or if more is required.

Because the essay is about only one work—and one topic about that work—it demonstrates the first approach to a problem in research, as outlined on page 1625. The essay is eclectic in dealing with the subject, introducing discussions of ideas, character, style, and structure. The goal is to cover the ground fairly completely, within the confines of the assignment, and hence the various topics may be justified. A shorter research assignment might deal with no more than, say, the Ghost's character, ignoring the other topics introduced into this essay. On the other hand, a longer essay might deal further with the philosophical and theological meanings of ghosts during the Elizabethan period, or a more detailed study of all the traits of the Ghost's character, and so on.

The central idea of the sample essay is stressed in paragraph 1, along with an assertion that the Ghost is a major influence in the play, together with a concession that the Ghost is only a minor character in the action. The research for this paragraph is derived primarily from a close reading of the play itself. Paragraph 2, continuing the exploration of the central idea. demonstrates that the Ghost figures in the major themes of *Hamlet*. Paragraph 3 is mainly functional, being used as the location of the thesis sentence.

Part II, containing paragraphs 4 through 6, deals with the Ghost's status as a spirit. Part III, with four paragraphs (7–10) is concerned with the Ghost's human rather than spiritual characteristics. Part IV, with paragraphs 11–13, deals with the significance of the Ghost in four of the major structures that dominate the play. Part V, with three paragraphs, considers the negative and inexorable influence the Ghost has upon the major figures of *Hamlet*, the emphasis being the character of Hamlet as the transferring agent of the Ghost's destructive revenge. The concluding paragraph (17) sums up the essay with the final idea of how the Ghost affects the tragic nature of *Hamlet*.

The list of works cited is the basis of all parenthetical references in the essay, in accordance with the *MLA Handbook for Writers of Research Papers*, 3rd ed. Using these references, an interested reader can consult the sources for the ideas expressed in the essay. The works cited can also serve as a springboard for expanded research.

Appendix D
Critical Approaches Important in the Study of Literature

A number of critical theories or approaches for understanding and interpreting literature are available to critics and students alike. Many of these have been developed during the twentieth century to create a discipline of literary studies comparable with disciplines in the natural and social sciences. Literary critics have often borrowed liberally from other disciplines (e.g., history, psychology, anthropology), but have primarily aimed at developing literature as a course of study in its own right.

At the heart of the various critical approaches have been many fundamental questions: What is literature? What does it do? Is its concern only to tell stories, or to express emotions? Is it private? Public? How does it get its ideas across? What more does it do than express ideas? How valuable was literature in the past and how valuable is it now? What can it contribute to intellectual, artistic, and social history? To what degree is literature an art, as opposed to an instrument for imparting knowledge? How is literature used, and how and why is it misused? What theoretical and technical expertise may be invoked to enhance literary studies?

Questions like these indicate that criticism is concerned not only with reading and interpreting stories, poems, and plays, but also with establishing theoretical understanding. Because of such extensive aims, you will understand that a full explanation and illustration of the approaches would fill the pages of a long book. Therefore the following descriptions are intended as no more than brief introductions. Bear in mind that in the hands of skilled critics, the approaches are so subtle, sophisticated, and complex that they are not only critical stances but also philosophies.

Although the various approaches provide widely divergent ways to study literature and literary problems, they reflect major tendencies rather than absolute straitjacketing. Even the most devoted practitioners of the methods do not pursue them rigidly, because not every approach is appropriate for every work, nor are the approaches always mutually exclusive. In addition, some of the approaches are more "user-friendly" for certain types of discovery than others. To a degree at least, most critics therefore utilize methods that technically belong to one or more of the other approaches. A critic stressing the topical/ historical approach, for example, might introduce the close study of a work that is associated with the method of the New Criticism. Similarly, a psychoanalytical critic might include details about archetypes. In short, a great deal of criticism is *pragmatic* or *eclectic* rather than rigid.

The approaches to be considered here are these: *Moral/Intellectual; Topical/Historical; New Critical/Formalist, Structuralist, Feminist; Economic Determinist/Marxist; Archetypal/Symbolic/Mythic; Deconstructionist;* and *Reader-Response.*

Following each description is a brief paragraph showing how Hawthorne's story "Young Goodman Brown" might be considered in the light of the particular approach. The paragraph following the discussion of structuralism, for example, shows how the structuralist approach can be applied to Goodman Brown and his story.

MORAL/INTELLECTUAL

The moral/intellectual approach is concerned with content and values (see Chapters 10 and 23). The approach is as old as literature itself, for literature is a traditional mode of imparting morality, philosophy, and religion. The concern in moral/intellectual criticism is not only to discover meaning, but also to determine whether works of literature are both *true* and *significant.*

To study literature from the moral/intellectual perspective is therefore to determine whether an individual work conveys a lesson or a message, and whether it can help readers lead better lives and improve their understanding of the world: What ideas does the work contain? How strongly does the work bring forth its ideas? What application do the ideas have to the work's characters and situations in the work? How may they be evaluated intellectually? Morally? A discussion based on such questions does not necessarily require a position of command or exhortation. Ideally, moral/intellectual criticism should differ from sermonizing to the degree that readers should always be left with their own decisions about whether they wish to assimilate the content of a work, and about whether this content is personally or morally acceptable.

Sophisticated critics have sometimes demeaned the moral/intellectual approach on the grounds that "message hunting" reduces a work's artistic value by treating it like a sermon or political speech. But the approach will be valuable as long as readers expect literature to be applicable to their own lives.

Example

"Young Goodman Brown" raises the issue of how an institution designed for human elevation, like the religious system of colonial Salem, can be so ruinous. Does the failure result from the system itself, or from the people who misunderstand it? Is what is true of religion as practiced by Brown also true of social and political institutions? Should any religious or political philosophy be given greater credence than good will and mutual trust? One of the major virtues of "Young Goodman Brown" is that it provokes questions like these. But at the same time it provides a number of satisfying answers. A particularly important one is that religious and moral beliefs should not be used to justify the condemnation of others. Another important answer is that attacks made from the refuge of a religion or group, such as Brown's puritanical judgment, is dangerous because it enables the judge to condemn without thought and without personal responsibility.

TOPICAL/HISTORICAL

This traditional approach stresses the relationship of literature to its historical period, and for this reason it has had a long life. Although much literature may be applicable to many places and times, much of it also directly reflects the intellectual and social worlds of the authors. When was the work written? What were the circumstances that produced it? What major issues does it deal with? How does it fit into the author's career? Blake's poem "London," for example, is a response to the oppression that Blake associated with the Industrial Revolution. Jeffers's "The Purse-Seine" describes the threat of modern environmental pollution.

The topical/historical approach investigates relationships of this sort, including the elucidation of words and concepts that today's readers may not immediately understand. Obviously, the approach requires the assistance of footnotes, dictionaries, histories, and handbooks.

A common criticism of the topical/historical approach is that in the extreme it deals with background knowledge rather than with literature itself. It is possible, for example, for a topical/historical critic to describe a writer's life, the period of the writer's work, and the social and intellectual ideas of the time—all without ever considering the meaning, importance, and value of the work itself.

Example

"Young Goodman Brown" is an allegorical story by Nathaniel Hawthorne (1804–1864), the New England writer who probed deeply into the relationships between religion and guilt. His ancestors had been involved in religious persecutions, including the Salem witch trials, and he, living 150 years afterward, wanted to probe the weaknesses and uncertainties of the sin-dominated religion of the earlier period. Not surprisingly, therefore, "Young Goodman Brown" takes place in Puritan, colonial Salem. Although the immediate concerns of the story belong to a vanished age, Hawthorne's treatment is still valuable because it is still timely.

NEW CRITICAL/FORMALIST

The New Criticism began in the 1930s and 1940s and has been a dominant force in twentieth-century literary studies. To the degree that New Criticism focuses upon literary texts as formal works of art, it departs from the topical/historical approach. The objection raised by the New Critics is that as topical/historical critics consider literary history, they avoid close contact with actual texts.

The inspiration for the Formalist or New-Critical approach was the French practice of *explication de texte*, a method that emphasizes detailed examination and explanation. The New Criticism is therefore at its most brilliant in the analysis of smaller units such as entire poems and short passages. The New Criticism also utilizes a number of techniques for the analysis of larger structures, many of which form the basis for the chapters in this book. Discussions of "point of view," "tone," "plot," "character," and "structure," for example, are ways of looking at literature derived from the New Criticism.

The aim of the formalist study of literature is to provide readers not only with the means of explaining the content of works ("What, specifically, does this say?"), but also with the critical tools needed for evaluating the artistic quality of individual works and writers ("How well is it said?"). A major aspect of New Critical thought is that content and form—including all ideas, ambiguities, subtleties, and even apparent contradictions—were originally within the conscious or subconscious control of the author. There are no accidents. It does not necessarily follow, however, that today's critic is able to define the author's intentions exactly, for such intentions require biographical details that can never be recovered and known. Each literary work therefore takes on its own existence and identity, and the critic's work is to discover a reading or readings that explain the facts of the text. Note that the New Critic does not claim infallible interpretations, and does not exclude the validity of multiple readings of identical works.

Dissenters from the New Criticism have noted a tendency by New Critics to ignore relevant knowledge that history and biography may bring to literary studies. In addition, the approach has been subject to the charge that stressing the examination of texts alone fails to deal with the value and appreciation of literature.

Example

A major aspect of Hawthorne's "Young Goodman Brown" is that the details are so vague and dreamlike that many readers are uncertain about what is happening. The action is a nighttime walk by the protagonist, Young Goodman Brown, into a deep forest, where he encounters a mysterious Satanic ritual that leaves him bitter and misanthropic. This much seems clear, but the precise nature of Brown's experience is not clear; nor is the identity of the stranger (father, village elder, devil) who accompanies Brown as he begins his walk. At the story's end Hawthorne's narrator states that the whole episode may have been no more than a dream or nightmare. Yet when morning comes, Brown walks back into town as though returning from an overnight trip, and he recoils in horror from his fellow villagers, including his wife Faith (paragraph 70). Could his attitude result from nothing more than a nightmare?

Even at the story's end, these uncertainties remain. For this reason one may conclude that Hawthorne deliberately creates the uncertainties to reveal how persons like Brown build defensive walls of judgment around themselves. The story thus implies that the real source of Brown's anger is as vague as his nocturnal walk. But he doesn't understand it in this way. Because both his vision and his judgment are absolute, he rejects everyone around him, even if the cost is a life of bitter suspicion and spiritual isolation.

STRUCTURALIST

The principle of *structuralism* stems from the attempt to find relationships and connections among elements that appear to be separate and discrete. Just as physical science reveals unifying universal principles of matter such as gravity and the forces of electromagnetism (and is constantly searching for a "unified field theory"), structuralism attempts to discover the forms unifying all literatures. Thus a structural description of Faulkner's "Barn Burning" would stress that the young boy, Sarty, is an *active* hero who undergoes a *test* (or series of tests), and emerges as a *victor*. The structural approach would apply the hero-test pattern, or some other pattern, to other works of literature, and determine that some protagonists are active or submissive, that they pass or fail their tests, or that they succeed or fail at other encounters. The key is that many apparently unrelated works reveal many common patterns, or contain similar structures with important variations.

The structural approach has become important because it enables critics to discuss works from widely separate cultures and historical periods. In this respect, critics have followed the leads of modern anthropologists, most notably Claude Lévi-Strauss (b. 1908). Along such lines, critics have undertaken the serious examination of folk tales and fairy tales. Some of the groundbreaking structuralist criticism, for example, was devoted to the structural principles underlying Russian folk tales. The method also bridges popular and serious literature, making little distinction between the two insofar as the description of the structures is concerned. Indeed, structuralism furnishes an ideal approach for comparative literature, and the method also enables critics to consolidate genres such as modern romances, detective tales, soap operas, and films.

Like the New Criticism, structuralism aims at comprehensiveness of description, and many critics would insist that the two are complementary and not separate. A distinction is that the New Criticism is at its best in dealing with smaller units of literature, whereas structuralism is best in the analysis of narratives and therefore larger units such as novels, myths, and stories. Because structuralism shows how fiction is organized into various typical situations, the approach merges with the *archetypal* approach (see below), and at times it is difficult to find any distinctions between structuralism and archetypalism.

Structuralism, however, deals not just with narrative structures, but also with structures of any type, wherever they occur. For example, structuralism makes great use of linguistics. Modern linguistic scholars have determined that there is a difference between "deep structures" and "surface structures" in language. A structuralist analysis of style, therefore, would stress the ways in which writers utilize such structures (see especially chapters 7 and 19). The structuralist interpretation of language also perceives distinguishing types or "grammars" of language that are recurrent in various types of literature. Suppose, for example, that you encounter opening passages like the following:

> Once upon a time a young prince fell in love with a young princess. He decided to tell her of his love, and early one morning he left his castle on his white charger, riding toward her castle home high in the mountains.

> Early that morning, Alan had found himself thinking about Anne. He had believed her when she said she loved him, but his feelings about her were not certain, and his thinking had left him still unsure.

The words of these two passages create different and distinct frames of reference. One is a fairy tale, the other the internalized reflection of feeling. The passages therefore demonstrate how language itself fits into predetermined patterns or structures. Similar uses of language structures can be associated with other types of literature.

Example

Young Goodman Brown is a hero who is passive, not active. Essentially, he is a witness, a receiver rather than a doer. His only action—taking his trip in the forest—occurs at the story's beginning. After that point, he no longer acts but instead is acted upon, and what he sees puts his life's beliefs to a test. Of course, many protagonists undergo similar testing (such as rescuing victims and slaying particularly terrible dragons), and they emerge triumphant. Not so with Goodman Brown. He is a responder who allows himself to be victimized by his own perceptions—or misperceptions. Despite all his previous experiences with his wife and with the good people of his village, he generalizes too hastily. He lets the single disillusioning experience of his nightmare govern his entire outlook on others, and thus he fails his test and turns his entire life into failure.

FEMINIST

The feminist approach holds that most of our literature presents a masculine-patriarchal view in which the role of women is negated or at best minimized. As an adjunct of the feminist movement in politics, the feminist critique of literature seeks to raise consciousness about the importance and unique nature of women in literature.

Specifically, the feminist view attempts (1) to show that writers of traditional literature have ignored women and have also transmitted misguided and prejudiced views of them, (2) to stimulate the creation of a critical milieu that reflects a balanced view of the nature and value of women, (3) to recover the works of women writers of past times and to encourage the publication of present women writers so that the literary canon may be expanded to recognize women as thinkers and artists, and (4) to urge transformations in the language to eliminate inequities and inequalities that result from linguistic distortions.

In form, the feminist perspective seeks to evaluate various literary works from the standpoint of the presentation of women. For works such as "Rape Fantasies" (story), "Conjoined" (poem) and *A Doll House* (play), a feminist critique would focus on how such works treat women and also on either the shortcomings or enlightenment of the author as a result of this treatment. When women appear as characters, how important are they, how individual in their own right? Are they credited with their own existence and their own character? In their relationships with men, how are they treated? Are they given equal status? Ignored? Patronized? Demeaned? Pedestalized? How much concern do the male characters exhibit about women's concerns?

Example

At the beginning of "Young Goodman Brown," Brown's wife Faith is only peripheral. In the traditional patriarchal spirit of wife-as-adjunct she asks her husband to stay at home and take his journey at another time. But Hawthorne does not give her the intelligence or dignity to let her explain her concern (or might he not have been interested in what she had to say?), and she therefore remains in the background with her pink hair ribbon as her distinguishing characteristic. During the mid-forest Satanic ritual, she appears again and is given power, but only the power to cause her husband to go astray. Once she is led in as a novice in the practice of demonism, her husband falls right in step. Unfortunately, by following her, Brown may conveniently excuse himself from guilt by claiming that "she" had made him do it, just as Eve "made" Adam eat the apple. Hawthorne's attention to the male hero, in other words, permits him to distort the female's role.

ECONOMIC DETERMINIST/MARXIST

The concept of cultural and economic determinism is one of the major political ideas of the last century. Karl Marx (1818–1883) emphasized that the primary influence on life was economic, and he saw society as an opposition between the capitalist and working classes. The literature that emerged from this kind of analysis features individuals in the grips of the class struggle. Often called "proletarian literature," it emphasizes persons of the lower class—

the poor and oppressed who spend their lives in endless drudgery and misery, and whose attempts to rise above their disadvantages usually result in renewed suppression.

While Marx's political ideas were never widely accepted in the United States, and have faded still more after the political breakup of the Soviet Union, the idea of economic determinism (and the related term "Social Darwinism") is still credible. As a result, much literature can be judged from an economic perspective: What is the economic status of the characters? What happens to them as a result of this status? How do they fare against economic and political odds? What other conditions stemming from their class does the writer emphasize (e.g., poor education, poor nutrition, poor health care, inadequate opportunity)? To what extent does the work fail by overlooking the economic, social, and political implications of its material? In what other ways does economic determinism affect the work? How should readers consider the story in today's developed or underdeveloped world? Seemingly, the specimen work "Young Goodman Brown" has no economic implications, but an economically oriented discussion might take the following turns:

Example

"Young Goodman Brown" is a fine story just as it is. It deals with the false values instilled by the skewed acceptance of sin-dominated religion. But it overlooks the economic implications of this situation. One suspects that the real story in the little world of Goodman Brown's Salem should be about survival and the disruption that an alienated member of society can produce. After Brown's condemnation and distrust of others forces him into his own shell of sick imagination, Hawthorne does not consider how such a disaffected character would injure the economic and public life of the town. Consider this, just for a moment: Why would the people from whom Brown recoils in disgust want to deal with him in business or personal matters? Would they want to follow his opinion in town meetings on crucial issues of public concern and investment? Would his preoccupation with sin and damnation make him anything more than a horror in his domestic life? Would his wife Faith be able to discuss household management with him, or how to take care of the children? All these questions of course are pointed toward another story—a story that Hawthorne did not write. They also indicate the shortcomings of Hawthorne's approach, because it is clear the major result of Young Goodman Brown's selfish preoccupation with evil would be a serious disruption of the economic and political affairs of his small community.

PSYCHOLOGICAL/PSYCHOANALYTIC[1]

The scientific study of the mind is a product of psychodynamic theory as established by Sigmund Freud (1856–1939) and of the psychoanalytic method practiced by his followers. Psychoanalysis provided a new key to the under-

---

[1] See also Chapter 4, "Characters: The People in Stories."

standing of character by claiming that behavior was caused by hidden and un-conscious motives and drives. It was greeted as a virtual revelation, and not surprisingly it had a profound effect on twentieth-century literature.

In addition, its popularity produced a psychological/psychoanalytic ap-proach to criticism. Some critics use the approach to explain fictional char-acters, as in the landmark interpretation by Freud and Ernest Jones that Shakespeare's Hamlet suffers from the "Oedipus Complex." Still other critics use it as a way of analyzing authors and the artistic process. For example, John Livingston Lowes's *The Road to Xanadu* presents a detailed examination of the mind, reading, and neuroses of Coleridge, the author of *Kubla Khan* (p. 637).

Critics using the psychoanalytic approach treat literature somewhat like information about patients in therapy. In the work itself, what are the obvi-ous and hidden motives that cause a character's behavior and speech? How much background (childhood trauma, adolescent memories, etc.) does the author reveal about a character? How purposeful is this information, with re-gard to the character's psychological condition? How much is important in analyzing and understanding the character?

In the consideration of authors, critics utilizing the psychoanalytic mode consider questions like these: What particular life experiences explain characteristic subjects or preoccupations? Was the author's life happy? mis-erable? upsetting? solitary? social? Can the death of someone in the author's family be associated with melancholy situations in that author's work? (All eleven of the brothers and sisters of the English poet Thomas Gray, for ex-ample, died before reaching adulthood. Gray was the only one to survive. In his poetry, Gray often deals with death, and he is therefore considered as one of the so-called "Graveyard School" of eighteenth-century poets. A psychoan-alytical critic might make much of this connection.)

Example

At the end of "Young Goodman Brown," Hawthorne's major character is no longer capable of normal existence. His nightmare should be read as a sym-bol of what in reality would have been lifelong mental subjection to the type of puritanical religion that emphasizes sin and guilt. Such preoccupation with sin is no hindrance to psychological health if the preoccupied people are con-vinced that God forgives them and grants them mercy. In their dealings with others, they remain healthy as long as they believe that other people have the same sincere trust in Divine forgiveness. If their own faith is short and uncer-tain, however, and they cannot believe in forgiveness, then they are likely to project their own guilt—really a form of personal terror—into others. They re-main conscious of their own sins, but they find it easy to claim that others are sinful—even those who are spiritually spotless, and even their own family, who should be dearest to them. When this process of projection occurs, then such people have created the rationale of condemning others because of their own guilt. The cost they pay is a life of gloom, a fate that Hawthorne makes for Goodman Brown after the nightmare about demons in human form.

ARCHETYPAL / SYMBOLIC / MYTHIC[2]

The archetypal approach, which is derived from the work of the Swiss psychoanalyst Carl Jung (1875–1961), presupposes that human life is built up out of patterns, or *archetypes* ("first molds" or "first patterns"), that are similar throughout various cultures and historical times. The approach is similar to the structuralist analysis of literature, for both approaches stress the connections that may be discovered in literature written in different times and in vastly different locations in the world.

In literary evaluation, the archetypal approach is used to support the claim that the very best literature is grounded in archetypal patterns. The archetypal critic therefore looks for archetypes such as God's creation of human beings, the sacrifice of a hero, or the search for paradise. How does an individual story/poem/play fit into any of the archetypal patterns? What truths does this correlation provide (particularly truths that cross historical, national, and cultural lines)? How closely does the work fit the archetype? What variations may be seen? What meaning or meanings do the connections have?

The most tenuous aspect of archetypal criticism is Jung's assertion that the recurring patterns provide evidence for a "universal human consciousness," which all of us, by virtue of our humanity, still retain in our minds and in our very blood.

Not all critics accept the hypothesis of a universal human consciousness, but they nevertheless consider the approach important for comparisons and contrasts (see Appendix B). Many human situations, such as adolescence, dawning love, the search for success, the reconciliation with one's mother and father, and the encroachment of age and death, are similar in structure and may be analyzed as archetypes. For example, the following situations may be seen as a pattern or archetype of *initiation:* A young man discovers his dedication to justice and fairness ("A & P,"); a young girl develops her sense of identity when thinking about her impoverished childhood ("The House on Mango Street"); young boys and girls begin to discover their sexual identities ("The Found Boat"); a speaker describes what it takes to join the writing profession ("How to Become a Writer"). The archetypal approach may also permit the analysis of variations on a single theme, as in Whitecloud's "Blue Winds Dancing" when the narrator abandons college (one sort of initiation) and returns to his native home (another sort).

Example

     In the sense that Brown undergoes a change from psychological normality to rigidity, the story is a reverse archetype of the initiation ritual. According to the archetype of successful initiation, initiates seek to demonstrate their worthiness to become full-fledged members of society. Telemachus in Homer's *Odyssey,* for example, is a young man who in the course of the epic goes through

[2] Symbolism and myths are also considered in Chapters 9, 21, and 22.

the initiation rituals of travel, discussion, and battle. But in "Young Goodman Brown" we see initiation in reverse, for just as there is an archetype of successful initiation, Brown's initiation leads him into failure. In the private areas of life on which happiness depends, he falls short. He sees evil in his fellow villagers, condemns his own minister, and shrinks even from his own wife. His life is one of despair and gloom. His suspicions are those of a Puritan of long ago, but the timeliness of Hawthorne's story is that the archetype of misunderstanding and condemnation has not changed. Today's headlines of misery and war are produced by the same kind of intolerance that is exhibited by Goodman Brown.

DECONSTRUCTIONIST

The *Deconstructionist* approach—which Deconstructionists explain not as an approach but rather as a performance—was developed by the French critic Jacques Derrida (b. 1930). In the 1970s and 1980s it became a major but also controversial mode of criticism. As a literary theory, Deconstructionism produces a type of analysis that stresses ambiguity and contradiction.

A major principle of Deconstructionism is that Western thought has been *logocentric*, that is, Western philosophers have assumed that central truth is knowable and entire. The Deconstructionist view is that there is no central truth because circumstances and time, which are changeable and sometimes arbitrary, govern the world of the intellect. This analysis leads to the declaration that "All interpretation is misinterpretation." That is, literary works cannot be encapsulated as organically unified entireties, and therefore there is not *one correct interpretation,* but only *interpretations,* each one possessing its own validity.

In "deconstructing" a work, therefore, the Deconstructionist critic raises questions about what other critics have claimed about the work. Is a poem accepted as a model of classicism? Then it also exhibits qualities of romanticism. Is a story about a young American Indian's flight from school commonly taken as a criticism of modern urban life? Then it may also be taken as a story of the failure of youth. In carrying out such criticism, Deconstructionist critics place heavy emphasis on the ideas contained in words like *ambivalence, discrepancy, enigma, uncertainty, delusion, indecision,* and *lack of resolution,* among others.

The Deconstructionist attack on "correct," "privileged," or "accepted" readings is also related to the principle that language, and therefore literature, is unstable. "Linguistic instability" means that the full understanding of words is never exact because there is a never-ending *play* between the words in a text and their many shades of meaning, including possible future meanings. That is, the words do not remain constant and produce a definite meaning, but instead call forth the possibility of "infinite substitutions" of meaning. Therefore, each work of literature is ambiguous and uncertain because its full meaning is constantly being *deferred*. This infinite deferral or semantic tension renders language unstable and makes correct or accepted readings impossible.

It is fair to state that Deconstructionism, among all the literary theories, has received intense criticism that has sometimes bordered on discrediting the theory entirely. A number of critics find that the position is elusive and vague. They grant that literary works are often ambiguous, uncertain, and apparently contradictory, but explain that the cause of these conditions is not linguistic instability but rather authorial intention. They also point out that the Deconstructionist linguistic analysis is derivative and misunderstood, and that it does not support Deconstructionist assertions about linguistic instability. In addition, they draw attention to the contradiction that Deconstructionism cannot follow its major premise about there being no "privileged readings," because it must recognize the privileged readings in order to invalidate or "subvert" them.

Example

There are many uncertainties in the details of "Young Goodman Brown." If one starts with the stranger on the path, one might conclude that he could be Brown's father, because he recognizes Brown immediately and speaks to him jovially. Or he could be the devil (he is recognized as such by Goody Cloyse) because of his wriggling walking stick. After disappearing, he also takes on the characteristics of an omniscient cult leader, because at the Satanic celebration he knows all the secret sins committed by Brown's neighbors and the community of greater New England. Additionally, he might represent a perverted conscience whose aim is to mislead and befuddle people by steering them into the holier-than-thou judgmentalism that Brown adopts. This method would be truly diabolical—to use religion in order to bring people to their own damnation. That he is an evil force is therefore clear, but the pathways of his evil are not as clear. He seems to work his mission of damnation by reaching souls like Goodman Brown through the means that are ordinarily attributed to conscience. But if he is a Satanic conscience, what are we to suppose that Hawthorne is asserting about what is considered real conscience?

READER-RESPONSE CRITICISM[3]

The Theory of Reader-Response is rooted in *phenomenology*, a branch of philosophy that deals with "the understanding of how things appear." The phenomenological idea of knowledge is that reality is to be found not in the external world itself but rather in the mental *perception* of externals. That is, all that human beings can know—actual *knowledge*—is our collective and personal understanding of the world and our conclusions about it.

[3] See "Responding to Literature: Likes and Dislikes" in Chapter 1 (pp. 37–44).

As a consequence of the phenomenological concept, Reader-Response theory holds that the reader is a necessary third party in the author-text-reader relationship that constitutes the literary work. The work, in other words, is not fully created until readers make a *transaction* with it by assimilating it and *actualizing* it in the light of their own knowledge and experience. The representative questions of the theory are these: What does this work mean to me, in my present intellectual and moral makeup? What particular aspects of my life may help me understand and appreciate the work? How can the work improve my understanding and widen my insights? How can my increasing understanding help me understand the work more deeply? The theory is that the free interchange or transaction that such questions bring about leads toward interest and growth, so that readers may assimilate literary works and accept them as part of their lives.

As an initial way of reading, the Reader-Response may be personal and anecdotal. In addition, by stressing response rather than interpretation, one of the leading exponents of the method (Stanley Fish) has raised the extreme question about whether texts, by themselves, have objective identity. These aspects have been cited as both a shortcoming and an inconsequentiality of the method.

It is therefore important to stress that the Reader-Response theory is *open*. It permits beginning readers to bring their own personal reactions to literature, but it also aims at increasing the discipline and skills of readers. The more that readers bring to literature through lifelong interests and disciplined studies, the more "competent" and comprehensive their responses will be. With cumulative experience, the disciplined reader will habitually adjust to new works and respond to them with increasing skill. If the works require special knowledge in fields like art, politics, science, philosophy, religion, or morality, competent readers will possess such knowledge or seek it out, and utilize it in improving their responses. Also, because students experience many similar intellectual and cultural disciplines, it is logical to conclude that responses will tend not to diverge but rather to coalesce; agreements result not from personal but from cultural similarities. The Reader-Response theory, then, can and should be an avenue toward informed and detailed understanding of literature, but the initial emphasis is the transaction between readers and literary works.

Example

"Young Goodman Brown" is a worrisome story because it shows so disturbingly that good intentions may cause harmful results. I think that a person with too high a set of expectations is ripe for disillusionment, just as Goodman Brown is. When people don't measure up to this person's standard of perfection, they can be thrown aside as though they are worthless. They may be good, but their past mistakes make it impossible for the person with high expectations to endure them. I have seen this situation occur among some of my friends and acquaintances, particularly in romantic relationships. Goodman Brown makes the same kind of misjudgment, expecting perfection and turning sour when he learns about flaws. It is not that he is not a good man, because he is shown at the start as a person of belief and stability. But he uncritically accepts his nightmare revelation that everyone else is evil (including his parents), and he finally distrusts everyone because of this enduring suspicion. He cannot look at his neighbors without avoiding them like an "anathema," and he turns away from his own wife "without a greeting" (paragraph 70). Brown's problem is that he confuses being human with being unworthy. By such a distorted standard of judgment, all of us fail, and that is what makes the story so disturbing.

Appendix E
Brief Biographies of the Poets in Part II

Leonard Adamé (b. 1947) A Californian, Adamé has contributed poems to *Revista Chicano-Riquena* and the *American Poetry Review*. His work was included in *Entrance: Four Chicano Poets* (1975), and also in *Piecework: Nineteen Fresno Poets* (1987). "My Grandmother Would Rock" was included in *From the Barrio: A Chicano Anthology* (1975).

A. R. Ammons (b. 1926) Archie Randolph Ammons was educated in North Carolina and California. He began teaching at Cornell University in 1964, the year in which his second poetry collection was published. Among his honors are the Bollingen Prize (1973–74) and a MacArthur Fellowship. Recent collections are *The Selected Poems: Expanded Edition* (1987) and *Sumerian Vistas* (1987). "80–Proof" was included in *Diversifications* (1975).

Maya Angelou (b. 1928) Born in St. Louis, Angelou acted and sang before becoming a writer. She is known as much for her fiction as for her poetry, and has also written plays. She achieved recognition with *I Know Why the Caged Bird Sings* (1970). *Just Give Me a Cool Drink of Water 'fore I Die* appeared in 1971, and she has published regularly since. Her national importance was recognized when she was chosen to read her poetry at the inauguration of President Bill Clinton in January, 1993. Recently she has spoken and sung in a number of Public television productions.

Matthew Arnold (1822–1888) One of the major Victorian poets, Arnold was brought up among books and learning, and eventually (1857) became Professor of Poetry at Oxford. In his Oxford lectures he described a loss of security and religious faith, and hence he stressed the need to recover absolutes—which to him was the major "function of criticism at the present time." "Dover Beach" is, along with "The Scholar Gypsy" and "Stanzas from the Grande Chartreuse," among his best-known poems.

Margaret Atwood (b. 1939) For a brief biography, see p. 301.

W. H. Auden (1907–1973) Wystan Hugh Auden was born in England, and lived permanently in the United States after the Spanish Civil War. A Marxist in his youth, he became a devout Christian in later years. He wrote prolifically, including collaborations with the dramatist Christopher Isherwood and the poet Louis MacNeice. Another notable collaboration is the libretto for Igor Stravinsky's opera *The Rake's Progress* (1951). He edited the *Oxford Book of Light Verse* (1938).

Imamu Amiri Baraka (LeRoi Jones, b. 1934)   Born in New Jersey, LeRoi Jones attended Rutgers, Howard, and Columbia Universities, and also the New School. After serving in the Air Force, he adopted the name Imamu Amiri Baraka. As a practical outgrowth of his devotion to African-American causes, he founded a community center—"Spirit House"—for African Americans in Newark, New Jersey. Among his many works are *Four Black Revolutionary Plays* (1969), and *African Revolution* (1973). His *Selected Poetry* appeared in 1979.

Marvin Bell (b. 1937)   Originally from New York, Bell teaches at the University of Iowa and has taught in Australia and Yugoslavia. He has published ten collections of poetry, the most recent being *Iris of Creation* and *Stars Which See: Stars Which Do Not See.*. *New and Selected Poems* was published in 1987. "Things We Dreamt We Died For" appeared in *A Probable Volume of Dreams* (1969).

Edmund Clerihew Bentley (1875–1956)   Bentley is an English writer known for his detective stories in which Philip Trent is an amateur sleuth reminiscent of Sherlock Holmes. Perhaps the best known of these works is *Trent's Last Case* (1912). Bentley is also known for the *clerihew,* a witty and brief form that he created for satiric squibs against political and historical persons.

Earle Birney (b. 1904)   One of the major modern Canadian writers, Birney was born in Calgary, Alberta. He is editor of *Twentieth Century Canadian Poetry* (1953). In 1975 his collected poetry was issued by McClelland and Stewart of Canada. By 1985 he had published more than twelve collections of poetry, in addition to his stories and plays.

Elizabeth Bishop (1911–1979)   Bishop was brought up by an aunt in Worcester, Massachusetts. She attended private schools and Vassar. During much of her life she lived in Brazil. She taught for a time at the University of Washington and then at Harvard. Her first collection of poems was *North and South* (1946), which she expanded in 1955 as *North and South—A Cold Spring*, for which she received the Pulitzer Prize in Poetry in 1956.

William Blake (1757–1827)   Blake was apprenticed to an engraver in London at the age of fourteen. Throughout his career he published his poems with his own engravings, and these original editions are now invaluable collector's items. Blake was a revolutionary at heart, who thought that humanity would flower if institutions were eliminated or at least redirected. *Songs of Experience*, from which "London" is taken, is a collection of poems on this theme, published in 1794, five years after the outbreak of the French Revolution. In this same year he published *Songs of Innocence*, from which "The Lamb" is taken.

Louise Bogan (1897–1970)   Born in Maine, Bogan spent most of her life in New York, writing regular reviews for *The New Yorker*. Her first volume of poems was *Body of This Death* (1923), in which "Women" appeared. Her *Collected Poems* (1954) was awarded the Bollingen Prize. Her major critical work was *Achievement in American Poetry, 1900–1950*, published in 1951. *Journey Around My Room* (1980) is a posthumous autobiographical work.

Arna Bontemps (1902–1973) Born in Louisiana, Bontemps by profession was a librarian (at Fisk University). In addition to poetry, he published a number of novels and works of children's fiction. *One Hundred Years of Negro Freedom* (1961), is a widely heralded historical work.

Anne Bradstreet (1612–1672) Born in England, Bradstreet married early and came to the American colonies when she was eighteen. Her career was that of wife and mother, and she bore eight children. Nevertheless she managed to write poems regularly, and kept them together in manuscript. In 1650 her brother-in-law had them published in London without her knowledge, and she was therefore unable to make corrections (see lines 3–6 of "The Author to Her Book"). The volume, entitled *The Tenth Muse,* was the first poetic publication in England by anyone living in colonial America. A second and corrected edition was considered in about 1666, and "The Author to Her Book" was composed in this expectation, but the new edition did not appear until six years after her death.

Robert Bridges (1844–1930) Bridges, an Englishman, studied at Oxford and became a practicing physician. He published his first book of poems in 1873, and eight years later gave up his practice to devote himself exclusively to literature. He was vitally interested in the "purity" of English and in the techniques of English prosody, and he devoted much skill to the fitting of poetic words to hymn tunes. He edited the poetry of Gerard Manley Hopkins (1918), with its unique prosodic techniques; thereby he helped establish Hopkins as a major poetic voice. In 1913 he became England's Poet Laureate.

Joseph Brodsky (Iosif Alexandrovich, b. 1940) Brodsky, a native Russian, was exiled in 1972 and came to the United States. Since then he has served as a Poet-in-Residence at a number of schools from Michigan to Massachusetts. He writes in Russian and translates his verse into English himself or with others. He has been distinguished with a MacArthur Foundation Fellowship, and was named American Poet Laureate in 1991. His verse is collected in *To Urania: Selected Poems 1965–1985* (1988).

Gwendolyn Brooks (b. 1917) Brooks was born in Chicago, where she has spent most of her life. Winner of the Pulitzer Prize for Poetry in 1950 (for *Annie Allen,* 1949), she is concerned with race in both her fictional and poetic works. "We Real Cool" exemplified this emphasis. In 1967 she began directing her work toward African-American readers, and has been involved in publishing a number of her poems in pamphlet form, of which *Primer for Blacks* (1980) is one.

Olga Broumas (b. 1949) Broumas is a native of Greece. Coming to America, she received her B.A. from the University of Pennsylvania in 1970, and her M.F.A. from the University of Oregon in 1973. She has taught English and writing at Oregon and Idaho, and now lives in Massachusetts. Some of her collections are *Caritas* (1976), *Pastoral Jazz* (1983), and *Black Holes, Black Stockings* (prose poems, 1985). "Circe" was included in *Beginning with O* (1977).

Elizabeth Barrett Browning (1806–1861) Elizabeth Barrett suffered a crippling spinal injury when still a girl in England. She was a recognized poet when she married Robert Browning in 1846. Because of her condition and the English climate, the Brownings moved to Italy, where they remained until Elizabeth's death. During her lifetime, her reputation as a poet eclipsed Robert's. Her *Cry of the Children* (1843) was an early poetic protest against the industrial exploitation of children. In 1850 she published *Sonnets from the Portuguese,* which she presented as a gift to her husband.

Robert Browning (1812–1889)   In his twenties and early thirties, Browning wrote a number of versified plays for the stage, but these were unsuccessful, and he did not achieve fame in his native England until he was well into his fifties. Because of his experience with drama, he found his poetic voice within the medium of the dramatic monologue, which he perfected to a high degree. Both "My Last Duchess" and "Soliloquy of the Spanish Cloister" appeared in his *Dramatic Lyrics* of 1842, exactly during the time when he was also writing his plays.

Robert Burns (1759–1796)   The best known and loved poet of Scotland, Burns gave up farming and taught himself to read and write English, French, and Latin. He published his first volume, *Scots Poems Chiefly in the Scottish Dialect*, in 1786. His use of the down-to-earth idiom of Scots peasants, together with joyous irreverence and frank lustiness, made him instantly famous.

George Gordon, Lord Byron (1788–1824)   One of the major English Romantic poets, Byron created the so-called "Byronic hero," a driven and solitary figure who is misunderstood by his fellow human beings. He published his semi-autobiographical poem "Childe Harolde's Pilgrimage" in 1811. In 1815 he published *Hebrew Melodies* (1815), in which "The Destruction of Sennacherib" appeared. That year, he left England and never returned. He continued writing poetry as he traveled, including the 16,000-line unfinished poem *Don Juan*. He died at Missolonghi, in Greece, while fighting for Greek independence.

Thomas Campion (1567–1620)   In his day, English poet Campion was known not only as a poet but also as a composer. He set many of his poems to music, including "Cherry Ripe." Two of his collections are *A Book of Airs* (1601) and *The Third and Fourth Books of Airs* (ca. 1617). His interest in the relationship between music and poetry prompted him to write a discourse on English metrics, *Observation in the Art of English Poesy* (1602).

Lewis Carroll (Charles L. Dodgson, 1832–1898)   Carroll is the pen name of English writer Charles L. Dodgson, who is famous for *Alice's Adventures in Wonderland* and *Through the Looking Glass*. Carroll was also a mathematician, lecturer, logician, and photographer. "Jabberwocky," from *Through the Looking Glass*, stems out of his interest in words. Some of the words he created in this poem, such as "chortle" and "whiffle," are now standard English.

Lucille Clifton (b. 1936)   Thelma Lucille Clifton was born and educated in New York. Her productivity as a writer began in the 1970s, and has been strong ever since. One of her earliest poetry collections was *An Ordinary Woman* (1974). Recently she published *Next: New Poems* (1987), and *Good Woman: Poems and a Memoir, 1969–1980* (1987). In addition to her poetry, she has written a number of stories and poems for children, such as *All Us Come Cross the Water* (1973).

Samuel Taylor Coleridge (1772–1834)   Coleridge was born in Devon, in southern England, and studied at Cambridge University but did not earn a degree. After a short stint as a soldier he fell into dire financial straits, from which he was rescued by the Wedgewood brothers (of ceramic fame), who provided him with an annuity so that he could devote himself to poetry. Wordsworth and he together published the *Lyrical Ballads* of 1798, a collection which is the benchmark of the English Romantic Movement. Coleridge contributed "The Rime of the Ancient Mariner," his most famous poem, and also "Kubla Khan." After 1802 he wrote little poetry, but his *Biographia Literaria* of 1817 is one of the major works of literary criticism of the early nineteenth century.

Billy Collins (b. 1941)   A native of New York, Collins received degrees at Holy Cross and the University of California at Riverside. He lives in New York and is a Professor of English at Lehman College. To date he has published four collections of poetry, including *The Apple that Astonished Paris* (1989), which includes "Schoolsville." A recent collection of poems, *Questions About Angels*, a winner in the National Poetry Series competition, was published in 1991.

Stephen Crane (1871–1900)   For a brief biography, see p. 93.

Richard Crashaw (1612–1649)   Crashaw left England when the English Civil War was beginning in 1642, and spent the remainder of his life in Italy. He is best known as a religious and devotional poet, although he also wrote on so conventional a topic as "Wishes to His Supposed Mistress." In 1646 he published *Steps to the Temple*, which contained "On Our Crucified Lord." Other works (with Latin titles) were *A Book of Holy Epigrams* (1634), and the posthumous *Poems to Our God* (1652).

Countee Cullen (1903–1946)   Poet, novelist, and writer of children's books, Cullen studied at New York University and Harvard, and became one of the leading figures in the Harlem Renaissance of the 1920s. He was a pioneer in dealing with the conditions and aspirations of African Americans. His earliest book of poems was *Color* (1925), which included "Yet Do I Marvel." Among his later collections were *The Ballad of the Brown Girl* (1927) and *The Black Christ and Other Poems* (1929).

E. E. Cummings (1894–1962)   Cummings studied at Harvard, receiving a Master's degree there. During World War I, he served in the Ambulance Corps in France, and, as a result of false charges of treason, was imprisoned—an experience he wrote about in his first work, *The Enormous Room* (1922). He began publishing poetry shortly thereafter, and continued doing so throughout his life. His collected poetry, consisting of more than a thousand poems, was published in 1992.

James Dickey (b. 1923)   A native of Georgia, Dickey served in World War II and afterwards spent a number of years writing advertising copy. Since 1969 he has been a full-time writer and teacher. His poems are narrative in structure, and often are based in his own knowledge and experiences with violence and tragedy, as in "The Performance" and "The Lifeguard." His best known novel is *Deliverance* (1970), which was made into a popular motion picture.

Emily Dickinson   For a brief biography, see p.877.

John Donne (ca. 1572–1631)   For a brief biography, see p. 865.

H. D. (Hilda Doolittle, 1886–1961)   Known by her initials, H. D., Doolittle was born in Pennsylvania, graduated from Bryn Mawr College, and after 1911 spent her life in England. As an early apostle and devotee of Ezra Pound, she espoused the manner of the "Imagist" school of poetry. Her first collection of poems was *Sea Garden* (1916). She also wrote *Tribute to Freud* (1956), a memoir of Sigmund Freud, whose patient she had been.

Rita Dove (b. 1952)   Dove was born in Ohio, and received degrees from Miami University and the University of Iowa. Her poetry has been collected in *The Yellow House on the Corner* (1980), *Museum* (1983), and *Thomas and Beulah* (1986). In 1985 she published a collection of stories, *Fifth Sunday*. She is Commonwealth Professor of English at the University of Virginia. In 1993 she became Poet Laureate of the United States, the first woman to be so honored.

Michael Drayton (1563–1631) Like his friend Shakespeare, Drayton was a native of Warwickshire. He became educated while serving in an aristocratic household. He was a versatile poet, writing not only sonnets but topographic poetry (*England's Heroical Epistles,* 1599), epic (*Nymphidia,* 1627), and satire (*The Owl,* 1604), in addition to popular ballads, myths, and scriptural paraphrases. "Since There's No Help" appeared in his sonnet sequence *Idea, the Shepherd's Garland* .

John Dryden (1631–1700) Poet Laureate from 1668 to 1688, Dryden was one of the foremost English poets and dramatists of the seventeenth century. His major poetic achievement was to fine-tune the heroic or neo-classic couplet, which he used for "To the Memory of Mr. Oldham." Nevertheless, he used blank verse for his best play, *All For Love* (1677), which deals with the same material as Acts IV and V of Shakespeare's *Antony and Cleopatra.* In 1688 he lost his official positions because he had been a supporter of the deposed James II. During the last twelve years of his life, therefore, he was forced to support himself mainly with translations, providing his contemporaries with poetic versions of Virgil, Ovid, Juvenal, and Chaucer.

Paul Laurence Dunbar (1872–1906) Dunbar was born in Ohio, the son of former slaves. During his brief life he rose to prominence as a poet, dramatist, and novelist. His first two collections of poems, *Oak and Ivy* (1893) and *Majors and Minors* (1895), in which "Sympathy" appeared, were favorably reviewed by William Dean Howells. His collected poems were published posthumously in 1913.

Richard Eberhart (b. 1904) Eberhart, the recipient of many awards, including the Pulitzer Prize in Poetry in 1966, was born in Minnesota and received his higher education at Dartmouth and Cambridge. His many works include *Collected Poems* of 1930 and 1976. In 1982 the governor of New Hampshire, Eberhart's home, proclaimed a "Richard Eberhart Day" in his honor.

T. S. Eliot (1888–1965) Born in Missouri, Thomas Stearns Eliot moved to England in 1914 and became a British citizen in 1927. With *The Waste Land* in 1922, he electrified the literary world because of his poetic use of colloquial speech and frank subject matter. Though he is considered a hyper-serious poet, his lighter side is shown in *Old Possum's Book of Practical Cats* (1939). These poems achieved popular fame in 1981 in the Broadway musical *Cats,* which was still running in early 1994.

James Emanuel (b. 1921) Emanuel was born in Nebraska and attended Howard University. He earned his Ph.D. at Columbia in 1962, and joined the faculty of English at the City College of New York. He has regularly published poems in journals such as *Phylon* and *Negro Digest.* An early collection of his poems is *Panther Man* (1970). More recent collections are *Black Man Abroad: The Toulouse Poems* (1978), *A Chisel in the Dark* (1980), and *The Broken Bowl* (1983).

John Engels (b. 1931) Engels has published poetry regularly since the 1970s. Early collections are *Signals from the Safety Coffin* (1975) and *Blood Mountain* (1977). *Vivaldi in Early Fall* (1981) includes "Naming the Animals." His most recent collection is *Cardinals in the Ice Age* (1987). His comprehensive volume is *Weather-Fear: New and Selected Poems, 1958–1982* (1983).

Mari Evans (b. 1923)   Evans has written fiction and criticism in addition to a major collection of poems, *I Am a Black Woman* (1970). *JD* (1975) is a collection of four stories about a young boy living in an urban housing project. Her *Black Women Writers (1950–1980): A Critical Evaluation* appeared in 1984.

Edward Field (b. 1924)   A native of Brooklyn, Field studied at New York University, and also, for a time, studied method acting at the Moscow Art Theatre. "Icarus" is taken from his first collection of poems, *Stand Up, Friend, with Me* (1963). Another of his collections is *Stars in My Eyes* (1979). In 1990 he edited *Head of a Sad Angel*, stories by Alfred Chester, with an introduction by Gore Vidal.

Anne Finch, Countess of Winchilsea (1671–1720)   Born in southern England, Anne Kingsmill Finch became an attendant of Mary D'Este of Modena, who reigned as Queen of England from 1685 to 1688. After King James II was deposed in 1688, Finch and her husband, Colonel Heneage Finch, were forced into political obscurity. During these years she wrote much poetry but kept it in manuscript. Once her husband and she became Earl and Countess of Winchilsea in 1712, she arranged for anonymous publication as *Miscellany Poems on Several Occasions*, which appeared in 1713.

Carolyn Forché (b. 1950)   Forché is a native of Detroit. After her first volume of poems in the Yale Younger Poets series (*Gathering the Tribes* [1976]) she spent two years in El Salvador as a journalist for Amnesty International. In 1982 she translated Claribel Alegria's *Flowers for the Volcano* in an English-Spanish edition. Her next volume of poetry was *The Country Between Us* in 1982, which includes "Because One Is Always Forgotten." In 1993 she published *Against Forgetting: Twentieth-Century Poetry of Witness*, an anthology of poems protesting against repression and genocide.

Robert Frost (1874–1963)   For a brief biography, see p. 89.

Isabella Gardner (1915–1981)   Isabella Stewart Gardner was born in Massachusetts. During her lifetime, she acted, edited *Poetry* magazine (1952–1956), taught, published four volumes of poems, and gave frequent poetry readings. She declared herself "a poet who is woman first and poet second." Two years before her death, she published much of her poetry in *Isabella Gardner: The Collected Poems*.

John Gay (1685–1732)   English poet and playwright John Gay was born and educated in Devon. As a young boy he was apprenticed to a silk mercer, but freed himself to become a writer in London. For a time in the late 1720s, he was a gentleman-in-waiting to the young Duke of Cumberland, for whom he wrote his *Fables*, which were among the most popular poems in the eighteenth century. His most famous play is *The Beggar's Opera* (1728), which at a stroke created *ballad opera*—a form featuring spoken dialogue and songs sung to popular music. "Let Us Take the Road" is from this play, and the music is the March in the opera *Rinaldo* (1711) by Georg Friderich Handel.

Dan Georgakas (b. 1938)   A native of Detroit, Georgakas received degrees at Wayne State University and the University of Michigan. Since 1978 he has been on the faculty of New York's Empire State College. His publications are varied, dealing with the film industry, radical American publications, the International Workers of the World, and American Indians. His poetry collection *Happy Man* (1968) includes "Hiroshima Crewman." Also in 1968 he edited and published *Z: An Anthology of Revolutionary Poetry*.

Allen Ginsberg (b. 1926)   One of the major voices of the "beat generation" of the fifties and sixties, Ginsberg was born in New Jersey and lived in San Francisco for a time. He is now a Distinguished Professor at Brooklyn College. His landmark poetry collection was *Howl and Other Poems* (1956), which occasioned a court case when certain persons sued, unsuccessfully, to suppress it on the grounds of obscenity. Ironically, his collection of 1973, *The Fall of America: Poems of These States*, received a National Book Award.

Nikki Giovanni (Yolande Cornelia Giovanni, Jr., b. 1943)   Giovanni, a poet whose reputation has coincided with the development of African-American consciousness and pride, was born in Tennessee. She has written poems for children, and has also published interviews with James Baldwin and Alice Walker. Among her collections of poetry are *Black Feeling, Black Talk* (1968), *Black Judgment* (1968), and *Cotton Candy on a Rainy Day* (1978). Recent works are *Those Who Ride the Night Winds* (1983) and *Sacred Cows—and Other Edibles* (1988).

Robert Graves (1895–1985)   Graves fought in the British Army in World War I and was badly wounded. His early autobiographical memoir, *Good-Bye to All That* (1929), deals in part with his war experiences. He became famous in the 1970s, when the BBC and PBS dramatized his historical novels about the life and times of Roman Emperor Claudius. His studies of mythology, *The White Goddess* (1947) and *The Greek Myths* (1955), explained the meaning of ancient religion to a generation of students.

Thomas Gray (1716–1771)   Gray was a Professor of History at Cambridge University. His poetic output was small, but nevertheless in 1757 he was offered the honor of Poet Laureate, which he refused. The "Elegy Written in a Country Churchyard" has been called one of the most often quoted poems of the English language. Another of Gray's frequently quoted poems is the "Ode on a Distant Prospect of Eton College," which concludes with the familiar lines "Where ignorance is bliss / 'Tis folly to be wise."

Marilyn Hacker (b. 1942)   Hacker, a native of New York City, has been the recipient of a National Book Award (1975) and a Guggenheim Fellowship. Her collections of poems include *Separations* (1976) and *Taking Notice* (1980), which includes "Sonnet Ending with a Film Subtitle." In 1990 she published a new collection of poems, *Going Back to the River,* and in the same year she included new and selected poems in *The Hang-Glider's Daughter.* In 1989 the composer Dennis Riley set five of her poems to music for soprano and chamber ensemble.

John Haines (b. 1936)   Born in Virginia, Haines served in the Navy during World War II, receiving a number of battle stars. He lives in Alaska, where at various times he has supported himself by working as a hunter, gardener, fisherman, and trapper, in addition to his writing. If any modern American writer can lay claim to being a poet of Nature and the frontier, it is Haines. He has published a number of collections, including *News From the Glacier: Selected Poems* (1982).

Donald Hall (b. 1928)   Hall was born in Connecticut. In addition to his devotion to poetry, he is a literary and art critic, a collector of literary anecdotes, and a student of baseball. He has published a number of poetry collections, including *The Alligator Bride* (1969), *Kicking the Leaves* (1978), and *The Happy Man* (1986). His *The One Day* was the winning poetry collection of the National Book Critics Circle Award in 1988.

Daniel Halpern (b. 1945)   Halpern was born and raised in New York, and is currently a Professor in the graduate writing program of Columbia University. He has lived on both the east and west coasts, and also has a residence in Morocco. He has produced seven volumes of poetry, including *Traveling on Credit, Seasonal Rights,* and *Foreign Neon* (1991), and he has also done work in editing and translating. Uniquely interesting about him is that he has co-authored a cookbook, *The Good Food: Soups, Stews, and Pastas* (1985). He has also written a tourist's guide to the "Essential Restaurants of Italy" (1990).

H. S. Hamod (b. 1936)   Sam Hamod is a Lebanese American who was born in Indiana. He received a Ph.D. from the Writer's Workshop of the University of Iowa, and is currently director of the National Communications Institute in Washington, D.C. He has published eight books of poetry, including *Dying with the Wrong Name* (1980), from which "Leaves" is selected.

Thomas Hardy (1840–1928)   Hardy was born in Dorsetshire, in southwest England, which he called "Wessex" in his novels and poems. He began a career as an architect, but gave it up to become a novelist. In 1898, after he had published more than a dozen novels, including *Tess of the D'Urbervilles, The Return of the Native,* and *Jude the Obscure,* he gave up novels and devoted himself to poetry. Before his death in 1928, he had published eight volumes of verse, which were collected and published posthumously in 1931.

Frances E. W. Harper (1825–1911)   Born a slave, Harper did not begin to write until after the Civil War. She began with *Moses: A Story of the Nile* (1869) and *Sketches of Southern Life* (1872). Her fictional work, *Iola Leroy, or Shadows Uplifted* (1892), was well received, and was included as part of a collection of fiction by African-American writers. One of her better known poetry collections is *Atlanta's Offering,* published in 1895. In 1988 her reputation as a poet was established by the publication of a complete edition of her poems.

Michael S. Harper (b. 1938)   Born in Brooklyn, the American poet Michael S. Harper should not be confused with the English writer Michael Harper. Harper has held distinguished visiting professorships at Carlton College and at Colgate, and has received both a Guggenheim Fellowship and an NEA Creative Writing Award. He currently teaches at Brown. Some of his collections of poems are *Dear John* (1970), *Images of Kin* (1977), and *Healing Songs for the Inner Ear* (1985). "Called" is from *Nightmare Begins Responsibility* (1975).

Robert Hayden (1913–1980)   Born in Detroit and educated at the University of Michigan, Hayden became a Professor of English at both Fisk and Michigan. His earliest collection of poems was *Heart-Shape in the Dust* (1940). He received a special prize for *A Ballad of Remembrance* at the World Festival of Negro Arts held in Senegal in 1962. His *Words in the Mourning Time* (1970) included laments for the assassinated leaders Martin Luther King and Robert Kennedy, together with poems opposing the Vietnamese war.

Seamus Heaney (b. 1939)   Heaney lives in Northern Ireland, which for many decades has been beset with Catholic-Protestant strife. The tensions of this situation have permeated some of his work, as in "Valediction," which is from his *Death of a Naturalist* (1966). Among Heaney's other collections of verse are *Wintering Out* (1972) and *Field Work* (1979).

Anthony Hecht (b. 1923)   Poet, critic, translator, and Pulitzer Prize winner (1967), Anthony Hecht was born in New York and is a Professor at Georgetown University. He has regularly published new collections of poems, such as *A Summoning of Stones* (1954), *The Hard Hours* (1967), *The Venetian Vespers* (1979), and *The Transparent Man* (1990). His *Collected Earlier Poems* was published in 1990. With John Hollander he published *Jiggery-Pokery: A Compendium of Double Dactyls* in 1967.

George Herbert (1593–1633)   Herbert, whose brother was an English lord, became a priest in 1630 after a career in governmental service. He died in 1633, leaving his poems to a friend, Nicholas Ferrar, who had them printed in 1633 as *The Temple*. The intricacy of Herbert's thought, illustrated in poems like "The Pulley" and "The Collar," has caused later critics to classify him as a "metaphysical" poet. In the twentieth century a number of church-music composers have set many of his lyrics as choral anthems.

Robert Herrick (1591–1674)   Herrick attended Cambridge, and became an Anglican priest in 1627. During the English Civil War he remained loyal to King Charles I, for which he was removed from service in 1647, but he resumed his duties after the Restoration of Charles II in 1660. His major collection of poems was *Hesperides,* published in 1648. A number of persons expressed disapproval because of his frank subject matter, but, as he said, though his muse was jocund, his spirit was chaste. "Corinna's Going A-Maying" is perhaps one of the best-known poems in the *carpe diem* tradition.

William Heyen (b. 1940)   Heyen's father came to America from Germany in 1928. Two uncles who remained in Germany became Nazis, and were killed in combat when serving in the German army. Heyen's concern with the Holocaust is thus a complex product of his ethnic ties and his anguish over Nazi atrocities. "The Hair: Jacob Korman's Story" was published in *Erika: Poems of the Holocaust* (1984). Among his volumes of poems are *The City Parables* (1980), *Pterodactyl Rose: Poems of Ecology*, and *Ribbons: The Gulf War.*

Roberta Hill (b. 1947)   Hill, of the Oneida Indian tribe, teaches writing and Native American literature at the University of Wisconsin at Eau Claire. In 1991 she was also studying for a Ph.D. at the University of Minnesota. Her first collection of poetry, *Star Quilt* (1985), received a Wisconsin Writers award.

John Hollander (b. 1929)   Hollander was born in New York, received his Ph.D. from the University of Indiana, and has taught at Hunter College and Yale University. He is a remarkably energetic and diversified poet, writing shaped verse (such as "Swan and Shadow"), children's verse, and nonsense verse. His musical-critical study, *The Untuning of the Sky: Ideas of Music in English Poetry, 1500–1700*, appeared in 1961. In 1967 he published *Jiggery-Pokery: A Compendium of Double Dactyls*, in collaboration with Anthony Hecht. His *Rhyme's Reason*, of 1981, is a guide to the various forms of English verse, which he illustrates with his own examples.

Gerard Manley Hopkins (1844–1889)   Hopkins was an English poet gifted not only in poetry but also in music and art. At the age of twenty-two he converted to Roman Catholicism and became a Jesuit priest. Although he published the long poem *The Wreck of the Deutschland* in 1875, the poems linking his devotion to Nature, on which his reputation now rests, were not published until early in the twentieth century. Hopkins coined the term "sprung rhythm" for his metrical system (see Glossary / Index).

A. E. Housman (1859–1936) Housman was a professor of Classics at Cambridge University. He created one major book of verse, *A Shropshire Lad* (1896), a collection of poems stressing the brevity and fragility of youth and love. His major scholarly pursuit was a study of the ancient Latin writer Manilius, whose works he edited. His *More Poems* was published posthumously, and his *Complete Poems* was published in 1956.

Julia Ward Howe (1819–1910) Julia Ward married Samuel Howe, and with him edited the Boston *Commonwealth*, a journal devoted to humanitarian causes. She became an activist for women's liberation, world peace, and the abolition of slavery, and she was the first woman elected to the American Academy of Arts and Letters. According to tradition, she wrote the "Battle Hymn of the Republic" after watching troops marching to battle. The poem was immediately popular among Union soldiers, and since that time it has remained her most popular poem and one of America's representative patriotic songs (sung to the music of "John Brown's Body").

Barbara Howes (b. 1914) Howes was born in New York City and received her B.A. from Bennington in 1937. She has lived in Italy, France, and Haiti, but has been a resident of Vermont for many years. Among her many poetry collections are *The Undersea Farmer* (1948) and *The Blue Garden* (1972). "Death of a Vermont Farm Woman," first printed in 1954, was included in her collection *Light and Dark* (1959).

Langston Hughes (1902–1967) See p. 1437 for a short biography.

Richard Hugo (1923–1982) Hugo was born in Seattle. He served in Italy during World War II, after which he concentrated on an academic life. In 1979 he published *Selected Poems,* and in 1980 he published *White Center* and *The Right Madness on Skye.* His poetry was collected and published posthumously, in 1984, as *Making Certain It Goes On.*

Josephine Jacobsen (b. 1908) A Canadian by birth, Jacobsen now lives alternately in New Hampshire and Maryland. In her distinguished career as a poet she has published nine poetry collections, including *For the Unlost* (1946), *The Instant of Knowing* (1974), *The Chinese Insomniacs* (1981), and *The Sisters: New and Selected Poems* (1987).

Randall Jarrell (1914–1965) Jarrell was born in Tennessee. He received his B.A. and M.A. degrees from Vanderbilt University. He wrote poetry, criticism, a novel, and children's fiction. His 1945 collection of poems, *Little Friend, Little Friend,* which includes "The Death of the Ball Turret Gunner," resulted from his service in the Army Air Corps during World War II. He published a number of other verse collections, including *Selected Poems* (1955) and *The Woman at the Washington Zoo* (1960).

Robinson Jeffers (1887–1962) Jeffers was born in Pittsburgh and spent most of his life in California. He used negative and often brutal subject matter in his poetry, for example, fratricide, in *Give Your Heart to the Hawks* (1933), betrayal, in *Dear Judas, and Other Poems* (1929), and infidelity, in *Thurso's Landing, and Other Poems* (1932). His adaptation of Euripides' *Medea* (1947), starring Judith Anderson in the title role, won him wide national recognition. "The Answer" and "The Purse-Seine" appeared in his *Selected Poetry* (1938).

Ben Jonson (1573–1637) Jonson was raised in the household of his stepfather, a bricklayer, and young Ben began his working life in that trade. He was able to free himself to attend the Westminster School, where he began acquiring his immense store of knowledge. After brief service as a soldier, he embarked upon a stage career. After Shakespeare retired in 1611, Jonson became the major practicing dramatist in England. In 1616 he published his non-dramatic poems, *Epigrams* and *The Forrest*. He became England's first Poet Laureate in 1619.

Donald Justice (b. 1925)   Born in Florida, Justice received his B. A. from the University of Miami (1945). He received his Ph.D. from the University of Iowa, and became a member of the faculty there. His collections of poetry include *The Summer Anniversaries* (1959), *Departures* (1973), and *Selected Poems* (1979), for which he was awarded the Pulitzer Prize in 1980. A generous selection of his work has been included in the recent publication, *A Donald Justice Reader*.

John Keats (1795–1821)   Keats is one of the major English Romantic poets. Both his parents died when he was still a child, and at the age of fifteen he was apprenticed to an apothecary-surgeon. In 1816 he received his license to practice medicine, but almost immediately he gave up that career in order to become a full-time poet. In the following five years he created a magnificent body of poetry. Mortally afflicted with tuberculosis, he went to Rome, where he took rooms next to the Spanish Steps. He died in Rome at the age of 26, and is buried in the English Cemetery near the Pyramid of Sestus Sextus.

X. J. Kennedy (Joseph Charles Kennedy, b. 1929)   Kennedy is a New Jersey native. He received an M.A. from Columbia, and a *Certificat* from the University of Paris (1956). His first book of verse was *Nude Descending a Staircase* (1961), and since then he has published eight major poetry collections. "Old Men Pitching Horseshoes" is from *Cross Ties* (1985), which received the *Los Angeles Times* Book Award for Poetry in 1985. "John While Swimming" is selected from the 1986 "juvenile" collection entitled *Brats.*

Mary Noël Kernan, S.C. (b. 1924)   Sister Noël's poems have been published in many journals and magazines. She teaches at Seton Hill College in Greensburg, Pennsylvania, and edits the newsletter of the National Catholic Center for Holocaust Education, of which she is a co-director.

Henry King (1592–1669)   King became Bishop of Chichester in 1642, and held this position for the rest of his life. He had been a friend of John Donne, and was likely one of Donne's early editors. During his lifetime he published two volumes of his own verse, one a poetic rendering of the Psalms, and the other an edition of *Poems, Elegies, Paradoxes, and Sonnets* (1657). His collected poems were published in 1965.

Carolyn Kizer (b. 1925)   Born in Spokane, Washington, Kizer studied at the University of Washington with Theodore Roethke. One of her specialties is the adaptation of poems from China and Japan. "Night Sounds," from *Mermaids in the Basement* (1984), is an example. Since 1959 she has published seven volumes of poetry, two of which are *Knock Upon Silence* (1965) and *Midnight Was My Cry* (1971). In 1985 her collection of poems *Yin* (1984) received the Pulitzer Prize for Poetry.

Knight, Etheridge (1931–1991)   Knight was born in Mississippi, and educated himself in various jails and prisons. He was convicted of robbery and was sent to the Indiana State Prison (1960–1966). When there he was visited by **Dudley Randall**, who persuaded him that his salvation lay in the development of his power to write. One of the products was the set of haiku included here, which were included in his first book, *Po-*

ems from Prison. Knight went on to write and teach at the University of Pittsburgh. His collection *Belly Song and Other Poems* was published in 1973, and earned him a nomination for both the Pulitzer Prize and a National Book Award.

Maxine Kumin (b. 1925)   Maxine Winokur Kumin was born in Philadelphia and now lives in New Hampshire. She received B.A. and M.A. degrees at Radcliffe. In addition to poetry she has written novels, stories, children's books (two in collaboration with Anne Sexton), and essays. Her fourth collection of poetry, *Up Country: Poems of New England* (1972) received the 1973 Pulitzer Prize. *Our Ground Time Here Will Be Brief* appeared in 1982. Recently she has published a new collection, *Looking for Luck.*

Joanne Kyger (b. 1934)   Kyger is known as a leading poet in California, her home state. Her first collection of poems was *The Tapestry and the Web* (1965). Up to 1981 she had published eleven poetry collections. Her comprehensive volume *Going On: Selected Poems 1958–1980* was published in 1983 as a part of the National Poetry Series. Her comically bold poem "Destruction" is taken from *The Wonderful Focus of You* (1980).

Philip Larkin (1922–1985)   A novelist, editor, and reviewer as well as a poet, Larkin was born in northern England and attended Oxford. His first collection of verse was *The North Ship* (1946), followed nine years later by *The Less Deceived,* in which "Next Please" was printed. In 1964 he published *The Whitsun Weddings,* and in 1974 *High Windows.*

Irving Layton (b. 1912)   Since 1945 Layton, one of Canada's major poets, has published more than fifty books. A comprehensive selection of his poems, *A Wild Peculiar Joy: Selected Poems 1945–1982,* was published in 1983. *The Love Poems of Irving Layton* and *Dance with Desire: Love Poems* were published in 1984 and 1986. In 1982 and 1983 he was one of those nominated for the Nobel Prize in Literature.

C. Day Lewis (1904–1972)   Irish by birth, Cecil Day-Lewis was educated at Oxford and became politically active in the 1930s. Some of his poetic collections are *From Feathers to Iron* (1931), *The Gate* (1962), and *Selections from His Poetry* (1967). In addition to writing poems, he made translations from Latin and French, and also wrote detective stories. In the 1950s he served as Professor of Poetry at Oxford, and became Poet Laureate in 1968.

Alan P. Lightman (b. 1948)   Lightman teaches science at the Massachusetts Institute of Technology, and is best known for his scientific writings.

Audre Lorde (b. 1934)   Lorde is a New Yorker whose parents are from Jamaica. She was educated at the National University of Mexico, Hunter College, and Columbia. Recent poetry collections are *Chosen Poems Old and New* (1982) and *Our Dead Behind Us* (1986).

Richard Lovelace (1618–ca. 1657)   One of the best-known "Cavalier" poets of the early seventeenth century, Lovelace served King Charles I in the Civil Wars and was twice imprisoned by the Parliament side. Stripped of his wealth, he died obscurely and in poverty. A collection of his poems was published posthumously, and his collected works were published in 1925.

Amy Lowell (1874–1925)   Lowell was one of the leaders of the "Imagist" school of poetry early in the twentieth century. Her earliest collection of poems was *A Dome of Many-Colored Glass* (1912). Later collections were *Sword Blades and Poppy Seed* (1914) and *Legends* (1921). "Patterns" appeared in her collection *Men, Women, and Ghosts* (1916).

Cynthia MacDonald (b. 1928)   MacDonald is a native of New York. She received her B.A. at Bennington and her M.A. at Sarah Lawrence (1970). For a time she was an opera and concert singer, but since 1979 she has been teaching at the University of Houston. Among her published poetry collections are *Amputations* (1972), *Transplants* (1976), *(W)holes* (1980), *Alternate Means of Transport* (1985), and *Living Wills* (1991).

Archibald MacLeish (1892–1982)   A native of Illinois, MacLeish graduated from Yale and had a varied public career during the years when he was also writing poetry. He received a Pulitzer Prize three times, twice for his poetry (1932, for *Conquistador*, and 1952, for *Collected Poems, 1917–1952*). In 1944 and 1945 he served President Franklin D. Roosevelt as an Assistant Secretary of State. Among his many poetry collections are *Songs for a Summer Day* (1915), *Songs for Eve* (1954), and *New and Collected Poems 1917–1976* (1976). "Ars Poetica" appeared in *Streets of the Moon* (1926).

Louis MacNeice (1907–1963)   A native of Ireland, MacNeice was a friend of W. H. Auden, C. Day Lewis, and other British writers during the 1930s and 40s. His poetic interests were less political than those of his friends, and more speculative and psychological. His first poetry collection was *Blind Fireworks* (1929). Later collections were *Holes in the Sky* (1948) and *The Burning Perch* (1961). His *Collected Poems* was published in 1966, three years after his death. "Snow" first appeared in his *Poems* of 1935.

Christopher Marlowe (1564–1593)   Marlowe is known as the major English dramatist before Shakespeare (*Tamberlaine the Great, Dr. Faustus, The Jew of Malta, Edward II*), and he may have collaborated with Shakespeare in some of the earliest plays. His unfinished poem *Hero and Leander* was completed by George Chapman and published in 1598. "Come Live with Me and Be My Love" was first published in 1599 in *The Passionate Pilgrim*, and was republished with Sir Walter Raleigh's accompanying poem in *England's Helicon* in 1600. A definitive edition of Marlowe's poems appeared in 1968.

Andrew Marvell (1621–1678)   Marvel, one of the major Metaphysical poets of the seventeenth century, lived during the Civil Wars of 1642–1649, the Commonwealth, the Protectorate of Oliver Cromwell, and the Restoration of King Charles II (1660). During his long career, which he began as a tutor in an aristocratic household, he assisted Milton (who served as Latin Secretary for the English Commonwealth), and he also was a Member of Parliament. His poems were not published until three years after his death. A modern edition of his *Poems and Letters* was published in 1971.

John Masefield (1878–1967)   The English poet John Masefield, though not an academic, was a compulsive reader and writer. His youth was spent as a merchant seaman and worker at odd jobs in the United States. Eventually he published fifty volumes of poems, together with many plays and novels, and he became Poet Laureate of England in 1930. His two best-known poems are "I Must Go Down to the Sea Again," included in *Salt-Water Ballads* (1902), and "Cargoes," which appeared in *Ballads and Poems* (1910).

Heather McHugh (b. 1948)   McHugh is a native Californian who has taught in Washington, North Carolina, and Iowa, and lived in Maine. Her B.A. is from Radcliffe; her

M.A. from Denver University. Her poetry was first collected in *Dangers* (1977) and *A World of Difference* (1981). More recent collections are *Shades* and *To the Quick*.

Claude McKay (1890–1948)   McKay, one of the important voices in the Harlem Renaissance of the 1920s, was born in Jamaica, emigrated to the United States in 1912, and settled in Harlem in 1914. He wrote a number of novels, including *Home to Harlem* (1928), and short stories, published in *Gingertown* (1932). His poems were collected in *Songs of Jamaica* (1911), *Spring in New Hampshire and Other Poems* (1920), and *Harlem Shadows* (1922), where we find "In Bondage" and "The White City."

James Merrill (b. 1926)   A native of New York City, Merrill now lives in Connecticut and Florida, depending on the season. He has earned many awards, including two Pulitzer Prizes (1971 and 1977), the Bollingen Prize, and two National Book Awards. Lately he has published *Late Settings* (1985) and *The Inner Room* (1988). "Laboratory Poem" was published in *The Country of a Thousand Years of Peace* (1970).

W. S. Merwin (b. 1927)   William Stanley Merwin was born in New York and raised in New Jersey and Pennsylvania. He published *Selected Translations 1948–1968* in 1968 and was distinguished by a PEN translation prize for this work. In 1988 he published two collections of poems: *The Rain in the Trees* and *Selected Poems*. He received the Pulitzer Prize in Poetry for *The Carriers of Ladders* (1970). "Odysseus" appeared in one of his early collections, *The Drunk in the Furnace* (1960).

Edna St. Vincent Millay (1892–1950)   Known as a free spirit at Vassar, Millay matured quickly, receiving the Pulitzer Prize for Poetry—the first woman to do so—for *The Harp Weaver and Other Poems* (1923), which contained "What Lips My Lips Have Kissed." Her maturing concerns were reflected in *Make Bright the Arrows* (1940) and especially *The Murder of Lidice* (1942), which she wrote for radio presentation after the Nazi extermination of that Czech village. She published her *Collected Sonnets* in 1941. *Edna St. Vincent Millay: Collected Poems*, a centenary edition, was published in 1993.

Vassar Miller (b. 1924)   Miller is a native of Houston and still a resident there. Her earliest published collections of verse were *Adam's Footprint* (1956) and *Wage War on Silence* (1960). She has cerebral palsy, a fact that may account for the poignancy of her verse. "Loneliness" is taken from *My Bones Being Wiser* (1963).

John Milton (1608–1674)   Milton is acknowledged as one of the greatest English poets. His fame rests largely on the epic poem *Paradise Lost*, which he wrote in 1667, long after he became blind. He led a varied career, and wrote extensively in both verse and prose, including many Latin poems. His most important political position was as Latin Secretary to Oliver Cromwell during the Interregnum (1649–1660). Latin at that time was the language of diplomacy, and a good Latinist like Milton was essential. Milton's *Poems* was published in 1645, and he issued a second edition in 1673.

Judith Minty (b. 1937)   Minty is of Finnish, Irish, and Mohawk descent. She resides in Arcata, California and teaches at Humboldt State University. Among her poetry collections are *Lake Songs and Other Fears* (1974), *In the Presence of Mothers* (1981), and *Counting the Losses, Jazz* (1986). A recent poetry collection is *Dancing the Fault*.

Marianne Moore (1887–1972)   A native of Missouri, Moore went to college at Bryn Mawr, in Pennsylvania. Her first poetry collection, *Poems*, was published without her knowledge in 1921. Later she published *Selected Poems* (1935), *Nevertheless* (1944), and

Collected Poems (1951), for which she received a Pulitzer Prize. In 1967 she put together all the poems on which she wished her reputation to rest, and published the collection as *Complete Poems*.

Thomas Moore (1779–1852) Moore was phenomenally popular in the nineteenth century with his many graceful lyric poems. He wrote poems for traditional tunes, and constantly added them to his poetry collections which he entitled *Irish Melodies* and published for many years (1807–1835). In addition to "Believe Me, If All Those Endearing Young Charms," his best recognized verses today are "The Minstrel Boy" and "The Last Rose of Summer." He published a biography of his friend Byron in 1730; he was entrusted with Byron's memoirs, but regrettably, permitted them to be destroyed.

Edwin Morgan (b. 1920) Morgan is a native and resident of Glasgow, Scotland, and taught for many years at Glasgow University. Since 1952 he has produced more than twenty volumes of poetry, including *The Vision of Cathkin Braes* (1952), *The Horseman's Word: A Sequence of Concrete Poems* (1972), and *Glasgow Sonnets* (1972). Among his many accomplishments are translations from Old English, Russian, and Hungarian.

Carol Muske (b. 1945) Muske lives in California with her husband, the actor David Dukes. A recent collection of her poems is *Applause*, and a recent novel is *Dear Digby*. *Red Trousseau* is a new collection of her poetry. *The American Poetry Review* published seven poems from *Red Trousseau* in the July/August, 1991, issue.

Ogden Nash (1902–1971) Nash is most closely associated with *The New Yorker*, which he served as an editor for many years. His verse is characterized by wit, humor, and satire, with an emphasis on original and funny rhymes and rhythms. Students of music may remember his voice on a 1950s recording of Saint-Saens's *Carnival of the Animals*. His many poetry collections include *Free Wheeling* (1931), *The Bad Parents' Garden of Verse* (1936), *You Can't Get There from Here* (1957), *Everyone But Thee and Me* (1962), and *Bed Riddance* (1970).

Jim Northrup (b. 1943) Northrup is a Chippewa Indian and lives with his family on the Fond du Lac Reservation in Minnesota. He has published a number of stories, and his poems have been published mainly in magazines and journals. His major poetry collection, which also contains stories, is *Walking the Rez Road* (1993). He writes a syndicated column and also works as an artist.

Howard Nemerov (1920–1991) Nemerov graduated from Harvard and served in World War II. After the war he taught at a number of colleges and began publishing his many essays, stories, plays, and poems. His poetry collections include *The Image and the Law* (1947), *The Western Approaches: Poems 1973–1975* (1975), and *Inside the Onion* (1985). He was honored as Poet Laureate by the Library of Congress from 1986 to 1988.

Naomi Shihab Nye (b. 1952) Nye, a Palestinian American, has been recognized not only as a poet but also as a folk singer. She has published her poetry in a number of collections, including *Tatooed Feet* (1977), *Different Ways to Pray* (1980), *Hugging the Jukebox* (1982), *Yellow Glove* (1986), and, as one of four poets, *Texas Poets in Concert: A Quartet* (1990).

Frank O'Hara (1926–1966) Both a poet and a playwright, O'Hara was a native of Baltimore but spent much of his life in New York City, where he worked for the Museum of Modern Art. In a freak accident in the summer of 1966, he was struck and killed by a dune buggy. During his short life he published a large number of poetry collections, including *A City, Winter, and Other Poems* (1952), *Meditations in an Emergency* (1957), from which "Poem" is taken, and *Love Poems* (1965). *In Memory of My Feelings: A Selection of Poems* (1967) and *The Collected Poems of Frank O'Hara* (1971) are posthumous collections.

Arthur O'Shaughnessy (1844–1881)   A minor English poet, O'Shaughnessy's collections are *Epic of Women and Other Poems* (1870) and *Music and Moonlight* (1874). His professional life was devoted to work at the British Museum, and he numbered the poet Dante Gabriel Rossetti among his friends. The death of his wife in 1879 was the occasion of "A Love Symphony," which was included in the posthumous *Songs of a Worker* in 1881.

Sharon Olds (b. 1942)   Born in San Francisco, Olds received her Ph.D. from Columbia in 1972, and has taught at New York University, Sarah Lawrence, Brandeis, and Columbia. In a recent informal survey among members of the Academy of American Poets, she was named most often as their favorite contemporary American poet. Her early poetry collections are *Satan Says* (1980) and *The Dead and the Living* (1984), which contains "35/10." Recent collections are *The Gold Cell* (1987) and *The Father* (1992).

Simon Ortiz (b. 1941)   Ortiz, of the Acoma Pueblo Indian Nation, was born in New Mexico. He attended the Universities of New Mexico and Iowa. His first volume of poetry was *Naked in the Wind* (1971). In 1991 he published the collection *After and Before the Lightning*. *Woven Stone*, a three-in-one volume of poems containing a memoir, appeared in 1992. His best-known collection of stories is *Howbah Indians* (1978).

Wilfred Owen (1893–1918)   A native of Shropshire, England, Owen became a British Army officer and was killed in France in 1918, just a week before the Armistice. He published only four poems in his lifetime, but after his death Siegfried Sassoon issued a collection of twenty-four poems (1920). Benjamin Britten used a number of Owen's poems, including "Anthem for Doomed Youth," as texts for his *War Requiem* (1962). The popular band "10,000 Maniacs" recorded a version of both "Anthem for Doomed Youth" and "Dulce et Decorum Est" on their album *Hope Chest* (Elektra 9-60962-2).

Dorothy Parker (1893–1967)   Parker became legendary because of her many witty "one-liners" and also because of her often caustic book and drama reviews for *The New Yorker* in the period between the World Wars. Her first volume of poetry was *Enough Rope* (1926), which included "Resumé." "Penelope" was included in her comprehensive collection *Not So Deep as a Well* (1936). She wrote many short stories, and served as a correspondent during the Spanish Civil War in the late 1930s.

Linda Pastan (b. 1932)   Pastan was born in New York. She received a B.A. from Radcliffe and an M.A. from Brandeis. Among her eight volumes of verse are *A Perfect Circle of Sun* (1971), *Setting the Table* (1980), *Waiting for My Life* (1981), *PM/AM: New and Selected Poems* (1983), and *A Fraction of Darkness* (1985).

Marge Piercy (b. 1936)   A native of Detroit, Piercy received her B.A. from the University of Michigan (1957) and M.A. from Northwestern (1958). She now lives in Cape Cod. Among her novels are *Braided Lives* (1980) and *Fly Away Home* (1984). The first of her many poetry collections was *Breaking Camp* (1968). Others are *The Moon Is Al-*

ways Female (1980), in which "Will We Work Together" appeared, *Circles on the Water: Selected Poems* (1982), including "A Work of Artifice" and "The Secretary Chant," and *Available Light* (1988), which includes "Wellfleet Sabbath."

Sylvia Plath (1932–1963)   One of the most confessional of poets, Plath was born in Massachusetts. After graduating from Smith College in 1955 she received a Fulbright Scholarship to England. She spent 1955–1956 in Cambridge, where she married Ted Hughes (now Poet Laureate). The following years brought overpowering emotional distress, and she took her life in 1963. Her poetry during these final years reflects the personal anguish that led to her suicide. Plath's *The Collected Poems* (1981) was awarded the 1982 Pulitzer Prize in Poetry.

Edgar Allan Poe (1809–1849)   See p. 254 for a brief biography.

Katha Pollitt (b. 1949)   A native of New York, Pollitt received her B.A. at Radcliffe. She has been an editor for the weekly magazine *The Nation* for many years, and serves as an associate faculty member of the Bennington Writing Seminars Program. She has also achieved wide recognition as an essayist. Her first book of poems was *Antarctic Traveller* (1982).

Alexander Pope (1688–1744)   Pope is the eminent eighteenth-century English poet acknowledged as master of the neo-classic couplet. A childhood accident deformed his spine and retarded his physical growth, but it did not hinder his poetic gifts. Because his family was Roman Catholic, he was not sent to school but was educated at home. By age 23 he had completed *An Essay on Criticism* (1711), the leading English work of criticism in poetic form. After 1725 he devoted himself principally to writing satire, producing *The Dunciad* (1728, rev. 1743), the *Moral Essays* (1731–35), *An Epistle to Dr. Arbuthnot* (1735), and other satiric works, including the *Epilogues to the Satires* in dialogue form (1738). One of his life's plans was to publish a major philosophic work in poetry, but the only part he completed was the *Essay on Man* (1734).

Ezra Pound (1885–1972)   A native of Idaho, Pound was educated at the University of Pennsylvania and spent most of his life in Europe. He was the leading exponent of poetic "Imagism" (cf. H. D., and Amy Lowell). During World War II he broadcast pro-Axis propaganda from Rome. After the war he was prosecuted for this, but was exonerated on the grounds of insanity. Pound is as much known for his influence on other poets as for his own poetry (T. S. Eliot acknowledged him as "the better maker" in the dedication to *The Waste Land*). He did publish many collections, however, such as *Exultations* (1909), *Canzoni* (1911), and *Cathay* (1915), which contained his versions of Chinese poems (see p. 978). His major work was the *Cantos*, which he worked on throughout his life after publishing the first portion in 1925.

Salvatore Quasimodo (1901–1968)   A native of Italy, Quasimodo's early work was part of the so-called Italian "hermetic" period prior to World War II. That is, his poetry was highly imagistic and personal. During the war he became militantly anti-fascist, and for this reason Mussolini sent him to prison. After the war he became deeply concerned with the conditions of common people. In addition, he translated many works into Italian. He was the recipient of the Nobel Prize for Literature in 1959. His *Complete Poems* was published in 1984.

Sir Walter Raleigh (ca. 1552–1618)   Raleigh was a courtier, explorer, and adventurer who alternately pleased and displeased Queen Elizabeth I. During the reign of James I he was imprisoned for thirteen years in the Tower of London. He was released to go on an expedition to South America, which proved disastrous. In 1618 he was executed for treason. Like many aristocrats he wrote extensively but circulated his poetry mostly in manuscript, with rare exceptions such as "The Nymph's Reply to the Shepherd." His collected poems were edited and published in 1951.

Dudley Randall (b. 1914)   A native of Washington, D. C., Randall spent five years working in the foundry at the Ford River Rouge plant in Michigan. He became a librarian after that, and became a head librarian in Michigan. In 1965 he founded the Broadside Press, an important and valuable publisher for African-American writers. One of the first poems from the press was "Ballad of Birmingham," which had earlier (1963) been set to music and made popular by the folk singer Jerry Moore. Randall's major poetry collections are *More to Remember: Poems of Four Decades* (1971) and *A Litany of Friends: New and Selected Poems* (1981).

John Crowe Ransom (1888–1974)   Along with Robert Penn Warren, Alan Tate, and Cleanth Brooks, Ransom was one of the important exponents of the New Criticism (see Appendix D). He founded the *Kenyon Review* and edited it for twenty years. His major poetry collections are *Chills and Fever* (1924), *Two Gentlemen in Bonds* (1927), and *Selected Poems* (1945, revised in 1963 and 1969).

Henry Reed (1914–1986)   Reed was English and received a degree from the University of Birmingham. He became best known in England for his translations and radio dramas. His major book of poems was *A Map of Verona* (1946), which contains "Naming of Parts." His radio plays were published in *The Streets of Pompeii* (1971), five plays in verse, and *Hilda Tablet and Others* (1971), four comedies in prose.

Edwin Arlington Robinson (1869–1935)   Robinson began his career inauspiciously with various jobs in New York City. The publication of *The Children of the Night* (1897) and *Captain Craig* (1902) impressed President Theodore Roosevelt, who arranged a position for him as clerk in the New York Customs House. After the publication of *The Town Down the River* in 1910, he was able to support himself with his poetry. "Tilbury Town," where many of his poetic characters reside, is modeled on Gardiner, Maine, the town where he grew up. He is particularly notable because he received the first Pulitzer Prize for poetry ever to be awarded (1922). He received the prize twice more, in 1924 and 1928.

Theodore Roethke (1908–1963)   Roethke was born in Saginaw, Michigan, where his father operated a greenhouse. His first collection of poems was *The Lost Son* (1948), which included "My Papa's Waltz." He achieved wide recognition before his death in 1963. In addition to distinguishing himself, he also taught other poets, numbering James Wright and Richard Hugo among his students at the University of Washington.

Christina Rossetti (1830–1894)   English-born Christina Rossetti's religious lyrics and ballads have made her a favorite with composers such as Gustav Holst and John Rutter. Painters of the Pre-Raphaelite Brotherhood, of whom her brother Dante Gabriel Rossetti was a leading figure, frequently called upon her to pose for their paintings. Ill health forced her to forsake a career as a governess, and after 1874 she became a virtual invalid. Some of her poetry collections are *Goblin Market and Other Poems* (1862), *The Prince's Progress and Other Poems* (1866), and *A Pageant and Other Poems* (1872). A modern edition of her *Complete Poems* was published in 1979.

Muriel Rukeyser (1913–1980)   A *poète engagée*, Rukeyser was arrested in Alabama in the 1930s for demonstrating in favor of the Scottsboro Nine. Later, she wrote on behalf of an imprisoned Korean poet in *The Gates* (1976). She published many collections, including *Theory of Flight* (1935), *Beast in View* (1944), *Body of Waking* (1958), and *Collected Poems* (1979).

Luis Omar Salinas (b. 1937)   Salinas was born in Texas. He attended Fresno State University from 1967 to 1972, and now lives in California. His first volume of poems was *Crazy Gypsy* (1970). In 1975 he was one of four poets included (along with Leonard Adamé and Gary Soto) in *Entrance: Four Chicano Poets*. Since then he has been regularly productive. One of his major volumes was *The Sadness of Days: Selected and New Poems*, which appeared in 1987.

Sonia Sanchez (b. 1934)   Sanchez was born in Alabama. She received a B.A. from Hunter College in 1955, and for a time after that she worked for the Congress of Racial Equality. Currently she teaches at Temple University. Early volumes of poetry were *Homecoming* (1969) and *We a BaddDDD People* (1970). More recently she published *homegirls & handgrenades* (1984) and *Under a Soprano Sky* (1987).

Carl Sandburg (1878–1967)   It is fair to say that Sandburg "knocked around" a good deal in his youth before working his way through Knox (then Lombard) College in Galesburg, Illinois, his home town. He published a volume of poetry in 1904, but did not gain recognition until 1914, when *Poetry* printed some of his poems. Later he published *Chicago Poems* (1916), *Smoke and Steel* (1920), *Selected Poems* (1926), and *Good Morning, America* (1928). He received the Pulitzer Prize in History (1939) for his biography of Abraham Lincoln, and the Pulitzer Prize in Poetry (1951) for his *Complete Poems* of 1950.

Siegfried Sassoon (1886–1967)   Sassoon served as an officer in World War I, was wounded twice, and got two medals for bravery (one of which he threw away). He is most widely recognized for his anti-war collections *The Old Huntsman* (1917) and *Counter-Attack and Other Poems* (1918), which contains "Dreamers." Neither of these books was well received. Later, Sassoon turned to spiritual subjects, as shown in *Vigils* (1935) and *Sequences* (1956). His *Collected Poems* was published in 1961.

Virginia Scott (b. 1937)   Canadian born, Scott received her degrees at Boston University and Wisconsin. She created, edited, and managed the Sunbury Press, a small press, and received a national award for this work in 1980. She has published poetry widely in journals. Her collected poems appear in *The Witness Box* (1985) and *Toward Appomatox* (1992). She has taught at Lehman College for many years, and is currently preparing a new collection of poems and also doing research into the work of Canadian poet Alden Nolan.

Alan Seeger (1886–1916)   Seeger was born in New York and was educated at Harvard. When World War I began he joined the French Foreign Legion. He was killed in the Battle of the Somme in 1916. His war poems were published in *Collected Poems* (1916).

Brenda Serotte (b. 1946)   Serotte's Sephardic-Jewish grandparents came to the United States from Turkey in 1918. Born and educated in New York, Serotte worked as a secretary, but after receiving a Bachelor's degree she taught junior high school, an experience which has inspired many of her poems. She has published in *The Friends Journal*, and is currently working on a book of poems based on the experiences of her extended family.

Anne Sexton (1928–1974)   Massachusetts born, Sexton is one of the more personal confessional poets. *To Bedlam and Part Way Back* (1960), for example, developed out of a nervous breakdown, and her posthumous *The Awful Rowing Toward God* (1975) describes some of the feelings leading to her suicide in 1974. Her collection *Live or Die* (1966) was awarded the Pulitzer Prize in Poetry for 1967.

William Shakespeare (1564–1616)   For biographical material, see pp. 1128–29 and 1323–25.

Karl Shapiro (b. 1913)   Baltimore born, Shapiro has lived in Nebraska and California. He was recognized early in his distinguished career as a poet and critic—his *V-Letter and Other Poems* (1944) receiving the 1945 Pulitzer Prize. Among his many poetry collections are *Essay on Rime* (1945), *Poems of a Jew* (1958), *Selected Poems* (1968), and *Selected Poems: 1940–1977* (1978). He edited *Poetry* magazine for five years, and *Prairie Schooner* for ten.

Percy Bysshe Shelley (1792–1822)   Shelley is one of the major English Romantic poets. He was a quintessential revolutionary, and suffered expulsion from Oxford as a result of an early pamphlet entitled *The Necessity of Atheism*. He married before he was twenty but within three years left his wife and went to Italy with Mary Godwin (1797–1851), the author of *Frankenstein*. The two were married in 1816. Throughout these years Shelley was writing his best-known short poems. He was working on his long philosophic poem *The Triumph of Life* in 1922 when he was drowned in a storm at sea. There are many excellent modern editions of his works, including the Houghton-Mifflin Cambridge edition and the Oxford edition.

Jane Shore (b. 1947)   Shore was born in New Jersey and took her M.A. at the University of Iowa in 1971. Her poems have been widely circulated in journals and magazines, and the general merit of her work is shown by frequent prizes and awards, including a grant from the NEA. Her poetry collections are *Lying Down in the Olive Press* (1969), *Eye Level* (1977), and *The Minute Hand* (1987).

Sir Philip Sidney (1554–1586)   Sidney's life was short but exemplary. He was a model scholar and courtier, and died during a war in Flanders under the command of his uncle, the Earl of Leicester. His most important prose work was *An Apologie for Poetrie* (1580, 1595), a landmark of Renaissance criticism. He composed the sonnet sequence *Astrophil and Stella* from 1580 to 1584. Its posthumous publication in 1591 created such great interest in the form that many later poets—notably Shakespeare, Spenser, Milton, Wordsworth, and Keats—created many of their poems as sonnets.

Jon Silkin (b. 1930)   Silkin is a native of London and has made his home in Newcastle, in northern England. He has been a publishing poet since 1954, when his *The Peaceable Kingdom* appeared. Other collections are *The Re-ordering of the Stones* (1961), *Flower Poems* (1965), *Amana Grass* (1971), which included "Worm," and *The Principle of Water* (1974). His *Selected Poems* was published in 1980.

Leslie Marmon Silko (b. 1948)   A Native American, Leslie Marmon Silko was brought up in Laguna Pueblo, New Mexico. She has taught at the University of Arizona and also at the University of New Mexico, and she has been honored with a MacArthur Foundation Fellowship. The topic in most of her works is the tradition of the Navajo People, which she treats with great love and understanding, as in "Where Mountain Lion Lay Down with Deer" (p. 988), which connects the individual with the past, the land, and Nature.

Dave Smith (b. 1942) Smith, a native of Virginia, earned his B.A. from the University of Virginia in 1965, and for a time taught high school, including the coaching of football. He received his Ph.D. at Ohio University in 1976. He now teaches at the University of Utah in Salt Lake City. Some of his collections are *Bull Island* (1970), *Goshawk, Antelope* (1979), and *The Roundhouse Voice: Poems 1970–1985* (1985). "Bluejays" is from *Homage to Edgar Allan Poe* (1981).

Stevie Smith (1902–1971) Stevie Smith, the pen name of Florence Margaret Smith, was a native of Hull, in Yorkshire. During her life she worked in publishing, and in addition she became well known as a radio personality because of her many poetry readings for the BBC. Some of her poetry collections were *A Good Time Was Had by All* (1937) and *Not Waving but Drowning* (1957). Posthumous collections of her work are *Scorpion and Other Poems* (1972) and *Collected Poems* (1975).

W. D. Snodgrass (b. 1926) Snodgrass is a native of Pennsylvania. He received his B.A. from the University of Iowa, and also did graduate study there. He taught at Wayne State University in Detroit (1959–1967), and was there when he published *Heart's Needle*, for which he received the 1960 Pulitzer Prize in Poetry. Among his other collections are *Gallows Songs of Christian Morgenstern* (1967), *After Experience* (1968), *If Birds Build with Your Hair* (1979), *The Fuehrer Bunker* (1977), which he later modified as a play (1981), and *Each in His Season* (1993).

Mary Ellen Solt (b. 1920) Solt was born in Iowa. She received degrees from Iowa State Teachers College (1941) and the University of Iowa (1948). For a time (1944–1946) she taught high school in Estherville, a small Iowa town. In 1970 she began teaching literature and composition at the University of Indiana. Her major collection of formed verse is *Flowers in Concrete* (1966). Her edited works include *Concrete Poetry: A World View* (1968).

Cathy Song (b. 1955) A native of Honolulu, Cathy Song received her B.A. at Wellesley College and her M.A. from Boston University. She lives and teaches in Hawaii. Her first volume of verse was *Picture Bride* (1983), for which she received both the Yale Series of Younger Poets Award and a National Book Critics Circle Award.

Gary Soto (b. 1952) Soto is a native of Fresno, California, and was educated in California. Since 1980 he has taught at Berkeley. Because of his native city he has sometimes been grouped with a "Fresno" school of poets. His first poetry collection was *The Elements of San Joaquin* (1977). Later collections are *The Tale of Sunlight* (1978), *Where Sparrows Work Hard* (1981), and *Black Hair* (1985).

Sir Stephen Spender (b. 1909) After leaving Oxford, Spender lived for a time in Germany. He joined the Communist Party for a few weeks in the 1930s, but later renounced this affiliation (in *The God that Failed* [1950]). His first poems were collected in a small book entitled *Twenty Poems* in 1930. Later collections were *Poems of Dedication* (1947), and *Collected Poems 1928–1953* (1955).

Edmund Spenser (ca. 1552–1599) Spenser, for whom poetry was the highest form of art, was educated at Cambridge and spent the greater part of twenty years working as a secretary to the English Lord Deputy of Ireland. His first important poem was *The Shepherds' Calendar* (1579), but his major work was *The Faerie Queene*, which reached six books in the publication of 1596. His *Amoretti*, consisting of eighty-eight sonnets, were his love poems to Elizabeth Boyle, whom he married in 1594—an event he celebrates in the *Epithalamion* (1595).

William E. Stafford (1914–1993)   Stafford, who published more than two dozen volumes of verse, was born in Kansas. He received his Ph.D. from Iowa State in 1955. In 1975 he was named Poet Laureate of Oregon, and at his death in 1993 he was a Professor Emeritus at Lewis and Clark College. For *Traveling through the Dark* (1962), his second volume of poetry, he won the National Book Award for Poetry in 1963. Among his many poetry collections are *Wyoming* (1985) and *An Oregon Message* (1987). With Marvin Bell, he published *Segues* in 1983.

Maura Stanton (b. 1946)   Stanton was born in Illinois. She took her B.A. at the University of Minnesota (1969) and her M.F.A. at the University of Iowa (1971). Since 1982 she has taught at the University of Indiana. Her major collections of poems are *Snow on Snow* (1975), which includes "The Conjurer," *Cries of Swimmers* (1984), and *The Country I Come From* (1988). Her major novel is *Molly Companion* (1977).

Gerald Stern (b. 1925)   Stern was born in Pittsburgh and became a faculty member of the University of Iowa's Writer's Workshop. He was honored by three grants from the NEA and by a Guggenheim Fellowship. His *Lucky Life* (1977), which contains "Burying an Animal," received the Lamont Prize in Poetry in 1977. Most recently he published *Leaving Another Kingdom: Selected Poems* (1990) and *Bread Without Sugar* (1992).

Wallace Stevens (1879–1955)   Stevens spent his professional life in business rather than academia. He wrote most of his poems after the age of fifty, but he included "The Emperor of Ice-Cream" and "Disillusionment of Ten O'Clock," both earlier poems, in the first edition of *Harmonium* in 1923. Some of his poetic collections are a second version of *Harmonium* (1931), and also *The Auroras of Autumn* (1950) and *Collected Poems* (1954).

Mark Strand (b. 1934)   Strand was born in Canada, on Prince Edward Island, and is currently a Professor at the University of Utah. He has been honored with a John D. and Catherine T. MacArthur Foundation Fellowship, and in 1990 he was named American Poet Laureate. His most recent collection of poems is *The Continuous Life* (1990). "The Remains" appeared in *Selected Poems* (1980), and had been published in *The New Yorker* in 1969.

May Swenson, (1919–1989)   Swenson was born in Utah and was of Swedish ancestry. She experimented constantly in her poetry, not only in content but also in form, as is shown in her work with shaped verse. Her *Iconographs* (1970) was a collective of formed poetry. The formed poem "Women" was included in her collection *New and Selected Things Taking Place* (1978). She also did translations from Swedish, as represented by *Windows and Stones* (1972).

Jonathan Swift (1667–1745)   Swift was born in Ireland. He became Dean of St. Patrick's Cathedral in Dublin, a position in which he served for thirty-one years. His most famous prose works are *A Tale of a Tub* (1704), *Gulliver's Travels* (1726) and *A Modest Proposal* (1729). Throughout his life, however, he constantly wrote poetry, and he devoted himself almost exclusively to poetry after 1730. His poems were edited by Harold Williams and published in three volumes in 1937.

James Tate (b. 1943)   Tate was born in Kansas City, earning degrees from the Universities of Kansas and Iowa. He now is a Professor of English at the University of Massachusetts. Since his first collection, *The Lost Pilot*, published when he was only 23, he has published two dozen volumes of verse. "The Blue Booby" is selected from *The Oblivion Ha-Ha* (1970), his second major collection. More recent works include *Viper Jazz* (1976), *Riven Doggeries* (1979), *Reckoner* (1986), *Distances from Loved Ones* (1990) and *Selected Poems* (1991).

Alfred, Lord Tennyson (1809–1892)   One of the most popular of the Victorian poets, Tennyson became Poet Laureate in 1850. His earliest verse was published in collaboration with his brother, *Poems by Two Brothers* (1827). Some of his other collections were *Poems* (1842), *Locksley Hall* (1842), *The Princess* (1847), *Maud, and Other Poems* (1855) and *Idylls of the King* (1857–1891). He wrote *In Memoriam*, in which the well known phrase "nature red in tooth and claw" appears, from 1833 to 1850. A collected and annotated edition of his poetry was published in 1969, but there are also many other useful editions.

Dylan Thomas (1914–1953)   A native of Wales, Thomas published his first collection, *Eighteen Poems*, in 1934. After World War II he became immensely popular in America as a speaker and lecturer because of the incantatory power with which he read his own poems. Fortunately, many of his readings survive on records available in college libraries. Thomas's *Collected Poems 1934–1952* was published in 1952 and was a commercial success. *The Poems of Dylan Thomas*, a definitive edition, was published in 1971. In the 1980s, the musician John Cale set "Do Not Go Gentle" to music as part of his *Falklands Suite* (found on Cale's *Words for the Dying*, Opal/Warner Bros. 9-26024-2).

Francis Thompson (1859–1907)   An English poet, Thompson tried to qualify for the Roman Catholic priesthood and also for the profession of medicine, but was unsuccessful in both attempts. For a number of years he struggled with poverty and addiction, but was rescued by friends. He became productive after 1893 with the publication of his *Poems*, and afterward he published *Sister Songs* (1895) and *New Poems* (1897).

Jean Toomer (1894–1967)   Toomer was born in Washington, D.C., studied at five colleges, and eventually settled in the African-American community in Sparta, Georgia. An important voice in the Harlem Renaissance, Toomer published his only book, *Cane*, a collection of stories, poems, and a play, in 1923. A collection of his works may be found in *The Wayward and the Seeking* (1980).

Chase Twichell (b. 1950)   Twichell, born in Connecticut, received her B.A. from Trinity College in Hartford and her M.A. from the University of Iowa. For a time she did editorial work. She has taught at both the University of Alabama and Hampshire College. Her poetry collections are *Northern Spy* (1981) and *The Odds* (1986).

Mona Van Duyn (b. 1921)   Van Duyn is a native of Iowa and received her college degrees there. She taught for a time at the University of Washington, and has been considered a "Northwest" poet for this reason. Among her poetry collections are *Valentines to the Wide World* (1959), *Merciful Disguises* (1973), and *Near Changes* (1990).

Tino Villanueva (b. 1941)   Villanueva was born in San Marcos, Texas. He received his B.A. from Southwest Texas State University in 1969, and his M.A. from SUNY Buffalo in 1971. He currently teaches at Wellesley College. In addition to the works he has written in Spanish, he contributed to Philip Ortego's *We Are Chicanos: An Anthology of Mexican-American Literature* (1974). His most recent collection of poetry is *Scene from the Movie GIANT* (1993).

Judith Viorst (b. 1931)   Viorst is a native of New Jersey and received her degrees from Rutgers and the Washington Psychoanalytic Institute. She is known for her wry humor. Her first major volume was *It's Hard to Be Hip over Thirty and Other Tragedies of Married Life* in 1968. Her *Necessary Losses* (1986) is a collection of poems and anecdotes. She also writes children's fiction.

Shelly Wagner (b. ca. 1948)   Wagner received her B.A. from Old Dominion University, after which she worked as an interior designer and social worker. Her younger son Andrew drowned in 1984, and it was five years later that she began her cycle of elegiac poems, *The Andrew Poems*, including "Boxes," which was published in 1994. Before this she had published poetry in publications like *American Poetry Review* and *Poetry East*. With her husband, she lives in Norfolk, Virginia.

David Wagoner (b. 1926)   Wagoner was born in Ohio. In 1954 he began teaching at the University of Washington, where he was a colleague, and later an editor, of Theodore Roethke. He has been extremely productive both as poet and novelist. A few of his many poetry collections are *Dry Sun, Dry Wind* (1953), *Staying Alive* (1966), *Collected Poems* (1976), and *Landfall* (1981).

Diane Wakoski (b. 1937)   Wakoski was born in California and graduated from Berkeley in 1960. Since 1967 she has been a member of the faculty of Michigan State University. Her selected collection of verse *Emerald Ice: Selected Poems, 1962–1988* (1988) indicates that by 1988 she had published thirty-nine separate books, including *The George Washington Poems* (1967) and *The Motorcycle Betrayal Poems* (1971).

Alice Walker (b. 1944)   Walker, whose hobby is gardening, was born in Georgia and attended Sarah Lawrence College, graduating in 1965. In addition to teaching at Yale and Wellesley, among other schools, she has been constantly productive in fiction, poetry, biography, and editing. Some of her poetry collections are *Goodnight, Willie Lee, I'll See You in the Morning* (1979) and *Horses Make a Landscape Look More Beautiful* (1984). For the collection *Revolutionary Petunias* (1973), she received a Wall Book Award nomination. Her best known work is the novel *The Color Purple* (1982), which was made into an Academy-Award-winning movie in 1985.

Edmund Waller (1606–1687)   Waller, whom Dryden constantly praised for the quality and originality of his poetic couplets, was a Royalist during the English Civil Wars of 1642–1649, and for his efforts was forced into exile. He returned in 1651 after swearing loyalty to Oliver Cromwell. After the Restoration, he supported King Charles II. His major collections of poetry were *Poems* (1645) and *Divine Poems* (1685).

Robert Penn Warren (1905–1989)   Three-time winner of the Pulitzer Prize (1947, 1957, 1978), and the first American Poet Laureate (1985), Warren was one of the leaders of the New Criticism (see Appendix D), and was also a leading exponent of Southern literature and culture. With Cleanth Brooks, his *Understanding Poetry, Understanding Drama,* and *Understanding Fiction* series of textbooks taught the techniques of New Criticism to a generation of graduate and undergraduate students. His novel *All the King's Men* (1946) was made into a successful motion picture in 1950. During his teaching career he taught at the University of Minnesota and then at Yale. Some of his poetry collections are *Thirty-Six Poems* (1935), *Promises* (1957), and *New and Selected Poems* (1985).

Bruce Weigl (b. 1949)   Weigl, who teaches at Penn State, was born in Ohio. He took his B.A. at Oberlin (1974), and his Ph. D. at the University of Utah (1979). His poetry collections include *Like a Sack Full of Old Quarrels* (1976), *Executioner* (1977), *A Romance* (1979), *The Monkey Wars* (1984), *Song of Napalm* (1988), and *What Saves Us* (1992).

Phyllis Wheatley (ca. 1753–1784) Wheatley was born in Africa. She was captured by slave traders and sold to John Wheatley, a Boston merchant, who treated her virtually as a daughter and saw to it that she was educated. When she published her *Poems on Various Subjects, Religious and Moral* (1773), however, the temper of the times made it necessary to include prefaces by Massachusetts men verifying that she was qualified to write poetry, and that she had indeed written the poems in the collection. Although she wrote a second volume of poetry, she could not find a publisher for it during her lifetime. Her collected works were published in 1988.

Walt Whitman (1819–1892) Whitman, who became a legend during his lifetime, is one of America's major poets. He was born in New York, and lived with his family in both Long Island and Brooklyn. At various times he worked as a printer, teacher, reporter, and government bureaucrat. In addition, he served as a nurse during the Civil War. His major work was *Leaves of Grass*, which he first published as a collection of twelve poems in 1855, and to which he added as time went on. Many editions were published in his lifetime, the last one in 1892. *Drum Taps*, poems based on his Civil War experiences, was published in 1865; a second edition contained "When Lilacs Last in the Dooryard Bloom'd," his poem on the death of Lincoln.

Cornelius Whur (1782–1853) Whur was a Methodist minister in Suffolk, England. In 1837 he published a poetry collection, *Village Musings on Moral and Religious Subjects*, which included "The First-Rate Wife." In his obituary notice he was recognized not only as a "distinguished" poet but also as a gardener.

Richard Wilbur (b. 1921) Wilbur was born in New York. He has published a number of poetry collections, including *New and Collected Poems* (1988), for which he was awarded the Pulitzer Prize in Poetry. In 1988 he was distinguished as the second American Poet Laureate (the first being Robert Penn Warren). "Ballade for the Duke of Orleans" appeared in *Advice to a Prophet and Other Poems* (1961), and "The Sirens" appeared in *Ceremony and Other Poems* (1950).

William Carlos Williams (1883–1963) Williams spent his career as a practicing pediatrician, but he early became friendly with Ezra Pound and Hilda Doolittle. He developed a second career as a writer, producing poems, plays, stories, novels, and essays. He published poems throughout his life, beginning with *Poems* (1913) and *Tempers* (1913), and ending with *Pictures from Brueghel* (1963), for which he was posthumously awarded the Pulitzer Prize.

David Wojahn (b. 1953) Wojahn is a native of Minnesota who received degrees from the Universities of Minnesota and Arizona. He teaches at the University of Arkansas, where he is also poetry editor of the journal *Crazy Horse*. His first volume of verse was *Icehouse Lights* (1981), which was distinguished by the Yale Series of Younger Poets Award. More recently he published *Mystery Train* (1990), which contains "It's Only Rock and Roll, But I Like It."

William Wordsworth (1770–1850) Along with Coleridge, Wordsworth was the first of the English Romantic poets. In 1798 the two men published *Lyrical Ballads*, containing poems which emphasized the importance of imagination in developing meaning from ordinary events. One of Wordsworth's major ideas was that poetry grows from "emotions recollected in tranquillity," and also that poetic diction should consist of the everyday language used by real people. Throughout much of his adult life Wordsworth worked on writing and revising his long poem, *The Prelude*, which was intended to show how the mysterious "wisdom and spirit of the universe" reached him through imagination. He became Poet Laureate in 1843.

James Wright (1927–1980)   Wright was born in Martins Ferry, Ohio, and received his Ph.D. at the University of Washington, where he was a student of Theodore Roethke. In 1966 he began teaching at Hunter College, and remained there until his death in 1980. His first poetry collection, *The Green Wall*, appeared in 1957, and after that he published collections regularly, receiving the 1972 Pulitzer Prize in Poetry for his *Collected Poems* (1971). *This Journey* was published posthumously in 1982, and *Above the River: The Complete Poems* appeared in 1990.

Sir Thomas Wyatt (ca. 1503–1542)   Wyatt was a courtier in the service of King Henry VIII. He is credited with introducing the sonnet form into English as a result of his translations of the sonnets of the Italian sonneteer Petrarch. He circulated his poems in manuscript, although a number of them were anthologized after his death in *The Court of Venus* (1542) and *Seven Penitential Psalms* (1549). Modern editions of his poems were published in 1969, 1975, and 1978.

William Butler Yeats (1865–1939)   The foremost Irish poet of the twentieth century, Yeats was instrumental in the founding of the Abbey Theatre in Dublin in 1899. An unorthodox thinker, he developed his poems out of his vast reading and his special interest in spiritualism. He published many volumes of poems, including *The Green Helmet* (1910), *The Wild Swans at Coole* (1917), *The Winding Stair* (1929), and *The Collected Poems* (1932). He was awarded the Nobel Prize for Literature in 1923.

Paul Zimmer (b. 1934)   Zimmer, whose sister is the science-fiction writer Marion Zimmer Bradley, was born in Canton, Ohio, and received his B.A. from Kent State. He has managed bookstores and university presses, at the present time serving at the University of Iowa Press. Among his many volumes of poems are *A Seed on the Wind* (1960), *The Ribs of Death* (1967), *Family Reunion* (1983), *The Great Bird of Love* (1989), and *Big Blue Train* (1993). His "Zimmer" poems are collected in *The Zimmer Poems* (1976), *Earthbound Zimmer* (1983), and *The American Zimmer* (1984).

GLOSSARY

This glossary presents brief definitions of terms boldfaced in the text. Page references indicate where readers may find additional detail and illustration, together with discussions about how the concepts may be utilized in studying literature and, ultimately, in writing about literature.

Abstract diction Language describing qualities that are rarefied and theoretical (e.g., "good," "interesting," "neat," and so on); distinguished from *concrete diction*. 266, 605

Accentual rhythm See *sprung rhythm*.

Actions or **incidents** The events or occurrences in a work. 52, 88, 1073

Allegory A complete *narrative* that may also be applied to a parallel set of external situations that may be political, moral, religious, or philosophical. 58, 322–60, 325, 1025

Alliteration (prosody) The repetition of identical consonant sounds (most often the sounds beginning words) in close proximity (e.g., "pensive poets," "grown grey"). 704, 712

Allusion Unacknowledged reference and quotations. Authors assume that readers will recognize the original sources, and relate their meaning to the new context. 327, 794

Amphibrach (prosody) A three-syllable poetic *foot* consisting of a light, heavy, and light stress. 709

Amphimacer or **Cretic (prosody)** A three-syllable *foot* consisting of a heavy, light, and heavy stress. 709

Anagnorisis or **recognition** Aristotle's term describing the point in a play, usually the *climax*, when a character experiences understanding. 1074

Analytical sentence outline A scheme or plan for an essay, arranged according to topics (A, B, C, etc.) and with the topics expressed in sentences. 23

Analyzed rhyme See *inexact rhyme*.

Anapaest (prosody) A three-syllable *foot* consisting of two light stresses climaxed by a heavy stress. 708

Anaphora ("to carry again or repeat") The repetition of the same word or phrase throughout a work or a section of a work. The effect is to lend weight and emphasis. 609, 654

Antagonist The person, idea, force, or general set of circumstances opposing the *protagonist*, an essential element of *plot*. 52, 88, 134, 1021

Anticipation See *procatalepsis*.

Antimetabole See *chiasmus*.

Antithesis A rhetorical device of opposition, in which one idea or word is established, and then the opposite idea or word is expressed, as in "I *burn* and *freeze*" and "I *love* and *hate*." 609, 751

Apostrophe The addressing of a discourse to a real or imagined person who is not present; also, a speech to an abstraction. 654

Apron or **thrust stage** A stage that projects into the auditorium area, thus increasing the space for action; a characteristic feature of Elizabethan theaters and many recent ones. 1016, 1233, 1427

Archetype A character, action, or situation that is a prototype or pattern of human life generally; a situation that occurs over and over again in literature, such as a quest, an initiation, or an attempt to overcome evil. Many *myths* are archetypes. 820

Archetypal / Symbolic / Mythic critical approach An interpretive approach explaining literature in terms of archetypal patterns (e.g., God's creation of human beings, the sacrifice of a hero, or the search for paradise). 1659

Arena stage or **Theater in the round** A theater arrangement, often outdoors, in which the audience totally surrounds the stage, with all actors entering and exiting along the same aisles used by the audience. 1016, 1233, 1427,

Argument The development of an idea, including the introduction of a hypothesis or major idea, supporting details, and logical conclusions. 26, 1307

Aside A short speech delivered by a character to another character or to the audience, the convention being that the other characters on stage cannot hear it; the speaker usually reveals his or her thoughts or plans. 1023, 1127

Assertion A sentence putting an *idea* (the subject) into operation (the predi-

cate); necessary for both developing and understanding the idea. 361

Assonance (prosody) The repetition of identical vowel sounds in different words in close proximity, as in the *deep green sea*. 704, 712

Atmosphere, or **mood** The emotional aura invoked by a work. 56, 234

Audience or **intended reader** (1) The people attending a theatrical production. 1077 (2) The intended group of readers for whom a writer writes. 18, 32, 296, 1016

Auditory images References to sounds. 630

Authorial voice The *voice* or *speaker* used by authors when seemingly speaking for themselves. The use of the term makes it possible to discuss a narration or presentation without identifying the ideas absolutely with those of the author. See also *Speaker, Point of view*, and *Third-Person Point of View*. 55, 181, 194

Bacchius, or **Bacchic (prosody)** A three-syllable *foot* consisting of a light stress followed by two heavy stresses, as in "a new song." 709

Ballad, Ballad Measure (prosody) A narrative poem composed of *quatrains* in which lines of iambic tetrameter alternate with iambic trimeter, rhyming *x-a-x-a*. 717, 753

Beast fable A fable featuring animals with human characteristics. 326

Beat, or **Accent (prosody)** The heavy stresses or accents in lines of poetry. The number of beats in a line usually dictates the meter of the line (five beats in a pentameter line, etc.). 705

Blank verse (prosody) Unrhymed iambic pentameter. 750

Blocking In the performance of a play, the grouping and movement of characters on stage. 1016

Blocking agent   A person, circumstance, or attitude that obstructs the union of lovers. 1318

Box set   In the modern theater, a realistic setting of a single room from which the "fourth wall" is missing, so that the stage resembles a three-dimensional picture. 1233

Brainstorming   The exploration, discovery, and development of details to be used in a composition. 14

Breve (prosody)   A mark in the shape of a bowl-like half circle (◡) to indicate a light stress or unaccented syllable. 706

Business, or **stage business**   The gestures, expressions, and general activity (beyond blocking) of actors on stage. Usually, business is designed to create laughter. It is often spontaneous. 1016

Buskins   Elegantly laced boots (*kothorni* or *cothurni*) worn by the actors in ancient Greek tragedy. Eventually the buskins became elevator shoes to stress the royal status of actors by making them tall. 1079

Cacophony (prosody)   Meaning "bad sound," *cacophony* refers to words combining sharp or harsh sounds. 713

Cadence group (prosody, style)   A coherent word group spoken as a single rhythmical unit, such as a noun phrase ("our sacred honor") or prepositional phrase ("of parting day"). 710

Caesura, caesurae (prosody)   The pause(s) separating phrases within lines of poetry, an important aspect of poetic *rhythm*. 709–10

Carpe diem poetry   Poetry concerned with the shortness of life and the need to act in or enjoy the present. *Carpe diem* means "seize the day." 843

Catastrophe   The "turning downward" of the dramatic plot, the fourth stage in the structure after the climax. The dé-

nouement of a play, in which things are explained and put into place. 1021

Catharsis (purgation)   Aristotle's concept that tragedy, by arousing pity and fear (*eleos* and *phobos*), brings about a "proper **purgation**" or catharsis of these emotions. 1074

Central idea   (1) The thesis or main idea of an essay. (2) The theme of a literary work. 53

Character   An extended verbal representation of a human being, the inner self that determines thought, speech, and behavior. 51, 131–179, 569–603, 1021

Chiasmus, or **antimetabole**   A rhetorical pattern in which words and ideas are repeated in the sequence A-B-B-A, as in "I *sing* of *love* and *love* to *sing*." 270, 609

Choragos   The sponsor or financial backer of a classical Greek dramatic production. Often the *choragos* was honored by serving as the leader (*koryphaios*) of the chorus. 1077

Choric figure   A character who remains detached from the action and who provides commentary. See also *raisonneur*. 1022

Chorus   In ancient Athenian drama, the chorus consisted of a group of young men who chanted in unison and performed dance movements to a flute accompaniment. 1069

Chronology ("logic of time")   The sequence of events in a work, with emphasis upon the complex intertwining of cause and effect. See also *sequence*. 52

Clerihew   A humorous closed-form poem in four lines, rhyming *A-A-B-B*, usually about a real or literary person. 756

Cliché rhymes (prosody)   Trite and widely used rhymes, such as *moon* and *June* or *trees* and *breeze*. 714

Climax (Greek for *ladder*) The high point of *conflict* and tension preceding the resolution of a drama or story; the point of decision, of inevitability and no return. The climax is sometimes merged with the *crisis* in the consideration of dramatic and narrative structure. 91, 1021

Closed-form poetry Poetry written in specific and traditional patterns produced through rhyme, meter, line-length, and line groupings. 749

Commedia dell'arte Broadly humorous farce developed in sixteenth-century Italy, featuring stock characters, stock situations, and much improvised dialogue. 1322

Comedy A literary genre which like tragedy originated in the Dionysiac festivals of ancient Athens. Derived from the Greek "komos" songs or "songs of merrymakers," the first comedies were wildly boisterous. Subsequently comedies became more subdued and realistic. In typical comedies today, confusions and doubts are resolved satisfactorily if not happily, and usually comedies are characterized by smiles and laughter. 1018, 1316–1423

Comedy of the Absurd A modern form of comedy dramatizing the apparent pointlessness, ambiguity, uncertainty, and absurdity of existence. 1323

Comedy of manners A form of comedy, usually regular (five acts or three acts), in which attitudes and customs are examined and satirized in the light of high intellectual and moral standards. The dialogue is witty and sophisticated, and characters are often measured according to their linguistic and intellectual powers. 1322

Commentary, analysis, or **interpretation** Passages of explanation and reflection about the meaning of actions, thoughts, dialogue, historical movements, and so on. 57

Common ground of assent Those interests, concerns, and assumptions that the writer assumes in common with readers so that an effective and persuasive tone may be maintained. 682

Common measure (prosody) A closed poetic quatrain, rhyming A-B-A-B, in which lines of iambic tetrameter alternate with iambic trimeter. See also *ballad measure*. 753

Comparison-contrast A technique of analyzing two or more works in order to determine similarities and differences in topic, treatment, and quality. *Appendix A,* 1609–23

Complex sentence A main clause together with a subordinate or dependent clause. 269

Complication A stage of narrative and dramatic structure in which the major *conflicts* are brought out; the *rising action* of a *drama*. 91, 1021

Compound sentence Two simple sentences joined by a conjunction. 269

Compound-complex sentence A compound sentence also integrating one or more dependent or subordinate clauses. 269

Concrete diction Words that describe exact and particular conditions or qualities, such as *cold, sweet,* and *creamy* in reference to an ice-cream sundae. These words are *concrete*, while the application of *good* or *neat* to the sundae is *abstract*. See also *abstract diction*. 55, 266, 605

Concrete poetry Poetry depicting visual shapes in addition to ideas and emotions. 761

Conflict The opposition between two characters, between large groups of people, or between *protagonists* and larger forces such as natural objects, ideas, modes of behavior, public opinion, and the like. Conflict may also be internal and psychological, involving choices facing a *protagonist*. It is the essence of *plot*. 52, 88, 1020

Connotation   The meanings that words suggest beyond their bare dictionary definitions. 267, 610

Consonant   segments   Consonant sounds; sounds produced as a result of the touching or close proximity of the tongue or the lips in relation to the teeth or palate (e.g., *m, n, p, f, sh, ch*); contrasted with *vowel segments*. 705, 712

Contextual symbol   See *Private Symbol*.

Convention   An accepted feature of a genre, such as the point of view in a story, the form of a poem (e.g., sonnet, ode), the competence or brilliance of the detective in detective fiction, the impenetrability of disguise and concealment in a Shakespearean play, or the chorus in Greek drama. 16

Corpus Christi play   A type of medieval drama that enacts events from the Bible, such as the killing of Abel by Cain, the problems of Noah, the anger of Herod, and so on. The word is derived from the religious festival of *Corpus Christi* ("Christ's body"), held in the spring of each year. Also called *mystery plays*. 1018, 1123

Cosmic irony (irony of fate)   *Situational irony* that is connected to a pessimistic or fatalistic view of life. 300

Costumes   The clothes worn by actors, designed to indicate historical periods, social status, economic levels, etc. 1016, 1079

Cothurni   See *buskins*.

Couplet   (prosody)   Two successive rhyming lines. 750

Crisis   The point of uncertainty and tension—the *turning point*—that results from the *conflicts* and difficulties brought about through the complications of the *plot*. The crisis leads to the *climax*—that is, to the decision made by the protagonist to resolve the conflict. Sometimes the *crisis* and the *climax* are considered as two elements of the same stage of plot development. 91, 1021

Cultural (universal) symbols   *Symbols* recognized and shared as a result of a common social and cultural heritage. See *Private symbols*. 324, 791, 1025

Cycle   (1) A group of closely related works. (2) In medieval religious drama, the complete set of plays performed during the Corpus Christi festival, from the creation of the world to the resurrection. As many as forty or fifty plays could make up the cycle. See also *Corpus Christi Plays*. 1123

Dactyl (prosody)   A three-syllable *foot* consisting of a heavy stress followed by two lights, such as "Notable parables." 707

Dactylic, or **triple rhyme (prosody)**   Rhyming *dactyls*. 715

Deconstructionist critical approach   An interpretive literary approach that rejects absolute interpretations and stresses ambiguities and contradictions. 1660

Decorum   The convention or expectation that words and subjects should be exactly appropriate—high or formal words for serious subjects (e.g., epic poems, tragedy), and low or informal words for low subjects (e.g., limericks, farce). 607

Denotation   The standard dictionary meaning of a word. 267, 610

Dénouement (untying) or **resolution**   The final stage of *plot* development, in which mysteries are explained, characters find their destinies, and the work is completed. Usually the dénouement is done as speedily as possible, for it occurs after all conflicts are ended. 92, 1021

Description The exposition of scenes, actions, attitudes, and feelings. 56

Device A rhetorical figure or strategy. 16

Deus ex machina ("A god out of the machine; *theos apo mechanes* **in Greek)** In ancient Greek drama, the entrance of a god to unravel the problems in a play. Today, the phrase *deus ex machina* refers to the artificial and illogical solution of problems. 1079

Dialect The speech of a particular region or social group, usually characterized by unique words, expressions, and pronunciation. When a dialect becomes widespread in government, business, education, and literature, it is claimed as the standard of the particular language. 606

Dialogue The speeches of two or more characters in a story, play, or poem. 56, 572, 1015, 1023

Diction Word choice, types of words, and the level of language. 264, 604–26

Diction, formal or **high** Proper, elevated, elaborate, and often polysyllabic language. 605

Diction, informal or **low** Relaxed, conversational, and familiar language, utilizing contractions and elisions, and sometimes employing slang and grammatical mistakes. 606

Diction, neutral or **middle** Correct language characterized by directness and simplicity. 606

Digraph (prosody) Two alphabetical letters spelling one sound, as in *digraph*, where *ph* spells the *f* sound, *stick*, where *ck* spells the *k* sound, and *thumb*, where *mb* spells the *m* sound. 704

Dilemma Two choices facing a protagonist, usually in a tragic situation, with either choice being unacceptable or damaging; a cause of both internal and external conflict. 89, 1077

Dimeter (prosody) A line of two metrical feet. 706

Dionysia The religious festivals of ancient Athens held to celebrate the god Dionysius. Both tragedy and comedy developed as major features of these festivals. 1070

Dipody, dipodic foot, or **syzygy (prosody)** The submergence of two normal *feet*, usually iambs or trochees, under a stronger beat, so that a "galloping" or "rollicking" rhythm results. 709

Director The person in charge of guiding and instructing all persons involved in a dramatic production. 1016

Dithyramb An ancient Athenian poetic form sung by choruses during the earliest Dionysiac festivals. The first tragedies originated from the dithyrambs. 1070

Domestic tragedy A tragedy of domestic life usually involving middle-class characters. 1076

Donnée (French for "given") The given action of set of assumptions on which a work of literature is based. 50

Double dactyl A comic closed-form poem in two quatrains, written in dactylic dimeter. The second line must be a proper name, and the sixth or seventh a single word. 756

Double entendre ("double meaning") Deliberate ambiguity, often sexual and usually humorous. 299

Double or **trochaic rhyme (prosody)** Two-syllable trochaic rhymes. 715

Double plot Two different but related lines of action, often in a play. 1020

Drama An individual play; also plays considered as a group; one of the three major *genres* of literature. 1015

Dramatic convention See *Convention*.

Dramatic irony A special kind of *situational irony* in which a character perceives his or her plight in a limited way while the audience and one or more of the other characters understand it entirely. 58, 300, 683, 1025, 1077

Dramatic monologue A type of poem, derived from the theater, in which a speaker addresses an internal listener or the reader at length. The form is related to the soliloquy. 573

Dramatic (objective) point of view A third-person *narration* reporting speech and action, but excluding commentary on the actions and thoughts of the characters. 55, 184–85, 187, 1022

Dying rhyme (prosody) See *falling rhyme*.

Dynamic character A character who undergoes adaptation, change, or growth, unlike the *static character,* who remains constant. In a *short story*, there is usually only one dynamic character, whereas in a *novel* there may be many. 134, 1021

Echoic words (prosody) Words echoing the actions they describe, such as *buzz*, *bump*, and *slap*; important in the device of *onomatopoeia*.. 713

Economic Determinist / Marxist critical approach An interpretive approach based on the theories of Karl Marx (1818–1883), stressing that literature is to be judged from an economic perspective. 1656

Editing See *Montage*.

Enclosing method See *Framing method*.

End-stopped line (prosody) A line ending in a full pause, usually indicated with a period or semi-colon. 710

English (Shakespearean) sonnet A fourteen-line poem, in iambic pentameter, composed of three quatrains and a couplet, rhyming *A-B-A-B, C-D-C-D, E-F-E-F, G-G*. 753

Enjambement, or run-on line (prosody) A line having no end punctuation but running over to the next line. 710

Epic A long narrative poem elevating character, speech, and action. 2, 47

Epigram A short and witty poem, usually in couplets, that makes a humorous or satiric point. 755

***Episodia* or episodes** The acting scenes or sections of Greek Tragedy, divided by the *stasima*, or choral sections. 1081

Epitaph Lines composed to mark someone's death, a special type of epigram. 755

Euphony (prosody) Meaning "good sound," *euphony* refers to word groups containing consonants that permit an easy and pleasant flow of spoken sound; opposite of *cacophony*. 713

Exact rhyme (prosody) Rhyming words in which both the vowel and consonant sounds rhyme; also called *perfect rhyme*. It is important to note that rhymes result from *sound* rather than spelling; words do not have to be spelled the same way or look alike to rhyme. 713

Exodos The final episode in a Greek tragedy, occurring after the last choral ode. 1081

Explication A complete and detailed analysis of a work of literature, often word-by-word and line-by-line. 563

Exposition The stage of dramatic or narrative structure which introduces all things necessary for the development of the *plot*. 91, 1021

Eye rhyme (prosody) Words which seem to rhyme because parts of them are spelled identically but pronounced differently (e.g., *bear, fear, fury, bury; stove, shove; wonder, yonder*). 714, 716

Fable A brief *story* illustrating a moral truth, most often associated with the ancient Greek writer Aesop. 48, 326

Falling Action See *Catastrophe.*

Falling rhyme Trochaic rhymes, such as *dying* and *crying,* and also dactylic rhymes, such as *flattery* and *battery.* 715

Fantasy The creation of events that are dreamlike or fantastic, departing from ordinary understanding of reality because of apparently illogical location, movement, causation, and chronology. 50

Farce *Farce,* a word derived from the Latin word *farsus,* meaning "stuffed," is an outlandish physical comedy overflowing with silly characters, improbable happenings, wild clowning, extravagant language, and bawdy jokes. 1019, 1322

Feminine rhyme See *Falling rhyme.*

Feminist critical approach An interpretive approach designed to raise consciousness about the importance and unique nature of women in literature. 1655

Fiction *Narratives* based in the imagination of the author, not in literal, reportorial facts; one of the three major *genres* of literature. 2, Chapter 2

Figurative language Words and expressions that conform to a particular pattern or form, such as *metaphor, simile,* and *parallelism.* 2, 649

Figures, rhetorical See *Figurative language.*

Film script The written dramatic text on which a film is based, including directions for movement and expression. 1576

Film Motion pictures, movies. 1576–98

First-person point of view The use of an "I," or first-person, *speaker* or *narrator* who tells about things that he/she has seen, done, spoken, heard, thought, and also learned about in other ways. 55, 183–84, 187

Flashback A method of *narration* in which past events are introduced into a present action. 92

Flat character A character, usually minor, who is not individual, but rather useful and structural, static and unchanging; distinguished from *round character.* 134, 1021

Foil A character, usually minor, designed to highlight qualities of a major character. 1022

Foot (prosody) Measured combinations of heavy and light *stresses,* such as the iamb, which contains a light and a heavy stress. 705

Form, poetic The various shapes and organizational modes of poetry. 749–88

Formal Substitution See *Substitution.*

Formalist critical approach See *New Critical / Formalist critical approach.*

Framing (enclosing) method The same features of topic or setting used at both the beginning and ending of a work so as to "frame" or "enclose" the work. 234

Free verse (prosody) Poetry based on the natural rhythms of phrases and normal pauses, not metrical feet. 759

French scene A numbering system for a play in which a new scene is numbered whenever characters enter or leave the stage. (As in Molière's *Love Is the Doctor.*) 1017

Freytag Pyramid A diagram showing how the five stages of dramatic plot structure go up and down like the sides of a pyramid. 1020

Full-length play A drama, either a tragedy or comedy (usually not a farce) designed for a full evening's performance, containing either five acts, three acts, or a long series of separate scenes. See also *regular play.* 1017

Gallery   The upper seats at the back and sides of a theater. 1125

General language   Words referring to broad classes of persons, objects, or phenomena; distinguished from *specific language*. 266, 605

Genre   A type of literature, such as *fiction* and *poetry*; also a type of work, such as detective fiction, epic poetry, tragedy, etc. 2

Graph, Graphics (spelling)   Writing or spelling; the appearance of words on a page, as opposed to their actual sounds. 704

Gustatory images   References to impressions of taste. 631

Haiku   A poetic form derived from Japanese, traditionally containing three lines of 5, 7, and 5 syllables. 2, 754

Half rhyme   See *Inexact rhyme.*

Hamartia   A Greek word (meaning "insolence, contemptuous violence," or "pride") describing the error or frailty that causes the downfall of a tragic protagonist. 1071, 1075

Heavy-stress rhyme   A *rhyme*, such as rhyming iambs or anapests, ending with a strong stress. 714

Heptameter, or the septenary (prosody)   A line consisting of seven metrical *feet*. 706

Hero, heroine   The major male and female *protagonists* in a narrative or drama; the terms are often used to describe leading characters in adventures and romances. 133

Heroic couplet (prosody)   Also called the *neoclassic couplet*. Two successive rhyming lines of iambic pentameter; the second line is usually end-stopped. Couplets written between 1660 and 1800 are usually called "heroic" regardless of their topic matter. 750

Hexameter (prosody)   A line consisting of six metrical *feet*. 706

High comedy   Elegant comedies characterized by wit and sophistication, in which the complications grow out of character; also, a *comedy of manners*. 1321

Historical critical approach   See *Topical / Historical critical approach.*

Hovering accent   See *Spondee.*

Hubris   See *Hamartia.*

Humor   The capacity to cause laughter. 297

Hymn (prosody)   A religious song, consisting of one and usually many more replicating rhythmical stanzas. 753

Hyperbole   A rhetorical figure in which emphasis is achieved through exaggeration. 299, 657

Iamb (prosody)   A two-syllable *foot* consisting of a light stress followed by a heavy stress (e.g., *the winds*). 706

Iambic pentameter (prosody)   A line consisting of five iambic *feet*. 706

Idea   A concept, thought, opinion, or belief; in literature, a unifying, centralizing conception or *theme*. 361–413, 839–64

Identical rhyme (prosody)   The use of the same words in rhyming positions, such as *veil* and *veil*, or *stone* and *stone*. 714, 716

Idiom   Usage that produces unique words and phrases within regions, classes, or groups; e.g., standing *on* line or *in* line; carrying a *pail* or a *bucket*; drinking *pop* or *soda*. Also, the habits and structures of particular languages. 606

Image, Imagery   Images are references that trigger the mind to fuse together memories of sights (*visual*), sounds (*auditory*), tastes (*gustatory*), smells (*olfactory*), and sensations of touch (*tactile*). "Image" refers to a single mental creation. "Imagery" refers to images throughout a work or throughout the works of a writer or group of writers. Images may be *literal* (descriptive and pictorial) and *metaphorical* (figurative and suggestive). 2, 627–48

Imaginative literature   Literature based in the imagination of the writer, usually *fiction, poetry,* and *drama.* 2

Imitation   The theory that literature is derived from life and is an imaginative duplication of experience; closely connected to *realism* and *verisimilitude.* 50

Imperfect foot (prosody)   A metrical *foot* consisting of a single syllable, either heavily or lightly stressed. 707

Incidents   See *Actions*

Incongruity   A discrepancy between what is ordinarily or normally expected and what is experienced. The resulting gap is a cause of amusement. 298

Inexact rhyme (prosody)   Rhymes that are created out of words with similar but not identical sounds. In most of these instances, either the vowel segments are different while the consonants are the same, or vice versa. This type of rhyme is variously called *slant rhyme, near rhyme, half rhyme, off rhyme, analyzed rhyme,* or *suspended rhyme.* 716

Inside speaker   The speaker of a poem presented in the first-person point of view. 569–70

Intellectual critical approach   See *Topical / Intellectual critical approach.*

Internal rhyme   The occurrence of rhyming words within a single line of verse. 716

Intrigue plot   The dramatic rendering of how a young woman and her lover foil the blocking mechanisms of a parent or guardian, often aided by a maidservant or *soubrette.* 1318

Invention   The process of discovering and determining materials to be included in a composition, whether an essay or an imaginative work; a vital phase of *prewriting.* 50

Ironic comedy   A form of comedy in which characters seem to be in the grips of uncontrollable, cosmic forces. The dominant tone is therefore ironic. 1323

Irony   Broadly, a means of indirection. Language that states the opposite of what is intended is *verbal irony.* The placement of characters in a state of ignorance is *dramatic irony,* while an emphasis on powerlessness is *situational irony.* 58, 235, 299, 683–85, 1076

Italian or **Petrarchan sonnet**   An iambic pentameter poem of fourteen lines, divided between the first eight lines (the *octet*) and the last six (the *sestet*). 752

Jargon   Words and phrases characteristic of a particular profession, trade, or pursuit such as medicine, sociology, football, or the military. 608

Journal   A notebook or word-processor file for recording observations, here, about reading. 10

Kinesthetic images   Words describing human or animal motion and activity. 632

Kinetic images   Words describing general motion. 632

Kothorni   See *Buskins.*

Lighting (stage)   The general word describing the many types, positions, directions, and intensities of artificial lights used in the theater. 1016

Limerick   A five-line closed poetic form in which two lines of anapaestic trimeter are followed by two in anapaestic dimeter and a final line in trimeter, rhyming *3a-*

3a-2b-2b-3a, often used in comic and bawdy verse. 755

Limited, or **limited-omniscient point of view** A third-person narration in which the actions and thoughts of the protagonist are the focus of attention. 55, 185, 187

Listener (internal audience) A character or characters imagined as the audience to whom a poem or story is spoken, and as a result one of the influences on the content of the work, as in Browning's "My Last Duchess" or Paley's "Goodbye and Good Luck." 572

Literature Written or oral compositions that tell stories, dramatize situations, express emotions, and analyze and advocate ideas. Literature is designed to engage readers emotionally as well as intellectually, with the major genres being *fiction, poetry, drama,* and *nonfiction prose,* and with many separate sub-forms. 1

Longshot (film) A distant camera view, including not only characters but also their surroundings; distinguished from a *closeup.* 1580

Low comedy Crude, violent, and physical comedies and farces, characterized by sight gags, bawdy jokes, and outrageous situations. 1322

Lyric A short poem written in a repeating stanzaic form, often designed to be set to music; a *song.* 753

Main plot The central and major line of causation and action in a literary work. 1020

Major mover A major participant in a work's action, who either causes things to happen or who is the subject of major events. If the first-person narrator is also a major mover, such as the *protagonist,* that fact gives first-hand authenticity to the narration.187

Makeup The materials, such as cosmetics, wigs, and padding, applied to an actor to change appearance for a specific role, such as a youth, an aged person, or a hunchback. 1016

Malapropism The comic use of an improperly pronounced word, so that what comes out is another but incorrect word. Examples are *odorous* for *odious* (Shakespeare), or *pineapple* for *pinnacle* (Sheridan). The new word must be close enough to the correct word so that the resemblance is immediately recognized, along with the error. See also *Pun.* 298

Marxist critical approach See *Economic Determinist / Marxist critical approach.*

Masculine rhyme (prosody) See *Rising rhyme.*

Mask Ancient Athenian actors wore facial masks to define their characters. 1080

Meaning That which is to be understood in a work; the total combination of ideas, actions, descriptions, and effects. 839–64

Mechanics of verse See *Prosody*

Melodrama A sentimental dramatic form with an artificially happy ending. 1019

Metaphor (a "carrying out a change") *Figurative language* that describes something as though it actually were something else, thereby enhancing understanding and insight. 16, 56, 649

Metaphorical language See *Figurative language*

Metaphysical conceit An elaborate and extended metaphor or simile that links two apparently unrelated fields or subjects. The term is commonly applied to the metaphorical language of a number of early seventeenth-century poets, particularly John Donne. 867

Meter (prosody) The number of *feet* within a line of traditional verse, such as *iambic pentameter* referring to a line containing five *iambs*. 706

Metonymy A rhetorical figure in which one thing is used as a substitute for another with which it is closely identified. 655

Metrical foot See *Foot*.

Metrics See *Prosody*.

Middle Comedy The Greek comedies written in the first two-thirds of the fourth Century B.C. Middle Comedy lessened or eliminated the chorus, and did away with the exaggerated costumes of the Old Comedy. No Middle Comedies survive from antiquity. 1317

Miracle play A medieval play dramatizing a miracle or miracles performed by a saint. An outgrowth of the earlier medieval *Corpus Christi* play. 1124

Monologue A long speech spoken by a single character to himself or herself, to the audience, or to an off-stage character. 1015

Monometer A line consisting of one metrical foot. 706

Montage The editing or assembling of the various camera "takes," or separate filmed scenes, to make a continuous film. 1579

Mood See *Atmosphere*.

Moral/Intellectual critical approach An approach to the interpretation of literature that is concerned primarily with content and values. 1651

Morality play A type of medieval and early Renaissance play that dramatizes the way to live a pious life. 1018, 1124

Motif Meaning "something that moves," a *motif* is sometimes used in reference to a main idea or theme in a single work or in many works, such as a *carpe*

diem theme, or a comparison of lovers to little worlds. See also *Archetype*. 839–64

Music of poetry (prosody) Broadly, the rhythms, sounds, and rhymes of poetry. See *Prosody*.

Muthos See *plot*.

Mystery plays See *Corpus Christi plays*.

Myth, Mythology, Mythos A *myth* is a story that deals with the relationships of gods to humanity , or with battles among heroes. A myth may also be a set of beliefs or assumptions among societies. *Mythology* refers collectively to all the stories and beliefs, either of a single group or number of groups. A system of beliefs and religious or historical doctrine is a *mythos*. 327, 817–38

Mythical reader See *Audience*.

Mythic critical approach See *Archetypal / Symbolic / Mythic critical approach*.

Mythopoeic The propensity to create myths and to live in terms of them. 818

Narration, narrative fiction The relating or recounting of a sequence of events or actions. While a *narration* may be reportorial and historical, *narrative fiction* is primarily creative and imaginative. 2, 47, 54, 88

Narrative ballad A poem in ballad measure telling a story. 554

Narrative fiction See *Prose fiction*.

Narrator See *Speaker*.

Near rhyme See *Inexact rhyme*.

New comedy The Greek comedy that developed at the end of the fourth century B.C., stressing wit, romanticism, and twists of plot. 1318

New Critical / Formalist critical approach An approach to the interpretation of literature based on the French practice of *explication de texte*, stressing the form and details of literary works. 1653

Nonfiction prose A *genre* consisting of essays, articles, and books that are concerned with real as opposed to fictional things; one of the major *genres* of literature. 2

Nonrealistic character An undeveloped and often symbolic character without full motivation or individual identity. 1022

Nonrealistic drama Dreamlike, fantastic, symbolic, and otherwise artificial plays that make no attempt to present an imitation of everyday reality. 1023, 1424–1575

Novel A long work of prose fiction. 49

Objective point of view See *Dramatic point of view.*

Octameter (prosody) A line of eight metrical feet. 706

Octave (prosody) The first eight lines of an Italian sonnet, unified by rhythm, rhyme, and topic. 752

Ode (prosody) A stanzaic poetic form (usually long, to contrast it with the *song*) with varying line lengths and sometimes intricate *rhyme* schemes. 753

Off rhyme See *Inexact rhyme.*

Old comedy The Athenian comedies of the fifth century B.C., featuring song, dance, ribaldry, satire, and invective. 1317

Olfactory imagery Images referring to smell. 631

Omniscient point of view A *third-person narrative* in which the *speaker* or *narrator*, with no apparent limitations, may describe intentions, actions, reactions, locations, and speeches of any or all of the characters, and may also describe their innermost thoughts (when necessary). 55, 185, 187

One-act play See *Short plays.*

Onomatopoeia (prosody) A blending of consonant and vowel sounds designed to imitate or suggest the activity being described. 713

Open-form poetry Poems that avoid traditional structural patterns, such as rhyme or meter, in favor of other methods of organization. 759

Orchestra (theaters) (1) In ancient Greek theaters, the *orchestra*, or dancing place, was the central circle where the chorus performed. (2) The word now refers to the ground floor or first-floor in a modern theater where the audience sits. 1078

Organic unity The interdependence of all elements of a work, including character, actions, speeches, descriptions, thoughts, and observations. 52

Outline A formal pattern for a written composition. 23

Outside speaker The speaker of a poem presented in a third-person point of view. 184

Overstatement See *Hyperbole.*

Parable A short *allegory* designed to illustrate a religious truth, most often associated with Jesus as recorded in the Gospels. 2, 327

Parados (1) A *parados* was either of the two aisles on each side of the orchestra in ancient Greek theaters, along which the performers could enter or exit. (2) The entry and first lyrical ode of the chorus in Greek tragedy, after the prologue. 1080

Paradox A rhetorical figure embodying a seeming contradiction that is nevertheless true. 653

Parallelism (style) A rhetorical structure in which the same grammatical forms are repeated. 269, 609, 751

Paranomasia See *Pun.*

Paraphrase A brief restatement, in one's own words, of all or part of a literary work; a *précis.*562

Pentameter (prosody) A line of five metrical *feet.* 706

Perfect rhyme See *Exact rhyme.*

Performance An individual production of a play, either for an evening or for an extended period, comprising acting, movement, lighting, sound effects, staging and scenery, ticket sales, and the accommodation of the audience. 1015

Peripeteia, or **reversal** Aristotle's term for a sudden reversal, when the action of a work, particularly a play, veers around quickly to its opposite. 1073, 1466

Persona (Latin for **mask** [**prosopon** in Greek.]) The narrator or speaker of a story or poem. See also *Speaker.* 55, 180

Personification A rhetorical figure in which human characteristics are attributed to nonhuman things or abstractions. 655

Petrarchan sonnet See *Italian sonnet.*

Phonetic, phonetics (prosody) The actual pronunciation of sounds, as distinguished from spelling or *graphics.* 704

Plausibility See *Verisimilitude.*

Play See *Drama.*

Playwright A writer of plays. 1015

Plot The plan or groundwork for a story, with the actions resulting from believable and authentic human responses to a *conflict.* It is causation, conflict, response, opposition, and interaction that make a *plot* out of a series of *actions.* Aristotle's word for plot is *muthos.* 88, 1020, 1073

Poem, poet, poetry A variable literary genre which is, foremost, characterized by the rhythmical qualities of language.

While poems may be short (including *epigrams* and *haiku* of just a few lines) or long (*epics* of thousands of lines), the essence of poetry is compression, economy, and force, in contrast with the expansiveness of prose. There is no bar to the topics that poets may consider, and poems may range from the personal and lyric to the public and discursive. A *poem* is one poetic work. A *poet* is a person who writes poems. *Poetry* may refer to the poems of one writer, to poems of a number of writers, to all poems generally, or to the aesthetics of poetry considered as an art. 2, 547

Point of view The *speaker, voice, narrator,* or *persona* of a work; the position from which details are perceived and related; a centralizing mind or intelligence; not to be confused with *opinion* or *belief.* 55, 180–229, 570, 1022

Point-of-view character The central figure or *protagonist* in a *limited-point-of-view narration,* the character about whom events turn, the focus of attention in the narration. 185

Postulate or **premise** The assumption on which a work of literature is based, such as a level of absolute, literal reality, or as a dreamlike, fanciful set of events. See also *Donnée.* 50

Précis A shortening, or cutting down, of a narrative into its essential parts—a synopsis, abridgment, paraphrase, condensation, or epitome. 81–86

Private or **contextual symbol** A symbol which is derived not from common historical, cultural, or religious materials, but which is rather developed within the context of an individual work. See *Cultural symbols.* 324, 791, 1025

Probability or **plausibility** The standard that literature should be about what is probable, common, normal, and usual. 136

Problem A question or issue about the interpretation or understanding of a work. 1304

Problem play A type of play dealing with a problem, whether personal, social, political, environmental, or religious. 1464

Procatalepsis or **anticipation** A rhetorical strategy whereby the writer raises an objection and then answers it; the idea is to strengthen an argument by dealing with possible objections before a dissenter can raise them. 1306

Producer The person in charge of practical matters connected with a stage production, such as securing finances, arranging for theater use, furnishing materials, renting or making costumes and properties, guaranteeing payments, and so on. 1016

Prologue In Greek tragedy, the introductory action and speeches before the *parados*, or first entry of the chorus. 1080

Props or **properties** The objects, furniture, and the like used on stage during a play. 1016

Proscenium, proscenium stage (1) See *proskenion*. (2) An arch that frames a *box set* and holds the curtain, thus creating the invisible fourth wall through which the audience sees the action of the play. 1016

Prose fiction Imaginative prose narratives (short stories and novels) that focus on one or a few characters who undergo a change or development as they interact with other characters and deal with their problems. 2, Chapters 2–12 of the book.

Prose poem A short work, written in prose, but employing the methods of verse, such as imagery, for poetic ends. 759

Proskenion A raised stage built in front of the *skene* in ancient Greek theaters to separate the actors from the chorus and make them more prominent. 1078

Prosody The sounds and rhythms of poetry. 703–48

Protagonist The central character and focus of interest in a *narrative* or *drama*. 52, 88, 134, 1021

Psychological / Psychoanalytic critical approach An interpretive literary approach stressing how psychology may be used in the explanation of both authors and literary works. 1657

Public (universal) mythology Widely known mythic systems that have been well established over a long period of time, such as Greco-Roman mythology and Germanic mythology. 821

Pun, or **paranomasia** A witty word-play which reveals that words with different meanings have similar or even identical sounds. See also *Malapropism*. 656

Purgation See *catharsis*.

Pyrrhic (prosody) A metrical *foot* consisting of two unaccented syllables. 708

Quatrain (1) A four-line stanza or poetic unit. (2) In an *English* or *Shakespearean* sonnet, a group of four lines united by rhyme. 717, 752

Raisonneur A character who remains detached from the action a provides reasoned commentary; a choric character. 1022

Reader-Response critical approach An interpretive approach based in the proposition that literary works are not fully created until readers make *transactions* with them by *actualizing* them in the light of their own knowledge and experience. 1661

Realism, or **verisimilitude** The use of true, lifelike, or probable situations and concerns. Also, the theory underlying the use of reality in literature. 50, 233

Realistic character   The accurate imitation of individualized men and women. 1022

Realistic comedy   See *Ironic comedy.*

Realistic drama   Plays that dramatize characters and situations in line with the world as we know it. 1023, 1232, 1424–1575

Realistic setting   A setting designed to resemble places that actually exist or that might exist. The settings of Ibsen's *A Doll House* are realistic. 1023, 1428

Regular play   A play, usually of three or five acts, that conforms to the various *rules* of drama. 1020

Recognition   See *Anagnorisis.*

Repetition   See *anaphora.*

Representative character   A *flat character* with the qualities of all other members of a group (i.e., clerks, cowboys, detectives, etc.); a *stereotype.* 134

Research, literary   The systematic use of primary and secondary sources for assistance in studying a literary problem. 1624–49

Resolution   See *Dénouement.*

Response   A reader's intellectual and emotional reactions to a literary work. 37

Revenge tragedy   A popular type of English Renaissance drama, developed by Thomas Kyd, in which a person is called upon (often by a ghost) to avenge the murder of a loved one. Shakespeare's *Hamlet* is in the tradition of revenge tragedy. 1128

Reversal   See *Peripeteia.*

Rhetoric   The art of persuasive writing; broadly, the art of all effective writing. 268, 649

Rhetorical figure   See *Figurative language.*

Rhetorical substitution   See *Substitution.*

Rhyme (prosody)   The repetition of identical concluding syllables in different words, most often at the ends of lines. 704, 713–17

Rhyme scheme (prosody)   The pattern of *rhyme,* usually indicated by assigning a letter of the alphabet to each rhyming sound. 717

Rhythm (prosody)   The varying speed, intensity, elevation, pitch, loudness, and expressiveness of speech, especially poetry. 704

Rising action   The action in a play before the climax. 1028

Rising rhyme (prosody)   Rhymes produced with one syllable words, like *sky* and *fly,* or with multisyllabic words in which the accent falls on the last syllable, such as *decline* and *confine. 714*

Romance   (1) Lengthy Spanish and French stories of the sixteenth and seventeenth centuries. (2) Modern formulaic stories describing the growth of an enthusiastic love relationship. 2, 49

Romantic comedy   Sympathetic comedy that presents the adventures of young lovers trying to overcome opposition and achieve a successful union. 1321

Round character   A character who profits from experience and undergoes a change or development; usually but not necessarily the *protagonist.* 133, 1021

Run-on line   See *Enjambement.*

Satire   An attack on human follies or vices, as measured positively against a normative religious, moral, or social standard. 685–87

Satiric comedy   A form of comedy designed to correct social and individual behavior by ridiculing human vices and follies. 1322

Satyr play A comic and burlesque play submitted by the ancient Athenian tragic dramatists along with their trilogies of tragedies. On each day of tragic performances, the satyr play was performed after the three tragedies. See also *Trilogy*. 1072

Scansion (prosody) The act of determining the prevailing *rhythm* of a poem. 705

Scene (1) In a play, a part or division (of an act, as in *Hamlet*, or entire play, as in *Death of a Salesman*) in which there is a unity of subject, setting, and (often) actors. (2) In a film, a unit of continuous action in one location. 1017

Scenery The artificial environment created on stage to produce the illusion of a specific or generalized place and time. 1016, 1023

Second-person point of view A *narration* in which a second-person listener ("you") is the *protagonist* and the speaker is someone with knowledge the protagonist does not possess or understand about his or her own actions (e.g., doctor, parent, rejected lover, etc.). 184, 187

Segment (prosody) The smallest meaningful unit of sound, such as the *l, uh,* and *v* sounds making up the word "love." Segments are to be distinguished from spellings. 703

Semivowel segments Midway between the consonant and vowel segments, the semivowel segments are *y, w,* and *h.* 705

Septenary See *Heptameter.*

Sequence (literally, "a following") The events in a work as they take place in time, from beginning to end. 88

Sestet (1) A six-line stanza or unit of poetry. (2) The last six lines of an *Italian* sonnet. 752

Sets The physical objects used in a theatrical production. 1016, 1023

Setting The natural, manufactured, and cultural environment in which characters live and move, including all the artifacts they use in their lives. 230–63

Shakespearean sonnet See *English sonnet.*

Shaped verse Poetry written so that the lines or words of the poem form a recognizable shape, such as a pair of wings or a geometrical figure. 761

Short plays Short plays usually contain one act, and are not commercially self-sustaining unless two or three of them are put together for an entire evening. One-act plays are ideal for classrooms or for film or television. 1017

Short story A compact, concentrated work of narrative fiction that may also contain description, dialogue, and commentary. Poe used the term "brief prose tale" for the short story, and emphasized that it should create a major, unified impact. 2, 49

Sight rhyme See *Eye rhyme.*

Simile A figure of comparison, using "like" with nouns and "as" with clauses, as in "the trees were bent by the wind *like actors bowing after a performance.*" 16, 649

Simple sentence (style) A complete sentence containing one subject and one verb, together with modifiers and complements. 269

Situational irony A type of *irony* emphasizing that human beings are enmeshed in forces beyond their comprehension and control. 58, 300, 683, 1025, 1077

Skene In ancient Greek theaters, the *skene* ("tent," "hut") was a building in front of the orchestra which contained front and side doors from which actors could make entrances and exits. It served a variety of purposes, including the storage of costumes and props. 1078

Slang   Informal and substandard vocabulary. Some slang is a permanent part of the language (e.g., phrases like "I'll be damned," "Go jump in the lake," and our many four-letter words). Other slang is spontaneous, rising within a group (jargon), and often then being replaced when new slang emerges. 607

Slant rhyme (prosody)   A *near rhyme,* in which the concluding consonant sounds are identical, but not the vowels, such as "should" and "food," "slim" and "ham." 714, 716

Slapstick comedy   A type of low farce in which the humor depends almost entirely on physical actions and sight gags. 1323

Social drama   A type of problem play that deals with current social issues and the place of individuals in society. 1019

Soliloquy   A speech made by a character, alone on stage, directly to the audience, the convention being that the character is revealing thoughts and feelings. A soliloquy is to be distinguished from an *aside,* which is made to the audience (or confidentially to another character) when other characters are present. 1023, 1127

Song (prosody)   A lyric poem with a number of repeating stanzas, written to be set to music. 753

Sonnet   A poem of fourteen lines in *iambic pentameter.* 752

Sound   The phonetics of language, collectively and separately considered. See *Prosody.*

Speaker   The *narrator* of a story or poem, the *point of view,* often an inde-

pendent character who is completely imagined and consistently maintained by the author. In addition to narrating the essential events of the work (justifying status as the *narrator*), the speaker may also introduce other aspects of his or her knowledge, and may interject judgments and opinions. Often the character of the speaker is of as much interest as the *actions* or *incidents.* 180, 569–70

Specific language (style)   Words referring to objects or conditions that may be perceived or imagined; distinguished from *general language.* 55, 266, 605

Speeches   See *Dialogue.*

Spondee (prosody)   A two-syllable foot consisting of successive, equally heavy accents (e.g., *slow time, men's eyes*). 707

Sprung, or **accentual rhythm (prosody)**   A method of accenting, developed by Gerard Manley Hopkins, in which major stresses are "sprung" from the poetic line. 708

Stage business   See *Business.*

Stage convention   See *Convention.*

Stage directions   A playwright's instructions concerning lighting, scenery, blocking, tone of voice, action, entrances and exits, and the like. 1015

Stanza (prosody)   A group of poetic lines corresponding to paragraphs in prose; the meters and rhymes are usually repeating or systematic. 717, 749

Stasima (singular *stasimon*)   Choral odes separating the episodes in Greek tragedies. 1081

Static character   A character who undergoes no change; contrasted with a *dynamic character.* 134, 1021

Stereotype   A character who is so ordinary and unoriginal that he/she seems to have been cast in a mold; a *representative* character. 134, 1022

Stichomythy In Greek tragedies, dialogue consisting of one-line speeches designed for rapid delivery. 1081

Stock character A *flat character* in a standard role with standard *traits*, such as the irate police captain, the bored hotel clerk, etc.; a *stereotype*. 134, 1022

Stop sound The consonant sound produced by the momentary stoppage and release of breath either when the lips touch each other or when the tongue touches the teeth or palate. The stop sounds in English are *p, t,* and *k* and *b, d,* and *g.* 705

Story A narrative, usually fictional, centering on a major character, and rendering a complete action. 49

Stress (prosody) The emphasis given to a syllable, either strong or light. See also *beat.* 704–706

Strong-stress rhythm See *Heavy-stress rhythm.*

Structuralist critical approach An interpretive approach attempting to find relationships and connections among elements that appear to be separate and discrete. 1654

Structure The arrangement and placement of materials in a work. 53, 90–93

Style The manipulation of language, the placement of words in the service of content. 55, 264–93

Subject The topic that a literary work addresses, such as love, marriage, war, death, and the like. 552, 841, 1026

Subplot A secondary line of action in a literary work that often comments directly or obliquely on the main plot. 1020

Substitution (prosody) *Formal substitution* is the use of an actual variant foot within a line, such as an anapaest being used in place of an iamb. *Rhetorical substitution* is the manipulation of the *caesura*

to create the effect of a series of differing feet. 710

Suspended rhyme See *Inexact rhyme.*

Syllable (prosody) A separately pronounced part of a word (e.g., the *eat* and *ing* parts of "eating") or, in some cases, a complete word (e.g., *the, when, flounced*). 704

Symbol, symbolism A specific word, idea, or object that may stand for ideas, values, persons, or ways of life. 56, 58, 322–60, 789–816, 1025

Symbolic character A character whose primary function is symbolic, even though the character also retains normal or realistic qualities. 1022

Symbolic critical approach See *Archetypal / Symbolic / Mythic critical approach.*

Synecdoche A rhetorical figure in which a part stands for a whole, or a whole for a part. 655

Synæsthesia A rhetorical figure uniting or fusing separate sensations or feelings; the description of one type of perception or thought with words that are appropriate to another. 656

Syntax Word order and sentence structure. A mark of style is a writer's syntactical patterning (regular patterns and variations), depending on the rhetorical needs of the literary work. 608

Syzygy See *Dipody.*

Tactile imagery Images of touch and feeling. 631

Tenor (figurative language) The sense, or meaning, of a *metaphor, symbol* or other rhetorical figure. See *Vehicle.* 652

Tercet A three-line unit or stanza of poetry, often rhyming *A-A-A* or *A-B-A.* 751

Terza rima (prosody) A three-line stanza form with the pattern *A-B-A, B-C-B,* etc. 752

Tetrameter (prosody)   A line consisting of four metrical *feet*. 706

Theater in the Round   See *Arena stage*.

Theme   (1) The major or central idea of a work. (2) An essay, a short composition developing an interpretation or advancing an argument. (3) The main point or idea that a writer of an essay asserts and illustrates. 53, 552, 839–64, 1026

Thesis statement, or **thesis sentence**   An introductory sentence which names the topics to be developed in the body of an essay. 21

Third-person point of view   A third-person method of *narration* (i.e., *she, he, it, they, them*, etc.), in which the *speaker* or *narrator* is not a part of the story, as with the *first-person point of view*. Because the third-person speaker may exhibit great knowledge and understanding, together with other qualities of character, he or she is often virtually identified with the author, but this identification is not easily decided. See also *Authorial Voice, Omniscient Point of View*. 55, 184–85, 187

Third-person objective point of view   See *Dramatic point of view*.

Thrust stage   See *Apron stage*.

Tiring house   An enclosed area in an Elizabethan theater in which actors changed costumes and awaited their cues, and in which stage properties were kept. 1125

Tone   The techniques and modes of presentation that reveal or create attitudes. 58, 294–321, 678–702, 1024

Topic sentence   The sentence determining the subject matter of a paragraph. 22

Topical / Historical critical approach   An interpretive approach that stresses the relationship of literature to its historical period. 1652

Traditional poetry   See *Closed-form poetry*.

Tragedy   A drama or other literary work that recounts the fall of an individual who, while undergoing suffering, deals responsibly with the situations and dilemmas that he or she faces, and who thus demonstrates the value of human effort. 1018, 1069–1315

Tragic flaw   See *Hamartia*.

Tragicomedy   A literary work—drama or story—containing a mixture of tragic and comic elements. 1019

Trait, traits   A typical mode of behavior; the study of major traits provides a guide to the description of *character*. 132

Trilogy   A group of three literary works, usually related or unified. For the ancient Athenian Dionysiac festivals, each competing dramatist submitted a *trilogy* (three tragedies), together with a *satyr play*. 1072

Trimeter (prosody)   A line consisting of three metrical *feet*. 706

Triple rhyme   See *Dactylic rhyme*.

Triplet See *Tercet*.

Trochaic (double) rhyme   Rhyming trochees such as *flower* and *shower*. 715

Trochee, trochaic (prosody)   A two-syllable *foot* consisting of a heavy followed by a light stress. 707

Trope   A short dramatic dialogue inserted into the Church mass during the early middle ages. 1018, 1122

Tudor interlude   Short tragedies, comedies, or historical plays performed by both professional actors and students during the reigns of Henry VII and Henry VIII (i.e., the first half of the sixteenth century). They sometimes featured abstract and allegorical characters and provided opportunities for both music and farcical action. 1124

Understatement The deliberate underplaying or undervaluing of a thing to create emphasis. 299, 657

Unit set A series of platforms, rooms, stairs, and exits that form the locations for all of a play's actions. A unit set enables scenes to change rapidly, without the drawing of a curtain and the placement of new sets. 1023

Unities The concept, related to *verisimilitude*, that literary works should comprise a single major action, take place in as little time as possible, and be confined to a single location (*action, time,* and *place*). During the Renaissance some critics considered the unities to be essential aspects of *regular drama*. Later critics considered the unity of action important, but minimized the unities of place and time. 1082

Universal symbol See *Cultural symbols.*

Value, values The expression of an idea or ideas that concurrently asserts their importance and desirability as goals, standards, and ideals. 363

Vehicle The image or reference of a rhetorical figure, such as a *metaphor* or *simile*; it is the vehicle that carries or embodies the *tenor.* 649

Verbal irony Language stressing the importance of an idea by stating the opposite of what is meant. 58, 299, 683, 1025

Verisimilitude (i.e., **"like truth"**) or **realism** A characteristic whereby the setting, circumstances, characters, dialogue, actions, and outcomes in a work are designed to seem true, lifelike, real, plausible, and probable. 50, 136, 233

Versification See *Prosody.*

Villanelle A closed poetic form of nineteen lines, composed of five triplets and a concluding quatrain. The form requires that whole lines be repeated in a specific order and that only two rhyming sounds occur throughout. 752, 781

Virgule (prosody) A slashmark (/) indicating the boundaries of poetic feet. 706

Visual image Language describing visible objects. 629

Visual poetry Poetry that draws much of its power from the appearance of the verse on the page. See also *Concrete verse* and *Shaped verse.* 761

Voice See *Speaker.*

Vowel rhyme (prosody) The use of any vowels in rhyming positions, as in *day* and *sky,* or *key* and *play.* 717

Vowel sounds, or **segments** Continuant sounds produced by the resonation of the voice in the space between the tongue and the top of the mouth, such as the *ee* in *feel,* the *eh* in *bet,* and the *oo* in *cool.* 705

Well-made play (*la pièce bien faite*) A form developed and popularized in nineteenth-century France by Eugène Scribe (1791–1861) and Victorien Sardou (1831–1908). Typically, the well made play is built on both secrets and the timely arrivals of new characters and threats. The protagonist overcomes adversity and ultimately overcomes it. Ibsen's *A Doll House* exhibits many characteristics of a well-made play. 1465

Word counts (style) An elementary method of describing a writer's style by counting and then explaining the lengths of words, sentences, and paragraphs. 268

PHOTO CREDITS

The following list represents the photo credits for all the author portraits in the book:

Chapter 8
page 301 - Margaret Atwood (UPI/Bettmann)
page 308 - Kate Chopin (Missouri Historical Society)

Chapter 9
page 330 - Nathaniel Hawthorne (Bettmann)
page 346 - John Steinbeck (UPI/Bettmann)

Chapter 10
page 387 - D. H. Lawrence (Bettmann)
page 399 - James Joyce (Bettmann)
page 403 - Irene Zabytko (Gil Ihrig)

Chapter 12
page 475 - Stephen Dixon (Courtesy of Henry Holt Co., Inc.)
page 486 - Gabriel García Márquez (AP/Wide World Photos)
page 491 - Charlotte Perkins Gilman (Culver Pictures, Inc.)
page 502 - Doris Lessing (Reuters/Bettmann)
page 510 - Flannery O'Connor (Bettmann)
page 520 - Frank O'Connor (G. Paul Bishop/Alfred A. Knopf, Inc.)
page 526 - Tillie Olsen (Courtesy of Feminist Press)
page 531 - Grace Paley (Gentil & Heyers, © 1994 Farrar, Straus and Giroux)
page 537 - Katherine Anne Porter (UPI/Bettmann)

Chapter 26
page 1027 - Anton Chekhov (Bettmann)
page 1038 - Susan Glaspell (AP/Wide World Photos)
page 1053 - Eugene O'Neill (UPI/Bettmann)

Chapter 27
page 1081 - Sophocles (Alinari/Art Resource)
page 1128 - William Shakespeare (Giraudon/Art Resource)
page 1233 - Arthur Miller (AP/Wide World Photos)

Chapter 28
pages 1403 - Beth Henley (Courtesy of William Morris Agency, Inc.)

Chapter 29
page 1430 - Edward Albee (New York Times Pictures)
page 1437 - Langston Hughes (UPI/Bettmann)
page 1463 - Henrik Ibsen (Bettmann)
page 1518 - Tennessee Williams (Friedman-Abeles Collection, New York Public Library at Lincoln Center)

Index of Authors, Titles, and First Lines

Alphabetical arrangement is letter-by-letter. Authors' names are printed in **bold** type, titles in *italic* type, and first lines in roman type.

INDEX OF KEY TERMS